*fourth edition*
*revised by Zena Sutherland*

# THE ARBUTHNOT ANTHOLOGY
## OF CHILDREN'S LITERATURE

Special contributors
"Guiding Literary Experience" by Sam Leaton Sebesta, University
of Washington, and Dianne L. Monson, University of Washington
"Illustrations in Children's Books" by Donnarae MacCann and Olga
Richard, University of California, Los Angeles

Illustrators
Rainey Bennett, Arthur Paul, John Averill,
Wade Ray, Seymour Rosofsky, and Debi Sussman

Lothrop, Lee & Shepard Company
A Division of William Morrow & Company, Inc., New York

*fourth edition*
*revised by Zena Sutherland, The University of Chicago*

# THE ARBUTHNOT ANTHOLOGY
## OF CHILDREN'S LITERATURE

*May Hill Arbuthnot*

*and*

*Dorothy M. Broderick*
*Dalhousie University*

*Shelton L. Root, Jr.*
*University of Georgia*

*Mark Taylor*

*Evelyn L. Wenzel*
*University of Florida*

Cover art by Ivan Rabuzin: *The Great Forest, 1960*.
Photograph courtesy of the artist.

Arbuthnot, May Hill, 1884–1969, comp.
  The Arbuthnot anthology of children's literature.

  Bibliography: pp. 985–1061.
  Includes indexes.
  SUMMARY: A collection of poetry, folklore, short
stories, biographies, and other nonfiction. Includes
a history and discussion of children's literature
with suggestions for using this literature.
  1. Children's literature. [1. Literature—Collections]
I. Bennett, Rainey.  II. Sutherland, Zena.  III. Title.
PZ5.A64Ar13       808. 8′99282        75–29998

ISBN: 0–688–41725–6

Trade edition first published 1976

# PREFACE
# TO THE FOURTH EDITION

*The Arbuthnot Anthology* was originally planned as a source book for classes in children's literature and as a collection of materials to be enjoyed with children in groups or individually. Like the first three editions, the Fourth Edition offers a balanced selection of different types of literature for children of all ages and a wide range of styles and subjects for their differing tastes. The book contains a great variety of poems, folk tales, modern fantasy, myths, epics, fables, realistic stories, historical fiction, biography, and informational writing. They are funny, provocative, tender, informative, exciting; there are old favorites and delightful new authors. Few activities, whether in the home, the library, or the classroom, are as rewarding as reading aloud, which brings listeners closer to each other and to the reader as they share a selection, and which can be a door to further inquiry, a stimulus for discussion, and an invitation to read more of the work of an individual author.

The selections in this revision are grouped into three main parts—Part One, Time for Poetry; Part Two, Time for Magic: Old and New; Part Three, Time for Realism: Facts and Fiction.

Part One, Time for Poetry, includes over 500 poems. Many of them are from the third edition and were originally in *Time for Poetry*,[1] compiled by May Hill Arbuthnot and Shelton L. Root, Jr. A fresh group of poems and poets have been added in the Fourth Edition, with selections that include traditional and contemporary writing as well as fine poems in English

translation. These new poems represent urban and ethnic voices heard increasingly in poetry for young people. Inevitably, some poems from the earlier edition have had to be omitted to make space for the new.

Part Two, Time for Magic: Old and New, is a collection of folk tales, fables, myths, epics, hero tales, and modern fantasy. Many of the selections are from the third edition, which drew on *Time for Old Magic*[2] and *Time for New Magic*,[3] compiled by Mrs. Arbuthnot and Mark Taylor. In this Fourth Edition the large collection of folklore from around the world has been enriched with the addition of several new tall tales and a black tale from the United States, an American Indian story, and folk tales from Africa, Estonia, Latvia, the Dominican Republic, Guatemala, Uruguay, Mexico, Puerto Rico, Scotland, Sweden, Denmark, Finland, and Canada.

Part Two also contains a rich collection of fantasy. The selections include short stories as well as excerpts from longer works. As in Part One, Time for Poetry, selections often fit into more than one category; animal stories may have elements of enchantment, tales of enchantment may also be humorous, humorous tales may also be science fiction. An effort has been made here and throughout the Fourth Edition to represent new materials and contemporary authors; there are old favorites like E. B. White's *Charlotte's Web* or stories by Hans Christian Andersen and new favorites like Rich-

[1]Scott, Foresman, 1968

[2]Scott, Foresman, 1970
[3]Scott, Foresman, 1971

ard Adams' *Watership Down*, Betty Brock's *No Flying in the House*, or Penelope Lively's *The Ghost of Thomas Kempe*.

Part Three, Time for Realism: Facts and Fiction, consists of realistic stories, historical fiction, biography, and informational books. Some of the material is from the third edition and was chosen from *Time for Stories of the Past and Present*[4] and *Time for Biography*[5] both compiled by Mrs. Arbuthnot and Dorothy M. Broderick, and from *Time for Discovery: Informational Books*,[6] compiled by Mrs. Arbuthnot and Evelyn L. Wenzel.

Today's children face contemporary problems and take our changing world in their stride. There is a new candor in their literature that is reflected in much of the fiction and biography of Part Three. Also reflected there is the need for representation of minority groups and current social issues. The historical fiction excerpts are arranged chronologically as is the section of biography; in these sections, as in informational books, the Fourth Edition shows the diversity of interests and the high quality of the able authors who are writing for children and young people today.

The introductions to all of the sections should be of special help to students and to all adults who would like to know about the books, authors, and artists so beloved by children. They give some history of the various types of books being considered and provide criteria for evaluating them. Almost all of the selections are preceded by informative headnotes. Generally, selections within each section are arranged in ascending order of difficulty and maturity.

Part Four, Time for Children's Literature, opens with "Milestones in Children's Literature," which furnishes not merely dates and a chronology of landmarks, but gives clues to relationships, innovations, and trends. Many of the books that are cited as milestones are represented by selections in the *Anthology*.

"Illustrations in Children's Books," written especially for the Fourth Edition by Donnarae MacCann and Olga Richard, traces the historical development of illustrated books for children from the early books with their small, crude woodcuts to today's lavishly illustrated picture books. A variety of media techniques is explained, children's responses to art are discussed, and the elements of visual language are explained. The work of individual artists is analyzed and is represented by illustrations in both color and black and white. The section concludes with a glossary of terms and a bibliography.

The third section of Part Four, "Guiding Literary Experience," was written for this edition by Sam Sebesta and Dianne Monson. They discuss such elements of literature as setting, characterization, and plot, and such aspects of guidance as reading interests and readability. Specific and useful suggestions are given for reading aloud, engaging children in discussion, and involving them in such activities as choral reading, dramatization, and storytelling, with descriptions of techniques used to stimulate and enhance literary experiences. Separate bibliographies are provided for each subsection.

The final sections of Part Four are a listing of winners of children's book awards, with a brief history of the awards, and an extensive annotated bibliography. The bibliography is in three parts: a section of sources of audiovisual materials, a list of books that provide background readings and reference sources for adults, and lists of books for children and young people, organized to correspond with sections of Parts One, Two, and Three.

The subject matter index has been expanded; it brings together selections that are on the same subject but in different literary genres, and it suggests some of the less tangible components of the excerpts. This is in addition to the index of authors, illustrators, and titles.

In addition to the eight-page color section and the black-and-white illustrations in "Illustrations in Children's Books," the section on historical milestones includes work by well-known artists. And a small sample of illustrations from informational books is included with the selections from those books.

Numerous illustrations drawn especially for *The Arbuthnot Anthology* accompany the selec-

[4]Scott, Foresman, 1968
[5]Scott, Foresman, 1969
[6]Scott, Foresman, 1971

tions throughout. These are the work of Arthur Paul, John Averill, Wade Ray, Seymour R. Rosofsky, Debi Sussman, and Rainey Bennett.

All of the people mentioned in this preface have contributed in great measure to the third edition of the book and therefore to whatever has been retained in this revision. The *Anthology* owes much, above all, to the discrimination and enthusiasm of May Hill Arbuthnot, whose book reflected an abiding dedication to and love of good literature, an understanding of children, and an informed concern for bringing the two together. I should like, also, to express appreciation for the patience and wisdom of my editors, JoAnn Johnson and Anne Gwash.

Zena Sutherland

# CONTENTS

The titles within the text that appear
in brackets were supplied by the
compilers for untitled chapters or
excerpts.

*part one*

# TIME FOR POETRY

People

Animals

Traveling

Play

Humor

Magic and Make-Believe

Wind and Water

Days and Seasons

Wisdom and Beauty

The range of poetry is so vast, its forms so diverse, and its pleasures so gratifying, that no child should grow up without being given an opportunity to appreciate it. In order to appreciate it, children should not be "taught" poetry but should be exposed to it.

Some adults do not like poetry because, in their childhood, they were required to learn it by rote and to perform dry dissections, or because they were exposed to poems too complex for their understanding, or to poems ineptly read.

Very young children respond with delight to the rhyme and rhythm of nursery rhymes, and they can move easily from Mother Goose to poems that have similar qualities. Children enjoy action, humor, nonsense, a narrative element, and what Walter de la Mare calls the "tune and runningness" of poetry's melodic quality. They are pleased by repetition, cumulation, and alliteration. As they become able to read by themselves, they may enjoy doggerel, which has many of the same appeals as nursery rhymes. It is incumbent on adults to provide them with poetic experiences that take them beyond the easy appeals of doggerel.

One way to do this is to read aloud, to guide their listening even after children can read in-

# POETRY

dependently. For one thing, good taste is usually a matter of exposure and experience. Children will not necessarily seek out the best, nor will they necessarily recognize it, so it is important to give them the best and thereby to let them hear the differences, to train their ears. For another thing, there are many children who find the appearance of poetry on the printed page a visual obstacle. This is perhaps even more true today than in the past, since contemporary poets use print in free patterns. Hearing poetry read well helps children get beyond that initial distraction.

Poetry is at its best as an aural experience, and the adult should select poetry for reading aloud that he or she reads well and enjoys. A droning voice or a sing-song delivery can spoil any poem. It's best to avoid complex figures of speech, arcane or obsolete words, imagery or symbolism that are complicated, to eschew poems with forced rhymes or inverted phrasing. Children enjoy poetry less if it is used to teach a lesson or as a reading exercise, or if they are required to memorize it or are quizzed about it.

On the other hand, older children may enjoy discussions about interpretations of the poet's meaning, or about the ways in which poets choose and use words to accentuate a mood or establish pace, but such discussions should not be forced and they should never be allowed to degenerate into an interrogation. Some poets have a message to convey and the subjects of their poems may lend themselves to discussion, but the primary appeal of poetry is emotional rather than intellectual; to dissect a poem may very well result in undermining this appeal.

What is this appeal? What is it that constitutes the special pleasure of the poem? It is in part the precision with which poets select words, choosing an unexpected adjective, like Robert Frost's "glassed-in" children watching a winter owl at sunset, or the imagery that stimulates our senses, like Carl Sandburg's picture of a slippery active baby playing in the bathtub: a "fish-child." It is in part the pattern of the language, the way the words are put together, whether the poem is in bound verse, pleasing in its metric form, or free verse that flows. Some of the appeal is in the melodic line, some—if rhyme is used—in the ingenious and natural flow of the rhyme. But more than that pleases us, for those aspects are the craft of the poet, the polished tools of poetic art. What reaches the reader or listener most deeply is the poet's insight, the poet's ability to capture the quintessence of a mood, an emotion, a scene. It is the ability to define these if they are unfamiliar to the reader, or to redefine them if they are familiar, in such a way that we see the scene or grasp the concept more clearly or more deeply than ever before.

In choosing poetry to read to children, one should look for these qualities. The poem should open new vistas or give new depth or meaning to the familiar; it should be melodic, the rhythm and language should fit the subject, and the diction should be distinguished—or at least distinctive—with a rich use of language whether the poem is serious or whether it is as blithe and crisp as David McCord's "The Pickety Fence."

Poetry is, said Robert Frost, "a stay against confusion." One may recall with pleasure a beloved folktale or a favorite novel, but—save for storytellers who have memorized some tales— it is only poems that can be remembered in full, remembered exactly as the poet wrote them. This pleasure, Robert Scholes wrote, is in a sense a game, a game that "takes two—a writer and a reader—to play it. If the reader is reluctant, it will not work."

This sharing by the reader, this feeling of participation rather than reluctance, is not restricted to poetry; there is lyric prose that can give the same satisfaction, but it exists in no other genre to the same extent. Perhaps this is in some measure the reason for the remarkable upsurge of the writing of poetry by children and young people in recent years.

Children are enthralled by the discovery that they can capture the essence of a mood, that they can play with words until they find exactly the right one, that their poetry can be a vehicle for expressing love or fear, joy or anger. Some of their poetry explores the beauty of the world around them; much of their writing is an expression of protest against its injustice.

Writing is one way to learn appreciation of the power of language. It can, like hearing poetry read aloud, sharpen our sensitivity to style. These are worthy goals, but they are not the primary goals of reading poetry to children. The literature of the English-speaking peoples is a rich heritage that adults can share with children, and its poetry is an abiding joy. To bring children this gift is to enable them to own a portion of that heritage for all of their lives.

## FATHER
*Frances Frost*

My father's face is brown with sun,
His body is tall and limber.
His hands are gentle with beast or child
And strong as hardwood timber.

My father's eyes are the colors of sky,
Clear blue or gray as rain:
They change with the swinging change of days
While he watches the weather vane.

That galleon, golden upon our barn,
Veers with the world's four winds.
My father, his eyes on the vane, knows when
To fill our barley bins,

To stack our wood and pile our mows
With redtop and sweet tossed clover.
He captains our farm that rides the winds,
A keen-eyed brown earth-lover.

# PEOPLE

*Christina Georgina Rossetti*

Mother shake the cherry-tree,
  Susan catch a cherry;
Oh how funny that will be,
  Let's be merry!

One for brother, one for sister,
  Two for mother more,
Six for father, hot and tired,
  Knocking at the door.

## ANDRE
*Gwendolyn Brooks*

I had a dream last night. I dreamed
I had to pick a Mother out.
I had to choose a Father too.
At first, I wondered what to do,
There were so many there, it seemed,
Short and tall and thin and stout.

But just before I sprang awake,
I knew what parents I would take.

And *this* surprised and made me glad:
They were the ones I always had!

## SO RUN ALONG AND PLAY
*David McCord*

You might think I was in the way.
*So run along*—along with what?
There isn't much that I have got
To run along with or beside.
The door, of course, is open wide;
The day, of course, is clear and fine;
The time right now, I guess, is mine.

But what is there to run to?
It wouldn't be much fun to
Run along—well, just to run.
O.K. for two or three; I'm *one*,
I'm all alone. I guess I'll walk
Along. I'll stop somewhere and talk;
Perhaps I'll think where I can walk to,
Because that's where there's what I'll talk to.
I'll walk along, but I won't play;
I won't play I am playing. Way
Beyond the third house one block back's
Another house with funny cracks
Across the paint. It seems to me
That's where some painter ought to be.

He should have been there years ago;
Maybe they don't like painters, though.
Or maybe he has my complaint:
They said "So run along and paint."

Well, if he ran along like me,
I'll bet I may know where he'll be.

## LITTLE
*Dorothy Aldis*

I am the sister of him
And he is my brother.
He is too little for us
To talk to each other.

So every morning I show him
My doll and my book;
But every morning he still is
Too little to look.

## GIRLS' NAMES
*Eleanor Farjeon*

What lovely names for girls there are!
There's Stella like the Evening Star,
And Sylvia like a rustling tree,
And Lola like a melody,
And Flora like a flowery morn,
And Sheila like a field of corn,
And Melusina like the moan
Of water. And there's Joan, like Joan.

## BOYS' NAMES
*Eleanor Farjeon*

What splendid names for boys there are!
There's Carol like a rolling car,
And Martin like a flying bird,
And Adam like the Lord's First Word,
And Raymond like the Harvest Moon,
And Peter like a piper's tune,
And Alan like the flowing on
Of water. And there's John, like John.

## THE PEOPLE

*Elizabeth Madox Roberts*

The ants are walking under the ground,
And the pigeons are flying over the steeple,
And in between are the people.

## PORTRAIT BY A NEIGHBOR

*Edna St. Vincent Millay*

Before she has her floor swept
    Or her dishes done,
Any day you'll find her
    A-sunning in the sun!

It's long after midnight
    Her key's in the lock,
And you never see her chimney smoke
    Till past ten o'clock!

She digs in her garden
    With a shovel and a spoon,
She weeds her lazy lettuce
    By the light of the moon.

She walks up the walk
    Like a woman in a dream,
She forgets she borrowed butter
    And pays you back cream!

Her lawn looks like a meadow,
    And if she mows the place
She leaves the clover standing
    And the Queen Anne's lace!

## AUNT SUE'S STORIES

*Langston Hughes*

Aunt Sue has a head full of stories.
Aunt Sue has a whole heart full of stories.
Summer nights on the front porch
Aunt Sue cuddles a brown-faced child to her
    bosom
And tells him stories.

Black slaves
Working in the hot sun,
And black slaves
Walking in the dewy night,
And black slaves
Singing sorrow songs on the banks of a mighty
    river
Mingle themselves softly
In the flow of old Aunt Sue's voice,
Mingle themselves softly
In the dark shadows that cross and recross
Aunt Sue's stories.

And the dark-faced child, listening,
Knows that Aunt Sue's stories are real stories.
He knows that Aunt Sue never got her stories
Out of any book at all,
But that they came
Right out of her own life.

The dark-faced child is quiet
Of a summer night
Listening to Aunt Sue's stories.

## MISS NORMA JEAN PUGH, FIRST GRADE TEACHER

*Mary O'Neill*

        Full of oatmeal
        And gluggy with milk
        On a morning in springtime
        Soft as silk
        When legs feel slow
        And bumble bees buzz
        And your nose tickles from
        Dandelion fuzz
        And you long to
        Break a few
        Cobwebs stuck with
        Diamond dew
        Stretched right out
        In front of you—
        When all you want
        To do is *feel*

Until it's time for
Another meal,
Or sit right down
In the cool
Green grass
And watch the
Caterpillars pass . . .
Who cares if
Two and two
Are four or five
Or red or blue?
Who cares whether
Six or seven
Come before or after
Ten or eleven?
Who cares if
C-A-T
Spells cat or rat
Or tit or tat
Or ball or bat?
Well, I do
But I didn't
Used to—
Until MISS NORMA JEAN PUGH!
She's terribly old
As people go
Twenty-one-or-five-or-six
Or so
But she makes a person want to
KNOW!

## CLASS ASSIGNMENT
*Marci Ridlon*

Man, I don't wanna write no poem.
I mean, like, what's ta say?
Should I say, maybe, that Mrs. Perez
always smells of garlic
or that her kids
run up and down the halls
screamin'
till I think I'm gonna find me

the elevator shaft
and jump right in?
Ha, ha. How about this?
"The house is dirty,
the halls is dirty,
the street is dirty,
I'm dirty."
Pretty good, huh?
Or maybe you'd like me to
write down that
I'm getting pretty sick of
talkin' to you
and that I just don't feel
like writin' down nothing.
I ain't got nothing pretty ta say.
A poem's gotta be pretty, ain't it?

## ANCIENT HISTORY
*Arthur Guiterman*

I hope the old Romans
Had painful abdomens.

I hope that the Greeks
Had toothache for weeks.

I hope the Egyptians
Had chronic conniptions.

I hope that the Arabs
Were bitten by scarabs.

I hope that the Vandals
Had thorns in their sandals.

I hope that the Persians
Had gout in all versions.

I hope that the Medes
Were kicked by their steeds.

They started the fuss
And left it to us!

## FORTUNE

*Lawrence Ferlinghetti*

Fortune
        has its cookies to give out

which is a good thing

        since it's been a long time since

        that summer in Brooklyn
when they closed off the street
        one  hot  day
        and the

### FIREMEN

                        turned on their hoses
and all the kids ran out in it

        in the middle of the street

and there were

        maybe a couple dozen of us

                        out there
with the water squirting up
                to the

                sky

                        and all over
                                us
there was maybe only six of us
                        kids altogether
running around in our
                        barefeet and birthday
        suits
        and I remember Molly but then
the firemen stopped squirting their hoses
        all of a sudden and went
                back in
                their firehouse

and
        started playing pinochle again
                just as if nothing
                had ever
                        happened
while I remember Molly
                looked at me and

        ran in

because I guess really we were the only ones there

## THE SHEPHERD

*William Blake*

How sweet is the shepherd's sweet lot!
From the morn to the evening he strays;
He shall follow his sheep all the day,
And  his  tongue  shall  be  filléd  with  praise.


For he hears the lambs' innocent call,
And he hears the ewes' tender reply;
He is watchful while they are in peace,
For they know when their shepherd is nigh.

## MISS T.

*Walter de la Mare*

        It's a very odd thing—
            As odd as can be—
        That whatever Miss T. eats
            Turns into Miss T.;
        Porridge and apples,
            Mince, muffins and mutton,
        Jam, junket, jumbles—
            Not a rap, not a button
        It matters; the moment
            They're out of her plate,
        Though shared by Miss Butcher
            And sour Mr. Bate;
        Tiny and cheerful,
            And neat as can be,
        Whatever Miss T. eats
            Turns into Miss T.

## TWO FRIENDS

*David Ignatow*

I have something to tell you.
I'm listening.
I'm dying.
I'm sorry to hear.
I'm growing old.
It's terrible.
It is, I thought you should know.
Of course and I'm sorry. Keep in touch.
I will and you too.
And let me know what's new.
Certainly, though it can't be much.
And stay well.
And you too.
And go slow.
And you too.

## MOTHER TO SON

*Langston Hughes*

Well, son, I'll tell you:
Life for me ain't been no crystal stair.
It's had tacks in it,
And splinters,
And boards torn up,
And places with no carpet on the floor—
Bare.
But all the time
I'se been a-climbin' on,
And reachin' landin's,
And turnin' corners,
And sometimes goin' in the dark
Where there ain't been no light.
So, boy, don't you turn back.
Don't you set down on the steps
'Cause you finds it kinder hard.
Don't you fall now—
For I'se still goin', honey,
I'se still climbin',
And life for me ain't been no crystal stair.

## OLD JAKE SUTTER

*Kaye Starbird*

Old Jake Sutter has a cabin-hut,
Beneath some willows where the river bends.
His beard is longer than I don't know what,
And woodland creatures are his only friends.
He lives on butternuts and fish and such.
His clothes are faded and are mostly tatters;
But old Jake Sutter doesn't worry much.
He's fed and covered, which is all that matters.

Old Jake Sutter has an outdoor chair,
(A car-seat borrowed from the village dump)
And summer evenings he relaxes there
And talks to sparrows on a nearby stump,
While coons and rabbits or a passing skunk
Serenely amble through his open door
To sniff the stuffing on his sagging bunk
Or knock his frying-pan upon the floor.

## LULLABY

*Thule Eskimo*

It is my big baby
That I feel in my hood
Oh how heavy he is!
*Ya ya! Ya ya!*

When I turn
He smiles at me, my little one,
Well hidden in my hood,
Oh how heavy he is!
*Ya ya! Ya ya!*

How sweet he is when he smiles
With two teeth like a little walrus.
Ah, I like my little one to be heavy
And my hood to be full.

## FRIDAY MOM IS HOME PAYDAY

*Lucille Clifton*

Swishing one finger
in the foam
of Mama's glass
when she gets home
is a very
favorite thing to do.
Mama says
foam is a comfort,
Everett Anderson
says so too.

## WE REAL COOL

*Gwendolyn Brooks*

THE POOL PLAYERS.
SEVEN AT THE GOLDEN SHOVEL.

We real cool. We
Left school. We

Lurk late. We
Strike straight. We

Sing sin. We
Thin gin. We

Jazz June. We
Die soon.

## MR. BEECHER

*N. M. Bodecker*

Homer Beecher
(Spanish teacher)
taught his students
in a bleacher.
In the snows
that blow
and vanish,
in the rains
he taught them
Spanish,
till the students
went away
(went to proms
and far away).
When they told him:
"Mister Beecher,
durable
but frozen teacher,
not a soul is left.
Just look!"
Teacher Beecher
closed his book.

## TO HIS COUSIN

*Doris Orgel*

One has to take what Nature gives—
One cannot choose one's relatives—
But do not think, son of my aunt,
That I can stand you, 'cause I can't!

## TAUGHT ME PURPLE

*Evelyn Tooley Hunt*

My mother taught me purple
Although she never wore it.
Wash-grey was her circle,
The tenement her orbit.

My mother taught me golden
    And held me up to see it,
Above the broken molding,
    Beyond the filthy street.

My mother reached for beauty
    And for its lack she died,
Who knew so much of duty
    She could not teach me pride.

### POEM FOR FLORA
*Nikki Giovanni*

when she was little
and colored and ugly with short
straightened hair
and a very pretty smile
she went to sunday school to hear
'bout nebuchadnezzar the king
of the jews

and she would listen

shadrach, meshach and abednego in the fire

and she would learn

how god was neither north
nor south east or west
with no color but all
she remembered was that
Sheba was Black and comely

and she would think

i want to be
like that


### THE RAGGLE, TAGGLE GYPSIES
*(Old Folk Song)*

There were three gypsies a-come to my door,
    And downstairs ran this lady, O.

One sang high and another sang low,
    And the other sang "Bonnie, Bonnie Bis-
    kay, O."

Then she pulled off her silken gown,
    And put on hose of leather, O.
With the ragged, ragged rags about her door
    She's off with the Raggle, Taggle Gypsies, O.

'Twas late last night when my lord came home,
    Inquiring for his lady, O.
The servants said on every hand,
    "She's gone with the Raggle, Taggle Gyp-
    sies, O."

"Oh, saddle for me my milk-white steed,
    Oh, saddle for me my pony, O,
That I may ride and seek my bride
    Who's gone with the Raggle, Taggle Gyp-
    sies, O."

Oh, he rode high and he rode low,
    He rode through woods and copses, O,
Until he came to an open field,
    And there he espied his lady, O.

"What makes you leave your house and lands?
    What makes you leave your money, O?
What makes you leave your new-wedded lord
    To go with the Raggle, Taggle Gypsies, O?"

"What care I for my house and lands?
    What care I for my money, O?
What care I for my new-wedded lord?
    I'm off with the Raggle, Taggle Gypsies, O."

"Last night you slept on a goose-feather bed,
    With the sheet turned down so bravely, O.
Tonight you will sleep in the cold, open field,
    Along with the Raggle, Taggle Gypsies, O."

"What care I for your goose-feather bed,
    With the sheet turned down so bravely, O?
For tonight I shall sleep in a cold, open field,
    Along with the Raggle, Taggle Gypsies, O."

"The Raggle, Taggle Gypsies." *Why did the lady run away? Could she have been a gypsy herself? This is exciting to speak with one group of voices for the narrative, another group for the frightened servants, and single voices for the lord and the lady.*

## SIR PATRICK SPENCE

*(Ballad)*

The king sits in Dumferling town,
 Drinking the blood-red wine:
"O where will I get a good sailor,
 To sail this ship of mine?"

Up and spoke an elderly knight,
 (Sat at the king's right knee),
"Sir Patrick Spence is the best sailor
 That sails upon the sea."

The king has written a broad letter,
 And signed it with his hand,
And sent it to Sir Patrick Spence,
 Was walking on the sand.

The first line that Sir Patrick read,
 A loud laugh laughed he;
The next line that Sir Patrick read,
 A tear blinded his eye.

"O who is this has done this deed,
 This ill deed done to me,
To send me out this time of year,
 To sail upon the sea!

"Make haste, make haste, my merry men all,
 Our good ship sails the morn:"
"O say not so, my master dear,
 For I fear a deadly storm.

"Late late yestereven I saw the new moon
 With the old moon in her arm,
And I fear, I fear, my master dear,
 That we will come to harm."

O our Scotch nobles were right loathe
 To wet their cork-heeled shoes;
But long after the play was played
 Their hats floated into view.

O long, long may their ladies sit,
 With their fans within their hand,
Or ever they see Sir Patrick Spence
 Come sailing to the land.

O long, long may their ladies stand,
 With their gold combs in their hair,
Waiting for their own dear lords,
 For they'll see them never more.

Half o'er, half o'er to Aberdour,
 It's fifty fathoms deep,
And there lies good Sir Patrick Spence,
 With the Scotch lords at his feet.

*"Sir Patrick Spence." This is a close translation of old English words into modern. Even so, like all the traditional ballads, it leaves much unsaid. It is possible that this ballad refers to the shipwreck and drowning of a number of Scottish nobles who in 1281 were returning from accompanying Margarét, daughter of the king of Scotland, to Norway, where she was to be married to King Eric.*

## A SONG OF SHERWOOD

*Alfred Noyes*

Sherwood in the twilight, is Robin Hood awake?
Grey and ghostly shadows are gliding through
 the brake,
Shadows of the dappled deer, dreaming of the
 morn,
Dreaming of a shadowy man that winds a shadowy horn.

Robin Hood is here again: all his merry thieves
Hear a ghostly bugle-note shivering through the
 leaves,
Calling as he used to call, faint and far away,
In Sherwood, in Sherwood, about the break of
 day.

Merry, merry England has kissed the lips of
    June:
All the wings of fairyland were here beneath the
    moon,
Like a flight of rose-leaves fluttering in a mist
Of opal and ruby and pearl and amethyst.

Merry, merry England is waking as of old,
With eyes of blither hazel and hair of brighter
    gold:
For Robin Hood is here again beneath the burst-
    ing spray
In Sherwood, in Sherwood, about the break of
    day.

Love is in the greenwood building him a house
Of wild rose and hawthorn and honeysuckle
    boughs:
Love is in the greenwood, dawn is in the skies,
And Marian is waiting with a glory in her eyes.

Hark! The dazzled laverock climbs the golden
    steep!
Marian is waiting: is Robin Hood asleep?
Round the fairy grass-rings frolic elf and fay,
In Sherwood, in Sherwood, about the break of
    day.

Oberon, Oberon, rake away the gold,
Rake away the red leaves, roll away the mould,
Rake away the gold leaves, roll away the red,
And wake Will Scarlett from his leafy forest bed.

Friar Tuck and Little John are riding down to-
    gether
With quarter-staff and drinking-can and grey
    goose-feather.
The dead are coming back again, the years are
    rolled away
In Sherwood, in Sherwood, about the break of
    day.

Softly over Sherwood the south wind blows.
All the heart of England hid in every rose

Hears across the greenwood the sunny whisper
    leap,
Sherwood in the red dawn, is Robin Hood
    asleep?

Hark, the voice of England wakes him as of old
And, shattering the silence with a cry of brighter
    gold,

Bugles in the greenwood echo from the steep,
*Sherwood in the red dawn, is Robin Hood
    asleep?*

Where the deer are gliding down the shadowy
    glen
All across the glades of fern he calls his merry
    men—
Doublets of the Lincoln green glancing through
    the May
In Sherwood, in Sherwood, about the break of
    day—

Calls them and they answer: from aisles of oak
    and ash
Rings the *Follow! Follow!* and the boughs begin
    to crash,
The ferns begin to flutter and the flowers begin
    to fly,
And through the crimson dawning the robber
    band goes by.

*Robin! Robin! Robin!* All his merry thieves
Answer as the bugle-note shivers through the
    leaves,
Calling as he used to call, faint and far away,
In Sherwood, in Sherwood, about the break of
    day.

# THE HIGHWAYMAN

*Alfred Noyes*

The wind was a torrent of darkness among the
    gusty trees.
The moon was a ghostly galleon tossed upon
    cloudy seas.
The road was a ribbon of moonlight over the
    purple moor,
And the highwayman came riding—
    Riding—riding—
The highwayman came riding, up to the old inn-
    door.

He'd a French cocked-hat on his forehead, a bunch
    of lace at his chin,
A coat of the claret velvet, and breeches of brown
    doe-skin.
They fitted with never a wrinkle. His boots were
    up to the thigh.
And he rode with a jewelled twinkle,
    His pistol butts a-twinkle,
His rapier hilt a-twinkle, under the jewelled sky.

Over the cobbles he clattered and clashed in the
    dark inn-yard.
He tapped with his whip on the shutters, but all
    was locked and barred.
He whistled a tune to the window, and who should
    be waiting there
But the landlord's black-eyed daughter,
    Bess, the landlord's daughter,
Plaiting a dark red love-knot into her long black
    hair.

And dark in the dark old inn-yard a stable-wicket
    creaked
Where Tim the ostler listened. His face was white
    and peaked.
His eyes were hollows of madness, his hair like
    mouldy hay,
But he loved the landlord's daughter,
    The landlord's red-lipped daughter.
Dumb as a dog he listened, and he heard the
    robber say—

"One kiss, my bonny sweetheart, I'm after a prize
    to-night,
But I shall be back with the yellow gold before
    the morning light;
Yet, if they press me sharply, and harry me
    through the day,
Then look for me by moonlight,
    Watch for me by moonlight,
I'll come to thee by moonlight, though hell
    should bar the way."

He rose upright in the stirrups. He scarce could
    reach her hand,
But she loosened her hair in the casement. His
    face burnt like a brand
As the black cascade of perfume came tumbling
    over his breast;
And he kissed its waves in the moonlight,
    (O, sweet black waves in the moonlight!)
Then he tugged at his rein in the moonlight, and
    galloped away to the west.

He did not come in the dawning. He did not
    come at noon;
And out of the tawny sunset, before the rise of
    the moon,
When the road was a gypsy's ribbon, looping
    the purple moor,
A red-coat troop came marching—
    Marching—marching—
King George's men came marching, up to the old
    inn-door.

They said no word to the landlord. They drank
    his ale instead.
But they gagged his daughter, and bound her, to
    the foot of her narrow bed.
Two of them knelt at her casement, with muskets
    at their side!
There was death at every window;
    And hell at one dark window;
For Bess could see, through her casement, the
    road that *he* would ride.

They had tied her up to attention, with many a
    sniggering jest.
They had bound a musket beside her, with the
    muzzle beneath her breast!

"Now, keep good watch!" and they kissed her.
  She heard the doomed man say—
*Look for me by moonlight;*
  *Watch for me by moonlight;*
*I'll come to thee by moonlight, though hell should*
  *bar the way!*

She twisted her hands behind her; but all the
  knots held good!
She writhed her hands till her fingers were wet
  with sweat or blood!
They stretched and strained in the darkness, and
  the hours crawled by like years,
Till, now, on the stroke of midnight,
  Cold, on the stroke of midnight,
The tip of one finger touched it! The trigger at
  least was hers!

The tip of one finger touched it. She strove no
  more for the rest.
Up, she stood up to attention, with the muzzle
  beneath her breast.
She would not risk their hearing; she would not
  strive again;
For the road lay bare in the moonlight;
  Blank and bare in the moonlight;
And the blood of her veins, in the moonlight,
  throbbed to her love's refrain.

*Tlot-tlot; tlot-tlot!* Had they heard it? The horse-
  hoofs ringing clear;
*Tlot-tlot, tlot-tlot,* in the distance? Were they
  deaf that they did not hear?
Down the ribbon of moonlight, over the brow
  of the hill,
The highwayman came riding—
  Riding—riding—
The red-coats looked to their priming! She stood
  up, straight and still.

*Tlot-tlot,* in the frosty silence! *Tlot-tlot,* in the
  echoing night!
Nearer he came and nearer. Her face was like
  a light.
Her eyes grew wide for a moment; she drew one
  last deep breath,

Then her finger moved in the moonlight,
  Her musket shattered the moonlight,
Shattered her breast in the moonlight and warned
  him—with her death.

He turned. He spurred to the west; he did not
  know who stood
Bowed, with her head o'er the musket, drenched
  with her own blood!
Not till the dawn he heard it, and his face grew
  grey to hear
How Bess, the landlord's daughter,
  The landlord's black-eyed daughter,
Had watched for her love in the moonlight, and
  died in the darkness there.

Back, he spurred like a madman, shouting a
  curse to the sky,
With the white road smoking behind him and
  his rapier brandished high.
Blood-red were his spurs in the golden noon;
  wine-red was his velvet coat;
When they shot him down on the highway,
  Down like a dog on the highway,
And he lay in his blood on the highway, with a
  bunch of lace at his throat.

*And still of a winter's night, they say, when the*
  *wind is in the trees,*
*When the moon is a ghostly galleon tossed upon*
  *cloudy seas,*
*When the road is a ribbon of moonlight over the*
  *purple moor,*
*A highwayman comes riding—*
  *Riding—riding—*
*A highwayman comes riding, up to the old*
  *inn-door.*

*Over the cobbles he clatters and clangs in the*
  *dark inn-yard.*
*He taps with his whip on the shutters, but all is*
  *locked and barred.*
*He whistles a tune to the window, and who*
  *should be waiting there*
*But the landlord's black-eyed daughter,*
  *Bess, the landlord's daughter,*
*Plaiting a dark red love-knot into her long black*
  *hair.*

## THE PIED PIPER OF HAMELIN

*Robert Browning*

Hamelin Town's in Brunswick
By famous Hanover city;
 The river Weser, deep and wide,
 Washes its wall on the southern side;
 A pleasanter spot you never spied;
But, when begins my ditty,
 Almost five hundred years ago,
 To see the townsfolk suffer so
  From vermin was a pity.

          Rats!

They fought the dogs, and killed the cats,
 And bit the babies in the cradles,
And ate the cheeses out of the vats,
 And licked the soup from the cook's own
  ladles,
Split open the kegs of salted sprats,
Made nests inside men's Sunday hats,
And even spoiled the women's chats,
 By drowning their speaking
 With shrieking and squeaking
In fifty different sharps and flats.

 At last the people in a body
 To the Town Hall came flocking:
 " 'Tis clear," cried they, "our Mayor's a noddy;
 And as for our Corporation—shocking
 To think that we buy gowns lined with ermine
 For dolts that can't or won't determine
 What's best to rid us of our vermin!
 You hope, because you're old and obese,
 To find in the furry civic robe ease?
 Rouse up, sirs! Give your brain a racking
 To find the remedy we're lacking,
 Or, sure as fate, we'll send you packing!"
At this the Mayor and Corporation
Quaked with a mighty consternation.

An hour they sat in council,
 At length the Mayor broke silence:
"For a guilder I'd my ermine gown sell;
 I wish I were a mile hence!
It's easy to bid one rack one's brain—
I'm sure my poor head aches again
I've scratched it so, and all in vain,
 Oh for a trap, a trap, a trap!"
Just as he said this, what should hap
At the chamber door but a gentle tap?
 "Bless us," cried the Mayor, "what's that?"
(With the Corporation as he sat,
Looking little though wondrous fat;
Nor brighter was his eye, nor moister,
Than a too-long-opened oyster,
Save when at noon his paunch grew mutinous
For a plate of turtle green and glutinous),
"Only a scraping of shoes on the mat?
Anything like the sound of a rat
Makes my heart go pit-a-pat!"

"Come in!"—the Mayor cried, looking bigger:
And in did come the strangest figure.
His queer long coat from heel to head
Was half of yellow and half of red;
And he himself was tall and thin,
With sharp blue eyes, each like a pin,
And light loose hair, yet swarthy skin,
No tuft on cheek nor beard on chin,
But lips where smiles went out and in—
There was no guessing his kith and kin!
And nobody could enough admire
The tall man and his quaint attire.
Quoth one: "It's as my great grandsire,
Starting up at the Trump of Doom's tone,
Had walked this way from his painted tomb-
 stone."

He advanced to the council-table:
And, "Please, your honours," said he, "I'm able,

By means of a secret charm, to draw
All creatures living beneath the sun,
That creep, or swim, or fly, or run,
After me so as you never saw!
And I chiefly use my charm
On creatures that do people harm,
The mole, and toad, and newt, and viper;
And people call me the Pied Piper."
(And here they noticed round his neck
  A scarf of red and yellow stripe,
To match with his coat of the selfsame cheque;
  And at the scarf's end hung a pipe;
And his fingers, they noticed, were ever straying
As if impatient to be playing
Upon this pipe, as low it dangled
Over his vesture so old-fangled.)
  "Yet," said he, "poor piper as I am,
  In Tartary I freed the Cham,
  Last June, from his huge swarms of gnats;
  I eased in Asia the Nizam
  Of a monstrous brood of vampire bats:
  And, as for what your brain bewilders,
  If I can rid your town of rats
  Will you give me a thousand guilders?"
  "One? fifty thousand!"—was the exclamation
Of the astonished Mayor and Corporation.

Into the street the Piper stept,
  Smiling first a little smile,
As if he knew what magic slept
  In his quiet pipe the while;
Then, like a musical adept,
To blow the pipe his lips he wrinkled,
And green and blue his sharp eyes twinkled
Like a candle-flame where salt is sprinkled;
And ere three shrill notes the pipe uttered,
You heard as if an army muttered;
And the muttering grew to a grumbling;
And the grumbling grew to a mighty rum-
  bling;
And out of the house the rats came tumbling.
Great rats, small rats, lean rats, brawny rats,
Brown rats, black rats, gray rats, tawny rats,
Grave old plodders, gay young friskers,
  Fathers, mothers, uncles, cousins,
Cocking tails and pricking whiskers,
  Families by tens and dozens,
Brothers, sisters, husbands, wives—
Followed the Piper for their lives.
From street to street he piped advancing,

And step by step they followed dancing,
Until they came to the river Weser
Wherein all plunged and perished
—Save one, who, stout as Julius Caesar,
Swam across and lived to carry
(As he the manuscript he cherished)
To Rat-land home his commentary,
Which was, "At the first shrill notes of the
  pipe,
I heard a sound as of scraping tripe,
And putting apples, wondrous ripe,
Into a cider press's gripe;
And a moving away of pickle-tub boards,
And a drawing the corks of train-oil flasks,
And a breaking the hoops of butter casks;
And it seemed as if a voice
(Sweeter far than by harp or by psaltery
Is breathed) called out, Oh, rats! rejoice!
The world is grown to one vast drysaltery!
To munch on, crunch on, take your nuncheon,
Breakfast, supper, dinner, luncheon!
And just as a bulky sugar puncheon,
All ready staved, like a great sun shone
Glorious scarce an inch before me,
Just as methought it said, come, bore me!
—I found the Weser rolling o'er me."

You should have heard the Hamelin people
Ringing the bells till they rocked the steeple.
  "Go," cried the Mayor, "and get long poles!
  Poke out the nests and block up the holes!
  Consult with carpenters and builders,
  And leave in our town not even a trace
  Of the rats!"—when suddenly up the face
  Of the Piper perked in the market-place,
With a, "First, if you please, my thousand
  guilders!"

A thousand guilders! The Mayor looked blue;
So did the Corporation too.
For council dinners made rare havoc
With Claret, Moselle, Vin-de-Grave, Hock;
And half the money would replenish
Their cellar's biggest butt with Rhenish.
To pay this sum to a wandering fellow
With a gipsy coat of red and yellow!
  "Beside," quoth the Mayor, with a knowing
  wink,
  "Our business was done at the river's brink;

We saw with our eyes the vermin sink,
And what's dead can't come to life, I think.
So, friend, we're not the folks to shrink
From the duty of giving you something to
    drink,
And a matter of money to put in your poke,
But, as for the guilders, what we spoke
Of them, as you very well know, was in joke.
Besides, our losses have made us thrifty;
A thousand guilders! Come, take fifty!"

The piper's face fell, and he cried,
"No trifling! I can't wait, beside!
I've promised to visit by dinnertime
Bagdad, and accepted the prime
Of the Head Cook's pottage, all he's rich in,
For having left the Caliph's kitchen,
Of a nest of scorpions no survivor—
With him I proved no bargain-driver,
With you, don't think I'll bate a stiver!
And folks who put me in a passion
May find me pipe to another fashion."

"How?" cried the Mayor, "d'ye think I'll brook
Being worse treated than a Cook?
Insulted by a lazy ribald
With idle pipe and vesture piebald?
You threaten us, fellow? Do your worst,
Blow your pipe there till you burst!"

Once more he stept into the street;
    And to his lips again
Laid his long pipe of smooth straight cane;
    And ere he blew three notes (such sweet
Soft notes as yet musicians cunning
    Never gave the enraptured air),
There was a rustling, that seemed like a bustling
Of merry crowds justling, at pitching and hus-
    tling,
Small feet were pattering, wooden shoes clatter-
    ing,
Little hands clapping, and little tongues chatter-
    ing,
And, like fowls in a farmyard when barley is
    scattering,
Out came the children running.
All the little boys and girls,
With rosy cheeks and flaxen curls,
And sparkling eyes and teeth like pearls,

Tripping and skipping, ran merrily after
The wonderful music with shouting and laugh-
    ter.

The Mayor was dumb, and the Council stood
As if they were changed into blocks of wood,
Unable to move a step, or cry
To the children merrily skipping by—
And could only follow with the eye
That joyous crowd at the Piper's back.
But how the Mayor was on the rack,
And the wretched Council's bosoms beat,
As the piper turned from the High Street
To where the Weser rolled its waters
Right in the way of their sons and daughters!
However, he turned from South to West,
And to Koppelberg Hill his steps addressed,
And after him the children pressed;
Great was the joy in every breast.
    "He never can cross that mighty top!
    He's forced to let the piping drop
    And we shall see our children stop!"
When lo! As they reached the mountain's side,
A wondrous portal opened wide,
As if a cavern was suddenly hollowed;
And the Piper advanced and the children fol-
    lowed,
And when all were in to the very last,
The door in the mountain-side shut fast.
Did I say all? No! one was lame,
And could not dance the whole of the way;
And in after years, if you would blame
His sadness, he was used to say:
    "It's dull in our town since my playmates left;
    I can't forget that I'm bereft
    Of all the pleasant sights they see,
    Which the Piper also promised me;
    For he led us, he said, to a joyous land,
    Joining the town and just at hand,
Where waters gushed and fruit trees grew,
And flowers put forth a fairer hue,
And everything was strange and new.
The sparrows were brighter than peacocks here,
And their dogs outran our fallow deer,
And honey-bees had lost their stings;
And horses were born with eagle's wings;
And just as I became assured
My lame foot would be speedily cured,
The music stopped, and I stood still,

And found myself outside the Hill,
Left alone against my will,
To go now limping as before,
And never hear of that country more!"

Alas, alas for Hamelin!
  There came into many a burger's pate
  A text which says, that Heaven's Gate
Opes to the Rich at as easy rate
As the needle's eye takes a camel in!
The Mayor sent East, West, North and South,
To offer the Piper by word of mouth,
  Wherever it was men's lot to find him,
Silver and gold to his heart's content,
If he'd only return the way he went,
  And bring the children all behind him.
But when they saw 'twas a lost endeavour,
And Piper and dancers were gone forever
They made a decree that lawyers never
  Should think their records dated duly
If, after the day of the month and year,
These words did not as well appear,
  "And so long after what happened here
  On the twenty-second of July,
  Thirteen hundred and seventy-six:"
And the better in memory to fix
The place of the Children's last retreat,
They called it, the Pied Piper's street—
Where anyone playing on pipe or tabor,
Was sure for the future to lose his labour.
Nor suffered they hostelry or tavern
To shock with mirth a street so solemn;
But opposite the place of the cavern
  They wrote the story on a column,
And on the great church window painted
The same, to make the world acquainted
How their children were stolen away;
And there it stands to this very day.
And I must not omit to say
That in Transylvania there's a tribe
Of alien people that ascribe
The outlandish ways and dress,
On which their neighbours lay such stress,
To their fathers and mothers having risen
Out of some subterraneous prison,
Into which they were trepanned
Long time ago in a mighty band
Out of Hamelin town in Brunswick land,
But how or why they don't understand.

## "HOW THEY BROUGHT THE GOOD NEWS FROM GHENT TO AIX"

*Robert Browning*

I sprang to the stirrup, and Joris, and he;
I galloped, Dirck galloped, we galloped all three;
"Good speed!" cried the watch, as the gatebolts
    undrew;
"Speed!" echoed the wall to us galloping
    through;
Behind shut the postern, the lights sank to rest,
And into the midnight we galloped abreast.

Not a word to each other; we kept the great pace
Neck by neck, stride by stride, never changing
    our place;
I turned in my saddle and made its girths tight,
Then shortened each stirrup, and set the pique
    right,
Rebuckled the cheek-strap, chained slacker the
    bit,
Nor galloped less steadily Roland a whit.

'Twas moonset at starting; but while we drew
    near
Lokeren, the cocks crew and twilight dawned
    clear;
At Boom, a great yellow star came out to see;
At Düffeld, 'twas morning as plain as could be;
And from Mecheln church-steeple we heard the
    half-chime,
So Joris broke silence with, "Yet there is time!"

At Aershot, up leaped of a sudden the sun,
And against him the cattle stood black every one,
To stare through the mist at us galloping past,
And I saw my stout galloper Roland at last,
With resolute shoulders, each butting away
The haze, as some bluff river headland its spray;

And his low head and crest, just one sharp ear
    bent back
For my voice, and the other pricked out on his
    track;

And one eye's black intelligence—ever that
    glance
O'er its white edge at me, his own master,
    askance!
And the thick heavy spume-flakes which aye and
    anon
His fierce lips shook upwards in galloping on.

By Hasselt, Dirck groaned; and cried Joris, "Stay
    spur!
Your Roos galloped bravely, the fault's not in
    her,
We'll remember at Aix"—for one heard the
    quick wheeze
Of her chest, saw the stretched neck and stagger-
    ing knees,
And sunk tail, and horrible heave of the flank,
As down on her haunches she shuddered and
    sank.

So we were left galloping, Joris and I,
Past Looz and past Tongres, no cloud in the sky;
The broad sun above laughed a pitiless laugh,
'Neath our feet broke the brittle bright stubble
    like chaff;
Till over by Dalhem a dome-spire sprang white,
And "Gallop," gasped Joris, "for Aix is in sight!"

"How they'll greet us!"—and all in a moment his
    roan
Rolled neck and croup over, lay dead as a stone;
And there was my Roland to bear the whole
    weight
Of the news which alone could save Aix from her
    fate,
With his nostrils like pits full of blood to the
    brim,
And with circles of red for his eye-sockets' rim.

Then I cast loose my buffcoat, each holster let
    fall,
Shook off both my jack-boots, let go belt and all,
Stood up in the stirrup, leaned, patted his ear,
Called my Roland his pet-name, my horse with-
    out peer;
Clapped my hands, laughed and sang, any noise,
    bad or good,
Till at length into Aix Roland galloped and
    stood.

And all I remember is—friends flocking round
As I sat with his head 'twixt my knees on the
    ground;
And no voice but was praising this Roland of
    mine,
As I poured down his throat our last measure of
    wine,
Which (the burgesses voted by common consent)
Was no more than his due who brought good
    news from Ghent.

## A LADY COMES TO AN INN

*Elizabeth Coatsworth*

Three strange men came to the Inn.
One was a black man, pocked and thin,
one was brown with a silver knife,
and one brought with him a beautiful wife.

That lovely woman had hair as pale
as French champagne or finest ale,
that lovely woman was long and slim
as a young white birch or a maple limb.

Her face was like cream, her mouth was a rose,
what language she spoke nobody knows,
but sometimes she'd scream like a cockatoo
and swear wonderful oaths that nobody knew.

Her great silk skirts like a silver bell
down to her little bronze slippers fell,
and her low-cut gown showed a dove on its nest
in blue tattooing across her breast.

Nobody learned the lady's name,
nor the marvelous land from which they came,
but still they tell through the countryside
the tale of those men and that beautiful bride.

## A SONG OF GREATNESS

*Mary Austin*

When I hear the old men
Telling of heroes,
Telling of great deeds
Of ancient days,

When I hear that telling
Then I think within me
I too am one of these.

When I hear the people
Praising great ones,
Then I know that I too
Shall be esteemed,
I too when my time comes
Shall do mightily.

## OPEN RANGE

*Kathryn and Byron Jackson*

Prairie goes to the mountain,
    Mountain goes to the sky.
The sky sweeps across to the distant hills
And here, in the middle,
    Am I.

Hills crowd down to the river,
    River runs by the tree.
Tree throws its shadow on sunburnt grass

And here, in the shadow,
    Is me.

Shadows creep up the mountain,
    Mountain goes black on the sky,
The sky bursts out with a million stars
And here, by the campfire,
    Am I.

## COTTONWOOD LEAVES

*Badger Clark*

Red firelight on the Sioux tepees,
    (Oh, the camp-smoke down the wind!)
Red firelight on the cottonwood trees
That clap, clap, clap in the dry night breeze.
    (Oh, the camp-smoke down the wind!)

Red-skinned braves in the circling dance;
    (Oh, the bright sparks toward the stars!)
The moccasined feet that stamp and prance
And the brandished knife and the lifted lance.
    (Oh, the bright sparks toward the stars!)

"A Song of Greatness" from *The Children Sing in the Far West* by Mary Austin. Copyright renewed 1956 Kenneth M. Chapman and Mary C. Wheelwright. Reprinted by permission of the publisher, Houghton Mifflin Company
"Open Range." From *Cowboys and Indians* by Kathryn and Byron Jackson. © 1948 by Western Publishing Company, Inc. Reprinted by permission of the publisher
"Cottonwood Leaves" by Badger Clark from *Sky Lines and Wood Smoke* by Badger Clark. The Chronicle Shop, Custer, South Dakota, 1947. Reprinted by permission of the *Custer County Chronicle*

Eagle plumes in the swirling troop,
  (Oh, the wild flame leaping high!)
And the painted bodies ramp and stoop
To the drum's hot thump and the vaunting
    whoop.
  (Oh, the wild flame leaping high!)

Back where the darkness drops its veil
  (Oh, the sad smoke drifting low!)
The far wolves howl and the widows wail
For the graveless dead on the grim war trail.
  (Oh, the sad smoke drifting low!)

Night on the plains, and the dreams it weaves,
  (Oh, the embers black and cold!)
Where painted ghosts with the step of thieves
Dance to the clap of the cottonwood leaves.
  (Oh, the embers black and cold!)


## HIAWATHA'S CHILDHOOD

*Henry Wadsworth Longfellow*

By the shores of Gitche Gumee,
By the shining Big-Sea-Water,
Stood the wigwam of Nokomis,
Daughter of the Moon, Nokomis.
Dark behind it rose the forest,
Rose the black and gloomy pine-trees,
Rose the firs with cones upon them;
Bright before it beat the water,
Beat the clear and sunny water,
Beat the shining Big-Sea-Water.

There the wrinkled, old Nokomis
Nursed the little Hiawatha,
Rocked him in his linden cradle,
Bedded soft in moss and rushes,
Safely bound with reindeer sinews;
Stilled his fretful wail by saying,
"Hush! the Naked Bear will hear thee!"
Lulled him into slumber, singing,
"Ewa-yea! my little owlet!
Who is this, that lights the wigwam?
With his great eyes lights the wigwam?
Ewa-yea! my little owlet!"

Many things Nokomis taught him
Of the stars that shine in heaven;
Showed him Ishkoodah, the comet,
Ishkoodah, with fiery tresses;

Showed the Death-Dance of the spirits,
Warriors with their plumes and war-clubs,
Flaring far away to northward
In the frosty nights of Winter;
Showed the broad, white road in heaven,
Pathway of the ghosts, the shadows,
Running straight across the heavens,
Crowded with the ghosts, the shadows.

At the door on summer evenings
Sat the little Hiawatha;
Heard the whispering of the pine-trees,
Heard the lapping of the water,
Sounds of music, words of wonder;
"Minne-wawa!" said the pine-trees,
"Mudway-aushka!" said the water.

Saw the fire-fly, Wah-wah-taysee,
Flitting through the dusk of evening,
With the twinkle of its candle
Lighting up the brakes and bushes,
And he sang the song of children,
Sang the song Nokomis taught him:
"Wah-wah-taysee, little fire-fly,
Little, flitting, white-fire insect,
Little, dancing, white-fire creature,
Light me with your little candle,
Ere upon my bed I lay me,
Ere in sleep I close my eyelids!"

Saw the moon rise from the water,
Rippling, rounding from the water,
Saw the flecks and shadows on it,
Whispered, "What is that, Nokomis?"
And the good Nokomis answered:

"Once a warrior, very angry,
Seized his grandmother, and threw her
Up into the sky at midnight;
Right against the moon he threw her;
'T is her body that you see there."

Saw the rainbow in the heaven,
In the eastern sky, the rainbow,
Whispered, "What is that, Nokomis?"
And the good Nokomis answered:

" 'T is the heaven of flowers you see there;
All the wild flowers of the forest,
All the lilies of the prairie,
When on earth they fade and perish,
Blossom in that heaven above us."

When he heard the owls at midnight,
Hooting, laughing in the forest,
"What is that?" he cried in terror;
"What is that?" he said, "Nokomis?"

And the good Nokomis answered:
"That is but the owl and owlet,
Talking in their native language,
Talking, scolding at each other."
  Then the little Hiawatha
Learned of every bird its language,
Learned their names and all their secrets,
How they built their nests in Summer,
Where they hid themselves in Winter,
Talked with them whene'er he met them,
Called them "Hiawatha's Chickens."
  Of all beasts he learned the language,
Learned their names and all their secrets,
How the beavers built their lodges,
Where the squirrels hid their acorns,
How the reindeer ran so swiftly,
Why the rabbit was so timid,
Talked with them whene'er he met them,
Called them "Hiawatha's Brothers."

### THE PIONEER

*Arthur Guiterman*

Long years ago I blazed a trail
  Through lovely woods unknown till then
And marked with cairns of splintered shale
  A mountain way for other men;

For other men who came and came:
  They trod the path more plain to see,
They gave my trail another's name
  And no one speaks or knows of me.

The trail runs high, the trail runs low
  Where windflowers dance or columbine;
The scars are healed that long ago
  My ax cut deep on birch and pine.

Another's name my trail may bear,
  But still I keep, in waste and wood,
My joy because the trail is there,
  My peace because the trail is good.

### BUFFALO DUSK

*Carl Sandburg*

The buffaloes are gone.
And those who saw the buffaloes are gone.
Those who saw the buffaloes by thousands and
    how they pawed the prairie sod into dust
    with their hoofs, their great heads down
    pawing on in a great pageant of dusk,
Those who saw the buffaloes are gone.
And the buffaloes are gone.

### THE GOOD JOAN

*Lizette Woodworth Reese*

  Along the thousand roads of France,
  Now there, now here, swift as a glance,
  A cloud, a mist blown down the sky,
  *Good Joan of Arc goes riding by.*

  In Domremy at candlelight,
  The orchards blowing rose and white
  About the shadowy houses lie;
  *And Joan of Arc goes riding by.*

  On Avignon there falls a hush,
  Brief as the singing of a thrush
  Across old gardens April-high;
  *And Joan of Arc goes riding by.*

  The women bring the apples in,
  Round Arles when the long gusts begin,

Then sit them down to sob and cry;
*And Joan of Arc goes riding by.*

Dim fall the hoofs down old Calais;
In Tours a flash of silver-gray,
Like flaw of rain in a clear sky;
*And Joan of Arc goes riding by.*

Who saith that ancient France shall fail,
A rotting leaf driv'n down the gale?
Then her sons knew not how to die;
Then good God dwells no more on high,

Tours, Arles, and Domremy reply!
*For Joan of Arc goes riding by.*

## COLUMBUS
*Annette Wynne*

An Italian boy that liked to play
In Genoa about the ships all day,
With curly head and dark, dark eyes,
That gazed at earth in child surprise;
And dreamed of distant stranger skies.

He watched the ships that came crowding in
With cargo of riches; he loved the din
Of the glad rush out and the spreading sails
And the echo of far-off windy gales.

He studied the books of the olden day;
He studied but knew far more than they;
He talked to the learned men of the school—
So wise he was they thought him a fool,
A fool with the dark, dark, dreamful eyes,
A child he was—grown wonder-wise.

Youth and dreams are over past
And out, far out he is sailing fast
Toward the seas he dreamed;—strange lands
    arise—
The world is made rich by his great emprise—
And the wisest know he was more than wise.

## COLUMBUS
*Joaquin Miller*

Behind him lay the gray Azores,
    Behind the Gates of Hercules;
Before him not the ghost of shores,
    Before him only shoreless seas.
The good mate said: "Now must we pray,
    For lo! the very stars are gone.
Brave Admiral, speak, what shall I say?"
    "Why, say 'Sail on! sail on! and on!'"

"My men grow mutinous day by day;
    My men grow ghastly wan and weak."
The stout mate thought of home; a spray
    Of salt wave washed his swarthy cheek.
"What shall I say, brave Admiral, say,
    If we sight naught but seas at dawn?"
"Why, you shall say at break of day,
    'Sail on! sail on! sail on! and on!'"

They sailed and sailed, as winds might blow,
    Until at last the blanched mate said,
"Why, now not even God would know
    Should I and all my men fall dead.
These very winds forget their way,
    For God from these dread seas is gone.
Now speak, brave Admiral, speak and say"—
    He said: "Sail on! sail on! and on!"

They sailed. They sailed. Then spake the
    mate:
    "This mad sea shows his teeth tonight.
He curls his lip, he lies in wait,
    With lifted teeth, as if to bite!
Brave Admiral, say but one good word:
    What shall we do when hope is gone?"
The words leapt like a leaping sword:
    "Sail on! sail on! sail on! and on!"

Then, pale and worn, he kept his deck,
    And peered through darkness. Ah, that
    night
Of all dark nights! And then a speck—
    A light! a light! a light! a light!

It grew, a starlit flag unfurled!
    It grew to be Time's burst of dawn.
He gained a world; he gave that world
    Its grandest lesson: "On! sail on!"

## ATLANTIC CHARTER,
### A.D. 1620-1942

*Francis Brett Young*

What are you carrying Pilgrims, Pilgrims?
What did you carry beyond the sea?
    *We carried the Book, we carried the Sword,*
    A steadfast heart in the fear of the Lord,
    And a living faith in His plighted word
    *That all men should be free.*

What were your memories, Pilgrims, Pilgrims?
What of the dreams you bore away?
    We carried the songs our fathers sung
    By the hearths of home when they were young,
    And the comely words of the mother-tongue
    In which they learnt to pray.

What did you find there, Pilgrims, Pilgrims?
What did you find beyond the waves?
    A stubborn land and a barren shore,
    Hunger and want and sickness sore:
    All these we found and gladly bore
    Rather than be slaves.

How did you fare there, Pilgrims, Pilgrims?
What did you build in that stubborn land?
    We felled the forest and tilled the sod
    Of a continent no man had trod
    And we established there, in the Grace of God,
    The rights whereby we stand.

What are you bringing us, Pilgrims, Pilgrims?
Bringing us back in this bitter day?
    The selfsame things we carried away:
    The Book, the Sword,
    The fear of the Lord,
    And the boons our fathers dearly bought:
    Freedom of Worship, Speech and Thought,
    Freedom from Want, Freedom from Fear,
    The liberties we hold most dear,
    And who shall say us Nay?

## THE LANDING
## OF THE PILGRIM FATHERS
### (November 19, 1620)

*Felicia Dorothea Hemans*

The breaking waves dashed high
    On a stern and rock-bound coast,
And the woods, against a stormy sky,
    Their giant branches tossed;

And the heavy night hung dark
    The hills and waters o'er,
When a band of exiles moored their bark
    On the wild New England shore.

Not as the conquerer comes,
    They, the true-hearted came:
Not with the roll of the stirring drums,
    And the trumpet that sings of fame;

Not as the flying come,
    In silence and in fear,—
They shook the depths of the desert's gloom
    With their hymns of lofty cheer.

Amidst the storm they sang,
    And the stars heard, and the sea;
And the sounding aisles of the dim woods rang
    To the anthem of the free!

The ocean-eagle soared
    From his nest by the white waves' foam,
And the rocking pines of the forest roared;
    This was their welcome home!

There were men with hoary hair
    Amidst that pilgrim-band;
Why had they come to wither there,
    Away from their childhood's land?

There was woman's fearless eye,
    Lit by her deep love's truth;
There was manhood's brow, serenely high,
    And the fiery heart of youth.

What sought they thus afar?
    Bright jewels of the mine?
The wealth of seas, the spoils of war?—
    They sought a faith's pure shrine!

Aye, call it holy ground,
    The soil where first they trod!
They have left unstained what there they
        found—
    Freedom to worship God!

## PAUL REVERE'S RIDE

*Henry Wadsworth Longfellow*

Listen, my children, and you shall hear
Of the midnight ride of Paul Revere,
On the eighteenth of April, in seventy-five;
Hardly a man is now alive
Who remembers that famous day and year.
He said to his friend, "If the British march
By land or sea from the town tonight,
Hang a lantern aloft in the belfry arch
Of the North Church tower as a signal light,—
One, if by land, and two, if by sea;
And I on the opposite shore will be,
Ready to ride and spread the alarm
Through every Middlesex village and farm,
For the country folk to be up and to arm."

Then he said, "Good Night!" and with muffled
    oar
Silently rowed to the Charleston shore,
Just as the moon rose over the bay,
Where swinging wide at her moorings lay
The *Somerset*, British man-of-war;
A phantom ship, with each mast and spar
Across the moon like a prison bar,
And a huge black hulk, that was magnified
By its own reflection in the tide.

Meanwhile, his friend, through alley and street,
Wanders and watches with eager ears,
Till in the silence around him he hears
The muster of men at the barrack door,
The sound of arms, and the tramp of feet,
And the measured tread of the grenadiers,
Marching down to their boats on the shore.

Then he climbed the tower of the Old North
    Church
By the wooden stairs, with stealthy tread,
To the belfry-chamber overhead,
And startled the pigeons from their perch
On the somber rafters, that round him made
Masses and moving shapes of shade,—
By the trembling ladder, steep and tall,
To the highest window in the wall,
Where he paused to listen and look down
A moment on the roofs of the town
And the moonlight flowing over all.

Beneath in the churchyard, lay the dead,
In their night-encampment on the hill,
Wrapped in silence so deep and still
That he could hear, like a sentinel's tread,
The watchful night-wind, as it went
Creeping along from tent to tent,
And seeming to whisper, "All is Well!"
A moment only he feels the spell
Of the place and the hour, and the secret dread
Of the lonely belfry and the dead;
For suddenly all his thoughts are bent
On a shadowy something far away,
Where the river widens to meet the bay,—
A line of black that bends and floats
On the rising tide, like a bridge of boats.

Meanwhile, impatient to mount and ride,
Booted and spurred, with a heavy stride
On the opposite shore walked Paul Revere.
Now he patted his horse's side,
Now gazed at the landscape far and near,
Then, impetuous, stamped the earth,
And turned and tightened his saddle-girth;
But mostly he watched with eager search
The belfry-tower of the Old North Church,
As it rose above the graves on the hill,
Lonely and spectral and somber and still.
And lo! as he looks, on the belfry's height
A glimmer, and then a gleam of light!
He springs to the saddle, the bridle he turns,
But lingers and gazes, till full on his sight
A second lamp in the belfry burns!

A hurry of hoofs in a village street,
A shape in the moonlight, a bulk in the dark,
And beneath, from the pebbles, in passing, a
    spark
Struck out by a steed flying fearless and fleet:
That was all! And yet, through the gloom and
    the light,
The fate of a nation was riding that night;
And the spark struck out by that steed, in his
    flight
Kindled the land into flame with its heat.
He has left the village and mounted the steep,
And beneath him, tranquil and broad and deep,
Is the Mystic, meeting the ocean tides;
And under the alders that skirt its edge,
Now soft on the sand, now loud on the ledge,
Is heard the tramp of his steed as he rides.

It was twelve by the village clock,
When he crossed the bridge into Medford town.
He heard the crowing of the cock,
And the barking of the farmer's dog,
And felt the damp of the river fog,
That rises after the sun goes down.
It was one by the village clock,
When he galloped into Lexington.
He saw the gilded weathercock
Swim in the moonlight as he passed.
And the meeting-house windows, blank and bare,
Gaze at him with a spectral glare,
As if they already stood aghast
At the bloody work they would look upon.

It was two by the village clock,
When he came to the bridge in Concord town.
He heard the bleating of the flock,
And the twitter of birds among the trees,
And felt the breath of the morning breeze
Blowing over the meadows brown.
And one was safe and asleep in his bed
Who at the bridge would be first to fall,
Who that day would be lying dead,
Pierced by a British musket-ball.

You know the rest. In the books you have read,
How the British Regulars fired and fled,—
How the farmers gave them ball for ball,
From behind each fence and farmyard wall,
Chasing the red-coats down the lane,
Then crossing the fields to emerge again
Under the trees at the turn of the road,
And only pausing to fire and load.

So through the night rode Paul Revere;
And so through the night went his cry of alarm
To every Middlesex village and farm,—
A cry of defiance and not of fear,
A voice in the darkness, a knock at the door,
And a word that shall echo forevermore!
For, borne on the night-wind of the Past,
Through all our history, to the last,
In the hour of darkness and peril and need,
The people will waken and listen to hear
The hurrying hoof-beats of that steed,
And the midnight message of Paul Revere.

## BALLAD OF JOHNNY APPLESEED

*Helmer O. Oleson*

Through the Appalachian valleys, with his kit
    a buckskin bag,
Johnny Appleseed went plodding past high peak
    and mountain crag.
Oh, his stockings were of leather, and his moc-
    casins were tough;
He was set upon a journey where the going
    would be rough.
        See him coming in the springtime,
        Passing violets in the glade.
        Many apple trees are needed,
        And the pioneers want shade.
Johnny carried many orchards in the bag upon
    his back,
And the scent of apple blossoms always lingered
    in his track.
Over half a fertile continent he planted shiny
    seed;
He would toss them in the clearings where the
    fawn and yearling feed.
        In the summer see him tramping
        Through the windings of the wood.
        Big red apples in the oven
        Make the venison taste good.
He would wander over mountain; he would
    brave a raging stream,
For his eyes were filled with visions like an an-
    cient prophet's dream.
He would travel after nightfall, start again at
    early morn;
He was planting seeds of apples for the children
    yet unborn.
    Where the autumn leaves turned crimson,
    He was eager to explore.
    Apple dumplings never blossomed
    On a shady sycamore.
Johnny traveled where the war whoop of the
    painted tribes rang loud;
And he walked among grim chieftains and their
    hot-eyed warrior crowd.
He told them of his vision, of his dream that
    would not die,
So he never was molested, and the settlers had
    their pie.
        Bitter winter found him trudging,
        Not for glory or applause,
        Only happy for the winesaps
        In tomorrow's applesauce!

## WASHINGTON
### *Nancy Byrd Turner*

He played by the river when he was young,
He raced with rabbits along the hills,
He fished for minnows, and climbed and swung,
And hooted back at the whippoorwills.
Strong and slender and tall he grew—
And then, one morning, the bugles blew.

Over the hills the summons came,
Over the river's shining rim.
He said that the bugles called his name,
He knew that his country needed him,
And he answered, "Coming!" and marched away
For many a night and many a day.

Perhaps when the marches were hot and long
He'd think of the river flowing by
Or, camping under the winter sky,
Would hear the whippoorwill's far-off song.
Working or playing, in peace or strife,
He loved America all his life!

## THOMAS JEFFERSON
## 1743–1826
### *Rosemary Carr and Stephen Vincent Benét*

Thomas Jefferson,
What do you say
Under the gravestone
Hidden away?

"I was a giver,
I was a molder,
I was a builder
With a strong shoulder."

Six feet and over,
Large-boned and ruddy,
The eyes grey-hazel
But bright with study.

The big hands clever
With pen and fiddle
And ready, ever,
For any riddle.

From buying empires
To planting 'taters,
From Declarations
To trick dumb-waiters

"I liked the people,
The sweat and crowd of them,
Trusted them always
And spoke aloud of them.

"I liked all learning
And wished to share it
Abroad like pollen
For all who merit.

"I liked fine houses
With Greek pilasters,
And built them surely,
My touch a master's.

"I liked queer gadgets
And secret shelves,
And helping nations
To rule themselves.

"Jealous of others?
Not always candid?

But huge of vision
And open-handed.

"A wild-goose-chaser?
Now and again,
Build Monticello,
You little men!

"Design my plow, sirs,
They use it still,
Or found my college
At Charlottesville.

"And still go questing
New things and thinkers,
And keep as busy
As twenty tinkers.

"While always guarding
The people's freedom—
You need more hands, sir?
I didn't need 'em.

"They call you rascal?
They called me worse,
You'd do grand things, sir,
But lack the purse?

'I got no riches.
I died a debtor.
I died free-hearted
And that was better.

"For life was freakish
But life was fervent,
And I was always
Life's willing servant.

"Life, life's too weighty?
Too long a haul, sir?
I lived past eighty.
I liked it all, sir."

"Benjamin Franklin, 1706–1790." From: *A Book of Americans* by Rosemary and Stephen V. Benét. Holt, Rinehart and Winston, Inc. Copyright, 1933 by Stephen Vincent Benét. Copyright renewed, 1961, by Rosemary Carr Benét. Reprinted by permission of Brandt & Brandt

## BENJAMIN FRANKLIN
### 1706–1790

*Rosemary Carr and
Stephen Vincent Benét*

Ben Franklin munched a loaf of bread while
    walking down the street
And all the Philadelphia girls tee-heed to see
    him eat,
A country boy come up to town with eyes as big
    as saucers
At the ladies in their furbelows, the gempmum
    on their horses.

Ben Franklin wrote an almanac, a smile upon
    his lip,
It told you when to plant your corn and how to
    cure the pip,
But he salted it and seasoned it with proverbs sly
    and sage,
And people read "Poor Richard" till Poor Rich-
    ard was the rage.

Ben Franklin made a pretty kite and flew it in
    the air
To call upon a thunderstorm that happened to
    be there,
—And all our humming dynamos and our electric
    light
Go back to what Ben Franklin found the day he
    flew his kite.

Ben Franklin was the sort of man that people
    like to see,
For he was very clever but as human as could be.
He had an eye for pretty girls, a palate for good
    wine,
And all the court of France were glad to ask him
    in to dine.

But it didn't make him stuffy and he wasn't
    spoiled by fame
But stayed Ben Franklin to the end, as Yankee as
    his name.

"Nancy Hanks, 1784–1818." From: *A Book of Americans* by Rosemary and Stephen V. Benét. Holt, Rinehart and Winston, Inc. Copyright, 1933 by Stephen Vincent Benét. Copyright renewed, 1961, by Rosemary Carr Benét. Reprinted by permission of Brandt & Brandt

"He wrenched their might from tyrants and its
    lightning from the sky."
And oh, when he saw pretty girls, he had a tak-
    ing eye!

## NANCY HANKS
## 1784–1818

*Rosemary Carr and
Stephen Vincent Benét*

If Nancy Hanks
Came back as a ghost,
Seeking news
Of what she loved most,
She'd ask first
"Where's my son?
What's happened to Abe?
What's he done?"

"Poor little Abe,
Left all alone
Except for Tom,
Who's a rolling stone;
He was only nine
The year I died.
I remember still
How hard he cried.

"Scraping along
In a little shack,
With hardly a shirt
To cover his back,
And a prairie wind
To blow him down,
Or pinching times
If he went to town.

"You wouldn't know
About my son?
Did he grow tall?
Did he have fun?
Did he learn to read?
Did he get to town?
Do you know his name?
Did he get on?"

"A Reply to Nancy Hanks" by Julius Silberger from
*Children and Books*. Scott, Foresman and Company, Chi-
cago, 1947
"I Saw a Ghost" by Joan Boilleau from *Children and*

## A REPLY TO NANCY HANKS

*Julius Silberger*

Yes, Nancy Hanks,
The news we will tell
Of your Abe
Whom you loved so well.
You asked first,
"Where's my son?"
He lives in the heart
Of everyone.

## I SAW A GHOST

*Joan Boilleau*

As twilight fell
O'er the river's banks,
I saw the ghost
Of Nancy Hanks
Floating in mist
O'er the river's banks.

I told the ghost
Of Nancy Hanks
Floating in mist
O'er the river's banks,
How Abe saved our nation
And kept it one,
How slaves were made free
By a great man; her son.

As moonlight fell
O'er the river's banks,
The smiling ghost
Of Nancy Hanks
Faded in mist
O'er the river's banks.

## LINCOLN

*Nancy Byrd Turner*

There was a boy of other days,
A quiet, awkward, earnest lad,
Who trudged long weary miles to get
A book on which his heart was set—
And then no candle had!

*Books*. Scott, Foresman and Company, Chicago, 1947
"Lincoln" by Nancy Byrd Turner from *Child Life*
(February 1929). Reprinted by permission of Rev. Mel-
vin Lee Steadman, Jr.

He was too poor to buy a lamp
But very wise in woodmen's ways.
He gathered seasoned bough and stem,
And crisping leaf, and kindled them
Into a ruddy blaze.

Then as he lay full length and read,
The firelight flickered on his face,
And etched his shadow on the gloom.
And made a picture in the room,
In that most humble place.

The hard years came, the hard years went,
But, gentle, brave, and strong of will,
He met them all. And when to-day
We see his pictured face, we say,
"There's light upon it still."

## ABRAHAM LINCOLN

*Mildred Plew Meigs*

Remember he was poor and country-bred;
  His face was lined; he walked with awkward
    gait.
Smart people laughed at him sometimes and
    said,
  "How can so very plain a man be great?"

Remember he was humble, used to toil.
  Strong arms he had to build a shack, a fence,
Long legs to tramp the woods, to plow the soil,
  A head chuck full of backwoods common
    sense.

Remember all he ever had he earned.
  He walked in time through stately White
    House doors;
But all he knew of men and life he learned
  In little backwoods cabins, country stores.

Remember that his eyes could light with fun;
  That wisdom, courage, set his name apart;
But when the rest is duly said and done,
  Remember that men loved him for his heart.

## ABRAHAM LINCOLN
## 1809–1865

*Rosemary Carr and*
*Stephen Vincent Benét*

Lincoln was a long man.
He liked out of doors.
He liked the wind blowing
And the talk in country stores.

He liked telling stories,
He liked telling jokes.
"Abe's quite a character,"
Said quite a lot of folks.

Lots of folks in Springfield
Saw him every day,
Walking down the street
In his gaunt, long way.

Shawl around his shoulders,
Letters in his hat.
"That's Abe Lincoln."
They thought no more than that.

Knew that he was honest,
Guessed that he was odd,

Knew he had a cross wife
Though she was a Todd.

Knew he had three little boys
Who liked to shout and play,
Knew he had a lot of debts
It took him years to pay.

Knew his clothes and knew his house.
"That's his office, here.
Blame good lawyer, on the whole,
Though he's sort of queer.

"Sure, he went to Congress, once,
But he didn't stay.
Can't expect us all to be
Smart as Henry Clay.

"Need a man for troubled times?
Well, I guess we do.
Wonder who we'll ever find?
Yes—I wonder who."

That is how they met and talked,
Knowing and unknowing.
Lincoln was the green pine.
Lincoln kept on growing.

### AND YET FOOLS SAY
*George S. Holmes*

He captured light and caged it in a glass,
Then harnessed it forever to a wire;
He gave men robots with no backs to tire
In bearing burdens for the toiling mass.

He freed the tongue in wood and wax and brass,
Imbued dull images with motions' fire,
Transmuted metal into human choir—
These man-made miracles he brought to pass.

Bulbs banish night along the Great White Way,
Thin threads of copper throb with might un-
seen;
On silver curtains shadow-actors play
That walk and talk from magic-mouthed ma-
chine,

While continents converse through skies o'er-
head—
And yet fools say that Edison is dead!

### ALEXANDER GRAHAM BELL DID NOT INVENT THE TELEPHONE
*Robert P. Tristram Coffin*

Alexander Graham Bell
Did not invent the telephone,
No good thing was ever yet
The work of any man alone.

My old Grandmother Sarah Bates,
Halfway out from coast to sky,
On Bates's Island, had a fine
Hand in that electric pie.

Grandma Bates with a small child
On her lap with quick hot breath

"And Yet Fools Say" by George S. Holmes. Reprinted by
permission of Scripps-Howard Newspapers
"Alexander Graham Bell Did Not Invent the Telephone." Reprinted with permission of Macmillan Pub-

lishing Co., Inc. from *Collected Poems* by Robert P.
Tristram Coffin. Copyright 1943 by Macmillan Publishing
Co., Inc., renewed 1971 by Margaret Coffin Halvosa, Alice
Westcott, Robert P. Tristram Coffin and Richard N.
Coffin

Willed the telephone to be
As she sat and stood off death.

Another grandmother I had,
Her head all over gimlet curls,
Ran that road of whispers to
Three other merry little girls.

Your Grandmother Fisher with her man
Down with fever of the lung
Willed that wiry line of life
Through the woodlands to be hung.

Your other Grandma Mary Snow,
Miles from your tall father's sire,
Sent out her love so stout, so straight,
It turned into a singing wire.

Little lonely barefoot boys
Aching for their freckled kind,
Old farmers through long nights of snow
Unrolled that wire from their mind.

Alexander Graham Bell
Had lots of help at his strange labor,
Maybe an arm down through the clouds
Helped him make the whole world neighbor.

# I HEAR AMERICA SINGING

*Walt Whitman*

I hear America singing, the varied carols I hear,
Those of the mechanics, each singing his as it
   should be blithe and strong,
The carpenter singing his as he measures his
   plank or beam,
The mason singing his as he makes ready for
   work or leaves off work,
The boatman singing what belongs to him in his
   boat, the deck hand singing on the steamboat deck,
The shoemaker singing as he sits on his bench,
   the hatter singing as he stands,
The wood-cutter's song, the ploughboy's on his
   way in the morning, or at noon intermission
   or at sundown,
The delicious singing of the mother, or the
   young wife at work, or the girl sewing or
   washing,
Each sings what belongs to him or her and to
   none else,
The day what belongs to the day—at night the
   party of young fellows, robust, friendly,
Singing with open mouths their strong melodious songs.

## I SING FOR THE ANIMALS

*Teton Sioux*
*(North America)*

> Out of the earth
> I sing for them,
> A Horse nation
> I sing for them.
> Out of the earth
> I sing for them,
> The animals
> I sing for them.

*Christina Georgina Rossetti*

> Pussy has a whiskered face,
> Kitty has such pretty ways;
> Doggie scampers when I call,
> And has a heart to love us all.

# ANIMALS

## MEDITATIO

*Ezra Pound*

When I carefully consider the curious habits of
    dogs
I am compelled to conclude
That man is the superior animal.

When I consider the curious habits of man
I confess, my friend, I am puzzled.

"I Sing for the Animals" by Frances Densmore from *Bureau of American Ethnology*, Bulletin 61, Smithsonian Institution. Reprinted by permission

"Pussy has a whiskered face." From *Sing-Song* by Christina Georgina Rossetti

"Meditatio." Ezra Pound, *Personae* (British title: *Collected Shorter Poems of Ezra Pound*). Copyright 1926 by Ezra Pound. Reprinted by permission of New Directions Publishing Corporation and Faber and Faber Ltd.

## VERN

*Gwendolyn Brooks*

When walking in a tiny rain
Across the vacant lot,
A pup's a good companion—
If a pup you've got.

And when you've had a scold,
And no one loves you very,
And you cannot be merry,
A pup will let you look at him,
And even let you hold
His little wiggly warmness—

And let you snuggle down beside.
Nor mock the tears you have to hide.

## A MALTESE DOG

*(Greek, second century* B.C.*)*

*Trans. by Edmund Blunden*

He came from Malta; and Eumêlus says
He had no better dog in all his days.
We called him Bull; he went into the dark.
Along those roads we cannot hear him bark.

## THE BUCCANEER

*Nancy Byrd Turner*

Danny was a rascal,
  Danny was a scamp;
He carried off a lady doll
  And left her in the damp.

He took her off on Monday;
  On Wednesday in he came
And dumped her gayly on the floor
  Without a bit of shame.

He was not sad or humble,
  He begged nobody's pardon;
He merely barked: "A lady doll
  I found out in the garden!"

## MY DOG

*Marchette Chute*

His nose is short and scrubby;
  His ears hang rather low;
And he always brings the stick back,
  No matter how far you throw.

He gets spanked rather often
  For things he shouldn't do,
Like lying-on-beds, and barking,
  And eating up shoes when they're new.

He always wants to be going
  Where he isn't supposed to go.
He tracks up the house when it's snowing—
  Oh, puppy, I love you so.

## TOM'S LITTLE DOG

*Walter de la Mare*

Tom told his dog called Tim to beg,
  And up at once he sat,
His two clear amber eyes fixed fast,
  His haunches on his mat.

Tom poised a lump of sugar on
  His nose; then, "Trust!" says he;
Stiff as a guardsman sat his Tim;
  Never a hair stirred he.

"Paid for!" says Tom; and in a trice
  Up jerked that moist black nose;
A snap of teeth, a crunch, a munch,
  And down the sugar goes!

## HOW?
*Aileen Fisher*

I

How do they know—
the sparrows and larks—
when it's time to return
to the meadows and parks?

How do they know
when fall is still here
it's the "thing" to go south
that time of the year?

Do you think that a bird
is just smart, or, instead,
that he carries a calendar
'round in his head?

II

How do they know—
the hornets and bees—
what direction to take
through the woods and the trees,

How far they should go,
how long they should roam,
and which way to turn
when it's time to go home?

Do you think that a bee
knows north from northwest—
or has he a compass
tucked under his vest?

*(Mother Goose)*

"Pussy-cat, pussy-cat,
  Where have you been?"
"I've been to London
  To visit the Queen."
"Pussy-cat, pussy-cat,
  What did you there?"
"I frightened a little mouse
  Under the chair."

## A KITTEN
*Eleanor Farjeon*

He's nothing much but fur
And two round eyes of blue,
He has a giant purr
And a midget mew.

He darts and pats the air,
He starts and cocks his ear,
When there is nothing there
For him to see and hear.

He runs around in rings,
But why we cannot tell;
With sideways leaps he springs
At things invisible—

Then half-way through a leap
His startled eyeballs close,
And he drops off to sleep
With one paw on his nose.

## CAT AND THE WEATHER
*May Swenson*

Cat takes a look at the weather.
Snow.
Puts a paw on the sill.
His perch is piled, is a pillow.

Shape of his pad appears.
Will it dig? No.
Not like sand.
Like his fur almost.

But licked, not liked.
Too cold.
Insects are flying, fainting down.
He'll try

to bat one against the pane.
They have no body and no buzz.
And now his feet are wet;
it's a puzzle.

Shakes each leg,
then shakes his skin
to get the white flies off.
Looks for his tail,

tells it to come on in
by the radiator.
World's turned queer
somehow. All white,

no smell. Well, here
inside it's still familiar.
He'll go to sleep until
it puts itself right.

**CAT**
*Mary Britton Miller*

The black cat yawns,
Opens her jaws,
Stretches her legs,
And shows her claws.

Then she gets up
And stands on four
Long stiff legs
And yawns some more.

She shows her sharp teeth,
She stretches her lip,
Her slice of a tongue
Turns up at the tip.

Lifting herself
On her delicate toes,
She arches her back
As high as it goes.

She lets herself down
With particular care,
And pads away
With her tail in the air.

*Elizabeth Coatsworth*

"Who are *you?*" asked the cat of the bear.
"I am a child of the wood,
I am strong with rain-shedding hair,
I hunt without fear for my food,
The others behold me and quail."
Said the cat, "You are lacking a tail."

What can you *do?*" asked the cat.
"I can climb for the honey I crave.
In the fall when I'm merry and fat
I seek out a suitable cave
And sleep till I feel the spring light."
Said the cat, "Can you see in the night?"

Said the cat, "*I* sit by man's fire,
But I am much wilder than you.
I do the thing I desire
And do nothing I don't want to do.
I am small, but then, what is that?
My spirit is great," said the cat.

*Christina Georgina Rossetti*

Wrens and robins in the hedge,
    Wrens and robins here and there;
Building, perching, pecking, fluttering,
    Everywhere!

*Shiki*

When my canary
flew away, that was the end
of spring in my house.

## THE WOODPECKER

*Elizabeth Madox Roberts*

The woodpecker pecked out a little round hole
And made him a house in the telephone pole.

One day when I watched he poked out his head,
And he had on a hood and a collar of red.

When the streams of rain pour out of the sky,
And the sparkles of lightning go flashing by,

And the big, big wheels of thunder roll,
He can snuggle back in the telephone pole.

## MAYBE THE BIRDS

*June Jordan*

Maybe the birds are worried
by the wind

they scream like people
in the hallway

wandering among the walls

*Emily Dickinson*

A bird came down the walk:
He did not know I saw;
He bit an angle-worm in halves
And ate the fellow, raw.

And then he drank a dew
From a convenient grass,
And then hopped sidewise to the wall
To let a beetle pass.

## MRS. PECK-PIGEON

*Eleanor Farjeon*

Mrs. Peck-Pigeon
Is picking for bread,
Bob-bob-bob
Goes her little round head.
Tame as a pussy-cat
In the street,
Step-step-step
Go her little red feet.
With her little red feet
And her little round head,
Mrs. Peck-Pigeon
Goes picking for bread.

## WILD GEESE

*Elinor Chipp*

I heard the wild geese flying
In the dead of the night,
With beat of wings and crying
I heard the wild geese flying,
And dreams in my heart sighing
Followed their northward flight.
I heard the wild geese flying
In the dead of the night.

## THE SANDHILL CRANE

*Mary Austin*

Whenever the days are cool and clear
The sandhill crane goes walking
Across the field by the flashing weir
Slowly, solemnly stalking.
The little frogs in the tules hear
And jump for their lives when he comes near,
The minnows scuttle away in fear,
When the sandhill crane goes walking.

The field folk know if he comes that way,
Slowly, solemnly stalking,
There is danger and death in the least delay
When the sandhill crane goes walking.
The chipmunks stop in the midst of their play,
The gophers hide in their holes away
And hush, oh, hush! the field mice say,
When the sandhill crane goes walking.

## CROWS
### David McCord

I like to walk
And hear the black crows talk.

I like to lie
And watch crows sail the sky.

I like the crow
That wants the wind to blow:

I like the one
That thinks the wind is fun.

I like to see
Crows spilling from a tree,

And try to find
The top crow left behind.

I like to hear
Crows caw that spring is near.

I like the great
Wild clamor of crow hate

Three farms away
When owls are out by day.

I like the slow
Tired homeward-flying crow;

I like the sight
Of crows for my good night.

## PARROT
### Alan Brownjohn

Sometimes I sit with both eyes closed,
But all the same, I've heard!
They're saying, 'He won't talk because
He is a *thinking* bird.'

I'm olive-green and sulky, and
The family say, 'Oh yes,
He's silent, but he's *listening*,
He *thinks* more than he *says!*

'He ponders on the things he hears,
Preferring not to chatter.'
—And this is true, but *why* it's true
Is quite another matter.

I'm working out some shocking things
In order to surprise them,
And when my thoughts are ready I'll
Certainly *not* disguise them!

I'll wait, and see, and choose a time
When everyone is present,
And clear my throat and raise my beak
And give a squawk and start to speak
And go on for about a week
*And it will not be pleasant!*

### Elizabeth Coatsworth

The sea gull curves his wings,
The sea gull turns his eyes.
Get down into the water, fish!
(If you are wise.)

The sea gull slants his wings,
The sea gull turns his head.
Get down into the water, fish!
(Or you'll be dead.)

## MICE
### Rose Fyleman

I think mice
Are rather nice.

　Their tails are long,
　Their faces small,
　They haven't any
　Chins at all.
　Their ears are pink,
　Their teeth are white,
　They run about
　The house at night.
　They nibble things
　They shouldn't touch
　And no one seems
　To like them much.

But *I* think mice
Are nice.

## THE MOUSE
### Elizabeth Coatsworth

I heard a mouse
Bitterly complaining
In a crack of moonlight
Aslant on the floor—

"Little I ask
And that little is not granted.
There are few crumbs
In this world any more.

"The bread-box is tin
And I cannot get in.

"The jam's in a jar
My teeth cannot mar.

"The cheese sits by itself
On the pantry shelf—

"All night I run
Searching and seeking,
All night I run
About on the floor,

"Moonlight is there
And a bare place for dancing,
But no little feast
Is spread any more."

## MESSAGE FROM A MOUSE, ASCENDING IN A ROCKET
### Patricia Hubbell

Attention, architect!
Attention, engineer!
A message from mouse,
Coming clear:

"Suggesting installing
Spike or sprocket
Easily turned by
A mouse in a rocket;
An ejection gadget
Simple to handle
To free mouse quickly
From this space-age ramble.
Suggest packing
For the next moon trip
A mouse-sized parachute
Somewhere in the ship,
So I can descend
(When my fear comes strong)
Back to earth where I was born.
Back to the cheerful world of cheese
And small mice playing,
And my wife waiting."

## THE RABBIT

*Elizabeth Madox Roberts*

When they said the time to hide was mine,
I hid back under a thick grapevine.

And while I was still for the time to pass,
A little gray thing came out of the grass.

He hopped his way through the melon bed
And sat down close by a cabbage head.

He sat down close where I could see,
And his big still eyes looked hard at me,

His big eyes bursting out of the rim,
And I looked back very hard at him.

## THE RABBITS' SONG OUTSIDE THE TAVERN

*Elizabeth Coatsworth*

We, who play under the pines,
We, who dance in the snow
That shines blue in the light of the moon,
Sometimes halt as we go—
Stand with our ears erect,
Our noses testing the air,
To gaze at the golden world
Behind the windows there.
Suns they have in a cave,
Stars, each on a tall white stem,
And the thought of a fox or an owl
Seems never to trouble them.
They laugh and eat and are warm,
Their food is ready at hand,
While hungry out in the cold
We little rabbits stand.

But they never dance as we dance!
They haven't the speed nor the grace.
We scorn both the dog and the cat
Who lie by their fireplace.

We scorn them licking their paws,
Their eyes on an upraised spoon—
We who dance hungry and wild
Under a winter's moon.

## FOUR LITTLE FOXES

*Lew Sarett*

Speak gently, Spring, and make no sudden sound;
For in my windy valley, yesterday I found
New-born foxes squirming on the ground—
Speak gently.

Walk softly, March, forbear the bitter blow;
Her feet within a trap, her blood upon the snow,
The four little foxes saw their mother go—
Walk softly.

Go lightly, Spring, oh, give them no alarm;
When I covered them with boughs to shelter
them from harm,
The thin blue foxes suckled at my arm—
Go lightly.

Step softly, March, with your rampant hurricane;
Nuzzling one another, and whimpering with
pain,
The new little foxes are shivering in the rain—
Step softly.

## LITTLE THINGS

*James Stephens*

Little things, that run, and quail,
And die, in silence and despair!

Little things, that fight, and fail,
And fall, on sea, and earth, and air!

All trapped and frightened little things,
The mouse, the coney, hear our prayer!

As we forgive those done to us,
—The lamb, the linnet, and the hare—

Forgive us all our trespasses,
Little creatures, everywhere!

## FIREFLY

*Elizabeth Madox Roberts*

A little light is going by,
Is going up to see the sky,
A little light with wings.

I never could have thought of it,
To have a little bug all lit
And made to go on wings.

## BUTTERFLY

*William Jay Smith*

Of living creatures most I prize
Black-spotted yellow Butterflies
Sailing softly through the skies,

Whisking light from each sunbeam,
Gliding over field and stream—
Like fans unfolding in a dream,

Like fans of gold lace flickering
Before a drowsy elfin king
For whom the thrush and linnet sing—

Soft and beautiful and bright
As hands that move to touch the light
When Mother leans to say good night.

## SNAIL

*Langston Hughes*

Little snail,
Dreaming you go.
Weather and rose
Is all you know.

Weather and rose
Is all you see,
Drinking
The dewdrop's
Mystery.

## SNAIL

*Maxine W. Kumin*

No one writes a letter to the snail.
He does not have a mailbox for his mail.
He does not have a bathtub or a rug.
There's no one in his house that he can hug.
There isn't any room when he's inside.

And yet they say the snail is satisfied.

## THE LITTLE TURTLE

*Vachel Lindsay*

There was a little turtle.
He lived in a box.
He swam in a puddle.
He climbed on the rocks.

He snapped at a mosquito.
He snapped at a flea.
He snapped at a minnow.
And he snapped at me.

He caught the mosquito.
He caught the flea.
He caught the minnow.
But he didn't catch me.

## THE NEWT

*David McCord*

The little newt
Is not a brute,
A fish or fowl,
A kind of owl:
He doesn't prowl
Or run or dig
Or grow too big.
He doesn't fly
Or laugh or cry—
He doesn't try.

The little newt
Is mostly mute,
And grave and wise,
And has two eyes.
He lives inside,
Or likes to hide;
But after rain
He's out again
And rather red,
I should have said.

The little newt
Of great repute
Has legs, a tail,
A spotted veil.
He walks alone
From stone to stone,
From log to log,
From bog to bog,
From tree to tree,
From you to me.

The little newt
By grass or root
Is very kind
But hard to find.
His hands and feet
Are always neat:
They move across
The mildest moss.
He's very shy,
He's never spry—
Don't ask me why.

## SNAKE

*D. H. Lawrence*

A snake came to my water-trough
On a hot, hot day, and I in pyjamas for the
    heat,
To drink there.

In the deep, strange-scented shade of the great
    dark carob-tree
I came down the steps with my pitcher
And must wait, must stand and wait, for there
    he was at the trough before me.

He reached down from a fissure in the earth-wall
    in the gloom
And trailed his yellow-brown slackness soft-
    bellied down, over the edge of the stone
    trough
And rested his throat upon the stone bottom,
And where the water had dripped from the tap,
    in a small clearness,
He sipped with his straight mouth,
Softly drank through his straight gums, into his
    slack long body,
Silently.

Someone was before me at my water-trough,
And I, like a second comer, waiting.

He lifted his head from this drinking, as cattle do,
And looked at me vaguely, as drinking cattle do,
And flickered his two-forked tongue from his lips,
    and mused a moment,
And stooped and drank a little more,
Being earth brown, earth golden from the burn-
    ing burning bowels of the earth
On the day of Sicilian July, with Etna smoking.

The voice of my education said to me
He must be killed,
For in Sicily the black, black snakes are innocent,
    the gold are venomous.

And voices in me said, If you were a man
You would take a stick and break him now, and
    finish him off.

"The Newt." From *Far and Few* by David McCord
(British title: *Mr. Bidery's Spidery Garden*). Copyright
1952 by David McCord. Reprinted by permission of Little,
Brown and Co., and George G. Harrap & Company Ltd.
"Snake" from *The Complete Poems of D. H. Lawrence,*
edited by Vivian de Sola Pinto and F. Warren Roberts.
Copyright © 1964, 1971 by Angelo Ravagli and C. M.
Weekly, Executors of The Estate of Frieda Lawrence
Ravagli. Reprinted by permission of The Viking Press,
Inc., Laurence Pollinger Ltd. and The Estate of Frieda
Lawrence Ravagli.

But I must confess how I liked him,
How glad I was he had come like a guest in
    quiet, to drink at my water-trough
And depart peaceful, pacified, and thankless,
Into the burning bowels of this earth.

Was it cowardice, that I dared not kill him?
Was it perversity, that I longed to talk to him?
Was it humility, to feel so honoured?
I felt so honoured.

And yet those voices:
*If you were not afraid, you would kill him!*

And truly I was afraid, I was most afraid,
But even so, honoured still more
That he should seek my hospitality
From out the dark door of the secret earth.

He drank enough
And lifted his head, dreamily, as one who has
    drunken,
And flickered his tongue like a forked night on
    the air, so black,
Seeming to lick his lips,
And looked around like a god, unseeing, into
    the air,
And slowly turned his head,
And slowly, very slowly, as if thrice adream,
Proceeded to draw his slow length curving round
And climb again the broken bank of my wall-
    face.

And as he put his head into that dreadful hole,
And as he slowly drew up, snake-easing his
    shoulders, and entered farther,

A sort of horror, a sort of protest against his
    withdrawing into that horrid black hole,
Deliberately going into the blackness, and slowly
    drawing himself after,
Overcame me now his back was turned.

I looked round, I put down my pitcher,
I picked up a clumsy log
And threw it at the water-trough with a clatter.

I think it did not hit him,
But suddenly that part of him that was left be-
    hind convulsed in undignified haste,
Writhed like lightning, and was gone
Into the black hole, the earth-lipped fissure in
    the wall-front,
At which, in the intense still noon, I stared with
    fascination.

And immediately I regretted it.
I thought how paltry, how vulgar, what a mean
    act!
I despised myself and the voices of my accursed
    human education.

And I thought of the albatross,
And I wished he would come back, my snake.

For he seemed to me again like a king,
Like a king in exile, uncrowned in the under-
    world,
Now due to be crowned again.
And so, I missed my chance with one of the
    lords
Of life.
And I have something to expiate;
A pettiness.

## THE ANT VILLAGE

*Marion Edey and Dorothy Grider*

Somebody up in the rocky pasture
  Heaved the stone over.
Here are the cells and a network of furrows
  In the roots of the clover.

Hundreds of eggs lie fitted in patterns,
  Waxy and yellow.
Hundreds of ants are racing and struggling.
  One little fellow

Shoulders an egg as big as his body,
  Ready for hatching.
Darkness is best, so everyone's rushing,
  Hastily snatching

Egg after egg to the lowest tunnels.
  And suddenly, where
Confusion had been, there now is nothing.
  Ants gone. Cells bare.

## HAIKU

*Issa*

A few flies
And I
Keep house together
In this humble home.

A mosquito bit me
Under the cherry tree,
And I spoke ill
Even of the blossoms.

All the while
I pray to Buddha
I keep on killing
Mosquitoes.

*Mary Britton Miller*

A son just born
To a duck is a drake,
And the child of a goose
Is called gosling,
And the moment when
The little chick steps
From the egg of a hen
A chicken is born.
But who knows the name
Of the new-born son
Of the beautiful swan?

           (Cygnet)

## DUCKS' DITTY

*Kenneth Grahame*

All along the backwater,
Through the rushes tall,
Ducks are a-dabbling,
Up tails all!

Ducks' tails, drakes' tails,
Yellow feet a-quiver,
Yellow bills all out of sight
Busy in the river!

Slushy green undergrowth
Where the roach swim—
Here we keep our larder,
Cool and full and dim.

Everyone for what he likes!
*We* like to be
Heads down, tails up,
Dabbling free!

High in the blue above
Swifts whirl and call—
*We* are down a-dabbling
Up tails all!

## THE NEW BABY CALF

*Edith H. Newlin*

Buttercup, the cow, had a new baby calf,
    a fine baby calf,
        a strong baby calf,
Not strong like his mother
But strong for a calf,
For *this* baby calf was so *new!*

Buttercup licked him with her strong warm
    tongue,
Buttercup washed him with her strong warm
    tongue,
Buttercup brushed him with her strong warm
    tongue,
    And the new baby calf *liked that!*

The new baby calf took a very little walk,
    a tiny little walk,
        a teeny little walk,
But his long legs wobbled
When he took a little walk,
    And the new baby calf fell down.

Buttercup told him with a low soft "Moo-oo!"
That he was doing very well for one so very new
And she talked very gently, as mother cows do,
    And the new baby calf *liked that!*

The new baby calf took another little walk,
    a little longer walk,
        a little stronger walk,
He walked around his mother and he found the
    place to drink.
    And the new baby calf liked *that!*

Buttercup told him with another low moo
That drinking milk from mother was a fine thing
    to do,
That she had lots of milk for him and for the
farmer too,
    And the new baby calf liked *that!*

The new baby calf drank milk every day,
His legs grew so strong that he could run and
    play,
He learned to eat grass and then grain and hay,
    And the big baby calf grew fat!

## THE PASTURE

*Robert Frost*

I'm going out to clean the pasture spring;
I'll only stop to rake the leaves away
(And wait to watch the water clear, I may):
I shan't be gone long.—You come too.

I'm going out to fetch the little calf
That's standing by the mother. It's so young
It totters when she licks it with her tongue.
I shan't be gone long.—You come too.

## THE YOUNG CALVES

*Robert P. Tristram Coffin*

A hush had fallen on the birds,
    And it was almost night,
When I came round a turn and saw
    A whole year's loveliest sight.

Two calves that thought their month of life
    Meant June through all the year
Were coming down the grassy road
    As slender as young deer.

They stopped amazed and took me in,
    Putting their ears out far,
And in each of four round eyes
    There was an evening star.

They did not breathe, they stared so hard,
    Brother close to brother,
Then their legs awoke, and they
    Turned flank to flank for mother.

A small boy in torn knickers came
  And caught them as they fled,
He put a slender arm around
  Each slender, startled head.

He never looked at me at all,
  I was not in his mind;
The three of them went down the road
  And never glanced behind.

## FOAL

*Mary Britton Miller*

Come trotting up
Beside your mother,
Little skinny.

Lay your neck across
Her back, and whinny,
Little foal.

You think you're a horse
Because you can trot—
But you're not.

Your eyes are so wild,
And each leg is as tall
As a pole;

And you're only a skittish
Child, after all,
Little foal.

## PONY CLOUDS

*Patricia Hubbell*

My pony trots around the track,
She doesn't ask me why,
While I upon her back look up
At ponies in the sky.
I wonder if the pony clouds

Ever tumble down
Or step into a star hole
As they prance about their town?
I wonder why the pony clouds
Go rushing by so fast?
They gallop so much swifter
Than my pony on the grass.
I wonder why the pony clouds
Are always white or grey,
And never ever chestnut or a warm, bright bay?
I wonder why the pony clouds
Have to disappear,
Turn into a steamboat or a big reindeer?

## MY MOTHER SAW A DANCING BEAR

*Charles Causley*

My mother saw a dancing bear
By the schoolyard, a day in June.
The keeper stood with chain and bar
And whistle-pipe, and played a tune.

And bruin lifted up its head
And lifted up its dusty feet,
And all the children laughed to see
It caper in the summer heat.

They watched as for the Queen it died.
They watched it march. They watched it halt.
They heard the keeper as he cried,
'Now, roly-poly!' 'Somersault!'

And then, my mother said, there came
The keeper with a begging-cup,
The bear with burning coat of fur,
Shaming the laughter to a step.

They paid a penny for the dance,
But what they saw was not the show;
Only, in bruin's aching eyes,
Far distant forests, and the snow.

"Foal" by Mary Britton Miller from *Menagerie* by Mary Britton Miller. Copyright 1928 by The Macmillan Company. Reprinted by permission of the author
"Pony Clouds" by Patricia Hubbell from *The Apple Vendor's Fair*. Copyright © 1963 by Patricia Hubbell.

Used by permission of Atheneum Publishers
"My Mother Saw a Dancing Bear." From the book *Figgie Hobbin* by Charles Causley. Published by Walker & Company, Inc. New York, N.Y. Text copyright © 1973 by Charles Causley. Reprinted by permission of the publishers

## THE TIGER
*William Blake*

Tiger! Tiger! burning bright
In the forests of the night,
What immortal hand or eye
Could frame thy fearful symmetry?

In what distant deeps or skies
Burnt the fire of thine eyes?
On what wings dare he aspire?
What the hand dare seize the fire?

And what shoulder, and what art,
Could twist the sinews of thy heart?
And when thy heart began to beat,
What dread hand? and what dread feet?

What the hammer? what the chain?
In what furnace was thy brain?
What the anvil? what dread grasp
Dare its deadly terrors clasp?

When the stars threw down their spears,
And watered heaven with their tears,
Did He smile His work to see?
Did He who made the Lamb make thee?

Tiger! Tiger! burning bright
In the forests of the night,
What immortal hand or eye
Dare frame thy fearful symmetry?

## THE WOLF AND THE CRANE
*Ennis Rees*

A wolf with a bone in his throat
Requested help from a goat,
But the goat was unable to aid him.
He then met a crane and paid him
To pull the bone out with his beak.
So the good crane first took a peek,
Then stuck his whole head down the gulf
That yawned past the jaws of the wolf,
And before his patient could groan
He pulled his head out with the bone.

But the wolf, without a kind word,
Took back his pay from the bird.
"You ought to be thankful," he said,
"That you, friend, still have a head,
Having had it so deep in the jaws
Of a wolf with teeth like a saw's!"

## BATS
*Randall Jarrell*

A bat is born
Naked and blind and pale.
His mother makes a pocket of her tail
And catches him. He clings to her long fur
By his thumbs and toes and teeth.
And then the mother dances through the night
Doubling and looping, soaring, somersaulting—
Her baby hangs on underneath.
All night, in happiness, she hunts and flies.
Her high sharp cries
Like shining needlepoints of sound
Go out into the night and, echoing back,
Tell her what they have touched.
She hears how far it is, how big it is,
Which way it's going:
She lives by hearing.
The mother eats the moths and gnats she
        catches
In full flight; in full flight
The mother drinks the water of the pond
She skims across. Her baby hangs on tight.
Her baby drinks the milk she makes him
In moonlight or starlight, in mid-air.
Their single shadow, printed on the moon
Or fluttering across the stars,
Whirls on all night; at daybreak
The tired mother flaps home to her rafter.
The others all are there.
They hang themselves up by their toes,
They wrap themselves in their brown wings.
Bunched upside-down, they sleep in air.
Their sharp ears, their sharp teeth, their
        quick sharp faces
Are dull and slow and mild.
All the bright day, as the mother sleeps,
She folds her wings about her sleeping child.

"The Tiger" by William Blake
"The Wolf and the Crane" reprinted from *Poems*,
p. 100, by Ennis Rees, by permission of the University of
South Carolina Press. Copyright © 1964 by the University
of South Carolina Press

"Bats." Reprinted with permission of Macmillan Publishing Co., Inc. from *The Bat-Poet* by Randall Jarrell.
Copyright © Macmillan Publishing Co., Inc., 1963, 1964

## THE BAT

*Theodore Roethke*

By day the bat is cousin to the mouse.
He likes the attic of an aging house.

His fingers make a hat about his head.
His pulse beat is so slow we think him dead.

He loops in crazy figures half the night
Among the trees that face the corner light.

But when he brushes up against a screen,
We are afraid of what our eyes have seen:

For something is amiss or out of place
When mice with wings can wear a human face.

## SEAL

*William Jay Smith*

See how he dives
 From the rocks with a zoom!
See how he darts
 Through his watery room
 Past crabs and eels
 And green seaweed,
 Past fluffs of sandy
 Minnow feed!
See how he swims
 With a swerve and a twist,
 A flip of the flipper,
 A flick of the wrist!
 Quicksilver-quick,
 Softer than spray,
 Down he plunges
 And sweeps away;
 Before you can think,
 Before you can utter
 Words like "Dill pickle"
 Or "Apple butter,"
 Back up he swims
 Past sting-ray and shark,

Out with a zoom,
 A whoop, a bark;
 Before you can say
 Whatever you wish,
 He plops at your side
 With a mouthful of fish!

## THE PRAYER OF THE CAT

*Carmen Bernos de Gasztold*

Lord,
I am the cat.
It is not, exactly, that I have something to ask
 of You!
No—
I ask nothing of anyone—
but,
if You have by some chance, in some celestial
 barn,
a little white mouse,
or a saucer of milk,
I know someone who would relish them.
Wouldn't You like someday
to put a curse on the whole race of dogs?
If so I should say,

                                    Amen

## THE PRAYER OF THE LITTLE DUCKS

*Carmen Bernos de Gasztold*

Dear God,
 give us a flood of water.
 Let it rain tomorrow and always.
 Give us plenty of little slugs
 and other luscious things to eat.
 Protect all folk who quack
 and everyone who knows how to swim.

                         Amen

"The Bat," copyright 1938 by Theodore Roethke from the book *The Collected Poems of Theodore Roethke.* Reprinted by permission of Doubleday & Company, Inc., and Faber and Faber Ltd.

"Seal" from *Boy Blue's Book of Beasts* by William Jay Smith. Copyright, © 1956, 1957 by William Jay Smith.

Reprinted by permission of William Jay Smith
"The Prayer of the Cat" and "The Prayer of the Little Ducks." From *Prayers from the Ark* by Carmen Bernos de Gasztold translated by Rumer Godden. Copyright © 1962 Rumer Godden. Reprinted by permission of the Viking Press, Inc. and Macmillan & Co., Ltd.

*William Shakespeare*

> Jog on, jog on, the foot-path way,
>     And merrily hent the stile-a:
> A merry heart goes all the day,
>     Your sad tires in a mile-a.

## A MODERN DRAGON

*Rowena Bastin Bennett*

A train is a dragon that roars through the dark.
He wriggles his tail as he sends up a spark.
He pierces the night with his one yellow eye,
And all the earth trembles when he rushes by.

# TRAVELING

## NIGHT TRAIN

*Robert Francis*

> Across the dim frozen fields of night
> Where is it going, where is it going?
> No throb of wheels, no rush of light,
> Only a whistle blowing, blowing.
> Only a whistle blowing.
>
> Something echoing through my brain,
> Something timed between sleep and waking,
> Murmurs, murmurs this may be the train
> I must be sometime, somewhere taking,
> I must be sometime taking.

# FROM A RAILWAY CARRIAGE

*Robert Louis Stevenson*

Faster than fairies, faster than witches,
Bridges and houses, hedges and ditches;
And charging along like troops in a battle
All through the meadows the horses and cattle:
All of the sights of the hill and the plain
Fly as thick as driving rain;
And ever again, in the wink of an eye,
Painted stations whistle by.

Here is a child who clambers and scrambles,
All by himself and gathering brambles;
Here is a tramp who stands and gazes;
And there is the green for stringing the daisies!
Here is a cart run away in the road
Lumping along with man and load;
And here is a mill, and there is a river:
Each a glimpse and gone for ever!

## TRAINS AT NIGHT

*Frances M. Frost*

I like the whistle of trains at night,
The fast trains thundering by so proud!
They rush and rumble across the world,
They ring wild bells and they toot so loud!

But I love better the slower trains.
They take their time through the world instead,
And whistle softly and stop to tuck
Each sleepy blinking town in bed!

## TRAINS

*James S. Tippett*

Over the mountains,
Over the plains,
Over the rivers,
Here come the trains.

Carrying passengers,
Carrying mail,
Bringing their precious loads
In without fail.

Thousands of freight cars
All rushing on
Through day and darkness,
Through dusk and dawn.

Over the mountains,
Over the plains,
Over the rivers,
Here come the trains.

## THE WAYS OF TRAINS

*Elizabeth Coatsworth*

I hear the engine pounding
in triumph down the track—
trains take away the ones you love
and then they bring them back!

trains take away the ones you love
to worlds both strange and new
and then, with care and courtesy,
they bring them back to you.

The engine halts and snuffs and snorts,
it breathes forth smoke and fire,
then snatches crowded strangers on—
but leaves what you desire!

## TRAVEL

*Edna St. Vincent Millay*

The railroad track is miles away,
   And the day is loud with voices speaking,
Yet there isn't a train goes by all day
   But I hear its whistle shrieking.

All night there isn't a train goes by,
   Though the night is still for sleep and dream-
      ing
But I see its cinders red on the sky,
   And hear its engine steaming.

My heart is warm with the friends I make,
   And better friends I'll not be knowing,
Yet there isn't a train I wouldn't take,
   No matter where it's going.

## GEOGRAPHY LESSON

*Zulfikar Ghose*

When the jet sprang into the sky,
it was clear why the city
had developed the way it had,
seeing it scaled six inches to the mile.
There seemed an inevitability
about what on ground had looked haphazard,
unplanned and without style
when the jet sprang into the sky.

When the jet reached ten thousand feet,
it was clear why the country
had cities where rivers ran
and why the valleys were populated.
The logic of geography—
that land and water attracted man—
was clearly delineated
when the jet reached ten thousand feet.

When the jet rose six miles high,
it was clear that the earth was round

and that it had more sea than land.
But it was difficult to understand
that the men on the earth found
causes to hate each other, to build
walls across cities and to kill.
From that height, it was not clear why.

## TAKING OFF

*Unknown*

     The airplane taxis down the field
     And heads into the breeze,
     It lifts its wheels above the ground,
     It skims above the trees,
     It rises high and higher
     Away up toward the sun,
     It's just a speck against the sky
     —And now it's gone!

## AT THE AIRPORT

*Howard Nemerov*

Through the gate, where nowhere and night
   begin,
A hundred suddenly appear and lose
Themselves in the hot and crowded waiting
   room.
A hundred others herd up toward the gate,
Patiently waiting that the way be opened
To nowhere and night, while a voice recites
The intermittent litany of numbers
And the holy names of distant destinations.

None going out can be certain of getting there.
None getting there can be certain of being loved
Enough. But they are sealed in the silver tube
And lifted up to be fed and cosseted,
While their upholstered cell of warmth and
   light
Shatters the darkness, neither here nor there.

"Travel" from *Collected Poems, Harper & Row*. Copyright 1921, 1922, 1923, 1948, 1950, 1951 by Edna St. Vincent Millay and Norma Millay Ellis

"Geography Lesson" by Zulfikar Ghose from *Jets from Orange* by Zulfikar Ghose. (Macmillan & Co. Ltd., 1967). Reprinted with the permission of Macmillan, London and Basingstoke

"Taking Off." Anonymous. From *Very Young Verses*. Published by Houghton Mifflin Company

"At the Airport" by Howard Nemerov from *The Blue Swallows* by Howard Nemerov. Copyright © 1967 by Howard Nemerov. Reprinted by permission of Margot Johnson Agency

## SONIC BOOM

*John Updike*

I'm sitting in the living room,
When, up above, the Thump of Doom
Resounds. Relax. It's sonic boom.

The ceiling shudders at the clap,
The mirrors tilt, the rafters snap,
And Baby wakens from his nap.

"Hush, babe. Some pilot we equip,
Giving the speed of sound the slip,
Has cracked the air like a penny whip."

Our world is far from frightening; I
No longer strain to read the sky
Where moving fingers (jet planes) fly.
Our world seems much too tame to die.

And if it does, with one more pop,
I shan't look up to see it drop.

## COCKPIT IN THE CLOUDS

*Dick Dorrance*

Two thousand feet beneath our wheels
The city sprawls across the land
Like heaps of children's blocks outflung,
In tantrums, by a giant hand.
To east a silver spire soars
And seeks to pierce our lower wing.
Above its grasp we drift along,
A tiny, droning, shiny thing.

The noon crowds pack the narrow streets.
The el trains move so slow, so slow.
Amidst their traffic, chaos, life,
The city's busy millions go.
Up here, aloof, we watch them crawl.
In crystal air we seem to poise
Behind our motor's throaty roar—
*Down there, we're just another noise.*

## NIGHT PLANE

*Frances M. Frost*

The midnight plane with its riding lights
looks like a footloose star
wandering west through the blue-black night
to where the mountains are,

a star that's journeyed nearer earth
to tell each quiet farm
and little town, "Put out your lights,
children of earth. Sleep warm."

## WHISTLES

*Rachel Field*

I never even hear
The boats that pass by day;
By night they seem so near,
A-whistling down the bay,
That I can almost understand
The things their whistles say.

I've waked sometimes all warm
In my bed, when eerily
I have heard them out of the dark
A-whistling cheerily
To tell the sleepy folk on land
All's well at sea.

## ADVENTURE

*Harry Behn*

It's not very far to the edge of town
Where trees look up and hills look down,
We go there almost every day
To climb and swing and paddle and play.

It's not very far to the edge of town,
Just up one little hill and down,
And through one gate, and over two stiles—
But coming home it's miles and miles.

*Elizabeth Coatsworth*

A horse would tire,
But I, I do not tire.
A stag would turn,
But I still keep my course.
A bird must rest,
And ashes follow fire,
But I excel
Flame, bird, or deer, or horse.

Only the wind
Do I require for ration,
Only the waves
Beneath my forefoot curled.
Eager I run
From nation unto nation
And seek my harbor
Halfway round the world.

## SEA-FEVER

*John Masefield*

I must go down to the seas again, to the lonely
sea and the sky,
And all I ask is a tall ship and a star to steer
her by,
And the wheel's kick and the wind's song and the
white sail's shaking
And a gray mist on the sea's face and a gray dawn
breaking.

I must go down to the seas again, for the call of
the running tide
Is a wild call and a clear call that may not be
denied;

And all I ask is a windy day with the white
clouds flying,
And the flung spray and the blown spume, and
the sea-gulls crying.

I must go down to the seas again to the vagrant
gypsy life,
To the gull's way and the whale's way where the
wind's like a whetted knife;
And all I ask is a merry yarn from a laughing
fellow-rover,
And quiet sleep and a sweet dream when the
long trick's over.

## CARGOES

*John Masefield*

Quinquireme of Nineveh from distant Ophir
Rowing home to haven in sunny Palestine,
With a cargo of ivory,
And apes and peacocks,
Sandalwood, cedarwood, and sweet white wine.

Stately Spanish galleon coming from the Isth-
mus,
Dipping through the Tropics by the palm-green
shores,
With a cargo of diamonds,
Emeralds, amethysts,
Topazes, and cinnamon, and gold moidores.

Dirty British coaster with a salt-caked smoke-
stack
Butting through the Channel in the mad March
days,
With a cargo of Tyne coal,
Road-rails, pig-lead,
Firewood, iron-ware, and cheap tin trays.

## MOTOR CARS

*Rowena Bastin Bennett*

From a city window, 'way up high,
I like to watch the cars go by.
They look like burnished beetles, black,
That leave a little muddy track
Behind them as they slowly crawl.
Sometimes they do not move at all
But huddle close with hum and drone
As though they feared to be alone.
They grope their way through fog and night
With the golden feelers of their light.

## THE BIRTHDAY BUS

*Mary Ann Hoberman*

My birthday is coming and I will be six,
I'd like a new bike and some peppermint sticks;
But if someone decided to give me a bus,
I'd accept it at once without making a fuss.

I'd tell all of my friends to come quickly inside
And I'd take them all out for a wonderful ride.
If somebody wanted to stop, he'd just buzz
And I'd stop in a minute, wherever I was;
And if somebody had somewhere special to go,
I'd drive there at once and I'd never say no.

The ride would be free; they would each have a
    seat;
And every half hour I'd hand out a treat.
I'd pull up at a bus stop; I'd put on the brake
And I'd pass around ice cream and soda and cake.
Then when they were finished, I'd call out, "Hi
    Ho!
Hold on to your hats, everybody! Let's go!"
(But if anyone asked me to please let him drive,
I'd say driving is dangerous for children of five.)

My birthday is coming and I will be six;
I'd like a new bike and some peppermint sticks;
But if someone decided to give me a bus,
I'd accept it at once without making a fuss.

"Motor Cars" from *Songs from Around a Toadstool Table* by Rowena Bennett. Copyright © 1967 by Rowena Bennett. Used by permission of Follett Publishing Company, a division of Follett Corporation
"The Birthday Bus" from *Hello and Good-By* by Mary Ann Hoberman. Copyright © 1959 by Mary Ann Hoberman. Reprinted by permission of Russell & Volkening, Inc., as agents of the author

## from ALL AROUND THE TOWN

*Phyllis McGinley*

J's the jumping Jay-walker,
  A sort of human jeep.
He crosses where the lights are red.
  Before he looks, he'll leap!
Then many a wheel
Begins to squeal,
  And many a brake to slam.
He turns your knees to jelly
  And the traffic into jam.

## TAXIS

*Rachel Field*

Ho, for taxis green or blue,
  Hi, for taxis red,
They roll along the Avenue
  Like spools of colored thread!

    *Jack-o'-Lantern yellow,*
    *Orange as the moon,*
    *Greener than the greenest grass*
    *Ever grew in June.*
    *Gayly striped or checked in squares,*
    *Wheels that twinkle bright,*
    *Don't you think that taxis make*
    *A very pleasant sight?*
    *Taxis shiny in the rain,*
    *Scudding through the snow,*
    *Taxis flashing back the sun*
    *Waiting in a row.*

Ho, for taxis red and green,
  Hi, for taxis blue,
I wouldn't be a private car
  In sober black, would you?

## from ALL AROUND THE TOWN

*Phyllis McGinley*

    B's the Bus,
    The bouncing Bus,
      That bears a shopper store-ward.

"J's the jumping Jay-walker" and "B's the Bus." From *All Around the Town* by Phyllis McGinley. Copyright 1948 by Phyllis McGinley. Reprinted by permission of J. B. Lippincott Company and Curtis Brown, Ltd.
"Taxis" copyright 1926 by Doubleday & Company, Inc. from the book *Taxis and Toadstools* by Rachel Field. Reprinted by permission of Doubleday & Company, Inc. and World's Work Ltd.

It's fun to sit
In back of it
　　But seats are better forward.
Although it's big as buildings are
　　And looks both bold and grand,
It has to stop obligingly
　　If you but raise your hand.

from **ALL AROUND THE TOWN**
*Phyllis McGinley*

E is the Escalator
　　That gives an elegant ride.
You step on the stair
With an easy air
　　And up and up you glide.
It's nicer than scaling ladders
　　Or scrambling 'round a hill,
For you climb and climb
But all the time
　　You're really standing still.

from **ALL AROUND THE TOWN**
*Phyllis McGinley*

R is for the Restaurant—
　　A really special treat.
(We do respect the relative
　　Who takes us there to eat.)
The waiters rush with plates of rolls,
　　They run to hold one's chair,
And always seem
To read ice-cream
　　Upon the bill-of-fare.

**MOVING**
*Eunice Tietjens*

I like to move. There's such a feeling
Of hurrying
　　and scurrying,
And such a feeling
Of men with trunks and packing cases,
Of kitchen clocks and mother's laces,
Dusters, dishes, books and vases,
Toys and pans and candles.

I always find things I'd forgotten,
An old brown Teddy stuffed with cotton,
Some croquet mallets without handles,
A marble and my worn-out sandals,
A half an engine and a hat . . .
And I like that.

I like to watch the big vans backing,
And the lumbering
　　and the cumbering,
And the hammering and the tacking.
I even like the packing!

And that will prove
I like to move!

**COUNTRY TRUCKS**

*Monica Shannon*

Big trucks with apples
　　And big trucks with grapes
Thundering through the mountains
　　While every wild thing gapes.

Thundering through the valley,
　　Like something just let loose,
Big trucks with oranges
　　For city children's juice.

Big trucks with peaches,
　　And big trucks with pears,
Frightening all the rabbits
　　And giving squirrels gray hairs.

Yet, when city children
　　Sit down to plum or prune,
They know more trucks are coming
　　As surely as the moon.

**CITY STREETS AND COUNTRY ROADS**

*Eleanor Farjeon*

　　The city has streets—
　　　　But the country has roads.

"E is the Escalator" and "R is for the Restaurant—."
From *All Around the Town* by Phyllis McGinley. Copyright 1948 by Phyllis McGinley. Reprinted by permission of J. B. Lippincott Company and Curtis Brown, Ltd.
　　"Moving" by Eunice Tietjens from *Child Life Magazine,* Copyright 1934, 1962 by Rand McNally & Company. Reprinted by permission of Marshall Head

"Country Trucks." From *Goose Grass Rhymes* by Monica Shannon. Copyright 1930 by Doubleday & Company, Inc. Reprinted by permission of the Publisher
　　"City Streets and Country Roads." Copyright 1926, renewed 1954 by Eleanor Farjeon. From *Poems for Children* by Eleanor Farjeon. Copyright 1951 by Eleanor Farjeon. Reprinted by permission of J. B. Lippincott Company and Harold Ober Associates Incorporated

In the country one meets
  Blue carts with their loads
Of sweet-smelling hay,
  And mangolds, and grain:
Oh, take me away
  To the country again!

In the city one sees,
  Big trams rattle by,
And the breath of the chimneys
  That blot out the sky,
And all down the pavements
  Stiff lamp-posts one sees—
But the country has hedgerows,
  The country has trees.

As sweet as the sun
  In the country is rain:
Oh, take me away
  To the country again!

## ROADS GO EVER EVER ON

*J. R. R. Tolkien*

Roads go ever ever on,
  Over rock and under tree,
By caves where never sun has shone,
  By streams that never find the sea;
Over snow by winter sown,
  And through the merry flowers of June,
Over grass and over stone,
  And under mountains in the moon.

## PARTING

*Wang Wei*

I watch you travel slowly down the mountains

And then the sun is gone. I close my thatched
  door.
Grasses will grow green again next spring;
But you, beloved friend, will you return?

## LONG TRIP

*Langston Hughes*

The sea is a wilderness of waves,
A desert of water.
We dip and dive,
Rise and roll,
Hide and are hidden
On the sea.
  Day, night,
  Night, day,
The sea is a desert of waves,
A wilderness of water.

## SAILING HOMEWARD

*Chan Fang-shēng*

Cliffs that rise a thousand feet
Without a break,
Lake that stretches a hundred miles
Without a wave,
Sands that are white through all the year,
Without a stain,
Pine-tree woods, winter and summer
Ever green,
Streams that for ever flow and flow
Without a pause,
Trees that for twenty-thousand years
Your vows have kept,
You have suddenly healed the pain of a traveler's
  heart,
And moved his brush to write a new song.

*(Mother Goose)*

Girls and boys, come out to play,
The moon doth shine as bright as day;
  Leave your supper, and leave your sleep,
And come with your playfellows into the street.
  Come with a whoop, come with a call,
Come with a good will or not at all.
  Up the ladder and down the wall,
A half-penny roll will serve us all.
  You find milk, and I'll find flour,
And we'll have a pudding in half an hour.


*(Mother Goose)*

Ride a cock horse
To Banbury Cross
To see a fair lady upon a white horse;

With rings on her fingers,
And bells on her toes,
She shall have music wherever she goes.

# PLAY

*Kate Greenaway*

School is over,
  Oh, what fun!
Lessons finished,
  Play begun.
Who'll run fastest,
  You or I?
Who'll laugh loudest?
  Let us try.

## RIDDLES FROM MOTHER GOOSE

As round as an apple, as deep as a cup,
And all the king's horses can't fill it up.
(*A Well*)

A riddle, a riddle, as I suppose,
A hundred eyes and never a nose!
(*A Sieve*)

Higher than a house,
Higher than a tree,
Oh! whatever can that be?
(*A Star*)

Lives in winter,
Dies in summer,
And grows with its roots upward!
(*An Icicle*)

A hill full, a hole full,
Yet you cannot catch a bowl full.
(*The Mist*)

Thirty white horses upon a red hill,
Now they tramp, now they champ,
Now they stand still.
(*The Teeth and Gums*)

Hick-a-more, Hack-a-more,
On the King's kitchen door;
All the King's horses,
And all the King's men,
Couldn't drive Hick-a-more,
Hack-a-more,
Off the King's kitchen door.
(*Sunshine*)

Old Mother Twitchett had but one eye,
And a long tail which she let fly;
And every time she went through a gap,
A bit of her tail she left in a trap.
(*A Needle and Thread*)

Little Nanny Etticoat
In a white petticoat,
And a red nose;
The longer she stands
The shorter she grows.
(*A Candle*)

Runs all day and never walks,
Often murmurs, never talks.
It has a bed but never sleeps, .
It has a mouth, but never eats.
(*A River*)

I have a little sister they call her "Peep-peep,"
She wades in the ocean deep, deep, deep.
She climbs up the mountain high, high, high,
The poor little thing hasn't got but one eye.
(*A Star*)

## RHYMING RIDDLES

*Mary Austin*

I come more softly than a bird,
And lovely as a flower;
I sometimes last from year to year
And sometimes but an hour.

I stop the swiftest railroad train
Or break the stoutest tree.
And yet I am afraid of fire
And children play with me.
(*Snow*)

I have no wings, but yet I fly,
I'm slender as a snake and straight as rain,
Who takes me in must die,
Who lets me quickly go will surest gain.
(*Arrow*)

"School is over. . . ." From *Under the Window* by Kate Greenaway. (London: Frederick Warne & Co., Ltd., 1910)
"Runs all day and never walks" and "I have a little sister they call her 'peep.'" From *The American Mother Goose* by Ray Wood. Copyright 1940 by Ray Wood.

Copyright © renewed 1968 by Willis J. Wood. Reprinted by permission of J. B. Lippincott Company
"Rhyming Riddles" from *The Children Sing in the Far West* by Mary Austin. Copyright renewed 1956 Kenneth M. Chapman and Mary C. Wheelwright. Reprinted by permission of the publisher, Houghton Mifflin Company

I never speak a word
But when my voice is heard
Even the mountains shake,
No hands I have
And yet great rocks I break.
                (*Thunder and Lightning*)


First I am frosted,
Second, I am beaten,
Third, I am roasted,
Fourth, I am eaten.
                (*Chestnut*)


(*Mother Goose*)

To market, to market, to buy a fat pig,
Home again, home again, jiggety jig.

To market, to market, to buy a fat hog,
Home again, home again, jiggety jog.

To market, to market, to buy a plum bun,
Home again, home again, market is done.


(*Mother Goose*)

The grand Old Duke of York
    He had ten thousand men,
He marched them up a very high hill
    And he marched them down again.
And when he was up he was up
    And when he was down he was down
And when he was only halfway up
    He was neither up nor down.


(*Mother Goose*)

Hippety hop to the barber shop,
    To get a stick of candy,
One for you and one for me,
    And one for Sister Mandy.


## HOPPITY

*A. A. Milne*

Christopher Robin goes
Hoppity, hoppity,
Hoppity, hoppity, hop.
Whenever I tell him
Politely to stop it, he
Says he can't possibly stop.

If he stopped hopping, he couldn't go anywhere,
Poor little Christopher
Couldn't go anywhere . . .
That's why he *always* goes
Hoppity, hoppity,
Hoppity,
Hoppity,
Hop.


## HUSKY HI

(*Norwegian*)

*Rose Fyleman*

Husky hi, husky hi,
Here comes Keery galloping by.
She carries her husband tied in a sack,
She carries him home on her horse's back.
Husky hi, husky hi,
Here comes Keery galloping by!


(*Mother Goose*)

Jack be nimble,
    Jack be quick,
Jack jump over
    The candlestick.

Jump it lively,
    Jump it quick,
But don't knock over
    The candlestick.

"Hoppity." From *When We Were Very Young* by A. A. Milne. Illustrated by Ernest H. Shepard. Copyright, 1924, by E. P. Dutton & Co., renewal, 1952, by A. A. Milne. Reprinted by permission of the publishers, E. P. Dutton & Co., Inc. and Curtis Brown Ltd. on behalf of the Estate of A. A. Milne

"Huski Hi." From *Picture Rhymes from Foreign Lands* by Rose Fyleman. Copyright 1935, © renewed 1963 by Rose Fyleman. Reprinted by permission of J. B. Lippincott Company

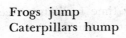

## JUMP OR JIGGLE
*Evelyn Beyer*

Frogs  jump
Caterpillars  hump

Worms  wiggle
Bugs  jiggle

Rabbits  hop
Horses  clop

Snakes  slide
Sea gulls  glide

Mice  creep
Deer  leap

Puppies  bounce
Kittens  pounce

Lions  stalk—
But—
*I  walk!*

## TIPTOE
*Karla Kuskin*

Yesterday I skipped all day,
The day before I ran,
Today I'm going to tiptoe
Everywhere I can.
I'll tiptoe down the stairway.
I'll tiptoe through the door.
I'll tiptoe to the living room
And give an awful roar
And my father, who is reading,
Will jump up from his chair
And mumble something silly like
"I didn't see you there."
I'll tiptoe to my mother
And give a little cough
And when she spins to see me
Why, I'll softly tiptoe off.
I'll tiptoe through the meadows,
Over hills and yellow sands

And when my toes get tired
Then I'll tiptoe on my hands.

## SLIDING
*Myra Cohn Livingston*

We can slide
            down
                    the
                        hill
        or
            down
                    the
                        stair
        or
            down
                    the
                        street
or anywhere.

Or down the roof
    where the shingles broke,
Or down the trunk
    of the back-yard oak.

Down
        the
            slide
                    or the ice
                    or the slippery street,

We can slide
            on our sled
            or our skates
            or our feet.

Oh, it's lots of fun to go outside
And slide
            and slide
                    and slide
                            and slide.

## CLIMBING
*Aileen Fisher*

            The trunk of a tree
            is the road for me
            on a sunny summer day.

Up the bark
that is brown and dark
through tunnels of leaves that sway
and tickle my knees
in the trembly breeze,
that's where I make my way.

Leaves in my face
and twigs in my hair
in a squeeze of a place,
but I don't care!

*Some* people talk
of a summer walk
through clover and weeds and hay.

*Some* people stride
where the hills are wide
and the rocks are speckled gray.

But the trunk of a tree
is the road for me
on a sunny summer day.

                                    David McCord

Every time I climb a tree
Every time I climb a tree
Every time I climb a tree
I scrape a leg
Or skin a knee
And every time I climb a tree
I find some ants
Or dodge a bee
And get the ants
All over me

And every time I climb a tree
Where have you been?
They say to me
But don't they know that I am free
Every time I climb a tree?
I like it best
To spot a nest
That has an egg
Or maybe three

And then I skin
The other leg
But every time I climb a tree
I see a lot of things to see
Swallows rooftops and TV
And all the fields and farms there be
Every time I climb a tree
Though climbing may be good for ants
It isn't awfully good for pants
But still it's pretty good for me
Every time I climb a tree

(*Mother Goose*)

Pease porridge hot,
    Pease porridge cold,
Pease porridge in the pot,
    Nine days old.
Some like it hot,
    Some like it cold,
Some like it in the pot,
    Nine days old.

(*Mother Goose*)

Higgledy, piggledy, my black hen,
    She lays eggs for gentlemen;
Sometimes nine, and sometimes ten,
    Higgledy, piggledy, my black hen.

(*Mother Goose*)

Intery, mintery, cutery corn,
Apple seed and apple thorn;
Wine, brier, limber lock,
Three geese in a flock,
One flew east, one flew west,
And one flew over the goose's nest.

(*Mother Goose*)

1, 2, 3, 4, 5!
I caught a hare alive;
6, 7, 8, 9, 10!
I let her go again.

*(Mother Goose)*

One, two,
Buckle my shoe;
Three, four,
Knock at the door;
Five, six,
Pick up sticks;
Seven, eight,
Lay them straight;
Nine, ten,
A good, fat hen;
Eleven, twelve,
Dig and delve;
Thirteen, fourteen,
Maids a-courting;
Fifteen, sixteen,
Maids in the kitchen;
Seventeen, eighteen,
Maids a-waiting;
Nineteen, twenty,
My plate's empty.

## THE A B C BUNNY

*Wanda Gág*

A for Apple, big and red
B for Bunny snug a-bed
C for Crash!
D for Dash!
E for Elsewhere in a flash
F for Frog—he's fat and funny
"Looks like rain," says he to Bunny
G for Gale!
H for Hail!
Hippy-hop goes Bunny's tail
I for Insects here and there
J for Jay with jaunty air
K for Kitten, catnip-crazy
L for Lizard—look how lazy
M for Mealtime—munch, munch, munch!
M-m-m these greens are good for lunch
N for Napping in a Nook
O for Owl with bookish look
P for prickly Porcupine

Pins and needles on his spine
Q for Quail
R for Rail
S for Squirrel Swishy-tail
T for Tripping back to Town
U for Up and Up-side-down
V for View
Valley too
W—"We welcome you!"
X for eXit—off, away!
That's enough for us today
Y for You, take one last look
Z for Zero—close the book!

## CHOOSING

*Eleanor Farjeon*

Which will you have, a ball or a cake?
A cake is so nice, yes, that's what I'll take.

Which will you have, a cake or a cat?
A cat is so soft, I think I'll take that.

Which will you have, a cat or a rose?
A rose is so sweet, I'll have that, I suppose.

Which will you have, a rose or a book?
A book full of pictures?—oh, do let me look!

Which will you have, a book or a ball?
Oh, a ball! No, a book; No, a—
    There! have them all!

### LAMPLIGHTER BARN

*Myra Cohn Livingston*

I can play
in the prickly hay
and I can find
where the chickens lay
and take off my shoes
and stay
and stay
in the tickly hay
on a rainy day.

### TEDDY BEAR

*Harry Behn*

I had to give Reginald a slap
For making a nuisance of himself.

When I was trying to take my nap
He had to go tumble off his shelf!

And when I honestly tried to sleep
He talked and talked, until I sneezed . . .

I really did my best to keep
Him quiet—but Mummy wasn't pleased.

### TELEGRAM

*William Wise*

I never got a telegram before;
But I went to the big front door,
And here was a man
Who wanted to see
Master Jonathan Blake!
So I said, "That's me."

And to make things clear,
He said, "Please sign here."
I never got a telegram before,
But I'd like to get at least a million more.

I never got a "wire" in my life;
So I sliced this one open with a knife.
Mother said most men
Prefer to use a cutter,
Since the knife I found
Was designed for butter.
But I never got a "wire" in my life!
So *naturally* I sliced it with a knife.

I never got a telegram before;
And when I went to the big front door,
It said: "Congratulations
On being six today
Every one of us loves you
That's all we can say."
I never got a telegram before,
But I'd like to get at least a *million* more!

### US TWO

*A. A. Milne*

Wherever I am, there's always Pooh,
There's always Pooh and Me.
Whatever I do, he wants to do,
"Where are you going to-day?" says Pooh:
"Well, that's very odd 'cos I was too.
Let's go together," says Pooh, says he.
"Let's go together," says Pooh.

"What's twice eleven?" I said to Pooh.
("Twice what?" said Pooh to Me.)
"I *think* it ought to be twenty-two."
"Just what I think myself," said Pooh.
"It wasn't an easy sum to do,
But that's what it is," said Pooh, said he.
"That's what it is," said Pooh.

"Lamplighter Barn." From *Wide Awake and Other Poems,* © 1959, by Myra Cohn Livingston. Reprinted by permission of Harcourt Brace Jovanovich, Inc.
  "Teddy Bear." From *The Wizard in the Well,* © 1956, by Harry Behn. Reprinted by permission of Harcourt Brace Jovanovich, Inc.
  "Telegram" from *Jonathan Blake* by William Wise. © William Wise, 1956. Reprinted by permission of Curtis

Brown, Ltd.
  "Us Two." From *Now We Are Six* by A. A. Milne, illustrated by Ernest H. Shepard. Copyright, 1927 by E. P. Dutton & Co., renewal © 1955 by A. A. Milne. Reprinted by permission of the publishers, E. P. Dutton & Co., Inc. and Curtis Brown Ltd. on behalf of the Estate of A. A. Milne

"Let's look for dragons," I said to Pooh.
"Yes, let's," said Pooh to Me.
We crossed the river and found a few—
"Yes, those are dragons all right," said Pooh.
"As soon as I saw their beaks I knew.
That's what they are," said Pooh, said he.
"That's what they are," said Pooh.

"Let's frighten the dragons," I said to Pooh.
"That's right," said Pooh to Me.
"*I'm* not afraid," I said to Pooh,
And I held his paw and I shouted "Shoo!
Silly old dragons!"—and off they flew.
"I wasn't afraid," said Pooh, said he,
"I'm *never* afraid with you."

So wherever I am, there's always Pooh,
There's always Pooh and Me.
"What would I do?" I said to Pooh,
"If it wasn't for you," and Pooh said: "True,
It isn't much fun for One, but Two
Can stick together," says Pooh, says he.
"That's how it is," says Pooh.

## SKATING

*Herbert Asquith*

When I try to skate,
My feet are so wary
They grit and they grate:
And then I watch Mary
Easily gliding,
Like an ice-fairy;
Skimming and curving,
Out and in,
With a turn of her head,
And a lift of her chin,
And a gleam of her eye,
And a twirl and a spin;
Sailing under
The breathless hush
Of the willows, and back

To the frozen rush;
Out to the island
And round the edge,
Skirting the rim
Of the crackling sedge,
Swerving close
To the poplar root,
And round the lake
On a single foot,
With a three, and an eight,
And a loop and a ring;
Where Mary glides,
The lake will sing!
Out in the mist
I hear her now
Under the frost
Of the willow-bough
Easily sailing,
Light and fleet,
With the song of the lake
Beneath her feet.

## DIFFERENT BICYCLES
*Dorothy Baruch*

When I ride my bicycle
I pedal and pedal
Knees up, knees down.
Knees up, knees down.

But when the boy next door
Rides his,
It's whizz—
A chuck   a chuck—

And away
He's gone
With his
Knees steady-straight
In one place . . .
Because—
    His bicycle has
    A motor fastened on.

"Skating." Reprinted with permission of Macmillan Publishing Co., Inc. and William Heinemann Ltd. Publishers from *Pillicock Hill* by Herbert Asquith

"Different Bicycles" by Dorothy Baruch from *I Like Machinery*. Permission granted by Bertha Klausner International Literary Agency, Inc.

## SKY DIVER
*Adrien Stoutenberg*

Grotesque, jumping out
like a clothed frog, helmet and glasses,
arms and legs wading the sky,
feet flapping before the cloth flower opens;
then suspended, poised,
an exclamation point upside-down,
and going down, swaying over corn and creeks
and highways scribbled
over the bones of fish and eagles.

There is the interim between air and earth,
time to study steeples
and the underwings of birds going over,
before the unseen chasm,
the sudden jaw open and hissing.

Lying here after the last jump
I see how fanatic roots are,
how moles breathe through darkness,
how deep the earth can be.

## SWING SONG
*Harry Behn*

Oh, I've discovered
A happy thing!
For every game
There's a song to sing,
Sometimes with words
Sometimes without,
It's easy to tell
What a song's about
From only a humming
Like wind at noon,
It needn't be even
Half a tune
If only it goes
With what you do,
If what you do
Is exactly true,
Or anyway if
It seems to you.

The time I discovered
This wonderful thing
I really was swinging
In a swing,
And the song I was singing
Was just as true
For all the flying
Sky-things too,
For seagulls and eagulls
And bees and bugs
And arrows and sparrows,
Enchanted rugs,
Clouds and balloons,
Balloons and bees—
A backward humming
A forward breeze,
Swinging without
Any tune you please.

## THE SWING
*Robert Louis Stevenson*

How do you like to go up in a swing,
　Up in the air so blue?
Oh, I do think it the pleasantest thing
　Ever a child can do!

Up in the air and over the wall,
　Till I can see so wide,
Rivers and trees and cattle and all
　Over the countryside—

Till I look down on the garden green,
　Down on the roof so brown—
Up in the air I go flying again,
　Up in the air and down!

"Sky Diver" by Adrien Stoutenberg from *A Short History of the Fur Trade*, by Adrien Stoutenberg. Copyright © 1968 by Adrien Stoutenberg. Reprinted by permission of the publisher, Houghton Mifflin Company and Andre Deutsch Limited, Publishers

"Swing Song." From *The Little Hill*, copyright, 1949, by Harry Behn. Reprinted by permission of Harcourt Brace Jovanovich, Inc.
"The Swing." From *A Child's Garden of Verses* by Robert Louis Stevenson

## MARCHING SONG

*Robert Louis Stevenson*

Bring the comb and play upon it!
   Marching, here we come!
Willie cocks his highland bonnet,
   Johnnie beats the drum.

Mary Jane commands the party,
   Peter leads the rear;
Feet in time, alert and hearty,
   Each a Grenadier!

All in the most martial manner
   Marching double-quick;
While the napkin, like a banner,
   Waves upon the stick!

Here's enough of fame and pillage,
   Great commander Jane!
Now that we've been round the village,
   Let's go home again.

## MY SHADOW

*Robert Louis Stevenson*

I have a little shadow that goes in and out
   with me,
And what can be the use of him is more than I
   can see.
He is very, very like me from the heels up to the
   head;
And I see him jump before me, when I jump into
   my bed.

The funniest thing about him is the way he likes
   to grow—
Not at all like proper children, which is always
   very slow;
For he sometimes shoots up taller like an India-
   rubber ball,
And he sometimes gets so little that there's none
   of him at all.

He hasn't got a notion of how children ought to
   play,
And can only make a fool of me in every sort of
   way.
He stays so close beside me, he's a coward you
   can see;
I'd think shame to stick to nursie as that shadow
   sticks to me!

One morning, very early, before the sun was up,
I rose and found the shining dew on every buttercup;
But my lazy little shadow, like an arrant sleepy-
   head,
Had stayed at home behind me and was fast
   asleep in bed.

## WHERE GO THE BOATS?

*Robert Louis Stevenson*

   Dark brown is the river,
      Golden is the sand.
   It flows along forever,
      With trees on either hand.

   Green leaves a-floating,
      Castles of the foam,
   Boats of mine a-boating—
      Where will all come home?

   On goes the river
      And out past the mill,
   Away down the valley,
      Away down the hill.

   Away down the river,
      A hundred miles or more,
   Other little children
      Shall bring my boats ashore.

"Marching Song." From *A Child's Garden of Verses* by
Robert Louis Stevenson
  "My Shadow." From *A Child's Garden of Verses* by

Robert Louis Stevenson
  "Where Go the Boats?" From *A Child's Garden of Verses* by Robert Louis Stevenson

## SNIFF

*Frances M. Frost*

When school is out, we love to follow
our noses over hill and hollow,
smelling jewelweed and vetch,
sniffing fern and milkweed patch.

The airy fifth of our five senses
leads us under, over, fences.
We run like rabbits through bright hours
and poke our noses into flowers!

## 74TH STREET

*Myra Cohn Livingston*

Hey, this little kid gets roller skates.
She puts them on.
She stands up and almost
flops over backwards.
She sticks out a foot like
she's going somewhere and
falls down and
smacks her hand. She
grabs hold of a step to get up and
sticks out the other foot and
slides about six inches and
falls and
skins her knee.

　　　　　And then, you know what?

She brushes off the dirt and the
blood and puts some
spit on it and then
sticks out the other foot

　　　　*again.*

## HAPPINESS

*A. A. Milne*

John had
Great Big
Waterproof
Boots on;
John had a
Great Big
Waterproof
Hat;
John had a
Great Big
Waterproof
Mackintosh—
And that
(Said John)
Is
That.

## THE BASE STEALER

*Robert Francis*

Poised between going on and back, pulled
Both ways taut like a tightrope-walker,
Fingertips pointing the opposites,
Now bouncing tiptoe like a dropped ball
Or a kid skipping rope, come on, come on,
Running a scattering of steps sidewise,
How he teeters, skitters, tingles, teases,
Taunts them, hovers like an ecstatic bird,
He's only flirting, crowd him, crowd him,
Delicate, delicate, delicate, delicate—now!

## THE LAND OF STORY-BOOKS

*Robert Louis Stevenson*

At evening when the lamp is lit,
Around the fire my parents sit;
They sit at home and talk and sing,
And do not play at anything.

Now, with my little gun, I crawl
All in the dark along the wall,
And follow round the forest track
Away behind the sofa back.

There, in the night, where none can spy,
All in my hunter's camp I lie,
And play at books that I have read
Till it is time to go to bed.

These are the hills, these are the woods,
These are my starry solitudes;
And there the river by whose brink
The roaring lions come to drink.

I see the others far away
As if in firelit camp they lay,
And I, like to an Indian scout,
Around their party prowled about.

So, when my nurse comes in for me,
Home I return across the sea,
And go to bed with backward looks
At my dear Land of Story-books.

On incandescent feet he falls
Unfalling, trailing white foam, white fire.

## THE PICKETY FENCE
*David McCord*

The pickety fence
The pickety fence
Give it a lick it's
The pickety fence
Give it a lick it's
A clickety fence
Give it a lick it's
A lickety fence
Give it a lick
Give it a lick
Give it a lick
With a rickety stick
Pickety
Pickety
Pickety
Pick

## SKIER
*Robert Francis*

He swings down like the flourish of a pen
Signing a signature in white on white.

The silence of his skis reciprocates
The silence of the world around him.

Wind is his one competitor
In the cool winding and unwinding down.

## THE UMPIRE
*Milton Bracker*

The umpire is a lonely man
Whose calls are known to every fan
Yet none will call him Dick or Dan
    In all the season's games.
They'll never call him Al or Ed
Or Bill or Phil or Frank or Fred
Or Jim or Tim or Tom or Ted—
    They'll simply call him names.

"Skier" by Robert Francis from *Come out into the Sun* by Robert Francis. Copyright © 1965 by Robert Francis. Reprinted by permission of the University of Massachusetts Press

"The Pickety Fence." From *Every Time I Climb a Tree* by David McCord (British title: *Mr. Bidery's Spidery Garden.*) Copyright 1952 by David McCord. Reprinted by permission of Little, Brown and Co., and George G. Harrap & Company Ltd.

"The Umpire" by Milton Bracker from *The New York Times*. Copyright © 1962 by The New York Times Company. Reprinted by permission

(*Mother Goose*)

Hey, diddle, diddle!
   The cat and the fiddle,
The cow jumped over the moon;
   The little dog laughed
   To see such sport,
And the dish ran away with the spoon.

# HUMOR

(*Mother Goose*)

Tom he was a piper's son,
He learned to play when he was young,
But all the tunes that he could play,
Was "Over the hills and far away."

Now Tom with his pipe made such a noise,
That he pleased both girls and boys,
And they stopped to hear him play
"Over the hills and far away."

Tom with his pipe did play with such skill,
That those who heard him could never keep
      still;
Whenever they heard they began for to dance,
Even pigs on their hind legs would after him
      prance.

## TWO FROM THE ZOO

*Eve Merriam*

There is an animal known as skink,
And no matter what you might happen to think
Or ever have thunk,

A skink—
Unlike a skunk—
Does not stink.
A skink is a skink.

If you go to the zoo
It may be on view
Alongside an aye-aye.

Aye, yes, that's right.
It's quite a sight.
Please take my word
That an aye-aye is not a sailor bird
Or anything else just as absurd.

No, it's truly
And zooly
A creature there.
Don't be afraid, since it's dulcet and docile
And not in the least
An unruly beast.

### *from* PERAMBULATOR POEMS

*David McCord*

When I was christened
they held me up
and poured some water
out of a cup.

The trouble was
it fell on me,
and I and water
don't agree.

A lot of christeners
stood and listened:
I let them know
that I was christened.

## THE GNU

*Theodore Roethke*

There's *this* to Remember about the Gnu:
He *closely* Resembles—but I *can't* tell *you!*

## THE DUEL

*Eugene Field*

The gingham dog and the calico cat
Side by side on the table sat;
'T was half-past twelve, and (what do you think!)
Nor one nor t' other had slept a wink!
    The old Dutch clock and the Chinese plate
    Appeared to know as sure as fate
There was going to be a terrible spat.
    (*I wasn't there; I simply state
    What was told to me by the Chinese plate!*)

The gingham dog went, "bow-wow-wow!"
And the calico cat replied, "mee-ow!"
The air was littered, an hour or so,
With bits of gingham and calico,
    While the old Dutch clock in the chimney-
    place
    Up with its hands before its face,
For it always dreaded a family row!
    (*Now mind: I'm only telling you
    What the old Dutch clock declares is true!*)

The Chinese plate looked very blue,
And wailed, "Oh, dear! what shall we do!"
But the gingham dog and the calico cat
Wallowed this way and tumbled that,
    Employing every tooth and claw
    In the awfullest way you ever saw—
And, oh! how the gingham and calico flew!
    (*Don't fancy I exaggerate—
    I got my news from the Chinese plate!*)

Next morning, where the two had sat
They found no trace of dog or cat;
And some folks think unto this day
That burglars stole that pair away!
    But the truth about the cat and pup

Is this: they ate each other up!
Now what do you really think of that!
   (*The old Dutch clock it told me so,*
   *And that is how I came to know.*)

## THE OWL AND THE PUSSY-CAT

*Edward Lear*

The Owl and the Pussy-Cat went to sea
  In a beautiful pea-green boat,
They took some honey, and plenty of money
  Wrapped up in a five-pound note.
The Owl looked up to the stars above,
  And sang to a small guitar,
"O lovely Pussy, O Pussy, my love,
  What a beautiful Pussy you are,
      You are,
      You are!
  What a beautiful Pussy you are!"


Pussy said to the Owl, "You elegant fowl,
  How charmingly sweet you sing!
Oh! let us be married, too long we have tarried:
  But what shall we do for a ring?"
They sailed away, for a year and a day,
  To the land where the Bong-tree grows;
And there in a wood a Piggy-wig stood,
  With a ring at the end of his nose,
      His nose,
      His nose,
  With a ring at the end of his nose.

"Dear Pig, are you willing to sell for one shilling
  Your ring?" Said the Piggy, "I will."
So they took it away, and were married next day
  By the Turkey who lives on the hill.
They dined on mince and slices of quince,
  Which they ate with a runcible spoon;
And hand in hand, on the edge of the sand,
  They danced by the light of the moon,
      The moon,
      The moon,
  They danced by the light of the moon.

"The Owl and the Pussy-cat" by Edward Lear from *The Owl and the Pussy-cat.*
"The Rum Tum Tugger." From *Old Possum's Book of Practical Cats,* copyright, 1939, by T. S. Eliot; renewed, 1967, by Esme Valerie Eliot. Reprinted by permission of Harcourt Brace Jovanovich, Inc. and Faber and Faber Ltd.

## THE RUM TUM TUGGER

*T. S. Eliot*

The Rum Tum Tugger is a Curious Cat:
If you offer him pheasant he would rather have
  grouse.
If you put him in a house he would much prefer
  a flat,
If you put him in a flat then he'd rather have a
  house.
If you set him on a mouse then he only wants a
  rat,
If you set him on a rat then he'd rather chase a
  mouse.
Yes the Rum Tum Tugger is a Curious Cat—
  And there isn't any call for me to shout it:
    For he will do
    As he do do
      And there's no doing anything about it!

The Rum Tum Tugger is a terrible bore:
When you let him in, then he wants to be out;
He's always on the wrong side of every door,
As soon as he's at home, then he'd like to get
  about.
He likes to lie in the bureau drawer,
But he makes such a fuss if he can't get out.
Yes the Rum Tum Tugger is a Curious Cat—
  And it isn't any use for you to doubt it:
    For he will do
    As he do do
      And there's no doing anything about it!

The Rum Tum Tugger is a curious beast:
His disobliging ways are a matter of habit.
If you offer him fish then he always wants a
  feast;
When there isn't any fish then he won't eat
  rabbit.
If you offer him cream then he sniffs and sneers,
For he only likes what he finds for himself;
So you'll catch him in it right up to the ears,
If you put it away on the larder shelf.
The Rum Tum Tugger is artful and knowing,
The Rum Tum Tugger doesn't care for a cud-
  dle;
But he'll leap on your lap in the middle of your
  sewing,
For there's nothing he enjoys like a horrible
  muddle.

Yes the Rum Tum Tugger is a Curious Cat—
   And there isn't any need for me to spout it:
     For he will do
     As he do do
       And there's no doing anything about it!

## MACAVITY: THE MYSTERY CAT

*T. S. Eliot*

Macavity's a Mystery Cat: he's called the Hidden
   Paw—
For he's the master criminal who can defy the
   Law.
He's the bafflement of Scotland Yard, the Flying
   Squad's despair:
For when they reach the scene of crime—*Macavity's not there!*

Macavity, Macavity, there's no one like Macavity,
He's broken every human law, he breaks the law
   of gravity.
His powers of levitation would make a fakir
   stare,
And when you reach the scene of crime—*Macavity's not there!*
You may seek him in the basement, you may
   look up in the air—
But I tell you once and once again, *Macavity's not there!*

Macavity's a ginger cat, he's very tall and thin;
You would know him if you saw him, for his eyes
   are sunken in.
His brow is deeply lined with thought, his head
   is highly domed;
His coat is dusty from neglect, his whiskers are
   uncombed.
He sways his head from side to side, with movements like a snake;
And when you think he's half asleep, he's always
   wide awake.

Macavity, Macavity, there's no one like Macavity,
For he's a fiend in feline shape, a monster of
   depravity.

You may meet him in a by-street, you may see
   him in the square—
But when a crime's discovered, then *Macavity's not there!*

He's outwardly respectable. (They say he cheats
   at cards.)
And his footprints are not found in any file of
   Scotland Yard's.
And when the larder's looted, or the jewel-case is
   rifled,
Or when the milk is missing, or another Peke's
   been stifled,
Or the greenhouse glass is broken, and the trellis
   past repair—
Ay, there's the wonder of the thing! *Macavity's not there!*

And when the Foreign Office find a Treaty's gone
   astray,
Or the Admiralty lose some plans and drawings
   by the way,
There may be a scrap of paper in the hall or on
   the stair—
But it's useless to investigate—*Macavity's not there!*
And when the loss has been disclosed, the Secret
   Service say:
"It *must* have been Macavity!"—but he's a mile
   away.
You'll be sure to find him resting, or a-licking of
   his thumbs,
Or engaged in doing complicated long division
   sums.

Macavity, Macavity, there's no one like Macavity,
There never was a Cat of such deceitfulness and
   suavity.
He always has an alibi, and one or two to spare:
At whatever time the deed took place—MACAV-
   ITY WASN'T THERE!
And they say that all the Cats whose wicked
   deeds are widely known,
(I might mention Mungojerrie, I might mention
   Griddlebone)
Are nothing more than agents for the Cat who
   all the time
Just controls their operations: the Napoleon of
   Crime!

## ALAS, ALACK!

*Walter de la Mare*

Ann, Ann!
    Come! Quick as you can!
There's a fish that *talks*
    In the frying-pan.
Out of the fat,
    As clear as glass,
He put up his mouth
    And moaned "Alas!"
Oh, most mournful,
    "Alas, alack!"
Then turned to his sizzling,
    And sank him back.

## THE ARMADILLO

*Jack Prelutsky*

The ancient armadillo
is as simple as the rain,
he's an armor-plated pillow
with a microscopic brain.

He's disinterested thoroughly
in what the world has wrought,
but spends his time in contemplative,
armadyllic thought.

## THREE LITTLE PUFFINS

*Eleanor Farjeon*

Three little puffins
    Were partial to muffins,
As partial as partial can be.
    They wouldn't eat nuffin
    But hot buttered muffin
For breakfast and dinner and tea.
    Pantin' and puffin'
    And chewin' and chuffin'

They just went on stuffin', dear me!
    Till the three little puffins
    Were chockful of muffins
And puffy as puffy can be,
            All three
    Were puffy as puffy can be.

## HOMEMADE BOAT

*Shel Silverstein*

This boat that we just built is just fine—
And don't try to tell us it's not.
The sides and the back are divine—
It's the bottom I guess we forgot. . . .

## THE OCTOPUS

*Ogden Nash*

Tell me, O Octopus, I begs,
Is those things arms, or is they legs?
I marvel at thee, Octopus;
If I were thou, I'd call me Us.

*Lewis Carroll*

How doth the little crocodile
    Improve his shining tail,
And pour the waters of the Nile
    On every golden scale!

How cheerfully he seems to grin,
    How neatly spreads his claws,
And welcomes little fishes in,
    With gently smiling jaws!

## HABITS OF THE HIPPOPOTAMUS

*Arthur Guiterman*

The hippopotamus is strong
  And huge of head and broad of bustle;
The limbs on which he rolls along
  Are big with hippopotomuscle.

He does not greatly care for sweets
  Like ice cream, apple pie, or custard,
But takes to flavor what he eats
  A little hippopotomustard.

The hippopotamus is true
  To all his principles, and just;
He always tries his best to do
  The things one hippopotomust.

He never rides in trucks or trams,
  In taxicabs or omnibuses,
And so keeps out of traffic jams
  And other hippopotomusses.

## HOW TO TELL THE WILD ANIMALS

*Carolyn Wells*

If ever you should go by chance
  To jungles in the East;
And if there should to you advance
  A large and tawny beast,
If he roars at you as you're dyin'
You'll know it is the Asian Lion.

Or if some time when roaming round,
  A noble wild beast greets you,
With black stripes on a yellow ground,
  Just notice if he eats you.
This simple rule may help you learn
The Bengal Tiger to discern.

If strolling forth, a beast you view,
  Whose hide with spots is peppered,

As soon as he has lept on you,
  You'll know it is the Leopard.
'Twill do no good to roar with pain,
He'll only lep and lep again.

If when you're walking round your yard,
  You meet a creature there,
Who hugs you very, very hard,
  Be sure it is the Bear.
If you have any doubt, I guess
He'll give you just one more caress.

Though to distinguish beasts of prey
  A novice might nonplus,
The Crocodiles you always may
  Tell from Hyenas thus:
Hyenas come with merry smiles;
But if they weep, they're Crocodiles.

The true Chameleon is small,
  A lizard sort of thing;
He hasn't any ears at all,
  And not a single wing.
If there is nothing on the tree,
'Tis the Chameleon you see.

*(American Mother Goose)*

I asked my mother for fifteen cents
To see the elephant jump the fence,
He jumped so high that he touched the sky
And never came back 'till the Fourth of July.

## ELETELEPHONY

*Laura E. Richards*

Once there was an elephant,
Who tried to use the telephant—
No! no! I mean an elephone
Who tried to use the telephone—
(Dear me! I am not certain quite

That even now I've got it right.)
Howe'er it was, he got his trunk
Entangled in the telephunk;
The more he tried to get it free,
The louder buzzed the telephee—
(I fear I'd better drop the song
Of elephop and telephong!)

## GRIZZLY BEAR

*Mary Austin*

If you ever, ever, ever meet a grizzly bear,
You must never, never, never ask him *where*
He is going,
Or *what* he is doing;
For if you ever, ever, dare
To stop a grizzly bear,
You will never meet *another* grizzly bear.

## JABBERWOCKY

*Lewis Carroll*

'Twas brillig, and the slithy toves
    Did gyre and gimble in the wabe:
All mimsy were the borogoves,
    And the mome raths outgrabe.

"Beware the Jabberwock, my son!
    The jaws that bite, the claws that catch!
Beware the Jubjub bird, and shun
    The frumious Bandersnatch!"

He took his vorpal sword in hand:
    Long time the manxome foe he sought—
So rested he by the Tumtum tree,
    And stood awhile in thought.

And, as in uffish thought he stood,
    The Jabberwock, with eyes of flame,
Came whiffling through the tulgey wood,
    And burbled as it came!

One, two! One, two! And through and through
    The vorpal blade went snicker-snack!

He left it dead, and with its head
    He went galumphing back.

"And hast thou slain the Jabberwock?
    Come to my arms, my beamish boy!
O frabjous day! Callooh! Callay!"
    He chortled in his joy.

'Twas brillig, and the slithy toves
    Did gyre and gimble in the wabe:
All mimsy were the borogoves,
    And the mome raths outgrabe.

## DON'T EVER CROSS A CROCODILE

*Kaye Starbird*

Don't ever cross a crocodile,
However few his faults.
Don't ever dare
A dancing bear
To teach you how to waltz.

Don't ever poke a rattlesnake
Who's sleeping in the sun
And say the poke
Was just a joke
And really all in fun.

Don't ever lure a lion close
With gifts of steak and suet.
Though lion-looks
Are nice in books,
Don't ever, ever do it.

## THE PURPLE COW

*Gelett Burgess*

I never saw a Purple Cow,
    I never hope to see one;
But I can tell you, anyhow,
    I'd rather see than be one.

ards. Copyright 1935 by Laura E. Richards; Copyright © 1960 by Hamilton Richards. Reprinted by permission of Little, Brown and Co.

"Grizzly Bear" from *The Children Sing in the Far West* by Mary Austin. Copyright renewed 1956 Kenneth M. Chapman and Mary C. Wheelwright. Reprinted by permission of the publisher, Houghton Mifflin Company

"Jabberwocky." *This sounds as convincing as if it made sense and it is wonderful to roll under your tongue.*
"Don't Ever Cross a Crocodile." From *Don't Ever Cross A Crocodile* by Kaye Starbird. Copyright © 1963 by Kaye Starbird. Reprinted by permission of J. B. Lippincott Company
"The Purple Cow" by Gelett Burgess from *The Burgess Nonsense Book* by Gelett Burgess. (New York: J. B. Lippincott Co., 1901)

## STATELY VERSE
*Unknown*

If Mary goes far out to sea,
  By wayward breezes fanned,
I'd like to know—can you tell me?—
  Just where would Maryland?

If Tenny went high up in air
  And looked o'er land and lea,
Looked here and there and everywhere,
  Pray what would Tennessee?

I looked out of the window and
  Saw Orry on the lawn;
He's not there now, and who can tell
  Just where has Oregon?

Two girls were quarrelling one day
  With garden tools, and so
I said, "My dears, let Mary rake
  And just let Idaho."

A friend of mine lived in a flat
  With half a dozen boys;
When he fell ill I asked him why.
  He said: "I'm Illinois."

An English lady had a steed.
  She called him 'Ighland Bay.
She rode for exercise, and thus
  Rhode Island every day.

## FISH STORY
*Richard Armour*

Count this among my heartfelt wishes:
To hear a fish tale told by fishes
And stand among the fish who doubt
The honor of a fellow trout,

And watch the bulging of their eyes
To hear of imitation flies
And worms with rather droopy looks
Stuck through with hateful, horrid hooks,
And fishermen they fled all day from
(As big as this) and got away from.

## TONY THE TURTLE

*E. V. Rieu*

Tony was a Turtle
  Very much at ease,
Swimming in the sunshine
  Through the summer seas,
And feeding on the fishes
Irrespective of their wishes,
With a "By your leave" and "Thank you"
  And a gentlemanly squeeze.

Tony was a Turtle
  Who loved a civil phrase;
Anxious and obliging,
  Sensitive to praise.
And to hint that he was snappy
Made him thoroughly unhappy;
For Tony was a Turtle
  With most engaging ways.

Tony was a Turtle
  Who thought, before he fed,
Of other people's comfort,
  And as he ate them said;
"If I seem a little grumpy,
It is *not* that you are lumpy."
For Tony was a Turtle
  Delicately bred.

"Fish Story." From *Light Armour* by Richard Armour. Copyright 1954 by Richard Armour. Used with permission of McGraw-Hill Book Company
"Tony the Turtle," "Night Thought of a Tortoise,"

*E. V. Rieu*

*Night Thought*
*of a*
*Tortoise*
*Suffering from*
*Insomnia*
*on a Lawn*

The world is very flat—
There is no doubt of that.

## THE FLATTERED FLYING FISH

*E. V. Rieu*

Said the Shark to the Flying Fish over the phone:
"Will you join me tonight? I am dining alone.
Let me order a nice little dinner for two!
And come as you are, in your shimmering blue."

Said the Flying Fish: "Fancy remembering me,
And the dress that I wore at the Porpoises' tea!"
"How could I forget?" said the Shark in his guile:
"I expect you at eight!" and rang off with a smile.

She has powdered her nose; she has put on her
    things;
She is off with one flap of her luminous wings.
O little one, lovely, light-hearted and vain,
The Moon will not shine on your beauty again!

## THE OSTRICH IS A SILLY BIRD

*Mary E. Wilkins Freeman*

The ostrich is a silly bird,
    With scarcely any mind.
He often runs so very fast,
    He leaves himself behind.

And when he gets there, has to stand
    And hang about till night,

and "The Flattered Flying Fish," by E. V. Rieu from *The Flattered Flying Fish* by E. V. Rieu. Copyright © 1962 by E. V. Rieu. Reprinted by permission of Penelope Rieu

Without a blessed thing to do
Until he comes in sight.

## THE BONNIE CRAVAT
*(Mother Goose)*

Jennie, come tie my,
Jennie, come tie my,
Jennie, come tie my bonnie cravat;
I've tied it behind,
I've tied it before,
I've tied it so often, I'll tie it no more.

*(Mother Goose)*

Ding, dong, bell!
Pussy's in the well!
Who put her in?
Little Johnny Green.
Who pulled her out?
Little Johnny Stout.

What a naughty boy was that
To try to drown poor pussy cat
Which never did him any harm,
But killed the mice in his father's barn!

*(Mother Goose)*

A diller, a dollar, a ten o'clock scholar!
What makes you come so soon?
You used to come at ten o'clock,
But now you come at noon.

*(Mother Goose)*

Bye, baby bunting,
Father's gone a-hunting,
Mother's gone a-milking,
Sister's gone a-silking,
And brother's gone to buy a skin
To wrap the baby bunting in.

"The Ostrich Is a Silly Bird" by Mary E. Wilkins Freeman. Reprinted from the August 1905 issue of *Harper's Magazine*

## REFLECTIONS DENTAL
### Phyllis McGinley

How pure, how beautiful, how fine
Do teeth on television shine!
No flutist flutes, no dancer twirls,
But comes equipped with matching pearls.
Gleeful announcers all are born
With sets like rows of hybrid corn.
Clowns, critics, clergy, commentators,
Ventriloquists and roller skaters,
M.C.s who beat their palms together,
The girl who diagrams the weather,
The crooner crooning for his supper—
All flash white treasures, lower and upper.
With miles of smiles the airwaves teem,
And each an orthodontist's dream.

'Twould please my eye as gold a miser's—
One charmer with uncapped incisors.


## THE PERFECT REACTIONARY
### Hughes Mearns

As I was sitting in my chair
I knew the bottom wasn't there,
Nor legs nor back, but *I just sat,*
Ignoring little things like that.


## SOMEBODY SAID
## THAT IT COULDN'T BE DONE
### Anonymous

Somebody said that it couldn't be done—
But he, with a grin, replied
He'd never be one to say it couldn't be done—
Leastways, not 'til he'd tried.
So he buckled right in, with a trace of a grin;
By golly, he went right to it.
He tackled The Thing That Couldn't Be Done!
And he couldn't do it.

## TOMBSTONE
### Lucia M. and James L. Hymes, Jr.

Here lies
A bully
Who wasn't so wise.
He picked on
A fellow
Who was his own size.

## MUMMY SLEPT LATE AND DADDY FIXED BREAKFAST
### John Ciardi

Daddy fixed the breakfast.
He made us each a waffle.
It looked like gravel pudding.
It tasted something awful.

"Ha, ha," he said, "I'll try again.
This time I'll get it right."
But what *I* got was in between
Bituminous and anthracite.

"A little too well done? Oh well,
I'll have to start all over."
*That* time what landed on my plate
Looked like a manhole cover.

I tried to cut it with a fork:
The fork gave off a spark.
I tried a knife and twisted it
Into a question mark.

I tried it with a hack-saw.
I tried it with a torch.
It didn't even make a dent.
It didn't even scorch.

The next time Dad gets breakfast
When Mommy's sleeping late,
I think I'll skip the waffles.
I'd sooner eat the plate!

# GLOSS

### David McCord

I know a little man both ept and ert.
An intro-? extro-? No, he's just a vert.
Sheveled and couth and kempt, pecunious, ane,
His image trudes upon the ceptive brain.

When life turns sipid and the mind is traught,
The spirit soars as I would sist it ought.
Chalantly then, like any gainly goof,
My digent self is sertive, choate, loof.

# THE FOLK WHO LIVE IN BACKWARD TOWN

### Mary Ann Hoberman

The folk who live in Backward Town
Are inside out and upside down.
They wear their hats inside their heads
And go to sleep beneath their beds.
They only eat the apple peeling
And take their walks across the ceiling.

# COUPLET COUNTDOWN

### Eve Merriam

6.
You'll find, in French, that couplet's
  a little word for two;

*Voici,* how little time before our couplet's
  through.

5.
Of all the forms of verse that can be shown,
The couplet is the shortest one that's known.

4.
Rain raineth and sun sunneth;
Behold how my couplet runneth
  over.

3.
One and one is or are two?
I never know: do you?

2.
Want your meter
Even neater?

1.
Terse
Verse.

# DIAMOND CUT DIAMOND

### Ewart Milne

Two cats
One up a tree
One under the tree
The cat up a tree is he
The cat under the tree is she
The tree is witch elm, just incidentally.
He takes no notice of she, she takes no notice of he.
He stares at the woolly clouds passing, she stares at the tree.
There's been a lot written about cats, by Old Possum, Yeats and Company
But not Alfred de Musset or Lord Tennyson or Poe or anybody
Wrote about one cat under, and one cat up, a tree.
God knows why this should be left for me
Except I like cats as cats be
Especially one cat up
And one cat under
A witch elm
Tree.

## THE STORY OF AUGUSTUS

*Heinrich Hoffmann*

Augustus was a chubby lad;
Fat ruddy cheeks Augustus had;
And every body saw with joy
The plump and hearty healthy boy.
He ate and drank as he was told,
And never let his soup get cold.
But one day, one cold winter's day,
He scream'd out—"Take the soup away!
O take the nasty soup away!
I won't have any soup to-day."

Next day, now look, the picture shows
How lank and lean Augustus grows!
Yet, though he feels so weak and ill,
The naughty fellow cries out still—
"Not any soup for me, I say:
O take the nasty soup away!
I won't have any soup to-day."

The third day comes; Oh what a sin!
To make himself so pale and thin.
Yet, when the soup is put on table,
He screams, as loud as he is able,—
"Not any soup for me, I say:
O take the nasty soup away!
I won't have any soup to-day."

Look at him, now the fourth day's come!
He scarcely weighs a sugar-plum;
He's like a little bit of thread,
And on the fifth day, he was—dead!

## THE MONKEYS AND THE CROCODILE

*Laura E. Richards*

Five little monkeys
  Swinging from a tree;
Teasing Uncle Crocodile,
  Merry as can be.
Swinging high, swinging low,
  Swinging left and right:
"Dear Uncle Crocodile,
  Come and take a bite!"

Five little monkeys
  Swinging in the air;
Heads up, tails up,
  Little do they care.
Swinging up, swinging down,
  Swinging far and near:
"Poor Uncle Crocodile,
  Aren't you hungry, dear?"

Four little monkeys
  Sitting in the tree;
Heads down, tails down,
  Dreary as can be.
Weeping loud, weeping low,
  Crying to each other:
"Wicked Uncle Crocodile,
  To gobble up our brother!"

## CURIOUS SOMETHING

*Winifred Welles*

If I could smell smells with my ears,
  If sounds came buzzing in my nose,
If in my lips were looks and tears,
  Tongues in my eyes, do you suppose
    That I should have this kind of face,
    Or something curious in its place?

"Gloss" from *Odds Without Ends* by David McCord. Copyright 1953, 1954 by David McCord. Reprinted by permission of Little, Brown and Co., and Curtis Brown, Ltd.

"The Folk Who Live in Backward Town" from *Hello and Good-By* by Mary Ann Hoberman. Copyright © 1959 by Mary Ann Hoberman. Reprinted by permission of Russell & Volkening, Inc., as agents of the author

"Couplet Countdown" from *It Doesn't Always Have to Rhyme* by Eve Merriam. Copyright © 1964 by Eve Mer-

riam. Used by permission of Atheneum Publishers

"Diamond Cut Diamond" by Ewart Milne from *Diamond Cut Diamond*. Reprinted by permission of The Bodley Head

"The Monkeys and the Crocodile" by Laura E. Richards from *Tirra Lirra* by Laura E. Richards. (Boston: Little, Brown & Co., 1932)

"Curious Something." From *Skipping Along Alone* by Winifred Welles. Reprinted by permission of State National Bank of Connecticut, Agent for James Welles Shearer

## ME (ALEXANDER SOAMES)

*Karla Kuskin*

"My nose is blue,
My teeth are green,
My face is like a soup tureen.
I look just like a lima bean.
I'm very, very lovely.
My feet are far too short
And long.
My hands are left and right
And wrong.
My voice is like the hippo's song.
I'm very, very,
Very, very,
Very, very
Lovely?"

## MRS. SNIPKIN AND MRS. WOBBLECHIN

*Laura E. Richards*

Skinny Mrs. Snipkin,
  With her little pipkin,
Sat by the fireside a-warming of her toes.
  Fat Mrs. Wobblechin,
  With her little doublechin,
Sat by the window a-cooling of her nose.

  Says this one to that one,
  "Oh! you silly fat one,
*Will* you shut the window down? You're freezing
    me to death!"
  Says that one to t' other one,
  "Good gracious, how you bother one!
There isn't air enough for me to draw my pre-
    cious breath!"

  Skinny Mrs. Snipkin,
  Took her little pipkin,
Threw it straight across the room as hard as she
    could throw;
  Hit Mrs. Wobblechin
  On her little doublechin,
And out of the window a-tumble she did go.

"Me" from *Alexander Soames: His Poems* by Karla Kuskin. Copyright © 1962 by Karla Kuskin. Reprinted by permission of Harper & Row, Publishers, Inc.
  "Mrs. Snipkin and Mrs. Wobblechin" by Laura E.

## GOING TOO FAR

*Mildred Howells*

A woman who lived in Holland, of old,
Polished her brass till it shone like gold.
She washed her pig after all his meals
In spite of his energetic squeals.
She scrubbed her doorstep into the ground,
And the children's faces, pink and round,
She washed so hard that in several cases
She polished their features off their faces—
Which gave them an odd appearance, though
She thought they were really neater so!
Then her passion for cleaning quickly grew,
And she scrubbed and polished the village
    through,
Until, to the rage of all the people,
She cleaned the weather-vane off the steeple.
As she looked at the sky one summer's night
She thought that the stars shone out less bright;
And she said with a sigh, "If I were there,
I'd rub them up till the world should stare."
That night a storm began to brew,
And a wind from the ocean blew and blew
Till, when she came to her door next day
It whisked her up, and blew her away—
Up and up in the air so high
That she vanished, at last, in the stormy sky.
Since then it's said that each twinkling star
And the big white moon, shine brighter far.
But the neighbors shake their heads in fear
She may rub so hard they will disappear!

*Lewis Carroll*

"You are old, Father William," the young man
    said,
  "And your hair has become very white;
And yet you incessantly stand on your head—
  Do you think, at your age, it is right?"

"In my youth," Father William replied to his
    son,
  "I feared it might injure the brain;

Richards from *Tirra Lirra* by Laura E. Richards. (Boston: Little, Brown & Co., 1932)
  "Going Too Far" by Mildred Howells from *St. Nicholas Magazine*. (Century Co., 1898)

But, now that I'm perfectly sure I have none,
    Why, I do it again and again."

"You are old," said the youth, "as I mentioned
        before.
    And have grown most uncommonly fat;
Yet you turned a back-somersault in at the
        door—
    Pray, what is the reason of that?"

"In my youth," said the sage, as he shook his
        grey locks,
    "I kept all my limbs very supple
By the use of this ointment—one shilling the
        box—
    Allow me to sell you a couple?"

"You are old," said the youth, "and your jaws are
        too weak
    For anything tougher than suet;
Yet you finished the goose, with the bones and
        the beak—
    Pray, how did you manage to do it?"

"In my youth," said his father, "I took to the law,
    And argued each case with my wife;
And the muscular strength, which it gave to my
        jaw
    Has lasted the rest of my life."

"You are old," said the youth, "one would hardly
        suppose
    That your eye was as steady as ever;
Yet you balanced an eel on the end of your
        nose—
    What made you so awfully clever?"

"I have answered three questions, and that is
        enough,"
    Said his father. "Don't give yourself airs!
Do you think I can listen all day to such stuff?
    Be off, or I'll kick you down-stairs!"

## THE PIRATE DON DURK OF DOWDEE

*Mildred Plew Meigs*

Ho, for the Pirate Don Durk of Dowdee!
He was as wicked as wicked could be,
But oh, he was perfectly gorgeous to see!
    The Pirate Don Durk of Dowdee.

His conscience, of course, was as black as a bat,
But he had a floppety plume on his hat
And when he went walking it jiggled—like that!
    The plume of the Pirate Dowdee.

His coat it was crimson and cut with a slash,
And often as ever he twirled his mustache
Deep down in the ocean the mermaids went
        splash,
    Because of Don Durk of Dowdee.

Moreover, Dowdee had a purple tattoo,
And stuck in his belt where he buckled it through
Were a dagger, a dirk and a squizzamaroo,
    For fierce was the Pirate Dowdee.

So fearful he was he would shoot at a puff,
And always at sea when the weather grew rough
He drank from a bottle and wrote on his cuff,
    Did Pirate Don Durk of Dowdee.

"The Pirate Don Durk of Dowdee" by Mildred Plew
Meigs from *Child Life* (March 1923). Reprinted by permission of Marion Plew Ruckel

Oh, he had a cutlass that swung at his thigh
And he had a parrot called Pepperkin Pye,
And a zigzaggy scar at the end of his eye
   Had Pirate Don Durk of Dowdee.

He kept in a cavern, this buccaneer bold,
A curious chest that was covered with mould,
And all of his pockets were jingly with gold!
   Oh jing! went the gold of Dowdee.

His conscience, of course, it was crook'd like a
   squash,
But both of his boots made a slickery slosh,
And he went through the world with a wonder-
   ful swash,
   Did Pirate Don Durk of Dowdee.

It's true he was wicked as wicked could be,
His sins they outnumbered a hundred and three,
But oh, he was perfectly gorgeous to see,
   The Pirate Don Durk of Dowdee.


## THE JUMBLIES

*Edward Lear*

They went to sea in a sieve, they did;
   In a sieve they went to sea:
In spite of all their friends could say,
On a winter's morn, on a stormy day,
   In a sieve they went to sea.
And when the sieve turned round and round,
And every one cried, "You'll all be drowned!"
They called aloud, "Our sieve ain't big;
But we don't care a button, we don't care a fig:
   In a sieve we'll go to sea!"
    Far and few, far and few,
      Are the lands where the Jumblies live:
     Their heads are green, and their hands are
      blue;
     And they went to sea in a sieve.


They sailed away in a sieve, they did,
   In a sieve they sailed so fast,
With only a beautiful pea-green veil
Tied with a ribbon, by way of a sail,

"The Jumblies" by Edward Lear from *The Owl and
the Pussy-cat*

To a small tobacco-pipe mast.
And every one said who saw them go,
"Oh! won't they be soon upset, you know?
For the sky is dark, and the voyage is long;
And, happen what may, it's extremely wrong
   In a sieve to sail so fast."
    Far and few, far and few,
      Are the lands where the Jumblies live:
     Their heads are green, and their hands are
      blue;
     And they went to sea in a sieve.

The water it soon came in, it did;
   The water it soon came in:
So, to keep them dry, they wrapped their feet
In a pinky paper all folded neat;
   And they fastened it down with a pin.
And they passed the night in a crockery-jar;
And each of them said, "How wise we are!
Though the sky be dark, and the voyage be long,
Yet we never can think we were rash or wrong,
   While round in our sieve we spin."
    Far and few, far and few,
      Are the lands where the Jumblies live:
     Their heads are green, and their hands are
      blue;
     And they went to sea in a sieve.


And all night long they sailed away;
   And when the sun went down,
They whistled and warbled a moony song,
To the echoing sound of a coppery gong,
   In the shade of the mountains brown.
"O Timballoo! How happy we are
When we live in a sieve and a crockery-jar!
And all night long, in the moonlight pale,
We sail away with a pea-green sail
   In the shade of the mountains brown."
    Far and few, far and few,
      Are the lands where the Jumblies live:
     Their heads are green, and their hands are
      blue;
     And they went to sea in a sieve.


They sailed to the Western Sea, they did,—
   To a land all covered with trees:
And they bought an owl, and a useful cart,
And a pound of rice, and a cranberry-tart,
   And a hive of silvery bees;

And they bought a pig, and some green jackdaws,
And a lovely monkey with lollipop paws,
And forty bottles of ring-bo-ree,
    And no end of Stilton cheese.
        Far and few, far and few,
            Are the lands where the Jumblies live:
        Their heads are green, and their hands are
            blue;
        And they went to sea in a sieve.


And in twenty years they all came back,—
    In twenty years or more;
And every one said, "How tall they've grown!


For they've been to the Lakes, and the Torrible
    Zone,
    And the hills of the Chankly Bore."
And they drank their health, and gave them a
    feast
Of dumplings made of beautiful yeast;
And every one said, "If we only live,
We, too, will go to sea in a sieve,
    To the hills of the Chankly Bore."
        Far and few, far and few,
            Are the lands where the Jumblies live:
        Their heads are green, and their hands are
            blue;
        And they went to sea in a sieve.


"small talk" copyright 1926 by P. F. Collier & Son Co.
from *The Lives and Times of Archy and Mehitabel*

## SMALL TALK
*Don Marquis*

i went into the flea circus
on broadway the other day
and heard a lot of fleas
talking and bragging to each other
one flea had been over to the swell dog show
and was boasting that he had bit
a high priced thoroughbred dog
yeah says another flea
that is nothing to get so proud of
a thoroughbred dog tastes just like a mongrel
i should think you would be more democratic
than to brag about that
go and get a reputation
said a third flea
i went into a circus last spring and bit a lion
i completely conquered him
i made him whine and cringe
he did not bite me back
get out of my way
i am the flea that licked a lion
i said to myself probably
that lion didnt even know he had been bitten
some insects are just like human beings
small talk i said to myself
and went away from there

                archy the cockroach

(British title: *Archy Does His Best*) by Don Marquis.
Reprinted by permission of Doubleday & Company, Inc.,
and Faber and Faber Ltd.

## FOR A MOCKING VOICE

*Eleanor Farjeon*

Who    calls?    Who    calls?    Who?
Did you call?    Did you?—
I call!    I call!    I!
Follow where I fly.—
Where?    O where?    O where?
On Earth or in the Air?—
Where you come, I'm gone!
Where you fly, I've flown!—
Stay! ah, stay! ah, stay,
Pretty Elf, and play!
Tell me where you are—
*Ha, ha, ha, ha, ha!*

*William Shakespeare*

Where the bee sucks, there suck I:
In a cowslip's bell I lie;
There I couch when owls do cry.
On the bat's back I do fly
After summer merrily.
Merrily, merrily, shall I live now
Under the blossom that hangs on the bough.

# MAGIC AND MAKE BELIEVE

## I KEEP THREE WISHES READY

*Annette Wynne*

I keep three wishes ready,
Lest I should chance to meet,
Any day a fairy
Coming down the street.

I'd hate to have to stammer,
Or have to think them out,
For it's very hard to think things up
When a fairy is about.

And I'd hate to lose my wishes,
For fairies fly away,
And perhaps I'd never have a chance
On any other day.

So I keep three wishes ready,
Lest I should chance to meet,
Any day a fairy
Coming down the street.

## COULD IT HAVE BEEN A SHADOW?

*Monica Shannon*

What ran under the rosebush?
  What ran under the stone?
Could it have been a shadow,
  Running away alone?
Maybe a fairy's shadow,
  Slipping away at dawn
To guard a gleaming pot of gold
  For a busy leprechaun.

## THE BEST GAME THE FAIRIES PLAY

*Rose Fyleman*

The best game the fairies play,
  The best game of all,
Is sliding down steeples—
  (You know they're very tall.)
You fly to the weathercock,
  And when you hear it crow
You fold your wings and clutch your things
  And then let go!

They have a million other games—
  Cloud-catching's one,
And mud-mixing after rain
  Is heaps and heaps of fun;
But when you go and stay with them
  Never mind the rest,
Take my advice—they're very nice,
  But steeple-sliding's best!

## YESTERDAY IN OXFORD STREET

*Rose Fyleman*

Yesterday in Oxford Street, oh, what d'you think,
    my dears?
I had the most exciting time I've had for years
    and years;
The buildings looked so straight and tall, the sky
    was blue between,
And, riding on a motor-bus, I saw the fairy
    queen!

Sitting there upon the rail and bobbing up and
    down,
The sun was shining on her wings and on her
    golden crown;
And looking at the shops she was, the pretty silks
    and lace—
She seemed to think that Oxford Street was quite
    a lovely place.

And once she turned and looked at me, and
    waved her little hand;
But I could only stare and stare—oh, would she
    understand?
I simply couldn't speak at all, I simply couldn't
    stir,
And all the rest of Oxford Street was just a shin-
    ing blur.

Then suddenly she shook her wings—a bird had
    fluttered by—
And down into the street she looked and up into
    the sky;
And perching on the railing on a tiny fairy
    toe,
She flashed away so quickly that I hardly saw
    her go.

I never saw her any more, altho' I looked all
    day;
Perhaps she only came to peep, and never meant
    to stay:
But oh, my dears, just think of it, just think what
    luck for me,
That she should come to Oxford Street, and I be
    there to see!

## THE CONJUROR

*Anonymous*

When I am a man and can do as I wish,
    With no one to ask if I may,
Although I'll play cricket a little and fish,
    I'll conjure the most of each day.

The conjuror's life is so easy and grand;
    He makes such superior jokes—
O, it's splendid to stand with a wand in your
    hand.
    And puzzle relations and folks.

If eggs should be wanted, you turn to a friend,
    And draw two or three from his hair;

If a rabbit is wished, and his hat he will lend,
    You wave, and behold, one is there!

To pound a gold watch into thousands of bits
    And restore it as good as before
Is a life that beats even a Major's to fits,—
    Apart from the absence of gore.

## OVERHEARD ON A SALTMARSH

*Harold Monro*

Nymph, nymph, what are your beads?

Green glass, goblin. Why do you stare at them?

Give them me.

        No.

Give them me. Give them me.

        No.

Then I will howl all night in the reeds,
Lie in the mud and howl for them.

Goblin, why do you love them so?

They are better than stars or water,
Better than voices of winds that sing,
Better than any man's fair daughter,
Your green glass beads on a silver ring.

Hush, I stole them out of the moon.

Give me your beads, I desire them.

        No.

I will howl in a deep lagoon
For your green glass beads, I love them so.
Give them me. Give them.

        No.

"The Conjuror." Anonymous. From *Poems of Magic and Spells*, edited by William Cole (New York: World Publishing Co., 1960)

"Overheard on a Saltmarsh" by Harold Monro from *Children of Love* (London: The Poetry Bookshop, 1913). Reprinted by permission of Lynn McGregor

## A SMALL DISCOVERY

*James A. Emanuel*

Father,
Where do giants go to cry?

To the hills
Behind the thunder?
Or to the waterfall?
I wonder.

(Giants cry.
I know they do.
Do they wait
Till nighttime too?)

## SLEEPYHEAD

*Walter de la Mare*

As I lay awake in the white moonlight,
I heard a faint singing in the wood,
    "Out of bed,
    Sleepyhead,
Put your white foot now,
    Here are we,
    Neath the tree
Singing round the root now!"

I looked out of window, in the white moonlight,
The trees were like snow in the wood—
    "Come away,
    Child, and play
Light with the gnomies;
    In a mound,
    Green and round,
That's where their home is.

    "Honey sweet,
    Curds to eat,
Cream and fruménty,
    Shells and beads,
    Poppy seeds,
You shall have plenty."

But soon as I stooped in the dim moonlight
To put on my stocking and my shoe,
The sweet, sweet singing died sadly away,
And the light of the morning peeped through:
Then instead of the gnomies there came a red
    robin
To sing of the buttercups and dew.

## CRAB-APPLE

*Ethel Talbot*

I dreamed the Fairies wanted me
    To spend my birth-night with them all;
And I said, "Oh, but you're so wee
    And I am so tremendous tall,
What could we do?"
    "Crab-apple stem!"
Said they, and I was just like them.

And then, when we were all the same,
    The party and the fun began;
They said they'd teach me a new game
    Of "Dew-ponds." "I don't think I can
Play that," I said.
    "Crab-apple blue!"
Said they, and I could play it too.

And then, when we had played and played,
    The Fairies said that we would dance;
And I said, "Oh, but I'm afraid
    That I've no shoes." I gave a glance
At my bare toes.
    "Crab-apple sweet!"
Said they, and shoes were on my feet.

And then we danced away, away,
    Until my birth-night all was done;
And I said, "I'll go home to-day;
    And thank you for my lovely fun,
I'll come again."
    "Crab-apple red!"
Said they, and I woke up in bed.

### STOCKING FAIRY

*Winifred Welles*

In a hole of the heel of an old brown stocking,
A little old Fairy sits rocking and rocking,
And scolding and pointing and squeaking and
    squinting,
Brown as a nut, a bright eye glinting,
She tugs at a thread, she drags up a needle,
She stamps and she shrills, she commences to
    wheedle,
To whine of the cold, in a fine gust of temper
She beats on my thumb, and then with a whim-
    per
She sulks in her shawl, she says I've forgotten
I promised to make her a lattice of cotton,
A soft, woven window, cozy yet airy,
Where she could sit rocking and peeking—Hush,
    Fairy,
Tush, Fairy, sit gently, look sweetly,
I'll do what I said, now, and close you in neatly.

### THE PLUMPUPPETS

*Christopher Morley*

When little heads weary have gone to their bed,
When all the good nights and the prayers have
    been said,
Of all the good fairies that send bairns to rest
The little Plumpuppets are those I love best.

*If your pillow is lumpy, or hot, thin and flat,*
*The little Plumpuppets know just what*
    *they're at;*
*They plump up the pillow, all soft, cool and*
    *fat—*
    *The little Plumpuppets plump-up it!*

The little Plumpuppets are fairies of beds:
They have nothing to do but to watch sleepy
    heads;
They turn down the sheets and they tuck you in
    tight,
And they dance on your pillow to wish you good
    night!

No matter what troubles have bothered the day,
Though your doll broke her arm or the pup ran
    away;
Though your handies are black with the ink that
    was spilt—
Plumpuppets are waiting in blanket and quilt.

*If your pillow is lumpy, or hot, thin and flat,*
*The little Plumpuppets know just what*
    *they're at;*
*They plump up the pillow, all soft, cool and*
    *fat—*
    *The little Plumpuppets plump-up it!*

### THE DREAM WOMAN

*Patricia Hubbell*

Early in the morning
Before the lights are on,
The dream woman scurries
Uptown and down.
Leaping in my window
She rushes to my bed,
Grasps at my dream
And wrings it from my head.
Quickly, quietly, she stuffs it in her bag,
Snaps shut the clasp
And runs from my side.
Out at the window,
Down a film of air,
The dream woman hurries
Lest the dawn appear.

When her bag is piled high
With dreams sad and gay,
She hurries to her home

To spin them all away.
She sits beside her spinning wheel,
She sits beside her loom,
And spins without ceasing
From morning until noon.

She gathers up the dreams
From her small black bag,
Shuffles them and sorts them
By color and by size,
Piles up the pink dreams,
Irons out the black,
Dyes a little white one
To match another scrap;
Gets out the darning needle,
Mends one that's torn,
And adds a slight embellishment
To one that's worn.

## THE HORSEMAN

*Walter de la Mare*

I heard a horseman
  Ride over the hill;
The moon shone clear,
  The night was still;
His helm was silver,
  And pale was he;
And the horse he rode
  Was of ivory.

## KIPH

*Walter de la Mare*

My Uncle Ben, who's been
To Bisk, Bhir, Biak—
Been, and come back:
To Tab, Tau, Tze, and Tomsk,
And home, by Teneriffe:
Who, brown as desert sand,
Gaunt, staring, slow and stiff,
Has chased the Unicorn
And Hippogriff,
Gave me a smooth, small, shining stone,
Called *Kiph*.

"Look'ee, now, Nevvy mine,"
He told me—"*If*
You'd wish a wish,
Just rub this smooth, small, shining stone,
Called *Kiph*."

Hide it did I,
In a safe, secret spot;
Slept, and the place
In dreams forgot.

One wish *alone*
Now's mine: Oh, if
I could but find again
That stone called *Kiph!*

## THE GNOME

*Harry Behn*

I saw a gnome
As plain as plain
Sitting on top
Of a weathervane.

He was dressed like a crow
In silky black feathers,
And there he sat watching
All kinds of weathers.

He talked like a crow too,
Caw caw caw,
When he told me exactly
What he saw,

Snow to the north of him
Sun to the south,
And he spoke with a beaky
Kind of a mouth.

But he wasn't a crow,
That was plain as plain
'Cause crows never sit
On a weathervane.

What I saw was simply
A usual gnome
Looking things over
On his way home.

"The Horseman" by Walter de la Mare from *Rhymes and Verses* by Walter de la Mare. Reprinted by permission of The Literary Trustees of Walter de la Mare, and The Society of Authors as their representative
"Kiph" by Walter de la Mare from *Rhymes and*

*Verses* by Walter de la Mare. Reprinted by permission of The Literary Trustees of Walter de la Mare, and The Society of Authors as their representative
"The Gnome." From *Windy Morning* by Harry Behn. Copyright 1953 by Harry Behn. Reprinted by permission of Harcourt Brace Jovanovich, Inc.

# THE BALLAD OF
# THE HARP-WEAVER

*Edna St. Vincent Millay*

"Son," said my mother,
    When I was knee-high,
"You've need of clothes to cover you,
    And not a rag have I.

"There's nothing in the house
    To make a boy breeches,
Nor shears to cut a cloth with
    Nor thread to take stitches.

"There's nothing in the house
    But a loaf-end of rye,
And a harp with a woman's head
    Nobody will buy,"
    And she began to cry.

That was in the early fall.
    When came the late fall,
"Son," she said, "the sight of you
    Makes your mother's blood crawl,—

"Little skinny shoulder-blades
    Sticking through your clothes!
And where you'll get a jacket from
    God above knows.

"It's lucky for me, lad,
    Your daddy's in the ground,
And can't see the way I let
    His son go around!"
    And she made a queer sound.

That was in the late fall.
    When the winter came,
I'd not a pair of breeches
    Nor a shirt to my name.

I couldn't go to school,
    Or out of doors to play.
And all the other little boys
    Passed our way.

"Son," said my mother,
    "Come, climb into my lap,
And I'll chafe your little bones
    While you take a nap."

And, oh, but we were silly
    For half an hour or more,
Me with my long legs
    Dragging on the floor,

A-rock-rock-rocking
    To a mother-goose rhyme!
Oh, but we were happy
    For half an hour's time!

But there was I, a great boy,
    And what would folks say
To hear my mother singing me
    To sleep all day,
    In such a daft way?

Men say the winter
    Was bad that year;
Fuel was scarce,
    And food was dear.

A wind with a wolf's head
    Howled about our door,
And we burned up the chairs
    And sat upon the floor.

All that was left us
    Was a chair we couldn't break,
And the harp with a woman's head
    Nobody would take,
    For song or pity's sake.

The night before Christmas
    I cried with the cold,
I cried myself to sleep
    Like a two-year-old.

And in the deep night
    I felt my mother rise,
And stare down upon me
    With love in her eyes.

I saw my mother sitting
    On the one good chair,
A light falling on her
    From I couldn't tell where,

Looking nineteen,
　　And not a day older,
And the harp with a woman's head
　　Leaned against her shoulder.

Her thin fingers, moving
　　In the thin, tall strings,
Were weav-weav-weaving
　　Wonderful things.

Many bright threads,
　　From where I couldn't see,
Were running through the harp-strings
　　Rapidly,

And gold threads whistling
　　Through my mother's hand.
I saw the web grow,
　　And the pattern expand.

She wove a child's jacket,
　　And when it was done
She laid it on the floor
　　And wove another one.

She wove a red cloak
　　So regal to see,
"She's made it for a king's son,"
　　I said, "and not for me."
　　But I knew it was for me.

She wove a pair of breeches
　　Quicker than that!
She wove a pair of boots
　　And a little cocked hat.

She wove a pair of mittens,
　　She wove a little blouse,
She wove all night
　　In the still, cold house.

She sang as she worked,
　　And the harp-strings spoke;
Her voice never faltered,
　　And the thread never broke.
　　And when I awoke,—

There sat my mother
　　With the harp against her shoulder,
Looking nineteen
　　And not a day older,

A smile about her lips,
　　And a light about her head,
And her hands in the harp-strings
　　Frozen dead.

And piled up beside her
　　And toppling to the skies,
Were the clothes of a king's son,
　　Just my size.

## TILLIE

*Walter de la Mare*

Old Tillie Turveycombe
Sat to sew,
Just where a patch of fern did grow;
There, as she yawned,
And yawn wide did she,
Floated some seed
Down her gull-e-t;
And look you once,
And look you twice,
Poor old Tillie
Was gone in a trice.
But oh, when the wind
Do a-moaning come,
'Tis poor old Tillie
Sick for home;
And oh, when a voice
In the mist do sigh,
Old Tillie Turveycombe's
Floating by.

## PERRY-THE-WINKLE

*J. R. R. Tolkien*

The Lonely Troll he sat on a stone
  and sang a mournful lay:
"O why, O why must I live on my own
  in the hills of Faraway?
My folk are gone beyond recall
  and take no thought of me;
alone I'm left, the last of all
  from Weathertop to the Sea."

"I steal no gold, I drink no beer,
  I eat no kind of meat;
but People slam their doors in fear,
  whenever they hear my feet.
O how I wish that they were neat,
  and my hands were not so rough!
Yet my heart is soft, my smile is sweet,
  and my cooking good enough."

"Come, come!" he thought, "this will not do!
  I must go and find a friend;
a-walking soft I'll wander through
  the Shire from end to end."
Down he went, and he walked all night
  with his feet in boots of fur;
to Delving he came in the morning light,
  when folk were just astir.

He looked around, and who did he meet
  but old Mrs. Bunce and all
with umbrella and basket walking the street;
  and he smiled and stopped to call:
"Good morning, ma'am! Good day to you!
  I hope I find you well?"
But she dropped umbrella and basket too,
  and yelled a frightful yell.

Old Pott the Mayor was strolling near;
  when he heard that awful sound,
he turned all purple and pink with fear,
  and dived down underground.
The Lonely Troll was hurt and sad:
  "Don't go!" he gently said,
but old Mrs. Bunce ran home like mad
  and hid beneath her bed.

The Troll went on to the market-place
  and peeped above the stalls;
the sheep went wild when they saw his face,
and the geese flew over the walls.
Old Farmer Hogg he spilled his ale,
  Bill Butcher threw a knife,
and Grip his dog, he turned his tail
  and ran to save his life.

The old Troll sadly sat and wept
  outside the Lockholes gate,
and Perry-the-Winkle up he crept
  and patted him on the pate.
"O why do you weep, you great big lump?
  You're better outside than in!"
He gave the Troll a friendly thump,
  and laughed to see him grin.

"O Perry-the-Winkle boy," he cried,
  "come, you're the lad for me!
Now if you're willing to take a ride,
  I'll carry you home to tea."
He jumped on his back and held on tight,
  and "Off you go!" said he;
and the Winkle had a feast that night,
  and sat on the old Troll's knee.

There were pikelets, there was buttered toast,
  and jam, and cream, and cake,
and the Winkle strove to eat the most,
  though his buttons all should break.
The kettle sang, the fire was hot,
  the pot was large and brown,
and the Winkle tried to drink the lot,
  in tea though he should drown.

When full and tight were coat and skin,
  they rested without speech,
till the old Troll said: "I'll now begin
  the baker's art to teach,
the making of beautiful cramsome bread,
  of bannocks light and brown;
and then you can sleep on a heather-bed
  with pillows of owlets' down."

"Young Winkle, where've you been?" they said.
  "I've been to a fulsome tea,
and I feel so fat, for I have fed
  on cramsome bread," said he.
"But where, my lad, in the Shire was that?
  Or out in Bree?" said they.

But Winkle he up and answered flat:
  "I ain't a-going to say."

"But I know where," said Peeping Jack,
  "I watched him ride away:
he went upon the old Troll's back
  to the hills of Faraway."
Then all the People went with a will,
  by pony, cart, or moke,
until they came to a house in a hill
  and saw a chimney smoke.

They hammered upon the old Troll's door.
  "A beautiful cramsome cake
O bake for us, please, or two, or more;
  O bake!" they cried, "O bake!"
"Go home, go home!" the old Troll said.
  "I never invited you.
Only on Thursdays I bake my bread,
  and only for a few."

"Go home! Go home! There's some mistake.
  My house is far too small;
and I've no pikelets, cream, or cake:
  the Winkle has eaten all!
You Jack, and Hogg, old Bunce and Pott
  I wish no more to see.
Be off! Be off now all the lot!
  The Winkle's the boy for me!"

Now Perry-the-Winkle grew so fat
  through eating of cramsome bread,
his weskit bust, and never a hat
  would sit upon his head;
for Every Thursday he went to tea,
  and sat on the kitchen floor,
and smaller the old Troll seemed to be,
  as he grew more and more.

The Winkle a Baker great became,
  as still is said in song;
from the Sea to Bree there went the fame
  of his bread both short and long.
But it weren't so good as the cramsome bread;
  no butter so rich and free,
as Every Thursday the old Troll spread
  for Perry-the-Winkle's tea.

## BEHIND THE WATERFALL
*Winifred Welles*

A little old woman
  In a thin white shawl,
Stepped straight through the column
  Of the silver waterfall,
As if the fall of water
  Were not anything at all.
I saw her crook her finger,
  I heard her sweetly call.
Over stones all green and glossy
  I fled and did not fall;
I ran along the river
  And through the waterfall,
And that heavy curve of water
  Never hindered me at all.
The little old woman
  In the thin white shawl
Took my hand and laughed and led me
  Down a cool, still hall,
Between two rows of pillars
  That were glistening and tall.
At her finger's tap swung open
  A wide door in the wall,
And I saw the crystal city
  That's behind the waterfall.

## THE LITTLE GREEN ORCHARD
*Walter de la Mare*

Some one is always sitting there,
  In the little green orchard;
Even when the sun is high,
  In noon's unclouded sky,
And faintly droning goes
  The bee from rose to rose,
Some one in shadow is sitting there,
  In the little green orchard.

Yes, and when twilight's falling softly
  On the little green orchard;
When the grey dew distils
  And every flower-cup fills;
When the last blackbird says,
  "What—what!" and goes her way—ssh!

I have heard voices calling softly
   In the little green orchard.

Not that I am afraid of being there,
   In the little green orchard;
   Why, when the moon's been bright,
   Shedding her lonesome light,
   And moths like ghosties come,
   And the horned snail leaves home:
I've sat there, whispering and listening there,
   In the little green orchard;

Only it's strange to be feeling there,
   In the little green orchard;
   Whether you paint or draw,
   Dig, hammer, chop, or saw;
   When you are most alone,
   All but the silence gone . . .
Some one is waiting and watching there,
   In the little green orchard.

## SAM

*Walter de la Mare*

When Sam goes back in memory,
   It is to where the sea
Breaks on the shingle, emerald-green
   In white foam, endlessly;
He says—with small brown eye on mine—
   "I used to keep awake,
And lean from my window in the moon,
   Watching those billows break.
And half a million tiny hands,
   And eyes, like sparks of frost,
Would dance and come tumbling into the moon,
   On every breaker tossed.
And all across from star to star,
   I've seen the watery sea,
With not a single ship in sight,
   Just ocean there, and me;
And heard my father snore . . . And once,
   As sure as I'm alive,
Out of those wallowing, moon-flecked waves
   I saw a mermaid dive;
Head and shoulders above the wave,

Plain as I now see you,
Combing her hair, now back, now front,
   Her two eyes peeping through;
Calling me, 'Sam!'—quietlike—'Sam!' . . .
   But me . . . I never went,
Making believe I kind of thought
   'Twas someone else she meant . . .
Wonderful lovely there she sat,
   Singing the night away,
All in the solitudinous sea
   Of that there lonely bay.
P'raps," and he'd smooth his hairless mouth,
   "P'raps, if 'twere *now*, my son,
P'raps, if I heard a voice say, 'Sam!' . . .
   Morning would find me gone."

## SOUTHBOUND ON THE FREEWAY

*May Swenson*

   A tourist came in from Orbitville,
   parked in the air, and said:

   The creatures of this star
   are made of metal and glass.

   Through the transparent parts
   you can see their guts.

   Their feet are round and roll
   on diagrams or long

   measuring tapes, dark
   with white lines.

   They have four eyes.
   The two in back are red.

   Sometimes you can see a five-eyed
   one, with a red eye turning

   on the top of his head.
   He must be special—

   the others respect him
   and go slow

when he passes, winding
among them from behind.

They all hiss as they glide,
like inches, down the marked

tapes. Those soft shapes,
shadowy inside

the hard bodies—are they
their guts or their brains?

### THE UNICORN
*Ella Young*

While yet the Morning Star
Flamed in the sky
A Unicorn went mincing by,
Whiter by far than blossom of the thorn:
His silver horn
Glittered as he danced and pranced
Silver-pale in the silver-pale morn.

The folk that saw him, ran away.
Where he went, so gay, so fleet,
Star-like lilies at his feet
Flowered all day,
Lilies, lilies in a throng,
And the wind made for him a song:

But he dared not stay
Over-long!

### INTRODUCTION
### to SONGS OF INNOCENCE
*William Blake*

Piping down the valleys wild,
  Piping songs of pleasant glee,
On a cloud I saw a child,
  And he laughing said to me:

"Pipe a song about a Lamb!"
  So I piped with merry cheer.
"Piper, pipe that song again";
  So I piped; he wept to hear.

"Drop thy pipe, thy happy pipe;
  Sing thy songs of happy cheer!"
So I sang the same again,
  While he wept with joy to hear.

"Piper, sit thee down and write
  In a book, that all may read."
So he vanished from my sight;
  And I plucked a hollow reed,

And I made a rural pen,
  And I stained the water clear,
And I wrote my happy songs
  Every child may joy to hear.

### THE SONG OF
### WANDERING AENGUS
*William Butler Yeats*

I went out to the hazel wood,
Because a fire was in my head,
And cut and peeled a hazel wand,
And hooked a berry to a thread;
And when white moths were on the wing,
And moth-like stars were flickering out,
I dropped a berry in a stream
And caught a little silver trout.

When I had laid it on the floor
I went to blow the fire aflame,
But something rustled on the floor,
And some one called me by my name:
It had become a glimmering girl
With apple blossom in her hair
Who called me by my name and ran
And faded through the brightening air.

Though I am old with wandering
Through hollow lands and hilly lands,
I will find out where she has gone,
And kiss her lips and take her hands;
And walk among long dappled grass,
And pluck till time and times are done
The silver apples of the moon,
The golden apples of the sun.

"The Unicorn" by Ella Young from *The Horn Book* (March-April 1939). Reprinted by permission of The Horn Book, Inc.

Introduction to *Songs of Innocence* by William Blake, from *Songs of Innocence*

"The Song of Wandering Aengus." Reprinted with permission of Macmillan Publishing Co., Inc., M. B. Yeats, Miss Anne Yeats, Macmillan of London & Basingstoke from *Collected Poems* by William Butler Yeats. Copyright 1906 by Macmillan Publishing Co., Inc., renewed 1934 by William Butler Yeats

*William Shakespeare*

With hey, ho, the wind and the rain,—
For the rain—it raineth every day.

## WEATHER

*Hilda Conkling*

Weather is the answer
When I can't go out into flowery places;
Weather is my wonder
About the kind of morning
Hidden behind the hills of sky.

## WATER

*Hilda Conkling*

The world turns softly
Not to spill its lakes and rivers.
The water is held in its arms
And the sky is held in the water.
What is water,
That pours silver,
And can hold the sky?

# WIND AND WATER

*Kate Greenaway*

Little wind, blow on the hill-top,
Little wind, blow down the plain;
Little wind, blow up the sunshine,
Little wind, blow off the rain.

(*Mother Goose*)

Blow wind, blow, and go mill, go,
That the miller may grind his corn;
That the baker may take it,
And into bread bake it,
And bring us a loaf in the morn.

## WINDY WASH DAY

*Dorothy Aldis*

The wash is hanging on the line
And the wind's blowing—
Dresses all so clean and fine,
Beckoning
And bowing.

Stockings twisting in a dance,
Pajamas very tripping,
And every little pair of pants
Upside down
And skipping.

## A KITE

*Unknown*

I often sit and wish that I
Could be a kite up in the sky,
And ride upon the breeze and go
Whichever way I chanced to blow.

*Christina Georgina Rossetti*

Who has seen the wind?
  Neither I nor you:
But when the leaves hang trembling
  The wind is passing thro'.

Who has seen the wind?
  Neither you nor I:
But when the trees bow down their heads
  The wind is passing by.

## THE WIND

*Robert Louis Stevenson*

I saw you toss the kites on high
And blow the birds about the sky;
And all around I heard you pass,
Like ladies' skirts across the grass—
  O wind, a-blowing all day long,
  O wind, that sings so loud a song!

I saw the different things you did,
But always you yourself you hid.
I felt you push, I heard you call,
I could not see yourself at all—
  O wind, a-blowing all day long,
  O wind, that sings so loud a song!

O you that are so strong and cold,
O blower, are you young or old?
Are you a beast of field and tree,
Or just a stronger child than me?
  O wind, a-blowing all day long,
  O wind, that sings so loud a song!

## THE KITE

*Harry Behn*

How bright on the blue
Is a kite when it's new!

With a dive and a dip
It snaps its tail

Then soars like a ship
With only a sail

As over tides
Of wind it rides,

Climbs to the crest
Of a gust and pulls,

Then seems to rest
As wind falls.

When string goes slack
You wind it back

And run until
A new breeze blows

And its wings fill
And up it goes!

How bright on the blue
Is a kite when it's new!

But a raggeder thing
You never will see

When it flaps on a string
In the top of a tree.

## SEASCAPE

*Barbara Juster Esbensen*

Like an echo
For the eye,
The mountain reaches blue
From a bright, exploding sea.
Snow crown
And breaker
Dazzle the wind,
And a gull hangs
Like an icy flake
Between.

## WINDY MORNING

*Harry Behn*

Who minds if the wind whistles and howls
    When sun makes a wall of pleasant light,
Who minds if beyond the wind owls
    Are hooting as if it still were night!

I know the night is somewhere stalking
    Singing birds, and high in tall
Far away air owls are talking,
    But I don't care if they do at all.

Inside a wall of pleasant sun,
    Inside a wall of the wind's noise
My room is still, and there's much to be done
    With paper and paste and trains and toys.

## HOLIDAY

*Ella Young*

    Where are you going
    Little wind of May-time?

    *To the silver-branched wood*
    *For an hour's playtime.*

"Seascape." From *Swing Around the Sun* by Barbara Juster Esbensen. Reprinted by permission of Lerner Publications Company, Minneapolis, 1965
"Windy Morning." From *Windy Morning* by Harry

Behn. Copyright 1953 by Harry Behn. Reprinted by permission of Harcourt Brace Jovanovich, Inc.
"Holiday" by Ella Young. Published by arrangement with the author

O, who'll be in the naked wood
To keep you company?

*Ruby-branched and silver-thorned*
*I'll find a wild rose-tree.*

What games will you play,
Little wind?

*Any game that chance sends:*
*I'll run in the tall tree-tops,*
*And dance at the branch-ends.*

Whom will you take for comrade,
Little wind so gaily going?

*Anyone who finds the path,*
*Without my showing.*

## WINDY NIGHTS

*Robert Louis Stevenson*

Whenever the moon and stars are set,
  Whenever the wind is high,
All night long in the dark and wet,
  A man goes riding by.
Late in the night when the fires are out,
Why does he gallop and gallop about?

Whenever the trees are crying aloud,
  And ships are tossed at sea,
By, on the highway, low and loud,
  By at the gallop goes he:
By at the gallop he goes, and then
By he comes back at the gallop again.

*Christina Georgina Rossetti*

The wind has such a rainy sound
  Moaning through the town,
The sea has such a windy sound,—
  Will the ships go down?

The apples in the orchard
  Tumble from their tree.—
Oh, will the ships go down, go down,
  In the windy sea?

## WIND-WOLVES

*William D. Sargent*

Do you hear the cry as the pack goes by,
The wind-wolves hunting across the sky?
Hear them tongue it, keen and clear,
Hot on the flanks of the flying deer!

Across the forest, mere, and plain,
Their hunting howl goes up again!
All night they'll follow the ghostly trail,
All night we'll hear their phantom wail,

For tonight the wind-wolf pack holds sway
From Pegasus Square to the Milky Way,
And the frightened bands of cloud-deer flee
In scattered groups of two and three.

## DO YOU FEAR THE WIND?

*Hamlin Garland*

Do you fear the force of the wind,
The slash of the rain?
Go face them and fight them,
Be savage again.
Go hungry and cold like the wolf,
Go wade like the crane:
The palms of your hands will thicken,
The skin of your cheek will tan,
You'll grow ragged and weary and swarthy,
But you'll walk like a man!

"Windy Nights." From *A Child's Garden of Verses* by Robert Louis Stevenson

"The wind has such a rainy sound." From *Sing-Song* by Christina Georgina Rossetti

"Wind-Wolves." Reprinted by permission of Scholastic Magazines, Inc. Copyright 1926 by Scholastic Magazines, Inc.

"Do You Fear the Wind?" by Hamlin Garland from *Silver Pennies,* compiled by Blanche Jennings Thompson. Reprinted by permission of Constance Garland Doyle and Isabel Garland Lord

## STORM

*Hilda Doolittle Aldington*

You crash over the trees,
you crack the live branch—
the branch is white,
the green crushed,
each leaf is rent like split wood.

You burden the trees
with black drops,
you swirl and crash—
you have broken off a weighted leaf
in the wind,
it is hurled out,
whirls up and sinks,
a green stone.

*Christina Georgina Rossetti*

O wind, why do you never rest,
    Wandering, whistling to and fro,
Bringing rain out of the west,
    From the dim north bringing snow?

*(Unknown)*

White sheep, white sheep,
On a blue hill,
When the wind stops
You all stand still.
When the wind blows
You walk away slow.
White sheep, white sheep,
Where do you go?

*(Mother Goose)*

Rain, rain, go away,
    Come again another day;
Little Johnny wants to play.

*(Mother Goose)*

One misty moisty morning,
    When cloudy was the weather,
I chanced to meet an old man,
    Clothed all in leather.
He began to compliment
    And I began to grin.
How do you do? And how do you do?
    And how do you do again?

*Mary Ann Hoberman*

Windshield wipers wipe the windshield
    Wipe the water off the pane

| This way | That way |
| This way | That way |
| This way | That way |

In the rain

## THE RAIN

*(Unknown)*

Rain on the green grass,
    And rain on the tree,
And rain on the house-top,
    But not upon me!

## RAIN

*Robert Louis Stevenson*

The rain is raining all around,
    It falls on field and tree,
It rains on the umbrellas here,
    And on the ships at sea.

## MUD
### Polly Chase Boyden

Mud is very nice to feel
All squishy-squash between the toes!
I'd rather wade in wiggly mud
Than smell a yellow rose.

Nobody else but the rosebush knows
How nice mud feels
Between the toes.

## THE RAINS OF SPRING
### Lady Ise (Arranged by Olive Beaupré Miller)

The rains of spring
Which hang to the branches
Of the green willow,
Look like pearls upon a string.

## SPRING RAIN
### Marchette Chute

The storm came up so very quick
It couldn't have been quicker.
I should have brought my hat along,
I should have brought my slicker.

My hair is wet, my feet are wet,
I couldn't be much wetter.
I fell into a river once
But this is even better.

## THE REASON
### Dorothy Aldis

Rabbits and squirrels
Are furry and fat,
And all of the chickens
Have feathers and that

Is why when it's raining
They need not stay in
The way children do who have
Only their skin.

## GALOSHES
### Rhoda W. Bacmeister

Susie's galoshes
Makes splishes and sploshes
And slooshes and sloshes,
As Susie steps slowly
Along in the slush.

They stamp and they tramp
On the ice and concrete,
They get stuck in the muck and the mud;
But Susie likes much best to hear

The slippery slush
As it slooshes and sloshes,
And splishes and sploshes,
All round her galoshes!

## from ALL AROUND THE TOWN
### Phyllis McGinley

U is for Umbrellas
That bloom in rainy weather,
Like many-colored mushrooms,
Sprouting upward altogether.
How useful an umbrella is!
But still I often wonder
If a roof on stormy evenings
Isn't nicer to be under.

"The Reason." Reprinted by permission of G. P. Putnam's Sons from *Everything and Anything* by Dorothy Aldis. Copyright 1925, 1926, 1927 by Dorothy Aldis

"Galoshes" from *Stories to Begin On* by Rhoda W. Bacmeister. Copyright, 1940 by E. P. Dutton & Co., Renewal © 1968 by Rhoda W. Bacmeister. Reprinted by permission of the publishers, E. P. Dutton & Co., Inc.

"U." From *All Around the Town* by Phyllis McGinley. Copyright 1948 by Phyllis McGinley. Reprinted by permission of J. B. Lippincott Company and Curtis Brown, Ltd.

"Mud" by Polly Chase Boyden from *Child Life* (April, 1930). Reprinted by permission of Barbara Boyden Jordan

"The Rains of Spring." From *Little Pictures of Japan* by Olive Beaupré Miller. Reprinted by permission of The Book House For Children

"Spring Rain." From *Around and About* by Marchette Chute. Copyright, © 1957 by Marchette Chute. Reprinted by permission of the publishers, E. P. Dutton & Co., Inc.

## LITTLE RAIN

*Elizabeth Madox Roberts*

When I was making myself a game
Up in the garden, a little rain came.

It fell down quick in a sort of rush,
And I crawled back under the snowball bush.

I could hear the big drops hit the ground
And see little puddles of dust fly round.

A chicken came till the rain was gone;
He had just a very few feathers on.

He shivered a little under his skin,
And then he shut his eyeballs in.

Even after the rain had begun to hush
It kept on raining up in the bush.

One big flat drop came sliding down,
And a ladybug that was red and brown

Was up on a little stem waiting there
And I got some rain in my hair.

## SPRING RAIN

*Harry Behn*

Leaves make a slow
Whispering sound
As down the drops go
Drip to the ground
  Peace, peace, says the tree.

Good wet rain!
Shout happy frogs,
Peepers and big green
Bulls in bogs,
  Lucky, lucky are we!

On a bough above,
Head under wing,
A mourning dove
Waits time to sing.
  Ah me, she sighs, ah me!


*Nobuyuki Yuasa*

A drop of rain!
The frog wiped his forehead
With his wrist.

## CITY RAIN

*Rachel Field*

Rain in the city!
  I love to see it fall
Slantwise where the buildings crowd
  Red brick and all.
Streets of shiny wetness
  Where the taxis go,
With people and umbrellas all
  Bobbing to and fro.

Rain in the city!
  I love to hear it drip
When I am cosy in my room
  Snug as any ship,
With toys spread on the table,
  With a picture book or two,
And the rain like a rumbling tune that sings
  Through everything I do.

## RAIN RIDERS
### Clinton Scollard

Last night I heard a *rat-tat-too;*
  'Twas not a drum-beat, that was plain;
I listened long, and then I knew
  It was the Riders of the Rain.

But with the rising of the dawn
  There was no sound of any hoofs;
The Riders of the Rain had gone
  To tramp on other children's roofs.

## THE RAIN
### William Henry Davies

I hear leaves drinking rain;
  I hear rich leaves on top
Giving the poor beneath
  Drop after drop;
'Tis a sweet noise to hear
These green leaves drinking near.

And when the Sun comes out,
  After this rain shall stop,
A wondrous light will fill
  Each dark, round drop;
I hope the Sun shines bright;
'Twill be a lovely sight.

## IN TIME OF SILVER RAIN
### Langston Hughes

In time of silver rain
The earth
Puts forth new life again,
Green grasses grow
And flowers lift their heads,
And over all the plain
The wonder spreads
  Of life,
  Of life,
  Of life!

In time of silver rain
The butterflies
Lift silken wings
To catch a rainbow cry,
And trees put forth
New leaves to sing
In joy beneath the sky
As down the roadway
Passing boys and girls
Go singing, too,
In time of silver rain
  When spring
  And life
  Are new.

## APRIL RAIN SONG
### Langston Hughes

Let the rain kiss you.
Let the rain beat upon your head with silver
  liquid drops.
Let the rain sing you a lullaby.

The rain makes still pools on the sidewalk.
The rain makes running pools in the gutter.
The rain plays a little sleep-song on our roof at
  night—

And I love the rain.

## FOG
### Carl Sandburg

     The fog comes
     on little cat feet.

     It sits looking
     over harbor and city
     on silent haunches
     and then moves on.

## THE FOG

*William Henry Davies*

I saw the fog grow thick,
  Which soon made blind my ken;
It made tall men of boys,
  And giants of tall men.

It clutched my throat, I coughed;
  Nothing was in my head
Except two heavy eyes
  Like balls of burning lead.

And when it grew so black
  That I could know no place,
I lost all judgment then,
  Of distance and of space.

The street lamps, and the lights
  Upon the halted cars,
Could either be on earth
  Or be the heavenly stars.

A man passed by me close,
  I asked my way, he said,
'Come, follow me, my friend'—
  I followed where he led.

He rapped the stones in front,
  'Trust me' he said 'and come';
I followed like a child—
  A blind man led me home.


*Christina Georgina Rossetti*

Boats sail on the rivers,
  And ships sail on the seas;
But clouds that sail across the sky
  Are prettier far than these.

There are bridges on the rivers,
  As pretty as you please;
But the bow that bridges heaven,

And overtops the trees,
And builds a road from earth to sky,
  Is prettier far than these.

## THE RAINBOW

*Walter de la Mare*

I saw the lovely arch
Of Rainbow span the sky,
The gold sun burning
As the rain swept by.

In bright-ringed solitude
The showery foliage shone
One lovely moment,
And the Bow was gone.

*William Wordsworth*

My heart leaps up when I behold
  A rainbow in the sky:
So was it when my life began;
So is it now I am a man;
So be it when I shall grow old,
  Or let me die!

*Eleanor Farjeon*

The tide in the river,
The tide in the river,

The tide in the river runs deep.
  I saw a shiver
  Pass over the river
As the tide turned in its sleep.

## THE NOISE OF WATERS

*James Joyce*

All day I hear the noise of waters
  Making moan,
Sad as the sea-bird is, when going
  Forth alone,
He hears the winds cry to the waters'
  Monotone.

The grey winds, the cold winds are blowing
  Where I go.
I hear the noise of many waters
  Far below.
All day, all night, I hear them flowing
  To and fro.

## COMPOSED UPON WESTMINSTER BRIDGE

*William Wordsworth*

Earth has not anything to show more fair:
Dull would he be of soul who could pass by
A sight so touching in its majesty:
This City now doth like a garment wear
The beauty of the morning; silent, bare,

Ships, towers, domes, theaters, and temples lie
Open unto the fields, and to the sky;
All bright and glittering in the smokeless air.
Never did sun more beautifully steep
In his first splendor valley, rock, or hill;
Ne'er saw I, never felt, a calm so deep!
The river glideth at his own sweet will:
Dear God! the very houses seem asleep;
And all that mighty heart is lying still!

## BROOKLYN BRIDGE AT DAWN

*Richard Le Gallienne*

Out of the cleansing night of stars and tides,
Building itself anew in the slow dawn,
The long sea-city rises: night is gone,
Day is not yet; still merciful, she hides
Her summoning brow, and still the night-car
    glides
Empty of faces; the night-watchmen yawn
One to the other, and shiver and pass on,
Nor yet a soul over the great bridge rides.

Frail as a gossamer, a thing of air,
A bow of shadow o'er the river flung,
Its sleepy masts and lonely lapping flood;
Who, seeing thus the bridge a-slumber there,
Would dream such softness, like a picture hung,
Is wrought of human thunder, iron and blood?

## THE BIG CLOCK

*(Unknown)*

Slowly ticks the big clock;
Tick-tock, tick-tock!
But Cuckoo clock ticks double-quick;
Tick-a-tock-a, tick-a-tock-a,
Tick-a-tock-a, tick!

## THE SUN

*John Drinkwater*

I told the Sun that I was glad,
    I'm sure I don't know why;
Somehow the pleasant way he had
    Of shining in the sky,
Just put a notion in my head
    That wouldn't it be fun
If, walking on the hill, I said
    "I'm happy" to the Sun.

# DAYS AND SEASONS

*(Mother Goose)*

Cocks crow in the morn
    To tell us to rise,
And he who lies late
    Will never be wise;

For early to bed
   And early to rise,
Is the way to be healthy
   And wealthy and wise.

## A CHILD'S DAY, PART II

*Walter de la Mare*

Softly, drowsily,
Out of sleep;
Into the world again
Ann's eyes peep;
Over the pictures
Across the walls
One little quivering
Sunbeam falls.
A thrush in the garden
Seems to say,
Wake, little Ann,
'Tis day, 'tis day!
Faint sweet breezes
The casement stir,
Breathing of pinks
And lavender.
At last from her pillow,
With cheeks bright red,
Up comes her round little
Tousled head;
And out she tumbles
From her warm bed.

## SINGING TIME

*Rose Fyleman*

I wake in the morning early
And always, the very first thing,
I poke out my head and I sit up in bed
And I sing and I sing and I sing.

"The Sun" by John Drinkwater from *All About Me* by John Drinkwater. Reprinted by permission of the publisher, Houghton Mifflin Company

"Softly, Drowsily" by Walter de la Mare from *A Child's Day* by Walter de la Mare. Reprinted by permission of The Literary Trustees of Walter de la Mare and The Society of Authors as their representative

"Singing Time," copyright 1923 by George H. Doran Company from the book *The Fairy Green* by Rose Fyleman. Reprinted by permission of Doubleday & Company, Inc. and The Society of Authors as the literary representative of the Estate of Rose Fyleman

## A SUMMER MORNING

*Rachel Field*

I saw dawn creep across the sky,
And all the gulls go flying by.
I saw the sea put on its dress
Of blue mid-summer loveliness,
And heard the trees begin to stir
Green arms of pine and juniper.
I heard the wind call out and say:
"Get up, my dear, it is to-day!"

## GETTING UP

*Rose Burgunder*

At seven sharp the morning rings,
the shades go up, and frosty things
(like printed windowpanes and boughs
and, on the frozen hillside, cows)
call us back to sleep.

All night the shades went up, it seemed,
on moon mosaics while I dreamed
that churchbells, schoolbells, chimed and chimed.
How shall the paths to day be climbed,
their way so steep?

## *from* ALL AROUND THE TOWN

*Phyllis McGinley*

W's for Windows.
   Watch them welcome in the night.
How they twinkle, twinkle, twinkle
   With the waning of the light!
There's nothing half so wonderful
   In all the wond'rous town
As a million winking Windows
   When the dusk is coming down.

"A Summer Morning." Reprinted with permission of Macmillan Publishing Co., Inc. from *Poems* by Rachel Field. Copyright 1924, 1930 by Macmillan Publishing Co., Inc.

"Getting Up." From *From Summer to Summer* by Rose Burgunder. Copyright © 1965 by Rose Styron. All rights reserved. Reprinted by permission of The Viking Press, Inc.

"W." From *All Around the Town* by Phyllis McGinley. Copyright 1948 by Phyllis McGinley. Reprinted by permission of J. B. Lippincott Company and Curtis Brown, Ltd.

*(American Mother Goose)*

Star-light, star-bright
First star I've seen tonight;
I wish I may, I wish I might
Get the wish I wish tonight.

*Elizabeth Coatsworth*

Hard from the southeast blows the wind
    Promising rain.
The clouds are gathering, and dry leaves
    Tap at the pane.

Early the cows come wandering home
    To shadowy bars,
Early the candles are alight
    And a few stars.

Now is the hour that lies between
    Bright day and night,
When in the dusk the fire blooms
    In tongues of light,

And the cat comes to bask herself
    In the soft heat,
And Madame Peace draws up her chair
    To warm her feet.

### SETTING THE TABLE

*Dorothy Aldis*

Evenings
When the house is quiet
I delight
To spread the white
Smooth cloth and put the flowers on the table.

I place the knives and forks around
Without a sound.
I light the candles.

I love to see
Their small reflected torches shine
Against the greenness of the vine
And garden.

Is that the mignonette, I wonder,
Smells so sweet?

And then I call them in to eat.

### EVENING HYMN

*Elizabeth Madox Roberts*

The day is done;
The lamps are lit;
Woods-ward the birds are flown.
Shadows draw close,—
Peace be unto this house.

The cloth is fair;
The food is set.
God's night draw near.
Quiet and love and peace
Be to this, our rest, our place.

### PRELUDE I

*T. S. Eliot*

The winter evening settles down
With smell of steaks in passageways.
Six o'clock.
The burnt-out ends of smoky days.
And now a gusty shower wraps
The grimy scraps
Of withered leaves about your feet
And newspapers from vacant lots;
The showers beat
On broken blinds and chimney-pots,
And at the corner of the street
A lonely cab-horse steams and stamps.
And then the lighting of the lamps.

## THE STAR

*Jane Taylor*

Twinkle, twinkle, little star,
How I wonder what you are!
Up above the world so high,
Like a diamond in the sky.

## UNTIL WE BUILT A CABIN

*Aileen L. Fisher*

When we lived in a city
(three flights up and down)
I never dreamed how many stars
could show above a town.

When we moved to a village
where lighted streets were few,
I thought I could see ALL the stars,
bŭt, oh, I never knew—

Until we built a cabin
where hills are high and far,
I never knew how many
        many
             stars there really are!

## THE FALLING STAR

*Sara Teasdale*

I saw a star slide down the sky,
Blinding the north as it went by,
Too burning and too quick to hold,
Too lovely to be bought or sold,
Good only to make wishes on
And then forever to be gone.

## STARS

*Sara Teasdale*

Alone in the night
On a dark hill

With pines around me
    Spicy and still,

And a heaven full of stars
    Over my head,
White and topaz
    And misty red;

Myriads with beating
    Hearts of fire
That aeons
    Cannot vex or tire;

Up the dome of heaven
    Like a great hill,
I watch them marching
    Stately and still,

And I know that I
    Am honored to be
Witness
    Of so much majesty.

## FULL MOON

*Walter de la Mare*

One night as Dick lay fast asleep,
    Into his drowsy eyes
A great still light began to creep
    From out the silent skies.
It was the lovely moon's, for when
    He raised his dreamy head,
Her surge of silver filled the pane
    And streamed across his bed.
So, for awhile, each gazed at each—
    Dick and the solemn moon—
Till, climbing slowly on her way,
    She vanished, and was gone.

## GOOD NIGHT
*Dorothy Mason Pierce*

On tip-toe comes the gentle dark
To help the children sleep
And silently, in silver paths,
The slumber fairies creep.

Then overhead, God sees that all
His candles are a-light,
And reaching loving arms to us
He bids His world Good Night.

*(Unknown)*

I see the moon,
And the moon sees me;
God bless the moon,
And God bless me.

## CRESCENT MOON
*Elizabeth Madox Roberts*

And Dick said, "Look what I have found!"
And when we saw we danced around,
And made our feet just tip the ground.

We skipped our toes and sang, "Oh-lo.
Oh-who, oh-who, oh what do you know!
Oh-who, oh-hi, oh-loo, kee-lo!"

We clapped our hands and sang, "Oh-ee!"
It made us jump and laugh to see
The little new moon above the tree.

## THE WHITE WINDOW
*James Stephens*

The Moon comes every night to peep
  Through the window where I lie:

But I pretend to be asleep;
  And watch the Moon go slowly by,
—And she never makes a sound!

She stands and stares!  And then she goes
  To the house that's next to me,
Stealing by on tippy-toes;
  To peep at folk asleep maybe
—And she never makes a sound!

## SILVER

*Walter de la Mare*

Slowly, silently, now the moon
Walks the night in her silver shoon;
This way, and that, she peers, and sees
Silver fruit upon silver trees;
One by one the casements catch
Her beams beneath the silvery thatch;
Couched in his kennel, like a log,
With paws of silver sleeps the dog;
From their shadowy cote the white breasts peep
Of doves in a silver-feathered sleep;
A harvest mouse goes scampering by,
With silver claws, and silver eye;
And moveless fish in the water gleam,
By silver reeds in a silver stream.

## LAST SONG
*James Guthrie*

To the Sun
Who has shone
  All day,
To the Moon
Who has gone
  Away,
To the milk-white,

"Goodnight" from *The Susannah Winkle Book* by Dorothy Mason Pierce. Copyright, 1935, by E. P. Dutton & Co., renewal © 1963 by Dorothy Mason Pierce. Reprinted by permission of the publishers, E. P. Dutton & Co., Inc.

"Crescent Moon." *Notice how different the mood of this moon poem is from that of the De la Mare poem, "Full Moon."* From *Under the Tree* by Elizabeth Madox Roberts. Copyright 1922 by B. W. Huebsch, Inc., 1950 by Ivor S. Roberts. Reprinted by permission of The Viking Press, Inc., New York

"The White Window." Reprinted with permission of Macmillan Publishing Co., Inc., Mrs. Iris Wise; Macmillan London & Basingstoke; and The Macmillan Company of Canada Limited from *Collected Poems* by James Stephens. Copyright 1915 by Macmillan Publishing Co., Inc., renewed 1943 by James Stephens

"Silver" by Walter de la Mare from *Collected Poems 1901–1918* by Walter de la Mare. Copyright 1920, Henry Holt and Co., Inc., 1948 by Walter de la Mare. Reprinted by permission of The Literary Trustees of Walter de la Mare and The Society of Authors as their representative

"Last Song" by James Guthrie. Reprinted by permission of Basil Blackwell, Publisher

Silk-white,
Lily-white Star
A fond goodnight
Wherever you are.

## FINIS

*Sir Henry Newbolt*

Night is come,
    Owls are out,
Beetles hum
    Round about:

Children snore
    Safe in bed,
Nothing more
    Need be said.

## THE PATH ON THE SEA

*Inna Muller*

The moon this night is like a silver sickle
Mowing a field of stars.
It has spread a golden runner
Over the rippling waves.
With its winking shimmer
This magic carpet lures me
To fly to the moon on it.

## ON A NIGHT OF SNOW

*Elizabeth Coatsworth*

Cat, if you go outdoors you must walk in the
    snow.
You will come back with little white shoes on
    your feet,
Little white slippers of snow that have heels
    of sleet.
Stay by the fire, my Cat. Lie still, do not go.
See how the flames are leaping and hissing low.
I will bring you a saucer of milk like a
    marguerite,

So white and so smooth, so spherical and so
    sweet.
Stay with me, Cat. Outdoors the wild winds
    blow.

Outdoors the wild winds blow, Mistress, and
    dark is the night.
Strange voices cry in the trees, intoning
    strange lore,
And more than cats move, lit by our eyes' green
    light,
On silent feet where the meadow grasses hang
    hoar—
Mistress, there are portents abroad of magic
    and might,
And things that are yet to be done. Open the
    door!

## SNOW TOWARD EVENING

*Melville Cane*

Suddenly the sky turned gray,
The day,
Which had been bitter and chill,
Grew intensely soft and still.
Quietly
From some invisible blossoming tree
Millions of petals cool and white
Drifted and blew,
Lifted and flew,
Fell with the falling night.

## ONE LEAF
*Kaye Starbird*

At least a month away from the autumn season
I saw a leaf from the maple break and fall,
Fluttering down for no apparent reason
One windless day when nothing else moved at all.

A sea gull cried in notes that tended to linger.
A sailboat lay becalmed on the summer ocean.
I reached to touch the falling leaf with my finger
And asked myself what fate had put it in motion.

Now in the scarlet glory of late September
As leaves drift down, too many to notice well,
It's odd how often and clearly I remember
The summer day when the single green leaf fell.

*(Mother Goose)*

January brings the snow,
  Makes our feet and fingers glow.
February brings the rain,
  Thaws the frozen lake again.
March brings breezes loud and shrill,
  Stirs the dancing daffodil.

April brings the primrose sweet,
  Scatters daisies at our feet.
May brings flocks of pretty lambs,
  Skipping by their fleecy dams.
June brings tulips, lilies, roses,
  Fills the children's hands with posies.

Hot July brings cooling showers,
  Apricots and gillyflowers.
August brings the sheaves of corn,
  Then the harvest home is borne.
Warm September brings the fruit,
  Sportsmen then begin to shoot.

Fresh October brings the pheasant,
  Then to gather nuts is pleasant.
Dull November brings the blast,
  Then the leaves are whirling fast.
Chill December brings the sleet,
  Blazing fire and Christmas treat.

## FALL
*Aileen L. Fisher*

The last of October
We lock the garden gate.
(The flowers have all withered
That used to stand straight.)

The last of October
We put the swings away
And the porch looks deserted
Where we liked to play.

The last of October
The birds have all flown,
The screens are in the attic,
The sandpile's alone:

Everything is put away
Before it starts to snow—
I wonder if the ladybugs
Have any place to go!

"One Leaf" from *The Pheasant on Route Seven* by Kaye Starbird. Copyright © 1968 by Kaye Starbird. Re-

printed by permission of J. B. Lippincott Company
"Fall" by Aileen Fisher from *The Coffee-Pot Face* by Aileen Fisher. Reprinted by permission of the author

*Emily Dickinson*

The morns are meeker than they were,
The nuts are getting brown;
The berry's cheek is plumper,
The rose is out of town.

The maple wears a gayer scarf,
The field a scarlet gown.
Lest I should be old-fashioned,
I'll put a trinket on.

## SEPTEMBER

*Edwina Fallis*

A road like brown ribbon,
A sky that is blue,
A forest of green
With that sky peeping through.

Asters, deep purple,
A grasshopper's call,
Today it is summer,
Tomorrow is fall.

## AUTUMN FIRES

*Robert Louis Stevenson*

In the other gardens
    And all up the vale,
From the autumn bonfires
    See the smoke trail!

Pleasant summer over
    And all the summer flowers.
The red fire blazes,
    The gray smoke towers.

Sing a song of seasons!
    Something bright in all!
Flowers in the summer,
    Fires in the fall!

## DOWN! DOWN!

*Eleanor Farjeon*

Down, down!
Yellow and brown
The leaves are falling over the town.

## AUTUMN WOODS

*James S. Tippett*

I like the woods
    In autumn
When dry leaves hide the ground,
When the trees are bare
And the wind sweeps by
With a lonesome rushing sound.

I can rustle the leaves
    In autumn
And I can make a bed
In the thick dry leaves
That have fallen
From the bare trees
Overhead.

## SPLINTER

*Carl Sandburg*

The voice of the last cricket
across the first frost
is one kind of good-by.
It is so thin a splinter of singing.

## TRICK OR TREAT
### Carson McCullers

Trick or treat, trick or treat.
We Halloweeners roam the street,
Scaring old ladies with our false faces.
We poke out big sacks and pillowcases.
And if people refuse to open the door,
Or give us an apple or nothing much more;
We soap their windows
And soap their doors.
So bring out your dainties
And all things sweet
For this is the night of
Trick or Treat.

## THEME IN YELLOW
### Carl Sandburg

I spot the hills
With yellow balls in autumn.
I light the prairie cornfields
Orange and tawny gold clusters
And I am called pumpkins.
On the last of October
When dusk is fallen
Children join hands
And circle round me
Singing ghost songs
And love to the harvest moon;
I am a jack-o'-lantern
With terrible teeth
And the children know
I am fooling.

## THIS IS HALLOWEEN
### Dorothy Brown Thompson

Goblins on the doorstep,
  Phantoms in the air,
Owls on witches' gateposts
  Giving stare for stare,
Cats on flying broomsticks,
  Bats against the moon,
Stirrings round of fate-cakes
  With a solemn spoon,
Whirling apple parings,
  Figures draped in sheets
Dodging, disappearing,
  Up and down the streets,
Jack-o'-lanterns grinning,
  Shadows on a screen,
Shrieks and starts and laughter—
  This is Halloween!

## SOMETHING TOLD THE WILD GEESE
### Rachel Field

Something told the wild geese
  It was time to go.
Though the fields lay golden
  Something whispered, "Snow."
Leaves were green and stirring,
  Berries, luster-glossed,
But beneath warm feathers
  Something cautioned, "Frost."
All the sagging orchards
  Steamed with amber spice,
But each wild breast stiffened
  At remembered ice.
Something told the wild geese
  It was time to fly—
Summer sun was on their wings,
  Winter in their cry.

## PREDICTION
### Barbara Juster Esbensen

Yesterday,
It was not there,
This pointed flavor
In the air.

Yesterday,
We gathered leaves
To wear like emblems
On our sleeves.

But now there is
A different feel:
The silver sky
Has rims of steel.

And in the night,
(I know! I know!)
The snow will fly!
The snow! The snow!

## THOSE WINTER SUNDAYS
*Robert Hayden*

Sundays too my father got up early
and put his clothes on in the blueblack cold,
then with cracked hands that ached
from labor in the weekday weather made
banked fires blaze. No one ever thanked him.

I'd wake and hear the cold splintering, breaking.
When the rooms were warm, he'd call,
and slowly I would rise and dress,
fearing the chronic angers of that house,

Speaking indifferently to him,
who had driven out the cold
and polished my good shoes as well.
What did I know, what did I know
of love's austere and lonely offices?

## ICE
*Dorothy Aldis*

When it is the winter time
I run up the street

And I make the ice laugh
With my little feet—
"Crickle, crackle, crickle
Crrreeet, crrreeet, crrreeet."

## WINTER POEM
*Nikki Giovanni*

once a snowflake fell
on my brow and i loved
it so much and i kissed
it and it was happy and called its cousins
and brothers and a web
of snow engulfed me then
i reached to love them all
and i squeezed them and they became
a spring rain and i stood perfectly
still and was a flower

## CYNTHIA IN THE SNOW
*Gwendolyn Brooks*

It SUSHES.
It hushes
The loudness in the road.
It flitter-twitters,
And laughs away from me.
It laughs a lovely whiteness,
And whitely whirs away,
To be
Some otherwhere,
Still white as milk or shirts.
So beautiful it hurts.

## SNOW
### Dorothy Aldis

The fenceposts wear marshmallow hats
On a snowy day;
Bushes in their night gowns
Are kneeling down to pray—
And all the trees have silver skirts
And want to dance away.


### Ralph Waldo Emerson

Announced by all the trumpets of the sky,
Arrives the snow, and, driving o'er the fields,
Seems nowhere to alight: the whited air
Hides hills and woods, the river and the heaven,
And veils the farm-house at the garden's end.
The sled and traveller stopped, the courier's feet
Delayed, all friends shut out, the housemates sit
Around the radiant fireplace, enclosed
In a tumultuous privacy of storm.


## FOR HANUKKAH
### H. N. Bialik

Father lighted candles for me;
    Like a torch the Shamash shone.
In whose honor, for whose glory?
    For Hanukkah alone.

Teacher bought a big top for me,
    Solid lead, the finest known.
In whose honor, for whose glory?
    For Hanukkah alone.

Mother made a pancake for me,
    Hot and sweet and sugar-strewn.
In whose honor, for whose glory?
    For Hanukkah alone.

Uncle had a present for me,
    An old penny for my own.
In whose honor, for whose glory?
    For Hanukkah alone.


## DREIDEL SONG
### Efraim Rosenzweig

Twirl about, dance about,
    Spin, spin, spin!
Turn, Dreidel, turn—
    Time to begin!

Soon it is Hanukkah—
    Fast Dreidel, fast!
For you will lie still
    When Hanukkah's past.


## A SONG OF ALWAYS
### Efraim Rosenzweig

The Temple is clean
    The lamp burns bright;
Judah the leader,
    Has started the light.

The sun shines by days,
    And dark is the night;
But always and always
    The lamp burns bright.


## BLESSINGS FOR CHANUKAH
### Jessie E. Sampter

Blessed art Thou, O God our Lord,
Who made us holy with his word,
And told us on this feast of light
To light one candle more each night.

(Because when foes about us pressed
  To crush us all with death or shame,
The Lord his priests with courage blest
To strike and give his people rest
And in the House that he loved best
  Relight our everlasting flame.)

Blest are Thou, the whole world's King,
Who did so wonderful a thing
For our own fathers true and gold
At this same time in days of old!

## AN OLD CHRISTMAS GREETING

*(Unknown)*

Sing hey! Sing hey!
For Christmas Day;
Twine mistletoe and holly,
For friendship glows
In winter snows,
And so let's all be jolly.

## CHRISTMAS

*(Mother Goose)*

Christmas is coming, the geese are
  getting fat,
Please to put a penny in an old
  man's hat;
If you haven't got a penny a
  ha'penny will do,
If you haven't got a ha'penny, God
  bless you.

## THE CHRISTMAS PUDDING

*(Unknown)*

Into the basin put the plums,
Stirabout, stirabout, stirabout!

Next the good white flour comes,
Stirabout, stirabout, stirabout!

Sugar and peel and eggs and spice,
Stirabout, stirabout, stirabout!

Mix them and fix them and cook them twice,
Stirabout, stirabout, stirabout!

*Sir Walter Scott*

Heap on more wood!—the wind is chill;
But let it whistle as it will,
We'll keep our Christmas merry still.

*Christina Georgina Rossetti*

But give me holly, bold and jolly,
Honest, prickly, shining holly;
Pluck me holly leaf and berry
For the day when I make merry.

## BUNDLES

*John Farrar*

A bundle is a funny thing,
It always sets me wondering;
For whether it is thin or wide
You never know just what's inside.

Especially on Christmas week,
Temptation is so great to peek!
Now wouldn't it be much more fun
If shoppers carried things undone?

"Christmas." From *The Real Mother Goose*. Rand McNally & Company, Chicago, 1916
"But give me holly, bold and jolly." From *Sing-Song* by Christina Georgina Rossetti

"Bundles" by John Farrar from *Songs for Parents* by John Farrar. Copyright 1921 by Yale University Press. Reprinted by permission of Yale University Press

## A VISIT FROM ST. NICHOLAS

*Clement C. Moore*

"Twas the night before Christmas, when all
    through the house
Not a creature was stirring, not even a mouse;
The stockings were hung by the chimney with
    care,
In hopes that St. Nicholas soon would be there;
The children were nestled all snug in their beds
While visions of sugar-plums danced in their
    heads;
And Mamma in her 'kerchief, and I in my cap,
Had just settled our brains for a long winter's
    nap,
When out on the lawn there arose such a clatter,
I sprang from my bed to see what was the matter.
Away to the window I flew like a flash,
Tore open the shutters and threw up the sash.
The moon on the breast of the new-fallen snow
Gave a lustre of midday to objects below,
When, what to my wondering eyes did appear,
But a miniature sleigh and eight tiny reindeer,
With a little old driver, so lively and quick,
I knew in a moment it must be St. Nick.
More rapid than eagles his coursers they came,
And he whistled, and shouted, and called them
    by name:
"Now, Dasher! now, Dancer! now, Prancer and
    Vixen!
On, Comet! on, Cupid! on, Donder and Blitzen!
To the top of the porch! to the top of the wall!
Now dash away! dash away! dash away, all!"
As dry leaves that before the wild hurricane fly,
When they meet with an obstacle, mount to the
    sky,
So up to the housetop the coursers they flew,
With the sleigh full of toys, and St. Nicholas too.
And then, in a twinkling, I heard on the roof
The prancing and pawing of each little hoof.

As I drew in my head, and was turning around,
Down the chimney St. Nicholas came with a
    bound.
He was dressed all in fur, from his head to his
    foot,
And his clothes were all tarnished with ashes and
    soot;
A bundle of toys he had flung on his back,
And he looked like a peddler just opening his
    pack.
His eyes—how they twinkled! his dimples, how
    merry!
His cheeks were like roses, his nose like a cherry!
His droll little mouth was drawn up like a bow,
And the beard on his chin was as white as the
    snow;
The stump of a pipe he held tight in his teeth,
And the smoke, it encircled his head like a
    wreath;
He had a broad face and a little round belly
That shook, when he laughed, like a bowl full of
    jelly.
He was chubby and plump, a right jolly old elf,
And I laughed when I saw him, in spite of my-
    self;
A wink of his eye and a twist of his head,
Soon gave me to know I had nothing to dread;
He spoke not a word, but went straight to his
    work,
And filled all the stockings; then turned with a
    jerk,
And laying his finger aside of his nose,
And giving a nod, up the chimney he rose.
He sprang to his sleigh, to his team gave a
    whistle,
And away they all flew like the down of a thistle.
But I heard him exclaim, ere he drove out of
    sight,
"HAPPY CHRISTMAS TO ALL,
AND TO ALL A GOOD-NIGHT!"

## HERE WE COME A-CAROLING

### (An Old Christmas Carol)

Here we come a-caroling
   Among the leaves so green;
Here we come a-wand'ring
   So fair to be seen.

*Love and joy come to you*
*And a joyful Christmas, too;*
*And God bless you and send*
*You a Happy New Year—*
*And God send you a Happy New Year.*

We are not daily beggars
   That beg from door to door;
But we are neighbors' children
   That you have seen before.

*Love and joy come to you*
*And a joyful Christmas, too;*
*And God bless you and send*
*You a Happy New Year—*
*And God send you a Happy New Year.*

God bless the master of the house
   Likewise the mistress, too;
And all the little children
   That round the table go.

*Love and joy come to you*
*And a joyful Christmas, too;*
*And God bless you and send*
*You a Happy New Year—*
*And God send you a Happy New Year.*

## CEREMONIES FOR CHRISTMAS

*Robert Herrick*

Come, bring with a noise,
   My merry, merry boys,
The Christmas log to the firing;

While my good dame, she
   Bids ye all be free;
And drinks to your hearts' desiring.

With the last year's brand
   Light the new block, and
For good success in his spending,
   On your psaltries play,
   That sweet luck may
Come while the log is a-tending.

Drink now the strong beer,
   Cut the white loaf here,
The while the meat is a-shredding;
   For the rare mince-pie
   And the plums stand by
To fill the paste that's a-kneading.

## IN THE WEEK WHEN CHRISTMAS COMES

*Eleanor Farjeon*

This is the week when Christmas comes.

Let every pudding burst with plums,
And every tree bear dolls and drums,
   In the week when Christmas comes.

Let every hall have boughs of green,
With berries glowing in between,
   In the week when Christmas comes.

Let every doorstep have a song
Sounding the dark street along,
   In the week when Christmas comes.

Let every steeple ring a bell
With a joyful tale to tell,
   In the week when Christmas comes.

*Children* by Eleanor Farjeon. Copyright 1951 by Eleanor Farjeon. Reprinted by permission of J. B. Lippincott Company and Harold Ober Associates Incorporated

"In the Week When Christmas Comes." Copyright 1927, © renewed 1955 by Eleanor Farjeon. From *Poems for*

Let every night put forth a star
To show us where the heavens are,
   In the week when Christmas comes.

Let every stable have a lamb
Sleeping warm beside its dam,
   In the week when Christmas comes.

This is the week when Christmas comes.

## CHRISTMAS IN THE WOODS

*Frances M. Frost*

Tonight when the hoar frost falls on the wood,
And the rabbit cowers, and the squirrel is cold,
And the horned owl huddles against a star,
And the drifts are deep, and the year is old,
All shy creatures will think of Him.
The shivering mouse, the hare, the wild young
    fox,
The doe with the startled fawn,
Will dream of gentleness and a Child:

The buck with budding horns will turn
His starry eyes to a silver hill tonight,
The chipmunk will awake and stir
And leave his burrow for the chill, dark mid-
    night,
And all timid things will pause and sigh, and
    sighing, bless
That Child who loves the trembling hearts,
The shy hearts of the wilderness.

*William Shakespeare*

Some say, that ever 'gainst that season comes
Wherein our Savior's birth is celebrated,
The bird of dawning singeth all night long:
So hallow'd and so gracious is the time.

## SONG

*Eugene Field*

    Why do bells for Christmas ring?
    Why do little children sing?

    Once a lovely, shining star,
    Seen by shepherds from afar,
    Gently moved until its light
    Made a manger's cradle bright.

    There a darling baby lay,
    Pillowed soft upon the hay;
    And its mother sang and smiled,
    "This is Christ, the holy child!"

    Therefore bells for Christmas ring,
    Therefore little children sing.

## CRADLE HYMN

*Martin Luther*

    Away in a manger,
    No crib for a bed,
    The little Lord Jesus
    Lay down his sweet head;
    The stars in the heavens
    Looked down where he lay,
    The little Lord Jesus
    Asleep in the hay.

    The cattle are lowing,
    The poor baby wakes,
    But little Lord Jesus
    No crying he makes.
    I love thee, Lord Jesus,
    Look down from the sky,
    And stay by my cradle
    Till morning is nigh.

"Christmas in the Woods" from *Christmas in the Woods* by Frances Frost. Copyright 1942 by Frances Frost, renewed © 1970, by Paul Blackburn. Reprinted by permission of Mrs. Paul Blackburn

"Some say, that ever 'gainst that season comes." From *Hamlet*, Act I, Sc. 1
"Song" by Eugene Field from *Sharps and Flats* by Eugene Field. Copyright 1900, 1928 by Julia Sutherland Field. Published by Charles Scribner's Sons

## NEW YEAR'S DAY
*Rachel Field*

Last night, while we were fast asleep,
  The old year went away.
It can't come back again because
  A new one's come to stay.


*Elizabeth Coatsworth*

Cold winter now is in the wood,
The moon wades deep in snow.
Pile balsam boughs about the sills,
And let the fires glow!

The cows must stand in the dark barn,
The horses stamp all day.
Now shall the housewife bake her pies
And keep her kitchen gay.

The cat sleeps warm beneath the stove,
The dog on paws outspread;
But the brown deer with flinching hide
Seeks for a sheltered bed.

The fox steps hungry through the brush,
The lean hawk coasts the sky.
"Winter is in the wood!" the winds
In the warm chimney cry.


## WINTER NIGHT
*Mary Frances Butts*

Blow, wind, blow!
Drift the flying snow!
Send it twirling, whirling overhead!
  There's a bedroom in a tree
  Where, snug as snug can be,
The squirrel nests in his cozy bed.

Shriek, wind, shriek!
Make the branches creak!
Battle with the boughs till break o' day!

In a snow-cave warm and tight,
Through the icy winter night
The rabbit sleeps the peaceful hours away.

  Call, wind, call,
  In entry and in hall,
Straight from off the mountain white and wild!
  Soft purrs the pussy-cat,
  On her little fluffy mat,
And beside her nestles close her furry child.

  Scold, wind, scold,
  So bitter and so bold!
Shake the windows with your tap, tap, tap!
  With half-shut dreamy eyes
  The drowsy baby lies
Cuddled closely in his mother's lap.


## STOPPING BY WOODS
## ON A SNOWY EVENING
*Robert Frost*

Whose woods these are I think I know.
His house is in the village, though;
He will not see me stopping here
To watch  his woods fill up with snow.

My little horse must think it queer
To stop without a farmhouse near
Between the woods and frozen lake
The darkest evening of the year.

He gives his harness bells a shake
To ask if there is some mistake.
The only other sound's the sweep
Of easy wind and downy flake.

The woods are lovely, dark, and deep,
But I have promises to keep,
And miles to go before I sleep,
And miles to go before I sleep.

"New Year's Day." From *A Little Book of Days* by Rachel Field. Copyright 1927 by Doubleday & Company, Inc. Reprinted by permission of the publisher
"Cold Winter Now Is in the Woods." Reprinted with permission of Macmillan Publishing Co., Inc. and Blackie & Son Limited from *Away Goes Sally* by Elizabeth Coatsworth. Copyright 1934 by Macmillan Publishing Co., Inc., renewed 1962 by Elizabeth Coatsworth Beston

"Winter Night" by Mary Frances Butts from *The Outlook.* (New York: The Outlook Publishing Co., 1897)
"Stopping by Woods on a Snowy Evening." From *The Poetry of Robert Frost* edited by Edward Connery Lathem. Copyright 1923, 1939, © 1967, 1969 by Holt, Rinehart and Winston, Inc. Copyright 1951 by Robert Frost. Reprinted by permission of Holt, Rinehart and Winston, Inc., and Jonathan Cape Ltd., on behalf of the Estate of Robert Frost

## VELVET SHOES

*Elinor Wylie*

Let us walk in the white snow
  In a soundless space;
With footsteps quiet and slow,
  At a tranquil pace,
  Under veils of white lace.

I shall go shod in silk,
  And you in wool,
White as a white cow's milk,
  More beautiful
  Than the breast of a gull.

We shall walk through the still town
  In a windless peace;
We shall step upon white down,
  Upon silver fleece,
  Upon softer than these.

We shall walk in velvet shoes:
  Wherever we go
Silence will fall like dews
  On white silence below.
  We shall walk in the snow.

## WINTER NIGHT

*Collister Hutchison*

A tree may be laughter in the spring
Or a promise
Or conceit.

In the summer it may be anything
Lazy and warm with life,
Complete.

In the fall
It is the answer
To a long-forgotten call.

But on a lonely winter night
In still air
When it takes the shape of a candle flame
Springing dark from a hill all white,
It is a dare.

## WAITING

*Harry Behn*

Dreaming of honeycombs to share
With her small cubs, a mother bear
Sleeps in a snug and snowy lair.

Bees in their drowsy, drifted hive
Sip hoarded honey to survive
Until the flowers come alive.

Sleeping beneath the deep snow
Seeds of honeyed flowers know
When it is time to wake and grow.

## A SURE SIGN

*Nancy Byrd Turner*

Here's the mail, sort it quick—
Papers, letters, notes,
Postcard scenes,
Magazines;
Our hearts are in our throats.
Something there,
White and square,
Sealed with wax, and bumpy—
At the edges flat and thin,
In the middle lumpy.

When you feel the envelope,
Do your fingers trace
Something narrow,
Like an arrow?
Or a part
Of a heart?
Or a Cupid's face?
Is your name across the back
In a crooked line?
Hurry, then; that's a sign
Someone's sent a valentine!

## A VALENTINE

*Eleanor Hammond*

Frost flowers on the window glass,
Hopping chickadees that pass,
Bare old elms that bend and sway,
Pussy willows, soft and gray,

Silver clouds across the sky,
Lacy snowflakes flitting by,
Icicles like fringe in line—
That is Outdoor's valentine!

## MY VALENTINE

*Mary Catherine Parsons*

I have a little valentine
    That some one sent to me.
It's pink and white and red and blue,
    And pretty as can be.

Forget-me-nots are round the edge,
    And tiny roses, too;
And such a lovely piece of lace—
    The very palest blue.

And in the center there's a heart,
    As red as red can be!
And on it's written all in gold,
    "To You, with Love from Me."

## HEARTS WERE MADE TO GIVE AWAY

*Annette Wynne*

Hearts were made to give away
    On Valentine's good day;
Wrap them up in dainty white,
Send them off the thirteenth night,
Any kind of heart that's handy—
    Hearts of lace, and hearts of candy,
    Hearts all trimmed with ribbands fine
    Send for good St. Valentine.
Hearts were made to give away
On Valentine's dear day.

## VALENTINES

*Henry Dumas*

Forgive me if I have not sent you
a valentine
but I thought you knew
that you already have my heart
Here take the space where my
heart goes
I give that to you too

## WISE JOHNNY

*Edwina Fallis*

Little Johnny-jump-up said,
    "It must be spring,

"A Valentine" by Eleanor Hammond from *Child Life* (February 1927). Reprinted by permission of Eleanor H. Doar

"My Valentine" by Kitty Parsons from *Youth's Companion*. Reprinted by permission of the author

"Hearts Were Made to Give Away." From *For Days and Days* by Annette Wynne. Copyright 1919 by J. B. Lippincott Company. Copyright renewed 1947 by Annette Wynne. Reprinted by permission of J. B. Lippincott Company

"Valentines." From *Play Ebony, Play Ivory*, by Henry Dumas, edited by Eugene B. Redmond. Copyright © 1974 by Loretta Dumas. Reprinted by permission of Random House, Inc.

"Wise Johnny" from *Sung Under the Silver Umbrella* by Edwina Fallis. (New York: Macmillan Publishing Co., Inc., 1935)

I just saw a lady-bug
And heard a robin sing."

(*Mother Goose*)

Daffadowndilly
  Has come up to town,
In a yellow petticoat
  And a green gown.

### DAFFODILS
*Kikuriō*

In spite of cold and chills
That usher in the early spring
We have the daffodils.

*Christina Georgina Rossetti*

Growing in the vale
  By the uplands hilly,
Growing straight and frail,
  Lady Daffadowndilly.

In a golden crown,
And a scant green gown
  While the spring blows chilly,
Lady Daffadown,
  Sweet Daffadowndilly.

### SEEDS
*Walter de la Mare*

The seeds I sowed—
For weeks unseen—
Have pushed up pygmy
Shoots of green;
So frail you'd think
The tiniest stone

Would never let
A glimpse be shown.

But no; a pebble
Near them lies,
At least a cherry-stone
In size,
Which that mere sprout
Has heaved away,
To bask in sunshine
And see the Day.

### SPRING
*Harry Behn*

The last snow is going,
Brooks are overflowing,
And a sunny wind is blowing
  Swiftly along.

Through the sky birds are blowing,
On earth green is showing,
You can feel earth growing
  So quiet and strong.

A sunny wind is blowing,
Farmer's busy sowing,
Apple trees are snowing,
  And shadows grow long.

Now the wind is slowing,
Cows begin lowing,
Evening clouds are glowing
  And dusk is full of song.

### from THE SONG OF SONGS

For, lo, the winter is past,
The rain is over and gone;
The flowers appear on the earth;
The time of the singing of birds is come,
And the voice of the turtle is heard in our land.

"Daffodils" by Kikurio from *A Year of Japanese Epigrams* edited and translated by William N. Porter and published by Oxford University Press. Reprinted by permission of the publisher

"Growing in the vale." From *Sing-Song* by Christina Georgina Rossetti

"Seeds" by Walter de la Mare from *Rhymes and Verses* by Walter de la Mare. Reprinted by permission of The Literary Trustees of Walter de la Mare, and The Society of Authors as their representative

"Spring." From *The Little Hill*, copyright, 1949, by Harry Behn. Reprinted by permission of Harcourt Brace Jovanovich, Inc.

"For, lo, the winter is past." The Song of Songs, 2:11, 12. *"The voice of the turtle" refers to the bird, the turtle dove.*

*William Shakespeare*

. . . daffodils,
That come before the swallow dares, and take
The winds of March with beauty . . .

## CROCUSES

*Jōsa*

The sunrise tints the dew;
The yellow crocuses are out,
And I must pick a few.

## WRITTEN IN MARCH

*William Wordsworth*

The Cock is crowing,
The stream is flowing,
The small birds twitter,
The lake doth glitter,
The green field sleeps in the sun;
The oldest and youngest
Are at work with the strongest;
The cattle are grazing,
Their heads never raising;
There are forty feeding like one!

Like an army defeated
The snow hath retreated,
And now doth fare ill
On the top of the bare hill;
The ploughboy is whooping—anon—anon:
There's joy in the mountains;
There's life in the fountains;
Small clouds are sailing,
Blue sky prevailing;
The rain is over and gone!

## I WILL GO WITH MY FATHER A-PLOUGHING

*Joseph Campbell*

I will go with my Father a-ploughing
To the Green Field by the sea,
And the rooks and crows and seagulls
Will come flocking after me.
I will sing to the patient horses
With the lark in the shine of the air,
And my Father will sing the Plough-Song
That blesses the cleaving share.

I will go with my Father a-sowing
To the Red Field by the sea,
And blackbirds and robins and thrushes
Will come flocking after me.
I will sing to the striding sowers
With the finch on the flowering sloe,
And my Father will sing the Seed-Song
That only the wise men know.

I will go with my Father a-reaping
To the Brown Field by the sea,
And the geese and pigeons and sparrows
Will come flocking after me.
I will sing to the weary reapers
With the wren in the heat of the sun,
And my Father will sing the Scythe-Song
That joys for the harvest done.

## ROBIN'S SONG

*E. L. M. King*

Robin's song is crystal clear
Cold as an icicle,
Sharp as a spear.
I have seen Spring lift her head,
Snowdrops a-shivering,
Winter dead.

## SPRING
*William Blake*

Sound the flute!
Now it's mute;
Birds delight,
Day and night,
Nightingale
In the dale,
Lark in sky,—
Merrily,
Merrily, merrily, to welcome in the year.

Little Boy,
Full of joy;
Little Girl,
Sweet and small;
Cock does crow,
So do you;
Merry voice,
Infant noise,
Merrily, merrily, to welcome in the year.

Little Lamb,
Here I am;
Come and lick
My white neck;
Let me pull
Your soft Wool;
Let me kiss
Your soft face;
Merrily, merrily, we welcome in the year.

## MEETING THE EASTER BUNNY
*Rowena Bastin Bennett*

On Easter morn at early dawn
  before the cocks were crowing,
I met a bob-tail bunnykin
  and asked where he was going,
" 'Tis in the house and out the house
  a-tipsy, tipsy-toeing,
'Tis round the house and 'bout the house
  a-lightly I am going."
"But what is that of every hue

you carry in your basket?"
" 'Tis eggs of gold and eggs of blue;
  I wonder that you ask it.
'Tis chocolate eggs and bonbon eggs
  and eggs of red and gray,
For every child in every house
  on bonny Easter Day."
He perked his ears and winked his eye
  and twitched his little nose;
He shook his tail—what tail he had—
  and stood up on his toes.
"I must be gone before the sun;
  the east is growing gray;
'Tis almost time for bells to chime."—
So he hippety-hopped away.

## ON THE ROAD TO NARA
*Matsuo Bashō*

Oh, these spring days!
  A nameless little mountain,
    wrapped in morning haze!

## SOUTH WIND
*Tu Fu*

The days grow long, the mountains
Beautiful. The south wind blows
Over blossoming meadows.
Newly arrived swallows dart
Over the steaming marshes.
Ducks in pairs drowse on the warm sand.

## APRIL
*Sara Teasdale*

The roofs are shining from the rain,
  The sparrows twitter as they fly,
And with a windy April grace
  The little clouds go by.

Yet the back-yards are bare and brown
  With only one unchanging tree—
I could not be so sure of Spring
  Save that it sings in me.

"Meeting the Easter Bunny" from *Songs from Around a Toadstool Table* by Rowena Bennett. Copyright © 1967 by Rowena Bennett. Used by permission of Follett Publishing Company, a division of Follett Corporation
"On the Road to Nara." From *An Introduction to Haiku* by Harold G. Henderson. Copyright © 1958 by Harold G. Henderson. Reprinted by permission of Doubleday & Company, Inc.

"South Wind" by Tu Fu. From *One Hundred Poems from the Chinese,* edited by Kenneth Rexroth. Copyright © 1971 by Kenneth Rexroth. All Rights Reserved. Reprinted by permission of New Directions Publishing Corporation
"April." Reprinted with permission of Macmillan Publishing Co., Inc. from *Collected Poems* by Sara Teasdale. Copyright 1915 by Macmillan Publishing Co., Inc., renewed 1943 by Mamie T. Wheless

## EASTER

*Hilda Conkling*

On Easter morn
Up the faint cloudy sky
I hear the Easter bell,
   *Ding dong . . . ding dong . . .*
Easter morning scatters lilies
On every doorstep;
Easter morning says a glad thing
Over and over.
Poor people, beggars, old women
Are hearing the Easter bell . . .
   *Ding dong . . . ding dong . . .*

## KNOXVILLE, TENNESSEE

*Nikki Giovanni*

I always like summer
best
you can eat fresh corn
from daddy's garden
and okra
and greens
and cabbage
and lots of
barbecue
and buttermilk
and homemade ice-cream
at the church picnic
and listen to
gospel music
outside
at the church
homecoming
and go to the mountains with
your grandmother
and go barefooted
and be warm
all the time
not only when you go to bed
and sleep

## TREES

*Harry Behn*

Trees are the kindest things I know,
They do no harm, they simply grow

And spread a shade for sleepy cows,
And gather birds among their boughs.

They give us fruit in leaves above,
And wood to make our houses of,

And leaves to burn on Hallowe'en,
And in the Spring new buds of green.

They are the first when day's begun
To touch the beams of morning sun,

They are the last to hold the light
When evening changes into night,

And when a moon floats on the sky
They hum a drowsy lullaby,

Of sleepy children long ago . . .
Trees are the kindest things I know.

*Christina Georgina Rossetti*

The days are clear,
   Day after day,
When April's here,
   That leads to May,
And June
Must follow soon:
   Stay, June, stay!—
If only we could stop the moon
And June!

## LILIES

*Shikō (Arranged by Olive Beaupré Miller)*

I thought I saw white clouds, but no!—
Bending across the fence,
White lilies in a row!

## THAT MAY MORNING

*Leland B. Jacobs*

That May morning—very early—
As I walked the city street,
Not a single store was open
Any customer to greet.

That May morning—it was early—
As I walked the avenue,
I could stop and stare and window-shop,
And hear the pigeons coo.

Early, early that May morning
I could skip and jump and run
And make shadows on the sidewalk,
Not disturbing anyone.

All the windows, all the lamp posts,
Every leaf on every tree
That was growing through the sidewalk
Seemed to be there just for me.

## DANDELION

*Hilda Conkling*

O little soldier with the golden helmet,
What are you guarding on my lawn?
You with your green gun
And your yellow beard,
Why do you stand so stiff?
There is only the grass to fight!

"Lilies." From *Little Pictures of Japan* by Olive Beaupré Miller. Reprinted by permission of The Book House For Children

"That May Morning." From *Is Somewhere Always Far Away?* by Leland B. Jacobs. Copyright © 1967 by Leland B. Jacobs. Reprinted by permission of Holt, Rinehart and Winston, Inc.

"Dandelion" from *Poems by a Little Girl* by Hilda Conkling. Copyright 1920 by J. B. Lippincott Company. Reprinted by permission of the author

## DANDELIONS

*Frances M. Frost*

Over the climbing meadows
Where swallow-shadows float,
These are the small gold buttons
On earth's green, windy coat.

## MILLIONS OF STRAWBERRIES

*Genevieve Taggard*

Marcia and I went over the curve,
Eating our way down
Jewels of strawberries we didn't deserve,
Eating our way down.
Till our hands were sticky, and our lips painted,
And over us the hot day fainted,
And we saw snakes,
And got scratched,
And a lust overcame us for the red unmatched
Small buds of berries,
Till we lay down—
Eating our way down—
And rolled in the berries like two little dogs,
Rolled
In the late gold.
And gnats hummed,
And it was cold,
And home we went, home without a berry,
Painted red and brown,
Eating our way down.

## THE LITTLE ROSE TREE

*Rachel Field*

Every rose on the little tree
Is making a different face at me!

Some look surprised when I pass by,
And others droop—but they are shy.

These two whose heads together press
Tell secrets I could never guess.

"Dandelions" from *Pool in the Meadow* by Frances Frost. Boston, Mass.: Houghton Mifflin Company

"Millions of Strawberries" by Genevieve Taggard. Reprinted by permission; © 1929, 1957 Genevieve Taggard. Originally in *The New Yorker*

"The Little Rose Tree." Reprinted with permission of Macmillan Publishing Co., Inc. from *Poems* by Rachel Field. Copyright 1924, 1930 by Macmillan Publishing Co., Inc.

Some have their heads thrown back to sing,
And all the buds are listening.

I wonder if the gardener knows,
Or if he calls each just a rose?

## THAT WAS SUMMER

*Marci Ridlon*

Have you ever smelled summer?
Sure you have.
Remember that time
when you were tired of running
or doing nothing much
and you were hot
and you flopped right down on the ground?
Remember how the warm soil smelled
and the grass?
That was summer.

Remember that time
when you were trying to climb
higher in the tree
and you didn't know how
and your foot was hurting in the fork
but you were holding tight
to the branch?
Remember how the bark smelled then—
all dusty dry, but nice?
That was summer.

Remember that time
when the storm blew up quick
and you stood under a ledge
and watched the rain till it stopped
and when it stopped
you walked out again to the sidewalk,
the quiet sidewalk?
Remember how the pavement smelled—
all steamy warm and wet?
That was summer.

If you try very hard
can you remember that time

when you played outside all day
and you came home for dinner
and had to take a bath right away,
right away?
It took you a long time to pull
your shirt over your head.
Do you remember smelling the sunshine?
That was summer.

## FOURTH OF JULY NIGHT

*Dorothy Aldis*

Pin wheels whirling round
Spit sparks upon the ground,
And rockets shoot up high
And blossom in the sky—
Blue and yellow, green and red
Flowers falling on my head,
And I don't ever have to go
To bed, to bed, to bed!

*Christina Georgina Rossetti*

What is pink? a rose is pink
By the fountain's brink.
What is red? a poppy's red
In its barley bed.
What is blue? the sky is blue
Where the clouds float thro'.
What is white? a swan is white
Sailing in the light.
What is yellow? pears are yellow,
Rich and ripe and mellow.
What is green? the grass is green,
With small flowers between.
What is violet? clouds are violet
In the summer twilight.
What is orange? why, an orange,
Just an orange!

### HAPPY THOUGHT
*Robert Louis Stevenson*

The world is so full of a number of things,
I'm sure we should all be as happy as kings.

### I AM
*Hilda Conkling*

I am willowy boughs
For coolness;
I am gold-finch wings
For darkness;
I am a little grape
Thinking of September,
I am a very small violet
Thinking of May.

### LESSON FROM A SUN-DIAL
*(from the German adapted by Louis Untermeyer)*

Ignore dull days; forget the showers;
Keep count of only shining hours.

### OF QUARRELS
*Arthur Guiterman*

No Quarrel ever Stirred
Before the Second Word.

# WISDOM AND BEAUTY

### OF GIVING
*Arthur Guiterman*

Not what you Get, but what you Give
Is that which proves your Right to Live.

## SHORT SERMON

*(from the German adapted by Louis Untermeyer)*

To give—and forgive—
Is a good way to live.

## OF COURTESY

*Arthur Guiterman*

Good Manners may in Seven Words be found:
Forget Yourself and think of Those Around.

## GOOD ADVICE

*(from the German adapted by Louis Untermeyer)*

Don't shirk
Your work
For the sake of a dream;
A fish
In the dish
Is worth ten in the stream.

## MOTTO

*(from the German adapted by Louis Untermeyer)*

However they talk, whatever they say,
Look straight at the task without dismay—
And if you can do it, do it today.

## DAY-DREAMER

*(from the German adapted by Louis Untermeyer)*

Too much thought:
Too little wrought.

*Elizabeth Coatsworth*

He who has never known hunger
Has never known how good
The taste of bread may be,
The kindliness of food.

## COLLECTION OF PROVERBS

*(Proverbs 16:32)*

He that is slow to anger is better than the
mighty;
And he that ruleth his spirit than he that taketh
a city.

*(Proverbs 15:1)*

A soft answer turneth away wrath:
But grievous words stir up anger.

*(Ecclesiastes 11:1)*

Cast thy bread upon the waters:
For thou shalt find it after many days.

*(II Timothy 1:7)*

For God hath not given us the spirit of fear;
But of power, and of love, and of a sound mind.

*(Isaiah 40:31)*

But they that wait upon the Lord shall renew
their strength;
They shall mount up with wings as eagles;

They shall run, and not be weary;
*And* they shall walk, and not faint.

*(Philippians 4:8)*

Whatsoever things are true,
Whatsoever things are honest,
Whatsoever things are just,
Whatsoever things are pure,
Whatsoever things are lovely,
Whatsoever things are of good report;
If there be any virtue,
And if there be any praise,
I will think on these things.

*Christina Georgina Rossetti*

An emerald is as green as grass;
   A ruby red as blood;
A sapphire shines as blue as heaven;
   A flint lies in the mud.

A diamond is a brilliant stone,
   To catch the world's desire;
An opal holds a fiery spark;
   But a flint holds fire.

## SELECTIONS FROM THE PSALMS

*(Psalm 37)*

Fret not thyself because of evildoers,
Neither be thou envious against the workers of
   iniquity.
For they shall soon be cut down like the grass,
And wither as the green herb.
I have seen the wicked in great power,
And spreading himself like a green bay tree.
Yet he passed away, and, lo, he was not:
Yea, I sought him, but he could not be found.
Trust in the Lord, and do good;
So shalt thou dwell in the land,
And verily thou shalt be fed.

*(Psalm 150)*

Praise ye the Lord.
Praise God in his sanctuary:
Praise him in the firmament of his power.
Praise him for his mighty acts:
Praise him according to his excellent greatness.
Praise him with the sound of the trumpet:
Praise him with the psaltery and harp.
Praise him with the timbrel and dance:
Praise him with stringed instruments and organs.
Praise him upon the loud cymbals:
Praise him upon the high sounding cymbals.
Let every thing that hath breath praise the
   Lord.
Praise ye the Lord.

*(Psalm 100)*

Make a joyful noise unto the Lord, all ye lands.
Serve the Lord with gladness:
Come before his presence with singing.
Know ye that the Lord he is God:
It is he that hath made us, and not we ourselves;
We are his people, and the sheep of his pasture.
Enter into his gates with thanksgiving,
And into his courts with praise:
Be thankful unto him, and bless his name.
For the Lord is good; his mercy is everlasting;
And his truth endureth to all generations.

*(Psalm 103)*

Bless the Lord, O my soul:
And all that is within me, bless his holy name.
Bless the Lord, O my soul,
And forget not all his benefits:
Who forgiveth all thine iniquities;
Who healeth all thy diseases;
Who redeemeth thy life from destruction;
Who crowneth thee with loving-kindness and
   tender mercies;
Who satisfieth thy mouth with good things;
So that thy youth is renewed like the eagle's.
Bless the Lord, O my soul:
And all that is within me, bless his holy name.

"An emerald is as green as grass." From *Sing-Song* by
Christina Georgina Rossetti

*(Psalm 147)*

Praise ye the Lord:
For it is good to sing praises unto our God;
For it is pleasant; and praise is comely.
Great is our Lord, and of great power:
Who covereth the heaven with clouds,
Who prepareth rain for the earth,
Who maketh grass to grow upon the mountains.
He giveth to the beast his food,
And to the young ravens which cry.
He giveth snow like wool:
He scattereth the hoarfrost like ashes.
He casteth forth his ice like morsels:
Who can stand before his cold?
He sendeth out his word, and melteth them:
He causeth his wind to blow, and the waters flow.
Sing unto the Lord with thanksgiving;
Praise ye the Lord.

*(Psalm 24)*

The earth *is* the Lord's, and the fulness
    thereof;
The world, and they that dwell therein.
For he hath founded it upon the seas,
And established it upon the floods.
Who shall ascend into the hill of the Lord?
Or who shall stand in his holy place?
He that hath clean hands, and a pure heart;
Who hath not lifted up his soul unto vanity,
Nor sworn deceitfully.
He shall receive the blessing from the Lord,
And righteousness from the God of his salvation.
This is the generation of them that seek him,
That seek thy face, O Jacob.
Lift up your heads, O ye gates;
And be ye lifted up, ye everlasting doors;
And the King of glory shall come in.
Who is this King of glory?
The Lord strong and mighty,
The Lord mighty in battle.
Lift up your heads, O ye gates;
Even lift them up, ye everlasting doors;
And the King of glory shall come in.
Who is this King of glory?

The Lord of hosts,
He *is* the King of glory.

*(Psalm 23)*

The Lord is my shepherd; I shall not want.
He maketh me to lie down in green pastures:
He leadeth me beside the still waters.
He restoreth my soul:
He leadeth me in the paths of righteousness for
    his name's sake.
Yea, though I walk through the valley of the
    shadow of death,
I will fear no evil: for thou art with me;
Thy rod and thy staff they comfort me.
Thou preparest a table before me in the presence
    of mine enemies:
Thou anointest my head with oil; my cup run-
    neth over.
Surely goodness and mercy shall follow me all
    the days of my life:
And I will dwell in the house of the Lord for
    ever.

## THE PILGRIM

*William Blake*

The Sword sang on the barren heath,
    The Sickle in the fruitful field:
The Sword he sang a song of death,
    But could not make the Sickle yield.

## GOOD NIGHT

*Victor Hugo*

Good night! Good night!
Far flies the light;
But still God's love
Shall flame above,
Making all bright.
Good night! Good night!

## A RED, RED ROSE

*Robert Burns*

O my Luve's like a red, red rose
    That's newly sprung in June:
O my Luve's like the melodie
    That's sweetly play'd in tune!

As fair art thou, my bonnie lass,
    So deep in luve am I:
And I will luve thee still, my dear,
    Till a' the seas gang dry:

Till a' the seas gang dry, my dear,
    And the rocks melt wi' the sun;
I will luve thee still, my dear,
    While the sands o' life shall run.

And fare thee weel, my only Luve
    And fare thee weel awhile!
And I will come again, my Luve,
    Tho' it were ten thousand mile.

## LIES

*Yevgeny Yevtushenko*

Telling lies to the young is wrong.
Proving to them that lies are true is wrong.
Telling them that God's in his heaven
and all's well with the world is wrong.
The young know what you mean. The young are
    people.
Tell them the difficulties can't be counted,
and let them see not only what will be
but see with clarity these present times.
Say obstacles exist they must encounter
sorrow happens, hardship happens.
The hell with it. Who never knew
the price of happiness will not be happy.
Forgive no error you recognize,
it will repeat itself, increase,
and afterwards our pupils
will not forgive in us what we forgave.

## A CHARM FOR SPRING FLOWERS

*Rachel Field*

Who sees the first marsh marigold
Shall count more wealth than hands can hold.

Who bends a knee where violets grow
A hundred secret things shall know.

Who finds hepatica's dim blue
Shall have his dearest wish come true.

Who spies on lady-slippers fair
Shall keep a heart as light as air.

But whosoever toucheth not
One petal, sets no root in pot,

He shall be blessed of earth and sky
Till under them he, too, shall lie.

*Emily Dickinson*

I'm nobody! Who are you?
Are you nobody too?
Then there's a pair of us—don't tell!
They'd banish us, you know.

How dreary to be somebody!
How public, like a frog
To tell your name the livelong day
To an admiring bog.

## NIGHT

*Sara Teasdale*

Stars over snow,
    And in the west a planet
Swinging below a star—
    Look for a lovely thing and you will
        find it,
It is not far—
    It never will be far.

## LOVELINESS

*Hilda Conkling*

Loveliness that dies when I forget
Comes alive when I remember.

## BE LIKE THE BIRD

*Victor Hugo*

Be like the bird, who
Halting in his flight
On limb too slight
Feels it give way beneath him,
Yet sings
Knowing he hath wings.

## I NEVER SAW A MOOR

*Emily Dickinson*

I never saw a moor,
I never saw the sea;
Yet know I how the heather looks,
And what a wave must be.

I never spoke with God,
Nor visited in heaven;
Yet certain am I of the spot
As if the chart were given.

## A BLACKBIRD SUDDENLY

*Joseph Auslander*

Heaven is in my hand, and I
Touch a heart-beat of the sky,
Hearing a blackbird's cry.

Strange, beautiful, unquiet thing,
Lone flute of God, how can you sing
Winter to spring?

You have outdistanced every voice and word,
And given my spirit wings until it stirred
Like you—a bird!

## DUST OF SNOW

*Robert Frost*

The way a crow
Shook down on me
The dust of snow
From a hemlock tree

Has given my heart
A change of mood
And saved some part
Of a day I had rued.

## I HEARD A BIRD SING

*Oliver Herford*

I heard a bird sing
  In the dark of December
A magical thing
  And sweet to remember.

"We are nearer to Spring
  Than we were in September,"
I heard a bird sing
  In the dark of December.

## THE COIN
*Sara Teasdale*

Into my heart's treasury
  I slipped a coin
That time cannot take
  Nor a thief purloin,—
Oh, better than the minting
  Of a gold-crowned king
Is the safe-kept memory
  Of a lovely thing.

## TRULY MY OWN
*Vanessa Howard*

I think if I searched a thousand lands
and twice the number in rainbows,
I'd never find one human being
who chose the things that I chose
a person who wanted the things I wanted
or sought what I sought to be

I'd never find one human being
like or comparison to me
and if I traveled seven seas
I still would be alone
for there is no one who thinks like me
for my dreams are truly my own.

*Sia*

Let our children live and be happy.
Send us the good south winds.
Send us your breath over the lakes that
    our great world may be made beautiful
    and our people may live.
There, far off, my Sun Father arises, as-
    cends the ladder, comes from his place.
May all complete the road of life, may all
    grow old.

May the children inhale more of the sacred
    breath of life.
May all my children have corn that they
    may complete the road of life.
Here sit down; here remain: we give you
    our best thoughts.
Hasten over the meal road; we are jealous
    of you.
We inhale the sacred breath through our
    prayer plumes.

## LISTEN CHILDREN
*Lucille Clifton*

listen children
keep this in the place
you have for keeping
always
keep it all ways

we have never hated black

listen
we have been ashamed
hopeless    tired    mad
but always
all ways
we loved us

we have always loved each other
children    all ways

pass it on

*Elizabeth Coatsworth*

Swift things are beautiful:
Swallows and deer,
And lightning that falls
Bright-veined and clear,
Rivers and meteors,

Wind in the wheat,
The strong-withered horse,
The runner's sure feet.

And slow things are beautiful:
The closing of day,
The pause of the wave
That curves downward to spray,
The ember that crumbles,
The opening flower,
And the ox that moves on
In the quiet of power.

*Vanessa Howard*

I am frightened that
the flame of hate
will burn me
will scorch my pride
scar my heart
it will burn and i
cannot put it out
i cannot call the fire department
and they cannot put out the fire within
    my soul
i am frightened that the flame
of hate will burn me
if it does
i will die

### HEAVEN
*Langston Hughes*

Heaven is
The place where
Happiness is
Everywhere.

### THE CREATION
*James Weldon Johnson*

And God stepped out on space,
And he looked around and said:
I'm lonely—
I'll make me a world.

And as far as the eye of God could see
Darkness covered everything,
Blacker than a hundred midnights
Down in a cypress swamp.

Then God smiled,
And the light broke,
And the darkness rolled up on one side,
And the light stood shining on the other,
And God said: That's good!

Then God reached out and took the light in his
    hands,
And God rolled the light in his hands
Until he made the sun;
And he set that sun a-blazing in the heavens.
And the light that was left from making the sun
God gathered it up in a shining ball
And flung it against the darkness,
Spangling the night with the moon and stars.
Then down between
The darkness and the light

He hurled the world;
And God said: That's good!

Then God himself stepped down—
And the sun was on his right hand,
And the moon was on his left;
The stars were clustered about his head,
And the earth was under his feet.
And God walked, and where he trod
His footsteps hollowed the valleys out
And bulged the mountains up.

Then he stopped and saw
That the earth was hot and barren.
So God stepped over to the edge of the world
And he spat out the seven seas—
He batted his eyes, and the lightnings flashed—
He clapped his hands, and the thunders rolled—
And the waters above the earth came down,
The cooling waters came down.

Then the green grass sprouted,
And the little red flowers blossomed,
The pine tree pointed his finger to the sky,
And the oak spread out his arms,
The lakes cuddled down in the hollows of the
    ground,
And the rivers ran down to the sea;
And God smiled again,
And the rainbow appeared,
And curled itself around his shoulder.

Then God raised his arm and waved his hand,
Over the sea and over the land,
And he said: Bring forth! Bring forth!
And quicker than God could drop his hand,
Fishes and fowls
And beasts and birds
Swam the rivers and the seas,
Roamed the forests and the woods,

And split the air with their wings.
And God said: That's good!

Then God walked around,
And God looked around
On all that he had made.
He looked at his sun,
And he looked at his moon,
And he looked at his little stars;
He looked on his world
With all its living things,
And God said: I'm lonely still.

Then God sat down—
On the side of a hill where he could think;
By a deep, wide river he sat down;
With his head in his hands,
God thought and thought,
Till he thought: I'll make me a man!

Up from the bed of the river
God scooped the clay;
And by the bank of the river
He kneeled him down;
And there the great God Almighty
Who lit the sun and fixed it in the sky,
Who flung the stars to the most far corner of the
    night,
Who rounded the earth in the middle of his
    hand;
This great God,
Like a mammy bending over her baby,
Kneeled down in the dust
Toiling over a lump of clay
Till he shaped it in his own image;

Then into it he blew the breath of life,
And man became a living soul.
Amen. Amen.

## WISDOM
### Langston Hughes

I stand most humbly
Before man's wisdom,
Knowing we are not
Really wise:

If we were
We'd open up the kingdom
And make earth happy
As the dreamed of skies.

### Walt Whitman

I believe a leaf of grass is no less than the jour-
  ney-work of the stars,
And the pismire is equally perfect, and a grain of
  sand, and the egg of the wren,
And the tree-toad is a chef-d'oeuvre for the highest,
And the running blackberry would adorn the
  parlors of heaven,
And the narrowest hinge in my hand puts to
  scorn all machinery,
And the cow crunching with depress'd head sur-
  passes any statue,
And a mouse is miracle enough to stagger sextil-
  lions of infidels.

### Elizabeth Coatsworth

How gray the rain
And gray the world
And gray the rain clouds overhead,
When suddenly
Some cloud is furled
And there is gleaming sun instead!

The raindrops drip
Prismatic light,
And trees and meadows burn in green,

And arched in air
Serene and bright
The rainbow all at once is seen.

Serene and bright
The rainbow stands
That was not anywhere before,
And so may joy
Fill empty hands
When someone enters through a door.

### Elizabeth Coatsworth

The warm of heart shall never lack a fire
However far he roam.
Although he live forever among strangers
He cannot lack a home.

For strangers are not strangers to his spirit,
And each house seems his own,
And by the fire of his loving-kindness
He cannot sit alone.

## HOUSE BLESSING
### Arthur Guiterman

Bless the four corners of this house,
  And be the lintel blest;
And bless the heart and bless the board
  And bless each place of rest;
And bless the door that opens wide
  To stranger as to kin;
And bless each crystal window-pane
  That lets the starlight in;
And bless the rooftree overhead
  And every sturdy wall.
The peace of man, the peace of God,
  The peace of Love on all!

## TO THE WAYFARER

*Unknown*

*A Poem Fastened to Trees in the Portuguese Forests*

Ye who pass by and would raise your hand
against me, hearken ere you harm me.

I am the heat of your hearth on the cold winter
nights, the friendly shade screening you
from summer sun, and my fruits are refreshing draughts, quenching your thirst as you
journey on.

I am the beam that holds your house, the board
of your table, the bed on which you lie, the
timber that builds your boat.

I am the handle of your hoe, the door of your
homestead, the wood of your cradle, and the
shell of your coffin.

I am the bread of kindness and the flower of
beauty.
Ye who pass by, listen to my prayer: harm me
not.

*Greenland Eskimo*

My eyes are tired,
my worn-out eyes,
which never more will follow the narwhal
when shooting up from the deep,
in order to break the waves of the sea,
and my muscles will nevermore tremble
when I seize the harpoon,
ijaja—a—ijaja—aje.

Wish that the souls
of the great sea animals I killed
would help me to get
my heavy thoughts to a distance.
Wish that the memory
of all my great hunts
might lift me out of the weakness of old age.
ijaja—a—ijaja—aje.

Let my breath blow a song
Of all this which calls to mind
my youth.
My song breaks from my throat
with the breath of my life.

*Emily Dickinson*

Hope is the thing with feathers
That perches in the soul,
And sings the tune without the words,
And never stops at all,

And sweetest in the gale is heard;
And sore must be the storm
That could abash the little bird
That kept so many warm.

I've heard it in the chillest land,
And on the strangest sea;
Yet, never, in extremity,
It asked a crumb of me.

## A WORD

*Emily Dickinson*

A word is dead
When it is said,
  Some say.

I say it just
Begins to live
That day.

## THE WONDERFUL WORLD

*William Brighty Rands*

Great, wide, beautiful, wonderful World,
With the wonderful water round you curled,

"My eyes are tired. . . ." Copyright © 1972 by James Houston. From *Songs of the Dream People: Chants and Images from the Indians and Eskimos of North America*, edited and illustrated by James Houston (A Margaret K. McElderry Book). Used by permission of Atheneum Publishers, Inc. and Longman Canada Limited
"Hope is the thing with feathers . . . ," and "A Word." From *The Poems of Emily Dickinson*, edited by Thomas H. Johnson. Cambridge, Mass.: Harvard University Press

And the wonderful grass upon your breast,
World, you are beautifully dressed.

## MY LAND IS FAIR FOR ANY EYES TO SEE

*Jesse Stuart*

My land is fair for any eyes to see—
Now look, my friends—look to the east and west!
You see the purple hills far in the west—
Hills lined with pine and gum and black-oak
    tree—
Now to the east you see the fertile valley!
This land is mine, I sing of it to you—
My land beneath the skies of white and blue.
This land is mine, for I am part of it.
I am the land, for it is part of me—
We are akin and thus our kinship be!
It would make me a brother to the tree!
And far as eyes can see this land is mine.
Not for one foot of it I have a deed—
To own this land I do not need a deed—
They all belong to me—gum, oak, and pine.

## THE NEGRO SPEAKS OF RIVERS

*Langston Hughes*

I've known rivers:
I've known rivers ancient as the world and older
    than the flow of human blood in human
    veins.

My soul has grown deep like the rivers.

I bathed in the Euphrates when dawns were
    young.
I built my hut near the Congo and it lulled me to
    sleep.
I looked upon the Nile and raised the pyramids
    above it.
I heard the singing of the Mississippi when Abe
    Lincoln went down to New Orleans, and
    I've seen its muddy bosom turn all golden
    in the sunset.

I've known rivers:
Ancient, dusky rivers.

My soul has grown deep like the rivers.

## TO DARK EYES DREAMING

*Zilpha Keatley Snyder*

Dreams go fast and far
    these days.
They go by rocket thrust.
They go arrayed
    in lights
        or in the dust of stars.
Dreams, these days,
    go fast and far.
Dreams are young, these days,
    or very old,
They can be black
    or blue or gold.
They need no special charts,
    nor any fuel.
It seems, only one rule applies,
    to all our dreams—
They will not fly except in open sky.
    A fenced-in dream
        will die.

## THE GOLDEN HIVE

*Harry Behn*

Here you have morning bursting buds
    Of bluebells,
A beetle in green metallic armor,
Swallows darting and dipping, shadows
    Of thunder coiling over hills,
    Raindrops, and sun again,
        And butterflies.

In a golden hive these bees are yours,
    Tracing
Tides of clover down indolent winds,
Dry cicadas ticking and droning,

Hens dozing in sunny dust,
All these are yours, your own,
  To remember forever!

## THE LAKE ISLE OF INNISFREE

*William Butler Yeats*

I will arise and go now, and go to Innisfree,
And a small cabin build there, of clay and
  wattles made;
Nine bean rows will I have there, a hive for
  the honey-bee,
And live alone in the bee-loud glade.

And I shall have some peace there, for peace
  comes dropping slow,
Dropping from the veils of the morning to
  where the cricket sings;
There midnight's all a glimmer, and noon a
  purple glow,
And evening full of the linnet's wings.

I will arise and go now, for always night and
  day
I hear lake water lapping with low sounds by
  the shore;
While I stand on the roadway, or on the pavements gray,
I hear it in the deep heart's core.

## SONG OF THE SKY LOOM

*Tewa (North America)*

O our Mother the Earth, O our Father
  the Sky,
Your children are we, and with tired backs
We bring you the gifts you love.
Then weave for us a garment of brightness;
May the warp be the white light of morning,

May the weft be the red light of evening,
May the fringes be the falling rain,
May the border be the standing rainbow.
Thus weave for us a garment of brightness,
That we may walk fittingly where birds
  sing,
That we may walk fittingly where grass is
  green,
O our Mother the Earth, O our Father
  the Sky.

## from MANIFESTO

*Nicanor Parra*
*translated by Miller Williams*

Ladies and gentlemen
This is our final word
—Our first and final word—
The poets have come down from Olympus.

For the old folks
Poetry was a luxury item
But for us
It's an absolute necessity
We couldn't live without poetry.

Unlike our elders
—And I say this with all respect—
We maintain this
A poet is no alchemist
A poet is a man like all men
A bricklayer building his wall:
A maker of windows and doors.

We talk
with everyday words
We don't believe in cabalistic signs.

And one thing more:
The poet is there
To see to it the tree does not grow crooked. . . .

## THE SPLENDOR FALLS ON CASTLE WALLS

*Alfred, Lord Tennyson*

The splendor falls on castle walls
  And snowy summits old in story;
The long light shakes across the lakes,
  And the wild cataract leaps in glory.
Blow, bugle, blow, set the wild echoes flying,
Blow, bugle; answer, echoes, dying, dying, dying.

O hark, O hear! how thin and clear,
  And thinner, clearer, farther going!
O sweet and far from cliff and scar
  The horns of Elfland faintly blowing!
Blow, let us hear the purple glens replying,
Blow, bugle; answer, echoes, dying, dying, dying.

O love, they die in yon rich sky,
  They faint on hill or field or river;
Our echoes roll from soul to soul,
  And grow forever and forever.
Blow, bugle, blow, set the wild echoes flying,
And answer, echoes, answer, dying, dying, dying.

# part two

# TIME FOR MAGIC: OLD AND NEW

*Folk Tales*

*Fables*

*Myths*

*Epics and Hero Tales*

*Modern Fantasy*

In all tongues and all times since humanity began, the most familiar words of childhood have probably been *tell me a story*. And the stories have been told, not really for children but for adults. As they always do, children have listened in, beyond the edge of the fire's light, to hear what tales were being told. Those they could grasp, they took to themselves, until, over the stretch of centuries, certain stories have become their own. Unfortunately, with the rise of the modern world, grownups have increasingly abandoned the folk tales of simpler times and quieter places as fit only for the young. Now folk tales are mainly the province of children and scholars, but surely anyone who knows the folk tales will agree with Horace: "Change the name and the tale is about you." The *tale* is all tales humans have ever told; the *you* is all of us.

# FOLK TALES

It is curious in an age as realistic and mechanized as ours that the magic of the folk tales still casts its spell on modern children. Witches and dragons, talking beasts and rebellious pancakes, flying carpets and cloaks of darkness, fairies and wise women, spells and enchantments are accepted as casually by children as airplanes and television.

It is true that the modern child becomes interested in fairy tales later than people used to think, and perhaps wears them out a little sooner. Except for a few of the simplest nursery tales of "The Little Red Hen" and "The Story of the Three Little Pigs" variety, the peak of children's interest in tales of magic seems to be reached around eight or nine years of age and not earlier. After nine there is a continued but steadily diminishing interest in such stories through the ages of ten, eleven, and twelve years.

Only a small fraction of the folk tales were composed for and told to children. A majority of the tales mirror the mature lives, customs, beliefs, and emotions of peoples all over the world, and their adult themes make large numbers of them totally unsuited to children. There still remain, however, enough stories with lively plots, plenty of action, and conclusions which satisfy children's liking for justice and successful achievement, to account for their continued popularity with young people.

The arrangement of the folk tales in this section is an arbitrary one that is calculated to assist the user of this volume and not to reflect scholarly schematics. As indicated in the table of contents, the five broad divisions are continents and geographical regions—Europe, Africa, Asia, Oceania and Australia, North and South America. Within these broad divisions (excepting those of Africa and Oceania and Australia, which are not subdivided), the tales are grouped (1) according to geographical proximity, an example being the Danish, Norwegian, and Swedish tales grouped under Scandinavia; (2) by individual countries, such as Spain or Czechoslovakia; and (3) according to cultural identity, for example, "United States: Tall Tales."

A quick glance will show that most of the folk tales presented here are from Europe and lands colonized by Europeans. Until recently, the most thorough investigation and recording of folk tales took place in Europe and in countries closely bound to her by language and tradition. Even today, when we speak of folk and fairy tales, most people immediately think of such stories as "The Story of the Three Bears," "Cinderella," and "Snow-White and the Seven Dwarfs." Happily, all this is changing. As new nations arise in the world, students of literature, folklore, and the arts are taking an interest in the culture of "new" peoples. Just in the nick of time, they are writing down and tape-recording the old tales before the rush of the twentieth century sweeps away the old patterns of life and with them all the tales and songs which were once a vital part of the daily life of a people. How fortunate that they are doing so, for after the tidal wave of modernism has changed the cultural contours of a group, the scholar can sometimes find only battered remnants in the debris of a folk-tale tradition.

For the most part, the folk tales in this book are the simpler, merrier ones from the great collections. Each of the large groups, such as the English, French, German, and Norwegian, begins with easier stories, most of them with nursery tales for the youngest children. They progress through tales of magic for the sevens, eights, and nines to the more mature stories which will command the respect of the elevens and twelves.

Grownups will discover likenesses in some of the stories from the different national and racial groups, and these likenesses sometimes interest children. Note the similarities between "Tom Tit Tot" and "Rumpelstiltzkin"; "Cinderella," "Tattercoats," and "Little Burnt-Face"; "Beauty and the Beast" and "East o' the Sun and West o' the Moon"; "Sadko" and "Urashima Taro and the Princess of the Sea."

Remember that the folk tales were created and kept alive by the oral tradition of gifted storytellers. Read them aloud if you must, but tell them if you can, for in the spontaneity of good storytelling, these tales come most vividly to life for you and your children.

Of course, tales of magic should never be used exclusively or in too great numbers, but in balanced proportion to realistic fiction and informational reading. Use the folk tales in connection with the study of a people—the Chinese, English, or East Indian, for example. Use them to stimulate the children's creative urge to paint or dramatize or write. The tall tales have often set children to creating their own "whoppers" and illustrating them.

Above all, use these stories for sheer delight. They have humor, nonsense, romance, and poetic beauty. They will help to break up the tight literalness that overtakes some children. They also reiterate moral truths that are important for children to know. "Be of good cheer," these stories seem to say. "Use your head, keep a kindly heart, a civil tongue, and a fearless spirit and you will surely find the water of life and your heart's desire."

# Great Britain

*Nowhere, amid the grand diversity of English, Scottish, Welsh, and Cornish folklore, together with that of Northern Ireland, can one find the typical British tale. Furthermore, it is pointless to try to determine from the texts available to children the salient features of English folklore, say, as against Cornish folklore. We do know that the Piskies are a fairy folk found frequently in Cornish tales, but they are next of kin to English brownies and Scottish kelpies. What is important is that from the various corners of the British Isles there come to us tales like those found in this anthology. Our greatest selection of stories is from English folklore. Most of the tales were garnered in the late nineteenth century and were retold most notably by Joseph Jacobs. His retelling of these tales has given generations of children access to the essence of the English oral narrative, with its memorably intrepid giant-killers (not included here) and its classics of the nursery—the accumulative tale like "The Old Woman and Her Pig," the humorous anecdote as found in "Master of All Masters," and the simple talking beast story like "The Story of the Three Little Pigs." Jacobs had a child audience in mind and intended, he said, "to write as a good old nurse will speak, when she tells Fairy Tales." How well he succeeded! The humor, the swinging prose rhythms, and the blending of practicality and wonder in the tales still provide a rare and indispensable literary treat for successive generations of four- to ten-year-old youngsters.*

## THE STORY OF THE THREE BEARS

### (English)

*This version of "The Three Bears" is from the tale as originally written by Robert Southey (1774–1843). Although the version by Flora Annie Steel remains the better known, the Southey original has a saucy verve which, after more than a century since its first appearance, is refreshing. Here is an example of an authored story which was taken into oral tradition. You may prefer to substitute the more universally known Goldilocks for the old Woman and to eliminate the remark about sending her to the House of Correction.*

"The Story of the Three Bears." From *English Fairy Tales*, collected by Joseph Jacobs. Third edition, revised. David Nutt, London, 1907

Once upon a time there were three bears who lived together in a house of their own in a wood. One of them was a Little, Small, Wee Bear; one was a Middle-sized Bear; and the other was a Great, Huge Bear. They had each a pot for their porridge: a little pot for the Little, Small, Wee Bear; a middle-sized pot for the Middle Bear; and a great pot for the Great, Huge Bear. And they had each a chair to sit in: a little chair for the Little, Small, Wee Bear; a middle-sized chair for the Middle Bear; and a great chair for the Great, Huge Bear. And they had each a bed to sleep in: a little bed for the Little, Small, Wee Bear; a middle-sized bed for the Middle Bear; and a great bed for the Great, Huge Bear.

One day, after they had made the porridge for their breakfast and poured it into their porridge-pots, they walked out into the wood while the porridge was cooling, that they might not burn their mouths by beginning too soon to eat it. And while they were walking, a little old Woman came to the house. She could not have been a good, honest old Woman, for first she looked in at the window and then she peeped in at the keyhole, and, seeing nobody in the house, she lifted the latch. The door was not fastened, because the bears were good bears, who did nobody any harm and never suspected that anybody would harm them. So the little old Woman opened the door and went in, and well pleased she was when she saw the porridge on the table. If she had been a good little old Woman, she would have waited till the bears came home, and then, perhaps, they would have asked her to breakfast, for they were good bears—a little rough or so, as the manner of bears is, but for all that very good-natured and hospitable. But she was an impudent, bad old Woman and set about helping herself.

So first she tasted the porridge of the Great, Huge Bear, and that was too hot for her, and she said a bad word about that. Then she tasted the porridge of the Middle Bear, and that was too cold for her, and she said a bad word about that too. And then she went to the porridge of the Little, Small, Wee Bear and tasted that, and that was neither too hot nor too cold, but just right. She liked it so well that she ate it all up, but the naughty old Woman said a bad word about the little porridge-pot, because it did not hold enough for her.

Then the little old Woman sat down in the chair of the Great, Huge Bear, and that was too hard for her. Then she sat down in the chair of the Middle Bear, and that was too soft for her. And then she sat down in the chair of the Little, Small, Wee Bear, and that was neither too hard nor too soft, but just right. So she seated herself in it, and there she sat till the bottom of the chair came out, and down she came, plump upon the ground. And the naughty old Woman said a wicked word about that too.

Then the little old Woman went upstairs into the bedchamber in which the three bears slept. And first she lay down upon the bed of the Great, Huge Bear, but that was too high at the head for her. Next she lay down upon the bed of the Middle Bear, and that was too high at the foot for her. And then she lay down upon the bed of the Little, Small, Wee Bear, and that was neither too high at the head nor too high at the foot, but just right. So she covered herself up comfortably and lay there till she fell fast asleep.

By this time the three bears thought their porridge would be cool enough, so they came home to breakfast. Now the little old Woman had left the spoon of the Great, Huge Bear, standing in his porridge.

"SOMEBODY HAS BEEN AT MY PORRIDGE!" said the Great, Huge Bear in his great, rough, gruff voice. And when the Middle Bear looked at his, he saw that the spoon was standing in it too. They were wooden spoons; if they had been silver ones, the naughty old Woman would have put them in her pocket.

"SOMEBODY HAS BEEN AT MY PORRIDGE!" said the Middle Bear in his middle voice.

Then the Little, Small, Wee Bear looked at his, and there was the spoon in the porridge-pot, but the porridge was all gone.

"Somebody has been at my porridge and has eaten it all up!" said the Little, Small, Wee Bear in his little, small, wee voice.

Upon this the three bears, seeing that some one had entered their house and eaten up the Little, Small, Wee Bear's breakfast, began, to look about them. Now the little old Woman had not put the hard cushion straight when she rose from the chair of the Great, Huge Bear.

"SOMEBODY HAS BEEN SITTING IN MY CHAIR!" said the Great, Huge Bear in his great, rough, gruff voice.

And the little old Woman had squatted down the soft cushion of the Middle Bear.

"SOMEBODY HAS BEEN SITTING IN MY CHAIR!" said the Middle Bear in his middle voice.

And you know what the little old Woman had done to the third chair.

"Somebody has been sitting in my chair and has sat the bottom out of it!" said the Little, Small, Wee Bear in his little, small, wee voice.

Then the three bears thought it necessary that they should make farther search, so they went upstairs into their bedchamber. Now the little old Woman had pulled the pillow of the Great, Huge Bear out of its place.

"SOMEBODY HAS BEEN LYING IN MY BED!" said the Great, Huge Bear in his great, rough, gruff voice.

And the little old Woman had pulled the bolster of the Middle Bear out of its place.

"SOMEBODY HAS BEEN LYING IN MY BED!" said

the Middle Bear in his middle voice.

And when the Little, Small, Wee Bear came to look at his bed, there was the bolster in its place, and the pillow in its place upon the bolster; and upon the pillow was the little old Woman's ugly, dirty head—which was not in its place, for she had no business there.

"Somebody has been lying in my bed—and here she is!" said the Little, Small, Wee Bear in his little, small, wee voice.

The little old Woman had heard in her sleep the great, rough, gruff voice of the Great, Huge Bear, but she was so fast asleep that it was no more to her than the roaring of wind or the rumbling of thunder. And she had heard the middle voice of the Middle Bear, but it was only as if she had heard some one speaking in a dream. But when she heard the little, small, wee voice of the Little, Small, Wee Bear, it was so sharp and so shrill that it awakened her at once. Up she started and when she saw the three bears on one side of the bed, she tumbled herself out at the other and ran to the window. Now the window was open, because the bears, like good, tidy bears, as they were, always opened their bedchamber window when they got up in the morning. Out the little old Woman jumped; and whether she broke her neck in the fall, or ran into the wood and was lost there, or found her way out of the wood and was taken up by the constable and sent to the House of Correction for a vagrant as she was, I cannot tell. But the three bears never saw anything more of her.

## THE STORY
## OF THE THREE LITTLE PIGS

*(English)*

*It is likely that this story is the top favorite of all five-year-olds who know it.*

Once upon a time when pigs spoke rhyme
And monkeys chewed tobacco,
And hens took snuff to make them tough,
And ducks went quack, quack, quack, O!

"The Story of the Three Little Pigs." From *English Fairy Tales,* collected by Joseph Jacobs. Third edition, revised. David Nutt, London, 1907

There was an old sow with three little pigs, and as she had not enough to keep them, she sent them out to seek their fortune. The first that went off met a man with a bundle of straw and said to him:

"Please, man, give me that straw to build me a house."

Which the man did, and the little pig built a house with it. Presently came along a wolf who knocked at the door and said:

"Little pig, little pig, let me come in."

To which the pig answered:

"No, no, by the hair of my chinny chin chin."

The wolf then answered to that:

"Then I'll huff, and I'll puff, and I'll blow your house in."

So he huffed, and he puffed, and he blew the house in and ate up the little pig.

The second little pig met a man with a bundle of furze and said:

"Please, man, give me that furze to build a house."

Which the man did, and the pig built his house. Then along came the wolf and said:

"Little pig, little pig, let me come in."

"No, no, by the hair of my chinny chin chin."

"Then I'll puff, and I'll huff, and I'll blow your house in."

So he huffed, and he puffed, and he puffed, and he huffed, and at last he blew the house down, and he ate up the little pig.

The third little pig met a man with a load of bricks, and said:

"Please, man, give me those bricks to build a house with."

So the man gave him the bricks, and the pig built his house with them. So the wolf came, as he did to the other little pigs, and said:

"Little pig, little pig, let me come in."

"No, no, by the hair of my chinny chin chin."

"Then I'll huff, and I'll puff, and I'll blow your house in."

Well, he huffed, and he puffed, and he huffed, and he puffed, and he puffed and huffed; but he could *not* get the house down. When he found that he could not, with all his huffing and puffing, blow the house down, he said:

"Little pig, I know where there is a nice field of turnips."

"Where?" said the little pig.

"Oh, in Mr. Smith's home-field. If you will be ready tomorrow morning, I will call for you, and we will go together and get some for dinner."

"Very well," said the little pig, "I will be ready. What time do you mean to go?"

"Oh, at six o'clock."

Well, the little pig got up at five and got the turnips before the wolf came (which he did about six) and said:

"Little pig, are you ready?"

The little pig said, "Ready! I have been and come back again, and got a nice potful for dinner."

The wolf felt very angry at this, but thought that he would be up to the little pig somehow or other, so he said:

"Little pig, I know where there is a nice apple tree."

"Where?" said the pig.

"Down at Merry-garden," replied the wolf, "and if you will not deceive me, I will come for you at five o'clock tomorrow, and we will get some apples."

Well, the little pig bustled up the next morning at four o'clock and went off for the apples, hoping to get back before the wolf came; but he had further to go and had to climb the tree, so that just as he was coming down from it, he saw the wolf coming, which, as you may suppose, frightened him very much. When the wolf came up he said:

"Little pig! What! Are you here before me? Are they nice apples?"

"Yes, very," said the little pig. "I will throw one down to you."

And he threw it so far that while the wolf was gone to pick it up, the little pig jumped down and ran home. The next day the wolf came again, and said to the little pig:

"Little pig, there is a fair at Shanklin this afternoon. Will you go?"

"Oh yes," said the pig, "I will go. What time shall you be ready?"

"At three," said the wolf. So the little pig went off before the time as usual and got to the fair

and bought a butter-churn, which he was going home with, when he saw the wolf coming. Then he could not tell what to do. So he got into the churn to hide and by so doing turned it round, and it rolled down the hill with the pig in it, which frightened the wolf so much that he ran home without going to the fair. He went to the little pig's house and told him how frightened he had been by a great round thing which came down the hill past him. Then the little pig said:

"Hah, I frightened you then. I had been to the

fair and bought a butter-churn, and when I saw you, I got into it and rolled down the hill."

Then the wolf was very angry indeed. He declared he *would* eat up the little pig and that he would get down the chimney after him. When the little pig saw what the wolf was about, he hung on the pot full of water and made up a blazing fire and, just as the wolf was coming down, took off the cover, and in fell the wolf. So the little pig put on the cover again in an instant, boiled him up, and ate him for supper and lived happy ever afterwards.

### HENNY-PENNY

#### (English)

*Here is the perfect example of a story whose ancestry reaches far back in time—all the way back to the early Buddhistic literature of India. It has something to say to all ages, yet, like its cousins "The Pancake" and "The Gingerbread Boy," it is a favorite of very young children. Versions of it are to be found in many lands, and its gentle lesson is always contemporary.*

One day Henny-Penny was picking up corn in the cornyard when—whack!—something hit her upon the head. "Goodness gracious me!" said Henny-Penny. "The sky's a-going to fall. I must go and tell the king."

So she went along, and she went along, and she went along, till she met Cocky-Locky. "Where are you going to, Henny-Penny?" said Cocky-Locky.

"Oh! I'm going to tell the king the sky's a-falling," said Henny-Penny.

"May I come with you?" said Cocky-Locky.

"Certainly," said Henny-Penny. So Henny-Penny and Cocky-Locky went to tell the king the sky was falling.

They went along, and they went along, and they went along, till they met Ducky-Daddles. "Where are you going to, Henny-Penny and Cocky-Locky?" said Ducky-Daddles.

"Oh! We're going to tell the king the sky's a-falling," said Henny-Penny and Cocky-Locky.

"May I come with you?" said Ducky-Daddles.

"Certainly," said Henny-Penny and Cocky-Locky. So Henny-Penny, Cocky-Locky, and Ducky-Daddles went to tell the king the sky was a-falling.

So they went along, and they went along, and they went along, till they met Goosey-Poosey. "Where are you going to, Henny-Penny, Cocky-Locky, and Ducky-Daddles?" said Goosey-Poosey.

"Oh! We're going to tell the king the sky's a-falling," said Henny-Penny and Cocky-Locky and Ducky-Daddles.

"May I come with you?" said Goosey-Poosey.

"Certainly," said Henny-Penny, Cocky-Locky, and Ducky-Daddles. So Henny-Penny, Cocky-Locky, Ducky-Daddles, and Goosey-Poosey went to tell the king the sky was a-falling.

So they went along, and they went along, and they went along, till they met Turkey-Lurkey. "Where are you going, Henny-Penny, Cocky-Locky, Ducky-Daddles, and Goosey-Poosey?" said Turkey-Lurkey.

"Oh! We're going to tell the king the sky's a-falling," said Henny-Penny, Cocky-Locky, Ducky-Daddles, and Goosey-Poosey.

"May I come with you, Henny-Penny, Cocky-

"Henny-Penny." From *English Fairy Tales,* collected by Joseph Jacobs. Third edition, revised. David Nutt, London, 1907

Locky, Ducky-Daddles, and Goosey-Poosey?" said Turkey-Lurkey.

"Oh, certainly, Turkey-Lurkey," said Henny-Penny, Cocky-Locky, Ducky-Daddles, and Goosey-Poosey. So Henny-Penny, Cocky-Locky, Ducky-Daddles, Goosey-Poosey, and Turkey-Lurkey all went to tell the king the sky was a-falling.

So they went along, and they went along, and they went along, till they met Foxy-Woxy, and Foxy-Woxy said to Henny-Penny, Cocky-Locky, Ducky-Daddles, Goosey-Poosey, and Turkey-Lurkey: "Where are you going, Henny-Penny, Cocky-Locky, Ducky-Daddles, Goosey-Poosey, and Turkey-Lurkey?"

And Henny-Penny, Cocky-Locky, Ducky-Daddles, Goosey-Poosey, and Turkey-Lurkey said to Foxy-Woxy: "We're going to tell the king the sky's a-falling."

"Oh! But this is not the way to the king, Henny-Penny, Cocky-Locky, Ducky-Daddles, Goosey-Poosey, and Turkey-Lurkey," said Foxy-Woxy. "I know the proper way. Shall I show it to you?"

"Oh certainly, Foxy-Woxy," said Henny-Penny, Cocky-Locky, Ducky-Daddles, Goosey-Poosey, and Turkey-Lurkey. So Henny-Penny, Cocky-Locky, Ducky-Daddles, Goosey-Poosey, Turkey-Lurkey, and Foxy-Woxy all went to tell the king the sky was a-falling.

So they went along, and they went along, and they went along, till they came to a narrow and dark hole. Now this was the door of Foxy-Woxy's cave. But Foxy-Woxy said to Henny-Penny, Cocky-Locky, Ducky-Daddles, Goosey-Poosey, and Turkey-Lurkey: "This is the short way to the king's palace. You'll soon get there if you follow me. I will go first, and you come after, Henny-Penny, Cocky-Locky, Ducky-Daddles, Goosey-Poosey, and Turkey-Lurkey."

"Why of course, certainly, without doubt, why not?" said Henny-Penny, Cocky-Locky, Ducky-Daddles, Goosey-Poosey, and Turkey-Lurkey.

So Foxy-Woxy went into his cave, and he didn't go very far, but turned round to wait for Henny-Penny, Cocky-Locky, Ducky-Daddles, Goosey-Poosey, and Turkey-Lurkey.

So at last at first Turkey-Lurkey went through the dark hole into the cave. He hadn't got far when "Hrumph," Foxy-Woxy snapped off Turkey-Lurkey's head and threw his body over his left shoulder. Then Goosey-Poosey went in, and "Hrumph," off went her head, and Goosey-Poosey was thrown beside Turkey-Lurkey. Then Ducky-Daddles waddled down, and "Hrumph," snapped Foxy-Woxy, and Ducky-Daddles' head was off, and Ducky-Daddles was thrown alongside Turkey-Lurkey and Goosey-Poosey. Then Cocky-Locky strutted down into the cave and he hadn't gone far when "Snap, Hrumph!" went Foxy-Woxy, and Cocky-Locky was thrown alongside of Turkey-Lurkey, Goosey-Poosey, and Ducky-Daddles.

But Foxy-Woxy had made two bites at Cocky-Locky, and when the first snap only hurt Cocky-Locky, but didn't kill him, he called out to Henny-Penny. But she turned tail and off she ran home, so she never told the king the sky was a-falling.

## THE COCK, THE MOUSE, AND THE LITTLE RED HEN

(English)

*"It's never too late to mend," said the little Red Hen. Her cheerful philosophy and unbegrudging ways are the very antidote to laziness and evil. Félicité LeFèvre's retelling is a small classic.*

Once upon a time there was a hill, and on the hill there was a pretty little house.

It had one little green door, and four little windows with green shutters, and in it there lived a COCK, and A MOUSE, and A LITTLE RED HEN. On another hill close by, there was another little house. It was very ugly. It had a door that wouldn't shut, and two broken windows, and all the paint was off the shutters. And in this house there lived A BOLD BAD FOX and FOUR BAD LITTLE FOXES.

One morning these four bad little foxes came to the big bad Fox and said:

"Oh, Father, we're so hungry!"

"We had nothing to eat yesterday," said one.

"And scarcely anything the day before," said another.

"The Cock, the Mouse, and the Little Red Hen." By Félicité LeFèvre

The big bad Fox shook his head, for he was thinking. At last he said in a big gruff voice:

"On the hill over there I see a house. And in that house there lives a Cock."

"And a Mouse!" screamed two of the little foxes.

"And a little Red Hen," screamed the other two.

"And they are nice and fat," went on the big bad Fox. "This very day I'll take my sack and I will go up that hill and in at that door, and into my sack I will put the Cock, and the Mouse, and the little Red Hen."

So the four little foxes jumped for joy, and the big bad Fox went to get his sack ready to start upon his journey.

But what was happening to the Cock, and the Mouse, and the little Red Hen, all this time?

Well, sad to say, the Cock and the Mouse had both got out of bed on the wrong side that morning. The Cock said the day was too hot, and the Mouse grumbled because it was too cold.

They came grumbling down to the kitchen, where the good little Red Hen, looking as bright as a sunbeam, was bustling about.

"Who'll get some sticks to light the fire with?" she asked.

"I shan't," said the Cock.

"I shan't," said the Mouse.

"Then I'll do it myself," said the little Red Hen.

So off she ran to get the sticks. "And now, who'll fill the kettle from the spring?" she asked.

"I shan't," said the Cock.

"I shan't," said the Mouse.

"Then I'll do it myself," said the little Red Hen.

And off she ran to fill the kettle.

"And who'll get the breakfast ready?" she asked, as she put the kettle on to boil.

"I shan't," said the Cock.

"I shan't," said the Mouse.

"I'll do it myself," said the little Red Hen.

All breakfast time the Cock and the Mouse quarrelled and grumbled. The Cock upset the milk jug, and the Mouse scattered crumbs upon the floor.

"Who'll clear away the breakfast?" asked the poor little Red Hen, hoping they would soon leave off being cross.

"I shan't," said the Cock.

"I shan't," said the Mouse.

"Then I'll do it myself," said the little Red Hen.

So she cleared everything away, swept up the crumbs, and brushed up the fireplace.

"And now, who'll help me to make the beds?"

"I shan't," said the Cock.

"I shan't," said the Mouse.

"Then I'll do it myself," said the little Red Hen.

And she tripped away upstairs.

But the lazy Cock and Mouse each sat down in a comfortable arm-chair by the fire, and soon fell fast asleep.

Now the bad Fox had crept up the hill and into the garden, and if the Cock and Mouse hadn't been asleep, they would have seen his sharp eyes peeping in at the window.

"Rat tat tat! Rat tat tat!" the Fox knocked at the door.

"Who can that be?" said the Mouse, half opening his eyes.

"Go and look for yourself, if you want to know," said the rude Cock.

"It's the postman perhaps," thought the Mouse to himself, "and he may have a letter for me." So without waiting to see who it was, he lifted the latch and opened the door.

As soon as he opened it, in jumped the big Fox.

"Oh! oh! oh!" squeaked the Mouse, as he tried to run up the chimney.

"Doodle doodle do!" screamed the Cock, as he jumped on the back of the biggest arm-chair.

But the Fox only laughed, and without more ado he took the little Mouse by the tail, and popped him into the sack, and seized the Cock by the neck and popped him in too.

Then the poor little Red Hen came running downstairs to see what all the noise was about, and the Fox caught her and put her into the sack with the others.

Then he took a long piece of string out of his pocket, wound it round, and round, and round the mouth of the sack, and tied it very tight indeed. After that he threw the sack over his back, and off he set down the hill, chuckling to himself.

"Oh, I wish I hadn't been so cross," said the

Cock, as they went bumping about.

"Oh! I wish I hadn't been so lazy," said the Mouse, wiping his eyes with the tip of his tail.

"It's never too late to mend," said the little Red Hen. "And don't be too sad. See, here I have my little work-bag, and in it there is a pair of scissors, and a little thimble, and a needle and thread. Very soon you will see what I am going to do."

Now the sun was very hot, and soon Mr. Fox began to feel his sack was heavy, and at last he thought he would lie down under a tree and go to sleep for a little while. So he threw the sack down with a big bump, and very soon fell fast asleep.

Snore, snore, snore, went the Fox.

As soon as the little Red Hen heard this, she took out her scissors, and began to snip a hole in the sack just large enough for the Mouse to creep through.

"Quick," she whispered to the Mouse, "run as fast as you can and bring back a stone just as large as yourself."

Out scampered the Mouse, and soon came back, dragging the stone after him.

"Push it in here," said the little Red Hen, and he pushed it in, in a twinkling.

Then the little Red Hen snipped away at the hole, till it was large enough for the Cock to get through.

"Quick," she said, "run and get a stone as big as yourself."

Out flew the Cock, and soon came back quite out of breath, with a big stone, which he pushed into the sack too.

Then the little Red Hen popped out, got a stone as big as herself, and pushed it in. Next she put on her thimble, took out her needle and thread, and sewed up the hole as quickly as ever she could.

When it was done, the Cock and the Mouse and the little Red Hen ran home very fast, shut the door after them, drew the bolts, shut the shutters, and drew down the blinds and felt quite safe.

The bad Fox lay fast asleep under the tree for some time, but at last he awoke.

"Dear, dear," he said, rubbing his eyes and then looking at the long shadows on the grass, "how late it is getting. I must hurry home."

So the bad Fox went grumbling and groaning down the hill, till he came to the stream. Splash! In went one foot. Splash! In went the other, but the stones in the sack were so heavy that at the very next step, down tumbled Mr. Fox into a deep pool. And then the fishes carried him off to their fairy caves and kept him a prisoner there, so he was never seen again. And the four greedy little foxes had to go to bed without any supper.

But the Cock and the Mouse never grumbled again. They lit the fire, filled the kettle, laid the breakfast, and did all the work, while the good little Red Hen had a holiday, and sat resting in the big arm-chair.

No foxes ever troubled them again, and for all I know they are still living happily in the little house with the green door and green shutters, which stands on the hill.

## MASTER OF ALL MASTERS

*(English)*

*Most youngsters find this story absolutely rib-tickling—especially if you say or read the last paragraph as fast as you can.*

A girl once went to the fair to hire herself for servant. At last a funny-looking old gentleman engaged her and took her home to his house. When she got there, he told her that he had something to teach her, for that in his house he had his own names for things.

He said to her, "What will you call me?"

"Master or mister, or whatever you please, sir," says she.

He said, "You must call me 'master of all masters.' And what would you call this?" pointing to his bed.

"Bed or couch, or whatever you please, sir."

"No, that's my 'barnacle.' And what do you call these?" said he, pointing to his pantaloons.

"Breeches or trousers, or whatever you please, sir."

"You must call them 'squibs and crackers.' And what would you call her?" pointing to the cat.

"Master of All Masters." From *English Fairy Tales*, collected by Joseph Jacobs. Third edition, revised. David Nutt, London, 1907

"Cat or kit, or whatever you please, sir."

"You must call her 'white-faced simminy.' And this now," showing the fire, "what would you call this?"

"Fire or flame, or whatever you please, sir."

"You must call it 'hot cockalorum,' and what this?" he went on, pointing to the water.

"Water or wet, or whatever you please, sir."

"No, 'pondalorum' is its name. And what do you call all this?" asked he, as he pointed to the house.

"House or cottage, or whatever you please, sir."

"You must call it 'high topper mountain.' "

That very night the servant woke her master up in a fright and said: "Master of all masters, get out of your barnacle and put on your squibs and crackers. For white-faced simminy has got a spark of hot cockalorum on its tail, and unless you get some pondalorum, high topper mountain will be all on hot cockalorum" . . . . .
. . . . . . . That's all.

· **TATTERCOATS**

*(English)*

*This is one of the prettiest of the 300 or more variants of the "Cinderella" theme.*

In a great palace by the sea there once dwelt a very rich old lord, who had neither wife nor children living, only one little granddaughter, whose face he had never seen in all her life. He hated her bitterly, because at her birth his favourite daughter died; and when the old nurse brought him the baby, he swore that it might live or die as it liked, but he would never look on its face as long as it lived.

So he turned his back and sat by his window, looking out over the sea and weeping great tears for his lost daughter, till his white hair and beard grew down over his shoulders and twined round his chair and crept into the chinks of the floor, and his tears, dropping on to the window-ledge, wore a channel through the stone and

"Tattercoats." From *More English Fairy Tales,* collected and edited by **Joseph Jacobs.** David Nutt, London, 1894

ran away in a little river to the great sea. And, meanwhile, his granddaughter grew up with no one to care for her or clothe her; only the old nurse, when no one was by, would sometimes give her a dish of scraps from the kitchen or a torn petticoat from the rag-bag; while the other servants of the palace would drive her from the house with blows and mocking words, calling her "Tattercoats" and pointing at her bare feet and shoulders, till she ran away crying, to hide among the bushes.

And so she grew up, with little to eat or to wear, spending her days in the fields and lanes, with only the gooseherd for a companion, who would play to her so merrily on his little pipe, when she was hungry or cold or tired, that she forgot all her troubles and fell to dancing, with his flock of noisy geese for partners.

But one day people told each other that the king was travelling through the land, and in the town nearby was to give a great ball to all the lords and ladies of the country, when the prince, his only son, was to choose a wife.

One of the royal invitations was brought to the palace by the sea, and the servants carried it up to the old lord who still sat by his window, wrapped in his long white hair and weeping into the little river that was fed by his tears.

But when he heard the king's command, he dried his eyes and bade them bring shears to cut him loose, for his hair had bound him a fast prisoner and he could not move. And then he sent them for rich clothes and jewels, which he put on; and he ordered them to saddle the white horse with gold and silk, that he might ride to meet the king.

Meanwhile, Tattercoats had heard of the great doings in the town, and she sat by the kitchen door, weeping because she could not go to see them. And when the old nurse heard her crying, she went to the lord of the palace and begged him to take his granddaughter with him to the king's ball.

But he only frowned and told her to be silent, while the servants laughed and said, "Tattercoats is happy in her rags, playing with the gooseherd. Let her be—it is all she is fit for."

A second, and then a third time, the old nurse begged him to let the girl go with him, but she was answered only by black looks and fierce words, till she was driven from the room by the jeering servants, with blows and mocking words.

Weeping over her ill-success, the old nurse went to look for Tattercoats; but the girl had been turned from the door by the cook and had run away to tell her friend, the gooseherd, how unhappy she was because she could not go to the king's ball.

But when the gooseherd had listened to her story, he bade her cheer up and proposed that they should go together into the town to see the king and all the fine things; and when she looked sorrowfully down at her rags and bare feet, he played a note or two upon his pipe, so gay and merry that she forgot all about her tears and her troubles, and before she well knew, the herdboy had taken her by the hand, and she and he, and the geese before them, were dancing down the road towards the town.

Before they had gone very far, a handsome young man, splendidly dressed, rode up and stopped to ask the way to the castle where the king was staying; and when he found that they too were going thither, he got off his horse and walked beside them along the road.

The herdboy pulled out his pipe and played a low sweet tune, and the stranger looked again and again at Tattercoats' lovely face till he fell deeply in love with her and begged her to marry him.

But she only laughed and shook her golden head.

"You would be finely put to shame if you had a goose-girl for your wife!" said she. "Go and ask one of the great ladies you will see tonight at the king's ball, and do not flout poor Tattercoats."

But the more she refused him, the sweeter the pipe played and the deeper the young man fell in love; till at last he begged her, as a proof of his sincerity, to come that night at twelve to the king's ball, just as she was, with the herdboy and his geese, and in her torn petticoat and bare feet, and he would dance with her before the king and the lords and ladies, and present her to them all, as his dear and honoured bride.

So when night came, and the hall in the castle was full of light and music, and the lords and ladies were dancing before the king, just as the clock struck twelve, Tattercoats and the herdboy, followed by his flock of noisy geese, entered at the great doors and walked straight up the ballroom, while on either side the ladies whispered, the lords laughed, and the king seated at the far end stared in amazement.

But as they came in front of the throne, Tattercoats' lover rose from beside the king and came to meet her. Taking her by the hand, he kissed her thrice before them all and turned to the king.

"Father!" he said, for it was the prince him-

self, "I have made my choice, and here is my bride, the loveliest girl in all the land, and the sweetest as well!"

Before he had finished speaking, the herdboy put his pipe to his lips and played a few low notes that sounded like a bird singing far off in the woods; and as he played, Tattercoats' rags were changed to shining robes sewn with glittering jewels, a golden crown lay upon her golden hair, and the flock of geese behind her became a crowd of dainty pages, bearing her long train.

And as the king rose to greet her as his daughter, the trumpets sounded loudly in honour of the new princess, and the people outside in the street said to each other:

"Ah! Now the prince has chosen for his wife the loveliest girl in all the land!"

But the gooseherd was never seen again, and no one knew what became of him; while the old lord went home once more to his palace by the sea, for he could not stay at court, when he had sworn never to look on his granddaughter's face.

So there he still sits by his window, if you could only see him, as you some day may, weeping more bitterly than ever, as he looks out over the sea.

## TOM TIT TOT

### (English)

*This is a humorous variant of the German "Rumpelstiltzkin." No one knows which came first. Children who hear both generally like this one best, and it is unquestionably one of the finest tales from English oral tradition. Try to keep its touch of Suffolk dialect, which Jacobs skillfully "reduced."*

Once upon a time there was a woman, and she baked five pies. And when they came out of the oven, they were that overbaked the crusts were too hard to eat. So she says to her daughter:

"Darter," says she, "put you them there pies on the shelf, and leave 'em there a little, and they'll come again." She meant, you know, the crust would get soft.

"Tom Tit Tot." From *English Fairy Tales*, collected by Joseph Jacobs. Third edition, revised. David Nutt, London, 1907

But the girl, she says to herself, "Well, if they'll come again, I'll eat 'em now." And she set to work and ate 'em all, first and last.

Well, come supper time the woman said, "Go you, and get one o' them there pies. I dare say they've come again now."

The girl went and she looked, and there was nothing but the dishes. So back she came and says she, "Noo, they ain't come again."

"Not one of 'em?" says the mother.

"Not one of 'em," says she.

"Well, come again, or not come again," said the woman, "I'll have one for supper."

"But you can't, if they ain't come," said the girl.

"But I can," says she. "Go you, and bring the best of 'em."

"Best or worst," says the girl, "I've ate 'em all, and you can't have one till that's come again."

Well, the woman she was done, and she took her spinning to the door to spin, and as she span she sang:

"My darter ha' ate five, five pies to-day.
My darter ha' ate five, five pies to-day."

The king was coming down the street, and he heard her sing, but what she sang he couldn't hear, so he stopped and said:

"What was that you were singing, my good woman?"

The woman was ashamed to let him hear what her daughter had been doing, so she sang, instead of that:

"My darter ha' spun five, five skeins to-day.
My darter ha' spun five, five skeins to-day."

"Stars o' mine!" said the king, "I never heard tell of anyone that could do that."

Then he said: "Look you here, I want a wife, and I'll marry your daughter. But look you here," says he, "eleven months out of the year she shall have all she likes to eat, and all the gowns she likes to get, and all the company she likes to keep; but the last month of the year she'll have to spin five skeins every day, and if she don't I shall kill her."

"All right," says the woman, for she thought what a grand marriage that was. And as for the five skeins, when the time came, there'd be plenty of ways of getting out of it, and likeliest, he'd have forgotten all about it.

Well, so they were married. And for eleven months the girl had all she liked to eat, and all the gowns she liked to get, and all the company she liked to keep.

But when the time was getting over, she began to think about the skeins and to wonder if he had 'em in mind. But not one word did he say about 'em, and she thought he'd wholly forgotten 'em.

However, the last day of the last month he takes her to a room she'd never set eyes on before. There was nothing in it but a spinning-wheel and a stool. And says he: "Now, my dear, here you'll be shut in tomorrow with some victuals and some flax, and if you haven't spun five skeins by the night, your head'll go off."

And away he went about his business.

Well, she was that frightened, she'd always been such a gatless girl that she didn't so much as know how to spin, and what was she to do tomorrow with no one to come nigh her to help her? She sat down on a stool in the kitchen, and law! how she did cry!

However, all of a sudden she heard a sort of a knocking low down on the door. She upped and oped it, and what should she see but a small little black thing with a long tail. That looked up at her right curious, and that said:

"What are you a-crying for?"

"What's that to you?" says she.

"Never you mind," that said, "but tell me what you're a-crying for."

"That won't do me no good if I do," says she.

"You don't know that," that said, and twirled that's tail round.

"Well," says she, "that won't do no harm, if that don't do no good," and she upped and told about the pies, and the skeins, and everything.

"This is what I'll do," says the little black thing, "I'll come to your window every morning and take the flax and bring it spun at night."

"What's your pay?" says she.

That looked out of the corner of that's eyes, and that said, "I'll give you three guesses every night to guess my name, and if you haven't guessed it before the month's up, you shall be mine."

Well, she thought she'd be sure to guess that's name before the month was up. "All right," says she, "I agree."

"All right," that says, and law! how that twirled that's tail.

Well, the next day, her husband took her into the room, and there was the flax and the day's food.

"Now there's the flax," says he, "and if that ain't spun up this night, off goes your head." And then he went out and locked the door.

He'd hardly gone, when there was a knocking against the window.

She upped and she oped it, and there sure enough was the little old thing sitting on the ledge.

"Where's the flax?" says he.

"Here it be," says she. And she gave it to him.

Well, come the evening a knocking came again to the window. She upped and she oped it, and there was the little old thing with five skeins of flax on his arm.

"Here it be," says he, and he gave it to her.

"Now, what's my name?" says he.

"What, is that Bill?" says she.

"Noo, that ain't," says he, and he twirled his tail.

"Is that Ned?" says she.

"Noo, that ain't," says he, and he twirled his tail.

"Well, is that Mark?" says she.

"Noo, that ain't," says he, and he twirled his tail harder, and away he flew.

Well, when her husband came in, there were the five skeins ready for him. "I see I shan't have to kill you tonight, my dear," says he. "You'll have your food and your flax in the morning," says he, and away he goes.

Well, every day the flax and the food were brought, and every day that there little black impet used to come mornings and evenings. And all the day the girl sat trying to think of names to say to it when it came at night. But she never hit on the right one. And as it got towards the end of the month, the impet began to look so maliceful, and that twirled that's tail faster and faster each time she gave a guess.

At last it came to the last day but one. The impet came at night along with the five skeins, and that said:

"What, ain't you got my name yet?"

"Is that Nicodemus?" says she.

"Noo, t'ain't," that says.

"Is that Sammle?" says she.

"Noo, t'ain't," that says.

"A-well, is that Methusalem?" says she.

"Noo, t'ain't that neither," that says.

Then that looks at her with that's eyes like a coal o'fire, and that says, "Woman, there's only tomorrow night, and then you'll be mine!" And away it flew.

Well, she felt that horrid. However, she heard the king coming along the passage. In he came, and when he sees the five skeins, he says, says he:

"Well, my dear," says he. "I don't see but what you'll have your skeins ready tomorrow night as well, and as I reckon I shan't have to kill you, I'll have supper in here tonight." So they brought supper, and another stool for him, and down the two sat.

Well, he hadn't eaten but a mouthful or so, when he stops and begins to laugh.

"What is it?" says she.

"A-why," says he, "I was out a-hunting today, and I got away to a place in the wood I'd never seen before. And there was an old chalk-pit. And I heard a kind of a sort of a humming. So I got off my hobby, and I went right quiet to the pit, and I looked down. Well, what should there be but the funniest little black thing you ever set eyes on. And what was that doing, but that had a little spinning wheel, and that was spinning wonderful fast, and twirling that's tail. And as that span that sang:

> "Nimmy nimmy not
> My name's Tom Tit Tot."

Well, when the girl heard this, she felt as if she could have jumped out of her skin for joy, but she didn't say a word.

Next day that there little thing looked so maliceful when he came for the flax. And when night came, she heard that knocking against the window panes. She oped the window, and that come right in on the ledge. That was grinning from ear to ear, and Oo! that's tail was twirling round so fast.

"What's my name?" that says, as that gave her the skeins.

"Is that Solomon?" she says, pretending to be afeard.

"Noo, t'ain't," that says, and that came further into the room.

"Well, is that Zebedee?" says she again.

"Noo, 'tain't," says the impet. And then that laughed and twirled that's tail till you couldn't hardly see it.

"Take time, woman," that says; "next guess, and you're mine." And that stretched out that's black hands at her.

Well, she backed a step or two, and she looked at it, and then she laughed out, and says she, pointing her finger at it:

> "Nimmy nimmy not
> Your name's Tom Tit Tot."

Well, when that heard her, that gave an awful shriek and away that flew into the dark, and she never saw it any more.

## THE BLACK BULL OF NORROWAY

*(English)*

*Here is a somber and beautiful story of a black spell which is broken at last by the faithful love of a girl. The rhymes add much to its charm.*

Long ago in Norroway there lived a lady who had three daughters. Now they were all pretty, and one night they fell a-talking of whom they meant to marry.

And the eldest said, "I will have no one lower than an Earl."

And the second said, "I will have no one lower than a Lord."

But the third, the prettiest and the merriest, tossed her head and said, with a twinkle in her eye, "Why so proud? As for me I would be content with the Black Bull of Norroway."

At that the other sisters bade her be silent and

"The Black Bull of Norroway." Reprinted with permission of Macmillan Publishing Co., Inc. and Macmillan, London and Basingstoke from *English Fairy Tales* by Flora Annie Steel. Copyright 1918 by Macmillan Publishing Co., Inc., 1946 by Flora Annie Steel.

not talk lightly of such a monster. For, see you, is it not written:

> To wilder measures now they turn,
> The black black Bull of Norroway;
> Sudden the tapers cease to burn,
> The minstrels cease to play.

So, no doubt, the Black Bull of Norroway was held to be a horrid monster.

But the youngest daughter would have her laugh, so she said three times that she would be content with the Black Bull of Norroway.

Well! It so happened that the very next morning a coach-and-six came swinging along the road, and in it sat an Earl who had come to ask the hand of the eldest daughter in marriage. So there were great rejoicings over the wedding, and the bride and bridegroom drove away in the coach-and-six.

Then the next thing that happened was that a coach-and-four with a Lord in it came swinging along the road; and he wanted to marry the second daughter. So they were wed, and there were great rejoicings, and the bride and bridegroom drove away in the coach-and-four.

Now after this there was only the youngest, the prettiest and the merriest, of the sisters left, and she became the apple of her mother's eye. So you may imagine how the mother felt when one morning a terrible bellowing was heard at the door, and there was a great big Black Bull waiting for his bride.

She wept and she wailed, and at first the girl ran away and hid herself in the cellar for fear, but there the Bull stood waiting, and at last the girl came up and said:

"I promised I would be content with the Black Bull of Norroway, and I must keep my word. Farewell, mother, you will not see me again."

Then she mounted on the Black Bull's back, and it walked away with her quite quietly. And ever it chose the smoothest paths and the easiest roads, so that at last the girl grew less afraid. But she became very hungry and was nigh to faint when the Black Bull said to her, in quite a soft voice that wasn't a bellow at all:

> "Eat out of my left ear,
> Drink out of my right,

> And set by what you leave
> To serve the morrow's night."

So she did as she was bid, and, lo and behold! the left ear was full of delicious things to eat, and the right was full of the most delicious drinks, and there was plenty left over for several days.

Thus they journeyed on, and they journeyed on, through many dreadful forests and many lonely wastes, and the Black Bull never paused for bite or sup, but ever the girl he carried ate out of his left ear and drank out of his right, and set by what she left to serve the morrow's night. And she slept soft and warm on his broad back.

Now at last they reached a noble castle where a large company of lords and ladies were assembled, and greatly the company wondered at the sight of these strange companions. And they invited the girl to supper, but the Black Bull they turned into the field, and left to spend the night after his kind.

But when the next morning came, there he was ready for his burden again. Now, though the girl was loth to leave her pleasant companions, she remembered her promise, and mounted on his back, so they journeyed on, and journeyed on, and journeyed on, through many tangled woods and over many high mountains. And ever the Black Bull chose the smoothest paths for her and set aside the briars and brambles, while she ate out of his left ear and drank out of his right.

So at last they came to a magnificent mansion where Dukes and Duchesses and Earls and Countesses were enjoying themselves. Now the company, though much surprised at the strange companions, asked the girl in to supper; and the Black Bull they would have turned into the park for the night, but that the girl, remembering how well he had cared for her, asked them to put him into the stable and give him a good feed.

So this was done, and the next morning he was waiting before the hall-door for his burden; and she, though somewhat loth at leaving the fine company, mounted him cheerfully enough, and they rode away, and they rode away, and they rode away, through thick briar brakes and up fearsome cliffs. But ever the Black Bull trod the brambles underfoot and chose the easiest paths, while she ate out of his left ear and drank out of his right, and wanted for nothing, though he had neither bite nor sup. So it came to pass that he grew tired and was limping with one foot when, just as the sun was setting, they came to a beautiful palace where Princes and Princesses were disporting themselves with ball on the green grass. Now, though the company greatly wondered at the strange companions, they asked the girl to join them, and ordered the grooms to lead away the Black Bull to a field.

But she, remembering all he had done for her, said, "Not so! He will stay with me!" Then seeing a large thorn in the foot with which he had been limping, she stooped down and pulled it out.

And, lo and behold! in an instant, to every one's surprise, there appeared, not a frightful monstrous bull, but one of the most beautiful Princes ever beheld, who fell at his deliverer's feet, thanking her for having broken his cruel enchantment.

A wicked witch-woman who wanted to marry him had, he said, spelled him until a beautiful maiden of her own free will should do him a favour.

"But," he said, "the danger is not all over. You have broken the enchantment by night; that by day has yet to be overcome."

So the next morning the Prince had to resume the form of a bull, and they set out together; and they rode, and they rode, and they rode, till they came to a dark and ugsome glen. And here he bade her dismount and sit on a great rock.

"Here you must stay," he said, "while I go yonder and fight the Old One. And mind! move neither hand nor foot whilst I am away, else I shall never find you again. If everything around you turns blue, I shall have beaten the Old One; but if everything turns red, he will have conquered me."

And with that, and a tremendous roaring bellow, he set off to find his foe.

Well, she sat as still as a mouse, moving neither hand nor foot, nor even her eyes, and waited, and waited, and waited. Then at last everything turned blue. But she was so overcome with joy to think that her lover was victorious that she forgot to keep still, and lifting one of her feet, crossed it over the other!

So she waited, and waited, and waited. Long she sat, and aye she wearied; and all the time he was seeking for her, but he never found her.

At last she rose and went she knew not whither, determined to seek for her lover through the whole wide world. So she journeyed on, and she journeyed on, and she journeyed on, until one day in a dark wood she came to a little hut where lived an old, old woman who gave her food and shelter, and bid her Godspeed on her errand, giving her three nuts, a walnut, a filbert, and a hazel nut, with these words:

"When your heart is like to break,
    And once again is like to break,
Crack a nut and in its shell
    That will be that suits you well."

After this she felt heartened up, and wandered on till her road was blocked by a great hill of glass; and though she tried all she could to climb it, she could not; for aye she slipped back, and slipped back, and slipped back; for it was like ice.

Then she sought a passage elsewhere, and round and about the foot of the hill she went sobbing and wailing, but ne'er a foothold could she find. At last she came to a smithy; and the smith promised if she would serve him faithfully for seven years and seven days, that he would make her iron shoon wherewith to climb the hill of glass.

So for seven long years and seven short days she toiled, and span, and swept, and washed in the smith's house. And for wage he gave her a pair of iron shoon, and with them she clomb the glassy hill and went on her way.

Now she had not gone far before a company of fine lords and ladies rode past her talking of all the grand doings that were to be done at the young Duke of Norroway's wedding. Then she passed a number of people carrying all sorts of good things which they told her were for the Duke's wedding. And at last she came to a palace castle where the courtyards were full of cooks and bakers, some running this way, some running that, and all so busy that they did not know what to do first.

Then she heard the horns of hunters and cries of "Room! Room for the Duke of Norroway and his bride!"

And who should ride past but the beautiful Prince she had but half unspelled, and by his side was the witch-woman who was determined to marry him that very day.

Well! at the sight she felt that her heart was indeed like to break, and over again was like to break, so that the time had come for her to crack one of the nuts. So she broke the walnut, as it was the biggest, and out of it came a wonderful wee woman carding wool as fast as ever she could card.

Now when the witch-woman saw this wonderful thing she offered the girl her choice of anything in the castle for it.

"If you will put off your wedding with the Duke for a day, and let me watch in his room to-night," said the girl, "you shall have it."

Now, like all witch-women, the bride wanted everything her own way, and she was so sure she had her groom safe, that she consented; but before the Duke went to rest she gave him, with her own hands, a posset so made that any one who drank it would sleep till morning.

Thus, though the girl was allowed alone into the Duke's chamber, and though she spent the livelong night sighing and singing:

> "Far have I sought for thee,
> Long have I wrought for thee,
> Near am I brought to thee,
> Dear Duke o' Norroway;
> Wilt thou say naught to me?"

the Duke never wakened, but slept on. So when day came the girl had to leave him without his ever knowing she had been there.

Then once again her heart was like to break, and over and over again like to break, and she cracked the filbert nut, because it was the next biggest. And out of it came a wonderful wee, wee woman spinning away as fast as ever she could spin. Now when the witch-bride saw this wonderful thing she once again put off her wedding so that she might possess it. And once again the girl spent the livelong night in the Duke's chamber sighing and singing:

> "Far have I sought for thee,
> Long have I wrought for thee,
> Near am I brought to thee,

> Dear Duke o' Norroway;
> Wilt thou say naught to me?"

But the Duke, who had drunk the sleeping-draught from the hands of his witch-bride, never stirred, and when dawn came the girl had to leave him without his ever knowing she had been there.

Then, indeed, the girl's heart was like to break, and over and over and over again like to break, so she cracked the last nut—the hazel nut —and out of it came the most wonderful wee, wee, wee-est woman reeling away at yarn as fast as she could reel.

And this marvel so delighted the witch-bride that once again she consented to put off her wedding for a day, and allow the girl to watch in the Duke's chamber the night through, in order to possess it.

Now it so happened that when the Duke was dressing that morning he heard his pages talking amongst themselves of the strange sighing and singing they had heard in the night; and he said to his faithful old valet, "What do the pages mean?"

And the old valet, who hated the witch-bride, said:

"If the master will take no sleeping-draught to-night, mayhap he may also hear what for two nights has kept me awake."

At this the Duke marvelled greatly, and when the witch-bride brought him his evening posset, he made excuse it was not sweet enough, and while she went away to get honey to sweeten it withal, he poured away the posset and made believe he had swallowed it.

So that night when dark had come, and the girl stole in to his chamber with a heavy heart thinking it would be the very last time she would ever see him, the Duke was really broad awake. And when she sat down by his bedside and began to sing:

> "Far have I sought for thee,"

he knew her voice at once, and clasped her in his arms.

Then he told her how he had been in the power of the witch-woman and had forgotten everything, but that now he remembered all and that the spell was broken for ever and aye.

So the wedding feast served for their marriage, since the witch-bride, seeing her power was gone, quickly fled the country and was never heard of again.

## THE BRIDE WHO OUT TALKED THE WATER KELPIE

*(Scottish)*

*One of a special kind of Scottish tales, this is a sgeulachdan (skale-ak-tan), a story that is not written down but is told at special gatherings by a master storyteller. The performance was prefaced by a long introduction into which the storyteller wove teasing hints about the participants, especially when the occasion was a wedding. The wedding sgeulachdan here is from Perthshire. Sorche Nic Leodhas (the pen name of LeClaire Alger) was herself a master storyteller, capturing to perfection the cadence and idiom of Scottish speech. Her tales need no adaptation, although they are best told by those who can manage a Scottish burr. This story about a bride bewitched introduces that mischievous little creature of Scottish lore, the kelpie.*

A soldier there was once, and he was coming home from the foreign wars with his heart light and free, and his bagpipes under his arm. He was marching along at a good pace, for he had a far way to go, and a longing in his heart to get back to his home again. But as the sun lowered to its setting, he could plainly see that he'd

not get there by that day's end so he began to be thinking about a place where he could bide for the night.

The road had come to the top of a hill and he looked down to see what lay at the foot of it. Down at the bottom was a village, and there was a drift of smoke rising from the chimneys where folks were getting their suppers, and lights were beginning to twinkle on here and there in the windows.

"There'll be an inn down there, to be sure," said the soldier, "and they'll have a bite of supper for me and a place for me to sleep."

So down the hill he went at a fast trot with his kilt swinging, and the ribbons on his bagpipes fluttering in the wind of his going.

But when he got near the foot of the hill, he stopped short. There by the road was a cottage and by the door of the cottage was a bench and upon the bench sat a bonny lass with black hair and blue eyes, taking the air in the cool of the evening.

He looked at her and she looked at him, but neither of them said a word, one to the other. Then the soldier went on his way again, but he was thinking he'd ne'er seen a lass he fancied so much.

At the inn they told him that they could find him a place to sleep and he could have his supper too, if he'd not be minding the wait till they got it ready for him. That wouldn't trouble him at all, said he. So he went into the room and laid off his bagpipes and sat down to rest his legs from his day's journey.

While the innkeeper was laying the table, the soldier and he began talking about one thing or another. At last the soldier asked, "Who is the bonny lass with the hair like the wing of a blackbird and eyes like flax flowers who bides in the house at the foot of the hill?"

"Och, aye," said the innkeeper. "That would be the weaver's lass."

"I saw her as I passed by on the road," said the soldier, "and I ne'er saw a lass that suited me so fine."

The innkeeper gave the soldier a queer sort of look, but said naught.

"I'm minded to talk to her father," the soldier said, "and if she could fancy me as I do her, happen we could fix it up to wed."

"Happen you'd better not," said the innkeeper.

"Why not, then?" asked the soldier. "Is she promised to someone already?"

"Nay, 'tis not that," the innkeeper replied quickly. "Only . . . Och, well! You see she's not a lass to be talking o'ermuch."

"'Tis not a bad thing for a lass to be quiet," the soldier said. "I ne'er could abide a woman with a clackiting tongue."

The innkeeper said no more, so that was the end o' that.

When he'd had his supper, the soldier went out of the house and back up the road till he came to the cottage again. The bonny lass was still sitting on the bench by the door.

"I'll be having a word with your father, my lass," said the soldier. She rose from the bench and opened the door and stood aside to let him go in. When he had gone in, she shut the door and left him standing in the room on one side of the door and herself outside on the other. But not a word did she say the while.

The soldier looked about the room, and saw at the far side a man who was taking a web of cloth from the loom.

"Is it yourself that's the weaver?" asked the soldier.

"Who else would I be?" asked the man, starting to fold the cloth.

"Then I've come to ask about your daughter."

The man laid the cloth by, and came over to the soldier. "What would you be asking then?" he asked.

"'Tis this," the soldier said, coming to the point at once. "I like the looks of your lass and if you've naught to say against it, I'd like to wed with her."

The weaver looked at the soldier, but said nothing at all.

"You need not fear I could not fend for her," the soldier said. "She'd want for naught. I have a good wee croft waiting for me at home and a flock of sheep and some bits of gear of my own. None so great, of course, but it would do fine for the lass and me, if she'd have me."

"Sit ye down," said the weaver.

So the two of them sat down at either side of the fire.

"I doubt ye'll be at the inn?" the weaver asked.

"Where else would one from a far place stay?" asked the soldier.

"Och, aye. Well, happen the folks at the inn were telling you about my lass?"

"What could they say that I could not see for myself?" the soldier said. "Except that she doesn't talk o'ermuch. They told me that."

"O'ermuch!" exclaimed the weaver. "She doesn't talk at all!"

"Not at all?" the soldier asked.

"Och, I'll tell you about it," said the weaver. "She went out to walk in the gloaming a year or two ago, and since she came home that night, not a word has come from her lips. Nobody can say why, but folks all say she's bewitched."

"Talk or no," said the soldier, "I'll have her if she'll take me." So they asked her and she took him.

Then they were married, and the soldier took the lass away with him to his own croft.

They settled in, she to keep the house and look after the hens and do the cooking and baking and spinning, and he to tend his sheep and keep the place outside up good and proper.

The lass and he were well pleased with each other and all went well for a while. Though she did not talk, she was good at listening and it took a time for the soldier to tell her all about himself. Then she had a light hand with the baking and a quick hand at the spinning, and she kept the house tidy and shining clean. And she had a ready smile that was sweet as a song. The soldier was off and away most of the day, tending his sheep or mending his walls or working about the croft. When he came home to the lass, the smile and the kiss he got from her were as good as words.

But when the year turned toward its end, and the days grew short and the nights long and dark, the sheep were penned in the fold and the soldier was penned in the house because of the winter weather outside. Then 'twas another story. The house was that quiet you'd be thinking you were alone in it. The soldier stopped talking, for the sound of his own voice going on and on all by itself fair gave him the creeps.

She was still his own dear lass and he loved her dearly, but there were times he felt he had to get out of the house and away from all that silence.

So he took to going out at night just to hear the wind blowing and the dead leaves rustling and a branch cracking in the frost or maybe a tyke barking at some croft over the hill. It was noisy outside compared to the way it was in the house.

One night he said to the lass, "The moonlight's bright this night. I'll be going down the road a piece to walk." So after he'd had his tea, he went out of the house and started down the road. He paid little heed to where he was going, and that's how it happened he nearly walked into the horse. The horse stopped with a jingle of harness and then the soldier saw that the horse was hitched to a cart, and the cart was filled with household gear—furniture and the like. There were two people on the seat of the cart, a man and a woman. The man called out to him, "Are we on the road to Auchinloch?"

"Och, nay!" the soldier said. "You're well off your way. If you keep on this way you'll land in Crieff—some forty miles on. And not much else but hills between here and there."

"Och, me!" said the woman. "We'll have to go back."

"Poor lass," the man said tenderly, "and you so weary already."

"I'm no wearier than yourself," the woman replied. " 'Twas you I was thinking of."

Suddenly the soldier said, "You're far out of your way and you'll never get there this night. Why do you not bide the night with us and start out fresh in the morn? Your horse will have a rest and so will you, and you'll travel faster by light of day, and you'll not be so much out in the end."

But it was not so much for them, he asked it, as for himself, just to be hearing other voices than his own in the house.

They saw he really meant it, so they were soon persuaded. It wasn't long till he had them in his house, and their horse with a feed of oats in his barn. They were friendly, likeable folks, and it was easy to get them talking, which was just what the soldier wanted. They were flitting because their old uncle had left them his croft, and they wouldn't have come at such an unseasonable time, if they hadn't wanted to settle in before the lambing began. Besides, they'd never had a place of their own, and they couldn't wait to get there. So they talked and the soldier talked, and the lass sat and smiled. But if they noticed she had naught to say, neither of them mentioned it.

The next morning they got ready to leave, and the soldier came out to the gate to tell them how to go. After he'd told them, the woman leaned over and said, "What's amiss with your wife? Does she not talk at all?"

"Nay," said the soldier. "She's spoken not a single word for two years past."

"Och, me!" the woman said. "She's not deaf, is she?"

"That she's not!" the soldier told her. "She hears all one says. The folks where she comes from say that she's bewitched."

"I thought it might be that," the woman said. "Well, I'll tell you what to do. Back where we dwelt there's a woman that has the second sight and she's wonderful for curing folks of things. She cured my own sister after the doctors gave her up. It was ten years ago and my sister's living yet. You take your wife over there and see what she can do." She told the soldier where to find the old body, and as they drove away, she said, "You needn't be afraid of her for she's as good as gold. She'll never take anything for helping anybody, and if she's a witch, nobody ever laid it against her. She's just a good old body that has the second sight."

The soldier went into the house and told his lass to get herself ready, for they were going visiting. He did not tell her why, in case it all came to naught, for he couldn't bear to have her disappointed if the old body couldn't help her at all.

He hitched his own wee horse to his cart, and he and the lass drove off to the place where the folks that were going to Auchinloch had dwelt.

They found the old body without any trouble right where the woman said she'd be. She was little and round and rosy and as merry and kind as she could be. The only thing strange about her was her eyes, for they were the sort that made you feel that nothing in the world could ever be unseen if she took the trouble to look at it, no matter where it was hidden.

When she heard the soldier's story, she said at once that she'd be glad to help them if she could. Folks were probably right when they said the lass was bewitched, but what she'd have to find out was how it had happened. That might take time because the lass couldn't help her, since she couldn't talk.

Then the old woman told the soldier to take himself off for a walk and leave the lass with her and not to come back too soon for if he did, she'd just send him away again.

The soldier walked around and around, and at last he found the village that belonged to the place. There was a blacksmith shop and an old stone church and a post office and a pastry shop and a little shop with jars of sweeties in the windows, that sold everything the other shops didn't have. When he'd seen them all, he went and sat in the only other place there was, which was the tavern, and the time went very slow. But at last he thought it must be late enough for him to go back and fetch his lass. Maybe he'd been foolish to bring her to the old body after all. He'd not go back if the old woman sent him away again. He'd just pack up his lass in the cart and take her home and keep her the way she was. If he'd known what was going to happen, maybe that's what he'd have done.

They were waiting for him when he got back to the little old woman's cottage, and the old body told him at once she'd found where the trouble lay.

"'Tis plain enough," said she. "Your wife has offended the water kelpie. When she went to walk in the gloaming, she drank from the well where the water kelpie bides. And as she leaned over to drink, one of the combs from her hair dropped into the water and she never missed it. The comb fouled the water, and the kelpie can bide in the well no more till she takes it out again. So angry he was, that while she drank of it, he laid a spell on the water that took her speech away."

"But what shall we do now?" asked the soldier.

"All you need to do," said the old woman, "is take your lass back to the well and have her take the comb from the water."

"And she'll talk then?" the soldier asked.

"Och, aye! She'll talk. But watch out for the water kelpie, lest he do her more harm for he's a queer creature always full of wicked mischief and nobody knows what he may do."

The lass and the soldier were so full of joy that they hardly knew how to contain it. The soldier wanted to pay the old woman for what she'd done, but she said it was nothing at all, and in any case she never took pay for doing a kindly service. So the soldier thanked her kindly, and he and his lass went home.

When they had found somebody to look after the croft, they started off to take the spell off the lass's tongue. When they got to the place, the soldier and the lass went out to find the well in the woods. The lass bared her arm and reached down into the water and felt around till she found the comb. She put it back in her hair, and as soon as she did, she found she could talk again.

The first thing she said was, "Och, my love, I can talk to you now!" And the second thing she said was, "Och, I have so much to say!"

They went back to the weaver's house, and when he found that his daughter could talk, he was that pleased. He ran about the village telling everybody, "My lass has found her tongue again!" 'Twas a rare grand day for the weaver. And of course for the soldier, too.

The weaver and the soldier couldn't hear enough of her chatter. They took to following her about just to listen to her as if it were music they were hearing.

After a day or two, she began to grow restless, for she wanted to go home to their own wee croft. So off they set, and she chattered to him every mile of the way. The sound of her voice was the sweetest sound he'd ever heard.

So they came home. It was still winter, and the sheep were still penned in the fold and the soldier in the house, but there wasn't a bit of silence in the cottage. There was this that she had to tell him, and something else she must say. The soldier could hardly slip a word in edgewise, but he still thought it was wonderful to hear her.

After a month or two had gone by and the winter was wearing off toward spring, he began to notice something he had not noticed before. And that was that his bonny wee wife talked away from morn to night, and he wasn't too sure that she did not talk in her sleep. He found he had in his house what he'd told the innkeeper he never could abide—a lass with a clackiting tongue.

He would not have had her silent again; ne'er the less, a little quiet now and then would not have come amiss. But he still loved her dearly, and she was his own dear lass.

So one fine morn after the lambing was over and the sheep were out on the hillside with their dams, he went off to see the old woman who had the second sight to find out if she could do aught about it.

"Deary me!" said she. "I misdoubted the kelpie would find a way to turn things against you."

"That he did!" said the soldier, "or I'd not be here."

"Did she drink of the water again?" the old body asked.

"She did not," said the soldier. "Not even a drop."

" 'Twas not that way he got at her then," said the old woman. "Well, tell me what she did do then?"

"She took the comb from the water and she stuck it in her hair," the soldier told her, "and that's all she did do."

"Did she wipe it off first?" the old body asked anxiously.

"Nay. She did not," said the soldier.

"I see it plain," the old body said. "The water that was on the comb was bewitched again. Och, there's not a fairy in the land so full of malice as the water kelpie."

So the old woman sat and thought and thought, and the soldier waited and waited. At last the old woman said, "A little is good, but too much is more than enough. We'll give the kelpie a taste of his own medicine. Take your lass back to the well. Set her beside it and bid her to talk down the well to the kelpie the livelong day. The kelpie must answer whoever speaks to him, so the one of them that tires first will be the loser."

" 'Twill not be my lass," said the soldier. "I'll back her to win the day."

So he took his wife back to the well and sat her down beside it, and bade her call the kelpie and talk to him until he came back for her.

So she leaned over the well as he told her to and called to the kelpie. "Kelpie! Kelpie! I'm here!" cried she.

"I'm here!" answered the kelpie from the bottom of the well.

"We'll talk the whole of the day," the lass said happily into the well.

"The whole of the day," the kelpie agreed.

"I've such a lot to tell you," the lass went on.

"A lot to tell you," the kelpie said in return.

The soldier went away, leaving the lass by the well talking so fast that her words tripped over themselves, with the kelpie answering her back all the time.

He came back when the sun had set and the gloaming lay over the wood, to find the lass still sitting there, bending over the well. She was still talking, but very slow, and he could hardly hear the kelpie answer at all.

Well, now that the day was safely over, the soldier laid his hand on her shoulder. "Come away, lass," said he. She looked at him so weary-like that his heart turned over with pity. He'd just take her the way she was from now on, silent or clackiting, he told himself.

She looked up and smiled at him, and then she called down the well. "I bid you good day, kelpie. 'Tis time for me to go home."

There wasn't a sound from the well for a moment. Then in a great loud angry voice the kelpie shouted, "GO HOME!"

So the soldier gave his arm to the lass, and they started to walk back through the woods to her father's house. She said only two things on the way home.

The first thing she said was, "I'm awful thirsty," but she drank no water from the well. The soldier made sure of that!

And the second thing she said was, "I'm tired of talking."

Well, from that time on, she neither talked too little or too much but just enough. The soldier was content, for she was his own dear lass, and he loved her dearly.

Since the old body with the second sight would never let them pay her for the good she'd done them, they invited her to be godmother when their first bairn was born. That pleased her more than if they'd given her a sack of gold. But never again in all her days did the wife go out alone in the gloaming or drink from a fairy well.

## SKERRY-WERRY

### (Cornish)

*A good Cornish tale is hard to find—at least in print and in a collection for children. "Skerry-Werry" is a haunted and haunting tale, brimful of Cornish words and the Cornish fairies that are known by such names as* piskies *and* dinkies. *Retold from traditional sources by a Cornish writer who loved these tales, "Skerry-Werry" has the mystery and dark beauty appropriate to the Celtic spirit and isolated mood of "the land outside England."*

On a great wind-swept moor in King Arthur's country stood a gray stone cottage with a shaggy roof of straw. The cottage was occupied by a widow woman named Nance Pencarrow. Nance was up in years, but in spite of her age her heart was young and she loved children dearly. She was also fond of animals, especially of her golden cat whom she called Tommie Cat.

The moor was a lonely spot, but Nance had gone there when she was first married, and now that she was old she did not want to live anywhere else. Besides, she was too busy to feel the loneliness for she had to get her own living which she did by spinning wool and flax.

When her day's work was done and she had had her supper, she went outside her cottage to enjoy the view. The moor was beautiful to her in all seasons and in all weathers, but particularly so at sundown when the setting sun made the brown moorland streams like rivers of gold.

One evening late in the summer, when the moor was like amethyst fire with heather, there was an unusually fine sunset. The sky behind the sinking sun was a background of pale yellow on which stood out, in sharp relief, great clouds of all wonderful shapes and sizes and every color. Nance watched, enchanted, until the sun was a mere speck on the distant, glittering sea. She was so charmed that she never thought of going into her cottage till the last glimmer of the afterglow had pulsed out of the sky and the stars began to show themselves.

"Skerry-Werry" by Enys Tregarthen from *Piskey Folk* by Elizabeth Yates. Copyright © 1940 by Elizabeth Yates by permission of The John Day Company, publisher

The night seemed unnaturally dark after such splendor, and, as the old woman turned to go in, she was startled to hear a little voice piping, "I've got no mammie to mammie me. Oh dear, what shall I do?"

"My dear senses!" Nance ejaculated. "Whatever is that crying?"

The voice, small as it was, seemed to fill all the silence, and the despair in it went straight to the old woman's kind heart. She listened intently but could not tell whence the cry came. One minute it seemed to be on her right, the next on her left, then it seemed to be away in the distance.

"The little mammieless thing is like a quail, you never can tell where it is," said Nance to herself as the tiny voice once more piped its mournful pipe.

"I'll go in and light my lantern and try to find the poor little cheeld," said the old woman as she hastened into the cottage. Entering it she noticed that her fire had burned down, so she poked it into a blaze, threw on furze and turf, lit her lantern, and went out again on to the moor. The fire leaped and flamed as she went and sent a warm glow after her through the open door.

"Where be 'ee, my little dear?" called the old woman, holding her lantern close to the ground.

As she held it the tiny voice wailed out again, "I've got no mammie to mammie me. Oh dear, what shall I do?"

Nance looked down and close to her feet, on a small bank of wild thyme, was a white face set in a frame of wind-blown hair. Tiny as the eyes were, Nance could see that they were blue as bluest milkworts.

"Why, you be a little bit of a cheeld!" cried Nance astonished. "You be that small 'twas no wonder I couldn't see 'ee. How did 'ee get out here on this lone moor all by your little self?"

The tiny creature with shining hair and blue eyes made no answer but again wailed out, "I've got no mammie to mammie me. Oh dear——"

"Where is your mammie?" interrupted Nance in great concern. "Shame upon her to leave 'ee in this lone place, if she did leave 'ee," Nance added as the child did not speak. "You be a little woman-cheeld by the looks of 'ee."

"I've got no——" began the tiny voice once

more while the pathos in it filled Nance's kind heart with pity.

"I shall mammie you if you will let me," she said, going down on her knees beside the little creature. "I shall dearly love to mammie you for I have nothing of my own to love except Tommie, my cat, an' the little moor birds."

"Will you really mammie me?" asked the child softly.

"Iss fy, I will, the same as if you was my own cheeld. You shall lack for nothing if I can help it."

"Then you shall mammie me till you can't hold me on your lap," said the child.

"That's a bargain," cried Nance, smiling all over her comely old face. "Come along with me into my cottage an' warm your dinky self by the fire."

The tiny creature tripped lightly after the old woman into the cottage. At the door they were met by the big golden cat, who held his tail aloft and purred loudly.

"Tommie Cat is pleased to see 'ee," said Nance in great delight. "He is a very particular gentleman an' don't like anybody except his ould mistress. So you must be in his good graces."

The child, who was not much taller than the golden cat when he stood on his hind legs, went straight to the fire and sat down on a small cricket. Tommie Cat sat by her side and purred yet more loudly while Nance gave the child a slice of buttered brown bread and a cup of goat's milk.

The little maid took it gratefully. When she had eaten and drank, she looked up at Nance and said, "Please, what must I call you?"

"Call me Mammie Pencarrow, if you please, my dear," returned the old woman.

"I will," replied the child. "Now, will you take me upon your lap and mammie me, Mammie Pencarrow?"

"Gladly," cried Nance, and seating herself in her elbow-chair she lifted the tiny creature onto her ample lap.

"My dear life, how heavy you be!" she exclaimed. "Whoever would have believed you was such a lump of a cheeld!"

The old woman, holding the child, petted her and called her by every endearing name she could think of till the fire died down and the cat began to mew.

"Tommie Cat thinks 'tis time we was in bed," said Nance at last. "'Tis just upon midnight, I reckon."

"I never sleep in a bed," said the child. "I sleep on the heather."

"I picked some heather only yesterday to dry for my fire," replied Nance. "I shall make a bed with it in the corner of my little chamber, an' I'll cover 'ee over with a quilt which the Small People made for my ould grandmother's firstborn."

"Then I shall be snug and warm," said the child, "and safer than little moorbirds under their mothers' wings."

Nance made haste to make a bed of heather, then she took the quilt from a chest, and soon the tiny stranger was lying fast asleep under the coverlet which was many-hued like the bow in the cloud and almost as soft. The child did not sleep long, and almost before the larks left their nests in the dewy turf she was awake, merry as a grig with her talk and laughter.

All that day Nance could hardly spin for watching the child dancing, until at last she exclaimed to her, "You can dance like the Dinkies!"

"Did you ever see the Dinkies dance?" the child asked quickly.

"No, but my ould grannie did," Nance replied. "I sometimes wish I had the gift of second sight as she had."

"Do you?" cried the little maid. "Perhaps you will grow new eyes, Mammie Pencarrow, and see even more wonderful things than your grannie saw."

When evening came Nance put aside her spinning wheel and got the supper ready for herself, the child, and Tommie Cat. After they had eaten, all three went to the door of the cottage and looked out over the great moor. The child soon got tired of standing still and began to dance like a gnat in the sunshine. As twilight spread over the earth the child ceased from her dancing and gazed toward the east where great boulder-crowned hills stood up against the evening sky.

"Be 'ee looking for your mammie?" asked Nance, noticing her eager gaze.

"No, I am looking for something I think you

will like to see. It is traveling fast over the moors from the tor country. Look, Mammie Pencarrow, look."

Mammie Pencarrow looked but saw nothing save the will-o'-the-wisp. "I can see nothing but Piskey lights whipping along," she said laughing. "I have seen Piskey lights times without number."

"Look, all the same," begged the child, "and keep your eyes fixed on the first light."

The old woman did as she was bidden and saw a teeny tiny white hand holding a lantern the size of a sloan.

"My goodness gracious," Nance exclaimed, "if my ould eyes didn't deceive me, I saw a dinky hand holding a teeny tiny light flip by my door. 'Twas a lovely little hand, sure 'nough, an' white as a moon daisy."

"You have begun to grow new eyes," laughed the child, clapping her hands.

"The dinky hand must be the hand of a Little Body like my ould grannie used to see," said Nance. "How I wish I could see the rest of her!"

"You will see lots of wonderful things if you get new eyesight," the child murmured.

The following evening again found the old woman, the little maid, and Tommie Cat outside the cottage. The child danced till the sun had set and the stars were reflected in all their silvery whiteness in the moorland pools. Then the dancing ceased, and the child sent her glance toward the tor country.

"There is something coming along," she said softly. "It will be here in a minute. Look hard at it when it comes near."

The old woman looked hard. When it came close to the cottage she exclaimed, "My dear life, I see two dinky feet dancing along! The feet do match the hand I saw yesterday eve. What darling little feet they be!"

"They are dancing like the Dinkies you told me about yesterday," said the child. "Oh, I am so glad you have seen the little feet for now I know that you are growing new eyes."

The next day it was wet. The rain fell quietly on the moor, bringing out the fragrance of the wild thyme, the mints, and many another moorland plant till the great open space with its multitude of flowers was full of sweetness.

"I'm afraid the Piskey lights won't come whipping over the moor in the dummuts this evening for 'tis raining an' will rain till tomorrow if I can tell the weather," said Nance as she sat at her spinning wheel and watched the child playing with the yellow cat. "An' I do so want to see the Little Body. I want to see her all to once unless she goes about in bits!"

The rain did not leave off, and the sun went down behind gray clouds. At eventide, when they went to the door and looked out, there was nothing to be seen save a heavy veil of mist.

"The mist is as thick as a hedge," said Nance. "We may as well go in an' sit by the fire."

"We will," cried the child, "and you shall hold me on your lap."

When the old woman had taken her seat in the elbow-chair she took the child on her lap, but to her astonishment she found her grown heavier. "Why, if you get much heavier I shan't be able to hold 'ee," Nance exclaimed. "I can't understand how you're such a great weight. You en't growing no bigger nuther. If my ould eyes tell me true, you have gone smaller!"

The child laughed mischievously.

"Somebody must have stepped over 'ee when you was a croom of a baby," Nance went on, "or you have stepped over a ling broom. If that was the case, you will always be a little go-by-the-ground like the Small People." Then she added tenderly, "but you will always be a little skerry-werry."

"What is a skerry-werry?" asked the child.

"A little body, quick an' light on her feet," said the old woman, "an' you be ever so quick on your dinky feet. I think I shall call 'ee Skerry-Werry."

"Do," said the child, "it is a nice name. Now, sing to me, Mammie Pencarrow, sing to Skerry-Werry."

Nance began to sing, but her voice was so loud and harsh that the cat left the hearthstone and jumped up on the window seat, and the child put her hands over her ears.

"My voice is harsher than corncraiks," said the old woman, "but I was willing to oblige 'ee, my dear. Sing to Mammie Pencarrow instead, won't 'ee now?"

Nothing loath, the little maid opened wide her red mouth and began to sing. Her voice was so bewitching that the old woman could not keep still. Her head went niddle noddle, her hands tried to keep time to the tune, the crock on the brandis went twirling, and the cloam on the gaily painted dresser started to dance, the cricket tapped on the floor, and Tommie Cat stood on his legs in the window seat.

"Stop singing, I beg of 'ee," Nance implored, "or I don't know what will happen. My little house will go dancing away over the moor unless 'ee stop."

The child stopped but she seemed surprised. "Was my voice harsh as a corncraik's?" she asked.

"No fy, it wasn't, I never heard such singing in all my life, but what it was about I have no more idea than Tommie Cat. You sang in a strange language, my dear, there wasn't a word of Cornish in it!"

The day that followed was a beautiful one. Skerry-Werry danced till Nance's head went spinning like her wheel and the big golden cat sat on his tail and looked amazed. At the setting of the sun all three went out on the moor. The child did not dance and the cat was as still as if he were sitting by a mousehole. The twilight came quickly after the sun had dropped into the sea.

"The Piskey lights have left the tor country," the child said. "Look, Mammie Pencarrow, look."

The Piskey lights came nearer and nearer. When they were quite close, Nance saw a teeny tiny woman about the height of her thumb at the head of the lights. Her face was white and shiny like a wren's egg fresh from the nest, her hair was as yellow as a sunbeam and as silky as cotton grass. Her dress was green and all of a glimmer like glowworm light. In her hand she held a lantern the size of a sloan, and the light that came from it was as silvery as the dew's crystal beads. She smiled as the old woman gazed down at her when she whipped past.

"My dear soul an' body, what a lovely little lady!" Nance exclaimed. "She must have been one of the Small People my ould grannie used to see."

"I'm ever so glad you have seen a Dinky," cried Skerry-Werry. "You really are getting your grandmother's gift, Mammie Pencarrow, the gift of second sight."

"There's more Piskey lights traveling over the moor," said the old woman, and keeping her gaze fixed on them she saw a teeny tiny horse's head with a golden mane which the head tossed as it flew by the cottage.

"My dear senses, whatever shall I see next?" laughed Nance with the glee of a child. "Now I wish I could see the rest of the little horse, his little tail and all! He must be a handsome critter judging by his head."

"I'm so glad you have seen the head of a dinky horse," piped the child, "for now I am certain that you have grown your new eyes."

For a long time they kept their faces turned toward the east, but they saw no more that night, and when the dummuts changed to darkness they went into the cottage.

The next evening, when the sun had gone under the water, the old woman faced the tor country to watch for Piskey lights. For a long time she watched in vain, then out of the twilight appeared four tiny lights which came galloping over the ground. When they came near she saw four horse's feet.

"I expect 'tis the feet of the dinky horse whose head I saw last night," cried Nance, holding up her hands.

"I wonder what you will see next," said Skerry-Werry.

"I wonder," echoed the old woman.

The next day it was misty, but for heat and not for rain. The mist lay white as hoar frost on the turf and heather, and the great hills were wrapped in gray.

"This sort of weather won't prevent the Piskey lights from whipping about if they're so minded," said Nance as she sat at her wheel.

"They will be minded, Mammie Pencarrow."

"How do you know, Skerry-Werry?" Nance asked.

"Because you mammied me," was the answer.

The moment supper was over and the things put away, Mammie Pencarrow, Skerry-Werry, and Tommie Cat went outside the cottage. The setting sun shone behind a thin veiling of mist. Through an eyelet in the fog could be seen the curve of the new moon. The evening was hot and sultry even on the open moor.

"I fear there won't be anything out of the

common for my ould eyes to see tonight," said Nance.

"Perhaps not for your *old* eyes to see, but there may be something lovely for your *new* eyes."

As Skerry-Werry was speaking, out of the mist came a teeny tiny prancing horse as bright as the crescent moon, with a golden tail that swept the ground. He was not half so big as Tommie Cat, but he was perfect, bare as a colt and as full of life and grace. His golden mane flew out as he came, and he galloped so fast that he was out of sight almost as soon as they saw him.

"My dear heart alive, I have seen the whole of the dinky horse!" Nance exclaimed. "Whoever would have believed there were such things as horses not so big as Tommie Cat!"

"It isn't everybody who can see a dinky horse," said Skerry-Werry. "Not one in a million. But the fog is lifting, and in the clearness I can see something coming. Look, Mammie Pencarrow, look."

Nance, sending her glance to where the child pointed, saw a long train of golden light coming over the turf. The cat shot out his ears, and his eyes became balls of green fire. The light was many yards in length and out of it appeared a hundred tiny horses. On every horse rode a tiny horseman dressed in a bright green coat and breeches and a red hat.

The old woman was too astonished to utter a word and sat, staring, with her eyes and mouth wide open. Behind the horses, which all had long manes and sweeping tails, came a teeny tiny carriage drawn by twelve horses as white as ewe's cream. In the carriage sat a teeny tiny woman with a very sad face. She looked so sorrowful that Nance's kind eyes filled with tears. As she gazed at her, the golden carriage and the prancing horses were almost lost sight of in her pity for the sad-faced woman.

"Nobody is too dinky to have sorrow," said the old woman softly to herself, "an' even the Small People must have their little sorrows, I s'pose."

"You have got the second sight," cried Skerry-Werry, "and you have seen more than your grandmother ever saw!"

"How do you know what my ould grannie saw or did not see?" asked Nance, gazing at the child.

"You're only a croom of a cheeld, or look like one, but you do talk like an ancient woman. You be'nt one of the Little Ancients, be 'ee, Skerry-Werry?"

"Why, Mammie Pencarrow, what will you say next?" laughed the child. "Shall we go into the cottage?"

"If you please," murmured the old woman.

Into the little dwelling they went, taking their places by the fire which was blazing on the hearthstone and sending a warm glow over the room.

"Won't you mammie me and call me pretty names like you did the first night I came?" asked the child.

Nance smiled. "I love to mammie you and say pretty things to you." Stooping down, she lifted the child on her lap, but the tiny maid was so heavy it nearly broke Nance's back.

"What a terrible weight you be," she groaned. "I don't believe I shall be able to hold 'ee on my lap more than a minute. The weight of 'ee is breaking my poor ould knees. 'Tis fine an' queer that a little bit of a cheeld like you should be so heavy. You be getting smaller as you be getting heavier. I can't understand it. There! my ould knees have given out already, iss fy, they have!"

As Nance spoke, Skerry-Werry slipped from her knees and fell face down on the cat, who looked as flat as a baking iron when the dinky maid picked herself up.

"I hope I did not hurt you, Tommie Cat," she whispered, patting him, "but I can't have hurt you so much as it hurts me to know that Mammie Pencarrow can no longer hold me on her lap and mammie me."

"I can mammie you in everything else," said Nance stoutly. "Sit on your cricket now an' warm your toes by the fire before we go to bed."

The child seated herself on the stool and sat gazing into the fire, her tiny white face resting on her hands. Her hair, which looked wind-blown even indoors, was a cloud of gold above her brow. The old woman sat and watched her. The cat, who had quickly recovered being fallen upon, got up and sat at his mistress' feet, but he did not purr.

Nance and Skerry-Werry were silent a long

time, and everything was very still in the cottage and out. The fire blazed brighter and brighter, its shine and the shadows playing on the whitewashed walls. Suddenly the silence was broken by a sad voice crying outside.

"I have lost my little cheeld-whidden. Ah me, what shall I do?"

The old woman started but said never a word. The cat looked toward the door. The child did not move.

In a little while the silence was again broken by the small, sad voice. "I have lost my little cheeld-whidden. Ah me, what shall I do?"

The old woman clutched the elbows of her chair. The cat turned his face to the door. The child sat still, gazing into the fire.

Suddenly Skerry-Werry looked up and said, "Whoever was that crying outside the door?"

"I don't know, my dear, unless it was a nighthawk," returned the old woman.

"I thought a nighthawk's note was a *churrrr*, and now and again a *wh-ip, wh-ip*," said the child. "The voice I heard outside the door was not like a nighthawk's."

"Perhaps it was a moorhen calling her children to her," said the old woman.

"Perhaps it was," said the child, "but I thought a moorhen's call was *krek-rerk-rerk*. The voice outside the door did not cry *krek-rerk-rerk*."

"Maybe it was a quail," said the old woman. "His voice is almost as sweet as a flute."

"I know it is," said the child, "for I have heard him often. But, all the same, it is not half so sweet as the voice I heard crying outside the door."

"Perhaps it was a horny-wink," said the old woman.

"I think it could not have been a horny-wink," said the child, "for a horny-wink cries *pet-wit, pet-wit*."

"It might have been a moor owl we heard."

"The moor owl's flight is soft and silent, but his cry is a scream."

"Perhaps it was a great black raven we heard," said the old woman, "as he was flying across the moors to his home on the cliffs."

"Perhaps it was," said the child, "but I thought a raven's voice was hoarse and loud, and that he called *cawk, cawk*. The voice I heard out-side the door was crying as if it had *lost* something."

"Then it must have been a poor mother cow crying out for her baby calf," said the old woman.

"The cow mother says *moo-moo-moo*, and the voice we heard was not crying like that. But perhaps we shall hear the voice again, Mammie Pencarrow."

"I hope not," said the old woman, "for it do hurt like pain."

"Did I hurt you like pain when I cried and said I had no mammie to mammie me?" asked the child.

"No fy, you didn't. I wanted only to find the little mammieless thing."

"Did you?" said the child, gazing up into Nance's face, which was looking troubled.

As she was gazing at the old woman, the sad voice was heard again outside the door. "I have lost my little cheeld-whidden. Ah me, what shall I do?"

"It is surely a shorn lamb shivering on the moor, bleating an' crying for its warm soft fleece," said the old woman loud and quickly as if she wanted to drown the voice outside her door.

"I thought a shorn lamb said *baa, baa, b-a-a*," said the child. "The voice we heard did not say *baa, b-a-a*."

"It must have been a mare whinnying for its foal," said the old woman louder and quicker than before.

"The voice I heard did not whinny," said the child.

"Then what did it say?" cried the old woman. "I want you to tell me."

"P'raps it was the cry of a hare caught in the cruel teeth of a gin," said the old woman.

"If you thought that, you would go out in the dark and set the poor hare free," said the child.

"P'raps it's your own mammie come back to mammie you," said the old woman, and her voice was almost as full of sadness as the little voice she had heard outside.

"Look and see," said the child.

Nance turned her face toward the door. There, standing on the drexel, was a beautiful little lady, the same little lady she had sitting in the golden carriage drawn by the twelve white horses. As she looked at her, the teeny tiny person lifted up her voice and wrung her hands, "Ah me, I have lost my little cheeld-whidden, what shall I do?" Her voice, pathetic in its woe yet sweeter than music, went straight to Nance's heart.

"If you be her little cheeld-whidden— an' I believe you be," she said, turning to the child, "why don't you run to her? She have got the greater right to you, my little Skerry-Werry," Nance added with a sob in her voice.

"I am her little cheeld-whidden," said the child, "and now that I am too heavy for you to hold on your lap I will go to her to mammie me."

Skerry-Werry got up from the cricket and went toward the door, and as she went she grew visibly smaller. By the time she had reached the little lady standing on the drexel she was only daisy high.

"My little cheeld, my own dear teeny tiny skilly-widden," cried the yearning voice of the mother. "I have found you at last."

The gladness in her voice filled Nance's heart with gladness, and Tommie Cat purred as he had never purred before.

"I must have mammied a Little Body's cheeld," said the old woman softly. "I'm fine an' glad she has got her own dinky mammie instead of me but, oh dear, oh dear, whatever shall I do without my little Skerry-Werry?"

Nance Pencarrow and Tommie Cat went to the door and looked out into the night. At first they saw nothing save the dark and the soft shining of stars. Then, out of the darkness, came the sound of silvery voices and happy laughter. As the old woman looked toward the sound, she saw that the darkness was lit up with a pale green light. Sitting on the turf were hundreds and hundreds of Small People and there in the center, dancing like a butterfly, was her Skerry-Werry!

# *Ireland*

*How is it possible to characterize the hero tales, the sorrowful romances, the drolls, the strange half-world of faëry with its enchantments and spells that mark the Celtic fairy tales? Great variety of plot and beauty of style have come from the lips of Irish storytellers, and far less humor than most people seem to expect. Indeed, so few and far between are the drolls and so numerous the somber tales of heroism and romance which come to tragic ends that the Irish tales are almost more popular with adults than with children. Ireland stands alone in the zeal and thoroughness with which its folk tales are sought out from among the people and recorded. The three examples given here differ widely in plot and style. "King O'Toole" is amusing and reflects a widespread European Catholic convention, while "The Peddler of Ballaghadereen" is, according to Ruth Sawyer who brought it to this country, traceable to Hebrew legend and was a tale told by the Irish seanachies. "Connla and the Fairy Maiden" is much more representative of the purely Gaelic tradition—pagan, romantic, and bardic.*

## KING O'TOOLE AND HIS GOOSE

*Stories of the saints walking the earth and taking part in men's affairs were fairly common in the Middle Ages. Usually they were serious stories, but here is an amusing exception. In spite of the unfamiliar and rather difficult nineteenth-century Irish style of speech, older children will get the sense and the humor of the tale.*

Och, I thought all the world, far and near, had heerd of King O'Toole—well, well, but the darkness of mankind is untellible! Well, sir, you must know, as you didn't hear it afore, that there was a king, called King O'Toole, who was a fine old king in the old ancient times, long ago; and it was he that owned the churches in the early days. The king, you see, was the right sort; he was the real boy and loved sport as he loved his life, and hunting in particular; and from the rising o' the sun, up he got, and away he went over the mountains after the deer; and fine times they were.

Well, it was all mighty good, as long as the king had his health; but, you see, in the course of time the king grew old, by raison he was stiff in his limbs, and when he got stricken in years, his heart failed him, and he was lost entirely for want o' diversion, because he couldn't go a-hunting no longer; and, by dad, the poor king was obliged at last to get a goose to divert him. Oh, you may laugh, if you like, but it's truth I'm telling you; and the way the goose diverted him was this-a-way: You see, the goose used to swim across the lake, and go diving for trout, and catch fish on a Friday for the king, and flew every other day round about the lake, diverting the poor king. All went on mighty well until, by dad, the goose got stricken in years like her master, and couldn't divert him no longer, and then it was that the poor king was lost entirely. The king was walkin' one mornin' by the edge of the lake, lamentin' his cruel fate, and thinking of drowning himself, that could get no diversion in life, when all of a sudden, turning round the corner, who should he meet but a mighty decent young man coming up to him.

"God save you," says the king to the young man.

"God save you kindly, King O'Toole," says the young man.

"True for you," says the king. "I am King O'Toole," says he, "prince and plennypenny-tinchery of these parts," says he; "but how came ye to know that?" says he.

"Oh, never mind," says St. Kavin.

You see it was Saint Kavin, sure enough—the saint himself in disguise, and nobody else. "Oh, never mind," says he, "I know more than that. May I make bold to ask how is your goose, King O'Toole?" says he.

"King O'Toole and His Goose." From *Celtic Fairy Tales*, selected and edited by Joseph Jacobs. David Nutt, London, 1892

"Blur-an-agers, how came ye to know about my goose?" says the king.

"Oh, no matter; I was given to understand it," says Saint Kavin.

After some more talk the king says, "What are you?"

"I'm an honest man," says Saint Kavin.

"Well, honest man," says the king, "and how is it you make your money so aisy?"

"By makin' old things as good as new," says Saint Kavin.

"Is it a tinker you are?" says the king.

"No," says the saint; "I'm no tinker by trade, King O'Toole; I've a better trade than a tinker," says he. "What would you say," says he, "if I made your old goose as good as new?"

My dear, at the word of making his goose as good as new, you'd think the poor old king's eyes were ready to jump out of his head. With that the king whistled, and down came the poor goose, just like a hound, waddling up to the poor cripple, her master, and as like him as two peas. The minute the saint clapt his eyes on the goose, "I'll do the job for you," says he, "King O'Toole."

"By *Jaminee!*" says King O'Toole, "if you do, I'll say you're the cleverest fellow in the seven parishes."

"Oh, by dad," says St. Kavin, "you must say more nor that—my horn's not so soft all out," says he, "as to repair your old goose for nothing; what'll you gi' me if I do the job for you?—that's the chat," says St. Kavin.

"I'll give you whatever you ask," says the king; "isn't that fair?"

"Divil a fairer," says the saint; "that's the way to do business. Now," says he, "this is the bargain I'll make with you, King O'Toole: will you gi' me all the ground the goose flies over, the first offer, after I make her as good as new?"

"I will," says the king.

"You won't go back o' your word?" says St. Kavin.

"Honour bright!" says King O'Toole, holding out his fist.

"Honour bright!" says St. Kavin, back agin, "it's a bargain. Come here!" says he to the poor old goose, "come here, you unfortunate ould cripple, and it's I that'll make you the sporting bird." With that, my dear, he took up the goose by the two wings. "Criss o' my cross an you," says he, markin' her to grace with the blessed sign at the same minute—and throwing her up in the air, "whew," says he, jist givin' her a blast to help her; and with that, my jewel, she took to her heels, flyin' like one o' the eagles themselves, and cutting as many capers as a swallow before a shower of rain.

Well, my dear, it was a beautiful sight to see the king standing with his mouth open, looking at his poor old goose flying as light as a lark, and better than ever she was; and when she lit at his feet, patted her on the head, and *"Ma vourneen,"* says he, "but you are the *darlint* o' the world."

"And what do you say to me," says Saint Kavin, "for making her the like?"

"By Jabers," says the king, "I say nothing beats the art o' man, barring the bees."

"And do you say no more nor that?" says Saint Kavin.

"And that I'm beholden to you," says the king.

"But will you gi'e me all the ground the goose flew over?" says Saint Kavin.

"I will," says King O'Toole, "and you're welcome to it," says he, "though it's the last acre I have to give."

"But you'll keep your word true," says the saint.

"As true as the sun," says the king.

"It's well for you, King O'Toole, that you said that word," says he; "for if you didn't say that word, the divil the bit o' your goose would ever fly agin."

When the king was as good as his word, Saint Kavin was pleased with him, and then it was that he made himself known to the king. "And," says he, "King O'Toole, you're a decent man, for I only came here to try you. You don't know me," says he, "because I'm disguised."

"Musha! then," says the king, "who are you?"

"I'm Saint Kavin," said the saint, blessing himself.

"Oh, queen of heaven!" says the king, making the sign of the cross between his eyes, and falling down on his knees before the saint; "is it the great Saint Kavin," says he, "that I've been discoursing all this time without knowing it," says he, "all as one as if he was a lump of a *gossoon*—and so you're a saint?" says the king.

"I am," says Saint Kavin.

"By Jabers, I thought I was only talking to a dacent boy," says the king.

"Well, you know the difference now," says the saint. "I'm Saint Kavin," says he, "the greatest of all the saints."

And so the king had his goose as good as new, to divert him as long as he lived; and the saint supported him after he came into his property, as I told you, until the day of his death—and that was soon after; for the poor goose thought he was catching a trout one Friday; but, my jewel, it was a mistake he made—and instead of a trout, it was a thieving horse-eel; and instead of the goose killing a trout for the king's supper

—by dad, the eel killed the king's goose—and small blame to him; but he didn't ate her, because he darn't ate what Saint Kavin had laid his blessed hands on.

## CONNLA AND
## THE FAIRY MAIDEN

*This is an ancient story that goes back to the pre-Christian times of the Druids. Its roots not only reach even further back in time, but run through much of the world's folklore. The gift of the apple, according to Robert Graves, "records an ancient ritual situation, outgrown by the time of Homer and Hesiod," [1] thus dating back to the neolithic and Bronze ages. The theme of the hero traveling to the Land of the Ever Young is found in a later Irish legend about the hero Oisin, and in the Japanese tale of Urashima Taro (see p. 338).*

Connla of the Fiery Hair was son of Conn of the Hundred Fights. One day as he stood by the side of his father on the height of Usna, he saw a maiden clad in strange attire towards him coming.

"Whence comest thou, maiden?" said Connla.

"I come from the Plains of the Ever Living," she said, "there where is neither death nor sin. There we keep holiday alway, nor need we help from any in our joy. And in all our pleasure we have no strife. And because we have our homes in the round green hills, men call us the Hill Folk."

The king and all with him wondered much to hear a voice when they saw no one. For save Connla alone, none saw the Fairy Maiden.

"To whom art thou talking, my son?" said Conn the king.

Then the maiden answered, "Connla speaks to a young, fair maid, whom neither death nor old age awaits. I love Connla, and now I call him away to the Plain of Pleasure, Moy Mell, where Boadag is king for aye, nor has there been sorrow

"Connla and the Fairy Maiden." From *Celtic Fairy Tales*, selected and edited by Joseph Jacobs. David Nutt, London, 1892
[1] Robert Graves, *The Greek Myths*, Volume One, George Braziller, Inc., 1955, page 21

or complaint in that land since he held the kingship. Oh, come with me, Connla of the Fiery Hair, ruddy as the dawn, with thy tawny skin. A fairy crown awaits thee to grace thy comely face and royal form. Come, and never shall thy comeliness fade, nor thy youth, till the last awful day of judgment."

The king in fear at what the maiden said, which he heard though he could not see her, called aloud to his Druid, Coran by name.

"Oh, Coran of the many spells," he said, "and of the cunning magic, I call upon thy aid. A task is upon me too great for all my skill and wit, greater than any laid upon me since I seized the kingship. A maiden unseen has met us, and by her power would take from me my dear, my comely son. If thou help not, he will be taken from thy king by woman's wiles and witchery."

Then Coran the Druid stood forth and chanted his spells towards the spot where the maiden's voice had been heard. And none heard her voice again, nor could Connla see her longer. Only as she vanished before the Druid's mighty spell, she threw an apple to Connla.

For a whole month from that day Connla would take nothing, either to eat or to drink, save only from that apple. But as he ate, it grew again and always kept whole. And all the while there grew within him a mighty yearning and longing after the maiden he had seen.

But when the last day of the month of waiting came, Connla stood by the side of the king his father on the Plain of Arcomin, and again he saw the maiden come towards him, and again she spoke to him.

"'Tis a glorious place, forsooth, that Connla holds among shortlived mortals awaiting the day of death. But now the folk of life, the ever-living ones, beg and bid thee come to Moy Mell, the Plain of Pleasure, for they have learnt to know thee, seeing thee in thy home among thy dear ones."

When Conn the king heard the maiden's voice he called to his men aloud and said:

"Summon swift my Druid Coran, for I see she has again this day the power of speech."

Then the maiden said: "Oh, mighty Conn, Fighter of a Hundred Fights, the Druid's power is little loved; it has little honour in the mighty land, peopled with so many of the upright. When the Law comes, it will do away with the Druid's magic spells that issue from the lips of the false black demon."

Then Conn the king observed that since the coming of the maiden, Connla his son spoke to none that spake to him. So Conn of the Hundred Fights said to him, "Is it to thy mind what the woman says, my son?"

" 'Tis hard upon me," said Connla; "I love my own folk above all things; but yet a longing seizes me for the maiden."

When the maiden heard this, she answered and said: "The ocean is not so strong as the waves of thy longing. Come with me in my curragh, the gleaming, straight-gliding crystal canoe. Soon can we reach Boadag's realm. I see the bright sun sink, yet far as it is, we can reach it before dark. There is, too, another land worthy of thy journey, a land joyous to all that seek it. Only wives and maidens dwell there. If thou wilt, we can seek it and live there alone together in joy."

When the maiden ceased to speak, Connla of the Fiery Hair rushed away from his kinsmen and sprang into the curragh, the gleaming, straight-gliding crystal canoe. And then they all, king and court, saw it glide away over the bright sea towards the setting sun, away and away, till eye could see it no longer. So Connla and the Fairy Maiden went forth on the sea and were no more seen, nor did any know whither they came.

## THE PEDDLER
## OF BALLAGHADEREEN

*This story was learned by Ruth Sawyer from an Irish seanachie (storyteller), and it is another example of a widespread European folklore theme. Ruth Sawyer has recorded this tale, telling it as she heard it told.*

More years ago than you can tell me and twice as many as I can tell you, there lived a peddler in Ballaghadereen. He lived at the crossroads, by

"The Peddler of Ballaghadereen." From *The Way of the Storyteller* by Ruth Sawyer. Copyright 1942, © 1970 by Ruth Sawyer. Reprinted by permission of The Viking Press, Inc.

himself in a bit of a cabin with one room to it, and that so small that a man could stand in the middle of the floor and, without taking a step, he could lift the latch on the front door, he could lift the latch on the back door, and he could hang the kettle over the turf. That is how small and snug it was.

Outside the cabin the peddler had a bit of a garden. In it he planted carrots and cabbages, onions and potatoes. In the center grew a cherry tree—as brave and fine a tree as you would find anywhere in Ireland. Every spring it flowered, the white blossoms covering it like a fresh falling of snow. Every summer it bore cherries as red as heart's blood.

But every year, after the garden was planted the wee brown hares would come from the copse near by and nibble-nibble here, and nibble-nibble there, until there was not a thing left, barely, to grow into a full-sized vegetable that a man could harvest for his table. And every summer as the cherries began to ripen the blackbirds came in whirling flocks and ate the cherries as fast as they ripened.

The neighbors that lived thereabouts minded this and nodded their heads and said: "Master Peddler, you're a poor, simple man, entirely. You let the wild creatures thieve from you without lifting your hand to stop them."

And the peddler would always nod his head back at them and laugh and answer: "Nay, then, 'tis not thieving they are at all. They pay well for what they take. Look you—on yonder cherry tree the blackbirds sing sweeter nor they sing on any cherry tree in Ballaghadereen. And the brown hares make good company at dusk-hour for a lonely man."

In the country roundabout, every day when there was market, a wedding, or a fair, the peddler would be off at ring-o'-day, his pack strapped on his back, one foot ahead of the other, fetching him along the road. And when he reached the town diamond he would open his pack, spread it on the green turf, and, making a hollow of his two hands, he would call:

"Come buy a trinket—come buy a brooch—
Come buy a kerchief of scarlet or yellow!"

In no time at all there would be a great crowding of lads and lasses and children about him, searching his pack for what they might be wanting. And like as not, some barefooted lad would hold up a jack-knife and ask: "How much for this, Master Peddler?"

And the peddler would answer: "Half a crown."

And the lad would put it back, shaking his head dolefully. "Faith, I haven't the half of that, nor likely ever to have it."

And the peddler would pull the lad over to him and whisper in his ear: "Take the knife—'twill rest a deal more easy in your pocket than in my pack."

Then, like as not, some lass would hold up a blue kerchief to her yellow curls and ask: "Master Peddler, what is the price of this?"

And the peddler would answer: "One shilling sixpence."

And the lass would put it back, the smile gone from her face, and she turning away.

And the peddler would catch up the kerchief again and tie it himself about her curls and laugh and say: "Faith, there it looks far prettier than ever it looks in my pack. Take it, with God's blessing."

So it would go—a brooch to this one and a top to that. There were days when the peddler took in little more than a few farthings. But after those days he would sing his way homeward; and the shrewd ones would watch him passing by and wag their fingers at him and say: "You're a poor, simple man, Master Peddler. You'll never be putting a penny by for your old age. You'll end your days like the blackbirds, whistling for crumbs at our back doors. Why, even the vagabond dogs know they can wheedle the half of the bread you are carrying in your pouch, you're that simple."

Which likewise was true. Every stray, hungry dog knew him the length and breadth of the county. Rarely did he follow a road without one tagging his heels, sure of a noonday sharing of bread and cheese.

There were days when he went abroad without his pack, when there was no market-day, no wedding or fair. These he spent with the children, who would have followed him about like the dogs, had their mothers let them. On these days he would sit himself down on some doorstep and when a crowd of children had gathered he would tell them tales—old tales of Ireland—tales of the good folk, of the heroes, of the saints. He knew them all, and he knew how to tell them, the way the children would never be forgetting one of them, but carry them in their hearts until they were old.

And whenever he finished a tale he would say, like as not, laughing and pinching the cheek of some wee lass: "Mind well your manners, whether you are at home or abroad, for you can never be telling what good folk, or saint, or hero you may be fetching up with on the road—or who may come knocking at your doors. Aye, when Duirmuid, or Fionn or Oisin or Saint Patrick walked the earth they were poor and simple and plain men; it took death to put a grand memory on them. And the poor and the simple and the old today may be heroes tomorrow—you never can be telling. So keep a kind word for all, and a gentling hand."

Often an older would stop to listen to the scraps of words he was saying; and often as not he would go his way, wagging his finger and mumbling: "The poor, simple man. He's as foolish as the blackbirds."

Spring followed winter in Ireland, and sum-

mer followed close upon the heels of both. And winter came again and the peddler grew old. His pack grew lighter and lighter, until the neighbors could hear the trinkets jangling inside as he passed, so few things were left. They would nod their heads and say to one another: "Like as not his pockets are as empty as his pack. Time will come, with winter at hand, when he will be at our back doors begging crumbs, along with the blackbirds."

The time did come, as the neighbors had prophesied it would, smug and proper, when the peddler's pack was empty, when he had naught in his pockets and naught in his cupboard. That night he went hungry to bed.

Now it is more than likely that hungry men will dream; and the peddler of Ballaghadereen had a strange dream that night. He dreamed that there came a sound of knocking in the middle of the night. Then the latch on the front door lifted, the door opened without a creak or a cringe, and inside the cabin stepped Saint Patrick. Standing in the doorway the good man pointed a finger; and he spoke in a voice tuned as low as the wind over the bogs. "Peddler, peddler of Ballaghadereen, take the road to Dublin town. When you get to the bridge that spans the Liffey you will hear what you were meant to hear."

On the morrow the peddler awoke and remembered the dream. He rubbed his stomach and found it mortal empty; he stood on his legs and found them trembling in under him; and he said to himself: "Faith, an empty stomach and weak legs are the worst traveling companions a man can have, and Dublin is a long way. I'll bide where I am."

That night the peddler went hungrier to bed, and again came the dream. There came the knocking on the door, the lifting of the latch. The door opened and Saint Patrick stood there, pointing the road: "Peddler, peddler of Ballaghadereen, take the road that leads to Dublin Town. When you get to the bridge that spans the Liffey you will hear what you were meant to hear!"

The second day it was the same as the first. The peddler felt the hunger and the weakness stronger in him, and stayed where he was. But when he woke after the third night and the third

coming of the dream, he rose and strapped his pack from long habit upon his back and took the road to Dublin. For three long weary days he traveled, barely staying his fast, and on the fourth day he came into the city.

Early in the day he found the bridge spanning the river and all the lee-long day he stood there, changing his weight from one foot to the other, shifting his pack to ease the drag of it, scanning the faces of all who passed by. But although a great tide of people swept this way, and a great tide swept that, no one stopped and spoke to him.

At the end of the day he said to himself: "I'll find me a blind alley, and like an old dog I'll lay me down in it and die." Slowly he moved off the bridge. As he passed by the Head Inn of Dublin, the door opened and out came the landlord.

To the peddler's astonishment he crossed the thoroughfare and hurried after him. He clapped a strong hand on his shoulder and cried: "Arra, man, hold a minute! All day I've been watching you. All day I have seen you standing on the bridge like an old rook with rent wings. And of all the people passing from the west to the east, and of all the people passing from the east to the west, not one crossing the bridge spoke aught with you. Now I am filled with a great curiosity entirely to know what fetched you here."

Seeing hunger and weariness on the peddler, he drew him toward the inn. "Come; in return for having my curiosity satisfied you shall have rest in the kitchen yonder, with bread and cheese and ale. Come."

So the peddler rested his bones by the kitchen hearth and he ate as he hadn't eaten in many days. He was satisfied at long last and the landlord repeated his question. "Peddler, what fetched you here?"

"For three nights running I had a dream——" began the peddler, but he got no further.

The landlord of the Head Inn threw back his head and laughed. How he laughed, rocking on his feet, shaking the whole length of him!

"A dream you had, by my soul, a dream!" He spoke when he could get his breath. "I could be telling you were the cut of a man to have dreams, and to listen to them, what's more. Rags on your back and hunger in your cheeks and age upon you, and I'll wager not a farthing in your pouch. Well, God's blessing on you and your dreams."

The peddler got to his feet, saddled his pack, and made for the door. He had one foot over the sill when the landlord hurried after him and again clapped a hand on his shoulder.

"Hold, Master Peddler," he said, "I too had a dream, three nights running." He burst into laughter again, remembering it. "I dreamed there came a knocking on this very door, and the latch lifted, and, standing in the doorway, as you are standing, I saw Saint Patrick. He pointed with one finger to the road running westward and he said: 'Landlord, Landlord of the Head Inn, take *that* road to Ballaghadereen. When you come to the crossroads you will find a wee cabin, and beside the cabin a wee garden, and in the center of the garden a cherry tree. Dig deep under the tree and you will find gold—much gold.' "

The landlord paused and drew his sleeve across his mouth to hush his laughter.

"Ballaghadereen! I never heard of the place. Gold under a cherry tree—whoever heard of gold under a cherry tree! There is only one dream that I hear, waking or sleeping, and it's

the dream of gold, much gold, in my own pocket. Aye, listen, 'tis a good dream." And the landlord thrust a hand into his pouch and jangled the coins loudly in the peddler's ear.

Back to Ballaghadereen went the peddler, one foot ahead of the other. How he got there I cannot be telling you. He unslung his pack, took up a mattock lying near by, and dug under the cherry tree. He dug deep and felt at last the scraping of the mattock against something hard and smooth. It took him time to uncover it and he found it to be an old sea chest, of foreign pattern and workmanship, bound around with bands of brass. These he broke, and lifting the lid he found the chest full of gold, tarnished and clotted with mold; pieces-of-six and pieces-of-eight and Spanish doubloons.

I cannot begin to tell the half of the goodness that the peddler put into the spending of that gold. But this I know. He built a chapel at the crossroads—a resting-place for all weary travelers, journeying thither.

And after he had gone the neighbors had a statue made of him and placed it facing the crossroads. And there he stands to this day, a pack on his back and a dog at his heels.

## Germany

*The German folk tales were known to English-speaking children in translation long before the tales of the British Isles and of other parts of the Western world were available. Since their first translation into English, the fairy tales of Jacob and Wilhelm Grimm have been published in most of the languages of the civilized world and are the beloved heritage of children everywhere. Because the Grimms were students of the German language, they collected their tales either directly from the lips of untutored story-tellers or, as they were able to get them, from reliable printed sources. It can be said that with their work the science of folklore was born, and that they did much to shape its early methods. Although at the outset they insisted on setting down the tales exactly as they were told, they eventually began to rewrite the tales from a number of oral and printed sources, so that some of their best-loved stories, like "Snow White and the Seven Dwarfs," represent their own literary retelling and not the folk teller's. The stories range from simple little tales for the nursery to mature themes for adults. They are dramatic, exciting, and full of suspense and smashing climaxes. Indeed, over the years many adults have questioned some of the more violent and cruel episodes. But children have made the Grimms' original and scholarly work their own possession, and these now classic tales are some of the most popular and best fairy tales ever told.*

## HANSEL AND GRETTEL

*A prime fear of many children is one of being abandoned. Here it is dealt with bluntly, but the aesthetic distance it acquires in story form, together with its happy ending, reassures youngsters. This is a favorite story to illustrate and dramatize.*

Once upon a time there dwelt on the outskirts of a large forest a poor woodcutter with his wife and two children; the boy was called Hansel and the girl Grettel. He had always little enough to live on, and once, when there was a great famine in the land, he couldn't even provide them with daily bread. One night, as he was tossing about in bed, full of cares and worry, he sighed and said to his wife: "What's to become of us? How are we to support our poor children, now that we have nothing more for ourselves?"

"I'll tell you what, husband," answered the woman, who was the children's step-mother. "Early tomorrow morning we'll take the children out into the thickest part of the wood; there we shall light a fire for them and give them each a piece of bread; then we'll go on to our work and leave them alone. They won't be able to find their way home, and we shall thus be rid of them."

"No, wife," said her husband, "that I won't do; how could I find it in my heart to leave my children alone in the wood? The wild beasts would soon come and tear them to pieces."

"Oh! you fool," said she, "then we must all four die of hunger, and you may just as well go and plane the boards for our coffins"; and she left him no peace till he consented.

"But I can't help feeling sorry for the poor children," added the husband.

The children, too, had not been able to sleep for hunger, and had heard what their step-mother had said to their father. Grettel wept bitterly and spoke to Hansel: "Now it's all up with us."

"No, no, Grettel," said Hansel, "don't fret yourself; I'll be able to find a way of escape, no fear." And when the old people had fallen asleep

"Hansel and Grettel." From *The Blue Fairy Book*, edited by Andrew Lang. Longmans, Green, and Co., London, 1889

he got up, slipped on his little coat, opened the back door and stole out.

The moon was shining clearly, and the white pebbles which lay in front of the house glittered like bits of silver. Hansel bent down and filled his pocket with as many of them as he could cram in. Then he went back and said to Grettel, "Be comforted, my dear little sister, and go to sleep. God will not desert us"; and he lay down in bed again.

At daybreak, even before the sun was up, the woman came and woke the two children: "Get up, you lie-abeds, we're all going to the forest to fetch wood." She gave them each a bit of bread and spoke: "There's something for your luncheon, but don't eat it up before, for it's all you'll get."

Grettel took the bread under her apron, as Hansel had the stones in his pocket. Then they all set out together on the way to the forest. After they had walked for a little, Hansel stood still and looked back at the house, and this manœuvre he repeated again and again.

His father observed him, and spoke: "Hansel, what are you gazing at there, and why do you always remain behind? Take care, and don't lose your footing."

"Oh! Father," said Hansel, "I am looking back at my white kitten, which is sitting on the roof, waving me a farewell."

The woman exclaimed: "What a donkey you are! That isn't your kitten, that's the morning sun shining on the chimney." But Hansel had not looked back at his kitten, but had always dropped one of the white pebbles out of his pocket onto the path.

When they had reached the middle of the forest the father said: "Now, children, go and fetch a lot of wood, and I'll light a fire that you mayn't feel cold."

Hansel and Grettel heaped up brushwood till they had made a pile nearly the size of a small hill. The brushwood was set fire to, and when the flames leaped high the woman said: "Now lie down at the fire, children, and rest yourselves; we are going into the forest to cut down wood; when we've finished we'll come back and fetch you."

Hansel and Grettel sat down beside the fire, and at midday ate their little bits of bread. They heard the strokes of the axe, so they thought their father was quite near. But it was no axe they heard, but a bough he had tied onto a dead tree, and that was blown about by the wind. And when they had sat for a long time their eyes closed with fatigue, and they fell fast asleep. When they awoke at last, it was pitch dark.

Grettel began to cry, and said: "How are we ever to get out of the wood?"

But Hansel comforted her. "Wait a bit," he said, "till the moon is up, and then we'll find our way sure enough." And when the full moon had risen he took his sister by the hand and followed the pebbles, which shone like new threepenny bits, and showed them the path. They walked all through the night, and at daybreak reached their father's house again.

They knocked at the door, and when the woman opened it she exclaimed: "You naughty children, what a time you've slept in the wood! We thought you were never going to come back." But the father rejoiced, for his conscience had reproached him for leaving his children behind by themselves.

Not long afterwards there was again great dearth in the land, and the children heard their step-mother address their father thus in bed one night: "Everything is eaten up once more; we have only half a loaf in the house, and when that's done it's all up with us. The children must be got rid of; we'll lead them deeper into the wood this time, so that they won't be able to find their way out again. There is no other way of saving ourselves."

The man's heart smote him heavily, and he thought: "Surely it would be better to share the last bite with one's children!" But his wife wouldn't listen to his arguments, and did nothing but scold and reproach him. If a man yields once, he's done for, and so, because he had given in the first time, he was forced to do so the second.

But the children were awake, and had heard the conversation. When the old people were asleep Hansel got up, and wanted to go out and pick up pebbles again, as he had done the first time; but the woman had barred the door, and Hansel couldn't get out. But he consoled his little sister, and said: "Don't cry, Grettel, and sleep peacefully, for God is sure to help us."

At early dawn the woman came and made the children get up. They received their bit of bread, but it was even smaller than the time before. On the way to the wood Hansel crumbled it in his pocket, and every few minutes he stood still and dropped a crumb on the ground.

"Hansel, what are you stopping and looking about you for?" said the father.

"I'm looking back at my little pigeon, which is sitting on the roof waving me a farewell," answered Hansel.

"Fool!" said the wife. "That isn't your pigeon, it's the morning sun glittering on the chimney." But Hansel gradually threw all his crumbs onto the path. The woman led the children still deeper into the forest, farther than they had ever been in their lives before.

Then a big fire was lit again, and the step-mother said: "Just sit down there, children, and if you're tired you can sleep a bit; we're going into the forest to cut down wood, and in the evening when we're finished we'll come back to fetch you."

At midday Grettel divided her bread with Hansel, for he had strewed his all along their path. Then they fell asleep, and evening passed away, but nobody came to the poor children.

They didn't awake till it was pitch dark, and Hansel comforted his sister, saying: "Only wait, Grettel, till the moon rises, then we shall see the bread crumbs I scattered along the path; they will show us the way back to the house." When the moon appeared they got up, but they found no crumbs, for the thousands of birds that fly about the woods and fields had picked them all up.

"Never mind," said Hansel to Grettel. "You'll see, we'll still find a way out." But all the same they did not.

They wandered about the whole night, and the next day, from morning till evening, but they could not find a path out of the wood. They were very hungry, too, for they had nothing to eat but a few berries they found growing on the ground. And at last they were so tired that their legs refused to carry them any longer, so they lay down under a tree and fell fast asleep.

On the third morning after they had left their father's house they set about their wandering again, but only got deeper and deeper into the wood, and now they felt that if help did not come to them soon they must perish. At midday they saw a beautiful little snow-white bird sitting on a branch, which sang so sweetly that they stopped still and listened to it. And when its song was finished it flapped its wings and flew on in front of them. They followed it and came to a little house, on the roof of which it perched; and when they came quite near they saw that the cottage was made of bread and roofed with cakes, while the window was made of transparent sugar.

"Now we'll set to," said Hansel, "and have a regular blow-out. I'll eat a bit of the roof, and you, Grettel, can eat some of the window, which you'll find a sweet morsel."

Hansel stretched up his hand and broke off a little bit of the roof to see what it was like, and Grettel went to the casement and began to nibble at it. Thereupon a shrill voice called out from the room inside:

> "Nibble, nibble, little mouse,
> Who's nibbling my house?"

The children answered:

> " 'Tis Heaven's own child,
> The tempest wild,"

and went on eating, without putting themselves about. Hansel, who thoroughly appreciated the roof, tore down a big bit of it, while Grettel pushed out a whole round window-pane, and sat down the better to enjoy it. Suddenly the door opened, and an ancient dame leaning on a staff hobbled out. Hansel and Grettel were so terrified that they let what they had in their hands fall.

But the old woman shook her head and said: "Oh, ho! you dear children, who led you here? Just come in and stay with me, no ill shall befall you." She took them both by the hand and led them into the house, and laid a most sumptuous dinner before them—milk and sugared pancakes, with apples and nuts. After they had finished, two beautiful little white beds were prepared for them, and when Hansel and Grettel lay down in them they felt as if they had got into heaven.

The old woman had appeared to be most friendly, but she was really an old witch who had waylaid the children, and had only built the little bread house in order to lure them in. When anyone came into her power she killed, cooked, and ate him, and held a regular feast-day for the occasion. Now witches have red eyes, and cannot see far, but, like beasts, they have a keen sense of smell, and know when human beings pass by. When Hansel and Grettel fell into her hands she laughed maliciously, and said jeeringly: "I've got them now; they shan't escape me."

Early in the morning, before the children were awake, the old woman rose up, and when she saw them both sleeping so peacefully, with their round rosy cheeks, she muttered to herself, "That'll be a dainty bite."

Then she seized Hansel with her bony hand and carried him into a little stable, and barred the door on him. He might scream as much as he liked, it did him no good.

Then she went to Grettel, shook her till she awoke, and cried: "Get up, you lazy-bones, fetch water and cook something for your brother. When he's fat I'll eat him up." Grettel began to cry bitterly, but it was of no use: she had to do what the wicked witch bade her.

So the best food was cooked for poor Hansel, but Grettel got nothing but crab-shells. Every morning the old woman hobbled out to the stable and cried: "Hansel, put out your finger, that I may feel if you are getting fat." But Hansel always stretched out a bone, and the old dame, whose eyes were dim, couldn't see it, and thinking always it was Hansel's finger, wondered why he fattened so slowly. When four weeks passed and Hansel still remained thin, she lost patience and determined to wait no longer.

"Hi! Grettel," she called to the girl, "be quick and get some water. Hansel may be fat or thin, I'm going to kill him tomorrow and cook him." Oh! how the poor little sister sobbed as she carried the water, and how the tears rolled down her cheeks!

"Kind heaven help us now!" she cried. "If only the wild beasts in the wood had eaten us, then at least we should have died together."

"Just hold your peace," said the old hag. "Crying won't help you."

Early in the morning Grettel had to go out

and hang up the kettle full of water, and light the fire. "First we'll bake," said the old dame. "I've heated the oven already and kneaded the dough." She pushed Grettel out to the oven, from which fiery flames were already issuing. "Creep in," said the witch, "and see if it's properly heated, so that we can shove in the bread." For when she had got Grettel in she meant to close the oven and let the girl bake, that she might eat her up too.

But Grettel perceived her intention, and spoke: "I don't know how I'm to do it; how do I get in?"

"You silly goose!" said the hag. "The opening is big enough. See, I could get in myself." And she crawled toward it, and poked her head into the oven. Then Grettel gave her a shove that sent her right in, shut the iron door, and drew the bolt. Gracious! how she yelled! it was quite horrible; but Grettel fled, and the wretched old woman was left to perish miserably.

Grettel flew straight to Hansel, opened the little stable-door, and cried: "Hansel, we are free; the old witch is dead."

Then Hansel sprang like a bird out of a cage when the door is opened. How they rejoiced, and fell on each other's necks, and jumped for joy, and kissed one another! And as they had no longer any cause for fear, they went into the old hag's house, and there they found, in every corner of the room, boxes with pearls and precious stones.

"These are even better than pebbles," said Hansel, and crammed his pockets full of them.

Grettel said: "I too will bring something home"; and she filled her apron full.

"But now," said Hansel, "let's go and get well away from the witches' wood."

When they had wandered about for some hours they came to a big lake. "We can't get over," said Hansel; "I see no bridge of any sort or kind."

"Yes, and there's no ferry-boat either," answered Grettel; "but look, there swims a white duck; if I ask her she'll help us over"; and she called out:

"Here are two children, mournful very,
Seeing neither bridge nor ferry;

Take us upon your white back,
And row us over, quack, quack!"

The duck swam toward them, and Hansel got on her back and bade his little sister sit beside him.

"No," answered Grettel, "we should be too heavy a load for the duck; she shall carry us across separately."

The good bird did this, and when they were landed safely on the other side and had gone on for a while, the wood became more and more familiar to them, and at length they saw their father's house in the distance. Then they set off to run and, bounding into the room, fell on their father's neck. The man had not passed a happy hour since he left them in the wood, but the woman had died. Grettel shook out her apron so that the pearls and precious stones rolled about the room, and Hansel threw down one handful after the other out of his pocket. Thus all their troubles were ended, and they all lived happily ever afterwards.

My story is done. See! there runs a little mouse. Anyone who catches it may make himself a large fur cap out of it.

## CLEVER ELSIE

*This story is pure slapstick. Elsie is such a dolt she provokes amused protest, but she has a host of equally weak-minded cousins in folk tales around the world.*

There was once a man who had a daughter who was called Clever Elsie. And when she had grown up, her father said, "We will get her married." "Yes," said the mother, "if only any one would come who would have her." At length a man came from a distance and wooed her, who was called Hans; but he stipulated that Clever Elsie should be really wise. "Oh," said the father, "she's sharp enough"; and the mother said, "Oh, she can see the wind coming up the street, and hear the flies coughing." "Well," said Hans, "if she is not really wise, I won't have her." When they were sitting at dinner and had eaten, the

"Clever Elsie." From *Grimm's Household Tales*, translated by Margaret Hunt

mother said, "Elsie, go into the cellar and fetch some beer."

Then Clever Elsie took the pitcher from the wall, went into the cellar, and tapped the lid briskly as she went, so that the time might not appear long. When she was below she fetched herself a chair, and set it before the barrel so that she had no need to stoop, and did not hurt her back or do herself any unexpected injury. Then she placed the can before her, and turned the tap, and while the beer was running she would not let her eyes be idle, but looked up at the wall, and after much peering here and there, saw a pick-axe exactly above her, which the masons had accidently left there.

Then Clever Elsie began to weep and said, "If I get Hans, and we have a child, and he grows big, and we send him into the cellar here to draw beer, then the pick-axe will fall on his head and kill him." Then she sat and wept and screamed with all the strength of her body, over the misfortune which lay before her. Those upstairs waited for the drink, but Clever Elsie still did not come. Then the woman said to the servant, "Just go down into the cellar and see where Elsie is." The maid went and found her sitting in front of the barrel, screaming loudly. "Elsie, why do you weep?" asked the maid. "Ah," she answered, "have I not reason to weep? If I get Hans, and we have a child, and he grows big, and has to draw beer here, the pick-axe will perhaps fall on his head, and kill him." Then said the maid, "What a clever Elsie we have!" and sat down beside her and began loudly to weep over the misfortune.

After a while, as the maid did not come back, and those upstairs were thirsty for the beer, the man said to the boy, "Just go down into the cellar and see where Elsie and the girl are." The boy went down, and there sat Clever Elsie and the girl both weeping together. Then he asked, "Why are you weeping?" "Ah," said Elsie, "have I not reason to weep? If I get Hans, and we have a child, and he grows big, and has to draw beer here, the pick-axe will fall on his head and kill him." Then said the boy, "What a clever Elsie we have!" and sat down by her, and likewise began to howl loudly.

Upstairs they waited for the boy, but as he still did not return, the man said to the woman, "Just go down into the cellar and see where Elsie is!" The woman went down, and found all three in the midst of their lamentations, and inquired what was the cause; then Elsie told her also that her future child was to be killed by the pick-axe, when it grew big and had to draw beer, and the pick-axe fell down. Then said the mother likewise, "What a clever Elsie we have!" and sat down and wept with them.

The man upstairs waited a short time, but as his wife did not come back and his thirst grew ever greater, he said, "I must go into the cellar myself and see where Elsie is." But when he got into the cellar, and they were all sitting together crying, and he heard the reason, and that Elsie's child was the cause, and that Elsie might perhaps bring one into the world some day, and that he might be killed by the pick-axe, if he should happen to be sitting beneath it, drawing beer just at the very time when it fell down, he cried, "Oh, what a clever Elsie!" and sat down, and likewise wept with them.

The bridegroom stayed upstairs alone for a long time; then as no one would come back he thought, "They must be waiting for me below: I too must go there and see what they are about." When he got down, the five of them were sitting screaming and lamenting quite piteously, each out-doing the other. "What misfortune has happened then?" asked he. "Ah, dear Hans," said Elsie, "if we marry each other and have a child, and he is big, and we perhaps send him here to draw something to drink, then the pick-axe which has been left up there might dash his brains out if it were to fall down, so have we not reason to weep?" "Come," said Hans, "more understanding than that is not needed for my household; as you are such a clever Elsie, I will have you," and he seized her hand, took her upstairs with him, and married her.

After Hans had had her some time, he said, "Wife, I am going out to work and earn some money for us; go into the field and cut the corn that we may have some bread." "Yes, dear Hans, I will do that." After Hans had gone away, she cooked herself some good broth and took it into the field with her. When she came to the field she said to herself, "What shall I do; shall I cut first, or shall I eat first? Oh, I will eat first." Then she drank her cup of broth, and when she was fully satisfied, she once more said, "What shall I do? Shall I cut first, or shall I sleep first? I will sleep first." Then she lay down among the corn and fell asleep. Hans had been at home for a long time, but Elsie did not come; then said he, "What a clever Elsie I have; she is so industrious that she does not even come home to eat."

But when evening came and she still stayed away, Hans went out to see what she had cut, but nothing was cut, and she was lying among the corn asleep. Then Hans hastened home and brought a fowler's net with little bells and hung it round about her, and she still went on sleeping. Then he ran home, shut the house-door, and sat down in his chair and worked.

At length, when it was quite dark, Clever Elsie awoke and when she got up there was a jingling all round about her, and the bells rang at each step which she took. Then she was alarmed, and became uncertain whether she really was Clever Elsie or not, and said, "Is it I, or is it not I?" But she knew not what answer to make to this, and stood for a time in doubt; at length she thought: "I will go home and ask if it be I, or if it be not I, they will be sure to know." She ran to the door of her own house, but it was shut; then she knocked at the window and cried, "Hans, is Elsie within?" "Yes," answered Hans, "she is within."

Hereupon she was terrified, and said, "Ah, heavens! Then it is not I," and went to another door; but when the people heard the jingling of the bells they would not open it, and she could get in nowhere. Then she ran out of the village, and no one has seen her since.

## SNOW-WHITE AND
## THE SEVEN DWARFS

*This may well be one of the most famous of folk tales, and Snow-White truly belongs in the distinguished company of Cinderella and Sleeping Beauty.*

It was in the middle of winter, when the broad flakes of snow were falling around, that a certain queen sat working at a window, the frame of which was made of fine black ebony; and as she was looking out upon the snow, she pricked her finger, and three drops of blood fell upon it. Then she gazed thoughtfully upon the red drops which sprinkled the white snow, and said, "Would that my little daughter may be as white as that snow, as red as the blood, and as black as the ebony window-frame!"

And so the little girl grew up. Her skin was as white as snow, her cheeks as rosy as blood, and her hair as black as ebony; and she was called Snow-White.

But this queen died; and the king soon married another wife, who was very beautiful, but so proud that she could not bear to think that any one could surpass her. She had a magical mirror, to which she used to go and gaze upon herself in it, and say,

"Mirror, Mirror on the wall
Who is fairest of us all?"

And the glass answered,

"Thou, queen, art fairest of them all."

But Snow-White grew more and more beautiful; and when she was seven years old, she was as

"Snow-White and the Seven Dwarfs." From *Grimm's Popular Stories*, translated by Edgar Taylor (slightly adapted)

bright as the day, and fairer than the queen herself. Then the glass one day answered the queen, when she went to consult it as usual,

"Queen, you are full fair, 'tis true,
But Snow-White fairer is than you."

When the queen heard this she turned pale with rage and envy; and called to one of her servants and said, "Take Snow-White away into the wide wood, that I may never see her more." Then the servant led Snow-White away; but his heart melted when she begged him to spare her life, and he said, "I will not hurt thee, thou pretty child." So he left her by herself, and though he thought it most likely that the wild beasts would tear her in pieces, he felt as if a great weight were taken off his heart when he had made up his mind not to kill her, but leave her to her fate.

Then poor Snow-White wandered along through the wood in great fear; and the wild beasts roared about her, but none did her any harm. In the evening she came to a little cottage, and went in there to rest herself, for her little feet would carry her no further. Everything was spruce and neat in the cottage. On the table was spread a white cloth, and there were seven little plates with seven little loaves, and seven little glasses, and knives and forks laid in order; and by the wall stood seven little beds. Then, as she was very hungry, she picked a little piece off each loaf, and drank a very little from each glass; and after that she thought she would lie down and rest. So she tried all the little beds; and one was

too long, and another was too short, till at last the seventh suited her; and there she laid herself down, and went to sleep.

Presently in came the masters of the cottage, who were seven little dwarfs that lived among the mountains, and dug and searched about for gold. They lighted up their seven lamps, and saw directly that all was not right. The first said, "Who has been sitting on my stool?" The second, "Who has been eating off my plate?" The third, "Who has been picking my bread?" The fourth, "Who has been meddling with my spoon?" The fifth, "Who has been handling my fork?" The sixth, "Who has been cutting with my knife?" The seventh, "Who has been drinking from my glass?" Then the first looked round and said, "Who has been lying on my bed?" And the rest came running to him, and every one cried out that somebody had been upon his bed. But the seventh saw Snow-White, and called all his brethren to come and see her; and they cried out with wonder and astonishment, and brought their lamps to look at her, and said, "Oh, what a lovely child she is!" And they were delighted to see her, and took care not to wake her; and the seventh dwarf slept an hour with each of the other dwarfs in turn, till the night was gone.

In the morning Snow-White told them all her story; and they pitied her, and said if she would keep all things in order, and cook and wash, and knit and spin for them, she might stay where she was, and they would take good care of her. Then they went out all day long to their work, seeking for gold and silver in the mountains; and Snow-White remained at home; and they warned her,

and said, "The queen will soon find out where you are, so take care and let no one in."

But the queen, now that she thought Snow-White was dead, believed that she was certainly the handsomest lady in the land; and she went to her mirror and said,

"Mirror, Mirror on the wall
Who is fairest of us all?"

And the mirror answered,

"Queen, thou art of beauty rare,
But Snow-White living in the glen
With the seven little men,
Is a thousand times more fair."

Then the queen was very much alarmed; for she knew that the glass always spoke the truth, and was sure that the servant had betrayed her. And she could not bear to think that any one lived who was more beautiful than she was; so she disguised herself as an old pedlar and went her way over the hills to the place where the dwarfs dwelt. Then she knocked at the door, and cried, "Fine wares to sell!" Snow-White looked out at the window, and said, "Good-day, good-woman; what have you to sell?" "Good wares, fine wares," said she; "laces and bobbins of all colors." "I will let the old lady in; she seems to be a very good sort of body," thought Snow-White; so she ran down, and unbolted the door. "Bless me!" said the old woman, "how badly your stays are laced! Let me lace them up with one of my nice new laces." Snow-White did not dream of any mischief; so she stood up before the old woman, who set to work so nimbly, and pulled the lace so tight, that Snow-White lost her breath, and fell down as if she were dead. "There's an end of all thy beauty," said the spiteful queen, and went away home.

In the evening the seven dwarfs returned; and I need not say how grieved they were to see their faithful Snow-White stretched upon the ground motionless, as if she were quite dead. However, they lifted her up, and when they found what was the matter, they cut the lace; and in a little time she began to breathe, and soon came to life again. Then they said, "The old woman was the queen herself; take care another time, and let no one in when we are away."

When the queen got home, she went straight to her glass, and spoke to it as usual; but to her great surprise it still said,

"Queen, thou art of beauty rare,
But Snow-White living in the glen
With the seven little men,
Is a thousand times more fair."

Then the blood ran cold in her heart with spite and malice to see that Snow-White still lived; and she dressed herself up again in a disguise, but very different from the one she wore before, and took with her a poisoned comb. When she reached the dwarfs' cottage, she knocked at the door, and cried, "Fine wares to sell!" But Snow-White said, "I dare not let any one in." Then the queen said, "Only look at my beautiful combs"; and gave her the poisoned one. And it looked so pretty that Snow-White took it up and put it into her hair to try it. But the moment it touched her head the poison was so powerful that she fell down senseless. "There you may lie," said the queen, and went her way. But by good luck the dwarfs returned very early that evening, and when they saw Snow-White lying on the ground, they guessed what had happened, and soon found the poisoned comb. When they took it away, she recovered, and told them all that had passed; and they warned her once more not to open the door to any one.

Meantime the queen went home to her glass, and trembled with rage when she received exactly the same answer as before; and she said, "Snow-White shall die, if it costs me my life." So she went secretly into a chamber, and prepared a poisoned apple. The outside looked very rosy and tempting, but whoever tasted it was sure to die. Then she dressed herself up as a peasant's wife, and travelled over the hills to the dwarfs' cottage, and knocked at the door; but Snow-White put her head out of the window and said, "I dare not let any one in, for the dwarfs have told me not." "Do as you please," said the old woman, "but at any rate take this pretty apple; I will make you a present of it." "No," said Snow-White, "I dare not take it." "You silly girl!" answered the other, "what are you afraid of? Do you think it is poisoned? Come! Do you eat one part, and I will eat the other." Now the apple was so prepared that one side was good, though the other side was poisoned. Then Snow-White was very much tempted to taste, for the apple looked exceedingly nice; and when she saw the old woman eat, she could refrain no longer. But she had scarcely put the piece into her mouth, when she fell down dead upon the ground. "This time nothing will save you," said the queen; and she went home to her glass and at last it said,

"Thou, queen, art the fairest of them all."

And then her envious heart was glad, and as happy as such a heart could be.

When evening came, and the dwarfs returned home, they found Snow-White lying on the ground. No breath passed her lips, and they were afraid that she was quite dead. They lifted her up, and combed her hair, and washed her face with water; but all was in vain, for the little girl seemed quite dead. So they laid her down upon a bier, and all seven watched and bewailed her three whole days; and then they proposed to bury her; but her cheeks were still rosy, and her face looked just as it did while she was alive; so they said, "We will never bury her in the cold ground." And they made a coffin of glass, so that they might still look at her, and wrote her name upon it, in golden letters, and that she was a king's daughter. And the coffin was placed upon the hill, and one of the dwarfs always sat by it and watched. And the birds of the air came too, and bemoaned Snow-White; first of all came an owl, and then a raven, but at last came a dove.

And thus Snow-White lay for a long, long time, and still looked as though she were only asleep; for she was even now as white as snow, and as red as blood, and as black as ebony. At last a prince came and called at the dwarfs' house; and he saw Snow-White, and read what was written in golden letters. Then he offered the dwarfs money, and earnestly prayed them to let him take her away; but they said, "We will not part with her for all the gold in the world." At last, however, they had pity on him, and gave him the coffin; but the moment he lifted it up to carry it home with him, the piece of apple fell from between her lips, and Snow-White awoke, and said, "Where am I?" And the prince an-

swered, "Thou art safe with me." Then he told her all that had happened, and said, "I love you better than all the world. Come with me to my father's palace, and you shall be my wife." And Snow-White consented, and went home with the prince; and everything was prepared with great pomp and splendour for their wedding.

To the feast was invited, among the rest, Snow-White's old enemy, the queen; and as she was dressing herself in fine rich clothes, she looked in the glass, and said,

"Mirror, Mirror on the wall,
Who is fairest of us all?"

And the glass answered,

"O Queen, although you are of beauty rare
The young queen is a thousand times more
fair."

When she heard this, she started with rage; but her envy and curiosity were so great, that she could not help setting out to see the bride. And when she arrived, and saw that it was no other than Snow-White, who, as she thought, had been dead a long while, she choked with passion, and fell ill and died. But Snow-White and the prince lived and reigned happily over that land many, many years.

## THE FISHERMAN AND HIS WIFE

*There is another version of the rhyme, by Wanda Gág, that goes: "Manye, Manye, Timpie Tee,/Fishye, Fishye in the sea,/Ilsebill my wilful wife/Does not want my way of life." Try that to create a somber spell in the telling. You may want to cut an episode or two from the story to keep it from seeming unduly long. Its moral has a lifelong application.*

There was once upon a time a Fisherman who lived with his wife in a miserable hovel close by the sea, and every day he went out fishing. And once as he was sitting with his rod, looking at the clear water, his line suddenly went down, far

"The Fisherman and His Wife." From *Grimm's Household Tales,* translated by Margaret Hunt down below, and when he drew it up again, he brought out a large Flounder. Then the Flounder said to him, "Hark you, Fisherman, I pray you, let me live. I am no Flounder really, but an enchanted prince. What good will it do you to kill me? I should not be good to eat. Put me in the water again, and let me go." "Come," said the Fisherman, "there is no need for so many words about it—a fish that can talk I should certainly let go, anyhow." With that he put him back again into the clear water, and the Flounder went to the bottom, leaving a long streak of blood behind him. Then the Fisherman got up and went home to his wife in the hovel.

"Husband," said the woman, "have you caught nothing to-day?" "No," said the man, "I did catch a Flounder, who said he was an enchanted prince, so I let him go again," "Did you not wish for anything first?" said the woman. "No," said the man; "what should I wish for?" "Ah," said the woman, "it is surely hard to have to live always in this dirty hovel; you might have wished for a small cottage for us. Go back and call him. Tell him we want to have a small cottage; he will certainly give us that." "Ah," said the man, "why should I go there again?" "Why," said the woman, "you did catch him, and you let him go again; he is sure to do it. Go at once." The man still did not quite like to go, but did not like to oppose his wife either, and went to the sea.

When he got there the sea was all green and yellow, and no longer so smooth; so he stood and said,

> "Flounder, flounder in the sea,
>   Come, I pray thee, here to me;
>   For my wife, good Ilsabil,
>   Wills not as I'd have her will."

Then the Flounder came swimming to him and said: "Well, what does she want then?" "Ah," said the man, "I did catch you, and my wife says I really ought to have wished for something. She does not like to live in a wretched hovel any longer; she would like to have a cottage." "Go, then," said the Flounder, "she has it already."

When the man went home, his wife was no longer in the hovel, but instead of it there stood a small cottage, and she was sitting on a bench be-

fore the door. Then she took him by the hand and said to him, "Just come inside. Look, now isn't this a great deal better?" So they went in, and there was a small porch, and a pretty little parlour and bedroom, and a kitchen and pantry, with the best of furniture, and fitted up with the most beautiful things made of tin and brass, whatsoever was wanted. And behind the cottage there was a small yard, with hens and ducks, and a little garden with flowers and fruit. "Look," said the wife, "is not that nice!" "Yes," said the husband, "and so we must always think it—now we will live quite contented." "We will think about that," said the wife. With that they ate something and went to bed.

Everything went well for a week or a fortnight, and then the woman said, "Hark you, husband, this cottage is far too small for us, and the garden and yard are little; the Flounder might just as well have given us a larger house. I should like to live in a great stone castle; go to the Flounder, and tell him to give us a castle." "Ah, wife," said the man, "the cottage is quite good enough; why should we live in a castle?" "What!" said the woman; "just go there, the Flounder can always do that." "No, wife," said the man, "the Flounder has just given us the cottage. I do not like to go back so soon; it might make him angry." "Go," said the woman, "he can do it quite easily, and will be glad to do it; just you go to him."

The man's heart grew heavy, and he would not go. He said to himself, "It is not right," and yet he went. And when he came to the sea the water was quite purple and dark-blue, and grey and thick, and no longer so green and yellow, but it was still quiet. And he stood there and said,

> "Flounder, flounder in the sea,
>   Come, I pray thee, here to me;
>   For my wife, good Ilsabil,
>   Wills not as I'd have her will."

"Well, what does she want, then?" said the Flounder. "Alas," said the man, half scared, "she wants to live in a great stone castle." "Go to it, then, she is standing before the door," said the Flounder.

Then the man went away, intending to go home, but when he got there, he found a great stone palace, and his wife was just standing on the steps going in, and she took him by the hand and said: "Come in." So he went in with her, and in the castle was a great hall paved with marble, and many servants, who flung wide the doors; and the walls were all bright with beautiful hangings, and in the rooms were chairs and tables of pure gold, and crystal chandeliers hung from the ceiling, and all the rooms and bedrooms had carpets, and food and wine of the very best were standing on all the tables, so that they nearly broke down beneath it. Behind the house, too, there was a great court-yard, with stables for horses and cows, and the very best of carriages; there was a magnificent large garden, too, with the most beautiful flowers and fruit-trees, and a park quite half a mile long, in which were stags, deer, and hares, and everything that could be desired. "Come," said the woman, "isn't that beautiful?" "Yes, indeed," said the man, "now let it be; and we will live in this beautiful castle and be content." "We will consider about that," said the woman, "and sleep upon it"; thereupon they went to bed.

Next morning the wife awoke first, and it was just daybreak, and from her bed she saw the beautiful country lying before her. Her husband was still stretching himself, so she poked him in the side with her elbow, and said, "Get up, husband, and just peep out of the window. Look you, couldn't we be the King over all that land? Go to the Flounder; we will be the King." "Ah, wife," said the man, "why should we be King? I do not want to be King." "Well," said the wife, "if you won't be King, I will; go to the Flounder, for I will be King." "Ah, wife," said the man, "why do you want to be King? I do not like to say that to him." "Why not?" said the woman; "go to him this instant; I must be King!" So the man went, and was quite unhappy because his wife wished to be King. "It is not right; it is not right," thought he. He did not wish to go, but yet he went.

And when he came to the sea, it was quite dark-grey, and the water heaved up from below, and smelt putrid. Then he went and stood by it, and said,

"Flounder, flounder in the sea,
Come, I pray thee, here to me;

For my wife, good Ilsabil,
Wills not as I'd have her will."

"Well, what does she want, then?" said the Flounder. "Alas," said the man, "she wants to be King." "Go to her; she is King already."

So the man went, and when he came to the palace, the castle had become much larger, and had a great tower and magnificent ornaments, and the sentinel was standing before the door, and there were numbers of soldiers with kettle-drums and trumpets. And when he went inside the house, everything was of real marble and gold, with velvet covers and great golden tassels. Then the doors of the hall were opened, and there was the court in all its splendour, and his wife was sitting on a high throne of gold and diamonds, with a great crown of gold on her head, and a sceptre of pure gold and jewels in her hand, and on both sides of her stood her maids-in-waiting in a row, each of them always one head shorter than the last.

Then he went and stood before her, and said: "Ah, wife, and now you are King." "Yes," said the woman, "now I am King." So he stood and looked at her, and when he had looked at her thus for some time, he said, "And now that you are King, let all else be. Now we will wish for nothing more." "No, husband," said the woman, quite anxiously, "I find time passes very heavily. I can bear it no longer. Go to the Flounder—I am King, but I must be Emperor, too." "Oh, wife, why do you wish to be Emperor?" "Husband," said she, "go to the Flounder. I will be Emperor." "Alas, wife," said the man, "he cannot make you Emperor; I may not say that to the fish. There is only one Emperor in the land. An Emperor the Flounder cannot make you! I assure you he cannot."

"What!" said the woman, "I am the King, and you are nothing but my husband; will you go this moment? Go at once! If he can make a king he can make an emperor. I will be Emperor; go instantly." So he was forced to go. As the man went, however, he was troubled in mind, and thought to himself: "It will not end well; it will not end well! Emperor is too shameless! The Flounder will at last be tired out."

With that he reached the sea, and the sea was quite black and thick, and began to boil up from below, so that it threw up bubbles, and such a sharp wind blew over it that it curdled, and the man was afraid. Then he went and stood by it, and said,

"Flounder, flounder in the sea,
Come, I pray thee, here to me;
For my wife, good Ilsabil,
Wills not as I'd have her will."

"Well, what does she want, then?" said the Flounder. "Alas, Flounder," said he, "my wife wants to be Emperor." "Go to her," said the Flounder; "she is Emperor already."

So the man went, and when he got there the whole palace was made of polished marble with alabaster figures and golden ornaments, and soldiers were marching before the door blowing trumpets, and beating cymbals and drums; and in the house, barons, and counts, and dukes were going about as servants. Then they opened the doors to him, which were of pure gold. And when he entered, there sat his wife on a throne, which was made of one piece of gold, and was quite two miles high; and she wore a great golden crown that was three yards high, and set with diamonds and carbuncles, and in one hand she had the sceptre, and in the other the imperial orb; and on both sides of her stood the yeomen of the guard in two rows, each being smaller than the one before him, from the biggest giant, who was two miles high, to the very smallest dwarf, just as big as my little finger. And before it stood a number of princes and dukes.

Then the man went and stood among them, and said, "Wife, are you Emperor now?" "Yes," said she, "now I am Emperor." Then he stood and looked at her well, and when he had looked at her thus for some time, he said, "Ah, wife, be content, now that you are Emperor." "Husband," said she, "why are you standing there? Now, I am Emperor, but I will be Pope too; go to the Flounder." "Oh, wife," said the man, "what will you not wish for? You cannot be Pope; there is but one in Christendom; he cannot make you Pope." "Husband," said she, "I will be Pope. Go immediately; I must be Pope this very day." "No, wife," said the man, "I do not like to say that to him; that would not do. It

is too much; the Flounder can't make you Pope." "Husband," said she, "what nonsense! If he can make an emperor, he can make a pope. Go to him directly. I am Emperor, and you are nothing but my husband; will you go at once?"

Then he was afraid and went; but he was quite faint, and shivered and shook, and his knees and legs trembled. And a high wind blew over the land, and the clouds flew, and towards evening all grew dark, and the leaves fell from the trees, and the water rose and roared as if it were boiling, and splashed upon the shore; and in the distance he saw ships which were firing guns in their sore need, pitching and tossing on the waves. And yet in the midst of the sky there was still a small bit of blue, though on every side it was as red as in a heavy storm. So, full of despair, he went and stood in much fear and said,

"Flounder, flounder in the sea,
Come, I pray thee, here to me;
For my wife, good Ilsabil,
Wills not as I'd have her will."

"Well, what does she want, now?" said the Flounder. "Alas," said the man, "she wants to be Pope." "Go to her then," said the Flounder; "she is Pope already."

So he went, and when he got there, he saw what seemed to be a large church surrounded by palaces. He pushed his way through the crowd. Inside, however, everything was lighted up with thousands and thousands of candles, and his wife was clad in gold, and she was sitting on a much higher throne, and had three great golden crowns on, and round about her there was much ecclesiastical splendour; and on both sides of her was a row of candles the largest of which was as tall as the very tallest tower, down to the very smallest kitchen candle, and all the emperors and kings were on their knees before her, kissing her shoe. "Wife," said the man, and looked attentively at her, "are you now Pope?" "Yes," said she, "I am Pope." So he stood and looked at her, and it was just as if he was looking at the bright sun. When he had stood looking at her thus for a short time, he said: "Ah, wife, if you are Pope, do let well alone!" But she looked as stiff as a post, and did not move or show any signs of life. Then said he, "Wife, now that you are Pope, be satisfied; you cannot become anything greater now." "I will consider about that," said the woman. Thereupon they both went to bed, but she was not satisfied, and greediness let her have no sleep, for she was continually thinking what there was left for her to be.

The man slept well and soundly, for he had run about a great deal during the day; but the woman could not fall asleep at all, and flung herself from one side to the other the whole night through, thinking always what more was left for her to be, but unable to call to mind anything else. At length the sun began to rise, and when the woman saw the red of dawn, she sat up in bed and looked at it. And when, through the window, she saw the sun thus rising, she said, "Cannot I, too, order the sun and moon to rise?" "Husband," she said, poking him in the ribs with her elbows, "wake up! Go to the Flounder, for I wish to be even as God is." The man was still half asleep, but he was so horrified that he fell out of bed. He thought he must have heard amiss, and rubbed his eyes, and said, "Alas, wife, what are you saying?" "Husband," said she, "if I can't order the sun and moon to rise, and have to look on and see the sun and moon rising, I can't bear it. I shall not know what it is to have another happy hour, unless I can make them rise myself." Then she looked at him so terribly that a shudder ran over him, and said, "Go at once; I wish to be like unto God." "Alas, wife," said the man, falling on his knees before her, "the Flounder cannot do that; he can make an emperor and a pope; I beseech you, go on as you are, and be Pope." Then she fell into a rage, and her hair flew wildly about her head, and she cried, "I will not endure this, I'll not bear it any longer; will you go this instant?" Then he put on his trousers and ran away like a madman. But outside a great storm was raging, and blowing so hard that he could scarcely keep his feet; houses and trees toppled over, the mountains trembled, rocks rolled into the sea, the sky was pitch black, and it thundered and lightened, and the sea came in with black waves as high as church-towers and mountains, and all with crests of white foam at the top. Then he cried, but could not hear his own words,

> "Flounder, flounder in the sea,
> Come, I pray thee, here to me;

> For my wife, good Ilsabil,
> Wills not as I'd have her will."

"Well, what does she want, then?" said the Flounder. "Alas," said he, "she wants to be like unto God." "Go to her, and you will find her back again in the dirty hovel." And there they are still living to this day.

## RUMPELSTILTZKIN

*This makes a splendid story for dramatization with puppets, either string puppets or hand. The children can cast the story into acts, line up their characters, and as they make the puppets, try out the dialogue with them. With children under ten years old, hand puppets are easier to make and the dialogue is usually kept fluid. Children over ten may want to write parts of their dialogue or all of it.*

There was once upon a time a poor miller who had a very beautiful daughter. Now it happened one day that he had an audience with the King, and in order to appear a person of some importance he told him that he had a daughter who could spin straw into gold.

"Now that's a talent worth having," said the King to the miller. "If your daughter is as clever as you say, bring her to my palace to-morrow, and I'll put her to the test."

When the girl was brought to him he led her into a room full of straw, gave her a spinning-wheel and spindle, and said: "Now set to work and spin all night till early dawn, and if by that time you haven't spun the straw into gold you shall die." Then he closed the door behind him and left her alone inside.

So the poor miller's daughter sat down, and didn't know what in the world she was to do. She hadn't the least idea of how to spin straw into gold, and became at last so miserable that she began to cry.

Suddenly the door opened, and in stepped a

"Rumpelstiltzkin." From *The Blue Fairy Book,* edited by Andrew Lang. Longmans, Green, and Co., London, 1889

tiny little man and said: "Good-evening, Miss Miller-maid; why are you crying so bitterly?"

"Oh!" answered the girl, "I have to spin straw into gold, and haven't a notion how it's done."

"What will you give me if I spin it for you?" asked the manikin.

"My necklace," replied the girl.

The little man took the necklace, sat himself down at the wheel, and whir, whir, whir, the wheel went round three times, and the bobbin was full. Then he put on another, and whir, whir, whir, the wheel went round three times, and the second too was full; and so it went on till the morning, when all the straw was spun away, and all the bobbins were full of gold.

As soon as the sun rose the King came, and when he perceived the gold he was astonished and delighted, but his heart only lusted more than ever after the precious metal. He had the miller's daughter put into another room full of straw, much bigger than the first, and bade her, if she valued her life, spin it all into gold before the following morning.

The girl didn't know what to do, and began to cry; then the door opened as before, and the tiny little man appeared and said: "What'll you give me if I spin the straw into gold for you?"

"The ring from my finger," answered the girl. The manikin took the ring, and whir! round went the spinning-wheel again, and when morning broke he had spun all the straw into glittering gold.

The King was pleased beyond measure at the sight, but his greed for gold was still not satisfied, and he had the miller's daughter brought into a yet bigger room full of straw, and said: "You must spin all this away in the night; but if you succeed this time you shall become my wife."

"She's only a miller's daughter, it's true," he thought; "but I couldn't find a richer wife if I were to search the whole world over."

When the girl was alone the little man appeared for the third time, and said: "What'll you give me if I spin the straw for you once again?"

"I've nothing more to give," answered the girl.

"Then promise me when you are Queen to give me your first child."

"Who knows what mayn't happen before that?" thought the miller's daughter; and besides, she saw no other way out of it, so she promised the manikin what he demanded, and he set to work once more and spun the straw into gold. When the King came in the morning, and found everything as he had desired, he straightway made her his wife, and the miller's daughter became a queen.

When a year had passed a beautiful son was born to her, and she thought no more of the little man, till all of a sudden one day he stepped into her room and said, "Now give me what you promised." The Queen was in a great state, and offered the little man all the riches in her kingdom if he would only leave her the child.

But the manikin said: "No, a living creature is dearer to me than all the treasures in the world."

Then the Queen began to cry and sob so bitterly that the little man was sorry for her, and said: "I'll give you three days to guess my name, and if you find it out in that time you may keep your child."

Then the Queen pondered the whole night over all the names she had ever heard, and sent a messenger to scour the land and to pick up far and near any names he should come across. When the little man arrived on the following day she began with Kasper, Melchior, Belshazzar, and all the other names she knew, in a string, but at each one the manikin called out, "That's not my name."

The next day she sent to inquire the names of all the people in the neighbourhood, and had a long list of the most uncommon and extraordinary for the little man when he made his appearance. "Is your name, perhaps, Sheepshanks, Cruickshanks, Spindleshanks?"

But he always replied, "That's not my name."

On the third day the messenger returned and announced: "I have not been able to find any new names, but as I came upon a high hill round the corner of the wood, where the foxes and hares bid each other good night, I saw a little house, and in front of the house burned a fire, and round the fire sprang the most grotesque little man, hopping on one leg and crying:

'To-morrow I brew, to-day I bake,
And then the child away I'll take;
For little deems my royal dame
That Rumpelstiltzkin is my name!' "

You may imagine the Queen's delight at hearing the name, and when the little man stepped in shortly afterwards and asked, "Now, my lady Queen, what's my name?" she asked first: "Is your name Conrad?"

"No."

"Is your name Harry?"

"No."

"Is your name, perhaps, Rumpelstiltzkin?"

"Some demon has told you that, some demon has told you that," screamed the little man, and in his rage drove his right foot so far into the ground that it sank in up to his waist. Then in a passion he seized the left foot with both hands and tore himself in two.

# THE ELVES
## AND THE SHOEMAKER

*This story has an excellent plot and appears in similar form in many lands, but the style here is rather dull, unless one turns the narrative into direct conversation. It lends itself well to simple dramatization or to a puppet play. Adrienne Adams' The Shoemaker and the Elves gives it added charm and substance as a picture story.*

There was once a shoemaker who worked very hard and was very honest; but still he could not earn enough to live upon, and at last all he had in the world was gone, except just leather enough to make one pair of shoes.

Then he cut them all ready to make up the next day, meaning to get up early in the morning to work. His conscience was clear and his heart light amidst all his troubles; so he went peaceably to bed, left all his cares to heaven, and fell asleep.

In the morning, after he had said his prayers, he set himself down to his work, when to his great wonder, there stood the shoes, all ready made, upon the table. The good man knew not what to say or think of this strange event. He looked at the workmanship; there was not one false stitch in the whole job, and all was so neat and true that it was a complete masterpiece.

That same day a customer came in, and the shoes pleased him so well that he willingly paid a price higher than usual for them; and the poor shoemaker with the money bought leather enough to make two pairs more. In the evening he cut out the work, and went to bed early that he might get up and begin betimes next day. But he was saved all the trouble, for when he got up in the morning the work was finished ready to his hand.

Presently in came buyers, who paid him handsomely for his goods, so that he bought leather enough for four pairs more. He cut out the work again over night, and found it finished in the morning as before; and so it went on for some time; what was got ready in the evening was always done by daybreak, and the good man soon

"The Elves and the Shoemaker." From *Grimm's Popular Stories,* translated by Edgar Taylor became thriving and prosperous again.

One evening about Christmas time, as he and his wife were sitting over the fire chatting together, he said to her, "I should like to sit up and watch to-night, that we may see who it is that comes and does my work for me." The wife liked the thought; so they left a light burning, and hid themselves in the corner of the room behind a curtain and watched to see what would happen.

As soon as it was midnight, there came two little naked dwarfs; and they sat themselves upon the shoemaker's bench, took up all the work that was cut out, and began to ply with their little fingers, stitching and rapping and tapping away at such a rate that the shoemaker was all amazement, and could not take his eyes off for a moment. And on they went till the job was quite finished, and the shoes stood ready for use upon the table. This was long before daybreak; and then they bustled away as quick as lightning.

The next day the wife said to the shoemaker, "These little wights have made us rich, and we ought to be thankful to them, and do them a good office in return. I am quite vexed to see them run about as they do; they have nothing upon their backs to keep off the cold. I'll tell you what, I will make each of them a shirt, and a coat and waistcoat, and a pair of pantaloons into the bargain; do you make each of them a little pair of shoes."

The thought pleased the good shoemaker very much; and one evening, when all the things were ready, they laid them on the table instead of the work that they used to cut out, and then went and hid themselves to watch what the little elves would do.

About midnight the elves came in and were going to sit down to their work as usual; but when they saw the clothes lying for them, they

laughed and were greatly delighted. Then they dressed themselves in the twinkling of an eye, and danced and capered and sprang about as merry as could be, till at last they danced out at the door and over the green; and the shoemaker saw them no more; but everything went well with him from that time forward, as long as he lived.

## THE FOUR MUSICIANS

*This story is wonderful to tell, to illustrate, and to dramatize! It has many variants and is universally popular and funny. In another amusing version, the cock crows, "Cuck, cuck, cuck, cucdoo-oo!" and the robber thinks a fellow is calling, "Cut the man in two-oo!" The story lends itself to simple dramatization by six- or seven-year-olds in a classroom, playroom, or yard. A few bandannas will make the robbers, and the animals may be costumed or not, depending upon the formality or spontaneity of the occasion.*

There was once a donkey who had worked for his master faithfully many years, but his strength at last began to fail, and every day he became more and more unfit for work. Finally his master concluded it was no longer worth while to keep him and was thinking of putting an end to him. But the donkey saw that mischief was brewing and he ran away.

"I will go to the city," said he, "and like enough I can get an engagement there as a musician; for though my body has grown weak, my voice is as strong as ever."

So the donkey hobbled along toward the city, but he had not gone far when he spied a dog lying by the roadside and panting as if he had run a long way. "What makes you pant so, my friend?" asked the donkey.

"Alas!" replied the dog, "my master was going to knock me on the head because I am old and weak and can no longer make myself useful to him in hunting. So I ran away; but how am I to gain a living now, I wonder?"

"Hark ye!" said the donkey. "I am going to

"The Four Musicians." From *The Oak Tree Fairy Book*, edited by Clifton Johnson, copyright 1933. Reprinted by permission of Roger Johnson

the city to be a musician. You may as well keep company with me and try what you can do in the same line."

The dog said he was willing, and they went on together. Pretty soon they came to a cat sitting in the middle of the road and looking as dismal as three wet days. "Pray, my good lady," said the donkey, "what is the matter with you, for you seem quite out of spirits?"

"Ah me!" responded the cat, "how can I be cheerful when my life is in danger? I am getting old, my teeth are blunt, and I like sitting by the fire and purring better than chasing the mice about. So this morning my mistress laid hold of me and was going to drown me. I was lucky enough to get away from her; but I do not know what is to become of me, and I'm likely to starve."

"Come with us to the city," said the donkey, "and be a musician. You understand serenading, and with your talent for that you ought to be able to make a very good living."

The cat was pleased with the idea and went along with the donkey and the dog. Soon afterward, as they were passing a farmyard, a rooster flew up on the gate and screamed out with all his might, "Cock-a-doodle-doo!"

"Bravo!" said the donkey, "upon my word you make a famous noise; what is it all about?"

"Oh," replied the rooster, "I was only foretelling fine weather for our washing-day; and that I do every week. But would you believe it! My mistress doesn't thank me for my pains, and she has told the cook that I must be made into broth for the guests that are coming next Sunday."

"Heaven forbid!" exclaimed the donkey; "come with us, Master Chanticleer. It will be better, at any rate, than staying here to have your head cut off. We are going to the city to be musicians; and—who knows?—perhaps the four of us can get up some kind of a concert. You have a good voice, and if we all make music together, it will be something striking. So come along."

"With all my heart," said the cock; and the four went on together.

The city was, however, too far away for them to reach it on the first day of their travelling, and when, toward night, they came to a thick woods, they decided to turn aside from the highway and pass the night among the trees. So they found a dry, sheltered spot at the foot of a great oak and the donkey and dog lay down on the ground beneath it; but the cat climbed up among the branches, and the rooster, thinking the higher he sat the safer he would be, flew up to the very top. Before he went to sleep the rooster looked around him to the four points of the compass to make sure that everything was all right. In so doing he saw in the distance a little light shining, and he called out to his companions, "There must be a house no great way off, for I can see a light."

"If that be the case," said the donkey, "let us get up and go there. Our lodging here is not what I am used to, and the sooner we change it for better the more pleased I shall be."

"Yes," said the dog, "and perhaps I might be able to get a few bones with a little meat on them at that house."

"And very likely I might get some milk," said the cat.

"And there ought to be some scraps of food for me," said the rooster.

So the cat and the rooster came down out of the tree and they all walked off with Chanticleer in the lead toward the spot where he had seen the light.

At length they drew near the house, and the donkey, being the tallest of the company, went up to the lighted window and looked in.

"Well, what do you see?" asked the dog.

"What do I see?" answered the donkey. "I see that this is a robber's house. There are swords and pistols and blunderbusses on the walls, and there are chests of money on the floor, and all sorts of other plunder lying about. The robbers are sitting at a table that is loaded with the best of eatables and drinkables, and they are making themselves very comfortable and merry."

"Those eatables and drinkables would just suit us," declared the rooster.

"Yes, indeed they would," said the donkey, "if we could only get at them; but that will never be, unless we can contrive to drive away the robbers first."

Then they consulted together and at last hit on a plan. The donkey stood on his hind legs with his forefeet on the window-sill, the dog got on the donkey's shoulders, the cat mounted the back of the dog, and the rooster flew up and perched on the back of the cat. When all was ready they began their music.

"Hehaw! hehaw! hehaw!" brayed the donkey.

"Bow-wow! bow-wow!" barked the dog.

"Meow! meow!" said the cat.

"Cock-a-doodle-doo!" crowed the rooster.

Then they all burst through the window into the room, breaking the glass with a frightful clatter. The robbers, not doubting that some hideous hobgoblin was about to devour them, fled to the woods in great terror.

The donkey and his comrades now sat down at the table and made free with the food the robbers had left, and feasted as if they had been hungry for a month. When they had finished they put out the lights and each sought a sleeping-place to his own liking. The donkey laid himself down on some straw in the yard, the dog stretched himself on a mat just inside the door, the cat curled up on the hearth near the warm ashes, and the rooster flew up on the roof and settled himself on the ridge beside the chimney. They were all tired and soon fell fast asleep.

About midnight the robbers came creeping back to the house. They saw that no lights were burning and everything seemed quiet. "Well, well," said the robber captain, "we need not have been so hasty. I think we ran away without reason. But we will be cautious. The rest of you stay here while I go and find out if we are likely to have any more trouble."

So he stepped softly along to the house and entered the kitchen. There he groped about until he found a candle and some matches on the mantel over the fireplace. The cat had now waked up and stood on the hearth watching the robber with shining eyes. He mistook those eyes for two live coals and reached down to get a light by touching a match to them. The cat did not fancy that sort of thing and flew into his face, spitting and scratching. Then he cried out in fright and ran toward the door, and the dog, who was lying there, bit the robber's leg. He managed, however, to get out in the yard, and there the donkey struck out with a hind foot and gave him a kick that knocked him down, and Chanticleer who had been roused by the noise, cried out "Cock-a-doodle-doo! Cock-a-doodle-doo!"

The robber captain had barely strength to crawl away to the other robbers. "We cannot live at that house any more," said he. "In the kitchen is a grewsome witch, and I felt her hot breath and her long nails on my face, and by the door there stood a man who stabbed me in the leg, and in the yard is a black giant who beat me with a club, and on the roof is a little fellow who kept shouting, 'Chuck him up to me! Chuck him up to me!'"

So the robbers went away and never came back, and the four musicians found themselves so well pleased with their new quarters that they did not go to the city, but stayed where they were; and I dare say you would find them there at this very day.

## MOTHER HOLLE

*One little girl approved the justice of the conclusion of this tale by remarking sternly, "It served that girl right to get pitch on her. She was a real mean girl." This tale may easily be traced from one of its earliest appearances in print (in Perrault's collection of French fairy tales in 1697) to English folklore and on to the Appalachian and Ozark mountains of the United States where, in one version from Arkansas, it is called "The Good Girl and the Ornery Girl."*

There was once a widow who had two daughters—one of whom was pretty and industrious, whilst the other was ugly and idle. But she was much fonder of the ugly and idle one, because she was her own daughter; and the other, who was a step-daughter, was obliged to do all the work, and be the Cinderella of the house. Every day the poor girl had to sit by a well, in the highway, and spin and spin till her fingers bled.

Now it happened that one day the shuttle was marked with her blood, so she dipped it in the well, to wash the mark off; but it dropped out of her hand and fell to the bottom. She began to weep, and ran to her step-mother and told her of the mishap. But she scolded her sharply, and was so merciless as to say, "Since you have let the shuttle fall in, you must fetch it out again."

"Mother Holle." From *Grimm's Household Tales*, translated by Margaret Hunt

So the girl went back to the well, and did not know what to do; and in the sorrow of her heart she jumped into the well to get the shuttle. She lost her senses; and when she awoke and came to herself again, she was in a lovely meadow where the sun was shining and many thousands of flowers were growing. Across this meadow she went, and at last came to a baker's oven full of bread, and the bread cried out, "Oh, take me out! take me out! or I shall burn; I have been baked a long time!" So she went up to it, and took out all the loaves one after another with the bread-shovel. After that she went on till she came to a tree covered with apples, which called out to her, "Oh, shake me! shake me! we apples are all ripe!" So she shook the tree till the apples fell like rain, and went on shaking till they were all down, and when she had gathered them into a heap, she went on her way.

At last she came to a little house, out of which an old woman peeped; but she had such large teeth that the girl was frightened, and was about to run away. But the old woman called out to her, "What are you afraid of, dear child? Stay with me; if you will do all the work in the house properly, you shall be the better for it. Only you must take care to make my bed well, and to shake it thoroughly till the feathers fly—for then there is snow on the earth. I am Mother Holle."

As the old woman spoke so kindly to her, the girl took courage and agreed to enter her service. She attended to everything to the satisfaction of her mistress, and always shook her bed so vigorously that the feathers flew about like snowflakes. So she had a pleasant life with her; never an angry word; and to eat she had boiled or roast meat every day.

She stayed some time with Mother Holle, before she became sad. At first she did not know what was the matter with her, but found at length that it was home-sickness: although she was many thousand times better off here than at home, still she had a longing to be there. At last she said to the old woman: "I have a longing for home; and however well off I am down here, I cannot stay any longer; I must go up again to my own people." Mother Holle said, "I am pleased that you long for your home again, and as you have served me so truly, I myself will take you up again." Thereupon she took her by the hand, and led her to a large door. The door was opened, and just as the maiden was standing beneath the doorway, a heavy shower of golden rain fell, and all the gold remained sticking to her, so that she was completely covered over with it.

"You shall have that because you have been so industrious," said Mother Holle; and at the same time she gave her back the shuttle which she had let fall into the well. Thereupon the door closed, and the maiden found herself up above upon the earth, not far from her mother's house.

And as she went into the yard the cock was sitting on the well, and cried——

> "Cock-a-doodle-doo!
> Your golden girl's come back to you!"

So she went in to her mother, and as she arrived thus covered with gold, she was well received, both by her and her sister.

The girl told all that had happened to her; and as soon as the mother heard how she had come by so much wealth, she was very anxious to obtain the same good luck for the ugly and lazy daughter. She had to seat herself by the well and spin; and in order that her shuttle might be stained with blood, she stuck her hand into a thorn bush and pricked her finger. Then she threw her shuttle into the well, and jumped in after it.

She came, like the other, to the beautiful meadow and walked along the very same path. When she got to the oven the bread again cried, "Oh, take me out! take me out! or I shall burn; I have been baked a long time!" But the lazy thing answered, "As if I had any wish to make myself dirty!" and on she went. Soon she came to the apple-tree, which cried, "Oh, shake me! shake me! we apples are all ripe!" But she answered, "I like that! one of you might fall on my head," and so went on.

When she came to Mother Holle's house she was not afraid, for she had already heard of her big teeth, and she hired herself to her immediately.

The first day she forced herself to work diligently, and obeyed Mother Holle when she told her to do anything, for she was thinking of all the gold that she would give her. But on the second day she began to be lazy, and on the third day still more so, and then she would not get up in the morning at all. Neither did she make Mother Holle's bed as she ought, and did not shake it so as to make the feathers fly up. Mother Holle was soon tired of this, and gave her notice to leave. The lazy girl was willing enough to go, and thought that now the golden rain would come. Mother Holle led her also to the great door; but while she was standing beneath it, instead of the gold a big kettleful of pitch was emptied over her. "That is the reward for your service," said Mother Holle, and shut the door.

So the lazy girl went home; but she was quite covered with pitch, and the cock by the well-side, as soon as he saw her, cried out——

"Cock-a-doodle-doo!
Your pitchy girl's come back to you!"

But the pitch stuck fast to her, and could not be got off as long as she lived.

## RAPUNZEL

*When it is well told, this grave, romantic tale creates a somber spell that lingers long after the final lines have been spoken.*

In a little German village lived a man and his wife. They had long wished for a child, and now at last they had reason to hope that their wish would be granted.

In their back yard was a shed which looked out upon their neighbor's garden. Often the woman would stand and look at this garden, for it was well kept and flourishing, and had lovely flowers and luscious vegetables laid out in the most tempting manner. The garden was surrounded by a high stone wall but, wall or no wall, there was not much danger of any one entering it. This was because it belonged to Mother Gothel, who was a powerful witch and was feared in all the land.

One summer's day, as the witch's garden was at its very best, the woman was again gazing from the window of her little shed. She feasted her eyes on the gay array of flowers, and she looked longingly at the many kinds of vegetables which were growing there. Her mouth watered as her eyes traveled from the long, crisp beans to the fat, green peas; from the cucumbers to the crinkly lettuce; from the carrots to the waving turnip tops. But when her glance fell upon a fine big bed of rampion (which in that country is called *rapunzel*) a strange feeling came over her. She had always been fond of rampion salad, and these plants in the witch's garden looked so fresh, so green, so tempting, that she felt she must have some, no matter what the cost.

But then she thought to herself, "It's no use. No one can ever get any of the witch's vegetables. I might as well forget about it."

Still, try as she would, she could not, could not forget. Every day she looked at the fresh green rampion, and every day her longing for it increased. She grew thinner and thinner, and began to look pale and miserable.

Her husband soon noticed this, and said, "Dear wife, what is the matter with you?"

"Oh," said she, "I have a strange desire for some of that rampion in Mother Gothel's garden, and unless I get some, I fear I shall die."

At this the husband became alarmed and as he loved her dearly, he said to himself, "Before you let your wife die, you'll get her some of those

"Rapunzel." Reprinted by permission of Coward, McCann & Geoghegan, Inc. from *Tales From Grimm* by Wanda Gág. Copyright 1936 by Wanda Gág. Copyright renewed

plants, no matter what the risk or cost."

Therefore, that evening at twilight, he climbed over the high wall and into the witch's garden. Quickly he dug up a handful of rampion plants and brought them to his ailing wife. She was overjoyed, and immediately made a big juicy salad which she ate with great relish, one might almost say with greed.

In fact she enjoyed it so much that, far from being satisfied, her desire for the forbidden vegetable had now increased threefold. And although she looked rosier and stronger after she had eaten the rampion salad, in a few days she became pale and frail once more.

There was nothing for the man to do but go over to the witch's garden again; and so he went, at twilight as before. He had reached the rampion patch and was about to reach out for the plants, when he stopped short, horrified. Before him stood the witch, old Mother Gothel herself!

"Oh, Mother Gothel," said the man, "please be merciful with me. I am not really a thief and have only done this to save a life. My wife saw your rampion from that window yonder, and now her longing for it is so strange and strong that I fear she will die if she cannot get some of it to eat."

At this the witch softened a little and said, "If it is as you say, I will let you take as many of the plants as are needed to make her healthy again. But only on one condition: when your first child is born, you must give it to me. I won't hurt it and will care for it like a mother."

The man had been so frightened that he hardly knew what he was doing, and so in his terror, he made this dreadful promise.

Soon after this, the wife became the mother of a beautiful baby girl, and in a short time Mother Gothel came and claimed the child according to the man's promise. Neither the woman's tears nor the man's entreaties could make the witch change her mind. She lifted the baby out of its cradle and took it away with her. She called the girl Rapunzel after those very plants in her garden which had been the cause of so much trouble.

Rapunzel was a winsome child, with long luxuriant tresses, fine as spun gold. When she was twelve years old, the witch took her off to the woods and shut her up in a high tower. It had neither door nor staircase but at its very top was one tiny window. Whenever Mother Gothel came to visit the girl, she stood under this window and called:

Rapunzel, Rapunzel,
Let down your hair.

As soon as Rapunzel heard this, she took her long braids, wound them once or twice around a hook outside the window, and let them fall twenty ells downward toward the ground. This made a ladder for the witch to climb, and in that way she reached the window at the top of the tower.

Thus it went for several years, and Rapunzel was lonely indeed, hidden away in the high tower.

One day a young Prince was riding through the forest when he heard faint music in the distance. That was Rapunzel, who was trying to lighten her solitude with the sound of her own sweet voice.

The Prince followed the sound, but all he found was a tall, forbidding tower. He was eager to get a glimpse of the mysterious singer but he looked in vain for door or stairway. He saw the little window at the top but could think of no way to get there. At last he rode away, but Rapunzel's sweet singing had touched his heart so deeply that he came back evening after evening and listened to it.

Once, as he was standing there as usual, well hidden by a tree—he saw a hideous hag come hobbling along. It was old Mother Gothel. She stopped at the foot of the tower and called:

Rapunzel, Rapunzel,
Let down your hair.

Now a pair of golden-yellow braids tumbled down from the window. The old hag clung to them and climbed up, up, up, and into the tower window.

"Well!" thought the Prince. "If that is the ladder to the songbird's nest then I, too, must try my luck some day."

The next day at dusk, he went back to the tower, stood beneath it and called:

Rapunzel, Rapunzel,
Let down your hair.

The marvelous tresses were lowered at once. The Prince climbed the silky golden ladder, and stepped through the tiny window up above.

Rapunzel had never seen a man, and at first she was alarmed at seeing this handsome youth enter her window. But the Prince looked at her with friendly eyes and said softly, "Don't be afraid. When I heard your sweet voice, my heart was touched so deeply that I could not rest until I had seen you."

At that Rapunzel lost her fear and they talked happily together for a while. Then the Prince said, "Will you take me for your husband, and come away with me?"

At first Rapunzel hesitated. But the youth was so pleasant to behold and seemed so good and gentle besides, that she thought to herself: "I am sure he will be much kinder to me than Mother Gothel."

So she laid her little hand in his and said, "Yes, I will gladly go with you, but I don't know how I can get away from here. If you come every day, and bring each time a skein of silk, I will weave it into a long, strong ladder. When it is finished I will climb down on it, and then you can take me away on your horse. But come only in the evening," she added, "for the old witch always comes in the daytime."

Every day the Prince came and brought some silk. The ladder was getting longer and stronger, and was almost finished. The old witch guessed nothing, but one day Rapunzel forgot herself and said, "How is it, Mother Gothel, that it takes you so long to climb up here, while the Prince can do it in just a minute—oh!"

"What?" cried the witch.

"Oh nothing, nothing," said the poor girl in great confusion.

"You wicked, wicked child!" cried the witch angrily. "What do I hear you say? I thought I had kept you safely hidden from all the world, and now you have deceived me!"

In her fury, she grabbed Rapunzel's golden hair, twirled it once or twice around her left hand, snatched a pair of scissors with her right, and ritsch, rotsch, the beautiful braids lay on the floor. And she was so heartless after this, that she dragged Rapunzel to a waste and desolate place, where the poor girl had to get along as best she could, living in sorrow and want.

On the evening of the very day in which Rapunzel had been banished, the old witch fastened Rapunzel's severed braids to the window hook, and then she sat in the tower and waited. When the Prince appeared with some silk, as was his wont, he called:

Rapunzel, Rapunzel,
Let down your hair.

Swiftly Mother Gothel lowered the braids. The Prince climbed up as usual, but to his dismay he found, not his dear little Rapunzel, but the cruel witch who glared at him with angry, venomous looks.

"Aha!" she cried mockingly. "You have come to get your dear little wife. Well, the pretty bird is no longer in her nest, and she'll sing no more. The cat has taken her away, and in the end that same cat will scratch out your eyes. Rapunzel is lost to you; you will never see her again!"

The Prince was beside himself with grief, and in his despair he leaped out of the tower window. He escaped with his life, but the thorny thicket into which he fell, blinded him.

Now he wandered, sad and sightless, from place to place, ate only roots and berries, and could do nothing but weep and grieve for the loss of his dear wife.

So he wandered for a whole year in deepest misery until at last he chanced upon the desolate place whither Rapunzel had been banished. There she lived in wretchedness and woe with her baby twins—a boy and a girl—who had been born to her in the meantime.

As he drew near, he heard a sweet and sorrowful song. The voice was familiar to him and he hurried toward it.

When Rapunzel saw him, she flew into his arms and wept with joy. Two of her tears fell on the Prince's eyes—in a moment they were healed and he could see as well as before.

Now they were happy indeed! The Prince took his songbird and the little twins too, and together they rode away to his kingdom. There they all lived happily for many a long year.

# *France*

*France has given us not only several of the best-known and most popular of folk tales, but also what is probably the first great collection of folk tales published for young people. This was the famous book of eight fairy tales published by Charles Perrault in 1697 (popularly known as* Contes de ma Mère l'Oye—Tales of Mother Goose) *, which anticipated by more than a hundred years the work of the Brothers Grimm and the serious interest in folklore which swept Europe afterwards. Of those first bright tales from Perrault we have here "The Sleeping Beauty in the Wood," "Cinderella," and "The Master Cat." Of the three other stories, two—"Beauty and the Beast" and "The White Cat"—are by well-known French women of the eighteenth century and stand somewhere between the folk tale and the modern fanciful tale. Mme. de Beaumont wisely kept her "Beauty and the Beast" close to the simplicity of the traditional tale. "The White Cat," by Mme. d'Aulnoy, is more elaborate and sophisticated but still retains a basic folk-tale construction. Little has been done in this century toward compiling French folk tales that are suitable for children and of recent vintage. Barbara Leonie Picard's collection is almost the only one to offer "new" French stories in English. It is to be hoped that someday soon the immortal tales of Perrault will be joined by equally splendid folk tales of France that reflect more recent expressions of the humorous wisdom of her people.*

## THE SLEEPING BEAUTY
## IN THE WOOD

*The idea of an enchanted sleep reaches back to Greek mythology and beyond. Here is its most perfect and romantic expression. This version omits the second episode in which the ogress proposes to eat up Beauty's children and threatens Beauty. Although such barbarism has a humorous undertone in Perrault's telling, it is neither suitable nor necessary for children. The adult is well advised to read this and the other seven Perrault tales in their original form.*

There were formerly a king and a queen who were so sorry that they had no children; so sorry that it cannot be expressed. They went to all the waters in the world; vows, pilgrimages, all ways were tried, and all to no purpose.

At last, however, the Queen had a daughter. There was a very fine christening; and the Princess had for her god-mothers all the fairies they could find in the whole kingdom (they found

"The Sleeping Beauty in the Wood." From *The Blue Fairy Book,* edited by Andrew Lang. Longmans, Green, and Co., London, 1889

seven), that every one of them might give her a gift, as was the custom of fairies in those days. By this means the Princess had all the perfections imaginable.

After the ceremonies of the christening were over, all the company returned to the King's palace, where was prepared a great feast for the fairies. There was placed before every one of them a magnificent cover with a case of massive gold, wherein were a spoon, knife, and fork, all of pure gold set with diamonds and rubies. But as they were all sitting down at the table they saw come into the hall a very old fairy, whom they had not invited because it was over fifty years since she had been out of a certain tower, and she was believed to be either dead or enchanted.

The King ordered her a cover, but could not furnish her with a case of gold as the others, because they had seven only made for the seven fairies. The old Fairy fancied she was slighted, and muttered some threats between her teeth. One of the young fairies who sat by her overheard how she grumbled and, judging that she might give the little Princess some unlucky gift, went, as soon as they rose from table, and hid herself behind the hangings, that she might speak last and repair, as much as she could, the evil which the old Fairy might intend.

In the meanwhile all the fairies began to give their gifts to the Princess. The youngest gave her for gift that she should be the most beautiful person in the world; the next, that she should have the wit of an angel; the third, that she should have a wonderful grace in everything she did; the fourth, that she should dance perfectly well; the fifth, that she should sing like a night-ingale; and the sixth, that she should play all kinds of music to the utmost perfection.

The old Fairy's turn came next. With her head shaking more with spite than age, she said that the Princess should have her hand pierced with a spindle and die of the wound. This terrible gift made the whole company tremble, and everybody fell a-crying.

At this very instant the young Fairy came out from behind the hangings, and spake these words aloud:

"Assure yourselves, O King and Queen, that your daughter shall not die of this disaster. It is true, I have no power to undo entirely what my elder has done. The Princess shall indeed pierce her hand with a spindle; but, instead of dying, she shall only fall into a profound sleep, which shall last a hundred years, at the expiration of which a king's son shall come and awake her."

The King, to avoid the misfortune foretold by the old Fairy, caused immediately proclamation to be made, whereby everybody was forbidden, on pain of death, to spin with a distaff and spindle, or to have so much as any spindle in their houses. About fifteen or sixteen years after, the King and Queen being gone to one of their houses of pleasure, the young Princess happened one day to divert herself by running up and down the palace; when going up from one apartment to another, she came into a little room on the top of the tower, where a good old woman, alone, was spinning with her spindle. This good woman had never heard of the King's proclamation against spindles.

"What are you doing there, goody?" said the Princess.

"I am spinning, my pretty child," said the old woman, who did not know who she was.

"Ha!" said the Princess, "this is very pretty; how do you do it? Give it to me, that I may see if I can do so."

She had no sooner taken it than it ran into her hand, and she fell down in a swoon.

The good old woman, not knowing very well what to do in this affair, cried out for help. People came in from every quarter in great numbers; they threw water upon the Princess' face, unlaced her, struck her on the palms of her hands, and rubbed her temples with Hungary-water, but nothing would bring her to herself.

And now the King, who came up at the noise, bethought himself of the prediction of the fairies, and, judging very well that this must necessarily come to pass, since the fairies had said it, caused the Princess to be carried into the finest apartment in his palace, and to be laid upon a bed all embroidered with gold and silver.

One would have taken her for a little angel, she was so very beautiful, for her swooning away had not diminished one bit of her complexion: her cheeks were carnation, and her lips were coral; indeed her eyes were shut, but she was heard to breathe softly, which satisfied those about her that she was not dead. The King commanded that they should not disturb her, but let her sleep quietly till her hour of awakening was come.

The good Fairy who had saved her life by condemning her to sleep a hundred years was in the kingdom of Matakin, twelve thousand leagues off, when this accident befell the Princess; but she was instantly informed of it by a little dwarf, who had boots of seven leagues, that is, boots with which he could tread over seven leagues of ground in one stride. The Fairy came away immediately, and she arrived, about an hour after, in a fiery chariot drawn by dragons.

The King handed her out of the chariot, and she approved everything he had done; but as she had very great foresight, she thought when the Princess should awake she might not know what to do with herself, being all alone in this old palace; and this was what she did: she touched with her wand everything in the palace—except the King and the Queen—governesses, maids of honour, ladies of the bedchamber, gentlemen, officers, stewards, cooks, undercooks, scullions, guards, with their beefeaters, pages, footmen; she likewise touched all the horses which were in the stables, the great dogs in the outward court, and pretty little Mopsey too, the Princess' little spaniel, which lay by her on the bed.

Immediately upon her touching them they all fell asleep that they might not awake before their mistress and that they might be ready to wait upon her when she wanted them. The very spits at the fire, as full as they could hold of partridges and pheasants, did fall asleep also. All this was done in a moment. Fairies are not long in doing their business.

And now the King and the Queen, having kissed their dear child without waking her, went out of the palace and put forth a proclamation that nobody should dare to come near it.

This, however, was not necessary, for in a quarter of an hour's time there grew up all round about the park such a vast number of trees, great and small, bushes and brambles, twining one within another, that neither man nor beast could pass through; so that nothing could be seen but the very top of the towers of the palace; and that either, unless it was a good way off. Nobody doubted but the Fairy gave herein a very extraordinary sample of her art, insuring that the Princess, while she continued sleeping, might have nothing to fear from any curious people.

When a hundred years were gone and passed, the son of the King then reigning, who was of another family from that of the sleeping Princess, being gone a-hunting on that side of the country, asked:

"What were those towers I saw in the middle of a great thick wood?"

Everyone answered according as they had heard. Some said that it was a ruinous old castle, haunted by spirits; others, that all the sorcerers and witches of the country kept there their sabbath or night's meeting. The common opinion was that an ogre lived there and that he carried thither all the little children he could catch, without anybody being able to follow him because only he had the power to pass through the wood.

The Prince was at a stand, not knowing what to believe, when a very aged countryman spake to him thus:

"May it please your royal highness, it is now about fifty years since I heard from my father, who heard my grandfather say, that there was then in this castle a princess, the most beautiful was ever seen; that she must sleep there a hundred years, and should be waked by a king's son, for whom she was reserved."

The young Prince was all on fire at these words, believing, without weighing the matter, that he could put an end to this rare adventure; and, pushed on by love and honour, resolved that moment to look into it.

Scarce had he advanced towards the wood when all the great trees, the bushes, and brambles gave way of themselves to let him pass through; he walked up to the castle, which he saw at the end of a large avenue, and he went in. What a little surprised him was that none of his people could follow him, because the trees closed again as soon as he had passed through them. However, he did not cease from continuing his way; a young and amorous prince is always valiant.

He came into a spacious outward court, where everything he saw might have frozen up the most fearless person with horror. There reigned over all a most frightful silence; the image of death everywhere showed itself, and there was nothing to be seen but stretched-out bodies of men and animals, all seeming to be dead. He, however, very well knew, by the ruby faces and pimpled noses of the beefeaters, that they were only asleep; and their goblets, wherein still remained some drops of wine, showed plainly that they fell asleep in their cups.

He then crossed a court paved with marble, went up the stairs, and came into the guard chamber, where guards were standing in their ranks, with their muskets upon their shoulders, and snoring as loud as they could. After that he went through several rooms full of gentlemen and ladies, all asleep, some standing, others sitting. At last he came into a chamber all gilded with gold, where he saw upon a bed, the curtains of which were all open, the finest sight was ever beheld—a princess, who appeared to be about fifteen or sixteen years of age, and whose bright and, in a manner, resplendent beauty, had somewhat in it divine. He approached with trembling and admiration, and fell down before her upon his knees.

And now, as the enchantment was at an end,

the Princess awaked, and looking on him with eyes more tender than the first view might seem to admit of:

"Is it you, my Prince?" said she to him. "You have waited a long while."

The Prince, charmed with these words, and much more with the manner in which they were spoken, knew not how to show his joy and gratitude. He assured her that he loved her better than he did himself. Their discourse was not well connected, they did weep more than talk— little eloquence, a great deal of love. He was more at a loss than she, and we need not wonder at it: she had time to think on what to say to him, for it is very probable (though history mentions nothing of it) that the good Fairy, during so long a sleep, had given her very agreeable dreams. In short, they talked four hours together, and yet they said not half what they had to say.

In the meanwhile all the palace awaked; everyone thought upon their particular business, and as all of them were not in love they were ready to die for hunger. The chief lady of honour, being as sharp set as other folks, grew very impatient, and told the Princess aloud that supper was served up. The Prince helped the Princess to rise. She was entirely dressed, and very magnificently, but his royal highness took care not to tell her that she was dressed like his great-grandmother and had a point band peeping over a high collar. She looked not a bit the less charming and beautiful for all that.

They went into the great hall of looking-glasses, where they supped, and were served by the Princess' officers. The violins and hautboys played old tunes, but very excellent, though it was now above a hundred years since they had played. And after supper, without losing any time, the lord almoner performed the wedding ceremony for Beauty and the Prince in the chapel of the castle. A short time thereafter, the Prince took Beauty to his own kingdom where they lived happily ever after.

## CINDERELLA or

## THE LITTLE GLASS SLIPPER

*Here is the favorite theme of fiction writers of every age—the misunderstood, lowly maiden who finally comes into her own. It is no wonder that in 1893 Marian Cox was able to list 345 variants of this story. The count has undoubtedly grown since then. Although Perrault's version is the best known, the story had already appeared in somewhat similar form in Italy and has since been retold by many others, most notably Walter de la Mare.*

Once there was a gentleman who married, for his second wife, the proudest and most haughty woman that was ever seen. She had, by a former husband, two daughters of her own humour, who were, indeed, exactly like her in all things. He had likewise, by another wife, a young daughter, but of unparalleled goodness and sweetness of temper, which she took from her mother, who was the best creature in the world.

No sooner were the ceremonies of the wedding over but the step-mother began to show herself in her true colours. She could not bear the good qualities of this pretty girl, and the less because they made her own daughters appear the more odious. She employed her in the meanest work of the house. The girl scoured the dishes, tables, etc., and scrubbed madam's chamber, and those of misses, her daughters; she lay up in a sorry garret, upon a wretched straw bed, while her sisters lay in fine rooms, with floors all inlaid, upon beds of the very newest fashion, and where they had looking-glasses so large that they might see themselves at their full length from head to foot.

The poor girl bore all patiently and dared not tell her father, who would have rattled her off; for his wife governed him entirely. When she had done her work, she used to go into the chimney-corner and sit down among cinders and ashes, which made her commonly be called *Cinderwench;* but the youngest, who was not so rude and uncivil as the eldest, called her Cinderella. However, Cinderella, notwithstanding her mean apparel, was a hundred times handsomer than her sisters, though they were always dressed very richly.

It happened that the King's son gave a ball,

"Cinderella or The Little Glass Slipper." From *The Blue Fairy Book*, edited by Andrew Lang. Longmans, Green, and Co., London, 1889

and invited all persons of fashion to it. Our young misses were also invited, for they cut a very grand figure among the quality. They were mightily delighted at this invitation, and wonderfully busy in choosing out such gowns, petticoats, and head-clothes as might become them. This was a new trouble to Cinderella; for it was she who ironed her sisters' linen, and plaited their ruffles; they talked all day long of nothing but how they should be dressed.

"For my part," said the eldest, "I will wear my red velvet suit with French trimming."

"And I," said the youngest, "shall have my usual petticoat; but then, to make amends for that, I will put on my gold-flowered manteau and my diamond stomacher, which is far from being the most ordinary one in the world."

They sent for the best tire-woman they could get to make up their head-dresses and adjust their double pinners, and they had their red brushes and patches from Mademoiselle de la Poche.

Cinderella was likewise called up to them to be consulted in all these matters, for she had excellent notions, and advised them always for the best, nay, and offered her services to dress their heads, which they were very willing she should do. As she was doing this, they said to her:

"Cinderella, would you not be glad to go to the ball?"

"Alas!" said she, "you only jeer me; it is not for such as I am to go thither."

"Thou art in the right of it," replied they; "it would make the people laugh to see a Cinder-wench at a ball."

Anyone but Cinderella would have dressed their heads awry, but she was very good, and dressed them perfectly well. They were almost two days without eating, so much they were transported with joy. They broke above a dozen laces in trying to be laced up close, that they might have a fine slender shape, and they were continually at their looking-glass. At last the happy day came; they went to court, and Cinderella followed them with her eyes as long as she could, and when she had lost sight of them, she fell a-crying.

Her godmother, who saw her all in tears, asked her what was the matter.

"I wish I could—I wish I could——" she was not able to speak the rest, being interrupted by her tears and sobbing.

This godmother of hers, who was a fairy, said to her, "You wish you could go to the ball; is it not so?"

"Y—es," cried Cinderella, with a great sigh.

"Well," said her godmother, "be but a good girl, and I will contrive that you shall go." Then she took her into her chamber, and said to her, "Run into the garden, and bring me a pumpkin."

Cinderella went immediately to gather the finest she could get, and brought it to her godmother, not being able to imagine how this pumpkin could make her go to the ball. Her godmother scooped out all the inside of it, having left nothing but the rind; which done, she struck it with her wand, and the pumpkin was instantly turned into a fine coach, gilded all over with gold.

She then went to look into her mouse-trap, where she found six mice, all alive, and ordered Cinderella to lift up a little the trapdoor, when, giving each mouse, as it went out, a little tap with her wand, the mouse was that moment turned into a fine horse, which altogether made a very fine set of six horses of a beautiful mouse-coloured dapple-grey. Being at a loss for a coachman, Cinderella said, "I will go and see if there is never a rat in the rat-trap—we may make a coachman of him."

"You are right," replied her godmother; "go and look."

Cinderella brought the trap to her, and in it there were three huge rats. The fairy made choice of one of the three which had the largest beard, and, having touched him with her wand, he was turned into a fat, jolly coachman, who had the smartest whiskers eyes ever beheld.

After that, she said to her: "Go again into the garden, and you will find six lizards behind the watering-pot. Bring them to me."

She had no sooner done so but her godmother turned them into six footmen, who skipped up immediately behind the coach, with their liveries all bedaubed with gold and silver, and clung as close behind each other as if they had done nothing else their whole lives. The fairy then said to Cinderella:

"Well, you see here an equipage fit to go to

the ball with; are you not pleased with it?"

"Oh! yes," cried she; "but must I go thither as I am, in these nasty rags?"

Her godmother only just touched her with her wand, and, at the same instant, her clothes were turned into cloth of gold and silver, all beset with jewels. This done, she gave her a pair of glass slippers, the prettiest in the whole world. Being thus decked out, she got up into her coach; but her godmother, above all things, commanded her not to stay till after midnight, telling her, at the same time, that if she stayed one moment longer, the coach would be a pumpkin again, her horses mice, her coachman a rat, her footmen lizards, and her clothes become just as they were before.

She promised her godmother she would not fail of leaving the ball before midnight; and then away she drove, scarce able to contain herself for joy. The King's son, who was told that a great princess, whom nobody knew, was come, ran out to receive her; he gave her his hand as she alighted from the coach, and led her into the hall, among all the company. There was immediately a profound silence. The dancing stopped, and the violins ceased to play, so eager was everyone to contemplate the singular beauties of the unknown new-comer. Nothing was then heard but a confused noise of: "Ha! how handsome she is! Ha! how handsome she is!"

The King himself, old as he was, could not help watching her and telling the Queen softly that it was a long time since he had seen so beautiful and lovely a creature.

All the ladies were busied in considering her clothes and head-dress, that they might have some made next day after the same pattern, provided they could meet with such fine materials and as able hands to make them.

The King's son conducted her to the most honourable seat, and afterwards took her out to dance with him; she danced so very gracefully that they all more and more admired her. A fine collation was served up, whereof the young prince ate not a morsel, so intently was he busied in gazing on her.

She went and sat down by her sisters, showing them a thousand civilities, giving them part of the oranges and citrons which the Prince had presented her with, which very much surprised

them, for they did not know her. While Cinderella was thus amusing her sisters, she heard the clock strike eleven and three-quarters, whereupon she immediately made a curtsy to the company and hastened away as fast as she could.

Upon arriving home, she ran to seek out her godmother, and, after having thanked her, she said she could not but heartily wish she might go next day to the ball, because the King's son had invited her.

As she was eagerly telling her godmother whatever had passed at the ball, her two sisters knocked at the door, which Cinderella ran and opened.

"How long you have stayed!" cried she, gaping, rubbing her eyes and stretching herself as if she had been just waked out of her sleep; she had not, of course, had any inclination to sleep since they went from home.

"If you had been at the ball," said one of her sisters, "you would not have been tired with it. There came thither the finest princess, the most beautiful ever was seen with mortal eyes; she showed us a thousand civilities, and gave us oranges and citrons."

Cinderella seemed very indifferent in the matter; indeed, she asked them the name of that princess; but they told her they did not know it, and that the King's son was very uneasy on her account and would give all the world to know who she was. At this Cinderella, smiling, replied:

"She must, then, be very beautiful indeed; how happy you have been! Could not I see her? Ah! dear Miss Charlotte, do lend me your yellow suit of clothes which you wear every day."

"Ay, to be sure!" cried Miss Charlotte; "lend my clothes to such a dirty Cinderwench as you! I should be a fool."

Cinderella, indeed, expected well such answer, and was very glad of the refusal; for she would have been sadly put to it if her sister had lent her what she asked for jestingly.

The next day the two sisters were at the ball, and so was Cinderella, but dressed more magnificently than before. The King's son was always by her, and never ceased his compliments and kind speeches to her; to whom all this was so far from being tiresome that she quite forgot what her godmother had recommended to her; so that she, at last, counted the clock striking twelve when she took it to be no more than eleven; she then rose up and fled, as nimble as a deer. The Prince followed, but could not overtake her. She left behind one of her glass slippers, which the Prince took up most carefully. She got home, but quite out of breath, and in her nasty old clothes, having nothing left her of all her finery but one of the little slippers, fellow to that she dropped.

The guards at the palace gate were asked if they had not seen a princess go out. They said they had seen nobody go out but a young girl, very meanly dressed, who had more the air of a poor country wench than a gentlewoman.

When the two sisters returned from the ball Cinderella asked them if they had been well diverted, and if the fine lady had been there. They told her that she had, but that she hurried away immediately when it struck twelve, and with so much haste that she dropped one of her little glass slippers, the prettiest in the world, which the King's son had taken up; that he had done nothing but look at her all the time at the ball, and that most certainly he was very much in love with the beautiful person who owned the glass slipper.

What they said was very true; for a few days after, the King's son caused it to be proclaimed, by sound of trumpet, that he would marry her whose foot this slipper would just fit. They whom he employed began to try it upon the princesses, then the duchesses and all the court, but in vain; it was brought to the two sisters, who did all they possibly could to thrust their foot into the slipper, but they could not effect it.

Cinderella, who saw all this, and knew her slipper, said to them, laughing: "Let me see if it will not fit me."

Her sisters burst out a-laughing, and began to banter her. The gentleman who was sent to try the slipper looked earnestly at Cinderella, and, finding her very handsome, said it was but just that she should try, and that he had orders to let everyone make trial.

He obliged Cinderella to sit down, and, putting the slipper to her foot, he found it went on very easily, and fitted her as if it had been made of wax. The astonishment of her two sisters was excessively great, but still abundantly greater when Cinderella pulled out of her pocket the

other slipper and put it on her foot. Thereupon, in came her godmother, who, having touched with her wand Cinderella's clothes, made them richer and more magnificent than any of those she had before.

And now her two sisters found her to be that fine, beautiful lady whom they had seen at the ball. They threw themselves at her feet to beg pardon for all the ill-treatment they had made her undergo. Cinderella took them up, and, as she embraced them, cried that she forgave them with all her heart, and desired them always to love her.

She was conducted to the young Prince, dressed as she was; he thought her more charming than ever and, a few days after, married her. Cinderella, who was no less good than beautiful, gave her two sisters lodgings in the palace, and that very same day matched them with two great lords of the court.

## THE MASTER CAT or PUSS IN BOOTS

*Of all the wise and resourceful fairy animals of the folk tales, Puss in Boots is the cleverest. It will be interesting to compare Gustave Doré's romantic illustration of Puss with the one shown here and with the interpretations of two distinguished modern illustrators, Marcia Brown and Hans Fischer, each of whom has published the story in picture-book form. There is good reason to believe that Perrault invented the boots for Puss, a brilliant stroke if so!*

There was a miller who left no more estate to the three sons he had than his mill, his ass, and his cat. The partition was soon made. Neither the scrivener nor attorney was sent for. They would soon have eaten up all the poor patrimony. The eldest had the mill, the second the ass, and the youngest nothing but the cat.

The poor young fellow was quite comfortless at having so poor a lot. "My brothers," said he, "may get their living handsomely enough by joining their stocks together; but, for my part,

"The Master Cat or Puss in Boots." From *The Blue Fairy Book*, edited by Andrew Lang. Longmans, Green, and Co., London, 1889

when I have eaten up my cat, and made me a muff of his skin, I must die of hunger."

The cat, who heard all this, but made as if he did not, said to him with a grave and serious air: "Do not thus afflict yourself, my good master; you have nothing else to do but to give me a bag, and get a pair of boots made for me, that I may scamper through the dirt and the brambles, and you shall see that you have not so bad a portion of me as you imagine."

The cat's master did not build very much upon what he said; he had, however, often seen him play a great many cunning tricks to catch rats and mice; as when he used to hang by the heels, or hide himself in the meal, and make as if he were dead; so that he did not altogether despair of his affording him some help in his miserable condition. When the cat had what he asked for, he booted himself very gallantly, and, putting his bag about his neck, he held the strings of it in his two forepaws, and went into a warren where was great abundance of rabbits. He put bran and sow-thistle into his bag, and, stretching out at length, as if he had been dead, he waited for some young rabbits, not yet acquainted with the deceits of the world, to come and rummage his bag for what he had put into it.

Scarce had he lain down but he had what he wanted: a rash and foolish young rabbit jumped into his bag, and Monsieur Puss, immediately drawing close the strings, took and killed him without pity. Proud of his prey, he went with it to the palace, and asked to speak with his majesty. He was shown upstairs into the king's apartment, and, making a low reverence, said to him:

"I have brought you, sir, a rabbit of the warren, which my noble Lord, the Master of Carabas"—for that was the title which Puss was pleased to give his master—"has commanded me to present to Your Majesty from him."

"Tell thy master," said the king, "that I thank him, and that he does me a great deal of pleasure."

Another time he went and hid himself among some standing corn, holding his bag open; and, when a brace of partridges ran into it, he drew the strings, and so caught them both. He went and made a present of these to the king, as he had done before with the rabbit which he took

in the warren. The king, in like manner, received the partridges with great pleasure, and ordered some money to be given to Puss.

The cat continued for two or three months thus to carry his majesty, from time to time, game of his master's taking. One day in particular, when he knew for certain that he was to take the air along the river-side with his daughter, the most beautiful princess in the world, he said to his master:

"If you will follow my advice your fortune is made. You have nothing else to do but go and wash yourself in the river, in that part I shall show you, and leave the rest to me."

The Marquis of Carabas did what the cat advised him to, without knowing why or wherefore. While he was washing, the king passed by, and the cat began to cry out: "Help! help! My Lord Marquis of Carabas is going to be drowned."

At this noise the king put his head out of the coach-window, and, finding it was the cat who had so often brought him such good game, he commanded his guards to run immediately to the assistance of his lordship the Marquis of Carabas. While they were drawing the poor marquis out of the river, the cat came up to the coach and told the king that, while his master was washing, there came by some rogues who went off with his clothes, though he had cried out: "Thieves! thieves!" several times, as loud as he could.

This cunning cat had hidden them under a great stone. The king immediately commanded the officers of his wardrobe to run and fetch one of his best suits for the Lord Marquis of Carabas.

The fine clothes the king had given him extremely set off his good mien (for he was well made and very handsome in his person), and the king's daughter took a secret inclination to him, and the Marquis of Carabas had no sooner cast two or three respectful and somewhat tender glances but she fell in love with him to distraction. The king would needs have him come into the coach and take part of the airing.

The cat, quite over-joyed to see his project begin to succeed, marched on before and, meeting with some countrymen who were mowing a meadow, he said to them: "Good people, you who are mowing, if you do not tell the king that the meadow you mow belongs to my Lord Marquis of Carabas, you shall be chopped as small as herbs for the pot."

The king did not fail asking of the mowers to whom the meadow they were mowing belonged.

"To my Lord Marquis of Carabas," answered they altogether, for the cat's threats had made them terribly afraid.

"You see, sir," said the marquis, "this is a meadow which never fails to yield a plentiful harvest every year."

The Master Cat, who went still on before, met with some reapers and said to them:

"Good people, you who are reaping, if you do not tell the king that all this corn belongs to the Marquis of Carabas, you shall be chopped as small as herbs for the pot."

The king, who passed by a moment after, would needs know to whom all that corn, which he then saw, did belong.

"To my Lord Marquis of Carabas," replied the reapers, and the king was very well pleased with it, as well as the marquis, whom he congratulated thereupon. The Master Cat, who went always before, said the same words to all he met, and the king was astonished at the vast estates of my Lord Marquis of Carabas.

Monsieur Puss came at last to a stately castle, the master of which was an ogre, the richest had ever been known; for all the lands which the king had then gone over belonged to this castle.

The cat, who had taken care to inform himself who this ogre was and what he could do, asked to speak with him, saying he could not pass so near his castle without having the honour of paying his respects to him.

The ogre received him as civilly as an ogre could do, and made him sit down.

"I have been assured," said the cat, "that you have the gift of being able to change yourself into all sorts of creatures you have a mind to; you can, for example, transform yourself into a lion, or elephant, and the like."

"That is true," answered the ogre very briskly "and to convince you, you shall see me now become a lion."

Puss was so sadly terrified at the sight of a lion so near him that he immediately got into the gutter, not without abundance of trouble and danger, because of his boots, which were of no use at all to him in walking upon the roof tiles. Shortly after, when Puss saw that the ogre had resumed his natural form, he came down, and owned he had been very much frightened.

"I have been moreover informed," said the cat, "but I know not how to believe it, that you have also the power to take on you the shape of the smallest animals; for example, to change yourself into a rat or a mouse; but I must own to you I take this to be impossible."

"Impossible!" cried the ogre; "you shall see that presently."

And at the same time he changed himself into a mouse, and began to run about the floor. Puss no sooner perceived this but he fell upon him and ate him up.

Meanwhile the king, who saw, as he passed, this fine castle of the ogre's, had a mind to go into it. Puss, who heard the noise of his majesty's coach running over the draw-bridge, ran out, and said to the king: "Your Majesty is welcome to this castle of my Lord Marquis of Carabas."

"What! my Lord Marquis," cried the king, "and does this castle also belong to you? There can be nothing finer than this court and all the stately buildings which surround it; let us go into it, if you please."

The marquis gave his hand to the princess, and followed the king, who went first. They passed into a spacious hall, where they found a magnificent collation, which the ogre had prepared for his friends, who were that very day to visit him, but dared not to enter, knowing the king was there. His majesty was perfectly charmed with the good qualities of my Lord Marquis of Carabas, as was his daughter, who had fallen in love with him, and, seeing the vast estate he possessed, said to him: "It will be owing to yourself only, my Lord Marquis, if you are not my son-in-law."

The marquis, making several low bows, accepted the honour which his majesty conferred upon him, and forthwith, that very same day, married the princess.

Puss became a great lord, and never ran after mice any more but only for his diversion.

## BEAUTY AND THE BEAST

*This story, very similar in theme to the Norse "East o' the Sun and West o' the Moon" and the Greek "Cupid and Psyche," has a unique charm of its own. Perhaps part of its appeal lies in Beauty's compassion for her poor Beast and her ability to see beyond his ugly exterior to his goodness. Andrew Lang derived his telling from that of Mme. Villeneuve (printed sometime between 1785 and 1789), a widely read adaptation of Mme. de Beaumont's earlier telling.*

Once upon a time, in a very far-off country, there lived a merchant who had been so fortunate in all his undertakings that he was enormously rich. As he had, however, six sons and six daughters, he found that his money was not too much to let them all have everything they fancied, as they were accustomed to do.

But one day a most unexpected misfortune befell them. Their house caught fire and was speedily burnt to the ground, with all the splendid furniture, the books, pictures, gold, silver, and precious goods it contained; and this was only the beginning of their troubles. Their father, who had until this moment prospered in all ways, suddenly lost every ship he had upon the sea, either by dint of pirates, shipwreck, or fire. Then he heard that his clerks in distant countries, whom he trusted entirely, had proved unfaithful; and at last from great wealth he fell into the direst poverty.

"Beauty and the Beast." From *The Blue Fairy Book*, edited by Andrew Lang. Longmans, Green, and Co., London, 1889

All that he had left was a little house in a desolate place at least a hundred leagues from the town in which he had lived, and to this he was forced to retreat with his children, who were in despair at the idea of leading such a different life. Indeed, the daughters at first hoped that their friends, who had been so numerous while they were rich, would insist on their staying in their houses now they no longer possessed one. But they soon found that they were left alone. Their former friends even attributed their misfortunes to their own extravagance and showed no intention of offering any help. So nothing was left for them but to take their departure to the cottage, which stood in the midst of a dark forest and seemed to be the most dismal place upon the face of the earth. As they were too poor to have any servants, the girls had to work hard and the sons, for their part, cultivated the fields to earn their living. Roughly clothed and living in the simplest way, the girls regretted unceasingly the luxuries and amusements of their former life; only the youngest tried to be brave and cheerful. She had been as sad as anyone when misfortune first overtook her father, but, soon recovering her natural gaiety, she set to work to make the best of things, to amuse her father and brothers as well as she could, and to try to persuade her sisters to join her in dancing and singing. But they would do nothing of the sort, and because she was not as doleful as themselves, they declared that this miserable life was all she was fit for. But she was really far prettier and cleverer than they were; indeed, she was so lovely that she was always called Beauty. After two years, when they were all beginning to get used to their new life, something happened to disturb their tranquillity. Their father received the news that one of his ships, which he had believed to be lost, had come safely into port with a rich cargo. All the sons and daughters at once thought that their poverty was at an end and wanted to set out directly for the town; but their father, who was more prudent, begged them to wait a little, and, though it was harvest-time and he could ill be spared, determined to go himself first, to make inquiries. Only the youngest daughter had any doubt but that they would soon again be as rich as they were before, or at least rich enough to live comfortably in some town where they would find amusement and gay companions once more. So they all loaded their father with commissions for jewels and dresses which it would have taken a fortune to buy; only Beauty, feeling sure that it was of no use, did not ask for anything. Her father, noticing her silence, said: "And what shall I bring for you, Beauty?"

"The only thing I wish for is to see you come home safely," she answered.

But this reply vexed her sisters, who fancied she was blaming them for having asked for such costly things. Her father, however, was pleased, but as he thought that at her age she certainly ought to like pretty presents, he told her to choose something.

"Well, dear Father," she said, "as you insist upon it, I beg that you will bring me a rose. I have not seen one since we came here, and I love them so much."

So the merchant set out and reached the town as quickly as possible, but only to find that his former companions, believing him to be dead, had divided between them the goods which the ship had brought; and after six months of trouble and expense he found himself as poor as when he started, having been able to recover only just enough to pay the cost of his journey. To make matters worse, he was obliged to leave the town in the most terrible weather, so that by the time he was within a few leagues of his home he was almost exhausted with cold and fatigue. Though he knew it would take some hours to get through the forest, he was so anxious to be at his journey's end that he resolved to go on; but night overtook him, and the deep snow and bitter frost made it impossible for his horse to carry him any further. Not a house was to be seen; the only shelter he could get was the hollow trunk of a great tree, and there he crouched all the night, which seemed to him the longest he had ever known. In spite of his weariness the howling of the wolves kept him awake, and even when at last the day broke he was not much better off, for the falling snow had covered up every path, and he did not know which way to turn.

At length he made out some sort of track, and though at the beginning it was so rough and slippery that he fell down more than once, it presently became easier, and led him into an avenue of trees which ended in a splendid castle. It seemed to the merchant very strange that no snow had fallen in the avenue, which was entirely composed of orange trees, covered with flowers and fruit. When he reached the first court of the castle he saw before him a flight of agate steps. He went up them and passed through several splendidly furnished rooms. The pleasant warmth of the air revived him, and he felt very hungry; but there seemed to be nobody in all this vast and splendid palace whom he could ask to give him something to eat. Deep silence reigned everywhere, and at last, tired of roaming through empty rooms and galleries, he stopped in a room smaller than the rest, where a clear fire was burning and a couch was drawn up cosily close to it. Thinking that this must be prepared for someone who was expected, he sat down to wait till he should come, and very soon fell into a sweet sleep.

When his extreme hunger wakened him after several hours, he was still alone; but a little table, upon which was a good dinner, had been drawn up close to him, and, as he had eaten nothing for twenty-four hours, he lost no time in beginning his meal, hoping that he might soon have an opportunity of thanking his considerate entertainer, whoever it might be. But no one appeared, and even after another long sleep, from which he awoke completely refreshed, there was no sign of anybody, though a fresh meal of dainty cakes and fruit was prepared upon the little table at his elbow. Since he was naturally timid, the silence began to terrify him, and he resolved to search once more through all the rooms; but it was of no use. Not even a servant was to been seen; there was no sign of life in the palace! He began to wonder what he should do and to amuse himself by pretending that all the treasures he saw were his own and considering how he would divide them among his children. Then he went down into the garden, and though it was winter everywhere else, here the sun shone, the birds sang, the flowers bloomed, and the air was soft and sweet. The merchant, in ecstasies with all he saw and heard, said to himself:

"All this must be meant for me. I will go this minute and bring my children to share all these delights."

In spite of being so cold and weary when he reached the castle, he had taken his horse to the stable and fed it. Now he thought he would saddle it for his homeward journey, and he turned down the path which led to the stable. This path had a hedge of roses on each side of it, and the merchant thought he had never seen or smelt such exquisite flowers. They reminded him of his promise to Beauty, and he stopped and had just gathered one to take to her when he was startled by a strange noise behind him. Turning round, he saw a frightful Beast, which seemed to be very angry and said, in a terrible voice:

"Who told you that you might gather my roses? Was it not enough that I allowed you to be in my palace and was kind to you? This is the way you show your gratitude, by stealing my flowers! But your insolence shall not go unpunished." The merchant, terrified by these furious words, dropped the fatal rose, and, throwing himself on his knees, cried: "Pardon me, noble sir. I am truly grateful to you for your hospitality, which was so magnificent that I could not imagine that you would be offended by my taking such a little thing as a rose." But the Beast's anger was not lessened by this speech.

"You are very ready with excuses and flattery," he cried; "but that will not save you from the death you deserve."

"Alas!" thought the merchant, "if my daughter Beauty could only know what danger her rose has brought me into!"

And in despair he began to tell the Beast all his misfortunes, and the reason of his journey, not forgetting to mention Beauty's request.

"A king's ransom would hardly have procured all that my other daughters asked," he said; "but I thought that I might at least take Beauty her rose. I beg you to forgive me, for you see I meant no harm."

The Beast considered for a moment, and then he said, in a less furious tone:

"I will forgive you on one condition—that is, that you will give me one of your daughters."

"Ah!" cried the merchant, "if I were cruel enough to buy my own life at the expense of one of my children's, what excuse could I invent to bring her here?"

"No excuse would be necessary," answered the Beast. "If she comes at all she must come willingly. On no other condition will I have her. See if any one of them is courageous enough and

loves you well enough to come and save your life. You seem to be an honest man, so I will trust you to go home. I give you a month to see if any of your daughters will come back with you and stay here, to let you go free. If none of them is willing, you must come alone, after bidding them good-bye for ever, for then you will belong to me. And do not imagine that you can hide from me, for if you fail to keep your word I will come and fetch you!" added the Beast grimly.

The merchant accepted this proposal, though he did not really think any of his daughters would be persuaded to come. He promised to return at the time appointed, and then, anxious to escape from the presence of the Beast, he asked permission to set off at once. But the Beast answered that he could not go until the next day.

"Then you will find a horse ready for you," he said. "Now go and eat your supper, and await my orders."

The poor merchant, more dead than alive, went back to his room, where the most delicious supper was already served on the little table which was drawn up before a blazing fire. But he was too terrified to eat, and only tasted a few of the dishes, for fear the Beast should be angry if he did not obey his orders. When he had finished he heard a great noise in the next room, which he knew meant that the Beast was coming. As he could do nothing to escape his visit, the only thing that remained was to seem as little afraid as possible; so when the Beast appeared and asked roughly if he had supped well, the merchant answered humbly that he had, thanks to his host's kindness. Then the Beast warned him to remember their agreement and to prepare his daughter exactly for what she had to expect.

"Do not get up to-morrow," he added, "until you see the sun and hear a golden bell ring. Then you will find your breakfast waiting for you here, and the horse you are to ride will be ready in the courtyard. He will also bring you back again when you come with your daughter a month hence. Farewell. Take a rose to Beauty, and remember your promise!"

The merchant was only too glad when the Beast went away, and though he could not sleep for sadness, he lay down until the sun rose. Then, after a hasty breakfast, he went to gather Beauty's rose, and mounted his horse, which carried him off so swiftly that in an instant he had lost sight of the palace, and he was still wrapped in gloomy thoughts when it stopped before the door of the cottage.

His sons and daughters, who had been very uneasy at his long absence, rushed to meet him, eager to know the result of his journey, which, seeing him mounted upon a splendid horse and wrapped in a rich mantle, they supposed to be favourable. But he hid the truth from them at first, only saying sadly to Beauty as he gave her the rose:

"Here is what you asked me to bring you; you little know what it has cost."

But this excited their curiosity so greatly that presently he told them his adventures from beginning to end, and then they were all very unhappy. The girls lamented loudly over their lost hopes, and the sons declared that their father should not return to this terrible castle, and began to make plans for killing the Beast if it should come to fetch him. But he reminded them that he had promised to go back. Then the girls were very angry with Beauty, and said it was all her fault, and that if she had asked for something sensible this would never have happened, and complained bitterly that they should have to suffer for her folly.

Poor Beauty, much distressed, said to them:

"I have indeed caused this misfortune, but I assure you I did it innocently. Who could have guessed that to ask for a rose in the middle of summer would cause so much misery? But as I did the mischief it is only just that I should suffer for it. I will therefore go back with my father to keep his promise."

At first nobody would hear of this arrangement, and her father and brothers, who loved her dearly, declared that nothing should make them let her go; but Beauty was firm. As the time drew near she divided all her little possessions among her sisters, and said good-bye to everything she loved, and when the fatal day came she encouraged and cheered her father as they mounted together the horse which had brought him back. It seemed to fly rather than gallop, but so smoothly that Beauty was not frightened; indeed, she would have enjoyed the journey if she had not feared what might happen to her at the end of it. Her father still tried to persuade

her to go back, but in vain. While they were talking the night fell, and then, to their great surprise, wonderful coloured lights began to shine in all directions, and splendid fireworks blazed out before them; all the forest was illuminated by them, and even felt pleasantly warm, though it had been bitterly cold before. This lasted until they reached the avenue of orange trees, where were statues holding flaming torches, and when they got nearer to the palace they saw that it was illuminated from the roof to the ground, and music sounded softly from the courtyard. "The Beast must be very hungry," said Beauty, trying to laugh, "if he makes all this rejoicing over the arrival of his prey."

But, in spite of her anxiety, she could not help admiring all the wonderful things she saw.

The horse stopped at the foot of the flight of steps leading to the terrace, and when they had dismounted her father led her to the little room he had been in before, where they found a splendid fire burning, and the table daintily spread with a delicious supper.

The merchant knew that this was meant for them, and Beauty, who was rather less frightened now that she had passed through so many rooms and seen nothing of the Beast, was quite willing to begin, for her long ride had made her very hungry. But they had hardly finished their meal when the noise of the Beast's footsteps was heard approaching, and Beauty clung to her father in terror, which became all the greater when she saw how frightened he was. But when the Beast really appeared, though she trembled at the sight of him, she made a great effort to hide her horror, and saluted him respectfully.

This evidently pleased the Beast. After looking at her he said, in a tone that might have struck terror into the boldest heart, though he did not seem to be angry: "Good-evening, old man. Good-evening, Beauty."

The merchant was too terrified to reply, but Beauty answered sweetly: "Good-evening, Beast."

"Have you come willingly?" asked the Beast. "Will you be content to stay here when your father goes away?"

Beauty answered bravely that she was quite prepared to stay.

"I am pleased with you," said the Beast. "As

you have come of your own accord, you may stay. As for you, old man," he added, turning to the merchant, "at sunrise to-morrow you will take your departure. When the bell rings get up quickly and eat your breakfast, and you will find the same horse waiting to take you home; but remember that you must never expect to see my palace again."

Then turning to Beauty, he said:

"Take your father into the next room, and help him to choose everything you think your brothers and sisters would like to have. You will find two travelling-trunks there; fill them as full as you can. It is only just that you should send them something very precious as a remembrance of yourself."

Then he went away, after saying, "Good-bye, Beauty; good-bye, old man;" and though Beauty was beginning to think with great dismay of her father's departure, she was afraid to disobey the Beast's orders; and they went into the next room, which had shelves and cupboards all round it. They were greatly surprised at the riches it contained. There were splendid dresses fit for a queen, with all the ornaments that were to be worn with them; and when Beauty opened the cupboards she was quite dazzled by the gorgeous jewels that lay in heaps upon every shelf. After choosing a vast quantity, which she divided between her sisters—for she had made a heap of the wonderful dresses for each of them—she opened the last chest, which was full of gold.

"I think, Father," she said, "that as the gold will be more useful to you, we had better take out the other things again and fill the trunks with it." So they did this; but the more they put in, the more room there seemed to be, and at last they put back all the jewels and dresses they had taken out, and Beauty even added as many more of the jewels as she could carry at once; and then the trunks were not too full, but they were so heavy that an elephant could have not have carried them!

"The Beast was mocking us," cried the merchant; "he must have pretended to give us all these things, knowing that I could not carry them away."

"Let us wait and see," answered Beauty. "I cannot believe that he meant to deceive us. All we can do is to fasten them up and leave them ready."

So they did this and returned to the little room, where, to their astonishment, they found breakfast ready. The merchant ate his with a good appetite, as the Beast's generosity made him believe that he might perhaps venture to come back soon and see Beauty. But she felt sure that her father was leaving her forever, so she was very sad when the bell rang sharply for the second time, and warned them that the time was come for them to part. They went down into the courtyard, where two horses were waiting, one loaded with the two trunks, the other for him to ride. They were pawing the ground in their impatience to start, and the merchant was forced to bid Beauty a hasty farewell; and as soon as he was mounted he went off at such a pace that she lost sight of him in an instant. Then Beauty began to cry, and wandered sadly back to her own room. But she soon found that she was very sleepy, and as she had nothing better to do she lay down and instantly fell asleep. And then she dreamed that she was walking by a brook bordered with trees and lamenting her sad fate, when a young prince, handsomer than anyone she had ever seen and with a voice that went straight to her heart, came and said to her, "Ah, Beauty! you are not so unfortunate as you suppose. Here you will be rewarded for all you have suffered elsewhere. Your every wish shall be gratified. Only try to find me out, no matter how I may be disguised, as I love you dearly, and in making me happy you will find your own happiness. Be as true-hearted as you are beautiful, and we shall have nothing left to wish for."

"What can I do, Prince, to make you happy?" said Beauty.

"Only be grateful," he answered, "and do not trust too much to your eyes. And, above all, do not desert me until you have saved me from my cruel misery."

After this she thought she found herself in a room with a stately and beautiful lady, who said to her:

"Dear Beauty, try not to regret all you have left behind you, for you are destined to a better fate. Only do not let yourself be deceived by appearances."

Beauty found her dreams so interesting that she was in no hurry to awake, but presently the clock roused her by calling her name softly twelve times, and then she got up and found her dressing-table set out with everything she could possibly want; and when her toilet was finished she found dinner was waiting in the room next to hers. But dinner does not take very long when you are all by yourself, and very soon she sat down cosily in the corner of a sofa, and began to think about the charming Prince she had seen in her dream.

"He said I could make him happy," said Beauty to herself.

"It seems, then, that this horrible Beast keeps him a prisoner. How can I set him free? I wonder why they both told me not to trust to appearances? I don't understand it. But, after all, it was only a dream, so why should I trouble myself about it? I had better go and find something to do to amuse myself."

So she got up and began to explore some of the many rooms of the palace.

The first she entered was lined with mirrors, and Beauty saw herself reflected on every side, and thought she had never seen such a charming room. Then a bracelet which was hanging from a chandelier caught her eye, and on taking it down she was greatly surprised to find that it held a portrait of her unknown admirer, just as she had seen him in her dream. With great delight she slipped the bracelet on her arm and went on into a gallery of pictures, where she soon found a portrait of the same handsome Prince, as large as life, and so well painted that as she studied it he seemed to smile kindly at her. Tearing herself away from the portrait at last, she passed through into a room which contained every musical instrument under the sun, and here she amused herself for a long while in trying some of them, and singing until she was tired. The next room was a library, and she saw everything she had ever wanted to read, as well as everything she had read, and it seemed to her that a whole lifetime would not be enough even to read the names of the books, there were so many. By this time it was growing dusk, and wax candles in diamond and ruby candlesticks were beginning to light themselves in every room.

Beauty found her supper served just at the time she preferred to have it, but she did not see anyone or hear a sound, and, though her father had warned her that she would be alone, she began to find it rather dull.

But presently she heard the Beast coming and wondered tremblingly if he meant to eat her up now.

However, as he did not seem at all ferocious, and only said gruffly, "Good-evening, Beauty," she answered cheerfully and managed to conceal her terror. Then the Beast asked her how she had been amusing herself, and she told him all the rooms she had seen.

Then he asked if she thought she could be happy in his palace; and Beauty answered that everything was so beautiful that she would be very hard to please if she could not be happy. And after about an hour's talk Beauty began to think that the Beast was not nearly so terrible as she had supposed at first. Then he got up to leave her, and said in his gruff voice:

"Do you love me, Beauty? Will you marry me?"

"Oh! what shall I say?" cried Beauty, for she was afraid to make the Beast angry by refusing.

"Say yes or no without fear," he replied.

"Oh! no, Beast," said Beauty hastily.

"Since you will not, good-night, Beauty," he said.

And she answered, "Good-night, Beast," very glad to find that her refusal had not provoked him. And after he was gone she was very soon in bed and asleep, and dreaming of her unknown Prince. She thought he came and said to her:

"Ah, Beauty! why are you so unkind to me? I fear I am fated to be unhappy for many a long day still."

And then her dreams changed, but the charming Prince figured in them all; and when morning came her first thought was to look at the portrait and see if it was really like him, and she found that it certainly was.

This morning she decided to amuse herself in the garden, for the sun shone, and all the fountains were playing; but she was astonished to find that every place was familiar to her, and presently she came to the brook where the myrtle trees were growing where she had first met the Prince in her dream, and that made her think more than ever that he must be kept a prisoner by the Beast. When she was tired she went back to the palace, and found a new room full of materials for every kind of work—ribbons to make into bows, and silks to work into flowers. Then there was an aviary full of rare birds, which were so tame that they flew to Beauty as soon as they saw her, and perched upon her shoulders and her head.

"Pretty little creatures," she said, "how I wish that your cage was nearer to my room, that I might often hear you sing!"

So saying she opened a door, and found to her delight that it led into her own room, though she had thought it was quite the other side of the palace.

There were more birds in a room farther on, parrots and cockatoos that could talk, and they greeted Beauty by name; indeed, she found them so entertaining that she took one or two back to her room, and they talked to her while she was at supper; after which the Beast paid her his usual visit, and asked the same questions as before, and then with a gruff "good-night" he took his departure, and Beauty went to bed to dream of her mysterious Prince. The days passed swiftly in different amusements, and after a while Beauty found out another strange thing in the palace, which often pleased her when she was tired of being alone. There was one room which she had not noticed particularly; it was empty, except that under each of the windows stood a very comfortable chair; and the first time she had looked out of the window it had seemed to her that a black curtain prevented her from seeing anything outside. But the second time she went into the room, happening to be tired, she sat down in one of the chairs, when instantly the curtain was rolled aside, and a most amusing pantomine was acted before her; there were dances, and coloured lights, and music, and pretty dresses, and it was all so gay that Beauty was in ecstasies. After that she tried the other seven windows in turn, and there was some new and surprising entertainment to be seen from each of them, so that Beauty never could feel lonely any more. Every evening after supper the Beast came to see her, and always before saying good-night asked her in his terrible voice:

"Beauty, will you marry me?"

And it seemed to Beauty, now she understood him better, that when she said, "No, Beast," he went away quite sad. But her happy dreams of the handsome young Prince soon made her forget the poor Beast, and the only thing that at all disturbed her was to be constantly told to distrust appearances, to let her heart guide her, and not her eyes, and many other equally perplexing things, which, consider as she would, she could not understand.

So everything went on for a long time, until at last, happy as she was, Beauty began to long for the sight of her father and her brothers and sisters; and one night, seeing her look very sad, the Beast asked her what was the matter. Beauty had quite ceased to be afraid of him. Now she knew that he was really gentle in spite of his ferocious looks and his dreadful voice. So she answered that she was longing to see her home once more. Upon hearing this the Beast seemed sadly distressed, and cried miserably:

"Ah! Beauty, have you the heart to desert an unhappy Beast like this? What more do you want to make you happy? Is it because you hate me that you want to escape?"

"No, dear Beast," answered Beauty softly, "I do not hate you, and I should be very sorry never to see you any more, but I long to see my father again. Only let me go for two months, and I promise to come back to you and stay for the rest of my life."

The Beast, who had been sighing dolefully while she spoke, now replied:

"I cannot refuse you anything you ask, even though it should cost me my life. Take the four boxes you will find in the room next to your own, and fill them with everything you wish to take with you. But remember your promise and come back when the two months are over, or you may have cause to repent it, for if you do not come in good time you will find your faithful Beast dead. You will not need any chariot to bring you back. Only say good-bye to all your brothers and sisters the night before you come away, and when you have gone to bed turn this ring round upon your finger and say firmly: 'I wish to go back to my palace and see my Beast again.' Good-night, Beauty. Fear nothing, sleep peacefully, and before long you shall see your father once more."

As soon as Beauty was alone she hastened to fill the boxes with all the rare and precious things she saw about her, and only when she was tired of heaping things into them did they seem to be full.

Then she went to bed, but could hardly sleep for joy. And when at last she did begin to dream of her beloved Prince she was grieved to see him stretched upon a grassy bank sad and weary, and hardly like himself.

"What is the matter?" she cried.

But he looked at her reproachfully, and said: "How can you ask me, cruel one? Are you not leaving me to my death perhaps?"

"Ah! don't be so sorrowful," cried Beauty; "I am only going to assure my father that I am safe and happy. I have promised the Beast faithfully that I will come back, and he would die of grief if I did not keep my word!"

"What would that matter to you?" said the Prince. "Surely you would not care?"

"Indeed I should be ungrateful if I did not care for such a kind Beast," cried Beauty indignantly. "I would die to save him from pain. I assure you it is not his fault that he is so ugly."

Just then a strange sound woke her—someone was speaking not very far away; and opening her eyes she found herself in a room she had never seen before, which was certainly not nearly so splendid as those she was used to in the Beast's palace. Where could she be? She got up and dressed hastily, and then saw that the boxes she had packed the night before were all in the room. While she was wondering by what magic the Beast had transported them and herself to this strange place she suddenly heard her father's voice, and rushed out and greeted him joyfully. Her brothers and sisters were all astonished at her appearance, as they had never expected to see her again, and there was no end to the questions they asked her. She had also much to hear about what had happened to them while she was away, and of her father's journey home. But when they heard that she had only come to be with them for a short time, and then must go back to the Beast's palace forever, they lamented loudly. Then Beauty asked her father what he thought could be the meaning of her strange dreams, and why the Prince constantly begged her not to trust to appearances. After much consideration he answered: "You tell me yourself that the Beast, frightful as he is, loves you dearly, and deserves your love and gratitude for his gentleness and kindness; I think the Prince must mean you to understand that you ought to reward him by doing as he wishes you to, in spite of his ugliness."

Beauty could not help seeing that this seemed very probable; still, when she thought of her dear Prince who was so handsome, she did not feel at all inclined to marry the Beast. At any rate, for two months she need not decide, but could enjoy herself with her sisters. But though they were rich now, and lived in a town again, and had plenty of acquaintances, Beauty found that nothing amused her very much; and she often thought of the palace, where she was so happy, especially as at home she never once dreamed of her dear Prince, and she felt quite sad without him.

Then her sisters seemed to have got quite used to being without her, and even found her rather in the way, so she would not have been sorry when the two months were over but for her father and brothers, who begged her to stay and seemed so grieved at the thought of her departure that she had not the courage to say good-bye to them. Every day when she got up she meant to say it at night, and when night came she put it off again, until at last she had a dismal dream which helped her to make up her mind. She thought she was wandering in a lonely path in the palace gardens, when she heard groans which seemed to come from some bushes hiding the entrance of a cave, and running quickly to see what could be the matter, she found the Beast stretched out upon his side, apparently dying. He reproached her faintly with being the cause of his distress, and at the same moment a stately lady appeared, and said very gravely:

"Ah! Beauty, you are only just in time to save his life. See what happens when people do not keep their promises! If you had delayed one day more, you would have found him dead."

Beauty was so terrified by this dream that the next morning she announced her intention of going back at once, and that very night she said good-bye to her father and all her brothers and sisters, and as soon as she was in bed she turned her ring round upon her finger, and said firmly:

"I wish to go back to my palace and see my Beast again," as she had been told to do.

Then she fell asleep instantly, and only woke up to hear the clock saying, "Beauty, Beauty," twelve times in its musical voice, which told her at once that she was really in the palace once more. Everything was just as before, and her birds were so glad to see her! But Beauty thought she had never known such a long day, for she was so anxious to see the Beast again that she felt as if supper-time would never come.

But when it did come and no Beast appeared she was really frightened; so, after listening and waiting for a long time, she ran down into the garden to search for him. Up and down the paths and avenues ran poor Beauty, calling him in vain, for no one answered, and not a trace of him could she find; until at last, quite tired, she stopped for a minute's rest, and saw that she was standing opposite the shady path she had seen in her dream. She rushed down it, and, sure enough, there was the cave, and in it lay the Beast—asleep, as Beauty thought. Quite glad to have found him, she ran up and stroked his head, but to her horror he did not move or open his eyes.

"Oh! he is dead; and it is all my fault," said Beauty, crying bitterly.

But then, looking at him again, she fancied he still breathed, and, hastily fetching some water from the nearest fountain, she sprinkled it over his face, and to her great delight he began to revive.

"Oh! Beast, how you frightened me!" she cried. "I never knew how much I loved you until just now, when I feared I was too late to save your life."

"Can you really love such an ugly creature as I am?" said the Beast faintly. "Ah! Beauty, you only came just in time. I was dying because I thought you had forgotten your promise. But go back now and rest, I shall see you again by-and-by."

Beauty, who had half expected that he would be angry with her, was reassured by his gentle voice, and went back to the palace, where supper was awaiting her; and afterwards the Beast came in as usual, and talked about the time she had spent with her father, asking if she had enjoyed herself and if they had all been very glad to see her.

Beauty answered politely, and quite enjoyed telling him all that had happened to her. And when at last the time came for him to go, and he asked, as he had so often asked before:

"Beauty, will you marry me?" she answered softly:

"Yes, dear Beast."

As she spoke a blaze of light sprang up before the windows of the palace; fireworks crackled and guns banged, and across the avenue of orange trees, in letters all made of fire-flies, was written: "Long live the Prince and his Bride."

Turning to ask the Beast what it could all mean, Beauty found that he had disappeared, and in his place stood her long-loved Prince! At the same moment the wheels of a chariot were heard upon the terrace, and two ladies entered the room. One of them Beauty recognized as the stately lady she had seen in her dreams; the other was also so grand and queenly that Beauty hardly knew which to greet first.

But the one she already knew said to her companion:

"Well, Queen, this is Beauty, who has had the courage to rescue your son from the terrible enchantment. They love one another, and only your consent to their marriage is wanting to make them perfectly happy."

"I consent with all my heart," cried the Queen. "How can I ever thank you enough, charming girl, for having restored my dear son to his natural form?"

And then she tenderly embraced Beauty and the Prince, who had meanwhile been greeting the Fairy and receiving her congratulations.

"Now," said the Fairy to Beauty, "I suppose you would like me to send for all your brothers and sisters to dance at your wedding?"

And so she did, and the marriage was celebrated the very next day with the utmost splendour, and Beauty and the Prince lived happily ever after.

## THE WHITE CAT

The White Cat and Other Old French Fairy Tales *is a handsome book illustrated by Elizabeth MacKinstry and serves as the source of this version. It was reissued in a facsimile edition in 1967.*

Once upon a time there was a King who had three sons. The day came when they were grown so big and strong that he began to fear they would be planning to rule in his place. This would cause trouble among themselves and his subjects. Now the King was not so young as he once had been but nevertheless he had no notion of giving up his kingdom then and there. So after much thought he hit upon a scheme which should keep them too busily occupied to interfere in the affairs of state. Accordingly he called the three into his private apartments where he spoke to them with great kindliness and concern of his plans for the future.

"I am planning to retire from the affairs of state. But I do not wish my subjects to suffer from this change. Therefore, while I am still alive, I shall transfer my crown to one of you. I shall not follow the usual custom of leaving the crown to my eldest son, but whichever one of you shall bring me the handsomest and most intelligent little dog shall become my heir."

The Princes were greatly surprised by this strange request, but they could not very well refuse to humor their father's whim; and since there was luck in it for the two younger sons and the elder of the three was a timid, rather spiritless fellow, they agreed readily enough. The King then bade them farewell after first distributing jewels and money among them and adding that a year from that day at the same place and hour they should return to him with their little dogs.

Within sight of the city gates stood a castle where the three often spent many days in company with their young companions. Here they agreed to part and to meet again in a year before proceeding with their trophies to the King; and so having pledged their good faith, and changing their names that they might not be known, each set off upon a different road.

It would take far too long to recount the adventures of all three Princes so I shall tell only of those that befell the youngest, for a more gay and well-mannered Prince never lived, nor one

"The White Cat." Reprinted with permission of The Macmillan Company from *The White Cat and Other Old French Fairy Tales* by Mme. La Comtesse D'Aulnoy, arranged by Rachel Field. Copyright 1928 by The Macmillan Company. Used by permission of Arthur Pederson

so handsome and accomplished.

Scarcely a day passed that he did not buy a dog or two, greyhounds, mastiffs, bloodhounds, pointers, spaniels, water dogs, lapdogs; but the instant he found a handsomer one he let the first go and kept the new purchase, since it would have been impossible for him to carry them all on his journeyings. He went without fixed plan or purpose and so he continued for many days until at last darkness and a terrible storm overtook him at nightfall in a lonely forest. Thunder and lightning rumbled and flashed; rain fell in torrents; the trees seemed to close more densely about him until at last he could no longer find his way. When he had wandered thus for some time he suddenly saw a glint of light between the tree trunks. Feeling certain that this must mean a shelter of some sort he pressed on till he found himself approaching the most magnificent castle he had ever seen. The gate was of gold and covered with jewels of such brilliance that it was their light which had guided him to the spot. In spite of the rain and storm he caught glimpses of walls of finest porcelain decorated with pictures of the most famous fairies from the beginning of the world up to that very day: Cinderella, Graciosa, Sleeping Beauty, and a hundred others. As he admired all this magnificence he noticed a rabbit's foot fastened to the golden gates by a chain of diamonds. Marveling greatly at such a lavish display of precious gems, the young Prince pulled at the rabbit's foot and straightway an unseen bell of wonderful sweetness rang; the gate was opened by hundreds of tiny hands and others pushed him forward while he hesitated amazed upon the threshold. He moved on wonderingly, his hand on the hilt of his sword until he was reassured by two voices singing a welcome. Again he felt himself being pushed, this time toward a gate of coral opening upon an apartment of mother-of-pearl from which he passed into others still more richly decorated and alight with wax candles and great chandeliers sparkling with a thousand rainbows.

He had passed through perhaps sixty such rooms when the hands that guided him made a sign for him to stop. He saw a large armchair moving by itself toward a fireplace at the same moment that the fire began to blaze and the hands, which he now observed to be very small and white, carefully drew off his wet clothes and handed him others so fine and richly embroidered they seemed fit for a wedding day. The hands continued to dress him, until at last, powdered and attired more handsomely than he had ever been in his life before, the Prince was led into a banquet hall. Here the four walls were decorated solely with paintings representing famous cats, Puss-in-Boots and others whom he was quick to recognize. Even more astonishing than this was the table set for two with its gold service and crystal cups.

There was an orchestra composed entirely of cats. One held a music book with the strangest notes imaginable; another beat time with a little baton; and all the rest strummed tiny guitars.

While the Prince stared in amazement, each cat suddenly began to mew in a different key and to claw at the guitar strings. It was the strangest music ever heard! The Prince would have thought himself in bedlam had not the palace itself been so marvelously beautiful. So he stopped his ears and laughed heartily at the various poses and grimaces of these strange musicians. He was meditating upon the extraordinary sights he had already seen in the castle, when he beheld a little figure entering the hall. It was scarcely more than two feet in height and wrapped in a long gold crêpe veil. Before it walked two cats dressed in deep mourning and wearing cloaks and swords, while still others followed, some carrying rat-traps full of rats and mice in cages.

By this time the Prince was too astonished to think. But presently the tiny pink figure approached him and lifted its veil. He now beheld the most beautiful little white cat that ever was or ever will be. She had such a very youthful and melancholy air and a mewing so soft and sweet that it went straight to the young Prince's heart.

"Son of a King," she said to him, "thou art welcome; my mewing Majesty beholds thee with pleasure."

"Madam," responded the Prince, bowing as low as possible before her, "it is very gracious of you to receive me with so much attention, but you do not appear to me to be an ordinary little cat. The gift of speech which you have and this superb castle you inhabit are certainly evidence to the contrary."

"Son of a King," rejoined the White Cat, "I pray that you will cease to pay me compliments. I am plain in my speech and manners, but I have a kind heart. Come," she added, to her attendants, "let them serve supper and bid the concert cease, for the Prince does not understand what they are singing."

"And are they singing words, madam?" he asked incredulously.

"Certainly," she answered, "we have very gifted poets here, as you will see if you remain long enough."

Supper was then served to them by the same hands that had guided him there, and a very strange meal it was. There were two dishes of each course—one soup, for instance, being of savory pigeons while the other had been made of nicely fattened mice. The sight of this rather took away the Prince's appetite until his hostess, who seemed to guess what was passing in his mind, assured him that his own dishes had been specially prepared and contained no rats and mice of any kind. Her charming manners convinced the Prince that the little Cat had no wish to deceive him, so he began to eat and drink with great enjoyment. During their meal he happened to observe that on one paw she wore a tiny miniature set in a bracelet. This surprised him so that he begged her to let him examine it more closely. He had supposed it would be the picture of Master Puss, but what was his astonishment to find it the portrait of a handsome young man who bore a strange resemblance to himself! As he stared at it, the White Cat was heard to sigh so deeply and with such profound sadness that the Prince became even more curious; but he dared not question one so affected. Instead he entertained her with tales of court life, with which, to his surprise, he found her well acquainted.

After supper the White Cat led her guest into another Hall, where upon a little stage twelve cats and twelve monkeys danced in the most fantastic costumes. So the evening ended in great merriment; and after the Cat had bade the Prince a gracious good night the same strange hands conducted him to his own apartment, where in spite of the softness of his bed he spent half the night trying to solve the mystery of the castle and his extraordinary little hostess.

But when morning came he was no nearer to an answer to his questionings, so he allowed the pair of hands to help him dress and lead him into the palace courtyard. Here a vast company of cats in hunting costume were gathering to the sound of the horn. A fête day indeed! The White Cat was going to hunt and wished the Prince to accompany her. Now the mysterious hands presented him with a wooden horse. He made some objection to mounting it, but it proved to be an excellent charger, and a tireless galloper. The White Cat rode beside him on a monkey, the handsomest and proudest that ever was seen. She had thrown off her long veil and wore a military cap which made her look so bold that she frightened all the mice in the neighborhood. Never was there a more successful hunt. The cats outran all the rabbits and hares and a thousand skillful feats were performed to the gratification of the entire company. Tiring of the hunt at last the White Cat took up a horn no bigger than the Prince's little finger and blew upon it with so loud and clear a tone it could be heard ten leagues away. Scarcely had she sounded two or three flourishes when all the cats in the countryside seemed to appear. By land and sea and through the air they all came flocking to her call, dressed in every conceivable costume. So, followed by this extraordinary train, the Prince rode back with his hostess to the castle.

That night the White Cat put on her gold veil again and they dined together as before. Being very hungry the Prince ate and drank heartily, and this time the food had a strange effect upon him. All recollection of his father and the little dog he was to find for him slipped from his mind. He no longer thought of anything but of gossiping with the White Cat and enjoying her kind and gracious companionship. So the days passed in pleasant sport and amusement and the night in feasting and conversation. There was scarcely one in which he did not discover some new charm of the little White Cat. Now he had forgotten even the land of his birth. The hands continued to wait upon him and supply every want till he began to regret that he could not become a cat himself to live forever in such pleasant company.

"Alas," he confessed to the White Cat at last,
"how wretched it makes me even to think of leaving you! I have come to love you so dearly. Could you not become a woman or else make me a cat?"

But though she smiled at his wish, the look she turned upon him was very strange.

A year passes away quickly when one has neither pain nor care, when one is merry and in good health. The Prince took no thought of time, but the White Cat was not so forgetful.

"There are only three days left to look for the little dog you were to bring to the King, your father," she reminded him. "Your two brothers have already found several very beautiful ones."

At her words the Prince's memory returned to him and he marveled at his strange forgetfulness.

"What spell would have made me forget what was most important to me in the whole world?" he cried in despair. "My honor and my fortune are lost unless I can find a dog that will win a kingdom for me and a horse swift enough to carry me home again in this short time!"

So, believing this to be impossible, he grew very sorrowful. Then the White Cat spoke to him with great reassurance.

"Son of a King," she said, "do not distress yourself so. I am your friend. Remain here another day, and though it is five hundred leagues from here to your country the good wooden horse will carry you there in less than twelve hours' time."

"But it is not enough for me to return to my father, dear Cat," said the Prince. "I must take him a little dog as well."

"And so you shall," replied she. "Here is a walnut which contains one more beautiful than the Dog Star."

"Your Majesty jests with me," he protested.

"Put the walnut to your ear then," insisted the Cat, "and you will hear it bark."

He obeyed her, and as he held the walnut to his ear a faint "Bow-wow" came from within, more tiny and shrill than a cricket on a winter night. The Prince could scarcely believe his ears or contain his curiosity to see so diminutive a creature. But he was wise enough to follow the White Cat's advice not to open the walnut till he should reach his father's presence.

It was a sad leave-taking between the Prince and the White Cat. A thousand times he thanked her, but though he urged her to return to court with him, she only shook her head and sighed deeply as upon the night of his arrival. So he galloped away at last on the wooden horse, which bore him more swiftly than the wind to the appointed place.

He reached the castle even before his two brothers and enjoyed the sight of their surprise at seeing a wooden horse champing at the bit in the courtyard. The two brothers were so busy telling of their various adventures that they took little note of their younger brother's silence concerning his, but when the time came to show one another their dogs the two were vastly amused at sight of an ugly cur which the young Prince had brought along, pretending to consider it a marvel of beauty. Needless to say the elder Princes smiled with secret satisfaction to think how far superior were their own dogs, for though they wished their brother no ill luck, they had no wish to see him ruling over the kingdom.

Next morning the three set out together in the same coach. The two eldest brothers carried baskets filled with little dogs too delicate and beautiful to be touched, while the youngest carried the poor cur as if it also was precious. By no outward sign did he betray the presence of the walnut with its precious occupant which was safely hidden in his pocket. No sooner did the three set foot in the palace than all the court crowded around to welcome the returned travelers and see the results of their journeyings. The King received them with great joy, professing delight over the little dogs his two elder sons brought out for his inspection. But the more he studied their merits, the more puzzled he became, so nearly were they alike in beauty and grace. The two brothers were already beginning to dispute with one another as to which deserved the crown when the younger brother stepped forward, holding upon the palm of his hand the walnut so lately presented to him by the White Cat. Opening it without more ado, he revealed a tiny dog lying upon cotton. So perfectly formed was it and so small that it could pass through a little finger ring without touching any part of it. It was more delicate than thistledown and its coat shone with colors of the rainbow. Nor was this all; immediately it was released from its kennel, the little creature arose on its hind legs and

began to go through the steps of a tarantella, with tiny castanets and all the airs and graces of a Spanish dancer!

The King was dumbfounded and even the two brothers were forced to acknowledge that such a beautiful and gifted dog had never been seen before. But their father was in no mood to give up his kingdom, so he announced that he had decided upon another test of their skill. This time he would give them a year to travel over land and sea in search of a piece of cloth so fine it would pass through the eye of the finest Venetian-point lace needle.

So the Prince remounted his wooden horse and set off at full speed, for now he knew exactly where he wanted to go. So great was his eagerness to see the beautiful White Cat once more that he could scarcely contain himself until her castle came into view. This time every window was alight to welcome him and the faithful pair of hands which had waited on him so well before were ready to take the bridle of the wooden horse and lead it back to the stable while the Prince hurried to the White Cat's private apartments.

He found her lying on a little couch of blue satin with many pillows. Her expression was sad until she caught sight of him. Then she sprang up and began to caper about him delightedly.

"Oh, dear Prince," cried she, "I had scarcely dared to hope for your return. I am generally so unfortunate in matters that concern me."

A thousand times must the grateful Prince caress her and recount his adventures, which perhaps she knew more about than he guessed. And now he told her of his father's latest whim—how he had set his heart upon having a piece of cloth that could pass through the eye of the finest needle. For his own part he did not believe it was possible to find such a thing, but he believed that if any one could help him in this quest it would be his dear White Cat. She listened attentively to all he told her and finally explained with a thoughtful air that this was a matter demanding careful consideration. There were, it seemed, some cats in her castle who could spin with extraordinary skill, and she added that she would also put a paw to the work herself so that he need not trouble himself to search farther.

The Prince was only too delighted to accept

this offer and he and his charming hostess sat down to supper together, after which a magnificent display of fireworks was set off in his honor. And once more the days passed in enchanted succession. The ingenious White Cat knew a thousand different ways of entertaining her guest, so that he never once thought of missing human society. Indeed, he was probably the first person in the world to spend a whole year of complete contentment with only cats for company.

The second year slipped away as pleasantly as the first. The Prince could scarcely think of anything that the tireless hands did not instantly supply, whether books, jewels, pictures, old things or new. In short, he had but to say, "I want a certain gem that is in the cabinet of the Great Mogul, or the King of Persia, or such and such a statue in Corinth or any part of Greece," and he saw it instantly before him, without knowing how it came or who brought it. It is not unpleasant at all to find oneself able to possess any treasure in the world. No wonder our Prince was happy!

But the White Cat who was ever watchful of his welfare, warned him that the hour of departure was approaching and that he might make himself easy in his mind about the piece of cloth, for she had a most wonderful one for him. She added that it was her intention this time to furnish him with an equipage worthy of his high birth, and without waiting for his reply, beckoned him to the window overlooking the castle courtyard. Here he saw an open coach of gold and flame-color with a thousand gallant devices to please the mind and eye. It was drawn by twelve horses as white as snow, four-and-four abreast, with harnesses of flaming velvet embroidered with diamonds and gold. A hundred other coaches, each with eight horses and filled with superbly attired noblemen followed, escorted by a thousand bodyguards whose uniforms were so richly embroidered you could not see the material beneath. But the most remarkable part of this cavalcade was that a portrait of the White Cat was to be seen everywhere, in coach device, uniform, or worn as a decoration on the doublets of those who rode in the train, as if it were some newly created order that had been conferred upon them.

"Go now," said the White Cat to the Prince.

"Appear at the court of the King, your father, in such magnificence that he cannot fail to be impressed and to bestow upon you the crown which you deserve. Here is another walnut. Crack it in his presence and you will find the piece of cloth you asked of me."

"Oh, dear White Cat," he answered tenderly, "I am so overcome by your goodness that I would gladly give up my hopes of power and future grandeur to stay here with you the rest of life."

"Son of a King," she answered, "I am convinced of your kindness of heart. A kind heart is a rare thing among princes who would be loved by all, yet not love any one themselves. But you are the proof that there is an exception to this rule. I give you credit for the affection you have shown to a little white cat that after all is good for nothing but to catch mice."

So the Prince kissed her paw and departed.

This time the two brothers arrived at their father's palace before him, congratulating themselves that their young brother must be dead or gone for good. They lost no time in displaying the cloths they had brought, which were indeed so fine that they could pass through the eye of a large needle but not through the small eye of the needle the King had already selected. At this there arose a great murmuring at court. The friends of the two Princes took sides among themselves as to which had fulfilled the bargain better. But this was interrupted by a flourish of trumpets announcing the arrival of their younger brother.

The magnificence of his train fairly took away the breath of the King and his court, but their astonishment grew even greater when, after saluting his father, the young Prince brought out the walnut. This he cracked with great ceremony only to find, instead of the promised piece of cloth, a cherry stone. At sight of this the King and the court exchanged sly smiles. Nothing daunted, the Prince cracked the cherry stone, only to find a kernel inside. Jeers and murmurs ran through the great apartment. The Prince must be a fool indeed! He made no answer to them, but even he began to doubt the White Cat's words as he found next a grain of wheat and within that the smallest millet seed. "Oh, White Cat, White Cat! Have you betrayed me?"

he muttered between his teeth. Even as he spoke he felt a little scratch upon his hand, so sharp that it drew blood. Taking this to be some sort of sign, the Prince proceeded to open the millet seed. Before the incredulous eyes of the whole court he drew out of it a piece of cloth four hundred yards long and marvelously embroidered with colored birds and beasts, with trees and fruits and flowers, with shells and jewels and even with suns and moons and countless stars. There were also portraits of Kings and Queens of the past upon it and of their children and children's children, not forgetting the smallest child, and each dressed perfectly in the habit of his century.

The sight of this was almost too much for the King. He could scarcely find the needle. Through its eye the wonderful piece of cloth was able to pass not only once, but six times, before the jealous gaze of the two older Princes. But the King was still far from ready to give up his kingdom. Once more he turned to his children.

"I am going to put your obedience to a new and final test," he told them. "Go and travel for another year and whichever one of you brings back with him the most beautiful Princess shall marry her and be crowned King on his wedding day. I pledge my honor that after this I shall ask no further favors of you."

So off the three went again, the youngest Prince still in a good humor although he had the least cause to be since he had twice been the acknowledged winner of the wager. But he was not one to dispute his father's will, so soon he and all his train were taking the road back to his dear White Cat. She knew the very day and hour of his arrival, and all along the way flowers had been strewn and perfume made the air sweet. Once more the castle gate was opened to him and the strange hands took him in charge while all the cats climbed into the trees to welcome their returning visitor.

"So, my Prince," said the White Cat when he reached her side at last, "once more you have returned without the crown. But no matter," she added as he opened his lips to explain. "I know that you are bound to take back the most beautiful Princess to court and I will find one for you, never fear. Meantime, let us amuse ourselves and be merry."

The third year passed for the young Prince as had the two others, and since nothing runs away faster than time passed without trouble or care, it is certain that he would have completely forgotten the day of his return to court had not the White Cat reminded him of it. This time, however, she told him that upon him alone depended his fate. He must promise to do whatever she asked of him. The Prince agreed readily enough until he heard her command him to cut off her head and tail and fling them into the fire.

"I!" cried the Prince, aghast, "I be so barbarous as to kill my dear White Cat? This is some trick to try my heart, but you should be sure of its gratitude."

"No, no, Son of a King," she answered, "I know your heart too well for that. But fate is stronger than either of us, and you must do as I bid you. It is the only way; and you must believe me, for I swear it on the honor of a Cat."

Tears came into the eyes of the Prince at the mere thought of cutting off the head of so amiable and pretty a creature. He tried to say all the most tender things he could think of, hoping to distract her. But she persisted that she wished to die by his hand because it was the only means of preventing his brothers from winning the crown. So piteously did she beg him that at last, all of a tremble, he drew his sword. With faltering hand he cut off the head and tail of his dear White Cat.

Next moment the most remarkable transformation took place before his very eyes. The body of the little White Cat suddenly changed into that of a young girl, the most graceful ever seen. But this was as nothing compared to the beauty and sweetness of her face, where only the shining brightness of the eyes gave any hint of the cat she had so recently been. The Prince was struck dumb with surprise and delight. He opened his eyes wider still to look at her, and what was his amazement to behold a troop of lords and ladies entering the apartment, each with a cat's skin flung over an arm. They advanced, and throwing themselves at the feet of their Queen, expressed their joy at seeing her once more restored to her natural form. She received them with great affection, but presently she desired them to leave her alone with the Prince.

"Behold, my dear Prince," she said as soon as

they had done so, "I am released of a terrible enchantment, too long a tale to tell you now. Suffice it to say that this portrait which you saw upon my paw when I was a cat, was given to me by my guardian fairies during the time of my trial. I supposed it was of my first, unhappy love who was so cruelly taken from me and whose resemblance to you is so striking. Conceive my joy then, to find that it is of the Prince who has my entire heart and who was destined to rescue me from my enchantment."

And she bowed low before our Prince, who was so filled with joy and wonder that he would have remained there forever telling her of his love, had she not reminded him that the hour for his return to his father's court was almost upon them. Taking him by the hands, she led him into the courtyard to a chariot even more magnificent than the one she had provided before. The rest were equally gorgeous, the horses shod with emeralds held in place by diamond nails, with such gold and jeweled trappings as were never seen before or since. But the young Prince had eyes for nothing beyond the beauty of his companion.

Just before they reached the outskirts of the city, they sighted the Prince's two brothers with their trains driving toward them from opposite directions. At this the Princess hid herself in a small throne of rock crystal and precious gems while the Prince remained alone in the coach. His two brothers, each accompanied by a charming lady, greeted him warmly but expressed surprise and curiosity that he should be alone. To these questions he replied that he had been so unfortunate as not to have met with any lady of sufficient beauty to bring with him to court. He added, however, that he had instead a very rare and gifted White Cat. At this the brothers laughed loudly and exchanged pleased glances,

for now they were convinced that he was indeed a simpleton and they need have no fears of his outwitting them a third time.

Through the streets of the city the two elder Princes rode with their ladies in open carriages, while the youngest Prince came last. Behind him was borne the great rock crystal, at which every one gazed in wonder.

The two Princes eagerly charged up the palace stairs with their Princesses, so anxious were they for their father's approval. The King received them graciously, but once more had difficulty in deciding which should have the prize. So he turned to his youngest son, who stood alone before him. "Have you returned empty-handed this time?" he asked.

"In this rock your Majesty will find a little White Cat," he answered, "one which mews so sweetly and has such velvet paws that you cannot but be delighted with it."

But before the surprised King could reach the crystal, the Princess touched an inner spring. It flew open revealing her in all her beauty, more dazzling than the sun itself. Her hair fell in golden ringlets; she was crowned with flowers and she moved with incomparable grace in her gown of white and rose-colored gauze. Even the King himself could not resist such loveliness, but hastened to acknowledge her undisputed right to wear the crown.

"But I have not come to deprive your Majesty of a throne which you fill so admirably," she said, bowing before him graciously. "I was born the heiress to six kingdoms of my own, so permit me to offer one to you and to each of your elder sons. I ask no other favors of you than your friendship and that your youngest son shall be my husband. Three kingdoms will be quite enough for us."

And so in truth they found them.

## The Scandinavian Countries

*The Scandinavian folk tales can be traced as a continuous tradition
for more than a thousand years, but the first serious study and collection of them
was begun in Sweden in 1630. When we speak of Scandinavia we
mean the present-day countries of Norway, Sweden, and Denmark (Iceland and
Finland not included), although the Norse traditions reach into
Finland, Iceland, Russia, the British Isles, and Northern Europe. The tales and*

*myths from the Scandinavian peoples are among the most prominent
in European literature. Although the temper of Scandinavian folk tales is, in the
main, serious, the stories have a drollery that equals that of the English tales.
Peter Christian Asbjörnsen and Jörgen Moe, like the Grimm brothers, collected
their stories from the lips of old storytellers, thus capturing the dramatic and
forthright quality that invariably characterizes such spontaneous narration. These
tales were also fortunate in their translator, Sir George Webbe Dasent, who
put them into such clear, vigorous English that their folk flavor and even the
feeling of spontaneity are preserved. These qualities make them easy to
tell and the stories should not be read if it is possible to learn them for telling.*

## THE MOST OBEDIENT WIFE

### (Danish)

*This tale is among those collected by Svend
Grundtvig, a well-known Danish folklorist of the
nineteenth century. The Danes, to all who know
them, exhibit a remarkable sense of humor,
which seems to be almost a national trait.*

Long ago there was a rich farmer who had
three daughters, all grown up and marriageable,
and all three very pretty. The eldest of them was
the prettiest, and she was also the cleverest, but
she was so quarrelsome and obstinate, that there
was never any peace in the house. She constantly
contradicted her father, who was a kind, peace-
loving man, and she quarrelled with her sisters,
although they were very good-natured girls.

Many wooers came to the farm, and one of
them wished to marry the eldest daughter. The
farmer said that he had no objection to him as a
son-in-law, but at the same time he thought it his
duty to tell the suitor the truth. Accordingly he
warned him that his eldest daughter was so violent and strong-minded that no one could live in
peace with her. As some compensation for these
faults, she would receive three hundred pounds
more in her dowry than would her two sisters.
That was, of course, very attractive, but the
young man thought over the matter and, after he
had been visiting the house for some time, he altered his mind and asked for the hand of the second daughter. The daughter accepted him, and,
as her father was willing, the two became man

"The Most Obedient Wife." From *Danish Fairy Tales*
by Svendt Grundtvig. Reprinted by permission of the
publishers, Thomas Y. Crowell Company, Inc.

and wife and lived very happily together.

Then came another wooer, from another part
of the country, and he also wanted to marry the
eldest daughter. The father warned him, as he
had cautioned the first wooer; telling him that
she would receive three hundred pounds more
than· her youngest sister, but that he must be
careful, for she was so stubborn and quarrelsome
that nobody could live in peace with her. So the
second wooer changed his mind and asked for
the hand of the youngest daughter. They married shortly after and lived happily and peacefully together.

The eldest sister was now alone with her father, but she did not treat him any better than
before, and grew even more ill-humoured because her two sisters had found favour in the
eyes of the first two wooers. She was obstinate
and quarrelsome, violent and bad-tempered, and
she grew more so from day to day.

At last another wooer came, and he was neither from their own district nor even from their
country, but from a distant land. He went to the
farmer and asked for the hand of his eldest
daughter. "I do not want her to marry at all,"
said the father. "It would be a shame to allow
her to do so; she is so ill-tempered and violent
that no human being could live in peace with
her and I do not want to be the cause of such unhappiness." But the wooer remained firm; he
wanted her, he said, whatever her faults might
be. At length the father yielded, provided that
his daughter were willing to marry the young
man, for, after all, he would be glad to get rid of
her, and as he had told the suitor the whole
truth about her, his conscience was clear. Accordingly, the young man wooed the girl, and she did
not hesitate long, but accepted the offer, for she

was tired of sitting at home a despised and spurned spinster.

The wooer said that he had no time to remain with them just then, as he must return home at once, and, as soon as the wedding day was fixed, he rode away. He also told them not to wait for him at the farm on the day of the wedding, he would appear in good time at the church. When the day came the farmer drove with his daughter to the church, where a great company of wedding guests had assembled; the bride's sisters and brothers-in-law were there, and all the village people arrived in their Sunday clothes. The bridegroom was there also, but in ordinary travelling garments; and so the couple walked up to the altar and were married.

As soon as the ceremony was over, the bridegroom took his young wife by the hand and led her out of the church. He sent a message to his father-in-law asking him to excuse their absence from the marriage feast, as they had no time to waste. He had not driven in a coach, as is the custom at weddings, but travelled on horseback, on a fine big grey horse, with an ordinary saddle, and a couple of pistols in the saddlebags. He had brought no friends or relations with him, only a big dog, that lay beside the horse during the ceremony. The bridegroom lifted his bride on to the pommel, as if she had been a feather, jumped into the saddle, put the spurs to his horse and rode off with the dog trotting behind. The marriage party standing at the church door looked after them, and shook their heads in amazement. Then they got into their carriages, drove back to the house, and partook of the marriage feast without bride or bridegroom.

The bride did not like this at all, but as she did not want to quarrel with her bridegroom so soon, she held her tongue for a time; but as he did not speak either, she at last broke the ice and said that it was a very fine horse they were riding. "Yes," he replied; "I have seven other horses at home in my stables, but this is my favourite; it is the most valuable of all, and I like it best." Then she remarked that she liked the beautiful dog also. "It is indeed a jewel of a dog," he said, "and has cost me a lot of money."

After a while they came to a forest, where the bridegroom sprang from his horse and cut a thin switch from a willow-tree. This he wound three times round his finger, then tied it with a thread and gave it to his bride, saying: "This is my wedding gift to you. Take good care of it, and carry it about with you always! You will not repent it." She thought it a strange wedding gift, but put it in her pocket, and they rode on again. Presently the bride dropped her glove, and the bridegroom said to the dog: "Pick it up, Fido!" But the dog took no notice, and left the glove on the ground. Then his master drew his pistol from the holster, shot the dog, and rode on, leaving it lying dead. "How could you be so cruel?" said his bride. "I never say a thing twice," was the reply, and they journeyed on in silence.

After some time they came to a running stream that they had to cross. There being only a ford, and no bridge, the man said to his horse: "Take good care! Not a drop must soil my bride's dress!" When they had crossed, however, the dress was badly soiled, and the husband lifted his bride from the horse, drew out the other pistol and shot the horse, so that it fell dead to the ground. "Oh, the poor horse!" cried the bride. "Yes, but I never say a thing twice," answered her husband. Then he took saddle, bridle, and cover from the horse; bridle and cover he carried himself, but the saddle he gave to his young wife, and said: "You can carry that; we shall soon be home." He walked on in silence, and the bride quickly put the saddle on her back and followed him; she had no desire to make him say it twice.

Soon they arrived at his dwelling place, a very fine farm. The menservants and maidservants rushed to the door and received them, and the husband said to them: "See, this is my wife and your mistress. Whatever she tells you, you are to do, just as if I had ordered it." Then he led her indoors and showed her everything—living-rooms and bedrooms, kitchen and cellar, brew-house and dairy—and said to her: "You will look after everything indoors, I attend to everything out-of-doors," and then they sat down to supper, and soon after went to bed.

Days, weeks and months passed; the young wife attended to all household matters while her husband looked after the farm, and not a single angry word passed between them. The servants had been accustomed to obey their master implicitly, and now they obeyed their mistress likewise, and so six months passed without there having arisen any necessity for the husband to say the same thing twice to his wife. He was always kind and polite to her, and she was always gentle and obedient.

One day he said to her: "Would you not like to visit your relations?" "Yes, dear husband, I should like to do so very much, if it is convenient," she replied. "It is quite convenient," he said, "but you have never mentioned it. It shall be done at once; get ready, while I have the horses put to the carriage." He went to the stable and saw to everything, while his wife ran upstairs to dress as quickly as possible for the journey. The husband drove up, cracked his whip and asked: "Are you ready?" "Yes, dear," came the reply, and she came running out and entered the carriage. She had not quite finished dressing and carried some of her things in her hand, and these she put on in the carriage.

Then they started. When they had driven nearly half the distance, they saw a great flock of ravens flying across the road. "What beautiful white birds!" said the husband. "No, they are black, dear!" said his wife. "I think it is going to rain," he said, turned the horses, and drove home again. She understood perfectly why he had done so; it was the first time that she had contradicted him, but she showed no resentment, and the two conversed in quite a friendly fashion all the way home. The horses were put into the stable—and it did not rain.

When a month had passed, the husband said one morning: "I believe it is going to be fine to-day. Would you not like to visit your relations?" She wished to do so very much indeed, and she hastened a little more than the last time, so that when her husband drove up and cracked his whip, she was quite ready and mounted the carriage beside him. They had driven considerably more than half the distance, when they met a large flock of sheep and lambs. "What a fine pack of wolves!" said the husband. "You mean sheep, dear!" said the wife. "I think it will rain before evening," said the husband, looking up at the sky. "It will be better for us to drive home again." With these words he turned the horses and drove back home. They conversed in a friendly manner until they reached home; but it

did not rain.

When another month had passed, the husband said one morning to his wife: "We really must see whether we cannot manage to visit your relations. What do you say to our driving across to-day? It looks as though the day would be fine." His wife thought so too; she was ready very soon and they set out. They had not travelled far when they saw a great flock of swans flying along over their heads. "That was a fine flock of storks," said the husband. "Yes, so it was, dear," said his wife, and they drove on; there was no change in the weather that day, so that they reached her father's farm in due course. He received them joyfully and sent at once for his two other daughters and their husbands, and a very merry family meeting it was.

The three married sisters went into the kitchen together, because they could talk more freely there, and they had a great deal to tell each other; the two younger ones in particular had many questions to ask their elder sister, because they had not seen her for a very long time. Then they helped to prepare the dinner; it goes without saying that nothing was too good for this festive occasion.

The three brothers-in-law sat meanwhile with their father-in-law in the sitting-room and they, too, had much to tell and ask each other. Then said the old farmer: "This is the first time that you have all three been gathered together under my roof, and I should like to ask you frankly how you are pleased with your wives." The husbands who had married the two younger, good-tempered sisters said at once that they were perfectly satisfied and lived very happily. "But how do you get on with yours?" the father-in-law asked the husband of the eldest sister. "Nobody ever married a better wife than I did," was the reply. "Well, I should like to see which of you has the most obedient wife," said the father-in-law, and then he fetched a heavy silver jug and filled it to the top with gold and silver coins. This he placed in the middle of the table before the three men, and said that he would give it to him who had the most obedient wife.

They put the matter to the test at once. The husband who had married the youngest sister went to the kitchen door and called: "Will you come here a moment, Gerda, please; as quickly as possible!" "All right, I am coming," she answered, but it was some time before she came, because as she explained, she had first to talk about something with one of her sisters. "What do you want with me?" she asked. The husband made some excuse, and she went out again.

Now it was the turn of the man who had married the middle sister. "Please come here a moment, Margaret!" he called. She also answered: "Yes, I am coming at once," but it was a good while before she came; she had had something in her hands and was compelled to put it down first. The husband invented some excuse, and she went out again.

Then the third husband went to the kitchen door, opened it slightly and just said: "Christine!"—"Yes!" she answered, as she stood there with a large dish of food in her hands. "Take this from me!" she said quickly to her sisters, but they looked at her in amazement and did not take the dish. Bang! she dropped it right on the middle of the kitchen floor, rushed into the room and asked: "What do you wish, dear?"—"Oh, I only wanted to see you," he said, "but since you are here, you may as well take that jug standing on the table; it is yours, with all that is in it.—You might also show us what you got from me as a marriage gift on your wedding day."—"Yes, dear, here it is," she said, and drew the willow ring from her bosom, where she had kept it ever since. The husband handed it to his father-in-law and asked: "Can you put that ring straight?"—No, that was impossible without breaking it. "Well, you see now," said the husband, "if I had not bent the twig when it was green, I could not have made it into this shape."

After that they sat down to a merry meal, then the husband of the oldest sister returned home with her, and they lived for many years very happily together.

### THE TALKING POT
### (Danish)

*This is a particularly good story to read or tell to younger children, and it lends itself well to dramatization. The vigorous action, the direct dialogue, the repeated phrases, and the triumph of the poor man and his wife over the rich man—all are typical folk tale elements and particularly effective in storytelling or dramatizing.*

Once upon a time there was a man so poor that he had nothing in the world but a wife, a house, and one lone cow. And after a time, he got even poorer than that, and so he had to take the cow to market and sell her.

On the way he met a fine-faced stranger. "Well, my good man," said the stranger, "whither away with that fat cow?"

"To market, and thank you," said the man, though the cow was far from fat.

"Then perhaps you will sell her to me," said the stranger.

Yes, the farmer would sell and gladly, provided the price were twenty dollars or more.

The stranger shook his head. "Money I cannot give you," he said. "But I have a wonderful pot that I will trade you," and he showed the farmer a three-legged iron pot with a handle that was tucked under his arm.

Now, truth to tell, there was nothing at all wonderful-looking about the pot, and it might have hung in any chimney in the country. Besides, the poor man had nothing to put in it, neither food nor drink, so he declined to make the trade. "Money I need, and money I must have," he said, "so you may keep your wonderful pot."

But hardly had he said these words than the pot began to speak. "Take me, take me," cried the pot, "and you'll never have cause to rue it." And so the man changed his mind and made the trade, for if the pot could talk, then surely it could do other things, too.

Home he now returned, and when he reached there, he hid the pot in the stable where the cow had always been kept, for he wanted to surprise his wife. Then he went inside. "Well, good wife," he said, "fetch me a bit to eat and a sup to drink, for I've walked a long mile and back today."

But his wife would do none of it till she heard about her husband's success at the market. "Did you make a fine bargain?" she asked.

"The Talking Pot." From *13 Danish Tales* by Mary C. Hatch, copyright, 1947, by Harcourt Brace Jovanovich, Inc.; renewed, 1975, by Edgun Wulff. Reprinted by permission of the publishers

"Fine as fine," said her husband.

"That is well," nodded the wife, "for we've a hundred places to use the money."

But it wasn't a money bargain. No indeed, exclaimed her husband.

Not a money bargain! Well, pray then, what had the good man gotten for the cow, cried the wife, and she would not rest till her husband had taken her to the barn and showed her the three-legged pot tied up to the stall.

And then the good wife *was* angry! Trading a fine, fat cow—though truth to tell it was neither fine nor fat—for a common black pot that might hang in anyone's chimney.

"You are stupid as a goose," cried the wife. "Now what will we do for food and drink? If you were not so tough, I do believe I would stew you!" And she started to shake her husband. But before she could do the poor man much damage, the pot began to speak again.

"Clean me, and shine me, and put me on the fire," said the pot, and at that the woman sang a different tune. "Well!" she said. "If you can talk, perhaps you can do other things, too." And she took the pot and scrubbed it and polished it, and then hung it over the fire.

"I will skip, I will skip," said the pot.

"How far will you skip?" asked the woman.

"Up the hill, and down the dale, and into the rich man's house," cried the little pot, and with that, it jumped down from the hook, and skipping across the room, went out the door, and up the road to the rich man's house. Here the rich man's wife was making fine cakes and puddings, and the pot jumped up on the table and settled there still as a statue.

"Well!" exclaimed the rich man's wife. "You are just what I need for my finest pudding." Then she stirred in sugar and spices, and raisins and nuts, a whole host of good things, and the pot took them all without a murmur. In a few minutes, the pudding was made, and the woman picked up the pot and put it on the fire. But down the pot jumped and skipped to the door.

"Dear me," exclaimed the woman. "What are you doing, and where are you going?"

"I'm bound for home to the poor man's house," cried the little pot, and away it went skipping up the road till it was back at the poor man's little cottage.

When the couple saw that the pot had brought them a fine pudding, the finest they had ever seen, they were very pleased, and the farmer said, "Now, my good wife, did I not make a good bargain when I traded our poor old cow for this wonderful pot?"

"Indeed you did," said his wife, and she fell to eating the pot's fine pudding.

The next morning, the pot again cried, "I will skip, I will skip!" And the wife said, "How far will you skip?"

"Up hill and down dale, and into the rich man's barn," the little pot replied, and out the house and up the road it went skipping, straight to the rich man's barn.

The rich man's servants were threshing grain, and the pot skipped to the center of the floor and stood there still as a statue.

"Well!" said one of the threshers. "Here is just the pot to hold a bushel of grain," and he poured in a sackful. But this took up no room at all, and so he poured in another and another till there was not a grain of anything left in the whole barn.

"A most peculiar pot!" exclaimed the men. "Though it looks as if it had hung in any number of chimneys." And then they tried to lift it, but it slid away from them and went skipping across the floor.

"Dear me," cried the men. "What are you doing, and where are you going?"

"I'm bound for home to the poor man's house," said the pot, and out the door it skipped, and though the men ran after it, they were left huffing and puffing far behind.

When the little pot reached home again, it poured out the wheat in the poor man's barn, and there was enough to make bread and cakes for years to come.

But that was not the end of its good deeds, for on the third morning it said again, "I will skip, I will skip!" And the old wife asked, "Where will you skip?" And it answered, "Up hill and down dale to the rich man's house," and out the house it ran at once.

Now the rich man was in his counting house counting out his money, and when the little pot arrived, up it jumped on the table, right in the midst of all the gold pieces.

"What a fine pot," cried the rich man. "Just

the thing for my money." And into the pot he tossed handful after handful of money till not one piece was left loose on the table. Then he picked up his treasure to hide it in his money cupboard, but the pot slipped from his fingers and hopped to the door.

"Stop, stop," cried the rich man. "You have all my money."

"But not yours for long," said the pot. "I carry it home to the poor man's house," and out the room it skipped and back to the poor man's cottage. There it poured out the golden treasure, and the old couple cried aloud with delight.

"Now you have enough," said the pot, and indeed they did, enough and more, too, and so the wife washed the pot carefully and put it aside.

But in the morning, the pot was off again, straight for the rich man's house, and when the rich man saw it, he cried, "There is the wicked pot that stole my wife's pudding, and my wheat, and all my gold. But it shall bring everything back, every last farthing and more." Then he grabbed the pot, but bless my soul, if he didn't stick fast! And though he tugged and he pulled, he couldn't get free.

"I will skip, I will skip," said the pot.

"Well, skip to the North Pole," cried the man, still furiously trying to free himself, and at that, away went the pot and the man with it. Up the hill they waltzed and down the hill, and never once did they stop, not even to say hello or good-bye at the old couple's cottage, for the pot was in a great hurry. The North Pole, you know, is far, far away, even for a fast-skipping pot.

## THE THREE
## BILLY-GOATS GRUFF
### (Norwegian)

*This is a matchless little tale to tell, admirable in plot and economy of words. Consider the first two paragraphs: scene, characters, conflict are all laid out briefly and vividly, an introduction that is a masterpiece of brevity.*

Once on a time there were three billy-goats, who were to go up to the hill-side to make themselves fat, and the name of all three was "Gruff."

On the way up was a bridge over a burn they had to cross; and under the bridge lived a great ugly troll, with eyes as big as saucers, and a nose as long as a poker.

So first of all came the youngest billy-goat Gruff to cross the bridge.

"Trip, trap! trip, trap!" went the bridge.

"WHO'S THAT tripping over my bridge?" roared the troll.

"Oh, it is only I, the tiniest billy-goat Gruff; and I'm going up to the hill-side to make myself fat," said the billy-goat, with such a small voice.

"Now, I'm coming to gobble you up," said the troll.

"Oh, no! pray don't take me. I'm too little, that I am," said the billy-goat. "Wait a bit till the second billy-goat Gruff comes. He's much bigger."

"Well, be off with you;" said the troll.

A little while after came the second billy-goat Gruff to cross the bridge.

"TRIP, TRAP! TRIP, TRAP! TRIP, TRAP!" went the bridge.

"WHO'S THAT tripping over my bridge?" roared the troll.

"Oh, it's the second billy-goat Gruff, and I'm going up to the hill-side to make myself fat," said the billy-goat, who hadn't such a small voice.

"Now I'm coming to gobble you up," said the troll.

"Oh, no! don't take me. Wait a little till the big billy-goat Gruff comes. He's much bigger."

"Very well! be off with you," said the troll.

But just then up came the big billy-goat Gruff.

"TRIP, TRAP! TRIP, TRAP! TRIP, TRAP!" went the bridge, for the billy-goat was so heavy that the bridge creaked and groaned under him.

"The Three Billy-Goats Gruff." From *Popular Tales from the Norse*, by Peter Christian Asbjörnsen and Jörgen Moe, translated by Sir George Webbe Dasent. David Douglas, Edinburgh, 1888

"WHO'S THAT tramping over my bridge?" roared the troll.

"IT'S I! THE BIG BILLY-GOAT GRUFF," said the billy-goat, who had an ugly hoarse voice of his own.

"Now I'm coming to gobble you up," roared the troll.

"Well, come along! I've got two spears,
And I'll poke your eyeballs out at your ears;
I've got besides two curling-stones,
And I'll crush you to bits, body and bones."

That was what the big billy-goat said; and so he flew at the troll, and poked his eyes out with his horns, and crushed him to bits, body and bones, and tossed him out into the burn, and after that he went up to the hill-side. There the billy-goats got so fat they were scarce able to walk home again; and if the fat hasn't fallen off them, why, they're still fat; and so—

"Snip, snap, snout.
This tale's told out."

## THE PANCAKE
### (Norwegian)

*How many versions of this tale there are!— such as the Russian "Mr. Bun" and Ruth Sawyer's* Journey-Cake, Ho! *Although the beginning here is rather long and exacting, one can simplify it for very young children to "Once there was a mother who had seven hungry children."*

*The ending is much more effective if the story-teller, as he utters the pig's "Ouf, ouf," will mime the pig's gulping down the hapless, haughty pancake.*

Once on a time there was a goody who had seven hungry bairns, and she was frying a pancake for them. It was a sweet-milk pancake, and there it lay in the pan bubbling and frizzling so thick and good, it was a sight for sore eyes to look at. And the bairns stood round about, and the goodman sat by and looked on.

"Oh, give me a bit of pancake, mother, dear; I am so hungry," said one bairn.

"Oh, darling mother," said the second.

"Oh, darling good mother," said the third.

"Oh, darling, good, nice mother," said the fourth.

"Oh, darling, pretty, good, nice mother," said the fifth.

"Oh, darling, pretty, good, nice, clever mother," said the sixth.

"Oh, darling, pretty, good, nice, clever, sweet mother," said the seventh.

So they begged for the pancake all round, the one more prettily than the other; for they were so hungry and so good.

"Yes, yes, bairns, only bide a bit till it turns itself,"—she ought to have said "till I can get it turned,"—"and then you shall all have some—a lovely sweet-milk pancake; only look how fat and happy it lies there."

When the pancake heard that, it got afraid, and in a trice it turned itself all of itself, and tried to jump out of the pan; but it fell back into it again t'other side up, and so when it had been fried a little on the other side too, till it got firmer in its flesh, it sprang out on the floor and rolled off like a wheel through the door and down the hill.

"Holloa! Stop, pancake!" and away went the goody after it, with the frying-pan in one hand and the ladle in the other, as fast as she could, and her bairns behind her, while the goodman limped after them last of all.

"The Pancake." From *Tales from the Fjeld,* from the Norse of Peter Christian Asbjörnsen and Jörgen Moe, translated by Sir George Webbe Dasent. Chapman and Hall, London, 1874

"Hi! won't you stop? Seize it. Stop, pancake," they all screamed out, one after the other, and tried to catch it on the run and hold it; but the pancake rolled on and on, and in the twinkling of an eye it was so far ahead that they couldn't see it, for the pancake was faster on its feet than any of them.

So when it had rolled awhile it met a man.

"Good-day, pancake," said the man.

"God bless you, Manny Panny!" said the pancake.

"Dear pancake," said the man, "don't roll so fast; stop a little and let me eat you."

"When I have given the slip to Goody Poody, and the goodman, and seven squalling children, I may well slip through your fingers, Manny Panny," said the pancake, and rolled on and on till it met a hen.

"Good-day, pancake," said the hen.

"The same to you, Henny Penny," said the pancake.

"Pancake, dear, don't roll so fast; bide a bit and let me eat you up," said the hen.

"When I have given the slip to Goody Poody, and the goodman, and seven squalling children, and Manny Panny, I may well slip through your claws, Henny Penny," said the pancake, and so it rolled on like a wheel down the road.

Just then it met a cock.

"Good-day, pancake," said the cock.

"The same to you, Cocky Locky," said the pancake.

"Pancake, dear, don't roll so fast, but bide a bit and let me eat you up."

"When I have given the slip to Goody Poody, and the goodman, and seven squalling children, and to Manny Panny, and Henny Penny, I may well slip through your claws, Cocky Locky," said the pancake, and off it set rolling away as fast as it could; and when it had rolled a long way it met a duck.

"Good-day, pancake," said the duck.

"The same to you, Ducky Lucky."

"Pancake, dear, don't roll away so fast; bide a bit and let me eat you up."

"When I have given the slip to Goody Poody, and the goodman, and seven squalling children, and Manny Panny, and Henny Penny, and Cocky Locky, I may well slip through your fingers, Ducky Lucky," said the pancake, and with

that it took to rolling and rolling faster than ever; and when it had rolled a long, long while, it met a goose.

"Good-day, pancake," said the goose.

"The same to you, Goosey Poosey."

"Pancake, dear, don't roll so fast; bide a bit and let me eat you up."

"When I have given the slip to Goody Poody, and the goodman, and seven squalling children, and Manny Panny, and Henny Penny, and Cocky Locky, and Ducky Lucky, I can well slip through your feet, Goosey Poosey," said the pancake, and off it rolled.

So when it had rolled a long, long way farther, it met a gander.

"Good-day, pancake," said the gander.

"The same to you, Gander Pander," said the pancake.

"Pancake, dear, don't roll so fast; bide a bit and let me eat you up."

"When I have given the slip to Goody Poody, and the goodman, and seven squalling children, and Manny Panny, and Henny Penny, and Cocky Locky, and Ducky Lucky, and Goosey Poosey, I may well slip through your feet, Gander Pander," said the pancake, which rolled off as fast as ever.

So when it had rolled a long, long time, it met a pig.

"Good-day, pancake," said the pig.

"The same to you, Piggy Wiggy," said the pancake, which, without a word more, began to roll and roll like mad.

"Nay, nay," said the pig, "you needn't be in such a hurry; we two can then go side by side and see one another over the wood; they say it is not too safe in there."

The pancake thought there might be something in that, and so they kept company. But when they had gone awhile, they came to a brook. As for piggy, he was so fat he swam safe across, it was nothing to him; but the poor pancake couldn't get over.

"Seat yourself on my snout," said the pig, "and I'll carry you over."

So the pancake did that.

"Ouf, ouf," said the pig, and swallowed the pancake at one gulp; and then, as the poor pancake could go no farther, why—this story can go no farther either.

## PRINCESS ON
## THE GLASS HILL

### (Norwegian)

*If this story seems overly long, let Boots find only the horse with the golden trappings and ride up the hill only once.*

Once on a time there was a man who had a meadow, which lay high up on the hill-side, and in the meadow was a barn, which he had built to keep his hay in. Now, I must tell you there hadn't been much in the barn for the last year or two, for every St. John's night, when the grass stood greenest and deepest, the meadow was eaten down to the very ground the next morning, just as if a whole drove of sheep had been there feeding on it over night. This happened once, and it happened twice; so at last the man grew weary of losing his crop of hay, and said to his sons—for he had three of them, and the youngest was nicknamed Boots, of course—that now one of them must just go and sleep in the barn in the outlying field when St. John's night came, for it was too good a joke that his grass should be eaten, root and blade, this year, as it had been the last two years. So whichever of them went must keep a sharp lookout; that was what their father said.

Well, the eldest son was ready to go and watch the meadow; trust him for looking after the grass! It shouldn't be his fault if man or beast, or the fiend himself, got a blade of grass. So, when evening came, he set off to the barn, and lay down to sleep; but a little later on in the night came such a clatter, and such an earthquake, that walls and roof shook, and groaned, and creaked; then up jumped the lad, and took to his heels as fast as ever he could; nor dared he once look round till he reached home; and as for the hay, why it was eaten up this year just as it had been twice before.

The next St. John's night, the man said again it would never do to lose all the grass in the outlying field year after year in this way, so one

"Princess on the Glass Hill." From *Popular Tales from the Norse*, by Peter Christian Asbjörnsen and Jörgen Moe, translated by Sir George Webbe Dasent. David Douglas, Edinburgh, 1888

of his sons must just trudge off to watch it, and watch it well too. Well, the next oldest son was ready to try his luck, so he set off, and lay down to sleep in the barn as his brother had done before him; but as night wore on there came on a rumbling and quaking of the earth, worse even than on the last St. John's night, and when the lad heard it he got frightened, and took to his heels as though he were running a race.

Next year the turn came to Boots; but when he made ready to go, the other two began to laugh, and to make game of him, saying,

"You're just the man to watch the hay, that you are; you who have done nothing all your life but sit in the ashes and toast yourself by the fire."

But Boots did not care a pin for their chattering, and stumped away, as evening drew on, up the hill-side to the outlying field. There he went inside the barn and lay down; but in about an hour's time the barn began to groan and creak, so that it was dreadful to hear.

"Well," said Boots to himself, "if it isn't worse than this, I can stand it well enough."

A little while after came another creak and an earthquake, so that the litter in the barn flew about the lad's ears.

"Oh!" said Boots to himself, "if it isn't worse than this, I daresay I can stand it out."

But just then came a third rumbling, and a third earthquake, so that the lad thought walls and roof were coming down on his head; but it passed off, and all was still as death about him.

"It'll come again, I'll be bound," thought Boots; but no, it did not come again; still it was and still it stayed; but after he had lain a little while he heard a noise as if a horse were standing just outside the barn-door, and cropping the grass. He stole to the door, and peeped through a chink, and there stood a horse feeding away. So big, and fat, and grand a horse, Boots had never set eyes on; by his side on the grass lay a saddle and bridle, and a full set of armour for a knight, all of brass, so bright that the light gleamed from it.

"Ho, ho!" thought the lad; "it's you, is it, that eats up our hay? I'll soon put a spoke in your wheel; just see if I don't."

So he lost no time, but took the steel out of his tinder-box, and threw it over the horse; then it had no power to stir from the spot, and became so tame that the lad could do what he liked with it. So he got on its back and rode off with it to a place which no one knew of, and there he put up the horse. When he got home his brothers laughed and asked how he had fared.

"You didn't lie long in the barn, even if you had the heart to go so far as the field."

"Well," said Boots, "all I can say is, I lay in the barn till the sun rose, and neither saw nor heard anything; I can't think what there was in the barn to make you both so afraid."

"A pretty story!" said his brothers; "but we'll soon see how you have watched the meadow"; so they set off; but when they reached it, there stood the grass as deep and thick as it had been over night.

Well, the next St. John's eve it was the same story over again; neither of the elder brothers dared to go out to the outlying field to watch the crop; but Boots, he had the heart to go, and everything happened just as it had happened the year before. First a clatter and an earthquake, then a greater clatter and another earthquake, and so on a third time; only this year the earthquakes were far worse than the year before. Then all at once everything was as still as death, and the lad heard how something was cropping the grass outside the barn-door, so he stole to the door, and peeped through a chink; and what do you think he saw? Why, another horse standing right up against the wall, and chewing and champing with might and main. It was far finer and fatter than that which came the year before, and it had a saddle on its back, and a bridle on its neck, and a full suit of mail for a knight lay by its side, all of silver, and as grand as you would wish to see.

"Ho, ho!" said Boots to himself; "it's you that gobbles up our hay, is it? I'll soon put a spoke in your wheel"; and with that he took the steel out of his tinder-box, and threw it over the crest of the horse, which stood as still as a lamb. Well, the lad rode this horse, too, to the hiding-place where he kept the other one, and after that he went home.

"I suppose you'll tell us," said one of his brothers, "there's a fine crop this year too, up in the hayfield."

"Well, so there is," said Boots; and off ran the others to see, and there stood the grass thick and deep, as it was the year before; but they didn't give Boots softer words for all that.

Now, when the third St. John's eve came, the two elder still hadn't the heart to lie out in the barn and watch the grass, for they had got so scared at heart the night they lay there before, that they couldn't get over the fright; but Boots, he dared to go; and, to make a long story short, the very same thing happened this time as had happened twice before. Three earthquakes came, one after the other, each worse than the one which went before, and when the last came, the lad danced about with the shock from one barn wall to the other; and after that, all at once, it was still as death. Now when he had lain a little while he heard something tugging away at the grass outside the barn, so he stole again to the door-chink, and peeped out, and there stood a horse close outside—far, far bigger and fatter than the two he had taken before.

"Ho, ho!" said the lad to himself, "it's you, is it, that comes here eating up our hay? I'll soon stop that—I'll soon put a spoke in your wheel." So he caught up his steel and threw it over the horse's neck, and in a trice it stood as if it were nailed to the ground, and Boots could do as he pleased with it. Then he rode off with it to the hiding-place where he kept the other two, and then went home. When he got home his two brothers made game of him as they had done before, saying they could see he had watched the grass well, for he looked for all the world as if he were walking in his sleep, and many other spiteful things they said, but Boots gave no heed to them, only asking them to go and see for themselves; and when they went, there stood the grass as fine and deep this time as it had been twice before.

Now, you must know that the king of the country where Boots lived had a daughter, whom he would only give to the man who could ride up over the hill of glass, for there was a high, high hill, all of glass, as smooth and slippery as ice, close by the king's palace. Upon the tip-top of the hill the king's daughter was to sit, with three golden apples in her lap, and the man who could ride up and carry off the three golden apples was to have half the kingdom, and the Princess to wife. This the king had stuck up on all the church-doors in his realm, and had given it out in many other kingdoms besides. Now, this Princess was so lovely that all who set eyes on her fell over head and ears in love with her whether they would or no. So I needn't tell you how all the princes and knights who heard of her were eager to win her to wife, and half the kingdom beside; and how they came riding from all parts of the world on high prancing horses, and clad in the grandest clothes, for there wasn't one of them who hadn't made up his mind that he, and he alone, was to win the Princess.

So when the day of trial came, which the king had fixed, there was such a crowd of princes and knights under the glass hill, that it made one's head whirl to look at them; and everyone in the country who could even crawl along was off to the hill, for they all were eager to see the man who was to win the Princess. So the two elder brothers set off with the rest; but as for Boots, they said outright he shouldn't go with them, for if they were seen with such a dirty changeling, all begrimed with smut from cleaning their shoes and sifting cinders in the dusthole, they said folk would make game of them.

"Very well," said Boots, "it's all one to me. I can go alone, and stand or fall by myself."

Now when the two brothers came to the hill of glass the knights and princes were all hard at it, riding their horses till they were all in a foam; but it was no good, by my troth; for as soon as ever the horses set foot on the hill, down they slipped, and there wasn't one who could get a yard or two up; and no wonder, for the hill was as smooth as a sheet of glass, and as steep as a house-wall. But all were eager to have the Princess and half the kingdom. So they rode and slipped, and slipped and rode, and still it was the same story over again. At last all their horses were so weary that they could scarce lift a leg, and in such a sweat that the lather dripped from them, and so the knights had to give up trying any more. So the king was just thinking that he would proclaim a new trial for the next day, to see if they would have better luck, when all at once a knight came riding up on so brave a steed that no one had ever seen the like of it in his born days, and the knight had mail of brass, and the horse a brass bit in his mouth, so bright that the sunbeams shone from it. Then all the others

called out to him he might just as well spare himself the trouble of riding at the hill, for it would lead to no good; but he gave no heed to them, and put his horse at the hill, and went up it like nothing for a good way, about a third of the height; and when he had got so far, he turned his horse round and rode down again. So lovely a knight the Princess thought she had never yet seen; and while he was riding, she sat and thought to herself,

"Would to heaven he might only come up, and down the other side."

And when she saw him turning back, she threw down one of the golden apples after him, and it rolled down into his shoe. But when he got to the bottom of the hill he rode off so fast that no one could tell what had become of him. That evening all the knights and princes were to go before the king, that he who had ridden so far up the hill might show the apple which the Princess had thrown, but there was no one who had anything to show. One after the other they all came, but not a man of them could show the apple.

At even the brothers of Boots came home too, and had such a long story to tell about the riding up the hill.

"First of all," they said, "there was not one of the whole lot who could get so much as a stride up; but at last came one who had a suit of brass mail, and a brass bridle and saddle, all so bright that the sun shone from them a mile off. He was a chap to ride, just! He rode a third of the way up the hill of glass, and he could easily have ridden the whole way up, if he chose; but he turned round and rode down, thinking, maybe, that was enough for once."

"Oh! I should so like to have seen him, that I should," said Boots, who sat by the fireside, and stuck his feet into the cinders as was his wont.

"Oh!" said his brothers, "you would, would you? You look fit to keep company with such high lords, nasty beast that you are, sitting there amongst the ashes."

Next day the brothers were all for setting off again, and Boots begged them this time, too, to let him go with them and see the riding; but no, they wouldn't have him at any price, he was too ugly and nasty, they said.

"Well, well!" said Boots; "if I go at all, I must go by myself. I'm not afraid."

So when the brothers got to the hill of glass, all the princes and knights began to ride again, and you may fancy they had taken care to shoe their horses sharp; but it was no good—they rode and slipped, and slipped and rode, just as they had done the day before, and there was not one who could get so far as a yard up the hill. And when they had worn out their horses, so that they could not stir a leg, they were all forced to give it up as a bad job. So the king thought he might as well proclaim that the riding should take place the day after for the last time, just to give them one chance more; but all at once it came across his mind that he might as well wait a little longer, to see if the knight in brass mail would come this day too. Well, they saw nothing of him; but all at once came one riding on a steed, far, far, braver and finer than that on which the knight in brass had ridden, and he had silver mail, and a silver saddle and bridle, all so bright that the sunbeams gleamed and glanced from them far away. Then the others shouted out to him again, saying he might as well hold hard, and not try to ride up the hill, for all his trouble would be thrown away; but the knight paid no heed to them, and rode straight at the hill, and right up it, till he had gone two-thirds of the way, and then he wheeled his horse round and rode down again. To tell the truth, the Princess liked him still better than the knight in brass, and she sat and wished he might only be able to come right up to the top, and down the other side; but when she saw him turning back, she threw the second apple after him, and it rolled down and fell into his shoe. But as soon as ever he had come down from the hill of glass, he rode off so fast that no one could see what became of him.

At even, when all were to go in before the king and the Princess, that he who had the golden apple might show it, in they went, one after the other, but there was no one who had any apple to show, and the two brothers, as they had done on the former day, went home and told how things had gone, and how all had ridden at the hill and none got up.

"But, last of all," they said, "came one in a silver suit, and his horse had a silver saddle and a silver bridle. He was just a chap to ride; and he got two-thirds up the hill, and then turned back. He was a fine fellow and no mistake; and the Princess threw the second gold apple to him."

"Oh!" said Boots, "I should so like to have seen him too, that I should."

"A pretty story!" they said. "Perhaps you think his coat of mail was as bright as the ashes you are always poking about and sifting, you nasty dirty beast."

The third day everything happened as it had happened the two days before. Boots begged to go and see the sight, but the two wouldn't hear of his going with them. When they got to the hill there was no one who could get so much as a yard up it; and now all waited for the knight in silver mail, but they neither saw nor heard of him. At last came one riding on a steed, so brave that no one had ever seen his match; and the knight had a suit of golden mail, and a golden saddle and bridle, so wondrous bright that the sunbeams gleamed from them a mile off. The other knights and princes could not find time to call out to him not to try his luck, for they were amazed to see how grand he was. So he rode right at the hill, and tore up it like nothing, so that the Princess hadn't even time to wish that he might get up the whole way. As soon as ever he reached the top, he took the third golden apple from the Princess' lap, and then turned his horse and rode down again. As soon as he got down, he rode off at full speed, and was out of sight in no time.

Now, when the brothers got home at even, you may fancy what long stories they told, how the riding had gone off that day; and amongst other things, they had a deal to say about the knight in golden mail.

"He just was a chap to ride!" they said; "so grand a knight isn't to be found in the wide world."

"Oh!" said Boots, "I should so like to have seen him; that I should."

"Ah!" said his brothers, "his mail shone a deal brighter than the glowing coals which you are always poking and digging at; nasty dirty beast that you are."

Next day all the knights and princes were to pass before the king and the Princess—it was too late to do so the night before, I suppose—that he who had the gold apple might bring it forth; but one came after another, first the princes and then the knights, and still no one could show the gold apple.

"Well," said the king, "some one must have it, for it was something that we all saw with our own eyes, how a man came and rode up and bore it off."

So he commanded that every one who was in the kingdom should come up to the palace and see if they could show the apple. Well, they all came, one after another, but no one had the golden apple, and after a long time the two brothers of Boots came. They were the last of all, so the king asked them if there was no one else in the kingdom who hadn't come.

"Oh, yes," said they; "we have a brother, but he never carried off the golden apple. He hasn't stirred out of the dust-hole on any of the three days."

"Never mind that," said the king; "he may as well come up to the palace like the rest."

So Boots had to go up to the palace.

"How, now," said the king; "have you got the golden apple? Speak out!"

"Yes, I have," said Boots; "here is the first, and here is the second, and here is the third too"; and with that he pulled all three golden apples out of his pocket, and at the same time threw off his sooty rags, and stood before them in his gleaming golden mail.

"Yes!" said the king; "you shall have my daughter, and half my kingdom, for you well deserve both her and it."

So they got ready for the wedding, and Boots got the Princess to wife, and there was great merry-making at the bridal-feast, you may fancy, for they could all be merry though they couldn't ride up the hill of glass; and all I can say is, if they haven't left off their merry-making yet, why, they're still at it.

## GUDBRAND ON THE HILL-SIDE

### (Norwegian)

*This story was retold in inimitable fashion by Hans Christian Andersen in his "What the Good-Man Does Is Sure to Be Right!" and is also found in the folklore of many European countries. The sly humor and tenderness of "Gud-brand on the Hill-Side" are beautifully interpreted by Mrs. Gudrun Thorne-Thomsen in her recording of it for the American Library Association.*

Once on a time there was a man whose name was Gudbrand; he had a farm which lay far, far away, upon a hill-side, and so they called him Gudbrand on the Hill-side.

Now, you must know this man and his good-wife lived so happily together, and understood one another so well, that all the husband did the wife thought so well done, there was nothing like it in the world, and she was always glad whatever he turned his hand to. The farm was their own land, and they had a hundred dollars lying at the bottom of their chest, and two cows tethered up in a stall in their farmyard.

So one day his wife said to Gudbrand, "Do you know, dear, I think we ought to take one of our cows into town and sell it; that's what I think; for then we shall have some money in hand, and such well-to-do people as we ought to have ready money like the rest of the world. As for the hundred dollars at the bottom of the chest yonder, we can't make a hole in them, and I'm sure I don't know what we want with more than one cow. Besides, we shall gain a little in another way, for then I shall get off with only looking after one cow, instead of having, as now, to feed and litter and water two."

Well, Gudbrand thought his wife talked right good sense, so he set off at once with the cow on his way to town to sell her; but when he got to the town, there was no one who would buy his cow.

"Well, well! never mind," said Gudbrand, "at the worst, I can only go back home again with my cow. I've both stable and tether for her, I should think, and the road is no farther out than in"; and with that he began to toddle home with his cow.

But when he had gone a bit of the way, a man met him who had a horse to sell, so Gudbrand thought 'twas better to have a horse than a cow, so he swopped with the man. A little farther on he met a man walking along and driving a fat

"Gudbrand on the Hill-Side." From *Popular Tales from the Norse*, by Peter Christian Asbjörnsen and Jörgen Moe, translated by Sir George Webbe Dasent. David Douglas, Edinburgh, 1888

pig before him, and he thought it better to have a fat pig than a horse, so he swopped with the man. After that he went a little farther, and a man met him with a goat; so he thought it better to have a goat than a pig, and he swopped with the man that owned the goat. Then he went on a good bit till he met a man who had a sheep, and he swopped with him too, for he thought it always better to have a sheep than a goat. After a while he met a man with a goose, and he swopped away the sheep for the goose; and when he had walked a long, long time, he met a man with a cock, and he swopped with him, for he thought in this wise, " 'Tis surely better to have a cock than a goose." Then he went on till the day was far spent, and he began to get very hungry, so he sold the cock for a shilling, and bought food with the money, for, thought Gudbrand on the Hill-side, " 'Tis always better to save one's life than to have a cock."

After that he went on home till he reached his nearest neighbour's house, where he turned in.

"Well," said the owner of the house, "how did things go with you in town?"

"Rather so so," said Gudbrand. "I can't praise my luck, nor do I blame it either," and with that he told the whole story from first to last.

"Ah!" said his friend, "you'll get nicely called over the coals, that one can see, when you get home to your wife. Heaven help you, I wouldn't stand in your shoes for something."

"Well," said Gudbrand on the Hill-side, "I think things might have gone much worse with me; but now, whether I have done wrong or not, I have so kind a goodwife, she never has a word to say against anything that I do."

"Oh!" answered his neighbour, "I hear what you say, but I don't believe it for all that."

"Shall we lay a bet upon it?" asked Gudbrand on the Hill-side. "I have a hundred dollars at the bottom of my chest at home; will you lay as many against them?"

Yes, the friend was ready to bet; so Gudbrand stayed there till evening, when it began to get dark, and then they went together to his house, and the neighbour was to stand outside the door and listen, while the man went in to see his wife.

"Good evening!" said Gudbrand on the Hill-side.

"Good evening!" said the goodwife. "Oh, is that you? Now God be praised."

Yes, it was he. So the wife asked how things had gone with him in town.

"Oh, only so so," answered Gudbrand; "not much to brag of. When I got to the town there was no one who would buy the cow, so you must know I swopped it away for a horse."

"For a horse," said his wife; "well, that is good of you; thanks with all my heart. We are so well-to-do that we may drive to church, just as well as other people; and if we choose to keep a horse we have a right to get one, I should think. So run out, child, and put up the horse."

"Ah!" said Gudbrand, "but you see I've not got the horse after all; for when I got a bit farther on the road I swopped it away for a pig."

"Think of that, now!" said the wife; "you did just as I should have done myself; a thousand thanks! Now I can have a bit of bacon in the house to set before people when they come to see me, that I can. What do we want with a horse? People would only say we had got so proud that we couldn't walk to church. Go out, child, and put up the pig in the stye."

"But I've not got the pig either," said Gudbrand; "for when I got a little farther on I swopped it away for a milch goat."

"Bless us!" cried his wife, "how well you manage everything! Now I think it over, what should I do with a pig? People would only point at us and say, 'Yonder they eat up all they have got.' No! now I have got a goat, and I shall have milk and cheese, and keep the goat too. Run out, child, and put up the goat."

"Nay, but I haven't got the goat either," said Gudbrand, "for a little farther on I swopped it away, and got a fine sheep instead."

"You don't say so!" cried his wife; "why, you do everything to please me, just as if I had been with you; what do we want with a goat! If I had it I should lose half my time in climbing up the hills to get it down. No, if I have a sheep, I shall have both wool and clothing, and fresh meat in the house. Run out, child, and put up the sheep."

"But I haven't got the sheep any more than the rest," said Gudbrand; "for when I had gone a bit farther I swopped it away for a goose."

"Thank you! thank you! with all my heart," cried his wife; "what should I do with a sheep? I have no spinning-wheel, nor carding-comb, nor should I care to worry myself with cutting and shaping and sewing clothes. We can buy clothes now, as we have always done; and now I shall have roast goose, which I have longed for so often; and, besides, down to stuff my little pillow with. Run out, child, and put up the goose."

"Ah!" said Gudbrand, "but I haven't the goose either; for when I had gone a bit farther I swopped it away for a cock."

"Dear me!" cried his wife, "how you think of everything! just as I should have done myself. A cock! think of that! why it's as good as an eight-day clock, for every morning the cock crows at four o'clock, and we shall be able to stir our stumps in good time. What should we do with a goose? I don't know how to cook it; and as for my pillow, I can stuff it with cotton-grass. Run out, child, and put up the cock."

"But after all I haven't got the cock," said Gudbrand; "for when I had gone a bit farther, I got as hungry as a hunter, so I was forced to sell the cock for a shilling, for fear I should starve."

"Now, God be praised that you did so!" cried his wife; "whatever you do, you do it always just after my own heart. What should we do with the cock? We are our own masters, I should think, and can lie a-bed in the morning as long as we like. Heaven be thanked that I have got you safe back again; you who do everything so well that I want neither cock nor goose; neither pigs nor kine."

Then Gudbrand opened the door and said, "Well, what do you say now? Have I won the hundred dollars?" and his neighbour was forced to allow that he had.

## THE HUSBAND WHO WAS TO MIND THE HOUSE

(*Norwegian*)

*Wanda Gág made a delightful little book of this story and called it* Gone Is Gone. *There is also an American folk-song version called "The Old Man in the Wood."*

Once on a time there was a man, so surly and cross, he never thought his wife did anything right in the house. So one evening, in hay-making time, he came home, scolding and swearing, and showing his teeth and making a dust.

"Dear love, don't be so angry; there's a good man," said his goody; "to-morrow let's change our work. I'll go out with the mowers and mow, and you shall mind the house at home."

Yes, the husband thought that would do very well. He was quite willing, he said.

So, early next morning, his goody took a scythe over her neck, and went out into the hay-field with the mowers and began to mow; but the man was to mind the house, and do the work at home.

First of all he wanted to churn the butter; but when he had churned a while, he got thirsty, and went down to the cellar to tap a barrel of ale. So, just when he had knocked in the bung, and was putting the tap into the cask, he heard overhead the pig come into the kitchen. Then off he ran up the cellar steps, with the tap in his hand, as fast as he could, to look after the pig, lest it

"The Husband Who Was to Mind the House." From *Popular Tales from the Norse*, by Peter Christian Asbjørnsen and Jörgen Moe, translated by Sir George Webbe Dasent. David Douglas, Edinburgh, 1888

should upset the churn; but when he got up he saw that the pig had already knocked the churn over and was routing and grunting amongst the cream, which was running all over the floor. He got so wild with rage that he quite forgot the ale-barrel, and ran at the pig as hard as he could. He caught it, too, just as it ran out of doors, and gave it such a kick that piggy lay for dead on the spot. Then all at once he remembered he had the tap in his hand; but when he got down to the cellar, every drop of ale had run out of the cask.

Then he went into the dairy and found enough cream left to fill the churn again, and so he began to churn, for butter they must have at dinner. When he had churned a bit, he remembered that their milking cow was still shut up in the byre, and hadn't had a bit to eat or a drop to drink all the morning, though the sun was high. Then all at once he thought 'twas too far to take her down to the meadow, so he'd just get her up on the house-top—for the house, you must know, was thatched with sods, and a fine crop of grass was growing there. Now their house lay close up against a steep down, and he thought if he laid a plank across to the thatch at the back he'd easily get the cow up.

But still he couldn't leave the churn, for there was his little babe crawling about on the floor, and "if I leave it," he thought, "the child is safe to upset it." So he took the churn on his back, and went out with it; but then he thought he'd better first water the cow before he turned her out on the thatch; so he took up a bucket to draw water out of the well; but, as he stooped down at the well's brink, all the cream ran out of the churn over his shoulders, and so down into the well.

Now it was near dinner-time, and he hadn't even got the butter yet; so he thought he'd best boil the porridge. He filled the pot with water and hung it over the fire. When he had done that, he thought the cow might perhaps fall off the thatch and break her legs or her neck. So he got up on the house to tie her up. One end of the rope he made fast to the cow's neck, and the other he slipped down the chimney and tied round his own thigh; and he had to make haste, for the water now began to boil in the pot, and he had still to grind the oatmeal.

So he began to grind away; but while he was hard at it, down fell the cow off the house top after all, and as she fell, she dragged the man up the chimney by the rope. There he stuck fast; and as for the cow, she hung halfway down the wall, swinging between heaven and earth, for she could neither get down nor up.

And now the goody had waited seven lengths and seven breadths for her husband to come and call them home to dinner; but never a call they had. At last she thought she'd waited long enough, and went home. But when she got there and saw the cow hanging in such an ugly place, she ran up and cut the rope in two with her scythe. But as she did this, down came her husband out of the chimney; and so when his old dame came inside the kitchen, there she found him standing on his head in the porridge-pot.

## THE PRINCESS WHO COULD NOT BE SILENCED

### (Norwegian)

*For once a woman does not have the last word!—but no one much minds, since the ending is obviously happy for everybody. As in "Boots and His Brothers," the punishment of ear clipping or ear branding is one which children easily accept, if it is told matter-of-factly. Besides, the focus here is on the marvelous wit of the genial and intrepid Espen. Tell this with all the offhand dash of Espen himself.*

There was once a king, and he had a daughter who was so cross and crooked in her words that no one could silence her, and so he gave it out that he who could do it should marry the princess and have half the kingdom, too. There were plenty of those who wanted to try it, I can tell you, for it is not every day that you can get a princess and half a kingdom. The gate to the king's palace did not stand still a minute. They came in great crowds from the East and the

"The Princess Who Could Not Be Silenced." From *East o' the Sun and West o' the Moon* by Gudrun Thorne-Thomsen. Reprinted with permission of Harper & Row, Publishers, Evanston

West, both riding and walking. But there was not one of them who could silence the princess.

At last the king had it given out that those who tried, and failed, should have both ears marked with the big red-hot iron with which he marked his sheep. He was not going to have all that flurry and worry for nothing.

Well, there were three brothers, who had heard about the princess, and, as they did not fare very well at home, they thought they had better set out to try their luck and see if they could not win the princess and half the kingdom. They were friends and good fellows, all three of them, and they set off together.

When they had walked a bit of the way, Espen picked up something.

"I've found—I've found something!" he cried.

"What did you find?" asked the brothers.

"I found a dead crow," said he.

"Ugh! Throw it away! What would you do with that?" said the brothers, who always thought they knew a great deal.

"Oh, I haven't much to carry, I might as well carry this," said Espen.

So when they had walked on a bit, Espen again picked up something.

"I've found—I've found something!" he cried.

"What have you found now?" said the brothers.

"I found a willow twig," said he.

"Dear, what do you want with that? Throw it away!" said they.

"Oh, I haven't much to carry, I might as well carry that," said Espen.

So when they had walked a bit, Espen picked up something again. "Oh, lads, I've found—I've found something!" he cried.

"Well, well, what did you find this time?" asked the brothers.

"A piece of a broken saucer," said he.

"Oh, what is the use of that? Throw it away!" said they.

"Oh, I haven't much to carry, I might as well carry that," said Espen.

And when they had walked a bit farther, Espen stooped down again and picked up something else.

"I've found—I've found something, lads!" he cried.

"And what is it now?" said they.

"Two goat horns," said Espen.

"Oh! Throw them away. What could you do with them?" said they.

"Oh, I haven't much to carry, I might as well carry them," said Espen.

In a little while he found something again.

"Oh, lads, see, I've found—I've found something," he cried.

"Dear, dear, what wonderful things you do find! What is it now?" said the brothers.

"I've found a wedge," said he.

"Oh, throw it away. What do you want with that?" said they.

"Oh, I haven't much to carry, I might as well carry that," said Espen.

And now, as they walked over the fields close up to the King's palace, Espen bent down again and held something in his fingers.

"Oh, lads, lads, see what I've found!" he cried.

"If you only found a little common sense, it would be good for you," said they. "Well, let's see what it is now."

"A worn-out shoe sole," said he.

"Pshaw! Well, that was something to pick up! Throw it away! What do you want with that?" said the brothers.

"Oh, I haven't much to carry, I might as well carry that, if I am to win the princess and half the kingdom," said Espen.

"Yes, you are likely to do that—you," said they.

And now they came to the king's palace. The eldest one went in first.

"Good-day," said he.

"Good-day to you," said the princess, and she twisted and turned.

"It's awfully hot here," said he.

"It is hotter over there in the hearth," said the princess. There lay the red-hot iron ready awaiting. When he saw that he forgot every word he was going to say, and so it was all over with him.

And now came the next eldest one. "Good-day," said he.

"Good-day to you," said she, and she turned and twisted herself.

"It's awfully hot here," said he.

"It's hotter over there in the hearth," said she. And when he looked at the red-hot iron he, too, couldn't get a word out, and so they marked his ears and sent him home again.

Then it was Espen's turn. "Good-day," said he.

"Good-day to you," said she, and she twisted and turned again.

"It's nice and warm in here," said Espen.

"It's hotter in the hearth," said she, and she was no sweeter, now the third one had come.

"That's good, I may bake my crow there, then?" asked he.

"I'm afraid she'll burst," said the princess.

"There's no danger; I'll wind this willow twig around," said the lad.

"It's too loose," said she.

"I'll stick this wedge in," said the lad, and took out the wedge.

"The fat will drop off," said the princess.

"I'll hold this under," said the lad, and pulled out the broken bit of the saucer.

"You are crooked in your words, that you are," said the princess.

"No, I'm not crooked, but this is crooked," said the lad, and he showed her the goat's horn.

"Well, I never saw the like!" cried the princess.

"Oh, here is the like of it," said he, and pulled out the other.

"Now, you think you'll wear out my soul, don't you?" said she.

"No, I won't wear out your soul, for I have a sole that's worn out already," said the lad, and pulled out the shoe sole.

Then the princess hadn't a word to say.

"Now, you're mine," said Espen. And so she was.

## LITTLE FREDDY
## WITH HIS FIDDLE
### (Norwegian)

*The Scandinavian tales are full of magic objects which assist those resourceful persons who learn how to use them. Freddy's fiddle is one of the gayest of these.*

Once on a time there was a cottager who had an only son, and this lad was weakly and hadn't much health to speak of; so he couldn't go out to work in the field.

His name was Freddy, and undersized he was, too; and so they called him Little Freddy. At home there was little either to bite or sup, and so his father went about the country trying to bind him over as a cowherd or an errand-boy; but there was no one who would take his son till he came to the sheriff, and he was ready to take him, for he had just packed off his errand-boy, and there was no one who would fill his place, for the story went that he was a skinflint.

But the cottager thought it was better there than nowhere: Freddy would get his food, for all he was to get was his board—there was nothing said about wages or clothes. So when the lad had served three years he wanted to leave, and then the sheriff gave him all his wages at one time. He was to have a penny a year. "It couldn't well be less," said the sheriff. And so he got threepence in all.

As for little Freddy, he thought it was a great sum, for he had never owned so much; but for all that he asked if he wasn't to have something more.

"You have already had more than you ought to have," said the sheriff.

"Sha'n't I have anything, then, for clothes?" asked little Freddy; "for those I had on when I came here are worn to rags, and I have had no new ones."

And, to tell the truth, he was so ragged that the tatters hung and flapped about him.

"When you have got what we agreed on," said the sheriff, "and three whole pennies beside, I have nothing more to do with you. Be off!"

But for all that he got leave just to go into the kitchen and get a little food to put in his scrip; and after that he set off on the road to buy himself more clothes. He was both merry and glad, for he had never seen a penny before; and every now and then he felt in his pockets as he went along to see if he had them all three. So when he

"Little Freddy with His Fiddle." From *Tales from the Fjeld,* from the Norse of Peter Christian Asbjörnsen and Jörgen Moe, translated by Sir George Webbe Dasent. Chapman and Hall, London, 1874

had gone far, and farther than far, he got into a narrow dale, with high fells on all sides, so that he couldn't tell if there were any way to pass out; and he began to wonder what there could be on the other side of those fells, and how he ever should get over them.

But up and up he had to go, and on he strode; he was not strong on his legs, and had to rest every now and then—and then he counted and counted how many pennies he had got. So when he had got quite up to the very top, there was nothing but a great plain overgrown with moss. There he sat him down, and began to see if his money were all right; and before he was aware of him a beggarman came up to him—and he was so tall and big that the lad began to scream and screech when he got a good look of him and saw his height and length.

"Don't you be afraid," said the beggarman; "I'll do you no harm; I only beg for a penny, in God's name."

"Heaven help me!" said the lad. "I have only three pennies, and with them I was going to the town to buy clothes."

"It is worse for me than for you," said the beggarman. "I have got no penny, and I am still more ragged than you."

"Well! then you shall have it," said the lad.

So when he had walked on awhile he got weary, and sat down to rest again. But when he looked up there he saw another beggarman, and he was still taller and uglier than the first; and so when the lad saw how very tall and ugly and long he was he fell a-screeching.

"Now, don't you be afraid of me," said the beggar; "I'll not do you any harm. I only beg for a penny, in God's name."

"Now, may heaven help me!" said the lad. "I've only got two pence, and with them I was going to the town to buy clothes. If I had only met you sooner, then——"

"It's worse for me than for you," said the beggarman. "I have no penny, and a bigger body and less clothing."

"Well, you may have it," said the lad.

So he went awhile farther, till he got weary, and then he sat down to rest; but he had scarce sat down than a third beggarman came to him. He was so tall and ugly and long, that the lad had to look up and up, right up to the sky. And when he took him all in with his eyes, and saw how very, very tall and ugly and ragged he was he fell a-screeching and screaming again.

"Now, don't you be afraid of me, my lad," said the beggarman. "I'll do you no harm; for I am only a beggarman, who begs for a penny in God's name."

"May heaven help me!" said the lad. "I have only one penny left, and with it I was going to the town to buy clothes. If I had only met you sooner, then—"

"As for that," said the beggarman, "I have no penny at all—that I haven't, and a bigger body and less clothes, so it is worse for me than for you."

"Yes!" said little Freddy, he must have the penny then—there was no help for it; for so each would have what belonged to him, and he would have nothing.

"Well!" said the beggarman, "since you have such a good heart that you gave away all that you had in the world, I will give you a wish for each penny." For you must know it was the same beggarman who had got them all three; he had only changed his shape each time, that the lad might not know him again.

"I have always had such a longing to hear a fiddle go, and see folk so glad and merry that they couldn't help dancing," said the lad; "and so, if I may wish what I choose, I will wish myself such a fiddle, that everything that has life must dance to its tune."

"That you may have," said the beggarman; "but it was a sorry wish. You must wish something better for the other two pennies."

"I have always had such a love for hunting and shooting," said little Freddy; "so if I may wish what I choose, I will wish myself such a gun that I shall hit everything I aim at, were it ever so far off."

"That you may have," said the beggarman; "but it was a sorry wish. You must wish better for the last penny."

"I have always had a longing to be in company with folk who were kind and good," said little Freddy; "and so, if I could get what I wish, I would wish it to be so that no one can say nay to the first thing I ask."

"That wish was not so sorry," said the beggarman; and off he strode between the hills, and he saw him no more. And so the lad laid down to sleep, and the next day he came down from the fell with his fiddle and his gun.

First he went to the storekeeper and asked for clothes, and at one farm he asked for a horse, and at another for a sledge; and at this place he asked for a fur-coat, and no one said him nay—even the stingiest folk were all forced to give him what he asked for. At last he went through the country as a fine gentleman, and had his horse and his sledge; and so when he had gone a bit he met the sheriff with whom he had served.

"Good-day, master," said little Freddy, as he pulled up and took off his hat.

"Good-day," said the sheriff. And then he went on, "When was I ever your master?"

"Oh, yes!" said little Freddy. "Don't you remember how I served you three years for three pence?"

"Heaven help us!" said the sheriff. "How you have got on all of a hurry! And pray how was it that you got to be such a fine gentleman?"

"Oh, that's telling!" said little Freddy.

"And are you full of fun, that you carry a fiddle about with you?" asked the sheriff.

"Yes! yes!" said Freddy. "I have always had such a longing to get folk to dance; but the funniest thing of all is this gun, for it brings down almost anything that I aim at, however far it may be off. Do you see that magpie yonder, sitting in the spruce fir? What'll you bet I don't bag it, as we stand here?"

On that the sheriff was ready to stake horse and groom, and a hundred dollars besides, that he couldn't do it; but, as it was, he would bet all the money he had about him; and he would go to fetch it when it fell—for he never thought it

possible for any gun to carry so far.

But as the gun went off down fell the magpie, and into a great bramble thicket; and away went the sheriff up into the brambles after it, and he picked it up and showed it to the lad. But in a trice little Freddy began to scrape his fiddle, and the sheriff began to dance, and the thorns to tear him; but still the lad played on, and the sheriff danced and cried and begged till his clothes flew to tatters, and he scarce had a thread to his back.

"Yes!" said little Freddy; "now I think you're about as ragged as I was when I left your service. So now you may get off with what you have got."

But, first of all, the sheriff had to pay him what he had wagered that he could not hit the magpie.

So when the lad came to the town he turned aside into an inn, and he began to play, and all who came danced, and he lived merrily and well. He had no care, for no one could say him nay to anything he asked.

But just as they were all in the midst of their fun, up came the watchmen to drag the lad off to the town-hall; for the sheriff had laid a charge against him, and said he had waylaid him and robbed him, and nearly taken his life. And now he was to be hanged—they would not hear of anything else. But little Freddy had a cure for all trouble, and that was his fiddle. He began to play on it, and the watchmen fell a-dancing, till they lay down and gasped for breath.

So they sent soldiers and the guard on their way; but it was no better with them than with the watchmen. As soon as ever little Freddy scraped his fiddle, they were all bound to dance,

so long as he could lift a finger to play a tune; but they were half dead long before he was tired. At last they stole a march on him, and took him while he lay asleep by night; and when they had caught him he was doomed to be hanged on the spot, and away they hurried him to the gallows-tree.

There a great crowd of people flocked together to see this wonder, and the sheriff, too, was there; and he was so glad at last at getting amends for the money and the skin he had lost, and that he might see him hanged with his own eyes. But they did not get little Freddie to the gallows very fast, for he was always weak on his legs, and now he made himself weaker still. His fiddle and his gun he had with him also—it was hard to part him from them; and so, when he came to the gallows and had to mount the steps, he halted on each step; and when he got to the top he sat down, and asked if they could deny him a wish, and if he might have leave to do one thing? He had such a longing, he said, to scrape a tune and play a bar on his fiddle before they hanged him.

"No! no!" they said. "It were sin and shame to deny him that." For, you know, no one could gainsay what he asked.

But the sheriff he begged them, for God's sake, not to let him have leave to touch a string, else it was all over with them altogether; and if the lad got leave, the sheriff begged them to bind him to the birch that stood there.

So little Freddy was not slow in getting his fiddle to speak, and all that were there fell a-dancing at once—those who went on two legs, and those who went on four; both the dean and the parson, and the lawyer, and the bailiff, and the sheriff; masters and men, dogs and swine, they all danced and laughed and screeched at one another. Some danced till they lay for dead; some danced till they fell into a swoon. It went badly with all of them, but worst of all with the sheriff, for there he stood bound to the birch, and he danced and scraped great bits off his back against the trunk. There was not one of them who thought of doing anything to little Freddy, and away he went with his fiddle and his gun, just as he chose; and he lived merrily and happily all his days, for there was no one who could say him nay to the first thing he asked for.

# EAST O' THE SUN AND WEST O' THE MOON

*(Norwegian)*

*This story, which is "Cupid and Psyche" in Norse dress, might well be a fragment of an ancient myth, with the polar bear an obvious symbol of winter in a northern country. The tale is also pure romance and fulfills the usual desires for food, warmth, luxury, security, and love.*

Once on a time there was a poor husbandman who had so many children that he hadn't much of either food or clothing to give them. Pretty children they all were, but the prettiest was the youngest daughter, who was so lovely there was no end to her loveliness.

So one day, 'twas on a Thursday evening late at the fall of the year, the weather was so wild and rough outside, and it was so cruelly dark, and rain fell and wind blew, till the walls of the cottage shook again. There they all sat round the fire busy with this thing and that. But just then, all at once something gave three taps on the window-pane. Then the father went out to see what was the matter; and, when he got out of doors, what should he see but a great big White Bear.

"Good evening to you," said the White Bear.

"The same to you," said the man.

"Will you give me your youngest daughter? If you will, I'll make you as rich as you are now poor," said the Bear.

Well, the man would not be at all sorry to be so rich; but still he thought he must have a bit of a talk with his daughter first; so he went in and told them how there was a great White Bear waiting outside, who had given his word to make them so rich if he could only have the youngest daughter.

The lassie said "No!" outright. Nothing could get her to say anything else; so the man went out and settled it with the White Bear, that he should come again the next Thursday evening and get an answer. Meantime he talked his daughter over, and kept on telling her of all the riches they would get, and how well off she would be herself; and so at last she thought bet-

"East o' the Sun and West o' the Moon." From *Popular Tales from the Norse,* by Peter Christian Asbjörnsen and Jörgen Moe, translated by Sir George Webbe Dasent. David Douglas, Edinburgh, 1888

ter of it, and washed and mended her rags, made herself as smart as she could, and was ready to start. I can't say her packing gave her much trouble.

Next Thursday evening came the White Bear to fetch her, and she got upon his back with her bundle, and off they went. So, when they had gone a bit of the way, the White Bear said, "Are you afraid?"

No! she wasn't.

"Well! mind and hold tight by my shaggy coat, and then there's nothing to fear," said the Bear.

So she rode a long, long way, till they came to a great steep hill. There, on the face of it, the White Bear gave a knock, and a door opened, and they came into a castle, where there were many rooms all lit up; rooms gleaming with silver and gold; and there too was a table ready laid, and it was all as grand as grand could be. Then the White Bear gave her a silver bell; and when she wanted anything, she was only to ring it, and she would get it at once.

Well, after she had eaten and drunk, and evening wore on, she got sleepy after her journey, and thought she would like to go to bed, so she rang the bell; and she had scarce taken hold of it before she came into a chamber, where there was a bed made, as fair and white as any one would wish to sleep in, with silken pillows and curtains, and gold fringe. All that was in the room was gold or silver; but when she had gone to bed, and put out the light, she heard someone come into the next room. That was the White Bear, who threw off his beast shape at night; but she never saw him, for he always came after she had put out the light, and before the day dawned he was up and off again. So things went on happily for a while, but at last she began to get silent and sorrowful; for there she went about all day alone, and she longed to go home to see her father and mother and brothers and sisters. So one day, when the White Bear asked what it was that she lacked, she said it was so dull and lonely there that she longed to go home to see her father and mother and brothers and sisters, and that was why she was so sad and sorrowful, because she couldn't get to them.

"Well, well!" said the Bear, "perhaps there's a cure for all this; but you must promise me one thing, not to talk alone with your mother, but only when the rest are by to hear; for she'll take you by the hand and try to lead you into a room alone to talk; but you must mind and not do that, else you'll bring bad luck on both of us."

So one Sunday the White Bear came and said now they could set off to see her father and mother. Well, off they started, she sitting on his back; and they went far and long. At last they came to a grand house, and there her brothers and sisters were running about out of doors at play, and everything was so pretty, 'twas a joy to see.

"This is where your father and mother live now," said the White Bear; "but don't forget what I told you, else you'll make us both unlucky."

"No! bless me, I'll not forget." And when she had reached the house, the White Bear turned right about and left her.

Then when she went in to see her father and mother, there was such joy, there was no end to it. None of them thought they could thank her enough for all she had done for them. Now, they had everything they wished, as good as good could be, and they all wanted to know how she got on where she lived.

Well, she said, it was very good to live where she did; she had all she wished. What she said besides I don't know; but I don't think any of them had the right end of the stick, or that they got much out of her. But so in the afternoon, after they had done dinner, all happened as the White Bear had said. Her mother wanted to talk with her alone in her bed-room; but she minded what the White Bear had said, and wouldn't go up stairs.

"Oh, what we have to talk about will keep," she said, and put her mother off. But somehow or other, her mother got round her at last, and she had to tell her the whole story. So she said that every night, when she had gone to bed, someone came into the next room as soon as she had put out the light, and that she never saw him, because he was always up and away before the morning dawned; and how she went about woeful and sorrowing, for she thought she should so like to see him, and that all day long she walked about there alone, and that it was dull and dreary and lonesome.

"My!" said her mother; "it may well be a troll you heard! But now I'll teach you a lesson how to set eyes on him. I'll give you a bit of candle, which you can carry home in your bosom; just light that while he is asleep, but take care not to drop the tallow on him."

Yes! she took the candle, and hid it in her bosom, and as night drew on, the White Bear came and fetched her away.

But when they had gone a bit of the way, the White Bear asked if all hadn't happened as he had said.

Well, she couldn't say it hadn't.

"Now, mind," said he, "if you have listened to your mother's advice, you have brought bad luck on us both, and then, all that has passed between us will be as nothing."

"No," she said, "I didn't listen to my mother's advice."

So when she reached home, and had gone to bed, it was the old story over again. There came someone into the next room; but at dead of night, when she heard he slept, she got up and struck a light, lit the candle, went into the room, and let the light shine on him, and so she saw that he was the loveliest prince one ever set eyes on, and she fell so deep in love with him on the spot, that she thought she couldn't live if she didn't give him a kiss there and then. And so she did, but as she kissed him, she dropped three hot drops of tallow on his shirt, and he woke up.

"What have you done?" he cried; "now you have made us both unlucky, for had you held out only this one year, I had been freed. For I have a stepmother who has bewitched me, so that I am a white bear by day, and a man by night. But now all ties are snapt between us; now I must set off from you to her. She lives in a castle which stands EAST O' THE SUN AND WEST O' THE MOON, and there, too, is a princess, with a nose three ells long, and she's the wife I must have now."

She wept and took it ill, but there was no help for it; go he must.

Then she asked if she mightn't go with him.

No, she mightn't.

"Tell me the way, then," she said, "and I'll search you out; *that* surely I may get leave to do."

"Yes, you might do that," he said; "but there is no way to that place. It lies EAST O' THE SUN AND WEST O' THE MOON, and thither you'd never find your way."

So next morning, when she woke up, both prince and castle were gone, and then she lay on a little green patch, in the midst of the gloomy thick wood, and by her side lay the same bundle of rags she had brought with her from her old home.

So when she had rubbed the sleep out of her eyes, and wept till she was tired, she set out on her way, and walked many, many days, till she came to a lofty crag. Under it sat an old hag, who played with a gold apple which she tossed about. Her the lassie asked if she knew the way to the prince, who lived with his stepmother in the castle that lay EAST O' THE SUN AND WEST O' THE MOON, and who was to marry the princess with a nose three ells long.

"How did you come to know about him?" asked the old hag; "But maybe you are the lassie who ought to have had him?"

Yes, she was.

"So, so; it's you, is it?" said the old hag. "Well, all I know about him is that he lives in the castle that lies EAST O' THE SUN AND WEST O' THE MOON, and thither you'll come, late or never; but still you may have the loan of my horse, and on him you can ride to my next neighbour. Maybe she'll be able to tell you; and when you get there, just give the horse a switch under the left ear, and beg him to be off home; and, stay, this gold apple you may take with you."

So she got upon the horse, and rode a long, long time, till she came to another crag, under which sat another old hag, with a gold carding-comb. Her the lassie asked if she knew the way to the castle that lay EAST O' THE SUN AND WEST O' THE MOON, and she answered, like the first old hag, that she knew nothing about it, except it was east o' the sun and west o' the moon.

"And thither you'll come, late or never; but you shall have the loan of my horse to my next neighbour; maybe she'll tell you all about it; and when you get there, just switch the horse under the left ear, and beg him to be off home."

And this old hag gave her the golden carding-comb; it might be she'd find some use for it, she said. So the lassie got up on the horse, and rode a far, far way, and a weary time; and so at last she came to another great crag, under which sat another old hag, spinning with a golden spinning-wheel. Her, too, she asked if she knew the way to the prince, and where the castle was that lay EAST O' THE SUN AND WEST O' THE MOON. So it was the same thing over again.

"Maybe it's you who ought to have had the prince?" said the old hag.

Yes, it was.

But she, too, didn't know the way a bit better than the other two. "East o' the sun and west o' the moon it was," she knew—that was all.

"And thither you'll come, late or never; but I'll lend you my horse, and then I think you'd best ride to the East Wind and ask him; maybe he knows those parts, and can blow you thither. But when you get to him, you need only give the horse a switch under the left ear, and he'll trot home of himself."

And so, too, she gave her the gold spinning-wheel. "Maybe you'll find a use for it," said the old hag.

Then on she rode many, many days, a weary time, before she got to the East Wind's house, but at last she did reach it, and then she asked the East Wind if he could tell her the way to the prince who dwelt east o' the sun and west o' the moon. Yes, the East Wind had often heard tell of it, the prince, and the castle, but he couldn't tell the way, for he had never blown so far.

"But, if you will, I'll go with you to my brother the West Wind. Maybe he knows, for he's much stronger. So, if you will just get on my back, I'll carry you thither."

Yes, she got on his back, and I should just think they went briskly along.

So when they got there, they went into the West Wind's house, and the East Wind said the lassie he had brought was the one who ought to have had the prince who lived in the castle EAST O' THE SUN AND WEST O' THE MOON; and so she had set out to seek him, and how he had come with her, and would be glad to know if the West Wind knew how to get to the castle.

"Nay," said the West Wind, "so far I've never blown; but if you will, I'll go with you to our brother the South Wind, for he's much stronger than either of us, and he has flapped his wings far and wide. Maybe he'll tell you. You can get

on my back, and I'll carry you to him."

Yes! she got on his back, and so they travelled to the South Wind, and weren't so very long on the way, I should think.

When they got there, the West Wind asked him if he could tell her the way to the castle that lay EAST O' THE SUN AND WEST O' THE MOON, for it was she who ought to have had the prince who lived there.

"You don't say so! That's she, is it?" said the South Wind.

"Well, I have blustered about in most places in my time, but so far have I never blown; but if you will, I'll take you to my brother the North Wind; he is the oldest and strongest of the whole lot of us, and if he doesn't know where it is, you'll never find any one in the world to tell you. You can get on my back, and I'll carry you thither."

Yes! she got on his back, and away he went from his house at a fine rate. And this time, too, she wasn't long on her way.

So when they got to the North Wind's house, he was so wild and cross, cold puffs came from him a long way off.

"BLAST YOU BOTH, WHAT DO YOU WANT?" he roared out to them ever so far off, so that it struck them with an icy shiver.

"Well," said the South Wind, "you needn't be so foul-mouthed, for here I am, your brother, the South Wind, and here is the lassie who ought to have had the prince who dwells in the castle that lies EAST O' THE SUN AND WEST O' THE MOON, and now she wants to ask you if you ever were there, and can tell her the way, for she would be so glad to find him again."

"YES, I KNOW WELL ENOUGH WHERE IT IS," said the North Wind. "Once in my life I blew an aspen-leaf thither, but I was so tired I couldn't blow a puff for ever so many days after. But if you really wish to go thither, and aren't afraid to come along with me, I'll take you on my back and see if I can blow you thither."

Yes! with all her heart; she must and would get thither if it were possible in any way; and as for fear, however madly he went, she wouldn't be at all afraid.

"Very well, then," said the North Wind, "but you must sleep here to-night, for we must have the whole day before us, if we're to get thither at all."

Early next morning the North Wind woke her, and puffed himself up, and blew himself out, and made himself so stout and big, 'twas gruesome to look at him; and so off they went high up through the air, as if they would never stop till they got to the world's end.

Down here below there was such a storm; it threw down long tracts of wood and many houses, and when it swept over the great sea, ships foundered by hundreds.

So they tore on and on—no one can believe how far they went—and all the while they still went over the sea, and the North Wind got more and more weary, and so out of breath he could scarce bring out a puff, and his wings drooped and drooped, till at last he sunk so low that the crests of the waves dashed over his heels.

"Are you afraid?" said the North Wind.

No, she wasn't.

But they weren't very far from land; and the North Wind had still so much strength left in him that he managed to throw her up on the shore under the windows of the castle which lay EAST O' THE SUN AND WEST O' THE MOON; but then he was so weak and worn out, he had to

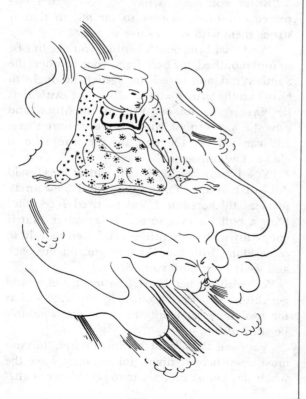

stay there and rest many days before he could get home again.

Next morning the lassie sat down under the castle window, and began to play with the gold apple; and the first person she saw was the long-nose who was to have the prince.

"What do you want for your gold apple, you lassie?" said the long-nose, and threw up the window.

"It's not for sale, for gold or money," said the lassie.

"If it's not for sale for gold or money, what is it that you will sell it for? You may name your own price," said the princess.

"Well! if I may get to the prince, who lives here, and be with him to-night, you shall have it," said the lassie whom the North Wind had brought.

Yes! she might; that could be done. So the princess got the gold apple; but when the lassie came up to the prince's bed-room at night he was fast asleep; she called him and shook him, and between whiles she wept sore; but all she could do she couldn't wake him up. Next morning as soon as day broke, came the princess with the long nose, and drove her out again.

So in the day-time she sat down under the castle windows and began to card with her golden carding-comb, and the same thing happened. The princess asked what she wanted for it; and she said it wasn't for sale for gold or money, but if she might get leave to go up to the prince and be with him that night, the princess should have it. But when she went up she found him fast asleep again, and all she called, and all she shook, and wept, and prayed, she couldn't get life into him; and as soon as the first gray peep of day came, then came the princess with the long nose and chased her out again.

So in the day-time the lassie sat down outside under the castle window, and began to spin with her golden spinning-wheel, and that, too, the princess with the long nose wanted to have. So she threw up the window and asked what she wanted for it. The lassie said, as she had said twice before, it wasn't for sale for gold or money; but if she might go up to the prince who was there, and be with him alone that night, she might have it.

Yes! she might do that and welcome. But now

you must know there were some folk who had been carried off thither, and as they sat in their room, which was next the prince, they had heard how a woman had been in there, and wept and prayed, and called to him two nights running, and they told that to the prince.

That evening, when the princess came with her sleepy drink, the prince made as if he drank, but threw it over his shoulder, for he could guess it was a sleepy drink. So, when the lassie came in, she found the prince wide awake; and then she told him the whole story how she had come thither.

"Ah," said the Prince, "you've just come in the very nick of time, for to-morrow is to be our wedding-day; but now I won't have the long-nose, and you are the only woman in the world who can set me free. I'll say I want to see what my wife is fit for, and beg her to wash the shirt which has the three spots of tallow on it; she'll say yes, for she doesn't know 'tis you who put them there; but that's a work only for Christian folk, and not for such a pack of trolls, and so I'll say that I won't have any other for my bride than the woman who can wash them out, and ask you to do it."

Next day, when the wedding was to be, the prince said, "First of all, I'd like to see what my bride is fit for."

"Yes!" said the step-mother, with all her heart.

"Well," said the prince, "I've got a fine shirt which I'd like for my wedding shirt, but somehow or other it has got three spots of tallow on it, which I must have washed out; and I have sworn never to take any other bride than the woman who's able to do that. If she can't, she's not worth having."

Well, that was no great thing they said, so they agreed, and she with the long nose began to wash away as hard as she could, but the more she rubbed and scrubbed, the bigger the spots grew.

"Ah!" said the old hag, her mother, "you can't wash; let me try."

But she hadn't long taken the shirt in hand, before it got far worse than ever, and with all her rubbing and wringing and scrubbing, the spots grew bigger and blacker, and the darker and uglier was the shirt.

Then all the other trolls began to wash, but the longer it lasted, the blacker and uglier the shirt grew, till at last it was as black all over as if it had been up the chimney.

"Ah!" said the prince, "you're none of you worth a straw; you can't wash. Why there, outside, sits a beggar lassie. I'll be bound she knows how to wash better than the whole lot of you. COME IN, LASSIE!" he shouted.

Well, in she came.

"Can you wash this shirt clean, lassie, you?" said he.

"I don't know," she said, "but I think I can."

And almost before she had taken it and dipped it in the water, it was as white as driven snow, and whiter still.

"Yes; you are the lassie for me," said the prince.

At that the old hag flew into such a rage, she burst on the spot, and the princess with the long nose after her, and the whole pack of trolls after her—at least I've never heard a word about them since.

As for the prince and princess, they set free all the folk who had been carried off and shut up there; and they took with them all the silver and gold, and flitted away as far as they could from the castle that lay EAST O' THE SUN AND WEST O' THE MOON.

## LINDA-GOLD AND THE OLD KING
### (Swedish)

*This is a tale without magic, unless it is the magic of love. For it is the innocent love of a small child that overcomes the bitter grief of the old king in this rather sentimental tale. Often in folklore or fairy tales, a young person who is good and humble is lifted to high position, but this is usually by test or quest. Linda-Gold*

"Linda-Gold and the Old King" by Anna Wahlenberg. From *Great Swedish Fairy Tales*, translated by Holger Lundbergh and selected by Elsa Olenius. Swedish Edition Copyright © 1966 by Albert Bonniers Forlag. English translation Copyright © 1973 by Dell Publishing Co., Inc. By permission of Delacorte Press and Chatto & Windus Ltd.

Long, long ago there lived an old king who was rather eccentric. People said he was odd because he had had many sorrows, poor old king. His queen and children had died, and he himself said his heart had been torn apart. Who had done that and how it had happened, he never told; but it was someone with claws, he said, and since then he imagined that everyone had claws on his hands.

No one was allowed to come nearer than two arms' lengths to the king. His valets were not allowed to touch him, and his dining-room steward had to place his food at the very edge of the table. The king had not shaken anyone's hand for many, many years. If people were careless enough not to remember about the two arms' lengths, and came an inch closer, the king had them put in irons for a week to refresh their memory.

In all other ways, the old king was a good king. He governed his subjects well and justly. Everyone was devoted to him, and the only thing his people regretted was that he had not found a new queen, or appointed anyone prince or princess to inherit the realm. When they asked him about this, however, he always said, "Show me someone who does not have claws, and I will let that person be my heir."

But no one ever appeared who, in the king's mind, did not have claws. The claws might be under the fingernails, or curled in the palm, but they were always there, he believed.

Now one day it happened that the old king was walking alone in the forest. He grew tired and sat down to rest on the moss and listen to the birds singing in the trees. Suddenly a small girl rushed up the path, her hair streaming behind. And when the king looked up, he saw in the trees a shaggy grey beast with flashing eyes and a grinning red mouth. It was a wolf, who wanted the little girl for breakfast. The old king rose and drew his sword, and straightaway the wolf turned in fear and ran back into the forest.

When the wolf had gone, the little girl began to weep and tremble. "Now you must walk home with me, too," she said, "or else the wolf will

chase me again."

"Must I?" asked the king, who was not accustomed to taking orders.

"Yes. And my mother will give you a loaf of white bread for your trouble. My name is Linda-Gold, and my father is the miller on the other side of the forest."

What she said was right, the king decided. He couldn't very well let her be killed by the wolf, and so he was obliged to accompany her.

"You go first," he said. "I will follow behind you."

But the little girl did not dare walk first. "May I hold your hand?" she asked, and moved closer to him.

The king started, and looked closely at the little hand raised to his. "No, I am sure you have claws, too, though you are so small," he said.

Linda-Gold's eyes filled with tears, and she hid her hands behind her back. "My father says that, when all I have done is forgotten to cut my nails." She felt ashamed and looked at the ground. But then she asked if she might at least take hold of his mantle, and the king agreed to that. He simply could not make himself tell her to keep two arms' lengths away, for she was only a small child who would not understand.

So she skipped along beside him and told him of her cottage and all her toys. She had so many beautiful things she wanted to show him. There was a cow made of pine cones, with match sticks for legs; a boat made from an old wooden shoe, with burdock leaves for a sail; and then best of all was a doll her mother had sewn for her from an old brown apron and stuffed with yarn. It had a skirt made from the sleeve of a red sweater, and a blue ribbon at the neck, and her big brother had drawn a face on it with coal and put on a patch of leather for a nose.

It was odd, but the king listened patiently to all her chattering, and smiled. He was sure the little hand had claws, yet he let it pull and jerk at his mantle as much as it wished. But when Linda-Gold and the king came to the highway, and the mill was not far away, the king said good-bye. Now Linda-Gold could go home by herself.

But Linda-Gold was disappointed. She did not want to say good-bye so soon. She clung to his arm and tugged it, and begged him. How could he *not* want white bread, which was so good? It couldn't be true that he did not want to look at her fine toys! She would let him play with her doll all the evening, if only he would come home with her. She would give him a present—the boat with the burdock-leaf sails—because he had saved her from the wolf.

When none of this helped, she at last asked the king where he lived.

"In the castle," he said.

"And what is your name?"

"Old Man Greybeard."

"Good. Then I will come to visit you, Old Man Greybeard." And she took off her little blue checked scarf, and stood waving it as long as the king could see her—and he turned to look back quite often because he thought her the sweetest little girl he had met in a long time.

Even after he had returned to the castle, he still thought of Linda-Gold, wondering if she really would come to visit him. He was worried because she did not want to keep her little hands at a respectful distance, but he could not deny that he longed to see her.

The king was still thinking of Linda-Gold the next morning, and feeling sure that she would not dare venture out so far for fear of the wolf, when he heard a clear child's voice calling from the palace yard. He went to the balcony and saw Linda-Gold with a rag doll under her arm. She was arguing with the gatekeeper. She said she must speak to Old Man Greybeard about something very important.

But the gatekeeper just laughed at her and replied that no Old Man Greybeard lived there. Then Linda-Gold got angry. He mustn't say that, she insisted, for she herself knew very well Old Man Greybeard did live there. He had told her so himself.

Next she went up to a lady-in-waiting who had just come outside, and asked her advice. No, the lady-in-waiting had never heard of Old Man Greybeard, either, and she too laughed heartily.

But Linda-Gold did not give up. She asked the cook, she asked the steward of the household, and she asked all the courtiers, who had begun to gather in the courtyard to stare at her. She turned red in the face as they all laughed, and her lower lip began to tremble. Her eyes were full of tears, but she still maintained firmly in a clear voice, "He must be here, because he told me so himself."

The king called from his balcony, "Yes, here I am, Linda-Gold."

Linda-Gold looked up, gave a shout of joy, and jumped up and down in excitement. "Do you see, do you see!" she called in triumph. "I told you he was here."

The courtiers could do nothing but stare in surprise. The king had to command twice that Linda-Gold be brought to him before anyone obeyed. Then it was no less a person than the royal court's Master of Ceremonies who led her to the king's chamber. When the door opened, Linda-Gold ran straight to the king and set her rag doll on his knee.

"I will give you this instead of the boat," she said, "because I thought that since you saved me from the wolf you should have the best thing of all."

The rag doll was the ugliest, most clumsy little bundle imaginable, but the old king smiled as if he were quite delighted with it.

"Isn't she sweet?" asked Linda-Gold.

"Yes, very."

"Kiss her, then."

And so the king had to kiss the doll on its black, horrible mouth.

"Since you like her, you should thank me, don't you think?"

"Thank you," said the king, nodding in a friendly way.

"That wasn't right," said Linda-Gold.

"Not right? How should it be then?"

"When you say thank you, you must also pat my cheek," said Linda-Gold.

And so the king had to pat her on the cheek; but it was a warm, soft little cheek, and not at all unpleasant to pat.

"And now—" said Linda-Gold.

"Is there something more?" asked the king.

"Yes, I would like to pat your cheek, too."

Here the king hesitated. This was really too much for him.

"Because, you see," Linda-Gold went on, "I cut my fingernails," and she held up both her small chubby hands for the king to see. He had to look at them whether he liked it or not.

And truly, he could not see anything unusual

on the pink fingertips. The nails were cut as close as a pair of scissors could do it, and there wasn't the trace of a claw.

"You can't say I have claws now, Greybeard," said Linda-Gold.

"No . . . hmm . . . well, pat me, then."

Linda-Gold flew up on his lap and stroked the old sunken cheeks and kissed them, and soon a couple of tears came rolling down. It was so long since the old king had known love.

Now he took Linda-Gold in his arms and carried her to the balcony. "Here you see the one you have always longed for," he called to those in the courtyard.

A loud cry of joy broke out among them. "Hurrah for our little princess. Hurrah! Hurrah!" they shouted.

Surprised and bewildered, Linda-Gold turned to the king and asked him what this meant.

"It means they like you because you have fine small hands which never scratch and have no claws," he said. Then he kissed the two little hands so that everyone could see, and from below the people shouted again, "Hurrah for our little princess!"

And that is how Linda-Gold became a princess and in the course of time inherited the realm of the old king.

## *Finland*

*Of all the national groups, the Finns are said to have the largest collection of folk tales in manuscript form. Unfortunately for us, most of these materials are in Finnish or German or Swedish. The history of folklore and folk-tale study in Finland is impressive and, as one scholar has said, predates the actual establishment of Finland as an independent nation. The outstandingly great name in the Finnish folklore study movement is that of Elias Lönnrot, who published the illustrious* Kalevala, *a collection in two volumes of ancient poetry and incantations. They make up a great folk epic that influenced the meter of Longfellow's* Hiawatha. *Almost every Finn knows the* Kalevala *and owns a copy of it. The Finnish "historic-geographic" method for folk-tale research and study, developed in the late nineteenth century, has shaped much of the folklore research that goes on in Europe, the United States, and other parts of the world. Thirty thousand of their tales have been collected, but not all have been published. The first collection of Finnish folk tales was* Fables and Tales of the Finnish Nation, *compiled by Eero Salmelainen. The stories in* Tales from a Finnish Tupa, *the collection best known in this country, are from that book, from Iivo Härkönen's collection,* Fables of the Finnish Nation, *and from storytellers heard by Bowman and Bianco. Perhaps because many of the tales are long and descriptive, Finnish folklore has not been as well known in this country or as much used as the Scandinavian tales have been. For the highly literate Finns, as for no other people, folklore and folk tales and folk songs are part and parcel of the national spirit, education, and pride.*

## THE PIG-HEADED WIFE
### (Finnish)

*This is one of the droll stories from* Tales from a Finnish Tupa. *A* tupa, *by the way, is a Finnish cottage, whose kitchen boasts an open fire and is the center of most household life. In the story of Matti's triumph over his obstinate wife Liisa, it is Liisa's supremacy in the kitchen that he cunningly challenges. Children enjoy being able to predict the wife's reaction to her husband's sly suggestions as much as they do the ending of the tale. Because the joke is saved until the very last word and because the tale is brief, it's just right for an encore.*

When Matti married Liisa, he thought she was the pleasantest woman in the world. But it wasn't long before Liisa began to show her real character. Headstrong as a goat she was, and as fair set on having her own way.

Matti had been brought up to know that a husband should be the head of his family, so he tried to make his wife obey. But this didn't work with Liisa. It just made her all the more stubborn and pig-headed. Every time that Matti asked her to do one thing, she was bound to do the opposite, and work as he would she generally got her own way in the end.

Matti was a patient sort of man, and he put up with her ways as best he could, though his friends were ready enough to make fun of him for being henpecked. And so they managed to jog along fairly well.

But one year as harvest time came round, Matti thought to himself:

"Here am I, a jolly good-hearted fellow, that likes a bit of company. If only I had a pleasant sort of wife, now, it would be a fine thing to invite all our friends to the house, and have a nice dinner and drink and a good time. But it's no good thinking of it, for as sure as I propose a feast, Liisa will declare a fast."

And then a happy thought struck him.

"I'll see if I can't get the better of Liisa, all the same. I'll let on I want to be quiet, and then she'll be all for having the house full of guests." So a few days later he said:

"The harvest holidays will be here soon, but don't you go making any sweet cakes this year. We're too poor for that sort of thing."

"Poor! What are you talking about?" Liisa snapped. "We've never had more than we have this year. I'm certainly going to bake a cake, and a good big one, too."

"It works," thought Matti. "It works!" But all he said was:

"Well, if you make a cake, we won't need a pudding too. We mustn't be wasteful."

"Wasteful, indeed!" Liisa grumbled. "We shall have a pudding, and a big pudding!"

Matti pretended to sigh, and rolled his eyes.

"Pudding's bad enough, but if you take it in your head to serve stuffed pig again, we'll be ruined!"

"You'll kill our best pig," quoth Liisa, "and let's hear no more about it."

"But wine, Liisa," Matti went on. "Promise me you won't open a single bottle. We've barely enough to last us through the winter as it is."

Liisa stamped her foot.

"Are you crazy, man? Who ever heard of stuffed pig without wine! We'll not only have wine, but I'll buy coffee too. I'll teach you to call me extravagant by the time I'm through with you!"

"Oh dear, oh dear," Matti sighed. "If you're going to invite a lot of guests, on top of everything else, that'll be the end of it. We can't possibly have guests."

"And have all the food spoil with no one to eat it, I suppose?" jeered Liisa. "Guests we'll have, and what's more, you'll sit at the head of the table, whether you like it or not."

"Well, at any rate I'll drink no wine myself," said Matti, growing bolder. "If I don't drink the others won't, and I tell you we'll need that wine to pull us through the winter."

Liisa turned on him, furious.

"You'll drink with your guests as a host should, till every bottle is empty. There! Now will you be quiet?"

When the day arrived, the guests came, and great was the feasting. They shouted and sang round the table, and Matti himself made more noise than any of his friends. So much so, that long before the feast was over Liisa began to suspect he had played a trick on her. It made her furious to see him so jolly and carefree.

As time went on she grew more and more contrary, until there was no living with her. Now, it happened one day in the spring when all the streams were high, that Matti and Liisa were crossing the wooden bridge over the little river which separated two of their meadows. Matti crossed first, and noticing that the boards were badly rotted, he called out without thinking:

"Look where you step, Liisa! The plank is rotten there. Go lightly or you'll break through."

"Step lightly!" shouted Liisa. "I'll do as . . ."

But for once Liisa didn't finish what she had to say. She jumped with all her weight on the rotted timbers, and fell plop into the swollen stream.

Matti scratched his head for a moment: then he started running upstream as fast as he could go.

Two fishermen along the bank saw him, and called: "What's the matter, my man? Why are you running upstream so fast?"

"My wife fell in the river," Matti panted, "and I'm afraid she's drowned."

"You're crazy," said the fisherman. "Anyone in his right mind would search downstream, not up!"

"Ah," said Matti, "but you don't know my Liisa! All her life she's been so pig-headed that even when she's dead she'd be bound to go against the current!"

## TIMO AND THE PRINCESS VENDLA
### (Finnish)

*Magic is an essential part of most Finnish lore, but it is often the magic of words. A peaceful people, the Finns avoid violence in their stories as they do in life. The tale is a familiar theme of a king who offers the hand of his daughter to a suitor who can solve a problem, but the punishment for failure is mild, and there are no rivals. The Finns, a pastoral people, reflect this by the one magic device of the story, the speaking animals. The story, however, is of wisdom—both Timo's and Vendla's.*

There was once a proud King who had an only daughter named Vendla. He said:

"My daughter shall be different from any other woman in the world. I want her to be wiser than anyone else, in order that she will do me honor."

So he sent for all the most famous teachers, and told them to teach his daughter every language in the world. After Vendla had learned French and English and German and Spanish and Greek and Latin and Chinese and all the other languages as well, so that she could talk to the courtiers of the world each in his own tongue, the King called his heralds and said:

"Go forth throughout the whole kingdom, and say to the people: 'The King will give the Princess Vendla in marriage to the man who can speak a new tongue that she does not understand. But let everyone beware, for any man who dares to woo the Princess without speaking a new tongue shall be flung into the Baltic Sea.'"

It happened that there dwelt in the kingdom a young shepherd lad named Timo. Timo was a dreamer who spent his time wandering about the deep wild forest talking to the birds and the beasts. And by talking to them he had learned to understand their language, and they his.

When Timo heard the King's proclamation he laughed.

"It shouldn't be so hard to win the Princess Vendla. There are many tongues in the world. Even the wisest men and women cannot understand them all."

So he started on his way to the King's castle. Before he had gone very far he met a sparrow.

"Where are you going with such a happy face, Timo?" the sparrow chirped.

"I am going to marry the Princess Vendla. Come with me and I'll give you a ride in my fine leather pouch."

"Surely I'll go with you," said the sparrow. And he hopped into the pouch, while Timo went his way.

Presently Timo met a squirrel that sat under his fluffy tail and nibbled at a hazelnut.

"Where are you going with such a happy face, Timo?" chattered the squirrel.

"I am going to marry the learned Princess Vendla."

"How wonderful!"

"Come with me and I'll give you a ride in my fine leather pouch."

The squirrel hopped into the pouch, and Timo strode gaily onward. Soon he met a crow, then a raven, then an owl. Each in turn asked him where he was going, and each in turn hopped into Timo's leather pouch to keep him company. On he strode, and before he knew it he came to the gates of the King's castle.

"Halt! Who are you?" boomed one of the King's soldiers.

"I am Timo, and I've come to woo the fair and learned Princess Vendla."

"Why, you're only a shepherd boy," cried the guard. "What's more, you're a fool as well."

"You must be in a hurry to taste the Baltic Sea!" laughed another of the soldiers.

"You can't even speak your own tongue properly, let alone others," cried a third soldier. "Where you come from, the people all talk as if they had a hot potato in their mouth!"

"You'd better run along back to your flocks while you've still got a chance," added the first soldier.

But Timo stood his ground.

"I come to woo the most beautiful and learned Princess Vendla," he said again. "Open the gates and let me in, for I can speak a dozen tongues that the Princess has never even heard."

"Well, remember we warned you," said the guard as he slowly opened the gates. "Next thing you know, we'll be giving you a ride to the Baltic Sea!"

Vendla was seated beside her father on a high golden throne. Her hair was decked with jewels and her face was so beautiful that when Timo saw her he fell on his knees.

"Is it true, most beautiful and learned Princess, that you will marry the man who can speak a language you do not understand?"

"This must be a brave man," thought the Princess as she looked at Timo standing there with his leather pouch across his shoulder.

"Yes," she said, "it is true."

"Do you know what will happen to you if you dare to woo the Princess, and fail to speak this unknown tongue you talk about?" thundered the King.

"I would swim a dozen seas bigger than the Baltic for such a Princess," cried Timo as he looked into Vendla's blue eyes.

"Then let us hear this fine language of yours," said the King.

Timo turned to the Princess.

"Listen, most beautiful Princess, and tell me if you understand."

As he spoke Timo thrust his hand into the leather pouch, and touched the sparrow softly. The bird woke up and chirped:

"*Tshiu, tshiu, tshiu, tshiu!* What do you want, Timo?"

"What tongue is that?" Timo asked.

"Truly," said the Princess, "it is a language I have never heard."

"So you don't understand all the tongues in the world!" Timo laughed. He touched the squirrel's tail.

"*Rak-rak-rak! Rak-rak! Ka-ka-ka-ka-ka-ka!* Leave me alone!" chattered the squirrel.

"Do you understand that?" Timo asked.

"I do not," said the Princess meekly.

Then Timo touched the crow.

"*Vaak, vaak, vaak—ak-ak!* Don't disturb me!" cawed the crow.

The Princess shook her head in amazement. Neither could she understand the "*thiuu, thiuu, thiuu*" of the woodpecker, nor the "*kronk, kronk, kronk*" of the raven.

"It is all most strange," said the Princess. "I cannot understand why my teachers never taught me these words!"

"You see, there are many languages that even the wisest men on earth do not know," said Timo, smiling.

"Vendla, I thought you the most learned woman in the world," cried the King furiously, "yet you let a country lad make fools of us both!"

"O King, this is not so," Timo pleaded. "Vendla is still the most learned lady in the land, for she has admitted her ignorance, and truly the greatest wisdom is to know that one does not know everything."

The Princess was pleased with Timo's honest eyes and his understanding words. She was glad that he had won her hand.

"O King," asked Timo, "will you now keep your bargain with me?"

"Take Vendla for your bride," answered the King. "You have won her, and with her I give you the half of my kingdom. May you always be as wise in the future as you have shown yourself today!"

Then the Princess climbed down from her high throne, and Timo took her in his arms and kissed her cheek.

The King proclaimed a glorious holiday with feasting throughout the land, and Timo and Vendla lived happily ever after.

# *Spain*

*The folklore of Spain, as well as that of Portugal, is richly varied, laced as it is with strong strains from the Moorish and Moslem civilizations that have been a part of the cultures of the Iberian peninsula in the past and from a fervent, deep-reaching Christian heritage. Spain has also exerted a tremendous influence on the language, literature, and lore of Spanish-speaking peoples of North and South America and various island groups. In turn, its folklore has been influenced by New World folklore as well as by the general European traditions. Although the collections of Spanish folk tales for children are rather few in number, folklore research in Spain is well organized and thorough, and folklore has been under investigation for a very long time. Although this facet of Spanish folklore is not evident in the tales chosen for this section, one notable feature is the frequent occurrence of stories about the saints, stories that are marked by a deep faith and a strong sense of morality. More evident here is the robust humor of Spain, the delight in using wit to outsmart others. A typically Spanish beginning for the tales is often used by Ruth Sawyer: "Once there was and was not. . . ." It makes an effective beginning and offers a change from "Once upon a time. . . ."*

## THE HALF-CHICK

*This selfish creature has his counterparts in many folk tales. The tale is really a variant of the English "The Old Woman and Her Pig," or perhaps it is the other way around. Before telling it, explain what a weather vane is and show children the picture of the weathercock (p. 266).*

Once upon a time there was a handsome black Spanish hen, who had a large brood of chickens. They were all fine, plump little birds, except the youngest, who was quite unlike his brothers and sisters. Indeed, he was such a strange, queer-look-

"The Half-Chick." From *The Green Fairy Book*, edited by Andrew Lang. Longmans, Green, and Co., London, 1892

ing creature, that when he first chipped his shell his mother could scarcely believe her eyes, he was so different from the twelve other fluffy, downy, soft little chicks who nestled under her wings. This one looked just as if he had been cut in two. He had only one leg, and one wing, and one eye, and he had half a head and half a beak. His mother shook her head sadly as she looked at him and said:

"My youngest born is only a half-chick. He can never grow up a tall handsome cock like his brothers. They will go out into the world and rule over poultry yards of their own; but this poor little fellow will always have to stay at home with his mother." And she called him Medio Pollito, which is Spanish for half-chick.

Now though Medio Pollito was such an odd, helpless-looking little thing, his mother soon found that he was not at all willing to remain under her wing and protection. Indeed, in character he was as unlike his brothers and sisters as he was in appearance. They were good, obedient chickens, and when the old hen chicked after them, they chirped and ran back to her side. But Medio Pollito had a roving spirit in spite of his one leg, and when his mother called to him to return to the coop, he pretended that he could not hear, because he had only one ear.

When she took the whole family out for a walk in the fields, Medio Pollito would hop away by himself, and hide among the Indian corn. Many an anxious minute his brothers and sisters had looking for him, while his mother ran to and fro cackling in fear and dismay.

As he grew older he became more self-willed and disobedient, and his manner to his mother was often very rude, and his temper to the other chickens very disagreeable.

One day he had been out for a longer expedition than usual in the fields. On his return he strutted up to his mother with the peculiar little hop and kick which was his way of walking, and cocking his one eye at her in a very bold way he said:

"Mother, I am tired of this life in a dull farm-yard, with nothing but a dreary maize field to look at. I'm off to Madrid to see the King."

"To Madrid, Medio Pollito!" exclaimed his mother; "why, you silly chick, it would be a long journey for a grown-up cock, and a poor little

thing like you would be tired out before you had gone half the distance. No, no, stay at home with your mother, and some day, when you are bigger, we will go a little journey together."

But Medio Pollito had made up his mind, and he would not listen to his mother's advice, nor to the prayers and entreaties of his brothers and sisters.

"What is the use of our all crowding each other up in this poky little place?" he said. "When I have a fine courtyard of my own at the King's palace, I shall perhaps ask some of you to come and pay me a short visit," and scarcely waiting to say good-bye to his family, away he stumped down the high road that led to Madrid.

"Be sure that you are kind and civil to everyone you meet," called his mother, running after him; but he was in such a hurry to be off, that he did not wait to answer her, or even to look back.

A little later in the day, as he was taking a short cut through a field, he passed a stream. Now the stream was all choked up and overgrown with weeds and water-plants, so that its waters could not flow freely.

"Oh! Medio Pollito," it cried, as the half-chick hopped along its banks, "do come and help me by clearing away these weeds."

"Help you, indeed!" exclaimed Medio Pollito, tossing his head, and shaking the few feathers in his tail. "Do you think I have nothing to do but to waste my time on such trifles? Help yourself, and don't trouble busy travellers. I am off to Madrid to see the King," and hoppity-kick, hoppity-kick, away stumped Medio Pollito.

A little later he came to a fire that had been left by some gypsies in a wood. It was burning very low, and would soon be out.

"Oh! Medio Pollito," cried the fire, in a weak, wavering voice as the half-chick approached, "in a few minutes I shall go quite out, unless you put some sticks and dry leaves upon me. Do help me, or I shall die!"

"Help you, indeed!" answered Medio Pollito. "I have other things to do. Gather sticks for yourself, and don't trouble me. I am off to Madrid to see the King," and hoppity-kick, hoppity-kick, away stumped Medio Pollito.

The next morning, as he was getting near Madrid, he passed a large chestnut tree, in whose branches the wind was caught and entangled.

"Oh! Medio Pollito," called the wind, "do hop up here, and help me to get free of these branches. I cannot come away, and it is so uncomfortable."

"It is your own fault for going there," answered Medio Pollito. "I can't waste all my morning stopping here to help you. Just shake yourself off, and don't hinder me, for I am off to Madrid to see the King," and hoppity-kick, hoppity-kick, away stumped Medio Pollito in great glee, for the towers and roofs of Madrid were now in sight.

When he entered the town he saw before him a great splendid house, with soldiers standing before the gates. This he knew must be the King's palace, and he determined to hop up to the front gate and wait there until the King came out. But as he was hopping past one of the back windows the King's cook saw him:

"Here is the very thing I want," he exclaimed, "for the King has just sent a message to say that he must have chicken broth for his dinner," and opening the window he stretched out his arm, caught Medio Pollito, and popped him into the broth-pot that was standing near the fire. Oh! how wet and clammy the water felt as it went over Medio Pollito's head, making his feathers cling to his side.

"Water, water!" he cried in his despair, "do have pity upon me and do not wet me like this."

"Ah! Medio Pollito," replied the water, "you would not help me when I was a little stream away on the fields; now you must be punished."

Then the fire began to burn and scald Medio Pollito, and he danced and hopped from one side of the pot to the other, trying to get away from the heat, and crying out in pain:

"Fire, fire! do not scorch me like this; you can't think how it hurts."

"Ah! Medio Pollito," answered the fire, "you would not help me when I was dying away in the wood. You are being punished."

At last, just when the pain was so great that Medio Pollito thought he must die, the cook lifted up the lid of the pot to see if the broth was ready for the King's dinner.

"Look here!" he cried in horror, "this chicken is quite useless. It is burnt to a cinder. I can't send it up to the royal table." And opening the window he threw Medio Pollito out into the street. But the wind caught him up, and whirled him through the air so quickly that Medio Pollito could scarcely breathe, and his heart beat against his side till he thought it would break.

"Oh, wind!" at last he gasped out, "if you hurry me along like this you will kill me. Do let me rest a moment, or——" but he was so breathless that he could not finish his sentence.

"Ah! Medio Pollito," replied the wind, "when I was caught in the branches of the chestnut tree you would not help me; now you are punished." And he swirled Medio Pollito over the roofs of the houses till they reached the highest church in the town, and there he left him fastened to the top of the steeple.

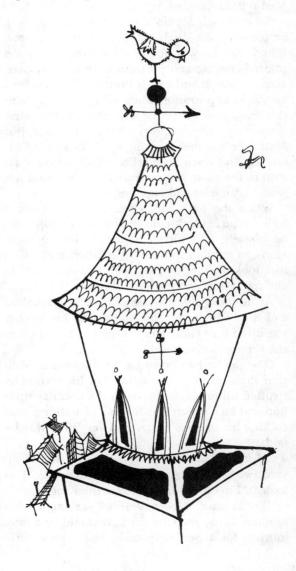

And there stands Medio Pollito to this day. And if you go to Madrid, and walk through the streets till you come to the highest church, you will see Medio Pollito perched on his one leg on the steeple, with his one wing drooping at his side, and gazing sadly out of his one eye over the town.

## THE JOKES OF SINGLE-TOE

*Padre Porko is a unique character in Spanish folklore. He is the gentlemanly pig, wise, witty, and urbane. He solves his own and his neighbors' problems with nonchalance. Look up the other stories in the book that bears his name. They are all good to tell.*

"Chestnuts are ripening and falling on the other side of the canal," said the black-headed sparrow, teetering on the edge of the table.

"Oh, but it's too early for chestnuts," observed the Padre. "It takes two or three frosty nights to open the prickles."

"Well, if you can't believe me," said the sparrow, ruffling his collar, "ask the squirrel. He keeps track of the nuts."

So the Padre asked Single-Toe (so named because he had only one on his left front foot). The squirrel put his paw beside his nose as though he were trying to think up an answer to a riddle. "I'll try to let you know in three days," he mumbled, "but don't do anything about chestnuts until you see me again." And he went off in such a rush that even the good Padre grew suspicious.

An hour later he laid down his pipe and beckoned to Mrs. Wren. "Do you mind having a little fly around the wood to see what the squirrel family is up to this morning?"

She came back twittering all over. "The squirrels, for miles around, are all in the grove across the canal, throwing down the chestnuts for dear life. Single-Toe is making them work all the harder, and giggling at something he seems to think very funny."

"Oh, the rascal," chuckled the Padre. "The sly

little one-toed sinner! He will give me an answer in three days, will he? Yes, indeed, after he has gathered all the best nuts." He called to his housekeeper. "Mrs. Hedge-Hog, bring me three of the oatmeal sacks from the cupboard and some strong string." And folding the bags inside his belt, he trotted off, pushing his wheelbarrow.

Up among the leaves, busy pulling the polished nuts out of the burrs, Single-Toe and his relatives did not hear the Padre arrive. Patter, plop, plop, plop, patter—the brown nuts were falling on the grass.

"What a lark," beamed the Padre, stuffing four or five into his mouth at once. "And this year they are sweeter and juicier than they have been for a long time." He made little piles of the biggest ones, and began filling his sacks. Finally he had all the wheelbarrow would carry. Bouncing the last bag up and down so he could tie the string around the top, he called out in his silkiest voice, "Many thanks, Single-Toe. You will see that I have taken only the big ones. I do hope that the prickers haven't made your paws sore."

There was a sudden calm in the chestnut grove. The squirrels came leaping down to a low bough, from where they could send sour looks after the Padre, trundling his barrow along toward the bridge. He was singing,

> With chestnuts roasting in a row,
>   I love to hear them sizzle.
> I care not how the winds may blow,
>   Nor how the rain-drops drizzle.
> I welcome every Jack and Jill
>   Who knocks upon my door.
> We toast our toes and eat our fill,
>   For there are plenty more.

One day three or four weeks later the Padre was doing a little carpentering under the umbrella pine, when something behind him sniffed. He jumped, and dropped two nails out of his mouth. There, under the table, tears running down their noses, were Mrs. Single-Toe and the four children.

"Bless my blue-eyed buttons," exclaimed the Padre, spitting out the rest of the nails. "What can be as wrong as all that?"

"It's Papa," said the oldest boy. "He's been in a hole by the old oak for four days, and is almost starved."

"But why doesn't he come home?" said the Padre. "The oak isn't far away."

"The fox won't let him," sobbed Madame Single-Toe.

"And why not?"

"He's mad because of Papa's jokes," the youngest child explained.

The Padre's mouth opened in a wide grin. "More of the jokes that other people don't find funny, eh? Well, I'll take a stroll by the twisted oak and have a talk with the fox." As he started off, he called over his shoulder, "Mrs. Hedge-Hog, you might give these youngsters a couple of the pickled chestnuts we keep for company." He winked solemnly at Mrs. Single-Toe, who blushed.

The fox was lying with his muzzle just an inch from the hole. He did not budge, nor lift his eye when the Padre wished him good morning. "I've got him this time," he snarled. "Four days I've been watching this hole. My mother brings my meals and keeps guard while I eat. He'll not get away *this* time!"

"He is a nuisance with his jokes, I admit," said the Padre peaceably, "but he doesn't do any real harm. Don't you think a good scare would be enough for him?"

"No, I don't," snapped the fox. "And don't you mix in this business, Padre, with your talk about kindness. What I've suffered from that little pest you'd never believe. First he dropped a tomato on my nose—a tomato that was too ripe. And then he dribbled pitch all over my head and neck while I was asleep. So don't waste your time." The fox advanced his red tongue hungrily to the very edge of the hole.

The Padre walked away, deep in thought. His generous heart was very unhappy. What should he say to the near-orphans in his kitchen? There must be some way to save him. Suddenly he saw some crows gossiping in a dead pine. "Will one of you black boys do me a favor, in a great hurry?" he called.

"Certainly, Don Porko," they all cawed.

"Fly low through the woods, and tell every rabbit you see that I want their road commissioner to come to my house for dinner. Say that I'm going to have celery root and cabbage, chopped in parsley."

The Padre's guest was promptness itself. He used a turnip leaf as a napkin, and when he had wiped his whiskers, ate the napkin. "It makes less for Ma'am Hedge-Hog to clear up," he explained.

"Now for serious business," said the Padre, leading the way to the garden, when they had finished their second glass of dandelion wine. "I have invited you here as an expert. We will draw a map." He made a cross in the soft earth with a stick. "Here is the oak that the lightning split. And here in front of it, so, is a rabbit hole that was begun, but never finished. Do you follow me?"

The road commissioner nodded. "I know it perfectly. The workman was caught by an owl when he came up with some dirt."

"Now," continued the Padre, "how far is the bottom of this unfinished hole from one of your regular tunnels, and how long would it take to dig up to it?"

"About half a jump," replied the road commissioner. "The 'Alley to the Ivy Rock' runs very close to that unfinished hole. A good digger can do a medium-sized jump of tunnel in half a day. I should say it would take two hours to dig upwards from 'Ivy Rock Alley' and join the hole."

The Padre beckoned the road commissioner to follow him to the cellar. Scraping away the sand, he laid bare ten carrots, each as smooth and straight as an orange-colored candle. "These are yours, Mr. Commissioner, if you will do this little job of digging for me."

The bargain was soon struck. "One thing more," said the Padre, as the commissioner was lolloping away. "You will find a friend of mine in the unfinished hole. Don't let him make a noise, but bring him here the moment you can get him free. I'll be waiting."

Daylight was fading when the rabbit returned, covered with damp earth to his armpits. He was supporting a hoarse, hungry, and grimy red squirrel. The Padre welcomed them, pointing to the cupboard. "Sh-h-h-sh, go and see what's inside, Single-Toe."

One might have thought a hundred squirrels were behind the cupboard door, such was the hugging and chattering, the rubbing of noses, and the scratching of ears. Single-Toe was invited to stay for a light lunch, even after the road commissioner had left for his burrow, the biggest carrot in his mouth.

Safe, fed, and warmed, the red squirrel became his own gay self again. He began to chuckle, then to shake with merriment. "Ha, ha, ha! That silly old fox is still there, watching an empty hole! Won't it be a priceless joke, if I climb the oak and drop a rotten egg on his nose?"

At the word "joke," Mrs. Single-Toe, the four little squirrels, and the good Padre, all stiffened.

"Don't you ever say that word again," said his wife. "Do you hear, no more jokes, never, never."

Single-Toe wilted. "Yes," he confessed, not daring to meet the Padre's eye, "jokes aren't always so terribly funny, are they? Not even for the joker."

# *Italy*

*Italy figures as the place in Europe where predecessors of many famous folk tales first appeared in print. In the work of Giambattista Basile (Il Pentamerone) and of Giovanni Francesco Straparola (Le Piacevoli Notti) we can find the prefigurings of "Cinderella," "Puss in Boots," and many others. But until recent years, Italian folk tales compiled for English-speaking children were few and seemed to be more generally European than typically Italian. This was mainly because few of the primary source materials were, or are, available in English. Also, it would be hard to find a "typical" Italian folk tale when one considers the various Italian provinces which were once independent kingdoms, and the islands of Corsica, Sardinia, and Sicily. "March and the Shepherd" and "The Most Precious Possession" are from Domenico Vittorini's Old Italian Tales, a treasury for the storyteller. Some of the stories are adapted from oral sources, but one is taken from Boccaccio (whose stories were from oral tradition and from his own imagination and cannot always be identified as having come from one or the other). The entire Vittorini collection of twenty tales has unusual variety, an earthy sort of humor, and a vigorous sense of justice. Told with simplicity and with respect for sources, these lively tales prove again how little human nature differs from country to country. "King Clothes" is from Jagendorf's The Priceless Cats, which, with other compilations like Haviland's Favorite Fairy Tales Told in Italy, adds to the number of good Italian folk tales retold for young people's enjoyment.*

## MARCH AND THE SHEPHERD

*This duel of wits between two tricksters, with the shepherd always the winner, makes the wry humor of the conclusion quite acceptable.*

One morning, in the very beginning of spring, a shepherd led his sheep to graze, and on the way he met March.

"March and the Shepherd." Reprinted by permission of David McKay Company, Inc., from *Old Italian Tales*, retold by Domenico Vittorini; copyright © 1958 by Domenico Vittorini

"Good morning," said March. "Where are you going to take your sheep to graze today?"

"Well, March, today I am going to the mountains."

"Fine, Shepherd. That's a good idea. Good luck." But to himself March said, "Here's where I have some fun, for today I'm going to fix you."

And that day in the mountains the rain came down in buckets; it was a veritable deluge. The shepherd, however, had watched March's face very carefully and noticed a mischievous look on it. So, instead of going to the mountains, he had remained in the plains. In the evening, upon returning home, he met March again.

"Well, Shepherd, how did it go today?"

"It couldn't have been better. I changed my mind and went to the plains. A very beautiful day. Such a lovely warm sun."

"Really? I'm glad to hear it," said March, but he bit his lip in vexation. "Where are you going tomorrow?"

"Tomorrow I'm going to the plains, too. With this fine weather, I would be crazy if I went to the mountains."

"Oh, really? Fine! Farewell."

And they parted.

But the shepherd didn't go to the plains again; he went to the mountains. And on the plains March brought rain and wind and hail—a punishment indeed from heaven. In the evening he met the shepherd homeward bound.

"Good evening, Shepherd. How did it go today?"

"Very well indeed. Do you know? I changed my mind again and went to the mountains after all. It was heavenly there. What a day! What a sky! What a sun!"

"I'm really happy to hear it, Shepherd. And where are you going tomorrow?"

"Well, tomorrow I'm going to the plains. I see dark clouds over the mountains. I wouldn't

want to find myself too far from home."

To make a long story short, whenever the shepherd met March, he always told him the opposite of what he planned to do the next day, so March was never able to catch him. The end of the month came and on the last day, the thirtieth, March said to the shepherd, "Well, Shepherd, how is everything?"

"Things couldn't be any better. This is the end of the month and I'm out of danger. There's nothing to fear now; I can begin to sleep peacefully."

"That's true," said March. "And where are you going tomorrow?"

The shepherd, certain that he had nothing to fear, told March the truth. "Tomorrow," he said, "I shall go to the plains. The distance is shorter and the work less hard."

"Fine. Farewell."

March hastened to the home of his cousin April and told her the whole story. "I want you to lend me at least one day," he said. "I am determined to catch this shepherd." Gentle April was unwilling, but March coaxed so hard that finally she consented.

The following morning the shepherd set off for the plains. No sooner had his flock scattered when there arose a storm that chilled his very heart. The sharp wind howled and growled; snow fell in thick icy flakes; hail pelted down. It was all the shepherd could do to get his sheep back into the fold.

That evening as the shepherd huddled in a corner of his hearth, silent and melancholy, March paid him a visit.

"Good evening, Shepherd," he said.

"Good evening, March."

"How did it go today?"

"I'd rather not talk about it," said the shepherd. "I can't understand what happened. Not even in the middle of January have I ever seen a storm like the one on the plains today. It seemed as if all the devils had broken loose from hell. Today I had enough rough weather to last me the whole year. And, oh, my poor sheep!"

Then at last was March satisfied.

And from that time on March has had thirty-one days because, as it is said in Tuscany, the rascal never returned to April the day he borrowed from her.

## THE MOST PRECIOUS
## POSSESSION

*This tale starts off as if it were to be a variant of "Dick Whittington" without the rags-to-riches theme, but the conclusion is different. The story is also similar to "The Priceless Cats" in Jagendorf's collection of the same name.*

There was a time when Italian traders and explorers, finding the way to the East blocked by the Turks, turned west in their search for new lands to trade with—a search that led to the discovery of the New World.

In those days there lived in Florence a merchant by the name of Ansaldo. He belonged to the Ormanini family, known not only for its wealth but for the daring and cunning of its young men. It happened that on one of his trips in search of adventure and trade, Ansaldo ventured beyond the Strait of Gibraltar and, after battling a furious storm, landed on one of the Canary Islands.

The king of the island welcomed him cordially, for the Florentines were well known to him. He ordered a magnificent banquet prepared and arranged to have it served in the sumptuous hall, resplendent with mirrors and gold, in which he had received Ansaldo.

When it was time to serve the meal, Ansaldo noticed with surprise that a small army of

"The Most Precious Possession." Reprinted by permission of David McKay Company, Inc., from *Old Italian Tales,* retold by Domenico Vittorini; copyright © 1958 by Domenico Vittorini

youths, carrying long stout sticks, entered and lined up against the walls of the banquet hall. As each guest sat down, one of the youths took up a place directly behind him, the stick held in readiness to strike.

Ansaldo wondered what all this meant and wracked his brain for some clue to these odd goings-on. He didn't have long to wait. Suddenly, a horde of huge ferocious rats poured into the hall and threw themselves upon the food that was being served. Pandemonium broke loose as the boys darted here and there, wielding the sticks.

For many years the Florentines had enjoyed the reputation of being the cleverest people on earth, able to cope with any situation. Ansaldo saw a chance to uphold the tradition. He asked the king's permission to go back to his ship, and returned shortly with two big Persian cats. These animals were much admired and loved by the Florentines and Venetians who had first seen them in the East and who had brought many of them back to Italy. Ever since, one or two cats always completed the crew of a ship when it set out on a long journey.

Ansaldo let the cats go and before long the entire hall was cleared of the revolting and destructive rats.

The astonished and delighted king thought he was witnessing a miracle. He could not find words enough to thank Ansaldo whom he hailed as the saviour of the island, and when Ansaldo made him a present of the cats, his gratitude knew no bounds.

After a pleasant visit, Ansaldo made ready to

sail for home. The king accompanied him to his ship and there he showered him with rich and rare gifts, much gold and silver, and many precious stones of all kinds and colors—rubies, topazes, and diamonds.

Ansaldo was overwhelmed not only by these costly gifts but by the king's gratitude and the praises he heaped upon him and on the cats. As for the latter, they were regarded with awe by all the islanders and as their greatest treasure by the king and the entire royal household.

When Ansaldo returned home he regaled his friends with the account of his strange adventure. There was among them a certain Giocondo de' Fifanti who was as rich in envy as he was poor in intelligence. He thought: "If the island king gave Ansaldo all these magnificent gifts for two mangy cats, what will he not give me if I present him with the most beautiful and precious things that our city of Florence has to offer?" No sooner said than done. He purchased lovely belts, necklaces, bracelets studded with diamonds, exquisite pictures, luxurious garments and many other expensive gifts and took ship for the now famous Canary Islands.

After an uneventful crossing he arrived in port and hastened to the royal palace. He was received with more pomp than was Ansaldo. The king was greatly touched by the splendor of Giocondo's gifts and wanted to be equally generous. He held a long consultation with his people and then informed Giocondo happily that they had decided to let him share with his visitor their most precious possession. Giocondo could hardly contain his curiosity. However, the day of departure finally arrived and found Giocondo on his ship, impatiently awaiting the visit of the king. Before long, the king, accompanied by the entire royal household and half the islanders, approached the ship. The king himself carried the precious gift on a silken cushion. With great pride he put the cushion into Giocondo's outstretched greedy hands. Giocondo was speechless. On the cushion, curled up in sleepy, furry balls, were two of the kittens that had been born to the Persian cats Ansaldo had left on the island.

The old story does not go on to say whether Giocondo, on his return to Florence, ever regaled his friends with the tale of *his* adventure!

# KING CLOTHES

*No happy ending here! The tale is a rather sharp commentary on certain human foibles. There are many stories in Italy about the peasant boy who is both foolish and wise, and his name varies from one area to the next. In Sicily he is called Giufa.*

It is told that years ago there lived in Sicily, the largest island in all the Mediterranean, a young fellow named Giufa, who was so silly that, as the saying goes, he wasn't sure of the weather when it was raining in buckets. That is what folks said, but I'm not sure they were right. For people lived in Sicily before they lived anywhere in Italy, and there must have been silly fellows before him.

Giufa wore rags for clothes and never had shoes, so the dust on the road jumped between his toes. And who looks at a fellow who is dressed in rags? Nobody. Doors were closed in his face, and sometimes people wouldn't ever talk to him. He was never asked to a wedding or a feast. Life was not too pleasant for Giufa.

One sunny day his mother sent him to take something to the farm that was next to theirs.

Giufa went off whistling, kicking the dust on the road. Sometimes he stopped to speak to a bird or a butterfly. Soon he came to the farmhouse. At the gate stood the wife of the farmer.

"Good day, mistress," Giufa said politely. "My mother sent me to give you this," and he held out a basket to her.

The woman took one look at his ragged clothes and dusty face and feet.

"Drop it right there," she cried, "and go quickly. You look like a scarecrow, and the dogs will be after you."

Giufa did not say anything. What could he say? Besides, it was dinnertime just then, and his stomach was empty and growling. So he turned sadly toward home.

Though kith and kin said he was a noodlehead, he had sense enough to think that the

Reprinted from *The Priceless Cats and Other Italian Stories* by M. A. Jagendorf by permission of the publisher, Vanguard Press, Inc. Copyright © 1956 by M. A. Jagendorf

farmwoman could have been a little nicer and could have asked him in to have a piece of bread and cheese.

When he reached home he told his mother how he had been treated, adding: "I could smell the bean soup out at the gate. They could have been good Christians and asked me to have a plate. They talk to me like that because I don't wear fine breeches and a velvet coat."

Giufa's mother worried about this, and a few weeks later she once again had to send her son with something to that same farm. Not wanting to put the boy to shame, she dressed him in a fine white shirt, good breeches, a nice blue coat, and good shoes.

You should have seen Giufa! He looked like a different fellow. He almost could not recognize himself.

Off he went, whistling gaily and joking with bird and beast until he came to the farmer's house. There stood both the farmer and his wife, and neither one recognized Giufa in his fine clean clothes.

"I have something for you," he cried.

It was noon then, and so they greeted him pleasantly and invited him into the farmhouse.

They asked him to sit down to hot steaming minestrone soup that was filled with fresh vegetables and good sharp cheese. With it came crisp fresh bread and rich red wine.

Giufa ate and joked and had the best time of his life. At the end of the meal, the farmer sat back and asked the boy to tell him about this and that. But instead of doing so, Giufa stood up and put some of the cheese and bread in the pockets of his coat and breeches and into his hat. The farmer and his wife laughed because they thought this was so funny. Then Giufa bowed low and, looking down at his bulging pockets and over at his hat, said:

"Here is food for you, my good clothes and fine hat, and I want to thank you from the bottom of my heart, for it is you who were treated like a king, and it is because of you, my good clothes and fine hat, that I had a fine meal. When I came here the last time without you, fine clothes, I was treated like a crazy dog."

Then he turned around and walked out. You can guess what the farmer and his wife thought and said! Maybe they remembered the saying: "Dress up a stick and folks'll think it's a nobleman."

# *Poland*

*If the Polish people seem to have their roots in things both Slavic and German, so does Polish folklore. The tales of Poland are distinctly Polish, but that Polish-ness is enriched by Jewish folklore, by the folk-tale traditions of various Slavic countries, and by the traditions of Germany and Western Europe. The tales, which seem to be mostly about the common folk who use their cleverness to get ahead, are enlivened with laughter and a warm, graceful piety. Tailors, peasant boys, kings, princesses, saints, and sinners make up the human parade in the stories, accompanied by a generous mixture of animals, witches, ghosts, and devils. Perhaps the going and coming of invaders has done painful things to Polish territory, but it has also enriched the tales of a gentle land whose people persist though their country's borders tremble and shift with the crosscurrents of history. There are few collections of Polish tales in English. The best known are those retold by Lucia Borski, as she presented them from her own background to boys and girls in the United States. Josephine Bernhard also compiled Polish tales in the 1930's. Some of the Borski and Bernhard tales are to be found in Virginia Haviland's more recent* Favorite Fairy Tales Told in Poland.

## KING BARTEK

*In this romantic story a royal disguise serves to reveal both the haughty hypocrite and the true-hearted maiden.*

On the outskirts of a village, in a hut fallen almost to ruins, there lived a very poor widow with her two daughters, Bialka and Spiewna. Both of them were so beautiful that their fame spread over seven mountains, over seven seas. Even at the King's palace the rumors were heard. Many of the knights wished to go at once and woo the girls.

The King disliked to lose his knights, as he had planned a great war, and besides he did not have much faith in the rumors. Instead of granting permission to the knights to go, he sent some of his faithful messengers to see the maidens and bring back pictures of Bialka and Spiewna.

The rumors were true. The pictures brought back by the messengers exceeded everybody's expectations. Spiewna was a true sister to the lily; Bialka, to the red rose. The first had azure eyes, the other, eyes dark as the Black Sea; one was proud of her long, golden braids, the other of her raven black braids. The first one had the beauty of a sunny day in her face, the other, the charm of a May night. The knights became enamored of the maidens; no one could keep them from departing. Even the King himself, as he was young and thought of marriage, scratched himself behind the ear and looked at the pictures with great pleasure. The war was put off, the court was desolated, and only the King and his Jester, Pieś, who was old and ugly like the seven mortal sins, were left there.

For a long, long time the knights did not come back. They were enjoying themselves; or it might be the other way around, Bialka and Spiewna, sure of their beauty, might be taking their time picking and choosing, like sparrows in poppy seeds. The knights in love unwound entangled thread, killed partridges in the air, and sang serenades. Be it as it may, their long ab-

"King Bartek." Reprinted by permission of David McKay Company, Inc., from *The Jolly Tailor and Other Fairy Tales Translated from the Polish* by Lucia Merecka Borski and Kate B. Miller. Copyright 1928, 1956 by Lucia Merecka Borski and John F. Miller

sence annoyed the King and he grew impatient and ill-tempered.

"Pieś," he once addressed the Jester, "do you know what I am thinking about?"

"I know, Your Lordship!"

"How?"

"Because our thoughts walk the same paths."

"I wonder!" laughed the King.

"Your Lordship wishes to go to the widow's daughters."

"You guessed!" cried the young King, rejoicing.

"Then we shall go together," said Pieś. "But we must change our places; I, a King; Your Lordship, a Jester."

"What an idea!" said the young ruler, shocked a bit.

"There won't be much of a difference," smiled the Jester.

"No, I shall not do it! You may, if you wish, become a King, but I shall put on a peasant's garb and call myself Bartek."

"As you please!" answered Pieś. "Something unpleasant may come of it though."

"Why?" asked the King, now Bartek.

"A King, be he as ugly and humpbacked as I am, will always have preference over Bartek. And then who knows? Your Highness may fall in love with either Spiewna or Bialka."

The youthful lord became alarmed.

"So much the better!" he said after a while, and added in a whisper, "The heart that loves will not fool itself."

They went on their journey.

In the meantime the widow's hut was as noisy as a beehive. One brought musicians, another singers. The hut changed into a music box adorned with garlands and flowers, as if in celebration of a holiday. The knights reveled, the girls danced, song followed song, and jokes, one after another. The mother's white bonnet swung on her white hair from one ear to the other from happiness.

Bialka liked Przegoń (Pshegon) more than all the others. Spiewna chose none as yet. Neither her mother's persuasion nor her sister's scoffs did any good. The girl's heart had not awakened yet, and without love she did not wish to marry even the richest of knights.

The betrothal of Przegoń to Bialka was announced. She had her wedding dress made, goods for which were brought by Przegoń. The jewelry, one could not describe, it could be gathered in measures.

Bialka was overwhelmed with joy, was triumphant with her success. She looked down on her sister with haughtiness and consoled her mother with scornful words.

"Do not worry, Mother! Spiewna awaits a prince. She will become wiser when she has to grow rue, and then I, Przegoń's wife, will try to get her an organist. Also I shall find a suitable nook for you, Mother."

Her mother's heart grieved, but what could she answer?

Then one day a golden carriage drove up before the door. All three of them ran quickly to the window, and Bialka shouted:

"The King has come!"

Sudden confusion possessed the hut. The old widow trotted to the kitchen to prepare some fowl for His Majesty, the King, while Bialka snatched a hand-mirror and a comb and turning to her sister called in a commanding voice:

"Don't you dare to call the King's attention to yourself!"

Spiewna stopped in astonishment.

"Do you hear me?" shouted Bialka.

"I hear, but I don't understand."

"You don't understand—you don't understand!"

"For—how—" began Spiewna.

"Don't dare to call the King's attention to yourself!"

"What do you care about the King when you have Przegoń?"

"Have I or not, that is nothing to you!" grumbled Bialka. "And better take my advice, otherwise—you shall see!"

His Majesty, the King, was far from good looking. He was ugly, old, his right arm was higher than the left, and he was also limping. But all this was covered with the golden crown, was concealed by the purple cloak and was straightened by the long robe richly embroidered with pearls. Upon seeing the sisters, he at once laid his royal gifts at their feet, and loaded them with compliments. Spiewna refused all the gifts; she accepted only a white rose, which she pinned into her hair.

"How beautiful he is!" whispered Bialka.

"How ridiculous he is!" replied Spiewna.

Bialka looked at her with anger.

Among the King's numerous attendants, there was a young and handsome page, called Bartek. Spiewna's eyes met the youth's gaze. Bartek, dazzled with the girl's beauty, did not take his eyes off her, and when the King offered jewels to Bialka, he came near Spiewna and said:

"All my riches is this fife. It plays beautifully and the time will come when I shall present you with its song."

Spiewna, standing on the threshold, blushed like a rose, and Bialka seeing this, maliciously whispered in her ear:

"Just the kind of a husband for you. Keep away from the King!"

"And Przegoń?" questioned Spiewna.

"You may have him," threw out Bialka.

Przegoń did not see the King, but he learned of his arrival and of his gifts to Bialka. He wished to speak to Bialka, but she, busy with her guest, who exaggerated his compliments and promised golden mountains, did not care to see him. He stayed away from his unfaithful sweetheart and waited to see what time would bring forth.

One night, and 'twas a night with the full moon, a scented intoxicating night, under the window of the room where both sisters slept, there came sounds of a guitar accompanied by a song.

"The King!" murmured Bialka and she jumped to the window.

The King sang:

*Out of the mist thou shalt have palaces,*
*For thy comfort and pleasures I will care*
*And pay with gold for thy every smile.*
*Attired, bejewelled like a peacock*
*Thou shalt be Queen in the royal gardens.*

"Do you hear, do you hear?" said Bialka to Spiewna. "Thus sings the King!"

Then later under the window fluted the country fife. Bialka looked out of the window and noticed Bartek. Seeing her sister moved by the sad and sweet tones of the fife, she roared with laughter.

The fife stopped playing and they heard this song:

*Do not come to me with pretense*
*But with love in thy pure eyes*
*That knows another's love.*
*Be not touched with a royal gown*
*That is worn by a fool's soul,*
*A soul that knows not what is love.*

"Thus sings Bartek!" called Spiewna.

"Ha-ha-ha!" rang out Bialka's venomous laughter. She leaned over the window and called aloud into the silent night:

"Drive away the fool, Your Majesty, who has the boldness to interrupt your song and insult your royal soul! Order him away, for he steals from us this beautiful night!"

"I will punish him more severely than you think," was the answer, "because to-morrow he will marry your sister."

"And when we?" asked Bialka.

"Even now. Come to me!"

Bialka jumped out of the window, and there she met face to face with Przegoń.

"What are you doing here?" she asked him haughtily.

"I came to wish you happiness with this— king's Jester," replied Przegoń pointing to Pieś.

"What? What?" cried Bialka, looking with frightened eyes at the splendid dress, like a king's.

And in the room, where Spiewna remained, Bartek's fife rang out followed by a song:

*'Tis hard to find true love*
*Under an alluring purple gown,*
*Infirmity shall remain in heart*
*With all the roses torn aside.*
*Ugly looks and lameness and a hump*
*May all be covered with a royal cloak.*
*The King wished for a true heart;*
*The fool desired fun and laughter;*
*And both are satisfied.*
*Therefore the fool dressed like a King;*
*The King put on the peasant's garb.*
*Now, maiden, cry for thy alluring loss*
*And understand these prophesying words:*
*That people are not judged by looks*
*But by their hearts and deeds.*

The golden carriage came to the door, a thousand torches were lighted, a thousand knights with Przegoń at the head surrounded the royal carriage, into which Spiewna was led with her bridesmaids, and they all went to the King's palace to celebrate the wedding. The mother rejoiced at Spiewna's happiness, but she grieved over the neglected Bialka, who had to grow sixteen beds of rue before she married an old organist.

# Czechoslovakia

*Present-day Czechoslovakia is the home of several groups of people—*
*the largest groups being the Czechs and Moravians in the west and the Slovaks in*
*the east. They are Slavic peoples, but for a long part of their history*
*they were dominated by the Magyars of Hungary. At different times Germany*
*also greatly influenced Czech life and customs. All this is reflected in*
*Czechoslovakian folklore, although it is not easily discernible in the folk tales.*
*Only one collection of Czechoslovakian tales is relatively recent,*
*Virginia Haviland's* Favorite Fairy Tales Told in Czechoslovakia *(1966), and*
*its five tales are from collections made before 1930. Fortunately, Parker*
*Fillmore's* The Shoemaker's Apron *(1920), in which the two selections here first*
*appeared, gave us fine stories told in clear, vigorous English that*
*preserves the Czechoslovakian folk feeling with its strong current of humor.*

## BUDULINEK

There was once a little boy named Budulinek. He lived with his old Granny in a cottage near a forest.

Granny went out to work every day. In the morning when she went away she always said:

"There, Budulinek, there's your dinner on the table and mind, you mustn't open the door no matter who knocks!"

One morning Granny said:

"Now, Budulinek, today I'm leaving you some soup for your dinner. Eat it when dinner time comes. And remember what I always say: don't open the door no matter who knocks."

She went away and pretty soon Lishka, the sly old mother fox, came and knocked on the door.

"Budulinek!" she called. "You know me! Open the door! Please!"

Budulinek called back:

"No, I mustn't open the door."

But Lishka, the sly old mother fox, kept on knocking.

"Listen, Budulinek," she said: "if you open the door, do you know what I'll do? I'll give you a ride on my tail!"

Now Budulinek thought to himself:

"Oh, that would be fun to ride on the tail of Lishka, the fox!"

So Budulinek forgot all about what Granny said to him every day and opened the door.

Lishka, the sly old thing, came into the room and what do you think she did? Do you think she gave Budulinek a ride on her tail? Well, she didn't. She just went over to the table and gobbled up the bowl of soup that Granny had put

there for Budulinek's dinner and then she ran away.

When dinner time came Budulinek hadn't anything to eat.

In the evening when Granny came home, she said:

"Budulinek, did you open the door and let anyone in?"

Budulinek was crying because he was so hungry, and he said:

"Yes, I let in Lishka, the old mother fox, and she ate up all my dinner, too!"

Granny said:

"Now, Budulinek, you see what happens when you open the door and let some one in. Another time remember what Granny says and don't open the door."

The next morning Granny cooked some porridge for Budulinek's dinner and said:

"Now, Budulinek, here's some porridge for your dinner. Remember, while I'm gone you must not open the door no matter who knocks."

Granny was no sooner out of sight than Lishka came again and knocked on the door.

"Oh, Budulinek!" she called. "Open the door and let me in!"

But Budulinek said:

"No, I won't open the door!"

"Oh, now, Budulinek, please open the door!" Lishka begged. "You know me! Do you know what I'll do if you open the door? I'll give you a ride on my tail! Truly I will!"

Budulinek thought to himself:

"This time maybe she will give me a ride on her tail."

So he opened the door.

Lishka came into the room, gobbled up Budulinek's porridge, and ran away without giving him any ride at all.

When dinner time came Budulinek hadn't anything to eat.

In the evening when Granny came home she said:

"Budulinek, did you open the door and let anyone in?"

Budulinek was crying again because he was so hungry, and he said:

"Yes, I let in Lishka, the old mother fox, and she ate up all my porridge, too!"

"Budulinek, you're a bad boy!" Granny said. "If you open the door again, I'll have to spank you! Do you hear?"

The next morning before she went to work, Granny cooked some peas for Budulinek's dinner.

As soon as Granny was gone he began eating the peas, they were so good.

Presently Lishka, the fox, came and knocked on the door.

"Budulinek!" she called. "Open the door! I want to come in!"

But Budulinek wouldn't open the door. He took his bowl of peas and went to the window and ate them there where Lishka could see him.

"Oh, Budulinek!" Lishka begged. "You know me! Please open the door! This time I promise you I'll give you a ride on my tail! Truly I will!"

She just begged and begged until at last Budulinek opened the door. Then Lishka jumped into the room and do you know what she did? She put her nose right into the bowl of peas and gobbled them all up!

Then she said to Budulinek:

"Now get on my tail and I'll give you a ride!"

So Budulinek climbed on Lishka's tail and Lishka went running around the room faster and faster until Budulinek was dizzy and just had to hold on with all his might.

Then, before Budulinek knew what was happening, Lishka slipped out of the house and ran off swiftly into the forest, home to her hole, with Budulinek still on her tail! She hid Budulinek down in her hole with her own three children and she wouldn't let him out. He had to stay there with the three little foxes and they all teased him and bit him. And then wasn't he sorry he had disobeyed his Granny! And, oh, how he cried!

When Granny came home she found the door open and no little Budulinek anywhere. She looked high and low, but no, there was no little Budulinek. She asked everyone she met had they seen her little Budulinek, but nobody had. So poor Granny just cried and cried, she was so lonely and sad.

One day an organ-grinder with a wooden leg began playing in front of Granny's cottage. The music made her think of Budulinek.

"Organ-grinder," Granny said, "here's a penny for you. But, please, don't play any more. Your music makes me cry."

"Why does it make you cry?" the organ-grinder asked.

"Because it reminds me of Budulinek," Granny said, and she told the organ-grinder all about Budulinek and how somebody had stolen him away.

The organ-grinder said:

"Poor Granny! I tell you what I'll do: as I go around and play my organ I'll keep my eyes open for Budulinek. If I find him I'll bring him back to you."

"Will you?" Granny cried. "If you bring me back my little Budulinek I'll give you a measure of rye and a measure of millet and a measure of poppy seed and a measure of everything in the house!"

So the organ-grinder went off and everywhere he played his organ he looked for Budulinek. But he couldn't find him.

At last one day while he was walking through the forest he thought he heard a little boy crying. He looked around everywhere until he found a fox's hole.

"Oho!" he said to himself. "I believe that wicked old Lishka must have stolen Budulinek! She's probably keeping him here with her own three children! I'll soon find out."

So he put down his organ and began to play. And as he played he sang softly:

"One old fox
    And two, three, four,

And Budulinek
    He makes one more!"

Old Lishka heard the music playing and she said to her oldest child:

"Here, son, give the old man a penny and tell him to go away because my head aches."

So the oldest little fox climbed out of the hole and gave the organ-grinder a penny and said:

"My mother says, please will you go away because her head aches."

As the organ-grinder reached over to take the penny, he caught the oldest little fox and stuffed him into a sack. Then he went on playing and singing:

"One old fox
    And two and three
    And Budulinek
    Makes four for me!"

Presently Lishka sent out her second child with a penny and the organ-grinder caught the second little fox in the same way and stuffed it also into the sack. Then he went on grinding his organ and softly singing:

"One old fox
    And another for me,
    And Budulinek
    He makes the three."

"I wonder why that old man still plays his organ," Lishka said and sent out her third child with a penny.

So the organ-grinder caught the third little fox and stuffed it also into the sack. Then he kept on playing and singing softly:

"One old fox—
    I'll soon get you!—
    And Budulinek
    He makes just two."

At last Lishka herself came out. So he caught her, too, and stuffed her in with her children. Then he sang:

"Four naughty foxes
Caught alive!
And Budulinek
He makes the five!"

The organ-grinder went to the hole and called down:

"Budulinek! Budulinek! Come out!"

As there were no foxes left to hold him back, Budulinek was able to crawl out.

When he saw the organ-grinder he cried and said:

"Oh, please, Mr. Organ-Grinder, I want to go home to my Granny!"

"I'll take you home to your Granny," the organ-grinder said, "but first I must punish these naughty foxes."

The organ-grinder cut a strong switch and gave the four foxes in the sack a terrible beating until they begged him to stop and promised that they would never again do anything to Budulinek.

Then the organ-grinder let them go and he took Budulinek home to Granny.

Granny was delighted to see her little Budulinek and she gave the organ-grinder a measure of rye and a measure of millet and a measure of poppy seed and a measure of everything else in the house.

And Budulinek never again opened the door!

## CLEVER MANKA

*This is a good example of the humor in Czech stories. It especially delights girls after hearing "The Most Obedient Wife." Riddles abounded in songs, tales, and morality plays during the Middle Ages, and this tale is but one example of how they have persisted and shaped later folk tales. Generally the riddles had to do with Christ and the Devil playing for a poor sinner's soul. Echoes of this may also be found in the Ethiopian tale "The Fire on the Mountain" and in the American tale "Young Melvin," though it is unlikely that they have any connection whatsoever with medieval moralities.*

"Clever Manka." Copyright, 1920, by Parker Fillmore; renewed 1948 by Louise Fillmore. From *The Shepherd's Nosegay* by Parker Fillmore, edited by Katherine Love and reprinted by permission of Harcourt Brace Jovanovich, Inc.

There was once a rich farmer who was as grasping and unscrupulous as he was rich. He was always driving a hard bargain and always getting the better of his poor neighbors. One of these neighbors was a humble shepherd who in return for service was to receive from the farmer a heifer. When the time of payment came the farmer refused to give the shepherd the heifer and the shepherd was forced to lay the matter before the burgomaster.

The burgomaster, who was a young man and as yet not very experienced, listened to both sides and when he had deliberated he said:

"Instead of deciding this case, I will put a riddle to you both and the man who makes the best answer shall have the heifer. Are you agreed?"

The farmer and the shepherd accepted this proposal and the burgomaster said:

"Well then, here is my riddle: What is the swiftest thing in the world? What is the sweetest thing? What is the richest? Think out your answers and bring them to me at this same hour tomorrow."

The farmer went home in a temper.

"What kind of a burgomaster is this young fellow!" he growled. "If he had let me keep the heifer I'd have sent him a bushel of pears. But now I'm in a fair way of losing the heifer for I can't think of any answer to his foolish riddle."

"What is the matter, husband?" his wife asked.

"It's that new burgomaster. The old one would have given me the heifer without any argument, but this young man thinks to decide the case by asking us riddles."

When he told his wife what the riddle was, she cheered him greatly by telling him that she knew the answers at once.

"Why, husband," said she, "our gray mare must be the swiftest thing in the world. You know yourself nothing ever passes us on the road. As for the sweetest, did you ever taste honey any sweeter than ours? And I'm sure there's nothing richer than our chest of golden ducats that we've been laying by these forty years."

The farmer was delighted.

"You're right, wife, you're right! That heifer remains ours!"

The shepherd when he got home was downcast and sad. He had a daughter, a clever girl named Manka, who met him at the door of his cottage and asked:

"What is it, father? What did the burgomaster say?"

The shepherd sighed.

"I'm afraid I've lost the heifer. The burgomaster set us a riddle and I know I shall never guess it."

"Perhaps I can help you," Manka said. "What is it?"

So the shepherd gave her the riddle and the next day as he was setting out for the burgomaster's, Manka told him what answers to make.

When he reached the burgomaster's house, the farmer was already there rubbing his hands and beaming with self-importance.

The burgomaster again propounded the riddle and then asked the farmer his answers.

The farmer cleared his throat and with a pompous air began:

"The swiftest thing in the world? Why, my dear sir, that's my gray mare, of course, for no other horse ever passes us on the road. The sweetest? Honey from my beehives, to be sure. The richest? What can be richer than my chest of golden ducats!"

And the farmer squared his shoulders and smiled triumphantly.

"H'm," said the young burgomaster, dryly. Then he asked:

"What answers does the shepherd make?"

The shepherd bowed politely and said:

"The swiftest thing in the world is thought for thought can run any distance in the twinkling of an eye. The sweetest thing of all is sleep for when a man is tired and sad what can be sweeter? The richest thing is the earth for out of the earth come all the riches of the world."

"Good!" the burgomaster cried. "Good! The heifer goes to the shepherd!"

Later the burgomaster said to the shepherd:

"Tell me, now, who gave you those answers? I'm sure they never came out of your own head."

At first the shepherd tried not to tell, but when the burgomaster pressed him he confessed that they came from his daughter, Manka. The burgomaster, who thought that he would like to make another test of Manka's cleverness, sent for ten eggs. He gave them to the shepherd and said:

"Take these eggs to Manka and tell her to have them hatched out by tomorrow and to bring me the chicks."

When the shepherd reached home and gave Manka the burgomaster's message, Manka laughed and said: "Take a handful of millet and go right back to the burgomaster. Say to him: 'My daughter sends you this millet. She says that if you plant, grow it, and have it harvested by to-morrow, she'll bring you the ten chicks and you can feed them the ripe grain.'"

When the burgomaster heard this, he laughed heartily.

"That's a clever girl of yours," he told the shepherd. "If she's as comely as she is clever, I think I'd like to marry her. Tell her to come to see me, but she must come neither by day nor by night, neither riding nor walking, neither dressed nor undressed."

When Manka received this message she waited until the next dawn when night was gone and day not yet arrived. Then she wrapped herself in a fishnet and, throwing one leg over a goat's back and keeping one foot on the ground, she went to the burgomaster's house.

Now I ask you: did she go dressed? No, she wasn't dressed. A fishnet isn't clothing. Did she go undressed? Of course not, for wasn't she covered with a fishnet? Did she walk to the burgomaster's? No, she didn't walk for she went with one leg thrown over a goat. Then did she ride? Of course she didn't ride for wasn't she walking on one foot?

When she reached the burgomaster's house she called out:

"Here I am, Mr. Burgomaster, and I've come neither by day nor by night, neither riding nor walking, neither dressed nor undressed."

The young burgomaster was so delighted with Manka's cleverness and so pleased with her comely looks that he proposed to her at once and in a short time married her.

"But understand, my dear Manka," he said, "you are not to use that cleverness of yours at my expense. I won't have you interfering in any of my cases. In fact if ever you give advice to any one who comes to me for judgment, I'll turn you out of my house at once and send you home to your father."

All went well for a time. Manka busied herself

in her house-keeping and was careful not to interfere in any of the burgomaster's cases.

Then one day two farmers came to the burgomaster to have a dispute settled. One of the farmers owned a mare which had foaled in the marketplace. The colt had run under the wagon of the other farmer and thereupon the owner of the wagon claimed the colt as his property.

The burgomaster, who was thinking of something else while the case was being presented, said carelessly:

"The man who found the colt under his wagon is, of course, the owner of the colt."

As the owner of the mare was leaving the burgomaster's house, he met Manka and stopped to tell her about the case. Manka was ashamed of her husband for making so foolish a decision and she said to the farmer:

"Come back this afternoon with a fishing net and stretch it across the dusty road. When the burgomaster sees you he will come out and ask you what you are doing. Say to him that you're catching fish. When he asks you how you can expect to catch fish in a dusty road, tell him it's just as easy for you to catch fish in a dusty road as it is for a wagon to foal. Then he'll see the injustice of his decision and have the colt returned to you. But remember one thing: you mustn't let him find out that it was I who told you to do this."

That afternoon when the burgomaster chanced to look out the window he saw a man stretching a fishnet across the dusty road. He went out to him and asked: "What are you doing?"

"Fishing."

"Fishing in a dusty road? Are you daft?"

"Well," the man said, "it's just as easy for me to catch fish in a dusty road as it is for a wagon to foal."

Then the burgomaster recognized the man as the owner of the mare and he had to confess that what he said was true.

"Of course the colt belongs to your mare and must be returned to you. But tell me," he said, "who put you up to this? You didn't think of it yourself."

The farmer tried not to tell but the burgomaster questioned him until he found out that Manka was at the bottom of it. This made him very angry. He went into the house and called his wife.

"Manka," he said, "do you forget what I told you would happen if you went interfering in any of my cases? Home you go this very day. I don't care to hear any excuses. The matter is settled. You may take with you the one thing you like best in my house for I won't have people saying that I treated you shabbily."

Manka made no outcry.

"Very well, my dear husband, I shall do as you say: I shall go to my father's cottage and take with me the one thing I like best in your house. But don't make me go until after supper. We have been very happy together and I should like to eat one last meal with you. Let us have no more words but be kind to each other as we've always been and then part as friends."

The burgomaster agreed to this and Manka prepared a fine supper of all the dishes of which her husband was particularly fond. The burgomaster opened his choicest wine and pledged Manka's health. Then he set to, and the supper was so good that he ate and ate and ate. And the more he ate, the more he drank until at last he grew drowsy and fell sound asleep in his chair. Then without awakening him Manka had him carried out to the wagon that was waiting to take her home to her father.

The next morning when the burgomaster opened his eyes, he found himself lying in the shepherd's cottage.

"What does this mean?" he roared out.

"Nothing, dear husband, nothing!" Manka said. "You know you told me I might take with me the one thing I liked best in your house, so of course I took you! That's all."

For a moment the burgomaster rubbed his eyes in amazement. Then he laughed loud and heartily to think how Manka had outwitted him.

"Manka," he said, "you're too clever for me. Come on, my dear, let's go home."

So they climbed back into the wagon and drove home.

The burgomaster never again scolded his wife but thereafter whenever a very difficult case came up he always said:

"I think we had better consult my wife. You know she's a very clever woman."

# Union of Soviet Socialist Republics

*The folk tales of the Soviet Union present a formidable subject for study.*
*The great collection by A. N. Afanasiev,* Russian Fairy Tales *(1855–1864), is held*
*to be as much a landmark in Russian folk-tale study as was the work of the*
*Grimms in Germany, although Afanasiev took his tales largely from those already*
*collected by others. Since the 1950's a movement has been underway in the*
*Soviet Union to publish its collected folklore in a series that will run to perhaps*
*a hundred volumes or more. Just the strictly Russian folk tales, folk*
*epics, and folk songs would fill many volumes, but the folklore of the other*
*hundred or so nationalities in the Soviet Union is also being systematically*
*recorded. Russian folklore is as dazzling as the history of Russia and is so imagi-*
*natively rich that opera and ballet have drawn frequently on its themes*
*and episodes. Violence, beauty, and strangeness are some of the elements that*
*color the tales. Although numerous Russian folk tales are available to*
*children in English, they scarcely do justice to the variety of tales that one may*
*find within Soviet borders. The Bibliography reveals that many individual*
*stories are found in picture-book form, while several other titles are collections*
*that represent separately Armenia, Latvia, Russia, and the Ukraine. A*
*more wide-ranging selection of tales may be found in* Tales of Faraway Folk *and*
More Tales of Faraway Folk, *by Babette Deutsch and Avrahm Yarmolin-*
*sky. These two books gather up twenty-five tales from Central Asia, Eastern*
*Russia, Estonia, and the Baltic and Caucasus regions.*

## THE FOOLISH MAN

### (Armenian)

*Only part of the Armenian people live in the*
*Soviet Union (Armenian Soviet Socialist Repub-*
*lic) because their ancient homeland is now di-*
*vided among Turkey, Iran, and the Soviet*
*Union. Most of the Armenian tales have been*
*unknown to children in this country, but the*
*book from which our selection was taken,* Once
There Was and Was Not, *does something to*
*change that. It is a rare bonanza for storytellers*
*and a beautiful reflection of the Armenian mind*
*and life. This tale is one with a bite, figuratively*
*and literally!*

Once there was and was not in ancient Armenia a poor man who worked and toiled hard
from morn till night, but nevertheless remained
poor.

Finally one day he became so discouraged that

he decided to go in search of God in order to ask
Him how long he must endure such poverty—
and to beg of Him a favor.

On his way, the man met a wolf.

"Good day, brother man," asked the wolf.
"Where are you bound in such a hurry?"

"I go in search of God," replied the man. "I
have a complaint to lodge with Him."

"Well," said the wolf, "would you do me a
kindness? When you find God, will you complain to Him for me, too? Tell Him you met a
half-starved wolf who searches the woods and
fields for food from morning till night—and
though he works hard and long, still finds nothing to eat. Ask God why He does not provide for
wolves since He created them?"

"I will tell Him of your complaint," agreed
the poor man, and continued on his way.

As he hurried over the hills and through the
valleys, he chanced to meet a beautiful maid.

"Where do you go in such a hurry, my
brother?" asked the maid.

"I go in search of God," replied the man.

"Oh, kind friend, when you find God, would
you ask Him something for me? Tell Him you
met a maid on your way. Tell Him she is young

and fair and very rich—but very unhappy. Ask God why she cannot know happiness. What will become of her? Ask God why He will not help her to be happy."

"I will tell Him of your trouble," promised the poor man, and continued on his way.

Soon he met a tree which seemed all dried up and dying even though it grew by the side of a river.

"Where do you go in such a hurry, O traveler?" called the dry tree.

"I go in search of God," answered the man. "I have a complaint to lodge with Him."

"Wait a moment, O traveler," begged the tree, "I, too, have a question for God.

"Please ask Him why I am dry both in summer and winter. Though I live by this wet river, my leaves do not turn green. Ask God how long I must suffer. Ask Him that for me, good friend," said the tree.

The man listened to the tree's complaint, promised to tell God, and continued once again upon his way.

Finally, the poor man reached the end of his journey. He found God seated beneath the ledge of a cliff.

"Good day," said the man as he approached God.

"Welcome, traveler," God returned his greeting. "Why have you journeyed so far? What is your trouble?"

"Well, I want to know why there is injustice in the world. Is it fair that I toil and labor from morn till night—and yet never seem to earn enough for a full stomach, while many who do not work half as hard as I live and eat as rich men do?"

"Go then," replied God. "I present you the Gift of Luck. Go find it and enjoy it to the end of your days."

"I have yet another complaint, my Lord," continued the man—and he proceeded to list the complaints and requests of the starved wolf, the beautiful maid, and the parched tree.

God gave appropriate answers to each of the three complaints, whereupon the poor man thanked Him and started on his way homeward.

Soon he came upon the dry, parched tree.

"What message did God have for me?" asked the tree.

"He said that beneath your trunk there lies a pot of gold which prevents the water from seeping up your trunk to your leaves. God said your branches will never turn green until the pot of gold is removed."

"Well, what are you waiting for, foolish man!" exclaimed the tree. "Dig up that pot of gold. It will make you rich—and permit me to turn green and live again!"

"Oh, no," protested the man. "I have no time to dig up a pot of gold. God has given me the Gift of Luck. I must hurry and search for it." And he hurried on his way.

Presently, he met the beautiful maid who was waiting for him. "Oh, kind friend, what message did God have for me?"

"God said that you will soon meet a kind man who will prove to be a good life's companion to you. No longer will you be lonely. Happiness and contentment will come to you," reported the poor man.

"In that case, what are you waiting for, foolish man?" exclaimed the maid. "Why don't you stay here and be my life's companion."

"Oh, no! I have no time to stay with you. God has given me the Gift of Luck. I must hurry and search for it." And the man hurried on his way.

Some distance away, the starving wolf impatiently awaited the man's coming, and hailed him with a shout.

"Well, what did God say? What message did He send to me?"

"Brother wolf, so many things have happened since I saw you last," said the man. "I hardly know where to begin. On my way to seek God, I met a beautiful maid who begged me to ask God the reason for her unhappiness. And I met a parched tree who wanted God to explain the dryness of its branches even though it stood by a wet river.

"I told God about these matters. He bade me tell the maid to seek a life's companion in order to find happiness. He bade me warn the tree about a pot of gold buried near its trunk which must be removed before the branches can receive nourishment from the earth.

"On my return, I brought God's answers to the maid and to the tree. The maid asked me to stay and be her life's companion, while the tree asked me to dig up the pot of gold.

"Of course, I had to refuse both since God gave me the Gift of Luck—and I must hurry along to search for it!"

"Ah-h-h, brother man, and what was God's reply to me?" asked the starving wolf.

"As for you," replied the man, "God said that you would remain hungry until you met a silly and foolish man whom you could eat up. Only then, said God, would your hunger be satisfied."

"Hmmmmmm," mused the wolf, "where in the world will I find a man more silly and stupid than you?"

And he ate up the foolish man.

## THE CLEVER THIEVES
### (Armenian)

*Like many Armenian tales, this is a story of common folk, a tale of outwitting that has no magic, and that is an example of the kind of peasant humor found in the literature of many cultures. Its blithe humor and brevity are a boon for the storyteller with little time left.*

Once there was and was not in ancient Armenia a hard-working peasant who had hitched his two mules to the plow and was working his field.

Two thieves chanced to pass by and decided to steal one of the poor man's mules. The first thief hid behind a large rock at the edge of the field near where the peasant was working. The second thief walked to the far end of the field. He began to wave his arms about and mutter, "I can't believe it . . . I can't believe it . . ."

Of course, the peasant noticed the peculiar actions of the stranger. He left his plow and walked the length of the field toward the thief.

In the meantime, unseen by the peasant, the first thief crept out from behind the rock, released one mule from the plow, and made off with it.

"Ho there, stranger," said the peasant, upon reaching the far end of his field. "Why do you wave your arms thus? And why do you mutter, 'I can't believe it . . . I can't believe it . . .' What is it you cannot believe?"

"I can't believe that any intelligent farmer would work his field with only one mule hitched to a plow," replied the thief.

The farmer turned around. He looked at his plow and at the one mule hitched to it.

"I can't believe it . . . I can't believe it . . ." muttered the astonished peasant, rubbing his eyes and waving his arms in amazement.

"Well," said the thief. "Now tell me. Why are *you* shouting 'I can't believe it . . . I can't believe it . . .' What can't *you* believe?"

"Oh-h-h," said the witless peasant hopelessly. "I can't believe that my two poor mules have shrunk to one."

Three apples fell from heaven: one for the teller, one for the listener, and one for all the peoples of the world.

## THE OLD TRAVELER
### (Estonian)

*The first collectors of Estonian folk tales were German scholars of the mid-nineteenth century since the country then was dominated by the German barons. This began a national movement for preservation of Estonian lore. The tale of the traveler uses the familiar theme of rewarding kindness.*

Once upon a time, a poor old traveler was walking along the road. It was dusk, and night was fast approaching. The old man decided to seek shelter, as the darkness was kept company by a bone-chilling cold. He came upon a large house and knocked at the window.

The woman of the house, who happened to be very rich, came out. "Why do you rap upon my window, you dirty old tramp?" she exclaimed.

"Please, could you give me shelter for the night, good lady?" he asked quietly.

She began to scold and shout at him. "I'll let the dogs loose on you! Then you'll think twice about asking to stay the night! Get away from here!"

The old man walked wearily on into the darkening night. The wind was beginning to rise and a few flakes of snow touched his face. Soon he came to another house. This one was small and squat, but from inside came happy shouts, and the windows gave off a cheerful glow. Perhaps I might stay the night here, he thought, knocking at the door.

A woman opened it.

"Please, could you give me shelter for the night, good lady?" the old man asked.

"Come in, come in," the woman replied in friendly tones. "You are welcome here, though it's noisy and there is not much room."

The stranger entered and found himself in the midst of many children, all playing happily although their clothing was tattered and worn.

"Your children's clothing is in bad condition," said the traveler. "Why don't you make them new shirts?"

"Ah, but I cannot," the woman replied. "My husband has gone to his rest, and I must bring up my children alone. We have barely enough money for bread, to say nothing of clothing."

Soon the woman laid out supper on the table and invited the stranger to join in the meal, such as it was. But the old traveler refused. "No, thank you," he said, "I ate but a short while ago." Then, untying his sack, he took out all the food he possessed and treated the children to it.

Afterward he lay down and at once fell asleep. In the morning the old man arose, thanked the mistress of the house for her hospitality, and said in parting, "That which you do in the morning, you will do until evening."

The woman did not understand his words and soon forgot them. She saw him to the gate and then returned to the house. If even that poor old man says my children are ragamuffins, what do all the other folk say? she thought. I will make at least one shirt out of the last piece of cloth I have left in the house.

She went to the house of her neighbor, the rich woman, to borrow a yardstick to see if even that piece would be enough. Then she returned to her house and began measuring. As she meas-

ured, the cloth seemed to get longer and longer. The more she measured, the more there was. There seemed no end to it.

She spent the whole day measuring, and in the evening she found that there was enough cloth to make clothes for her family for the rest of their lives. At last she realized what the old traveler had meant by his parting words.

That night, when she returned the yardstick to her neighbor, she told her the whole story. The rich woman was beside herself with fury. What a fool I was, she thought. I could have fulfilled my every desire!

Calling a servant, she ordered him to harness a horse. "Quickly, ride after that old tramp and bring him back here! The poor man should be helped; I have always said so!"

The servant caught up with the traveler on the following day, but the old man refused to go back. The servant became very upset. "If I don't bring you back," said he, "my mistress will drive me away without my wages!"

"Then don't fret, my lad," the old man said. "I will return with you." And he climbed into the cart.

The rich woman stood impatiently at the gate as they arrived. She met the old man with bows and smiles and, leading him into the house, gave him food and drink and made up a soft bed for him. "Lie down, Father, and rest," she said with a simper.

The old man lived in the rich woman's house for a day, and then for another, and then for a third. He ate and drank and slept and smoked his pipe, all very comfortably because the rich woman treated him so kindly.

But inwardly she was fuming. When will this old good-for-nothing get out of here? she said to herself. But she dared not turn him out, for then all the trouble she had gone to on his account would be wasted. To her great joy, on the morning of the fourth day the old man began to pack his sack in preparation for leaving.

The rich woman went outside to see him off. The old traveler walked to the gate in silence, and in silence he passed through it. The rich woman could restrain herself no longer. "Tell me, tell me, what am I to do today?" she cried.

The old man looked at her for a long time. Finally he said, "That which you do in the morning, you will do until evening."

The rich woman rushed into the house, flew up the stairs, and opened her linen closet. She pulled all the cloth from the top shelf, raising a huge cloud of dust, and took out her money jar. She brought it down and sat on the floor with it. But just as she was about to begin counting, the dust she had raised tickled her nose, and she sneezed three times. When she sneezed she raised another cloud of dust, and she sneezed three times again, somewhat louder. Each time she sneezed, more dust was raised and she sneezed again.

*A-tishoo! A-tishoo! A-tishoo!* This time the chickens in the yard fluttered off in all directions, feathers flying.

*A-tishoo! A-tishoo! A-tishoo!* The cows and horses broke out of their stalls and scampered over the hill.

*A-tishoo! A-tishoo! A-tishoo!* The servants ran out of the house, their hands over their ears.

*A-tishoo! A-tishoo! A-tishoo!* The windows shattered out of their frames and cracks appeared in the plaster.

And so it went. *A-tishoo! A-tishoo! A-tishoo!* Until at the end of the day, when the sun had set, the rich woman sat alone in the dark hallway, her house tumbled in ruins about her ears.

### THE MAGIC MILL

#### (Latvian)

*A felicitous blend of many folklore themes, this has a magic object, a greedy brother and a modest one, and an ogre. It's a "why" story, too.*

Once upon a time long ago there lived two brothers. One was rich, but the other was quite poor. The rich brother thought only of himself and hated the sight of his poor brother.

One day the poor brother, without even a penny in his pocket, ran out of bread. All his cupboards were bare and he was hungry. He

went to his brother to ask for help. But the minute the rich brother saw him coming, he shouted gruffly, "Come to me, indeed!" He threw a moldy pork-bone out the window to him. "Here, take this pork-bone and run to hell. Sell it to the devil. Then you will get your pennies!"

The poor brother thanked him and ran off, in tears, to find the underworld. Soon a saintly man, as white as sunlight, walked beside him. "Why are you crying?" he asked.

"Because my brother sent me to hell to sell this pork-bone. But how will I ever find the way? And who down there would ever buy a bone?"

"Well, now," smiled the man, "why let such a simple thing discourage you? Nonsense! It will be easy to trade the bone, for the demons in the underworld are greedy for tidbits of pork. And to find the way, that is even easier. Look," he pointed, "simply follow down this path. It leads directly to the underworld. But remember one thing. Do not ask pennies for that pork-bone. Instead, ask for something worth having. Ask for the mill which lies cast aside in a corner."

The poor brother thanked him and went on his way. He walked and walked. Truly, it was a long way down to the world of the dead. Behind him were the sunny green fields and sweet, sparkling streams. The path became barren, hot, and dark.

At long last he reached the underworld, but a great, rusty, iron gate blocked his way. He knocked on the gate. Out came the devil's servant, a three-headed ogre.

"What do you want?" said the ogre gruffly.

"Look, I have this pork-bone to trade."

"A pork-bone, you say!" The three heads all shouted, "How splendid! What do you want for it?"

"Not much. Let me have the mill that lies cast aside in the corner there. That will do."

"No no no! Not that! Ask for something else."

"I need nothing else," said the poor brother. "I will only trade for the mill."

"Not that! No no no!" The ogre shook his three heads stubbornly.

But the poor brother, seeing the three heads all lick their lips for the pork-bone, was determined not to give up.

At that, the ogre's three heads whispered to

each other that no living man could keep the mill for long. Since men were no less greedy than demons, the sly heads whispered, the mill would soon come back to the underworld. So at last the ogre gave the poor brother the mill.

Wonderful! The greedy ogre ran back into hell with his precious pork-bone and locked the great gate from inside. And the poor brother hurried home with the mill. On the way he met the white man again.

"Did you get the mill?" he asked.

"I did," said the brother. "But what am I ever to do with it? I have nothing to grind."

"Listen," said the man, "you will never say such things when you learn what the mill can do. It is a most wonderful mill! Simply ask it for anything you need, anything at all. Tell it what you wish, and at once it will spin with a roar and pour out all kinds of blessings. But its power is terrible, like fire or water, so be sure you use it well. I will teach you the words to stop its spinning, but this power must be yours alone. Tell no one else these holy words."

He taught the poor brother everything he needed to know to use the magic mill well. Then the man vanished.

Now happy days began for the poor brother. Every day the mill supplied him with the very best meals. It heaped up wealth and blessings of all kinds. And at last it ground him so much gold that he built a splendid, golden castle. He built it near the sea. It shone in the sun, and could be seen for miles around.

As soon as the rich brother saw the castle, he came running like mad to his brother. He was crazy with greed. There was nothing he would not do to get as much gold for himself.

"Gracious me!" he cried. "Where did you get your hands on so much gold? Why don't I have such a castle? Oh," he purred, "what a good and splendid brother you are! I simply can't tell you how fond I am of you. Tell me, where did you get the gold?"

So his brother told him about the magic mill.

"You say the mill did it?" asked the rich brother. "Can this really be true? Listen, dear little brother, sell me your mill. For heaven's sake, do sell it! I won't go until you do."

Well, his brother did not want money for the mill. And he was quite unselfish. So he said, "I will gladly give you the mill. I have enough wealth and blessings from the mill already. Now it is your turn."

The rich brother seized the mill and ran home with it, huffing and grunting and puffing. He ran all the way and was out of breath when he got home, trembling and shouting for joy.

Since he ran so hard, his wife wondered what terrible misfortune had come to him. But he puffed and panted and showed her the mill and told her what it had done for his brother.

The next morning the rich brother got ready to take his workers to the fields. His wife, of course, wanted to stay at home to cook oatmeal for breakfast. "No such thing!" he told her. She would come along with the men to help in the fields, he insisted. And he, at breakfast time, would run home and grind oatmeal with the mill in a jiffy. So they both went to the fields.

At breakfast time, the rich brother dropped his scythe and ran home to make the oatmeal.

"Oatmeal!" he commanded. The mill spun with a roar and began to grind. It ground and ground oatmeal. Now all the pots were full of it.

"Enough!" he commanded. But the mill ground and ground. My, how it did grind!

"Enough!" he shouted. "Enough, enough!"

It was no use. The mill ground and ground. Already the whole room was full of oatmeal and still the mill ground. Now the oatmeal oozed out into his courtyard. Still the mill ground. My, how it did grind!

Terrified, the rich brother hauled the mill out behind the courtyard gate. More and more oatmeal poured out. It heaped higher and higher. It surged into the neighboring shops and houses, and soon the whole village was full of it. Oatmeal flooded over the meadow, turning sweet grass to mush. It made the streams a gummy mess.

"Devil take it!" he cried. "Look what a mess that infernal mill has gotten me into!"

Finally he seized the madly spinning mill and ran with it back to his brother.

"Here!" he said angrily. "You can do what you want with your mill!"

His brother only laughed when he saw the heaping oatmeal. Very quietly, he spoke the words to stop it. There was no more oatmeal.

For some while after, the poor brother received many more blessings from the magic mill.

Then one day a ship came in sight of his golden castle. This was a time, of course, when the sea was pure, sweet water. All the creatures of the Earth could drink from it.

On this bright, sunny day, the sailors saw the castle glittering. Wonder of wonders, they whispered among themselves, what sort of castle was this? They left their ship and came to inspect it. From its floors right up to its towering spires, they found it to be pure, solid gold. Truly, it must belong to a powerful lord.

"Whose castle is this?" they asked the poor brother.

"It is mine," he said.

"Where did you get such a noble castle?"

So he told them about the magic mill.

"You say the mill did it?" they asked, hardly believing their ears. "This simple little trifle of a mill?" They gazed about with looks of respectful wonder. But they were thorough scoundrels and cheats. That night they stole the mill.

In the morning the poor brother looked for his mill, growing angry and sad. But it was nowhere to be found. The sailors were far at sea.

In their greed, the sailors could not agree what to make the mill grind first. But while the others put their heads together and argued, one sailor—simply for a chicken-brained joke—shouted, "Hey mates! We've got no salt. We left it home. Let's see the mill grind salt first. Salt! We can't eat a thing without it!"

So be it. The mill spun with a roar. It began to grind salt. In a moment a dish was full.

"Enough!" said the sailors, but it was no use. The mill roared like crazy. Madly, it whirled. Nothing they did could stop it.

"What have we done?" they all shouted. They jumped on it, every man. They clutched it with their hands. But nothing, nothing could stop it.

In an instant the ship was full of salt.

It sank. Down, down to the bottom of the sea it sank with all of the sailors and the mill. Yet under the sea the mill was grinding, grinding salt. It still grinds today.

And that, you see, is why sea water is now so very salty.

# THE DEVIL'S BRIDE

*(Latvian)*

*There's good even in a thief in the story of a bride claimed by Satan, one of many amusing Latvian tales in which the devil is bested.*

A long time ago there lived on a farm a farm hand and a milkmaid. They never saw eye to eye, and they fought together like cat and dog. The people around them would watch and smile and say, "Just wait and see! You will marry in the end. Once old John and Lisel, who live on the next farmstead, were just the same. Then they could scarce wait until fall when working people have time to marry. Just at oak-cutting time, the pastor announced their marriage banns, and after three weeks the wedding was celebrated. Now they have grown children who themselves are ready for marriage. Just wait! You will marry in the end!"

Now, the farm hand was no ordinary farm hand. During the winter he served as overseer to the baron's kiln house. He had a horse of his own and money besides. When he heard his neighbors' talk, he would say, "If I take the milkmaid as my wife, may a thief steal my horse!"

And the milkmaid would say, "If I marry the farm hand, may the devil take my soul!"

But indeed! In just a short time, there they were, the farm hand and the milkmaid, married and celebrating their wedding feast.

After the wedding the bride was driven from the church to her new home. It was then that the devil appeared to claim her soul; and it was then that a thief appeared to steal the farm hand's horse. The two met behind the garden fence.

"Where are you going?" asked the devil of the thief.

"I am going to steal that horse," answered the thief. "And where are you going?" asked the thief of the devil.

"I am here to claim the soul of the milkmaid," answered the devil. "But I cannot do it alone. You must help me. When we get inside, I will crawl under the bench, and you will hide behind the stove. The bride will sit on the bench at the head of the table. I will step on her foot. Immediately, she will sneeze, and you are to say, 'The devil take the bride's soul!' After you say this three times, the bride will die, and I can claim her soul. There will be great confusion. Everyone will run about with endless lamenting. In the meantime, you can steal the horse with no trouble at all."

The devil and the thief entered the house where the devil noticed a red-berry tree switch. "Of that, I am afraid. If someone were to flail me with that switch, my bones would shatter into dust."

Once inside the house, the devil crawled under the bench, and the thief hid behind the stove. Just then the bride came into the room and sat down on the bench at the head of the table. The devil stepped on her foot; the bride sneezed so loudly that the entire room resounded. Everyone stood about as though bewitched or dumbstruck. No one had wit enough to say, "God help you!" Only the thief, from behind the stove, called out in a loud voice, "God help you!"

The devil was angry but thought, "Let him say it thus this time; it does not matter so long as the third time he says, 'The devil take the bride's soul!' That will do."

The devil stepped on the bride's foot a second time. The bride sneezed again as loudly as the first time. No one said, "God help you!"—no one but the thief who was still hiding behind the stove. "God help you!"

The devil grew so angry that he was ready to devour the thief. Still, he thought, "There is the third time." He stepped on the bride's foot for the third time. She sneezed so loudly that the entire room trembled, but the wonder of it was no one, not even a chicken, had the sense to say, "God help you!" The bride turned pale. At this, the thief put his head around the corner of the stove and exclaimed at the top of his voice, "God help you!" Immediately, the bride recovered, got up, and started to dance.

The devil turned blue with anger and shouted, "People! People! Look there is a thief behind the stove!"

And the thief called out, "People! People! The devil is under the bride's bench!"

No one looked for the thief. All eyes turned to the bench. No one save the thief could see the devil. Suddenly, the thief remembered what the devil had said about the red-berry tree switch. The thief seized the switch and started to whip the devil. Dust flew in all directions; the devil was driven out of the door never to be seen again. Everyone surrounded the thief, asking him how he had become mixed up with the devil.

"Why, it was the doing of the farm hand and the milkmaid. Did he not say, 'If I take the milkmaid as my wife, may a thief steal my horse'? And did she not say, 'If I marry the farm hand, may the devil take my soul'?"

The young couple were happy that their quarreling had taken such a happy turn, and they gave the horse to the thief as a wedding-guest gift. They forgot that they did not see eye to eye, and they forgot to fight like cat and dog. So it was that they lived a long and contented life together.

## SADKO
### (Russian)

*A poignant story that lends itself to dramatization, either with puppets or human actors.*

In Novgorod in the old days there was a young man—just a boy he was—the son of a rich merchant who had lost all his money and died. So Sadko was very poor. He had not a kopeck in the world, except what the people gave him when he played his dulcimer for their dancing. He had blue eyes and curling hair, and he was strong, and would have been merry; but it is dull work playing for other folk to dance, and Sadko dared not dance with any young girl, for he had no money to marry on, and he did not want to be chased away as a beggar. And the young women of Novgorod, they never looked at the handsome Sadko. No; they smiled with their bright eyes at the young men who danced with them, and if they ever spoke to Sadko, it was just to tell him sharply to keep the music going or to play faster. So Sadko lived alone with his dulcimer, and

"Sadko" from *Old Peter's Russian Tales*, retold in English by Arthur Ransome. Copyright 1917 by Thomas Nelson & Sons Limited and reprinted with their permission

made do with half a loaf when he could not get a whole, and with crust when he had no crumb. He did not mind so very much what came to him, so long as he could play his dulcimer and walk along the banks of the little river Volkhov [1] that flows by Novgorod, or on the shores of the lake, making music for himself, and seeing the pale mists rise over the water, and dawn or sunset across the shining river.

"There is no girl in all Novgorod as pretty as my little river," he used to say, and night after night he would sit by the banks of the river or on the shores of the lake, playing the dulcimer and singing to himself.

Sometimes he helped the fishermen on the lake, and they would give him a little fish for his supper in payment for his strong young arms.

And it happened that one evening the fishermen asked him to watch their nets for them on the shore, while they went off to take their fish to sell them in the square at Novgorod.

Sadko sat on the shore, on a rock, and played his dulcimer and sang. Very sweetly he sang of the fair lake and the lovely river—the little river that he thought prettier than all the girls of Novgorod. And while he was singing he saw a whirlpool in the lake, little waves flying from it across the water, and in the middle a hollow down into the water. And in the hollow he saw the head of a great man with blue hair and a gold crown. He knew that the huge man was the Tzar of the Sea. And the man came nearer, walking up out of the depths of the lake—a huge, great man, a very giant, with blue hair falling to his waist over his broad shoulders. The little waves ran from him in all directions as he came striding up out of the water.

Sadko did not know whether to run or stay; but the Tzar of the Sea called out to him in a great voice like wind and water in a storm,—

"Sadko of Novgorod, you have played and sung many days by the side of this lake and on the banks of the little river Volkhov. My daughters love your music, and it has pleased me too. Throw out a net into the water, and draw it in, and the waters will pay you for your singing.

[1] The Volkhov would be a big river if it were in England, and Sadko and old Peter called it little only because they loved it.

And if you are satisfied with the payment, you must come and play to us down in the green palace of the sea."

With that the Tzar of the Sea went down again into the waters of the lake. The waves closed over him with a roar, and presently the lake was as smooth and calm as it had ever been.

Sadko thought, and said to himself: "Well, there is no harm done in casting out a net." So he threw a net out into the lake.

He sat down again and played on his dulcimer and sang, and when he had finished his singing the dusk had fallen and the moon shone over the lake. He put down his dulcimer and took hold of the ropes of the net, and began to draw it up out of the silver water. Easily the ropes came, and the net, dripping and glittering in the moonlight.

"I was dreaming," said Sadko; "I was asleep when I saw the Tzar of the Sea, and there is nothing in the net at all."

And then, just as the last of the net was coming ashore, he saw something in it, square and dark. He dragged it out, and found it was a coffer. He opened the coffer, and it was full of precious stones—green, red, gold—gleaming in the light of the moon. Diamonds shone there like little bundles of sharp knives.

"There can be no harm in taking these stones," says Sadko, "whether I dreamed or not."

He took the coffer on his shoulder, and bent under the weight of it, strong though he was. He put it in a safe place. All night he sat and watched by the nets, and played and sang, and planned what he would do.

In the morning the fishermen came, laughing and merry after their night in Novgorod, and they gave him a little fish for watching their nets; and he made a fire on the shore, and cooked it and ate it as he used to do.

"And that is my last meal as a poor man," says Sadko. "Ah me! who knows if I shall be happier?"

Then he set the coffer on his shoulder and tramped away for Novgorod.

"Who is that?" they asked at the gates.

"Only Sadko, the dulcimer player," he replied.

"Turned porter?" said they.

"One trade is as good as another," said Sadko, and he walked into the city. He sold a few of the stones, two at a time, and with what he got for them he set up a booth in the market. Small things led to great, and he was soon one of the richest traders in Novgorod.

And now there was not a girl in the town who could look too sweetly at Sadko. "He has golden hair," says one. "Blue eyes like the sea," says another. "He could lift the world on his shoulders," says a third. A little money, you see, opens everybody's eyes.

But Sadko was not changed by his good fortune. Still he walked and played by the little river Volkhov. When work was done and the traders gone, Sadko would take his dulcimer and play and sing on the banks of the river. And still he said, "There is no girl in all Novgorod as pretty as my little river." Every time he came back from his long voyages—for he was trading far and near, like the greatest of merchants—he went at once to the banks of the river to see how his sweetheart fared. And always he brought some little present for her and threw it into the waves.

For twelve years he lived unmarried in Novgorod, and every year made voyages, buying and selling, and always growing richer and richer. Many were the mothers of Novgorod who would have liked to see him married to their daughters. Many were the pillows that were wet with the tears of the young girls, as they thought of the blue eyes of Sadko and his golden hair.

And then, in the twelfth year since he walked into Novgorod with the coffer on his shoulder, he was sailing a ship on the Caspian Sea, far, far away. For many days the ship sailed on, and Sadko sat on deck and played his dulcimer and sang of Novgorod and of the little river Volkhov that flows under the walls of the town. Blue was the Caspian Sea, and the waves were like furrows in a field, long lines of white under the steady wind, while the sails swelled and the ship shot over the water.

And suddenly the ship stopped.

In the middle of the sea, far from land, the ship stopped and trembled in the waves, as if she were held by a big hand.

"We are aground!" cry the sailors; and the captain, the great one, tells them to take soundings. Seventy fathoms by the bow it was, and seventy fathoms by the stern.

"We are not aground," says the captain, "unless there is a rock sticking up like a needle in the middle of the Caspian Sea!"

"There is magic in this," say the sailors.

"Hoist more sail," says the captain; and up go the white sails, swelling out in the wind, while the masts bend and creak. But still the ship lay shivering, and did not move, out there in the middle of the sea.

"Hoist more sail yet," says the captain; and up go the white sails, swelling and tugging, while the masts creak and groan. But still the ship lay there shivering and did not move.

"There is an unlucky one aboard," says an old sailor. "We must draw lots and find him, and throw him overboard into the sea."

The other sailors agreed to this. And still Sadko sat, and played his dulcimer and sang.

The sailors cut pieces of string, all of a length, as many as there were souls in the ship, and one of those strings they cut in half. Then they made them into a bundle, and each man plucked one string. And Sadko stopped his playing for a moment to pluck a string, and his was the string that had been cut in half.

"Magician, sorcerer, unclean one!" shouted the sailors.

"Not so," said Sadko. "I remember now an old promise I made, and I keep it willingly."

He took his dulcimer in his hand, and leapt from the ship into the blue Caspian Sea. The waves had scarcely closed over his head before the ship shot forward again, and flew over the waves like a swan's feather, and came in the end safely to her harbour.

"And what happened to Sadko?" asked Maroosia.

"You shall hear, little pigeon," said old Peter, and he took a pinch of snuff. Then he went on.

Sadko dropped into the waves, and the waves closed over him. Down he sank, like a pebble thrown into a pool, down and down. First the water was blue, then green, and strange fish with goggle eyes and golden fins swam round him as he sank. He came at last to the bottom of the sea.

And there, on the bottom of the sea, was a palace built of green wood. Yes, all the timbers of all the ships that have been wrecked in all the seas of the world are in that palace, and they are all green, and cunningly fitted together, so that the palace is worth a ten days' journey only to see it. And in front of the palace Sadko saw two big kobbly sturgeons, each a hundred and fifty feet long, lashing their tails and guarding the gates. Now, sturgeons are the oldest of all fish, and these were the oldest of all sturgeons.

Sadko walked between the sturgeons and through the gates of the palace. Inside there was a great hall, and the Tzar of the Sea lay resting in the hall, with his gold crown on his head and his blue hair floating round him in the water, and his great body covered with scales lying along the hall. The Tzar of the Sea filled the hall—and there is room in that hall for a village. And there were fish swimming this way and that in and out of the windows.

"Ah, Sadko," says the Tzar of the Sea, "you took what the sea gave you, but you have been a long time in coming to sing in the palaces of the sea. Twelve years I have lain here waiting for you."

"Great Tzar, forgive," says Sadko.

"Sing now," says the Tzar of the Sea, and his voice was like the beating of waves.

And Sadko played on his dulcimer and sang.

He sang of Novgorod and of the little river Volkhov which he loved. It was in his song that none of the girls of Novgorod were as pretty as the little river. And there was the sound of wind over the lake in his song, the sound of ripples under the prow of a boat, the sound of ripples on the shore, the sound of the river flowing past the tall reeds, the whispering sound of the river at night. And all the time he played cunningly on the dulcimer. The girls of Novgorod had never danced to so sweet a tune when in the old days Sadko played his dulcimer to earn kopecks and crusts of bread.

Never had the Tzar of the Sea heard such music.

"I would dance," said the Tzar of the Sea, and he stood up like a tall tree in the hall.

"Play on," said the Tzar of the Sea, and he strode through the gates. The sturgeons guarding the gates stirred the water with their tails.

And if the Tzar of the Sea was huge in the hall, he was huger still when he stood outside on the bottom of the sea. He grew taller and taller, towering like a mountain. His feet were like small hills. His blue hair hung down to his waist, and he was covered with green scales. And he began to dance on the bottom of the sea.

Great was that dancing. The sea boiled, and ships went down. The waves rolled as big as houses. The sea overflowed its shores, and whole towns were under water as the Tzar danced mightily on the bottom of the sea. Hither and thither rushed the waves, and the very earth shook at the dancing of that tremendous Tzar.

He danced till he was tired, and then he came back to the palace of green wood, and passed the sturgeons, and shrank into himself and came through the gates into the hall, where Sadko still played on his dulcimer and sang.

"You have played well and given me pleasure," says the Tzar of the Sea. "I have thirty daughters, and you shall choose one and marry her, and be a Prince of the Sea."

"Better than all maidens I love my little river," says Sadko; and the Tzar of the Sea laughed and threw his head back, with his blue hair floating all over the hall.

And then there came in the thirty daughters of the Tzar of the Sea. Beautiful they were, lovely, and graceful; but twenty-nine of them passed by, and Sadko fingered his dulcimer and thought of his little river.

There came in the thirtieth, and Sadko cried out aloud. "Here is the only maiden in the world as pretty as my little river!" says he. And she looked at him with eyes that shone like stars reflected in the river. Her hair was dark, like the river at night. She laughed, and her voice was like the flowing of the river.

"And what is the name of your little river?" says the Tzar.

"It is the little river Volkhov that flows by Novgorod," says Sadko; "but your daughter is as fair as the little river, and I would gladly marry her if she will have me."

"It is a strange thing," says the Tzar, "but Volkhov is the name of my youngest daughter."

He put Sadko's hand in the hand of his youngest daughter, and they kissed each other. And as they kissed, Sadko saw a necklace round her neck, and knew it for one he had thrown into the river as a present for his sweetheart.

She smiled, and "Come!" says she, and took him away to a palace of her own, and showed him a coffer; and in that coffer were bracelets and rings and earrings—all the gifts that he had thrown into the river.

And Sadko laughed for joy, and kissed the youngest daughter of the Tzar of the Sea, and she kissed him back.

"O my little river!" says he; "there is no girl in all the world but thou as pretty as my little river."

Well, they were married, and the Tzar of the Sea laughed at the wedding feast till the palace shook and the fish swam off in all directions.

And after the feast Sadko and his bride went off together to her palace. And before they slept she kissed him very tenderly, and she said,—

"O Sadko, you will not forget me? You will play to me sometimes, and sing?"

"I shall never lose sight of you, my pretty one," says he; "and as for music, I will sing and play all the day long."

"That's as may be," says she, and they fell asleep.

And in the middle of the night Sadko happened to turn in bed, and he touched the Princess with his left foot, and she was cold, cold, cold as ice in January. And with that touch of cold he woke, and he was lying under the walls of Novgorod, with his dulcimer in his hand, and one of his feet was in the little river Volkhov, and the moon was shining.

"O grandfather! And what happened to him after that?" asked Maroosia.

"There are many tales," said old Peter. "Some say he went into the town, and lived on alone until he died. But I think with those who say that he took his dulcimer and swam out into the middle of the river, and sank under water again, looking for his little Princess. They say he found her, and lives still in the green palaces of the bottom of the sea; and when there is a big storm, you may know that Sadko is playing on his dulcimer and singing, and that the Tzar of the Sea is dancing his tremendous dance, down there, on the bottom, under the waves."

"Yes, I expect that's what happened," said Ivan. "He'd have found it very dull in Novgorod, even though it is a big town."

## THE FIRE-BIRD, THE HORSE OF POWER, AND THE PRINCESS VASILISSA

*(Russian)*

*One wonders at the young archer's readiness for despair when he has the horse of power to solve all his problems. But no matter, for this story has the color and the extravagant magic of an Oriental tale that spins on and on. It makes a good introduction to Stravinsky's "Firebird" and indicates how folk tales have inspired musicians and artists. Children may enjoy making a puppet play out of this tale.*

Once upon a time a strong and powerful Tzar ruled in a country far away. And among the servants was a young archer, and this archer had a horse—a horse of power—such a horse as belonged to the wonderful men of long ago—a great horse with a broad chest, eyes like fire, and hoofs of iron. There are no such horses nowadays. They sleep with the strong men who rode them, the bogatirs, until the time comes when Russia has need of them. Then the great horses will thunder up from under the ground, and the valiant men leap from the graves in the armour they have worn so long. The strong men will sit those horses of power, and there will be swinging of clubs and thunder of hoofs, and the earth will be swept clean from the enemies of God and the Tzar. So my grandfather used to say, and he was as much older than I as I am older than you, little ones, and so he should know.

Well, one day long ago, in the green time of the year, the young archer rode through the forest on his horse of power. The trees were green; there were little blue flowers on the ground under the trees; the squirrels ran in the branches, and the hares in the undergrowth; but no birds sang. The young archer rode along the forest path and listened for the singing of the birds, but there was no singing. The forest was silent, and the only noises in it were the scratching of four-footed beasts, the dropping of fir cones, and the heavy stamping of the horse of power in the soft path.

"What has come to the birds?" said the young archer.

He had scarcely said this before he saw a big curving feather lying in the path before him. The feather was larger than a swan's, larger than an eagle's. It lay in the path, glittering like a flame; for the sun was on it, and it was a feather of pure gold. Then he knew why there was no singing in the forest. For he knew that the fire-bird had flown that way, and that the feather in the path before him was a feather from its burning breast.

The horse of power spoke and said,

"Leave the golden feather where it lies. If you take it you will be sorry for it, and know the meaning of fear."

But the brave young archer sat on the horse of power and looked at the golden feather, and wondered whether to take it or not. He had no wish to learn what it was to be afraid, but he thought, "If I take it and bring it to the Tzar my master, he will be pleased; and he will not send me away with empty hands, for no tzar in the world has a feather from the burning breast of the fire-bird." And the more he thought, the more he wanted to carry the feather to the Tzar. And in the end he did not listen to the words of the horse of power. He leapt from the saddle, picked up the golden feather of the fire-bird, mounted his horse again, and galloped back through the green forest till he came to the palace of the Tzar.

He went into the palace, and bowed before the Tzar and said,—

"O Tzar, I have brought you a feather of the fire-bird."

The Tzar looked gladly at the feather, and then at the young archer.

"Thank you," says he; "but if you have brought me a feather of the fire-bird, you will be able to bring me the bird itself. I should like to see it. A feather is not a fit gift to bring to the Tzar. Bring the bird itself, or, I swear by my sword, your head shall no longer sit between your shoulders!"

The young archer bowed his head and went out. Bitterly he wept, for he knew now what it was to be afraid. He went out into the courtyard, where the horse of power was waiting for him, tossing its head and stamping on the ground.

"Master," says the horse of power, "why do you weep?"

"The Tzar has told me to bring him the fire-bird, and no man on earth can do that," says the young archer, and he bowed his head on his breast.

"I told you," says the horse of power, "that if you took the feather you would learn the meaning of fear. Well, do not be frightened yet, and do not weep. The trouble is not now; the trouble lies before you. Go back to the Tzar and ask him to have a hundred sacks of maize scattered over the open field, and let this be done at midnight."

The young archer went back into the palace and begged the Tzar for this, and the Tzar ordered that at midnight a hundred sacks of maize should be scattered in the open field.

Next morning, at the first redness in the sky, the young archer rode out on the horse of power, and came to the open field. The ground was scattered all over with maize. In the middle of the field stood a great oak with spreading boughs. The young archer leapt to the ground, took off the saddle, and let the horse of power loose to wander as he pleased about the field. Then he climbed up into the oak and hid himself among the green boughs.

The sky grew red and gold, and the sun rose. Suddenly there was a noise in the forest round the field. The trees shook and swayed, and almost fell. There was a mighty wind. The sea piled itself into waves with crests of foam, and the fire-bird came flying from the other side of the world. Huge and golden and flaming in the sun, it flew, dropped down with open wings into the field, and began to eat the maize.

The horse of power wandered in the field. This way he went, and that, but always he came a little nearer to the fire-bird. Nearer and nearer came the horse. He came close up to the fire-bird, and then suddenly stepped on one of its spreading fiery wings and pressed it heavily to the ground. The bird struggled, flapping mightily with its fiery wings, but it could not get away. The young archer slipped down from the tree, bound the fire-bird with three strong ropes, swung it on its back, saddled the horse, and rode to the palace of the Tzar.

The young archer stood before the Tzar, and his back was bent under the great weight of the fire-bird, and the broad wings of the bird hung on either side of him like fiery shields, and there was a trail of golden feathers on the floor. The young archer swung the magic bird to the foot of the throne before the Tzar; and the Tzar was glad, because since the beginning of the world no tzar had seen the fire-bird flung before him like a wild duck caught in a snare.

The Tzar looked at the fire-bird and laughed with pride. Then he lifted his eyes and looked at the young archer, and says he,

"As you have known how to take the fire-bird, you will know how to bring me my bride, for whom I have long been waiting. In the land of Never, on the very edge of the world, where the red sun rises in flame from behind the sea, lives the Princess Vasilissa. I will marry none but her. Bring her to me, and I will reward you with silver and gold. But if you do not bring her, then, by my sword, your head will no longer sit between your shoulders!"

The young archer wept bitter tears, and went

out into the courtyard where the horse of power was stamping the ground with its hoofs of iron and tossing its thick mane.

"Master, why do you weep?" asked the horse of power.

"The Tzar has ordered me to go to the land of Never, and to bring back the Princess Vasilissa."

"Do not weep—do not grieve. The trouble is not yet; the trouble is to come. Go to the Tzar and ask him for a silver tent with a golden roof, and for all kinds of food and drink to take with us on the journey."

The young archer went in and asked the Tzar for this, and the Tzar gave him a silver tent with silver hangings and a gold-embroidered roof, and every kind of rich wine and the tastiest of foods.

Then the young archer mounted the horse of power and rode off to the land of Never. On and on he rode, many days and nights, and came at last to the edge of the world, where the red sun rises in flame from behind the deep blue sea.

On the shore of the sea the young archer reined in the horse of power, and the heavy hoofs of the horse sank in the sand. He shaded his eyes and looked out over the blue water, and there was the Princess Vasilissa in a little silver boat, rowing with golden oars.

The young archer rode back a little way to where the sand ended and the green world began. There he loosed the horse to wander where he pleased, and to feed on the green grass. Then on the edge of the shore, where the green grass ended and grew thin and the sand began, he set up the shining tent, with its silver hangings and its gold-embroidered roof. In the tent he set out the tasty dishes and the rich flagons of wine which the Tzar had given him, and he sat himself down in the tent and began to regale himself, while he waited for the Princess Vasilissa.

The Princess Vasilissa dipped her golden oars in the blue water, and the little silver boat moved lightly through the dancing waves. She sat in the little boat and looked over the blue sea to the edge of the world, and there, between the golden sand and the green earth, she saw the tent standing, silver and gold in the sun. She dipped her oars, and came nearer to see it the better. The nearer she came the fairer seemed the tent, and at last she rowed to the shore and grounded her little boat on the golden sand, and stepped out daintily and came up to the tent. She was a little frightened, and now and again she stopped and looked back to where the silver boat lay on the sand with the blue sea beyond it. The young archer said not a word, but went on regaling himself on the pleasant dishes he had set out there in the tent.

At last the Princess Vasilissa came up to the tent and looked in.

The young archer rose and bowed before her. Says he—

"Good-day to you, Princess! Be so kind as to come in and take bread and salt with me, and taste my foreign wines."

And the Princess Vasilissa came into the tent and sat down with the young archer, and ate sweetmeats with him, and drank his health in a golden goblet of the wine the Tzar had given him. Now this wine was heavy, and the last drop from the goblet had no sooner trickled down her little slender throat than her eyes closed against her will, once, twice, and again.

"Ah me!" says the Princess, "it is as if the night itself had perched on my eyelids, and yet it is but noon."

And the golden goblet dropped to the ground from her little fingers, and she leant back on a cushion and fell instantly asleep. If she had been beautiful before, she was lovelier still when she lay in that deep sleep in the shadow of the tent.

Quickly the young archer called to the horse of power. Lightly he lifted the Princess in his strong young arms. Swiftly he leapt with her into the saddle. Like a feather she lay in the hollow of his left arm, and slept while the iron hoofs of the great horse thundered over the ground.

They came to the Tzar's palace, and the young archer leapt from the horse of power and carried the Princess into the palace. Great was the joy of the Tzar; but it did not last for long.

"Go, sound the trumpets for our wedding," he said to his servants; "let all the bells be rung."

The bells rang out and the trumpets sounded, and at the noise of the horns and the ringing of the bells the Princess Vasilissa woke up and looked about her.

"What is this ringing of bells," says she, "and this noise of trumpets? And where, oh, where is the blue sea, and my little silver boat with its golden oars?" And the princess put her hand to her eyes.

"The blue sea is far away," says the Tzar, "and for your little silver boat I give you a golden throne. The trumpets sound for our wedding, and the bells are ringing for our joy."

But the Princess turned her face away from the Tzar; and there was no wonder in that, for he was old, and his eyes were not kind.

And she looked with love at the young archer; and there was no wonder in that either, for he was a young man fit to ride the horse of power.

The Tzar was angry with the Princess Vasilissa, but his anger was as useless as his joy.

"Why, Princess," says he, "will you not marry me, and forget your blue sea and your silver boat?"

"In the middle of the deep blue sea lies a great stone," says the Princess, "and under that stone is hidden my wedding dress. If I cannot wear that dress I will marry nobody at all."

Instantly the Tzar turned to the young archer, who was waiting before the throne.

"Ride swiftly back," says he, "to the land of Never, where the red sun rises in flame. There—do you hear what the Princess says?—a great stone lies in the middle of the sea. Under that stone is hidden her wedding dress. Ride swiftly. Bring back that dress, or, by my sword, your head shall no longer sit between your shoulders!"

The young archer wept bitter tears, and went out into the courtyard, where the horse of power was waiting for him, champing its golden bit.

"There is no way of escaping death this time," he said.

"Master, why do you weep?" asked the horse of power.

"The Tzar has ordered me to ride to the land of Never, to fetch the wedding dress of the Princess Vasilissa from the bottom of the deep blue sea. Besides, the dress is wanted for the Tzar's wedding, and I love the Princess myself."

"What did I tell you?" says the horse of power. "I told you that there would be trouble if you picked up the golden feather from the fire-bird's burning breast. Well, do not be afraid. The trouble is not yet; the trouble is to come. Up! into the saddle with you, and away for the wedding dress of the Princess Vasilissa!"

The young archer leapt into the saddle, and the horse of power, with his thundering hoofs, carried him swiftly through the green forests and over the bare plains, till they came to the edge of the world, to the land of Never, where the red sun rises in flame from behind the deep blue sea. There they rested, at the very edge of the sea.

The young archer looked sadly over the wide waters, but the horse of power tossed its mane and did not look at the sea, but on the shore. This way and that it looked, and saw at last a huge lobster moving slowly, sideways, along the golden sand.

Nearer and nearer came the lobster, and it was a giant among lobsters, the tzar of all the lobsters; and it moved slowly along the shore, while the horse of power moved carefully and as if by accident, until it stood between the lobster and the sea. Then, when the lobster came close by, the horse of power lifted an iron hoof and set it firmly on the lobster's tail.

"You will be the death of me!" screamed the lobster—as well he might, with the heavy foot of the horse of power pressing his tail into the sand. "Let me live, and I will do whatever you ask of me."

"Very well," says the horse of power; "we will let you live," and he slowly lifted his foot. "But this is what you shall do for us. In the middle of the blue sea lies a great stone, and under that stone is hidden the wedding dress of the Princess Vasilissa. Bring it here."

The lobster groaned with the pain in his tail. Then he cried out in a voice that could be heard all over the deep blue sea. And the sea was disturbed, and from all sides lobsters in thousands made their way towards the bank. And the huge lobster that was the oldest of them all and the tzar of all the lobsters that live between the rising and the setting of the sun, gave them the order and sent them back into the sea. And the young archer sat on the horse of power and waited.

After a little time the sea was disturbed again, and the lobsters in their thousands came to the shore, and with them they brought a golden casket in which was the wedding dress of the Princess Vasilissa. They had taken it from under the great stone that lay in the middle of the sea.

The tzar of all the lobsters raised himself pain-fully on his bruised tail and gave the casket into the hands of the young archer, and instantly the horse of power turned himself about and galloped back to the palace of the Tzar, far, far away, at the other side of the green forests and beyond the treeless plains.

The young archer went into the palace and gave the casket into the hands of the Princess, and looked at her with sadness in his eyes, and she looked at him with love. Then she went away into an inner chamber, and came back in her wedding dress, fairer than the spring itself. Great was the joy of the Tzar. The wedding feast was made ready, and the bells rang, and flags waved about the palace.

The Tzar held out his hand to the Princess, and looked at her with his old eyes. But she would not take his hand.

"No," says she; "I will marry nobody until the man who brought me here has done penance in boiling water."

Instantly the Tzar turned to his servants and ordered them to make a great fire, and to fill a great cauldron with water and set it on the fire, and, when the water should be at its hottest, to take the young archer and throw him into it, to do penance for having taken the Princess Vasilissa away from the land of Never.

There was no gratitude in the mind of that Tzar.

Swiftly the servants brought wood and made a mighty fire, and on it they laid a huge cauldron of water, and built the fire around the walls of the cauldron. The fire burned hot and the water steamed. The fire burned hotter, and the water bubbled and seethed. They made ready to take the young archer, to throw him into the cauldron.

"Oh, misery!" thought the young archer. "Why did I ever take the golden feather that had fallen from the fire-bird's burning breast? Why did I not listen to the wise words of the horse of power?" And he remembered the horse of power, and he begged the Tzar,

"O lord Tzar, I do not complain. I shall presently die in the heat of the water on the fire. Suffer me, before I die, once more to see my horse."

"Let him see his horse," says the Princess.

"Very well," says the Tzar. "Say good-bye to

your horse, for you will not ride him again. But let your farewells be short, for we are waiting."

The young archer crossed the courtyard and came to the horse of power, who was scraping the ground with his iron hoofs.

"Farewell, my horse of power," says the young archer. "I should have listened to your words of wisdom, for now the end is come, and we shall never more see the green trees pass above us and the ground disappear beneath us, as we race the wind between the earth and the sky."

"Why so?" says the horse of power.

"The Tzar has ordered that I am to be boiled to death—thrown into that cauldron that is seething on the great fire."

"Fear not," says the horse of power, "for the Princess Vasilissa has made him do this, and the end of these things is better than I thought. Go back, and when they are ready to throw you in the cauldron, do you run boldly and leap yourself into the boiling water."

The young archer went back across the courtyard, and the servants made ready to throw him into the cauldron.

"Are you sure that the water is boiling?" says the Princess Vasilissa.

"It bubbles and seethes," said the servants.

"Let me see for myself," says the Princess, and she went to the fire and waved her hand above the cauldron. And some say there was something in her hand, and some say there was not.

"It is boiling," says she, and the servants laid hands on the young archer; but he threw them from him, and ran and leapt boldly before them all into the very middle of the cauldron.

Twice he sank below the surface, borne around with the bubbles and foam of the boiling water. Then he leapt from the cauldron and stood before the Tzar and the Princess. He had become so beautiful a youth that all who saw cried aloud in wonder.

"This is a miracle," says the Tzar. And the Tzar looked at the beautiful young archer and thought of himself—of his age, of his bent back, and his gray beard, and his toothless gums. "I too will become beautiful," thinks he, and he rose from his throne and clambered into the cauldron, and was boiled to death in a moment.

And the end of the story? They buried the Tzar, and made the young archer Tzar in his place. He married the Princess Vasilissa, and lived many years with her in love and good fellowship. And he built a golden stable for the horse of power, and never forgot what he owed him.

## THE CLEVER JUDGE

*(Russian)*

*Babette Deutsch, one of the authors of* Tales of Faraway Folk, *from which this story is taken, identifies "The Clever Judge" as a Kirghiz folk tale. In the introduction she says: "The people who tell this tale live on the vast steppes or prairies of southwestern Asia. They are herders of cattle, sheep, and goats. And they are clever fellows, too, as you shall see."*

There lived a man in the steppes who was famous for his justice and wisdom. At that time if a man was known for his fairness, people came to him from far and wide to ask him to settle their disputes. And so it was that one day two villagers appeared before this wise man and asked him to settle their quarrel.

"Tell me your story," the judge said to the plaintiff.

"I had to leave my village," said the plaintiff, "for I had business elsewhere. And all my wealth was a hundred gold coins. I did not come by them easily. I had to work hard for them, and I did not want them to be stolen while I was away. Nor did I care to carry so much money with me on my journey. So I entrusted these gold coins for safekeeping to this man here. When I got back from my journey, he denied that he had ever received the money from me."

"And who saw you give him these hundred gold coins?" asked the judge.

"No one saw it. We went together to the heart of the forest and there I handed him the coins."

"What have you to say to this?" the judge asked, turning to the defendant.

The defendant shrugged his shoulders.

"I don't know what he is talking about," said

the man. "I never went to the forest with him. I never saw his gold coins."

"Do you remember the place where you handed over the money?" the judge asked the plaintiff.

"Of course I do. It was under a tall oak. I remember it very well. I can point it out with no trouble at all."

"So you do have a witness, after all," said the judge. "Here, take my signet ring, go to the tall tree under which you stood when you handed over the money, set the seal of my signet ring against the trunk, and bid the tree appear before me to bear out the truth of your story."

The plaintiff took the signet ring and went off to carry out the demand of the judge. The defendant remained behind and waited for his return.

After some time had passed, the judge turned to the defendant and asked, "Do you think he has reached the oak by this time?"

"No, not yet," was the answer.

After further time had passed, the judge again turned to the defendant and asked, "Do you think he has reached the tree by this time?"

"Yes," was the answer, "by now he must have reached it."

Not long after that the plaintiff returned.

"Well?" asked the judge.

"I did just as you said," replied the plaintiff. "I walked as far as the forest and then I went on until I came to the tall oak under which we stood when I handed over my gold coins. I set the seal of your signet ring against the trunk of the tree and I bade it appear before you as a witness. But the tree refused to budge."

"Never mind," said the judge. "The oak has appeared before me and it has borne witness in your favor."

At that the defendant exclaimed, "How can you say such a thing! I have been here all this while and no tree has stalked into the place."

"But," replied the judge, "you said that you had not been in the forest at all. And yet when I asked you whether the plaintiff had reached the oak, first you answered that he could not have reached it, and the second time you said that he must surely have reached it. Therefore, you *were* in the forest and you remembered where the oak was under which you stood when the plaintiff handed his gold coins to you for safekeeping. Now you must not only return him his hundred gold pieces, but you must also pay a fine for having tried to cheat him."

So the tree was a witness without budging, and justice was done.

# Turkey

*Turkish folklore has an impressive scope and vitality. Until the 1920's, sung-spoken narratives about folk heroes, tales of wonder and magic, ballads, songs, and traditional folk-theater plays were a living legacy of Turkish folkways. However, much of the recorded folklore exists only in Arabic, and with the establishment of the Turkish republic many of the old customs, such as the folk theater, have passed away within the last two generations. The books listed in the Bibliography provide many fine stories from Turkish folklore, the most popular being, as they are in Turkey, the tales of the Hodja.*

## HOW MANY DONKEYS?

*Fortunately, many tales about the irresistibly popular Nasr-ed-Din Hodja (spellings will vary) are available in several books for English-speaking boys and girls. The Turks love humorous*

*stories, and the Hodja anecdotes have provided them with a rare character whose adventures*

"How Many Donkeys?" Reprinted by permission of David McKay Company, Inc., from *Once the Hodja* by Alice Geer Kelsey; copyright, 1943, by Alice Geer Kelsey

*have been told and laughed over for at least five centuries. He is their Paul Bunyan and their Three Sillies all in one. His mixture of wisdom and folly strike such sympathetic chords in us all that he is easily one of the most lovable figures in world folklore.*

There was the tinkle of tiny bells, the sharp clip of small hoofs, the throaty drone of a solitary singer. Nasr-ed-Din Hodja was bringing the donkeys back from the mill, their saddlebags filled with freshly ground wheat. The hot Turkish sun beat down on his turbaned head. The brown dust from the donkeys' hoofs puffed about him. The staccato trot of his donkey jiggled him back and forth. But Nasr-ed-Din Hodja was too pleased to be uncomfortable.

"I'll show them," he chuckled. "They gave me plenty of advice about taking care of their donkeys and their wheat. As though I did not know more about donkeys than any man in Ak Shehir."

His eyes rested lazily on the road ahead. At first it followed the brook running away from Mill Valley, the brook that turned the heavy stones to grind the wheat. Then the road disappeared over a hilltop.

"Just over that hill," he mused contentedly, "is Ak Shehir, where they are waiting for their donkeys. There is not a scratch or a bruise on one of the little creatures. No donkeys in all Turkey have had better treatment today than these nine."

Idly he began counting them.

"What?" he gasped. "Eight donkeys?"

He jumped from his donkey and ran hither and yon, looking behind rocks and over hilltops, but no stray donkey could he see. At last he stood beside the donkeys and counted again. This time there were nine. With a sigh of relief he climbed onto his own donkey and went swinging along the road. His long legs in their baggy pantaloons swung easily back and forth in time to the donkey's trot. Passing through a cluster of trees he thought it time to count the donkeys again.

"One—two—three—" and up to eight he counted, but no ninth donkey was to be seen. Down from his donkey's back he came. Behind all the trees he peered. Not a hair of a donkey could he find.

Again he counted, standing beside his donkeys. There they all were—nine mild little donkeys waiting for orders to move on. Nasr-ed-Din Hodja scratched his poor head in bewilderment. Was he losing his mind or were the donkeys all bewitched? Again he counted. Yes, surely there were nine.

"Ughr-r-r-r," Nasr-ed-Din Hodja gave the low guttural which is Turkish for "Giddap." As he rode on, he looked about him for the evil spirits which must be playing tricks on him. Each donkey wore the blue beads which should drive away the evil spirits. Were there evil spirits abroad stronger even than the blue beads?

He was glad to see a friend coming toward him down the road.

"Oh, Mustapha Effendi," he cried. "Have you seen one of these donkeys? I have lost a donkey and yet I have not lost it."

"What can you mean, Hodja Effendi?" asked Mustapha.

"I left the mill with nine donkeys," explained the Hodja. "Part of the way home there have been nine and part of the way there have been eight. Oh, I am bewitched! Help me! Help me!"

Mustapha was used to the queer ways of the Hodja, but he was surprised. He counted the donkeys silently.

"Let me see you count the donkeys," he ordered the Hodja.

"One—two—three," began the Hodja, pointing at each one as he counted up to eight.

As he said the last number, he stopped and looked at his friend with a face full of helplessness and terror. His terror turned to amazement as Mustapha slapped his knee and laughed until he almost fell from his donkey.

"What is so funny?" asked the Hodja.

"Oh, Hodja Effendi!" Mustapha laughed. "When you are counting your brothers, why, oh why, do you not count the brother on whom you are riding?"

Nasr-ed-Din Hodja was silent for a moment to think through this discovery. Then he kissed the hand of his deliverer, pressed it to his forehead and thanked him a thousand times for his help. He rode, singing, on to Ak Shehir to deliver the donkeys to their owners.

# A Tale from "Arabian Nights"

*The source of the* Arabian Nights *is lost in antiquity. Some of the tales seem to stem from ancient India, others from North Africa, and others from Persia. In the Moslem world, where they were preserved, they were not considered polite literature but circulated in the market places or the coffee houses. The first translation of the stories into French, in 1704, was made by Antoine Galland from a manuscript that came from Syria but was written in Egypt. However confused their source, the "thousand and one tales" have been spellbinding young readers ever since. Today, perhaps because of rival media of entertainment, they are not so much read. Their interminable length is undoubtedly the chief obstacle to their popularity, for they contain stories within stories, episodes upon episodes, magic and more magic. Modern adapters of these tales have practiced an economy of incident that was lacking in the original, but even greatly cut versions have a color, dramatic plot construction, and a use of magic that remain weird and enthralling. Perhaps this sample will send some of the children to a collection of the tales for further reading.*

## ALADDIN AND THE WONDERFUL LAMP

*This version of "Aladdin and the Wonderful Lamp," by Andrew Lang, is based on his translation from the French of Galland. Until fairly recently, scholars had cause to believe that the story of Aladdin was not part of the original* Arabian Nights *but rather had been added by Galland himself from other sources. For the full flavor and spread of the* Arabian Nights, *the adult will do well to turn to the masterful translation from the Arabic by Sir Richard Francis Burton (1821–1890), which is now a literary classic in its own right. It has been published in a three-volume edition (1965) that includes Burton's fascinating scholarly notes.*

There once lived a poor tailor who had a son called Aladdin, a careless, idle boy who would do nothing but play all day long in the streets with little idle boys like himself. This so grieved the father that he died; yet, in spite of his mother's tears and prayers, Aladdin did not mend his ways. One day, when he was playing in the streets as usual, a stranger asked him his age, and if he was not the son of Mustapha the tailor.

"Aladdin and the Wonderful Lamp." From *The Blue Fairy Book,* edited by Andrew Lang. Longmans, Green, and Co., London, 1889

"I am, sir," replied Aladdin; "but he died a long while ago."

On this the stranger, who was a famous African magician, fell on his neck and kissed him, saying: "I am your uncle, and knew you from your likeness to my brother. Go to your mother and tell her I am coming." Aladdin ran home and told his mother of his newly found uncle.

"Indeed, child," she said, "your father had a brother, but I always thought he was dead."

However, she prepared supper, and bade Aladdin seek his uncle, who came laden with wine and fruit. He presently fell down and kissed the place where Mustapha used to sit, bidding Aladdin's mother not to be surprised at not having seen him before, as he had been forty years out of the country. He then turned to Aladdin and asked him his trade, at which the boy hung his head, while his mother burst into tears. On learning that Aladdin was idle and would learn no trade, he offered to take a shop for him and stock it with merchandise. Next day he bought Aladdin a fine suit of clothes and took him all over the city, showing him the sights, and brought him home at nightfall to his mother, who was overjoyed to see her son so fine.

Next day the magician led Aladdin into some beautiful gardens a long way outside the city gates. They sat down by a fountain and the magician pulled a cake from his girdle, which he divided between them. They then journeyed onwards till they almost reached the mountains. Aladdin was so tired that he begged to go back, but the magician beguiled him with pleasant stories and led him on in spite of himself. At last they came to two mountains divided by a narrow valley.

"We will go no farther," said the false uncle. "I will show you something wonderful; only do you gather up sticks while I kindle a fire."

When it was lit the magician threw on it a powder he had about him, at the same time saying some magical words. The earth trembled a little and opened in front of them, disclosing a square flat stone with a brass ring in the middle to raise it by. Aladdin tried to run away, but the magician caught him and gave him a blow that knocked him down.

"What have I done, uncle?" he said piteously; whereupon the magician said more kindly:

"Fear nothing, but obey me. Beneath this stone lies a treasure which is to be yours, and no one else may touch it, so you must do exactly as I tell you."

At the word *treasure* Aladdin forgot his fears, and grasped the ring as he was told, saying the names of his father and grandfather. The stone came up quite easily, and some steps appeared.

"Go down," said the magician; "at the foot of those steps you will find an open door leading into three large halls. Tuck up your gown and go through them without touching anything, or you will die instantly. These halls lead into a garden of fine fruit trees. Walk on till you come to a niche in a terrace where stands a lighted lamp. Pour out the oil it contains, and bring it to me." He drew a ring from his finger and gave it to Aladdin, bidding him prosper.

Aladdin found everything as the magician had said, gathered some fruit off the trees and, having got the lamp, arrived at the mouth of the cave. The magician cried out in a great hurry: "Make haste and give me the lamp." This Aladdin refused to do until he was out of the cave. The magician flew into a terrible passion, and throwing some more powder on to the fire, he said something, and the stone rolled back into its place.

The magician left Persia for ever, which plainly showed that he was no uncle of Aladdin's, but a cunning magician, who had read in his magic books of a wonderful lamp, which would make him the most powerful man in the world. Though he alone knew where to find it, he could only receive it from the hand of another. He had picked out the foolish Aladdin for this purpose, intending to get the lamp and kill him afterwards.

For two days Aladdin remained in the dark, crying and lamenting. At last he clasped his hands in prayer, and in so doing rubbed the ring, which the magician had forgotten to take from him. Immediately an enormous and frightful genie rose out of the earth, saying: "What wouldst thou with me? I am the Slave of the Ring, and will obey thee in all things."

Aladdin fearlessly replied: "Deliver me from this place!" whereupon the earth opened, and he found himself outside.

As soon as his eyes could bear the light he went home, but fainted on the threshold. When he came to himself he told his mother what had passed, and showed her the lamp and the fruits he had gathered in the garden, which were in reality precious stones. He then asked for some food.

"Alas! child," she said, "I have nothing in the house, but I have spun a little cotton and will go and sell it."

Aladdin bade her keep her cotton, for he would sell the lamp instead. As it was very dirty she began to rub it, that it might fetch a higher price. Instantly a hideous genie appeared, and asked what she would have. She fainted away, but Aladdin, snatching the lamp, said boldly: "Fetch me something to eat!" The genie returned with a silver bowl, twelve silver plates containing rich meats, two silver cups, and two bottles of wine.

Aladdin's mother, when she came to herself, said: "Whence comes this splendid feast?"

"Ask not, but eat," replied Aladdin. So they sat at breakfast till it was dinner-time, and Aladdin told his mother about the lamp. She begged him to sell it, and have nothing to do with devils.

"No," said Aladdin, "since chance hath made us aware of its virtues, we will use it, and the ring likewise, which I shall always wear on my finger."

When they had eaten all the genie had

brought, Aladdin sold one of the silver plates, and so on until none were left. He then had recourse to the genie, who gave him another set of plates, and thus they lived for many years.

One day Aladdin heard that an order from the Sultan proclaimed that everyone was to stay at home and close his shutters while the Princess, his daughter, went to and from the bath. Aladdin was seized by a desire to see her face, which was very difficult, as she always went veiled. He hid himself behind the door of the bath, and peeped through a chink. The Princess lifted her veil as she went in, and looked so beautiful that Aladdin fell in love with her at first sight. He went home so changed that his mother was frightened. He told her he loved the Princess so deeply that he could not live without her and meant to ask her in marriage of her father.

His mother, on hearing this, burst out laughing, but Aladdin at last prevailed upon her to go before the Sultan and carry his request. She fetched a napkin and laid in it the magic fruits from the enchanted garden, which sparkled and shone like the most beautiful jewels. She took these with her to please the Sultan, and set out, trusting in the lamp. The Grand Vizier and the lords of council had just gone in as she entered the hall and placed herself in front of the Sultan. He, however, took no notice of her. She went every day for a week, and stood in the same place.

When the council broke up on the sixth day the Sultan said to his Vizier: "I see a certain woman in the audience-chamber every day carrying something in a napkin. Call her next time, that I may find out what she wants."

Next day, at a sign from the Vizier, she went up to the foot of the throne and remained kneeling till the Sultan said to her: "Rise, good woman, and tell me what you want." She hesitated, so the Sultan sent away all but the Vizier, and bade her speak freely, promising to forgive her beforehand for anything she might say. She then told him of her son's violent love for the Princess.

"I prayed him to forget her," she said, "but in vain; he threatened to do some desperate deed if I refused to go and ask your Majesty for the hand of the Princess. Now I pray you to forgive not me alone, but my son Aladdin."

The Sultan asked her kindly what she had in the napkin, whereupon she unfolded the jewels and presented them. He was thunderstruck, and turning to the Vizier said: "What sayest thou? Ought I not to bestow the Princess on one who values her at such a price?"

The Vizier, who wanted her for his own son, begged the Sultan to withhold her for three months, in the course of which he hoped his son would contrive to make him a richer present. The Sultan granted this, and told Aladdin's mother that, though he consented to the marriage, she must not appear before him again for three months.

Aladdin waited patiently for nearly three months, but after two had elapsed his mother, going into the city to buy oil, found every one rejoicing, and asked what was going on.

"Do you not know," was the answer, "that the son of the Grand Vizier is to marry the Sultan's daughter to-night?"

Breathless, she ran and told Aladdin, who was overwhelmed at first, but presently bethought him of the lamp. He rubbed it, and the genie appeared, saying: "What is thy will?"

Aladdin replied: "The Sultan, as thou knowest, has broken his promise to me, and the Vizier's son is to have the Princess. My command is that to-night you bring hither the bride and bridegroom."

"Master, I obey," said the genie.

Aladdin then went to his chamber, where, sure enough, at midnight the genie transported the bed containing the Vizier's son and the Princess. "Take this new-married man," he said, "and put him outside in the cold, and return at daybreak." Whereupon the genie took the Vizier's son out of bed, leaving Aladdin with the Princess.

"Fear nothing," Aladdin said to her; "you are my wife, promised to me by your unjust father, and no harm shall come to you."

The Princess was too frightened to speak, and passed the most miserable night of her life, while Aladdin lay down beside her and slept soundly. At the appointed hour the genie fetched in the shivering bridegroom, laid him in his place, and transported the bed back to the palace.

Presently the Sultan came to wish his daughter good-morning. The unhappy Vizier's son jumped up and hid himself, while the Princess would not say a word, and was very sorrowful.

The Sultan sent her mother to her, who said: "How comes it, child, that you will not speak to your father? What has happened?"

The Princess sighed deeply, and at last told her mother how, during the night, the bed had been carried into some strange house, and what had passed there. Her mother did not believe her in the least, but bade her rise and consider it an idle dream.

The following night exactly the same thing happened, and next morning, on the Princess's refusing to speak, the Sultan threatened to cut off her head. She then confessed all, bidding him ask the Vizier's son if it were not so. The Sultan told the Vizier to ask his son, who owned the truth, adding that, dearly as he loved the Princess, he had rather die than go through another such fearful night, and wished to be separated from her. His wish was granted, and there was an end of feasting and rejoicing.

When the three months were over, Aladdin sent his mother to remind the Sultan of his promise. She stood in the same place as before, and the Sultan, who had forgotten Aladdin, at once remembered him and sent for her. On seeing her poverty the Sultan felt less inclined than ever to keep his word, and asked his Vizier's advice, who counselled him to set so high a value on the Princess that no man living could come up to it.

The Sultan then turned to Aladdin's mother, saying: "Good woman, a sultan must remember his promises, and I will remember mine, but your son must first send me forty basins of gold brimful of jewels, carried by forty black slaves, led by as many white ones, splendidly dressed. Tell him that I await his answer."

The mother of Aladdin bowed low and went home, thinking all was lost. She gave Aladdin the message, adding: "He may wait long enough for your answer!"

"Not so long, mother, as you think," her son replied. "I would do a great deal more than that for the Princess."

He summoned the genie, and in a few moments the eighty slaves arrived, and filled up the small house and garden. Aladdin made them set out to the palace, two and two, followed by his

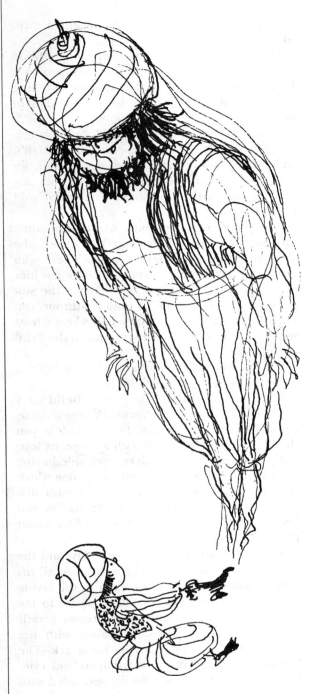

mother. They were so richly dressed, with such splendid jewels in their girdles, that everyone crowded to see them and the basins of gold they carried on their heads. They entered the palace, and, after kneeling before the Sultan, stood in a half-circle round the throne with their arms crossed, while Aladdin's mother presented them to the Sultan.

He hesitated no longer, but said: "Good woman, return and tell your son that I wait for him with open arms." She lost no time in telling Aladdin, bidding him make haste. But Aladdin first called the genie.

"I want a scented bath," he said, "a richly embroidered habit, a horse surpassing the Sultan's, and twenty slaves to attend me. Besides this, six slaves, beautifully dressed, to wait on my mother; and lastly, ten thousand pieces of gold in ten purses."

No sooner said than done. Aladdin mounted his horse and passed through the streets, the slaves strewing gold as they went. Those who had played with him in his childhood knew him not, he had grown so handsome. When the Sultan saw him, he came down from his throne, embraced him, and led him into a hall where a feast was spread, intending to marry him to the Princess that very day.

But Aladdin refused, saying, "I must build a palace fit for her," and took his leave.

Once home, he said to the genie: "Build me a palace of the finest marble, set with jasper, agate, and other precious stones. In the middle you shall build me a large hall with a dome, its four walls of massy gold and silver, each side having six windows, whose lattices, all except one which is to be left unfinished, must be set with diamonds and rubies. There must be stables and horses and grooms and slaves; go and see about it!"

The palace was finished by next day, and the genie carried him there and showed him all his orders faithfully carried out, even to the laying of a velvet carpet from Aladdin's palace to the Sultan's. Aladdin's mother then dressed herself carefully, and walked to the palace with her slaves, while he followed her on horseback. The Sultan sent musicians with trumpets and cymbals to meet them, so that the air resounded with music and cheers. She was taken to the Princess, who saluted her and treated her with great honour.

At night the Princess said good-bye to her father, and set out on the carpet for Aladdin's palace, with his mother at her side, and followed by the hundred slaves. She was charmed at the sight

of Aladdin, who ran to receive her.

"Princess," he said, "blame your beauty for my boldness if I have displeased you."

She told him that, having seen him, she willingly obeyed her father in this matter. After the wedding had taken place Aladdin led her into the hall, where a feast was spread, and she supped with him, after which they danced till midnight.

Next day Aladdin invited the Sultan to see the palace. On entering the hall with the four-and-twenty windows, with their rubies, diamonds, and emeralds, he cried: "It is a world's wonder! There is only one thing that surprises me. Was it by accident that one window was left unfinished?"

"No, sir, by design," returned Aladdin. "I wished your Majesty to have the glory of finishing this palace."

The Sultan was pleased, and sent for the best jewellers in the city. He showed them the unfinished window, and bade them fit it up like the others.

"Sir," replied their spokesman, "we cannot find jewels enough."

The Sultan had his own fetched, which they soon used, but to no purpose, for in a month's time the work was not half done. Aladdin, knowing that their task was vain, bade them undo their work and carry the jewels back, and the genie finished the window at his command. The Sultan was surprised to receive his jewels again, and visited Aladdin, who showed him the window finished. The Sultan embraced him, the envious Vizier meanwhile hinting that it was the work of enchantment.

Aladdin had won the hearts of the people by his gentle bearing. He was made captain of the Sultan's armies, and won several battles for him, but remained modest and courteous as before, and lived thus in peace and content for several years.

But far away in Africa the magician remembered Aladdin, and by his magic arts discovered that Aladdin, instead of perishing miserably in the cave, had escaped, and had married a princess, with whom he was living in great honour and wealth. He knew that the poor tailor's son could only have accomplished this by means of the lamp, and travelled night and day till he reached the capital of China, bent on Aladdin's ruin. As he passed through the town he heard people talking everywhere about a marvellous palace.

"Forgive my ignorance," he asked, "what is this palace you speak of?"

"Have you not heard of Prince Aladdin's palace," was the reply, "the greatest wonder of the world? I will direct you if you have a mind to see it."

The magician thanked him who spoke, and having seen the palace knew that it had been raised by the Genie of the Lamp, and became half mad with rage. He determined to get hold of the lamp, and again plunge Aladdin into the deepest poverty.

Unluckily, Aladdin had gone a-hunting for eight days, which gave the magician plenty of time. He bought a dozen copper lamps, put them into a basket, and went to the palace, crying: "New lamps for old!" followed by a jeering crowd. The Princess, sitting in the hall of four-and-twenty windows, sent a slave to find out what the noise was about, who came back laughing, so that the Princess scolded her.

"Madam," replied the slave, "who can help laughing to see an old fool offering to exchange fine new lamps for old ones?"

Another slave, hearing this, said: "There is an old one on the cornice there which he can have."

Now this was the magic lamp, which Aladdin had left there, as he could not take it out hunting with him. The Princess, not knowing its value, laughingly bade the slave take it and make the exchange.

She went and said to the magician: "Give me a new lamp for this."

He snatched it and, amid the jeers of the crowd, bade the slave take her choice. Little he cared, but left off crying his lamps, and went out of the city gates to a lonely place, where he remained till nightfall, when he pulled out the lamp and rubbed it. The genie appeared, and at the magician's command carried him, together with the palace and the Princess in it, to a lonely place in Africa.

Next morning the Sultan looked out of the window towards Aladdin's palace and rubbed his eyes, for it was gone. He sent for the Vizier

and asked what had become of the palace. The Vizier looked out too, and was lost in astonishment. He again put it down to enchantment, and this time the Sultan believed him, and sent thirty men on horseback to fetch Aladdin in chains. They met him riding home, bound him, and forced him to go with them on foot. The people, however, who loved him, followed, armed, to see that he came to no harm. He was carried before the Sultan, who ordered the executioner to cut off his head. The executioner made Aladdin kneel down, bandaged his eyes, and raised his scimitar to strike.

At that instant the Vizier, who saw that the crowd had forced their way into the courtyard and were scaling the walls to rescue Aladdin, called to the executioner to stay his hand. The people, indeed, looked so threatening that the Sultan gave way and ordered Aladdin to be unbound, and pardoned him in the sight of the crowd. Aladdin now begged to know what he had done.

"False wretch!" said the Sultan, "come hither," and showed him from the window the place where his palace had stood. Aladdin was so amazed that he could not say a word. "Where is my palace and my daughter?" demanded the Sultan. "For the first I am not so deeply concerned, but my daughter I must have, and you must find her or lose your head."

Aladdin begged for forty days in which to find her, promising if he failed, to return and suffer death at the Sultan's pleasure. His prayer was granted, and he went forth sadly from the Sultan's presence. For three days he wandered about like a madman, asking everyone what had become of his palace, but they only laughed and pitied him. He came to the banks of a river, and knelt down to say his prayers before throwing himself in. In so doing he rubbed the magic ring he still wore. The genie he had seen in the cave appeared, and asked his will.

"Save my life, genie," said Aladdin, "and bring my palace back."

"That is not in my power," said the genie; "I am only the Slave of the Ring; you must ask him of the lamp."

"Even so," said Aladdin, "but thou canst take me to the palace, and set me down under my dear wife's window." He at once found himself in Africa, under the window of the Princess, and fell asleep out of sheer weariness.

He was awakened by the singing of the birds, and his heart was lighter. He saw plainly that all his misfortunes were owing to the loss of the lamp, and vainly wondered who had robbed him of it.

That morning the Princess rose earlier than she had done since she had been carried into Africa by the magician, whose company she was forced to endure once a day. She, however, treated him so harshly that he dared not live there altogether. As she was dressing, one of her women looked out and saw Aladdin. The Princess ran and opened the window, and at the noise she made, Aladdin looked up. She called to him to come to her, and great was the joy of these lovers at seeing each other again.

After he had kissed her, Aladdin said: "I beg of you, Princess, in God's name, before we speak of anything else, for your own sake and mine, tell me what has become of an old lamp I left on the cornice in the hall of four-and-twenty windows, when I went a-hunting."

"Alas!" she said, "I am the innocent cause of our sorrows," and told him of the exchange of the lamp.

"Now I know," cried Aladdin, "that we have to thank the African magician for this! Where is the lamp?"

"He carries it about with him," said the Princess. "I know, for he pulled it out of his breast to show me. He wishes me to break my faith with you and marry him, saying that you were beheaded by my father's command. He is for ever speaking ill of you, but I only reply by my tears. If I persist, I doubt not but he will use violence."

Aladdin comforted her, and left her for a while. He changed clothes with the first person he met in the town, and having bought a certain powder returned to the Princess, who let him in by a little side door.

"Put on your most beautiful dress," he said to her, "and receive the magician with smiles, leading him to believe that you have forgotten me. Invite him to sup with you, and say you wish to taste the wine of his country. He will go for some and while he is gone I will tell you what to do."

She listened carefully to Aladdin and when he left her, arrayed herself gaily for the first time since she left China. She put on a girdle and head-dress of diamonds, and, seeing in a glass that she was more beautiful than ever, received the magician, saying, to his great amazement: "I have made up my mind that Aladdin is dead, and that all my tears will not bring him back to me, so I am resolved to mourn no more, and have therefore invited you to sup with me; but I am tired of the wines of China, and would fain taste those of Africa."

The magician flew to his cellar, and the Princess put the powder Aladdin had given her in her cup. When he returned she asked him to drink her health in the wine of Africa, handing him her cup in exchange for his, as a sign she was reconciled to him. Before drinking the magician made her a speech in praise of her beauty, but the Princess cut him short, saying: "Let us drink first, and you shall say what you will afterwards." She set her cup to her lips and kept it there, while the magician drained his to the dregs and fell back lifeless. The Princess then opened the door to Aladdin, and flung her arms round his neck; but Aladdin put her away, bidding her leave him, as he had more to do. He then went to the dead magician, took the lamp out of his vest, and bade the genie carry the palace and all in it back to China. This was done, and the Princess in her chamber only felt two little shocks, and little thought she was at home again.

The Sultan, who was sitting in his closet, mourning for his lost daughter, happened to look up, and rubbed his eyes, for there stood the palace as before! He hastened thither, and Aladdin received him in the hall of the four-and-twenty windows, with the Princess at his side. Aladdin told him what had happened, and showed him the dead body of the magician, that he might believe. A ten days' feast was proclaimed, and it seemed as if Aladdin might now live the rest of his life in peace; but it was not to be.

The African magician had a younger brother, who was, if possible, more wicked and more cunning than himself. He travelled to China to avenge his brother's death, and went to visit a pious woman called Fatima, thinking she might be of use to him. He entered her cell and clapped a dagger to her breast, telling her to rise and do his bidding on pain of death. He changed clothes with her, coloured his face like hers, put on her veil, and murdered her, that she might tell no tales. Then he went towards the palace of Aladdin, and all the people, thinking he was the holy woman, gathered round him, kissing his hands and begging his blessing. When he got to the palace there was such a noise going on round him that the Princess bade her slave look out of the window and ask what was the matter. The slave said it was the holy woman, curing people by her touch of their ailments, whereupon the Princess, who had long desired to see Fatima, sent for her. On coming to the Princess, the magician offered up a prayer for her health and prosperity. When he had done, the Princess made him sit by her, and begged him to stay with her always. The false Fatima, who wished for nothing better, consented, but kept his veil down for fear of discovery. The Princess showed him the hall, and asked him what he thought of it.

"It is truly beautiful," said the false Fatima. "In my mind it wants but one thing."

"And what is that?" said the Princess.

"If only a roc's egg," replied he, "were hung up from the middle of this dome, it would be the wonder of the world."

After this the Princess could think of nothing but the roc's egg, and when Aladdin returned from hunting he found her in a very ill humour. He begged to know what was amiss, and she told him that all her pleasure in the hall was spoilt for the want of a roc's egg hanging from the dome.

"If that is all," replied Aladdin, "you shall soon be happy." He left her and rubbed the lamp, and when the genie appeared commanded him to bring a roc's egg. The genie gave such a loud and terrible shriek that the hall shook.

"Wretch!" he cried, "is it not enough that I have done everything for you, but you must command me to bring my master and hang him up in the midst of this dome? You and your wife and your palace deserve to be burnt to ashes, but that this request does not come from you, but from the brother of the African magician, whom you destroyed. He is now in your palace disguised as the holy woman—whom he murdered. He it was who put that wish into your wife's head. Take care of yourself, for he means to kill you." So saying, the genie disappeared.

Aladdin went back to the Princess, saying his head ached, and requesting that the holy Fatima should be fetched to lay her hands on it. But when the magician came near, Aladdin, seizing his dagger, pierced him to the heart.

"What have you done?" cried the Princess. "You have killed the holy woman!"

"Not so," replied Aladdin, "but a wicked magician," and told her of how she had been deceived.

After this Aladdin and his wife lived in peace. He succeeded the Sultan when he died, and reigned for many years, leaving behind him a long line of kings.

# *Africa*

*Until as late as 1900 much of the African continent was still a mystery; since 1950 more than two dozen new independent African states have been established! This unique chapter in history has been reflected in the growing number of books of African tales. What has until recently been but a trickle promises to become a great stream of narrative, much of it printed in this country for a special audience of children. It must be emphasized, however, that in Africa, the content of the oral narrative represents not only a survival of earlier customs and thought but also the contemporary and vital expression of long-established communities and tribes. African storytellers are fond of using songs within the prose narration and of having a kind of chanted interchange of phrase and song with their listeners. Moralistic endings are a well-integrated feature of many of the tales. "Why" stories are frequent. We may also note a strong sense of ethics and a very sophisticated predilection for realism, sometimes bordering on the humorously cynical. Whether the tales are from the Pygmies of the Congo basin, the Bushmen of the Kalahari Desert, or the Guragé tribes of Ethiopia, they share these qualities. The stories here will help to some extent to make children aware of the variety, depth, and uniqueness of the Africans' life and thought, bringing into sharper focus the common humanity we all share, as well as their distinctive views.*

## ALLAH WILL PROVIDE

### (North African)

*It is possible even today to hear stories, maybe this very one, told by wandering storytellers in the Moslem countries of North Africa. "Allah Will Provide" poses a metaphysical question which it slyly does and does not answer! Bou Azza's conclusions and actions certainly seem foolish, but would he have received his good fortune had he behaved differently? This is good fun to dramatize with puppets or live actors.*

Bou Azza was an honest woodcutter who worked hard each day cutting down trees which he sold in the market place of a small North African village. His efforts were not highly rewarded, however, for he earned barely enough money to keep his young wife and himself in food and clothing.

Because he was getting old in body, Bou Azza wondered with each passing day how much

longer he would be able to work and who would take care of him and his wife when he was too old to do so.

One afternoon as the hot sun beat down on him, Bou Azza gathered together the logs he had cut that morning, fastened them with a piece of rope, and slung them over his shoulder. Then he set out down the hill toward his tiny house on the outskirts of the village.

Before reaching his home, Bou was forced to stop and rest beneath an olive tree near the road. As he wiped the perspiration from his forehead he suddenly noticed a horned viper curled up on the ground a few feet away from him. At first the old woodcutter was very frightened for he knew that a bite from this reptile would surely kill him. Carefully he climbed up to a high branch of the olive tree. But after watching the snake for a few seconds, Bou Azza realized that he had nothing to fear. The snake had other interests.

On one of the lower branches of the tree, not far from where Bou Azza was sitting, there was a small bird. The snake was staring at the bird with his beady black eyes, swaying its long, slender body back and forth, and occasionally spitting out its evil-looking, forked tongue.

At first the bird did not notice the snake, but

when she did, her small feathery body was seized with helpless terror. Gripping the fragile little twig on which she rested, she tried to move her wings, but they were frozen with fear. She also tried to sound an alarm, but her beak opened and shut without a sound coming out.

As the snake swayed back and forth, Bou Azza realized that the bird had been hypnotized by the viper's movements, and he watched the two animals with weird fascination.

As Bou Azza looked down, the viper held the bird in its merciless stare, swaying from side to side like the pendulum of a clock, while the helpless victim became more and more paralyzed. Then suddenly the little bird fell from the branch and landed just a few inches from the snake. As Bou Azza watched, the snake ate its prey whole—feathers and all. Then, satisfied, it crawled away looking for new victims.

Bou Azza, rested from his journey, but sickened by what he had just witnessed, headed for home with his wood on his back, and an idea in his head.

As Bou Azza walked home in the twilight, he thought more and more about his idea. After a time he said to himself, "I am a fool! The serpent finds much food without really working for it, thanks to Allah. Whereas I, a man, must work very hard in the hottest part of the day to earn just a mouthful of food. Allah alone is good, and with His help I will be like the serpent. No longer will I work so hard to get food when the serpent gets it for nothing. So shall it be."

And continuing on his way home, Bou Azza wore an expression of contentment over the new way of life that the serpent had revealed to him.

On the following morn, instead of rising before the sun made its way into the sky, Bou Azza stayed in bed until noon. Then he took his grass mat to the rear of the house where he sat under a fig tree.

His wife became worried at his strange behavior, and when she saw that he obviously had no plans to work for the day she went to him and said, "Bou Azza! What is wrong with you today? Are you not going to cut wood to sell in the market?"

"No, wife," said Bou Azza as he stretched in the sun. "I will not leave my mat even if I die of hunger. Yesterday I saw a serpent finding his food without working, and I have decided that if Allah feeds the serpents he will provide me with my bread."

His anxious wife had no idea what her husband was talking about and thought he had gone mad.

"Please get up," she cried, and she tugged at his clothing. But nothing she said or did made any difference, and when twilight came to Bou Azza's home, he was still resting on his mat.

The poor woman was sick with worry for she had always counted on her husband for food and money. But when she realized that he would not change his mind, she hurried to the woods while there was still light to see and looked for mushrooms to sell at the market in the village.

She looked for hours, scraping away leaves, digging under fallen logs, searching everywhere. Suddenly, as she dug into some soft earth her knife hit something hard buried beneath the surface of the ground. Rapidly she dug the dirt away and uncovered a metal cooking pot with a

lid. After working for some time she pried the lid off and discovered that the pot was filled with shimmering gold pieces.

The animals of the forest drew close to watch her struggle helplessly with the giant pot as she shouted with excitement. But it was too heavy for her to lift. She ran as fast as she could to the house crying with happiness. "Oh, Bou Azza," she shouted. "I have found a whole pot of gold. Come with me. Help me bring it to the house."

Actually Bou Azza was impressed with the thought of the gold. But he had made a promise to himself not to move, and now he could not lift his finger.

"Oh, wife," he said, without opening his eyes. "If Allah saw fit to let you find such a treasure surely he will give you the strength to carry it home. Personally I have decided not to move an inch!"

This reply made his wife furious. And she ran to the house of her brothers to see if they would help her carry the pot home. Naturally her brothers were delighted with the prospect of sharing so much gold, and they ran with Bou Azza's wife to the forest and helped her carry it home.

When she and her brothers reached her house, with the giant pot spilling over with gold, she felt sure that her husband would get off his mat and help her count their fortune.

"Get up, you lazy lout!" she shouted, as she stood over her husband who slept peacefully on his straw bed. "I hope you have enough energy to come and count your riches."

"Did I not tell you?" he said sleepily. "I am not going to lift a finger until Allah drops fortunes on my head just as he showered gifts on the serpent."

"Just as you like," the angry wife said, as she filled her skirt with hundreds of heavy gold pieces and poured them over her husband's head.

"Praise be to Allah!" her husband shouted as the gold pieces fell around him. "Praise be to the one and only Allah! Do you not now see, my wife, that serpents and men are all his creatures and he does provide for all of us?"

His wife did not understand, but she did know that for the rest of their lives she and her hus-

band would live in luxury and that Bou Azza would never have to work again.

And every time someone came to visit them, Bou Azza told them this story, ending each time with the words, "Why work? Allah will provide."

And although his listeners felt that he was wrong, no one could contradict him.

## THE FIRE ON THE MOUNTAIN

### (Ethiopian)

*The history and character of the Ethiopians are unique, and this fact is reflected in their tales. Like the ancient Egyptians, the Ethiopians were originally Hamites, people who invaded Africa from Asia. Known from Biblical times as Abyssinia, Ethiopia is one of the oldest Christian countries in Africa, but her people include Caucasians, Negroes, and Asians of varying languages and religions. "The Fire on the Mountain" is a magnificent ethical tale which avoids all preaching in favor of vividly dramatizing its point. Read Harold Courlander's introduction and notes in the excellent collection from which this story is taken.*

People say that in the old days in the city of Addis Ababa there was a young man by the name of Arha. He had come as a boy from the country of Guragé, and in the city he became the servant of a rich merchant, Haptom Hasei.

Haptom Hasei was so rich that he owned everything that money could buy, and often he was very bored because he had tired of everything he knew, and there was nothing new for him to do.

One cold night, when the damp wind was blowing across the plateau, Haptom called to Arha to bring wood for the fire. When Arha was finished, Haptom began to talk.

"How much cold can a man stand?" he said, speaking at first to himself. "I wonder if it would be possible for a man to stand on the highest peak, Mount Sululta, where the coldest winds blow, through an entire night without blankets or clothing and yet not die?"

"I don't know," Arha said. "But wouldn't it be a foolish thing?"

"Perhaps, if he had nothing to gain by it, it would be a foolish thing to spend the night that way," Haptom said. "But I would be willing to bet that a man couldn't do it."

"I am sure a courageous man could stand naked on Mount Sululta throughout an entire night and not die of it," Arha said. "But as for me, it isn't my affair since I've nothing to bet."

"Well, I'll tell you what," Haptom said. "Since you are so sure it can be done, I'll make a bet with you anyway. If you can stand among the rocks on Mount Sululta for an entire night without food or water, or clothing or blankets or fire, and not die of it, then I will give you ten acres of good farmland for your own, with a house and cattle."

Arha could hardly believe what he had heard. "Do you really mean this?" he asked.

"I am a man of my word," Haptom replied.

"Then tomorrow night I will do it," Arha said, "and afterwards, for all the years to come, I shall till my own soil."

But he was very worried, because the wind swept bitterly across that peak. So in the morning Arha went to a wise old man from the Guragé tribe and told him of the bet he had made. The old man listened quietly and thoughtfully, and when Arha had finished he said:

"I will help you. Across the valley from Sululta is a high rock which can be seen in the daytime. Tomorrow night, as the sun goes down, I shall build a fire there, so that it can be seen from where you stand on the peak. All night long you must watch the light of my fire. Do not close your eyes or let the darkness creep upon you. As you watch my fire, think of its warmth, and think of me, your friend, sitting there tending it for you. If you do this you will survive, no matter how bitter the night wind."

Arha thanked the old man warmly and went back to Haptom's house with a light heart. He told Haptom he was ready, and in the afternoon Haptom sent him, under the watchful eyes of other servants, to the top of Mount Sululta. There, as night fell, Arha removed his clothes and stood in the damp cold wind that swept

across the plateau with the setting sun. Across the valley, several miles away, Arha saw the light of his friend's fire, which shone like a star in the blackness.

The wind turned colder and seemed to pass through his flesh and chill the marrow in his bones. The rock on which he stood felt like ice. Each hour the cold numbed him more, until he thought he would never be warm again, but he kept his eyes upon the twinkling light across the valley, and remembered that his old friend sat there tending a fire for him. Sometimes wisps of fog blotted out the light, and then he strained to see until the fog passed. He sneezed and coughed and shivered, and began to feel ill. Yet all night through he stood there, and only when the dawn came did he put on his clothes and go down the mountain back to Addis Ababa.

Haptom was very surprised to see Arha, and he questioned his servants thoroughly.

"Did he stay all night without food or drink or blankets or clothing?"

"Yes," his servants said. "He did all of these things."

"Well, you are a strong fellow," Haptom said to Arha. "How did you manage to do it?"

"I simply watched the light of a fire on a distant hill," Arha said.

"What! You watched a fire? Then you lose the bet, and you are still my servant, and you own no land!"

"But this fire was not close enough to warm me, it was far across the valley!"

"I won't give you the land," Haptom said. "You didn't fulfill the conditions. It was only the fire that saved you."

Arha was very sad. He went again to his old friend of the Guragé tribe and told him what had happened.

"Take the matter to the judge," the old man advised him.

Arha went to the judge and complained, and the judge sent for Haptom. When Haptom told his story, and the servants said once more that Arha had watched a distant fire across the valley, the judge said:

"No, you have lost, for Haptom Hasei's condition was that you must be without fire."

Once more Arha went to his old friend with the sad news that he was doomed to the life of a servant, as though he had not gone through the ordeal on the mountaintop.

"Don't give up hope," the old man said. "More wisdom grows wild in the hills than in any city judge."

He got up from where he sat and went to find a man named Hailu, in whose house he had been a servant when he was young. He explained to the good man about the bet between Haptom and Arha, and asked if something couldn't be done.

"Don't worry about it," Hailu said after thinking for a while. "I will take care of it for you."

Some days later Hailu sent invitations to many people in the city to come to a feast at his house. Haptom was among them, and so was the judge who had ruled Arha had lost the bet.

When the day of the feast arrived, the guests came riding on mules with fine trappings, their servants strung out behind them on foot. Haptom came with twenty servants, one of whom held a silk umbrella over his head to shade him from the sun, and four drummers played music that signified the great Haptom was here.

The guests sat on soft rugs laid out for them and talked. From the kitchen came the odors of wonderful things to eat: roast goat, roast corn and durra, pancakes called injera, and many tantalizing sauces. The smell of the food only accentuated the hunger of the guests. Time passed. The food should have been served, but they didn't see it, only smelled vapors that drifted from the kitchen. The evening came, and still no food was served. The guests began to whisper among themselves. It was very curious that the honorable Hailu had not had the food brought out. Still the smells came from the kitchen. At last one of the guests spoke out for all the others:

"Hailu, why do you do this to us? Why do you invite us to a feast and then serve us nothing?"

"Why, can't you smell the food?" Hailu asked with surprise.

"Indeed we can, but smelling is not eating, there is no nourishment in it!"

"And is there warmth in a fire so distant that it can hardly be seen?" Hailu asked. "If Arha was warmed by the fire he watched while standing on Mount Sululta, then you have been fed by the smells coming from my kitchen."

The people agreed with him; the judge now saw his mistake, and Haptom was shamed. He thanked Hailu for his advice, and announced that Arha was then and there the owner of the land, the house, and the cattle.

Then Hailu ordered the food brought in, and the feast began.

## SON OF THE LONG ONE

*(East African)*

*Here is one of the typical tales from the many told about the hare (in some places called "Sungura"). It deftly builds suspense and has a surprise ending that is funny and satisfying. The storyteller can have a good time with this, and children may learn a point about being afraid of the unknown or about jumping to conclusions.*

Sungura, the hare, was out in his garden all morning. When he returned to his house under the roots of a big thorn tree, he saw some very strange-looking tracks in the dust of his doorway, long tracks, as if some huge animal had gone in. Sungura was frightened. He had never seen such tracks and was quite convinced that some monster was inside his house. He called out in a shaky voice, "Hodi, who is inside my house?"

A big voice replied, "I am the warrior son of the long one whose anklets became unfastened in a great battle and are dragging behind. I can crush the mighty rhinoceros to earth and the elephant trembles at my voice. Beware of me!"

Sungura was indeed frightened. What sort of monster is in my house? he thought. He shuddered at the thought of any creature whose anklets dragging could make these tracks. He must be huge and much too strong to be chased away by a hare. Sungura decided to get help from some of his friends and started off into the bush. He had gone only a few feet when he met the jackal, Mbweha. "Oh, clever Mbweha," he cried, "Please help me. Some strange, strong animal is in my house and refuses to come out. Perhaps you who are so cunning can get him to go away."

"Well, I'll talk to this mysterious intruder, but I'm not sure he'll listen."

"Son of the Long One." Reprinted from *Jambo, Sungura, Tales from East Africa,* by Eleanor B. Heady. By permission of Grosset & Dunlap, Inc.; Text Copyright © 1965 by Eleanor B. Heady

Sungura and Mbweha approached the door of the house. "See the tracks," said the hare. "Aren't they strange?"

"They are indeed," agreed the jackal. Then he called out, "Hodi, who is in the house of my friend, Sungura?"

Again the big voice answered, "I am the warrior son of the long one whose anklets became unfastened in a great battle and are dragging behind. I can crush the mighty rhinoceros to earth and the elephant trembles at my voice. Beware of me!"

Now Mbweha was as frightened as his friend. "He sounds very ferocious, Sungura. I think we better go away and leave him." So the hare and the jackal trotted into the bush, but Sungura was still determined to get the intruder out of his house.

Next they met a leopard. "Oh, Chui, my friend, I need your help," said Sungura. "Someone very strong is inside my house and refuses to come out."

"Refuses? It's your house, isn't it?"

"Of course, Chui, but he seems to think no one is strong enough to make him leave and now I have no place to sleep tonight. What shall I do?"

"I'll go have a talk with this fellow," said Chui. "Perhaps my reputation for cunning has come to his ears. He will probably go away when I arrive."

The three friends trotted back to the house of the hare and this time, Chui, the leopard, called out, "Who is in the house of my friend, Sungura?"

For a moment there was no answer, then just as before came this reply, "I am the warrior son of the long one whose anklets became unfastened in a great battle and are dragging behind. I can crush the mighty rhinoceros to earth. The elephant trembles at the sound of my voice. Beware of me!"

"What could one as strong as I do against him? He can crush the rhinoceros. I think we better go away and leave him," said Chui. "I have never met such a creature and I have no desire to do so."

"But he has my house," wailed Sungura.

"You'll just have to find another," said Mbweha.

"Of course, you'd be foolish to try to fight with the son of the long one," agreed Chui.

With that the jackal and the leopard ran into the bush, leaving the disappointed hare looking sadly at his house.

Sungura started out again, not quite sure where he was going. Find another house, indeed! That wasn't as easily done as some people seemed to suppose. Then he heard a booming voice above him, "Is that you way down there, Sungura? Thought you usually took a nap in the afternoon. Something wrong?"

Sungura looked up at the huge swaying trunk of Tembo, the elephant. "Something is very wrong, Tembo," he said. "Come with me and I'll show you."

As they walked toward the hare's home, Sungura told the elephant of the intruder and how he refused to leave. "I think I can make him go," said Tembo. "I am the largest animal in the bush. Surely he will be afraid of me."

When they reached the hare's tree Tembo called out, "Hodi, may I come in, you who have taken the house of my friend, Sungura. I am Tembo, king of the bush."

"Ha, ha, ha," laughed the big voice, "Come in indeed! Don't you know that you are much too large to come in? Besides, I am stronger than you. I am the warrior son of the long one whose anklets became unfastened in a great battle and are dragging behind. I can crush the mighty rhinoceros to earth and you, Tembo, should tremble at my voice for I am very mighty."

"I have never heard of such a creature," said Tembo shakily. "Perhaps you will have to let him stay in your house, Sungura. I wouldn't dare try to get him out. He is much too strong for me."

"Well thank you, Tembo," said the hare. "I guess there is no one to help." Sungura hopped sadly off into the bush and sat down on a round stone to think. A huge tear rolled down each cheek. "My lovely home," he sobbed. "How shall I ever find another?"

Just then there was a stirring in the grass and a small rasping voice asked, "What is the trouble? Perhaps I can help."

Sungura looked down into the funny ugly face of Chura, the frog. "Oh, my small friend, you cannot help. Some very strong creature is in my house and will not go away. Mbweha, Chui, and Tembo have all tried to get him to leave, but he refuses. He sounds so terrible. What shall I do?" Sungura began to cry harder.

"There, there, Sungura," croaked the frog. "Don't be so upset. There must be a way to get rid of this house-stealer. He can't be so very large, or he couldn't get into your house."

"True, I didn't think of that," said Sungura.

"Now let's go to your house and I'll see what I can do."

Sungura arose doubtfully and the two friends hopped back to the hole under the tree. The frog looked carefully at the strange tracks and then winked at his friend, calling out in a loud voice, "Who is in the house of my friend, Sungura?"

Once again the intruder replied, "I am the warrior son of the long one whose anklets became unfastened in a great battle. I can crush the mighty rhinoceros to earth and the elephant trembles at the sound of my voice. Beware of me!"

And Chura replied, "I am strong and a leaper. If you don't leave the house of my friend I shall leap upon you and off again before you can harm me. You will not like my leaping."

The voice that came from the hare's house was a much smaller one this time, a voice that sounded frightened. "Please, oh leaper, I am only Nyodu, the caterpillar. I shall come out if you promise not to harm me."

Sungura could hardly believe his eyes when the tiny furry creature crawled slowly out of his house. "And to think all of us were afraid of you —all but Chura, who is very brave."

"Not brave at all," laughed the frog. "I have learned never to believe a thief. If you'll remember that you will save yourself a lot of trouble."

## MEN OF DIFFERENT COLORS

(East African)

*From a collection of stories never before written down, gathered by Eleanor Heady in East Africa, "Men of Different Colors" is a "why" story, one of hundreds that explain how things were in the beginning. It is prefaced by the conjecture of village children of today about the strange appearance of a white man, the first they have ever seen. The importance of the village storyteller is evident in the fact that it is to Mama Semamingi that they go, for in rural Africa it has been the traditional role of the storyteller to be the historian, the preserver of the culture. Here's a tale that explains how the god Mungu first made people from the beautiful black clay, and how, for his own convenience, he made people of other colors.*

There was great excitement in the village. A stranger had stopped that day. He carried large sheets of white paper. On these he drew pictures, mostly pictures of animals, but some of people and villages and even trees. This was strange, but the strangest thing of all was the man himself. He was different, a different color, a very light red, declared Kambo. But Karioki and Gachui said he was nearer white or maybe the color of cream. His hair was different, too. It didn't stay curled neatly to his scalp the way proper hair should do, but stuck up like dry grass straw, straight and spiky. It was nearly the color of straw, too.

At first the children were frightened of the stranger. They ran away and hid. Then, as they watched from their hiding places, they discovered that he was friendly despite his looks. He talked and smiled with the elders, then he gave the children sweets wrapped in paper. The children had eaten these before when the men had come back from trips to the duka, or shop, of Hamed, the Indian.

All day long the talk was of the stranger. Who was he? Where had he come from? Why was he so different?

When evening came and they gathered for their story, the talk was still of the stranger.

"Let's ask Mama Semamingi about him," said Wakai. "She knows everything."

"Yes, yes," agreed the others.

When the grandmother joined the circle, the children were still talking.

"Men of Different Colors" from *When the Stones Were Soft* by Eleanor B. Heady. Copyright © 1968 by Eleanor B. Heady with permission of Funk & Wagnalls Publishing Company, Inc.

She smiled. "So you want to know about the stranger?"

"How did you know, Mama Semamingi?"

"I guessed," she said. "That is all anyone has been talking about today."

"Why is he so different?" asked one of the bigger boys.

"He was made that way, just as you were made as you are," answered the grandmother. "Did you know that people like Hamed, the Indian, are different, too?"

None of the children had been to the shop of Hamed. They had only heard of him. "No, is he red, too?" asked Kambo.

"He's not red, nor white, nor is he black. He is a brown man. My story tells about him, too."

"Tell us, please," said the children.

"Mzuri, good, here it is."

The great god Mungu lived in a white ice palace on the top of the high mountain, Kitingara. He became tired of his sparkling castle. He was lonely. *I must make a friend to live with me and to help with the thunder and lightning,* he thought. So the lonely mountain god set off downhill to look for some clay. He went down the mountain to the green forests below his palace.

In a little open place among the trees, he found a spring of bubbling water that sparkled off down the hillside in a little stream. On either side of this stream there was thick, dark clay, clay of a beautiful shiny blackness.

"Just the thing for my man," said Mungu. He knelt on the soft earth and began to work. For many hours he toiled. When at last he had finished, he arose, clapped his hands, and the still statue of a man opened his eyes, moved his head, and spoke to Mungu saying, "You are the great Mungu."

Mungu replied, "You shall be my helper and live with me in my white palace. I will call you Mutunyeusi, the black man."

For many weeks Mungu and Mutunyeusi, black like the clay from which he was made, lived in the ice palace. The man was cold at the top of the mountain. His clay became frozen so that he felt stiff and useless. He begged Mungu to allow him to go down below to the little streams and green valleys. "If you will

only let me go down to the green forests then I shall really be able to help you. I can care for the lower regions while you, oh master, guard the heavens."

Mungu granted the wish of Mutunyeusi. Down the black man went into the green valleys. He was happy there, hunting and living off wild berries and fruits, but he in his turn became lonely and returned to the top of Kitingara. "Please, oh great Mungu," he said. "Make another man for my companion, so that I shall not be lonely."

"That is easily done and quickly, too," replied Mungu. "Let us go at once to the stream with the black clay and make a friend for you."

They set off for the stream. When they arrived, Mutunyeusi helped his master make not one, but two, more men.

"Three will be less lonely than two," said Mungu. "And perhaps sometimes one of you can visit me on my lonely mountain top."

The great mountain god gazed into the distance, thinking. He was troubled. These three men were just alike. How could he tell them apart? He must devise some way to make them different. He returned to his mountain top, leaving the three men in the forest. There he thought and thought, trying to discover some way to make his men different.

One day when Mungu was out walking, he came upon a little pool of pure white water that stood in a hollow below the great river of ice on Kitingara. When he saw this water, he thought of a plan. He called his three black sons and said to them, "See that pool? I want each of you in turn to wash in it. Something wonderful will happen if you do."

"Very well, master," said Mutunyeusi, the first man. "Let my younger brothers wash before me." He pushed one black brother forward toward the water. In he went, the white liquid covering him completely; when he came out, wonder of wonders! He had lost his black color and was a shining, pinkish white!

"Oh, let *me* try!" cried the next brother, and ran into the shallow pool. Alas, there wasn't much water left and he was barely dampened. His color, when he came out, was a light brown. At last came the turn of Mutunyeusi, but there was so little of the water left in the pool that all he could wet was the palms of his hands and the soles of his feet, which turned a pinkish color.

Mungu was very pleased, "Now I shall always know my children apart," he said. "You, Mutunyeusi, shall remain black and be the father of a family of black children. You shall live in the plains and forests surrounding my mountain. You shall be closest because you were my first son." Then, turning to the one who had bathed first, Mungu said, "You shall be known as Muzungu, the white man, and to you and your children I give all the lands to the north. Go to them and be happy." And to the second brother he said, "You will be the father of the brown people, Muhindi, and to you I give all the lands to the east. May your people prosper there."

Down from the mountain went the brothers, now each so different from the other. They went into the lands their father had given them. That is why to this very day you will find brown people in the eastern lands, white people to the north, and black people around the lonely mountain.

## THE GREAT TUG-OF-WAR

### (Nigerian)

*This tale of a wheeling-dealing rabbit is one to tax the wits. It will surely remind many readers of the cunning ploys of Brer Rabbit, although Zomo is the name given to the ubiquitous and wily hare by the Hausa people of Nigeria. The story is given immediacy by the use of the present tense and by the crisp, colloquial dialogue. It incorporates an incident that is often told as a story in its own right, the episode of the tug-of-war. Hugh Sturton, the compiler of* Zomo, the Rabbit, *says that Zomo is indeed the direct ancestor of Brer Rabbit. Sturton has taken many liberties with the tales of Zomo in order to put them into acceptable and entertaining form. Even though folklorists may object, children will* enjoy the results; they know quite well that Zomo will never turn over a new leaf.

It happens one year that the rains come late and go early so the harvest is poor and food is scarce. Animals who usually reap a hundred baskets of corn find they have only fifty, and animals who usually reap fifty find they have only twenty-five. As for Zomo, who never reaps more than ten, even in the best of seasons, he is left with only five.

"When are you going to fetch the rest of it?" asks his wife when he brings home his five baskets.

"There isn't any more," says Zomo.

"D'you mean to tell me," says his wife, "that this is all we have to eat for the next twelve months?"

"We shall have to manage as best we can," says Zomo.

The corn lasts through most of the dry season but by the time the hot weather comes round, it is nearly finished. First Zomo tries to borrow some more, but the other animals say they have none to lend. Then he tries to borrow money so that he can buy corn in the market, but they remember the last time they lent him money, and so they are sorry but they can't oblige.

When his wife tells him that they have food for only two more days, Zomo reckons that the time has come for him to have a good think. So he goes and sits under the *chediya* tree with his thinking cap on, and in the evening, when his wife calls him in to supper, he tells her that he is going to go and see Giwa the Elephant, who has more corn than he knows what to do with.

Next morning, Zomo puts on his best gown and goes and calls on Giwa. When he reaches the house, he says that he has a message for the master and he is taken into the audience chamber where Giwa is receiving those who come to pay their respects.

"God give you long life," cries Zomo in a loud voice, doing obeisance and looking very respectful.

"Amen, Zomo," says Giwa, who likes to be buttered up.

"I have a message for you," says Zomo. "It is from Dorina the Hippopotamus."

"We don't see much of him since he's taken to living in the river," says Giwa. "Tell me," he goes on, "does he still have that black stallion?"

"That is what the message is about," says Zomo.

"Well, you can tell him from me," says Giwa, "that if he still wants to swap the black for my chestnut, there is nothing doing; but I will buy the black from him any time he likes."

"He is short of corn this year," says Zomo, "and he says that if you can let him have some, he will give you the black in exchange."

"Oho," says Giwa, "so that's how the land lies, is it? Well, how much does he want?"

"He says that he'll let him go for a hundred baskets," says Zomo, "so long as he can keep him until after the festival."

"Whatever does he want to do that for?" asks Giwa.

"He's his favorite mount," says Zomo, "and he likes to ride him in the procession."

"All right," says Giwa, "tell Dorina it's a bargain."

Without more ado, the elephant orders his wife and daughters to measure out a hundred baskets of corn.

"There you are, Zomo," he says when this is done. "If you lead the way, my boys will carry it for you. And tell Dorina," he goes on, "that he can keep the black until the festival, but no longer."

"I'll tell him that," says Zomo. So saying, he takes his leave and sets off with ten young elephants behind him who are each carrying ten baskets of corn.

"All right, put it down here, boys," says Zomo when they reach a place near his house. "You've done your share—I'll get those lazy young hippos to take it the rest of the way."

As soon as the young elephants have gone, Zomo calls to his wife and children and they carry the baskets into his house. When they have finished, his corn-stores are all full and running over.

"Where did you get all this?" asks Zomo's wife when they finish carting the corn.

"Giwa is my friend," says Zomo, "and when he hears that my corn is nearly finished, he insists on giving me some of his. 'Zomo,' he says. 'I won't have you going short.' Naturally I do not wish to offend him and so I accept."

When she hears this, Zomo's wife looks at him as if she doesn't believe a word he says, but she holds her tongue and says nothing.

Next morning, Zomo puts on his best gown again, and this time he makes for the river where Dorina the Hippopotamus has his house. Since Dorina lives in the water, the bad season does not hurt him and he has plenty of food.

When Zomo reaches Dorina's gate, he says that he has a message for him and is taken to the audience chamber.

"God give you victory," Zomo cries in a loud voice, doing obeisance and looking very respectful, just as he does with the elephant.

"Welcome, Zomo," says Dorina. "What brings you to these parts?"

"I have a message," says Zomo, "from Giwa the Elephant."

"Oh?" says Dorina. "What does Giwa want with me?"

"He wants to know," says Zomo, "whether you still want to buy his chestnut."

"Of course I do," says Dorina. "I even offer to swap my black for him, but Giwa will not have it."

"Well, he's changed his mind now," says Zomo, and tells Dorina the same tale that he already told Giwa, right down to the bit about Giwa wishing to keep the chestnut until the festival because it is the horse he likes to ride in the procession. Dorina is so pleased with the proposition that then and there he tells his wife and daughters to prepare a hundred baskets of dried fish.

When the fish is ready, Zomo takes his leave and sets off for dry land with twenty young hippos behind him, each carrying five baskets. By and by they reach a place near his house, and he tells them to put the stuff down and he will get the young elephants, who are fat and lazy he says, to carry it the rest of the way.

As soon as the young hippos have gone back to the river, Zomo fetches his wife and children and they carry the baskets home. Since the larder is already full of corn, the eight youngest rabbits

have to give up their hut to make room for the fish, which fills it right up to the thatch and makes it bulge like a pumpkin.

Soon after this, the rains come and all through the rainy season Zomo keeps his wife and children busy plaiting a rope. It is the biggest rope you ever saw and so strong that you can tie Giwa the Elephant up with it and he won't get loose. His old woman is always asking Zomo what they want with such a rope, but Zomo won't say.

By and by, when the rains are nearly over, the festival comes round. All the animals ride in the procession, and the elephant sees that the hippo is mounted on the black, and the hippo sees that the elephant is mounted on the chestnut.

Next day, bright and early, Zomo takes one end of his rope and sets out for the river. When he comes to the bank, he finds a fig tree and passes the rope round the trunk. Then he goes on to the hippo's house.

"Ah, Zomo," says Dorina when he is ushered into his presence, "you are just the man I wish to see. Do you bring news about my horse?"

"God give you long life," says Zomo, "here is the end of his tethering rope, which Giwa the Elephant tells me to bring to you. When the sun rises tomorrow, he will take him down to the river by the fig tree, and he says when you see the leaves of the fig tree begin to shake, it will be the signal to pull him in on the rope."

"Very well," says Dorina. "We'll be ready."

"God give you victory," Zomo goes on, "Giwa also says to tell you that this chestnut of his is a mighty strong horse and that he can't answer for it if you let him get away."

"Never fear," says Dorina, "my boys will take care of him."

When Zomo leaves the hippo, he goes and gets the other end of the rope and takes it to the elephant's house. "God give you long life," he says to Giwa, and then he spins him the same yarn, right down to the bit about the black being a mighty strong horse and Dorina not answering for it if he lets him get away.

"Not to worry," says Giwa. "My boys will look after him all right."

When Zomo gets home that evening, he tells his wife that people may come asking for him next day, and that if they do, she is to say that he is gone to Gwanja.

"But," says she, "you aren't going to Gwanja, are you?"

"Not I," says Zomo, "but this is what you must say. And furthermore," he goes on, "if they ask how long I shall be away, you are to say six months if not eight."

Early next morning, before the sun rises, Giwa the Elephant lines up his ten sons outside his house. He tells them that the hippo's black is mighty strong and that when he gives the signal they must heave on the rope with all their might. On the river bank Dorina the Hippo is doing the same thing with his twenty sons.

By and by the sun rises, the breeze springs up, and the leaves of all the trees along the river bank begin to shake. But Giwa and Dorina do not notice the other trees because they are only watching the fig tree. As soon as they see its leaves shaking, they both shout, "Heave," and then all the young elephants and all the young hippos begin to pull on the rope as if their lives depend on it.

At first the hippos gain some ground. When the old elephant sees this, he thinks that his horse is getting away and so he becomes very agitated and dances up and down and shouts to his sons to pull harder. Then the elephants begin to gain ground and it is the turn of the old hippo at the other end to become agitated and dance up and down and shout.

While this goes on, Zomo slips out of his house and hides himself in the branches of the fig tree. He has to hold on tight because the elephants and the hippos are pulling it this way and that and at one time he thinks that the tree will come up by the roots. But he waits until the tree is steady because both sides strain so hard, and then he takes out his knife and reaches down and cuts the rope.

When Zomo cuts the rope, the young hippos, who are up on the bank of the river, go toppling back into the water and make such a mighty splash that it stuns all the fish for miles around and even gives old Kada the Crocodile a headache.

As for the young elephants at the other end, they are right in front of their father's house, and so when the rope parts, they all go tumbling backward and knock down the ornamental gateway, which Giwa made for himself the year before, and then go rolling on into the compound where they flatten two huts and a corn-store.

When the old elephant and the old hippo see the rope part, they both think they will lose their horse, and so they both dash out to the fig tree to catch it and there they run into one another. Now Giwa, besides being surprised, is by no means pleased to see Dorina just now. He scowls at him and says that the black broke his tethering rope and that unless Dorina catches him and brings him back he will have to ask for the return of all his corn.

Dorina doesn't care to be scowled at at the best of times, let alone just now when he thinks that his horse has got away, and so he scowls right back and says that he doesn't know about any corn, all he knows is that the chestnut has broken his rope and got away and that unless Giwa catches him and brings him back he will have to ask for the return of all his fish.

Giwa is not used to being spoken to like this, even by Zaki the Lion, and doesn't care for it any more than Dorina cares to be scowled at. "Dorina," he says, "you get above yourself. You may be a great man among the frogs and fishes, but here on land we don't consider you any great shakes."

This makes Dorina madder than ever because he doesn't like to be reminded that he now lives with frogs and fishes. "Giwa," he says, "the only reason I leave dry land and live in the water is that your belly rumbles so loud at night that it disturbs my children and they don't get their proper sleep."

At this, Giwa calls the hippo a baseborn, bandy-legged bog-trotter, and Dorina says that the elephant is a beady-eyed, swivel-nosed, loppy-lugged lounge-about. If the other animals don't come running up at this moment, they will certainly come to blows but as it is, they are just parted in time.

Later both of them send for Zomo, but they are told that Zomo is gone to Gwanja and won't be back for six months, if not eight. In fact it is much longer than this before Giwa and Dorina are on speaking terms again.

As for Zomo, he lies low and keeps out of everybody's sight. But his wife and children get so fat on Giwa's corn and Dorina's fish that the other animals think that Zomo must be working in Gwanja and sending money back to his family.

"That Zomo," they say to one another, "I do declare that he has turned over a new leaf at last."

## ANANSI'S HAT-SHAKING DANCE
(West African)

*West Africa is the home of many nations and many tribes, among them the countries of Ghana, Guinea, Senegal, and Dahomey and such peoples as the Ashanti and the Wolofs. Kwaku Anansi, the West African spider-man, is becoming more and more popular in the United States, and "Anansi's Hat-Shaking Dance" is one of the best stories for revealing his vanity and his aversion to telling the truth. His character is not at all changed in the Jamaican stories about him.*

"Anansi's Hat-Shaking Dance." From *The Hat-Shaking Dance and Other Tales of the Gold Coast* by Harold Courlander and Albert Kofi Prempeh, © 1957 by Harold Courlander and reprinted with permission of Harcourt Brace Jovanovich, Inc. Originally based on one of the tales in Rattray's *Akan-Ashanti Folk Tales* (Clarendon Press)

*As a trickster-hero, a liar, and a thief, he is at the same time lovable and forgivable—for in Anansi we find not malice but mischief, not evil but devilment.*

If you look closely, you will see that Kwaku Anansi, the spider, has a bald head. It is said that in the old days he had hair, but that he lost it through vanity.

It happened that Anansi's mother-in-law died. When word came to Anansi's house, Aso, his wife, prepared to go at once to her own village for the funeral. But Anansi said to Aso: "You go ahead; I will follow."

When Aso had gone, Anansi said to himself: "When I go to my dead mother-in-law's house, I will have to show great grief over her death. I will have to refuse to eat. Therefore, I shall eat now." And so he sat in his own house and ate a huge meal. Then he put on his mourning clothes and went to Aso's village.

First there was the funeral. Afterwards there was a large feast. But Anansi refused to eat, out of respect for his wife's dead mother. He said: "What kind of man would I be to eat when I am mourning for my mother-in-law? I will eat only after the eighth day has passed."

Now this was not expected of him, because a man isn't required to starve himself simply because someone has died. But Anansi was the kind of person that when he ate, he ate twice as much as others, and when he danced, he danced more vigorously than others, and when he mourned, he had to mourn more loudly than anybody else. Whatever he did, he didn't want to be outdone by anyone else. And although he was very hungry, he couldn't bear to have people think he wasn't the greatest mourner at his own mother-in-law's funeral.

So he said: "Feed my friends, but as for me, I shall do without." So everyone ate—the porcupine, the rabbit, the snake, the guinea fowl, and the others. All except Anansi.

On the second day after the funeral they said to him again: "Eat, there is no need to starve."

But Anansi replied: "Oh no, not until the eighth day, when the mourning is over. What kind of man do you think I am?"

So the others ate. Anansi's stomach was empty, and he was unhappy.

On the third day they said again: "Eat, Kwaku Anansi, there is no need to go hungry."

But Anansi was stubborn. He said: "How can I eat when my wife's mother has been buried only three days?" And so the others ate, while Anansi smelled the food hungrily and suffered.

On the fourth day, Anansi was alone where a pot of beans was cooking over the fire. He smelled the beans and looked in the pot. At last he couldn't stand it any longer. He took a large spoon and dipped up a large portion of the beans, thinking to take it to a quiet place and eat it without anyone's knowing. But just then the dog, the guinea fowl, the rabbit, and the others returned to the place where the food was cooking.

To hide the beans, Anansi quickly poured them in his hat and put it on his head. The other people came to the pot and ate, saying again: "Anansi, you must eat."

He said: "No, what kind of man would I be?"

But the hot beans were burning his head. He jiggled his hat around with his hands. When he saw the others looking at him, he said: "Just at this very moment in my village the hat-shaking festival is taking place. I shake my hat in honor of the occasion."

The beans felt hotter than ever, and he jiggled his hat some more. He began to jump with pain, and he said: "Like this in my village they are doing the hat-shaking dance."

He danced about, jiggling his hat because of the heat. He yearned to take off his hat, but he could not because his friends would see the beans. So he shouted: "They are shaking and jiggling the hats in my village, like this! It is a great festival! I must go!"

They said to him: "Kwaku Anansi, eat something before you go."

But now Anansi was jumping and writhing with the heat of the beans on his head. He shouted: "Oh no, they are shaking hats, they are wriggling hats and jumping like this! I must go to my village! They need me!"

He rushed out of the house, jumping and pushing his hat back and forth. His friends followed after him saying: "Eat before you go on your journey!"

But Anansi shouted: "What kind of man do

you think I am, with my mother-in-law just buried?"

Even though they all followed right after him, he couldn't wait any longer, because the pain was too much, and he tore the hat from his head. When the dog saw, and the guinea fowl saw, and the rabbit saw, and all the others saw what was in the hat, and saw the hot beans sticking to Anansi's head, they stopped chasing him. They began to laugh and jeer.

Anansi was overcome with shame. He leaped into the tall grass, saying: "Hide me." And the grass hid him.

That is why Anansi is often found in the tall grass, where he was driven by shame. And you will see that his head is bald, for the hot beans he put in his hat burned off his hair.

All this happened because he tried to impress people at his mother-in-law's funeral.

## THE SLOOGEH DOG

## AND THE STOLEN AROMA

### (Congolese)

*Perhaps this tale originated in North Africa. It is certainly very close in its spirit and lesson to the Ethiopian "The Fire on the Mountain," and variants of it occur in Turkey and Switzerland.*

There was once a greedy African who through shrewd and sometimes dishonest dealings had become very rich. He was so rich in ivory that he had a fence of tusks all around his compound. He was so rich in sheep that he dared not count them, lest the evil spirits become jealous and destroy them.

He had so many wives that it took him from sunup to sundown just to walk past the doors of their huts. And he had so many daughters of marriageable age that he kept them in a herd guarded day and night by old women.

The favorite pastime of this rich man was eating. But no guest ever dipped the finger in the

"The Sloogeh Dog and the Stolen Aroma." Reprinted by permission of Coward-McCann, Inc., from *Tales from the Story Hat* by Verna Aardema. Copyright 1960 by Coward-McCann, Inc.

pot with him at mealtime. No pet sat near him waiting to pick up fallen crumbs.

He ate alone in the shade of a big tree near the ivory gate of his compound. He ate much food and he became very fat.

One day as he sat on his eating stool, a procession of wives filed over to him from the cookhouse. Each carried on her head a basket or platter or bowl of food.

Each put her offering before him and backed away to sit on her heels and watch him eat. This day among the delicacies were baked elephant's foot, fried locusts, and rice balls with peanut gravy.

A wonderful aroma came from the steaming food. It flooded the compound and seeped through and over the ivory fence.

Now it happened that, at the very moment the smell of the food was spreading through the jungle, the Sloogeh Dog was coming down a path near the rich man's gate. In his wanderings he had foolishly crossed the hot, barren "hungry country" and he was truly on the verge of starvation.

When the smell of the rich man's food met him, his head jerked up and saliva gathered at the corners of his mouth. New strength came into his long lean body. He trotted, following the scent, straight to the rich man's gate.

The Sloogeh Dog pushed on the gate. It was tied fast, so he peered between the ivory posts. Seeing the man eating meat off a big bone, he made polite little begging sounds deep in his throat.

Saliva made two long threads from the corners of his mouth to the ground.

The sight of the hungry creature at his very gate spoiled the rich man's enjoyment of his food. He threw a vex and bellowed, "Go away from my face, beggar!"

The Sloogeh Dog was outside the fence where anyone was free to be. He knew he didn't have to go away. But he had another idea. He trotted all the way around the compound searching for the pile of rich scraps which he was sure would be somewhere near the fence. He found not so much as a peanut shuck.

However, he didn't forget the wonderful smell of that food. Each day, at mealtime, he would come to sniff and drool at the rich man's gate.

Each day the man would drive him away. And every day his anger grew until one day he left his food and went straight to the Council of Old Men.

He told his story. Then he said, "I want you to arrest that beggar of a dog!"

"On what grounds?" asked one of the old men.

"For stealing the aroma of my food!" said the rich man.

So the dog was arrested, a judge was appointed, and a day was set for the trial.

On the day of the trial, the whole village gathered about the Tree of Justice. From the start, the sympathy of the people was all with the Sloogeh Dog, for there was scarcely one of them who had not been swindled by the rich man.

But the judge was a just man. "I agree that the aroma was part of the food and so belonged to the accuser," he said. "And since the dog came every day to enjoy the smell of the food, one must conclude that it was intentional."

Murmurs of pity came from the crowd.

The Sloogeh Dog yawned nervously.

The judge continued. "If he had stolen only once, the usual punishment would be to cut off his paws!"

The Sloogeh Dog's legs gave way under him and he slithered on his belly to a hiding place back of the Tree of Justice.

"However," cried the judge, "since the crime was a daily habit, I must think about it overnight before I decide on a suitable punishment."

At sunup the next morning the people gathered to hear the sentence. They became very curious when the judge came leading a horse. He dropped the reins to the ground and left the animal standing where the trail enters the village.

Was the horse part of the punishment? Was the judge taking a trip later? He only shrugged when the people questioned him.

The judge called the rich man and the Sloogeh Dog to come before him. Handing a kiboko to the rich man, he said, "The accused will be beaten to death by the accuser!"

The rich man took off his gold-embroidered robe. He made a practice swing through the air with the whip.

The judge held up his hand. "Wait!" he commanded.

Then he turned to the people. "Do the people

agree that it was the invisible part of the food, and therefore its spirit, that was stolen?"

"Ee, ee!" cried the people.

The judge held up his hand again. "Do the people agree that the spirit of the dog is his shadow?"

"Ee, ee!" they said.

"Then," boomed the judge, "since the crime was against the spirit of the food, *only* the spirit of the dog shall be punished!"

The people howled with laughter. Their feet drummed on the hard-packed earth. They slapped each other's backs and shouted, "Esu! Esu!"

The Sloogeh Dog leaped up and licked the judge's nose.

The judge turned to the rich man and, when he could be heard, he said, "The shadow is big now, but you must beat it until the sun is straight up in the sky. When there is nothing left of the shadow, we shall agree that it is dead."

The rich man threw down the whip, picked up his garment, and said, "I withdraw the charges."

The judge shook his head. "You caused the

arrest," he said. "You wanted the trial. Now administer justice. And if the kiboko touches so much as a hair of the Sloogeh Dog, it will be turned upon you!"

There was nothing for the rich man to do but swing the whip hour after hour. The people watched and laughed as the dog leaped and howled, pretending to suffer with his shadow.

As the sun climbed higher and higher, the shadow became smaller and smaller—and much harder to hit. The whip became heavier in the man's flabby hands. He was dripping with sweat and covered with dust stirred up by the whip.

When the man could hardly bear the ordeal any longer, the dog lay down. That made it necessary for the man to get on his knees and put his arm between him and the dog to keep from touching a hair. When he brought down the whip, he hit his arm.

The people screamed with laughter.

The rich man bellowed and threw the kiboko. Then he leaped to the back of the judge's horse and rode headlong out of the village.

"He won't come back," said the oldest Old Man. "He would get *his* paws chopped off if he did. He stole the judge's horse!"

The Sloogeh Dog slunk off toward the rich man's house, his long nose sniffing for a whiff of something cooking beyond the ivory gate.

### THE HONEY GATHERER'S
### THREE SONS

*(Congolese)*

*It would be more precise to refer to this story and the next as fables. They are only two out of hundreds that are employed to instruct children as well as to amuse all listeners. The ways in which various kinds of folklore are used to teach Congolese children are most interestingly explained in the preface to* The Magic Drum, *the collection from which this story is taken.*

A honey gatherer had three sons, all born at the same time. Their names were Hear-it-how-

"The Honey Gatherer's Three Sons" from *The Magic Drum* by W. F. P. Burton. Copyright © 1961 by W. F. P. Burton, by permission of The John Day Co., publishers, and A. M. Heath & Company Ltd. for W. F. P. Burton

ever-faint-the-sound, Follow-it-however-great-the-distance and Put-it-together-however-small-the-pieces. These names are sufficient to indicate the skill of these young men, but their friends called them simply Hear, Follow and Piece.

One day the honey gatherer went on a long, long journey into the forest until he came to a tree that was as high as a hill, and the bees that buzzed in and out showed clearly that it must be full of honey. He climbed up, but, treading on a rotten branch, fell to the ground and was broken into ten pieces.

Hear was sitting beside the hut in the village, but he promptly jumped to his feet, saying, "Father has fallen from a tree. Come! Let us go to his help."

His brother Follow set out and led them along the father's tracks until they came upon the body lying in ten pieces. Piece then put all the parts together, fastened them up, and the father walked home while the sons carried his honey.

Next day the honey gatherer again set out to look for honey, while his sons sat at home, each boasting that he was more important than the others.

"You could not have heard him without me," said Hear.

"Though you had heard him you could not have found him without me," said Follow.

"Even though you had found him, you could not have put him together without me," said Piece.

Meanwhile, the old honey gatherer had gone far into the forest till he came to a tree as high as the clouds, and the bees buzzing in and out showed clearly that it must be full of honey. He climbed up, but, treading on a rotten branch, fell to the ground and was broken into a hundred pieces. His sons were sitting at home boasting about their prowess, when Hear jumped up, saying, "Father has fallen!"

Follow reluctantly set out to follow the footprints, and found the hundred pieces on the ground. Pointing to them he said, "See how indispensable I am. I have found him for you."

Piece then put the hundred pieces together very grudgingly, saying, "I, and I alone, have restored Father."

Their father walked home, while the sons carried the honey.

Next day the old honey gatherer went farther than ever into the forest and he found a tree that reached to the stars. The bees buzzing in and out showed that it must be full of honey. He climbed up, but, treading on a rotten branch, fell to the ground and was broken into a thousand pieces.

Hear heard the fall, but would not tell his brothers. Follow knew that there must have been an accident since his father did not return, while Piece realized that his father needed his assistance, but would not condescend to ask his brothers to find him so that he might piece him together.

So the old honey gatherer died, because the selfish sons each thought more of his own reputation than of his father's. In truth, each needed the others, and none was wiser or better than the rest.

## LOOK BEHIND
## AS WELL AS BEFORE
*(Congolese)*

*Here, for older children, is the African cousin to "The Old Woman and Her Pig." It has an interesting counterpart in the picture book* The Camel Who Took a Walk, *by Jack Tworkov, which has been made into a filmstrip by Weston Woods Studios.*

The big white ant, the luswa, wanted to get married and was taking the bride-price to the parents of the girl to whom he was addressing his attentions. He was so occupied with his errand that he did not look behind, or he would have seen a frog following him. The frog was licking his lips as he went after the luswa, and was so intent on the prospect of a feast that he did not see a snake following him. Had the snake looked behind, he would have known that a wooden club was after him. The club was so eager to overtake the snake that he did not see the small white ants doggedly pursuing him. The small white ants, the tuswalandala, did not realize it, but a fowl was on their tracks. The fowl was anxious to feast off the small white ants, but did not know

that a wild cat was slinking after her. The wild cat had his eye on the fowl, otherwise he would have detected a trap that was in his path. The trap was thinking of nothing but the wild cat or he would have seen the bush fire rolling toward him. The bush fire was heaving up sparks and smoke and thus failed to realize that water was barring his way. The water only thought of attacking the fire, and so was not prepared for the drought that was on his heels.

The parents of the prospective bride had cooked a feast, but before they could sit down to it the frog began to eat the big white ant. The snake attacked the frog. The club struck down the snake. The small white ants gnawed into the club, the fowl snapped up the small white ants, the wild cat seized the fowl, the trap fell on the wild cat, the fire consumed the trap, the water put out the fire, the drought dried up the water, and all that was left was a dusty waste. How much better if the white ant had looked behind. And moreover, if you have cruel designs upon another, don't forget that others may have similar designs on you.

## WINDBIRD AND THE SUN
*(South African)*

*This typical* why *story has been very nicely retold and expanded by Josef Marais. Children might enjoy looking for other tales from around the world that tell why there are rainbows. "Windbird and the Sun" comes from the Hottentots, a rapidly disappearing people who are confined largely to the desert regions of South Africa.*

Once the Queen of the Fountains had a beautiful daughter. Her name was Thashira and the Queen was very proud of her and gave her all that she wished. But nothing made Thashira really happy except bright colors. Gaily-colored flowers, or blankets of yellow, green or blue, or necklaces made of gaudy stones—all these gave Thashira pleasure. Nothing else interested her

"Look Behind as Well as Before" from *The Magic Drum* by W. F. P. Burton. Copyright © 1961 by W. F. P. Burton, by permission of The John Day Co., publishers, and A. M. Heath & Company Ltd. for W. F. P. Burton

"Windbird and the Sun." From *Koos the Hottentot* by Josef Marais (New York: Alfred A. Knopf, Inc., 1945), pp. 53–62. Reprinted by permission of the author

—in fact the Queen's daughter for most of the time was sad and unpleasant to her friends. She would not help grind corn, or fashion clay pots, as the other girls of the kraal did. She would not take part in the dance ceremonies when harvest time came. All day Thashira sat and stared at the blue of the sky. Flowers seldom bloomed in the dry country and the thorntrees and bushes were mostly bare without any color to delight her eyes. The Queen herself was busy travelling up the mountains to see the fountains, and she was very worried knowing that her daughter was so sad.

The young men of the kraal left Thashira alone. "Who wants such a dull, unpleasant girl for a wife?" they said.

Sometimes Thashira went to the nearby vlei (when there was some water there) and plucked water lilies for a wreath to put on her head. Sometimes she gathered wild berries and decorated her body with the red juice. During these times she was happy and everyone said, "Thashira has found another color," and everyone would smile at her and nod and say, "How pretty you look!" Then she tried mixing the juice of plants with the brown or red clay near the vlei and with that she painted pictures on the rocks. But Thashira tired of all this and spent most of the days lying in the shade of a baobab tree and staring at the bright blue of the sky.

The Sun saw her there one day and said to her, "Beautiful Thashira, I know you love the blue color of the sky. That makes me happy because it is I who give the sky its color." She came out from under the branch of the baobab tree and looked up for a moment at the brilliant Sun and said, "Thank you, you are kind." Then she went back under the shade. She did not even smile.

The Sun sympathized with her, for he too liked colors. Every day he tried placing new and finer colors in the sky when the day was ending and he was ready to sink beyond the koppies to the west. This pleased Thashira and she made a habit of climbing the highest koppie to admire the Sun while he showed her his new glowing colors. So they became very fond of each other, the maiden and the Sun.

But Windbird fell in love with Thashira. As she lay half asleep under the baobab tree he ca-

ressed her hair and cooled her brow. It was not often that Windbird was so gentle. In the dry country he is always in a violent hurry. Most of the time Windbird is very busy journeying back and forth from the seacoast to the great lands in the interior of Africa. Above the ocean he chooses a large cloud and flies with it inland. If the mountains are very high he has to trail the cloud so high that he sometimes loses most of it on the way. Then the people are angry at him for bringing no clouds or rain. Windbird has a quick temper, and if he finds the people are angry and blaming him he gets angry too. Then he blows the dust over the Veld. And people hate him still more.

But when Windbird fell in love with the daughter of the Queen of the Fountains, he blew very gently for weeks. He brought clouds from as far as Cape Agulhas where the Indian and the Atlantic oceans meet. He tore off pieces of clouds while he flew them over the big mountains near the coast, for fear they were too big and might cause hailstones. Thus, just enough rain fell, and the flowers bloomed and the plants sprouted and there were lots of colors for the maiden to enjoy.

"That's all very well," growled Windbird to himself, "but Thashira doesn't know it is I who bring her this pleasure."

So one day while the girl was romping among the chinkerinchees, plucking bunches of the tiny white flowers with their green dotted petals, he approached her and said, "Thashira, I love you. That is why I have brought the clouds to water the ground and give you these fine flowers. I am great and strong. I am Windbird." He thought the maiden would be grateful and impressed by his prowess. But she glanced at him coolly and said, "Thank you, you are kind." Then she continued picking chinkerinchees. Windbird flew into a temper. He blew great blasts of air across the Veld so that the newly-grown grasses and plants swayed until their roots broke. The flowers were torn off their stems. The bushes were uprooted.

"Now you can see my strength," Windbird boasted, and the air currents whistled wildly across Veld and vlei. Thashira was heartbroken. All the brightly-colored plants and blossoms had disappeared. Once more the land was dusty and bare. Again she took to lying in the shade of her baobab tree and gazing at the only color that was left—the blue of the sky. When Windbird came to call on her she scornfully told him to go away.

The Queen of the Fountains returned and found her daughter sadder than ever. Thashira's only companion now was a little dove whose neck was decorated with gaily-colored feathers. When the Sun shone on the little dove her feathers reflected all the colors of the Sun's rays. The Queen saw that Thashira spent her days beneath the baobab tree. She watched Thashira whisper messages to the dove who then flew far away into the blue sky.

"Thashira, my daughter, you are so sad. True, life in this dry land is dreary. What can I do to make you happy?"

"Mother, I love the Sun for he makes the sky blue, and his warmth helps the colorful flowers to bloom."

"Is it to the Sun that you are sending your little dove with messages?" asked the Queen, and Thashira shyly nodded.

"Good—then I will order that a great ladder be built so that you may go up into the blue sky you love so much and stay forever with the Sun," cried the Queen.

The elephants and the hippos and the rhinos and the monkeys rushed to obey the Queen of the Fountains for they knew how much their lives depended on pleasing her. In the distant forests they pulled down the trees. Against all the rules of nature the Queen ordered the rivers to flood over the dry land even for a brief period so that they might bring the great logs to Thashira's home. The people built hundreds and hundreds of ladders and placed them one on top of the other. When they reached so high into the sky that the top ladder could not be seen Thashira sent her little dove with a final message to the Sun, and then while the crowds of people anxiously watched, she placed her foot on the first rung.

Suddenly from the distance came the horrible wail of the wind. Windbird was furious that the Sun had won Thashira. Now his moment for revenge had come.

"So!" Windbird roared in his anger. "You scorned the power of Windbird! Now you shall see who is stronger—the Sun or the Wind." And the dust and bushes flew across the Veld, the

loose stones whipped the bodies of the multitude of people. With a tremendous crack the great ladders came tumbling down to earth. The cries of the people mingled with the cruel whistling of Windbird.

The Queen of the Fountains wept for her daughter, Thashira. She wept and wept with sorrow and her tears floated upwards in a great, grey mist. Then the little dove returned from above with one of her wings almost broken from the strong winds; but the colors of her neck feathers were brighter than ever. She alighted on the shoulder of beautiful Thashira. The next moment Thashira with the little dove were floating upward, and the misty vapor from the Queen's tears enveloped them. The Sun burst out in all his brilliance. The whistling of Windbird died down to a whisper . . . then there was dead stillness. The people looked upward and across the sky shone a glorious rainbow of all the colors that anyone could wish.

Thashira is the rainbow and when the Sun

shines on her, she glows with happiness. Though Windbird tries and tries he cannot blow her away. From time to time Windbird breaks into one of his violent fits of temper, but Thashira remains steadfast in the sky proudly showing the Sun and the world her gorgeous colors. May Windbird never succeed in blowing Thashira. the rainbow, away!

## THE STEPCHILD AND THE FRUIT TREES
*(Ibo)*

*There's a strong sense of justice in the folk literature of every country, and here the unfair treatment meted out to Ijomah results in a victory over her unkind stepmother, a conclusion children find very satisfying. Like Cinderella, Ijomah's motherless state is compensated for by the protection of magic. The songs within the story are meant to be shared, and Ibo audiences participate in the performance when the familiar songs begin.*

Once upon a time there lived a family in a village where there were a lot of fruit trees. So many different kinds of fruit trees grew there that in every season, rainy or dry, there was always plenty of fruit in the market to sell. People came to the market from other villages and from the nearby town to buy the good fruit.

The father of the family in this fruit-tree village had four children, all of them girls. But one of the girls, Ijomah, was a stepchild. Her mother had died when Ijomah was twelve years old and her father had married again.

It was then that Ijomah's troubles began. Her stepmother, Nnekeh, never liked her. She only loved her own children and completely neglected Ijomah. Worse than that, she made the girl do all the hard work and did not even give her enough food.

Ijomah's father, Mazo, was too busy with his

trade to know what was going on. Even on weekends he was out on business. The few times he was at home Ijomah complained to him in secret, but Mazo never wanted to offend his second wife. Instead of talking the matter over with Nnekeh, he always asked Ijomah to be patient, and once in a while he gave her some money to buy food.

Ijomah's mother had loved to plant flowers. After she died, Ijomah continued to tend the garden. Nnekeh often sent her own children to pick all the brightest and most beautiful flowers, but always once a month Ijomah took roses to her mother's grave. She would have taken the roses more often, but Nnekeh never gave her the chance. At times Ijomah cried over the loss of her mother and over her own sad state. But things never changed.

One day Nnekeh went to the market and bought some red juicy fruit called *odala*. Children love to eat the pink pulpy flesh of the *odala,* and they play games of marbles with the hard black seeds. Of course Nnekeh only gave the fruit to her own children, and Ijomah had none. Ijomah had to be content with the two scanty meals she was given that day. But after her half sisters had eaten their *odala,* Ijomah saw that they had thrown away the seeds. She collected the seeds and planted them in her garden.

When she woke up one day, she found little plants sprouting from the seeds. She was very happy and took great care to make the plants grow up strong and healthy. Early every morning, long before the others stirred from their beds, Ijomah would go to her garden to water the plants. As she watered them she sang this song:

"My *odala!* grow
  Please
My *odala!* grow
  Please
Grow, grow, grow
  Please
My father's wife
  Please
Bought *odala* from the market
  Please
Ate, ate, ate

Please
Ate and did not give her stepdaughter
Please."

Each morning Ijomah sang her song and watered the *odala* plants she loved so much.

Soon the plants grew into trees, and one day Ijomah saw the first fruit beginning to grow. She was so happy she wanted to dance. She never stopped singing her song.

But when the fruit began to ripen, Nnekeh said the trees belonged to her children, not just to Ijomah. Ijomah was very unhappy. She told Nnekeh that the trees and fruit were hers, but Nnekeh said: "I bought the *odala* in the market, and without them you would have had no trees!"

As soon as the fruit were fully ripe, people came to Ijomah's garden to buy them. Very many people came because the *odala* were so big and sweet. Ijomah wanted to sell the fruit and have money to buy some of the beautiful things that her stepmother would never allow her to have.

Nnekeh was furiously angry. She raged at Ijomah and refused to let her sell the *odala*. She herself would be the one to sell them. Ijomah was so unhappy she could not sleep that night. Very, very early the following morning, just as the first rays of sunlight appeared, she crept to the garden, stood sadly by the *odala* trees, and started singing:

"My *odala!* die
Please
My *odala!* die
Please
Die, die, die
Please
My father's wife
Please
Bought *odala* from the market
Please
Ate, ate, ate
Please
Ate and did not give her stepdaughter
Please
My *odala!* die."

As she finished the song, the *odala* trees began to shrivel and shrivel until they were all withered up.

When daylight came, the people whom Nnekeh had told about the big juicy fruit went to the garden to buy some. But all that the people found were shriveled trees and withered fruit. Everyone was surprised and annoyed.

Nnekeh was so ashamed she wished the ground would open and swallow her up. She started shouting like an angry general in the army. She knew very well, she said, that her crafty stepdaughter had played a trick on her. Ijomah only laughed and told the villagers that the fruit trees were hers.

"But if Nnekeh wants to," Ijomah said, "she can bring the trees to life again. If the trees are hers, they will obey her! If they belong to me, they will obey me!"

Nnekeh looked at the shriveled trees, but there was nothing she could do. She tried to pounce on Ijomah, but the people grabbed her and pulled her away. Then they asked Ijomah whether she could do anything to the trees.

Ijomah smiled and started singing:

"My *odala!* grow
Please
My *odala!* grow
Please. . . ."

While she sang, the trees began to grow! New green leaves sprouted from the withered branches, and soon the trees were loaded with fruit, larger and riper than ever. When the villagers saw that, they knew the stepmother was wrong. The fruit belonged to Ijomah, and Nnekeh had been trying to take them away from her.

So the villagers bought fruit from Ijomah. They bought and bought. They carried away basketloads of fruit and still there was more to buy. No one had ever seen so many *odalà* or tasted fruit so fine and sweet. Soon Ijomah was the richest person in the village. She had money to buy all the things she wanted, and her stepmother never troubled her again.

# *China*

*Although China's history and literature reach back at least four thousand
years, we actually know very little of her folk tales. Chinese tales have long
appeared in collections for young people, but their validity is questionable,
since they may have been invented in large part, drawn from some of the few
texts of Chinese literature that have been translated into Western tongues,
or taken from accounts given by persons in this country—accounts that are not
verifiable. Chinese children had, however, not been entirely without
a literature since legacies from the oral tradition were available in many
forms. The stories were based chiefly on the deeds of heroes of legend
or folklore, and were standard fare for shadow plays and storytelling. Indeed,
the professional storyteller was judged on how well he could recall and
tell a favorite version. The scholar Lu Hsün, in the twentieth century, gathered
several collections of old fairy tales for children and translated many
from other lands. It was not until 1917 that efforts were begun to unlock the
great treasure of China's folk literature, but these efforts were sporadic
until the present Communist era. Now China's tales are assiduously collected
from every possible source and published widely for the people, but they
are rewritten and distorted to promote the Communist way of life. The two
stories here cannot be called true folk tales. They are both taken from
Alice Ritchie's* The Treasure of Li-Po, *a charming group of six stories that have
retained their popularity with American children for over twenty years
and that capture the spirit and inflection of pre-Communist China as we have
generally assumed it to be. The titles in the Bibliography are mainly of
compilations which purport to be actual folk tales taken from reliable printed
sources or from the lips of Chinese storytellers. In all of them we
see the China of long ago.*

## THE FOX'S DAUGHTER

*What a charming way to present a homily on
the virtue and reward of serious attention to
one's duties!*

Nothing is luckier than to be the child of a
fox, for, without taking the trouble to learn anything, foxes know as much magic as the man
who spends his whole life studying it, and when
a fox's child takes human form, as sometimes
happens, and becomes a boy or a girl, he knows
as much magic as his father.

Liu was a young student who should have
been working hard for his examinations, but he
was rather idle and much preferred wandering

"The Fox's Daughter." From *The Treasure of Li Po*
by Alice Ritchie, copyright, 1949 by Harcourt Brace
Jovanovich, Inc. and reprinted with their permission and
the permission of The Hogarth Press Ltd.

about his father's estate, or sailing in a boat on
the river which ran through it, to sitting indoors
over his books.

One day, when he was occupied—if it can be
called occupied—in this way, he saw the form of
a young girl among the reeds which grew upon a
little island in the river. Quickly he jumped into
his boat and hurried across the water, and, tying
the boat up to a willow tree, he began to search
the island for her.

For some time he saw nothing, but he heard
mocking laughter to the right and to the left,
and, running wildly first in one direction and
then in the other, he tore his silk robe and broke
the strap of one of his sandals. At last he succeeded in running her down, but she looked so
beautiful, leaning against a tree and smiling at
him, that even after he had got his breath back
he could not speak.

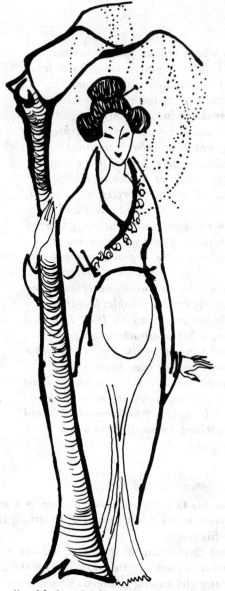

"Alas," said the girl in a clear low voice, looking at his torn robe and flapping sandal, "if Master Liu pursued his studies with the same zeal as he has pursued me, he would take a high place when the candidates go up to the Examination Hall, and some day he would be a man of great importance—but of course he will do nothing of the sort."

Liu eagerly asked her name and how she happened to know all about him, and also how she came to be upon the island, for he could see no boat except his own.

"My name is Feng-Lien," said the maiden, "but as to how I came here, I shall not tell you, and I can go away again as swiftly."

(This was not surprising, because of course she was a fox's daughter, and could appear and disappear at will.) And now she made a movement as if she meant to go, but Liu sprang forward with his hands spread out.

"I beg you to stay," he cried, "or at least tell me where we shall meet again, for you are the most beautiful person I have ever seen."

"Look for me in your books," said the maiden; then, seeing his face become clouded with disappointment, she took a little silver mirror from her girdle and gave it to him. "There," she said, "you shall have something which has belonged to me, but I warn you, you will never see me in it except through your books." And in a moment she had vanished.

Liu went back to his boat feeling very sad, and many times before he reached the house he looked longingly into the silver mirror, but all he saw was the back-view of the beautiful Feng-Lien standing as if she was watching someone going away from her.

As soon as he reached his room, remembering what she had said, he took out the heavy and difficult books which he had never had a mind to study, and laying them on the top of the mirror, he tried to see it through them, but of course he saw nothing, not even its silver handle, buried under those great volumes.

"Feng-Lien meant more than she said," he remarked to himself, and he removed the books from the mirror with a sigh and applied himself earnestly to reading them, refusing to see his friends when they came to the house and not accepting any invitations. After he had spent several days in this way, he looked into the mirror again, and there was Feng-Lien with her face turned towards him, smiling and nodding as if she was pleased.

For a month or more he did nothing but study, looking often into the mirror to be encouraged by the lovely face of Feng-Lien, but presently the fine summer weather came, and he could not force himself to stay in the house. He began once more to wander about the garden and the wild land beside the river, idly enjoying the scent of the newly opened flowers and the sight of the bright birds.

"Perhaps I shall see Feng-Lien again," he said. But he did not find her, and in his heart he knew she would not come while he behaved in this way. Then, one evening after he had been on a fishing expedition all day with some friends, when he pulled out the silver mirror he saw Feng-Lien crying bitterly, and the next morning she had her back turned to him.

"It is clear that there is only one thing to be done," he said to himself. "I must make a habit of working all the time."

He took the silver mirror and nailed it on the wall so that whenever he raised his eyes from his difficult reading he would see Feng-Lien's face. She always looked happy now. This went on for two years, and at the end of that time he went up to the Examination Hall and did so well that he took a high place in the final list.

"Now," he said, "at last, I shall surely be allowed to see Feng-Lien herself."

He took up the mirror and looked for a long time at her reflection, at the arched eyebrows and the beautiful eyes and the smiling mouth, until it seemed to him that her lips parted and she spoke, yes, she seemed to be speaking words of welcome and congratulation, and suddenly the mirror dissolved into a drop of dew and instead of her likeness, Feng-Lien herself stood before him.

"Really," she said, bowing very low, "I am quite frightened of this learned young man."

"The success I have had is entirely owing to you," said Liu.

So they were married, and Liu attained to one of the highest positions in China, but Feng-Lien never again had to use the magic she possessed by reason of being a fox's daughter. She found quite simple ways of keeping her husband, who continued to be by nature somewhat lazy, up to the mark.

## TWO OF EVERYTHING

*Whether you read aloud or tell this story, it will produce howls of laughter. It is easy to dramatize and guarantees a pleased audience.*

"Two of Everything." From *The Treasure of Li Po* by Alice Ritchie, copyright, 1949 by Harcourt Brace Jovanovich, Inc., and reprinted with their permission and the permission of The Hogarth Press Ltd.

Mr. and Mrs. Hak-Tak were rather old and rather poor. They had a small house in a village among the mountains and a tiny patch of green land on the mountain side. Here they grew the vegetables which were all they had to live on, and when it was a good season and they did not need to eat up everything as soon as it was grown, Mr. Hak-Tak took what they could spare in a basket to the next village which was a little larger than theirs and sold it for as much as he could get and bought some oil for their lamp, and fresh seeds, and every now and then, but not often, a piece of cotton stuff to make new coats and trousers for himself and his wife. You can imagine they did not often get the chance to eat meat.

Now, one day it happened that when Mr. Hak-Tak was digging in his precious patch, he unearthed a big brass pot. He thought it strange that it should have been there for so long without his having come across it before, and he was disappointed to find that it was empty; still, he thought they would find some use for it, so when he was ready to go back to the house in the evening he decided to take it with him. It was very big and heavy, and in his struggles to get his arms round it and raise it to a good position for carrying, his purse, which he always took with him in his belt, fell to the ground, and, to be quite sure he had it safe, he put it inside the pot and so staggered home with his load.

As soon as he got into the house Mrs. Hak-Tak hurried from the inner room to meet him.

"My dear husband," she said, "whatever have you got there?"

"For a cooking-pot it is too big; for a bath a little too small," said Mr. Hak-Tak. "I found it buried in our vegetable patch and so far it has been useful in carrying my purse home for me."

"Alas," said Mrs. Hak-Tak, "something smaller would have done as well to hold any money we have or are likely to have," and she stooped over the pot and looked into its dark inside.

As she stooped, her hairpin—for poor Mrs. Hak-Tak had only one hairpin for all her hair and it was made of carved bone—fell into the pot. She put in her hand to get it out again, and then she gave a loud cry which brought her husband running to her side.

"What is it?" he asked. "Is there a viper in the pot?"

"Oh, my dear husband," she cried. "What can be the meaning of this? I put my hand into the pot to fetch out my hairpin and your purse, and look, I have brought out two hairpins and two purses, both exactly alike."

"Open the purse. Open both purses," said Mr. Hak-Tak. "One of them will certainly be empty."

But not a bit of it. The new purse contained exactly the same number of coins as the old one —for that matter, no one could have said which was the new and which the old—and it meant, of course, that the Hak-Taks had exactly twice as much money in the evening as they had had in the morning.

"And two hairpins instead of one!" cried Mrs. Hak-Tak, forgetting in her excitement to do up her hair which was streaming over her shoulders. "There is something quite unusual about this pot."

"Let us put in the sack of lentils and see what happens," said Mr. Hak-Tak, also becoming excited.

They heaved in the bag of lentils and when they pulled it out again—it was so big it almost filled the pot—they saw another bag of exactly the same size waiting to be pulled out in its turn. So now they had two bags of lentils instead of one.

"Put in the blanket," said Mr. Hak-Tak. "We need another blanket for the cold weather." And, sure enough, when the blanket came out, there lay another behind it.

"Put my wadded coat in," said Mr. Hak-Tak, "and then when the cold weather comes there will be one for you as well as for me. Let us put in everything we have in turn. What a pity we have no meat or tobacco, for it seems that the pot cannot make anything without a pattern."

Then Mrs. Hak-Tak, who was a woman of great intelligence, said, "My dear husband, let us put the purse in again and again and again. If we take two purses out each time we put one in, we shall have enough money by tomorrow evening to buy everything we lack."

"I am afraid we may lose it this time," said Mr. Hak-Tak, but in the end he agreed, and they dropped in the purse and pulled out two, then

they added the new money to the old and dropped it in again and pulled out the larger amount twice over. After a while the floor was covered with old leather purses and they decided just to throw the money in by itself. It worked quite as well and saved trouble; every time, twice as much money came out as went in, and every time they added the new coins to the old and threw them all in together. It took them some hours to tire of this game, but at last Mrs. Hak-Tak said, "My dear husband, there is no need for us to work so hard. We shall see to it that the pot does not run away, and we can always make more money as we want it. Let us tie up what we have."

It made a huge bundle in the extra blanket and the Hak-Taks lay and looked at it for a long time before they slept, and talked of all the things they would buy and the improvements they would make in the cottage.

The next morning they rose early and Mr. Hak-Tak filled a wallet with money from the bundle and set off for the big village to buy more things in one morning than he had bought in a whole fifty years.

Mrs. Hak-Tak saw him off and then she tidied up the cottage and put the rice on to boil and had another look at the bundle of money, and made herself a whole set of new hairpins from the pot, and about twenty candles instead of the one which was all they had possessed up to now. After that she slept for a while, having been up so late the night before, but just before the time when her husband should be back, she awoke and went over to the pot. She dropped in a cabbage leaf to make sure it was still working properly, and when she took two leaves out she sat down on the floor and put her arms round it.

"I do not know how you came to us, my dear pot," she said, "but you are the best friend we ever had."

Then she knelt up to look inside it, and at that moment her husband came to the door, and, turning quickly to see all the wonderful things he had bought, she overbalanced and fell into the pot.

Mr. Hak-Tak put down his bundles and ran across and caught her by the ankles and pulled her out, but, oh, mercy, no sooner had he set her carefully on the floor than he saw the kicking legs of another Mrs. Hak-Tak in the pot! What was he to do? Well, he could not leave her there, so he caught her ankles and pulled, and another Mrs. Hak-Tak so exactly like the first that no one would have told one from the other, stood beside them.

"Here's an extraordinary thing," said Mr. Hak-Tak, looking helplessly from one to the other.

"I will not have a second Mrs. Hak-Tak in the house!" screamed the old Mrs. Hak-Tak.

All was confusion. The old Mrs. Hak-Tak shouted and wrung her hands and wept, Mr. Hak-Tak was scarcely calmer, and the new Mrs. Hak-Tak sat down on the floor as if she knew no more than they did what was to happen next.

"One wife is all *I* want," said Mr. Hak-Tak, "but how could I have left her in the pot?"

"Put her back in it again!" cried Mrs. Hak-Tak.

"What? And draw out two more?" said her husband. "If two wives are too many for me, what should I do with three? No! No!" He stepped back quickly as if he was stepping away from the three wives and, missing his footing, lo and behold, he fell into the pot!

Both Mrs. Hak-Taks ran and each caught an ankle and pulled him out and set him on the floor, and there, oh, mercy, was another pair of kicking legs in the pot! Again each caught hold of an ankle and pulled, and soon another Mr. Hak-Tak, so exactly like the first that no one could have told one from the other, stood beside them.

Now the old Mr. Hak-Tak liked the idea of his double no more than Mrs. Hak-Tak had liked the idea of hers. He stormed and raged and scolded his wife for pulling him out of the pot, while the new Mr. Hak-Tak sat down on the floor beside the new Mrs. Hak-Tak and looked as if, like her, he did not know what was going to happen next.

Then the old Mrs. Hak-Tak had a very good idea. "Listen, my dear husband," she said, "now, do stop scolding and listen, for it is really a good thing that there is a new one of you as well as a new one of me. It means that you and I can go on in our usual way, and these new people, who are ourselves and yet not ourselves, can set up house together next door to us."

And that is what they did. The old Hak-Taks built themselves a fine new house with money from the pot, and they built one just like it next door for the new couple, and they lived together in the greatest friendliness, because, as Mrs. Hak-Tak said, "The new Mrs. Hak-Tak is really more than a sister to me, and the new Mr. Hak-Tak is really more than a brother to you."

The neighbors were very much surprised, both at the sudden wealth of the Hak-Taks and at the new couple who resembled them so strongly that they must, they thought, be very close relations of whom they had never heard before. They said: "It looks as though the Hak-Taks, when they so unexpectedly became rich, decided to have two of everything, even of themselves, in order to enjoy their money more."

# Japan

*The ideals embodied in the Japanese tales are the ones by which the Japanese have lived for centuries, and the beliefs and customs pictured in the stories are very like the present-day ones. Storytellers do not abound in Japan as they do in Turkey or in Africa, but folklorists have found many farmers, villagers, and fishermen who were living repositories of the traditional tales and legends. The average Japanese knows many of his folk tales because they have long been printed in single-story and collected editions for children and because they inform so much of the artistic and cultural life of Japan. As in China, so in Japan much of the traditional folk literature provides the content for the sermons of Buddhist priests, for the plays in such traditional theaters as the Bunraku Doll Theater, and for the work of artists and poets. In reading the tales of Japan, one quickly comes very close to the spirit of her past and her present.*

## MOMOTARO:

## BOY-OF-THE-PEACH

*This is one of the most popular stories in Japan, where the word for ogres is "oni." It is uniquely Japanese and has been charmingly retold by Uchida.*

Once long, long ago, there lived a kind old man and a kind old woman in a small village in Japan.

One fine day, they set out from their little cottage together. The old man went toward the mountains to cut some firewood for their kitchen, and the old woman went toward the river to do her washing.

When the old woman reached the shore of the river, she knelt down beside her wooden tub and began to scrub her clothes on a round, flat stone. Suddenly she looked up and saw something very strange floating down the shallow river. It was a big, big peach; bigger than the round wooden tub that stood beside the old woman.

Rumbley-bump and a-bumpety-bump . . . Rumbley-bump and a-bumpety-bump. The big peach rolled closer and closer over the stones in the stream.

"My gracious me!" the old woman said to herself. "In all my long life I have never seen a peach of such great size and beauty. What a fine present it would make for the old man. I do think I will take it home with me."

Then the old woman stretched out her hand just as far as she could, but no matter how hard she stretched, she couldn't reach the big peach.

"If I could just find a long stick, I would be able to reach it," thought the old woman, looking around, but all she could see were pebbles and sand.

"Oh, dear, what shall I do?" she said to herself. Then suddenly she thought of a way to bring the beautiful big peach to her side. She began to sing out in a sweet, clear voice,

"The deep waters are salty!
The shallow waters are sweet!
Stay away from the salty water,
And come where the water is sweet."

She sang this over and over, clapping her hands in time to her song. Then, strangely enough, the big peach slowly began to bob along toward the shore where the water was shallow.

Rumbley-bump and a-bumpety-bump . . . Rumbley-bump and a-bumpety-bump. The big peach came closer and closer to the old woman and finally came to a stop at her feet.

The old woman was so happy, she picked the big peach up very carefully and quickly carried it home in her arms. Then she waited for the old man to return so she could show him her lovely present. Toward evening the old man came home with a big pack of wood on his back.

"Come quickly, come quickly," the old woman called to him from the house.

"What is it? What is the matter?" the old man asked as he hurried to the side of the old woman.

"Just look at the fine present I have for you," said the old woman happily as she showed him the big round peach.

"My goodness! What a great peach! Where in the world did you buy such a peach as this?" the old man asked.

The old woman smiled happily and told him how she had found the peach floating down the river.

"Well, well, this is a fine present indeed," said the old man, "for I have worked hard today and I am very hungry."

Then he got the biggest knife they had, so he could cut the big peach in half. Just as he was ready to thrust the sharp blade into the peach, he heard a tiny voice from inside.

"Wait, old man! Don't cut me!" it cried, and before the surprised old man and woman could say a word, the beautiful big peach broke in two, and a sweet little boy jumped out from inside. The old man and woman were so surprised, they could only raise their hands and cry out, "Oh, oh! My goodness!"

Now the old man and woman had always wanted a child of their own, so they were very, very happy to find such a fine little boy, and decided to call him "Momotaro," which means boy-of-the-peach. They took very good care of the little boy and grew to love him dearly, for he was a fine young lad. They spent many happy years together, and before long Momotaro was fifteen years old.

One day Momotaro came before the old man and said, "You have both been good and kind to me. I am very grateful for all you have done, and now I think I am old enough to do some good for others too. I have come to ask if I may leave you."

"You wish to leave us, my son? But why?" asked the old man in surprise.

"Oh, I shall be back in a very short time," said Momotaro. "I wish only to go to the Island of the Ogres, to rid the land of those harmful creatures. They have killed many good people, and have stolen and robbed throughout the country. I wish to kill the ogres so they can never harm our people again."

"That is a fine idea, my son, and I will not stop you from going," said the old man.

So that very day, Momotaro got ready to start out on his journey. The old woman prepared some millet cakes for him to take along on his trip, and soon Momotaro was ready to leave. The old man and woman were sad to see him go and called, "Be careful, Momotaro! Come back safely to us."

"Yes, yes, I shall be back soon," he answered. "Take care of yourselves while I am away," he added, and waved as he started down the path toward the forest.

He hurried along, for he was anxious to get to the Island of the Ogres. While he was walking through the cool forest where the grass grew long and high, he began to feel hungry. He sat down at the foot of a tall pine tree and carefully unwrapped the *furoshiki*[1] which held his little millet cakes. "My, they smell good," he thought. Suddenly he heard the tall grass rustle and saw something stalking through the grass toward him. Momotaro blinked hard when he saw what it was. It was a dog as big as a calf! But Momotaro was not frightened, for the dog just said, "Momotaro-san, Momotaro-san, what is it you are eating that smells so good?"

[1] Pronounced foo-ro-shee-kee, a square cloth used to wrap and carry articles.

"I'm eating a delicious millet cake which my good mother made for me this morning," he answered.

The dog licked his chops and looked at the cake with hungry eyes. "Please, Momotaro-san," he said, "just give me one of your millet cakes, and I will come along with you to the Island of the Ogres. I know why you are going there, and I can be of help to you."

"Very well, my friend," said Momotaro. "I will take you along with me," and he gave the dog one of his millet cakes to eat.

As they walked on, something suddenly leaped from the branches above and jumped in front of Momotaro. He stopped in surprise and found that it was a monkey who had jumped down from the trees.

"Greetings, Momotaro-san!" called the monkey happily. "I have heard that you are going to the Island of the Ogres to rid the land of these plundering creatures. Take me with you, for I wish to help you in your fight."

When the dog heard this he growled angrily. "Grruff," he said to the monkey. "*I* am going to help Momotaro-san. We do not need the help of a monkey such as you! Out of our way! Grruff, grruff," he barked angrily.

"How dare you speak to me like that?" shrieked the monkey, and he leaped at the dog, scratching with his sharp claws. The dog and the monkey began to fight each other, biting, clawing, and growling. When Momotaro saw this he pushed them apart and cried, "Here, here, stop it, you two! There is no reason why you both cannot go with me to the Island of the Ogres. I shall have two helpers instead of one!" Then he took another millet cake from his *furoshiki* and gave it to the monkey.

Now there were three of them going down the path to the edge of the woods. The dog in front, Momotaro in the middle, and the monkey walking in the rear. Soon they came to a big field and just as they were about to cross it, a large pheasant hopped out in front of them. The dog jumped at it with a growl, but the pheasant fought back with such spirit that Momotaro ran over to stop the dog. "We could use a brave bird such as you to help us fight the ogres. We are on our way to their island this very day. How would you like to come along with us?"

"Oh, I would like that indeed, for I would like to help you rid the land of these evil and dangerous ogres," said the pheasant happily.

"Then here is a millet cake for you, too," said Momotaro, giving the pheasant a cake, just as he had to the monkey and the dog.

Now there were four of them going to the Island of the Ogres, and as they walked down the path together, they became very good friends.

Before long they came to the water's edge and Momotaro found a boat big enough for all of them. They climbed in and headed for the Island of the Ogres. Soon they saw the island in the distance wrapped in gray, foggy clouds. Dark stone walls rose up above towering cliffs and large iron gates stood ready to keep out any who tried to enter.

Momotaro thought for a moment, then turned to the pheasant and said, "You alone can wing your way over their high walls and gates. Fly into their stronghold now, and do what you can to frighten them. We will follow as soon as we can."

So the pheasant flew far above the iron gates and stone walls and down onto the roof of the ogres' castle. Then he called to the ogres, "Momotaro-san has come to rid the land of you and your many evil deeds. Give up your stolen treasures now, and perhaps he will spare your lives!"

When the ogres heard this, they laughed and shouted. "HO, HO, HO! We are not afraid of a little bird like you! We are not afraid of little Momotaro!"

The pheasant became very angry at this, and flew down, pecking at the heads of the ogres with his sharp, pointed beak. While the pheasant was fighting so bravely, the dog and monkey helped Momotaro to tear down the gates, and they soon came to the aid of the pheasant.

"Get away! Get away!" shouted the ogres, but the monkey clawed and scratched, the big dog growled and bit the ogres, and the pheasant flew about, pecking at their heads and faces. So fierce were they that soon the ogres began to run away. Half of them tumbled over the cliffs as they ran and the others fell pell-mell into the sea. Soon only the Chief of the Ogres remained. He threw up his hands, and then bowed low to Momotaro. "Please spare me my life, and all our stolen trea-

sures are yours. I promise never to rob or kill anyone again," he said.

Momotaro tied up the evil ogre, while the monkey, the dog and the pheasant carried many boxes filled with jewels and treasures down to their little boat. Soon it was laden with all the treasures it could hold, and they were ready to sail toward home.

When Momotaro returned, he went from one family to another, returning the many treasures which the ogres had stolen from the people of the land.

"You will never again be troubled by the Ogres of Ogre Island!" he said to them happily.

And they all answered, "You are a kind and brave lad, and we thank you for making our land safe once again."

Then Momotaro went back to the home of the old man and woman with his arms full of jewels and treasures from Ogre Island. My, but the old man and woman were glad to see him once again, and the three of them lived happily together for many, many years.

## URASHIMA TARO AND THE PRINCESS OF THE SEA

*This tale, which can be traced back to the eighth century in Japan, bears striking resemblance to such European tales as the Gaelic story of Oisin's sojourn in the Land of the Ever-Young and the Russian "Sadko." It has aptly been called the Japanese "Rip Van Winkle." The simplicity and poetry of the tale have been captured by Taro Yashima in his picture-book version,* The Seashore Story, *a runner-up for the Caldecott Award in 1968.*

Long, long ago, in a small village of Japan, there lived a fine young man named Urashima Taro. He lived with his mother and father in a thatched-roof house which overlooked the sea. Each morning he was up before the sun, and went out to sea in his little fishing boat. On days when his luck was good, he would bring back large baskets full of fish which he sold in the village market.

"Urashimo Taro and the Princess of the Sea." From *The Dancing Kettle and Other Japanese Folk Tales,* copyright, 1949, by Yoshiko Uchida. Reprinted by permission of Harcourt Brace Jovanovich, Inc.

One day, as he was carrying home his load of fish, he saw a group of shouting children. They were gathered around something on the beach and were crying, "Hit him! Poke him!" Taro ran over to see what was the matter, and there on the sand he saw a big brown tortoise. The children were poking it with a long stick and throwing stones at its hard shell.

"Here, here," called Taro. "That's no way to treat him! Why don't you leave him alone, and let him go back to the sea?"

"But we found him," said one of the children. "He belongs to us!"

"Yes, yes, he is ours," cried all the children.

Now, because Urashima Taro was a fair and kindly young man, he said to them, "Suppose I give each of you something in return for the tortoise?" Then he took ten shiny coins out of a small bag of money and gave one to each child. "Now, isn't that a fair bargain?" he asked. "A coin for each of you, and the tortoise for me."

"Yes, yes. Thank you!" called the children, and away they ran to the village candy shop.

Taro watched the old tortoise crawl away slowly toward the sea and called, "You'd better stay at home in the sea from now on, old fellow!" Then, smiling happily because he had been able to save the tortoise, he turned to go home. There his mother and father were waiting for him with bowls of steaming rice and soup.

Several days passed, and Taro soon forgot all about the tortoise whom he had saved. One day he was sitting in his boat feeling very sad because he could catch no fish. Suddenly he heard a voice from the sea calling, "Urashima-san! Urashima-san!"

"Now who could be calling me here in the middle of the sea?" thought Urashima Taro. He looked high and low, but could see no one. Suddenly, from the crest of a big wave, out popped the head of the old tortoise.

"I came to thank you for saving me the other day," said the tortoise.

"Well, I'm glad you got away safely," said Taro.

"This time I would like to do something for you, Urashima-san," said the tortoise. "How would you like to visit the princess who lives in the Palace of the Sea?"

"The princess of the sea!" shouted Taro. "I have heard often of her beauty, and everyone says her palace is more lovely than any place on earth! But how can I go to the bottom of the sea, and how can I enter her palace?"

"Just leave everything to me," said the old tortoise. "Hop on my back and I will see that you get there safely. I will also take you into the palace, for I am one of the palace guards."

So Urashima Taro jumped onto the smooth round back of the tortoise, and away they went.

Swish, swish . . . the waves seemed to part and make a path for them as the tortoise swam on. Soon Taro felt himself going down . . . down . . . down . . . into the sea, but he wasn't getting wet at all. He heard the waves lapping gently about his ears. "That's strange," thought Taro. "This is just like a dream—a nice happy dream."

Before long, they were at the bottom of the big blue sea. Taro could see bright-colored fish playing hide and seek among the long strands of swaying seaweed. He could see clams and other shellfish shyly peeking out at him from their shells. Soon Taro saw something big and shiny looming in the hazy blue water.

"Is that the palace?" he asked anxiously. "It looks very beautiful."

"Oh, no," answered the tortoise. "That is just the outer gate."

They came to a stop and Taro could see that the gateway was guarded by a fish in armor of silver. "Welcome home," the guard called to the tortoise, as he opened the gate for them to enter.

"See whom I have brought back with me," the tortoise answered happily. The guard in the armor of silver turned to Urashima Taro and bowed most politely. Taro just had time to return the bow when he looked up and saw another gate. This one was even larger than the first, and was made of silver stones and pillars of coral. A row of fish in armor of gold was guarding the second gate.

"Now, Urashima-san, if you will get off and wait here, I will tell the princess that you have come," said the tortoise, and he disappeared into the palace beyond the gate. Taro had never seen such a beautiful sight in all his life. The silver stones in the gate sparkled and glittered as though they were smiling at him. Taro had to blink hard.

Soon the tortoise was back at his side telling him that the princess was waiting to see him. He led Taro through the gate of coral and silver, and up a path of golden stones to the palace. There in front of the palace stood the beautiful princess of the sea with her ladies-in-waiting.

"Welcome to the Palace of the Sea, Urashima Taro," she said, and her voice sounded like the tinkling of little silver bells. "Won't you come with me?" she asked.

Taro opened his mouth to answer, but not a

sound would come forth. He could only look at the beautiful princess and the sparkling emeralds and diamonds and rubies which glittered on the walls of the palace. The princess understood how Taro felt, so she just smiled kindly and led him down a hallway paved with smooth, white pearls. Soon they came to a large room, and in the center of the room was an enormous table and an enormous chair. Taro thought they might have been made for a great king.

"Sit down, Urashima-san," said the princess, and as he sat in the enormous chair, the ladies-in-waiting appeared from all sides. They placed on the table plate after plate of all the delicious things that Taro could think of. "Eat well, my friend," said the princess, "and while you dine, my maids will sing and dance for you." Soon there was music and singing and dancing. The room was filled with laughing voices. Taro felt

like a king now! He thought surely this was all a dream, and that it would end soon. But no, after he had dined, the princess took him all through the beautiful palace. At the very last, she brought him to a room that looked as though it were made of ice and snow. There were creamy pearls and sparkling diamonds everywhere.

"Now, how would you like to see all the seasons of the year?" whispered the princess.

"Oh, I would like that very much," answered Taro, and as he spoke, the east door of the room opened slowly and quietly. Taro could scarcely believe the sight before his eyes. He saw big clouds of pale pink cherry blossoms and tall green willow trees swaying in the breeze. He could hear bluebirds singing, and saw them fly happily into the sky.

"Ah, that is spring," murmured Taro. "What a lovely sunny day!" But before he could say more, the princess led him further on. As she opened the door to the south, Taro could see white lotus blossoms floating on a still green pond. It was a warm summer day, and he could hear crickets chirping lazily, somewhere in the distance. She opened the door to the west and he saw a hillside of maple trees. Their leaves of crimson and yellow were whirling and dancing down among golden chrysanthemums. He had seen such trees each fall in his own little village. When the princess opened the door to the north, Taro felt a blast of cold air. He shivered, and looked up to see snowflakes tumbling down from gray skies. They were putting white caps on all the fence posts and treetops.

"Now you have seen all the seasons of the year," said the princess.

"They were beautiful!" sighed Taro happily. "I have never seen such wonderful sights in all my life! I wish I could stay here always!"

Taro was having such a very good time that he forgot all about his home in the village. He feasted and danced and sang with his friends in the Palace of the Sea, and before he knew it, three long years had gone by. But to Taro they seemed to be just three short days.

At last Taro said to the princess, "Alas, I have been here much too long. I must go home to see my mother and father so they will not worry about me."

"But you will come back?" asked the princess.

"Oh, yes, yes. I will come back," answered Taro.

"Before you go I have something for you," said the princess, and she gave Taro a small jewel box studded with many precious stones.

"Oh, it is beautiful, Princess," said Taro. "How can I thank you for all you have done for me?"

But the princess went on, "There is just one thing about that box," she said. "You must never, never open it if you ever wish to return to the Palace of the Sea. Can you remember that, Urashima Taro?"

"I will never open it, no matter what happens," promised Taro. Then he said good-bye to all his friends in the palace. Once again he climbed on the back of the old tortoise and they sailed toward his village on the seacoast. The princess and her ladies-in-waiting stood at the coral gate and waved to Taro till he could no longer see them. The tortoise swam on and on, and one by one all the little bright-colored fish that had been following them began to turn back. Before long, Taro could see the seacoast where he used to go fishing, and soon they were back on the very beach where Taro had once saved the tortoise. Taro hopped off onto the smooth white sand. "Good-bye, old friend," he said. "You have been very good to me. Thank you for taking me to the most beautiful place I have ever seen."

"Farewell, Urashima-san," said the old tortoise. "I hope we may meet again some day." Then he turned and crawled slowly back into the sea.

Now that he was in his own village once more, Taro was most anxious to see his parents. He ran along the path which led to their house with his jewel box tucked securely under his arm. He looked eagerly at each person whom he passed. He wanted to shout a greeting to them, but each face seemed strange and new. "How odd!" thought Taro. "I feel as though I were in some other village than my own. I don't seem to know anyone. Well, I'll soon see Mother and Father," he said, and hurried on. When he reached the spot where the house should have been, there was no house to be seen. There was just an empty lot full of tall green weeds. Taro couldn't believe his eyes. "Why, what has happened to my home? Where are my parents?" he cried. He looked up and down the dusty path and soon saw an old, old woman coming toward him. "I'll ask her what has happened to my home," thought Taro.

"Old woman, please, can you help me?" asked Taro.

The old woman straightened her bent back and cocked her gray head, "Eh, what did you say?" she asked.

"Can you tell me what happened to Urashima Taro's home? It used to be right here," said Taro.

"Never heard of him," said the old woman, shaking her head.

"But you must have," Taro replied. "He lived right here, on this very spot where you are standing."

"Now let me see," she sighed. "Urashima Taro. Yes, it seems I have heard of him. Oh, I remember now. There is a story that he went out to sea in his fishing boat one day and never came back again. I suppose he was drowned at sea. Well, anyway, that was over three hundred years ago. My great-great-grandfather used to tell me about Urashima Taro when I was just a little girl."

"Three hundred years!" exclaimed Taro. His eyes were like saucers now. "But I don't understand."

"Well, I don't understand what you want with a man who lived three hundred years ago," muttered the old woman, and she trudged on down the road.

"So three years in the Palace of the Sea has really been three hundred years here in my village," thought Taro. "No wonder all my friends are gone. No wonder I can't find my mother or father!" Taro had never felt so lonely or so sad as he did then. "What can I do? What can I do?" he murmured to himself.

Suddenly he remembered the little jewel box which the princess had given him. "Perhaps there is something in there that can help me," he thought, and forgetting the promise he had made to the princess, he quickly opened the box. Suddenly, there arose from it a cloud of white smoke which wrapped itself around Taro so that he could see nothing. When it disappeared, Urashima Taro peered into the empty box, but he could scarcely see. He looked at his hands and they were the hands of an old, old man. His face was wrinkled; his hair was as white as snow. In that short moment Urashima Taro had become three hundred years older. He remembered the promise he had made to the princess, but now it was too late and he knew that he could never visit the Palace of the Sea again. But who knows, perhaps one day the old tortoise came back to the beach once more to help his friend.

## Korea

*Korea, once called the* Hermit Kingdom *during the long period between the late 1500's and late 1800's when she deliberately isolated herself from the world, is in many ways unknown to us. Most of the world knows of her, thanks to a recent long and terrible war, but few people are acquainted with her proud history, her contributions to world culture (such as the invention of movable metal printing type), and her fine artistic and literary traditions. Only one book of Korean folk tales for children exists to unshroud partially the mystery of her folklore. That is Eleanore M. Jewett's* Which Was Witch? *and from it we can see that Korean tales are full of ghosts and magic. As interpreted by Miss Jewett, the stories are beautiful in style and content and make a fine contribution to the storyteller's repertory.*

## WHICH WAS WITCH?

*Despite its witty title, this tale is a good eerie one—especially for Halloween.*

There was once a wise and learned man named Kim Su-ik. He lived just inside the south gate of Seoul but he might as well have lived anywhere for all the thought he gave the matter. His mind was entirely taken up with study and books, and one could say of him, as Im Bang said of another scholar, "He used to awake at first cockcrow, wash, dress, take up his book and never lay it aside. On his right were pictures, on his left were books, and he happy between. He rose to be a Prime Minister."

One night Kim Su-ik was absorbed in studying a Chinese classic when he suddenly felt hungry. He clapped his hands to summon a servant, and immediately the door of his room opened.

His wife stepped in.

"What does the master of the house desire?" said she.

"Food," he answered briefly, his attention already returned to the book in his lap.

"I have little in the house but a few roasted chestnuts. If that will suffice I will bring them to you myself. The servants have long since gone to their sleeping quarters."

Kim Su-ik grunted his approval and went on with his studies. In a very short time the door opened again and his wife came in bearing a brass bowl full of hot roasted chestnuts. He helped himself to one and was in the act of putting it into his mouth when once more the door opened and in stepped his wife with a brass bowl full of hot roasted chestnuts.

But his wife was already there, standing beside him with the bowl in her hands!

Kim Su-ik, his mouth still open and a chestnut half in it, looked in astonishment from one to the other of the identical women. They were as like as two pins—faces, features, figures, clothes, the way they stood, the way they used their fingers and moved their shoulders. Never were twins more completely alike. Kim Su-ik passed his hands before his eyes. He must have over-

done his studying, he thought to himself, read too late and too steadily. His eyes were playing tricks on him, that was all. He was seeing double.

But when he looked again the two women were still there, and what was stranger still, they seemed not to be aware of each other, but stood quietly, gracefully, their eyes fastened on him as if waiting to know his pleasure.

The scholar leaped to his feet, choking back the cry of terror that rose in his throat. He knew, suddenly, without a doubt, what this meant. It was midnight, the moon was at the full, ghosts, evil spirits, witches and goblins would be abroad, filled with power. One of these two creatures standing before him was his wife, known and loved by him all his wedded life—and perhaps not quite fully appreciated, he hastily decided. The other must be a witch, able to change into any form she chose in the twinkling of an eye. But *which was which?* How could he protect his wife and drive this evil double from beside her?

Being a quick thinker as well as a learned one, Kim Su-ik plunged into action. He seized the arm of one of the women with his right hand and before the other could realize what he was about, he had her arm fast in his left hand. They turned mildly reproachful eyes upon him but made no effort to free themselves.

"My dear," said one, "too much study has fevered your brain."

"My dear," said the other, "too much reading of books has affected your mind."

Kim Su-ik looked from one to the other. Not a particle of difference was there to give him a hint as to which was wife and which was witch. He shook them gently. They smiled indulgently as at a child. He shook harder. No resentment, no struggle to get free. He was tempted to relax his grip on the two arms, but he knew he must not for a moment do that, and hung on more firmly than ever.

Minutes went by, then hours, the dull slow moving hours between midnight and cockcrow. The three stood silent, motionless, in the same spot. Kim Su-ik grew weary beyond words. So, too, must his wife be weary, but neither of the two women he held so tightly by the arm said anything or showed by any movement or expression of the face that she was tired, puzzled or angry. His wife would have been tired and puzzled—angry, too, perhaps, but she would not have blustered or scolded. Any other woman would, were she witch or human. But surely his wife would say *something*. What in the world had got into her? Was she bewitched? Or walking in her sleep? Perhaps she was not either one of these two women. He wanted to rush into the other part of the house to see if she was there, thus proving that both of these were witches. But he did nothing, just hung on, grimly, silently.

At long last a cock crowed. Immediately the woman at his left tried to wrench her arm free. The other remained quiet. Kim Su-ik dropped the unresisting one and threw all his strength into a struggle with the other. Like a wild thing the creature fought, biting, snarling, spitting, leaping back and forth. Still the scholar held on to her and would not let go. The arm in his hand shrank and grew hairy. The whole figure

dwindled, the eyes grew round and green and blazed with fury.

Another cock crowed and another, and the first gray light of dawn melted the dark shadows out of doors. But Kim Su-ik had no thought or time to notice the coming of day. With a hideous shriek the creature changed before his very eyes into a powerful wildcat. In horror he loosed his hold, and she leaped through the window and was gone.

"I still think you are studying too much," said a quiet, familiar voice behind him, and there stood his wife, pale, trembling a little, but smiling confidently.

"Why didn't you let me know which was which?" demanded Kim Su-ik.

His wife laughed. "I don't know what you are talking about! You behaved very strangely, but then, one never knows what to expect of a scholar. Which was which what?"

"Witch!" said Kim Su-ik.

# Vietnam

*The land of Vietnam, like Korea, is much older than most of us realize.
While its first settlers may have been of Chinese origin, the Vietnamese people
are not Chinese; for many centuries they have clung to their land and
their customs in defiance of the older, more powerful civilization to the north. The
history of Vietnam has yet to be written for us, but in the folk tales of this
land we find echoes of that history and can discern the spirit of the people. The
two tales presented here, retold from oral and printed sources, are but an
indication of the unique quality of Vietnam's folklore.*

**THE LOVE CRYSTAL**

*This is one of the most exquisite tales to come
from the Orient. In Vietnam there is also a song,*

*equally exquisite, that accompanies the story. Although it is an adult kind of tale, it speaks movingly even to youngsters because of its imagery
and lyricism.*

Long ago in the Serene Land, a beautiful maiden lived in a palace beside a tranquil river. Her father was a great Mandarin. So great was her beauty that it was forbidden anyone but the members of the Mandarin's household to look upon her. In order to keep the girl from the gaze of all others, the Mandarin had her put in the top of a tower which rose above the river. There she passed the lonely hours embroidering and reading, waiting for the man who was destined to come and make her his bride.

Often she would gaze out upon the river below and dream of all the places the river had been in its winding course. As she watched the river one day, she saw a poor fisherman sailing his small boat. She could not see him well from such a height, but he looked from afar to be young and strong. He played a flute, and its melody rose sweet and clear to the tower where the Mandarin's daughter looked down on him. She was struck with joy and wonder at the plaintive sound. It was somehow sad and tender, and as she listened she was deeply moved. The music spoke to her of faraway places she would never see. It spoke to her of feelings for which there are no words. It spoke to her of all the things which make the earth beautiful.

Day after day the fisherman played his flute as his small boat passed beneath the tower where the lonely girl listened in rapture. The pure tones of the flute wound upward like a silver thread of sound. Perhaps, she thought, he was some prince in disguise whom fate meant to be her husband. For the songs he played were like songs of love, especially one which he played over and over until the girl heard it repeated nightly in her dreams. Although she was too shy to send for him, she threw down flower petals to show him her delight.

The fisherman knew that a maiden dwelt high in the tower, and when the flower petals drifted down to the water beside his boat, he knew that she liked his songs. He thought she must be beautiful, even though he had never clearly seen her face.

And so a bond grew between them, a bond

"The Love Crystal." Adapted from *The Fisherman and the Goblet* by Mark Taylor. Published in 1969 by Golden Gate Junior Books. Reprinted by permission of Childrens Press

made of his songs and her pleasure in them. It was enough. As she listened to his flute and as he caught the softly falling petals, each fancied only the best about the other.

One day the fisherman did not appear. He had learned that it was the Mandarin's daughter who lived in the tower; he dared not return. The girl waited until the sun departed from the sky and would not leave the window until the cool evening breeze swept across the empty river.

When the fisherman did not appear the next day, the girl felt despair. She refused to turn away from the window either to eat or to sleep. All that night she kept vigil with the moon, praying that the fisherman and his flute songs would return. But when the day dawned and waned and the fisherman never came, the girl at last wept. As one day followed after the other, she sat by the window growing pale and thin. At first she wept often; then she became silent. Her loveliness began to pale as does a flower which slowly wilts and fades.

The doctors were summoned in vain to find

the cause of her illness. The Mandarin and his wife were frantic. They were not bad people, they merely wanted to protect their beautiful daughter. Now all had somehow gone wrong and she was wasting away. Then the girl's maid could no longer be silent, and whether the Mandarin should be angry or not, she told him about the fisherman whose flute songs had charmed his daughter.

The Mandarin sent for the fisherman. He was brought to the palace. The poor fisherman was indeed young and strong as the girl had imagined, but his face was ugly.

"Although you are only a humble fisherman," said the Mandarin, "your songs hold the key to my daughter's well-being. Perhaps you are the man fate has destined to become her husband. Let us see if she will love you as she has loved your music."

The fisherman was distressed. "I do not want to have the power of life and death over your daughter," he said. "I only played my songs beneath the tower because she seemed to like them. I have never even gazed upon her face."

The fisherman was taken to the foot of the tower and bade to play his flute. When the girl heard the music, she was filled with joy. She rushed from the tower down the winding stairs to where the fisherman stood. Surely he would be as handsome as his songs were beautiful. Surely he was a prince in disguise. Alas, no! He was ugly. And as she tried to thank him for his music, the maiden turned away in dismay.

When the fisherman saw the Mandarin's daughter, he was struck with love for her. But when she turned from him, he knew such love was hopeless. Sadly he went away, and sadly the girl returned to the top of the tower. Although she was cured, something beautiful had gone from her life.

No more did the fisherman return in his boat. Never again did the girl hear his flute. In time she almost forgot him, except for the echo of his one most beautiful flute song in her dreams. A year passed, and still the girl lived in the tower, waiting for the prince who never came.

But long before the year had passed, the fisherman had died. For soon after he fell in love with the Mandarin's daughter, he died from the utter hopelessness of it. All his beauty was in his music and not in his face, and the girl wanted only his songs.

When the fisherman was to be buried, his family found beside him an exquisite crystal. Everyone realized that the crystal was made from his unanswered love. They put it in the prow of his boat as a remembrance of him whose flute would never be heard and enjoyed again. The flute they gave to the river.

One day, when the Mandarin was boating upon the river, he saw the fisherman's boat with the shining crystal fixed to its bow. When he learned how it came to be there, he was deeply moved and asked to buy it. A good price was paid for the crystal and the Mandarin had it taken to the turner and made into a teacup.

No cup more exquisite had ever been seen! But strange and wonderful to tell, when tea was poured into the cup an image would appear in it. It was the image of the dead fisherman in his boat. And as it sailed around the cup, one could faintly hear his flute.

Thinking to please his daughter, the Mandarin took her the crystal cup. When she saw the fisherman's image and heard the same flute song that haunted her dreams, she was overwhelmed with grief. Hiding her distress, however, she asked to be alone with the cup.

When all had left her, the girl poured tea in the cup and held it in her hands. As she gazed into it she saw the fisherman and heard—as clearly as though he were again on the river—his flute playing his song of love. Then she realized that a heart which can make music is more important than an ugly face. Our faces are given to us, but our hearts are fashioned by our own hands. She knew that the fisherman had loved her enough to die, and her indifference had brought him death.

Quietly the maiden wept, and as she did her tears fell into the cup. Slowly the crystal dissolved, for her tears were made of love and they at last brought peace to the fisherman's soul.

Later they found the girl sitting beside the window. Her soul had left her body, leaving her as still as stone. From the river they faintly heard the sound of someone unseen playing upon a flute. Then all knew that at last the Mandarin's beautiful daughter and the fisherman were together in happiness.

# India

*Until recent years, most of the Indian tales offered to children have
come from two literary classics,* The Panchatantra (*the oldest known collection
of Indian fables*) *and the* Jatakas (*fables about the many reincar-
nations of Gautama Buddha in animal forms*). *Both collections are readily
traced to the second and third centuries* B.C., *and both have informed
many of the later tales found in Europe as well as in India.
Of possibly more than 3000* Jataka *tales a fraction have been successfully retold for children. When references to the Buddha are omitted in these,
good talking-beast tales remain. Therefore selections from the* Jatakas
*have been included with the folk tales in this anthology. Recent compilations of
stories from India have moved away from the* Jatakas, The Panchatantra,
*and ancient epics like* The Ramayana, *and a feeling for the common folk of
India is to be found in the picture-book tale* The Valiant
Chattee-Maker, *a humorous retelling by Christine Price, and* The Beautiful
Blue Jay and Other Tales of India, *by John Spellman. By no means
will such books displace our interest in the old classics, but they will be of aid
in helping children sense something of life and thought in India today.*

## THE HARE THAT RAN AWAY

*These next three tales are from the Jatakas. In
each instance they are rather more gentle and
ethical than dramatic. "The Hare That Ran
Away" is obviously the ancestor of "Henny-
Penny." The story may begin without the reference to Buddha, "Once there was a wise Lion
who did much to help his fellow creatures and
he found there was much to be done. For instance, there was a little nervous Hare . . . ."*

And it came to pass that the Buddha (to be)
was born again as a Lion. Just as he had helped
his fellow-men, he now began to help his fellow-
animals, and there was a great deal to be done.
For instance, there was a little nervous Hare who
was always afraid that something dreadful was
going to happen to her. She was always saying:
"Suppose the Earth were to fall in, what would
happen to me?" And she said this so often that at
last she thought it really was about to happen.
One day, when she had been saying over and
over again, "Suppose the Earth were to fall in,
what would happen to me?" she heard a slight
noise: it really was only a heavy fruit which had

fallen upon a rustling leaf, but the little Hare
was so nervous she was ready to believe anything,
and she said in a frightened tone: "The Earth *is*
falling in." She ran away as fast as she could go,
and presently she met an old brother Hare, who
said: "Where are you running to, Mistress
Hare?"

And the little Hare said: "I have no time to
stop and tell you anything. The Earth is falling
in, and I am running away."

"The Earth is falling in, is it?" said the old
brother Hare, in a tone of much astonishment;
and he repeated this to *his* brother hare, and *he*
to *his* brother hare, and *he* to *his* brother hare,
until at last there were a hundred thousand
brother hares, all shouting: "The Earth is falling
in." Now presently the bigger animals began to
take the cry up. First the deer, and then the
sheep, and then the wild boar, and then the buffalo, and then the camel, and then the tiger, and
then the elephant.

Now the wise Lion heard all this noise and
wondered at it. "There are no signs," he said, "of
the Earth falling in. They must have heard
something." And then he stopped them all short
and said: "What is this you are saying?"

And the Elephant said: "I remarked that the
Earth was falling in."

"How do you know this?" asked the Lion.

"Why, now I come to think of it, it was the Tiger that remarked it to me."

And the Tiger said: "*I* had it from the Camel," and the Camel said: "*I* had it from the Buffalo." And the buffalo from the wild boar, and the wild boar from the sheep, and the sheep from the deer, and the deer from the hares, and the Hares said: "Oh! *we* heard it from *that* little Hare."

And the Lion said: "Little Hare, *what* made you say that the Earth was falling in?"

And the little Hare said: "I *saw* it."

"You saw it?" said the Lion. "Where?"

"Yonder by the tree."

"Well," said the Lion, "come with me and I will show you how——"

"No, no," said the Hare, "I would not go near that tree for anything, I'm *so* nervous."

"But," said the Lion, "I am going to take you on my back." And he took her on his back, and begged the animals to stay where they were until they returned. Then he showed the little Hare how the fruit had fallen upon the leaf, making the noise that had frightened her, and she said: "Yes, I see—the Earth is *not* falling in." And the Lion said: "Shall we go back and tell the other animals?"

And they went back. The little Hare stood before the animals and said: "The Earth is *not* falling in." And all the animals began to repeat this to one another, and they dispersed gradually, and you heard the words more and more softly: "The Earth is *not* falling in," etc., etc., etc., until the sound died away altogether.

## GRANNY'S BLACKIE

Once upon a time a rich man gave a baby Elephant to a woman.

She took the best of care of this great baby and soon became very fond of him.

The children in the village called her Granny, and they called the Elephant "Granny's Blackie."

The Elephant carried the children on his back

"Granny's Blackie." From *The Jataka Tales* by Ellen C. Babbitt, Copyright © 1912, Renewed Copyright © 1940. By permission of Prentice-Hall, Inc., Englewood Cliffs, New Jersey

all over the village. They shared their goodies with him and he played with them.

"Please, Blackie, give us a swing," they said to him almost every day.

"Come on! Who is first?" Blackie answered and picked them up with his trunk, swung them high in the air, and then put them down again, carefully.

But Blackie never did any work.

He ate and slept, played with the children, and visited with Granny.

One day Blackie wanted Granny to go off to the woods with him.

"I can't go, Blackie, dear. I have too much work to do."

Then Blackie looked at her and saw that she was growing old and feeble.

"I am young and strong," he thought. "I'll see if I cannot find some work to do. If I could bring some money home to her, she would not have to work so hard."

So next morning, bright and early, he started down to the river bank.

There he found a man who was in great trouble. There was a long line of wagons so heavily loaded that the oxen could not draw them through the shallow water.

When the man saw Blackie standing on the bank he asked, "Who owns this Elephant? I want to hire him to help my Oxen pull these wagons across the river."

A child standing near by said, "That is Granny's Blackie."

"Very well," said the man, "I'll pay two pieces of silver for each wagon this Elephant draws across the river."

Blackie was glad to hear this promise. He went into the river, and drew one wagon after another across to the other side.

Then he went up to the man for the money.

The man counted out one piece of silver for each wagon.

When Blackie saw that the man had counted out but one piece of silver for each wagon, instead of two, he would not touch the money at all. He stood in the road and would not let the wagons pass him.

The man tried to get Blackie out of the way, but not one step would he move.

Then the man went back and counted out another piece of silver for each of the wagons and put the silver in a bag tied around Blackie's neck.

Then Blackie started for home, proud to think that he had a present for Granny.

The children had missed Blackie and had asked Granny where he was, but she said she did not know where he had gone.

They all looked for him but it was nearly night before they heard him coming.

"Where have you been, Blackie? And what is that around your neck?" the children cried, running to meet their playmate.

But Blackie would not stop to talk with his playmates. He ran straight home to Granny.

"Oh, Blackie!" she said. "Where have you been? What is in that bag?" And she took the bag off his neck.

Blackie told her that he had earned some money for her.

"Oh, Blackie, Blackie," said Granny, "how hard you must have worked to earn these pieces of silver! What a good Blackie you are!"

And after that Blackie did all the hard work and Granny rested, and they were both very happy.

## THE BANYAN DEER

There was once a Deer the color of gold. His eyes were like round jewels, his horns were white as silver, his mouth was red like a flower, his hoofs were bright and hard. He had a large body and a fine tail.

He lived in a forest and was king of a herd of five hundred Banyan Deer. Near by lived another herd of Deer, called the Monkey Deer. They, too, had a king.

The king of that country was fond of hunting the Deer and eating deer meat. He did not like to go alone so he called the people of his town to go with him, day after day.

The townspeople did not like this for while they were gone no one did their work. So they decided to make a park and drive the Deer into it. Then the king could go into the park and

"The Banyan Deer" from *The Jataka Tales* by Ellen C. Babbitt © 1912, Renewed © 1940. By permission of Prentice-Hall, Inc., Englewood Cliffs, New Jersey

hunt and they could go on with their daily work.

They made a park, planted grass in it and provided water for the Deer, built a fence all around it and drove the Deer into it.

Then they shut the gate and went to the king to tell him that in the park near by he could find all the Deer he wanted.

The king went at once to look at the Deer. First he saw there the two Deer kings, and granted them their lives. Then he looked at their great herds.

Some days the king would go to hunt the Deer, sometimes his cook would go. As soon as any of the Deer saw them they would shake with fear and run. But when they had been hit once or twice they would drop down dead.

The King of the Banyan Deer sent for the King of the Monkey Deer and said, "Friend, many of the Deer are being killed. Many are wounded besides those who are killed. After this suppose one from my herd goes up to be killed one day, and the next day let one from your herd go up. Fewer Deer will be lost this way."

The Monkey Deer agreed. Each day the Deer whose turn it was would go and lie down, placing its head on the block. The cook would come and carry off the one he found lying there.

One day the lot fell to a mother Deer who had a young baby. She went to her king and said, "O King of the Monkey Deer, let the turn pass me by until my baby is old enough to get along without me. Then I will go and put my head on the block."

But the king did not help her. He told her that if the lot had fallen to her she must die.

Then she went to the King of the Banyan Deer and asked him to save her.

"Go back to your herd. I will go in your place," said he.

The next day the cook found the King of the Banyan Deer lying with his head on the block. The cook went to the king, who came himself to find out about this.

"King of the Banyan Deer! did I not grant you your life? Why are you lying here?"

"O great King!" said the King of the Banyan Deer, "a mother came with her young baby and told me that the lot had fallen to her. I could not ask any one else to take her place, so I came myself."

"King of the Banyan Deer! I never saw such kindness and mercy. Rise up. I grant your life and hers. Nor will I hunt any more the Deer in either park or forest."

## THE TIGER, THE BRAHMAN,
## AND THE JACKAL

*There is a series of jackal stories in which the jackal is generally the trickster who is finally caught and punished, but in this story the tables are turned. Children will be satisfied with the explanation that a brahman is a wise, good man. Further details are unnecessary.*

Once upon a time a tiger was caught in a trap. He tried in vain to get out through the bars, and rolled and bit with rage and grief when he failed.

By chance a poor Brahman came by. "Let me out of this cage, O pious one!" cried the tiger.

"Nay, my friend," replied the Brahman mildly, "you would probably eat me if I did."

"Not at all!" swore the tiger with many oaths; "on the contrary, I should be for ever grateful, and serve you as a slave!"

Now when the tiger sobbed and sighed and wept and swore, the pious Brahman's heart softened, and at last he consented to open the door of the cage. Out popped the tiger, and, seizing the poor man, cried, "What a fool you are! What is to prevent my eating you now, for after being cooped up so long I am just terribly hungry!"

In vain the Brahman pleaded for his life; the most he could gain was a promise to abide by the decision of the first three things he chose to question as to the justice of the tiger's action.

So the Brahman first asked a *pipal* tree what it thought of the matter, but the *pipal* tree replied coldly, "What have you to complain about? Don't I give shade and shelter to every one who passes by, and don't they in return tear down my branches to feed their cattle? Don't whimper—be a man!"

Then the Brahman, sad at heart, went farther afield till he saw a buffalo turning a well-wheel; but he fared no better from it, for it answered, "You are a fool to expect gratitude! Look at me! While I gave milk they fed me on cotton-seed and oil-cake, but now I am dry they yoke me here, and give me refuse as fodder!"

The Brahman, still more sad, asked the road to give him its opinion.

"My dear sir," said the road, "how foolish you are to expect anything else! Here am I, useful to

"The Tiger, the Brahman, and the Jackal." From *Tales of the Punjab* by Flora Annie Steel. Copyright 1933 by The Macmillan Company. Reprinted by permission of Macmillan, London and Basingstoke and The Bodley Head

everybody, yet all, rich and poor, great and small, trample on me as they go past, giving me nothing but the ashes of their pipes and the husks of their grain!"

On this the Brahman turned back sorrowfully, and on the way he met a jackal, who called out, "Why, what's the matter, Mr. Brahman? You look as miserable as a fish out of water!"

Then the Brahman told him all that had occurred. "How very confusing!" said the jackal, when the recital was ended; "would you mind telling me over again? for everything seems so mixed up!"

The Brahman told it all over again, but the jackal shook his head in a distracted sort of way, and still could not understand.

"It's very odd," said he sadly, "but it all seems to go in at one ear and out at the other! I will go to the place where it all happened, and then perhaps I shall be able to give a judgment."

So they returned to the cage, by which the tiger was waiting for the Brahman, and sharpening his teeth and claws.

"You've been away a long time!" growled the savage beast, "but now let us begin our dinner."

"*Our* dinner!" thought the wretched Brahman, as his knees knocked together with fright; "what a remarkably delicate way of putting it!"

"Give me five minutes, my lord!" he pleaded, "in order that I may explain matters to the jackal here, who is somewhat slow in his wits."

The tiger consented, and the Brahman began the whole story over again, not missing a single detail, and spinning as long a yarn as possible.

"Oh, my poor brain! oh, my poor brain!" cried the jackal, wringing his paws. "Let me see! how did it all begin? You were in the cage, and the tiger came walking by——"

"Pooh!" interrupted the tiger, "what a fool you are! *I* was in the cage."

"Of course!" cried the jackal, pretending to tremble with fright; "yes! I was in the cage—no, I wasn't—dear! dear! where are my wits? Let me see—the tiger was in the Brahman, and the cage came walking by—no, that's not it either! Well, don't mind me, but begin your dinner, for I shall never understand!"

"Yes, you shall!" returned the tiger, in a rage at the jackal's stupidity; "I'll *make* you understand! Look here—I am the tiger——"

"Yes, my lord!"
"And that is the Brahman——"
"Yes, my lord!"
"And that is the cage——"
"Yes, my lord!"
"And I was in the cage—do you understand?"
"Yes—no—Please, my lord——"
"Well?" cried the tiger, impatiently.
"Please, my lord!—how did you get in?"
"How!—why, in the usual way, of course!"
"Oh dear me!—my head is beginning to whirl again! Please don't be angry, my lord, but what is the usual way?"

At this the tiger lost patience, and jumping into the cage, cried, "This way! Now do you understand how it was?"

"Perfectly!" grinned the jackal, as he dexterously shut the door; "and if you will permit me to say so, I think matters will remain as they were!"

## THE CARTMAN'S STORIES

*One can see how this tale reflects the age-old experience and current wisdom of people. It is a great satisfaction to observe how the cartman turns his misfortune into good fortune by simply following three adages. John Spellman took these tales just as he heard them told by Indian mothers to their children.*

There once was a very poor farmer who had such a small farm that it was only with great difficulty that he was able to care for his family with its earnings. Still, like most Indian farmers, he lived a happy and contented life. Men are usually self-satisfied and contented with their lot whatever it may be. But that is never true of women. The farmer's wife was always grumbling about her fate and cursed him for his poverty. She urged him to do some side business to add to the small earnings of the farm.

One day he finally got tired of his wife's pestering and decided to do something about it. He took out his cart and put it up for hire. Fortunately he got a customer very soon. The village merchant wanted to take some merchandise to a nearby village, so he engaged the poor farmer.

After loading the merchandise they both started for the next village. On the way the cartman began to be bored by the complete silence of the merchant. He said to the merchant, "Sir, why don't you talk? Do you know any stories or yarns?"

The merchant was not a talkative fellow. He disliked talk. So, to avoid talking, he told the cartman, "Look, I will give you a story, but I will charge you one *rupee* for each story I tell."

The cartman took it as a joke and said, "Come! Come! Let us hear some nice stories from you. Nobody charges for friendly and free talk." The merchant would not agree and the cartman would not keep quiet. He kept nagging the merchant to tell a story.

The merchant thought he would teach him a good lesson.

"All right," he said. "Listen to my story.

"Never refuse or disobey a request made by the village council.

"My story is over," he said. "Pay me my rupee."

The cartman still thought it was all a joke, so he insisted on having another story. The merchant said, "All right. Listen to my second story.

"Never tell a secret or a truth to a woman.

"My story is over, give me another rupee."

The cartman still took it as a joke and insisted on a nice long yarn that would really entertain him.

The merchant said, "Very well, listen to my third story.

"Never tell a falsehood in a law court.

"My story is over. Give me my third rupee."

Still the cartman took it as a joke and insisted on a really good story. But the merchant would not tell one. He knew the poor cartman had no money to pay, and he did not want to waste his breath for nothing. The fare agreed for the trip was only three rupees. The merchant thought to recover it from the cartman as his payment for the three stories. For a long time he kept on arguing with the cartman, but he would not tell him any more stories.

At last they came to their destination. The cartman unloaded the goods and demanded his fare. The merchant said, "Pay me my three ru-pees for my three stories and I will pay you your fare."

The cartman never expected the joke would be carried so far and so seriously. He was so disappointed and dejected that he did not know what to do. He had no money for food or fodder for his bullocks. And worst of all, what would he tell his wife when he went home? He felt like drowning himself in the river. Dejected, disappointed and weary, the poor cartman started homeward. His fellow cartmen jeered at him for his foolishness, but he listened quietly to all the jeering.

On the way they all came to a village. A destitute beggar had died suddenly, and the village council had met to make arrangements for the disposal of the body. They wanted a cart to carry the body to the cremation ground, but nobody would agree to do it. They disliked the idea of carrying a dead body.

When our cartman was approached, he thought for a moment and then readily agreed, for he was very badly in need of money. Besides, he remembered the merchant's advice in his first story: "Never refuse or disobey a request made by a village council." He decided to see how true it was, since he had paid such a high price for it.

The village council members loaded the dead body into the cart and paid him a rupee for the freight. They told him to take the body to the cremation ground, burn it, throw the ashes into the holy river and then go to his home. The cartman transported the body, put it on the funeral bier, set fire to it and sat down to watch the burning body. When it had completely burned, he went to collect the ashes. To his great surprise he found many tiny, hot bits of glittering gold among the ashes. The gold had been around the waist of the body, hidden under the clothes, left there unknown to anybody. He quickly collected them, put them in his pocket, threw the ashes in the river, and went back to his home in the dead of night.

Before he returned, his companions had already reported the whole story to his wife, so the wife was waiting to scold him. She greeted him with very harsh words, but somehow the poor man succeeded in consoling her. He gave her the rupee he had earned and she was satisfied for the moment. When everybody was asleep he quietly got up and buried the gold in a secret place.

For several days he did not do any work at all but spent his time idling. His wife became very angry, but he did not pay any attention. One day he quietly took out a part of the hidden gold, sold it in the market and bought clothes and provisions for himself and his family.

People were astonished and very curious about his sudden wealth. When they asked him about it, he would say, "God comes in my dreams and gives me money." They would not believe him and planned to force the secret from his wife. But the wife did not know anything either. She was just as curious as the others, and she finally asked her husband. He thought for a time and then remembered the merchant's second story: "Never tell a secret or truth to womenfolk." So he said, "Look, dear, I go into the jungle and drink *dhattura* juice. Then my hairs

become gold and I pluck them and sell them."

Now everyone knows that dhattura juice is poisonous, but all the people started to drink it just the same. They all became seriously ill from the poison and some died. Complaints went to the police about this mishap. An enquiry was held and the source was traced to the cartman, who was arrested and put before the court.

When the judge asked the man to explain himself, he thought for a moment and told the whole truth from beginning to end, for he remembered 'the merchant's third story: "Never tell a falsehood in the law court."

The magistrate was greatly amused by his story and acquitted him, for he was quite innocent. He said, "It served the people right, for they did a foolish thing without considering the effects of their thoughtless actions."

Then the farmer lived very happily ever after.

## *Oceania and Australia*

*Although folklorists and anthropologists have been active for several centuries in recording the folklore of the peoples of the Pacific, we have few tales from Oceania and Australia. A great body of material has been gathered, but no really outstanding collection of tales from the islands is yet available for children. From Australia we have only a recent edition of Mrs. K. Langloh Parker's stories taken from the Aborigines of New South Wales, Australian Legendary Tales. These tales, first published in 1896, were recorded from the now-extinct Euahlayi people with whom Mrs. Parker played as a child. Although folklorists do not consider her work a primary contribution to scholarship, the stories are told simply and honestly as she heard them. It was no easy task to put Aborigine thoughts into English, and many tales in the Parker collection seem strange, falling short of what we think of as "good stories." But they are all we have from the Aborigines that will appeal to boys and girls in the upper grades. As for the folklore of the European settlers in Australia, nothing in the way of tales for children has appeared.*

### BEEREEUN THE MIRAGEMAKER

#### (*Australian*)

*Most why stories explain a single fact or phenomenon, but this one explains several. Moreover, the Aborigine words in it will amuse children with their strange, lyrical sounds and may serve as a small vocabulary study. Note how*

*much geography and natural history are conveyed by this rather rambling tale.*

Beereeun the lizard wanted to marry Bullai Bullai the green parrot sisters. But they did not

"Beereeun the Miragemaker." From *Australian Legendary Tales* collected and edited by H. Drake-Brockman. All Rights Reserved. Reprinted by permission of The Viking Press, Inc., and Angus & Robertson Ltd., Sidney

want to marry him. They liked Weedah the mockingbird better. Their mother said they must marry Beereeun, for she had pledged them to him at their births, and Beereeun was a great wirinun and would harm them if they did not keep her pledge.

When Weedah came back from hunting they told him what their mother had said, how they had been pledged to Beereeun, who now claimed them.

"Tomorrow," said Weedah, "old Beereeun goes to meet a tribe coming from the Springs country. While he is away we will go toward the Big River, and burn the track behind us. I will go out as if to hunt as usual in the morning. I will hide myself in the thick gidya scrub. You two must follow later and meet me there. We will then cross the big plain where the grass is now thick and dry. Bring with you a fire stick. We will throw it back into the plain, then no one can follow our tracks. On we will go to the Big River. There I have a friend who has a goombeelga, a bark canoe. Then shall we be safe from pursuit, for he will put us over the river. And we can travel on and on even to the country of the short-armed people if so we choose."

The next morning ere Goo-goor-gaga had ceased his laughter Weedah had started.

Some hours later, in the gidya scrub, the Bullai Bullai sisters joined him.

Having crossed the big plain they threw back a fire stick where the grass was thick and dry. The fire spread quickly through it, crackling and throwing up tongues of flame.

Through another scrub went the three, then across another plain, through another scrub and onto a plain again.

The day was hot, Yhi the sun was high in the sky. They became thirsty, but saw no water, and had brought none in their haste.

"We want water," the Bullai Bullai cried.

"Why did you not bring some?" said Weedah.

"We thought you had plenty, or would travel as the creeks run, or at least know of a goolagool, a water-holding tree."

"We shall soon reach water. Look even now ahead, there is water."

The Bullai Bullai looked eagerly toward where he pointed, and there in truth, on the far-side of the plain, they saw a sheet of water. They quickened their steps, but the farther they went, the farther off seemed the water, but on they went ever hoping to reach it. Across the plain they went, only to find that on the other side of a belt of timber the water had gone.

The weary girls would have lain down, but Weedah said that they would surely reach water on the other side of the wood. Again they struggled on through the scrub to another plain.

"There it is! I told you so! There is the water."

And looking ahead they again saw a sheet of water.

Again their hopes were raised, and though the sun beat fiercely, on they marched, only to be again disappointed.

"Let us go back," they said. "This is the country of evil spirits. We see water, and when we come where we have seen it there is but dry earth. Let us go back."

"Back to Beereeun, who would kill you?"

"Better to die from the blow of a boondi in your own country than of thirst in a land of devils. We will go back."

"Not so. Not with a boondi would he kill you, but with a gooweera, a poison stick. Slow would be your death, and you would be always in pain until your shadow was wasted away. But why talk of returning? Did we not set fire to the big plain? Could you cross that? Waste not your breath, but follow me. See, there again is water!"

But the Bullai Bullai had lost hope. No longer would they even look up, though time after time Weedah called out, "Water ahead of us! Water ahead of us!" only to disappoint them again and again.

At last the Bullai Bullai became so angry with him that they seized him and beat him. But even as they beat him he cried all the time, "Water is there! Water is there!"

Then he implored them to let him go, and he would drag up the roots from some water trees and drain the water from them.

"Yonder I see a coolabah. From its roots I can drain enough to quench your thirst. Or here beside us is a bingawingul; full of water are its roots. Let me go. I will drain them for you."

But the Bullai Bullai had no faith in his promises, and they but beat him the harder until they were exhausted.

When they ceased to beat him and let him go, Weedah went on a little way, then lay down, feeling bruised all over, and thankful that the night had come and the fierce sun no longer scorched them.

One Bullai Bullai said to her sister, "Could we not sing the song our Bargi used to sing, and make the rain fall?"

"Let us try, if we can make a sound with our dry throats," said the other.

"We will sing to our cousin Dooloomai the thunder. He will hear us, and break a rain cloud for us."

So they sat down, rocking their bodies to and fro, and beating their knees, sang:

> "Moogaray, Moogaray, May, May,
> Eehu, Eehu, Doon-gara."

> "Hailstones, hailstones, wind, wind,
> Rain, rain, lightning."

Over and over again they sang these words as they had heard their Bargi, or mother's mother, do. Then for themselves they added:

> "Eehu oonah wambaneah Dooloomai
> Bullul goonung inderh gingnee
> Eehu oonah wambaneah Dooloomai."

> "Give us rain, Thunder, our cousin,
> Thirsting for water are we,
> Give us rain, Thunder, our cousin."

As long as their poor parched throats could make a sound they sang this. Then they lay down to die, weary and hopeless. One said faintly, "The rain will be too late, but surely it is coming, for strong is the smell of the gidya."

"Strong indeed," said the other.

But even this sure sign to their tribe that rain is near roused them not. It would come, they thought, too late for them. But even then away in the north a thundercloud was gathering. It rolled across the sky quickly, pealing out thunder calls as it came to tell of its coming. It stopped right over the plain in front of the Bullai Bullai. One more peal of thunder, which opened the cloud, then splashing down came the first big drops of rain. Slowly and few they came

until just at the last, when a quick, heavy shower fell, emptying the thundercloud, and filling the gilguy holes on the plain.

The cool splashing of the rain on their hot, tired limbs gave new life to the Bullai Bullai and to Weedah. They all ran to the gilguy holes. Stooping their heads, they drank and quenched their thirst.

"I told you the water was here," said Weedah. "You see I was right."

"No water was here when you said so. If our cousin Dooloomai had not heard our song for his help, we should have died, and you too."

And they were angry. But Weedah dug them some roots, and when they ate they forgot their anger. When their meal was over they lay down to sleep.

The next morning on they went again. That day they again saw across the plains the same strange semblance of water that had lured them on before. They knew not what it could be, they knew only that it was not water.

Just at dusk they came to the Big River. There they saw Goolay-yali the pelican, with his canoe. Weedah asked him to put them over onto the other side. He said that he would do so one at a time, as the canoe was small. First he said he would take Weedah, that he might get ready a camp of the long grass in the bend of the river. He took Weedah over. Then back he came and, fastening his canoe, he went up to the Bullai Bullai, who were sitting beside the remains of his old fire.

"Now," said Goolay-yali, "you two will go with me to my camp, which is down in that bend. Weedah cannot get over again. You shall live with me. I shall catch fish to feed you. I have some even now in my camp cooking. There, too, have I wirrees of honey, and durri ready for the baking. Weedah has nothing to give you but the grass nunnoos he is but now making."

"Take us to Weedah," they said.

"Not so," said Goolay-yali, and he stepped forward as if to seize them.

The Bullai Bullai stooped and filled their hands with the white ashes of the burned-out fire, which they flung at him.

Handful after handful they threw at him until he stood before them white, all but his hands, which he spread out and shook, thus freeing

them from the cloud of ashes enveloping him and obscuring his sight.

Having thus checked him, the Bullai Bullai ran to the bank of the river, meaning to get the canoe and cross over to Weedah.

But in the canoe, to their horror, was Beereeun! Beereeun, whom to escape they had sped across plain and through scrub.

Yet here he was, while between them and Weedah lay the wide river.

They had not known it, but Beereeun had been near them all the while. He it was who had made the mirage on each plain, thinking he would lure them on by this semblance of water until they perished of thirst. From that fate Dooloomai, their cousin the thunder, had saved them. But now the chance of Beereeun had come.

The Bullai Bullai looked across the wide river and saw the nunnoos, or grass shelters, Weedah had made. They saw him running in and out of them as if he were playing a game, not thinking of them at all. Strange nunnoos they were too, having both ends open.

Seeing where they were looking, Beereeun said, "Weedah is womba, deaf. I stole his Doowi while he slept and put in its place a mad spirit. He knows naught of you now. He cares naught for you. It is so with those who look too long at the mirage. He will trouble me no more, nor you. Why look at him?"

But the Bullai Bullai could not take their eyes from Weedah, so strangely he went on, unceasingly running in at one end of the grass nunnoo, through it and out of the other.

"He is womba," they said, but yet they could not understand it. They looked toward him and called him, though he heeded them not.

"I will send him far from you," said Beereeun, getting angry. He seized a spear, stood up in the canoe and sent it swiftly through the air into Weedah, who gave a great cry, screamed "Water is there! Water is there!" and fell back dead.

"Take us over! Take us over!" cried the Bullai Bullai. "We must go to him, we might yet save him."

"He is all right. He is in the sky. He is not there," said Beereeun. "If you want him you must follow him to the sky. Look, you can see him there now." And he pointed to a star that the Bullai Bullai had never seen before.

"There he is, Womba."

Across the grass nunnoo the Bullai Bullai looked, but no Weedah was there. Then they sat down and wailed a death song, for they knew well they should see Weedah no more. They plastered their heads with white ashes and water; they tied on their bodies green twigs; then, cutting themselves till the blood ran, they lit some smoke branches and smoked themselves, as widows.

Beereeun spoke to Goolay-yali the pelican, saying, "There is no brother of the dead man to marry these women. In this country they have no relation. You shall take one, and I the other. To-night when they sleep we will each seize one."

"That which you say shall be," said Goolay-yali the pelican.

But the sisters heard what they said, though

they gave no sign and mourned the dead Wee-dah without ceasing. And with their death song they mingled a cry to all of their tribe who were dead to help them, and save them from these men who would seize them while they were still mourning, before they had swallowed the smoke water, or their tribe had heard the voice of their dead.

As the night wore on, the wailing of the women ceased. The men thought that they were at length asleep, and crept up to their camp. But it was empty! Gone were the Bullai Bullai!

The men heaped fuel on their fire to light up the darkness, but yet saw no sign of the Bullai Bullai.

They heard a sound, a sound of mocking laughter. They looked around, but saw nothing.

Again they heard a sound of laughter. Whence came it? Again it echoed through the air.

It was from the sky. They looked up. It was the new star Womba, mocking them. Womba who once was Weedah, who laughed aloud to see that the Bullai Bullai had escaped their enemies, for even now they were stealing along the sky toward him, which the men on earth saw.

"We have lost them," said Beereeun. "I shall make a roadway to the skies and follow them. Thence shall I bring them back, or wreak my vengeance on them."

He went to the canoe where were his spears. Having grasped them, he took, too, the spears of Goolay-yali, which lay by the smoldering fire.

He chose a barbed one. With all his force he threw it up to the sky. The barb caught there, the spear hung down. Beereeun threw another, which caught on to the first, and yet another, and so on, each catching the one before it, until he could touch the lowest from the earth. This he clutched hold of, and climbed up, up, up, until he reached the sky. Then he started in pursuit of the Bullai Bullai. And he is still pursuing them.

Since then the tribe of Beereeun have always been able to swarm up sheer heights. Since then, too, his tribe, the little lizards of the plains, make eer-dher, or mirages, to lure on thirsty travelers, only to send them mad before they die of thirst. Since then Goolay-yali the pelican has been white, for ever did the ashes thrown by the

Bullai Bullai cling to him; only where he had shaken them off from his hands are there a few black feathers. The tribe of Bullai Bullai are colored like the green of the leaves the sisters strung on themselves in which to mourn Weedah, with here and there a dash of whitish yellow and red, caused by the ashes and the blood of their mourning. And Womba the star, the mad star, still shines (our Canopus). And Weedah the mockingbird still builds grass nunnoos, open at both ends, in and out of which he runs, as if they were but playgrounds.

And the fire which Weedah and the Bullai Bullai made spread from one end of the country to the other, over ridges and across plains, burning the trees so that their trunks have been black ever since. Deenyi, the iron barks, smoldered the longest of all, and their trunks were so seared that the seams are deeply marked in their thick black bark still, making them show out grimly distinct on the ridges, to remind the Daens forever of Beereeun the miragemaker.

## THE PRISONER

(South Seas)

*Rarotonga, the island where this tale takes place, is part of the region of Polynesia. The story is a simple etiological tale and a humorous anecdote. Tapa cloth is made by pounding thin the soft inner bark of the mulberry tree.*

Once long ago, on the beautiful island of Rarotonga, there lived a girl named Rangi, who was very skillful in the making of tapa cloth from the wet bark of trees. She was especially good at cutting graceful designs with sharp shells on the tapa cloth she fashioned.

Her special place for working was on the open beach of the island, just by the shadow of some wild ginger plants that grew along the shore. Here, almost any day from early in the morning until sunset brought out the first stars, Rangi could be found working away at her tapa designs.

One day, while Rangi worked on the beach, a huge black grouper, a fish almost as big as a small whale, swam up to the edge of the reef from the deep sea. He peered over the reef at the shore, attracted by the splash of brightness made by the ginger blossoms. And when he looked over the reef at the ginger blossoms, he naturally couldn't help seeing Rangi near by, kneeling gracefully and wielding her tapa shells.

The great fish had never seen such a beautiful maiden as Rangi. He fell deeply in love with her in an instant, the way a beast or a fish can sometimes love a human being. And the grouper said to himself, "More than anything in the world, I would like to win that girl for my wife!"

So he set about wooing Rangi in the only way he knew: he swam over the reef into the lagoon on the next high tide, darted as fast as his sluggish body would go toward the beach where Rangi worked, and splashed at the water with his tail and his fins to draw the girl's attention to him.

Rangi looked up and saw him splashing there, near by. And since she was a very friendly girl, she said kindly, "Why, hello there. What a very large fish you are! And pretty, too. Do you mind if I copy some of your markings in my tapa cloth designs?"

"Not at all," returned the grouper, "if you will only consent to marry me."

"Marry you!" Rangi was quite surprised, needless to say. "I couldn't do that."

"Why not?"

"Because you're a fish and I'm a girl, that's why," said Rangi, laughing.

"Please," begged the fish. "I am madly in love with you!"

Rangi shook her head gently. "I'm sorry, fish," she said, "but I must refuse."

At these words, the grouper was very sad, and he slowly swam out toward the reef. Rangi thought he was swimming away forever and wouldn't bother her again, but she was wrong.

The fish swam only as far as the deep water under the reef. Then he went right down to the bottom and lay there, mourning in his heart for the beautiful girl who would not marry him. He decided that he could not give up Rangi as easily as that—he couldn't just swim away forever. So he determined to wait until the next high tide and try his luck again.

The second proposal of marriage, however, was no more successful than his first. Rangi smiled kindly at the grouper but steadfastly refused to consider marrying him. The fish pleaded and begged to no avail. Rangi could not be moved.

Still the fish would not give up. He *had* to have Rangi for his wife. Nothing else would satisfy him. So he decided on a bold plan.

When Rangi turned back to her work and was not looking at him, the fish stretched out a fin as big as a sail and gathered Rangi up in it. He flipped her from the beach into the sea in an instant. Before Rangi had time to do more than gasp and choke a little on the salt water she'd swallowed, the big grouper opened his enormous mouth wide and swallowed Rangi in one big swallow—tapa shells and all.

Rangi wasn't hurt. Not a bit. The fish loved her too much to hurt her. But he was determined to have Rangi for his own. He hoped to be able to talk her around to marrying him in the end. Once Rangi was safe and sound in his warm stomach, the fish swam rapidly through the pass into the open ocean and took her far, far from land.

"Let me out!" shouted Rangi angrily. "Let me out! You are a wicked fish to swallow me and steal me from my home."

"I love you," replied the fish, swimming faster than ever. "That's the only excuse I have. But I can't let you go."

"You must let me go," shouted Rangi up the fish's throat. "You must!"

"Oh, no," said the fish. "Not likely. Not until you agree to marry me."

Rangi, in despair, began to think about how she might escape from the fish's insides. She thought and thought for six days and nights without sleeping. And the only way she could think of to get out of the fish was to cut her way out. She still had with her the sharp cutting shells with which she patterned her tapa cloth. They were stuck into the girdle around her waist.

The first thing Rangi did was to examine very carefully the inside of her prison to find where the flesh was thinnest. She tapped around the walls of the fish's stomach, listening to the sound. She tapped the walls of the fish's throat. And at the upper end of his throat, not far below his enormous mouth, she found the thinnest part of the fish's body. So she began to cut there.

Hour after hour she toiled, drawing the sharp edges of her shells against the flesh of the fish's throat. She decided to make a cut on both sides of his throat, so that she would double her chances of escaping if she ever broke through. She worked very hard. *Cut, cut, cut, cut.*

At length the black grouper, feeling the pain in his throat, called out, "What are you doing in there, Rangi?"

"I'm cutting my way out of you, fish," reported Rangi honestly. "I'll stop if you'll let me out."

But the fish was stubborn. "Go ahead and cut me," he said. "I love you too much to let you out."

So Rangi cut some more.

On the fourth day of her work, she had cut so deeply into both sides of the fish's throat that she could see daylight through the gashes. Only a thin layer of skin now separated her from freedom.

She said to the fish, "You win, fish. I am weary to death of cutting. I shall never get out, I suppose, unless I agree to marry you. So take me to some near-by island where I can get ashore in safety, and I will reconsider marrying you."

"Do you mean it?" asked the grouper, overjoyed. "But how can I trust you?"

"I'm still your prisoner," Rangi reminded him. "How could I escape, even if I wanted to deceive you?"

"That's true," admitted the fish. He swam at once toward the nearest island. "I'm taking you to Mauke," said the fish. "Is that all right?"

"Perfect," said Rangi. "They have beautiful jasmine flowers on Mauke for my bridal bouquet. Let me know when we get there, will you, please?"

"Certainly," said the fish. "You have made me very happy." After an hour, he called out, "We are there, Rangi. Inside the reef at Mauke."

"Close to shore?" asked Rangi. She got her tapa shells ready to make the last cuts in the fish's throat.

"As close as I can get," said the fish.

"Then here I go!" cried Rangi, and slashed the final slash with her shells at each side of the fish's throat. The thin outer skin parted, and through the slits in the fish's gullet, Rangi could see blue sky and green water again. She looked out to see which of her windows in the fish's throat was nearest the shore and jumped quickly through it into the waters of the lagoon. Soon she rose to her feet in the shallow water and ran up on the shore, safely out of reach of her strange suitor.

As for the black grouper, once he became used to the water rushing in and out of his throat through Rangi's cuts, he found it rather a pleasant feeling. He sighed and swam slowly out to sea, vowing never to fall in love with a human girl again.

This story explains why *all* fish have gills in their throats today.

# *Canada*

*Aside from the Eskimo and Indian lore, which has been included in this anthology with the tales of all North American Indians, Canada's most distinguishable body of stories and songs comes from the folk literature of French-speaking Canadians. Not many collections are available for young people, however, and much remains to be discovered from the work of Canadian folklore scholars. Though the present offerings are few (see the Bibliography), in them live such unique figures as the* loup-garou, *a dangerous supernatural wolf created in the folk imagination, and those colorful, adventurous men out of Canada's early French history—the* voyageurs *and the* coureurs de bois. *They hold a firm place in the folk literature of Canada, and to those of imaginative mind it may seem that they wander still among her rivers, lakes, and forests.*

## LITTLE NICHET'S
## BABY SISTER

*The Nichet stories are traditional tales that
Natalie Carlson heard from her French-Canadian uncle. They are also realistic and suggest
the friendly spirit in the encounters between
Canada's Indians and the French settlers.*

That little Nichet, Jean LeBlanc's youngest
child, was one to keep his parents as busy as all
the other thirteen tied together.

One day the little fellow had a new question
for his wise father.

"Papa," said Nichet, "where did the Boulan-
gers get their new baby?"

"That is an easy question," answered Jean
LeBlanc. "The good Indians brought her, my little nest egg."

"Did the good Indians bring me to you?"
asked Nichet.

"Of course," answered his father. "The good
Indians bring all the babies."

Little Nichet thought about this for a while.

"Papa," he asked again, "will the good Indians
bring us another baby? I would like to have a little sister like Marie Boulanger."

"*Tatata!*" exclaimed Jean LeBlanc. "Already
the good Indians have brought us a houseful.
Thirteen brothers and sisters are quite enough
for such a little fellow as you. And if we had a
new baby, you would no longer be our little nest
egg."

But Nichet did not think that thirteen brothers and sisters were enough, especially when they
were all older and bigger than he.

One afternoon little Nichet wanted to ask his
father more about this. But his father and his
mother had driven to town in the two-wheeled
cart with his eight sisters squeezed together in
back.

It was a lonely day for Nichet because his five
brothers were out in the field working. And
Grandmère kept falling asleep over the rug she
was hooking.

So Nichet bravely decided to go to the Indian

"Little Nichet's Baby Sister" from *Sashes Red and Blue*
by Natalie Savage Carlson. Copyright © 1956 by Natalie
Savage Carlson. Reprinted by permission of Harper &
Row, Publishers, Inc.

village himself and ask the Indians if they didn't
have an extra baby for the LeBlancs.

Nichet started out on his own two short legs.
He walked down the river road. He walked up
the Indian trail.

At last he came to the Indian village with its
houses scattered over the ground like half-
melons.

The Indian village was deserted. The Indians
must have gone to town too. Then Nichet saw a
few squaws working among the corn sprouts on
the hillside. He started toward them.

But he never got as far as the cornfields. For
there, propped against a tree trunk, was exactly
what Nichet wanted. It was a little papoose laced
to its cradle board.

Nichet was so excited that he could scarcely
unlace the baby from the board. He lifted it
carefully in his arms. The baby did not cry like
the Boulanger's new Marie. Nichet looked at its
brown skin and its black eyes and its straight
black hair. He tried to decide whether it looked
more like his papa or his mamma.

The little baby waved its tiny brown arms at
him.

"You are my little sister," said Nichet. "I
think you look most like me. I will take you
home to your papa and mamma."

Nichet LeBlanc carried the papoose down the
trail to the river road. It was a long walk and Nichet was so tired he did not think he would ever
get the baby to its home. But his sturdy legs carried them both there at last.

Papa and Mamma and the girls had not returned from town yet. The boys were still in the
field. Nichet took the baby to show her to
Grandmère, but the old lady was asleep with her
mouth open and her glasses on the end of her
nose.

So little Nichet carried the baby into his parents' bedroom. He carefully laid it in the middle
of the bright quilt. Then he ran down the lane
to wait for his mamma and papa. He wanted to
be the first one to tell them the news that they
had a new baby.

At first his papa and mamma thought that little Nichet had a fever. Then they thought that
he had fallen asleep like Grandmère and had
had a bad dream. But when they saw the brown
baby with the black hair and black eyes lying on

the bed, they knew that Nichet had told the truth.

"Where did this baby come from?" cried Mamma LeBlanc.

"The Indians brought her," said little Nichet. "That is, I went and got her myself so they wouldn't give her to someone else."

Then there was a great *tohu-bohu* of chattering among the LeBlancs.

"We will have to take it right back," said Jean LeBlanc. "If the Indians think we have stolen their baby, they might burn down our house."

Little Nichet was brokenhearted. He begged and begged his parents to keep his little brown sister with the black hair and black eyes who looked so much like him.

But back to the Indians went the little sister. Little Nichet held her in his arms all the way there in the two-wheeled cart.

There was another *tohu-bohu* of chattering going on at the Indian village.

"A bear has carried off one of the babies," a young brave explained to Jean LeBlanc.

"We have your baby here," said Jean. "It was carried off by a very little bear."

Nichet cried and cried at the loss of his Indian sister. He began feeling sorry for himself. He began thinking that if his papa and mamma had returned the baby to the Indians, they might do the same with him someday.

Little Nichet began feeling sorrier than ever for himself. He decided to return to the Indians of his own free will. How his parents would cry when they found he was gone! They would come galloping to the Indian village. They would take him home again—and his baby sister too.

He packed his nightshirt and his willow whistle and his lynx tail into a sack and set out for the Indian village once more. He walked all the way down the river road. He follwed the trail to the houses that were like half-melons.

"I have come back to stay with my little sister," Nichet told one of the Indians.

Then the Indians were as worried as the LeBlancs had been.

"If we keep you here," said one of them, "your papa will think that we have stolen you. He will burn down our lodges."

Little Nichet refused to leave. "I want to stay here and be an Indian like my little sister," he said.

The Indians gathered together and talked their *micmac* talk, which Nichet could not understand. Then one of them turned to him.

"Can you shoot a bow and arrow?" he asked in Nichet's talk.

"No," said little Nichet.

"Can you skin a moose?"

"No," said little Nichet.

"Can you build a birch canoe?"

"No," said little Nichet.

"Then you cannot stay with us," said the brave. "An Indian must be able to do all those things."

So little Nichet sadly turned and started away. But another Indian came running to him with something furry in his hands.

"A gift for you," said the Indian. "A trade for the baby you returned to us."

He dropped a tiny baby animal into Nichet's arms. It had the head of a beaver, the body of a bear, and the tail of a rabbit.

"What is it?" asked Nichet.

"Your wise father will have a name for it," said the Indian, then he began talking his *micmac* talk that Nichet could not understand.

Nichet carried the baby animal home happily.

All the way his busy mind wondered if it was a fox or a beaver or a mink or what.

All the LeBlancs were happy to see that Nichet was home again. For truth, they didn't even know he had gone away until they saw the furry little animal in his arms.

"It is a little whistler," said his wise father, Jean LeBlanc. "Some people call them woodchucks and some people call them groundhogs. But the people back in France call them marmots."

"What is it good for?" asked Grandmère. "Will it give milk or pull a cart or lay eggs?"

"It is good for a lonesome little boy who needs a companion smaller than himself," said Jean LeBlanc. He leaned over Nichet and smiled at the new baby. "Across the ocean in France," he said, "chimney sweeps from the mountains keep whistlers for pets. They teach them to do a little dance like a bear's."

"Can I be a chimney sweep when I am bigger?" asked little Nichet.

"You may be a chimney sweep tomorrow," said Jean LeBlanc generously. "I am going to take down the stovepipe for your mamma and you may help me clean the soot out of it."

So little Nichet thought that he had made a very good trade with the Indians. The boy picked out the name of Pierrette for his tiny pet, and his father helped him to teach that whistler to dance.

Whenever Nichet whistled a special tune, Pierrette would sit up on her hindquarters and wave her forepaws from right to left as she did her dance of the bear. And from time to time she would make polite curtsies. You may be sure that Pierrette was as popular at the stay-awake parties as old Michel Meloche, the storyteller.

## THE CANOE IN THE RAPIDS

*This is a tale of woodsmen, but not of dashing heroes, for the two trappers are vanquished ignominiously in an amusing story with nonsense elements that delight children.*

"The Canoe in the Rapids." From *The Talking Cat and Other Stories of French Canada* by Natalie Savage Carlson. Copyright, 1952, by Natalie Savage Carlson. Reprinted by permission of Harper & Row, Publishers, Inc.

Once in another time, François Ecrette was an adventurer in the woods. Every winter he went north with Sylvain Gagnon. They trapped foxes, beavers, minks and any furred creature that would step into their traps.

When spring came and the ice in the river melted, the two men would load their furs into a canoe and paddle down the swift current to sell their winter's catch to the trader.

It was one such spring that François and Sylvain headed south with the finest catch that they had ever made. If only they could beat the other trappers to the trading post, they could make a fine bargain.

"A-ah, we will be rich men," said Sylvain, who already could hear the *tintin* of coins in his deep pockets.

"Yes," answered François, "if we get through the Devil's Jaws safely."

Nowhere on any of the rivers of Canada was there such a fearsome place. In the Devil's Jaws, there were waterfalls that roared and whirlpools that spun a boat about like a dry leaf. It was as if the river fell into a panic itself when squeezed into the Devil's Jaws and tried to run away in every direction.

"That's true," said Sylvain, "but you are lucky to have me for a partner. Nowhere in all Canada is there such a skillful boatman as Sylvain Gagnon."

Sylvain drew the cold air in through his nose and puffed out his chest with it.

So François Ecrette felt safe and happy, even though the worst ordeal of the long trip was ahead of them.

They loaded the canoe with their bundles of furs and their provisions. For days they paddled down the river, singing gay songs to pass away the long hours.

One late afternoon they beached their boat on the bank and made for a clearing on the hill. They built a campfire, and François started to roast a young rabbit he had shot. He hung it over the coals by spearing it on a green willow branch.

"We must eat well," said Sylvain, "for we are close to the Devil's Jaws. We will need all our strength for that pull and push."

"But it will soon be dark," François reminded him. "Shouldn't we camp here all night so we can go through the rapids in daylight?"

"Pou, pou," laughed Sylvain, "what a scared rabbit you are! I can paddle at night as well as by day. I could shoot the Devil's Jaws with my eyes closed and a beaver riding on my paddle."

François rubbed his stubbly chin.

"My faith," he exclaimed, "I am the luckiest man in the world to have you for a partner, Sylvain Gagnon. I don't believe you have fear of anything."

As if to test the truth of this, an angry growl came from behind the bushes. Both men jumped to their feet, François seizing his rifle as he did so. The bushes broke open and a big brown bear came through them. He walked slowly on all fours, shuffling from this paw to that paw, and from that paw to this paw. Straight toward the two trappers he came.

François lifted his rifle to his shoulder and took careful aim. He pulled the trigger. Plink! Nothing happened. There was no bullet in the rifle because it had been used on the rabbit.

The bear gave another angry growl. He rose on his hind legs and walked toward François like a man, shuffling from this paw to that paw.

François dropped the gun and ran for his life. Already Sylvain Gagnon was far ahead of him, his fur coat making him look like a bear that ran too fast to shuffle from this paw to that paw. François made for a big tree, but he didn't have time to climb it as the bear was almost on him. So around the tree he ran. And behind him followed the bear. Round and round and round the tree ran François and the bear. Any little bird looking down from the treetop wouldn't have known whether the bear was chasing François Ecrette or François was chasing the bear. The trapper ran so fast that he was more behind the bear than in front of him. And as the bear ran around the tree, he clawed the air angrily. But his sharp claws only tore the bark from the tree. And if François had anything at all to be thankful for, it was that the ragged shreds flying through the air were bark from the tree and not skin from his back.

Around and around and around went the man and the beast. The bear got dizzy first. He ran slower and slower. Finally he broke away from the tree and went staggering away, first to this side and then to that side. And as he reeled and stumbled, he knocked his head into one tree trunk after another. Bump—bump—bump.

François lost no time in finding another tree to climb, for the tree they had been running around had been stripped of its bark as far up as a bear could reach. As he climbed, he could hear the bump, bump, bump of the bear's head as he stumbled into tree trunks.

Panting and dizzy himself, François settled into a crotch of the tree. Now where was that false friend, Sylvain Gagnon, who had left him to face the bear alone? He called and called but there was no answer. Perhaps the bear had eaten Sylvain. A-tout-tou, what bad luck that would be when there was still the Devil's Jaws ahead! How could he ever get through those treacherous waters without the skillful boatman Sylvain Gagnon?

And how could he get safely from the tree to the boat? Perhaps the bear was waiting for him among the bushes. The sleepy sun soon went to bed and it grew dark. It became colder than ever. François Ecrette's arms and legs were numb.

At last he jerkily lowered himself from the tree. He looked about in every direction, but it was too dark to see anything. He sniffed and sniffed like a bear, for if a bear can smell a man, maybe a man can smell a bear. But all François could smell was the sharp, icy air of early spring. Slowly he made his way down the hill toward the place they had left the canoe.

Then great joy filled the heart of François Ecrette. Although the trees blackened the river, a faint moonlight glimmered through them. Its pale light fell upon a figure hunched in the bow of the canoe with the fur coat pulled up over its ears.

"Sylvain," cried François, "you are safe after all. Why didn't you come back to me?"

But Sylvain must have felt a deep shame, for he only put his head down between his arms and made a sad, apologetic sound.

"Believe me, my friend," said François, "I'm certainly glad you escaped, for we have a terrible ride ahead of us this night. Do you think we better try the rapids after all?"

But his companion resolutely straightened up and squared his shoulders in the fur coat. François pushed the boat into the stream, leaped aboard and grabbed a paddle. Silently they floated into the current; then the slender canoe headed for the dangers ahead.

"My faith, it is good to have you in this boat with me," cried François. "This current is like a bolt of lightning."

The boat raced faster and faster. Instead of paddling for speed, François had to spend his strength flattening the paddle like a brake. The trees made a dark tunnel of the river course so that François could barely see his companion's stout back.

On, on they went. The frail canoe sped in a zigzag flight like a swallow. François Ecrette's sharp ear caught the distant roar of the rapids.

"Brace yourself, Sylvain," he cried, "for the boat is now in your hands. I will help you as much as I can."

So he plied his paddle from this side to that side and from that side to this side. The river had become like an angry, writhing eel. He heard the waterfall ahead and began paddling like mad so the canoe would shoot straight and true. The least slant of the boat and the churning current would turn it over and over, and swallow them both.

François felt the icy wind and the cold spray on his face as they plunged over the waterfall and bobbed in the whirlpool below. He fought the churning, frothing waters that he could hear more than see. His muscles tightened like iron and the air blew up his lungs.

"My faith, but it's a good thing to have such a boatman as Sylvain Gagnon guiding this canoe," rejoiced François. "In such a current as this, no other man could bring a boat through safely. I will forget the way he deserted me when that big brown bear attacked us."

All danger was not over yet, for the stern of the canoe was sucked into the outer rim of a whirlpool. The lurch of the boat wrenched François Ecrette's back like a blow from a giant hammer. The canoe spun around completely. For fully ten minutes, there was such a battle with the churning waters as François had never known before. Around and around, up and down rocked the canoe, with François fiercely wielding his paddle. If it hadn't been for the soothing figure in front of him, he would have given up in fright.

Finally the canoe straightened out and leaped straight ahead. The roar of the rapids grew fainter. François let his paddle drag and relaxed.

"My faith," he gasped. "I thought that was the last of us for sure. You have saved us both, Sylvain Gagnon. No boatman in all Canada but you could have gotten us out of that Devil's trap."

But his modest companion only shrugged his shoulders and humped lower into the bow.

Then because François was worn out from his paddling, he decided to take a little nap. With no other partner but Sylvain would he have dared doze off. But Sylvain had proved his mettle in getting them through the rapids, and the waters ahead were slow and peaceful. So François rested his paddle, closed his eyes and fell into a deep sleep.

When he awoke, it was morning. The sun had chased the shadows out from under the trees, and the river sparkled in the friendliest kind of way.

François rubbed the sleep out of his eyes.

"Ah, Sylvain," he yawned, "what a night we had in the rapids. If it hadn't been for you—a-tou-tou-tou-tou!"

For François Ecrette's partner in the canoe was not Sylvain Gagnon, the great boatman, but the big brown bear of the clearing!

François jumped up and gave a bloodcurdling shriek. The bear slowly turned around and looked at him. He shook his great furry head as if to shake his brains back into their right place after they had been knocked apart by the tree trunks. He gave a low threatening growl.

François didn't wait any longer. He dived into the river and furiously swam through the icy water. After what seemed a sinner's life time, he reached the frosty shore. When he looked back at the river, he had a last glance of the canoe, full of furs, disappearing among the trees with the big brown bear standing in the bow.

Now this was a fine how-does-it-make of trouble. Here was François all alone in the wilderness without Sylvain, furs, provisions or even a dry match.

Luckily the trading post couldn't be too far away now. François gathered dry wood and started a fire in the Indian way, by rubbing two sticks together. Then he stood as close to the fire as he could, to dry out his clothes. He scorched and steamed like the uneaten rabbit back on the sharp stick in the clearing.

At last he was dry enough to brave the cold walk down the river bank. He set out slowly. The branches scratched his hands and face. His boots sloshed and squashed through the slush of early spring.

It was late afternoon by the time he reached the trader's village. Everyone seemed surprised to see him alive.

"Your canoe was found caught in a log jam below here, with bear tracks on the shore," said the trader. "We thought a bear had carried you off."

"But the furs," cried François. "What happened to them? Were they lost?"

"They are all safe," said the trader. "Your friend Sylvain Gagnon arrived only a little while ago. He helped me check through them."

Then a familiar face appeared in the crowd.

"François, my good friend," cried Sylvain. "I got a ride back with a party of Indians. But how did you ever get the canoe through the rapids all by yourself?"

"Sylvain, my false friend," retorted the trapper, "I was not alone. The big brown bear who chased me in the clearing was with me."

Then François Ecrette shivered and shook in a way that had nothing to do with the cold spring afternoon or his damp clothing.

So all turned out well for François Ecrette in the end. But he never went on any more trapping trips with Sylvain Gagnon. You see, my friends, one who turns into a big brown bear when you need him most is not a true friend.

# United States: Variants of European Folk Tales

*There is no such thing as a typical American folk tale. While we find scattered over the United States pockets of folklore that have grown out of definite ethnic, occupational, and regional situations, the stories in these groups are mostly American adaptations of traditional European tales. Although these have come out of untypical areas, such as the Southern Appalachians and the Ozarks, they are widely known because they have been assiduously recorded and retold in popular books that have delighted adults and children. But our best examples of the European variants are found in Richard Chase's* The Jack Tales *and* Grandfather Tales, *stories which may be traced back to Jacobs, the Grimms, Asbjörnsen and Moe, even to* The Odyssey *and* Beowulf. *In America the tales have changed their dress and picked up new comic vitality.*

### JOURNEY CAKE, HO!

*Although not strictly a folk tale, created as it was to be a picture book, this rollicking version of the well-known "The Pancake" and "The Gingerbread Boy" makes a fine addition to one's storytelling repertory. If you have the book, by all means share with children Robert McCloskey's genial, lively illustrations for the story.*

There were three of them: the old woman, Merry; the old man, Grumble; and Johnny, the bound-out boy. They lived in a log cabin, t'other side of Tip Top Mountain.

The old woman took care of the wool; she

*Journey Cake, Ho!* by Ruth Sawyer. Copyright 1953 by Ruth Sawyer and Robert McCloskey. Reprinted by permission of The Viking Press, Inc.

carded and spun and knit it. She laid the fire, tended the griddle, churned the butter, and sang at her work. The song she liked best ran this-wise:

"Ho, for a Journey Cake—
　Quick on a griddle bake!
　　Sugar and salt it,
　　Turn it and brown it,
　Johnny, come eat it with milk for your tea."

The old man tended the garden patch, sheared the sheep, milked the cow, felled the trees, sawed the logs, and grumbled at his work. The grumble he liked best was:

　　"A bother, a pest!
　　All work and no rest!
　　Come winter, come spring,
　　Life's a nettlesome thing."

And what about Johnny? He split the kindling, filled the woodbox, lugged the water, fed the creatures, fished the brook, and whistled at his work. One tune was as fine as another to Johnny.

Their whole world lay close about them. There were the garden patch, the brook, the logging road that ran down to the valley where the villagers lived, and the spruce woods.

On the tallest tree sat Raucus, the sentinel crow, watching and waiting to caw when surprise or trouble was near.

Nothing happened for a long, long time. They lived snug, like rabbits in their burrow. Then—

One night a fox carried off the hens. "Caw, caw!" called the crow. But it was too late. The next night a wolf carried off the sheep. "Caw, caw, caw!" called the crow. But it was too late.

There came a day when the pig wandered off and got himself lost. Last of all the cow fell into the brook and broke her leg.

All that day the crow cawed and cawed and cawed.

That night the old woman said, shaking her head, "Trouble has come. The meal chest is low, the bin is near empty. What will feed two will not feed three."

The old man grumbled and said, "Johnny, 'tis likely you'll be leaving us on the morrow and finding yourself a new master and a new ma'm."

The next morning by sunup the old woman had run together a piece of sacking and put straps to it, to hold Johnny's belongings—a knife, some gum from the spruce trees, his shoes and a washing-cloth. On top went the Journey Cake that had been baked for him. It was large, round, and crusty-hard. "Now be off with you!" said the old man, grumbling. "What must be, must be."

"Off with you—and luck follow after," said the old woman sadly.

Johnny said nothing at all. He left his whistle behind him and took the logging road down to the valley.

Right foot, left foot, right foot, left foot. He was halfway down and more when the straps on his sacking bag broke loose. Out bounced the Journey Cake.

It bumped and it bumped; it rolled over and over. Down the road it went, and how it hollered!

　　"Journey Cake, ho!
　　Journey Cake, hi!
　　Catch me and eat me
　　As I roll by!"

Away and away rolled the Journey Cake. Away and away ran Johnny.

Faster and faster. They passed a field full of cows. A brindle cow tossed her head and took after them. She mooed:

　　"At running I'll beat you.
　　I'll catch you and eat you!"

Faster and faster, faster and faster! They passed a pond full of ducks.

　　"Journey Cake, ho!
　　Journey Cake, hi!
　　Catch me and eat me
　　As I roll by!"

A white duck spread her wings, and away and away she went after them, quacking:

　　"At flying I'll beat you.
　　I'll catch and I'll eat you!"

Faster and faster, faster and faster! They came to a meadow where sheep were grazing. A white sheep and a black sheep took after them.

Now they were through the valley and the road began to climb. Slower and slower rolled the Journey Cake. Slower and slower ran Johnny, the brindle cow, the white duck, and the two sheep.

> "Journey Cake, hi!
> The journey is long.
> Catch me and eat me
> As I roll along."

They passed a wallows. A spotted pig heard and came a-grunting.

They passed a barnyard, and a flock of red hens flew over the stump fence, squawking. Slower and s-l-o-w-e-r, higher and higher.

At last they came to a mountain pasture where a gray donkey was feeding. Now the Journey Cake was huffing and puffing:

> "Journey Cake, hi!
> The journey is long.
> C-c-catch me and eat me—
> As I roll along."

The donkey was fresh. He kicked up his heels and brayed:

> "I'll show I can beat you.
> I'll catch you and eat you."

Higher went the road. Slower and slower, slower and slower rolled the Journey Cake— t'other side of Tip Top Mountain. Slower and slower and slower, slower and slower came the procession with Johnny at the head. Huffing and puffing, they circled the spruce woods. From his perch on the tallest tree, Raucus, the crow, let out his surprise warning: "Caw, caw, caw!"

Johnny heard. He stopped, all of a quickness. There was the brook; there was the garden patch; there was the log cabin.

He was home again. The Journey Cake had brought him to the end of his journey!

The Journey Cake spun around twice and fell flat. "I'm all of a tucker!" it hollered.

"We're all of a tucker," cried the others. The red hens found a house waiting for them. The cow found her tether rope; the pig found a sty; the duck found a brook; the sheep found a place for grazing, and the donkey walked himself into the shed.

The old woman came a-running.

The old man came a-running.

Johnny hugged them hard. He found his whistle again and took up the merriest tune. "Wheee—ew, wheee—ew!" he whistled. He hopped first on right foot, then on left foot. When he had his breath he said, "Journey Cake did it. Journey Cake fetched me-and-the-cow-and-the-white-duck-and-the-black-and-white-sheep-and-the-flock-of-red-hens-and-the-pig-and-the-gray-donkey. Now they are all yours!"

The old man forgot his best grumble. The old woman picked up the Journey Cake and went inside to freshen it up on the griddle. She went, singing the song she liked best:

> "Warm up the Journey Cake;
> From now on it's Johnny Cake.
> Johnny, come eat it
> With milk for your tea!"

## JACK AND THE ROBBERS

*The tens and elevens will readily recognize "The Four Musicians" in this homespun variant with the realistic conclusion. They should hear Richard Chase tell it in the laconic drawl of a mountain man.*

This here's another tale about Jack when he was still a small-like boy. He was about twelve, I reckon, and his daddy started tryin' to make him help with the work around the place. But Jack he didn't like workin' much. He would piddle around a little and then he'd go on back to the house, till one day his daddy whipped him. He just tanned Jack good. Jack didn't cry none, but he didn't like it a bit. So early the next mornin' he slipped off without tellin' his mother and struck out down the public road. Thought he'd go and try his fortune somewhere off from home.

"Jack and the Robbers" from *The Jack Tales*, edited by Richard Chase. Copyright © renewed 1971 by Richard Chase. Copyright 1943, by Richard Chase. Reprinted by permission of Houghton Mifflin Company

He got down the road a few miles and there was an old ox standin' in a field by a rail fence, a-bellowin' like it was troubled over somethin'—

"Um-m-m-muh!
Um-m-m—muh-h-h!"

"Hello!" says Jack. "What's the matter?"

"I'll just tell you," says the old ox. "I'm gettin' too old to plow and I heard the men talkin' about how they'd have to kill me tomorrow and get shet of me."

"Come on down here to the gap," says Jack, "and you can slip off with me."

So the old ox followed the fence to where the gap was at and Jack let the bars down and the old ox got out in front of Jack, and they went on down the public road.

Jack and the ox traveled on, and pretty soon they came where there was an old donkey standin' with his head hangin' down over the gate, a-goin'—

"Wahn-n-n-eh!
Wahn-n-n-eh!
Wahn-n-n-eh!"

"Hello," says Jack. "What's troublin' you?"

"Law me!" says the old donkey. "The boys took me out to haul in wood this mornin' and I'm gettin' so old and weak I couldn't do no good. I heard 'em say they were goin' to kill me tomorrow, get shet of me."

"Come on and go with us," says Jack.

So he let the old donkey out and they pulled on down the public road. The old donkey told Jack to get up on his back and ride.

They went on a piece, came to an old hound dog settin' in a man's yard. He would bark awhile and then howl awhile—

"A-woo! woo! woo!
A-oo-oo-oo!"

—sounded awful lonesome.

"Hello," says Jack. "What you a-howlin' so for?"

"Oh, law me!" says the old dog. "The boys took me coon-huntin' last night, cut a tree where the coon had got up in it. I got hold on the coon all right, but my teeth are all gone and hit got loose from me. They said they were goin' to kill me today, get shet of me."

"Come on, go with us," says Jack.

So the old dog scrouged under the gate.

The old donkey says to him, "Get up on my back and ride, if you want to."

Jack holp the old dog up behind him, and they went on down the public road.

Came to an old tomcat climbin' along the fence. Hit was a-squallin' and meowin', stop ever' now and then, sit down on the top rail—

"Meow-ow!
Meow-ow-ow!"

—sounded right pitiful.

"Hello!" says Jack. "What's the matter you squallin' so?"

"Oh, law!" says the old cat. "I caught a rat out in the barn this mornin', but my teeth are gettin' so old and bad I let him go. I heard 'em talkin' about killin' me to get shet of me, 'cause I ain't no good to catch rats no more."

"Come on and go with us," says Jack.

So the old cat jumped down off the fence.

The old donkey says, "Hop up there on my back and you can ride."

The old cat jumped up, got behind the dog, and they went on down the public road.

Came to where they saw an old rooster settin' on a fence post, crowin' like it was midnight, makin' the awfulest lonesome racket—

"Ur rook-a-roo!
Ur-r-r rook-a-roo-oo-oo!"

"Hello!" says Jack. "What's troublin' you?"

"Law me!" says the old rooster. "Company's comin' today and I heard 'em say they were goin' to kill me, put me in a pie!"

"Come on with us," says Jack.

Old rooster flew on down, got behind the cat, says, "All right, boys. Let's go!"

So they went right on down the highway. That was about all could get on the old donkey's back. The old rooster was right on top its tail and a-havin' a sort of hard time stayin' on. They traveled on, traveled on, till hit got plumb dark.

"Well," says Jack, "we got to get off the road and find us a place to stay tonight."

Directly they came to a little path leadin' off in the woods, decided to take that, see could they find a stayin' place in there. Went on a right smart piece further, and 'way along up late in the night they came to a little house, didn't have no clearin' around it. Jack hollered hello at the fence but there didn't nobody answer.

"Come on," says the old donkey. "Let's go investigate that place."

Well, there wasn't nobody ever came to the door and there wasn't nobody around back of the house, so directly they went on in. Found a right smart lot of good somethin' to eat in there.

Jack says, "Now, who in the world do you reckon could be a-livin' out here in such a wilderness of a place as this?"

"Well," says the old donkey, "hit's my o-pinion that a gang of highway robbers lives out here."

So Jack says, "Then hit looks like to me we might as well take up and stay here. If they've done stole all these vittles, we got as much right to 'em as they have."

"Yes," says the old dog, "that's exactly what I think, too. But if we stay, I believe we better get fixed for a fight. I expect they'll be comin' back in here about midnight."

"That's just what I was goin' to say," says the old cat. "I bet it's pretty close to midnight right now."

"Hit lacks about a hour," says the old rooster.

"Come on, then," says Jack. "Let's all of us get set to fight 'em."

The ox said he'd stay out in the yard. The old donkey said he'd take up his stand on the porch just outside the door. The dog said he'd get in behind the door and fight from there. The old tomcat got down in the fireplace, and the old rooster flew up on the comb of the roof, says, "If you boys need any help now, just call on me, call on me-e-e!"

They all waited awhile. Heard somebody comin' directly; hit was seven highway robbers. They came on till they got pretty close to the house, then they told one of 'em to go on in and start up a fire so's they could have a light to see to get in and so they could divide out the money they'd stole that day.

One man went on in the house, the other six waited outside the gate.

That man went to the fireplace, got down on his knees to blow up the fire. The cat had his head right down on the hearth-rock and that man thought its eyes was coals of fire. Time he blowed in that old cat's eyes, it reached out its claws right quick and scratched him down both cheeks. The robber hollered and headed for the door. The dog ran out and bit him in the leg. He shook it off and ran on the porch and the old donkey raised up and kicked him on out in the yard. The ox caught him up on its horns and ran to the fence and threw him out in the bresh. About that time the old rooster settin' up there on top of the house started in to crowin' right big.

The other robbers, time they heard all that racket, they put out from there just as fast as

they could run. The one they'd sent in the house finally got up and started runnin' like a streak, caught up with 'em in no time. They said to him, says, "What in the world was that in there?"

"Oh, I'm killed! I'm killed!" says the man. "I won't live over fifteen minutes!"

The other said, "Well, 'fore ye die, tell us what it was caused all that racket back yonder."

"Law me! That house is plumb full of men, and they've even got one on the roof. I went to blow up the fire and a man in the fireplace raked me all over the face with an awl. Started to run and a man behind the door took me in the leg with a butcher knife. Time I got out the door, a man out there hit me with a knot-maul, knocked me clean off the porch. A man standin' in the yard caught me on a pitchfork and threw me over the fence. And then that man up on the roof hollered out,

'Chunk him on up here!
Chunk him on up here.'

Ain't no use in us goin' back there with all of them men in the house. Let's leave here quick 'fore they come after us."

So them highway robbers ran for their life, and kept on runnin' till they were plumb out the country.

Jack and the ox and the old donkey and the dog and the cat and the rooster, they took possession of that house, and just had 'em a big time.

But the last time I was down that way, Jack had gone on back home to his folks. He was out in the yard a-cuttin' his mother a big pile of stovewood.

## YOUNG MELVIN

*This story seems solely a product of rural America, with its protagonist's naïveté and ultimate sly turning of the tables; but it has its counterparts in other lands and is an old theme in world literature. (See "The Mice That Ate Iron.") This is a perfect example of how a common motif or situation in folklore is adapted to fit the particular circumstances and character of a locality.*

After his pappy passed on Young Melvin decided he wanted to travel. He'd always lived back at the forks of the creek and he hadn't ever at no time been farther from there than the crossroads.

So Young Melvin put out the fire and hid the ax and skillet and called up his hound named Bulger and he was on his way. He went over the hill and a good piece further and he come to the crossroads. He went straight to Old Man Bill Blowdy's house there. He knocked on the door.

Old Man Bill Blowdy come to the door and stuck his nose out the crack. "Who's there?" says he, not daring to come out for fear it was somebody he'd beat in some deal.

"It's me," says Young Melvin. "Just me and my hound dog Bulger."

Old Man Bill Blowdy opened the door then and gave Young Melvin a sly look. "Come in and rest and eat a bite," he says, faint-like.

He was a great big fat red man that was always grinning and easy talking, like butter wouldn't melt in his mouth. And he was just about the slickest, double-dealingest old cooter in the country or anywhere else at all. Nobody could beat him in a deal—never had, anyway—or when it come to a law-suit. Always lawing somebody, Old Man Bill Blowdy was.

"Why don't you come in, Young Melvin?" he says.

"Because I'm on my way, Mister Old Man Bill Blowdy. I'm a-going to town for sure. It's forty miles and across two counties but I aim to see that town. That's why I come to see you."

Old Man Bill Blowdy started shutting the door. "Now, now, Young Melvin," he says. "I'm hard up for money right now. I couldn't loan my sweet mother, now in heaven praise be, so much as a penny."

"I don't want no money," says Young Melvin. "I ain't the borrowing kind."

So Old Man Bill Blowdy poked his head out again. "What can I do for you then?"

"Well, it's like this. You're my twenty-third cousin, my only kin in this world. I got a favor for you to do for me."

"Young Melvin." From *God Bless the Devil! Liars' Bench Tales* by James R. Aswell, et al. Copyright 1940 by The University of North Carolina Press, and reprinted with their permission

Old Man Bill Blowdy started sliding that door shut. "No, no favors. I make it a rule to do no favors and don't expect none from nobody."

"It's a favor I'm aiming to pay for," says Young Melvin.

"Oh," says Old Man Bill Blowdy, opening the door once more, "that's different now. Come right in, Young Melvin."

"No sir, no need to come in, for I'd just be coming out again. What I want you to do is keep my fox hound Bulger while I'm off on my travels. I'll pay his keep, I'll pay what's right when I come back to get him."

Old Man Bill Blowdy grinned all over his face. He thought he saw a way to make himself something extry or get him a fox hound one. Everybody knew Young Melvin was simple. Honest as the day's long but simple.

"Why yes," says Old Man Bill Blowdy. "Why yes, I'll keep Bulger for you, Young Melvin, and glad to."

So Young Melvin gave his hound dog over and bid Old Man Bill Blowdy farewell. "I'll be back next week or month or sometime. I don't know how long it'll be, for it's forty miles and across two counties to town."

Well, one day the week or month or anyhow sometime after that, here come Young Melvin down the pikeroad to the crossroads, limping and dusty and easy in mind. He went straight to Old Man Bill Blowdy's house and knocked his knuckles on the door.

Old Man Bill Blowdy stuck his nose out the crack and says, "Who's there?"

"It's me, it's Young Melvin."

"How are you, Young Melvin?"

"Fair to piddling. I walked to town and saw all the sights and then walked back here again. Forty miles and across two counties. Don't never want to roam no more. I'm satisfied now."

Old Man Bill Blowdy started shutting the door. "Glad to hear it, Young Melvin. Next time you come down to the crossroads, drop in and say hello. Any time, just any time, Young Melvin."

"Hold there! Wait a minute!" says Young Melvin.

"I'm busy," says the old man.

But Young Melvin got his foot in the door. "How about Bulger, Old Man Bill Blowdy? How about him?"

Old Man Bill Blowdy kept trying to shut the door and Young Melvin kept shoving his foot in.

"See here!" says Young Melvin. "I mean my fox hound."

"Oh him? Why, I declare to my soul I'd almost forgot that hound dog, Young Melvin. I sure almost had."

"Where is he at?" says Young Melvin, still trying to keep the old man from closing the door.

"I'll tell you," says Old Man Bill Blowdy, still trying to shut it, "I feel mighty bad about it, Young Melvin, but your Bulger is no more."

"How come? What do you mean?"

"Why, he's perished and gone, Young Melvin. The first night after you left I sort of locked him up in that little busted-down house over in the Old Ground. Well sir, Young Melvin, those last renters of mine that lived there was powerful dirty folks. They left the place just lousy with chinch bugs. Them bugs was mortal hungry by this time. So they just eat that Bulger of yours alive. Eat all but the poor thing's bones by morning—and the bones was pretty well gnawed.

"It was my fault in one way. I ought to known better than put your dog in there, Young Melvin. But I done it. So I won't charge you a penny for his keep the night I had him. I aim to do the fair thing."

Well, Old Man Bill Blowdy stuck his sly eye to the crack of the door to see how Young Melvin was taking it. He knew the boy was simple. He figured he had him. Because Old Man Bill Blowdy had Bulger hid out and he aimed to swap him for something to a man he knew in the next county.

So Young Melvin stood there looking like the good Lord had shaken him off His Christian limb. Tears come in his eyes and he sleeved his nose. "That dog was folks to me," he says. "Them chinch bugs don't know what they done to me."

He pulled his foot out of the door and he backed down the steps. He started towards home.

Old Man Bill Blowdy eased out on the porch to watch him go.

About that time Young Melvin turned around. "Mister Old Man Bill Blowdy," he says, "my place is way over the hill and a good piece further. I'm beat out and tired. Wonder if you'd loan me your mule to ride on? I'll bring it back tomorrow."

The old man knew Young Melvin was honest as the livelong day. Besides, he was so tickled with how he'd got him a good hound to swap and it not costing anything that he just called across the way to the crossroads store and got a witness to the loan and let Young Melvin take the mule. It was a fine mule, too, with the three hind ribs showing, the best sort of sign in a mule—shows he's a hard worker.

Next morning Young Melvin never showed up and Old Man Bill Blowdy got worried. He got worrieder still in the middle of the day when no sign of Young Melvin did he see.

But along about afternoon he saw Young Melvin come walking over the hill and down towards the crossroads. He run out on his porch and yelled, "Hey, Young Melvin, where's my mule?"

Young Melvin kept walking. He just shook his head. "I feel mighty bad about that mule, Mister Old Man Bill Blowdy," he called. "I sure do."

"Hey! Wait there!"

But Young Melvin went on, heading for the tore at the crossroads.

So Old Man Bill Blowdy was so mad he didn't wait to get his shoes. He just jumped off the porch and run across to Square Rogers, that good old man's house up the road a ways.

"Square," he says, "I want you to handle Young Melvin. He stole my mule."

The Square waked up his deputy and the deputy went down and brought in Young Melvin. Everybody at the crossroads come tagging along behind.

Square said, "Son, they tell me you stole a mule."

"No sir, Square Rogers, I never done it," says Young Melvin.

Old Man Bill Blowdy stomped his bare feet and shook his fists. "He's a bald-faced liar!"

"Curb yourself down, Old Man Bill Blowdy," says the Square, "and let the boy tell his side. Go ahead, Young Melvin."

So Young Melvin told his side, told how he borrowed the mule and started for home. "Well," he says, "you know I live over the hill and a good piece further. I rode that mule to the top of the hill. I was minding my own business and not giving nobody any trouble. Then all on a sudden I see a turkey buzzard dropping down out of the sky. Here it come, dropping fast and crowing like a game rooster.

"First thing I knew that old buzzard just grabbed Old Man Bill Blowdy's mule by the tail and started heaving and the mule's hind legs lifted off the ground and I went flying over his head and hit a rock head-on. I failed in my senses a minute. When I could see straight I saw that buzzard sailing away with the mule, most a mile high and getting littler all the time.

"And that's how it happened. I sure am sorry, but there ain't much you can do with a thing like that, Square."

"Hold on there!" says Square Rogers, that good old man. "I've seen many a turkey buzzard in my time, Young Melvin, but never a one that could crow."

"Well," says Young Melvin, "it surprised me some too. But in a county where chinch bugs can eat up a full-grown fox hound in one night, why I just reckon a turkey buzzard has a right to crow and fly off with a mule if he wants to."

So it all come out and Square Rogers, that good old man, made Old Man Bill Blowdy fork up Bulger and then Young Melvin gave back the mule.

Old Man Bill Blowdy was mocked down to nothing. He just grieved and pined away and it wasn't no more than ten years before he taken sick and wasted away and died.

# United States: Tall Tales

*England has its giant stories, but the United States of America, with
its national symbols a spread eagle and a super-tall figure of a man called "Uncle
Sam," has expressed its exuberant sense of bigness in a series of tall tales.
Nearly all the morally upright tall tale heroes are products not of the folk
imagination but of the imagination of publicists and writers. Pecos
Bill, a western cowboy; Paul Bunyan of the lumber camps; Stormalong, a New
England sailor, have little or no basis of origin among the folk, either
ethnically, regionally, or occupationally, as do Jesse James and Billy the Kid.
Such heroes as John Henry, Barney Beal of Maine, Casey Jones, Davy
Crockett, and Mike Fink were real people whose legends have outgrown their
biographies—again, thanks in part to the efforts of storytellers and
various writers who helped the legends along.
Two things are certain: first, the American tall tale is largely a manufactured
item; second, the imaginary figures of America's past have intrigued
the American mind and become mass culture heroes who embody what we like
to think of as American traits and philosophy. The general formula
for these stories is that the details shall be meticulously realistic and convincing,
and the whopping exaggeration shall be told with a straight face and
complete gravity. Perhaps the place of these tales in American life (no matter what
their origin and validity) has been best stated by Tristram P. Coffin:
"As a nation becoming almost universally literate before its national folk culture
could form, America had to provide itself with symbols and legends that other
nations would have found ready-made."* [1] We had to, and we did!*

## THE CAMP
## ON THE BIG ONION

*With this introduction to Paul Bunyan, the
mighty logger, children may want Glen Rounds'
delightful book,* Ol' Paul, the Mighty Logger. *A
casual manner in the reading or telling is best
for bringing out the humor of these tales.*

That first fall I was workin' for Paul was when
he got the big hotcake griddle. Always in the
woods in them days the boys was mighty fond of
hotcakes—just like men are pretty generally any-
wheres, I guess—and if there was anything could
be said for Paul it was that he tried to treat his
men right. And so, naturally, he wanted 'em to
have hotcakes if there was any way he could fix
it, and then besides, the way he ate 'em after-

wards, he was more'n a little fond of 'em himself.

Well, in camp before that they hadn't never
had hotcakes, because they didn't have no griddle big enough to cook 'em on, and no stove they
could of put the griddle on if they'd of had it
anyway, and so what they had for breakfast before that and what they was havin' when I went
to work for Paul was just sourdough biscuits.
And even so the cook used to have to get up
twenty-six hours before daylight to get the biscuits cooked in time because all he had to cook
'em on was one of them there drumhead stoves
they used to have and he couldn't only cook but
sixty-four drippin' pans full at a time.

But that year Paul made up his mind he was
goin' to have hotcakes for the men and he was
goin' to have a griddle big enough to cook 'em
on. And so he went down to the plow-works at
Moline, Illinois, and contracted for 'em to make
him one to suit him.

The steel that went into this griddle of Paul's
was what would have gone into two hundred
and sixty breakin' plows, and when it was done

[1] Tristram P. Coffin and Hennig Cohen, *Folklore in
America,* Doubleday, 1966, p. xx

"The Camp on the Big Onion." From *Paul Bunyan,*
copyright 1924, 1952 by Esther Shepard. Reprinted by
permission of Harcourt Brace Jovanovich, Inc.

finally, it measured two hundred and thirty-five foot across.

And then the men at the plow-works, of course, didn't have no way to ship it up to Paul and they was out there in the yard at the works figgurin' on how they could build some side-tracks and put several flatcars alongside each other and try to ship it up on them, when Paul happened to come along to see if his griddle wasn't finished yet.

"Never mind that," he says to the men when he seen 'em out there. "Never mind tryin' to build any extra tracks. We couldn't never get enough cars anyway, I don't believe. I'll just raise 'er up on edge and hitch my Blue Ox to 'er, and she'll roll right along."

And so after they'd got out of the way he raised 'er up, and hitched on, and started right out for home.

And when he come to within four or five miles of the camp, like he'd calculated it out beforehand, I guess, he just unhitched the Blue Ox and let the griddle spin on by itself. And here she come, rollin' right along. And when she got to just the right place, where he'd figgured to place her, she begun to spin round and round like spin-the-plate at a play-party and dug a nice big hole for the fire to go in under it, and settled right down and was all ready to go.

Paul had the bull-cooks pile in an acre or two of brush for a good fire, and him and Ole the Blacksmith rigged up a tank for the cook to make his batter in and a flume with a stop-cock in it, so's he could run it out onto the griddle and then shut it off whenever he had enough. Paul got flunkies with slabs of bacon strapped to their feet to skate around on the griddle to keep it greased, and a chicken wire fence all around for 'em to climb up on when the batter come in too thick. We rigged up a kind of block and tackle arrangement to haul the hotcake off with when it was done—that's on that first griddle. Afterwards, like in the camp in North Dakota, Paul, of course, always had donkey engines.

There was four hundred bull-cooks bringin' in the spruce-boughs for the bunks in the big bunkhouse at that first camp I was in; it had eighty tiers of bunks, most of 'em muzzle loaders but the two bottom layers, they was sidewinders. And the men used to go to bed in balloons at night and come down in parachutes in the mornin'.

A pretty sight it used to be to watch 'em comin' down.

"R-o-oo-ool out! Daylight in the swamp!" one of the cookees would yell, and then in a minute or two they'd all be rollin' out of their blankets, and the parachutes would open and they'd all come sailin' down. It sure was a pretty sight—about as fine a show as I ever laid eyes on.

Sometimes in the mornin' I used to stop at the door of the bunkhouse, on my way from the barn, to watch 'em. For Bill and I generally used to be on our way in to breakfast about that time, and Bill'd sometimes take the time to stop for a minute or so.

"I like to see 'em," he'd say to me. "Angus, that's a mighty fine show. They come faster now than they used to when it was just for sourdough biscuits. But we'll have to hustle along and get our hotcakes. We got to get back to the Ox."

That spring on the Big Onion we had an awful lot of trouble with the garlic that growed there where Garlic Crick joins the Big Onion River—a kind of V-shaped tract in there along the loggin' road, that was just full of it. The cook tried to use it all up seasonin' the soup but the Frenchies wouldn't stand for it in their pea-soup after the first week, and even with that he only got the top layer off and then there was four more layers growin' under that one. It beats all how thick that wild garlic can grow when it gets a good start. Everybody that even went by that place was seasoned so strong there wasn't nobody else could live with him and, worst of it, he couldn't stand to live with himself even. And we pretty near just had to break up camp, but then Paul heard that the Italian garlic crop was goin' to fail that year and so we grubbed up the whole piece, every last layer of it, and shipped it all to Italy and that way we got rid of it at last; just in time when a good many of us was goin' on the drive anyway, though.

## PECOS BILL

## AND HIS BOUNCING BRIDE

*Here is one of the children's favorites of all the made-up heroes. The "Western" has become one expression of the American culture, thanks to film and television stories which have little to do with the real cowboy or the real West. But Pecos Bill, in spite of all exaggerations, fits the clichés so dear to our hearts, and Slue-Foot Sue is a comic parody of the determined young lady who loses out to the cowboy's horse.*

There were two loves in the life of Pecos Bill. The first was his horse Widow-Maker, a beautiful creamy white mustang. The second, was a girl, a pretty, gay creature named Slue-Foot Sue.

Widow-Maker was the wildest pony in the West. He was the son of the White Mustang. Like his father he had a proud spirit which refused to be broken. For many years cowboys and *vaqueros* had tried to capture him. At last Pecos Bill succeeded. He had a terrible time of it. For a whole week he lay beside a water hole before he could lasso the white pony. For another week he had to ride across the prairies, in and out of canyons and briar patches, before he could bring the pony to a walk. It was a wild ride indeed. But after Bill's ride on the cyclone it was nothing.

At last the white stallion gave up the struggle. Pecos patted his neck gently and spoke to him in horse language. "I hope you will not be offended," he began as politely as possible, "but beauty such as yours is rare, even in this glorious state of Texas. I have no wish to break your proud spirit. I feel that together you and I would make a perfect team. Will you not be my partner at the I.X.L. Ranch?"

The horse neighed sadly. "It must be," he sighed. "I must give up my freedom. But since I must, I am glad that you are the man who has conquered me. Only Pecos Bill is worthy to fix a saddle upon the son of the great White Stallion, the Ghost King of the Prairie."

"I am deeply honored," said Pecos Bill, touched in his heart by the compliment.

"It is rather myself who am honored," replied the mustang, taking a brighter view of the situation.

The two of them went on for several hours saying nice things to each other. Before they were through, the pony was begging Pecos to be

"Pecos Bill and His Bouncing Bride" by Anne Burnett Malcolmson from *Yankee Doodle's Cousins.* Copyright 1941 by Anne Burnett Malcolmson. Reprinted by permission of Houghton Mifflin Company

his master. Pecos was weeping and saying he was not fit to ride so magnificent a beast. In the end, however, Pecos Bill made two solemn promises. He would never place a bit in the pony's mouth. No other human would ever sit in his saddle.

When Bill rode back to I.X.L. with his new mount, the second promise was broken. Old Satan, the former bad man, had not completely recovered from his badness. He was jealous of Bill. When he saw the beautiful white stallion he turned green and almost burst with jealousy. One night he stole out to the corral. Quietly he slipped up beside the horse and jumped into the saddle.

Pegasus, as the horse was called, knew right away that his rider was not Pecos Bill. He lifted his four feet off the ground and bent his back into a perfect semicircle. Old Satan flew off like an arrow from a bow. He flew up into the air, above the moon, and came down with a thud on top of Pike's Peak. There he sat howling with pain and fright until the boys at I.X.L. spotted him.

Bill was angry. He knew, however, that Old Satan had had enough punishment. In his kind heart he could not allow the villain to suffer any more than he had to. So he twirled his lasso around his head, let it fly, and roped Old Satan back to the Texas ranch. The former desperado never tried to be bad again.

The cowhands were so impressed by the pony's bucking they decided to change his name. From that time on they dropped the name of Pegasus and called him Widow-Maker. It suited him better.

The story of Bill's other love, Slue-Foot Sue, is a long one. It began with the tale of the Perpetual Motion Ranch. Bill had bought a mountain from Paul Bunyan. It looked to him like a perfect mountain for a ranch. It was shaped like a cone, with smooth sides covered with grassy meadows. At the top it was always winter. At the bottom it was always summer. In between it was always spring and fall. The sun always shone on one side; the other was always in shade. The cattle could have any climate they wished.

Bill had to breed a special kind of steer for his ranch. These had two short legs on one side and two long legs on the other. By traveling in one direction around the mountain, they were able to stand up straight on the steep sides.

The novelty wore off, however, and at last Bill sold the Perpetual Motion Ranch to an English duke. The day that the I.X.L. boys moved out, the lord moved in. He brought with him train-load after trainload of fancy English things. He had featherbeds and fine china and oil paintings and real silver and linen tablecloths and silk rugs. The cowboys laughed themselves almost sick when they saw these dude things being brought to a cattle ranch.

Pecos Bill didn't laugh. He didn't even notice the fancy things. All he could see was the English duke's beautiful daughter. She was as pretty as the sun and moon combined. Her hair was silky and red. Her eyes were blue. She wore a sweeping taffeta dress and a little poke bonnet with feathers on it. She was the loveliest creature Pecos Bill had ever seen.

She was as lively and gay as she was pretty. Bill soon discovered that Slue-Foot Sue was a girl of talent. Before anyone could say "Jack Robinson," she changed into a cowboy suit and danced a jig to the tune of "Get Along, Little Dogies."

Bill soon lost all his interest in cowpunching. He spent his afternoons at the Perpetual Motion Ranch, teaching Sue to ride a broncho. Sue could ride as well as anyone, but she pretended to let him teach her. After several months of Bill's lessons, she put on a show. She jumped onto the back of a huge catfish in the Rio Grande River and rode all the way to the Gulf of Mexico, bareback. Bill was proud of her. He thought she had learned her tricks all from him.

Sue's mother was terribly upset by her daughter's behavior. She didn't care much for Bill. She was very proper. It was her fondest hope that Sue would stop being a tomboy and marry an earl or a member of Parliament.

As soon as she realized that her daughter was falling in love with a cowboy, she was nearly heart-broken. There was nothing she could do about it, however. Slue-Foot Sue was a head-strong girl who always had her own way.

At last the duchess relented. She invited Bill to tea and began to lecture him on English manners. She taught him how to balance a teacup, how to bow from the waist, and how to eat scones and marmalade instead of beans and bacon. He learned quickly, and soon the duchess was pleased with him. She called him "Colonel."

When the boys from the I.X.L. Ranch saw what was going on they were disgusted. Here was their boss, their brave, big, cyclone-riding Pecos Bill, mooning around in love like a sick puppy. They laughed at his dude manners. They made fun of his dainty appetite. When he dressed up in his finery to call on his girl, they stood in the bunkhouse door. They simpered and raised their eyebrows and said to one another, "La-dee-da, dearie, ain't we fine today!"

But for all their kidding they were broken-hearted. None of them had anything against Sue. They admired the way she rode a horse and played a guitar and danced a jig. But the thought of losing Bill to a woman was too much. Even worse was the thought that Bill might get married and bring a woman home to live with them. That was awful.

In spite of their teasing and the duchess's lessons, Bill asked Slue-Foot Sue to marry him. She

accepted before he could back out. Her father, the lord, had always liked Bill and was terribly pleased at the match.

On his wedding day Pecos Bill shone like the sun in his new clothes. His boys were dressed in their finest chaps and boots for the occasion. Half of them were going to be groomsmen. The other half were going to be bridesmen. At first Bill asked them to be bridesmaids, but they refused. They said that was going too far.

They rode to the Perpetual Motion Ranch in a fine procession, Bill at the head on Widow-Maker. The white horse pranced and danced with excitement.

At the ranch house waited the rest of the wedding party. The lord had sent back to England for a bishop to perform the ceremony. There stood His Eminence in his lace robes. On his one hand stood the duke in a cutaway coat. On his other hand stood the duchess in a stiff purple gown right from Paris.

Down the stairs came the bride. She was a vision of beauty. She wore a white satin dress cut in the latest fashion. It had a long lace train, but its chief glory was a bustle. A bustle was a wire contraption that fitted under the back of the dress. It made the skirt stand out and was considered very handsome in those days.

As Slue-Foot Sue danced down the steps even the cowhands forgot their sorrow. They jumped down from their horses and swept their sombreros from their heads. Pecos Bill lost his head. He leapt down from Widow-Maker and ran to meet her. "You are lovely," he murmured. "I promise to grant you every wish you make."

That was a mistake. A devilish gleam twinkled in Sue's eye. For months she had been begging Bill to let her ride Widow-Maker. Bill, of course, had always refused.

Now Sue saw her chance. Before she allowed the wedding to proceed, she demanded that Bill give her one ride on his white mustang.

"No, no!" cried Pecos Bill. Before he could stop her Sue dashed down the drive and placed her dainty foot into the stirrup. The duchess screamed. The bishop turned pale.

Widow-Maker gave an angry snort. This was the second time the promise to him had been broken. He lifted his four feet off the ground and arched his back. Up, up, up shot Slue-Foot

Sue. She disappeared into the clouds.

"Catch her, catch her!" roared Bill at the boys. They spread themselves out into a wide circle. Then from the sky came a scream like a siren. Down, down, down fell Sue. She hit the earth with terrible force. She landed on her bustle. The wire acted as a spring. It bounced. Up again she flew.

Up and down, up and down between the earth and sky Sue bounced like a rubber ball. Every time she fell her bustle hit first. Back she bounced. This went on for a week. When at last she came back to earth to stay, she was completely changed. She no longer loved Pecos Bill.

The wedding was called off and the boys returned to the I.X.L. with their unhappy boss. For months he refused to eat. He lost interest in cowpunching. He was the unhappiest man Texas had ever seen.

At last he called his hands together and made a long speech. He told them that the days of real cowpunching were over. The prairie was being fenced off by farmers. These "nesters," as he called them, were ruining the land for the ranchers. He was going to sell his herd.

The I.X.L. had its last roundup. Bill gathered all the prime steers together and put them on the train for Kansas City. Then he divided the cows and calves among his boys. He himself mounted Widow-Maker and rode away.

The boys hated to see him go, but they knew how he felt. "Nesters" or no "nesters," the real reason for his going was his broken heart.

None of them ever saw him again. Some of them thought he had gone back to the coyotes. Others had an idea that Slue-Foot Sue had changed her mind and that she and Bill were setting up housekeeping in some private canyon. But they never knew.

Some years later an old cowhand claimed that Bill had died. The great cowpuncher had met a dude rancher at a rodeo. The dude was dressed up in an outfit he had bought from a movie cowboy. The dude's chaps were made of doeskin. His boots were painted with landscapes and had heels three inches high. The brim of his hat was broad enough to cover a small circus. Bill took a good look at him and died laughing.

## THE BOOMER FIREMAN'S
## FAST SOONER HOUND

*Children will enjoy Virginia Burton's pictures in Jack Conroy and Arna Bontemps' book* The Fast Sooner Hound. *They will also be entertained by that super horse, recorded in verse by Dick Jones and called* Platonia the Pride of the Plain.

In the days of the old railroad trains before diesel engines were ever thought of the fireman was an important man. A Boomer fireman could get him a job most anytime on most any railroad and was never long for any one road. Last year he might have worked for the Frisco, and this year he's heaving black diamonds for the Katy or the Wabash. He travelled light and travelled far and didn't let any grass grow under his feet when they got to itching for the greener pastures on the next road or the next division or maybe on the other side of the mountains. He didn't need furniture and he didn't need many clothes, and goodness knows he didn't need a family or a dog.

One day when one of these Boomer firemen pulled into the roadmaster's office looking for a job, there was that Sooner hound of his loping after him. That hound would sooner run than eat and he'd sooner eat than fight or do something useful like catching a rabbit. Not that a rabbit would have any chance if the Sooner really wanted to nail him, but that crazy hound dog didn't like to do anything but run and he was the fastest thing on four legs.

"I might use you," said the roadmaster. "Can you get a boarding place for the dog?"

"Oh, he goes along with me," said the Boomer. "I raised him from a pup just like a mother or father and he ain't never spent a night or a day or even an hour far away from me. He'd cry like his poor heart would break and raise such a ruckus nobody couldn't sleep, eat or hear themselves think for miles about."

"Well, I don't see how that would work out," said the roadmaster. "It's against the rules of the road to allow a passenger in the cab, man or beast, or in the caboose and I aim to put you on a freight run so you can't ship him by express. Besides, he'd get the idea you wasn't nowhere about and pester folks out of their wits with his yipping and yowling. You look like a man that could keep a boiler popping off on an uphill grade, but I just don't see how we could work it if the hound won't listen to reason while you're on your runs."

"Why he ain't no trouble," said the Boomer. "He just runs alongside, and when I'm on a freight run he chases around a little in the fields to pass the time away. It's a little bit tiresome on him having to travel at such a slow gait, but that Sooner would do anything to stay close by me, he loves me that much."

"Oh, is that so? Well, don't try to tell that yarn around here," said the roadmaster.

"I'll lay my first paycheck against a fin [1] that he'll be fresh as a daisy and his tongue behind his teeth when we pull into the junction. He'll run around the station a hundred times or so to limber up."

"It's a bet," said the roadmaster.

On the first run the Sooner moved in what was a slow walk for him. He kept looking up into the cab where the Boomer was shoveling in the coal.

"He looks worried," said the Boomer. "He thinks the hog law [2] is going to catch us, we're making such bad time."

The roadmaster was so sore at losing the bet that he transferred the Boomer to a local passenger run and doubled the stakes. The Sooner speeded up to a slow trot, but he had to kill a lot of time, at that, not to get too far ahead of the engine.

Then the roadmaster got mad enough to bite off a drawbar. People got to watching the Sooner trotting alongside the train and began thinking it must be a mighty slow road. Passengers might just as well walk; they'd get there just as fast. And if you shipped a yearling calf to market, it'd be a bologna bull before it reached the stockyards. Of course, the trains were keeping up

"The Boomer Fireman's Fast Sooner Hound," by Jack Conroy. From *A Treasury of American Folklore*, edited by B. A. Botkin. Reprinted by permission of Jack Conroy

[1] Five dollar bill.—J. C.
[2] Rule forbidding excessive over time.—J. C.

their schedules the same as usual, but that's the way it looked to people who saw a no-good mangy Sooner hound beating all the trains without his tongue hanging out an inch or letting out the least little pant.

It was giving the road a black eye, all right. The roadmaster would have fired the Boomer and told him to hit the grit with his Sooner and never come back again, but he was stubborn from the word go and hated worse than anything to own up he was licked.

"I'll fix that Sooner," said the roadmaster. "I'll slap the Boomer into the cab of the Cannon Ball, and if anything on four legs can keep up with the fastest thing on wheels I'd admire to see it. That Sooner'll be left so far behind it'll take nine dollars to send him a post card."

The word got around that the Sooner was going to try to keep up with the Cannon Ball. Farmers left off plowing, hitched up, and drove to the right of way to see the sight. It was like a circus day or the county fair. The schools all dismissed the pupils, and not a factory could keep enough men to make a wheel turn.

The roadmaster got right in the cab so that the Boomer couldn't soldier on the job to let the Sooner keep up. A clear track for a hundred miles was ordered for the Cannon Ball, and all the switches were spiked down till after that streak of lightning had passed. It took three men to see the Cannon Ball on that run: one to say, "There she comes," one to say, "There she is," and another to say, "There she goes." You couldn't see a thing for steam, cinders and smoke, and the rails sang like a violin for a half hour after she'd passed into the next county.

Every valve was popping off and the wheels three feet in the air above the roadbed. The Boomer was so sure the Sooner would keep up that he didn't stint the elbow grease; he wore the hinges off the fire door and fifteen pounds of him melted and ran right down into his shoes. He had his shovel whetted to a nub.

The roadmaster stuck his head out of the cab window, and —whosh!—off went his hat and almost his head. The suction like to have jerked his arms from their sockets as he nailed a-hold of the window seat.

It was all he could do to see, and gravel pinged against his goggles like hailstones, but he let out a whoop of joy.

"THE SOONER! THE SOONER!" he yelled. "He's gone! He's gone for true! Ain't *nowhere* in sight!"

"I can't understand that," hollered the Boomer. "He ain't *never* laid down on me yet. It just ain't like him to lay down on me. Leave me take a peek."

He dropped his shovel and poked out his head. Sure enough, the Sooner was nowhere to be seen. The Boomer's wild and troubled gaze swept far and wide.

"Don't see him, do you?" the roadmaster demanded. "He's at least seventy-six miles behind."

The Boomer didn't answer. He just threw his head back into the cab and began to shovel coal. He shoveled without much spirit, shaking his head sadly. There was no need for hard work, anyhow, for the Cannon Ball was puffing into the station at the end of the run.

Before the wheels had stopped rolling, the roadmaster jumped nimbly to the ground. A mighty cheer was heard from a group of people nearby. The roadmaster beamed as he drew near them.

"Here I am!" he shouted. "Where are the cameras? Do you want to take my picture in the cab?"

"Go way back and sit down!" a man shouted as he turned briefly toward the railroad official. "You might as well scrap that Cannon Ball. The Sooner has been here a good half hour and time has been hanging heavy on his hands. Look at him!"

The Sooner was loping easily around a tree, barking at a cat which had taken refuge in the branches and was spitting angrily. The Sooner didn't look even a mite tired, and his tongue was behind his teeth.

"I'm through! Enough is enough, boys!" the roadmaster sputtered. "The rule about passengers in the cab is a dead duck from now on. Let the Sooner ride in the cab as often and as far as he wants to."

The Cannon Ball chugged out of the station with the Boomer waving his shovel in salute and the Sooner yelping proudly beside him. The people cheered until the train disappeared around a bend.

## MIKE HOOTER AND THE SMART BEARS IN MISSISSIPPI

*Mike Hooter came to Yazoo County, Mississippi, in 1800. Hunter, fisherman, and enthusiastic preacher, he became one of the state's folk heroes, especially renowned as a hunter of bears. Mike is the observer in this humorous tale of a noodlehead hunter and a cunning bear.*

There are bears and bears—smart bears and foolish bears. Folks in Mississippi used to say Mississippi bears are the smartest bears in all these United States.

That's what Mike Hooter, the great Bear-Hunter Preacher of the Magnolia State, used to say when he was alive, and he sure knew all anybody ever knew about bears. Fact is, he was the greatest bear hunter ever was in Mississippi. Ask any man in the state and he'll agree mighty quick.

Some folks called him Mike Shouter, for he was forever roaring louder than ten waterfalls when he got to preaching sermons or when he was arguing about the smartness of the Mississippi bears. If you tried to argue the point about bears, he'd come 'round quick with the tale of Ike Hamberlin and his funny bear hunt in the cane. It's a good tale worth telling.

One time Mike Hooter and Ike Hamberlin got to talking about bear hunting and they planned to go out together one day after the big game. But Ike was monstrous jealous of Mike, so he thought he'd steal a march on his friend and go out alone before him. He set out early in the morning, he and his dogs, without Mike.

But Mike had got wind of this, so he got up crack early himself that morning, took his two-shooter, and went off looking for Ike. But he didn't take his dogs along.

After a time he sighted Ike and just followed him right along a ways off.

Ike had gone pretty deep in the canes when his dogs started growling and barking. Their

Reprinted from *Folk Stories of the South* by M. A. Jagendorf by permission of the publisher, Vanguard Press, Inc. Copyright © 1972 by M. A. Jagendorf

hairs began standing straight on their backs like tomcats in a fight. And there was another kind o' deep noise too, something a-tween a grunt and growl.

"Run, git 'm," Ike shouted to the dogs. But the dogs wouldn't. They just ran around Ike yapping and crying, as if they were scared to death, tails stuck a-tween the hind legs.

"Sic 'em! Sic 'em!" Ike kept on hollering to the dogs, but they minded him like birds in flight.

Mike was watching all the time, wondering what was coming next.

Ike was mad as a hornet, but he kept his temper, coaxing and coaxing the dogs to stir up the bear that was somewhere. Those dogs wasn't acting natural. Mike, watching, felt kind of sorry for Ike.

There was the man out hunting for bear! There was a bear for sure somewhere 'round the canebrake! There were bear-hunting dogs to stir the bear! And instead of doing their duty as good hunting dogs should, they just kept on whining, tail a-tween the legs. It sure was not right. You'd think a hant was on 'em.

Ike was mad fit to kill.

"I'll make you good-for-nothin' critters tend t' your business as you oughta," he shouted. Then he took his flintlock, leaned it against a tree, and ran to the creek and began picking up stones and throwing 'em at the dogs.

Well, when Ike Hamberlin got busy picking up stones and throwing them at the dogs that were howling t' heaven, there was suddenly heard an awful noise in the cane. A crackling and breaking and crashing like a hurricane, and out came the biggest and most powerful bear ever seen by Ike or Mike. He was a great giant standing on his hind legs. And what do you think that critter did! He just walked up to the tree where the gun was standing, picked it up with his front paws and looked at it, and then blowed into it with powerful breaths—blowing all the powder out!

Right then, Ike Hamberlin, his back to the bear, thought he'd thrown enough rocks at his cowardly or bewitched dogs and started out for his gun. When he turned around and saw the bear with it, he stood stock still. His hair stood up on his head, his mouth was wide open, and his eyes were ready to jump out of his head. And Mike, watching, was just as numb.

The bear looked at Ike with a bear grin, kind of plumb unconcerned, then he put the rifle back against the tree, turned around, and began easy loping off.

Ike rushed up to the gun, grabbed it, aimed straight at the bear, and snapped the lock! . . . Not a sound from the trusty old piece! But there was a sound of laughing afar off. Mike had seen what the bear had done and was laughing fit t' kill. The bear turned around and looked at the aiming Ike. His jaws opened wide in a bear laugh, one of his front paws went to his nose and—he thumbed his nose at good Ike, who was snapping and snapping. Then Ike turned the gun 'round and saw the powder was gone! His face looked like it'd been soaking in vinegar for six months. He shook his fist at the bear, shouted a few strong words, and turned 'round to go home. He'd had enough bear hunting for the day.

Mike turned home too, laughing till the tears ran out of his eyes.

He told the story for the rest of his life, just as I'm telling it to you. And it always brought a good laugh.

Now, wouldn't you say that Mississippi bears are mighty smart bears?

## IN ARKANSAS STICK TO BEARS: DON'T MESS WITH SWAMPLAND SKEETERS

*From the first collection of regional folklore drawn from those southern states that constituted the Confederacy, this story of the outsize mosquitoes of the Delta is typical of the American tall tale: an idiomatic use of language, colorful phrasing, and the straight-faced telling of whopping fibs.*

Reprinted from *Folk Stories of the South* by M. A. Jagendorf by permission of the publisher, Vanguard Press, Inc. Copyright © 1972 by M. A. Jagendorf

Back in the old days there lived a squatter in the Delta region not far from what is now the city of Helena. That squatter called himself Major Jones and he said he was slicker than a weasel, but his neighbors said he was a living bobcat that's dragged its tail through a briar patch. He wasn't a neighborly neighbor. He was forever complaining, but his biggest complaint was against Delta mosquitoes that were making life hard for man and beast.

They were as plentiful as ants at a picnic and big as wild turkeys. Some of them were nearly as big as deers in the woods.

One hot night the squatter set out to hunt bear. He was always bragging about his shooting strength. Truth to tell, he was lazy as pond water, so, instead of using his shooting piece on critters, he set bear traps deep in the swamps where he was sure bear were plentiful. After setting the contraptions he returned home. It was then nearly late candle-time, and it was mighty warm. Best time for mosquito-hunting. They were out thick as barn hay. They were zooming louder than frogs croaking. The squatter was hopping faster than a fox with a bumblebee in his tail, to steer clear of 'em. But those varmint mosquitoes smelled blood and they were hot after it. And I tell you when skeeters are on your trail, it's worse than snakes.

The man had come to his canoe, jumped in, and set down to paddle. But the crick skeeters were after him like a mighty army with banners, as it says in the Holy Book. Their zooming seemed like thunder in the springtime. The squatter fought them with paddle and gun to keep them off, but they were coming at him like a herd of buffalo. Major Jones was getting madder by the minute; he thought it was time to use powder and lead. He raised his hunting piece and began to fire. He brought down one or two of the zoomers and scared the rest, but only for a short time. Pretty soon they were at him again. By now he had come to where his cabin was. He leaped out of the canoe, ran to the door quicker than a jack rabbit, and put on the latch behind him, thanking the Lord for his safe escape.

The next morning early he went to the trap to see if it had caught a fat brown bear, for he was in need of meat and oil.

When he got there and saw what he saw, his face looked like soot on a stick.

That bear trap had caught . . . a skeeter the size of a young heifer.

Major Jones's face was fit to scare black cats at night. He held his teeth tight, threw a rope round the neck of the skeeter, tied a log to its borer, and hobbled its hind legs good. Then he got the varmint out of the trap and dragged it home slow-like. It wasn't easy, for that skeeter was bucking and rearing to beat running fire.

"Jest you keep on rearin' and buckin'! I'm gonna train you to be gentle as a lamb and I'm gonna train you to drill holes with that borer of yourn. Maybe I'll find oil."

In the end he got the varmint in the barn, but he put the boot on the wrong leg.

That critter began tearing and ripping around the barn like a bull with hornets all over. It was making such a racket with zooming, nobody could sleep. The third night the squatter couldn't stand it any longer.

"I'll teach that toad blister somethin'," he said to his wife. He took an old mule harness that was lying in the lot back of the cabin and went cautiously into the barn. With dodging and cross-running he got it on the skeeter, tied the skeeter to a post, and went to his cabin.

The mosquito didn't like the queer contraption one bit. So he began smashing it right and left and made enough noise to wake the dead. In the end Major Jones went to the door of the barn. Inside, the skeeter was banging and hitting away. Before Jones's hand touched the wooden latch, the door came down with a bang. The critter had broken the door and had got the harness off its neck.

Major Jones's eyes popped open big as goose eggs, for the next thing that happened no man in Arkansas had ever seen.

Before you could say Jehoshaphat that skeeter was up in the air flying in the moonlight. It was aiming straight for the pasture where the squatter's cow was mooing for the calf. Down went that critter in the pasture and, come gunpowder!, if it didn't get hold of that cow with its hind legs and begin lifting it off the grass.

Now, it is common knowledge in Arkansas that it needs two Bear State mosquitoes to carry off a fair-sized cow, and here just one skeeter was doing it! Major Jones was so flabbergasted that he didn't even run for his shooting piece. It wouldn't have done him any good anyway.

That skeeter with the cow in its hind legs was so high up by then, no lead could catch it.

"Wal!" Major Jones growled like a bobcat with a thorn in its leg, "wal, that'll teach me to stick to bears and not mess 'round skeeters in Arkansas swamplands."

# United States: Black Tales

*The talking-beast tales of Uncle Remus are a priceless treasury of Negro*
*folk tales. Although it is commonly believed that Joel Chandler Harris wrote*
*them down just as he heard them told, the truth is that he took elements*
*of the folk tales that he found among the Southern Negroes and molded them*
*into polished, literary gems which preserve a form of then current*
*Southern Negro dialect, a rich vein of humor, and a superb gift for storytelling.*
*The origins of these stories have been discussed ever since they first*
*appeared. Although Harris retold them to a great extent, the tales were in*
*common circulation among plantation Negroes. Folklorists now seem*
*generally agreed that the tales drew upon earlier African sources (there*
*are many stories about the hare in Africa), but that for the most part the*
*stories are from European predecessors. (The best and most authentic*
*examples of African folk tales in the New World are still the hundreds*
*of Anansi stories found in the West Indies.)*
*The hero of these stories is Brer Rabbit, the weakest of all the animals.*
*He is a trickster, but a lovable one, with no meanness in him, just a love of*
*playing pranks on his bigger neighbors. Occasionally they turn the*
*tables on him, but his wit and resourcefulness always save him. Those fortunate*
*people who can read and understand the rich dialect in which these*
*stories are recorded should always read or tell them in that form. When put into*
*everyday English, the tales lose their unique charm. The collection is too*
*rich for children to miss, and every effort should be made to keep these stories*
*in circulation. The recordings of some of them, made by Frances Clarke*
*Sayers for the American Library Association, are an especially fine way to hear*
*them as they might have been told.*

## THE WONDERFUL TAR-BABY STORY

*This is the best known of all the stories and a*
*perennial favorite with children. Be sure to tell*
*the sequel, "How Mr. Rabbit Was too Sharp*
*for Mr. Fox," in which Brer Rabbit, as usual,*
*gets out of his predicament.*

"Didn't the fox *never* catch the rabbit, Uncle
Remus?" asked the little boy the next evening.

"He come mighty nigh it, honey, sho's you
born—Brer Fox did. One day atter Brer Rabbit
fool 'im wid dat calamus root, Brer Fox went ter
wuk en got 'im some tar, en mix it wid some tur-

"The Wonderful Tar-Baby Story." From *Uncle Remus: His Songs and Sayings.* Copyright © 1908, © 1921, © 1935, Renewed © 1963 by Esther LaRose Harris. By permission of Prentice-Hall, Inc., Englewood Cliffs, New Jersey

kentime, en fix up a contrapshun wat he call a
Tar-Baby, en he tuck dish yer Tar-Baby en he
sot 'er in de big road, en den he lay off in de
bushes fer to see what de news wuz gwineter be.
En he didn't hatter wait long, nudder, kaze bimeby here come Brer Rabbit pacin' down de
road—lippity-clippity, clippity-lippity—dez ez
sassy ez a jay-bird. Brer Fox, he lay low. Brer
Rabbit come prancin' 'long twel he spy de Tar-
Baby, en den he fotch up on his behime legs like
he wus 'stonished. De Tar-Baby, she sot dar, she
did, en Brer Fox, he lay low.

" 'Mawnin'!' sez Brer Rabbit, sezee—'nice
wedder dis mawnin',' sezee.

"Tar-Baby ain't sayin' nothin', en Brer Fox,
he lay low.

" 'How duz yo' sym'tums seem ter segashuate?'
sez Brer Rabbit, sezee.

"Brer Fox, he wink his eye slow, en lay low, en
de Tar-Baby, she ain't sayin' nothin'.

" 'How you come on, den? Is you deaf?' sez

Brer Rabbit, sezee. 'Kaze if you is, I kin holler louder,' sezee.

"Tar-Baby stay still, en Brer Fox, he lay low.

" 'Youer stuck up, dat's w'at you is,' says Brer Rabbit, sezee, 'en I'm gwineter kyore you, dat's w'at I'm a gwineter do,' sezee.

"Brer Fox, he sorter chuckle in his stummick, he did, but Tar-Baby ain't sayin' nothin'.

" 'I'm gwineter larn you howter talk ter 'spect-tubble fokes ef hit's de las' ack,' sez Brer Rabbit, sezee. 'Ef you don't take off dat hat en tell me howdy, I'm gwineter bus' you wide open,' sezee.

"Tar-Baby stay still, en Brer Fox, he lay low.

"Brer Rabbit keep on axin' 'im, en de Tar-Baby, she keep on sayin' nothin', twel present'y Brer Rabbit draw back wid his fis', he did, en blip he tuck 'er side er de head. Right dar's what he broke his merlasses jug. His fis' stuck, en he can't pull loose. De tar hilt 'im. But Tar-Baby, she stay still, en Brer Fox, he lay low.

" 'Ef you don't lemme loose, I'll knock you agin,' sez Brer Rabbit, sezee, en wid dat he fotch 'er a wipe wid de udder han', en dat stuck. Tar-Baby, she ain't sayin' nothin', en Brer Fox, he lay low.

" 'Tu'n me loose, fo' I kick de natal stuffin' outen you,' sez Brer Rabbit, sezee, but de Tar-Baby, she ain't sayin' nothin'. She des hilt on, en den Brer Rabbit lose de use er his feet in de same way. Brer Fox, he lay low. Den Brer Rabbit

squall out dat ef de Tar-Baby don't tu'n 'im loose he butt 'er cranksided. En den he butted, en his head got stuck. Den Brer Fox, he sa'ntered fort', lookin' des ez innercent ez one er yo' mammy's mockin'-birds.

" 'Howdy, Brer Rabbit,' sez Brer Fox, sezee. 'You look sorter stuck up dis mawnin',' sezee, en den he rolled on de groun', en laughed en laughed twel he couldn't laugh no mo'. 'I speck you'll take dinner wid me dis time, Brer Rabbit. I done laid in some calamus root, en I ain't gwineter take no skuse,' sez Brer Fox, sezee."

Here Uncle Remus paused, and drew a two-pound yam out of the ashes.

"Did the fox eat the rabbit?" asked the little boy to whom the story had been told.

"Dat's all de fur de tale goes," replied the old man. "He mout, en den again he moutent. Some say Jedge B'ar come long en loosed 'im—some say he didn't. I hear Miss Sally callin'. You better run 'long."

## OLD MR. RABBIT,
## HE'S A GOOD FISHERMAN

*The humor here is superb, though it is more gentle than in some of the tales, as both Brer Rabbit and Brer Fox enjoy the joke each has played on the other. Take your time in reading or in telling this one.*

"Brer Rabbit en Brer Fox wuz like some chilluns w'at I knows un," said Uncle Remus, regarding the little boy, who had come to hear another story, with an affectation of great solemnity. "Bofe un um wuz allers atter wunner nudder, a prankin' en a pester'n 'roun', but Brer Rabbit did had some peace, kaze Brer Fox done got skittish 'bout puttin' de clamps on Brer Rabbit.

"One day, w'en Brer Rabbit, en Brer Fox, en Brer Coon, en Brer B'ar, en a whole lot un um wuz clearin' up a new groun' fer ter plant a roas'n'year patch, de sun 'gun ter git sorter hot, en Brer Rabbit he got tired; but he didn't let on, kaze he 'fear'd de balance un um'd call 'im lazy, en he keep on totin' off trash en pilin' up bresh, twel bimeby he holler out dat he gotter brier in his han', en den he take'n slip off, en hunt fer cool place fer ter res'. Atter w'ile he come 'crosst a well wid a bucket hangin' in it.

"'Dat look cool,' sez Brer Rabbit, sezee, 'en cool I speck she is. I'll des 'bout git in dar en take a nap,' en wid dat in he jump, he did, en he ain't no sooner fix hisse'f dan de bucket 'gun ter go down."

"Wasn't the Rabbit scared, Uncle Remus?" asked the little boy.

"Honey, dey ain't been no wusser skeer'd beas' sence de worril begin dan dish yer same Brer Rabbit. He fa'rly had a ager. He know whar he cum fum, en he dunner whar he gwine. Dreckly he feel de bucket hit de water, en dar she sot, but Brer Rabbit he keep mighty still, kaze he dunner w'at minnit gwineter be de nex'. He des lay dar en shuck en shiver."

"Old Mr. Rabbit, He's a Good Fisherman." From *Uncle Remus: His Songs and Sayings* © 1908, © 1921, © 1935, Renewed © 1963 by Esther LaRose Harris. By permission of Prentice-Hall, Inc., Englewood Cliffs, New Jersey

"Brer Fox allers got one eye on Brer Rabbit, en w'en he slip off fum de new groun', Brer Fox he sneak atter 'im. He know Brer Rabbit wuz atter some projick er nudder, en he tuck'n crope off, he did, en watch 'im. Brer Fox see Brer Rabbit come to de well en stop, en den he see 'im jump in de bucket, en den, lo en beholes, he see 'im go down outer sight. Brer Fox wuz de mos' 'stonish Fox dat you ever laid eyes on. He sot off dar in de bushes en study en study, but he don't make no head ner tails ter dis kinder bizness. Den he say ter hisse'f, sezee:

"'Well, ef dis don't bang my times,' sezee, 'den Joe's dead en Sal's a widder. Right down dar in dat well Brer Rabbit keep his money hid, en ef 'tain't dat den he done gone en 'skiver'd a gole-mine, en ef 'tain't dat, den I'm a gwineter see w'at's in dar,' sezee.

"Brer Fox crope up little nigher, he did, en lissen, but he don't year no fuss, en he keep on gittin' nigher, en yit he don't year nuthin'. Bimeby he git up close en peep down, but he don't see nuthin' en he don't year nuthin'. All dis time Brer Rabbit mighty nigh skeer'd outen his skin, en he fear'd fer ter move kaze de bucket might keel over en spill him out in de water. W'ile he sayin' his pra'rs over like a train er kyars runnin', ole Brer Fox holler out:

"'Heyo, Brer Rabbit! Who you wizzitin' down dar?' sezee.

"'Who? Me? Oh, I'm des a fishin', Brer Fox,' sez Brer Rabbit, sezee. 'I des say ter myse'f dat I'd sorter sprize you all wid a mess er fishes fer dinner, en so here I is, en dar's de fishes. I'm a fishin' fer suckers, Brer Fox,' sez Brer Rabbit, sezee.

"'Is dey many un um down dar, Brer Rabbit?' sez Brer Fox, sezee.

"'Lots un um, Brer Fox; scoze en scoze un um. De water is natally live wid um. Come down en he'p me haul um in, Brer Fox,' sez Brer Rabbit, sezee.

"'How I gwineter git down, Brer Rabbit?'

"'Jump inter de bucket, Brer Fox. Hit'll fetch you down all safe en soun'.'

"Brer Rabbit talk so happy en talk so sweet dat Brer Fox he jump in de bucket, he did, en, ez he went down, co'se his weight pull Brer Rabbit up. W'en dey pass one nudder on de half-way groun', Brer Rabbit he sing out:

" 'Good-by, Brer Fox, take keer yo' cloze,
    Fer dis-is de way de worril goes;
    Some goes up en some goes down,
    You'll git ter de bottom all safe en soun'." *

"W'en Brer Rabbit got out, he gallop off en tole de fokes w'at de well b'long ter dat Brer Fox wuz down in dar muddyin' up de drinkin' water, en den he gallop back ter de well, en holler down ter Brer Fox:
    " 'Yer come a man wid a great big gun—
    W'en he haul you up, you jump en run.' "

"What then, Uncle Remus?" asked the little boy, as the old man paused.

"In des 'bout half n'our, honey, bofe un um wuz back in de new groun' wukkin des like dey never heer'd er no well, ceppin' dat eve'y now'n den Brer Rabbit'd bust out in er laff, en ole Brer Fox, he'd git a spell er de dry grins."

## MASTER JAMES' NIGHTMARE
### Charles Chesnutt

*Charles Chesnutt's book* The Conjure Woman *was published in 1899 after appearing in* Atlantic Monthly *as short stories. A black educator and lawyer, Chesnutt wrote these tales of slaves and conjuring in a slave dialect, omitted here as is the framing material about Uncle Julius, who tells the tales.*

Way back, there was this man, James Mc-Lean, and when his daddy died, he left the plantation to Master James, and he was a *hard* man. Was no use living if you had to live 'round Master James. His slaves had to work from daylight to dark, and they didn't get much to eat. And what they did get was least. They couldn't

* As a Northern friend suggests that this story may be somewhat obscure, it may be as well to state that the well is supposed to be supplied with a rope over a wheel, or pulley, with a bucket at each end.

"Master James' Nightmare." Adapted by Zena Sutherland from "Master James' Nightmare," copyright 1899 by Charles W. Chesnutt. Published by Houghton Mifflin and Company

sing, or dance, or play the banjo. He wouldn't let them marry, wouldn't even let them go courting. Said he wasn't in the business of raising slaves, he was in the cotton business.

Any time he saw signs of courting, he'd sell one of the two. Anybody complained, they'd get whipped. Well, they didn't complain, but they sure enough didn't like it. They hoped for a bit there that things would get better, because Master James was courting himself, and love can change a man. He was going over every day and every night to see Miss Libbie, that was Master Marlboro's oldest gal. But it appears that when Miss Libbie heard about the goings-on at Master James' plantation, she said she just never could trust a man like that. Why, he might be so used to abusing his slaves that he'd get to abusing a wife after she'd been around a while.

The slaves were mighty sorry when the match was bust up, 'cause Master James was worse than ever. All the time he'd spent courting, he put in now on abusing his slaves, and all his bad feeling about Miss Libbie he worked off on them.

Now while he'd been courting and too busy to notice, two of the slaves had got to setting a heap of store by one another. One was named Solomon, and the other—well, I forget, but it's not important in this tale. Anyway, when Miss Libbie throwed Master James over, he found out about Solomon and the gal monstrous quick. He gave Solomon a whipping and sent the gal off to another plantation, and then he told the others that if he ever caught them at any more such foolishness, he'd skin them alive and tan their hides before their very eyes.

Sometimes Master James would go down to his other plantation for a week or more, and his overseer would look after the work. He was a poor white man, Nick Johnson. The slaves called him Master Johnson to his face, but behind his back they called him Old Nick. And that name suited him to a T. They didn't like the way Master James used them, but he was master and had a right to do as he pleased. All the slaves despised Old Nick as much as they hated him, 'cause he didn't own anybody. Was no better than a slave himself, and in those days any respectable person would rather be a slave than a poor white man.

Now, after Solomon's gal had been sent away,

he kept feeling more and more bad. Finally allowed that he was going to see if there couldn't be something done to get her back and to make Master James treat the slaves better. So he took a peck of corn out of the barn and went over to see Aunt Peggy, the free black conjure woman down by Wilmington Road.

Aunt Peggy, she listened to his tale and asked some questions, and then told him she'd work her roots and see what they said about it, and tomorrow night he should come back and fetch another peck of corn, and she'd have something for to tell him. So Solomon went back the next night, and sure enough, Aunt Peggy told him what to do. Gave him some stuff that looked like pounded-up roots and herbs.

"This here stuff," says she, "is a monstrous powerful kind of goopher. You take this home, give it to the cook if you can trust her, and tell her to put it in your master's soup the first cloudy day he has okra soup for dinner. Mind you follow the directions."

"Ain't going to poison him, is it?" asked Solomon, getting kind of scared; for he was a good man and didn't want to do nobody no real harm.

"Oh, no," says old Aunt Peggy, "it's going to do him good, but he'll have a monstrous bad dream first. A month from now you come down here and let me know how the goopher's working. For I ain't done much of this kind of conjuring of late, and I have to kind of keep track of it and see that it don't accomplish no more than I allow for it to do. And I have to be kind of careful about conjuring white folks; so you be sure and let me know, whatever you do, just what's going on around the plantation."

So Solomon said all right, and took the goopher mixture up to the big house and gave it to the cook, and told her what to do. Happened the next day was a cloudy day, so the cook made okra soup for Master James' dinner, and put Solomon's powder in it. She made it real good, so Master James ate a whole lot of it and appeared to enjoy it.

Next morning, he told the overseer he was going away on business to his other plantation, and expected he'd be gone a month or so.

"But," he says, "I want you to run this here plantation for all it's worth. The slaves are get-

ting monstrous trifling and lazy and careless. Can't depend on them. I want that to stop, and I want the expenses cut down while I'm away, and a heap more work done. Fact is, I want this plantation to make a record that'll show what kind of overseer you are."

Old Nick only said, "Yessir," but he grinned and showed his big yellow teeth, and he snapped the rawhide he carried around. Made cold chills run up and down the backbone of the slaves that heard Master James talking. And that night there was moaning and groaning down in the slave quarters, 'cause they all knew what was coming.

Well, next morning the trouble began, just as soon as Master James went away. Master Johnson, he started right off to see what he'd have to show Master James when he got back. He made the tasks bigger and the rations smaller, and when the slaves had worked the whole day, he'd find something for them to do to keep them busy until it was almost time for them to sleep.

About three or four days after Master James went away, young Master Duncan McSwayne rode up to the big house one day with a slave sitting behind him in the buggy, tied to the seat. Asked if Master James was home. Master Johnson, he said no.

"Well," says Master Duncan, "I fetched this slave over to Master McLean to pay a bet we made on a card game. I bet him a slave, and here's one I reckon will fill the bill. He was picked up t'other day for a stray slave; couldn't give an account of himself, and so he was sold at auction and I bought him. He's kind of brash, but I know your power, Master Johnson, and I reckon if anybody can make him toe the mark, you're the man."

Master Johnson grinned one of them grins that showed all his snaggled teeth and make the slaves say he looks like the devil, and he says to Master Duncan, "I reckon you can trust me to tame any black man that was born. The slave don't live what I can't take down in about four days."

Well, Old Nick had his hands full longer than that with that new slave. The rest of them, they were sorry for him but they allowed he kept Master Johnson so busy that they got along better than they would have if the new slave had never come. The first thing that happened, Master Johnson said to this new man, "What's your name, Sambo?"

"My name ain't Sambo," answered the new slave.

"Did I ask what your name wasn't?" says Master Johnson. "You want to be particular how you talk to me. Now. What's your name and where did you come from?"

"I don't know my name and I don't know where I come from. My head is all kind of mixed up."

"Yes, I reckon I'll have to give you something to clear your head. At the same time, I'll learn you some manners, and after this maybe you'll say 'sir' when you speak to me."

Well, Master Johnson hauled off with his rawhide and hit the new slave once. New slave looked at Master Johnson as if he didn't know what to make of this here kind of learning. But when the overseer raised his whip to hit him again, the new slave just hauled off and made for Master Johnson. If some of the other slaves hadn't stopped him, it appears as if he might have made it warm for Old Nick there for a while. But the overseer made the other slaves help tie the new man up, gave him forty lashes with a dozen or so thrown in for good measure. Old Nick never was stingy with *that* kind of rations. New slave went on at a terrible rate, just like a wild man, but he had to take his medicine, 'cause he was tied up and couldn't help himself.

Master Johnson locked the new slave in the barn and gave him nothing to eat for a day or so, 'til he got him kind of quieted down, and then he turned him loose and put him to work. New man said he wasn't used to working and wouldn't do it, so he got another forty lashes for impudence. Master Johnson let him fast a day or so more, then put him to work. The slave went to work, but he didn't appear to know how to handle a hoe. Took about half the overseer's time looking after him, and that poor slave got more lashing and cursing than any four others on the plantation. But he couldn't seem to get it through his mind that he was a slave and had to work and mind the white folks in spite of the fact that Old Nick gave him a lesson every day. Finally Master Johnson allowed he could do

nothing with him; if it was *his* slave, he'd break his spirit or break his neck, one way or the other.

Of course, he'd only been sent over on trial, so Master Johnson could send him back before he killed him. So he did, he tied him up and sent him back to Master Duncan.

Now Master Duncan McSwayne was one of these easy-going people who didn't like to have trouble with slaves or anyone else, and he knew that if Master Old Nick couldn't get along with the slave nobody could, so he took the slave into town that day and sold him to a trader who was getting up a gang of slaves to ship off to New Orleans.

Next day after the new man had been sent away, Solomon was working in the cotton field and when he looked up at the end of the row, who should he see but Aunt Peggy, who beckoned to him—the overseer was down the other side of the field—and she said, "Why ain't you come and reported to me like I told you?"

"Aunt Peggy, there ain't nothing to report. Master James went away the day after we gave him the goopher mixture, we haven't seen hide nor hair of him since, and of course we don't know what effect it had."

"I don't care nothing about your Master James now, what I want to know is what's been going on among the slaves. Been getting along any better on the plantation?"

"No, Aunt Peggy, worse. Master Johnson is stricter than ever, the poor slaves hardly have time to draw a breath, and they allow they might as well be dead as alive."

"Uh huh," says Aunt Peggy. "I told you that was a monstrous powerful goopher and its work don't appear all at once."

"Long as we had the new slave, he kept Master Johnson busy most of the time, but now he's gone away, I suppose the rest of us'll catch it worse than ever."

"What's going on with the new slave?" asked Aunt Peggy quickly, batting her eyes and straightening up.

"Old Nick has sent him back to Master Duncan, and I hear he's sold him to a slave trader who's going to ship him off with a gang tomorrow."

Aunt Peggy appeared to get really stirred up

when she heard this, and shook her stick at him.

"Why didn't you come and tell me about this new slave being sold away? Didn't you promise, if I gave you that goopher, that you' come and report to me everything that was going on at the plantation? By not doing it, I'm afraid you spoiled my conjuring. You come to my house tonight, and you do what I tell you or I'll put a spell on you that will make all your hair fall out, and your eyes drop out, and your ears grow up so you can't hear. When you're fooling around with a conjure woman like me, you mind your *P*s and *Q*s or there'll be trouble."

So of course Solomon went to Aunt Peggy's that night and she gave him a roasted sweet potato.

"You take this," says she, "I goophered it especially for the new slave—you better not eat it yourself or you'll wish you hadn't—you slip off to town and give it to him. He must eat it before morning if he doesn't want to be sold away to New Orleans."

"But suppose the patrollers catch me, Aunt Peggy, what am I going to do?" Solomon asked.

"The patrollers won't touch you, but if you don't find that slave, *I'm* going to get you, and you'll find I'm worse than the patrollers. I'll sprinkle some of this mixture on you so the patrollers can't see you, and you can rub your feet with the grease from this gourd so you can run fast. Rub some of it on your eyes so you can see in the dark, and then find that slave and give him the potato or you'll have more trouble than you ever had before in your life or ever will have."

So Solomon took the potato, went up the road as fast as he could go, and before long reached the town. He went right by the patrollers and they didn't appear to notice him, and by and by he found out where the strange slave was kept. He walked right past the guard and found him. Solomon could see the slave, asleep, and he put the sweet potato right in front of the man's nose. Well, he reached up in his sleep and took it and ate it. Never woke up. Then Solomon went back and told Aunt Peggy, and he got back to his cabin along about two in the morning.

Next day was Sunday. Solomon was disturbed in his mind about his gal, and was wondering what Aunt Peggy had to do with the new slave.

He sauntered into the woods to be by himself, when who should he see standing under a tree but a white man. Didn't know him at first, until the white man spoke up.

"Is that you, Solomon?" he says. Then Solomon recognized the voice.

"For the Lord's sake, Master James! Is that you?"

"Yes, Solomon," says his master, "this is me, or what's left of me."

No wonder Solomon hadn't known Master James at first, for he was dressed like a poor white man, and he was barefoot and looked kind of pale and peaked, as if he'd come through a hard spell of sickness.

"You look kind of poorly, Master James. Have you been sick, sir?"

"No, Solomon," says Master James, shaking his head slowly, "I haven't been sick, but I had a monstrous bad dream—in fact, a regular nightmare. But tell me how things have been going on at the plantation since I left."

So Solomon up and told him about the crops and the animals. And then when he started to tell about the new slave, Master James pricked up his ears, and every now and then he'd say, "Uh huh! Uh huh!" and nod his head. By and by, when he'd asked Solomon some questions, he says, "Now, Solomon, I don't want you to say a word to nobody about meeting me here, but I want you to slip up to the house and fetch me some shoes and some clothes. I forgot to tell you that a man robbed me back yonder on the road and swapped clothes with me without asking whether or no—but you needn't say anything about that, either. Go fetch some clothes here, don't let anyone see you, keep your mouth shut, and I'll give you a dollar."

Solomon was so astonished he like to fell over in his tracks when Master James promised to give him a dollar. Certainly was a change come over Master James when he offered one of his slaves that much money. Solomon began to suspect that Aunt Peggy's conjuration had been working monstrous strong.

Solomon fetched Master James some clothes and shoes, and that same evening Master James appeared at the house and let on like he just got home from the other plantation. Master Johnson was all ready to talk to him, but Master

James sent him word he wasn't feeling very well that night, and he'd see him tomorrow.

So next morning after breakfast, Master James sent for the overseer and asked him to give an account of his stewardship. Old Nick told Master James how much work had been done, and got the books and showed him how much money had been saved. Then Master James asked him how the slaves had been behaving, and Master Johnson said they had been behaving well, most of them, and them that didn't behave well at first changed their conduct after he got ahold of them a time or two.

"All," says he, "except the new slave Mr. Duncan brought over here and left on trial while you were gone."

"Oh, yes," answered Master James, "tell me all about that new slave. I heard a little about that queer new man last night and it was just ridiculous. Tell me all about him."

So, seeing Master James so good-natured about it, Master Johnson up and told him how he tied up the new hand the first day and gave him forty lashes because he wouldn't tell his name.

"Ha, ha, ha!" says Master James, laughing fit to kill, "But that's too funny for anything. Tell me more about the new slave."

So Master Johnson went on and told him how he had to starve the new slave before he could make him take hold of a hoe.

"That was the queerest notion for a slave," says Master James, "putting on airs just like he was a white man. And I reckon you didn't do nothing to him?"

"Oh, no sir," says the overseer, grinning like a Cheshire cat, "I didn't do nothing but take the hide off him."

Master James laughed and laughed, until it appeared like he was just going to bust. *Tell me some more about that new slave, oh, tell me some more. That new slave interests me, he does, and that's a fact."

Master Johnson didn't quite understand why Master James should make such a great admiration about the new slave, but of course he wanted to please the gentleman who hired him, so he explained all about how many times he'd had to cowhide the new slave, and how he made him do tasks twice as big as some of the other hands, and how he would chain him up in the barn at night and feed him on cornbread and water.

"Oh, but you're a monstrous good overseer; you're the best overseer in this country, Mr. Johnson," says Master James when the overseer got through with his tale, "and there ain't never been no slave breaker like you 'round here before. And you deserve great credit for sending that slave away before you spoilt him for the market. In fact, you're such a good overseer, and you got this plantation in such fine shape that I reckon I don't need you any more. You've got the slaves so well trained, I expect I can run them myself from this time on. But I wish you'd held on to that new slave until I got home, for I'd like to have seen him, I certainly should."

The overseer was so astonished he didn't hardly know what to say, but finally he asked Master James if he wouldn't give him a recommendation for another place.

"No sir," says Master James, "somehow or other I don't like your looks since I came back this time, and I'd much rather you wouldn't stay around here. Fact is, I'm afraid that if I met you alone in the woods sometime, I might want to harm you. But laying that aside, I've been over these here books of yours that you kept while I was away and for a year or so back, and there's some figures that just aren't clear to me. I haven't got time to talk about them now, but I expect before I settle with you for this last month, you'd better come up here tomorrow after I look over the books and accounts some more, and then we'll straighten our business all up."

Master James allowed afterward that he was just taking a shot in the dark when he said that about the books, but, howsoever, Master Nick Johnson left that neighborhood betwixt the next two suns, and nobody around there ever saw hide nor hair of him since. And all the slaves thanked the Lord and allowed it was good riddance to bad rubbish.

But all the things I done told you ain't nothing compared to the change that came over Master James from that time on. Aunt Peggy's goopher had made a new man of him entirely. Next day after he came back, he told the hands they need work only from sun to sun, and he cut their tasks down so nobody needed to stand over with a rawhide or a hickory. And he said if the slaves wanted to have a dance in the big barn any Saturday night, they could. And by and by, when Solomon saw how good Master James was, he asked him if he could please send down to the other plantation for his gal. Master James said certainly, and gave Solomon a pass and a note to the overseer on the other plantation, and sent him with a horse and buggy to fetch his gal back.

And Master James' own gal, Miss Libbie, heard about the new goings-on, and she changed her mind about Master James. And before long they had a fine wedding, and everyone on the plantation had a big feast, and there was fiddling and dancing and fun and frolic from sundown 'til morning.

## *North American Indian and Eskimo Tales*

*On the whole, the stories from the Indian peoples of the North American continent have not proved particularly appealing unless edited (and distorted) to a considerable degree. They often seem to us overly long and formless. The reason may be that too many collectors and interpreters of these native tales were unaware (perhaps deliberately uninformed) of the deep significance of the stories and their style. Taken out of context, the Indian tales have not translated successfully into our culture's terms. This gives us a biting example, however, of how necessary it is to understand a people's mind and ways in order to understand its tales, and not the other way round as has often been averred. To appreciate the Indian's myths and legends, we must first know the Indian.*

## GRAY MOSS ON GREEN TREES

*(Choctaw)*

*The French who came to the New World called the gray tree-moss of the South "Spanish beards" and the Spanish called it "French wigs." This is one of many "why" stories that explain it.*

The Indians tell a tale down in Louisiana. Maybe it's the Choctaw Indians, maybe it's the Chitimacha Indians, who battled with the French for many years when they were not busy making fine baskets and bright copper things. It might even be another tribe that tells this tale, or it may be all the tribes.

There was an Indian mother working in the field along the river. Near her, her two children played with bows and arrows, and with blue and purple flowers.

Suddenly, cold Wind came racing in the air through the trees. Then Rain came on, sharp rain, running in all directions. Water in the river rose, high and cold.

The mother took the children by the hand and ran toward her hut of palmetto leaves. But she could not run as fast as the flying Wind, or as fast as the racing Water. Water was all around her, coming higher and higher, and held her feet down.

The mother climbed up a thick oak tree, holding the younger child in her arms. The older one followed her slowly. Soon they were high up, where Water could not reach them.

Wind kept on howling and Water kept on rising. Then Rain stopped, but cold Wind still ran wildly in the trees and around the three high up in the branches. The mother and the children were very cold and the children began to cry.

"Mother, I am cold, my feet are cold."

"Mother, my hands are cold and I can't hold on to the branches."

Moon came out over the black, flying clouds. Its white light was sharp and bright.

"Mother, I am cold," both the children cried.

The mother, too, was very cold.

Reprinted from *Folk Stories of the South* by M. A. Jagendorf by permission of the publisher, Vanguard Press, Inc. Copyright © 1972 by M. A. Jagendorf

"Man in the Sky," the mother prayed, "my children are very cold and will die. I am very cold and I can't keep them warm. I don't want my children to die from the cold. Take pity on them, they are very young. Take pity on me, so I can be with them. Be kind to us and don't let us die."

So the Indian mother prayed to Moon, while black and gray clouds flew all around the sky.

Moon spoke to Clouds, and to Wind. They listened. Moon shone strong on the mother and the children, and they fell asleep. Then Moon wove and wove and wove. . . .

Morning came. The sky was clear and warm. The Indian mother and her children awoke and were warm. They looked on the branches and saw what they had never seen before. All over the trees, in the branches and around them, was a thick green-gray blanket that had covered them. It was not made of cloth, but of grass, and Moon had woven it. The Indian mother looked and looked, and so did the children.

"Mother," cried the older boy, "it's a blanket all around us. It kept us warm all night. Moon heard you pray and tore up the clouds to make a blanket for us. Moon hung it on the tree to keep us warm."

"Yes, son, that's what Moon did for us. The sky is clear and the clouds are now on the tree."

They came down and went home.

The "Cloud-Cloth," folks call Spanish moss. It has been on the trees in Louisiana ever since and has spread to trees in other states.

## LITTLE BURNT-FACE

*(Micmac)*

*Little Burnt-Face is the scorched face of the desert in the burning summer and the Great Chief, whose symbol is the arching rainbow, is the healing rain. Invisible for a long period of time, he comes at last and restores its original beauty to the face of the waiting earth child. This is typical of the folklore of many tribal cultures in the way that it uses symbolism and also in the concern it shows for natural phenomena.*

Once upon a time, in a large Indian village on the border of a lake, there lived an old man who was a widower. He had three daughters. The eldest was jealous, cruel, and ugly; the second was vain; but the youngest of all was very gentle and lovely.

Now, when the father was out hunting in the forest, the eldest daughter used to beat the youngest girl, and burn her face with hot coals; yes, and even scar her pretty body. So the people called her "Little Burnt-Face."

When the father came home from hunting he would ask why she was so scarred, and the eldest would answer quickly: "She is a good-for-nothing! She was forbidden to go near the fire, and she disobeyed and fell in." Then the father would scold Little Burnt-Face and she would creep away crying to bed.

By the lake, at the end of the village, there was a beautiful wigwam. And in that wigwam lived a Great Chief and his sister. The Great Chief was invisible; no one had ever seen him but his sister. He brought her many deer and supplied her with good things to eat from the forest and lake, and with the finest blankets and garments. And when visitors came all they ever saw of the Chief were his moccasins; for when he took them off they became visible, and his sister hung them up.

Now, one Spring, his sister made known that her brother, the Great Chief, would marry any girl who could see him.

Then all the girls from the village—except Little Burnt-Face and her sisters—and all the girls for miles around hastened to the wigwam, and walked along the shore of the lake with his sister.

And his sister asked the girls, "Do you see my brother?"

And some of them said, "No"; but most of them answered, "Yes."

Then his sister asked, "Of what is his shoulder-strap made?"

And the girls said, "Of a strip of rawhide."

"And with what does he draw his sled?" asked his sister.

And they replied, "With a green withe."

Then she knew that they had not seen him at all, and said quietly, "Let us go to the wigwam."

So to the wigwam they went, and when they entered, his sister told them not to take the seat next the door, for that was where her brother sat.

Then they helped his sister to cook the supper, for they were very curious to see the Great Chief eat. When all was ready, the food disappeared, and the brother took off his moccasins, and his sister hung them up. But they never saw the Chief, though many of them stayed all night.

One day Little Burnt-Face's two sisters put on their finest blankets and brightest strings of beads, and plaited their hair beautifully, and slipped embroidered moccasins on their feet. Then they started out to see the Great Chief.

As soon as they were gone, Little Burnt-Face made herself a dress of white birch-bark, and a cap and leggings of the same. She threw off her ragged garments, and dressed herself in her birch-bark clothes. She put her father's moccasins on her bare feet; and the moccasins were so big that they came up to her knees. Then she, too, started out to visit the beautiful wigwam at the end of the village.

Poor Little Burnt-Face! She was a sorry sight! For her hair was singed off, and her little face was as full of burns and scars as a sieve is full of holes; and she shuffled along in her birch-bark clothes and big moccasins. And as she passed through the village the boys and girls hissed, yelled, and hooted.

And when she reached the lake, her sisters saw her coming, and they tried to shame her, and told her to go home. But the Great Chief's sister received her kindly, and bade her stay, for she saw how sweet and gentle Little Burnt-Face really was.

Then as evening was coming on, the Great Chief's sister took all three girls walking beside the lake, and the sky grew dark, and they knew the Great Chief had come.

And his sister asked the two elder girls, "Do you see my brother?"

And they said, "Yes."

"Of what is his shoulder-strap made?" asked his sister.

"Of a strip of rawhide," they replied.

"And with what does he draw his sled?" asked she.

And they said, "With a green withe."

Then his sister turned to Little Burnt-Face and asked, "Do you see him?"

"I do! I do!" said Little Burnt-Face with awe. "And he is wonderful!"

"And of what is his sled-string made?" asked his sister gently.

"It is a beautiful Rainbow!" cried Little Burnt-Face.

"But, my sister," said the other, "of what is his bow-string made?"

"His bow-string," replied Little Burnt-Face, "is the Milky Way!"

Then the Great Chief's sister smiled with delight, and taking Little Burnt-Face by the hand, she said, "You have surely seen him."

She led the little girl to the wigwam, and bathed her with dew until the burns and scars all disappeared from her body and face. Her skin became soft and lovely again. Her hair grew long and dark like the Blackbird's wing. Her eyes were like stars. Then his sister brought from her treasures a wedding-garment, and she dressed Little Burnt-Face in it. And she was most beautiful to behold.

After all this was done, his sister led the little girl to the seat next the door, saying, "This is the Bride's seat," and made her sit down.

And then the Great Chief, no longer invisible, entered, terrible and beautiful. And when he saw Little Burnt-Face, he smiled and said gently, "So we have found each other!"

And she answered, "Yes."

Then Little Burnt-Face was married to the Great Chief, and the wedding-feast lasted for days, and to it came all the people of the village. As for the two bad sisters, they went back to their wigwam in disgrace, weeping with shame.

## HOW THE LITTLE OWL'S NAME WAS CHANGED

*(Eskimo)*

*This is one of the better and more felicitously styled stories from Charles Gillham's collection of Eskimo tales. It is a why story which echoes one of mankind's oldest reasons for rejoicing— the return of spring. Even in the bleak far north, as in the warm climes of ancient Greece, the owl is a symbol of life and renewal.*

Every spring in Alaska a little owl would come north with the other birds. It was a tiny owl and flew noiselessly over the tundra on its soft, downy wings. At first the Eskimos called him Anipausigak, which meant "the little owl." Later, after the Eskimos knew more about the bird, they called him Kerayule, which means in their language "the owl that makes no noise when he flies."

In the very early days, before the white men came to Alaska, the Eskimos had no matches and it was very difficult for them to have a fire. Also there was very little wood in the Eskimo country.

One spring there was one family living all by themselves that had a bit of fire, but there was no place where they could get any if this went out. In the middle of the igloo was a pit, or hole, in the floor. Here a tiny little fire was kept burning at all times. Always someone watched it and tended it. The smoke went curling out of the window in the top of the igloo.

In this igloo were a little boy and a little girl with their mother and father. All times of the day and night someone had to stay in the house and watch the tiny fire. One day when the little girl was all alone—her folks were out hunting seals—some bad people came to the igloo.

"Oh, so you are all alone, little girl," one of them said. "I suppose you are watching the fire so that it does not go out?"

"Yes," said the little girl. "It would be very bad if we lost our fire. We would be very cold and would have nothing to cook by. I must watch it carefully so that when my parents come home there will be a warm house here to greet them."

The bad man laughed. "You will not have to watch your fire any more, little girl, for we have no fire in our igloo and we are going to take yours with us."

How frightened the little girl was and how badly she felt to think she was going to lose the fire! She thought quickly. "Can't I make you some fire on another stick, Mr. Man?" she asked. "Then you can take it with you and I will still have some left for my mother and father and my little brother when they come home from hunting seals."

"I haven't time to wait for you to make new fire," the bad man said, "and, besides, I do not care if you are cold and hungry." With that he grabbed the fire and went away with it, leaving the poor little girl crying and all her fire gone.

When the mother and father and little brother came home they found the igloo cold, and the little girl told them what had happened. Hastily the father took his bow and arrow and set out to the igloo of the bad men to get his fire. When he got there, however, he found that they had two men who guarded the fire day and night. They were big men and had big spears, and bows and arrows too. So the poor man could not get his fire away from them. He begged them to let him

have just a little of it to carry back to his wife and children, but they only laughed at him.

So for several days the good Eskimos had a terrible time. It was very cold and they could not make a fire with anything. At last, one night, the father Eskimo thought of a plan. He called for the little owl, Kerayule, who makes no noise when he flies.

"Please, little owl, will you help us?" the Eskimo man asked him. "You see we have no fire, and we are cold. Please will you get our fire back for us from the bad men who took it away?"

"How can I do that?" asked the little owl. "I would like to help you, but they have spears and bows and arrows. Besides, they are much stronger than I am. Just how do you think I could get the fire?"

"You make no noise when you fly," the Eskimo man replied. "They will not hear you coming in the night. Also you can see in the darkness, and you can go straight to their igloo. The window in the top of it will be open, and you can look in and see how you can get the fire for us."

"I never thought of that," said the little owl. "I think, maybe, I can get the fire for you. I *can* see in the darkness and I make no noise at all when I fly."

So the little owl set off through the dark night to the igloo where the bad men lived.

Carefully the owl flew over the igloo and he did not make a sound. He looked into the window in the top where the smoke came out. He saw the fire—just one small stick burning in the fire pit. Also he saw one of the bad men sitting by it. He seemed to be asleep. The little owl hovered lower and alighted without a sound on the edge of the window. Silently, like a great soft feather, the little owl fluttered down into the igloo.

Right by the fire pit, the little owl landed on the floor and the man did not see him. Maybe he was asleep, but the owl was not sure. Hopping softly across to the stick of fire, the little owl took the unburned end in his mouth and, with a great flutter, flew straight up through the open window in the top of the igloo. As he did, the man awakened. He grabbed his bow and arrow to shoot the little owl, but was too late. Out into the night sailed the little owl, through the black darkness. He flew straight to the igloo of the good Eskimos.

The children were watching for the little owl, and soon they saw the fire come flying through the black sky.

"Look!" shouted the little girl. "See the *sparkling fire* coming!"

And to this day the Eskimos at Hooper Bay call the little owl "sparkling fire owl," or Kennreirk in their language. Sometimes in the springtime, when the sparkling fire owl comes to Hooper Bay and hovers around the people, they will listen closely to see if they can hear him make any noise. Sometimes—very rarely—he makes a little snapping with his beak, or a flutter with his wings. If the people can hear him make any noise they are very glad, for that is the best of good omens. They say the little sparkling fire owl is sending them good luck. If they go hunting they are sure to get a seal, or an eider duck, or a fat fish.

The Eskimo people love the little sparkling fire owl because he brings them good luck and, too, when they see him they know the springtime has come to stay.

# *The West Indies*

*In the folklore of the West Indies we find a remarkable fusion of the Old and New Worlds. Anansi stories, direct from Africa, have over the centuries become intermingled with themes from European folk tales. The stories of Uncle Bouqui and Ti Malice, saucy with French overtones, show the European influence, even while containing elements of the rabbit tales from Africa. And some of the tales of Puerto Rico and Cuba reflect the early Spanish dominance in the Caribbean.*

*The study of West Indian folklore seems rather neglected, but the nuggets of West Indian tales found in collections for children indicate a rich mine to be worked. From the tales of Anansi, of Uncle Bouqui, of the frog in Puerto Rico, and of Juan Bobo as he appears here and there, it would seem that some of the characteristics of the people who inhabit these islands are an irrepressible wit, a delight in harmless trickery, and a love of laughter.*

**BANDALEE**

*(Jamaican)*

*From Aesop to Anansi—or, from Asia to Europe to Africa to the West Indies! Here is the familiar tale of the race between the hare and the*

tortoise now firmly a part of Anansi folklore. *This story illustrates again that basic themes are found throughout world folklore, giving us historical evidence that tales have traveled from one continent to the other, even though we cannot always say when or why or how. Older children will enjoy De la Mare's "The Hare and the Hedgehog."*

Whispers went through the forest.

Whenever two of the forest creatures met they put their heads together and whispered. Even those that usually kept far apart could be seen whispering in each other's ears—even Tiger and Goat, Mongoose and Chicken, Dog and Cat were busy whispering to each other.

It was all about Land Turtle. They whispered to each other that Land Turtle had become a very rich man.

Anansi heard the whispers. He believed that they were true, and he made up his mind that he would get some of Land Turtle's money. His eyes shone when he heard of all the money that Land Turtle had. Surely it would not be hard to trick Land Turtle, who looked so slow and stupid.

"I never knew that Land Turtle was so rich," said Anansi to himself. "I thought he was a poor man. He hasn't any sense either, so he has no right to be rich. I've never seen anyone move as slowly as Land Turtle, except Brother Worm. It won't be hard to take some of his money from him."

Anansi crawled under his bed and pulled out from the darkest corner an old calabash that he used to hide his savings. Slowly he counted it, and the counting did not take long because there was so little money. "I must get to work," said Anansi, and he set off for the bank. He lodged his money in the bank and then went to Land Turtle's house.

Now it happened that Land Turtle was a much wiser creature than he seemed. He moved slowly, but he could think fast. When he saw Anansi coming he guessed that there was some reason for the visit, and so he told his wife and children to hide themselves while he talked with Anansi.

"Good morning, Brother Land Turtle," said Mr. Anansi, who was a little breathless because he had walked so fast. "It's a long time since we two met."

Land Turtle bowed but said nothing.

"It's a long time since I paid you a friendly visit," said Anansi.

Land Turtle bowed again, but said nothing.

"Yes, a long time," said Anansi. "To tell you the truth, you would not have seen me today at all; but I went for a long walk, and, as I was tired, I turned in here on my way home to rest a while. Yes, I went to the bank to put in some money because if we do not save we will never have anything."

"That is true," said Land Turtle, who was still wondering why Anansi had come.

"You know, Land Turtle," said Anansi, "perhaps we could make a bargain. You have money in the bank. I have money in the bank. I want more, and you want more. Now suppose we agree to run a race to the bank. The one that wins will get all the money belonging to the two of us."

Land Turtle was silent for a few minutes. He saw through Anansi's scheme.

"That's not fair, Anansi," he said. "Look how fast you walk and how slow I am. You'd get to the bank long before me. But I'll agree to race you if you promise you will run as a spider, and not change yourself into a man." It was well known that Anansi could change himself whenever he wished.

"I'll agree to run the race as a spider," Anansi said.

He knew that even in his spider form, running along his rope, he could run faster than Land Turtle. What a fool Land Turtle was, thought Anansi, to dream of racing me.

"Well, Brother Anansi," said Land Turtle, "since we have made the bargain, the next thing is to decide where we shall start from. As you know, there are two roads that lead to the bank."

"Pshaw," said Anansi, "a road is a road. One is just as long as the other. We can talk about that tomorrow. Let's go to the bank and tell the banker that the one of us that gets there first tomorrow is to have the money, yours and mine put together."

So they went to the bank and explained it all to the banker, and then they went home to get a good night's sleep. Land Turtle called his wife and his sons and his daughters, and told them about the race. "Anansi is very cunning," he said, "but this time Land Turtle is going to be cunning, too. But I will need your help." And then he told them what they must do.

Now Land Turtle knew that Anansi would suggest that each should go by a different road. One road followed the river, and another ran up on the bank a little way. Every little while, there was a crossing that joined the two. Early in the morning of the day of the race, Mr. Land Turtle and his children walked along the river road; and wherever there was a crossing, one of the children sat down to wait. For old Brother Land Turtle and his children looked so much alike that nobody could tell one from another. Mr. Land Turtle's oldest son went to meet Anansi at the starting place, and Mr. Land Turtle himself took up his station at the last crossroads. As soon as he was sure that the race had begun, he planned to run to the bank, get all the money, and go back home through the woods.

All the animals had come out to see the race. Some stood at the starting place, some waited outside the bank. Soon Anansi came along, all smiles and confidence. He could almost feel the weight of Land Turtle's money in his pocket.

Stupid old Land Turtle. Look at him, thought Anansi, as he looked at what he thought was Mr. Land Turtle, but what was in fact Mr. Land Turtle's oldest son.

Just as Land Turtle had thought, Anansi suggested that they run by different roads and call out to each other from time to time. Land Turtle's son nodded his head, to show that he agreed; and Anansi called out—one, two, three—and away they went. Soon Anansi was well ahead of Land Turtle, yet when he came to the first crossing and called out, "You Turtle, you Turtle," he heard a voice reply: "Anansi oh, Anansi oh, bandalee, bandalee."

"Well," thought Anansi, "Land Turtle isn't far behind." And he ran faster. At the next crossing he called out again, "You Turtle, you Turtle," and one of Land Turtle's children answered: "Anansi oh, Anansi oh, bandalee, bandalee."

"I never thought Land Turtle could run so fast," said Anansi to himself. "I must run faster if I'm to get the gold." And away he went.

Once again at the third crossing Anansi called out, "You Turtle, you Turtle!" And once again

one of Land Turtle's children called out, "Anansi oh, Anansi oh, bandalee, bandalee."

"Faster still, faster still," thought Anansi to himself. He began to feel anxious. By the time he got to the last crossing he hardly had enough breath to call out, "You Turtle, you Turtle."

This time no answer came.

"At last," said Anansi to himself, "at last I am well ahead. Now for the money at the bank." But at that very moment Land Turtle was leaving the bank with his own money and with the few pence that belonged to Anansi.

Anansi was sure that he had left Land Turtle far behind, so he slowed down and walked into the bank as if he owned it. He asked for his money and Land Turtle's, but the banker told him that he had already given the money to Land Turtle.

"What," panted Anansi, "do you mean that Land Turtle got here first?"

"Yes," said the banker. "Land Turtle came in fifteen minutes ago."

"Are you sure that it was Land Turtle?" asked Anansi.

"Quite sure," said the banker. "I know Land Turtle well, and I gave him the money."

Out rushed Anansi as fast as his legs could carry him. In the distance he could see Land Turtle toiling along.

"To think that slow coach beat me in a race," cried Anansi. "Stop, Turtle, stop."

Turtle did not stop, but Anansi soon caught up with him.

"So you won the race," said Anansi. "Well, well, who could have thought it. Let us walk home together."

Poor Land Turtle was very frightened. However, Anansi was so friendly that soon Land Turtle was calm again. Quietly they walked along until they came to a pond. Anansi saw his chance.

"Let's both dive in," he said, "and see who can stay under the water longest."

Land Turtle was pleased to see how well Anansi had taken his defeat, and he readily agreed. Besides that, he was proud of his diving. This was the one thing in which he felt certain that he could beat Anansi every time. He put down his bag of gold at the edge of the pond, and both Anansi and Turtle dived at the same time.

Land Turtle stayed under for as long as he possibly could. Surely Anansi would lose for the second time in one day. Then he came up but, alas, both Anansi and the money had gone.

## UNCLE BOUQUI
## AND GODFATHER MALICE
### (Haitian)

*Again we find that delightful blending of European and African tales. This is nothing more nor less than a variant of the Grimms' "Cat and Mouse Keep House." Compare the two and see how well each pictures the people and place from which it came. Uncle Bouqui's fate is considerably better than that of the mouse in the Grimms' tale.*

One time Bouqui and Malice were farming together in the Red Mountains. Every day they went out to their fields with their hoes and machetes, and they worked until the middle of the afternoon when the sun was broiling hot.

Uncle Guinéda, who lived in the village, had chopped down a tree full of honey, and he gave Bouqui a big gourd full of it because Bouqui was godfather to Guinéda's youngest child. Bouqui was very proud and jealous of that gourd of honey, and he hung it up in the rafters of his house, intending to save it for a big holiday, such as Christmas or Dessaline's Day.

Now Ti Malice liked honey just about better than anything. His mouth watered at the sight of that gourd hanging there in the rafters. Four or five times he politely suggested that they sit down and have a glass of honey, but Bouqui shook his head and made an ugly face.

"I'm saving that honey for an occasion," Bouqui said.

"When two good friends get together that *is* an occasion," Malice said.

"Do you think I'm a rich man?" Bouqui said. "I can't eat honey every day."

One hot morning they were out in the field cultivating corn. The earth was dry, and the sun

"Uncle Bouqui and Godfather Malice" from *Uncle Bouqui of Haiti* by Harold Courlander. Copyright 1942 by Harold Courlander. Reprinted by permission of the author

was hot, and Malice became thirstier and thirstier. He began to think of that cool gourd of honey hanging in the rafters of Bouqui's house. Two or three times he stood very still and closed his eyes, just so he could imagine the honey.

Finally he dropped his hoe on the ground.

"Wah!" he said. "Someone is calling me."

"I didn't hear anything but a lamb baaing," Bouqui said, "and it didn't sound like 'Malice.' "

"Wah! There it is again," Malice said. "I'll have to go to see who it is."

He picked up his hat and marched over the hill, and when he was out of Bouqui's sight he turned and headed for Bouqui's house. He went inside and climbed up into the rafters and took down the honey gourd. He poured some honey in a glass, mixed it with water, and drank it. Then he mixed some more and drank it. He kept mixing and drinking until he was so full he couldn't swallow another drop. Then he hung the gourd back in the rafters and went back to the field.

Bouqui was working away with his hoe, and he was mighty hot. He pushed out his lips and made an ugly face.

"You certainly were gone long enough! What happened to you?"

"Wah, Bouqui! Everyone wants me to be godfather to their children. Nobody leaves me alone. I had to go to a baptism."

"Woy, that's different!" Bouqui said, breaking into a smile. "Is it a boy or girl?"

"A girl, and a very nice one indeed," Malice said, licking the honey off his chin.

"Wonderful!" Bouqui said, beaming and resting his arms on the hoe handle. "I like babies. What's her name?"

"Her name?" Malice said. "Oh, yes. Well, I named her *Début*." (Début means "beginning" in Creole.)

"*Début!*" Bouqui gasped. "Woy, what an elegant name! How did you ever think of it?"

"It just came to me," Ti Malice said modestly. And he picked up his hoe and went back to work.

The next day they were weeding the garden with their machetes, and the sun got hotter and hotter, and Malice got thirstier and thirstier. He tried to keep his mind on his work, but all he could think of was that honey gourd hanging in

Uncle Bouqui's rafters. Suddenly he stood up straight and cocked his ear and said:

"Wah, Bouqui, did someone call me?"

"I don't think so," Bouqui answered. "I heard a calf bawling on the next hill, but I don't think he mentioned your name."

"There!" Malice said. "There it is again! I'll have to go see who wants me." He stuck his machete into his belt and marched over the hill.

Bouqui shook his head and mumbled to himself. He rapped his right ear with his knuckles, and then he took hold of his left ear and tweaked it.

"My ears are asleep," he said. "I didn't hear a thing!"

As soon as he was out of sight, Malice turned and ran for Bouqui's house. He climbed up into the rafters and brought down the honey gourd and fixed himself a big drink. He fixed another, and another. He drank and drank and drank until he felt ready to burst. Then he hung the gourd in the rafters again and went down to the field where Bouqui was chopping away in the hot sun.

"Well, what happened?" Bouqui asked impatiently. "You were gone a tremendously long time!"

"Uncle Bouqui, my friends just won't leave me alone. They're always bothering me. It's always Malice-this and Malice-that. They needed me to come and baptise another baby."

"That's a different matter," Bouqui said with a grin. "Boy or girl?"

"A boy this time," Malice said, licking honey off his fingers.

"What's his name?" Bouqui said. "I certainly like babies."

"His name? Oh, well, I called this one *Dèmi*," Malice said. (Dèmi means "halfway" in Creole.)

"*Dèmi!* What a fine name! You certainly have a wonderful imagination. *Dèmi!* It's mighty sweet."

"It certainly is," Malice answered. "There's probably just one more as sweet as that one." And they picked up their machetes and went back to work.

The next day they were out cultivating again. The sun got hotter and hotter. Malice started to sing to keep his mind off the honey, but it was no use. He threw his hoe down on the ground.

"Wah!" he said. "What an imposition!"

"What's the matter?"

"Didn't you hear?" Malice said.

"No, only some dogs barking."

"Someone's calling me again. What do you think they want?"

"People certainly are having babies!" Bouqui said. "Don't be gone long!" He twisted and jerked his ears. "They're half dead," he muttered. "I didn't hear anything but the dogs."

Malice headed over the hill, and then he scrambled for Uncle Bouqui's house. He took down the honey gourd and drank and drank. He drank until the gourd was empty. He stuck his tongue inside and licked it clean as far as he could reach. When he was through, the gourd was dry as an old cornstalk. He hung it up in the rafters and went back to where Uncle Bouqui was sweating and making dark faces in the hot sun.

"Well," Bouqui said, "what was it?"

"Another baby," Ti Malice said. "A girl. I think it's the last one."

"Wonderful!" Bouqui said. "What did you name it?"

"Name it? Oh. Well, I named this one *Sèche*," Malice said. (Sèche means "dry" in Creole.)

"*Sèche!* What an unusual name!" Bouqui said. "Woy, you are just about the best baby-namer in Haiti."

When they went home after work that night Bouqui said, "You know, I think we should celebrate all those babies tonight. Why should I save the honey until Christmas? If we don't drink it the flies will."

He reached up in the rafters and took down the gourd. He stood there a long time looking into it. Then he carried it outside and looked again. He closed his eyes for a minute, then opened them. He turned the gourd upside-down, but nothing happened. He licked the edges, but they didn't even taste like honey. He smelled the gourd, but there wasn't even an odor left.

"Oh-oh!" he said at last. "It's gone!"

He turned around, but somehow Malice seemed to have disappeared too. Uncle Bouqui sat down to think. He thought, thought, thought. He mumbled and argued with himself. He scratched his head first, and then he scratched his chin. He just couldn't make any

sense out of it. Suddenly he began to tingle. For a moment he sat very still, tingling from head to toe. Then he leaped into the air and howled.

"Wah! The first one was named *Début!* And the second was named *Dèmi!* And the third was named *Sêche!* Beginning, Halfway, and Dry! Wah!" he wailed. "And all the time I was out there working! Beginning, Halfway, and Dry— *of my honey!*"

That night Uncle Bouqui waited until Ti Malice was asleep on his mat, and then he crawled into the house quietly on his hands and knees. "Beginning, Halfway, Dry," he kept saying over and over to himself. When he got to Malice's mat, Bouqui opened his mouth wide and—*pimme!* He clamped his teeth down hard on Malice's big toe. Malice let out a wild yowl and sprang into the air, but Bouqui hung on.

"Ouch!" Malice yelled. "Stop it, you're killing me!"

Bouqui let go with his teeth, and Malice's yelling died down to a moan.

"Uncle Bouqui!" he whimpered. "Uncle Bouqui! What do you call that, anyway?"

"I call that one *Début!*" Bouqui shouted. And he lunged forward, *pamme!* He caught Malice's other big toe right between his teeth.

Malice leaped and jerked and howled, but Bouqui held on. Malice hopped and crawled and jumped, but Uncle Bouqui wouldn't let go.

"Wah!" Malice screamed. "I'm hurt for life!"

Bouqui opened his mouth and made a ferocious face at Malice.

"Uncle Bouqui, Uncle Bouqui!" Malice groaned. "What do you call this business, anyway?"

"I call this one *Dèmi!*" Bouqui shouted. And he lunged forward to get another one of Malice's toes with his teeth.

But Ti Malice came to life. He sprang across the room as though he were running on hot coals. In no time at all he was outside, racing off into the hills.

"Wah!" he howled as he went through the gate. "Wah! There's one thing you'll never do, Bouqui! You'll never be godfather to *Sêche!* Not unless you catch me first!" And he disappeared into the darkness without another word.

Bouqui stood listening until the sound of Malice's feet slapping against the trail had died away. He got to thinking.

"*Sêche,*" he said. "It's a mighty unusual name, at that."

## WHO RULES THE ROOST?

*(Dominican)*

*This is a realistic folk tale—that is, if one can accept the readiness of José and Francisco to give up so much to settle an argument.*

In a small town of the Dominican Republic there once lived two men who were good friends. Both were merchants. One, José, sold yucca and corn. The other, Francisco, sold yams. These two often talked together, about this, that, and the other.

One day José, the older of the two, said to his friend Francisco, "From the oldest days, from the days when the world began, from the first days Christopher Columbus saw our blessed Island of Hispaniola, and right on down to our

Reprinted from *The King of the Mountains* by M. A. Jagendorf and R. S. Boggs by permission of the publisher, Vanguard Press, Inc. Copyright © 1960 by M. A. Jagendorf and R. S. Boggs

day, woman has been the ruler of the house. She is not only queen of the house, but also king."

"Now, José," said Francisco, "I say you are wrong. True, I am not married, as you are, but I say man rules the house, and woman follows. The man heads his home, and his wife obeys him."

"My good friend Francisco! You are a thousand times wrong. Am I not married? I should know! Look around you, right here in our town, and on all the farms around the town. Look as far as you like, for that matter. You will always find that I am right, no matter where you look in this world. Woman rules the roost!"

"You are wrong, José, dead wrong. I tell you man is the rooster of the house, and woman just cackles."

And so they argued, but neither convinced the other he was right. It got so that every evening after their work was done they would look for each other and begin to argue the same question over and over.

One evening the argument became livelier than usual, and José said he would *prove* he was right.

"I'll tell you what we'll do, Francisco. You say that man rules the house, I say that woman rules the roost. We can argue this question until Judgment Day, and we'll get nowhere. Let us put the matter to a test. Whichever of us wins, the other must admit that he was wrong. Agreed?"

"I agree," said Francisco.

"Here's what we'll do. I'll take a dozen horses, and you take a dozen cows. We'll go from house to house and talk to people and find out whether the man of each house or his wife is master. If it's the woman, we'll give her a cow. If it's the man, we'll give him a horse. What do you say to that?"

"That's a good plan. I agree!" said Francisco.

Bright and early the next morning, José was at the meeting place with his dozen horses, and Francisco with his cows. They set out with the animals behind them. "Remember," said Francisco, "the first one who gives away all his animals loses."

When they came near the first house, they could hear before they ever reached the door who was master there. The woman was screaming at her husband for not having locked up the pigs the night before. The husband stood with head bowed and did not open his mouth.

"Give her a cow!" said José victoriously. And Francisco sadly did so without saying a word.

They went to the next house. While they were still out in the road they heard a woman shout, "Go and get the bread! Be quick about it, and don't argue with me!"

Francisco looked at José in despair and meekly gave that woman a cow.

And so they went from house to house, and quickly found out who was the head—the woman, of course! Poor Francisco had to give away cow after cow. Finally he had just one cow left, but José still had his twelve horses. Francisco's face had grown longer and longer, and José's smile had grown broader and broader.

At last they came to the house where the judge of the town lived. The judge was home, but his wife was out.

"Good morning, *buenos días, Señor Juez,*" they both said respectfully. "We are trying to find out who is the master of the house in the different homes of our community, the man or his wife."

"I say the woman always rules the house," said José with great certainty.

"And I said the man is master in his home," said Francisco sadly.

To his surprise, the judge said, "You are right, Francisco. Here in my house *I* am the head and master. Whatever I say goes. *My* wife does as I say."

"I'm glad to hear that, Señor Judge," said José.

"Yes, it's been that way from the day we were married," the judge said proudly.

"You're a lucky man, Señor Judge," said José. "The Lord has blessed you."

"It's really quite simple," continued the judge, encouraged by this respect and admiration. "All you have to do is to begin the very first hour you are married to show your wife that you are the head of the house."

"You are the first man we have found to say that," said Francisco, his spirits rising.

"In this house, my word is law," continued

the judge.

"I'm delighted to hear that, indeed," said José, "even though I lose a horse by it. You see, Señor Judge, we decided to give a horse to each man who is master of his house. You are the first to get one. I have a dozen horses here. Please come out and choose the one you like best."

"Do you really mean this?" asked the judge.

"Yes, I do," said José. "Come and take the one that pleases you most."

"This is my lucky day," said the judge joyfully. "You say there are twelve to choose from?"

"That's right!" said José. "See, here they are."

The judge came out and looked them over carefully. "Just look at that black one," he said. "He looks as if he could run a good race. But that brown one! He looks strong and healthy. And that spotted one! He is certainly a handsome horse. Well, well, well! It's really hard to choose. I tell you, José, just wait until my wife comes back. She's a fine judge of horses. Besides, I'd like to please her. It's funny, but she's right most of the time."

"Father in heaven!" cried José. "He's no better than the rest. Give him your last cow, Francisco. Unfortunately for us men, I win. You can easily see who rules the house here."

Francisco did not say one word. Sadly he handed over his last cow to the judge. Then he turned to José and said just two words: "You win!"

Now everyone knows who rules the roost in the Dominican Republic, just as in all the rest of the world: the woman!

## THE THREE FAIRIES
### (Puerto Rican)

*Are the three crones really fairies, or are they part of Mama's careful arrangements to provide a good life for her child? It makes little difference to the enjoyment of this blithe tale, for the fun is in the trick played on the bridegroom, and in the colloquial ease of the dialogue.*

There was once a widow who had a very pretty,

kind and good daughter. Being sickly, the woman worried much about dying and leaving her daughter alone in the world. Every night she prayed that the girl would find a good husband who would care for and protect her.

The girl was indeed virtuous and industrious. But not flirtatious at all. Nor yet coy. Nor coquettish. So the young men of the town, being more jocund than judicious, avoided her.

There was in that place a wealthy *señor* who was looking for a girl to marry. A hardworking girl. A comely girl. A good girl. Well, you say, so there's the story. The *señor* married the widow's daughter, and that was that. Nooooo . . . there were complications, and that was *not* that. At least not right away.

True, the *señor* did come to visit the widow. True, he admired the daughter greatly—and said so. True, the widow was most encouraging, pointing out her daughter's attractions: her quietness, her diligence, her tenderness, her flawless complexion, her honey-hued hair, the beauty mark on her chin, and on and on.

"But," inquired the *señor*, who had been pondering, "can she spin? Can she sew? Can she embroider? For in my business there is much of cotton and silk."

"*Por supuesto,* naturally she can sew, spin and embroider to a fare-thee-well. There is nothing that girl cannot do. She spins a thread as fine as a spider's. Her stitches are smaller than the footprints of a fly. She can embroider a bird so you reach to stroke its feathers."

"In that case," announced the *señor*, "it is settled. If she is *that* good a spinner, a sewer, an embroiderer, I will marry her. I shall arrange at once for the wedding." And away he went.

The widow was overjoyed. You would have thought *she* was the one getting married. And what did the daughter have to say? (Though it was by now rather late for her to say anything, even about her own marriage.)

"Mama, I heard what you said. How could you be so foolish? I know little of sewing, noth-

"The Three Fairies." Copyright © 1974 by Dorothy Sharp Carter. From *Greedy Mariani and Other Folktales of the Antilles* selected and edited by Dorothy Sharp Carter (A Margaret K. McElderry Book). Used by permission of Atheneum Publishers and Curtis Brown, Ltd.

ing of embroidery, and less of spinning. What will that *señor* think of me when we are married?"

"You are the foolish one, daughter. Surely there is a solution to the problem. All you have to do is think of it. I did this for your good, you well know."

When she went to bed that night the poor girl wept a thousand or more tears thinking of the terrible lies her mother had told. Not to speak of what might befall *her* for having deceived the *señor*. She had just resolved to go to him early the next day and confess the truth about herself when she heard a slight noise. Sitting up, she saw three strangers. On top of everything else! The poor girl wept harder than ever.

However, the strangers assured her they were fairies and had come to help her. Their only condition, they said, would be an invitation to her wedding. The girl was only too happy to consent, saying they could come as her dearest relatives. They disappeared, and the girl fell asleep.

Days passed and preparations were made for the wedding. The girl informed her *novio* that she had invited a few of her cousins whom she loved very much to come to the wedding feast.

The day of the celebration arrived, passed and died away. That night all the wedding guests sat down at the table for dinner. Three chairs remained vacant.

"For whom are these reserved?" asked the groom.

At that moment came a knock at the door. It opened and three old horrors entered whom the girl introduced as her cousins.

Dinner was served, and the whole world was content and ate tremendously. When it was over the husband arose and went to speak to the girl's kin, who were now his cousins as well as his wife's.

He asked the first, "Hear me, cousin. Will you tell me why you are so humped and one-eyed?" (A blunt man, the bridegroom.)

"*Ay,* my son! From all the embroidery I did in my life."

The husband whispered to his wife, "From now on I forbid you to embroider. I can pay to have this done and I do not wish you to be so deformed as your unlucky cousin."

Then he asked the second, "And why is it your two arms are so unequal?"

"Because I have spent my whole life spinning."

The *señor* took his wife's hand. "Nevermore will you spin, my love."

And finally he questioned the third of the cousins. "What is the matter with your eyes, that they burst from your head as grapes from their skins?"

"Ah, so would yours if your life had been spent sewing and reviewing tiny stitches."

"This, my dear, shall not happen to you," said the *señor*, turning to his wife. "You are to do no more sewing. None at all."

The very next day the husband gathered up all his wife's sewing equipment and hurled it out the door, since he cared more for his wife's beauty than all the work she could do. The two lived most happily and the girl never had to grieve herself to explain away the lies her poor mother had told.

# Latin America

*On the whole, the Latin American folk tales available for children that have been published in this country are not very satisfying. Charles Finger's* Tales from Silver Lands *and* The King of the Mountains; A Treasury of Latin American Folk Stories *by Moritz Jagendorf and R. S. Boggs are among the best collections in print; still it is comparatively difficult to find first-rate tales that have drama, local color, and appeal for children. The few tales chosen for this section hardly do justice to the wealth of material in the folklore archives of some Latin American countries. However, much of the best song and story material has not been translated into English. As is typical of the folk literature of all the Americas, from northern Canada to southern Chile, that of Latin America is a mixture of native Indian, African, European, and some Asiatic traditions. Out of the material available to us we can give children a feeling for certain aspects of these cultures and traditions, but little of it reflects the people as they are now. Our neighbors to the south have much to tell us in their tales and their music. We are only just beginning to lend them an ear.*

## THE KING OF THE MOUNTAINS

### (Bolivian)

*This traditional Indian story was told to Mr. Jagendorf by a Bolivian who was visiting in New York.*

The sun, all gold in the sky, and the condor,[1] the great and strong bird of the high mountains, are worshiped and loved in many parts of Andean South America. Beautiful temples were built to the sun, and large monuments were erected with the condor as the symbol of the land.

There are many stories about both the bird and the sun everywhere in that vast land, and here is one from Bolivia.

This happened long, long ago, soon after the earth first came into being. The birds in Bolivia wanted to have a king. But who would be king?

Reprinted from *The King of the Mountains* by M. A. Jagendorf and R. S. Boggs by permission of the publisher, Vanguard Press, Inc. Copyright © 1960 by M. A. Jagendorf and R. S. Boggs.

[1] The condor is one of the largest birds in existence. With its wings open in flight, it measures from nine to ten feet. It is also one of the most graceful birds when flying and can go for nearly half an hour without moving its wings—just sailing beautifully through the air. The bird with jet-black feathers, save for a white frill around the base of the neck, inhabits the high mountains of the Andes.

There was so much chattering and arguing among them about this that the leaves got tired of listening. There was screaming and whistling and singing without end. Every bird wanted to be king.

Finally one wise old bird said, "Let Pachacámac, the great king of the earth, decide; or, better yet, let the one who comes nearest the sun, where Pachacámac has his golden palace, be king of the birds."

This made sense to all the birds, and they agreed, for no one was wiser than Pachacámac. The birds screamed their desire to Pachacámac, and the king of the earth spoke: "Yes, let the bird who flies highest and who comes nearest the sun and my palace be king. The bird who does this will have to be very brave."

Then, at a given signal, all the birds rose into the sky. They were like a great cloud of many colors, and there were so many of them that the sun could not be seen.

Up and up they went, streaking and circling about. Soon some dropped down. Others rose higher and higher. Then more dropped down.

The higher they went, the fewer there were. These few circled still higher. And still more dropped down until there were only three left in the great blue heaven with the gleaming sun. They were the eagle, the hawk, and the condor. Just these three, circling slowly, rising and rising, getting nearer and nearer to the sun.

Up they went, while all the birds below watched in silence. All the animals were watching, too, for it was a sight worth seeing, those three—the fearless eagle, the keen hawk, and the majestic condor—winging their way silently upward.

Soon those watching below saw one of the three becoming larger and larger, and the other two becoming smaller and smaller. It was the hawk who was coming down, while the eagle and condor kept going up.

"I am beaten by those who are stronger and more fearless than I. The heat was too strong for me," said the hawk.

The birds did not hear. They were watching the two left circling and soaring, soaring and circling, rising higher and higher. The birds and the animals on earth watched silently. Which one would win?

Sometimes the eagle looked at the condor; sometimes the condor looked at the eagle. The eagle looked more often. He was feeling hotter and hotter. His skin was burning dry, his eyes were burning hot. He had to shut them; he could no longer stand the golden fire of the sun, and he began to drop. The condor saw him falling. All the birds and the animals saw him coming down. A great stream of pride surged through the condor's body, and he did not feel the heat at all. He had won!

"I must get nearer the sun!" he cried. So he kept circling, circling, closer and closer to the great, shining sun. The feathers on his head were burned. He kept rising, rising, slowly. The feathers on his neck were burned. It was hard for him to breathe the fiery air, but he kept on rising! His eyes became red as fire! Still, he kept them open and kept on rising.

"I must rise to the sun! It matters not what pain I may feel."

Then, suddenly, there was a cool, sweet wind coming from the yellow, gleaming brightness. There was the Golden City of the Sun. And there, in the center, was Pachacámac, the father of all, sitting on his golden throne.

"Hail, great Malleu, Condor, bird of the sun! Only you had the courage to come so high."

The condor was speechless before all that glory.

"No bird has ever come so close to my City of the Sun. For this you deserve to be king of the birds. You are the king, strong and fearless. Only the strong and fearless can stand the light of the sun that wounds the sight and burns the eyes. You are like me, so I shall take your form when I visit the earth or fly through the air. I am the great king of all that is on the earth, and you will be the great king of all the flying birds. My home is the City of the Sun. Yours will be the highest mountains that are nearest to the sun. Your palace of snow and ice will gleam like my palace of gold. And when you leave the earth, you will come here to me."

Since that time the people of Bolivia know, just as the birds know, that the condor is not only king of all the birds, but that he is sometimes even Pachacámac, king of the earth, flying in the form of the condor; and when they see Malleu, the condor, they look upon him with love, respect, and worship.

To this day wonderful monuments are still built in Bolivia with the condor on top, wings spread wide, as if it were flying to the sun.

## THE WITCHES' RIDE

### (Costa Rican)

*Here is as lively a Halloween story as anyone could ask for. It has a familiar theme—the simpleton who comes out on top—and it is an example of a European tale in Latin America, so untouched by the native culture that it is hardly even Costa Rican in feeling. The Irish "The Voyage of the Wee Red Cap" offers an interesting parallel to this story.*

Once, in the days of long ago, there lived in Costa Rica a widow who had an only son. Now this son was considered a *bobo*, or simpleton, because he was lazy and, more than that, because in one way or another he muddled everything he set out to do.

One day the bobo's mother was preparing to cook the *chayote* hash and rice which were to be their supper. She went to the shed for wood to burn in the stove, but the shed was empty. So she told the bobo to go to the forest yonder and bring her some sticks for the fire.

Since it was already late afternoon and a chill wind was blowing, the bobo wrapped himself up in a coarse old blanket, wearing it like a cape. Then he set off. He soon entered the forest, but there were no broken branches at hand and since he had no machete, or long, sharp knife, with him to cut branches from the trees, he went on farther and farther, from one thicket to another. Before long he was deep in the forest.

Soon it grew dark and he lost the path. As he groped his way through the dense underbrush and hanging vines, not knowing which way to turn, he suddenly came upon a hut. He was glad to find a shelter and knocked a good round knock. No one answered. So he opened the door and went in. Finding the hut deserted, he proceeded to make himself at home. In a corner behind a pile of straw he found an old mat woven of reeds, and there he snuggled down. Soon, in good comfort, he was fast asleep.

He slept and slept till at the hour of midnight

he was awakened with a start by the sound of merry voices. He raised his head a wee bit and looked around with one eye.

Through the open window of the hut the moonlight shone on the clay floor, turning it white. There the bobo saw twelve black shadows—the shadows of twelve old witches. They were jesting and laughing and having altogether a merry time as each witch took a sip from a big drinking gourd, then smacked her lips and passed it on.

Meantime, the bobo lay quiet and still behind the pile of straw, scarcely daring to draw his breath lest the witches find him and change him into some bird or beast.

And the riot and revelry went on until the gourd ran dry. Then without any warning at all, a witch cried out in a croaking voice, "Time to be off!" At the same moment she picked up a broom from a pile on the floor, placed herself nimbly upon it, and said these magic words:

"Fly me faster than a fairy,
    Without God—without Saint Mary!"

Away out of the window she flew and soared gracefully up into the air. The others followed quickly—each pouncing upon a broomstick from the pile, then repeating the magic words.

High in the night sky they flew, one behind the other, like a long black waving ribbon. They circled once and again around the big yellow moon and then vanished swiftly from sight beyond the tall mountain peaks.

"A week of Sundays!" cried the bobo in surprise. "Wasn't that neatly done! I wouldn't mind doing it myself! And why not?"

Well, as soon as the last witch had disappeared, up sprang the bobo from the reed mat and straightway went to the corner where the pile of brooms had been. He hoped that the witches might have left one behind. And they had! He snatched it up, and fastening the blanket around his shoulders good and tight, he placed himself upon the stick. Then he shouted with all his might:

"Fly me faster than a fairy,
    Without God—without Saint Mary!"

These words were scarcely out of his mouth when up he shot into the air like a whizzing arrow, and out of the window he flew. Faster and faster he soared, low over the treetops and high toward the moon, like a bird. And he flew and flew and flew, and the higher he went, the more he liked it—so much that every once in a while he would say the magic words again to the broom.

But, alas, he was not called a bobo for nothing. In his great glee he muddled the words, and said to the broomstick:

"Fly me faster than a fairy,
Fly with God and good Saint Mary!"

No sooner were these words out of his mouth than the broom began to fall. Fast—and faster than fast—it dropped. The poor bobo had no time to think of the right magic words as he tumbled and somersaulted through the air.

Now then, it so happened that some robbers were hiding at the edge of the forest that night. Their booty was spread out on a large cloth, and they were seated around it, counting out each one's share of the treasure by the weak light of their lantern.

"Ho! The Devil himself must have been with us today," cried one of the robbers in delight. "Hope he doesn't take a fancy to drop in for his share!"

And at this very moment the bobo, who was coming down full tilt, saw the group and shouted, "Out of the way! Look out there, all of you! Make way for this poor devil!"

The robbers looked up, each and all of them afraid of the strange sight the bobo made. For his blanket flapped and danced behind him like two big black wings as he plunged down upon them. They sprang up in great fear, thinking they had the Devil on their backs.

"The Devil! The Devil is loose! Here he comes!" they cried in terror. "Run! Let us fly! Away . . . away!" They took to their heels as if they were running a race. And they left their booty behind.

The bobo came down in one enormous swoop upon the pile of riches—*plump!* There he sat, gazing rapturously at the heap of gold and silver coins. "Bless my soul! Bless my little soul!" he cried.

Straightway he jumped up and piled the coins together again in the center of the large cloth. Then he made a bundle out of it, slung it over his shoulder, and hobbled home very happy, humming a merry tune.

And as for the robbers, they were never seen again.

## OVERSMART IS BAD LUCK
*(Uruguayan)*

*Since this is a folklore plot that is common to many European countries, it appears to be a variant. Brief and pithy, the story of the clever rooster and the gullible fox has the quality of a fable, especially with its moral tag.*

Señor Rooster was a fine bird, and he lived in a village in Uruguay. He was smart, too, and he liked to take walks beyond the village to see the world.

One day he took a long walk and wandered deep into the forest. He came to a tall tree and decided to fly high up into the branches and look at the whole world from there. So he flew up into the tree, branch after branch, until he got high, high up.

Now Señor Fox came walking through the woods. As he passed under the tree he heard Señor Rooster flapping his wings in the branches, and he looked up. He saw the feathers of Señor Rooster and his fat body, and he thought what a fine dinner he would make. But Señor Fox had no wings and could not fly up into the tree. Nor could he climb. Well, he remembered that good words often pave good roads.

"My dear, dear friend, Señor Rooster!" he cried. "How are you today? I see you are all alone up there. It seems very strange for a famous gentleman like you to be all alone. I'm sure all the fine fat hens in the henhouse are worried about you, wondering where you have gone, and are anxious to see you."

"Good Señor Fox," replied Señor Rooster,

Reprinted from *The King of the Mountains* by M. A. Jagendorf and R. S. Boggs by permission of the publisher, Vanguard Press, Inc. Copyright © 1960 by M. A. Jagendorf and R. S. Boggs

"just let them wait. The longer they wait, the happier they will be to see me when I return."

"You're a smart gentleman, Señor Rooster, and very wise. But I wouldn't let the poor hens wait too long. Come down and we'll walk together to the henhouse. I'm going that way."

"Ha, ha, ha!" laughed the rooster. "What sweet and honeyed words you use to catch me! Do you really think I'll come down so you can make a good dinner of me? Sweet words catch fools."

"Don't say that, Señor Rooster. Maybe in my former days of sin I was guilty of such things, but no more . . . no more. . . . I've reformed completely. Besides, haven't you heard the news? Don't you know about the new decree now in force in our forest? No animal can eat another; all are to be friends. That's the new law. Anyone who breaks it will be punished severely. I'm surprised you haven't heard about it. Everyone knows it."

"Well, that's news to me, Señor Fox."

"I wouldn't dare to eat you now, even if I were starving to death, my good friend. Honestly. On my honor."

"Well, it must be so, when you talk like that."

"It's the absolute truth, Señor Rooster. So you see, you can come down now."

"Really!" said Señor Rooster, but still he did not come down. Instead, he looked around in all directions. Suddenly he saw a hunter approaching with his dogs. That gave him an idea. He began to count slowly: "One . . . two . . . three . . . four . . ."

"What are you counting, good friend Rooster?"

"Five . . . six . . ."

"What *are* you counting? Tell me, friend."

Señor Rooster pretended he hadn't heard, and said, "Six fine big hunting dogs running this way, and a man with a gun behind them!"

"Dogs! What dogs? Coming this way? With a hunter?"

"Yes, Señor Fox, all coming this way!"

"From which direction are they coming? Please tell me quickly! From where?"

"They're coming from over that way," and he pointed with his wing in exactly the opposite direction from which he saw them.

"I'd better run along now," cried Señor Fox.

"I'm in a hurry." And off he ran, as fast as his legs would carry him.

"Señor Fox! Señor Fox!" called Señor Rooster. "Don't run away! Don't go! You can tell the dogs and the hunter about the new decree among the animals in the forest."

Señor Fox ran into the dogs, and Señor Rooster sat in the tree.

If you dig a pit to catch someone innocent, you often fall into it yourself. Oversmart is bad luck.

## THE FIRST FLUTE
### (Guatemalan)

*Almost every tribe and nation has a tale in which a princess, pining, is restored by the efforts of a suitor. In this Mayan tale set in the days before the Spanish conquest, a god helps a minstrel make the flute that enchants.*

During the glory of the Mayan civilization, years before the coming of the Spanish, there lived a *cacique* who had a beautiful daughter, the Princess Nima-Cux, whom he loved dearly.

Not only was Nima-Cux beautiful, she was possessed of talents. She could plait grass into fine baskets. She could mold little animals out of clay—and you even knew exactly which animals they were supposed to be. The coati had a long ringed tail. The puma had an open mouth showing sharp teeth. The tapir's snout was definitely snoutish. The snake wound round and round and round—and if you unwound him, he reached from Nima-Cux's toes to her earplugs.

Above all, Nima-Cux could sing like a bird. Her voice tripped up and down the scale as easily as her feet tripped up and down the steps. The *cacique* sat back and counted his blessings. They all had to do with Nima-Cux, her beauty, her baskets, her clay work, and, especially, her voice.

As princesses should, Nima-Cux had everything she asked for—besides some things she hadn't thought of requesting. There were finely carved dolls, necklaces of rare shells, a cape of

"The First Flute." From *The Enchanted Orchard and Other Folktales of Central America,* copyright © 1973 by Dorothy Sharp Carter. Reprinted by permission of Harcourt Brace Jovanovich, Inc.

bright parrot feathers, an enormous garden filled with flowers and blossoming trees and singing birds and pet animals. No wonder Nima-Cux was happy.

Thus life flowed along, contentedly for everyone in the household until Nima-Cux neared her sixteenth birthday. Suddenly she became sad and melancholy. Nothing made her happy. Then again, nothing made her unhappy. She just *was*, for no reason at all, she said.

The *cacique* was greatly agitated. He strode up and down the garden, wondering, wondering what would please Nima-Cux. Another doll? A bright fish? A golden plate for her breast-of-pheasant? But to whatever he proposed, Nima-Cux would only murmur politely, "No. But thank you, Papa."

The cook sent boys scampering up the tallest palm trees to bring back heart of palm for Nima-Cux's dinner.

Hunters were ordered into the jungle to capture monkeys. "Mind you, *funny* monkeys to entertain the princess. Not a sad one in the crowd —or off comes your head."

Maidens roamed the royal gardens gathering orchids to ornament the princess' bedchamber.

What happened? Nima-Cux would peer at the rare *palmito* and moan softly, "I am not hungry."

She would stare at the monkeys cavorting on the branches while the royal household screamed in amusement and whisper, "Yes, yes, very comical," and sigh deeply. The household would hush its laughter and echo her sighs.

The orchids went unnoticed until they dropped to the floor with a dry rustle.

Herb doctors came. Witch doctors came. Old hunched crones said to know the secrets of life came. They all said, "But she seems quite well and normal. A bit pale. A trifle listless. Perhaps a good tonic . . ."

Nima-Cux was annoyed enough to argue about the tonic. "That smelly stuff? I won't even taste it."

Finally a sorcerer somewhat wiser than the others spoke to the *cacique*. "After all, the princess is practically sixteen. Other girls her age are married. Find a good husband for the Princess Nima-Cux—and she will again shine radiant as a star."

The *cacique* shook his head. A *husband*? How could a mere husband bring her happiness if her own father could not? A poor suggestion. What were sorcerers coming to?

He peeked once more at Nima-Cux's dismal face—and in desperation sent messengers throughout his kingdom. The young man skillful enough to impress the princess and coax a smile to her lips would become her husband. In a week the first tournament would be held.

During the next week the roads were worn into holes by the thousands of footsteps. Everyone in the kingdom hurried to the palace either to take part or to watch the take-parters (or is it takers-part?). Seats were constructed for the nobility. Those not so noble found a patch of thick grass, a loop of vine, or a high branch. The *cacique* and Nima-Cux sat on a canopied stand. The tournaments began.

The first contestant marched out proud and arrogant in his gold tunic, attended by a troop of warriors. A handsome youth he was. Maidens fainted with joy at the sight of him. The rest of the contestants growled and trembled.

But Nima-Cux frowned and asked, "What can he *do*? Besides prance and preen, worse than any *quetzal*?"

The *cacique* sighed and made a sign for the warrior to display his talents—if any. The soldiers stood before the young man and threw ears of corn into the air. With his bow and arrows the warrior shot kernels from the ears in regimental procession. One row, then the next and next until all the kernels were gone.

The spectators cheered and shouted with admiration. Such skill—and such elegance! Ayyyyyyy! The other contestants ground their teeth and sobbed.

Nima-Cux yawned and asked politely, "May we see the second match, Papa? The first has taken up *so* much time."

The *cacique* sighed again and motioned for the tournament to continue.

The second competitor strode out as confident and proud as the first. He walked alone, bearing a large basket. When he set it down, out slithered a tremendous snake of a poisonous variety, its eyes glaring with malevolence.

The spectators gasped with horror. Maidens fainted with fear. The remaining rivals watched with relish.

The youth engaged the angry snake in combat, artfully evading its deadly fangs. The spectators held their breaths.

"How boring!" muttered Nima-Cux, staring into the distance.

"Really? Really, daughter? You don't like it?" asked the *cacique* with regret. (He was enjoying the contests immensely.)

He motioned for more action. The youth complied by squeezing the life from the snake. Then he bowed to the applause of the crowd. Or most of the crowd. Nima-Cux was already on her way to the palace and her couch with a headache.

For days the tournaments continued. The most handsome and courageous of the Mayan youth competed with each other for the favor of Nima-Cux—favor that was nowhere to be seen. Certainly not on her lips, which remained clamped in a sulky line. Nor in her eyes, which gazed sadly at the competition without seeing it.

Finally the last contestant appeared, a merry boy wearing the tattered dress of a minstrel. The spectators smiled. The other contestants laughed scornfully. With a quick bow to the princess, the boy began to sing. He sang of the lakes, the forests, the hills of the highlands. He sang of the crystal stars flashing from the dark river of night. He sang of love.

Not bad, not bad, nodded the *cacique*. Not, of course, to compare with Nima-Cux's singing. He glanced at his daughter. What astonishment! Her eyes resembled the crystal of the song. Her lips were open and curving—upward. She was smiling! The *cacique* sat back and pondered the puzzle of life and love.

"I like him, Papa. We can sing together. I will marry him. Only first, he must learn the song of each bird of the forest. Then he can teach me."

The minstrel was happy to oblige. He had *meant* it when he sang of love. At once he disappeared into the jungle.

Day after day he practiced, imitating this bird, then that one. But Guatemala is home to hundreds, thousands of birds. Some whistle a complicated tune. The minstrel began to despair of his task.

The god of the forest, after listening for days to the young minstrel's efforts, took pity on him. Also on the birds and other wild inhabitants of the woods—not to mention himself. He appeared before the minstrel, wearing a kindly smile.

"Perhaps I can help you," he offered. "It is a difficult exercise you are engaged in."

Severing a small limb from a tree, the god removed the pith and cut a series of holes in the tube. "Now attend carefully," he said. And he instructed the young man exactly how to blow into one end while moving his fingers over the holes. The notes of the birds tumbled out, clear and sweet.

With a torrent of thanks, the minstrel flew on his way, carrying the *chirimia,* or flute. Just in time. Nima-Cux, anxious that the chore she had assigned her lover had been impossible, was on the point of another decline. She received the youth with joy. Enchanted she was with the flute and its airs . . . with the minstrel and his airs.

The two were married and lived long and happily in the palace of the *cacique*. And today the Indians of Guatemala will point to the *chirimia,* the most typical of native instruments, and tell you this is the way it came about.

## THE SACRED DRUM OF TEPOZTECO
### (Mexican)

*This story is a portion of the great narrative cycle of the gods and heroes of Mexico, but it is also an explanation of a natural phenomenon.*

Long ago, in the valley of Tepoztlán, a valley in Mexico where there is much copper, Tepozteco was born. He was born to be different from other children, for he was destined to be a god.

In a short time he was a fully grown man, rich in wisdom and great in strength and speed. He could hunt better than other men, and he gave counsel that brought success. So the people made him king. And as he grew in wisdom and under-

Reprinted from *The King of the Mountains* by M. A. Jagendorf and R. S. Boggs by permission of the publisher, Vanguard Press, Inc. Copyright © 1960 by M. A. Jagendorf and R. S. Boggs

standing and strength, they worshiped him and made him a god.

He was known for his virtues even to the farthest corners of his kingdom, and he was loved and respected by all. The other kings feared him, although they never dared to say so.

One day the king of Ilayacapan asked Tepozteco to come to a great feast to be given in his honor. Other kings and nobles and men of strength were also invited.

The king told his cooks to prepare food such as had never been eaten before. He had new dishes painted in bright colors, and he ordered new blankets of lovely designs.

And the most beautiful blanket of all was to be for Tepozteco to sit upon. This was to be a feast of feasts.

On the appointed day, the kings and nobles arrived wearing their richest robes and jewels of jade and gold. It was a wonderful sight to see the great company seated on the many-colored mats, with the richly painted dishes before them. All around were beautiful servants ready to bring the fine food.

They sat and they sat. They were waiting for the great guest, Tepozteco.

They waited and they waited. After a long time they heard the *teponaztli*, the drum that always announced the coming of Tepozteco.

Soon he was seen, approaching with his followers. But he was not dressed for the feast. He was dressed in hunting clothes, with an ocelot skin thrown over his shoulders and weapons in his hands. His followers also were dressed in hunting clothes.

The king and his guests looked at them in silent surprise. Then the king spoke.

"Noble Tepozteco," he said, "you have put shame on me and my land and my guests. This feast was in your honor, and we came properly dressed to honor you, but you have come in your hunting clothes and not in your royal garments."

Tepozteco looked at the king and his company and did not say a word. For a long time he was silent. Then he spoke.

"Wait for me. I shall soon return in my royal clothes."

Then he and his followers vanished into the air like a cloud.

Again the company waited a long time, and finally the drum of Tepozteco was heard once again. Suddenly the whole company saw him.

He was alone, dressed more beautifully than anyone there. He was all covered with gold. From his shoulders hung a mantle in colors that gleamed more richly than birds in the sunlight. His headdress was of the most brilliant quetzal feathers ever seen. Gold bands bound his arms and jade beads encircled his neck. In his hand he held a shield studded with jewels and richly colored stones.

The king and his company were greatly pleased at the sight.

"Now you are dressed in a manner befitting this noble gathering in your honor. Let the food be served."

Tepozteco did not answer. He seated himself on a mat, and the food was served by beautiful maidens. Everyone ate except Tepozteco, who took the dishes and poured his food on his mantle.

Everyone stopped eating and looked at the guest of honor in surprise.

"Why do you do this?" asked the king.

"I am giving the food to my clothes, because it was they, not I, that you wanted at your feast. I was not welcome here in whatever clothes I chose to wear. Only when I came in these, my feast-day clothes, were you pleased. Therefore this feast is for them, not for me."

"Leave my palace," said the king sharply.

Tepozteco rose and left.

When he had gone, a great cry of anger rose from all the guests.

"He is not fit to live among us," they cried. "We must destroy him!"

Everyone agreed to this, and the kings and nobles gathered a great army of warriors and marched on Tepoztlán.

Tepozteco knew he could not do battle against this great army, for his soldiers were too few. So he went up on the Montaña del Aire—the Mountain in the Air—where a vast temple had been built for him by his people.

There he stood, drawn up to his full height, almost reaching the sky. He raised his hands and waved them in all directions. The earth quaked and trembled and roared. Trees fell and rocks flew in every direction. Masses of earth rose into the air. Everything fell on the army that had come to destroy Tepozteco and his people, and the enemy was wiped out.

The temple of Tepozteco still stands on that mountain, and at night, when the wind screams through the canyons that the earthquake created along the Montaña del Aire, one can hear the sacred drum of Tepozteco, telling his people he is still there to guard and protect his city.

## PANCHO VILLA AND THE DEVIL
### (Mexican)

*Pancho Villa is one of the outstanding figures in Mexican history, and some of the stories about him have acquired the supernatural quality that accrues to folk heroes the world over. The tale also reflects the deep piety of the Mexican people.*

Do you want to hear a story about the Mexican people? Then I shall tell you one about a man who is *all* the Mexican people. He is a great hero whom every Mexican loves: Pancho Villa.

He was stronger than any Mexican who ever lived—that is what people say. He knew everything—just ask any Mexican. He understood all things about men and animals, and he was not afraid of anything in the world. He was not even afraid of the Devil himself. Yes, that's right; not even of the Devil himself.

People say he sold himself to the Devil, and the Devil, in return, made him strong and brave. Maybe he did, but that was just to fool the Devil in the end, for that is exactly what Pancho Villa finally did. All his life he waited for the chance, and in the end he got it.

Pancho Villa had a horse with feet like dancing flames. Not only was this horse as swift as a tornado, but it was also as smart as a hare. It was a horse for a hero of Mexico—for Pancho Villa.

Reprinted from *The King of the Mountains* by M. A. Jagendorf and R. S. Boggs by permission of the publisher, Vanguard Press, Inc. Copyright © 1960 by M. A. Jagendorf and R. S. Boggs

Villa's horse was always helping him. When he was hungry, the horse would lead him to a place where he could find something to eat. When he was thirsty, it would lead him to water. When he would lose contact with his soldiers, it would show him where they were.

To tell the truth, that horse actually *was* the Devil, waiting to carry off Pancho Villa to . . . you know where I mean.

Do you think Pancho Villa did not know who that horse really was? Of course he knew! And he was just waiting for the right time to show him which one of them was the smarter. He let the horse do everything for him. He gave it plenty of food. But he kept his eyes wide open, just the same.

Things went on that way for a long, long time, the horse doing everything for Pancho Villa, and the great hero accepting it but always watching, watching.

Now, you know they finally killed Pancho Villa. The fools! They did not know he was the greatest Mexican who ever lived. Ask any true Mexican, and he will tell you.

The only one who knew he was going to be killed was that horse, the Devil. It could talk, but it never said a word. It just kept waiting to carry him off to the Hill of Box, where the Devil lived, just north of San Juan del Río. It was there that Pancho Villa sold his soul, so he would become a great hero.

As soon as Pancho Villa was shot, the horse spoke.

He said, "Now, you come with me. I have kings and princes in my hill, but I don't have anyone there as fearless as you."

But that Devil-horse had forgotten one thing.

Said Pancho Villa, "You are right. I am fearless, and I am not afraid of anything, not even of *you*, Devil! I have gone to church ever since I gave up soldiering, and now you can't take me. I have a cross around my neck, so you can't touch me. You go back to your hill and I'll go the other way, where all good Mexicans go."

The Devil-horse couldn't answer that, so he galloped off, screaming and neighing, in the opposite direction. Fire and brimstone shot from his hoofs.

And Pancho Villa went off in the other direction, to heaven, where he really belongs.

Of all forms of fiction, the fable is the most pedantic and the least appealing to children. It is a lesson in behavior, a kind of sugar-coated moral pill, large doses of which are hard to take. Yet presented occasionally, among other and livelier kinds of stories, fables are not unpalatable. They offer a shrewd appraisal of motives and behavior. Their canny and satiric comments on folly are amusing, and wise behavior is picturesquely presented. Such fables as "The Dog in the Manger," "The Fox and the Crow" and "The Hare and the Tortoise" are never forgotten. These and many others have come to occupy a permanent place in our thinking and our speech. Children

# FABLES

should know the fables because they contain the distilled wisdom of the ages in memorable form.

Fables might be defined as brief narratives which attempt to make abstract ideas of good or bad, wise or foolish behavior, concrete and sufficiently striking to be understood and remembered. But because they are concerned with abstract ideas they are not readily understood by most children until the episodes and their significance have been talked over. Sometimes the characters are men, sometimes the elements, but chiefly, they are animals. Whatever they are, the characters of a fable are as impersonal as an algebraic equation. It is never Peter Rabbit with his little brothers and sisters, Flopsy, Mopsy, and Cottontail. It is merely RABBIT, and you never care whether RABBIT has a family or is an orphan. He is simply RABBIT. This abstract, impersonal quality of the fable does not appeal to small children, and the obvious intention of teaching a moral lesson grows tiresome if the fables are used too often or with too heavy a hand.

Since Caxton first published Aesop's fables in English, there have been many editions for children and young people. As one looks through them, it becomes apparent that each editor or compiler of fables had his own notion of what the *moral* for each fable was. Sometimes it was religious, sometimes merely ethical, sometimes highly political. It would seem that fables allow for a wide latitude of interpretation and application. For this reason, then, if for no other, it would be wise not to insist that the children glean one interpretation only from any given fable.

Today there are many editions of Aesop's fables, several of them illustrated by distinguished artists. We also have numerous editions of the fables of La Fontaine, and at least one edition from the Russian fables of Krylov. (See the Bibliography.) Joseph Jacobs' *The Fables of Aesop* has long been a favorite edition and was once practically a household item. His versions are still fun to read. They are spare in treatment and faithful to the Aesopic text of earlier translators from the Latin and Greek manuscripts. James Reeves' *Fables from Aesop* with illustrations in color, sets a much livelier note by having the animals speaking directly. Possibly one of the best renderings of Aesop, however, especially for contemporary children, is to be found in Louis Untermeyer's *Aesop's Fables,* handsomely illustrated by the Provensens. Although only forty fables are included, they are full of verve and humor and present Aesop in a most refreshing manner.

## *Aesop's Fables*

*"The Lion and the Mouse" and "The Town Mouse and the Country Mouse" are well liked by the five- and six-year-olds because they are simple little stories and the morals are not too obtrusive. The other fables might well appear in almost any order you like, three or four a year. Perhaps the morals of "The Fox and the Grapes" and "The Dog in the Manger" are a little too subtle for young children and are better reserved for the oldest children. Be sure to bring along also some of the many illustrated editions of the fables. In some instances, the fables will lead directly into certain folk tales which are either similar in their point or are expansions of them (such as "Henny-Penny" and "Bandalee"). Many of the fables will also serve to give the children a point of departure for writing and staging brief plays.*

### THE HARE
### WITH MANY FRIENDS

A hare was very popular with the other beasts who all claimed to be her friends. But one day she heard the hounds approaching and hoped to escape them by the aid of her many friends. So she went to the horse, and asked him to carry her away from the hounds on his back. But he declined, stating that he had important work to do for his master. He felt sure, he said, that all her other friends would come to her assistance. She

"The Hare with Many Friends." From *The Fables of Aesop,* selected, told anew, and their history traced by Joseph Jacobs. Macmillan & Co., London, 1894

then applied to the bull, and hoped that he would repel the hounds with his horns.

The bull replied: "I am very sorry, but I have an appointment with a lady; but I feel sure that our friend the goat will do what you want."

The goat, however, feared that his back might do her some harm if he took her upon it. The ram, he felt sure, was the proper friend to apply to. So she went to the ram and told him the case.

The ram replied: "Another time, my dear friend. I do not like to interfere on the present occasion, as hounds have been known to eat sheep as well as hares."

The hare then applied, as a last hope, to the calf, who regretted that he was unable to help her, as he did not like to take the responsibility upon himself, as so many older persons than himself had declined the task. By this time the hounds were quite near, and the hare took to her heels and luckily escaped.

*He that has many friends, has no friends.*

## THE ANT
## AND THE GRASSHOPPER

In a field one summer's day a grasshopper was hopping about, chirping and singing to its heart's content. An ant passed by, bearing along with great toil an ear of corn he was taking to the nest.

"Why not come and chat with me," said the grasshopper, "instead of toiling and moiling in that way?"

"I am helping to lay up food for the winter," said the ant, "and recommend you to do the same."

"Why bother about winter?" said the grasshopper. "We have got plenty of food at present." But the ant went on its way and continued its toil. When the winter came the grasshopper had no food, and found itself dying of hunger, while it saw the ants distributing every day corn and grain from the stores they had collected in the summer. Then the grasshopper knew—

*It is best to prepare for the days of necessity.*

"The Ant and the Grasshopper," "The Shepherd's Boy," and "The Lion and the Mouse." From *The Fables of Aesop*, selected, told anew, and their history traced by Joseph Jacobs. Macmillan & Co., London, 1894

## THE SHEPHERD'S BOY

There was once a young shepherd boy who tended his sheep at the foot of a mountain near a dark forest. It was rather lonely for him all day, so he thought upon a plan by which he could get a little company and some excitement. He rushed down towards the village calling out "Wolf, wolf," and the villagers came out to meet him, and some of them stopped with him for a considerable time. This pleased the boy so much that a few days afterwards he tried the same trick, and again the villagers came to his help. But shortly after this a wolf actually did come out from the forest, and began to worry the sheep, and the boy of course cried out "Wolf, wolf," still louder than before. But this time the villagers, who had been fooled twice before, thought the boy was again deceiving them, and nobody stirred to come to his help. So the wolf made a good meal off the boy's flock, and when the boy complained, the wise man of the village said:

*"A liar will not be believed, even when he speaks the truth."*

## THE LION AND THE MOUSE

Once when a lion was asleep a little mouse began running up and down upon him; this soon wakened the lion, who placed his huge paw upon him, and opened his big jaws to swallow him. "Pardon, O King," cried the little mouse; "forgive me this time, I shall never forget it. Who knows but what I may be able to do you a turn some of these days?" The lion was so tickled at the idea of the mouse being able to help him, that he lifted up his paw and let him go. Some time after, the lion was caught in a trap, and the hunters, who desired to carry him alive to the king, tied him to a tree while they went in search of a waggon to carry him on. Just then the little mouse happened to pass by, and seeing the sad plight in which the lion was, went up to him and soon gnawed away the ropes that bound the king of the beasts. "Was I not right?" said the little mouse.

*Little friends may prove great friends.*

heartily welcome. Beans and bacon, cheese and bread, were all he had to offer, but he offered them freely. The town mouse rather turned up his long nose at this country fare, and said: "I cannot understand, Cousin, how you can put up with such poor food as this, but of course you cannot expect anything better in the country; come you with me and I will show you how to live. When you have been in town a week you will wonder how you could ever have stood a country life." No sooner said than done: the two mice set off for the town and arrived at the town mouse's residence late at night. "You will want some refreshment after our long journey," said the polite town mouse, and took his friend into the grand dining-room. There they found the re-

### THE FOX AND THE CROW

A fox once saw a crow fly off with a piece of cheese in its beak and settle on a branch of a tree. "That's for me, as I am a fox," said Master Renard, and he walked up to the foot of the tree. "Good-day, Mistress Crow," he cried. "How well you are looking to-day: how glossy your feathers; how bright your eye. I feel sure your voice must surpass that of other birds, just as your figure does; let me hear but one song from you that I may greet you as the Queen of Birds." The crow lifted up her head and began to caw her best, but the moment she opened her mouth the piece of cheese fell to the ground, only to be snapped up by Master Fox. "That will do," said he. "That was all I wanted. In exchange for your cheese I will give you a piece of advice for the future—do not trust flatterers."

*The flatterer doth rob by stealth,*
*His victim, both of wit and wealth.*

### THE TOWN MOUSE
### AND THE COUNTRY MOUSE

Now you must know that a town mouse once upon a time went on a visit to his cousin in the country. He was rough and ready, this cousin, but he loved his town friend and made him

"The Fox and the Crow," "The Town Mouse and the Country Mouse." From *The Fables of Aesop*, selected, told anew, and their history traced by Joseph Jacobs. Macmillan & Co., London, 1894

from its afternoon work, came up to the manger and wanted to eat some of the straw. The dog in a rage, being awakened from its slumber, stood up and barked at the ox, and whenever it came near attempted to bite it. At last the ox had to give up the hope of getting at the straw, and went away muttering:

*"Ah, people often grudge others what they cannot enjoy themselves."*

mains of a fine feast, and soon the two mice were eating up jellies and cakes and all that was nice. Suddenly they heard growling and barking. "What is that?" said the country mouse. "It is only the dogs of the house," answered the other. "Only!" said the country mouse. "I do not like that music at my dinner." Just at that moment the door flew open, in came two huge mastiffs, and the two mice had to scamper down and run off. "Good-bye Cousin," said the country mouse. "What! going so soon?" said the other. "Yes," he replied;

*"Better beans and bacon in peace than cakes and ale in fear."*

### THE DOG IN THE MANGER

A dog looking out for its afternoon nap jumped into the manger of an ox and lay there cosily upon the straw. But soon the ox, returning

### BELLING THE CAT

Long ago, the mice held a general council to consider what measures they could take to outwit their common enemy, the cat. Some said this, and some said that; but at last a young mouse got up and said he had a proposal to make, which he thought would meet the case. "You will all agree," said he, that our chief danger consists in the sly and treacherous manner in which the enemy approaches us. Now, if we could receive some signal of her approach, we could easily escape from her. I venture, therefore, to propose that a small bell be procured,

"The Dog in the Manger" and "Belling the Cat," from *The Fables of Aesop,* selected, told anew, and their history traced by Joseph Jacobs. Macmillan & Co., London, 1894

and attached by a ribbon round the neck of the cat. By this means we should always know when she was about, and could easily retire while she was in the neighbourhood."

This proposal met with general applause, until an old mouse got up and said: "That is all very well, but who is to bell the cat?" The mice looked at one another and nobody spoke. Then the old mouse said:

*"It is easy to propose impossible remedies."*

## THE WIND AND THE SUN

The wind and the sun were disputing which was the stronger. Suddenly they saw a traveller coming down the road, and the sun said: "I see a way to decide our dispute. Whichever of us can cause that traveller to take off his cloak shall be regarded as the stronger. You begin." So the sun retired behind a cloud, and the wind began to blow as hard as it could upon the traveller. But the harder he blew the more closely did the traveller wrap his cloak round him, till at last the wind had to give up in despair. Then the sun came out and shone in all his glory upon the traveller, who soon found it too hot to walk with his cloak on.

*Kindness effects more than Severity.*

## THE FOX AND THE GRAPES

One hot summer's day a fox was strolling through an orchard till he came to a bunch of grapes just ripening on a vine which had been trained over a lofty branch. "Just the thing to quench my thirst," quoth he. Drawing back a few paces, he took a run and a jump, and just missed the bunch. Turning round again with a one, two, three, he jumped up, but with no greater success. Again and again he tried after the tempting morsel, but at last had to give it up, and walked away with his nose in the air,

"The Wind and the Sun," "The Fox and the Grapes," "The Crow and the Pitcher." From *The Fables of Aesop*, selected, told anew, and their history traced by Joseph Jacobs. Macmillan & Co., London, 1894

saying: "I am sure they are sour."

*It is easy to despise what you cannot get.*

## THE CROW AND THE PITCHER

A crow, half-dead with thirst, came upon a pitcher which had once been full of water; but when the crow put its beak into the mouth of the pitcher he found that only very little water was left in it and that he could not reach far enough down to get at it. He tried, and he tried, but at last had to give up in despair. Then a thought came to him, and he took a pebble and dropped it into the pitcher. Then he took another pebble and dropped it into the pitcher. Then he took another pebble and dropped that into the pitcher. Then he took another pebble and dropped that into the pitcher. Then he took another pebble and dropped that into the pitcher. Then he took another pebble and dropped that into the pitcher. At last, at last, he saw the water mount up near him; and after casting in a few more pebbles he was able to quench his thirst and save his life.

*Little by little does the trick.*

## THE HARE AND THE TORTOISE

The hare was once boasting of his speed before the other animals. "I have never yet been beaten," said he, "when I put forth my full speed. I challenge any one here to race with me."

The tortoise said quietly: "I accept your challenge."

"That is a good joke," said the hare; "I could dance round you all the way."

"Keep your boasting till you've beaten," answered the tortoise. "Shall we race?"

So a course was fixed and a start was made. The hare darted almost out of sight at once, but soon stopped and, to show his contempt for the tortoise, lay down to have a nap. The tortoise plodded on and plodded on, and when the hare awoke from his nap, he saw the tortoise just near the winning-post and could not run up in time to save the race. Then said the Tortoise:

*"Plodding wins the race."*

# The Panchatantra

*The fables in the East Indian collections are much longer and more like stories with morals than they are like the spare little abstractions we know as Aesop's fables. The Panchatantra was really a textbook on "the wise conduct of life" and contained stories within stories. Maude Barrows Dutton retold thirty-four of the best-known tales from The Panchatantra and, with the inimitable illustrations of E. Boyd Smith, made an attractive little book called The Tortoise and the Geese and Other Fables of Bidpai. The Bidpai fables are the Arabic versions of The Panchatantra. The other source of Indian fables is the group called the Jatakas, already described in connection with the folk tales of India. As explained, the selections from the Jatakas are included with the folk tales because they become good talking-beast tales when references to the Buddha are omitted.*

## THE PARTRIDGE AND THE CROW

A Crow flying across a road saw a Partridge strutting along the ground.

"What a beautiful gait that Partridge has!" said the Crow. "I must try to see if I can walk like him."

She alighted behind the Partridge and tried for a long time to learn to strut. At last the Partridge turned around and asked the Crow what she was about.

"Do not be angry with me," replied the Crow. "I have never before seen a bird who walks as beautifully as you can, and I am trying to learn to walk like you."

"Foolish bird!" responded the Partridge. "You are a Crow, and should walk like a Crow. You would look silly indeed if you were to strut like a partridge."

But the Crow went on trying to learn to strut, until finally she had forgotten her own gait, and she never learned that of the Partridge.

## THE TYRANT WHO BECAME A JUST RULER

In olden times there lived a King who was so cruel and unjust towards his subjects that he was always called The Tyrant. So heartless was he that his people used to pray night and day that they might have a new king. One day, much to their surprise, he called his people together and said to them,——

"The Hare and the Tortoise" from *The Fables of Aesop*, selected, told anew and their history traced by Joseph Jacobs. Macmillan & Co., London, 1894

"The Partridge and the Crow" and "The Tyrant Who Became a Just Ruler" from *The Tortoise and the Geese and Other Fables of Bidpai* by Maude Barrows Dutton. Reprinted by permission of Houghton Mifflin Company

"My dear subjects, the days of my tyranny are over. Henceforth you shall live in peace and happiness, for I have decided to try to rule henceforth justly and well."

The King kept his word so well that soon he was known throughout the land as The Just King. By and by one of his favorites came to him and said,——

"Your Majesty, I beg of you to tell me how it was that you had this change of heart towards your people?"

And the King replied,——

"As I was galloping through my forests one afternoon, I caught sight of a hound chasing a fox. The fox escaped into his hole, but not until he had been bitten by the dog so badly that he would be lame for life. The hound, returning home, met a man who threw a stone at him, which broke his leg. The man had not gone far when a horse kicked him and broke his leg. And the horse, starting to run, fell into a hole and broke his leg. Here I came to my senses, and resolved to change my rule. 'For surely,' I said to myself, 'he who doeth evil will sooner or later be overtaken by evil.' "

## THE MICE THAT ATE IRON

*The theme of this fable is found among the folk tales of many countries. An American variant, "Young Melvin," appears on pages 374–76.*

In a certain town lived a merchant named Naduk, who lost his money and determined to travel abroad. For

> The meanest of mankind is he
> Who, having lost his money, can
> Inhabit lands or towns where once
> He spent it like a gentleman.

And again:

> The neighbor gossips blame
> His poverty as shame
> Who long was wont to play
> Among them, proud and gay.

In his house was an iron balance-beam inher-

"The Mice That Ate Iron." From *The Panchatantra* by Arthur W. Ryder. Copyright 1925 by the University of Chicago Press. Reprinted by permission of the University of Chicago Press

ited from his ancestors, and it weighed a thousand *pals*. This he put in pawn with Merchant Lakshman before he departed for foreign countries.

Now after he had long traveled wherever business led him through foreign lands, he returned to his native city and said to Merchant Lakshman: "Friend Lakshman, return my deposit, the balance-beam." And Lakshman said: "Friend Naduk, your balance-beam has been eaten by mice."

To this Naduk replied: "Lakshman, you are in no way to blame, if it has been eaten by mice. Such is life. Nothing in the universe has any permanence. However, I am going to the river for a bath. Please send your boy Money-God with me, to carry my bathing things."

Since Lakshman was conscience-stricken at his own theft, he said to his son Money-God: "My dear boy, let me introduce Uncle Naduk, who is going to the river to bathe. You must go with him and carry his bathing things." Ah, there is too much truth in the saying:

> There is no purely loving deed
> Without a pinch of fear or greed
> Or service of a selfish need.

And again:

> Wherever there is fond attention
> That does not seek a service pension,
> Was there no timid apprehension?

So Lakshman's son took the bathing things and delightedly accompanied Naduk to the river. After Naduk had taken his bath, he thrust Lakshman's son Money-God into a mountain cave, blocked the entrance with a great rock, and returned to Lakshman's house. And when Lakshman said: "Friend Naduk, tell me what has become of my son Money-God who went with you," Naduk answered: "My good Lakshman, a hawk carried him off from the river-bank."

"Oh, Naduk!" cried Lakshman. "You liar! How could a hawk possibly carry off a big boy like Money-God?" "But, Lakshman," retorted Naduk, "the mice could eat a balance-beam made of iron. Give me my balance-beam, if you want your son."

Finally, they carried their dispute to the palace gate, where Lakshman cried in a piercing tone: "Help! Help! A ghastly deed! This Naduk person has carried off my son—his name is Money-God."

Thereupon the magistrates said to Naduk: "Sir, restore the boy to Lakshman." But Naduk pleaded: "What am I to do? Before my eyes a hawk carried him from the river-bank." "Come, Naduk!" said they, "you are not telling the truth. How can a hawk carry off a fifteen-year-old boy?" Then Naduk laughed outright and said: "Gentlemen, listen to my words.

> Where mice eat balance-beams of iron
> A thousand *pals* in weight,
> A hawk might steal an elephant;
> A boy is trifling freight."

"How was that?" they asked, and Naduk told them the story of the balance-beam. At this they laughed and caused the restoration of balance-beam and boy to the respective owners.

# Fables of La Fontaine

*In France the fables were turned into verse by a skilled poet, Jean de La Fontaine, a contemporary of Charles Perrault. The sources used by La Fontaine were Latin versions of Aesop and The Fables of Bidpai, and the versions of Marie de France, who introduced the fable into France in the twelfth century. La Fontaine's rhymed moralities were so popular in the France of his day that people called him le fablier, "the fable-teller." To translate his witty French verses into English verse is to lose some of their gaiety and charm, so they are usually translated into prose. "The Grasshopper and the Ant" is an example of a metrical translation, and "The Fox and the Crow" and "The Cricket and the Ant" are in the vigorous prose of Margaret Wise Brown. In "The Fox and the Crow" she has used a sing-and-say style that suggests the original verse form but tells the story clearly.*

## THE FOX AND THE CROW

Mister Crow sat on the limb of a tree with a big piece of cheese in his mouth.

Old Mister Fox smelled the cheese from a long way off. And he came to the foot of the tree and spoke to the crow.

> "Good morning, Mr. Coal Black Crow,
> How beautiful and shining your feathers grow,
> Black as the night and bright as the sun,
> If you sing as well, your fortune is won."

At these words Mr. Crow joyously opened his beak to sing his creaky old crow song.

And the cheese fell down to the ground. The fox snapped it up in his mouth.

As he ran away he called back over his bushy tail, "My dear Mr. Crow, learn from this how every flatterer lives at the expense of anybody who will listen to him. This lesson is well worth the loss of a cheese to you."

## THE CRICKET AND THE ANT

All through the summer the cricket sang. He sang in the grass when they planted the seed. And he sang in the grass when the flowers bloomed. Why should a cricket work on a sunny day, when he could sing and dance and play? In the early fall when the seeds were blowing in the air the cricket chirped his song. But when winter came and the cold winds blew, the merry little cricket had nothing to eat and nowhere to go.

So he hopped to the house of his neighbor, the ant, who had worked all summer storing up her food for the winter. He knocked at the door and cried, "Oh, dear! Oh, dear! I am starving, hungry, starving! Kind ant, will you lend me some seeds to live on until spring? And I will give you five seeds in the spring for every seed that you give me today."

But the ant was practical—as ants are.

"What did you do in the summer when the days were warm and the flowers were going to seed?" asked the ant. "What did you do in the early fall when the seeds were blowing through the air?"

"Night and day I sang," said the cricket.

"You sang!" said the ant. "Then now you can dance to your own music. I will eat the seed I gathered and the house I have built will keep me warm. Maybe your dancing will keep you warm in the snow."

## THE GRASSHOPPER AND THE ANT

A grasshopper gay
Sang the Summer away,
And found herself poor
By the winter's first roar.
Of meat and of bread,
Not a morsel she had!
So a-begging she went,
To her neighbour the ant,
    For the loan of some wheat,

Which would serve her to eat,
Till the season came round.
    "I will pay, you," she saith
    "On an animal's faith,
Double weight in the pound
Ere the harvest be bound."
The ant is a friend
    (And here she might mend)
    Little given to lend.
"How spent you the summer?"
    Quoth she, looking shame
    At the borrowing dame.
"Night and day to each comer
I sang if you please."
    "You sang! I'm at ease;
For 'tis plain at a glance,
Now, Ma'am, you must dance."

"The Grasshopper and the Ant." From *A Hundred Fables* by Jean de la Fontaine. Reprinted by permission of The Bodley Head

Myth and epic are a part of that anonymous stream of folklore which includes the folk tales and the fables. All these once helped to weld people together with a body of common beliefs, customs, morals, and hero cults. They were indeed the "cement of society," holding it together with a moral code and giving it a certain identity.

However, in the light of modern historical and anthropological research, much of what was once thought about myths, their origin and significance, has been called into question. The more that has been discovered about the ancient

# MYTHS

Greeks, the more we have had to give up our rather simplistic and romantic notions about what their myths meant and what purpose they served. But old notions take a long time to die, and in almost all popularly written books or articles on myths, these older views predominate. It is difficult to understand the full evolution and significance of myths and mythology, and we should be prepared to delve deep and long if we try to do so.

In the meantime, when we speak of myths as literature for children, we refer principally to the myths of the Greeks, Romans, and Norsemen. All peoples have some form of mythology, but the Greeks and Scandinavians created myths that have shaped the mentality, language, and literature of Western humanity. Not a day passes, hardly an hour of conversation occurs, that we do not use a word or think a thought that draws upon the concepts and tales of these two great mythologies. This is why Shelley could say of us: *"We are all Greeks."* He might have added that we are partly Norse as well.

The origins and possible significance of myths are adult concerns that arise only if one begins to wonder why a myth exists in the first place. Otherwise, the myth may be viewed, as is usually the case, as a kind of ancient adult fairy tale which now appeals more to young people and students of literature than to anyone else. Even so, there are problems about when to introduce the myth to young people and which versions or retellings to use.

Myths generally contain themes which are too adult for young children in the primary grades. Some myths are fables and *pourquoi* tales that may be put into simple form for boys and girls— "Echo and Narcissus," for example. A few myths read like fairy tales, even in their original version, such as "King Midas" or "Baucis and Philemon," and are therefore suitable for the eight- and nine-year-olds. But most myths have complexities that make them more suitable for young people in the upper grades and high school. No blanket decision can be made about them. On the other hand, one must be cautious about those well-intended attempts to adapt and simplify the myths. Such attempts are usually disastrous, sacrificing the spirit of the original and destroying style for the sake of bare plot. The reteller's attitude must also be considered. Hawthorne, in *A Wonder-Book for Girls and Boys* and *Tanglewood Tales for Girls and Boys*, made the myths

read like sentimental Gothic fairy tales. Robert Graves, a noted scholar of mythology and a great poet, gave his versions of the myths for young people a decidedly irreverent and cynical flavor. Padraic Colum, in contrast, achieved a bardic feeling in his approach.

The selections here are from older editions in which the writers achieved a good style that will appeal to young people while adhering closely to the more standard translations of the myths as they have come down to us through the writings of Greek and Roman poets, dramatists, and literary commentators. Various editions of the myths are listed in the Bibliography, and by consulting the annotations you can determine which editions are most suitable for your specific purposes. Ultimately, however, if one steeps oneself in the myths by reading many versions and commentaries, one will come to have one's own versions, unique to one's understanding of these great tales, and to one's attitude toward them.

It is hoped that this small selection of myths will send teachers, parents, and children to whole books of mythology to be used in connection with their study of a people or just for delight in the stories themselves. For to know the beauty of Olympus or Valhalla and to encounter the gods at their best is to dream again some of humanity's ancient dreams of how grand life may be for those who dare greatly. There are admirable dreams in the myths. How they came about and whether they are dreams of the past or auguries of the future matters little, for they are couched in symbols whose meaning will grow with children's maturity.

# *Greek and Roman Myths*

*When we turn to the Greek myths, Edith Hamilton's observation is undeniable: "The myths as we have them are the creation of great poets." And it was one of the great accomplishments of the Greeks that their myths for the most part did away with the irrational and fearful elements which characterize many primitive mythologies. Indeed, they acknowledged that the gods were cruel and capricious and that human life was beset by tragedy, but in their myths they made these facts seem understandable and even beautiful. It may be that in making the gods in their own image, they made them not more comprehensible but less fearful, until in time they came to associate with various gods the better aspects and reaches of human reason and virtue.*

## CLYTIE

*The maiden in the process of transformation is an interesting subject for illustration.*

Clytie was a water-nymph and in love with Apollo, who made her no return. So she pined away, sitting all day long upon the cold ground, with her unbound tresses streaming over her shoulders. Nine days she sat and tasted neither food nor drink, her own tears and the chilly dew her only food. She gazed on the sun when he rose, and as he passed through his daily course to his setting; she saw no other object, her face turned constantly on him. At last, they say, her limbs rooted in the ground, her face became a flower (sunflower), which turns on its stem so as always to face the sun throughout its daily course; for it retains to that extent the feeling of the nymph from whom it sprang.

## ARACHNE

*The gods seem to be especially hard on conceit and boastfulness.*

Not among mortals alone were there contests of skill, nor yet among the gods, like Pan and Apollo. Many sorrows befell men because they grew arrogant in their own devices and coveted divine honors. There was once a great hunter, Orion, who outvied the gods themselves, till they took him away from his hunting-grounds and set him in the heavens, with his sword and belt, and his hound at his heels. But at length jealousy invaded even the peaceful arts, and disaster came of spinning!

There was a certain maiden of Lydia, Arachne by name, renowned throughout the country for her skill as a weaver. She was as nimble with her fingers as Calypso, that nymph who kept Odysseus for seven years in her enchanted island. She was as untiring as Penelope, the hero's wife, who wove day after day while she watched for his return. Day in and day out, Arachne wove too. The very nymphs would gather about her loom,

"Clytie." From *The Age of Fable; or Beauties of Mythology,* by Thomas Bulfinch. J. E. Tilton and Company, Boston, 1863

naiads from the water and dryads from the trees.

"Maiden," they would say, shaking the leaves or the foam from their hair, in wonder, "Pallas Athena must have taught you!"

But this did not please Arachne. She would not acknowledge herself a debtor, even to that goddess who protected all household arts, and by whose grace alone one had any skill in them.

"I learned not of Athena," said she. "If she can weave better, let her come and try."

The nymphs shivered at this, and an aged woman, who was looking on, turned to Arachne.

"Be more heedful of your words, my daughter," said she. "The goddess may pardon you if you ask forgiveness, but do not strive for honors with the immortals."

Arachne broke her thread, and the shuttle stopped humming.

"Keep your counsel," she said. "I fear not Athena; no, nor anyone else."

As she frowned at the old woman, she was amazed to see her change suddenly into one tall, majestic, beautiful—a maiden of gray eyes and golden hair, crowned with a golden helmet. It was Athena herself.

The bystanders shrank in fear and reverence; only Arachne was unawed and held to her foolish boast.

In silence the two began to weave, and the nymphs stole nearer, coaxed by the sound of the shuttles, that seemed to be humming with delight over the two webs,—back and forth like bees.

They gazed upon the loom where the goddess stood plying her task, and they saw shapes and images come to bloom out of the wondrous colors, as sunset clouds grow to be living creatures when we watch them. And they saw that the goddess, still merciful, was spinning, as a warning for Arachne, the pictures of her own triumph over reckless gods and mortals.

In one corner of the web she made a story of her conquest over the sea-god Poseidon. For the first king of Athens had promised to dedicate the city to that god who should bestow upon it the most useful gift. Poseidon gave the horse. But Athena gave the olive,—means of livelihood,—

"Arachne" from *Old Greek Folk Stories Told Anew* by Josephine Preston Peabody. Reprinted by permission of Houghton Mifflin Company

symbol of peace and prosperity, and the city was called after her name. Again she pictured a vain woman of Troy, who had been turned into a crane for disputing the palm of beauty with a goddess. Other corners of the web held similar images, and the whole shone like a rainbow.

Meanwhile Arachne, whose head was quite turned with vanity, embroidered her web with stories against the gods, making light of Zeus himself and of Apollo, and portraying them as birds and beasts. But she wove with marvelous skill; the creatures seemed to breathe and speak, yet it was all as fine as the gossamer that you find on the grass before rain.

Athena herself was amazed. Not even her wrath at the girl's insolence could wholly overcome her wonder. For an instant she stood entranced; then she tore the web across, and three times she touched Arachne's forehead with her spindle.

"Live on, Arachne," she said. "And since it is your glory to weave, you and yours must weave forever." So saying, she sprinkled upon the maiden a certain magical potion.

Away went Arachne's beauty; then her very human form shrank to that of a spider, and so remained. As a spider she spent all her days weaving and weaving; and you may see something like her handiwork any day among the rafters.

## ORPHEUS AND EURYDICE

*This has been one of the more popular of the myths with writers and dramatists, and many European folk tales echo its sorrowful theme.*

When gods and shepherds piped and the stars sang, that was the day of musicians! But the triumph of Phoebus Apollo himself was not so wonderful as the triumph of a mortal man who lived on earth, though some say that he came of divine lineage. This was Orpheus, that best of harpers, who went with the Grecian heroes of the great ship *Argo* in search of the Golden Fleece.

"Orpheus and Eurydice" from *Old Greek Folk Stories Told Anew* by Josephine Preston Peabody. Reprinted by permission of Houghton Mifflin Company

After his return from the quest, he won Eurydice for his wife, and they were as happy as people can be who love each other and every one else. The very wild beasts loved them, and the trees clustered about their home as if they were watered with music. But even the gods themselves were not always free from sorrow, and one day misfortune came upon that harper Orpheus whom all men loved to honor.

Eurydice, his lovely wife, as she was wandering with the nymphs, unwittingly trod upon a serpent in the grass. Surely, if Orpheus had been with her, playing upon his lyre, no creature could have harmed her. But Orpheus came too late. She died of the sting, and was lost to him in the Underworld.

For days he wandered from his home, singing the story of his loss and his despair to the helpless passers-by. His grief moved the very stones in the wilderness, and roused a dumb distress in the hearts of savage beasts. Even the gods on Mount Olympus gave ear, but they held no power over the darkness of Hades.

Wherever Orpheus wandered with his lyre, no one had the will to forbid him entrance; and at length he found unguarded that very cave that leads to the Underworld where Pluto rules the spirits of the dead. He went down without fear. The fire in his living heart found him a way through the gloom of that place. He crossed the Styx, the black river that the gods name as their most sacred oath. Charon, the harsh old ferryman who takes the Shades across, forgot to ask of him the coin that every soul must pay. For Orpheus sang. There in the Underworld the song of Apollo would not have moved the poor ghosts so much. It would have amazed them, like a star far off that no one understands. But here was a human singer, and he sang of things that grow in every human heart, youth and love and death, the sweetness of the Earth, and the bitterness of losing aught that is dear to us.

Now the dead, when they go to the Underworld, drink of the pool of Lethe; and forgetfulness of all that has passed comes upon them like a sleep, and they lose their longing for the world, they lose their memory of pain, and live content with that cool twilight. But not the pool of Lethe itself could withstand the song of Orpheus; and in the hearts of the Shades all the old dreams awoke wondering. They remembered once more the life of men on Earth, the glory of the sun and moon, the sweetness of new grass, the warmth of their homes, all the old joy and grief that they had known. And they wept.

Even the Furies were moved to pity. Those, too, who were suffering punishment for evil deeds ceased to be tormented for themselves, and grieved only for the innocent Orpheus who had lost Eurydice. Sisyphus, that fraudulent king (who is doomed to roll a monstrous boulder uphill forever), stopped to listen. The daughters of Danaus left off their task of drawing water in a sieve. Tantalus forgot hunger and thirst, though before his eyes hung magical fruits that were wont to vanish out of his grasp, and just beyond reach bubbled the water that was a torment to his ears; he did not hear it while Orpheus sang.

So, among a crowd of eager ghosts, Orpheus came, singing with all his heart, before the king and queen of Hades. And the queen Proserpina wept as she listened and grew homesick, remembering the fields of Enna and the growing of the wheat, and her own beautiful mother, Demeter. Then Pluto gave way.

They called Eurydice and she came, like a young guest unused to the darkness of the Underworld. She was to return with Orpheus, but on one condition. If he turned to look at her once before they reached the upper air, he must lose her again and go back to the world alone.

Rapt with joy, the happy Orpheus hastened on the way, thinking only of Eurydice, who was following him. Past Lethe, across the Styx they went, he and his lovely wife, still silent as a Shade. But the place was full of gloom, the silence weighed upon him, he had not seen her for so long; her footsteps made no sound; and he could hardly believe the miracle, for Pluto seldom relents. When the first gleam of upper daylight broke through the cleft to the dismal world, he forgot all, save that he must know if she still followed. He turned to see her face, and the promise was broken!

She smiled at him forgivingly, but it was too late. He stretched out his arms to take her, but she faded from them, as the bright snow, that none may keep, melts in our very hands. A murmur of farewell came to his ears—no more. She was gone.

He would have followed, but Charon, now on guard, drove him back. Seven days he lingered there between the worlds of life and death, but after the broken promise, Hades would not listen to his song. Back to the Earth he wandered, though it was sweet to him no longer. He died young, singing to the last, and round about the place where his body rested, nightingales nested in the trees. His lyre was set among the stars; and he himself went down to join Eurydice, unforbidden.

Those two had no need of Lethe, for their life on earth had been wholly fair, and now that they are together they no longer own a sorrow.

## PROSERPINE

*This myth, sometimes called "Demeter and Persephone," the Greek names for the mother and child, is the story of winter and summer, of the grains maturing below ground in darkness. Robert Graves gives a rather saucy version of it. (See the Bibliography.)*

When Jupiter and his brothers had defeated the Titans and banished them to Tartarus, a new enemy rose up against the gods. They were the giants Typhon, Briareus, Enceladus, and others. Some of them had a hundred arms, others breathed out fire. They were finally subdued and buried alive under Mount Ætna, where they still sometimes struggle to get loose, and shake the whole island with earthquakes. Their breath comes up through the mountain, and is what men call the eruption of the volcano.

The fall of these monsters shook the earth, so that Pluto was alarmed, and feared that his kingdom would be laid open to the light of day. Under this apprehension, he mounted his chariot, drawn by black horses, and took a circuit of inspection to satisfy himself of the extent of the damage.

While he was thus engaged, Venus, who was sitting on Mount Eryx playing with her boy Cupid, espied him, and said, "My son, take your darts with which you conquer all, even Jove himself, and send one into the breast of yonder dark monarch, who rules the realm of Tartarus. Why should he alone escape? Seize the opportunity to extend your empire and mine. Do you not see that even in heaven some despise our power? Minerva the wise, and Diana the huntress, defy us; and there is that daughter of Ceres, who threatens to follow their example. Now do you, if you have any regard for your own interest or mine, join these two in one."

The boy unbound his quiver, and selected his sharpest and truest arrow; then, straining the bow against his knee, he attached the string, and, having made ready, shot the arrow with its

"Proserpine." From *The Age of Fable; or Beauties of Mythology*, by Thomas Bulfinch. J. E. Tilton and Company, Boston, 1863

barbed point right into the heart of Pluto.

In the vale of Enna there is a lake embowered in woods, which screen it from the fervid rays of the sun, while the moist ground is covered with flowers, and Spring reigns perpetual. Here Proserpine was playing with her companions, gathering lilies and violets, and filling her basket and her apron with them, when Pluto saw her, loved her, and carried her off. She screamed for help to her mother and her companions; and when in her fright she dropped the corners of her apron and let the flowers fall, childlike she felt the loss of them as an addition to her grief. The ravisher urged on his steeds, calling them each by name, and throwing loose over their heads and necks his iron-colored reins. When he reached the River Cyane, and it opposed his passage, he struck the riverbank with his trident, and the earth opened and gave him a passage to Tartarus.

Ceres sought her daughter all the world over. Bright-haired Aurora, when she came forth in the morning, and Hesperus, when he led out the stars in the evening, found her still busy in the search. But it was all unavailing. At length weary and sad, she sat down upon a stone, and continued sitting nine days and nights, in the open air, under the sunlight and moonlight and falling showers. It was where now stands the city of Eleusis, then the home of an old man named Celeus. He was out in the field, gathering acorns and blackberries, and sticks for his fire. His little girl was driving home their two goats, and as she passed the goddess, who appeared in the guise of an old woman, she said to her, "Mother,"—and the name was sweet to the ears of Ceres,—"why do you sit here alone upon the rocks?"

The old man also stopped, though his load was heavy, and begged her to come into his cottage, such as it was. She declined, and he urged her.

"Go in peace," she replied, "and be happy in your daughter; I have lost mine." As she spoke, tears—or something like tears, for the gods never weep,—fell down her cheeks upon her bosom.

The compassionate old man and his child wept with her. Then said he, "Come with us, and despise not our humble roof; so may your daughter be restored to you in safety."

"Lead on," said she, "I cannot resist that appeal!" So she rose from the stone and went with them.

As they walked he told her that his only son, a little boy, lay very sick, feverish and sleepless. She stooped and gathered some poppies. As they entered the cottage, they found all in great distress, for the boy seemed past hope of recovery. Metanira, his mother, received her kindly, and the goddess stooped and kissed the lips of the sick child. Instantly the paleness left his face, and healthy vigor returned to his body.

The whole family were delighted—that is, the father, mother, and little girl, for they were all; they had no servants. They spread the table, and put upon it curds and cream, apples, and honey in the comb. While they ate, Ceres mingled poppy juice in the milk of the boy. When night came and all was still, she arose, and taking the sleeping boy, moulded his limbs with her hands, and uttered over him three times a solemn charm, then went and laid him in the ashes. His mother, who had been watching what her guest was doing, sprang forward with a cry and snatched the child from the fire. Then Ceres assumed her own form, and a divine splendor shone all around.

While they were overcome with astonishment, she said, "Mother, you have been cruel in your fondness to your son. I would have made him immortal, but you have frustrated my attempt. Nevertheless, he shall be great and useful. He shall teach men the use of the plough, and the rewards which labor can win from the cultivated soil." So saying, she wrapped a cloud about her, and mounting her chariot rode away.

Ceres continued her search for her daughter, passing from land to land, and across seas and rivers, till at length she returned to Sicily, whence she at first set out, and stood by the banks of the River Cyane, where Pluto made himself a passage with his prize to his own dominions. The river nymph would have told the goddess all she had witnessed, but dared not, for fear of Pluto; so she only ventured to take up the girdle which Proserpine had dropped in her flight, and waft it to the feet of the mother. Ceres, seeing this, was no longer in doubt of her loss, but she did not yet know the cause, and laid the blame on the innocent land.

"Ungrateful soil," said she, "which I have en-dowed with fertility and clothed with herbage and nourishing grain, no more shall you enjoy my favors."

Then the cattle died, the plough broke in the furrow, the seed failed to come up; there was too much sun, there was too much rain; the birds stole the seeds—thistles and brambles were the only growth.

Seeing this, the fountain Arethusa interceded for the land. "Goddess," said she, "blame not the land; it opened unwillingly to yield a passage to your daughter. I can tell you of her fate, for I have seen her. . . . While I passed through the lower parts of the earth, I saw your Proserpine. She was sad, but no longer showing alarm in her countenance. Her look was such as became a queen—the queen of Erebus; the powerful bride of the monarch of the realms of the dead."

When Ceres heard this, she stood for a while like one stupefied; then turned her chariot towards heaven, and hastened to present herself before the throne of Jove. She told the story of her bereavement, and implored Jupiter to interfere to procure the restitution of her daughter. Jupiter consented on one condition, namely, that Proserpine should not during her stay in the lower world have taken any food; otherwise, the Fates forbade her release. Accordingly, Mercury was sent, accompanied by Spring, to demand Proserpine of Pluto. The wily monarch consented; but alas! the maiden had taken a pomegranate which Pluto offered her, and had sucked the sweet pulp from a few of the seeds. This was enough to prevent her complete release; but a compromise was made, by which she was to pass half the time with her mother, and the rest with her husband Pluto.

Ceres allowed herself to be pacified with this arrangement, and restored the earth to her favor. Now she remembered Celeus and his family, and her promise to his infant son Triptolemus. When the boy grew up, she taught him the use of the plough, and how to sow the seed. She took him in her chariot, drawn by winged dragons, through all the countries of the earth, imparting to mankind valuable grains, and the knowledge of agriculture. After his return, Triptolemus built a magnificent temple to Ceres in Eleusis, and established the worship of the goddess, under the name of the Eleusinian mysteries, which, in the splendor and solemnity of their observance, surpassed all other religious celebrations among the Greeks.

## ICARUS AND DAEDALUS

*Here would seem to be, according to some people, a lesson for us on the dangers of putting too much stock in our own powers.*

Among all those mortals who grew so wise that they learned the secrets of the gods, none was more cunning than Daedalus.

He once built, for King Minos of Crete, a wonderful Labyrinth of winding ways so cunningly tangled up and twisted around that, once inside, you could never find your way out again without a magic clue. But the king's favor veered with the wind, and one day he had his master architect imprisoned in a tower. Daedalus managed to escape from his cell; but it seemed impossible to leave the island, since every ship that came or went was well guarded by order of the king.

At length, watching the sea-gulls in the air—the only creatures that were sure of liberty—he thought of a plan for himself and his young son Icarus, who was captive with him.

Little by little, he gathered a store of feathers great and small. He fastened these together with thread, moulded them in with wax, and so fashioned two great wings like those of a bird. When they were done, Daedalus fitted them to his own shoulders, and after one or two efforts, he found that by waving his arms he could winnow the air and cleave it, as a swimmer does the sea. He held himself aloft, wavered this way and that with the wind, and at last, like a great fledgling, he learned to fly.

Without delay, he fell to work on a pair of wings for the boy Icarus, and taught him carefully how to use them, bidding him beware of rash adventures among the stars. "Remember," said the father, "never to fly very low or very high, for the fogs about the earth would weigh you down, but the blaze of the sun will surely melt your feathers apart if you go too near."

"Icarus and Daedalus" from *Old Greek Folk Stories Told Anew* by Josephine Preston Peabody. Reprinted by permission of Houghton Mifflin Company

For Icarus, these cautions went in at one ear and out by the other. Who could remember to be careful when he was to fly for the first time? Are birds careful? Not they! And not an idea remained in the boy's head but the one joy of escape.

The day came, and the fair wind that was to set them free. The father bird put on his wings, and, while the light urged them to be gone, he waited to see that all was well with Icarus, for the two could not fly hand in hand. Up they rose, the boy after his father. The hateful ground of Crete sank beneath them; and the country folk, who caught a glimpse of them when they were high above the tree-tops, took it for a vision of the gods—Apollo, perhaps, with Cupid after him.

At first there was a terror in the joy. The wide vacancy of the air dazed them—a glance downward made their brains reel. But when a great wind filled their wings, and Icarus felt himself sustained, like a halcyon-bird in the hollow of a wave, like a child uplifted by his mother, he forgot everything in the world but joy. He forgot Crete and the other islands that he had passed over: he saw but vaguely that winged thing in the distance before him that was his father Daedalus. He longed for one draught of flight to quench the thirst of his captivity: he stretched out his arms to the sky and made towards the highest heavens.

Alas for him! Warmer and warmer grew the air. Those arms, that had seemed to uphold him, relaxed. His wings wavered, drooped. He fluttered his young hands vainly—he was falling—and in that terror he remembered. The heat of the sun had melted the wax from his wings; the feathers were falling, one by one, like snowflakes; and there was none to help.

He fell like a leaf tossed down the wind, down, down, with one cry that overtook Daedalus far away. When he returned, and sought high and low for the poor boy, he saw nothing but the bird-like feathers afloat on the water, and he knew that Icarus was drowned.

The nearest island he named Icaria, in memory of the child; but he, in heavy grief, went to the temple of Apollo in Sicily, and there hung up his wings as an offering. Never again did he attempt to fly.

## CUPID AND PSYCHE

*The theme of this beautiful story is similar to that of "East o' the Sun" and other stories of maidens who doubt and lose their loves but search for them faithfully and successfully.*

Once upon a time, through that Destiny that overrules the gods, Love himself gave up his immortal heart to a mortal maiden. And thus it came to pass.

There was a certain king who had three beautiful daughters. The two elder married princes of great renown; but Psyche, the youngest, was so radiantly fair that no suitor seemed worthy of her. People thronged to see her pass through the city, and sang hymns in her praise, while strangers took her for the very goddess of beauty herself.

This angered Venus, and she resolved to cast down her earthly rival. One day, therefore, she called hither her son Love (Cupid, some name him), and bade him sharpen his weapons. He is an archer more to be dreaded than Apollo, for Apollo's arrows take life, but Love's bring joy or sorrow for a whole life long.

"Come, Love," said Venus. "There is a mortal maid who robs me of my honors in yonder city. Avenge your mother. Wound this precious Psyche, and let her fall in love with some churlish creature mean in the eyes of all men."

Cupid made ready his weapons, and flew down to earth invisibly. At that moment Psyche was asleep in her chamber; but he touched her heart with his golden arrow of love, and she opened her eyes so suddenly that he started (forgetting that he was invisible), and wounded himself with his own shaft. Heedless of the hurt, moved only by the loveliness of the maiden, he hastened to pour over her locks the healing joy that he ever kept by him, undoing all his work. Back to her dream the princess went, unshadowed by any thought of love. But Cupid, not so light of heart, returned to the heavens, saying not a word of what had passed.

Venus waited long; then, seeing that Psyche's heart had somehow escaped love, she sent a spell

"Cupid and Psyche" from *Old Greek Folk Stories Told Anew* by Josephine Preston Peabody. Reprinted by permission of Houghton Mifflin Company

upon the maiden. From that time, lovely as she was, not a suitor came to woo; and her parents, who desired to see her a queen at least, made a journey to the Oracle, and asked counsel.

Said the voice: "The princess Psyche shall never wed a mortal. She shall be given to one who waits for her on yonder mountain; he overcomes gods and men."

At this terrible sentence the poor parents were half distraught, and the people gave themselves up to grief at the fate in store for their beloved princess. Psyche alone bowed to her destiny. "We have angered Venus unwittingly," she said, "and all for sake of me, heedless maiden that I am! Give me up, therefore, dear father and mother. If I atone, it may be that the city will prosper once more."

So she besought them, until, after many unavailing denials, the parents consented; and with a great company of people they led Psyche up the mountain,—as an offering to the monster of whom the Oracle had spoken,—and left her there alone.

Full of courage, yet in a secret agony of grief, she watched her kindred and her people wind down the mountain-path, too sad to look back, until they were lost to sight. Then, indeed, she wept, but a sudden breeze drew near, dried her tears, and caressed her hair, seeming to murmur comfort. In truth, it was Zephyr, the kindly West Wind, come to befriend her; and as she took heart, feeling some benignant presence, he lifted her in his arms, and carried her on wings as even as a sea-gull's, over the crest of the fateful mountain and into a valley below. There he left her, resting on a bank of hospitable grass, and there the princess fell asleep.

When she awoke, it was near sunset. She looked about her for some sign of the monster's approach; she wondered, then, if her grievous trial had been but a dream. Nearby she saw a sheltering forest, whose young trees seemed to beckon as one maid beckons to another; and eager for the protection of the dryads, she went thither.

The call of running waters drew her farther and farther, till she came out upon an open place, where there was a wide pool. A fountain fluttered gladly in the midst of it, and beyond there stretched a white palace wonderful to see.

Coaxed by the bright promise of the place, she drew near, and, seeing no one, entered softly. It was all kinglier than her father's home, and as she stood in wonder and awe, soft airs stirred about her. Little by little the silence grew murmurous like the woods, and one voice, sweeter than the rest, took words. "All that you see is yours, gentle high princess," it said. "Fear nothing; only command us, for we are here to serve you."

Full of amazement and delight, Psyche followed the voice from hall to hall, and through the lordly rooms, beautiful with everything that could delight a young princess. No pleasant thing was lacking. There was even a pool, brightly tiled and fed with running waters, where she bathed her weary limbs; and after she had put on the new and beautiful raiment that lay ready for her, she sat down to break her fast, waited upon and sung to by the unseen spirits.

Surely he whom the Oracle had called her husband was no monster, but some beneficent power, invisible like all the rest. When daylight waned, he came, and his voice, the beautiful voice of a god, inspired her to trust her strange destiny and to look and long for his return. Often she begged him to stay with her through the day, that she might see his face; but this he would not grant.

"Never doubt me, dearest Psyche," said he. "Perhaps you would fear if you saw me, and love is all I ask. There is a necessity that keeps me hidden now. Only believe."

So for many days Psyche was content; but when she grew used to happiness, she thought once more of her parents mourning her as lost, and of her sisters who shared the lot of mortals while she lived as a goddess. One night she told her husband of these regrets, and begged that her sisters at least might come to see her. He sighed, but did not refuse.

"Zephyr shall bring them hither," said he. And on the following morning, swift as a bird, the West Wind came over the crest of the high mountain and down into the enchanted valley, bearing her two sisters.

They greeted Psyche with joy and amazement, hardly knowing how they had come hither. But when this fairest of the sisters led them through her palace and showed them all the treasures that were hers, envy grew in their hearts and choked their old love. Even while they sat at feast with her, they grew more and more bitter; and hoping to find some little flaw in her good fortune, they asked a thousand questions.

"Where is your husband?" said they. "And why is he not here with you?"

"Ah," stammered Psyche. "All the day long— he is gone, hunting upon the mountains."

"But what does he look like?" they asked; and Psyche could find no answer.

When they learned that she had never seen him, they laughed her faith to scorn.

"Poor Psyche," they said. "You are walking in a dream. Wake, before it is too late. Have you forgotten what the Oracle decreed,—that you were destined for a dreadful creature, the fear of gods and men? And are you deceived by this show of kindliness? We have come to warn you. The people told us, as we came over the mountain, that your husband is a dragon, who feeds you well for the present, that he may feast the better, some day soon. What is it that you trust? Good words! But only take a dagger some night, and when the monster is asleep go, light a lamp, and look at him. You can put him to death easily, and all his riches will be yours—and ours."

Psyche heard this wicked plan with horror. Nevertheless, after her sisters were gone, she brooded over what they had said, not seeing their evil intent; and she came to find some wisdom in their words. Little by little, suspicion ate, like a moth, into her lovely mind; and at nightfall, in shame and fear, she hid a lamp and a dagger in her chamber. Toward midnight, when her husband was fast asleep, up she rose, hardly daring to breathe; and coming softly to his side, she uncovered the lamp to see some horror.

But there the youngest of the gods lay sleeping,—most beautiful, most irresistible of all immortals. His hair shone golden as the sun, his face was radiant as dear Springtime, and from his shoulders sprang two rainbow wings.

Poor Psyche was overcome with self-reproach. As she leaned toward him, filled with worship, her trembling hands held the lamp ill, and some burning oil fell upon Love's shoulder and awakened him.

He opened his eyes, to see at once his bride and the dark suspicion in her heart.

"O doubting Psyche!" he exclaimed with sudden grief,—and then he flew away, out of the window.

Wild with sorrow, Psyche tried to follow, but she fell to the ground instead. When she recovered her senses, she stared about her. She was alone, and the place was beautiful no longer. Garden and palace had vanished with Love. Over mountains and valleys Psyche journeyed alone until she came to the city where her two envious sisters lived with the princes whom they had married. She stayed with them only long enough to tell the story of her unbelief and its penalty. Then she set out again to search for Love.

As she wandered one day, travel-worn but not hopeless, she saw a lofty palace on a hill near by, and she turned her steps thither. The place seemed deserted. Within the hall she saw no human being,—only heaps of grain, loose ears of corn half torn from the husk, wheat and barley, alike scattered in confusion on the floor. Without delay, she set to work binding the sheaves together and gathering the scattered ears of corn in seemly wise, as a princess would wish to see them. While she was in the midst of her task, a voice startled her, and she looked up to behold Demeter herself, the goddess of the harvest, smiling upon her with good will.

"Dear Psyche," said Demeter, "you are worthy of happiness, and you may find it yet. But since you have displeased Venus, go to her and ask her favor. Perhaps your patience will win her pardon."

These motherly words gave Psyche heart, and she reverently took leave of the goddess and set out for the temple of Venus. Most humbly she offered up her prayer, but Venus could not look at her earthly beauty without anger.

"Vain girl," said she, "perhaps you have come to make amends for the wound you dealt your husband; you shall do so. Such clever people can always find work!"

Then she led Psyche into a great chamber heaped high with mingled grain, beans, and lentils (the food of her doves), and bade her separate them all and have them ready in seemly fashion by night. Heracles would have been helpless before such a vexatious task; and poor Psyche, left alone in this desert of grain, had not courage to begin. But even as she sat there, a moving thread of black crawled across the floor from a crevice in the wall; and bending nearer, she saw that a great army of ants in columns had come to her aid. The zealous little creatures worked in swarms, with such industry over the work they like best, that, when Venus came at night, she found the task completed.

"Deceitful girl!" she cried, shaking the roses out of her hair with impatience, "this is my son's work, not yours. But he will soon forget you. Eat this black bread if you are hungry, and refresh your dull mind with sleep. To-morrow you will need more wit."

Psyche wondered what new misfortune could be in store for her. But when morning came, Venus led her to the brink of a river, and, pointing to the wood across the water, said, "Go now to yonder grove where the sheep with the golden fleece are wont to browse. Bring me a golden lock from every one of them, or you must go your ways and never come back again."

This seemed not difficult, and Psyche obediently bade the goddess farewell, and stepped into the water, ready to wade across. But as Venus disappeared, the reeds sang louder and the nymphs of the river, looking up sweetly, blew bubbles to the surface and murmured: "Nay, nay, have a care, Psyche. This flock has not the gentle ways of sheep. While the sun burns aloft, they are themselves as fierce as flame; but when the shadows are long, they go to rest and sleep, under the trees; and you may cross the river without fear and pick the golden fleece off the briers in the pasture."

Thanking the water-creatures, Psyche sat down to rest near them, and when the time came, she crossed in safety and followed their counsel. By twilight she returned to Venus with her arms full of shining fleece.

"No mortal wit did this," said Venus angrily. "But if you care to prove your readiness, go now, with this little box, down to Proserpina and ask her to enclose in it some of her beauty, for I have grown pale in caring for my wounded son."

It needed not the last taunt to sadden Psyche. She knew that it was not for mortals to go into Hades and return alive; and feeling that Love had forsaken her, she was minded to accept her doom as soon as might be.

But even as she hastened toward the descent, another friendly voice detained her. "Stay, Psyche, I know your grief. Only give ear and you shall learn a safe way through all these trials." And the voice went on to tell her how one might avoid all the dangers of Hades and come out unscathed. (But such a secret could not pass from mouth to mouth, with the rest of the story.)

"And be sure," added the voice, "when Proserpina has returned the box, not to open it, however much you may long to do so."

Psyche gave heed, and by this device, whatever it was, she found her way into Hades safely, and made her errand known to Proserpina, and was soon in the upper world again, wearied but hopeful.

"Surely Love has not forgotten me," she said. "But humbled as I am and worn with toil, how shall I ever please him? Venus can never need all the beauty in this casket; and since I use it for Love's sake, it must be right to take some." So saying, she opened the box, heedless as Pandora! The spells and potions of Hades are not for mortal maids, and no sooner had she inhaled the strange aroma than she fell down like one dead, quite overcome.

But it happened that Love himself was recovered from his wound, and he had secretly fled from his chamber to seek out and rescue Psyche. He found her lying by the wayside; he gathered into the casket what remained of the philter, and awoke his beloved.

"Take comfort," he said, smiling. "Return to our mother and do her bidding till I come again."

Away he flew; and while Psyche went cheerily homeward, he hastened up to Olympus, where all the gods sat feasting, and begged them to intercede for him with his angry mother.

They heard his story and their hearts were touched. Zeus himself coaxed Venus with kind words till at last she relented, and remembered that anger hurt her beauty, and smiled once more. All the younger gods were for welcoming Psyche at once, and Hermes was sent to bring her hither. The maiden came, a shy newcomer among those bright creatures. She took the cup that Hebe held out to her, drank the divine ambrosia, and became immortal.

Light came to her face like moonrise, two radiant wings sprang from her shoulders; and even as a butterfly bursts from its dull cocoon, so the human Psyche blossomed into immortality.

Love took her by the hand, and they were never parted any more.

## ATALANTA'S RACE

Even if Prince Meleager had lived, it is doubtful if he could ever have won Atalanta to be his wife. The maiden was resolved to live unwed, and at last she devised a plan to be rid of all her suitors. She was known far and wide as the swiftest runner of her time; and so she said that she would only marry that man who could outstrip her in the race, but that all who dared to try and failed must be put to death.

This threat did not dishearten all of the suitors, however, and to her grief, for she was not cruel, they held her to her promise. On a certain day the few bold men who were to try their fortune made ready, and chose young Hippomenes as judge. He sat watching them before the word was given, and sadly wondered that any brave man should risk his life merely to win a bride. But when Atalanta stood ready for the contest, he was amazed by her beauty. She looked like Hebe, goddess of young health, who is a glad serving-maiden to the gods when they sit at feast.

The signal was given, and, as she and the suitors darted away, flight made her more enchanting than ever. Just as a wind brings sparkles to the water and laughter to the trees, haste fanned her loveliness to a glow.

Alas for the suitors! She ran as if Hermes had lent her his wingèd sandals. The young men, skilled as they were, grew heavy with weariness and despair. For all their efforts, they seemed to lag like ships in a calm, while Atalanta flew before them in some favoring breeze—and reached the goal!

To the sorrow of all on-lookers, the suitors were led away; but the judge himself, Hippomenes, rose and begged leave to try his fortune. As Atalanta listened, and looked at him, her heart was filled with pity, and she would willingly have let him win the race to save him from defeat and death; for he was comely and younger than the others. But her friends urged her to rest and make ready, and she consented, with an unwilling heart.

Meanwhile Hippomenes prayed within himself to Venus: "Goddess of Love, give ear, and send me good speed. Let me be swift to win as I have been swift to love her."

Now Venus, who was not far off,—for she had already moved the heart of Hippomenes to love, —came to his side invisibly, slipped into his hand three wondrous golden apples, and whispered a word of counsel in his ear.

The signal was given; youth and maiden started over the course. They went so like the wind that they left not a footprint. The people cheered on Hippomenes, eager that such valor should win. But the course was long, and soon fatigue seemed to clutch at his throat, the light shook before his eyes, and, even as he pressed on, the maiden passed him by.

At that instant Hippomenes tossed ahead one of the golden apples. The rolling bright thing caught Atalanta's eye, and full of wonder she stooped to pick it up. Hippomenes ran on. As he heard the flutter of her tunic close behind him, he flung aside another golden apple, and another moment was lost to the girl. Who could pass by such a marvel? The goal was near and Hippomenes was ahead, but once again Atalanta caught up with him, and they sped side by side like two dragon-flies. For an instant his heart failed him; then, with a last prayer to Venus, he flung down the last apple. The maiden glanced at it, wavered, and would have left it where it had fallen, had not Venus turned her head for a second and given her a sudden wish to possess it. Against her will she turned to pick up the golden apple, and Hippomenes touched the goal.

So he won that perilous maiden; and as for Atalanta, she was glad to marry such a valorous man. By this time she understood so well what it was like to be pursued, that she had lost a little of her pleasure in hunting.

## BAUCIS AND PHILEMON

*Stories of gods walking the earth in disguise have, in the Christian era, become tales of saints walking the earth in disguise. Two good examples are found in Richard Chase's "Wicked John and the Devil" and in "King O'Toole and His Goose."*

"Atalanta's Race" from *Old Greek Folk Stories Told Anew* by Josephine Preston Peabody. Reprinted by permission of Houghton Mifflin Company

"Baucis and Philemon." From *The Age of Fable; or Beauties of Mythology,* by Thomas Bulfinch. J. E. Tilton and Company, Boston, 1863

On a certain hill in Phrygia stand a linden tree and an oak, enclosed by a low wall. Not far from the spot is a marsh, formerly good habitable land, but now indented with pools, the resort of fen-birds and cormorants. Once on a time, Jupiter, in human shape, visited this country, and with him his son Mercury (he of the caduceus) without his wings. They presented themselves as weary travellers, at many a door, seeking rest and shelter, but found all closed, for it was late, and the inhospitable inhabitants would not rouse themselves to open for their reception. At last a humble mansion received them, a small thatched cottage, where Baucis, a pious old dame, and her husband Philemon, united when young, had grown old together. Not ashamed of their poverty, they made it endurable by moderate desires and kind dispositions. One need not look there for master or for servant; they two were the whole household, master and servant alike.

When the two heavenly guests crossed the humble threshold, and bowed their heads to pass under the low door, the old man placed a seat, on which Baucis, bustling and attentive, spread a cloth, and begged them to sit down. Then she raked out the coals from the ashes, and kindled up a fire, fed it with leaves and dry bark, and with her scanty breath blew it into a flame. She brought out of a corner split sticks and dry branches, broke them up, and placed them under the small kettle. Her husband collected some pot-herbs in the garden, and she shred them from the stalks, and prepared them for the pot. He reached down with a forked stick a flitch of bacon hanging in the chimney, cut a small piece, and put it in the pot to boil with the herbs, setting away the rest for another time. A beechen bowl was filled with warm water, that their guests might wash. While all was doing, they beguiled the time with conversation.

On the bench designed for the guests was laid a cushion stuffed with sea weed; and a cloth, only produced on great occasions, but ancient and coarse enough, was spread over that. The old lady, with her apron on, with trembling hand set the table. One leg was shorter than the rest, but a piece of slate put under restored the level. When fixed, she rubbed the table down with some sweet-smelling herbs. Upon it she set some of chaste Minerva's olives, some cornel ber-

ries preserved in vinegar, and added radishes and cheese, with eggs lightly cooked in the ashes. All were served in earthen dishes, and an earthenware pitcher, with wooden cups, stood beside them. When all was ready, the stew, smoking hot, was set on the table. Some wine, not of the oldest, was added; and for dessert, apples and wild honey; and over and above all, friendly faces, and simple but hearty welcome.

Now while the repast proceeded, the old folks were astonished to see that the wine, as fast as it was poured out, renewed itself in the pitcher, of its own accord. Struck with terror, Baucis and Philemon recognized their heavenly guests, fell on their knees, and with clasped hands implored forgiveness for their poor entertainment. There was an old goose, which they kept as the guardian of their humble cottage; and they bethought them to make this a sacrifice in honor of their guests. But the goose, too nimble, with the aid of feet and wings, for the old folks, eluded their pursuit, and at last took shelter between the gods themselves. They forbade it to be slain; and spoke in these words: "We are gods. This inhospitable village shall pay the penalty of its impiety; you alone shall go free from the chastisement. Quit your house, and come with us to the top of yonder hill."

The old couple hastened to obey, and, staff in hand, labored up the steep ascent. They had reached to within an arrow's flight of the top, when turning their eyes below, they beheld all the country sunk in a lake, only their own house left standing. While they gazed with wonder at the sight, and lamented the fate of their neighbors, that old house of theirs was changed into a *temple*. Columns took the place of the corner posts, the thatch grew yellow and appeared a gilded roof, the floors became marble, the doors were enriched with carving and ornaments of gold.

Then spoke Jupiter in benignant accents: "Excellent old man, and woman worthy of such a husband, speak, tell us your wishes; what favor have you to ask of us?"

Philemon took counsel with Baucis a few moments; then declared to the gods their united wish. "We ask to be priests and guardians of this your temple; and since here we have passed our lives in love and concord, we wish that one and the same hour may take us both from life, that I may not live to see her grave, nor be laid in my own by her." Their prayer was granted. They were the keepers of the temple as long as they lived.

When grown very old, as they stood one day before the steps of the sacred edifice, and were telling the story of the place, Baucis saw Philemon begin to put forth leaves, and old Philemon saw Baucis changing in like manner. And now a leafy crown had grown over their heads, while exchanging parting words, as long as they could speak. "Farewell, dear spouse," they said together, and at the same moment the bark closed over their mouths. The Tyanean shepherd still shows the two trees, standing side by side, made out of the two good old people.

## PEGASUS AND THE CHIMAERA

When Perseus cut off Medusa's head, the blood sinking into the earth produced the winged horse Pegasus. Minerva caught and tamed him, and presented him to the Muses. The fountain Hippocrene, on the Muses' mountain Helicon, was opened by a kick from his hoof.

The Chimæra was a fearful monster, breathing fire. The fore part of its body was a compound of the lion and the goat, and the hind part a dragon's. It made great havoc in Lycia, so that the king Iobates sought for some hero to destroy it. At that time there arrived at his court a gallant young warrior, whose name was Bellerophon. He brought letters from Prœtus, the son-in-law of Iobates, recommending Bellerophon in the warmest terms as an unconquerable hero, but added at the close a request to his father-in-law to put him to death. The reason was that Prœtus was jealous of him, suspecting that his wife Antea looked with too much admiration on the young warrior. (From this instance of Bellerophon being unconsciously the bearer of his own death-warrant, the expression "Bellerophontic letters" arose, to describe any species of commu-

"Pegasus and the Chimaera." From *The Age of Fable; or Beauties of Mythology,* by Thomas Bulfinch. J. E. Tilton and Company, Boston, 1863

nication which a person is made the bearer of, containing matter prejudicial to himself.)

Iobates, on perusing the letters, was puzzled what to do, not willing to violate the claims of hospitality, yet wishing to oblige his son-in-law. A lucky thought occurred to him, to send Bellerophon to combat with the Chimæra. Bellerophon accepted the proposal, but before proceeding to the combat consulted the soothsayer Polyidus, who advised him to procure if possible the horse Pegasus for the conflict. For this purpose he directed him to pass the night in the temple of Minerva. He did so, and as he slept Minerva came to him and gave him a golden bridle. When he awoke the bridle remained in his

hand. Minerva also showed him Pegasus drinking at the well of Pirene, and at sight of the bridle, the winged steed came willingly and suffered himself to be taken. Bellerophon mounted him, rose with him into the air, soon found the Chimæra, and gained an easy victory over the monster.

After the conquest of the Chimæra, Bellerophon was exposed to further trials and labors by his unfriendly host, but by the aid of Pegasus he triumphed in them all; till at length Iobates, seeing that the hero was a special favorite of the gods, gave him his daughter in marriage and made him his successor on the throne. At last Bellerophon by his pride and presumption drew upon himself the anger of the gods; it is said he even attempted to fly up into heaven on his winged steed; but Jupiter sent a gadfly which stung Pegasus and made him throw his rider, who became lame and blind in consequence. After this Bellerophon wandered lonely through the Aleian field, avoiding the paths of men, and died miserably.

## MIDAS

*This is the meager source (in translation) from which Hawthorne spun the better-known version that follows it.*

Bacchus, on a certain occasion, found his old schoolmaster and foster-father, Silenus, missing. The old man had been drinking, and in that state wandered away, and was found by some peasants, who carried him to their king, Midas. Midas recognized him, and treated him hospitably, entertaining him for ten days and nights with an unceasing round of jollity. On the eleventh day he brought Silenus back, and restored him in safety to his pupil. Whereupon Bacchus offered Midas his choice of a reward, whatever he might wish. He asked that whatever he might touch should be changed into gold. Bacchus consented, though sorry that he had not made a better choice. Midas went his way, rejoicing in his new-acquired power, which he hastened to put to the test. He could scarce believe his eyes when

"Midas." From *The Age of Fable; or Beauties of Mythology*, by Thomas Bulfinch. J. E. Tilton and Company, Boston, 1863

he found a twig of an oak, which he plucked from the branch, become gold in his hand. He took up a stone; it changed to gold. He touched a sod; it did the same. He took an apple from the tree; you would have thought he had robbed the garden of the Hesperides. His joy knew no bounds, and as soon as he got home, he ordered the servants to set a splendid repast on the table. Then he found to his dismay that whether he touched bread, it hardened in his hand; or put a morsel to his lips, it defied his teeth. He took a glass of wine, but it flowed down his throat like melted gold.

In consternation at the unprecedented affliction, he strove to divest himself of his power; he hated the gift he had lately coveted. But all in vain; starvation seemed to await him. He raised his arms, all shining with gold, in prayer to Bacchus, begging to be delivered from his glittering destruction.

Bacchus, merciful deity, heard and consented. "Go," said he, "to the River Pactolus, trace the stream to its fountain-head, there plunge your head and body in, and wash away your fault and its punishment." He did so, and scarce had he touched the waters before the gold-creating power passed into them, and the river sands became changed into gold, as they remain to this day.

Thenceforth Midas, hating wealth and splendor, dwelt in the country, and became a worshipper of Pan, the god of the fields. On a certain occasion Pan had the temerity to compare his music with that of Apollo, and to challenge the god of the lyre to a trial of skill. The challenge was accepted, and Tmolus, the mountain god, was chosen umpire. The senior took his seat, and cleared away the trees from his ears to listen.

At a given signal Pan blew on his pipes, and with his rustic melody gave great satisfaction to himself and his faithful follower Midas, who happened to be present. Then Tmolus turned his head toward the Sun-god, and all his trees turned with him. Apollo rose; his brow wreathed with Parnassian laurel, while his robe of Tyrian purple swept the ground. In his left hand he held the lyre, and with his right hand struck the strings. Ravished with the harmony, Tmolus at once awarded the victory to the god of the lyre, and all but Midas acquiesced in the judgment.

He dissented, and questioned the justice of the award. Apollo would not suffer such a depraved pair of ears any longer to wear the human form, but caused them to increase in length, grow hairy, within and without, and movable on their roots; in short, to be on the perfect pattern of those of an ass.

Mortified enough was King Midas at this mishap; but he consoled himself with the thought that it was possible to hide his misfortune, which he attempted to do by means of an ample turban or head-dress. But his hair-dresser of course knew the secret. He was charged not to mention it, and threatened with dire punishment if he presumed to disobey. But he found it too much for his discretion to keep such a secret; so he went out into the meadow, dug a hole in the ground, and stooping down, whispered the story, and covered it up. Before long a thick bed of reeds sprang up in the meadow, and as soon as it had gained its growth, began whispering the story, and has continued to do so, from that day to this, every time a breeze passes over the place.

## THE GOLDEN TOUCH

Once upon a time, there lived a very rich king whose name was Midas; and he had a little daughter, whom nobody but myself ever heard of, and whose name was Marygold.

This King Midas was fonder of gold than of anything else in the world. He valued his royal crown chiefly because it was composed of that precious metal. If he loved anything better, or half so well, it was the one little maiden who played so merrily around her father's footstool. But the more Midas loved his daughter, the more did he desire and seek for wealth. He thought, foolish man! that the best thing he could possibly do for this dear child would be to bequeath her the immensest pile of yellow, glistening coin, that had ever been heaped together since the world was made. Thus, he gave all his thoughts and all his time to this one purpose. If ever he happened to gaze for an instant at the gold-tinted clouds of sunset, he wished that they were real gold, and that they could be squeezed

"The Golden Touch." From *A Wonder Book for Girls and Boys* by Nathaniel Hawthorne

safely into his strong box. When little Marygold ran to meet him, with a bunch of buttercups and dandelions, he used to say, "Poh, poh, child! If these flowers were as golden as they look, they would be worth the plucking!"

And yet, in his earlier days, before he was so entirely possessed of this insane desire for riches, King Midas had shown a great taste for flowers. He had planted a garden, in which grew the biggest and beautifullest and sweetest roses that any mortal ever saw or smelt. These roses were still growing in the garden, as large, as lovely, and as fragrant, as when Midas used to pass whole hours in gazing at them, and inhaling their perfume. But now, if he looked at them at all, it was only to calculate how much the garden would be worth if each of the innumerable rose-petals were a thin plate of gold. And though he once was fond of music the only music for poor Midas, now, was the chink of one coin against another.

At length Midas had got to be so exceedingly unreasonable, that he could scarcely bear to see or touch any object that was not gold. He made it his custom, therefore, to pass a large portion of every day in a dark and dreary apartment, under ground, at the basement of his palace. It was here that he kept his wealth. To this dismal hole —for it was little better than a dungeon—Midas betook himself, whenever he wanted to be particularly happy. Here, after carefully locking the door, he would take a bag of gold coin, or a gold cup as big as a washbowl, or a heavy golden bar, or a peck-measure of gold-dust, and bring them from the obscure corners of the room into the one bright and narrow sunbeam that fell from the dungeon-like window. He valued the sunbeam for no other reason but that his treasure would not shine without its help. And then would he reckon over the coins in the bag, toss up the bar, and catch it as it came down; sift the gold-dust through his fingers; look at the funny image of his own face, as reflected in the burnished circumference of the cup; and whisper to himself, "O Midas, rich King Midas, what a happy man art thou!"

Midas was enjoying himself in his treasure-room, one day, as usual, when he perceived a shadow fall over the heaps of gold; and, looking suddenly up, what should he behold but the figure of a stranger, standing in the bright and narrow sunbeam! It was a young man, with a cheerful and ruddy face. Whether it was that the imagination of King Midas threw a yellow tinge over everything, or whatever the cause might be, he could not help fancying that the smile with which the stranger regarded him had a kind of golden radiance in it. Certainly, although his figure intercepted the sunshine, there was now a brighter gleam upon all the piled-up treasure than before. Even the remotest corners had their share of it, and were lighted up, when the stranger smiled, as with tips of flame and sparkles of fire.

As Midas knew that he had carefully turned the key in the lock, and that no mortal strength could possibly break into his treasure-room, he, of course, concluded that his visitor must be something more than mortal. Midas had met such beings before now, and was not sorry to meet one of them again.

The stranger gazed about the room; and when his lustrous smile had glistened upon all the golden objects that were there, he turned again to Midas.

"You are a wealthy man, friend Midas!" he observed. "I doubt whether any other four walls, on earth, contain so much gold as you have contrived to pile up in this room."

"I have done pretty well,—pretty well," answered Midas, in a discontented tone. "But, after all, it is but a trifle, when you consider that it has taken me my whole life to get it together. If one could live a thousand years, he might have time to grow rich!"

"What!" exclaimed the stranger. "Then you are not satisfied?"

Midas shook his head.

"And pray what would satisfy you?" asked the stranger. "Merely for the curiosity of the thing, I should be glad to know."

Midas paused and meditated. He felt a presentiment that this stranger, with such a golden lustre in his good-humored smile, had come hither with both the power and the purpose of gratifying his utmost wishes. Now, therefore, was the fortunate moment, when he had but to speak, and obtain whatever possible, or seemingly impossible thing, it might come into his head to ask. So he thought, and thought, and thought, and heaped up one golden mountain upon another, in his imagination, without being able to imagine them big enough. At last, a bright idea occurred to King Midas. It seemed really as bright as the glistening metal which he loved so much.

Raising his head, he looked the lustrous stranger in the face.

"Well, Midas," observed his visitor, "I see that you have at length hit upon something that will satisfy you. Tell me your wish."

"It is only this," replied Midas. "I am weary of collecting my treasures with so much trouble, and beholding the heap so diminutive, after I have done my best. I wish everything that I touch be changed to gold!"

The stranger's smile grew so very broad, that it seemed to fill the room like an outburst of the sun, gleaming into a shadowy dell, where the yellow autumnal leaves—for so looked the lumps and particles of gold—lie strewn in the glow of light.

"The Golden Touch!" exclaimed he. "You certainly deserve credit, friend Midas, for striking out so brilliant a conception. But are you quite sure that this will satisfy you?"

"How could it fail?" said Midas.

"And will you never regret the possession of it?"

"What could induce me?" asked Midas. "I ask nothing else, to render me perfectly happy."

"Be it as you wish, then," replied the stranger, waving his hand in token of farewell. "Tomorrow, at sunrise, you will find yourself gifted with the Golden Touch."

The figure of the stranger then became exceedingly bright, and Midas involuntarily closed his eyes. On opening them again, he beheld only one yellow sunbeam in the room, and all around him, the glistening of the precious metal which he had spent his life in hoarding up.

Whether Midas slept as usual that night, the story does not say. At any rate, day had hardly peeped over the hills, when King Midas was broad awake, and stretching his arms out of bed, began to touch the objects that were within reach. He was anxious to prove whether the Golden Touch had really come, according to the stranger's promise. So he laid his finger on a chair by the bedside, and on various other things, but was grievously disappointed to perceive that they remained of exactly the same substance as before. Indeed, he felt very much afraid that he had only dreamed about the lustrous stranger, or else that the latter had been making game of him. And what a miserable affair would it be, if after all his hopes, Midas must content himself with what little gold he could scrape together by ordinary means, instead of creating it by a touch!

All this while, it was only the gray of the morning, with but a streak of brightness along the edge of the sky, where Midas could not see it. He lay in a very disconsolate mood, regretting the downfall of his hopes, and kept growing sadder and sadder, until the earliest sunbeam shone through the window, and gilded the ceiling over his head. It seemed to Midas that this bright yellow sunbeam was reflected in rather a singular way on the white covering of the bed. Looking more closely, what was his astonishment and delight, when he found that this linen fabric had been transmuted to what seemed a woven texture of the purest and brightest gold! The Golden Touch had come to him with the first sunbeam!

Midas started up, in a kind of joyful frenzy, and ran about the room, grasping at everything that happened to be in his way. He seized one of the bed-posts, and it became immediately a fluted golden pillar. He pulled aside a window-curtain, in order to admit a clear spectacle of the wonders which he was performing; and the tassel grew heavy in his hand,—a mass of gold. He took up a book from the table. At his first touch, it assumed the appearance of such a splendidly bound and gilt-edged volume as one often meets with, nowadays; but, on running his fingers through the leaves, behold! It was a bundle of thin golden plates, in which all the wisdom of the book had grown illegible. He hurriedly put on his clothes, and was enraptured to see himself in a magnificent suit of gold cloth, which retained its flexibility and softness, although it burdened him a little with its weight. He drew out his handkerchief, which little Marygold had hemmed for him. That was likewise gold, with the dear child's neat and pretty stitches running all along the border, in gold thread!

Somehow or other, this last transformation did not quite please King Midas. He would rather that his little daughter's handiwork should have remained just the same as when she climbed his knee and put it into his hand.

But it was not worth while to vex himself about a trifle. Midas now took his spectacles from his pocket, and put them on his nose, in order that he might see more distinctly what he was about. In those days, spectacles for common people had not been invented, but were already worn by kings; else, how could Midas have had any? To his great perplexity, however, excellent as the glasses were, he discovered that he could not possibly see through them. But this was the most natural thing in the world; for, on taking them off, the transparent crystals turned out to be plates of yellow metal, and, of course, were worthless as spectacles, though valuable as gold. It struck Midas as rather inconvenient that, with all his wealth, he could never again be rich enough to own a pair of serviceable spectacles.

"It is no great matter, nevertheless," said he to himself, very philosophically. "We cannot expect any great good, without its being accompanied with some small inconvenience. The Golden Touch is worth the sacrifice of a pair of spectacles, at least, if not of one's very eyesight. My own eyes will serve for ordinary purposes, and little Marygold will soon be old enough to read to me."

King Midas went down stairs, and smiled, on observing that the balustrade of the staircase became a bar of burnished gold, as his hand passed over it, in his descent. He lifted the door-latch (it was brass only a moment ago, but golden when his fingers quitted it), and emerged into the garden. Here, as it happened, he found a great number of beautiful roses in full bloom, and others in all the stages of lovely bud and blossom. Very delicious was their fragrance in the morning breeze. Their delicate blush was one of the fairest sights in the world; so gentle, so modest, and so full of sweet tranquillity, did these roses seem to be.

But Midas knew a way to make them far more precious, according to his way of thinking, than roses had ever been before. So he took great pains in going from bush to bush, and exercised his magic touch most indefatigably; until every individual flower and bud, and even the worms at the heart of some of them, were changed to gold. By the time this good work was completed, King Midas was summoned to breakfast; and as the morning air had given him an excellent appetite, he made haste back to the palace.

On this particular morning, the breakfast consisted of hot cakes, some nice little brook-trout, roasted potatoes, fresh boiled eggs, and coffee, for King Midas himself, and a bowl of bread and milk for his daughter Marygold.

Little Marygold had not yet made her appearance. Her father ordered her to be called, and, seating himself at table, awaited the child's coming, in order to begin his own breakfast. To do Midas justice, he really loved his daughter, and loved her so much the more this morning, on account of the good fortune which had befallen him. It was not a great while before he heard her coming along the passageway crying bitterly. This circumstance surprised him, because Marygold was one of the cheerfullest little people whom you would see in a summer's day, and hardly shed a thimbleful of tears in a twelve-month. When Midas heard her sobs, he determined to put little Marygold in better spirits, by an agreeable surprise; so, leaning across the table, he touched his daughter's bowl (which was a China one, with pretty figures all around it), and transmuted it to gleaming gold.

Meanwhile, Marygold slowly and disconsolately opened the door, and showed herself with her apron at her eyes, still sobbing as if her heart would break.

"How now, my little lady!" cried Midas. "Pray what is the matter with you, this bright morning?"

Marygold, without taking the apron from her eyes, held out her hand, in which was one of the roses which Midas had so recently transmuted.

"Beautiful!" exclaimed her father. "And what is there in this magnificent golden rose to make you cry?"

"Ah, dear father!" answered the child, as well as her sobs would let her; "it is not beautiful, but the ugliest flower that ever grew! As soon as I was dressed I ran into the garden to gather some roses for you; because I know you like them. But, oh dear, dear me! What do you think has happened? Such a misfortune! All the beautiful roses, that smelled so sweetly and had so many lovely blushes, are blighted and spoilt! They are grown quite yellow, as you see this one, and have no longer any fragrance! What can have been the matter with them?"

"Poh, my dear little girl,—pray don't cry about it!" said Midas, who was ashamed to confess that he himself had wrought the change which so greatly afflicted her. "Sit down and eat your bread and milk! You will find it easy enough to exchange a golden rose like that (which will last hundreds of years) for an ordinary one which would wither in a day."

"I don't care for such roses as this!" cried Marygold, tossing it contemptuously away. "It has no smell, and the hard petals prick my nose!"

The child now sat down to table, but was so occupied with her grief for the blighted roses that she did not even notice the wonderful transmutation of her China bowl. Perhaps this was all the better; for Marygold was accustomed to take pleasure in looking at the queer figures, and strange trees and houses, that were painted on the circumference of the bowl; and these ornaments were now entirely lost in the yellow hue of the metal.

Midas, meanwhile, had poured out a cup of coffee, and, as a matter of course, the coffee-pot, whatever metal it may have been when he took it up, was gold when he set it down. He thought to himself, that it was rather an extravagant style of splendor, in a king of his simple habits, to breakfast off a service of gold, and began to be puzzled with the difficulty of keeping his treasures safe. The cupboard and the kitchen would no longer be a secure place of deposit for articles so valuable as golden bowls and coffee-pots.

Amid these thoughts, he lifted a spoonful of coffee to his lips, and, sipping it, was astonished to perceive that, the instant his lips touched the liquid, it became molten gold, and, the next moment, hardened into a lump!

"Ha!" exclaimed Midas, rather aghast.

"What is the matter, father?" asked little Marygold, gazing at him, with the tears still standing in her eyes.

"Nothing, child, nothing!" said Midas. "Eat your milk, before it gets quite cold."

He took one of the nice little trouts on his plate, and, by way of experiment, touched its tail with his finger. To his horror, it was immediately transmuted from an admirably fried brook-trout into a gold-fish. A very pretty piece of work, as you may suppose; only King Midas, just at that moment, would much rather have had a real trout in his dish than this elaborate and valuable imitation of one.

"I don't quite see," thought he to himself, "how I am to get any breakfast!"

He took one of the smoking-hot cakes, and had scarcely broken it, when, to his cruel mortification, though, a moment before, it had been of the whitest wheat, it assumed the yellow hue of Indian meal. Almost in despair, he helped himself to a boiled egg, which immediately underwent a change similar to those of the trout and the cake. The egg, indeed, might have been mistaken for one of those which the famous goose, in the story-book, was in the habit of laying; but King Midas was the only goose that had had anything to do with the matter.

"Well, this is a quandary!" thought he, leaning back in his chair, and looking quite enviously at little Marygold, who was now eating her bread and milk with great satisfaction. "Such a costly breakfast before me, and nothing that can be eaten."

Hoping that, by dint of great dispatch, he might avoid what he now felt to be a considerable inconvenience, King Midas next snatched a hot potato, and attempted to cram it into his mouth, and swallow it in a hurry. But the Golden Touch was too nimble for him. He found his mouth full, not of mealy potato, but of solid metal, which so burnt his tongue that he roared aloud, and, jumping up from the table, began to dance and stamp about the room, both with pain and affright.

"Father, dear father!" cried little Marygold, who was a very affectionate child, "pray what is the matter? Have you burnt your mouth?"

"Ah, dear child," groaned Midas, dolefully, "I don't know what is to become of your poor father!"

Already, at breakfast, Midas was excessively hungry. Would he be less so by dinner-time? And how ravenous would be his appetite for supper, which must undoubtedly consist of the same sort of indigestible dishes as those now before him.

These reflections so troubled wise King Midas, that he began to doubt whether, after all, riches are the one desirable thing in the world. But this was only a passing thought. So fascinated was Midas with the glitter of the yellow metal, that he would still have refused to give up the Golden Touch for so paltry a consideration as a breakfast.

Nevertheless, so great was his hunger, and the perplexity of his situation, that he again groaned aloud, and very grievously too. Our pretty Marygold could endure it no longer. She sat, a moment, gazing at her father, and trying, with all the might of her little wits, to find out what was the matter with him. Then, with a sweet and sorrowful impulse to comfort him, she started from her chair, and, running to Midas, threw her arms affectionately about his knees. He bent down and kissed her. He felt that his little daughter's love was worth a thousand times more than he had gained by the Golden Touch.

"My precious, precious Marygold!" cried he.

But Marygold made no answer.

Alas, what had he done? The moment the lips of Midas touched Marygold's forehead, a change had taken place. Her sweet, rosy face, so full of affection as it had been, assumed a glittering yellow color, with yellow tear-drops, congealing on her cheeks. Her beautiful brown ringlets took the same tint. Her soft and tender little form grew hard and inflexible within her father's encircling arms. Oh, terrible misfortune! The victim of his insatiable desire for wealth, little Marygold was a human child no longer, but a golden statue!

Yes, there she was, with the questioning look of love, grief, and pity, hardened into her face. It was the prettiest and most woeful sight that ever mortal saw. All the features and tokens of Marygold were there; even the beloved little dimple remained in her golden chin. But, the more perfect was the resemblance, the greater was the father's agony at beholding this golden image, which was all that was left him of a daughter. It had been a favorite phrase of Midas, whenever he felt particularly fond of the child, to say that she was worth her weight in gold. And now the phrase had become literally true. And now, at last, when it was too late, he felt how infinitely a warm and tender heart, that loved him, exceeded in value all the wealth that could be piled up betwixt the earth and sky!

Midas, in the fulness of all his gratified desires, began to wring his hands and bemoan himself; and now he could neither bear to look at Marygold, nor yet to look away from her. Except when his eyes were fixed on the image, he could not possibly believe that she was changed to gold. But, stealing another glance, there was the precious little figure, with a yellow tear-drop on its yellow cheek, and a look so piteous and tender, that it seemed as if that very expression must needs soften the gold, and make it flesh again. This, however, could not be.

While Midas was in this tumult of despair, he suddenly beheld a stranger standing near the door. Midas bent down his head, without speaking; for he recognized the same figure which had appeared to him, the day before, in the treasure-room, and had bestowed on him this disastrous faculty of the Golden Touch. The stranger's countenance still wore a smile, which seemed to shed a yellow lustre all about the room, and gleamed on little Marygold's image, and on the other objects that had been transmuted by the touch of Midas.

"Well, friend Midas," said the stranger, "pray how do you succeed with the Golden Touch?"

Midas shook his head.

"I am very miserable," said he.

"Very miserable, indeed!" exclaimed the stranger. "And how happens that? Have I not faithfully kept my promise with you? Have you not everything that your heart desired?"

"Gold is not everything," answered Midas. "And I have lost all that my heart really cared for."

"Ah! So you have made a discovery, since yesterday?" observed the stranger. "Let us see, then. Which of these two things do you think is really worth the most,—the gift of the Golden Touch, or one cup of clear cold water?"

"O blessed water!" exclaimed Midas. "It will never moisten my parched throat again!"

"The Golden Touch," continued the stranger, "or a crust of bread?"

"A piece of bread," answered Midas, "is worth all the gold on earth!"

"The Golden Touch," asked the stranger, "or your own little Marygold, warm, soft, and loving as she was an hour ago?"

"Oh, my child, my dear child!" cried poor Midas, wringing his hands. "I would not have given that one small dimple in her chin for the power of changing this whole big earth into a solid lump of gold!"

"You are wiser than you were, King Midas!" said the stranger, looking seriously at him. "Your own heart, I perceive, has not been entirely changed from flesh to gold. Were it so, your case would indeed be desperate. But you appear to be still capable of understanding that the commonest things, such as lie within everybody's grasp, are more valuable than the riches which so many mortals sigh and struggle after. Tell me, now, do you sincerely desire to rid yourself of this Golden Touch?"

"It is hateful to me!" replied Midas.

A fly settled on his nose, but immediately fell to the floor; for it, too, had become gold. Midas shuddered.

"Go, then," said the stranger, "and plunge into the river that glides past the bottom of your garden. Take likewise a vase of the same water, and sprinkle it over any object that you may desire to change back again from gold into its former substance. If you do this in earnestness and sincerity, it may possibly repair the mischief which your avarice has occasioned."

King Midas bowed low; and when he lifted his head, the lustrous stranger had vanished.

You will easily believe that Midas lost no time in snatching up a great earthen pitcher (but, alas me! it was no longer earthen after he touched it), and hastening to the river-side. As he scampered along, and forced his way through the shrubbery, it was positively marvellous to see how the foliage turned yellow behind him, as if the autumn had been there, and nowhere else. On reaching the river's brink, he plunged headlong in, without waiting so much as to pull off his shoes.

"Poof! poof! poof!" snorted King Midas, as his head emerged out of the water. "Well, this is really a refreshing bath, and I think it must have quite washed away the Golden Touch. And now for filling my pitcher!"

As he dipped the pitcher into the water, it gladdened his very heart to see it change from gold into the same good, honest earthen vessel which it had been before he touched it. He was conscious, also, of a change within himself. A cold, hard, and heavy weight seemed to have gone out of his bosom. Perceiving a violet, that grew on the bank of the river, Midas touched it with his finger, and was overjoyed to find that the delicate flower retained its purple hue, instead of undergoing a yellow blight. The curse of the Golden Touch had, therefore, really been removed from him.

King Midas hastened back to the palace; and, I suppose, the servants knew not what to make of it when they saw their royal master so carefully bringing home an earthen pitcher of water. But that water, which was to undo all the mischief that his folly had wrought, was more precious to Midas than an ocean of molten gold could have been. The first thing he did, as you need hardly be told, was to sprinkle it by handfuls over the golden figure of little Marygold.

No sooner did it fall on her than you would have laughed to see how the rosy color came back to the dear child's cheek! And how she began to sneeze and sputter!—and how astonished she was to find herself dripping wet, and her father still throwing more water over her!

"Pray do not, dear father!" cried she. "See how you have wet my nice frock, which I put on only this morning!"

For Marygold did not know that she had been a little golden statue; nor could she remember anything that had happened since the moment when she ran with outstretched arms to comfort poor King Midas.

Her father did not think it necessary to tell his beloved child how very foolish he had been, but contented himself with showing how much wiser he had now grown. For this purpose, he led little Marygold into the garden, where he sprinkled all the remainder of the water over the rose-bushes, and with such good effect that above five thousand roses recovered their beautiful bloom. There were two circumstances, however, which as long as he lived, used to put King Midas in mind of the Golden Touch. One was, that the sands of the river sparkled like gold; the other, that little Marygold's hair had now a golden tinge, which he had never observed in it before she had been transmuted by the effect of his kiss.

When King Midas had grown quite an old man, and used to trot Marygold's children on his knee, he was fond of telling them this marvellous story, pretty much as I have now told it to you. And then would he stroke their glossy ringlets, and tell them that their hair, likewise, had a rich shade of gold, which they had inherited from their mother.

"And to tell you the truth, my precious little folks," quoth King Midas, diligently trotting the children all the while, "ever since that morning, I have hated the very sight of all other gold, save this!"

# Norse Myths

*One notices very quickly a difference in mood between the Greek and
Norse myths. Greek myth has the bright beauty of a southern country, but Norse
myth is somber on a grand and heroic scale. One senses in the tales of
Odin and Balder a world before this world, a world somehow doomed. The
Greek myths can be humorous and lighthearted on occasion. The
Norse myths, while they have joyfulness here and there, are never light-
hearted. Can this be due to their having originated in a northern clime? Quite
possibly, for the striking change of seasons did not occur in Greece, and
it would seem to follow that Norsemen were much more grimly aware of the
mystery of ever recurring cycles of life and seeming death in most living
things, faced as they were with the stark contrast between flower-filled, light-filled
summers, and winters of deepest cold and great darkness. The myth of
Balder and his death is an exquisite evocation of that sense of the tragedy of
death and the mystery of rebirth, and it is a more despairing symbol of the
change of seasons than the Greek story of Demeter and Persephone.*

## HOW THOR FOUND HIS HAMMER

*Rarely does one find outright humor in a
Norse myth, and this one is one of the exceptions. There are undertones even to this tale,
however, which belong to the province of archaeologists and anthropologists, and it may be that
humor was not intended here.*

The frost-giants were always trying to get into
Asgard. For more than half the year they held
the world in their grasp, locking up the streams
in their rocky beds, hushing their music and the
music of the birds as well, and leaving nothing
but a wild waste of desolation under the cold
sky. They hated the warm sunshine which stirred
the wild flowers out of their sleep, and clothed
the steep mountains with verdure, and set all the
birds a-singing in the swaying tree-tops. They
hated the beautiful god Balder, with whose presence summer came back to the ice-bound earth,
and, above all, they hated Thor, whose flashing
hammer drove them back into Jotunheim, and
guarded the summer sky with its sudden gleam-
ings of power. So long as Thor had his hammer
Asgard was safe against the giants.

"How Thor Found His Hammer." From *Norse Stories*
by Hamilton Wright Mabie. Published by Dodd, Mead &
Company

One morning Thor started up out of a long,
deep sleep, and put out his hand for the hammer; but no hammer was there. Not a sign of it
could be found anywhere, although Thor anxiously searched for it. Then a thought of the
giants came suddenly in his mind; and his anger
rose till his eyes flashed like great fires, and his
red beard trembled with wrath.

"Look, now, Loke," he shouted, "they have
stolen Mjolner by enchantment, and no one on
earth or in heaven knows where they have hidden it."

"We will get Freyja's falcon-guise and search
for it," answered Loke, who was always quick to
get into trouble or to get out of it again. So they
went quickly to Folkvang and found Freyja surrounded by her maidens and weeping tears of
pure gold, as she had always done since her husband went on his long journey.

"The hammer has been stolen by enchantment," said Thor. "Will you lend me the falcon-
guise that I may search for it?"

"If it were silver, or even gold, you should
have it and welcome," answered Freyja, glad to
help Thor find the wonderful hammer that kept
them all safe from the hands of the frost-giants.

So the falcon-guise was brought, and Loke put
it on and flew swiftly out of Asgard to the home
of the giants. His great wings made broad shadows over the ripe fields as he swept along, and

the reapers, looking up from their work, wondered what mighty bird was flying seaward. At last he reached Jotunheim, and no sooner had he touched ground and taken off the falcon-guise than he came upon the giant Thrym, sitting on a hill twisting golden collars for his dogs and stroking the long manes of his horses.

"Welcome, Loke," said the giant. "How fares it with the gods and the elves, and what has brought you to Jotunheim?"

"It fares ill with both gods and elves since you stole Thor's hammer," replied Loke, guessing quickly that Thrym was the thief; "and I have come to find where you have hidden it."

Thrym laughed as only a giant can when he knows he has made trouble for somebody.

"You won't find it," he said at last. "I have buried it eight miles under ground, and no one shall take it away unless he gets Freyja for me as my wife."

The giant looked as if he meant what he said, and Loke, seeing no other way of finding the hammer, put on his falcon-guise and flew back to Asgard. Thor was waiting to hear what news he brought, and both were soon at the great doors of Folkvang.

"Put on your bridal dress, Freyja," said Thor bluntly, after his fashion, "and we will ride swiftly to Jotunheim."

But Freyja had no idea of marrying a giant just to please Thor; and, in fact, that Thor should ask her to do such a thing threw her into such a rage that the floor shook under her angry tread, and her necklace snapped in pieces.

"Do you think I am a weak lovesick girl, to follow you to Jotunheim and marry Thrym?" she cried indignantly.

Finding they could do nothing with Freyja, Thor and Loke called all the gods together to talk over the matter and decide what should be done to get back the hammer. The gods were very much alarmed, because they knew the frost-giants would come upon Asgard as soon as they knew the hammer was gone. They said little, for they did not waste time with idle words, but they thought long and earnestly, and still they could find no way of getting hold of Mjolner once more. At last Heimdal, who had once been a Van, and could therefore look into the future, said: "We must have the hammer at once or As-

gard will be in danger. If Freyja will not go, let Thor be dressed up and go in her place. Let keys jingle from his waist and a woman's dress fall about his feet. Put precious stones upon his breast, braid his hair like a woman's, hang the necklace around his neck, and bind the bridal veil around his head."

Thor frowned angrily. "If I dress like a woman," he said, "you will jeer at me."

"Don't talk of jeers," retorted Loke; "unless that hammer is brought back quickly, the giants will rule in our places."

Thor said no more, but allowed himself to be dressed like a bride, and soon drove off to Jotunheim with Loke beside him disguised as a servant-maid. There was never such a wedding journey before. They rode in Thor's chariot and the goats drew them, plunging swiftly along the way, thunder pealing through the mountains and the frightened earth blazing and smoking as they passed. When Thrym saw the bridal party coming he was filled with delight.

"Stand up, you giants," he shouted to his companions; "spread cushions upon the benches and bring in Freyja, my bride. My yards are full of golden-horned cows, black oxen please my gaze whichever way I look, great wealth and many treasures are mine, and Freyja is all I lack."

It was evening when the bride came driving into the giant's court in her blazing chariot. The feast was already spread against her coming, and with her veil modestly covering her face she was seated at the great table, Thrym fairly beside himself with delight. It wasn't every giant who could marry a goddess!

If the bridal journey had been so strange that any one but a foolish giant would have hesitated to marry a wife who came in such a turmoil of fire and storm, her conduct at the table ought certainly to have put Thrym on his guard; for never had a bride such an appetite before. The great tables groaned under the load of good things, but they were quickly relieved of their burden by the voracious bride. She ate a whole ox before the astonished giant had fairly begun to enjoy his meal. Then she devoured eight large salmon, one after the other, without stopping to take breath; and having eaten up the part of the feast specially prepared for the hungry men, she turned upon the delicacies which had been made for the women, and especially for her own fastidious appetite.

Thrym looked on with wondering eyes, and at last, when she had added to these solid foods three whole barrels of mead, his amazement was so great that, his astonishment getting the better of his politeness, he called out, "Did any one ever see such an appetite in a bride before, or know a maid who could drink so much mead?"

Then Loke, who was playing the part of a serving-maid, thinking that the giant might have some suspicions, whispered to him, "Freyja was so happy in the thought of coming here that she has eaten nothing for eight whole days."

Thrym was so pleased at this evidence of affection that he leaned forward and raised the veil as gently as a giant could, but he instantly dropped it and sprang back the whole length of the hall before the bride's terrible eyes.

"Why are Freyja's eyes so sharp?" he called to Loke. "They burn me like fire."

"Oh," said the cunning serving-maid, "she has not slept for a week, so anxious has she been to come here, and that is why her eyes are so fiery."

Everybody looked at the bride and nobody envied Thrym. They thought it was too much like marrying a thunder-storm.

The giant's sister came into the hall just then, and seeing the veiled form of the bride sitting there went up to her and asked for a bridal gift. "If you would have my love and friendship give me those rings of gold upon your fingers."

But the bride sat perfectly silent. No one had yet seen her face or heard her voice.

Thrym became very impatient. "Bring in the hammer," he shouted, "that the bride may be consecrated, and wed us in the name of Var."

If the giant could have seen the bride's eyes when she heard these words he would have sent her home as quickly as possible, and looked somewhere else for a wife.

The hammer was brought and placed in the bride's lap, and everybody looked to see the marriage ceremony; but the wedding was more strange and terrible than the bridal journey had been. No sooner did the bride's fingers close round the handle of Mjolner than the veil which covered her face was torn off and there stood Thor, the giant-queller, his terrible eyes blazing with wrath.

The giants shuddered and shrank away from those flaming eyes, the sight of which they dreaded more than anything else in all the worlds; but there was no chance of escape. Thor swung the hammer round his head and the great house rocked on its foundations. There was a vivid flash of lightning, an awful crash of thunder, and the burning roof and walls buried the whole company in one common ruin.

Thrym was punished for stealing the hammer, his wedding guests got crushing blows instead of bridal gifts, and Thor and Loke went back to Asgard, where the presence of Mjolner made the gods safe once more.

## THE DEATH OF BALDER

*Here is the Norse equivalent of the Greek myth of Demeter and Persephone, but in much more stark and moving terms. Balder the beautiful, the sun, drifts away in the fiery flames of autumn, leaving the world in darkness.*

There was one shadow which always fell over Asgard. Sometimes in the long years the gods almost forgot it, it lay so far off, like a dim cloud

"The Death of Balder." From *Norse Stories* by Hamilton Wright Mabie. Published by Dodd, Mead & Company

in a clear sky; but Odin saw it deepen and widen as he looked out into the universe, and he knew that the last great battle would surely come, when the gods themselves would be destroyed and a long twilight would rest on all the worlds; and now the day was close at hand. Misfortunes never come singly to men, and they did not to the gods. Idun, the beautiful goddess of youth, whose apples were the joy of all Asgard, made a resting place for herself among the massive branches of Ygdrasil, and there every evening came Brage, and sang so sweetly that the birds stopped to listen, and even the Norns, those implacable sisters at the foot of the tree, were softened by the melody. But poetry cannot change the purposes of fate, and one evening no song was heard of Brage or birds, the leaves of the world-tree hung withered and lifeless on the branches, and the fountain from which they had daily been sprinkled was dry at last. Idun had fallen into the dark valley of death, and when Brage, Heimdal, and Loke went to question her about the future she could answer them only with tears. Brage would not leave his beautiful wife alone amid the dim shades that crowded the dreary valley, and so youth and genius vanished out of Asgard forever.

Balder was the most god-like of all the gods, because he was the purest and the best. Wherever he went his coming was like the coming of sunshine, and all the beauty of summer was but the shining of his face. When men's hearts were white like the light, and their lives clear as the day, it was because Balder was looking down upon them with those soft, clear eyes that were open windows to the soul of God. He had always lived in such a glow of brightness that no darkness had ever touched him; but one morning, after Idun and Brage had gone, Balder's face was sad and troubled. He walked slowly from room to room in his palace Breidablik, stainless as the sky when April showers have swept across it because no impure thing had ever crossed the threshold, and his eyes were heavy with sorrow. In the night terrible dreams had broken his sleep, and made it a long torture. The air seemed to be full of awful changes for him, and for all the gods. He knew in his soul that the shadow of the last great day was sweeping on; as he looked out and saw the worlds lying in light

and beauty, the fields yellow with waving grain, the deep fiords flashing back the sunbeams from their clear depths, the verdure clothing the loftiest mountains, and knew that over all this darkness and desolation would come, with silence of reapers and birds, with fading of leaf and flower, a great sorrow fell on his heart.

Balder could bear the burden no longer. He went out, called all the gods together, and told them the terrible dreams of the night. Every face was heavy with care. The death of Balder would be like the going out of the sun, and after a long, sad council the gods resolved to protect him from harm by pledging all things to stand between him and any hurt. So Frigg, his mother, went forth and made everything promise, on a solemn oath, not to injure her son. Fire, iron, all kinds of metal, every sort of stone, trees, earth, diseases, birds, beasts, snakes, as the anxious mother went to them, solemnly pledged themselves that no harm should come near Balder. Everything had promised, and Frigg thought she had driven away the cloud; but fate was stronger than her love, and one little shrub had not sworn.

Odin was not satisfied even with these precautions, for whichever way he looked the shadow of a great sorrow spread over the worlds. He began to feel as if he were no longer the greatest of the gods, and he could almost hear the rough shouts of the frost-giants crowding the rainbow bridge on their way into Asgard. When trouble comes to men it is hard to bear, but to a god who had so many worlds to guide and rule it was a new and terrible thing. Odin thought and thought until he was weary, but no gleam of light could he find anywhere; it was thick darkness everywhere.

At last he could bear the suspense no longer, and saddling his horse he rode sadly out of Asgard to Niflheim, the home of Hel, whose face was as the face of death itself. As he drew near the gates, a monstrous dog came out and barked furiously, but Odin rode a little eastward of the shadowy gates to the grave of a wonderful prophetess. It was a cold, gloomy place, and the soul of the great god was pierced with a feeling of hopeless sorrow as he dismounted from Sleipner, and bending over the grave began to chant weird songs, and weave magical charms over it. When he had spoken those wonderful words which could waken the dead from their sleep, there was an awful silence for a moment, and then a faint ghost-like voice came from the grave.

"Who are thou?" it said. "Who breaketh the silence of death, and calleth the sleeper out of her long slumbers? Ages ago I was laid at rest here, snow and rain have fallen upon me through myriad years; why dost thou disturb me?"

"I am Vegtam," answered Odin, "and I come to ask why the couches of Hel are hung with gold and the benches strewn with shining rings?"

"It is done for Balder," answered the awful voice; "ask me no more."

Odin's heart sank when he heard these words; but he was determined to know the worst.

"I will ask thee until I know all. Who shall strike the fatal blow?"

"If I must, I must," moaned the prophetess. "Hoder shall smite his brother Balder and send him down to the dark home of Hel. The mead is already brewed for Balder, and the despair draweth near."

Then Odin, looking into the future across the open grave, saw all the days to come.

"Who is this," he said, seeing that which no mortal could have seen,—"who is this that will not weep for Balder?"

Then the prophetess knew that it was none other than the greatest of the gods who had called her up.

"Thou art not Vegtam," she exclaimed, "thou art Odin himself, the king of men."

"And thou," answered Odin angrily, "art no prophetess, but the mother of three giants."

"Ride home, then, and exult in what thou has discovered," said the dead woman. "Never shall my slumbers be broken again until Loke shall burst his chains and the great battle come."

And Odin rode sadly homeward knowing that already Niflheim was making itself beautiful against the coming of Balder.

The other gods meanwhile had become merry again; for had not everything promised to protect their beloved Balder? They even made sport of that which troubled them, for when they found that nothing could hurt Balder, and that all things glanced aside from his shining form, they persuaded him to stand as a target for their weapons; hurling darts, spears, swords, and battle-axes at him, all of which went singing through the air and fell harmless at his feet. But Loke, when he saw these sports, was jealous of Balder, and went about thinking how he could destroy him.

It happened that as Frigg sat spinning in her house Fensal, the soft wind blowing in at the windows and bringing the merry shouts of the gods at play, an old woman entered and approached her.

"Do you know," asked the newcomer, "what they are doing in Asgard? They are throwing all manner of dangerous weapons at Balder. He stands there like the sun for brightness, and against his glory, spears and battle-axes fall powerless to the ground. Nothing can harm him."

"No," answered Frigg joyfully; "nothing can bring him any hurt, for I have made everything in heaven and earth swear to protect him."

"What!" said the old woman, "has everything sworn to guard Balder?"

"Yes," said Frigg, "everything has sworn except one little shrub which is called Mistletoe, and grows on the eastern side of Valhal. I did not take an oath from that because I thought it was too young and weak."

When the old woman heard this a strange light came into her eyes; she walked off much faster than she had come in, and no sooner had she passed beyond Frigg's sight than this same old feeble woman grew suddenly erect, shook off her woman's garments, and there stood Loke himself. In a moment he had reached the slope east of Valhal, and plucked a twig of the unsworn Mistletoe, and was back in the circle of the gods, who were still at their favorite pastime with Balder. Hoder was standing silent and alone outside the noisy throng, for he was blind. Loke touched him.

"Why do you not throw something at Balder?"

"Because I cannot see where Balder stands, and have nothing to throw if I could," replied Hoder.

"If that is all," said Loke, "come with me. I will give you something to throw, and direct your aim."

Hoder, thinking no evil, went with Loke and did as he was told.

The little sprig of Mistletoe shot through the air, pierced the heart of Balder, and in a moment the beautiful god lay dead upon the field. A shadow rose out of the deep beyond the worlds and spread itself over heaven and earth, for the light of the universe had gone out.

The gods could not speak for horror. They stood like statues for a moment, and then a hopeless wail burst from their lips. Tears fell like rain from eyes that had never wept before, for Balder, the joy of Asgard, had gone to Niflheim and left them desolate. But Odin was saddest of all, because he knew the future, and he knew that peace and light had fled from Asgard forever, and that the last day and the long night were hurrying on.

Frigg could not give up her beautiful son, and when her grief had spent itself a little, she asked who would go to Hel and offer her a rich ransom if she would permit Balder to return to Asgard.

"I will go," said Hermod; swift at the word of Odin, Sleipner was led forth, and in an instant Hermod was galloping furiously away.

Then the gods began with sorrowful hearts to make ready for Balder's funeral. When the once beautiful form had been arrayed in grave-clothes they carried it reverently down to the deep sea, which lay, calm as a summer afternoon, waiting for its precious burden. Close to the water's edge lay Balder's Ringhorn, the greatest of all the ships that sailed the seas, but when the gods tried to launch it they could not move it an inch. The great vessel creaked and groaned, but no one could push it down to the water. Odin walked about it with a sad face, and the gentle ripple of the little waves chasing each other over the rocks seemed a mocking laugh to him.

"Send to Jotunheim for Hyrroken," he said at last; and a messenger was soon flying for that mighty giantess.

In a little time, Hyrroken came riding swiftly on a wolf so large and fierce that he made the gods think of Fenrer. When the giantess had alighted, Odin ordered four Berserkers of mighty strength to hold the wolf, but he struggled so angrily that they had to throw him on the ground before they could control him. Then Hyrroken went to the prow of the ship and with one mighty effort sent it far into the sea, the rollers underneath bursting into flame, and the whole earth trembling with the shock. Thor was so angry at the uproar that he would have killed the giantess on the spot if he had not been held back by the other gods. The great ship floated on the sea as she had often done before, when Balder, full of life and beauty, set all her sails and was borne joyfully across the tossing seas. Slowly and solemnly the dead god was carried on board, and as Nanna, his faithful wife, saw her husband borne for the last time from the earth which he had made dear to her and beautiful to all men, her heart broke with sorrow, and they laid her beside Balder on the funeral pyre.

Since the world began no one had seen such a funeral. No bells tolled, no long procession of mourners moved across the hills, but all the worlds lay under a deep shadow, and from every quarter came those who had loved or feared Balder. There at the very water's edge stood Odin himself, the ravens flying about his head, and on his majestic face a gloom that no sun would ever lighten again; and there was Frigg, the desolate mother, whose son had already gone so far that he would never come back to her; there was Frey standing sad and stern in his chariot; there was Freyja, the goddess of love, from whose eyes fell a shining rain of tears; there, too, was Heimdal on his horse Goldtop; and around all these glorious ones from Asgard crowded the children of Jotunheim, grim mountain-giants seamed with scars from Thor's hammer, and frost-giants who saw in the death of Balder the coming of that long winter in which they should reign through all the worlds.

A deep hush fell on all created things, and every eye was fixed on the great ship riding near the shore, and on the funeral pyre rising from the deck crowned with the forms of Balder and Nanna. Suddenly a gleam of light flashed over the water; the pile had been kindled, and the flames, creeping slowly at first, climbed faster and faster until they met over the dead and rose skyward. A lurid light filled the heavens and shone on the sea, and in the brightness of it the gods looked pale and sad, and the circle of giants grew darker and more portentous. Thor struck the fast burning pyre with his consecrating hammer, and Odin cast into it the wonder ring Draupner. Higher and higher leaped the flames, more and more desolate grew the scene; at last they began to sink, the funeral pyre was consumed. Balder had vanished forever, the summer was ended, and winter waited at the doors.

Meanwhile Hermod was riding hard and fast on his gloomy errand. Nine days and nights he rode through valleys so deep and dark that he could not see his horse. Stillness and blackness and solitude were his only companions until he came to the golden bridge which crosses the river Gjol. The good horse Sleipner, who had carried Odin on so many strange journeys, had never travelled such a road before, and his hoofs rang drearily as he stopped short at the bridge, for in front of him stood its porter, the gigantic Modgud.

"Who are you?" she asked, fixing her piercing eyes on Hermod. "What is your name and parentage? Yesterday five bands of dead men rode across the bridge, and beneath them all it did not shake as under your single tread. There is no colour of death in your face. Why ride you hither, the living among the dead?"

"I come," said Hermod, "to seek for Balder. Have you seen him pass this way?"

"He has already crossed the bridge and taken his journey northward to Hel."

Then Hermod rode slowly across the bridge that spans the abyss between life and death, and found his way at last to the barred gates of Hel's dreadful home. There he sprang to the ground, tightened the girths, remounted, drove the spurs deep into the horse, and Sleipner, with a mighty leap, cleared the wall. Hermod rode straight to the gloomy palace, dismounted, entered, and in a moment was face to face with the terrible queen of the kingdom of the dead. Beside her, on a beautiful throne, sat Balder, pale and wan, crowned with a withered wreath of flowers, and close at hand was Nanna, pallid as her husband, for whom she had died. And all night long, while ghostly forms wandered restless and sleepless through Helheim, Hermod talked with Balder and Nanna. There is no record of what they said, but the talk was sad enough, doubtless, and ran like a still stream among the happy days in Asgard when Balder's smile was morning over the earth and the sight of his face the summer of the world.

When the morning came, faint and dim, through the dusky palace, Hermod sought Hel, who received him as cold and stern as fate.

"Your kingdom is full, O Hel!" he said, "and without Balder, Asgard is empty. Send him back to us once more, for there is sadness in every heart and tears are in every eye. Through heaven and earth all things weep for him."

"If that is true," was the slow, icy answer, "if every created thing weeps for Balder, he shall return to Asgard; but if one eye is dry he remains henceforth in Helheim."

Then Hermod rode swiftly away, and the decree of Hel was soon told in Asgard. Through all the worlds the gods sent messengers to say that all who loved Balder should weep for his return, and everywhere tears fell like rain. There was weeping in Asgard, and in all the earth there was nothing that did not weep. Men and women and little children, missing the light that had once fallen into their hearts and homes, sobbed with bitter grief; the birds of the air, who had sung carols of joy at the gates of the morning since time began, were full of sorrow; the beasts of the fields crouched and moaned in their desolation; the great trees, that had put on their robes of green at Balder's command, sighed as the wind wailed through them; and the sweet flowers, that waited for Balder's footstep and sprang up in all the fields to greet him, hung their frail blossoms and wept bitterly for the love and the warmth and the light that had gone out. Throughout the whole earth there was nothing but weeping, and the sound of it was like the wailing of those storms in autumn that weep for the dead summer as its withered leaves drop one by one from the trees.

The messengers of the gods went gladly back to Asgard, for everything had wept for Balder; but as they journeyed they came upon a giantess, called Thok, and her eyes were dry.

"Weep for Balder," they said.

"With dry eyes only will I weep for Balder," she answered. "Dead or alive, he never gave me gladness. Let him stay in Helheim."

When she had spoken these words a terrible laugh broke from her lips, and the messengers looked at each other with pallid faces, for they knew it was the voice of Loke.

Balder never came back to Asgard, and the shadows deepened over all things, for the night of death was fast coming on.

Epics, sagas, and hero tales grow out of and along with myth. They consist of cycles of stories, each cycle centering on a human hero, buffeted by gods and humans, who suffers greatly and endures staunchly to the end. Myth is still with us in the early epics, for the gods apparently leave their own affairs in Olympus and Asgard for the express purpose of interfering with human adventures on earth. But in the epics the center of interest shifts from the gods to the human heroes, from Olympus to earth. After both the

# EPICS AND HERO TALES

gods and Olympus had faded from human dreams, culture heroes still excited human imagination and gained belief. Tales of greatness would cluster about a single name until a Roland or a Robin Hood assumed the impressive stature of the epic hero even without the background of warring gods.

The *epic* is strongly national in its presentation of human character. Odysseus is the embodiment of the Greek ideals of manly courage, sagacity, beauty, and endurance. Sigurd is the personification of the Norse code of heroism. King Arthur has come to represent Norman-English chivalry, and Robin Hood, the English love of freedom and justice as well as the ideal of lusty, jovial manhood. Study the epic hero of a nation and you will learn a great deal about the moral code of that nation and era.

Not all epics are suitable for children, but some of them provide a literary and emotional experience as unforgettable as it is precious. *Robin Hood* is certainly the prime favorite with elementary-school children, with the *Odyssey* next in appeal. It is probable that *King Arthur*, *Roland*, the *Iliad*, and perhaps the *Sigurd Saga* are better postponed for the days of adolescence, although if *told* to children, the Sigurd stories are well liked and so are many of the Arthur cycle. The personification of a great ideal in one hero, the sweep and excitement of epic action, the continuity of the adventures, and the nobility of the stories—these are epic qualities for which there are no substitutes.

Often the epic can be associated with some great poet, who may also have been a bard or minstrel, and this is to be expected when one recalls that the epic is basically defined as a poem which tells the story of heroic figures and their deeds. Thus, we think of the Homeric tradition (which was a tradition encompassing many poets and periods of time) in the person of Homer, the blind poet who composed, in elevated poetic style, his account of the Greek and Trojan wars and the wanderings of Odysseus. Taillefer was the great minstrel to William the Conqueror and is said to have accompanied him onto the battlefield at Hastings, reciting to him the *Chanson de Roland*. During certain ages the minstrels did accompany heroes and sovereigns onto the fields of battle that they might later set it all to verse and music.

The *saga*, if we wish to be exact in our terms, is very much like the epic, except that it is in prose and is a term originally applied to the heroic tales of medieval Iceland. As for the *hero tale*, so-called, while it may be either an epic or a saga, it is more likely a story about a rather recent hero or heroine (Robin Hood, Countess Jeanne) whose biographical data can more or less be verified, even though the tale may have gone far beyond the realities of his or her life and acquired much material straight out of myth and folk tale.

Reading epics will give young people some idea of the great antiquity of the epic form and of its enduring appeal. In the epics we can also find much that parallels our own times. After reading of Roland and Robin Hood, older boys and girls may well ask themselves and us: "Who will be *our* epic heroes?" What shall we answer?

## from GILGAMESH

### Bernarda Bryson

Gilgamesh, *from which this selection is taken, is the oldest written epic known, first recorded in cuneiform nearly 3000 years before Christ. It prefigures much of what was to come later in the Old Testament and in the Greek myths.*

### The Monster Humbaba

Perfect was the friendship of Gilgamesh and Enkidu. The wild man asked only to be the servant of the King, but Gilgamesh called him "my younger brother," and Ninsun, the queen, looked upon him almost as a son. Everywhere, they went together and everywhere they were admired. They took part in feats of strength and daring, winning all prizes and all praise. And in all this Enkidu was content.

Not so, Gilgamesh. On one occasion he said to his friend, "Day and night I dream of a great enterprise. Whenever I close my eyes, voices come to me and say: 'Arouse yourself, Gilgamesh, there are great things to be done!'"

Enkidu's mind was full of foreboding.

"You and I, Enkidu, we will climb the mountain and destroy the monster Humbaba!"

Enkidu's eyes filled with tears and he turned away.

"Why should you cry, O Enkidu? Are you not the bravest of men? Are you no longer my friend and brother whom I admire more than anyone at all?"

Enkidu spoke: "I knew the presence of Humbaba even when I was a wild man on the steppes and in the forest. I could hear the sighing of his voice rise over the sound of thunder and high winds. I could hear the beating of his heart and feel the heat of his breath at a distance of five-hundred shar. I do not fear beast or mortal man, O Gilgamesh, but Humbaba is not mortal; he is the appointed servant of the gods, the guardian of the wild cows and the cedar forest. Whoever comes near him will grow weak. He will become paralyzed and will fail."

"The monster is an everlasting evil," said Gilgamesh. "It oppresses the people. Day and night it spreads fires and spews its ashes over the town. It is hated by great Shamash, constantly obscuring his face. O Enkidu, shall my life be as an empty wind? What am I, if I turn aside from the things I want to do? I am nothing, only someone waiting for death! But if I do this thing, O Enkidu, even though I should fail, then they will say, 'Gilgamesh died a hero's death! He died defending his people.' I will have made an everlasting name for myself and my life will not be as an empty wind!"

Still Enkidu turned away.

Gilgamesh then called in the armorers, the makers of spears and shields and axes. They cast for him swords of bronze inlaid with silver and gold. They made powerful long-bows and arrows tipped with stone, and most beautiful of all, a spear with a handle of lapis lazuli and gold inset with many glittering jewels.

Gilgamesh called Enkidu and laid the weapons before him, hoping to tempt him with their beauty. And still Enkidu said no.

Gilgamesh was downcast. "My brother has grown soft and timid. He no longer loves daring; he has forgotten adventure; I will go alone!"

The elders of Uruk, who had long ago forgotten their hatred of the King, now came to him: "O Gilgamesh, do not undertake this thing. You are young; your heart has carried you away. Settle down, O King; take a bride to yourself; let your life be tranquil!"

Gilgamesh laughed. "Save your wise counsel for my friend, Enkidu. He'll listen. You waste your words on me, good fathers!"

The elders came in secret to Enkidu. "If the King stubbornly insists on doing this thing, risking danger and defying the gods, then Enkidu you must accompany him!"

"Indeed, you must go ahead of him," a second elder said, "for it is known that whoever first enters the cedar gate will be the first killed."

"Besides, it is you who know the way, Enkidu. It is you who have trodden the road!"

"May Shamash stand beside you!"

"May he open the path for you!"

Enkidu went to Gilgamesh. "My head is bowed, O King. I am your brother and your servant; wherever you will go, I will go."

Tears came into the eyes of Gilgamesh; his faith in Enkidu was restored. "Now, my brother, we will go to Ninsun; we will tell our plan and ask her to petition the gods for our success!"

Pale as she was, Ninsun turned more pale. But since she could not dissuade her son, she merely kissed him, giving him her blessing. To Enkidu she said, "Even though you are not my son, O Enkidu, you are like a son to me, and I shall petition the gods for you as for Gilgamesh. But remember, please, that as a man protects his own person, so must he guard the life of his companion!"

The people of Uruk walked with the two friends through the streets admiring their weapons and praising their bold plan: "Praise be to Gilgamesh who dares everything! Praise be to Enkidu who will safeguard his companion!" But Harim the priestess mourned, "May your feet carry you back safely to the city, Enkidu!" And thus they set out.

Ninsun dressed herself in her finest garments. She attached the golden pendants to her ears and set the divine tiara upon her head. She anointed herself with perfumes and carried in her hand an incense that would carry its pleasant odors into the sky. Mounting with stately grace to the roof of her palace, she raised her voice to its highest pitch and called out, "O Shamash, listen to me!" Then waiting a little for her voice to reach the ears of the god, she went on: "O Shamash, why have you given my son Gilgamesh such a restless heart? Why have you made him so eager for adventure? Now he has gone up to fight with the indestructible monster Humbaba. Why have you sent him, O Shamash, to wipe out the evil that you abhor? It is all your plan! It is you who have planted the idea in his head! May you not sleep, O Shamash, until Gilgamesh and his friend Enkidu return to Uruk. If they fail, may you never sleep again!"

Ninsun extinguished the small blaze from under the incense and descended from the roof of the palace.

Gilgamesh and Enkidu walked toward the mountain of the cedar forest. At a distance of twenty double-hours they sat down beside the path and ate a small amount of food. At a distance of thirty double-hours, they lay down to sleep, covering themselves with their garments. On the following day they walked a distance of fifty double-hours. Within three days' time, they covered a distance that it would have taken ordinary men some fifteen days to cover. They reached the mountain and saw before them a towering and magnificent gate of cedar wood.

"Here," said Gilgamesh, "we must pour meal upon the earth, for that will gain us the goodwill of the gods; it will persuade them to reveal their purpose in our dreams!"

They poured meal on the ground and lay down to sleep. After some time Gilgamesh wakened his friend. "Enkidu, I have had a dream; it went like this: We were standing in a deep gorge beside a mountain. Compared to it, we were the size of flies! Before our very eyes the mountain collapsed; it fell in a heap!"

"The meaning of that seems very clear," said Enkidu. "It means that Humbaba is the mountain and that he will fall before us!"

They closed their eyes again and slept. After some time, Gilgamesh again awakened his friend. "I've had another dream, Enkidu. I saw the same mountain this time, and again it fell, but it fell on me. However, as I lay struggling, a beautiful personage appeared. He took me by my feet and dragged me out from under the mountain. Now I wonder what this means? Is it that you will rescue me from the monster, or will someone else come along?"

They pondered a little and went back to sleep. Next Enkidu wakened his brother, Gilgamesh. "Has a cold shower passed over us? Did the lightning strike fires, and was there a rain of ashes?"

"The earth is dry and clean," said Gilgamesh, "you must have dreamed!" But since neither of them could understand the meaning of this dream, they fell asleep again, and soon the day came.

They approached the magnificent gate. "Let's open it, Enkidu! Let's be on our way!"

For a last time, Enkidu tried to persuade his friend to turn back. But since the King would not listen, it was he who went first and placed his hand against the gate to push it open. Enkidu was thrown backward with such violence that he fell to the earth. He rose to his feet. "Gilgamesh, wait! My hand is paralyzed!"

"Put it on my arm, Enkidu! It will take strength from my arm because I am not afraid."

When the two friends threw their weight against the gate, however, it swung inward.

They walked up the mountainside through the sacred trees. And these became closer and thicker until the sky was blotted out. They could hear the giant heartbeat of Humbaba and smell the smoke from his lungs.

To show his daring, Gilgamesh cut one of the cedar trees. The blows of his axe rang out, and from afar the terrible Humbaba heard the sound.

With a crashing of timbers and a rolling of loose stones, Humbaba came down upon them. His face loomed among the treetops, creased and grooved like some ancient rock. The breath he breathed withered the boughs of cedar and set small fires everywhere.

Enkidu's fears now vanished and the two heroes stood side by side as the monster advanced.

He loomed over them, his arms swinging out like the masts of a ship. He was almost upon them when suddenly the friends stepped apart. The giant demon lurched through the trees, stumbled, and fell flat. He rose to his feet bellowing like a bull and charged upon Enkidu. But the King brought down his axe on the toe of Humbaba so that he whirled about roaring with pain. He grasped Gilgamesh by his flowing hair, swung him round and round as if to hurl him through the treetops, but now Enkidu saw his giant ribs exposed and he thrust his sword into the monster's side. Liquid fire gushed from the wound and ran in small streams down the mountainside. Gilgamesh fell to the earth and lay still, trying to breathe. But meanwhile Humbaba grasped the horns of Enkidu and began to flail his body against a tree. Surely the wild man would have died, but now Gilgamesh roused himself. He lanced into the air his long spear with its handle of lapis lazuli and gold. The spear caught Humbaba in the throat and remained there poised and glittering among the fires that had ignited everywhere.

The giant loosened his hold on Enkidu; he cried out. The earth reverberated with the sound, and distant mountains shook.

Gilgamesh felt pity in his heart. He withdrew his sword and put down his axe, while the monster Humbaba crept toward him grovelling and wailing for help. Now Enkidu perceived that the monster drew in a long breath in order to spew forth his last weapon—the searing fire that would consume the King. He leaped on the demon and with many sword thrusts released the fire, so that it bubbled harmlessly among the stones.

Humbaba was dead; the two heroes, black with soot and dirt, were still alive. They hugged each other; they leaped about; and singing and shouting, they descended the mountainside. Gentle rains fell around them and the land was forever free from the curse of the giant Humbaba.

## from  THE ODYSSEY

*This excerpt from the great Greek epic,* The Odyssey, *is one of the most interesting episodes in the life of the hero Odysseus, whose wanderings lasted for ten years.*

### The Curse of Polyphemus

Of all the heroes that wandered far and wide before they came to their homes again after the fall of Troy, none suffered so many hardships as Odysseus. Ten years did he fight against Troy, but it was ten years more before he came to his home and his wife Penelope and his son Telemachus.

Odysseus set out from Troy with twelve good ships. He touched first at Ismarus, where his first misfortune took place, and in a skirmish with the natives he lost a number of men from each ship's crew.

A storm then drove them to the land of the Lotus-Eaters, a wondrous people, kindly and content, who spend their lives in a day-dream and care for nothing else under the sun. No sooner had the sailors eaten of this magical lotus than they lost all their wish to go home, or to see their wives and children again. By main force, Odysseus drove them back to the ships and saved them from the spell.

Thence they came one day to a beautiful strange island, a verdant place to see, deep with soft grass and well watered with springs. Here they ran the ships ashore, and took their rest and feasted for a day. But Odysseus looked across to the mainland, where he saw flocks and herds, and smoke going up softly from the homes of men; and he resolved to go across and find out what manner of people lived there. Accordingly, next morning, he took his own ship's company and they rowed across to the mainland.

Now, fair as the place was, there dwelt in it a race of giants, the Cyclopes, great rude creatures, having each but one eye, and that in the middle of his forehead. One of them was Polyphemus, the son of Poseidon. He lived by himself as a shepherd, and it was to his cave that Odysseus came, by some evil chance. It was an enormous grotto, big enough to house the giant and all his flocks, and it had a great courtyard without. But Odysseus, knowing nought of all this, chose out twelve men, and with a wallet of corn and a goatskin full of wine they left the ship and made

"The Curse of Polyphemus" from *Old Greek Folk Stories Told Anew* by Josephine Preston Peabody. Reprinted by permission of Houghton Mifflin Company

a way to the cave, which they had seen from the water.

Much they wondered who might be the master of this strange house. Polyphemus was away with his sheep, but many lambs and kids were penned there, and the cavern was well stored with goodly cheeses and cream and whey.

Without delay, the wearied men kindled a fire and sat down to eat such things as they found, till a great shadow came dark against the doorway, and they saw the Cyclops near at hand, returning with his flocks. In an instant they fled into the darkest corner of the cavern.

Polyphemus drove his flocks into the place and cast off from his shoulders a load of young trees for firewood. Then he lifted and set in the entrance of the cave a gigantic boulder of a doorstone. Not until he had milked the goats and ewes and stirred up the fire did his terrible one eye light upon the strangers.

"What are ye?" he roared then, "robbers or rovers?" And Odysseus alone had heart to answer.

"We are Achaens of the army of Agamemnon," said he. "And by the will of Zeus we have lost our course, and are come to you as strangers. Forget not that Zeus has a care for such as we, strangers and suppliants."

Loud laughed the Cyclops at this. "You are a witless churl to bid me heed the gods!" said he. "I spare or kill to please myself and none other. But where is your cockle-shell that brought you hither?"

Then Odysseus answered craftily: "Alas, my ship is gone! Only I and my men escaped alive from the sea."

But Polyphemus, who had been looking them over with his one eye, seized two of the mariners and dashed them against the wall and made his evening meal of them, while their comrades stood by helpless. This done, he stretched himself through the cavern and slept all night long, taking no more heed of them than if they had been flies. No sleep came to the wretched seamen, for, even had they been able to slay him, they were powerless to move away the boulder from the door. So all night long Odysseus took thought how they might possibly escape.

At dawn the Cyclops woke, and his awakening was like a thunderstorm. Again he kindled the fire, again he milked the goats and ewes, and again he seized two of the king's comrades and served them up for his terrible repast. Then the savage shepherd drove his flocks out of the cave, only turning back to set the boulder in the doorway and pen up Odysseus and his men in their dismal lodging.

But the wise king had pondered well. In the sheepfold he had seen a mighty club of olivewood, in size like the mast of a ship. As soon as the Cyclops was gone, Odysseus bade his men cut off a length of this club and sharpen it down to a point. This done, they hid it away under the earth that heaped the floor; and they waited in fear and torment for their chance of escape.

At sundown, home came the Cyclops. Just as he had done before, he drove in his flocks, barred the entrance, milked the goats and ewes, and made his meal of two more hapless men, while their fellows looked on with burning eyes. Then Odysseus stood forth, holding a bowl of the wine that he had brought with him; and, curbing his horror of Polyphemus, he spoke in friendly fashion: "Drink, Cyclops, and prove our wine, such as it was, for all was lost with our ship save this. And no other man will ever bring you more, since you are such an ungentle host."

The Cyclops tasted the wine and laughed with delight so that the cave shook. "Ho, this is a rare drink!" said he. "I never tasted milk so good, nor whey, nor grape-juice either. Give me the rest, and tell me your name, that I may thank you for it."

Twice and thrice Odysseus poured the wine and the Cyclops drank it off; then he answered: "Since you ask it, Cyclops, my name is Noman."

"And I will give you this for your wine, Noman," said the Cyclops; "you shall be eaten last of all!"

As he spoke his head drooped, for his wits were clouded with drink, and he sank heavily out of his seat and lay prone, stretched along the floor of the cavern. His great eye shut and he fell asleep.

Odysseus thrust the stake under the ashes till it was glowing hot; and his fellows stood by him, ready to venture all. Then together they lifted the club and drove it straight into the eye of Polyphemus and turned it around and about.

The Cyclops gave a horrible cry, and, thrusting

away the brand, he called on all his fellow-giants near and far. Odysseus and his men hid in the uttermost corners of the cave, but they heard the resounding steps of the Cyclopes who were roused, and their shouts as they called, "What ails thee, Polyphemus? Art thou slain? Who has done thee any hurt?"

"Noman!" roared the blinded Cyclops; "Noman is here to slay me by treachery."

"Then if no man hath hurt thee," they called again, "let us sleep." And away they went to their homes once more.

But Polyphemus lifted away the boulder from the door and sat there in the entrance, groaning with pain and stretching forth his hands to feel if any one were near. Then, while he sat in double darkness, with the light of his eye gone out, Odysseus bound together the rams of the flock, three by three, in such wise that every three should save one of his comrades. For underneath the mid ram of each group a man clung, grasping his shaggy fleece; and the rams on each side guarded him from discovery. Odysseus himself chose out the greatest ram and laid hold of his fleece and clung beneath his shaggy body, face upward.

Now, when dawn came, the rams hastened out to pasture, and Polyphemus felt of their backs as they huddled along together; but he knew not that every three held a man bound securely. Last of all came the kingly ram that was dearest to his rude heart, and he bore the king of Ithaca. Once free of the cave, Odysseus and his fellows loosed their hold and took flight, driving the rams in haste to the ship, where, without delay, they greeted their comrades and went aboard.

But as they pushed from shore, Odysseus could not refrain from hailing the Cyclops with taunts, and at the sound of that voice Polyphemus came forth from his cave and hurled a great rock after the ship. It missed and upheaved the water like an earthquake. Again Odysseus called, saying: "Cyclops, if any shall ask who blinded thine eye, say that it was Odysseus, son of Laertes of Ithaca."

Then Polyphemus groaned and cried: "An Oracle foretold it, but I waited for some man of might who should overcome me by his valor— not a weakling! And now"—he lifted his hands and prayed—"Father, Poseidon, my father, look upon Odysseus, the son of Laertes of Ithaca, and grant me this revenge—let him never see Ithaca again! Yet, if he must, may he come late, without a friend, after long wandering, to find evil abiding by his hearth!"

So he spoke and hurled another rock after them, but the ship outstripped it, and sped by to the island where the other good ships waited for Odysseus. Together they put out from land and hastened on their homeward voyage.

But Poseidon, who is lord of the sea, had heard the prayer of his son, and that homeward voyage was to wear through ten years more, with storm and irksome calms and misadventure.

## from THE MERRY ADVENTURES OF ROBIN HOOD

### Howard Pyle

*The Robin Hood cycle is a little less "heroic" than the Greek and Germanic epics, but children love Robin Hood and should not miss the stories. Howard Pyle consulted the actual early ballads in order to make his masterful prose version. Anne Malcolmson's* Song of Robin Hood *gives us those ballads with their music. The teacher or parent who can sing and play a guitar can give children a unique experience by singing one of the ballads in its entirety.*

### Little John and the Tanner of Blyth

It often comes about in this world that unlucky happenings fall upon one in such measure that it seems, as the saying is, that every cat that one strokes flies into one's face. Thus it was with Little John one bright day in the merry Maytime; so listen and you shall hear how Dame Luck so buffeted him that his bones were sore for many a day thereafter.

One fine day, not long after Little John had left abiding with the Sheriff and had come back, with his worship's cook, to the merry greenwood, as has just been told, Robin Hood and a few chosen fellows of his band lay upon the soft sward beneath the greenwood tree where they dwelt.

"Little John and the Tanner of Blyth." From *The Merry Adventures of Robin Hood* by Howard Pyle

The day was warm and sultry, so that whilst most of the band were scattered through the forest upon this mission and upon that, these few stout fellows lay lazily beneath the shade of the tree, in the soft afternoon, passing jests among themselves and telling merry stories, with laughter and mirth.

All the air was laden with the bitter fragrance of the May, and all the bosky shades of the woodlands beyond rang with the sweet song of birds,—the throstle-cock, the cuckoo, and the wood-pigeon,—and with the song of birds mingled the cool sound of the gurgling brook that leaped out of the forest shades, and ran fretting amid its rough, gray stones across the sunlit open glade before the trysting tree. And a fair sight was that halfscore of tall, stout yeomen, all clad in Lincoln green, lying beneath the broad-spreading branches of the great oak tree, amid the quivering leaves of which the sunlight shivered and fell in dancing patches upon the grass.

The good old times have gone by when such men grow as grew then; when sturdy quarterstaff and longbow toughened a man's thews till they were like leather. Around Robin Hood that day there lay the very flower of English yeomanrie. Here the great Little John, with limbs as tough as the gnarled oak, yet grown somewhat soft from good living at the Sheriff's house in Nottingham Town; there Will Stutely, his face as brown as a berry from sun and wind, but, for all that, the comeliest yeoman in the mid-country, only excepting Allan a Dale the minstrel, of whom you shall hear anon. Beside these was Will Scathelock, as lank as a greyhound, yet as fleet of foot as a buck of three years' growth; young David of Doncaster, with great stout limbs only less than those of Little John in size, the tender beard of early youth now just feathering his chin, and others of great renown both far and near.

Suddenly Robin Hood smote his knee.

"By Saint Dunstan," quoth he, "I had nigh forgot that quarter-day cometh on apace, and yet no cloth of Lincoln green in all our store. It must be looked to, and that in quick season. Come, busk thee, Little John! stir those lazy bones of thine, for thou must get thee straightway to our good gossip, the draper, Hugh Longshanks of Ancaster. Bid him send us

straightway twentyscore yards of fair cloth of Lincoln green; and mayhap the journey may take some of the fat from off thy bones, that thou hast gotten from lazy living at our dear Sheriff's."

"Nay," muttered Little John (for he had heard so much upon this score that he was sore upon the point), "nay, truly, mayhap I have more flesh upon my joints than I once had, yet, flesh or no flesh, I doubt not that I could still hold my place and footing upon a narrow bridge against e'er a yeoman in Sherwood, or Nottinghamshire, for the matter of that, even though he had no more fat about his bones than thou hast, good master."

At this reply a great shout of laughter went up, and all looked at Robin Hood, for each man knew that Little John spake of a certain fight that happened between their master and himself, through which they first became acquainted.

"Nay," quoth Robin Hood, laughing louder than all, "Heaven forbid that I should doubt thee, for I care for no taste of thy staff myself, Little John. I must needs own that there are those of my band can handle a seven-foot staff more deftly than I; yet no man in all Nottinghamshire can draw gray-goose shaft with my fingers. Nevertheless, a journey to Ancaster may not be ill for thee; so go thou, as I bid, and thou hadst best go this very evening, for since thou hast abided at the Sheriff's[1] many know thy face, and if thou goest in broad daylight, thou mayest get thyself into a coil with some of his worship's men-at-arms. Bide thou here till I bring thee money to pay our good Hugh. I warrant he hath no better customers in all Nottinghamshire than we." So saying, Robin left them and entered the forest.

Not far from the trysting tree was a great rock in which a chamber had been hewn, the entrance being barred by a massive oaken door two palms' breadth in thickness, studded about with spikes, and fastened with a great padlock. This was the treasure-house of the band, and thither Robin Hood went, and, unlocking the door, entered the chamber, from which he brought forth a bag of gold, which he gave to Little John, to pay Hugh

[1] The expression *to abide at the Sheriff's* means "to be in jail."

Longshanks withal, for the cloth of Lincoln green.

Then up got Little John, and, taking the bag of gold, which he thrust into his bosom, he strapped a girdle about his loins, took a stout pikestaff full seven feet long in his hand, and set forth upon his journey.

So he strode whistling along the leafy forest path that led to Fosse Way, turning neither to the right hand nor the left, until at last he came to where the path branched, leading on the one hand onward to Fosse Way, and on the other, as well Little John knew, to the merry Blue Boar Inn. Here Little John suddenly ceased whistling, and stopped in the middle of the path. First he looked up and then he looked down, and then, tilting his cap over one eye, he slowly scratched the back part of his head. For thus it was: at the sight of these two roads, two voices began to alarum within him, the one crying, "There lies the road to the Blue Boar Inn, a can of brown October, and a merry night with sweet companions such as thou mayst find there"; the other, "There lies the way to Ancaster and the duty thou art sent upon." Now the first of these two voices was far the louder, for Little John had grown passing fond of good living through abiding at the Sheriff's house; so, presently, looking up into the blue sky, across which bright clouds were sailing like silver boats, and swallows skimming in circling flight, quoth he, "I fear me it will rain this evening, so I'll e'en stop at the Blue Boar till it passes by, for I know my good master would not have me wet to the skin." So, without more ado, off he strode down the path that lay the way of his likings. Now there was no sign of any foul weather, but when one wishes to do a thing, as Little John did, one finds no lack of reasons for the doing.

Four merry wags were at the Blue Boar Inn; a butcher, a beggar, and two barefoot friars. Little John heard them singing from afar, as he walked through the hush of the mellow twilight that was now falling over hill and dale. Right glad were they to welcome such a merry blade as Little John. Fresh cans of ale were brought, and with jest and song and merry tales the hours slipped away on fleeting wings. None thought of time or tide till the night was so far gone that Little John put by the thought of setting forth upon his journey again that night, and so bided at the Blue Boar Inn until the morrow.

Now it was an ill piece of luck for Little John that he left his duty for his pleasure, and he paid a great score for it, as we are all apt to do in the same case, as you shall see.

Up he rose at the dawn of the next day, and, taking his stout pikestaff in his hand, he set forth upon his journey once more, as though he would make up for lost time.

In the good town of Blyth there lived a stout tanner, celebrated far and near for feats of strength and many tough bouts at wrestling and the quarterstaff. For five years he had held the mid-country champion belt for wrestling, till the great Adam o' Lincoln cast him in the ring and broke one of his ribs; but at quarterstaff he had never yet met his match in all the country about. Beside all this, he dearly loved the longbow, and a sly jaunt in the forest when the moon was full and the dun deer in season; so that the King's rangers kept a shrewd eye upon him and his doings, for Arthur a Bland's house was apt to have a plenty of meat in it that was more like venison than the law allowed.

Now Arthur had been to Nottingham Town the day before Little John set forth on his errand, there to sell a halfscore of tanned cowhides. At the dawn of the same day that Little John left the Inn, he started from Nottingham, homeward for Blyth. His way led, all in the dewy morn, past the verge of Sherwood Forest, where the birds were welcoming the lovely day with a great and merry jubilee. Across the Tanner's shoulders was slung his stout quarterstaff, ever near enough to him to be gripped quickly, and on his head was a cap of double cowhide, so tough that it could hardly be cloven even by a broadsword.

"Now," quoth Arthur a Bland to himself, when he had come to that part of the road that cut through a corner of the forest, "no doubt at this time of year the dun deer are coming from the forest depths nigher to the open meadow lands. Mayhap I may chance to catch a sight of the dainty brown darlings thus early in the morn." For there was nothing he loved better than to look upon a tripping herd of deer, even when he could not tickle their ribs with a cloth-yard shaft. Accordingly, quitting the path, he went peeping this way and that through the underbrush, spying now here and now there, with all the wiles of a master woodcraft, and of one who had more than once donned a doublet of Lincoln green.

Now as Little John stepped blithely along, thinking of nothing but of such things as the sweetness of the hawthorn buds that bedecked the hedgerows, or the crab trees that stood here and there all covered with fair pink blossoms, or gazing upward at the lark, that, springing from the dewy grass, hung aloft on quivering wings in the yellow sunlight, pouring forth its song that fell like a falling star from the sky, his luck led him away from the highway, not far from the spot where Arthur a Bland was peeping this way and that through the leaves of the thickets. Hearing a rustling of the branches, Little John stopped, and presently caught sight of the brown cowhide cap of the Tanner moving amongst the bushes.

"I do much wonder," quoth Little John to himself, "what yon knave is after, that he should go thus peeping and peering about. I verily believe that yon scurvy varlet is no better than a thief, and cometh here after our own and the good King's dun deer." For by much roving in the forest, Little John had come to look upon all the deer in Sherwood as belonging to Robin Hood and his band as much as to good King Harry. "Nay," quoth he again, after a time, "this matter must e'en be looked into." So, quitting the highroad, he also entered the thickets, and began spying around after stout Arthur a Bland.

So for a long time they both of them went hunting about, Little John after the Tanner, and the Tanner after the deer. At last Little John trod upon a stick, which snapped under his foot, whereupon, hearing the noise, the Tanner turned quickly and caught sight of the yeoman. Seeing that the Tanner had spied him out, Little John put a bold face upon the matter.

"Hilloa," quoth he, "what art thou doing here, thou naughty fellow? Who art thou that comest ranging Sherwood's paths? In very sooth thou hast an evil cast of countenance, and I do think, truly, that thou art no better than a thief, and comest after our good King's deer."

"Nay," quoth the Tanner boldly,—for, though taken by surprise, he was not a man to be frightened by big words,—"thou liest in thy teeth. I am no thief, but an honest craftsman. As for my countenance, it is what it is; and for the matter of that, thine own is none too pretty, thou saucy fellow."

"Ha!" quoth Little John, in a great loud voice, "wouldst thou give me backtalk? Now I have a great part of mind to crack thy pate for thee. I would have thee know, fellow, that I am, as it were, one of the King's foresters. Leastwise," muttered he to himself, "I and my friends do take good care of our good sovereign's deer."

"I care not who thou art," answered the bold Tanner, "and unless thou hast many more of thy kind by thee, thou canst never make Arthur a Bland cry 'A mercy.'"

"Is that so?" cried Little John in a rage. "Now, by my faith, thou saucy rogue, thy tongue hath led thee into a pit thou wilt have a sorry time getting out of; for I will give thee such a drubbing as ne'er hast thou had in all thy life before. Take thy staff in thy hand, fellow, for I will not smite an unarmed man."

"Marry come up with a murrain!" cried the Tanner, for he, too, had talked himself into a fume. "Big words ne'er killed so much as a

mouse. Who art thou that talkest so freely of cracking the head of Arthur a Bland? If I do not tan thy hide this day as ne'er I tanned a calf's hide in all my life before, split my staff into skewers for lamb's flesh and call me no more brave man! Now look to thyself, fellow!"

"Stay!" said Little John; "let us first measure our cudgels. I do reckon my staff longer than thine, and I would not take vantage of thee by even so much as an inch."

"Nay, I pass not for length," answered the Tanner. "My staff is long enough to knock down a calf; so look to thyself, fellow, I say again."

So, without more ado, each gripped his staff in the middle, and, with fell and angry looks, they came slowly together.

Now news had been brought to Robin Hood how that Little John, instead of doing his bidding, had passed by duty for pleasure, and so had stopped over night with merry company at the Blue Boar Inn, instead of going straight to Ancaster. So, being vexed to his heart by this, he set forth at dawn of day to seek Little John at the Blue Boar, or at least to meet the yeoman on the way, and ease his heart of what he thought of the matter. As thus he strode along in anger, putting together the words he would use to chide Little John, he heard, of a sudden, loud and angry voices, as of men in a rage, passing fell words back and forth from one to the other. At this, Robin Hood stopped and listened. "Surely," quoth he to himself, "that is Little John's voice, and he is talking in anger also. Methinks the other is strange to my ears. Now Heaven forfend that my good trusty Little John should have fallen into the hands of the King's rangers. I must see to this matter, and that quickly."

Thus spoke Robin Hood to himself, all his anger passing away like a breath from the window-pane, at the thought that perhaps his trusty right-hand man was in some danger of his life. So cautiously he made his way through the thickets whence the voices came, and, pushing aside the leaves, peeped into the little open space where the two men, staff in hand, were coming slowly together.

"Ha!" quoth Robin to himself, "here is merry sport afoot. Now I would give three golden angels from my own pocket if yon stout fellow would give Little John a right sound drubbing! It would please me to see him well thumped for having failed in my bidding. I fear me, though, there is but poor chance of my seeing such a pleasant sight." So saying, he stretched himself at length upon the ground, that he might not only see the sport the better, but that he might enjoy the merry sight at his ease.

As you may have seen two dogs that think to fight, walking slowly round and round each other, neither cur wishing to begin the combat, so those two stout yeomen moved slowly around, each watching for a chance to take the other unaware, and so get in the first blow. At last Little John struck like a flash, and, "rap," the Tanner met the blow and turned it aside, and then smote back at Little John, who also turned the blow; and so this mighty battle began. Then up and down and back and forth they trod, the blows falling so thick and fast that, at a distance, one would have thought that half a score of men were fighting. Thus they fought for nigh a half an hour, until the ground was all ploughed up with the digging of their heels, and their breathing grew labored like the ox in the furrow. But Little John suffered the most, for he had become unused to such stiff labor, and his joints were not as supple as they had been before he went to dwell with the Sheriff.

All this time Robin Hood lay beneath the bush, rejoicing at such a comely bout of quarter-staff. "By my faith!" quoth he to himself, "never had I thought to see Little John so evenly matched in all my life. Belike, though, he would have overcome yon stout fellow before this had he been in his former trim."

At last Little John saw his chance, and, throwing all the strength he felt going from him into one blow that might have felled an ox, he struck at the Tanner with might and main. And now did the Tanner's cowhide cap stand him in good stead, and but for it he might never have held staff in hand again. As it was, the blow he caught beside the head was so shrewd that it sent him staggering across the little glade, so that, if Little John had had the strength to follow up his vantage, it would have been ill for stout Arthur. But he regained himself quickly, and at arm's length, struck back a blow at Little John, and this time the stroke reached its mark, and down went Little John at full length, his cudgel flying from his hand as he fell. Then, raising his staff, stout Arthur dealt him another blow upon the ribs.

"Hold!" roared Little John. "Wouldst thou strike a man when he is down?"

"Ay, marry would I," quoth the Tanner, giving him another thwack with his staff.

"Stop!" roared Little John. "Help! hold, I say! I yield me! I yield me, I say, good fellow!"

"Hast thou had enough?" asked the Tanner, grimly, holding his staff aloft.

"Ay, marry, and more than enough."

"And thou dost own that I am the better man of the two?"

"Yea, truly, and a murrain seize thee!" said Little John, the first aloud and the last to his beard.

"Then thou mayst go thy ways; and thank thy patron saint that I am a merciful man," said the Tanner.

"A plague o' such mercy as thine!" said Little John, sitting up and feeling his ribs where the Tanner had cudgelled him. "I make my vow, my ribs feel as though every one of them were broken in twain. I tell thee, good fellow, I did think there was never a man in all Nottinghamshire could do to me what thou hast done this day."

"And so thought I, also," cried Robin Hood, bursting out of the thicket and shouting with laughter till the tears ran down his cheeks. "O man, man!" said he, as well as he could for his mirth, " 'a didst go over like a bottle knocked from a wall. I did see the whole merry bout, and never did I think to see thee yield thyself so, hand and foot, to any man in all merry England. I was seeking thee, to chide thee for leaving my bidding undone; but thou hast been paid all I owed thee, full measure, pressed down and overflowing, by this good fellow. Marry, 'a did reach out his arm full length whilst thou stood gaping at him, and, with a pretty rap, tumbled thee over as never have I seen one tumbled before." So spoke bold Robin, and all the time Little John sat upon the ground, looking as though he had sour curds in his mouth. "What may be thy name, good fellow?" said Robin, next, turning to the Tanner.

"Men do call me Arthur a Bland," spoke up the Tanner, boldly; "and now what may be thy name?"

"Ha, Arthur a Bland!" quoth Robin, "I have heard thy name before, good fellow. Thou didst break the crown of a friend of mine at the fair at Ely last October. The folk there call him Jock o'Nottingham; we call him Will Scathelock. This poor fellow whom thou hast so belabored is counted the best hand at the quarterstaff in all merry England. His name is Little John, and mine Robin Hood."

"How!" cried the Tanner, "art thou indeed the great Robin Hood, and is this the famous Little John? Marry, had I known who thou art, I would never have been so bold as to lift my hand against thee. Let me help thee to thy feet, good Master Little John, and let me brush the dust from off thy coat."

"Nay," quoth Little John, testily, at the same time rising carefully, as though his bones had been made of glass, "I can help myself, good fellow, without thy aid; and, let me tell thee, had it not been for that vile cowskin cap of thine, it would have been ill for thee this day."

At this Robin laughed again, and, turning to the Tanner, he said, "Wilt thou join my band, good Arthur? for I make my vow thou art one of the stoutest men that ever mine eyes beheld."

"Will I join thy band?" cried the Tanner, joyfully; "ay, marry, will I! Hey for a merry life!" cried he, leaping aloft and snapping his fingers, "and hey for the life I love! Away with tanbark and filthy vats and foul cowhides! I will follow thee to the ends of the earth, good master, and not a herd of dun deer in all the forest but shall know the sound of the twang of my bowstring."

"As for thee, Little John," said Robin, turning to him and laughing, "thou wilt start once more for Ancaster, and we will go part way with thee, for I will not have thee turn again to either the right hand or the left till thou hast fairly gotten away from Sherwood. There are other inns that thou knowest yet, hereabouts." Thereupon, leaving the thickets, they took once more to the highway, and departed upon their business.

### from THE HOUND OF ULSTER

*Rosemary Sutcliff*

*This selection from* The Hound of Ulster *describes the settlement of a long quarrel among the three heroes and comrades (Laery, Conall, and Cuchulain) as to which of them should be called the "Champion of all the Heroes of Ireland." The quarrel was brought about by the lies and maneuverings of the chieftain, Bricrieu, a wily troublemaker. In this episode the three heroes are finally sent by their king, Conor, to Curoi of Kerry, to have him decide the matter, all previous attempts at arbitration having failed.*

### The Championship of Ireland

And when Conor the King could make himself heard, he said, coldly angry, 'Then here is my word. You shall go to Curoi of Kerry with this accursed claim; his sight is deeper and his powers older even than those of the Druids, and it may be that he can settle the thing once and for all. Meanwhile, let me hear no more of it.'

So next day the three heroes and their charioteers set out to lay the matter before Curoi the Lord of Kerry.

He was gone from home when they came clattering up the chariot way into the great Dūn on its coastwise headland where he had his palace. But Blanid his wife greeted them softly and warmly, lifting long eyelids at each in turn. And when she had heard what brought them to Dūn Curoi, she said 'Surely that is a thing that can be settled easily enough. But my lord will be three nights from home, and though he has left warriors set about me, I am a foolish woman and grow nervous when he is not by my side. Therefore, let me beg of you as a favour that each of you in turn will watch one night outside the stockade of the Dūn. In that way I shall feel safe.'

That night, when the time came for the warriors to seek their sleeping places, Laery, who was so much the eldest of the three, claimed the first watch, and took up his position outside the big thorn bush that closed the stockade. And Curoi's Queen went to her own chamber and lit a small fire in a brazier and fed it with strange and unholy things until it burned blue; and began to comb her crow-black hair and sing, weaving the

"The Championship of Ireland." From *The Hound of Ulster* by Rosemary Sutcliff. Copyright © 1963 by Rosemary Sutcliff. Reprinted by permission of the publishers, E. P. Dutton & Co., Inc. and The Bodley Head

charm that guarded the gate from all comers after nightfall—and other spells besides.

The night wore on quietly, and Laery was almost asleep leaning on his spear, when he saw a great shadow rising from the sea. Denser and darker and more menacing it grew, until it took the shape of a monstrous human figure, and the moonlight was blotted out behind its shoulders. And Laery saw with a thrill of horror that it carried two war spears whose shafts were branch-stripped oak trees.

'This is a bad night for Ulster,' said the Shadow Giant, and the voice of him boomed hollow as the sea in a cave. And on the word he flung both his spears at Laery the Triumphant; but they passed him by, one on either side, and stood quivering in the massive timber ramparts of the Dūn. Then Laery flung his own spears, and though they were better aimed, he might as well have thrown at a thundercloud as at the great mass towering over him; and with a boom of laughter the monster stooped and caught him up, gripping him so hard in one hand as almost to crush his ribs like egg-shells, and tossed him over the ramparts of the Dūn.

The tumult roused the warriors within, and they came running with Cuchulain and Conall at their head, and found Laery lying just inside the stockade, half dead with his bruises and bubbling for breath; and beyond the stockade the moonlight shining bright and unhindered as before.

The next night Conall took the watch, and all happened in the same way. And when the warriors came running to his aid, he told them of the fight with the giant, just as Laery had done, but like Laery, he could not bring himself to tell how the giant had tossed him contemptuously like a bundle of old rags over the wall. And so, knowing of the spell that Blanid the Queen set every night on the gateway, all men believed that both had jumped the high stockade.

The third night Cuchulain, the youngest, took up his watch outside the Dūn, and the Queen went to her chamber and made her blue fire and let down her black hair to weave the same spells as before, but this time she braided her hair into strange patterns and with each pattern she made another spell that she had not woven last night nor the night before, and little winds ran about the place and small shapeless things squeaked in the corners.

And Cuchulain, leaning on his spear before the gateway, had a quiet watch until midnight. And then he thought he saw nine grey shadows creeping towards him. 'Who comes?' he shouted. 'If you be friends, stand where you are; if you be foes, come on!'

And the nine shadow-warriors raised a great shout and sprang upon him all together, like hounds pulling down a stag; and he fought them all together, shouting his war-cry that made the very timbers of the Dūn shudder behind him, and slew them or drove them back into mist or hacked them into the ground. Then nine more of the shadows leapt upon him, and for the third time, nine more, and all of them Cuchulain dealt with; and then spent and breathless, sat down on a boulder beside the gate to rest.

And as he sat with his head sunk on his breast, he heard a great boom and crash of waves as though of a winter storm beating on the shore, though all about him the night was still. And looking up, he saw a monstrous dragon threshing up from the water. Higher and higher into the air it rose in an arching blaze of fearful glory like a shooting star, and its wings spread half across the sky as it sank with terrible open jaws towards Cuchulain.

Cuchulain's weariness dropped from him like a threadbare cloak, and he sprang to his feet, then made the Hero's Salmon Leap straight up to meet the winged terror, and thrust the full length of his arm down its throat. It was as though his arm was engulfed to the shoulder in living fire, and the hot stinking breath of the creature beat in his face. His hand found the huge pulsing heart and tore it out by the roots.

The monster fell out of the air, black blood bursting from its mouth, and the blaze of its eyes dying out like the red gleeds of a sinking fire. Cuchulain sprang upon the body of the dead monster, and smiting off its head, set it on the pile of three times nine grey snarling warriors' heads he had raised already. And again he sank down on the boulder.

It was almost dawn when he became aware of the shadow coming up from the sea that both Laery and Conall had encountered. Cuchulain rose to his feet and stood waiting while the shadow darkened and took on giant shape.

'This is a bad night for Ulster,' said the shape, raising the first of the two great spears.

'Yet it may be a worse night for you!' Cuchulain cried.

And the two spears came whistling one after the other, missing him as narrowly as they had missed Laery and Conall, to crash deep into the timber walls of Dūn Curoi; and the monster stooped to grapple with him. But in the same instant Cuchulain sprang up, sword in hand, and leaping as high as the giant's head, flashed in a mighty blow that brought him tumbling to his knees. The giant roared out in a great anguished voice, and with the cry still hanging in the air, was gone like a curl of wood-smoke that the wind whips away.

The first faint light of dawn was broadening over the sea, and Cuchulain knew that there would be no more comers that night, and weary as he was, he thought to go back into the Dūn and rest. But the spells that held the gateway would not yield until the first rays of the sun touched the threshold, and if, as he believed, the other two had leapt the stockade, then so could he. Twice he tried the leap, and twice, with his weariness on him, he failed; and then a great rage rose in him that he could not do what his comrades had done, and with the rage, his utmost strength came upon him, and the Hero light began to flicker like summer lightning about his head, and he took a little run, and vaulting on his spear, went up and over, so high and far that the leap carried him not merely across the wall but into the heart of the Dūn, and he landed on his feet again in the inner court, on the very threshold of Curoi's hall.

He sank down on the door sill, and leaning against the painted doorpost, heaved a great slow sigh.

And Curoi's wife came out from the hall behind him and stooped to touch his shoulder, letting the darkness of her hair trail all across his face. 'That is the sigh of a weary conqueror, not of a beaten man,' she said. 'Come in now, and eat and rest.'

Later, she showed to all three the pile of heads that lay at her gate and said, 'Those are beside the Shadow Giant, who leaves no trace. Now are you content to yield to Cuchulain the Champion's Portion?' she said.

But still the other two would not yield the victory, Laery out of hot jealousy and Conall because by that time he was growing ashamed, and shame always made him the more stubborn. 'No!' said Laery. 'And how should we be content? All men know that Cuchulain was fathered within the Hollow Hills. His own kin among the Lordly People have aided him in this; therefore the contest is an unfair one.'

'Then there is no more that I can do to help you settle the thing,' said Blanid; and she looked just as any other woman whose patience is worn into holes, save that the dark hair on the head of her lifted and crackled like the fur of a black cat that is stroked the wrong way when there is thunder in the air. 'Go home now to Emain Macha, and wait there until my Lord Curoi himself brings you his judgement. But see that you keep the peace with each other while you wait, and whatever the judgement of Curoi may be, see that you accept it, lest Ulster become a laughing stock to Munster and Leinster and Tara and Connacht, for this child's quarrel among her greatest heroes!'

So the three returned to King Conor with the quarrel still unhealed between them, but they kept the peace as Curoi's wife had commanded.

And the days went by and the days went by with no word from Curoi of Kerry. And then one evening when all the Red Branch Warriors were at meat in the King's Hall, save for Conall who was off hunting and his foster brother Cuchulain who had driven down to his own lands of Murthemney to see how the work went on the new house that his men were raising within the old ring-banks of Dūn Dealgan, the door flew open as though at a great blast from the first of the winter gales that was howling like a wolf pack outside. And as all eyes leapt towards it, a terrible figure strode through into the wind-scurried firelight. A creature like a man but taller than any mortal man, horrible to see, and with the yellow eyes of a wolf that glared about the hall as he came. He was clad only in wolfskins roughly sewn together, and a grey mantle over them, and shaded himself from the light of fire and torches with a young oak tree torn up by the roots; and in his free hand he swung a mighty

axe with a keen and cruelly shining edge.

Up the hall strode the horrifying visitor, where every warrior had sprung to his feet, and leaned himself against the massive carved and painted roof-tree beside the central hearth.

'Who are you?' asked Cethern Son of Findtan, striving to make a jest of it. 'Are you come to be our candlestick, or would you burn the house down? Go farther down the hall, my large and hairy friend.'

'Men call me Uath the Stranger, and I am come for neither of those purposes,' returned the giant, in a voice as terrible as his looks. 'I come to see whether, here among the Red Branch Warriors of Ulster, I may find the thing that I have failed to find elsewhere in all Ireland.'

'And what would that be?' demanded Conor the King.

'A man to keep the bargain that he makes with me.'

'And this bargain? Is it then so hard to keep?'

The stranger hunched his great skin-clad shoulders. 'It would seem so.' Then he swung up

the great axe he carried, and held it high, so that all might see the glitter of the firelit blade. 'Behold this axe of mine, is she not fair? But always she is hungry—hungry for the blood of men. Any man bold enough to grasp her tonight may use her to cut my head from my shoulders—provided that he comes here to meet me again tomorrow night that I may return the blow.'

A low murmur of voices, half awed, half angry, sounded all down the crowded benches of the hall; and the stranger looked round him with eyes that blazed like a wolf's when they catch the edge of the firelight. 'The Heroes of the Red Branch are accounted foremost in all Ireland for courage, honour, strength and truth; therefore, let you prove it by finding me, from among you, a man to keep this bargain with me —any man save the King.' His voice rose to a roar like that of a gale among trees. 'If you fail to find me such a champion, then must I say before all men that Ulster has lost her courage and is dishonoured!'

Hardly had he made an end than Laery sprang from his seat. 'Not yet is Ulster without a champion! Give me the axe, and kneel down, fellow!'

'Not so fast! Not so fast, manikin!' Uath the Stranger laughed and began to caress the gleaming axe blade, murmuring over it in a tongue that was strange to all men there. Then handing the weapon to Laery, he knelt and laid his neck over a mighty oak log beside the fire. Laery stood over him, swinging the great axe to test its weight and balance, then brought it crashing down with such force that the stranger's head leapt apart from his body, and the blade bit deep into the log.

Then a horrified gasp broke from all beholders, for as Laery the Triumphant stood back, the body of the stranger twitched, then rose and pulled the axe from the block and picked up its own head from where it had rolled against the hearthstone, and strode down the hall and out into the wild night; and it seemed that the very flames of the torches burned blue behind his passing.

And Laery stood beside the fire, looking as though he had been struck blind.

Next evening the Red Branch Warriors sat at supper in the King's Hall. But they ate little and talked little; and all eyes were turned towards the door. It burst open as before, and in strode Uath the Stranger, with his hideous head set as firmly as ever on his shoulders, and the huge axe swinging in his hand.

As before, he came and leaned against the rooftree and looked about him with yellow eyes under his brows. 'Where is the warrior with whom I last night made a bargain?'

And King Conor Mac Nessa demanded also of his warriors, 'Where is Laery the Triumphant?'

And up and down the benches the warriors looked at each other, but no man had seen Laery the Triumphant that evening.

'So not even among the flower of the Ulster Warriors is there one to keep his word! Never think again to hold your heads high among the Chariot Chiefs of the world, oh small whipped curs of Ulster who cannot count among you one champion whose honour counts as much with him as a whole skin.'

Conall had returned from his hunting and was in the hall that night, and he sprang up, crying, 'Make the bargain afresh, oh Uath the Stranger; make it with me, and you shall not have cause a second time to cry shame on the men of Ulster!''

So the stranger laughed again, and made his magic in a strange tongue, and knelt for Conall as he had knelt for Laery. And again when the blow had been struck, he rose and took up the axe and his own severed head and strode out into the night.

The next evening Conall took his accustomed place among the warriors at supper, white and silent, but determined on his fate. Only when the door burst open as before, and the dreadful figure came striding up the hall, his own courage broke, for it was one thing to die in the red blaze of battle, with company on the journey, and quite another to lay one's head on the block in cold blood, for such an executioner; and he slipped down behind the benches and made for the small postern doorway of the hall.

So when Uath the Stranger called for Conall of the Victories, there was no answer save the click of the falling door pin.

Then Uath looked about him at the shamed and angry faces of King and warriors. 'A pitiful thing it is to see how men such as the Red

Branch Warriors hanker after a great name and yet lack the courage to deserve it! Great warriors indeed you are, who cannot furnish forth *one* man to keep his faith with me! Truly even Cuchulain, though he is nothing but a boy that must stain his chin with bramble juices when he wishes to seem a man, one would think too proud to behave as these two mighty heroes have behaved!'

Cuchulain rose from his place among the Royal kinsmen, and flung his defiance down the hall in a trumpet shout, 'Young I may be, Uath the Stranger, but I keep my word!'

'Come you and prove it, then,' said Uath the Stranger, 'for it is one thing to say and another to do!'

And with a great cry Cuchulain came leaping down the hall and seized the axe from the giant's hand, and springing up from the floor, smote the Stranger's head from his shoulders without even waiting for him to kneel down.

Uath the Stranger lurched like an oak tree in a gale, then steadied, and took back the axe from Cuchulain as though there were nothing odd in the way of it at all, and strode after his head which had bounced like a great hurley ball far off under one of the benches; and so walked down the hall and out into the night, the flames of the torches burning blue behind him.

Next night Cuchulain took his usual place among the warriors. And though the rest, watching him, saw that he was very white and that he scarcely touched the food but drank more than usual of the mead, he had not the look of a man who would take one step backward from the thing that he had come to meet.

Late into the evening, once again the wind rose and the door burst open, and in strode Uath the Stranger, wearing his terrible majesty like a cloud of darkness upon him, and cried out, striking the butt of his axe against the roof-tree, 'Where is Cuchulain? Let him come out to me now, if he would keep his bargain!'

Cuchulain rose in his place and stepped forward. 'I am here.'

'The sadness is in your voice,' Uath said, 'and who shall wonder. Let it be a comfort to you when the axe falls, that you have redeemed the honour of Ulster.' He fingered the axe edge with head cocked, as a harper tuning his instrument.

'Kneel down, now.'

Cuchulain cast one last look round the great hall, seeing Emer's white stone-still face among the women's benches, and the faces of the King, and his friends, and the hounds that he had loved. Then he knelt and laid his head on the great log beside the fire.

'Stretch out your neck farther,' said the voice of Uath, tree-tall above him.

'You are playing with me as a cat plays with a bird!' Cuchulain said angrily. 'Kill me swiftly, for I did not torment you with waiting last night!'

The stranger swung up his axe until the butt of it broke through the rafters with a crash like that of a great tree falling in a storm, then brought it sweeping down in a glittering arc; and the crash of the blow seemed to make the whole hall jump on its foundations. And of the men watching, some covered their eyes, and some could not look away from the horror.

But the young warrior knelt perfectly unharmed, and beside him, no longer the hideous stranger, stood Curoi of Kerry, leaning on his great axe which had bitten deep into the paved floor, smashing the flagstones within a hand's breadth of Cuchulain's head.

'Did I not send you the word through my Queen that I would bring you my decision by and by?' said Curoi. 'Rise up now, Cuchulain.' And as Cuchulain got slowly to his feet and looked about him, as though he were not sure even now that his head was secure upon his shoulders, he said, 'Is the thing still in doubt? Here stands the Champion of all the Heroes of Ireland. The only one among you all, who dared to keep his bargain with death because he gave his word. There is none among the Heroes of Ulster to equal the Hound for courage and truth and honour, and therefore to him I adjudge the Championship and the Champion's Portion at any feast where he may be present, and to Emer his wife, the first place among the princesses of Emain Macha.' For an instant he seemed almost as terrible as Uath the Stranger had been. 'This is the word of Curoi of Kerry, and woe to any warrior who shall dispute it!'

And as he spoke, suddenly it was only his voice that was there, and the firelight shining through the place where he had been. And with the last words spoken, nothing was left of Curoi at all, only the foredoor of the hall crashed shut as though a great wind had blown it to.

For the time that a man might take to draw seven breaths, no one spoke or moved in the hall of Conor the King. And then men began to leave their places and crowd round Cuchulain where he still stood beside the hearth.

Laery came with the rest, and Conall of the Victories to set his arm about Cuchulain's shoulders.

'Why did you speak evil words of me to such as Bricrieu Poison Tongue?' Cuchulain said.

And in the same instant Conall said, 'Why did you speak poison of me to Bricrieu the Gadfly? I would not have spoken so of *you*.'

And Laery grumbled in his russet beard, 'Young cubs, you are, to say scornful things of me to that bird of ill omen, Bricrieu! But I am older, and should have had some wisdom.'

And they looked from one to another in sudden understanding. 'Bricrieu! Of course!' and then began to laugh, and the laughter spread all up and down the hall and broke in waves of mirth against the rafters.

And from that time forward, Cuchulain was acknowledged by all men to be Champion of all the Heroes of Ireland.

### *from* HERO TALES FROM THE AGE OF CHIVALRY
#### *Grant Uden*

*Retold from the Froissart Chronicles, the tale of the valorous Jeanne de Montfort is based, as are all his histories, in part on observation and in part on conversations with participants in events. This was the period of the Hundred Years' War between France and England; it was the time when the nobility observed an elaborate code of chivalry. Countess Jeanne, a doughty heroine of Brittany, led an army in her husband's absence to save his honor and his hope for a ducal throne.*

#### *The Adventure of the Countess Jeanne*

Let us today take the case of the Countess Jeanne of Montfort, wife of Count John. . . .

I hope that some day you will come to know the fair duchy of Brittany, far to the northwest from Chimay; a land of proud, sturdy, fierce men, always quick to fight beneath their ermine banner; a land of sunny streams and smiling villages on the one hand, and on the other, of battlefields and fortified towns. Chief among the towns is Rennes, where the black-a-vised young Bertrand of Brittany, only twenty years old, rode incognito in a great tournament and broke fifteen lances. Then his own father, not recognizing his son in his borrowed armor, rode against this presumptuous unknown knight, who pulled his horse aside and refused the challenge rather than lift weapon against his sire.

It was in the cathedral at Rennes, just before that tournament, that a great wedding took place between Countess Jeanne, niece of old Duke John of Brittany, and Charles, Count of Blois and nephew of King Philip of France. In the congregation that day, amid all the noblest blood of Brittany, was another Countess Jeanne, wife of the Count of Montfort, half brother to old Duke John.

A puzzle of names and relationships, is it not? But keep the two Jeannes and their husbands distinct in your mind, for, assuredly, they were very separate in life. Duke John died. And who should succeed to the throne of the duchy? The King of France, ever ready to get some grasp over the fair domain of Brittany, strongly supported his nephew Charles of Blois and his Breton bride. But, on the other hand, Count John of Montfort laid his claim, backed by his proud wife. And where should the lord of Montfort look for support? Where better than across the Channel to the ancient foe of the King of France, the King of England?

Edward III was ready enough to help any defiance of King Philip of France. So it came to war, with, ranged on one side, the King of France and Charles of Blois, and on the other the King of England and John of Montfort—oh! and Countess Jeanne of Montfort. Let us never forget this Countess Jeanne, for, faith, she was not a lady to allow herself to be forgotten.

I will not weary you with all the struggle so far as John of Montfort is concerned. He was captured in Nantes by a great French army and carried off captive to Paris, where he was held for three years.

When this happened, the Countess of Montfort was in Rennes, where they brought her the news of her husband's defeat. Though she was sorrowful enough of heart, she did not waste time in useless pining, for she had the courage of a man and the heart of a lion. She immediately set about rallying her friends and all the soldiers she could muster, showing them her little son John, named after his father, and saying, "Sirs, do not be so cast down by the loss of my lord the Count. He is one man, and here is another, who shall restore his father and shall be sufficient leader to you all. I have money enough to pay all the soldiers and captains I need."

Having thus put good heart into those at Rennes, Countess Jeanne set out for all her other garrisons and fortresses in Brittany, taking with her always her young son, making the same plea, putting spirit into her followers, and paying them liberally into the bargain. Then she settled down for the winter in Hennebon, a fortress on the river Blavet near the coast, so that she could keep in touch with her ally the King of England across the water. And all through the winter she periodically sent to the other garrisons, paying them generous wages and keeping up their spirits for the next campaigning season.

With the coming of spring the armies stirred again and Charles of Blois came into Brittany with a great host, intent on subduing the duchy. The first place he tackled was Rennes which, you will remember, had been the city where he had been married in the cathedral; the place, too, where Countess Jeanne had begun her courageous tour of defiance. She had left there a strong Breton captain, Sir Walter Cadoudel, who held out with great valor and for a time inflicted much damage on the attackers.

Unfortunately, the citizens became so weary of the struggle and saw so little hope of relief that they implored Sir Walter to surrender, and when he would not consent, seized him and flung him into prison, after which they gave up the city to Charles of Blois on condition that all the Montfort followers could leave unharmed. This, Charles agreed to, and Sir Walter was able to make his way to Hennebon to continue his fight for Countess Jeanne who, immediately she knew of the invasion of Charles of Blois, had sent another of her knights, Sir Amery de Clisson, to England to beg the assistance of King Edward. He was very ready to give it and appointed Sir Walter Manny, one of the greatest English captains, to lead an army. Sir Walter embarked with a company of knights and some six thousand of the best archers in England. This was an encouraging start, but they ran into heavy gales and were at sea nearly six weeks before they could land in France.

Things had not begun well for my lady Jeanne. Sir Walter Manny hovered on the high seas, so near and yet so far, and Rennes had fallen. Moreover, Charles of Blois was sweeping triumphantly on to Hennebon, resolved to capture the Countess and bring the whole war to a quick end.

Inside Hennebon there was a great bustle. The alarm bell was rung and every man was ordered to arm and prepare for the defense of the town. When Charles of Blois arrived he encamped his forces, and some of the young bloods immediately tried a skirmish at the town barriers. They were dealt with sharply by the defenders and retired with little luck.

The third day a major attack was mounted, from early morning till noon. The first onslaught was repulsed with heavy losses to the attackers. Charles's captains, when they saw their men giving ground, were in a great rage and sent them in to try again more furiously than before.

Jeanne, Countess of Montfort, was everywhere at once. She put on armor, mounted a great warhorse, and rode from street to street, cheering on the citizens to the battle. Neither did she confine her efforts to the men. Under her orders the girls and womenfolk cut their gowns short, loaded themselves with stones from the streets, and staggered with them to the walls so that they could be hurled down on the attackers. They also carried up pots full of lime to burn and choke any who tried to scale the walls.

All this would have been more than enough

for most women. But not Countess Jeanne. She climbed the top of a tower to see how the French army was faring outside. As she looked out over the plain, with its press of steel-clad men storming to the attack, its shouting captains urging on the siege engines, she noticed one thing that interested her greatly. The camp was deserted. The long lines of tents and pavilions were emptied of soldiers. Only boys and camp servants were to be seen moving about. She came quickly down from the tower still in her armor, and called for her great courser again. She summoned three hundred mounted men and rode with them to one of the town gates that was free from attack. They flung it open, and at the head of her three hundred she dashed straight for the deserted enemy camp. There they slashed the tent ropes, demolished the fine lodgings of Charles of Blois and his lords, and set fire to the whole encampment.

The frightened camp servants scattered and fled.

Hearing the din, the French knights looked back from Hennebon to see the rising columns of smoke. Shouting "Treason! Treason!" they left the assault on the town and made their way back to what was left of their base.

The Countess Jeanne looked through the billowing smoke and saw the knights and men-at-arms crowding back. Her return to Hennebon was cut off! Rallying her force she turned her horse, skirted the town, and rode hard for the port of Brest some seventy miles away.

When the marshal of the French army saw the Countess and her company galloping away, he set off in pursuit with a great force and managed to cut off a few that were not so well horsed as the rest. But most of them, riding hell-for-leather, got safely to Brest with the Countess Jeanne and were received by the garrison with great joy.

The disconsolate French, left with their camp and all their stores burned, wondered if they could make do with lodgings made of boughs and leaves from the trees outside Hennebon. Those inside the town, not knowing what had become of their valiant Countess, were desperately worried. For five days they heard nothing. Then at sunrise the watchers saw the distant light strike on bridle and armor. My lady Mont-

fort came riding rapidly around the edge of the French army with five hundred men behind her. Leaving Brest at midnight, they had returned to the defense of Hennebon. With a great wave of cheering and a blare of trumpets, the defenders threw open the gates. The astonished French, who thought they had seen the last of this unusual captain, watched helplessly. By the time they had recovered their wits, the gates were slammed and barred again.

The French army tried one more fierce assault on the town, struggling till noon, but with as little success as before. Then Charles of Blois called off the attack and held a council of war. In the end they decided to split forces. Count Charles marched off with half the host to besiege the castle of Aurai. The rest stayed on at Hennebon but made no further assaults. They sent to Rennes, however, for a dozen large siege engines they had left there, and with their aid kept up a bombardment of stones day and night. This harassed the defenders and was less expensive in lives than making direct attacks. Indeed, they made such good progress with their ceaseless battering that the courage of some of the defenders began to falter and a group of them talked of surrender on condition that they might keep their goods. This did not suit the lionhearted Countess Jeanne. She begged the Breton lords, for the love of God, not to give up, saying she was certain that before three days had passed relief would come.

But counsels against her were strong and made so deep an impression on the chief citizens that they were on the point of yielding up the town and had allowed the French to advance close to the walls for the purpose of taking it over.

Then came the final surprise of this surprising tale.

My lady Montfort, sick at heart that all her efforts should come to nothing, climbed a stair in the castle of Hennebon and, with little spirit left, stared out to sea. She could scarcely believe her eyes. For she saw a distant crowd of sail standing into harbor. Her joyful cries brought the townsfolk running. They crowded to the ramparts and saw for themselves the host of ships, great and small, making for hard-pressed Hennebon.

Sir Walter Manny and his storm-tossed fleet

from England had at last arrived.

That is really the end of the story. If I wished, I could dwell on the reception the Countess gave to Sir Walter Manny when he landed with all his captains. I could tell of the feasting and jollity that made it difficult to remember the town was still under siege.

They did, however, receive a frequent reminder, for the French, furious at the collapse of the surrender negotiations, brought up their largest machine as near as possible to the walls and hurled great stones over them day and night.

In the end, Sir Walter Manny, that great knight who carried the golden lion on the black chevronels, had had enough of the unmannerly machine. He led out a company of archers and men-at-arms who shot down the men who were firing and then broke the siege engine in pieces. For good measure, before the laggard French host was properly astir, they set fire to the camp again! This was too much. The French commander struck camp and straggled off to rejoin Charles of Blois at Aurai.

The Countess Jeanne came down from the castle with a blithesome heart and in her excitement kissed Sir Walter Manny and his companions two or three times, one after the other. It must have been a formidable experience!

Some of the qualities that make folk tales so appealing to children are the same ones they enjoy in modern fanciful stories. Both have action and adventure, and both have that delectable ingredient, magic. To children, especially to younger children, there is no great difference between the old tales and the newer fantasies. They are alluring in the same way, because what happens in them cannot possibly happen in real life, or because the people (or toys, or animals, or machines) in them are either fabulous and cannot exist, or they cannot exist and speak in the way they do. Trains talk, hobbits and borrowers struggle to survive, dinosaurs make themselves invisible at will, and children encounter ghosts from the past or they move into the past, the future, or other worlds conceived by an author's imagination.

Modern fantasy began in the seventeenth century with adaptations of traditional tales. The stories of Charles Perrault, elaborated versions of simple folklore, became immensely popular in French court circles. After him came Mme. d'Aulnoy and Mme. Leprince de Beaumont in the eighteenth century; their tales were didactic or romantic fairy tales, the most enduring of which has been the latter's "Beauty and the Beast."

Hans Christian Andersen also began with

# MODERN FANTASY

adaptations of folk tales, but the imaginative qualities of his writing and its distinctive style contributed to his position as the true originator of the modern fairy tale. In Andersen's stories, both those he adapted and those he created, there is a variety never equaled by any other writer of fanciful fiction, a freshness and vitality achieved by few.

Some of the finest fantasy written for children has been about animals. This is not surprising, for children and animals seem to have a natural affinity. Generally speaking, animals embody a kind of lost innocence, and their very natures serve as models for what is worst and best in human character. When human faults and virtues are exemplified by animals, we seem to see ourselves rather more clearly.

Then there are countless animal fantasies in which the animals are merely disguised people. Such use of animal characters appears commonly in comic strips and in animated film cartoons. Mickey Mouse is no mouse, and Petunia is no goose. However, we enjoy them immensely. They are the modern equivalent of Aesop, for better or worse. The range of stories in this category is very great, and the quality of stories varies from very good to very bad.

Many writers of animal fantasy, while managing to preserve the natural qualities of the creatures they write about, nevertheless have them behave as though they were people, as do Beatrix Potter, Russell Hoban in the "Frances" stories, and Arnold Lobel. We see this approach in Kipling's *Jungle Book* and in E. B. White's *Charlotte's Web,* books in which animals think and converse like people but never seem to lose their animal qualities.

The personification of inanimate objects is a familiar device in the fairy tale, the modern picture book, and the film cartoon. Not only do young children invest things with life and personality, but so do primitives and perfectly sane civilized adults. We know that primitive people believe demons and gods reside in rocks, trees, lakes, and the forces of nature. But we ourselves give names to our automobiles, boats, and airplanes and talk about them as if they had minds of their own!

Try to enumerate a long list of writers who have successfully brought the inanimate to life so well that readers *believe* it. It is impossible. Only a handful of men and women have had the genius to turn a fairly familiar literary device into the kind of art which sustains a story or a book and achieves credibility. There is no end of storybooks in which the inanimate lives, but there are few such stories that live in our hearts. Who does not believe in Pooh and Pinocchio? Who is not convinced of the passion and faithfulness of the steadfast tin soldier?

Stories about inanimate objects seem to have been Andersen's invention and his special delight. They are good stories, although many of them are sad and adult in theme and therefore not always popular with children. Modern authors have picked up Andersen's innovation and put it to happier and more childlike uses, as Edward Ormondroyd has done in *Theodore* and Rumer Godden has done in her doll series.

The great test for this kind of fantasy is whether or not we are convinced that a love-struck tin soldier really feels or that a small teddy bear is a person to love and cherish. It seems an easy task to pretend that such things live, but it is immensely difficult to accomplish. Writers who wish to animate the inanimate must never shock our sense of credibility. By succeeding in making us believe that objects live, they attune us to other possible dimensions of the familiar world.

Children need a certain degree of experience and maturity before they can appreciate incongruity, which is a key ingredient in most humor and nonsense. The teacher, the librarian, and the parent must thus trust to time and, to some extent, luck in finding stories and books which boys and girls will find funny. Above all things, do not press the search, force the issue, or foist upon unwilling youngsters books they *ought* to laugh over. Leave the matter up to chance for the most part. Humor found by accident and enjoyed with spontaneity is the best and the rarest, and turns up where least expected. Maybe that is the secret!

Humor is, of course, an appealing element of any kind of literature, prose or poetry, fantasy or realism, but not every child responds to every kind of humor. Nonsense may enchant one child, wit another, puns or slapstick still another. Or a child may enjoy the humor of a book one year that he or she would not have appreciated the year before. One of the best ways to extend children's horizons in the enjoyment of humor in fantasy is reading aloud to a group, because the peer influence is strong. It's hard not to laugh when all your friends or classmates are finding a book uproariously enjoyable. One teacher who read Scott Corbett's *Ever Ride a Dinosaur?* to a fourth grade class when it was first published reports that he has had to read it every year since. The grapevine has established the fact that one of the attractions of fourth grade is that funny dinosaur book.

The dilemmas of the Peterkin family have

cheered several generations of children, but some people find the Peterkins stupid rather than hilarious. Such varying reactions merely point up the difficulty of determining what is humorous and what isn't. The humor in those stories is based on the bland obtuseness of the Peterkins, who are direct descendants of the noodleheads of folk tales. In Lloyd Alexander's Prydain cycle, the humor depends on the exaggerated character traits and the dialogue, especially in such characters as Gurgi, with his rhyming words and extravagant emotionalism, or on the outrageous fibbing of the harpist, Fflewddur Flam.

The use of names like Fflewddur Flam is in itself appealing to most children, whether the character is human or invented. Joan Aiken and Leon Garfield, whose stories may be realistic, fantastic, or borderline writing, use colorful names with relish and abandon. And surely some of the creatures of Middle-earth are the more satisfying literary creations because of their names: Belladonna Took is funny even if you know nothing of the character, and so is Bilbo Baggins.

The names are used to help establish character in many books, but while they can add humor to a mediocre fantasy, they cannot in themselves establish character. It is possible to write a good fantasy without solid characterization; it is not possible to write a great fantasy without it. The strength of characterization in the Prydain cycle is what gives it depth. Taran, the protagonist, moves through the five books in a realistic progression in which he changes from a shallow, self-seeking boy to a young man who has learned that a human being's worth is in himself, not in his lineage, and who is more concerned with helping others than with personal gain. The hobbit, Bilbo Baggins, is a conventional little creature whose devotion to his friends and whose resolute courage on their behalf are all the more convincing because he is *not* an adventurous, swashbuckling hero.

The characterization in fantasy must, as it must in other forms of fiction, develop with consistency and in relation to the situations and the events that develop in the story. Hazel, the rabbit who is the leader of the warren in *Watership Down*, learns to make decisions and to handle dissent because he is thrust into the position of having to do so. He does not begin as a heroic chieftain, but he becomes one through a believable chain of events.

No matter how good a fanciful story is, it will not be enjoyed by all children, for there are some who prefer realistic fiction to the exclusion of all other kinds. As with those children who are unmoved by certain varieties of humor, the answer may lie in reading aloud. One may begin with a story that is based in realism in order to draw them toward the genre, a story like *The Ghost of Thomas Kempe*, in which there is strong characterization, humor, a well-constructed plot, and the very real problems of a boy whose reputation for pranks makes it difficult for him to prove his innocence.

Science fiction, which often is very serious and realistic within the fantasy framework, can be a good introduction for the reluctant reader of fanciful tales. *A Wrinkle in Time*, for example, has not only the appeals of magic and beings of another world, but a warm family situation and the same conflict between good and evil that distinguishes much of our folk literature.

Some children—and some adults—object to fantasy because it isn't true, but fantasy has, save perhaps for the tall tales of writers such as Sid Fleischman, some truth in it, whether it is the obvious reality of the daily life of the animals in *Rabbit Hill* or the deeper truths of *A Wrinkle in Time*.

Fantasy is, in one sense, its own best advocate. It is in the realm of the imaginative, and children are imaginative. It stretches and tests the imagination more than any other kind of writing, both with its inner logic and with its more obvious appeals of time-shifts, invented new worlds, supernatural creatures, and magic spells and talismans. Children seldom distinguish, as many adults do, between what is possible and what is impossible. They know, of course, that they are reading about something that cannot happen, but they lose themselves in their reading. They *believe* in the miniature world of the borrowers, in Charlotte changed into Claire, in a girl badger who talks. To introduce them to the variety of stories excerpted here is to widen their horizons.

# Animals and Toys

*from* CHARLOTTE'S WEB

*E. B. White*

*Ask adults to name a children's book, and they are likely to say* Charlotte's Web, *even ahead of* Alice's Adventures in Wonderland.

*When E. B. White was given the prestigious Laura Ingalls Wilder Award [1] in 1970, it was written of* Charlotte's Web: *"When a book has almost universal acclaim from adult critics, and almost universal acceptance by children, it is rarest of the rare.* Charlotte's Web, *E. B. White's second book for children, is such a one. This fantasy about a pig and a spider and about the bittersweet realities of friendship rings real to children, is relished by adults for its wit and poignancy and for the truth which distills from the story, and is becoming a touchstone for imaginative writing for children in our times." [2]*

*In the following selection, Wilbur and the reader first meet Charlotte.*

## Charlotte

The night seemed long. Wilbur's stomach was empty and his mind was full. And when your stomach is empty and your mind is full, it's always hard to sleep.

A dozen times during the night Wilbur woke and stared into the blackness, listening to the sounds and trying to figure out what time it was. A barn is never perfectly quiet. Even at midnight there is usually something stirring.

The first time he woke, he heard Templeton gnawing a hole in the grain bin. Templeton's teeth scraped loudly against the wood and made quite a racket. "That crazy rat!" thought Wil-

[1] The Laura Ingalls Wilder Award is presented once every five years "to an author or illustrator whose works, published in the United States, have over a period of years made a substantial and lasting contribution to literature for children."

[2] Winnifred Moffett Crossley, Chairman, Laura Ingalls Wilder Award Committee, 1970

bur. "Why does he have to stay up all night, grinding his clashers and destroying people's property? Why can't he go to sleep, like any decent animal?"

The second time Wilbur woke, he heard the goose turning on her nest and chuckling to herself.

"What time is it?" whispered Wilbur to the goose.

"Probably-obably-obably about half-past eleven," said the goose. "Why aren't you asleep, Wilbur?"

"Too many things on my mind," said Wilbur.

"Well," said the goose, "that's not *my* trouble. I have nothing at all on my mind, but I've too many things under my behind. Have you ever tried to sleep while sitting on eight eggs?"

"No," replied Wilbur. "I suppose it *is* uncomfortable. How long does it take a goose egg to hatch?"

"Approximately-oximately thirty days, all told," answered the goose. "But I cheat a little. On warm afternoons, I just pull a little straw over the eggs and go out for a walk."

Wilbur yawned and went back to sleep. In his dreams he heard again the voice saying, "I'll be a friend to you. Go to sleep—you'll see me in the morning."

About half an hour before dawn, Wilbur woke and listened. The barn was still dark. The sheep lay motionless. Even the goose was quiet. Overhead, on the main floor, nothing stirred: the cows were resting, the horses dozed. Templeton had quit work and gone off somewhere on an errand. The only sound was a slight scraping noise from the rooftop, where the weather-vane swung back and forth. Wilbur loved the barn when it was like this—calm and quiet, waiting for light.

"Day is almost here," he thought.

Through a small window, a faint gleam appeared. One by one the stars went out. Wilbur could see the goose a few feet away. She sat with head tucked under a wing. Then he could see the sheep and the lambs. The sky lightened.

"Oh, beautiful day, it is here at last! Today I

shall find my friend."

Wilbur looked everywhere. He searched his pen thoroughly. He examined the window ledge, stared up at the ceiling. But he saw nothing new. Finally he decided he would have to speak up. He hated to break the lovely stillness of dawn by using his voice, but he couldn't think of any other way to locate the mysterious new friend who was nowhere to be seen. So Wilbur cleared his throat.

"Attention, please!" he said in a loud, firm voice. "Will the party who addressed me at bedtime last night kindly make himself or herself known by giving an appropriate sign or signal!"

Wilbur paused and listened. All the other animals lifted their heads and stared at him. Wilbur blushed. But he was determined to get in touch with his unknown friend.

"Attention, please!" he said. "I will repeat the message. Will the party who addressed me at bedtime last night kindly speak up. Please tell me where you are, if you are my friend!"

The sheep looked at each other in disgust.

"Stop your nonsense, Wilbur!" said the oldest sheep. "If you have a new friend here, you are probably disturbing his rest; and the quickest way to spoil a friendship is to wake somebody up in the morning before he is ready. How can you be sure your friend is an early riser?"

"I beg everyone's pardon," whispered Wilbur. "I didn't mean to be objectionable."

He lay down meekly in the manure, facing the door. He did not know it, but his friend was very near. And the old sheep was right—the friend was still asleep.

Soon Lurvy appeared with slops for breakfast. Wilbur rushed out, ate everything in a hurry, and licked the trough. The sheep moved off down the lane, the gander waddled along behind them, pulling grass. And then, just as Wilbur was settling down for his morning nap, he heard again the thin voice that had addressed him the night before.

"Salutations!" said the voice.

Wilbur jumped to his feet. "Salu-*what?*" he cried.

"Salutations!" repeated the voice.

"What are *they,* and where are *you?*" screamed Wilbur. "Please, *please,* tell me where you are. And what are salutations?"

"Salutations are greetings," said the voice. "When I say 'salutations,' it's just my fancy way of saying hello or good morning. Actually, it's a silly expression, and I am surprised that I used it at all. As for my whereabouts, that's easy. Look up here in the corner of the doorway! Here I am. Look, I'm waving!"

At last Wilbur saw the creature that had spoken to him in such a kindly way. Stretched across the upper part of the doorway was a big spiderweb, and hanging from the top of the web, head down, was a large grey spider. She was about the size of a gumdrop. She had eight legs, and she was waving one of them at Wilbur in friendly greeting. "See me now?" she asked.

"Oh, yes indeed," said Wilbur. "Yes indeed! How are you? Good morning! Salutations! Very pleased to meet you. What is your name, please? May I have your name?"

"My name," said the spider, "is Charlotte."

"Charlotte what?" asked Wilbur, eagerly.

"Charlotte A. Cavatica. But just call me Charlotte."

"I think you're beautiful," said Wilbur.

"Well, I *am* pretty," replied Charlotte. "There's no denying that. Almost all spiders are rather nice-looking. I'm not as flashy as some, but I'll do. I wish I could see you, Wilbur, as clearly as you can see me."

"Why can't you?" asked the pig. "I'm right here."

"Yes, but I'm near-sighted." replied Charlotte. "I've always been dreadfully near-sighted. It's good in some ways, not so good in others. Watch me wrap up this fly."

A fly that had been crawling along Wilbur's trough had flown up and blundered into the lower part of Charlotte's web and was tangled in the sticky threads. The fly was beating its wings furiously, trying to break loose and free itself.

"First," said Charlotte, "I dive at him." She plunged headfirst toward the fly. As she dropped, a tiny silken thread unwound from her rear end.

"Next, I wrap him up." She grabbed the fly, threw a few jets of silk around it, and rolled it over and over, wrapping it so that it couldn't move. Wilbur watched in horror. He could hardly believe what he was seeing, and although he detested flies, he was sorry for this one.

"There!" said Charlotte. "Now I knock him out, so he'll be more comfortable." She bit the fly. "He can't feel a thing now," she remarked. "He'll make a perfect breakfast for me."

"You mean you *eat* flies?" gasped Wilbur.

"Certainly. Flies, bugs, grasshoppers, choice beetles, moths, butterflies, tasty cockroaches, gnats, midges, daddy longlegs, centipedes, mosquitoes, crickets—anything that is careless enough to get caught in my web. I have to live, don't I?"

"Why, yes, of course," said Wilbur. "Do they taste good?"

"Delicious. Of course, I don't really eat them. I drink them—drink their blood. I love blood," said Charlotte, and her pleasant, thin voice grew even thinner and more pleasant.

"Don't say that!" groaned Wilbur. "Please don't say things like that!"

"Why not? It's true, and I have to say what is true. I am not entirely happy about my diet of flies and bugs, but it's the way I'm made. A spider has to pick up a living somehow or other, and I happen to be a trapper. I just naturally build a web and trap flies and other insects. My mother was a trapper before me. Her mother was a trapper before her. All our family have been trappers. Way back for thousands and thousands of years we spiders have been laying for flies and bugs."

"It's a miserable inheritance," said Wilbur, gloomily. He was sad because his new friend was so bloodthirsty.

"Yes, it is," agreed Charlotte. "But I can't help it. I don't know how the first spider in the early days of the world happened to think up this fancy idea of spinning a web, but she did, and it was clever of her, too. And since then, all of us spiders have had to work the same trick. It's not a bad pitch, on the whole."

"It's cruel," replied Wilbur, who did not intend to be argued out of his position.

"Well, *you* can't talk," said Charlotte. "*You* have your meals brought to you in a pail. Nobody feeds me. I have to get my own living. I live by my wits. I have to be sharp and clever, lest I go hungry. I have to think things out, catch what I can, take what comes. And it just so happens, my friend, that what comes is flies and insects and bugs. And *further*more," said

Charlotte, shaking one of her legs, "do you realize that if I didn't catch bugs and eat them, bugs would increase and multiply and get so numerous that they'd destroy the earth, wipe out everything?"

"Really?" said Wilbur. "I wouldn't want *that* to happen. Perhaps your web is a good thing after all."

The goose had been listening to this conversation and chuckling to herself. "There are a lot of things Wilbur doesn't know about life," she thought. "He's really a very innocent little pig. He doesn't even know what's going to happen to him around Christmastime; he has no idea that Mr. Zuckerman and Lurvy are plotting to kill him." And the goose raised herself a bit and poked her eggs a little further under her so that they would receive the full heat from her warm body and soft feathers.

Charlotte stood quietly over the fly, preparing to eat it. Wilbur lay down and closed his eyes. He was tired from his wakeful night and from the excitement of meeting someone for the first time. A breeze brought him the smell of clover—the sweet-smelling world beyond his fence. "Well," he thought, "I've got a new friend, all right. But what a gamble friendship is! Charlotte is fierce, brutal, scheming, bloodthirsty—everything I don't like. How can I learn to like her, even though she is pretty and, of course, clever?"

Wilbur was merely suffering the doubts and fears that often go with finding a new friend. In good time he was to discover that he was mistaken about Charlotte. Underneath her rather bold and cruel exterior, she had a kind heart, and she was to prove loyal and true to the very end.

### from RABBIT HILL
*Robert Lawson*

*Rabbit Hill was the name of Robert Lawson's home in Connecticut, and the multitude of small animals that inhabited the grounds gave him the idea for what has become a book loved by many*

*children. The sequel to* Rabbit Hill *is* The Tough Winter, *which never became as popular as the first story of the animals of the Hill.*

### Willie's Bad Night

It was Bluegrass that almost proved the undoing of Willie Fieldmouse. He was on the window sill, as usual, watching and listening to the Folks. This evening, having finished their gardening plans, they were talking of grass seed. Willie was not especially interested and was only half listening when he was suddenly electrified by a familiar word.

"This book," the Man was saying, "recommends a mixture of Red Top, White Clover and Kentucky Bluegrass."

*Bluegrass! Kentucky Bluegrass!* Wouldn't Father Rabbit be pleased! He must be told at once!

Haste and excitement made Willie inexcusably careless. He should have remembered that the lid of the rainwater barrel was old and rotted, that there were several dangerous holes in it. He did not, and his leap from the window sill landed him squarely in one of the holes. He grabbed frantically as he went through, but the rotten wood crumbled under his claws and with a sickening shock he plunged into the icy water.

He came up gasping. The cold seemed to have driven all the air from his lungs but he managed one wild squeak for help before the water closed over him again. He was very feeble when he came up this time. He struggled weakly toward the side of the barrel but the walls were slippery with moss and his paws too numbed to get a hold. Faintly he squeaked once more—why didn't someone help him—Father or Little Georgie or Phewie? As the water closed over him for the last time he was dimly conscious of a noise and a brilliant glare of light. Then the light went out, everything went out.

A long time later, he never knew how long, Willie's eyes fluttered open. He dimly realized that he was still wet, that uncontrollable fits of shivering shook him. He seemed to be lying in a nest of some soft white stuff which was very comfortable, he could see the glow of dancing flames and feel a gentle warmth. Then he closed his eyes again.

Later they opened and he saw the faces of the Folks bending over his bed. It was terrifying to see Folks this close. They looked enormous, like something in a nightmare. He tried to burrow into the soft cotton when his nose suddenly caught the smell of warm milk. Someone was holding a medicine dropper before his face—on the end of it a white drop hung. Weakly, Willie licked at it—it was delicious. There was something else in the milk, something that coursed hotly through all his body. He felt stronger already and sucked at the dropper until it was completely empty. Ah, that was better! His stomach was swollen with the comforting warm food, his eyelids drooped and again he slept.

There was consternation among the Animals when Willie failed to report to the group waiting at the burrow. Father and Uncle Analdas immediately organized a searching party but were unable to find any trace of him.

Phewie, who had been enjoying the freedom of the garbage pail, reported that he had heard a mouse-cry, had seen the Folks emerge from the house with flashlights and do something at the rain barrel. Just what, he did not know.

Willie's oldest cousin climbed to the window sill but found the window closed. The Gray Squirrel was wakened and sent to the roof to investigate. He listened at all the upstairs windows without discovering anything unusual.

"It's that dingblasted old Cat," shouted Uncle Analdas. "The sneakin', deceitful, hypocritical scoundrel, makin' out he's old and harmless. Wish I'd kicked him in the face like I planned to."

Porkey was inclined to blame Tim McGrath. "It's him and his traps," he argued. "Always talkin' traps he is, and poisons. Likely he led them Folks into settin' a trap fer Willie."

Father said little, but all the night through he, Uncle Analdas and Little Georgie coursed the Hill like setter dogs, searching every inch of field and wall, looking under every shrub and bush. Not till dawn approached did they admit defeat and return wearily to the burrow where Mother, very red-eyed and sniffly, had a hot breakfast waiting for them.

But of all the Animals the Mole's rage and grief were the most moving. His pal, his Eyes, were lost and he was helpless to join in the search!

"I'll fix 'em," he said grimly. "I'll fix 'em.

There won't never a blade of grass take root on this place—never! Never a bulb or a shrub stay set neither. I'll tear 'em up and I'll root 'em out, I'll dig and I'll heave and I'll burrow, I'll fetch in every friend and relation from here to Danbury way and tear this place apart till they wish they'd never—"

His threats were muffled as he plunged frantically into the neatly rolled front lawn. All night the other Animals could hear his grunting, could see the surface of the ground ripple and heave like troubled waters.

It was gray dawn when Willie woke again. The room was chilly but on the hearth a few embers still smouldered and the bricks gave out a comforting warmth. He eased himself out of the cardboard box where he had slept and drew closer to the glowing coals. All his muscles felt stiff and sore, he was still a little wobbly but otherwise he felt very well. He bathed a bit and stretched himself, feeling better all the time. That warm milk and whatever was in it had certainly tasted good. He wished he had some more. He ought to be getting along home but there was no way out—the doors and windows were all closed.

The sun had risen before he heard footsteps approaching through the house. He caught a whiff of the Man's pipe smell, heard the soft pad of Mr. Muldoon's paws. Wildly he looked for a hiding place but no good one offered. On either side of the fireplace bookshelves extended from floor to ceiling and in desperation he leaped to the top of the first row of books and crouched back into the darkest corner just as the door opened.

The Folks came in and at once inspected the box. "Well, well, he's gone," said the Man. "Must be feeling better. Wonder where he is?"

The Lady did not answer. She was watching Mr. Muldoon who had wandered idly over to the bookshelves.

Willie backed as far into the corner as he could squeeze, his heart pounding wildly as the great cat drew closer and closer. The head seemed huge now, the mouth was opening, two rows of white fangs showed, his eyes were gleaming yellow coals. Willie, petrified with fear, could only watch helplessly as the red jaws opened wider and wider. He could feel the hot breath, strong with the odor of canned salmon.

Then Mr. Muldoon sneezed.

"There he is," the Lady said quietly, "on the books, in the corner. Come, Mullie, don't worry the poor little thing. He's had enough trouble already." She seated herself and the cat strolled stiffly over, leaped to her lap and settled down for a nap. The Man opened the outside door and also sat down.

It was some time before Willie's breath came back and his heart returned to normal. When it did he ventured forth, an inch at a time. Nothing happened, so he began the long circuit of the room, staying close to the wall and pausing under each piece of furniture. He was almost to the doorway now and gave one quick survey before the final dash.

The Lady still continued to sit quietly, her fingers slowly stroking Mr. Muldoon's jowls. He snored faintly, with a sound not unlike the steady, gurgling wheeze of the Man's pipe.

One wild scurry and Willie burst out into the sunlight. Across the terrace he went, but even in the excitement of his newly won freedom he was forced to pause at the appearance of the front lawn. The smoothly rolled surface was striped and circled and crisscrossed with a perfect crazy-quilt pattern of mole runs, scarcely a foot of it undisturbed. He skipped to the nearest run, made two digs and plunged beneath the surface.

"Mole! Mole!" he cried as he galloped through the echoing tunnel. "Here I am, Mole, it's me—Little Willie."

Tim McGrath, hands on hips, stood on the front lawn surveying the wreckage of his careful labor. His jaws were a deep, purplish red, his neck seemed swollen with suppressed rage.

"Look at it!" he sputtered, "*Just look at it!* What did I tell you about them moles? But no. No traps, of course not. No poison, oh dear me, no! *Now look!*"

The Man sucked on his pipe rather apologetically. "It is quite a mess, isn't it?" he admitted. "I guess we'll just have to roll it down again."

Tim McGrath gazed at the sky and whispered softly. "*We'll* have to roll it again! *We'll have to roll it again!* Oh Lord, give me strength." Wearily he trudged away to fetch the rake and roller.

## THE ELEPHANT'S CHILD

### Rudyard Kipling

*When well told, this story is priceless, and one can hear a good telling of it by Boris Karloff on Caedmon Records. The hilarious* Just So Stories *are drolls in the manner of* pourquoi *tales. Probably only adults will fully appreciate Kipling's amusing parodies on the processes of evolution; but children will enjoy them as fantastic and funny stories. "The Elephant's Child" is a favorite with children, doubtless because now and then all children yearn for the day when they can safely spank their relatives.*

In the high and Far-Off times the Elephant, O Best Beloved, had no trunk. He had only a blackish, bulgy nose, as big as a boot, that he could wriggle about from side to side; but he couldn't pick up things with it. But there was one Elephant—a new Elephant—an Elephant's Child—who was full of 'satiable curtiosity, and that means he asked ever so many questions. *And* he lived in Africa, and he filled all Africa with his 'satiable curtiosities. He asked his tall aunt, the Ostrich, why her tail-feathers grew just so, and his tall aunt the Ostrich spanked him with her hard, hard claw. He asked his tall uncle, the Giraffe, what made his skin spotty, and his tall uncle, the Giraffe, spanked him with his hard, hard hoof. And still he was full of 'satiable curtiosity! He asked his broad aunt, the Hippopotamus, why her eyes were red, and his broad aunt, the Hippopotamus, spanked him with her broad, broad hoof; and he asked his hairy uncle, the Baboon, why melons tasted just so, and his hairy uncle, the Baboon, spanked him with his hairy, hairy paw. And *still* he was full of 'satiable curtiosity! He asked questions about everything that he saw, or heard, or felt, or smelt, or touched, and all his uncles and his aunts spanked him. And still he was full of 'satiable curtiosity!

One fine morning in the middle of the Precession of the Equinoxes this 'satiable Elephant's Child asked a new fine question that he had

"The Elephant's Child." From *Just So Stories* by Rudyard Kipling. Reprinted by permission of Mrs. George Bambridge, Doubleday & Company, Inc., and Macmillan of London & Basingstoke

never asked before. He asked, "What does the Crocodile have for dinner?" Then everybody said, "Hush!" in a loud and dretful tone, and they spanked him immediately and directly, without stopping for a long time.

By and by, when that was finished, he came upon Kolokolo Bird sitting in the middle of a wait-a-bit thorn-bush, and he said, "My father has spanked me, and my mother has spanked me; all my aunts and uncles have spanked me for my 'satiable curtiosity; and *still* I want to know what the Crocodile has for dinner!"

Then Kolokolo Bird said, with a mournful cry, "Go to the banks of the great grey-green, greasy Limpopo River, all set about with fever-trees, and find out."

That very next morning, when there was nothing left of the Equinoxes, because the Precession had preceded according to precedent this 'satiable Elephant's Child took a hundred pounds of bananas (the little short red kind), and a hundred pounds of sugarcane (the long purple kind), and seventeen melons (the greeny-crackly kind), and said to all his dear families, "Good-bye. I am going to the great grey-green, greasy Limpopo River, all set about with fever-trees, to find out what the Crocodile has for dinner." And they all spanked him once more for luck, though he asked them most politely to stop.

Then he went away, a little warm, but not at all astonished, eating melons, and throwing the rind about, because he could not pick it up.

He went from Graham's Town to Kimberley, and from Kimberley to Khama's Country, and from Khama's Country he went east by north, eating melons all the time, till he at last came to the banks of the great grey-green, greasy Limpopo River, all set about with fever-trees, precisely as Kolokolo Bird had said.

Now you must know and understand, O Best Beloved, that till that very week, and day, and hour, and minute, this 'satiable Elephant's Child had never seen a Crocodile, and did not know what one was like. It was all his 'satiable curtiosity.

The first thing that he found was a Bi-Coloured-Python-Rock-Snake curled round a rock.

"'Scuse me," said the Elephant's Child most politely, "but have you seen such a thing as a

Crocodile in these promiscuous parts?"

"*Have* I seen a Crocodile?" said the Bi-Coloured-Python-Rock-Snake, in a voice of dretful scorn. "What will you ask me next?"

"'Scuse me," said the Elephant's Child, "but could you kindly tell me what he has for dinner?"

Then the Bi-Coloured-Python-Rock-Snake uncoiled himself very quickly from the rock, and spanked the Elephant's Child with his scalesome, flailsome tail.

"That is odd," said the Elephant's Child, "because my father and my mother, and my uncle and my aunt, not to mention my other aunt, the Hippopotamus, and my other uncle, the Baboon, have all spanked me for my 'satiable curtiosity—and I suppose this is the same thing."

So he said good-bye very politely to the Bi-Coloured-Python-Rock-Snake, and helped to coil him up on the rock again, and went on, a little warm, but not at all astonished, eating melons, and throwing the rind about because he could not pick it up, till he trod on what he thought was a log of wood at the very edge of the great grey-green, greasy Limpopo River, all set about with fever-trees.

But it was really the Crocodile, O Best Beloved, and the Crocodile winked one eye—like this!

"'Scuse me," said the Elephant's Child most politely, "but do you happen to have seen a Crocodile in these promiscuous parts?"

Then the Crocodile winked the other eye, and lifted half his tail out of the mud; and the Elephant's Child stepped back most politely, because he did not wish to be spanked again.

"Come hither, Little One," said the Crocodile. "Why do you ask such things?"

"'Scuse me," said the Elephant's Child most politely, "but my father has spanked me, my mother has spanked me, not to mention my tall aunt, the Ostrich, and my tall uncle, the Giraffe, who can kick ever so hard, as well as my broad aunt, the Hippopotamus, and my hairy uncle, the Baboon, *and* including the Bi-Coloured-Python-Rock-Snake, with the scalesome, flailsome tail, just up the bank, who spanks harder than any of them; and *so,* if it's quite all the same to you, I don't want to be spanked any more."

"Come hither, Little One," said the Crocodile, "for I am the Crocodile," and he wept crocodile-tears to show it was quite true.

Then the Elephant's Child grew all breathless, and panted, and kneeled down on the bank and said, "You are the very person I have been looking for all these long days. Will you please tell me what you have for dinner?"

"Come hither, Little One," said the Crocodile, "and I'll whisper."

Then the Elephant's Child put his head down close to the Crocodile's musky, tusky mouth, and the Crocodile caught him by his little nose, which up to that very week, day, hour, and minute, had been no bigger than a boot, though much more useful.

"I think," said the Crocodile—and he said it between his teeth, like this—"I think today I will begin with Elephant's Child!"

At this, O Best Beloved, the Elephant's Child was much annoyed, and he said, speaking through his nose, like this, "Led go! You are hurtig be!"

Then the Bi-Coloured-Python-Rock-Snake scuffled down from the bank and said, "My young friend, if you do not now, immediately and instantly, pull as hard as ever you can, it is my opinion that your acquaintance in the large-pattern leather ulster" (and by this he meant the Crocodile) "will jerk you into yonder limpid stream before you can say Jack Robinson."

This is the way Bi-Coloured-Python-Rock-Snakes always talk.

Then the Elephant's Child sat back on his little haunches, and pulled, and pulled, and pulled, and his nose began to stretch. And the Crocodile floundered into the water, making it all creamy with great sweeps of his tail, and *he* pulled, and pulled, and pulled.

And the Elephant's Child's nose kept on stretching; and the Elephant's Child spread all his little four legs and pulled, and pulled, and pulled, and his nose kept on stretching; and the Crocodile threshed his tail like an oar, and *he* pulled, and pulled, and pulled, and at each pull the Elephant's Child's nose grew longer and longer—and it hurt him hijjus!

Then the Elephant's Child felt his legs slipping, and he said through his nose, which was now nearly five feet long, "This is too butch for be!"

Then the Bi-Coloured-Python-Rock-Snake came down from the bank, and knotted himself in a double-clove-hitch round the Elephant's Child's hind legs, and said, "Rash and inexperienced traveller, we will now seriously devote ourselves to a little high tension, because if we do not, it is my impression that yonder self-propelling man-of-war with the armour-plated upper deck" (and by this, O Best Beloved, he

meant the Crocodile), "will permanently vitiate your future career."

That is the way all Bi-Coloured-Python-Rock-Snakes always talk.

So he pulled, and the Elephant's Child pulled, and the Crocodile pulled; but the Elephant's Child and the Bi-Coloured-Python-Rock-Snake pulled hardest; and at last the Crocodile let go of the Elephant's Child's nose with a plop that you could hear all up and down the Limpopo.

Then the Elephant's Child sat down most hard and sudden; but first he was careful to say "Thank you" to the Bi-Coloured-Python-Rock-Snake; and next he was kind to his poor pulled nose, and wrapped it all up in cool banana leaves, and hung it in the great grey-green, greasy Limpopo to cool.

"What are you doing that for?" said the Bi-Coloured-Python-Rock-Snake.

" 'Scuse me," said the Elephant's Child, "but my nose is badly out of shape, and I am waiting for it to shrink."

"Then you will have to wait a long time," said the Bi-Coloured-Python-Rock-Snake. "Some people do not know what is good for them."

The Elephant's Child sat there for three days waiting for his nose to shrink. But it never grew any shorter, and besides, it made him squint. For, O Best Beloved, you will see and understand that the Crocodile had pulled it out into a really truly trunk same as all Elephants have to-day.

At the end of the third day a fly came and stung him on the shoulder, and before he knew what he was doing he lifted up his trunk and hit that fly dead with the end of it.

" 'Vantage number one!" said the Bi-Coloured-Python-Rock-Snake. "You couldn't have done that with a mere-smear nose. Try and eat a little now."

Before he thought what he was doing the Elephant's Child put out his trunk and plucked a large bundle of grass, dusted it clean against his forelegs, and stuffed it into his own mouth.

" 'Vantage number two!" said the Bi-Coloured-Python-Rock-Snake. "You couldn't have done that with a mere-smear nose. Don't you think the sun is very hot here?"

"It is," said the Elephant's Child, and before he thought what he was doing he schlooped up a schloop of mud from the banks of the great grey-green, greasy Limpopo, and slapped it on his head, where it made a cool schloopy-sloshy mud-cap all trickly behind his ears.

" 'Vantage number three!" said the Bi-Coloured-Python-Rock-Snake. "You couldn't have done that with a mere-smear nose. Now how do you feel about being spanked again?"

" 'Scuse me," said the Elephant's Child, "but I should not like it at all."

"How would you like to spank somebody?" said the Bi-Coloured-Python-Rock-Snake.

"I should like it very much indeed," said the Elephant's Child.

"Well," said the Bi-Coloured-Python-Rock-Snake, "you will find that new nose of yours very useful to spank people with."

"Thank you," said the Elephant's Child, "I'll remember that; and now I think I'll go home to all my dear families and try."

So the Elephant's Child went home across Africa frisking and whisking his trunk. When he wanted fruit to eat he pulled fruit down from a tree, instead of waiting for it to fall as he used to do. When he wanted grass he plucked grass up from the ground, instead of going on his knees as he used to do. When the flies bit him he broke off the branch of a tree and used it as a fly-whisk; and he made himself a new, cool, slushy-squshy mud-cap whenever the sun was hot. When he felt lonely walking through Africa he sang to himself down his trunk, and the noise was louder than several brass bands. He went especially out of his way to find a broad Hippopotamus (she was no relation of his), and he spanked her very hard, to make sure that the Bi-Coloured-Python-Rock-Snake had spoken the truth about his new trunk. The rest of the time he picked up the melon rinds that he had dropped on his way to the Limpopo—for he was a Tidy Pachyderm.

One dark evening he came back to all his dear families, and he coiled up his trunk and said, "How do you do?" They were very glad to see him, and immediately said, "Come here and be spanked for your 'satiable curtiosity."

"Pooh," said the Elephant's Child. "I don't think you peoples know anything about spanking; but I do, and I'll show you."

Then he uncurled his trunk and knocked two of his dear brothers head over heels.

"O Bananas!" said they, "where did you learn that trick, and what have you done to your nose?"

"I got a new one from the Crocodile on the banks of the great grey-green, greasy Limpopo River," said the Elephant's Child. "I asked him what he had for dinner, and he gave me this to keep."

"It looks very ugly," said his hairy uncle, the Baboon.

"It does," said the Elephant's Child. "But it's very useful," and he picked up his hairy uncle, the Baboon, by one hairy leg, and hove him into a hornet's nest.

Then that bad Elephant's Child spanked all his dear families for a long time, till they were very warm and greatly astonished. He pulled out his tall Ostrich aunt's tail-feathers; and he caught his tall uncle, the Giraffe, by the hind leg, and dragged him through a thorn-bush; and he shouted at his broad aunt, the Hippopotamus, and blew bubbles into her ear when she was sleeping in the water after meals; but he never let anyone touch Kolokolo Bird.

At last things grew so exciting that his dear families went off one by one in a hurry to the banks of the great grey-green, greasy Limpopo River, all set about with fever-trees, to borrow new noses from the Crocodile. When they came back nobody spanked anybody any more; and ever since that day, O Best Beloved, all the Elephants you will ever see, besides all those that you won't, have trunks precisely like the trunk of the 'satiable Elephant's Child.

## from THE WIND IN THE WILLOWS

### Kenneth Grahame

*Kenneth Grahame started telling the stories about Ratty, Mole, and all the other denizens of the river bank to his small son at bedtime. When the child did not want to go to the seashore without his father, Grahame promised to send him*

stories. *A perceptive nurse who read the install-
ments of* The Wind in the Willows *to the boy,
recognized their worth and saved the letters.
From them, the book grew and was finally put
together for publication. It remains one of the
great juvenile classics in the English language.
This does not mean that every child is going to
like it, but children should be exposed to its
beauty and humor in the hope that the conta-
gion will "take."*

### The Open Road

"Ratty," said the Mole suddenly, one bright
summer morning, "if you please, I want to ask
you a favour."

The Rat was sitting on the river bank, singing
a little song. He had just composed it himself,
so he was very taken up with it, and would not
pay proper attention to Mole or anything else.
Since early morning he had been swimming in
the river in company with his friends the ducks.
And when the ducks stood on their heads suddenly, as ducks will, he would dive down and
tickle their necks just under where their chins
would be if ducks had chins, till they were
forced to come to the surface again in a hurry,
spluttering and angry and shaking their feathers
at him, for it is impossible to say quite *all* you
feel when your head is under water. At last they
implored him to go away and attend to his own
affairs and leave them to mind theirs. So the
Rat went away, and sat on the river bank in the
sun, and made up a song about them, which he
called

DUCKS' DITTY

All along the backwater,
Through the rushes tall,
Ducks are a-dabbling,
Up tails all!

Ducks' tails, drakes' tails,
Yellow feet a-quiver,
Yellow bills all out of sight
Busy in the river!

"The Open Road" from *The Wind in the Willows* by
Kenneth Grahame is reprinted by permission of Charles
Scribner's Sons, the Bodleian Library, Oxford and
Methuen Children's Books Ltd.

Slushy green undergrowth
Where the roach swim—
Here we keep our larder,
Cool and full and dim.

Every one for what he likes!
*We* like to be
Heads down, tails up,
Dabbling free!

High in the blue above
Swifts whirl and call—
*We* are down a-dabbling
Up tails all!

"I don't know that I think so *very* much of
that little song, Rat," observed the Mole cautiously. He was no poet himself and didn't care
who knew it; and he had a candid nature.

"Nor don't the ducks neither," replied the
Rat cheerfully. "They say, '*Why* can't fellows be
allowed to do what they like *when* they like and
*as* they like, instead of other fellows sitting on
banks and watching them all the time and making remarks, and poetry and things about them?
What *nonsense* it all is!' That's what the ducks
say."

"So it is, so it is," said the Mole, with great
heartiness.

"No, it isn't!" cried the Rat indignantly.

"Well then, it isn't, it isn't," replied the Mole
soothingly. "But what I wanted to ask you was,
won't you take me to call on Mr. Toad? I've
heard so much about him, and I do so want to
make his acquaintance."

"Why, certainly," said the good-natured Rat,
jumping to his feet and dismissing poetry from
his mind for the day. "Get the boat out, and
we'll paddle up there at once. It's never the
wrong time to call on Toad. Early or late he's
always the same fellow. Always good-tempered,
always glad to see you, always sorry when you
go!"

"He must be a very nice animal," observed
the Mole, as he got into the boat and took the
sculls, while the Rat settled himself comfortably
in the stern.

"He is indeed the best of animals," replied
Rat. "So simple, so good-natured, and so affectionate. Perhaps he's not very clever—we can't
all be geniuses; and it may be that he is both

boastful and conceited. But he has got some great qualities, has Toady." Rounding a bend in the river, they came in sight of a handsome, dignified old house of mellowed red brick, with well-kept lawns reaching down to the water's edge.

"There's Toad Hall," said the Rat; "and that creek on the left, where the notice-board says, 'Private. No landing allowed,' leads to his boat-house, where we'll leave the boat. The stables are over there to the right. That's the banqueting-hall you're looking at now—very old, that is. Toad is rather rich, you know, and this is really one of the nicest houses in these parts, though we never admit as much to Toad."

They glided up the creek, and the Mole shipped his sculls as they passed into the shadow of a large boat-house. Here they saw many handsome boats, slung from the cross-beams or hauled up on a slip, but none in the water; and the place had an unused and deserted air.

The Rat looked around him. "I understand," said he. "Boating is played out. He's tired of it, and done with it. I wonder what new fad he has taken up now? Come along and let's look him up. We shall hear all about it quite soon enough."

They disembarked, and strolled across the gay flower-decked lawns in search of Toad, whom they presently happened upon resting in a wicker garden-chair, with a preoccupied expression of face, and a large map spread out on his knees.

"Hooray!" he cried, jumping up on seeing them, "this is splendid!" He shook the paws of both of them warmly, never waiting for an introduction to the Mole. "How *kind* of you!" he went on, dancing round them. "I was just going to send a boat down the river for you, Ratty, with strict orders that you were to be fetched up here at once, whatever you were doing. I want you badly—both of you. Now what will you take? Come inside and have something! You don't know how lucky it is, your turning up just now!"

"Let's sit quiet a bit, Toady!" said the Rat, throwing himself into an easy chair, while the Mole took another by the side of him and made some civil remark about Toad's "delightful residence."

"Finest house on the whole river," cried Toad boisterously. "Or anywhere else, for that matter," he could not help adding.

Here the Rat nudged the Mole. Unfortunately the Toad saw him do it, and turned very red. There was a moment's painful silence. Then Toad burst out laughing. "All right, Ratty," he said. "It's only my way, you know. And it's not such a very bad house, is it? You know you rather like it yourself. Now, look here. Let's be sensible. You are the very animals I wanted. You've got to help me. It's most important!"

"It's about your rowing, I suppose," said the Rat, with an innocent air. "You're getting on fairly well, though you splash a good bit still. With a great deal of patience, and any quantity of coaching, you may—"

"O, pooh! boating!" interrupted the Toad, in great disgust. "Silly boyish amusement. I've given that up *long* ago. Sheer waste of time, that's what it is. It makes me downright sorry to see you fellows, who ought to know better, spending all your energies in that aimless manner. No, I've discovered the real thing, the only genuine occupation for a lifetime. I propose to devote the remainder of mine to it, and can only regret the wasted years that lie behind me, squandered in trivialities. Come with me, dear Ratty, and your amiable friend also, if he will be so very good, just as far as the stable-yard, and you shall see what you shall see!"

He led the way to the stable-yard accordingly, the Rat following with a most mistrustful expression; and there, drawn out of the coach-house into the open, they saw a gipsy caravan, shining with newness, painted a canary-yellow picked out with green, and red wheels.

"There you are!" cried the Toad straddling and expanding himself. "There's real life for you, embodied in that little cart. The open road, the dusty highway, the heath, the common, the hedgerows, the rolling downs! Camps, villages, towns, cities! Here to-day, up and off to somewhere else to-morrow! Travel, change, interest, excitement! The whole world before you, and a horizon that's always changing! And mind, this is the very finest cart of its sort that was ever built, without any exception. Come inside and look at the arrangements. Planned 'em all myself, I did!"

The Mole was tremendously interested and excited, and followed him eagerly up the steps and into the interior of the caravan. The Rat only snorted and thrust his hands deep into his pockets, remaining where he was.

It was indeed very compact and comfortable. Little sleeping-bunks—a little table that folded up against the wall—a cooking-stove, lockers, bookshelves, a bird-cage with a bird in it; and pots, pans, jugs and kettles of every size and variety.

"All complete!" said the Toad triumphantly, pulling open a locker. "You see—biscuits, potted lobster, sardines—everything you can possibly want. Soda-water here—baccy there—letter-paper, bacon, jam, cards and dominoes—you'll find," he continued, as they descended the steps again, "you'll find that nothing whatever has been forgotten, when we make our start this afternoon."

"I beg your pardon," said the Rat slowly, as he chewed a straw, "but did I overhear you say something about 'we' and 'start' and 'this afternoon'?"

"Now, you dear good old Ratty," said Toad imploringly, "don't begin talking in that stiff and sniffy sort of way, because you know you've got to come. I can't possibly manage without you, so please consider it settled, and don't argue—it's the one thing I can't stand. You surely don't mean to stick to your dull fusty old river all your life, and just live in a hole in a bank, and boat? I want to show you the world! I'm going to make an animal of you, my boy!"

"I don't care," said the Rat doggedly. "I'm not coming, and that's flat. And I am going to stick to my old river, and live in a hole, and boat, as I've always done. And what's more, Mole's going to stick to me and do as I do, aren't you, Mole?"

"Of course I am," said the Mole loyally. "I'll always stick to you, Rat, and what you say is to be—has got to be. All the same, it sounds as if it might have been—well, rather fun, you know!" he added wistfully. Poor Mole! The Life Adventurous was so new a thing to him, and so thrilling; and this fresh aspect of it was so tempting; and he had fallen in love at first sight with the canary-coloured cart and all its little fitments.

The Rat saw what was passing in his mind, and wavered. He hated disappointing people, and he was fond of the Mole, and would do almost anything to oblige him. Toad was watching both of them closely.

"Come along in and have some lunch," he said diplomatically, "and we'll talk it over. We needn't decide anything in a hurry. Of course, I don't really care. I only want to give pleasure to you fellows. 'Live for others!' That's my motto in life."

During luncheon—which was excellent, of course, as everything at Toad Hall always was—the Toad simply let himself go. Disregarding the Rat, he proceeded to play upon the inexperienced Mole as on a harp. Naturally a voluble animal, and always mastered by his imagination, he painted the prospects of the trip and the joys of the open life and the roadside in such glowing colours that the Mole could hardly sit in his chair for excitement. Somehow it soon seemed taken for granted by all three that the trip was a settled thing; and the Rat, though still unconvinced in his mind, allowed his good-nature to override his personal objections. He could not bear to disappoint his two friends, who were already deep in schemes and anticipations, planning out each day's separate occupation for several weeks ahead.

When they were quite ready, the now triumphant Toad led his companions to the paddock and set them to capture the old grey horse, who, without having been consulted, and to his own extreme annoyance, had been told off by Toad for the dustiest job in this dusty expedition. He frankly preferred the paddock, and took a deal of catching. Meantime Toad packed the lockers still tighter with necessaries, and hung nose-bags, nets of onions, bundles of hay, and baskets from the bottom of the cart. At last the horse was caught and harnessed, and they set off, all talking at once, each animal either trudging by the side of the cart or sitting on the shaft, as the humour took him. It was a golden afternoon. The smell of the dust they kicked up was rich and satisfying; out of thick orchards on either side the road, birds called and whistled to them cheerily; good-natured wayfarers, passing them, gave them "Good day," or stopped to say nice things about their beautiful cart; and rabbits, sitting at their front doors in the hedgerows, held up their fore paws, and said, "O my! O my! O my!"

Late in the evening, tired and happy and miles from home, they drew up on a remote common far from habitations, turned the horse loose to graze, and ate their simple supper sitting on the grass by the side of the cart. Toad talked big about all he was going to do in the days to come, while stars grew fuller and larger all around them, and a yellow moon, appearing suddenly and silently from nowhere in particular, came to keep them company and listen to their talk. At last they turned into their little bunks in the cart; and Toad, kicking out his legs, sleepily said, "Well, good night, you fellows! This is the real life for a gentleman! Talk about your old river!"

"I *don't* talk about my river," replied the patient Rat. "You *know* I don't, Toad. But I *think* about it," he added pathetically, in a lower tone: "I think about it—all the time!"

The Mole reached out from under his blanket, felt for the Rat's paw in the darkness, and gave it a squeeze. "I'll do whatever you like, Ratty," he whispered. "Shall we run away to-morrow morning, quite early—*very* early—and go back to our dear old hole on the river?"

"No, no, we'll see it out," whispered back the Rat. "Thanks awfully, but I ought to stick by Toad till this trip is ended. It wouldn't be safe for him to be left to himself. It won't take very long. His fads never do. Good night!"

The end was indeed nearer than even the Rat suspected.

After so much open air and excitement the Toad slept very soundly, and no amount of shaking could rouse him out of bed next morning. So the Mole and Rat turned to, quietly and manfully, and while the Rat saw to the horse, and lit a fire, and cleaned last night's cups and platters and got things ready for breakfast, the Mole trudged off to the nearest village, a long way off, for milk and eggs and various necessaries the Toad had, of course, forgotten to provide. The hard work had all been done, and the two animals were resting, thoroughly exhausted, by the time Toad appeared on the scene, fresh and gay, remarking what a pleasant easy life it was they were all leading now, after the cares and worries and fatigues of housekeeping at home.

They had a pleasant ramble that day over grassy downs and along narrow by-lanes, and camped, as before, on a common, only this time the two guests took care that Toad should do his fair share of work. In consequence, when the time came for starting next morning, Toad was by no means so rapturous about the simplicity of the primitive life, and indeed attempted to resume his place in his bunk, whence he was hauled by force. Their way lay, as before, across country by narrow lanes, and it was not till the afternoon that they came out on the high road, their first high road; and there disaster, fleet and unforeseen, sprang out on them—disaster momentous indeed to their expedition, but simply overwhelming in its effect on the after-career of Toad.

They were strolling along the high road easily, the Mole by the horse's head, talking to him, since the horse had complained that he was being frightfully left out of it, and nobody considered him in the least; the Toad and the Water Rat walking behind the cart talking together—at least Toad was talking, and Rat was saying at intervals, "Yes, precisely; and what did *you* say to *him?*"—and thinking all the time of something very different, when far behind them they heard a faint warning hum, like the drone of a distant bee. Glancing back, they saw a small cloud of dust, with a dark centre of energy, advancing on them at incredible speed, while from out the dust a faint "Poop-poop!" wailed like an uneasy animal in pain. Hardly regarding it, they turned to resume their conversation, when in an instant (as it seemed) the peaceful scene was changed, and with a blast of wind and a whirl of sound that made them jump for the nearest ditch, it was on them! The "Poop-poop" rang with a brazen shout in their ears, they had a moment's glimpse of an interior of glittering plate-glass and rich morocco, and the magnificent motor-car, immense, breath-snatching, passionate, with its pilot tense and hugging his wheel, possessed all earth and air for the fraction of a second, flung an enveloping cloud of dust that blinded and enwrapped them utterly, and then dwindled to a speck in the far distance, changed back into a droning bee once more.

The old grey horse, dreaming, as he plodded

along, of his quiet paddock, in a new raw situation such as this simply abandoned himself to his natural emotions. Rearing, plunging, backing steadily, in spite of all the Mole's efforts at his head, and all the Mole's lively language directed at his better feelings, he drove the cart backwards towards the deep ditch at the side of the road. It wavered an instant—then there was a heart-rending crash—and the canary-coloured cart, their pride and their joy, lay on its side in the ditch, an irredeemable wreck.

The Rat danced up and down in the road, simply transported with passion. "You villains!" he shouted, shaking both fists. "You scoundrels, you highwaymen, you—you—road-hogs! —I'll have the law of you! I'll report you! I'll take you through all the Courts!" His home-sickness had quite slipped away from him, and for the moment he was the skipper of the canary-coloured vessel driven on a shoal by the reckless jockeying of rival mariners, and he was trying to recollect all the fine and biting things he used to say to masters of steam-launches when their wash, as they drove too near the bank, used to flood his parlour carpet at home.

Toad sat straight down in the middle of the dusty road, his legs stretched out before him, and stared fixedly in the direction of the disappearing motor-car. He breathed short, his face wore a placid, satisfied expression, and at intervals he faintly murmured "Poop-poop!"

The Mole was busy trying to quiet the horse, which he succeeded in doing after a time. Then he went to look at the cart, on its side in the ditch. It was indeed a sorry sight. Panels and windows smashed, axles hopelessly bent, one wheel off, sardine-tins scattered over the wide world, and the bird in the bird-cage sobbing pitifully and calling to be let out.

The Rat came to help him, but their united efforts were not sufficient to right the cart. "Hi! Toad!" they cried. "Come and bear a hand, can't you!"

The Toad never answered a word, or budged from his seat in the road; so they went to see what was the matter with him. They found him in a sort of trance, a happy smile on his face, his eyes still fixed on the dusty wake of their destroyer. At intervals he was still heard to murmur "Poop-poop!"

The Rat shook him by the shoulder. "Are you coming to help us, Toad?" he demanded sternly.

"Glorious, stirring sight!" murmured Toad, never offering to move. "The poetry of motion! The *real* way to travel! The *only* way to travel! Here to-day—in next week to-morrow! Villages skipped, towns and cities jumped—always somebody else's horizon! O bliss! O poop-poop! O my! O my!"

"O *stop* being an ass, Toad!" cried the Mole despairingly.

"And to think I never *knew!*" went on the Toad in a dreamy monotone. "All those wasted years that lie behind me, I never knew, never even *dreamt!* But *now*—but now that I know, now that I fully realize! O what a flowery track lies spread before me, henceforth! What dust-clouds shall spring up behind me as I speed on my reckless way! What carts I shall fling carelessly into the ditch in the wake of my magnificent onset! Horrid little carts—common carts—canary-coloured carts!"

"What are we to do with him?" asked the Mole of the Water Rat.

"Nothing at all," replied the Rat firmly. "Because there is really nothing to be done. You see, I know him from of old. He is now possessed. He has got a new craze, and it always takes him that way, in its first stage. He'll continue like that for days now, like an animal walking in a happy dream, quite useless for all practical purposes. Never mind him. Let's go and see what there is to be done about the cart."

A careful inspection showed them that, even if they succeeded in righting it by themselves, the cart would travel no longer. The axles were in a hopeless state, and the missing wheel was shattered into pieces.

The Rat knotted the horse's reins over his back and took him by the head, carrying the bird-cage and its hysterical occupant in the other hand. "Come on!" he said grimly to the Mole. "It's five or six miles to the nearest town, and we shall just have to walk it. The sooner we make a start the better."

"But what about Toad?" asked the Mole anxiously, as they set off together. "We can't leave him here, sitting in the middle of the road by himself, in the distracted state he's in! It's not safe. Supposing another Thing were to come along?"

"O, *bother* Toad," said the Rat savagely; "I've done with him!"

They had not proceeded very far on their way, however, when there was a pattering of feet behind them, and Toad caught them up and thrust a paw inside the elbow of each of them; still breathing short and staring into vacancy.

"Now, look here, Toad!" said the Rat sharply; "as soon as we get to the town, you'll have to go straight to the police-station, and see if they know anything about that motor-car and who it belongs to, and lodge a complaint against it. And then you'll have to go to a blacksmith's or wheelwright's and arrange for the cart to be fetched and mended and put to rights. It'll take time, but it's not quite a hopeless smash. Meanwhile, the Mole and I will go to an Inn and find comfortable rooms where we can stay till the cart's ready, and till your nerves have recovered from their shock."

"Police-station! Complaint!" murmured Toad dreamily. "Me *complain* of that beautiful, that heavenly vision that has been vouchsafed me! *Mend* the *cart!* I've done with carts forever. I never want to see the cart, or to hear of it, again. O, Ratty! You can't think how obliged I am to you for consenting to come on this trip! I wouldn't have gone without you, and then I might never have seen that—that swan, that sunbeam, that thunderbolt! I might never have heard that entrancing sound, or smelt that bewitching smell! I owe it all to you, my best of friends!"

The Rat turned from him in despair. "You see what it is?" he said to the Mole, addressing him across Toad's head: "He's quite hopeless. I give it up—when we get to the town we'll go to the railway-station, and with luck we may pick up a train there that'll get us back to River Bank tonight. And if ever you catch me going a-pleasuring with this provoking animal again!" —He snorted, and during the rest of that weary trudge addressed his remarks exclusively to Mole.

On reaching the town they went straight to the station and deposited Toad in the second-class waiting-room, giving a porter twopence to keep a strict eye on him. They then left the horse at an inn stable, and gave what directions they could about the cart and its contents. Eventually, a slow train having landed them at a station not very far from Toad Hall, they escorted the spell-bound, sleep-walking Toad to his door, put him inside it, and instructed his housekeeper to feed him, undress him, and put him to bed. Then they got out their boat from the boat-house, sculled down the river home, and at a very late hour sat down to supper in their own cosy riverside parlour, to the Rat's great joy and contentment.

The following evening the Mole, who had risen late and taken things very easy all day, was sitting on the bank fishing, when the Rat, who had been looking up his friends and gossiping, came strolling along to find him. "Heard the news?" he said. "There's nothing else being talked about, all along the river bank. Toad went up to Town by an early train this morning. And he has ordered a large and very expensive motor-car."

### *from* WINNIE-THE-POOH
*A. A. Milne*

*Young children like the Pooh books, but sometimes miss part of their humor. In many families parents begin reading Pooh stories to the five- or six-year-olds and are still reading them when the children are ten. Although* Winnie-the-Pooh *is known and loved around the world, one must be careful about using it with too young a group of children in school. It is* not *for children of kindergarten age, unless five-year-olds and their parents share it quietly together; but a group of third-graders may have great fun with it and may even make replicas of Pooh, Piglet, and all the rest or dramatize some of the episodes.*

### In Which Pooh Goes Visiting and Gets Into a Tight Place

Edward Bear, known to his friends as Winnie-the-Pooh, or Pooh for short, was walking through the forest one day, humming proudly to himself. He had made up a little hum that very morning, as he was doing his Stoutness Exercises in front of the glass: *Tra-la-la, tra-la-la,* as he stretched up as high as he could go, and then *Tra-la-la, tra-la—oh, help!—la,* as he tried to reach his toes. After breakfast he had said it over and over to himself until he had learnt it off by heart, and now he was humming it right through, properly. It went like this:

*Tra-la-la, tra-la-la,*
*Tra-la-la, tra-la-la,*
*Rum-tum-tiddle-um-tum.*
*Tiddle-iddle, tiddle-iddle,*
*Tiddle-iddle, tiddle-iddle,*
*Rum-tum-tum-tiddle-um.*

Well, he was humming this hum to himself, and walking along gaily, wondering what everybody else was doing, and what it felt like, being somebody else, when suddenly he came to a sandy bank, and in the bank was a large hole.

"Aha!" said Pooh. (*Rum-tum-tiddle-um-tum.*) "If I know anything about anything, that hole means Rabbit," he said, "and Rabbit means Company," he said, "and Company means Food and Listening-to-Me-Humming and such like. *Rum-tum-tum-tiddle-um.*"

So he bent down, put his head into the hole, and called out:

"Is anybody at home?"

There was a sudden scuffling noise from inside the hole, and then silence.

"What I said was, 'Is anybody at home?' " called out Pooh very loudly.

"No!" said a voice; and then added, "You needn't shout so loud. I heard you quite well the first time."

"Bother!" said Pooh. "Isn't there anybody here at all?"

"Nobody."

Winnie-the-Pooh took his head out of the hole, and thought for a little, and he thought to himself, "There must be somebody there, because somebody must have *said* 'Nobody.' " So he put his head back in the hole, and said:

"Hallo, Rabbit, isn't that you?"

"No," said Rabbit, in a different sort of voice this time.

"But isn't that Rabbit's voice?"

"I don't *think* so," said Rabbit. "It isn't *meant* to be."

"Oh!" said Pooh.

He took his head out of the hole, and had another think, and then he put it back, and said:

"Well, could you very kindly tell me where Rabbit is?"

"He has gone to see his friend Pooh Bear, who is a great friend of his."

"But this *is* Me!" said Bear, very much surprised.

"What sort of Me?"

"Pooh Bear."

"Are you sure?" said Rabbit, still more surprised.

"Quite, quite sure," said Pooh.

"Oh, well, then, come in."

So Pooh pushed and pushed and pushed his way through the hole, and at last he got in.

"You were quite right," said Rabbit, looking at him all over. "It *is* you. Glad to see you."

"Who did you think it was?"

"Well, I wasn't sure. You know how it is in the Forest. One can't have *anybody* coming into one's house. One has to be *careful*. What about a mouthful of something?"

Pooh always liked a little something at eleven o'clock in the morning, and he was very glad to see Rabbit getting out the plates and mugs; and when Rabbit said, "Honey or condensed milk with your bread?" he was so excited that he said, "Both," and then, so as not to seem greedy, he added, "But don't bother about the bread, please." And for a long time after that he said nothing . . . until at last, humming to himself in a rather sticky voice, he got up, shook Rabbit lovingly by the paw, and said that he must be going on.

"Must you?" said Rabbit politely.

"Well," said Pooh, "I could stay a little longer if it—if you—" and he tried very hard to look in the direction of the larder.

"As a matter of fact," said Rabbit, "I was going out myself directly."

"Oh, well, then, I'll be going on. Good-bye."

"Well, good-bye, if you're sure you won't have any more."

"*Is* there any more?" asked Pooh quickly.

Rabbit took the covers off the dishes, and said, "No, there wasn't."

"I thought not," said Pooh, nodding to himself. "Well, good-bye. I must be going on."

So he started to climb out of the hole. He pulled with his front paws, and pushed with his back paws, and in a little while his nose was out in the open again . . . and then his ears . . . and then his front paws . . . and then his shoulders . . . and then——

"Oh, help!" said Pooh. "I'd better go back."

"Oh, bother!" said Pooh. "I shall have to go on."

"I can't do either!" said Pooh. "Oh, help *and* bother!"

Now by this time Rabbit wanted to go for a walk too, and finding the front door full, he went out by the back door, and came round to Pooh, and looked at him.

"Hallo, are you stuck?" he asked.

"N-no," said Pooh carelessly. "Just resting and thinking and humming to myself."

"Here, give us a paw."

Pooh Bear stretched out a paw, and Rabbit pulled and pulled and pulled. . . .

"*Ow!*" cried Pooh. "You're hurting!"

"The fact is," said Rabbit, "you're stuck."

"It all comes," said Pooh crossly, "of not having front doors big enough."

"It all comes," said Rabbit sternly, "of eating too much. I thought at the time," said Rabbit, "only I don't like to say anything," said Rabbit, "that one of us was eating too much," said Rabbit, "and I knew it wasn't *me*," he said. "Well, well, I shall go and fetch Christopher Robin."

Christopher Robin lived at the other end of the Forest, and when he came back with Rabbit, and saw the front half of Pooh, he said, "Silly old Bear," in such a loving voice that everybody felt quite hopeful again.

"I was just beginning to think," said Bear, sniffing slightly, "that Rabbit might never be able to use his front door again. And I should *hate* that," he said.

"So should I," said Rabbit.

"Use his front door again?" said Christopher Robin. "Of course he'll use his front door again."

"Good," said Rabbit.

"If we can't pull you out, Pooh, we might push you back."

Rabbit scratched his whiskers thoughtfully, and pointed out that, when once Pooh was pushed back, he was back, and of course nobody was more glad to see Pooh than *he* was, still there it was, some lived in trees and some lived underground, and——

"You mean I'd *never* get out?" said Pooh.

"I mean," said Rabbit, "that having got *so* far, it seems a pity to waste it."

Christopher Robin nodded.

"Then there's only one thing to be done," he said.

"We shall have to wait for you to get thin again."

"How long does getting thin take?" asked Pooh anxiously.

"About a week, I should think."

"But I can't stay here for a *week!*"

"You can *stay* here all right, silly old Bear. It's getting you out which is so difficult."

"We'll read to you," said Rabbit cheerfully. "And I hope it won't snow," he added. "And I say, old fellow, you're taking up a good deal of room in my house—*do* you mind if I use your back legs as a towel-horse? Because, I mean, there they are—doing nothing—and it would be very convenient just to hang the towels on them."

"A week!" said Pooh gloomily. "*What about meals?*"

"I'm afraid no meals," said Christopher Robin, "because of getting thin quicker. But we *will* read to you."

Bear began to sigh, and then found he couldn't because he was so tightly stuck; and a tear rolled down his eye, as he said:

"Then would you read a Sustaining Book, such as would help and comfort a Wedged Bear in Great Tightness?"

So for a week Christopher Robin read that sort of book at the North end of Pooh, and Rabbit hung his washing on the South end . . . and in between Bear felt himself getting slenderer and slenderer. And at the end of the week Christopher Robin said, "*Now!*"

So he took hold of Pooh's front paws and Rabbit took hold of Christopher Robin, and all Rabbit's friends and relations took hold of

Rabbit, and they all pulled together. . . .

And for a long time Pooh only said *"Ow!"*

And *"Oh!"* . . .

And then, all of a sudden, he said *"Pop!"* just as if a cork were coming out of a bottle.

And Christopher Robin and Rabbit and all Rabbit's friends and relations went head-over-heels backwards . . . and on the top of them came Winnie-the-Pooh—free!

So, with a nod of thanks to his friends, he went on with his walk through the forest, humming proudly to himself. But, Christopher Robin looked after him lovingly, and said to himself, "Silly Old Bear!"

## from THE ADVENTURES OF PINOCCHIO

### Carlo Lorenzini

*Carlo Collodi was the pen name of a witty Italian by the name of Carlo Lorenzini. Since Italians and Sicilians have always loved puppets, it is not surprising that Lorenzini should write a story about a puppet that comes to life. Anyone who has ever made puppets or played with them has experienced the uncanny feeling that the creatures really do have a life of their own and may take to their heels any minute. This episode finds Pinocchio in a terrible fix. He has run away from school, failed to keep his promises, and is now so conspicuously punished for his sins that he is repenting for dear life.*

### Pinocchio's Ears Become Like Those of a Donkey

Every one, at one time or another, has found some surprise awaiting him. Of the kind which Pinocchio had on that eventful morning of his life, there are but few.

What was it? I will tell you, my dear little readers. On awakening, Pinocchio put his hand up to his head and there he found—

Guess!

He found that, during the night, his ears had grown at least ten full inches!

You must know that the Marionette, even from his birth, had very small ears, so small indeed that to the naked eye they could hardly be seen. Fancy how he felt when he noticed that overnight those two dainty organs had become as long as shoe brushes!

He went in search of a mirror, but not finding any, he just filled a basin with water and looked at himself. There he saw what he never could have wished to see. His manly figure was adorned and enriched by a beautiful pair of donkey's ears.

I leave you to think of the terrible grief, the shame, the despair of the poor Marionette.

He began to cry, to scream, to knock his head against the wall, but the more he shrieked, the longer and the more hairy grew his ears.

At those piercing shrieks, a Dormouse came into the room, a fat little Dormouse, who lived upstairs. Seeing Pinocchio so grief-stricken, she asked him anxiously:

"What is the matter, dear little neighbor?"

"I am sick, my little Dormouse, very, very sick—and from an illness which frightens me! Do you understand how to feel the pulse?"

"A little."

"Feel mine then and tell me if I have a fever."

The Dormouse took Pinocchio's wrist between her paws and, after a few minutes, looked up at him sorrowfully and said:

"My friend, I am sorry, but I must give you some very sad news."

"What is it?"

"You have a very bad fever."

"But what fever is it?"

"The donkey fever."

"I don't know anything about that fever," answered the Marionette, beginning to understand even too well what was happening to him.

"Then I will tell you all about it," said the Dormouse. "Know then that, within two or three hours, you will no longer be a Marionette, nor a boy."

"What shall I be?"

"Within two or three hours you will become a real donkey, just like the ones that pull the fruit carts to market."

"Oh, what have I done? What have I done?" cried Pinocchio, grasping his two long ears in his hands and pulling and tugging at them angrily, just as if they belonged to another.

"My dear boy," answered the Dormouse to cheer him up a bit, "why worry now? What is done cannot be undone, you know. Fate has decreed that all lazy boys who come to hate books and schools and teachers and spend all their days with toys and games must sooner or later turn into donkeys."

"But is it really so?" asked the Marionette, sobbing bitterly.

"I am sorry to say it is. And tears now are useless. You should have thought of all this before."

"But the fault is not mine. Believe me, little Dormouse, the fault is all Lamp-Wick's."

"And who is this Lamp-Wick?"

"A classmate of mine. I wanted to return home. I wanted to be obedient. I wanted to study and to succeed in school, but Lamp-Wick said to me, 'Why do you want to waste your time studying? Why do you want to go to school? Come with me to the Land of Toys. There we'll never study again. There we can

enjoy ourselves and be happy from morn till night.' "

"And why did you follow the advice of that false friend?"

"Why? Because, my dear little Dormouse, I am a heedless Marionette—heedless and heartless. Oh! If I had only had a bit of heart, I should never have abandoned that good Fairy, who loved me so well and who has been so kind to me! And by this time, I should no longer be a Marionette. I should have become a real boy, like all these friends of mine! Oh, if I meet Lamp-Wick I am going to tell him what I think of him—and more too!"

After this long speech, Pinocchio walked to the door of the room. But when he reached it, remembering his donkey ears, he felt ashamed to show them to the public and turned back. He took a large cotton bag from a shelf, put it on his head, and pulled it far down to his very nose.

Thus adorned, he went out. He looked for Lamp-Wick everywhere, along the streets, in the squares, inside the theaters, everywhere; but he was not to be found. He asked every one whom he met about him, but no one had seen him.

In desperation, he returned home and knocked at the door.

"Who is it?" asked Lamp-Wick from within.

"It is I!" answered the Marionette.

"Wait a minute."

After a full half hour the door opened. Another surprise awaited Pinocchio! There in the room stood his friend, with a large cotton bag on his head, pulled far down to his very nose.

At the sight of that bag, Pinocchio felt slightly happier and thought to himself:

"My friend must be suffering from the same sickness that I am! I wonder if he, too, has donkey fever?"

But pretending he had seen nothing, he asked with a smile:

"How are you, my dear Lamp-Wick?"

"Very well. Like a mouse in a Parmesan cheese."

"Is that really true?"

"Why should I lie to you?"

"I beg your pardon, my friend, but why then are you wearing that cotton bag over your ears?"

"The doctor has ordered it because one of my knees hurts. And you, dear Marionette, why are you wearing that cotton bag down to your nose?"

"The doctor has ordered it, because I have bruised my foot."

"Oh, my poor Pinocchio!"

"Oh, my poor Lamp-Wick!"

An embarrassingly long silence followed these words, during which time the two friends looked at each other in a mocking way.

Finally the Marionette, in a voice sweet as honey and soft as a flute, said to his companion:

"Tell me, Lamp-Wick, dear friend, have you ever suffered from an earache?"

"Never! And you?"

"Never! Still, since this morning my ear has been torturing me."

"So has mine."

"Yours, too? And which ear is it?"

"Both of them. And yours?"

"Both of them, too. I wonder if it could be the same sickness."

"I'm afraid it is."

"Will you do me a favor, Lamp-Wick?"

"Gladly! With my whole heart."

"Will you let me see your ears?"

"Why not? But before I show you mine, I want to see yours, dear Pinocchio."

"No. You must show yours first."

"No, my dear! Yours first, then mine."

"Well, then," said the Marionette, "let us make a contract."

"Let's hear the contract!"

"Let us take off our caps together. All right?"

"All right."

"Ready then!"

Pinocchio began to count, "One! Two! Three!"

At the word "Three!" the two boys pulled off their caps and threw them high in air.

And then a scene took place which is hard to believe, but it is all too true. The Marionette and his friend, Lamp-Wick, when they saw each other both stricken by the same misfortune, instead of feeling sorrowful and ashamed, began to poke fun at each other, and after much nonsense, they ended by bursting out into hearty laughter.

They laughed and laughed, and laughed again —laughed till they ached—laughed till they cried.

But all of a sudden Lamp-Wick stopped laughing. He tottered and almost fell. Pale as a ghost, he turned to Pinocchio and said:

"Help, help, Pinocchio!"

"What is the matter?"

"Oh, help me! I can no longer stand up."

"I can't either," cried Pinocchio; and his laughter turned to tears as he stumbled about helplessly.

They had hardly finished speaking, when both of them fell on all fours and began running and jumping around the room. As they ran, their arms turned into legs, their faces lengthened into snouts, and their backs became covered with long gray hairs.

This was humiliation enough, but the most horrible moment was the one in which the two poor creatures felt their tails appear. Overcome with shame and grief, they tried to cry and bemoan their fate.

But what is done can't be undone! Instead of moans and cries, they burst forth into loud donkey brays, which sounded very much like, "Haw! Haw! Haw!"

At that moment, a loud knocking was heard at the door and a voice called to them:

"Open! I am the Little Man, the driver of the wagon which brought you here. Open, I say, or beware!"

### from THE RETURN OF THE TWELVES

*Pauline Clarke*

*Pauline Clarke is a versatile English writer whose books range from stories for young children to tales of adventure, historical fiction, and fantasy for older children. Her* Return of the Twelves *received the Carnegie Medal in England. It is one of the most deftly handled fan-*

Reprinted by permission of Coward, McCann & Geoghegan, Inc. and Faber and Faber Ltd. from *The Return of the Twelves* (British title: *The Twelve and the Genii*) by Pauline Clarke. Text copyright © 1962 by Pauline Clarke tasies to have appeared, telling how the toy soldiers that once belonged to the Brontë children returned to their original and rightful home at Haworth, which is now the Brontë museum. One of the unique aspects of this book is that the two worlds of here-and-now and make-believe seem perfectly fused; also, these soldiers actually exist, and the boundaries between the past and the present are crossed as the reader comes to know each of the soldiers as a small idiosyncratic personality. This is the second chapter, which serves as a most intriguing introduction!

### The Patriarch

Max waited until he heard the car doors slam and the engine purr and sing. Then he raced down to his own room and leaned out of the window in time to see the back of the station wagon disappear out of the driveway. For a minute he felt sorry and lonely.

He went quickly up the attic stairs and looked through the keyhole again.

The wooden soldiers stood exactly as he had seen them when Jane interrupted. They hadn't moved a tenth of an inch. They were as dead as ninepins. They had frozen again. Max sighed, enraged. It would be miserable if he had kept himself from going with the others for nothing.

All the same, he didn't give up hope. He had seen them move twice now, and what you saw you believed. (Like everyone else, Max also believed many things he didn't see.)

The candy ball was getting more manageable now, and as he knelt there Max turned it over and over in his mouth. Suddenly he crunched it all up with determination and impatience. He decided to go in.

He wandered around the attic, pretending to be busy looking at things, but all the while keeping a cautious eye on them. It felt to him as though they were keeping cautious eyes on him too. It was like two cats casually looking away from each other, but each really wondering if the other was going to pounce.

Max felt as though he and his family had always lived in this house. He remembered the time they first came up here to the attic, carrying the stool, the boat and the drum.

Mrs. Morley had said, "Now, we won't banish Great-Grandpa's Ashanti things forever, but since I don't know quite where they're going, will you take them carefully up to the attic, please?"

Philip, Jane and Max were only too eager to explore the attic. Philip had seized the heavy carved wooden stool with its curved seat; Jane had clasped the curious-shaped, skin-covered drum to her chest; Max had taken the carved model canoe. Their great-grandfather had been a missionary on the Gold Coast of West Africa. He had gone up the Niger River farther than any other missionary before him, no doubt in just such a boat. He had talked to kings who thought it was quite all right to kill people for sacrifices. He had seen the pits where they threw them and huts that were full of skulls.

Now Max came to the stool, sat down on its curve—which fitted him so comfortably—and looked squarely at the soldiers. On just such a stool, their mother had often told them, the kings of Ashanti were crowned. She had been told by Grandma, who was the daughter of the missionary.

Max had stayed behind that first time, to explore thoroughly. He had stamped around the attic just as he had seen the contractor do, jumping on boards and tapping walls. He had been rewarded by finding the loose board near the window. Max never left things half explored. He got his knife, pried up the board, and found the dirty roll of torn rag in which the old soldiers were. Twelve of them.

"After all," said Max aloud, "I did rescue you from a living death."

He thought this was a fine expression; he had read it in a book lately. Although they were so old and battered, it was exciting and mysterious to find them hidden and to wonder who had hidden them. Added to this, when he brought them to show the family, his mother was quite impressed.

"Max, how interesting! Take care of them, because I should think they're really old. They ought to be in a museum."

"How old, Mummy? How old, Daddy?" Max asked, clutching the soldiers in his two hands.

"Careful! They look a bit frail," his father had said. He took one and scrutinized it. "Not much face left, or paint. He has a sort of high black cap on. I should think they're Napoleonic, or probably Wellington, being English, from what you can see of their clothes."

"Well, *how* old, Daddy?" Max persisted.

"Over a hundred years, if I'm right, Max. Take care of them, please. I don't know that you should be allowed to play with them."

"But I found them!" Max exploded. And of course, because they were admired and valued, Max quickly became devoted to them. Jane said they were shabby, and Philip said they were worm-eaten (which wasn't true; it was only because he hadn't found them himself). But Max adored them. One or two still had a round flat stand with two holes in it for their feet. They weren't all the same size; some were taller than others. And although their faces were blurred and rubbed, you could still tell that each was different. Mrs. Morley said this was delightful because it proved they were handmade, each carved with his own face. Max agreed.

But all this was nothing compared to the time, two days ago, when Max had set them out on the attic floor, and lying on his tummy, had beat with his fingers on the Ashanti drum, so that they could march to it. Before his startled eyes, one of them, a tallish fellow—and at once noticed for his sly, birdlike alertness—hopped and twirled into life at the sound of the drum. He threw his tiny arms in the air, as if he were glad to feel life again. He skipped along the ranks, punching some in the jaw, tweaking the noses of others, and tripping the feet of the most stolid. Then once more he found his place in line, and all twelve stood to surprised attention and took at least ten tiny steps forward over the boards.

When Max half started to his feet in excitement, they stopped. They froze like a toad does when you meet him crossing the lawn. Even the lively fellow froze.

Then today, Max had heard their tiny noises and seen them at it. Before Jane had come and spoiled everything.

Now he knew he must be gentle and careful and not do sudden things. Max was a persistent boy and patient for his age (which isn't a patient age), so he just sat there on the Ashanti stool, with his hands on his thin knees, wondering if an Ashanti king had been crowned on it.

Max could wait as long as they could. They would trust him sooner or later. Surely they knew he loved them?

If he were an Ashanti king, the first person he would sacrifice would be Anthony Gore. He knew that it was wrong to make human sacrifices, but then, if he were an Ashanti king in those old days, he *wouldn't* know this, so it would be all right. He supposed. When the Ashanti kings knew better, they stopped doing it. Max wondered if they missed it very much.

Max sighed and tried smiling at the soldiers. Then with two fingers he tapped out the rhythm of a song on the drum which stood beside him. He started to sing it, almost in a whisper, so as not to frighten them.

"Oh, the brave old Duke of York,
   He had ten thousand men;
   He marched them up to the top of the hill,
   And he marched them down again."

It was the only marching song he could think of about old soldiers.

"And when they were up, they were up,
   And when they were down, they were down,
   And when they were only halfway up,
   They were neither up nor down."

Max piped it very quietly, soft as a pin. To his joy, the soldiers broke ranks and clustered together in a little band. Again he heard that faint crackling, whisking sound which was their talk. He wasn't surprised this time, because he'd been expecting it. He kept still.

One of them turned away from the others and came boldly across the attic floor to Max. Behind this one, prancing from side to side as if to urge him on, came the lively soldier Max had first seen move. The lively one finally gave the other a good push, but the first one seemed to be a stately and dignified character and he didn't lose his balance. Then they all bowed low from the waist, and the one in front lifted his arms and waggled his head.

Now, does he want me to pick him up? Max wondered. Did he dare? Would it frighten them?

He gently put out his hand, leaned down, and grasped the dignified little soldier by the waist. It was no bigger than that lizard he had picked up on the moor the other day. The fellow waved his arms, but didn't struggle.

Max brought him close up to his face. Perhaps the soldier wanted to say something. Max held him close to his ear. There was a crackle. Max closed his eyes and listened very hard, holding his breath. The crackle came again, in more of a pattern. Max brought the soldier a little nearer. The third time, he could hear and understand.

"Are you one of the Genii?" asked the creature.

Max had read *The Arabian Nights,* so he knew all about the Genii, those spirits who preside over a person's destiny all his life. If these soldiers wanted him to be a Genie to them, he didn't mind.

"Yes," he said, very solemnly and quietly. He was surprised to hear a sudden faint sprinkle of sound like rice falling on the floor. The soldiers were clapping.

"I am Butter Crashey," said the small fellow Max held. Max didn't know what to say to this. Should he say How do you do? Or I like you very much? Or How old are you? Or Where did you come from? None of these seemed quite right, and the last two seemed rude.

"I like your name," he said at last. "How did you get it?"

"I fell into the butter long ago," said his friend.

"I thought you must have," said Max.

"I am the patriarch of the Twelves," he went on, "and my age is one hundred and forty."

Max had a vague idea that if a person was very old, it was proper to congratulate him. "Good for you," he said. Then he thought this didn't sound old-fashioned enough, so he added, "Allow me to congratulate you upon being full of years and wisdom."

This was the way Philip spoke sometimes. Max felt pleased with it and so, it was clear, did Butter Crashey. He bent his head to acknowledge the compliment. Now that he was alive, his face had become sharp and detailed. It was no longer blurred and featureless with being so old. It was like bringing a scene properly into focus through a pair of field glasses. Max looked at all the others and saw that the same was true

of them. The jaunty soldier seemed to have particularly piercing eyes, and he made a face as Max looked. Max was delighted.

"Under your protection," announced Butter Crashey, "we propose to make a journey of discovery, as we once set forth under the four Genii to carve out a kingdom among the Ashanti."

"That's a very good idea," said Max, who was longing to see the soldiers moving around downstairs. He put the patriarch gently down with the others and went to the attic door. He opened it and stood to one side. The twelve soldiers formed into a column and marched toward the door and out onto the landing.

## THE STEADFAST TIN SOLDIER
### Hans Christian Andersen

*Andersen was gifted in his ability to write tales that endowed inanimate objects with life. These personifications probably grew in part out of his lonely childhood and his lifelong delight in puppets. However, the adult Andersen, being a keen observer of people, used these perfectly fashioned tales about darning needles, tops, and balls as vehicles for superb humor and briskly penetrating commentary on human foibles. They have consequently become gems of wit and wisdom for all times.*

There were once five and twenty tin soldiers, all brothers, for they were the offspring of the same old tin spoon. Each man shouldered his gun, kept his eyes well to the front, and wore the smartest red and blue uniform imaginable. The first thing they heard in their new world, when the lid was taken off the box, was a little boy clapping his hands and crying, "Soldiers, soldiers!" It was his birthday and they had just

"The Steadfast Tin Soldier." From Hans Andersen's *Fairy Tales.* Translated by Mrs. Edgar Lucas. Everyman's Library Edition. Reprinted by permission of E. P. Dutton & Co., Inc. and J. M. Dent & Sons Ltd.

been given to him; so he lost no time in setting them up on the table. All the soldiers were exactly alike with one exception, and he differed from the rest in having only one leg. For he was made last, and there was not quite enough tin left to finish him. However, he stood just as well on his one leg, as the others on two, in fact he is the very one who is to become famous. On the table where they were being set up, were many other toys; but the chief thing which caught the eye was a delightful paper castle. You could see through the tiny windows, right into the rooms. Outside there were some little trees surrounding a small mirror, representing a lake, whose surface reflected the waxen swans which were swimming about on it. It was altogether charming, but the prettiest thing of all was a little maiden standing at the open door of the castle. She, too, was cut out of paper, but she wore a dress of the lightest gauze, with a dainty little blue ribbon over her shoulders, by way of a scarf, set off by a brilliant spangle, as big as her whole face. The little maid was stretching out both arms, for she was a dancer, and in the dance, one of her legs was raised so high into the air that the tin soldier could see absolutely nothing of it, and supposed that she, like himself, had but one leg.

"That would be the very wife for me!" he thought; "but she is much too grand; she lives in a palace, while I only have a box, and then there are five and twenty of us to share it. No, that would be no place for her! but I must try to make her acquaintance!" Then he lay down full length behind a snuff box, which stood on the table. From that point he could have a good look at the little lady, who continued to stand on one leg without losing her balance.

Late in the evening the other soldiers were put into their box, and the people of the house went to bed. Now was the time for the toys to play; they amused themselves with paying visits, fighting battles, and giving balls. The tin soldiers rustled about in their box, for they wanted to join the games, but they could not get the lid off. The nutcrackers turned somersaults, and the pencil scribbled nonsense on the slate. There was such a noise that the canary woke up and joined in, but his remarks were in verse. The only two who did not move were the tin soldier and the little dancer. She stood as stiff as ever on tip-toe, with her arms spread out; he was equally firm on his one leg, and he did not take his eyes off her for a moment.

Then the clock struck twelve, when pop! up flew the lid of the snuff box, but there was no snuff in it, no! There was a little black goblin, a sort of Jack-in-the-box.

"Tin soldier!" said the goblin, "have the goodness to keep your eyes to yourself."

But the tin soldier feigned not to hear.

"Ah! you just wait till to-morrow," said the goblin.

In the morning when the children got up they put the tin soldier on the window frame, and, whether it was caused by the goblin or by a puff of wind, I do not know, but all at once the window burst open, and the soldier fell headforemost from the third story.

It was a terrific descent, and he landed at last, with his leg in the air, and rested on his cap, with his bayonet fixed between two paving stones. The maid-servant and the little boy ran down at once to look for him; but although they almost trod on him, they could not see him. Had the soldier only called out, "Here I am," they would easily have found him, but he did not think it proper to shout when he was in uniform.

Presently it began to rain, and the drops fell faster and faster, till there was a regular torrent. When it was over two street boys came along.

"Look out!" said one; "there is a tin soldier! He shall go for a sail."

So they made a boat out of a newspaper and

put the soldier into the middle of it, and he sailed away down the gutter; both boys ran alongside clapping their hands. Good heavens! what waves there were in the gutter, and what a current, but then it certainly had rained cats and dogs. The paper boat danced up and down, and now and then whirled round and round. A shudder ran through the tin soldier, but he remained undaunted, and did not move a muscle, only looked straight before him with his gun shouldered. All at once the boat drifted under a long wooden tunnel, and it became as dark as it was in his box.

"Where on earth am I going to now!" thought he. "Well, well, it is all the fault of that goblin! Oh, if only the little maiden were with me in the boat it might be twice as dark for all I should care!"

At this moment a big water rat, who lived in the tunnel, came up.

"Have you a pass?" asked the rat. "Hand up your pass!"

The tin soldier did not speak, but clung still tighter to his gun. The boat rushed on, the rat close behind. Phew, how he gnashed his teeth and shouted to the bits of stick and straw.

"Stop him, stop him, he hasn't paid the toll! he hasn't shown his pass!"

But the current grew stronger and stronger, the tin soldier could already see daylight before him at the end of the tunnel; but he also heard a roaring sound, fit to strike terror to the bravest heart. Just imagine! Where the tunnel ended the stream rushed straight into the big canal. That would be just as dangerous for him as it would be for us to shoot a great rapid.

He was so near the end now that it was impossible to stop. The boat dashed out; the poor tin soldier held himself as stiff as he could; no one should say of him that he even winced.

The boat swirled round three or four times, and filled with water to the edge; it must sink. The tin soldier stood up to his neck in water, and the boat sank deeper and deeper. The paper became limper and limper, and at last the water went over his head—then he thought of the pretty little dancer, whom he was never to see again, and this refrain rang in his ears:

"Onward! Onward! Soldier!
For death thou canst not shun."

At last the paper gave way entirely and the soldier fell through—but at the same moment he was swallowed by a big fish.

Oh! how dark it was inside the fish, it was worse than being in the tunnel even; and then it was so narrow! But the tin soldier was as dauntless as ever, and lay full length, shouldering his gun.

The fish rushed about and made the most frantic movements. At last it became quite quiet, and after a time, a flash like lightning pierced it. The soldier was once more in the broad daylight, and some one called out loudly, "A tin soldier!" The fish had been caught, taken to market, sold, and brought into the kitchen, where the cook cut it open with a large knife. She took the soldier up by the waist, with two fingers, and carried him into the parlour, where everyone wanted to see the wonderful man, who had travelled about in the stomach of a fish; but the tin soldier was not at all proud. They set him up on the table, and, wonder of wonders! he found himself in the very same room that he had been in before. He saw the very same children, and the toys were still standing on the table, as well as the beautiful castle with the pretty little dancer.

She still stood on one leg, and held the other up in the air. You see she also was unbending. The soldier was so much moved that he was ready to shed tears of tin, but that would not have been fitting. He looked at her, and she looked at him, but they said never a word. At this moment one of the little boys took up the tin soldier, and without rhyme or reason, threw him into the fire. No doubt the little goblin in the snuff box was to blame for that. The tin soldier stood there, lighted up by the flame, and in the most horrible heat; but whether it was the heat of the real fire, or the warmth of his feelings, he did not know. He had lost all his gay color; it might have been from his perilous journey, or it might have been from grief, who can tell?

He looked at the little maiden, and she looked at him; and he felt that he was melting away, but he still managed to keep himself erect, shouldering his gun bravely.

A door was suddenly opened, the draught caught the little dancer and she fluttered like a sylph, straight into the fire, to the soldier, blazed up and was gone!

By this time the soldier was reduced to a mere lump, and when the maid took away the ashes next morning she found him, in the shape of a small tin heart. All that was left of the dancer was her spangle, and that was burnt as black as coal.

## Stories of Enchantment

**THE REAL PRINCESS**

*Hans Christian Andersen*
*This is an allegory, a satire on the absurdity* of believing in the special delicacy of blue-bloodedness. But children take it literally as a funny story. They enjoy illustrating the princess atop her twenty mattresses.

There was once a prince, and he wanted a princess, but then she must be a *real* princess. He travelled right round the world to find one, but there was always something wrong. There were plenty of princesses, but whether they were real princesses he had great difficulty in discovering; there was always something which was not quite right about them. So at last he had to come home again, and he was very sad because he wanted a real princess so badly.

One evening there was a terrible storm; it thundered and lightened and the rain poured down in torrents; indeed it was a fearful night.

In the middle of the storm somebody knocked at the town gate, and the old King himself went to open it.

It was a princess who stood outside, but she was in a terrible state from the rain and the storm. The water streamed out of her hair and her clothes, it ran in at the top of her shoes and out at the heel, but she said that she was a real princess.

"Well, we shall soon see if that is true," thought the old Queen, but she said nothing. She went into the bedroom, took all the bed-clothes off and laid a pea on the bedstead; then she took twenty mattresses and piled them on the top of the pea, and then twenty feather beds on the top of the mattresses. This was where the princess was to sleep that night. In the morning they asked her how she had slept.

"Oh, terribly badly!" said the princess. "I have hardly closed my eyes the whole night! Heaven knows what was in the bed. I seemed to be lying upon some hard thing, and my whole body is black and blue this morning. It is terrible!"

They saw at once that she must be a real princess when she had felt the pea through twenty mattresses and twenty feather beds. Nobody but a real princess could have such a delicate skin.

So the prince took her to be his wife, for now he was sure that he had found a real princess,

"The Real Princess." From Hans Andersen's *Fairy Tales.* Translated by Mrs. Edgar Lucas. Everyman's Library Edition. Reprinted by permission of E. P. Dutton & Co., Inc. and J. M. Dent & Sons Ltd.

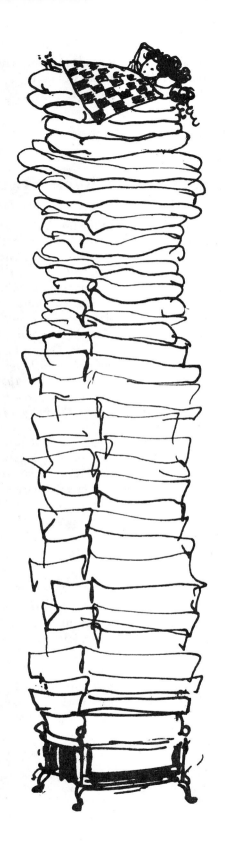

and the pea was put into the Museum, where it may still be seen if no one has stolen it.

Now this is a true story.

## from TALES FROM MOOMINVALLEY
### Tove Jansson

*Tove Jansson received the Hans Christian Andersen International Children's Book Medal in 1966, in recognition of the outstanding value of her work. Interestingly, it is only within the last five to ten years that her books have begun to receive attention in the United States. "The Invisible Child" stands as an independent story but gives a good feeling for the Moomins themselves and for Miss Jansson's easy and whimsical style. Some critics complain that nothing much ever happens in the Moomin books and that one never quite knows what Moomins are really like. However, each reader must be the judge of that. One cannot really describe in any important concrete detail a state of happiness, and for those who know and love them the Moomins are a state of happiness whether their adventures are small or big. Some very concrete proofs of that are the seven books about the Moomins, a large following of children in Europe, and the adult enthusiasm which brought Tove Jansson the Hans Christian Andersen Medal.*

### The Invisible Child

One dark and rainy evening the Moomin family sat around the verandah table picking over the day's mushroom harvest. The big table was covered with newspapers, and in the centre of it stood the lighted kerosene lamp. But the corners of the verandah were dark.

"My has been picking pepper spunk again," Moominpappa said, "Last year she collected flybane."

"Let's hope she takes to chanterelles next autumn," said Moominmamma. "Or at least to something not directly poisonous."

"Hope for the best and prepare for the worst," Little My observed with a chuckle.

They continued their work in peaceful silence.

Suddenly there were a few light taps on the glass pane in the door, and without waiting for an answer Too-ticky came in and shook the rain off her oilskin jacket. Then she held the door open and called out in the dark: "Well, come along!"

"Whom are you bringing?" Moomintroll asked.

"It's Ninny," Too-ticky said. "Yes, her name's Ninny."

She still held the door open, waiting. No one came.

"Oh, well," Too-ticky said and shrugged her shoulders. "If she's too shy she'd better stay there for a while."

"She'll be drenched through," said Moominmamma.

"Perhaps that won't matter much when one's invisible," Too-ticky said and sat down by the table. The family stopped working and waited for an explanation.

"You all know, don't you, that if people are frightened very often, they sometimes become invisible," Too-ticky said and swallowed a small egg mushroom that looked like a little snowball. "Well. This Ninny was frightened the wrong way by a lady who had taken care of her without really liking her. I've met this lady, and she was horrid. Not the angry sort, you know, which would have been understandable. No, she was the icily ironical kind."

"What's ironical?" Moomintroll asked.

"Well, imagine that you slip on a rotten mushroom and sit down on the basket of newly picked ones," Too-ticky said. "The natural thing for your mother would be to be angry. But no, she isn't. Instead she says, very coldly: 'I understand that's your idea of a graceful dance, but I'd thank you not to do it in people's food.' Something like that."

"How unpleasant," Moomintroll said.

"Yes, isn't it," replied Too-ticky. "This was the way this lady used to talk. She was ironic all day long every day, and finally the kid started to turn pale and fade around the edges, and less and less was seen of her. Last Friday one couldn't catch sight of her at all. The lady gave her away to me and said she really couldn't take care of relatives she couldn't even see."

"And what did you do to the lady?" My asked with bulging eyes. "Did you bash her head?"

"That's of no use with the ironic sort," Too-ticky said. "I took Ninny home with me, of course. And now I've brought her here for you to make her visible again."

There was a slight pause. Only the rain was heard, rustling along over the verandah roof. Everybody stared at Too-ticky and thought for a while.

"Does she talk?" Moominpappa asked.

"No. But the lady has hung a small silver bell around her neck so that one can hear where she is."

Too-ticky arose and opened the door again. "Ninny!" she called out in the dark.

The cool smell of autumn crept in from the garden, and a square of light threw itself on the wet grass. After a while there was a slight tinkle outside, rather hesitantly. The sound came up the steps and stopped. A bit above the floor a small silver bell was seen hanging in the air on a black ribbon. Ninny seemed to have a very thin neck.

"All right," Too-ticky said. "Now, here's your new family. They're a bit silly at times, but rather decent, largely speaking."

"Give the kid a chair," Moominpappa said. "Does she know how to pick mushrooms?"

"I really know nothing at all about Ninny," Too-ticky said. "I've only brought her here and told you what I know. Now I have a few other things to attend to. Please look in some day, won't you, and let me know how you get along. Cheerio."

When Too-ticky had gone the family sat quite silent, looking at the empty chair and the silver bell. After a while one of the chanterelles slowly rose from the heap on the table. Invisible paws picked it clean from needles and earth. Then it was cut to pieces, and the pieces drifted away and laid themselves in the basin. Another mushroom sailed up from the table.

"Thrilling!" My said with awe. "Try to give her something to eat. I'd like to know if you can see the food when she swallows it."

"How on earth does one make her visible again," Moominpappa said worriedly. "Should we take her to a doctor?"

"I don't think so," said Moominmamma. "I believe she wants to be invisible for a while. Too-ticky said she's shy. Better leave the kid alone until something turns up."

And so it was decided.

The eastern attic room happened to be un-occupied, so Moominmamma made Ninny a bed there. The silver bell tinkled along after her upstairs and reminded Moominmamma of the cat that once had lived with them. At the bedside she laid out the apple, the glass of juice and the three striped pieces of candy everybody in the house was given at bedtime.

Then she lighted a candle and said:

"Now have a good sleep, Ninny. Sleep as late as you can. There'll be tea for you in the morning any time you want. And if you happen to get a funny feeling or if you want anything, just come downstairs and tinkle."

Moominmamma saw the quilt raise itself to form a very small mound. A dent appeared in the pillow. She went downstairs again to her own room and started looking through her Granny's old notes about Infallible Household Remedies. Evil Eye. Melancholy. Colds. No. There didn't seem to be anything suitable. Yes, there was. Towards the end of the notebook she found a few lines written down at the time when Granny's hand was already rather shaky. "If people start getting misty and difficult to see." Good. Moominmamma read the recipe, which was rather complicated, and started at once to mix the medicine for little Ninny.

The bell came tinkling downstairs, one step at a time, with a small pause between each step. Moomintroll had waited for it all morning. But the silver bell wasn't the exciting thing. That was the paws. Ninny's paws were coming down the steps. They were very small, with anxiously bunched toes. Nothing else of Ninny was visible. It was very odd.

Moomintroll drew back behind the porcelain stove and stared bewitchedly at the paws that passed him on their way to the verandah. Now she served herself some tea. The cup was raised in the air and sank back again. She ate some bread and butter and marmalade. Then the cup and saucer drifted away to the kitchen, were washed and put away in the closet. You see, Ninny was a very orderly little child.

Moomintroll rushed out in the garden and shouted: "Mamma! She's got paws! You can see her paws!"

I thought as much, Moominmamma was thinking where she sat high in the apple tree. Granny knew a thing or two. Now when the medicine starts to work we'll be on the right way.

"Splendid," said Moominpappa. "And better still when she shows her snout one day. It makes me feel sad to talk with people who are invisible. And who never answer me."

"Hush, dear," Moominmamma said warningly. Ninny's paws were standing in the grass among the fallen apples.

"Hello Ninny," shouted My. "You've slept like a hog. When are you going to show your snout? You must look a fright if you've wanted to be invisible."

"Shut up," Moomintroll whispered, "she'll be hurt." He went running up to Ninny and said:

"Never mind My. She's hardboiled. You're really safe here among us. Don't even think about that horrid lady. She can't come here and take you away . . ."

In a moment Ninny's paws had faded away and become nearly indistinguishable from the grass.

"Darling, you're an ass," said Moominmamma. "You can't go about reminding the kid about those things. Now pick apples and don't talk rubbish."

They all picked apples.

After a while Ninny's paws became clearer again and climbed one of the trees.

It was a beautiful autumn morning. The shadows made one's snout a little chilly but the sunshine felt nearly like summer. Everything was wet from the night's rain, and all colours were strong and clear. When all the apples were

picked or shaken down Moominpappa carried the biggest apple mincer out in the garden, and they started making apple-cheese.

Moomintroll turned the handle, Moominmamma fed the mincer with apples, and Moominpappa carried the filled jars to the verandah. Little My sat in a tree singing the Big Apple Song.

Suddenly there was a crash.

On the garden path appeared a large heap of apple-cheese, all prickly with glass splinters. Beside the heap one could see Ninny's paws, rapidly fading away.

"Oh," said Moominmamma. "That was the jar we use to give to the bumble-bees. Now we needn't carry it down to the field. And Granny always said that if you want the earth to grow something for you, then you have to give it a present in the autumn."

Ninny's paws appeared back again, and above them a pair of spindly legs came to view. Above the legs one could see the faint outline of a brown dress hem.

"I can see her legs!" cried Moomintroll.

"Congrats," said little My, looking down out of her tree. "Not bad. But the Groke knows why you must wear snuff-brown."

Moominmamma nodded to herself and sent a thought to her Granny and the medicine.

Ninny padded along after them all day. They became used to the tinkle and no longer thought Ninny very remarkable.

By evening they had nearly forgotten about her. But when everybody was in bed Moominmamma took out a rose-pink shawl of hers and made it into a little dress. When it was ready she carried it upstairs to the eastern attic room and cautiously laid it out on a chair. Then she made a broad hair ribbon out of the material left over.

Moominmamma was enjoying herself tremendously. It was exactly like sewing doll's clothes again. And the funny thing was that one didn't know if the doll had yellow or black hair.

The following day Ninny had her dress on. She was visible up to her neck, and when she came down to morning tea she bobbed and piped:

"Thank you all ever so much."

The family felt very embarrassed, and no one

found anything to say. Also it was hard to know where to look when one talked to Ninny. Of course one tried to look a bit above the bell where Ninny was supposed to have her eyes. But then very easily one found oneself staring at some of the visible things further down instead, and it gave one an impolite feeling.

Moominpappa cleared his throat. "We're happy to see," he started, "that we see more of Ninny today. The more we see the happier we are . . ."

My gave a laugh and banged the table with her spoon. "Fine that you've started talking," she said. "Hope you have anything to say. Do you know any good games?"

"No," Ninny piped. "But I've heard about games."

Moomintroll was delighted. He decided to teach Ninny all the games he knew.

After coffee all three of them went down to the river to play. Only Ninny turned out to be quite impossible. She bobbed and nodded and very seriously replied, quite, and how funny, and of course, but it was clear to all that she played only from politeness and not to have fun.

"Run, run, can't you!" My cried. "Or can't you even jump?"

Ninny's thin legs dutifully ran and jumped. Then she stood still again with arms dangling. The empty dress neck over the bell was looking strangely helpless.

"D'you think anybody likes that?" My cried. "Haven't you any life in you? D'you want a biff on the nose?"

"Rather not," Ninny piped humbly.

"She can't play," mumbled Moomintroll.

"She can't get angry," little My said. "That's what's wrong with her. Listen, you," My continued and went close to Ninny with a menacing look. "You'll never have a face of your own until you've learned to fight. Believe me."

"Yes, of course," Ninny replied, cautiously backing away.

There was no further turn for the better.

At last they stopped trying to teach Ninny to play. She didn't like funny stories either. She never laughed at the right places. She never laughed at all, in fact. This had a depressing effect on the person who told the story. And she was left alone to herself.

Days went by, and Ninny was still without a face. They became accustomed to seeing her pink dress marching along behind Moominmamma. As soon as Moominmamma stopped, the silver bell also stopped, and when she continued her way the bell began tinkling again. A bit above the dress a big rose-pink bow was bobbing in thin air.

Moominmamma continued to treat Ninny with Granny's medicine, but nothing further happened. So after some time she stopped the treatment, thinking that many people had managed all right before without a head, and besides perhaps Ninny wasn't very good-looking.

Now everyone could imagine for himself what she looked like, and this can often brighten up a relationship.

One day the family went off through the wood down to the beach. They were going to pull the boat up for winter. Ninny came tinkling behind as usual, but when they came in view of the sea she suddenly stopped. Then she lay down on her stomach in the sand and started to whine.

"What's come over Ninny? Is she frightened?" asked Moominpappa.

"Perhaps she hasn't seen the sea before," Moominmamma said. She stooped and exchanged a few whispering words with Ninny. Then she straightened up again and said:

"No, it's the first time. Ninny thinks the sea's too big."

"Of all the silly kids," little My started, but Moominmamma gave her a severe look and said: "Don't be a silly kid yourself. Now let's pull the boat ashore."

They went out on the landing-stage to the bathing hut where Too-ticky lived, and knocked at the door.

"Hullo," Too-ticky said, "how's the invisible child?"

"There's only her snout left," Moominpappa replied. "At the moment she's a bit startled but it'll pass over. Can you lend us a hand with the boat?"

"Certainly," Too-ticky said.

While the boat was pulled ashore and turned keel upwards Ninny had padded down to the water's edge and was standing immobile on the wet sand. They left her alone.

Moominmamma sat down on the landing-stage and looked down into the water. "Dear me, how cold it looks," she said. And then she yawned a bit and added that nothing exciting had happened for weeks.

Moominpappa gave Moomintroll a wink, pulled a horrible face and started to steal up to Moominmamma from behind.

Of course he didn't really think of pushing her in the water as he had done many times when she was young. Perhaps he didn't even want to startle her, but just to amuse the kids a little.

But before he reached her a sharp cry was heard, a pink streak of lightning shot over the landing-stage, and Moominpappa let out a scream and dropped his hat into the water. Ninny had sunk her small invisible teeth in Moominpappa's tail, and they were sharp.

"Good work!" cried My. "I couldn't have done it better myself!"

Ninny was standing on the landing-stage. She had a small, snub-nosed, angry face below a red tangle of hair. She was hissing at Moominpappa like a cat.

"Don't you *dare* push her into the big horrible sea!" she cried.

"I see her, I see her!" shouted Moomintroll. "She's sweet!"

"Sweet my eye," said Moominpappa, inspecting his bitten tail. "She's the silliest, nastiest, badly-brought-uppest child I've ever seen, with or without a head."

He knelt down on the landing-stage and tried to fish for his hat with a stick. And in some mysterious way he managed to tip himself over, and tumbled in on his head.

He came up at once, standing safely on the bottom, with his snout above water and his ears filled with mud.

"Oh dear!" Ninny was shouting. "Oh, how great! Oh, how funny!"

The landing-stage shook with her laughter.

"I believe she's never laughed before," Too-ticky said wonderingly. "You seem to have changed her, she's even worse than little My. But the main thing is that one can see her, of course."

"It's all thanks to Granny," Moominmamma said.

from **THE BORROWERS**

*Mary Norton*

*If you know exactly where you put your favorite pencil, but it is not there when you return for it, then probably your house has* THEM *—the* BORROWERS. *They are tiny ingenious folk who live under the floor and who borrow what they need from "human beans"—such as a thimble for a kettle, or a stamp for a portrait to hang on their walls. Their greatest danger is being seen by the giant humans. In this chapter, Pod returns from a borrowing expedition, thoroughly frightened—he has been seen!*

### [Danger!]

Pod came in slowly, his sack on his back; he leaned his hat pin, with its dangling name-tape, against the wall and, on the middle of the kitchen table, he placed a doll's tea cup; it was the size of a mixing bowl.

"Why, Pod—" began Homily.

"Got the saucer too," he said. He swung down the sack and untied the neck. "Here you are," he said, drawing out the saucer. "Matches it."

He had a round, currant-bunny sort of face; tonight it looked flabby.

"Oh, Pod," said Homily, "you do look queer. Are you all right?"

Pod sat down. "I'm fair enough," he said.

"You went up the curtain," said Homily. "Oh, Pod, you shouldn't have. It's shaken you—"

Pod made a strange face, his eyes swiveled round toward Arrietty. Homily stared at him, her mouth open, and then she turned. "Come along, Arrietty," she said briskly, "you pop off to bed, now, like a good girl, and I'll bring you some supper."

"Oh," said Arrietty, "can't I see the rest of the borrowings?"

"Your father's got nothing now. Only food. Off you pop to bed. You've seen the cup and saucer."

Arrietty went into the sitting room to put away her diary, and took some time fixing her candle on the upturned drawing pin which served as a holder.

"Whatever are you doing?" grumbled Homily. "Give it here. There, that's the way. Now off to bed and fold your clothes, mind."

"Good night, Papa," said Arrietty, kissing his flat white cheek.

"Careful of the light," he said mechanically, and watched her with his round eyes until she had closed the door.

"Now, Pod," said Homily, when they were alone, "tell me. What's the matter?"

Pod looked at her blankly. "I been 'seen,' " he said.

Homily put out a groping hand for the edge of the table; she grasped it and lowered herself slowly on to the stool. "Oh, Pod," she said.

There was silence between them. Pod stared at Homily and Homily stared at the table. After a while she raised her white face. "Badly?" she asked.

Pod moved restlessly. "I don't know about badly. I been 'seen.' Ain't that bad enough?"

"No one," said Homily slowly, "hasn't never been 'seen' since Uncle Hendreary and he was the first they say for forty-five years." A thought struck her and she gripped the table. "It's no good, Pod, I won't emigrate!"

"No one's asked you to," said Pod.

"To go and live like Hendreary and Lupy in a badger's set! The other side of the world, that's where they say it is—all among the earthworms."

"It's two fields away, above the spinney," said Pod.

"Nuts, that's what they eat. And berries. I wouldn't wonder if they don't eat mice—"

"You've eaten mice yourself," Pod reminded her.

"All draughts and fresh air and the children growing up wild. Think of Arrietty!" said Homily. "Think of the way she's been brought up. An only child. She'd catch her death. It's different for Hendreary."

"Why?" asked Pod. "He's got four."

"That's why," explained Homily. "When you've got four, they're brought up rough. But never mind that now. . . . Who saw you?"

"A boy," said Pod.

"A what?" exclaimed Homily, staring.

"A boy." Pod sketched out a rough shape in the air with his hands. "You know, a boy."

"But there isn't—I mean, what sort of a boy?"

"I don't know what you mean 'what sort of a boy.' A boy in a night-shirt. A boy. You know what a boy is, don't you?"

"Yes," said Homily, "I know what a boy is. But there hasn't been a boy, not in this house, these twenty years."

"Well," said Pod, "there's one here now."

Homily stared at him in silence, and Pod met her eyes. "Where did he see you?" asked Homily at last.

"In the schoolroom."

"Oh," said Homily, "when you was getting the cup?"

"Yes," said Pod.

"Haven't you got eyes?" asked Homily. "Couldn't you have looked first?"

"There's never nobody in the schoolroom. And what's more," he went on, "there wasn't today."

"Then where was he?"

"In bed. In the night-nursery or whatever it's called. That's where he was. Sitting up in bed. With the doors open."

"Well, you could have looked in the nursery."

"How could I—halfway up the curtain!"

"Is that where you was?"

"Yes."

"With the cup?"

"Yes. I couldn't get up or down."

"Oh, Pod," wailed Homily, "I should never have let you go. Not at your age!"

"Now, look here," said Pod, "don't mistake me. I got up all right. Got up like a bird, as you might say, bobbles or no bobbles. But"—he leaned toward her—"afterwards—with the cup in me hand, if you see what I mean. . . ." He picked it up off the table. "You see, it's heavy like. You can hold it by the handle, like this . . . but it drops or droops, as you might say. You should take a cup like this in your two hands. A bit of cheese off a shelf, or an apple—well, I drop that . . . give it a push and it falls and I climbs down in me own time and picks it up. But with a cup—you see what I mean? And coming down, you got to watch your feet. And, as I say, some of the bobbles was missing. You didn't know what you could hold on to, not safely. . . ."

"Oh, Pod," said Homily, her eyes full of tears, "what did you do?"

"Well," said Pod, sitting back again, "he took the cup."

"What do you mean?" exclaimed Homily, aghast.

Pod avoided her eyes. "Well, he'd been sitting up in bed there watching me. I'd been on that curtain a good ten minutes, because the hall clock had just struck the quarter—"

"But how do you mean—'he took the cup'?"

"Well, he'd got out of bed and there he was standing, looking up. 'I'll take the cup,' he said."

"Oh!" gasped Homily, her eyes staring, "and you give it him?"

"He took it," said Pod, "ever so gentle. And then, when I was down, he give it me." Homily put her face in her hands. "Now don't take on," said Pod uneasily.

"He might have caught you," shuddered Homily in a stifled voice.

"Yes," said Pod, "but he just give me the cup. 'Here you are,' he said."

Homily raised her face. "What are we going to do?" she asked.

Pod sighed. "Well, there isn't nothing we can do. Except—"

"Oh, no," exclaimed Homily, "not that. Not emigrate. Not that, Pod, now I've got the house so nice and a clock and all."

"We could take the clock," said Pod.

"And Arrietty? What about her? She's not like those cousins. She can *read,* Pod, and sew a treat—"

"He don't know where we live," said Pod.

"But they look," exclaimed Homily. "Remember Hendreary! They got the cat and—"

"Now, now," said Pod, "don't bring up the past."

"But you've got to think of it! They got the cat and—"

"Yes," said Pod, "but Eggletina was different."

"How different? She was Arrietty's age."

"Well, they hadn't told her, you see. That's where they went wrong. They tried to make her believe that there wasn't nothing but was under the floor. They never told her about Mrs. Driver or Crampfurl. Least of all about cats."

"There wasn't any cat," Homily pointed out, "not till Hendreary was 'seen.'"

"Well, there was, then," said Pod. "You got to tell them, that's what I say, or they try to find out for themselves."

"Pod," said Homily solemnly, "we haven't told Arrietty."

"Oh, she knows," said Pod; he moved uncomfortably. "She's got her grating."

"She doesn't know about Eggletina. She doesn't know about being 'seen.'"

"Well," said Pod, "we'll tell her. We always said we would. There's no hurry."

Homily stood up. "Pod," she said, "we're going to tell her now."

## from TISTOU OF THE GREEN THUMBS

### Maurice Druon

*Druon's allegory is one of the most charming in years, distinguished by the Gallic gift for understatement. This episode in which Tistou transforms a prison and yet humbly takes advice from his secret adviser, the old gardener Moustache, is one children will enjoy, and they may appreciate a discovery he makes in a later chapter: " 'I have discovered a most extraordinary thing,' whispered Tistou. 'Flowers prevent evil things from happening.' "*

### In Which Tistou Has a Bad Dream and What Happens as a Result of It

Certainly Tistou asked too many questions; he even went on asking them in his sleep.

The night after his lesson on order, he had an appalling nightmare. Of course, dreams are only dreams, and their importance should not be exaggerated. But one can't stop oneself dreaming.

So Tistou saw in his sleep his pony Gymnast, his head shaved, walking round and round in a circle between high, dark walls. And behind him the roan thoroughbreds, their heads shaved too, dressed in striped clothes, wearily dragging their feet along in ridiculous boots. Suddenly Gymnast, having first looked to right and left to see that no one was watching him, made a dash for the gates and tried to jump over them. But he fell back on the iron spikes. His ridiculous boots beat the air, and he neighed in the most lamentable way.

Tistou woke up with a start, his forehead was damp and his heart beating hard.

"Luckily it was only a dream," he said to himself very quickly. "Gymnast is in the stables and so are the thoroughbreds."

But he couldn't go to sleep again.

"What would be so hard on horses must be even worse for men," he thought. "Why should the poor prisoners be made to look so ugly; they

won't become any the better for it. I know quite well that, if I were shut up inside there, even if I had done nothing wrong before, I should most certainly become very wicked indeed. What can be done to make them less unhappy?"

He heard eleven o'clock and then midnight strike on the Mirepoil church clock. But he went on asking himself questions.

And, quite suddenly, he had the glimmerings of an idea.

"Supposing the poor prisoners were surrounded with flowers? Order would be a less ugly thing, and perhaps the prisoners would become better. Supposing I tried my green thumbs? I'll suggest it to Mr. Turnbull. . . ."

But then he thought that Mr. Turnbull would merely turn red in the face. And he remembered Moustache's advice not to speak of his green thumbs.

"I shall have to do it alone, without anyone knowing."

Once an idea has taken possession of one's mind it becomes a resolve. And a resolve never leaves one in peace till it has been acted upon. Tistou felt that he could not go to sleep again till he had put his plan into execution.

He got out of bed and searched for his slippers; one of them had hidden itself under the chest of drawers. But where was the other? The other was laughing at him, hanging from the window-latch. That's what comes of throwing your slippers about!

Tistou crept out of the room; the thick carpet deadened the sound of his steps.

He silently reached the banisters and slid down them on his stomach.

Outside, the moon was full. The man in the moon was blowing out his cheeks with fresh air.

On the whole, the moon is kind to people who go out into the night. Hardly had he seen Tistou crossing the lawn in his long white night-shirt, than he polished up his face with a cloud that happened to be in reach of his hand.

"If I don't watch over that boy," he said to himself, "he'll end up by falling into a ditch."

The moon reappeared, brighter than ever, and even sent a message to the stars of the Milky Way asking them to twinkle as brightly as they could.

Protected by the moon and the stars, Tistou, half walking, half running through the deserted streets, reached the prison without incident.

He was a little bit nervous, of course. This was his first adventure.

"If only my green thumbs work properly!" he thought. "If only Moustache hasn't made a mistake!"

Tistou poked his thumbs wherever he could, into the earth, into the crack between the wall and the pavement, into the crevices between the stones, into the sockets of each prison bar. He worked very conscientiously. He didn't even neglect the keyhole of the entrance gate, or the sentry-box where a guard was asleep.

When he had finished, he went home and fell asleep at once.

Indeed, Carolus had considerable difficulty in waking him in the morning.

"Wake up, Tisti! Sun shine bright!" We have already mentioned the fact that Carolus spoke with a foreign accent.

There was a question on the tip of Tistou's tongue, but he dared not ask it. All the same, he did not have to wait long to know the result of his experiment.

For, goodness me, what had happened to the prison? If Mr. Turnbull had fired a big gun in the middle of Mirepoil Square, he couldn't have created more excitement! Imagine the bewilderment of the whole town at the spectacle of such a wonder! Imagine the astonishment of the people when they saw their prison transformed into a castle of flowers, into a palace of marvels!

Before ten o'clock, the whole town had heard the fabulous news. By midday the whole population was gathered in front of the high wall covered with roses and the bars transformed into arbors.

There was not a window in the prison, not a single bar which had not received its share of flowers. Creepers climbed and clung and hung down; while the horrid spikes on the walls had been replaced by cacti.

The most odd sight of all was perhaps the sentry-box over which honeysuckle had grown so thickly that the guard was imprisoned inside. The plants had used his rifle as a prop and had blocked the entrance. The astonished crowd gazed at the guard, who was calmly and resignedly smoking his pipe in the shelter of a bower.

No one could explain the miracle. No one except, of course, Moustache, who came to have a look like everyone else and then went off without a word.

But that afternoon, when Tistou put on his straw hat for his second gardening lesson and went in search of him, Moustache greeted him with, "Oh, so there you are! Not bad, not bad at all! For a start, you've done very well."

Tistou felt rather embarrassed.

"Without you, Mr. Moustache, I should never have known I had green thumbs," said Tistou, by way of rendering thanks.

But Moustache did not like people to be effusive.

"All right, all right," he said. "But you've used too much honeysuckle. And you must beware of aristolochia. It's a fast-growing creeper but its leaves are dark. Next time, use rather more morning-glory; it'll add a note of gaiety."

Thus Moustache became Tistou's secret adviser.

## from THE BOOK OF THREE
### Lloyd Alexander

The Book of Three *is the first of five books that stirringly recount the chronicles of the land of Prydain and the high destiny of Taran, the impetuous and impatient Pig-Keeper. It was selected as an A.L.A. Notable Book, and the final book in the cycle,* The High King, *was awarded the Newbery Medal. In this chapter of the first book, we meet Gurgi, a seemingly repugnant creature who, nevertheless, becomes Taran's follower and ultimately obtains for him a priceless treasure of knowledge. Gurgi's strangeness, his courage, and his essential goodness are so well delineated and made so plausible that he emerges, in this outstanding fantasy, as a unique character to be much loved and long remembered. It is also in this chapter that the dimensions of the Prydain epic begin to take their shape.*

### Gurgi

By the time Taran woke, Gwydion had already saddled Melyngar. The cloak Taran had slept in was damp with dew. Every joint ached from his night on the hard ground. With Gwydion's urging, Taran stumbled toward the horse, a white blur in the gray-pink dawn. Gwydion hauled Taran into the saddle behind him, spoke a quiet command, and the white steed moved quickly into the rising mist.

Gwydion was seeking the spot where Taran had last seen Hen Wen. But long before they had reached it, he reined up Melyngar and dismounted. As Taran watched, Gwydion knelt and sighted along the turf.

"Luck is with us," he said. "I think we have struck her trail." Gwydion pointed to a faint circle of trampled grass. "Here she slept, and not too long ago." He strode a few paces forward, scanning every broken twig and blade of grass.

Despite Taran's disappointment at finding the Lord Gwydion dressed in a coarse jacket and mud-spattered boots, he followed the man with growing admiration. Nothing, Taran saw, escaped Gwydion's eyes. Like a lean, gray wolf, he moved silently and easily. A little way on, Gwydion stopped, raised his shaggy head and narrowed his eyes toward a distant ridge.

"The trail is not clear," he said, frowning. "I can only guess she might have gone down the slope."

"With all the forest to run in," Taran queried, "how can we begin to search? She might have gone anywhere in Prydain."

"Not quite," answered Gwydion. "I may not know where she went, but I can be sure where she did *not* go." He pulled a hunting knife from his belt. "Here, I will show you."

Gwydion knelt and quickly traced lines in the earth. "These are the Eagle Mountains," he

said, with a touch of longing in his voice, "in my own land of the north. Here, Great Avren flows. See how it turns west before it reaches the sea. We may have to cross it before our search ends. And this is the River Ystrad. Its valley leads north to Caer Dathyl.

"But see here," Gwydion went on, pointing to the left of the line he had drawn for the River Ystrad, "here is Mount Dragon and the domain of Arawn. Hen Wen would shun this above all. She was too long a captive in Annuvin; she would never venture near it."

"Was Hen in Annuvin?" Taran asked with surprise. "But how . . ."

"Long ago," Gwydion said, "Hen Wen lived among the race of men. She belonged to a farmer who had no idea at all of her powers. And so she might have spent her days as any ordinary pig. But Arawn knew her to be far from ordinary, and of such value that he himself rode out of Annuvin and seized her. What dire things happened while she was prisoner of Arawn—it is better not to speak of them."

"Poor Hen," Taran said, "it must have been terrible for her. But how did she escape?"

"She did not escape," said Gwydion. "She was rescued. A warrior went alone into the depths of Annuvin and brought her back safely."

"That was a brave deed!" Taran cried. "I wish that I . . ."

"The bards of the north still sing of it," Gwydion said. "His name shall never be forgotten."

"Who was it?" Taran demanded.

Gwydion looked closely at him. "Do you not know?" he asked. "Dallben has neglected your education. It was Coll," he said. "Coll Son of Collfrewr."

"Coll!" Taran cried. "Not the same . . ."

"The same," said Gwydion.

"But . . . but . . . ," Taran stammered. "Coll? A hero? But . . . he's so bald!"

Gwydion laughed and shook his head. "Assistant Pig-Keeper," he said, "you have curious notions about heroes. I have never known courage to be judged by the length of a man's hair. Or, for the matter of that, whether he has any hair at all."

Crestfallen, Taran peered at Gwydion's map and said no more.

"Here," continued Gwydion, "not far from Annuvin, lies Spiral Castle. This, too, Hen Wen would avoid at all cost. It is the abode of Queen Achren. She is as dangerous as Arawn himself; as evil as she is beautiful. But there are secrets concerning Achren which are better left untold.

"I am sure," Gwydion went on, "Hen Wen will not go toward Annuvin or Spiral Castle. From what little I can see, she has run straight ahead. Quickly now, we shall try to pick up her trail."

Gwydion turned Melyngar toward the ridge. As they reached the bottom of the slope, Taran heard the waters of Great Avren rushing like wind in a summer storm.

"We must go again on foot," Gwydion said. "Her tracks may show somewhere along here, so we had best move slowly and carefully. Stay close behind me," he ordered. "If you start dashing ahead—and you seem to have that tendency—you will trample out any signs she might have left."

Taran obediently walked a few paces behind. Gwydion made no more sound than the shadow of a bird. Melyngar herself stepped quietly; hardly a twig snapped under her hoofs. Try as he would, Taran could not go as silently. The more careful he attempted to be, the louder the leaves rattled and crackled. Wherever he put his foot, there seemed to be a hole or spiteful branch to trip him up. Even Melyngar turned and gave him a reproachful look.

Taran grew so absorbed in not making noise that he soon lagged far behind Gwydion. On the slope, Taran believed he could make out something round and white. He yearned to be the first to find Hen Wen and he turned aside, clambered through the weeds—to discover nothing more than a boulder.

Disappointed, Taran hastened to catch up with Gwydion. Overhead, the branches rustled. As he stopped and looked up, something fell heavily to the ground behind him. Two hairy and powerful hands locked around his throat.

Whatever had seized him made barking and snorting noises. Taran forced out a cry for help. He struggled with his unseen opponent, twisting, flailing his legs, and throwing himself from one side to the other.

Suddenly he could breathe again. A shape sailed over his head and crashed against a tree trunk. Taran dropped to the ground and began rubbing his neck. Gwydion stood beside him. Sprawled under the tree was the strangest creature Taran had ever seen. He could not be sure whether it was animal or human. He decided it was both. Its hair was so matted and covered with leaves that it looked like an owl's nest in need of housecleaning. It had long, skinny, woolly arms, and a pair of feet as flexible and grimy as its hands.

Gwydion was watching the creature with a look of severity and annoyance. "So it is you," he said. "I ordered you not to hinder me or anyone under my protection."

At this, the creature set up a loud and piteous whining, rolled his eyes, and beat the ground with his palms.

"It is only Gurgi," Gwydion said. "He is always lurking about one place or another. He is not half as ferocious as he looks, not a quarter as fierce as he should like to be, and more a nuisance than anything else. Somehow, he manages to see most of what happens, and he might be able to help us."

Taran had just begun to catch his breath. He was covered with Gurgi's shedding hair, in addition to the distressing odor of a wet wolfhound.

"O mighty prince," the creature wailed, "Gurgi is sorry; and now he will be smacked on his poor, tender head by the strong hands of this great lord, with fearsome smackings. Yes, yes, that is always the way of it with poor Gurgi. But what honor to be smacked by the greatest of warriors!"

"I have no intention of smacking your poor, tender head," said Gwydion. "But I may change my mind if you do not leave off that whining and sniveling."

"Yes, powerful lord!" Gurgi cried. "See how he obeys rapidly and instantly!" He began crawling about on hands and knees with great agility. Had Gurgi owned a tail, Taran was sure he would have wagged it frantically.

"Then," Gurgi pleaded, "the two strengthful heroes will give Gurgi something to eat? Oh joyous crunchings and munchings!"

"Afterward," said Gwydion. "When you have answered our questions."

"Oh, afterward!" cried Gurgi. "Poor Gurgi can wait, long, long for his crunchings and munchings. Many years from now, when the great princes revel in their halls—what feastings—they will remember hungry, wretched Gurgi waiting for them."

"How long you wait for your crunchings and munchings," Gwydion said, "depends on how quickly you tell us what we want to know. Have you seen a white pig this morning?"

A crafty look gleamed in Gurgi's close-set little eyes. "For the seeking of a piggy, there are many great lords in the forest, riding with frightening shouts. *They* would not be cruel to starving Gurgi—oh, no—they would feed him . . ."

"They would have your head off your shoulders before you could think twice about it," Gwydion said. "Did one of them wear an antlered mask?"

"Yes, yes!" Gurgi cried. "The great horns! You will save miserable Gurgi from hurtful choppings!" He set up a long and dreadful howling.

"I am losing patience with you," warned Gwydion. "Where is the pig?"

"Gurgi hears these mighty riders," the creature went on. "Oh, yes, with careful listenings from the trees. Gurgi is so quiet and clever, and no one cares about him. But he listens! These great warriors say they have gone to a certain place, but great fire turns them away. They are not pleased, and they still seek a piggy with outcries and horses."

"Gurgi," said Gwydion firmly, "where is the pig?"

"The piggy? Oh, terrible hunger pinches! Gurgi cannot remember. Was there a piggy? Gurgi is fainting and falling into the bushes, his poor, tender head is full of air from his empty belly."

Taran could no longer control his impatience. "Where is Hen Wen, you silly, hairy thing?" he burst out. "Tell us straight off! After the way you jumped on me, you deserve to have your head smacked."

With a moan, Gurgi rolled over on his back and covered his face with his arms.

Gwydion turned severely to Taran. "Had you followed my orders, you would not have been jumped on. Leave him to me. Do not make him any more frightened than he is." Gwydion looked down at Gurgi. "Very well," he asked calmly, "where is she?"

"Oh, fearful wrath!" Gurgi snuffled, "a piggy has gone across the water with swimmings and splashings." He sat upright and waved a woolly arm toward Great Avren.

"If you are lying to me," said Gwydion, "I shall soon find out. Then I will surely come back with wrath."

"Crunchings and munchings now, mighty prince?" asked Gurgi in a high, tiny whimper.

"As I promised you," said Gwydion.

"Gurgi wants the smaller one for munchings," said the creature, with a beady glance at Taran.

"No, you do not," Gwydion said. "He is an Assistant Pig-Keeper and he would disagree with you violently." He unbuckled a saddlebag and pulled out a few strips of dried meat, which he tossed to Gurgi. "Be off now. Remember, I want no mischief from you."

Gurgi snatched the food, thrust it between his teeth, and scuttled up a tree trunk, leaping from tree to tree until he was out of sight.

"What a disgusting beast," said Taran. "What a nasty, vicious . . ."

"Oh, he is not bad at heart," Gwydion answered. "He would love to be wicked and terrifying, though he cannot quite manage it. He feels so sorry for himself that it is hard not to be angry with him. But there is no use in doing so."

"Was he telling the truth about Hen Wen?" asked Taran.

"I think he was," Gwydion said. "It is as I feared. The Horned King has ridden to Caer Dallben."

"He burned it!" Taran cried. Until now, he had paid little mind to his home. The thought of the white cottage in flames, his memory of Dallben's beard, and the heroic Coll's bald head touched him all at once. "Dallben and Coll are in peril!"

"Surely not," said Gwydion. "Dallben is an old fox. A beetle could not creep into Caer Dallben without his knowledge. No, I am certain the fire was something Dallben arranged for unexpected visitors.

"Hen Wen is the one in greatest peril. Our quest grows ever more urgent," Gwydion hastily continued. "The Horned King knows she is missing. He will pursue her."

"Then," Taran cried, "we must find her before he does!"

"Assistant Pig-Keeper," said Gwydion, "that has been, so far, your only sensible suggestion."

## from THE WHISPER OF GLOCKEN

### Carol Kendall

*This book carries on the chronicles of the Minnipins from the isolated valley called the Land Between the Mountains, first recorded in* The Gammage Cup. *The earlier volume told of the five famous Outlaw Heroes who fought against conformity and defended the valley from the Mushrooms. In* The Whisper of Glocken *the valley is threatened when the waters of the Watercress River mysteriously flow backward. Five New Heroes are sent by the Old Heroes to learn why the river has changed direction. Glocken, the bell-ringer of the village of Water Gap, is one of the five reluctant companions. He also knows more than anyone else about the famous bell called the* Whisper of Glocken, *and his knowledge and the bell are integral to the story. In this selection the five New Heroes live through one of their many desperate moments, and it is the courageous action of Gam Lutie which saves them all as she does what she can to deal with the terrible egg-like creatures.*

### [A Long Night of Terror]

Bleakly staring at the mountain barrier flung against the sky, Gam Lutie felt a tremor of—could it be fear? Of course not, she told herself, but the tremor persisted, quivering up from her middle into her very throat. Fear? Gam Lutie afraid? Unthinkable!

"I expect," someone was saying, "that is, I really do think it is time to open this hamper."

Gam Lutie snapped her eyes away from the fearsome Barrier. "Don't speak foolishness at such a time!"

But Scumble had already thrown back the cover of the hamper.

"Have you left your senses behind?" demanded Gam Lutie. "Close up the treasure this—" The thin, whimpering cry from the hamper cut her off.

"Oh Scumble!" Silky cried. "Oh Scumble! You brought him!" Falling to her knees before the hamper, she tenderly lifted out the baby Digger. He blinked round at them with frightened greeny eyes.

Gam Lutie's throat went dry. The treasure . . . the treasure that was forever to be in her keeping, that she had brought so carefully with her to preserve it from harm. . . .

"Oh Scumble," Silky stopped her crooning sounds over the spidery creature long enough to say, "I can't tell you . . ."

"I can." Gam Lutie had found her voice, and a terrible voice it was. *"Where is the treasure?"*

Scumble had the grace to look shamefaced. "Tunnel," he mumbled.

She wanted to beat her fists on his head . . . to grind him into the iron hard ground . . . to. . . . With a tremendous gasp, she got hold of herself. It took every fiber of will she possessed to control the furious pounding in her temples. When at last she could trust herself to speak again, she had to push the words out between her teeth.

"There . . . is . . . no trust . . . in you."

Crustabread looked from the hamper to her. "You are wrong," he said. "Scumble is all trust. None of the rest of us was thinking with his brain. We might have starved here."

"When you're hungry," said Scumble modestly, "it's better to think with your stomach." With a tug, he brought out of the hamper a large moon-melon and laid it carefully on the ground. "There wasn't room for more than two." He had been avoiding Gam Lutie's eyes, but now he straightened and dared look back at her. "I'm sorry, Gam Lutie," he said after a nervous swallow. "I hid the bronze chest in a niche high up in the wall of the tunnel. I promise you it's safe."

"Shall I carve?" asked Glocken.

*I won't eat of it, I won't*, Gam Lutie repeated over and over to herself. *I will not be a partner to perfidy.* But when the pieces of melon were laid out, and the others respectfully waited for her to serve herself, her hand scarcely hesitated in reaching for a slice. Retiring a little from the rest, she forced herself to eat as though her throat wasn't a parched desert. Her aloofness had little effect on the others, who unashamedly slurped and gulped and smacked like noisy greedy sucking-fish.

*Listen to their noise. . . . Listen. . . .* Gam Lutie shrank back as she realized that her own lips were smacking over the melon as loudly as theirs. She must get hold of herself! She must!

They brought her fishcake and bread from their own shares, but she refused with what seemed the rightful degree of haughtiness, and then wished she had taken some, for her act of self-denial went unnoticed.

The moon was slipping away now, the earth darkening, and the cold more bitter. Only Gam Lutie's pride kept her from joining the huddled warmth of the others. Silky had wrapped the shivering baby Digger in a fold of her cloak, and she made odious cooing sounds over him the while she pushed bits of the moon-melon into his mouth. Glocken was fumbling with the scroll which Walter the Earl had given him, trying to make his numb fingers manage the charcoal-stick. Gam Lutie's eyes passed over Scumble the faithless.

Crustabread came to his feet, even in his weariness moving more like a woods animal than a Minnipin. "We must go on."

There was no argument. One by one they groaned upward, adjusted their packs. Silky laid the baby Digger in the hamper with the second moon-melon and lowered the lid. Without a word, Glocken picked up the hamper and plodded off after Crustabread. Gam Lutie fell in behind, then Silky, and last of all, Scumble.

They had picked their frozen way for perhaps half an hour when Glocken suddenly gave a great groan and doubled over, clutching his middle.

"What is it?" Gam Lutie hurried forward. "What's the matter with you?" She knelt beside him where he was squirming on the hard ground. Crustabread came running back.

"Something . . . biting . . . my middle," Glocken gasped. "Gam Lutie . . . I'm dying. . . ."

"Nonsense," said Gam Lutie with a certainty she wasn't at all certain of. She pushed his hair back and felt his forehead. Clammy. His feet suddenly thrashed out, and his whole middle arched like a bridge.

"What's wrong with him?" Silky whispered, horrified.

Gam Lutie pushed her aside. "I must have hot water, and at once. Crustabread, set fire to one of those dry, bushy plants. Silky, give me the herb basket. And get Glocken's water bottle out of his pack and wrap his cloak around him. Better get all the water bottles together and heat them—just in case."

"Just in case of *what?*" Silky's eyes were wide as she untied the herb basket from her belt.

"In case we need them. What else? Now move!" Gam Lutie tore at the fastenings of the herb basket. Fishcakes. She was sure it was the fishcakes, too long in the broiling sun at the tunnel's mouth yesterday. Fish-poisoning. Essence of Emptie, she muttered as she rummaged through the clay pots and bottles. Essence of Emptie. Her numbed fingers stumbled about until she found the right one. DANGER, shouted the label in blood-berry ink. NEVER USE FULL STRENGTH. USE ONLY IF ALL ELSE FAILS.

Idiot, Gam Lutie said between her teeth, if I wait to see all else failing, it will be too late for the Essence. Willing her hands to remain steady, she measured half a spoonful of the mud-brown liquid into the clay medicine cup.

Behind her, one of the dry bushes flamed up, and she heard Crustabread call to Scumble to uproot more of the bushes to feed the fire. The clinking sounds told her that Silky was propping the stone bottles around the flames.

Near at hand the baby Digger, spilled from the hamper when Glocken went sprawling, kept up a steady whimpering that grated on Gam Lutie's raw nerves.

Glocken suddenly began to shiver, but when Gam Lutie tried to wrap him closer in his cloak, he kicked it off again with his thrashing feet. When she tried to rub his icy hands, he jerked them away. Then Silky silently appeared and handed over a steaming flask wrapped round with folds of cloth. Carefully, Gam Lutie measured the water into the Essence of Emptie and watched it turn murky. She handed the flask back to Silky and waved her away.

"Glocken!" she commanded with all the authority in her, "stop this silly groaning and take your medicine. Sit up and drink this." She yanked him upright, and when he opened his mouth to protest, poured the murky liquid down his throat. He coughed and sputtered, but the Essence of Emptie stayed down, and Gam Lutie sat back on her heels. He would be sick, and when his stomach was empty, he would recover. Probably.

The baby Digger whimpered louder, and Gam Lutie, irritated, called to Silky to see to him since she had appointed herself his caretaker. There was no answer.

"Silky!" she repeated, fear sharpening her voice.

Nothing, except—was that a little cry above the snapping of the fire?

Alarmed, Gam Lutie sprang to her feet and stared round her in the half-light of the coming dawn. The fire still blazed, and wisps of steam curled up from the stone flasks encircling it. But the other Minnipins had disappeared as though wiped off the face of the desert.

"Crustabread! Silky! Scumble! Answer me!" Her voice disappeared after them into the frozen loneliness.

She stood stock-still for an instant, the fear gnawing at her, and then, when she felt certain that she could keep her legs from running wildly into the desert, she snatched up the herb basket and a water flask and began to circle the burning bush. The lightening sky revealed nothing but the ghostly shapes of desert plants.

But then Glocken called feebly, and she had to hurry back to where he was staggering to his feet. She led him off a few steps and held his head while he was sick.

"Better," he gasped, leaning heavily against her. "Cold . . ." and he began to shiver violently.

She dragged him back to the fire and wrapped his cloak securely about him. He gave her a twist of a smile and closed his eyes.

This time she made a wider cast around the fire, and then a still wider one, fanning out farther and farther into the desert from the mountain's base. It wasn't until the next semicircle that she stumbled over Silky. She was doubled up on the ground on the far side of the fire, and her breathing came in stutters.

Gam Lutie went swiftly to work, her mind in a ferment of dread. If Silky was this bad, would Scumble and Crustabread still be alive when she found them? It was a punishment, of course. And a just one. They had left behind the treasure and punished themselves by eating bad fishcakes. Certainly it was only justice that they pay for their perfidy with sick stomachs. But death . . . ? She finally had to pry Silky's teeth apart with the spoon and pour the medicine mixture down her throat.

She spent another precious minute striking a spark to a nearby dry bush to mark the spot, and then she hurried on with her herb basket, in an ever-widening fan, to find Scumble and Crustabread. The desert was a lighter gray now. Time . . . time . . .

A moment later she came upon Scumble, but the sight of him was horrifying. He was draped headfirst over a plant—he must have toppled into it when the sickness had taken him. Dried blood caked a hundred punctures where the thorns had punctured his skin. Thorns . . . ! Gam Lutie choked back a cry, for Scumble had keeled over into a death-plant.

Setting her teeth, she went to work to disentangle him. The thorns clung tenaciously to his clothing, resisting her pulls and tugs. She dared not think of what poisons were seeping into his blood. Her thoughts touched on the Mushroom salve that Silky had wasted on the baby Digger—and on the pot broken in the struggle for it—and shied away to Crustabread, still somewhere on the desert, still untreated. She raised her head to call out.

"Crustabread! Crustabread! Where are you!" But her voice was thin and useless in the vastness, and it ended on a sob.

Frenziedly she attacked the death-plant. Cruel barbs slashed at her, tore her hands. She ripped back, no longer caring what venoms she was releasing, only determined to overcome this baneful plant at last. But for every thorn that she pulled out of Scumble's clothes, two more snagged him. If she only had Hack the Butcher's long knife. . . .

Long knife. . . . Her jaw dropped. But she *had* a long knife—the sword of the Minnipins! What had gone wrong with her headpiece! She was acting as addled as a hooter-bird smoked out of a hollow tree.

The sword of the Minnipins sliced through the death-plant like a knife through a fresh stringy bean. In three whacks, Scumble came free from the plant's clutches and sagged against her. Dropping the sword, she lowered him to the hard ground and snatched the bottle of Essence from the herb basket.

He looked dead.

In desperation, Gam Lutie tilted the bottle and trickled Essence of Emptie directly into his mouth. NEVER USE FULL STRENGTH—the warning words shouted at her in the blood-berry ink. *I can't help it,* she half-sobbed, not knowing whether she spoke aloud or only thought the words. *He will surely die without it. If it burns out his voice, at least he will still live. . . .*

When she was sure that the Essence was down to stay, she tilted the water flask to Scumble's mouth to offset the searing effects of the strong medicine, but most of the water ran out. Gently she laid him on his side on the ground and struggled to her feet. There was nothing more she could do for him except to pluck the rest of the thorns from his clothing, and that could wait until she had found Crustabread. She knew it was surely too late to save Crustabread's life, but she must make the effort. She didn't take time to kindle another fire. There was enough light now to find her way back.

Grasping her sword and catching up the herb basket on the other arm, she struck out once more in an ever bigger arc from the mountain barrier.

They should never have come on this expedition, she thought bitterly. They weren't fitted for it. What could even a Gam Lutie do with a band of folk like these—fish oil, sarcen silk, and bells. And the other one? Who knew about Crustabread? He was silence and a queer little gulp. Despair seized her. Deep black despair such as she had never known, despair that was supposed to be alien to anybody carrying the Gam Lutie name. Was she no better then, under

a desert sky, than a Scumble or a Glocken or even a flittery Silky? It was a galling thought.

After a while, between one dreary step and the next, she thought of the book of Muggles' *Maxims* in the herb basket. "When all is despair, open this book and read what is there." She had no faith in the simple Muggles' ability to overcome a Gam Lutie's despondency, but it cost little effort to extract the book from the basket and let it fall open in her hands. When this was done, she bent her head and read in the early light, *The turtle soup doesn't burn until all the liquor has boiled away.*

For a moment she didn't take it in and read it again, her cracked lips moving with the words. Then she gave a snort and clapped the book to. *Very* helpful! Turtle soup, really! Clearly, the Muggles one was not in possession of all her head elements.

In any case, now she knew where she stood —alone. It is where a Gam Lutie always stood. Alone and dependable. All was not lost so long as Gam Lutie was still able to move! She lifted her head and stepped out more determinedly. Her right hand had begun to tingle, and she switched the sword to her left.

A moment later she faltered to a halt and stood staring down at the sword. There could be no doubt. The tingling, now in her left hand, was coming from the sword's hilt. It was warm to the touch. And the blackened blade— wasn't it less black now? Fearfully, she raised her head and, turning in a slow circle, scanned the desert reaches. There was nothing—nothing except the Barrier on one side and the endless scrubby growth of the desert floor. Nothing moved—and yet the sword grew warm in her hand. It was the secret of the swords—the secret that told of danger nearby as clearly as a shout.

With a last anguished scanning of the ground round her for a sight of Crustabread, she turned and fled back to the thread of smoke that marked the first campfire. She must gather her patients together, try to rouse them. She. . . . Suddenly her foot plunged through the hard crust of the earth, and she pitched to the ground, the sword knocked from her hand.

At the same moment an unearthly screech split the air.

Stumbling, scrambling, she wrenched her foot

out of the hole . . . *hole!* . . . snatched up the sword, and stumbled on.

Another shrill scream. It was the baby Digger, struggling on the ground against a—a thing that tore at the dressings on his hurt leg.

Without any will on Gam Lutie's part, the sword lifted and fell, cleaving the thing in two.

She was too stunned for a moment to move. The two splits lay at her feet, but in her mind she could still see the thing whole—a crusty, greenish-brown egg shape, flatter on the bottom, about the size of one of Prize the Baker's loaves. Where the sword had cut it through, it leaked a thick white substance. Its tearing claws were folded now, but Gam Lutie remembered with a shudder how powerfully they had shredded the wrappings of the baby Digger's leg. It had a tail. . . . Fighting against the sick feeling inside her, Gam Lutie bent closer. The tail was in segments—like the vine of the wild grape—and it snaked across the ground as far as Gam Lutie could see.

She caught her breath. There beyond Glocken —a faint movement, a shifting of the ground. . . . The hard earth bulged again, and once more, and then there slowly emerged another monstrous greenish-brown egg. It rested immobile for a moment before it slowly, slowly began to move, drawing its ropy tail out of the hole behind it. Gam Lutie held her breath as it got nearer to Glocken, but it crawled round him and headed directly for the baby Digger.

She let it get right up to the wounded leg before she brought the sword down. The thing died without sound and with only a twitch of its long tail.

Swaying over the two collapsed egg-shapes, Gam Lutie tried to think. The things had ignored Glocken, but had gone for the baby Digger's injured leg. What had called them forth from the ground? The smell of blood? Or simply the break of day? Or . . . ? Her eyes fell on the still-smouldering campfire, and she rubbed her forehead tiredly. Whatever had brought them forth, they traveled round Glocken to reach the baby Digger. The baby Digger's wounded leg. Did they only attack the injured, then? Were you safe from them as long as you had no open wounds?

Scumble! Scumble had a hundred open wounds where the thorns had pierced his skin!

Scooping the baby Digger into her arms, she fled toward the spot where she had left Scumble. She paused to look at Silky, unharmed and peacefully asleep. But what she saw near the smoking ashes of the fire she had made there, sent her lurching, staggering on. Pits—half a hundred pits in the ground where there had been none before—and from each of them an ominous tail stretched like a thin snake. They were all going in the same direction. Toward Scumble.

The baby Digger whimpered and struggled in her arms, she only held him tighter. She must hang on to him above all things, for it might be that she would have to use him to draw the egg-shapes away from Scumble.

The next moment, she was amongst them. The ground tilted and swayed with the army of murderous eggs. There was no mercy in Gam Lutie's sword as it hacked a way through the swarm to reach Scumble just beyond. The sword leaped in her hand, struck, and leaped again.

At last she was leaning over Scumble. None of the egg-shapes had reached him. Gam Lutie squeezed her eyes tight shut for an instant and drew a deep breath. She dared not think what would have happened had she lighted a fire near Scumble, for it was surely the heat of the fires which had drawn the egg-shapes from their beds to the attack. Had there been a fire closer than Silky's, the things could have broken ground and torn Scumble to shreds before she even knew of their existence. She wouldn't allow herself to think of Crustabread helpless somewhere on the desert. . . .

Turning abruptly, she waited for the rest of the egg-shapes to arrive. They paid no attention to their slain kin but moved over and round them to reach their own doom by the sword of the Minnipins. They came and came and came, and at last they came no more.

Stupid with fatigue, Gam Lutie let her sword tip touch the ground, its hilt once more cool in her palm. The dun earth was white with the thick substance that leaked from the egg-shapes, and she stepped back, sickened. Her mind was clotted with weariness and worry, but there was still so much to do. There was Crustabread. . . .

She called his name, feebly, hopelessly, knowing that he would not answer. The sky was flushed with color now. The sun, their enemy, had risen beyond the Barrier. When it topped the ridge, its full glare would sap her remaining strength. What must be done, must be done before the sun looked over the ridge.

She dropped to her knees beside Scumble and laid the baby Digger carefully on the ground. He made a soft whining noise, his eyes glazed with fear.

"It's all right," she said impatiently. The sound of her voice was strange after such a long silence—and oddly comforting. She went on talking, though of course the creature could have no idea of what she was saying. "We've got to get these thorns out of the way first. If the poison comes through the thorns, and Scumble so weakened already with the food poison. . . . And there is no more of the salve Muggles gave us. . . ."

The baby Digger lay watching her attentively, his greeny eyes wide and questioning.

Gam Lutie paused to pick a thorn from her own finger. The blood welled out. "If I had the salve," she went on, "I would put some on your leg too. I owe you that much, because if it hadn't been for your scream, the egg-shapes would have got Scumble before I knew they existed. Here, what are you trying to do? Lie still or you'll hurt your leg."

But the creature struggled to sit up, and seeing his determination, Gam Lutie stopped plucking thorns long enough to help him. He made peculiar little clicking sounds, and the greeny eyes bored into hers as though he would make her see into his mind. She nodded her head.

"Yes, yes, it's going to be all right."

The clicking came faster, and now he pointed at the cloven shells of the egg-shapes that lay behind her. Gam Lutie looked back fearfully, but nothing moved there.

"Yes, yes," she said irritably. "If any more of them come, I'll get rid of them." She put her hand to the hilt of the sword. It remained cool to her touch.

But now the baby Digger was pointing his needle-finger at her scratched and bloody hand, and his clicking cascaded over her. The finger swung back to the egg-shape, then once again to the scratches.

"What . . . ?" Gam Lutie sat back on her heels. "What are you trying to tell me? That the egg-shapes will come when they sense the blood? Yes, yes, I know that. I shall just—"

Scumble suddenly started thrashing about. Gam Lutie forgot the creature. She pulled and tugged Scumble upright and finally held his head while he got rid of the poisons in his stomach. Then she half-led, half-carried him a little distance away and lowered him to the ground between two of the poison-plants. He tried to say something to her, but his voice was the merest husk.

"It's all right," Gam Lutie said, hoping that it was. "Your throat is numb from the medicine, but it will pass. And you're stuck up with thorns, but I've got most of them out. Just go to sleep. I'll tuck you up." She pulled his cloak about him, wondering if Silky and Glocken were still covered. But dare she leave Scumble as long as there was danger of more egg-shapes appearing?

She went back to the spot where she had left the baby Digger. He wasn't there! She looked round frantically.

He was stretched out amongst the cloven shells, scooping up some of the thick white substance, which had flowed from them when the sword struck them in two. The thick white substance . . .

And then she knew! Knew what the little creature—the Wafer—had been trying to tell her.

She had found the source of the Mushroom's marvelous healing salve!

*from* **NO FLYING IN THE HOUSE**

*Betty Brock*

*Stories of children born of a mortal and a fairy are common in folk legendry, but they are seldom set in the present time as* No Flying in the House *is. The tiny dog, Gloria, is a fairy whose duty is the protection of little Annabel, the ward of Mrs. Vancourt, and in this chapter Annabel not only learns to fly but discovers that she is half fairy herself. Annabel is a precocious three-year-old who is orphaned, and she has come into the Vancourt home against its owner's wishes. It is Gloria who has insisted, after Mrs. Vancourt is impressed by the fact that the little dog talks, that if she stays, Annabel stays. Thus Annabel has become a ward, and at the close of the story, when the happy new flyer has found her parents, she also discovers that her guardian is her grandmother.*

### [I Can Fly!]

Christmas passed. The snows came, drifting on the terrace, icing the lawns and gardens with frosting as white as a wedding cake's. Using the terrace banisters as a ski slope, Gloria practiced jumps with her new Christmas skis. Annabel tried hers out on a gentler slope. Coasting with Beatrice took Annabel's mind off flying. The closest she had come to flying was swooshing downhill on her red sled with Gloria perched on her shoulder. When the ice was black on the reservoir, Gloria taught Annabel to skate. Though Gloria rode around close to Annabel's ear like a small snowball, she knew how to land on her feet when Annabel fell down.

Sometimes when the weather was bad, Annabel roamed about the house alone, looking for the gold pieces of cat which Miss Peach had locked away. She tried drawers and closets and cupboards, but Miss Peach had hidden the pieces well. The one place she was never able to search—which was always kept locked—was the long chest in the stair hall. It was an old chest, used to store extra linen, carved all over with flowers and faces of mischievous elves. Since Mrs. Vancourt had found the pieces of golden cat in a pile in the stair hall, the chest was a

Chapter 7 from *No Flying in the House* by Betty Brock. Text copyright © 1970 by Betty Brock. Reprinted by permission of Harper & Row, Publishers, Inc.

logical place to store them, Annabel figured, and she had tried the lid a dozen times.

One afternoon in late February when the snows were melted and hard rain drummed against the terrace doors, Annabel thought of the cat. Its first visit on that rainy day seemed so long ago. Wandering into the stair hall, she jiggled the chest's carved lid. It was still locked. Kneeling down, Annabel squinted into the empty keyhole. Inside, it was black. She blew into the keyhole, making a little whistle. She tapped on the sides of the chest. She rattled the lid.

"Why don't you try holding your breath?" said a voice from the windowsill.

Annabel whirled around. Crouched on the sill, swishing its golden tail, was the cat! Carefully, she stood up, wanting very much to grab it before it could disappear, not daring to move nearer for fear of frightening it.

"It's all in the breathing," the cat went on. "If you want to open the chest, hold your breath, close your eyes; then breathe out slowly, and you'll get a surprise."

Annabel tried to speak calmly, as though finding the cat again didn't matter. "Holding my breath will only make my face turn red," she said. "I've tried it. I think you have me mixed up with someone else."

"If one of us is mixed up," said the cat, "it isn't I."

Afraid that the cat would disappear if she argued, she decided to try its suggestion. "Promise you won't go away if I close my eyes."

"I'll do no such thing," said the cat haughtily. "I come and go as I like."

"Oh, very well," said Annabel. She took a deep breath and closed her eyes, forgetting that she had no reason for wanting the chest open now.

"Not enough," said the cat. "Shallow breathing leads inevitably to failure. Take a really deep breath."

Annabel sucked in hard.

"Deeper."

Annabel felt like a balloon.

"Now," said the cat, "let it out slowly and wish on the chest."

Annabel felt as if her insides had turned to liquid honey flowing syrupy down a golden river, and as they flowed away she became lighter and lighter until she felt light enough to ride on a butterfly's wing.

She heard a click.

"Now open your eyes," said the cat.

There stood the chest, its lid wide open! But much more incredible, Annabel was floating three feet off the floor!

"I can fly!" she cried.

Immediately she collapsed on the floor with a thump.

The cat laughed.

Annabel rubbed her elbow. "I was flying. I know I was!" she exclaimed. "What happened?"

"Floating isn't flying," said the cat. "Flying takes practice. Floating is only the first step."

Annabel closed her eyes and breathed deeply again. When she opened them, she was once more floating.

"Keep your breathing regular and even," said the cat. "No shouting until you get the hang of it."

Soon Annabel was able to stretch out flat in the air and roll over. "For months I've tried to fly," she said. "Why couldn't I before?"

"You didn't really think you could," said the cat. "Isn't it amazing the things we don't do simply because we think we can't do them? Wiggle your feet a bit. That's it. Away you go!"

To Annabel's delight, she shot up to the ceiling and sailed down again like a gull riding a fresh breeze.

"Can anyone be a fairy?" she asked. "My friend Beatrice Cox would be very interested—"

"Beatrice Cox is a mortal," said the cat.

"But so am I," said Annabel. Fortunately she was only a foot off the floor when she spoke, for immediately she fell.

The cat began to walk along the windowsill. "Stupid!" it spat at her.

"Don't leave!" called Annabel. "You always leave just when I want to ask you a question."

The cat sat down again. "If you weren't so stupid, you wouldn't need to ask questions."

Annabel decided to overlook its rudeness. "What you mean is if I believe I'm a fairy, I won't fall."

"Don't tell me what I mean," said the cat. "I know what I mean. You're the confused one."

"But if I'm a fairy now, wasn't I a mortal be-fore? Like Beatrice?"

"How could you be?" asked the cat with a sneer. "Your mother is Princess Felicia of the Western Kingdom."

Annabel tingled all over with excitement. "My very own mother is a princess? A fairy princess?" She hugged herself. "So *that's* why I'm a fairy!"

"You're only half," said the cat. "Felicia made the mistake of marrying a mortal named Tippens when she could have chosen any prince in the realm."

Annabel nodded. "Beatrice *said* Tippens didn't sound like a fairy name. So I'm half-mortal like my father and half-fairy like my mother!"

"Unfortunately, yes," said the cat. "A most unsatisfactory arrangement for casting spells or disappearing. I doubt that you'll ever be a really first-rate fairy."

"What about my parents? Do you know where they are?"

"In exile, of course. Felicia's marriage angered her father, the King, so much he exiled her and her mortal spouse to an island far away."

"Someday they will return," said Annabel carefully. That was what Gloria had always told her. "But why can't Gloria talk about them?"

"They wanted you brought up as a mortal," said the cat. "That's why Felicia assigned Gloria to bring you up in the mortal world. Gloria has orders never to tell you that you are part-fairy."

So that was Gloria's secret! No wonder she never talked about Felicia. Suddenly Annabel felt very kindly toward the cat. "And but for you, dear cat, I would have grown up never knowing that I could fly!"

"I understand children," said the cat. "They all want to fly. With practice, you can fly as low as a dragonfly."

"High, you mean," said Annabel. "I want to fly high."

"Anybody can fly high," said the cat. "It's low flying that requires skill. Try hovering over a whitecapped sea without wetting your feet, or following a rabbit's trail up a cliff thick with bayberry without getting a scratch."

Annabel zoomed up to the ceiling and dipped down again, hovering a few inches above the carpet. Then she zoomed under a table. But, trying to maneuver through the legs of a chair, she became hopelessly entangled.

"I see what you mean," she said, getting back into the air. "Don't you think I'm too big to follow a rabbit's trail without getting a scratch?" The cat didn't answer.

Looking down from the ceiling, Annabel couldn't see it anywhere. She flew down to investigate. On the windowsill, instead of the cat, glittered a neat pile of gold pieces, two of them studded with emeralds.

Thoughtfully, Annabel sifted the golden pieces through her fingers, listening to the clicking noise they made.

"It said it wasn't really a cat," she told herself, sweeping the golden pieces into her hand. Carefully, she placed them in the chest and closed the lid. Now it didn't matter about the cat. The discovery that she was half-fairy was enough. She didn't care if she never saw the cat again.

### from THE LION, THE WITCH, AND THE WARDROBE
#### C. S. Lewis

*One hardly expects to find Christian theology in a book for boys and girls, and a fantasy at that! But this is precisely what one does find in the Narnia books of C. S. Lewis, if one is looking. The children could not care less. For them these books are exciting adventures in which the great struggle between good and evil is clearly portrayed. Like Lucy, who stepped into the wardrobe to hide and found the world of Narnia all by accident, many grownups have been surprised to find a wealth of serious speculations and riddles about good and evil in these fantasies for children. Try this excerpt with the youngsters and see what happens.*

*The Lion, the Witch, and the Wardrobe is the first in the Narnia series.* Prince Caspian, The Voyage of the Dawn Treader, The Silver Chair, The Horse and His Boy, *and* The Magician's Nephew *continue the adventures in this strange, new world.* The Last Battle *concludes the series, and as the title implies, the loyal followers of the king of Narnia are making their last stand against the forces of evil. Children need not grasp the doctrinal content to thoroughly enjoy the intensely real world the author creates and the powerful conflict in which the four children are engaged.*

### Lucy Looks into a Wardrobe

Once there were four children whose names were Peter, Susan, Edmund and Lucy. This story is about something that happened to them when they were sent away from London during the war because of the air-raids. They were sent to the house of an old Professor who lived in the heart of the country, ten miles from the nearest railway station and two miles from the nearest post office. He had no wife and he lived in a very large house with a housekeeper called Mrs. Macready and three servants. (Their names were Ivy, Margaret and Betty, but they do not come into the story much.) He himself was a very old man with shaggy white hair, which grew over most of his face as well as on his head, and they liked him almost at once; but on the first evening when he came out to meet them at the front door he was so odd-looking that Lucy (who was the youngest) was a little afraid of him, and Edmund (who was the next youngest) wanted to laugh and had to keep on pretending he was blowing his nose to hide it.

As soon as they had said good night to the Professor and gone upstairs on the first night, the boys came into the girls' room and they all talked it over.

"We've fallen on our feet and no mistake," said Peter. "This is going to be perfectly splendid. That old chap will let us do anything we like."

"I think he's an old dear," said Susan.

"Oh, come off it!" said Edmund, who was tired and pretending not to be tired, which always made him bad-tempered. "Don't go on talking like that."

"Like what?" said Susan; "and anyway, it's time you were in bed."

"Trying to talk like Mother," said Edmund. "And who are you to say when I'm to go to bed? Go to bed yourself."

"Hadn't we all better go to bed?" said Lucy. "There's sure to be a row if we're heard talking here."

"No there won't," said Peter. "I tell you this is the sort of house where no one's going to mind what we do. Anyway, they won't hear us. It's about ten minutes' walk from here down to that dining room, and any amount of stairs and passages in between."

"What's that noise?" said Lucy suddenly. It was a far larger house than she had ever been in before and the thought of all those long passages and rows of doors leading into empty rooms was beginning to make her feel a little creepy.

"It's only a bird, silly," said Edmund.

"It's an owl," said Peter. "This is going to be a wonderful place for birds. I shall go to bed now. I say, let's go and explore to-morrow. You might find anything in a place like this. Did you see those mountains as we came along? And the woods? There might be eagles. There might be stags. There'll be hawks."

"Badgers!" said Lucy.

"Snakes!" said Edmund.

"Foxes!" said Susan.

But when next morning came, there was a steady rain falling, so thick that when you looked out of the window you could see neither the mountains nor the woods nor even the stream in the garden.

"Of course it *would* be raining!" said Edmund. They had just finished breakfast with the Professor and were upstairs in the room he had set apart for them—a long, low room with two windows looking out in one direction and

two in another.

"Do stop grumbling, Ed," said Susan. "Ten to one it'll clear up in an hour or so. And in the meantime we're pretty well off. There's a wireless and lots of books."

"Not for me," said Peter, "I'm going to explore in the house."

Everyone agreed to this and that was how the adventures began. It was the sort of house that you never seem to come to the end of, and it was full of unexpected places. The first few doors they tried led only into spare bedrooms, as everyone had expected that they would; but soon they came to a very long room full of pictures and there they found a suit of armour; and after that was a room all hung with green, with a harp in one corner; and then came three steps down and five steps up, and then a kind of little upstairs hall and a door that led out onto a balcony, and then a whole series of rooms that led into each other and were lined with books —most of them very old books and some bigger than a Bible in a church. And shortly after that they looked into a room that was quite empty except for one big wardrobe; the sort that has a looking-glass in the door. There was nothing else in the room at all except a dead blue-bottle on the window-sill.

"Nothing there!" said Peter, and they all trooped out again—all except Lucy. She stayed behind because she thought it would be worth while trying the door of the wardrobe, even though she felt almost sure that it would be locked. To her surprise it opened quite easily, and two moth-balls dropped out.

Looking into the inside, she saw several coats hanging up—mostly long fur coats. There was nothing Lucy liked so much as the smell and feel of fur. She immediately stepped into the wardrobe and got in among the coats and rubbed her face against them, leaving the door open, of course, because she knew that it is very foolish to shut oneself into any wardrobe. Soon she went further in and found that there was a second row of coats hanging up behind the first one. It was almost quite dark in there and she kept her arms stretched out in front of her so as not to bump her face into the back of the wardrobe. She took a step further in—then two or three steps—always expecting to feel woodwork against the tips of her fingers. But she could not feel it.

"This must be a simply enormous wardrobe!" thought Lucy, going still further in and pushing the soft folds of the coats aside to make room for her. Then she noticed that there was something crunching under her feet. "I wonder is that more moth-balls?" she thought, stooping down to feel it with her hands. But instead of feeling the hard, smooth wood of the floor of the wardrobe, she felt something soft and powdery and extremely cold. "This is very queer," she said, and went on a step or two further.

Next moment she found that what was rubbing against her face and hands was no longer soft fur but something hard and rough and even prickly. "Why, it is just like branches of trees!" exclaimed Lucy. And then she saw that there was a light ahead of her; not a few inches away where the back of the wardrobe ought to have been, but a long way off. Something cold and soft was falling on her. A moment later she found that she was standing in the middle of a wood at night-time with snow under her feet and snowflakes falling through the air.

Lucy felt a little frightened, but she felt very inquisitive and excited as well. She looked back over her shoulder and there, between the dark tree-trunks, she could still see the open doorway of the wardrobe and even catch a glimpse of the empty room from which she had set out. (She had, of course, left the door open, for she knew that it is a very silly thing to shut oneself into a wardrobe.) It seemed to be still daylight there. "I can always get back if anything goes wrong," thought Lucy. She began to walk forward, *crunch-crunch,* over the snow and through the wood towards the other light.

In about ten minutes she reached it and found that it was a lamp-post. As she stood looking at it, wondering why there was a lamp-post in the middle of a wood and wondering what to do next, she heard a pitter patter of feet coming towards her. And soon after that a very strange person stepped out from among the trees into the light of the lamp-post.

He was only a little taller than Lucy herself and he carried over his head an umbrella, white with snow. From the waist upwards he was like a man, but his legs were shaped like a goat's (the hair on them was glossy black) and instead of feet he had goat's hoofs. He also had a tail, but Lucy did not notice this at first because it was neatly caught up over the arm that held the umbrella so as to keep it from trailing in the snow. He had a red woollen muffler round his neck and his skin was rather reddish too. He had a strange, but pleasant little face with a short pointed beard and curly hair, and out of the hair there stuck two horns, one on each side of his forehead. One of his hands, as I have said, held the umbrella: in the other arm he carried several brown paper parcels. What with the parcels and the snow it looked just as if he had been doing his Christmas shopping. He was a Faun.

And when he saw Lucy he gave such a start of surprise that he dropped all his parcels.

"Goodness gracious me!" exclaimed the Faun.

### What Lucy Found There

"Good evening," said Lucy. But the Faun was so busy picking up his parcels that at first he did not reply. When he had finished he made her a little bow.

"Good evening, good evening," said the Faun. "Excuse me—I don't want to be inquisitive—but should I be right in thinking that you are a Daughter of Eve?"

"My name's Lucy," said she, not quite understanding him.

"But you are—forgive me—you are what they call a girl?" asked the Faun.

"Of course I'm a girl," said Lucy.

"You are in fact Human?"

"Of course I'm human," said Lucy, still a little puzzled.

"To be sure, to be sure," said the Faun. "How stupid of me! But I've never seen a Son of Adam or a Daughter of Eve before. I am delighted. That is to say—" and then he stopped as if he had been going to say something he had not intended but had remembered in time. "Delighted, delighted," he went on. "Allow me to introduce myself. My name is Tumnus."

"I am very pleased to meet you, Mr. Tumnus," said Lucy.

"And may I ask, O Lucy, Daughter of Eve," said Mr. Tumnus, "how you have come into Narnia?"

"Narnia? What's that?" said Lucy.

"This is the land of Narnia," said the Faun, "where we are now; all that lies between the lamp-post and the great castle of Cair Paravel on the eastern sea. And you—you have come from the wild woods of the west?"

"I—I got in through the wardrobe in the spare room," said Lucy.

"Ah!" said Mr. Tumnus in a rather melancholy voice, "if only I had worked harder at geography when I was a little Faun, I should no doubt know all about those strange countries. It is too late now."

"But they aren't countries at all," said Lucy, almost laughing. "It's only just back there—at least—I'm not sure. It is summer there."

"Meanwhile," said Mr. Tumnus, "it is winter in Narnia, and has been for ever so long, and we shall both catch cold if we stand here talking in the snow. Daughter of Eve from the far land of Spare Oom where eternal summer reigns around the bright city of War Drobe, how would it be if you came and had tea with me?"

"Thank you very much, Mr. Tumnus," said Lucy. "But I was wondering whether I ought to be getting back."

"It's only just round the corner," said the Faun, "and there'll be a roaring fire—and toast —and sardines—and cake."

"Well, it's very kind of you," said Lucy. "But I shan't be able to stay long."

"If you will take my arm, Daughter of Eve," said Mr. Tumnus, "I shall be able to hold the umbrella over both of us. That's the way. Now —off we go."

And so Lucy found herself walking through the wood arm in arm with this strange creature as if they had known one another all their lives.

They had not gone far before they came to a place where the ground became rough and there were rocks all about and little hills up and little hills down. At the bottom of one small valley Mr. Tumnus turned suddenly aside as if he were going to walk straight into an unusually large rock, but at the last moment Lucy found he was leading her into the entrance of a cave. As soon as they were inside she found herself blinking in the light of a wood fire. Then Mr. Tumnus stooped and took a flaming piece of wood out of the fire with a neat little pair of tongs, and lit a lamp. "Now we shan't be long," he said, and immediately put a kettle on.

Lucy thought she had never been in a nicer place. It was a little, dry, clean cave of reddish stone with a carpet on the floor and two little chairs ("one for me and one for a friend," said Mr. Tumnus) and a table and a dresser and a mantelpiece over the fire and above that a picture of an old Faun with a grey beard. In one corner there was a door which Lucy thought must lead to Mr. Tumnus' bedroom, and on one wall was a shelf full of books. Lucy looked at these while he was setting out the tea things. They had titles like *The Life and Letters of Silenus* or *Nymphs and Their Ways* or *Men, Monks and Gamekeepers; a Study in Popular*

*Legend* or *Is Man a Myth?*

"Now, Daughter of Eve!" said the Faun.

And really it was a wonderful tea. There was a nice brown egg, lightly boiled, for each of them, and then sardines on toast, and then buttered toast, and then toast with honey, and then a sugar-topped cake. And when Lucy was tired of eating the Faun began to talk. He had wonderful tales to tell of life in the forest. He told about the midnight dances and how the Nymphs who lived in the wells and the Dryads who lived in the trees came out to dance with the Fauns; about long hunting parties after the milk-white Stag who could give you wishes if you caught him; about feasting and treasure-seeking with the wild Red Dwarfs in deep mines and caverns far beneath the forest floor; and then about summer when the woods were green and old Silenus on his fat donkey would come to visit them, and sometimes Bacchus himself, and then the streams would run with wine instead of water and the whole forest would give itself up to jollification for weeks on end. "Not that it isn't always winter now," he added gloomily. Then to cheer himself up he took out from its case on the dresser a strange little flute that looked as if it were made of straw and began to play. And the tune he played made Lucy want to cry and laugh and dance and go to sleep all at the same time. It must have been hours later when she shook herself and said,

"Oh Mr. Tumnus—I'm so sorry to stop you, and I do love that tune—but really, I must go home. I only meant to stay for a few minutes."

"It's no good *now*, you know," said the Faun, laying down his flute and shaking his head at her very sorrowfully.

"No good?" said Lucy, jumping up and feeling rather frightened. "What do you mean? I've got to go home at once. The others will be wondering what has happened to me." But a moment later she asked, "Mr. Tumnus! Whatever is the matter?" for the Faun's brown eyes had filled with tears and then the tears began trickling down his cheeks, and soon they were running off the end of his nose; and at last he covered his face with his hands and began to howl.

"Mr. Tumnus! Mr. Tumnus!" said Lucy in great distress. "Don't! Don't! What is the matter? Aren't you well? Dear Mr. Tumnus, do tell me what is wrong." But the Faun continued sobbing as if his heart would break. And even when Lucy went over and put her arms round him and lent him her handkerchief, he did not stop. He merely took the handkerchief and kept on using it, wringing it out with both hands whenever it got too wet to be any more use, so that presently Lucy was standing in a damp patch.

"Mr. Tumnus!" bawled Lucy in his ear, shaking him. "Do stop. Stop it at once! You ought to be ashamed of yourself, a great big Faun like you. What on earth are you crying about?"

"Oh—oh—oh!" sobbed Mr. Tumnus, "I'm crying because I'm such a bad Faun."

"I don't think you're a bad Faun at all," said Lucy. "I think you are a very good Faun. You are the nicest Faun I've ever met."

"Oh—oh—you wouldn't say that if you knew," replied Mr. Tumnus between his sobs. "No, I'm a bad Faun. I don't suppose there ever was a worse Faun since the beginning of the world."

"But what have you done?" asked Lucy.

"My old father, now," said Mr. Tumnus, "that's his picture over the mantelpiece. He would never have done a thing like this."

"A thing like what?" said Lucy.

"Like what I've done," said the Faun. "Taken service under the White Witch. That's what I am. I'm in the pay of the White Witch."

"The White Witch? Who is she?"

"Why, it is she that has got all Narnia under her thumb. It's she that makes it always winter. Always winter and never Christmas; think of that!"

"How awful!" said Lucy. "But what does she pay *you* for?"

"That's the worst of it," said Mr. Tumnus with a deep groan. "I'm a kidnapper for her, that's what I am. Look at me, Daughter of Eve. Would you believe that I'm the sort of Faun to meet a poor innocent child in the wood, one that had never done me any harm, and pretend to be friendly· with it, and invite it home to my cave, all for the sake of lulling it asleep and then handing it over to the White Witch?"

"No," said Lucy. "I'm sure you wouldn't do anything of the sort."

"But I have," said the Faun.

"Well," said Lucy rather slowly (for she wanted to be truthful and yet not to be too hard on him), "well, that was pretty bad. But you're so sorry for it that I'm sure you will never do it again."

"Daughter of Eve, don't you understand?" said the Faun. "It isn't something I *have* done. I'm doing it now, this very moment."

"What do you mean?" cried Lucy, turning very white.

"You are the child," said Mr. Tumnus. "I had orders from the White Witch that if ever I saw a Son of Adam or a Daughter of Eve in the wood, I was to catch them and hand them over to her. And you are the first I ever met. And I've pretended to be your friend and asked you to tea, and all the time I've been meaning to wait till you were asleep and then go and tell *her*."

"Oh but you won't, Mr. Tumnus," said Lucy. "You won't, will you? Indeed, indeed you really mustn't."

"And if I don't," said he, beginning to cry again, "she's sure to find out. And she'll have my tail cut off, and my horns sawn off, and my beard plucked out, and she'll wave her wand over my beautiful cloven hoofs and turn them into horrid solid hoofs like a wretched horse's. And if she is extra and specially angry she'll turn me into stone and I shall be only a statue of a Faun in her horrible house until the four thrones at Cair Paravel are filled—and goodness knows when that will happen, or whether it will ever happen at all."

"I'm very sorry, Mr. Tumnus," said Lucy. "But please let me go home."

"Of course I will," said the Faun. "Of course I've got to. I see that now. I hadn't known what Humans were like before I met you. Of course I can't give you up to the Witch; not now that I know you. But we must be off at once. I'll see you back to the lamp-post. I suppose you can find your own way from there back to Spare Oom and War Drobe?"

"I'm sure I can," said Lucy.

"We must go as quietly as we can," said Mr. Tumnus. "The whole wood is full of *her* spies. Even some of the trees are on her side."

They both got up and left the tea things on the table, and Mr. Tumnus once more put up his umbrella and gave Lucy his arm, and they went out into the snow. The journey back was not at all like the journey to the Faun's cave; they stole along as quickly as they could, without speaking a word, and Mr. Tumnus kept to the darkest places. Lucy was relieved when they reached the lamp-post again.

"Do you know your way from here, Daughter of Eve?" said Tumnus.

Lucy looked very hard between the trees and could just see in the distance a patch of light that looked like daylight. "Yes," she said, "I can see the wardrobe door."

"Then be off home as quick as you can," said the Faun, "and—c-can you ever forgive me for what I meant to do?"

"Why, of course I can," said Lucy, shaking him heartily by the hand. "And I do hope you won't get into dreadful trouble on my account."

"Farewell, Daughter of Eve," said he. "Perhaps I may keep the handkerchief?"

"Rather!" said Lucy, and then ran towards the far-off patch of daylight as quickly as her legs would carry her. And presently instead of rough branches brushing past her she felt coats, and instead of crunching snow under her feet she felt wooden boards, and all at once she found herself jumping out of the wardrobe into the same empty room from which the whole adventure had started. She shut the wardrobe door tightly behind her and looked around, panting for breath. It was still raining and she could hear the voices of the others in the passage.

"I'm here," she shouted. "I'm here. I've come back, I'm all right."

## from ALICE'S ADVENTURES IN WONDERLAND

*Lewis Carroll*

*When an astonished England began investigating the author of Alice's Adventures in Wonderland, it was soon discovered that there was no such person as Lewis Carroll. The name con-*

"A Mad Tea-Party." From *Alice's Adventures in Wonderland* by Lewis Carroll *cealed a staid lecturer in mathematics at Oxford, Charles Lutwidge Dodgson. This young man liked children, and on one famous summer afternoon, he rowed three little girls up the River Cherwell. On the river bank, while they were having tea, the children asked for a story, and the young man told them his masterly concoction of sense and nonsense, nightmares and pleasant dreams, the world upside down and hindside before—fantasia unlimited! If the children enjoy this excerpt, try the whole book.*

### A Mad Tea-Party

There was a table set out under a tree in front of the house, and the March Hare and the Hatter were having tea at it: a Dormouse was sitting between them, fast asleep, and the other two were using it as a cushion, resting their elbows on it, and talking over its head. "Very uncomfortable for the Dormouse," thought Alice; "only, as it's asleep, I suppose it doesn't mind."

The table was a large one, but the three were all crowded together at one corner of it: "No room! No room!" they cried out when they saw Alice coming. "There's *plenty* of room!" said Alice indignantly, and she sat down in a large arm-chair at one end of the table.

"Have some wine," the March Hare said in an encouraging tone.

Alice looked all round the table, but there was nothing on it but tea. "I don't see any wine," she remarked.

"There isn't any," said the March Hare.

"Then it wasn't very civil of you to offer it," said Alice angrily.

"It wasn't very civil of you to sit down without being invited," said the March Hare.

"I didn't know it was *your* table," said Alice; "it's laid for a great many more than three."

"Your hair wants cutting," said the Hatter. He had been looking at Alice for some time with great curiosity, and this was his first speech.

"You should learn not to make personal remarks," Alice said with some severity: "It's very rude."

The Hatter opened his eyes very wide on hearing this; but all he *said* was, "Why is a raven like a writing-desk?"

"Come, we shall have some fun now!" thought Alice. "I'm glad they've begun asking riddles—I believe I can guess that," she added aloud.

"Do you mean that you think you can find out the answer to it?" said the March Hare.

"Exactly so," said Alice.

"Then you should say what you mean," the March Hare went on.

"I do," Alice hastily replied; "at least—at least I mean what I say—that's the same thing, you know."

"Not the same thing a bit!" said the Hatter. "Why, you might just as well say that 'I see what I eat' is the same thing as 'I eat what I see'!"

"You might just as well say," added the March Hare, "that 'I like what I get' is the same thing as 'I get what I like'!"

"You might just as well say," added the Dormouse, who seemed to be talking in his sleep, "that 'I breathe when I sleep' is the same thing as 'I sleep when I breathe'!"

"It *is* the same thing with you," said the Hatter, and here the conversation dropped, and the party sat silent for a minute, while Alice thought over all she could remember about ravens and writing-desks, which wasn't much.

The Hatter was the first to break the silence. "What day of the month is it?" he said, turning to Alice: he had taken his watch out of his pocket, and was looking at it uneasily, shaking it every now and then, and holding it to his ear.

Alice considered a little, and said, "The fourth."

"Two days wrong!" sighed the Hatter. "I told you butter wouldn't suit the works!" he added, looking angrily at the March Hare.

"It was the *best* butter," the March Hare meekly replied.

"Yes, but some crumbs must have got in as well," the Hatter grumbled: "you shouldn't have put it in with the bread-knife."

The March Hare took the watch and looked at it gloomily: then he dipped it into his cup of tea, and looked at it again: but he could think of nothing better to say than his first remark, "It was the *best* butter, you know."

Alice had been looking over his shoulder with some curiosity. "What a funny watch!" she remarked. "It tells the day of the month, and doesn't tell what o'clock it is!"

"Why should it?" muttered the Hatter. "Does *your* watch tell you what year it is?"

"Of course not," Alice replied very readily: "but that's because it stays the same year for such a long time together."

"Which is just the case with *mine*," said the Hatter.

Alice felt dreadfully puzzled. The Hatter's remark seemed to her to have no sort of meaning in it, and yet it was certainly English. "I don't quite understand you," she said, as politely as she could.

"The Dormouse is asleep again," said the Hatter, and he poured a little hot tea onto its nose.

The Dormouse shook its head impatiently, and said, without opening its eyes, "Of course, of course: just what I was going to remark myself."

"Have you guessed the riddle yet?" the Hatter said, turning to Alice again.

"No, I give it up," Alice replied: "what's the answer?"

"I haven't the slightest idea," said the Hatter.

"Nor I," said the March Hare.

Alice sighed wearily. "I think you might do something better with the time," she said, "than wasting it in asking riddles that have no answers."

"If you knew Time as well as I do," said the Hatter, "you wouldn't talk about wasting *it!* It's *him.*"

"I don't know what you mean," said Alice.

"Of course you don't!" the Hatter said, tossing his head contemptuously. "I dare say you never even spoke to Time!"

"Perhaps not," Alice cautiously replied: "but I know I have to beat time when I learn music."

"Ah! That accounts for it," said the Hatter. "He won't stand beating. Now, if you only kept on good terms with him, he'd do almost anything you liked with the clock.

"For instance, suppose it were nine o'clock in the morning, just time to begin lessons: you'd only have to whisper a hint to Time, and round goes the clock in a twinkling! Half-past one, time for dinner!"

("I only wish it was," the March Hare said to itself in a whisper.)

"That would be grand, certainly," said Alice thoughtfully; "but then—I shouldn't be hungry for it, you know."

"Not at first, perhaps," said the Hatter; "but you could keep it to half-past one as long as you liked."

"Is that the way *you* manage?" Alice asked.

The Hatter shook his head mournfully. "Not I!" he replied. "We quarreled last March—just before *he* went mad, you know—" (pointing with his teaspoon at the March Hare) "—it was at the great concert given by the Queen of Hearts, and I had to sing

'Twinkle, twinkle, little bat!
How I wonder what you're at!'

You know the song, perhaps?"

"I've heard something like it," said Alice.

"It goes on, you know," the Hatter continued, "in this way:—

'Up above the world you fly,
Like a teatray in the sky.
Twinkle, twinkle—' "

Here the Dormouse shook itself, and began singing in its sleep *"Twinkle, twinkle, twinkle, twinkle—"* and went on so long that they had to pinch it to make it stop.

"Well, I'd hardly finished the first verse," said the Hatter, "when the Queen bawled out 'He's murdering the time! Off with his head!' "

"How dreadfully savage!" exclaimed Alice.

"And ever since that," the Hatter went on in a mournful tone, "he won't do a thing I ask! It's always six o'clock now."

A bright idea came into Alice's head. "Is that the reason so many tea-things are put out here?" she asked.

"Yes, that's it," said the Hatter with a sigh: "it's always tea-time, and we've no time to wash the things between whiles."

"Then you keep moving round, I suppose?" said Alice.

"Exactly so," said the Hatter: "as the things get used up."

"But when you come to the beginning again?" Alice ventured to ask.

"Suppose we change the subject," the March

Hare interrupted yawning. "I'm getting tired of this. I vote the young lady tells us a story."

"I'm afraid I don't know one," said Alice, rather alarmed at the proposal.

"Then the Dormouse shall!" they both cried. "Wake up, Dormouse!" And they pinched it on both sides at once.

The Dormouse slowly opened his eyes. "I wasn't asleep," he said in a hoarse, feeble voice: "I heard every word you fellows were saying."

"Tell us a story!" said the March Hare.

"Yes, please do!" pleaded Alice.

"And be quick about it," added the Hatter, "or you'll be asleep again before it's done."

"Once upon a time there were three little sisters," the Dormouse began in a great hurry; "and their names were Elsie, Lacie, and Tillie; and they lived at the bottom of a well—"

"What did they live on?" said Alice, who always took a great interest in questions of eating and drinking.

"They lived on treacle," said the Dormouse, after thinking a minute or two.

"They couldn't have done that, you know," Alice gently remarked. "They'd have been ill."

"So they were," said the Dormouse; "*very* ill."

Alice tried a little to fancy to herself what such an extraordinary way of living would be like, but it puzzled her too much, so she went on: "But why did they live at the bottom of a well?"

"Take some more tea," the March Hare said to Alice, very earnestly.

"I've had nothing yet," Alice replied in an offended tone, "so I can't take more."

"You mean you can't take *less*," said the Hatter: "it's very easy to take *more* than nothing."

"Nobody asked *your* opinion," said Alice.

"Who's making personal remarks now?" the Hatter asked triumphantly.

Alice did not quite know what to say to this: so she helped herself to some tea and bread-and-butter, and then turned to the Dormouse, and repeated her question. "Why did they live at the bottom of a well?"

The Dormouse again took a minute or two to think about it, and then said, "It was a treacle-well."

"There's no such thing!" Alice was beginning very angrily, but the Hatter and the March

Hare went "Sh! Sh!" and the Dormouse sulkily remarked, "If you can't be civil, you'd better finish the story for yourself."

"No, please go on!" Alice said very humbly. "I won't interrupt you again. I dare say there may be *one*."

"One, indeed!" said the Dormouse indignantly. However, he consented to go on. "And so these three little sisters—they were learning to draw, you know—"

"What did they draw?" said Alice, quite forgetting her promise.

"Treacle," said the Dormouse, without considering at all this time.

"I want a clean cup," interrupted the Hatter: "let's all move one place on."

He moved on as he spoke, and the Dormouse followed him: the March Hare moved into the Dormouse's place, and Alice rather unwillingly took the place of the March Hare. The Hatter was the only one who got any advantage from the change: and Alice was a good deal worse off than before, as the March Hare had just upset the milk-jug into his plate.

Alice did not wish to offend the Dormouse again, so she began very cautiously: "But I don't understand. Where did they draw the treacle from?"

"You can draw water out of a water-well," said the Hatter; "so I should think you could draw treacle out of a treacle-well—eh, stupid?"

"But they were *in* the well," Alice said to the Dormouse, not choosing to notice this last remark.

"Of course they were," said the Dormouse— "well in."

This answer so confused poor Alice, that she let the Dormouse go on for some time without interrupting it.

"They were learning to draw," the Dormouse went on, yawning and rubbing his eyes, for it was getting very sleepy; "and they drew all manner of things—everything that begins with an M—"

"Why with an M?" said Alice.

"Why not?" said the March Hare.

Alice was silent.

The Dormouse had closed its eyes by this time, and was going off into a doze, but, on being pinched by the Hatter, it woke up again with a little shriek, and went on: "—that begins with an M, such as mousetraps, and the moon, and memory, and muchness—you know you say things are 'much of a muchness'—did you ever see such a thing as a drawing of a muchness?"

"Really, now you ask me," said Alice, very much confused, "I don't think—"

"Then you shouldn't talk," said the Hatter.

This piece of rudeness was more than Alice could bear: she got up in great disgust, and walked off: the Dormouse fell asleep instantly, and neither of the others took the least notice of her going, though she looked back once or twice, half hoping that they would call after her: the last time she saw them, they were trying to put the Dormouse into the teapot.

"At any rate I'll never go *there* again!" said Alice as she picked her way through the wood. "It's the stupidest tea-party I ever was at in all my life!"

Just as she said this, she noticed that one of the trees had a door leading right into it. "That's very curious!" she thought. "But everything's curious today. I think I may as well go in at once." And in she went.

Once more she found herself in the long hall, and close to the little glass table. "Now, I'll manage better this time," she said to herself, and began by taking the little golden key, and unlocking the door that led into the garden. Then she set to work nibbling at the mushroom (she had kept a piece of it in her pocket) till she was about a foot high: then she walked down the little passage: and *then*—she found herself at last in the beautiful garden, among the bright flowerbeds and the cool fountains.

## *from* THE CHILDREN OF GREEN KNOWE

*Lucy Maria Boston*

*This book is one of the most unusual and beautiful ghost stories ever written. It is about Toseland (Tolly), a lonely boy, staying with*

From *The Children of Green Knowe,* copyright 1954, © 1955 by L. M. Boston. Reprinted by permission of Harcourt Brace Jovanovich, Inc. and Faber and Faber Limited

*his great-grandmother in a big stone castle. It suggests witches, ghosts, and spells. Tolly encounters all three and comes to love the ghost children from the long, long ago of his own family. After reading this, children will want to read the other Green Knowe books as well.*

### [*Tolly's New Home*]

A little boy was sitting in the corner of a railway carriage looking out at the rain, which was splashing against the windows and blotching downward in an ugly, dirty way. He was not the only person in the carriage, but the others were strangers to him. He was alone as usual. There were two women opposite him, a fat one and a thin one, and they talked without stopping, smacking their lips in between sentences and seeming to enjoy what they said as much as if it were something to eat. They were knitting all the time, and whenever the train stopped the click-clack of their needles was loud and clear like two clocks. It was a stopping train—more stop than go—and it had been crawling along through flat flooded country for a long time. Everywhere there was water—not sea or rivers or lakes, but just senseless flood water with the rain splashing into it. Sometimes the railway lines were covered by it, and then the train-noise was quite different, softer than a boat.

"I wish it was *the* Flood," thought the boy, "and that I was going to the Ark. That would be fun! Like the circus. Perhaps Noah had a whip and made all the animals go round and round for exercise. What a noise there would be, with the lions roaring, elephants trumpeting, pigs squealing, donkeys braying, horses whinnying, bulls bellowing, and cocks and hens always thinking they were going to be trodden on but unable to fly up onto the roof where all the other birds were singing, screaming, twittering, squawking and cooing. What must it have sounded like, coming along on the tide? And did Mrs. Noah just knit, knit and take no notice?"

The two women opposite him were getting ready for the next station. They packed up their knitting and collected their parcels and then sat staring at the little boy. He had a thin face and very large eyes; he looked patient and rather sad. They seemed to notice him for the first time.

"What's your name, son?" asked the fat woman suddenly. "I've never seen you on this train before." This was always a question he dreaded. Was he to say his unexpected real name or his silly pet names?

"Toseland," he said.

"Toseland! That's a real old-fashioned name in these parts. There's Fen Toseland, and Toseland St. Agnes and Toseland Gunning. What's your Christian name?"

"That is it—Toseland."

"Do your mum and dad live round here, son?"

"No, they live in Burma."

"Fancy that now! That's a long way away. Where are you going, then?"

"I don't know. That is, I'm going to my great-grandmother Oldknow at Green Noah. The station in Penny Soaky."

"That's the next station after this. We get out here. Don't forget—the next station. And make sure there's some dry land before you get out of the train. The floods are bad there. Bye-bye, cheerio."

They got out, shouting and joking with the porters and kissing the people who had come to meet them. They started off into the hissing rain as if they loved it. Toseland heard the fat woman's loud voice saying, "Oh, I don't mind this. I like it, it's our home-rain, not like that dirty London water."

The train jogged on again and now Toseland was quite alone. He wished he had a family like other people—brothers and sisters, even if his father were away. His mother was dead. He had a stepmother but he hardly knew her and was miserably shy of her. He had been at a boarding-school, and for the last holidays he had been left behind to stay with the head mistress, Miss Spudd, and her old father. They meant to be kind to him, but they never spoke to him without saying "dear." It was "Finish up your porridge, dear, we don't want you to get thin," or "Put on your coat, dear, we don't want you to catch cold," or "Get ready for church, dear, we don't want you to grow up a heathen." And every day after breakfast, "Run along to your room, dear, we want to read the papers."

But now his great-grandmother Oldknow had written that he was to come and live with her. He had never seen her, but she was his own great-grandmother, and that was something. Of course she would be very old. He thought of some old people he had seen who were so old that it frightened him. He wondered if she would be frighteningly old. He began to feel afraid already, and to shake it off he thought about Green Noah and Penny Soaky. What queer names! Green Noah was pure mystery, but Penny Soaky was friendly like a joke.

Suddenly the train stopped, and the porters were shouting "Penny Soaky! Penny Soaky!" Toseland had no sooner got the door open than a man wearing a taxi-driver's hat came along calling:

"Anybody here for Green Noah? Are you Master Toseland for Green Noah?"

"Oh yes, please. It's me."

"This your luggage? Two more in the van? You stand here out of the rain while I get it."

There were a few houses to be seen on one side of the line, and on the other nothing but flooded fields with hedges standing in the water.

"Come along," said the taxi-man. "I've put all your luggage in the car. It'll be dark before we get there and we've got to go through a lot of water."

"Is it deep?"

"Not so deep, I hope, that we can't get through."

"If it rains forty days and forty nights will it be a real flood?"

"Sure enough it would."

Toseland sat by the driver and they set off. The windscreen wipers made two clear fans on the windscreen through which he could see the road half covered with water, with ditches brimming on either side. When they came near the bridge that crossed the river, the road disappeared under water altogether and they seemed to drive into the side of the river with a great splash that flew up against the windows; but it was only a few inches deep, and then they reached the humpbacked bridge and went up and over it, and down again into deeper water on the other side. This time they drove very carefully like bathers walking out into cold water. The car crept along making wide ripples.

"We don't want to stick here," said the driver, "this car don't float."

They came safely through that side too, and now the headlights were turned on, for it was growing dark, and Toseland could see nothing but rain and dazzle.

"Is it far?" he asked.

"Not very, but we have to go a long way round to get past the floods. Green Noah stands almost in the middle of it now, because the river runs alongside the garden. Once you get there you won't be able to get out again till the flood goes down."

"How will I get in, then?"

"Can you swim?"

"Yes, I did twenty strokes last summer. Will that be enough?"

"You'll have to do better than that. Perhaps if you felt yourself sinking you could manage a few more?"

"But it's quite dark. How will I know where to swim to?"

The driver laughed. "Don't you worry. Mrs. Oldknow will never let you drown. She'll see you get there all right. Now here we are. At least, I can't go any further." Toseland pushed the car door open and looked out. It had stopped raining. The car was standing in a lane of shallow water that stretched out into the dark in front and behind. The driver was wearing Wellington boots, and he got out and paddled round the car. Toseland was afraid that he would be left now to go on as best he could by himself. He did not like to show that he was afraid, so he tried another way of finding out.

"If I am going to swim," he said, "what will you do with my luggage?"

"You haven't got no gum boots, have you?" said the driver. "Come on, get on my shoulders and we'll have a look round to see if anyone's coming to meet you." Toseland climbed onto his shoulders and they set off, but almost at once they heard the sound of oars, and a lantern came round the corner of the lane rocking on the bows of a rowing boat. A man called out, "Is that Master Toseland?" The driver shouted back, "Is that Mr. Boggis?" but Toseland was speechless with relief and delight.

"Good evening, Master Toseland," said Mr. Boggis, holding up the lantern to look at him, while Toseland looked too, and saw a nice old cherry-red face with bright blue eyes. "Pleased to meet you. I knew your mother when she was your size. I bet you were wondering how you were going to get home?" It was nice to hear somebody talking about "home" in that way. Toseland felt much happier, and now he knew that the driver had been teasing him, so he grinned and said: "I was going to swim."

The boat was moored to somebody's garden gate while the two men put the trunk and tuck-box into it.

"You'll be all right now," said the taxi-man. "Goodnight to you both."

"Goodnight, and thank you," said Toseland.

Mr. Boggis handed him the lantern and told him to kneel up in the bows with it and shout if they were likely to bump into anything. They rowed round two corners in the road and then in at a big white gate. Toseland waved the lantern about and saw trees and bushes standing in the water, and presently the boat was rocked by quite a strong current and the reflection of the lantern steamed away in elastic jig-saw shapes and made gold rings round the tree trunks. At last they came to a still pool reaching to the steps of the house, and the keel of the boat grated on gravel. The windows were all lit up, but it was too dark to see what kind of a house it was, only that it was high and narrow like a tower.

"Come along in," said Mr. Boggis. "I'll show you in. I'd like to see Mrs. Oldknow's face when she sees you."

The entrance hall was a strange place. As they stepped in, a similar door opened at the far end of the house and another man and boy entered there. Then Toseland saw that it was only themselves in a big mirror. The walls round him were partly rough stone and partly plaster, but hung all over with mirrors and pictures and china. There were three big old mirrors all reflecting each other so that at first Toseland was puzzled to find what was real, and which door one could go through straight, the way one wanted to, not sideways somewhere else. He almost wondered which was really himself.

There were vases everywhere filled with queer flowers—branches of dry winter twigs out of which little tassels and rosettes of flower petals were bursting, some yellow, some white, some purple. They had an exciting smell, almost like something to eat, and they looked as if they had been produced by magic, as if someone had said "Abracadabra! Let these sticks burst into flower." "What if my great-grandmother is a witch!" he thought. Above the vases, wherever there was a beam or an odd corner or a doorpost out of which they could, as it were, grow, there were children carved in dark oak, leaning out over the flowers. Most of them had wings, one had a real bird's nest on its head, and all of them had such round polished cheeks they seemed to be laughing and welcoming him.

While he was looking round him, Boggis had taken his coat and cap from him and hung them up. "Your great-grandmother will be in here," he said, and led him to a little old stone doorway such as you might find in a belfry. He knocked on the door. "Come in," said a clear voice. Boggis gave Toseland a shove, and he found himself inside.

The room seemed to be the ground floor of a castle, much like the ruined castles that he had explored on school picnics, only this was not a ruin. It looked as if it never possibly could be. Its thick stone walls were strong, warm and lively. It was furnished with comfortable polished old-fashioned things as though living in castles was quite ordinary. Toseland stood just outside the door and felt it must be a dream.

His great-grandmother was sitting by a huge open fireplace where logs and peat were burning. The room smelled of woods and woodsmoke. He forgot about her being frighteningly old. She had short silver curls and her face had so many wrinkles it looked as if someone had been trying to draw her for a very long time and every line put in had made the face more like her. She was wearing a soft dress of folded velvet that was as black as a hole in darkness. The room was full of candles in glass candlesticks, and there was candlelight in her ring when she held out her hand to him.

"So you've come back!" she said, smiling, as he came forward, and he found himself leaning against her shoulder as if he knew her quite well.

"Why do you say 'come back'?" he asked, not at all shy.

"I wondered whose face it would be of all the faces I knew," she said. "They always come back. You are like another Toseland, your grandfather. What a good thing you have the right name, because I should always be calling you Tolly anyway. I used to call him Tolly. Have you got a pet name? I'm sure they don't call you Toseland at school."

"No, I get called Towser."

"And at home?"

"My stepmother calls me Toto, but I hate it. It's worse than Towser."

"I think I agree with you. Here we are all used to Toseland, it's the family name and doesn't seem queer to us. So you shan't be Toto here. Do you mind Tolly?"

"I like it. It's what my mother used to call me. What shall I call you?"

"Granny," she said. "What does one generation more or less matter? I'm glad you have come. It will seem lovely to me."

Tolly watched the flames tugging loose from the logs and leaping up the black chimney. They reminded him of bonfire flames wrestling and tearing and whistling in the sky on the fifth of November. Those had been frightening, but these were wonderful.

"Are these our flames?" he asked. "I mean, are they our own?"

"The blue ones are yours and the orange ones are mine."

"And the candle-flames?"

"All yours."

Tolly hesitated, then asked in a very little voice because he hardly dared, "Is it my house—I mean, partly?"

"Of course it is—partly, as you say. Well, now that you are here what shall we do first? Are you hungry?"

She rose and, standing, looked much older. Her figure was bent and shrunken, her face no higher than Tolly's own. The folds of her dress seemed both to weigh her down and hold her up. She brought a tray that was laid ready for him on the sideboard, and put it on a low table in front of the fire. There were egg sandwiches and chicken sandwiches and iced orange cake and jelly and chocolate finger biscuits.

Toseland ate happily and tried not to make crumbs.

"I came in a boat with a lantern," he said. "I played the house was Noah's Ark."

"Oh, the Ark! So you played it was the Ark."

"Yes. Do you think Noah had a whip like a circus man and made the animals run round and round for exercise?"

"Yes. And Ham juggled with clubs and plates to pass the time away, and Shem and Japhet were clowns and tried to make Mrs. Noah laugh. But she never did, because if she had done, all her buttons would have burst off. She was done up very tight."

At that moment the fire went *pop!* and shot a piece of wood out into the room. *Pop!* again.

"Buttons! Who said buttons? Poor Mrs. Noah." Tolly chased the sparks and trod on them to put them out.

"Why do you live in a castle?" he said, looking round.

"Why not? Castles were meant to live in."

"I thought that was only in fairy tales. Is it a real castle?"

"Of course."

"I mean, do things happen in it, like the castles in books?"

"Oh yes, things happen in it."

"What sort of things?"

"Wait and see! I'm waiting too, to see what happens now that you are here. Something will, I'm sure. Tomorrow you can explore the inside of the house up and down, and learn your way about and to feel at home in it, because you won't be able to go outside until the floods go down. And now you must come to see your own room, and you must go to bed early tonight."

She led him up winding stairs and through a high, arched room like a knight's hall, that she called the Music Room, and on up more stairs to the very top of the house. Here there was a room under the roof, with a ceiling the shape of the roof and all the beams showing. It was a long room with a triangle of wall at each end and no walls at the sides, because the sloping ceiling came down to the floor, like a tent. There were windows on three sides, and a little low wooden bed in the middle covered with a patchwork quilt, as unlike a school bed as anything could be. There was a low table, a chest of drawers and lots of smooth, polished, empty floor. At one side there was a beautiful old rocking-horse—not a "safety" rocking-horse hanging on iron swings from a centre shaft, but a horse whose legs were stretched to full gallop, fixed to long rockers so that it could, if you rode it violently, both rear and kick. On the other side was a doll's house. By the bed was a wooden box painted vermilion with bright patterns all over it, and next to it all Tolly's luggage piled up, making the room look really his. A wicker bird-cage hung from one of the beams. On the only side that had no window there hung a big mirror reflecting all the rest—the rafters, the wicker cage, the rocking-horse, the doll's house, the painted box, the bed.

"In this house," said Tolly, "everything is twice!" He tried the lid of the painted box, but could not open it.

"The key is lost," said Mrs. Oldknow. "I don't know what's in it. It used to be the children's toy-box."

He put his hand on the rocking-horse's mane, which was real horse-hair. Its tail was real hair too, black and soft and long. He started it rocking. It made a nice creaky sound, like a rocking-chair. He opened the front of the doll's house. "Why, it's this house!" he said. "Look, here's the knight's hall, and here's the stairs, and here's my room! Here's the rocking-horse and here's the red box, and here's a tiny bird-cage! But it's got four beds in it. Are there sometimes other children here?"

Mrs. Oldknow looked at him as if she would like to know everything about him before she answered.

"Yes," she said, "sometimes."

"Who are they?"

"You'll see when they come, if they come."

*from* **TOM'S MIDNIGHT GARDEN**
*Philippa Pearce*

*Deft writing and a carefully balanced mixture of reality and fantasy lend distinction to this story of a young boy's journey into the past—*

*namely, an old woman's childhood. While the basic idea is not new in literature, its appeal is strengthened by the plausibility of the dream-like moments which are tinged with nostalgia and seem so real to Tom.* Tom's Midnight Garden *received the Carnegie Medal as the outstanding children's book published in England in 1958. It promises to remain a favorite for years to come. In the two excerpts that follow, Tom discovers the beautiful garden and meets Hatty as a little girl in the late Victorian era.*

### *Through a Door*

Every night now Tom slipped downstairs to the garden. At first he used to be afraid that it might not be there. Once, with his hand already upon the garden door to open it, he had turned back, sick with grief at the very thought of absence. He had not dared, then, to look; but, later the same night, he had forced himself to go again and open that door: there the garden was. It had not failed him.

He saw the garden at many times of its day, and at different seasons—its favourite season was summer, with perfect weather. In earliest summer hyacinths were still out in the crescent beds on the lawn, and wallflowers in the round ones. Then the hyacinths bowed and died; and the wallflowers were uprooted, and stocks and asters bloomed in their stead. There was a clipped box bush by the greenhouse, with a cavity like a great mouth cut into the side of it: this was stacked full of pots of geraniums in flower. Along the sundial path, heavy red poppies came out, and roses; and, in summer dusk, the evening primroses glimmered like little moons. In the latest summer the pears on the wall were muffled in muslin bags for safe ripening.

Tom was not a gardener, however; his first interest in a garden, as Peter's would have been, was tree-climbing. He always remembered his first tree in this garden—one of the yews round

the lawn. He had never climbed a yew before, and was inclined to think ever afterwards that yews were best.

The first branches grew conveniently low, and the main trunk had bosses and crevices. With the toes of his left foot fitted into one of these last, Tom curved his hands round the branch over his head. Then he gave a push, a spring and a strong haul on the arms: his legs and feet were dangling free, and the branch was under his chest, and then under his middle. He drew himself still farther forward, at the same time twisting himself expertly: now he was sitting on the bough, a man's height above ground.

The rest of the ascent was easy but interesting: sometimes among the spreading, outermost branches; sometimes working close to the main trunk. Tom loved the dry feel of the bark on the main trunk. In places the bark had peeled away, and then a deep pink showed beneath, as though the tree were skin and flesh beneath its brown.

Up he went—up and up, and burst at last from the dim interior into an openness of blue and fiery gold. The sun was the gold, in a blue sky. All round him was a spreading, tufted surface of evergreen. He was on a level with all the yew-tree tops round the lawn; nearly on a level with the top of the tall south wall.

Tom was on a level, too, with the upper windows of the house, just across the lawn from him. His attention was caught by a movement inside one of the rooms: it came, he saw, from the same maid he had once seen in the hall. She was dusting a bedroom, and came now to the window to raise the sash and shake her duster outside. She looked casually across to the yewtrees as she did so, and Tom tried waving to her. It was like waving to the He in blind-man's-buff.

The maid went back into the depths of the room, to her dusting. She left the window open behind her, and Tom could now see more. There was someone else in the room besides the maid—someone who stood against the far wall, facing the window. The maid evidently spoke to her companion occasionally as she worked, for Tom could hear the faint coming and going of voices. He could not see the other figure at all clearly, except that it was motionless, and there was the whiteness and shape of a face that was always turned in his direction. That steadfastness of direction embarrassed Tom. Very gradually he began to draw his head downwards, and then suddenly ducked it below tree-level altogether.

Tom saw more people later, in the garden itself. He stalked them warily, and yet—remembering his invisibility to the house-maid—with a certain confidence too.

He was pretty sure that the garden was used more often than he knew. He often had the feeling of people having just gone—and an uncomfortable feeling, out of which he tried to reason himself, again and again, of someone who had *not* gone: someone who, unobserved, observed him. It was a relief really to see people, even when they ignored his presence: the maid, the gardener, and a severe-looking woman in a long dress of rustling purple silk, face to face with whom Tom once came unexpectedly, on a corner. She cut him dead.

Visibility . . . invisibility . . . If he were invisible to the people of the garden, he was not completely so at least to some of the other creatures. How truly they saw him he could not say; but birds cocked their heads at him, and flew away when he approached.

And had he any bodily weight in this garden, or had he not? At first, Tom thought not. When he climbed the yew-tree he had been startled to feel that no bough swung beneath him, and not a twig broke. Later—and this was a great disappointment to him—he found that he could not, by the ordinary grasping and pushing of his hand, open any of the doors in the garden, to go through them. He could not push open the door of the greenhouse or of the little heating-house behind it, or the door in the south wall by the sundial.

The doors shut against Tom were a check upon his curiosity, until he saw a simple way out: he would get through the doorways that interested him by following at the heels of the gardener. He regularly visited the greenhouse, the heating-house, and used the south wall door.

Tom concentrated upon getting through the south wall door. That entry promised to be the easiest, because the gardener went through so often, with his tools. There must be a tool-shed somewhere through there.

The gardener usually went through so quickly and shut the door so smartly behind him, that there was not time for anyone else to slip through as well. However, he would be slower with a wheelbarrow, Tom judged; and he waited patiently for that opportunity. Yet even then the man somehow only made a long arm to open the door ahead of the wheelbarrow, wheeled it very swiftly through, caught the door-edge with the toe of his boot as he passed and slammed the door in Tom's face.

Tom glared at the door that once more was his barrier. Once more, without hope, he raised his hand to the latch and pressed it. As usual, he could not move it: his fingers seemed to have no substance. Then, in anger, he pressed with all imaginable might: he knitted his brows, and brought all his will to bear upon the latch, until he felt that something had to happen. It did: his fingers began to go through the latch, as though the latch, and not his fingers, now, were without substance. His fingers went through the ironwork of the latch altogether, and his hand fell back into place by his side.

Tom stared down at that ever-memorable right hand. He felt it tenderly with his left, to see if it were bruised or broken: it was quite unhurt—quite as before. Then he looked at the latch: it looked as real as any latch he had ever seen anywhere.

Then the idea came to Tom that the door might be no more solid than the latch, if he really tried it.

Deliberately he set his side against the door, shoulder, hip and heel, and pressed. At first, nothing gave, either of himself or the door. Yet he continued the pressure, with still greater force and greater determination; and gradually he became aware of a strange sensation, that at first he thought was a numbness all down his side—but no, it was not that.

'I'm going through,' Tom gasped, and was seized with alarm and delight.

On the other side of the wall, the gardener had emptied his barrow-load of weeds and was sitting on the handle of his barrow, in front of a potting-shed, eating his midday dinner. If he had been able to see Tom at all he would have seen a most curious sight: a very thin slice of boy, from shoulder to foot, coming through a perfectly solid wooden door. At first the body came through evenly from top to bottom; then, the upper part seemed to stop, and the bottom part came through in its entirety, legs first. Then one arm came through, then another. Finally, everything was through except the head.

The truth was that Tom was now a little lacking courage. The passing through the door of so much of his body had not been without enormous effort and peculiar, if indescribable, sensations. 'I'm just resting a minute,' said Tom's head, on the garden side of the door; yet he knew that he was really delaying because he was nervous. His stomach, for instance, had felt most uncomfortable as it passed through the door; what would the experience be like for his head—his eyes, his ears?

On the other hand—and the new idea was even worse than the old—supposing that, like a locomotive-engine losing steam-pressure, he lost his present force of body and will-power in this delay? Then, he would be unable to move either forwards or backwards. He would be caught here by the neck, perhaps for ever. And just supposing someone came along, on the far side of the wall, who by some evil chance *could* see him—supposing a whole company came: they would see an entirely defenceless stern sticking out—an invitation to ridicule and attack.

With a convulsive effort, eyes closed, lips sealed, Tom dragged his head through the door, and stood, dizzy, dazed, but whole, on the far side of it.

When his vision cleared, he saw that he was standing directly in front of the potting-shed and the gardener. Tom had never been front to front with the gardener before: he was a large-framed young man, with a weather-reddened face, and eyes the colour of the sky itself—they now looked straight through Tom and far away. Into his mouth he was putting the last fragments of a thick bacon-and-bread sandwich. He finished the sandwich, closed his eyes and spoke aloud: 'For all good things I thank the Lord; and may He keep me from all the works

of the Devil that he hurt me not.'

He spoke with a country voice, clipping short his *t*'s and widening his vowels, so that Tom had to listen attentively to understand him.

The gardener opened his eyes again, and, reaching behind him, brought out another sandwich. Tom wondered, in some surprise, whether he said grace after every sandwich. Perhaps he never knew how many he was going to eat.

The gardener went on eating, and Tom turned away to look around him. He was in an orchard, that also served for the keeping of hens, the pegging out of washing and the kindling of a bonfire. Beyond the orchard were meadows and trees, from among which rose the roofs of what must be a village.

While he looked, Tom was also keeping a sharp eye upon the gardener. When the man had really finished his meal he grasped the handles of his wheelbarrow, to return to his work in the garden. In a moment, Tom was beside him. He had not at all enjoyed the experience of going through a shut door, and he did not now intend to have to repeat it. This time there was an easy way through: he got nimbly up into the empty barrow and was wheeled back into the garden in comfort.

It was a long time before Tom literally forced his way through a door again. Anyway, he had seen the orchard, and that was enough in that direction; other doors could wait. Meanwhile, he climbed the low wall at the bottom of the garden and explored the wood beyond. On the third side of the garden he wormed his way through the hedge again and crossed the meadow. The only surprise there was the boundary: a river, clear, gentle-flowing, shallow, and green with reeds and water-plants.

The garden and its surroundings, then, were not, in themselves, outside the natural order of things; nor was Tom alarmed by his own unnatural abilities. Yet to some things his mind came back again and again, troubled: the constant fine weather, the rapid coming and going of the seasons and the times of day, the feeling of being watched.

One night all his uneasiness came to a head. He had gone from his bed in the flat upstairs and crept down to the hall at about midnight, as usual; he had opened the garden door. He had found for the first time that it was night, too, in the garden. The moon was up, but clouds fled continuously across its face. Although there was this movement in the upper air, down below there was none: a great stillness lay within the garden, and a heavier heat than at any noon. Tom felt it: he unbuttoned his pyjama jacket and let it flap open as he walked.

One could smell the storm coming. Before Tom had reached the bottom of the garden, the moon had disappeared, obscured altogether by cloud. In its place came another light that seemed instantaneously to split the sky from top to bottom, and a few seconds later came the thunder.

Tom turned back to the house. As he reached the porch, the winds broke out into the lower air, with heavy rain and a deathly chilling of the temperature. Demons of the air seemed let loose in that garden; and, with the increasing frequency of the lightning, Tom could watch the foliage of the trees ferociously tossed and torn at by the wind, and, at the corner of the lawn, the tall, tapering fir-tree swinging to and fro, its ivy-wreathed arms struggling wildly in the tempest like the arms of a swaddling-child.

To Tom it seemed that the fir-tree swung more widely each time. 'It can't be blown over,' thought Tom. 'Strong trees are not often blown over.'

As if in answer to this, and while the winds still tore, there came the loudest thunder, with a flash of lightning that was not to one side nor even above, but seemed to come down into the garden itself, to the tree. The glare was blinding, and Tom's eyes closed against it, although only for a part of a second. When he opened them again, he saw the tree like one flame, and falling. In the long instant while it fell, there seemed to be a horrified silence of all the winds; and, in that quiet, Tom heard something—a human cry—an 'Oh!' of the terror he himself felt. It came from above him—from the window of one of the upper rooms.

Then the fir-tree fell, stretching its length —although Tom did not know this until much later—along the gravebeds of the asparagus in the kitchen-garden. It fell in darkness and the resumed rushing of wind and rain.

Tom was shaken by what he had seen and heard. He went back into the house and shut the garden door behind him. Inside, the grandfather clock ticked peacefully; the hall was still. He wondered if perhaps he had only imagined what he had seen outside. He opened the door again, and looked out. The summer storm was still raging. The flashes of lightning were distant now: they lit up the ugly gap in the trees round the lawn, where the fir-tree had stood.

The tree had fallen, that had been a sight terrible enough; but the cry from above troubled Tom more. On the next night came the greatest shock of all. He opened the garden door as usual, and surveyed the garden. At first, he did not understand what was odd in its appearance; then, he realized that its usual appearance was in itself an oddity. In the trees round the lawn there was no gap: the ivy-grown fir-tree still towered above them.

### Hatty

Tom only rarely saw the three boys in the garden. They would come strolling out with the air-gun, or for fruit. They came for apples on the second occasion of Tom's seeing them, which was only a few days after the first.

With a terrier at their heels, they sauntered out of the house and—apparently aimlessly— took the path by the greenhouse, and so came into the kitchen-garden. Then, suddenly, they bunched together and closed upon a young tree of early ripening apples.

'We were only told not to pick any,' said Hubert, 'Come on, lads! Shake the tree and make them fall!'

He and James set their hands to the tree-trunk and shook it to and fro. An apple dropped, and then several more. Edgar was gathering them up from the ground, when he paused, looked sharply across to the bushes, and cried: 'Spying!' There stood the child, Hatty. She came out into the open, then, as concealment had become pointless.

'Give me an apple, please,' she said.

'Or you'll tell, I suppose!' cried Edgar. 'Spy and telltale!'

'Oh, give her an apple—she means no harm!' said James. As Edgar seemed unwilling, he himself threw one to her, and she caught it in the bottom of her pinafore held out in front of her. 'Only don't leave the core on the lawn, Hatty, as you did last time, or you'll get yourself into trouble, and us too, perhaps.'

She promised, and, eating her apple, drew nearer to the group. Each boy had an apple now, and they were eating them hurriedly, scuffling the earth with their feet as they came away from the tree, to confuse the tracks they had made.

Now they halted again—and it happened to be quite near Tom, but with their backs to him —while they finished their apples. The terrier snuffed his way round their legs and so came to Tom's side of the group. He was closer to Tom than he had ever been before, and became—in some degree—aware of him. So much was clear from the dog's behaviour: he faced Tom; his hackles rose; he growled again and again. Hu-

bert said, 'What is it, Pincher?' and turned; he looked at Tom, and never saw him.

Edgar had turned quickly, at the same time: he looked more searchingly, through and through Tom. Then James turned, and lastly even Hatty. They all four stared and stared through Tom, while the dog at their feet continued his growling.

It was very rude of them, Tom felt, and very stupid, too. Suddenly he lost patience with the lot of them. He felt the impulse to be rude back, and gave way to it—after all, no one could see him: he stuck out his tongue at them.

In retort, the girl Hatty darted out her tongue at Tom.

For a moment, Tom was so astounded that he almost believed he had imagined it; but he knew he had not. The girl had stuck out her tongue at him.

She could see him.

'What did you stick out your tongue for, Hatty?' asked Edgar, who must be able to see things even out of the corners of his eyes.

'My tongue was hot in my mouth,' said Hatty, with a resourcefulness that took Tom by surprise. 'It wanted to be cool—it wanted fresh air.'

'Don't give pert, lying answers!'

'Let her be, Edgar,' said James.

They lost interest in the dog's curious behaviour, and in Hatty's. They began to move back to the house. The dog skulked along nervously beside them, keeping them between himself and Tom, and still muttering to himself deep in his throat; the girl walked slightly ahead of them all.

Tom followed, seething with excitement, waiting his chance.

They went in single file by the narrow path between the greenhouse and the large box-bush. Hatty went first, then the three boys. Tom followed behind the four of them; but, when he emerged from the path and came on to the lawn, there were only the three boys ahead of him.

'Where's Hatty?' James was asking. He had been the last of the three.

'Slipped off somewhere among the trees,' said Edgar, carelessly. The three boys continued upon their way back into the house.

Tom was left on the lawn, gazing about him in determination and anger. She thought she had slipped through his fingers, but she hadn't. He would find her. He would have this out with her.

He began his search. He looked everywhere that he could think of: among the bushes; up the trees; behind the heating-house; beyond the nut stubs; under the summerhouse arches; inside the gooseberry wire; beyond the beanpoles . . .

No . . . No . . . No . . . She was nowhere. At last, behind him, he heard her call, 'Coo-eee!'

She was standing there, only a few yards from him, staring at him. There was a silence. Then Tom—not knowing whether he was indeed speaking to ears that could hear him—said: 'I knew you were hiding from me and watching me, just now.'

She might have meant to pretend not to hear him, as, earlier, she must have pretended not to see him; but her vanity could not resist this opening. 'Just now!' she cried, scornfully. 'Why, I've hidden and watched you, often and often, before this! I saw you when you ran along by the nut stubs and then used my secret hedge tunnel into the meadow! I saw you when Susan was dusting and you waved from the top of the yew-tree! I saw you when you went right through the orchard door!' She hesitated, as though the memory upset her a little; but then went on. 'Oh, I've seen you often—and often —and often—when you never knew it!'

So that was the meaning of the footprints on the grass, on that first day; that was the meaning of the shadowy form and face at the back of the bedroom, across the lawn; that, in short, was the meaning of the queer feeling of being watched, which Tom had had in the garden so often, that, in the end, he had come to accept it without speculation.

A kind of respect for the girl crept into Tom's mind. 'You don't hide badly, for a girl,' he said. He saw at once that the remark angered her, so he hurried on to introduce himself: 'I'm Tom Long,' he said. She said nothing, but looked as if she had little opinion of that, as a name. 'Well,' said Tom, nettled, 'I know your name: Hatty—Hatty Something.' Into the saying he

threw a careless disdain: it was only tit for tat.

The little girl, with only the slightest hesitation, drew herself up into a stiffness, and said: 'Princess Hatty, if you please: I am a Princess.'

## from TIME AT THE TOP

### Edward Ormondroyd

*No elevator ride will ever be the same again for anyone who reads* Time at the Top. *In a finely constructed and believable fantasy of travel back in time, Edward Ormondroyd tells Susan Shaw's story just as if he had actually witnessed it, managing very deftly to deal with a slight altering of history. It is all made to seem perfectly natural that the friendly elevator in Susan's apartment building should deliver her into the past (but that is because Susan met a witch one morning without realizing it at the time). Fortunately, the following excerpt will make these things clear and introduce children to one of the best-reasoned fantasies to have been written in recent years for practical-minded young people.*

### The Elevator Misbehaves

That elevator always reminded me of a tired old horse. It groaned when it started and groaned when it stopped. It labored up or down the shaft at such a plodding gait that you wondered if you were ever going to arrive. The door sighed when it opened or shut. I once suggested to Mr. Bodoni that we should either put the poor thing out to pasture or have it shot. "Yeah," he said, not getting the joke but willing to be amiable about it.

Around the top of the inside walls was a little frieze of cast-metal rosettes and curlicues. Mr. Bodoni, inspired one year by both the Spring weather and a sudden urge to express himself, had begun to paint these red. I don't know which gave out first, his paint or his inspiration;

at any rate he stopped halfway through the fourteenth rosette, and has not finished the job to this day. The rest of the inside was painted buff.

There was the usual bank of buttons—ten of them, including the basement stop, the emergency stop, and the alarm—and a dial-and-arrow above the door to show which floor you were approaching. A yellow ticket assured anyone who wanted to read it that the mechanism had been inspected and found satisfactory by a Mr. Scrawl Blot Scribble, who I sincerely hope is a better inspector than he is a penman. Mr. Bodoni had also hung up a ticket, with *No Smokking in Elvater, Please!* thickly pencilled thereon. (His own cigar was always dead, and didn't count, of course.) Finally there was a metal plate which said *Capacity 1500 Lbs.* I remember that when I first met Susan she was staring at this, moving her lips and ticking off her fingers.

"How does it come out?" I asked.

"I can't make it come out right," she said. "If everybody weighed a hundred and fifty pounds you could get ten people in, but what if they all weighed two hundred pounds? I'm not very good at arithmetic."

"Hmm," I said, and I began to work on it too. But I'm not very good at arithmetic either, and she had gotten off at her floor before I arrived at an answer.

Going up the elevator now, Susan occupied her mind with the usual arithmetical speculations.

'Fifteen hundred ulbs,' she thought. 'Or is it libs? Almost a ton. Or is a ton one thousand? No, two thousand. Suppose everybody weighed a hundred and seventy-five. Let's see, one seventy-five into . . . um. I wish Mr. Bodoni'd learn to spell. One seventy-five into fifteen hundred, make it nine, nine times five is . . . um. At least Elsie Mautner's even dumber than I am in arithmetic. Try eight. Eight fives are forty, that's a zero, maybe it'll come out even, let's see, carry the four . . . um. Wonder how many people *do* weigh a hundred seventy-five? Pretty heavy. Oh well, almost at the top. I'll work it out on the way down.' For the arrow was creeping past six. Too bad there weren't

arrows in the classrooms at school to save you when you were stuck on a problem . . . The arrow plodded up to seven and stopped.

The elevator kept on going.

It was the strangest sensation—as if the elevator were forcing its way up through something sticky in the shaft, like molasses or chewing gum. There was a thin humming noise all around her, and the light dimmed. She was startled, and a little frightened. But of course there were only seven floors, so the elevator would have to stop at the seventh. The arrow must be out of order. She would have to tell Mr. Bodoni. He'd look mournful, the way he always did when something went wrong, as if it were all your fault.

Now the elevator stopped. The door said "Sighhh . . ." and opened. Susan clutched her hands together and said, "Oh!"

'They must be redecorating,' she thought in astonishment. 'No, that can't be it; you don't redecorate a hallway. Maybe it's a private suite? But why should the public elevator open into a—?'

It was a hallway she was looking into, but it certainly wasn't the seventh-floor hallway of the apartment building as she remembered it. For one thing, the floor, instead of being covered with brown carpeting, was bare parqueted wood, beautifully polished. For another thing, there were no numbered doors opposite; the wall there was solidly wainscotted with oak. Against it stood a marble-topped table with carved lyre-shaped legs, on which were a vase of paper flowers and a stuffed owl under a glass bell. Everything was glowing with—was it sunlight? Sunlight on a March evening like this?

She became aware of sounds. There must be a clock nearby, and a large one too: tock—tock —tock—a stately sound. A bird was singing; not a canary, something richer and wilder and much more inventive. And wait a minute—yes—no —chickens? Impossible! And another sound; a serene whispering murmur, rising and dying. It could only be one thing, a breeze rustling through foliage. And yet only a few minutes ago, downstairs in the apartment, she had heard the rattling gusts of March against the window.

The scent of flowers was very strong.

She stepped out of the elevator in a daze. Yes,

there was a clock, a grandfather one, with hunting scenes painted on its porcelain face. The sunlight came through a window to the right of the elevator. It was a funny kind of window, very tall and narrow, with two sets of curtains: straight-hanging white lace framed by drawn-back red velvet. It was open; all the strange scents and sounds were coming through it with the sunlight, irresistibly drawing her to investigate. She leaned her elbows on the sill and stared out, filling her lungs with warm sweet air and murmuring, "Oh my." She had never been any closer to the country than the seaside resort in New Jersey where her father took her during summer vacation. But this was countryside, all right: she could just tell, even though all she could see was a portion of hedged-in garden. The hedge was a tall tangle of roses and privet and honeysuckle. Hydrangeas grew under the window, lifting their pale blue pompons to the sill. The grass was badly in need of cutting, and had flowers growing in it. The base of one of the huge trees on the lawn was encircled by a white-painted iron settee.

'I'm dreaming, that's all there is to it,' she thought. 'I've fallen asleep over the newspaper. It's like *Alice in Wonderland.* I'll probably try to get into the garden, but the door will be too small, or the golden key will be lost, or something, and there'll be a little bottle with a label saying "Drink Me," and a White Rabbit—no, it's a black cat.' For a large black tom had emerged from the hedge, and was plowing nose-first through the grass like a ship through waves. The bird abruptly ceased its singing, and began to scold: "Mew! Mew!" 'A bird mewing like a cat?' she wondered. 'Maybe the cat sings like a bird . . . Oh well, pretty soon Mrs. Clutchett'll poke me with her broom and say, "C'mon, Susie, help me set the table." '

"Maw-w-w!" said a cow in the distance; and she wondered why she should dream that. 'Very realistic of me,' she thought.

The elevator door sighed, and trundled shut.

"No, wait!" she gasped. *"Ow!"* Springing back from the window, she cracked her head against the sash. Her eyes filled with tears. She wasn't dreaming—no dream could hurt like that. Through the blur she saw that the elevator was gone. There was no door in the wall. Solid, un-

broken wood paneling!

'Oh no, oh no!' she thought in a panic, searching for the button.

"Vicky!" a woman's voice called. "Vicky?"

Someone was coming. There was no button on the wall, and not enough time to recall the elevator anyhow. But she had no business being here! Quick! Where? The red curtains! She slipped behind the nearest one, and squeezed herself as thin as she could. Fortunately they reached all the way to the floor.

The footsteps came down the hallway, and with them a curious rustling sound as of long skirts. She could not resist a quick peek. What she saw made her catch her breath. It was a lovely, tall, slender woman with masses of rich chestnut hair piled on her head. Susan, always susceptible to beautiful ladies, felt her heart go out to this one at once: 'That's what I want to be like when I grow up,' she thought. And the woman must be an actress, too. Why else would she be in costume? She had on a grey dress whose skirt came down to the floor; it had a lot of material draped around the hips, but was tightly fitted from the waist up. All she needed was make-up to be ready to step out before the footlights.

"Vicky?" she called again, stopping by the grandfather clock.

"What's the matter, Mama?" Now a girl came running down the hallway from the opposite direction. She was slightly taller than Susan; her hair was a dark coppery brown, and fell in waves below her shoulders. She wore a dress similar to her mother's except that the skirt was shorter, and black cotton stockings.

"I just heard the strangest noise somewhere around here!" said the woman in a puzzled voice. "Did you hear anything?"

"No, I was talking with Maggie. What kind of noise?"

"Well, it's hard to say—a kind of rumble, I think it was, and then a thump . . ."

"Oh, I expect it was just Toby. Shall I look for him?"

"No, I don't think . . . it sounded like something rolling or sliding. And then a very distinct thump, like—oh, like a bird flying against the window."

"It must have been Toby, chasing that catbird

—they hate each other so."

"I suppose you're right . . . Well, I'm sorry I disturbed you for nothing."

"Oh, *Mama*. Maggie says supper is almost ready anyway. Doesn't the honeysuckle smell just glorious?"

"Mm, lovely."

They moved off down the hallway with their arms about each other.

"Mama, everything outside is getting so jungly. Why don't we have a gardener in?"

"Well, dear," Susan thought the woman's voice was a little evasive, "suppose we wait just a bit longer. Mr. Branscomb is coming tomorrow afternoon about the investments, and after he's gone I'll think about it . . ." Their voices faded down the end of the hall.

'Well, that's funny,' Susan thought. 'I never saw either of them before. If they lived up here I would have seen them in the elevator.' It had come to her that part of the seventh floor must have been converted into a very realistic stage set, and that the woman and the girl had been rehearsing their parts in a play. But no, that couldn't be it. No stage set that she had ever seen was so realistic that you could hear cows and smell flowers and feel the warmth of sunlight. And if this were the seventh floor of the apartment building, *why hadn't the woman recognized the sound of the elevator?* That rum-

bling sigh was unmistakable after you'd heard it once . . . Well, it was all very queer. Even as a dream it would have been the strangest she'd ever had.

She crept out from behind the curtain and began to look for the button again. If that elevator could come up here once—wherever "here" was—it could come up again. But there was no button. And while she was still peering and poking helplessly along the wainscotting she heard the sound of running feet approaching. This time she lost her head. She darted toward the window curtains, changed her mind and stepped back, glanced desperately about for a better hiding place, and at last, without a second to spare, threw her leg over the windowsill and dropped down the other side—falling through the hydrangeas with a tremendous thrashing and crackling. 'Good grief, what a racket!' she thought; 'like an *elephant!* I hope the bushes cover me.'

Apparently they did, for the girl's voice said, right over her, "All right, you naughty Toby cat! Breaking the bushes! Just wait till I catch you, that's all! And if I don't, Bobbie will tomorrow, and then see if you don't regret the day you were born!"

'Now I've really done it,' Susan sighed when Vicky had gone. 'Although I suppose I could go to the front door and say, "Pardon me, but there's an elevator in your house that you don't know about, and I have to use it." No, no—all that explaining . . . It's hard enough to explain when you know *what* you're explaining. I certainly don't have any idea of what this is all about. Well, I'll just have to wait till it's dark, and sneak in, and try to get that darned elevator up somehow. Poor Daddy'll worry when I don't show up for dinner. And Mrs. Clutchett will be snorting around and making things worse . . . How am I ever going to explain this to *anybody* without making them think I've gone absolutely insane . . . ?'

She might as well make herself comfortable for the wait. She snuggled down in the litter of dry leaves, murmuring, "What a day! What a stupid impossible crazy day! I should've stuffed my ears with cotton and gone back to bed and stayed there this morning." Wrapped in blankets, impervious to noise—the idea began to make her feel drowsy. The air was as warm as her own bedclothes; the stirring bushes lulled and hushed, more comfortable to the ear even than silence. 'It *is* a dream, really,' she thought, yawning. 'I hope I can remember it to tell Daddy . . .'

### The Meaning of Three

It was dark when she awakened. 'They've let me sleep through dinner,' she thought. Why should they do that? "Daddy?" she said. There was no answer. Something crackled under her as she shifted.

Then she remembered. It wasn't a dream after all.

She crawled out from under the hydrangeas as quietly as she could, and stood up on the lawn, and then caught her breath with wonder. The sky was ablaze with stars. Where had they all come from? She had never seen more than a few score, feebly competing with the city's neon; here they were beyond imagining in number. 'Why, that must be the Milky Way!' she thought, recognizing that glowing swath overhead from a picture in one of her science textbooks. And in gazing up at it she discovered something else that the city would never have let her find out. The night sky could be *heard*. It was like the sound of the sea in a shell, only much fainter, as though it had come to her

straining ears from as far away as the dimmest star.

There were other sounds too. The grass was full of crickets, who were chirping and rustling as they moved about through the stems, so that the whole lawn whispered with them. She was sure she heard frogs nearby. And suddenly in the distance a train said, "Way a *wayyy* oh-h-h-h-h," sweet crescendo, sad diminuendo.

'If I lived here,' she thought, 'I'd never go to bed, never. I'd just sit outside all night and look and listen . . .'

But she simply had to go back: her father would be worried sick by now, and furious with her for making him worry. All the windows of the house were dark. It was a very large house, she noticed now, tall and narrow and with a profile reminiscent of a castle. She would just have to hope that everyone was asleep, and that she could find an unlocked door. Slowly she began to grope her way through the shadows.

'Wish there was more moon,' she thought after five minutes of blundering. 'There seem to be hedges all over the place. Ouch! Thorns. Well, here's an opening. That sounds like frogs —must be a pond nearby.'

She was right. At the next step there was no ground under her foot; she sprawled forward clutching at the air, and *slosh!*—she was under. Fortunately the water was only waist-deep, and she was on her feet again immediately. The bottom was squdgy. Something cold and soft slithered across her bare knees. She shuddered, and scrambled up the stone bank.

"They'll all be ruined," she muttered, taking off her clothes and wringing them out. "Stupid place for a pond!" But she didn't want to stand about naked while they dried, so she put them on again. They clung to her, and her shoes squelched with every step. It was a good thing that the weather was so warm. What if it had been March here too? The very memory of the wind and sleet she had left behind—how long ago now?—made her shiver.

In another ten minutes she was clear of the hedges and shrubbery, and had found a flight of wooden stairs against the dark bulk of the house. She crept up them one step at a time, testing each tread for squeaks; and thank goodness! there was a door at the top, with a handle that turned easily and quietly.

'Now,' she thought, standing in the interior darkness, 'which side of the house am I on? I'm all mixed up. This might even be the wrong floor . . . I know, I'll listen for the grandfather clock. It was near the elevator.'

Room after room, all caves of shadow; windows that pretended to be doorways; doors that hid themselves in the darkest corners; sharp-cornered furniture everywhere. She groped along inch by inch, hardly daring to put her hands out for fear of knocking something over, and wincing at every move for fear of striking her face against some unseen projection. She could not hear the clock anywhere.

Eventually she found herself at the foot of a staircase. She felt her way across the bottom stair; encountered the newel post, all knobby with carving; felt her way around that, and met a table top; put her hand on something cold that gave under her touch; and *crash!*—the sound of a metal object bouncing on the floor. Not very loud, actually, but loud enough.

She crouched, suffocating.

A door opened softly upstairs. Pause. Then a whisper: "Toby!"

Pause.

"Toby?"

"Meow!" said Susan, with all the realism she could muster.

A long heart-pounding silence; then the upstairs door softly closed again.

She remained motionless for a few more minutes, to make sure that all was quiet above, then straightened up. Suddenly, somewhere to her left, a sweet melancholy chime struck the quarter hour.

'There it is!' she thought, sagging with relief. As quickly as the dark permitted she went toward the sound, discovered a doorway, and—yes! it was the hallway, all right. Up ahead was the dim patch of light that must be the window, and beyond it she heard the clock solemnly knocking each passing second on the head with its pendulum.

'Now for the button—there *must* be a button.'

She began to run her fingers over the wainscotting. There was no button. The wood seemed to be glowing somehow. Brighter and brighter—her shadow loomed and wavered

on the paneling—

She whirled around.

There stood Vicky in a nightgown, holding a trembling candle aloft and staring at her round-eyed with fright. She seemed on the verge of screaming.

Susan hissed, "Now don't yell or do anything silly! I'm not a ghost."

"Are-are you a burglar's accomplice?" Vicky faltered.

"Of course not. I'm just lost, that's all. Soon as I can find the elevator I'll go away. Do you know where the button is?"

Vicky stepped backward. "Button? What button?"

"The *elevator* button. Oh, I forgot—you don't know about the elevator, do you? Look, I know it doesn't make any sense, but I'm not crazy, really. Why do you keep staring at me like that?"

"Your *clothes.*"

"Well, what's the matter with them? They're just wet, that's all. I fell in your pond."

"It's not the wet . . ."

"What's the matter with you?" Susan burst out after a moment's silence. "You act like I was a freak or something!"

"It's your clothes," said Vicky. "They're the oddest I ever saw."

"Well, that nightgown of yours is pretty hilarious, too," Susan retorted. "And what about those dresses you and your mother were wearing this afternoon? I never saw such funny old-fashioned clothes in all my life."

"Why, they are *not* old-fashioned! Mama just bought that dress a month ago!"

"You mean for a play? Is she going to be in a play?"

"No, of course not—just to wear. Don't you know what people wear?"

"Certainly I know what people wear!" Susan said in exasperation. "And I know perfectly well that people don't wear clothes like that any more. In the Gay Nineties, maybe, but not in 19*60.*"

The other girl retreated a step, and the candle shook violently in her hand. "I think you're mad. I didn't say anything about 1960. I mean right now. This year."

"What do you mean, this year?" said Susan,

beginning to feel a bit frightened. "I'm *talking* about this year. It's 1960."

Vicky shook her head.

"Well then, for goodness sake, what year *is* it?"

"Don't you really know? It's 1881, of course."

"Oh!" Susan gasped. The shape of the house! The design of the dresses! The funny curtains by the window! All the oddities she had noticed in the last few hours clicked into place in her mind. "Eighteen—eighteen—oh no! What's happened? Where am I? What street are we on?"

"Street? It's not a street, it's a country road."

"All right, all right, but what's it called?"

"Ward Lane."

Well, that sounded right—or almost right. "But where's the city?"

"Don't you know? It's about five miles from here."

"Five *miles!*" Susan moaned, clutching her head. "Oh, am I lost! Am I ever lost! Listen—when I got on the elevator I was *in* the city, on Ward *Street,* and it was *1960!*"

"Nonsense," Vicky said faintly. "Things like that can't happen."

"I know they can't! Look, I don't want to argue: I just want to go back. I'm here whether it can happen or n—" Striking herself dramatically at the word *here,* she felt something hard in the pocket of her skirt. "Look!" she continued excitedly, "I can prove it—about being from the twentieth century, I mean. You know about dimes and quarters, don't you? Well, here, look at the dates. Oh, go on, take them, I'm not going to hurt you!"

Vicky hesitantly took the coins and held them close to the candle flame. "What funny designs they have! Oh! This one says 1953! 1945! 1960 —oh, my goodness! 1960! You—maybe you are from the twentieth century. But it's impos— how could you possibly *get* here?"

"I've been *telling* you, I came in the elevator. Do you know what an elevator is?"

"We may live in the country," Vicky said, "but we are not backward."

"All right, I'm sorry. I didn't know whether they'd been invented yet. Anyway, I got on this elevator where I live, just across the hall, and it let me out here instead of where I thought I

was going, and then it went down again and I can't call it back. You know, I'm beginning to think the stupid thing wants me to be here."

Vicky gave a sudden start. "*Wants* you to be here?"

"Oh, I know it sounds silly—it is silly. I just can't think why—"

"No," Vicky whispered. "No. It isn't silly." Her eyes were widening again, and the candle in her hand shook so much that it almost guttered out. "I just remembered something. The well! It must be the—yes, it has to be! *It worked!* Look, you don't have to go back right away, do you?"

"Well, I ought—"

"Look," Vicky interrupted with growing excitement, catching Susan by the sleeve, "you *can't* go back now, I simply must talk with you. Really, it's *essential.* Come up to my—are you hungry? I'll get something to eat. And we'll have to get those wet clothes off you. Oh, my heavens, talk about—! I was right, I was right— it's perfectly true, Maggie doesn't know what she's talking about! Here, wait, don't move a step, I'll be right back!"

She hurried soundlessly down the hallway, and returned in a minute carrying some slices of bread and a pot of jam.

"All I could find in a hurry, I'm afraid. Maggie's hidden everything because Bobbie's coming home tomorrow, and he always—Come on, you *must* tell me all about it, and I'll tell you about —oh, it's just unbelievable!—please be very careful on the stair, we mustn't wake Mama up."

Susan, utterly bewildered, allowed herself to be led on tiptoe up the stairs and cautiously along a second-floor hallway.

"Oh, what a lovely bed!" she exclaimed on entering Vicky's room. It was a high four-poster with a frilly arched canopy, and curtains at the head.

"Ssshh! You mustn't talk loud. Mama's a fairly sound sleeper, but Maggie has ears like an owl. Yes, isn't it a beauty? Grandmama left it to me in her will. Here, you can wear one of my nightgowns. Take off those wet things—I won't look. I'll put some jam on the bread. Oh pooh, I forgot the spoon. I guess we can just dip the slices in. Wish we had some tea. Does the nightgown fit all right? I'm a little taller than you."

"Yes, it's fine. Where shall I put my things?"

"Oh, over the back of the chair is all right, they'll dry soon. That's awfully nice material. What funny shoes! Does everybody wear such short skirts in the twentieth century?"

"Yes, why not?"

"It seems so immodest. But I suppose if everybody does it's all right. I don't wear corsets myself, neither does Mama. She says they're such a torture, and there's no sense in it if your waist is naturally slender. Thank goodness ours are! Here, sit on the bed, you can put your feet under the sheets if they're cold. Oh! My manners—you must forgive me, I'm so excited about the magic. I don't care if it *does* sound silly, it *is* magic. I'm Victoria Albertine Walker."

"Susan Shaw."

" 'Charmed to meet you, Miss Shaw. Isn't the weather delightful?' That's what we say in Deportment Class," she giggled. "Now! Please tell me what happened, and don't leave out *any*thing, because it may be of great importance."

So Susan recounted the events of the day. When she got to the part about the old woman with the runaway hat, Victoria's eyes grew rounder and rounder, and she hugged her knees; and as soon as the tale was finished she burst out:

"Yes, of course! The old woman was a witch, a good witch!"

"A witch?" Susan said. "That's craz—" She checked herself. Everything else was crazy—why not a witch? "She didn't look like one, anyway. I thought she might have been a gypsy or something."

"Of course she didn't look like one. They never do, that's just the point. If she looked like a witch you'd do whatever she asked, to get her blessings, and it wouldn't be any test of your character. You see? It's like that in lots of stories. But if they look like someone else, and they're troublesome, and you help them out of the kindness of your heart anyway, then they know that you're worthy."

"Hmm. Well, that could be it, I suppose. But I still can't figure out what she meant by giving me three. Three what?"

"Why, that's perfectly plain. They always give you three of something. She must have meant that you could have three trips in the elevator to here!"

"Ohhhh! That could be it, couldn't it? But why here?"

Victoria gave her a long speculative look. "That's what I wanted to talk to you about. I think I know why."

"Why? How can you know?"

"Because—oh, it's all so spooky! *You were sent here on purpose because I wished you here.*"

Susan felt a shiver race down her back. "Me? How did you know about me?"

"Oh, I didn't wish for you in particular; just —somebody." She hesitated a moment. "Cross your heart and hope to die you won't tell? It's a *very serious* secret."

"Cross my heart three times and hope to die."

"All right. Well, first I wished on a star. You know, 'Star light, star bright, first star I see to-night.' Do you do that in the twentieth century too? Anyway, it didn't work. Then I remembered there was an old abandoned well about half a mile down the lane, and I thought, 'Maybe it's a wishing well.' So I asked Maggie, she's Irish, but she said no it wasn't, that was all blasphemy, only God can grant your wishes and He doesn't do it very often because it's not for the good of your soul. And she believes in ghosts, too, can you imagine? But I don't care, it can't be blasphemy if you're wishing for someone else's sake—can it? So I went there this very afternoon, and I threw in the thing I love best, a little gold locket that Papa gave me when I was ten, and I marched around it three times, and I said, 'I wish someone would come and chase Mr. Sweeney away.' "

"And?"

"Well, I never dreamed it would happen this way—but here you are!" Victoria concluded triumphantly.

"Oh, now, wait a minute!" Susan protested. "I can't—who's Mr. Sweeney?"

"Oh, he's this perfectly dreadful man who's been absolutely hounding poor Mama to marry him."

"Oh! Is your father—?"

"Yes, poor Papa died two years ago."

"Why, so did my mother."

"Oh, I *am* sorry . . .

"Anyway," Victoria went on after an interval of silence, "I was hoping some handsome man with a noble brow would come along, and show Mr. Sweeney up for a scoundrel and give him a thrashing. But I'm sure you'll do just as well. You're from the future, after all, you must know an awful lot. Oh no," she added hastily, seeing that Susan was going to interrupt, "I don't mean *you* should thrash him. Maybe you could just— I don't know. Scare him away, maybe."

"Well, I don't know . . . Why doesn't your Mama turn him down?"

"Oh, she has. But he's so persistent. He's after her money, I'm certain of it, the scoundrel. Poor Papa left quite a lot . . . Sweeeeeney," she drawled in a savage falsetto. "Isn't that a dreadful name? I couldn't stand having a name like that."

"Why, your Mama could marry anyone she wanted to," Susan said warmly. "She's the most beautiful lady I ever saw. She's as beautiful as a movie star!"

"Oh, how poetic! 'Beautiful as a moving star.' I'll have to write that in my diary. Yes, she is. But, you know, she's been so—oh, resigned since Papa died. She sold our city house and buried herself out here because Papa loved it here so much, and she won't go out in society where she could meet suitable men. And Mr. Sweeney keeps lurking around and forcing his attentions on her and wearing her down, until I'm afraid she'll say yes just to have some peace . . . Well! We won't have to worry about it until tomorrow. My brother Bobbie's coming home from school tomorrow. We'll have to consult him first anyway, he's the man of the house now, even if he's only twelve. Robert Lincoln Walker. Don't ever call him Bobolink, it makes him furious."

"Oh, I can't stay till tomorrow. I have to go back."

"But Susan, you only have three trips, it's a shame to waste one."

"Yes, but my father is probably frantic by now."

"That's right, I forgot . . . But look, it's so late; surely a few more minutes won't matter?"

"Well . . . just a few."

"Good! Tell me about your Mama. You don't mind talking about it?"

So Susan told her all she could remember.

Then Victoria told Susan all about her late Papa. Devouring bread and jam by candlelight, they agreed that two parents seemed to be able to take care of themselves, but that one alone required careful management; which was a great responsibility, but no doubt worth it in the long run. Then Victoria swore Susan to secrecy, and brought out her diary, and read selected parts of it out loud; which proved so fascinating that Susan resolved to keep one of her own as soon as she could begin. (Although she determined that *her* style would be more brisk, and would not run so much to sad pure thoughts, and moonlight on marble gravestones, and noble breaking hearts and so on.) And of course certain passages in the diary brought them around to the subject of Boys; and Susan quite forgot about going home while they pursued that fascinating topic . . . Gradually their voices began to trail off—they yawned—the silences grew longer; and at last the two friends slept, curled up on the bed, while the candle burned down to a puddle of wax and put itself out.

## from WATERSHIP DOWN
### *Richard Adams*

*Winner of the Carnegie Medal, awarded by the British Library Association to the most distinguished children's book of each year,* Watership Down *proved to be equally popular with children and with adults when it was published in the United States. It is a very long book and, at times, very sophisticated, but it is a fresh and vital fantasy that gives a convincing picture of a whole society. The beauty of the Berkshire countryside is vividly evoked, the characterization is solid, the writing fluent. The heroes of this tale —and they are heroic—are a group of rabbits who have set out to found a new and safe community. Led by Hazel, they have come to Water-*

*ship Down and dug a home among the roots of the beech trees, a haven they call Honeycomb Hall.*

### A Honeycomb and a Mouse

The next day was as hot and cloudless as the last. Neither Pipkin nor Dandelion was at morning silflay; and Hazel relentlessly took the others up to the beech hanger to go on with the digging. He questioned Strawberry about the great burrow and learned that its ceiling, as well as being vaulted with a tangle of fibers, was strengthened by roots going vertically down into the floor. He remarked that he had not noticed these.

"There aren't many, but they're important," said Strawberry. "They take a lot of the load. If it weren't for those roots the ceiling would fall after heavy rain. On stormy nights you could sense the extra weight in the earth above, but there was no danger."

Hazel and Bigwig went underground with him. The beginnings of the new warren had been hollowed out among the roots of one of the beech trees. It was still no more than a small, irregular cave with one entrance. They set to work to enlarge it, digging between the roots and tunneling upward to make a second run that would emerge inside the wood. After a time Strawberry stopped digging and began moving about between the roots, sniffing, biting and scuffling in the soil with his front paws. Hazel supposed that he was tired and pretending to be busy while he had a rest, but at length he came back to them and said that he had some suggestions.

"It's this way," he explained. "There isn't a big spread of fine roots above here. That was a lucky chance in the great burrow and I don't think you can expect to find it again. But, all the same, we can do pretty well with what we've got."

"And what *have* we got?" asked Blackberry, who had come down the run while he was talking.

"Well, we've got several thick roots that go straight down—more than there were in the great burrow. The best thing will be to dig round them and leave them. They shouldn't be gnawed through and taken out. We shall need

them if we're going to have a hall of any size."

"Then our hall will be full of these thick, vertical roots?" asked Hazel. He felt disappointed.

"Yes, it will," said Strawberry, "but I can't see that it's going to be any the worse for that. We can go in and out among them and they won't hinder anyone who's talking or telling a story. They'll make the place warmer and they'll help to conduct sound from above, which might be useful some time or other."

The excavation of the hall (which came to be known among them as the Honeycomb) turned out to be something of a triumph for Strawberry. Hazel contented himself with organizing the diggers and left it to Strawberry to say what was actually to be done. The work went on in shifts and the rabbits took it in turns to feed, play and lie in the sun above ground. Throughout the day the solitude remained unbroken by noise, men, tractors or even cattle, and they began to feel still more deeply what they owed to Fiver's insight. By the late afternoon the big burrow was beginning to take shape. At the north end, the beech roots formed a kind of irregular colonnade. This gave way to a more open central space: and beyond, where there were no supporting roots, Strawberry left blocks of the earth untouched, so that the south end consisted of three or four separate bays. These narrowed into low-roofed runs that led away into sleeping burrows.

Hazel, much better pleased now that he could see for himself how the business was going to turn out, was sitting with Silver in the mouth of the run when suddenly there was a stamping of "Hawk! Hawk!" and a dash for cover by the rabbits outside. Hazel, safe where he was, remained looking out past the shadow of the wood to the open, sunlit grass beyond. The kestrel sailed into view and took up station, the black-edged flange of its tail bent down and its pointed wings beating rapidly as it searched the down below.

"But do you think it *would* attack us?" asked Hazel, watching it drop lower and recommence its poised fluttering. "Surely it's too small?"

"You're probably right," replied Silver. "All the same, would you care to go out there and start feeding?"

"I'd like to try standing up to some of these elil," said Bigwig, who had come up the run behind them. "We're afraid of too many. But a bird from the air would be awkward, especially if it came fast. It might get the better of even a big rabbit if it took him by surprise."

"See the mouse?" said Silver suddenly. "There, look. Poor little beast."

They could all see the field mouse, which was exposed in a patch of smooth grass. It had evidently strayed too far from its hole and now could not tell what to do. The kestrel's shadow had not passed over it, but the rabbits' sudden disappearance had made it uneasy and it was pressed to the ground, looking uncertainly this way and that. The kestrel had not yet seen it, but could hardly fail to do so as soon as it moved.

"Any moment now," said Bigwig callously.

On an impulse, Hazel hopped down the bank and went a little way into the open grass. Mice do not speak Lapine, but there is a very simple, limited *lingua franca* of the hedgerow and woodland. Hazel used it now.

"Run," he said. "Here; quick."

The mouse looked at him, but did not move. Hazel spoke again and the mouse began suddenly to run toward him as the kestrel turned and slid sideways and downward. Hazel hastened back to the hole. Looking out, he saw the mouse following him. When it had almost reached the foot of the bank it scuttered over a fallen twig with two or three green leaves. The twig turned, one of the leaves caught the sunlight slanting through the trees and Hazel saw it flash for an instant. Immediately the kestrel came lower in an oblique glide, closed its wings and dropped.

Before Hazel could spring back from the mouth of the hole, the mouse had dashed between his front paws and was pressed to the ground between his back legs. At the same moment the kestrel, all beak and talons, hit the loose earth immediately outside like a missile thrown from the tree above. It scuffled savagely and for an instant the three rabbits saw its round, dark eyes looking straight down the run. Then it was gone. The speed and force of the pounce, not a length away, were terrifying and Hazel leaped backward, knocking Silver off his balance. They picked themselves up in silence.

## from THE HOBBIT

*J. R. R. Tolkien*

*Bilbo Baggins isn't a picaresque hero; he's a sedate and respectable hobbit with no desire for adventure. But when the challenge of adventure comes to him, Bilbo rises to meet it. Surely this is an element of the book that has contributed to its great appeal to children, the very fact that it is a small, unassuming creature like themselves who copes with hostile goblins and the terrible dragon Smaug.*

### An Unexpected Party

In a hole in the ground there lived a hobbit. Not a nasty, dirty, wet hole, filled with the ends of worms and an oozy smell, nor yet a dry, bare, sandy hole with nothing in it to sit down on or to eat: it was a hobbit-hole, and that means comfort.

It had a perfectly round door like a porthole, painted green, with a shiny yellow brass knob in the exact middle. The door opened on to a tube-shaped hall like a tunnel: a very comfortable tunnel without smoke, with panelled walls, and floors tiled and carpeted, provided with polished chairs, and lots and lots of pegs for hats and coats—the hobbit was fond of visitors. The tunnel wound on and on, going fairly but not quite straight into the side of the hill—The Hill, as all the people for many miles round called it—and many little round doors opened out of it, first on one side and then on another. No going upstairs for the hobbit: bedrooms, bathrooms, cellars, pantries (lots of these), wardrobes (he had whole rooms devoted to clothes), kitchens, diningrooms, all were on the same floor, and indeed on the same passage. The best rooms were all on the lefthand side (going in), for these were the only ones to have windows, deep-set round windows looking over his garden, and meadows beyond, sloping down to the river.

This hobbit was a very well-to-do hobbit, and

his name was Baggins. The Bagginses had lived in the neighbourhood of The Hill for time out of mind, and people considered them very respectable, not only because most of them were rich, but also because they never had any adventures or did anything unexpected: you could tell what a Baggins would say on any question without the bother of asking him. This is a story of how a Baggins had an adventure, and found himself doing and saying things altogether unexpected. He may have lost the neighbors' respect, but he gained—well, you will see whether he gained anything in the end.

The mother of our particular hobbit—what is a hobbit? I suppose hobbits need some description nowadays, since they have become rare and shy of the Big People, as they call us. They are (or were) small people, smaller than dwarves (and they have no beards) but very much larger than lilliputians. There is little or no magic about them, except the ordinary everyday sort which helps them to disappear quietly and quickly when large stupid folk like you and me come blundering along, making a noise like elephants which they can hear a mile off. They are inclined to be fat in the stomach; they dress in bright colours (chiefly green and yellow); wear no shoes, because their feet grow natural leathery soles and thick warm brown hair like the stuff on their heads (which is curly); have long clever brown fingers, good-natured faces, and laugh deep fruity laughs (especially after dinner, which they have twice a day when they can get it). Now you know enough to go on with. As I was saying, the mother of this hobbit—of Bilbo Baggins, that is—was the famous Belladonna Took, one of the three remarkable daughters of the Old Took, head of the hobbits who lived across The Water, the small river that ran at the foot of The Hill. It had always been said that long ago one or other of the Tooks had married into a fairy family (the less friendly said a goblin family); certainly there was still something not entirely hobbitlike about them, and once in a while members of the Took-clan would go and have adventures. They discreetly disappeared, and the family hushed it up; but the fact remained that the Tooks were not as respectable as the Bagginses, though they were undoubtedly richer.

Not that Belladonna Took ever had any adventures after she became Mrs. Bungo Baggins. Bungo, that was Bilbo's father, built the most luxurious hobbit-hole for her (and partly with her money) that was to be found either under The Hill or over The Hill or across The Water, and there they remained to the end of their days. Still it is probable that Bilbo, her only son, although he looked and behaved exactly like a second edition of his solid and comfortable father, got something a bit queer in his make-up from the Took side, something that only waited for a chance to come out. The chance never arrived, until Bilbo Baggins was grown up, being about fifty years old or so, and living in the beautiful hobbit-hole built by his father, which I have just described for you, until he had in fact apparently settled down immovably.

By some curious chance one morning long ago in the quiet of the world, when there was less noise and more green, and the hobbits were still numerous and prosperous, and Bilbo Baggins was standing at his door after breakfast smoking an enormous long wooden pipe that reached nearly down to his woolly toes (neatly brushed) —Gandalf came by. Gandalf! If you had heard only a quarter of what I have heard about him, and I have only heard very little of all there is to hear, you would be prepared for any sort of remarkable tale. Tales and adventures sprouted up all over the place wherever he went, in the most extraordinary fashion. He had not been down that way under The Hill for ages and ages, not since his friend the Old Took died, in fact, and the hobbits had almost forgotten what he looked like. He had been away over The Hill and across The Water on businesses of his own since they were all small hobbit-boys and hobbit-girls.

All that the unsuspecting Bilbo saw that morning was a little old man with a tall pointed blue hat, a long grey cloak, a silver scarf over which his long white beard hung down below his waist, and immense black boots.

"Good Morning!" said Bilbo, and he meant it. The sun was shining, and the grass was very green. But Gandalf looked at him from under long bushy eyebrows that stuck out further than the brim of his shady hat.

"What do you mean?" he said. "Do you wish

me a good morning, or mean that it is a good morning whether I want it or not; or that you feel good this morning; or that it is a morning to be good on?"

"All of them at once," said Bilbo. "And a very fine morning for a pipe of tobacco out of doors, into the bargain. If you have a pipe about you, sit down and have a fill of mine! There's no hurry, we have all the day before us!" Then Bilbo sat down on a seat by his door, crossed his legs, and blew out a beautiful grey ring of smoke that sailed up into the air without breaking and floated away over The Hill.

"Very pretty!" said Gandalf. "But I have no time to blow smoke-rings this morning. I am looking for someone to share in an adventure that I am arranging, and it's very difficult to find anyone."

"I should think so—in these parts! We are plain quiet folk and have no use for adventures. Nasty disturbing uncomfortable things! Make you late for dinner! I can't think what anybody sees in them," said our Mr. Baggins, and stuck one thumb behind his braces, and blew out another even bigger smoke-ring. Then he took out his morning letters, and began to read, pretending to take no more notice of the old man. He had decided that he was not quite his sort, and wanted him to go away. But the old man did not move. He stood leaning on his stick and gazing at the hobbit without saying anything, till Bilbo got quite uncomfortable and even a little cross.

"Good morning!" he said at last. "We don't want any adventures here, thank you! You might try over The Hill or across The Water." By this he meant that the conversation was at an end.

"What a lot of things you do use Good morning for!" said Gandalf. "Now you mean that you want to get rid of me, and that it won't be good till I move off."

"Not at all, not at all, my dear sir! Let me see, I don't think I know your name?"

"Yes, yes, my dear sir!—and I do know your name, Mr. Bilbo Baggins. And you do know my name, though you don't remember that I belong to it. I am Gandalf, and Gandalf means me! To think that I should have lived to be good-morninged by Belladonna Took's son, as if I was selling buttons at the door!"

"Gandalf, Gandalf! Good gracious me! Not the wandering wizard that gave Old Took a pair of magic diamond studs that fastened themselves and never came undone till ordered? Not the fellow who used to tell such wonderful tales at parties, about dragons and goblins and giants and the rescue of princesses and the unexpected luck of widows' sons? Not the man that used to make such particularly excellent fireworks! I remember those! Old Took used to have them on Midsummer's Eve. Splendid! They used to go up like great lilies and snapdragons and laburnums of fire and hang in the twilight all evening!" You will notice already that Mr. Baggins was not quite so prosy as he liked to believe, also that he was very fond of flowers. "Dear me!" he went on. "Not the Gandalf who was responsible for so many quiet lads and lasses going off into the Blue for mad adventures, anything from climbing trees to stowing away aboard the ships that sail to the Other Side? Bless me, life used to be quite inter—I mean, you used to upset things badly in these parts once upon a time. I beg your pardon, but I had no idea you were still in business."

"Where else should I be?" said the wizard. "All the same I am pleased to find you remember something about me. You seem to remember my fireworks kindly, at any rate, and that is not without hope. Indeed for your old grandfather Took's sake, and for the sake of poor Belladonna, I will give you what you asked for."

## from THE GHOST OF THOMAS KEMPE
*Penelope Lively*

*There had been several odd occurrences by the time James found the message that began, "Wee must take paines to informe the neighbors that I doe once more practice my arte and cunninge in this howse." So the boy, who's been accused of leaving prankish messages, finally learns that a long-deceased sorcerer is haunting the cottage, leaving querulous notes that are at-*

*tributed to the innocent James. How can that be explained to parents who don't believe in ghosts? The fanciful and realistic elements are adroitly knit together, and the fantasy is treated in a matter-of-fact way that is quite believable*

### Messages from a Sorcerer

Surprisingly, James slept well. When he woke in the morning the church bells were ringing and the streets were Sundayish and quiet, with people cleaning cars instead of driving them and old ladies walking past in gloves and hats. For a moment he couldn't think what it was that nagged somewhere in his head, like a forgotten message or an undiscovered crime, and then he caught sight of the writing on the mirror, and everything came back with a rush. The writing had lost its initial impact now and merely looked scruffy. He rubbed it off with a handkerchief and got back into bed again to think about things.

*Sorcerie, astrologie, physicke. . .*
*Thou hast dygged up my spectacles. . . .*

He's got a very weird way of saying things, this person. Old-fashioned. Unless it's somebody putting it on, but it doesn't sound like that.

Nobody but me knows about the spectacles, because as it happens I didn't show them to anyone. Therefore they must have been his spectacles, or he couldn't have known about them.

If someone has spectacles, they are a real person. But those are very old specs.

*It was my first apprentice loste them in the yard. . . .*

The person who's writing these messages, thought James carefully, is someone who once lived in this house. He's getting in, somehow, without anyone noticing, and doing it. To have a go at me. For some reason. Because he's barmy or something.

He's getting in, and wandering around, and doing all this, and there are four of us living here and none of us have noticed him.

"No," he said out loud. "No." He got out of bed and dressed, slowly.

Tim goes mad every time anyone comes near the house. Postmen, and milkmen. He'd know. But he has been barking. At nothing.

He said firmly, aloud. "It's impossible. There aren't such things!" and went downstairs.

"Who lived here before us, Mum?"

"Oh, it was an elderly couple. A Mr. and Mrs. Rivers."

"Where did they go?"

"To Scotland, I think it was. They were going to live with their daughter. Mr. Rivers had bad arthritis. He couldn't get about much."

James said, "Had they lived here long?"

"Ages," said Mrs. Harrison. "Most of their lives, I think."

"They haven't been back lately, have they? Dropped in?"

"No, of course not. Why are you so interested in them all of a sudden?"

"I'm not," said James. "It doesn't matter."

It was like knowing you'd done something wrong. You skirted round the problem, and pretended it wasn't there in the hope that it would just go away, and then there it was again, sticking out and tripping you up so that you couldn't ignore it any more.

Somebody is doing this. But they can't be. Therefore. . . .

"There's something wrong with James," said Helen. "He hasn't said anything for ten minutes."

Mrs. Harrison said, "Are you feeling all right, James?"

"Yes, thanks."

"Perhaps he's getting something," said Helen. "Measles. There's measles at school."

"He's had them."

"It would be just like him to be the first person to get them twice. I mean, when you think of some of the things he's done. Falling through the bathroom ceiling and being the only boy on the school outing to get his arm stuck in a grating so they had to call the Fire Brigade. . . ."

"It wasn't my fault the loft didn't have a proper floor, was it? And how could I help it if I dropped my sherbert stick through the drain and the stupid bars were made too narrow?" said James belligerently.

"Personally," said Mr. Harrison, "I always think it better to draw a veil over James's past. May I have the marmalade please?"

James got up. "I'm going to see Simon."

"Be sensible."

"Yes."

Be sensible. Nothing, he thought grimly, walking down East End Lane, was very sensible at the moment. Nothing made any sense unless you explained it in a way that most people would say wasn't even possible.

James unfolded his story to Simon, incident by incident, repeating the text of the messages as best he could. When he had finished he looked at Simon expectantly.

There was a silence. Then Simon said, "I think someone's having you on."

"They can't be. I've told you. About the glasses and all that."

"Your sister?"

"My sister isn't clever enough to think of it. Not that old-fashioned writing and everything."

"But who could it be?"

"It's someone who lived in the house once."

"A real person?"

"Real," said James, "once."

There was a pause. Simon said cautiously, "Once?"

"Once."

"You mean," said Simon, "not real now?"

"That's right."

Simon hunched his nose. It was a thing he did every few minutes to push his glasses up again. He said, "If a person was real once but not now, but they're still going on doing things, then they're a ghost."

"Yes," said James.

Simon was silent for a moment. He looked away, blinked, looked back at James, and said, "You think it's a ghost that's doing all this?"

"There isn't anything else I can think. Is there?"

"I didn't *think* I believed in ghosts," said Simon.

"Neither did I. But I haven't got much choice now, have I?"

Simon said, "Are yo*u sure* there isn't someone getting in?"

"Quite sure," said James coldly, "I've told you."

"It's a bit weird, isn't it? I mean, you don't often hear about people having trouble with ghosts, do you?"

"Maybe it's not a thing they talk about. I can see why."

"You don't see headlines in the paper, after all. MAN COMPLAINS OF GHOST NUISANCE."

James put his hands in his pockets and began to walk away. "I'm going. You can come if you want, but I don't specially care."

"I'll come," said Simon cheerfully. He was the sort of person with whom it is difficult to prolong a disagreement, and after a while James's irritation began to ebb away as they wandered around Ledsham together. They did some exploring in the churchyard until chased away by the Vicar and finally ended up at the field just beyond the outskirts of the village where some archaeologists were excavating a Bronze Age settlement. It wasn't very interesting: two or three people in shirt sleeves were digging small round holes and sorting through enormous piles of stones and earth, but they were getting enviably dirty in the process. The boys thought it must be a pretty nice kind of job, being paid to dig holes all day: they offered to help, with winning smiles, but were rejected.

"Anybody'd think we were likely to break things, or get things muddled up," said James resentfully. "We were only being helpful."

They walked slowly home, past the school, the fire station, the pubs, the butcher's, the chemist's.

They went round the corner into Abbey Way, and past the police station. They paused for a moment to read the notice board. It was a dull notice board: no WANTED posters, no sinister criminal faces, front and profile, no Rewards Offered. Merely old, mildewed warnings about dog licenses and rear lights on bicycles. And, today, something else.

It was tacked to the wooden frame of the notice board with a rusty nail. Almost before James had read it he knew what was coming. The writing was larger this time, and the letters rather more carefully formed. It was obviously intended to be a notice, or, more precisely, an advertisement. It said:

For the discoverie of goodes loste by the crystalle or by booke & key or with the sieve & sheeres seeke me at my dwellynge which lyes at the extremetie of Easte Ende Lane. I have muche skille also in such artes as alchemie, astronomie etc. & in physicke & in the seekynge out of wytches & other eville persons. My apprentice, who dwells at the same howse, will bring me messages.

It was signed, rather flamboyantly, with much swirl and flourish.

Thos. Kempe Esq. Sorcerer

"There!" said James, with a mixture of triumph and despair. "There! Now do you believe me?"

Simon took his glasses off, scrubbed round them with his fingers, and read the notice for a second time. "Well," he said cautiously.

"Well, what?"

"Somebody could have put it there."

"Such as who?"

"I don't know."

"Such as me, perhaps?" said James in a freezing voice.

"No. Not you. You've been with me all morning. You know something?"

James didn't answer.

"If anyone sees it," Simon went on amiably, "they might sort of connect it with you. Because it mentions your house."

James's anger gave way to alarm. "What shall I do?"

Simon glanced up and down the street. There was no one in sight. The police station windows stared blankly down at them.

"Take it off. Quickly."

James hesitated. Then he darted forward, tweaked the notice from the nail, and began to walk quickly away down the road, stuffing it in his pocket. Simon caught up with him.

"Let's have another look."

Pulling the notice out again, James saw with indignation that his own red ballpoint had been used once more, and a page from his exercise book. He tore it into very small pieces and put it in a litter basket by the bus stop.

"Whoever he is, this person," said Simon, "he's got some pretty funny ideas, hasn't he? Jiggery-pokery with sieves and whatnot to find out who stole things. He'd make a pretty rotten policeman. And leaves for medicines and all that. It wouldn't work—not now there's penicillin and things."

"He just wants things done like they were in his time," said James. "With him doing them.

And me helping."

"Oh," said Simon, "I see." He sounded very polite. Too polite.

James said, "You don't believe he's a ghost, do you?"

"I didn't say I didn't."

"But you don't."

"I kind of half do and half don't," said Simon with great honesty. "I do when I'm with you but I think if I was by myself I wouldn't."

They walked on for a few minutes in silence. Then Simon said, "What are you going to do? I mean, whatever it is or whoever it is, he keeps getting you into trouble."

"I know. And I'm getting fed up with it. What can I do?"

"If he is—what you think," said Simon, "there's one thing you could try."

"What?"

"Ask him to stop it."

James stared. "Talk back to him?"

"That's it. Worth trying anyway."

"Yes. I s'pose it might be." Somehow that had not occurred to him. But, when you stopped and thought about it, there was no reason why this should be a one-way conversation. If he was here, this Thos. Kempe, Sorcerer, making a right nuisance of himself, then the best thing might well be to talk straight back to him. Maybe that was all that was needed. Just explain quietly and firmly that this sort of thing really wouldn't do, and he'd see reason and go away. Back where he came from, wherever that might be.

Feeling rather more hopeful about the future, James parted from Simon at his gate and went home for lunch.

A feeling of dissatisfaction hovered around the house. Mrs. Harrison was suffering one of her attacks of hay fever, which made her red-eyed and irritable. Mr. Harrison had fallen over a bucket of water standing in the porch, and was resignedly mopping up the mess as James arrived. He followed James into the kitchen, carrying bucket and cloth, which he dumped down by the sink.

"I don't want to interfere with the housekeeping arrangements," he said, "but I must point out that the best place for a full bucket of water is not the centre of the front porch."

"Not guilty," said his wife, sneezing violently.

"Must have been a child. And don't talk to me about water. I think I'm about to melt as it is." She began peeling potatoes, with vicious stabs.

"I've only just come in, haven't I?" said James.

"Good gracious!" said Mr. Harrison. "You don't imagine I'd ever suspect it might have been you, do you?" James gave him a suspicious look and went out into the garden to make sure Helen hadn't been interfering with his hole. He found that Tim had located a tributary to the original rat hole in the drain, and had spent a happy morning digging up a clump of irises. James hastily replanted them: Tim never seemed to understand that he was only living with them on sufferance as it was and might one day go too far. Mr. Harrison had several times said darkly, "That dog will have to go."

After lunch the pewter clouds that had been slowly massing above the village all morning opened up into determined, continuous rain. Mrs. Harrison said she felt as though she was being drowned from without as well as within, and went to bed with a book. Mr. Harrison went to sleep in an armchair. Helen went to see a friend.

James remembered he had some homework to do. He climbed up to his bedroom, closed the door, and sat down at his table. Tim padded round the room once or twice, jumped up on the bed, swirled the covers around several times until he achieved a satisfactory position, and went to sleep. Outside, the rain drummed on the roof and poured in oily rivers down the window.

James opened his project book, looked at his notes, and began to write. It was a project about ancient Greece, and he was enjoying it. He looked things up, and wrote, and stuck some pictures in, and thought about Alexander the Great, and drew a picture of a vase with blokes having a battle on it, and forgot about everything except what he was doing. Around him, the room rustled occasionally: a piece of paper floated to the floor, and a pen rolled across the table. Tim twitched in his sleep.

All of a sudden something nudged James's foot. It was a sheet from his exercise book. He picked it up and read:

I am glad to see thee at thy studies, though I lyke not thy bookes. Where is thy Latin? & where are thy volumes of Astrologie? But to our businesse. . . . I have putt out the water for people to knowe wee are seekynge thieves: it will doe for a crystalle. Thy father's baldnesse could be stayed by bathing with an ointment made from the leaves of Yarrow (a herb of Venus) but there is no cure for thy mother's ailments of the eyes for it is caused by wytcherie. Nothing will suffice save to seeke out the wytch & bringe her to justice. This muste wee doe with all haste.

James swung round in his chair. Then he got up and searched the room, even looking under the bed. There was nothing to be seen, and nothing moved.

He read the note again. The reference to his father's baldness he found particularly annoying. That was cheek, that was. In fact, he thought, he's a proper busybody, that's what he is.

And then he remembered Simon's suggestion. All right then, let's have a go. Let's try talking to him.

He cleared his throat, feeling distinctly foolish at addressing the empty room, even though there was no one to hear, and said "Er—Mr. Kempe."

Silence. Tim uncurled himself and looked up, yawning.

James took a deep breath and said firmly, "I'm afraid I can't do the things you want me to do because people don't go in much for sorcery nowadays. I don't think they'd really be very interested. You see we don't use those kind of medicines now because we've got penicillin and that and we've got policemen for finding out if anyone's pinched things and catching thieves and my mother gets hay fever every year and it really isn't anything to do with witchcraft it's because she's allergic to. . . ."

There was a loud crash behind him. He whirled round. One of his clay pots had fallen onto the floor and smashed. Even as he looked, a second one raised itself from the shelf, flew across the room, narrowly missing his right ear, and dashed itself against the opposite wall. Tim leapt from the bed and rushed about the room, barking furiously.

"Hey! Stop that!" shouted James.

A gust of wind swept wildly round the room, lifting all the papers on the table and whirling them about the floor. The ink bottle scuttered to the edge of the table and hung there till James grabbed hold of it with one hand while with the other he made ineffectual dabs at the flying pages from his project book.

"Here! Lay off! Cut it out!"

The door opened and banged itself shut again, twice. The windows rattled as though assaulted by a sudden thunderstorm. The calendar above the bed reared up, twitched itself from the hook, and flapped to the floor. A glass of water on the bedside table tipped over and broke, making a large puddle on the mat. Downstairs, James could hear the sitting room door open, and his father's footsteps cross the hall.

"Please!" he squeaked breathlessly, using one hand to steady the chair, which was bucking about like a ship in a storm, while with the other he warded off Volume I of *A Child's Encyclopaedia* which had risen from the bookshelf and hurled itself at his head.

"Please! Don't! Look, perhaps I could. . . ."

Mrs. Harrison's bedroom door opened and her voice could be heard saying something loud and not very friendly on the landing. Mr. Harrison was coming up the stairs.

The bedcover whisked off the bed, whirled round once or twice, and sank to the floor, engulfing a frantic Tim in its folds.

"All right!" shouted James, "all right! I'll do it. Anything. If you stop."

The room subsided. Tim struggled out from under the bedcover and dived for the shelter of the bed. The door opened and Mr. Harrison came in. James stood amid the wreckage of his room and waited for the storm to break.

### *from* CHARLOTTE SOMETIMES

#### *Penelope Farmer*

*Charlotte Makepeace had just arrived at boarding school the day before, and when she woke in the morning and looked out the window, it was odd. Where there had been a building yesterday, there was a tree! Charlotte is now Clare, and the time is World War I. This is one of the most deftly written time-shift stories for children; both settings are well drawn, and there's suspense even when the mystery ends.*

### When in the World Am I?

Charlotte shot back down the bed, hiding her head beneath the covers. It must be a dream. If she counted ten before looking out again, she would find she had imagined it. As a little girl she had often lain like that under the bedclothes, counting, but hoping to open her eyes on a different world—a palace perhaps, herself a princess—whereas now she merely wanted things the same as yesterday, the red brick building, the shadowed room; no sun, no tree. Having counted to a hundred just to make sure, she peered out again to find the sun still there with its colored, dusty beams; also the cedar tree.

Slowly, reluctantly, she turned her head to look into the room itself. Her sun-dazzled eyes could tell scarcely more at first than its shape and color, both still apparently the same. She could see black iron bedsteads, too, four of them, but as her sight cleared, saw that against the wall opposite where the fifth bed should have been was a huge white-painted cupboard with drawers underneath. All the proper chests of drawers had gone, and their photographs and ornaments, their dogs and cats and gnomes, their calendars and combs and hairbrushes; so had the curtained cubicle and the wash-basin with its shining taps. In place of that a white enamel basin stood on a stand, a white enamel jug inside it. On the chair beside Charlotte's bed, where her new book should have been, lay a little prayerbook in a floppy leather cover and a rather shabby Bible with gold-edged pages.

Janet and Vanessa must have got up early, Charlotte thought wildly, for two of the beds were empty, their coverings smooth as if not slept in at all. They must have made their beds and gone out so quietly that no one had awakened.

But that did not explain why the cupboard stood where Elizabeth's bed should have been, nor why the hair on Susannah's pillow next to her own was no longer dark like Susannah's hair but a lightish brown.

The hump beneath the blankets stirred. There was a little groaning and sighing, and a hand reached out, curling itself and uncurling again, terrifying Charlotte, because if she did not know who the hand belonged to and the light brown hair, how would that person know who Charlotte was, and however was she to explain her presence there?

The hump spoke.

"Clare," it said crossly. *"Clare."*

Charlotte looked wildly about but found no one still to answer, except herself.

*"Clare,* are you awake?" demanded the hump, more crossly than ever.

"I'm awake," Charlotte said, which was true, without her having to admit she was not Clare, whoever Clare might be.

"Well then, why didn't you say so before?"

"I . . ." began Charlotte. "Because I . . ." And then, to her horror, the girl in the other bed sat up abruptly. She was quite a little girl, much smaller than Susannah. Indeed she looked smaller than anyone Charlotte had seen so far at boarding school, though she wore the regulation nightdress. She had long hair and a round face, puzzled rather than cross and red and creased-looking on the side nearest Charlotte on which she must have been lying.

She looked at Charlotte as if she saw just whom she expected to see and said, "Is it early, Clare? Has the bell gone? Have we got to get up?"

"But I'm not Clare," Charlotte began to say hopelessly, then stopped herself, explanation being impossible, especially since this girl seemed to think so incredibly that she was Clare.

"What's the matter with you, Clare?" the little girl cried. "Why don't you answer me? Is it time to get up, is it, is it, *is* it?"

"I haven't heard a bell yet," Charlotte said.

"Oh well, then it can't be time to get up. We mustn't be late. Aunt Dolly said we'd get into fearful trouble if we were late for breakfast at school."

Charlotte was scarcely listening, thinking, horrified, that perhaps she was not Charlotte any more but had changed into someone else. That would explain why the little girl had greeted her as Clare.

She held out her hands to see. They did not look any different, but she wondered suddenly if she knew them well enough to tell. They were quite ordinary hands with fingers of medium length and no scars or marks to distinguish them. With her hands she stroked her hair, which was quite straight and fell some way below her shoulders just as it had done the day before. When she picked up a piece and drew it round, it seemed the same color, too, fairish, nondescript. She moved her hands rapidly over all her face—eyes, mouth, chin, cheeks, nose—and then again, more slowly. But it did not tell her very much. Could you just by feel, she wondered, recognize your own face? A blind person might, whose touch was sight, but she was not sure she could trust herself to do it. Her mouth, for instance, seemed wider than she'd thought; her nose felt narrower.

"What are you feeling your face for like that?" the little girl was asking curiously.

"Oh . . . oh . . . Nothing in particular. . . ." And at that moment, luckily, the bell went, an old-fashioned clanging bell, not the shrill electric one of the night before.

Charlotte jumped out of bed immediately, but the other huddled back into hers, saying, "I don't feel a bit like getting up, but of course you do what we ought, Clare, you always do."

Charlotte was so desperate by now that she did not care if the girl did find her odd. She ran to the only mirror in the room, a square, rather stained and pitted one hung just beside the door, and the relief that came when she saw her own face staring back at her was huger than she could have thought.

Except if she was Charlotte, why did the little girl take her for somebody else called Clare?

Just then the door opened and a woman came in; a tall, thin woman with her hair screwed up on her head under a white cap like a nurse's cap, her head very small like the knob on a knitting needle. Her big white apron was starched to shine; indeed, she shone all over as if newly polished: shoes, hair, apron, even her nose. Her skirt, Charlotte noticed, was so long that it stopped not far above her ankles.

"Emily? Isn't it?" she said to Charlotte. "Are you so vain, Emily, that you must stare at yourself before breakfast?"

Charlotte looked at her quite speechlessly, but Emily shot up in bed and said indignantly, "She's not Emily, she's Clare. *I'm* Emily."

"I do beg your pardon then, Emily," said the woman sarcastically. "Just to remind you, *I* am Nurse Gregory. Did you not hear the bell, Emily? Get out of your bed at once. Just because you sleep here as a convenience—" ("And what does that mean?" thought Charlotte.) "Just because you sleep here as a convenience does not mean you may take liberties or disregard the rules."

"Oh, I don't think she meant to. I don't think she knew you had to get up at once." Charlotte found herself automatically defending Emily, just as she had always defended her own sister Emma at home.

"But it's a whole half hour to breakfast," Emily was protesting on her own behalf. "It doesn't take me half an hour to get dressed." The nurse looked from her to Charlotte with a smile that had a glitter but no friendliness.

"Do I take it then you are a dirty little girl and never properly wash yourself?"

"I wash very well, indeed," cried Emily indignantly. "Don't I, Clare? Our Aunt Dolly says I wash very well . . ."

"Does she not also tell you, Emily, that it is rude to answer back? I shall return then in fifteen minutes and expect to find you both ready, save your hair, which I shall braid myself today."

"Clare always braids my hair for me."

"No doubt," said Nurse Gregory, turning to the door. "But I shall do it for today."

If Emily was rebellious, Charlotte was relieved at this, never having braided hair before. She was also (foolishly she thought and irrelevantly) quite pleased at the idea of having her hair in braids, which she had always wanted secretly and never been allowed, for her grandfather, with whom she lived, did not like girls to wear their hair that way. To think foolish, irrelevant thoughts was more comfortable than fighting her way through the impossible ones: what was happening to her, and why and how.

The uniform she had to wear was not unlike the one she had worn yesterday, if less well-fitting. Under it, despite the blaze of sun, went a thick woolen vest and bodice, thick navy-blue knickers, and thick black stockings. Charlotte had not worn stockings the day before.

All the while she dressed herself and helped Emily do up her buttons, all the while Nurse Gregory was combing and braiding their hair—using the comb more as if to dissect heads—and while afterwards she and Emily knelt on the chilly linoleum to say their prayers, Charlotte was trying in her mind to describe how things seemed to her that morning: the room, Nurse Gregory, the clothes she wore. There was some particular word she wanted. She could not, in these confusions, think what it was. Nurse Gregory had pulled her hair so tightly into its single braid, tied ribbon so tightly at top and bottom, that her scalp ached and prickled still, which made her brain seem to ache and prickle, too. The more she hunted for this word, the more confused she felt.

Outside the room was the same—or it looked the same—horde of blue-clad girls whose faces she did not know, the same thud of feet and clatter of voices, the same mazed passages and stairs as yesterday, except that she thought (or had she dreamed it) that the walls had been white then, while today they were brown. Yesterday they had eaten in a large white-walled room but today went beyond it to breakfast in a smaller brown-paneled one, where a picture hung of a man with eyes black as buttons and a stiff white clergyman's collar. She thought she recognized the picture, though she did not recognize the room. The trouble was that she had found everything so strange and confusing yesterday in a new school that now, even when she shut her eyes and tried to remember, she could not really tell what had changed about her and what had not. She began to wonder whether perhaps she had dreamed before or even was dreaming today.

The porridge for breakfast was brought round by maids in uniform. There had been no maids yesterday, Charlotte was sure. The uniforms were black and white and looked, she thought, as Nurse Gregory's had—and again she fumbled for the right word, but this time it swam into her head quite easily—they looked a little old-fashioned. Their skirts were rather too long for one thing, like Nurse Gregory's. Of course, she thought, some people just did wear longish skirts and old-fashioned clothes—Miss Gozzling for example, her grandfather's housekeeper. Old-fashioned was the word she wanted anyway; the one her mind had chased so uselessly before. Everything this morning seemed old-fashioned: in obvious ways, such as there being no washbasin, no electric bell; and in other less obvious ways. But then her home, Aviary Hall, was just as old-fashioned, if not more so, having been decorated and furnished many years ago and scarcely altered since. No doubt this school was the same, she told herself firmly. A different explanation that slid into her mind was so huge and impossible that she could not believe it, did not want to even. It frightened her. She turned her mind wildly away, thinking, "How funny, I haven't heard any airplanes this morning. I wonder why?"

## Humorous Tales

### THE EMPEROR'S NEW CLOTHES

#### Hans Christian Andersen

*This amusing tale is an allegory and a droll. It sounds much like a folk tale, but no folk tale ever had its wit and its tongue-in-cheek attitude toward the pompous incompetents of the world. Andersen in this story takes his revenge on the stupid people who made him suffer.*

Many years ago there was an Emperor who was so excessively fond of new clothes that he spent all his money on them. He cared nothing about his soldiers, nor for the theatre, nor for driving in the woods except for the sake of showing off his new clothes. He had a costume for every hour in the day, and instead of saying as one does about any other King or Emperor, "He is in his council chamber," here one always said, "The Emperor is in his dressing-room."

Life was very gay in the great town where he

"The Emperor's New Clothes." From Hans Andersen's *Fairy Tales*. Translated by Mrs. Edgar Lucas. Everyman's Library Edition. Reprinted by permission of E. P. Dutton & Co., Inc. and J. M. Dent & Sons Ltd.

lived; hosts of strangers came to visit it every day, and among them one day two swindlers. They gave themselves out as weavers, and said that they knew how to weave the most beautiful stuffs imaginable. Not only were the colours and patterns unusually fine, but the clothes that were made of these stuffs had the peculiar quality of becoming invisible to every person who was not fit for the office he held, or if he was impossibly dull.

"Those must be splendid clothes," thought the Emperor. "By wearing them I should be able to discover which men in my kingdom are unfitted for their posts. I shall distinguish the wise men from the fools. Yes, I certainly must order some of that stuff to be woven for me."

He paid the two swindlers a lot of money in advance so that they might begin their work at once.

They did put up two looms and pretended to weave, but they had nothing whatever upon their shuttles. At the outset they asked for a quantity of the finest silk and the purest gold thread, all of which they put into their own bags while they worked away at the empty looms far into the night.

"I should like to know how those weavers are getting on with the stuff," thought the Emperor; but he felt a little queer when he reflected that anyone who was stupid or unfit for his post would not be able to see it. He certainly thought that he need have no fears for himself, but still he thought he would send somebody else first to see how it was getting on. Everybody in the town knew what wonderful power the stuff possessed, and everyone was anxious to see how stupid his neighbor was.

"I will send my faithful old minister to the weavers," thought the Emperor. "He will be best able to see how the stuff looks, for he is a clever man and no one fulfils his duties better than he does!"

So the good old minister went into the room where the two swindlers sat working at the empty looms.

"Heaven preserve us!" thought the old minister, opening his eyes very wide. "Why, I can't see a thing!" But he took care not to say so.

Both the swindlers begged him to be good enough to step a little nearer, and asked if he did not think it a good pattern and beautiful colouring. They pointed to the empty loom, and the poor old minister stared as hard as he could but he could not see anything, for of course there was nothing to see.

"Good heavens!" thought he, "is it possible that I am a fool? I have never thought so and nobody must know it. Am I not fit for my post? It will never do to say that I cannot see the stuffs."

"Well, sir, you don't say anything about the stuff," said the one who was pretending to weave.

"Oh, it is beautiful! quite charming!" said the old minister looking through his spectacles; "this pattern and these colours! I will certainly tell the Emperor that the stuff pleases me very much."

"We are delighted to hear you say so," said the swindlers, and then they named all the colours and described the peculiar pattern. The old minister paid great attention to what they said, so as to be able to repeat it when he got home to the Emperor.

Then the swindlers went on to demand more money, more silk, and more gold, to be able to proceed with the weaving; but they put it all into their own pockets—not a single strand was ever put into the loom, but they went on as before weaving at the empty looms.

The Emperor soon sent another faithful official to see how the stuff was getting on, and if it would soon be ready. The same thing happened to him as to the minister; he looked and looked, but as there were only the empty looms, he could see nothing at all.

"Is not this a beautiful piece of stuff?" said both the swindlers, showing and explaining the beautiful pattern and colours which were not there to be seen.

"I know I am not a fool!" thought the man, "so it must be that I am unfit for my good post! It is very strange though! however, one must not let it appear!" So he praised the stuff he did not see, and assured them of his delight in the beautiful colours and the originality of the design. "It is absolutely charming!" he said to the Emperor. Everybody in the town was talking about this splendid stuff.

Now the Emperor thought he would like to see it while it was still on the loom. So, accompanied by a number of selected courtiers, among whom were the two faithful officials who had already seen the imaginary stuff, he went to visit the crafty impostors, who were working away as hard as ever they could at the empty looms.

"It is magnificent!" said both the honest officials. "Only see, Your Majesty, what a design! What colours!" And they pointed to the empty loom, for they thought no doubt the others could see the stuff.

"What!" thought the Emperor; "I see nothing at all! This is terrible! Am I a fool? Am I not fit to be Emperor? Why, nothing worse could happen to me!"

"Oh, it is beautiful!" said the Emperor. "It has my highest approval!" and he nodded his satisfaction as he gazed at the empty loom. Nothing would induce him to say that he could not see anything.

The whole suite gazed and gazed, but saw nothing more than all the others. However, they all exclaimed with His Majesty, "It is very beautiful!" and they advised him to wear a suit made of this wonderful cloth on the occasion of a great procession which was just about to take place. "It is magnificent! gorgeous! excellent!" went from mouth to mouth; they were all equally delighted with it. The Emperor gave each of the rogues an order of knighthood to be worn in their buttonholes and the title of "Gentlemen Weavers."

The swindlers sat up the whole night, before the day on which the procession was to take place, burning sixteen candles, so that people might see how anxious they were to get the Emperor's new clothes ready. They pretended to take the stuff off the loom. They cut it out in the air with a huge pair of scissors, and they stitched away with needles without any thread in them. At last they said, "Now the Emperor's new clothes are ready!"

The Emperor, with his grandest courtiers, went to them himself, and both the swindlers raised one arm in the air, as if they were holding something, and said, "See, these are the trousers, this is the coat, here is the mantle!" and so on. "It is as light as a spider's web. One might think one had nothing on, but that is the very beauty of it!"

"Yes!" said all the courtiers, but they could not see anything, for there was nothing to see.

"Will Your Imperial Majesty be graciously pleased to take off your clothes," said the imposters, "so that we may put on the new ones, along here before the great mirror."

The Emperor took off all his clothes, and the impostors pretended to give him one article of dress after the other, of the new ones which they had pretended to make. They pretended to fasten something round his waist and to tie on something; this was the train, and the Emperor turned round and round in front of the mirror.

"How well His Majesty looks in the new clothes! How becoming they are!" cried all the people round. "What a design, and what colours! They are most gorgeous robes!"

"The canopy is waiting outside which is to be carried over Your Majesty in the procession," said the master of the ceremonies.

"Well, I am quite ready," said the Emperor. "Don't the clothes fit well?" and then he turned round again in front of the mirror, so that he should seem to be looking at his grand things.

The chamberlains who were to carry the train stooped and pretended to lift it from the ground with both hands, and they walked along with their hands in the air. They dared not let it appear that they could not see anything.

Then the Emperor walked along in the procession under the gorgeous canopy, and everybody in the streets and at the windows exclaimed, "How beautiful the Emperor's new clothes are! What a splendid train! And they fit to perfection!" Nobody would let it appear that he could see nothing, for then he would not be fit for his post, or else he was a fool.

None of the Emperor's clothes had been so successful before.

"But he has got nothing on," said a little child.

"Oh, listen to the innocent," said its father; and one person whispered to the other what the child had said. "He has nothing on; a child says he has nothing on!"

"But he has nothing on!" at last cried all the people.

The Emperor writhed, for he knew it was true, but he thought "the procession must go on now," so he held himself stiffer than ever, and the chamberlains held up the invisible train.

# MRS. PETERKIN
# WISHES TO GO TO DRIVE
*Lucretia Hale*

*One account of the beginnings of these tales says that the episode of the lady who wished to go for a drive really happened and gave the author the idea for these tales. However they began, Lucretia, the gifted sister of Edward Everett Hale, learned to pick up every silly mistake which she or any of her friends blundered into, and turn it into a problem for the "lady from Philadelphia."*

One morning Mrs. Peterkin was feeling very tired, as she had been having a great many things to think of, and she said to Mr. Peterkin, "I believe I shall take a ride this morning!"

And the little boys cried out, "Oh, may we go too?"

Mrs. Peterkin said that Elizabeth Eliza and the little boys might go.

So Mr. Peterkin had the horse put into the carryall, and he and Agamemnon went off to their business, and Solomon John to school; and Mrs. Peterkin began to get ready for her ride.

She had some currants she wanted to carry to old Mrs. Twomly, and some gooseberries for somebody else, and Elizabeth Eliza wanted to pick some flowers to take to the minister's wife; so it took them a long time to prepare.

The little boys went out to pick the currants and the gooseberries, and Elizabeth Eliza went out for her flowers, and Mrs. Peterkin put on her cape-bonnet, and in time they were all ready. The little boys were in their india-rubber boots, and they got into the carriage.

Elizabeth Eliza was to drive; so she sat on the front seat, and took up the reins, and the horse started off merrily, and then suddenly stopped, and would not go any farther.

Elizabeth Eliza shook the reins, and pulled them, and then she clucked to the horse; and Mrs. Peterkin clucked; and the little boys whistled and shouted; but still the horse would not go.

"We shall have to whip him," said Elizabeth Eliza.

Now Mrs. Peterkin never liked to use the whip; but, as the horse would not go, she said she would get out and turn his head the other way, while Elizabeth Eliza whipped the horse, and when he began to go she would hurry and get in.

So they tried this, but the horse would not stir.

"Perhaps we have too heavy a load," said Mrs. Peterkin, as she got in.

So they took out the currants and the gooseberries and the flowers, but still the horse would not go.

One of the neighbors, from the opposite house, looking out just then, called out to them to try the whip. There was a high wind, and they could not hear exactly what she said.

"I have tried the whip," said Elizabeth Eliza.

"She says 'whips,' such as you eat," said one of the little boys.

"We might make those," said Mrs. Peterkin, thoughtfully.

"We have got plenty of cream," said Elizabeth Eliza.

"Yes, let us have some whips," cried the little boys, getting out.

And the opposite neighbor cried out something about whips; and the wind was very high.

So they went into the kitchen, and whipped up the cream, and made some very delicious whips; and the little boys tasted all round, and they all thought they were very nice.

They carried some out to the horse, who swallowed it down very quickly.

"That is just what he wanted," said Mrs. Peterkin; "now he will certainly go!"

So they all got into the carriage again, and put in the currants, and the gooseberries, and the flowers; and Elizabeth Eliza shook the reins, and they all clucked; but still the horse would not go!

"We must either give up our ride," said Mrs. Peterkin, mournfully, "or else send over to the lady from Philadelphia, and see what she will say."

The little boys jumped out as quickly as they could; they were eager to go and ask the lady from Philadelphia. Elizabeth Eliza went with them, while her mother took the reins.

They found that the lady from Philadelphia was very ill that day, and was in her bed. But when she was told what the trouble was she very kindly said they might draw up the curtain from the window at the foot of the bed, and open the blinds, and she would see. Then she asked for her opera-glass, and looked through it, across the way, up the street, to Mrs. Peterkin's door.

After she had looked through the glass she laid it down, leaned her head back against the pillow, for she was very tired, and then said, "Why don't you unchain the horse from the horse-post?"

Elizabeth Eliza and the little boys looked at one another, and then hurried back to the house and told their mother. The horse was untied, and they all went to ride.

## HOW THEY BRING BACK THE VILLAGE OF CREAM PUFFS WHEN THE WIND BLOWS IT AWAY

### Carl Sandburg

*When a poet turns to nonsense, something unusual is bound to result. Carl Sandburg, poet, newspaperman, and biographer, declared that he was tired of reading his little girls stories about castles and kings. Why not something American, something in a lingo they would understand? With this declaration of independence, he created his* Rootabaga Stories. *The fantastic nonsense about a boy who lived in the Village of Liver-and-Onions or about a Village of Cream Puffs that blew away sent his own three little girls into gales of laughter. Of course, they were luckier than the rest of us because they heard the author of the stories read them in his wonderful voice and manner. But the airy lightness of these tales carries over for any reader. You have to know them well to read them well because they run on like a patter-song with hardly a chance to catch your breath.*

A girl named Wing Tip the Spick came to the Village of Liver-and-Onions to visit her uncle and her uncle's uncle on her mother's side and her uncle and her uncle's uncle on her father's side.

It was the first time the four uncles had a chance to see their little relation, their niece. Each one of the four uncles was proud of the blue eyes of Wing Tip the Spick.

The two uncles on her mother's side took a long deep look into her blue eyes and said, "Her eyes are so blue, such a clear light blue, they are the same as cornflowers with blue raindrops shining and dancing on silver leaves after a sun shower in any of the summer months."

And the two uncles on her father's side, after taking a long deep look into the eyes of Wing Tip the Spick, said, "Her eyes are so blue, such

a clear light shining blue, they are the same as cornflowers with blue raindrops shining and dancing on the silver leaves after a sun shower in any of the summer months."

And though Wing Tip the Spick didn't listen and didn't hear what the uncles said about her blue eyes, she did say to herself when they were not listening, "I know these are sweet uncles and I am going to have a sweet time visiting my relations."

The four uncles said to her, "Will you let us ask you two questions, first the first question and second the second question?"

"I will let you ask me fifty questions this morning, fifty questions tomorrow morning, and fifty questions any morning. I like to listen to questions. They slip in one ear and slip out of the other."

Then the uncles asked her the first question first, "Where do you come from?" and the second question second, "Why do you have two freckles on your chin?"

"Answering your first question first," said Wing Tip the Spick, "I come from the Village of Cream Puffs, a little light village on the upland corn prairie. From a long ways off it looks like a little hat you could wear on the end of your thumb to keep the rain off your thumb."

"Tell us more," said one uncle. "Tell us much," said another uncle. "Tell it without stopping," added another uncle. "Interruptions nix nix," murmured the last of the uncles.

"It is a light little village on the upland corn prairie many miles past the sunset in the west," went on Wing Tip the Spick. "It is light the same as a cream puff is light. It sits all by itself on the big long prairie where the prairie goes up in a slope. There on the slope the winds play around the village. They sing it wind songs, summer wind songs in summer, winter wind songs in winter.

"And sometimes like an accident, the wind gets rough. And when the wind gets rough it picks up the little Village of Cream Puffs and blows it away off in the sky—all by itself."

"O-o-h-h," said one uncle. "Um-m-m-m," said the other three uncles.

"Now the people in the village all understand the winds with their wind songs in summer and winter. And they understand the rough wind who comes sometimes and picks up the village and blows it away off high in the sky all by itself.

"If you go to the public square in the middle of the village you will see a big roundhouse. If you take the top off the roundhouse you will see a big spool with a long string winding up around the spool.

"Now whenever the rough wind comes and picks up the village and blows it away off high in the sky all by itself then the string winds loose off the spool, because the village is fastened to the string. So the rough wind blows and blows and the string on the spool winds looser and looser the farther the village goes blowing away off into the sky all by itself.

"Then at last when the rough wind, so forgetful, so careless, has had all the fun it wants, then the people of the village all come together and begin to wind up the spool and bring back the village where it was before."

"O-o-h-h," said one uncle. "Um-m-m-m," said the other three uncles.

"And sometimes when you come to the village to see your little relation, your niece who has four such sweet uncles, maybe she will lead you through the middle of the city to the public square and show you the roundhouse. They call it the Roundhouse of the Big Spool. And they are proud because it was thought up and is there to show when visitors come."

"And now will you answer the second question second—why do you have two freckles on your chin?" interrupted the uncle who had said before, "Interruptions nix nix."

"The freckles are put on," answered Wing Tip the Spick. "When a girl goes away from the Village of Cream Puffs her mother puts on two freckles, on the chin. Each freckle must be the same as a little burnt cream puff kept in the oven too long. After the two freckles looking like two little burnt cream puffs are put on her chin, they remind the girl every morning when she combs her hair and looks in the looking glass. They remind her where she came from and she mustn't stay away too long."

"Oh-h-h-h," said one uncle. "Um-m-m-m," said the other three uncles. And they talked among each other afterward, the four uncles by themselves, saying:

"She has a gift. It is her eyes. They are so blue, such a clear light blue, the same as cornflowers with blue raindrops shining and dancing on silver leaves after a sun shower in any of the summer months."

At the same time Wing Tip the Spick was saying to herself, "I know for sure now these are sweet uncles and I am going to have a sweet time visiting my relations."

## from BEN AND ME

*Robert Lawson*

*Children who chuckle over this ridiculous biography of Benjamin Franklin, purportedly written by a mouse, should be urged to read a genuine biography of our "first civilized American." If they are nine or ten, give them Ingri and Edgar d'Aulaire's* Ben Franklin *(Doubleday, 1950; see* Part Three, Time for Realism*). If they are twelve, give them Enid Meadowcroft's* Story of Benjamin Franklin *(Grosset) and also the excellent, well-rounded, lavishly illustrated* Many Worlds of Benjamin Franklin, *by Frank Donovan and the editors of* American Heritage *(Harper, 1964).*

### Electricity

Ben never thereafter mentioned my little adventure in printing, so I tried to be somewhat more lenient about his maxims.

Trying though they were, however, they were nothing compared to an enthusiasm which beset him about this time. This was the study of what he called "Electricity."

It all started with some glass tubes and a book of instructions sent him by a London friend. These tubes he would rub with a piece of silk or fur, thereby producing many strange and, to me, unpleasant effects. When a tube was sufficiently rubbed, small bits of paper would spring from the table and cling to it, or crackling sparks leap from it to the finger of anyone foolish enough to approach.

Ben derived great amusement from rubbing a tube and touching it to the tip of my tail. Thereupon a terrible shock would run through my body, every hair and whisker would stand on end and a convulsive contraction of all my muscles would throw me several inches in the air.

This was bad enough, but my final rebellion did not come until he, in his enthusiasm, used the fur cap to rub the tube. And *I* was in the cap.

"Ben," said I, "this has gone far enough. From now on, kindly omit me from these experiments. To me they seem a perfectly senseless waste of time, but if they amuse you, all right, go ahead with them. Just leave me out."

"I fear that you are not a person of vision, Amos," said he. "You fail to grasp the world-wide, the epoch-making importance of these experiments. You do not realize the force—"

"Oh don't I?" I replied. "My tail is still tingling."

"I shall tear the lightning from the skies," he went on, "and harness it to do the bidding of man."

"Personally," said I, "I think the sky's an excellent place for it."

Nothing I could say, though, served to dampen Ben's enthusiasm.

Soon he received an elaborate machine that could produce much greater currents than the glass tubes. It was worked by a crank which he ground at happily for hours. Our room became cumbered with rods, wires, tubes, copper plates and glass jars filled with evil-smelling liquids. It was difficult to move about without touching something likely to produce one of those hair-stiffening shocks.

Ben even went so far as to organize a group of similarly obsessed people, calling it "the Philosophical Society." They gathered once a week, armed with their glass tubes, bits of silk and wires. They spent whole evenings fiddling with these things or listening to long speeches about the wonders of "electricity," mostly by Ben. I napped.

After he had played with the new apparatus for a few weeks and had it working well, Ben decided to give an exhibition of his achievements in this field.

A large hall having been secured for the occasion by the Philosophical Society, Ben spent several busy days arranging and testing his apparatus, planning various experiments, writing a speech and inviting prominent people.

Frankly, I was bored by the whole affair, but since Ben seemed rather hurt by my attitude I tried to take a little interest. I read his speech and the descriptions of all the various experiments. By noon I understood everything quite thoroughly.

While we ate a light lunch of bread and cheese I told Ben of my studies. He was delighted and quite touched by my interest.

In the afternoon he went to have his hair curled, leaving me in the hall, where I went on with my research. Determined that no errors should mar this performance, since it meant so much to Ben, I carefully went over each wire and piece of apparatus, comparing them with his diagrams and descriptions.

I discovered that he had apparently made several grave mistakes, for not a few of the wires were connected in a manner that seemed to me obviously incorrect. There were so many of these errors to rectify that I was kept quite busy all afternoon. My corrected arrangements seemed to leave several loose wires and copper plates with no place to go, so I just left them in one of the chairs on the stage. I was barely able to finish before Ben arrived from the hairdresser's.

As we hurried home for supper, he was so filled with pride and excitement that I had no opportunity to tell him how narrowly he had escaped ruining the exhibition by his carelessness.

When we arrived back at the hall in the evening the brilliantly lit auditorium was crowded. Seated in chairs on the stage were the Governor and his Lady; the Mayor; several of the clergy; and the Chief of the Volunteer Fire Brigade holding his silver trumpet.

Ben made his speech, and performed several simple experiments with the glass tubes. They were watched with great interest by the audience and generously applauded.

He then stepped to the new apparatus and signaled to a young apprentice from the print shop who was stationed at the crank. The lad turned with a will, and a loud humming sound came from the whirling wheel while blue sparks cracked about it.

"And now, my friends," said Ben proudly, "when I turn this knob you shall see, if my calculations are correct, a manifestation of electrical force never before witnessed on this continent."

They did.

As Ben turned the knob the Governor rose straight in the air in much the same manner that I used to when Ben applied the spark to my tail. His hair stood out just as my fur did. His second leap was higher and his hair even straighter. There was a noticeable odor of burning cloth.

On his third rising the copper plate flew from the chair, landing, unfortunately, in his Lady's lap. Her shriek, while slightly muffled by her wig, was, nevertheless, noteworthy.

The Fire Chief, gallantly advancing to their aid, inadvertently touched one of the wires with his silver trumpet. This at once became enveloped in a most unusual blue flame and gave off a strange clanging sound.

Ben leaped toward them, but I clamped on his ear. I had felt those shocks before.

"The boy—" I hissed. "Stop the machine!"

He sprang at the apprentice, who was still grinding merrily. The lad, not an admirer of the Governor, ceased his efforts with some reluctance.

The Governor was stiff and white in his chair, his Lady moaned faintly under her wig, the Fire Chief stared dazedly at his tarnished trumpet, and the audience was in an uproar.

"Never mind, Ben," I consoled as we walked home, "I feel certain that we'll succeed next time."

"Succeed!" shouted Ben. "SUCCEED! Why, Amos, don't you realize that I have just made the most successful, the most momentous experiment of the century? I have discovered the effects produced by applying strong electric shocks to human beings."

"Granted the Governor *is* one," I said, "we surely did."

## *from* THE PUSHCART WAR

*Jean Merrill*

*At first one might wonder why this book is thought of as fantasy—it seems so very ordinary in its setting, New York City in 1976. But just as in 1776 a small nation defied a growing empire, so in 1976 the much harassed pushcart peddlers fight the big trucks for their independence and livelihood. What follows is a mild satire for young people about several aspects of urban life. With humor and excellent character drawing, this story reflects the mood of protest which has swept American life in the 1960's and 1970's. The account of Mr. Jerusalem's blow for liberty is one of its best moments, and the edge of reality is never far away.*

### *The Pea Shooter Campaign—Phase I*

It took a week for the pushcart peddlers to prepare for their attack. Maxie Hammerman kept his shop open twenty-four hours a day, and the peddlers in teams of twenty men took turns putting the pins in peas.

Carlos made all five hundred and nine shooters himself. He cut them from a roll of yellow plastic tubing that a storekeeper had given him for taking away his cartons for ten years at no charge.

At last, everything was ready. The attack was set for the morning of March 23rd. The evening before, the peddlers all reported to Maxie Hammerman's shop to collect their shooters and twenty-four rounds of ammunition each.

General Anna outlined the plan of battle. Everyone was to go to the location where he usually did business. He was to wait there until 10:00 A.M., when the morning traffic would be well under way. At 10:00 sharp, he was to fire at the tires of any trucks that came in range.

Frank the Flower had wanted Wanda Gambling to fire the opening shot from in front of the Empire State Building, but General Anna felt that this would attract too much attention.

"Where there is a movie star," said General Anna, "There is a crowd. We do not want the trucks to know what is hitting them."

So the Pea Shooter Campaign began in quite an ordinary way. Between 10:05 A.M. and 10:10 A.M. on March 23rd, ninety-seven truck drivers in different parts of the city discovered that they had flat tires. Not one of the drivers knew what had hit him.

Ninety-seven hits (out of some five hundred pea-pins that were fired in the opening attack) is, according to the Amateur Weapons Association, a very good average, especially as many of the peddlers had never handled a pea shooter before. And there were a few, like Mr. Jerusalem, who had grave doubts about the whole idea.

Mr. Jerusalem's heart was not in the attack. Though he had voted with the other peddlers to fight the trucks, fighting of any sort went against his nature. Mr. Jerusalem's performance on the first morning of the Pea Shooter Campaign is, therefore, of special interest.

At the time of the Pushcart War, Mr. Jerusalem was already an old man. No one knew exactly how old. He was held in great respect by the other pushcart peddlers, because his cart was not only his business, but it was also his home.

Unlike the other peddlers, Mr. Jerusalem did not have a room where he went to sleep or cook his meals. Instead he had a small frying pan, a cup, and a tin plate which he hung neatly from the underside of his cart. He had a charcoal burner built into one corner of the cart so that he could cook for himself whenever he felt like a hot meal.

Mr. Jerusalem's favorite joke was: "Some people go out to dinner on special occasions. I eat out all the time." This was true. Mr. Jerusalem was often to be seen sitting on a curb eating a plate of beans or turnips that he had cooked himself.

At night Mr. Jerusalem dropped canvas sheets over the sides of his cart so that there was a sort of tent underneath the cart. Then he would park the cart under a tree or in a vacant lot, crawl under the cart, roll up in a quilt, and go to sleep. In the summer he often did not bother with the canvas sheets, but slept alongside the cart so that he could see the stars. He was usually the first peddler on the streets in the morning.

Mr. Jerusalem had lived this way for fifty or sixty years, and he had never picked a fight with anyone. His motto was: "I live the way I want. You don't bother me. And I won't bother you."

Having lived by this motto for so long, Mr. Jerusalem was not happy about the Pea Shooter Campaign. To be sure, he had a great deal more at stake than the other peddlers. In his case, it was not only his business, but his home that was in danger as long as the trucks continued to attack the pushcarts. Still it went against his deepest convictions to cause another man trouble.

"There are not troubles enough in the world?" he had asked himself as he had worked alongside the other peddlers, putting pins in the peas. "Why should I make more?"

Mr. Jerusalem was still asking himself this question as he set off down Delancey Street on the morning of March 23rd. Like the other peddlers, Mr. Jerusalem was fully armed, although no one walking down the street would have noticed.

Anyone glancing at Mr. Jerusalem would have taken the yellow plastic straw sticking from his coat pocket for a yellow pencil. And no one would have taken any notice at all of the two dozen peas with a pin stuck carefully through the center of each, which Mr. Jerusalem had pinned to the sleeve of his jacket.

Or, even if someone had noticed, he would have supposed that Mr. Jerusalem had twenty-four tiny sleeve buttons on his jacket. Mr. Jerusalem's clothes never looked like anyone else's anyway. He picked them up here and there, secondhand, and he had his own style of wearing them.

"A sleeveful of ammunition!" Mr. Jerusalem muttered to himself, as he set off on the morning of March 23rd to pick up a secondhand popcorn machine that he had arranged to buy. "Who would believe it?

"A man my age—going to war!" Mr. Jerusalem shook his head sadly. "I can hardly believe it myself.

"Fighting in the streets!" he continued. "A man of peace for eighty years is walking fully armed down Delancey Street. A man who does not care for fighting.

"It is not only that I do not care for fighting," he went on.

"Naturally, I do not care for fighting," he admitted. "But it is also that fighting a ten-ton truck with a pea shooter is a little crazy. I do not think it will work.

"But what else can we do?" he asked himself.

He could not think of anything else. "So I will fight," he said. "If I have to," he added.

All the same Mr. Jerusalem was relieved when at 10:00 o'clock, the hour the attack was to begin, there was no truck parked within a hundred feet of his cart. Mr. Jerusalem did not think he could hit the tire of a moving truck.

"Would General Anna want me to waste the ammunition?" he asked himself. "Or Maxie Hammerman? Or Miss Wanda Gambling who has been so kind as to pay for one ton of pins? Not to mention peas."

When Mr. Jerusalem arrived at the candy store where he was to pick up the popcorn machine, he parked his cart. He was just starting into the store, when someone shouted at him.

Mr. Jerusalem looked around and saw a Leaping Lema. The driver of the Leaping Lema was trying to back into a space in front of Mr. Jerusalem's cart. The truck was loaded with new glass-and-chromium popcorn machines.

Now if there was any kind of truck that Mr. Jerusalem did not like, it was a Leaping Lema. The reason for this was that Mr. Jerusalem had known Louie Livergreen's father.

Louie's father had been, before his death, one of the most-respected pushcart peddlers in the secondhand-clothes line. Mr. Jerusalem had often made a cup of tea on his charcoal burner for Solomon Livergreen when he and Solomon were working on the same street.

Mr. Jerusalem should have been glad that Solomon's son was a big success—people said Louie Livergreen now owned one hundred big trucks. But Mr. Jerusalem held it against Louie Livergreen that from the day Louie had got his first truck, he had never come to see his father again. So every time Mr. Jerusalem saw a Leaping Lema on the streets, he thought, "They are breaking up family life."

As he watched the Leaping Lema backing into the curb on the first day of the Pea Shooter Campaign, Mr. Jerusalem wondered what his old friend Solomon Livergreen would have thought of the Pushcart War. Would Solomon, he wondered, have shot at a truck belonging to his own son, Louie Livergreen? And what would

Solomon have wished his old friend Mr. Jerusalem to do?

"Shoot if you have to." That is what Solomon Livergreen would say, Mr. Jerusalem said to himself.

Mr. Jerusalem's conversation with Solomon Livergreen was interrupted by the driver of the Leaping Lema.

"Hey, Bud," shouted the driver. "Stop talking to yourself and move the baby buggy!" The driver was Little Miltie, a driver mentioned in the diary of Joey Kafflis.

Mr. Jerusalem frowned. It was bad enough that Little Miltie, a man one half the age of Mr. Jerusalem and not as tall, should call Mr. Jerusalem "Bud." But that Little Miltie should call Mr. Jerusalem's cart, which was also his home, a "baby buggy"—this was unnecessarily rude. However, Mr. Jerusalem answered courteously.

"I will only be a minute," he said.

"I can't wait a minute," said Little Miltie. "I got to deliver a popcorn machine."

"Well," said Mr. Jerusalem, "I have to pick up a popcorn machine. And until I pick up this secondhand popcorn machine, there will be no room in the store for a new machine such as you wish to deliver." And he turned to go about his business.

But as Mr. Jerusalem started into the candy store, Little Miltie raced his motor. Mr. Jerusalem hesitated. He remembered what had happened to Morris the Florist. He glanced over his shoulder.

"I'm backing up, Bud," Little Miltie said.

Mr. Jerusalem sighed and walked back to move his cart to the other side of the street.

Little Miltie grinned. "That's a good boy, Buster."

Mr. Jerusalem did not reply, but as Little Miltie was backing into the place Mr. Jerusalem had left, the old peddler took out his pea shooter. He looked at it doubtfully.

"A man my age—with a *pea shooter!*" he sighed. "Such a craziness on Delancey Street." However, he inserted one of the pea-pins, took careful aim—and fired.

For a moment nothing happened. Mr. Jerusalem felt foolish. "All right, I admit it," he said. "We are all crazy."

Mr. Jerusalem was about to drop his pea

shooter in the gutter when he heard a slight hissing sound—the sound of air escaping from a tire.

"Or perhaps not so crazy," said Mr. Jerusalem.

He put the pea shooter back in his pocket and went to collect the popcorn machine. When he came out of the candy store, one of Little Miltie's rear tires was quite flat. Little Miltie was stamping up and down in the street and speaking even more rudely to the tire than he had spoken to Mr. Jerusalem.

"What is the matter?" asked Mr. Jerusalem. "The Leaping Lema is not leaping so good? A little trouble maybe?"

But Little Miltie was too angry to reply.

"Believe me, Solomon, I had to do it," Mr. Jerusalem said, as if to his old friend Solomon Livergreen.

"The fact is, Solomon," he continued, as he roped the popcorn machine onto his cart, "to cause a little trouble now and then is maybe good for a man.

"But, Solomon," he asked as he set off down Delancey Street, "who would have thought a man of my age would be such a good shot?

"Naturally, it pays to use high-quality pins," he added.

Although Mr. Jerusalem knew where he could get a good price for the secondhand popcorn machine, he was now in no hurry to get there. He paused to look over every truck that had stopped for a traffic light or had pulled up to a curb to make a delivery.

Mr. Jerusalem chose his targets very carefully, and to his astonishment he hit four more trucks before he ran out of ammunition. At 2:30 in the afternoon, he headed back to Maxie Hammerman's for more pea-pins. He still had not got around to selling his popcorn machine.

#### from LITTLE OLD
#### MRS. PEPPERPOT
#### *Alf Proysen*

*Mrs. Pepperpot and the Little Old Woman are cousins surely, though the Atlantic Ocean lies between them. And Mrs. Pepperpot must undoubtedly be on good terms with the Bor-rowers. Just an ordinary housewife, she has two remarkable powers: she can shrink her size, and she can understand the speech of animals (which makes her an ally of the good Dr. Dolittle). Children appreciate Mrs. Pepperpot's shrewdness in solving problems, her derring-do, and her constant good spirits. "Mrs. Pepperpot at the Bazaar" demonstrates all these lovely qualities.*

### Mrs. Pepperpot at the Bazaar

One day Mrs. Pepperpot was alone in her kitchen. At least, she was not *quite* alone, because Hannah, the little girl who had had the doll for Christmas, was there as well. She was busy scraping out a bowl and licking the spoon, for the old woman had been making gingerbread shapes.

There was a knock at the door. Mrs. Pepperpot said, 'Come in.' And in walked three very smart ladies.

'Good afternoon,' said the smart ladies. 'We are collecting prizes for the lottery at the school bazaar this evening. Do you think you have some little thing we could have? The money from the bazaar is for the boys' brass band—they need new instruments.'

'Oh, I'd like to help with that,' said Mrs. Pepperpot, for she dearly loved brass bands. 'Would a plate of gingerbread be any use?'

'Of course,' said the smart ladies, but they laughed behind her back. 'We could take it with us now if you have it ready,' they said. But Mrs. Pepperpot wanted to go to the bazaar herself, so she said she would bring the gingerbread.

So the three smart ladies went away and Mrs. Pepperpot was very proud and pleased that she was going to a bazaar.

Hannah was still scraping away at the bowl and licking the sweet mixture from the spoon.

'May I come with you?' she asked.

'Certainly, if your father and mother will let you.'

'I'm sure they will,' said the child, 'because Father has to work at the factory and Mother is at her sewing all day.'

'Be here at six o'clock then,' said Mrs. Pepperpot, and started making another batch of gingerbread shapes.

But when Hannah came back at six the old woman was not there. All the doors were open, so she went from room to room, calling her. When she got back to the kitchen she heard an odd noise coming from the table. The mixing bowl was upside down, so she lifted it carefully. And there underneath sat her friend who was now again as small as a pepperpot.

'Isn't this a nuisance?' said Mrs. Pepperpot. 'I was just cleaning out the bowl after putting the gingerbread in the oven when I suddenly started shrinking. Then the bowl turned over on me. Quick! Get the cakes out of the oven before they burn!'

But it was too late; the gingerbread was burnt to a cinder.

Mrs. Pepperpot sat down and cried, she was so disappointed. But she soon gave that up and started thinking instead. Suddenly she laughed out loud and said:

'Hannah! Put me under the tap and give me a good wash. We're going to the bazaar, you and I!'

'But you can't go to the bazaar like that!' said Hannah.

'Oh yes, I can,' said Mrs. Pepperpot, 'as long as you do what I say.'

Hannah promised, but Mrs. Pepperpot gave her some very queer orders. First she was to fetch a silk ribbon and tie it round the old woman so that it looked like a skirt. Then she was to fetch some tinsel from the Christmas decorations. This she had to wind round and round to make a silver bodice. And lastly she had to make a bonnet of gold foil.

'Now you must wrap me carefully in cellophane and put me in a cardboard box,' said Mrs. Pepperpot.

'Why?' asked Hannah.

'When I've promised them a prize for the bazaar they must have it,' said Mrs. Pepperpot, 'so I'm giving them myself. Just put me down on one of the tables and say you've brought a mechanical doll. Tell them you keep the key in your pocket and then pretend to wind me up so that people can see how clever I am.'

Hannah did as she was told, and when she got to the bazaar and put the wonderful doll on the table, many people clapped their hands and crowded round to see.

'What a pretty doll!' they said. 'And what a lovely dress!'

'Look at her gold bonnet!'

Mrs. Pepperpot lay absolutely still in her cardboard box, but when she heard how everybody praised her, she winked at Hannah with one eye, and Hannah knew what she wanted. She lifted Mrs. Pepperpot very carefully out of the box and pretended to wind her up at the back with a key.

Everyone was watching her. But when Mrs. Pepperpot began walking across the table, picking her way through the prizes, there was great excitement.

'Look, the doll can walk!'

And when Mrs. Pepperpot began to dance they started shouting and yelling with delight, 'The doll is dancing!'

The three smart ladies who had been to see Mrs. Pepperpot earlier in the day sat in special seats and looked very grand. One of them had given six expensive coffee cups, the second an elegant table mat and the third a beautiful iced layer cake.

Mrs. Pepperpot decided to go over and speak to them for she was afraid they had recognized her and thought it queer that she hadn't brought the gingerbread.

The three smart ladies were very pleased when the doll came walking across the table to them.

'Come to me!' said the one who had given the coffee cups, and stretched her hand out towards Mrs. Pepperpot, who walked on to it obediently.

'Let me hold her a little,' said the lady with the elegant table mat, and Mrs. Pepperpot went over to her hand.

'Now it's my turn,' said the lady with the iced cake.

'I'm sure they know it's me,' thought Mrs. Pepperpot, 'that's why they stare at me so hard and hold me on their hands.'

But then the lady with the cake said, 'Well, I must say, this is a much better prize than the gingerbread that the odd old woman offered us today.'

Now she should never have said that; Mrs. Pepperpot leaped straight out of her hand

and landed PLOP! right in the middle of the beautiful iced layer cake. Then she got up and waded right through it. The cake lady screamed, but people were shouting with laughter by now.

'Take that doll away!' shrieked the second lady, but *squish, squash!* went Mrs. Pepperpot's sticky feet, right across her lovely table mat.

'Get that dreadful doll away!' cried the third lady. But it was too late; Mrs. Pepperpot was on the tray with the expensive coffee cups, and began to dance a jig. Cups and saucers flew about and broke in little pieces.

What a to-do! The conductor of the brass band had quite a job to quieten them all down. He announced that the winning numbers of the lottery would be given out.

'First prize will be the wonderful mechanical doll,' he said.

When Hannah heard that she was very frightened. What would happen if somebody won Mrs. Pepperpot so that she couldn't go home to her husband? She tugged at Mrs. Pepperpot's skirt and whispered, 'Shall I put you in my pocket and creep away?'

'No,' said Mrs. Pepperpot.

'But think how awful it would be if someone won you and took you home.'

'What must be must be!' said Mrs. Pepperpot.

The conductor called out the winning number, '311!' Everyone looked at their tickets, but no one had number 311.

'That's a good thing!' sighed Hannah with relief. There would have to be another draw. But just then she remembered she had a ticket in her hand; it was number 311!

'Wait!' she cried, and showed her ticket. The conductor looked at it and saw it was the right one.

So Hannah was allowed to take Mrs. Pepperpot home.

Next day the old woman was her proper size again and Hannah only a little girl, and Mrs. Pepperpot said, 'You're my little girl, aren't you?'

'Yes,' said Hannah, 'and you're my very own Mrs. Pepperpot, because I won you at the bazaar yesterday.'

And that was the end of Mrs. Pepperpot's adventures for a very long time.

# Science Fiction

*from* **DOWN TO EARTH**

*Patricia Wrightson*

*Australia provides the source and the setting for this well-written story of a Martian boy's visit to our planet. The tale seems completely credible, especially in picturing the concern and efforts of the children to keep Martin hidden until he can return to Mars. The children's ready acceptance of an "alien" who is only a glowing light at times, as well as that "alien's" view of humans, signals a carefully imagined and well-constructed tale of science fiction for middle-grade youngsters.*

## The Powerful Starer

George and Cathy stared at the strange boy, who stood quite still and smiled at them.

"Hello," he said encouragingly.

"Hello to you, too," said George with emphasis. "And what do you think you're doing here?"

The boy considered the question. "Do you mean just now or all the time?"

"I wouldn't give too much lip if I were you. I mean what do you think you're doing here?"

"Just now," said the boy obligingly, "I've been watching you and the others. And the cats." He smiled again.

"Have you, now? And do you think that's the proper thing to do, sneaking about and prying on people?"

The boy laughed a little, kindly. "I didn't want to talk to them all at once. I wanted to talk to you first. I've seen you before."

"I know you have. You cost me two bob."

The boy looked puzzled, but before he could ask any questions, Cathy Brimble broke in. Her eyes were still shining, and her red hair was electric with excitement.

"You've been here all the time, haven't you?

In the night too. Living here." The boy looked at her and nodded solemnly. She swung around eagerly to George. "See? I knew! I knew there was someone. Didn't I tell you?"

George nodded with rising satisfaction. "Poor old Day! If he ever starts thinking he doesn't know everything, it'll kill him. With a bit of luck." He looked again at the boy and grinned at his air of quiet pride. "What's the idea, anyhow? It must be pretty tough, living on your own in this place."

"It's a nice, quiet place," said the boy simply.

George grinned again. "Yeah? Where do you come from?"

"As a matter of fact," said the boy modestly, "I'm a spaceman. From another planet, you know. You can't see it from here."

Cathy gasped, and George gave a shout of laughter.

*"Honestly!"* said Cathy indignantly. "We could've called the police or anything, but we've been quite decent to you. I've had an eye on you for weeks and never said a word to anyone except this George Adams. How you could!" She stared at him with burning reproach.

"But don't you understand? A spaceman. I came in—" He hesitated and gazed intently at Cathy as if searching for something. "—in a spaceship."

George was still chuckling. "Come off it, mate. Whose leg do you think you're pulling? A flying saucer, I suppose, was it?"

The boy gave him a penetrating stare, turned stiffly, and strode off into the dimness of the shuttered garage.

George seized Cathy's arm and drew her outside. "Honestly!" said Cathy, allowing herself to be led to the gate. "What a nerve!"

"Sulking," said George. "On his dignity, poor little coot. You wouldn't credit it, would you?"

*"He's* on his dignity! What about us? It's downright insulting; that's what it is."

"I don't think so," said George tolerantly. "Poor little kid's a nut, that's all."

Cathy started. "Oh! Do you think that's it?"

"Well, don't you? There has to be something the matter. Even just living on his own in a place like this—well, is that normal? If he's really doing that, there must be something wrong."

"He might be dodging the police."

"Come off it, Cathy. If he had his senses and he was hiding from the police, would he tell us that yarn? He'd have to think up somthing better than flying saucers. That's if he *is* living in the place."

"Well, somebody is."

"I know; you said that before. But it mightn't be him. He might be having us on, just trying to be funny. Anyhow, I'm going to try and coax him out of his fit of the dignities and see what turns up."

They went back to the little room and stood in the doorway to the garage. There was nobody to be seen. George whispered, "He must be lying behind that can." Cathy nodded.

"Hey!" called George softly. "Hey, Spaceman!" He couldn't resist adding, "Hey, Martin the Martian! Are you there?" No answer. "Ar, come on, Spaceman. You took us by surprise, that's all."

In the gloom of the garage they suddenly saw the boy standing near the roller door. George went in to him.

"Come on, mate; I take it all back. Come and tell us about it." The boy didn't move. "It's just that you don't look like a spaceman, see? I mean, you don't look like what we thought you would. You just look like us."

The boy spoke with unexpected fierceness. "You don't think you can *see* me with your puny Earth eyes, do you?"

"Well," said George, at a loss, "can you see us with your puny Space ones?"

The boy hesitated for a moment. "No," he said at last. It sounded like a confession made rather sulkily.

"There you are, then," said George in his heartiest voice, leading the boy by degrees out of the garage to the daylight of the outer room. "None of us can see each other. We're all stone blind, only we don't know it. Come and tell us all about it, mate."

"You won't understand," said the boy, re-covering his calmness and with it his dignity. "You don't know enough. You *think* you can see me, but you can't really, because I'm quite outside the range of what your brain was built to see. But your mind realizes there's another mind there, a sort of person, so your mind makes the pictures it always does for that sort of thing and you think you're really seeing me. To you, I just look like an Earth person, because that's the only sort your brain can see."

"I get it," said George encouragingly. "And what about when you look at us?"

"The same thing," said the boy. It seemed to annoy him a little to admit it. "To me, you just look like us."

"What, spacemen?" demanded George, immensely tickled. "Are we purple? Have we got horns?"

"It's no use asking. Can't you understand? We can't even tell each other. Our minds can only take in what they can understand. I say you're not purple with horns, and you say you're not purple with horns, and we think we're saying the same thing, but perhaps we each mean something different."

"I see. So for all we know, we might really look exactly the same as each other?"

"Highly unlikely," began the boy learnedly. "The scientific evidence—"

"What evidence? How do you know your mind isn't playing the same sort of tricks with the evidence? I vote we really look the same as each other and save all the trouble. Then we can forget all about it. What do you say?" finished George coaxingly.

The boy said nothing but looked vexed and seemed to be trying to sort out his argument in order to put it more clearly.

Cathy had been sitting in the doorway in unusual silence, having no experience of the way to handle people who are mentally sick. Now she spoke sternly to George. "You're mixing him up, and it's not clever." She smiled winningly at the strange boy. "How did you get on here on your own? Tell us how you came to pick on this place."

The boy responded at once. "I needed somewhere private to sleep, you know, and there was no one here. I just moved in. It's quite comfortable."

"What do you live on? You know, I mean to eat."

"There's enough," said the boy vaguely.

George and Cathy exchanged a look, the same thought leaping into both their minds. Could a boy live on one sardine can of raw meat per night?

Cathy said carefully, "Do you ever see the Cat Woman?"

The boy smiled. "I listen for her every night, and the cats, too. She'd be surprised if she knew I was here." He added importantly, "I don't want too many people to know I'm here yet, until I've learned to manage properly. That's the only reason I haven't followed her to see the rest of her cats."

"We'll do that one night," said George heartily. "How long are you staying?"

"Oh, just till the next new moon, you know. This is my first trip, and I didn't plan to stay long this time."

"Bad luck. But you're doing pretty well for a first trip, aren't you? It's pretty good, learning to speak English the way you do, just in one little trip."

"I'm not speaking English," said the boy a little stiffly. "I'm speaking telepathy. We're rather good at that."

"Well, good for you. It sounds just like English."

Cathy broke in quickly. If the poor boy was weak in the head, it wasn't fair to get him tangled up in a net of arguments. "Were you the one that cleaned up that picture and took it upstairs?"

"Did I really clean it?" The boy sounded pleased. "I was trying to. And I tried to understand what it was about. I couldn't, though."

"And I don't blame you, mate," said George.

"I will," said the boy quickly, "if I look at it with someone else like you. I'll be able to tell what *you're* seeing. Will you come and look at it?"

"Sorry, not just now. Some other time. We've got to go now, haven't we, Cathy?" He looked at Cathy with so much meaning that she stood up reluctantly. George led the way toward the gate.

"Are you coming back?" called the boy. He looked small and wistful, standing alone in the doorway.

"Try and stop us," George assured him. "We haven't heard nearly enough yet. See you later." He hustled Cathy away through the gate.

"What are we rushing off for?" Cathy demanded.

George frowned forbiddingly and hurried her on toward the park. When they had gone a safe distance beyond the iron fence, he said, "What do you make of all that?"

Cathy tossed her frizzy head with spirit. "I don't think it's a bit clever to keep on making fun of a poor kid like that."

"You don't, eh? You don't reckon he was a bit too clever to be all that silly?"

"*I* didn't notice him being too clever. . . . I just don't know what a person ought to *do*. You don't like giving anyone away, do you? But how can you leave a poor thing like that all on his own there?"

They had reached the park. Several couples were briskly walking their dogs. An old man sat on a bench and gazed out to sea. A handful of boys of different sizes clambered about the low stone wall beside the water. George said nothing for a moment but walked on thoughtfully over the grass. A pigeon hopped nimbly out of the way and then resumed its own thoughtful walking.

"Don't you want to see the Cat Woman?" said George at last.

Cathy blinked. "Why? What's she got to do with it?"

"I just thought I might have a look at her. We could go down tonight and catch her at it. Might be able to see where she goes from there."

"I don't know if I can. I suppose I could try —but what for?"

"Well, I'm going down tonight to watch for the Cat Woman. You please yourself. But if you're coming, *don't* tell the spaceman. If we turn up about dark and he's there, that'll show he really is living there and we can start worrying what to do about it. And if he's not," finished George darkly, "then I reckon he's not too silly to be trying to put one over."

"Of course he'll be there! I keep on telling

you he's been there all the time. But if you have to go to all that trouble to prove it, you go ahead. *I* don't need to. Still, I might turn up if I can. Just to see the Cat Woman, of course."

"Half-past seven?"

"I might. Don't count on it."

George grinned annoyingly, and Cathy strode away over the grass, carrying her shoulders very straight and swinging her hips in a way that reminded George of his mother when she was vexed.

George himself was surprised to find that he, too, had a little trouble in getting away that evening. His mother was very interested to hear about the Cat Woman and said that he must be careful not to get in her way and that next time he must take her some meat for her cats. His father added that he was not to trail her all over town and must be home again by half-past nine.

"If I was going to a show, I'd be out till after eleven," George pointed out.

"That's a different thing altogether. It's one thing going up the street to the pictures and straight home again, and it's another thing hanging round the streets till all hours. Half-past nine at the latest."

"*All* right," grumbled George, and left at once to prevent further argument.

He hurried downstairs from his parents' apartment in a block that was neither old nor new and that no one had ever thought of calling cooperatives. From the quiet avenue he turned into the steep Bar Road. There was a Saturday night activity in all the irregular streets climbing up and down from the harbor. Cars sped along them like whining insects with bright staring eyes drawn to the lights of King's Cross. The streetlamps hung from their poles like drops of light. The buildings, all the mixed-up huddle of them, small and shabby, old and gracious, new and self-important, had retreated into the twilight and crouched there, blinking owlishly from lighted windows. The lights on the north shore made a phosphorous glow, and the bridge was a green-lit archway from shore to shore.

The park looked wide, empty, and shadowy. A rather stern woman in slacks was walking a dog. A man sitting erect on a bench was gazing over the dark water. The familiar driveway looked dark and adventurous. George hurried to the gate and quietly across the little yard. Now that he was here in the strangeness of evening, looking up at the odd little balcony with the dark, empty rooms behind it, he was full of excited curiosity. Would the strange boy really be here? A sort of Robinson Crusoe stranded alone in the midst of the city?

He hurried to the doorway of the lower room and hesitated. Before he could call, a shadow came forward from the darkness, and Cathy Brimble was there.

"Oh, it's you," she said shortly, sounding a little nervous. "I said you were coming." She hesitated while George strained his eyes and ears for a sign of anyone else in the room. "The Cat Woman hasn't turned up so far."

"What about Martin the Martian?"

The boy spoke from behind Cathy, who moved aside uneasily. "I'm glad you came." He said it so politely that George at once felt like a visitor. "She ought to be here soon. She comes every night."

"Right," said George. "We'd better get close to the door on each side, and we might get a glimpse without her spotting us."

Cathy and George stood close against the wall on one side of the door, and the strange boy moved silently to the other. Cathy's manner was surprising; George hadn't expected her to be nervous. Maybe the boy was odd, but she had been on his side all right before. George said conversationally, "I bet he was surprised when you turned up tonight, Cathy."

"He was," said Cathy with a polite giggle. "He was asleep. In the—in the garage."

"What's your name?" said George to the shadow on the other side of the doorway. "Can't keep on calling you Martin the Martian."

There was a pause. "Why not?" said the boy at last.

"If you say so."

"Funny," thought George. "He's almost too cagy to be stupid."

The boy stirred a little. "Here she comes."

Someone was pushing a handcart up the driveway on the other side of the fence. They could hear the slow whisper and creak of the wheels.

## from THE TWENTY-ONE BALLOONS

*William Pène du Bois*

*The "intermission" with which this story begins is in Professor Sherman's lecture on his escape from an island that exploded. In this part of his talk he describes one of his surprising adventures on the Island of Krakatoa.*

### Airy-Go-Round

During the intermission, the mayor and the Chief Surgeon of the San Francisco General Hospital rushed to Professor Sherman's bedside to see if he was all right. "Are you tired?" they asked in one voice. "Would you rather resume tomorrow?" asked the Mayor. "How do you feel?" asked the Chief Surgeon. "Is there anything we can do for you?"

"I feel fine," said Professor Sherman.

"Would you like one of the nurses to change the drinking water in your carafe?" asked the Chief Surgeon.

"I don't care, it tastes all right to me."

"Could I fetch you a little refreshment?" asked the Mayor. "Something to renew your strength?"

"If you insist," said the Professor. The Mayor ran off at a fast puffing trot while the Chief Surgeon busied himself tucking in the comforter on the Professor's bed. It should have been obvious to anyone, even two such important personages as the Mayor and Chief Surgeon, that all Professor Sherman wanted during this intermission he had called was a few minutes of rest.

The Mayor came back with a nip and the Professor swallowed it in one gulp. Then, looking at the Mayor and Surgeon, he said with a smile on his face, "You know, Gentlemen, this to me is very funny. A little over a month ago, I was an insignificant arithmetic teacher who would have found it almost impossible to get to see either one of you. Now you are waiting on me like a pair of well-trained valets. I thank you for your kind attention. It goes to show how wonderful ballooning can be. You never can tell where the winds will blow you, what fan-

tastic good fortune they can lead you to. *Long live balloons!*" he shouted. The Mayor and the Chief Surgeon joined in with a few sheepish giggles, then backed away.

By this time the fifteen minutes were up and Professor Sherman was gratified to see that the people of the audience had quietly returned to their seats and were sitting attentively. The packed auditorium wasn't making a sound. It was waiting anxiously to hear the end of his extraordinary story.

The Chief Surgeon saw, as before, that the Professor was comfortably propped up with pillows, and the Mayor walked over to the Professor's bedside. With one hand resting on the head of the bed, he turned to the audience and said:

"Again it gives me great pleasure to present Professor William Waterman Sherman."

The Professor thanked the Mayor, cleared his throat, and resumed his talk:

Mr. F. led me to the first invention he had promised to show me, the Balloon Merry-Go-Round. On our way I told Mr. F. that the name of the invention suggested something at an amusement park. "Just what is this invention for?"

"It is part of an amusement park," said Mr. F., "which the children of Krakatoa are planning for themselves. You see, our children now are between the ages of ten and fifteen. When we return from our trips to other countries, they help us unload our freighter with great interest. It suddenly dawned on them a year or so ago that it would be an excellent idea if a few boatloads were brought back full of supplies exclusively for them; for after all they do own a share in the mines, too. We agreed to give them two boatloads a year, so all of the children held a meeting to decide how best to fill their freighters. This amusement park they have started to build is the result of their planning. The Balloon Merry-Go-Round is their own invention, designed with but little help from us."

"Is there any school here?" I asked.

"The children have no formal schooling. We have taught them how to read and write, and we have tried to teach them a little arithmetic. They have all taken part in the building of our international houses—which is most educating in itself. But all in all, a school is sorely needed here. You aren't by any chance a teacher, are you? Just what does the title Professor stand for in your case?"

"Professor of, uh, Aeronautics," I stuttered. "I teach Balloon Theory at, uh, the San Francisco Lighter than Air School." I felt a flush of heat in my cheeks as I waded through this fabulous lie. I had no intention of getting involved again in teaching, the very thing from which this trip of mine was intended to take me.

"How interesting," said Mr. F. "That goes to show how quickly one gets out of touch with one's native city. I can't say that I even recall hearing of such an institution."

"It's one of the latest," I muttered, "practically brand new." Then quickly changing the subject, I asked what other forms of amusement could be found at the park.

"So far, they have just had time to design and build the Merry-Go-Round, but they have a lot more planned. Most of the usual rides found at amusement parks are impractical for Krakatoa because they are higher than the jungle life on the Island and would be visible from the sea. As a matter of fact, we only take rides on the Balloon Merry-Go-Round after thoroughly scanning the horizon for passing ships. We never use it if anything is in sight. Do you see that tall pole in the distance?"

"Yes, I do," I said. The pole was straight and the same width at the bottom as at the top. It was threaded like a gigantic screw and it was about seventy-five feet tall.

"That's part of the Balloon Merry-Go-Round, the axle around which it revolves to give it its spin when it is gaining altitude."

"Can't that be seen from the ocean?"

"Yes, it can. But one lone pole isn't enough to attract much attention from passing ships."

We came to a little forest of palm trees, the same sort of neatly kept little forest I had seen the day before, with freshly cut lawn instead of the usual jungle underbrush. We walked through this forest for a hundred yards or so and then came upon a clearing. In the middle of this clearing was what was apparently the Balloon Merry-Go-Round. There were eight little boats around the base of the pole, all joined together bow to stern. In the place of oarlocks, there were

two brass rings on these boats, and through these rings passed poles which all met at the main vertical pole of the Merry-Go-Round where they were screwed into the hub of another large brass ring around the pole, forming spokes of a giant wheel. Each boat was covered with a protective tarpaulin. Mr. F. removed one of the tarpaulins and showed me one. They were nice little centerboard sailboats, sturdy and quite seaworthy. The sails were neatly stowed in trim lockers. I didn't notice any masts, but there was definitely a place for them. Alongside of each of these boats was a large deflated balloon painted a pale sky-blue. Off to one side in the clearing there was a little shack made of bamboo which reminded me very much of my basket house. On its walls outside, eight silk hoses were hanging, neatly coiled up and in line. There was a bell on top of this little shack, which could be reached by climbing a ladder.

Mr. F. walked over to the shack, went inside, and came out again with a spyglass. He climbed up the ladder to the roof of the shack and carefully looked over the horizon around him, apparently for ships. "Would you care to risk a trip in it?" he asked me. "The weather today is ideal."

"As an ardent balloonist, I accept with enthusiasm; but as a sixty-six-year-old man I must confess that I accept with some trepidation. Is it safe?"

"Absolutely," answered Mr. F. "You don't believe that we would allow our children to make ascensions in dangerous contraptions, do you?"

"I guess not," I said, reassured. "I am sure that any invention using balloons and wind as motive power cannot but be enjoyable."

"Very well, then," said Mr. F. He then loudly rang the bell on top of the shack. This sound produced the same reaction, only considerably happier and more excited, as a school bell back home. We were shortly surrounded by children. These children didn't seem to need to be explained anything either; as soon as they arrived in the clearing they made themselves extremely busy readying the Balloon Merry-Go-Round. They took the tarpaulins off all the boats and rolled them up neatly. Four of the children ran into the shack where they prepared the hydrogen machine and pumps. Another eight each grabbed a silk hose, attached it to the hydrogen machine in the shack on one end, and to one of the balloons on the other. The balloons were all carefully unfolded and laid out flat on the ground, and the nets and ropes which attached them to the boats were carefully placed around and beside them so that they wouldn't get tangled up when the balloons were filled with gas. Slowly the balloons started to fill with hydrogen, the ones nearest the pumps filling faster than the others. They lazily lifted themselves off the ground with the children watching them carefully, constantly straightening the ropes so they wouldn't get tangled. Soon they were all full of hydrogen and straining at the boats which were roped to the ground. All forty children were present, working efficiently on the Merry-Go-Round, although it was apparent that there was only room for fourteen of them on this trip. There was room for two in each boat, making a total of sixteen seats, but Mr. F. and I were going to occupy two of the seats. There was no arguing among the children as to whose turn it was; they must have had some sort of passenger schedule they followed closely. I did notice that neither B-1 nor B-2 were among the children who climbed into the boats when they were ready. I suppose that this was because it was "B" Day of the Month of Lamb and they had plenty of work to do at their British chop house. I sat in a boat with Mr. F's son, F-1, and Mr. F. sat with a child in a boat which was on the opposite side of the big pole from ours. "This will make the Merry-Go-Round balance better," said F-1.

There were two children on the ground near each boat. When we were all aboard, they detached the silk hydrogen hoses and rolled them back up to the shack where they carefully hung them up. They then returned to us and one held a rope at the bow of each boat and the other held a rope at the boat's stern. One of the children passengers had a blank pistol, the sort used for starting races at track meets. He stood up and yelled in a high clear voice, *"Is everybody ready?"*

A shrill and deafening *"yes"* was heard, mixed with the deeper voices of Mr. F. and myself. At this signal, the children standing near the boats all gave their ropes a sharp pull, which seemed to unhook the boats from the ground, and they

all ran around the pole in the direction we were heading, giving us a good fast start.

The boats were joined together to form the rim of a wheel. The poles going through the brass oarlocks of the boats formed the spokes of this wheel. The spokes were attached to a big brass ring, or hub of the wheel, and this whole gigantic Merry-Go-Round revolved around the seventy-five-foot pole which was pointing straight up to the sky and was threaded like a screw. The balloons lifted the boats around and around the huge screw up into the air. The Balloon Merry-Go-Round gained speed as it gained altitude. The pole was well greased so that by the time we neared the top we were going very fast. I asked F-1 what happened when we reached the top of the pole. "Do we quickly deflate the balloons and revolve back down to the ground around the pole in the opposite direction?"

"Of course not," said F-1. "We fly right off the pole into the air."

"You'll see," he said.

We soon reached the top and the Merry-Go-Round lunged upward as it lost its grip on the pole. The wind immediately started to carry us off over the Island. We were gaining altitude fast and, of course, still spinning around at great speed. I must admit this was truly a delightful and exciting ride, unlike any other balloon experience I have ever had. I saw now how the boats were kept level. A child in each boat held the ripcord of his boat's balloon. Whenever a boat went a little higher than the others, the ripcord would be pulled releasing a little hydrogen until the boat was again on the same level.

"You must only be able to take short trips," I told F-1, "if you constantly have to release gas to keep the Merry-Go-Round level."

"That's right," he answered. "The length of our trips depends on many things such as the calmness of the weather, how well we distribute the weight in the boats, and how skillfully we control the ripcords. But you understand," he added, "the Balloon Merry-Go-Round wasn't built for travel but rather for short pleasure trips."

"Oh, of course," I said.

The Balloon Merry-Go-Round was heading directly for the mountain. I saw that we were going to fly over it. I asked F-1 if this were not dangerous.

"It isn't dangerous, but it's rather unfortunate because it always means a short trip."

"Why?" I asked.

"Because the huge crater of the volcanic mountain is full of hot air which forms sort of a vacuum. When we fly over the crater, the Merry-Go-Round is sucked downward rather violently and we always use up a lot of gas controlling it and keeping it level."

"Isn't this hazardous?" I asked.

"No," said F-1, "by the time we reach the mountain, we will be high enough to clear it by a great distance. The only danger in taking a ride in this is landing on the ground or on the mountain, or worst of all, in the mountain when the wind is calm. Krakatoa is a small island, and if there is any wind at all, it will carry the Merry-Go-Round out to sea. Once when we first got it, we took a trip on a very calm day. We went straight up, spun around a while, and gradually lost altitude, landing in a forest of palm trees. No one was hurt, but some of the boats were damaged and one of the balloons was torn. Since then, we have only risked trips when there is wind."

We were nearing the mountain and I leaned over the side of my boat to look down at the crater. There was a thick gray smoke crawling around inside. It was like looking into a horrible pit full of elephants. When we were directly over the mountain there was a sickening atmosphere of hot air permeated with sulphurous gases. The Merry-Go-Round started tossing around violently over the pit, and the children with the ripcords kept a careful watch directly across our giant wheel at opposite boats to keep the Merry-Go-Round as steady and level as possible. Hanging on tightly, I leaned over the side of the boat in order to have a direct look into the volcanic crater itself. In places where the smoke had cleared a bit I could see a lake of thick molten lava boiling and bubbling in slow motion. It was a sickening, frightening sight. As I was leaning over, the Merry-Go-Round suddenly plunged downward, then swayed from side to side as the children steadied it. I must have taken a deep gasp of breath, out of fear, I suppose, and my lungs were suddenly filled with

hot sulphurous fumes. The Merry-Go-Round was still spinning fast, as well as pitching and rocking in the air. I hastily drew my head back into the boat, shut my eyes, and lay down on the bottom of the boat. I could hear the rumbling of the mountain beneath me mixed with the hissing noise of hydrogen being released from the balloons. I think I was as close to being sick then as it is possible for anyone to be. We were soon over the mountain, and in fresh, calm air again and I sat up feeling considerably better.

"To tell you the truth, Sir," said F-1, who apparently could well see that I had nearly lost my British breakfast, "I was nearly sick myself that time. The mountain seems unusually violent this morning. I hope this isn't a bad sign."

I took this to be the remark of a younger balloonist comforting an older one who had nearly made a fool of himself. I told him that my behavior was quite inexcusable.

Flying over water in this spinning airship was

completely enjoyable. The magnificent seascape of the Pacific Ocean passed before your eyes half of the time, and Krakatoa in its entirety was beneath you for your careful observation with each turn of the Merry-Go-Round. The Island looked beautiful from the air. Its vegetation was so rich, warm, and soft-looking. The mountain looked so fearful and exciting. The magnificent houses of all nations looked like extraordinary doll's houses on felt lawns, and the Krakatoan crystal house shone like a jewel. The contrast between the trimmed interior and untrimmed ring of jungle around the Island was easy to see from our boats. The Island looked like a formal garden surrounded by a bushy untrimmed hedge.

After a flight lasting approximately thirty-five minutes we were near the surface of the water. The children, controlling their ripcords like experts, lowered the Merry-Go-Round gently and smoothly into the Ocean. We made one complete turn in the water and came slowly to a stop. "Well," I exclaimed, "that was undoubtedly the most thrilling and unusual trip I have ever had the pleasure of taking."

The children in the boats, Mr. F., and I then all leaned back and relaxed a while in the sun, looking up at the balloons which were now half empty and bobbing back and forth with the wind. Suddenly one of the boys, the same one who had fired the starting gun, stood up and said, "All right, everybody, let's go."

At this command the rest of the children stood up and carefully deflated their balloons and folded them up in their boats without letting any part of them touch water. They folded them lengthwise first, then rolled them from the top toward the bottom where the gas escape was, thus forcing all of the gas out of them and making small neat bundles. They opened the little lockers in the boats, where the sails were, took the sails out, and replaced them with the folded balloons. Each boat had one mainsail.

"How do you sail these boats when they are all attached together like a wheel?" I asked. "And what do you use for masts?" These were foolish questions, I immediately realized, for while I was asking them I managed to figure out these problems for myself.

First of all, the children detached the boats one from the other at their bows and sterns. When this was done, they were still attached to each other by the poles which formed the spokes of the giant wheel. These poles were obviously the masts when the boats were used for sailing. The children, two on each pole, all pushed together toward the center hub until the poles slid out through the brass oarlock rings on their boats. Then, still working two on each pole, they unscrewed the poles from the brass hub in the center. They all unscrewed their poles except one boy, the boy who gave the commands. He pulled his pole in with the hub still attached to it, unscrewed the hub in his boat, and put it away in a separate locker. Now that they each had their masts, it was a simple problem to put them into the mast holes. Mr. F. and I did our best to work as efficiently as any of the other crew members. Soon the mainsail was rigged up and we were ready to sail back to the Island. Only the need for a boom was absent from this compact invention. We lowered centerboards and lined up. It was evidently the custom to race home. The boy who gave the signals took out his gun, fired it, and we were homeward bound as fast as the wind would take us. I am afraid I was more of a hindrance than a capable assistant to young F-1. We finished the race last by about seven minutes. The boats were moored to a dock near the freighter in the hidden inlet and we assembled on shore. F-1 explained to me that the boy who had given the signals was the "Captain of the Day," some sort of honor each child received in turn.

The Captain of the Day told the rest of us that since this was my first trip in the Balloon Merry-Go-Round, the results of the boat race wouldn't count on the Official Scoring Sheet. F-1 let out a whooping cheer at this which made me feel quite badly. The Captain of the Day then took me aside and told me, in a most polite way, that he thought it would be an excellent idea if I learned a bit about sailing since I now found myself to be a citizen of Krakatoa. I assured him that I would.

The Captain of the Day then closed the meeting by saying that the Merry-Go-Round would be reassembled around the flying pole right after supper. "And I want you all to be here and help," he said, looking sternly in my direction.

After forty years of schoolteaching I found myself being ordered about by a child. I couldn't help but find this heretofore impossible turnabout amusing. I was indeed far away from the usual dull school routines I so disliked.

*"I'll be there!"* I said in a loud voice, as everybody looked at me and laughed.

The whole trip had taken about five hours and we had therefore missed lunch. I devoured an excellent supper at the B.'s chop house, and then Mr. F. and I reported to the flying pole. The Captain of the Day rang the bell on top of the shack assembling all of the children and we were divided into eight groups of five. (B-1 and B-2 were still busy.) With five on each boat, we had the Merry-Go-Round reassembled and ready to go in less than half an hour. I will confess, though, that after this busy second day on the fabulous Island, I was well ready for bed and slept like a top.

## from DOLPHIN ISLAND

### Arthur C. Clarke

*The exciting imagination of this prolific British author who lives in Malaya has not been denied young people. In* Dolphin Island, *Arthur Clarke tells an absorbing tale of very advanced research with dolphins in the twenty-first century. Shipwrecked, Johnny is rescued in this chapter by the dolphins themselves. He has a unique voyage to his new home and his new life on Dolphin Island. The scientific conjecture and theory here are sound and stimulating.*

### [Rescue!]

As those fins sliced toward the raft, cutting through the water with incredible speed, Johnny thought of all the gruesome tales he had read about sharks and shipwrecked sailors. He drew himself up into as little space as possible, at the center of the packing case. It wobbled alarmingly, and he realized how small a push would

be needed to turn it over. To his surprise, he felt little fear, only a kind of numbed regret and a hope that, if the worst came to the worst, it would all be over quickly. And it seemed a pity, too, that no one would ever know what had happened to him. . . .

Then the water around the raft was full of sleek, gray bodies, switchbacking along the surface in a graceful roller-coaster motion. Johnny knew almost nothing about the creatures of the sea, but surely, sharks did not swim in this fashion. And these animals were breathing air, just as he was; he could hear them wheezing as they went by, and he caught glimpses of blowholes opening and closing. Why, of course—they were dolphins!

Johnny relaxed and no longer tried to hide himself in the middle of his raft. He had often seen dolphins in movies or on television, and he knew that they were friendly intelligent creatures. They were playing like children among the wreckage of the *Santa Anna,* butting at the floating debris with their streamlined snouts, making the strangest whistling and creaking

noises as they did so. A few yards away, one had reared its head completely out of the water and was balancing a plank on its nose, like a trained animal in a circus act; it seemed to be saying to its companions, "Look at me—see how clever I am!"

The strange, unhuman but intelligent, head turned toward Johnny, and the dolphin dropped its plaything with an· unmistakable gesture of surprise. It sank back into the water, squeaking with excitement, and a few seconds later, Johnny was surrounded by glistening, inquisitive faces. They were smiling faces, too, for the mouths of the dolphins seemed to be frozen in a kind of fixed grin—one so infectious that Johnny found himself smiling back at them.

He no longer felt alone; now he had companionship, even though it was not human and could do nothing to help him. It was fascinating to watch the leathery, dove-gray bodies moving around him with such effortless ease as they hunted among the debris of the *Santa Anna*. They were doing this, Johnny soon realized, purely out of playfulness and fun; they were more like lambs gamboling in a spring meadow than anything he had ever expected to find in the sea.

The dolphins continued to bob up and to look at him from time to time, as if making sure that he had not run away. They watched with great curiosity as he pulled off his sodden clothing and spread it to dry in the sun, and they seemed to be giving the matter careful thought when Johnny asked them solemnly: "Well, what shall I do now?"

One answer to that question was obvious: he had to arrange some shelter from the tropical sun before it roasted him alive. Luckily, this problem was quickly solved; he was able to build a little wigwam from some pieces of driftwood which he lashed together with his handkerchief and then covered with his shirt. When he had finished, he felt quite proud of himself, and hoped that his audience appreciated his cleverness.

Now he could do nothing but lie down in the shade and conserve his strength while the wind and the currents carried him to an unknown fate. He did not feel hungry, and though his lips were already dry, it would be several hours before thirst became a serious problem.

The sea was much calmer now, and low, oily waves were rolling past with a gentle, undulating motion. Somewhere Johnny had come across the phrase, "Rocked in the cradle of the deep." Now he knew exactly what it meant. It was so soothing, so peaceful here that he could almost forget his desperate position; he was content to stare at the blue sea and the blue sky, and to watch the strange yet beautiful animals that glided and swooped around him, sometimes hurling their bodies clear out of the water in the sheer joy of life. . . .

Something jolted the raft, and he awoke with a start. For a moment he could hardly believe that he had been sleeping and that the sun was now almost overhead. Then the raft jerked again—and he saw why.

Four dolphins, swimming side by side, were pushing the raft through the water. Already it was moving faster than a man could swim, and it was still gaining speed. Johnny stared in amazement at the animals splashing and snorting only inches away from him; was this another of their games?

Even as he asked himself that question, he knew that the answer was No. The whole pattern of their behavior had changed completely; this was deliberate and purposeful. Playtime was over. He was in the center of a great pack of the animals, all now moving steadily in the same direction. There were scores, if not hundreds, ahead and behind, to right and left, as far as he could see. He felt that he was moving across the ocean in the midst of a military formation—a brigade of cavalry.

He wondered how long they would keep it up, but they showed no signs of slackening. From time to time, one of the dolphins would drop away from the raft, and another would immediately take its place, so that there was no loss of speed. Though it was very hard to judge how fast he was moving, Johnny guessed that the raft was being pushed along at over five miles an hour. There was no way of telling, however, whether he was moving north, south, east, or west; he could get no compass bearings from the almost vertical sun.

Not until much later in the day did he discover that he was heading toward the west, for the sun was going down in front of him. He was glad to see the approach of night, and looked forward to its coolness after the scorching day. By this time he was extremely thirsty; his lips were parched and cracked, and though he was tantalized by the water all around him, he knew that it would be dangerous to drink it. His thirst was so overpowering that he did not feel any hunger; even if he had some food, he would be unable to swallow it.

It was a wonderful relief when the sun went down, sinking in a blaze of gold and red. Still the dolphins drove on into the west, beneath the stars and the rising Moon. If they kept this up all through the night, Johnny calculated, they would have carried him the best part of a hundred miles. They *must* have a definite goal, but what could it be? He began to hope that there was land not far away, and that for some unknown reason these friendly and intelligent creatures were taking him to it. But why they were going to all this trouble he could not imagine.

The night was the longest that Johnny had ever known, for his growing thirst would not allow him to sleep. To add to his distress, he had been badly sunburned during the day, and he kept twisting and turning on the raft in a vain attempt to find a comfortable position. Most of the time he lay flat on his back, using his clothes to protect the sore spots, while the Moon and stars crept across the sky with agonizing slowness. Sometimes the brilliant beacon of a satellite would drift from west to east, traveling much more swiftly than any of the stars, and in the opposite direction. It was maddening to know that up on the space stations were men and instruments that could easily locate him—if they bothered to search. But, of course, there was no reason why they should.

At last the Moon went down, and in the brief darkness before dawn the sea once more came alight with phosphorescence. The graceful, superbly streamlined bodies all around the raft were outlined with fire; every time one of them shot into the air, the trajectory of its leap was a glowing rainbow in the night.

This time Johnny did not welcome the dawn; now he knew how pitiful his defenses were

against the tropical sun. He re-erected his little tent, crept beneath it, and tried to turn his thoughts away from drink.

It was impossible. Every few minutes he found himself picturing cold milk shakes, glasses of iced fruit juice, water flowing from faucets in sparkling streams. Yet he had been adrift for not more than thirty hours; men had survived without water for much longer than that.

The only thing that kept up his spirits was the determination and energy of his escort. The school still drove on into the west, carrying the raft before it with undiminished speed. Johnny no longer puzzled himself about the mystery of the dolphins' behavior; that was a problem that would solve itself in good time—or not at all.

And then, about midmorning, he caught his first glimpse of land. For many minutes he was afraid that it was merely a cloud on the horizon —but, if so, it was strange that it was the only cloud in the sky and that it lay dead ahead. Before long he could not doubt that it was an island, though it seemed to float clear of the water, and the heat haze made its outlines dance and shimmer against the skyline.

An hour later, he could see its details clearly. It was long and low and completely covered with trees. A narrow beach of dazzling white sand surrounded it, and beyond the beach there seemed to be a very wide, shallow reef, for there was a line of white breakers at least a mile out at sea.

At first Johnny could see no signs of life, but at last, with great relief, he spotted a thin stream of smoke rising from the wooded interior. Where there was smoke there were human beings—and the water for which his whole body was now craving.

He was still several miles from the island when the dolphins gave him a bad shock; they were turning aside as if to by-pass the land that was now so close. Then Johnny understood what they were doing. The reef was too great an obstacle; they were going to outflank it and approach the island from the other side.

The detour took at least an hour, but Johnny's mind was at rest, now that he felt sure that he was nearing safety. As the raft and its untiring escort swung around to the western side of the island, he saw first a small group of boats at anchor, then some low white buildings, then a collection of huts with dark-skinned people moving among them. There was a fairly large community here, on this lonely speck in the Pacific.

Now at last the dolphins seemed a little hesitant, and Johnny got the impression that they were reluctant to go into the shallow water. They pushed the raft slowly past the anchored boats, then backed off as if to say, "It's up to you now."

Johnny felt an overwhelming impulse to say some words of thanks, but his mouth was too dry for speech. So he stepped quietly off the raft, found himself in water only waist deep, and waded ashore.

There were people running along the beach toward him, but they could wait. He turned toward the lovely, powerful creatures who had brought him on this incredible journey, and waved them a grateful farewell. Already they were turning back toward their home, in the deep water of the open sea.

Then something seemed to happen to his legs, and as the sand came up to hit him, dolphins, island, and everything else vanished from his consciousness.

## from FARMER IN THE SKY

*Robert A. Heinlein*

*Robert Heinlein's books are usually listed for teen-age reading. They are not easy, but this sample is included because it has lasted over the years and appeals to children interested in space travel. Mr. Heinlein's books interest adults as well as young people. This episode has to do with the beginning of a journey to Ganymede, where the boy and his family are going to settle. Mr. Heinlein's later works have gone considerably further into space and into unusual concepts.*

### Space Ship Bifrost

I woke up hungry but I suddenly remembered that this was it!—my last day on Earth. Then I was too excited to be hungry. I got up, put on my Scout uniform and my ship suit over it.

I thought we would go right on board. I was wrong.

First we had to assemble under awnings spread out in front of the hotel near the embarking tubes. It wasn't air conditioned outside, of course, but it was early and the desert wasn't really hot yet. I found the letter "L" and sat down under it, sitting on my baggage. Dad and his new family weren't around yet; I began to wonder if I was going to Ganymede by myself. I didn't much care.

Out past the gates about five miles away, you could see the ships standing on the field, the *Daedalus* and the *Icarus,* pulled off the Earth-Moon run for this one trip, and the old *Bifrost* that had been the shuttle rocket to Supra-New-York space station as far back as I could remember.

The *Daedalus* and the *Icarus* were bigger but I hoped I would get the *Bifrost;* she was the first ship I ever saw blast off.

A family put their baggage down by mine. The mother looked out across the field and said, "Joseph, which one is the *Mayflower?*"

Her husband tried to explain to her, but she still was puzzled. I nearly burst, trying to keep from laughing. Here she was, all set to go to Ganymede and yet she was so dumb she didn't even know that the ship she was going in had been built out in space and couldn't land anywhere.

The place was getting crowded with emigrants and relatives coming to see them off, but I still didn't see anything of Dad. I heard my name called and turned around and there was Duck Miller. "Gee, Bill," he said, "I thought I'd missed you."

"Hi, Duck. No, I'm still here."

"I tried to call you last night but your phone answered 'service discontinued,' so I hooked school and came up."

"Aw, you shouldn't have done that."

"But I wanted to bring you this." He handed me a package, a whole pound of chocolates. I didn't know what to say.

I thanked him and then said, "Duck, I appreciate it, I really do. But I'll have to give them back to you."

"Huh? Why?"

"Weight. Mass, I mean. I can't get by with another ounce."

"You can carry it."

"That won't help. It counts just the same."

He thought about it and said, "Then let's open it."

I said, "Fine," and did so and offered him a piece. I looked at them myself and my stomach was practically sitting up and begging. I don't know when I've been so hungry.

I gave in and ate one. I figured I would sweat it off anyhow; it was getting hot and I had my Scout uniform on under my ship suit—and that's no way to dress for the Mojave Desert in June! Then I was thirstier than ever, of course; one thing leads to another.

I went over to a drinking fountain and took a very small drink. When I came back I closed the candy box and handed it back to Duck and told him to pass it around at next Scout meeting and tell the fellows I wished they were going along. He said he would and added, "You know, Bill, I wish I was going, I really do."

I said I wished he was, too, but when did he change his mind? He looked embarrassed but about then Mr. Kinski showed up and then Dad showed up, with Molly and the brat—Peggy—and Molly's sister, Mrs. van Metre. Everybody shook hands all around and Mrs. van Metre started to cry and the brat wanted to know what made my clothes so bunchy and what was I sweating about?

George was eyeing me, but about then our names were called and we started moving through the gate.

George and Molly and Peggy were weighed through and then it was my turn. My baggage was right on the nose, of course, and then I stepped on the scales. They read one hundred and thirty-one and one tenth pounds—I could have eaten another chocolate.

"Check!" said the weightmaster, then he looked up and said, "What in the world have you got on, son?"

The left sleeve of my uniform had started to unroll and was sticking out below the half sleeve of my ship suit. The merit badges were shining out like signal lights.

I didn't say anything. He started feeling the lumps the uniform sleeves made. "Boy," he said, "you're dressed like an arctic explorer; no wonder you're sweating. Didn't you know you weren't supposed to wear anything but the gear you were listed in?"

Dad came back and asked what the trouble was. I just stood there with my ears burning. The assistant weightmaster got into the huddle and they argued what should be done. The weightmaster phoned somebody and finally he said, "He's inside his weight limit; if he wants to call that monkey suit part of his skin, we'll allow it. Next customer, please!"

I trailed along, feeling foolish. We went down inside and climbed on the slide strip, it was cool down there, thank goodness. A few minutes later we got off at the loading room down under the rocket ship. Sure enough, it was the *Bifrost*, as I found out when the loading elevator poked

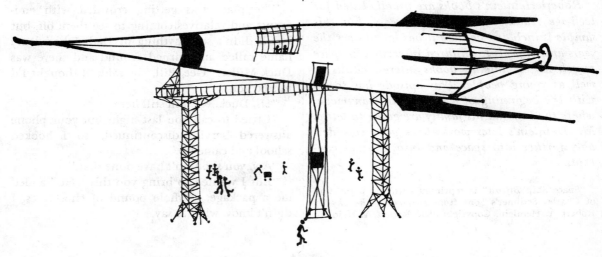

above ground and stopped at the passenger port. We filed in.

They had it all organized. Our baggage had been taken from us in the loading room; each passenger had a place assigned by his weight. That split us up again; I was on the deck immediately under the control room. I found my place, couch 14-D, then went to a view port where I could see the *Daedalus* and the *Icarus*.

A brisk little stewardess, about knee high to a grasshopper, checked my name off a list and offered me an injection against dropsickness. I said no, thanks.

She said, "You've been out before?"

I admitted I hadn't; she said, "Better take it."

I said I was a licensed air pilot; I wouldn't get sick. I didn't tell her that my license was just for copters. She shrugged and turned away. A loudspeaker said, "The *Daedalus* is cleared for blasting." I moved up to get a good view.

The *Daedalus* was about a quarter of a mile away and stood up higher than we did. She had fine lines and was a mighty pretty sight, gleaming in the morning sunshine. Beyond her and to the right, clear out at the edge of the field, a light shone green at the traffic control blockhouse.

She canted slowly over to the south, just a few degrees.

Fire burst out of her base, orange, and then blinding white. It splashed down into the ground baffles and curled back up through the ground vents. She lifted.

She hung there for a breath and you could see the hills shimmer through her jet. And she was gone.

Just like that—she was gone. She went up out of there like a scared bird, just a pencil of white fire in the sky, and was gone while we could still hear and feel the thunder of her jets inside the compartment.

My ears were ringing. I heard someone behind me say, "But I haven't had breakfast. The Captain will just have to wait. Tell him, Joseph."

It was the woman who hadn't known that the *Mayflower* was a space-to-space ship. Her husband tried to hush her up, but he didn't have any luck. She called over the stewardess. I heard her answer, "But, madam, you can't speak to the Captain now. He's preparing for blast-off."

Apparently that didn't make any difference. The stewardess finally got her quiet by solemnly promising that she could have breakfast after blast-off. I bent my ears at that and I decided to put in a bid for breakfast, too.

The *Icarus* took off twenty minutes later and then the speaker said, "All hands! Acceleration stations—prepare to blast off." I went back to my couch and the stewardess made sure that we were all strapped down. She cautioned us not to unstrap until she said we could. She went down to the deck below.

I felt my ears pop and there was a soft sighing in the ship. I swallowed and kept swallowing. I knew what they were doing: blowing the natural air out and replacing it with the standard helium-oxygen mix at half sea-level pressure. But the woman—the same one—didn't like it. She said, "Joseph, my head aches. Joseph, I can't breathe. Do something!"

Then she clawed at her straps and sat up. Her husband sat up, too, and forced her back down.

The *Bifrost* tilted over a little and the speaker said, "Minus three minutes!"

And then "Minus one minute!" and another voice took up the count:

"Fifty-nine! Fifty-eight! Fifty-seven!"

My heart started to pound so hard I could hardly hear it. But it went on: "—thirty-five! Thirty-four! Thirty-three! Thirty-two! Thirty-one! *Half!* Twenty-nine! Twenty-eight!"

And it got to be: *"Ten!"*

And "Nine!"

"Eight!

"Seven!

"And six!

"And five!

"And four!

"And three!

"And two—"

I never did hear them say "one" or "fire" or whatever they said. About then something fell on me and I thought I was licked. Once, exploring a cave with the fellows, a bank collapsed on me and I had to be dug out. It was like that —but nobody dug me out.

My chest hurt. My ribs seemed about to break. I couldn't lift a finger. I gulped and couldn't get my breath.

I wasn't scared, not really, because I knew we would take off with a high *g*, but I was awfully uncomfortable. I managed to turn my head a little and saw that the sky was already purple. While I watched, it turned black and the stars came out, millions of stars. And yet the Sun was still streaming in through the port.

The roar of the jets was unbelievable but the noise started to die out almost at once and soon you couldn't hear it at all. They say the old ships used to be noisy even after you passed the speed of sound; the *Bifrost* was not. It got as quiet as the inside of a bag of feathers.

There was nothing to do but lie there, stare out at that black sky, try to breathe, and try not to think about the weight sitting on you.

And then, so suddenly that it made your stomach turn flip-flops, you didn't weigh anything at all.

#### from A WRINKLE IN TIME

*Madeleine L'Engle*

*A Wrinkle in Time is an interesting combination of pure fantasy and science fiction, including space travel by the unique means of the tesseract, which works in the fourth dimension. It also offers musings on good and evil, and an Orwellian portrayal of a dark planet locked in the grip of IT, an all-controlling mind. These ideas are not exactly new, but they are tremendously exciting when young people first encounter them. In this excerpt, Meg is nursed to health by the strange "beasts" on an unknown planet, after she has been injured in escaping—just in the nick of time—from the evil clutch of IT.*

### Aunt Beast

"No!" Mr. Murry said sharply. "Please put her down."

A sense of amusement seemed to emanate from the beasts. The tallest, who seemed to be the spokesman, said, "We frighten you?"

"What are you going to do with us?" Mr. Murry asked.

The beast said, "I'm sorry, we communicate better with the other one." He turned toward Calvin. "Who are you?"

"I'm Calvin O'Keefe."

"What's that?"

"I'm a boy. A—a young man."

"You, too, are afraid?"

"I'm—not sure."

"Tell me," the beast said. "What do you suppose you'd do if three of *us* suddenly arrived on your home planet."

"Shoot you, I guess," Calvin admitted.

"Then isn't that what we should do with you?"

Calvin's freckles seemed to deepen, but he answered quietly. "I'd really rather you didn't. I mean, the earth's my home, and I'd rather be there than anywhere in the world—I mean, the universe—and I can't wait to get back, but we make some awful bloopers there."

The smallest beast, the one holding Meg, said, "And perhaps they aren't used to visitors from other planets."

"Used to it!" Calvin exclaimed. "We've never had any, as far as I know."

"Why?"

"I don't know."

The middle beast, a tremor of trepidation in his words, said, "You aren't from a dark planet, are you?"

"No." Calvin shook his head firmly, though the beast couldn't see him. "We're—we're shadowed. But we're fighting the shadow."

The beast holding Meg questioned, "You three are fighting?"

"Yes," Calvin answered. "Now that we know about it."

The tall one turned back to Mr. Murry, speaking sternly. "You. The oldest. Man. From where have you come? Now."

Mr. Murry answered steadily. "From a planet called Camazotz." There was a mutter from the three beasts. "We do not belong there," Mr. Murry said, slowly and distinctly. "We were strangers there as we are here. I was a prisoner there, and these children rescued me. My youngest son, my baby, is still there, trapped in the dark mind of IT."

Meg tried to twist around in the beast's arms to glare at her father and Calvin. Why were they being so frank? Weren't they aware of the danger? But again her anger dissolved as the gentle warmth from the tentacles flowed through her. She realized that she could move her fingers and toes with comparative freedom, and the pain was no longer so acute.

"We must take this child back with us," the beast holding her said.

Meg shouted at her father. "Don't leave me the way you left Charles!" With this burst of terror a spasm of pain wracked her body and she gasped.

"Stop fighting," the beast told her. "You make it worse. Relax."

"That's what IT said," Meg cried. "Father! Calvin! Help!"

The beast turned toward Calvin and Mr. Murry. "This child is in danger. You must trust us."

"We have no alternative," Mr. Murry said. "Can you save her?"

"I think so."

"May I stay with her?"

"No. But you will not be far away. We feel that you are hungry, tired, that you would like to bathe and rest. And this little—what is the word?" the beast cocked its tentacles at Calvin.

"Girl," Calvin said.

"This little girl needs prompt and special care. The coldness of the—what is it you call it?"

"The Black Thing?"

"The Black Thing. Yes. The Black Thing burns unless it is counteracted properly." The three beasts stood around Meg, and it seemed that they were feeling into her with their softly waving tentacles. The movement of the tentacles was as rhythmic and flowing as the dance of an undersea plant, and lying there, cradled in the four strange arms, Meg, despite herself, felt a sense of security that was deeper than anything she had known since the days when she lay in her mother's arms in the old rocking chair and was sung to sleep. With her father's help she had been able to resist IT. Now she could hold out no longer. She leaned her head against the beast's chest, and realized that the gray body was covered with the softest, most delicate fur imaginable, and the fur had the same beautiful odor as the air.

I hope I don't smell awful to it, she thought. But then she knew with a deep sense of comfort that even if she did smell awful the beasts would forgive her. As the tall figure cradled her she could feel the frigid stiffness of her body relaxing against it. This bliss could not come to her from a thing like IT. IT could only give pain, never relieve it. The beasts must be good. They had to be good. She sighed deeply, like a very small child, and suddenly she was asleep.

When she came to herself again there was in the back of her mind a memory of pain, of agonizing pain. But the pain was over now and her body was lapped in comfort. She was lying on something wonderfully soft in an enclosed chamber. It was dark. All she could see were occasional tall moving shadows which she realized were beasts walking about. She had been stripped of her clothes, and something warm and pungent was gently being rubbed into her body. She sighed and stretched and discovered that she *could* stretch. She could move again, she was no longer paralyzed, and her body was bathed in waves of warmth. Her father had not saved her; the beasts had.

"So you are awake, little one?" The words came gently to her ears. "What a funny little tadpole you are! Is the pain gone now?"

"All gone."

"Are you warm and alive again?"

"Yes, I'm fine." She struggled to sit up.

"No, lie still, small one. You must not exert yourself as yet. We will have a fur garment for you in a moment, and then we will feed you. You must not even try to feed yourself. You must be as an infant again. The Black Thing does not relinquish its victims willingly."

"Where are Father and Calvin? Have they gone back for Charles Wallace?"

"They are eating and resting," the beast said, "and we are trying to learn about each other and see what is best to help you. We feel now that you are not dangerous, and that we will be allowed to help you."

"Why is it so dark in here?" Meg asked. She tried to look around, but all she could see was shadows. Nevertheless there was a sense of openness, a feel of a gentle breeze moving lightly about, that kept the darkness from being oppressive.

Perplexity came to her from the beast. "What is this dark? What is this light? We do not understand. Your father and the boy, Calvin, have asked this, too. They say that it is night now on our planet, and that they cannot see. They have told us that our atmosphere is what they call opaque, so that the stars are not visible, and then they were surprised that we know stars, that we know their music and the movements of their dance far better than beings like you who spend hours studying them through what you call telescopes. We do not understand what this means, *to see*."

"Well, it's what things look like," Meg said helplessly.

"We do not know what things *look* like, as you say," the beast said. "We know what things *are* like. It must be a very limiting thing, this seeing."

"Oh, no!" Meg cried. "It's—it's the most wonderful thing in the world!"

"What a very strange world yours must be!" the beast said, "that such a peculiar-seeming thing should be of such importance. Try to tell me, what is this thing called *light* that you are able to do so little without?"

"Well, we can't see without it," Meg said, realizing that she was completely unable to ex-

plain vision and light and dark. How can you explain sight on a world where no one has ever seen and where there is no need of eyes? "Well, on this planet," she fumbled, "you have a sun, don't you?"

"A most wonderful sun, from which comes our warmth, and the rays which give us our flowers, our food, our music, and all the things which make life and growth."

"Well," Meg said, "when we are turned toward the sun—our earth, our planet, I mean, toward our sun—we receive its light. And when we're turned away from it, it is night. And if we want to see we have to use artificial lights."

"Artificial lights," the beast sighed. "How very complicated life on your planet must be. Later on you must try to explain some more to me."

"All right," Meg promised, and yet she knew that to try to explain anything that could be seen with the eyes would be impossible, because the beasts in some way saw, knew, understood, far more completely than she, or her parents, or Calvin, or even Charles Wallace.

"Charles Wallace!" she cried. "What are they doing about Charles Wallace? We don't know what IT's doing to him or making him do. Please, oh, please, help us!"

"Yes, yes, little one, of course we will help you. A meeting is in session right now to study what is best to do. We have never before been able to talk to anyone who has managed to escape from a dark planet, so although your father is blaming himself for everything that has happened, we feel that he must be quite an extraordinary person to get out of Camazotz with you at all. But the little boy, and I understand that he is a very special, a very important little boy—ah, my child, you must accept that this will not be easy. To go *back* through the Black Thing, *back* to Camazotz—I don't know. I don't know."

"But Father left him!" Meg said. "He's got to bring him back! He can't just abandon Charles Wallace!"

The beast's communication suddenly became crisp. "Nobody said anything about abandoning anybody. That is not our way. But we know that just because we want something does not mean that we will get what we want, and we still do not know *what* to do. And we cannot allow you, in your present state, to do anything that would jeopardize us all. I can see that you wish your father to go rushing back to Camazotz, and you could probably make him do this, and then where would we be? No. No. You must wait until you are more calm. Now, my darling, here is a robe for you to keep you warm and comfortable." Meg felt herself being lifted again, and a soft, light garment was slipped about her. "Don't worry about your little brother." The tentacles' musical words were soft against her. "We would *never* leave him behind the shadow. But for now you must relax, you must be happy, you must get well."

The gentle words, the feeling that this beast would be able to love her no matter what she said or did, lapped Meg in warmth and peace. She felt a delicate touch of tentacle to her cheek, as tender as her mother's kiss.

"It is so long since my own small ones were grown and gone," the beast said. "You are so tiny and vulnerable. Now I will feed you. You must eat slowly and quietly. I know that you are half starved, that you have been without food far too long, but you must not rush things or you will not get well."

Something completely and indescribably and incredibly delicious was put to Meg's lips, and she swallowed gratefully. With each swallow she felt strength returning to her body and she realized that she had had nothing to eat since the horrible fake turkey dinner on Camazotz which she had barely tasted. How long ago was her mother's stew? Time no longer had any meaning.

"How long does night last here?" she murmured sleepily. "It will be day again, won't it?"

"Hush," the beast said. "Eat, small one. During the coolness, which is now, we sleep. And, when you waken, there will be warmth again and many things to do. You must eat now, and sleep, and I will stay with you."

"What should I call you, please?" Meg asked.

"Well, now. First, try not to say any words for just a moment. Think within your own mind. Think of all the things you call people, different kinds of people."

While Meg thought, the beast murmured to her gently. "No, *mother* is a special, a one-name; and a father you have here. Not just friend, nor

teacher, nor brother, nor sister. What is *acquaintance?* What a funny, hard word. *Aunt.* Maybe. Yes, perhaps that will do. And you think of such odd words about me. *Thing,* and *monster! Monster,* what a horrid sort of word. I really do not think I am a monster. *Beast.* That will do. *Aunt Beast."*

"Aunt Beast," Meg murmured sleepily, and laughed.

"Have I said something funny?" Aunt Beast asked in surprise. "Isn't Aunt Beast all right?"

"Aunt Beast is lovely," Meg said. "Please sing to me, Aunt Beast."

If it was impossible to describe sight to Aunt Beast, it would be even more impossible to describe the singing of Aunt Beast to a human being. It was a music even more glorious than the music of the singing creatures on Uriel. It was a music more tangible than form or sight. It had essence and structure. It supported Meg more firmly than the arms of Aunt Beast. It seemed to travel with her, to sweep her aloft in the power of song, so that she was moving in glory among the stars, and for a moment she, too, felt that the words Darkness and Light had no meaning, and only this melody was real.

Meg did not know when she fell asleep within the body of the music. When she wakened Aunt Beast was asleep, too, the softness of her furry, faceless head drooping. Night had gone and a dull gray light filled the room. But she realized now that here on this planet there was no need for color, that the grays and browns merging into each other were not what the beasts knew, and that what she, herself, saw was only the smallest fraction of what the planet was really like. It was she who was limited by her senses, not the blind beasts, for they must have senses of which she could not even dream.

She stirred slightly, and Aunt Beast bent over her immediately, "What a lovely sleep, my darling. Do you feel all right?"

"I feel wonderful," Meg said. "Aunt Beast, what is this planet called?"

"Oh, dear," Aunt Beast sighed. "I find it not easy at all to put things the way your mind shapes them. You call where you came from Camazotz?"

"Well, it's where we came from, but it's not our planet."

"You can call us Ixchel, I guess," Aunt Beast told her. "We share the same sun as lost Camazotz, but that, give thanks, is all we share."

"Are you fighting the Black Thing?" Meg asked.

"Oh, yes," Aunt Beast replied. "In doing that we can never relax. We are the called according to His purpose, and whom He calls, them He also justifies. Of course we have help, and without help it would be much more difficult."

"Who helps you?" Meg asked.

"Oh, dear, it is so difficult to explain things to you, small one. And I know now that it is not just because you are a child. The other two are as hard to reach into as you are. What can I tell you that will mean anything to you? Good helps us, the stars help us, perhaps what you would call *light* helps us, love helps us. Oh, my child, I cannot explain! This is something you just have to know or not know."

"But—"

"We look not at the things which are what you would call seen, but at the things which are not seen. For the things which are seen are temporal. But the things which are not seen are eternal."

"Aunt Beast, do you know Mrs. Whatsit?" Meg asked with a sudden flooding of hope.

"Mrs. Whatsit?" Aunt Beast was puzzled. "Oh, child, your language is so utterly simple and limited that it has the effect of extreme complication." Her four arms, tentacles waving, were outflung in a gesture of helplessness. "Would you like me to take you to your father and your Calvin?"

"Oh, yes, please!"

"Let us go, then. They are waiting for you to make plans. And we thought you would enjoy eating—what is it you call it? oh, yes, breakfast—together. You will be too warm in that heavy fur, now. I will dress you in something lighter, and then we will go."

As though Meg were a baby, Aunt Beast bathed and dressed her, and this new garment, though it was made of a pale fur, was lighter than the lightest summer clothes on earth. Aunt Beast put one tentacled arm about Meg's waist and led her through long, dim corridors in which she could see only shadows, and shadows of shadows, until they reached a large, columned chamber. Shafts of light came in from an open skylight and converged about a huge, round, stone table. Here were seated several of the great beasts, and Calvin and Mr. Murry, on a stone bench that circled the table. Because the beasts were so tall, even Mr. Murry's feet did not touch the ground, and lanky Calvin's long legs dangled as though he were Charles Wallace. The hall was partially enclosed by vaulted arches leading to long, paved walks. There were no empty walls, no covering roofs, so that although the light was dull in comparison to earth's sunlight, Meg had no feeling of dark or of chill. As Aunt Beast led Meg in, Mr. Murry slid down from the bench and hurried to her, putting his arms about her tenderly.

"They promised us you were all right," he said.

While she had been in Aunt Beast's arms Meg had felt safe and secure. Now her worries about Charles Wallace and her disappointment in her father's human fallibility rose like gorge in her throat.

"I'm fine," she muttered, looking not at Calvin or her father, but at the beasts, for it was to them she turned now for help. It seemed to her that neither her father nor Calvin were properly concerned about Charles Wallace.

"Meg!" Calvin said gaily. "You've never tasted such food in your life! Come and eat!"

Aunt Beast lifted Meg up onto the bench and sat down beside her, then heaped a plate with food, strange fruits and breads that tasted unlike anything Meg had ever eaten. Everything was dull and colorless and unappetizing to look at, and at first, even remembering the meal Aunt Beast had fed her the night before, Meg hesitated to taste, but once she had managed the first bite she ate eagerly; it seemed that she would never have her fill again.

The others waited until she slowed down. Then Mr. Murry said gravely, "We were trying to work out a plan to rescue Charles Wallace. Since I made such a mistake in tessering away from IT, we feel that it would not be wise for me to try to get back to Camazotz, even alone. If I missed the mark again I could easily get lost and wander forever from galaxy to galaxy, and that would be small help to anyone, least of all to Charles Wallace."

Such a wave of despondency came over Meg that she was no longer able to eat.

"Our friends here," he continued, "feel that it was only the fact that I still wore the glasses your Mrs. Who gave you that kept me within this solar system. Here are the glasses, Meg. But I am afraid that the virtue has gone from them and now they are only glass. Perhaps they were meant to help only once and only on Camazotz. Perhaps it was going through the Black Thing that did it." He pushed the glasses across the table at her.

"These people know about tessering," Calvin gestured at the circle of great beasts, "but they can't do it onto a dark planet."

"Have you tried to call Mrs. Whatsit?" Meg asked.

"Not yet," her father answered.

"But if you haven't thought of anything else, it's the *only* thing to do! Father, don't you care about Charles at all!"

At that Aunt Beast stood up, saying, "Child," in a reproving way. Mr. Murry said nothing and Meg could see that she had wounded him deeply. She reacted as she would have reacted to Mr. Jenkins. She scowled down at the table, saying, "We've *got* to ask them for help now. You're just stupid if you think we don't."

Aunt Beast spoke to the others. "The child is distraught. Don't judge her harshly. She was almost taken by the Black Thing. Sometimes we can't know what spiritual damage it leaves even when physical recovery is complete."

Meg looked angrily around the table. The beasts sat there, silent, motionless. She felt that she was being measured and found wanting.

Calvin swung away from her and hunched himself up. "Hasn't it occurred to you that we've been trying to tell them about our ladies? What do you think we've been up to all this time? Just stuffing our faces? Okay, you have a shot at it."

"Yes. Try, child." Aunt Beast seated herself again, and pulled Meg up beside her. "But I do not understand this feeling of anger I sense in you. What is it about? There is blame going on, and guilt. Why?"

"Aunt Beast, don't you know?"

"No," Aunt Beast said. "But this is not telling me about—whoever they are you want us to know. Try."

Meg tried. Blunderingly. Fumblingly. At first she described Mrs. Whatsit and her man's coat and multicolored shawls and scarves, Mrs. Who and her white robes and shimmering spectacles, Mrs. Which in her peaked cap and black gown quivering in and out of body. Then she realized that this was absurd. She was describing them only to herself. This wasn't Mrs. Whatsit or Mrs. Who or Mrs. Which. She might as well have described Mrs. Whatsit as she was when she took on the form of a flying creature of Uriel.

"Don't try to use words," Aunt Beast said soothingly. "You're just fighting yourself and me. Think about what they *are*. This *look* doesn't help us at all."

Meg tried again, but she could not get a visual concept out of her mind. She tried to think of Mrs. Whatsit explaining tessering. She tried to think of them in terms of mathematics. Every once in a while she thought she felt a flicker of understanding from Aunt Beast or one of the others, but most of the time all that emanated from them was gentle puzzlement.

"Angels!" Calvin shouted suddenly from across the table. "Guardian angels!" There was a moment's silence, and he shouted again, his face tense with concentration, "Messengers! Messengers of God!"

"I thought for a moment—" Aunt Beast started, then subsided, sighing. "No. It's not clear enough."

"How strange it is that they can't tell us what they themselves seem to know," a tall, thin beast murmured.

One of Aunt Beast's tentacled arms went around Meg's waist again. "They are very young. And on their earth, as they call it, they never communicate with other planets. They revolve about all alone in space."

"Oh," the thin beast said. "Aren't they *lonely?*"

Suddenly a thundering voice reverberated throughout the great hall:

"WWEEE ARRE HHERRE!"

*part three*

# TIME FOR REALISM: FACTS AND FICTION

*Realistic Fiction*

*Historical Fiction*

*Biography*

*Informational Books*

Good books are concerned not so much with teaching the child reader as they are with offering children a new way of seeing the world, helping them discover the way things are, and making it easier for them to see the way things might be if we were all better people. Middle-class children can sympathize with Roosevelt Grady and his mother in their yearning for a settled life; children becoming aware of stereotyped sex roles can see in *Hello, Aurora* the conflict between old-fashioned attitudes and new, or even be made aware of the conflict for the first time.

The range of problems in realistic stories reflects the authors' understanding of the need to present material appropriate to a wide range of age levels. What is a problem to a five-year-old has little meaning for a ten-year-old; this is as it should be if the child is maturing normally. What appealed to children fifty years ago may not be the same, whether it is the writing style or the subject of a story, as what appeals to today's young readers. Animal stories, for example, are as popular as ever with young children, but there are fewer avid readers of animal stories in the middle and upper grades.

What is appropriate for the reader of any age depends on such factors as reading ability and

# REALISTIC FICTION

comprehension of concepts, subject interest, age and sex, and individual preferences for particular writing styles or kinds of humor. A book that a seven-year-old cannot read independently may be perfectly comprehensible—and enjoyable —when it is read aloud. Still another element of appropriateness is, in the opinion of many adults, the inclusion of material they feel is too sophisticated or too grim for young readers.

There is considerable dissension in the world of children's books today about the subject matter being handled in realistic books. A number of adults reject out of hand the idea that juvenile literature can—or should—cope with such things as menstruation (*The Long Secret* by Louise Fitzhugh), or a child murderer (*The Egypt Game* by Zilpha K. Snyder). These same adults would probably also reject children's books that deal with problems of divorce, alcoholism, and all social problems, whether they are brought about because of race, nationality, or religion.

Such adults think of themselves as protectors of youth. They are, in reality, merely protecting themselves from acknowledging the world around them as it exists today. They are also lacking in historical perspective, for many of the books they most cherish were highly controversial when they were first published. *The Adventures of Tom Sawyer* and *Adventures of Huckleberry Finn* were banned from libraries; even *Little Women* was considered unsuitable for children.

All of us have not only the right but the responsibility to reject any book which is badly written, but we should not confuse the author's ability to write with his or her choice of subject matter. It is how the subject is handled, not the subject matter *per se,* which is the crux of literary judgment. Thus, we should not ask, first, "What is the book about?" but rather, "How well written is the book?" Only after we have determined that a book meets literary standards do we then discuss it in terms of "values," for if there is one thing we do know, it is that all well-written books make some important statement about life.

The trouble is that the moment we begin to talk about a book's having values, we are accused of approving of didacticism. Perhaps we can put this controversy into perspective by analyzing the well-written book, which possesses values and makes important points pertinent to helping children grow.

A didactic book is one which is written to teach children a lesson, a type of book which has its roots in eighteenth- and nineteenth-century tracts. These tracts were written in story form with children as the central characters, and they were designed to teach the young to be pious, industrious, or honest.[1] One of the recurring religious lessons in these early tracts was that it was a great blessing to die young before one had time

[1] May Hill Arbuthnot and Zena Sutherland, *Children and Books,* 4th ed., Scott, Foresman, 1972

to sin, thus assuring oneself of a place in heaven. Over and over in the early books for children, one encounters painful death scenes followed by pious moralizing about the joys of dying. All character development and plot action were twisted in order that the author might make his —or more often, her—point.

As the harsh religiosity of the Puritans eased, it was followed by books which preached to the little daughter of the manor that it was wrong for her to play with the young son of the gardener, that she must learn her place and role in a rigidly constructed society. The action in such books was constantly interrupted by long lectures delivered in the most dogmatic tones.

For over two hundred years didacticism dominated juvenile literature. Then came *Hans Brinker, Heidi, The Adventures of Tom Sawyer,* and *Little Women,* bringing a fresh wind to the field. These remarkable books were thoroughly entertaining, moral but not moralizing, and so popular that their success would seem to have been sufficient to wipe out forever the juvenile tract type of story.

It didn't. Unhappily, didacticism in children's books seems to rise in one form or another in every generation. While much of the best modern realistic fiction includes some reflection of developmental values—those stages in the maturing child that are appropriate to his or her age—there are still books in which these values are stressed to the exclusion or detriment of literary quality. There is a vast difference between a story like *Peter and Veronica,* which is candid about the harm prejudice can do to a child, but which also has a sound structure, a good pace and style, and well-developed characters, and a didactic story written for the sole purpose of teaching a lesson about prejudice.

When reading such books, one can almost hear the author saying, "Pay attention to this point. Learn the lesson. This is important." Such books are dull books, and what devotees of didacticism have yet to learn is that an unread book does no good no matter how many lessons it is designed to teach.

In the area of race relations we have had some of our worst books in recent years, not because of faulty intentions, but because it takes a really good writer to depict the similarities while also showing the uniqueness of people. Being black in America is different from being a white person, not because of internal differences, but because of external pressures; the author who writes a book which states that race doesn't count is fooling himself or herself, not the readers. One hopes that race someday will not matter, but it does today and the author writes a dishonest book if he or she shows it otherwise.

Aside from an obvious difference in talent, the difference between a didactic author and one who writes good realistic books might be expressed in these terms: the didactic author writes glibly and dully about broad subjects (race relations, sibling rivalry), while the author of good realistic stories explores the growth and development of a few characters in a specific situation. The writer draws no great conclusions, but offers enough insight within the book so that the sensitive, thoughtful reader can draw his or her own conclusions.

In the attempt to portray the world as it is and thus make it recognizable to the young reader, the author of today's realistic stories must move into previously uncharted areas. This writer must listen to children when they do not know that they are being observed in order to capture the full flavor of the language they use, complete with its titillating use of profanity and its careful exploring of sex. He or she must see the ambivalent relationships among children and between children and parents. The author must absorb what the psychologists and child psychiatrists have to say. And finally, he or she must retain the ability to remember what it feels like to be a child. Remembering with as much honesty as an adult can muster, not yielding to the deceptive adult myth that childhood is the happiest time of our lives.

If an author does all this and has the ability to write, someday he or she will sit down and begin a story. The mysterious process of creative writing is at work—a process neither writer nor reader can describe or completely understand. All that a person is and has been, all that a person has seen and heard and read blend together, and out of this totality of one person's being comes a book which makes others feel more alive. Whether the book is happy or sad, whether it deals with people like ourselves or those differ-

ent from us, becomes irrelevant. We recognize a part of ourselves in the author's characters, and yet we also come to understand that no person is exactly like another. That is what books are all about: being able to see that "people" consists of a multitude of individuals, each one searching for his or her own particular way of life.

Examination of realistic stories shows that the authors pose a problem for the central character and allow the character to solve or resolve it in a thoroughly plausible way. There are no fairy godmothers in realistic stories; their place is taken by hard work and reasonable action on the part of the main characters.

Such stories can be as exciting as fairy tales and as full of humor, adventure, or romance as "nonrealistic" stories. The difference lies only in their plausibility and the absence of magical forces. The plot may turn simply upon a child's need to stoop down and tie his shoelace (see *Wait for William* by Marjorie Flack), or it may be as important as the search for a home by a boy so deprived that he lacks even a name of his own (see *The Loner* by Ester Wier). But whatever the action of the realistic story, it must carry the conviction of complete plausibility so that the reader can identify with the hero and believe in the hero's mistakes and triumphs as if they were one's own.

When books portray characters who have fears or problems similar to those of the reader, they can help point the way to adjustment or solution, and they ease the child reader's mind by showing that he or she is not alone in being afraid or resentful or discriminated against. Even a book that has good characterization and a fine writing style can, however, fail in convincing the reader if it offers an implausible solution that depends on contrivance or coincidence. An animal story like *Along Came a Dog* moves us to pity and affection because the dog is pictured without sentimentality or anthropomorphism; he inspires admiration because he is drawn with integrity.

The same kind of adherence to truth should be a part of all realistic fiction, whether the central characters are animals or people. In *Queenie Peavy*, the father would be less believable and the book weaker if he had come home a regenerated character; this is equally true of the adults in *Trouble in the Jungle*. The children in both stories learn to cope with their problems in an environment that remains constant.

A book like *Trouble in the Jungle* is important, too, because it shows characters who come from the lower class. Too many English books leave the impressions that all English people live in mansions with nannies and butlers. Like the varied people in the United States, the peoples of other lands are a diverse group. Stories set in other countries should reflect this diversity of cultures but should also reflect the similarities among all peoples. Children everywhere have the same needs and emotional responses. They need to love and be loved, to feel secure but experience change, to achieve and learn, to encounter beauty and knowledge. They all fear when they are threatened and pleased when they find approval.

By seeing both similarities and differences, children are laying the groundwork for a better understanding as adults. They can learn from books that the diversity of life is one of its miracles.

# Life in the United States

## from DID YOU CARRY THE FLAG TODAY, CHARLEY?

*Rebecca Caudill*

*The honor of carrying the flag of the Little School goes to the boy or girl who has been "specially good that day." Charley is sure from the beginning of his school career that he will carry the flag, but it is many a day before he can answer "Yes" when his family asks, "Did you carry the flag today, Charley?" In Charley, Rebecca Caudill has created one of the most delightful characters of recent times, a boy who will appeal to all age groups.*

### [The Thing]

Of all the rooms at Little School, the one Charley liked best was Mr. Sizemore's. Charley's group went there the last half hour of every Wednesday.

In Mr. Sizemore's room the children made things of clay. They colored with crayons. They painted pictures with their fingers on big sheets of paper. They built houses and fences and calf pens with blocks. One day a boy built a mountain with blocks. On the mountain top he put a little flag.

The blocks were in a small room just off Mr. Sizemore's classroom. On a low shelf in that room stood big jars of clay of many colors.

One Wednesday afternoon, Mr. Sizemore said, "Suppose we paint today."

All the boys and girls liked to paint with their fingers. Whenever they sat at the tables to paint, Mr. Sizemore placed a piece of drawing paper in front of each of them. Then he took a large jar from a shelf, and went around the room pouring a blob of starch on each piece of paper.

Charley was sitting at the end of his table. He laid both hands flat in the blob of starch and smeared, and smeared, around and around. "It feels slick, like ice," he said, and he smeared some more.

"Ready for the blue stuff, Mr. Sizemore," he called.

"Is everyone ready?" asked Mr. Sizemore.

Around the room Mr. Sizemore went from table to table, sprinkling a few drops of tempera paint on each paper. He sprinkled blue paint on some papers, red paint on some, and yellow paint on some.

"I want some of every color, Mr. Sizemore," said Charley.

Mr. Sizemore sprinkled blue and red and yellow on Charley's paper.

"You know what I'm painting?" Charley said to Vinnie who sat next to him.

"No. What?" asked Vinnie.

"A rainbow," said Charley.

"I saw a rainbow one time," said Vinnie.

"Where was it?" asked Charley.

"In the sky, of course," said Vinnie. "Where'd you think it would be?"

"I saw a rainbow on the ground one time," said Charley.

"Mr. Sizemore," said Vinnie, "you know what Charley said? He said he saw a rainbow on the ground one time. He didn't, did he?"

"I did, too," said Charley.

"Where was it, Charley?" asked Mr. Sizemore.

"In a puddle," said Charley. "At a filling station."

"You could have seen one there," said Mr. Sizemore. "In an oil puddle. It wouldn't have been exactly like the rainbow you see in the sky, but it could have had some of the same colors."

"See?" Charley said to Vinnie.

Charley smeared and smeared.

"Done, Mr. Sizemore," he called.

Mr. Sizemore wrote on one corner of Charley's paper in big black letters, CHARLEY.

"It's name is Rainbow in a Puddle at a Filling Station," said Charley.

Mr. Sizemore wrote on one edge of the paper, RAINBOW IN A PUDDLE AT A FILLING STATION. With two clothespins he fastened Charley's picture on a cord stretched along the wall. When it was dry he would put it in a big folder labeled CHARLEY with all the other pictures Charley had painted. On the last day of school, Charley could take the folder home and show his mother all his pictures.

"Now I want to make something out of clay," Charley said.

"All right," said Mr. Sizemore. "You may get some clay off the shelf."

Charley went to the block room and chose some pink clay. Back at the table he pinched off a piece of the clay and rolled it in his hands till it was as thin as a toothpick. He took another piece and rolled it as thin as a pencil, and pinched one end of each of the two together to make a straight line. He rolled another piece just a bit thicker, and pinched one end of it to the end of the second piece. To keep it in a straight line, he had

to move Vinnie's paper.

"Quit that, Charley!" scolded Vinnie.

Charley rolled another piece of clay, a little thicker still. To pinch the end of it to the third piece, he had to move Carl's paper.

"Mr. Sizemore, make Charley quit!" complained Carl.

"What's Charley doing?" asked Mr. Sizemore as he walked over to the table.

"He thinks the whole table belongs to him," said Carl and Vinnie.

"What are you making, Charley?" asked Mr. Sizemore.

"A Thing," said Charley as he rolled another piece.

"You come with me," Mr. Sizemore said. "Bring your clay."

Mr. Sizemore led the way to the room where the blocks were kept. The other children went on painting.

"Since the Thing is so long, why don't you work in here by yourself?" asked Mr. Sizemore. "We'll spread a newspaper on the floor, and you can make your Thing on the paper."

"It'll have to be a long newspaper, Mr. Sizemore," Charley told him. "Because this sure is a long Thing I'm making."

Together Mr. Sizemore and Charley spread newspaper on the floor from the middle of the room up to the door. Then Mr. Sizemore went back into the classroom where the other boys and girls were painting.

Alone in the room, Charley looked at the row of jars of clay standing on the shelf. He took down the jar containing the pink clay and went to work, rolling and rolling, each piece a little thicker than the one before, and pinching the ends together.

Soon Charley had used up all the pink clay there was, and the Thing was not finished. He took down the jar of black clay and went to work again, rolling and rolling, each piece thicker than the one before. He used all the black clay there was. Then he took down the jar of yellow clay and began rolling.

The Thing was finally as big around as Charley's arm. It had reached almost to the door when the bell rang for the end of the school day.

Charley heard the children in the next room putting away their papers. He heard them getting in line in the hall. He heard Miss Amburgey say, "If you're going to meet that three o'clock bus at Elkhorn, Mr. Sizemore, you'll have to leave right away. I'll take care of your group."

Charley heard more talking and more shuffling of feet down the hall. Then everything grew still.

It was the best day he'd had at Little School. Here he was, all alone, with nobody to tell him "Do this" and "Do that." And the Thing was growing longer and thicker. It was now as thick as a baseball bat, its front end yellow, its middle black, its tail pink.

Charley heard footsteps in Mr. Sizemore's room. For a few seconds everything was quiet. Charley listened. Then he heard the footsteps go away down the hall. He heard Mr. Webb's voice. "Charley! Charley Cornett!"

He'd have to hurry, thought Charley to himself.

He took one more piece of yellow clay, shaped it broad and flat, and fastened it to the piece as thick as a baseball bat. That was the Thing's head. The Thing's head lay across the doorsill into Mr. Sizemore's classroom.

Charley stood up and looked at the Thing. He laughed as he thought how scared Mr. Sizemore would be when he walked into his room the next morning and saw the Thing looking at him over the doorsill.

The Thing ought to have a tongue, decided Charley. He took from the jar of red clay one tiny piece. He shaped it thin and short and flat, and fastened it to the Thing's head. The tongue curved upward. Charley stood up to admire it.

He heard steps coming along the hall toward Mr. Sizemore's room. He looked around. There stood Miss Amburgey in the doorway.

"Charley," she scolded, "where have you been?"

"Here," said Charley.

"All the time since the bell rang?"

"Yes'm."

"Why didn't you come with the other children?"

"I wasn't with the other children," said Charley. "They were out here and I was in there."

"But you heard the bell, didn't you?"

"Yes'm."

"Don't you know that when the bell rings it says you must come?" asked Miss Amburgey.

"Yes'm."

"Why didn't you come then?"

"I hadn't finished."

"What hadn't you finished?"

"A Thing I was making."

"Whether you've finished or not, when the bell rings you're to put everything away and come at once. You can finish the next day. Do you know the bus left fifteen minutes ago?"

Charley's face grew serious.

"But I wasn't done," he said.

"What were you doing," asked Miss Amburgey, "that you couldn't leave till tomorrow?"

"I told you, Miss Amburgey, I was making a Thing."

"What kind of thing?"

"Miss Amburgey," said Charley, "shut your eyes and I'll take your hand and lead you to see it. But you won't tell Mr. Sizemore, will you?"

"Charley," said Miss Amburgey sternly, "you know very well—"

She stopped and looked down at Charley.

"All right," she said, and she shut her eyes. Charley took her hand and led her to the door of the room where the blocks stayed.

"Open!" said Charley.

Miss Amburgey opened her eyes.

"Charley! What a snake!" she gasped. "It looks like a real one, except, of course, it is an odd color."

"You know what kind of snake it is?" asked Charley. "It's a yellowblackpink snake and it bites. I'm going to leave it here to scare Mr. Sizemore in the morning."

"Well," said Miss Amburgey, "since you've taken such pains to make the Thing, I guess you may leave it. But come along now. Since the bus has left you, I'll have to take you home myself."

Charley followed her out of the schoolhouse and climbed into her jeep beside her.

What a place school was! thought Charley. He had made the Thing to scare Mr. Sizemore and now he was going to go jeeping home along the blacktop.

As Miss Amburgey turned the key and stepped on the gas pedal, Charley braced himself and ordered, "Now, Miss Amburgey, let 'er tear!"

"You really ought to have to walk home," said Miss Amburgey.

Charley was silent.

"I told Mr. Mullins to stop and tell your mother we couldn't find you, but that, as soon as we did, I'd bring you home. If she weren't worried, I'd let you out right here and start you walking."

They drove along in silence for another minute.

"Miss Amburgey," asked Charley, "how can snakes run so fast when they don't have legs?"

"They're made that way," said Miss Amburgey.

"A rope's made that way too," said Charley, "but it can't run."

They drove another minute in silence.

"You want me to name all the snakes I know?" asked Charley.

"Let's hear them," said Miss Amburgey.

"Rattlesnake. Copperhead snake. Black snake. Chicken snake. Blue racer snake. Garter snake. Water moccasin snake."

"There are books in the library that tell all about snakes," Miss Amburgey said. "And all kinds of snakes that you don't know about, like boa constrictors, and king cobras, and sidewinders. I suspect they even tell how a snake can run fast when it hasn't any legs."

"Sure enough, Miss Amburgey? Books tell you that?"

"They do," said Miss Amburgey. "That's what books are written for."

"Is that what books really do?" asked Charley. "Tell you about things?"

"Books tell you almost anything you will ever want to know," said Miss Amburgey. "Some things, of course, you'll have to find out for yourself."

"When do I go to the library again?" asked Charley.

"This is Wednesday," said Miss Amburgey. "You go to the library day after tomorrow. On Friday."

Miss Amburgey stopped the jeep in front of the Cornetts' mailbox. All the Cornetts were waiting anxiously.

"No need asking," said Claude as Charley climbed out. "You didn't carry the flag today, Charley."

"No," said Charley. "But I made a Thing. Boy, you ought to see it!"

## from EDDIE AND THE FIRE ENGINE
### Carolyn Haywood

*Once children discover Eddie, they will want to read all the* Eddie *books and the* Betsy *books too. No one writes about pleasant family life and the mild adventures of children 4 to 7 more happily than Carolyn Haywood.*

### Eddie Goes to Dancing School

One day when Eddie came home from school his mother said, "Eddie, Mrs. Wallace was here this afternoon."

"You mean Toothless's mother?" Eddie asked.

"Eddie, that's a dreadful way to speak of Anna Patricia," said Mrs. Wilson.

"Well, it's true!" said Eddie. "She hasn't had any front teeth for such a long time that I guess she's never going to get any. And anyway, Anna Patricia is a silly name. Why don't they call her Anna or Patricia? Or just Pat? If I had a name like that I'd make everybody call me Pat."

"I guess Anna Patricia likes to be called by her full name," said Eddie's mother.

"Well, in school we all call her Toothless," said Eddie.

"Mrs. Wallace is forming a dancing class," said his mother. "She came to invite you to join."

Eddie looked at his mother with a face filled with horror. "A dancing class!" he cried. "What would I want to do that for?"

"Now, Eddie," said Mrs. Wilson, "it will be very nice for you to learn to dance. Dancing school is fun."

"Fun for the girls maybe, but not for boys. Are Rudy and the twins going?"

"It's just for the children in your room in school," said his mother.

"That's tough," said Eddie. Then his face brightened. "I know, Mama! You tell her Papa can't afford to send me to dancing school."

"But it's free, Eddie," said his mother. "Only the girls have to pay."

"That's a mean trick," said Eddie. "And I bet I'll have to dance with Toothless. And she lisps!"

"Of course you'll dance with Anna Patricia," said Mrs. Wilson. "The dancing class is going to be held at her home."

Eddie sat down and held his head. "Ugh!" he said. "When?"

"Friday afternoon, at half past four," replied Mrs. Wilson.

"Friday afternoon!" wailed Eddie. "That's when we practice for the Saturday ball game."

"Eddie," said his mother, "you wouldn't want it to be on Saturday, would you?"

"Of course not," Eddie moaned. "But why does it have to be at all? Why do I have to learn to dance? Rudy and the twins don't have to learn to dance. Why do you pick on me?"

"Eddie, you will have a very nice time," said his mother. "Don't raise such a fuss. Go and see."

"If I don't like it can I stop?" Eddie asked.

"Yes, if you don't like it you can stop," his mother replied.

"O.K.!" said Eddie. "But don't tell Rudy and the twins that I have to go to dancing school."

"O.K.!" said Mrs. Wilson.

On Friday, when Eddie came home from school, his mother said, "Eddie, put on your best suit for dancing class."

"You mean my best Sunday suit?" said Eddie.

"Yes, dear," replied Mrs. Wilson.

"Golly! This dancing school business gets worse all the time," said Eddie.

Eddie washed his face and hands and soaked his hair with water. Then he took off his blue jeans and put on his best suit. "What will I do if I meet Rudy and the twins, all dressed up in my Sunday suit on Friday?" Eddie shrieked from his bedroom.

When he came downstairs his mother handed him a package. "These are your pumps, dear," she said.

"My what, Mama?" said Eddie, screwing up his nose.

"Your pumps," replied Mother, "your dancing pumps."

"What do I do with 'em?" Eddie asked.

"You wear them on your feet," said Mrs. Wilson.

"You mean I can't dance in my shoes?" Eddie cried.

"You would step on the little girls' feet, Eddie, in those clumsy shoes," said his mother.

"Serves 'em right!" said Eddie. "I'll walk all over Toothless's feet. Just let me at 'em."

"Eddie, do stop dawdling and get off," said his mother. "Have you money for bus fare? And don't forget to ask for a transfer."

Eddie pulled some change out of his pocket and looked at it. "O.K.," he said.

Just then he heard the twins coming in the front door. Eddie leaped like a deer and was out of the back door in a flash. He did not stop running until he reached his bus stop.

When the bus arrived Eddie stepped in. He knew the bus driver. He often rode with him. His name was Mike.

"Hi!" said Mike. "You look like a movie actor. All you need is a carnation in your buttonhole. Where you going, all dressed up?"

"Don't ask me," Eddie moaned. He flopped into the seat nearest the door.

"Come on, tell me. You'll feel better if you tell me," said Mike.

"You promise you won't tell anybody?" said Eddie.

"On my honor," said Mike.

Eddie got up and whispered in Mike's ear. "I'm going to dancing school. Isn't that horrible?"

"Oh! Cheer up!" said Mike. "I went to dancing school once. And look at me now."

"You did?" said Eddie, with a brighter face. He leaned over and whispered, "And did you have pumps?"

"Sure! Sure!" said Mike. "I was the best pumper in the crowd. You'll learn to pump. It's easy."

"No, Mike," said Eddie. "They're some kind of shoes. They're in this package."

"Oh, I thought that was your supper," said Mike. "Oh, sure! Pumps. Sure, you gotta have pumps."

"I have to change buses at Brewster Road," said Eddie.

"Righto!" said Mike. "Three more stops before we get there."

When the bus reached Brewster Road, Mike drew up to the curb. As Eddie stepped out he said, "So long, Mike."

"So long, pal!" said Mike. "I'll wait for you

to cross the street."

Eddie crossed the street in front of the bus. When he reached the opposite corner, he heard Mike calling, "Hey, Eddie!"

Eddie looked back and saw a package flying toward him. It landed at his feet. "Your pumps," Mike called out, as he started the bus.

Eddie picked up the parcel and put it under his arm. He stood on the corner and waited for the other bus. Across the street there was a used car lot. It belonged to Mr. Ward, a friend of Eddie's father. Eddie looked over the cars while he waited. Suddenly, he caught sight of something bright red. Eddie's heart began to beat faster. He ran across the street and over to the lot. Sure enough! It was just what he thought. There was the fire engine he had ridden on at the Fair. A man was lying under it, working with a hammer.

Eddie stooped down and looked under. There was Mr. Ward. "Hello, Mr. Ward!" said Eddie. "I rode on this fire engine once. It was super!"

"You did, Eddie?" said Mr. Ward, pushing himself out from between the wheels. "Well, how would you like to ride on it again?"

"Now?" said Eddie, his eyes shining.

"I want to see how it runs," said Mr. Ward. "I just put in a new part."

"Swell!" said Eddie, climbing right up into the front seat. "This is great!" he added, as the fire engine started.

Then Mr. Ward looked down on the ground. "Does that bundle belong to you?" he asked.

"Oh, golly! Yes," said Eddie. "Stop."

The fire engine stopped and Eddie got down. He ran back and picked up his package. Then he climbed up again. He put the package on the seat beside him and they started off. "I sure like this fire engine," he said.

"You going anywhere special?" Mr. Ward asked.

"Oh, not very special," Eddie replied.

"Got plenty of time?" said Mr. Ward.

"Oh sure!" said Eddie.

"Very well! She's going good. We'll take a spin around," said Mr. Ward.

Eddie held onto the seat and swung his legs. This was wonderful! "Can I pull the bell?" he asked.

"No, we can't ring the bell," said Mr. Ward.

"The fire company would object. Might look like a false alarm."

Mr. Ward drove Eddie way out into the country before he said, "I guess I had better get back. Where can I drop you?"

Eddie thought of dancing school for the first time since he had been on the bus. "Oh! I have to go to Beech Tree Road," he said.

"Beech Tree Road?" said Mr. Ward. "What's going on there? By the way, you look all slicked up."

"Yeah," said Eddie. "I forgot all about it. I'm going to dancing school."

"You don't say!" said Mr. Ward. "What have you got in the package?"

Eddie looked sheepish. "Aw, pumps," he said.

"Pumps!" said Mr. Ward. "What the heck are pumps?"

"I don't know," said Eddie. "Something you wear on your feet."

"Well, suppose I take you right over to the place," said Mr. Ward.

"Oh, that would be great!" said Eddie.

Mrs. Wallace was standing at the front door when Eddie drove up in the fire engine. As he jumped down she said, "Why, Eddie! You're very late. I've been wondering why you didn't get here."

"I guess I am a little late," said Eddie. "Mr. Ward gave me a lift."

Eddie could hear the boys and girls laughing. They were all in the dining room.

"It's too bad you missed the dancing class," said Mrs. Wallace. "The children are having their ice cream now."

Eddie's face shone. "Ice cream?" he said. "Gee, that's great!"

"Hello, Eddie!" the children called out when Eddie walked into the dining room.

"Hello!" said Eddie, sitting down at the table.

Mrs. Wallace handed him a large plate of ice cream and Eddie lost no time in eating it. Just as he swallowed the last spoonful, the doorbell rang. Mrs. Wallace went to the front door and opened it. Eddie heard Mr. Ward's voice say, "Is Eddie Wilson still here?"

"Yes, he is," said Mrs. Wallace.

"Well, here are his pumps," said Mr. Ward.

The children had caught a glimpse of the fire engine through the open door. They rushed to the door to look at it. "Oh, here's the fire engine that was at the Fair!" they cried.

"I had a ride on it this afternoon," said Eddie.

"Oh, can we have a ride?" the children shouted. "Can we have a ride?"

"You have on your best clothes," said Mrs. Wallace. "You can't go riding on a fire engine in your best clothes, in your dancing clothes."

"We won't hurt them," the children cried.

"I didn't hurt mine, did I?" said Eddie.

"I'll take them all home," said Mr. Ward.

The children rushed to the fire engine, the little girls in their ruffled dresses and the boys in their Sunday suits.

"Now, everybody sit still," said Mr. Ward. "You have to keep your clothes clean."

Just as everyone was settled Eddie jumped down. "Wait a minute," he said.

He ran into the house and came back with his package. He looked up at Mr. Ward and grinned. "Forgot my pumps," he said.

Mr. Ward dropped the children off, one by one. Eddie was the last. When he drove up to the house, the twins were looking out of the window. When they saw Eddie, they rushed to the front door.

"What's the idea," cried Joe, "riding on the fire engine?"

"Where have you been?" cried Frank.

"I've been to dancing school," said Eddie.

"Dancing school!" cried the twins in chorus.

"Gee, it's swell!" said Eddie, as he waved good-by to Mr. Ward.

When dinner was almost over, the doorbell rang. Mr. Wilson went to the door and opened it and everyone around the dining-room table heard Mr. Ward's voice say, "Here are Eddie's pumps. He left them on the fire engine."

When Mr. Wilson came back to the dining room, he was carrying a package. He put it on the window sill. "Here are your pumps, Eddie," he said.

"Pumps!" cried Rudy and the twins together. "What are pumps?"

"I don't know," said Eddie. "I haven't had time to look at 'em. But dancing school was swell, Mama. Dancing school was swell!"

## from ELLEN TEBBITS

*Beverly Cleary*

*Beverly Cleary's first book,* Henry Huggins, *was an instantaneous success. There are now several other books about Henry, all of them equally funny and popular. Ellen in* Ellen Tebbits *is the feminine counterpart of Henry. This book about Ellen's adventures is just as hilarious as the other books and is especially popular with girls. As American as supermarkets and completely true to child nature, Mrs. Cleary's stories are humorous commentaries on modern life.*

### Ellen Rides Again

The arrival of spring meant different things to different people. To Mrs. Tebbits it meant spring cleaning. To Mrs. Allen it meant planting seeds and setting out new flowers. To Ellen and Austine spring meant something much more important. It meant no more winter underwear.

The two girls were walking home from the library one warm spring afternoon. They felt light and carefree in their summer underwear.

It was a wonderful feeling. It made them want to do something exciting.

At the library Austine had been lucky enough to find two horse books. "I wish I could ride a horse sometime," she said.

"Haven't you ever ridden a horse?" asked Ellen.

"No. Have you?" Austine sounded impressed.

"Oh, yes," said Ellen casually. "Several times."

It was true. She had ridden several times. If she had ridden twice she would have said a couple of times. Three was several times, so she had told the truth.

"Where? What was it like? Tell me about it," begged Austine.

"Oh, different places." That was also true. She had ridden at the beach. Her father had rented a horse for an hour and had let Ellen ride behind him with her arms around his waist. The horse's back had been slippery and she had bounced harder than was comfortable, but she had managed to hang on.

And she had ridden at Uncle Fred's farm. Uncle Fred had lifted her up onto the back of his old plow horse, Lady, and led her twice around the barnyard. Lady didn't bounce her at all.

And then there was that other time when her father had paid a dime so she could ride a pony around in a circle inside a fence. It hadn't been very exciting. The pony seemed tired, but Ellen had pretended it was galloping madly. Yes, it all added up to several times.

"Why haven't you told me you could ride?" Austine demanded. "What kind of saddle do you use?" Austine knew all about different kinds of saddles, because she read so many horse books.

"Oh, any kind," said Ellen, who did not know one saddle from another. "Once I rode bareback." That was true, because Lady had no saddle.

"Golly," said Austine. "Bareback!"

Ellen was beginning to feel uncomfortable. She had not meant to mislead Austine. She really did not know how it all started.

"Oh, Ellen, you have all the luck," exclaimed Austine. "Imagine being able to ride horseback. And even bareback, too."

"Oh, it's nothing," said Ellen, wishing Austine would forget the whole thing.

But the next day at school Austine did not forget about Ellen's horseback riding. She told Linda and Amelia about it. They told Barbara and George. Barbara and George told other boys and girls. Each time the story was told, it grew.

Even Otis was impressed and he was a difficult boy to impress. When the girls started home after school, he was waiting on the edge of the school grounds. He had a piece of chalk and was busy changing a sign from "Bicycle riding forbidden at all times" to "Bicycle riding bidden at all times." Otis crossed out "for" every time he had a chance, but the rain always washed away the chalk marks.

"Hello, Ellen," he said, walking along beside her in his cowboy boots. Since Christmas Otis had worn boots instead of Oxfords. He was not wearing spurs today. Miss Joyce had asked him not to wear them to school.

Ellen and Austine ignored him.

Otis kicked at the grass along the edge of the sidewalk. "Say, Ellen, is it true you ride a lot? Even bareback?"

"Of course it's true," said Austine.

"I wish people would stop talking about it," said Ellen crossly. "What's so wonderful about riding a horse, for goodness' sake?"

"Gee whiz," said Otis enviously. "Some people have all the luck."

The girls continued to ignore him. He followed them for a while, kicking at the grass, and then turned down another street.

When the girls came to Austine's house, they found Mrs. Allen on her knees beside a flat box of pansy plants. She was taking them out of the box and setting them into a border along the driveway.

"Hello there," she said. "Since tomorrow is Memorial Day and there isn't any school, how would you like to go on a picnic?"

Ellen did not say anything. She thought Mrs. Allen meant her, too, but she was not sure. She hoped so. That was the trouble with the word *you*. Sometimes it meant one person and sometimes it meant a lot of people. Maybe Mrs. Allen was talking to Austine and not to both of them.

Mrs. Allen said, "Ellen, I have already asked your mother and she says you may go."

"Thank you. I'd love to go." Maybe a picnic would make Austine forget about horses. And if they went on a picnic, Austine couldn't come to

Ellen's house to play and perhaps say something about horseback riding in front of Mrs. Tebbits. Ellen was worried about what her mother would say if she found out how Ellen had exaggerated.

"Where are we going?" asked Austine.

"We're going to drive out toward Mount Hood. The rhododendrons are beginning to bloom, and I thought it would be nice to see them blooming in the woods."

The next morning at ten o'clock Ellen ran down Tillamook Street and around the corner to Austine's house. For her share of the picnic she carried eight deviled eggs carefully packed in a cardboard box. Mr. Allen was backing out the car. Mrs. Allen sat in the front seat and Austine in the back.

"Hop in," said Mr. Allen. "Bruce isn't going with us. The boy scouts are marching in a parade."

Ellen was glad she and Austine could each sit by a window. That made it easier to look for white horses and to play the alphabet game. The first one to see a white horse got to make a wish. Ellen was going to wish Austine would forget about her horseback riding.

The girls always played the alphabet game when they rode in a car. Each watched the signs on her own side of the road for the letters of the alphabet. Each letter had to be found in order or it did not count. The k in a Sky Chief Gasoline sign could not be used unless a j had already been seen. The girl who had a Burma Shave sign on her side of the road at the right time was lucky because it contained in the right order both u and v, two hard letters to find. The game went quickly at first, because there were lots of signs, but as they neared the mountains the signs became more scarce.

Ellen was looking for a Texaco filling station for an x when Austine shouted, "Look, a white horse! I've got dibs on it." She shut her eyes to wish.

Ellen was sorry she had not seen the horse first. She needed a wish. Finally both girls were down to z. By then the car was winding along the mountain roads.

"Z!" shouted Ellen. "I win. There was a sign by that bridge that said 'Zigzag River.'"

"That's all right," said Austine generously. "I'm going to get my wish."

It was a few more miles along the highway that Austine saw the horses. "Look, Daddy! Horses for rent, fifty cents an hour! Please stop," she begged.

Mr. Allen drew over to the side of the road near some horses in a makeshift corral. Austine scrambled out of the car and ran to the horses, while the others followed.

"Daddy, please let us go horseback riding. All my life I've wanted to ride a horse. Please, Daddy. You and Mother could go on and look at the rhododendrons and come back for us."

"Would it be safe for the girls to ride alone?" Mrs. Allen asked the man with the horses.

"Please, Mother," begged Austine. "Make my wish come true."

"Sure. Kids do it all the time," answered the man. "They ride up that dirt road as far as the old sawmill and turn around and come back. The horses know the way. Takes about half an hour. Road runs right along the highway."

"They won't be thrown from the horses?" asked Mrs. Allen.

"From these horses?" said the man. "No, lady. These horses worked at a riding academy for years."

"You're sure they're gentle?"

"Yes, ma'am. Gentle as kittens."

"The girls could hang onto the saddle horns," suggested Mr. Allen.

"Oh, Daddy, you aren't supposed to hang onto the saddle horns. Only tenderfoots, I mean tenderfeet, do that. We'll be safe, because Ellen has ridden a lot and I know all about riding from books."

Ellen wished Austine would keep still. She was not at all sure she wanted to ride, especially without a grownup along.

"I suppose it would be safe to let the girls ride for half an hour," said Mrs. Allen. "We could walk along the dirt road and look at the rhododendrons while they rode. That way they would be within shouting distance."

"All right, girls, which horses do you want to ride?" asked Mr. Allen, taking a handful of change out of his pocket.

Ellen thought she had better act brave even if she didn't feel that way. "The spotted horse is nice, but I think I'd rather have the brown one over in the corner of the pen." She thought the brown horse looked gentle.

"I'll take the pinto on this side of the corral," said Austine, glancing at Ellen.

Oh dear, thought Ellen. I've said the wrong thing. I wish I'd read some horse books.

Austine watched eagerly and Ellen watched uneasily while the man saddled and bridled the two horses. "O.K., kids," he said.

Ellen walked over to the brown horse and patted him gingerly. He seemed awfully big when she stood beside him. But he looked down at her with large gentle eyes, and Ellen felt braver.

The man held out his hand, palm up.

Oh, I wonder if he wants me to give him some money, thought Ellen. It must be that, but I'm sure Austine's father paid him. Or maybe he wants to shake hands. A sort of farewell.

"Come on, girlie. Step up," said the man. "Don't be scared. Brownie isn't going to hurt you."

My goodness, thought Ellen. I guess he expects me to step in his hand. I suppose it's all right. His hand is dirty anyway.

She put her foot into his hand and he boosted her onto the horse. The ground seemed a long way below her. And Ellen had forgotten how wide a horse was. The man shortened her stirrups and then helped Austine onto the pinto. Ellen patted Brownie on the neck. She was anxious to have him like her. If only she had a lump of sugar in her pocket.

"Look," cried Austine. "I'm really on a horse."

Ellen knew she was expected to take the lead. "Giddap," she said uncertainly. Brownie did not move.

The man gave each horse a light slap on the rump. They walked out of the corral and ambled down the dirt road as if they were used to going that way. Austine's mother and father followed on foot.

Ellen carefully held one rein in each hand. As she looked at the ground so far below, she hoped Brownie wouldn't decide to run.

"I'm going to call my horse Old Paint like in the song," said Austine, who never missed the Montana Wranglers on the radio and knew all about cowboy songs. "I wish I'd worn my cowboy neckerchief."

"Yes," said Ellen briefly. She didn't feel like making conversation.

When Austine's horse moved in front, Ellen took hold of the saddle horn. It wasn't so much that she was scared, she told herself. She just didn't want to take unnecessary chances.

"I wish we'd worn our pedal pushers," said Austine. "It's sort of hard to feel like a cowgirl in a dress."

"I wish we had, too."

Maybe this wasn't going to be so bad after all. The horses seemed to know the way, and Ellen found the rocking motion and the squeak of the saddle rather pleasant. She was even able to look around at the trees and enjoy the woodsy smell.

Then when they had gone around a bend in the road, Brownie decided it was time to go back to the corral. He turned around and started walking in the direction from which they had come.

"Hey," said Ellen anxiously. She pulled on the right rein, but Brownie kept on going. "Stop!" she ordered, more loudly this time.

"What are you going that way for?" asked Austine, turning in her saddle.

"Because the horse wants to," said Ellen crossly.

"Well, turn him around."

"I can't," said Ellen. "He won't steer."

Austine turned Old Paint and drew up beside Ellen. "Don't you know you're supposed to hold both reins in one hand?" Austine was scornful.

Ellen didn't know. "I just held them this way to try to turn him," she said. She took them in her left hand. They were so long she wound them around her hand.

Austine leaned over and took hold of Brownie's bridle with one hand. "Come on, Old Paint," she said, and turned her horse forward again. Brownie followed.

"Thanks," said Ellen. "My, you're brave."

"Oh, that's nothing," said Austine modestly. "You don't steer a horse," she added gently. "You guide him."

"Oh . . . I forgot." Ellen wondered how she would ever explain her ignorance to Austine. What would her best friend think when she found out how Ellen had misled her?

The horses plodded on down the woodsy road. Through the trees the girls could see the highway and hear cars passing. Austine's mother and father appeared around the bend, and Ellen began to feel brave again.

"Let's gallop," suggested Austine.

Ellen's legs were beginning to ache. "How do you make them gallop?"

"Dig your heels in," said Austine.

"Oh, I wouldn't want to hurt the horse," said Ellen.

"You won't hurt him, silly. Cowboys wear spurs, don't they?"

Ellen timidly prodded Brownie with her heels. Brownie ambled on.

Austine dug in her heels. Old Paint began to trot. At first Austine bounced, but soon she rode smoothly. Then her horse began to gallop.

When Old Paint galloped, Brownie began to trot. Ellen began to bounce. She hung onto the saddle horn as hard as she could. Still she bounced. Slap-slap-slap. Her bare legs began to hurt from rubbing against the leather of the saddle flap. Slap-slap-slap. Goodness, I sound awful, she thought. I hope Austine doesn't hear me slapping this way.

Austine's horse, after galloping a few yards, slowed down to a walk. "Whoa, Old Paint," cried Austine anyway, and pulled on the reins. Old Paint stopped and Austine panted a minute.

"I did it, Ellen!" she called. "It was just a few steps, but I really, truly galloped. I hung on with my knees and galloped just like in the movies."

"Wh-wh-oa-oa!" Ellen's voice was jarred out between bounces. Brownie trotted on. Slap-slap-slap.

Austine began to laugh. "I can see trees between you and the saddle every time you go up. Oh, Ellen, you look so funny!"

Slap-slap-slap. Ellen didn't think she could stand much more bouncing. It was worse than being spanked.

"Ellen Tebbits! I don't think you know a thing about horseback riding."

"Wh-wh-oa-oa!" When Brownie reached Old Paint he stopped. After Ellen got her breath, she gasped, "I do, too. It's just that the other horses I rode were tamer."

The horses walked on until the road curved down to the edge of a stream.

"Oh, look. There's a bridge," exclaimed Ellen, looking up.

"I guess the highway crosses to the other side of the stream," said Austine. "I wonder if the poor horses are thirsty."

There was no doubt about Brownie's wanting a drink. He left the road and picked his way down the rocky bank to the water.

"Poor horsie, you were thirsty," said Ellen, patting his neck.

But Brownie did not stop at the edge of the stream. He waded out into it.

"Whoa," yelled Ellen, above the rush of the water. "Austine, help!"

Brownie waded on.

"Austine! What'll I do? He's going swimming!"

"Here, Brownie! Here, Brownie!" called Austine from the bank. Her voice sounded faint across the surging water.

When Brownie had picked his way around the boulders to the middle of the stream, he stopped and looked around.

"Look, he's in over his knees!" Ellen looked down at the swirling water. "Giddap, Brownie!"

"Kick him in the ribs," yelled Austine from across the stream.

"I don't want to hurt him," called Ellen, but she did kick him gently. Brownie did not appear to notice.

"Slap him on the behind with the ends of the reins," directed Austine from the bank.

Ellen slapped. Brownie turned his head and looked at her reproachfully.

By this time some hikers had stopped on the bridge. Looking down at Ellen, they laughed and pointed. Ellen wished they would go away.

Brownie lowered his head to drink. Because Ellen had the reins wound around her hand, she could not let go. As she was pulled forward, the saddle horn poked her in the stomach.

"Oof," she said. Hanging over the horse's neck, she clung to his mane with one hand while she unwound her other hand.

Brownie looked at her with water dripping from his chin. Ellen thought it was his chin. Maybe on a horse it was called something else.

Austine broke a branch from a huckleberry bush that grew out of an old log at the edge of the stream. She waved it toward Brownie. "Here, horsie. Nice horsie."

Brownie glanced at her with mild interest.

"Oh, go on, Brownie," said Ellen in disgust. She kicked him hard this time. Brownie looked at her sadly and swished his tail.

A couple of cars stopped on the bridge and the occupants looked down at Ellen and laughed. "Yippie!" yelled one of the hikers and everyone laughed. "Ride 'em, cowboy!"

"Do something, Austine," Ellen called across the water. "Our half hour must be nearly up."

"Maybe I could ride back and get the man who owns the horses," Austine yelled back.

"No, Austine. Don't leave me here alone," begged Ellen. "Maybe I could get off and wade. I don't think the water would come up to my shoulders."

"The current's too strong," called Austine. "And anyway, we're supposed to bring the horses back. You can't go off and leave Brownie."

Austine was right. Ellen knew that she couldn't leave Brownie. She might lose him, and the man would probably make her pay for him. At least, she thought he would. She had never heard of anyone losing a horse, so she wasn't sure. "I can't stay here forever," she called.

"Mother and Daddy should catch up with us in a minute," Austine called. "They'll know what to do."

That was just what was worrying Ellen. She didn't want the Allens to see her in such a predicament. What would they think after Austine had told them she had ridden before? Maybe they had wandered off to look at rhododendrons and were lost in the woods by now.

Still Brownie did not move. Ellen wondered what it would be like to try to sleep on a horse. Again she wished she had brought some lumps of sugar. She could have eaten them herself when she became hungry.

One of the hikers climbed down the bank to the edge of the water. "Need some help, little girl?" he called.

"Oh yes, please," answered Ellen gratefully.

Jumping from boulder to boulder, the man drew near her, but he could not get close enough to reach Brownie's bridle. "Throw me the reins, little girl," he directed.

Ellen threw them as hard as she could. They fell into the water, but the man grabbed them as the current carried them toward him.

"Come on, old fellow," he said, pulling at the reins. Meekly Brownie began to pick his way around the boulders toward the bank.

"Oh, thank you," said Ellen, when they reached dry ground. "I guess I would have had to stay out there all day if you hadn't come for me."

"That's all right," said the man. "The trouble is, you let the horse know you were afraid of him. Let the old nag know you're boss and you won't have any trouble."

"Thank you, I'll try," said Ellen, taking a firm grip on the reins. "Good-by."

Just then Austine's mother and father appeared around the bend in the road. "Enjoying your ride, girls?" asked Mr. Allen.

"Oh, yes," said Austine. "We just stopped to give the horses a drink."

"It's time to turn back now," said Mrs. Allen.

"All right, Mother," said Austine.

The girls headed their horses toward the corral. Ellen was so embarrassed she didn't know quite what to say to Austine. What would Austine think of her after this? What would she tell the kids at school?

Finally, when Austine's mother and father were a safe distance behind, Ellen said in a low voice, "I guess I didn't know quite as much about horseback riding as I thought I did."

"Your horse was just hard to manage, that's all," said Austine generously.

"Austine?" said Ellen timidly.

"What?"

"You won't tell anybody, will you? You won't tell that Otis Spofford what happened, will you?"

Austine smiled at her. "Of course I won't tell. We're best friends, aren't we? It'll be a secret like the underwear. Giddap, Old Paint."

"Thank you, Austine," said Ellen gratefully. "You're a wonderful friend. And you know what? I'm going to look for some horse books the next time we go to the library."

The horses, knowing they were headed toward hay, showed more spirit. Ellen held the reins firmly. That Brownie was going to know who was boss. She began to enjoy herself. She pretended she was returning to a ranch after a hard day riding the range.

"I didn't know horses had such long hair," she remarked.

"It's their winter coat," explained Austine. "They'll shed it this summer."

Ellen laughed. "Just like winter underwear," she said.

### from THE SECRET LANGUAGE

*Ursula Nordstrom*

*A boarding school story by an eminent editor of children's books has become a perennial favorite. The situation is firmly set on the first page, involving the listener's or reader's attention immediately, and the plight of the homesick Victoria engages the sympathy of any child who has felt that emotion.*

### New Girl

Sooner or later everyone has to go away from home for the first time. Sometimes it happens when a person is young. Sometimes it happens when a person is old. But sooner or later it does happen to everyone. It happened to Victoria North when she was eight.

The other children in the Coburn Home School bus shouted at each other, and pushed each other, and ran up and down the aisle. But Victoria sat alone looking out the window.

The bus turned down a country road, and suddenly one of the boys cried, "There's the old dump!"

"Coburn School! Coburn Home School!" the bus driver called. "All out!"

A pale, bony girl stood waiting for the bus. "Victoria North!" she yelled. "Victoria North Victoria North Victoria Victoria North North! I'm looking for a new girl named Victoria North! Any new kids on this bus?" She looked at Victoria. "That you? Well, I'm your roommate. My name is Ann Spear. Come on and I'll show you our room." She walked toward a large brick building, and Victoria followed her. Yellow leaves lay across the graveled path, and in the distance the hills were blue with mist.

"This is the girls' dormitory," Ann said as she opened the front door. "It's called Wingate Hall. The boys live in Shippen Hall. Do you like boys?"

Victoria looked at Ann. She was too homesick to speak.

"Well, I don't," Ann said flatly, and started up a flight of stairs. "But we just see them in classes. We have separate dining rooms. I've been here for two years and I'm supposed to tell you about everything. Anyhow, the boys at this school are all awful, if you ask me."

At the head of the stairs Ann turned and led Victoria down a long hall. "This is our corridor," Ann said. "Our housemother is Miss Mossman, and she is very very very strict." She opened a door. "Here's our room."

Victoria's trunk, which someone had unlocked for her, stood next to one of the beds.

"You better unpack now," Ann said. "I'm going back down to see what other old girls came back. See you later."

Victoria hung her hat and coat in the closet and slowly unpacked her trunk. On every article of clothing her mother had sewn a name-tape, in accordance with the instructions in the Coburn Home School catalogue. At home Victoria had liked the way her name looked woven in red on the white tape. But now, in this new place, the name-tapes made even her most familiar possessions seem strange to her.

When she hung up her flannel bathrobe she found a note from her mother pinned to it. In the note her mother asked her to remember to wear clean underwear every day and to say her prayers every night. And then her mother said Christmas vacation would come soon. The note made Victoria more homesick than she had been before. After she put on her new dark blue dress she stood looking out the window, trying not to cry.

Ann came back in a little while. She looked at Victoria critically. "What's the matter with your *collar?*" she said impatiently. "My goodness, it's all twisted. Here, I'll fix it. My goodness, you can't even dress yourself yet!" Ann frowned as she pulled Victoria's collar straight.

There was a heavy knock at the door and a tall woman came in. "How do you do, Victoria?" she said. "I am your housemother, Miss Mossman." Miss Mossman was an ugly woman with straight black hair and little black eyes. "I'm glad to have you on my corridor," she said. "Ann will explain our rules and regulations to you, and I am sure you will find them easy to obey. I will see you at my table at supper."

Miss Mossman left, and Victoria sat down on her bed.

"We are not allowed to sit on the beds," Ann said sharply. "Sit on your chair. My goodness!"

Victoria went over to the window and carefully wrapped the cord of the shade around her thumb. She was trying not to cry in front of Ann.

In a few minutes a gong sounded, and Ann jumped up. "Come on," she said. "Supper! Hurry up!"

In the dining room Victoria followed Ann to one of the long tables and sat down next to her.

"Oh, you don't sit here, dopey," Ann said. "You're supposed to sit at Miss Mossman's table. She told you!"

Victoria stumbled to her feet. She didn't know which table was Miss Mossman's, and in the blur of strange faces she couldn't find the housemother. All the other children were at their places. At the sound of a bell all heads were lowered and grace was said aloud. "For what we are about to receive may the good Lord make us truly thankful." The words echoed around Victoria as she stood alone in the middle of the dining room. When grace was over, Victoria saw Miss Mossman beckoning to her.

"Girls," Miss Mossman said, "this is Victoria North, a new student this year. Victoria, there's your place, between Sue Burton and Eleanor Mindendorfer." She briefly introduced the other girls. Several of them looked up and said "Hi" as Victoria slid into her seat and stared at the plate of food in front of her. Sue Burton, who was fat and had red hair, said, "What's your name again?"

But Victoria didn't hear her.

"Please pass the bread," said Eleanor Mindendorfer loudly.

"How come you came back, Martha?" Sue said to a dark girl with bangs who sat opposite Victoria. "I thought you weren't coming back this year."

The dark girl scowled. "I'm probably only going to stay until Thanksgiving," she said.

"But I thought you weren't coming back at all this year," Sue insisted. "You did say you were going to live home. I remember. But I was sure you'd have to come back anyhow, though."

"M.Y.O.D.O.B. And that means Mind Your Own Dumb Old Business," Martha said clearly.

"Martha!" Miss Mossman said. "There is no need to be rude to Sue. Why, Victoria, you're not eating your supper. Here at Coburn School we eat what is placed in front of us, Victoria. Come, dear."

Victoria picked up her fork and tried to swallow some food.

"My little brother is coming to this school next year, Miss Mossman," Eleanor Mindendorfer announced.

"That's splendid, Eleanor. What is your brother's name?"

"His name is Sidney, and he's my little brother, and——"

"Oh, ick-en-spick," Martha said.

"What?" Eleanor looked at her. "What did

you say, Martha?"

"I said ick-en-spick," Martha repeated.

"Oh, Martha, you're so funny!" Eleanor began to giggle.

But Sue was indignant. "What kind of talk is that?" she asked. "It's crazy."

"Well, it isn't crazy."

"It certainly sounds crazy, if you ask me," Sue said.

"I didn't ask you, and it isn't crazy. Neither is ankendosh. Neither is leebossa."

"Martha Sherman, what are you talking about?" Sue was puzzled.

"I'm talking about a secret language I just happen to know."

"What do you mean? What secret language?"

"It's just my secret language, that's all," Martha said.

"What was that funny word you said?"

"Ick-en-spick."

"What does it mean? And what did that other funny word you said mean?"

"Wouldn't you like to know?" said Martha, and she made a hideous face at Sue.

"Now, Martha," said Miss Mossman from the head of the table. "You must stop being rude. Stop it at once."

"She's a big fat dope," Martha said.

"Martha! You must behave yourself, or I will have to ask you to leave the table. Eleanor, I know you must be looking forward to having your little brother here next year."

"Yes, I am, Miss Mossman. He is a year and two months younger than I am, and his name is Sidney, and——"

"Well, what's so wonderful about that?" Martha asked.

"Well! I guess I can talk about my brother if I want to!"

"Oh, all right. Tell some more. Go ahead." Martha shrugged. "His name is Sidney, and he's coming to this school next year."

"Yes, he is," Eleanor said.

"Poor old Sidney," said Martha heavily.

Everyone turned to look at the housemother. Two bright red spots appeared on Miss Mossman's cheeks, and her right eye began to twitch. She said sternly, "Martha, you may go to your room at once. Although you have been back at Coburn less than one day, I will have to give you

a demerit. Now go to your room immediately. I'll talk to you later."

Martha folded her napkin, pushed back her chair, and left the dining room slowly. She was still scowling.

"She's an awful girl," Sue said to the rest of the table. "She's the worst girl in this whole school."

"That will be enough, Susan," Miss Mossman said severely.

"I think she is the worst girl here," Sue whispered to Victoria. "Some people in this school think she is so wonderful, and she thinks she is too, but I think she is awful."

Victoria didn't answer.

"Victoria, you haven't touched your food," Miss Mossman said. "Now finish your supper at once."

Victoria stared at her plate.

"Victoria, did you hear me? Eat your supper at once. The rest of us are waiting for you."

Tears suddenly spilled over Victoria's cheeks. They ran down her face and fell on her clasped hands. She lowered her head. Everyone at the table looked at her.

"Victoria," Miss Mossman said sharply. "Look at me, Victoria."

Slowly Victoria turned toward the head of the table. With her eyes shut and her mouth twisted, she wept soundlessly. Several of the girls began to giggle.

Miss Mossman saw that Victoria was indeed unable to eat. "You may clear," she said to the maid.

After supper the children sat on folding chairs in the drawing room for an hour of singing.

"Turn, please, to page eighty-seven. 'A Capital Ship,'" Miss Mossman said as Miss Douglass sat down at the piano.

"A Capital Ship" was a gay song, and everyone loved it.

Next Miss Mossman announced, "Page forty-one. 'Now the Day Is Over.'"

To Victoria, sitting in the front row next to Ann, the slow music and the words—"Now the day is over. Night is drawing nigh. Shadows of the evening steal across the sky"—seemed the saddest she had ever heard. In the middle of the song she started again to cry.

"Oh, stop it!" Ann whispered. "Stop crying!" And she shook the songbook in exasperation.

The next song was "The Harp That Once Through Tara's Halls." It, too, was a sad song, and Victoria continued to cry. Finally Miss Mossman motioned to Ann to take Victoria out. Behind her disgusted and resentful roommate, Victoria stumbled slowly from the room.

Upstairs Ann stood with her hands on her hips and glared at Victoria. "You're an awful crybaby," Ann said. She picked up her towel and washcloth and flounced out of the room.

Victoria pulled off her dress and her shoes and got into bed in her underwear and her socks. She was shivering, though it was not a cold night. She did not even think of saying her prayers.

Ann came back. "Aren't you going to get washed?" she asked.

Victoria was crying and she couldn't answer.

"Are you just going to leave your dress on the floor?"

There was no answer.

"You'll get a demerit," Ann said spitefully. "Don't say I didn't tell you. Miss Mossman may even give you two demerits. I don't care, though."

The singing was over. Girls came upstairs noisily to get ready for bed. They shouted to each other in the corridor, banged doors, ran back and forth to the bathrooms. Suddenly there was a loud blast on a whistle, and then there was silence. Ann snapped out the light and got into bed.

Victoria tried to be quiet. But she was crying so hard that she had to gasp when she tried to catch her breath. Every time Victoria did that, Ann turned over noisily in bed and heaved an irritated sigh. Finally Ann sat up and whispered crossly, "Oh, stop *bawling!*" Then she flopped back down in her bed and sighed loudly again. After a while Ann went to sleep.

This was the first night Victoria had ever spent away from her mother, and it was worse than the worst nightmare she had ever had. Her mother couldn't have known it would be like this! Gasping and choking, Victoria rolled over on her back, stared up into the dark, and wept. The tears rolled down her cheeks into her ears, and she turned over on her side and wiped her face and her ears on the stiff sheet. Today had

been as awful as anything could be, and she had lived through it. She had lived through today, but what about tomorrow? What would she do tomorrow?

Finally, sobbing and gasping, she grew tired. After a long time, she turned over once more and put her head under the pillow. And then at last she fell asleep too.

### The Secret Language

"Wake up!" Ann cried. She shook Victoria's shoulder. "The whistle just blew. Hurry up for inspection!"

Victoria pulled on her bathrobe and hurried into the hall behind her roommate. At the end of the corridor the housemother stood waiting to see that everyone was out of bed. When all the girls were lined up two by two in front of their doors, Miss Mossman called, "Dismissed!" and blew the whistle again.

"Breakfast in half an hour!" Ann yelled, and ran down the hall to the bathroom. Victoria followed her slowly.

"My, your eyes are all red," Sue Burton remarked, looking at Victoria in the mirror over the washbasins. "I guess you cry an awful lot. Don't you like it here?"

Victoria shook her head and bent over a basin. Sue began to talk across her to Ann. "Miss Mossman is just as mean as ever, with all those whistles and morning inspection and everything," Sue said.

"Yes." Ann sighed. "That standing in the hall gives me a pain. She must have been a jail-mother before, not a housemother."

Victoria finished brushing her teeth, and as she straightened up, Sue and Ann both looked at her and giggled. Several other girls did too. Suddenly Martha, the girl who had been dismissed from the table the night before, came in, dragging a towel. "What's so funny?" she asked.

"I guess that new girl's homesick," Sue said. "She was crying during singing last night, and Ann had to take her out, and her face looks funny."

"Oh, ankendosh," Martha said. "How old are you, anyhow?" she said to Victoria.

Martha sounded friendly, but Victoria hurried past her without speaking and went back to her room to get dressed.

The day wore on. Victoria went to the school hall with Ann and the others, and met the teachers. No class work was done, but books were distributed and desks were assigned.

After the last class was dismissed, Victoria walked out of the school hall behind Ann, who was whispering and giggling with Eleanor Mindendorfer. As they went out the door Ann turned to Victoria and said crossly, "Oh, hang off me, will you? You've been hanging on me all day! Just please hang off me!" Then Ann walked away with Eleanor and some of the other old girls.

Victoria stood by the school hall and looked around her. She didn't know where to go or what to do. In a few minutes Miss Blanchard, the arithmetic teacher, came out the door. "Hello," she said. "You're Victoria North, aren't you? I think Victoria is a pretty name."

Victoria looked up at her, but could think of nothing to say.

"Why don't you go down to the swings for a while? That will be fun. In a few days you will know more of the other children and you'll be happier, Victoria. Really you will be. I know it is hard at first."

Victoria was silent, and finally Miss Blanchard turned and walked away. Victoria picked up some gravel and looked at it carefully, then let it fall slowly out of her hand. She examined the bark on a tree for a few minutes. Then she walked back to her room.

The first ten days at Coburn Home School were all lonely ones for Victoria. She didn't know anyone, and no one seemed to want to know her. Her mother wrote her every day, but the letters only made Victoria more homesick.

Then one afternoon, late in September, Victoria was alone down by the swings. Martha wandered by and saw her. "Hello," she said. She sat on the end of a slide. "That's some dumb table we're at," she added. "I wish I could be at Miss Blanchard's table."

Victoria was afraid to say something Martha might think was silly. So she said nothing. But she smiled.

"I hate this old school," Martha said.

"Oh, so do I!" Victoria said.

"I hate it," Martha repeated. "And it's worse than it was last year. But I only came back for a little while, anyhow. Pretty soon I'm going to live home and go to day school. Are you going home for Thanksgiving?"

Victoria shook her head. "I guess not."

"Well, I am, and I just bet I won't have to come back here. I'm going to tell my mother and father about this school. I'll tell them about the food. I'll tell them they give us horrible, disgusting, dirty, gluey purple stuff to eat and they call it oatmeal."

Victoria was startled but fascinated.

"Does your family live in New York?" Martha asked.

"My mother does, most of the time."

"What do you mean, most of the time?"

"Well, she has to go away once in a while. She works. That's way I can't go home for Thanksgiving."

"Where's she going?"

"Chicago."

"My father's an importer. What's yours?"

Victoria could hardly remember him. "I haven't any," she said.

"You just have a mother?"

"Yes."

"Oh. Lots of the kids here just have a mother, too. Or just a father. What's your favorite subject?"

"Reading. What's yours?"

"Arithmetic."

"Arithmetic!" Victoria was amazed. "Oh, I hate arithmetic!"

"Well, I hate reading," Martha said reasonably. "What are you going to be when you grow up?"

"I don't know yet. What are you?"

"Oh, I guess I'll be an inventor, or maybe a singer. Oh, I certainly hate this school," Martha repeated. "I hate all the buildings and all the rooms, and the food, and I even hate the swings, and I hate this dumb slide." She kicked the slide as she spoke.

"It's an awful old school," Victoria agreed. And she gave the slide a little kick too.

Suddenly Martha stood up and marched around one of the swings with her stomach stuck out in what seemed to Victoria an extremely amusing way. Then Martha sang in a piercing voice:

"Two more months to vacation.
Then I go to the station.
Back to civilization.
Back to Mother and Home."

"Did you make that up?" Victoria asked, impressed.

"Me? No! You never heard that before? I guess that's just because you never went to boarding school before. I can make up stuff, though, if I want to."

Victoria thought Martha was wonderful. They climbed up on a seesaw, and seesawed up and down in the darkening light. Then they went to the dormitory to get ready for dinner.

At the table that night Martha looked across at Victoria and said, "Hey, Vick, maybe we'll have ice cream tonight. That would be leebossa, wouldn't it?"

The other girls looked at Martha in surprise, and then at Victoria.

"Wouldn't it? Wouldn't it be leebossa?" Martha repeated, staring at Victoria.

"Yes, I guess so," Victoria said finally.

"After singing I'll tell you all about my secret language," Martha said. "But you'll have to promise you'll never tell anyone else!"

"I promise," said Victoria faintly.

The other girls looked at Victoria with new interest. Martha had never been so friendly to anyone else.

That night when singing was over, Martha waited in the hall for Victoria and they walked upstairs together.

"Ick-en-spick is for when something is silly," Martha explained. "Or like when someone is trying to get in good with a teacher, and is trying to be very sweet. You know. Goody-goody stuff is ick-en-spick."

Victoria nodded.

"Ankendosh," Martha went on, "is for something mean or disgusting. Ann Spear is usually very ankendosh."

"She certainly is," Victoria said.

"Now, leebossa is for when you like something. When something is just lovely or when something works out just right, it is leebossa. For anything especially nice you can say leelee-leeleebossa. But that's only for something really wonderful. Understand?"

"Yes, thank you for telling me. Are there any other words?"

"No. But maybe we can make up some more," Martha said.

"That would be leebossa," Victoria said, and Martha grinned at her.

From then on Martha and Victoria were friends. Whenever possible they did their homework with each other. They walked to and from the school hall together every day. And they sat next to each other at singing every night.

Being friends with Martha was wonderful, and Victoria was happier than she had been. But she was still afraid of Miss Mossman, and she still missed her mother, and she still counted the days to Christmas vacation.

## *from* JUSTIN MORGAN HAD A HORSE

*Marguerite Henry*

*No one has written more thrilling tales of different breeds of horses than has Mrs. Henry. King of the Wind, the story of the ancestor of the famous race horse, Man o' War, won the Newbery Medal in 1949. The episodes given here come from a book about the ancestor of a special breed of horses, the sturdy and willing Morgan horse. Little Bub, the horse hero, is given to the schoolmaster Justin Morgan in payment of a debt. Young Joel Goss, who has been apprenticed to Miller Chase and who is also a friend of the schoolmaster, loves the colt from the time he first sets eyes on him and undertakes to gentle him. The excerpts presented herein are taken from chapters seven and eight of the revised edition of Justin Morgan Had a Horse.*

### *Little Bub Is Rented Out*

Never was a creature more willing to be gentled. After but two lessons, he wore a halter as if it were a part of him. Like his forelock. Or his tail. Fastening two ropes to the halter, Joel drove him around and around in a circle, teaching him to "git up" and to "whoa."

Next Joel slipped a bit in the colt's mouth. At first Bub's ears went back in displeasure. He did not mind rope or leather things, but iron felt cold and hard to his tongue. One night Joel warmed the bit in his hands and coated it with maple syrup. From then on Little Bub accepted it each time, actually reaching out for it, jaws open wide.

Whenever the colt learned a new lesson, Joel told him what a fine, smart fellow he was. "Soon you'll be *big* for your size!" he would say. "And then you've got to be so smart and willing that even an ornery man won't have reason to whop ye. I couldn't abide that!" he added in dread.

Some nights Joel fastened a lantern to an old two-wheeled cart borrowed from Mister Jenks. Then, filling the cart with stones for weight, he drove Bub over the rolling hills. He practiced pulling him up short. He practiced walking him, trotting him, stopping and backing him.

The moon waned and became full again. By now Joel was galloping Little Bub, galloping him bareback across the fields. And Bub wanted to go! It was as if the clean, cold air felt good in his lungs, as if he liked the night and the wind and the boy.

One evening when Master Morgan remained late at school, Joel burst in on him so full of laughter he could scarcely talk. The other apprentice boys had gone long ago, and Joel's laughter rang out so heartily in the empty room that the schoolmaster joined in without knowing why.

Between spasms the boy managed to gasp, "You should've seed that little hound-dog run!"

"What little hound-dog?"

"Why, Mister Jenks's yellow one," giggled Joel, bursting into fresh laughter. "He come a-tearin' out the house, yammering at Little Bub, trying to nip his legs. Oh, ho, ho, ho!"

From *Justin Morgan Had a Horse* by Marguerite Henry. Copyright 1954 by Rand McNally & Co. Reprinted by permission

"What did Bub do?"

"What did he *do?*" shrieked Joel. "Why, he sprung forward like a cat outen a bag. And that idiot hound was too addled to go home. He streaked down the road with Bub after him."

Joel had to wipe away his tears before he could go on. "By and by," he chuckled, "the hound got so beat out I took pity on him and reined in."

Master Morgan's eyes twinkled. "I reckon Farmer Beane was right," he said. "Seems as if Little Bub and dogs just don't cotton to each other."

When Mister Goss first heard that Joel was training the schoolmaster's colt, he was furious. But later, when neighbors marveled at the boy's skill, he boasted and bragged about it: "All that boy knows about horses he got from me!"

The truth of the matter was that in watching his father train a colt Joel had learned what not to do, as well as what to do. While his father could break and train in a matter of hours, his horses often seemed broken in spirit, too. The boy was determined that this should not happen to his colt. And it had not. Little Bub's eyes were still dancy. He still tossed his mane and nosed the sky. He still had a frisky look about him. No, he had lost none of his spirit.

Even in the rough winds of winter, the colt's schooling went right on, night after night. And about the time when Joel began to think Little Bub might be his forever, a stranger came knocking at the schoolhouse door.

School was in full session. A dozen apprentice boys were bent over their copybooks. As if on one stem, a dozen heads turned around.

Master Morgan pushed his spectacles up on his forehead, brushed the chalk off his vest, and went to the door. "Come in, sir," he said.

A tall, gaunt man entered and sat down on the splint-bottomed chair which the schoolmaster offered. "Good evening," he said in a voice that rolled out strong. "I'm Ezra Fisk, a new settler, and word has come to my ear that you have a horse to rent."

Eleven pens stopped scratching and eleven pairs of eyes looked up with interest. Joel's pen skated wildly across the page as if his arm had been jolted out of its socket.

"You will continue with your work," the schoolmaster nodded to the boys. He could not bring himself to answer the man's question at once.

Mister Fisk filled in the silence that followed. "I've been watching a lad ride a smallish horse in the moonlight," he said in his trumpet of a voice, "and by inquiring at the inn, I understand the horse belongs to you, sir."

Justin Morgan made a steeple out of his fingers. His Yes was spoken through tight lips.

"You see," the newcomer explained, "I have a piece of wooded land along the White River. And Robert Evans, my hired hand, will need a horse to help clear it. This fellow, Evans, is a brawny man, and I figure he and a horse with some get-up-and-git could clear the land in a year's time."

Master Morgan hesitated a long moment before he spoke. "You would like to buy the horse, sir?"

"Tsk, tsk, Morgan. No, indeed! Who would buy such a *little* animal? As I said, I merely wish to rent him."

The schoolmaster stood up and looked questioningly at Joel. Ezra Fisk followed his glance. "That the boy who's been riding the colt?"

"Aye," Master Morgan said very softly. "And for his sake I am loathe to part with the animal."

The visitor now lowered his voice, too. "I understand," he said, leaning one arm on the desk, "that you are paid sometimes in Indian corn and sometimes the full sum of two dollars per week. Yet even the latter amount," he added knowingly, "covers no such extras as horses and harpsichords."

Joel sat forward, holding his breath, trying to hear the next words.

"But I, my good man," and now the voice waxed strong again, "stand ready to pay fifteen dollars a year, and the animal's keep, of course."

He said no more.

The noise of the scratching pens faded away. A stray flutter of smoke went up the chimney with a faint hiss. Joel was afraid he was going to cry. He wanted to run to Little Bub and hide him away somewhere deep in the woods. Perhaps this was all a bad dream. It *must* be a bad dream! Why else would his head drop forward in a nod, answering Yes to the schoolmaster's unspoken question?

The next afternoon Joel was setting a log in the sawmill when he heard the creaking of a wagon wheel and the cloppety-clop of hoofs coming down the road. This in itself was nothing to make him stop work, but from the uneven beat of the hoofs he could tell that the animals were not traveling in a team. And then, without looking up, he knew. He knew that the lighter hoofbeats were those of Little Bub. He started the saw, and then he turned and faced the road.

It *was* Little Bub, all right, not five rods away. He was tied to the back of a wagon pulled by a team of oxen. His reddish coat glinted in the sunlight, and he held his head high, as if he found nothing at all disgraceful in being tied to an oxcart.

The blood hammered in Joel's head. He might have called out, "Hi, Little Bub!" and felt the hot pride of having him nicker in reply. Instead, he kept hearing the schoolmaster's words: "I've got to pay off my debts before I die. Will you gentle the colt for me, lad?"

Well, Bub had been gentled, all right. Anyone could see that. With a heavy heart, Joel watched the procession as it passed him by, and then clattered over the log bridge and climbed up and up the steep hill. At last it disappeared over the brow, and nothing was left of it. Nothing, but a wisp of dust.

### The Pulling Bee

In the weeks that followed, it was hard for Joel to pay attention to his work. He kept seeing Little Bub in the back of his mind, seeing him go lickety-split after the hound-dog or just capering for the fun of it. And in the sound of the millwheel he kept hearing the high, bugling neigh. And often, when no one was looking, he would sniff his jacket to smell the very essence of Little Bub!

In whatever Joel was doing—gathering stones for fences, wielding a mattock on stumps in the highway, working inside or outside—the little horse nudged into his thoughts.

One day, when Joel was up inside the chimney sweeping away the soot, his ears picked out three names from the talk going on in the room below: Ezra Fisk, Robert Evans, Justin Morgan. Precariously his fingers clung to the bricks like a bird. If he made the least noise or if his bare feet slid into view, the talk might stop or take a new tack altogether. His toes found a narrow ledge of brick and caught a foothold. His whole body tensed with listening.

"Yup," a voice was saying, "the schoolmaster's little horse is turning out to be a crack puller. Already he's made a nice clearing of about five acres."

Another voice said, "So the little horse can pull, eh?"

"Yup," the first voice replied. "Evans brags that the critter can jerk a log right out of its bark!"

A loud guffaw greeted the remark.

In the dark of the chimney Joel smiled in pride. But what if—the smile faded, and worry crept in—what if Evans was working Little Bub too hard? What if he became swaybacked and old before his time?

Joel had to know. Quickly he slid down the chimney and dropped to the hearth. But he was too late. All he saw was the whisk of a coattail and the door to the public room swinging shut, and at the same time Mistress Chase coming at him with a broken lock to be mended.

As the days went by, Joel heard more and more about Little Bub's labors, and his worry sharpened. At last he talked things over with Miller Chase.

"Why, work don't hurt horses," Mister Chase said reassuringly. "It's t'other way around. Idleness is what really hurts 'em. Their muscles git soft and their lungs git so small they can't even run without wheezing."

And so Joel's mind was eased.

By the time spring came on, Joel and the miller were the best of friends. In the late afternoon while Mistress Chase napped, he often waved Joel away with a smile. "Be off with you now. Have a mite of fun," he would say.

Joel took delight in these free afternoon hours. At this time of day Chase's Mill was the liveliest spot on the White River. Farmers would congregate to chat as they waited for the big saw to cut their logs. And often they tested the strength of their horses with a log-pulling contest. Surely, Joel thought, Little Bub must show up some day.

It was on a late afternoon in April that his hopes were realized. The millstream had grown swollen with spring rains, and Mister Chase had taken on a helper to keep the mill sawing logs both night and day.

On this afternoon, when the yard was crowded with farmers, the miller called to Joel. "See the man studying that-there pine log? That's Nathan Nye. And if Nathan Nye is about, acting mighty important and bossy, you can be expecting most anything to happen. He was ever good at fixing pulling contests."

Joel watched the jerky-legged man hop from one group to another, like a puppet on a string.

"If I was a boy, now, with no chores to do," the miller smiled, "it seems like I'd skedaddle right out there and be in the center of things."

In no time at all Joel was helping Mister Nye wrap tug chains about the huge pine log. A big dappled mare stood waiting to have the chains hooked to her harness.

The mare's owner, Abel Hooper from Buttonwood Flats, was too busy bragging to be of any help. "A mighty lucky thing I'm first," he was saying. "Big Lucy and me'll pull this-here piece o' kindling onto the logway in one pull. Then you can all hyper on home afore lantern time."

Abel Hooper had to eat his words. Big Lucy tried hard. She dug her forefeet into the earth and tugged and tugged, but the log barely trembled. Even when he poked her with the prodding stick, she only looked around as if to tell him it was useless.

One after another the work horses had their turn. Yet no matter how whips cracked or masters yelled, the log seemed rooted to earth.

Nathan Nye made a megaphone of his hands. "Folks!" he shouted. "Guess it's just too hefty for a horse. You men with oxen can have a try now."

Just then a bearded farmer came riding up on a chunky young stallion. Joel's heart missed a beat. Could this be Little Bub? This unkempt, mud-coated horse? Why, small as he was, he looked to be a six- or even a seven-year-old! Then Joel grinned as the little stallion let out a high bugle and a rumbling snort.

"Wait!" called the big man astride the little horse. "Here's a critter wants to try."

A smile, half scorn, half amusement, crossed Nathan Nye's face. "Evans," he said, "ye're crazy as if ye'd burnt yer shirt. Look at Big Lucy. She's still blowin' from the try. And Biggle's Belgian— his muscles are still a-hitchin' and a-twitchin'.

Even Wiggins' beast failed. Can't none of 'em budge that log."

"None exceptin' my one-horse team!" crowed Evans.

Fear caught at Joel as a silence fell upon the crowd.

And then came the rain of words, mingled with laughter.

*That* little sample of a horse!"

"Why, his tail is long as a kite's!"

"Yeah, he's liable to get all tangled up and break a leg."

"Morgan's horse," Evans said slowly, "ain't exactly what you'd call a drafter, but whatever he's hitched to generally has to come."

Joel heard the sharp voice of Mistress Chase calling: "Boy! You come here!"

"Oh, rats!" he muttered under his breath. On the way to the inn he stopped long enough to put his cheek against Little Bub's. "I'll be back," he whispered. "I'll be right back."

Mistress Chase met him just inside the door with a kettle of hasty pudding. "Hang the kettle over the fire," she commanded, "and stir and stir until I tell you to quit."

He hung the kettle on the crane and set to work. "*Hasty* pudding!" Joel cried to himself. "It beats me how it got its name! Nothing quick about this!" Suddenly he heard the clump of boots and looked around to see Evans, followed by a little company of men, strut into the inn.

"Madam Innkeeper!" Evans called. "I'm wagering a barrel o' cider that my horse can move the pine log. But now, pour me a mugful. I'm dying of thirst."

Joel was stirring so vigorously he almost upset the pudding. Mistress Chase let out a shriek. "Boy! Mind what you're doing! Hasty pudding's not meant to feed the fire!"

For once he paid no heed. He tore across the room and grabbed Mister Evans by the sleeve. "Sir!" he cried. "Little Bub's been working hard all day. Please don't ask him to pull that big log."

Evans gulped his drink. "Go 'way," he snapped in annoyance. "When I want advice, I'll not ask it of a whipper-snapper. I know that horse!" He stomped out of doors, the others joking and laughing behind him.

While Joel stirred the pudding, he kept look-ing out the window. He could see Little Bub nibbling all the fresh green shoots within his range. And he could see the men sizing him up, feeling of his legs, then making their wagers.

One by one, the stars dusted the sky. Nathan Nye brought out a lantern so that Evans could see to fasten the tug chains to the log.

"I just *got* to go out there now!" Joel pleaded. "Ma'am, if you please, could I?"

Mistress Chase nodded. "You're stirring so strong that hasty pudding's heaving like a sea. Go on! Git out, afore ye upset it."

"Oh, thanks, ma'am," Joel murmured as he bolted for the door, vaulted over a barrel of cider, and ran to the mill, where Evans was stepping off ten rods.

"Aye, fellers!" he was saying. "Bub can do it—in two pulls." He turned around, almost stumbling over the boy. "A nettle hain't half as pesky as you," he growled. "Out of my way or I'll clout you!"

Nathan Nye shouted to Evans. "Mebbe you'd oughter listen to the lad. Want to give up afore you start?"

"No such-a-thing! Why, I'm actually ashamed to ask Morgan's horse to pull a splinter like this. Now, if you'll find me three stout men to sit astride the log, why, then I'll ask him."

Joel ran to Little Bub. "Oh, my poor little feller," he choked. "None of the big critters could do it, and now with three men besides!—Oh, Bub, Bub . . ."

Laughter was ringing up and down the valley. "Ho-ho-ho—that pint-sized cob to pull such a big log! Ho-ho . . ."

Nathan Nye had no trouble at all in finding three brawny volunteers. As the men straddled the log, they joked and laughed and poked one another in the ribs.

"Look to your feet, men!" warned Evans. "This horse means business. Something's got to give."

Nye held the lantern aloft. It lighted the huddle of faces. They were tense with excitement. Some of the men were placing last-minute bets. Some were chewing madly on wisps of hay. Others twirled their hats and wrung them nervously. Joel felt as if he were going to be sick.

Evans repeated his warning. "Look to your feet, men!"

Someone tittered.

Then the silence exploded as Evans roared, "Git up!"

The sharp word of command galvanized the little horse into action. His muscles swelled and grew firm. He backed ever so slightly. He lowered his head, doubling down into the harness. He lunged, half falling to his knees, straining forward, throwing his whole weight into the collar.

A hush closed around the gathering. It hung heavy and ominous. Suddenly the very earth seemed to shake. The chains were groaning, the log itself trembling as if it had come alive. It began to skid. It was moving! The stout man aboard laughed hysterically, then sobered, trying to balance himself, clutching onto the others. The log kept on moving. It was halfway to the mill!

The horse's breath whistled in his lungs. His nostrils flared red in exertion. Sweat broke out on his body, lathering at the collar and traces. Joel, too, was drenched in sweat. He was struggling, straining, panting as if he were yoked alongside Little Bub.

Now the terrible silence again as the horse stood to catch his wind. There was no sound at all from the crowd. Overhead a robin, trying to get settled for the night, chirped insistently.

Now Evans commanded again. And again the horse backed slightly, then snatched the log into motion. Again the log was sliding, sliding, sliding. This time it did not stop until it reached the sawmill!

Still none of the onlookers made a sound. The three men astride were as silent as the log they sat upon. Only the horse's breathing pierced the quiet.

Then as if a dike had opened, there was a torrent of noise. Everyone began shouting at once. "Hooray for Little Bub! Hooray for Evans and Justin Morgan! Hooray for the big-little horse!"

Joel rushed over and threw his arms around Bub's neck. His whole body ached, as if he had moved the log himself. "It's over! It's over! You did it, Bub! You did it!" he kept repeating, sobbing a little from exhaustion and relief.

The horse lipped Joel's cheek and neck. He almost tried to say, "It's all right, boy; don't be taking it so hard." He was winded and leg-weary, but it was good to be near the boy again. It was good.

He nickered softly.

*from* **THE MIDDLE MOFFAT**

*Eleanor Estes*

*Jane had never meant to introduce herself to anyone as the "mysterious middle Moffat"; it had just slipped out when she first met old Mr. Buckle, and he had solemnly agreed that anything in the middle was indeed mysterious. The game between the small girl and the very old man develops into a real friendship in this chapter. The ingenuous tone of the writing, the warmth and simplicity of the relationships, and Estes' ability to identify with the child's point of view have made the Moffats minor classics.*

### An Afternoon with the Oldest Inhabitant

Jane took the short cut across the huge, empty lot to the library. She was in a hurry because she had just gotten the idea that it would be fine to read every book in the library. Of course not all at once; just one at a time. She arrived there hot and panting. The best way to go about reading every book in the library, she thought, was to go to a certain section, take down the first book on the first shelf, get it stamped, take it home, read it, bring it back, and take out the very next book. In this way she would not miss one single book. She tiptoed over to one of the sections, took down the first book without looking to see what it was, and had it stamped at the desk. As she was about to leave she noticed Mr. Buckle in an armchair by the window.

"What book did you take, mysterious middle Moffat?" he asked her.

Jane showed him her book. She saw for the first time it was called "The Story of Lumber."

"H-m-m-m, 'The Story of Lumber' . . . very mystifying," he said, and he put his forefinger on the side of his nose like Hawkshaw, the detective.

Jane played her part, too; then she backed out on tiptoes, waving a reassuring good-by to Miss Lamb, the librarian, who watched her with a truly mystified expression.

Jane read "The Story of Lumber" as rapidly as possible. It was not very interesting. But if she were going to read every book in the library, she would have to take the bad along with the good. She brought "The Story of Lumber" back the next day and took the next book. The oldest inhabitant was sitting in the same place by the window. His soft white hair shone in the sunshine.

Again Jane showed him the new book she had borrowed and saw with a trace of dismay

"An Afternoon With the Oldest Inhabitant." From *The Middle Moffat,* copyright, 1942, 1970, by Eleanor Estes. Reprinted by permission of Harcourt Brace Jovanovich, Inc. and The Bodley Head

that this one was called "The Story of Cotton."

" 'The Story of Cotton' . . . more mystifying than ever," whispered Mr. Buckle.

Jane played Hawkshaw a trifle absent-mindedly. She sat down on the granite steps outside the library and read for a while. This book also was far from interesting. Evidently she had chosen the wrong section to begin on. Where were all the books like "Heidi"? Still if she read the bad ones first, the good ones would be like dessert.

When she brought back "The Story of Cotton" and saw that the next book was "The Story of Sugar," she decided to try something different. She still planned to read every book in the library but she would take the best ones first. Then, by the time she finished all the good ones, she would be such a good reader she could just tear through things like "The Story of Sugar" in a few minutes.

She chose a bound volume of *St. Nicholas* magazine. This was full of good things. As she left the library she met Mr. Buckle coming up the granite steps. He was supporting himself by means of the brass railing.

"Hello, Mr. Buckle," said Jane. "I am going to read every book in the library," she added, feeling exuberant again now that she had something good.

Mr. Buckle nodded his head up and down, beaming. He was out of breath and he was hanging onto the brass railing.

"Is it cheating," Jane demanded, "if I don't read every word in this big book? It's not really a book. It's a lot of magazines."

"Did you say to yourself, I am going to read every book and every magazine?"

"No . . . every book."

"Well, then, it's not cheating."

"But maybe a whole lot of magazines together makes a book."

"It is very mystifying," agreed Mr. Buckle, "but I think once a magazine, always a magazine."

Jane ran home the long way so she could race the trolley car to Ashbellows Place. She was a good runner and almost always beat the trolley to her corner. Running around to the back yard and climbing onto the high board fence, she peered through the apple trees. She hoped that

Nancy Stokes would have come home from her piano lesson by now. But Nancy was nowhere in sight. She must have had to go somewhere with her mother.

So Jane went around front and sat down on the little square porch to read her *St. Nicholas*. The first story began, "In the middle of the night . . ."

In the middle of the night . . . It reminded Jane of her own position in the Moffat family. It was now definitely established that she was the middle Moffat. Mama introduced her as "Jane, the middle Moffat" not only to the Gillespie girls but also to the new curate of the church for whom she was making vestments and cassocks.

Of course the only person to whom she had made that mistake about being the mysterious middle Moffat was Mr. Buckle. And, as it turned out, this had not proved to be such a grave error anyway. In fact, he seemed to enjoy the game of Hawkshaw, the detective, very much. And if he liked it, and he was the oldest inhabitant and the most important person in the town, it certainly had not done any harm, this calling herself the mysterious middle Moffat. It might even, by keeping him in such good spirits, help him live to be one hundred.

Jane was doing all she could about that. For instance, she sometimes followed him from a distance to see that he crossed the street safely and that no dogs jumped out at him unexpectedly and made him lose his balance. Whenever she heard of a new family moving to Cranbury, she checked up immediately to find out how old the oldest person in that family was. When she found that there was no one ninety-nine or over, she quickly told Mr. Buckle so he would know he was still the oldest inhabitant in town.

Janey tried to be near by whenever the oldest inhabitant was shuffling past the firehouse, because the Cranbury fire alarm was the loudest in the whole state. What a blast when it went off! And it was so sudden! There was no warning at all. Jane always said politely when she joined him here, "Don't we have the loudest fire alarm here in Cranbury?" This was just to remind him to be on guard and steel himself in case it blew.

Yes, she was doing everything she could to help him reach one hundred. Just this afternoon running home from the library, she had kicked

aside a fallen branch, a broken bottle, an orange peel, so the way would be clear when Mr. Buckle came home. She even occasionally carried around an old umbrella so that he would not get caught in the rain. Of course she could not spend her whole time this way, but she did as much as she could.

Once she had seen Mr. Buckle go out and she had followed at a distance with the Moffats' big old umbrella. She really thought it might rain because the sparrows were chattering in the big elm tree in front of the house. Somebody told her once this was a sure sign of rain. When she reached the Green, there he was blowing cotton to the birds. Puffs of cotton on the grass looked like dandelions gone to seed.

Just as Janey arrived, the sky actually, all of a sudden, did turn black all over. The rain came marching up the street. She reached the oldest inhabitant and opened the umbrella over his head just as the big drops started to fall on his side of the street.

"This is very mysterious," he said, "your being on hand with the umbrella." And they had walked home together in the rain.

Now, while Jane was rocking back and forth in the green rocker, and reading her *St. Nicholas* magazine, a fog began to roll in from the Sound. Jane looked up from her book. A fog! And it seemed to be growing thicker and thicker. She put her book down and watched it roll in. Soon she could hardly see the lot across the street. This was going to be a really heavy fog, perhaps as good a fog as they had in London.

She ran down the steps and up and down the Moffats' long lawn trying to separate the fog, as though it were a gauzy curtain. Then she could see what was going on in the world. As she reached the sidewalk, she slipped on some damp autumn leaves and ran into Miss Buckle, the daughter of the oldest inhabitant, who caught her in her arms.

"Goodness, Jane. What a start you gave me. I'm afraid I'm going to be late to P'fessor Fairweather's Browning Society. . . . Good-by, child."

And she set Jane firmly on the walk. Jane watched the oldest inhabitant's daughter disappear in the fog. P'fessor Fairweather . . . Jane liked the way she said that. She never said *Pro-*

fessor Fairweather. Just P'fessor Fairweather, very fast. That was nice, the way she talked. Everything she said sounded so important.

Well! Miss Buckle was going to the Browning Society, leaving the oldest inhabitant all alone. Jane hoped he had gotten home from the library in the fog safely. Supposing some witch who was exactly one hundred was jealous of him and had snatched him down under the squash vines that grew so thickly all over one corner of the lot. That's the way it might be if this were a fairy tale and not Ashbellows Place. However, fairy tale or not, she decided to spend the afternoon with the oldest inhabitant so he would not be tempted to go out in the fog.

Once the oldest inhabitant had said to her: "Come in and see my chicken-bone furniture some day."

Today would be a good chance to do this. Of course she would not say she had come to call on him to keep him from getting lost in the fog. But she would say she had come to see his chicken-bone furniture. Besides she really owed him a visit since he had come to her organ recital.

Jane ran into her house to get her knitting, for she intended to stay with the oldest inhabitant until the fog lifted. Then she marched up the street and onto Mr. Buckle's porch. She walked right in. She tiptoed through the little parlor with the black horse-hair chairs and sofa, and she went into the sitting-room, where the oldest inhabitant was bent over a big book. He balanced it halfway on his knees and halfway on the little oval-shaped table beside him.

"Hello, Mr. Buckle," said Jane politely.

"Hello, Jane," said the oldest inhabitant.

"I've come to see the bones," said Jane.

"Ah, yes," said the oldest inhabitant. "The chicken-bone furniture . . ."

Jane glanced around the room. She had never been in this house before. On one wall was a picture of the ruins of Pompeii, and on another was a picture of a lot of sheep huddled together in a blizzard. There was a picture exactly like this in Nancy's house. Jane preferred colored pictures such as the one the Moffats had in their green and white parlor of a milkmaid leading home the cows.

The oldest inhabitant showed her a little glass cabinet in a corner of the room. This held the furniture he had carved out of chicken bones. Jane stood with her hands behind her back so Mr. Buckle would not think she would touch things and break them. She looked at the chicken-bone furniture in amazement. What lovely little things! Tiny tables, chairs, cupboards, beds, a sofa, a bookcase with what looked like real little books, and even the tiniest of clocks!

"Oh, how nice!" exclaimed Jane.

"Yes . . . those are all carved out of chicken bones. Every piece. I did them all by hand."

"My," said Jane. "What a lot of chickens you must have eaten!"

"Yes . . ." said the oldest inhabitant. "They are very famous. Peabody Museum is asking for them all the time. My daughter frequently suggests that I give them to the Museum, but I like to keep them here."

Jane admired the chicken-bone furniture for quite some while. The oldest inhabitant sat down in his little rocking chair again. Now that Jane had seen the chicken-bone furniture, she wondered if the oldest inhabitant expected her to go home. He had gone home after the organ recital. But first they had had cookies and grape juice. He might think if she stayed longer that she wanted something to eat. But she had resolved to stay until the fog lifted or Miss Buckle came home. However, she couldn't look at the chicken-bone furniture the whole afternoon. And he might get alarmed if she sat down and took out her knitting. He might think, "Goodness! Is she going to stay all day?"

That's what the Moffats always thought when Mrs. Price arrived and sat down with her knitting. For she usually did spend the entire afternoon there, while everybody was wanting to do something else.

Fortunately the oldest inhabitant spoke just then and relieved Jane of her embarrassment. "Well, middle Moffat. Now we have seen the chicken-bone furniture. How would you like to look at pictures through the stereoscope?"

"That would be nice," agreed Jane.

The oldest inhabitant went to a little closet in the corner and came back with a pile of pictures and the stereoscope. He put the pile of pictures on the table beside him and sat down. Jane pulled up a chair.

"Now you fit the pictures in and we'll look," said Mr. Buckle.

So Jane fitted a picture in the stereoscope and passed it to the oldest inhabitant, who adjusted it to his eyes. He peered at it with his white head thrust a little forward. Then he handed it to Jane and she adjusted it to her eyes. One by one they went through all the pictures this way. When it was Jane's turn to look, she never knew exactly how long she should look. She didn't want to look too long and make the oldest inhabitant tired of waiting for the next picture. And she didn't want to look too little and give the impression she was not appreciating the beauty of the scene. At length she decided to count up to ten, slowly. There! That was a good polite time to look at each one, she thought.

It really was funny how these two same pictures on the cards jumped together into one picture when you looked at them through the stereoscope. In real life they looked like picture post cards with two identical pictures separated by a line down the middle. But through the stereoscope the two pictures hopped together into one.

How the man, walking along the woody path, suddenly jumped out at you! A real man in a straw hat! The mountains stood out from one another, and the waterfall looked as though it might splash you. A castle hidden in the trees suddenly emerged. You could almost pick the flowers, especially the edelweiss! There was a nearness and a farness to the pictures, as though you were standing on the top of Shingle Hill and looking at real scenery. But of course these scenes were of the Alps, not Shingle Hill. One picture showed an old Swiss with a long white beard sitting in front of his mountain cottage. Goats were nibbling the grass.

"Maybe the alms-uncle in 'Heidi,'" thought Jane.

"Another oldest inhabitant," said Mr. Buckle, laughing.

Jane smiled at him and looked a longer time, counting up to fifteen at this one.

When they had finished looking at the pictures, the oldest inhabitant said, "I see you have brought your knitting."

"Yes," said Jane. "A scarf for the soldiers in France."

She held it up for him to see. She wished she could knit red rows and blue rows for a change. Maybe she could change it into a helmet. It was not long enough for a scarf yet, but it was nearly long enough for a helmet.

"Would you change this into a helmet?" she asked the oldest inhabitant.

"It's supposed to be a scarf?"

"Yes."

"My goodness! Changing scarves into helmets! The mysterious middle Moffat!" exclaimed the oldest inhabitant.

Jane laughed, and whoops! she lost a stitch!

"Catch it! Catch it!" shouted the oldest inhabitant as though it were a runaway horse.

Jane sat down and clumsily recaptured the stitch.

"Narrow escape," said Mr. Buckle.

"My goodness," thought Jane. "He shouldn't shout like that. I better not drop any more stitches."

She knit one or two rows in silence. The oldest inhabitant watched her for a while and then he bent his head over his book. All you could hear now in the house was the sound of Janey's knitting needles clicking together, the soft breathing of the oldest inhabitant, and the tick-tock of the comfortable clock on the mantel. Mr. Buckle breathed in to the clock's tick and out to the clock's tock.

Jane knit and the clock tick-tocked. The quiet made her sleepy. She heard coal being dumped into Clara Pringle's cellar. Bag after bag rattled down the chute. What a lot of bags of coal they were getting, good hard black coal! Must be enough for a year at least. In the Moffats' house they never had more than one bag of coal at a time . . . She heard an occasional horse and wagon joggle by. Clop, clop. And she heard Joey call, "Ru-fus! Mama wants you to come home." All these noises sounded miles away.

Jane thought she would like to stretch her legs now and look out of the window, and see if she could see any of these things that were going on out there in the fog. But of course she did not do this. The oldest inhabitant might get it into his head that she did not like sitting here, or that he should offer her something to eat.

She looked at the oldest inhabitant to see if he had gone to sleep. But he hadn't, and he surprised her very much by saying, "How about a good game of double solitaire now?"

Double solitaire! Her favorite game! She and Joey and Rufus played it all the time. She nodded her head up and down. She would play slowly and let him win, she thought. She was the quickest double solitaire player of the Moffats. That was one thing, like running, that she was very good at. It made Rufus mad, she went so fast. She would be careful and not go too fast for the oldest inhabitant.

Mr. Buckle pushed aside the lamp, a small plaster model of the Yale Bowl, a copy of the *National Geographic,* and the red-fringed table-cloth. This table had a white marble top, wonderful for games! He pulled out a little drawer that was ordinarily hidden by the tablecloth and took out two decks of playing cards. Jane pulled her chair around opposite him, and they were ready to begin.

He gave her one deck of cards. "Shuffle!" he bade her.

Jane separated her pack of cards into two piles and shuffled one into the other. The oldest inhabitant did not like the way she shuffled.

"That is not the way to shuffle," he said. "This is the way to shuffle."

And he held the pack in his left hand, took some of the cards out with his right hand, and shuffled them back and forth so fast you couldn't see them. He was the fastest shuffler Jane had ever known.

"There," he said. "Now! We are ready to begin."

They laid out the cards neatly for the game and all was ready.

"Start!"

The oldest inhabitant bit out the words like a sergeant giving a command.

Start! The cards flew! Slap down the ace of hearts! Who would get the two on first? The oldest inhabitant! Slap on the three . . . the four. Ace of spades! Slap down the two . . . the three. Who'd get the four on first?

The oldest inhabitant!

He flipped the cards through the air between plays! The cards were flying! Slap on the jack . . . the queen . . . the king! Look at the diamonds! Build up the diamond pile. Who had the seven?

Janey!

Put it on quick. Down with the eight . . . the nine. The oldest inhabitant got his card there first almost every time. When he didn't, he put the card on the edge of the table, flipped it lightly in the air, making it turn a somersault, caught it neatly between thumb and forefinger, and returned it to its proper place while Jane was racing for the next card. Flying through the air, aces, spades, hearts, twos, threes, jacks, queens, everything!

Jane's head spun! Her eyes felt crossed. She played faster than she had ever played in her whole life in order to uphold the honor of the Moffats. Let the oldest inhabitant win! Pooh! Not to be licked hollow the way she licked Clara Pringle, that's all she hoped for now.

The oldest inhabitant was winning! And not because she was letting him either. Letting him! What a foolish thought! The oldest inhabitant, a veteran of the Civil War, who sat on the reviewing stand for every important occasion, and gave out the diplomas at graduation . . . soon to be one hundred years old. . . . What had she been thinking? Letting him win! Of course a man such as this would win.

Mr. Buckle flipped his last card, the king of hearts, into the air. It turned a neat somersault right smack down on the heart pile.

The oldest inhabitant had won!

"There!" he beamed, rocking back and forth in his chair, his hands on his knees, watching while Jane finished up her last cards.

"Gee . . ." gasped Jane. "You're some player!"

"Shall we have another game?" he asked. "Or is it time for Nellie? She doesn't like me to play doubles."

And at that very moment the front door opened. The oldest inhabitant swept all the cards into the little drawer, yanked the tablecloth back into place, and the Yale Bowl, too! Just in time!

"Hello, Father. And, why, hello, Jane!" said Miss Buckle, bustling into the room, the cherries on her hat shaking and rattling together. "I declare . . . P'fessor Fairweather. . . . What an inspiration! My . . ."

Jane backed out of the room and out of the house, scarcely able to say good-by. Goodness! What a game! Her head was whirling and she still felt dizzy. She must practice that card trick.

The one in which you flipped the card off the edge of the table and caught it neatly between thumb and forefinger. That would impress Joey and Rufus, and Nancy Stokes, too.

"Watch me!" she'd say. And the cards would flip through the air the way they had for the oldest inhabitant.

### from HOW MANY MILES TO BABYLON?
#### Paula Fox

*James is nine, he's black, he lives with his three aunts because his father has decamped and his mother's in the hospital. But he likes to imagine his mother is in Africa, that the cheap ring he found in the street was left by her as a sign of her love. He dreams of being an African prince. Trapped by bullies in the solitary game of make-believe that comforts him, James is drawn into their dog-stealing gang and held captive in a deserted Coney Island funhouse. The mood and the suspense are equally dramatic.*

#### [Trapped by the Gang]

"James Douglas! You're sleeping!" cried Miss Meadowsweet.

His hand was damp where his cheek had rested against it. For a second, he couldn't see clearly. Everyone was laughing except the teacher. "The fours," she said.

"Four times one is four," said James, still in a daze.

An eraser hit him. "Who did that?" Miss Meadowsweet shouted; the children roared.

"Four times two is eight," James said, brushing the chalk dust off his shirt.

No one heard him. Perhaps he had wakened up into a little corner of a dream. But he saw the dark scars on his desk, the faces drawn with red ink, the carved words, the little ditch for a pencil.

Then the milk and crackers came and he didn't have to finish the fours. What were fours for? Why did he get so sleepy every morning about this time? He yawned.

"Cover your mouth with your hand when you yawn," said Miss Meadowsweet. He didn't see how she could spot him yawning in a room full of kids—dozens, fifty maybe. He didn't even know half of them. There were Buddy and Karen and Lucky who sat right near him, and a new boy in front of him who couldn't even speak English. The children called him "Mira," because that's what he was always saying.

Lucky wasn't often in school because he liked to set the wastebasket on fire and he was always being sent home. Karen cried a lot. She cried when she got something wrong. She'd put her head down on her desk and say, "But I know the answer." Her notebook was full of gold stars and still she'd howl if she made just one little mistake. Buddy had used the masking tape Miss Meadowsweet kept on her desk to tape a knife to his arm. It was only a little knife but James could see where it bulged. Buddy would say, "You do what I say, James, or I cut you!" James didn't pay any attention because he knew it would take Buddy too long to get the masking tape off and get at the knife.

Then there was Ben. He was the biggest boy in the class. He wore a blue jacket and a necktie and he worked hard all the time. Ben never fooled around. He was Miss Meadowsweet's favorite—everybody knew that—but he didn't seem to care. She smiled at him, but Ben didn't smile at her. He just worked. At the end of the day he put his books in his canvas bag and he walked out of school, not looking to his left or right. He had such a stern expression on his face that even the older children made way for him in the corridors, and behind his back they called Ben "Deacon."

The Deacon was a different color from anyone else. There were light brown children in James' class, dark brown children like James and just a few white children. But Ben was pale brown as though he'd faded from some darker color, and he had golden freckles on his nose and his hair was reddish. James had seen him once in the church Aunt Grace and Aunt Althea took him to on Sunday. The church was just a little room you walked into right off the street and the Deacon had been sitting in the back. Right next to him was a little window with colored pieces of glass stuck into it, and the light fell on the Deacon's face so that his hair looked blue and his skin red.

After church, James saw the Deacon walking away between his father and mother. They were all dressed up in clothes that looked new, not like the clothes Aunt Grace and Aunt Althea brought back from the places where they worked. Aunt Paul never brought him old things. She said he had to have his own new clothes. She said she didn't want James walking around in somebody else's old raggedy pants and Aunt Althea had called her a dreamer.

It was reading time now. James opened his book. He didn't care much about clothes; it bothered him though when the pants were too big and slid down his hips, or when the shirts smelled funny as if they had been in the bottom of some dusty old bag.

"James Douglas! Come back to us!" He jumped in his seat and fumbled for his book which fell out of his hands to the floor.

"You leave it on the floor or I fix you," whispered Buddy. James paid no attention to him. Karen reached over and showed him the place where he was supposed to read. "Look, Jane, Look!" he read. Someone had drawn a little figure wearing a tall hat falling out of the window of Jane's and Dick's house. James made a mistake.

"Not *her*, James, but *here*. Come up to the blackboard and write out both words," said Miss Meadowsweet.

When he got to the blackboard he couldn't find any chalk.

"James, go to Mr. Johnson's room and ask Mr. Johnson to give you some chalk. Politely now!" said Miss Meadowsweet.

James left his classroom feeling sleepier than ever. He must have waked up last night. He remembered now that he had seen Aunt Paul and Aunt Grace sitting in two straight chairs in front of the television set. The light from the screen had fallen on their faces and had made them look scary, like people made of wood.

What was it that had waked him? Was it Aunt Grace pointing at something he couldn't see on the screen and whispering, "Look at that! Look at the way those people behave themselves." But he was used to the Aunts whispering all night long, back and forth across the room, until the sound was like a song that rocked him back to sleep. Maybe it was the noise next door, right up against the wall where his bed was, a noise like furniture breaking.

Mr. Johnson's room was way down at the end of the corridor near the school entrance. Sometimes a policeman stood there and leaned up against the door with his hat tipped over half his face. He was a special policeman, not like the ones who directed traffic or the ones who sometimes came at night to James' building. He wore a thick black leather holster strapped to his hip. It was hard for James to imagine real feet inside the policeman's shoes.

He shivered. The policeman wasn't there today.

James felt suddenly wide awake. He hardly thought about what he was doing, but he walked right past Mr. Johnson's room and out through the front door onto the street.

The sunlight was pale yellow now, the gray clouds all swept away into one corner of the sky, like the dust Aunt Grace swept into a corner of their room every evening. He was cold but he couldn't go back to get his jacket. No, he couldn't walk into the classroom and say to Miss Meadowsweet, "I've come to get my jacket before I go." Perhaps he'd never be able to get his jacket.

Right across the street there was a row of buildings just like the one he lived in. Two yellow dogs chased a gray cat under an old black car, and all the people leaning up against the steps laughed.

What if Miss Meadowsweet came with a policeman and chased him while his three Aunts stood and watched and cried into their hands? He wouldn't be able to dive under a car like that cat. But they wouldn't find him, not where he was going. He felt in his pocket to make sure the ring was still there and then set off along the avenue.

He was a good walker. He had discovered that if he told himself stories, he could cover a lot of ground without noticing how much time it took. Once last year, all the subways in New

York had stopped running because the men who ran the trains went on strike, and Aunt Paul had had to walk miles because the lady she worked for every day wouldn't pay her wages if she didn't show up. The subway workers wanted more money. That was easy for James to understand; everybody he knew wanted more money.

James' school was closed during the strike because the teachers couldn't get to it. So he and Aunt Paul had left early one morning, when the sun was barely up, and they had walked toward Flatbush Avenue with hundreds of people. When they finally got to the big apartment house where she worked, Aunt Paul said that she was just sick and hardly knew how she'd get through the day thinking about walking all the way back home. For the first time he could remember, Aunt Paul had been cross with him. She told him to sit down on a chair in the lady's kitchen and *not move* until she said he could.

Walking away from school now, looking at his feet as they moved, first one, then the other, he told himself the story of that day. He had sat in the kitchen with all those green plants lined up on the window sill and looked at everything until the toaster and the coffee pot and all the pots and pans and the stove became one big silver blur. Then Aunt Paul had come in and said the Missus had gone out and he could look at the other rooms. The whole place was like a big store except that there were no price tags on anything. All the time he was looking, his Aunt Paul was wiping furniture or running the vacuum clearner, or carrying a pail of water and a mop somewhere.

She had told him not to touch anything, but he did. He touched two white keys on the piano and he picked up a little carved sheep made out of some kind of white stone. The sheep had a bell that really rang tied around its neck. James wanted to put it in his pocket and take it home. Aunt Paul told him to put it right down. "She's very particular about her things," she had said. "If she catch you playing with that, I don't know what she'd do!"

Right inside that apartment there were two bathrooms, and so many closed doors he wondered if other families lived there. But most of the doors led to closets. "You can go into the boy's room," his Aunt had said, "but you stand right in the middle of the floor and don't hardly move."

The boy's room had shelves of toys and other shelves of books and a bicycle with its own stand in a corner. He couldn't bear that room, not while he had to be so still in the middle of the floor.

He had a piece of chocolate cake after his lunch. "Don't try to get it all in your mouth at once, Little Bits. There's plenty more," Aunt Paul had said.

Later that day the lady came back. She had on gloves and she patted his head. "Well . . . so this is *her* son," the lady had said to Aunt Paul. "Yes, ma'am. That's him," Aunt Paul had said. "Nice-looking," said the lady and she took a bunch of flowers from a vase and gave them to Aunt Paul. "You might catch a ride," she said. "I saw a lot of trucks stopping for people. Isn't it awful how this strike can tie up the whole city?" "Yes, ma'am," said Aunt Paul.

Aunt Paul filled her shopping bag with other paper bags and some balls of string, and she stuck the flowers in on top. Then they went down to the wide street which ran along beside a big park. They caught a ride too. A big truck with canvas flaps at the back stopped for them, and a lot of arms reached out and pulled them both in behind the flaps. James was so tired he had leaned against his Aunt. "That's where your mother worked before she got sick and had to go to the hospital," she said. The words woke him up. His mother had been in that same place and had known all about the bicycle and the little stone sheep with the bell. He sat in the dark thinking about those rooms with his mother walking through them, wondering why she had never told him about it, and smelling the funny sour smell of the flowers the lady had given Aunt Paul.

James had told himself the story of that day many times and each time he was able to remember more clearly what things had felt like and tasted like, how they had looked. It was the same with all the stories he told himself—whether they had really happened or not, they seemed to get clearer as he thought about them.

James looked up.

He had come to the street which his Aunts

had told him never to cross. It was a different part of town, they said. On the other side of the street were little apartment houses, light brown, with curtains in the windows and little skinny black fire escapes zig-zagging down to the street. Last time he had been here, he had seen some children his own age playing ball on the sidewalk. Some of them had hair the color of margarine. Aunt Paul had said that this was the kind of place she'd like to live in, and Aunt Althea had laughed and declared that Aunt Paul's mind was leaving her.

He turned right and walked two blocks and then right again and there was the empty house. James had found it almost a month ago, right after his birthday and two months after his mother had gone away. It was a real house made of wood with a sagging wooden porch and a doorbell hanging out on its wire near the door. It had a peaked roof and most of the windows were broken. There was a little rusty fence like a line of written "m's" all around the front, and a soft old black tire inside where there were little tufts of yellowed grass.

Before he took a step on the path, James looked up and down the street. A woman was pushing a baby carriage around the corner. The two gray buildings on either side of the house showed no sign of life. Nobody leaned out of the windows like people did in his building. Across the street was a place where you took laundry. He could see some women sitting in front of the washing machines looking at magazines. The only living thing on the street at the moment was a little brown dog tied up to a bus-stop sign by a long rope. The dog watched him silently.

James wished the dog was not looking at him. He didn't want to be seen going into the house, even by a dog. He *knew* he shouldn't go into the house—it wasn't his house. But that wasn't the reason why he wanted the street to be empty when he walked up the little path. What he knew and what he felt were two different things. He felt that going into that house had to be something he did secretly, as though it were night and he moved among shadows.

The door was open enough to let him slip in without pushing it. Sunlight didn't penetrate the dirty windows, so he stood still until his eyes grew accustomed to the darkness. Then, as he smelled the dusty old rooms and the dampness of the wallpaper that was peeling off the walls, other things he felt came swimming toward him through the gloom like fish.

James knew that his mother had gotten so sick one night that she had had to go away to a hospital. He knew that she couldn't write to him because she had to wait until she got better before she could do anything except lie flat and still. Sometimes Aunt Grace got a letter from the hospital telling how she was coming along. He knew that he had once lived in another room where there had been only three people, his father, his mother and himself, and that his father was mostly home and his mother was out working, and that one night the light which had hung from the middle of the ceiling, like the light in his Aunt's room, had never gone out. His mother had spent that night standing next to the window looking into the street. After that he had not seen his father again, and when he asked his mother about him she had said, "Gone, gone, gone. . . ." just like that, three times. Then they had moved in with the three Aunts, who were not really his Aunts but his father's. That same day someone had given him a bag of jelly beans.

That was the story of what had happened. But James had discovered another story hidden just beneath it. It was different from the first, but if he felt it, wasn't it true? When his Aunts talked about his mother being in the hospital, he wanted to tell them she was in Africa. Yet when he was walking along somewhere, thinking, or sitting at his desk in school, picturing her there in Africa, something in *him* said, no, she was sick and in the hospital. It was like having his arms yanked by two people going in different directions. But when he came to this house, the stories came together and were one.

Then James knew and felt the same thing! He was being guarded by those three old women so that no harm would come to him. His mother had gone across the ocean to their real country, and until she came back, no one was supposed to know who he really was. She had to fix everything. She had to see the people who lived in the deserts and the mountains, in the forests and the cities and tell them about him. But he knew he was not the only prince. He knew there were others. When everything was all right, all the princes would come together in a great clearing dressed in their long bright robes and their feathers, and after that everything would be different.

James knew how a prince would dress. He had seen pictures of princes and the villages they lived in. He had seen them dance on television and in the movies, but his mother had told him how the real life of all those princes had come to an end long ago, how they had been made to march for days and weeks through the wild forests, with their hands chained and their necks in ropes, until they came to a river where they were put in boats which carried them across the water.

Even though James had a good memory, he couldn't recall his mother ever telling him any other story except that one. She didn't talk much. But sitting there one morning across the table from him she had just begun, even though he wasn't looking at her. It was pouring rain outside and they were alone in the room. "What happened then?" he had asked her, because he was so afraid she would stop and not say any more, just get quiet the way she usually was and watch him and not speak. But she had gone on. She said that all those people would never recognize each other again, and no one knew who his own grandparents were.

But his mother must have found a secret paper that told all about James' great-great-great-grandfather who had been a king. She had left the ring for him so that he would know how hard she was working to make everything fine.

"King," he whispered to himself as he felt his way down the stairs to the basement. The word gave him courage. He hadn't gotten used to that basement yet, and some of the things he *knew* scared him: rats cannonballing out of corners, fanged like snakes, damp and gray; or the people who really owned the house suddenly coming back and finding him there, tying him up and sending him away to jail.

The basement was very cold. He fumbled around in the dark until his knees bumped up against the orange crate, then he reached in his pocket and took out a book of matches. He lit one and saw the soup can with the candle stub stuck in it. There was a strong draft blowing through the basement, so he had to light a lot of matches before he got the candle lit.

Great shadows swelled and sprang at the walls or shrank into dense black pools on the floor. James opened the box next to the can and took out the things he needed. There were some feathers from a duster, a little bottle of white paste and tubes and little jars of paint, blue and red and gray and white, that Aunt Althea had brought home one day in her shopping bag. There was a piece of red curtain he had found upstairs and a band with some feathers pasted on it and a pair of old slippers that Aunt Paul had thrown away.

When he had first come to the house, he had been able to go barefoot. But now it was too cold and the floor felt wet as though water had leaked in from the ground. The only sound he heard was the little noise he made opening jars. He began to paint his face, a line down his nose, across his forehead, slanting across his cheeks, but he didn't use very much because later he would have to rub it all off on the red curtain so that his Aunts wouldn't find a trace of it. Then he tied the band around his head, and the feathers hung down and tickled his cheeks. He stopped his work for a minute and ate a cheese cracker he found in his pocket. He wasn't scared now. He had even begun to feel quite warm. He tied the curtain around himself, making a big knot around his neck from two of the ends and pulling the other two in at his waist with a rope he'd found in the bathroom one morning. He took off his shoes and slid his feet into the slippers. Then, his heart beating faster, he took candle and ring and walked back to the other end of the basement.

The flicker of light showed him first the giant black boots, then the huge red-clothed legs, then the black belt with the silver buckle, then the white beard almost covering the face, the two apple cheeks, the small gleaming eyes, then the cap with the bell disappearing into the darkness above. He held the candle up high until he could see the whole giant cardboard figure, three times taller than he was, leaning up against the wall, the eyes staring straight ahead.

He put the candle down, placed the ring in front of the figure and clapped his hands softly, then harder. James began to dance, hopping on one foot and then the other, brushing his slippered feet on the floor, bending back and forward as far as he could. He never quite took his glance from the bright eyes of the figure. If the dance was right, those eyes would see him, recognize him, and his mother would know he had found the ring. Slowly his clapping grew louder; he bent and whirled until it seemed to him he was dancing before an immense fire that warmed and comforted him.

Then just when James thought the eyes had found him at last, he heard such a shriek that he spun on his heels and leapt back until he had fallen against the figure, his arms flung out, the feathered band falling over his face.

There was a second shriek, then shouts, and James realized that what he had heard was laughter.

"Look at—look at!" said a voice. "We got a Sandy Claus in our house!"

"Yeah. He got his dwarf with him too," said a second.

"Sandy Claus and his dwarf," said the first.

Two figures emerged from the darkness. One was tall and skinny and had a black cloth wrapped around his head. One earring gleamed in his ear. The other was short and plump and carried a torn umbrella, one of its metal ribs sticking straight out.

"Well, well, you never know, do you, Blue?" said the tall skinny one.

"No, Stick, you never do know."

"Can I go?" cried James, his voice trembling.

"The dwarf speaks English. Here I thought it'd speak Sandy Claus," said Stick.

"Yeah. That's just what I thought. Say a word in Sandy Claus, dwarf," said Blue.

"Please. Can I go?" pleaded James.

They stared down at him. They weren't so much bigger than he was after all, but big enough. Stick turned his head toward Blue.

"I just got an idea," said Stick. "We can use him to get the dogs."

"A whole idea?" said Blue. "You improving."

"We could use us a dwarf," said Stick, grinning.

"What's your name, dwarf?" asked Blue.

Thinking suddenly of his mother, her black hair tumbling down her back, dressed in a long white gown, stronger than anyone, thinking of the big clearing where all the people would come together, of the princes who would be there, James darted forward and picked up the ring. He held it out above the candle so they could see it. For a second he forgot what he knew, and only said what he felt.

"I'm a prince," he cried.

The two of them threw back their heads and shouted with laughter. They clutched themselves around their middles and staggered and stamped on the floor with their feet.

"A prince!" howled Blue.

"Yeah. A little black prince," yelled Stick. "Wait'll Gino hear this." Then they both stopped laughing at the same moment and Stick reached out and grabbed the ring from James' hand.

"Look here, he got himself a ring from a candy box. A ring for a black prince," said Stick.

"Let's see that valuable ring. Look at that! They let us in the subway for free if we flash this ring," said Blue. Then he threw the ring into the farthest corner of the basement.

James tore off the red curtain and ran for the stairs, but the big slippers tripped him up and Stick caught hold of his arm.

"No, no, Prince," said Blue. "You going to stay with us. We got work for you to do. If you be good, maybe we'll make you a king. We got the power, Prince. If you don't be good, we keep you a dwarf."

"Go get Gino," said Stick. "We got to change our plan."


## THE MIDNIGHT FOX
*Betsy Byars*

*Tom hadn't wanted to stay with his aunt and uncle while his parents were in Europe. He hadn't wanted to visit a farm; he didn't even like animals. But his imagination had been caught by the beauty and grace of the black fox, and in this episode he first sees her delightful cub.*

### The Search

The days and weeks passed quickly, long warm days in which I walked through the woods looking for the black fox.

The next time I saw her was in the late afternoon at the ravine.

This was my favorite place in the forest. The sides of the ravine were heavy dark boulders with mosses and ferns growing between the rocks, and at the bottom were trunks of old dead trees. The tree trunks were like statues in some old jungle temple, idols that had fallen and broken and would soon be lost in the creeping foliage. There was only an occasional patch of sunlight.

At the top of the ravine was a flat ledge that stuck out over the rocks, and I was lying there on my stomach this particular afternoon. The rock was warm because the sun had been on it since noon, and I was half asleep when suddenly I saw something move below me. It was the black fox. There was a certain lightness, a quickness that I could not miss.

She came over the rocks as easily as a cat. Her tail was very high and full, like a sail that was bearing her forward. Her fur was black as coal, and when she was in the shadows all I could see was the white tip of her tail.

As I watched, she moved with great ease over one of the fallen trees, ran up the other side of the ravine, and disappeared into the underbrush.

I stayed exactly where I was. My head was resting on my arms, and everything was so still I could hear the ticking of my watch. I wanted to sit up. I am sort of a bony person and after I have been lying on something hard for a long time, I get very uncomfortable. This afternoon, however, I did not move; I had the feeling that the fox was going to come back through the ravine and I did not want to miss seeing her.

While I was waiting I watched an ant run across the ledge with an insect wing. He was running so fast with this wing that he would make a little breeze and the wing would fly out of his grasp. Then he would go back and get the wing and start running again.

Then I watched some birds on the other side of the ravine circling over the rocks, catching insects as they skimmed the air. It was a beautiful sight, and I thought as I watched them, *That is what man had in mind when he first said, "I*

want to fly." And I thought about some old genius working up in a remote mountain valley actually making a little flying machine that he could strap on his back like a knapsack, and this old man would come down to a big air base and he would go out on the flight line and announce to everyone, "Folks, I have invented a flying machine." There would be a silence and then everyone would start laughing as if they would never stop, and finally the Captain would pause long enough to explain to the old man that flying machines had *already* been invented, that right over there—that big silver thing with the huge wings, *that* was a flying machine, and over there, those enormous bullet-shaped things, *those* were flying machines. "Well," the old man would say, shaking his head sadly, "I won't waste no more of your time. I'll just head on home," and he would press a button on his knapsack, and silently, easy as a bird, he would lift off the ground, and skimming the air, fly toward the hills. For a moment everyone would be too stunned to move, and then the General would cry, "Come back, come back," and everyone at the air base would run beneath the flying old man crying, "Wait, wait, come back, come back!" because that was the way every one of those men really wanted to fly, free and easy and silent as a bird. But the old man, who was a little hard of hearing, would not hear their cries and would fly off into the distance and never be seen again.

Right after I stopped thinking about this, the black fox came back. She came down the rocks the same way she had gone up, her white-tipped tail as light as a plume, and I remembered a black knight I saw once in the movies who was so tall and fine and brave you could see his black plume racing ahead of all the other knights when there was a battle.

She had something in her mouth that looked like a frog—it probably was, for the creek was low now and you could always find a frog if you wanted one. She trotted on, apparently concerned only with getting the frog home, and yet I had the feeling that she was missing nothing. She passed across the ravine in a zigzag line and then started up the other side.

I did not move, and yet all at once she looked up at me. She froze for a moment, her bright eyes looking at me with curiosity rather than fear, and she cocked her head to one side, listening.

I stayed perfectly still—I was getting good at this—and we looked at each other. Then she turned away and bounded up the side of the ravine, turning at the top and disappearing into the underbrush. I felt that somewhere in the shelter of the trees she had paused to see if I was going to follow. Perhaps she wanted me to follow so she could lead me back into the forest, but I stayed where I was. After a while, I got up and went back to the farm.

The next time I saw the fox, it was a marvelous accident. These don't happen very often in real life, but they do happen, and that's what this was. Like the time Petie and I were walking down the alley behind his house and there, on top of this lady's garbage, we saw a mayonnaise jar full of marbles—not just cat's-eye marbles but all different kinds, kinds I had never seen before. Petie and I turned them all out on the grass and first Petie chose one and then I chose one until they were all gone. And both of us right now, today, have every single one of those marbles.

This was an even better accident. For the past two weeks I had been practically tearing the woods apart looking for the den of the black fox. I had poked under rocks and logs and stuck sticks in rotted trees, and it was a wonder that some animal had not come storming out and just bitten my hand off.

I had found a hornet's nest like a huge gray shield in a tree. I had found a bird's nest, low in a bush, with five pale-blue eggs and no mother to hatch them. I had found seven places where chipmunks lived. I had found a brown owl who never moved from one certain limb of one certain tree. I had heard a tree, split by lightning years ago, suddenly topple and crash to the ground, and I ran and got there in time to see a disgruntled possum run down the broken tree and into the woods. But I did not find the place where the black fox lived.

Now, on this day, I did not go into the woods at all. I had gone up the creek where there was an old chimney, all that was left of somebody's cabin. I had asked Aunt Millie about it, but all she could remember was that some people named Bowden had worked on the farm a long time ago

and had lived here. I poked around the old chimney for a while because I was hoping I would find something that had belonged to the Bowdens, and then I gave that up and walked around the bend.

I sat on a rock, perfectly still, for a long time and looked down into the creek. There were crayfish in the water—I could see them, sometimes partly hidden beneath a covering of sand, or I could see the tips of their claws at the edge of a rock. There were fish in the water so small I could almost see through them. They stayed right together, these fish, and they moved together too.

After a while I looked across the creek and I saw a hollow where there was a small clearing. There was an outcropping of rocks behind the clearing and an old log slanted against the rocks. Soft grass sloped down to the creek bank.

I don't know how long I sat there—I usually forgot about my watch when I was in the woods —but it was a long time. I was just sitting, not expecting anything or waiting for anything. And the black fox came through the bushes.

She set a bird she was carrying on the ground and gave a small yapping bark, and at once, out of a hole beneath the rocks came a baby fox.

He did not look like his mother at all. He was tiny and woolly and he had a stubby nose. He tumbled out of the hole and fell on the bird as if he had not eaten in a month. I have never seen a fiercer fight in my life than the one that baby fox gave that dead bird. He shook it, pulled it, dragged it this way and that, all the while growling and looking about to see if anyone or anything was after his prize.

The black fox sat watching with an expression of great satisfaction. Mothers in a park sometimes watch their young children with this same fond, pleased expression. Her eyes were golden and very bright as she watched the tiny fox fall over the bird, rise, and shake it.

In his frenzy he dropped the bird, picked up an older dried bird wing in its place, and ran around the clearing. Then, realizing his mistake, he returned and began to shake the bird with even greater fierceness. After a bit he made another mistake, dropping the bird by his mother's tail, and then trying to run off with that.

In the midst of all this, there was a noise. It

was on the other side of the clearing, but the black fox froze. She made a faint sound, and at once the baby fox, still carrying his bird, disappeared into the den.

The black fox moved back into the underbrush and waited. I could not see her but I knew she was waiting to lead the danger, if there was any, away from her baby. After a while I heard her bark from the woods, and I got up quietly and moved back down the creek. I did not want the black fox to see me and know that I had discovered her den. Hazeline had told me that foxes will pick up their young like cats and take them away if they think someone has discovered their den.

I wondered if this was how the black fox had come to have only one baby. Perhaps her den had been the one discovered by Mr. Hunter. Perhaps she had started to move her cubs and had got only one to safety before Mr. Hunter had arrived with his dynamite.

I decided I would never come back here to bother her. I knew I would be tempted, because already I wanted to see that baby fox play with his bird some more, but I would not do it. If I was to see the black fox again, it would be in the woods, or in the pasture, or in the ravine, but I was not going to come to the den ever again. I did not know that an awful thing was going to happen which would cause me to break this resolution.

I went home and I put a tiny little mark on the edge of my suitcase with my penknife. I did this every time I saw the black fox. There were four marks on my suitcase now, and in the weeks to come, there were to be ten more. Fourteen times I saw the black fox and most of those fourteen she saw me too. I think she knew that I wasn't anything to be afraid of. She didn't exactly jump with joy when she saw me and she didn't trust me, but I know she was not afraid.

After I got home, my mom said, "What on earth happened to your brand-new suitcase? There are notches all over it."

And I said, "Let me see," as if I was surprised too, but if I had wanted to, I could have sat right down then and told her about every one of those notches, that this one was for when I saw the black fox carrying home a live mouse so her baby could start learning to hunt for him-

self, and that this one was for when I saw the fox walking down the stream, her black legs shining like silk, and this one was for when the fox passed me so closely that I could have put out my hand and touched her thick soft fur. The fifteenth notch I never put in the suitcase, for that was not a happy memory like the others but a painful one.

### from PETER AND VERONICA
*Marilyn Sachs*

*Peter and Veronica first met in* Veronica Ganz. *After their original enmity they have become close friends.*

### [A Small Miracle]

"Are you sure it's all right if I come?" Veronica asked.

"Sure I'm sure," Peter said, even though he wasn't sure at all. With only three weeks to go now, he and his family were still deadlocked over Veronica. He had spoken to Rabbi Weiss, and of course Rabbi Weiss had only said he must respect his parents' wishes. He had drawn Rosalie into the argument, and she had sided with him. But still his mother said no. Every night at his house there were more arguments, more scenes, more tears. The whole atmosphere began to feel more like a funeral, Peter thought, than a bar mitzvah.

So now, on this Friday afternoon, he had just gone ahead and invited her anyway. If his parents persisted in refusing to allow her to come, he had decided that he would ask them to call the whole thing off. But there was no point in going into details with Veronica. She knew how his mother felt about her. He knew how her mother (and Stanley), felt about him. Ever since their conversation on the library steps, it hadn't seemed necessary to discuss family matters any further.

"I mean—nobody'll mind if I come?" Veronica said carefully.

"Look," said Peter, "this is my party, and if I can't invite my friends, then it won't be much of a party. And I especially want you to come. As a matter of fact," Peter clenched his fists, "I want you to come more than anybody else. O.K.?"

"Well, thanks," Veronica said, her face thoughtful. "But what do I do? Where do I go?"

"First you come to the synagogue at nine o'clock in the morning. And then, after the services, you come to my house for the party."

"I've never been inside a synagogue before," Veronica said, twisting up her face. "Stop pulling my hand, Stanley! What do I have to do?"

"Nothing special. Just come and sit down. Oh, wear a hat and maybe a nice dress."

"Like church." Veronica nodded. "But what do I do inside?"

"It's easy. Sit down, and take a prayer book, and just do what everybody else is doing."

"Well, you know, Peter, I'm Lutheran, and I don't know if I'm supposed to do what everybody else is doing in a synagogue."

"Oh, that's right," said Peter. "Well, I guess you don't have to say or do anything if you don't want to. Some of the other kids who are coming aren't Jewish either. Just read the book or look around."

"What do you do?"

"I'm up in the front with the rabbi and the other boy who's being bar mitzvahed. The two of us read selections in Hebrew from the Torah —that's the first five books of the Bible—and then we make speeches."

"In front of everybody?"

"Uh, huh."

"Aren't you scared?"

"Nope." And he wasn't. Not about making the speech. It was going to be a good one, that he knew. Most bar-mitzvah speeches dealt with the debt of gratitude the boy owed to his parents and his teacher. Peter's speech would also contain the expected words of gratitude, but he had some other ideas he thought he might also like to include. This part of his speech he had not discussed with his teacher, preferring to develop it all by himself. The idea for it had actually grown out of his friendship with Veronica, and his struggle in her behalf. He had some polishing up to do, but by and large, the speech was completed. He was proud of it and of himself. It would be somewhat different from other bar-mitzvah speeches he had heard, some-

what more important, he thought. Of course, the way matters stood now, he might never get to give it at all.

"You just be there," he said grimly.

Stanley's skates skidded out from under him and he flopped down on the ground.

On this particular Friday, Stanley had again joined them, on skates, this time, and was occupied at present with clutching Veronica's hands, legs, skirts—whatever he could reach.

Veronica turned her attention to him. "Get up, Stanley, and don't hang on to me. You'll never learn to skate if you hang on."

Stanley remained seated on the ground. "If I don't hold on to you, you'll run away," he said pathetically.

"All right. I promise I won't run away. Now stand up. Here." She held out a hand to him. Stanley grabbed it with both hands and staggered to his feet.

"Now—let go!"

Stanley let go, swayed, skidded, and flopped again to the ground. He began hiccuping.

"Why don't we put him between us," Peter said, "and each of us hold one of his hands. That way we can balance him better."

"I'm not going to hold your hand," Stanley said, turning his special look of loathing on Peter.

"Now look," Veronica said sharply, "nobody wanted you along today, but you said you were just dying to skate. So get up, and you're going to skate whether you like it or not."

She pulled him to his feet, grabbed one hand, and motioned for him to give Peter his other hand. But Stanley's arm hung limply by his side. Peter put out his hand, took Stanley's and Stanley clenched his fist so that Peter ended up holding his thumb. The three of them began moving along, Veronica and Peter supporting Stanley between them.

"Who else is going to be there?" Veronica asked, continuing the conversation.

"Marv, and Paul, and I have to ask Bill, and I guess some of the girls, and . . ."

"I'm not coming," Stanley said, lurching into Veronica.

"Nobody asked you," Veronica said, yanking him upright.

Around the corner came Roslyn Gellert and Reba Fleming. Reba began giggling as soon as she saw them, and Roslyn seemed to be study- ing something in another direction. There was strength in numbers, and Peter decided that this would be a fine time to invite Roslyn to his bar mitzvah. And since one should not harbor thoughts of malice at such an important occa- sion, he might as well ask that drip, Reba, too.

"Hey, Roslyn, Reba," he yelled, letting go of Stanley's hand and skating in their direction.

Stanley's feet flew out from under him and he fell down.

"Aw," said Reba, "the poor little kid."

She and Roslyn hurried over and helped Stan- ley up.

"Hello, Veronica," Roslyn said. "Is this your brother?"

"Yeah."

"What a cute little boy!"

Stanley grabbed hold of Roslyn and held on for dear life.

"Roslyn," said Peter, "I'd like you to come to my bar mitzvah. It's three weeks from tomor- row. You too, Reba."

"Thanks," said Reba. "I can come."

Stanley had one arm around Roslyn's neck and the other around her waist.

"There you are, honey," Roslyn cooed. "You won't fall. Just let go of my neck."

"Let go of her neck, Stanley," Veronica or- dered.

But Stanley hung paralyzed where he was.

"You're choking me," gasped Roslyn.

Veronica grabbed Stanley and pulled. He hung on. She pulled harder.

"I can't breathe," Roslyn gurgled.

"Let go, Stanley," Peter yelled, and he tried to unfasten Stanley's fingers.

A strong yank from Veronica, and then Stan- ley came loose, and the two of them were rolling on top of each other on the ground.

"Roslyn," Peter repeated, "I'd like you to come to my bar mitzvah. It's going to be three weeks from tomorrow."

Roslyn's face was very pink. She looked at Stanley and Veronica twisted up together like a pretzel on the ground and suddenly began laughing. Peter followed her gaze. They sure did look funny, wrapped up in each other that way. He began snickering, too, and then Roslyn looked at him, and they smiled at each other,

and it was all very comfortable and friendly again.

"I'd love to come Peter. Thanks. I'm sure I can make it."

"Swell," Peter said enthusiastically, and then he added quickly, "How's everything? How are you doing in math?"

"O.K., I guess."

"Well now, don't forget, if you need any help, just ask me."

Roslyn looked away. "Thanks, Peter," she said softly, "I will." She took Reba's arm. " 'By now, 'By Veronica, 'By Stanley."

The living knot had disentangled itself and began to assume the vertical. Veronica's face was angry.

"Come on, Stanley, we're going home." She pulled Stanley to his feet and began skating away from Peter.

"Hey, wait," Peter yelled, going after her. "What's wrong?"

"You laughed," Veronica said sullenly.

"Well, so what? You sure looked funny, the two of you."

"If it was you, you wouldn't think it was so funny. I'm going home."

Peter put an arm on Veronica's shoulder. "Don't be like that, Veronica. I'm sorry if I laughed, but—here—this is what you looked like."

He began lurching back and forth, making crazy, clownlike gestures. Finally he let one skate skid and went down, twisting himself up as he went.

Veronica looked down at him coldly.

He crossed his eyes at her.

She pursed up her lips in disdain.

He made Mortimer Snerd noises at her. She blinked. Then he began waggling his tongue and trying to lick his nose. Veronica burst out laugh- ing, and Stanley said sadly, "Aren't we going home, Veronica?"

Peter leaned back on his hands and smiled fondly at Stanley. The kid had his good points after all, and now Roslyn and he were friends again.

"Come on, Stanley, let's skate," said Peter. He stood up, reached for Stanley's thumb where it hung limply at the end of an unresponsive arm, and the three of them were off again.

They came to a big hill, leading down to a busy thoroughfare. He and Veronica had zoomed down it many a time, turning sharply at the end of it to avoid the heavy traffic that always whizzed along the cross street. They stood on the crest, looking down hungrily, and Veronica said, "You sit here, Stanley, and we'll be back up in a second."

"No!" said Stanley.

She took him by both arms and sat him down, protesting, on the pavement.

"Let's go," she cried, and she and Peter flew down the hill with the wind and Stanley's cries spurring them on. At the bottom, each turned sharply in different directions, finding anchorage in the parked cars along the curb.

They climbed back up the hill and Stanley was waiting for them.

"I want to go down too," he said.

"No," said Veronica. "You can't even skate."

"You take me."

"No!"

Stanley hicced, and Peter said generously, grateful for Stanley's presence today, "Look, if I hold him by one hand and you hold him by the other, we can do it."

"No!"

"I wanna go," shouted Stanley. "I wanna go."

He offered his thumb to Peter, and Veronica smiled and said, "Well . . ."

"I wanna go."

"O.K.," said Veronica, "but don't fall."

The three of them stood poised at the top of the hill.

"Get ready," said Peter, "get set."

"Go," shouted Stanley.

And they were off. Peter tried hard to keep a tight grip on Stanley's thumb, but it kept wiggling. Stanley managed to skim along with them though, and at the bottom he yanked his thumb out of Peter's hand. Thinking that Stanley had gone along with Veronica, Peter made his sharp turn, anchored himself around a parked car, and turned, smiling, to look at Veronica and Stanley. There was only Veronica on the opposite side of the street, leaning against a parked car and looking at him in horror.

"Didn't he go with you?" she shouted.

"No—didn't he go with you?"

"Oh—no!"

For a moment he couldn't look. He just couldn't. All those cars and buses whizzing along, and little Stanley, poor, little Stanley who couldn't skate, somewhere lost under them.

And then Veronica began screaming, "Stanley! Stanley! Stanley!"

Peter took a deep, terrified breath and looked. The cars were still whizzing along, and from across the broad, busy street, Stanley stood on the sidewalk, waving and laughing and marvelously safe.

Peter got across first. "Are you all right?" he cried. "What happened?"

And then Veronica was there. She grabbed Stanley, and pulled him close to her, and said, "Stanley, Stanley, oh, Stanley!"

"I can skate," Stanley said, pushing her away. "Now, I can skate. Come on, Peter. Let's do it again."

He offered Peter his whole hand this time, which was, in this afternoon of miracles, the greatest miracle of all.

## from ALONG CAME A DOG
### Meindert DeJong

*A stray dog, hunting for a home and needing something or someone to love, has made himself the guardian of a small, crippled hen. The hen's owner had driven the dog away, but he crept back to care for the hen. The theme is simple, but it is handled with a superb blend of strength and delicacy; the author's descriptions of animal behavior are based on keen observation and unsentimental affection.*

### The Little Boss

When the man decided to go searching for the little hen in the darkening swamp, he unknowingly held the big dog trapped up in the hay barn. The dog could not come out of hiding—not with the man roving around the farm. Eyes glued to a chink between two boards in the barn wall, the dog watched the man stride across the field, straight toward the old fallen willow at

From *Along Came a Dog* by Meindert DeJong. Copyright © 1958 by Meindert DeJong. Reprinted by permission of Harper & Row, Publishers, Inc., and Lutterworth Press

the edge of the swampland.

There the man stopped, and there he stooped and searched, and once he picked up a rooster's long tail feather and dropped it again. The man had found the spot of the fearful thrashing! He came out of his stoop, and plunged straight on into the swamp. He went past the fallen willow and disappeared behind the tall brush and reeds that rimmed the swamp.

The man searched long. Even after the swamp and the fields had gone dark the beam of his flashlight flickered and ranged through the swamp. And once the dog heard him calling the little red hen, and the call sounded lost and lonely and helpless. The man's voice at once fell still, he did not call any more.

But though the swamp and the night had gone black the dog stayed, eyes glued to the chink, and still he waited. At last the beam of the flashlight came shining straight out of the swamp, and the man came past the willow again, came on across the field. He passed the barn, and went on into the house. The man was alone— he had not found the little hen.

Later the lights in the house went out, and then, at last, the dog dared plunge from the barn down into the dark wagon. He nosed a moment in the corner under the seat where the little hen always slept with him—even though he knew the little hen couldn't be there—but then he jumped down from the wagon and ran toward the spot of the fearful thrashing.

What the man had been unable to find, the dog's expert nose sniffed out in moments. He immediately snuffled out the short, zigzag trail of the little hen as she had worked and worried the egg toward the hidden nest under the tree. He did not merely smell the little hen's trail, he smelled the rolling trail of the egg. His egg—for he even smelled that it was the egg he had carried in his mouth.

It was a matter of seconds to find the little hen in the nest under the hanging tree. The big dog's tail wagged mightily. In his relief at finding the little hen he eagerly poked his nose into the nest to nuzzle her. For his trouble he got a swift, hard rap on the nose. After that one warning peck, the little hen immediately ducked back into the nest—sat dark and secret and still.

The dog waited. At last he understood that the little hen didn't intend to go to the wagon to sleep in her every-night spot, that she intended to stay in the nest all night. It puzzled him, but he finally wormed under the leaning tree trunk the best he could, and looped his big body around the nest to spend the night protecting and guarding the little hen.

In the early dawn of Sunday morning the dog got up. He poked his nose out of the overhanging branches and leaves of the willow tree. He immediately turned back to the nest as if to tell the little hen that morning and daylight had come to the farm and that he must go into hiding, and she must go to wait for the man at the kitchen door. But the little hen sat perfectly still, didn't show the slightest intention of running to the house as she did all other mornings.

The dog became nervous. He poked his nose toward the nest again. Still the little hen didn't make the slightest move to come up out of the nest. He stood before her almost quivering with anxiety and the need to go into hiding; trembling with a hungry impatience to see if the imprisoned hen in the barn had laid an egg for him. He suddenly nudged the little hen right up out of the nest. Then under her he saw the two eggs. He rammed the little hen out of his way with his head, reached into the nest, and pulled out the one egg—*his* egg.

Fury descended on his head in the nest. The little hen was a red ball of fury, every puffed-out feather quivering with rage, head swollen with hate and rage. She came right down on the dog's head, and her wings shivered as she rained vicious pecks on his soft nose.

Even with the egg in his mouth the big dog yelped out in surprise. He crawled back before her, but she didn't relent one moment, and he didn't defend himself. He backed away confused and meek—somehow knowing he had done a terrible wrong.

At last, in his confusion, he just opened his mouth and let the egg roll. Immediately the little hen's attack stopped, and she became all concern for the egg. Completely ignoring the dog, she began working the egg back to the nest. The dog lay watching and puzzling.

He lay guilty and humble, but he was not entirely unhappy. The tip of his tail even began to tremble a little as a glimmer of understanding crept into his mind. Then, as the little hen got up to turn the two eggs in the nest, he saw his egg again. The egg had been his. But the little hen had made his egg her egg. And that made her his boss. And then when he'd tried to take his egg out of the nest she had punished him for wrongdoing. That had made her his boss completely. The dog's tail twitched understanding.

The little hen, by punishing him, had made everything different. And much better! Now the little hen did not belong to him merely to guard and protect—she was his boss, he belonged to her. He belonged to someone! The dog swiped a big paw over his sore, pecked nose, and felt good. And he loved the little hen.

But in the nest the little hen had laid an egg. And now she came up out of the nest, paced before the dog, and cackled her triumph until it shrilled over the quiet Sunday morning fields— she the proud mother of a newly laid egg. But she settled back on the three eggs and became as silent and secret as she had been before.

Wide-eyed and pondering, the dog looked at the quiet little hen, and somehow he came to understand that she was guarding the eggs, and would not leave the nest, and that even he wasn't to be near. But then—if his little boss didn't want him here—it made him free to run to the barn to go look for an egg, and to go into hiding. He got up, wagged his tail in all respectful friendliness for the little hen, and gravely turned and ran toward the barn.

In his new happiness his tail went on wagging in friendliness at everything and nothing in the empty morning field. But when he ran into the barn, a chicken rose up in alarm under the hay loader. And as she rose the dog saw a chalky white egg under her. He immediately poked his nose toward the egg. But this chicken, too, stood her ground and struck out at him. And the dog pulled his head back, looked through the wide doorway at the distant willow tree, and wagged his tail.

The white hen also pecking him had made it sure. Whole eggs were not for him. Now he knew it surely, and he fitted it together with the other things he had learned, for he knew he was doing what his boss wanted. The little hen was his boss, and whole eggs were not for him, but belonged to his boss.

Then broken eggs were for him! He turned away and hurried up the hay loader, for up above in the hay barn was a chicken who laid broken, splattered eggs. He had never been punished for eating the broken eggs—so broken eggs were for him, whole eggs belonged to his little boss. He rammed the trap door open to look for a broken egg.

There was no egg for him in the upper barn. The white hen was fitting herself a nest in the loose hay near the big barn doors. She was making the contented little singsong sounds that meant the coming of an egg. In the middle of the barn the dog sat down on his haunches and waited hopefully for her to lay a broken egg for him.

## from THE HOUSE OF DIES DREAR

*Virginia Hamilton*

*Thomas knew that the large, old house to which his family had just moved had been set up as a station on the Underground Railroad by its original owner, the abolitionist Dies Drear. There was no complete set of plans, but Papa had said there were hidden rooms; in these chapters Thomas first senses the mystery and danger of the house, the secrets that are unveiled in an exciting final episode. Imaginative and dramatic, the book is a suspense-filled mystery about a black family and at the same time a story that incorporates historical facts.*

### [The Forbidding House]
Thomas did not wake in time to see the Ohio River. Mr. Small was glad he didn't, for through the gloom of mist and heavy rain, most of its

expanse was hidden. What was visible looked much like a thick mud path, as the sedan crossed over it at Huntington.

Thomas lurched awake a long time after. The car went slowly; there was hardly any rain now. His mother spoke excitedly, and Thomas had to shake his head rapidly in order to understand what she was saying.

"Oh dear! My heavens!" Mrs. Small said. "Why it's huge!"

Mr. Small broke in eagerly, turning around to face Thomas. "You've waited a long time," he said. "Take a good look, son. There's our new house!"

Thomas looked carefully out of his window. He opened the car door for a few seconds to see better, but found the moist air too warm and soft. The feel of it was not nice at all, and he quickly closed the door. He could see well enough out of the window, and what he saw made everything inside him grow quiet for the first time in weeks. It was more than he could have dreamed.

The house of Dies Drear loomed out of mist and murky sky, not only gray and formless, but huge and unnatural. It seemed to crouch on the side of a hill high above the highway. And it had a dark, isolated look about it that set it at odds with all that was living.

A chill passed over Thomas. He sighed with satisfaction. The house of Dies Drear was a haunted place, of that he was certain.

"Well," Mr. Small said, "what do you think of it, Thomas?"

"It must be the biggest house anyone ever built," Thomas said at last. "And to think—it's our new house! Papa, let's get closer, let's go inside!"

Smiling, Mr. Small kept the car on the highway that now curved up closer toward the house. In a short time they were quite near.

At the base of the hill on which the house sat, a stream ran parallel to the highway. It was muddy and swollen by rain; between it and the hill lay a reach of fertile land, lushly tangled with mullein weed and gold wildflower. The hill itself was rocky and mostly bare, although a thaw had come to the rest of the land and countryside. At the very top of the hill Thomas noticed a grove of trees, which looked like either pine or spruce.

The house of Dies Drear sat on an outcropping, much like a ledge, on the side of the hill. The face of the ledge was rock, from which gushed mineral springs. And these came together at the fertile land, making a narrow groove through it before emptying into the stream. Running down the face of the ledge, the springs coated the rock in their path with red and yellow rust.

Thomas stared so long at the ledge and springs, his eyes began to play tricks on him. It seemed as if the rust moved along with the spring waters.

"It's bleeding," he said softly. "It looks just like somebody cut the house open underneath and let its blood run out! That's a nice hill though," he added. He looked at the clumps of skinny trees at each side of the house. Their branches were bare and twisted by wind.

Thomas cleared his throat. "I bet you can see a lot from the top of that hill." He felt he ought to say this. The hill was hardly anything compared to the mountains at home. Otherwise the land in every direction was mostly flat.

"You can see the college from the top of the hill," Mr. Small said. "And you can see the town. It's quite a view. On a clear day those springs and colored rock make the hill and house look like a fairyland."

"All those springs!" Thomas said. He shook his head. "Where do they come from? I've never seen anything like them."

"You'll get used to the look of the land," Mr. Small said. "This is limestone country, and always with limestone in this formation you'll find the water table percolating through rock into springs. There are caves, lakes and marshes all around us, all because of the rock formations and the way they fault."

Mrs. Small kept her eye on the house. It was her nature to concentrate on that which there was a chance of her changing.

"No, it's not," she said softly. "Oh, dear, no, it will never be pretty!"

"Everything is seeping with rain," Mr. Small said to her. "Just try to imagine those rocks, that stream and the springs on a bright, sunny day. Then it's really something to see."

Thomas could imagine how everything looked

on a day such as his father described. His eyes shone as he said, "It must look just about perfect!"

They drove nearer. Thomas could see that the house lay far back from the highway. There was a gravel road branching from the highway and leading to the house. A weathered covered bridge crossed the stream at the base of the hill. Mr. Small turned off the highway and stopped the car.

"There's been quite a rain," he said, "I'd better check the bridge."

Now Thomas sat with his hands folded tightly beneath his chin, with his elbows on his knees. He had a moment to look at the house of Dies Drear, the hill and the stream all at once. He stared long and hard. By the time his father returned, he had everything figured out.

They continued up the winding road, the house with its opaque, watching windows drawing ever nearer.

The stream is the moat. The covered planks over it are the drawbridge, Thomas thought. And the house of Dies Drear is the castle.

But who is the king of all this? Who will win the war?

There was a war and there was a king. Thomas was as sure of this as he was certain the house was haunted, for the hill and house were bitten and frozen. They were separated from the rest of the land by something unkind.

"Oh dear," Mrs. Small was saying. "Oh dear. Dear!"

Suddenly the twins were scrambling over Thomas, wide awake and watching the house get closer. By some unspoken agreement, they set up a loud, pathetic wail at the same time.

"Look!" Thomas whispered to them. "See, over there is clear sky. All this mist will rise and get blown away soon. Then you'll feel better."

Sure enough, above the dark trees at the top of the hill was deep, clear sky. Thomas gently cradled the boys. "There are new kinds of trees here," he told them. "There will be nights with stars above trees like you've never known!" The twins hushed, as Thomas knew they would.

Up close the house seemed to Thomas even more huge, if that were possible. There were three floors. Above the top floor was a mansard roof with dormer windows jutting from its steep lower slopes. Eaves overhanging the second story dripped moisture to the ground in splattering beats. There was a veranda surrounding the ground floor, with pillars that rose to the eaves.

Thomas liked the house. But the chill he had felt on seeing it from the highway was still with him. Now he knew why.

It's not the gray day, he thought. It's not mist and damp that sets it off. There are things beyond weather. The house has secrets!

Thomas admired the house for keeping them so long.

But I'm here now, he thought happily. It won't keep anything from me.

The twins refused to get out of the car, so Thomas had to carry one while his mother carried the other. They cried loudly as soon as they were set on the veranda.

"They don't like the eaves dripping so close," Mr. Small said. "Move them back, Thomas."

Thomas placed the boys close to the oak door and then joined Mrs. Small in front of the house. His father was already busy unloading the trailer. The heavy furniture and trunks had come by van a week earlier. Thomas guessed all of it would be piled high in the foyer.

"It's old," Mrs. Small remarked, looking up at the dormers of the house. "Maybe when the sun comes out. . . ." Her voice trailed off.

Thomas placed his arm through hers. "Mama, it must be the biggest house for miles. And all the land! We can plant corn . . . we can have horses! Mama, it will be our own farm!"

"Oh, it's big," Mrs. Small said. "Big to clean and big to keep an eye on. How will I ever know where to find the boys?"

"I'll watch them," said Thomas. "Wait until it's warm weather for sure. They'll be with me all the time."

"Let's go inside now," Mr. Small said to them. He had unloaded cartons beside the twins on the veranda. "Thomas and I will have to set up the beds the first thing."

"And I'll have to get the kitchen ready," said Mrs. Small, "and you'll have to drive to town for food. Goodness, there's so much to do, I won't have time to look around." Then she smiled, as though relieved.

Mr. Small went first, and Mrs. Small held the door for the twins and Thomas. At once the boys began to cry. Thomas watched them, noticing that they avoided touching the house, especially the oak door trimmed with carved quatrefoils. Mrs. Small hadn't noticed, and Thomas said nothing. He scooped up the boys and carried them inside.

When the heavy door closed behind them, they were instantly within a place of twilight and stillness.

Thomas couldn't recall having been in a more shadowy place, nor had he ever felt such a silence that seemed to wait. There was no small entrance room, as Thomas had imagined, but a long, wide hall. One part of the hall was cut by stairs, which rose in a curve to disappear in darkness somewhere above. Beyond where Thomas' father stood, there was a wide doorway leading to another room. Thomas could make out cupboards there. It was the kitchen and it seemed to be very large. On either side of the hall were closed doors, which he guessed led into sitting rooms.

"Papa," Thomas said. He was growing uneasy just standing there. Mrs. Small motioned him to be quiet.

"What is it?" she whispered to Thomas' father. "What *is* it?"

Mr. Small softly cleared his throat. "Nothing," he said, "but I had expected the furniture from the van to be piled up in this hall."

The twins grew heavy in Thomas' arms. He found that he was leaning against a table. He had been for some time. "Here's some of the furniture," he said.

Billy turned to see and caught his ghostly reflection in a mirror by the table at the same moment as did Thomas. Billy screamed and cried. Thomas was so startled, he nearly dropped the boys. Mr. Small quickly found a light switch. Now they saw a grand, gilded mirror, on either side of which were two familiar end tables.

"Why, that looks beautiful!" said Mrs. Small. "Those are my tables, but whose mirror is it?"

"That mirror was there the first time I saw the place," Mr. Small said. "If you like it, I guess we can keep it."

He opened one of the doors off the hall, paused, and then beckoned them to come. He switched on a light inside. They saw that their livingroom furniture had been cleverly arranged to fit a much larger room.

"Who did all this?" Mrs. Small said. "How did they know I'd want it like this—it's just beautiful!"

"I don't know for certain who did it," said Mr. Small, "but I suspect it was Pluto. He's the only one who would think to do it."

They looked at the room. The two oversized easy chairs which Thomas had known for so long were placed side by side with a mahogany lamp table between them. No longer were they catercornered on either side of the couch, familiar, as they had been at home. They sat like soldiers on their guard.

The couch was placed across the room from the chairs. And between two of the floor to ceiling windows stood Mrs. Small's kitchen worktable.

Thomas gave Buster to Mrs. Small to hold. He went up to the worktable holding Billy, patting the boy, who still cried. The top of the table had been sanded smooth and rubbed with linseed oil. All the old nicks and gashes from all the meats his mother had prepared on it had been worked away. And placed at either end of the table were plants of ivy in the white china tureens his mother had never favored.

"Who would have dreamed my old table could look like that?" Mrs. Small said. "And I never would have thought to use those tureens that way."

"It makes a nice decoration," Mr. Small said. "The table and tureens belong to another time. Mr. Pluto saw that."

Thomas turned slowly around. At the far end of the room was a massive fireplace. Old Mr. Pluto hadn't thought to build a fire there. But on either side of the hearth he had arranged Billy's and Buster's little rocking chairs.

Mrs. Small laughed on seeing the chairs, and Mr. Small smiled.

"Look, boys, there're your chairs," said Mrs. Small. The boys looked and then turned to Thomas. Thomas was still wary, so the boys refused to sit just yet.

As soon as Thomas had entered the room, he understood what old Pluto had tried to do. He had arranged the furniture in a rigid progression, with the two long windows, not the open fireplace, as its focus. Thomas' eyes swept from the fireplace to the windows, then out into the gray day, on and on, until he could see no farther.

It's his warning, thought Thomas. He means for us to flee.

"I don't like it," Thomas said, "I don't like it at all. And who is this Mr. Pluto to work out the cuts in Mama's table? He's sure taken a lot on himself. He's got no business in our new house!"

"I would have placed that table in some corner of the kitchen," said Mrs. Small. "I don't know why I even bothered to bring it, it's so old. Thomas, I'm surprised at you."

"It was thoughtful of Mr. Pluto to put the house in order for us," said Mr. Small. "I certainly hadn't expected him to."

But Mr. Small would not meet Thomas' questioning gaze.

He doesn't like Mr. Pluto doing this any more than I do, Thomas thought. I know he doesn't. He just doesn't want to upset Mama.

"Come, let's take a look upstairs," Mr. Small said. "I would guess Mr. Pluto put the beds up. It will be interesting to see what rooms he chose."

"Papa, are you going to let him take over?" Thomas said. "How does he know what room I want?"

"We can change your room if you don't like it," said Mrs. Small. "But if Mr. Pluto took as much time with the bedrooms as he did with this room, they will do just fine."

Thomas was shocked. His mother and father were allowing a stranger, and a man who looked like the devil besides, to walk right in their house and fix it to suit himself. He wasn't even a relative. He wasn't anybody!

"I don't want to see any more right now," Thomas said glumly. "I think I'll go out and look at the rocks and springs."

He sat Billy down in his rocking chair. At once Billy began to cry, clinging to Thomas' leg. Buster, still cradled in his mother's arms, began to cry too.

"Well then," Mrs. Small said, "you go with Thomas. I don't know what's got into you."

"I think they're just tired out," said Mr. Small.

"Thomas, you keep an eye on them," Mrs. Small said. "I don't think you'll have much trouble if you sit them far back on the veranda."

Once outside, Thomas placed the boys on the dry veranda and squatted between them. He put an arm around each one until they hushed crying. After they had quieted, he stroked them gently.

"What do you suppose that old Pluto is up to?" Thomas said in a low voice. "Fixing things and arranging things. Maybe he hopes to get Papa to like him a lot . . . then he can rule everything. Well, he didn't count on us, did he? He's the devil and he won't be king!"

"Now," he said to the boys. "Mama and Papa are upstairs. We're all alone here. Tell me what it was about this door that caused you not to touch that pretty design. Remember? We came in the house through this door, and there was something about it you didn't like."

The twins stayed quiet. Thomas knew they couldn't tell him anything. But he was used to questioning them and finding answers in himself.

Thomas got up to examine the front steps. They were weathered but recently painted white as was the rest of the house. He examined the oak door and saw nothing unusual. He bent close to study the quatrefoil designs that were carved on the doorframe. They were shaped like petals. He was ready to turn away, when he found something. One petal, on a line with the doorknob, had a tiny, wood button in its center. Thomas checked, but not one of the other petals had such a button. He wouldn't have found this one if he hadn't been looking hard for something.

"So that's it," he said, "but how in the world did you all know?"

He took each twin by the hand, and led them up to the button. They bobbed from side to side, whimpering as if something hurt them. Thomas released them and let them sit on the veranda facing the barren lawn.

Cautiously he waved his hand over the button. There was a stream of cold air coming from around it. He glanced at the twins. When they stood, the air just about hit them in the face.

"It was chilly and you didn't like it," he said to them.

Carefully, and with a hand that was shaking, Thomas pushed the button. He pulled, he jerked, but nothing at all happened.

The twins fell into tantrums unlike anything Thomas had ever seen. They kicked their legs and flailed their arms wildly. They jumped up high and sat down hard, at the same time screaming at the tops of their lungs.

"You'll hurt yourselves!" Thomas warned them. He didn't touch them. He feared he might make matters worse. So he just stood there, looking down at them with his eyes darting all around.

"Quiet, kids! You'll have Mama come get you!"

It seemed that was exactly what they wanted, for they kept up the screaming.

"So you saw something!" Thomas whispered. His eyes were wide. "Something scary? Something I didn't see and couldn't take care of?"

Thomas thought of ghosts. Suddenly he was afraid, not for himself but for the twins, who could see but not say.

"Not very nice ghosts," he said, "if they have to go around scaring babies."

Thomas picked the boys up, balancing one on each hip. "But why would ghosts come just because I pushed a button?" he wondered out loud. "Ghosts?" he asked them. They whimpered and nestled against him.

"No," Thomas decided. "Something else a little more real." He hadn't the time to think what that might be, for his mother came then to see what was causing the twins to scream.

"They're just hungry, I guess," Thomas told her. "They were sitting there and then they started to cry."

"They're tired, too," Mrs. Small said. She took them from Thomas. "Now don't be long," she told him. "I'll have supper ready early. Mr. Pluto filled the refrigerator with food!"

Thomas held the door for his mother. He waited until she was in the kitchen with the twins before he closed the door hard.

Mr. Pluto, he thought. Always Mr. Pluto!

He stood on the veranda with his back to the oak door; he took in all there was to see—the grand pillars, eaves dripping wet onto the barren ground, and the circle of gray mist beyond the lawn.

When he looked carefully, Thomas was able to see through the mist. He could make out the downward slope of the hill, with its rocks and springs, and the fertile land lying along the stream. He thought he could see the bridge and the muddy roadbed that crossed over it. Somewhere beyond that lay the highway. He listened, but could hear no traffic. All was silent. The only movement was the stream, rapid and swollen with the long rain, and the springs rushing into it.

Thomas was satisfied that no one watched him. He turned around to face the oak door and pushed the button in the quatrefoil. Nothing happened. He looked left and right and, at last, craned his head to see behind him. At once he saw what must have caused the twins' tantrum. The front steps were poised about a foot off the ground and wide to the left of their proper place. Where the steps should have been was a black and jagged hole about three feet around.

Thomas stood as still as one of his wood carvings. With his back pressed against the oak door, he faced the steps and waited for whatever it was—ghosts, demons—that would rise up from the hole to challenge him. Instead, the sudden shock came from the side of the house.

He fell to his knees instinctively to hide himself. Coming forth now was the queerest sight he'd seen in all his life.

### [Thomas Meets the Ghost]

Out of the trees on the right side of the house came walking the blackest, biggest horse Thomas could remember seeing. Maybe it was not as huge as he thought at first, but he was closer to it than he had ever been to a horse. Riding on it was a tiny girl, sitting straight and tall. She had a white, frilly nightcap on her head and she wore red flannel pajamas with lace at the neck and sleeves. She had no shoes on her feet and she sat well forward, her toes clasped in the horse's mane. With her arms folded across her chest, she stared into the distance. She was serene and happy and seemed not to notice Thomas.

Following the horse was a big boy about Thomas' age. He was stronger and heavier than Thomas, and his arm muscles bulged as he pulled back on the horse's tail.

"Whoa, you black!" he said in a loud whisper. "You mean old devil! Let my Pesty off, you hear, before I break off your tailbone! Pesty, you get down off of him. Please? Come on, make him stop, I've got to get my supper before it's all gone!"

The little girl paid no attention to him. Once she laughed and then turned the horse with just her toes. She circled the lawn, with the big boy pulling hard on the horse's tail. The horse didn't seem to care. Soon they came toward the house again, right for the steps and Thomas.

Thomas felt for the button, but he couldn't find it unless he took his eyes off the little girl, the horse and the boy. They were very close, almost to the steps, and the boy was yelling for the girl to stop that horse.

"You want him to fall down under them steps? You going to walk him right through that door?"

But the child knew what she was doing. She gently nudged the horse; it stopped in front of the hole. She looked at Thomas as though she'd known he was there all the time, and smiled very sweetly at him.

Coming around the horse's flank, the boy bent delicately to look into the hole. He was aware of Thomas. Thomas could tell. Both children were playing a game with him, and he could not figure out the rules.

"Anybody go foolin' around down there maybe will get lost forever," the boy said. "Maybe get lost in one of Mr. Pluto's tunnels and never get found again."

"Nothing down there," said the child. "Nothing but sounds."

"Now how do you know that?" asked the boy. "I bet there's plenty down there nobody's run into yet."

"Mr. Pluto let me walk it," said the child, "and I know there is nothing."

"Pesty, how many times must I tell you not to get too close to Mr. Pluto? He's going to make you disappear one of these times, and then how will I ever get you home to supper?"

"I'll tell him to tie you up," said the child. "Leave you in one of those tunnels for the ghosts to play with."

"Do you intend to go down under there?"

asked the boy. "You planning on finding out how quick you can get scared in the dark?"

A few seconds passed before Thomas realized the boy was speaking to him. The boy still wouldn't look at Thomas, but pretended to be concerned with the hole.

"Who *are* you?" asked Thomas, still afraid and not at all eager to move from the safety of the door. "Who *are* you!"

The boy looked up at the child on the horse in mock amazement, then he quickly turned a polite, smiling face on Thomas.

"Well, how you been! How you feeling?" he said.

Now anger began slowly to take the place of Thomas' fear.

Then the boy said, "We are Darrow's children. I mean, I'm Mr. Darrow's youngest son, and that girl there, she follows me around so my Mama lets her stay. I call this girl Pesty. My Daddy calls her Sarah, and Mama calls her Sooky. Mr. Pluto, he calls her Little Miss Bee, and I guess you can make up a name, too, it won't matter to her."

"You mean to say she lives with you," Thomas said, slowly, "and follows you around—you all call her different names, but she isn't your sister?"

"I just have brothers," said the boy. He looked carefully at the child on the horse. "Still, she's as close to a sister as I guess I'll ever get."

"But where did she come from?" asked Thomas. Still on his knees, he had crawled out as far as the steps now, close to the boy and close to the horse. He didn't realize he had moved.

The child kicked the boy in the chest playfully and laughed.

"She came in a new tin tub," said the boy. "It was night, and I was sleeping. I was five and I don't remember it. But they say that Mama brought her in to show her off to Daddy. And the next day I saw her and I've been seeing her ever since."

Thomas wanted to ask more questions, but now the child was asking him a question.

"What you doing on Mr. Pluto's porch? He'll snatch you baldheaded if he finds you."

"He's liable to turn Pesty on you, too, and that's the worst thing could happen," said the boy.

"Mr. Pluto just works here," said Thomas angrily. "This is my father's house. We are going to live in it, and old Pluto is going to work for us."

The boy fell into a fit of laughter calculated to make Thomas even madder. He slithered on the wet ground and pounded his fists silently. Even Pesty was giggling softly into the horse's mane.

"I think you children just better get off my father's land," said Thomas. He stepped off the porch. "Part of the Underground Railroad must be under these steps. I've got work to do."

"There's no train tracks down there," said Pesty. "There never was none that I ever seen."

But Thomas was not stopping for them. The boy stood up, eyeing Thomas seriously now. Pesty backed the horse off so Thomas could kneel down by the hole.

"You fixing to go down under there? You want some company?" asked the boy.

"You'd just better get out of here," said Thomas, not looking at him. "I don't need any of your help."

"Well, I reckon that's true as far as it goes," said the boy. "But I suspect you'll be needing me later."

"We'll come back after awhile to see how you come out," said the child on the horse. And then she and the boy fell into more laughter.

"Naw," said the boy laughing. "Naw, Pesty, you can't come back today. You are all ready for bed in your pajamas, and after supper I'm going to lock you up so you can't bother this here new boy. How you like Pesty's pretty night clothes, new boy? She likes to wear red because Mr. Pluto told her red was the best color. Mr. Pluto likes red because it is the color of fire, and he is the keeper of fire. Pesty is the keeper's helper!" The boy laughed and laughed.

Thomas was excited at having met such odd children. But he hid his feelings from them by turning calmly away. "You get out of here," he said, "before I call my father!"

"Oh, we're going," said the boy. "And I'm M. C. Darrow, the youngest."

"I don't really care who you are," said Thomas right back at him. "I am Thomas Small, the oldest son of my father."

"But you can just call me Mac," said M. C. Darrow. "Everybody calls me Mac, even Mr. Pluto, when I let him get close enough."

Thomas didn't say anything. Lying flat on his stomach, he looked into the hole; his head and shoulders disappeared inside. It was then he lost his grip and fell head first into thin, black air. He landed some five feet down, on damp sod that smelled like a mixture of yellow grass and mildew. All the breath was knocked out of him. He lay there unable to move or think for at least ten seconds, until air seeped back into his lungs. Otherwise he seemed not to have hurt himself. He could hear Pesty and M. C. Darrow going away. Mac was talking quietly to the child. Then Thomas couldn't hear them anymore.

There was gray light filtering down from the opening of the steps to where Thomas lay, and he could see that he was at the edge of a steep stairway cut out of rock. The stairs were wet; he could hear water dripping down on them from somewhere.

"I could have rolled down those steps," he whispered. Mac Darrow and Pesty must have known there was a drop down to where Thomas now lay. But they hadn't told him. "They are not friends then," said Thomas softly. He cautioned himself to be more careful.

I was showing off, he thought. I hurried and I fell. That was just what they'd wanted.

"Move slowly. Think fast," Thomas whispered. "Keep in mind what's behind and look closely at what's in front."

Thomas always carried a pencil-thin flashlight, which he sometimes used for reading in the car. He sat up suddenly and pulled out the flashlight. It wasn't broken from the fall, and he flicked it on. He sat in a kind of circle enclosed by brick walls. In some places, the brick had crumbled into powder, which was slowly filling up the circle of sod.

That will take a long time, thought Thomas. He looked up at the underside of the veranda steps.

Thomas got to his feet and made his way down the rock stairway into darkness. At the foot of the stairs was a path with walls of dirt and rock on either side of it. The walls were so close, Thomas could touch them by extending his arms a few inches. Above his head was a low ceiling carved out of rock. Such cramped space made him uneasy. The foundation of the house had to be somewhere above the natural rock. The idea of the whole three-story house of Dies Drear pressing down on him caused him to stop a moment on the path. Since he had fallen, he hadn't had time to be afraid. He wasn't now, but he did begin to worry a little about where the path led. He thought of ghosts, and yet he did not seriously believe in them. "No," he told himself, "not with the flashlight. Not when I can turn back . . . when I can run."

And besides, he thought, I'm strong. I can take care of myself.

Thomas continued along the path, flickering his tiny beam of light this way and that. Pools of water stood in some places. He felt a coldness, like the stream of air that came from around the button on the oak doorframe. His shoes were soon soaked. His socks grew cold and wet, and he thought about taking them off. He could hear water running a long way off. He stopped again to listen, but he couldn't tell from what direction the sound came.

"It's just one of the springs," he said. His voice bounced off the walls strangely.

Better not speak. There could be tunnels leading off this one. You can't tell what might hear you in a place like this.

Thomas was scaring himself. He decided not to think again about other tunnels or ghosts. He did think for the first time of how he would get out of this tunnel. He had fallen five feet, and he wasn't sure he would be able to climb back up the crumbling brick walls. Still the path he walked had to lead somewhere. There had to be another way out.

Thomas felt his feet begin to climb; the path was slanting up. He walked slowly on the slippery rock; then suddenly the path was very wide. The walls were four feet away on either side, and there were long stone slabs against each wall. Thomas sat down on one of the slabs. It was wet, but he didn't even notice.

"Why these slabs?" he asked himself. "For the slaves, hiding and running?"

He opened and closed a moist hand around the flashlight. The light beam could not keep back the dark. Thomas had a lonely feeling, the kind of feeling running slaves must have had.

And they dared not use light, he thought. How long would they have to hide down here? How could they stand it?

Thomas got up and went on. He placed one foot carefully in front of the other on the path, which had narrowed again. He heard the faint sound of movement somewhere. Maybe it was a voice he heard, he couldn't be sure. He swirled the light around over the damp walls, and fumbled it. The flashlight slid out of his hand. For a long moment, he caught and held it between his knees before finally dropping it. He bent quickly to pick it up and stepped down on it. Then he accidentally kicked it with his heel, and it went rattling somewhere over the path. It hit the wall, but it had gone out before then. Now all was very dark.

"It's not far," Thomas said. "All I have to do is feel around."

He felt around with his hands over smooth, moist rock; his hands grew cold. He felt water, and it was icy, slimy. His hands trembled, they ached, feeling in the dark, but he could not find the flashlight.

"I couldn't have kicked it far because I wasn't moving." His voice bounced in a whisper off the walls. He tried crawling backward, hoping to hit the flashlight with his heels.

"It's got to be here . . . Papa?" Thomas stood, turning toward the way he had come, the way he had been crawling backward. He didn't at all like walking in the pitch blackness of the tunnel.

"I'll go on back," he said. "I'll just walk back as quick as I can. There'll be light coming from the veranda steps. I'll climb up that wall and then I'll be out of this. I'll get Papa and we'll do it together."

He went quickly now, with his hands extended to keep himself from hitting the close walls. But then something happened that caused him to stop in his tracks. He stood still, with his whole body tense and alert, the way he could be when he sensed a storm before there was any sign of it in the air or sky.

Thomas had the queerest notion that he was not alone. In front of him, between him and the steps of the veranda, something waited.

"Papa?" he said. He heard something.

The sound went, "Ahhh, ahhh, ahhh." It was not moaning, nor crying. It wasn't laughter, but something forlorn and lost and old.

Thomas backed away. "No," he said. "Oh please!"

"Ahhh, ahhh," something said. It was closer to him now. Thomas could hear no footsteps on the path. He could see nothing in the darkness.

He opened his mouth to yell, but his voice wouldn't come. Fear rose in him; he was cold, freezing, as though he had rolled in snow.

"Papa!" he managed to say. His voice was a whisper. "Papa, come get me . . . Papa!"

"Ahhhh." Whatever it was, was quite close now. Thomas still backed away from it, then he turned around, away from the direction of the veranda. He started running up the path, with his arms outstretched in front of him. He ran and ran, his eyes wide in the darkness. At any moment, the thing would grab him and smother his face. At any time, the thing would paralyze him with cold. It would take him away. It would tie him in one of the tunnels, and no one would ever find him.

"Don't let it touch me! Don't let it catch me!"

Thomas ran smack into a wall. His arms and hands hit first; then, his head and chest. The impact jarred him from head to foot. He thought his wrists were broken, but ever so slowly, painful feeling flowed back into his hands. The ache moved dully up to the sockets of his shoulders. He opened and closed his hands. They hurt so much, his eyes began to tear, but he didn't seem to have broken anything.

Thomas felt frantically along the wall. The wall was wood. He knew the feel of it right away. It was heavy wood, perhaps oak, and it was man made, man hewn. Thomas pounded on it, hurting himself more, causing his head to spin. He kept on, because he knew he was about to be taken from behind by something ghostly and cold.

"Help me! It's going to get me!" he called. "Help me!"

Thomas heard a high, clear scream on the other side of the wall. Next came the sound of feet scurrying, and then the wall slid silently up.

"Thomas Small!" his mother said. "What in heaven's name do you think you are doing inside that wall!"

*from*

# FROM THE MIXED-UP FILES OF

# MRS. BASIL E. FRANKWEILER

*E. L. Konigsburg*

*This winner of the 1968 Newbery Medal is the story of Claudia Kincaid and her brother Jamie, told by Mrs. Basil E. Frankweiler. Claudia was not running away from home permanently; she planned to return home "after everyone had learned a lesson in Claudia appreciation." But long after "everyone" had learned his lesson, Claudia and her brother were still hiding out in the Metropolitan Museum of Art, taking baths in the fountain, sleeping in a sixteenth-century bed, and being intrigued with the identification of the sculptor whose beautiful statue was on display. Mrs. Frankweiler, donor of the statue, holds the answer to Claudia's questions, and from her mixed-up files emerges the answer that finally allows Claudia and Jamie to return home. The following selection is Chapter 3 in the book; notice how Mrs. Frankweiler alternately "narrates" the story from the children's point of view and "tells" their story from her own point of view. The Saxonberg mentioned in this selection is Mrs. Frankweiler's lawyer, to whom she has sent these "files."*

## ["Checking-In" at the Museum]

As soon as they reached the sidewalk, Jamie made his first decision as treasurer. "We'll walk from here to the museum."

"Walk?" Claudia asked. "Do you realize that it is over forty blocks from here?"

"Well, how much does the bus cost?"

"The bus!" Claudia exclaimed. "Who said anything about taking a bus? I want to take a taxi."

"Claudia," Jamie said, "you are quietly out of your mind. How can you even think of a taxi? We have no more allowance. No more income. You can't be extravagant any longer. It's not my money we're spending. It's *our* money. We're in this together, remember?"

"You're right," Claudia answered. "A taxi is

expensive. The bus is cheaper. It's only twenty cents each. We'll take the bus."

"*Only* twenty cents each. That's forty cents total. No bus. We'll walk."

"We'll wear out forty cents worth of shoe leather," Claudia mumbled. "You're sure we have to walk?"

"Positive," Jamie answered. "Which way do we *go?*"

"Sure you won't change your mind?" The look on Jamie's face gave her the answer. She sighed. No wonder Jamie had more than twenty-four dollars; he was a gambler and a cheapskate. If that's the way he wants to be, she thought, I'll never again ask him for bus fare; I'll suffer and never, never let him know about it. But he'll regret it when I simply collapse from exhaustion. I'll collapse quietly.

"We'd better walk up Madison Avenue," she told her brother. "I'll see too many ways to spend *our* precious money if we walk on Fifth Avenue. All those gorgeous stores."

She and Jamie did not walk exactly side by side. Her violin case kept bumping him, and he began to walk a few steps ahead of her. As Claudia's pace slowed down from what she was sure was an accumulation of carbon dioxide in her system (she had not yet learned about muscle fatigue in science class even though she was in the sixth grade honors class), Jamie's pace quickened. Soon he was walking a block and a half ahead of her. They would meet when a red light held him up. At one of these mutual stops Claudia instructed Jamie to wait for her on the corner of Madison Avenue and 80th Street, for there they would turn left to Fifth Avenue.

She found Jamie standing on that corner, probably one of the most civilized street corners in the whole world, consulting a compass and announcing that when they turned left, they would be heading "due northwest." Claudia was tired and cold at the tips; her fingers, her toes, her nose were all cold while the rest of her was perspiring under the weight of her winter clothes. She never liked feeling either very hot or very cold, and she hated feeling both at the same time. "Head due northwest. Head due northwest," she mimicked. "Can't you simply say turn right or turn left as everyone else does? Who do you think you are? Daniel Boone? I'll bet no one's

used a compass in Manhattan since Henry Hudson."

Jamie didn't answer. He briskly rounded the corner of 80th Street and made his hand into a sun visor as he peered down the street. Claudia needed an argument. Her internal heat, the heat of anger, was cooking that accumulated carbon dioxide. It would soon explode out of her if she didn't give it some vent. "Don't you realize that we must try to be inconspicuous?" she demanded of her brother.

"What's inconspicuous?"

"Un-noticeable."

Jamie look all around. "I think you're brilliant, Claude. New York is a great place to hide out. No one notices no one."

"Anyone," Claudia corrected. She looked at Jamie and found him smiling. She softened. She had to agree with her brother. She was brilliant. New York was a great place, and being called brilliant had cooled her down. The bubbles dissolved. By the time they reached the museum, she no longer needed an argument.

As they entered the main door on Fifth Avenue, the guard clicked off two numbers on his people counter. Guards always count the people going into the museum, but they don't count them going out. (My chauffeur, Sheldon, has a friend named Morris who is a guard at the Metropolitan. I've kept Sheldon busy getting information from Morris. It's not hard to do since Morris loves to talk about his work. He'll tell about anything except security. Ask him a question he won't or can't answer, and he says, "I'm not at liberty to tell. Security.")

By the time Claudia and Jamie reached their destination, it was one o'clock, and the museum was busy. On any ordinary Wednesday over 26,000 people come. They spread out over the twenty acres of floor space; they roam from room to room to room to room to room. On Wednesday come the gentle old ladies who are using the time before the Broadway matinee begins. They walk around in pairs. You can tell they are a set because they wear matching pairs of orthopedic shoes, the kind that lace on the side. Tourists visit the museum on Wednesdays. You can tell them because the men carry cameras, and the women look as if their feet hurt; they wear high heeled shoes. (I always say that those who wear 'em deserve 'em.) And there are art students. Any day of the week. They also walk around in pairs. You can tell that they are a set because they carry matching black sketchbooks.

(You've missed all this, Saxonberg. Shame on you! You've never set your well-polished shoe inside that museum. More than a quarter of a million people come to that museum every week. They come from Mankato, Kansas, where they have no museums and from Paris, France, where they have lots. And they all enter free of charge because that's what the museum is: great and large and wonderful and free to all. And complicated. Complicated enough even for Jamie Kincaid.)

No one thought it strange that a boy and a girl, each carrying a book bag and an instrument case and who would normally be in school, were visiting a museum. After all, about a thousand school children visit the museum each day. The guard at the entrance merely stopped them and told them to check their cases and book bags. A museum rule: no bags, food, or umbrellas. None that the guards can see. Rule or no rule, Claudia decided it was a good idea. A big sign in the checking room said NO TIPPING, so she knew that Jamie couldn't object. Jamie did object, however; he pulled his sister aside and asked her how she expected him to change into his pajamas. His pajamas, he explained, were rolled into a tiny ball in his trumpet case.

Claudia told him that she fully expected to check out at 4:30. They would then leave the museum by the front door and within five minutes would re-enter from the back, through the door that leads from the parking lot to the Children's Museum. After all, didn't that solve all their problems? (1) They would be seen leaving the museum. (2) They would be free of their baggage while they scouted around for a place to spend the night. And (3) it was free.

Claudia checked her coat as well as her packages. Jamie was condemned to walking around in his ski jacket. When the jacket was on and zipped, it covered up that exposed strip of skin. Besides, the orlon plush lining did a great deal to muffle his twenty-four-dollar rattle. Claudia would never have permitted herself to become so overheated, but Jamie liked perspiration, a little bit of dirt, and complications.

Right now, however, he wanted lunch. Claudia wished to eat in the restaurant on the main floor, but Jamie wished to eat in the snack bar downstairs; he thought it would be less glamorous, but cheaper, and as chancellor of the exchequer, as holder of the veto power, and as tightwad of the year, he got his wish. Claudia didn't really mind too much when she saw the snack bar. It was plain but clean.

Jamie was dismayed at the prices. They had $28.61 when they went into the cafeteria, and only $27.11 when they came out still feeling hungry. "Claudia," he demanded, "did you know food would cost so much? Now, aren't you glad that we didn't take a bus?"

Claudia was no such thing. She was not glad that they hadn't taken a bus. She was merely furious that her parents, and Jamie's too, had been so stingy that she had been away from home for less than one whole day and was already worried about survival money. She chose not to answer Jamie. Jamie didn't notice; he was completely wrapped up in problems of finance.

"Do you think I could get one of the guards to play me a game of war?" he asked.

"That's ridiculous," Claudia said.

"Why? I brought my cards along. A whole deck."

Claudia said, "*Inconspicuous* is exactly the opposite of that. Even a guard at the Metropolitan who sees thousands of people every day would remember a boy who played him a game of cards."

Jamie's pride was involved. "I cheated Bruce through all second grade and through all third grade so far, and he still isn't wise."

"Jamie! Is that how you knew you'd win?"

Jamie bowed his head and answered, "Well, yeah. Besides, Brucie has trouble keeping straight the jacks, queens, and kings. He gets mixed up."

"Why do you cheat your best friend?"

"I sure don't know. I guess I like complications."

"Well, quit worrying about money now. Worry about where we're going to hide while they're locking up this place."

They took a map from the information stand; for free. Claudia selected where they would hide during that dangerous time immediately after the museum was closed to the public and before all the guards and helpers left. She decided that she would go to the ladies' room, and Jamie would go to the men's room just before the museum closed. "Go to the one near the restaurant on the main floor," she told Jamie.

"I'm not spending a night in a men's room. All that tile. It's cold. And, besides, men's rooms make noises sound louder. And I rattle enough now."

Claudia explained to Jamie that he was to enter a booth in the men's room. "And then stand on it," she continued.

"Stand on it? Stand on what?" Jamie demanded.

"You know," Claudia insisted. "Stand on it!"

"You mean stand on the toilet?" Jamie needed everything spelled out.

"Well, what else would I mean? What else is

there in a booth in the men's room? And keep your head down. And keep the door to the booth very slightly open," Claudia finished.

"Feet up. Head down. Door open. Why?"

"Because I'm certain that when they check the ladies' room and the men's room, they peek under the door and check only to see if there are feet. We must stay there until we're sure all the people and guards have gone home."

"How about the night watchman?" Jamie asked.

Claudia displayed a lot more confidence than she really felt. "Oh! there'll be a night watchman, I'm sure. But he mostly walks around the roof trying to keep people from breaking in. We'll already be in. They call what he walks, a cat walk. We'll learn his habits soon enough. They must mostly use burglar alarms in the inside. We'll just never touch a window, a door, or a valuable painting. Now, let's find a place to spend the night."

They wandered back to the rooms of fine French and English furniture. It was here Claudia knew for sure that she had chosen the most elegant place in the world to hide. She wanted to sit on the lounge chair that had been made for Marie Antoinette or at least sit at her writing table. But signs everywhere said not to step on the platform. And some of the chairs had silken ropes strung across the arms to keep you from even trying to sit down. She would have to wait until after lights out to be Marie Antoinette.

At last she found a bed that she considered perfectly wonderful, and she told Jamie that they would spend the night there. The bed had a tall canopy, supported by an ornately carved headboard at one end and by two gigantic posts at the other. (I'm familiar with that bed, Saxonberg. It is as enormous and fussy as mine. And it dates from the sixteenth century like mine. I once considered donating my bed to the museum, but Mr. Untermyer gave them this one first. I was somewhat relieved when he did. Now I can enjoy my bed without feeling guilty because the museum doesn't have one. Besides, I'm not that fond of donating things.)

Claudia had always known that she was meant for such fine things. Jamie, on the other hand, thought that running away from home to sleep in just another bed was really no challenge at all.

He, James, would rather sleep on the bathroom floor, after all. Claudia then pulled him around to the foot of the bed and told him to read what the card said.

Jamie read, "Please do not step on the platform."

Claudia knew that he was being difficult on purpose; therefore, she read for him, "State bed—scene of the alleged murder of Amy Robsart, first wife of Lord Robert Dudley, later Earl of . . ."

Jamie couldn't control his smile. He said, "You know, Claude, for a sister and a fussbudget, you're not too bad."

Claudia replied, "You know, Jamie, for a brother and a cheapskate, you're not too bad."

Something happened at precisely that moment. Both Claudia and Jamie tried to explain to me about it, but they couldn't quite. I know what happened, though I never told them. Having words and explanations for everything is too modern. I especially wouldn't tell Claudia. She has too many explanations already.

What happened was: they became a team, a family of two. There had been times before they ran away when they had acted like a team, but those were very different from *feeling* like a team. Becoming a team didn't mean the end of their arguments. But it did mean that the arguments became a part of the adventure, became discussions not threats. To an outsider the arguments would appear to be the same because feeling like part of a team is something that happens invisibly. You might call it *caring*. You could even call it *love*. And it is very rarely, indeed, that it happens to two people at the same time—especially a brother and a sister who had always spent more time with activities than they had with each other.

They followed their plan: checked out of the museum and re-entered through a back door. When the guard at that entrance told them to check their instrument cases, Claudia told him that they were just passing through on their way to meet their mother. The guard let them go,

knowing that if they went very far, some other guard would stop them again. However, they managed to avoid other guards for the remaining minutes until the bell rang. The bell meant that the museum was closing in five minutes. They then entered the booths of the rest rooms.

They waited in the booths until five-thirty, when they felt certain that everyone had gone. Then they came out and met. Five-thirty in winter is dark, but nowhere seems as dark as the Metropolitan Museum of Art. The ceilings are so high that they fill up with a lot of darkness. It seemed to Jamie and Claudia that they walked through miles of corridors. Fortunately, the corridors were wide, and they were spared bumping into things.

At last they came to the hall of the English Renaissance. Jamie quickly threw himself upon the bed forgetting that it was only about six o'clock and thinking that he would be so exhausted that he would immediately fall asleep. He didn't. He was hungry. That was one reason he didn't fall asleep immediately. He was uncomfortable, too. So he got up from bed, changed into his pajamas and got back into bed. He felt a little better. Claudia had already changed into her pajamas. She, too, was hungry, and she, too, was uncomfortable. How could so elegant and romantic a bed smell so musty? She would have liked to wash everything in a good, strong, sweet-smelling detergent.

As Jamie got into bed, he still felt uneasy, and it wasn't because he was worried about being caught. Claudia had planned everything so well that he didn't concern himself about that. The strange way he felt had little to do with the strange place in which they were sleeping. Claudia felt it, too. Jamie lay there thinking. Finally, realization came.

"You know, Claude," he whispered, "I didn't brush my teeth."

Claudia answered, "Well, Jamie, you can't always brush after every meal." They both laughed very quietly. "Tomorrow," Claudia reassured him, "we'll be even better organized."

It was much earlier than her bedtime at home, but still Claudia felt tired. She thought she might have an iron deficiency anemia: tired blood. Perhaps, the pressures of everyday stress and strain had gotten her down. Maybe she was light-headed from hunger; her brain cells were being robbed of vitally needed oxygen for good growth and, and . . . yawn.

She shouldn't have worried. It had been an unusually busy day. A busy and unusual day. So she lay there in the great quiet of the museum next to the warm quiet of her brother and allowed the soft stillness to settle around them: a comforter of quiet. The silence seeped from their heads to their soles and into their souls. They stretched out and relaxed. Instead of oxygen and stress, Claudia thought now of hushed and quiet words: glide, fur, banana, peace. Even the footsteps of the night watchman added only an accented quarter-note to the silence that had become a hum, a lullaby.

They lay perfectly still even long after he passed. Then they whispered good night to each other and fell asleep. They were quiet sleepers and hidden by the heaviness of the dark, they were easily not discovered.

(Of course, Saxonberg, the draperies of that bed helped, too.)

### from MY SIDE OF THE MOUNTAIN

*Jean George*

*Almost every human being, boy or girl, man or woman, occasionally wishes to escape the complexities of modern life and return to nature, but few follow through on their desires. Readers, young and old, can vicariously share such an experience in reading about Sam Gribley's adventures on his side of the mountain during the year he lived alone and off the land.*

### This Is about the Old, Old Tree

I knew enough about the Catskill Mountains to know that when the summer came, they were covered with people. Although Great-grandfather's farm was somewhat remote, still hikers and campers and hunters and fishermen were sure to wander across it.

Therefore I wanted a house that could not be

From the book *My Side of the Mountain* by Jean George. Copyright, ©, 1959 by Jean George. Reprinted by permission of E. P. Dutton & Co., Inc. and The Bodley Head

seen. People would want to take me back where I belonged if they found me.

I looked at that tree. Somehow I knew it was home, but I was not quite sure how it was home. The limbs were high and not right for a tree house. I could build a back extension around it, but that would look silly. Slowly I circled the great trunk. Halfway around, the whole plan became perfectly obvious. To the west, between two of the flanges of the tree that spread out to be roots, was a cavity. The heart of the tree was rotting away. I scraped at it with my hands; old, rotten insect-ridden dust came tumbling out. I dug on and on, using my ax from time to time as my excitement grew.

With much of the old rot out, I could crawl in the tree and sit cross-legged. Inside I felt as cozy as a turtle in its shell. I chopped and chopped until I was hungry and exhausted. I was now in the hard good wood, and chopping it out was work. I was afraid December would come before I got a hole big enough to lie in. So I sat down to think.

You know, those first days, I just never planned right. I had the beginnings of a home, but not a bite to eat, and I had worked so hard that I could hardly move forward to find that bite. Furthermore it was discouraging to feed that body of mine. It was never satisfied, and gathering food for it took time and got it hungrier. Trying to get a place to rest it took time and got it more tired, and I really felt I was going in circles and wondered how primitive man ever had enough time and energy to stop hunting food and start thinking about fire and tools.

I left the tree and went across the meadow looking for food. I plunged into the woods beyond, and there I discovered the gorge and the white cascade splashing down the black rocks into the pool below.

I was hot and dirty. I scrambled down the rocks and slipped into the pool. It was so cold I yelled. But when I came out on the bank and put on my two pairs of trousers and three sweaters, which I thought was a better way to carry clothes than in a pack, I tingled and burned and felt coltish. I leapt up the bank, slipped, and my face went down in a patch of dogtooth violets.

You would know them anywhere after a few looks at them at the Botanical Gardens and in colored flower books. They are little yellow lilies on long slender stems with oval leaves dappled with gray. But that's not all. They have wonderfully tasty bulbs. I was filling my pockets before I got up from my fall.

"I'll have a salad type lunch," I said as I moved up the steep sides of the ravine. I discovered that as late as it was in the season, the spring beauties were still blooming in the cool pockets of the woods. They are all right raw, that is if you are as hungry as I was. They taste a little like lima beans. I ate these as I went on hunting food, feeling better and better, until I worked my way back to the meadow where the dandelions were blooming. Funny I hadn't noticed them earlier. Their greens are good, and so are their roots—a little strong and milky, but you get used to that.

A crow flew into the aspen grove without saying a word. The little I knew of crows from following them in Central Park, they always have something to say. But this bird was sneaking, obviously trying to be quiet. Birds are good food. Crow is certainly not the best, but I did not know that then, and I launched out to see where it was going. I had a vague plan to try to noose it. This is the kind of thing I wasted time on in those days when time was so important. However, this venture turned out all right, because I did not have to noose that bird.

I stepped into the woods, looked around, could not see the crow, but noticed a big stick nest in a scrabbly pine. I started to climb the tree. Off flew the crow. What made me keep on climbing in face of such discouragement, I don't know, but I did, and that noon I had crow eggs and wild salad for lunch.

At lunch I also solved the problem of carving out my tree. After a struggle I made a fire. Then I sewed a big skunk cabbage leaf into a cup with grass strands. I had read that you can boil water in a leaf, and ever since then I had been very anxious to see if this were true. It seems impossible, but it works. I boiled the eggs in a leaf. The water keeps the leaf wet, and although the top dries up and burns down to the water level, that's as far as the burning goes. I was pleased to see it work.

Then here's what happened. Naturally, all this took a lot of time, and I hadn't gotten very far on my tree, so I was fretting and stamping out the fire when I stopped with my foot in the air.

The fire! Indians made dugout canoes with fire. They burned them out, an easier and much faster way of getting results. I would try fire in the tree. If I was very careful, perhaps it would work. I ran into the hemlock forest with a burning stick and got a fire going inside the tree.

Thinking that I ought to have a bucket of water in case things got out of hand, I looked desperately around me. The water was far across the meadow and down the ravine. This would never do. I began to think the whole inspiration of a home in the tree was no good. I really did have to live near water for cooking and drinking and comfort. I looked sadly at the magnificent hemlock and was about to put the fire out and desert it when I said something to myself. It must have come out of some book: "Hemlocks usually grow around mountain streams and springs."

I swirled on my heel. Nothing but boulders around me. But the air was damp, somewhere—I said—and darted around the rocks, peering and looking and sniffing and going down into pockets and dales. No water. I was coming back, circling wide, when I almost fell in it. Two sentinel boulders, dripping wet, decorated with flowers, ferns, moss, weeds—everything that loved water—guarded a bathtub-sized spring.

"You pretty thing," I said, flopped on my stomach, and pushed my face into it to drink. I opened my eyes. The water was like glass, and in it were little insects with oars. They rowed away from me. Beetles skittered like bullets on the surface, or carried a silver bubble of air with them to the bottom. Ha, then I saw a crayfish.

I jumped up, overturned rocks, and found many crayfish. At first I hesitated to grab them because they can pinch. I gritted my teeth, thought about how much more it hurts to be hungry, and came down upon them. I did get pinched, but I had my dinner. And that was the first time I had planned ahead! Any planning that I did in those early days was such a surprise to me and so successful that I was delighted with even a small plan. I wrapped the crayfish in leaves, stuffed them in my pockets, and went back to the burning tree.

Bucket of water, I thought. Bucket of water? Where was I going to get a bucket? How did I think, even if I found water, I could get it back to the tree? That's how cityfied I was in those days. I had never lived without a bucket before—scrub buckets, water buckets—and so when a water problem came up, I just thought I could run to the kitchen and get a bucket.

"Well, dirt is as good as water," I said and ran back to my tree. "I can smother the fire with dirt."

Days passed working, burning, cutting, gathering food, and each day I cut another notch on an aspen pole that I had stuck in the ground for a calendar.

### In Which I Meet One of My Own Kind and Have a Terrible Time Getting Away

Five notches into June, my house was done. I could stand in it, lie down in it, and there was room left over for a stump to sit on. On warm evenings I would lie on my stomach and look out the door, listen to the cicadas and crickets, and hope it would storm so that I could crawl into my tree and be dry. I had gotten soaked during a couple of May downpours, and now that my house was done, I wanted the chance to sit in my hemlock and watch a cloudburst wet everything but me. This opportunity didn't come for a long time. It was dry.

One morning I was at the edge of the meadow. I had cut down a small ash tree and was chopping it into lengths of about eighteen inches each. This was the beginning of my bed that I was planning to work on after supper every night.

With the golden summer upon me, food was much easier to get, and I actually had several hours of free time after supper in which to do other things. I had been eating frogs' legs, turtles, and best of all, an occasional rabbit. My snares and traps were set now. Furthermore, I had a good supply of cattail roots I had dug in the marsh.

If you ever eat cattails, be sure to cook them well, otherwise the fibers are tough and they take more chewing to get the starchy food from them than they are worth. However, they taste just like potatoes after you've been eating them a couple of weeks, and to my way of thinking are extremely good.

Well, anyway, that summer morning when I was gathering material for a bed, I was singing and chopping and playing a game with a raccoon I had come to know. He had just crawled in a hollow tree and had gone to bed for the day when I came to the meadow. From time to time I would tap on his tree with my ax. He would hang his sleepy head out, snarl at me, close his eyes, and slide out of sight.

The third time I did this, I knew something was happening in the forest. Instead of closing his eyes, he pricked up his ears and his face became drawn and tense. His eyes were focused on something down the mountain. I stood up and looked. I could see nothing. I squatted down and went back to work. The raccoon dove out of sight.

"Now what's got you all excited?" I said, and tried once more to see what he had seen.

I finished the posts for the bed and was looking around for a bigger ash to fell and make slats for the springs when I nearly jumped out of my shoes.

"Now what are you doing up here all alone?" It was a human voice. I swung around and stood face to face with a little old lady in a pale blue sunbonnet and a loose brown dress.

"Oh! gosh!" I said. "Don't scare me like that. Say one word at a time until I get used to a human voice." I must have looked frightened because she chuckled, smoothed down the front of her dress, and whispered, "Are you lost?"

"Oh, no, Ma'am," I stuttered.

"Then a little fellow like you should not be all alone way up here on this haunted mountain."

"Haunted?" said I.

"Yes, indeed. There's an old story says there are little men up here who play ninepins right down in that gorge in the twilight." She peered at me. "Are you one of them?"

"Oh, no, no, no, no," I said. "I read that story. It's just make-believe." I laughed, and she puckered her forehead.

"Well, come on," she said, "make some use of yourself and help me fill this basket with strawberries."

I hesitated—she meant *my* strawberry supply.

"Now, get on with you. A boy your age should be doing something worth while, 'stead of play-

ing mumbly peg with 'sticks. Come on, young man." She jogged me out into the meadow.

We worked quite a while before we said any more. Frankly, I was wondering how to save my precious, precious strawberries, and I may say I picked slowly. Every time I dropped one in her basket, I thought how good it would taste.

"Where do ye live?" I jumped. It is terribly odd to hear a voice after weeks of listening only to birds and crickets and raccoons, and what is more, to hear the voice ask a question like that.

"I live here," I said.

"Ye mean Delhi. Fine. You can walk me home."

Nothing I added did any good. She would not be shaken from her belief that I lived in Delhi. So I let it go.

We must have reaped every last strawberry before she stood up, put her arm in mine and escorted me down the mountain. I certainly was not escorting her. Her wiry little arms were like crayfish pinchers. I couldn't have gotten away if I had tried. So I walked and listened.

She told me all the local and world news, and it was rather pleasant to hear about the national league, an atom bomb test, and a Mr. Riley's three-legged dog that chased her chickens. In the middle of all this chatter she said, "That's the best strawberry patch in the entire Catskill

range. I come up here every spring. For forty years I've come to that meadow for my strawberries. It gits harder every year, but there's no jam can beat the jam from that mountain. I know. I've been around here all my life." Then she went right into the New York Yanks without putting in a period.

As I helped her across the stream on big boulders, I heard a cry in the sky. I looked up. Swinging down the valley on long pointed wings was a large bird. I was struck by the ease and swiftness of its flight.

"Duck hawk," she said. "Nest around here ever year. My man used to shoot 'em. He said they killed chickens, but I don't believe it. The only thing that kills chickens is Mr. Riley's three-legged dog."

She tipped and teetered as she crossed the rocks, but kept right on talking and stepping as if she knew that no matter what, she would get across.

We finally reached the road. I wasn't listening to her very much. I was thinking about the duck hawk. This bird, I was sure, was the peregrine falcon, the king's hunting bird.

"I will get one. I will train it to hunt for me," I said to myself.

Finally I got the little lady to her brown house at the edge of town.

She turned fiercely upon me. I started back.

"Where are you going, young man?"

I stopped. Now, I thought, she is going to march me into town. Into town? Well, that's where I'll go then, I said to myself. And I turned on my heel, smiled at her, and replied, "To the library."

### The King's Provider

Miss Turner was glad to see me. I told her I wanted some books on hawks and falcons, and she located a few, although there was not much to be had on the subject. We worked all afternoon, and I learned enough. I departed when the library closed. Miss Turner whispered to me as I left, "Sam, you need a haircut."

I hadn't seen myself in so long that this had not occurred to me. "Gee, I don't have any scissors."

She thought a minute, got out her library scissors, and sat me down on the back steps. She did a fine job, and I looked like any other boy who had played hard all day, and who, with a little soap and water after supper, would be going off to bed in a regular house.

I didn't get back to my tree that night. The May apples were ripe, and I stuffed on those as I went through the woods. They taste like a very sweet banana, are earthy and a little slippery. But I liked them.

At the stream I caught a trout. Everybody thinks a trout is hard to catch because of all the fancy gear and flies and lines sold for trout fishing, but, honestly, they are easier to catch than any other fish. They have big mouths and snatch and swallow whole anything they see when they are hungry. With my wooden hook in its mouth, the trout was mine. The trouble is that trout are not hungry when most people have time to fish. I knew they were hungry that evening because the creek was swirling, and minnows and everything else were jumping out of the water. When you see that, go fish. You'll get them.

I made a fire on a flat boulder in the stream, and cooked the trout. I did this so I could watch the sky. I wanted to see the falcon again. I also put the trout head on the hook and dropped it in the pool. A snapping turtle would view a trout head with relish.

I waited for the falcon patiently. I didn't have to go anywhere. After an hour or so, I was rewarded. A slender speck came from the valley and glided up the stream. It was still far away when it folded its wings and bombed the earth. I watched. It arose, clumsy and big—carrying food—and winged back to the valley.

I sprinted down the stream and made myself a lean-to near some cliffs where I thought the bird had disappeared. Having learned that day that duck hawks prefer to nest on cliffs, I settled for this site.

Early the next morning, I got up and dug the tubers of the arrow-leaf that grew along the stream bank. I baked these and boiled mussels for breakfast, then I curled up behind a willow and watched the cliff.

The hawks came in from behind me and circled the stream. They had apparently been out hunting before I had gotten up, as they were returning with food. This was exciting news. They were feeding young, and I was somewhere near the nest.

I watched one of them swing in to the cliff and disappear. A few minutes later it winged out empty-footed. I marked the spot mentally and said, "Ha!"

After splashing across the stream in the shallows, I stood at the bottom of the cliff and wondered how on earth I was going to climb the sheer wall.

I wanted a falcon so badly, however, that I dug in with my toes and hands and started up. The first part was easy; it was not too steep. When I thought I was stuck, I found a little ledge and shinnied up to it.

I was high, and when I looked down, the stream spun. I decided not to look down any more. I edged up to another ledge, and lay down on it to catch my breath. I was shaking from exertion and I was tired.

I looked up to see how much higher I had to go when my hand touched something moist. I pulled it back and saw that it was white—bird droppings. Then I saw them. Almost where my hand had been sat three fuzzy whitish-gray birds. Their wide-open mouths gave them a startled look.

"Oh, hello, hello," I said. "You are cute."

When I spoke, all three blinked at once. All three heads turned and followed my hand as I swung it up and toward them. All three watched my hand with opened mouths. They were marvelous. I chuckled. But I couldn't reach them.

I wormed forward, and *wham!*—something hit my shoulder. It pained. I turned my head to see the big female. She had bit me. She winged out, banked, and started back for another strike.

Now I was scared, for I was sure she would cut me wide open. With sudden nerve, I stood up, stepped forward, and picked up the biggest

of the nestlings. The females are bigger than the males. They are the "falcons." They are the pride of kings. I tucked her in my sweater and leaned against the cliff, facing the bulletlike dive of the falcon. I threw out my foot as she struck, and the sole of my tennis shoe took the blow.

The female was now gathering speed for another attack, and when I say speed, I mean 50 to 60 miles an hour. I could see myself battered and torn, lying in the valley below, and I said to myself, "Sam Gribley, you had better get down from here like a rabbit."

I jumped to the ledge below, found it was really quite wide, slid on the seat of my pants to the next ledge, and stopped. The hawk apparently couldn't count. She did not know I had a youngster, for she checked her nest, saw the open mouths, and then she forgot me.

I scrambled to the river bed somehow, being very careful not to hurt the hot fuzzy body that was against my own. However, Frightful, as I called her right then and there because of the difficulties we had had in getting together, did not think so gently of me. She dug her talons into my skin to brace herself during the bumpy ride to the ground.

I stumbled to the stream, placed her in a nest of buttercups, and dropped beside her. I fell asleep.

When I awoke my eyes opened on two gray eyes in a white stroobly head. Small pinfeathers were sticking out of the stroobly down, like feathers in an Indian quiver. The big blue beak curled down in a snarl and up in a smile.

"Oh, Frightful," I said, "you are a raving beauty."

Frightful fluffed her nubby feathers and shook. I picked her up in the cup of my hands and held her under my chin. I stuck my nose in the deep warm fuzz. It smelled dusty and sweet.

I liked that bird. Oh, how I liked that bird from that smelly minute. It was so pleasant to feel the beating life and see the funny little awkward movements of a young thing.

The legs pushed out between my fingers, I gathered them up, together with the thrashing wings, and tucked the bird in one piece under my chin. I rocked.

"Frightful," I said. "You will enjoy what we are going to do."

## from QUEENIE PEAVY

*Robert Burch*

*Set in rural Georgia during the depression era, Queenie's story reflects the impact of hard times on a community, but it is primarily a perceptive portrayal of a child molded by circumstance and rising above it by her own efforts. A troublemaker in school and out, Queenie has been in trouble with the law; defensive about the father who is in jail, she has been bitter toward her classmates in her loyalty to him. She comes to realize, in the course of the book, that she cannot expect help from him, but must help herself.*

### The Pride of the County

The next afternoon Queenie didn't try to catch Persimmon the way she had been doing. She decided not to risk making matters worse by getting into another scrap. She was still hurt that he had done her such a mean turn, but it was not nearly so important to her now. The thing that mattered was that her father had been paroled, and she hurried home to see him.

Her mother had taken half a day off from the canning plant, and was with her father in the house. They were sitting in her mother's room —only from now on it would be her father's room, too.

"Pa!" cried Queenie excitedly. "You're home!" She ran over to the rocking chair where he sat, planning to kiss him. But he did not reach out to her and she stopped abruptly and stood in front of him. She didn't know what to say next, so she said again, "You're home." This time she said it as if she couldn't quite believe it.

"Yes, I'm home," said her father, smiling at her.

"I'm glad you are," said Queenie. "I sure am glad you are."

"Me, too," said her father. "Anything beats the penitentiary." He got to his feet, and she thought maybe he was going to put his arms around her. Maybe he had been so overcome by seeing her again that he'd been too happy to

know what to do at first. But he started toward the kitchen. "I'm thirsty," he said. "Is the bucket still in the same place?"

"I'll get you a dipperful," said Queenie, hurrying to bring him the gourd filled with water.

When he took it, he noticed his daughter's height and said, "You get lankier and lankier, don't you, String Bean?"

Queenie laughed. "I sure do, Pa. Lankier and lankier."

"She's getting prettier," said her mother, while Mr. Peavy drank the water. "Why can't you tell her that?"

Her father handed back the dipper. "Cain't tell her anything I ain't noticed," he said, slapping Queenie on the back. Both of them laughed, but her mother did not. Her father continued, "Go do your night work, Queenie. We're gonna eat supper early and go into town."

"Are we really?" asked Queenie.

"Just your ma and me. We got to see some folks."

Queenie's smile disappeared as she started out. "Don't you want to come with me and see how the chickens are looking and all?"

"Cain't say that I do," said her father, sitting back in the rocker.

Queenie left, but she was sorry to be urged out of the house. She wanted to talk with her father—and just get to look at him for a while, too. And besides, it was early for doing the chores. She told Ol' Dominick, after she had fed the chickens, "You think I'm going crazy, don't you?—doing the night work ahead of time. And unless you tell 'em better, those dumb hens will be so confused they'll decide it's time to go to roost." He flew onto the post that held the clothesline, flapped his wings, and crowed. Queenie reached up and patted him. "Tell 'em again!" she said, and he crowed once more as she walked away.

Sweetheart was not at the gate or anywhere in sight, and Queenie walked down into the pasture. She brooded over being sent from the house until she thought of the most likely reason her father and mother were going into town. She guessed they would call on Sheriff Townsend and Deputy Ellins, and Judge Lewis, if they got there before he left his office, and maybe Cravey Mason's father, too, since it seemed that he was one of the main ones agitating for something to be done about her. She imagined her father was going to ask everybody to leave his daughter alone. He would assure them that his girl would be so good, now that he was home, that everyone in these parts would be proud of her. Queenie Peavy would be the pride of the county.

That's what she was thinking when she finally located Sweetheart on the far side of the pasture, eating kudzu through the barbed-wire fence. Amaryllis was there, too, and Queenie drove both cows to the barn. By the time she got there it was almost the usual milking time.

Elgin Corry came along soon, followed by Dover, Avis, and Matilda. Avis and Dover swung on the door of one of the stables and Matilda sat and watched them. Elgin said, "Children, don't make me have to tell you again that you're too heavy for such as that. You'll ruin the hinges." They went into another part of the barn and a few moments later the squeaking sounds of the feed-room door opening and closing indicated that they were swinging on it. But Elgin did not call to them. Instead, he told Queenie, "I hate to stay on 'em all the time. I can remember when I was their age it came natural to always be swinging on anything that would move."

Queenie got up from her milking stool to pour a pan of milk into the bucket. When she sat down again, she said, "Pa's home. Did you know that?"

"I heard he was coming. How's he getting along?"

"He's fine," she answered cheerily. "He sure is glad to get home and see me and Mamma again."

She waited for Elgin to say how pleased he was to hear the news; but instead he called to Avis and Dover, "Come here a minute, I want to talk to you." They came over and stood near him and he continued, "Queenie tells me that Mr. Peavy is home."

"Yes, sir," said Avis. "We heard. We were sitting over there in the feed room all the time."

Elgin laughed. "You were swinging on the feed-room door, you mean. But that's not why I called you. I want to remind you that you're not to be playing near Queenie's house any more. Do you hear me?"

"How come?" asked Dover.

" 'Cause I said not to," answered Elgin sternly. "And 'cause Mr. Peavy might not like it if you yell and holler and carry on with a lot of noise. His nerves may not be too good after all he's been through and——"

Queenie interrupted. "Oh, Pa's nerves are just fine. And if you suspect he's apt to get mad and chase Dover and Avis off, I'm sure he won't. Oh, I know some folks claim Pa's got a mean streak, but they don't know him, that's all."

Someone in the doorway of the barn said, "You tell 'em, String Bean!" and Queenie looked up to see her father coming inside. He spoke to Elgin, who had got up to turn Amaryllis into the lot.

"Howdy," greeted Elgin.

Queenie's father asked, "How's it going?"

"Fine, I reckon. Glad to see you back."

Dover and Avis began edging away, but Elgin stopped them. "Children," he said, "say 'hello' to Mr. Peavy."

Dover said, "Howdy-do, Mr. Peavy," but bashfulness suddenly came on Avis and she looked down at the ground and would not lift her head.

Queenie said, "They've grown a heap since you saw them, haven't they, Pa?"

"Not as much as you," he said pleasantly. "But I came to tell you that your ma and I are leaving for town."

"But what about your supper?"

"After you were so long getting back, we went ahead and ate."

"I had to hunt for Sweetheart," explained Queenie as her father left the stable.

He called back to her, "Your supper's on the stove."

Queenie felt cheated. Here he was home and she had barely seen or talked to him. She reminded herself, however, that it was probably on her account that he was so anxious to go into town. He must not be able to wait another minute to get started. She called after him, "Bye, Pa. Have a good time in town!" But if he heard her he did not turn around to answer.

Queenie ate supper by herself and then put away the dishes from the kitchen table and brought out her books. She planned to excel in her school work tomorrow. And she would behave so well, too, that everybody would see right off the change that had come over her the minute her father got home. Nobody was apt to say anything that would make her mad, she knew, since the remarks that unloosed her temper always had to do with her father's being in prison. Now that he was home, nobody could irritate her about it. But even if they could, she decided, she wouldn't let it upset her—because she was going to improve so drastically. She intended to astound everyone: Queenie Peavy would definitely be the pride of the county!

She studied her algebra problems for the next day, reworking each one until she understood it clearly, and then stopped to think more about her own situation. She wondered where her parents were at that moment. Had they seen Sheriff Townsend already? Had they arrived in town before Judge Lewis left? What about Cravey's father? She bet they would talk sense into everybody before the night was over, and she wouldn't any more have to go off to that ol' reformatory than a jack rabbit.

She got out her notebook and began writing sentences for English homework. "My rooster's name is Ol' Dominick," she wrote first. It showed the apostrophe being used to denote possession in one instance and to take the place of an omitted letter in another. "Well, how about that!" she said to herself, pleased that she had come across the second example accidentally.

Next, she began to read her science book. She read beyond the pages assigned for the lesson because she was not sleepy—and, too, she wanted to stay awake until her parents came home.

After a while she had studied her lessons until she was well prepared in all of them. But her mother and father were not home yet and she began to wonder what was taking them such a long time. She left her English book open on the table in front of her, and whenever she heard any kind of noise outside, she would bend over the book and appear to be reading it, deep in concentration. She wanted her parents to think she was sitting up late because she still had homework to do instead of because she was curious to find out what had happened in town. But the noises outside always turned out to be false alarms, twigs breaking or perhaps animals

from the woods scurrying about, not the return of Mr. and Mrs. Peavy.

At first she was not sleepy, but gradually she began to nod. Then suddenly there was a crackling noise on the dried leaves near the side of the house and she was wide awake once more. She bent over the English book and waited.

Several minutes passed and nothing happened. Then she heard the crackling noise again and could not pretend to study any longer. She ran to the door and opened it. "Ma?" she called into the yard. "Pa? Are you there?"

No answer came and then she saw the Corrys' hound standing near the steps. "Aw, Matilda!" she said dejectedly, "was that you crunching around out there?" and went back inside.

She gave up then, and got into bed. It was so long past her usual bedtime that she went to sleep almost by the time she pulled the cover under her chin.

During the night she heard, or thought she heard, her mother and father coming into the house, but she was too sleepy to rouse herself to say anything. Soon she drifted back to sleep, thinking she was overhearing them talk. Such phrases as "out of your mind drinking even one drop of whisky when you're on parole" and "no firearms" came from her mother. Her father's voice, sounding gruff, was low. He seemed to be telling his wife that he wished she would not nag at him on his first day home.

In the morning, Queenie overslept. She usually woke up the moment daylight came into the room, but this time the sun had cleared the horizon before she knew it had even begun to rise. She dressed quickly, got a fire started in the cookstove, and then hurried to the barn to do the milking—after tiptoeing into the next room and waking her mother.

It was a beautiful morning, and she felt refreshed and good until the thoughts came back to her about the conversations in the night. Then she decided she hadn't really heard them. She must have only dreamed them, the way she sometimes did when she was too anxious about anything.

Smoke was coming out of the chimney at Elgin Corry's house and Queenie could smell ham cooking. Nothing smelled quite as good on a crisp, clear morning. Elgin was leaving the barn when Queenie got to it. "Good morning," he said. "Sun-up comes early, don't it?"

Queenie smiled. "I thought I was later than I am." She was relieved to find that he wasn't too far ahead of her with his work. She bet he never overslept.

When she got home with the milk, her mother was in the kitchen. The fire was roaring hot now, and fatback and eggs were frying on top of the stove while biscuits from the day before were being warmed in the oven. Only two plates were on the table, and Queenie laughed. "You forgot to set a place for Pa!"

"He's still sleeping," answered Mrs. Peavy. "We'd better not wake him this time." She put the breakfast on the table and the two of them sat down.

Talking softly, so as not to wake her father, Queenie asked, "What did you find out last night?"

"About what?"

"About me. Is anybody still saying I need to be sent off? Wasn't that what you and Pa went to town about?"

Mrs. Peavy looked up. "No," she said. "That wasn't it. Your father wanted to see a few old friends. And you may just as well know it, he also wanted to see a few old enemies—ones he thinks should have lied in court to keep him out of jail." She broke the yellow of a fried egg and sopped at it with a biscuit. Then she continued the conversation. "But I've been trying all along to persuade the sheriff that the charges against you ought to be dropped. I had hoped to convince him that you'd do all right from now on."

"Did you sway him? Can't he see what a good effect Pa's being home will have on me?"

Her mother shook her head. "If your father obeys his parole officer and goes by the rules, it will help all of us in the long run. Of course, your behavior will count, too." She added slowly, "And I just as well . . ." She stopped there, as if she dreaded to say more. "Have some butter and pass it to me," she said briskly. "Let's finish breakfast."

Queenie ate in silence and then began getting ready for school. "I left my civics book on a chair in yonder," she said, motioning toward the other room.

"Tiptoe in and get it," said Mrs. Peavy, putting pieces of the fatback between biscuits for a lunch for Queenie and one for herself to take to the canning plant.

Queenie entered the other room quietly. Her father turned over in the bed as if he might be awake, but soon he was breathing heavily and she knew he was still asleep. She eased over to the corner where she had left the book. Her father's work jacket was hung on the back of the chair, and she reached over it and lifted the book without making a sound. But suddenly she saw something that made her gasp. She straightened up and stood motionless.

A second later she looked over at her father, but he had not awakened. Her gaze then returned to what had startled her. The sun shone in through the window and she saw clearly that she had not been mistaken. Sticking out of the jacket pocket was the handle of a pistol.

Queenie backed away from it—as if it were a snake or a wild animal that might not strike if she managed to back out of range without attracting its attention. At the door, she turned and hurried to the kitchen table.

"Ma!" she said, sitting down in one of the chairs.

"Here's your lunch," said Mrs. Peavy. "And your father's breakfast is in the warming closet. I'd better be on my way."

"Ma," said Queenie, "we better do all we can to help Pa not break any of his parole rules or anything."

"Yes, we'd better," agreed her mother, wrapping a piece of newspaper around her own lunch. "And before I leave, there's something else . . ." She hesitated, then started over. "I've been trying to tell you—the sheriff says his investigation of you proves there'll have to be a trial or a court hearing or something."

Queenie looked as if she had been slapped. Her eyes widened and her mouth dropped open and she put her hands to her head. She said nothing for a few seconds. Then she asked, "Will they put me in jail?"

"No," answered Mrs. Peavy. "I signed an appearance bond, which means I promised them you won't run away and that you'll appear at the hearing or the trial, whichever they decide to have."

## from A DOG ON BARKHAM STREET

*Mary Stolz*

*Edward Frost wants two things from life: a dog, and Martin Hastings, the bully next door, to disappear from his world. Mary Stolz, long recognized as an outstanding writer of stories for teenage girls, here turns her attention to a real boy with real problems.*

### [Edward Cleans His Room]

Edward stood at the window and watched the rain tossing in sudden gusts along the street when the wind caught it, then falling straight again. Once in a while a car went by, its tires hissing, and once a wet, ruffled robin bounded across the grass and then took to its wings and flew, apparently, over the roof.

Now a dog came running along, its nose to the ground, its back quite sleek with water. Edward watched it hopefully. There were no end of stories in which the boy wanted a dog but didn't get one until a wonderful dog came along and selected *him*. In the stories these dogs were either stray ones, or the people who owned them saw how the boy and the dog loved each other and gave the dog up.

In the stories the parents agreed to keep the dog, even if they'd been very much against the idea before.

Edward was always looking around for some dog that would follow him home from school and refuse to leave. In a case like that, he didn't see how his mother could refuse. He had even, a couple of times, tried to lure a dog to follow him. Whistling at it, snapping his fingers, running in a tempting way. But he must have picked dogs that already had homes and liked them. Now if this dog, this wet dog running along by itself in the rain, should suddenly stop at his house, and come up to the door and cry to be let in . . . wouldn't his mother be *sure* to let Edward have him? You couldn't leave a dog out in the rain, could you? The dog ran across the street, ran back, dashed halfway over the lawn, stopped to

From *A Dog on Barkham Street* by Mary Stolz. Copyright © 1960 by M. S. Stolz. Reprinted by permission of Harper & Row, Publishers, Inc. and Roslyn Targ Literary Agency

shove its nose in a puddling flowerpot, backed off sneezing, sat down and scratched its chin.

Edward held his breath, waiting. After a moment he tapped lightly on the windowpane. The dog cocked its head in an asking gesture, got to its feet, then wheeled around and continued down the street. Edward sighed. He was not at all surprised—the dog had a collar with at least four license tags dangling from it—but still he sighed. He was pretty sure he'd forgotten to make his bed and suspected that a hammer he'd been using yesterday was now lying in the back yard getting pretty wet. Mr. Frost was particular about his tools, and Edward felt that dogs, if they weren't getting further away from him, certainly weren't coming any nearer. He decided to go up and make his bed. He didn't see what there was to do about the hammer just now, since his mother would notice if he went out in the rain to get it.

The mailman turned the corner, and Edward lingered to watch him. Mr. Dudley had his mail sack and a tremendous black umbrella to juggle. He wore a black slicker that glistened in the rain and shining mud-splashed rubbers and a plastic cover on his hat. He was late already but he moved slowly, as if he were tired.

"Mr. Dudley's coming," Edward said, as his mother came in the room.

Mrs. Frost came over to the window. "Poor man," she said. "Stay and ask him if he'd like to come in for a cup of coffee."

Edward waited, and when Mr. Dudley turned up their walk, he ran to the front door and opened it. "Mother says do you want some coffee, Mr. Dudley," he asked, as he took the mail.

"Well now, that's a handsome offer," Mr. Dudley said, frowning down at his rubbers, "but does your mother know I'm just this side of drowned?"

"Oh, that's all right," Edward said cheerfully. "You take off your rubbers and raincoat here on the porch."

Mr. Dudley laid down the mail sack and his huge black umbrella. "Can't say a cup of coffee won't be welcome," he observed, as he and Edward made for the kitchen.

Mrs. Frost gave the mailman a sweet bun with his coffee, and Edward a cup of cocoa. They sat in the breakfast nook and the rain beat against the window, making things quite snug. Edward glanced out in the back yard. There was the hammer, all right. In perfectly plain view. He guessed his mother hadn't noticed it yet, and decided that rain or no rain he was going to have to go after it. It was too good a hammer to leave there until his father got home and saw it.

"Notice you have a letter there from Arizona, Mrs. Frost," said Mr. Dudley. He licked the sugar daintily from his fingers and Edward watched with admiring envy. He wondered if Mr. Dudley's mother had told him, when he was a little boy, "Don't lick your fingers, dear, use the napkin." He decided she probably had and now Mr. Dudley, all grown up, was doing as he pleased. It was satisfying to watch and look forward to. Edward was really looking forward to growing up. And the first thing I'll do, he said to himself now, is move to some city that Martin Hastings never heard of.

Mrs. Frost had picked up the letter from Arizona. Her forehead wrinkled the way it did when a pie came out of the oven not looking as she'd planned it to. Edward and Mr. Dudley waited for her to say who it was from. Or, perhaps, "How strange—who can it be from?" Or, "So it is—a letter from Arizona." But she said none of these things. She frowned at the letter, and then, in a funny gesture, put the other letters on top of it, and asked Mr. Dudley if he wanted another cup of coffee.

After the mailman had gone, Edward began to say, "Who is that letter from—" but his mother interrupted him. This was something she practically never did, since she was always telling Edward how he shouldn't, and it made him begin to be very curious about the letter. His mother asked if he'd made his bed and he said maybe he ought to go up and see, so he climbed the stairs to his room, wondering all the way (about the letter, not the bed), and found that sure enough everything was rumpled and tossed around just as he had left it.

Suddenly, because that possible dog was on his mind, and because there was nothing else to do, Edward decided to make a tremendous gesture. He would clean his entire room. He would stack the books that lay around so carelessly. He would straighten his toys and his clothes. He'd get out

the vacuum and do the rug. Maybe he'd even clean the closet. Yes, that was a great idea. He'd never cleaned the closet in his life. His mother would be so bowled over she'd probably offer him a St. Bernard on the spot.

He plunged in at once, dragging out clothes, books, fishing equipment, old forgotten trucks and games. He put the clothes on the still-unmade bed, shoved everything else out on the floor. It seemed to take an awfully long time to get the closet emptied, and then when he thought he was done he looked up, saw the shelves, and wished he'd never started.

They were absolutely jammed with junk. Well, maybe it wasn't all junk, but it looked it. And now his room was filled to brimming with things that would have to be put away again. He sat on his heels and stared around, thinking that the whole idea of cleaning up was pretty silly. Everything was just going to have to be put back in the closet, so what was the point of taking it out in the first place?

"My word, Edward," said his mother at the door, "what are you doing?"

"Cleaning my room," he said glumly.

"That's a good idea," she said, coming in. "Did all that come out of the closet?"

Edward nodded. "And it all has to go back," he said. "And I was just thinking, what's the point? I mean, where do you get *ahead?* I don't think I'll clean it after all."

"You can't leave it this way," said Mrs. Frost.

She picked up a battered green dump truck. "Do you ever use this?" When Edward said he didn't suppose so, at least he hadn't in a long time, she said, "Why don't you get a box from the cellar and put the things you don't really want in it, and we'll give it to the Salvation Army? They're marvelous at fixing things up for Christmas. It seems to me there must be a lot of things you've outgrown. When you get all that sorted out, you won't have so much to put back, and you'll be neater, *and* ahead. Sweep the closet out before you put your things away, of course, and put them away tidily. I see you hadn't made your bed after all."

There was no reasonable answer to this, so Edward stumped down to the basement for a box, wondering if dogs appreciated what people had to go through to get them. He paused at the cellar door, looking out. The rain hadn't slackened any. Or had it? He leaned forward, pressing his nose to the glass. He wasn't fifteen feet from that hammer, and his mother was busy upstairs, so if he just dashed out . . .

Pulling his sweater up so that it partly covered his head, he opened the door and dashed. The grass was sopping, the earth beneath it marshy, and, though he got the hammer all right, his shoulders and feet were drenched even in so short a run. Back in the cellar, he dried the hammer thoughtfully and stared at his shoes. Finally he removed them. The socks were dry enough. He took a towel from the hamper and rubbed his head and the sweater. Picking up the box, he went upstairs in his stocking feet, hoping his mother wouldn't notice anything.

"Here's the box," he said in a loud cheerful voice. "Think it's big enough?"

His mother had her back to him. She was on a chair, getting things down from the shelves. "I thought," she said, not turning around yet, "that I'd help you out a little. This is really quite a big job. Here, you take these things, and I'll hand you down some more—" She glanced around and stopped talking. Her eyes went from his head to his feet.

"I suppose," she said, "you had some reason for going out in the pouring rain? Aside from its nuisance value, that is?"

Edward wiggled his shoulders. He disliked that kind of remark, and would have preferred to have her come right out and ask what the heck he thought he was doing. But just saying something right out was a thing grownups rarely did. In this, as in so many matters concerning adults, Edward failed to see the reason but accepted the fact.

"Somebody had left the hammer out in the rain," he mumbled. "It might've got rusty."

"Somebody?" said Mrs. Frost, lifting one eyebrow.

Edward debated, and then said with inspiration, "Well, *I'm* somebody, aren't I?"

Mrs. Frost began to scowl, looked at the ceiling, half-smiled, turned back to the closet, and said, "How about all these jigsaw puzzles?"

"They're a bit on the simple side," said Edward. He almost added that they could get him some harder ones, but decided this wasn't the best time for requests of any sort. His mother was being very nice about the rain and the hammer, so there was no point in annoying her.

It was a funny thing, he mused, piling things in the box for the Salvation Army, that lots of times he asked for things not really much wanting them at all. For instance, jigsaw puzzles. He didn't actually want any, he didn't even like doing them very much when he got them, but the habit of *asking* was just one he sort of had. He asked for Good Humors if the Good Humor man happened to be around, clothes if he happened to be in a store where they sold them, toys if he happened to see them in an advertisement or a shop window. He guessed that one way and another he asked for something or other every single day whether he wanted it or not. Sometimes he got the thing and sometimes he didn't but anyone could see that the asking annoyed parents. Rod said he'd found that, too. Once Mr. Frost had said, "Edward, don't you ever bore yourself with these constant requests?" and Edward had said he didn't think so.

Still, thinking it over now, he wondered if it wouldn't be wiser to limit all the asking to a dog. If he concentrated on that, one of several things might happen. Either he'd wear them down so that at last they'd give in, or he'd impress them so much with how he wanted a dog and nothing else that they'd give in, or they'd get to be so sorry for him that they'd give in. Or—he had to admit—they'd get so irritated that he'd never see a dog until he was grown-up himself. He piled a fleet of little trucks in the box, and sat back on his heels to think.

"Problems?" said his mother, coming away from the closet to inspect the box. Edward nodded. "Could I help?" Mrs. Frost asked.

"Probably not," he said sadly. Then he looked up and met his mother's blue, friendly eyes. "*How* responsible do I have to be before I can have a dog?"

"Quite a bit, I'm afraid. Now, Edward . . . look at today. Bed unmade again, hammer out in the rain, *you* out in the rain—"

"But I'm cleaning my whole room," he protested.

"You started to," his mother reminded him.

"If you recall, you got everything out and then changed your mind."

"When I grow up," Edward said, "my boy will have a dog as soon as he asks for it. In fact, I bet having the dog will *teach* him to be responsible," he added hopefully.

"But suppose it doesn't? Suppose you get the dog, and he doesn't take care of it at all?"

"I wouldn't mind taking care of it myself."

"Well, that's where you and I differ," said Mrs. Frost. "I would mind."

Edward, realizing that he hadn't handled his end of the argument well at all, gave up for the time being.

So now he could either get on with the room because he'd started and ought to finish, or he could get on with it because his mother was perfectly sure to make him. He decided on the former, and, in as responsible a voice as he could manage, he said, "Guess I might as well finish up here, eh?"

"I guess you might as well," said Mrs. Frost with a smile. "I'll have to leave you. I'm making a lemon meringue pie."

"You are?" said Edward with pleasure. There were few things he preferred to lemon meringue pie. "Gee, that's great." He went and fetched the vacuum cleaner and set to work in a good humor, the matter of dogs dwindling to the back of his mind.

Even people who wanted something badly couldn't think about it every single minute.

## from THE ADVENTURES OF

## TOM SAWYER

*Mark Twain*

*This is one of the most famous scenes in American literature, and it should lead children to the book.*

### The Glorious Whitewasher

Saturday morning was come, and all the summer world was bright and fresh, and brimming with life. There was a song in every heart; and

From *The Adventures of Tom Sawyer* by Mark Twain (pseud. for Samuel L. Clemens), 1876

if the heart was young the music issued at the lips. There was cheer in every face and a spring in every step. The locust trees were in bloom and the fragrance of the blossoms filled the air. Cardiff Hill, beyond the village and above it, was green with vegetation, and it lay just far enough away to seem a Delectable Land, dreamy, reposeful, and inviting.

Tom appeared on the sidewalk with a bucket of whitewash and a long-handled brush. He surveyed the fence, and all gladness left him and a deep melancholy settled down upon his spirit. Thirty yards of board fence nine feet high. Life to him seemed hollow, and existence but a burden. Sighing he dipped his brush and passed it along the topmost plank; repeated the operation, did it again; compared the insignificant whitewashed streak with the far-reaching continent of unwhitewashed fence, and sat down on a tree-box discouraged. Jim came skipping out at the gate with a tin pail, and singing "Buffalo Gals." Bringing water from the town pump had always been hateful work in Tom's eyes, before, but now it did not strike him so. He remembered that there was company at the pump. White, mulatto, and Negro boys and girls were always there waiting their turns, resting, trading playthings, quarreling, fighting, skylarking. And he remembered that although the pump was only a hundred and fifty yards off, Jim never got back with a bucket of water under an hour—and even then somebody generally had to go after him. Tom said:

"Say, Jim, I'll fetch the water if you'll whitewash some."

Jim shook his head and said:

"Can't, Mars Tom. Ole missis, she tole me I got to go an' git dis water an' not stop foolin' roun' wid anybody. She say she spec' Mars Tom gwine to ax me to whitewash, an' so she tole me go 'long an' 'tend to my own business—she 'lowed *she'd* 'tend to de whitewashin'."

"Oh, never you mind what she said, Jim. That's the way she always talks. Gimme the bucket—I won't be gone only a minute. *She* won't ever know."

"Oh, I dasn't, Mars Tom. Ole missis she'd take an' tar de head off'n me. 'Deed she would."

"*She!* She never licks anybody—whacks 'em over the head with her thimble—and who cares for that, I'd like to know. She talks awful, but talk don't hurt—anyways it don't if she don't cry. Jim, I'll give you a marvel. I'll give you a white alley!"

Jim began to waver.

"White alley, Jim! And it's a bully taw."

"My! Dat's a mighty gay marvel, *I* tell you! But Mars Tom, I's powerful 'fraid ole missis —"

"And besides, if you will I'll show you my sore toe."

Jim was only human—this attraction was too much for him. He put down his pail, took the white alley, and bent over the toe with absorbing interest while the bandage was being unwound. In another moment he was flying down the street with his pail and a tingling rear, Tom was whitewashing with vigor, and Aunt Polly was retiring from the field with a slipper in her hand and triumph in her eye.

But Tom's energy did not last. He began to think of the fun he had planned for this day, and his sorrows multiplied. Soon the free boys would come tripping along on all sorts of delicious expeditions, and they would make a world of fun of him for having to work—the very thought of it burnt him like fire. He got out his worldly wealth and examined it—bits of toys, marbles, and trash; enough to buy an exchange of *work,* maybe, but not half enough to buy so much as half an hour of pure freedom. So he returned his straitened means to his pocket, and gave up the idea of trying to buy the boys. At this dark and hopeless moment an inspiration burst upon him! Nothing less than a great, magnificent inspiration.

He took up his brush and went tranquilly to work. Ben Rogers hove in sight presently—the very boy, of all boys, whose ridicule he had been dreading. Ben's gait was the hop-skip-and-jump —proof enough that his heart was light and his anticipations high. He was eating an apple, and giving a long, melodious whoop, at intervals, followed by a deep-toned ding-dong-dong, ding-dong-dong, for he was personating a steamboat. As he drew near, he slackened speed, took the middle of the street, leaned far over to starboard and rounded to ponderously and with laborious pomp and circumstance—for he was personating the *Big Missouri,* and considered himself to be drawing nine feet of water. He was boat and captain and engine-bells combined, so he had to im-

agine himself standing on his own hurricane-deck giving the orders and executing them:

"Stop her, sir! Ting-a-ling-ling!" The headway ran almost out and he drew up slowly toward the sidewalk.

"Ship up to back! Ting-a-ling-ling!" His arms straightened and stiffened down his sides.

"Set her back on the stabboard! Ting-a-ling-ling! Chow! ch-chow-wow! Chow!" His right hand, meantime, describing stately circles—for it was representing a forty-foot wheel.

"Let her go back on the labboard! Ting-a-ling-ling! Chow-ch-chow-chow!" The left hand began to describe circles.

"Stop the stabboard! Ting-a-ling-ling! Stop the labboard! Come ahead on the stabboard! Stop her! Let your outside turn over slow! Ting-a-ling-ling! Chow-ow-ow! Get out that head-line! *Lively* now! Come—out with your spring-line—what're you about there! Take a turn round that stump with the bight of it! Stand by that stage, now—let her go! Done with the engines, sir! Ting-a-ling-ling! *Sh't! s'h't! sh't!*" (trying the gaugecocks).

Tom went on whitewashing—paid no attention

to the steamboat. Ben stared a moment and then said:

"Hi-*yi! You're* up a stump, ain't you!"

No answer. Tom surveyed his last touch with the eye of an artist, then he gave his brush another gentle sweep and surveyed the result, as before. Ben ranged up alongside of him. Tom's mouth watered for the apple, but he stuck to his work. Ben said:

"Hello, old chap, you got to work, hey?"

Tom wheeled suddenly and said:

"Why, it's you, Ben! I warn't noticing."

"Say—*I'm* going in a-swimming, *I* am. Don't you wish you could? But of course you'd druther *work*—wouldn't you? Course you would!"

Tom contemplated the boy a bit, and said:

"What do you call work?"

"Why, ain't *that* work?"

Tom resumed his whitewashing, and answered carelessly:

"Well, maybe it is, and maybe it ain't. All I know is, it suits Tom Sawyer."

"Oh come, now, you don't mean to let on that you *like* it?"

The brush continued to move.

"Like it? Well, I don't see why I oughtn't to like it. Does a boy get a chance to whitewash a fence every day?"

That put the thing in a new light. Ben stopped nibbling his apple. Tom swept his brush daintily back and forth—stepped back to note the effect—added a touch here and there—criticized the effect again—Ben watching every move and getting more and more interested, more and more absorbed. Presently he said:

"Say, Tom, let *me* whitewash a little."

Tom considered, was about to consent; but he altered his mind:

"No—no—I reckon it wouldn't hardly do, Ben. You see, Aunt Polly's awful particular about this fence—right here on the street, you know—but if it was the back fence I wouldn't mind and *she* wouldn't. Yes, she's awful particular about this fence; it's got to be done very careful; I reckon there ain't one boy in a thousand, maybe two thousand, that can do it the way it's got to be done."

"No—is that so? Oh come, now—lemme just try. Only just a little—I'd let *you*, if you was me, Tom."

"Ben, I'd like to, honest injun; but Aunt Polly —well, Jim wanted to do it, but she wouldn't let him; Sid wanted to do it, and she wouldn't let Sid. Now don't you see how I'm fixed? If you was to tackle this fence and anything was to happen to it——"

"Oh, shucks, I'll be just as careful. Now lemme try. Say—I'll give you the core of my apple."

"Well, here— No, Ben, now don't. I'm afeared——"

"I'll give you *all* of it!"

Tom gave up the brush with reluctance in his face, but alacrity in his heart. And while the late steamer *Big Missouri* worked and sweated in the sun, the retired artist sat on a barrel in the shade close by, dangled his legs, munched his apple, and planned the slaughter of more innocents. There was no lack of material; boys happened along every little while; they came to jeer, but remained to whitewash. By the time Ben was fagged out, Tom had traded the next chance to Billy Fisher for a kite, in good repair; and when *he* played out, Johnny Miller bought in for a dead rat and a string to swing it with—and so on, and so on, hour after hour. And when the middle of the afternoon came, from being a poor poverty-stricken boy in the morning, Tom was literally rolling in wealth. He had beside the things before mentioned, twelve marbles, part of a jews'-harp, a piece of blue bottle-glass to look through, a spool cannon, a key that wouldn't unlock anything, a fragment of chalk, a glass stop-

per of a decanter, a tin soldier, a couple of tadpoles, six firecrackers, a kitten with only one eye, a brass door-knob, a dog-collar—but no dog—the handle of a knife, four pieces of orange-peel, and a dilapidated old window-sash.

He had had a nice, good, idle time all the while—plenty of company—and the fence had three coats of whitewash on it! If he hadn't run out of whitewash, he would have bankrupted every boy in the village.

Tom said to himself that it was not such a hollow world, after all. He had discovered a great law of human action, without knowing it—namely, that in order to make a man or a boy covet a thing, it is only necessary to make the thing difficult to attain. If he had been a great and wise philosopher, like the writer of this book, he would now have comprehended that Work consists of whatever a body is *obliged* to do, and that Play consists of whatever a body is not obliged to do. And this would help him to understand why constructing artificial flowers or performing on a treadmill is work, while rolling tenpins or climbing Mont Blanc is only amusement. There are wealthy gentlemen in England who drive four-horse passenger-coaches twenty or thirty miles on a daily line, in the summer, because the privilege costs them considerable money; but if they were offered wages for the service, that would turn it into work and then they would resign.

The boy mused awhile over the substantial change which had taken place in his worldly circumstances, and then wended toward headquarters to report.

#### from HARRIET THE SPY

##### *Louise Fitzhugh*

*Having learned from her friend Janie that they are destined to go to dancing school, Harriet Welsch, girl spy and author-in-training, decides to take the initiative in getting her parents to change their minds about dancing school.*

*The response of her parents, the way Ole Golly copes, and the relationships among the children are seen in this excerpt. Harriet's arrival in the book world was like an atomic explosion; some adults strongly object to the book. Other adults and most children find Harriet believable and unforgettable.*

### [*Harriet Changes Her Mind*]

That night at dinner everything was going along as usual, that is, Mr. and Mrs. Welsch were having an interminable, rambling conversation about nothing in particular while Harriet watched it all like a tennis match, when suddenly Harriet leaped to her feet as though she had just then remembered, and screamed, "I'll be *damned* if I'll go to dancing school."

"Harriet!" Mrs. Welsch was appalled. "How dare you use words like that at the table."

"Or any other place, dear," interjected Mr. Welsch calmly.

"All right, I'll be FINKED if I'll go to dancing school." Harriet stood and screamed this solidly. She was throwing a fit. She only threw fits as a last resort, so that even as she did it she had a tiny feeling in the back of her brain that she had already lost. She wouldn't, however, have it said that she went down without a try.

"Where in the world did you learn a word like that?" Mrs. Welsch's eyebrows were raised almost to her hairline.

"It's not a verb, anyway," said Mr. Welsch. They both sat looking at Harriet as though she were a curiosity put on television to entertain them.

"I *will not*, I *will not*, I *will not*," shouted Harriet at the top of her lungs. She wasn't getting the right reaction. Something was wrong.

"Oh, but you will," said Mrs. Welsch calmly. "It really isn't so bad. You don't even know what it's like."

"I hated it," said Mr. Welsch and went back to his dinner.

"I *do so* know what it's like." Harriet was getting tired of standing up and screaming. She wished she could sit down but it wouldn't have done. It would have looked like giving up. "I went there once on a visit with Beth Ellen because she had to go and I was spending the night, and you have to wear party dresses and all the boys are too short and you feel like a *hippopotamus.*" She said this all in one breath and screamed "hippopotamus."

Mr. Welsch laughed. "An accurate description, you must admit."

"Darling, the boys get taller as you go along."

"I just *won't.*" Somehow, indefinably, Harriet felt she was losing ground all the time.

"It isn't so bad." Mrs. Welsch went back to her dinner.

This was too much. The point wasn't coming across at all. They had to be roused out of their complacency. Harriet took a deep breath, and in as loud a voice as she could, repeated, "I'll be *damned* if I'll go!"

"All right, that does it." Mrs. Welsch stood up. She was furious. "You're getting your mouth washed out with soap, young lady. Miss Golly, Miss Golly, step in here a minute." When there was no response, Mrs. Welsch rang the little silver dinner bell and in a moment Cook appeared.

Harriet stood petrified. *Soap!*

"Cook, will you tell Miss Golly to step in here a minute." Mrs. Welsch stood looking at Harriet as though she were a worm, as Cook departed. "Now Harriet, to your room. Miss Golly will be up shortly."

"But . . ."

"Your *room,*" said Mrs. Welsch firmly, pointing to the door.

Feeling rather like an idiot, Harriet left the dining room. She thought for half a second about waiting around and listening outside but decided it was too risky.

She went up to her room and waited. Ole Golly came in a few minutes later.

"Well, now, what is this about dancing school?" she asked amiably.

"I'm not going," Harriet said meekly. There was something that made her feel ridiculous when she shouted at Ole Golly. Maybe because she never got the feeling with Ole Golly that she did with her parents that they never heard anything.

"Why not?" Ole Golly asked sensibly.

Harriet thought a minute. The other reasons weren't really it. It was that the thought of being in dancing school somehow made her feel undignified. Finally she had it. *"Spies* don't go to dancing school," she said triumphantly.

"Oh, but they do," said Ole Golly.

"They do *not,*" said Harriet rudely.

"Harriet"—Ole Golly took a deep breath and sat down—"have you ever thought about how spies are trained?"

"Yes. They learn languages and guerrilla fighting and everything about a country so if they're captured they'll know all the old football scores and things like that."

"That's *boy* spies, Harriet. You're not thinking."

Harriet hated more than anything else to be told by Ole Golly that she wasn't thinking. It was worse than any soap. "What do you mean?" she asked quietly.

"What about *girl* spies? What are they taught?"

"The same things."

"The same things and a few more. Remember that movie we saw about Mata Hari one night on television?"

"Yes . . ."

"Well, think about that. Where did she operate? Not in the woods guerrilla fighting, right? She went to parties, right? And remember that scene with the general or whatever he was—she was dancing, right? Now how are you going to be a spy if you don't know how to dance?"

There must be some answer to this, thought Harriet as she sat there silently. She couldn't think of a thing. She went "Hmmmph" rather loudly. Then she thought of something. "Well, do I have to wear those silly dresses? Couldn't I wear my spy clothes? They're better to learn to dance in anyway. In school we wear our gym suits to learn to dance."

"Of course not. Can you see Mata Hari in a gym suit? First of all, if you wear your spy clothes everyone knows you're a spy, so what have you gained? No, you have to look like everyone else, then you'll get by and no one will suspect you."

"That's true," said Harriet miserably. She couldn't see Mata Hari in a gym suit either.

"Now"—Ole Golly stood up—"you better march downstairs and tell them you changed your mind."

"What'll I say?" Harriet felt embarrassed.

"Just say you've changed your mind."

Harriet stood up resolutely and marched down the steps to the dining room. Her parents were having coffee. She stood in the doorway and said in a loud voice, "I've changed my mind!" They looked at her in a startled way. She turned and left the doorway abruptly. There was nothing further to be said. As she went back up the steps she heard them burst out laughing and then her father said, "Boy, that Miss Golly is magic, sheer magic. I wonder where we'd be without her?"

Harriet didn't know how to approach Janie about her defection, but she decided she must. At lunch Sport and Janie sat laughing over the new edition of *The Gregory News* which had just come out. *The Gregory News* was the school paper. There was a page reserved for every grade

in the Middle School and every grade in the Upper School. The Lower School were such idiots they didn't need a page.

"Look at that. It's ridiculous." Janie was talking about Marion Hawthorne's editorial about candy wrappers everywhere.

"She just did that because Miss Whitehead talked about them on opening day," Harriet sneered.

"Well, what else? She hasn't got the sense to think of anything original." Sport bit into a hard-boiled egg. Sport made his own lunch and it was usually hard-boiled eggs.

"But it's so dumb and boring," Harriet said. "Listen to this: 'We must not drop our candy wrappers on the ground. They must be put into the wastebaskets provided for this purpose.' It's not even news; we hear it practically every day."

"I'll put *her* in a wastebasket," said Janie with satisfaction.

"My father says you have to catch the reader's attention right at first and then hold it," said Sport.

"Well, she just lost it," said Harriet.

"You oughta write it, Harriet, you're a writer," said Sport.

"I wouldn't do it now if they paid me. They can have their dumb paper." Harriet finished her sandwich with a frown.

"They should be blown up," said Janie.

They ate in silence for a moment.

"Janie . . ." Harriet hesitated so long that they both looked up at her. "I think they've got me," she said sadly.

"What? Was that sandwich poisoned?" Janie stood up. The egg fell right out of Sport's mouth.

"No," Harriet said quickly. Now it was anticlimactic. "I mean dancing school," Harriet said grimly.

Janie sat down and looked away as though Harriet had been impolite.

"Dancing school?" Sport squeaked, picking the egg out of his lap.

"Yes," said Janie grimly.

"Oh, boy, am I glad. My father never even *heard* of that." Sport grinned around his egg.

"Well," said Harriet sadly, "It looks like I'm gonna have to if I'm gonna be a spy."

"Who ever heard of a dancing spy?" Janie

was so furious she wouldn't even look at Harriet.

"Mata Hari," Harriet said quietly; then when Janie didn't turn around she added very loudly, "I can't *help* it, Janie."

Janie turned and looked at her. "I know," she said sadly, "I'm going too."

It was all right then, and Harriet ate her other tomato sandwich happily.

After school, when Harriet went home for her cake and milk, she remembered that it was Thursday and that Thursday was Ole Golly's night out. As she was running down the steps to the kitchen she was struck by a thought so interesting that it made her stop still on the steps. If Ole Golly had a boy friend and she went out on her night out—wouldn't she meet the boy friend? And . . . if she were to meet the boy friend—couldn't Harriet follow her and see what he looked like? Extraordinary thought. She decided that she would have to be extra careful and terribly crafty to find out when, where, and with whom Ole Golly was spending her free evening. If Ole Golly went to places like the Welsches did, like night clubs, Harriet wouldn't be able to follow. Out of the question. She would have to wait until she was Mata Hari for that.

But *IF*, for instance, this boy friend were to come to the house and pick up Ole Golly. *THEN* Harriet could at least see what he looked like. She decided to pursue this as she clattered down the rest of the way into the kitchen. Ole Golly was having her tea. The cook put out the cake and milk as Harriet slipped into place at the table.

"Well," said Ole Golly in a friendly manner.

"Well?" said Harriet. She was looking at Ole Golly in a new way. What was it like for Ole Golly to have a boy friend? Did she like him the way Harriet liked Sport?

"Well, iffen it don't rain, it'll be a long dry spell," Ole Golly said softly, then smiled into her tea.

Harriet looked at her curiously. That was one thing about Ole Golly, thought Harriet, she never, never said dull things like, 'How was school today?' or 'How did you do in arithmetic?' or 'Going out to play?' All of these were unanswerable questions, and she supposed that Ole Golly was the only grown-up that knew that.

# HATSUNO'S GREAT-GRANDMOTHER

*Florence Crannell Means*

Told Under the Stars and Stripes, *from which this story is taken, is one of several collections compiled by the Association for Childhood Education International. The stories in* Told Under the Stars and Stripes *reflect the many racial and ethnic groups which live together under the flag of the United States.*

Hatsuno Noda walked alone in the crowd of girls and boys pouring out of school. She held her head so straight that her chubby black braids spatted her trim shoulders, and her step was so brisk that you would have thought she enjoyed walking by herself. Hatsuno could not bear to let anyone guess how lonesome she felt in the gay throng.

Brother Harry and six-year-old brother Teddy were deep in clumps of their schoolmates, but the girls from Hattie's class streamed by her without pausing. Behind her Patty White, whom she liked best of all, skipped along between Sue and Phyllis, giggling and talking. Hattie wondered what they were talking about. Often they were chattering about Hattie's secret dream; but today it sounded as if they were discussing the Mother's Day tea next month. This morning the teacher had appointed Patty chairman of the decorating committee.

Hattie could have helped decorate. Her slim fingers knew how to fold amazing Japanese paper birds, flowers, dolls. And at the old school the teacher would have had her do colored drawings on the blackboard, along with Tommy Lin, who was Chinese, and Consuelo, who was Mexican. The three drew better than any of the "plain Americans." But in this new school, where almost all were "plain Americans," no one knew what Hattie's fingers could do.

No, the girls were not talking about the tea. "If you join now," Patty was saying, "you can

"Hatsuno's Great-Grandmother," by Florence Crannell Means, from *Told Under the Stars and Stripes*, copyright 1945 The Macmillan Company, New York, New York. Reprinted by permission of the author and the Association for Childhood Education International, 3615 Wisconsin Avenue, N.W., Washington, D.C. 20016

go up to camp this summer—"

Oh, if only Patty were saying it to Hatsuno! But she wasn't. She broke off as she danced past with the others.

"Hi, Hattie!" she called, wrinkling her uptilted nose in a smile and tossing back her thistledown curls.

Hattie smiled a small, stiff smile, though she ached to shout "Hi!" and fall in step with Patty. Then maybe Patty would think to ask her.

"Join"—"camp": those words were the keys to one of Hattie's dearest dreams.

Hatsuno had never been in the mountains. All her life she had lived where she could see them, stretching like a purple wall across the end of the dingy downtown street. They were beautiful, with snow-capped peaks shining pink and lavender and gold in the sunrise, and Hatsuno had always longed to explore them; but though they looked so near, they were miles and miles away.

The new school had given her hope. In the new school there was a Camp Fire group; and every summer it spent a few days at a camp far up in the mountains. Hattie had seen pictures of its bark-covered lodges climbing steeply among the tall evergreens beside a sparkling stream. She had heard Patty tell of the campfires and the horse-back rides. For Patty was a Camp Fire girl, and Patty's mother was the guardian of the group. Yet, friendly though Patty was, she never spoke of Hattie's joining. And Hattie was far too shy to bring up the subject.

In her old home she had not been so shy; but the old house had grown too small, and they had had to move to a larger one. Hattie, the first Noda baby, had been followed by five boys, and, as Harry said, each child shrunk the house a little bit more. This spring brought not only a new baby but a new grandmother, and the house was as small as Hattie's year-before-last coat. Even Mother couldn't let out its hems enough to make it do.

Mother could manage almost anything. During the depression, when Father was out of work, Mother had kept the children neat as wax and even stylish. She was always up, working, when Hattie woke in the morning, always up, mending and making over, when Hattie went to sleep at night. Mother was proud that even in the bad years Denver had few Japanese Americans "on relief": almost as few as in jail.

Even Mother could not stretch the house enough for the new baby and Great-Grandmother. So the Nodas had moved, uprooting the children from neighborhood and school. The new school was pleasant; Hattie's teacher, Miss Bender, was lovely; Patty White was the gayest, prettiest girl Hattie had ever met. But Hattie didn't fit in.

So here she was, walking home alone, with Camp Fire and the mountains as far away as ever. Teddy overtook her, making noises like a machine gun—like a railway train—like an airplane. Teddy's face was as round as a button, his eyes as black as coal, his teeth as white as rice.

"Last one home's a lame duck!" he chirped at her.

She did not hurry as once she would have done. Home was a changed place now; changed by Grandmother as well as by the new house.

Though Great-Grandmother had come from Japan ten years ago, Hattie had never seen her till this month. Great-Grandmother had lived with Aunt Kiku in San Francisco, until Aunt Kiku's death had left Grandmother alone.

She was not at all what Hattie had expected; not at all like grandmothers in books, comfortable, plump people who loved to spoil their grandchildren. No, Grandmother was not that kind.

Hattie slowly opened the door, which still quivered from Teddy's banging it. Little gray Grandmother sat stiffly erect, only her head bent toward the sock she was darning, her small feet dangling.

"How do you do, Grandmother?" said Hattie.

"How do you do, Elder Daughter?" Grandmother responded. There is no easy way to say "granddaughter" in Japanese.

Under their folded lids Grandmother's eyes traveled down Hattie. Hattie, feeling prickly, smoothed her hair, straightened her collar, twitched her checked skirt, and finally shifted her weight to one knee as Grandmother reached her feet.

"A cold day for bare legs," Grandmother observed. Hattie thought her look added, *And a great girl twelve years old should wear long stockings.*

Self-consciously Hattie's eyes pulled free

from Grandmother's. "Oh," she cried, "Dicky's climbed on the piano again." She ran over and replaced the box of satiny white wood in which her latest—and last—doll always stood on view, fairly safe from the six boys. It was an enchanting doll, with glossy black hair and a silk kimono. "The other boys at least keep off the piano," Hattie scolded, "but not Dicky."

Grandmother's cool eyes seemed to say, *Boys have to be excused, since they're so much more important than girls. And why should a great girl of twelve care about dolls?*

Hattie hurried on into the good-smelling kitchen. "Mother," she complained, "Grandmother doesn't understand that we're Americans, not Japanese. I bet she'd like me to flop down on my knees and bump my head on the floor the way you used to have to, and say, 'Honorable Grandmother, I have returned.'"

"Wash your hands," said Mother, "and help me get dinner on the table."

Hattie slapped her shoes down hard, as she went to the sink to wash. She wished her heels weren't rubber; they didn't make enough noise to express her feelings.

"Of course you will give proper courtesy to the old," Mother said quietly.

"Why? She doesn't even like me." The question was useless. Hattie had grown up knowing that politeness to the old was as much a law as honesty, industry, self-control—and minding parents.

Mother only said, "Stop and buy grapefruit on your way from school. Be sure to pick out heavy ones."

"Of course," Hattie grumbled. Hadn't she known how to choose good fruit and vegetables since she was nine?

Dinner was Japanese American. Seven Nodas —and Grandmother—crowded around an ordinary American table; but the utensils were chopsticks instead of knives and forks. The fish soup and the pickled radish were Japanese; the *pakkai* were American spareribs and the fluffy white rice was international. Bread and butter were pure American, and the dessert was Japanese gelatin, too firm to quiver. "It's not so nervous as American jelly," Harry said, and made Teddy laugh till his eyes went shut.

Only Grandmother seemed all Japanese; in the way she sipped her soup and tea, with a noise that was polite in Japan but not in America; in the way she refused bread and butter; in the way she greeted an old neighbor of the Nodas', who came in as they were finishing the meal.

Grandmother shuffled across the room, toeing in, because for sixty-five of her seventy-five years she had worn clogs; and she bowed the deep bow of old Japan, her withered hands sliding down to her knees. Why couldn't Grandmother be more American?

The neighbor had come to remind them that tonight was the festival called Buddha's Birthday. Grandmother's eyes brightened at the news. But Mother apologized: she could not go with Grandmother, for Saburo the new baby was feverish, and she could never bear to leave her babies when they were sick. Father? He had to work tonight. Thoughtfully Grandmother looked at Hattie. Hattie excused herself and hurried back to school.

Right up to the time school opened, she kept seeing Grandmother's eyes brighten and grow dull. If Hattie had been with Patty and the others on the schoolground, as she longed to be, she might have forgotten Grandmother. But sitting lonesomely at her desk, pretending to read, she could not forget.

Maybe it was good, after all, to have a rule about being kind to old people whether they like you or not. Hattie thought of Mother, taking care of her and her brothers when they were young and helpless. How dreadful if, when Mother grew old and helpless, they did not take turn about and care for her! Hattie frowned at her book, thinking.

"Mad, Hattie? My, but you're scowling!" teased Patty, pausing as she came in from the schoolground.

Hattie shook her head and smiled. If only Patty would sit down beside her and say the thrilling words, "Oh, Hattie, wouldn't you like to join Camp Fire?" If she would even say, "Can't you come over after school?"

But after school Hattie walked home alone, as usual, stopping for the grapefruit on her way. When she had put them in the home cooler, she hunted up Grandmother, and ducked her head in a shy bow. "Grandmother," she said, "if you want to go to Buddha's Birthday tonight, I'm sure Mother will let Harry and me go with you."

The Nodas were Methodists, so the Buddhist church was strange to Hattie and Harry. Tonight it was crowded, and all through the program small children trotted in and out and climbed over people's feet, with nobody minding. There were songs and dances and pantomimes, graceful kimonos, stately poses, dignified steps; and voices in the high falsetto which was the proper tone for Japanese actors, but which gave Hattie a funny, embarrassed feeling. "Such squeaky doors!" Harry whispered comically.

Coming home by street-car and bus, the three arrived so late that the house was all sleeping. Harry bade Grandmother good-night and stumbled drowsily to his room, but Grandmother lingered, eyes bright and cheeks flushed.

Hattie hunted for something to say. "The dancing was lovely," she said. "And the kimonos."

"I have one old kimono," Grandmother said, turning toward her door. With Hattie at her heels, she opened a dresser drawer and took out a silken bundle which she unfolded and held out, smiling faintly at Hattie's gasp of admiration.

"Chrysanthemums, for your aunt's name, Kiku, Chrysanthemum," said Grandmother. Gorgeous blossoms in many rich colors grew across the heavy blue crepe. "It was the only one saved from the great San Francisco fire. She wrapped it round one of her doll boxes." Grandmother motioned toward the drawer and a white wood box that lay there.

"Could I see?" Hattie stuttered.

"You may," Grandmother answered.

When Hattie slid open the box the breath of the Orient puffed out into her nostrils. She lifted the bag that protected the doll's hair and face, and gazed at the miniature lady, exquisitely moulded, and robed in brocades, padded, corded, embroidered. Clasping the box to her breast with one hand, Hattie pulled out a chair for Grandmother. "I don't know much about the doll festival," she coaxed shyly. "Here in Denver we don't."

She curled up on the floor at Grandmother's feet. "O Kiku San brought her doll set with her," Grandmother said, "when she married and came to America. This one is more than a hundred years old. We were taught to take care of things. The girls' festival—O Hina Matsuri—was a great day. It was play, but it taught us history and manners."

Looking from the doll to Grandmother, Hattie listened with all her might. She missed some words, for the Japanese the Nodas used at home was simple, and, to Hattie's relief, there had been no Japanese Language School for some years now. Still, she could follow the story, and it made pictures for her in the quiet night: little-girl-Grandmother wearing enchanting kimonos, in charming rooms carpeted with cushiony mats; spending long hours learning to serve tea just so, to arrange flowers just so, to paint the difficult Japanese letters just so; learning to hold her face and voice calm no matter how she felt. Girl-Grandmother, writing poems with her friends and going to view the full moon, valuing beauty above riches. Grandmother, hearing about America, and longing to go where life was free for women. Grandmother, never able to come until she was too old to fit herself into this new land.

When the parlor clock struck one, Grandmother stopped short. "A girl of twelve should be asleep!" she said severely.

Next morning Hattie wondered if she had dreamed that companionable midnight visit, for Grandmother looked coldly at Hattie's bare knees and said, "Since you must run and jump like a boy, I suppose those ugly short clothes are necessary." But even while Hattie was biting her lip uncomfortably, Grandmother added, "Hatsuno, the chrysanthemum kimono and the doll are to be yours. After all, you are our only girl."

Home was beginning to seem homelike again.

That was fortunate for Hattie, since neighborhood and school were still strange. It was a relief to go back to their old district on Sundays, to the Japanese Methodist Church. And once Mother took the older children to an evening carnival at their old school. On the way they stopped at the store where they used to buy Japanese food, dishes, cloth. Clean and bright itself, it was jammed in among grimy second-hand stores and pawn shops. It was queer, Hattie thought, but no matter how clean people were, or what good citizens, if they happened to be born Chinese or Japanese or Mexican, they were expected to live down on these dirty, crowded streets, with the trucks roaring past. Yes, the new neighborhood and school were far pleasanter than the old—if only Hatsuno could fit in.

As Mother's Day approached, Hattie felt lonelier than ever. When she came into school two days before the tea, Patty, Sue and Phyllis were huddled round the teacher's desk. Miss Bender smiled approvingly at Hattie, who was already top student in Seventh Grade. Patty smiled, too, and looked at .her expectantly. Hattie's heart thumped with the wish to push herself in amongst them. But how could she? She smoothed her starched skirt under her, sat down, and pretended to clean out her desk.

"It's such a late spring," Miss Bender was saying, "the lilacs aren't out. But I'll bring sprays of cherry-blossoms. And we must find out how many mothers to expect. I hope your mother is coming, Hattie."

"No, ma'am," Hattie said soberly. "The baby has chickenpox, and Mother just won't leave a sick baby."

"Haven't you an aunt or grandmother who could come in her place?"

Oh, dear! Grandmother would be so different from the rest. What would Patty think of her? Then Hattie's head came up. "I'll ask Great-Grandmother," she said.

She thought Grandmother would refuse. She hoped Grandmother would refuse. Instead, Grandmother asked, "Every girl should have mother or grandmother at this tea?"

"Yes, Grandmother."

"And your mother will not leave the baby. Elder daughter, you went with me to Buddha's Birthday. I go with you to school."

Hattie swallowed a lump in her throat. Grandmother was doing this because she thought Hattie wished it. Tea—Grandmother would sip it in Japanese fashion. Would she notice if the girls giggled? She would hide the fact if she did. Hattie thought of Grandmother's long training in the concealment of pain or disappointment. Well, that was a good heritage for anybody. Hattie would use it now. "Thank you, Grandmother," she said. "I will come and get you Friday, after school."

When the two came into the schoolroom that afternoon, the mothers were all there and having their tea, and it seemed to Hattie that everyone stopped talking and turned to gaze. Well, she and Grandmother must look pretty funny, Hattie thought.

Hattie was dressed like the other girls, in white sweater and short white skirt, her white anklets folded neatly above her oxfords, and her black hair out of its braids and done in another favorite style of the season. Grandmother, as short and slim as Hattie, wore a dress nicely made over from a kimono, but looking a little strange; and her gray hair was combed straight back from the withered little face with its slanting eyes.

Politely Hattie introduced Miss Bender to Grandmother, and pulled up one of the visitor's chairs, since Grandmother had never been to a tea where people stood up and balanced the dishes on their hands. Patty brought her a plate, Phyllis the sandwiches, Sue a cup of tea. Then Patty returned, pulling her mother after her. "Mom," she said, "here's Hattie. And here's her great-grandma." Patty dropped her mother's hand and stood beaming.

Hattie looked anxiously at Grandmother. She could not speak a word of English, nor the others a word of Japanese. But, instead of words, Seventh Grade and its mothers were bringing sandwiches and cakes till Grandmother's plate was heaped. And Grandmother sat there, as stately and self-possessed and smiling as if she went to seven teas a week.

Hattie studied her more closely. Others might think Grandmother's little face a mask, but Hattie saw that the eyes were bright again, and that the wrinkled cheeks were pink. Grandmother liked it! Grandmother felt happy and at home!

Maybe even a great-grandmother could be lonesome, especially when she was too old to learn the ways of a new land. Thinking so happily of Grandmother that she forgot all about her own shyness, Hattie squeezed Patty's arm, just as she might have squeezed Teddy's on some rare occasion when he was sweet instead of maddening.

Patty squeezed back—quickly, as if she had been waiting for the chance. "Mother!" she stuttered, in a voice that matched her gay fluff of curls. "Mother, I think maybe I was mistaken. I think Hattie might like to—" She looked eagerly up into her mother's questioning eyes—"You ask her, Mother!" she begged.

"About Camp Fire? Hattie, would you like to join our Camp Fire group?"

Hattie was silent from pure joy and astonishment.

"If I got your name in this week," Mrs. White continued, "you could go to camp with us. A camp in the mountains; do you know about it?"

"Oh, yes, ma'am, *I know*," Hattie said with shining eyes. "Oh, yes, ma'am!"

## from ELLEN GRAE

### Vera and Bill Cleaver

*Few readers who meet Ellen Grae are likely to forget her. Ellen is a real creative artist, and her story leaves readers with much to think and talk about. How much of what she says is true? Everyone recognizes that the tale of Fortis Alonzo Gridley is a story, but what about Ira's account of his parents' death? Around that question the authors have written a short but provocative book that is humorous and at the same time seriously explores the question of moral responsibility.*

### [Ellen Tells a Story and Hears a Story]

Mrs. McGruder isn't a religious person especially, although she and Mr. McGruder attend the Methodist Church every Sunday and when I live with her I have to leave off being a Pantheist and turn Methodist too. But she likes to have people talk to her about religion.

So, wanting to please her, I told her that I had learned to be most truly, humbly grateful for all the benevolences God had seen fit to bestow upon me.

She turned a light green gaze upon me and asked, "Oh? What brought that on?"

"Nothing brought it on," I explained. "I just started feeling grateful toward Him. I feel grateful toward you too, Mrs. McGruder. For letting me come back down here and stay with you while I go to school. I vow that I've changed since last year and won't be as much trouble to you this year as I was last."

She said, "Well, if that's true it'll be my turn to be grateful. Like what, for instance, have you changed?"

"Well, for one thing I take a bath every night now without anybody hollering at me to do it and for another I've stopped swearing. I don't even say hell any more. I think that the use of profanity is a vocabulary deficiency, don't you?"

"At the moment I can't think," Mrs. McGruder said, handing me a freshly sugared doughnut. "I'm too busy counting my blessings."

"I know a girl whose father, they said, dropped dead from swearing. Her name's Opal Gridley. Her father's name was Fortis Alonzo and I think that's what killed him."

"I'm really trying but I don't get the connection," Mrs. McGruder said.

"You will in a minute. Well, anyway, he was a meter reader for the gas company and I guess that and his having a name like Fortis Alonzo burdened him heavily and made him feel unimportant."

"I think Fortis Alonzo is rather a pretty name," Mrs. McGruder murmured.

"Do you? Well, that's what it was. Fortis Alonzo Gridley. He used to drive around with all the windows in his car rolled up. Even when everybody else was standing around pouring sweat and with their tongues hanging out having trouble breathing because it was so hot, Mr. Gridley would get in his car and roll up all the windows and drive around and wave to people."

"I'm still trying," Mrs. McGruder said.

"His wife was fat and could sing Italian. She practiced every night after supper. If you listened it was sadly pretty but nobody did. They'd all come out on their porches and stand around and laugh and this made Mr. Gridley mad. He'd run out of his house and shake his fist at them and swear. When he died everybody said that's what caused it. They said God struck him dead for swearing so much. But do you know something?"

"I'm beginning to think not," Mrs. McGruder said.

"Mr. Fortis Alonzo Gridley died at his own hand. Trying to make people think he was rich enough to have an air-conditioned car. He didn't have it though and that's what killed him. The heat and no air at all. I was the one who got to him first the night he collapsed. Gridley's house was next door to ours and when I saw Mr. Gridley drive up weaving and wobbling I ran over and jerked the door of his car open and he fell out. He didn't have time to say one word. Just blew a bubble and died."

"What do you mean he blew a bubble?"

"He blew a bubble while he was dying. It looked like glass. Mrs. McGruder?"

"Yes, Ellen Grae?"

"Was that telegram that came a few minutes ago from Rosemary?"

"It was from her father. She'll be in on the ten o'clock train. Are you ready for more breakfast now?"

"No thanks. I still hate breakfast; I haven't changed that much. Will I have to room with her again?"

"That's my plan. Why?"

"Oh, nothing. It's just that I was thinking it might be better if I could have a room to myself this year. I forgot to tell you and I'll bet Grace did too that lately I have these strange seizures."

"Seizures? What kind of seizures?"

"Seizures. You know. They always come at night. I get up and crash around and cry out. I know when I'm doing it but I can't stop myself. Jeff says it's a very frightening thing to watch. He says it's almost as if I was disembodied. I was just thinking it might be better if Rosemary could be spared the sight. You know how frail she is."

"No, I hadn't noticed," Mrs. McGruder said, setting two scrambled eggs and a glass of milk in front of me. "I'll be on the lookout for one of your attacks but in the meantime could you just oblige me and eat so that we can get on to more important things?"

Mrs. McGruder is a MORE person. Everything, no matter what it is, always should be MORE.

Together we went down the hall to the room that I was again to share with Rosemary and Mrs. McGruder looked at my bed and said that the sheets and spread could stand a little MORE smoothing and the pillow a little MORE plumping. Then she watched while I finished unpacking my suitcases which contained MORE books than clothes and said that I should have brought MORE dresses and that those I did bring needed MORE starch.

She looked at my white shoes and made a noise with her tongue against the roof of her mouth. "Who polished these shoes, Ellen Grae?"

"I did. Don't they look nice?"

"Yes. Except they've got MORE white on the soles than on the tops."

About ten o'clock we drove down to the village of Thicket to meet Rosemary's train but as usual it was late. Mrs. McGruder parked the car off to one side and tried to settle down to reading a magazine which she had had the foresight to bring along but couldn't because I was there.

"Goodness, Ellen Grae. Stop fidgeting."

"I'm not fidgeting. I'm itching myself. It's all those baths I've been taking. Wouldn't some boiled peanuts taste good right about now? Just to take our minds off things?"

Mrs. McGruder frowned but when she turned her head to look at me there was a gentleness in her eyes. "Oh, honey, you don't really want any boiled peanuts now, do you?"

"Some nice, salty, juicy ones. The way Ira fixes them. While we're just sitting here waiting for Rosemary I could just hop over to his stand and get us a couple of bags. I'd hurry."

Mrs. McGruder sighed but reached into her handbag and found her change purse and extracted a quarter. "All right but don't make me come after you. And watch when you cross the street."

She meant for cars, of course, but there were only three parked ones. First Street lay hot and quiet under the September sun. The only humans in sight were the clerk from Sangster's Grocery Store who was busy letting down the green window awnings, a man in white coveralls who had his head stuck in the door of the barber shop, and Ira who was setting up his stand in its customary oak-shaded spot.

A lot of people in Thicket think that Ira is crazy but he's not. He's just different. He never wears shoes even when the cold winds come sweeping down from the north, he can't read or write and he lives in a two-room tin shack down near the river bend all by himself. Mrs. McGruder told me that once upon a time Ira had a mother and father, at least a stepfather, but that one day they just picked up and left and never came back. Nobody knows how old Ira is. Mrs. McGruder says maybe thirty but I think maybe he's older because he's got white in his black hair and sometimes his dark eyes have a very old man's sadness in them. Ira lives on what money he can make selling boiled and parched peanuts and sometimes somebody patient will pay him to mow a yard. He could make a lot of money mowing yards because he's neat and careful but he won't talk to people. He just nods and points which makes everybody nervous. Even when he goes into a store to buy something that's all he does. Mrs. McGruder told me that in all the years she's been seeing Ira around town she's never heard him speak. I reckon nobody has except me. He talks to me all the time.

I skipped up to his stand and whacked the board that was his counter and said, "Hey, Ira."

He turned around and gave me his slow, quiet look. "Hey, Ellen Grae. I wuz hopin' you'd come by to see me this mornin'. I saw you yistiddy when you come on the train."

"You did? I didn't see you. Why didn't you holler?"

"They wuz people around. Ellen Grae, I got me a goat now."

"Oh, Ira, that's wonderful!"

"When can you come and see her?"

"I don't know. Maybe Sunday after church. I'll get Grover to come with me. I brought back a whole pile of books with me. If you want me to I'll bring one when I come and read you a story. What's your goat's name?"

"Missouri."

"Missouri? That's a funny name for a goat."

"My mother's name wuz Missouri," Ira explained softly, setting two waxed paper bags of boiled peanuts up on the counter. "My goat reminds me of my mother. Did I ever tell you what happened to my mother, Ellen Grae?"

I laid my quarter on the counter and waited for Ira to lay back a nickel change but he didn't. Which wasn't unusual. Ira didn't know how to make change. If you handed him a dollar for one bag of peanuts he'd keep the whole thing. But,

by the same token, if you only handed him a penny for a half dozen bags that was all right too. So, if you traded with him for any length of time, things kind of evened themselves out.

"Yes, you told me what happened to your mother, Ira. Listen, I have to go now. Mrs. McGruder and I just came down to the train station to meet Rosemary. When Grover and I come over Sunday afternoon I'll read to you."

"She died in the swamp, she and her husband. While they wuz tryin' to run away from me. They had 'em this ol' rattler in a box and they wuz draggin' me alongside an' pokin' at him with a stick but instead of bitin' me like he wuz suppose' to, he stuck his ol' head out 'n bit 'em. They swoll up and threshed around some afterward but they wa'n't nothin' I could do for 'em. We wuz too far back in the swamp. So I buried 'em 'longside of that ol' snake. I killed the snake first so he wouldn't bite 'em no more. I didn't tell you 'bout this before, did I, Ellen Grae?"

"No, I reckon this is the first time, Ira. Listen, I'll see you Sunday." I picked up the two bags of peanuts and started to turn away and leave but something in the way Ira looked caused me to turn back. "Listen, Ira, you feel all right, don't you? You aren't sick or anything, are you?"

For a second I thought there were tears on Ira's black lashes but it was only the sun glinting on them. He said, "No, I'm not sick, Ellen Grae. Just tuckered out from talkin' so much."

Poor Ira. He has these hallucinations.

## from HOMER PRICE

### Robert McCloskey

*The doughnut episode in* Homer Price *has long been a favorite of readers of Robert McCloskey's amusing stories. He won the Caldecott Medal in 1942 for* Make Way for Ducklings, *and in 1958 for* Time of Wonder. *Any one of his other picture-stories might also have won it—* Lentil, Blueberries for Sal, *or* One Morning in Maine. *His illustrations for* Trigger John's Son *by Tom Robinson are equally delightful.*

## The Doughnuts

One Friday night in November Homer overheard his mother talking on the telephone to Aunt Agnes over in Centerburg. "I'll stop by with the car in about half an hour and we can go to the meeting together," she said, because tonight was the night the Ladies' Club was meeting to discuss plans for a box social and to knit and sew for the Red Cross.

"I think I'll come along and keep Uncle Ulysses company while you and Aunt Agnes are at the meeting," said Homer.

So after Homer had combed his hair and his mother had looked to see if she had her knitting instructions and the right size needles, they started for town.

Homer's Uncle Ulysses and Aunt Agnes have a very up and coming lunch room over in Centerburg, just across from the court house on the town square. Uncle Ulysses is a man with advanced ideas and a weakness for labor saving devices. He equipped the lunch room with automatic toasters, automatic coffee maker, automatic dish washer, and an automatic doughnut maker. All just the latest thing in labor saving devices. Aunt Agnes would throw up her hands and sigh every time Uncle Ulysses bought a new labor saving device. Sometimes she became unkindly disposed toward him for days and days. She was of the opinion that Uncle Ulysses just frittered away his spare time over at the barber shop with the sheriff and the boys, so, what was the good of a labor saving device that gave you more time to fritter?

When Homer and his mother got to Centerburg they stopped at the lunch room, and after Aunt Agnes had come out and said, "My, how that boy does grow!" which was what she always said, she went off with Homer's mother in the car. Homer went into the lunch room and said, "Howdy, Uncle Ulysses!"

"Oh, hello, Homer. You're just in time," said Uncle Ulysses. "I've been going over this automatic doughnut machine, oiling the machinery and cleaning the works . . . wonderful things, these labor saving devices."

"Yep," agreed Homer, and he picked up a cloth and started polishing the metal trimmings while Uncle Ulysses tinkered with the inside workings.

"Opfwo-oof!!" sighed Uncle Ulysses and, "Look here, Homer, you've got a mechanical mind. See if you can find where these two pieces fit in. I'm going across to the barbershop for a spell, 'cause there's somethin' I've got to talk to the sheriff about. There won't be much business here until the double feature is over and I'll be back before then."

Then as Uncle Ulysses went out the door he said, "Uh, Homer, after you get the pieces in place, would you mind mixing up a batch of doughnut batter and put it in the machine? You could turn the switch and make a few doughnuts to have on hand for the crowd after the movie . . . if you don't mind."

"O.K." said Homer, "I'll take care of everything."

A few minutes later a customer came in and said, "Good evening, Bud."

Homer looked up from putting the last piece in the doughnut machine and said, "Good evening, Sir, what can I do for you?"

"Well, young feller, I'd like a cup o' coffee and some doughnuts," said the customer.

"I'm sorry, Mister, but we won't have any doughnuts for about half an hour, until I can mix some dough and start this machine. I could give you some very fine sugar rolls instead."

"Well, Bud, I'm in no real hurry so I'll just have a cup o' coffee and wait around a bit for the doughnuts. Fresh doughnuts are always worth waiting for is what I always say."

"O.K." said Homer, and he drew a cup of coffee from Uncle Ulysses' super automatic coffee maker.

"Nice place you've got here," said the customer.

"Oh, yes," replied Homer, "this is a very up and coming lunch room with all the latest improvements."

"Yes," said the stranger, "must be a good business. I'm in business too. A traveling man in outdoor advertising. I'm a sandwich man, Mr. Gabby's my name."

"My name is Homer. I'm glad to meet you, Mr. Gabby. It must be a fine profession, traveling and advertising sandwiches."

"Oh no," said Mr. Gabby, "I don't advertise sandwiches, I just wear any kind of an ad, one sign on front and one sign on behind, this way. . . . Like a sandwich. Ya know what I mean?"

"Oh, I see. That must be fun, and you travel too?" asked Homer as he got out the flour and the baking powder.

"Yeah, I ride the rods between jobs, on freight trains, ya know what I mean?"

"Yes, but isn't that dangerous?" asked Homer.

"Of course there's a certain amount a risk, but you take any method a travel these days, it's all dangerous. Ya know what I mean? Now take airplanes for instance . . ."

Just then a large shiny black car stopped in front of the lunch room and a chauffeur helped a lady out of the rear door. They both came inside and the lady smiled at Homer and said, "We've stopped for a light snack. Some doughnuts and coffee would be simply marvelous."

Then Homer said, "I'm sorry, Ma'm, but the doughnuts won't be ready until I make this batter and start Uncle Ulysses' doughnut machine."

"Well now aren't you a clever young man to know how to make *doughnuts!*"

"Well," blushed Homer, "I've really never done it before but I've got a receipt to follow."

"Now, young man, you simply must allow me to help. You know, I haven't made doughnuts for years, but I know the best receipt for doughnuts. It's marvelous, and we really must use it."

"But Ma'm . . ." said Homer.

"Now just *wait* till you taste these doughnuts," said the lady. "Do you have an apron?" she asked, as she took off her fur coat and her rings and her jewelry and rolled up her sleeves. "Charles," she said to the chauffeur, "hand me that baking powder, that's right, and, young man, we'll need some nutmeg."

So Homer and the chauffeur stood by and handed things and cracked the eggs while the lady mixed and stirred. Mr. Gabby sat on his stool, sipped his coffee, and looked on with great interest.

"There!" said the lady when all of the ingredients were mixed. "Just *wait* till you taste these doughnuts!"

"It looks like an awful lot of batter," said Homer as he stood on a chair and poured it into the doughnut machine with the help of the chauffeur. "It's about *ten* times as much as Uncle Ulysses ever makes."

"But wait till you taste them!" said the lady

with an eager look and a smile.

Homer got down from the chair and pushed a button on the machine marked, "Start." Rings of batter started dropping into the hot fat. After a ring of batter was cooked on one side an automatic gadget turned it over and the other side would cook. Then another automatic gadget gave the doughnut a little push and it rolled neatly down a little chute, all ready to eat.

"That's a simply *fascinating* machine," said the lady as she waited for the first doughnut to roll out.

"Here, young man, *you* must have the first one. Now isn't that just *too* delicious!? Isn't it simply marvelous?"

"Yes, Ma'm, it's very good," replied Homer as the lady handed doughnuts to Charles and to Mr. Gabby and asked if they didn't think they were simply divine doughnuts.

"It's an old family receipt!" said the lady with pride.

Homer poured some coffee for the lady and her chauffeur and for Mr. Gabby, and a glass of milk for himself. Then they all sat down at the lunch counter to enjoy another few doughnuts apiece.

"I'm so glad you enjoy my doughnuts," said the lady. "But now, Charles, we really must be going. If you will just take this apron, Homer, and put two dozen doughnuts in a bag to take along, we'll be on our way. And, Charles, don't forget to pay the young man." She rolled down her sleeves and put on her jewelry, then Charles managed to get her into her big fur coat.

"Good night, young man, I haven't had so much fun in years. I *really* haven't!" said the lady, as she went out the door and into the big shiny car.

"Those are sure good doughnuts," said Mr. Gabby as the car moved off.

"You bet!" said Homer. Then he and Mr. Gabby stood and watched the automatic doughnut machine make doughnuts.

After a few dozen more doughnuts had rolled down the little chute, Homer said, "I guess that's about enough doughnuts to sell to the after theater customers. I'd better turn the machine off for a while."

Homer pushed the button marked *Stop* and

there was a little click, but nothing happened. The rings of batter kept right on dropping into the hot fat, and an automatic gadget kept right on turning them over, and another automatic gadget kept right on giving them a little push and the doughnuts kept right on rolling down the little chute, all ready to eat.

"That's funny," said Homer, "I'm sure that's the right button!" He pushed it again but the automatic doughnut maker kept right on making doughnuts.

"Well I guess I must have put one of those pieces in backwards," said Homer.

"Then it might stop if you pushed the button marked *Start*," said Mr. Gabby.

Homer did, and the doughnuts still kept rolling down the little chute, just as regular as a clock can tick.

"I guess we could sell a few more doughnuts," said Homer, "but I'd better telephone Uncle Ulysses over at the barber shop." Homer gave the number and while he waited for someone to answer he counted thirty-seven doughnuts roll down the little chute.

Finally someone answered, "Hello! This is the sarber bhop, I mean the barber shop."

"Oh, hello, sheriff. This is Homer. Could I speak to Uncle Ulysses?"

"Well, he's playing pinochle right now," said the sheriff. "Anythin' I can tell 'im?"

"Yes," said Homer. "I pushed the button marked *Stop* on the doughnut machine but the rings of batter keep right on dropping into the hot fat, and an automatic gadget keeps right on turning them over, and another automatic gadget keeps giving them a little push, and the doughnuts keep right on rolling down the little chute! It won't stop!"

"O.K. Wold the hire, I mean, hold the wire and I'll tell 'im." Then Homer looked over his shoulder and counted another twenty-one doughnuts roll down the little chute, all ready to eat. Then the sheriff said, "He'll be right over. . . . Just gotta finish this hand."

"That's good," said Homer. "G'by, sheriff."

The window was full of doughnuts by now so Homer and Mr. Gabby had to hustle around and start stacking them on plates and trays and lining them up on the counter.

"Sure are a lot of doughnuts!" said Homer.

"You bet!" said Mr. Gabby. "I lost count at twelve hundred and two and that was quite a while back."

People had begun to gather outside the lunch room window, and someone was saying, "There are almost as many doughnuts as there are people in Centerburg, and I wonder how in tarnation Ulysses thinks he can sell all of 'em!"

Every once in a while somebody would come inside and buy some, but while somebody bought two to eat and a dozen to take home, the machine made three dozen more.

By the time Uncle Ulysses and the sheriff arrived and pushed through the crowd, the lunch room was a calamity of doughnuts! Doughnuts in the window, doughnuts piled high on the shelves, doughnuts stacked on plates, doughnuts lined up twelve deep all along the counter, and doughnuts still rolling down the little chute, just as regular as a clock can tick.

"Hello, sheriff, hello, Uncle Ulysses, we're having a little trouble here," said Homer.

"Well, I'll be dunked!" said Uncle Ulysses.

"Dernd ef you won't be when Aggy gits home," said the sheriff.

"Mighty fine doughnuts though. What'll you do with 'em all, Ulysses?"

Uncle Ulysses groaned and said, "What will Aggy say? We'll never sell 'em all."

Then Mr. Gabby, who hadn't said anything for a long time, stopped piling doughnuts and said, "What you need is an advertising man. Ya know what I mean? You got the doughnuts, ya gotta create a market . . . Understand? . . . It's balancing the demand with the supply . . . That sort of thing."

"Yep!" said Homer. "Mr. Gabby's right. We have to enlarge our market. He's an advertising sandwich man, so if we hire him, he can walk up and down in front of the theater and get the customers."

"You're hired, Mr. Gabby!" said Uncle Ulysses.

Then everybody pitched in to paint the signs and to get Mr. Gabby sandwiched between. They painted "SALE ON DOUGHNUTS" in big letters on the window too.

Meanwhile the rings of batter kept right on dropping into the hot fat, and an automatic gadget kept right on turning them over, and another automatic gadget kept right on giving them a little push, and the doughnuts kept right on rolling down the little chute, just as regular as a clock can tick.

"I certainly hope this advertising works," said Uncle Ulysses, wagging his head. "Aggy'll certainly throw a fit if it don't."

The sheriff went outside to keep order, because there was quite a crowd by now—all looking at the doughnuts and guessing how many thousand there were, and watching new ones roll down the little chute, just as regular as a clock can tick. Homer and Uncle Ulysses kept stacking doughnuts. Once in a while somebody bought a few, but not very often.

Then Mr. Gabby came back and said, "Say, you know there's not much use o' me advertisin' at the theater. The show's all over, and besides almost everybody in town is out front watching that machine make doughnuts!"

"Zeus!" said Uncle Ulysses. "We must get rid of these doughnuts before Aggy gets here!"

"Looks like you will have ta hire a truck ta waul 'em ahay, I mean haul 'em away!!" said the sheriff who had just come in. Just then there was a noise and a shoving out front and the lady from the shiny black car and her chauffeur came pushing through the crowd and into the lunch room.

"Oh, gracious!" she gasped, ignoring the doughnuts, "I've lost my diamond bracelet, and I know I left it here on the counter," she said, pointing to a place where the doughnuts were piled in stacks of two dozen.

"Yes, Ma'm, I guess you forgot it when you helped make the batter," said Homer.

Then they moved all the doughnuts around and looked for the diamond bracelet, but they couldn't find it anywhere. Meanwhile the doughnuts kept rolling down the little chute, just as regular as a clock can tick.

After they had looked all around the sheriff cast a suspicious eye on Mr. Gabby, but Homer said, "He's all right, sheriff, he didn't take it. He's a friend of mine."

Then the lady said, "I'll offer a reward of one hundred dollars for that bracelet! It really *must* be found! . . . it *really* must!"

"Now don't you worry, lady," said the sheriff. "I'll get your bracelet back!"

"Zeus! This is terrible!" said Uncle Ulysses.

"First all of these doughnuts and then on top of all that, a lost diamond bracelet . . ."

Mr. Gabby tried to comfort him, and he said, "There's always a bright side. That machine'll probably run outta batter in an hour or two."

If Mr. Gabby hadn't been quick on his feet Uncle Ulysses would have knocked him down, sure as fate.

Then while the lady wrung her hands and said, "We must find it, we *must!*" and Uncle Ulysses was moaning about what Aunt Agnes would say, and the sheriff was eyeing Mr. Gabby, Homer sat down and thought hard.

Before twenty more doughnuts could roll down the little chute he shouted, "SAY! I know where the bracelet is! It was lying here on the counter and got mixed up in the batter by mistake! The bracelet is cooked inside one of these doughnuts!"

"Why . . . I really believe you're right," said the lady through her tears. "Isn't that *amazing?* Simply *amazing!*"

"I'll be durn'd!" said the sheriff.

"OhH-h!" moaned Uncle Ulysses. "Now we have to break up all of these doughnuts to find it. Think of the *pieces!* Think of the *crumbs!* Think of what *Aggy* will say!"

"Nope," said Homer. "We won't have to break them up. I've got a plan."

So Homer and the advertising man took some cardboard and some paint and printed another sign. They put this sign

FRESH DOUGHNUTS
2 for 5¢
WHILE THEY LAST
$100.00 PRIZE
FOR FINDING
A BRACELET
INSIDE A DOUGHNUT
P.S. You have to give the
bracelet back

in the window, and the sandwich man wore two more signs that said the same thing and walked around in the crowd out front.

THEN . . . The doughnuts began to sell! *Everybody* wanted to buy doughnuts, *dozens* of doughnuts!

And that's not all. Everybody bought coffee to dunk the doughnuts in too. Those that didn't buy coffee bought milk or soda. It kept Homer and the lady and the chauffeur and Uncle Ulysses and the sheriff busy waiting on the people who wanted to buy doughnuts.

When all but the last couple of hundred doughnuts had been sold, Rupert Black shouted, "I GAWT IT!!" and sure enough . . . there was the diamond bracelet inside of his doughnut!

Then Rupert went home with a hundred dollars, the citizens of Centerburg went home full of doughnuts, the lady and her chauffeur drove off with the diamond bracelet, and Homer went home with his mother when she stopped by with Aunt Aggy.

As Homer went out of the door he heard Mr. Gabby say, "Neatest trick of merchandising I ever seen," and Aunt Aggy was looking sceptical while Uncle Ulysses was saying, "The rings of batter kept right on dropping into the hot fat, and the automatic gadget kept right on turning them over, and the other automatic gadget kept right on giving them a little push, and the doughnuts kept right on rolling down the little chute just as regular as a clock can tick—they just kept right on a comin', an' a comin', an' a comin', an' a comin'."

## from THE EGYPT GAME

### Zilpha K. Snyder

*While never definitely labeled, the setting of this story is Berkeley, California, a college community where children of all races and nationalities play together with only the ordinary conflicts of childhood present. Once launched into "the Egypt game," Melanie and April plunge themselves into ancient times with all the enthusiasm of youth. In this selection, Melanie and April meet, and April is introduced to "the imagining games." The Egypt Game was a runner-up for the 1968 Newbery Medal.*

### Enter Melanie—and Marshall

On that same day in August, just a few minutes before twelve, Melanie Ross arrived at the door of Mrs. Hall's apartment on the third floor. Melanie was eleven years old and she had lived in the Casa Rosada since she was only seven. During that time she'd welcomed a lot of new people to the apartment house. Apartment dwellers, particularly near a university, are apt to come and go. Melanie always looked forward to meeting new tenants, and today was going to be especially interesting. Today, Melanie had been sent up to get Mrs. Hall's granddaughter to come down and have lunch with the Rosses. Melanie didn't know much about the new girl except that her name was April and that she had come from Hollywood to live with Mrs. Hall who was her grandmother.

It would be neat if she turned out to be a real friend. There hadn't been any girls the right age in the Casa Rosada lately. To have a handy friend again, for spur-of-the-moment visiting, would be great. However, she had overheard something that didn't sound too promising. Just the other day she'd heard Mrs. Hall telling Mom that April was a strange little thing because she'd been brought up all over everywhere and never had much of a chance to associate with other children. You wouldn't know what to expect of someone like that. But then, you never knew what to expect of any new kid, not really. So Melanie knocked hopefully at the door of apartment 312.

Meeting people had always been easy for Melanie. Most people she liked right away, and they usually seemed to feel the same way about her. But when the door to 312 opened that morning, for just a moment she was almost speechless. Surprise can do that to a person, and at first glance April really was a surprise. Her hair was stacked up in a pile that seemed to be more pins than hair, and the whole thing teetered forward over her thin pale face. She was wearing a big, yellowish-white fur thing around her shoulders, and carrying a plastic purse almost as big as a suitcase. But most of all it was the eyelashes. They were black and bushy looking, and the ones on her left eye were higher up and sloped in a different direction. Melanie's mouth opened and closed a few times before anything came out.

April adjusted Dorothea's old fur stole, patted up some sliding strands of hair and waited—warily. She didn't expect this Melanie to like her—kids hardly ever did—but she *did* intend to

From *The Egypt Game.* Copyright © 1967 by Zilpha Keatley Snyder. Used by permission of Atheneum Publishers

make a very definite impression; and she could see that she'd done that all right.

"Hi," Melanie managed after that first speechless moment. "I'm Melanie Ross. You're supposed to have lunch with us, I think. Aren't you April Hall?"

"April Dawn," April corrected with an off-hand sort of smile. "I was expecting you. My grandmother informed me that—uh, she said you'd be up."

It occurred to Melanie that maybe kids dressed differently in Hollywood. As they started down the hall she asked, "Are you going to stay with your grandmother for very long?"

"Oh no," April said. "Just till my mother finishes this tour she's on. Then she'll send for me to come home."

"Tour?"

"Yes, you see my mother is Dorothea Dawn—" she paused and Melanie racked her brain. She could tell she was supposed to know who Dorothea Dawn was. "Well, I guess you haven't happened to hear of her way up here, but she's a singer and in the movies, and stuff like that. But right now she's singing with this band that travels around to different places."

"Neat!" Melanie said. "You mean your mother's in the movies?"

But just then they arrived at the Ross's apartment. Marshall met them at the door, dragging Security by one of his eight legs.

"That's my brother, Marshall," Melanie said.

"Hi, Marshall," April said. "What in the heck is that?"

Melanie grinned. "That's Security. Marshall takes him everywhere. So my dad named him Security. You know. Like some little kids have a blanket."

"Security's an octopus," Marshall said very clearly. He didn't talk very much, but when he did he always said exactly what he wanted to without any trouble. He never had fooled around with baby talk.

Melanie's mother was in the kitchen putting hot dog sandwiches and fruit salad on the table. When Melanie introduced April she could tell that her mother was surprised by the eyelashes and hairdo and everything. She probably didn't realize that kids dressed a little differently in Hollywood.

"April's mother is a movie star," Melanie explained.

Melanie's mother smiled. "Is that right, April?" she asked.

April looked at Melanie's mother carefully through narrowed eyes. Mrs. Ross looked sharp and neat, with a smart-looking very short hairdo like a soft black cap, and high winging eyebrows, like Melanie's. But her smile was a little different. April was good at figuring out what adults meant by the things they didn't quite say—and Mrs. Ross's smile meant that she wasn't going to be easy to snow.

"Well," April admitted, "not a star, really. She's mostly a vocalist. So far she's only been an extra in the movies. But she almost had a supporting role once, and Nick, that's her agent, says he has a big part almost all lined up."

"Gee, that's neat!" Melanie said. "We've never known anyone before whose mother was an extra in the movies, have we Mom?"

"Not a soul," Mrs. Ross said, still smiling.

During lunch, April talked a lot about Hollywood, and the movie stars she'd met and the big parties her mother gave and things like that. She knew she was overdoing it a bit but something made her keep on. Mrs. Ross went right on smiling in that knowing way, and Melanie went right on being so eager and encouraging that April thought she must be kidding. She wasn't sure though. You never could tell with kids—they didn't do things in a pattern, the way grown-ups did.

Actually Melanie knew that April was being pretty braggy, but it occurred to her that it was probably because of homesickness. It was easy to see how much she'd like to be back in Hollywood with her mother.

While they were having dessert of ice cream and cookies, Mrs. Ross suggested that April might like to look over Melanie's books to see if there was anything she'd like to borrow.

"Do you like to read?" Melanie asked. "Reading is my favorite occupation."

"That's for sure." Mrs. Ross laughed. "A full-time occupation with overtime. Your grandmother tells me that you do a lot of reading, too."

"Well, of course, I'm usually pretty busy, with all the parties and everything. I do read some though, when I have a chance."

But after lunch when Melanie showed April her library, a whole bookcase full in her bedroom, she could tell that April liked books more than just a little. She could tell just by the way April picked a book up and handled it, and by the way she forgot about acting so grown-up and Hollywoodish. She plopped herself down on the floor in front of the bookcase and started looking at books like crazy. For a while she seemed to forget all about Melanie. As she read she kept propping up her eyelashes with one finger.

All of a sudden she said, "Could you help me get these darn things off? I must not have put them on the right place or something. When I look down to read I can't even see the words."

So Melanie scratched the ends of the eyelashes loose with her longest fingernail, and then April pulled them the rest of the way off. They were on pretty tight, and she said, "Ouch!" several times and a couple of other words that Melanie wasn't allowed to say.

"— —!" said April, looking in the mirror. "I think I pulled out most of my real ones. Does it look like it to you?"

"I don't think so," Melanie said. "I still see some. Is this the first time you've worn them? The false ones, I mean?"

April put back on her haughty face. "Of course not. Nearly everybody wears them in Hollywood. My mother wears them all the time. It's just that these are new ones, and they must be a different kind."

April put her eyelashes away carefully in her big bag and they went back to looking at books. Melanie showed her some of her favorites, and April picked out a couple to borrow. It was then that April took a very special book off the shelf.

It was a very dull-looking old geography book that no one would be interested in. That was why Melanie used it to hide something very special and secret. As April opened the book some cutout paper people fell out on the floor.

"What are those?" April asked.

"Just some old things of mine," Melanie said, holding out her hand for the book, but April kept on turning the pages and finding more bunches of paper people.

"Do you really still play with paper dolls?" April asked in just the tone of voice that Melanie had feared she would use. Not just because she was April, either. It was the tone of voice that nearly anyone would use about a sixth grade girl who still played with ordinary paper dolls.

"But they're not really paper dolls," Melanie said, "and I don't really play with them. Not like moving them around and dressing them up and everything. They're just sort of a record for a game I play. I make up a family and then I find people who look like them in magazines and catalogues. Just so I'll remember them better. I have fourteen families now. See they all have their names and ages written on the back. I make up stuff about their personalities and what they do. Sometimes I write it down like a story, but usually I just make it up."

April's scornful look was dissolving. "Like what?"

"Well," Melanie said, "this is the Brewster family. Mr. Brewster is a detective. I had to cut him out of the newspaper because he was the only man I could find who looked like a detec-

tive. Don't you think he does?"

"Yeah, pretty much."

"Well anyway, he just—that is, I just made up about how he solved this very hard mystery and caught some dangerous criminals. And then the criminals escaped and were going to get revenge on Mr. Brewster. So the whole family had to go into hiding and wear disguises and everything."

April spread the Brewsters out on the floor. Her eyes were shining and without the eyelashes they were pretty, wide and blue. "Have they caught the criminals yet?" she asked. Melanie shook her head. "Well, how about if the kids catch them. They could just happen to find out where the criminals were hiding?"

"Neat!" Melanie said. "Maybe Ted," she pointed to the smallest paper Brewster, "could come home and tell the other kids how he thinks he saw one of the criminals, going into a certain house."

"And then," April interrupted, "the girls could go to the house pretending to sell Girl Scout cookies, to see if it really was the crooks."

From the Girl-Scout-cookies caper, the game moved into even more exciting escapades, and when Mrs. Ross came in to say that Marshall was down for his nap and that she was leaving for the university where she was taking a summer course for schoolteachers, the criminals were just escaping, taking one of the Brewster children with them as a hostage. An hour later, when Marshall came in sleepy-eyed and dragging Security, several of the other paper families had been brought into the plot. Marshall seemed content to sit and listen, so the game went on with daring adventures, narrow escapes, tragic illnesses and even a romance or two. At last, right in the middle of a shipwreck on a desert island, April noticed the time and said she'd have to go home so she'd be there when Caroline got back from work.

As they walked to the door Melanie said, "Do you want to play some more tomorrow?"

April was adjusting her fur stole around her shoulders for the trip upstairs. "Oh, I guess so," she said with a sudden return to haughtiness.

But Melanie was beginning to understand about April's frozen spells, and how to thaw her out. You just had to let her know she couldn't make you stop liking her that easily. "None of my friends know how to play imagining games the way you do," Melanie said. "Some of them can do it a little bit but they mostly don't have any very good ideas. And a lot of them only like ball games or other things that are already made up. But I like imagining games better than anything."

April was being very busy trying to get her stole to stay on because the clasp was a little bit broken. All at once she pulled it off, wadded it all up and tucked it under her arm. She looked right straight at Melanie and said, "You know what? I never did call them that before, but imagining games are just about all I ever play because most of the time I never have anybody to play with."

She started off up the hall. Then she turned around and walked backward waving her fur stole around her head like a lasso. "You've got lots of good ideas, too," she yelled.

## from ROOSEVELT GRADY

*Louisa R. Shotwell*

*There are two things in life Roosevelt Grady wants: to find a place to "stay put," and to learn what happens to the leftover number when "putting into" doesn't come out evenly. Neither dream seems so much to ask from life, unless you are a child in a migrant worker's family.*

### Putting Into

Roosevelt bunched his sweater underneath him to soften the jouncing floor of the moving truck. He leaned his head back against his mother's arm. If the air got any chillier, he'd have to take his sweater out from under him and put it on to keep warm, but it wasn't quite that cold. Not yet.

Along with three other families, the Gradys rode in the back of the truck. All but Papa, who sat up front to spell Cap Jackson. Cap was the regular driver and he was the crew leader, too. He owned the truck and in it he carried the people to places where crops were ready for picking.

"We're heading for beans and cucumbers," Cap Jackson said.

Roosevelt's mother sat straight up on the flat side of the family suitcase. It was made of metal and it was slippery, so she had her feet planted wide apart and flat on the floor to brace herself. On her lap she held Princess Anne, sleeping.

Between Mamma's feet lay Sister. She was seven years old and dainty, with dimples. Her smile, Papa always said, could charm a snake out of a tree.

"Honest, could it?" Roosevelt asked him once.

"Well, I tell you, Roosevelt," Papa said, "the first time we find a snake in a tree, we'll get Sister to smile at him and we'll see what happens." So far they hadn't found a tree with a snake in it.

On the other side of Mamma slumped Matthew, who was only five and chubby. Matthew had a lame foot, but that didn't keep him from enjoying life. He was great on making jokes, and he didn't miss a thing.

The truck had a canvas roof. The roof sloped up on each side to a peak like the top of a barn, and it kept you from seeing the sky. Anyway, it was dark outside. It was the middle of the night, but the truck kept right on going.

Between sleeping and waking, Roosevelt thought about putting into. He thought about that special thing he wanted to know. The question kept running around his head the way a mosquito teases you in the dark.

This was his question: When you put something into something else and it doesn't come out even, what do you do with what's left over?

What happened yesterday was exactly what had happened at the school where he'd first heard about putting into. The teacher came to where it seemed she must explain it the very next day. And then what? That time it wasn't beans that ran out. It was celery, but it didn't matter what the crop was. If it ran out, it ran out, and that was the end. The whole family packed up and piled into Cap Jackson's sputtery old truck and away they went to find a place where onions or tomatoes or some old thing was coming along ready to harvest. And same as yesterday, Roosevelt never got back to school to hear what the teacher had to say.

Some places there wouldn't be any school at all. Or else there'd be a school and the bean-picker boys and girls didn't get to go to it. The school would be for residents, and bean-picker families weren't residents. They didn't belong.

Once there was a school and it was closed when they got there. It was closed because the crop was ripe. A crop vacation, folks called this, and everybody picked, young ones and grown-ups and old people. Everybody except, of course, Princess Anne. Over in Louisiana she sat by herself in a fruit crate at the end of the strawberry rows and sucked her thumb, cute as a bug.

Roosevelt rubbed his eyes, leaned his head against Mamma's knee, and tried hard to go to sleep. He'd almost made it when buzz went that old mosquito again, nagging at him about putting into. Like 3 into 17. You can't say 17's got six 3's in it, because six 3's need 18. So the answer has to be five 3's. But that's only 15. So what do you do with the poor little 2 that gets left over?

Roosevelt liked to have things come out even.

He liked to have a place to put every piece of whatever it was he had. He liked to pick all the ripe beans quick and clean off one plant and then move along that row to the next. He liked to fill his basket just full enough so it was even across the top. If one bean stuck up in the air, he'd pull it out and make a little hole among the other beans and poke it carefully down in. He liked to make a pan of corn bread and cut it into exactly enough squares to make one piece for everybody in the family. Except Princess Anne. Her teeth hadn't come through far enough yet to chew anything crusty. Sometimes Mamma would break off a little of her piece of corn bread and dunk it in her coffee to soften it. Then she gave that to Princess Anne.

Bouncing along through the dark, Roosevelt got to thinking some more about numbers. Take nine. Right now nine was an important number in his life. He was nine years old. His birthday was the ninth day of September, and if you began to count the months with January one and February two and so on, what did September turn out to be? Why, nine!

To be perfectly sure, he whispered the months over to himself, counting on his fingers. Sure enough, nine came out to be September.

How many different schools had he been to in his lifetime? He counted to himself. Six, seven, eight . . . and nine. There was that nine again. Different schools, that is. If you counted twice the schools he'd been to and then gone back to, they made thirteen, but Roosevelt didn't want to count that way. He didn't like the number thirteen. Papa said thirteen was unlucky. Mamma said she didn't believe in lucky or unlucky, but there was no use tempting fate.

"What's tempting fate?" Roosevelt asked her.

"It means trying to outsmart the devil," Mamma said. "And he's really smart. You're best off to stay clean away from thirteen this and thirteen that. You can just as easy make it twelve or fourteen and not take any chances."

One day a while back, Roosevelt had asked Papa about putting into and the poor little left-over number. He had laughed and said: "Just throw it away."

But Roosevelt couldn't feel right doing that.

What would become of it?

Another day he had asked Mamma. She said: "Save it till you need it."

"What do you do with it," Roosevelt wanted to know, "while you're waiting to need it?"

Mamma didn't laugh nearly so often as Papa did, but she laughed that time.

"Put it in your pocket," she said, "and go fetch me a bucket of water."

### The Secret

The truck jerked to a stop, and the motor coughed and went still. From the driver's seat, Cap Jackson called out:

"Anybody want a drink? There's a spring here at the edge of the woods."

The people stirred. Cap came around and let down the tailgate and put up the ladder. Roosevelt experimented with a swallow and his mouth felt dry, so he clambered down. The stars were bright. The air was cold and it had a piney smell, clean and fresh. He waited his turn in line in front of a pipe with water bubbling out of it. In the starlight the pipe looked rusty. The men had to stoop over to reach it, but it was exactly the right height for Roosevelt. He didn't have to bend down or stand on his toes, either one.

When his turn came, the water was cool and he took a big gulp, but it didn't taste good. Not good at all. It tasted like a bad egg.

"Sulphur water," said one of the men.

Roosevelt spit his mouthful out on the ground. He shivered. When he climbed back into the truck, he put his sweater on and sat right flat down on the boards.

As the motor wheezed and the truck began to move, Sister and Matthew both woke up and wiggled. Roosevelt was glad they'd waked up. He felt like having company.

"Talk to us, Mamma," said Matthew. "Tell us a story."

"Hush," said Mamma. "Other folks want to go to sleep."

"Talk to us soft-like," begged Matthew. "Whisper to us about . . . you know . . ."

Roosevelt knew what was coming. Matthew always asked for the same story. It was Roosevelt's favorite story, too.

". . . about the olden days. And the dog run."

"All right," said Mamma. "Lean close and I'll tell it to you short. Then you go to sleep."

And she did. She didn't make it too short either. About the little house in the cotton field in Georgia, how it sat up on stilts and was a house in two parts like, with this comfortable sitting-out place in between and a roof over the whole thing. The sitting-out place was the dog run, and it had a rocking chair like President Kennedy's.

The Gradys had a dog there too, a hound, sort of. Named Nellie. She had short tan hair and floppy ears and brown eyes. Her eyes were wistful.

"What's wistful?" Matthew demanded.

"Wistful is you want something and you don't know what," said Mamma.

They had chickens, too, and two big pigs and a litter of little pigs. And a goat. And growing out back they had sweet potatoes and collards and mustard greens.

Roosevelt moved his tongue around to see if he could make himself remember the taste of a sweet potato. He couldn't.

Now it was Sister's turn. Was she still awake? She was.

"Take us back to your wedding day, Mamma," she said. "Tell us about your white dress and what Papa said."

"There was this magnolia tree," said Mamma, "right ouside the Pink Lily Baptist Church. And it was brim full of waxy white blossoms. I wore a shiny white dress with a green sash and long streamers and I had a veil, all cloudy, made of net. Your papa told me I was almost the prettiest thing in the whole county.

" 'Almost the prettiest? Why almost?' I said, kind of sniffy and jealous."

"Jealous," said Sister. "Tell us what's jealous."

"Jealous is you're scared somebody you like likes somebody else better than you," Mamma explained. "Now don't interrupt me any more. And your papa said, 'You or that magnolia tree. I can't make up my mind which one is prettier. But I'll pick you.' So off we went to live in the little house in the cotton field."

"Now tell us why we left the little house in the cotton field," insisted Matthew. "Why did we go away and leave our dog Nellie and the little pigs and the dog run all behind us?"

"Why we left? Why, honey, the machines came

along. The tractors got bigger and bigger and they did more and more of the work the people used to do. Mr. Wilson let us stay on a while and your papa got some work in the sawmill six miles off. But pretty soon Mr. Wilson plain had to tear down our house to plant more cotton. So that's when we went on the season, looking for work wherever we could find it."

She stopped a minute. When she went on, her voice sounded different. Angry, almost.

"Some folks say now they've even got a machine that knows how to pick cotton. A big red monster. With fingers."

Sister sighed, a long whishy sigh that meant she was on her way to sleep again. Roosevelt waited. When Matthew breathed so even it seemed certain he must be asleep too, Roosevelt sat up close to Mamma's ear.

"Now let's you and me talk about our secret," he whispered.

"Hush," said Mamma.

"Please," said Roosevelt.

Mamma didn't say anything right away, and Roosevelt sat stiff and still. Then she spoke, not whispering but still so low he could hardly hear. She said just what he knew she'd say.

"Someday we'll find ourselves a house in a place where there's work for your papa every one of all twelve months in the year. Maybe the house won't have a dog run, but it'll sure enough be a home. And you and Sister and Matthew will go to school, the same school right along, day in, day out, fall and winter and right on to the end of spring."

"And Princess Anne?" asked Roosevelt.

"Princess Anne, too, soon as she's big enough. You'll all go right along with the children that belong. Because we'll be in a place where we'll all belong. We'll be right out of this bean-picking rat race and we'll stay put."

"How will we find this place?" asked Roosevelt anxiously, even though he'd asked this before and knew what the answer would be.

"I don't know how," said Mamma, "but we'll know it when we see it. There'll be something about it so we'll know it. And don't you forget. This is our secret."

"It's our secret," said Roosevelt, and he dropped his head in the crook of Mamma's elbow and fell sound asleep.

## from GUESTS IN THE PROMISED LAND
### Kristin Hunter

*"Two's Enough of a Crowd," one of eleven short stories for older children, is both funny and tender, a love story in which two black adolescents find each other. But it's also a story in which two young people find themselves, a plea against conformity that has a universal application.*

### Two's Enough of a Crowd

I used to blame all my troubles on being a nondancer. I thought if I could learn to wiggle and shake, I'd be popular.

One flashy minute on the floor, and whammo! I'd be the Dream Lover. Instead of a tall, skinny, nervous cat who's always trying to disappear into a wall.

It took Amy to show me I was different in other ways too.

Like my name. Most black cats are named James or William or Leroy. And they're called Cool Breeze or Poor Boy or Pots and Pans.

*Nobody* black is named Maurice. Except me. And nobody ever called me anything else.

(Of course, nobody black is named *Amy*, either. Now that there's two of us, it's not so bad.)

But in the old days, I felt mighty sorry for myself. I thought I was the only black person in the world with two left feet and no sense of rhythm.

If you're white, you don't have to dance. All you got to do is talk that talk, program them computers, and count that money.

But to be black and a nondancer is like being a blind brain surgeon. Or a one-armed violinist.

Most black kids are born knowing how to dance. They boogaloo into this world and funky chicken into their mothers' arms. Even in my family.

At twelve months my little brother started walking. At fourteen months, he was slopping.

I was so disgusted, I never spoke to the little monster again.

Here I thought my bad dancing was something I'd *inherited,* like a long head and pointed ears.

Don't tell me dancing isn't important. Old folks always say that. They say not dancing leaves you more time to study. Well, that just shows how much *they* know. I'd sell my straight A average tomorrow if I could do the monkey.

Don't tell me to take dancing lessons, either. I tried. I found out three things.

One, only the first lesson is free. After that, they charge you a fortune.

Two, they only teach nowhere dances like the fox-trot and the samba.

Three, ain't no school in the world can teach soul dancing. Sure, they can draw marks on the floor to show where your feet go. But those marks don't show you how to move the rest of your body. And *that's* where it's at, baby.

The knees and the hips and the waist and the arms are all part of the action. And they all got to move *together.* You're either born knowing how, or you're not. If you got it, flaunt it.

If you haven't got it, hide behind the biggest piece of furniture. Which is what I usually do at parties.

At Keeno Robinson's Christmas party, I headed for the Christmas tree as soon as the first record started playing. The tree was only five feet high, and I'm six-one. But by scrunching down, I managed to hide.

Then I peered through the branches. The floor was frantic. Every couple deserved to be on TV. But the best were Stretch Hankins and LaTanya Harris.

LaTanya is the world's foxiest chick. She wears extra hair, falsh eyelashes and skin-tight sweaters. I don't really like her. But I'd have given anything to dance with her the way Stretch was doing.

The only time I danced with LaTanya, I stepped on her foot. She laughed at me. I haven't asked her to dance since.

I thought I was the only one at the party not dancing. Then I spotted someone else. I couldn't believe my eyes.

Over in the opposite corner sat this *beautiful* girl. All by herself. *Reading.*

Crossing the floor to get to her wasn't easy. It was like walking through a roomful of guided missiles. But I managed to get there without any bruises.

She looked just as good close up. And it was all real. Hair, eyelashes, everything. "What's your name?" I asked.

"Amy, Amy Livingston."

I told her mine. Then I asked what she was reading.

"Oh, just a book."

"Why did you hide it when I came over?"

"I thought you might laugh at me. It's not relevant."

Now, "relevant" is a very big word in our crowd. If a thing isn't relevant, it's nowhere. As far as I can figure out, "relevant" means something you know already. Like how to comb a natural, and where to buy neck bones.

I finally got the title out of her. *Green Mansions,* by W. H. Hudson.

"It's just a romantic story about a girl who lives in the woods. There aren't any black people in it or anything. It isn't even about anything that could have really happened. It's not at *all* relevant."

"Do you like it?" I asked.

"Very much."

"Well then," I said, "it's relevant to *you.*"

She smiled. It was delightful. All pearls and dimples. "Thank you for saying that. I never thought of that before."

"But why aren't you dancing?" I wanted to know.

"Oh, nobody ever asks me to dance." She wasn't feeling sorry for herself. She just said it straight. Like, "Oh, it never rains around here in October."

But she had to be putting me on. She looked like somebody on a magazine cover.

Idiot that I am, I couldn't resist. "Well, someone is now." Here we go, Mister Clumsy Chump, I thought.

"We'll have to wait for a slow record," she said. And looked down sideways, toward her right foot.

I saw that she had on a heavy, built-up shoe.

"I was born with one leg shorter than the other," she explained.

"Just be glad you were born," I said. It came

out sounding hard and tough. I hadn't meant it to.

So I added, "Because *I* am."

I got the full, dazzling smile that time. It almost blinded me.

"Oh, what a nice thing to say. I *am* glad. Especially now that I can walk. I couldn't always, you know."

The athletes and acrobats were finally taking a rest. A slow record started playing. And we started moving around the floor.

It was just as easy as that. I found I didn't have to worry about the beat. She dragged one foot slowly. So I dragged both of mine. It left me free to concentrate on other things, like her perfume. It smelled like lilacs, and got me a little drunk.

"You're a great dancer," she said afterward.

Now, anyone who tells me *that* has a friend for life. But the trouble with me is I'm honest.

"Girl, you're a lovely liar," I said. "I can't dance at all."

"Really?" she said with a mischievous grin. "What else can't you do?"

I gave it some serious thought. Finally I admitted, "I can't curse."

It's quite a problem. Most of my friends turn the air blue with every other sentence. But *my* folks are so strict, I have trouble saying heck and darn.

"You think that's bad? I can't even use *slang*," she said.

She really had my sympathy. First of all, it's not "slang," it's "jive talk." And in our crowd, it's your first language. English is your second.

"I had eight operations," she explained. "I spent four years in the hospital, off and on. Nobody to talk to but white doctors and nurses. Now all the kids say I talk white. They make fun of me. So I mostly keep quiet."

"I love the way you talk. Don't you dare stop," I said.

It was jungle time again. James Brown was grunting and shouting over three speakers. And LaTanya was going into her act. She danced so violently you'd have thought she was in a hurricane.

Keeno appointed himself a one-man cheering section. "Work out, mama," he urged. "Take it easy, but go greasy. Shake it but don't break it,

cause if you bruise it, you can't use it! Oh, I feel so *attitudinous!* My vines are fine, my choppers shine, I'm full of wine, and this pad is *mine!* Pull back your jibs, peasants, and let me pass! OobydoobyshoobyOW!"

"I think he's happy," I translated for Amy.

"Monkeys love bananas. Maybe somebody just gave him one," she said with a giggle.

I laughed too. Suddenly, the crowd at the party didn't seem like the World's Most Important People. They were just people.

Another person was what made the difference. Or so I was discovering. When you're alone, the center of the crowd seems like the only place to be.

But when there are two of you, you can sit back and watch without feeling left out. You feel very cozy because you've got your *own* crowd.

"Do you like soul food?" I asked. Some platters were appearing.

"I hate it," she said. "All that grease. *Ugh.*"

My sentiments exactly. Why had I been forcing myself to swallow it all those years?

Because I had been alone, that's why. And, alone, I didn't have the courage to say "no thank you."

I was getting curious about this girl. I asked her more questions. "Do you hate honkies?"

"What are they?" she asked.

Too much. Too everlasting much. I explained.

She shuddered. "Oh, no. My doctor is white. He *helped* me. Besides, I don't hate anybody."

"But don't you feel oppressed?"

"I guess I *should,*" she said, looking troubled. "But the truth is, I feel free as a bird. Ever since I started walking."

"Do you like James Brown?" was my next question.

"No," she admitted. "He doesn't sing. He screams."

Now, James Brown is the High Priest of What's Happening. The Sultan of Soul. Not liking him is like drawing a funny mustache on a picture of Malcolm X.

I cheered her courage. "Hooray. Who *is* your favorite musician?"

"Schubert," she said. "And after him, Brahms."

Too unbelievable much! "What else do you

like that's unrelevant?"

"The word is *irrelevant*," she corrected gently. "And the answer is 'everything.' "

The steamy odor of stewed innards was filling Keeno's rec room. Our host was about to pass out the chitlins. "Wrinkled steads, everybody!" he hollered gleefully.

"It's not polite to refuse food," I said. "Let's go, before they make us *eat* those horrible things."

Boy, I felt brave. And free. Like it was 1865, and I'd just kicked off my chains. The ones put on me by my own people.

Amy's house was just like Amy. Different. There were no zebra-striped pillows. No plaster heads of Africans. No orange ceramic cats. Strangest of all, no plastic slipcovers. And no wall-to-wall Spanish-style stereo.

Just worn, comfortable furniture. Old, soft rugs. Lots of books. And a fine, foreign turntable sitting on top of a speaker.

It worked too, which is more than I can say for some stereos. The *Great Symphony* by Schubert lived up to its name. So did the *Fantastic* one by Berlioz.

When they had finished playing, I said, "You're a brave girl, to be so different."

"Not really," she said. "If you're different, you just *are*. You can't be any other way. You have no choice."

So it was as simple as that! After all those years of hiding and pretending to be like the crowd. This girl was amazing.

"But how did you get to be this way?"

"I told you. I had all those operations. They put me behind in school. I've never had much time to run with the crowd. I have to read and study a lot, if I want to catch up and go to college."

"What do you plan to take up? Black studies?"

"Promise not to tell."

I promised.

"English writers. The early ones. Like Chaucer."

Now, how irrelevant can you get? I almost kissed her *then*. "Why did you make me promise not to tell?" I asked.

"Because they'd put me down."

"Who?"

"Keeno. And Cool Breeze. And Sheryl. And Stretch. And LaTanya."

"Well, who put them in charge of the world?" I asked. "Who made *them* the dictators?"

"Nobody. But they *are*."

"Let me tell you about me," I said. "I have this thing about cells and germs. I love to look at them under a microscope."

"Maybe you'll discover a cure for sickle cell anemia. That's a disease only black people have. That would be relevant."

"Maybe *you'll* discover Chaucer was black."

We laughed ourselves absolutely silly over that one.

Then we got serious. We promised never to let the others know our secrets. Not that we're scared or ashamed. It's just more fun that way.

"Listen, Amy," I said. "This spring my class is having a prom. Not my scene at all. I wasn't planning to go. But I will if you'll go with me."

"I'd love to, Maurice," she said. She made my name sound better than a nickname. When all those years, I'd wished for one.

"I warn you," I said. "I can't do the slop, the wobble, the monkey, or the funky chicken."

"My favorite dance," she said, "is the waltz."

I *had* to kiss her that time. First, for being so different. Second, for showing me I was, too. Third, for proving it didn't matter. Because there were *two* of us now, and we didn't need the dictators. We didn't need to dance, either. How important is dancing, compared to walking?

So we'll go to the prom. And when the others rap and rave, we'll keep quiet. While they jump and shake, we'll sit on the sidelines and smile. And keep our secrets.

Because we've found out that nothing's as relevant as love.

## Life in Other Lands

**from HELLO, AURORA**
*Anne-Cath. Vestly*

*In their old neighborhood, everyone had known that Aurora's family was different, that*

*Mother worked as a lawyer and that Father stayed home to take care of Aurora and baby Socrates because he was earning a doctorate and could work at home. Now they had moved to a big apartment building where the housewives look askance at a man doing the shopping and caring for the children. Aurora, already timid about being a new girl, had been distressed by the prying of the mothers of Brit-Karen and Nusse. In this chapter, one of the many humorous episodes in the story, there is a quality of warmth, a simplicity typical of this delightful Norwegian story.*

### Father in the Laundry Room

Mother had gone to work, and Father was doing his best to find the things that needed washing. "Let's see, here are the sheets and towels and so on, and here are all our sweaters, Mummy's heavy ski sweater and mine, too. We'll take them all, because those large machines can take a big load, you know. I'll have to make several trips with them, and we'll have Socrates with us too."

"There's an awful lot," said Aurora.

"Listen, I'll go down first with the sheets and put them in the machine, and you can wait here. Then we'll feed and change Socrates, and you can take him out in his baby carriage while I'm in the laundry room."

"All right," said Aurora.

Father went off with a heavy suitcase full of laundry, and Aurora was left behind. Maybe she could try to do the dishes while he was away. She was sure he'd be pleased.

Aurora got a nice, solid kitchen chair to stand on. She tied on an apron and put the right amount of soap in the water. There was plenty of hot water in this building, so doing the dishes was fun, and it would be nice to surprise Daddy.

Just as she was getting started, there was a ring at the door. She gave an impatient little sigh. There seemed to be no peace. Anyway,

should she open the door when she was alone? Daddy hadn't said anything about that. If only she had had one of those peepholes in the door now, she could have seen who was standing outside.

The bell rang again and Aurora said: "Who is it?"

"It's Nusse's mother," said a voice outside.

That was safe enough. Aurora managed to open the door although her fingers were covered with soap and slipped on the smooth handle.

"Hello, Aurora," said Nusse's mother. Aurora hadn't seen her since the time when she was going into town with Brit-Karen and Nusse, and was so angry because Nusse had been playing in the sandbox. But she certainly wasn't thinking of that today.

"I wondered if you would come up and keep Nusse company while I go shopping?"

"Oh no," said Aurora. "I can't today."

"Perhaps Nusse could come up here?" said her mother. "She can be up for a little while even if she isn't allowed to go out."

"No," said Aurora, "because I won't be here. I have to take Socrates out while Daddy is in the laundry room."

"Oh, is that so? Can't you take him—what was it you called him?"

"Socrates," said Aurora.

"Socrates, yes. Can't you take Socrates up to Nusse? She has such a bad cold I don't dare take her shopping with me, but she doesn't like being alone, you know."

Aurora understood that very well. Nobody liked to be left alone when the grownups went shopping. Still, everybody had to put up with it when they were sick.

"What about Brit-Karen?" said Aurora. "She can come and stay with Nusse, can't she?"

"Her parents are afraid of her catching cold," said Nusse's mother, "so Brit-Karen isn't allowed to come. I went to ask her first for they are supposed to be such good friends, but no luck. Her mother was quite upset at the idea and wouldn't let Brit-Karen go. But then we thought that maybe you would come, since you are alone so much."

Aurora looked at Nusse's mother. Her eyes were hard, too, just like the other woman's had been. She wanted Aurora to stay with Nusse and take Socrates with her. But Nusse had a cold, and Mummy had said that she must be very careful to keep Socrates away from anyone who was coughing and sneezing, because it was no laughing matter when such tiny babies caught a cold.

"No, I can't," said Aurora.

"But it will only be for a little while, while I'm at the store," said Nusse's mother. "Surely you can do me that little service." Aurora felt desperate; it was so confusing. But then she remembered her mother saying that Daddy and Socrates and she and Mommy were a group on their own, and must look after each other, and so she said: "No, I can't, because there are things called cold germs and they mustn't come near Socrates."

"Oh well, I just thought you might enjoy getting out for a little while," said Nusse's mother, "but I won't press you, of course."

She turned and went. Aurora could see from her back that she wasn't pleased. The dishes didn't seem so much fun now, either.

A little later, Father came upstairs at full speed. "So far so good," he said. "I hope I've done it right. There were instructions but it all seemed so complicated. Anyway, the clothes can go on washing themselves while I check on Socrates. Why, bless your heart. Have you begun the dishes?"

"They would be finished if the doorbell hadn't rung," said Aurora.

"Was it someone selling raffle tickets for the Sausage Eaters' Association?" said Father.

"It was Nusse's mother," Aurora answered. "She wanted me to keep Nusse company while she went shopping."

"Of course you couldn't," said Father, and went around snatching up more dirty clothes.

Socrates obviously sensed that Father was extra busy today, for he wasn't in a good mood. He kicked and screamed, and Father had to stop and say "bsbsbsbsbsbsbs" many times before he calmed down. Not until Aurora brought his bottle did he become really good-tempered and smiling.

"We're helping Daddy do the washing," said Aurora, "so you must be a good boy when I take you out in the baby carriage, understand?"

Socrates looked as if he wanted to think about

it first, but then he drank his milk, burped twice, and seemed to have no objection to being put in his baby carriage.

"Now I'll carry the suitcase with the sweaters and we'll put the bag of dirty linen on top of you, Socrates. Wrap up well, Aurora, it's cold outside."

It was a long way to the laundry room and they had a heavy load, but fortunately Socrates didn't seem to mind his carriage being used as a laundry truck. When they came to the door of the laundry room, Father said: "Well, so long, Aurora. Don't go too far."

He didn't look happy as he went off with his load.

"It's only for today, you know," said Aurora, wheeling Socrates away.

Father came into the laundry room and was dismayed to see a stream of soapsuds flowing from the washing machine he was using.

Luckily there was a woman there who was doing her washing, too, and she calmed Father down and said he had just used too much soap powder. She showed him how to set the machine for rinsing, and finally she helped him to put the clothes in the spin dryer to get most of the water out. Everything was all right as long as the woman was there. She was calm and collected and Father understood everything she said. But unfortunately she had finished her own washing. She had started early in the morning and was ready to go now. Father thought the place seemed deserted after she had gone. But she had done a lot already. Soon he could put all their sweaters in the machine. He had to laugh when he remembered how last year Mother had struggled to wash the thick sweaters in a small tub. She hadn't had much water either, poor soul. No, this really was much better.

These machines weren't bad when you got used to them. Father began to whistle to himself, and to think about how people washed clothes in the olden days and in many parts of the world today. The women stood on the riverbank and beat the clothes clean, and stooped down to rinse them. Perhaps they sang too. Father could picture the women doing the washing for him while he sat and watched them and thought about it all.

He wondered what Aurora was doing now. He put the sweaters in the machine, turned the knobs to set it going, and went out to look for her.

Aurora had been wheeling Socrates up and down for quite a long time. Now and then she had peeped into the low windows of the laundry room and seen her father standing in front of the washing machine, but he hadn't seen her for he was so terribly busy. Socrates was quiet because he was asleep.

"Hello, Aurora," said Father. "All right?"

"Yes," whispered Aurora. "Will you be finished soon?"

"No, not for a while," said Father. "Our sweaters are being washed this very minute. Are you tired of pushing the carriage? If you want to you can leave it for a few minutes and play in the snow."

"Mmmm," said Aurora. There was a lot of snow here. Perhaps she could make something really important; a snowman, or maybe an animal that she could sit on would be better. Lovely. She began to roll the snow into big round balls, working away with all her might, and Father went in to his washing.

He stood for a minute looking at the machine that was washing the sweaters. He ought to rinse them now, but he had to get rid of the soapy water first. The water that came out was boiling hot. Oh dear! He had set the machine at boiling. Maybe that wasn't right for washing woolens. Of course it made them nice and clean, but he would keep quiet about it all the same. The washing that was hanging in the drying cupboard was already dry enough for ironing, so he would have to start that. It was an electric mangle iron and there was something that had to be turned on here, too. The rollers had some kind of material around them, and Father set the iron going to see if they really did turn by themselves.

They did, but apparently they didn't like to have nothing to iron, for suddenly there was a very hot smell. Father was so frightened that he turned the iron off as fast as he could. He went out to Aurora. "That iron is hard to use," he said. "I wonder if the super is around."

Aurora looked up from the large snow animal she was making. She didn't see the superintendent, but she saw that Father looked upset. Then she caught sight of Knut. He was coming home from school with some other boys. She tried to wave to him without the others noticing. Clearly he had seen her, for he went a little farther and then suddenly jumped, shouting something or other, ran back the way he had come, sprang quickly to one side, and made for the laundry room.

"Do you know where the super is, Knut?" asked Father. "I can't figure out how to work that iron."

"I can," said Knut proudly. "I've done the washing several times when Mother was too busy."

"Are you allowed in the laundry room?" asked Aurora.

"It's only small children who aren't allowed," answered Knut. He went in with Father, and Aurora stood outside and thought how lucky it was that Knut knew all about knobs. He showed Father what to do and stayed with him until all the ironing was finished.

The woolens were ready to come out of the spin dryer. Father took one garment out after another and Knut said: "Aurora and Socrates have a lot of sweaters."

"Well, yes, but these are not only theirs," said Father. "There are ski sweaters belonging to my wife and me as well."

"Oh," said Knut, looking at the sweaters Father was talking about. They were just the right size for Aurora and even Socrates.

"Hmmn," said Father. "They do seem to be smaller. Maybe they'll stretch again while they're drying. That's probably what happens."

Knut looked at Father. "Did you boil them?" he asked.

Father was embarrassed, but he looked Knut straight in the eyes and said: "That's just what I did."

"They've shrunk," said Knut. "I did that the first time, too."

"Oh dear, what can we do about it?" said Father.

"You can dry them in my apartment," said Knut, "and then we can . . ." He whispered, although there were only the two of them in the laundry room now.

"Yes," said Father, "and then we can buy Mother a new sweater for Christmas. Thank you for all your help, Knut. I don't know what I would have done if you hadn't been here."

That, thought Knut, was a thing worth hearing. He helped Father carry all the washing upstairs.

Aurora was working on the animal she was making. She was not sure what kind of animal it was, because on one side it was a little like a camel and on the other it was more like a sheep.

"It's most like a camel," she said to herself, "and now I'm riding my camel over the desert, and there are camels in front of me and behind me, too. We stick together so we won't be attacked by desert robbers."

She didn't notice the two boys who were standing there looking at her.

"What's that ugly thing?" said one of them. "It spoils the looks of the whole building."

"Be quiet," said Aurora, "you'll wake up Socrates."

"I'll talk as much as I want. We live here, too, you know."

"Mmmn," said Aurora. She sat quiet as a mouse on her splendid camel and didn't dare say any more. Then Knut appeared.

Aurora remembered what he had said, so she petted her camel's head and didn't look at him at all.

"Hi, Knurre, will you help us knock down the scarecrow this kid has made?"

"That's a silly game," said Knut. His voice sounded quite different now than when he spoke to Aurora and her father. "No—come on, you guys, let's go and see if the slide behind the building is any good."

They ran off and Aurora went home with Socrates. She found her father there. "Isn't Knut with you?" he said. "I promised him an extra good lunch today because he was such a help."

"He had to help me with some boys," said Aurora, "so he went away with them."

"That's too bad," said Father.

He and Aurora were eating their sandwiches, and Socrates was lying in his carriage thinking about his last bottle, when Knut arrived.

"I'm a little late," he said, "but I couldn't get here any sooner."

"Lunch is served," said Father. "I really am glad there are some men living in this building, Knut."

"So am I," said Knut, and he took a large bite of bread and cheese.

### from FROM ANNA

*Jean Little*

*A new country, Canada, a new school, a new language—all terrify Anna. After her initial fears, Anna finds herself among sympathetic classmates and befriended by a kindly doctor and a teacher who understand how much patience and understanding a handicapped child may need. The book is permeated by a sense of community and by a conviction of the need for freedom.*

#### The Second Day

Anna watched her feet walking along.

One . . . two . . . one . . . two . . .

Soon she would be at the school. Maybe she could even see it now if she looked up. She did not look up.

It was a long walk but there was no way to get lost. You just kept going straight ahead after you got to the first big street and turned left. Mama had watched until Anna had made that first turn safely. So she was not lost.

She felt lost though.

One . . . two . . . one . . . two . . .

Yesterday at school they had been nice but she was new yesterday. Today she would probably be Awkward Anna again. Miss Williams would not smile.

Today she'll want me to read from a book, Anna told herself, getting ready for the worst.

"Hi, Anna," a boy's voice called.

Anna looked up without stopping to think. The next instant, she felt silly. Nobody knew her. There must be another Anna. She glanced around quickly. There were no other girls in sight. Only a tall boy coming along the sidewalk from the opposite direction.

From *From Anna* by Jean Little. Copyright © 1972 by Jean Little. Reprinted by permission of Harper & Row, Publishers, Inc.

Anna dropped her gaze hastily and quickened her steps. She was almost sure he had been looking right at her and smiling but her new glasses must be playing tricks. She did not know that boy.

They met where the walk led into the school building.

"What's the matter? You deaf?" the boy asked.

He was laughing a little.

Anna darted another glance up at him and then stared at her shoes again.

It's Bernard, she thought, feeling sick.

She was not positive, but she had better answer. Bernard was Rudi's size exactly.

"I am not deaf," she told him.

Her voice was thin and small.

"Good," the boy said. "Hey, why don't you look at me."

Obediently, Anna lifted her head. He was still laughing. Sometimes when Rudi teased, he laughed too.

"That's better," the boy said. "Now I'm going to do you a favor."

Anna had no idea what he was talking about. She was certain now, though, that he was Bernard. She longed to run but something firm in the way he spoke to her made her stay facing him, waiting.

"This will be your first lesson in being a good Canadian," he went on.

"Lesson?" Anna repeated like a parrot.

Her voice was a little stronger now.

"Yeah, lesson. When you hear somebody say 'Hi, Anna,' the way I did, you say 'Hi' back again."

He paused. Anna stared up at him.

"You say 'Hi, Bernard!' " he prompted.

Anna just stood, still not understanding, still not quite brave enough to run.

"Come on or we're both going to be late," he urged. "Just say 'Hi, Bernard.' That's not so hard to say, is it?"

"Hi," Anna heard herself whisper.

She could not manage to add his name. What did "Hi" mean anyway?

Bernard grinned.

"That's a start," he said. "See you in class, kid."

He loped up the walk, leaving her behind.

Anna followed slowly.

Somehow she had done the right thing. Bernard had not been mean. But what had it all been about?

She was so puzzled that she was inside the school before she remembered how afraid she was.

Then the nightmare began. She could not find the right classroom. She wandered up one long hall, down another. Through open doorways, she caught sight of groups of children but she recognized nobody. Several boys and girls hurried past her. They all knew exactly where they were going. If one had stopped long enough, she might have been able to ask the way but nobody seemed to see her.

A bell clanged. Anna jumped. Then everywhere the doors were closed.

She went on walking past the tall shut doors. She tried not to think of Papa. She tried not to think at all. She just walked and walked and walked.

"Anna! Anna! This way!"

Footsteps clattered after her. Angel footsteps! But the angel was Isobel, her ringlets bouncing, her eyes warm with sympathy.

"Bernard said he'd seen you so we guessed you must be lost," she explained.

She grabbed Anna's cold hand and squeezed it.

"I know exactly how you feel," she told the new girl, tugging her along, not seeming to mind that Anna could not speak a word in return. "I got lost six times my first week here. This school is so big and all the halls look the same. At recess, I'll show you a sure way to remember. You just have to come in the right door, climb two sets of stairs, turn right and you're there. Here, I mean," she finished.

Before them, like a miracle, was the right door. It stood open. Nobody was working. Benjamin wasn't even in his desk. He was at the door watching for them. In an instant, Miss Williams was there too.

"Oh, Anna, I'm sorry I wasn't there to meet you," she said.

Anna let Isobel lead her to her desk. She sank into her seat. She listened. Apparently everyone in the class had been lost at least once in the school building. Nobody blamed Anna.

Not once did anyone say, "How stupid of you not to have paid better attention yesterday!"

"I got lost once just coming back from the bathroom," Ben said and blushed.

The rest laughed. Ben didn't seem to mind. He smiled himself.

"I expect you were daydreaming, Ben," Miss Williams commented.

"I was figuring out whether a person could dig a tunnel under the Atlantic Ocean," Benjamin admitted.

The class laughed again. Anna stopped trembling. Here in Canada, she thought, maybe it is all right to make mistakes.

"Now it's time we stopped gossiping," Miss Williams told them. "Take your place, Ben."

Ben went to his desk. Miss Williams moved to stand at the front of the room. As she opened her mouth to begin, a voice spoke up.

"Hi, Anna," Bernard said.

Anna looked at him. Then she looked at the teacher. Miss Williams was smiling, waiting. Anna gripped the edge of her desk.

"Hi, Bernard," she said, still in a whisper.

"I'm teaching her to be a Canadian," Bernard explained.

Miss Williams did not look surprised.

"Good," she said simply. "Class, stand."

When it was time for recess, Isobel did not forget. Ben came along too. They took Anna to the door through which she would enter the school.

"It's the door you'd come to naturally, walking from your place," Isobel said.

Anna's surprise showed on her face. How did Isobel know where the Soldens lived?

"I heard Dr. Schumacher tell Miss Williams your address yesterday," Isobel confessed. "I live on the same street, two blocks this way. Now listen, you come in here . . ."

"Cross-eyed . . . cross-eyed!" a voice in the playground sang out.

Anna did not know what the words meant. Until she saw her stiffen, she did not know they had anything to do with Isobel.

"Ignore them, Isobel," Ben urged. "Pretend you don't even hear, like Miss Williams said."

"Four-eyes . . . four-eyes!" another voice took up the mocking chant.

Isobel let the school door close, shutting the three of them safely inside. She smiled shakily at Ben.

"Ignore them yourself, Benjamin," she advised.

"I hate them!" Ben said, through clenched teeth.

"Me too . . . but hating doesn't help," Isobel said. "It would if we were a lot bigger."

She caught the bewilderment on Anna's face.

"She doesn't know what they mean," she said to Ben.

She explained about crossed eyes. Anna did not get all the words but she understood the gestures. Isobel's eyes did cross sometimes but they were nice eyes, brown and kind. Anna remembered the brightness in them that morning when Isobel had found her. She, like Ben, hated whoever called Isobel names.

"Four-eyes" meant glasses. Ben pointed to his eyes and then to each of his round lenses, counting them up.

"Four," he finished.

Anna looked at his earnest face. She hesitated. Could she make herself understood? Then she tried.

"Maybe I was it," she told him.

Ben looked at Isobel for help.

"What did you say?" Isobel asked Anna.

That hateful English! She should have known better than to attempt it. Then in a flash, Anna knew what to do. She imitated Ben, pointing to her own eyes and lenses as she counted.

"Ohhhh," Ben and Isobel said together. They laughed, the tension leaving their faces.

"Join the crowd," Isobel said.

As she spoke, she put her arm around Anna's shoulders and hugged her quickly, lightly.

"Come on. We're showing her how to find the room," Ben reminded them.

Anna followed her guides. She did not know what "join the crowd" meant exactly, but she was suddenly glad she had tried out her English.

Then, as she climbed the stairs with the other two, she remembered the tormenting singsong voices outside and she scowled. So there were boys like Rudi in Canada too. She had been wrong about Bernard, but there were others.

She had been very wrong about Bernard. He spoke to her again that afternoon when school was over and he was about to leave.

"So long, Anna," he said.

Anna did not know it but she reminded Bernard of a stray cat. He had rescued so many stray cats that his mother had refused to let him in the door with one ever again. Now he waited for Anna to answer him. He did not hurry her. You had to be gentle and patient with strays.

At last Anna responded.

"So long?" she said, making a question out of it.

"It just means 'Good-bye till later,'" the boy explained. She understood—it meant *"Auf wiedersehen."*

He smiled at her and left, forgetting her the moment she was out of sight.

Anna did not forget. All the way to Papa's store, she thought and thought about Bernard.

A bell chimed when she opened the door. Anna listened for it. It was as though the store said "Hi, Anna."

It is a Canadian store, she thought.

Papa was busy. Anna did not mind. She drifted back to a shadowy corner and perched on an upended orange crate. Already she had chosen this dim room, so crowded with things and yet so peaceful, as a refuge. Even Papa did not have a lot of time to notice her here. Sometimes it was nice not being noticed. Sometimes you had things to think about, private things.

She could see Papa weighing some cheese for a plump lady. She watched him count oranges into a bag. But she was not thinking about him.

"Hi, Bernard," whispered Anna. "So long, Bernard."

Now Papa was climbing up a set of steps to get down a mousetrap.

I could say it to the others too maybe, Anna thought. Hi, Isobel. So long, Ben.

She gasped at her own daring. Yet one of these days, she might.

The stout lady said, "Thank you, Mr. Solden," and went out.

Isobel put her arm around me, remembered Anna.

Papa was the only person who hugged her. When anyone else tried, she went stiff and jerked away. She could not help it. Sometimes she did not even want to. But she still did.

"Anna's not a loving child," Mama had said once to Aunt Tania when Anna had squirmed away from a kiss.

But today, with Isobel, it had been different. No fuss, thought Anna. Just nice.

Papa had turned. He was peering through the shadows, looking for her. Anna waited for him to find her in her corner. They smiled at each other across the store.

"Good afternoon, Anna," her father said.

She looked at him. In all her world, he was the kindest person. He would not laugh at her even if she got it wrong. Papa never laughed at her when he knew she was serious. She took a deep breath.

"Hi, Papa," said Anna in a loud, brave voice. It sounded fine.

## from HEIDI

*Johanna Spyri*

*Heidi is a homeless, forlorn child trying to make a place for herself. In this selection, Heidi arrives at her grandfather's and gets acquainted with him and his surroundings. This is a reassuring book, and the gallant spirit of the little girl is unforgettable.*

### At the Grandfather's

After Dete had disappeared, the uncle sat down again on the bench and blew great clouds of smoke from his pipe, while he kept his eyes fixed on the ground without saying a word. Meanwhile Heidi was content to look about her. She discovered the goats' shed built near the hut and peeped into it. It was empty.

The child continued hunting about and came to the fir trees behind the hut. The wind was blowing hard, and it whistled and roared through the branches, high up in the tops. Heidi stood still and listened. When it stopped somewhat she went round to the other side of the hut and came back to her grandfather. When she found him in the same place where she had left him, she

From *Heidi* by Johanna Spyri, translated by Helen B. Dole. Used by permission of the publishers, Ginn and Company

placed herself in front of him, put her hands behind her, and gazed at him. Her grandfather looked up.

"What do you want to do?" he asked, as the child continued standing in front of him without moving.

"I want to see what you have in the hut," said Heidi.

"Come along, then!" and the grandfather rose and started to go into the hut.

"Bring your bundle of clothes," he said as he entered.

"I shan't want them any more," replied Heidi.

The old man turned round and looked sharply at the child, whose black eyes shone in expectation of what might be inside the hut.

"She's not lacking in brains," he said half to himself. "Why won't you need them any more?" he asked aloud.

"I'd rather go like the goats, with their swift little legs."

"So you shall, but bring the things along," commanded the grandfather; "they can be put into the cupboard."

Heidi obeyed. The old man opened the door, and Heidi followed him into a good-sized room, which occupied the whole hut. In it were a table and a chair; in one corner was the grandfather's bed, in another the fireplace where hung the large kettle; on the other side, in the wall, was a large door, which the grandfather opened; it was the cupboard. There hung his clothes, and on one shelf lay his shirts, stockings, and linen; on another were plates, cups, and glasses, and on the topmost a loaf of bread, smoked meat, and cheese. Everything the Alm-Uncle owned and needed for his living was kept in this closet. As soon as he had opened the door, Heidi came running with her bundle and pushed it in, as far back of her grandfather's clothes as possible, that it might not be easy to find it again. Then she looked carefully round the room and said:

"Where shall I sleep, grandfather?"

"Wherever you like," he replied.

This was quite to Heidi's mind. She looked into every nook and corner to see where would be the best place for her to sleep. In the corner by her grandfather's bed stood a little ladder, which led to the hayloft. Heidi climbed this.

There lay a fresh, fragrant heap of hay, and through a round window one could look far down into the valley below.

"This is where I will sleep," Heidi called down; "it is lovely! Just come and see how lovely it is up here, grandfather!"

"I know all about it," sounded from below.

"I am going to make a bed," called out the child again as she ran busily to and fro in the loft; "but you must come up here and bring a sheet, for the bed must have a sheet for me to sleep on."

"Well, well," said the grandfather below; and after a few moments he went to the cupboard and rummaged about; then he drew out from under his shirts a long, coarse piece of cloth, which might serve for a sheet. He came up the ladder and found that a very neat little bed had been made in the hayloft; the hay was piled up higher at one end to form the pillow, and the bed was placed in such a way that one could look from it straight out through the round open window.

"That is made very nicely," said the grandfather; "next comes the sheet; but wait a moment,"—and he took up a good armful of hay and made the bed as thick again, in order that the hard floor might not be felt through it; "there, now put it on."

Heidi quickly took hold of the sheet, but was unable to lift it, it was so heavy; however, this made it all the better because the sharp wisps of hay could not push through the firm cloth. Then the two together spread the sheet over the hay, and where it was too broad or too long Heidi quickly tucked it under. Now it appeared quite trim and neat, and Heidi stood looking at it thoughtfully.

"We have forgotten one thing, grandfather," she said.

"What is that?" he asked.

"The coverlet; when we go to bed we creep in between the sheet and the coverlet."

"Is that so? But supposing I haven't any?" asked the old man.

"Oh, then it's no matter," said Heidi soothingly; "we can take more hay for a coverlet"; and she was about to run to the haymow again, but her grandfather prevented her.

"Wait a moment," he said, and went down

the ladder to his own bed. Then he came back and laid a large, heavy linen bag on the floor.

"Isn't that better than hay?" he asked. Heidi pulled at the bag with all her might and main, trying to unfold it, but her little hands could not manage the heavy thing. Her grandfather helped, and when it was finally spread out on the bed, it all looked very neat and comfortable, and Heidi, looking at her new resting-place admiringly, said:

"That is a splendid coverlet, and the whole bed is lovely! How I wish it were night so that I could lie down in it!"

"I think we might have something to eat first," said the grandfather. "What do you say?"

In her eagerness over the bed, Heidi had forgotten everything else; but now that eating was suggested to her, a great feeling of hunger rose within her, for she had taken nothing all day, except a piece of bread and a cup of weak coffee early in the morning, and afterward she had made the long journey. So Heidi heartily agreed, saying:

"Yes, I think so too."

"Well, let us go down, since we are agreed," said the old man and followed close upon the child's steps. He went to the fireplace, pushed the large kettle aside and drew forward the little one that hung on the chain, sat down on the three-legged wooden stool with the round seat and kindled a bright fire. Almost immediately the kettle began to boil, and the old man held over the fire a large piece of cheese on the end of a long iron fork. He moved it this way and that, until it was golden yellow on all sides. Heidi looked on with eager attention. Suddenly a new idea came to her mind; she jumped up and ran to the cupboard, and kept going back and forth. When the grandfather brought the toasted cheese to the table, it was already nicely laid with the round loaf of bread, two plates, and two knives, for Heidi had noticed everything in the cupboard, and knew that all would be needed for the meal.

"That is right, to think of doing something yourself," said the grandfather, laying the cheese on the bread and putting the teapot on the table; "but there is something still lacking."

Heidi saw how invitingly the steam came out of the pot, and ran quickly back to the cupboard. But there was only one little bowl there. Heidi was not long puzzled; behind it stood two glasses;

the child immediately came back with the bowl and glasses and placed them on the table.

"Very good. You know how to help yourself; but where are you going to sit?"

The grandfather himself was sitting in the only chair. Heidi shot like an arrow to the fireplace, brought back the little three-legged stool and sat down on it.

"Well, you have a seat, sure enough, only it is rather low," said the grandfather; "but in my chair also you would be too short to reach the table; still you must have something anyway, so come!"

Saying which he rose, filled the little bowl with milk, placed it on the chair, and pushed it close to the three-legged stool, so that Heidi had a table in front of her. The grandfather laid a large slice of bread and a piece of the golden cheese on the chair and said:

"Now eat!"

He seated himself on the corner of the table and began his dinner. Heidi grasped her bowl and drank and drank without stopping, for all the thirst of her long journey came back to her. Then she drew a long breath and set down the bowl.

"Do you like the milk?" asked her grandfather.

"I never tasted such good milk before," answered Heidi.

"Then you must have some more"; and the grandfather filled the bowl again to the brim and placed it before the child, who looked quite content as she began to eat her bread, after it had been spread with the toasted cheese soft as butter. The combination tasted very good, with frequent drinks of milk.

When the meal was over, the grandfather went out to the goat-shed to put it in order, and Heidi watched him closely as he first swept it clean with a broom and then laid down fresh straw for the animals to sleep on. Then he went to his little shop, cut some round sticks, shaped a board, made some holes in it, put the round sticks into them, and suddenly it was a stool like his own, only much higher. Heidi was speechless with amazement as she saw his work.

"What is this, Heidi?" asked the grandfather.

"It is a stool for me, because it is so high; you made it all at once," said the child, still deeply astonished.

"She knows what she sees; her eyes are in the right place," remarked the grandfather to himself as he went round the hut driving a nail here and there; then he repaired something about the door, and went from place to place with hammer, nails, and pieces of wood, mending and clearing away wherever it was needed. Heidi followed him step by step and watched him with the closest attention, and everything he did interested her very much.

Evening was coming on. It was beginning to blow harder in the old fir trees, for a mighty wind had sprung up and was whistling and moaning through their thick tops. It sounded so beautiful in Heidi's ears and heart that she was quite delighted, and skipped and jumped under the firs as if she were feeling the greatest pleasure of her life. The grandfather stood in the doorway and watched the child.

A shrill whistle sounded. Heidi stopped her jumping, and the grandfather stepped outside. Down from above came goat after goat, leaping like a hunting train, and Peter in the midst of them. With a shout of joy Heidi rushed in among the flock and greeted her old friends of the morning one after the other.

When they reached the hut, they all stood still, and two lovely slender goats—one white, the other brown—came out from the others to the grandfather and licked his hands, in which he held some salt to welcome them. This he did each evening. Peter disappeared with his flock. Heidi gently stroked first one goat and then the other and ran round them to stroke them on the other side; she was perfectly delighted with the little creatures.

"Are they ours, grandfather? Are they both ours? Will they go into the shed? Will they stay with us always?" asked Heidi, one question following the other in her delight. When the goats had finished licking their salt, the old man said:

"Go and bring out your little bowl and the bread."

Heidi obeyed, and came back at once. The grandfather milked the goat and filled the bowl and cut off a piece of bread, saying:

"Now eat your supper and then go up to bed! Your Aunt Dete left a bundle for you; your nightgowns and other things are in it. You will find it downstairs in the closet if you need it.

I must attend to the goats now; so sleep well!"

"Good night, grandfather! Good night—what are their names, grandfather? what are their names?" cried the child, running after the old man and the goats as they disappeared into the shed.

"The white one is named Schwänli[1] and the brown one Bärli,"[2] answered the grandfather.

"Good night, Schwänli! good night, Bärli!" called Heidi at the top of her voice. Then Heidi sat down on the bench and ate her bread and drank her milk; but the strong wind almost blew her off the seat; so she finished hastily, then went in and climbed up to her bed, in which she immediately fell asleep and slept as soundly and well as if she had been in the loveliest bed of some royal princess.

Not long after, even before it was entirely dark, the grandfather also went to bed; for he was always up with the sun, and it came climbing over the mountain very early in the summer

---

[1] Schwänli = little swan
[2] Bärli = little bear

---

time. In the night the wind blew with such force that its blasts made the whole hut tremble, and every rafter creaked. It howled and groaned down the chimney like voices in distress, and outside in the fir trees it raged with such fury that now and then a bough was broken off.

In the middle of the night the grandfather rose and said half aloud to himself: "She may be afraid."

He climbed the ladder and went to Heidi's bedside. The moon outside shone brightly in the sky for a moment and then disappeared behind the driving clouds, and everything grew dark. Then the moonlight came again brightly through the round opening and fell directly on Heidi's couch. Her cheeks were fiery red as she slept under the heavy coverlet, and she lay perfectly calm and peaceful on her little round arm. She must have been dreaming happy dreams, for a look of happiness was on her face. The grandfather gazed long at the sweetly sleeping child until the moon went behind a cloud again and it was dark. Then he went back to his own bed.

## from THE FAMILY
## UNDER THE BRIDGE

*Natalie Savage Carlson*

*After World War II, there was a time in Paris when there were not enough houses and apartments for people to live in. The poor lived in tents, slept in doorways, or made homes for themselves under bridges. In this selection old Armand, the hobo, first encounters the children. Before the story is finished they have had some funny, some sad, and some exciting adventures together. Get the book and enjoy the wonderful illustrations by Garth Williams along with the heart-warming story.*

### [A Hobo Adventure]

Once there was an old hobo named Armand who wouldn't have lived anywhere but in Paris. So that is where he lived.

Everything that he owned could be pushed around in an old baby buggy without any hood, so he had no worries about rents or burglars. All the ragged clothing he owned was on his back, so he didn't need to bother with trunks or dry-cleaners.

It was easy for him to move from one hidey-hole to another so that is what he was doing one late morning in December. It was a cold day with the gray sky hanging on the very chimney pots of Paris. But Armand did not mind because he had a tickly feeling that something new and exciting was going to happen to him today.

He hummed a gay tune to himself as he pushed his buggy through the flower market at the side of Notre Dame cathedral. The flowers reminded him that someday it would be spring even though it wasn't bad winter yet.

There were pots of fragile hyacinths and tulips crowded together on planks in front of the stalls. There were pink carnations and oleanders in great tin pails. Most of all there were bouquets of red-beaded holly, clumps of white-pearled mistletoe and little green fir trees because it would soon be Christmas.

Armand's keen eye caught sight of a pile of broken branches and wilted flowers swept away from one stall. "Anabel" was the name written over the stall, and Armand touched his black beret to the stocky woman whose blue work apron hung below her wooly coat.

"By your leave and in gratitude for your generosity, madame," he said to the woman who was surely Anabel. He piled the broken branches on top of his belongings in the baby buggy. Then he fastidiously picked a sprig of dried holly from the litter and pulled it through his torn buttonhole. He wanted to look his best for whatever gay adventure was waiting for him this day.

The woman who must have been Anabel only frowned at Armand as he trundled his buggy toward the Rue de Corse. Past the ancient buildings he shuffled, his buggy headed for the far branch of the Seine River.

But as he entered the square in front of Notre Dame, a hand grasped his arm from behind.

"Your fortune, monsieur," wheedled a musical voice. "You will meet with adventure today."

Armand let go of the handle of the buggy and whirled around to face a gypsy woman in a short fur coat and full, flowered skirt.

He gave her a gap-toothed smile. "You, Mireli," he greeted her. "Your people are back in Paris for the winter?"

The gypsy woman's dark face beamed under the blue scarf. "Doesn't one always spend the winters in Paris?" she asked, as if she were a woman of fashion. "But have you taken to the streets so early?"

Armand shrugged his shoulders under the long overcoat that almost reached to his ankles. "It's back under the bridge for me," he answered. "I've had enough of the crowded corners and tight alleys in the Place Maubert. And I'm tired of sorting rags for that junk dealer. I'm ready for that adventure you're promising me."

Mireli could understand. "That courtyard we rent seems like a cage after the freedom of the long, winding roads," she said, "but the men have found plenty of work for the winter. A city with as many restaurants as Paris has more than enough pots and pans to be mended. Of course the children can talk of nothing but the fields and woods of spring."

"I can't abide children," grumped Armand. "Starlings they are. Witless, twittering, little pests."

Mireli shook her finger at him. "You think you don't like children," she said, "but it is only that you are afraid of them. You're afraid the sly little things will steal your heart if they find out you have one."

Armand grunted and took the handle of the buggy again. Mireli waved him away, swaying on bare feet squeezed into tarnished silver sandals. "If you change your mind about the bridge, you can come to live with us," she invited. "We're beyond the Halles—where they're tearing down the buildings near the old Court of Miracles."

Armand tramped under the black, leafless trees and around the cathedral by the river side without even giving it a glance.

In the green park behind the flying buttresses, some street urchins were loitering. Two of them played at dueling while a third smaller one watched, munching a red apple. The swordsmen, holding out imaginary swords, circled each other. Closer and closer came the clenched fists, then the boys forgot their imaginary swords and began punching each other.

They stopped their play as Armand went by. "Look at the funny old tramp!" one cried to his playmates.

Armand looked around because he wanted to see the funny old tramp too. It must be that droll Louis with his tall black hat and baggy pants. Then he realized that he was the funny old tramp.

"Keep a civil tongue in your head, starling," he ordered. He fingered the holly in his lapel. "If you don't, I'll tell my friend Father Christmas about your rude manners. Then you'll get nothing but a bunch of sticks like these on my buggy."

The boys looked at him with awe. Father Christmas is the Santa Claus of France. He rides down from the north on his little gray donkey and leaves presents for good children.

The small boy held out his half-eaten apple. "Are you hungry, monsieur?" he asked. "Would you like the rest of this apple?"

But the biggest boy mockingly punched the air with his fist. "Pouf!" he scoffed. "There's no Father Christmas. He's just make-believe."

"If you doubt my word," said Armand with dignity, "just take a look in the Louvre store. You'll find him on the mezzanine floor."

He grinned like one of the roguish gargoyles on the cathedral. There really was a Father Christmas and it was his friend Camille, who felt the urge to work when the weather turned cold.

"I believe you, monsieur," said the boy with the apple. "I saw Father Christmas outside the store yesterday. He was eating hot chestnuts on the street."

Armand hunched his shoulders and quickly walked toward the bridge. Mireli was right. These starlings would steal your heart if you didn't keep it well hidden. And he wanted nothing to do with children. They meant homes and responsibility and regular work—all the things he had turned his back on so long ago. And he was looking for adventure.

Down a few blocks was the bridge under which he lived when the weather wasn't too raw. And plenty of company he had during the summer with all the homeless of Paris staking their claims to this space or that.

"But first I must have dinner," he told him-self, looking up at the restaurant across the street. He licked his thumb and held it up. "The wind is just right," he decided.

So he parked his buggy beside the low wall and settled himself in the breeze that came from the restaurant. He pulled all the kitchen smells deep into his lungs. "Ah, steak broiled over charcoal," he gloated. "And the sauce is just right. But they scorched the potatoes."

For two hours Armand sat on the curb enjoying the food smells because that is the length of time a Frenchman allows himself for lunch in the middle of the day.

Then he daintily wiped his whiskered lips with his cuff and rose to his knobby shoes. "And just keep the change, waiter," he said generously, although there wasn't a white-uniformed waiter in sight. "You'll need it for Christmas."

He started down the steps that dropped from the street to the quay beside the Seine. He bounced the back wheels of the buggy down each step. "I am really quite stuffed," he told himself, "but I wish I had taken that apple. It would have been the right dessert after such a rich sauce."

Down the quay he pushed the buggy toward the bridge tunnel that ran along the shore. On the cobbled quay a man was washing his car with the free Seine water. A woman in a fur coat was airing her French poodle. A long barge, sleek as a black seal, slid through the river. It was like coming home after a long absence, thought Armand. And anything exciting could happen under a Paris bridge.

As he neared the tunnel, his eyes widened with surprise and anger. A gray canvas was propped over the niche that had always been his own. And a market pushcart was parked by the pillar.

He raced his buggy across the cobblestones toward the arch. When he arrived there, he reached up and angrily tore down the canvas with one swoop of his arm. Then he jumped back in surprise and horror.

"Oh, là, là!" he cried. "Starlings! A nest full of them!"

Because three startled children snuggled into a worn quilt looked up at him with eyes as surprised as his own. The little girl and the boy cowered deeper into the quilt. But the older girl quickly jumped to her feet. She had direct blue eyes and they matched her determined chin and snubbed nose and bright red hair.

"You can't take us away," she cried, clenching her fists. "We're going to stay together because we're a family, and families have to stick together. That's what mama says."

As Armand glared at the children, a shaggy dog that should have been white came bounding across the quay. It protectively jumped between the tramp and the children, barking fiercely at Armand. The hobo quickly maneuvered his buggy between himself and the dog.

"If that beast bites me," he cried, "I'll sue you for ten thousand francs."

The girl called the dog to her. "Here, Jojo!

Come, Jojo! He won't take us away. He's only an old tramp."

The dog stopped barking and sniffed at the wheels of Armand's baby buggy.

The man was insulted. "I'll have you know that I'm not just any old tramp," he said. And he wasn't. "I'm not friendless, and I could be a workingman right now if I wanted. But where

are your parents and who are you hiding from? The police?"

He studied the children closely. Redheads they were, all of them, and their clothes had the mismatched, ill-fitting look of poverty.

The older girl's eyes burned a deep blue. "Our landlady put us out because we don't have enough money to pay for the room since papa died," she explained. "So mama brought us here because we haven't any home now. And she told us to hide behind the canvas so nobody could see us, or they'd take us away from her and put us in a home for poor children. But we're a family, so we want to stay together. I'm Suzy and they're Paul and Evelyne."

The boy swaggered a little. "If I was bigger, I'd find a new place for us to live," he boasted.

"It looks to me like you've already found a new place," said Armand, "and it's my old place. You've put me out of my home just like that landlady did to you."

Suzy was apologetic. She moved the pushcart over and measured Armand with one eye closed. Then she carefully drew a long rectangle on the concrete with a piece of soft coal.

"That's your room," she said. "You can live with us." On second thought, she scrawled a small checkered square at the foot of the rectangle. "There's a window," she said gravely, "so you can look out and see the river."

Armand grumbled to himself and pulled his coat tighter across his chest as if to hide his heart. Oh, this starling was a dangerous one. He'd better move on. Paris was full of bridges, the way the Seine meandered through it. No trouble finding another one. But as he started away, the girl ran over and clutched him by his torn sleeve.

"Please stay," she begged. "We'll pretend you're our grandfather."

Armand snorted. "Little one," he said, "next to a millionaire, a grandfather is the last thing I hope to be." But even as he grumbled, he began unpacking his belongings.

He stacked the branches and twigs, and made a pile of the dead leaves he had gathered. He pulled out a dirty canvas and a rusty iron hook. He set a blackened can with a handle near the leaves. He sorted some bent spoons and knives. Last of all, he pulled out an old shoe with a hole in the sole.

"Might come across its mate one of these days," he explained to the children. "And it fits me just right."

The children wanted to help him. Oh, these starlings were clever. They knew how to get around an old man. Lucky he wasn't their grandfather. But he laid his canvas over the rectangle Suzy had made for him.

He started a fire with the branches and dead leaves. Then he hung a big can over the fire. Into it he dropped scraps of food he unwrapped from pieces of newspaper.

"In the good old days of Paris," he told the children, "they used to ring bells in the market places at the close of day so the tramps would know they were welcome to gather up the leftovers. But no more. Nowadays we have to look after ourselves."

They watched him eating his food. Even the dog that should have been white watched each morsel that went into his mouth and drooled on the concrete. Armand wriggled uneasily. "What's the matter?" he asked gruffly. "Haven't you ever seen anybody eat before?" They said nothing in reply, but four pairs of eyes followed each move of his tin spoon. "I suppose you're hungry," he growled. "Starlings always have to be eating. Get your tinware."

Suzy pulled some stained, cracked bowls and twisted spoons from the pushcart. Armand carefully divided the food, even counting in the dog.

It was dark by the time the children's mother joined them. The lights of Paris were floating in the river, but the only light in the tunnel flickered from a tiny fire Armand had made. He could not see the woman's face well, but he felt the edge of her tongue.

"What are you doing here?" she demanded of the hobo.

Armand was angered. "And I might ask you the same, madame," he retorted. "You have taken my piece of the bridge."

"The bridges don't belong to anybody," said the woman. "They're the only free shelter in Paris."

Suzy tried to make peace. "He's a nice, friendly old tramp, mama," she explained, "and he's going to live with us."

"I'm not a friendly old tramp," said Armand indignantly. "I'm a mean, cranky old tramp, and I hate children and dogs and women."

"Then if you hate us," said Paul, "why did you give us some of your food?"

"Because I'm a stupid old tramp," replied Armand. "Because I'm a stupid, soft-hearted old tramp." Oh, là, là! There it was. He had let slip that he really had a heart. Now this homeless family would surely be after that too.

The mother was displeased to hear that the children had accepted the hobo's food. "We are not beggars," she reminded them. "I have a steady job at the laundry, and that is more than he can say."

She went to work warming a pan of soup and breaking a long loaf of bread that she had brought with her. Armand sat in the rectangle marked by Suzy and thought that this woman's trouble was pride, and that pride and life under the bridge weren't going to work out well together.

By the dying light of the fire, the woman went back and forth to her pushcart, pulling out moth-eaten blankets and making bed-places on the concrete. Just overhead the automobiles roared, lights garlanded the bridge and people walking along the higher quay laughed lightly. But it could have been a million miles away from the little group under the bridge.

"You ought to put the starlings in some charity home until you find a place of your own, madame," suggested Armand, after the children had dropped off to sleep. "This life is not for them. Now, you wouldn't want them to end up like me, would you?"

"Families should stick together through the lean times as well as the fat," replied the woman. "And I have hopes. I'm going to see my sister-in-law soon. She may know of a place for us out in Clichy."

Armand stretched out on his canvas without bothering about any covering. He was used to the cold. He never felt it any more. But he was sure these children would feel it. As he lay on the hard concrete an uneasy thought worried him, like a mouse gnawing at his shoestring. Now that he had befriended these starlings, his life would never again be completely his own.

from AVALANCHE!

*A. Rutgers van der Loeff*

*Natural disaster is our sternest teacher. When nature intrudes upon our organized lives, whether it is a flood, a hurricane, or an avalanche in a Swiss village, we are tested seemingly beyond human endurance. In this excerpt, Werner, the hero, has returned from helping rescue people buried beneath tons of snow. Physically weakened by his efforts and mentally worn out from worrying about his own family, Werner asks the question we all ask, "Why do all these things happen?" The answer he receives provides one of the most important messages in juvenile literature within the framework of a thoroughly spellbinding book.*

### Where Do We Go from Here?

When he came to, he was lying on his camp bed in the station restaurant at Brachen. It was broad daylight and only one or two people here and there were sitting or lying on their beds. The place seemed less full than before. He looked at the corner over by the coffee machines to see if Klaus were lying there, but the bed had been taken away.

He looked round slowly. He had a queer, light-headed feeling and wondered how long he had been asleep.

Paolo was in the next bed. He was asleep, but his hands moved restlessly on the coverlet, and now and then he muttered something. Farther along, Nikolai and Giuseppe lay fast asleep.

The camp beds of the others had been tidily made. They were empty. The boys must have gone off to the village. Werner raised himself on one elbow and gave a little grunt of pain. All his muscles hurt. He looked round a bit farther. Then he saw Hans Peter sitting behind him a little distance away. He was sitting on a pile of knapsacks between two beds with his back against the wall, staring gloomily before him. Werner beckoned, but Hans Peter did not see. He was sunk in thought.

Was he angry at their having gone off without

him? He would have been a great help, but he could never have given Mr. Hutamäki the slip like the rest of them. Would he know how Klaus and Marie were? And whether their parents had been found?

Werner heaved himself up a bit farther and all his muscles seemed to protest. He was aching everywhere—back, shoulders, arms.

"Hans Peter!" he said in an urgent whisper.

Hans Peter jumped. He stood up rather reluctantly and came over to Werner's bed. "How do you feel?" he asked gruffly.

"I'm fine. How are the others?"

"I've been left here as watchdog," said Hans Peter. "You're none of you to get up till the doctor says you may. He's coming back this afternoon. There was no room for you in the hospital."

"But there's nothing wrong with us!" exclaimed Werner in surprise.

Hans Peter did not answer.

"How long have we been asleep?" asked Werner.

"Two nights and a day and a half."

Werner's jaw dropped.

"They gave you injections to make you sleep. You were suffering from exhaustion or something. They made quite a song and dance about you."

"But I feel fine," protested Werner. "My muscles ache a bit, that's all."

Hans Peter shrugged his shoulders. "Well, you looked pretty moldy, all the lot of you, when they brought you in here the day before yesterday. You all had jabs at the hospital. You looked more dead than alive, I can tell you, and Hutamäki had the scare of his life. It was a mean trick you played us, creeping out while we were asleep, instead of taking us with you."

"We couldn't help that," said Werner. "Mr. Hutamäki would never have approved of your coming and you might have let on to him about us."

"Honestly, I don't know what I should have done," Hans Peter admitted. He was not so gruff now. "But I've never been so angry in all my life."

Werner glanced over to the corner where he had expected to see Klaus. He hesitated and then asked, "How are Klaus and his sister?"

Hans Peter looked uncomfortable. He began

to say something and then stopped, looking away so as not to meet Werner's eyes.

"D'you mean it was all for nothing?" Werner asked suddenly, with his heart in his mouth.

Hans Peter shook his head. "Marie's alive, but they don't know if she'll pull through." He paused. "They found the parents; they were both dead." He paused again and it was a minute before he added, "And Klaus is very ill. He's delirious."

Werner felt the blood beating in his temples. His heart was thumping. He felt dizzy and lay down again on his back.

"Everyone here is getting on fine," Hans Peter went on presently, in a flat, expressionless voice. "Most of them are out now. It's visiting time at the hospital. And the trains are running again. A lot of the evacuees have left."

But Werner was not listening any more. He could see Klaus, and Marie's pinched white face. Should not he and the other boys have done what they did? Had they just been crazy fools?

Then he remembered Klaus when he was brought in that evening, sobbing and kicking because he had had to leave the place where his parents were buried. He had kept on shouting, but no one had listened to him. He had known they had been searching in the wrong place. In his helplessness there was nothing Klaus could do but howl. But later he had dug frantically for hours.

And had it all been wrong? Had they just caused more misery? Klaus was delirious, his parents were dead after all, and Marie . . . .

"What exactly is wrong with Marie?" he asked. Hans Peter hesitated, but after a bit he answered. "She bled an awful lot inside," he said. "She's got to have an operation. They wanted to do it yesterday afternoon, but they couldn't because they hadn't any blood for her."

"No blood?" asked Werner, puzzled.

"She's got to have a blood transfusion before the operation, and after it's over. But they couldn't find anyone that had exactly the same kind of blood. As a rule it isn't so tricky, but with Marie it was very difficult. A lot of us went over to let them test our blood. They tried me and Mr. Hutamäki and Bartel. But our blood wasn't right either. There were two doctors and three nurses working on us, and word kept on coming up from the lab that it wasn't the right kind of blood. And you'll never guess who had the right kind in the end."

"Who?" demanded Werner excitedly.

"Your Aunt Augusta. First they wouldn't try her. They said she was too old and her blood pressure wasn't high enough, or something. She was so cross with the doctors when they wouldn't try her that they gave in. And then they found she had exactly the right kind."

"Well, what happened?" Werner asked. "Were they in time?"

"I'm not quite sure about what happened after that. They took Aunt Augusta away with them and we were all sent back here."

"Have they operated on Marie?"

"Yesterday evening, but they don't know yet if it was successful or not. It should have been done much sooner. Your aunt had to stay in the hospital."

Werner lay quite still on his back. It was all too much for him to take in at once. Aunt Augusta and Marie . . . it was all so wonderful. He knew just what his father would have said about it—"It was meant."

He tried to think. If he and his father had not brought the boys down from the hut above Urteli, they would not have been evacuated together. If they had not come here to Brachen, Klaus would not have been able to take them up to his home. In that case Marie would be dead by now, for she could have lasted only a couple of hours longer. And if Aunt Augusta had not been evacuated with them she would not have been able to give her blood. It was meant!

But what about the avalanches? Were they meant too? That could not be right. There must be something wrong somewhere. All those people killed and injured, all that grief and suffering! His whole heart revolted against the idea of so much pain. It was senseless for the snow to come hurtling down from the mountains. Why did it happen? Why? Why? Why did Klaus and Marie have to lose their father and mother?

"*I* don't know," he muttered suddenly half aloud.

"What is it?" asked Hans Peter. "What don't you know?"

"Why do all these things happen? Why can't people just live happy and ordinary lives?"

"Happy and ordinary aren't the same," said Hans Peter slowly. "I believe you're only happy if you *know* you're happy. And you only know that after you've been miserable. A lot of us in the Children's Village have learned that."

Werner said nothing. Hans Peter went on rather uncertainly, "The head of our Village told us something once. He said misfortune shakes you awake, and it's only when you're awake that life becomes quite real, because then you've learned what it's worth."

## from THE BUSHBABIES

### William Stevenson

*This is much more than the story of a foolish young girl's attempt to return her beloved bushbaby to its natural habitat. As the journey to return the bushbaby progresses across Africa, Jackie is faced with a growing awareness of the danger in which she has placed Tembo—everyone thinks he has kidnaped her—since the orders are to shoot him on sight. But she also comes to appreciate his tremendous knowledge of the country and to understand that numerous skills are required for survival in different environments. The Bushbabies is one of the few juvenile books which lay the groundwork for the young adult to read with compassion Alan Paton's* Cry the Beloved Country.

### [Kamau Goes Home]

"Are you the little girl with the bushbaby?" asked the second engineer of the United States motor vessel *Thoreau*.

Jackie, picking her way between coils of tarred rope, said: "Yes. Want to see him?"

She lifted the lid to the basket which was his second home, displaying Kamau asleep in his nest of old sweaters.

"That's a rare 'un," said the engineer. "Worth his weight in gold, I bet."

He stood in front of her, face red against the brilliant white of his starched shirt and shorts. "You've got a game permit, of course."

"Of course," Jackie replied quickly, and flushed.

"Good kid." The engineer let her pass. "It'd be a bad thing if all the rare animals of Africa were taken away, eh?" he called after her.

But Jackie was already running, gripped by the sudden fear that she had forgotten the vital permit with the impressive words: *"Granting permission hereby for the export of one bushbaby— to wit:* galagos senegalensis zanzibaricus." She could remember even the Latin name. Where had she put the permit?

She flew to her cabin and hooked the door shut. Then she threw open her suitcase and whirled through its contents.

The permit was nowhere to be found.

She searched Sally's bag on the adjacent bunk. She went carefully through all her own pockets. She combed her memory.

She had no recollection of packing the permit. With growing certainty and alarm, she knew she had left it behind.

Her heart flipped.

She tried to remember the restriction on animals leaving Africa. Of one thing she was sure. It would be illegal to keep Kamau.

There was a knock at the door. Trembling, she unhooked it.

"I come to make bunks ready." It was the Swahili steward. He moved to the two-tiered bunks and saw the basket.

"Little missie has *galago,* bushbaby?"

"You know?"

"All the ship knows."

She thought in that case it would be impossible to keep Kamau as a stowaway.

"Does the captain know?"

"The captain." He paused, crouching over the coverlet, eyes dark and expressionless. "The captain will find out, missie. He is not liking animals on board. One time he makes the ship's carpenter leave a pet monkey behind, in Madagascar."

This was worse news still.

"Please don't tell him."

"Why for should I tell the captain?" The steward gave her an indignant look. "I do my work. Captain does his." He turned and busied himself with the blankets.

Jackie picked up the basket and took it into the small shower room. She closed the door and lifted Kamau gently out. He disliked being disturbed and drew back his ears, blowing between sharp little teeth with a sound like a muted roar.

From outside came the whine and screech of cranes. Soon the ship must sail. She had to think fast. If she tried to keep Kamau hidden, the captain was bound to find out. If she somehow deceived the captain, there would be customs men to face later. Either way she would certainly lose her bushbaby.

She let him leap to the rail of the shower curtain, where he clung upside down, head twisted so that he could watch her.

She remembered how her father had gone to some trouble to get Kamau's export license from the Kenya Game Department.

And now she had forgotten the permit.

She remembered, too, going to the public library and reading: "These are among the strangest animals in existence. Their relatives of the *tarsier* family are found only in equatorial forests of Asia. The animal commonly called the bushbaby, however, has been known to survive in cold climates."

Jackie winced. Here she was, planning to expose Kamau to the wintry blasts of a northern climate. Yet she could not even preserve the piece of paper that protected his life.

She heard the outer door clunk open again.

"Daddy!" She rushed to meet him.

"What is it?" He caught the urgency in her voice and looked at her with such frank and honest eyes that she faltered.

"Nothing." She was suddenly afraid to mention the permit. Her father was a square sort of man; square of shoulders and with a face that seemed to be chiseled from stone. He had an old-fashioned square-dealing approach to life. She could see no way of enlisting his help in breaking regulations.

"Come on deck and join the others." Trapper Rhodes took her arm in the belief that her evident distress was due to the tension of recent days.

She let him lead her to the main deck, her mind working furiously. There was only one solution that she could see. Kamau must be released here, in Mombasa dockyard.

Shrinking from the thought, she took her place at the rail. The dock was almost deserted. The last of the cargo had swung aboard. Big arc lights swayed in the humid night breeze, casting an eerie glow on the greasy concrete below. Chains rattled. Davits creaked.

A voice behind her said: "We'll be another coupla hours before sailing."

It was the second engineer talking quietly to Rhodes.

"In that case," said Penny firmly, "we'd better get some sleep." She herded the children together. "It's been a long day. And truth to tell, I'd sooner not be here when we cast off. We'll say goodbye to Africa tomorrow, at a good long distance."

Later when they were all bunked down, Penny said to her husband: "Did you see how upset Jackie was?"

His answer was lost in the metallic whir of the fan.

"You know," Penny continued, "that girl has changed a great deal since we gave her the bushbaby. She's still awfully clumsy. And forgetful. She breaks cups and trips over her own legs, which are certainly too long for her age. She's awkward and dreamy and moves like a young colt. But she's a gentle child," said Penny, closing her eyes. "And a kind heart is worth a ton of cleverness."

In the next cabin Jackie waited until she heard Sally's breathing deepen into slumber.

Then she crept into the shower room. Kamau squatted beside the dish of milk and corn flakes she had smuggled from the cook's galley. He was clasping a mint candy, licking it with rapture in his eyes. She knew from long experience that mints had an almost hypnotic power over him, glueing his attention just as firmly as his twig-fingers were glued to the candy itself.

With a movement so swift it was scarcely perceptible, she scooped him up.

"*Kek-kek-kek!*" His screech was somewhat muffled by the mint. She bundled him into the basket, crammed down the lid, and pegged it into place.

She checked again that Sally was asleep, and slipped into the clothes she had worn in the train; riding breeches, a yellow shirt, and a brown whipcord jacket. Into a pocket of the jacket she stuffed a paper bag full of Kamau's remaining mints.

She tied her long golden hair at the back hastily, using an old piece of blue ribbon. She donned her favorite chukka boots made from the ear of an elephant. Finally, on impulse, she bent and kissed Sally. "Back soon," she whispered, and slipped away.

The gangway was down and still unattended. Men scurried about the decks, absorbed in their own pursuits. Jackie was grateful that nobody had come to see them off. All farewells, except for Tembo's, had been made upcountry. And Tembo, once he saw the baggage safely stowed away, had not lingered to drag out the agony.

Jackie scampered down the gangway and stood for a moment in the shadows. A stumpy locomotive of the port railway fussed along the gleaming metal of the line. A group of stevedores, bared backs glistening in the artificial light, stood arguing in a group.

She waited, and when the way seemed clear, she ran to the shelter of a nearby godown. There, in the thick smell of diesel oil and coffee, Jackie took stock.

She could let Kamau out of his basket now, and pray that somehow he would find his way safely back to the highland forests that were his natural home.

But then she thought of all his enemies. The hooting owls. The giggling hyena. The fish eagle whose harsh cry sounded across the marshes. The baboons who worked in teams, so clever and ruthless they could tear a leopard to pieces, never mind a bushbaby.

She shuddered.

Her mind went back to the very first time she had seen the basket she now clutched in her arms.

It had been their last Christmas Day in Africa.

The African workers and their children were gathered under the tall pine tree growing outside the bungalow. The tree was decorated with lights, and gifts were scattered on the grass below.

She had seen nothing at first but the straw basket tied with red ribbon.

"How do I open it?"

Jackie remembered how her father had bent down and freed the ribbon. "It will open itself."

The lid of the basket had lifted a fraction, making her jump.

And then, for the first time in her life, she had seen a bushbaby.

A tiny hand had groped along the basket's edge, followed by a face like a furry walnut.

"What is it?"

"Galago." Tembo's deep voice boomed in her ear.

She clapped her hands. "What a super, super surprise."

At the sound of her voice the bushbaby had jumped clean out of the basket and into her lap, tail thrashing like a propeller.

"His name is Kamau." Again it was Tembo who spoke. "The sprite who lives in the jungle. Kamau."

Now, as Jackie peered out of the darkness of the godown, she smiled sadly at the recollection of those happy months that followed. Kamau had been comforted by the warmth of her body, and made a permanent haven inside her shirt. She had to teach him to give up his nocturnal habits, for he was by nature a night animal.

"He's got the face of a fox, the ears of a bat, the eyes of an owl," Jackie had written to a distant uncle. "He's the color of a squirrel and he grins like a monkey and he's got the fingers of an old man. And he jumps like a kangaroo!"

She listened to him now, astir in the basket.

She stood alone on the dockside, in an agony

of doubt, and heard the locomotive come clattering and clanging down the line again. It stopped and there was a moment of silence.

Away in the distance she caught faint notes of a toy harmonica. At first she thought the sound came from the ship. She heard Kamau scratching to be let out of the basket, and she lifted the lid. The bushbaby scrambled onto her arm and stiffened, his big paper thin ears pricked forward, his head twisting in every direction to pick up the sound.

Tembo!

She knew it must be Tembo, for the bushbaby had responded to the same harmonica notes.

Long ago, her father had said: "The most constructive thing the army ever taught Tembo was to play the mouth organ." And he had given the African headman a big old-fashioned German harmonica made of engraved metal and carved walnut. In camp, at night, Tembo would play this impressive instrument while the women husked coconuts or pounded the evening meal of posho made from corn meal.

Now, straining her ears like Kamau, the girl was sure she recognized the notes. They were lost again in the deep and sudden thunder of the *Thoreau*'s siren.

It reminded her of the foghorn near the family cottage, a few miles along the coast from Mombasa. Its desolating thunder made her think of shipwrecks and storm-tossed seas. When it stopped, and the echoes dwindled away, she listened again for the notes of a mouth organ, but heard nothing.

Kamau slipped under her shirt and, hugging the basket, she ran the length of the godown. Part of her mind insisted that she had imagined the mouth organ. Deep down inside herself, she was not so sure.

Again the ship's siren blew, and still she felt this strange compulsion to run away from it. She slipped her hand inside the basket and felt the comforting furry warmth of the bushbaby. She stopped running, and looked back.

There was a great deal of activity now around the *Thoreau*. She saw figures moving about the stern and on the fantail. A rope snaked astern and fell with a clear splash into the murky water.

She stood, breathing fast.

A loud clatter drew her attention to the gang-way. It was moving away from the ship's hull. Mesmerized, she saw more ropes curl through the air. Her legs were rooted to the ground. Common sense told her to shout, to run to the trundling gangway some fifty yards away.

But nothing on earth would have made her drop Kamau.

The ship's propellers began to churn. She heard small waves slap against the wharfside.

As if in a bad dream she saw the ship detach itself from the black density of the docks. Lights twinkled along the hull. The gap between the *Thoreau* and the quay began to widen with surprising speed. The ship had moved so slowly at first. Now it surged forward in a great hurry to be free from Africa. In the wake came a stench of fuel and tar, of stale cooking pots and sacks of coffee. A stream of garbage shot through a chute in the stern, and again the siren blew.

The girl stared unbelievingly at the black and deepening gulf between herself and her family. The basket in her arms, however, was like an anchor. While her head spun with the enormity of her situation, her legs refused to move. And then, quite slowly at first, came a wave of relief. Kamau was safe. He was still with her.

When she heard the notes of the harmonica again, she was certain it must be Tembo.

She followed the sound, half-sobbing, until she came to the end of the main wharf. There she saw him, seated on a bollard, silhouetted against the city's glow.

"Tembo!" She was still too far away to be heard. He was playing a mournful African song. Jackie had heard it many times when he crouched over the charcoal brazier at night. It was a song of his own people, made long ago when Arab slavers laid waste this part of the continent. The song was a lament for the lost freedom of the chained African slaves, and for the slaughtered children they left behind. It was a dirge that recalled the endless march of the slaves, and in it were echoes of the wide horizons and the great forests they would never see again.

Tembo stopped. Moving softly, anxious not to alarm him, Jackie whispered: "Hullo, old friend. It's me. Do not be disturbed. Tembo?"

She spoke in Swahili.

The man jumped to his feet. His eyes shone, whites gleaming. He was on the very edge of the shifting pool of light cast by the swinging flood lamps, and he peered dubiously into the surrounding dark.

"Baba?" His voice was a hiss. "What are you doing here. *Wafanyajee?*"

"Come quickly, Tembo, out of the light."

He took a firm grip on the short club hanging from his wrist and moved toward her.

"Is it really you?"

"It is me, Tembo. I want your help." She touched his arm.

When his eyes had adjusted to the dark, and he saw truly that the girl stood there, the man sucked his breath. "What have you done?" He dropped to one knee and pressed her face between his callused hands. Then he saw the basket.

"Kamau?"

"Yes." She began to explain.

The African groaned. "You have done this thing for the galago? You have left the ship?"

"There was nothing else I could do," Jackie said simply. She hesitated. "I must get him home, to the place where he was caught. To the Place of the Hippopotamus."

Until this moment she had given no thought to such a plan. It rose unbidden to her mind. At once, however, she saw what a sensible solution it would be. Among his own family, he would be safe.

"That is a long way," Tembo was saying. "It is beyond Ndi." He added slowly: "Your father will be angry."

"He will understand." She spoke with more confidence than she felt. "If I had stayed on the ship, Kamau would die."

Tembo nodded slowly. He had never pretended to share the Rhodes' curious love of animals. As a young Kamba warrior, one of the fleetest hunters in his village, he regarded animals as either a nuisance or as a source of food. He passed no judgments on white-skinned foreigners who took a different view. He thought of them quite simply as mad. There was no telling how far they might go in their craziness.

He fingered the bracelet on his scarred wrist. It was made from the hairs plucked from a lion's tail, and it was the most powerful of his charms. He turned it slowly between his thick fingers, standing there in the darkness while the girl waited patiently at his side.

"How will the bushbaby make such a long journey?" he asked.

"With your help."

His friendship with Trapper Rhodes went back a long way. He had not expected to have it tested so severely by the daughter.

"You will help?" she persisted.

She was interrupted by a long blast from the ship's siren and she waited, head cocked, watching Tembo's face.

He was wearing the old desert kepi, with a neck flap at the back, that he used on safari. Over his thin shoulders he had flung an army greatcoat, worn like a cloak. His feet were thrust into black boots that were several sizes too large. The leather was cracked and the boots lacked laces. In these clothes he had gladly suffered the most acute discomfort, considering them to be appropriate to the sad occasion of parting.

The siren echoed across the harbor, and faded. Again the girl remembered the foghorn, and her father's cottage.

"I know!" She seemed to explode with the idea. "We will go to the cottage at Vipingo. It's a short bus journey from here. And tomorrow, when the

post office is open, I will send a telegram—a letter by radio—to the ship."

She saw the doubt lingering in his face.

"You have not seen the cottage but it is beside the farm of Major Bob."

Tembo's face cleared slightly. He knew about Major Bob and felt less apprehensive.

"Is it not possible to take the northern train?"

"No." She spoke decisively, detecting from his voice that the battle was half won. "In the cottage at Vipingo we shall be safe tonight. Major Bob will tell us what to do in the morning. If we go to the train, there will be questions at the barrier. There will be white policemen."

She knew the beefy red-faced police. They seldom understood small girls as her African friends did. The red-faced whites were too busy blustering around. Her family's cottage, on the other hand, was far off the beaten track. There she could plan her next move.

Tembo wiped his harmonica across the knee of his torn pants. Perhaps if he humored the girl now, she would see sense in the morning. "You are sure this is what you wish?"

"I am sure, old friend." She slipped her free hand into his gnarled fist. "Remember when we all went climbing on Kilimanjaro?"

Tembo chuckled softly.

"And we got lost in the mist, you and I?" She grinned up at him. Behind her, the Thoreau's lights twinkled in the harbor mouth. "We had such fun, just the two of us, singing and shouting down the mountain. It will be like that, Tembo, like climbing a mountain together."

The African smiled and hunched his shoulders under the greatcoat. It was a coat far too big, and much too warm, but he wore it with pride. He wore it as he had once worn the skin of the colobus monkey, in days when he carried a spear and shield, before he went to war in the service of a foreign king. The coat was a link with those distant days when he shouldered a rifle to fight the white king's enemies.

He looked down at the towheaded child. His days as an askari in the King's African Rifles had taught him many things. His days as a tribal warrior had also taught him much. He had learned to accept the passing of these days—the great days of hunting the lion; and other, more bewildering days, marching against an unknown army. Time had taught him never to grieve over his lost youth; never to look back in sadness at what had gone beyond recall. Despite this he had been sitting on the dockside in great despair as the ship sailed away with those he had served with loyalty and affection. A few minutes ago, the world had seemed a forlorn and lonely place. Age had come creeping into his bones.

He held the girl's hand and felt a warm surge of joy. Jackie's mother had once said he would follow the girl to the end of the earth; and he himself had believed this; and hidden his unhappiness when he saw that the girl had no further need of him. Foolishly, he had nursed a secret hope that Trapper Rhodes would take him away too. But the ship had sailed, with no word said. A little time ago he was blaming himself for being a failure. Now fate had provided him with an opportunity to show that, if need be, he would follow this girl anywhere.

He laughed, the deep booming laugh that Jackie knew so well. He was a religious man, respectful of tribal gods, and devoted to the biblical figures he had learned about at the mission school. He released the girl's hand and cupped the harmonica between his horny palms.

There was a marching song they both remembered, played on ceremonial parades by the King's African Rifles. It was called: "When the Saints Go Marching In."

He squared his shoulders. "Come, then, baba. You will be my captain-bwana and give me orders." He blew out his cheeks, the wooden club dangling by a thong from his wrist. "Let us go." He sucked in a lungful of air and began to play.

"Forward!" cried Jackie, falling into the spirit of the game. "To the bus for Vipingo."

On the hot sticky night of October the twenty-fourth a puzzled Sikh policeman patrolling the Kilindini dockyard in Mombasa heard the strains of a familiar military march float down the tarmac road by the ferry. He thought he saw an African in flowing robes, accompanied by a slender blond girl, flit in the shadows between the street lamps. He was sure he had heard "When the Saints Go Marching In" when the record was played several days later. By that time the unusual spectacle had assumed an importance that even the most efficient Sikh officer could never have foreseen.

*Reginald Ottley*

*The opening chapter of this powerful book reflects all of its qualities. There are the harshness of life on the Australian desert, the lack of sentimentality characteristic of such a rugged life, and the gentleness of those who love things smaller and weaker than themselves—the boy's love for the pup, and the small touches of friendship for the boy shown by those around him. Although it is set in the Australia of the 1930's, the mixture of harshness and tenderness needed to survive in such an environment is universal. Ottley's* Roan Colt *is a worthy sequel.*

### Kanga's Choice

The boy crouched, to peer under the huge feed-bin. In a scooped-out hole, he could see a bitch being nuzzled by newborn pups. The little mites were wiggling, crawling blindly on top of each other.

Gentle-handed, the boy reached under the bin. When the bitch's tongue licked wetly on his fingers, he rubbed her ears. "It's all right, Brolga," he whispered. "It's on'y me. I'm jus' feelin' in, t' count 'em." As he said it, he slid his fingers along her sleek body. Lightly, he touched each squirming pup. Their eagerness choked him in the throat. He wanted to stay there. Just him, the bitch, and the pups. But he couldn't. He could sense the tall old man staring down.

Slowly, the boy straightened. Worry lines creased his freckles. "There's seven of 'em, Kanga," he said. "Seven little beauts. An' they're all snuggin' up." He hoped to sound confident, but his voice broke.

Kanga's lean height stooped. His hard, wide shoulders brushed down past the boy. Stiffly, the old man groped, to pull out the seven pups. One after the other, he set them on the strawed floor. When the seven squirmed in a line, he rolled each one with a finger. The finger was calloused, yet its touch on the pups was light. The mites

wriggled, then scratched fatly at their bellies.

The boy watched every movement. His heart seemed swollen inside his shirt. "Cor," he thought, "I wish I could grab 'em all an' run, run, run. But there ain't nowhere to go. Just sand an' waste an' desert. You couldn't get far before old Kanga'd have you." He waited while the pups wheezed faintly.

Finally, Kanga towered to his height. The boy saw a pup in the old man's hand. "This 'un 'll do," Kanga said. "He's got the most bone. You'd best git rid of the others." He slid the pup onto the boy's cupped palms. Dejectedly, the boy held it close to his chest. "Come on, little feller," he said with a sigh, "I'll put you back with your mum." He knelt to slip the pup under the bitch. She whimpered, calling to the rest of her litter.

The boy swiveled around. The six remaining pups squirmed at his feet. He tucked them together, pushing each little ball against the other. "Couldn't she keep 'em, Kanga?" he whispered. "Couldn't she keep 'em all, jus' for a while?"

Kanga rubbed tobacco in his hand. The battered felt hat masked his gaunt, seamed face. He had the tobacco tamped in his pipe when he said, "There's enough strife about for a good dawg, son; never mind for them that ain't wanted. An' if you want a 'king' dawg, you have t' rear 'im right. On 'is own, so he'll grow big an' strong."

The boy stroked the pups. They wriggled when he bunched them. Their tiny heads reached in search of their mother's teats. He wished they were his, to give back to the bitch. Kanga struck a match. Through encircling hands, he puffed and drew on the pipe. The bowl glowed as he added, "You'd better get a shovel an' bucket. I'll have 'em set when you git back."

The boy choked. He tried to speak, but words blurred in his throat. With a final pat, he re-bunched the pups and walked toward the door. Kanga watched the boy go.

When he returned, the shed had darkened. Kanga knelt with his back to the feedbin. In front of him lay the now still pups. Blindly, the boy gave the bucket to Kanga and kept the spade.

Kanga took the bucket with one hand and lifted the pups with the other. They settled limply, piled in a soft-skinned heap. Rising, he gave the bucket to the boy. "Here you are," he said. "They're better orf out of it. Take 'em out t' the sandhills an' dig a hole. They'll be right when you tip 'em into it."

For a long, long moment the boy stared up at Kanga, then down at the bucket. Slowly, he turned and went out through the doorway again. Kanga heard him stumble on the rough timber step.

Outside, the sun had set. Under the peppercorn trees surrounding the homestead, it was already dark. The boy saw a light glitter brightly in the kitchen. Up in the trees, galah cockatoos scrambled for their roosts. "They're all alive," he thought. "Warm, an' waitin' for t'morrow. Yet the pups—they're all dead. All except one. You can't understand a man like Kanga. He's like an old tree that doesn't think or feel." Clear of the peppercorns, the boy trudged westward.

Where the red-earthed plains merged into drifting sand, he set down the bucket, then leaned on the spade. The handle felt cool and smooth to his grasp. Overhead, an odd star or two began to show through the haze. Slowly, the boy dug a hole. He finished it with his hands, making the sides clean and straight. Then he lined the hole with dry, withered tussock grass. "You'll be right, there," he said, and gently placed the pups, side by side, in the hole. "An' when I cover you, I won't press hard. That way"—he wiped a hand under his eyes—"you won't feel bad. You'll know that the light ain't too far away." He covered the pups by letting sand trickle down. When he leveled the top, the hole was lost in a vast sea of desert.

Trudging back, he thought of many things: the mystery of death when it comes; the quick way life has of going. One minute the pups were warm and wriggling; the next they were limp and still. And where had it gone? Life, as it's called. The boy didn't know. But he *did* know the pups were dead. They were nice little fellers. Every one a beaut. He set down the bucket to rub a hand under his eyes.

At the bunkhouse, he left the spade and bucket outside. In his room, the air felt hot and heavy. Through the window came the whisper of leaves rustling on the peppercorns. Sprawled flat on his bunk, the boy let tears flow freely. He didn't mind when nobody was there to see.

But on the other side of a timber partition, old Kanga heard. He puffed his pipe, then shook the ash. The bowl glowed redly in his hand. Hard-knuckled, he rapped the partition. "You there, boy?" he said. "You ain't ate yet. Your tucker's in the kitchen. Mrs. Jones was askin' for you."

The boy wiped his face. His boots clumped when he sat up. "Yeah," old Kanga went on, "there's pie an' cream. I saw it on your table." He lay back and closed his teeth on the pipe.

The boy wavered. "I'd just as soon stay," he thought. "But if I do, she'll be over for me. Then I'll have to go, or she'll think I'm crook an' send for the boss." His feet shuffled as he edged toward the door. It was dark in the room, and he couldn't see too well. "Thanks, Kanga," he said. "I nearly forgot. The trouble was that job I had t' do." He went out through the doorway and clumped down the steps. On his bunk, old Kanga puffed. Smoke drifted up in the darkness.

In the kitchen, Mrs. Jones rolled dough to fit the bread tins. She smiled when the boy came in. "Set down," she told him. "Your tea's cold. I'll make a fresh pot." She wiped her hands on her apron.

The boy pulled out a chair. He had a knife and fork in his hands when he said, "It don't matter, Mrs. Jones. A feller c'n drink it cold, the same as if it's hot. I'm sorry I'm late in for tea." He paused and looked up. Mrs. Jones saw the smudge where he'd rubbed his eyes. She had heard from Kanga about the pups. She wished there was more she could do. "Never mind," she said. "You couldn't help it. Now pass me that pot. I can't have you drink cold tea."

Later, the boy stood up. The pie crust and cream tasted sweet in his mouth; he'd scraped the last crumb from the plate. "Do you want me," he asked, "to give you a hand? Help with the washin' up?" He reached for the door as he spoke; one leg held it partly open.

Mrs. Jones smiled. She liked the ways he had. Always willing to help, yet always half away somewhere else. "No," she told him, "there's not much to do. You go along, an' don't get worrying. Good night. An' make sure you wash. There's dust still on your face."

The boy nodded. "It ain't dust," he thought. "It's sand from them sandhills. I had it on me hands."

"Good night, Mrs. Jones," he said. "I'll be around early t' get wood t' cook breakfast." He let the door rub, sliding across his back, as he went out.

In the morning, Kanga rode away before dawn. Behind him trotted his rabbit-hunting pack of thirty-four dogs. At his side, loose-muscled and scarred, loped Skipper, his "king" dog. Kanga couldn't see him but knew he was there. He always had been, since his training as a pup; he always would be, until he died, unless Kanga chained him to a peg or whistled him to control the dogs. Then Skipper would hurtle to rip and slash, to bring the pack to order. The dog was Kanga's life. If he knew love, it was for the dog. If the dog knew love, it was for Kanga. The two were inseparable, except by chain or command.

An hour after Kanga had gone, Yamboorah homestead stirred. Stockmen came from the buildings to yard their saddle horses. Wild galahs, squawking in the peppercorn trees, woke the boy. As a rule, he liked to hear them. They flocked in great numbers on Yamboorah, and the big old trees were a favorite roosting place. But this morning their angry chattering seemed more raucous. "Get out," he shouted, as he pulled on his boots, "an' start the day right. You've all got rotten tempers." Then he thought about Brolga and the pup. Under a tap, he splashed his face with water, then went out through the gateway.

Near the stables, he waited while horses galloped by. An aboriginal stockman riding behind them waved and smiled; his white teeth flashed over the bobbing rumps. The boy saw the whip in his hand swing up, then down. As it cracked, the big mob of horses surged. Squint-eyed in the dust, the boy entered the shed. Its door hung open, propped by a stone.

On the floor, he settled on hands and knees. Brolga was still there, under the bin. The pup was asleep, curled in a ball. A tiny snuffle sniffled through its jaws.

The bitch nuzzled the boy's hands for scent of her pups. "I'm sorry," he whispered, "but I couldn't do a thing. You know how it is with Kanga. He's hard, Brolga. Hard as a Mulga log." Unknowing of words but keen to the boy's tone, Brolga licked his hand. She pushed her muzzle deep into the cupped palm. The scent of her pups stayed strong on the boy's skin.

He let her push. His fingers touched her warm jaws. "So there it is," he thought. "She loved her pups, but I buried 'em. Lay 'em deep in that round sandy hole. An' all because Kanga wants to breed a 'king' dog—a dog that'll fight an' kill if the old man wants him to." The boy stroked the bitch, then scrambled up. "I'll get you a feed," he said, "an' something to drink. It's me best, Brolga. I tried t' save 'em, but I didn't have a chance."

At the door, he bumped into a man. Ross, the overseer, stood craglike on the step. "Good day, son," he said with a nod. "You're about bright an' fresh. How's the bitch an' her brood?" He held a bridle hooked on his arm, a stockwhip coiled on his shoulder.

The boy sighed. "She's right," he said, "but there's only one pup. Kanga killed the rest, an' I had t' bury 'em." He said it the way he felt— as if he'd helped to kill them.

Ross nodded. He rolled a cigarette and stared over the boy's shoulder at the horse yards. A stockman was saddling a young horse; the horse bucked and threw the saddle from its back. Ross held the cigarette. "Git hold of 'is ear," he shouted, then looked down at the boy. "Yeah," he said, in a softer voice, "that's how it is with Kanga. He's got t' rear a pup t' take the place of Skipper. He's gittin' old an' mightn't last much longer. Believe me, old Kanga knows his dawgs. Now git on over t' see the cook. She might want some wood or something." His face creased as the boy left. A smile blurred the set, weathered lines. "An' keep that chin up," he added. "Then you won't knock into a man. You ain't safe, with your head down." He heel-rocked toward the stables, chuckling. He stood six foot and weighed fifteen stone.

At the woodheap, the boy split a log into short, neat lengths, then trundled them to the kitchen. As he set down the barrow, he sniffed the warm, still air. The smell of bread, fresh-baked from the oven, drifted out through the door. When he opened it, the smell grew richer. Frying chops added to the odor. Arm-loaded, he carried in the wood. Mrs. Jones bustled near the fire. Pans of bread glowed brownly on their racks. The wood rattled as the boy dumped it down. He noticed the box was empty. Mrs. Jones must have used the last stick to bake her bread. "I'm late," he said, "an' I promised you. But I had t' look at Brolga. She's doin' fine with her pup." He stared at the chops sizzling in the pan.

Mrs. Jones fussed with a turning fork. "Don't worry," she told him. "I had enough. There's a mug of tea there, waiting on the table." Fat hissed when she turned a chop.

The boy nodded. Near the mug stood another pan of chops, salted but uncooked. Reaching for the mug, he inched a chop into his hand, along with the mug. Carefully he carried both outside. Mrs. Jones glanced over when the door had closed. The smile grew broader across her face. "That's one less," she thought. "But God bless his soul. He'll put it to good use. It'll help make milk for Brolga's puppy." She turned the rest of the chops, then lifted the other pan from the table.

Outside, the boy gulped his tea. It washed down hot and tasty. Mrs. Jones always sugared it just right.

With the chop rammed into his pocket, he headed for the stables. A group of stockmen, coming in for their breakfasts, said the usual "Good day, son." But the boy just nodded. The chop felt greasy and cold in his pocket; he could feel it sticky against his leg. "They might see the bulge," he thought. "These trousers are pretty tight."

The men walked on, bowlegged, on their heels. One of them rubbed his chin. "He looked kind of scary-like," he said. "An' not too good in the gait. Seemed t' have a limp." He spat as he went through the gateway.

In the shed, the boy hunkered down against the wall. He eased the chop until the bone end showed. The raw red tip poked out invitingly. "Come on, Brol'," he said. "Come an' see what's here." He pulled the chop to show another inch. Excitement made him jerky. The chop almost fell, and he had to push it back.

Brolga crawled slowly, mindful of her pup. Her head showed first, then her sleek, slender body. Tail held low, she feathered straw on the floor. Close to the boy, she crouched, nuzzling his hands. The scent of meat overpowered all other—even that of her pups. And hunger made her drool.

The boy chuckled. He twisted over, till his pocket was fully showing. The chop protruded on his lean, boyish rump. "You ain't lookin'," he told her. "You're in the wrong place. Jus' sniff along till you find it."

Brolga sniffed. Then she lifted her head to sniff again. Inquiringly, she snuffled along his trousers, into every crease and wrinkle. Near the pocket she questioned the boy. Her soft eyes begged for permission. The boy nodded. His hand slid over her ears. "Sure," he whispered, "I brought it for you. You an' your little bloke, asleep under there." He nodded again, this time toward the bin.

Sight of the bin reminded him. He had two horses to feed, as well as Brolga. Patches and Powder were gray Arabs, kept especially for the boss. He could hear them stamping in their stalls. Scuffle-footed, he scrambled up from the wall. "You see how it is," he said to Brolga. "I look after you an' forget them. They'll kick down their stalls if I don't feed 'em."

The bitch wagged her tail. Jaws clamped on the chop, she crept under the bin. The boy heard her crunch as he threw up the lid. With stomach flattened, he hung over, groping for two buckets. He buried them in chaff, then pulled them out. The short golden stems overflowed when he lifted. Carefully, he plodded toward the door. The buckets swung as he turned, before going out. "I'll be back," he called. "Jes' you stay there. Next time I'll bring some water." The crunch of bone was Brolga's answer.

In the stalls he worked fast. Patches nipped him on the trousers, right where the chop had been. Powder tried to bump him. The boy dodged neatly. "I'm awake to you," he told them. "An' don't think I ain't. If you'll give me time, I'll tip it in." While they ate, he cleaned their stalls. The floors were raked and the straw bedding stacked when he slapped each snowy rump. "So long," he said. "You're right for another day. The boss'll feed you lunchtime." He ducked and scurried away when each took a flying kick.

After breakfast, Mrs. Jones wanted eggs. "It's cake day today," she said, while the boy wiped his plate. "And I'll need some eggs. A billyful will do." The boy was halfway through the doorway when she added, "You could look along the hedge. But be careful of the nests. I want fresh eggs, not stale." The boy let the door close. He flipped up the billycan, then caught it as he walked along the path. "She talks a lot," he thought, "but means her best. A feller knows not to touch the broodies. You c'n tell 'em by their feathers an' the shine they put on their eggs."

Under the hedge, he scraped and crawled. The rough limbs clawed his back. He kept one eye searching for eggs, the other for slithering snakes. Goannas he didn't mind; they hissed and spat, but you could hunt them away. Snakes reared up to strike; you had to be quick to get away in time.

The billy was full when he saw a snake in the dust. A long, thin tongue flickered questing from its jaws. Startled, the boy pushed backwards. The gaping head seemed almost under his chin. He heard it hiss as he crawled on backwards. "Phew!" he gasped as, clear of the hedge, he scrambled upright. "You made me puff. Another yard and I'd 've touched you." The thought made him shiver. He was glad of the sun flaring down on his shoulders. Glad, too, that he'd balanced the billy. Not an egg was cracked or broken.

In the kitchen, Mrs. Jones lifted out the eggs, then set them in a bowl. "They're lovely," she said. "Lovely and fresh. Did you have any trouble finding them?"

The boy shook his head. A leaf or two still clung to his hair. "No," he told her. "They were jus' lyin' about. I didn't go near the broodies. There's a few of 'em, too. On their nests."

Mrs. Jones nodded. Broody hens meant more chickens. More chickens meant more fowls for the table. "That's good," she said with a smile. "We must look out for them. There's a pen in the garden to put them in." She rinsed the billy under a tap.

The boy watched her hands. They were large and white, with smooth round fingers. He'd seen them often lift great steaming pots. "She's strong," he thought: "though her arms look soft. You can't see any muscle." The billy was back in his grasp when he said, "Yeah, I like the little 'uns. They're all fluff an' wool." He remembered the snake, beady-eyed and waiting. "But they get a rough trot if a snake gets at 'em."

Mrs. Jones came from Sydney, far away on the New South Wales coast. She had read about snakes but seldom seen one—only in Taronga Zoo. The thought of them made her cold. "Yes," she agreed. "I believe they *are* bad. We'll have to be careful." She looked directly at the boy. "And you be careful, too."

The boy chuckled. "I will," he said, and left

her wondering if he really would. Later, she talked about it to Ross, the overseer. He was sitting straddle-legged in the men's dining room. The back of the chair poked up through his arms; his chin hung over the top. He liked to sit that way after a day in the saddle; it rested his legs, he said.

He rocked up straight when she entered. The chair legs squeaked on the hard, bare floor. Crag-faced, he listened while she talked. "Don't worry, ma'am," he told her. "He'll live t' grow. But I'll talk to him just the same—if it'll help to ease your mind." He added the last in the hope she would smile. It lighted her face when she did.

"Thank you," she said, "I thought you would," and left him holding the chair.

## from THE INCREDIBLE JOURNEY
### Sheila Burnford

*This is Chapter 2 of the story of three heroic animals—a young Labrador retriever, a Siamese cat, and an old bull terrier—who travel through two hundred and fifty miles of Canadian wilderness to the place and people that mean home and love to them. Young children will listen enraptured to its being read aloud, while older children and adults will find pleasure in reading it to themselves.*

### [The Beginning of the Journey]

There was a slight mist when John Longridge rose early the following morning, having fought a losing battle for the middle of the bed with his uninvited bedfellow. He shaved and dressed quickly, watching the mist roll back over the fields and the early morning sun break through. It would be a perfect fall day, an Indian summer day, warm and mellow. Downstairs he found the animals waiting patiently by the door for their early morning run. He let them out, then cooked and ate his solitary breakfast. He was out in the driveway, loading up his car when the dogs and cat returned from the fields. He fetched some biscuits for them and they lay by the wall of the house in the early sun, watching him. He threw the last item into the back of the car, thankful that he had already packed the guns and hunting equipment before the Labrador had seen them, then walked over and patted the heads of his audience, one by one.

"Be good," he said. "Mrs. Oakes will be here soon. Good-by, Luath," he said to the Labrador, "I wish I could have taken you with me, but there wouldn't be room in the canoe for three of us." He put his hand under the young dog's soft muzzle. The golden-brown eyes looked steadily into his, and then the dog did an unexpected thing: he lifted his right paw and placed it in the man's hand. Longridge had seen him do this many a time to his own master and he was curiously touched and affected by the trust it conveyed, almost wishing he did not have to leave immediately just after the dog had shown his first responsive gesture.

He looked at his watch and realized he was already late. He had no worries about leaving the animals alone outside, as they had never attempted to stray beyond the large garden and the adjacent fields; and they could return inside the house if they wished, for the kitchen door was the kind that closed slowly on a spring. All that he had to do was shoot the inside bolt while the door was open, and after that it did not close properly and could be pushed open from the outside. They looked contented enough, too—the cat was washing methodically behind his ears—the old dog sat on his haunches, panting after his run, his long pink tongue lolling out of his grinning mouth; and the Labrador lay quietly by his side.

Longridge started the car and waved to them out of the window as he drove slowly down the drive, feeling rather foolish as he did so. "What do I expect them to do in return?" he asked himself with a smile, "Wave back? Or shout 'Good-by'? The trouble is I've lived too long alone with them and I'm becoming far too attached to them."

The car turned around the bend at the end of the long tree-lined drive and the animals heard the sound of the engine receding in the distance. The cat transferred his attention to a hind leg; the old dog stopped panting and lay down; the

young dog remained stretched out, only his eyes moving and an occasional twitch of his nose.

Twenty minutes passed by and no move was made; then suddenly the young dog rose, stretched himself, and stood looking intently down the drive. He remained like this for several minutes, while the cat watched closely, one leg still pointing upwards; then slowly the Labrador walked down the driveway and stood at the curve, looking back as though inviting the others to come. The old dog rose too, now, somewhat stiffly, and followed. Together they turned the corner, out of sight.

The cat remained utterly still for a full minute, blue eyes blazing in the dark mask. Then, with a curious hesitating run, he set off in pursuit. The dogs were waiting by the gate when he turned the corner, the old dog peering wistfully back, as though he hoped to see his friend Mrs. Oakes materialize with a juicy bone; but when the Labrador started up the road he followed. The cat still paused by the gate, one paw lifted delicately in the air—undecided, questioning, hesitant; until suddenly, some inner decision reached, he followed the dogs. Presently all three disappeared from sight down the dusty road, trotting briskly and with purpose.

About an hour later Mrs. Oakes walked up the driveway from her cottage, carrying a string bag with her working shoes and apron, and a little parcel of tidbits for the animals. Her placid, gentle face wore a rather disappointed look, because the dogs usually spied her long before she got to the house and would rush to greet her.

"I expect Mr. Longridge left them shut inside the house if he was leaving early," she consoled herself. But when she pushed open the kitchen door and walked inside, everything seemed very silent and still. She stood at the foot of the stairs and called them, but there was no answering patter of running feet, only the steady tick-tock of the old clock in the hallway. She walked through the silent house and out into the front garden and stood there calling with a puzzled frown.

"Oh, well," she spoke her thoughts aloud to the empty, sunny garden, "perhaps they've gone up to the school. . . . It's a funny thing, though," she continued, sitting on a kitchen chair a few minutes later and tying her shoelaces, "that Puss isn't here—he's usually sitting on the window sill at this time of the day. Oh, well, he's probably out hunting—I've never known a cat like that for hunting, doesn't seem natural somehow!"

She washed and put away the few dishes, then took her cleaning materials into the sitting room. There her eye was caught by a sparkle on the floor by the desk, and she found the glass paperweight, and after that the remaining sheet of the note on the desk. She read it through to where it said: "I will be taking the dogs (and Tao too of course!) . . .", then looked for the remainder. "That's odd," she thought, "now where would he take them? That cat must have knocked the paperweight off last night—the rest of the note must be somewhere in the room."

She searched the room but it was not until she was emptying an ash tray into the fireplace that she noticed the charred curl of paper in the hearth. She bent down and picked it up carefully, for it was obviously very brittle, but even then most of it crumbled away and she was left with a fragment which bore the initials J. R. L.

"Now, isn't that the queerest thing," she said to the fireplace, rubbing vigorously at the black marks on the tiles. "He must mean he's taking them all to Heron Lake with him. But why would he suddenly do that, after all the arrangements we made? He never said a word about it on the telephone—but wait a minute, I remember now—he was just going to say something about them when the line went dead; perhaps he was just going to tell me."

While Mrs. Oakes was amazed that Longridge would take the animals on his vacation, it did not occur to her to be astonished that a cat should go along too, for she was aware that the cat loved the car and always went with the dogs when Longridge drove them anywhere or took them farther afield for walks. Like many Siamese cats, he was as obedient and as trained to go on walks as most dogs, and would always return to a whistle.

Mrs. Oakes swept and dusted and talked to the house, locked it and returned home to her cottage. She would have been horrified to the depths of her kindly, well-ordered soul if she had known the truth. Far from sitting sedately in the back of a car traveling north with John Longridge,

as she so fondly visualized, the animals were by now many miles away on a deserted country road that ran westward.

They had kept a fairly steady pace for the first hour or so, falling into an order which was not to vary for many miles or days; the Labrador ran always by the left shoulder of the old dog, for the bull terrier was very nearly blind in the left eye, and they jogged along fairly steadily together—the bull terrier with his odd, rolling, sailorlike gait, and the Labrador in a slow lope. Some ten yards behind came the cat, whose attention was frequently distracted, when he would stop for a few minutes and then catch up again. But, in between these halts, he ran swiftly and steadily, his long slim body and tail low to the ground.

When it was obvious that the old dog was flagging, the Labrador turned off the quiet, graveled road and into the shade of a pinewood beside a clear, fast-running creek. The old dog drank deeply, standing up to his chest in the cold water; the cat picked his way delicately to the edge of an overhanging rock. Afterwards they rested in the deep pine needles under the trees, the terrier panting heavily with his eyes half closed, and the cat busy with his eternal washing. They lay there for nearly an hour, until the sun struck through the branches above them. The young dog rose and stretched, then walked towards the road. The old dog rose too, stiff-legged, his head low. He walked toward the waiting Labrador, limping slightly and wagging his tail at the cat, who suddenly danced into a patch of sunlight, struck at a drifting leaf, then ran straight at the dogs, swerving at the last moment, and as suddenly sitting down again.

They trotted steadily on, all that afternoon—mostly traveling on the grassy verge at the side of the country road; sometimes in the low overgrown ditch that ran alongside, if the acute hearing of the young dog warned them of an approaching car.

By the time the afternoon sun lay in long, barred shadows across the road, the cat was still traveling in smooth, swift bursts, and the young dog was comparatively fresh. But the old dog was very weary, and his pace had dropped to a limping walk. They turned off the road into the bush at the side, and walked slowly through a clearing in the trees, pushing their way through the tangled undergrowth at the far end. They came out upon a small open place where a giant spruce had crashed to the ground and left a hollow where the roots had been, filled now with drifted dry leaves and spruce needles.

The late afternoon sun slanted through the branches overhead, and it looked invitingly snug and secure. The old dog stood for a minute, his heavy head hanging, and his tired body swaying slightly, then lay down on his side in the hollow. The cat, after a good deal of wary observation, made a little hollow among the spruce needles and curled around in it, purring softly. The young dog disappeared into the undergrowth and reappeared presently, his smooth coat dripping water, to lie down a little way apart from the others.

The old dog continued to pant exhaustedly for a long time, one hind leg shaking badly, until his eyes closed at last, the labored breaths came further and further apart, and he was sleeping—still, save for an occasional long shudder.

Later on, when darkness fell, the young dog moved over and stretched out closely at his side and the cat stalked over to lie between his paws; and so, warmed and comforted by their closeness, the old dog slept, momentarily unconscious of his aching, tired body or his hunger.

In the nearby hills a timber wolf howled mournfully; owls called and answered and glided silently by with great outspread wings; and there were faint whispers of movement and small rustling noises around all through the night. Once an eerie wail like a baby's crying woke the old dog and brought him shivering and whining to his feet; but it was only a porcupine, who scrambled noisily and clumsily down a nearby tree trunk and waddled away, still crying softly. When he lay down again the cat was gone from his side—another small night hunter slipping through the unquiet shadows that froze to stillness at his passing.

The young dog slept in fitful, uneasy starts, his muscles twitching, constantly lifting his head and growling softly. Once he sprang to his feet with a full-throated roar which brought a sudden splash in the distance, then silence—and who knows what else unknown, unseen or unheard passed through his mind to disturb him further? Only

one thing was clear and certain—that at all costs he was going home, home to his own beloved master. Home lay to the west, his instinct told him; but he could not leave the other two—so somehow he must take them with him all the way.

## from TROUBLE IN THE JUNGLE

### John Rowe Townsend

*The story of children in a ghetto neighborhood in northern England is candid and lively, with a quick establishment of the setting, good characterization, and rapid pace. The children, left on their own, cope resourcefully until the delinquent adults return, helping to rout a gang of thieves while they keep house for themselves.*

### [On Their Own]

It was a fine spring day, not warm but with a sort of hazy sunshine, and I was walking through the Jungle with my sister Sandra and my friend Dick. The Jungle isn't a real jungle, it's a district off the Wigan Road in the city of Cobchester. We call it the Jungle because all the streets are named after tropical flowers—like Orchid Grove, where we live. That may sound gay and colorful, but there's nothing colorful about the Jungle. It's a dirty old place, and one of these days the Corporation is going to pull it all down—if it doesn't fall down of its own accord first.

But on this sunny Saturday morning, as we walked home to our lunch, even the Jungle seemed a cheerful place. Summer was coming, the blades of grass were showing between the cobblestones, and soon the weeds would blossom on the empty sites. The days were getting longer. Next week perhaps we would be playing cricket after school. There was a dog in Mimosa Row that I was getting very friendly with. I was going to make a soap-box car for my cousin Harold. Life was full of interesting things to do.

We walked three abreast, with Sandra in the

middle. And as we turned into Orchid Grove I felt happy and burst out singing.

"Hark at him!" said Sandra. "Not a care in the world."

"Poor old Kevin!" said Dick, with mock sympathy. "He's got a pain. Where does it hurt, Kevin?"

"I'll hurt *you* in a minute!" I said.

"Oh, yes? You and who else?"

"Do you think I couldn't?"

"Yes, I do think you couldn't."

"Well, I'll show you." And we started a friendly scuffle, the kind that happens a dozen times a day.

I generally get the worse of any fight with Dick. He's fourteen, a year older than I am, and quite a bit bigger. He's a cheerful redheaded boy, very good-looking, and the only thing wrong with him is that he's bossy. He thinks he's a born leader (which he may be) and he thinks he's always right (which he isn't). And now he held me off with one hand, grinning in a way that he knew would annoy me.

"Break it up, you two!" said Sandra. Small and thin, with sharp determined face, she stepped between us. "Fight when you're on your own, not when you're with me. Kevin, what did you start it for? It's all your fault."

Sandra always blames me—partly because I'm her brother and partly because in her eyes Dick can do no wrong.

"Just wait a minute, Sandra," said Dick. "Give me time to bash his brains out. Oh, no, I was forgetting, he hasn't any. . . ."

"Oh, leave off!" said Sandra again; and then, as something caught her eye, she added, "Just look what's happening over there!"

Dick and I broke it up, and looked the way she was pointing.

Along the other side of the street came the two grown-ups from our house. First Doris, in her best coat and headscarf, stalking ahead as fast as she could walk. Then Walter, with a battered suitcase, scurrying after her.

Walter is our uncle. When our parents died Sandra and I went to live with Walter and his two young children, Harold and Jean. Walter's wife had left him, and Sandra had to act as mother to the younger ones. It was hard work for her. She's only twelve herself.

When Doris, a friend of Walter's, came to live with us, it looked as though things might get better. But not for long. Doris was a blonde, bulky woman with a round, puddingy face. She was always padding about the house in slippers, a cigarette in her mouth, grousing and not getting anything done. She didn't like us children, and she tried to take it out on Walter. Every few days they'd have a row and she'd threaten to go away.

"I'm leaving you," she'd say. "I'm not staying in this house another minute."

"All right, then," Walter would say. "Hop it, and good riddance."

He knew she wouldn't hop it, because she'd nowhere else to go.

"You'll say that once too often, Walter Thompson," she'd tell him, and then she'd go on grumbling: "What with you and them brats, it's enough to drive me barmy. . . ." But it would all die down. By evening they'd be round at the George, the pub in the next street, just as if nothing had happened. Sandra would put Harold and Jean to bed, and then she and I would sit up and do what we liked for a bit, until Walter and Doris came back.

But now, this Saturday midday, the two of them were hurrying along Orchid Grove in a very strange manner. Doris strode ahead, looking neither left nor right. Walter caught up with her and tried to say something, but she ignored him. Neither of them took any notice of us.

I was mildly puzzled. "What's up with them?" I said. "I've never seen them go off like this before. And at lunchtime, too."

Sandra looked quite alarmed. She ran across the street and caught Doris by the arm.

"Will you be out for lunch?" she asked.

Doris shook herself free. "I will that!" she said fiercely.

"What shall we have?"

"You can fend for yourselves, can't you?"

"When will you be back?" asked Sandra.

But Walter had now caught up. "Ask no questions and you'll be told no lies!" he snapped. "Now get out of the road!"

And the two of them—Doris with her head in the air, and Walter hurrying alongside, still trying to make her listen to him—turned out of Orchid Grove into Hibiscus Street.

As they disappeared round the corner, three or four heads poked out of doorways, and puzzled or knowing looks were exchanged. I shrugged my shoulders.

"They might keep their quarrels to themselves, instead of putting on a show for the neighbors," I said.

But Sandra still looked anxious.

"There's something behind all this," she said. "I've felt for a few days there was real trouble coming. And this has got me worried."

"Cheer up, love," said Dick. "Look on the bright side. They're out of the way for a bit. Enjoy the peace while you've got it."

"I wish I felt sure it was only a bit," said Sandra.

"Well, they wouldn't walk out on you, would they?"

"I don't know," said Sandra thoughtfully. "I don't know. . . . Anyway, come on, Kevin, we'd better get something to eat."

"And I'd better get home," said Dick. He lives just the other side of Hibiscus Street. "Don't worry, they'll turn up like a pair of bad pennies. See you later." And off he went whistling.

We went into the house. The younger children, Harold and Jean, had appeared from nowhere and were squabbling mildly in the kitchen.

"Give us a butty, Sandra!" urged Jean. (A butty is a slice of bread and butter.) She danced around us, twirling her skirt, a roly-poly, round-faced, cheeky child of six.

"A butty, a butty, a red jam butty!" she chanted. I aimed a clout at her, but missed.

Harold slouched off into a chair and said nothing. At eight he was almost the image of his father Walter: small, slightly built, with wispy fair hair and blue eyes. He seemed to have gone off into his private dream world; but after a minute he got up again and went to the cupboard. He took out a big loaf and put it on the table between Sandra and Jean as if to quieten the row once and for all.

Sandra took the breadknife, and in a minute had sent the two children out with a thick slice of bread and jam in each hand. Then, putting the kettle on, she turned to me.

"I bet they've hooked it!" she said savagely. "I bet they've hooked it!"

"I don't think Walter would walk out on us," I said. "In fact I don't really think Doris would. You know what she is. All talk. She's always planning to do this and that, but nothing ever comes of it. I don't know what they're up to, but I bet they'll be at the George tonight as usual."

But I didn't feel quite as confident as I tried to sound. I remembered that Doris had been particularly cross and shrill for the last few days. It had begun when Walter came home one evening and said he'd been offered a job in Yorkshire but he'd turned it down because there wouldn't be anywhere for us to live. Doris was furious and had been taking it out of everybody ever since. She'd kept saying she was sick of this house and sick of this town and sick of him and sick of us. What if she'd really gone? And if so, had Walter gone, too?

I comforted myself with what Dick had said. Surely they'd be coming back. It was common sense after all. And by the time I'd eaten a few slices of bread and jam and drunk a mug of tea I felt much better.

Afterwards I went to the soccer match with Dick and his father, while Sandra saw to some mending and the youngsters played out in the street. It was a splendid match, the last day of the league championship, and United won 3–1. They were top of the table already, and this last performance capped it all. I came home full of the afternoon's play and hoarse with shouting, and I'd quite forgotten we had any worries.

Saturday teatime was usually the high point of the week at 40 Orchid Grove. Walter generally went to the match, too—though he never took me with him—and Doris went to see a friend, and they both used to come home for a hot tea before going round to the George to spend the evening. It would be a good tea with sausages or beans or tomatoes, and there'd be a big fire, and if United had won Walter would be in a happy mood. He'd even been known to hand out sixpences and shillings (which we spent at once in case he tried to take them back next day).

But today was a chilly contrast. There was no fire in the hearth, no meal on the table. As I stood in the doorway, my spirits sinking, Sandra came in from the street with a child on each hand. She looked grim but calm.

"Light a fire, Kevin, if there's some coal," she said. "We're on our own this evening."

Everybody was hungry. After having only a bread-and-jam lunch, Harold and Jean were whimpering a bit and wiping their faces with grubby hands. So we had a good look round to see what there was to eat, and we found quite a lot of things. There was some bacon that had gone off a bit, but wasn't too bad. There were potatoes. There was a whole jar of jam. There were several milk bottles with varying amounts of milk in the bottom, all sour. But there was a can of condensed milk and there was plenty of tea. In fact the cupboard was better stocked than usual. And we had one surprising bit of luck. We found a ten-shilling note under the tea-jar that Doris must have forgotten. Sandra pocketed that. "You never know when we'll need it," she said.

We had coal and candles, too, so really we were much better off than we might have been. There was no electricity in the house, and we'd no shillings for the gas, but I soon made a good fire and we had a fine fry-up of bacon and potatoes. There was enough for us all to feel full. Then we stoked the fire up again and sat round it.

"Tell us a story, Kevin," said Sandra. So I made up a story, all about children cast away on a desert island. And we imagined it was us, and that we could hear the waves beating all round us. And we pretended to be alone and in peril, instead of warm and comfortable in our home at Cobchester. I went on with the story for quite a while, because once I get started it's no trouble to make up stories. They just come to me. But after a while we noticed that Jean was nodding, and Harold was getting tired, too. So Sandra told them both to go to bed. Then there was a lot of arguing, and Jean cheeked both of us, and Sandra belted her, not hard, but she squawked as if she was being murdered. And Harold did a go-slow and took twenty minutes to get his shoes and socks off, and every time we

looked the other way he stopped getting undressed and did something else. And even when they were in bed in a corner of the room they kept grousing and cheeking us and pinching each other and bawling, and it was a long time before we got any peace.

In the end they both went to sleep. We didn't know the time, but it was getting dark. By now I had persuaded myself that Walter and Doris would be in the pub as usual, and I told Sandra so.

"Well, if they are, they won't come out before closing-time," said Sandra.

"Dick was right, it's peaceful without them," I said. I'd quite enjoyed my evening. "It won't be peaceful when they come in, though."

We both grimaced, for this was the one drawback to Saturday. Not that Walter and Doris were violent when they came home on Saturday night, like a couple we knew in the next street, but there was often a lot of shouting and quarreling, and Sandra and I would get cuffed it we put a foot wrong, or even sometimes if we didn't.

So we decided we would go to bed, to be out of the way.

Our house, like all the others in Orchid Grove, had a living room and a scullery and two bedrooms. Our back bedroom was in a bad state because the roof needed repairing, so we four children all slept downstairs in the living room. We had a big iron bedstead, and Harold and I slept with our heads at one end and Sandra and Jean at the other. There was room for all of us, and we had some blankets and old coats to keep us warm, and it was a very good arrangement. Sandra and I were awake for quite a time, listening to footsteps going past and people singing and shouting, and wondering whether Walter and Doris were coming. Then Sandra fell asleep, but I lay quietly watching the red embers in the grate and thinking how well we'd managed. And eventually I dozed off, too, and I didn't know anything more until next morning.

Sandra was shaking me. "They haven't come!" she said. "They haven't come!"

When children are very young, last week seems long ago and the next town may seem very far away. Developing perspective about time and space is one of the signs of increasing maturity in children. Many adults have had the experience of seeing a child show wide-eyed amazement upon learning that television has not always existed. Or, they have met children who associate Franklin Roosevelt, say, with the Civil War. We may laugh about such incidents, but behind them lies an important point: children need guidance in developing a sense of time and place in history.

Children need to come to understand that the world did not begin with their birth and will not end with their death. They need to learn that their lives are a part of the continuity of existence, and that what is the present for them will be history for future generations.

In the 1961 edition of *Time for True Tales*, it was noted that the reading tastes of children often parallel adult tastes. We have seen this point dramatically illustrated in the intervening years when the publication of adult historical fiction has declined. Although there has been good historical fiction published to celebrate the bicentennial of the American Revolution, the emphasis in children's books is on nonfiction— as it is in the world of adult books.

# HISTORICAL FICTION

Of course good historical fiction continues to be written and published. It will always be possible to entrance children with accounts of times past; they are intrigued by a world without electricity or jet planes, and there is a romantic fascination in reliving through books the times when Indians rode the plains of our country and when primitive tribes occupied England.

Good fiction makes bare facts in the history textbook come alive, and good teachers have always supplemented the dates of battles and treaties with stories in order to help children see that history *is* people.

## Three types of historical fiction

There are three distinct levels or types of books within the category called historical fiction. Authenticity is the only criterion they have in common. They should be true to place, period, and the people who lived during the time in which the book is set. It is impossible to overemphasize the importance of authenticity, since without it the book is valueless; with it, a less than perfect style or inadequate characterization can be, and often is, forgiven.

The purest type of historical fiction is that in which history itself is the center of interest, no matter how thrilling the plot or how well developed the characters. Such books can be written only about pivotal points in human history; they are set in periods when the old way was giving way to the new. It is fairly easy to recognize such books. One has only to ask the question: could this plot and these characters have been superimposed upon any other period of history? When the answer is a resounding No, as it is in *The Capricorn Bracelet* by Rosemary Sutcliff and in *Johnny Tremain* by Esther Forbes, we know that these books represent historical fiction at its very finest.

The majority of such books come from England. This is not to denigrate the efforts of American writers; it is merely to observe that Britain has had more pivotal points about which to write; and, being a much older nation, England—and many other countries—can look at history with a degree of objectivity and a sense of perspective few Americans can match. Aside from the American Revolution, only the Civil War has actually been pivotal, and it is still too close to us; the scars are still too raw for it to be written about in the grand manner.

The second type of historical fiction can best be analyzed in relationship to some of these books produced about the Civil War. Factual history here takes a back seat to the reporting of human values. The real point of books like William O. Steele's *Perilous Road* or Harold Keith's *Rifles for Watie* is not the war itself, or not even the issues which led to that war, but rather the fact that men of good will and intelligence fought on both sides of the conflict. This point is important and must be made repeatedly, not only for children but for adults as well, since the human tendency is to divide the world into good guys and bad guys; good guys being those who agree with us and bad guys being those who don't. The same point needs to be made in books about the American Indian; for all too many years, juvenile fiction failed to depict the Indian as a human being with his or her own sense of values and own civilization. Indians were worthy of being exterminated if they resisted acceptance of white culture. Now, all good books about Indians strive to show that, while they did not have white society's values, they had their own, and the best of the books suggest that certain aspects of Indian culture were superior to those of the white society.

In short, this second type of historical fiction is more concerned with human aspects of history than with events themselves—a concern which does not make the category less important than the first, just different.

The third category is often classified in libraries as "Frontier and Pioneer Life Stories," which means that the books are set in the past but that no historical event is involved. An excellent example of such a book is *Caddie Woodlawn*, which takes place during the Civil War but the impact of the war plays no part in the lives of the characters. (One knows only incidentally the time period involved.)

All three types of books are important. They are differentiated here only because they serve different purposes and have greater appeal to varied age levels, although there are individual situations and individual children's abilities that extend the usual limitations. Younger children, for example, often enjoy books from the third group when they are read aloud, books like *Caddie Woodlawn*. They should begin their independent reading with books in this category, like Alice Dalgliesh's *The Courage of Sarah Noble*. These are stories that will introduce them gradually to a way of life far different from their own. As they reach the fifth or sixth grades and United States history begins to take on form and meaning for them, they are ready for books in the second category; they can begin trying to understand that "right" is never the exclusive property of one side in a conflict. Finally, they should progress to books in the first category, to an understanding that there are certain landmark periods in history when the entire course of events is altered.

The major defect to watch for in evaluating books with historical settings is the tendency, on the part of authors who have done inadequate historical research, to attribute modern speech patterns or modern attitudes to characters from other historical periods. One of the joys in reading history stems from the fact that it shows how much progress humankind has made, despite the imperfect record: people are no longer burned at the stake for deviate opinions, strides have been made toward recognizing the dignity of all persons. We do a disservice to children if we let them think that such progress comes as a matter of course.

Betty Baker's *Walk the World's Rim* is a fine book to demonstrate this progress throughout the years. The Spaniards in the book see nothing wrong in Esteban's being a slave; for them, slavery is an accepted way of life. But the young Indian, Chakoh, has been taught that slaves are only slaves because they are cowardly and unworthy of freedom. Miss Baker makes it obvious that Chakoh would have immediately rejected Esteban as a friend if he had known Esteban as a slave from their first meeting. It takes the entire book for Chakoh to learn that Esteban was never a slave within his own heart, the place where real slavery begins. The point is made, and made well, but within the framework of authentic attitudes of the time. There is no distortion of history, no sentimentality.

This emphasis on avoiding historical distortion and sentimentality brings us back to authenticity. An author who knows history well writes books which convey to the youthful reader both the joys and hardships of life in times past. There is the joy of little Laura's listening to Papa tell the story of the time he met the bear; there is the pain of picking up and moving on because the present homestead will not support the family (see *Little House in the Big Woods*, Laura Ingalls Wilder).

Another criterion for historical fiction is the smoothness with which the author incorporates information. It is possible to have authentic material based on careful research but to weaken a story either by presenting background information in such long, solid passages that the flow of the narrative is halted, or by using facts in conversations in an unnatural way, so that the readers are aware that the exchange of dialogue between characters is solely for the benefit of the reading audience.

Historical fiction, after all, is fiction. For all the added interest the historical aspect may give, it is the story that appeals to most young readers, the dramatic events or the problems that confront the characters. The children of today, many of whom have traveled more than their parents and grandparents, and all of whom are more exposed to the mass media, are to a far greater degree aware of, and often concerned about, peoples of other regions and other countries than their own, or about those of differing racial or religious backgrounds. Historical fiction can help them realize the importance of the heritage of other cultures as well as of their own.

Before the technological revolution, all people, from primitive times on, worked from dawn to sunset clearing land, planting crops, and fight-off enemies. There were queens and emperors who lived a different life, explorers and adventurers and heads of state who escaped the humdrum existence of ordinary men and women. Children need to know that history is made by both the ordinary people and the extraordinary. History has lessons to tell, and historical fiction can make the lessons come alive.

## from THE CAPRICORN BRACELET
### Rosemary Sutcliff

*This is the second of six episodes about a family heirloom, the Capricorn bracelet, first awarded to Lucius Calpurnius for service in the Eagles, part of the Roman Legions in Britain. Each family member speaks of his own time, and the exciting episodes span three centuries.*

*The second Lucius describes the building of Hadrian's Wall, giving a colorful picture of that period—Rosemary Sutcliff at her superb best.*

### A.D. 123: Rome Builds a Wall

Lucius Calpurnius, Senior Centurion of the Sixth Victrix, that's me. Lucius after my grandfather, who was the first of our family to follow the Eagles. *His* father was a wine merchant in Londinium, killed when Boudicca and her tribesmen sacked the city. My grandfather—he was only a boy at the time—escaped somehow, and hitched himself onto the nearest Legion (you know the rag, tag and bobtail that every Legion trails behind it). And as soon as he was old enough he joined up properly, in the Second Augustan. He served with Agricola on his great Caledonian campaigns, and won himself a military bracelet for distinguished conduct—bringing off an ambushed patrol more or less in one piece and getting them back to the main body of the Legion. His most treasured possession, that bracelet was; but not for the obvious reason. He told me once that a Capricorn was his father's personal device, which he used for sealing the necks of his wine jars. And so, though this he never told me in so many words, I think he felt the broad silver band with its embossed Augustan Capricorn to be some kind of link with his father. A family thing as well as a military one.

At all events, when he came to die, he didn't have it buried with him according to the usual custom but left it to me, my own father, his son, being already dead. So, it's mine now, and when my time comes I shall hand it on to my son after me.

My grandfather and I were always good friends, and I remember well how, when I was a boy and eager for stories as most boys are, he used to tell me about those northern campaigns. Very bitter he used to get, about the way Agricola was recalled to Rome with his work half done. "We could have set our frontier on the northernmost seashore," he used to say. "Nothing beyond it to the world's end. A frontier that

From *The Capricorn Bracelet.* © 1973 Rosemary Sutcliff. Used by permission of Henry Z. Walck, Inc. and Oxford University Press, Publishers

would have been safe for all time. As it is, what have we?" And he'd start to rub his left thigh in the way that he had, where an old spear wound still ached when the wind was in the east. "A handful of frontier forts strung out into the wilderness, on supply lines so long and thin that they could be cut any dark night by three men and a boy with a dream and a blunt sword between them. Might as well build a wall across from Luguvallium to Segedunum and cut our losses north of it."

Well, we've not cut our losses, we still hold our garrisons in Lowland Caledonia, though we had to let the Highland forts go. But after that last rising, when the whole of the north went up in flames and the re-formed Ninth Legion was lost without trace, we did build our wall.

Hadrian's Wall, they call it now, because it was on the Emperor Hadrian's orders that it was built. Eighty odd miles from coast to coast across the north of Britain. Seventeen forts, with milecastles and signal towers between, and the Wall itself, striding along the high ground, stringing them all together into one great frontier line.

Oh yes, I knew the Wall; knew it on winter nights when the sleet blows in your face as you pace the ramparts on sentry duty; knew it in green spring dawns, with the plover crying on the wind—there's always a wind blowing up there. Knew it with the distant hills a'shimmer in the August heat haze and the heather honey-scented and tall enough to hide a Pictish raiding party. Knew it before most of it was there at all, for I had a hand in building it. All three of the Legions in Britain had a hand in it, sending up each a couple of cohorts at a time. We've always been our own builders and roadmakers, we who follow the Eagles.

Anyway, there I was, just back from service in Germany, and newly promoted Centurion—young for it, too, though I says it that shouldn't —and my men behind me, tramp, tramp, tramping along the road toward Cilurnum at the day's end. Oh yes, the road was there already, looping along from hillcrest to hillcrest between the remains of an older frontier ditch and the new beginnings of the Wall. We came marching up the last slope, into the eye of a low sunset, and checked before a timber gateway; and I was the proud man when I answered the sentry's challenge.

"Tenth Century, Tenth Cohort, Victrix. Detailed for Wall building duty."

So the gate guard passed us through, and we marched into the big quarter-built fort, and grounded our spears before the row of wooden shacks that would be stone barrack rows one day. And there we were at Cilurnum, more or less on the edge of nowhere. I went and reported to the Fort Commander, and the next day, straight from the long march north, we started work.

It was the third working season, and the forts and mile-castles were beginning to take shape, and in places even the Wall itself was a course or two up from its foundations. Each Century worked on its own section; mine had the section running down to Cilurnum bridge, where a river came out through the Wall from the north. Handy, that was, because there was no bathhouse up there as yet; and when the day's work was done, and we were hot and gritty from head to foot, with the stone dust even in our eyebrows, a plunge in the river was the next best thing to a regular bath.

The only trouble was that the fort's Asturian Cavalry, whose job was to guard us while we worked, came down to water their horses at about the same time.

It was a trouble I ran into on my very first day. We'd stripped off and taken to the water. Oh, but it felt cold and good on our hot gritty hides! I was plunging and rolling like a porpoise, my ears so full of water and the sound of my own splashing that I did not hear the trampling horses' hooves and the jink of accouterments, until a bit of shouting started, and I came up and shook the water out of my ears and eyes, and saw the Cavalry Troop among the alder and hazel scrub on the bank. The shouting was going to and fro between them and some of my own lads close inshore, and there seemed to be a trifle of unpleasantness starting up. So I waded ashore, and addressed myself to the thickset young man who seemed to be in command.

"What might be the trouble?"

He rounded on me, answering my question with another, "What in the name of Hades do you think you're doing?"

"Taking a bath," I said, scrambling up the bank. I've often noticed that the simple truth annoys people. It seemed to annoy him even more than he was annoyed already.

"Upstream of the watering place! Do you expect my horses to drink the water you've been washing your filthy selves in?"

I grabbed at what dignity I could—which isn't much, when you're stark naked and dripping wet, and confronting a fully-caparisoned cavalryman—and said, "Do you know who you're talking to?" or something equally stupid.

He nodded. "I saw you march in. You're the new Centurion, and you command sixty men to my thirty. Not, if I may say so, that it shows at the moment."

Suddenly I began to get a glimmer of an idea that the thing was funny. "If you'll just give me time to dry off and put on some clothes, maybe I can make a better showing."

He said encouragingly, "You do that, you put on your fine feathery helmet and I'll call you 'Sir' and salute you; but meanwhile, call your lads off from fouling my horses' drinking water. There's all the river downstream for bathing in."

"I do beg your pardon," I said, "I'm fresh from Castra Regina. We have baths there and no problem with the Cavalry drinking the bath water."

I found that I had begun to laugh. And he looked at me a moment, trying not to join in; then the corners of his mouth started to twitch and he gave up trying.

And that was how I made my first friend at Cilurnum. Felix, who commanded our single troop of Asturian horse.

The next evening, Frontinus rode in on one of his visits of inspection. And a foul evening it was, too, with half a gale from the southwest driving gray swaths of rain across the moors. The sort of weather when you can't see a Pictish warband half a bowshot away. (Not that you ever see a Pictish warband anyway, until it's on top of you!)

The only bright spot anywhere was that Sextus, one of the senior Centurions, had been out hunting a few days since, and the stag he had killed was just ripe for eating, so there would be a good supper in Mess that night.

But I did not eat in Mess that night. I was

Duty Centurion. When you're Duty Centurion for the night, you spend a good deal of it doing rounds; and in between whiles you sit with your drawn sword on the table before you, in the little lighted room—the Sacellum we call it—where the Cohort Standard and the pay chest are housed; and you eat your supper there too, in solitary state. Well, so I did First Rounds, and there ate my solitary share of Sextus's kill, and began to write up the reports and such that always fall to the Duty Centurion's lot.

Except for the pacing steps of the sentry that came and went along the colonnade outside, there was nothing to be heard but the wind and the rain. I might have been alone in a dead fort, with nothing moving, save the ghosts when the drafts set the lamp-flame jumping. And then the trumpet sounded for the second watch of the night, and I turned the hourglass, and presently it was time for Second Rounds.

I got up and slammed my sword into its sheath, flung on my cloak, and went out. The wind and rain swooped into my face as I slammed the Sacellum door behind me, and passed the sentry outside. Night rounds especially in rough weather, have a strangeness about them, a great loneliness, that is in some way akin to the loneliness of the Mysteries. Indeed I have felt much the same thing in the Bull Cave during the Raising Ceremony, as though one had come to some borderland between this world and another; but one is not sure whether it is oneself or the sentries challenging out of the stormy darkness who are the ghosts.

I made my way from guardpoint to guardpoint, sentry post to sentry post; at each one, the alert movement of a shadow in the night, the sound of a pilum butt grounded in salute.

"Who comes?"

"Duty Centurion. All's well?"

"All's well, Sir."

And the exchange of the password for the night.

And then on again, to the next point, and the next, and the next.

Lastly, that night, huddling my cloak around my ears, I made my way out along the line of the Wall toward the bridge. The blockhouse was not properly finished yet, but we kept a guard there, because the iron grills for closing the space under the bridge were not yet fixed, and until that was done it was a weak place in the defenses. The blockhouse made a square of blackness against the shifting lesser dark of the river and the storm-drenched night. There was a glimmer of torchlight from an open doorway, and again the sentry's challenge.

"Who comes?"

"Duty Centurion. All's well?"

I shouldered in for a few moments' shelter by the fire. The blockhouse was a shell of warmth and light, the dark and the storm pressing in on all sides.

"What a night!" someone said.

"It certainly isn't the kind you'd expect to find anyone abroad on—except maybe the Wild Hunt."

And at that very instant, between gust and gust of the wind, we heard the high protesting squeal of a scared horse, coming as it seemed from almost under our feet.

In the torchlit guard post men looked at each other, in a split moment of utter stillness lapped around by the tumult of the storm. Then the sentry was in the doorway. "Horses, Sir—under the bridge."

I nodded. "After me, all of you—quick."

Then we were outside and crouching in the lea of the blockhouse wall, with the steep drop on the bank below us, and the water running yeasty under the bridge. And against the yeastiness of the water, half-blinded as I was by the rain, I could just make out a movement of dark shapes. There was a splashing and a trampling of horses, and a muffled curse. I drew the Optio back to the corner of the blockhouse. "Ulpins, get back to the fort, and report horse raiders trying to break through under the bridge. Trumpeter—sound the alarm. The rest of you, out swords and follow me!"

And as the trumpet brayed, the high notes teased out and flung away by the wind, we went plunging down to the attack. The raiders met us at the water's edge. We fought among the storm-lashed alders on the bank; we fought in the water itself, the horses swirling and plunging about us before they broke away. It was a small vicious struggle, confused as a fight in the ragged end of a dream; a flurry of slash and stab in the dark. I was caught in a tangle of blows with somebody, a black shadow like all the rest, until a gleam of light from the blockhouse showed me his face for an instant as we reeled to and fro. And it was Conn!

I shouted, "Conn! *You!*"

And he laughed, and shouted back, "Did you not say we needed fresh blood to improve the breed?" His blade slashed past my cheek and turned on my shoulder-piece, (the metal had to be beaten out afterward, and I carried the mark for many a long day) and he slipped in the mud and my point took him under the collarbone as he went down.

That was pretty near the end of it.

They might have got through, if that one horse hadn't taken scare and squealed. As it was, well, the Quarter Guard was down to our help and the thing was over before it was well begun. And our lads were rounding up the scattered horses; and Conn and a couple more of the tribesmen were sprawled dead on the river bank, and the rest had gotten away.

I heard the voice of the Senior Centurion somewhere, lifted above the storm. "Let them go, we've got the horses."

But I didn't take much notice. I was squatting close under the blockhouse wall, where there was a little shelter from the wind and rain, with the Chief Engineer propped against my knee. Someone had brought a torch, and we could see that there wasn't anything to be done. He'd taken a stab wound between the ribs—he had no harness on, no protection but his leather tunic, just as he'd come from the Mess table— and was bubbling blood with every breath he drew.

"Gods!" someone said. "It's Frontinus!"

I nodded.

"What in the name of the Black One did the old fool want to get mixed up in this lot for?"

Frontinus looked up at us with a flicker of humor. "Would you have—had me sit on my rump in the—fort, while a mob of misbegotten horse thieves cut the picket lines and—broke out through—*my Wall?*"

"Your Wall!" I said furiously. I think I was weeping.

"*My Wall.*" Frontinus's voice was going, and I had to bend close to catch what he said above the tumult of the storm. "Someone else will—

have to finish it. But—it will be a good wall— all the same." He tried to laugh. "Ah now, never look so woebegone! Better this way than— slowly—rusting out at Aquae Sulis—after all."

He gave a small wet choking sound, and his head fell sideways against my shoulder.

I laid him down and got to my feet. I gave the necessary orders, and by and by I went back to the Sacellum, and fell to cleaning my sword, which was red when I laid it on the table.

We finished building Hadrian the Wall he had ordered, though under a new Engineer. I don't suppose many people remember Frontinus now, except those of us who served under him, and our ranks are thinning as the years go by. But his Wall will stand while Rome lasts. Maybe longer.

## from MASTER ROSALIND

*John and Patricia Beatty*

*Orphaned Rosalind Broome, kidnapped and taken to London, had been dressed as a boy while on an errand, for the roads were unsafe in Elizabethan times. Called "Robin," she finds work at the Globe theater—playing girls' parts— and meets many of the prominent theater people of the period—Shakespeare, Jonson, Burbage.*

### Copyist

Rosalind supped that evening far more grandly than ever before. The food was marvelous and came not from wooden trenchers but from heavy pewter dishes. The two young maids piled her plate high and vowed she ate as heartily as the brawny young servingman. Then they sent her climbing through the well-furnished house to inspect the bedchamber on the third floor. To her way of thinking, the "last lad" in this house had been no servant. Had he been a player? This chamber was better than hers in Cowley. It had a featherbed and a walnut bedstead with blue canopy and hangings, a table and brass ewer, and, to her utter astonishment, a looking glass. She had never seen such a wondrous thing before. She spent long moments gazing by candlelight at her clean face. Yes, she made a passing fair boy, slim, with the square jaw of the Broomes, as her grandfather had told her, and the same dark brows. And Moll had cut her hair well. She had misled people in Oxfordshire and the rogues, too. But now she had gulled the practiced eyes of players into thinking she was Robin, not Rosalind. She laughed for an instant, then thought of Helen and Ned, caught that morning in the goldsmith's house. She thought of her flight through Blackfriars, of the forger, of Moll's friendship and Tom o' Bedlam's wrath, of the Earl of Essex, the play, Master Gulliford, and now Thomas Pope. What a day it had been! Yet she was not tired. She had never felt so alive in all her days.

Suddenly her mirror gazing was interrupted by Pope's shouting from below. "Robin, 'tis time to ride back to the playhouse."

Rosalind found the stage of the Curtain lit by candles set on the floor outlining its rim and by many torches in sconces at its rear. It was chill inside for all that it was late summer. Ice-white stars glittered through the opening at the Curtain's top. She was grateful for the warmth of the cloak Dame Gillet had given her, as she went about the chars Pope set her. In the tiring room she learned that an efficient company of players readied properties and costumes long before a play was performed. Tonight while the tiring men ironed and mended garments, Rosalind dusted off and repainted the face of the severed head she'd seen earlier that day. As she daubed paint on it, she watched Master Burbage striding about rehearsing gestures. He was crowned with a gilt circle, adorned with a false gray beard, and clad in the long scarlet gown of a king. What king, Rosalind had no idea. Then

as she finished the head, she was called by Pope to attend Master Gulliford, who required his face to be painted again for another lady's part.

"What do I use?" she asked Gulliford as she looked bewildered at the many ointment pots on the table before him.

Seated on a high stool, he giggled. "The white paint. The white is the jawbones of a sow, burned, then mixed with oil of white poppy. Paint me first with the white. I shall darken my eyes with kohl and drop belladonna into them with this feather." He held up a white pigeon's feather, then glared across the tiring room at his uncle, who spoke with Master Will. Gulliford went on, "When I have donned my wig, I trust these players will think me a great lady enough for this old play. We only rehearse tonight. Master Burbage says he wishes to see how I will suit the lady's part. It is a new part for me."

As Rosalind began to stroke white onto the boy's face, she said, "I have met Dame Gillet. She is all that you say she is."

The boy player nodded sagely. "Do as I told you, Robin. Carry yourself cleverly. Master Pope may make a player of you yet. We have some need of boy players now. There are often too few of us. We come here as small lads and play women's roles until we are twenty years, if we can manage our voices that long. Some of us grow too tall much too quickly and grow beards." He smiled into the looking glass at his reflection. "Other boy players depart the company."

"Do all boys live with older players?"

"Aye, all do. I am older than you, Robin, near to sixteen. I shall not play court ladies much longer. I grow too old. I must have an eye to my future."

Rosalind had not guessed him to be so old. He was not tall. She went on smoothing the white stuff over his face, then asked, "Why do boys play women's parts?"

Gulliford did a strange thing. He pinched his stark white nose with his fingers and said, whining through it, " 'Boys must play women's parts. 'Tis a more scandalous thing for a woman to play a woman's part.' This is how many churchmen of London preach against us from their churches. They hate plays and players, but still we play. Someone must play women's parts.

Authors keep writing parts into plays for women and girls. So boys and men must play them. Lads play pretty maidens and queens. Men play old women." He laughed. "You should see your good Master Pope play a fat old hag. You would not know him to be Master Pope at all."

Rosalind's work done with the white paint, the boy player waved her aside, motioned toward a scroll of paper, and then pulled a small pot of vermilion to him and began to paint his cheeks and lips with a brush. "Master Pope tells me you can read. I want to practice my lines for this play. Hear me recite them to you, Robin."

Rosalind unrolled the scroll. It was made up of sheets of paper pasted together. She saw lines of writing on it and in the left-hand margin instructions, "Enter," "Exit."

"Give me my cues," Gulliford commanded.

She felt helpless. "I do not know what cues are."

"They are the other player's closing lines to their speeches. Commence with the fourth line from the top. It should say, 'I'll win this Lady Margaret. For whom? Why, for my king. Tush! That's a wooden thing!' "

After Rosalind recited, Gulliford spoke his lines in an ice-sweet girlish treble. " 'He talks of wood; it is some carpenter!' Now, Robin, you read the next line you see to me. After you have read it, I speak again."

For a half hour Rosalind coached Master Gulliford, who complained more than once that he was "slow of study." Then, snatching up a fan, the player, garbed as a dazzling, bewigged lady in a violet gown, swept out of the tiring room onto the stage.

All had gone out there now except for the tiring men, who folded costumes into chests. They paid no heed to Rosalind as she took up a candle and began to wander around the playhouse. First she read the pasteboard plot of *The Taming of the Shrew* hanging from a peg, listing the players' names. Then she found stairs leading down below the stage. There, as she listened to Burbage's resonant voice from above, she saw more steps. These steps led up to a trapdoor cut into the stage floor. Rosalind yearned to open it and poke her head through it to surprise the players but discarded the idea. She suspected Burbage would not approve if she

interrupted his rehearsal. Because it was dark and gloomy under the stage, she soon left. She went back to the tiring room and began to climb another set of stairs she'd also spied out. They led above the stage to the hut. In it over the stage's ceiling, which was painted to represent a blue but clouded sky, she found a remarkable variety of things—a winch and a chairlike throne on ropes, a gray rain cloud of painted canvas, gunpowder in small casks, cannonballs, and a small cannon.

Also to her surprise she found Master Will seated at a small table, writing, flanked by two candles blowing slantwise in the August breeze.

Rosalind apologized, backing toward the steep flight of steps. "I did not mean to disturb you, sir."

He put his finger to his lips. "Do not tell anyone that I am here. I came up without their knowing it. They think I have gone home. Here I have some peace. In the tiring room I am besieged by players who say to me 'Alter this line for me' or 'Why have you given me but one song to sing in your new play?' " He laughed, then asked, "How do you fare with Master Pope?"

"I like him very well. I hope he may make a player of me. I would rather be a player than a servant."

The playwright nodded. "He has made players of other boys before. I am told you are a pastor's grandson, of good birth, read and write, and know Latin and Greek."

Rosalind felt her face grow hot. She could only nod. Master Pope had said much of her to the company in a very short time, it seemed, while she had repainted the earl's cut-off head.

He pushed a piece of blank paper over to her, then offered her his quill and ink. "Write these words for me as I speak them, Robin. Write in your very fairest hand."

Leaning over his table, Rosalind wrote as fast as she could in the hand her grandfather had taught her.

> But when the blast of war blows in our ears,
> Then imitate the action of the tiger;
> Stiffen the sinews, summon up the blood. . . .

Master Will took the paper, looked at it, then nodded. "It is a fair secretary hand, the Italian hand. I write but the common English hand. Yours is by far the clearest I have seen of this company, and it is well spelled, too. Tell Master Pope for me that I shall require you to copy out the players' parts for the cue sheets for the play I now write."

Rosalind felt a pang of disappointment. First servant's work, now a clerk's.

"You do not wish to be a copyist for me?" Master Will seemed to have read her mind.

"If I am to be a servant to one player and a copyist to another, when am I to be a player?"

The playwright laughed. "Before you are a player, you will do many, many things. You will learn to starch ruffs, take playbills to the printer, nail them up on London Bridge, send this throne of the gods down out of our painted heavens by means of the winch, and push ghosts up through the trapdoor so their draperies will not get caught on the steps. Perhaps you will even set flame to the touch-hole of our cannon when the play calls for cannon fire, though I trust you will not send a ball through the roof or set the playhouse afire. Players must know all about the theater." The dark-eyed man rose, went to one end of the hut, and with his foot sent the cannonball rolling noisily across the floor. He put his finger to his lips again for silence.

"You up there in the hut! Cease that. We require no thunder in this play!" came Richard Burbage's angry roaring from the stage below.

Master Will waited until Rosalind had stopped laughing, then said, "Tell Dame Gillet to have your face washed well at the moon's wane with elder leaves distilled in May. You have country freckles, Robin."

Rosalind grinned; he but teased her. "'Tis near September now, and I'm not often out-of-doors. Freckles will go away."

"Yes, it is near autumn. Soon the Queen will return to London to spend the winter. She goes from London in the summer when the plague is most fierce."

"Do common folk ever see her, Master Will?"

"All London may see her if they choose to when she returns. She comes riding into the city with her court about her."

"Lord Essex, too? I saw him today."

The man's wise eyes were fixed on her face.

"Aye, Essex, too. I do not know what business brought him here today. He is mostly with the Queen. You love him then?"

"Yes, he is the greatest man in England. My father was in Spain with him."

"Aye, the greatest man in England." His face grave, Master Will looked down at the papers of his unfinished play. "Many young men and all London lads love Essex well today. Tomorrow he may not fare so well."

## from CALICO BUSH

*Rachel Field*

*The period of the French and Indian War is the setting for the story of Marguerite Ledoux, a French orphan "bound out" to Joel and Dolly Sargent, early settlers in Maine. She had traveled with them, shared their hardships without complaint, and loved them, yet they never made her feel that she was one of them. This Christmas excerpt from "Winter" has about it the poignant loneliness of the outsider.*

### Winter

It was a fairly warm day for December and she went out with Debby to watch him split the wood. It was pleasant to see his ax come down so swift and sure each time, and sometimes when he paused to rest he would talk to her for a minute or two. The baby was so well wrapped in a woolen shawl that she looked like a brownish caterpillar with a pink nose and tufts of light hair showing at one end.

"What time of year is it now?" Marguerite asked as Ira stopped to draw his sleeve across his streaming forehead.

"Let's see," he answered going over to the post where he still made his daily notches, dividing the months by means of long horizontal strokes.

"Well, I declare, if it ain't got to be the middle o' December! Yes, tomorrow's the seventeenth, time I finished that beaver cap I promised Abby."

"Is it for Christmas?" asked Marguerite.

But he shook his head. "No," he said. "Our folks don't hold with such foolishness. We went to meetin' back in Marblehead on Christmas, I recollect, but there was a Dutch boy I knew told me how they had all kinds o' doin's where he come from."

"You mean, it will be no different from other days?" Marguerite's eyes grew wide with disappointment. "No carols, and no cakes, and no gifts from one to another?"

"I guess that's about right," he told her and went on with the chopping.

If Ira gave her no encouragement in Christmas festivities she knew it would be useless to expect more of Dolly and Joel Sargent. She tried to put the thought from her mind, but as each day came bringing it nearer she found herself remembering more and more the happy preparations for it she had helped to make at home. She dreamed of the Christmas cakes Grand'mère had always baked with such pride, of the seeded raisins and the picked nut-meats stirred ceremoniously in the rich batter. And then there were the carols, with the Sisters in the convent beating time and making sure that not a single "Noël" was left out when all their pupils' voices were lifted together. She tried to tell the children of the tiny carved statues of the Virgin and Joseph and the little Christ Child in the manger, with cattle and sheep and shepherds all painted as perfectly as life, that were brought out on Christmas Eve in the candle-lit chapel. Unfortunately Dolly had overheard part of this recital and had chided her roundly.

"I'll thank you to keep your Popishness to yourself," she had told her. "We may be in too God-forsaken a spot for a meetin' house, but that's no reason to put ideas in the children's heads."

And so it came to be Christmas Eve in the log cabin on Sargent's point with no smell of spice cakes, or incense, or candles, and none to feel the lack of them but Marguerite Ledoux.

She had been out to the post herself that noon, counting the month's notchings to be sure. There could be no doubt—tomorrow would make twenty-five. She would not have missed the holiday preparations so much, she thought, if she might have gone over to see Aunt Hepsa; but she knew there was no chance of this with such a high sea running and snow left in patches from last week's fall. It was rare, Joel had said, to have much fall near the sea. A bad winter ahead, Seth Jordan had predicted, and it looked as if he were right. Frost had covered the little square panes of glass with such feathery patternings, it required much breathing and scratching to make even a little hole to see out. Marguerite was tired of doing this. The room was almost dark, but she knew that outside there was still half an hour or so left of twilight. She went over to the pegs behind the door and took down the brown cloak and hood.

"What are you doin'?" Dolly asked her as she had her hand on the door.

"I'm—I want to bring more cones," she hazarded, grasping at the first idea that came into her head. "There are not so many left in the basket."

"Well, all right, then," Dolly told her, "only don't fetch in the wet ones that make the fire smoke. Pick 'em from underneath. No, Jacob," she added at a question from the child, "you can't go along—it's too cold."

Marguerite buckled on the shoes Aunt Hepsa had given her, tied on her cloak, and went out basket in hand. Once she shut the door behind her some of the depression which had weighed upon her spirit all day left her. It was impossible to feel so sad out in the snow with the pointed trees and all their shiny dark-green needles. They smelled of Christmas to her. There had been branches of evergreen in the chapel sometimes. Perhaps if she hunted at the edge of the tall woods behind the spring she might find some red partridge berries to bring back to the children. It was bad luck if you gave nothing on Christmas, and they need not know the reason for such a gift.

As she turned into the wood path behind the house she looked across the water to Sunday Island. White places showed on the cleared field round the Jordan house where the snow remained, and the trees above it on the upper pasture where she and Aunt Hepsa had gathered bayberry looked more dark and bristling than ever in the winter twilight. She was glad that a curl of smoke rose from the chimney. Aunt Hepsa must be cooking supper, she told herself, and she paused to send her a Christmas wish across the water.

"I wonder if she's begun her new quilt yet?" she thought as she struck into the wood path. "She had the indigo dye Ethan brought her all ready to make a blue pot."

There were no red berries under the snow in the clearing by the spring where she had hoped to find them, so she went on farther along the blazed trail. It was very still there, with only a light wind stirring the spruce and fir boughs overhead. The light stayed longer there than she had expected, for the snow helped prolong the winter afternoon. Sometimes she stooped to gather cones, taking care to shake off the snow as Dolly Sargent had bidden her. The cold was intense, but her blood was quick and the old homespun cloak and hood enveloped her warmly. There was no sound except her footfalls in the snow. A sudden impulse came upon her to sing one of the carols which she knew the Sisters in the convent must even then be teaching other voices to raise.

She set down the half-filled basket of cones, folded her hands piously under the cloak, and began the first simple little chant that she had ever learned.

"Noël—Noël—Noël!"

Her own voice startled her in the stillness. Then at the sound of the familiar words she grew confident and began the one that had been Grand'mère's favorite because she also had sung it when she was a girl in the little village where she had lived.

"J'entends le ciel retentir
 Des cantiques des Saints Anges,
 Et la terre tressaillir
 Des transports de leurs louanges.
 C'est l'Oinct qui devoit venir,
 Il est déjà dans ses langes.
 Miracle! prodige nouveau,
 Le fils de Dieu dans le berceau!
 Mais plus grand prodige encore,
 Ce grand Roi, que le ciel adore,
 Doit expirer sur un poteau.
 Noël! Noël! Noël!"[1]

As she sang there in the deepening twilight, she felt strangely comforted. The French words that had lain so long forgotten welled up out of her mind as easily as if she had been with the Sisters in the candle-lit chapel and not alone these thousands of miles away in a snowy wood.

"Noël! Noël!" she cried once more to the ranks of spruces, and then as she turned to retrace her steps something dark and swift moved towards her from behind a tree trunk.

There was not time enough to run away. The words were hardly cool on her lips before he stood beside her—a tall Indian in skins, with a musket that went oddly with his fringes and bright feathers. So silently did he come that not a twig snapped under his foot. He seemed not to dent the snow as he moved over it. His eyes showed bright in the copper of his skin, and a deep scar ran crookedly across one cheek. He

[1] This old carol may be freely rendered as follows:—
I hear the heavens resound
To such angelic song
That trembling stirs the ground,
While rolls the news along—
The Heavenly Child is found,
To Whom all praise belong.
Oh! wondrous miracle,
A God in his cradle!
Yet must we wonder more,
This King the heavens adore
Must die upon a cross.

came so close that she saw it plainly, and yet she could not move so much as an inch. Her feet seemed rooted in the snow, and if her heart continued to beat, she could not feel it. For what seemed like ages he continued to regard her fixedly with his black, unblinking eyes, while she waited for him to seize the tomahawk from his belt and make an end of her. But he did not move to do so. Instead, his lips parted in a queer smile.

"Noël!" he said, pronouncing the word carefully in a deep, guttural voice. "Noël!"

Marguerite felt her heart begin to beat again, though her knees were still numb and she continued to stare at him incredulously. Surely this must be a miracle, more extraordinary than any bestowed on Saint Catherine or Saint Elizabeth! A savage had come out of the woods to greet her in her own tongue on Christmas Eve! She forced herself to smile back and answer him.

His words were meager and hard to catch, but she made out from them and his signs that he had lived with the French in Quebec. He was bound there now, or so she guessed from his

pointing finger. She could not tell how many of her words he understood, but whenever she said "Noël" his eyes would brighten with recognition and he would repeat it after her. "Les Pères Gris," he told her, had cured him. He touched the scar as he spoke and crossed his two lean forefingers to make a cross.

It was almost dark now; only a faint light lingered between the spruces. Pumpkin barked in the distance and Marguerite knew she must hurry back lest they grow alarmed. What would they think, Joel and Dolly Sargent and the rest, if they should come upon her there in the woods holding converse with an Indian? Prompted by an impulse she pulled the cord out from under her dress and jerked off Oncle Pierre's gilt button. It glittered in her hand as she held it out to the tall figure before her.

"Pour un souvenir de Noël," she said as she laid it in his hand before she turned and sped off towards the clearing.

Her heart was still pounding as she came out

of the woods and in sight of the log house. Pumpkin bounded to meet her as she paused to put back the cord and its only remaining treasure. She had not thought to make such a Christmas gift, but surely she could not have done less. She could not but feel that somehow it was a fortunate sign, this strange meeting. Perhaps Le Bon Dieu had Himself arranged it that she might be less lonely on Christmas Eve. But she knew there must not be a word of it to the rest. She would never be able to make them understand what she scarcely understood herself. As for Caleb, she could well guess what he would say and that he would think ill of her ever after.

Dolly Sargent scolded her roundly for staying away so long.

"I declare you deserve a beatin'," she told her hotly, "strayin' so far at this time o' night. I vow Debby's got more sense 'n you show sometimes."

There was no mention made of Christmas next day save that Joel asked a lengthier blessing over their breakfast cornmeal than was usual with him. But Marguerite no longer minded. Had she not had her miracle the night before?

### from JOHNNY TREMAIN
*Esther Forbes*

*The first episode given here reveals the patience of the British soldiers with the rebellious colonists and the deadly earnestness of the rebels during the American Revolution. The second provides a glimpse of the plotters, their ideals and activities.*

#### ["That a Man Can Stand Up"]

Along down Old Country Road, marching through the meager, half-light of the new day, came a company of Minute Men up and out early, drilling for coming battles before it was yet the hour to get to their chores. Left, right, left, right, left . . . they did not march too well. A boy no bigger than Dusty Miller had put a fife to his lips, was trying to blow it. He made awkward little tootles. The men marched on past the defaced gates of the Lytes' country seat, never turning to look at them or Doctor Warren's chaise with Cilla and Johnny under the hood.

Oh, God help them, thought Johnny. They haven't seen those British troops in Boston. I have. They haven't seen the gold lace on the generals, those muskets—all so alike, and every-one has a bayonet. They haven't seen . . .

The chaise overtook and passed the marching farmers.

That musket which Rab did not have both-ered Johnny. However, the soldiers never car-ried them while loitering about alehouses and wharves, or the stables of the Afric Queen. They stood guard with them. They drilled with them. They practiced marksmanship (very badly, Rab said), and now and then over at the foot of the Common they executed a deserter with them, but never, not once, as far as Johnny could make out, did they leave them about. Drilling, shooting, marching over, they stacked them at their bar-racks and there was always at least a sergeant guarding these stacked guns.

Johnny and Rab dropped their voices, even in the privacy of their attic, when they discussed these muskets. The Yankee gunsmiths were work-ing from dawn to dusk preparing guns, making new ones, but as long as Rab had a weapon and was, after all, little more than a boy, he believed he had no chance for a modern gun unless he got it for himself from the British.

"How soon," Johnny whispered, "before they march out . . . and the war begins?"

"God knows," Rab murmured. "God and Gen-eral Gage. Maybe not until next spring. Armies always move in the spring. But before then I must have a good gun in my hands. A man can stand up to anything with a good weapon in his hands. Without it, he's but a dumb beast."

Johnny had never seen Rab so blocked by any-thing. Apparently he went through every situa-tion without friction, like a knife going through cheese. Now he was blocked and it made him restless, possibly less canny. One day he told Johnny that he had a contract with a farmer from Medway who was making a business of buying muskets from the British privates and selling them to Minute Men. Rab did not like to ask his aunt for so large a sum. She had little enough to buy food. But she had said, "Weapons before food."

One morning Johnny knew Rab was meeting the farmer at market. He knew that the soldier, returning from guard duty, was going, absent-mindedly, to leave his musket on a pile of straw. It had all been worked out. But when he heard yells and shouts from the market-place and the rattle of British drums calling up reserves, he tore over to Dock Square. He had a feeling that the turmoil was over Rab's gun. He was right.

A solid block of redcoats faced out, presenting their muskets at the market people and inhabi-tants. The Captain was yelling to the churning hundreds. "Get back, stand back, good people of Boston. This is our own private affair."

"What's happened?" Johnny asked an old henwife.

"They've caught one of their own men selling a musket to a farmer."

"Happens he comes from Medway?"

"So 'tis said."

"Happens they caught more than the farmer and the soldier?"

"They caught three in all. They are taking them over to the Province House—for General Gage."

"Gage is in Salem."

"For some colonel, then."

No mob gathered to rescue the two Yankees. All, by now, felt a certain confidence in the Brit-ish way of doing things. A general, or even a colo-nel, had the right to punish a soldier caught sell-ing his arms, and also anyone who tempted him.

Johnny tagged the marching soldiers, but it was not until they turned into the Province House that he saw the three prisoners. The Brit-ish soldier was grinning, and Johnny guessed that he had been put up to this game merely to snare "the yokels."

The farmer was in his market smock. He had long, straight gray hair and a thin, mean mouth. You could tell by looking at him he had gone into this little business for the love of money, not for the love of freedom. Rab had been shaken out of his usual nice balance between quick action and caution by his passionate desire for a good gun. Otherwise he would not have mixed himself up with such a man. Rab himself was looking a little sullen. He was not used to defeat. What would they do to him? They might imprison him. They might flog him. Worst of all, they might turn him over to some tough top sergeant to be taught "a lesson." This informal punishment would doubtless be the worst.

The Province House was a beautiful building and as Johnny hung about the front of it he had a chance to admire it for over an hour. It stood well back from the rattle and bustle of Marlborough Street, with its glassy-eyed copper Indian on top of the cupola and its carved and colored lion and unicorn of Britain over the door. Behind the house he heard orders called and soldiers were hallooing—but worst of all they were laughing. And that was Colonel Nesbit's boy bringing around the Colonel's charger. There was a large group of people still standing in the street. The hilarity of the British soldiers did not ease their fears as to the fate of the prisoners. Johnny could hear the rattle of the men's muskets as they came to attention, and then, all together, four drummers let their sticks fall as one.

Out onto Marlborough Street, with the drummers in black bearskin caps first, and then Colonel Nesbit on horseback, came almost the entire Forty-Seventh Regiment, surrounding a cart. In the cart sat a hideous blackbird, big as a man, shaped like a man, with head hung forward like a moulting crow. It was a naked man, painted with tar and rolled in feathers. Three times already the Whigs had tarred and feathered enemies and carted them through the streets of Boston. Now it was the British turn. The redcoats marched. The Colonel's horse pranced. The cart with its shameful burden bumped over the cobbles. One glance had convinced Johnny this was not Rab. The hideous blackbird had a paunch. Rab had none.

Before the Town House, Colonel Nesbit ordered a halt, and an orderly came forward and read a proclamation. It merely explained what was being done and why, and threatened like treatment to the next buyer of stolen weapons. Then (Colonel Nesbit was evidently a newspaper reader) the regiment went to Marshall Lane and stopped before the office of the *Spy*. The threat was made that the editor of that paper would soon be treated like the bird in the cart. Then they were heading for Edes and Gill's office. Johnny guessed the *Observer* would come next after the *Boston Gazette*, and ran to Salt Lane to warn Uncle Lorne. He jumped into the shop, slamming the door after him, looking wildly about for the printer. Rab, in his printer's apron, was standing at his bench, quietly setting type.

"Rab! How'd you do it? How'd you get away?"

Rab's eyes glittered. In spite of his great air of calm, he was angry.

"Colonel Nesbit said I was just a child. 'Go buy a popgun, boy,' he said. They flung me out the back door. Told me to go home."

Then Johnny laughed. He couldn't help it. Rab had always, as far as Johnny knew, been treated as a grown man and always looked upon himself as such.

"So all he did was hurt your feelings."

Rab grinned suddenly, but a little thinly. Johnny told of the tar-and-feathering of the farmer and also that he expected in a short time the Forty-Seventh Regiment would come marching down Salt Lane and stop before the door to read that proclamation about tar-and-feathering seditious newspaper publishers.

"And here they come—those dressed-up red monkeys. But they don't dare do anything but stop, read a proclamation, and move on."

When this was over and the troops moved on down the lane to Union, Johnny and Rab stood in the street and watched them.

"Luckily," said Rab, "I didn't give my money in advance. I'll return it to Aunt Jenifer."

But he still stood in the street watching the stiff rhythm of the marching troops, the glitter of their guns and bayonets, the dazzle of the white and scarlet disappearing at the bottom of the lane.

"They'll make good targets, all right," he said absent-mindedly. "Out in Lexington they are telling us, 'Pick off the officers first, then the sergeants.' Those white crosses on their chests are easy to sight on . . ."

His words frightened Johnny a little. Lieutenant Stranger, Sergeant Gale, Major Pitcairn . . .

Johnny could not yet think of them as targets. Rab could.

. . . . . . . . . . . . . . . . . . . . . . . . . . . . . . . . . . .

It was fall, and for the last time Sam Adams bade Johnny summon the Observers for eight o'clock that night.

"After this we will not meet again, for I believe Gage knows all about us. He might be moved to arrest Mr. Lorne. He might send soldiers to arrest us all."

"I hardly think they would hang the whole club, sir. Only you and Mr. Hancock."

Johnny had meant this for a compliment, but Sam Adams looked more startled than pleased.

"It has been noticed that every so often many of us are seen going up and down Salt Lane, entering the printing shop. We must, in the future, meet in small groups. But once more, and for the last time . . . And make as good a punch for us as you can."

. . . . . . . . . . . . . . . . . . . . . . . . . . . . . . . . . . .

It would be a small meeting, for of the twenty-two original members many had already left town to get away from the threat of arrest by the British. Josiah Quincy was in England. Of the three revolutionary doctors, only Church and Warren remained. Doctor Young had gone to a safer spot. James Otis was at the moment in Boston. Johnny had not notified him, although he had founded this club in the first place. Ever since he had grown so queer, the other members did not wish him about, even in his lucid periods. He talked and talked. Nobody could get a word in edgewise when James Otis talked.

This, the last meeting, started with the punch bowl on the table instead of ending with it. There was no chairman nor was there any time when the two boys were supposed to withdraw. They were talking about how Gage had at last dared send out a sortie beyond the gate of Boston and, before the Minute Men got word of their plans, they had seized cannon and gunpowder over in Charlestown, got into their boats and back to Boston. Not one shot had been fired and it was all too late when the alarm had been spread and thousands of armed farmers had ar-

rived. By then the British were safe home again. Yet, Sam Adams protested, this rising up of an army of a thousand from the very soil of New England had badly frightened General Gage. Once the alarm spread that the British had left Boston, the system of calling up the Minute Men had worked well indeed. The trouble had been in Boston itself.

"In other words, gentlemen, it was our fault. If we could have known but an hour, two hours, in advance what the British were intending, our men would have been there before the British troops arrived instead of a half-hour after they left."

Johnny had been told off to carry letters for the British officers, to keep on good terms with their grooms and stable boys over at the Afric Queen. Somehow he had failed. He hadn't known. Nobody had known that two hundred and sixty redcoats were getting into boats, slipping off up the Mystic, seizing Yankee gunpowder, and rowing it back to Castle Island for themselves.

Paul Revere was saying, "We must organize a better system of watching their movements—but in such a way that they will not realize they are being watched."

. . . . . . . . . . . . . . . . . . . . . . . . . . . . . . . . . . .

There was a heavy footstep across the floor of the shop below. Rab leaped to the ladder's head.

"James Otis," he reported to the men standing about Adams.

"Well," said Sam Adams, a little crossly, "no one needs stay and listen to *him*. He shot his bolt years ago. Still talking about the natural rights of man—and the glories of the British Empire! You and I, John, had as well go home and get a good night's sleep before leaving at dawn tomorrow."

Otis pulled his bulk up the ladder. If no one was glad to see him, at least no one was so discourteous as to leave. Mr. Otis was immediately shown every honor, given a comfortable armchair and a tankard of punch. Seemingly he was not in a talkative mood tonight. The broad, ruddy, good-natured face turned left and right, nodding casually to his friends, taking it for granted that he was still a great man among them, instead of a milestone they all believed they had passed years before.

He sniffed at his punch and sipped a little.

"Sammy," he said to Sam Adams, "my coming interrupted something you were saying . . . 'We will fight,' you had got that far."

"Why, yes. That's no secret."

"For what will we fight?"

"To free Boston from these infernal redcoats and . . ."

"No," said Otis. "Boy, give me more punch. That's not enough reason for going into a war. Did any occupied city ever have better treatment than we've had from the British? Has one rebellious newspaper been stopped—one treasonable speech? Where are the firing squads, the jails jammed with political prisoners? What about the gallows for you, Sam Adams, and you, John Hancock? It has never been set up. I hate those infernal British troops spread all over my town as much as you do. Can't move these days without stepping on a soldier. But we are not going off into a civil war merely to get them out of Boston. Why are we going to fight? Why, why?"

There was an embarrassed silence. Sam Adams was the acknowledged ringleader. It was for him to speak now.

"We will fight for the rights of Americans. England cannot take our money away by taxes."

"No, no. For something more important than the pocketbooks of our American citizens."

Rab said, "For the rights of Englishmen—everywhere."

"Why stop with Englishmen?" Otis was warming up. He had a wide mouth, crooked and generous. He settled back in his chair and then he began to talk. It was such talk as Johnny had never heard before. The words surged up through the big body, flowed out of the broad mouth. He never raised his voice, and he went on and on. Sometimes Johnny felt so intoxicated by the mere sound of the words that he hardly followed the sense. That soft, low voice flowed over him; submerged him.

". . . For men and women and children all over the world," he said. "You were right, you tall, dark boy, for even as we shoot down the British soldiers we are fighting for rights such as they will be enjoying a hundred years from now.

". . . There shall be no more tyranny. A handful of men cannot seize power over thousands. A man shall choose who it is shall rule over him.

". . . The peasants of France, the serfs of Russia. Hardly more than animals now. But because we fight, they shall see freedom like a new sun rising in the west. Those natural rights God has given to every man, no matter how humble . . ." He smiled suddenly, and said . . . "or crazy," and took a good pull at his tankard.

". . . The battle we win over the worst in England shall benefit the best in England. How well are they over there represented when it comes to taxes? Not very well. It will be better for them when we have won this war.

"Will French peasants go on forever pulling off their caps and saying 'Oui, Monsieur,' when the gold coaches run down their children? They will not. Italy. And all those German states. Are they nothing but soldiers? Will no one show them the rights of good citizens? So we hold up our torch—and do not forget it was lighted upon the fires of England—and we will set it as a new sun to lighten a world . . ."

Sam Adams, anxious to get that good night's sleep before starting next day for Philadelphia, was smiling slightly, nodding his gray head, seeming to agree. He was bored. It does not matter, he was thinking, what James Otis says these days—sane or crazy.

Joseph Warren's fair, responsive face was aflame. The torch Otis had been talking about seemed reflected in his eyes.

"We are lucky men," he murmured, "for we have a cause worth dying for. This honor is not given to every generation."

"Boy," said Otis to Johnny, "fill my tankard."

It was not until he had drained it and wiped his mouth on the back of his hand that he spoke

again. All sat silently waiting for him. He had, and not for the first time, cast a spell upon them.

"They say," he began again, "my wits left me after I got hit on the head by that customs official. That's what you think, eh, Mr. Sam Adams?"

"Oh, no, no, indeed, Mr. Otis."

"Some of us will give our wits," he said, "some of us all our property. Heh, John Hancock, did you hear that? *Property*—that hurts, eh? To give one's silver wine-coolers, one's coach and four, and the gold buttons off one's sprigged satin waistcoats?"

Hancock looked him straight in the face and Johnny had never before liked him so well.

"I am ready," he said. "I can get along without all that."

"You, Paul Revere, you'll give up that silver-craft you love. God made you to make silver, not war."

Revere smiled. "There's a time for the casting of silver and a time for the casting of cannon. If that's not in the Bible, it should be."

"Doctor Warren, you've a young family. You know quite well, if you get killed they may literally starve."

Warren said, "I've thought of all that long ago."

"And you, John Adams. You've built up a very nice little law practice, stealing away my clients, I notice. Ah, well, so it goes. Each shall give according to his own abilities, and some—" he turned directly to Rab—"some will give their lives. All the years of their maturity. All the children they never live to have. The serenity of old age. To die so young is more than merely dying; it is to lose so large a part of life."

Rab was looking straight at Otis. His arms were folded across his chest. His head flung back a little. His lips parted as though he would speak, but he did not.

"Even you, my old friend—my old enemy? How shall I call you, Sam Adams? Even you will give the best you have—a genius for politics. Oh, go to Philadelphia! Pull all the wool, pull all the strings and all the wires. Yes, go, go! And God go with you. We need you, Sam. We must fight this war. You'll play your part—but what it is really about . . . you'll never know."

James Otis was on his feet, his head close against the rafters that cut down into the attic, making it the shape of a tent. Otis put out his arms.

"It is all so much simpler than you think," he said. He lifted his hands and pushed against the rafters.

"We give all we have, lives, property, safety, skills . . . we fight, we die, for a simple thing. Only that a man can stand up."

With a curt nod, he was gone.

Johnny was standing close to Rab. It had frightened him when Mr. Otis had said, "Some will give their lives," and looked straight at Rab. Die so that "a man can stand up."

Once more Sam Adams had the center of attention. He was again buttoning up his coat, preparing to leave, but first he turned to Revere.

"Now *he* is gone, we can talk a moment about that spy system you think you can organize in Boston."

Paul Revere, like his friend, Joseph Warren, was still slightly under the spell of James Otis.

"I had not thought about it that way before," he said, not answering Sam Adams's words. "You know my father had to fly France because of the tyranny over there. He was only a child. But now, in a way, I'm fighting for that child . . . that no frightened lost child ever is sent out a refugee from his own country because of race or religion." Then he pulled himself together and answered Sam Adams's remarks about the spy system.

That night, when the boys were both in bed, Johnny heard Rab, usually a heavy sleeper, turning and turning.

"Johnny," he said at last, "are you awake?"

"Yes."

"What was it he said?"

"That a man can stand up."

Rab sighed and stopped turning. In a few moments he was asleep. As often had happened before, it was the younger boy who lay wide-eyed in the darkness.

"That a man can stand up."

He'd never forget Otis with his hands pushed up against the cramping rafters over his head.

"That a man can stand up"—as simple as that.

And the strange new sun rising in the west. A sun that was to illumine a world to come.

from AMERICA TRAVELS

*Alice Dalgleish*

*The period during which people traveled by canal boats comes as vividly to life in this story as do the children in it, two determined little girls who both know what they want and are determined to get it.*

### The Kitten on the Canal Boat

Harriet lay in her narrow bunk watching pictures move slowly past, framed in the small, square window. Each morning the pictures were different: sometimes a patch of blue sky, white clouds, or green fields, sometimes sheep grazing or cows lying lazily under a tree. Harriet was quite accustomed to moving scenery, for all of her nine summers had been spent on a canal boat. In the winter months Harriet lived in a house, but she much preferred the time spent on the canal where something interesting and different was always happening.

Now the sun was coming in the small, square window and it was time to get up. Harriet jumped out of bed and climbed on a box to look out. The *Red Lion of the West* was nosing slowly along the canal and there was nothing to be seen but fields full of buttercups. Harriet was glad that it was a fine day, for it meant that as the *Red Lion* passed through the next town gay picnic parties might come on board.

Two kinds of people traveled on the sturdy slow-moving canal boats. There were serious people who were really going somewhere. These slept on the boat and either brought their food with them or had their meals cooked by Harriet's mother in the tiny kitchen. These travelers sometimes were moving from one town or village to another, so they brought with them many bundles and baskets, with a large part of their household belongings. Then there were the gay people who were not really going anywhere but who thought it fun to take a trip on the boat. Harriet loved these picnic parties with laughing ladies who held little parasols over their heads to keep the sun from spoiling their beautiful complexions. They always carried the most interesting

lunches put up in dainty baskets.

When Harriet was dressed she went to the kitchen. It was a neat little kitchen with red-checked curtains and a red geranium in the window. These matched the rest of the *Red Lion* which was a trim boat painted red and white with a black stripe. As Harriet entered the kitchen a good smell of crisp bacon came from the frying pan on the small stove. There were other important things to be done, however, so she did not waste much time over breakfast. From a basket in the corner she took two kittens, a gray one and a black one. With a kitten tucked under each arm she went out on the roof of the boat, which was quite flat, like a deck. There she stood and watched her brother, who was walking along the towpath beside Jerry and Jim, the mules that pulled the boat. At the stern stood Harriet's father with his hand on the tiller; it was his job to steer the boat.

Harriet put the kittens down on the deck and sat looking along the canal. This was an exciting day, for on this day the *Red Lion* passed the *Blossoming Bough,* the boat on which lived Harriet's friend, Alice. As the boats passed each other Harriet and Alice waved, and even had time to talk. Now, as Harriet watched, the *Blossoming Bough* turned the corner and came slowly down the canal. She was a pretty boat, as trim as the *Red Lion* but painted green and white with a touch of yellow. As the boats came near each other the *Blossoming Bough* drew off to one side to allow the *Red Lion* to pass. The tow lines were dropped so that the mules pulling the *Red Lion* could step over them.

Harriet stood as close to the edge of the deck as she dared. There was Alice close to the edge of *her* boat. It was well to be careful, for the deck had no railing and canal water was dark and cold.

"Harriet!" called Alice, "I have a new dress."

"What is it like?" asked Harriet.

"Oh, it's white, for Sundays. I'm not allowed to wear it on week days."

"I'm going to have a new dress soon," said Harriet.

"A Sunday dress?"

"Yes, I think it will be white like yours."

The *Red Lion* had slipped past the *Blossoming Bough.*

"Good-by, Harriet!"

"Good-by, Alice!"

There would be no more excitement now until the *Red Lion of the West* reached the next town. Harriet sat on the deck and played with the kittens. Suddenly her father put a horn to his lips and blew a long blast. Harriet ducked her head, for this meant that they were about to pass under a low bridge. It seemed no time at all until they reached the town—and there was a picnic party! It was a particularly interesting picnic party.

There were two pretty ladies with parasols, and two gentlemen, their hats tied to their buttonholes with string to keep them from blowing away. And there was a little girl. Harriet thought, as the little girl stepped daintily onto the deck, that she had never seen anything so beautiful or so exactly like a picture come to life. The little girl had blue eyes, yellow curls, and pink cheeks. Her dress was of the palest pink, and below it showed white lace-trimmed pantalettes. Harriet stood there feeling very dark and solid and different in her calico dress. She could not take her eyes off the little girl. There above the golden curls was a bonnet, a dainty straw bonnet trimmed with pink roses and tied under its owner's chin with a pink bow.

The ladies moved gracefully to a seat, arranged their skirts and sat chatting with the gentlemen. The little girl's mother called her to sit beside her. For five minutes the little girl sat there as prim and as quiet as a china ornament on a shelf. Then she saw the kittens.

"Oh, Mamma!" she said, "look at the darling kittens! A black one and a gray one. The gray one is just the kitten I want!"

"They belong to the little girl who lives on the boat," said her mother.

"Oh, but I *want* one," said the pink child, who had always had what she wanted. "I *want* one, Mamma, I want the gray one. It's my birthday, you know." Two large tears came into the blue eyes.

"Mercy, Florence," said her mother, looking worried, "don't cry! Let's ask the little girl if she will sell us the gray kitten."

"Little girl," said Florence, "will you sell us the gray kitten?"

"No!" said Harriet, her brown eyes very large, her feet planted firmly on the deck.

"But I *want* her," fretted the child.

"He's my favorite kitten," said Harriet.

"She's my favorite *kind* of kitten," said Florence even more fretfully. Then, as suddenly as the sun comes out from behind a cloud, she changed her tone and began to coax. "Won't you let me have her? Please?"

"Well," said Harriet, weakening, "perhaps I will. But *you* must give *me* something that I want very much."

"Oh, I *will!*" smiled Florence. "What is it?"

"Your lovely pink bonnet," answered Harriet.

There was a moment of chatter and fluttering.

"My pink bonnet?"

"Your lovely pink bonnet!"

"Your *new* pink bonnet. Florence, you *can't*."

But Florence usually had her own way and this was her birthday. Once more two big tears came into her eyes. This time they fell and splashed on the pink dress. Slowly one hand began to untie the strings of the pink bonnet.

"No, Florence."

"Oh, please, Mamma."

"The sun is much too hot."

"Mamma, it's such a lovely day and I can share your parasol." By this time the bonnet was untied. Harriet picked up the gray kitten. With one hand she took the bonnet, with the other she gave up the gray kitten. Then she hurried into the kitchen to find her mother.

Mother shook her head over the queer ways of little girls, but at last she was persuaded that the exchange was a fair one. It was well that she thought so, for by this time wild horses could not have dragged the kitten from Florence's arms.

When the picnic was over a little girl without a bonnet stood on the shore and waved to another little girl on the deck of the canal boat.

"I'll be very kind to your nice gray kitten," called Florence. "And I'm going to call her Velvet."

"*His* name is Tom!" shouted Harriet, but the *Red Lion* was too far along the canal for the pink child to hear. This was just as well, for never in the world could she have owned a kitten with the plain name of Tom.

It was Sunday morning when next the *Red Lion of the West* passed the *Blossoming Bough*. The sound of church bells came faintly across the fields. It was very quiet on the canal. The boats slipped silently along, for on Sundays they were not allowed to blow their horns. Harriet stood as close to the edge of the deck as she dared. Alice stood close to the edge too. Each little girl was wearing a Sunday dress. Each dress was white, with white pantalettes. Alice's hair was blowing in the breeze, but on Harriet's head there was a bonnet, a dainty straw bonnet with pink roses and pink ribbons tied under the chin.

"Look at my Sunday dress!" screamed Alice.

"Look at mine!"

"Why, Harriet, you have a pink bonnet!"

"Yes, isn't it beautiful?"

There was quite a long silence while Alice took in all the glory of the pink bonnet.

"It's the most beautiful bonnet I ever saw."

Harriet turned around to show the back of the bonnet.

"Did your mother give it to you?"

"No, I got it from a little girl in exchange for a kitten."

"For *what*?" The boats had passed each other. "*For a kitten!*"

But the *Red Lion of the West* was now too far away from the *Blossoming Bough*. There was nothing to do but wait until they passed again, then Harriet and Alice could finish their conversation. It was often like that!

## MARTIN AND ABRAHAM LINCOLN

*Catherine Cate Coblentz*

*The year before her death, Catherine Coblentz wrote a wonderful fairy tale,* The Blue Cat of Castle Town, *which should be read aloud. It embodies her own spirit of service to the "bright enchantment" of "beauty, content and peace." This touching story,* Martin and Abraham Lincoln, *is a true incident of the Civil War.*

"Flour and sugar and butter and eggs. Flour and sugar and butter and eggs." Martin Emery kept saying the words over to himself as he went slowly up the lane.

He had heard his mother whispering them again and again these past days. The words reminded him of the songs which his friend, Snowden, sang. Only Martin felt sure Mother's words were not a song but a prayer. For Mother needed so many things for Martin, for Maria, and Amanda, and Anna, the baby.

Martin gulped. When Father was at the Fort near by he had seen to it that Mother had these things. But he was gone. He would be gone for a long time. Somehow or other Martin felt he must take his place and help. After all he wore a new uniform now with shiny buttons. It was just like the one Father was wearing the last time Martin had seen him.

By this time Martin had come to the end of the lane. So he climbed up on the big rock by the roadside. Then he turned about and waved at the little gray house. Maria and Amanda and Anna, the baby, were standing in the doorway. They all waved back. Though Maria had to start Anna's hand going.

Then Martin looked up the road. It was Saturday and time for Snowden and Nellie to appear around the curve. Pretty soon he saw Nellie's long white ears. He heard the bell on Nellie's neck, and the jingle of her harness. He heard the creaking wheels on Nellie's cart. He saw the baskets of fresh vegetables in the back.

He saw Snowden, but Snowden didn't see Martin. Snowden was bent over on the front seat. In his hand was a stub of a pencil; on his knee a piece of paper. He kept frowning and looking at the paper. "I sure got to make a lot of money today," he said loud enough for Martin to hear him. "I sure got to. There's flour to get for Rosebell, and sugar and butter and eggs."

But if Snowden didn't see Martin, Nellie did. As soon as she came to the rock, Nellie stopped still. She looked at Martin. Then she turned her head and looked at Snowden. Then she flicked her ears.

When Nellie flicked her ears it was a sign. As soon as Martin saw it, he began scrambling over the wheel. He climbed up on the seat beside Snowden. Snowden blinked with surprise.

"May I go to Washington with you?" Martin asked.

Snowden started to nod. Then he stopped and asked, "Does your mother know?"

"She knows," said Martin. "That's why she let me wear my new suit." He stood up so Snowden could see the suit better. He stretched his shoulders as high as he could.

Snowden looked him up and down. He didn't miss a quirk of the soldier-like cap or a single shiny button. "Hmm," he said. "Nice, Martin. Just like your father's."

"Father's regiment brought Mother the cloth," said Martin, "and the buttons."

"Snowden," began Martin, as the cart moved on toward Washington, "how do you get flour and sugar and butter and eggs?"

Snowden sighed, "Sometimes I declare I don't know myself, Martin. Rosebell and the children need so many things." He took up the pencil once more. When he put it down again, Martin asked another question.

"When the war is over, will my father come home, Snowden?"

Snowden drew a deep breath. "All the war prisoners will come home then, Martin. All those that the northern army has taken will go back south to their homes. And all those that the southern army has taken will go back to their homes."

"I wish the war was over now," burst out Martin.

Snowden looked at him. "So do I," he said. "Abraham Lincoln does, too, I reckon."

Martin knew who Abraham Lincoln was. His picture was in the little gray house at the end of the lane. He never could decide which picture he liked better, that of his father or of Abraham Lincoln. His mother said they were both very important people. "Mr. Lincoln is the best President this country ever had, Martin," she said. "And your father is the best cobbler."

*Best cobbler, best cobbler* went Nellie's iron shoes, as they thumped, thumped across the bridge that led from Alexandria into Washington. Martin kicked his feet back to feel whether the empty basket was under the seat. It was. Martin knew why it was there. He knew, too, what would happen to that basket.

At the very first house, Snowden began his morning song. Martin waited to hear what the song was. It was a different one every week. This week it was a good song. Martin joined in after the first time. He sang as loud as he could:

> Squash and beans and 'taters,
> Garden fresh, garden fresh,
> Beans and squash and 'taters.

After every sale, Snowden would put a scoop of beans or 'taters, or maybe a big squash into the basket under the seat.

The faster Snowden sold what he had, the bigger the gifts to the basket. And when everything else was sold that basket would be quite full. When Snowden and Martin and Nellie went home, Snowden would stop at the little gray house at the end of the lane.

"Got some left overs, Mrs. Emery." Snowden would say. "Thought maybe you'd help me out by using them." Then he always added, "Martin was a big help to me today, Mrs. Emery."

Had it not been for Snowden's left overs, Martin knew that he and Maria and Amanda and Anna would be hungry oftener than they were. Now, if they only had flour and sugar and butter and eggs, Mother wouldn't need to worry.

So on this Saturday Martin tried harder than ever to help Snowden as much as he could. He called:

Squash and beans and 'taters,

at the top of his lungs. Earlier in the season it had been:

Rhubarb and radishes, ripe and red.

Later there would be cabbages and parsnips and turnips, and Snowden would make up new songs for them to call.

"You are good at making up songs," said Martin as the cart rattled along the wide streets.

"And you are good at singing them," replied Snowden. "Words said over and over make a good song."

Words said over and over! That made Martin think of his mother, and the words she made into a prayer. He drew a long, quivering sigh.

"Wars, which put fathers in prison when they are needed at home, are a bad thing," Snowden said. He had been watching Martin closely.

Martin nodded. He swallowed the lump in his throat and called:

Squash and beans and 'taters,
Garden fresh, garden fresh,
Beans and squash and 'taters.

However, his voice didn't sound nearly as cheerful as it usually did. Toward the end of the morning it began trailing after Snowden's like a small echo.

Squash and beans and 'taters,

Snowden would sing.

Beans and 'taters,

would come Martin's echo.

Snowden glanced at Martin several times. It was very hot. Martin looked pale. Snowden made

up his mind he would take him to a cool spot, while he went off to buy the groceries which Rosebell needed.

So a little before noon, Snowden turned Nellie about. And when they came to a big parklike place filled with shade trees, Snowden pulled the reins.

"Whoa, Nellie," he said.

"Now, Martin," he went on, "you just stay here in the shade and rest until Nellie and I come back. It's a good place for anyone in a uniform like yours. There's been lots of soldiers on this lawn, I can tell you. I've seen them sleeping here at night sometimes. And all over the place in the day. And I've seen them jump up and stand just as proud and straight when Abraham Lincoln came along."

"Came along here, Snowden? Abraham Lincoln?"

"Of course, Martin. See that building there? That's the Capitol, Martin—our Capitol."

Martin stood on the ground and stared. Snowden and Nellie started to leave. Then Nellie stopped and flicked her ears. That made Snowden remember something. He reached in his pocket.

"I most forgot," he said. "Rosebell gave me a sandwich for you, Martin. And an apple."

"I have a sandwich." Martin pointed to his pocket. He did not take it out, for he did not want Snowden to see how small and thin that sandwich was. There was no butter on the bread, only a smear of molasses.

"You'd better take this," urged Snowden. "Rosebell made it special."

"Thank you," said Martin, reaching for the thick sandwich and the apple. He would just take a bite or two out of the sandwich and save the rest for Maria and Amanda and Anna. He would save the apple, too, most of it.

When Snowden and Nellie were gone, and when the last sound of Nellie's bell, the jingle of her harness, and the creaking of the cart wheels faded in the distance, Martin wandered about for a little. Then he climbed on a bench. He ate his thin sandwich. He ate a little of Snowden's thick one. It was so good. Half of it was gone before he knew it. He re-wrapped it in the paper Rosebell had put about it, and laid it on the bench. When Martin wasn't looking a fat squirrel slipped up on the bench and grabbed at it. Martin felt the squirrel touch his hand. He jumped. The squirrel jumped. The sandwich fell and landed in a puddle.

Martin could have cried when he saw that. But he didn't. He would save all the apple, he decided, for Maria and Amanda and Anna. He would not take even a bite.

The sun was hot. Martin went over and sat down on the stone steps of the Capitol. The steps were clean and cool. His eyes closed a little as he leaned back, his head resting against the stone at one side.

Then, as always when he was alone and it was still, Martin began thinking about his father. The lump in his throat began to grow.

He heard someone coming down the steps in back of him. But there was plenty of room so Martin didn't move. He just sat there and watched dreamily as a long shadow moved over the step he was on, and went slither-sliding down the step ahead. And the next. And the next. And the next.

Then the shadow stopped still and stayed in one place. A voice just in back of Martin said, "Well, well! How's my little soldier?"

Soldier! When his father's friends said that, Martin had always done as his father had taught him, jumped to his feet and saluted. So, forgetting how tired and sad he had been, he sprang to his feet, flinging his head back and his hand up at the same time.

As his fingers touched the visor of his little blue cap, Martin's heart began to thud like a drum. For Abraham Lincoln was standing there looking down at him, his sad face losing its look of worry, and breaking slowly into a smile. Abraham Lincoln, himself!

"What is your name, soldier?" the great man asked, gravely returning the salute.

Martin told him.

"Where were you born, Martin?"

"In Vermont. In a log cabin."

The man nodded. "I was born in a log cabin, too."

"I know, Mother told me. She said some day I might get to be President like you."

"All mothers say that, Martin. What does your father say?"

"I don't know." Martin's voice slowed. "You see, he is away. He used to be a cobbler, but now he is your soldier."

"What regiment? And where is he now?"

The lump in Martin's throat was growing worse. It was difficult to make the words come. "The First Vermont—" he managed. And then the sobs had him. "He's in Andersonville Prison," he jerked.

But the great man was bending over. Strong arms were lifting Martin. In another moment the man had taken Martin's place on the steps. Martin was folded into his lap.

The boy's face was hidden now, in Abraham Lincoln's vest.

Abraham Lincoln just sat there, holding the little boy whose sobbing had been so long kept back. A great hand patted him gently and understandingly between the shoulders. When Martin grew quieter the man began to talk.

"So your father is a cobbler. Is he a good cobbler, Martin?"

Martin nodded his head so hard that his nose

went up and down against Abraham Lincoln's ribs.

"Good cobblers are mighty important," said the man. "Never made a pair of shoes myself. But I saw a boy once that needed some mighty bad." The President settled his back a little more comfortably into the corner of the step and the wall.

"It happened when I was postmaster back in Illinois," he went on. "People didn't write many letters in those days, so I carried them in my hat. One cold day as I was going along with the letters in my hat, I saw Ab Trout. He was barefoot as the day he was born and chopping a pile of logs from an old barn that had been torn down. The logs were gnarled and tough. And Ab's ax kept going slower and slower.

"'What do you get for this job, Ab?' I asked him.

"'A dollar.'

"'What do you aim to do with it?'

"'Buy a pair of shoes,' he said.

"'You'll never get one shoe at this rate, Ab,' I told him. 'Better go in and warm yourself and you'll work faster.' So he did. Funniest thing, Martin. When Ab came out, that wood was all chopped! Now, what do you think of that?"

Martin sat up and looked straight at Abraham Lincoln. "I think you chopped that wood," he said.

"Maybe you're right," smiled Lincoln. "After all, folks must help each other."

Martin nodded. "I help my mother all I can," he said. "I fix the rough places when they come in the shoes of Maria and Amanda and Anna. I can do it most as well as Father did. Mother says it helps a lot."

"I am sure it does." The President nodded.

"Vermont is a long way off," he went on. "Tell me, how do you happen to be here, Martin?"

Martin wiped the last tear from his cheek with the handkerchief Mr. Lincoln handed him. He could talk now. He wanted to.

"Father went to war," he began. "He was stationed at a fort near Alexandria. So, after a time he found a house near the fort, and sent for Mother and me and Maria and Amanda and Anna. We came on the train. At first we saw Father often. Then one night when some of the soldiers were sent out to take a railroad bridge, Father was captured. He was sent to prison."

"How does your mother manage to take care of you?" asked Abraham Lincoln.

"Well, it's like you said. Folks help. The soldiers—Father's friends—bring their mending to her. They ask her to cook for them. And sometimes they bring their washing for her to do. They pay as much as they can. The soldiers give us cloth for our clothes, too.

"And Snowden helps. Snowden is my friend. He sells vegetables and I help him call. Snowden fills the basket under the seat with vegetables and calls them left overs. He gives the basket to Mother. But the vegetables aren't left overs. Not really."

Martin didn't tell about his mother's prayer for flour and sugar and butter and eggs. He didn't need to. For Abraham Lincoln seemed to know all about that prayer.

"Hmm!" he began. "It seems to me, Martin, that part of this job of helping belongs to the army—your father's army, and mine. I will speak to somebody, and I'm pretty sure there will be food from the army stores every week for your mother. Things that Snowden and the soldiers can't supply, like butter and bacon and other things."

There wasn't any lump in Martin's throat now. He felt wonderful. But for some reason the tears began to pour down his face.

The man pretended not to see. Instead, he raised himself to his feet, and a sudden frown grew deep between his eyes. "It's my shoe, Martin," he explained. "There's a nail sticking right into my foot. And I keep forgetting to have it fixed."

"Oh, wait," cried Martin. "I can help you." He darted off to a pile of stones by the steps. Luckily he found the kind he wanted right away. When he came back Abraham Lincoln sat on the steps with his shoe off, waiting to be helped.

Martin sat down beside him. He slipped one stone inside the great shoe. With the other he pounded hard on the sole.

"My father showed me how," be boasted between pounds. "He is a good cobbler."

Abraham Lincoln smiled. "I'd like to be a cobbler myself, Martin. A good cobbler."

"That's what I am going to be," nodded Martin.

Down the street he could hear the sound of Nellie's bell, the jingle of her harness and the creaking of the wheels on Nellie's cart. But he finished the shoe and gave it to Abraham Lincoln.

The man put on the shoe. He stood up and set the foot, where the nail had been, down carefully. He pressed harder, while Martin watched his face. There was no frown between Abraham Lincoln's eyes.

"It's a good job, Martin," he praised. "It feels just fine." He paused and looked over Martin's head far into the distance. The worry had gone now from the President's face. "You have helped me, Martin," he said, "more than you know!"

Martin said nothing. He only slipped his hand inside Abraham Lincoln's. They came down the steps together.

They were waiting when Snowden and Nellie arrived.

Snowden's mouth popped wide open. Nellie stopped. She flicked her ears and Snowden swept off his hat.

The man beside Martin lifted his gravely in return. Then he bent and raised Martin high in the air and put him on the seat beside Snowden.

"Good-by, soldier," he said.

Martin saluted. Snowden saluted. Abraham Lincoln saluted. Nellie started toward home.

### from JED

#### Peter Burchard

*Although he was only sixteen, Jed had already fought in the battle of Shiloh. Loyal to the Union, Jed was disturbed by some of the things the Yankee soldiers did. Foraging, to him, was just another name for stealing. In this excerpt, he finds a small, belligerent child who is hurt and who announces defiantly that his father is a Confederate soldier. In befriending the child and later, in helping the family, Jed proves that not all enemies are ruthless. Burchard has made the*

Reprinted by permission of Coward, McCann & Geoghegan, Inc. from *Jed: The Story of a Yankee Soldier and a Southern Boy* by Peter Burchard. Copyright © 1960 by Coward-McCann, Inc.

*ethical value of Jed's conduct significant without making it moralistic in this simple but touching story of the Civil War period.*

#### [A Yankee Meets a Young Confederate]

Right after reveille Sergeant Charlie came around. "Well, Jed," Charlie said, "did you break up any Rebel raids this morning?"

"Only a little one," Jed said. "How does it happen you didn't come around before this?"

"Now, I'm sorry, Jed," Charlie said. "If I'd a knowed it would worry you so I'd have come around earlier."

"I'll forgive you just this once," Jed said. "But don't let it happen again."

Charlie smiled and walked toward the next picket.

Jed heard Charlie whistling a little tune. Almost as soon as the sound of Charlie's whistling died away Jed heard something else. At first he thought it might be the dog working his way out of the thicket, but he soon realized that a little dog couldn't make that much noise.

Jed curled his finger around the trigger of his rifle and stood stock-still, trying to see into the waves of light, rolling mist that veiled the lowland. For a minute he heard nothing, and then he heard the crackle of dead branches and a crash as if someone had fallen down.

"Halt!" Jed called. "Who is that out there?"

There was no answer.

"Come forward and make yourself known," Jed called, "or I'll start shooting."

Then a voice spoke up. It was a child's voice. "Go ahead, Yankee," the voice said.

Jed lowered his rifle. "You come out here fast," he yelled.

There was no answer. Jed held his rifle loosely in one hand and moved forward. It came to him that maybe this was some kind of trap. He found his way to where the dog had been, but he wasn't there any more. He stood listening. Suddenly the dog began to yelp. Jed moved forward, following the sound. He went through the thicket to a little clearing on the other side. There he saw a young boy sitting on a log and looking mad enough to chew nails. He was bareheaded, his hair was the color of corn silk and his eyes were blue. The little dog was sitting at his feet and didn't make a sound as Jed walked up.

"What are you doing here?" Jed asked him.

The boy tilted his tan face up to Jed and looked at him with pure hate in his eyes. "Nothin' that matters to you," he said. "I woke up early and went out with my dog."

"It matters plenty to me," Jed said. "You should stay clear of this camp. It's lucky you didn't get shot."

"I need no Yankee mercy, soldier," the boy said.

Jed could feel himself getting hot under the collar. "You mind your tongue, boy," he said. "There are pickets all around this camp and some of them have itching trigger fingers."

"I hate Yankees," the boy said, "and most of all I hate Yankee soldiers. My pa's a Confederate soldier."

"Then I don't blame you for hating Yankee soldiers," Jed said, "but there's no call to get yourself shot to prove it."

He looked down at the blond head and at the dog sitting trustingly by the boy's feet. "Now you get up and cut out of here as fast as your legs will carry you," he said. "I go off duty soon and you'd best not be here when the next man comes around."

The dog got up and limped toward Jed, wagging his tail and looking up. He leaned down and gave the dog a pat. "Now take your dog and git," he said. "Walk straight out that way. Don't circle around or you're liable to get shot by one of the other pickets."

The boy sat on the log, not saying a word or making a move. Finally he said, "I can't walk. I fell in a chuckhole and when I walk my leg near kills me."

Jed faced the boy, holding his rifle in one hand, his other hand in a fist on his hip. He gazed at him thoughtfully.

"How far do you live from here?" he asked.

"Two or three miles I guess," the boy said, "but I'm not likely to tell you which way. You'd bring those other Yankees around to steal our pigs and chickens and burn our buildings."

"Well, you can't crawl home," Jed said. "Maybe your leg is broken. I better take you to our surgeon and get him to fix you up."

"If you're a mind to shoot me," the boy said, "shoot me here. No use to drag me back to that Yankee camp."

Jed found it hard to keep a straight face. "Now don't be a fool," he said. "Even Yankees don't shoot children."

He moved forward and reached out his hand so the boy could hang on and hop to the willow tree. "Come on," he said, "there's no use fighting me."

The boy drew back his hand. "Not while there's a breath in me," he said.

Jed turned on his heel. "You can't go far on a broken leg," he said, "and I don't have the heart to leave a tad like you to starve. You think things over. I'll come back later to see if you've changed your mind."

He walked back to the willow tree and looked around and listened and settled back against the tree.

His relief came about half an hour later when the sun had burned the mist away and stood like a red ball in the east.

"Well, how you been, Davy?" Jed asked the boy.

"Fine, Jed boy," his relief said. "I thought maybe you died of the fever, I haven't seen you for so long."

Davy was no taller than Jed, but he was thicker, and he had a bullet-shaped head. Jed looked him up and down. "I have a fever that makes me ache to get out of here and fight this war to a finish," he said.

"You ain't just waggin' your tongue, Jed boy," Davy said. "Most anything is better than this."

Jed hesitated and looked into Davy's eyes. "Davy," he said.

"What is it, boy?" Davy asked.

"Well, it might be hard to believe," Jed said, suddenly talking very fast, "but there's a little boy out there past that thicket. He's hurt his leg and I got to take him to the surgeon to get him fixed up. Maybe the surgeon can figure out a way to get him home without kicking up a fuss with Captain Pike and all. I'd like it if you could keep this a secret."

"Why, all right." Davy said. "How old is the boy?"

" 'Bout eight or nine I guess," Jed said. "I haven't heard him stir since I found him, so he must still be there."

"Maybe it's some trick," Davy said.

"I thought of that," Jed said, "but I can't figure out what kind of trick it would be. Anyway I don't think he's play-acting."

"Well, go ahead and get him," Davy said. "If it was me I'd let the little Rebel crawl back home."

"Now you don't mean that, surely," Jed said.

## from FARMER BOY

### Laura Ingalls Wilder

*Farmer Boy is the one book in the Wilder series devoted to the Wilder family. The other seven, beginning with* Little House in the Big Woods, *are concerned with the adventures of the Ingalls family as it pioneers westward into new country. In the last three books, beginning with* The Long Winter, *the Ingalls family and Almanzo Wilder meet and share the same vicissitudes and adventures. Laura marries Almanzo and later writes this wonderful series of books, a saga of pioneering in this country. The Fourth of July described in the following episode must have been about 1867. One of the important things Almanzo Wilder's father did for his son was to give him a sense of values. Children will be interested perhaps in a comparison of prices then and now.*

### Independence Day

Almanzo was eating breakfast before he remembered that this was the Fourth of July. He felt more cheerful.

It was like Sunday morning. After breakfast he scrubbed his face with soft soap till it shone, and he parted his wet hair and combed it sleekly down. He put on his sheep's-gray trousers and his shirt of French calico, and his vest and his short round coat.

Mother had made his new suit in the new style. The coat fastened at the throat with a little flap of the cloth, then the two sides slanted back to show his vest, and they rounded off over his trousers' pockets.

He put on his round straw hat, which Mother

had made of braided oat-straws, and he was all dressed up for Independence Day. He felt very fine.

Father's shining horses were hitched to the shining, red-wheeled buggy, and they all drove away in the cool sunshine. All the country had a holiday air. Nobody was working in the fields, and along the road the people in their Sunday clothes were driving to town.

Father's swift horses passed them all. They passed by wagons and carts and buggies. They passed gray horses and black horses and dappled-gray horses. Almanzo waved his hat whenever he sailed past anyone he knew, and he would have been perfectly happy if only he had been driving that swift, beautiful team.

At the church sheds in Malone he helped Father unhitch. Mother and the girls and Royal hurried away. But Almanzo would rather help with the horses than do anything else. He couldn't drive them, but he could tie their halters and buckle on their blankets, and stroke their soft noses and give them hay.

Then he went out with Father and they walked on the crowded sidewalks. All the stores were closed, but ladies and gentlemen were walking up and down and talking. Ruffled little girls carried parasols, and all the boys were dressed up, like Almanzo. Flags were everywhere, and in the Square the band was playing "Yankee Doodle." The fifes tooted and the flutes shrilled and the drums came in with rub-a-dub-dub.

"Yankee Doodle went to town,
Riding on a pony,
He stuck a feather in his hat,
And called it macaroni!"

Even grown-ups had to keep time to it. And there, in the corner of the Square, were the two brass cannons!

The Square was not really square. The railroad made it three-cornered. But everybody called it the Square, anyway. It was fenced, and grass grew there. Benches stood in rows on the grass, and people were filing between the benches and sitting down as they did in church.

Almanzo went with Father to one of the best front seats. All the important men stopped to shake hands with Father. The crowd kept coming till all the seats were full, and still there were people outside the fence.

The band stopped playing, and the minister prayed. Then the band tuned up again and everybody rose. Men and boys took off their hats. The band played, and everybody sang.

> "Oh, say, can you see by the dawn's early light,
>     What so proudly we hailed at the twilight's
>         last gleaming,
>     Whose broad stripes and bright stars through
>         the perilous night,
>         O'er the ramparts we watched were so gal-
>             lantly streaming?"

From the top of the flagpole, up against the blue sky, the Stars and Stripes were fluttering. Everybody looked at the American flag, and Almanzo sang with all his might.

Then everyone sat down, and a Congressman stood up on the platform. Slowly and solemnly he read the Declaration of Independence.

"When in the course of human events it becomes necessary for one people . . . to assume among the powers of the earth the separate and equal station. . . . We hold these truths to be self-evident, that all men are created equal. . . ."

Almanzo felt solemn and very proud.

Then two men made long political speeches. One believed in high tariffs, and one believed in free trade. All the grown-ups listened hard, but Almanzo did not understand the speeches very well and he began to be hungry. He was glad when the band played again.

The music was so gay; the bandsmen in their blue and red and their brass buttons tootled merrily, and the fat drummer beat rat-a-tat-tat on the drum. All the flags were fluttering and everybody was happy, because they were free and independent and this was Independence Day. And it was time to eat dinner.

Almanzo helped Father feed the horses while Mother and the girls spread the picnic lunch on the grass in the churchyard. Many others were picnicking there, too, and after he had eaten all he could Almanzo went back to the Square.

There was a lemonade-stand by the hitching-posts. A man sold pink lemonade, a nickel a glass, and a crowd of the town boys were standing around him. Cousin Frank was there. Almanzo

had a drink at the town pump, but Frank said he was going to buy lemonade. He had a nickel. He walked up to the stand and bought a glass of the pink lemonade and drank it slowly. He smacked his lips and rubbed his stomach and said:

"Mmmm! Why don't you buy some?"

"Where'd you get the nickel?" Almanzo asked. He had never had a nickel. Father gave him a penny every Sunday to put in the collection-box in church; he had never had any other money.

"My father gave it to me," Frank bragged. "My father gives me a nickel every time I ask him."

"Well, so would my father if I asked him," said Almanzo.

"Well, why don't you ask him?" Frank did not believe that Father would give Almanzo a nickel. Almanzo did not know whether Father would, or not.

"Because I don't want to," he said.

"He wouldn't give you a nickel," Frank said.

"He would, too."

"I dare you to ask him," Frank said. The other boys were listening. Almanzo put his hands in his pockets and said:

"I'd just as lief ask him if I wanted to."

"Yah, you're scared!" Frank jeered. "Double dare! Double dare!"

Father was a little way down the street, talking to Mr. Paddock, the wagon maker. Almanzo walked slowly toward them. He was faint-hearted, but he had to go. The nearer he got to Father, the more he dreaded asking for a nickel. He had never before thought of doing such a thing. He was sure Father would not give it to him.

He waited till Father stopped talking and looked at him.

"What is it, son?" Father asked.

Almanzo was scared. "Father," he said.

"Well, son?"

"Father," Almanzo said, "would you—would you give me—a nickel?"

He stood there while Father and Mr. Paddock looked at him, and he wished he could get away. Finally Father asked:

"What for?"

Almanzo looked down at his moccasins and muttered:

"Frank had a nickel. He bought pink lemonade."

"Well," Father said, slowly, "if Frank treated you, it's only right you should treat him." Father put his hand in his pocket. Then he stopped and asked:

"Did Frank treat you to lemonade?"

Almanzo wanted so badly to get the nickel that he nodded. Then he squirmed and said:

"No, Father."

Father looked at him a long time. Then he took out his wallet and opened it, and slowly he took out a round, big silver half-dollar. He asked:

"Almanzo, do you know what this is?"

"Half a dollar," Almanzo answered.

"Yes. But do you know what half a dollar is?"

Almanzo didn't know it was anything but half a dollar.

"It's work, son," Father said. "That's what money is; it's hard work."

Mr. Paddock chuckled. "The boy's too young, Wilder," he said. "You can't make a youngster understand that."

"Almanzo's smarter than you think," said Father.

Almanzo didn't understand at all. He wished he could get away. But Mr. Paddock was look-ing at Father just as Frank looked at Almanzo when he double-dared him, and Father had said Almanzo was smart, so Almanzo tried to look like a smart boy. Father asked:

"You know how to raise potatoes, Almanzo?"

"Yes," Almanzo said.

"Say you have a seed potato in the spring, what do you do with it?"

"You cut it up," Almanzo said.

"Go on, son."

"Then you harrow—first you manure the field, and plow it. Then you harrow, and mark the ground. And plant the potatoes, and plow them, and hoe them. You plow and hoe them twice."

"That's right, son. And then?"

"Then you dig them and put them down cel-lar."

"Yes. Then you pick them over all winter; you throw out all the little ones and the rotten ones. Come spring, you load them up and haul them here to Malone, and you sell them. And if you get a good price, son, how much do you get to show for all that work? How much do you get for half a bushel of potatoes?"

"Half a dollar," Almanzo said.

"Yes," said Father. "That's what's in this half-dollar, Almanzo. The work that raised half a bushel of potatoes is in it."

Almanzo looked at the round piece of money that Father held up. It looked small, compared with all that work.

"You can have it, Almanzo," Father said. Almanzo could hardly believe his ears. Father gave him the heavy half-dollar.

"It's yours," said Father. "You could buy a sucking pig with it, if you want to. You could raise it, and it would raise a litter of pigs, worth four, five dollars apiece. Or you can trade that half-dollar for lemonade, and drink it up. You do as you want, it's your money."

Almanzo forgot to say thank you. He held the half-dollar a minute, then he put his hand in his pocket and went back to the boys by the lemon-ade-stand. The man was calling out,

"Step this way, step this way! Ice-cold lemon-ade, pink lemonade, only five cents a glass! Only half a dime, ice-cold pink lemonade! The twentieth part of a dollar!"

Frank asked Almanzo:

"Where's the nickel?"

"He didn't give me a nickel," said Almanzo, and Frank yelled:

"Yah, yah! I told you he wouldn't! I told you so!"

"He gave me half a dollar," said Almanzo.

The boys wouldn't believe it till he showed them. Then they crowded around, waiting for him to spend it. He showed it to them all, and put it back in his pocket.

"I'm going to look around," he said, "and buy me a good little sucking pig."

The band came marching down the street, and they all ran along beside it. The flag was gloriously waving in front, then came the buglers blowing and the fifers tootling and the drummer rattling the drumsticks on the drum. Up the street and down the street went the band, with all the boys following it, and then it stopped in the Square by the brass cannons.

Hundreds of people were there, crowding to watch.

The cannons sat on their haunches, pointing their long barrels upward. The band kept on playing. Two men kept shouting, "Stand back! Stand back!" and other men were pouring black powder into the cannons' muzzles and pushing it down with wads of cloth on long rods.

The iron rods had two handles, and two men pushed and pulled on them, driving the black powder down the brass barrels. Then all the boys ran to pull grass and weeds along the railroad tracks. They carried them by armfuls to the cannons, and the men crowded the weeds into the cannons' muzzles and drove them down with the long rods.

A bonfire was burning by the railroad tracks, and long iron rods were heating in it.

When all the weeds and grass had been packed tight against the powder in the cannons, a man took a little more powder in his hand and carefully filled the two little touchholes in the barrels. Now everybody was shouting.

"Stand back! Stand back!"

Mother took hold of Almanzo's arm and made him come away with her. He told her:

"Aw, Mother, they're only loaded with powder and weeds. I won't get hurt, Mother. I'll be careful, honest." But she made him come away from the cannons.

Two men took the long iron rods from the fire.

Everybody was still, watching. Standing as far behind the cannons as they could, the two men stretched out the rods and touched their red-hot tips to the touchholes. A little flame like a candle-flame flickered up from the powder. The little flames stood there burning; nobody breathed. Then—BOOM!

The cannons leaped backward, the air was full of flying grass and weeds. Almanzo ran with all the other boys to feel the warm muzzles of the cannons. Everybody was exclaiming about what a loud noise they had made.

"That's the noise that made the Redcoats run!" Mr. Paddock said to Father.

"Maybe," Father said, tugging his beard. "But it was muskets that won the Revolution. And don't forget it was axes and plows that made this country."

"That's so, come to think of it," Mr. Paddock said.

Independence Day was over. The cannons had been fired, and there was nothing more to do but hitch up the horses and drive home to do the chores.

That night when they were going to the house with the milk, Almanzo asked Father,

"Father, how was it axes and plows that made this country? Didn't we fight England for it?"

"We fought for Independence, son," Father said. "But all the land our forefathers had was a little strip of country, here between the mountains and the ocean. All the way from here west was Indian country, and Spanish and French and English country. It was farmers that took all that country and made it America."

"How?" Almanzo asked.

"Well, son, the Spaniards were soldiers, and high-and-mighty gentlemen that only wanted gold. And the French were fur-traders, wanting to make quick money. And England was busy fighting wars. But we were farmers, son; we wanted the land. It was farmers that went over the mountains, and cleared the land, and settled it, and farmed it, and hung on to their farms.

"This country goes three thousand miles west, now. It goes 'way out beyond Kansas, and beyond the Great American Desert, over mountains bigger than these mountains, and down to the Pacific Ocean. It's the biggest country in the world, and it was farmers who took all that country and made it America, son. Don't you ever forget that."

## from SING DOWN THE MOON

### Scott O'Dell

*The peaceful Navahos of Canyon de Chelly had been threatened by Spanish slavers and then by white soldiers in 1864. Their crops destroyed by the white men, the Indians were forced to march to Fort Sumner, the "long march" of tragedy. Taut and direct, the story is told by Bright Morning, a young woman of indomitable spirit, who convinces her husband to escape to a hidden canyon and live again in peace.*

### [The Long Knives Come]

In the morning guards were set again at the head of the trail. Running Bird and I crawled to our places near the piñon tree and crouched there as the sun rose and shone down on the camp of the Long Knives. Other lookouts hid themselves along the rim of the mesa, among the rocks and brush.

Nothing had changed in the night. There were the same number of tents among the trees and the same number of horses tethered on the riverbank. Our hogans were deserted. No smoke rose from the ovens or the fire pits. There was no sound of sheep bells.

The camp of the Long Knives was quiet until the sun was halfway up the morning sky. Men strolled about as if they had nothing to do. Two were even fishing in the river with long willow poles. Then—while Running Bird and I watched a squirrel in the piñon tree, trying to coax him down with a nut—I saw from the corner of an eye a puff of smoke rise slowly from our village. It seemed no larger than my hand. A second puff rose in the windless air and a third.

"Our homes are burning!"

The word came from the lookout who was far out on the mesa rim, closest to the village. It

From *Sing Down the Moon* by Scott O'Dell. Copyright © 1970 by Scott O'Dell. Reprinted by permission of the publishers, Houghton Mifflin Company and Hamish Hamilton Children's Books Ltd.

was passed from one lookout to the other, at last to me, and I ran with it back to our camp and told the news to my father.

"We will build new homes," he said. "When the Long Knives leave we will go into the forest and cut timber. We will build hogans that are better than those the soldiers burned."

"Yes," people said when they heard the news, "we will build a new village."

Tall Boy said nothing. He sat working on his lance, using his teeth and one hand, and did not look up.

I went back to the piñon and my father went with me. All our homes had burned to the ground. Only gray ashes and a mound of earth marked the place where each had stood. The Long Knives were sitting under a tree eating, and their horses cropped the meadow grass.

My father said, "They will ride away now that they have destroyed our village."

But they did not ride away. While we watched, ten soldiers with hatchets went into our peach orchard, which still held its summer leaves. Their blades glinted in the sunlight. Their voices drifted up to us where we were huddled among the rocks.

Swinging the hatchets as they sang, the soldiers began to cut the limbs from the peach trees. The blows echoed through the canyon. They did not stop until every branch lay on the ground and only bare stumps, which looked like a line of scarecrows, were left.

Then, at the last, the Long Knives stripped all the bark from the stumps, so that we would not have this to eat when we were starving.

"Now they will go," my father said, "and leave us in peace."

But the soldiers laid their axes aside. They spurred their horses into a gallop and rode through the cornfield, trampling the green corn. Then they rode through the field of ripening beans and the melon patch, until the fields were no longer green but the color of the red earth.

"We will plant more melons and corn and beans," my father said.

"There are no seeds left," I said. "And if we had seeds and planted them they would not bear before next summer."

We watched while the soldiers rode back to their camp. We waited for them to fold their tents and leave. All that day and the next we watched from the rim of the mesa. On the third day the soldiers cut alder poles and made a large lean-to, which they roofed over with the branches. They also dug a fire pit and started to build an oven of mud and stones.

It was then we knew that the Long Knives did not plan to leave the canyon.

"They have learned that we are camped here," my father said. "They do not want to climb the cliff and attack us. It is easier to wait there by the river until we starve."

### [Into Captivity]

Clouds blew up next morning and it began to rain. We cut brush and limbs from the piñon pines and made shelters. That night, after the rain stopped, we went to the far side of the mesa where our fires could not be seen by the soldiers and cooked supper. Though there was little danger that the soldiers would attack us, my father set guards to watch the trail.

We were very careful with our jars of water, but on the sixth day the jars were empty. That night my father sent three of us down the trail to fill the jars at the river. We left soon after dark. There was no moon to see by so we were a long time getting to the river. When we started back up the trail we covered our tracks as carefully as we could. But the next day the soldiers found that we had been there. After that there were always two soldiers at the bottom of the trail, at night and during the day.

The water we carried back lasted longer than the first. When the jars were nearly empty it rained hard for two days and we caught water in our blankets and stored it. We also discovered a deep stone crevice filled with rainwater, enough for the rest of the summer. But the food we had brought with us, though we ate only half as much as we did when we were home in the village, ran low. We ate all of the corn and slaughtered the sheep we had brought. Then we ground up the sheep bones and made a broth, which was hard to swallow. We lived on this for two days and when it was gone we had nothing to eat.

Old Bear, who had been sick since we came to the mesa, died on the third day. And that night the baby of Shining Tree died. The next night was the first night of the full moon. It was then that my father said that we must leave.

Dawn was breaking high over the mesa when we reached the bottom of the trail. There was no sign of the soldiers.

My father led us northward through the trees, away from our old village and the soldiers' camp. It would have been wiser if we had traveled in the riverbed, but there were many who were so weak they could not walk against the current.

As soon as it grew light we found patches of wild berries among the trees and ate them while we walked. The berries were ripe and sweet and gave us strength. We walked until the sun was overhead then, because four of the women could go no farther, we stopped and rested in a cave.

We gathered more berries and some roots and stayed there until the moon came up. Then we started off again, following the river northward, traveling by the moon's white glow. When it swung westward and left the canyon in darkness we lay down among the trees. We had gone no more than two leagues in a day and part of a night, but we were hopeful that the soldiers would not follow us.

In the morning we built a small fire and roasted a basket of roots. Afterward the men held council to decide whether to go on or to stay where we were camped.

"They have burned our homes," my father said. "They have cut down the trees of our orchard. They have trampled our gardens into the earth. What else can the soldiers do to us that they have not already done?"

"The Long Knives can drive us out of the canyon," my uncle said, "and leave us to walk the wilderness."

At last it was decided that we stay.

We set about the cutting of brush and poles to make shelters. About mid-morning, while we were still working on the lean-tos, the sound of hoofs striking stone came from the direction of the river.

Taking up his lance, Tall Boy stepped behind a tree. The rest of us stood in silence. Even the children were silent. We were like animals who hear the hunter approach but from terror cannot flee.

The Long Knives came out of the trees in

single file. They were joking among themselves and at first did not see us. The leader was a young man with a red cloth knotted around his neck. He was looking back, talking to someone, as he came near the place where Tall Boy stood hidden.

Tall Boy stepped from behind the tree, squarely in his path. Still the leader did not see him.

Raising the lance, Tall Boy quickly took aim and drew back, ready to send it toward the leader of the Long Knives. He had practiced with the lance before we came down the mesa, time after time during all of one day, trying to get used to throwing it with his left hand. With his right hand he had been the best of all the warriors. It was with a lance that he had killed the brown bear beyond Rainbow Mountain, a feat of great skill.

But now, as the iron-tipped weapon sped from his grasp, it did not fly straight. It wobbled and then curved upward, struck the branch of a tree, and fell broken at the feet of the soldier's horse.

The horse suddenly stopped, tossing its head. Only then did the soldier turn to see the broken lance lying in front of him. He looked around, searching for the enemy who had thrown it. He looked at my father, at my uncle, at me. His eyes swept the small open space where we stood, the women, the children, the old people, all of us still too frightened to move or speak.

Tall Boy, as soon as he had thrown the lance, dodged behind the tree where he had hidden before, backed away into the brush and quietly disappeared. I saw his face as he went past me. He no longer looked like a warrior. He looked like a boy, crushed and beaten, who flees for his life.

The rest of the Long Knives rode up and surrounded us. They searched us one by one, making certain that no one carried a weapon, then they headed us down the canyon.

We passed the ruined fields of beans and corn and melons, the peach trees stripped of their bark and branches, our burned-out homes. We turned our eyes away from them and set our faces. Our tears were unshed.

Soon we were to learn that others bore the same fate, that the whole nation of the Navahos was on the march. With the Long Knives at their backs, the clans were moving—the Bitter-Water, Under-His-Cover, Red-House, Trail-to-the-Garden, Standing-House, Red-Forehead, Poles-Strung-Out—all the Navahos were marching into captivity.

## from SAMURAI OF GOLD HILL
*Yoshiko Uchida*

*This story of the small band of Japanese colonists who came to California in 1869, after a bitter war and the collapse of the Japanese feudal system, is based on historical fact. In "Gold Hill at Last," young Koichi and his father, a samurai, first arrive at the community where they hope to start new and peaceful lives. They start a farm they plan as a sanctuary for the feudal lord they have served and to whom they are still loyal, but they find the climate and the hostility of some of their neighbors are obstacles, even though they make some friends.*

### Gold Hill at Last
The room was big and bare, with two large brass beds and a marble-top washstand bearing a basin and pitcher. Koichi had somehow expected more of his first American room.

"I thought . . ." he began and then he stopped. He really didn't know what he thought it would be like. Perhaps he had expected silken screens painted with silver and gold, or lacquered tables inlaid with mother-of-pearl. He had been dreaming of the elegant rooms of the castle at Wakamatsu and thinking America would be even more rich and golden and beautiful.

Their room smelled of stale tobacco and the horses stabled next door.

"Come, Koichi-san, let us go out and inspect this city of the hills," Rintaro said in his loud cheerful voice. "Your father and Herr Schnell have already gone to see about buying supplies and shipping our trees and plants to Gold Hill."

Rintaro asked the other men if they would like to go along, but none of them did. "We will wait here for Herr Schnell," they said cautiously. "We will wait until later."

But Koichi and Rintaro couldn't wait to see the city. They strode out of the hotel together, Rintaro with a short sword thrust in his sash and Koichi with Grandfather's sword dangling at his side.

"Look straight ahead," Rintaro told Koichi. "Do not meet their stares and they will leave us alone."

They marched with their eyes straight ahead past a carriage shop and a warehouse heaped with tallow and hides. But Koichi could not keep looking ahead for long, for now they came to buildings of stone and granite, some of them three stories high, and there were banks and courthouses and theaters and shops on all sides. Koichi simply had to stop at the windows to gaze at the shawls and jewels and tortoise-shell combs for the ladies and the hats and shirts and collars for men.

The streets were full of people, all rushing about as though they were late for appointments. They all took time, however, to stare at the strange-looking pair. Even people in horse-drawn wagons and carriages leaned out to stare as though they couldn't quite believe their eyes.

Rintaro led Koichi up and down the cobbled streets, pausing now and then in front of a saloon where the sound of laughter and music came cascading out into the streets. He licked his lips, looked longingly at the doorway and then at Koichi and, with a sigh, continued to walk straight ahead.

"You can go in if you want to. I won't tell Father," Koichi said loyally.

But Rintaro shook his head. "No," he said. "Today I do no drinking. Besides," he added with a quick grin, "I have only coins of Japan, and here they would not even buy me an empty wine cup."

They walked up and down the streets of San Francisco until they were too hungry to go further. When they got back to their hotel, they discovered that Herr Schnell had ordered a dinner of boiled potatoes, corned beef and cab-

bage and coffee for them all.

"Ugh," Koichi groaned, as he drank the steaming black liquid. It was bitter and so hot, the tears came rushing to his eyes. And when he picked up the heavy fork and ate a mouthful of corned beef, he could almost hear his Grandmother scolding, *"Mah, mah,* my grandson, eating the meat of a cow!"

"Papa says the meat will make us grow big and strong," Toyoko said as she watched Koichi poking about at his meat.

But when Koichi looked around the table, he saw that all the others were having trouble swallowing their meat as well. Only Herr Schnell was chewing and swallowing busily as though it were a meal fit for Lord Matsudaira himself.

Early the next morning, they boarded another side-wheeler. This time it was a smaller ship called *The Sitka,* and it was to take them up the river to Sacramento.

"From Sacramento we will rent wagons to Placerville," Herr Schnell explained. "And from Placerville, we shall go on to our final destination, Gold Hill."

Koichi liked the name. It sounded as though the hillsides were laden with veins of gold, and even though Herr Schnell had told them the gold rush was over, perhaps he could find just a little gold that no one had discovered before.

The little *Sitka* crept slowly up the river, passing other riverboats and barges laden with wheat coming out from the valleys.

"How dry the countryside looks," Father said, for as far as they could see, the low curved hills, dotted with dark clumps of live oak, were the color of golden sand or ripened wheat.

"There has been no rain here," the farmers said anxiously. "The earth is as dry as a bleached bone."

"Strange that it should be so in the sixth month," Rintaro mused, for in Japan this was the time for the rainy season. Rain fell from dull leaden skies for weeks and weeks, until the land was like a soaking sponge. It was a dreary time of year, but the farmers were glad for the rain-filled paddies where the rice plants would thrive green and strong.

America was not only bigger and noisier, it seemed brighter and sharper, and Koichi felt as though he had come from a land of soft gray mist to a land of eternal harsh sun.

"What about the silkworm eggs?" he asked. "Since it is so warm, won't they hatch and die before we can feed them?"

"I have been thinking of them too," Father said, "but there is nothing we can do. I don't even know if they are on this same ship with us."

"How much farther?" Koichi asked Herr Schnell.

"Not far now," he answered reassuringly, but it was almost dusk when they reached Sacramento, and it was not until early the next morning that Herr Schnell rented three wagons for the ride to Placerville almost fifty miles away.

The crack of the driver's whip sent the horses dashing down the dusty Green Valley road. It was a long bumpy ride, for the road was worn with ruts made by the hundreds of wagons and coaches that had traveled over it during the rush for silver and gold, and by the thundering horses of the pony express.

The horses kicked up a fine spray of red dust, and only Herr Schnell seemed to have the inclination to talk with the driver of the wagon, who was happy to have someone listen to his memories of how it had been during the busy gold rush years. He told of the days when there had been so many wagons moving down the road that if one pulled off the road in the morning, it couldn't get back in line until late at night. He pointed out each village they passed, the old pony express stops and the first farm that owned a mechanical plow.

They moved on, passing clumps of willow and poplar and buckeye and, once in a while, tall pines quite unlike the gnarled trees that stood near the temple at Wakamatsu. Sometimes a rabbit or squirrel would skitter across the road, or a deer would bound away into the woods at the sound of the horses, and once, Koichi saw a large brown bear lumbering slowly into the thickets.

The wagons rumbled on through the heat of the day and came at last to a busy town where they stopped in front of an old two-storied hotel.

"Well, here we are in Placerville," Herr Schnell called out.

Koichi knew it was a fairly big city, for the driver had told them there were over eight good mountain roads running in all directions from it, and on the main street, he had seen banks and newspaper offices and even a telegraph company.

They climbed wearily from the wagons, covered with dust. Mrs. Schnell coughed and fanned herself with a small folding fan. Her beautiful silk kimono was full of wrinkles and her hair grayed with dust.

"Mama, I ache all over," Toyoko groaned.

Koichi felt exactly the same.

"Wait here," Herr Schnell instructed the dreary group. "I must find new wagons to take us to Gold Hill." And he went off down the dusty street.

The terrible searing heat of the afternoon felt like the breath of an angry dragon.

"A nice long soak in a tub would feel good right now," Rintaro sighed, stretching his aching legs.

"And a bowl of rice and pickles," Koichi added.

"I'd rather have a sweet bean-paste cake," Toyoko said.

But Okei was not thinking of food or hot baths. "See how they all stare at us," she murmured. "I do not like the look in their eyes."

"I do not either," Toyoko's mother said, and she drew her child closer to her.

Everyone who went by stopped to stare at them, and one man even spat in the dust at their feet.

"Why do they hate us?" Koichi asked. "What have we done?"

"It is just that they don't know us, that is why they dislike us," Father explained. "When we have built our fine tea and silk farm it will be different. You'll see." Father tried to sound cheerful, but his face was drawn and creased with lines of weariness.

When Herr Schnell came back at last, he had only one wagon and he looked glum. "No one will rent wagons to us," he said darkly.

"Why?" they all wondered.

"Because we are Japanese."

"Ah. And that is bad?"

"They do not know us, so they do not trust us. It is always bad to be different. I was once different too, in your country." Herr Schnell looked tired and discouraged and Koichi suddenly felt sorry for him.

Koichi looked down on the ground because he didn't know what to say. Presently, he noticed an enormous pair of boots beside him. He looked up at the face that belonged to the boots and saw a tall fair-haired man wearing the working clothes of a farmer. His nose was sprinkled with freckles and his eyes were a friendly blue. He wiped his forehead with a big handkerchief and asked, "Say, ain't you the folks from Japan who're coming up to the Graner place in Gold Hill?"

"We are. We are," Herr Schnell answered eagerly.

"Heard you was coming," the man said. "My name's Thomas Whitlow. I'm ranching close by the Graner place." He held out an enormous hand which Herr Schnell shook vigorously.

"We're in need of two more wagons," Herr Schnell explained.

"I can take some of you," Thomas Whitlow offered. "We could do it in two wagons if you folks don't mind squeezing in some."

The gods had sent this kind man just in time, for now the sun was dropping in the sky and the air was growing dusky.

The road to Gold Hill was as bumpy as the Green Valley road, but now the horses jogged along gently for there weren't many miles to go. They passed small villages and farms and dozens of orchards filled with trees bearing apples and plums and peaches and almonds. And on the hillsides were vineyards climbing as high as the water could go.

As they bumped along, Koichi's head dropped to his chest, and the rumbling wagon lulled him to an exhausted sleep. The shadowy trees moved by like silent ghosts and the sounds of the buzzing cicadas began to fill the air.

Koichi dreamed he was in Japan, riding to a great battle to win back the castle. The battle was almost won and Koichi was waving the Matsudaira banner in the air when the wagon pulled off the road and came to a stop.

"Here we are," Mr. Whitlow's voice sang out in the warm darkness. "This here's the Graner place."

They had finally come to the end of their journey. This was the Graner house and this was Gold Hill. The Wakamatsu Colony of Japan had arrived at last.

## from PETROS' WAR

*Alki Zei*

*Ten-year-old Petros had been filled with elation and pride in October, watching the Greek soldiers march out of Athens. Surely they would quickly defeat the Italians. Here, with the German enemy within the gates, the weary remnants of the Greek forces return, and Petros learns what war is really like. What Alki Zei achieves, in addition to telling an exciting tale of the Underground work in which Petros participates, is to show the truth of the Roman comment, ". . . the enemy with hatred in its eyes is the most powerful."*

### Within the Gates

A tiny ray of light crept between the bars of the shutters and rested on Petros' bed; then it traveled on to caress Theodore's domed shell. Petros had brought the tortoise up to his room the night before because everyone said that at any moment now the Germans would be entering Athens. It was not that Theodore was in any special danger; Petros just wanted him for company. The odd thing was that Antigone made no objection when Petros suggested it.

Petros opened his eyes and watched the dust motes stirring in the rays of sunlight. It was Sunday. But with the war on, one day was no longer any different from another. Sunday, Monday, Tuesday: they were all the same, workday or holiday. That, Petros reflected, was one good thing about going to school. With school, Sunday was special, something you waited for eagerly. Now, if it weren't for the calendar in their room, with Sunday marked on it in red, you'd never even notice when it arrived. Every morning, whoever woke up first could tear off the page with the date and read the verse or the proverb that was printed on the back of it. He glanced over at Antigone's bed. She wasn't there. She must be up. Petros hastened to tear off the page before she could get back to the room and do it.

Sunday
27
April
1941

The proverb for today was a funny one: "Either the compass is out of order or else the boat is going in the wrong direction."

He was one up on Antigone, he thought, and hid the bit of paper in a book.

Theodore was wandering about the room, bumping his shell against the furniture. Petros stretched his arms, yawned, and gave the bedclothes a kick. Then he had an inspiration.

He leapt out of bed, searched furiously among Antigone's paints, found a tube of red paint, grabbed Theodore, who was trying vainly to squeeze under the chest of drawers, and, with a brush, he wrote on Theodore's shell: *April 27, 1941*. Then he set the tortoise down on the floor. It was a great idea to have a living calendar roaming around the room! It might even amuse Antigone so much that she wouldn't make him take Theodore back down to the cellar. . . . What had happened to make his sister get up so early?

From the dining room came the sound of the radio. They were playing the national anthem at full blast.

"Grandfather," a voice called, "turn it down! You'll have the whole neighborhood on its feet." Petros heard the rush of footsteps. He turned and saw Mama and Antigone standing in the doorway. Antigone had her hair pulled back, and it was tied with a black ribbon. Where, Petros wondered, was the cauliflower coiffure like Deanna Durbin's this morning? He started to say something, but Mama's frightened voice broke in.

"Can you hear it?"

Antigone ran to the window and listened.

"It sounds like the tanks," she whispered.

"The Germans are coming!" Petros cried. And he too ran toward the window. He started to fling open the shutters.

"No!" his mother cried. "Leave them closed!"

They pressed together and peered through the bars. The streets were deserted. All the shutters in all the houses were closed. Except that you knew that behind those shutters other eyes were staring out.

". . . When the victorious Marcus Claudius Marcellus entered the city, he found the houses barred and the streets deserted. There was not even a single dog, or a cat, not a living soul. . . . He was aware only of thousands of eyes watching them from behind the pierced shutters. And then Marcus Claudius Marcellus understood that the enemy without arms, the enemy with hatred in its eyes, is the most powerful. . . ."

Petros remembered reading that, in some book at school, in history class. And for a moment, he felt as though he were in ancient Syracuse when the conquering Romans took over the city.

Everyone in the house was silent. You'd think the enemy was hidden in every corner, watching. His father took down the map with the little flags and tore it into pieces. The radio went silent: it was as though it too refused to surrender. With no one daring to utter a word, it was like having an invalid in the house. He remembered how, just before Sotiris' grandfather died, everyone had gone about on tiptoe. Sotiris had walked in stocking feet.

There was a sudden sound of rapping.

Everyone started.

It was Theodore, who had reached the door.

"Look at that!" exclaimed Antigone, pointing at Theodore's shell. Then she said that tortoises are supposed to live for a hundred years; and so everyone would recall, a century later, that it was on that day the Germans entered Athens.

For the first three days no one left the house. Petros went back and forth between their apartment and Sotiris', where the two boys stayed in a tiny room that just barely held Sotiris' bed. They climbed up on it and peered between the bars of the shutters at the German soldiers in the street, with their green uniforms, their shaved heads, and their blank eyes.

On the morning of the second day Petros and Sotiris climbed secretly out onto the balcony, by way of the spiral iron service staircase. The house was on a small rise; from the balcony they could see the whole city, as far as the Acropolis.

"Look!" Sotiris cried. "What's happening to the flag?"

The wind was blowing. The flag that hung from a thin pole at the eastern end of the Acropolis seemed no larger than a dot. The wind blew stronger, and suddenly the flag was blown out so that the whole of it could be seen.

"Holy Mother of God!" Sotoris exclaimed.

Instead of the white and sky-blue emblem of Greece spread out on the wind, the flag they beheld was red with an enormous black swastika, like the claws of an angry bird of prey, in its center.

They stared out at it, their hearts strange and heavy in their chests. Then they crept down from the balcony on tiptoe so as not to be seen.

During those days the grown-ups all went about with swollen eyes. No one dared mention Uncle Angelos' name because then Grandfather's hands started to tremble and he looked a hundred years old. Sotiris' father had not come back from the front either.

And Antigone had begun to write poetry. She sat on her bed with a notebook on her knees, a big notebook with a cherry-colored cover. Of course she never showed Petros what she was writing. But once in a while she would ask him a question.

"Tell me a word that rhymes with 'conquered.'"

Petros couldn't think of one. The only words that came to his mind didn't rhyme, like "barley" and "lentils." They were eating lentils for the third day. Every time she reheated them, Mama added more water; and they kept getting more and more tasteless. No one had any appetite at meals and yet Petros was always hungry. He was ashamed that nothing seemed to stem his appetite; not even the stamping of German boots on the sidewalk outside, under the windows.

The evening when he and Sotiris saw a German car come to a halt outside their door, they held their breaths. Their eyes nearly popping out of their heads, they watched while a husky German soldier jumped out, held open the rear door of the car, and stood there like a ramrod.

Out of the car stepped Mrs. Leventi's daughter Lela, her hair bleached yellow as straw; and another German, an officer with pale blond hair. The chauffeur followed them into the house, carrying a huge cardboard carton that looked just like the ones that Michael, Lela's English fiancé, used to bring.

Petros left Sotiris there and ran off to tell the news to Antigone. As he pelted down the stairs he heard the sound of footsteps coming up. He bent over the railing to see who was coming. A Greek soldier in a ragged uniform with a rough stubble of beard on his face waved a grimy hand at him. The soldier's eyes were bloodshot. Petros felt a shiver of fear. He started running back up the stairs to Sotiris'.

"Petraki!"

He turned. Then he leaped into the arms of the ragged, dirty soldier.

The soldier pushed him away.

"Don't," he said. "You'll only catch my lice."

The glittering medals, the shiny boots, the white horse, the sword flashing like lightning, the victories and the valorous deeds of heroism that Petros had awaited with the return of his uncle, all swept across his mind and vanished.

"Well," Angelos asked in a weary voice, "aren't you glad to see me?"

Then Petros noticed that one of his uncle's feet was bandaged in filthy rags. With a single bound he reached the door of their apartment and banged at it with his fists.

"Open the door!" he shouted. "Open up! Uncle Angelos has come home!"

A man with hollow, freshly shaven cheeks and red sunken eyes sat on Grandfather's couch. He was wearing Papa's pajamas. They seemed much too big for him. One stockingless foot was stuffed into a green slipper of Mama's (Papa was wearing his and there wasn't another pair in the house) with his heel sticking out of it. The other foot was bare, the big toe bandaged in clean gauze.

What could Petros say now to Sotiris, who was waiting impatiently to hear all about Uncle Angelos' valiant deeds at the front? How could he tell Sotiris that all Angelos could talk about were the woolen stockings and sweaters that never reached the front lines, the shoes into which the water leaked, and the chilblains? Angelos didn't say, "The bullets slaughtered us." What he said was, "It was the frostbite that knocked us out." How could Petros admit that Angelos had made his way home covered with lice, his boots in shreds, going from village to village begging for bread? And in those villages, others had been there before him. The villages had been stripped bare of food—or else the villagers were hiding what was left. Could he tell Sotiris that Angelos had swapped Rita's gold locket for half a loaf of stale bread?

"All the same," Petros said stubbornly, "we beat the Italians!"

"That's all over now," Uncle Angelos said in a tired voice. Then he asked if he could go into the bedroom now and lie down, because he hadn't slept for days.

Petros would tell Sotiris that Angelos hadn't told them any of his feats of war because he had been too tired. Or he'd make up something himself: how his uncle had returned on a horse —fortunately Sotiris hadn't seen him when he arrived—and described to them how he had whirled his sword around his head and the Italians had fled like rabbits.

But there was no need to lie to Sotiris. The next day when they went outdoors the streets were full of ragged soldiers begging for old clothes or a little food. But Sotiris' father never came back, not even in rags or crippled.

"What are we going to say to Rita?" Antigone asked Petros when they were getting ready for bed and she was tying up her hair in curling rags.

"About her locket?" Petros asked.

"No. About his not coming home a hero."

"If he had been wounded in battle, that wouldn't be so bad," Petros reflected. "But to get frostbite!"

They turned off the light. But before they fell asleep, they jumped up. From Mama's bedroom they could hear a hoarse wild voice: "The machine gun—get the machine gun! It's to the right!" And then came Mama's soothing voice: "Calm yourself, Angelos."

"He did fight, all the same," Antigone whispered happily.

"He's having nightmares about the battle," Petros rejoined enthusiastically.

After that they both fell into a deep, peaceful sleep, and they didn't hear Uncle Angelos shout, "Don't! Don't beat him! He's a prisoner!"

Imaginative as children are, there are times when they, like adults, prefer to turn to fact. Facts are the essence of biography, giving the truth of history with more drama than it is possible to convey in most other nonfiction. Biographies tell of real people and real events and so may stir emulation; in depicting the difficulties and achievements of others, children may get a clearer picture of their own problems and goals —or lack of goals. Because of their reality, biographies can help clarify and focus youthful ambitions.

Furthermore, biographies can recreate a period or crisis for young readers as straight historical accounts can rarely do. If children have discovered the charm of Washington's early peaceful and luxurious life, the great parties at the mansions, the pleasant visiting back and forth between the big plantations, they sense at once the sacrifice it must have been for him to give up this life and line up with the ragged colonists in their hazardous rebellion against tyranny. And the bloody massacres are seen in a new light when a young reader follows Crazy Horse through the hard discipline of his childhood to his mature decision to save the land for his

# BIOGRAPHY

people. It is the concrete episodes and the individual human beings that bring the past to life for children.

The best biographies are the result of a combination of factors. Authors do depth research; they carefully select their audiences; and they adjust their styles of writing to insure the utmost clarity for the proposed audience. Most of all, somewhere along the way, they have become so excited about their subjects that they are able to convey to their readers their own enthusiasm.

The qualities essential to sound biography for adults are equally important in good biographies for children and young people. For both, biography must be authentic—that is, the story should be true to place, period, and people—and observe historical truth, but in juvenile biographies conversations may legitimately be manufactured and episodes may be dramatized which are not in the record but are merely based on the implications of the record. It is known that Admiral Penn bitterly opposed his son William's conversion to the Quaker way of life, and so in her biography of Penn, Elizabeth Janet Gray has created a scene of great dramatic intensity between father and son—a scene in which the talk, though imaginary, is true to the spirit of the historical record and to the nature and relationship of father and son. The trial scene which has been chosen for this book is handled in the same way. So, in these fictionalized biographies we are permitted to know the thoughts, motives, and conversations of the heroes and heroines, although these are not to be found in the historical record.

The worth of fictionalized biography depends upon the honesty of the author in utilizing verifiable historical facts and in his or her ability to write imaginary scenes and dialogue in the spirit of the times and the characters involved.

Good adult biography tries to give its readers the whole person, with faults, weaknesses, and failures and the ability to conquer or rise above them to greatness. This practice is not as true of juvenile biographies as it should be. The biographies of musicians in the series by Opal Wheeler and Sybil Deucher follow a pleasant pattern—the child musician displays the qualities that are to make him notable as a man, there are a few childish pranks or mistakes which are amusing but not serious, and life flows along with a series of successes and never a hint of the grueling struggle and toil or the handicaps and tragedies. It is too neat a pattern; life does not move like that as some of the better biographies for children make clear. To be sure, the Wheeler-Deucher biographies are for children of nine or thereabouts, and most of them are as delightful as they are popular. But even at that level, life should not look too easy and too smooth. Carl Sandburg in his *Abe Lincoln Grows Up,* for children of eleven years old and older, gives the sorrows, the privations, and the limitations of Lincoln's early years. His was not a normal, joy-ous childhood but quite the reverse.

Some authors of juvenile biographies disregard the childhood of their heroes and heroines, and boldly present the person. In MacKinlay Kantor's *Lee and Grant at Appomattox,* for example, children read about the failures and the drinking which clouded General Grant's early manhood. These, in contrast to Lee's honor and nobility, actually increase the reader's respect for Grant's achievements later and for the generous and noble heights to which he rose in the hour of the surrender.

A good biography shows its subject to be a multi-faceted person; not all good or all bad. A person of any substance is disliked as well as admired, argues with other great people of his or her time about issues, and is sometimes wrong. A good book is able to portray people's weaknesses and mistakes without lessening their importance to history. Early biographies of George Washington made him a stereotype for honesty and courage. More recent books present him as a backwoods boy who rose to greatness in spite of his limitations. To try to minimize or omit the tragedies of George Washington Carver's early days is to falsify the record, but the shadows over his childhood point up the brilliance of his later achievements.

This brings up the point of the author's selectivity in choice of details and emphasis. We would not like to see juvenile biography descend to the level of many "popular" adult biographies in which the subject's every indiscretion is dwelt upon. On the other hand, we do not wish to see important causal factors suppressed because they pose problems of presentation. The author has an obligation to determine when an event was of real importance to the character's subsequent behavior and achievements and when it would be interesting (to adults) but irrelevant.

Learning to recognize that elusive quality known as style is an important step in evaluating biographies. It is style that makes for writing greatness, for there are untold hundreds of books that are factually accurate without achieving the status of literature.

The best biographies are distinguished literature as truly as are great novels, poems, or short stories. And the style of writing, the author's choice and arrangement of words, is as important as the events recorded. No matter how accurate the facts, an author cannot produce a good book if he or she uses sweet, flowery prose to tell of vigorous frontiersmen like Boone or about the adventures of Lewis and Clark. On the other hand, Edna St. Vincent Millay's biography would quite properly be written in a poetic style; Emily Dickinson's in an introspective one. An inappropriate style may suggest to readers that the author never quite came to understand the essence of the person he or she was writing about.

Many juvenile biographies give rich details of life in other days which help children to relive the past and feel close kinship with their heroes and heroines. These lives of great people are unusually well written on the whole, with a sense of pattern and style in the narrative and of unity in the life described. Publishers are selecting eminent writers to produce the new biography, and this has resulted in a decided swing away from the all-sweetness-and-light school of writing to a sensible and truthful realism. Indeed historical facts are so competently and conscientiously handled that the popularity of these juvenile biographies is something to be thankful for and to be encouraged.

## *from* THE SEVEN QUEENS OF ENGLAND

### Geoffrey Trease

*In both the biographies and the historical fiction he has written, Geoffrey Trease has demonstrated a distinctive ability to bring history to life, to invest his stories with a sense of excitement. In the book from which this selection is taken, he presents brief biographical sketches that dramatically describe the seven women who have ruled England. In the story of Maud (1102–1167), that strong-willed mother of Henry II, he draws a fascinating picture of the complexities of court intrigue that is historically accurate yet enthusiastic in admiration of it and of her.*

Reprinted by permission of the publisher, Vanguard Press, Inc., from *Seven Queens of England* by Geoffrey Trease. Copyright, 1953 by Geoffrey Trease

## Maud, Mother of the Plantagenets

Young widows, in those days, could do one of two things: marry again or become nuns. Only seldom were they able to keep their independence.

Maud obviously could not disappear into a convent, so, very soon, King Henry arranged for her to marry Geoffrey Plantagenet, whose father was Count of Anjou, a small area of France bordering Brittany. This time, the bridegroom was ten years younger than the bride. Geoffrey was barely sixteen. He was a good-looking boy, nicknamed "the Handsome," but inclined to be self-willed and conceited. This conceit was made worse a year later when his father went off to seek his fortune in Palestine (where he remained as King of Jerusalem) and the boy found himself Count of Anjou.

It was not likely that a strong-minded young woman like Maud, who had worn the crown of an empress, was going to submit meekly to a boy-husband, and the marriage was rather a stormy affair, with quarrels and separations. But these were patched up, and in 1133 a son was born to them at Le Mans who was destined to become Henry II, one of England's strongest kings, and to establish the royal line of the Plantagenets. Maud shed tears of happiness at his christening. It was the only time in her life, say the historians, that she was seen to weep.

Other children followed quickly: Geoffrey in 1134 and William in 1136. Unfortunately, these otherwise happy events could hardly have come at a worse time from the political point of view. King Henry died suddenly on December 1, 1135. Maud should have ridden posthaste to Normandy, crossed to England by the swiftest ship available, and had herself proclaimed Queen of England. Her babies and her own health (she had been seriously ill the previous year) made this impossible.

Stephen of Blois saw his chance and took it. He hurried to London, where he was popular with the citizens, and thence to Winchester, the old capital, where he seized the royal treasure and the late King's crown. Two days before Christmas, that crown was placed on his head in Westminster Abbey, and his supporters were hailing him as King.

It was a long time before Maud could counter these rapid moves. Her hands were tied. She appealed to the Pope: the result was vague, but unfavorable to her as far as it went. Her uncle, King David of Scotland, invaded the North of England to support her claim. He was bought off the first time, and, on his second appearance, crushingly defeated at the Battle of the Standards, at Northallerton, by Stephen's supporter, the fighting Archbishop of York. In Normandy —the other part of the disputed inheritance— Stephen fought a campaign against Maud's husband. The only effect of this was to make both the rivals equally unpopular with the people they claimed as subjects. It was not until nearly four years after King Henry's death, when Stephen had squandered most of the royal treasure, quarreled with his leading supporters in the Church and the government, and reduced his own affairs to confusion, that Maud's long-delayed opportunity arrived. Inspired by her half brother, Robert, Earl of Gloucester, the West of England flared into revolt against the usurper, and in October, 1139, Maud herself landed at Portsmouth with a small force of a hundred and forty knights.

For some reason, hard to understand now, she did not make straight for the West Country where her support lay. Instead, she rode to the great castle of Arundel, in Sussex, where her stepmother (now herself remarried) gave her a friendly welcome. This visit was nearly fatal to Maud's chances. Suddenly Stephen, who had been besieging Corfe Castle in Dorset, appeared with his army beneath the walls of Arundel.

Arundel Castle might well have withstood a siege. But would the garrison, apart from Maud's own knights, resist? Adelicia's new husband, d'Albini, had no wish to quarrel with Stephen. The outlook for Maud was black. Stephen could have made her prisoner and either held her or deported her across the Channel, where, he considered, she belonged.

Stephen's easygoing character saved her. He was a kindly man, generous and chivalrous, but he had no foresight, no intellectual grasp, no ability to distinguish good advice from bad. In this present situation it was against his knightly instincts to make war on women; and at the same time (in contradiction of these instincts)

he listened to the foolish argument that, if he left Maud free to gather her supporters in the West, he would be better able to smash them at a single blow.

So Maud rode forth from Arundel with all honor, with Stephen's safe-conduct and his own brother to escort her, and went to Bristol, the chief stronghold of her party.

There is no point in chronicling the detailed ebb and flow of the long civil war which devastated England for the next few years. Neither claimant could win over a really overwhelming majority of supporters. Stephen was liked, but he did not inspire people. He excelled in personal contacts and was, if anything, too familiar. He was fairly described as "no king, only the first and best of the barons." Maud, on the other hand, offended Englishmen by being too cold and distant, in the German manner which had been forced upon her as a child. With this was joined the hardness and pride of her Norman ancestry and the traditional obstinacy of the Saxon. She had the courage and enterprise of a man. Perhaps if her more feminine qualities had not been so thwarted when she was young, she might have won more support in England.

However, she made a good beginning.

Setting up her capital in Bristol, she quickly restored order in the territory she controlled. This was a period when local barons—seeing the breakdown of national government—became a law to themselves and turned their castles into robber-strongholds. As the *Anglo-Saxon Chronicle* records in a famous passage:

> "When the castles were made they filled them with devils and evil men. Then they took those men whom they deemed to have any possessions, husbandmen and women, and put them in prison for gold and silver and tortured them with unspeakable torture. They put them in dungeons in which there were adders and snakes and toads. . . . They robbed and burned all the towns, so thou mightest well go all a day's journey and thou wouldest never find a man settled in a town, nor the land tilled . . . ."

But at least the area directly controlled by Maud was well governed.

In the course of the next year or two, support for her spread through other parts of the country. Two of her followers seized Lincoln Castle by a trick. Stephen marched to Lincoln, and was there met by Maud's growing army, under the Earl of Gloucester. This included a strong force of Welsh infantry and a body of picked shock troops, known as "the Disinherited" because they had all lost their lands by supporting Maud and had everything to gain by her victory.

Stephen's chief supporters ran away. Stephen, who was certainly no coward, was left dismounted, defending himself with a Danish battle-ax he had snatched up. Seeing matters were hopeless, he surrendered. Maud hurried to Winchester, received the crown, and proclaimed herself Queen.

At this critical moment, Maud's pride was her undoing. Her rival was safely imprisoned in her own stronghold at Bristol, but his very able wife still had an unbeaten army in Kent. London, as always, favored Stephen. There were countless people to be handled tactfully and won over to her side—churchmen and barons and the citizens of her capital—before Maud could be formally crowned at Westminster.

She never was. For some mysterious reason which can never now be understood—unless it was the state of her health at the time, affecting her moods and behavior, and the natural reaction after so many years of waiting—Maud's common sense seemed to desert her during those few vital months. She had shown herself a wise and patient woman before; she was a wise and patient woman afterward; but just then, on the eve of her coronation, she managed to offend all the people whose help she most needed.

Worst of all, she talked to the free and independent Londoners as though she were still the Holy Roman Empress. Their answer was revolt. As she sat down to dinner in the Palace of Westminster on Midsummer Day, feeling perfectly secure, she was astounded to learn that London had risen and that Stephen's wife was leading an army through the gates.

There was just time to mount a horse and escape. Maud and her party rode hell-for-leather to Oxford, sixty miles away. She held one ace in her hand: Stephen himself, still captive at Bristol. Otherwise, the civil war must be fought

and won again.

It was fought, but it was never won. Maud led her army with the courage and energy of her grandfather, William the Conqueror. She surprised the old castle at Winchester, laid siege to the new one, and was herself besieged. When supplies ran short, she resolved to make a dash for it. She rode out early one morning, to be followed later by her half brother. As the country was alive with enemy troops, the two parties went by different routes. The Earl was the unlucky one: he was attacked as he was crossing the little Hampshire river, Test, and taken prisoner. Pausing at Ludgershall for him to overtake her, Maud realized that something had gone wrong and that she herself was in mortal danger. She remounted and galloped for Devizes, thirty miles away. She arrived there exhausted, unable to keep in the saddle any longer. But it would have been folly to rest, with Stephen's followers scouring the countryside for her, and her iron will forced her on. She had herself strapped in a litter between two horses and carried to Gloucester with all speed. There, in her loyal West Country, she would be safe.

It was not the last of her dramatic escapes. The capture of her half brother forced her, after some hard bargaining, to release Stephen in exchange. In the autumn of 1142, Stephen besieged her in Oxford Castle, and this resulted in the most famous episode of her life.

Again the garrison's supplies were running short, and again Maud decided to make a dash for it, knowing that the main object of the siege was to capture her. Even the gentlemanly Stephen had got over his reluctance to make war on a lady, if that lady was his cousin Maud.

This time conditions were very different. Christmas was near, and the weather was unusually bitter. Not only was the foggy Thames valley deep in snow, but the river itself was covered with thick ice, which seldom happens more than once in ten or twenty winters.

Dressed all in white, with three knights similarly camouflaged, Maud was let down by ropes from the ramparts. Stephen's men held the town to the east of the fortress, but the way was clear to the riverbank. The four ghostly figures passed noiselessly and unchallenged through the silvery gloom. The ice held. The

Thames wound dimly in front of them between its low hills, offering them a highway to safety. The snow formed a thick carpet even over the ice, but at least the going was easier than through the deep drifts on land. Seven or eight miles of hard trudging through the night brought them to the great abbey of Abingdon, where they got horses to continue their journey to Wallingford.

So, with sieges and escapes, marchings and countermarchings, the civil war went on its weary way. England was in a state of anarchy. Maud controlled some areas and Stephen others, but whole regions took little notice of either. Lords changed sides as suited them, and might was right. Neither of the royal rivals could ever muster sufficient strength to crush the other.

As Maud never recaptured London, her coronation at Westminster never took place, but this fact cannot, by itself, weaken her claim to be the lawful sovereign during those years. Sometimes she styled herself *Anglorum regina*, "Queen of the English," but more often, *Anglorum domina*, "Lady of the English." But whatever form of words she used, she left no doubt in anyone's mind that she considered herself the rightful ruler of both England and Normandy, where her husband kept up a warfare parallel with her own against Stephen's Norman supporters. Maud's early training by the German archbishop had given her a clear vision of political power. She always knew that the real thing was something much more than words and titles.

She showed this when, in 1153, the two sides had fought themselves to a standstill. Her faithful half brother had died of fever and her other chief allies were dead. Stephen, on the other hand, had lost his son and heir, and it may be that Maud guessed that her rival himself had not long to live. At all events, she agreed to make peace by the Treaty of Wallingford. She resigned the crown to Stephen while he lived. On his death, it was to come to her eldest son, Henry, now a forceful young knight of twenty.

So it came about. Stephen died in the following year, and on the nineteenth of December, in Westminster Abbey, the crown was placed upon the close-cropped, reddish head of Henry II, first of the Plantagenet kings who were to rule England until the end of the Middle Ages.

Maud had no reason to feel that her long struggle had been in vain. In giving up the crown for a little while, she had made it safe for her son and her son's sons.

Nor, though she now withdrew into the background, did she relax her energies. She was a help to Henry throughout the first ten years of his reign, and undoubtedly it was her wisdom and experience which saved him from worse mistakes than he did make and enabled him to become one of the greatest medieval kings. He, passionate and strong-willed though he was, listened to his mother when he would listen to no one else. The martyr Becket might never have been murdered had Maud lived longer.

She died in 1167, at Rouen, in Normandy. In her last years, as befitted an elderly lady in those days, she busied herself with good works. She had always been generous to churches and monasteries; now she was even more active, building and endowing. She gave Rouen a magnificent new stone bridge, crossing the Seine by thirteen arches. But such charities were not enough to absorb the tireless energies of one who had been both queen and empress, and she spent her last months, bedridden and feeble though she was, collecting military intelligence in the war against King Louis of France. Her chief agent was the Prior of St. Barbara's, near Lisieux, who collected information about French troop movements from a network of his own spies, and passed it to Maud for transmission to her son. The regular go-between was a monk, and the actual papers were hidden in his luxuriant beard.

So Maud died, a fighter to the end, and was buried as she had always meant to be, in the abbey church of Bec, in Normandy. Nearly four centuries passed before another woman tried to govern England.

### from PENN

*Elizabeth Janet Gray*

*England's illustrious admiral, Sir William Penn, was bitterly disappointed when his son William (1644–1718) became a convert to the Quaker way of worship and life. During the sev-*

*enteenth century, England was not a country to tolerate religious differences, and young William's Quaker faith kept him from attaining any favors from the court. Father and son quarreled bitterly over the issue, although they had a deep affection for each other. Then, William was cast into prison and brought to trial for conducting a Quaker meeting "to the great disturbance of his [the king's] peace." Even though the jury acquitted him, Penn's future was bleak in England, so he journeyed to the New World where his personal integrity and high ideals led to the successful establishment of Pennsylvania, a proprietary colony.*

### The Trial

On Thursday the first of September 1670, a sergeant and his yeomen came early in the morning to escort Penn and Mead out of Newgate and down the street called the Old Bailey to the Sessions House, where the court sat at seven. It was a "fair and stately building," with large galleries for spectators.

There were ten justices on the bench. Several of them young William Penn already knew. Sir Samuel Starling was Chief Justice. The Admiral's "buffle-headed" old friend, Sir John Robinson, the Lord Lieutenant of the Tower, was another—and good reason William had for remembering him! A third, Sir Richard Brown, had been particularly brutal in his raids on the Friends' meeting-houses a few years ago, and two more were well known as zealous churchmen and persecutors of Non-Conformists. Altogether they were about as arrogant, puffing, choleric, muddleheaded, prejudiced a lot of judges as one could find anywhere.

The jury was sworn in, twelve slow-witted, plain citizens, with good plain English names, John and James and William and Henry. There was an Edward Bushell, and Thomas Veer was foreman.

The prisoners were brought before the bar, and the indictment read. It was an astonishing piece of writing: a single sentence of two hundred and fifty words looped and bunched to-

From *Penn* by Elizabeth Janet Gray. Copyright 1938 by Elizabeth Janet Gray, © 1966 by Elizabeth Gray Vining. Reprinted by permission of The Viking Press, Inc.

gether in alternately legal and hysterical phrases. The gist of it was that "William Penn, gent., and William Mead, linen-draper, the fifteenth day of August, with force and arms unlawfully and tumultuously did assemble, and the aforesaid William Penn by agreement between him and William Mead before made, then and there in the open street did take upon himself to preach and speak, by reason whereof a great concourse and tumult of people in the street, a long time did remain and continue in contempt of the Lord the King and of his law, to the great disturbance of his peace and to the great terror of many of his liege subjects."

The Clerk then asked: "What say you, William Penn and William Mead? Are you guilty as you stand indicted, or not guilty?"

They pleaded "Not guilty," and the court was adjourned till afternoon.

While they were waiting, they discussed the errors in the indictment. To begin with, the date was wrong; the day of the meeting was Sunday the fourteenth of August, not the fifteenth. In the second place, they did not meet with force and arms. Nobody had arms except the soldiers. Nobody used force except the soldiers. Then, since they had never seen each other before, they obviously could not have met by agreement before made. And finally, they did not remain and continue in contempt of the King and his law, for the chief officer who came to take them had allowed the meeting to go on after Mead promised that Penn would go with them at the end of it.

In the afternoon they were brought back to the Sessions House, but instead of going on with their trial, the court, "both to affront and to tire them," kept them waiting there for five long hours while trials of felons and murderers were held, and at the end of the time adjourned.

September second they cooled their heels in Newgate.

September third was a Saturday. The sergeant and his yeomen came for them again before seven. Just as they went into the courtroom one of the officers, on a kindly impulse, took off their hats for them. Sir Samuel Starling was quick to see.

"Sirrah," he thundered, "who bid you put their hats off? Put them on again."

So, hats on, they stood before the bar. Ten judges in wigs and robes sat in a portentous row upon the bench and looked down with hostile eyes, while the chief among them proceeded solemnly to fine the prisoners forty marks apiece for wearing their hats in court.

It was childish; it was contemptible. William Penn, who was twenty-five, looked straight into all those hard and prejudiced old eyes, and said calmly: "I desire it may be observed that we came into the court with our hats off (that is, taken off), and if they have been put on since, it was by order from the Bench, and therefore not we, but the Bench, should be fined."

There being no answer to that, the jury was sworn again. Sir John Robinson objected to the way Edward Bushell took the oath. Bushell was known to be a man of tender conscience and tough will, and the judges were a little uneasy about him. They had no good excuse, however, for getting rid of him, and so the trial went forward.

The first witness was called and sworn to tell "the truth, the whole truth, and nothing but the truth, so help me God."

Lieutenant Cook, in command of the soldiers, testified that he saw Mr. Penn speaking to the people but could not hear what he said. Two others said that they saw Penn preaching to some four hundred people and Mead talking to Lieutenant Cook, but could not hear what either Penn or Mead said. There was no further evidence.

Then Penn spoke up and said: "I desire you would let me know by what law it is you prosecute me, and upon what law you ground my indictment."

The Recorder of London, who was the legal expert on the case, answered promptly: "The common law."

At once Penn asked: "What is that common law?" but the legal expert could not produce a definition or an example of it. The other justices on the bench began to shout at Penn, and the Recorder snapped:

"The question is whether you are guilty of this indictment."

Penn corrected him. "The question is not whether I am guilty of this indictment, but whether the indictment be legal." He pointed out that if the common law was so hard to understand it was very far from being common, and he quoted Coke and the Magna Carta.

The Recorder, losing his temper completely, shouted: "Sir, you are an arrogant fellow, and it is not for the honor of the court to suffer you to go on!" To which Penn answered mildly: "I have asked but one question, and you have not answered me; though the rights and privileges of every Englishman are concerned in it."

"If I should suffer you to ask questions till tomorrow morning," replied the Recorder huffily, "you would never be the wiser."

And young Penn could not resist the temptation to retort: "That is according as the answers are."

That was too much for the judges; they turned purple with rage.

"I desire no affront to the court but to be heard in my just plea. . . ."

The Mayor and the Recorder both broke out in indignant shouts: "Take him away! Take him away! Turn him into the bale-dock."

The bale-dock was a sort of pen at the far end of the courtroom, open at the top but enclosed by high palings so that the prisoners could not see or hear what was going on. Before he was dragged off to this coop, William Penn delivered a ringing challenge:

"Is this justice or true judgment? Must I therefore be taken away because I plead for the fundamental laws of England? However, this I leave upon your consciences, who are of the jury and my sole judges, that if these ancient fundamental laws which relate to liberty and property (and are not limited to particular persuasions in the matter of religion) must not be indispensably maintained and observed, who can say he hath a right to the coat upon his back?"

"Be silent there."

"I am not to be silent in a case wherein I am so much concerned, and not only myself but many ten thousand families besides."

Roughly they pulled him off to the bale-dock. Mead had his turn, stood his ground well, quoted a Latin tag, defined a riot, and was also consigned for his pains to the bale-dock.

There, stuck away in the dimness, they could not hear what was going on in the court, but one of the officers whispered to them that the Recorder was charging the jury. It was absolutely against the law to charge the jury in the absence of the prisoners. Penn flung himself on the palings and pulled himself up so that he could shout over the top of them:

"I appeal to the jury who are my judges!" Loudly as he could, he quoted the law, and he called to the jury to take notice that he had not been heard in his own defense.

"Pull that fellow down, pull him down," bawled the Recorder.

The people in the galleries craned their necks and rustled and buzzed.

"I say these are barbarous and unjust proceedings!" shouted Penn, clinging to the side of the bale-dock.

"Take them away to the hole," commanded the Recorder.

To the hole they went, a sort of dungeon in the Sessions House, a stinking hole, Penn said, and one that the Lord Mayor would not consider a fit sty for his swine. There they stayed while the jury deliberated.

They were a long time at it. After an hour and a half, eight of them returned to the court, and four who disagreed remained in the jury chamber above. The four, of whom Edward Bushell was recognized as the leader, were brought down and scolded and threatened by the court. All twelve of them were then sent back to reach a conclusion, and this time, after more deliberation, they brought the unanimous verdict that William Penn was guilty of speaking in Gracechurch Street.

This of course was equal to an acquittal. There was no law against speaking in Gracechurch Street. The Mayor tried to make them say "speaking to an unlawful assembly," but they refused. Determined to have a different verdict, he ordered them back to the jury chamber, and they asked for pen, ink, and paper to take with them.

In a little more than half an hour they returned, Penn and Mead were brought back to the bar, and the jury handed in its verdict again, this time written and signed. "We do find William Penn to be guilty of speaking or preaching to an assembly met together in Gracechurch Street, the fourteenth of August last, 1670, and that William Mead is not guilty of the said indictment."

Whereupon the Mayor called Bushell "an impudent, canting fellow," and the Recorder told them all:

"Gentlemen, you shall not be dismissed till we have a verdict the court will accept; and you shall be locked up without meat, drink, fire, and tobacco. You shall not think thus to abuse the court; we will have a verdict, or by the help of God you shall starve for it."

Before the jury departed again, Penn got his

word in, and the voice of this young man of twenty-five, whom the Lord Mayor later called "that wild, rambling colt," was the only calm and authoritative voice in the whole amazing, hysterical courtroom.

"My jury, who are my judges, ought not to be thus menaced. Their verdict should be free and not compelled. The bench ought to wait upon them but not forestall them."

But the court was ready to break up for the day and "huddle the prisoners to the jail and the jury to their chamber." As the second day of the trial ended, Penn turned to the jury and said:

"You are Englishmen; mind your privileges, give not away your right."

To which Bushell stanchly made reply: "Nor will we ever do it."

And that night the jury was shut up without "meat, drink, fire, nor any other accommodation."

The next day was Sunday, and it was illegal to hold court. Nevertheless, at seven, the court sat.

The foreman of the jury read the verdict again: "William Penn is guilty of speaking in Gracechurch Street."

The Mayor prompted him: "To an unlawful assembly?" and Edward Bushell answered for him: "No, my lord, we give no other verdict than what we gave last night; we have no other verdict to give."

Another of the justices, Sir Thomas Bludworth, commented gloomily: "I knew Mr. Bushell would not yield," and the Recorder threatened again: "I will have a positive verdict, or you will starve for it." After the night they had just spent, the jury could not look on this as an empty threat.

Penn desired to ask one question: Did the court accept the verdict "Not guilty," given of William Mead?

"It cannot be a verdict," said the Recorder, "because you are indicted for a conspiracy; and one being found guilty and not the other, it could not be a verdict."

Penn's answer was quick. "If not guilty be not a verdict, then you make of the jury and Magna Carta a mere nose of wax. . . . And if William Mead be not guilty, it consequently follows that I am clear, since you have indicted us of a conspiracy, and I could not possibly conspire alone."

But for the third time the verdict was rejected and the jury sent back to find another. Again it returned with the one answer it had to give.

The court was well-nigh beside itself with rage. It threatened to set a mark on Edward Bushell, to have an eye on him, to cut his nose. And now Penn's voice rings out:

"It is intolerable that my jury should be thus menaced. Is this according to the fundamental law? Are they not my proper judges by the great charter of England? What hope is there of ever having justice done, when juries are threatened and their verdicts rejected? I am concerned to speak and grieved to see such arbitrary proceedings. Did not the Lieutenant of the Tower render one of them worse than a felon? And do you not plainly seem to condemn such for factious fellows who answer not your ends? Unhappy are those juries who are threatened to be fined and starved and ruined if they give not in their verdicts contrary to their consciences."

The Recorder had nothing to say in answer but: "My lord, you must take a course with that fellow."

"Jailer, bring fetters," commanded the Chief Justice, "and stake him to the ground."

"Do your pleasure," replied Penn superbly, "I matter not your fetters."

And now the Recorder's rage did what Penn was later to tell his children anger always does: it threw him into a desperate inconvenience. He made a speech that echoed around London and that he bitterly regretted afterwards.

"Till now," he said, "I never understood the reason of the policy and prudence of the Spaniards in suffering the Inquisition among them. And certainly it will never be well with us till something like the Spanish Inquisition be in England."

It was a dreadful thing to say. The torture and terror of the Spanish Inquisition were fresh in men's minds—Penn's grandfather, Giles Penn, had suffered from it—and in England Popery was more feared and detested than non-conformity.

For the fourth time the jury was ordered to go find another verdict; this time they refused to go, saying there was no other verdict. The Recorder in a passion left the bench, sputtering: "I protest I will sit here no longer to hear these things," but the Mayor called to him to stay while he uttered a few more threats, had the sheriff take the jury up to their room, and adjourned the court.

The prisoners were sent back to Newgate, where at least they had more freedom and comfort than the jury.

At seven o'clock on the morning of Monday, September fifth, the court sat again. The jury staggered in, wan, white, hungry, thirsty, and disheveled.

"Look upon the prisoners," said the Clerk. "What say you, is William Penn guilty or not guilty?"

"Not guilty."

"What say you? Is William Mead guilty, or not guilty?"

"Not guilty."

It was plain and definite this time. There was nothing the Bench could do except to call the roll and make each juror give his verdict separately. Everyone answered firmly: "Not guilty."

The people in the galleries were pleased, so pleased that they "made a kind of hymn about it." All over the courtroom there were little murmurs of satisfaction.

But the affair was not over. The Recorder had his last word. "I am sorry, gentlemen, you have followed your own judgments and opinions rather than the good and wholesome advice which was given you. God keep my life out of your hands: but for this the court fines you forty marks a man, and imprisonment till paid."

They had been threatened with fines and imprisonment, they had faced the ugly temper of the Bench, they must have known this was coming. But forty marks was a lot of money, about twenty-six pounds sterling, in a day when a lieutenant in the Plymouth colony, for instance, got an annual salary of twenty marks, and women worked in the hayfields for a penny a day.

Penn then stepped up toward the Bench and demanded his liberty. He was told that he too was in for fines—the forty mark fine imposed at the beginning of the session for wearing his hat. He began to quote the Magna Carta again, but the Recorder had had all he could stand. "Take

him away," he implored, "take him away, take him out of the court."

But before he went young William Penn had one thing more to say. He said it. "I can never urge the fundamental laws of England but you cry: 'Take him away, take him away.' But it is no wonder, since the Spanish Inquisition hath so great a place in the Recorder's heart. God Almighty, who is just, will judge you for these things."

So the prisoners who had been acquitted, and the jury who had acquitted them, went together to Newgate prison.

That night Penn wrote to his father. "Because I cannot come, I write." He told him the story of the trial, ending: "I am more concerned at thy distemper and the pains that attend it, than at my own mere imprisonment, which works for the best."

The next day he wrote: "I entreat thee not to purchase my liberty. They will repent them of their proceedings. I am now a prisoner notoriously against law."

And the next: "I am persuaded some clearer way will suddenly be found to obtain my liberty, which is no way so desirable to me as on the account of being with thee. . . . My present restraint is so far from being humor that I would rather perish than release myself by so indirect a course as to satiate their revengeful, avaricious appetites. The advantage of such freedom would fall very far short of the trouble of accepting it."

To pay the fine would be to admit its justice. What he wanted was either to be released by the court, or to bring suit against the judges for illegal imprisonment. In this way a principle could be established. This was the course the jury was taking. Every six hours they demanded their freedom, and when at length they were released on bail, they brought suit against the judges—and won their case. The whole body of judges in the King's Bench Court decided that no jury could be fined for its verdict. So it was that as a result of the trial of William Penn the sacredness of trial by jury was established for all time.

But that was nearly a year later.

The Admiral could not wait. He was dying, and he wanted to see his beloved son William again. He secretly paid his fine, and Mead's too, and they were set free.

## *from* BENJAMIN FRANKLIN

### *Ingri and Edgar Parin d'Aulaire*

*This is a selection from one of the d'Aulaires' biographies for young readers eight to ten. In this selection, the sturdy, intelligent Ben (1706–1790) comes to life. All the picture-biographies of this husband-and-wife team are worth looking up:* George Washington, Abraham Lincoln *(Caldecott Medal)*, Leif the Lucky, *and* Pocahontas.

### [Boy into Man]

At the time when the King of England ruled over the American colonies there stood a small house on Milk Street in Boston.

In this house there lived a candlemaker whose name was Josiah Franklin. He was a good and pious man, and the Lord had given him a virtuous wife and a blessing of seventeen children, all counted.

Three times each Sunday he led all his children to church and he taught them to be honest and hard-working and satisfied with little.

"He who knows his trade does not have to stand except for kings," said Josiah Franklin. He looked proudly at his ten husky sons and hoped that someday they would all be good tradesmen.

The youngest of his sons was Benjamin. He was born in 1706. He was different from his brothers. He was only knee-high to a grasshopper when he first learned to read and he wondered and asked questions from morning till night. He was a merry little fellow with stocky legs and a bright mind, busy with flights of fancy and practical ideas. He thought it was a pity that his father, who was so busy working to keep them all in food and clothes, should waste so much time saying a long grace every time he ate.

"Father," he said one day as they were sitting down to table, "think of all the time you could save if you would thank the Lord, once and for all, for the whole larder."

His father was pious and serious but he could not help smiling, and when he told his friends what a clever young son he had, they laughed with him and agreed that Benjamin was so

bright he might even become a minister. And on the next holiday one of the friends filled Benjamin's little coat pocket with copper pennies. Benjamin had never had a penny of his own before and joyfully he ran to a toy shop, where he offered all his money for a whistle he had set his heart on. He ran home and marched through the house shrilly blowing it while the rest of his family stopped up their ears.

When his sisters and brothers found out that he had spent all of his pennies for the whistle, he was the one who stopped up his ears. They teased him and called him a spendthrift till he wept. He had spent four times as much as the whistle was worth. That was the only time Benjamin ever spent a penny unwisely.

Benjamin lived near the sea, and he early learned to swim and sail. He never grew tired of watching the wind carry the boats over the water, just as it carried his kite up into the sky. One day, while he was swimming, he fastened the kite to himself as if it were a sail and he were a boat. It carried him gently over the water while his friends, who were kicking and splashing, looked on in astonishment. Because he had so many ideas like this, he was usually the leader among his playmates.

Like any boy, he sometimes led them into mischief. Once he got all of his playmates together at the shore where they liked best to fish. The ground was swampy, but near by Benjamin had found a big pile of stones that were to be used for building a house. He and his friends took these stones and built a fine wharf. But when the workmen came and found the stones gone, it helped Benjamin little to plead the usefulness of their work.

After he had been soundly spanked by his father, Benjamin was convinced that nothing is useful that is not honest.

When Benjamin was eight years old, his father sent him to grammar school. He rose to the head of his class in reading and writing, and he read every book he could lay his hands upon. But he was poor in arithmetic. His father began to think that perhaps Benjamin should be a tradesman like his brothers. So, when Benjamin was ten years old, he was taken out of school to learn his father's trade of candlemaking.

Benjamin hated dipping candles and cutting

wicks the whole day long. He read and he dreamed. More and more he dreamed about ships and voyages to faraway ports. His father began to fear that his son might become a sailor and be lost at sea. Hoping to find Benjamin a trade that he would really like, he took him to call on joiners and braziers and cutlers and bricklayers in their workshops. Benjamin learned much about these trades but he did not want to follow any of them. At last his worried father persuaded him that, since he was so fond of books, he should become a printer's apprentice. Then he could look at the printed word all day long.

His older brother James had a printing shop and, when Benjamin was twelve, he moved from his father's house and bound himself to be his brother's apprentice for nine years. In return, James was to teach him to print and to give him his board and clothes.

James was a strict master. When his young brother answered back with his quick wit and ready tongue, he boxed his ears severely. Benjamin had to sweep the floor, wash the type, and do all the dirty work while he watched his brother and his helpers print pamphlets and books. By and by James taught him to set type and print.

Benjamin was a hard-working boy and he learned fast. In a few years he was his brother's best worker. He would have liked life in the printing shop very much if he had had more time to read all the books around him. One day he had one of his practical ideas. He asked his brother to give him half of the money he paid for Benjamin's board so he could get his own meals and eat them in the shop when the others went out. James did not mind. He saved money. And Benjamin was happy. Now he had time to read books in peace while he ate his gruel and munched an apple. He did not care much what he ate as long as it was cheap and wholesome. He soon found that he could save half of the money his brother gave him for food. With that he bought books.

Benjamin wanted very much to become a writer himself. When he read something he liked especially well, he rewrote it in his own words. And sometimes he would be hanged if he didn't think that he was better than the author.

One of the things James printed was a newspaper. Benjamin's fingers were itching to write for it, for who does not want to see his own words in print? But he knew that his brother would only laugh and say he was getting too big for his breeches and give him a whack into the bargain. So he kept his writing secret.

One morning his brother found under his door a letter to the newspaper signed Widow Dogood. James did not recognize Benjamin's writing, for he had disguised it. Benjamin chuckled and was very pleased with himself when not only his brother and his friends but also the readers of the paper highly praised the widow's good sense and learning. His brother had many letters from the virtuous lady and printed them all before Benjamin confessed that he was the widow.

James was angry. After that he was stricter than ever with Benjamin. In his eyes Benjamin was a fresh little sprout who believed he could both print and write better than his master.

Benjamin thought he was now too big to be thrashed by his brother. He had been his apprentice for five years and had become a very good printer. Yes, he had even run the printing shop alone while his brother was away. He asked his brother please to let him go so that he could find work for himself elsewhere. But James said no, he must stay till his nine years were up.

Then Benjamin made up his mind to run away. He knew it was wrong but he could no longer stand his brother's harsh treatment. He sold some of his cherished books to get a little money, and late one night he secretly boarded a ship bound for New York. He stood at the rail watching his native town vanish into the night. He felt small and lonesome. His parents would be sad and his brother would be angry. He was only seventeen and he did not know a soul in New York who might help him.

The winds were fair, but even so the trip to New York took three days. During a lull the sailors fished and made a big haul of cod. They invited Benjamin to eat with them, but Benjamin said no, thank you, he ate neither flesh nor fish, for he had read in a book that it was murder to kill and eat creatures that had done him no harm. But he loved codfish and, when the fish was cooking and the good smells reached his nose, he began to hunt about in his mind for a reason to share the sailors' meal. He remembered that when the codfish were cut open he had seen small fish in their stomachs. If big fish ate small fish, why should he not eat big fish? Then he ate heartily and thought to himself how lucky he was to be a thinking creature who could find a good reason for doing what he wanted to do. After that Benjamin always ate what was set before him.

Benjamin liked the sea voyage. When he arrived in New York, he stood at the wharf for a while and thought. He could go to sea if he still wanted to, but he had become a printer, and a printer he would be.

New York was a very small town in 1723 and there was but one printer. He had no work for Benjamin and advised him to go to Philadelphia. Philadelphia was a larger town.

So Benjamin set off for Philadelphia. He had very little money left and could not afford to travel all the way by ship. He stuffed what he could into his pockets and shipped the rest of his belongings. A few pennies paid his passage on a ramshackle old boat that was about to cross to the Jersey shore.

Halfway across, a gale blew up and the rotten sails went to pieces. In the storm a Dutchman fell overboard. Benjamin quickly grabbed him by the hair and pulled him back into the boat. The dripping Dutchman pulled a book out of his pocket and asked Benjamin to dry it for him. It was the most beautiful book Benjamin had ever seen. It had been printed in Europe with fine type and many pictures. That was the kind of book he would like to print.

He had plenty of time to enjoy the book, for the boat pitched and tossed in the bay of New York for thirty hours. At last the crew managed to bring her to port on the Jersey shore and, cold and wet, Benjamin started to walk. It was a long way on foot, for it is a hundred miles from New York to Philadelphia.

For days he trudged through ruts and mud, in rain and storm, and he began to be sorry he had ever run away. When he reached the Delaware River, he was lucky. A small boat came sailing downstream and the crew took him on board. But soon the wind died down. Benjamin had to help row the boat till his hands were covered with blisters. He looked so bedraggled and for-

lorn, it was a wonder he was not sent home as a runaway bound boy.

That is the way he arrived in Philadelphia early on a Sunday morning. People in their Sunday-go-to-meeting clothes were walking through the streets, Benjamin walked along with them, looking this way and that till he came to an open bakeshop. He was very hungry and went in and asked the baker for three pennies' worth of bread. To his surprise, the baker handed him three huge buns, for bread was very cheap in Philadelphia. It was three times more than he could eat! The people turned their heads to hide their smiles when they saw Benjamin walking up Market Street with his pockets stuffed with clothes and his arms full of bread. A pretty girl standing in a doorway snickered and giggled out loud.

He followed the people in the street until he came to a Quaker meetinghouse, which he entered. He was so exhausted that he fell asleep the

moment he sat down. He had come to the city of brotherly love, so nobody woke him till the meeting was over. Then a kind Quaker showed him to an inn where he could rest and eat.

Scrubbed and refreshed, Benjamin went out the next morning, and soon he found work as a printer's helper. Nobody laughed at his looks any longer, but everybody laughed at his jokes. It was not long before the people of Philadelphia were telling one another how lucky it was that such a good printer and fine young fellow had settled in their town. Many of them made friends with him. The governor of Pennsylvania came to see if Benjamin was really as clever as people said. He asked him out to dine with him and was much taken by his good sense. He advised Benjamin to go back to Boston and ask his father's forgiveness for running away and his help in setting up a printing shop of his own. Then he, the governor, would help him to get printing to do. That sounded like good advice to Benjamin.

Eight months after he had run away, he sailed back to Boston for a visit. He was dressed in a fine new suit. He had a watch, and silver coins jingled in his pocket. His parents were happy that he had done so well, and readily forgave him. But his father thought he was still too young to have a shop of his own and told him to return to his well-paid work as a printer's helper. His brother would not forgive him and it was not till many years later that the two brothers were friends again.

## from GEORGE WASHINGTON, LEADER OF THE PEOPLE

### Clara Ingram Judson

*George Washington's boyhood has had a mythlike quality for most children. This selection re-creates the period, the customs, the family, and, above all, young George Washington (1732–1799) and his idolized older brother, Lawrence Washington. Clara Ingram Judson's*

"By the Rappahannock" and "Many Changes" from *George Washington, Leader of the People,* copyright 1951, by Clara Ingram Judson, reprinted by permission of Follett Publishing Company

*biographies can be relied upon for their careful historical details. Her many books about American immigrants* (They Came from Sweden, They Came from Scotland, *and others*) *and her exciting story about Chicago's Chinatown—The Green Ginger Jar—illustrate her appreciative understanding of widely different people and her profound concern for everything that goes into making our American culture rich and sound.*

### By the Rappahannock

The farm by the river was the lush green of June in Virginia. The air was warm, fine for growing things. A mocking bird sang in the linden tree and the chatter of wrens mingled with domestic noises of roosters, hens, and ducks in the chicken yard.

A house, high above the Rappahannock, had a comfortable look against a line of tall trees. Nearby, a barn, the kitchen, poultry house, storeroom, smithy and quarters for the slaves made a little settlement such as was usually found on prosperous Virginia farms in that year 1739.

At the horse lot a boy tugged at the heavy gate bar, while his pony, Whitefoot, pawed impatiently, eager to be gone.

"Want help?" Tim, the stableman, called.

"No, I can do it myself," George Washington said quickly. As he tugged again, he noticed that Whitefoot was suddenly still, ears cocked as though he heard a new sound.

"Someone coming, Whitefoot?" George asked, listening. The rhythmic sound of hoofbeats came from far down the lane leading to the main road to Fredericksburg.

George climbed onto the fence for a look. He was sturdy and tall for a boy in his eighth year. Freckles sprinkled his straight nose, and his hands were tanned from long hours out of doors. Now he brushed a lock of sandy-colored hair from his forehead and squinted his gray-blue eyes down the lane.

"It's *Lawrence!*" he cried excitedly. "Whitefoot! Lawrence is coming!"

George jumped down from the fence, pulled out the gate bar, which suddenly seemed lighter, threw himself onto his pony and dashed off down the lane.

A visit from George's twenty-one-year-old

half-brother was a thrilling surprise. Lawrence Washington had been home from England only a few months. George admired this tall, handsome brother and saw him far too little.

Lawrence waved as George drew near and grinned with amusement when the boy pulled Whitefoot up short with a flourish that sent pebbles flying.

"Oh, Lawrence! I am so glad to see you!" George cried breathlessly. "I didn't know you were coming today!"

"I started early; I have meant to come for several days," Lawrence said. "Is Father here?"

"No," George told him. "I think he is at the iron works. Maybe you had better ride over and see him?"

"No, my errand is here," Lawrence said. "And I doubt if your mother would let you ride over with me in any case. Where are you bound now?"

"To school," George told him in a bored tone. "That Master Hobby is a tiresome man, Lawrence. He teaches the same thing over and over."

"Perhaps it is a good thing that I came today," Lawrence remarked as they rode along toward the house.

"Did you come about *me?*" George was astonished. But Lawrence merely shook his head and laughed mysteriously.

"I must talk to your mother now," he said. "And you should shut that gate, George. You will be in trouble if a colt gets into the field."

Reluctantly George stopped to close and fasten the gate while Lawrence rode to the hitching post near the house.

George turned Whitefoot into the lot, fastened the gate and called to a stableboy to care for Lawrence's mount. But his manner was absent-minded; his thoughts were on Lawrence. Something was up, that was certain, something that concerned George. But what could be important enough to bring Lawrence on a thirty-mile ride from Hunting Creek farm? In June, too, when a farmer had work to oversee.

Shouts of small children and the bark of a dog guided George to the lawn in front of the house. There, on the high bank Lawrence had joined Mrs. Washington and the younger children, Betty, Sam, and Jack. They had been watching their father's scow as it crossed the river.

"It is a good thing you came today, Lawrence," Mrs. Washington was saying to her stepson as George came near. "While you are in Fredericksburg about George, you can attend to the delivery of my boxes. I saw the ship from England arrive yesterday."

"Am I going to Fredericksburg?" George exclaimed. Many times he had looked toward the white steeple of the church across the river and wondered what was beneath the thick trees. "I have never been to a town," he added.

"That is not surprising," Lawrence said casually. "Virginia has few towns. But you shall see Fredericksburg today, for my errand there is for you. Father thinks it is high time. . . ."

"George! Run to the house and put on your best coat," Mrs. Washington interrupted. "Lawrence can explain your father's plan while you are on the ferry. It comes now." The scow had reached the landing at the foot of the ravine.

George glanced down at his shirt and knee-pants. The garments were clean and good enough for Hobby's little school. But he did look shabby compared with Lawrence's elegant coat and breeches, trimmed with shining buttons and buckles. He hurried into the house, brushed his hair and put on his best coat and the shoes with buckles. Lawrence was strolling toward the ravine when he returned and together they hurried to the wharf.

"Lawrence! Tell the captain to have a care for my boxes," Mrs. Washington called after them. "The last time your father ordered goblets, every one was broken on the way."

"I shall see to it," Lawrence promised. "Come, George!"

The children left behind began to fuss.

"I want to ride on the ferry," six-year-old Betty teased.

"I want to go!" Sam planted his feet wide apart and yelled.

Jack was too young to understand but he yelled too.

"Quiet, all of you!" Mrs. Washington commanded. "Better be gone quickly, Lawrence," she called over her shoulder, "or these children will be heard in Fredericksburg."

Laughing, Lawrence and George hurried away. In a few minutes they were aboard the clumsy ferry.

As they pulled away, George looked expectantly at Lawrence.

"So you want to know what this is about?" Lawrence said. "The last time Father came to Hunting Creek, he told me that he was not pleased with Hobby's teaching. A one-room neighborhood school is good for a time. It is convenient and gives you a start. But Father heard that a better school might be opened in Fredericksburg. He wants to know if the rumor is true. We shall not count on it until we see."

The crossing was brief. Before George had time for many questions, the ferry tied up near the sailing ship from England. Lawrence went at once to attend to Mrs. Washington's boxes.

George marveled that Lawrence knew exactly what to say and do as invoices were checked and boxes marked "Fragile" were moved to the ferry under his watchful eye.

"I am lucky to have a brother as wonderful as Lawrence," George thought humbly. "I wonder if I can ever be as smart and as handsome?" It seemed doubtful.

"Now we can leave," Lawrence said in relief. And the two climbed the steep cobblestone road to the town.

George looked around with keen curiosity. He saw the church with the familiar steeple, many houses, a stone jail with iron-barred windows, shops, and people strolling about.

Lawrence inquired of one of these for the residence of the Reverend James Marye and was directed to the parsonage, by the church. The rector was at home, and Lawrence introduced himself and George and accepted the invitation to come inside.

"My father had hoped to call upon you, sir, about the education of my young brother," he explained as they all sat down. "But because of his many duties at his iron works and the task of managing his three plantations, the matter has been postponed. My father has heard that you may open a school. If this is your intention, we would like to enroll my brother."

The Reverend Marye had looked keenly from one Washington to the other while Lawrence was speaking.

"Where did you receive your education?" he asked.

"At Appleby in England," Lawrence told him.

"My father lived in England and attended Appleby. Others of our family went to that school and my brother Augustine, Jr., who is near my age, is there. At the proper time my father plans to take George to England, too. Meanwhile, my brother needs good preparation which my father hopes you can give him."

"Have you had any schooling, George?" Marye asked.

"Yes, sir. Master Hobby teaches me reading and writing and sums," George answered respectfully.

Marye turned to his desk and selected a bit of paper and a quill pen.

"Let me see your writing," he said.

George sat down, took the quill, and wrote his name in his best style. The result was not remarkable. Marye eyed it, frowning.

"Those field schools," he began. Then he paused and rubbed his chin thoughtfully. It was plain he was not favorably impressed with George's instruction. The term "field school" which he used was often applied to a small one-room schoolhouse erected by a group of neighbors. One gave a part of his field, others labor, materials, or tobacco for buying books. The great problem was to find a suitable teacher; the colony of Virginia lacked such men.

"I do better with sums," George ventured to speak up when the silence grew long. "I like arithmetic."

"I hope we are not too late to enter my brother," Lawrence remarked, now a bit anxious at the turn the interview was taking.

"On the contrary, you are too early," Marye answered more cheerfully. "I shall not open my school before autumn, perhaps not until next year. Um-m-m, I wonder if your father has considered the cost of textbooks as well as tuition?"

"My father will not object to any proper charge," Lawrence answered, with due caution about committing his father's purse. "Perhaps you will be good enough to send Father word when your school is about to open?"

"You may count on that," Marye said, now reassured. "Meanwhile, have the boy continue his studies."

The visitors bowed out politely. As they

walked down the street, George sighed with relief.

"The Reverend Marye must be a *very* learned man," he said. "He is so very solemn."

"Never mind!" Lawrence answered. "You have to be prepared for Appleby, and Hobby could never do it. Where shall we go now? The ferry can wait."

"I would like to go to the Apothecary's Shop, Lawrence," George said, eagerly. "Our smith has told me about it. The window has two big urns, one red, one green. Candy is for sale," George added hopefully.

Lawrence was willing, and soon they saw the small but enchanting window. Inside, the shop had a luscious fragrance.

"We have some excellent sugar which has just arrived from England," the apothecary told them. He opened a case and took out a shallow wooden bowl in which hunks of a taffylike substance were piled. George's mouth watered as he admired the rich caramel color and watched Lawrence expectantly.

"I shall take two pounds," Lawrence ordered. The apothecary reached for his iron sugar clippers; he used them like tongs to cut off individual portions and place them on the scale.

"Two pounds," he repeated.

"Can you direct us to a baker's shop?" Lawrence asked as he paid for the sugar and handed the sack to George.

"Down the street by the corner there is a good place," the man said.

At the baker's, Lawrence bought caraway comfits. George ate two on the ferry and found them delicious.

"I shall take the rest home for a treat," he decided.

The dining table was set in the wide hall. The stone fireplace was empty this June day, but the hearth was cheerful with bright brasses and an embroidered fire screen. A gold-framed mirror hung on one wall and opposite a handsome floor clock ticked off seconds. Leather-bottomed chairs were set up to a large table covered with a linen tablecloth and set with china and pewter. The children stood by their chairs as their mother entered.

"We saw the ferry coming so we waited dinner," she said. "George has learned to say grace,

Lawrence. We are ready, son."

They stood with bowed heads while George recited: "God bless us for what we are about to receive." Then they sat down.

A young serving maid hovered over the children, tying bibs, while an older woman brought food from the kitchen. In Virginia this was often a separate building; the danger of fire was less and flies, drawn by cooking, were kept from the dining room.

The woman set a large platter before Lawrence, who carved the two roast chickens. Then she brought sliced ham, a bowl of greens cooked with bacon, blackberry jam, butter, hot cornbread and handleless cups of hot tea. Later she passed wheat bread and a large bowl piled with fruit picked that morning; early plums, cherries and red currants.

As they were finishing the meal, Lawrence winked at George, who promptly produced the comfits and the sugar.

"I shall persuade Father to take *me* to town soon," Betty announced as she found the last crumb and plunked it into her mouth. George chuckled. They both knew their father had no time for shopping journeys.

The other children drifted out of doors. George sat quietly as Lawrence talked with Mrs. Washington about the school and left messages for his father. Until last winter the Washingtons had all lived at Hunting Creek farm and Mrs. Washington was interested in the place.

"Perhaps your father will come to Hunting Creek soon," she remarked as Lawrence rose to leave.

"I wish he would bring George with him," Lawrence said. "That is, if you can spare him?" George's face brightened and Mrs. Washington half promised.

Striding along by Lawrence, George went to the horse lot where he mounted Whitefoot to ride as far as the main road.

"I wish you could stay longer, Lawrence," George said.

"And who would do my work at Hunting Creek?" scoffed Lawrence. "Lucky for me the day is long so I can get home before dark. But you will be coming to visit me, George. Don't tease Father. Better be surprised when he mentions a visit. Then you may say that I will teach you farming and care of the stock. He will like that, and you will enjoy it more than school." Laughing, Lawrence touched his horse slightly and was on his way.

George rode back to the barn. The Washingtons had slaves to do the work at Ferry farm, but Mr. Washington had told George that a boy old enough to have his own horse must take care of it. That was no hardship; George liked keeping Whitefoot's stall clean, bedding the pony with fresh straw, and measuring out the feed. Usually he talked as he curried and cared for his pony. But today his thoughts were with Lawrence. The prospect of a visit at Hunting Creek farm was far more interesting than a new school.

. . . . . . . . . . . . . .

### Many Changes

After months without word from the West Indies a letter that Lawrence had written in Jamaica arrived. George was astonished that Lawrence wrote more about smallpox and yellow fever than about glorious battles. After more months word came that the war had turned to Georgia; the fleet was not needed, and Virginians were coming home.

Lawrence arrived late in 1742 and was received with honor by the colony. Later the governor appointed him military adjutant in recognition of his war service, an office that gave him charge of the militia of Virginia.

The returned warrior found changes at Ferry farm. The baby sister had died. Austin, Lawrence's brother who had expected to study law in England, had come home to help his father. He was learning to manage the farm at Pope's Creek.

"I had George visit me for a time," Austin told Lawrence. "He is good company." Lawrence saw that the two got on well.

But George soon showed his family that no one took Lawrence's place in his affections. Now his hero was more fascinating than ever; he had seen foreign places and could tell tales of ships and battles. Lawrence had served on the flagship and was the friend of a real admiral. George followed his brother around and begged to be allowed to go back with him to Hunting Creek.

"And leave school?" Lawrence exclaimed. "Are you failing?"

"Oh, no, Lawrence!" George was shocked. "But I could learn more with you."

Lawrence grinned understandingly. But George stayed in school.

After gay holidays with six sons and daughter Betty crowding the modest house, the older sons went back to work. At Pope's Creek, Austin was trying to set up a business of raising fine horses, much needed in the colony. Lawrence, at Hunting Creek, planned to erect a few needed buildings and clear more fields for growing tobacco. He had told his father that he hoped to marry Anne Fairfax in the spring. As for Gus Washington, he continued his heavy round of duties at his Accokeek Iron Works, Hunting Creek, Pope's Creek, and Ferry farm.

The iron business had first been successful in America in 1717, with a Maryland furnace owned by an English firm. There Gus Washington learned how to take ore from the ground, smelt it, and ship it to England. Colonists were not allowed to make durable goods; that profitable business was reserved for England.

Washington built furnaces, prepared wood for charcoal from his own forest and built ships for transport. All this required scores of laborers who must be housed and fed. Wagons, tools, and all sorts of supplies were needed, and craftsmen, too; wagonwrights, blacksmiths, millers, sawyers, carpenters, and others. Slaves could be trained to work under a skilled manager, but this last was a hard job to fill. Gus Washington had to be his own manager much of the time.

As for George, he did so well in school that his father planned an Easter vacation for him—a visit to his cousins in another county. George was there, in the midst of a day of sports, when a messenger arrived from Ferry farm.

"Your father is ill—very ill!" the man cried as he slid from his exhausted horse. "You are to come home at once."

George dashed for Whitefoot. The messenger was loaned a fresh mount and the two galloped home. George arrived in time to see his strong father stretched flat on his bed, too ill to know his son or to speak. Mrs. Washington let him stand there a few minutes, then she motioned him away.

Soon Lawrence came into the hall. "Father is dead."

"*Dead!*" George exclaimed incredulously. His strong handsome father, the man who had more energy than any person George had ever known—dead? But it was true. This sad loss came a few weeks after George's eleventh birthday.

During those next sad days George thought often of the ride with his father nearly four years before. He was glad to have had that trip and their talk to remember.

After Augustine Washington had been buried in the family burying ground a mile from Pope's Creek, his will was read. George's father had thought of the future of all his children.

Lawrence, the oldest son, was to have the largest plantation, Hunting Creek farm. That was still the custom in the colony. Austin inherited Pope's Creek farm. George was to have Ferry farm when he was twenty-one and also some other land. Sam and Jack and Charles were each given tracts of several hundred acres and Betty's inheritance was in money. The forty-nine slaves were divided among the heirs, and each child and the mother were given shares in the iron company. Mrs. Washington was to hold and manage her children's property until they became of age.

When this legal business was finally settled, Lawrence and Austin went back to their homes, and life at Ferry farm settled down. George missed Lawrence more than ever because now he had no father.

In July of that year, 1743, Lawrence married Anne Fairfax and the family reassembled for the wedding. The event, so soon after Mr. Washington's death, was not as festive as it might have been, but George thought it very grand. The social life of Virginia was the most elegant of all the colonies.

This marriage brought many changes in George's life. Lawrence's bride invited him for a long visit; she told him to call her Nancy, as Lawrence did. George's mother was willing to have George stay at Hunting Creek now that Lawrence had a bride of distinction.

Nancy's father, Colonel William Fairfax, continued his liking for George. Fairfax was one of the richest and most distinguished men in Virginia; he was a burgess, then a member of the higher body, the Council, and a year after the wedding was made President of the Council.

Next to the governor's palace, his home, Belvoir, was the meeting place of the greatest men in the colony.

George was now eleven and a half and naturally quick to observe people and manners. This association with the Fairfax family had taught him fine manners and habits of graciousness; in a measure, it took the place of the training his father had intended him to have in England.

Lawrence and Nancy lived in the story-and-a-half house that was probably built by Gus Washington before he moved there in the seventeen-thirties. It had a center hall and four rooms downstairs and rooms with dormer windows above. They added furniture and hangings, and Nancy had handsome silver and other choice things. George thought the place very elegant, though, of course, it was not large and handsome like Belvoir.

When the pretty things were all in place, Nancy told George they were giving the place a new name.

"This is no longer Hunting Creek farm, George," she said. "We call it Mount Vernon; Mount for the high bank above the river, Vernon for Lawrence's good friend the admiral."

"Mount Vernon," George repeated the words, testing the sound. "That is a good name, Nancy. I like it."

A few days later the Lawrence Washingtons gave a dinner party as a housewarming. The slaves worked early and late with the preparations. They polished silver, washed and ironed linens, and washed the china and every window in the house.

George wondered if a boy going on twelve would be allowed at the table. Nancy soon relieved his mind about that.

"Lawrence thinks this is a good chance for you to learn about grown-up affairs," she said. "Wear that new suit Lawrence ordered from London. Better try it on today, George, and let Lawrence see if it needs any changes. And, George, will you tell Chloe that I shall be out to inspect every duck myself when she has finished cleaning them? Everything is to be perfect at my first party!"

She bustled about happily, keys clicking at her belt like an experienced housewife. George did the errand and then ran upstairs to try on the suit. It had come only that morning.

The guests were very fashionable. The dinner was delicious, George thought, though he was so excited he could not eat as much as usual—well, not quite as much. When the ladies retired to the drawing room to talk of fashions and household matters, Colonel Fairfax motioned for George to sit by him. The men were talking, at the moment, about war.

"You must feel a satisfaction, Lawrence," a guest across the table remarked, "to know that you could serve the king when he needed you." Lawrence nodded and bowed modestly.

"His majesty needs service in peacetime, too," a man in a green satin coat said. The others looked at him.

"I am thinking of the land west of the mountains," he explained. "Your relative, Lord Fairfax, owns vast acreage. I believe you manage it for him, Fairfax?"

"If you can call it managing," Colonel Fairfax waved his hand casually. "Actually wilderness land has little value. King Charles the Second would not have given it away, years ago, if he had thought well of it."

"You speak of the Fairfax Proprietary, I take it?" a guest in a bright-blue coat and stylish periwig inquired.

"Yes." Fairfax smiled. "An elegant name for a wild, unsurveyed stretch of country. I had a letter from Lord Fairfax the other day—he asks whether there is a demand by settlers for his land. I do not know what to tell him."

"No demand at all, I'd say," some one spoke up. "Not with Indians only a short journey away. Now if the Indians could be persuaded to move west of the Allegheny Range a lively trade in land might open up."

"At great profit to us all," Fairfax laughed and raised his glass. The talk went on until the guests' carriages arrived.

That was only the first of many dinner parties at Mount Vernon. How much of the talk —business, military, and political—a boy of twelve could understand, George himself could hardly have told. But he was a thoughtful lad. He turned men's words over in his mind and began growing up.

Occasionally George rode with Lawrence to see Austin at Pope's Creek. This brother urged George to live with him.

"You like to work with horses, George," he said. "And there are boys your own age nearby —the Lee family, and others." But though George did go for one or two visits, he was always glad to return to Mount Vernon. He loved that place.

When he stayed at Ferry farm he found that life very different from either brother's. There, small children, school, and daily tasks under his mother's supervision kept him busy.

Mrs. Washington had considerable help, both slaves and indentured servants. Still, the mother of five children and manager of a farm had a great deal to do. She must guard the children from daily hazards: poison ivy on the river slope, measles, warts, croup (the terror of those days), and chicken pox. She was also the doctor, and she made her own medicines from herbs grown in her garden or searched out in the forest.

The blacksmith was the dentist, though of course the mother pulled "baby teeth." She tied a string from tooth to doorknob and held the child while some one slammed the door—and pulled the tooth. The blacksmith was called in when a "second tooth" ached. Mother held the patient flat on the table while the smith, with a dramatic flourish of black pincers and sheer strength, yanked out the tooth—and often some bone along with it.

The children all rode horses, too. So the mother must be ready to tie red meat over bruises or set broken bones. It was a busy life, full of surprises.

At school, George studied the classics, writing, algebra, and geometry. Reverend Marye was most particular about writing. He had George copy one hundred and ten rules from an old English volume called *The Rules of Conduct*.

"Write each rule over and over until you have it perfect," the master ordered. "I shall accept no carelessly made letters."

So George wrote in his copybook:

"Mock not, nor jest at anything of importance; break no jests that are sharp biting, and if you deliver anything witty or pleasant, abstain from laughing at it yourself.

"When you see a crime punished, you may be inwardly pleased; but always show pity to the suffering offender.

"Labor to keep alive in your breast that little spark of celestial fire called conscience."

This chore of copying over and over to satisfy his teacher taught George the easy, flowing handwriting that was to be so important to him later.

One Saturday his mother set him at the tedious task of cleaning the storehouse. This was a small building, near the kitchen, where countless articles were put when not in daily use. He moved boxes and bundles. He scrubbed and sorted under her keen eye until someone called her away. While alone, George rummaged in a dark corner. There he found an odd thing made up of iron rods and chains. As his mother returned she heard the sounds he made examining the thing.

"Now what have you there?" she demanded.

"I don't know, Mother," George said. "Do you?"

When she saw what he was holding, she laughed. "Of course I know! That's your father's surveying chain; did you never see it before? His compass is in the desk. Your father always surveyed property he bought to make sure of the boundaries."

"Father knew everything, didn't he?" George said quietly.

Something in the lad's tone caught his mother's attention. She put her hand on his shoulder in a rare gesture of affection.

"Not everything, son," she answered kindly. "But he was a fine man. He had more knowledge than most men in the colony. But a chain is no good to us now. Take it to the smith; he can use the metal." Mary Washington was her practical self again.

"May I keep it because it was Father's?" George asked.

"Oh, yes, if you like. After you have scrubbed the floor, put it in the corner, there. It does not take much room."

She bustled away, the keys at her belt jingling. "He will soon forget," she thought. "Then the smith can have it."

George finished the scrubbing and put the brush and bucket away. As he laid the long chain in the corner he made a promise to himself.

"Monday I shall begin to learn surveying."

### from AMERICA'S PAUL REVERE

*Esther Forbes*

*When Henry Wadsworth Longfellow wrote his poem "The Midnight Ride of Paul Revere," he created a legend about Revere (1735–1818) that has not yet died. The "midnight rider" has supplanted the real man in most people's minds, which is unfortunate, for Revere was more than a sentinel whose job it was to warn the Massachusetts countryside of the coming of British troops. He was an extremely talented man and a dedicated patriot, as Esther Forbes' fine biography shows.*

### [The Express Rider]

Always on March fifth, there was a big mass meeting to commemorate the Boston Massacre.

It was held in Old South Church and orations were given. These were violently anti-British. It had been tyranny five years before to land two regiments down on Boston—and naturally bloodshed had been the result. Now, in 1775, there were six times as many soldiers—the tyranny six times as bad. Most people suspected that more blood soon would be shed. People were saying Gage would prohibit the meeting, but he did not. Then they said he was waiting to get all the most prominent Whigs in one building and arrest them all. They were not arrested. But some of his young officers decided to attend and interrupt the speakers and make what trouble they could. But people treated them politely, and the meeting went off without any violence. Paul Revere's close friend, Doctor Joseph Warren, was the orator that year. And Sam Adams and John Hancock both sat on the platform. It took courage for them to appear publicly and denounce British rule. This meeting should be remembered as an example of 'freedom of speech.' What was said was close to treason. Any time he wanted, Gage could arrest the leaders and send them to London. King George was angry that he did not, and there was a rhyme the British soldiers liked:

'As for their King John Hancock
And Adams, if they're taken,
Their heads for signs shall hang on high
Upon that hill called "Beacon." '

Soon afterward both Adams and Hancock left Boston. Joseph Warren and Paul Revere stayed on.

And so it was the eighteenth of April in the year seventeen-seventy-five. People wondered if this was the day General Gage would send out his men to seize John Hancock and Sam Adams, who were at Lexington, and capture the military supplies the Patriots had hidden at Concord and other inland towns. The spy system reported that the British were preparing boats, and that six hundred of the best of the regulars were being held ready for *something*. Was it for an attack?

Paul Revere had suggested that if the regulars left by land, one lantern would be shown in the spire of Christ Church. If by sea, two. The British would try to stop all messengers from Boston who might warn the Minute Men. However, two men would try to get out. One was Billy Dawes, who would leave by the town gate. The other, Paul Revere, who would, if he did not get caught, cross the Charles River to Charlestown.

That afternoon he saw that the *Somerset,* British man-o'-war, was being moved into the mouth of the Charles to stop people like himself who might want to cross the river. As soon as it was dark, from all over Boston, groups of British regulars marched stealthily toward the foot of the Common and got into boats. At ten o'clock, Joseph Warren sent word for Billy Dawes to start, and Paul Revere told Robert Newman to show two lanterns in the steeple. If neither he nor Dawes got past the British, the lanterns would at least give some warning.

When he had sent Newman off, he went home to say goodbye to his family and get his riding boots. North Square, where he lived, was already full of troops, waiting to march. He was careful that no one saw what he was doing.

Two of Revere's friends rowed him over to Charlestown.

Charlestown had seen the tiny lights in the steeple. The Patriots there were expecting Revere, and had a fast horse saddled and waiting. Revere flung himself on the horse, and so alone down the dark road and through the bright white moonlight he rode to spread the alarm. At Lexington, John Hancock and Sam Adams were staying with the Clarks. He wished to warn them they might be seized for high treason. He later said that at Medford, 'I alarmed the Captain of the Minute Men, and after that I alarmed almost every house till I got to Lexington. Up flew windows and out popped heads. "The regulars are out." "What? How's that?" "The regulars are out." '

Bells rang and drums beat. Men mounted and galloped off to warn other towns. Minute Men jumped from their beds, grabbed muskets, and hastened to the rendezvous.

It was midnight, when Revere woke John Hancock and Sam Adams to tell them the regulars were out and they had best hide themselves. Half an hour later, Dawes arrived. The two messengers ate together, rested their horses, and decided to continue to Concord. Everyone knew

Concord had a large supply of military equipment. The Sunday before, Revere had told them they had better begin hiding it, because in Boston people thought the regulars would soon try to capture the supplies. Young Doctor Prescott said he would go with them. The three left Lexington together. One would stop and knock at one door, and another at the next. By now, they knew that General Gage had sent out, very secretly the day before, a number of British officers, who, as soon as the regulars left Boston, were to hide in the bushes along the roads leading to Concord and stop all messengers. Revere had already met two of them when he left Charlestown, but his fast Yankee horse had quickly left them behind. When the three men were only halfway to Concord, they met another group of officers. Paul Revere was on the road. They jumped out of the darkness at him with drawn pistols almost before he saw them, but he had time to call a warning to Dawes and Prescott, who were knocking at farmhouse doors. An officer raced to catch them, but Dawes broke through and fell off his horse. Doctor Prescott jumped a wall and was off for Concord, leaving no danger that Concord would be surprised. The Minute Men were well aroused. It was the group of ten British officers who were in danger of being captured by the Minute Men if they did not quickly join the British troops come out from Boston.

They questioned Revere.

'How far is Cambridge? What is your name?'

'Revere.'

'What, *Paul* Revere?'

They knew they had caught Boston's most famous express rider. Soon they let the other men

whom they had picked up that night go, and hurried as fast as they could for Lexington, hoping to join the troops. A sergeant led Revere's horse. An officer kept a pistol pointed at his head.

'If you attempt to run or we are insulted, we'll blow out your brains,' he said.

'You may do as you please,' Revere said. He knew his mission was accomplished.

But when the British found they had to hurry, they could not bother with a prisoner. They took Revere's horse away and let him go free. As he was already in Lexington, he decided to go to the Clarks' parsonage and see if he could help Hancock and Adams. He found they were just leaving, and went with them. Then Hancock remembered he had left a trunk full of papers, which must not fall into the hands of the British, at Buchman Tavern on Lexington Green, so Revere and Hancock's clerk went back to save them. In Lexington, there was great excitement. People said the British regulars were very close. Revere saw the thin line of Minute Men standing on the Green waiting for them. He and the clerk hurried to the tavern. As they were carrying the trunk out of the tavern door, they saw the scarlet flood of British regulars come to a halt before the handful of Minute Men. The British officers galloped ahead to order the Minute Men to disperse. Revere walked through the lines carrying his half of the dangerous trunk. He heard a shot and then a volley, cries of wounded men, and the huzzahing of the exultant troops, passing through the handful of men who thought to oppose them, as they headed now for Concord. The first shot of the American Revolution had been fired.

### from TEN BRAVE MEN

*Sonia Daugherty*

*The time was 1765, the scene Virginia; the "shot heard 'round the world" was ten years off, the Declaration of Independence would not see light until 1776, but already people were restless with England's constant demands upon the*

*Colonies. Voices were beginning to be raised in protest; one that was heard most clearly was that of Patrick Henry (1736–1799). The roughneck from the backwoods was born with the power to move people with his words once he felt in his heart the righteousness of his cause. Young readers who thrill to Henry's eloquence should be introduced to Nardi Reeder Campion's full-length biography (see Bibliography).*

### Patrick Henry

"I know not what course others may take; but as for me, give me liberty, or give me death!"

It was early morning. The sun was shining and birds were singing in the gnarled old oak tree on the bank of the river. The water ran so smoothly and quietly, you could hardly hear it. A man in a coonskin cap was sitting under the oak tree fishing. He listened to the birds and to the river, and watched the silver trout under the water, but his thoughts were far away. His tall shaggy horse nibbled at the grass nearby and waited patiently. He was hungry and the grass was mostly weeds, but he was used to that and he seemed not to mind it.

An old wagon rumbled down the road and slowed up. The man in the wagon looked around and waved his hand. But the fisherman was not looking in his direction and did not see him. The man in the wagon shook his head, and clucked to his horse to go on. He was in a hurry to get to the store, to trade the pelt of the fox he had trapped on his mountain farm, for nails he needed to fix his roof.

"I saw Patrick Henry fishing," he told the storekeeper, later.

"I thought Patrick went to Williamsburg to sit in the House of Burgesses," exclaimed a wiry little man sorting seeds he wanted for his garden.

"So did I," said the farmer. "But there he was sitting on the bank of the South Anna fishing."

"Maybe Louisa County made a mistake to elect Patrick to the House," said the little man.

"Maybe so," said the farmer. "Patrick failed as a storekeeper and he failed as a farmer. He may fail as a politician."

The storekeeper shook his head. Everybody in Hanover came to his store to buy and to trade, and stayed to talk about this one and that one. "Folks think well of Patrick," he said at last. "Patrick is a good lawyer."

"Patrick studied law only six weeks," laughed the little man.

"He is a mighty good lawyer," said the storekeeper again. "He won that 'Parson's Cause' case right over lawyer Lyons' head. People are expecting big things of Patrick."

A rider in buckskin breeches and a coonskin cap over his tousled red hair, pulled up his horse at the door at this moment, and entered the store, carrying a fishing basket over his shoulder. "Good morning," he called out in a friendly voice.

"Good morning, Patrick Henry," said the storekeeper. "We thought maybe you went to Williamsburg."

"I should be on my way there now," admitted Patrick. "But there isn't a better place to think things over than sitting with a fishing rod in your hand and a fish nibbling at the bait."

The men crowded around the newcomer to examine the silvery trout shining against the sides of the basket.

"I'll trade you a new rod for the catch," offered the storekeeper.

"I guess Sally will want half of it," smiled Patrick. "And you take the rest."

The storekeeper went to fetch a basket to transfer his share of the fish while Patrick scanned the shelf. "It isn't a fishing rod I want this morning, but a little present to leave with my wife and the children while I am away to Williamsburg," he said after a while. His eyes fell on a crock of wild honey on the counter, as he spoke. "That's just the thing," he nodded.

"Jim Hastings found a honey tree the other day. It's the best honey I've had in a long while," said the storekeeper, measuring off a generous chunk of golden honey into a container.

Patrick fitted the small crock of honey into the pocket of his hunting jacket, flung the basket of fish to his shoulder and rode away as suddenly as he had come. Humming a tune and weighing in his mind the things he had been thinking about when fishing, he hardly noticed how his horse galloped to get home to breakfast.

"Father is coming, Mother!" Little Martha ran shouting into the house where Sally was preparing her spinning wheel for the day. Sally and her two younger daughters, Ann and Betsy, came out on the porch where Billy, the young terrier, was barking a wild welcome at his master. Patrick lifted his little daughters, one after the other, for a swing high above his shoulders. They screamed and laughed, and asked to do it again.

"What?" he cried, pretending to be angry. "Away with you. You are making me work too hard." But they knew he was only pretending and that he would swing them again. They laughed and danced about him and hung on to his hunting jacket.

"I nearly forgot to tell you in this commotion," said Patrick, "I bumped right into a honey tree."

"A honey tree?" shouted little Martha.

"A honey tree, a honey tree," sang the little girls reaching for the crock of honey.

"Help, help," cried Patrick capturing the crock, and handing it to Sally. "The honey tree sent it to you with compliments."

Sally laughed, and took the honey jar. "We were waiting breakfast for you," and she led the family to the belated breakfast.

They gathered around the table and listened wide eyed to Patrick's account of his adventure —"Shandy, the horse, found a four-leaf clover in the weeds. The birds were so pleased they began to sing a dance tune, and would you believe it, the trout in the brook danced to the tune." The little girls shouted with delight. They were used to his stories. But suddenly he stopped talking, got up from the table and began to pack a bundle, to take with him to Williamsburg: a homespun coat and a fresh shirt to wear to the House of Burgesses. "They will be elegant folks there," he said to Sally, pointing with pretended disapproval at the hunting shirt he was wearing.

"They may be dressed in elegant coats, but you'll measure up to the best of them," said Sally with confidence.

"Play us a tune, father," begged little Martha.

"Yes, yes, play us a tune," chimed in Ann and Betsy.

"Who ever heard of it, a tune so early in the morning?" Patrick pretended to look outraged.

"A good-by tune," said little Martha.

"I'll play you a weepy tune then," said Patrick, brushing away imaginary tears.

"A dance tune, father, a merry tune," cried the little girls clapping their hands.

"So? A dance tune? Very well," he said, still pretending to weep. His fiddle in his hands now, he began to play one tune after another. The children danced around him in circles, singing the tunes to keep time. Then his face became stern. He stopped playing, laid the fiddle in its case and tied it into his bundle.

Jack White, his young Negro servant, brought the shaggy horse to the door now.

"There," cried Patrick, "Jack knows I should be on my way."

"Must you go? Do you have to go away?" The little girls clung to his legs and to his arms.

"Be good, be extra good while I am away." He lifted each one for another high swing and a kiss.

Sally walked beside him to where the impatient horse was pawing the ground, eager to be off.

"There will be important questions to decide," said Patrick quietly.

"You will be equal to whatever comes up," Sally assured him.

He leaned over, kissed her good-by, and jumped on his horse. The young terrier ran barking after him as the horse trotted away.

The sun was high in the blue sky, the air was sweet with honeysuckle and wild orange. It was a beautiful morning. Patrick Henry sat on his horse, lost in thought. He had not been in Williamsburg since the day he went there to ask Wythe and Peyton Randolph to sign his license to practice law. He smiled now as he remembered it all—Wythe, the learned scholar, refused even to listen to his arguments.

"You say you studied law alone, and only for six weeks?" asked Wythe with a frown. "Go to college, young man, and study with proper teachers," he told him.

It was a great good fortune for him, mused Patrick, that the venerable Peyton Randolph became interested in his arguments and consented to sign his license to practice law. And two other lawyers did likewise. They believed in him. Why? wondered Patrick, gratefully. He promised them that he would continue to read and to study. But that was not the reason they believed in him; he understood it better now. They were convinced he could be a lawyer by the way he argued his own case with them. "Yes," he cried aloud, and the lean horse under him bounced forward to a quicker pace, raising a cloud of red dust on the bumpy road. "I proved it, I proved I am a good lawyer."

The sun was hot on his shoulders. Patrick took off his cap and mopped his forehead. He felt excited and happy and a little uneasy at the same time. He was going to sit in the House of Burgesses. It was an honor, but more important, he thought soberly, was the opportunity he would now have to help shape events, make changes for the better for the people in the colonies.

It was dusk by the time his horse turned into Duke of Gloucester Street. After Hanover, Williamsburg seemed very elegant to Patrick. Fashionable ladies in silks and velvets passed him by in elegant carriages. Patrick galloped down the entire length of the street from William and Mary College at one end, to the Capitol at the other. He turned about to trot back to the Raleigh Tavern. The uncurtained windows of the tavern sparkled with candlelight. Patrick reined his horse, and watched the parade of gentlemen in powdered wigs, frilled shirts, velvet coats and knee breeches, coming and going in and out of the wide doors of the tavern. It would be a pleasant place to stay the night, but as he jingled his meager purse in his hand, he decided he must find himself a cheaper place. He thought of Sally and his little daughters snug at home. He felt lonely now, wondering where he could find a bed to sleep.

Two men came out of the tavern talking and laughing, and stopped to try a new dance step on the green in front of the tavern. Patrick pulled his violin out of his bundle and started to play a dance tune. A horseman galloped by, and came back presently. A tall slender young man with sandy red hair leaned forward from the saddle— "Patrick Henry," he called out in a surprised voice. "I was wondering who it could be, playing like that."

"Thomas Jefferson," exclaimed Patrick in a delighted voice.

"What are you doing in Williamsburg?" asked Jefferson.

"I guess you haven't heard I've been elected to the House of Burgesses from Louisa County," said Patrick with a slow smile.

"Then you've come to Williamsburg to sit in the House of Burgesses. Stay the night at my house," invited Jefferson.

"Thank you," said Patrick with a wide smile. "I was just wondering where I'd sleep this night."

"I'll hurry and tell Caesar there will be company, and you come along," Jefferson called over his shoulder as he galloped away in the dusk.

Patrick finished playing his tune, and went to find a stable to put his horse away for the night.

Caesar, Jefferson's young slave, was waiting for him at the door when he arrived, the bundle under his arm. "Come right in, sir, come right in." Caesar beamed a wide smile as he led the way into Jefferson's bachelor apartment. It was a pleasant room to come into out of the night. Candles were lit on the fine mahogany table. The white cloth and the silver sparkled in the candlelight. Book shelves crowded with books lined the walls: law books, histories, poetry. Patrick put his bundle on the sofa, took off his coonskin cap, and went to wash the dust from his hands and face.

Jefferson came in from an inner room now, his sandy hair freshly combed, his white face shining with a genial smile. He was seven years younger than Patrick, and he was still a student, studying law at William and Mary College, but already he was a finished gentleman. "You are just in time," he exclaimed gaily. "Caesar is waiting to give us our supper."

The cold meat and hot corn bread tasted good to Patrick after his long ride. There were many things to talk about, pleasant things they both remembered as they sat in the soft candlelight— "Do you remember the first time we met?" asked Jefferson in his slow genial voice. "'Twas a house party at Captain Daindridge's house."

"Ay, at Hanover, at Captain Nathaniel West Daindridge's house. It was Christmas holiday," reminisced Patrick with a wide smile.

"I still remember the dance tunes you played," smiled Jefferson. "But I hear you have become a great lawyer now," he added, shortly.

"I wouldn't claim that." Patrick looked very serious now, and pleased at the same time, that Jefferson had heard a flattering report of him.

"The learned lawyers, here in Williamsburg, talk with much wonder of the way you pleaded that 'Parson's Cause' case," said Jefferson.

"The lawyers are surprised I won the case, because they know I studied by myself, and only for six weeks," grinned Patrick.

"Well, yes," admitted Jefferson. "It's a wonder to us all; and what's more to wonder at is that you win every case you take."

"The 'Parson's Cause' case was my first case," said Patrick. "I was mighty anxious to win that case for my clients. I read and studied in the law books, and prepared my case carefully to make sure my arguments would be correct. But first I made sure I was in the right. When I know a thing is right, I plead from the heart."

"From the heart, I like that," exclaimed Jefferson. "Maybe you didn't need to read law books as long as we all do at college."

"As to that, I promised Peyton Randolph when he signed my license that I would read and study, and I do," said Patrick.

"When you are not fishing and hunting," laughed Jefferson.

"It is true, I'd rather fish and hunt," confessed Patrick with a wide smile. Caesar came in now to clear the table. Jefferson took his violin from the top shelf of his bookcase and began to tune it.

"That 'Parson's Cause' case," said Patrick, "gave me a chance to show the Parliament in England that they can't tell us here in the colonies, what we should pay our clergy. The Parliament in England is running us high handed, what with taxes and trade regulations."

"That's true," Jefferson nodded, his face clouded now. "But we can't deny that England has a right to tax her colonies and that's what we are, a colony to England."

"Nevertheless, they go too far, and now there is that Stamp Act. It's not only a nuisance, but a hardship," cried Patrick, with such heat that Jefferson stopped tuning his violin, and stood waiting to hear what he had on his mind. "We'll have to pay for a stamp every time we use a legal paper, and every time we buy a newspaper or sign a document. Are we going to submit to that?"

Jefferson scratched a few notes on his violin, his face grave and thoughtful. He felt embarrassed that he had not given the question much thought. Patrick seemed to know and to understand things he had hardly thought about. "No one likes the Stamp Act, but what can we do about it?" he asked after a while.

Patrick fumbled in his bundle for his violin and struck up one of the tunes they had played together at the Christmas house party in Hanover. It was a merry tune; they broke out into a song, and began to dance. Another tune came to their minds, and then another. They forgot England, and the tax and law books. Their voices rang out through the windows into the starlit night. Suddenly there was a loud banging on the door. Jefferson stopped playing and went to the door still holding the fiddle in his hand. A man in a nightshirt and a night cap over his head was shivering in the night air on the doorstep.

"Sir," he cried indignantly. "The whole neighborhood is waiting for you to stop fiddling. It is long past midnight. No one can sleep with such noise going on."

"I am right sorry, sir," apologized Jefferson. "I had no idea it was that late."

"Look at the clock, look at the clock," roared the man, as he turned to go to his house.

Jefferson tiptoed back into his rooms and went to bed. Patrick took off his dusty boots and curled up on the sofa to sleep.

The sun was just rising when Patrick wakened. This was the *day,* he remembered instantly, his first day to sit in the House of Burgesses. He tiptoed noiselessly into the dressing room to wash and dress himself with particular care.

When Jefferson wakened a little later, he saw Patrick sitting at the window dressed in the new homespun coat he had brought with him, his red unruly hair carefully groomed. He was too engrossed, writing on the flyleaf of an old book, to notice Jefferson standing in the doorway.

"I hope you don't mind," he called out when he looked up presently and saw Jefferson watching him with an amused smile.

"Not in the least," Jefferson assured him. "The book is in tatters."

"I didn't want to waken you to ask for paper," explained Patrick, as he tore the leaf from the book, folded it carefully, and put it in his pocket.

Caesar came in with breakfast now, and Jefferson wondered what Patrick had to write down in such a hurry that he couldn't wait to ask for paper. But Patrick Henry didn't offer to tell him.

The Capitol building was crowded to the door for there were many people in Williamsburg who were anxious to hear the debate on the Stamp Act. The law students from William and Mary College were obliged to stand in the doorway to listen to the discourses in the House of Burgesses. Patrick lingered in the entrance for a parting word with Jefferson before he pushed his way through the crowd into the courtroom. Speaker of the House Robinson, was already in his place at the front. The leaders of the House, wealthy plantation owners in powdered wigs and broadcloth coats, were talking in little clusters, laughing at each other's pleasantries.

They didn't seem at all preoccupied with the important question that was to be discussed, marveled Patrick Henry. He was glad to recognize George Johnston, of Fairfax County, standing near by. Here was someone he could sound out—"What will be done about the Stamp Act, sir?" he asked Johnston.

"Nothing more can be done about it," Johnston shrugged his shoulders. "The Stamp Act's been passed. We don't like it, but what can we do about it?" he demanded.

"We can protest," cried Patrick hotly.

"Protest?" Johnston looked surprised.

"If we accept the Stamp Act without a protest it's a sign we've no spirit. That's what they'll think about us in England, and they'll be right. And they'll levy more taxes on us. We'll be taxed and taxed and taxed again and again."

"We have no redress. We can't stop them taxing us. We're subject to the crown," reasoned Johnston.

Patrick pulled out a folded paper from his pocket and handed it to Johnston. "I've written out seven resolutions, sir, if you would care to read them. You might be willing also to second them."

Johnston took the paper and read it slowly. An excited look came into his eyes. "I'm with you, sir, I'll second your resolutions," he cried.

Speaker Robinson was now pounding the table with his silver mace. Patrick slouched into his seat on the long wooden bench with the other burgesses. Two men on the bench beside him were talking in low grumbling voices. "We force the soil so as to grow bigger crops of tobacco so as to pay taxes to England," one of the men was saying.

"Ay, and if we keep on forcing the soil, there'll be no life left in it," said the other man. "It's getting poorer all the time."

"That's it," exclaimed a man in a nearby seat. "Can't raise crops on poor soil."

"I've no glass in my windows, but I must pay taxes to the crown before I spend money on window glass," broke in a third man.

"If we spent some of that tax money on fixing our roads—" mumbled another burgess from the up country.

"The meeting please come to order," cried the clerk.

A gentleman in a powdered wig and a handsome coat, stood up now and began to talk. He looked very imposing as he stood there, talking in a loud voice—"The Stamp Act seems to have caused much talk," he measured every word carefully. "The fact is, this tax is so small it is but a trifle. I see it more as a nuisance rather than a hardship to complain about."

"The cost of the stamp may be small, but it's an extra tax, and it's a tax too much," cried a voice from the back seat in the row of benches.

No one paid attention to the interruption. A

stout man with many ruffles of fine lace on his shirt stood up now and began to explain the reason why the colonies should pay the tax with good grace—"The English Parliament deems it necessary to fix the Stamp Act, therefore we, the loyal subjects to the crown, are willing to obey."

"The two gentlemen hold the welfare of the crown before the welfare of the colonies, it seems to me," Patrick whispered to Johnston.

"Governor Fauquier is a Tory as you may have heard, and he has many admirers in the House," Johnston whispered back.

Patrick listened to the speeches of the leaders of the House with a frown, and shifted uneasily in his seat. Suddenly he stood up and began to talk. His voice sounded frightened at the first few words:

"The English Parliament is interfering with the affairs of the colonies," he exclaimed. "The misrule of the English Parliament has brought great hardships to the colonies," Patrick's voice grew louder and firmer.

"Who is this buckskin gentleman, giving his views?" cried an indignant voice from the front.

"An ignorant fellow from the backwoods," said one of the lawyers with a shrug.

Patrick went on talking as if he had not heard them. He was talking about something he understood and treasured. He was talking about liberty, the right of men to govern themselves. His eyes glowed, his voice rang. A spell fell on the assembly as they listened to his arguments—"We submit to taxation without representation," he cried in a challenging voice.

Peyton Randolph frowned. He was a proud Virginia gentleman, and he was also attorney general to the king of England.

"This thing must be stopped," he said to Pendleton. Wythe shook his head. A debate started up now as leaders of the House rose to interrupt Patrick at every word—"Is this new member from Louisa County claiming Virginia has a right to make laws to resist the English Parliament?" demanded an indignant voice.

In answer Patrick unfolded the piece of paper he was holding in his hand and began to read what he had scribbled there early that morning:

"The first adventurers who settled in America brought with them the right of franchise," Patrick pronounced each word in a high fiery voice.

"What's that?" interrupted an angry man at the front. Patrick straightened his shoulders and went on reading from his paper, explaining the rights of the colonies.

"Two royal charters were granted by King James the First that entitled the colonies to all privileges, liberties and immunities . . . as if they were living within the realm of England. . . ."

"Patrick Henry may be from the backwoods," called out a burgess from the benches, "but it's Patrick Henry, this man from the backwoods, and not our learned lawyers who is saying what we need to know."

"Yes, that's true," said Wythe to Peyton Randolph. "I now wish I had signed his license to practice law."

Peyton Randolph frowned, his face red and angry.

"Resolved therefore," Patrick went on—"Resolved that the general assembly of this colony have the only sole and exclusive rights and power to lay taxes and impositions upon the inhabitants of this colony."

"This is sedition," cried out a Tidewater gentleman.

"Sedition, sedition," cried out several leaders of the House.

"No person that is not in the general assembly of the colonies has a right to impress taxation on the people of the colonies; such a person should be considered an enemy. Caesar had his Brutus and Charles the First his Cromwell and George the Third—"

"Shame, shame," interrupted the Speaker of the House, pounding his mace on the table.

"Treason," cried an indignant voice. "Shame, treason, treason," resounded from all sides.

Patrick looked around him slowly, noting the frightened faces. His eyes flashed—"And George the Third may profit by their example." His voice rang and echoed in the ceiling. "If this be treason, make the most of it."

The whole House buzzed with excited voices now. The burgesses crowded around Patrick to congratulate him, clapping him on the shoulder, shaking his hand.

"Who was Caesar?" a farmer was asking.

"Caesar was a dictator in olden times in Rome. He ruled the people of Rome without their consent exactly, and Brutus killed him. And Charles the First tried to rule England without Parliament; Cromwell and his army beheaded him," explained a more informed burgess with a knowing wink.

At the front of the House, Tidewater gentlemen were talking in troubled voices. Many of them agreed with what Patrick said, but they were not ready to say aloud what might bring on war.

Patrick listened to the buzz of many voices all talking at once. There was to be a vote. They were going to vote on his resolves. The burgesses from the back country were in high spirits, making jokes and laughing. They gave their vote fearlessly; come what might, they were ready for it in their own minds. Patrick listened to the vote as it was taken—Some of the burgesses had gone home to their mountain farms to look after the spring plowing, but there were enough left who would vote for his resolves. "We'll win by a small majority," he whispered to Johnston. He looked very sober now. Virginia must not lose this chance to stand up, and show the English Parliament that the colonies had a spirit in them to resist oppression.

The clerk cleared his throat and announced the vote. The resolves had passed. That meant that the colonies would offer a protest based on what they knew was their right.

The House adjourned. The burgesses could go home now to their plowing. They lingered a while to talk— This was an important day. They all only dimly guessed how important it was. They left the Capitol at last. There was a lot to think about on the way home. This day, May 29, 1765, was a day to remember.

Patrick went now to find his bundle which he had left in a corner of the entry.

"You spoke with courage and with wisdom." Jefferson came up now to press his hand warmly. "From today, I shall take note of the affairs in the colonies."

"You spoke for all Virginia," one of the leaders of the House stopped to say to Patrick as he was leaving the Capitol.

"I hope so, sir," Patrick bowed. He could bow with as much grace as any Tidewater gentleman when he chose. But now he was thinking of going home. He went to get his horse. He could

go fishing with an easy mind now, and he might hunt in the woods, and trap a bear, as he once did— But his foremost thought would remain with meetings in Louisa County, and in the Hanover Courthouse, where he would raise his voice to challenge men's minds to think of freedom as a gift already theirs to claim.

His lean horse trotted briskly over the red clay road. Patrick clicked his tongue to spur him on. He was in a hurry to get home to share his happiness with Sally. He had spoken for Virginia. He felt proud of that, but in the back of his thoughts was the hope that all the other colonies might hear of it, and arise to speak for their rights.

## from ABE LINCOLN GROWS UP
### Carl Sandburg

*Carl Sandburg was both a poet and an authority on Lincoln lore. From the first volume of his* Lincoln (1809–1865) *biography he made a cutting for children and young people called* Abe Lincoln Grows Up, *excerpted here.*

### "Peculiarsome" Abe

The farm boys in their evenings at Jones's store in Gentryville talked about how Abe Lincoln was always reading, digging into books, stretching out flat on his stomach in front of the fireplace, studying till midnight and past midnight, picking a piece of charcoal to write on the fire shovel, shaving off what he wrote, and then writing more—till midnight and past midnight. The next thing Abe would be reading books between the plow handles, it seemed to them. And once trying to speak a last word, Dennis Hanks said, "There's suthin' peculiarsome about Abe."

He wanted to learn, to know, to live, to reach out; he wanted to satisfy hungers and thirsts he couldn't tell about, this big boy of the backwoods. And some of what he wanted so much, so deep down, seemed to be in the books. Maybe in books he would find the answers to dark questions pushing around in the pools of his thoughts and the drifts of his mind. He told Dennis and other people, "The things I want to know are in books; my best friend is the man who'll git me a book I ain't read." And sometimes friends answered, "Well, books ain't as plenty as wildcats in these parts o' Indianny."

This was one thing meant by Dennis when he said there was "suthin' peculiarsome" about Abe. It seemed that Abe made the books tell him more than they told other people. All the other farm boys had gone to school and read "The Kentucky Preceptor," but Abe picked out questions from it, such as "Who has the most right to complain, the Indian or the Negro?" and Abe would talk about it, up one way and down the other, while they were in the cornfield pulling fodder for the winter. When Abe got hold of a storybook and read about a boat that came near a magnetic rock, and how the magnets in the rock pulled all the nails out of the boat so it went to pieces and the people in the boat found themselves floundering in water, Abe thought it was funny and told it to other people. After Abe read poetry, especially Bobby Burns's poems, Abe began writing rhymes himself. When Abe sat with a girl, with their bare feet in the creek water and she spoke of the moon rising, he explained to her it was the earth moving and not the moon—the moon only seemed to rise.

John Hanks, who worked in the fields barefooted with Abe, grubbing stumps, plowing, mowing, said: "When Abe and I came back to the house from work, he used to go to the cupboard, snatch a piece of corn bread, sit down, take a book, cock his legs up high as his head, and read. Whenever Abe had a chance in the field while at work, or at the house, he would stop and read." He liked to explain to other people what he was getting from books; explaining an idea to some one else made it clearer to him. The habit was growing on him of reading out loud; words came more real if picked from the silent page of the book and pronounced on the tongue; new balances and values of words stood out if spoken aloud. When writing letters for his father or the neighbors, he read the words out loud as they got written. Before writing a letter he asked questions such as: "What do you want to say in the letter? How do you want to say it? Are you sure that's the best way to say it? Or do you think we can fix up a better way to say it?"

As he studied his books his lower lip stuck out; Josiah Crawford noticed it was a habit and joked Abe about the "stuck-out lip." This habit too stayed with him.

He wrote in his Sum Book or arithmetic that Compound Division was "When several numbers of Divers Denominations are given to be divided by 1 common divisor," and worked on the exercise in multiplication; "If 1 foot contain 12 inches I demand how many there are in 126 feet." Thus the schoolboy.

What he got in the schools didn't satisfy him. He went to three different schools in Indiana, besides two in Kentucky—altogether about four months of school. He learned his A B C, how to spell, read, write. And he had been with the other barefoot boys in butternut jeans learning "manners" under the schoolteacher, Andrew Crawford, who had them open a door, walk in, and say, "Howdy do?" Yet what he tasted of books in school was only a beginning, only made him hungry and thirsty, shook him with a wanting and a wanting of more and more of what was hidden between the covers of books.

He kept on saying, "The things I want to know are in books; my best friend is the man who'll git me a book I ain't read." He said that

to Pitcher, the lawyer over at Rockport, nearly twenty miles away, one fall afternoon, when he walked from Pigeon Creek to Rockport and borrowed a book from Pitcher. Then when fodder-pulling time came a few days later, he shucked corn from early daylight till sundown along with his father and Dennis Hanks and John Hanks, but after supper he read the book till midnight, and at noon he hardly knew the taste of his corn-bread because he had a book in front of him. It was a hundred little things like these which made Dennis Hanks say there was "suthin' peculiarsome" about Abe.

Besides reading the family Bible and figuring his way all through the old arithmetic they had at home, he got hold of "Aesop's Fables," "Pilgrim's Progress," "Robinson Crusoe," and Weems's "The Life of Francis Marion." The book of fables, written or collected thousands of years ago by the Greek slave, known as Aesop, sank deep in his mind. As he read through the book a second and third time, he had a feeling there were fables all around him, that everything he touched and handled, everything he saw and learned had a fable wrapped in it somewhere. One fable was about a bundle of sticks and a farmer whose sons were quarreling and fighting.

There was a fable in two sentences which read, "A coachman, hearing one of the wheels of his coach make a great noise, and perceiving that it was the worst one of the four, asked how it came to take such a liberty. The wheel answered that from the beginning of time, creaking had always been the privilege of the weak." And there were shrewd, brief incidents of foolery such as this: "A waggish, idle fellow in a country town, being desirous of playing a trick on the simplicity of his neighbors and at the same time putting a little money in his pocket at their cost, advertised that he would on a certain day show a wheel carriage that should be so contrived as to go without horses. By silly curiosity the rustics were taken in, and each succeeding group who came out from the show were ashamed to confess to their neighbors that they had seen nothing but a wheelbarrow."

The style of the Bible, of Aesop's fables, the hearts and minds back of those books, were much in his thoughts. His favorite pages in them he read over and over. Behind such proverbs as,

"Muzzle not the ox that treadeth out the corn," and "He that ruleth his own spirit is greater than he that taketh a city," there was a music of simple wisdom and a mystery of common everyday life that touched deep spots in him, while out of the fables of the ancient Greek slave he came to see that cats, rats, dogs, horses, plows, hammers, fingers, toes, people, all had fables connected with their lives, characters, places. There was, perhaps, an outside for each thing as it stood alone, while inside of it was its fable.

One book came, titled, "The Life of George Washington, with Curious Anecdotes, Equally Honorable to Himself and Exemplary to His Young Countrymen. Embellished with Six Steel Engravings, by M. L. Weems, formerly Rector of Mt. Vernon Parish." It pictured men of passion and proud ignorance in the government of England driving their country into war on the American colonies. It quoted the far-visioned warning of Chatham to the British parliament, "For God's sake, then, my lords, let the way be instantly opened for reconciliation. I say instantly; or it will be too late forever."

The book told of war, as at Saratoga. "Hoarse as a mastiff of true British breed, Lord Balcarras was heard from rank to rank, loud-animating his troops; while on the other hand, fierce as a hungry Bengal tiger, the impetuous Arnold precipitated heroes on the stubborn foe. Shrill and terrible, from rank to rank, resounds the clash of bayonets—frequent and sad the groans of the dying. Pairs on pairs, Britons and Americans, with each his bayonet at his brother's breast, fall forward together faint-shrieking in death, and mingle their smoking blood." Washington, the man, stood out, as when he wrote, "These things so harassed my heart with grief, that I solemnly declared to God, if I know myself, I would gladly offer myself a sacrifice to the butchering enemy, if I could thereby insure the safety of these my poor distressed countrymen."

The Weems book reached some deep spots in the boy. He asked himself what it meant that men should march, fight, bleed, go cold and hungry for the sake of what they called "freedom."

"Few great men are great in everything," said the book. And there was a cool sap in the passage: "His delight was in that of the manliest sort, which, by stringing the limbs and swelling the muscles, promotes the kindliest flow of blood and spirits. At jumping with a long pole, or heaving heavy weights, for his years he hardly had an equal."

Such book talk was a comfort against the same thing over again, day after day, so many mornings the same kind of water from the same spring, the same fried pork and corn-meal to eat, the same drizzles of rain, spring plowing, summer weeds, fall fodder-pulling, each coming every year, with the same tired feeling at the end of the day, so many days alone in the woods or the fields or else the same people to talk with, people from whom he had learned all they could teach him. Yet there ran through his head the stories and sayings of other people, the stories and sayings of books, the learning his eyes had caught from books; they were a comfort; they were good to have because they were good by themselves; and they were still better because they broke the chill of the lonesome feeling.

He was thankful to the writer of Aesop's fables because that writer stood by him and walked with him, an invisible companion, when he pulled fodder or chopped wood. Books lighted lamps in the dark rooms of his gloomy hours. . . . Well—he would live on; maybe the time would come when he would be free from work for a few weeks, or a few months, with books, and then he would read. . . . God, then he would read. . . . Then he would go and get at the proud secrets of his books.

His father—would he be like his father when he grew up? He hoped not. Why should his father knock him off a fence rail when he was asking a neighbor, passing by, a question? Even if it was a smart question, too pert and too quick, it was no way to handle a boy in front of a neighbor. No, he was going to be a man different from his father. The books—his father hated the books. His father talked about "too much eddication"; after readin', writin', 'rithmetic, that was enough, his father said. He, Abe Lincoln, the boy, wanted to know more than the father, Tom Lincoln, wanted to know. Already Abe knew more than his father; he was writing letters for the neighbors; they hunted out the Lincoln farm to get young Abe to find his bottle of ink with blackberry brier root and copperas in it, and his pen made from a turkey buzzard feather, and

write letters. Abe had a suspicion sometimes his father was a little proud to have a boy that could write letters, and tell about things in books, and outrun and outwrestle and rough-and-tumble any boy or man in Spencer County. Yes, he would be different from his father; he was already so; it couldn't be helped.

In growing up from boyhood to young manhood, he had survived against lonesome, gnawing monotony and against floods, forest and prairie fires, snake-bites, horse-kicks, ague, chills, fever, malaria, "mill-sick."

A comic outline against the sky he was, hiking along the roads of Spencer and other counties in southern Indiana in those years when he read all the books within a fifty-mile circuit of his home. Stretching up on the long legs that ran from his moccasins to the body frame with its long, gangling arms, covered with linsey-woolsey, then the lean neck that carried the head with its surmounting coonskin cap or straw hat—it was, again, a comic outline—yet with a portent in its shadow. His laughing "Howdy," his yarns and drollery, opened the doors of men's hearts.

Starting along in his eleventh year came spells of abstraction. When he was spoken to, no answer came from him. "He might be a thousand miles away." The roaming, fathoming, searching, questioning operations of the minds and hearts of poets, inventors, beginners who take facts stark, these were at work in him. This was one sort of abstraction he knew; there was another: the blues took him; coils of multiplied melancholies wrapped their blue frustrations inside him, all that Hamlet, Koheleth, Schopenhauer have uttered, in a mesh of foiled hopes. "There was absolutely nothing to excite ambition for education," he wrote later of that Indiana region. Against these "blues," he found the best warfare was to find people and trade with them his yarns and drolleries. John Baldwin, the blacksmith, with many stories and odd talk and eye-slants, was a help and a light.

Days came when he sank deep in the stream of human life and felt himself kin of all that swam in it, whether the waters were crystal or mud.

He learned how suddenly life can spring a surprise. One day in the woods, as he was sharpening a wedge on a log, the ax glanced, nearly took his thumb off, and left a white scar after healing.

"You never cuss a good ax," was a saying in those timbers.

## from WE ALCOTTS

### Aileen Fisher and Olive Rabe

*In writing the story of Louisa May Alcott's family from the viewpoint of her mother, the "Marmee" of* Little Women, *the authors have compiled a biography that is interesting as a background for the family life portrayed in the story and that is equally interesting as a picture of the intellectual and political ferment in New England. The Bronson Alcott family's friends included Thoreau, Emerson, Whitman, Parker, and other leaders of literary and philosophical circles. The father of the family was an idealist who experimented in new ways to teach children and whose family cheerfully participated in such experiments in living at the Fruitlands Commune. Much of the story is about Louisa (1832–1888): her stormy moods, her sense of responsibility, her joy in writing.*

### [My Kingdom]

After her fourteenth birthday, Louisa tried harder than ever to curb her temper and shake off her moods. Having a room of her own where she could sit and think and write made more difference than I thought possible.

One of the first poems Louisa wrote with the new pen was on this very subject. She called it "My Kingdom," a long poem of thirty-two lines, which I thought read exceedingly well. I was surprised and delighted, for I had many a time read poems in the papers that did not come up to this standard. How well she summarized her theme in the last stanza!

> "I do not ask for any crown
> But that which all may win,
> Nor seek to conquer any world
> Except the one within.
> Be thou my guide until I find,
> Led by a tender hand,

> Thy happy kingdom in myself,
> And dare to take command."

Mr. Alcott and I were happy to think that both Louisa and Anna had a natural gift for writing. Their practice in collaborating on the plays that they produced and acted in, gave them a feeling for the dramatic in stories. Louisa had a further flair for the fanciful. If only, I often thought, their father had some of the girls' spontaneity and freedom in writing, if only he could write as naturally and easily as he could talk! His staid, scholarly style made his work formidable and hard to read, to say nothing of making it hard to sell.

Ever since Mr. Emerson had adversely criticized a manuscript of Mr. Alcott's years before, a manuscript on which months of toil had been lavished, my husband had resigned himself to the conviction that he could never succeed as a writer. Perhaps it was true. It did seem that words that flowed so fluently from my husband's lips became stilted as soon as he put them on paper.

His own lack of skill in writing did not in the least dull his pleasure in the girls' accomplishments. After reading "My Kingdom," he exclaimed, his face alight, "It seems we have a poet in the family!"

I doubt if there ever lived a father more devoted to a family of girls. The boy in him was never too old to play with them, even though the man's hair was turning white. Often he entered into their games in the barn and in the house, and walked with them through fields and woods and up the hill. From their earliest childhood he read aloud to them—*Pilgrim's Progress* every year, and other books like the *Faerie Queene* whose inward meanings needed explaining. He habitually planned their dresses because he had greater talent for design than I. When the girls were ill, he helped to nurse them. He often cooked their meals. He gave them lessons and encouraged them in their work. With kindness but firmness he disciplined them. And in return, one and all, they loved him.

As the girls grew older, the differences between them became more pronounced. Anna, our dependable quiet one, inherited her father's patience and shyness. Louisa might scold and fume over a disappointment, but Anna would accept it philosophically, confident that everything would turn out all right. Like her father, she was tall, blonde, and graceful, and she always seemed to retain her dignity. Anna had another characteristic that ever endeared her to me. From earliest childhood she was like a little mother, watching over Louy—when Louy would let her—and later mothering Elizabeth and Abba May with unending warmth and love.

Of all our girls, Elizabeth was most like her father. If I had to put it in one word, I should say "lovable." She had an even, serene temperament and the same kind of deep religious feeling her father had. They both *lived* it. The rapport between the two of them was a delight to see. Lizzie's talent for music, though, came through the Mays. She loved music and played the piano well, and with expression. Though not as hardy as the others, she was a sunny child and filled a special niche in all our hearts.

Our Abba May, with her sparkling temperament, was the most social of the four. Being the baby, she was, I am afraid, somewhat spoiled. Her fair complexion, light wavy hair, and blue eyes made her an unusually attractive child, except when impulsiveness or impatience ruled her. Like Louisa and me, she had a quick temper . . . and a quick repentance. Abba, whom we soon were to call May at her request, inherited her father's artistic sensitiveness and manual skill, and was never happier than when she had crayon or paintbrush in her hand.

Louisa . . . what shall I say about Louisa, who was always big for her age both in mind and body? Above all, she was her mother's child in ways besides appearance and temperament. She had my energetic constitution and practical outlook on life, and, my husband always said, my wit and tenderness. Yet one characteristic of her father's she had more strongly than any of the girls—a complete dedication to her ideals. Because she was like me in so many ways, I understood her far better than her father did, and felt especially close to her. She might be difficult at times, but she was always my Louy, full of vigor and ideas and surprises.

She often came to me in the kitchen to tell about a run she had had in the fields or woods, where "the moss was like velvet," and the trees made arches of bright leaves. Once she told how she stopped at the end of a woodsy walk and saw sunshine over the meadows. "It seemed like going through a dark life or grave into heaven beyond. A very strange and solemn feeling came over me as I stood there, with no sound but the rustle of the pines, no one near me, and the sun so glorious, as for me alone. It seemed as if I *felt* God as I never did before, and I prayed in my heart that I might keep that happy sense of nearness all my life."

One day, after she had been quiet in her room for several hours, she ran out to help me take down the washing. A gentle breeze was blowing through the bright green tops of the trees, and the grounds around Hillside, tended so lovingly by my husband, made the place look like a corner of paradise. "We won't ever have to move again, will we?" Louisa demanded suddenly. "Because if we move I'll have to give up my room. And it's the best thing I ever had."

I had been going through my usual struggle with finances that week. "I *hope* we can stay at Hillside," I answered. I did not want her to count on it too heavily. "It seems to be a habit of the Alcotts to move, though, Louy."

She looked at me closely. She must have seen the worry-lines on my face. "I'll get the other clothes basket," she said. In a few minutes she was back, carrying the basket by one handle, her other hand behind her back. She let the basket thump to the ground. "Guess what I've got, Marmee," she said.

"One of your 'beautiful' bugs?"

She opened her hand. It was full of small hoarded coins, fifty cents in all, which she had earned sewing doll clothes. "It's not much. But it's a start. I'll put everything I earn toward staying here at Hillside."

My voice quavered a little as I thanked her. She was learning about family straits early in life.

But our financial troubles were only part of our life. We had books to read aloud and discuss, and our table talk, and social times with the Emersons and other friends, and walks, and reform movements in which we were interested. We had, of course, kept up our active interest in the abolitionist issue. I belonged to the Women's Anti-Slavery Society in Concord and took part in its activities with great conviction and enthusiasm.

The second summer we lived at Hillside the women held their annual picnic, commemorating the freeing of the West Indian slaves, at Henry Thoreau's little house at Walden Pond. For years Henry's mother had been one of the prime movers of the Society, and Henry himself was an ardent abolitionist and conductor on the Underground Railroad. Often he took runaways to his mother's in the dark at night, and from there conducted them along their way toward Canada.

In February of '47 we Alcotts had a runaway slave from Maryland with us for two weeks. He had made several stops on the Underground Railroad before reaching Hillside, and we suggested that he needed a good rest before proceeding on his journey. I warned the girls not to breathe a word to their friends about the stranger at our house.

Louisa sensed the drama of the situation immediately, and asked in an anxious whisper, "But what if they come looking for him? Where can we hide him?" I had been wondering about that myself. "I know!" Louisa continued, her dark eyes sparkling with excitement. "There's that secret closet in the back bedroom next to the chimney. No one would think of looking there."

As it turned out we had no need for a hiding place. Our dark friend, with cap pulled down, even helped Mr. Alcott saw and pile wood in perfect safety. I was sure that Louisa kept careful watch from some vantage point, ready to give warning if anyone approached.

The runaway was about thirty years old, strong and self-reliant and full of courage. His tales of the wrongs and sufferings he had endured in Maryland made a deep impression on the girls and reinforced their feeling of the dreadful injustice of slavery. After he had been with us about two weeks, he felt he should be on his way to Canada and freedom, and we did what we could to help him toward his goal.

The third year we lived at Hillside our financial problems seemed worse than ever. Louisa sensed my worry more than any of the other girls. One day when we were alone together she asked suddenly, "Do you know what my greatest wish in life is?"

"To be famous? To make a happy marriage? To travel in Europe?"

"Bigger than any of those," Louisa replied. "To make enough money to pay off *all our debts.*"

I laughed. "Aren't you a little young to be thinking of making so much money, Louy?"

I kept hoping that we would, in some way, be able to remain at Hillside. "Hope, and keep busy," I had found was the best motto for a family like ours. While we hoped for money to come in, we kept busy, forgetting our needs in our accomplishments.

I had long since discovered that no matter how poor one was there were always those who were poorer. The girls came home one day telling of a little girl they had talked to on the way to the village. The child had had nothing to eat all day. Next morning we decided to carry our breakfast to the starving family, and although it was only simple fare, to them it was a feast.

We were not the only ones beset with financial troubles that year. In August the dream of George and Sophia Ripley came to an end when Brook Farm, in its seventh year of life, dissolved. They had lost all their money in the venture and were heavily in debt besides.

"What will become of them now?" I asked my husband.

"I understand they are going to New York. Mr. Ripley will keep on with his writing, and his wife hopes to find a teaching position. Somehow or other they say they will pay off their debts."

"My heart goes out to them," I murmured.

Along with debts, Louisa was a problem. She was in a particularly difficult stage, posing a trial especially for her father, who found it hard to understand his dark-eyed daughter. She would be moodily silent for hours, even days at a time, not even answering when spoken to. Then again she would burst forth so crossly and tempestuously we wished she were silent again. For a while her father thought she must be possessed by the devil, bound in chains that she seemed unable to break. I thought her actions not too difficult to explain. She was obviously much under the spell of the romantic reading she was doing, and she let her emotions get the upper hand.

A change for the better set in when she had her first taste of Goethe. In Mr. Emerson's library she came upon a volume of Goethe's letters to a young girl, Bettine, who had formed a romantic attachment for the great poet when he was nearly sixty years old. The romance fascinated Louisa. I learned years later that she immediately put herself in Bettine's place and Mr. Emerson in Goethe's place.

She became romantic, under the spell of the book, reading and writing poetry, keeping a "heart-journal" and wandering in the moonlight. She wrote long, endearing letters to Mr. Emerson, which she never sent. Later she told how she would sit in a tall cherry tree at midnight and sing romantic songs to the moon until the owls scared her to bed.

Of course, Mr. Alcott and I, and Mr. Emerson, were blissfully unconscious of the romance he was inspiring. But the venture into the romantic softened Louisa's moods and released some of the chains that my husband thought bound her.

The pressure of worry over family finances lifted for Mr. Alcott that summer, not because we came into a fortune, but because Mr. Emerson provided him with a congenial task. Mr. Emerson had been improving his grounds for years, adding plum, pear, and apple trees to his orchard, and having Mr. Thoreau and Mr. Hosmer bring pines and hemlocks and other trees to transplant around the house. He often sat and talked of an evening in Mr. Alcott's summerhouse, one of the many improvements my husband had made on our own place, and it occurred to our good friend and neighbor that a summerhouse on his own grounds would be an attractive addition.

Mr. Alcott was delighted to undertake the work. He felt pure joy in the task of creating an unusual little building in the Emerson garden. Mr. Emerson paid him fifty dollars, and as always the money was a godsend. But it seemed to me the work went on endlessly. For more than three months my husband put in long days, working on a bower in which he said his friend was to entertain the Muses, symbolized by nine upright posts. He went with Mr. Emerson and Henry Thoreau to Walden Woods to cut the hemlocks for these posts, and Henry helped for a day or two with the building. But the design was too original to suit him. It called for curved rafters, sweeping brackets under the cornice, and pointed arches over the openings and doorways.

My husband continued to work on this project almost till Thanksgiving Day. With amusement he listened to the comments of townspeople who kept coming to examine the building. Few saw it as an artistic achievement. "They say it's odd, Abba," he told me more than once. "They say it's the strangest thing they ever saw. A whirligig. But to me it has a beautiful simplicity. I prefer the curved line over the straight line in building. But Henry, now . . ." He chuckled. "Henry's geometrically-minded. He likes straight lines."

The summerhouse was still unfinished when Mr. Emerson sailed for Europe in October. In a way I dreaded to see him go. He was such an understanding friend, making books available to us all, taking us on walks and for drives in his carriage, asking us to his home on social occasions to meet his celebrated friends. Besides, he was ever willing to lend a hand in an unobtrusive way. We kept our financial troubles to ourselves, but he knew, of course, how little money we had coming in.

And how kind he was to the children, to Louisa particularly! She was an avid reader, and he gave her the run of his extensive library, letting her come and go like a member of the family. I could not imagine what life at Hillside would be like without the Emersons near by.

The day Mr. Emerson sailed, his wife, Henry Thoreau, my husband, and I went along to the wharf in Boston to see him off. The ship looked none too safe to me, nor to Henry either. We eyed it disdainfully when it could not even get out to sea by raising its own sails, but had to be ignominiously towed out. Mrs. Emerson stood bravely on the wharf waving good-bye. Behind my fluttering handkerchief I felt hot tears on my face. What if something happened to Mr. Emerson!

My load of misgiving and sadness continued until we learned that he had landed safely in England.

During his absence of over eight months,

Henry Thoreau again lived with the Emerson family. He had left Walden Pond the month before, after more than two years in his "hut," and was looking for a publisher for his manuscript on the Concord and Merrimack River trip. The Emerson children loved him, and so did Mrs. Emerson in her grateful motherly way.

The children loved our girls, too, and spent much time at Hillside. Our barn, which we never used for sheltering cows or horses, turned out to be an invaluable haven for them all. They used it not only for a theater, but for "playing school," with Anna and Louisa for teachers. The summer Louisa was fifteen, she started what she called a "real school" in the barn when Anna was off in New Hampshire on a visit. Ellen and Edith Emerson, who were nine and six that summer, were especially eager pupils. They hung on Louisa's words when she read them stories she wrote about flowers or ants or spiders. Besides, she conscientiously taught them the three R's, even though she had never been good at arithmetic or spelling. The money she earned she turned over to me proudly, and I accepted it in the same spirit.

"Do you think you'll be a teacher, Louy?" I asked.

She shook her head. "Some of it I like—the stories, the nature walks. But I don't like all that sitting down over lessons. I don't honestly think I'm cut out to be a teacher, Mother." She stared out of the window for a few minutes, then turned to me pensively. "Do you think anyone would ever pay me for writing stories?"

"That would involve a great deal of sitting down, too, wouldn't it?"

"Oh, but when I'm writing stories, I don't *know* I'm sitting," she replied quickly. "I don't even know when I'm hungry."

Fall in Concord was a beautiful time of year, and I somehow always found the peace of mind to enjoy the changing colors. But in late October of the year 1848 a disturbing wistfulness mingled with my peace as the yellows and reds deepened on the elms and maples. Soon winter would be closing in on us again, with its bitter cold and dwindling food supplies.

My heart clung to the happiness we had known for three years in our own home in Hillside, yet my head told me that the time had come when we must make a change. We had so often scraped the bottom of the barrel I expected it to fall apart any minute. What Mr. Alcott and I could earn in Concord simply wasn't enough to keep the family going. We had to face it. In Boston our chances might be better.

November was bitingly cold that year, the coldest the villagers could remember. I was beside myself with worry and uncertainty. One morning when the girls were at their lessons and Mr. Alcott at the woodpile, I did not make an effort to hold back my tears. Sitting at the kitchen table, I put my head on my arms and wept.

It was just at that moment that my old friend Maria Child arrived on a surprise visit. She had come to Boston on business, and decided to take the stage to Concord to see me. I looked up through my tears. She put her arms around me and urged me to tell her what was troubling me. I quickly regained my composure, except that the sight of my dear friend after many years, almost made me weep again from sheer joy.

I could not resist confiding in her. She was at once sympathetic and businesslike about our family straits. "Come to Boston," she said, "and let me help find work for you before I return to New York." Her confidence gave me hope.

Before the week was out, I had a position, and we Alcotts were beginning to pack our belongings.

One of the benevolent societies had hired me to visit the poor and decide where charity should be distributed. The work paid poorly and was very demanding, but I felt it was worthwhile. Without having a great deal to distribute, I had already been visiting the poor for many years. Now I had a chance to do it on a large scale. With gratitude I looked forward to returning to my home city, although it was a wrench to leave the home where we had been so happy, the first home of our own. We had lived at Hillside three and a half years, far longer than we had lived in any other house.

"Well, at least it isn't summer," Louisa remarked, as she went about gathering up her possessions. "It's easier to move when the leaves are down and everything is bleak and cold and gray. I just hope our prospects in Boston will be brighter than the November sky in Concord."

## from HARRIET TUBMAN: CONDUCTOR ON THE UNDERGROUND RAILROAD

*Ann Petry*

*Unlike most of the slaves who fled the South, Harriet Tubman (1821?–1913) occasionally hired out as a domestic servant to help others escape. Physically and emotionally, hers was a hard life since the sleeping spells caused by a wound to her head never left her, and she was unable to persuade her unyielding husband to go to the North with her. But the spirit she demonstrated gave faith to thousands of slaves, both those she conducted along the Underground Railroad and those who were forced to stay behind.*

### Minta Becomes Harriet

There was panic in the quarter. The master was dead. Would the slaves be sold? Would all these families be separated and scattered about the countryside? The older slaves whispered to each other, saying: "Did he free us as he promised?"

Harriet, conscience-stricken, believing that her prayers had killed Edward Brodas, ignored the fear in the voices, the faces, of the slaves. She said, later, of this period, "It appeared like I would give the world full of silver and gold, if I had it, to bring that poor soul back. . . . I would give *myself;* I would give everything!"

The slaves were quickly reassured. The overseer told them that the plantation was to remain intact. It had been willed to an heir who was too young to administer it. It would be managed by the young master's guardian, Dr. Anthony Thompson, a minister in Bucktown. According to the master's will, none of the slaves could be sold outside the state of Maryland.

This information ended the whispered, panicky conversations in the quarter. It did nothing to end Harriet's feeling of guilt. Her common sense told her that her prayers could not possibly have killed the master. Yet she was not quite certain. This incident of the master's death follow-

ing so swiftly after her reiterated plea, *Kill him, Lord,* left her with the conviction that prayer was always answered.

She was uneasy, too. She knew that she was no longer regarded as a desirable slave. There was always the possibility that Dr. Thompson, once he heard the story of the way in which she had defied an overseer, would decide to sell her, lest she transmit to the other slaves the same spirit of rebellion.

Once again she toyed with the idea of running away. Somehow the urgency was gone. Old Rit and Ben were here on the plantation. So were her brothers and sisters. All of them had joyously accepted the announcement that nothing was to be changed.

But who could be certain? The master had promised to free Old Rit, but he hadn't. He had never been cruel to his slaves. But he hired them out to men who were cruel. He sold them whenever the need arose. He had tried to sell her when she was sick and worthless. No one could know what this temporary master, Doc Thompson, as he was known in Bucktown, would be like. He would probably continue the old master's practice of hiring out slaves.

She knew what it was like to be hired out. One moment she had been a laughing child, running through the woods, chasing rabbits, playing with the other small children in the quarter, and the next moment she had been picked up and taken to the house of James Cook and set to work doing jobs that a child should not have been expected to do.

She would always remember Miss Susan and the whip that she kept on the little shelf behind her bed, always remember how desperately tired she got because she never had enough sleep. She could see herself a child, rocking a baby in a cradle, rock, rock, rock; could see herself sick with the measles, walking the length of Cook's trap line, in winter, shivering, eyes watering. She remembered how she had hated the scaly tails of the muskrats, the wild smell of them, and yet did not want to find them caught fast in the traps.

Long afterward, she said of this period in her life, "They [the slaveholders] don't know any better, it's the way they were brought up. 'Make the little slaves mind you, or flog them,' was what they said to their children, and they were brought up with the whip in their hands. Now that wasn't the way on all plantations; there were good masters and mistresses, as I've heard tell, but I didn't happen to come across any of them."

After the terrible wound in her head had healed, she became aware of the admiration of the other slaves. Even the old ones listened to her opinions, deferred to her. Though Old Rit continued to deplore the audacity, the boldness in Harriet that made her defy an overseer, she stopped calling her Minta or Minty. So did the others.

She was Harriet now to all of them. It was as though the pet names, the diminutives, were no longer suitable for a teen-aged girl who bore on her forehead a great scar, ineradicable evidence of the kind of courage rarely displayed by a grownup.

Though the wound in her head had healed, she was subject to periods of troubled sleep, she had strange dreams which recurred night after night. These dreams had a three-dimensional quality in which people and places were seen more clearly, more sharply than in her waking moments. At night, in the quarter, she described these dreams or visions, as she called them, to the other slaves. Even in the telling, something of the reality of the dream came through to the others, so that they were awed by her.

As soon as she was able to work again, Doc Thompson hired out Harriet and her father, Ben, to John Stewart, a builder. At first Harriet worked in his house, doing the housework that she despised.

There was no question but what she was well enough to work, though she sometimes had severe headaches, especially if she got very tired. Then the ache was like a pounding inside her skull. The headaches did not bother her as much as the sudden onset of that deep trancelike sleep which still occurred without warning.

Whenever she thought of running away, not so often now, the knowledge of this awful weakness stopped her. She knew that she might be found asleep by the side of the road, and brought back immediately. The deep scar on her forehead made her easily recognized.

She was afraid to leave and yet she could not bear the life she led, inside all day, sweeping and dusting, making beds, washing clothes. The house was so near the woods that she could hear the ring of the axes, hear the crash as a great tree came down.

After three months of housework, she asked Stewart, her temporary master, if she could work in the woods with the men. "I always did field work," she explained. "So I can swing a ax just like a man."

Stewart knew she was strong. He had seen her bring in big logs for the fireplaces, had once stopped to watch in unconcealed amazement as she carried a tremendous iron caldron filled with hot water from the cookhouse to a nearby stream. He did not have to pay her old master, Doc Thompson, very much for her hire because she was a woman. If she could do a man's work, felling trees, splitting logs, he'd be getting a bargain.

"We can try it," he said. "If it don't work out why you'll have to go back to cooking and cleaning."

But it did work out. Harriet was delighted. She knew that Stewart was pleased with the new arrangement, for shortly afterward he allowed her to "hire her time." This was a privilege which was extended to trustworthy slaves who were good workers. It meant that Harriet could find jobs for herself, and would pay Stewart fifty or sixty dollars a year. Whatever she earned over and beyond this sum, she was allowed to keep.

She sought and found jobs that would keep her out of doors. She hauled logs, plowed fields, drove an oxcart. She became a familiar figure in the fields—a slender, muscular young woman, with her skirts looped up around her waist and a vivid bandanna tied on her head. Dressed in this fashion, she did the rough hard work of a prime field hand.

During this period, she often worked with Ben, her father. John Stewart placed Ben in charge of the slaves who cut the timber which was to be sent by boat to the Baltimore shipyard. For weeks at a time Harriet swung a broadax in the woods as part of Ben's crew, cutting half a cord of wood a day just like a man.

She learned most of the woods lore that she knew from Ben: the names of birds, which berries were good to eat and which were poisonous, where to look for water lilies, how to identify the hemlocks and the plant that he called cranebill, wild geranium or crane's bill. For these things—bark of hemlock, root of water lily, leaf of crane's bill—had medicinal value. The slaves used them to cure all sorts of ailments, fevers and intestinal disorders.

Harriet was an apt pupil. Ben said that her eyes were sharper than his. She said, "No. It's not just my eyes. It's my hands, too." She thought her hands seemed to locate the root or herb she was seeking before she actually saw it.

Ben taught her how to pick a path through the woods, even through the underbrush, without making a sound. He said, "Any old body can go through a woods crashing and mashing things down like a cow. That's easy. You practice doing it the hard way—move so quiet even a bird on a nest don't hear you and fly up."

Neither of them ever discussed the reasons why it was desirable to be able to go through the woods soundlessly. Discussion wasn't necessary. Deep inside herself Harriet knew what Ben was doing. He was, in his own fashion, training her for the day when she might become a runaway, and a successful flight would depend on the stealth of her movements through the woods that bordered all the roads.

When she was nineteen, Ben rewarded her efforts with praise. She had followed him through the woods and though he moved quietly himself, he had not heard her, although she was close behind him. When they reached a clearing, she came up in back of him and touched him lightly on the arm. He jumped, startled, and then laughed when he saw Harriet standing beside him.

He said, "Hat, you walk like a Injun. Not even a leaf make a rustle, not even a twig crack back on itself when you come through there."

She was tremendously pleased by this. She thought if only her master, John Stewart, would stop having her exhibit her strength for the entertainment of his guests, she would be content to spend the rest of her life on this plantation hiring herself out. The work was hard, yes, but now that she was grown, she could do the most back-breaking jobs without effort. Besides the workday was lightened and shortened by moments of fun, by words of praise like those of

Ben's, by the endless wonder and beauty of the woods.

Unfortunately, Stewart had long since discovered that she was as strong as any of the men on the plantation. She could lift barrels of produce,

could shoulder heavy timbers. Whenever he had visitors, he gave orders that she was to be hitched to a boat loaded with stone and was to drag it behind her as she walked along the edge of the river. She could hear cries of astonishment, laughter, applause from the men who stood on the bank watching. This audience of fashionably dressed planters made her feel that she was little better than a trained animal, brought out for their amusement.

Though Stewart continued to have her perform for his friends, she remained with him, hiring her time, for six years.

In Boston, on October 21, 1835, William Lloyd Garrison, publisher of *The Liberator*, was rescued from a mob of some two thousand well-dressed, eminently respectable men who were intent on hanging him. The mayor and the constables got

Garrison away from the crowd and finally lodged him in the Leverett Street Jail for safety.

That night, thin, bespectacled William Lloyd Garrison wrote on the wall of his cell: "William Lloyd Garrison was put into this cell on Monday afternoon, October 21, 1835, to save him from the violence of a respectable and influential mob, who sought to destroy him for preaching the abominable and dangerous doctrine that all men are created equal, and that all oppression is odious in the sight of God."

### The Patchwork Quilt

In 1843, Harriet Ross began to make a patchwork quilt. She had trouble finding the brilliantly colored pieces of cotton cloth she needed. Sewing the quilt together was even harder.

The needle kept slipping through her fingers. Sometimes she did not know that she had lost it, until she tried to take a stitch and found that she held only a long piece of thread. Time and again she hunted for the needle on the dirt floor of the cabin. It was difficult to find it there, difficult for fingers accustomed to grasping the handle of a broadax to pick up an object as tiny as a needle.

It seemed as though she would never be able to master the art of sewing, to make the needle go through the material in the places where she wanted it to go. It was the hardest task she had ever undertaken.

Yet as the quilt pattern developed, she thought it was as beautiful as the wild flowers that grew in the woods and along the edge of the roads. The yellow was like the Jerusalem flower, and the purple suggested motherwort, and the white pieces were like water lily, and the varying shades of green represented the leaves of all the plants, and the eternal green of the pine trees.

For this was no ordinary quilt. It would be trousseau, and the entire contents of what under different circumstances would have been a hope chest. Harriet had fallen in love. She was going to marry a young man named John Tubman. He was a tall, well-built fellow, with a ready laugh, and a clear lilting whistle.

When she worked on the quilt, head bent, awkward fingers guiding the needle carefully through the material, she experienced a strange, tender feeling that was new to her. The quilt became a symbol of the life that she would share with John. She thought about him while she sewed, how tall he was, how sweet the sound of his whistling. She was so short she had to look up to him. She looked up to him for another reason, too. He was free. He had always been free. Yet he wanted to marry her and she was a slave. So she felt humble, too.

They were married in 1844. Harriet went to live in his cabin, taking with her her one beautiful possession, the patchwork quilt.

The knowledge that she was still a slave bothered her more and more. If she were sold, she would be separated from John. She truly loved him. She had asked him how he came to be free. He said it was because his mother and father had been freed by their master, at the time of the master's death.

This made Harriet wonder about her own family, especially about Old Rit, who was forever talking about the promises of freedom that had been made to her. She paid five dollars to a lawyer to look up the wills of the various masters to whom Old Rit had belonged. It had taken her years to save five dollars; she had hoarded pennies to accumulate such a sum. But it seemed to her the information she received was well worth the cost. She found that Old Rit had originally been willed to a young woman named Mary Patterson, with the provision that she was to be freed when she was forty-five. Mary Patterson died shortly afterward, still unmarried. According to the lawyer, Old Rit should have been freed long ago. Instead she remained a slave, and so, of course, her children were slaves. Old Rit had been sold and resold many times.

After this, Harriet grew more and more discontented. She felt that she was a slave only because Old Rit had been tricked and deceived, years ago.

Times were hard the year that Harriet married John Tubman. And the next year, too. In the quarter she heard a great deal of talk about the reasons for this. One of the house servants said the trouble was due to the difference in the price of cotton. Dr. Thompson had said so. He said cotton brought thirteen cents a pound in 1837, and when it was high, the slave traders paid as much as a thousand dollars for prime field hands. Then cotton started going down,

down, down, until now in 1845 it was bringing only five cents a pound, and the slave traders gave less than five hundred dollars for young strong slaves.

Harriet decided that from the dilapidated look of the plantation—fields lying fallow, the Big House in need of repair—Doc Thompson would soon be selling slaves again. He wouldn't be able to get much for them in Maryland, so in spite of the old master's will, he would sell them South.

She told John Tubman this. Every time she said it, she spoke of going North, of running away, following the North Star.

He warned her against such foolishness. What would she find there that she didn't have here? She hired her time, and so she always had a little money of her own. They had a cabin to themselves. Maryland was a good place to live. It never got too cold. There were all the coves and creeks where one could fish and set traps.

He said that if she went North, she'd freeze to death. Besides, what happened to the ones who went there? None of them came back to tell what it was like. Why was that? Because they couldn't. They died there. They must have. If they were still alive, they would have returned to show the way to some of the rest of the slaves. None returned. None sent back word. What would she have there that she didn't have here?

Her reply was always the same: "I'd be free."

She told him about the dreams she had, how night after night, she dreamed that men on horseback came riding into the quarter, and then she heard the shrieks and screams of women and children, as they were put into the chain gang, that the screaming of the women made her wake up. She would lie there in the dark of the cabin, sweating, feeling cold because the fire was out, and the chill from the dirt floor seemed to have reached her very bones, and, though awake, she could still hear the echo of screams.

When she went back to sleep she would dream again. This time she was flying. She flew over cotton fields and cornfields, and the corn was ripe, the tassels waving all golden brown in the wind, and then she flew over Cambridge and the Choptank River, and she could see the gleam of the water, like a mirror, far down, under her, and then she came to a mountain and flew over that. At last she reached a barrier, sometimes it was a fence, sometimes a river, and she couldn't fly over it.

She said, "It appeared like I wouldn't have the strength, and just as I was sinking down, there would be ladies all dressed in white over there, and they would put out their arms and pull me across—"

John Tubman disliked these dreams. When she retold them, her husky voice pitched low, she made them sound as though they had really happened. He thought this showed how restless and impatient she had become. He laughed at her, finally. He said that she must be related to Old Cudjo, who was so slow-witted he never laughed at a funny story until a half hour after it was told. Because only a slow-witted person would have the same dream all the time.

In spite of his derision, she kept telling him about her dreams. She said that on clear nights the North Star seemed to beckon to her. She was sure she could follow that star. They could go North together. Then she would be free too. Nothing could part them then.

He decided he would put an end to this talk of escape, of the North, and freedom. He asked what she would do when the sky was dark. Then how would she know which way was North? She couldn't read the signs along the road. She wouldn't know which way to go. He would not go with her. He was perfectly satisfied where he was. She would be alone, in the dark, in the silence of the deep woods. What would she eat? Where would she get food?

She started to say: in the woods. She could live a long time on the edible berries and fruit that she had long ago learned to recognize. And yet—she had seen many a half-starved runaway brought back in chains, not enough flesh left on him to provide a decent meal for a buzzard. Perhaps she, too, would starve. She remembered the time she ran away from Miss Susan's and crawled into a pigpen, remembered the squealing and grunting of the pigs, the slops thrown into the trough, and fighting with the pigs, pushing them away, to get at the trough. After four days she had been indistinguishable from the pigs, filthy, foul-smelling—and starving. So she had gone back to Miss Susan. The memory of this experience made her avoid John's eyes, not answer him.

Perhaps her silence made him angry. He may have interpreted it as evidence of her stubbornness, her willfulness, her utter disregard of all his warnings, and so made a threat which would put a stop to this crazy talk about freedom.

He shouted at her, "You take off and I'll tell the Master. I'll tell the Master right quick."

She stared at him, shocked, thinking, he couldn't, he wouldn't. If he told the master that she was missing, she would be caught before she got off the plantation. John knew what happened to runaways who were caught and brought back. Surely he would not betray his own wife.

And yet—she knew that there were slaves who had betrayed other slaves when they tried to escape. Sometimes they told because they were afraid of the master, it was always hard on the ones who were left behind. Sometimes the house servants were the betrayers, they were closest to the masters, known to be tattletales, certain to be rewarded because of their talebearing.

But John Tubman was free. And free Negroes helped the runaways. It was one of the reasons the masters disliked and distrusted them. Surely John would not deny freedom to her, when he had it himself. Perhaps he was afraid he would be held responsible for her escape, afraid the master would think John had incited her to run away. Besides, he was satisfied here, he had said so, and men disliked change, or so Old Rit had told her, saying also that women thrived on it.

Then she thought, frowning, but if a man really loved a woman, wouldn't he be willing to take risks to help her to safety? She shook her head. He must have been joking, or speaking through a sudden uncontrollable anger.

"You don't mean that," she said slowly. But he did mean it. She could tell by the way he looked at her.

For the tall young man with the gay laugh, and the merry whistle, had been replaced by a hostile stranger, who glared at her as he said, "You just start and see."

She knew that no matter what words she might hear during the rest of her life, she would never again hear anything said that hurt like this. It was as though he had deliberately tried to kill all the trust and the love and the deep devotion she had for him.

That night as she lay beside him on the floor of the cabin, she felt that he was watching her, waiting to see if this was the night when she would try to leave.

From that night on, she was afraid of him.

In the spring of the same year, Thomas Garrett, Quaker, who since 1822 had been offering food and shelter to runaway slaves in Wilmington, Delaware, was tried and found guilty of breaking the law covering fugitive slaves. Found guilty with him was John Hunn, a stationmaster of the Underground Railroad in Middletown, Delaware, and a much younger man.

The trial was held in the May Term of the United States Court, at New Castle, before Chief Justice Taney and Judge Hall.

The fines and damages that Garrett had to pay took every dollar of his property. His household effects and all his belongings were sold at public auction. The sheriff who conducted the sale turned to Garrett and said, "Thomas, I hope you'll never be caught at this again."

Garrett, who was then sixty years old, answered: "Friend, I haven't a dollar in the world, but if thee knows a fugitive anywhere on the face of the earth who needs a breakfast, send him to me."

During the operation of the Underground Railroad, twenty-five hundred slaves passed through Garrett's "station" in Wilmington.

## from AMERICA'S OWN MARK TWAIN

*Jeanette Eaton*

*Mark Twain's (1835–1910)* The Adventures of Tom Sawyer *and* Adventures of Huckleberry Finn *are still widely read and show no signs of declining popularity. The books were the author's re-creation of his own early days in Hanni-*

bal, Missouri, as this chapter from Jeanette Eaton's biography clearly shows. Twain was a very complex man, his famous sense of humor partially concealing the ability to deeply analyze people and their place on earth. Eaton's portrait of the man, his successes and failures, his joys and heartbreaks, should increase a young person's appreciation of one of America's greatest and most talented authors.

## [Childhood Days]

It was school that Sam dreaded. The very next day after the family was reunited at Hannibal he had to set out to the little log house on Main Street. Mrs. Elizabeth Horr was the teacher—the keeper of Sam's jail. From afar he saw her standing in the doorway to greet her pupils with a smile. But she and Sam met in a spirit of mutual suspicion. "Here is the mischief-maker" was the message of her glance. His sulky pout declared, "The old tyrant looks as mean as ever."

As he plumped down on a bench at the back of the room he rehearsed his first day of school the year before. During the first hour he had pulled so many pigtails, tickled so many boys' shins, and made so many funny faces to inspire giggles that Mrs. Horr used up her complete store of reproofs and sent him out to get a switch for his own punishment. After a long disappearance he returned with a fragile shaving which had blown into the schoolyard from a nearby carpenter's shop. To the accompaniment of general laughter he gravely handed it to his teacher. "Samuel Langhorne Clemens," she cried. "I'm ashamed of you." Immediately she had sent one of the bigger boys out to cut something that looked like switch. It felt like one, too, as it descended on Sam. Since he had never suffered such a punishment at home, he raged inwardly at the indignity. From then on he spent most of his school hours in planning vengeance. He became such an adept at contriving mischief which could not be pinned on him that his punishments were actually few. Facing his second year now, he wondered how the battle would go.

Classes always began with a prayer and a reading from the Bible. These selections, like the sermons Sam heard on Sundays, usually dealt with sinners and their awful fate. The Book of Job was a favorite choice. Sternly Mrs. Horr would read a passage describing God's punishment of a wicked person.

"He shall flee from the iron weapon, and the bow of steel shall strike him through. A fire that no man lit shall consume him. The heavens shall reveal his iniquity; and the earth shall rise up against him."

Listening with inward shudders, Sam felt tumult in his soul. On the one hand, he became convinced that God was only a fierce avenger. On the other, he had a guilty feeling that his own iniquities might justly be written on the sky and that fire might well devour him. However, once the arithmetic lesson began, such dark forebodings vanished, and he gleefully pulled the pigtail of the little girl in front of him.

Almost against his will the little rebel learned to read that year. That helped long winter days to pass swiftly. Bad colds and stomach upsets that kept him home proved boons to learning. Basking in his mother's anxious care, he pored over tales of adventure. Spring days with windows open were the enemies of schoolbooks. Then ears and eyes attended only to the trill of warblers, bursting cherry blossoms, and drifting sunlit clouds. During the recreation periods in the yard, however, he abandoned dreams to chase the girls, fight enemies, and cement friendships with boys who admired his pranks. Sometimes, with one or two other daring truants, he would slip away to visit the river or steal into the woods to spy on old Indian Joe's tumble-down cabin.

It was the May Day celebration, put on belatedly in June, which aroused sudden loyalty to the school. For this occasion boys were dressed in their Sunday jackets and best nankeen pants. Girls wore ruffled dresses just short enough to show embroidered pantalets. To the toot and thump of the municipal band, the pupils marched along Main Street, which was lined with applauding parents and lesser citizens. A Maypole dance, songs, and declamations by the older children were performed in the grassy corner of an ancient graveyard. The finale was a lavish picnic dinner spread for the heroes and heroines of a nine-month scholastic struggle.

In May, 1842, however, no one in the Clemens family had the heart to join the celebration. Benjamin, the gentlest, sweetest-tempered member of the family, was suddenly stricken with a mortal illness. On the night Sam learned from Pamela that their brother could not get well, he tossed all night in despairing sleeplessness. Before him arose every occasion when he had teased Ben or persuaded him to mischief. The realization that he could never redeem such wickedness was crushing. Early in the morning he tiptoed into the room where his brother lay. One glance at the sheeted figure told him that Benjamin was dead. His mother sat beside the cot with her head in her hands.

In a soundless rush Sam reached her side. "Oh, Ma," he moaned. "Oh, Ma!"

Her soft hand touched his head. In a tear-choked voice she said, "Yes, Sammy, he is gone. We can't understand it. But we can still say, 'The Lord gave and the Lord hath taken away.'" Sam shook his head. He could only kneel in awe and fear and beg forgiveness for all his sins. Weeks passed before he could either sleep or eat normally.

Due to his shattered state, his mother lengthened the summer visit at the Quarles farm to late autumn. The coming of frost brought new sources of delight to Sam. The spacious sitting room was warmed by crackling logs in the huge fireplace and after dark all the family gathered there. Uncle John sat smoking his pipe in a rush-bottomed chair in one chimney corner and Aunt Patsy sat knitting opposite him. Mrs. Clemens worked on a piece of fine embroidery beside the kerosene lamp. Tabitha and Sam and often little Henry and several neighbor children romped and laughed in the shadows.

Three times, when the moon was full, Sam stole off to join the Negroes on a hunt for coons. Excited hounds sniffing, racing, and barking; boys and men with guns and lanterns tramping through the woods; voices calling and the bang of the guns—here were all the elements of a thrilling chase.

On rainy evenings old soft-spoken Uncle Daniel was persuaded to come in and entertain everyone with stories. He could send chills down youthful spines with witch stories. But he himself preferred to relate "How de Mean Old Fox Got His Comeuppance" or "How Bunny Rabbit Done Fooled Mr. Houn' Dog."

When he got home again Sam not only retold to Pamela these fascinating legends, but invented many of his own. When he could make her laugh or bring the glow of interest into her eyes, he would bounce with pride in his creations. He wondered if he could ever inspire an equal response in Orion. This vain hope made him miss Benjamin more than ever. He would have listened!

Orion was no longer in Hannibal. His father had secured him an apprenticeship in a printing firm in St. Louis. When he came home for holidays he seemed to Sam strangely old and silent. One evening when his mother asked him why he was so melancholy, Sam put down his book to hear the answer.

"Well, Ma," said Orion slowly, "how could you expect me to like my kind of employment? Our people weren't laborers like me. How often you've told us how your family descended from an English earl. And look at Pa! He had an ancestor who sat in Parliament. Seems to me I ought to be in a profession."

Tossing her red head, Mrs. Clemens replied, "Yes, our heritage is of the best—except in one respect. We weren't left good money to go with good blood, nor even the ability to make it. So we just have to do what we can. I was brought up to be a fine lady." Instinctively she stretched out her slender white fingers. "But now I'm going to keep boarders until things get better for your father. If you learn the printing trade, Orion, you may reach out to something else. Remember how Benjamin Franklin got on."

A deep voice from the corner of the room said, "Don't ever forget, my children, our lands in Tennessee. If anything happens to me, you will inherit those one hundred thousand acres. There are riches in them." Judge Clemens leaned toward his wife and the lamplight on his face revealed dreamy satisfaction.

With a little shrug, Jane Clemens tossed the vast Tennessee tract into the limbo of illusion. Her husband had bought it for four hundred dollars not long after they were married and there it lay useless, demanding taxes every year.

Sam stared at his mother's expression of scorn. Why didn't she think it wonderful to own so much land? It was queer that she even hated to have it mentioned. Giving up the puzzle, he spoke to Orion. "Say, I'm going to skate on the river tomorrow with Will Bowen. Want to come along? It's frozen hard clear across to Illinois."

Orion acknowledged the invitation with a gentle smile, but reminded his brother that he had to leave early in the morning with a pork packer who was driving his big wagon down to St. Louis. Everyone turned sorrowing looks upon him. But this was an undemonstrative family and no one said anything. Only his mother was up to give him breakfast at dawn and say good-by. She remained in the kitchen to be sure Sam ate something before he strode off with skates under his arm to speed across the vast ice field of the Mississippi.

With his closest chum, Will Bowen, and several other boys, Sam often spent half the day enjoying this sport. Not only were racing and playing tag exhilarating, there was something wondrous in the sight of the mighty river held motionless in winter's grip. On sunny days the blue sheen of a surface usually a dingy brown, the splendor of clouds overhead, the glitter of frozen branches on the tree-lined shores of mainland and islands, composed a scene of such beauty that even the boys were aware of it.

Uncle John's farm and the great river provided Sam with a wide variety of enchanting amusements—sometimes mixed with strange and even frightening experiences. In the fall of 1843, for example, Sam was almost scared into believing that truancy was a sin, after a magnificent afternoon of forbidden freedom ended late at night in terror.

A few moments after he had sneaked away from the schoolyard that day, Sam met Tom Blankenship. Tom was the most envied eight-year-old in Hannibal. He didn't go to school. He went barefoot from early spring until snowfall. He could fish, swim, and paddle a canoe all day if he chose. On the other hand, he had no mother and his reprobate of a father often beat him in a drunken rage. He went about unwashed and dressed in rags, he seldom had enough to eat, and sometimes, when his father was drunk, he had to sleep in some overturned barrel. But this untrammeled freedom gave him an aura of romance in the eyes of his contemporaries. Besides, since the mothers of well-brought-up children sternly forbade all association with Tom, it was peculiarly tempting to seek the company of this easygoing, pleasant-tempered, plucky, and highly experienced individual.

"Hi, Tom, where you going?" asked Sam.

"Oh, fishin', I reckon. I got a skiff hid on shore that was washed up in the storm last week. It don't leak much. Wisht you didn't have to go to that old school and could come along."

"Shucks, I'll come! I'm sick of school already after three weeks of it."

It was the perfect afternoon to put conscience to sleep. Sam liked to be on the Mississippi better than anywhere else in the world. To paddle against the current was exhilarating and to let the boat drift downstream with no effort except steering was blissful. Every time they passed one of the great rafts that carried lumber from the North, shouted greetings were exchanged. Once they had to paddle furiously to avoid the path of a big steamer.

In the shallows each boy caught two fish and in the late afternoon they landed, built a fire, and cooked them. After a delightful swim they stretched out on the grass, chatting or communing in silence. Glorious sunset clouds drifted southward and later a moon rose above the trees. "Say, Tom," asked Sam suddenly, "do you suppose your pa knows where you are?"

"Nope. Anyway he wouldn't care where I was, except maybe he wants me to fetch him a quart of whiskey. What about your folks?"

Ah, there lurked the dregs in this delicious cup. Sam confessed that probably all his family were combing the town to find him. Silently he pictured his arrival at home and the storm of disapproval that would meet him. It was just too much to face. "I know what I'll do," he said. "I won't go home at all. I'll crawl into Pa's law office and sleep there. Maybe in the morning they'll be so glad I ain't drowned or choked to death by Injun Joe that they'll let me off easy."

"That's a good idea," said Tom, and began to shove off the skiff.

At the corner of two shadowy streets they parted with whispered farewells. Sam found it easy to push up a window in his father's small office. A shabby couch stood right beside it. Kicking off his shoes, Sam stretched out and was asleep in a few seconds. Perhaps it was the bright moonlight slanting through the window that waked him. He sat up with a jerk, looked around, and stared in surprised recognition of his whereabouts.

But what was that on the floor? Choking down a scream, the boy stared at the man's figure stretched out full length on the wooden boards. Who was it? Was he asleep? Couldn't be a robber in this little hole! Just as Sam was able to breathe again, moonlight flooded down on the motionless figure. Oh, heavens! It couldn't be! What he saw was the marble face of a dead man.

Sam got into his shoes and crawled out of the window! Up the moonlit streets he ran a swift race from the dreadful unknown. No light shone in the Clemens house. Stealthily he climbed to the upper porch and found his bedroom window wide-open. Soundlessly stripping off his clothes, Sam lay down beside Henry and by a mighty effort kept his tense body from jerking and thrashing about as he lay there, sleepless.

Next morning he screwed up his courage to face his parents. To his surprise, questions and comments were brief. Unasked, they told him of a shocking murder. Two Spanish travelers from the Southwest had hardly landed in Hannibal when they started a drunken brawl. Knives were flashed and one was driven through the breast of the smaller man. Judge Clemens came on the scene in time to have the murderer caught and dragged into the jail. The judge then consented to give shelter to the dead man in his empty office. Today the killer would be charged with the crime.

Sam listened to the account with his stomach rising and falling. He knew he was going to be haunted by the dead man's ghost. And so he was, in uneasy dreams. To rid himself of the awful apparition, he tried to be a model pupil at school and for nearly a month had a perfect record of attendance.

In the boy's ninth year his father's fortunes improved somewhat. He built a more convenient small house on Hill Street and provided Pamela with a piano, on which she practiced diligently. The family often gathered around to sing familiar ditties to her accompaniment. Sam, who had

a sweet treble voice, loved these sessions. Watching him, his mother would remark to her husband that no one would suspect their angelic-looking son of being the imp he was.

Sam had gradually drawn around him a group of boys ready to follow his impetuous lead anywhere at any time. One of the many exciting opportunities afforded by Hannibal was its famous cave. When the family first moved into the town Sam heard of its wonders, and while he was a little tot he had his first glimpse of its dark interior. Taken by his mother to a church picnic, he was allowed to join the young people on a visit to the cave. A good-humored youth promised to look after him.

A walk straight up a hill brought them to the entrance on its steep side. An unbolted heavy door of oak had been opened for visitors, and they pushed into the large, dusky entrance chamber. Sam's wondering eyes turned from the uneven rocky floor to the dripping walls and up to the rough ceiling.

"Oh, it's a big cave, ain't it!" he exclaimed.

A girl clinging to the young man's arm giggled at this. "Big! Why it's miles long and miles deep, boy! Nobody's ever been all through it. Wait till we light our candles and you'll see."

Down the sloping passage the chattering procession, with candles lifted high to shine on the strange, glistening walls, moved slowly. Sam was shown how one narrow corridor after another opened off the main path. They turned right into a huge cell hollowed out of solid rock and had to retrace their steps. Laughter and talk echoed merrily through the darkness. But as they kept going down, down, down until he felt they must have reached the very center of the earth, the little boy asked timorously, "Couldn't you get lost in this cave?"

He was told that you could indeed. For this reason visitors always kept close together and carried plenty of candles. Some few persons had managed to find lakes and foaming streams, and precipices that dropped down to indefinite depths. One misstep on the moist, slippery path might mean death. Although Sam said nothing, this information produced a trembling inside of him that did not cease until he was finally led out of the fearsome labyrinth and could take a deep breath of fresh air and look gratefully around at the sunny meadows. Nevertheless, on the way home he remarked to his mother that he meant to explore the cave from top to bottom some day.

At the time Mrs. Clemens only laughed at her small son, but some four years later she remembered the boast with a sinking heart. One morning her friend Mrs. Bowen came in with frightening news. Her son Will had inadvertently revealed that several times after school he had been exploring the cave with Jimmy McDaniel, John Garth, and Sam Clemens. "Imagine those young fools!" gasped Will's mother. "They'll get lost some day sure as you live—if not drowned or smashed up in a fall. What are we going to do?"

Jane Clemens heard this report with mingled fear and indignation. For half an hour the two women exchanged their worries, which was lucky for Sam. By the time he got back from school his mother had expended most of her emotion, and she greeted her son in a mood of loving concern.

"Oh, Sam," she concluded, with a sob in her voice, "do you want to break my heart? Last year you nearly drowned trying to swim in the river during a storm. Now you want to get lost forever in the cave!"

Shocked as he was that his cave explorations were no longer a secret, the boy was touched by his mother's anxiety. "Oh, Ma," he said, "don't take on so. We won't get lost. We do just the way Theseus did when he went through the labyrinth after the Minotaur. You remember—his lady, Ariadne, gave him a silk string and kept one end herself at the door. All Theseus had to do after killing the Minotaur was to go back the way the string led. We tie a strong kite string to a piece of rock on the main corridor and unwind it while we explore, and then we follow it back again. We always keep close together. So don't you worry!"

Mrs. Clemens was not impressed. Sternly she forbade him ever to enter the cave again. Theseus of Hannibal was appalled. Grownups! What did they know about the thrill of discovery? Why, only yesterday he and the other boys had found the prettiest bubbling spring hundreds of feet below the surface. He would never promise not to explore the cave. No! Not if he were tortured like the early Christians. Of course he

couldn't announce his defiance. What he must do was to distract her attention. By extraordinary good fortune he had the perfect means of doing so.

With his most disarming smile he said, "I'm sorry you got so scared about me, Ma. I think a lot of you, Ma. I've got a present for you in my pocket. Hold out your hand!"

Smiling girlishly in pleased expectation, she did so. Sam's hand came from his pocket and opened within hers. A scream followed. "What is it? Oh, my heavens, it's a bat! Oh, you dreadful boy! Oh, the horrid thing!"

As she rushed to the window to fling away her present, the donor skipped swiftly from the room.

The explorers agreed that it would be diplomatic to avoid the cave for several weeks. But thanks to their ingenious leader, they soon engaged in a most interesting project. It concerned a monster boulder perched on the very crest of Holliday Hill. Sam's proposal was to dig it from its deep bed, push it over the brink, and watch it bounce its long way down. The idea met with warm approval. Armed with borrowed shovels and spades, the boys met on the hill several times a week. Hours were spent in work so arduous that if it had been required by parents, the boys would have revolted in fury.

"This big thing is like an iceberg," muttered Sam one day, as he peered down the excavation. "Three quarters of it is underground, same as an iceberg is more'n three quarters below water."

At last one afternoon the cone-shaped monster moved a little. With cheers the boys smoothed away the front of the crater they had dug. Slowly the rock fell forward upon the runway. "Now push!" shouted the boss. So near the edge of the short, steep precipice, so ready to tumble was the boulder, that a push by eight sturdy hands was enough to topple it over the brink. Tense with excitement, the boys knelt on the cliff's edge to watch the monster's progress. There were no big trees in its path. Weeds, bushes, tender saplings went down before it like toothpicks. Smaller rocks crumbled under its weight. "Look at her go!" yelled Sam.

But above the crash of the wild descent rose a frightened scream from Will Bowen. "Look! A dray is comin' along the road down there!"

Fear struck chill to four hearts. They were almost afraid to watch. Then they roared with glee. The boulder's momentum, as it reached the last sheer drop, had carried it sailing over the cart like a mammoth bird. It demolished a neat woodpile at the far edge of the lane—and then bounded straight into the side of a small shop! Half the structure collapsed like kindling, and out of the door rushed three terrified workmen.

"It's the cooper's shop!" gasped John Garth.

The horrified boys saw the men turn from their inspection of the ruin to gaze upward at Holliday Hill. With common accord they wriggled into the bushes like crabs. At last they could safely stand up behind a big oak tree.

"Anyway," panted Sam, "nobody was even hurt!" Challenged as to why he was so sure, he explained. "Why, those men just stood there scratching their heads and looking. If anybody'd been hurt, they'd have carried him out. Just the same, let's get away quick! Grab your shovels and picks!"

Down the far side of the hill the boys scurried. Each agreed to return his borrowed tools and then slip home. Then immediately after supper they would go, one at a time, to see what was left of the cooper's shop. By that time the weird accident of the boulder's fall had become the talk of the town. There were crowds at the scene of destruction. As hour after hour the workmen had related the tale of the sudden crash and their miraculous escape from death, they reaped so many congratulations, so much sympathy, and such lavish promises of aid in restoring the shop that they obviously felt like heroes. Late that evening the boys met in the Bowens' back yard to express in cautious whispers their mutual relief and their triumph in putting through an exciting project.

Nevertheless, a violent thunderstorm that night shook Sam's complacence. Lightning seemed to hover right over his bed. From moment to moment the frightened sinner expected to be struck down. To the howling wind he confessed his guilt and promised that if only his life were spared, he would take no more risks with the life and property of others. The pact did not, however, include renouncing personal risks of his own. Before a year had gone by he deliberately put his life in grave danger.

In the summer of 1845 measles was the stylish disease in Hannibal. One by one all Sam's pals were stricken, until finally he had nobody to play with. Jane Clemens was determined to keep the infection from her household, and she watched her irrepressible son's every move with the stern air of an army sergeant. Like other healthy boys with anxious mothers, Sam was forbidden to leave home. For a time he accepted boredom and devoted himself to books. But when he heard that Will Bowen, in spite of equal isolation, had the measles, he resolved to get the disease too.

One day while his mother was busy with dinner, he went to his friend's house and knocked at the closed door. Mrs. Bowen refused to let him in. Next he hid in the Bowens' yard until he saw her go out of the front door, and then he sneaked up to Will's room. After only ten minutes of a delightful chat Mrs. Bowen found him and sternly sent him home. Finally Sam achieved a night assault. He climbed up a wisteria trellis to Will's window, slipped into the room, undressed, and got into bed beside him. Their whispered conversation went unheard. Unfortunately he slept late. In the morning he was personally conducted back to his alarmed mother. Next day he was covered from head to toe with red spots.

For a while he felt only satisfaction to be sharing the scourge with his pals. Then as he burned with fever and his bones ached, he wondered whether he had made a mistake. Yet it was interesting to be the center of constant attention. After a week of high fever he learned from his mother's frightened face that she expected him to die, and in a vague way he believed he might. Pamela wore an air of mourning when she came in to feed him soup. Even his father spent some time sitting silently by his bed.

But Sam eventually began to get well. The best part of his convalescence was a long stay at the Quarles farm. He didn't even mind making up for lost lessons at the country school a few miles from the farm. A morning walk through the woods and meadows was charming. The luncheon he carried in his knapsack was always delicious. Moreover, he had a teacher who made history lessons vividly interesting by paying small attention to the dull textbook, which offered only bare facts and hundreds of dates.

## from CRAZY HORSE

### Shannon Garst

*Shannon Garst was one of the earliest authors to write about American Indians with empathy and appreciation for the special qualities of their lives. The rigorous training of Indian youths began early; the code of behavior expected of them was exacting; the price of failure was to be ridiculed and treated as an outcast. To become a respected warrior, a man had to be valorous; to become a chief, a man had to be an extraordinary warrior. Crazy Horse (1844?–1877), who led the Sioux in their last stand against the white invaders of their Dakota territory, was such a warrior. This excerpt shows the resourcefulness and intelligence Crazy Horse had as a youngster as well as the weaknesses he had to overcome to become a great leader.*

### The Earned Name

As the hunters rode into the Oglala village, laughing and jabbering, the Indian women came out to meet them and ran beside their horses. Has-ka's sister, Laughing One, and his stepmother, Gathers-Her-Berries, ran beside his horse chattering like magpies over his kill.

Reaching camp the women seized the meat and threw the hunks onto beds of leaves while they deftly sliced it into strips which they threw over pole racks to dry, out of reach of the dogs.

That night the campfires sputtered and blazed as the buffalo fat dripped onto them. The air was savory with fine smells of roasting hump and ribs. The Oglalas ate until they were stuffed. Never had food tasted so good to Has-ka. The fact that he had helped in providing meat for the camp made him feel pleasantly important and he was still elated over the fact that Hump had singled him out.

He purposely walked through the camp to see if he would be noticed. He was. Men pointed to him and said, "There goes Has-ka. His arrow brought down a buffalo. He was the youngest one on the hunt."

It was very agreeable to be pointed out and no-

ticed this way. He almost forgot that Hump had to come to his rescue just in time.

When the Oglalas had eaten so much that they could not cram down another mouthful, they danced to the throbbing drums until the food was jounced down enough so that they could eat some more. Has-ka ate and danced with them. He was aware of No Water's glowering, envious glances upon him but this only increased his feeling of triumph. The older boy had gone along on the hunt, but only as one of the boys who led a pack horse on which to bring back the meat. He had had no part in the kill and no one after the hunt had pointed him out as he walked through the village.

Has-ka gorged himself and danced until he grew so sleepy that he crawled off to his sleeping robes. However, he was up at dawn the next morning, eager for more excitement.

Mock buffalo hunts were always a favorite pastime of Sioux youngsters. After one of the real hunts there were often buffalo calves left behind on the plains, which had been unable to keep up with the herd after it had been stampeded. It was the delight of the boys to chase these calves, shooting at them with the blunt arrows they used in their games.

Has-ka, filled with elation over his first buffalo hunt, joined in the noisy horseback chase of one of these young calves. Strongheart was the first to catch up with it. With a yell of triumph the boy shouted, "I, Has-ka the buffalo hunter, will ride this calf!"

Leaning over, he grabbed a handful of the

woolly hair of the hump and threw himself onto the calf's back. More frightened than ever by this new terror, the young buffalo increased his speed so that the Indian boys' ponies could scarcely keep up. But what they lacked in speed, they made up for in yelling as they gave chase.

The calf suddenly stopped running and tried by bucking to rid itself of the strange and frightening thing clinging to its back. Has-ka found this change of pace not at all to his liking. His head was rammed down between his shoulders. With each jump that jounced him first to one side, then to the other, he thought he could not stick on, but he righted himself and managed. His companions were not going to be given a chance to laugh at him. He must not lose the importance he had gained. Most of all he dreaded giving No Water another opportunity to ridicule him. Once he was tipped clear over to the side of the calf. It was only the realization of how his comrades would whoop with glee if he were thrown that gave him the determination to right himself and hang grimly on.

Gradually the bucking eased off, then ceased, when the calf became tired.

"I, Has-ka, did ride the buffalo calf," he cried, raising his hand in triumph.

"Has-ka did ride the buffalo calf," his companions chanted.

"I, Has-ka, will ride the buffalo calf into the village," he shouted.

"*Hoka hey! Hoka hey!*" his friends cried, crowding their ponies close to the buffalo calf and driving it toward the Oglala camp. The riderless Strongheart trotted at the rear of the yelling horde.

Drawn by the shouts of the boys the people came from their tepees to see the procession led by young Has-ka riding the buffalo calf.

"Has-ka did ride the buffalo calf!" his friends shouted.

The warrior Hump stood in front of his lodge laughing at the sight. "The buffalo calf seems too tame a mount for you, my friend," he said.

"He was wild enough out there on the hills," young Hump said. "You should have seen Has-ka ride. I thought the calf's bucking would snap his head off as we snap off the head of a grouse."

"It was easy," Has-ka said modestly. A new hope, however, was born within him that his people would now give him a man-like earned name such as Rides the Buffalo Calf instead of the one he so detested.

But the next day he was still called Has-ka.

The incident, though, did reawaken Hump's interest in him and the warrior made him his adopted son, according to the Sioux custom, and taught him the lore of his people, the best way to make weapons and the secrets of warfare, finding in the eager boy an apt pupil.

His own son, young Hump, was restless and had not Has-ka's ambition to become a leader and his father often lost patience with him. The warrior and his pupil, however, were so often together that their tribesmen spoke of them as the "grizzly and his cub."

Was ever another boy so fortunate, Has-ka wondered, as to have so fine a teacher? In every way he strove to make himself like his hero. Yet he never found courage to speak to Hump of his high ambitions for fear of being laughed at. The man, however, at times possessed an uncanny ability to sense what was in the boy's mind.

One day they were returning from a hunt, jogging along in silence. Has-ka had been completely lost in his thoughts, imagining himself leading a band of Oglala warriors against the Crow tribe.

Suddenly Hump said, "To be a leader of your people you must listen often and in silence to the Great Holy Mystery. The day is not too far away when you will go alone to the hills for the Vision Quest."

Has-ka looked startled. He was surprised that Hump knew what was in his mind, and it pleased him that his teacher considered him worthy of the test which would prove whether or not the *Wakan Tanka* would guide him to leadership.

"You think—I may someday be a leader?" Has-ka's tone was hopeful.

Hump gave him a long, strange look, and for a moment did not speak. Finally he said, "The desire for prominence among our people is always in your heart. Why?"

Has-ka met his friend's glance with a questioning look.

"Why?" Hump asked again. "Why is the wish for greatness always with you?"

"Because—" Has-ka floundered for words. "It

is a good thing to be great. To be pointed out. To be a leader—"

It was not easy to put into words the reasons for his deepest desire. A shadow of disappointment crossed the warrior's face and Has-ka saw that he was not pleased.

"Your reasons are selfish ones," Hump's tone was harsh. "Leadership is a gift from the *Wakan Tanka*. To be used for the good of the people—not because one would be pointed out."

Has-ka felt humbled. "How does one know if he is singled out for leadership—to serve his people?" he persisted.

"At the time of the Vision Quest," Hump repeated. "It is time you were thinking about getting ready."

As the preliminary step of training for the sterner ordeal ahead, Hump one day ordered him to do without food for an entire day. The warrior blackened Has-ka's face with charred wood as the sign that he was fasting. His comrades pranced about him, tantalizing him by holding juicy chunks of savory buffalo meat close to his mouth, or by offering him *wasna*, dried ground buffalo meat mixed with ground-up plums—a favorite food of the Indians.

He wore a solemn expression on his blackened face as he went about the camp. The holy, set-apart feeling he had today was very pleasant—not like the old set-apart feeling he used to have because of his light complexion and his lack of sureness in himself. In those days the feeling had been so painful and unbearable sometimes that he had wanted to crawl off like a wounded animal.

He kept to himself the entire day, not being in a mood to join the other boys in their rough fun. He wandered along Lodge Pole Creek, then lay on the warm grass with his hands under his head, staring at the lazy clouds floating above him until he drifted off into deep sleep. In his dreams he saw himself single-handed driving off the pony herds of the enemy—slaying enemy chiefs —saving his hero, Hump, from the scalping knife. He saw himself being called upon to stand up beside the campfire to tell of his remarkable coups. Saw his record being painted upon a white buffalo robe. Saw the feathered crown of a chieftain being placed upon his head.

When he awoke he struggled to recapture those pleasant dreams, but now he was wide awake. He got to his feet and strolled along the stream, then wandered to the top of a hill. By now the sun was dipping beyond the western horizon in a blaze of brilliant colors. Lightheaded from hunger, Has-ka stretched his hands toward the sinking sun. "A vision, *Wakan Tanka*," he murmured. "Grant me a vision of greatness. Show me the path I must take."

In his dizzy, elated state he fully expected the golden clouds to part, revealing the *Wakan Tanka*.—Or the Holy Mystery would send one of His animal spirits with a message telling Has-ka that he was truly destined for greatness and that he would be powerful among the Sioux. All of the men who were leaders among Has-ka's people had received such visions or messages at some time or other—usually following a fast.

He stood until his outstretched arms ached— and his soul ached, too, with the waiting. But no vision—no message came. The sun sank. A veil of darkness fell over the world, and Has-ka's spirits sank with the sun. Perhaps he was not destined for greatness after all! His arms fell to his sides and he walked slowly back to the village.

Two sleeps following Has-ka's fast, No Water raced through the village shouting, *"Che-hoo-hoo! Che-hoo-hoo!* All who are brave and strong, line up for *che-hoo-hoo.*"

This was a wrestling game in which the Sioux boys chose sides, each boy picking his own opponent. When a wrestler's shoulders were forced to the ground, he was "dead."

Young Hump was one of the leaders; No Water, as usual, was the other. Hump chose Has-ka to be on his side. Has-ka looked over the "enemy" line to pick out someone about his own size and weight to challenge.

He was startled when he heard No Water shout his own name.

"I, No Water," the enemy leader yelled, "do challenge the One Who Cries When the Wasps Sting Him."

The older boy could not have chosen a surer way of arousing Has-ka to anger than with this almost-forgotten taunt. Sudden fury boiled through his veins, yet he was no fool. No Water was larger and heavier—had every chance of winning. But, of course, he had to accept the challenge or be disgraced in the eyes of his comrades.

Soon enemy was upon enemy and the ground was covered with writhing, struggling pairs. Has-ka braced himself as No Water seized him. He fought with every ounce of strength that was in him and when his breath rasped in his throat and he was so exhausted that every muscle felt limp, he gritted his teeth and kept on struggling and straining until unknown reserves of strength came to his help. But grit and determination were not sufficient against superior strength and weight.

At last when many shoulders were pinned to the ground, the victors pretended to take the scalps of those whom they had defeated. It was not until most of the pairs had ended their struggles that No Water managed to throw Has-ka and leap upon him to pin his shoulders to the ground. According to the rules of the game that was supposed to be the end of it, except for the pretended scalping, but No Water knelt on Has-ka's shoulders while his thumbs pressed the beaten boy's windpipe.

Has-ka's breath came out with a gurgling groan—almost a cry. His good friend, He Dog, pulled No Water off.

The *che-hoo-hoo* winners danced the victory dance about the defeated enemy who hunched sullenly in the center of the ring. No Water pointed triumphantly to Has-ka and shouted, *"Hopo!* I, No Water, did beat my enemy He-Who-Cries-When-the-Wasps-Sting. And I did make him cry out again. Has-ka has not the brave heart! Has-ka is a girl!"

The beaten boy's spirits sank to his moccasins. He had thought he was making headway in gaining the respect of his comrades. Now, even though he had done his best, he had disgraced himself again. He had given his rival another chance to gloat over him. Why did the older boy hate him so? Why did he always try to belittle him before his companions?

Disgraced and unhappy Has-ka shunned his comrades until an exciting event made him forget his personal troubles.

An unknown disease had swept through the pony herd the previous winter and there was talk of the need of new horses. Has-ka listened eagerly. He hoped that a pony-stealing expedition was afoot.

The easiest method of acquiring new horses

and the one the Sioux liked best because of the excitement it afforded, was to creep at night into some camp of their enemy, the Crows, and drive their tamed horses away. But now the Crows were far beyond the Big Horns, so the Oglalas must round up wild horses to replenish their herds. This method was harder work, for the horses so caught must be broken and the Sioux would be denied the sly pleasure of besting the enemy Crows.

An excited longing swept through Has-ka as he listened to the plans for the wild horse hunt. He made up his mind to go along.

Nearly all of the men, and some of the boys who were old enough, joined the wild horse hunt. Scouts rode out ahead toward the sand hills to see if they could locate a herd of wild horses and after riding for nearly half a sun they gave the blanket signal from a hilltop that they had discovered a herd in the valley below. The Indians scattered, circling the valley, but staying out of sight of the horses. Has-ka was riding Strongheart. He quivered with excitement as his group waited beneath the brow of the hill for the signal to advance.

When the surround was complete, several of the hunters on the south side rode over the hill yelling. The wild horses stampeded in the opposite direction, where Has-ka and his companions were waiting. Some of the hunters strung out across their path. The horses galloped in another direction only to have more hunters block their way. Finding every direction of escape closed to them, the frightened, bewildered animals started circling. When they were milling in a compact bunch, the hunters closed in on them and started thrusting their long sticks with hair rope loops over the heads of the horses they wanted to capture.

Has-ka caught sight of a pony the color of a red autumn leaf. It carried its small, well-shaped head high, nostrils distended. Its eyes were wide open but there was more a look of fight in them than of fear. The instant he saw the red stallion, Has-ka knew that it was a spirited and intelligent animal and he wanted it with all of his heart. So also did Lone Bear and he thrust out his loop trying to get it over the animal's head, but missed. Has-ka thrust out his loop, but he missed, too, for even though the red horse was frightened he was wise and wary.

Finally Lone Bear gave up with a grunt of disgust and concentrated his efforts on a less crafty animal, but no other would satisfy Has-ka. Already some of his comrades were riding toward home trailing their mustangs, which they called crazy horses, tied to the tails of their tame ponies.

At last his loop settled over the neck of the red horse and with a yell of triumph he jerked on the willow pole, drawing the loop tight. The animal reared and snorted, but could not rid itself of the thing around its neck that was fast choking its breath from it.

Has-ka edged Strongheart close to the wild pony and then he did a daring thing. He threw himself onto the red pony's back, with nothing in the world with which to control it but the hair loop around its neck.

With a shrill whinny of rebellion the red horse broke loose from the herd, galloped into the open, bucking, rearing, turning, twisting, omitting none of the tricks a wild horse knows in an effort to dislodge its rider. He sunfished and galloped, but Has-ka clung to his mane, tightening the noose around its neck when necessary, but giving the magnificent animal its head as much as possible. A wild sense of elation swept through the boy. He yelled and his heels pounded the sides of the wild horse. He would ride this horse and finally conquer him.

The hunters stopped trying to capture mustangs to watch the performance that went on all over the hillside between Has-ka and the wild horse, until it was flecked with foam and finally stood with drooping head and heaving sides, too spent to struggle longer. It recognized a master.

Has-ka was spent, too, yet a thrill of triumph swept through him. He had conquered this splendid beast. Loosening his noose he reached forward and grasping an ear he turned the pony's head, his heels pounding its sides. Slowly the red pony obeyed his master's will and stumbled in the direction Has-ka wanted him to go.

When Has-ka, astride the horse he had conquered, rode up to his companions, they shouted, "He has ridden a crazy horse! *Tashunka-Witko!* Crazy Horse! Crazy Horse! His name shall be *Tashunka-Witko!* Crazy Horse!"

The boy's heart beat faster. At last he had an earned name—and a splendid one. The name of his father, but one which he himself had earned. To the Indians the name meant an untamed, splendid horse of great spirit and courage. He could not have earned a finer name, even if he had chosen it.

Crazy Horse made his rope into a halter and tied the horse to Strongheart's tail. Neither animal liked being tied to the other, but Strongheart was trained to obey and the wild horse was tired, so they got along well enough.

When the horse hunters reached their village, the first thing they did was to rope and throw the mustangs they had captured. The right fore foot was tied to the left hind foot and the horse allowed to struggle to his feet. Now the ponies could not kick and the process of taming them started at once.

Every day Crazy Horse went to the corral and roped this new horse he named Warrior. He stroked him and talked to him, breaking and training him as he had Strongheart, until finally the spirited pony yielded to the stronger will. Crazy Horse grinned with pleasure, for there were not two finer ponies in the Oglala camp than Strongheart and Warrior—and well he knew there wasn't a better horseman.

Never was there a day when the boys of Crazy Horse's band were not practicing riding in some form or other. There were races in the early evening, but Crazy Horse's favorite sport and the one he always wanted was the riding contest in which the boys chose sides. When Crazy Horse would gallop his stallion at its utmost speed, past his admiring companions, making it zigzag in its course, with just the tip of his heel showing over its neck, they would cry, *"Tashunka-Witko—* Crazy Horse rides without being seen!" "Crazy Horse was invisible to the enemy!" "Crazy Horse is the finest rider in the Oglala camp!"

## from EMMELINE AND HER DAUGHTERS

*Iris Noble*

*Over half a century ago, Emmeline Pankhurst (1858–1928) and her three daughters led the struggle of some English women who believed that they should have the right to vote. They are still referred to as "the Pankhurst suffragettes." It had been Emmeline's husband who led this respectable Victorian matron to understand the importance of the cause, and after his death she had devoted her life to women's suffrage. Laughed at when they began, Pankhurst's army soon was taken seriously enough by officials that there were reprisals: women were clubbed when they demonstrated, jailed when they became activists, and force-fed when they went on hunger strikes in prison. In writing of Emmeline Pankhurst and her daughters (Adela, Christabel, and Sylvia), Iris Noble also gives a splendidly detailed and well-researched history of the women's suffrage movement in England. Their story is told with objectivity and candor, needing no drama other than the facts.*

## [We Shall Sleep in Prison Tonight]

As Emmeline listened to Christabel explain her idea, it was as if she heard the echo of her husband's voice—"why don't you *force* us to give you the vote?"—because that was the essence of her daughter's thinking.

"We need a new organization," said Christabel, standing in the center of the small sitting room and addressing her family. "One that will act boldly and go out and talk to women and convince them it is their right to have the vote. The league and all the other woman suffrage organizations are either too polite or too tied in political parties to act with independence. Politicians just take advantage of us. If we'll work for their elections, they promise to bring into the House of Commons Father's bill for franchise—but do they do it? Never."

"Mr. Hardie does," said Adela.

But Christabel brushed aside the interruption. "He is one man, and he hasn't the power to do much for us. What we need is an organization *of* women *for* women, one that will lead all the

Reprinted by permission of Julian Messner, A Division of Simon & Schuster, Inc., and McIntosh and Otis, Inc. from *Emmeline and Her Daughters: The Pankhurst Suffragettes* by Iris Noble. Copyright © 1971 by Iris Noble

women of Britain into militant action. There are millions of women, and if they speak with one voice they will get the vote. But our organization must have no other purpose but that. We must drive, single-minded, to achieve that one purpose and no other—the vote. And with the vote we will raise women to equality in work and in education and before the law!"

Emmeline felt herself alive with excitement. Her mind went leaping ahead. "Oh, Christabel is right, I know she is! I am tired of waiting, tired of having men tell me to be patient, fobbing me off with promises that are never kept. Why should men give us something when we haven't the strength to demand it?"

"But what about all the other reforms Father wanted?" asked Adela.

"First things first," replied her mother. "Once women have the vote and can be elected to Parliament, they will be in a position to make all kinds of reforms. Christabel's plan is superb—and you know why? Because it is so simple. It has the virtue of simplicity. Women who are divided among themselves on other matters can join an organization that calls for only one thing, for suffrage. Women of all ranks of society, from the educated and wealthy to the uneducated working woman, can join together in a crusade so clear-cut that all can understand and sympathize with it."

"And another thing," Christabel still had the floor and she was not finished, "is that we must make a noise. We must get into the newspapers. We must be *heard*. We must make men so uncomfortable that they will give us what we want if only to get rid of us."

This made even Emmeline pause and think. Publicity was foreign to women. Nice women, gentlewomen, did not do things that would attract unfavorable notice in newspapers or journals. But she met the challenge and smiled at Christabel. "I've had that sort of notoriety, and it has not hurt me. I don't think it will prevent women from joining us. We've been quiet too long."

Surprisingly, Adela agreed. "History books are full of how men have achieved what they wanted, and they didn't do it sitting at home. They organized and went out into the streets; they gathered in mobs before the Houses of

Parliament; they forced governments to give way to them."

Emmeline started to speak, but stopped. She gave Christabel an eloquent glance that bade her be still. Adela must think things out for herself; if she thought Christabel was trying to persuade her she would very likely take the opposite view.

The plainest of the Pankhurst girls, resembling her father more than her mother, Adela was a puzzle to all of them. Until she was past three years old she had suffered from a disease of the leg and been unable to walk. She had therefore been a solitary child, sitting and rocking and making up stories to amuse herself. She was not the least bit shy, like Sylvia, but she liked to think her own thoughts and make up her own mind.

Emmeline was the only person who had a real influence on her, and sometimes that influence failed. As for Christabel, Adela seemed to resent her older sister and rebelled at any direction from her.

"I suppose," said Adela, thoughtfully, staring into the fire, "that we must cut any political ties with any political party. We have to be free to criticize as well as support any candidate. But to think we can achieve what we want without the cooperation of men, of leading politicians, is not sensible." Though she was only seventeen, she was apt to speak like an echo of her father, in his scholarly way. "Suffrage can only be granted by Parliament and by whichever political party is in power there. I grant you we can expect nothing from the Conservatives, but we have many friends in the Liberal Party and even more in the Labor members of the House."

"Oh, agreed," said Christabel, impatiently. "But just because the Liberals say they are for woman suffrage they think they can count on our support and keep us quiet. I say they can't —from now on. They'll have to come to us, support us, *do* something for us, before we'll work for them."

Adela slowly nodded, and Emmeline knew she was won over. It was time to get down to practical matters. It flashed through her mind how absurd it was for one widow and two young daughters to be planning an organization that would lead all British women to the winning of

the vote—when they didn't know if even one other woman would follow them—but she quickly pushed that thought out of her mind. After all, they were the Pankhurst family and not like any other.

When Christabel and Emmeline worked out the details of the organization, Adela was appalled at their undemocratic ideas, but at last she grudgingly admitted the necessity of them.

There was to be no constitution, no by-laws, no elections. The founders would choose the leadership, and those leaders would be permanent ones. Their orders must be obeyed without question; their instructions would be binding upon everyone.

"If the membership doesn't like it, they can leave the organization as easily as they can join it," declared Christabel. "We aren't building a political party; we're building an army. Generals in an army don't waste time discussing with privates how the battle is to be waged, and neither shall we."

But it was Emmeline's argument that convinced Adela. "You've seen for yourself the endless haggling and quarreling that goes on in every other suffrage group. At every election time they split into factions, and when it is over there is always bitterness because some favorite candidate didn't get chosen. We can't have quarrels. We can't have a divided organization, or we're finished before we start."

Adela capitulated. She also readily approved the conditions of membership, because they would enable working women to join as easily as rich ones. Any woman could become a member by paying a shilling, and there would be no yearly dues demanded. Salaries paid to the leaders would be the bare minimum needed for the work. Any large expenses would have to be paid by donations and gifts, or collections taken up at meetings, but no one was to be forced to give or made ashamed if they could not.

Men could not join, but they would be encouraged to attend meetings and help in any way they could.

Each new member would sign a declaration of adherence to the organization's policy, to work for woman suffrage and to promise she would work for no other group until suffrage was won. Any member could be instantly expelled for disagreeing with this policy, or if she came to a meeting and tried to drag in other causes, no matter how worthy those causes were. No member could ask the others to help her in some particular charity or to work against some particular injustice—not until the cause of suffrage was won.

Not until the last details had been worked out and it was time for bed did Emmeline realize that Harry had sat quietly throughout the whole discussion, saying nothing.

"What do you think, son?" she asked, turning low the wick in the oil lamp and handing it to him to light himself to his room.

"I?" he blushed. "Whatever you think, Mamma. You always know what is right."

The next day Emmeline sent out invitations to all the women in Manchester who were particularly interested in suffrage matters—except for those who were jealous heads of their own organizations. The result was a farly large gathering at her house.

She had expected shock and disapproval over a new organization and over the rules, and some of the women did express alarm that it should be so autocratic and undemocratic. But she was unprepared, in spite of her natural optimism, for the enthusiasm. It started small, then spread like a wave throughout the room, with everyone exclaiming at once that the idea was brilliant.

Suffrage, and only suffrage! These women, too, were tired of seeing their efforts going for nothing, frittered away without getting one step nearer to their goal. A very few women left, saying they weren't interested, but the majority vied with each other to see who could be the first to find a shilling in her handbag and sign the pledge.

So the Women's Social and Political Union was born.

Mrs. Jacob Bright and Christabel were chosen as leaders, but when Emmeline's name was put forward she quite sincerely objected. One Pankhurst was enough. She held to this for a few months, but when she realized that all the women looked to her for leadership, insisted she take the chair at meetings and would belong only if she were in charge, she gave in.

From the first moment of organization, the members were swept into activities new to them. No longer could they stay cosily in their own homes, holding meetings among themselves. They had to go out to where people were—on street corners, to outside social gatherings or to political meetings—and force themselves to speak about woman suffrage. Timid ladies found themselves standing on stools, while other ladies steadied them, and braving the jeers and laughter of street-corner bullies as they spoke of injustice to women.

Emmeline and Christabel were by far the best speakers, though Adela soon developed an earnest style of her own. Christabel's striking combination of a charming face and figure along with the logic of her legal brain always commanded attention, but it was Emmeline Pankhurst who could quiet the most unruly audience and bring unknown women to her afterwards, with their shillings in their hands.

When men shouted at her: "Go get yourself a husband, and stay at home where you belong!" or "If you had a handful of kids you wouldn't be bothering about votes!" and when conservative women who had paused to listen for a moment, shuddered and said: "What an unnatural female!" she was ready with answers for them. She had been a beloved wife, she was the mother of four children, she held the home together for them and she had nothing but praise for wifehood or motherhood.

"Can you say the same?" she demanded of her hecklers. "Do you honor the mother who bore you, or your own wife, when you deny them what you look upon as a right for yourself? When you treat them as creatures beneath you?"

Membership in the Women's Social and Political Union, or the Union, or the W.S.P.U., as it was often called, grew steadily, by ones and twos and threes. New faces were seen at the Pankhurst home; new, and younger, women began calling to find out what they could do.

From London, Sylvia made her contribution by sending them more of her scholarship money than she kept for herself. At this time in her life she could have broken away from her family and devoted herself solely to art, but she was too emotionally tied to her mother. She often criticized Emmeline, but unwillingly she adored her. Sylvia did not then have the self-confidence to make a new life and new friends; instead, she tried to win Emmeline's favor by denying herself every comfort and living in a miserable room.

Her only London friend was Keir Hardie, who was like a second father to her. When he talked to her of his hard, bitter life as a miner's child and of how much he hoped to do for working people in his seat in Parliament, Sylvia wondered if her art was not an indulgence and her duty was to political causes. So she cut down on food, bought no clothes and sent everything she could to her mother.

Emmeline was glad of the money, but she had little idea of what a great sacrifice this was for a twenty-year-old girl. How could she? To Emmeline, nothing was too much for anyone to give for the cause of woman suffrage; no one gave more than she did, herself.

What Christabel did seemed more to the point, because the older girl was so active, rushing from classes to meetings. One day she reported to her mother an interesting success.

The Oldham Trades Council of Labour Party men had arranged a special meeting for Christabel to speak on woman suffrage to workers in the Oldham district. After her speech was over, three young girls waited and asked to talk to her. They were sisters named Kenney, cotton factory workers, and their spokesman was sister Annie, small, quick, eager and lively.

Could they join the W.S.P.U.? They handed over their shillings, but that was not all. Could Miss Pankhurst come and talk to the women at their factory? They would make all the arrangements. Christabel agreed to come.

Christabel had no faith that Annie Kenney knew anything about making suitable arrangements for a meeting, but when she arrived on the appointed day she was agreeably astonished. Annie was a born organizer. She had talked to the cotton-mill women and persuaded them to stay late, tired as they were after a day's work; she had bullied the foreman into giving her a room for the meeting.

It was a success. Almost all the women enthusiastically joined the W.S.P.U. and pledged themselves to talk to others.

The real success was the association between Annie and Christabel, which was to last almost their lifetimes. Every general needs a competent aide, and Annie became that to Christabel. Any young girl as deprived by birth and education as Annie, eager as she was to escape the dreariness of her cotton-mill life, needed an ideal and an idol to inspire her, and Christabel was that to Annie.

Nor did Annie care how little she had to live on if it meant she could become part of the Pankhurst world.

It was she who suggested the next move that would widen the field of suffrage work. A traveling fair, called the Lancashire Wakes, went from town to town through Lancashire and Yorkshire counties. People flocked to the fair. They came for pleasure and fun, but they were also accustomed to speakers from the Salvation Army and other serious groups who gave talks on the sidelines. Why shouldn't the W.S.P.U. do the same?

They did—as often as Emmeline could get away from work, Christabel and Adela from school, or they could persuade other members to take their places. And they found that, in spite of some rough heckling from men who were too full of beer to mind their manners, they attracted larger crowds than anyone.

Emmeline discarded all complicated slogans in favor of the simple one: *Votes for Women!* This was on the banner they held over the speaker's chair and on all the leaflets they distributed. Most of the audience gathered around them as they would for any free and exciting sideshow, but always there were women—and some men—who showed their sympathy and donated some money.

For two years the W.S.P.U. worked and grew, making itself known throughout the two counties and finding that the ripples of their work were spreading even beyond. Letters came to the Pankhurst home from unexpected sources. The newspapers mentioned them, and Christabel pushed hard for publicity—any kind, whether it was favorable or not.

She was developing a shrewd sense of the value of making woman suffrage a thing that was talked about. At night she and Harry would go out and chalk up in bold letters on city sidewalks notices of meetings or just *Votes for Women!*

Late in 1904 Keir Hardie wrote Emmeline that there was a chance he could introduce Dr. Pankhurst's bill for woman suffrage in the next session of Parliament. Although the Conservative Party still held the offices of Prime Minister and Cabinet, Liberal and Labour Party strength in the House of Commons was growing, and most of those members had promised to support him.

So, in February of 1905, Emmeline got a few days' leave from her job and went to London to help him. Sylvia accompanied her to Parliament and waited with her in the anteroom of the House of Commons. Then Keir Hardie came and explained what would happen. On this Wednesday there would be the usual custom of balloting to see which favorite bills of which members would be permitted to be heard in this session. He was hopeful for a place for the Suffrage Bill.

When he went back into the House, Emmeline did not stand idly by. She sent in her name to various politicians whom she considered her friends or who were indebted to her and Dr. Pankhurst for help given in their elections. When they came out to greet her, she wasted no time in telling them where their duty lay and why they had to support Mr. Hardie.

By now, from all her husband's teachings and from Christabel's legal studies, she knew her facts about the injustices done to women regarding inheritances, property rights and marital status. From her own experiences as registrar and, especially, from Annie Kenney's stories, she also knew that the claim that women were better off under mens' chivalry was a pack of lies.

A cotton-mill manufacturer might put his own wife and mother up on a pedestal, but that did not stop him from exploiting the poor women who worked for him. There was no chivalry and no protection there. He worked them terribly long hours, at less pay than men got, with no safeguards for their health.

The whole basis of argument that women should not be treated the same as men because they were too weak in brains and bodily strength was brutally exploded when it came to profits. In mills and factories women slaved alongside of men and were expected to be as fast and capable as men; as much was demanded of them, and far less was given to them.

As Emmeline talked, her cheeks' flushed and her eyes sparkling, her daughter marveled at her. She knew that her mother's elegant appearance was only made possible by her exquisite sewing, by borrowing a ribbon from Christabel and a brooch from Adela, and this did not surprise her. Emmeline Pankhurst always had a flair for style. But Sylvia had seen little of her in the past few years and was unprepared for how young she had grown.

The W.S.P.U. had brought new life to Emmeline. She did not try to dress youthfully or pretend to be less than her forty-six years, but there was a zest and excitement about her that made her daughter feel drab by comparison.

When Hardie came out of the House chamber, he was troubled. He had not won a place; he could not introduce a bill that session, but his good friend Bramford Slack had won a place for another measure. If Slack could be persuaded to substitute the bill for woman suffrage instead of the one he had proposed, he would have the right to do this.

Emmeline went into a whirlwind of action, dragging Sylvia with her. Bramford Slack was not to be found at Parliament, but that did not stop her. She went to his house and pleaded with his wife, to such good purpose that that lady persuaded her husband to make the substitution.

One step had been won, and Emmeline's hopes were high. Before she left London she got in touch with the National Union of Women's Suffrage Societies, a committee that tried to coordinate the work and bring about cooperation among all the suffrage groups in Britain. The National Union was delighted to hear that Mr. Slack would actually propose votes for women during that session, and promised to do all they could to help.

Friday, May 12, was the day set for Mr. Slack to introduce the measure. It would have to be heard that day and given a preliminary passing for future debate, or it would go by default and he could not speak again.

Emmeline again came to London. When she and Sylvia reached the entrance to the House of Commons, they were overjoyed to see the street and lobby and anterooms crowded with women, many of whom Emmeline already knew. They greeted her with smiling faces. "A great day for us, Mrs. Pankhurst," said little, elderly Mrs. Wolstenholme Elmy, a pioneer suffrage worker, "and we have you to thank for it."

"The battle isn't won yet," warned Emmeline, but her hopes were high.

Those hopes dwindled as the hours dragged on. None of the women had thought to secure seats for themselves in the small section of the House Visitors' Gallery allotted to women, so none of them knew what was happening. Keir Hardie came out to report, and he was worried. Mr. Slack's proposal was to be the last on the day's schedule, and it seemed that discussion of prior bills was being deliberately prolonged. Time was running out.

Emmeline sent in a note to the Conservative Party leader, Mr. A. J. Balfour, threatening him that no woman would work for his party in the next general election unless Slack's bill was heard. It was an empty threat. Most of the women supported the Liberal Party anyway.

There was only one hour, then a half-hour, then ten minutes left. The door of the House opened as Keir Hardie strode out, and behind him Emmeline could hear a roar of laughter from the House chamber.

"It's all over," Hardie told the women, bitterly. "We've lost. They talked the time away, deliberately arguing and laughing about trifles —anything to prevent the bill from being proposed this session."

"I heard them laughing. Were they laughing at *us?*" Emmeline was shocked and furious.

"It amounts to the same thing. They were carrying on a ridiculous argument about tail lights, saying that if a cart had to carry a red light at the rear, why shouldn't a horse have one on his tail? But the real reason for the laughter was that they were enjoying themselves, killing time and mocking us. Grown men acting like children—just to prevent woman suffrage being discussed this session!" Hardie was indignant. "The Liberals were as bad as the rest!"

He had to go back to the House for a moment, but the women were in no mood to go home. Their spirits were sore with resentment. They wanted to discuss what had happened. They left the lobby, but near a statue outside the House of Lords they gathered to talk. Mrs. Elmy, the pioneer who had suffered so many rebuffs, tried to make a speech.

Policemen converged on them. Not even Mrs. Elmy's age and white curls could affect them in what they considered their duty: the women must leave. The police attitude became threatening, but when Keir Hardie appeared—a member of Parliament—they were more polite and led the women across the street to Broad Sanctuary in front of Westminster Abbey.

There the women could have their impromptu meeting, and there they passed a strong resolution of protest to the House of Commons for its shameful actions that day.

That night, in Sylvia's shabby room, Emmeline paced up and down as she did when she was agitated, wringing her hands and venting her feelings in angry denunciations and tragic exclamations.

"The wretches—laughing at us! When I think of the promises the Liberal Party made to your father and to me! Oh, when I think of them, and think how we must go on enduring such humiliations, year after year—it's too much! It's more than the spirit can stand . . ." Suddenly, in the midst of her dramatics, she caught sight of her daughter's face and saw that Sylvia was really suffering. It flashed across her mind that this sensitive girl truly thought her mother was in despair.

She stopped pacing, laughed and reached out to pat Sylvia's cheek. "Don't look at me like that. Bless you, your old mother likes it. This is what I call life!"

It was true. Disappointed as she was, she was in the center of a conflict, in the heart of a storm, and that was life to her. The worse the disappointment, the stronger she rose to meet the next challenge.

Sylvia could not understand such a temperament, so foreign to her own. She knew her mother too well to think that such extravagant behavior was any evidence of insincerity, yet she was incapable of matching it with the same kind of dramatics. The events of the day made her feel just wretched. Would she ever be the daughter Emmeline wanted?

When Emmeline returned to Manchester she found Christabel knew all about the Parliamentary failure, and her response was the same as her mother's. The Liberals would find they could not get away with this betrayal! Her anger was satisfying to Emmeline, but when she announced her next move her mother was horrified.

"I am going to prison," said Christabel, and hurried to explain before Emmeline could voice her shocked protest. "Annie and I have talked it over, and we have decided it is the only way to call public attention to the Liberals' treatment of us—because it will be the Liberals who will put us in jail."

"You are going to get yourself deliberately arrested? Why?" Part of Emmeline's mind was leaping ahead to the significance of the action; part was pulling back, trying to say that this must not happen to Christabel.

Quickly, Christabel outlined her plans. A nationwide general election was coming up. The Liberal Party intended to make a strong bid to take over the Government. A great meeting was scheduled in the Free Trade Hall of Manchester, where the Liberals would launch their campaign and throw down the gauntlet to the Conservatives.

Christabel and Annie would be at that meeting.

If they were allowed to speak and present the case for woman suffrage, well and good. But if not, they were resolved to make a disturbance that would get them sent to jail. The newspapers would be full of it. Then let the Liberal leaders answer to the women who supported them why they had sent a daughter of Dr. Pankhurst, one of the Liberal Party founders, to jail!

Emmeline listened. The plan was good. But she said: "I shall go with Annie—not you, Christabel."

"The plan wouldn't work with you, Mother. They wouldn't dare arrest you, not in Manchester. They wouldn't let you speak, but they would be polite and shut you up," said her daughter. And Emmeline had to admit that it was true.

On the night of the meeting the two girls were gay and full of little nervous jokes, and Emmeline tried hard to answer them in the same spirit. She teased Annie about the bulge under her coat, where she was carrying a rolled-up banner which read "Will You Give Votes to Women?" She even smiled as Christabel walked out the door and laughingly called back to her mother: "We shall sleep in prison tonight!"

Then Emmeline was left alone in her private agony. Her favorite child was going into danger, and all she could do was wait and pray through the long and miserable hours.

This was something she would have to face, not only for Christabel but for her son and other daughters. If love for them made a coward out of her, she would be ruthless with that love. She would steel herself to their sacrifice. She would honor them by giving them the same privilege she demanded for herself, of suffering for a cause they all believed in.

Otherwise, in some crisis, she might weaken and falter, try to hold them back and thus fall back herself.

## from THE ONE BAD THING ABOUT FATHER

*Ferdinand Monjo*

*In an invented diary of Theodore Roosevelt's son Quentin, Ferdinand Monjo succeeds in capturing both the robust personality of President Roosevelt (1858–1919) and the somewhat biased viewpoint of his child. While the book is intended for readers in the primary grades, it can be read aloud with enjoyment because of the humor and the direct style. Historically accurate, the biography is fictionalized just enough to give narrative interest yet remain consistent with facts.*

### Archie and I

I'm Quentin.
Here's my brother Archie.
And here's Father.
There's just one bad thing about Father.
He's President of the United States.

That means he has to live in the White House.
And all the rest of us—
Mother
Alice
Ted
Kermit
Ethel
Archie
and me—
we all have to live there too.
There's one thing Archie and I
can't understand about Father.
I mean, Father could have been
a boxer or a wrestler.
He can even do jujitsu.
Mother says
he could have headed the police force
in New York City forever if he had wanted to.
Our brother Ted says
Father could have kept on being a cowboy
on his ranch in the West.
Father showed Archie and me his brand
for branding cattle. Here it is:

Father could have been a general.
Our sister Alice says
Father was a brave soldier and
helped win a war in Cuba.
And Father could have been a hunter.
Our brother Kermit says
Father knows how to catch
wildcats and bears.
Now if Father can do all these things,
what Archie and I would like to know is
how come he'd rather be President?

Being President can practically
ruin your whole life.
Presidents have to read lots of books.
They have to shake hands with congressmen.

They have to tell jokes to policemen.
They have to make lots of speeches.
They have to play tennis with senators.
They have to work out with prizefighters.
They have to go horseback riding
with cowboys.
And they have to have dinner
with lots of foreign princes.
Archie and I don't get to see
half enough of Father.
Father feels pretty bad about it too.
He lets us come to his office
every afternoon at four.
And for an hour or so
he does whatever we want him to do.
Sometimes
we take the hose
and flood the sandbox.
Father draws a map for us with his
umbrella and tells us all about the war.
He shows us where the Russians and
the Japanese are fighting each other.
Then we get our boats.
Archie is the Russian navy,
and I am the Japanese navy.
I always get to sink Archie's fleet
because the Japanese
are beating the Russians.
That's what Father says.
He's trying to get them to stop fighting.
Sometimes we visit
our blue parrot, Eli Yale.
Sometimes when Father rides his horse, Renown,
he lets Ethel and Archie and me
take turns riding our pony, Algonquin.
Algonquin has a soft nose.
Charlie Lee takes care of him.
Sometimes we visit our other pets.
We say hello to Jonathan, the rat,
to our white guinea pig, Dewey, Jr.,
to our hens, Baron Speckle and Fierce,
and to Josiah, the badger.
Father brought Josiah home from
one of his hunting trips.
Josiah likes milk and potatoes.
Sometimes we feed the dogs,
Cuba
and Skip
and Jack
and Sailor Boy.

And that's all the pets
we have—
except for the two kangaroo rats,
the turtle,
the flying squirrel,
and Tom Quartz, the kitten.
One time I gave Tom Quartz a bath
in the bathtub. He nearly drowned.

### Government Property

We like to have Father around.
But Mother says we have to let Father
have a few hours to himself every day
or he will never be able to run the country.


So Archie and I get this gang
of ours together.
Father calls us The White House Gang.
And we find stuff to do.
But when you live in the White House,
you have to be careful.
Things don't really *belong* to you.
Nearly everything is government property.
Suppose you are riding your express wagon
in the hall, having a race
with your dog, Skip.
Suppose the wagon turns over and
your hand goes through a picture.
It's Mrs. Benjamin Harrison,
wife of the twenty-third President.
And that picture is government property!
Nobody likes it when you slide downstairs
on tin trays either.
"By Godfrey!" says Father. "Don't you
bunnies know how dangerous that could be?
Suppose some senator got hurt?"


Suppose you and Archie and everybody
are having a stilt race on the lawn
and you happen to run
through a flower bed.
Here come the Secret Service men
and the White House police.
You have to get right out
of that flower bed.
It's government property too!
If Father catches you putting

spitballs on Andrew Jackson, he gets mad.
Andrew Jackson was the *seventh* President.
He's government property too!


Suppose you and your gang slide down
the awning over the front portico.
It's too steep to climb back up.
The police pull you back by a rope.
By Godfrey!
You can't play with awnings.
They're government property too.
You can't even visit your brother
when he's sick.
When Archie had the measles,
he was upstairs in his bedroom.
He hadn't seen Algonquin for weeks.
So I went to Charlie Lee, and we
sneaked Algonquin into the basement,
past the White House police.
We rang for the freight elevator.
Then we all got on.
Charlie and I had to *push* Algonquin.
We all went upstairs and
had a long visit with Archie.
It cheered him up a lot.
But the minute Father found out,
he sent Algonquin
right back to the stable.
"By Godfrey, Quentin! How can you be
such a muttonhead! It's preposterous!
You know perfectly well you can't
bring a pony into the White House
on the freight elevator!
It's *government property!*"


### At Oyster Bay

Archie and I have much more fun
in summer at our house on Oyster Bay.
Nothing is government property there.
Our big brothers, Ted and Kermit,
are home from school.
And sometimes our big sister, Alice,
is there too.
Alice usually helps Father run the country.
Alice isn't here this summer though.
Father says she's on a junket.
A junket is a trip to China and Japan.
Father likes to write letters to us.

Here's a picture Father drew
in a letter to Alice.

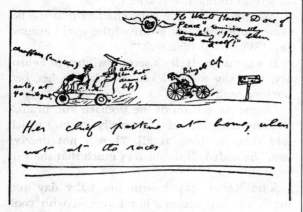

He drew the bicycle cop because
Alice loves to speed.
She races her car along
at twenty-five miles an hour!
Alice has her picture in the paper
practically every day.
Some man once asked Father why
he didn't do something about Alice.
Father said, "I can do one of two things.
I can be President of the United States.
Or I can control Alice.
I cannot possibly do both."
This summer, while Alice is away,
Archie and I are helping
Father run things.
This way we may get to see
more of Father.
If the Russians and the Japanese
would quit fighting,
Father would be pleased as punch.
And so would we.
Father sent a telegram to Russia,
asking them to stop fighting.
He sent another telegram to Japan,
asking them to stop fighting too.
Soon after that, a big ship came
to Oyster Bay.
Two Russians got off.
They wanted to see Father
about ending the war.
Archie and I were waiting

for them on the dock.
We pretended we were fishing.
But we were watching
every move they made.
And we reported their arrival to Father.
We knew some Japanese gentlemen were coming.
They wanted to talk to Father too
about ending the war.
Archie and I went to town.
We hung around and hitched
a ride home with them.
And then we reported their arrival
to Father.
The peace talks are coming along
quite nicely, thanks to Archie and me.

## *from* THE HELEN KELLER STORY
*Catherine Owens Peare*

Helen Keller's (1880–1968) *triumph over
blindness and deafness is one of the most stirring
success stories of all time. Her intelligence
needed only to be unlocked and, thanks to the
dedication of Anne Sullivan, her teacher, Miss
Keller lived a long and productive life. Children
with both sight and hearing should find themselves inspired by Helen Keller's life to do more
with these senses that they take for granted.
Older children will want to read Miss Keller's
own book,* The Story of My Life.

### Pupil and Teacher

The baby was pretty and bright and quick. At
six months she was almost talking. "Tea, tea,
tea!" she said, or "wah-wah! wah-wah!" when she
wanted a drink of water. By the time she was a
year old she was trying to walk, a few steps and a
tumble, a few steps and a tumble.

In the long, mild summers of the South, where
shrubs and flowers grew luxuriantly, she learned
quickly to love the out-of-doors. She reached out
for dancing leaves, buried her nose in the roses,
or cocked her head at the song of a bird.

"My daughter will be a lovely young lady some day," said her mother, holding the baby high. "She's a Boston Adams on my side, and her father is a Southern gentleman of distinction."

Captain Arthur Keller looked the part of a distinguished Southerner with his full mustache and goatee and straight posture. He had been an officer in the Confederate Army during the Civil War, and he was distantly related to Robert E. Lee.

"I can scarcely believe he is twenty years older than I," Kate Adams Keller thought as she handed him his jouncing, lively daughter.

"My first little girl," he said, as the child tugged at his whiskers, "has a mind of her own."

Captain Keller already had two sons by a former marriage: James who was nineteen, almost as old as his stepmother; and Simpson who was in his early teens.

The little girl with a mind of her own had been born on June 27, 1880, in the town of Tuscumbia, Alabama, in a two-room house on the Keller farmlands where her parents were spending the first few years of their married life. The rest of the Keller family lived very near by in the main house, "Ivy Green."

"What will you call her?" had been the question of family and neighbors who crowded into the little annex to see the new baby.

"She is to be named after my mother, Helen Everett," said Mrs. Keller.

"I like the name of Mildred," said Captain Keller, but his remark was lost in the gay confusion.

When the day of the baby's christening arrived, Kate Keller looked proudly at her husband as he stood before the minister holding the tiny creature in a long white dress. But when the minister asked the baby's name, Captain Keller had a lapse of memory. He could remember only that she was to be named for her grandmother.

"She is to be called Helen Adams Keller," he told the minister, and Helen Adams Keller she became.

Kate Keller sighed and resigned herself to the error. Apparently her husband had a keen enough memory to be editor of their paper, the *North Alabamian,* but not keen enough to remember his own daughter's name.

Helen thrived and grew rapidly, passed her first summer, then her second, and her mother recited the old superstition, "When a baby passes its second summer, it is safe."

"Tea, tea, tea!" the baby chattered, as she became more and more aware of the world around her. "Wah-wah! Wah-wah!"

It was during Helen's second winter, in February, that she was stricken and lay in her bed burning with fever.

"Acute congestion of the stomach and brain," was the diagnosis of the family doctor, which told them nothing at all. "I will not deceive you," he added. "I doubt very much that she will recover."

Kate Keller stayed with her baby day and night, soothed Helen's hot forehead with cool, wet cloths, whispered and hummed to her when she fretted. By some miracle the baby did recover, so far as anyone could see at the time, but the Kellers soon realized that the fever had destroyed Helen's sight and hearing.

Helen Keller became another kind of child. Since she could not hear, she could not learn to talk, and only emitted an occasional squeal or cry. Since she could not see, she became baffled by her environment, and would walk only when she could cling to her mother's long skirts. Because she was baffled, she became bad-tempered, contrary, hostile, unmanageable.

As she passed her second, third, and fourth birthdays, her disposition grew worse and worse. She wanted to communicate with the world around her and could not. She had devised a few signs of her own. She would nod for *yes* and shake her head for *no*. If she wanted bread and butter, she would act out the slicing of bread with a knife. If she wanted her mother, she stroked her cheek.

"She has intelligence," the heartbroken mother insisted. "I can see that she has intelligence."

But there were others who thought differently.

"You ought to have her put away, Kate," said one relative. "She's too odd to have around. The sight of her makes everyone unhappy."

She was certainly not a pleasant sight, even though she was a healthy, husky child, quite tall for her age. She was sullen and disheveled, often refusing to let anyone comb her hair or straighten her clothing.

All the while Kate and her husband inquired in every direction for doctors and specialists, the child's temper tantrums grew more violent, and her acts of mischief more dangerous.

Kate knew in her heart that she could expect to have the child taken away from her. What happened to a child that was "taken away"? Where would she be placed? Who would endure her willfulness like her own mother?

Captain and Mrs. Keller had moved out of the annex into the main house by the time Helen was five. Surely there was plenty of room for one handicapped child! And Mr. Keller had been appointed marshal of northern Alabama, which increased their income. Surely they could afford to give Helen some kind of care.

When Helen was six Mrs. Keller had a second child, Mildred.

Helen, surrounded by darkness and silence, was used to rushing to her mother's arms and her mother's lap whenever she felt insecure or lost or aggrieved. Suddenly there was another child in Mother's lap. Helen was accustomed to Mother's time whenever she wished, and now Mother was dividing her time, even pushing Helen away when she was attending to the new creature.

One day in a fit of resentment Helen darted at Mildred's cradle and tipped it over, sending Mildred tumbling out. Maybe the new child would break, the way her dolls sometimes broke when she dashed them to the floor.

Then, while the stamping and remorseless Helen felt hands pulling her away and guiding her out of the room, the distraught mother had to listen once more to the grim advice.

"You ought to put her away, Kate. She's mentally defective."

"No, no, no! She's intelligent. She learns easily. I can tell."

Something had to be done. The situation had to be faced and solved.

In the quiet of a late evening, when Mr. and Mrs. Keller were sitting in the living room and both children were asleep, an idea suddenly did occur to Mrs. Keller. She had been reading Charles Dickens's *American Notes*.

"Listen to this!" she said suddenly to her husband. "When Charles Dickens was in Boston he visited a place called the Perkins Institution for the Blind. He says, 'The children were at their daily tasks in different rooms, except a few who were already dismissed, and were at play. . . . Good order, cleanliness, and comfort pervaded every corner of the building. The various classes, who were gathered round their teachers, answered the questions put to them with readiness and intelligence, and in a spirit of cheerful contest for precedence which pleased me very much. . . . In a portion of the building set apart for that purpose are workshops for blind persons whose education is finished, and who have acquired a trade. . . . Several people were at work here, making brushes, mattresses, and so forth; and the cheerfulness, industry, and good order discernible in every other part of the building extended to this department also. On the ringing of a bell, the pupils all repaired, without any guide or leader, to a spacious music-hall, where they took their seats . . . and listened with manifest delight to a voluntary on the organ.' "

"My dear!" her husband interrupted her. "Have you forgotten that Helen is also deaf? Bells? Music halls? Organs? She could not be reached in that way."

"I know, I know!" replied Kate Keller. "But there's more. Dickens discovered something else. Listen to this."

Mrs. Keller read on: " 'The thought occurred to me as I sat down in another room, before a girl, blind, deaf, and dumb; destitute of smell, and nearly so of taste: before a fair young creature with every human faculty, and hope, and power of goodness and affection, enclosed within her delicate frame, and but one outward sense—the sense of touch. There she was, before me; built up, as it were, in a marble cell, impervious to any ray of light or particle of sound; with her poor white hand peeping through a chink in the wall, beckoning to some good man for help, that an immortal soul might be awakened. . . . Her face was radiant with intelligence and pleasure. Her hair, braided by her own hands, was bound about a head whose intellectual capacity and development were beautifully expressed in its graceful outline and its broad open brow; her dress, arranged by herself, was a pattern of neatness and simplicity. The work she had knitted lay beside her; her writing-book was on the desk she leaned upon. . . . She was seated in a little enclosure, made by school-desks and forms, writing her daily journal. . . . Her name is Laura Bridgman.' "

Arthur Keller had put down his own book and was looking off into space, thinking deeply as he listened.

"How did they communicate with her?" he asked.

"With a finger alphabet of some sort—entirely through her sense of touch, which is about all Laura Bridgman has. Helen is not as afflicted as Laura. Helen can taste and smell."

"I don't know," said Captain Keller. "Charles Dickens likes to dramatize things to the hilt. I think it would be wise to check up on the Perkins Institution in some other way."

A few days later a peddler came through town selling harnesses, and he knocked at the door of "Ivy Green." The minute Mrs. Keller heard his accent she asked, "Are you from New England?"

"Boston, ma'am."

"Have you ever heard of the Perkins Institution for the Blind?"

"No, ma'am, but I'll inquire about it when I return home," he promised.

Maybe he kept his promise; maybe he forgot. Anyway, the Kellers never heard from him again.

In a town as small as Tuscumbia everyone knew everyone else, and many of the neighbors worried about the deaf-blind child who was growing up half wild.

"I've heard of an eye specialist in Baltimore, a Dr. Chisholm," one of them dropped by to say. "He has cured many cases of blindness that were thought to be hopeless. Why don't you take your little girl to see him?"

Anxiously Kate Keller and the Captain took Helen on the long train trip to Baltimore, only to have Dr. Chisholm say,

"I can do nothing for her. She is permanently blind."

"But what becomes of people like Helen?" Mrs. Keller asked in desperation. "She won't always have us."

"While you are this far north," said Dr. Chisholm, "why don't you stop at the national capital on the way home and see Alexander Graham Bell? He knows a great deal about the teaching of deaf children, and he is a very sympathetic and understanding man."

With fading courage they went on to Washing-

ton, scarcely speaking a word to one another on the way, so sunken were they in black despair. A first child, a lovely child with silken, wavy hair, yet not a child, not really a human being.

Kate Keller thought Dr. Bell the kindliest man she had ever met. He was tall and attractive, with black hair and beard and large eyes. Not yet forty, he had ten years earlier demonstrated his telephone at the Chicago World's Fair.

Dr. Bell put the Kellers at their ease at once and lifted the little girl to his knee while he talked with them.

"She's obviously a bright child, a very teachable child," said Dr. Bell as Helen explored his vest buttons with her fingers.

"Yes, Dr. Bell, but how? How?" begged Mrs. Keller, and she was almost in tears.

"Have you ever heard of the Perkins Institution in Boston?" he asked.

Kate and Arthur Keller looked at each other. Yes, they had!

"My wife read about it in Dickens's *American Notes*," the Captain told Dr. Bell.

"Oh, then you know of the case of Laura Bridgman?"

They nodded.

"The man who taught Laura Bridgman, Dr. Samuel Gridley Howe, is dead, but his successor, Mr. Michael Anagnos, is doing splendid work with handicapped children. I suggest that you write to him about Helen."

Both Kellers thanked him profusely. Their spirits had risen steadily from the moment they had begun to talk with him.

"How did you happen to become interested in this sort of thing, Dr. Bell?" asked Mrs. Keller.

"My grandfather, my father, and I have all been interested in speech, in elocution, and in teaching articulation to deaf persons."

"It must be frightful to be deaf or blind," said Mrs. Keller.

"Oh, not necessarily," replied Dr. Bell in a very matter-of-fact tone. "My wife has been deaf since she was four, when she lost her hearing as a result of scarlet fever. We are very happy."

Kate Keller could have bitten off her own tongue for having said such a careless thing, but Dr. Bell didn't seem perturbed.

"The only thing we have to fear," he went on, "is ignorance, Mrs. Keller. In olden times the deaf-blind were legally classified as idiots, because no one understood them. We are beginning to overcome our ignorance of these matters. We are beginning to learn that what the handicapped need is education at the hands of well-trained and sympathetic teachers. Beethoven lost his hearing, you will remember, but he went right on composing music. Homer, the Greek poet, was blind. John Milton wrote his greatest poetry after he had lost his sight. And Thomas Edison, who has perfected the electric light bulb and is developing the electric power plant, is quite deaf. When he and his wife go to the theater, she taps out the dialogue on his knee in Morse code. We really don't need all of our senses to live successfully."

Dr. Bell smiled at the little girl sitting on his knee, and he set his watch so that its alarm would ring and placed it in her hands. When she felt the vibration in her finger tips, she began to jounce and swing her feet happily.

"I can easily detect a great deal of intelligence in this little brown head," said Dr. Bell. "I am sure she can be educated. She is certainly bright enough to learn the finger alphabet."

The Kellers left his office filled with hope.

"Write the letter to Mr. Anagnos immediately," Mrs. Keller said as soon as they were home.

Captain Keller did just that, sending a detailed description of Helen, and a reply came from Perkins Institution very soon after. Before the summer ended, Mr. Anagnos had selected one of his own former students, twenty-year-old Anne Sullivan, to be Helen Keller's governess.

Anne Sullivan had come to Perkins as a blind child, he explained to the Kellers, and later her vision had been partially restored by surgery. She wanted to spend the winter weeks studying Dr. Howe's records on Laura Bridgman, before going to Alabama, and so they could expect her on the first of March.

"Just a few more months," thought Kate Keller. "Just a few more months, and there will be someone to take care of my little girl."

And while the robust and undisciplined Helen tyrannized the household with her pranks—locking doors and hiding keys, yanking tablecloths filled with dishes to the floor—Kate Keller fastened her hopes on Anne Sullivan and the first of March.

"James will drive you to the station to meet her," said the Captain when the day came.

Anxious and tense, Mrs. Keller sat on the front seat of the carriage beside her stepson. He allowed the reins to lie slack on the back of the motionless horse, and they both stared along the railway tracks watching for that first puff of soft-coal smoke in the distance.

"How will we know her?" Mrs. Keller wondered aloud.

"She will probably be the only passenger, Mother. It will be all right. Don't worry."

"She is coming such a long way to help us!"

James noticed the train first.

"There it is," he said and climbed out of the carriage.

The train pulled in and ground to a stop before the little wooden station house. A man in the baggage compartment tossed a sack of mail to the local agent, and the train pulled out. No passenger disembarked.

Without a word James Keller climbed back into his seat, jerked the reins, and turned the horse's head toward home. Kate Keller fumbled for a handkerchief and began to cry.

"What can you expect from a Yankee?" James snapped. "I hope she never sets foot in Alabama."

"There's another train this afternoon, and we are going to meet it!" declared Mrs. Keller firmly.

Anne Sullivan didn't appear on the first of March, nor on the second.

"We are going to meet every train until she comes!" insisted Helen's mother.

On the third of March, 1887, Kate and James sat in the carriage at the railway station once more, waiting for a late afternoon train. This time a passenger did get off, a young girl dressed in burdensome woolen clothing, looking frightened and tired, her eyes red from weeping and the irritation of the soft-coal dust.

"Miss Sullivan?"

"Yes."

James helped her into the carriage, and placed her bag and trunk in the back.

"We were afraid you weren't coming," said Mrs. Keller.

"I am sorry," said Anne Sullivan. "I had the

wrong kind of ticket somehow, and I had to change trains at Philadelphia and Baltimore. Then I had to wait over a whole day at Washington for a train coming to Tuscumbia."

"Oh, that is too bad."

"It's all right, now," said Miss Sullivan. "I'm only thinking of your little girl. I want to see my pupil as soon as possible."

The carriage drew into the yard at last and Captain Keller came forward to help them down. Miss Sullivan didn't seem to be listening to the introduction. She was looking at the open doorway of the house where a young mortal stood—blank-faced and hostile—nearly seven years old.

Miss Sullivan left the Kellers and hurried forward to gather the little "phantom" into her arms.

### Miracle at the Pump House

"Phantom"—Helen Keller's own name for herself as a child—stood in the doorway sensing the excitement of a new arrival. She felt the vibration of a strange footstep on the porch, then another footstep, coming closer. Strangers were often enemies. She bent her head down and charged into the newcomer, and the newcomer fell back. Again the footsteps came toward her, and the stranger tried to put arms around her. Helen drove off Miss Sullivan's embrace with kicks and punches.

She discovered that the stranger had a bag, and she grabbed the bag and darted into the house. When her mother caught up with her and tried to take the bag away she fought, because she knew her mother would give in. Mother always gave in.

But Anne Sullivan encouraged her to keep the bag and carry it up the stairs. Soon a trunk was brought into the room, and Helen flung herself against it, exploring the lid with her fingers until she found the lock. Miss Sullivan gave her the key and allowed her to unlock it and lift the lid. Helen plunged her hands down into the contents, feeling everything.

The newcomer lifted a doll out of the trunk and laid it in Helen's arms, and after that she did something very strange indeed. She held one of Helen's hands and in its palm formed curious figures with her own fingers. First she held her

own thumb and middle finger together while her index finger stood upright. Then she formed a circle by joining her thumb and first finger, and finally she spread her thumb and index finger as far apart as they would go.

With a sudden wild leap Helen darted for the door, but the stranger caught hold of her and brought her back, forcing her into a chair. Helen fought and raged, but the stranger was strong. She did not give in like family and servants. Helen was startled to feel a piece of cake being placed in her hand, and she gobbled it down quickly before it could be taken away. The stranger did another trick with her fingers. On Helen's palm she formed an open circle with thumb and first finger, next closed her fist for a moment, following that by placing her thumb between her second and third fingers and curling her last two fingers under, and finally held all her finger tips together against her thumb.

That was enough! Helen tore loose and bolted out of the room and down the stairs, to Mother, to Father, to her stepbrother, to the cook, to anybody whom she could manage.

But at dinner the stranger sat next to her. Helen had her own way of eating, and no one had ever tried to stop her. She stumbled and groped her way from place to place, snatching and grabbing from other people's plates, sticking her fingers into anything at all. When she came to the visitor, her hand was slapped away. Helen reached out for the visitor's plate again. Another slap! She flung herself forward and was lifted bodily back. Now she was being forced into her own chair again, being made to sit there, and once more she was raging, fighting, kicking. She broke away and found all the other chairs empty. Her family had deserted her, left her alone with this enemy!

Again the enemy took hold of her, made her sit down, forced a spoon into her hand, made her eat from her own plate.

When the ordeal finally ended, she broke away and ran out of the dining room—to Mother, to Mother's arms. Mother's eyes were wet. Mother was crying. Mother was sorry.

Every day there were battles with the newcomer. There were battles when she had to take her bath, comb her hair, button her shoes. And always those finger tricks; even Mother and

Father were doing them. Since the trick for cake usually brought her a piece of cake, Helen shrewdly began to learn others.

If battles with her new governess grew too unbearable, Helen could seek out Martha Washington, a child her own age, daughter of their Negro cook, and bully and boss her. Martha's pigtails were short because Helen had once clipped them off with a pair of scissors.

Or she could simply romp with her father's hunting dogs and forget there was such a thing in the house as a governess. She could help feed the turkey gobblers, or go hunting for the nests of the guinea hens in the tall grass. She loved to burrow her way in amongst the big flowering shrubs; completely surrounded by the prickly leaves of the mimosa she felt safe and protected.

There was real comfort in revenge. She knew about keys and locks, and she found a day when she could lock the awful intruder in her room and run away with the key. The big day of revenge came when, in one of the enemy's unguarded moments, Helen raised her fists in the air and brought them down on Miss Sullivan's face. Two teeth snapped off.

An abrupt change occurred in her life right after that.

Miss Sullivan took her by the hand and they went for a carriage drive. When the carriage stopped, they alighted and entered a different house. Helen groped her way about the room, recognizing nothing, until her companion placed one of her own dolls in her arms. She clung to the familiar thing. But as soon as Helen realized that she was alone with the stranger in a strange place, that no amount of rubbing her cheek would bring her mother, she flung the doll away in a rage. She refused to eat, refused to wash, and gave the governess a long, violent tussle when it came time to go to bed.

The governess did not seem very tall, but she was strong and stubborn, and for the first time in her life Helen began to experience defeat. She grew tired, wanted to lie down and sleep, but still she struggled against the stranger's will. She would sleep on the floor, or in the chair! But each time she was dragged back to the bed. At last Helen felt herself giving in, and, exhausted by her own efforts, and huddled close to the farthest edge of the big double bed, she fell asleep.

When Helen awoke in the morning, she flung herself out of bed prepared to give further resistance, but somehow her face was washed with less effort than the night before, and after she had dressed and eaten her breakfast she felt her companion's determined but gentle hands guiding her fingers over some soft, coarse yarn, guiding them again along a thin bone shaft with a hooked end. In a very little while Helen had grasped the idea of crocheting, and as she became interested in making a chain she forgot to hate Anne Sullivan.

Each day in the new house after that brought new skills to be learned—cards to sew, beads to string.

After about two weeks, Helen had begun to accept her routine, her table manners, her tasks, her companion. The whole world seemed to grow gentler as her own raging disposition subsided.

She cocked her head suddenly one afternoon and sniffed the air, detecting a new odor in the room, something familiar—one of her father's dogs! Helen groped about until she found the silken, long-haired setter, Belle. Of all the dogs on the farm, Belle was Helen's favorite, and she quickly lifted one of Belle's paws and began to move the dog's toes in one of the finger tricks. Miss Sullivan patted Helen's head, and the approval made her feel almost happy.

Miss Sullivan soon took her by the hand and led her out the door, across a yard, to some front steps, and instantly Helen realized where she was. She was home! She had been in the little annex near home all this time. Mother and Father had not been far away. She raced up the steps and into the house and flung herself at one adult after another. She was home! Scrambling up the stairs to the second floor, she found her own room just the same, and when she felt Miss Sullivan standing behind her she turned impulsively and pointed a finger at her and then at her own palm. Who was she?

"T-e-a-c-h-e-r," Anne Sullivan spelled into her hand.

But the finger trick was too long to be learned at once.

Every day after that Teacher and Helen were

constant companions indoors and out, and gradually Helen learned to see with her fingers. Teacher showed her how to explore plants and animals without damaging them—chickens, grasshoppers, rabbits, squirrels, frogs, wildflowers, butterflies, trees. Grasshoppers had smooth, clear wings; the wings of a butterfly were powdery. The bark of a tree had a curious odor, and through its huge trunk ran a gentle humming vibration.

Hand-in-hand they wandered for miles over the countryside, sometimes as far as the Tennessee River where the water rushed and churned over the mussel shoals.

For everything she felt or did there was a finger trick: wings, petals, river boats—walking, running, standing, drinking.

One morning when she was washing her face and hands, Helen pointed to the water in the basin, and Teacher spelled into her hand: "w-a-t-e-r." At the breakfast table later Helen pointed to her mug of milk, and Teacher spelled: "m-i-l-k." But Helen became confused. "D-r-i-n-k" was milk, she insisted. Helen pointed to her milk again and Teacher spelled, "m-u-g." Was m-u-g d-r-i-n-k? In another second Helen's mind was a jumble of wiggling fingers. She was frustrated, bewildered, angry, a bird trapped in a cage and beating her wings against the bars.

Quickly Teacher placed an empty mug in her hand and led her out-of-doors to a pump that stood under a shed in the yard. Helen stood before the pump, mug in hand, as Teacher indicated, and felt the rush of cold water over her hands. Teacher took one of her hands and spelled, "w-a-t-e-r." While water rushed over one hand Helen felt the letters, w-a-t-e-r, in the other.

Suddenly Helen was transfixed, and she let her mug crash to the ground forgotten. A new, wonderful idea . . . back into her memory rushed that infant's word she had once spoken: "wah-wah." She grew excited, her pulse raced, as understanding lighted her mind. Wah-wah was w-a-t-e-r. It was a word! These finger tricks were words! There were words for everything. That was what Teacher was trying to tell her.

She felt Teacher rush to her and hug her, and Teacher was as excited as she, crying and laughing, because at last Helen understood the concept of words.

Joyfully they ran back into the house, and Helen was surrounded by an excited household. All the rest of the day she demanded words, words, words. What was this? What was that? Even the infant Mildred? What was that? "B-a-b-y." And once more Helen pointed a persistent finger at Miss Sullivan and demanded the word that would identify *her*.

"T-e-a-c-h-e-r," Anne Sullivan spelled. "T-e-a-c-h-e-r."

The last shred of hostility and hate vanished from Helen's soul as she glowed with her sudden happiness. She felt her fingers being lifted to Teacher's face to explore its expression. The corners of the mouth were drawn up and the cheeks were crinkled. Helen imitated the expression, and when she did her face was no longer blank, because Helen Keller was smiling.

When bedtime finally arrived, she put her hand willingly into Teacher's and mounted the stairs, and before climbing into bed she slipped her arms around Teacher's neck and kissed her —for the first time.

## *from* SHIRLEY CHISHOLM

### Susan Brownmiller

*When Shirley Chisholm (1924–   ) was elected to Congress in 1968, she was the first black person ever elected from Brooklyn, New York, and the first black woman elected to Congress in the history of our nation. "Unbought and unbossed" was her slogan, and she's lived up to her campaign sobriquet of "fighting Shirley Chisholm." Born in Brooklyn, Shirley and her sisters had been sent to Barbados as small children; there their education was so good that when they came back to the United States to rejoin their parents, the girls were skipped a grade. An excellent student, Shirley became interested in black history while she was in high school, and she became aware of the struggle for women's rights. While this biography gives a brief, lively account of her childhood, it stresses Shirley Chisholm's concern for education, her growing interest in local politics, and her emergence as a national figure.*

### "Jamaican Men Always Want the Best"

Shirley graduated from Brooklyn College in 1946. The war had been over for one year. Mr. St. Hill had managed during the war years to save a sizable amount of money for the first time in his life because of overtime work at the factory. He put down $10,000 on a fine three-story brick row house on Prospect Place on the edge of Bedford-Stuyvesant. The St. Hills became homeowners in Brooklyn at last!

Mrs. St. Hill was overjoyed. The house had a full basement and a garden out in front, and there was an imposing flight of concrete steps leading up to the front door. It was a world away from the cold, steamless, overcrowded tenement apartment that she had taken her daughters to when they came from Barbados in 1934.

Shirley had little time to spend at the new house, however. And for the time being she had to put aside Professor Warsoff's ideas and suggestions for the future. For the moment, Shirley had enough to do—she had to get a job, earn her living. And, at the same time, she knew she wanted to get further training. Politics—and the challenge of that sort of work, which Shirley knew she would enjoy—would have to wait.

Early each morning Shirley took the subway train up to Harlem where she had found a job as a nursery school teacher at the Mount Calvary Child Care Center. After her day's work with the children, she barely had time for a quick bite to eat before she took the train farther uptown to Washington Heights and Columbia University. To improve her skills, she enrolled in the evening classes at Columbia's School of Education, working for a master's degree.

After her evening classes at Columbia, she got back on the train for the ride back to Brooklyn each night. The long train rides each day were tiring, but Shirley got into the habit of opening her books and studying on the train, unmindful of the other passengers.

The schedule Shirley set up for herself—rushing from job to school and then back home again to sleep—was a rugged one. It left her no time for a social life. She planned her weekends so she could devote most of her time to studying. But she still loved to dance, and once in a great while she would take time to go dancing.

At one of those rare Saturday night dances that Shirley allowed herself to attend, she was introduced by friends to a pipe-smoking, solidly built young graduate student from Jamaica named Conrad Chisholm. They chatted for a while between dances, and before she knew it, Shirley was telling Conrad about her job with the children at the Harlem nursery. He seemed interested in what she had to say, so Shirley went on and described to him the classes she was taking at Columbia.

The young man suddenly broke into her monologue. "Don't you ever stop to have any fun?" he asked gently.

Shirley was taken aback. "That's a rather fresh question," she retorted. "I happen to enjoy my work, and I love going to Columbia."

"There are other things in life besides work and school," Conrad replied with a twinkle in his eye. "How about having dinner with me one night this week?"

"I never take time off during the week for socializing," Shirley said rather primly. "I can't afford to fall behind in my studies." She was sorry she was being so stand-offish with this nice young man from Jamaica with his soft, lilting accent, but he didn't look the sort of fellow who would have difficulty finding some other young lady to take out to dinner.

To her surprise, Conrad Chisholm refused to take no for an answer. "I happen to know a good Jamaican restaurant that I think you'd like," he went on with a confident smile.

"You Jamaican men are pretty sure of yourselves, aren't you?" Shirley said with a laugh. She was beginning to enjoy sparring with this fellow.

"Jamaican men always want the best," Conrad Chisholm replied. "And I'm going to take you out to dinner."

He did just that. The two spent a long evening discussing the relative merits of Barbados and Jamaica. As West Indians, Conrad and Shirley discovered that they had a lot in common. The conversation never seemed to run out.

"Who is this man who can upset my vital day-to-day plans?" Shirley asked herself that night after Conrad had taken her home. "Could he become important to me?"

He could. A year later they were married. Shirley was twenty-five years old. One of the first things she did was to get some stationery printed up with her new name, Shirley Chisholm. She liked the sound of it, and she liked the way it looked printed on the paper.

"You always said Jamaican men want the best," Shirley told her husband. "So you just *had* to marry a Bajan girl."

Conrad and Shirley rented a small house in Brooklyn not far from Shirley's parents. Shirley, her master's degree from Columbia under her belt, was appointed director of a private nursery school in Brownsville.

"See," she told Conrad gaily. "No more long subway rides for me. When you first met me all I did, it seemed, was ride the subways morning and night."

"Somehow I can't imagine my wife not on the move," Conrad answered. Shirley glowed. Her husband always knew just what to say to her. His calm personality was a wonderful foil for her excitable nature. Whenever anything went wrong at the nursery, and Shirley come home upset, she would talk it over with Conrad, who always managed to cheer her up.

Yes, Conrad was an unusual man, Shirley thought. She couldn't imagine being married to anyone else. Some of her girl friends had husbands who didn't want their wives to have any independent life at all. They were actually jealous of their wives' careers. But Conrad understood that a career of her own was important to *his* wife, and he always encouraged her to do her best.

Shirley decided that one of the reasons why her husband was different was that Conrad was deeply involved with his own job, which he thoroughly enjoyed. Conrad Chisholm had gone into private detective work shortly after he met Shirley. When he told Shirley about some of the cases he was investigating, they sounded as exciting as anything out of a detective story.

Conrad's reputation as a private investigator was growing and he was offered a good job doing investigation work for a big railroad company. He came home and discussed the offer with Shirley.

"It sounds like a good job," he said, drawing on his pipe. "I'll be working on cases of rail-road men who claim they were injured on the job, and who are suing the railroad company for damages. My job will be to determine if they really are injured, and how seriously, without letting them know, of course, that I represent the railroad. Some of these men fake their injuries and then try to sue the company for a quarter of a million dollars. It will be tricky work—getting them to talk to me, talking to their neighbors, things like that, without letting them know that I'm really investigating them."

"So far, so good," Shirley said. "Why are you hesitating?"

"Well, the railroad company told me I'd be traveling a lot. They'd be sending me to places like Chicago. When I'm on a case, it might take more than two weeks to get all the facts for my report. That means that I'll be away from home for long periods of time. How do you feel about that?"

"I won't like it, certainly. But I think the job sounds too good to turn down."

"Good. That's what I hoped you'd say." Conrad smiled broadly. "We must promise each other that one of us will never interfere with the other's career."

"And always help each other to the best of our ability," Shirley added.

"It's a deal."

Shirley did miss Conrad when he was away from home, but soon she had an important new job to keep her busy. She was appointed director of the Hamilton-Madison Child Care Center on the Lower East Side of Manhattan.

The Hamilton-Madison Center was located right in the middle of a huge housing project. Shirley had more than 150 black and Puerto Rican children who came to the nursery each day. Working under her were several assistant teachers and social workers.

When Conrad came home from his trips, Shirley would fill him in on what had gone on that week at the center. "The Puerto Rican children are adorable—they're teaching me Spanish," she told her husband at one point. "They teach me Spanish and I teach them English. We have no trouble communicating at all. Actually, my only problems are with some of the social workers. Their ideas on education and mine are somewhat different."

"What do you mean?" Conrad asked his wife.

"Well, I think that the children should be on a strict schedule. They should take their naps at a certain hour, get up at a certain hour, and even have their milk and cookies at a certain hour each day. I have some people working for me who don't care about schedules at all. Now, when I was growing up in Barbados, Granny was very strict with us children. We were sent to school at age three and a half. It worked for me, and I think it would work for these children too."

"Do you tell that to the social workers?" Conrad asked.

"Oh yes," Shirley laughed. "I call staff meetings all the time, and we have very interesting discussions. I'm in charge and they know it, so they're coming around to doing things my way."

"You sound like a tough boss, Shirley," Conrad said to his wife. He smiled. "Now forget your problems and let me tell you what happened to me this week in Chicago."

After a half hour of listening to Conrad, Shirley felt totally relaxed. She forgot about the problems at Hamilton-Madison Child Care Center.

The evenings were the difficult part of Shirley's life when Conrad was away on the road, although he always remembered to keep in touch with her by telephone. She wasn't the sort of person who could sit quietly at home watching television, and there were just so many books a person could read in one week.

Something was stirring in her neighborhood of Bedford-Stuyvesant, and Shirley got wind of it. In 1953 a local Negro lawyer named Lewis Flagg decided to run for judge in the next election. The white bosses who controlled Brooklyn's Democratic Party machine brought in a white lawyer from outside the neighborhood as their candidate for the judgeship.

"Isn't that just like those corrupt politicians," Shirley told Conrad on the telephone one night. "Bedford-Stuyvesant is now an almost all-black neighborhood, and those politicians won't let a black man get the job."

"Does Flagg have any organization working for him?" Conrad asked.

"I hear there's something called the Bedford-Stuyvesant Political League," Shirley answered. "They've opened up a headquarters in an empty store in the neighborhood. I passed it on the way to the subway this morning."

"Why don't you go down and look into it?" Conrad suggested. "They probably need someone with your organizing abilities."

"Maybe you're right," Shirley replied. "It just makes me mad the way these white politicians act so highhanded."

The following evening, Shirley walked over to the store front where the Bedford-Stuyvesant Political League was located. She asked who was in charge, and was introduced to a tall and courtly black man named Wesley Holder.

Holder wasted no time in asking Shirley if she was a registered Democrat. When she told him she was, he asked if she had signed a nominating petition for Lewis Flagg. Shirley hadn't, but she promptly signed the petition when Holder presented it to her.

"Do you know if your friends and neighbors are registered Democrats, Mrs. Chisholm?" Holder asked.

"I'm pretty sure my friends are all registered voters," Shirley replied. "I don't know if they're all Democrats."

"Would you like to take a nominating petition home with you and ask your friends to sign for Lewis Flagg? The only way we can get him on the ballot is if we have enough signatures. Since Mr. Flagg is running in the Democratic primary, all the signers must be registered Democrats."

Shirley took the nominating petition home with her. She liked this Wesley Holder. He struck her as a shrewd person who knew what he was doing. She smiled to herself. "I'm getting mixed up in politics," she thought. "Sort of edging in. Professor Warsoff was right."

Two evenings later, Shirley walked into the League's headquarters with fifteen signatures on the nominating petition Holder had given her.

"It wasn't as easy as I thought it would be," Shirley told Holder. "I had to ring a lot of doorbells to get these fifteen signatures. Some people whom I just assumed were registered voters turned out not to be registered at all. And some of those who were registered said we were crazy

—that a black man would never get to be a judge in Brooklyn."

"That's our problem, Mrs. Chisholm," Holder told her. "Most of the black people in this neighborhood are not registered to vote, and many of the others don't think we stand a chance. One of our jobs will be to get hundreds of new people registered so they can vote for Flagg in the general election. I know we can do it, and I hope you'll continue to help us."

Shirley nodded. "Give me another one of those nominating petitions," she said suddenly. "I just thought of some more people I can ask to sign."

Holder looked at Shirley with surprise. "When you take on a project, Mrs. Chisholm, you really work at it, don't you?" he said.

"That's how I approach everything in life, Mr. Holder," Shirley replied. "And I like to be on the winning team."

Shirley and Wesley Holder grew to be good friends during the Flagg campaign. Shirley liked the well-mannered politician from British Guiana, and he, in turn, gave her more and more responsibility as the campaign wore on. The campaign was a bitter one, but when it was over, Lewis Flagg had been elected judge.

Shirley Chisholm had gotten her feet wet in politics—and she *had* been on the winning team.

Informational books, emerging historically from textbook and didactic tract, have had their ups and downs on the way to establishing themselves firmly as a part of the body of literature for children and youth. Like other types of books, they range in literary quality from works of negligible significance to ones that have survived with distinction over the years. They communicate to the reader in ways quite different from imaginative literature. This difference is important and needs to be understood, but does not put informational books in an inferior position as sometimes assumed or implied.

The major purpose of informational books is to inform, not to tell a story, though affective means may be employed and a story framework is sometimes used as a device to interest the reader. The information presented is factual, though the best of this material goes beyond simple presentation of facts to the presentation of principles, concepts, and theories, and to interpretation, persuasion, and evaluation.

# INFORMATIONAL BOOKS

People read informational books for many reasons: the practical need to find answers, a human desire to know and understand, and simply for relaxation and entertainment. Writers employ diversified styles and techniques to engage readers' interests on as many levels as possible.

Informational literature may be defined, then, as nonfiction prose concerned with presenting, interpreting, and evaluating facts on any subject, for a multitude of purposes and audiences. The best of this material gives high priority to accuracy, clarity, and interest. It may, in addition, be characterized by beauty of form and expression and universality of interest. Like all other kinds of literature, informational books fall on a continuum ranging from poor to excellent. This category, like all other categories, needs to be evaluated by general criteria applicable to all kinds of literature and also by specific criteria appropriate to its type.

Informational books must be *accurate* in their presentation, interpretation, and evaluation of facts. This obvious criterion cannot be overemphasized in evaluating informational books for children, as accuracy has sometimes been sacrificed to interest. Our confidence in a book's accuracy is bolstered when we note that the author is a specialist in the field he or she writes about or that the writer is a professional who has had the manuscript checked by experts. Important, too, are careful documentation and indication of the use of original sources. Book reviews prepared by specialists in various disciplines are helpful in appraising the accuracy of these books.

The illustrations as well as the text of an informational book must be accurate. Not only do they clarify the text, but they may add information also. The full range of graphic processes is available to enable information to be carried as much in illustration as in text (sometimes even more), not only in picture books for young children, but in those for older students and adults. The illustrations included with the following selections are a small sampling of the work that accompanies outstanding informational writing.

Good informational books must be *up-to-date*, not only in content but in the methods cited and used in the collection of facts. And these facts should be related so as to build concepts and principles and should be presented in language and contexts close to children's own experience.

Suggesting activities for observation, experimentation, and discovery serves to inform children and young people of the *methods of science*, not just its factual content. To simplify with respect for children and for the integrity of the subject matter means going as deep as possible into a subject without boring the intended readers or losing them in masses of technical detail. It means making precise decisions about what can be omitted without sacrificing scientific accuracy. It means, too, avoidance of explanations of natural phenomena in terms of purpose on the part of "mother nature," for example, or of diety. It means dealing objectively with animals and plants, *not* attributing human characteristics to them as, for example, suggesting that a queen ant is "lonely" in her underground room.

Readers of scientifically sound informational books will not only learn about the methods of science but will understand the *tentativeness of answers* and the *spirit of scientific endeavor*. For scientists ask more questions than they answer, fail as well as succeed, work under all kinds of conditions, and are subject to the full range of human emotions about their work. The books about them, then, should build attitudes that eventually may dissipate the confusion and controversy about the role of science.

Children, says Ben W. Bova, "have one utterly ruthless weapon they can—and do—use against any book: they put it down the moment it stops being interesting." [1]

No amount of scientific accuracy by itself can guarantee reader interest. Children voluntarily browsing may choose an informational book for their own pleasure. They may be attracted, initially, by illustration or content, but whether they stay with it depends, in part, on the holding power of the author's style. On the other hand, children seeking specific information—what to feed a turtle or the identity of a shell—or preparing an assigned report, say, on air pollution, will value such helps as an index, chapter headings, center and side headings, pictures and other graphic devices, and a glossary.

Beyond providing accurate, current information in ways that will interest the reader, some informational books are set apart by the freshness and originality of style and by an overall design that results in a unified, artistic whole. Some authors prefer a straightforward, objective style with little or no intrusion of their own point of view, while others are subjective and personal. Use of first, second, or third person produces variations of formality and informality, while a writer's attitude toward his or her subject and reader is subtly revealed by the tone —light, humorous, or flippant; serious, impersonal, matter-of-fact. A thin line sometimes separates styles distinguished by vivid, rhythmic, warmly human yet dispassionate writing from those characterized by an overuse of metaphor and emotionally charged language.

Informational books should be carefully evaluated by all editors, reviewers, teachers, and librarians. Each assessment should include consideration of the book in terms of its accuracy, its appeal to its intended reader, and its literary and artistic quality. The relative importance of each criterion can be determined only at the point of contact of a single book with an individual reader. This reader's interest, experience, reading ability, and taste all contribute to answering the question: "Is this a good book?"

## BENNY'S ANIMALS

*Millicent E. Selsam*

*Millicent Selsam's science books are always accurate and informative, whether they are fiction or nonfiction, for young children or older readers. In this book for the beginning reader, the style is brisk and humorous, but the author presents lucidly such concepts as observation and classification.*

Benny was very neat.
He liked everything to be in its place.
He had a place for his large books.
He had a place for his small books.
And he had another place for his middle-sized books.
If he had money, he would put the pennies in one pile.
He would put the nickels in another pile and the dimes in another pile.
Once his mother said to his father, "Do you think Benny is all right?
David's mother says David throws his things on the floor.

And John's mother says John never puts his things away.
But you know Benny.
He puts every little thing in its place."
"Don't worry about him," said Benny's father.
"He is just a neat boy."
One day Benny went for a walk on the beach.
He found many things.
He put them in a paper bag.
When he got home, he took them out of the bag and looked at them.

Some looked like this.

Some looked like this.

A few looked like this.

One looked like this.

And one looked like this.

Benny called to his mother.

"Mother," he said, "do you know what these things are?"

"They are the shells of animals," said his mother.

"I did not know shells came from animals," said Benny.

"Well, they do," said his mother.

"Some animals can take minerals from the sea water to build shells.

This one is a clam.

And this one is a scallop.

I'm not sure what that round one is.

Let's look it up."

She gave Benny a book with pictures of animals that live in the sea.

Benny looked at the pictures.

He found the round shell.

It was a moon snail.

He found the shell with points.

It was a starfish.

And he found the shell with legs.

It was a crab.

Benny went back to his room.

He put all the clams in one pile.

He put the scallops in another pile.

He put the moon snails together.

He kept the starfish by itself.

He kept the crab by itself.

Then he made a sign:

ANIMALS FROM THE SEA.

Benny's friend John came to see him.

He looked at Benny's sign.

"Why do you call these things animals?" he asked.

"Because they are animals," said Benny.

"That's not what I call an animal," said John.

"All right," said Benny, "what is an animal?"

"A horse is an animal," said John.

"So is a zebra. And a cat.

And an elephant.

Animals all have heads and bodies and four legs."

"How about birds?" said Benny.

"They only have two legs."

"Birds are birds, not animals," said John.

"How about fish?" asked Benny.

"They have no legs at all."

"Fish are fish," said John.

"I don't call them animals."

Then Benny asked, "How about a butterfly?"

"That I know," said John.

"They are insects, not animals."

"But my mother said these clams and snails were animals," said Benny.

"Hmmmm," said John.

"Let's go ask her again."

They went to Benny's mother.

"Didn't you say my clams and snails were animals?" asked Benny.

"Yes," said Benny's mother.

"Any living thing that is not a plant is an animal."

"So what is a living thing?" asked Benny.

"Well," said his mother, "our cat is a living thing.

But a rock is not.

Can you tell me how a rock is different from a cat?"

"A rock doesn't eat," said Benny.

"A rock can't grow," said John.

"A rock can't breathe," said Benny.

"Very good," said Benny's mother.

"And a rock can't make more rocks like itself.

Your clams and snails can do all of this, and they are not plants."

"So I guess they really are animals," said John.

"So my sign is right," said Benny.

That night Benny had dinner with his mother, his father, and his little brother, Eddie.

"Father," said Benny, "are we animals?"

"Well . . ." said his father.

"Well," said Benny, "we are alive.

We eat and breathe, don't we?

And we are not plants, right?"

"Right," said his father.

"So we are animals," said Benny.

"You are right," said his mother.

"But how are we different from other animals?" asked his father.

"We can talk, and they can't," said Benny.

"And Eddie is just like other animals because he can't talk either."

Just then Eddie said, "Da—da."

"See," said Benny's mother, "Eddie is learning to talk.

So he is not just like other animals."

"But right now—" said Benny.

"Hush," said his mother.

"There's a big difference even now."

"Let's think of all the animals we know," said Benny.

"Not right now," said Benny's mother.

"I have a better idea.

Why don't you look at our old magazines?

You can cut out all the animal pictures."

Benny got John to help him.

They both looked for pictures of animals.

They cut out pictures of tigers and butterflies and lions and snakes.

They cut out pictures of worms and frogs and dogs.

They found pictures of monkeys and whales and birds and fish and lobsters and snails.

Soon they had a big pile of pictures.

"Let's put the ones that look alike together," said Benny.

"All right," said John.

In one pile Benny put birds, butterflies, and bats.

"That's because they all have wings," he said.

In another pile he put worms and snakes.

"That's because they are long and thin," said Benny.

In another pile he put all animals with four feet.

"I'm putting all these water animals together," said John.

And he showed Benny a pile of fish, clams, lobsters, snails, and jellyfish.

"Well, they don't look alike," said Benny.

"I know," said John, "but they all live in the sea."

"That's no good," said Benny.

"I want them to look alike."

Benny's father came into the room.

"Well, how many animals did you find?" he asked.

"Lots," said Benny. "Look.

We put the ones that look alike together."

Benny's father looked at the piles.

"These are sort of mixed up," he said.

"Why did you put birds, butterflies, and bats in one pile?"

"Because they all have wings," said Benny.

"But a bird has feathers," said Benny's father.

"And a bat has fur.

And a butterfly has scales.

I don't think they belong together at all."

"How can we make sure?" asked Benny.

"I'll take you to the museum," said Benny's father.

"Maybe somebody there can help you out."

The next Saturday, Benny's father took Benny and John to the museum.

"Can someone here help us arrange these animals?"

Benny's father asked the man at the door.

"Go to the fourth floor and ask for Professor Wood," said the man.

When they found Professor Wood, Benny spoke first.

"We have all these piles of animals, and we are trying to put the same kinds together.

Can you help us, please?"

"Let me see your pictures," said Professor Wood.

Benny showed the professor the pile with worms and snakes.

"These do not go together," said Professor Wood.

"Why not?" asked Benny.

"They look alike."

"That is not the important thing," said Professor Wood.

"We put animals together if they have the same *structure*."

"Structure?" asked Benny.

"What is that?"

"It means the kinds of parts an animal has and how the parts are put together," said Professor Wood.

"The first question we ask is, Does the animal have a backbone?

All animals either have a backbone or they do not.

And this puts all the animals into two big groups."

"Only two groups!" said Benny.

"That's just the beginning," said the professor.

"Why don't you go home and put all your pictures into two piles—a backbone pile and a no-backbone pile.

Remember, any animal with bones has a backbone.

Then come back here and I'll have a look at them."

"All right," said Benny.

"Good," said John.

"Thank you," said Benny's father.

"Good-bye," said Professor Wood.

The next day Benny and John looked at the pictures again.

"Do birds have backbones?" asked Benny.

"Sure. Didn't you ever eat a chicken?" said John.

"Oh, that's right—bones," said Benny.

He put the bird picture in the backbone pile.

"How about butterflies?" asked John.

"No backbone," said Benny.

"You can squeeze them."

"Jellyfish?" asked John.

"All soft as jelly," said Benny.

"Snakes?" asked John.

"Fred has a snake skeleton—backbone pile," said Benny.

"Worms?" asked John.

"No backbone," said Benny.

"Fish?" asked John.

"Never mind. I know where it goes.

I see the backbone every time I eat a fish."

"What about these shell animals?" asked Benny.

"Those shells are on the outside," said John. "I once ate a clam.

It was all soft inside."

"Did you like it?" asked Benny.

"What's the difference?" said John.

"Put it in the no-backbone pile."

"I once ate a scallop," said Benny.

"It was soft inside too."

"All right—no-backbone pile," said John.

They put monkeys, tigers, lions, elephants, deer, dogs, and cats in the backbone pile.

"I am sure they all have bones," said Benny.

Benny and John did not know what to do with some other animals.

They put them in pile number three.

Benny and John and Benny's father went back to see Professor Wood.

The professor looked at the pictures.

"Very good. But what's the third pile?" he asked.

"We did not know where these animals belong," said Benny.

Professor Wood looked at the pictures in the third pile.

"The crabs and starfish go with the no-backbone group.

They are hard on the outside but have no bones inside.

And the frogs go with the backbone group," he said.

Then he picked up the whole backbone pile.

"Remember what I said?

This is just the beginning.

Now we can divide this pile into five different piles.

One pile will be fish.

Another pile will be amphibians—animals that live in the water when they are young and on land when they are grown up.

Those are your frogs and toads.

A third pile will be reptiles—your snakes, lizards, turtles, and alligators.

Pile number four will be birds—they all have feathers.

And the last pile will be mammals—they have hair or fur.

When you go home, divide your backbone pile into these five groups: fish, amphibians, reptiles, birds, and mammals."

"What about the no-backbone pile?" asked Benny.

"You have enough to do now," said the professor.

"Can we come back later to work on the no-backbone pile?" asked John.

"Certainly," said Professor Wood.

"Then we'll know everything about how to arrange animals," said Benny.

"Everything?" said Professor Wood.

"Not at all. You will know a little bit.

Then you will have to find out how to divide each of the smaller piles into still smaller piles."

"Do you mean that after we divide the backbone pile into five piles, we can make still smaller piles?" asked Benny.

"Oh, yes," said Professor Wood.

"There are about 17,000 kinds of fish.

Besides, knowing the separate groups is not the most important thing."

"What is most important?" asked Benny.

"Well, you are learning how to separate one group of animals from another," said the professor.

"That's right," said Benny.

"But I spend my time learning how to bring them together," said Professor Wood.

"How can you bring them together?" asked John.

"I mean that I find out how animals are related to each other," said the professor.

"Do you mean animals have relatives?" asked Benny. "Like cousins?"

"Yes," said Professor Wood, "but not each animal. Each *kind* of animal has relatives."

"Oh," said Benny.

"Do you have any cousins that look like you?" asked the professor.

"Yes," said Benny. "I have a cousin that looks a little like me."

"Do you know why?" asked the professor.

"No, I don't," said Benny.

"Don't you have the same grandfather?" asked Professor Wood.

Benny thought.

"Only one of them is the same," he said.

"True," said the professor.

"Now can you tell me why two different kinds of animals might have structures that look alike?"

"Because they had the same grandfather?" asked John.

"Sort of," said the professor, "if by 'grandfather' you mean a kind of animal that lived millions of years ago.

I'll tell you a true story.

About fifty million years ago there was an animal that lived in the forest.

It had a long body like a weasel.

It had a head like a fox.

It had a long tail.

It had sharp claws and teeth.

From that kind of animal came lions, tigers, and leopards, as well as small wildcats and housecats.

All these animals are relatives."

"I see," said Benny.

"You mean animals are relatives if you can trace them back to—to—"

"A common ancestor," said the professor.

"Well," said John, "first we will put these animals in order."

"Then," said Benny, "we will become ancestor detectives."

"I never thought of that," said Professor Wood.

"That is really what I am."

## HIDE AND SEEK FOG

*Alvin Tresselt*

*From* Hide and Seek Fog, *information seeps into the reader like the fog Tresselt describes. The text is in prose, but it looks and sounds like poetry. On the page, the author breaks sentences comfortably between phrases, and he uses imagery and even some words of his own invention. When read aloud well, the text informs young children through their senses while it also provides a few simple facts about those who work and those who vacation on the seashore.*

*Roger Duvoisin's illustrations for this book are perfect visual accompaniments of Tresselt's words. They, too, inform sensually, even while they define, through pictures, such words as buoys, lobster pots, and terns.*

*The following text is complete and, as nearly as possible, is set up line for line as in the original. Readers should examine the handsome book and illustrations for themselves.*

The lobsterman first saw the fog
as it rolled in from the sea.
He watched it turn off the sun-sparkle on the
    waves,
and he saw the water turn gray.
Carefully he set his last lobster pot,
and headed his boat back to shore.

The dampness touched the crisp white sails
of the racing sailboats,
and suddenly the wind left them in the middle
    of the race.
The sailboats had to creep home
around the islands and across the bay,
ahead of the rolling fog.

In long straight lines
the seagulls and terns flew back
to their roosts on the craggy rocks.
They knew the fog was coming, too.
Now the water of the bay was gray like the sky,
and the end of the beach was gone.

Now the afternoon sun turned to a pale daytime
    moon,
then vanished into the bank of fog.

On the beach, the sand was suddenly cold and
    sticky.
The mothers and fathers
gathered up blankets and picnic baskets.
They called—"Cathy! John! Come out of the
    water!
We're going now!"
The children ran in and out one more time,
blue-lipped and shivering.
They scurried about looking for lost pails and
    shovels.
They scooped up one more pretty shell
and a gray seagull feather.
Then everyone trudged across the chilly sand
    and cold rocks,
back to cars and cottages.

The lobsterman delivered his lobsters to the fish-
    ing wharf.
He hurried home through winding streets,
just as the fog began to hide the town.
The sailboats bobbled like corks
on the dull gray water of the cove.
Their sails were wrapped for the night,
and the sailors rowed through the misty fog back
    to land.
But indoors in the seaside cottages
the children toasted marshmallows over a drift-
    wood fire,
while the fog tip-toed past the windows
and across the porch.
And the fog stayed three days.

On the first day the lobsterman spent his time
painting buoys and mending lobster pots.
He could hear the mournful lost voices of the
    foghorns
calling across the empty grayness of the bay.
The fathers read books and took naps.
Then they got out their cars and drove the
    mothers
into town so they could do their marketing . . .
creeping, creeping . . . along the strange and
    hidden roads.
The streets of the town were so full of fog

that the people bumped into one another
with their arms full of bundles.

Only the children liked the fog. They played
hide-and-seek
in and out among the gray-wrapped rocks.
They spoddled in the lazy lapping waves on the
beach,
and they got lost—right in front of their own
cottages!

On the second day the lobsterman talked about
the weather
down on the fishing wharf.
"The worst fog in twenty years," the lobsterman
said.
And no one could go out after fish.

The fathers scowled and complained
about spending their vacations
in the middle of a cloud.
The mothers tried to cheer everyone up.
They put on gay bright clothes, and they helped
the children
make scrapbooks by the driftwood fire.

But out of doors the fog
twisted about the cottages like slow-motion
smoke.
It dulled the rusty scraping of the beach grass.
It muffled the chattery talk of the low tide waves.
And it hung, wet and dripping,
from the bathing suits and towels on the
clothesline.

Then on the third afternoon
there was suddenly a warm glow in the foggy air.
And before everyone's eyes
the damp cotton-wool thinned out.
The western sun slanted through, under the fog,
changing the islands in the bay to gold.
A breeze sprang up out of no place and gently,
gently,
rolled back the fog, back to the wide and empty
ocean.
Once more the water sparkled, beyond the islands,
across the wide bay to the edge of the world.

The lobsterman went down to check his boat

and make sure that everything was all ready for
the morning.
The sailors made plans for a sailboat race next
day,
in and out among the islands.

Then at last the mothers and fathers and all the
children
came out of the shut-in cottages
into the fresh, clean air. And the families
gathered
for a clambake on the beach.

*from* HERE COME THE DOLPHINS!

*Alice E. Goudey*

*Alice Goudey has written a number of books in
the "Here Come the . . ." series that includes
bears, beavers, bees, deer, elephants, lions, raccoons, and wild dogs. The series is distinguished
for qualities well illustrated in this selection
from* Here Come the Dolphins! *Factual information is presented very skillfully in a way to interest younger children, though fictionalizing
and humanizing the animals are carefully
avoided. The dolphins are named (Old Scarsides and Grayback), but they communicate
only in ways characteristic of their species. Short
sentences and paragraphs reduce reading difficulty, and the organization of the information
around an event (the birth and growth of a
dolphin) makes the text interesting to readers
of all ages. Garry MacKenzie's pictures in black
and white and ocean blue add color and excitement to the narrative.*

### [A Baby Is Born]

Small waves ripple quietly across the blue-
green water of the ocean.

The air is clear and the first rays of morning
sunlight dance on the waves like a million
twinkling lights.

Three kittiwakes fly above the sparkling water.

"Kittiwake! Kittiwake! Kittiwake!" they call,

as if glad to be alive on such a wonderful day.

Suddenly a dolphin leaps from the quiet surface of the water. Then another one leaps into the air. Soon, all about, dolphins are leaping high in the air.

Young, happy looking dolphins of different sizes chase one another and then leap upward.

Mother dolphins join the young ones.

Even Old Scarsides, who is almost twelve feet long, leaps out, showing the scars of many battles on his gray, rubbery skin.

But one dolphin, Grayback, does not join the others in their play. She stays quietly by herself a short distance away.

Two companions stay with Grayback. They swim slowly around her. Now and then they touch her with their noses as if uneasy about her safety.

It is almost noon before the dolphin herd leaves the open water and starts swimming toward the bay. With strong downward movements of their flat tails, or flukes, they send their streamlined bodies through the water.

Up and down, up and down, their dark gray backs move through the water with even, rolling motions.

When they enter the bay the laughing gulls see the dolphins as their rounded backs break the surface of the water.

"Keeow! Keeow! Keeow!" The gulls scream their noisy greeting.

Grayback is the last to enter the bay. Her companions swim close beside her.

Not far away, two long, gray, shadowy forms circle slowly about.

Old Scarsides makes a clapping sound with his powerful jaws when he sees them.

Two hungry tiger sharks!

But he will leave them alone as long as they do not bother any member of the herd.

The dolphins are hungry now. They have not eaten since early morning.

Just ahead of them they hear a school of little mullets.

Flip! Flip! Splash! The little fish flop in and out of the water.

The dolphins dash in among them and snap them up as they jump above the water.

The hungry dolphins swallow the mullets in one gulp. Even though they have almost a hundred teeth in their jaws they seldom use them for chewing. They use their teeth for catching and holding their prey or for nipping and biting one another and their enemies.

The laughing gulls swoop down on outstretched wings. They, too, gobble up the little fish when they flop out of the water.

It is almost sundown when the gulls look down into the clear water of the bay and see a little dolphin by Grayback's side.

Grayback's first baby has been born!

"Keeow! Keeow! Keeow!" the gulls scream.

We might imagine the gulls are saying, "Just another big fish. Just another big fish in the ocean. Too big for us to swallow. *Much* too big for us to swallow."

It is true that Grayback's baby looks like a big fish. But he does not belong to the fish family. He belongs to the great family of mammals.

He cannot get oxygen from the air dissolved in water as the fishes do. He must get his oxygen from the air above the water.

Now the gulls see him swim quickly toward the surface of the water. Grayback swims just below him, ready to push him up if he needs her help. If he does not get air quickly he cannot live.

The gulls see his small, rounded head come above the water.

At last he is breathing!

He draws the fresh air into his lungs through a hole on the top of his head. It is called a *blow hole*.

When the baby dolphin has filled his lungs with air he closes his little blow hole and goes beneath the water again to rest quietly at his mother's side.

If he did not close his blow hole, water would run into his lungs and he would drown.

But he does not rest for long. In about thirty seconds he rises to the surface again.

Woo-OOf! Woo-oof! He blows the old air out of his lungs with a rushing sound and again draws in fresh, clean air.

Like all dolphins, he could stay under the water for about six minutes but he, and all the dolphin family, usually come up for air two or three times each minute.

Grayback and her companions stay close beside the baby. It is well that they do because, as night comes on, the two shadowy forms of the tiger sharks circle closer and closer to them.

The sharks are not alone. Little pilot fish swim close to them. The pilot fish are waiting to gobble up bits of food that the sharks drop while they are eating.

Also, two shark suckers cling to the sides of the sharks and get a free ride. These strange creatures hold onto the sharks' rough skin with little suction discs on the tops of their heads. They, too, snatch up bits of food that the sharks drop.

A baby dolphin would make a good meal for the sharks, the pilot fish and the shark suckers!

The sharks make quick turns and swim in figure eights, turning this way and that way, as if hunting for something.

They cannot see very well but their sense of smell leads them toward Grayback and her baby.

Now their turns become quicker and quicker and more frantic and their small eyes glitter with excitement.

Grayback and her companions encircle the baby dolphin, and Old Scarsides whistles shrilly as the sharks dart toward them.

Then the whole herd of dolphins shoot through the water like torpedoes. They are upon the sharks in an instant, ramming them with their hard, bony snouts and slamming them with their tails.

Water flies in all directions!

The dolphins whistle shrilly and Old Scarsides snaps his powerful jaws again and again as he rushes forward for another poke with his snout.

The noise of the battle can be heard across the bay.

A night heron, flying across the bay, hears it. "Quok! Quok!" he cries.

The gulls, rocking on the water, hear it and fly up and circle about and sound their alarm cry.

And the fish under the water scoot away to a safer place.

One of the sharks sinks his notched saw-teeth in the side of a dolphin. Blood flows from the wound and stains the water.

The taste and smell of the blood makes the sharks fight more wildly than ever.

At last Old Scarsides strikes one of the sharks a hard blow behind one of his gills. The shark sinks to the bottom of the bay.

When this happens the other shark whirls quickly and heads out toward the open water.

Grayback's baby is safe at last.

But it takes some time for the dolphins to quiet down. They are uneasy and swim about, whistling and snapping their jaws.

It is not very often that they must fight the sharks in the ocean. It is usually only when a baby dolphin is born or when a dolphin is wounded and there is the taste and smell of blood in the water.

The sharks are quick, and their saw-teeth are dangerous, but they do not have hard, bony skeletons to protect their bodies. Their skeletons are of cartilage which is somewhat like gristle and much softer than the hard bones of the dolphins. The blows of the dolphins' snouts can send them to the bottom of the ocean.

Now that the battle is over, the dolphin herd is tired and, like all other animals, needs sleep. They take little catnaps, never sleeping for long at a time. Even while sleeping, with their eyes partly or completely closed, they swim slowly about just below the surface of the water. With slow movements of their flat tails they go up and down, up and down as they rise to the surface to breathe.

The moon throws her light across the water and all is quiet as the dolphins rest.

### from THE STORY OF MANKIND

*Hendrik Willem Van Loon*

*In 1922, the first Newbery Medal was awarded to Dutch-born Hendrik Van Loon for his* The Story of Mankind, *a book considered revolu-*

Reprinted from *The Story of Mankind* by Hendrik Willem Van Loon (New and Enlarged Edition) by permission of Liveright Publishing Corporation, New York. Copyright 1967, 1951 by Liveright Publishing Corporation

*tionary at the time for its way of presenting history to young people. Unlike many histories of the period with their dull, chronological reporting of events,* The Story of Mankind *is organized around significant happenings, conditions, institutions, and people. In "Feudalism" and "Chivalry," the selections that follow, note how the past is related to the present (knights are described as the civil servants of their day) ; principles are pointed up ("Like all human institutions, Knighthood was doomed to perish as soon as it had outlived its usefulness") ; interpretations are freely made (it is suggested that the spirit of knighthood persisted long after the institution had disappeared) . Van Loon's writing style is informal (he addresses the reader as "you" and refers to himself as "I") , and there are touches of ironical humor (knights, Van Loon said, were to befriend all—except Mohammedans, who were to be killed on sight) . Such qualities do not seem revolutionary now, but they were regarded so in the early twenties, and Van Loon is at least partially responsible for the subsequent changes in the treatment of history for young people.*

### Feudalism

How Central Europe, attacked from three sides, became an armed camp and why Europe would have perished without those professional soldiers and administrators who were part of the Feudal System.

The following, then, is the state of Europe in the year one thousand, when most people were so unhappy that they welcomed the prophecy foretelling the approaching end of the world and rushed to the monasteries, that the Day of Judgement might find them engaged upon devout duties.

At an unknown date, the Germanic tribes had left their old home in Asia and had moved westward into Europe. By sheer pressure of numbers they had forced their way into the Roman Empire. They had destroyed the great western empire, but the eastern part, being off the main route of the great migrations, had managed to survive and feebly continued the traditions of

Rome's ancient glory.

During the days of disorder which had followed (the true "dark ages" of history, the sixth and seventh centuries of our era), the German tribes had been persuaded to accept the Christian religion and had recognised the Bishop of Rome as the Pope or spiritual head of the world. In the ninth century, the organising genius of Charlemagne had revived the Roman Empire and had united the greater part of western Europe into a single state. During the tenth century this empire had gone to pieces. The western part had become a separate kingdom, France. The eastern half was known as the Holy Roman Empire of the German nation, and the rulers of this federation of states then pretended that they were the direct heirs of Cæsar and Augustus.

Unfortunately the power of the kings of France did not stretch beyond the moat of their royal residence, while the Holy Roman Emperor was openly defied by his powerful subjects whenever it suited their fancy or their profit.

To increase the misery of the masses of the people, the triangle of western Europe was for ever exposed to attacks from three sides. On the south lived the ever dangerous Mohammedans. The western coast was ravaged by the Northmen. The eastern frontier (defenceless except for the short stretch of the Carpathian mountains) was at the mercy of hordes of Huns, Hungarians, Slavs and Tartars.

The peace of Rome was a thing of the remote past, a dream of the "Good Old Days" that were gone for ever. It was a question of "fight or die," and quite naturally people preferred to fight. Forced by circumstances, Europe became an armed camp and there was a demand for strong leadership. Both King and Emperor were far away. The frontiersmen (and most of Europe in the year 1000 was "frontier") must help themselves. They willingly submitted to the representatives of the king who were sent to administer the outlying districts, *provided they could protect them against their enemies.*

Soon central Europe was dotted with small principalities, each one ruled by a duke or a count or a baron or a bishop, as the case might be, and organised as a fighting unit. These dukes and counts and barons had sworn to be faithful to the king who had given them their "feudum" (hence our word "feudal") in return for their loyal services and a certain amount of taxes. But travel in those days was slow and the means of communication were exceedingly poor. The royal or imperial administrators therefore enjoyed great independence, and within the boundaries of their own province they assumed most of the rights which in truth belonged to the king.

But you would make a mistake if you supposed that the people of the eleventh century objected to this form of government. They supported Feudalism because it was a very practical and necessary institution. Their Lord and Master usually lived in a big stone house erected on the top of a steep rock or built between deep moats, but within sight of his subjects. In case of danger the subjects found shelter behind the walls of the baronial stronghold. That is why they tried to live as near the castle as possible and it accounts for the many European cities which began their career around a feudal fortress.

But the knight of the early Middle Ages was much more than a professional soldier. He was the civil servant of that day. He was the judge of his community and he was the chief of police. He caught the highwaymen and protected the wandering pedlars who were the merchants of the eleventh century. He looked after the dikes so that the countryside should not be flooded (just as the first noblemen had done in the valley of the Nile four thousand years before). He encouraged the Troubadours who wandered from place to place telling the stories of the ancient heroes who had fought in the great wars of the migrations. Besides, he protected the churches and the monasteries within his territory, and although he could neither read nor write (it was considered unmanly to know such things), he employed a number of priests who kept his accounts and who registered the marriages and the births and the deaths which occurred within the baronial or ducal domains.

In the fifteenth century the kings once more became strong enough to exercise those powers which belonged to them because they were "anointed of God." Then the feudal knights lost their former independence. Reduced to the rank of country squires, they no longer filled a need and soon they became a nuisance. But Europe would have perished without the "feudal system" of the dark ages. There were many bad knights as there are many bad people to-day. But generally speaking, the rough-fisted barons of the twelfth and thirteenth century were hard-working administrators who rendered a most useful service to the cause of progress. During that era the noble torch of learning and art which had illuminated the world of the Egyptians and the Greeks and the Romans was burning very low. Without the knights and their good friends, the monks, civilisation would have been extinguished entirely, and the human race would have been forced to begin once more where the cave-man had left off.

### Chivalry

It was quite natural that the professional fighting-men of the Middle Ages should try to establish some sort of organisation for their mutual benefit and protection. Out of this need for close organisation, Knighthood or Chivalry was born.

We know very little about the origins of Knighthood. But as the system developed, it gave the world something which it needed very badly—a definite rule of conduct which softened the barbarous customs of that day and made life more livable than it had been during the five hundred years of the Dark Ages. It was not an easy task to civilise the rough frontiersmen who had spent most of their time fighting Mohammedans and Huns and Norsemen. Often they were guilty of backsliding, and having vowed all sorts of oaths about mercy and charity in the morning, they would murder all their prisoners before evening. But progress is ever the result of slow and ceaseless labour, and finally the most unscrupulous of knights was forced to obey the rules of his "class" or suffer the consequences.

These rules were different in the various parts of Europe, but they all made much of "service" and "loyalty to duty." The Middle Ages regarded service as something very noble and beautiful. It was no disgrace to be a servant, provided you were a good servant and did not slacken on the job. As for loyalty, at a time when life depended upon the faithful performance of many unpleasant duties, it was the chief virtue of the fighting man.

A young knight therefore was asked to swear that he would be faithful as a servant to God and as a servant to his King. Furthermore, he promised to be generous to those whose need was greater than his own. He pledged his word that he would be humble in his personal behaviour and would never boast of his own accomplishments and that he would be a friend of all those who suffered (with the exception of the Mohammedans, whom he was expected to kill on sight).

Around these vows, which were merely the Ten Commandments expressed in terms which the people of the Middle Ages could understand, there developed a complicated system of manners and outward behaviour. The knights tried to model their own lives after the example of those heroes of Arthur's Round Table and Charlemagne's court of whom the Troubadours had told them. . . . They hoped that they might prove as brave as Lancelot and as faithful as Roland. They carried themselves with dignity and they spoke careful and gracious words that they might be known as True Knights, however humble the cut of their coat or the size of their purse.

In this way the order of Knighthood became a school of those good manners which are the oil of the social machinery. Chivalry came to mean courtesy and the feudal castle showed the rest of the world what clothes to wear, how to eat, how to ask a lady for a dance and the thousand and one little things of every-day behaviour which help to make life interesting and agreeable.

Like all human institutions, Knighthood was doomed to perish as soon as it had outlived its usefulness.

The crusades, about which one of the next chapters tells, were followed by a great revival of trade. Cities grew overnight. The townspeople became rich, hired good school teachers and soon were the equals of the knights. The invention of gun-powder deprived the heavily armed "Chevalier" of his former advantage and the use of mercenaries made it impossible to conduct a battle with the delicate niceties of a chess tournament. The knight became superfluous. Soon he became a ridiculous figure, with his devotion to ideals that had no longer any practical value. It was said that the noble Don Quixote de la Mancha had been the last of the true knights. After his death, his trusted sword and his armour were sold to pay his debts.

But somehow or other that sword seems to have fallen into the hands of a number of men. Washington carried it during the hopeless days of Valley Forge. It was the only defence of Gordon, when he had refused to desert the people who had been entrusted to his care, and stayed to meet his death in the besieged fortress of Khartoum.

And I am not quite sure but that it proved of invaluable strength in winning the Great War.

### from THE NEW LAND

#### Phillip Viereck

*The fact that the northeastern part of our country was explored for over a hundred years before the Pilgrims arrived is seldom given much attention in elementary-school history classes. Original sources, too, are seldom used in teaching history to children. In order to remedy this situation, Phillip Viereck, a teacher, brought out* The New Land, *which provides an account of the "Discovery, Exploration, and Early Settlement of Northeastern United States, from Earliest Voyages to 1621, Told in the Words of the Explorers Themselves" in journals, logbooks, letters, and other accounts. According to the Preface, "Journals, maps and a minimum of editorial bridging passages are interwoven to tell the story" and "Marginal notes and illustrations, the results of years of research, are added to clarify obscure passages or archaic wording." Viereck compiled and edited the book and wrote the running commentary, and his wife, Ellen, prepared the illustrations.*

*Superior readers in fifth and sixth grades can read this remarkable history for themselves. However, because of the unique quality of the language, it might well be read aloud to chil-*

*dren. The marginal notes (in the following selection placed in brackets within the text) should be included in the reading, for their explanations and for their occasional touches of humor. Especially interesting in this selection ("the letter of Giovanni da Verrazano to Francis Ist, King of France") is Verrazano's very favorable impression of the Indians—quite different from the impressions of many later explorers and also quite different from the impression Verrazano himself gained of some Indians he encountered later on in his journey.*

*The following selection from* The New Land *exactly reproduces the text but gives no notion of the handsome format. The illustrations from only the first page are reproduced (the original has sketches on every page), and the marginal notes appear here in brackets within the text.*

#### Giovanni da Verrazano: The First Thorough Exploration, 1524

Verrazano, born in Florence, Italy, was a child of the Age of Exploration. While he was yet a boy, Columbus discovered the Caribbean islands, and during his early teens the first ship rounded Africa and reached India. Cabot, the Corte Reals, Vespucci, and others expanded man's concept of the size and shape and the very nature of his planet. The increasingly accepted notion that the world was round was at last proved true in 1522 when Del Cano sailed the one remaining ship of Magellan's fleet back into port after circling the globe. And in 1524, having earned a reputation as a pilot and adventurer, Verrazano sailed with a commission from the French king to explore the coast of the New Land in search of a passage to the Orient.

The seventeenth of January of the year 1524, by the Grace of God we departed from the deserted rock by the Isle of Madera with 50 men, with victuals, weapons, and other ship-munition very well provided and furnished for 8 months. Sailing westward with a fair easterly wind, in 25 days we ran 800 leagues [*Some early sources say 500 leagues. A league is a little over three miles.*] , and the 20th of February we were overtaken with as sharp and terrible a tempest as ever any sailors suffered, whereof with the divine help and merciful assistance of Almighty God,

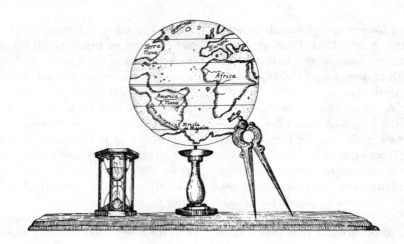

and the goodness of our ship, accompanied with the good hap of her fortunate name. [*Named the* DAUPHINE *after the eldest son of the king.*], we were delivered, and with a prosperous wind followed our course west and by north. And in another 25 days we made above 400 leagues more, where we discovered a new land [*Land must have been sighted at either North or South Carolina.*], never before seen of any man either ancient or modern.

At the first sight it seemed somewhat low, but being within a quarter of a league of it, we perceived by the great fires that we saw by the sea coast, that it was inhabited and saw that the land stretched to the southwards. In seeking some convenient harbor wherein to anchor and also to gain knowledge of the place, we sailed fifty leagues in vain, and seeing the land to run still to the southwards, we resolved to return back again towards the north, where we found ourselves troubled with the like difficulty. [*They may have sailed as far south as northern Florida before turning around.*]

At length being in despair to find any port, we cast anchor upon the coast, and sent our boat to shore [*The "ship's boat" was large enough to hold 25 men, with 8 or 10 oars and a sail.*], where we saw great store of people which came to the sea side. Seeing us approach, they fled away, and sometimes would stand still and look back, beholding us with great admiration, but afterwards being animated and assured with signs that we made them, some of them came down to the seaside, seeming to rejoice very much at the sight of us, and marveling greatly at our apparel, shape and whiteness. They showed us by sundry signs where we might most commodiously come aland with our boat, offering us also of their victuals to eat.

The people are of color russet, and not much unlike the Saracens—their hair black, thick and not very long, which they tie together in a knot behind and wear it like a little tail. They are well featured in their limbs, of mean stature, and commonly somewhat bigger than we—broad breasted, strong armed, their legs and other parts of their bodies well fashioned. We saw many of them handsome, having black and great eyes, with a cheerful and steady look, not strong of body, yet sharp witted, nimble and exceed-

ing great runners, as far as we could learn by experience. In those two last qualities they are like to the people of the East parts of the world, and especially to them of the uttermost parts of China. [*Noting the similarity between Indians and Orientals, Verrazano was perhaps hoping that the expedition was nearing Asia.*] We could not learn of this people their manner of living, nor their particular customs, by reason of the short abode we made on the shore, our company being but small, and our ship riding far off in the sea. [*Historians believe that Verrazano had been a corsair or pirate before this expedition, capturing many Spanish ships, including some loaded with Cortes's treasure from Mexico. Thus his ship was probably larger than those of most of the later explorers. He often had to anchor far from the land.*]

Sailing forwards, we found certain small rivers and arms of the sea, that fall down by certain creeks, washing the shore on both sides as the coast lies. And beyond this we saw the open country rising in height above the sandy shore with many fair fields and plains, full of mighty great woods, some very thick, and some thin, replenished with divers sorts of trees, as pleasant and delectable to behold, as is possible to imagine. And the land is full of many beasts,—stags, deer and hares, and likewise of lakes and pools of fresh water, with great plenty of fowls, convenient for all kind of pleasant game.

We departed from this place, still running along the coast, which we found to trend toward the east. We saw everywhere very great fires, by reason of the multitude of the inhabitants. While we rode on that coast, partly because it had no harbor, and because we wanted water, we sent our boat ashore with 25 men. By reason of great and continual waves that beat against the shore, being an open coast, without protection, none of our men could possibly go ashore without wrecking our boat. We saw there many people which came unto the shore, making divers signs of friendship, and showing that they were content we should come aland. By trial we found them to be very courteous and gentle, as your Majesty shall understand by the success.

To the intent we might send them of our things, which the Indians commonly desire and esteem, as sheets of paper, glasses, bells, and such like trifles, we sent a young man, one of our mariners ashore, who swimming towards them, and being within 3 or 4 yards of the shore, not trusting them, cast the things upon the sand. Seeking afterwards to return, he was with violence of the waves beaten upon the shore, so bruised that he lay there almost dead.

The Indians perceiving, ran to catch him, and drawing him out, they carried him a little way off from the sea. The young man being at the first dismayed, began then greatly to fear, and cried out piteously. The Indians which did accompany him, went about to cheer him and to give him courage, and then setting him on the ground at the foot of a little hill against the sun, they began to behold him with great admiration, marvelling at the whiteness of his flesh. Taking off his clothes, they made him warm at a great fire, not without our great fear who remained in the boat, that they would have roasted him at that fire, and have eaten him.

The young man having recovered his strength, and having stayed a while with them, showed them by signs that he was desirous to return to the ship. They with great love clapping him fast about with many embracings, accompanied him to the sea, and to put him in more assurance, leaving him alone, went unto a high ground and stood there, beholding him until he was entered into the boat. [*Here is a fine example of a first contact between the old world and the new, in which European distrust was shown to be unnecessary.*] This young man observed, as we did also, that these are of color inclining to black as the others were, with their flesh very shining, of mean stature, handsome visage, and delicate limbs, and of very little strength, but of prompt wit. We observed no more than that.

Departing from hence, following the shore which trended somewhat toward the north, in 50 leagues space we came to another land which showed much more fair and full of woods, being very great, where we rode at anchor, so that we might have some knowledge thereof, we sent 20 men aland, who entered into the country about 2 leagues. They found that the people were fled to the woods for fear. They saw only one old woman with a young maid of 18 or 20 years, who seeing our company, hid themselves in the grass for fear. The old woman carried two infants on her shoulders, and behind her neck a child of eight. The young woman was laden likewise with as many. When our men came unto them, the women cried out. The old woman made signs that the men were fled unto the woods. As soon as they saw us to quiet them and to win their favor, our men gave them such victuals as they had with them to eat, which the old woman received thankfully. But the young woman disdained them all, threw them with contempt on the ground. We took a child from the old woman to bring to France. Going about to take the young woman who was very beautiful and of tall stature, we could not possibly, for the great outcries that she made, bring her to the sea. Having great woods to pass through and being far from the ship, we decided to leave her behind, bearing away the child only. [*Never underestimate the power of a woman!*]

We found those folks to be more white than those that we found before, being clad with certain leaves that hang on boughs of trees, which they sew together with threads of wild hemp. Their hair was trussed up after the same manner as the former were. Their ordinary food is of pulse [*"Pulse" could mean edible seeds such as peas and beans.*], whereof they have great store, differing in color and taste from ours, of good and pleasant taste. Moreover they live by fishing and fowling, which they take with gins [*"Gins" may refer to nets or snares.*], and bows made of hard wood, the arrows of canes, being headed with the bones of fish and other beasts. The beasts in these parts are much wilder than in our Europe, by reason they are continually chased and hunted. We saw many of their boats made of one tree 20 feet long, and 4 feet broad, which are not made with iron or stone, or any other kind of metal (because that in all this country for the space of 200 leagues which we ran, we never saw one stone of any sort). They help themselves with fire, burning so much of the tree as is sufficient for the hollowness of the boat. They do the same in making the stern and the forepart, until it be fit to sail upon the sea. [*Birch bark canoes were used farther north, but these large dugouts were found along most of the coast. The natives were able to launch them through the breakers.*]

We saw in this country many vines growing naturally, which growing up, took hold of the trees as they do in Lombardy, which if by husbandmen they were dressed in good order, without all doubt they would yield excellent wines. Having oftentimes seen the fruit thereof dried, which was sweet and pleasant and not differing from ours, we think those here do esteem the same, because in every place where they grow, they take away the under branches growing round about, that the fruit thereof may ripen better. [*Here is evidence that the Indians knew how to make raisins.*]

We found also roses, violets, lilies, and many sort of herbs, and sweet and odoriferous flowers different from ours.

Having made our abode three days in this country, and riding on the coast for want of harbors, we concluded to depart trending along the shore between the north and the east, sailing only in the daytime, and riding at anchor by night. In the space of 100 leagues sailing we found a very pleasant place situated amongst certain little steep hills. From amidst the hills there ran down into the sea an exceeding great stream of water, which in the mouth was very deep, and from the sea to the mouth of the same with the tide which we found to rise 8 feet, any great ship laden may pass up. [*New York Harbor, Lower Bay. Verrazano noted in the margin that he named the land "Angoulême," which had been the principality of Francis before he became King.*]

But because we rode at anchor in a place well fenced from the wind, we would not venture ourselves without knowledge of the place. We passed up with our boat only into the said river [*Through the narrows which now bears his name.*], and saw the country very well peopled. The people are almost like unto the others, and are clad with the feathers of fowls of divers colors. They came towards us very cheerfully, making great shouts of admiration, showing us where we might come to land most safely with our boat. We entered up the said river into the land about half a league, where it made a most pleasant lake about 3 leagues in compass. [*Upper*

*Bay of New York Harbor. He named it "Bay of St. Marguerite," after the elder sister of King Francis.*] The people rowed from the one side to the other to the number of 30 of their small boats, wherein were many people which passed from one shore to the other to come and see us. And behold upon the sudden a contrary flaw of wind coming from the sea, we were forced to return to our ship, leaving this land to our great discontentment, for the great commodity and pleasantness thereof, which we suppose is not without some riches, all the hills showing mineral matters in them. [*Hudson, 85 years later, also noted that the hills seemed to contain minerals.*]

We weighed anchor, and sailed toward the east, for so the coast trended. And so always for 50 leagues being in the sight thereof, we discovered an island in form of a triangle, distant from the mainland 10 leagues, about the bigness of the Island of Rhodes. It was full of hills covered with trees, well peopled, for we saw fires all along the coast. We gave it the name of your Majesty's mother, not staying there by reason of the weather being contrary. [*It is impossible to be certain whether Luisa Island was Block Island, Martha's Vineyard or Nantucket. None fits the description exactly. Tall trees must have made the islands appear much larger then. Best bet is Block Island.*]

And we came to another land being 15 leagues distant from the island, where we found a passing good haven, wherein being entered, we found about 20 small boats of the people. [*This haven, in which the expedition spent two weeks, was lower Narragansett Bay.*] With divers cries and wonderings they came about our ship, coming no nearer than 50 paces towards us. They stayed and beheld the artificialness [*The word "artificial" at that time did not mean false, but referred to artfulness, or skillful handwork.*] of our ship, our shape and apparel. Then they all made a loud shout together, declaring that they rejoiced. When we had somewhat encouraged them, using their gestures, they came so near us, that we cast them certain bells and glasses, and many toys, which when they had received, they looked on them with laughing, and came without fear aboard our ship.

There were amongst these people 2 kings of so goodly stature and shape as is possible to declare. The eldest was about 40 years of age, the second was a young man of 20 years. Their apparel was on this manner: the elder had upon his naked body a hart's skin wrought artificially with divers branches like damask. His head was bare with the hair tied up behind with divers knots. About his neck he had a large chain, garnished with divers stones of sundry colors. The young man was almost appareled after the same manner.

This is the goodliest people, and of the fairest conditions that we have found in this our voyage. They exceed us in bigness. [*Almost all of the early explorers remarked that the Indians were taller than Europeans.*] They are of the color of brass, some of them incline more to whiteness, others are of yellow color, of comely visage, with long and black hair, which they are very careful to trim and deck up. They are black and quick eyed, and of sweet and pleasant countenance, imitating much the old fashion. I write not to your Majesty of the other parts of their body, having all such proportion as appertains to any handsome man.

The women are of the like conformity and beauty, very handsome and well favored, of pleasant countenance, and comely to behold. They are as well mannered and modest as any women, and of good education. They are all naked save their privy parts, which they cover with a deerskin branched or embroidered as the men use. There are also some of them which wear on their arms very rich skins of luserns. [*A "lusern" was a lynx.*] They adorn their heads with divers ornaments made of their own hair, which hang down before on both sides their breasts. Others use other kinds, dressing themselves like unto the women of Egypt and Syria. These are of the elder sort, and when they are married, they wear divers decorations according to the usage of the people of the East, as well men as women. [*Verrazano had traveled to the Near East as a child.*]

Among them we saw many plates of wrought copper [*Several other explorers found that the natives of this area were wearing copper items.*], which they esteem more than gold, which for the color they make no account of, they make most account of azure and red. The things that they esteem most of all those which we gave them, were bells, crystals of azure color, and other toys to hang at their ears or about their neck. They did not desire cloth of silk or of gold, much less of any other sort, neither cared they for things made of steel and iron, which we often showed them in our armor which they made no wonder at, and in beholding them they only asked the art of making them. The like they did at our glasses ["*Glasses refers to mirrors.*], which when they beheld, they suddenly laughed and gave them us again. They are very liberal, for they give that which they have. We became great friends with these.

One day we entered into the haven with our ship, whereas before we rode a league off at sea by reason of the contrary weather. They came in great companies of their small boats unto the ship with their faces all bepainted with divers colors, showing us that it was a sign of joy, bringing us of their victuals. They made signs unto us where we might safest ride in the haven for the safeguard of our ship. [*Most likely Newport, R.I. The name given by the expedition was "Refugio," or Port of Refuge.*]

After we were come to an anchor, we bestowed 15 days in providing ourselves many necessary things. Every day the people repaired to see our ship bringing their wives with them, whereof they were very jealous. They themselves entering aboard the ship and staying there a good space, caused their wives to stay in their boats, and for all the entreaty we could make, offering to give them divers things, we could never obtain that they would suffer them to come aboard our ship.

And oftentimes one of the two kings coming with his queen, and many gentlemen for their pleasure to see us, sending a small boat to give us intelligence of their coming, saying they would come to see our ship. This they did in token of safety, and as soon as they had answer from us, they came immediately, and having stayed a while to behold it, they wondered at hearing the cries and noises of the mariners. [*Although it is not clear here it seems as if he is saying that (in true sailor fashion) the crew called and made noises at the women, and thus the Indian men kept their wives and daughters away from the ship.*] The queen and her maids stayed in a very light boat, at an island a quarter of a league off, while the king abode a long space in our ship uttering favorable opinions and making gestures, viewing with great admiration all the furniture of the ship, demanding the property of every thing particularly. He took likewise great pleasure in beholding our apparel, and in tasting our meats and so courteously taking his leave departed.

And sometimes our men staying 2 or 3 days on a little island near the ship for divers necessaries (as it is the use of seamen) he returned with 7 or 8 of his gentlemen to see what we did. He asked of us oftentimes if we meant to make any long abode there, offering us of their provision. Then the king drawing his bow and running up and down with his gentlemen, made much sport to gratify our men.

We were oftentimes within the land 5 or 6 leagues, which we found as pleasant as is possible to declare, very apt for any kind of husbandry of corn [*The word "corn" at the time meant any grain.*], wine and oil, for there are plains broad, open and without impediment, of trees of such fruitfulness, that any seed being sown therein, will bring forth most excellent fruit. We entered afterwards into the woods, which we found so great and thick, that any army were it ever so great might have hid itself therein, the trees whereof are oaks, cypress trees [*This port is far to the north of the natural limit of cypress trees. Verrazano was probably seeing red cedars, a variety of juniper.*], and other sorts unknown in Europe. We found apple, plum trees, and nut trees, and many other sorts of fruit differing from ours. There are beasts in great abundance, as harts, deer, luzerns, and other kinds which they take with their nets and bows which are their chief weapons. The arrows which they use are made with great cunning, and instead of iron, they head them with flint, with jasper stone and hard marble & other sharp stones which they use instead of iron to cut trees, and to make their boats of one whole piece of wood, making it hollow with great and wonderful art, wherein 10 or 12 men may sit commodiously. Their oars are short and broad at the end, and they use them in the sea without any danger, and by main force of arms, with as great speediness as they wish. [*This describes paddling as opposed to rowing.*]

We saw their houses made in circular or round form 10 or 12 paces in compass, made with half circles of timber, separate one from another without any order of building, covered with mats of straw wrought cunningly together, which save them from the wind and rain. If they had the order of building and perfect skill of workmanship as we have, there were no doubt but that they would also make great and stately buildings, for all the seacoasts are full of clear and glistening stones and alabaster, and therefore it is full of good havens and harbors for ships.

They move the foresaid houses from one place to another according to the commodity of the place and season wherein they will make their abode, and only taking off the mats, they have other houses built easily. The father and the whole family dwell together in one house in great number: in some of them we saw 25 or 30 persons.

They feed as the others do aforesaid of pulse which grow in that country with better order of husbandry then in the others. They observe in their sowing the course of the moon and of the rising of certain stars, and divers other customs spoken of by antiquity. Moreover they live by hunting and fishing. They live long and are seldom sick, and if they chance to fall sick at any time, they heal themselves with fire without any physician, and they say that they die of old age. [*"Heal themselves with fire" may refer to the Indian habit of smoking tobacco. It is curious that Verrazano never mentioned it otherwise.*] They are full of pity and charity for their neighbors. At their departure out of life, they use mourning mixed with singing, which continues for a long space. This is as much as we could learn of them.

## *from* THE AMERICAN REVOLUTION 1775–83: A BRITISH VIEW

*Clorinda Clarke*

*It takes a generous measure of imagination to see a war from the enemies' point of view. And that is just what Clorinda Clarke, an American-born writer who studied at Oxford, tried to do*

*when she wrote a history of the American Revolution for young people in England. For the information for her book she consulted contemporary British as well as American sources, and for many of her illustrations she used newspapers, letters, cartoons, and pictures of the period. The American Revolution 1775–83 was published in England in 1964 and in the United States in 1967. This selection, the final chapter, describes what happened after the war to the Loyalists, those who opposed the Revolution, and it offers older students an opportunity to compare this account with American accounts of the same period.*

### The Fate of the Loyalists

"Oh, God, it is all over," Lord North cried when he heard about Cornwallis's surrender at Yorktown. But it was not all over! Two years passed before the Treaty of Paris ended the Revolution.

In those two years Washington held his hungry, unpaid, mutinous army together. Fighting in the United States dwindled to a few skirmishes in the south. In those two years England put all her strength into winning at sea. She won so well —against the French in the West Indies and the Spanish at Gibraltar—that by 1783 she could have set much stiffer terms than she did.

The Treaty of Paris, signed on September 3, 1783, gave the territory between the Allegheny Mountains and the Mississippi River to the United States. The Canadian–American boundary was much as it is now. Florida went to Spain.

Some very important questions had to be answered before the Treaty was signed. They concerned the Loyalists. What was to become of them? Must the Rebels give them back the property they had stolen? If the Rebels did not return the property, must they repay the Loyalists for their losses?

To the chief American negotiator, Benjamin Franklin, the Loyalists were America's "bitterest enemies." He warned England that if she wanted a peace treaty she had better "drop all mention of the refugees." By 1783 England wanted a peace treaty very much. She was sick of the American war. She wanted to end the American–French alliance. The English government also knew that, without fighting again, it could not force the Americans to repay the Loyalists for their losses.

Richard Oswald, an English negotiator, thought of a compromise which Congress accepted. He suggested that Congress should recommend that each state investigate the seizures of Loyalist property and, if they seemed unfair, to correct them.

Who were the Loyalists? What happened to them after the Revolution? The Loyalists (or as their enemies called them, the Tories) were Americans who after the Declaration of Independence in July 1776 wanted America to remain in the British Empire. Certain sorts of people were often Loyalists, such as government officials, lawyers, doctors, Anglican clergymen, large landowners in the north, small landowners in the southern states.

American legend had it that all Loyalists were rich and powerful, people who feared the Revolution would deprive them of their wealth and influence. Historians now know there were Loyalists among all groups, laborers and weavers as well as lawyers and landowners. Negro slaves

Loyalist recruiting poster

became Loyalist when England promised them their freedom if they fought in the British army. Surprisingly, people who were not of English descent were more apt to be Loyalist than those whose ancestors had come from England.

Loyalist strength differed in each colony. They were strong in North Carolina, weak in South Carolina. Weakest in Massachusetts and Virginia, they were very strong in Pennsylvania and New York. If Loyalist New York and Pennsylvania had not been "put in awe" by strongly Rebel Massachusetts to the north, and Virginia to the south, they well might not have joined the Revolution at all! From the end of 1776 until after the Treaty of 1783 New York City remained in British hands. If the British had not yielded her up peacefully, it would have been almost impossible to get them out by force.

As in all civil wars the American Revolution broke up long friendships and loving families. The Rebel leader Benjamin Franklin never forgave his son William for remaining a Loyalist.

But nobody suffered more from the bitter feelings than the prisoners of war. At first the British did not treat their captives as prisoners of war, but as rebels and traitors. Only when many of their own men fell into American hands and they feared reprisals did they change their attitude and become somewhat less harsh.

The Rebels, by the same token, after the Declaration of Independence, considered the Loyalists traitors and criminals against the state, and treated them accordingly.

During the Revolution the Americans took about 15,000 prisoners, the British about 10,000. Neither side had the facilities to take care of their captives properly. Prisoners were packed into stinking jails made over from crowded warehouses, rotting ships and open mine shafts. They died from disease, filth, cold and hunger. Ill-treatment of prisoners, like the Indian raids, did much to increase American bitterness against the British and to harden feelings toward the Loyalists after the Revolution was over.

How many Loyalists were there? No one knows exactly, but there were Loyalists in every colony. Probably about one third of all the people who took an active part in the Revolution were Loyalist in sympathy.

Why, if there were Loyalists everywhere, and

Great Britain's army and navy were behind them, did their side lose? The Loyalists never worked together as well as the Rebels did. They laughed at Sam Adams's Committees of Correspondence but never got together themselves so that Loyalists in one colony could exchange ideas and news, or even find out who were Loyalists in the other colonies.

Most important: before the Declaration of Independence many Loyalists and Rebels agreed politically on many things. They both resented the King's ministers. They both opposed taxation without representation. They both wanted a restoration of their Englishmen's rights. What they disagreed about was independence itself. The Loyalists feared the "mob rule" independence might bring far more than they resented Parliament's new taxes.

Since the two parties agreed on so much, the Loyalists were caught off guard when, in July 1776, independence was declared. Suddenly, after July 4, they were no longer considered law-abiding citizens, but traitors to their native land! And if their wealth and position made them the objects of envy, Rebel mobs threatened them with tar and feathers, and they fled out of the country.

Also, during the Revolution, some Loyalists seem to have been willing to let the British army

*Tory cartoon showing how Rebels treated Loyalists*

do the fighting for them. Admiral Howe's secretary once complained, "They all prate and profess much, but when you call upon them they do nothing."

On the other hand, when early in the war the Massachusetts Loyalists wanted to form their own regiments, the British army would not let them. But as the war dragged on and British losses mounted, Loyalist regiments were set up. Over 50,000 Loyalists fought. The names of some of their regiments were the British Legion, the King's Orange Rangers and the Maryland Loyalists.

What became of the Loyalists after the Revolution?

If their position did not excite envy in their neighbors, if they kept their political opinions to themselves, if they never fought against the Rebels, they could live quietly, without being attacked, right through the Revolution and afterwards. This was particularly true in New York, North Carolina and other states where there were Loyalist communities. Many of them continued to live much as they had before the Revolution started, and became leaders in the young American republic. But if they left the country during the Revolution or joined the British army, their lands and property were confiscated.

Early in the Revolution, 1,000 Massachusetts Loyalists sailed with Howe from Boston to Halifax. Thousands more migrated later to Nova Scotia and Quebec. They created the province of New Brunswick. The descendants of the 60,000 exiles to Canada became very strong there. They did much to keep Canada in the British Empire and Commonwealth. Known as United Empire Loyalists, they have given Canada statesmen, warriors and educators.

Southern Loyalists traveled to the West Indies —where their heirs have preserved British traditions. The wealthiest Loyalists went to England. As early as 1775 they were dining together each week at the New England Club, meeting at the New England Coffee House on Threadneedle Street in London.

Though many Loyalists felt they had been betrayed, England generally treated them fairly and generously. By 1782 annual pensions totaling £70,000 were being awarded to them. After a Royal Commission was set up in 1783 to examine their claims, £3,000,000 more were distributed among them. In addition, £26,000 were given each year to Loyalists' widows and children. Settlers in Canada received almost £26,000,000.

After the Revolution some of the Loyalists prospered in England and on the Continent. Among these were the painters Gilbert Stuart and John Singleton Copley. (Copley's son became Lord Chancellor.) James Thompson from Massachusetts was a renowned scientist and inventor, an adviser to the King of Bavaria and a count of the Holy Roman Empire. (He took the title Count Rumford.)

But many of the 100,000 refugees grew homesick and some managed to go home again. Many more, however, stayed in exile, like all political refugees full of wrongs, dreams and stories of the old days. So numerous were they, one Loyalist wrote: "There will scarcely be a village in England without some American dust in it by the time we are all laid to rest."

Why were these Loyalists afraid to go home to America after the Revolution was over and the Peace Treaty signed? Why did a man like Washington call them "parricides" (father-murderers)? First, after the Declaration of Independence most Rebels automatically considered all Loyalists traitors to the United States. Second, during the war, Loyalists often had spied for the British army—on their Rebel friends and relatives. Worse, some Loyalists not only organized the brutal Indian raids along the frontiers, but put on war paint and led them. Also, the savage warfare in the southern states during the final years of the war (though the Loyalists were no crueller than the Rebels) left long and bitter memories behind.

These are some of the reasons why the Loyalists were resented by Rebels during their lives, and why, for generations afterward, they were condemned in American history and literature.

Few Englishmen—and certainly not George III—wanted to be tyrants or to oppress the colonies. In 1788, after it was all over, George III said about the Revolution: "We meant well to the Americans—just to punish them with a few bloody noses, and then make bows for the mutual happiness of the two countries. But want of principle got into the army, want of skill and energy in the First Lord of the Admiralty, and want of unanimity at home. We lost America."

Englishmen who valued their personal liberty eventually realized that the defeat at Yorktown had really done good because it had checked their country's "drift towards despotism." They came to see that the American colonies had not been lost in vain. As Horace Walpole put it: "Let us save the constitution. If England is free, and America is free, though disunited, the whole world will not be in vassalage." So, after the Revolution, while the new United States was making a new kind of government, England, under the leadership of William Pitt, Lord Chatham's son, became strong once more.

## from GEORGE WASHINGTON'S WORLD

*Genevieve Foster*

*Almost twenty years after Hendrik Van Loon, in* The Story of Mankind, *was hailed as an innovator in the writing of history for children, another author received a similar accolade.* George Washington's World *was the book, and Genevieve Foster was the author and illustrator. The six parts of the book discuss, respectively, the periods when George Washington was a boy, a soldier, a farmer, a commander, a citizen, and the President. Each period tells not only what was happening to George Washington but what was going on all over the world. Preceding each part is a pictorial overview of some of the famous people and many of the important events of the time. The first selection, from the period "When George Washington Was a Soldier," tells what was going on in far-off China between 1756 and 1763. The second selection, from the period "When George Washington Was Just a Citizen," covers a story, dateline Paris, 1783, about a perilous experiment that did indeed have repercussions down through the years, exactly as predicted by a well-known witness and reporter.*

*Seeing historical events together on a horizontal time line is not only an interesting way for anyone to study history but is particularly appropriate for middle-grade and junior-high students who have had some experience in studying history. In order to enliven her text, Genevieve Foster often details actions or dialogues that might have taken place. She also takes some liberties in characterizing historical figures. George Washington's World and others of her books with a similar pattern provide a wealth of fascinating details that interested and capable students may want to check for accuracy. For example, did the English (as the first of the following selections suggests) introduce opium to the Chinese people?*

### Ch'ien Lung and the "Barbarians"

Half way around the world from the American colonies where the young nation of the United States had not yet come into being, lay the oldest nation in the world, the great and ancient Empire of China. There when George Washington was four years old, Ch'ien Lung, a young Manchu prince, had ascended the red Dragon Throne in the Purple City of Peking, to become China's Emperor. On that coronation day, as he stood in his embroidered robes and the princes of the realm kowtowed before him, Ch'ien Lung made a wish that he be permitted to reign for sixty years. If so, he vowed, he would then abdicate in favor of a son. With his wish granted, Ch'ien Lung was to go down in history as the last great Emperor of China.

That China might prosper under his reign, Ch'ien Lung from the beginning tried to fulfill what the Chinese held to be a ruler's foremost duty, that of setting a good example to his people. Faithfully he observed the ancient customs. Each year at the time of Winter Solstice he went to the Temple of Heaven and gave thanks for the blessings of the year gone by, and prayed to rule so wisely in the year to come that he might truly deserve to be called the Father of his People. In the spring, on the Day of Pure

Ch'ien
Lung

Brightness, he took his offering to the tablet of Shen-nung, the "divine" Farmer King, the one who had first taught the people of China how to till their fields.

These and all other time-honored customs, Ch'ien Lung faithfully observed, for though a Manchu and a descendant of one of China's conquerors, he was as truly Chinese as those whose ancestors had always lived within the Great Wall, and tilled their fields along Huang-Ho, the Yellow River.

Ch'ien Lung was steeped in China's culture, and proud of her long continuous history, one beginning twenty-four hundred years before the birth of Christ. At the time that Julius Cæsar found only wild tribes in France and England, China had been for centuries the eastern center of the world's civilization. When Rome fell, and the Dark Ages blotted out Europe, China's culture continued to go steadily on. In 1755, more books had been written and printed in Chinese than in all other languages put together.

No Chinese book of history, however, told of what had happened outside of Asia. To the black-haired people, China was truly, as they called it, "All-That-Is-Under-Heaven." In Ch'ien Lung's thought, Europeans were merely "outside barbarians," not differing greatly from the wild tribes of Asia.

Too many Europeans, he thought, were coming to China in these later years, bringing things to trade that Chinese people had no use for. They were becoming a nuisance, those red-faced people with their beaklike noses and their pale bulging eyes. Every year more of the "Holan devils," as the people called them, and more of the "red-haired devils," who called their country England, came pushing into China's harbors, sailing up her rivers, and clamoring in their loud voices for silk, for porcelains, and especially for tea.

In ancient days when travellers from Europe had come only overland, China had been well protected from them, as well as from the wild tribes on the western border, by the mountains, the desert and the Great Wall. But now that they were coming by water, a new means had to be found to protect the peace of China from these disturbing "devils." So in 1757, the Hongs of Canton were created.

"From now on," said Ch'ien Lung, "Canton shall be the only place in our empire where Europeans shall be allowed to trade."

Europeans, however, were not to be allowed to enter the city of Canton itself. Outside the walls, along the river, buildings called Hongs were built, where the Europeans might have their living quarters, their storehouses and their offices. A special group of Chinese Mandarins, the Hong Merchants, was appointed to carry on all the dealings with the foreigners. Since the Europeans were not allowed to learn Chinese, and since the Chinese cared to learn no more than necessary of that barbaric language which had so many difficult tongue-twisting sounds, business between the English and the Chinese was carried on in a ridiculous jargon which came to be known as pidgin English.

"No likee silk?" they would say, or "Me sellee number one tea."

The English were most annoyed by the whole arrangement. They protested but it did no good. Ch'ien Lung remained firm. It was best so. Foreigners had no understanding of China's laws and customs, nor did they follow the wisdom of her great teachers. Besides that, having nothing at first to offer that his people wanted, English traders had hit upon a dreadful drug that Chinese people could be made to buy. It was opium made from poppies grown in India. Therefore it seemed best to Ch'ien Lung to restrict the trade. What could "outside barbarians" from the Western Ocean bring to China but discord and evil?

So while the Hong Merchants dealt with the barbarians, the people of China were undisturbed by them. Life went on as it had for centuries. Chinese farmers tilled their neat fields and governed themselves in their small villages, as independently as people in Massachusetts, Pennsylvania, or Virginia. China was an empire, but it was at heart, as it had always been, a democratic country.

The farmers of China were still singing in the year 1755 the same old song good King Yao had heard his people singing 2000 years B.C.:

"We rise at dawn
 And rest at sunset,
 We dig wells and drink,

We till our fields and eat:
What is the power of the Emperor to us?"

Back in England, wares brought from China were so popular that English manufacturers began to copy them. Dishes decorated with the well-known bright blue "willow" pattern were made by Mr. Spode and Mr. Wedgwood, while chairs, cabinets and lacquer screens were designed in Chinese fashion by the furniture maker, Thomas Chippendale.

### Aviation Is Born

Balloons were the main topic of conversation in Paris the winter of 1783. In September three unsuspecting barnyard animals, a cock, a sheep and a duck, had been sent up in a balloon into what was supposed to be the "dangerous upper air," and to every one's amazement had come down again quite unharmed by their strange experience. Since that day, Paris and Versailles had talked of almost nothing but balloons.

No one was more interested in the subject than the old philosopher, Benjamin Franklin. Some one lacking imagination asked him why.

"Of what use is a balloon?" inquired the literal-minded gentleman.

"Of what use is a newborn baby?" answered Benjamin Franklin, who could see that, as surely as a baby grows to be a man, these first balloon experiments would develop into the great science of aviation.

"Yet I fear," said he, for he was nearly seventy-eight years old, "I fear that it will hardly be a common carriage in my time."

He could not help thinking how much more comfortable it would be than bumping over the cobblestones in a coach. That was so painful to him now that to his great disappointment he had not been able to make the trip to Versailles the day the animals went up, but he never missed any of the following balloon ascensions when he was well enough to go. He was also very much interested in hearing of how the two brothers had come to make their first balloon.

Joseph and Stephen Montgolfier, the inventors of the balloon, had grown up in a small town in southern France.

Looking up into the summer sky one day, the younger brother had said, "I believe that if one

of those clouds could be captured in a paper bag it would carry the bag up and an extra weight besides." Later, the idea had occurred to the brothers that they might make a paper bag rise by filling it with hot air and smoke. They made several trial balloons and then in June, 1783, announced a public demonstration in the market place of their home town. The curious crowd, gathered from far and wide, saw a huge blue paper bag, hanging over an open fire, swell to its full spherical size, break the ropes which held it and before their astonished eyes rise into the air and sail away! Like a thing bewitched! News of the experiment spread like wildfire. Scientists wrote and invited the Montgolfiers to come to Paris, after which Louis XVI summoned them to bring the balloon to Versailles that he too and his court also might see this interesting invention.

One afternoon in November, Benjamin Franklin set out in his coach, for a balloon ascension, in as great excitement as an old gentleman could possibly be, for he was about to witness the first voyage in the air ever taken by man. A daring young fellow, by name of de Rozier, had volunteered to make the flight and a friend had offered to go with him. This is part of the account of it which Benjamin Franklin sent to the Royal Society of London:

Nov. 21, 1783.

"Dear Sir:

"Enclosed is a copy of the Experiment made yesterday in the Garden of the Palace where the Dauphin now resides, which being near my House, I was present. The Balloon was larger than that which carried the Sheep Etc. Its Bottom was open and in the middle of the Opening was fixed a kind of Basket Crate in which Faggots and Sheaves of Straw were burnt. When it went over our Heads we could see the Fire which was very considerable. There was a vast Concourse of Gentry in the Garden, who had great Pleasure in seeing the Adventurers go off so cheerfully, & applauded them by Clapping etc., but there was at the same time a good deal of Anxiety for their Safety. Multitudes in Paris saw the Balloon passing, but did not know that there were Men with it, it being then so high that they could not see them. One of these courageous Philosophers did me the honor to call upon me in the Evening after the Experiment with Mr. Montgolfier, the very ingenious Inventor. I was happy to see him safe. Improvement in the management of Balloons has already made a rapid progress and one cannot say how far it may go. A few months since the idea of witches riding through the air upon a broomstick and that of Philosophers upon a bag of smoke would have appeared equally impossible and ridiculous. This Experiment is by no means a trifling one. With great and sincere esteem, I am, sir, your most obedient and humble servant."

*B. Franklin*

"I begin to be almost sorry I was born so soon," he remarked to himself as he dusted what he had written with sand, laid down his quill and removed his spectacles, "since I cannot have the Happiness of Knowing what will be known a hundred years from now."

## from WOMEN'S RIGHTS

*Janet Stevenson*

*This brisk history of the struggle for equal rights for women in America is preceded by several biographical sketches of early fighters in the suffrage movement. Stevenson is lucid and objective in discussion of the nature of the opposition to the suffragettes, and candid in evaluating the results of the victory that was achieved in 1920. The crisp, direct writing is often lightened by wry humor.*

### Background to Battle

The idea that the right to vote (or suffrage, or the franchise, as it also is sometimes called) is a natural right of all citizens did not originate with Susan Anthony, although the amendment that finally guaranteed the right in America was called the Anthony Amendment.

In the beginning of what became the United States of America, the thirteen British colonies followed the old English Common Law in this matter of suffrage. Under that system, only people who owned property and paid taxes on it could vote. Women who owned property (and some did) had the same voting privileges as men.

At the time of the American Revolution, many states had passed laws that restricted the franchise to male property-owners. But in 1776, women could still vote in New York, Massachusetts, New Hampshire, and New Jersey. In New Jersey they could and did vote as late as the presidential election of 1804. They lost the privilege in 1807, and from then until Wyoming entered the Union in 1890, any woman who dropped a marked ballot in a ballot box was defying the law.

The excuse for this undemocratic side of the world's first democracy was that women didn't need the vote. They were protected by men: by their fathers while they were young; by their husbands when they married; by their sons, if they were widowed; or by brothers, cousins, uncles, or some other male guardian who could substitute for their "natural" protector. It was for their own good. Women weren't endowed by their Creator with the abilities that would make the ballot useful to them. There were exceptions, of course, but a "normal" woman wouldn't know what to do with independence or citizenship if they were given to her.

For much the same sort of reason women lacked many other rights. In some states, married women lost their property (even that which they inherited) as soon as they married. In some they had no right to keep wages they earned outside the home. They were seldom allowed to keep their children in case of a divorce, no matter who was at fault. Women could be sentenced to death by a court in which they were not permitted to be a witness. And so on and on.

According to Sir William Blackstone, the most widely respected writer on the British Common Law, a woman stopped being a separate individual—a human being—at the moment of her marriage. She suffered civil death.

Neither Blackstone nor the Common Law had the last word on the rights of women in America, but the legal system of most states was founded on a set of assumptions about the natures of both women and men that led to a very different set of rights and responsibilities being assigned to each. The system never worked well in practice because many of these assumptions were false.

Some men were good providers and protectors of their wives and families. Some men were not. Like women, men are not all either strong or weak, bright or dull, responsible or irresponsible. The law gave them a heavy burden to carry, including "full responsibility for a wife's behavior!" (And with that, the right to punish her for bad behavior!) Some men proved too weak or foolish or cruel to carry such responsibilities. Everyone knew of abuses, where, for example, a husband became a drunkard and spent not only his wife's inheritance, but money she earned to feed herself and her children. Or where a woman was granted a divorce from such a mate, but he continued to be the guardian of their children.

No one knew how to cure such abuses without changing the law in ways that seemed positively revolutionary. But the colonies were engaged in a revolution in 1776, and some people thought women's grievances should be considered along with others.

When John Adams was in Philadelphia, helping to draft the Declaration of Independence and the laws that would govern the new nation, his wife, Abigail, wrote him, half-jokingly:

> Do not put such unlimited power into the hands of the husbands. Remember, all men would be tyrants if they could. . . . If particular care and attention is not paid to the ladies, we are determined to foment a rebellion, and will not hold ourselves bound by any laws in which we have no voice or representation.

She was only *half*-joking, as Mr. Adams must have known. For she was one of many women who were having to run their own homes and farms and businesses, as well as bring up and educate their children, while their husbands were away fighting and not available for duty as protectors.

That women like Abigail Adams could do the job of both partners and do it well was proof of some natural ability that was not getting much encouragement from the kind of education offered to girls. Another Massachusetts matron, Mrs. Judith Murray, at about the same time, wrote the first serious plea for equal opportunity in education ever to appear in English.

Mrs. Murray noticed that the "difference" in the intelligence of men and women did not show at the start of their lives. No one expected a boy-child of two to be "superior in judgment" to a girl of the same age. "But from that period, what partiality! How is the one exalted and the other depressed by the contrary modes of education that are adopted. The one is taught to aspire, the other is early confined and limited."

What women needed, she said, was a chance to exercise their minds on something more challenging than "the mechanism of a pudding." Until they got that right, there would be little use in their pressing for citizenship.

*from* THE LONG FREEDOM ROAD

*Janet Harris*

*The long struggle of black Americans for freedom and civil rights can be told as a sequence of milestones in history. As history accumulates, the small details and the everyday people who are caught up in the large movements and memorable events tend to be forgotten. The following selection records the name of Rosa Parks and the incident that initiated a yearlong bus strike; it also records the name of E. D. Nixon, who made a call to a new minister in town, a man whose name is in no danger of being omitted from histories of the future. This illustrates an important kind of material for young people—history recorded almost as it is being lived and introducing as present-day heroes and heroines the little people who are, in their own way, influencing its direction. Such a person is the author herself, who has worked with NAACP, CORE, and the President's Commission on Fair Housing in Long Island. Her writing is forthright and factual but often dramatic.*

### The Montgomery Bus Boycott

"I woke up this mornin' with my mind set on freedom. Hallelu, hallelu, hallelujah."

There is no plaque in Montgomery, Alabama, as there is at Bunker Hill, to mark it as the birthplace of a revolution. Yet as surely as the shots fired on Bunker Hill were heard round the world, the steady footsteps of Montgomery's Negroes walking to their jobs during the whole year of 1956 echoed through America.

In the Negro revolution, as in the American Revolution, the idea of freedom was dramatically translated into action. Montgomery was not the first site of such action. Insurrections, mass movements, and riots of one sort or another had erupted periodically in many places, in many guises, since 1658, when slaves in Connecticut rebelled, killed their masters, and fled

to live among the Indians.

But the quiet revolution that began in Montgomery was different from the hundreds of earlier flareups. Montgomery became the testing ground for a new means of revolt—"nonviolent protest."

How did it all come about? What exactly is nonviolence? Who were the people in the story? What sort of a place is Montgomery? What were the reasons for the revolt?

Montgomery, the capital of Alabama, is a traditional Southern city. It was once the capital of the Confederacy. Jefferson Davis, the President of the Confederacy, stood on the portico of the Capitol there to receive the oath of office. There the Confederate flag was first unfurled.

Montgomery is also a modern city, with large office buildings and with a section of the business district devoted to state administration. It is an important center for cotton, livestock, and lumber, but there is little heavy industry. Because there are few jobs available, most Negroes find menial positions as domestic workers, porters, or unskilled laborers. There is a small class of Negro professionals, but most Negroes in Montgomery are poor.

Though the United States Supreme Court had decided in 1954 that segregation—in schools, at least—was unconstitutional, in only a few places, such as Washington, D.C., had any changes occurred. Like every other Southern city, Montgomery was as strictly segregated in 1955 as it had been since the end of Reconstruction.

There were separate schools for white and for Negro children. Separate restaurants, barber shops, and theaters served the white community and the Negro community. There were special playgrounds, parks, and swimming pools for whites. Negroes were not admitted to "white" wards in hospitals. Even the toilets and water fountains in public places were marked "white" and "colored," and no thirsty Negro youngster dared to drink from the "white" spigot!

Nowhere were the lines of segregation harder to cross than on the local buses, where the front of each vehicle was strictly reserved for whites, the rear for Negroes.

One of the daily riders of these segregated

buses was a Negro woman named Rosa Parks. On December 1, 1955, tired from her day's work as a seamstress in a downtown department store, she boarded a bus to travel home.

She was lucky because there was an empty seat. With a sigh of relief, she sat down and eased her aching feet out of her snug shoes.

After a few stops, the bus became crowded. Mrs. Parks looked up to find a white man standing over her. He demanded that she give up her seat.

Mrs. Parks hesitated. It was against the law for a Negro to refuse such an order. Yet almost as though it were not her own voice, she heard herself answer, quietly but firmly, "No, I'm sorry."

The driver stopped the bus and called a policeman. Within a few minutes, Mrs. Parks was arrested, booked, and put into jail.

In a matter of hours, many of Montgomery's Negroes heard the news. Mrs. Parks was popular and well known. She had been secretary of the local NAACP. She had helped organize church suppers and bazaars, and she was a familiar figure at prayer meetings.

As they spread word of Rosa Parks's arrest, people remembered what had happened the year before. Claudette Colvin, a pretty Negro high school sophomore, had also refused to surrender her seat on a bus. She, too, was whisked to jail. The Negro community attempted to change the system. They appointed a citizen's committee to talk to the manager of the bus company and to the Montgomery City Commission, which ran the local government.

The bus company officials and the police commissioner, representing the city commission, said they were sorry about what had happened and promised changes. Claudette was tried, found guilty, and given a suspended sentence. The changes promised by the city commission never came about.

Now, Mrs. Parks's friends decided, enough was enough! The Supreme Court had supported Linda Brown's right to attend school with her white playmates. The pattern of "separate but equal" had been challenged in the Supreme Court, and the Supreme Court had ruled segregation unconstitutional. It was time for the segregation on Montgomery's buses to end too!

Later that evening, E. D. Nixon, a burly former Pullman porter who had been president of the Alabama NAACP, signed bond for Mrs. Parks. As soon as he saw her safely home, he started telephoning the other leaders of the Negro community.

Early the next morning, he called the new minister of the Dexter Avenue Baptist Church. Without so much as a "Hello," Nixon plunged into the story of Mrs. Parks's arrest. "We have taken this type of thing too long already," he said, his voice shaking with emotion. "The time has come to boycott the buses. Only through a boycott can we make the white folks understand that we will not accept this kind of treatment any longer."

It was a fateful telephone call. The man to whom E. D. Nixon spoke that morning was the Reverend Martin Luther King.

Martin Luther King was then twenty-seven years old. He was born in Atlanta, Georgia, the son of a minister and grandson of a sharecropper. Once, when he was a small boy, his father took him to a downtown shoe store. They sat down in the first empty seats, in the front of the store.

A young white clerk went over to them and said politely, "I'll be happy to wait on you if you'll just move to the rear of the store."

"We're comfortable *here*," his father replied.

"Sorry," said the clerk, "but you'll have to move."

"We'll either buy shoes sitting here, or we won't buy shoes at all," Reverend King replied, and taking Martin by the hand, he walked out of the store. "I don't care how long I have to live with this system," he said angrily to his son. "I will never accept it."

Martin Luther King knew he could never accept it, either. He worked hard in school. He went to Crozer Theological Seminary in Chester, Pennsylvania, and then to Boston University. While he was studying in Boston and taking additional courses in philosophy at Harvard, he met a beautiful girl, Coretta Scott. She was a music student at New England Conservatory. They were married in 1953.

Coretta King's home was in Marion, Alabama. She, too, grew up with prejudice. So when young Dr. King was offered the pastorate of the Dexter Avenue Church, deep in the South, they both knew what their problems would be. Coretta would have little opportunity for a singing career in Montgomery. Their children would have to attend segregated schools. But the young couple decided to return to the South. As educated Negroes, they felt a moral obligation to help their people acquire real freedom and equality.

The Dexter Avenue Baptist Church to which Dr. King came is a handsome red brick building standing on one corner of a square near the center of downtown Montgomery. There were influential and respected citizens in the congregation. Like many Southern churches, this church was more than a place in which to worship God, it was a community center as well.

The planning meeting for the bus boycott was called for 7:30 P.M. on Friday, December 2, the day after Mrs. Parks was arrested. When Dr. King entered the large meeting room, he found it already filled. In the room were physicians, schoolteachers, lawyers, businessmen, postal workers, union leaders, and clergymen—people from every segment of Negro life—all of them willing and anxious to lend their support to the boycott.

The committee worked feverishly that night and the following day. Telephones hummed as news of the boycott spread through the community. A committee of women mimeographed leaflets, to be distributed by Monday, when the boycott was to begin:

DON'T RIDE THE BUS TO WORK, TO TOWN, TO SCHOOL, OR ANY PLACE MONDAY, DECEMBER 5.

ANOTHER NEGRO WOMAN HAS BEEN ARRESTED AND PUT IN JAIL BECAUSE SHE REFUSED TO GIVE UP HER BUS SEAT.

DON'T RIDE THE BUSES. IF YOU WORK, TAKE A CAB, OR SHARE A RIDE, OR WALK.

COME TO A MASS MEETING, MONDAY AT 7:00 P.M. AT THE HOLT STREET BAPTIST CHURCH FOR FURTHER INSTRUCTION.

Dr. King was up and dressed by 5:30 Monday morning. At 6 his wife called to him, "Martin, come quickly." The first bus had gone by—and it had been empty!

Together they watched the second and the third bus. Not a single Negro passenger!

On December 5, 90 percent of the Negroes who usually rode the buses stayed off them.

Bus after bus, empty except for a handful of self-conscious white passengers, rolled down streets crowded with domestic workers and laborers patiently walking miles to work.

Children ran and leaped after the buses, shouting "No riders today!"

Policemen on motorcycles trailed the buses. In the white community, the false rumor spread that "goons," strong-armed Negroes, were to prevent Negroes from boarding the buses.

The bus boycott was a tremendous success that Monday. Now Dr. King and his associates had to make a decision. Should they continue the boycott? Perhaps it would be better to call it off rather than run the risk of a fizzle. But when they reached the Monday night mass meeting, arranged by Ralph Abernathy, minister of the Holt Street Church, their fears were quelled.

Traffic was jammed for five blocks around the building. In the dark night, police cars circled the church. People, ten deep, stood quietly on the streets outside the packed church. Loudspeakers were hooked up to the outside of the building.

As he walked into the church, Dr. King hesitated. He had not had the time to prepare a speech, and he had much to say. Dr. King wanted his people to know that this boycott was not like the other boycotts that had been used in the South. White segregationist groups had often boycotted Negroes who had asked for fair treatment by "blacklisting" them. Once branded a "troublemaker," a Negro was not likely to be able to find work. White businessmen who were in sympathy with Negroes had been boycotted, too, and as a result of campaigns by segregationists, some of them had been unable to keep their businesses going.

But this boycott was different. "Our concern," Dr. King said later, "was not to put the bus company *out* of business, but to put *justice in business.* We are saying to the white community: 'We can no longer lend our cooperation to an evil system. "

To change the "evil system," Dr. King proposed a program of nonviolent protest or resistance. It was a philosophy he had come to believe in while he was still a theological student. It was derived from the Sermon on the Mount: Love thine enemy. It had roots in Thoreau's theory of civil disobedience: Take dramatic action to protest unfair laws. And finally, it had been spelled out in the theory of passive resistance, as conceived by Mahatma Gandhi in India's successful struggle for independence from Britain.

Dr. King knew he was asking his people to embark on a difficult path. Would his people walk quietly and not give in to anger even if they were jeered at and beaten? Could they win the understanding of the segregationists? Could the Negroes accept suffering without returning hurt for hurt? Could they end hatred—simply by refusing to re-create it? If they gave in to violence, Montgomery would be the home of one more futile, bloody episode.

With these thoughts in mind, Dr. King climbed the platform to the pulpit. And there he found he needed no prepared speech. The words came from his heart:

"There comes a time," he said, "that people get tired."

"Yes, yes," the people murmured.

"We are tired of being segregated and humiliated."

"Amen."

"Tired of being kicked about."

"Yes, yes."

"We have no alternative but to protest. We are protesting for the birth of justice in the community. In our protest there will be no cross burnings. No white person will be taken from his home by a hooded Negro mob and brutally murdered. There will be no threats and intimidation.

"Love must be our ideal. Love your enemies, bless them, and pray for them. Let no man pull you so low as to make you hate him.

"If you will protest courageously, and yet with dignity and Christian love, when the history books are written in future generations the historians will say, 'There lived a great people—a black people—who gave new meaning and dignity to civilization.' "

The Negroes of Montgomery voted for brotherly love and for protest. They voted, that night, to ask for courteous treatment by the bus operators; to ask to be seated on a first-come, first-served basis, with Negroes seated from the back of the bus and whites seated from the front; and to ask for Negro bus drivers on mainly Negro lines. They voted to stay off the buses until their demands were met.

The boycott continued, for the modest requests made to the bus company were not granted. The walkers trudged on. Private car pools were organized. A druggist volunteered to dispatch cars from a downtown parking lot. A fleet of fifteen new station wagons was added, each car registered as the property of a different church, with the church name written on it. Every morning as these wagons carried their loads of passengers to work, startled passersby heard the sound of hymn singing drifting from the open windows.

The costs of operating the boycott were enormous. Help poured in—first dimes and nickels from the Negroes of Montgomery, then contributions from all over the world. Donations came from Tokyo, from Singapore. The largest donations were made by church groups, both Negro and white.

The owners of the bus company grew panicky as they saw only empty buses and empty coin boxes. In desperation, the city officials acted. On February 22, 1956, Dr. King and nearly one hundred others were arrested on a charge of "conspiracy to conduct an illegal boycott." Friends posted bail, and the boycott leaders returned to their work while they awaited trial.

Another meeting was held, this time in the First Baptist Church. Dr. Abernathy, Dr. King's close friend, officiated. Two thousand people attended.

"Do you want to keep on walking?" Dr. Abernathy asked the boycotters.

"Yes, yes!" they shouted.

In March, Dr. King was convicted and fined $1,000. Eventually the fine was paid, and the other cases were dropped, but the arrests increased the determination of the boycotters.

Violence fed the boycott, too. In contrast to the quiet behavior of the strikers, the segregationists responded with acts of terror. Four Negro churches were bombed on January 10, along with the houses of two ministers—one white, one Negro. On January 30, Dr. King's house was bombed. Although the family was home, miraculously no one was hurt.

By March, Dr. King's house had been bombed three times. "Kill me, but know that if you do, you have fifty thousand more to kill," Dr. King warned from his pulpit.

Spring came, bringing with it drenching, warm rain. The boycotters continued to walk. A reporter questioned one of the walkers, a tiny, bent old woman. "Aren't you tired?" he asked.

"My feets is tired," she said softly. "But my soul is rested."

Some whites preferred to place the blame on Communists and outside agitators. Many a domestic, quietly attending to her tasks in the home of her white employer, was questioned about the movement. One Negro girl described the situation: "Our white families [employers] say to us, it's such a terrible thing that a man like that Reverend King comes here and gets the colored people all stirred up, and we say, 'No, ma'am, the reverend, he didn't stir us up, we've been stirred up a mighty long time.' But our white folks, they just don't seem to hear us."

But the voices of Montgomery's Negroes were heard—in the courts, as well as on the streets. An appeal by Aurelia Browder, who, like Mrs. Parks, had been arrested and convicted for refusing to comply with "Jim Crow" bus regulations, was filed in the United States District Court. When the Court ruled against bus segregation, Montgomery's officials took the case to the United States Supreme Court.

Mrs. Browder's lawyers questioned whether or not a community could establish and enforce Jim Crow laws, since the Supreme Court had ruled in favor of Oliver Brown in the school segregation case. And the Supreme Court, on November 13, 1956, agreed that segregation was just as illegal on buses as it had been in schools. The state laws which required segregation on Montgomery's buses were declared invalid. The Montgomery boycotters had won their case!

On December 20, more than a year after Rosa Parks's arrest, the decision reached Montgomery, and the buses were desegregated. Dr. King, Dr. Abernathy, E. D. Nixon, and the Reverend Glenn Smiley, a white Southern ally, rode the first integrated bus.

The bus driver greeted the group with a warm smile as they took their seats in the front of the bus. "We are glad to have you with us this morning," he said.

The success of the bus boycott was an important victory for civil rights, though the fight was just beginning. The victory went far beyond the original battle for a bus seat. The boycott was a way for Negroes to express the feelings that they could not put into words.

"We are tired of being segregated and humiliated," Dr. King had thundered from his pulpit. "We will walk the streets until the walls of segregation are finally battered by the forces of justice." And Negroes listened, and were aroused. They followed the leader who taught them to protest against poverty and injustice through the persuasive power of brotherly love. When Martin Luther King was awarded the Nobel Prize for Peace eight years later, it was as "the first person in the Western World to have shown that a struggle can be waged without violence."

The boycott focused the attention of white Americans on their colored fellow citizens. Public opinion, spurred on by acts of civil disobedience such as the Montgomery boycott, was shifting. Though most white citizens were preoccupied with their own affairs, changes were taking place, not only on the streets of the South but in the Supreme Court and in the halls of Congress where the law of the land was decided.

### from THE CONSUMER MOVEMENT
*James Haskins*

*Author of* Diary of a Harlem Schoolteacher *and books on such diverse topics as witchcraft, street gangs, religion, and black history, James*

Pp. 34–41 from *The Consumer Movement* by James S. Haskins. Copyright © 1975 by James S. Haskins. Reprinted by permission of Franklin Watts, Inc.

*Haskins is a skilled researcher whose writing is always clear and straightforward, balanced in coverage, and informal in tone. In* The Consumer Movement, *he defines the consumers and their needs, and discusses the ways in which they can be taken advantage of. The remainder of the book considers various industries and areas of particular concern: the cigarette industry, drugs, food, clothing, credit buying, big business, and toys. In the selection chosen here, Haskins describes the startling facts about toys that may teach violence and others that have maimed children.*

### The Consumer Movement and the Toy Industry

Today, the average American over the age of sixteen spends about $21 a year on toys. In 1972, the toy industry ranked with the auto industry in sales volume. But the auto industry must obey federal safety regulations in making cars, and on the highways traffic regulations try to insure that cars are used safely and correctly. There are few such federal regulations upon the toy industry, and once a toy is purchased there are no traffic lights or STOP signs to insure protection against dangerous playthings. The United States Public Health Service has estimated that toys alone injure some 700,000 children every year. Why hasn't something been done about it? The consumer movement is working to make toys more safe, but like its work in other areas, it is finding many barriers in its way.

One barrier is time. While the hazards of flammable fabrics, for example, were recognized as far back as the early 1950's, the American toy industry and thus the number of dangerous toys, was just beginning to grow. In 1954, the toy industry's sales volume was $516 million; in 1969 it was well over $2 billion. Between 1955 and 1956 the toy industry was one of the fastest growing industries in America. After World War II there was a "baby boom"—many, many babies were born. By 1955, all these babies were old enough to play with toys. Also, by 1955 the country had entered a period of prosperity, and people had lots of money to spend on toys. Toy manufacturers fell over each other in their efforts to provide toys for the boom babies and to get the consumers' money. In their rush, they paid little attention to safety, but it would be wrong to describe toy makers as evil or as deliberately endangering America's children. The general attitude about accidents with toys, like the attitude about accidents with cars, was that human beings, not the toys or cars themselves, were at fault. If a little boy took the rubber tip off his toy arrow and accidentally put out a friend's eye, or if a little girl was burned playing with her toy electric oven, it was the parents' fault for not watching the children more closely.

By the middle 1960's, these attitudes had begun to change. Too many accidents involving toys were occurring, too many toys were causing deaths and injuries. Dolls with flammable hair caused little girls to receive painful burns; little girls' jewelry made of poisonous seeds or beans caused poisoning and death; the "harpoon" eyes, which were stuck in stuffed toys with a long pin or sharp piece of metal, were often removed to become dangerous weapons; play chemistry sets actually contained chemicals that, when mixed together, caused large explosions. Consumers began to demand legal protection from such toys, and in 1966 the Child Protection Act was passed.

The Child Protection Act was, of course, a step in the right direction, but it was not a very bold step. It barred the sale of toys too dangerous for common use, but it was weak in its definition of "common use." Of course, poisonous beads were too dangerous for common use, but what about toy ovens that could become hot enough to burn a child or whose electrical coils could be dangerously exposed by lifting off an easily removable panel? Then, too, the act provided for the removal of products once they were on the market, but not for the prevention of such products being placed on the market. The act did not provide enough money for government testing of new toys. Thus, in 1967, the year *after* the act was passed, "sonic boom" toys were being sold that should never have been allowed on the market in the first place. Consumers Union tested a Sonic Blaster, which looked like a bazooka gun, and reported that the toy fired compressed air with a "deafening" blast and could permanently damage the hearing of a youngster using it or of a person standing in front of the muzzle. Consumers Union's magazine, *Consumer Reports* advised: "If your child has one, the only sensible course is to throw it out. But destroy it first so that it will not fall into the hands of some other child."

One thing the act did do was to cause toy manufacturers to begin emphasizing the "safety" of their toys and, if there was some possible danger in a particular toy, to put warnings on the packaging. The only trouble was, the claims of safety were not always true, and the warnings on the labels were not always obvious or clear. One example of untrue claims of safety was given in Chapter I: B-B guns were said to be perfectly safe to use inside, despite the fact that accidents from ricochets often occurred. Another untrue claim was the exploding cap device advertised as "harmless." The toy was a feathered projectile, something like a badminton "birdie," with one or several caps inside. The object was to throw it into the air and to watch it explode on contact with the ground. This "harmless" toy caused a number of children to be permanently blinded in one eye.

In many cases where warning labels were placed on toys, the warnings might just as well not have been there. While " 'Snippy' Safe Electric Paper Scissors" was among the first electrical toys to point out that it was, after all, a real electrical appliance, the warning was not prominent. The outside of the cardboard box claimed "Safe—NO SHARP POINTS!" Only after the toy was removed from the box could the buyer see the warning: "Caution! The National Safety Council warns never to use any electrical appliance in or near water, or with wet hands. Remember, Snippy is an electrical appliance just like a radio, iron, or electric razor."

The "Magic Cool Oven" was another example. On the outside of the box were the words: "Outside safe for little fingers to touch." Hidden on the inside of the oven was a warning, stamped in the metal and hard to read, that said: "Caution, contact with hands inside of oven or inside of cooling chamber may cause burns." And only if you tipped the oven completely over would you find on its bottom the words, "Do not immerse in water and clean with damp cloth only." Even the most concerned parent would have had to go over the toy with a magnifying glass like a detective to find these warnings.

Dangerous toys continued to be sold, injuries and deaths continued to result, and it was obvious that the 1966 Child Protection Act was not enough. Thus, in 1969, a stronger law was passed, the Child Protection and Toy Safety Act. In many ways it strengthened the 1966 law. Instead of setting up exclusive and particular standards, it set up flexible standards and gave the Secretary of Health, Education and Welfare great leeway in deciding which toys presented hazards. The toy industry had fought this flexibility, but fortunately they were not successful. The act provided for funds for increased governmental testing of products, making more possible the discovery of dangerous new products before they were placed on the market. Finally, the act narrowed the definition of "normal use" to mean normal use by children, taking into account that children behave a lot differently than adults. But although the 1969 act could have done much to make toys more safe, it did not do enough. Agencies whose duty it was to test products did not receive enough money, and even those toys proved to be hazardous were not removed from the market quickly enough. Months after the 1969 act was passed, the National Commission on Product Safety reported:

Dolls still have pins to hold their hair ribbons on, little girls can still bake their own cakes in their own electric ovens, a little boy can make a design with his glass screen Etch-A-Sketch toy—and run the risk of sketching a permanent scar design somewhere on his body.

Not until 1972 was a strong and enforceable act passed. Called the Consumer Product Safety Act of 1972, it established a five-man, full-time Consumer Product Safety Commission with strong powers to pull dangerous products off the market immediately and to require premarket testing for all products. But as with every other area of consumer concern, it is still up to the consumer to raise the kind of protest that will shake up the toy industry and that will keep the government doing what its laws enable it to do. Right now, with the consumer movement strong and popular, this is being done. Let us hope this success will continue.

People who buy toys for children must shop around for safe toys. If they find children playing with toys that are not safe, they should take them away, substituting safe toys in their place. They should complain both to the retailer and the manufacturer, and they should register their complaints with local and national consumer protection agencies. If individual consumers become more responsible consumers in the area of toy safety, the consumer movement will be free to go on to other areas.

The consumer movement has made progress in the area of physical safety of toys, toys that can burn or injure a child's body. But there is a growing concern with another type of toy safety, a type of safety that has to do with children's minds; that, so far, nothing has been done about. Indeed, there is a question about whether or not any actual laws could be passed to make toys safer for children's minds.

What type of toy is harmful to a child's mind? A toy that teaches the child about violence, or a toy that frightens the child, or a toy that teaches the child bad habits. Many consumers object to the sale of candy cigarettes. After all, if the Surgeon General of the United States has required health warnings on packages of real cigarettes, isn't it wrong to teach children that cigarettes are good, like candy? Antismoking ads for young people try to show that smoking and excellence in sports do not go together. Yet candy cigarette manufacturers often put free toy baseballs in their bags of candy cigarette packages.

Other toys teach violence. Lakeside Toys makes "Crashmobile," a "motorized, exploding car." Is this manufacturer trying to teach children who will someday drive cars that crashes are fun? Chemtoy Company invented a toy called "Bounce Your Eyeball." "High bouncing, realistically colored and veined 'Eye Balls,'" the package announced. Another toy, "Pieces of Body," depicted on the package two surgeons in blood-spattered smocks performing an operation and surrounded by bloody feet, ears, noses, fingers, and inner organs. Isn't there a risk that children will not know the difference between real eyeballs and toy eyeballs or that they will look at the picture of the surgeons on the "Pieces of Body" game and think it is real?

The strongest case in the area of harmful toys of this type is against toy guns. Sometimes tragedy results because the toy gun looks real and is used in hold-ups and robberies, and then a real gun is used against the robber. At other times a real gun is assumed to be a toy by a child. In 1973, a nine-year-old New York City boy brought what he thought was a toy gun to school and, while showing it to one of his classmates, shot him. Many people object to toy guns because they feel that children who play with toy guns become adults who play with real guns. Perhaps, these people suggest, if there were no toy guns there would be fewer than the 20,000 gun-related deaths every year in the United States. In a letter to a New York newspaper one woman urged, "Let the children point their fingers and say 'bang-bang,' which is just what they do when they have no guns. Because we adults accept the fact that children are aggressive, it does not logically follow that we should provide them with realistic replicas of murder weapons." The woman ended her letter: "The toy makers proudly claim that toys are the learning tools of childhood. Then where do guns fit in?"

There is not much hope that these consumers can obtain any legal curbs on such toys. After all, it is very hard to *prove* that playing with toy eyeballs teaches a child violence or that buying a child candy cigarettes will influence him to smoke real cigarettes when he grows up. If, in the United States, the lobby of gun manufacturers and rifle clubs is so strong that it has been able to prevent the passage of laws that would control the possession of real guns by adults, it is not very realistic to expect the government to ban toy guns from the market. Concerned citizens continue to push for gun control laws. Many feel that if the powerful auto industry was successfully fought in many areas by the consumer movement, then the gun lobby, which is not as strong as the auto industry, can be fought successfully as well. But even if this could be done, there is no guarantee that controls on real guns would be followed by controls on the sale of toy guns.

All concerned consumers can do is make the public aware of the possible harmful effects of these toys. But even if they were able to reach everyone, some people would disagree with them. Some would laugh at the idea that a child would confuse candy with real cigarettes. Others would think the bouncing eyeballs were just funny. Fathers who hunted or belonged to rifle clubs would resent the idea that toy guns should be banned. For them, guns are a hobby and a sport; toy guns are a way for children to become interested in that hobby or sport early. In this area, perhaps more than in any other area of consumer concern, those who are against such toys can expect little help from outside. They probably must be content with refusing to buy these toys for their own or others' children, and with trying to convince other adults that these toys are, in their own way, just as dangerous as ovens that burn, chemistry sets that explode, and metal cars with sharp edges.

## from WRAPPED FOR ETERNITY
### *Mildred Mastin Pace*

*One of the acid tests of good informational writing is the smooth incorporation of material based on research; in Pace's discussion of the mummies of Egypt, the text has almost a narrative quality. The facts about mummification, tomb robberies, and the work of scientists in finding and restoring mummies are dramatic, and the informal writing sets them off in the oral tradition of the skilled storyteller. Pace does full justice to a fascinating subject.*

### Where Did All the Mummies Go?

A mummy must be pretty tough.

We have seen how the thirty royal mummies survived the damage by graverobbers, the hasty rewrapping by tomb priests, a hurried transfer to another tomb in antiquity, and finally, in modern times, the trip by boat to Cairo. Even unwrapped, a mummy will continue to exist if kept with reasonable care, the temperature constant, humidity low.

Why then, out of the tremendous number of mummies made by the ancient Egyptians over a period of twenty-five centuries, are there only

a comparatively few left? Obviously, they were destroyed.

Some were destroyed by carelessness and ignorance, some by accident. A few, a very few, were destroyed in scientific study and experimentation. But many were destroyed on purpose, for profit.

The greatest destruction of mummies for profit occurred over a period of four hundred years, when mummies were used as medicine. From the early thirteenth century A.D. well into the seventeenth century, Egyptian tombs were stripped of their mummies, the mummies chopped up and sold in Europe to be fed to the sick and ailing.

While the ancient thieves favored the tombs of the royal and the rich, these later looters took any and all mummies they could find. For them, the communal tombs of the poor, stacked with mummies, were bonanzas.

Taking "mummy" to cure their ills was not just a practice of the superstitious and ignorant. Far from it! Sir Frances Bacon, the great English philosopher of Shakespeare's day, took it and recommended it particularly "for the staunching of blood." Whether Shakespeare used it or not, we don't know. But he mentions it as medicine in several of his plays. And it is one of the magic ingredients in the witches' brew in *Macbeth*.

King François I of France always carried a little packet of mummy in case of sudden illness or an accident.

Most all the doctors of those centuries prescribed it and believed in it as a cure for many diseases.

The loathsome practice would never have gotten started if people had known how mummies were really made. They thought bitumen —a kind of mineral pitch—was used in the wrappings to preserve the bodies. It never was. What they saw in the wrappings was not bitumen but resins that had turned black and glass-like, resembling the mineral.

For several centuries before they began using cut-up mummies for medicine, pure bitumen was prized as a cure-all. However, it was hard to get. There was a mountain in Persia where bitumen, called *mummia* by the Persians, oozed out of cracks in the rocks. It was considered so precious, the mountain was guarded night and day and the mineral was stored in the Royal Treasury. There were other sources—the Dead Sea, for one. But these sources were very difficult to work, and the amounts extracted after tremendous hard labor were small.

Doctors, apothecaries, the sick, and the suffering demanded it. Merchants dishonestly stretched the precious stuff by mixing it with pitch. Smugglers and thieves trafficked in it. Another source was desperately needed.

Then came the rumor, wild and inaccurate: In Egypt there were thousands, probably hundreds of thousands, of ancient bodies wrapped in bandages that were heavy with bitumen. Travelers had seen them. Why not remove the bandages and reclaim the substance?

At the very first this is what was done. The body itself was not used. And because the Persians called the substance mummia, the Arabs began calling the bandaged body a mummy. Thus the word mummy was never known to the Egyptians who practiced mummification. It was coined in the early centuries after Christ. It is actually a misnomer for a wrapped corpse.

As soon as the "bitumen" (which was really resin) from the wrappings came into use, doctors and surgeons everywhere proclaimed it far better, far more effective, than the natural bitumen, or mummia, had ever been. It was believed that the human body around which it had been wrapped gave the drug, in some unknown way, greater curing powers. Now the doctors asked: If this is so, why not go one step further and use the entire wrapped body?

Without doubt, those who dealt in the drug found it much easier to chop up the whole mummy. It must have been a bit difficult to unwrap the body, soak the bandages, and reclaim the hard black substance. Also, there would be a much greater volume of salable drug if the whole body were used.

A lot was needed! Not only did doctors prescribe mummy for all kinds of ailments and diseases, but also for bone fractures, concussions, paralysis—even as an antidote for poison. It became a standard drug on the shelves of apothecary shops all over Europe.

Demand was so great, so many mummies were being destroyed to make the drug, that Egyptian officials finally realized along in the late sixteenth century that their land would soon be mummy-less if steps weren't taken. So it was made illegal to transport mummies. They must be left in their tombs.

This led to a most unsavory fraud, practiced on a wide and dangerous scale in Egypt. Greedy and dishonest men began to manufacture mummies. They took any bodies they could lay their hands on. Some were executed criminals. Others were slaves who had died and whose bodies had not been claimed. Some were paupers who had died without funds or friends to bury them.

These facts mattered not at all to the mummy manufacturers as they went about the business of making a mummy. First they filled the body's natural openings with a cheap blackish material, asphaltum. Then incisions were cut in the muscular part of the limbs and asphaltum packed in. The bodies were then tightly bound up and placed in the sun. The heat of the sun and the arid atmosphere dried them out sufficiently so they looked like mummies. And as mummies they were sold.

A prominent French physician, visiting Egypt late in the sixteenth century, saw one of these "mummy factories." He reported that he saw forty or more mummies newly made and ready for sale. He asked the owner of the factory if any of these people had died of infectious diseases, especially the plague. The owner said he neither knew nor cared. As long as he could get the bodies, it mattered not to him how the person died. These were the bodies that would turn up as mummies in apothecary jars in Europe!

When the physician returned to France, he told a friend, a well-known surgeon, what he had seen. They both publicly denounced the use of mummy as medicine and refused to prescribe it. Whether they influenced others in their profession is not known.

In any event, the use of mummy medicine was on its way out. But not because the medical men and their patients had lost faith in it as a cure-all.

The fraudulent mummy-makers in Egypt were in trouble. It started in one small town where money was sorely needed to meet local expenses. The town officials learned that a certain citizen was getting rich making false mummies and transporting them for sale. They had him arrested, fined him a large sum, and let him go. But not for long. A few mummies later he was again arrested and again the fine was a big one.

Other towns and cities heard of this simple method of raising funds and tried it—with success. Soon the heavy fines became too much for the crooks. They could not afford to continue their mummy hoax and went out of business. With no mummies available—real or false—mummy as medicine gradually disappeared.

But for a long time after, the mummia from Mummy Mountain in Persia was still considered magical and more precious than gold. In 1809 the King of Persia, wishing to bestow an important gift on the Queen of England and the Empress of Russia, sent each lady a small gold box full of the bitumen. While traveling in Persia a few years later, Sir William Ouseley, an English writer, met a trader who offered a dab of the mountain's mummia—about enough to fill an English walnut shell—for the price of eight pounds sterling. He did not buy it. The price was too high.

### from GREAT IDEAS OF SCIENCE
*Isaac Asimov*

*A prolific and versatile writer, Isaac Asimov is as esteemed for his science fiction as for his books on history and science. He writes for young children, adolescents, and adults, and a distinguishing feature of his writing is the combination of wit and erudition.*

#### Lavoisier and Gases

It's hard to believe that air is really something. You can't see it and normally you don't feel it, and yet it's there. If it moves quickly enough, it becomes a storm blast that can wreck ships and blow down trees. Its presence can't be denied.

Is air the only substance that can't be seen?

Reprinted by permission of *Scholastic Magazines, Inc.,* from *Great Ideas of Science,* © 1969 by Isaac Asimov. Originally appeared in *Science World*

The alchemists of the Middle Ages seemed to think so. When their concoctions gave off colorless bubbles or vapors, they recorded that they had formed "an air."

If alchemists existed today, we would not take many of their findings seriously. After all, alchemy was a false science that was more interested in converting other metals to gold than in adding to our knowledge of matter. However, some able alchemists observed and studied the behavior of the metals and other substances they worked with. In this way, they made important discoveries that contributed to modern chemistry.

### An Able Alchemist

One of these talented alchemists was Jan Baptista van Helmont. Actually, he was a physician and only dabbled in alchemy. About 1630, van Helmont felt dissatisfied with the notion that all colorless vapors were really air. The "airs" he found bubbling out of his mixtures just didn't seem to be air at all.

For instance, when he placed bits of silver into a strong chemical called nitric acid, the silver dissolved and a red vapor bubbled up and curled into the space above the surface of the liquid. Was this air? Who had ever heard of red air? Who had ever heard of air that could be seen?

Then, when van Helmont added limestone to vinegar, bubbles rose to the top of the liquid again. These at least were colorless and looked just like air bubbles. But if he held a lighted candle above the liquid's surface, the flame went out. What kind of air was it in which a candle would not burn? The same flame-quenching vapors rose from fermenting fruit juice and from smoldering wood.

So, the so-called airs that van Helmont and other alchemists produced were not really air. But they were so much like air that they fooled everyone—that is, everyone but van Helmont. He decided that air was just one example of a group of airlike substances.

These substances were harder to study than ordinary materials, which could easily be seen and felt. Ordinary substances had definite shapes and took up definite amounts of room. They came in pieces and quantities—a lump of sugar, half a glass of water. The airlike substances did not. They seemed to spread out thinly everywhere and to have no structure.

## From "Chaos" to "Gas"

A new group of substances needed a name. Van Helmont knew the Greek myth that the universe began with thin matter without structure that spread out everywhere. The Greeks called that original matter *chaos*. There was a good word! But van Helmont was Flemish—that is, he lived in what is now Belgium—and he pronounced the old Greek word in good Flemish fashion. He spelled it as he pronounced it, and the word became "gas."

Van Helmont was the first to realize that air was but one kind of gas and that there also were other kinds of gas. Nowadays, we call his red gas nitrogen dioxide and his flame-quenching gas carbon dioxide.

Van Helmont found it difficult to study the gases because as soon as they formed, they mixed with air and faded away. However, about one hundred years later an English minister, Stephen Hales, thought of a way to prevent that diffusion.

Hales let the gas bubbles form in a vessel whose only opening was a bent pipe. The pipe led under water, into the mouth of an upsidedown water-filled bottle. The bubbles traveled through the pipe and up into the bottle, forcing out the water, giving Hales a bottle full of some particular gas, with which he could then experiment.

## Priestley's New Drink

Unfortunately, some gases could not be collected in a water-filled bottle because they dissolve in water. However, about 1770, another English minister, Joseph Priestley, substituted mercury for water. Gases did not dissolve in mercury, so it could be used to collect any gas.

Priestley collected van Helmont's two gases by using mercury. He was particularly interested in carbon dioxide. Once he had collected the gas over mercury, he dissolved some in water and found that a pleasant drink resulted. He had invented soda water.

Priestley also collected the gases ammonia, hydrogen chloride, and sulfur dioxide and he discovered oxygen. Obviously, there were dozens of different gases.

## A Burning Issue

About the same time that Priestley was discovering gases, in the 1770's, the French chemist Antoine-Laurent Lavoisier (lah-vwah-ZYAY) was wrapped up in the problem of combustion. Combustion—that is, the burning or rusting of substances in air—was a process that nobody really understood.

Of course, Lavoisier wasn't the first to study combustion. But he had an advantage over his predecessors: He firmly believed that accurate measurements were important in an experiment. The idea of making careful measurements was not new. It had been introduced two hundred years before by Galileo. However, it was Lavoisier who extended the idea to chemistry.

Therefore, Lavoisier didn't just watch substances burning and examine the ash that was left behind. And he didn't just watch metals rusting and examine the rust, that is, the dull or crumbly substance that formed on their surface. Before a substance burned or rusted, he carefully measured its weight. And after combustion he weighed it again.

At first these measurements brought only confusion. Wood burned and the ash it left behind was much *lighter* than the original wood. A candle burned and was gone altogether; nothing at all was left behind. Lavoisier and some friends bought a small diamond and heated it until it also burned. That vanished, too. Did burning a material destroy part or all of its substance?

On the other hand, Lavoisier found that when metals rusted, the rust was *heavier* than the original metal. Additional solid material seemed to come from nowhere. Why should rusting add matter, while burning seemed to destroy it?

## A Weighty Problem

Earlier chemists had not worried very much about such things because they weren't acustomed to weighing their chemicals. Lighter? Heavier? What difference did it make?

But Lavoisier worried about it. Did burned material vanish into thin air? Ah, perhaps that was it. If substances formed gases when they burned, wouldn't those gases do just that? Wouldn't they mix with the air and vanish into it?

Van Helmont had shown that burning wood produced carbon dioxide. Lavoisier had obtained the same gas from his burning diamond. Thus, it was certain that combustion could produce gas. But *how much* gas was formed? Was it enough to make up for the loss of weight?

Lavoisier thought that might be the case. About twenty years earlier a Scottish chemist, Joseph Black, had heated limestone (calcium carbonate) and found that it released carbon dioxide. The limestone lost weight, but the weight of the gas produced equaled that lost weight.

"Well then," Lavoisier thought, "suppose a burning substance loses weight because it releases a gas. Then what about metals? Did they gain weight when they rust because they combine with a gas?"

Black's work again provided a clue. He had bubbled carbon dioxide gas through limewater (a solution of calcium hydroxide), and the gas and calcium hydroxide combined to form powdered limestone. If calcium hydroxide could combine with a gas to form another substance, Lavoisier thought, then perhaps metals did the same.

*Locking Air Out*

Thus, Lavoisier had good reason to suspect that gases were behind the weight changes that resulted from combustion. But how would he prove his suspicion? Weighing ashes and rusts was not enough; he also would have to weigh the gases.

However, the wide blanket of air that encircles the earth created a problem. How could he weigh gases that escaped from burning objects into the air? On the other hand, how could he determine the amount of gas that left the air to combine with a metal, when more air would rush in to take its place?

The answer, Lavoisier realized, was to lock in the gases and lock out all but a definite amount of air. He could do both by conducting his chemical reactions in a sealed container. Then, if a substance inside it burned and released gases, they would be captured in the container. If a substance rusted and combined with gases, they would come only from the air inside the container.

*Weighing the Evidence*

Lavoisier began by carefully weighing the container with the solid substance and air sealed inside it. He heated the enclosed substance by focusing sunlight on it with a large magnifying glass or by building a fire under it. When the substance had burned or rusted, he again weighed the container with its contents.

He repeated the process with a number of different substances. In every case, regardless of what it was that burned or rusted, the sealed container showed no change in weight.

Suppose, for example, a piece of wood burned to an ash, which of course weighed less than the wood. The weight of the gas released by the wood made up the missing weight. Therefore, the weight of the container remained the same.

Suppose a piece of iron absorbed gas from the air in the container and changed into rust. The rust was heavier than the iron. However, the weight gained was exactly offset by the air's loss of weight. Again, the weight of the container did not change.

Lavoisier's experiments and measurements had a great influence on the development of chemistry. They laid the groundwork for his interpretation of combustion, the interpretation we still use today. The experiments also led him to conclude that matter could be neither created nor destroyed; it could only change from one form to another (for example, from solid substance to gas).

This is the famous "law of conservation of matter." This idea that matter is indestructible made it easier to accept, thirty years later, the theory that matter is made up of indestructible atoms.

Both the law of conservation of matter and the atomic theory have been improved and slightly changed in the twentieth century. On the whole, however, they form the strong and sturdy platform on which modern chemistry stands. For his part in building this platform, Lavoisier is commonly called the "father of modern chemistry."

## from THE LIVING COMMUNITY: A VENTURE INTO ECOLOGY

### S. Carl Hirsch

*This selection provides a provocative statement about man's plight and his potential for extricating himself from the intricate network of problems he has created. In this final chapter of* The Living Community, *which won the Thomas Alva Edison Award for the best science book of the year, Hirsch points out the significance of ecological balance in determining the future of man on earth. His distinguished prose is used to good advantage in ending the book on an optimistic and inspirational note.*

### No Place Like Oikos[1]

No man is an island, entire of itself; every man is a piece of the continent, a part of the main; if a clod be washed away by the sea, Europe is the less, as well as if a promontory were, as well as if a manor of thy friends or of thine own were. . . .
—John Donne, *Devotions*

Great men seem to free us from a narrow and short-sighted view of things.

Columbus sailed boldly toward the riddle beyond the rim of the sea. Galileo extended man's vision to the distant stars.

Charles Darwin gave life on earth its true dimension of time. His measuring units were not years but generations, thousands of them. And after Darwin, man could at last look back and see how far the road of evolution stretched behind him.

Darwin also disclosed the unity of all life on the planet by showing how organisms relate to one another. Out of Darwin's insight came a new era in biology—and the beginnings of the science of ecology.

In the latter half of the nineteenth century,

[1] "The name 'ecology' was formed about a hundred years ago out of the Greek word *oikos*, which means 'home.' Ecology is the study of the home life of living things, how they relate to one another and to their nonliving environment." *The Living Community*, p. 19

the life sciences moved ahead rapidly. During this period it was proved that organisms come only from other living organisms. The cell theory was expanded to explain the structure of all living things. The germ theory explained the cause of many diseases and revealed parasitic life in its smallest forms.

In this setting of discovery, the science of ecology began its own special approach to life. Ecology is rooted in the truth that neither man nor any species can live alone. And its chief concern is with the ways of living together.

Living beings are dependent on one another, linked by food chains. They are joined by cycles which circulate the energy and the chemical substances needed for life. Species act as a check on one another, so that populations are kept within livable limits. Species tend to find the niches in which they can live satisfactorily. And they can sometimes adapt to new niches when and where they are available.

These are some of the principles with which the ecologist works. He studies life within the structure of the living community. Just as one cell is a unit within a multi-celled organism, so is a single community a unit of nature. The community can exist in an area as small as a drop of pond water or a bit of soil, or in a territory as wide as the earth. It is always possible to draw a larger circle around a smaller one. Similarly, the community can always be considered not only as an individual unit but also as a part of a larger unit.

Today, the science of ecology, still very young, offers much to the person who will enter its many fields of search and service. It is no longer possible to find new continents in sailing ships, but the undiscovered worlds of ecology remain.

One may travel around the world, as Darwin did, or like Thoreau, stay close to home.

To Thoreau, there were a thousand fascinating worlds of nature right in his own community. "I have traveled widely around Concord," he once said.

The intricate patterns of ecology may be traced in a woodlot or a millpond. The experiments of ecology can be homemade in a backyard garden, in a miniature zoo, in a classroom aquarium. Countless living communities may be studied without any need to capture, kill, or collect.

There are mysteries in the marsh. There are the strange and special ecologies of whales and wasps, of insect-eating plants and slave-keeping ants. There is the desert, with its moisture-holding plants and dry-skinned animals that seem to come alive only after the blazing sun has burned itself down on the horizon. There are the fascinating surface waters of the sea, where plant and animal life shimmers in the night—a world that intrigued young Darwin as he dragged a net from the stern of the *Beagle*.

While other branches of biology go deeply into the details of life processes, ecology offers a broader, far-ranging view. Other biologists reduce living matter to smaller and smaller fragments for study, but ecologists are concerned with the larger and more complex levels of organized living.

In dealing with the way that individuals and groups react to one another and to their surroundings, the ecologist is faced with the greatest challenge of all in his attempt to comprehend the role man plays today in changing the environment on a global scale.

Ecology devotes itself to studying, describing, and understanding the total community. This young science is called on increasingly to help *solve* the urgent problems of a man-transformed world.

The handprint of man can be found on almost every landscape. If the result is ugly in some places, it is pleasing in others.

Nature has its way with the land. But there is also man-made beauty in a hedgerow of willows, in a peaceful village, in a patchwork of grain fields and orchards.

Man's works include the rice terraces in the Philippines and the towers of the great cities, the lemon groves reclaimed from the Sahara Desert and the tulip beds that Holland won back from the sea.

Some of man's best efforts are those that blend with nature. And these include the great public parks of America, the sanctuaries for wildlife, and the growing number of areas set aside as wilderness.

"We need the tonic of wilderness," Thoreau once wrote, "to wade sometimes in marshes where the bittern and the meadow-hen lurk, and hear the booming of the snipe; to smell the whispering sedge where only some wilder and more solitary fowl builds her nest, and the mink crawls with its belly close to the ground."

These wild areas are where we can learn most about nature. The wilderness is a matchless laboratory. Its value is boundless. This is also where we fulfill the deep human need for a warmer kinship with the creatures and the vegetation with which we share the planet.

And yet, few of us can wander off at will to some woodland Walden where life is primitive and simple. We have new ways of life and will not return to the past.

Modern man is part of a more complex society that has built new modes of living. The man-made communities grow larger and more remote from the wild world of nature. In building an advancing civilization, man is carried forward to new environments.

Each day brings new inventions and improved technology that modify the conditions of life. But there are a number of unwanted changes that follow in the stream of progress as well.

For example, the air and water of many cities and industrial communities have been fouled and polluted. Dirty streams and lakes are not only ugly but also injurious to health. Foul air is not only unpleasant but poisonous as well.

A thick gray veil hangs over many cities. It carries smoke and fumes, dust and ash. Many of the noxious substances are the products of burning fuels. Some of the most dangerous of all pollutants cannot be seen. They travel invisibly across the globe. Traces of the insect poison DDT have shown up throughout the world, wherever samples of the atmosphere have been analyzed. Radioactive substances, the products of nuclear-bomb tests, have appeared in varying quantities on every continent.

Some of the dangerous substances not only travel in the atmosphere but also enter into food chains. Insecticides have been traced from plants to birds and mammals. Radioactive substances originating in the explosions of nuclear weapons fall out of the atmosphere onto the grass of a cow pasture, and then appear in cow's milk.

Many human ailments can be traced directly or indirectly to contaminated air and water.

There may be unknown long-range effects on health as well.

In the record of life on earth, no species has survived in a changing environment for which it was not fitted. Certain plants and animals find it impossible to live in modern cities. Lichens, hardy enough to survive in some of the most difficult environmental conditions on earth, have long been disappearing from industrial areas.

Can such communities be made safe and healthful? Can their residents be assured of the clean air and fresh water that are so essential to human life?

It may require man's highest intelligence to solve such problems. It may take the full resources of the sciences—including the science of ecology.

As a science, ecology has no hard boundaries. It is naturally linked with many neighboring sciences.

The work of ecologists brings them into contact with the scientists who study the land and the sea and the climates of the earth. They share ideas with biologists who probe the structure and behavior and development of organisms.

In turn, other scientists have found great value in the viewpoint of ecology. For example, medical scientists see the importance of applying the ecological approach to the problems of disease and health. Typhus carried by fleas that infest rats could be controlled only through some understanding of the ecology of rats. The mosquitoes that spread malaria cannot be dealt with apart from their full natural environment.

Gradually the idea has taken hold that the health of nature carries along with it the health of mankind. Man survives only as a member of the total community. His food, safety, and well-being are linked with the welfare of all other living things.

In some branches of science, man acquires immense power to change the earth. In other scientific studies—such as ecology—he can find greater wisdom in using that power for the benefit of earth's living community.

By scientifically prolonging human life, man has rapidly increased his numbers on earth—without solving the problem of feeding them all. In applying the principles of ecology to food production, there is greater hope for the half of the earth's people who still live in hunger and want.

Modern man's advances in technology have led to the pollution of the air and water of many regions. Ecology offers some guidance in restoring healthful conditions.

In modern times, man has become the greatest challenge to his own survival. With nuclear weapons, he has become capable of turning vast areas—or even the earth itself—into an environment where nothing can live. Ecology points instead toward goals which sustain life. Every shred of truth that this science has gathered affirms that the earth can be a peaceful and orderly community, based on the interdependence which unites the human species and links mankind with all other living things.

Man has shown great skill both in adjusting to changes in his environment and in creating new conditions in which he can live. In fact, he has made himself at home in some of the most improbable places. He can survive for long periods in the deep seas, in the frigid Antarctic, in altitudes high above the earth. He is venturing into new space environments. Man is even preparing now to transport livable communities with him to the moon, or to Mars. He is solving fantastic problems in space biology and in space ecology.

But as we face the exciting prospects of this last third of the twentieth century, many of the old problems remain. The Greek word *oikos* embraced the idea of the entire world as man's home. And there is no escape from the housekeeping duties on earth. "What is the use of a house," Thoreau asked, two hundred years ago, "if you haven't got a tolerable planet to put it on?"

As we explore new worlds, we are obliged to keep this old one livable. Man is superbly fitted for the earth. It is up to him to keep it a fit place in which to live.

### from WORKSHOPS IN SPACE

*Ben Bova*

*Ben Bova, author of many books on science as well as science fiction, has—as many of the best science writers do—an ability to communi-cate his own sense of excitement in the wonders of his subject without ever insisting that his readers enjoy it, too. Therefore we are free to enjoy it all the more. In this selection from* Workshops in Space, *he describes in vigorous prose the Skylab launch and the urgent repair mission, but the focus of the book is on the information that has already been gathered, on the usefulness of that information for solving geological, agricultural, and meteorological problems. Bova ends with a discussion of the costs of space flight and the possibility of lower-ing them by using a reusable space shuttle.*

### The Lessons of Skylab

Ever since the earliest days of the space pro-gram, experts have argued that space exploration should be carried out entirely by unmanned spacecraft.

They point out that it is difficult for a man to live and work in space. And dangerous. Un-manned spacecraft can carry instruments and sensors without risking the lives of human as-tronauts. Humans must be protected against harmful radiation, cradled in padded couches, covered with bulky pressure suits. They need oxygen, water, food. Manned spacecraft are a hundred times more expensive and intricate than unmanned ones.

In exploring the Moon, the Soviet Union used unmanned vehicles that were remotely con-trolled from Earth. These robot vehicles even collected rock samples and returned them to Russia. There is no doubt that the Russian lunar exploration effort was less expensive than our Apollo program. Certainly it risked no lives.

Yet the Apollo program brought back far more information, performed many more varied experiments, and captured the imaginations of people all across the world. The Apollo astro-nauts were able to see more, learn more, do

From *Workshops in Space* by Ben Bova. Copyright © 1974 by Ben Bova. Reprinted by permission of the pub-lishers, E. P. Dutton & Co., Inc. and Robert P. Mills, Ltd., Literary Agency

more on the Moon's rugged surface than any remotely controlled piece of machinery could accomplish.

And when most people think of space ex-ploration, they think in terms of human astro-nauts doing the exploring. Of course, unmanned probes go first to scout the way. But ultimately the thrill of exploring space comes when human beings step out into new territory.

Is this sheer emotionalism? Would it be better to use only unmanned space probes, and forget about sending astronauts into the unknown? The results of the Apollo program seem to show that the astronauts collected far more knowledge about the Moon than the Russian robot probes. But was the extra information worth the extra cost?

In Phase II of the space program, where our attention is focused on our own planet Earth, this question is still extremely important. Should we concentrate our Phase II efforts on un-manned satellites, or would we get more for our money by sending astronauts into orbit?

The Skylab program was, in part, an attempt to answer that question.

The broad goals of Skylab were to place sev-eral teams of astronauts into Earth orbit for periods of one to three months for four main objectives: 1) studying the Earth from orbit; 2) studying the Sun; 3) studying the perform-ance of human beings under long-term con-ditions of weightlessness; and 4) examining new manufacturing processes that utilize the advan-tages of weightlessness.

Almost immediately, things started to go wrong.

The Skylab launch was originally set for late 1972. This date was postponed several times, until the Skylab was finally launched May 14, 1973.

The plan was to launch the Skylab itself and place it in orbit, then on the following day launch the first three-man team of astronauts. All of the hardware involved in the program, incidentally, came out of the Apollo program. The Skylab boosters were Saturn rockets that hadn't been used during the Apollo effort. The astronauts' spacecraft were Apollo Command Modules, the same craft that carried men to the Moon and returned them to safe splashdowns here on Earth. The Skylab itself was a specially modified section of an upper stage of a Saturn IV-B rocket.

The trouble came early.

It came from a relatively minor error. But it caused major difficulties.

The Skylab's main section—called the Orbital Workshop—was protected by meteoroid shields. These are sheets of aluminum foil, only .06 centimeter thick (.025 inch), which will stop microscopic particles of space dust from hitting the main walls of the Workshop. While the chances of having the Skylab hit by a meteor big enough to puncture the main walls were practically nil, there is a constant hail of what astronomers call meteoric dust; and the meteoroid shield was designed to keep these microscopic particles from grinding against the Workshop's hull and eventually damaging it.

The shields were designed to swing away from the Workshop's hull a distance to 12.7 centimeters (5 inches) when the Skylab was safely in orbit. One of the shields accidentally swung out only 63 seconds after launch, while the booster rocket was still climbing through the atmosphere. The shield was immediately ripped away, just as a raindrop is sluiced off the windshield of a fast-moving car.

When the meteoroid shield pulled off, it jammed one of the solar panels and ripped the other one off the Workshop completely. The solar panels are arrays of specially designed solar cells (or batteries) that convert sunlight into electricity. The jammed solar panel couldn't be extended when orbit was achieved, and so couldn't catch sunlight and produce electricity for Skylab's equipment. So Skylab went into orbit with only a fraction of its planned 10.5 kilowatts of electric power available.

Not only that, but the meteoroid shield also served as a heat (or thermal) insulator for the interior of the Workshop. Up in orbit, a spacecraft that's exposed to the Sun's unfiltered intensity will quickly heat up to impossible temperatures, unless it has the proper thermal insulation. Without the "sunshade" protection of the meteoroid shield, the Workshop quickly became too hot to live in.

If Skylab had been an unmanned craft, the entire mission would have ended right there—63 seconds after launch. The Skylab got into orbit, but it only had half its electrical power, and it was getting too hot to be used. Not only was it too hot for astronauts to live in, but the heat threatened to fog the film in Skylab's cameras and damage or destroy many other sensitive pieces of equipment. In its damaged condition, Skylab was useless.

And that's where the astronauts came to the rescue: as repairmen. Eleven days after Skylab's launch, on May 25, 1973, astronauts Charles ("Pete") Conrad, Paul Weitz, and Joseph Kerwin were launched from Kennedy Space Flight Center. Their primary mission was to save the billion-dollar Skylab from complete failure.

It had been a frantic eleven days. At several National Aeronautics and Space Administration (NASA) centers, engineers and the astronauts worked madly to find ways to fix the damaged Workshop. The astronauts practiced making the needed repairs in a huge water-filled tank that contained a complete Skylab spacecraft. Wearing their spacesuits, and buoyed by the water to simulate the zero-gravity conditions in orbit, the astronauts and their colleagues worked out the techniques for repairing the Workshop.

Within a few hours of their arrival in the orbiting Skylab, a new "solar parasol" was protecting the Workshop from the Sun's heat. Things were getting down to normal. After several attempts, the astronauts freed the jammed solar panel, and the electrical power in the Workshop went up dramatically. The astronauts worked and lived in zero gravity for the remainder of their planned mission, then successfully returned to Earth.

The Skylab's second and third three-man teams also had their share of difficulties during their 56-day and 83-day missions in orbit. But they overcame them and concluded the Skylab program successfully.

It may sound strange to say that the first job for Skylab's astronauts was that of repairmen, but this is precisely one of the main reasons why men are needed in orbit. Unmanned spacecraft can become useless because one key component— a transistor or a solar panel—has failed. The unmanned spacecraft cannot repair itself. Human astronauts can find out what is wrong, and then fix it.

*part four*

# TIME FOR CHILDREN'S LITERATURE

*Milestones in Children's Literature*

*Illustrations in Children's Books*

*Guiding Literary Experience*

*Children's Book Awards*

*Bibliography*

# MILESTONES IN CHILDREN'S LITERATURE[1]

**1484**  Aesop's Fables, translated and printed by William Caxton

Illustration by William Caxton for *Aesop's Fables*

These fables were originally intended for adult reading, but the children probably heard them read aloud and took them over. Later, in 1692, Sir Roger l'Estrange put out a special children's edition.

**c. 1600**  Hornbooks and battledores

From the fifteenth through the eighteenth centuries these were used to teach children the alphabet and numbers. Their importance lies in the fact that for the first time printed, educational material was put into children's own hands.

**1646**  Spiritual Milk for Boston Babes, John Cotton

This tedious theological treatise in catechism form was designed, alas, for the edification of the young; it is important only because it was one of the earliest children's books to be imported from England.

**1657 or 1658**  Orbis Pictus, Comenius

Generally considered to be the earliest picture book for children, *Orbis Pictus (The World Illustrated)* was certainly the first book we know to use explanatory pictures to amplify a word's meaning, much as the modern primer does.

**1678**  Pilgrim's Progress, John Bunyan

Children probably skipped the long, moralizing interludes and read with pleasure the dramatic story which was intended for adults. For generations it inspired children to act out its episodes and artists to illustrate many editions.

[1] These dates have been checked and double-checked, but agreement over precise dates is apparently impossible because some sources give the date of writing, others the date of copywriting or first publication or publication in the United States.

**1691**  The New England Primer

Almost as depressing as the *Spiritual Milk,* this little primer inducted New England children into the joys of reading.

**1697**  Contes de ma Mère l'Oye, Perrault

In France appeared *Histoires ou Contes du Temps Passé avec des Moralités,* popularly called *Contes de ma Mère l'Oye.* These eight famous folk tales—The Sleeping Beauty, Cinderella, Puss in Boots, Little Red Riding Hood, Bluebeard, Riquet with the Tuft, Little Thumb, Diamonds and Toads—are still beloved by children.

**1715**  Divine and Moral Songs for Children, Isaac Watts

Realizing that poetry makes words easily remembered, Watts fashioned moralistic verses and wonderful hymns, the former for children, the latter for all ages. *Divine and Moral Songs* was originally titled *Divine Songs Attempted in Easy Language for the Use of Children.*

**1719**  Robinson Crusoe, Daniel Defoe

Adventure at last! Defoe, pamphleteer and satirist, in trouble politically and religiously most of his life, turned out the memorable story of a lone man, marooned on an island, creating and controlling a savage world.

**1726**  Gulliver's Travels, Jonathan Swift

A political satire by the famous Dean of the Dublin Cathedral, *Gulliver's Travels* was not intended for children, but was appropriated by them, in part at least. The miniature world of the Lilliputians is their favorite section and the double meanings do not trouble them.

**1729**  Tales of Mother Goose (first English translation of Perrault's Contes de ma Mère l'Oye)

Perhaps it was from this pioneer translation of the popular folk tales that John Newbery got the idea for the title of his nursery rhyme book.

**1744**  A Little Pretty Pocket-Book

John Newbery's famous first venture into the field of book publishing for children was highly successful. This little miscellany included games, proverbs, fables, a rhymed alphabet, and two moral letters to children signed by Jack the Giant-Killer.

**1765**  Mother Goose's Melody, or Sonnets for the Cradle

The publication date of this work has been open to question, but the Opies (*Oxford Dictionary of Nursery Rhymes*) place it as 1765. However, no copy earlier than T. Carmen's edition of 1780 survives.

**1765** **The History of Little Goody Two-Shoes**
Almost as famous as *A Little Pretty Pocket-Book* and *Mother Goose* is this little novel of the life, sufferings, and successes of the enterprising Margery Meanwell.

**1779** **A Pretty Book of Pictures for Little Masters and Misses; or, Tommy Trip's History of Beasts and Birds, Thomas Bewick**
Bewick's woodcuts were the first book illustrations of high artistic quality and skill for children.

**1785** **Mother Goose's Melodies (Isaiah Thomas edition)**
Publisher W. H. Whitmore vouches for the fact that this was the first American edition of Mother Goose, pirated from Newbery. The 1899 Whitmore edition was titled *The Original Mother Goose's Melody.*

**1789** **Songs of Innocence, William Blake**
Authentic poetry began for children with William Blake's remarkable book. It was followed by *Songs of Experience* in 1794.

**1803** **First public library for children**
Caleb Bingham, author of school texts, remembering the lack of books in his own childhood, gave a children's library to Salisbury, Connecticut. By 1900, many public libraries had children's rooms directed by such great pioneers as Anne Carroll Moore, Caroline Hewins, and Frances Jenkins Olcott.

**1804** **Original Poems for Infant Minds, Ann and Jane Taylor**
In the gently moralistic vein of Isaac Watts, these sisters wrote children's verses that were much loved in their day. In 1806 *Rhymes for the Nursery* appeared.

**1807** **The Butterfly's Ball, William Roscoe**
Enormously popular in its day, this long picture-poem has no story but is full of amusing descriptions of dressy insects, pictured with human faces. William Mulready's illustrations were engraved and then hand-colored in each copy.

**1822** **A Visit from St. Nicholas, Clement C. Moore**
This lively narrative poem has attracted many major artists whose imaginative illustrations have proved as spellbinding as the spirited verse. It was written in 1822, but not published until 1823.

**1823** **Grimm's Popular Stories (translated into English by Edgar Taylor)**
Published in two volumes between the years 1823 and 1826, these unforgettable old tales caught the imagination of English children and of adults as well. The books contained etchings by George Cruikshank, the first English artist to combine fine drawing with imaginative humor in illustrations for children.

**1843** **A Christmas Carol, Charles Dickens**
Perhaps this classic was intended for adults, but how wise children are when they appropriate books that speak to them.

**1846** **Book of Nonsense, Edward Lear**

Illustration from Edward Lear's *Book of Nonsense*

Hilarious jingles with equally absurd pictures constituted England's first contribution to laughter in the evolution of children's books.

**1846** **Fairy Tales, Hans Christian Andersen (first English translation)**
These beautiful stories, sometimes adaptations of folk themes, sometimes completely original, mark the beginning of the modern fanciful tale.

**1846** **Struwwelpeter, Heinrich Hoffmann**
Translated from the German in 1848, *Slovenly Peter* added its humorous exaggerations both in picture and verse to the child's sense of the comic. Here was tongue-in-cheek moralizing about untidiness or fussiness or haughtiness that set both children and grownups chuckling.

**1852** **A Wonder-Book for Girls and Boys, Nathaniel Hawthorne**
Hawthorne's famous retelling of the Greek myths, popular for a long time because of its imaginative and storytelling qualities, is now little used, perhaps because the author reduced the Olympians to child size, sacrificing the stern adult meanings.

**1865** **Alice's Adventures in Wonderland, Lewis Carroll (Charles Lutwidge Dodgson)**

Illustration by Sir John Tenniel for *Through the Looking-Glass* by Lewis Carroll

One of the world's great fantasies came from an Oxford don, a lecturer in logic and mathematics. The nonsensical adventures of Alice in her mad world have a curious logic that is not wholly child-like.

**1865   Hans Brinker, or the Silver Skates, Mary Mapes Dodge**

Written by an American who had never been to Holland, this story of Dutch life and adventure is still good reading and has enjoyed long popularity.

**1865-1876   Sing a Song of Sixpence, illustrated by Walter Crane**

Since Crane's Toy Books were never dated, 1865–1876 is only an approximation of the years in which his picture books appeared. His work marked the beginning of modern color printing and fine design applied to children's books.

**1868-1869   Little Women, Louisa M. Alcott**

This notably realistic classic of family life has been read, reread, laughed and cried over by girls for generations. Issued originally in two parts.

**1872   Sing-Song, Christina Rossetti**

A gifted poet wrote these tender and lovely lyrics for children, their first collection of lyric verse since William Blake.

**1873   St. Nicholas Magazine**

This monthly magazine, edited by Mary Mapes Dodge and published until 1940, was the all-time oustanding periodical for children. It was distinguished for the high quality of its fiction and for its policy of not sermonizing. Alcott, Burnett, Palmer Cox, Kipling, Pyle, Longfellow, and Lucretia Hale were some of the well-known contributors.

**1876   The Adventures of Tom Sawyer, Mark Twain (Samuel Clemens)**

Here is realism and Americana for young readers, written in the vernacular by a great humorist who, in Tom, remembered his own boyhood.

**1877   Black Beauty, Anna Sewell**

Although the horse is overly humanized, this famous book marks the beginning of the popularity of stories about the vicissitudes of animals, both pets and wild creatures.

**1878   Under the Window, Kate Greenaway**

Undistinguished verses about children's play activities are recorded on pages that are pictorial lyrics. The quaint costumes of the characters influenced children's clothes over much of the world.

**1878   The House That Jack Built and The Diverting History of John Gilpin, illustrated by Randolph Caldecott**

Illustration from *Randolph Caldecott's Picture Book*

Continuing in the tradition of Walter Crane, Randolph Caldecott brought the picture book new distinction with his humorous, lively illustrations.

**1880   The Peterkin Papers, Lucretia Hale**

Told with a straight face, these "moron stories" are as fantastic as any of the "Clever Elsies" or sillies of the folk tales.

**1880   The Adventures of Pinocchio, Carlo Lorenzini (pseudonym, C. Collodi)**

From *Le Adventure di Pinocchio* by C. Collodi, illustration by Attilio Mussino. C/E Giunti Bemporad Marzocco, Florence, Italy

This is the children's own epic, themselves in wood, first translated into English and published in the United States in 1892. The beautiful Italian edition illustrated by Attilio Mussino was published in 1929 in this country, opening the way to the rich international exchange of children's books.

**1883   Treasure Island, Robert Louis Stevenson**

Mystery, unforgettable characters, and hair-raising action make this absorbing story by a great storyteller as spellbinding today as ever.

**1883**   Nights with Uncle Remus, Joel Chandler
Harris

Joel Chandler Harris, © 1908, Esther La Rose Harris, *Uncle Remus: His Songs and His Sayings*. Reprinted by permission of Prentice-Hall, Inc. Englewood Cliffs, N.J.

These stories of quickwitted, mischievous Brer Rabbit and his pranks are reminiscent of talking-beast tales of other countries.

**1883**   The Merry Adventures of Robin Hood,
Howard Pyle

Illustration by Howard Pyle for *The Merry Adventures of Robin Hood* by Howard Pyle, Charles Scribner's Sons. Reproduced by permission

For years this was the favorite version of these enchanting hero tales. Pyle's meticulous and beautiful illustrations greatly enhanced the book.

**1884**   Heidi, Johanna Spyri (date of English translation)

The story of the little Swiss girl, her grandfather, and her goats has become a classic. Heidi's great love for the peace and beauty of her mountains speaks to every young reader.

**1884**   The Adventures of Huckleberry Finn, Mark
Twain (Samuel Clemens)

This work is considered by many critics to be the greatest of all Twain's books, but *Tom Sawyer* still holds first place with most young readers.

**1885**   A Child's Garden of Verses, Robert Louis
Stevenson

Said to have been inspired by one of Kate Greenaway's little books, *A Child's Garden of Verses* contains poems as fresh today as ever. Their singing quality and the subject matter make the book a real treasure.

**1889**   The Blue Fairy Book, Andrew Lang

This was the first of Andrew Lang's long series of folk tale collections, named for various colors. His excellent versions popularized the tales.

**1894**   The Jungle Book, Rudyard Kipling

Children were fascinated by this tale of a boy who was raised by wolves and who knew the languages and laws of the jungle.

**1899**   The Story of the Treasure-Seekers, E. Nesbit

This was the first of the much-loved series of stories about the Bastable children, forever intent on restoring the fortune of the family.

**1901**   The Tale of Peter Rabbit, Beatrix Potter

Because this book was written and circulated before the idea of publication occurred to the author there is a conflict about the dates. Percy Muir (*English Children's Books*) insists that the author's own date, 1900, is wrong and 1901 is correct. We know at least that this small picture-story is written and illustrated with consummate skill.

**1903**   Johnny Crow's Garden, L. Leslie Brooke

And the Pig
Danced a Jig

Illustration from *Johnny Crow's Garden*, by L. Leslie Brooke, reproduced by permission of the publisher, Frederick Warne and Company

Leslie Brooke is known for this and for *Ring o' Roses,* a delightful Mother Goose book. Sly humor, excellent drawing, and good use of color mark his picture books.

**1908  Wind in the Willows, Kenneth Grahame**

Written by a master of prose style, *Wind in the Willows* is pure enchantment. It is rich in sensory appeal, peopled with unforgettable characters, full of humor, kindliness, and warmth.

**1919  First children's book department in the United States**

Macmillan was the first American publisher to set up a separate children's book department and Louise Seaman Bechtel was its first editor.

**1919  Children's Book Week**

This week, initiated by Franklin K. Matthews, Chief Librarian of the Boy Scouts, and Frederic G. Melcher of the American Booksellers Association, is still observed annually in schools, libraries, and bookstores.

**1921  The Story of Mankind, Hendrik Willem van Loon**

The first book to receive the Newbery Medal tells the history of man's slow march toward civilization. Van Loon brought to informational writing a whole new approach.

**1921  Here and Now Story Book, Lucy Sprague Mitchell**

Realizing that for children under five there were few if any stories concerned with the child himself and his daily experiences, Mrs. Mitchell set out to supply these tales. Her stories and those of her imitators dispensed with plot and centered on the child's activities, using much of his own talk. These experience stories mostly passed into oblivion but stimulated publishers to provide books for the preschool child.

**1922  Newbery Medal**

Frederic G. Melcher, an American editor and publisher, created this award, which is given annually to the author of the year's "most distinguished contribution to American literature for children," and he named it appropriately for John Newbery, first English publisher of books for children.

**1924  The Horn Book Magazine**

This excellent and discriminating magazine, edited by Bertha Mahony Miller and Elinor Whitney Field, is devoted wholly to the books and reading of children and young people.

**1924  When We Were Very Young, A. A. Milne**

With these deft verses, Christopher Robin joined the juvenile immortals and went gaily on through *Now We Are Six* (1927).

**1926  Winnie-the-Pooh, A. A. Milne**

From *The House at Pooh Corner* by A. A. Milne, illustrations by Ernest H. Shepard. Copyright 1928 by E. P. Dutton & Co.; renewal © 1956 by A. A. Milne. Reproduced by permission of the publishers, E. P. Dutton & Co., Inc.

After the first book of verse, Christopher Robin and Pooh Bear set off on a series of prose adventures that are the essence of straight-faced humor. *The House at Pooh Corner* followed in 1928.

**1926  Smoky, the Cow Horse, Will James**

Written in cowboy vernacular, this is a genuinely moving story of the vulnerability of animals at the hands of unscrupulous men.

**1928  Millions of Cats, Wanda Gág**

Illustration by Wanda Gág. Reprinted by permission of Coward, McCann & Geoghegan, Inc. from *Millions of Cats* by Wanda Gág. Copyright 1928 by Wanda Gág. Copyright renewed 1956 by Wanda Gág

Told and illustrated by an artist steeped in folk tales, *Millions of Cats* paved the way for the "golden years" of the thirties when picture books achieved a new importance.

**1928  Abe Lincoln Grows Up, Carl Sandburg**

Illustration by James Daugherty from *Abe Lincoln Grows Up* by Carl Sandburg, copyright, 1925, 1928 by Harcourt Brace Jovanovich, Inc.; renewed, 1954, 1956 by Carl Sandburg. Reproduced by permission of the publishers

No young person should miss this poignant story cut from the author's adult biography of Lincoln.

**1932    Little House in the Big Woods, Laura Ingalls Wilder**

This is the first of a series of eight books which describe the pioneer experiences of the Ingalls family. The series was reissued in 1953 with splendid, authentic illustrations by Garth Williams.

**1938    Caldecott Medal**

Named in honor of Randolph Caldecott, the English artist and illustrator, this award is given annually to the illustrator of the year's "most distinguished American picture book for children."

**1937    The Hobbit, J. R. R. Tolkien**

In this book, which stands as a milestone in fantasy, and in the succeeding trilogy, *Lord of the Rings,* Tolkien has created an ancient world of small people which is completely fascinating to young and adult readers alike.

**1941    George Washington's World, Genevieve Foster**

This is the first of the author's *World* books which give a horizontal view of life around the world at the different periods of each man's life. These books provide children with a rounded sense of period, seldom found in a textbook.

**1941    Paddle-to-the-Sea, Holling C. Holling**

With simple and dramatic text and glowing illustrations there are combined anthropology, geography, science, history, and imagination, all of which give Holling's books timeless interest and values.

**1943    Homer Price, Robert McCloskey**

Illustration from *Homer Price* by Robert McCloskey. Copyright 1943, copyright © renewed 1971 by Robert McCloskey. Reprinted by permission of The Viking Press, Inc.

McCloskey wrote and illustrated this humorous classic about and for today's children.

**1943    Johnny Tremain, Esther Forbes**

The story of a silversmith's apprentice during the Revolutionary War marks a high point in American historical fiction for children.

**1944    The Hundred Dresses, Eleanor Estes**

The sad story of Wanda Petronski, who is scorned by her classmates, is one of the first fine stories of a child who is different.

**1947    Canadian Library Awards**

Given annually to outstanding children's books, one in English and, since 1954, one in French. An award for illustration was added in 1971.

**1950    The Lion, the Witch, and the Wardrobe, C. S. Lewis**

C. S. Lewis, English scholar and theologian, wrote seven entrancing fantasies (this is the first) about the mythical land of Narnia.

**1952    Charlotte's Web, E. B. White**

Illustration by Garth Williams from *Charlotte's Web* by E. B. White. Copyright © 1952 by E. B. White. Reprinted by permission of Harper & Row, Publishers, Inc., and Hamish Hamilton Children's Books Ltd., London (U.K. publishers)

Quite probably the best-loved American book for children written this century! The warmth, humor, and pathos of the story of Charlotte's efforts to save Wilbur have endeared it to all ages.

**1952    Anne Frank: Diary of a Young Girl**

It is possible that this haunting diary of a little Jewish girl who lived from her thirteenth to fifteenth year in a wretched hideout and finally died in the Nazi camp at Bergen-Belsen will be too poignant for some young readers to endure.

**1954** **Laura Ingalls Wilder Award**
Given at five-year intervals to an author or illustrator whose books published in the United States have made a lasting contribution to literature for children, this award was first presented to Laura Ingalls Wilder for her "Little House" books.

**1954** **U.S. Supreme Court decision barring segregation in the public schools**
Since the Court decision and along with the growth in the civil rights movement, an increasing number of children's books by and about blacks have been published—poetry, fiction, picture books, biography, and informational books.

**1956** **Hans Christian Andersen Award**
The first international book award was established to be presented every two years to a living author who has made an outstanding contribution to children's literature. In 1966 the award was expanded to include an illustrator as well.

**1957** **The Cat in the Hat, Dr. Seuss (pseudonym for Theodor Seuss Geisel)**

Illustration from *The Cat in the Hat,* by Dr. Seuss. Copyright © 1957 by Dr. Seuss. Reprinted by permission of Random House, Inc., and Wm. Collins & Co. Ltd., London

This preposterous fantasy pioneered the way for easy-to-read books, which aim to give readers a sense of fluency and a growing confidence in their own ability.

**1958** **The Sea Around Us, Rachel Carson**
This outstanding science writer's fascinating story of the sea, first published in 1951, appeared in an adaptation for young readers.

**1960s** **Children's paperback books**
Flexibility, wide choice, economy, and informality are some of the reasons for the great impact of paperbacks on children's reading, a growing trend that began in the '60s.

**1962** **The Snowy Day, Ezra Jack Keats**
The innovative illustrations in this book won the Caldecott Award for the author-artist; however, of more significance was the fact that this was one of the first picture books with which black children could identify.

**1962** **The Work of Meindert DeJong**
For the body of his work, DeJong was awarded the Hans Christian Andersen Medal.

**1964** **The Book of Three, Lloyd Alexander**
In this first book and the succeeding ones in the series about the mythical kingdom of Prydain, Lloyd Alexander has written some of the finest fantasy of our time. The fifth and final book, *The High King,* won the Newbery Award.

**1964** **Harriet the Spy, Louise Fitzhugh**
Completely contemporaneous! Harriet is popular with children and heartily disliked by some adults. Whether or not Harriet survives is not important; it is her very immediacy that gives her significance.

**1964** **Consultant in Children's Literature, Library of Congress**
The establishment of this position gave national recognition to the importance of the field of children's literature.

**1966** **Mildred L. Batchelder Award**
The American Library Association established an annual award for the most outstanding translation of a book first published in a foreign language in a foreign country.

**1968** **Council on Interracial Books for Children Award**
Awards are made annually for unpublished manuscripts in each of five minority groups.

**1969** **National Book Award for Children's Literature**
Beginning this year, an award was presented annually to the most distinguished children's book written by an American citizen and published in the United States in the preceding year.

**1970** **The Work of Maurice Sendak**
For the body of his work, Sendak was awarded the Hans Christian Andersen Medal.

**1972** **The Children's Book Showcase**
The Children's Book Council established an

annual exhibit of books chosen as the best designed and illustrated titles of the previous year.

**1972**  **The Work of Scott O'Dell**

For the body of his work, O'Dell was awarded the Hans Christian Andersen Medal.

**1972**  **Watership Down, Richard Adams**

Winner of Britain's Carnegie Medal, the book was published in the United States in 1974; in both countries it became an instant classic.

**1974**  **M. C. Higgins, the Great, Virginia Hamilton**

This was the first book to win both the Newbery Medal and the National Book Award.

# ILLUSTRATIONS IN CHILDREN'S BOOKS

*by Donnarae MacCann and Olga Richard*

Children have an extraordinary capacity for visual discovery and enjoyment. Watch young children's involvement with good picture books and see how thoroughly their eyes explore everything on the page, how responsive they are to the artist's ingenuity and skill. Pictures in children's books should include the vitality, imagination, and good craftsmanship which sustain and increase this visual pleasure.

Many artists have made a serious effort to develop the picture space with impressive arrangements of colors, lines, shapes, and textures. Children who see these illustrations encounter the keen perception and originality that characterize art. They encounter, as well, a delightful form of diversion.

Bringing children and books together is an opportunity which should be used to full advantage; this can happen only if we are able to discern good book illustrations as well as good texts. Adults often describe illustrations as beautiful, charming, vigorous, sweet, humorous, and so on. Such terms do indicate some qualities evident in good graphic art, but they do not convey the uniqueness of the individual artist's work. In order to assess any illustrations, we need to consider the elements of the visual language and the specific way in which they are used. Before a drawing can be "vigorous," it must be an assemblage of certain art elements such as line, color, shape, or pattern. For example, the artist may have chosen to use line or shape. So we ask, did he or she assemble these lines or shapes in an original, personal manner? Have these elements alone been used? If so, how? Is the style different from the style used by another artist, or do we have the feeling that we have seen such illustrations before? Is the artist consistent from one illustration to the next or do some look as if he or she has spent more time on some than on others? Is there a visual continuity as one turns the pages—that is, has the same assortment of elements been used? Has the artist shown concern for all the picture space; does it all have visual interest?

These seven questions can be used to initiate a visual inquiry for almost any illustration and any book. It is only through this kind of close analysis that one can understand how illustrations happen to be vigorous or tranquil, creative or stereotyped. Our emotional reaction does not happen by chance but is the result of deliberate choices made by the artist.

This kind of approach was used for this survey of illustrations in children's books, irrespective of the historical era under consideration. It was the basis for appraising new books because no other criteria are as valid for estimating the long-range importance and lasting significance of a book's graphic art. If illustrations do not hold up well in the mainstream of the visual arts, the book's longevity will depend upon other factors. It may rest upon the book's literary strength—plot and characterization, for example, and whatever the illustrations contribute to the pictorialization of these elements. In such cases, the pictures offer pale reflections of literary content rather than new, vital extensions of that content.

Only a few examples of children's book illustrations are reproduced here in this chapter. To sharpen your perceptions and acquaint yourself with some of the excellent work that has been and is being done in this area, browse frequently in libraries and bookstores. The artists and books cited here are a good starting point.

## THE CHILD AUDIENCE

As in literature, where such elements as originality and sensitive characterization are desirable in books for both children and adults, in the field of graphic art there are overlapping criteria. We look for spontaneity, a compelling design, and a close coordination with the text in illustrations intended for any audience. But it is worth noting distinctive qualities important in books for children. The child's age makes a difference in a book's literary features because very young children usually require brevity and a direct, concrete presentation. But their response to pictures is not affected by a short attention span; the various features in a work of graphic art are there to be seen all at once. This makes even intricate illustrations accessible at an early age. It is impossible to list standards of "attractiveness" which appeal to all children, other than the purely aesthetic standards which are used to assess the worth of all visual art. Anything else runs into a barrier of bias conditioned by time, geography, personal backgrounds, and individual idiosyncrasies.

The children's book illustrator does not forget the particular way children perceive and respond to the world around them, and the most fundamental aspect of the child's view is that it is an uninhibited vision. One children's book illustrator, Roger Duvoisin, has noted that while adults have long practiced the habit of seeing only what interests them, children see practically everything. He writes,

> The child's interests are infinite and he sees the tiniest details of his world as well as the biggest forms. And he does not say, "I do not understand." He looks and sees. He lives among wonders and the children's book artist only has to take him by the hand, so to speak, to lead him toward the most imaginative adventures.[1]

This receptivity is seen in the fact that there are popular books whose pictures are relatively complex (Leo Lionni's *Swimmy,* 1963), simple (Bruno Munari's *ABC,* 1960), colorful (Brian Wildsmith's *The Lion and the Rat,* 1963), black and white (Wanda Gág's *Millions of Cats,* 1928), abstract (Saul Bass' *Henri's Walk to Paris,* text by Leonore Klein, 1962), realistic (Lynd Ward's *The Biggest Bear,* 1952), impressionistic (Hans Fischer's *The Traveling Musicians,* 1955), and expressionistic (Antonio Frasconi's *The House That Jack Built,* 1958).

Another quality of childhood reflected in books is the child's keen appreciation of humor. This is not a limitation on illustrators, but simply one facet of their audience which they may wish to cater to. When the humor in a book depends upon associations or incongruities of some kind, authors and illustrators must remember what a typical child's background includes in order to make the associations clear. This requirement was not realized in the book that surprisingly won the National Book Award in children's literature in 1971: *The Slightly Irregular Fire Engine, or the Hithering Thithering Djinn* by author-illustrator Donald Barthelme. To fully enjoy this book the child would need

Illustration from *Snail, Where Are You?* by Tomi Ungerer. Copyright © 1962 by Tomi Ungerer

Ungerer makes a simple, direct, large brown shape to portray a mountain goat's head, neck, and shoulders. He outlines and also details the interior of the shape with a brush-like line that varies in thickness. This is an uncluttered, almost stark, image with a strong visual impact. The snail form appears in the scroll detail of the horns (as it appears in the tail of a pig, on the caps of waves, elsewhere in simple disguises on every page).

[1] Roger Duvoisin. "Children's Book Illustration: The Pleasures and Problems," in *Top of the News,* November 1965, p. 31.

an adult's historical perspective because the humor stems from nineteenth-century magazine illustrations or facsimiles. These are scattered across the pages alongside nineteenth-century advertisements for patent medicines and other things ("Hydrath of Cloral . . . Balm of Peace to Nervous Spirits"). The effect is bizarre enough to offer some interest, but the humorous point will escape many children.

It must be admitted that Barthelme approached this book in the spirit of play, and this is one of the general characteristics of the child's relation to the world. The children's book illustrator needs to remember his or her own childhood playfulness and observe the play of modern children. This is not difficult because the fine arts, including graphics in books, are involved with many of the same features that characterize play: challenge, discipline, improvisation, curiosity, discovery, excitement, anticipation, fulfillment, interest. Paul Rand, book illustrator and professor of art at Yale, has discussed the play principle in its relation to design, and some of his children's books, with texts by Ann Rand, are excellent models: *I Know a Lot of Things* (1956) and *Sparkle and Spin* (1957).[2] Rand reveals for the child the possible interplay between a known object such as a mushroom or cartload of wood and these objects as they are imagined and handled whimsically.

In an interesting research project, a child's drawing proved less interesting to children of five and six years of age than a picture which presented a more complete rendering. A carefully planned experiment by psychologist Wolfgang Metzger showed that children were extremely inattentive to drawings by other children, and from this he has deduced that they would not find self-conscious imitations of children's drawings attractive.[3] When such imitations appear in books, the illustrator's approach has undoubtedly been a superficial one. The pictures are affectations and lack the significant

characteristics of children's art works: "spontaneous invention, emotional intensity, a natural use of the visual language." These qualities are singled out by the distinguished book illustrator Joseph Low as earmarks of what children create themselves and what others should create for them. He writes,

> We need to . . . put before [children] work which matches theirs in imagination and vitality, which does not imitate it in mannerism, certainly, but matches it in kind and goes beyond it in range and clarity.[4]

# ILLUSTRATED BOOKS AND PICTURE BOOKS: EARLY HISTORY

The modern "picture book" is a type of publication which branched off from the "illustrated book." It can be a picture story in the purest sense, with every scene, object, or idea conveyed visually; or it can have illustrations which do not present the entire plot line, but still take more space than in the "illustrated book." The designer of an illustrated book has a predominance of printed text to plan for and only a few illustrations.

Even the earliest printed books in the fifteenth century included some pictures and decorations. The quality of this ornamentation, then as now, depended upon the artist's imagination, commitment to good craftsmanship, and understanding of bookmaking as a unique art. To create a sense of unity on the page—a primary criterion for book illustration and design—the pictures had to blend harmoniously with the appearance of the text. In simplest terms, a drawing or painting had to be visually coordinated with the linear nature of the letters of the alphabet printed in parallel lines in black ink on white paper. This remained the fundamental design problem until

[2] Paul Rand. "Design and the Play Instinct," in *The Education of Vision*, edited by Gyorgy Kepes. Braziller, 1965, p. 174.

[3] Wolfgang Metzger. "The Influence of Aesthetic Examples," in *The Education of Vision*, p. 26.

[4] Joseph Low. "Picture Books," in *The Horn Book Magazine*, December 1967, p. 715.

# THE CROCODILE.

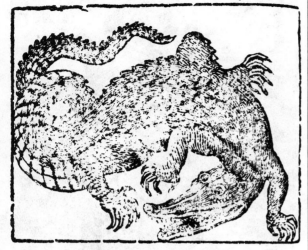

Illustration by Thomas Bewick from *Morning's Amusement; Or Tales of Quadrupeds* by Mrs. C. Mathews. Thomas Wilson & Sons, York, 1809

Bewick's crocodile is dynamic with its varied surface texture and its big, squirmy, swirly shape on a plain white ground.

the invention of photographic processes reproducing colored art works. Then the situation was practically reversed. The unity of the page is still largely affected by the written text in an "illustrated book" because that text dominates the space, but in many children's books since the 1860s the page has consisted primarily of pictures. These pictures often have great complexity of color, texture, and composition, so the problem now in achieving unity on the page is one of handling that black and white linear typeface in some subordinate but harmonious way—especially when this printed text may be only a few words.

Referring to the need for a text to be truly "illustrated" or lighted up, Sir Francis Meynell noted that "book pictures remained no more than 'graphic reminiscences' of the text until the end of the eighteenth century, when the miniature and the giant geniuses of Bewick and Blake possessed the books they decorated." [5]

Thomas Bewick revitalized the woodcut medium and pleased both adults and children in such books as *The History of Quadrupeds*

(1790) and *British Birds* (1797). In his best illustrations he created a dramatic feeling by dividing the background into strong white and gray areas against which simple objects were placed in asymmetrical arrangement. Tonalities (the shadings in the composition) were developed by increasing the distance between lines for lighter areas, and bringing them close together for darker areas. His method of cutting against the grain on hard wood permitted varied textural effects which he utilized simply and sparingly, preferring to leave the object static and stiff. [6] An exception is a spontaneously curved crocodile in the book *Mornings' Amusement; or Tales of Quadrupeds* (1809)—a contrast to the formalized treatment of people and architecture.

George Cruikshank produced animated illustrations, making full use of the tonal effects and fluent line that are characteristic of the etching. In *Grimm's Fairy Tales* (1824), he revealed his skill in creating many modeled forms, using crosshatchings and white to sculpt objects. His pictures include few true blacks except for foreground accents, as in a scarf or shoe. He was a satirical artist—a social crusader—and therefore the ideal illustrator for Charles Dickens's *Oliver Twist* in 1846.

Lithography was first used in book illustrating in the 1820s and it marked a substantial technical advance. Of all the processes available at this date, lithography permitted the least interference with the artist's original design, for it could remain unhampered by a commercial engraver—the professional copier who prepared the printing plates and who was sometimes indifferent to the quality of the original art work. [7] Two books of particular importance, Edward Lear's *Book of Nonsense* (1846) and William Nicholson's *An Alphabet* (1898), were produced by this process, although original designs were also cut in wood. Lear's line was cartoonish, spontaneous, and simple. His proportions were often clumsy and

---

[5] Sir Francis Meynell. *English Printed Books*, 2nd ed. Collins, 1948, pp. 37–38.

[6] A glossary at the end of this chapter provides a definition of "textural effects," "crosshatching," and other terms which may be unfamiliar. Also the technical processes such as etching, lithography, engraving, etc., are simply defined.

[7] Philip James. *English Book Illustration: 1800–1900*. King Penguin Books, 1947, p. 65.

awkward, but his groupings of objects, their size changes, and varying perspectives were refreshing. Nicholson emphasized the shapes of objects in *An Alphabet* by contrasting the light and dark areas sharply. He used few detail lines and those were simple, bold, and heavy—usually culminating in a dark area.

The technology leading to the "picture book" as a distinct category of children's literature developed out of experiments with printing inks and with superimposing wood blocks to reproduce full color paintings in adult picture magazines.[8] Artists who illustrated important children's books found their chief employment on the staffs of such magazines (for example, George Cruikshank, Richard Doyle, Randolph Caldecott).

Edmund Evans, the English printer and wood engraver, began experimenting with color printing in the 1850s. He employed artists Walter Crane, Kate Greenaway, and Randolph Caldecott to make picture books for children, the first notable success being achieved in 1866 with Walter Crane's *Sing a Song of Sixpence*. The modern picture book was now launched as a financially feasible venture.[9]

During this period, as in the previous century, wood engravings were being used creatively in children's illustrated books by such artists as Sir John Tenniel (in Lewis Carroll's *Alice's Adventures in Wonderland* and *Through the Looking Glass,* 1865 and 1871), Richard Doyle (in William Allingham's *In Fairyland,* 1870), and Arthur Hughes (in George Macdonald's *At the Back of the North Wind,* 1871). In *Alice,* Tenniel developed illustrations with hundreds of short, controlled, crosshatched lines. Rich tonalities were achieved, strong mood feelings, and a clear sense of focus and direction in the composition. The book design, however, suffered from insufficient white space around each illustration.

Richard Doyle used close tonalities for the pictures in *In Fairyland,* with tints of soft yel-

Illustration by William Nicholson from *An Alphabet,* circa 1898. Courtesy of the Estate of William Nicholson

Nicholson's light and dark areas are strongly defined as shapes, and the treatment of both line and shape is so minimal as to create partial silhouettes. This simplification of design was a mark of originality in nineteenth-century English illustration.

lows, oranges, blues, and greens to add interest to his simply organized compositions. In a typical illustration that depicts a musical elf teaching young birds to sing, Doyle placed a light oval area in the center of the picture space. The elf is in the upper center of the oval, surrounded by birds, grasses, leaves. All the lines in these objects served to direct the eye to the elf as the center of interest. Each drawing is botanically perfect, and the meticulously drawn lines create richly textured surfaces such as the intricate vein detail on curving leaves. This book, printed by Edmund Evans, was a beneficiary of Evans's successful experiments in color printing with superimposed wood blocks. In earlier wood-engraved books, color had been added by hand by a cheap labor force—frequently young children following a hand-colored model of the illustration.

[8] David Bland. *A History of Book Illustration.* University of California Press, 1969, p. 254.
[9] *Orbis Pictus* or *Visible World* (1658) by John Comenius is commonly referred to as the first children's picture book, but it was an isolated example of a book resembling the picture encyclopedia. It did not establish a trend.

Arthur Hughes used a tight, controlled line for both object outline and interior development in the Macdonald book. Textural effects have been included for all objects (particularly in loose, wind-tossed hair), and he has left white areas throughout each picture to give a quality of light and to build a feeling of shape and depth. His overall design for each illustration is freer and more ingenious than the treatment of the objects used in the composition.

By the 1880s several photographic processes were being used to transfer designs to wood blocks, and new techniques such as the line-block and the three-color process were utilized in children's books.[10] The line-block permits no tonal variation but achieves an exceptional fineness of line, as can be seen in Laurence Housman's illustrations for Christina Rossetti's *Goblin Market* (1893). Housman twisted and distorted objects to fit planned areas of space. The lines are elegant, curving, and used as outline or for the breaking up of larger objects into smaller shapes. Abstract designs, including such elements as strawberries and peacock tails, are inventively used as rhythmic border decorations. The book as a whole was designed as well as illustrated by Housman with just the right space allotted to pictures, ornamentation, and type.

Beatrix Potter was among the early artists using watercolors for pictures to be reproduced by the three-color process. She was a realist whose simple, sketchy line was used to outline objects and capture their characteristic qualities. *The Tale of Peter Rabbit* (1901) is a typical example and shows her understanding of how to use action-filled scenes to complement a very succinct text.

In contrast to Potter's style, Arthur Rackham's illustrations contained close tonalities with many varying, animated lines. In books such as *Grimm's Fairy Tales* (1900), *Rip Van Winkle* (1905), and even his last book, *Wind in the Willows* (1939), the effect of this style was a fanciful and mystical mood. In his vignettes for *Rip Van Winkle,* he used a small, thin, nervous, broken line—sometimes adding another agitated line beside it—all creating a feeling of movement. This mood is carefully presented in the book, with generous amounts of space around each small vignette.

The illustrators mentioned so far in this historical summary were all British. Their books were usually published in America at about the same time they appeared in England, sometimes with credit and payment extended to the original British publisher and sometimes without this acknowledgment of the book's origin. Such "pirating" was fairly common prior to the twentieth century.

Among American illustrators, Howard Pyle was perhaps the most influential in both the old and new graphic techniques. His illustrations in

Illustration by Arthur Hughes from *At the Back of the North Wind* by George Macdonald. Reprinted by permission of the University of California, Los Angeles Library

Hughes' "North Wind" enters the picture space from the side and in the midst of swirling drapery and hair. This treatment is characteristic of the work of Pre-Raphaelite illustrators. Hughes leaves many white areas throughout the picture to suggest the quality of light to build depth.

[10] James, *English Book Illustration,* pp. 47, 49.

*The Merry Adventures of Robin Hood* (1883) and *The Wonder Clock* (1888) were wood engravings inspired by the work of Albrecht Dürer. He later used a wash method of painting in black and white which made use of the photographic reproductive process, the halftone. In *The Wonder Clock,* Pyle created elegant, stylish page decorations throughout the book—sometimes freely curving lines to create symmetrical vines and flowers and occasionally a vivid and striking "doodle." In large illustrations, he arranged objects around a center of interest and detailed such objects realistically with great specificity and technical skill, but with the same emphasis on stylishness and elegance.

Maxfield Parrish illustrated *The Arabian Nights* (1909) with painted illustrations, and N. C. Wyeth illustrated Robert Louis Stevenson's *Treasure Island* (1911) with this same technique. The halftone and three-color process led to this popular style of color illustration in books and magazines, as well as to the multi-colored painted poster.

Parrish created immensely popular escapist art—never-never lands, wonder worlds with castles, urns, porticoes, and Renaissance maidens. With early training in architectural engineering, he arranged his visual statements systematically: a large central figure dominated the picture space, and landscape details on a greatly diminishing scale made up the background. His figures were static and studio-posed in unreal, craggy landscapes. His luminous colors were achieved by applying layers of alternating transparent paint and glazes.

N. C. Wyeth, in *Treasure Island,* used much the same format as Parrish but Wyeth's arrangements are more varied. There is a stronger contrast in the lights and darks used; the backgrounds of trees, sky, and architectural objects are more commonplace and are detailed and treated in a more realistic manner. Color was not as important to Wyeth as to Parrish. Wyeth concentrated on varied composition, on light and dark contrast, and on textured surfaces to create strong moods of believable yet romantic environments.

During the early years of the twentieth century, a number of distinguished folktale collections were published for children with illustrations deriving some of their inspiration from the English Art Nouveau movement and from Japanese prints. The work of the French illustrator Edmund Dulac expressed a combination of both influences in his *Arabian Nights* (1913). The Danish illustrator Kay Nielsen acknowledged a similar kind of inspiration, having seen many drawings and carvings from China. The collection of Scandinavian tales *East of the Sun, West of the Moon* (1913) includes a representative sample of his work. Illustrations by both Dulac and Nielsen evoke the world of magic in its most exotic aspect and with a strong feeling for its strange, untamable forces.

W. Heath Robinson's version of *Old-Time Stories* by Charles Perrault (1921) reveals the influence of his famous English compatriot, Aubrey Beardsley, but it is in no way derivative.[11] An eerie quality of light enhances the supernatural aspect of the stories.

# MODERN BOOK ILLUSTRATION

The illustrated book was the forerunner of that nineteenth-century invention, the picture book, and today both are influenced by some long-lasting trends. As in the past, much of the best graphic work is reserved for folktales, poetry anthologies, and occasionally a work of fiction. This stems from a publishing policy extending back into the eighteenth century: the exploitation of the "gift book" trade. Children's books which appeared elaborate, "arty," and expensive were desired by the public for gift giving at holiday time, and the content needed to be something that had status or familiarity in the mind of the general public. Fine illustrations were therefore commissioned for books by authors who were very well known and for familiar folktales or established poetry. This holiday trade still affects children's book publishing today to a degree.

[11] David Larkin. *The Fantastic Kingdom: A Collection of Illustrations from the Golden Days of Storytelling.* Ballantine, 1974. Prefatory notes for Plate 13.

Illustration Copyright © 1963 by Joseph Low from *Smiling Duke,* by permission of Houghton Mifflin Company, Publishers

Low alters the quality of his line by changing its thickness from a thin waver to lumpiness. By doing this, he creates a feeling of bulk and texture in his four various-shaped birds. This changing quality of line also creates animation, energy, and vitality—all distinguishing traits of a Low drawing. The unity of the page is maintained by pulling the color wash over casually into the page containing the typeface. When the type appears on the page with the illustration, the printed words are placed to function as line detail. This works well because of the arrangement and also because line details on wings and bodies are similar to, but stronger than, the linear typeface.

The challenge to the illustrator of an illustrated book is what it has always been: to respond to the textual content and achieve a sense of harmony with it, but not to let it subdue graphic ideas to the point where pictures become characterless. At the same time, the illustrator needs to consider the printed blocks of type that nearly fill the book space in an illustrated book. Illustrators must either integrate their illustrations with these large expanses of type, or separate the illustrations in their placement in the book so that the eye finds no disquieting conflict. If the pictures are exceptionally good, they will have a strength and unity of design that makes them not only a pleasurable, unique dimension in the book, but also a well-balanced part of the whole.

Some of the well-designed and illustrated books published in recent times include Countee Cullen's *The Lost Zoo* illustrated by Joseph Low (1968), Verna Aardema's *Behind the Back of the Mountain: Black Folktales from Southern Africa* illustrated by Leo and Diane Dillon (1973), and Christie Harris's *Once Upon a Totem* illustrated by J. Fraser Mills (1963). The designer of the Cullen book has used soft, warm paper tones as background for Joseph Low's muted color illustrations, and there is a liberal framing of both text and pictures. According to the whimsical introduction, the verses in *The Lost Zoo* (telling about animals who missed boarding Noah's ark) are a collaboration between the poet, Countee Cullen, and his feline companion Christopher Cat. The affection between these two is expressed in the warm, mellow quality in the book as a whole.

In *Behind the Back of the Mountain,* the patterns, tonal variations, and unusual ways of framing are delightful in themselves, and the African association is created with designs on clothing and jewelry and in the portrayal of tribal architecture and African animal life. A supernatural dimension, present in every story, is suggested by the frequent use of gray images in the background which evoke the spirit world, in contrast to foreground figures in sharp black and white.

The collection of five heroic legends from North Pacific Coast Indian tribes, *Once Upon a Totem,* demonstrates the successful accommodation of heavy blacks in the strong woodcuts to vertical panels of type.

### The picture book tradition

The picture book, as we know it today, emerged as a genre when technology made color illustrations less expensive. Illustrators like Crane, Greenaway, and Caldecott could now become prolific picture-book artists. The public responded so enthusiastically to the work of these three illustrators that the foundations of the genre were firmly established. The early traditions then developed in many new, advantageous directions as the children's book field underwent general expansion and became international in character.

The Greenaway tradition is the most limited one, and yet it has countless admirers. Kate Greenaway, in *Under the Window* (1878) and other books, created quaintly dressed child figures grouped usually in a pastoral setting. She used a delicate, careful, restrained line to outline objects and to texture them just enough to suggest that there were differences between areas. The textures were not strong enough to make one feel any surface animation. The groupings were well planned, but the figures were bland, prim, neat, and posed. The effect was mainly decorative, with careful attention given to borders, ornamental designs, and patterns on costumes.

This style is represented in the twentieth century by illustrators such as Marguerite de Angeli (*Book of Nursery and Mother Goose Rhymes*, 1954), Tasha Tudor (*A Is for Annabelle*, 1954), Elizabeth Orton Jones (*Small Rain: Verses from the Bible* by Jessie Orton Jones, 1944), and Joan Anglund (*A Friend Is Someone Who Likes You,* 1958). More than some other conventions in children's books, this style tends to limit itself through preoccupation with adult sentiment and nostalgia about childhood. The soft, pastel, demure figures are often repeated in monotonous fashion, and while they are not totally lacking in interest, they seem wan and static in comparison with the many vigorous characters in children's books. Artists with a broader view of both childhood and the art of illustration have produced pictures with greater vitality.

Randolph Caldecott's draftsmanship has been called "an extreme instance of instinctive drawing." [12] This liveliness was displayed in *The Three Jovial Huntsmen* (1880), where his line was particularly spontaneous in developing animal figures. But although his animal groups were well arranged, the proportions and scale of other objects were often awkward, as if each item were drawn separately with no concern for the unity of everything on the page.

Illustration from *R. Caldecott's Picture Book,* No. 2 by Randolph Caldecott, 1881. Reprinted by permission of Frederick Warne & Co., Inc., Publishers

Caldecott has created in this book several small, animated vignettes in which the graphic ideas are nicely unified. The quality of techniques and craftsmanship is consistently high with both the landscape details and the foreground objects. His line is sketchy, he outlines horses and riders in a loose but knowledgeable manner, and accents hats, boots, and mane to create tonal contrast. The lines develop a casual, graceful quality as they flow from riders to horse and back to riders.

Artists in the twentieth century who use line for comic, genial characterizations are more or less in the Caldecott tradition: Leslie Brooke at the beginning of this century (*Johnny Crow's Garden,* 1903), and today Arnold Lobel in *A Zoo for Mr. Muster* (1962), John Goodall in *The Adventures of Paddy Pork* (1968), and more. [13]

Walter Crane was the most innovative of these nineteenth-century picture book artists, although his illustrations were usually too crowded with irrelevant detail. In *The Story of the Three Bears* (probably about 1873), Crane used short,

[12] Bertha E. Mahony, and others. *Illustrators of Children's Books, 1744–1945.* The Horn Book, 1947, p. 71.

[13] The annual prize for the best illustrations in a picture book published in the United States is called the Caldecott Medal. The list of winners is at the back of this book.

repetitious lines to create forms and thereby to supply texture as well as shape.[14] The style is sketchy with some tonalities developed, but with no feeling of solidity. The quality is uneven because he is not uniformly attentive to all parts of the illustrations.

Crane was a member of the Pre-Raphaelite group of William Morris and Sir Edward Burne-Jones and was a leading theorist, teacher, and writer about book design, furniture design, and textile design. There is no noticeable connection between Crane's style and the work of such prominent twentieth-century illustrators as James Daugherty (*Andy and the Lion*, 1938) or Ludwig Bemelmans (*Madeline*, 1939), yet Crane deserves credit for that approach to illustration which is ambitious in scope and relates the tasks of the illustrator to the goals of the fine arts.

### The expansion of the picture book tradition

In the early and mid-twentieth century, many artists continued the example set by Crane, Caldecott, and Greenaway for intricate, fully developed illustrations. As in the previous era, artists were attracted to the expressive application of various visual elements. Line was the predominant stress in the books illustrated by Adrienne Adams (*The Shoemaker and the Elves*, 1960), Roger Duvoisin (*Veronica*, 1961), Marc Simont (*A Tree Is Nice*, by Janice Udry, 1956), and in many books by Marcia Brown (*Puss in Boots*, 1952, or *Cinderella*, 1954). Textural effects in a realistic mode were typical in works by Leonard Weisgard (*Nibble, Nibble*, by Margaret Wise Brown, 1959), Robert Lawson (*The Story of Ferdinand*, by Munro Leaf, 1936), Robert McCloskey (*Blueberries for Sal*, 1948), and Barbara Cooney (*Chanticleer and the Fox*, 1958). Simple contour lines with colored, flat shapes characterized Jean deBrunhoff's books about Babar (*The Story of Babar, the Little Elephant*, 1933);[15] and lines meandering, bisecting, and encircling each other created shapes which func-

Reprinted with the permission of Farrar, Straus & Giroux, Inc. from *Overhead the Sun*, Lines from Walt Whitman, illustrated by Antonio Frasconi, Copyright © 1969 by Antonio Frasconi

The Expressionist quality in this illustration is derived from the soberness of the facial features—the intent, dynamic, questioning look. Strong lines are cut into the face shape for the details of the eyes, nose, mouth, and hair. The illustration has four light areas: two yellows on each side of the child, the child's head, and the sun. The sky surface is textured, but remains as background because of the close shades of blue and black combining to create a neutral ground. The head and sun dominate the illustration.

tion as pattern in Wanda Gág's *Millions of Cats* (1928), and Virginia Lee Burton's *Katy and the Big Snow* (1943).

Between approximately 1920 and 1950 the range of graphic art in picture books expanded as the result of European and Asian artists emigrating to the United States. Also European and Japanese picture books have been imported in greater numbers in recent years, and co-production by European, British, and American publishers developed throughout the 1950s and 1960s. These events brought to the picture book

---

[14] Percy Muir. *Victorian Illustrated Books.* Praeger, 1971, p. 177.

[15] DeBrunhoff's *The Travels of Babar* (1937) should be avoided because of the racist treatment of Africans in illustrations and text.

Illustration by Nicolas Mordvinoff is reproduced by permission of Harcourt Brace Jovanovich, Inc., from *The Little Tiny Rooster* by Will and Nicolas, © 1960 by William Lipkind and Nicolas Mordvinoff

Mordvinoff uses spontaneous, provocative line and no closed contours. The broken lines create a suggestion of movement and animation. He develops various techniques to define textural differences in the rooster's body: dots speckle the comb, short curved lines are repeated irregularly and overlap for the breast, short curved lines are used again for the legs but the lines are thinner and are repeated in a vertical pattern.

audience a fresh and more elaborate decorative sense, a more asymmetrical handling of space, a more fanciful and dramatic treatment of color, and an unconventional use of line.

The seven questions suggested at the beginning of this chapter as the basis for a visual inquiry receive the most positive affirmation in the works of some of these internationally oriented artists. Especially is the quality of a unique, personal style recognizable in their illustrations, whether they have emphasized line, color, shape, texture, or unusual approaches to composition.

*Treatment of Line.* For example, Boris Artzybasheff's treatment of line is unmistakably his own. In *The Seven Simeons* (1937), he uses a simple, precise, clean, ornamental line for outlining and repeating objects to make a decorative page design. The final impression is one of neatness, tidiness, everything carefully in posi-

tion but ornately embellished, a style appropriate for an elaborate Russian fairy tale.

In contrast to Artzybasheff, Nicolas Mordvinoff loosely constructs objects with many lines of varied lengths and dispositions. In *The Little Tiny Rooster* by William Lipkind (1960), he creates an expressive, energetic, adventurous little rooster whose texture and structure are formed with hundreds of animated lines. The story relates how this tiny creature must prove its extraordinary courage to a disdainful, unsympathetic barnyard community.

Bill Sokol has a highly individual style in *The Emperor and the Nightingale* by Hans Christian Andersen (1959). He creates both thick and thin line qualities within a single pen stroke. His line seems to stop every now and then to allow the ink to blot a bit and thicken the line; then he moves it on again. This lumpy quality builds mass, pattern, and texture. The total effect highlights the satiric side of Andersen as he describes the absurdity in an emperor's court.

Copyright © 1959 by William Sokol. Reprinted from *The Emperor and the Nightingale*, by Hans Christian Anderson, illustrated by William Sokol, by permission of Pantheon Books, a Division of Random House, Inc.

Sokol's bird is essentially linear yet it suggests (with its dots, black brush strokes in the wings, and gentle, softly curving strokes for the body) a simple but substantial and solid form. The lumpy quality of the line is decorative while also suggestive of texture.

*Treatment of Shape.* Artists who are particularly attracted to the qualities in shapes have also devised new pictorial styles. Jan Balet, in *Joanjo; A Portuguese Tale* (1967), builds a base of solidly colored, simple shapes and then decorates them with boldly contrasting colors and patterns. The shapes are clean-edged, static, puppet-like, but the rich embellishment animates the picture surface to create a bright, vital effect.[16] The tale concerns Joanjo's elaborate dream about himself as a hero and therefore lends itself to a fanciful, colorful interpretation.

Nicholas Sidjakov, in *Baboushka and the Three Kings* by Ruth Robbins (1960), also decorates surfaces, but unlike Balet, he relies not on color but on line for this function. His shapes are made with heavy line contours and the same kind of heavy line patterns the interior of each shape. Like Balet, his outlines are static in order to accommodate the varied, rich line details. The inspiration of Christmas is expressed vibrantly, but there is also that simplicity that we can easily associate with an aged peasant woman like Baboushka.

Leo Lionni, in *Inch by Inch* (1960), uses textured shapes as collage materials. They contain patterns which are unrelated to the object (for example, a textile fabric for the form of a bird). These shapes are cut and pasted in overlapping arrangements and the whole effect is playful—suitably whimsical for the story of a clever inchworm.

*Treatment of Texture.* Surface treatments, or textures, are a mark of contemporary book illustration. An artist such as Fritz Eichenberg develops the surface in a sculptural manner with traditional shading and modeling techniques (as in the counting book *Dancing in the Moon,* 1956). Ludwig Bemelmans uses line to stipple, pattern, suggest movements, and add color to the Parisian settings in *Madeline's Rescue* (1953). Antonio Frasconi, in the Mother Goose verse *The House That Jack Built* (1958), leaves many ridges in the woodcut to break up a surface with irregular lines. This produces an overall

---

[16] An example of clean-edged shapes can be seen in the illustration in this chapter from Jacob Lawrence's *Harriet and the Promised Land.*

animation and expressive quality which are excellent background textures for his strong, dynamic forms.

In *Swimmy* (1963), Leo Lionni makes textural shifts of color and surface by blotting, rubbing, and stamping with muted colors. The result is a mysterious, damp, enigmatic environment that one easily associates with the underwater world of a tiny, heroic fish. In *Umbrella* (1958)—about a three-year-old's daily walk to nursery school and her love of the rainy days—Taro Yashima creates warmth and a glowing quality in his surfaces. The technique involves a strong contrast of light and dark shapes. The edges and interiors of shapes are often textured with varied colors: a dark and rich sgrafitto process which makes a good contrast with the white areas and creates a luminous quality for the entire picture.

*Treatment of Space.* With respect to composition or the treatment of space, many contemporary illustrators have defied traditional notions of proper balance and creatively developed their own. For example, Lionni has the forms in *Inch by Inch* freely entering and leaving the picture plane. He achieves an unerring sense of balance through asymmetrical arrangements. Tomi Ungerer, in *The Three Robbers* (1962), makes unusual groupings of shapes in whatever portion of the page he wishes—top, bottom, or at the side—and balances them with strong, clear, contrasting colors. The effect is stark, bold, dramatic.

*The broadening international scope of picture books*

The European and Asian artists mentioned above for their exceptional use of graphic elements came to America as either full-time or part-time residents. A concurrent development was the translation of many books into English and their publication in the United States, as well as in the country of their origin. Books illustrated by André Francois and "Laurence" (Laurence Cruse) (France), Reiner Zimnik (Germany), Bruno Munari (Italy), Hans Fischer, Felix Hoffman, Alois Carigiet, Paul Nussbaumer, and Celestino Piatti (Switzerland)

Reprinted with permission of Macmillan Publishing Co., from *Hildilid's Night* by Cheli Duran Ryan, Illustrated by Arnold Lobel, Copyright © 1971 by Arnold Lobel

Lobel's lines form shapes and build patterns, as in the horizontal and vertical striping effect in the ground areas around the house. Distance is suggested by the diminishing shapes. This is consistently high quality pen and ink work, using black and white lines on yellow overlays of color.

are among the most important. British artists such as Edward Ardizzone, Brian Wildsmith, John Burningham, David McKee, Michael Foreman, and Pat Hutchins have their books published regularly in the United States, or sometimes work directly for an American publisher. The work of all these artists has been important in establishing a high status and high quality for children's book illustration. Some examples are shown in this chapter; the others deserve further comment.

In *Roland* by Nelly Stéphane (1958), André Francois has created a joyful, original picture book with an emphasis on elaborate decoration. He stripes, dots, speckles, and flowers every conceivable surface in his room interiors. Laurence Cruse takes the reader on a tour of a small French town in *A Village in Normandy* (1968). The images have a primitive simplicity coupled with a whimsical treatment of detail, as in the row of tiny, fragile dots to represent the chain on a postman's bicycle. A humorous effect is also achieved through the playful treatment of size relationships and perspective; the tiniest miniature figures are scattered across certain pages and add a sense of busyness to this attractive village.

Bruno Munari's style in his *ABC* (1960) provides the specific textural treatment which relates to the object—the walnut, orange, onion, etc. He emphasizes clean-edged shapes in a spacious arrangement on the page. In contrast, Alois Carigiet, in *The Pear Tree, the Birch Tree, and the Barberry Bush* (1967), uses an open, sketchy, airy style for this Alpine story and is more interested in suggesting texture, depth, and animation than in being precise or specific with detail. Another Swiss artist, Paul Nussbaumer, depicts the same kind of scenery in *William Tell and His Son* (1967) and *Barry, the Story of a Brave St. Bernard* (1968), texts by Bettina Hürlimann. He uses many dramatic white highlights and dozens of textured surfaces, as in the hand-hewn wood interiors, cobblestone streets, and fancy trimmings on the costumes of noblemen in the William Tell legend.

Hans Fischer's fanciful, decorative line is well suited to the depiction of feasts and pageants being enjoyed by cats, dogs, rabbits, and goats—festivities which are the climax in *Pitschi* (1953), *The Birthday* (1954), and *The Traveling Musicians* (1955). Fischer uses intricately crosshatched illustrations to capture the intense feeling in suspenseful night scenes—for example, when the wolf threatens Pitschi, the cat.

David McKee is unusually playful in his treatment of perspective, line, and shape. In the book called *123456789 Benn* (1970), the angle at which we see several city blocks makes it necessary to turn the book upside down if we want to see the shops on the opposite side of a boulevard in a right-side-up position. Another stretch of shops is turned on its side. Black and white illustrations are richly patterned with line, and the pages in color are bold in shapes or color contrasts. The story tells of Mr. Benn's imaginary confinement in a prison where he helps decorate each prisoner's costume and cell.

Michael Foreman uses what appears to be corrugated brown paper for his collage figures in *The Two Giants* (1967). He also includes colorful paint-over-paint landscapes, providing a

light-hearted aura for his story of quarreling giants who throw boulders at each other.

*Changes, Changes* (1971) by Pat Hutchins is the best of many recent books by this author-illustrator. The story without words presents a boy and girl who arrange and rearrange blocks: cylinders, rectangles, triangles, etc. They put out a fire with a fire truck formed from blocks, then make a ship from the blocks and sail out to sea. They land and change the block-ship to a block-truck, then to a train, then to a house. All the shapes have textured surfaces within simple, strong outlines, and the total effect is tight, stiff, and amusing.

Impressive books have been imported from Japan and published in American editions. Yutaka Sugita's *Wake Up, Little Tree* (1969) is similar in style to *Have You Seen My Mother?* (1969), but quieter in tone to match its reverent Christmas story. (See the illustration from *Have You Seen My Mother?* in this chapter.) Many other fine examples could be mentioned but *Suho and the White Horse* by Yuzo Otsuka and illustrated by Suekichi Akaba (1969) is exceptional in its style and design. Akaba creates large but gentle panoramic environments using color in close tonalities. On subtle, muted background colors, he uses simple shapes with soft edges and then applies line in muted colors to further define objects.[17] These techniques seem ideally suited to this tragic, understated Mongolian legend which tells how a horse and its young owner are separated and how the horse later asks the boy in a dream to use its bones and its hide for the creation of a fine musical instrument.[18]

*A few new talents*

Many of the artists discussed so far have been working for a decade or more as prolific chil-

[17] An example of soft-edged shapes can be seen in the illustrations from *Have You Seen My Mother?* and *All Us Come Cross the Water* reproduced in this chapter.

[18] Students should examine the two issues of the Swiss publication, *Graphis, The International Journal of Graphic Art and Applied Art,* which were devoted to "An International Survey of Children's Book Illustration," *Graphis* no. 131 (1967) and no. 155 (1971). The magazine has an English as well as a French and German text, and excellent children's book illustrations from all over the world have been reproduced.

dren's book illustrators. Other artists have recently joined the field with exceptional books. Susan Jeffers, in her version of the Mother Goose rhyme *The Three Jovial Huntsmen* (1973), uses many fine lines to create panoramic views of animals in a forested landscape. Horizontal, curved lines are painstakingly employed to sculpt every tree trunk. The three hunters are purposely treated so that they appear alien to this botanically perfect environment. They are tightly drawn, clean-edged figures.

A book with delightful color is *Wim of the Wind* by Antoine de Vinck, illustrated by Miche Wynants (1974). It contains no outlines; colors create the forms and the textures and they change subtly in shade and tone to produce light and dark areas on the page. Wim is a clever basket weaver who hears the sea wind telling him to create windmills—tiny pinwheels to amuse his child and huge windmills to help the peasants.

Jutta Ash's illustrations for *Chicken Licken* by Kenneth McLeish (1973) are designed to create a feeling of density throughout the whole book. This is the folktale about the scatterbrained chicken who predicts the end of the world, and Ash's version captures both its nonsensical aspect (with endless fancy patterns), and its dramatic aspect (with a crowded array of fowls and menacing foxes). However, her style would have been better displayed if about two more inches had been added to the page space.

Robert Andrew Parker has recently illustrated many books, but his most effective collaboration with an author is in *Pop Corn and Ma Goodness* by Edna Mitchell Preston (1969). Parker uses a sketchy, airy style that serves to suggest objects and movements rather than define them with precision. Each painting has the kind of naive appearance which suits perfectly the nonsensical, melodic frontier story.

An astute handling of composition is seen in Jacqueline Gachet's *The Ladybug* (1970). Every page is deliberately organized in a fresh, unpredictable manner. Objects have been translated into geometric shapes and arranged against a ground which is also divided geometrically. Patterns are of the right color to keep them subordinate and within the shape edge. The story is a moral tale which condemns militarism and

From *Sam, Bangs & Moonshine* written and illustrated by Evaline Ness. Copyright © 1966 by Evaline Ness. Reproduced by permission of Holt, Rinehart and Winston, Publishers

Ness creates sensitive portraits of children. This one is simply done, with thin, spare lines for hair texture and thicker ones for legs, jars, and doorsteps. Shaded, dark areas give depth to the body of the cat. Ness has a strong design sense and a special talent for pulling facing pages together with either line and shape, line and pattern, or line, shape, and texture. Almost every page has a ground texture like brayer rolling or rubbings of one kind or another. Over this she adds a strong, knowledgeable line and depicts a great variety of objects with ease, grace, and freedom.

war. This is not an easy theme to put across in a children's book, and Gachet's strong illustrations seem essential to the clarity and potency of this briefly presented message.

The use of space is also the refreshing aspect of *The Cat and Mouse Who Shared a House* illustrated by Ruth Hürlimann (1973). A huge textured cat—sculptural and solid looking—fills an entire page; in fact goes off the page on all sides. Something very large is in every illustration, as when a tile roof takes up two thirds of the area with the cat perched on the top. Patterns are made from the tile designs and the texture of the cat. The ancient tale (retold here from the Grimm Brothers version) concerns a cat and mouse who make an agreement to live together. The unreliable cat finally eats her roommate and the truism is stated plainly: "The cat and mouse can never really be friends."

Jeffers, Wynants, Ash, Parker, Gachet, and Hürlimann are among the many illustrators who are proving how lively and varied the picture book continues to be. The perception and style of each one is highly personal, their chosen medium is handled with consummate skill, and the overall tone of their work is humorous or serious in conjunction with the mood of each text.

### Elements of book design

The artist's skill and style are announced on the book jacket, end papers, title page, and the book's first illustration. He or she is then obliged to maintain this level of skill—and the same style—throughout the book. We are jarred visually if this is not accomplished. Visual continuity is as significant to the book's success as the verbal logic of the story. The basic question, therefore, when evaluating book design, is whether the book appears to be the work of one talent or of collaborators who view the book similarly. In this sense, a book is like a good film where the impression reaching the viewer indicates a work produced, written, and directed by one creative person.

Many picture books contain illustrations in both black and white and in color, but as can be seen in Paul Nussbaumer's illustrations for *William Tell and His Son,* the basic style is maintained even when the medium changes. Nussbaumer's emphasis upon light and dark contrasts is as evident in the black and white sketches as in the full-color drawings.

Besides continuity, there are qualities in the physical makeup of a book that make the whole either more or less inviting. The paper color and texture, the size and shape of the book, the type, the arrangement of the illustrations and printed text, the uniformity and size of the margins, the binding—all these elements either enhance or diminish the work of the illustrator and author. The second basic question is therefore, How have the different parts of the book been embellished or given suitable attention? In other words, are the end papers and title page decorative and in harmony with the overall style and tone of the book? Is there a frontispiece or tailpiece that adds an introductory or concluding note? Is the framing, the space surrounding illustrations and blocks of type, sufficient to avoid a crowded feeling? Is the type unobtrusive, and each page well balanced? Are facing pages well balanced? If tinted paper is used, what is its relation to the book as a whole?

Although photographs are not part of our discussion in this chapter, the kinds of questions we are asking here concerning the relation of illustration to overall book design are as useful in evaluating those books illustrated with photos as those with drawings or paintings.

There are well-designed books with no illustrations at all, but when illustrations are included, we can safely say that there is no good design unless those illustrations are original, engaging, and skillfully executed. We could say that a good picture can exist without a good text, but in such a case there is no point in having it in a book. The picture would be better in a gallery or portfolio. Texts and illustrations are part of a unit and children use books as a unit. A certain level of quality is therefore necessary in these two basic parts of a book.

### Some design problems

The number of carelessly designed books is baffling, considering how unnecessary this negligence is. Both well-designed and poorly designed books usually cost the same to the buyer in a book store. The problem seems to be one of low commitment and insufficient attention to detail rather than cost.

The bindings of children's books are influenced by library usage. An excessively tight, heavy-duty sewing damages all the images in the center of a double-page spread, but this is viewed as a helpful concession to libraries, with their need for long-wearing books. The artist or book designer can compensate for this but apparently is not often given technical advice to cope with the problem.

Conflicting images on the facing left- and right-hand pages cause a problem in many books. This occurs in N. M. Bodecker's excellent group of rhymes, *It's Raining Said John Twaining* (1973). On the page about "Squire McGuire," the patterns on clothing and architecture require something either subdued on the opposite page or something that repeats a similar pictorial idea so that the eye can encompass the whole design. As it is, the opposite page contains a more abstract style of patterning on three large trees, and this strong, decorative approach competes with the busyness of the line work and the many varied shapes on the page featuring Squire McGuire.

This kind of problem is seen in nearly every picture book illustrated by the English artist, Charles Keeping, with the exception of *The Christmas Story* (1968). In that distinguished book every page is a double-page spread, and along with the book's neutral colors, this allows the luxuriant, abstract textures to be seen and relished without annoying distraction. In his other picture books, the colors and textures on facing pages clash, and the blocks of type are squeezed in here and there with no consistent plan.

Inadequate framing and margins diminish the interesting illustrations in Maurice Sendak's *Mr. Rabbit and the Lovely Present* (text by Charlotte Zolotow, 1962). In Ed Emberley's *Simon's Song* (text by Barbara Emberley, 1969), the layout on each page is distressingly crowded, whereas generous space has been allowed for the delicate drawings in his book *London Bridge Is*

Illustration by Thomas Daly from *Joel and the Wild Goose,* by Helga Sandburg. Reprinted by permission of the Dial Press

Daly works with both shape and line in unelaborate poetic arrangements. About twenty small, bare-branched trees mark the horizon line separating the large snow areas from a gently shaded sky area, and they serve to blend the two and suggest quiet, bleak winter distances. Joel is a solid shape made by contour lines, pattern, and solid areas. Six large trees are treated in silhouette, and one of the branches partially encircles him, directing the viewer to the footsteps in the snow.

*Falling Down: The Song and the Game* (1967).

The artist who is intent upon making the best book possible faces a number of practical problems in achieving his goal. Many decisions about page space, typeface, size, and so on are out of the illustrator's hands. Yet any offensive quality resulting from crowded pages reflects on the artist rather than the publisher. Because the offense is visual, we tend to think the artist is responsible for the poorly planned book.

### Good models

Some interesting examples of book design in illustrated books were mentioned earlier in this chapter. Among picture books a particularly good example is *Joel and the Wild Goose* by Helga Sandburg, illustrated by Thomas Daly (1963). The front endpapers contain a heavily bordered snowscape and the back endpapers show the same scene in springtime. This snowscape is a bird's-eye view of the bleak farm terrain, and on the title page one sees it at a slightly closer range. A real "close-up" of the farmer's house appears opposite the first page of text. All illustrations are bordered in black and vary in size and placement on the page. There is no feeling of clutter. Since the type is framed with a black border in squares or rectangles, it too becomes a significant part of the page design. Everything is so well composed that a serene feeling is established for the book as a whole.

Two books illustrated by Margot Zemach are particularly notable for their design: *Mazel and Shlimazel or the Milk of a Lioness,* text by Isaac Bashevis Singer, translated by Elizabeth Shub (1967), and *The Judge,* text by Harve Zemach (1969). The frontispiece of *Mazel and Shlimazel* is a village street scene, drawn with a vigorous line and with the perspective treated in a fanciful manner. The title page is a neatly blocked arrangement of several typefaces, and the first page leads into the story with a landscape vignette. Liberal amounts of space surround each block of text and the vignettes which are often included on the same page. The tailpiece shows just the hero's back as he leaves the book in what is clearly a jaunty, contented mood. In *The Judge* the endpapers consist of the same

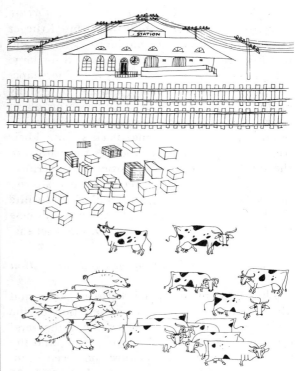

Illustration by Reiner Zimnik from *The Crane,* © 1970. Reprinted by permission of Harper and Row

There is a sense of glee in some of Zimnik's panoramic landscapes. One is reminded of a child who has an endless assortment of building materials to group and arrange—blocks, buildings, animals, fences, signs. With meticulous, precise line, Zimnik groups cows, pigs, boxes, two rows of fencing, a station, and six telephone poles. The wires of the telephone poles serve to top the whole picture elegantly. Zimnik achieves rhythmic repetition in the slats of the fencing, the telephone wires, and so on.

wallpaper pattern that we see throughout the book. An Old English typeface is used for the announcement of the title preceding the title page, and is combined with a pleasing assortment of typefaces on that page. The frontispiece is a portrait of the grumpy, tyrannical judge. Each illustration is neatly framed with a very light beige or gold or pinkish line and the text is on the opposite page until we reach the three climactic double-page spreads at the end. These three illustrations provide a splendidly farcical conclusion to what Harve Zemach called his "untrue tale."

Ed Young, in *The Golden Swans, A Picture Story from Thailand*, retold by Kermit Krueger (1969), has effectively employed colored and textured papers to serve as the ground for large shapes denoting people and swans. The shapes have an inkblot appearance, and flow diagonally off the page to suggest even larger forms off in space. The title page is highly dramatic with a group of swiftly ascending black swans. Their frightened appearance introduces the pathos of the tale, which concerns a swan who sacrifices herself to preserve the secret that the swans are spirits. On the following page a black and white illustration, reminiscent of ancient Chinese brush paintings, establishes the Oriental setting.

### Correlation of text and illustration

The harmony of mood between story and illustration depends upon the selection of the right illustrator. In many cases the author and illustrator are one and the same person, and the correlation of text and pictures has been spontaneous from the outset. For example, the naivete and childlike directness of the text in *Harry Is a Scaredy Cat* by Byron Barton (1974) suits perfectly his skillful adaptation of comic book techniques, with extra dialogue placed in balloons and simple, uniform outlines to delineate objects.

John Burningham's stylized animals blend ideally with the frolicsome mood and the slapstick climax of the picnic in *Mr. Gumpy's Outing* (1971). The animals each have different, but equally playful patterns (as on the chickens) or textures (as on the sheep) or colors (as on the cat). *The Winter Picnic* (1970) has a separate author (Robert Welber) and illustrator (Deborah Ray) but the festive mood of that picnic is handsomely embodied in the brilliant hues of color and ornate floral patterns on caps, scarves, and coats.

A case in which two highly skilled illustrators have treated the same story with a different emphasis and mood is the Hans Christian Andersen story, *The Nightingale*. Nancy Ekholm Burkert illustrated it in 1965 in a style that suggests Oriental screen paintings. This gave a geographical and historical emphasis to the story and a literal dimension that played down its allegori-

cal aspect. Bill Sokol illustrated it in 1959 in a way that captured the satiric element and the fanciful and universal aspect of the story as a fable. Sokol's blotchy kind of line is a whimsical counterpart to Andersen's tongue-in-cheek dialogue and narration. It also conveys a similar subtlety.

The picture book author and illustrator Roger Duvoisin has described the principles upon which text and illustrations best complement each other and interact:

> Literature is an art which has its own conceptions and its own means of expressions. It does not need help from another art, unless the writer himself has planned it that way. Illustrations which impose the artist's conception of a novel with definitiveness and precise literalness come like a screen between the author and his readers. The illustrations interfere in a very unpleasant way with the readers' own dreams.
>
> But illustrations, as done by the superior artists, are related to the text in a free, loose, subtle way; they leave the reader free to interpret the writing with complete freedom. And he has the added pleasure of doing the same with the illustrations.[19]

Duvoisin is not implying that in a book like *Madeline* (1939) Ludwig Bemelmans could have depicted eleven instead of twelve "little girls in two straight lines," after describing twelve in the text. But when Bemelmans used these small figures playfully as shapes and patterns, rather than painting conventional portraits, he gave the child the pleasure of witnessing an imaginative, dynamic style.

### Cartoonists and the art of storytelling

If a description of the modern picture book ended at this point, many of the books most popular with children would remain unmentioned. Dr. Seuss, a cartoonist, is probably one of the most popular author-illustrators with young children and this popularity is fully deserved. All his work meets the demand made on every cartoon: the demand to be humorous or satirical. After his first children's book, *And to*

---

[19] Duvoisin, "Children's Book Illustration," p. 30.

*Think That I Saw It on Mulberry Street* (1937), he created many more which can justifiably be termed classics; that is, they have delighted several generations of children and there is no sign that their popularity is slowing down. *Thidwick the Big-Hearted Moose* (1948), *Horton Hears a*

Illustration from *Father Fox's Penny Rhymes* by Clyde Watson, Copyright © 1971 by Wendy Watson from *Father Fox's Penny Rhymes* by Clyde Watson and Wendy Watson with permission of Thomas Y. Crowell Co., Inc.

A neatly planned book: tidy, compact, and full of things which extend the story. Watson deals with myriads of objects and casually leaves the impression that there is still room for a hundred thousand more. Note the receding landscape, with miles and miles suggested by the tiny dots.

*Who* (1954), *The Sneetches and Other Stories* (1961), *I Had Trouble Getting to Solla Sollew* (1965)—these have all been highly successful with English-speaking children. But the pleasure in these books stems not from what is seen per se. It is derived more from the charm and credibility of the characters, the excitement in the plots, the humorous predicaments, the fanciful worlds, and the rhythm and energy of verbal, not visual, language.

Other picture books which have been popular over several decades include Hardie Gramatky's *Little Toot* (1939), H. A. and Margaret Rey's *Curious George* (1941), and Gene Zion and Margaret Bloy Graham's *Harry the Dirty Dog* (1956). *Hubert's Hair-Raising Adventure* by Bill Peet (1959), has a similar appeal, and recent books such as *Piggy in a Puddle* by Charlotte Pomerantz, illustrated by James Marshall (1974) or *Herman the Helper* by Robert Kraus, illustrated by Jose Aruego and Ariane Dewey (1974) would seem to be in this same tradition.

In all these books the drawings are important, but not in the same way we have discussed the importance of artwork earlier in this chapter. The cartoon drawings of illustrators such as Dr. Seuss or Hardie Gramatky are important in the degree that they are humorous, and in the way they embody the characterization that has been shaped through the actions in the story. In addition, the drawings function as a means of moving the story from one episode to the next; the tale unravels through a related series of pictures and can be understood through the logical development of action seen from page to page. The pictures thus help the child who has not yet learned to read to discover plot, or what the story is about.

Besides helping with the visual progression of the plot and the depiction of characters, some cartoonists have captured a character's personality in a manner that is inimitable. For example, it is hard to imagine any other delineation for Harry, the hero of *Harry the Dirty Dog* (1956), *No Roses for Harry* (1958), and *Harry by the Sea* (1965) than the one Margaret Bloy Graham has provided. Harry is a pampered, bourgeois pet who has a streak of romantic daring and naughtiness in him. Graham gives him a rather shapeless form (in the anatomical

sense), and a solid, undistinguished appearance (spots and thin, scraggly fur) which make Harry's combination of conformity and impetuosity all the more entertaining.

Usually the inimitable aspect of a cartoon stems from the quality of the line, as in Edward Koren's *Don't Talk to Strange Bears* (1969), William Steig's *Roland, the Minstrel Pig* (1968) and *Sylvester and the Magic Pebble* (1969), and in some of James Marshall's books such as *Miss Dog's Christmas Treat* (1973). But in the Zion and Graham books our enjoyment springs from the many moods achieved by the cartoonist with a minimum of visual means. Using only the dog's simple, nondescript form and a line or two to suggest eyes and mouth, Graham makes Harry convincingly surprised, dejected, content, scheming, disgusted, proud, ashamed, smug—in short, very much alive and very human in his range of emotions.

An artist like Ludwig Bemelmans was both an expert cartoonist and a master of book illustration as a branch of the fine arts. This can be said of Nicolas Mordvinoff, André Francois, Joseph Low, Reiner Zimnik, John Burningham, and a number of others who are able to embody a characterization accurately, develop a story line pictorially, and at the same time contribute something visually ingenious, humorous, and harmonious.

The important point about cartoonists as well as other illustrators is that when their style includes a unique treatment of lines, colors, or shapes, the viewer crosses "the frontier into the new region which the pictorial art as such has added to the world." [20]

# A SUMMARY OF OLD AND NEW TRENDS

A number of generalizations can be made about the changing fashions in children's book illustration. Some changes stem from the poten-

[20] C. S. Lewis. *An Experiment in Criticism.* Cambridge University Press, 1961, pp. 21–22.

Illustration from *A Kiss for Little Bear* by Else Holmelund Minarik, illustrated by Maurice Sendak. Text copyright © 1968 by Else Holmelund Minarik. Pictures copyright © 1968 by Maurice Sendak

The forms of the cat and skunk, as well as the foliage,
are created with thousands of short, varied lines. The
light and dark areas are carefully controlled so that tonal
contrasts help build the forms as well as suggest depth.
There is a quiet, low-keyed feeling of movement created
by the rich, varied surface animation of sky, shrub,
ground, and animal textures. The landscape is lush (with
the feeling of another time and place)—an appropriate
fantasy environment for this mixture of animals.

tial inherent in new printing technology; and
some stem from the spirit of experimentation
that characterizes twentieth-century art in general. For example, the contemporary illustrator
often makes color his most vital concern (as a
way to build a background and define an area),
regardless of the line used later to define an
object. Color is used frankly and freely for its
own sake. An illustration by Brian Wildsmith
shouts "Color!" before anything else is noticed.

Today's artists draw people with no special
deference or compulsion to render them "perfect." Human forms are treated in the same
manner as the surrounding landscape and architecture, as in Monika Laimgruber's *The Em-*

*peror's New Clothes* by Hans Christian Andersen
(1973). In this book thousands of dots build
the shape outlines, tonal contrasts, densities, and
patterns whether an object is flora, fauna, architectural structure, or human being. Laimgruber's
work is highly stylized, tight, static, rich, and
kinesthetic in its feeling of surface movement.

Although there are still many books which
offer banal, simpering faces of children, a larger
variety of characterization is evident in the best
modern illustrations. Charles Keeping and Antonio Frasconi both depict many serious, contemplative faces, and Keeping emphasizes urban
children in urban environments.

There are today more asymmetrical compositions and more varied size relationships within
this asymmetry. Since the picture space is the
artists' undisputed domain, they utilize colors,
lines, and shapes to instill the entire area with
visual interest; they permit themselves greater
distortion (as in Abe Birnbaum's *Green Eyes,*
1953) to bring this about.

Contemporary books contain less page decoration in the form of flower and vine doodles,
vignettes, and other extraneous ornamentation.
Today's artist usually extends his or her visual
idea into all the available space—often as a
double-page spread—and this makes for a more
integral, unified appearance. The books of
Evaline Ness are particularly notable in the
way the double page is integrated, but this illustrator has also created some handsome vignettes and miscellaneous ornamentations in
*Coll and His White Pig* by Lloyd Alexander
(1965). Either method of page design can be
interesting and tasteful.

Many picture books reflect the contemporary
magazine convention in which large photographs
spill over the edge of the page and leave no
margins. This is the case in *Henri's Walk to
Paris* by Lenore Klein and illustrated by Saul
Bass (1962), but Bass allows liberal format
space in the interior of his pages by using large
expanses of solid color. Incorporating the type
into the design has also enabled him to achieve
a spacious layout. William Wondriska has a
similarly bold, contemporary feeling in *Puff*
(1960), where he uses bright red color sections
and strong horizontal lines to pull the viewer's
eye off all the pages.

*A Little Book of Beasts*, Illustrated by Peter Parnall, Copyright © 1973. Reprinted by permission of Simon and Schuster, Children's Book Division

Parnall's squirrel consists of hundreds of short, small, thin klines which follow the animals contour and build form and texture. The lines are shorter in the head detail and become longer in the tail portion, adding illusion of depth. The nuts are treated differently, outlined with line detail over a brown wash. The cranny consists of elegant long lines which enclose the cluster of nuts.

Finally, there is today a breadth of styles. Romanticism is the style of Nancy Ekholm Burkert in her version of *Snow White and the Seven Dwarfs* (1972). Expressionism characterizes the work of Jacob Lawrence in *Harriet and the Promised Land* (1968) and all of Frasconi's books. Superrealism is the style of Feodor Rojankovsky's best animal portraits in *Animals in the Zoo* (1962); and there is an abstract, almost nonobjective, approach to illustrating in Janina Domanska's *If All the Seas Were One Sea* (1971), Bernard Waber's *A Firefly Named Torchy* (1970), and Joseph Domjan's *The Little Cock* (a tale retold by Jeanne B. Hardendorff, 1969).[21]

[21] Even surrealism (which utilizes fantastic, dreamlike images) can be found in children's books, usually in the publications of Harlin Quist, Inc. *Number 24* (1973) by Guy Billout and *The Endless Party* (1967) by Etienne Delessert and Eleanore Schmid are good examples of this style. There is some question as to whether the Harlin Quist books are not too ironical for the typical child audience, but this issue relates to texts and to a book's overall conception more than to the style of the illustrations per se.

Modern books share some characteristics with earlier ones. For example, a sense of mood and drama is created by using strong light and dark contrasts. This is typical of Sir John Tenniel's illustrations for *Alice in Wonderland,* and also characterizes many illustrations by Taro Yashima (*Umbrella,* 1958) and Maurice Sendak (*The Moon Jumpers,* text by Janice Udry, 1959). Creating rich textural surfaces is a technique that many modern artists exploit, but it is found also in Arthur Hughes's illustrations for *At the Back of the North Wind* which was published in 1871.

The impulse to decorate is seen in the early illustrations of Laurence Housman for *Goblin Market* (1893) and in books like Pat Hutchins' *The Surprise Party* (1969). The botanically perfect illustration is seen in Richard Doyle's work for *In Fairyland* (1870) and in the modern work of Peter Parnall. There have always been cartoonish, amusing drawings which emphasize the "what" rather than the "how" in an illustration. For example, Edward Lear directs the viewer's attention to a large nose simply by grossly exaggerating its size. In this case he gives little attention to the aesthetic implications. This is the approach in the illustrations of Dr. Seuss also.

Finally, the tendency to romanticize and idealize is noticeable in all eras and it is not a problem in children's books if there is some visual gain or the creation of a powerful mood. Striking examples include *The Little Match Girl* by Hans Christian Andersen, illustrated by Blair Lent (1968), as well as the major works of Nancy Ekholm Burkert, Felix Hoffmann, and Susan Jeffers.

# THE TREATMENT OF WOMEN AND RACIAL GROUPS

Sexism in children's books has been recognized as a form of conditioning that affects expectations and self-esteem. "By sexist we [the Feminist Collective on Children's Media] mean predetermining social roles on the basis of sex alone." [22] A larger number of male characters in books has caused speculation about whether children inadvertently learn to believe in superior male importance. Also traditional male activities are clearly differentiated from those supposedly suitable for women, and the young reader may be learning to gauge the "rightness" of his or her own behavior from this information.

In 1971 Alleen Pace Nilsen analyzed eighty Caldecott prize-winning picture books and honor books and found that male names appeared in the titles more than three times as often as female names. One fourth of the books contained only token female characters, and the total representation of women declined over the past twenty years. A survey by one of Nilsen's college

Reprinted with permission of Macmillan Publishing Co., Inc. from *About Wise Men & Simpletons: Twelve Tales from Grimm* by Nonny Hogrogian, translated by Elizabeth Shub, Copyright © 1971 by Nonny Hogrogian

Hogrogian's line is lean, minimal, sculptured. It suggests bulk, solidity, and clothing drapery with the simplest of means. The figures fill the entire page: mother's hair touching the top edge, her body touching the side edge, and her shoe the bottom and right edge. A few interior lines break up the large outline into smaller, but still simple, varied shapes. The book design is excellent. The illustration rectangle uses a gray ground and balances, quietly with the block of type the same size on the facing page.

students showed that in the influential Dr. Seuss books, males outnumbered females seven to one. [23]

There are a number of good books in which no mention is made of a character's sex (as in *Green Eyes* where a cat tells his/her own story and his/her sex is never known); but there are too few books that allow you to see a woman without an apron when a woman is included.

[22] "Only You, Dick Daring! Survival Report of National Book Association Week," in *Publishers Weekly*, March 22, 1971, p. 20.

[23] Alleen Pace Nilsen. "Women in Children's Literature," in *College English*, May 1971, pp. 918, 926.

Among the books mentioned in this chapter, *Winter Picnic, Rrra-ah, Harry Is a Scaredy Cat,* and many more show mothers in the traditional domestic position. Being always at home, mothers are typically shown disciplining children, while fathers are almost inevitably playing with them. In *The Run, Jump, Bump Book* by Robert Brooks (1971), a mother is always saying "pick things up," "be quiet," "be careful." The protagonist's remark when her father takes her to the playground tells something about the attitude pervading the book: "But *sometimes* it was different." There is a clear implication that a child's associations with father are happier than those with mother.

Letty C. Pogrebin, editor of children's features of *Ms. Magazine,* has written about the need to portray women in the business and professional world, where forty percent of them actually are: "No one is asking for complete role reversal between sexes. Balanced variety, that's all." Famous author-illustrators such as Dr. Seuss, Jean deBrunhoff, and Maurice Sendak have brought a tradition-confined male perception into their books, and for them this was probably inevitable. Creativity is dependent upon honest perceptions, whatever they may be. Pogrebin says she doesn't deprive her own daughters of the imaginative deBrunhoff or Sendak books, but writes: "What's to be gained from a visit to Richard Scarry's unimaginative animal community, where aproned mother bears are forever dishing up breakfast treats and pushing shopping carts?"[24]

Changes in the pictorial depiction of masculine and feminine roles in children's books will follow the changes in texts, changes which can be made now without misrepresenting present life styles and attitudes. For example, in *Christina, Katerina and the Box* by Patricia Lee Gauch (1971), a girl is shown as an inventive child who devises interesting games with a huge, cast-off box. She is not the timid observer who has been repeatedly presented in children's stories in marked contrast to energetic, clever boys.

When psychologist Kenneth B. Clark discussed the need for black American representation in

books and elsewhere, he was stating the rationale for a balanced and authentic representation of the feminine also:

> The individual child develops an awareness of his own personality through recognizing his own physical characteristics and learning what value others in the society place on those characteristics. This becomes an important part of what he thinks about himself.

Clark noted further that "children respond more to the concrete realities they perceive than to the abstract ideas and explanations they are offered."[25]

The centuries-long exclusion of black Americans from children's books is now well known. There were four black characters in picture books between 1939 and 1950, and only seven in the 1950s. Following the inner-city riots in the 1960s, thirty-eight blacks appeared in picture books, still a small percentage in relation to the number published over a ten-year period.[26]

Racism has taken other forms besides the exclusion of blacks and other Third World groups. Africans and black Americans have been typically depicted by demeaning caricatures as in *Epaminondas and His Auntie* by Sara Cone Bryant, illustrated by Inez Hogan (1938), and *No Mules* by William Papas (1967), or with Caucasian facial features and hairstyles (as in *Mississippi Possum* by Miska Miles, illustrated by John Schoenherr, 1965, or *Corduroy* by Don Freeman, 1968). A variety of physical characteristics provides an accurate reflection of the Afro-American population, but unless a book includes consistency and specificity in its ethnic identification, it is simply a sophisticated caricature or the work of a careless illustrator.

Authenticity is possible in either realistic or abstract modes of art. In John Steptoe's illustrations, the dynamic quality provided by the colors and shapes is in sharp contrast to the everyday schoolroom and household environments depicted. Steptoe proves that the strongest realism

[24] Letty C. Pogrebin. "Girls' Liberation," in *The New York Times Book Review,* May 6, 1973, p. 4.

[25] Kenneth B. Clark. *Prejudice and Your Child.* 2nd ed. enlarged. Beacon Press, 1963; pp. 23, 32.

[26] Joan Baronberg *Black Representation in Children's Books.* Horace Mann-Lincoln Institution; Teachers College, Columbia University; ERIC Information Retrieval Center on the Disadvantaged, 1971, p. 9.

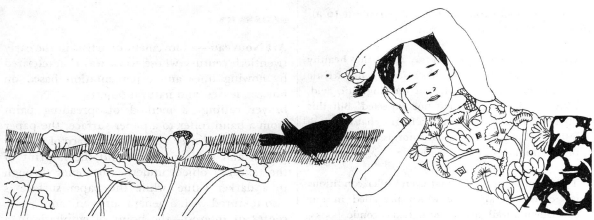

Illustration from *A Wish for Little Sister,* written and illustrated by Jacqueline Ayer is reproduced by permission of Harcourt Brace Jovanovich, Inc., © 1960 by Jacqueline Ayer

Ayer's figures use a combination of contour line and reliance on tonal contrasts for structure. The short strokes

of line that build the grass area also form the edge of "little sister's" upper arm, while the rest of the arms, head, and body have a thin, clean line subtly defining their form. The same kind of line patterns the blouse, while the skirt is a white pattern on a black ground, balancing the black mynah bird and "little sister's" black hair.

does not rely on photographic accuracy, but on depth of feeling and the ability to project this feeling through the creative use of the visual elements. For example, the simplicity of the portraiture, the unpretentiousness of people and environment, plus the tension created by contrasting, vivid colors—these features make *All Us Come Cross the Water* by Lucille Clifton with illustrations by Steptoe (1973) a strong, visual experience.

With respect to other Third World groups, representation is extremely deficient. In 1972 the Council on Interracial Books for Children analyzed 100 children's books about Puerto Ricans and found not one which presented an authentic portrayal of Puerto Rican self-awareness. In 1975 the Council published a similar study of Chicano culture in children's books.[27]

As in the case of women, Third World book characters need to be shown in unstereotyped roles. The illustrator is confined to what is provided in a text and can extend it only so far with background material. However, even when no central Third World characters appear in a story, the inclusion of authentic, multiracial scenes as part of the environment gives the child a solid, visual verification of our multiethnic nation. When such environments go beyond the much criticized gimmick of a few shaded-in faces, they present the visible evidence

which is instructive for children.

## CONCLUSION: THE INFLUENCE OF QUALITY

Prior to the nineteenth century, not many books were created exclusively for children for they did not constitute a sizeable and reliable market for publishers. The influential bookseller of the 1700s, John Newbery, started the trend of making attractive books for child readers. But literacy was not widespread, and the demand for gift books was seasonal. Today there is a large, steady, enthusiastic child audience to receive an illustrator's or writer's work. Not many research studies have been undertaken to answer questions about the child's aesthetic responses. But in the anthology *The Education of Vision,* studies are described which show how these responses change under the impact of the environment. The carefully documented evidence compiled by psychologist Wolfgang Metz-

[27] "100 Children's Books about Puerto Ricans: A Study in Racism, Sexism, and Colonialism," in *Interracial Books for Children,* Spring 1972, p. 1. (Vol. 5, no. 7 and 8, 1975, on Chicano culture). The Council is a valuable source of information on books dealing with all Third World groups, and it is now combating sexism as well as racism.

ger led to conclusions which are pertinent to all those involved with children:

> We . . . are now able to say that the healthy child is endowed with a basic feeling for artistic merit—both in the visual and the linguistic field. This is something we had not expected. But this predisposition is apparently so fragile that responsibility for the growth of artistic norms does rest with the environment.

> There can be no doubt that even under conditions less extreme than those which prevailed in our experiment, wall decorations, texts, comic books, etc., exert a corresponding effect on the child, especially because the child is under their influence for such an extended period of time. Now that this is known, the influences can be controlled.[28]

Metzger states that there is now "a conclusive argument against all . . . who consider superfluous, or even oppose, a controlled influence or appreciation of style in the visual and linguistic arts." His findings enable educators and parents to refute those who "do not believe that it is necessary to be very discriminating in the choice of texts, illustrations, and room decorations for children, and who allow business and industry to dictate the shape of the world in which their children grow."[29]

Today's illustrator has this audience with "a basic feeling for artistic merit" to speak to in visual terms, plus various media to draw upon. The only limiting factor appears to be the inhibition placed upon illustrators by publishers who are sometimes concerned for the acceptance of an unfamiliar style. This limitation can be progressively overcome if many styles of art are examined, discussed, and seen to be appreciated. The artist will then be free to treat the book like any other fine arts medium. Illustrators who work consistently in this framework are helping sustain children's sensitivity to art, and revealing what immeasurable pleasures are to be found within books. With this background children retain their realization that the world at large is something to be uniquely perceived.

[28] Wolfgang Metzger. "The Influence of Aesthetic Example," p. 26.
[29] Ibid.

## GLOSSARY

**Art Nouveau**—a movement of artists in the early twentieth century whose work was characterized by flowing lines and ornamentation based on flowers, leaves, and natural objects.

**brayer rolling**—a method of spreading paint from a hand roller to a paper surface; the paper is often placed over a textured surface of strings, leaves, and similar objects and the imprint of the textured object underneath comes through in a darker value, while the paper surface is also textured with a general uneven tone.

**center of interest**—the point of emphasis in a picture, the point of attraction.

**clean-edged shapes**—a form in which the external edge is clean, sharp, precise.

**collage**—an assemblage of different materials on a picture plane; an arrangement in which the visual elements are cut from cloth, newspapers, wallpapers, fur, etc.

**composition**—the organization and arrangement of the physical and visual elements in a work of art; since we must respond to the visual units in a picture as related units—not perceived in isolation—it follows that the space around each object is as important as the objects themselves.

**contour line**—the outline of an object; the external boundary of a form as defined by a line.

**crosshatching**—the crossing of lines at various angles, usually in pen and ink, with which an artist constructs his tonal areas, or shadows, or modeling.

**double-page spread**—a single composition which includes both the left and right pages of an opened book.

**etching**—the process in which a design is scratched through an acid-resisting coat (like wax) on a metal plate. The plate is then submerged in a shallow bath of acid which slowly eats into the exposed lines and areas. After the plate is cleaned of the acid-resistant coat, it is covered with printer's ink and then wiped clean, so that the ink remains only in the incised lines. The plate is then printed (using considerable pressure) on damp paper.

**expressionism**—art which freely expresses the artist's inner or subjective emotions and response to events and to his or her environment.

**framing**—to enclose as in a frame with orna-

Illustration from *The Lazy Bear* by Brian Wildsmith. Copyright © 1973 by Brian Wildsmith. Reprinted by permission of Franklin Watts, Inc. and Oxford University Press, London

Wildsmith puts two styles together in this book: a flat, decorative, clean-edged abstract mode for dealing with the landscape, and a textured style for the animals in which form is created with varying line and color. The direction and color of these lines change subtly to create a feeling of round mass and of fur texture. On the other hand, leaf and flower forms are flat, clean-edged, and decorative with strong color contrasts and rich patterning. They are a powerful foil for the animals, who nonetheless hold their own very well with their tonalities.

Piatti blocks off the picture space into seven major areas of subtle colors: a light blue-white textured sky area and various greens ranging from ochres to blue-greens. He tex-tures and patterns these areas with sponge-like impres-sions, muted colored stripes, speckles, and dots to make a variety of surfaces. The caravan, disappearing over the horizon, is the accent, with the brightest and the lightest colors.

Steptoe breaks objects into shapes and boldly identifies them with vivid colors, sometimes overlapping with a contrasting color in such a way as to leave edges of the foundation color remaining in irregular slivers. His heavy line defines each object precisely and unifies the entire picture. It moves around the whole composition—joining, changing direction, creating a vitality of movement. Although the colors are raw, the tonalities are close. The white negative space of irregular shapes provides the needed contrast to the brilliance and closeness of the colors.

The artist, Sugita, uses a very simple tiger shape, with minimal form change in the contour. This shape is created with rich, luminous yellow-oranges, which contrast brilliantly with the subtly changing dark browns of the textured background area. The tiger's stripes create a rounded form and flow into the dark ground. These stripes, along with the eye and mouth detail, make vivid decorations on the luminous yellows. None of the colors are flat or clean-edged and they therefore produce an agitated surface and a textured quality throughout the book.

The space is planned by Keith with four horizontal bands: lavender at the top and bottom, plus a green band infiltrated with lavender and a blue band with both green and lavender. The only white in the picture is in the bottom band, yet there is a feeling of air and flow within these four areas. This is accomplished with free forms—shadowy, indistinct edges and close halftones of muted colors. A bright, perfectly round orange sun is a sharp note of raw color which reflects as lavender in the blue water. The lavenders, greens, blues, and oranges are delicately hued, gentle, soft, and varied.

Illustration from *The Girl Who Loved the Wind* by Jane Yolen, Copyright © 1972 by Ed Young from *The Girl Who Loved the Wind* by Jane Yolen and Ed Young with permission of Thomas Y. Crowell Co., Inc.

Young uses a soft cool tint of gray for the ground color, sometimes a plain wash and sometimes a subtle pattern of the same gray. On this he creates tree and shrub shapes with a wide range of greens, and patterns them with tiny, precise, jewel-like leaves and flowers. They create an overall quivering texture to the entire surface of the page. The girl is an accent of scarlet, and the red color is delicately suggested in the tree trunks to the left of her, in the warm band of a wall above her, and in the other pinks distributed throughout the pattern. The book designer has blocked the areas of type on color grounds which blend well with the illustrations.

Burningham develops three distinct areas in this picture space. He engages the eye with a unique textural quality in each area and yet fuses them into a synthesis of soft greens. Lines are emphasized in the background (uniform, overlapping yellow-green lines) and foreground (freely placed curved lines building a foliage mass). The cat is a solid, simple shape in the middle, and the dark, velvety greens of his body fade and blend into the foreground foliage. The sole color accents are in the cat's face (black eyes and a bold orange glow) and in the flower petals.

*Harriet and the Promised Land,* Copyright © 1968, by Jacob Lawrence, Reprinted by permission of Windmill Books, Inc. Simon & Schuster, Inc.

Lawrence uses many clean-edged shapes and overlaps them to create strong color and value contrasts. A large, exaggerated human figure dominates the picture space, but it is divided into several color areas. The skirt is patterned with smaller shapes that echo the colors in the figures high on the page. Although the shapes are static, a feeling of movement is achieved through vigorous opposing directions in the arms, shovel handle, and shadows in the foreground, all moving diagonally and creating strong, dramatic contrasts.

mental or decorative design elements, or with color, line, or space within the page.

**glazes**—transparent or semi-transparent films of colors applied over dry, lighter colors.

**ground**—the surface (the color, the kind of paper, etc.) on which the picture is painted or drawn.

**halftone**—a method of achieving different shades of grays in which the entire surface of the picture is broken up into tiny dots of various sizes, by using grids or screens in front of the picture in the photographing process. The lightest areas have the smallest black dots with much white space surrounding them, the medium grays look like a checkerboard of black and white dots, and the darkest areas have white dots on a black area. The merging of these microscopic dots, to the unaided eye, creates the quality of varying tones.

**impressionism**—art which captures the impression of light and airy atmosphere by means of colors and shapes as they might be seen at a glance.

**Japanese prints**—pictures which exerted a great influence on Western artists in the last hundred years because of the colors used and the high degree of integration and feeling even though the Japanese artists did not cut blocks themselves but only supplied a brush drawing to specialized craftsmen, printers, and publishers.

**kinesthetic**—the sum of the images representing movement to the mind; the sensation of sight in which movement is represented to the mind although not actually experienced.

**layout**—the arrangement or plan for all the graphic elements on a book, magazine, or newspaper page; it includes both pictures and type.

**line-block**—a process involving a photographic negative printed in positive on a sensitized emulsion on a sheet of zinc. The light passes through the transparent parts of the negative, which corresponds to the lines of the drawing, and hardens the emulsion on those parts only. After the plate is etched it is mounted on a wooden block and printed.

**lithography**—a method of reproduction in which a drawing is made on a prepared lithographic stone with a greasy crayon or ink, and prints are taken. For color lithography, a different stone is needed for each color.

**metal-engraving**—a method of engraving (drawing on metal by a process of incising lines) in which the line is incised directly into the metal plate with a tool called a Graver or Burin, and the "burr" removed so that a clean, sharp, metallic line can be printed. The "burr"—the ridge of metal ploughed up by the Graver or Burin—may be left on the plate, as in the process called drypoint. When printed, this ridge produces a softer quality.

**modeled forms**—representation of roundness of form in any medium so that the object assumes the appearance of natural relief.

**muted color**—a lightened or softened shade of a color.

**nonobjective art**—a mode of art in which the artist arranges visual elements of color, shape, line, and textures in a nonliteral manner, with no object from nature intended or depicted.

**picture plane**—the two-dimensional surface within which the artist makes his or her picture.

**romanticism**—art characterized by picturesque strangeness or by imaginary notions conceived and treated with much freedom of fancy and high drama.

**scale**—varying dimensions and positions of objects on the picture plane, used to give the impression of distance or scope.

**sculptural**—a graphic work in which forms are made to appear round.

**sgraffito**—a method of scratching away the top layer of paint to expose the undercoat of dry paint. The undercoat appears as lines or stripes or varied textures.

**stipple**—to apply paint in dots or short strokes.

**textural effects**—the changing characteristics of the paint surface, accomplished by blending elements, by brushwork, etc.; or the representation of varying physical characteristics of particular surfaces such as fabric, wood, hair, sand.

**three-color process**—the color version of the halftone process where the original drawing is split up into dots. A glass color filter allows only one primary color (red, yellow, or blue) to pass into the camera. From each of the three color negatives a halftone block is made and the three overlapping impressions (red over yellow, blue over yellow, red over blue) can create a full-color illustration. A fourth block printed in black enables the tones to be stronger, so the process has evolved into the four-color process.

**tints**—light shades of any color.

**tonalities or tonal effects**—the interrelationships of lights and shades of colors in the composition.

**transparent paint**—transparent pigment such as watercolor as opposed to opaque pigment such as oil paint.

**type**—the name given to all printed letters; the many different styles these letters come in are called "typefaces."

**vignette**—a small, decorative design or illustration.

**watercolors**—a very finely ground pigment combined with a binding material (glycerine or gum), diluted with water; its qualities are transparency, vividness, luminosity.

**woodcut**—a method of cutting designs from the surface of a wood block in which the grain runs parallel to the length of the board. The parts of the design which are not to be printed are cut away. The wood surface is then inked and printed.

**wood engraving**—a method of incising a drawing or design on a wooden block in which the grain runs vertically to the plank (an end-grain block). The lines are made by pressing in and forcing the grain to the sides. More delicate lines and details are obtained than in the woodcut. The block is inked and printed.

# BIBLIOGRAPHY

ALDERSON, BRIAN, *Looking at Picture Books*, 1973. Catalogue for an exhibition arranged by Great Britain's National Book League. Distributed in the United States by the Children's Book Council, 67 Irving Place, New York, N.Y. 10003. Alderson is doctrinaire in his advocacy of traditional English book illustration and those working today within these conservative conventions. Yet he is usually a stimulating and perceptive critic, and this catalogue provides us with his comments about 371 picture books and several picture-book filmstrips.

THE ARTIST AND THE BOOK, 1860–1960, Museum of Fine Arts, Boston, and Harvard College Library, 1961. A catalogue of an exhibition of original graphic art published in book form. Most of the materials were taken from limited, expensive editions or were originally portfolios of prints by such artists as Daumier, Courbet, Manet, Toulouse-Lautrec, Derain, Dufy, Picasso, Braque, Rouault, and Matisse. There are some children's book illustrators represented, illustrators whose works were published at normal prices and distributed through commercial channels; for example, Jean Charlot, Hans Fischer, Antonio Frasconi, Rockwell Kent, Edward Lear, Joseph Low, William Nicholson, Howard Pyle, John Tenniel. This exhibition served to place good illustration where it belongs—in the realm of the fine arts.

BLAND, DAVID, *A History of Book Illustration: The Illuminated Manuscript and the Printed Book*, rev. ed., University of California Press, 1969. A comprehensive description of important books from every part of the world and the trends in book illustration and design that they represent. Technical printing developments and social changes that affected bookmaking are covered. Children's books are discussed as part of the mainstream of general book publishing.

*The Illustration of Books*, Pantheon, 1952. Discusses principles which should be applied to illustrated books, whether juvenile or adult.

CIANCIOLO, PATRICIA, *Illustrations in Children's Books*, Brown, 1970. This book contains a thorough survey of the different graphic media used by many picture book illustrators. It is intended for elementary school teachers and will direct their attention to some excellent examples of picture book art CHILDREN'S BOOK COUNCIL. *The Children's Book Showcase Catalogs*, 1972, 1973, 1974, 1975. Distributed by The Children's Book Council, New York. Describes graphic techniques and includes thoughtful evaluations of approximately thirty children's books judged each year as the best in terms of illustration, book design, and production. Prominent illustrators, designers, and editors comprise the jury.

HÜRLIMANN, BETTINA, *Picture-Book World*, World, 1969. Useful mainly for the many examples reproduced from good picture books from twenty-four different countries.

JAMES, PHILIP, *English Book Illustration: 1800–1900*, King Penguin Books, 1947. A succinct survey of the most important English books and illustrators of the nineteenth century. Describes straightforwardly the techniques used by illustrators and assesses the results.

KINGMAN, LEE, *Newbery and Caldecott Medal Books, 1956–1965*, Horn Book, 1965. Continues the collection of speeches and biographical notes about prize-winning children's book illustrators published earlier by Bertha Mahony Miller and Elinor Field (*Caldecott Medal Books, 1938–1957*).

KLEMIN, DIANA, *The Art of Art for Children's Books: A Contemporary Study*, Potter, 1966. Like the Hürlimann book, this is valuable for its selection of examples from modern picture books.

LARKIN, DAVID, *The Fantastic Kingdom: A Collection of Illustrations from the Golden Days of Storytelling*, Ballantine, 1974. Forty color reproductions from early twentieth-century children's books in the field of folklore and fantasy. Brief biographical notes are included about each illustrator, plus a few qualitative comments about style. Included are Edmund Dulac, W. Heath Robinson, Kay Nielsen, Dorothy Lathrop, Maxfield Parrish, Arthur Rackham, and others.

MACCANN, DONNARAE, and OLGA RICHARD, *The Child's First Books: A Critical Study of Pictures and Texts*, Wilson, 1973. An attempt to trace the relationship between children's book illustration and art history in general, explaining the negative effect of graphic stereotypes, and discussing specifically the visual elements (color, line, texture, shape, and composition) and the literary elements (originality of concept, drama, plot, humor, characterization, and style). Thirty-nine examples from contemporary picture books are included, and there is a critical discussion of the American prize for children's book illustration, the Caldecott Award.

MAHONY, BERTHA E., LOUISE PAYSON LATIMER, and BEULAH FOLMSBEE, *Illustrators of Children's Books, 1744–1945*, Horn Book, 1947. An extensive history of children's book illustration which includes 250 illustrations, a biographical section about artists, and a bibliography of illustrators and authors. Supplementary volumes of this work—*Illustrators of Children's Books, 1946–1956* by Ruth Hill Viguers, Marcia Dalphin, and Bertha Mahony Miller, and *Illustrators of Children's Books, 1957–1966* by Lee Kingman, Joanna Foster, and Ruth Giles Lontoft—are also valuable.

MUIR, PERCY, *Victorian Illustrated Books*, Praeger, 1971. Includes reproductions that provide a clear view of both the talent and the restrictive traditions of the Victorian era; miscellaneous information about personalities, techniques, and the general history of book-making.

PITZ, HENRY C., *Illustrating Children's Books: History, Technique, Production*, Watson-Guptill, 1963. A short history of illustration in children's books in America, England, and Western Europe; but particularly useful for its simple description of the processes for reproducing illustrations and techniques involved in page design and other aspects of bookmaking. The illustrations selected to reproduce in this book are uneven in quality.

SMITH, JANET ADAM, *Children's Illustrated Books*, Collins, 1948. A brief, laudatory discussion of famous English children's books. Informative in its descriptions of early books and some early publishing trends.

# GUIDING LITERARY EXPERIENCE

by *Sam Leaton Sebesta* and *Dianne L. Monson*

## CHOOSING LITERATURE WITH CHILDREN

Literature has its own reason for being. It is evidence of humankind's enduring aesthetic achievement, of the striving for perfectibility. Literary value in and of itself, then, is cause for celebration. The works sampled in this anthology can be experienced as part of that celebration, with growing respect for the contribution of children's literature to the vast aesthetic realm of all literature, of all art.

Literature helps assure children that the world is their home. The world disclosed through literature may be filled with pleasure, or it may be a world in which exist possibilities for pleasure yet to be realized. It may be a world in great disorder—but with hope that disorder can be in part righted through one's efforts. Whatever its tone and theme, literature reaches out to the reader or listener, giving assurance, reducing alienation, bringing a sense of being.

Viewed this way, literature is seldom totally escapist. It may give sanctuary, turning thoughts and feelings away from unpleasant conditions; but, even then, it offers positive confrontation with reality. The slight but significant difficulties between James Marshall's *George and Martha* show us that problems in hippopotamus—and human—relationships can be ironed out. Beverly Cleary's *Henry Huggins* and her *Ramona the Brave* show that life contains many kinds of trouble, but the troubles faced by Henry and Ramona are mixed with laughter. Carol Kendall's *The Gammage Cup,* delightful in its otherworld fantasy, turns us gently back to our own viewpoint concerning the balance between conformity and individuality. There is pleasure in these works as in nearly all works of literature. There is reassurance in them. There is knowledge that the world, despite and sometimes because of its difficulties, is a good place to be.

Children do not ask that their literature make the world seem easy or perfect, but they have a right to honest literature that clarifies the way.

They will follow Tien Pao in DeJong's *The House of Sixty Fathers* through the desolation of war. They will starve with him and rejoice with him when he finds solace through companionship. Their quest for honesty will let them journey with Paula Fox's *The Slave Dancer* through unlightened horror to emerge with vicarious understanding of one grim aspect of history. Now as in the past they may even suffer some "improving" books whose didacticism or ill-conceived messages discredit their ability to weigh alternatives and to make their own choices. But if given the opportunity for wide literary experience, they will respond to the best that literature has to offer. They will draw upon the experience to find the world their home.

There are ways you can help children to experience literature. The first is by helping them make choices in literature—not by choosing for them, but by assisting them in their choices. The second is by aiding literary response—again, not by dictating response to them, but by helping them discover ways of responding from which they may choose.

### Literature and Human Development

As you help children choose their literature, consider the effect of their choices upon their development in terms of human needs. It is not that need-fulfillment alone is the criterion for determining literary selection—literary quality is broader than that—but this criterion will serve to begin our discussion.

Inevitably, children must meet the challenges of change, hence the needs they experience along the way to adulthood. But not all needs are future-oriented: childhood, though temporary, has its own intensive needs of the moment. Over the years, experts have attempted to define both types of needs and to relate them to literary choice. Sometimes these needs focus upon the child's personal development and sometimes upon the child's social development. A modern viewpoint is that these ways of discerning needs for human development are compatible.

The opening chapter of *Children and Books* presents a framework of children's needs together with examples of books that help satisfy their hungers.[1] Here is a summary, drawn from this not-to-be-missed chapter:

1. The need for physical well-being (*The Secret Garden, Behind the Magic Line,* etc.)
2. The need to love and be loved (*Queenie Peavy, A Stranger at Green Knowe,* etc.)
3. The need to belong (*Santiago, The Hundred Dresses, The Soul Brothers and Sister Lou,* etc.)
4. The need to achieve (*Let the Balloon Go, Crow Boy,* etc.)
5. The need to change (*The Borrowers, Charlotte's Web,* etc.)
6. The need to know (biographies, accounts of true adventures, etc.)
7. The need for beauty and order (Shirley Glubok's series about art objects, books about music, etc.)

And, finally, there is the need for a variety of good books promoting the literary experience—to embrace literature as a value in itself.

This list of needs and examples is open-ended: you can proceed from it to more detailed descriptions of children's needs, drawing upon your interaction with children. As you read children's literature, consider how or whether a selection relates to needs and fosters human development.

You are likely to find some surprises. A decade ago some adults wondered whether Maurice Sendak's *Where the Wild Things Are* might terrify children. Instead, the book delighted them. Its monster-defeating hero imparts a sense of well-being and achievement! The wordless pages at the climax of the story have a dance-like beauty that is need-satisfying. Similarly, books such as Louise Fitzhugh's *Harriet the Spy* and E. L. Konigsburg's *From the Mixed-up Files of Mrs. Basil E. Frankweiler* have raised questions about meeting children's needs. Their popularity and value have been attested through the quantity and quality of children's responses.

This is not to say that every popular book can be defended. Sensationalism and taboo-breaking may arouse interest while selling readers short

in the more stable domains of wholesome need-fulfillment and entertainment. It is important to examine children's responses carefully, to ask whether a selection really does meet defensible needs when children experience it. Thus, to understand children's needs and the way literature answers these needs will aid you in helping children choose books.

An ultimate human need, as discussed by the late Abraham Maslow, is *self-actualization*—the need to become "everything that one is capable of becoming." [2] Maslow believed that a social system might be evaluated according to its ability to foster self-actualization in its members. Other needs might be temporarily laid aside in the motivated individual's quest for self-actualization, although in the main they contribute to his or her fulfillment. The value of this concept for choosing literature is unmistakable. Does a book that helps satisfy, say, needs for change and achievement also contribute to the reader's vision of the best person he or she is capable of becoming? And, if it seems to do so, does it make this contribution to human development in an effective way? An aid to judging the effectiveness of a piece of literature is to examine the quality of literary elements in the prospective choice, a matter we'll now discuss.

*Literature and Its Elements*

The variety of literature, past and present, offers a wide choice. Sometimes a child or a helping adult becomes so engrossed in one literary type that others are forgotten. The folk tale and other folklore, the modern picture book, poetry, fanciful and realistic fiction, biography, and other informational materials—all have unique ways of combining elements of literature to achieve a unified, stimulating effect.

*Settings*—the places where incidents occur—need to be considered in relation to a literary work as a whole. That the visual setting should be clear and in some way noteworthy goes without saying. But consider other factors in setting as well. Does the setting appeal to all the senses? How well does it establish a book's mood? Does the author invest the work with psychological effect through setting? It is sometimes main-

---

[1] May Hill Arbuthnot and Zena Sutherland, *Children and Books,* fourth edition (Scott, Foresman, 1972).

[2] Abraham H. Maslow, *Toward a Psychology of Being,* (Van Nostrand, 1962).

tained that children read only for plot, but this is not true; they are eager for a sense of place, the "atmosphere" of a book communicated through its setting.

In the folk tale, for example, settings may be minimal, enhancing the universal quality of the tale. Or, in the hands and eyes of a picture book artist, the folk tale setting may be explicit, filled with detail to particularize the story. Artists such as Gerald McDermott and Blair Lent contribute to folk tales in this way, adding to the sense of place.

Authors of fantasy and science fiction must create settings that differ from places we know and yet maintain believability. For some children, these other worlds are an entry to literary wonder, evidence that imagination can enter where limited experience cannot. Such a discovery as this may have led a generation of young people to read avidly the works of J. R. R. Tolkien and C. S. Lewis. The precise detail of setting in Mary Norton's *Borrowers* series creates a miniature world that impels us to look more closely at everyday things around us. Realistic episodes, too, need to be "seen" in significant settings. Notice, then, how settings are presented in the various literary forms in this anthology.

*Character* in poetry, fiction, and biography is another element to be noted in choosing and using books. Well-delineated characters in literature give more than pale reflections of real life. Through a skilled author's structured presentation we discover thoughts and motives behind actions and so find the roots of empathy, sympathy, and antipathy toward living things. The spastic child in Ivan Southall's *Let the Balloon Go,* the retarded boy in Betsy Byars' *The Summer of the Swans,* and the troubled but spirited heroes and heroines in the books of Marilyn Sachs are characters who bring understanding of unique qualities in others. In addition, since all experience has commonalities, we gain insight into ourselves.

Although much has been said about the ways authors should or should not present characters, there is really no right and wrong to the matter. Toad, in *The Wind in the Willows,* one of the most beloved of all fictional characters, violates the rules of consistency: he changes size and even appearance whenever the story calls for it. Mod-

ern authors often attempt to present character through actions, speech, and thoughts; yet it is sometimes refreshing to hear directly about a character's qualities through the author's description, as in Virginia Hamilton's works. A good way to develop your sensitivity for characterization in literature is to go back and examine works you and children love. Ask, how did the author achieve a characterization that stays in the mind and heart?

Settings in narrative literature give the background for action. Characters are the "doers" of the action. The structure of action itself is called the *plot.* Children read or listen to a narrative to see how the plot thickens: how incidents build to a climax usually followed by some sort of resolution. They experience the plot—the set of actions—by being involved with the characters in their settings, sharing their dilemmas, discovering the courses of action chosen and the results of those choices. This is free experience. When we lay the story aside, it should be with a satisfaction that we have added to our accumulation of life experience. A need for refreshment or enlightenment should have been fulfilled.

Of course, not all literature is narrative. Informational books may or may not contain plot. Their structure, as Zena Sutherland has pointed out, may derive from the author's choice and ordering of facts.[3] Some poetry avoids plot, its structure based instead on direct communication of an image or idea.

In choosing literature, consider whether the structure of a work fits the author's purpose. If the purpose seems to be to impart factual information, consider the organization of facts, not necessarily through plot. If the intent is to convey a mood—for instance, the quiet and mystical charm of a summer twilight—then you may not expect or insist on heavy action and deep characterization. The variety in literary structure makes it impossible for all works to conform to a single set of criteria.

All of these elements—setting, characters, and plot or other organization—contribute to the *theme* of a literary work. Theme is the term used to describe the work's significance, its unified meaning. The theme may or may not be directly

[3] Zena Sutherland, "Information Pleases—Sometimes," *Wilson Library Bulletin,* October 1974, pp. 161–73.

stated. Whether it is or not, the reader brings his or her own interpretation to it, drawing upon previous experience. To state a book's theme or to discuss a theme directly often requires a level of abstraction that lacks meaning for a child. At worst, abstract talk about themes becomes a foray into moralizing; the work itself gets lost. Nevertheless, the concept of theme can help you in choosing literature and in suggesting activities that are relevant to theme.

Theme needs to be considered in relation to two other unifying elements in literature: *tone* and *style*. The author's tone—his or her attitude toward the material—conveys the seriousness or playfulness behind the theme. Style—the manner of writing—includes word choices, sentence constructions, the rhythm, the "feeling" unique to the author's craft. As such, style is integral to the manner in which the theme is set forth.

The style of Scott O'Dell's *Sing Down the Moon* (see pp. 767–70) is simple and understated. The historical account of Navaho subjugation is told in the words of Bright Morning. Through her eyes, through her simple but formal words and cadences, we see the mesas and canyons of the Southwest; we experience the hunger and cold as she and her people are driven from their grazing lands into captivity. Characters and physical settings are woven together as is natural in a culture so dependent upon the land.

A tone emerges as we follow Bright Morning through the two main episodes of enslavement that comprise the plot. It is not the tone of violent anger one might expect from a twentieth-century author recounting inhuman events. Rather, it is the tone of respect and admiration for a practical young woman who survived; who suffered much and learned that endurance and survival are chosen alternatives to outrage and self-destruction. Endurance through hardship becomes the book's theme—ultimately, the muted triumph of all subjugated people who refuse to surrender their spirit. All of the book's elements point to this theme, making it powerful.

Used in this way, a knowledge of elements in literature can help you to comprehend a work, to decide if it is a good choice, and to consider ways to help others comprehend it. The aim is not to pick it apart but quite the opposite: to experience its totality. Before you attempt some of the activities suggested in the following pages, stop a moment and consider the contribution of literary elements to some of your favorite selections in the *Anthology*. Then, with renewed understanding of the workings of literature, decide which of the activities will aid literary experience with specific selections.

*Interests, Taste, and Readability*

Interest plays an important role in literary enjoyment. When a child expresses strong approval of a selection, an *interest* seems indicated. You may help the budding reader or listener by pointing out similar works, with the aim of appealing to interest. That seems wise—but tread softly when drawing conclusions about modern children's interests! Why?

First, we cannot assume, as so many studies of children's interests have assumed, that the topic of a work is the reason for its appeal. The theme, the tone, and even the organization of a prized selection may be the basis for enthusiasm. A liking for Guiterman's "Ancient History" (p. 7) may not indicate a liking for "The Capricorn Bracelet" (pp. 738–42) even though the two might appear on the same subject list! A love for dog stories or mysteries or biography won't always indicate that these topics or types alone will appeal: there are elements within such selections—suspense, bravery, careful decision-making—that help account for interest beyond the superficial subject listing. These elements—sometimes as much as the subject—are often helpful clues to exploring interests, and hence to aiding choice.

Second, interests vary and change. The seeking of a healthy child can lead to wide exploration, well beyond the bounds of expressed interests. The interest studies of the past, attempting to discover "norms" of interest for groups of children, may give us clues to how to study interests, but they tell us little about the actual interests of children today. For example, some such studies once indicated that boys prefer adventure and action, while girls prefer mystery, romance, and "quiet" fare. Well, don't be surprised to find a boy today entranced by *The Secret Garden* or a girl asking for the latest book on karate.

Third, literature doesn't always need to serve a passive role in meeting preconceived interests.

Few children are fortunate enough to live in an environment that lets them know first-hand about architecture, archaeology, Ali Baba, ballet, or bionics; yet books containing these topics have proved again and again to be high interest-arousers. Look, for example, at David Macaulay's *Cathedral: The Story of Its Construction* and *City: A Story of Roman Planning and Construction* as books likely to create interest even if they do not meet ready-made ones.

Finally, the attempt to meet interests does not dictate levels of *taste*. The starved imagination may be anesthetized with the midnight horror movie and the Saturday morning cartoon, or it may be richly fed with Natalie Babbitt's *The Devil's Storybook,* the wilder things of Sendak, William Steig's loving donkeys, and all the things that go bump in the night that you'll find in this collection. Whatever the interests, taste can be developed and guided. The literature exists for doing so.

A word about *readability* should be added to these remarks about interests and taste. Because an interest often indicates some familiarity with a topic, type, or element, children are at times able to read high-interest materials considerably above their general reading level.[4] This does not mean, however, that, once interest is met, a child can read anything! At times, a book, however intrinsically interesting, must be left for later years because of its difficulty. At times, the reading must be a shared activity. This is why our presentation of techniques and activities for enhancing literary experience begins with some aid in reading aloud.

# READING ALOUD

Why read aloud? Children's reading interests can certainly be expanded through a well-planned program of oral reading. Reading aloud to children can also create enjoyment of prose and poetry and give information to the listeners. And the reader performs another, very impor-

[4] Thomas H. Estes and Joseph L. Vaughan, Jr., "Reading Interest and Comprehension: Implications," *The Reading Teacher,* November 1973, pp. 149–53.

tant function—providing a model so that children see and hear the techniques of good oral reading in operation. If literature is to be read aloud, it should be read effectively.

*Preparation for Reading*

In order to heighten reader-listener interaction during an oral reading session, librarians, teachers, and parents need time for their own preparation. They also need time with the children prior to the reading in order to establish a mood for listening and the right kind of attitude toward the material to be read.

Consider some kinds of preparation that can enhance the reading. First, selecting good material is essential but it takes time. Generally speaking, a selection for oral reading should be related to interests of most children in the group, it should be of good literary quality so that the listeners have an opportunity to acquire taste for good literature, and it should be interesting to the reader. The latter is important. Few readers other than skilled actors can give a passage its best interpretation unless there is some degree of emotional involvement. If you don't care for a selection, can you really expect the children to? An adult, searching for material, needs to read at least part of a book, passage, or poem, judging whether it meets the above qualifications and reads well aloud. You may not always have to read an entire book aloud, although that may sometimes be absolutely demanded by children because they like it so well. A poem should be read completely, of course, but often reading a chapter or passage from a book will stimulate the curiosity of listeners so that they will finish the book independently.

Once the material has been selected, the reader must become familiar with it. A scanning of the section to be read shows an experienced reader immediately the key ideas that should be emphasized as well as the general tone of the passage (humorous, exciting, mysterious, sad, etc.) and important stylistic features such as pauses or words to be emphasized. At this point, a person inexperienced in oral reading would be wise to read the entire passage aloud, practicing to get the most appropriate effect. The practice also makes it possible to maintain some eye contact with the listeners during the later reading. Tape recording the practice session, analyzing it during playback, and practicing again with attention to punctuation and key words in a phrase or sentence will lead to a more interesting interpretation. Similarly, practicing a short dialogue passage so as to give each speaker a definitive style (a deep, booming voice for the troll and a thin, high voice for the tiny billygoat Gruff) will do much to enhance the presentation and to provide children with ideas for interpreting characters. Remember that the extensive prereading described here is not necessary for each selection. Intensive practice on a few selections will help to develop skill and cut down on preparation time later.

Although adult preparation is generally done well ahead of time, a few minutes just prior to the reading period should be set aside to prepare children. When a book is introduced, it is worthwhile to let children discuss the title with attention to what it tells about the book. Information about the author may also be of interest, especially if the children have enjoyed other books by that same person. Succeeding sessions, devoted to continuation of the story, should be preceded by a very brief resume of the story thus far, or of the last episode. The resume may be given by the adult or, better still, by one of the children. In addition to providing necessary background for any children who missed the last reading, it gives listeners experience in identifying the main ideas of a story and developing a succinct summary.

### Reading Prose Passages Aloud

Prose passages should be read so as to give listeners a feel for the pace of the story and for the motives of characters. The reader develops the mood of the story and, in a sense, represents the author to the listeners by giving as accurate an interpretation of the story as possible. In order to do this, the reader must be keenly aware of the major and minor themes and of the buildup of conflict in the plot. The reader should be able to interpret characters by varying voice quality and tone when reading dialogue passages. In addition, more subtle characteristics such as a teasing mood, a threatening stance, or the general unpleasantness of a character should

be evident from the interpretation. For example, in "The Thing" (p. 605) from Rebecca Caudill's *Did You Carry the Flag Today, Charley?* Miss Amburgey's tone changes from distinct scolding to what must be a mixture of dismay and amusement. A good reader is aware that setting, characterization, and style interact with plot to influence the tone of a selection. The small town doughnut shop setting, the contrast of local characters with a wealthy traveler, and the author's style in "The Doughnuts" (pp. 605–608) from Robert McCloskey's *Homer Price* produce a general tone of easy-going, almost slapstick, humor. In contrast, " 'Checking-In' at the Museum" (pp. 655–60) from E. L. Konigsburg's *From the Mixed-Up Files of Mrs. Basil E. Frankweiler* is set in a large city museum, and the characterization reveals two rather sophisticated children. The author's style contributes to a general tone that is subtly humorous, yet underlined with a strong sense of adventure. Because the different elements of a good story work toward a unified effect, that should be evident in the oral interpretation.

Any background information necessary for listeners to fully comprehend the story should be presented during the prereading period. If vocabulary in the story is abstract or simply beyond the sophistication of listeners, that should be dealt with. New words may be presented and discussed prior to the reading, or the reader may follow a word with a brief definition, as "the *vociferous* old man (who talked far more than he should) said. . . ."

A book that is otherwise good for oral reading may have some long narrative passages that move too slowly to hold the attention of young children. In that case, it is preferable to omit a passage, substituting a brief summary of the contents so that the listeners do not lose the momentum of the plot. Such passages can only be identified by adult prereading, another argument for such preparation.

Selections from the *Anthology* offer excellent material for oral reading. Most of them are excerpted from longer works and carefully chosen so as to include interesting and readable passages. They can usually be read at a single sitting, and will often spark an interest in listeners so that they will want to read the rest of the book. If possible, copies of books should be available in the classroom or in the library following oral reading of a passage from those books.

Realistic fiction is a good source of oral reading material as are carefully chosen folk tales, and there are selections in the *Anthology* suitable for use with children of almost any age. "The Thing" from *Did You Carry the Flag Today, Charley?* is a story that children in the early grades will enjoy. As introduction to the story, you might spend a few minutes talking about the title of the book. Charley, the five-year-old main character, has a difficult time adjusting to the rigor of school. The best child in the class is allowed to carry the flag to the school bus each day after school but Charley never manages to behave well enough to attain that honor. Months go by and Charley has to say "no" when his older brothers and sisters ask every day whether he carried the flag. The excerpt, "The Thing," gives some insight into Charley's wants and his frustrations at school. It shows a little boy wanting to work things out in his own way and at his own speed. The story is told with humor and with sympathy for an independent five-year-old. Charley's needs are those of children of any age and his story holds their attention.

A selection for older children, approximately ages eight to ten, is "Motherless Lamb" from Kate Seredy's *The Good Master*. Kate, in the story, is the proverbial tomboy, sent to the country to live with her uncle and his family because her widowed father simply cannot handle her. She seems fairly harmless, a child who has reportedly been in ill health and is in need of fresh country air. Then she disappears, just after handing her aunt a letter from her father telling about the real Kate and the reason for sending her to the farm. The total inaccuracy of their early description of her as a "motherless lamb" becomes clear as the entire family searches in vain for her only to find that she has outwitted them for the second time during her very brief visit. The story offers fine opportunity for character interpretation, character contrast, and change in the attitude of Kate's uncle from anger to forgiving gentleness.

A story for upper-grade children, Sheila Burnford's *The Incredible Journey*, evokes a great sense of adventure and of the interdependence of three animals. The body of the book is entirely narrative, as is the selection included in the *Anthology*, for it is the story of three faithful pets in search of a beloved master. The reading is enlivened by excellent descriptions of the animals and of the contrast in their actions. The old dog, especially, makes a good subject because the reader is encouraged to recreate for listeners the great desire to see his master that drives the old, tired dog to continue the journey. Each of the selections described here represents an author's commitment to create a thought-provoking situation and each selection offers a challenge to the reader to interpret the situation for listeners.

There are a number of oral reading techniques that may be applied to the three excerpts just discussed. An oral reader must be aware of the mechanics of vocal production and the means of varying inflection. There are certain cues that speakers use along with words to signal meaning to listeners. Those cues have to do with changes in voice pitch and intensity (accenting certain important words more strongly than others) and with the use of pauses between words. In written language, such pauses are signaled to the reader by means of punctuation marks which signify pauses of different lengths. Similarly, punctuation marks signal changes in voice intensity and pitch to a reader. A person reading the sentence, "Where did you put my shoes?" is likely to emphasize the word, "shoes," and raise the voice on that word to inflect the question. In order to become more familiar with the range of sounds and vocal techniques available, it is fun for teacher and students to read together a sentence such as, "I hope you can come," emphasizing "I" in the first reading, "hope" in the second reading, "you" in the third, and so forth. Tape recording the reading and playing back each rendition makes clear the number of different interpretations that can be produced by changes in the use of the voice. An expert reader learns to scan ahead and to emphasize the key word in a sentence or phrase as well as to utilize punctuation marks as signals.

Analysis of "The Thing" shows a need for the reader to separate the narration from the sections of dialogue and occasional monologue. Voice changes are necessary for the bit parts of Mr.

Sizemore and Mr. Webb. There is a lengthy section of dialogue between Charley and Miss Amburgey, with Miss Amburgey changing her tone from one of reproof to one of information, telling Charley of the wonderful resources available in the library. There are opportunities to interpret passages that end with exclamation marks ("Charley! What a snake!") and to interpret Charley's thoughts as he works on "The Thing."

"Motherless Lamb" gives an opportunity to portray an angry Uncle Marton, a smug Kate, and a sympathetic aunt. Seredy makes liberal use of exclamation marks, useful signs to a reader, and she also uses all capital letters for Uncle Marton's final, very loud, "COME DOWN!" There are also many descriptive words that make good oral reading, as in these sentences spoken by Kate's aunt, "I just know her poor little heart is broken. And you two looking at her as if she were a bug. It's enough to kill a child!"

A reader who is able to scan ahead and prepare for dramatic passages should be successful in holding the attention of the group *if* the material has been well chosen and the reader is able to maintain eye contact with the listeners from time to time during the reading.

### Reading Poetry Aloud

Nearly all children like poetry if they are fortunate enough to hear good poems read aloud well. As with prose, adults have a responsibility to select carefully and to read effectively. The selection process is important because it should result in a poem chosen to suit reader as well as listener. Most people read best when they like the material and, for that reason, you should select poetry that you enjoy for oral reading. Many teachers and librarians like to keep a card file of favorite poems. You might find it useful to read through the poetry section of the *Anthology,* reading *aloud,* if possible, to determine which poems are most appealing to you. Favorite poems are then noted with page numbers in a card file that may also include notes about the theme of the poem and about special occasions when the poem might be read. For example, you might have a card titled "People" with listings of the page numbers of your favorite poems. Other poems with that theme, but not included in the *Anthology,* may be noted on attached cards. The cards serve as a good source for that day when children seem to be especially interested in themselves as people with special concerns or for a day which is the birthdate of a famous person. You have a variety of poems that you like, so now you can find one quickly to read at the right moment. The file may also be made available for children to use on their own.

It is important to seize the opportune moment to introduce a poem. When you sense a "right" mood pervading the room, perhaps an atmosphere of playfulness, that is the time to read a poem that will add to the spirit of the occasion. Carroll's "You are Old, Father William" (p. 82) suits a day when everything seems to be at sixes and sevens, but good-humoredly so. Roethke's "The Gnu" (p. 71) would also be appropriate for a lively day and, like most poems, deserves more than one reading. The second reading gives children a chance to enjoy the characteristics of poetry that they find most appealing. Children in the early grades respond well to rhythm, rhyme, and the sound of words, and those are apparently favorite poetic elements with children in the intermediate grades, too.[5]

When you have found poems that you like, you need to turn to the second criterion for choosing poems to read aloud—children's interests. Intermediate grade children favor modern poetry, particularly poetry with contemporary language, over traditional poetry.[6] Poems from the *Anthology* such as "Friday Mom Is Home Payday" by Lucille Clifton (p. 10), "We Real Cool" by Gwendolyn Brooks (p. 10), "Poem for Flora" by Nikki Giovanni (p. 11), and "Sky Diver" by Adrien Stoutenberg (p. 66) are appealing because of the language. The content of such poems also appeals to many children because they like poems about familiar, enjoyable experiences.[7]

Humorous poetry and poems about animals are enjoyed by many children.[8] The *Anthology*

[5] Ann Terry, *Children's Poetry Preferences* (National Council of Teachers of English), p. 48.
[6] Ibid., p. 49.
[7] Ibid.
[8] Ibid.

contains many poems that will appeal to those interests. "Mice" by Rose Fyleman (p. 40), "The Little Turtle" by Vachel Lindsay (p. 42), "The Rabbits' Song Outside the Tavern" by Elizabeth Coatsworth (p. 41), "Bats" by Randall Jarrell (p. 48), and "The Prayer of the Cat" by Carmen Bernos de Gasztold (p. 49) are good selections for oral reading. These and others in the *Anthology* are also useful to have available when children tell about their pets. Poems such as "Eletelephony" by Laura E. Richards (p. 75), "Reflections Dental" by Phyllis McGinley (p. 79), and "Mummy Slept Late and Daddy Fixed Breakfast" by John Ciardi (p. 79) exemplify the kind of humor children enjoy in poetry. You will discover many other favorites as you use poems from this collection with children.

Teachers who like poetry can make a practice of reading a poem or two whenever there are spare minutes in the school day. Children can develop a love for poetry if short periods before and after lunch are used for sharing of good poems. Library story hours can also include time for poetry. A poem related to the season of the year or to the theme of a story hour makes an effective introduction to the session. An anthology poetry section which is organized by theme is a good source of material. For example, on a day when some child has a new dog, choose a poem such as "My Dog" by Marchette Chute (p. 35) or another poem from the collection of animal poems. On a gray, rainy day, read one of the poems in the "humor" section. You have a variety of things to choose from, including "Eletelephony" (p. 75), "The Armadillo" by Jack Prelutsky (p. 74), or "Homemade Boat" by Shel Silverstein (p. 74). Or, if you prefer to match poetry to weather, read "Water" by Hilda Conkling (p. 98), "Windshield Wipers Wipe the Windshield" by Mary Ann Hoberman (p. 102), or "Galoshes" by Rhoda W. Bacmeister (p. 103).

Good oral reading of poetry is an art which can become a reality with concentrated practice. You must be aware that each word in a good poem is carefully chosen so that it contributes maximally to the sense of the whole piece. Words are not used lavishly; a poem is compact. When you read poems aloud, you must be aware of the general mood, whether humorous, rollicking, pensive, or whimsical. The mood should be conveyed to the listener by tone of voice, and also by emphasizing the rhyme, rhythm, and, often, by the inflection of key words in each line.

"Seal" by William Jay Smith (p. 49) is a poem about an animal and it is humorous. It also has a good strong rhythm and a regular rhyme scheme. All of those characteristics point to a poem that should appeal to children. The *shape* of the poem on the page is a guide to the tone it deserves. It has a slow curve, the shape of a seal's path in the water. The oral reader, by varying pitch of voice, can achieve an interpretation of the glide from one side to the other, under, over, that a seal displays. Words in the selection also supply cues for effective oral reading. There are many action words that are fun to read aloud—zoom, darts, swerve, twist, flick, flip, plops. The rhyme scheme (ABCB) suggests a good steady swing to the poem, a swing that is also indicated by the poem's curving shape. If you are not an experienced reader of poetry, "The Seal" is a good beginning.

"The Prayer of the Cat" by de Gasztold (p. 49) is a lovely little nonrhymed poem which allows the reader to change tone from the beginning to the end of the poem. The opening, "Lord, I am the cat," reflects the dignity we associate with cats. The last line is probably as much a plea as any thought a cat might have. "Wouldn't you like someday to put a curse on the whole race of dogs?" deserves to be read with yearning touched with just a bit of slyness. The effect suggests that this is a conversation between equals or near-equals. All through the reading, "I" must be emphasized in order to develop the egocentric quality of the cat. "Mouse" is spoken with some relish so that it is obviously a treasured object, and "dogs" are spoken of with disgust, fear, or a combination of the two. Studying the poem and reading it aloud several times before presenting it to children will help to sharpen the interpretation.

The importance of reading a poem several times to children cannot be overestimated. A second or third reading often gives them a chance to understand a figure of speech that was not clear the first time. If some words in a poem are too obscure for most children but must be understood if the poem is to be enjoyed, you should introduce them before the first reading, perhaps when the title is read. This applies particularly to foreign terms, such as "bairn," which may be completely unfamiliar to children. An option is to pause after the first reading, discuss the meaning of difficult words, and read the poem a second time so that children can attach meaning to the words when they hear them in context.

In general, then, you prepare for oral reading of poetry with many of the same things in mind as when you prepare for oral reading of prose. You must decide on the mood the poem represents and then must interpret the lines to establish that mood. In a poem with strong rhythm, emphasize that rhythm. Pick out and emphasize qualities such as alliteration (produced by using a series of words with a recurring initial sound). An inexperienced oral reader should practice reading poetry aloud and, if possible, tape record the reading. Playback helps in hearing awkward places or ineffective treatment of rhythm or rhyme.

Oral reading is a challenge but also a very rewarding activity. Children have an opportunity to hear a good model when a teacher or librarian or parent reads aloud effectively. Oral reading can extend a literature or reading program so that children become acquainted with material of good literary quality which may be too difficult for them to read independently. Most important, children have opportunities to practice the skills of good oral reading if they are given occasion to read aloud for the entertainment of others—peers, parents, or younger children. The sections on "Speaking Literature Together" and "Readers Theatre" develop some ideas for oral reading practice.

### Selected Bibliography for Reading Aloud

For additional references, see "Storytelling and Reading Aloud" in the General Bibliography at the back of this book.

BAMMAN, HENRY A., MILDRED A. DAWSON, and ROBERT J. WHITEHEAD, *Oral Interpretation of Children's Literature,* Brown, 1964. Guidelines for improving student oral reading and oral interpretation of poetry which may be helpful to adults as well. Recommended poems and records included.

BROWN, JENNIFER, "Reading Aloud," *Elementary English,* (April 1973), pp. 635–36. Good discussion of the values of oral reading and a useful annotated bibliography of recommended books to use with children.

ROEDER, HAROLD H., and NANCY LEE, "Twenty-five Teacher-tested Ways to Encourage Voluntary Reading," *Reading Teacher,* (October 1973), pp. 48–50. Includes a number of good ideas that relate to oral reading.

TERRY, ANN, *Children's Poetry Preferences: A National Survey of Upper Elementary Grades.* NCTE Research Report No. 16. Urbana, Ill.: NCTE, 1974. Discusses currently reported poetry interests in terms of content, stylistic features, and specific poems.

THORNLEY, GWENDELLA, "Reading Poetry to Children," *Elementary English,* (November 1962), pp. 691–98+. Guidelines for oral reading and an extensive bibliography of recommended sources of poetry.

WHITEHEAD, ROBERT, *Children's Literature: Strategies of Teaching,* Prentice, 1968. Practical suggestions for oral reading techniques and lists of recommended books to read aloud to children in K-7.

WITUCKE, VIRGINIA, *Poetry in the Elementary School,* Brown, 1970. Recommendations for a poetry program in the elementary school, including listings of selected poems.

# ORAL INTERPRETATION TECHNIQUES

The foregoing information to help you read literature aloud will also be helpful as we extend our discussion to include techniques for sharing literature orally. As you experiment with these techniques—choral speaking, readers theatre, and storytelling—keep in mind the suggestions and their aim: to bring the joy of literary experience to children through vivid interpretation.

### Speaking Literature Together

Many values are claimed for speaking literature together. These include stimulation of interest in prose and poetry, the unique experience of shared community spirit, the impetus to interpretation, and improved speech and poise.[9] An additional advantage, unfashionable but worth considering, is that literature spoken together encourages effortless and productive memorization.

[9] Martha Dallmann, *Teaching the Language Arts in the Elementary School,* (Brown, 1971), pp. 326–27.

Without being urged, the young child discovers the joy of speaking literature from memory. Mother Goose rhymes, Milne's "Hoppity" (p. 60), a bit of Lear or Carroll or Stevenson or Aldis—these slide effortlessly from ear to memory to tongue if the child is given half an opportunity. The sound and sense of simple poems honed over generations continue to appeal—even, it must be admitted, when some of the words and referents have become unfamiliar in everyday parlance. Lacking such material, the young child attempts to fulfill the need to speak literature aloud, perhaps with the less permanently appealing jingles from commercial television.

Poetry, of course, is easiest—that is, poetry with built-in memory aids such as rhyme, meter, and mouth-watering turns of phrase. Prose, too, has cadence; its artful language may echo in the memory and find a permanent place there. The refrains of the simplest folk tales, the exquisitely precise and economical language of the best-written picture books are fuel for the memory to kindle into the joy of speaking literature aloud.

This initial ability of memory and the " 'satiable curtiosity" that drives it may be lost as the child grows older. A few decades ago the loss might be blamed on forced memorization and formalized, tiresomely elaborate "verse choirs." Today the loss is more likely to be the result of neglect. So much has been said *against* asking anyone to memorize anything that the advantages and pleasures of memory are almost forgotten. The speaking choirs comprised of children of a half-century ago suffered a similar fate. In the words of their foremost proponent, Marjorie Gullan of Scotland: "Severe setbacks to the choral speaking movement have resulted from the bad impression made on educators by bad choral speaking, demonstrated by incompetent, untrained teachers." [10]

Whether or not one wishes to revive a choral speaking movement may be open to question. The main values of speaking literature together can be attained informally and perhaps with less technical training than was once supposed. A

[10] Agnes Curren Hamm, *Choral Speaking Technique*, (Tower, 1946), p. 5.

few selections suitable for speaking aloud and an open atmosphere for sharing them will start you off on a worthwhile exploration of the art.

Begin, then, with one or two promising poems or brief prose passages. Read them to yourself aloud until they are familiar, until parts of them stick in your memory. Read or recite them to a group of children. Invite discussion about their meaning and interpretation (see "Questions for Eliciting Discussion," pp. 958–61). Then, without fanfare, invite children to join you in speaking the passages aloud.

It is probably best to begin with unison speaking—that is, everyone is given the opportunity to speak the lines together. Later, as a selection seems to warrant such variation, try division into parts. Choral speaking gains power as voices are arranged into high, medium, and low. Some poems provide a refrain or echo for the total group, with solo voices or solo choirs speaking the rest. For examples, see "The Good Joan" (p. 23), "Mice" (p. 40), and "The Jumblies" (p. 84). A question-and-answer poem naturally invites a two-part division: one subchorus to do the questioning and one to speak the reply:

How many miles to Babylon?
*Three score and ten.*
Shall I get there by candle-light?
*Yes and back again;*
*If your feet are nimble and light*
*You will get there by candle-light.*

The contrast of meaning or mood in some passages fits an antiphonal division so that subgroups represent extremes, as in "Swift things are beautiful," (p. 138) and the magnificent dialogue of "The Story of the Three Little Pigs" (p. 152).

Sequential speaking, each member or subgroup taking its turn in reading an assigned part, is also effective in the right place, as in the buildup of stanzas in "The Creation" (p. 139). In certain cases a running accompaniment may form an orchestralike background as the passage is spoken. In Laura E. Richards' "The Baby Goes to Boston," as spoken by one group, a few members recited the "Jiggle joggle" accompaniment throughout the poem:

What does the train say?
    Jiggle joggle, jiggle joggle!
What does the train say?
    Jiggle joggle jee!
Will the little baby go
Riding with the locomo?
Loky moky poky stoky
Smoky choky chee! . . .[11]

Whatever the final arrangement, emphasis must be given to informal interpretation—to enjoying the work and communicating its tone and meaning rather than to creating a formalized do-as-the-leader-says atmosphere.

A good sequence for most choral speaking sessions begins with brief vocal warmups in order that the group may experiment with its potential as an instrument for interpreting literature. A tongue-twister or alliterative poem such as "Galoshes" (p. 103), a brief exercise for practicing dynamics (loud and soft) such as "The Base Stealer" (p. 68), and a spirited review of a few familiar works set the tone for enjoyment and productive practice. Then move to less familiar, more challenging fare: a new poem or prose passage selected for the purpose by a leader and several participants. Finish the session with a selection that has stood the test of enjoyment.

Vary the procedure. Use scripts sometimes; at other times invite recitation from memory. The tonal effect will probably be enhanced if the group stands straight and tall, but there are times to speak literature aloud while reclining and relaxing! Most verse choir experts recommend that an assigned leader conduct with the hand, as if the group were a singing chorus or orchestra, but this practice, too, should be varied. Sometimes a musical background or the use of slides and other visuals will enhance the session, though these at other times are distracting.[12]

The best indication of success is that children enjoy choral speaking and want to try it again and again. Consider also whether the sessions seem to produce heightened taste and quality of

response. Finally, do not dismiss too lightly the advantage of memory: that pleasure-filled choral speaking sessions may induce children to place good literature in their memory pockets for a lifetime of enjoyment.

## Selected Bibliography for Speaking Literature Together

First, here are seven books containing poems conducive to speaking aloud. Your own favorites and those of the children with whom you work should be added to this list.

ADOFF, ARNOLD, ed., *I Am the Darker Brother*, Macmillan, 1968. The strong feelings expressed with notable lack of singsong verse make this collection a fine one for the choral speaking group.
ALDIS, DOROTHY, *All Together*, Putnam, 1952. The simple language conveying honesty of tone in such poems as "The Little Hat," "No," and "Bad" makes this a timeless collection, and the poems are easily memorized and retained.
BENÉT, ROSEMARY and STEPHEN VINCENT, *A Book of Americans*, Holt, 1933, 1961. Lilting, loving portraits of some famous Americans, including Abigail Adams, Dolly Madison, Nancy Hanks, Columbus, De Soto, and Woodrow Wilson.
CIARDI, JOHN, *I Met a Man*, Houghton, 1961. Selections such as "The Cat Heard the Cat-Bird" make fine warmups.
KUSKIN, KARLA, *Any Me I Want to Be*, Harper, 1972. Poems spoken by a snake, a parrot, a dragon, and others—these are fine for varying the tone of a group.
LIVINGSTON, MYRA COHN, *The Malibu and Other Poems*, Atheneum, 1972. Great variety in subject and tone appears in these poems, hence a chance for contrasting interpretations. See in particular "Only a Little Litter," "Time to Practice," and "Goldfish Whisper."
MERRIAM, EVE, *It Doesn't Always Have to Rhyme*, Atheneum, 1964. The title poem and many that follow provide an expressive way to examine the workings of poetry while speaking it.

Selected adult references are listed on pages 986–87.

*Readers Theatre*

Readers Theatre has been defined as "a medium in which two or more oral interpreters through their oral reading cause an audience to experience literature."[13] Although Readers The-

[11] Laura E. Richards, "The Baby Goes to Boston," from *Tirra Lirra: Rhymes Old and New*, originally published by Dana Estes & Co., 1902.
[12] Myra Weiger, "Getting Together with Poetry," *Elementary English*, January 1975, pp. 105–07.

[13] Leslie Irene Coger and Melvin R. White, *Readers Theatre Handbook: A Dramatic Approach to Literature* (Scott, Foresman, 1967), p. 8.

atre can involve physical movements of the readers, the interpretation is often done with voice, facial expression, and limited use of the body. In fact, many productions are staged with the readers perched on stools or standing behind lecterns. The emphasis is definitely on the use of the voice to convey interpretation. Costumes, scenery, and props are usually not used. Readers do use scripts which are placed so that they are as unobtrusive as possible. They can be held in black loose-leaf binders or placed on music stands in front of the readers.

After reading the foregoing description, you may wonder whether Readers Theatre is too formal to use with elementary age children. The fact is that it can be adapted easily to an informal situation. All you need are a good story and enough children to take the parts of the characters and the narrator. The only other needs are story copies for each reader and time set aside for them to study the material. Eventually you might want to provide readers with an audience, but that is not necessary for elementary children. You will find that children enjoy the group reading so much that they request an audience only when they think the story is unusually interesting.

Oral interpretation can succeed or fail on the basis of the material you select. Stories must have interesting, well-paced dialogue with few long, narrative parts. Beyond that, they should have strongly contrasting characters so that children can work for distinctive vocal tone and quality for each character and so they can use facial and bodily expressions that make the characterization convincing.

Contrast comes with "good" and "bad" characters, of course, but the contrast between seriousness and teasing, young and old, or accused and accuser can also provide good opportunities for interpretation. Characters in strong conflict also offer good material. A number of selections in the *Anthology* are good for Readers Theatre productions. "The Doughnuts" (pp. 687–91) from *Homer Price* will give children plenty of options for character interpretation. It requires seven readers: Homer, Uncle Ulysses, Mr. Gabby (customer whose name suggests an interpretation), the wealthy lady, the sheriff, Rupert Black, and the narrator. McCloskey writes dialogue with

punctuation marks and descriptive words that clue the reader: "OhH—h!" moaned Uncle Ulysses. ". . . Think of the *pieces!* Think of the *crumbs!* Think of what *Aggie* will say!" The italics and exclamation marks in this case indicate a part that is fun to read. Some other selections that satisfy the criteria of good dialogue and contrasting characters are "Ellen Rides Again" (pp. 611–17) from *Ellen Tebbits*, "Enter Melanie—and Marshall" (pp. 691–95) from *The Egypt Game*, "Troubles with a Penguin" from *Mr. Popper's Penguins*, and "A Mad Tea-Party" (pp. 531–35) from *Alice in Wonderland*.

Folk tales that are effective in Readers Theatre are "The Four Musicians" (pp. 200–202), "Clever Elsie" (pp. 188–90), "Budulinek" (pp. 277–80), and "The Tiger, the Brahman, and the Jackal" (pp. 350–51). "The Cock, the Mouse, and the Little Red Hen" works well if an adult reads the narrator's part.

You should guide children's prereading and study of the material much as you would prepare for your own oral reading of a story. Be sure they are aware of striking character traits and moods and they catch the author's punctuation cues. Once the readers have been chosen for a particular selection, each one should read through the piece silently several times, concentrating on the general tone and on the relationships between characters. You might find it helpful to give the readers a few questions to guide their analysis of character relationships. For example, for "Troubles with a Penguin" you can ask: How does the repairman act toward Mr. Popper at the beginning? (He has come to do a job and simply wants instructions.) When does he change and begin to be suspicious that Mr. Popper is crazy? (When Mr. Popper says that he wants a handle on the inside of the refrigerator door and then refuses to tell the man why.) How should your voice sound if you are the repairman? How would Mr. Popper sound?

Prereading and study can also give children time to note changes that are called for in the pace of the reading. Some speeches need fast reading in order to convey excitement or fear; others are best read slowly so as to establish a character as slow-moving or to build up gradual suspense. You will need to point out such situations in literature and give children practice with them. The warmup suggestions that follow can help to focus attention on important cues.

Singers move through a carefully planned series of warmups before presenting a concert and even before serious practice. Speakers also need to warm up before a presentation if they want to make the best possible use of their vocal powers. You will find in working with children that they enjoy warmups and, as a result, they relax and are able to enjoy the reading that follows.

There are several guidelines that can improve the quality of a warmup period. First, be sure that you plan several activities with the last one most nearly related to the stories that will later be read; second, try to include at least one activity that will give children opportunity to explore the boundaries (high and low, loud and soft) of their voices; and, third, plan to include an activity that will guide children's thinking about the personalities, feelings, and motives of the characters they will be interpreting. A sample, ten-minute warmup session is described below.

Step One: An adult leads children in exercises for loosening up the tongue and jaw. First, tell them to move the tongue all around the inside of the mouth, polishing front and back of each tooth. Following that, they are to open their mouths as wide as possible and put out their tongues as far as they can. You can pace the rhythm by saying, "jaw open, tongue out" five or six times. The effect is amusing to an observer but the exercise does wonders for tongue and jaw flexibility.

Step Two: The adult leads and children take part in "Halloween" or a similar story. Whenever a word appears in bold-faced type, the reader (usually an adult) pauses long enough for children to make the appropriate sound. It is a good idea to present the bold-faced words and sounds before reading the story, allowing children to practice each sound as the stimulus word is spoken by the leader. Upper-grade children will be able to work as a large group, everyone making all sounds. Younger children may find it difficult to remember all of the sounds. Therefore, it is better to assign a part to a small group of two or three children. The major purpose of the activity, of course, is to give opportunity to vary pitch and volume.

### Halloween

Sounds needed:
HALLOWEEN—all of the sounds that follow are made simultaneously
WITCH—Hee, hee!
OWLS—Whooooooo!
SKELETONS—knock quickly on desks or use rattle
GHOST—Boooo!
CROW—Awk! Awk!
CAT—Miaow!
DOG—Woof, woof, woof! Yip, yip!
CHILDREN—Help! Oh, help!
SUDDENLY—Ah!!

One HALLOWEEN a strange thing happened in CROW Hollow. During the school HALLOWEEN party, one of the teachers disappeared. She disappeared while they were playing "Find the SKELETON." The CHILDREN were sitting quietly in the room with their eyes closed while she hid the SKELETON. She didn't come back for a long time. Someone said, "Maybe she's really a WITCH!" And the CHILDREN all laughed.

But it was getting dark outside and the CHILDREN were frightened. SUDDENLY, they heard a DOG bark out in the woods and closer to the school they heard OWLS hooting from all the nearby trees. Two CATS jumped in through a window and another CAT ran in through the open door, followed by a DOG. All of the animals ran wildly around the room as the CHILDREN tried to catch them. SUDDENLY, the door blew shut with a bang! All the CHILDREN stopped where they were and looked! There, right in front of them, was a big white GHOST, waving its arms and shouting, "It's HALLOWEEN! It's HALLOWEEN!"

The white GHOST floated over to the teacher's desk and disappeared underneath it. Nobody moved until they heard a familiar voice say, "There now, wasn't that fun? That was my surprise to you. Go home and have a Happy HALLOWEEN!"

Step Three: Prepare a short exercise to help children concentrate on the story to be read. In preparation for "The Tiger, the Brahman, and the Jackal," you might use a transparency like that shown below:

Think of the words that best describe each character.
The Brahman is ———. He is also ——— and
———. The Brahman would talk like ———
———.

The tiger is ——— and ———.
The tiger would talk like ———.
The jackal is ——— and ———.
The jackal would talk like ———.

(The above character analyses assume that children have read the story silently.)
Now, study the jackal's speech below. Decide how it should be read, where you would pause, and which words you would emphasize.
"Of course!" cried the jackal, pretending to tremble with fright, "yes! I was in the cage—no, I wasn't—dear! dear! where are my wits? Let me see—the tiger was in the Brahman, and the cage came walking by—no, that's not it either! Well, don't mind me, but begin your dinner, for I shall never understand!"

When the warmups are finished, let children spend some time studying their scripts and practicing reading aloud. At this point, tape recording of individual parts and of dialogue between characters can help children to refine their attempts at interpretation. This stage of the practice may conclude with the reading of the entire story done for the pleasure of the group involved and without the benefit of an audience.

Some selections will be so well liked by children that they will want to present them to others. In those cases, you will need to consider the staging of the production. Children can decide whether they will want costumes or props, although neither is usually necessary. Material like Seuss's *The King's Stilts,* however, is well suited to the use of a few props such as a plume-tipped pen and a pair of stilts. The reading situation must be planned so that you have script holders that are not distracting to readers or audience and so that readers have some plan for their formation on the "stage." The simplest staging is usually the most effective. Readers can remain seated during the production or each one can rise while reading. Or children can stand at

the rear of the stage area and step forward while reading. Alternatives are for the readers to stand behind boxes or lecterns during the entire reading or to stand facing, but to the side of, the narrator (see diagram). In any case, the production should begin simply, with the narrator reading the title and supplying background information on the story (or resume of preceding sections), if it is required.

◁

△

READERS          ◁  NARRATOR

▽

◁

Sound effects can add flavor to a Readers Theatre presentation. However, they should never be used so liberally that they overpower the effect of the vocal interpretation. Readers Theatre is not dramatization and the emphasis is upon the literature rather than dramatic effects. Sound effects must be an accompaniment to the reading, if they are used at all. They can help to create mood. Children can produce marvelous sounding nizzards, whole flocks of them, for Seuss's *The King's Stilts,* and for "The Doughnuts" they can manage a very good doughnut machine noise for subtle background sound by raiding their fathers' tool chests. Wise use of sound effects can help to create a more finished production if the reading is to be presented to an audience.

## Selected Bibliography for Oral Interpretation Techniques

ANDERSON, PAUL S., *Language Skills in Elementary Education,* 2nd ed., Macmillan, 1972, pp. 128–49. Excellent selections with specific directions for using them comprise the very practical information provided in this source. The author has obviously spent time experimenting with speaking-aloud-together techniques.
ARTLEY, A. STERL, "Oral Reading as a Communication Process," *The Reading Teacher,* 26 (October 1972), pp. 46–51. Identifies a number of classroom occasions for oral interpretation. There is a good description of teacher-guided interpretation of a scene from Beverly Cleary's *Henry Huggins.*
BRIDGE, ETHEL B., "Hickory Dickory Dock: Prelude to Choral Speaking," *Elementary English,* 49 (December 1972), pp. 1169–70. Describes techniques for developing choral reading sessions based on four poems.
COGER, LESLIE IRENE and WHITE, MELVIN R.,

*Readers Theatre Handbook*, 2nd ed., Scott, Foresman, 1973. A useful guide for teachers who want to adapt Readers Theatre for classroom use; includes sample scripts and recommendations for casting and rehearsing.

FENIMORE, FLORA, "Choral Reading as a Spontaneous Experience," *Elementary English*, (November 1971), pp. 870–76. Outlines five approaches for involving upper grade children with poetry.

POST, ROBERT M., "An Oral Interpreter's Approach to the Teaching of Elementary School Literature," *The Speech Teacher*, 20 (September 1971), pp. 167–73. Recommends instructional techniques and materials for introducing a variety of oral interpretation situations to elementary grade children.

RASMUSSEN, CARRIE, *Let's Say Poetry Together*, Burgess, 1963. A booklet addressed to girls and boys who want to help themselves to a wide variety of poems, with suggestions for speaking them well.

TAYLOR, LOREN E., *Choral Drama*, Burgess, 1965. A selection of materials, including drama, for choral speaking; a list of values for such activity; suggestions for the speaker including use of "frontal speech" in which placement enhances articulation.

# STORYTELLING

"To hold 'children from play, and old men from the chimney corner'—nothing short of this, I take it, can be called storytelling."—Ruth Sawyer.[14]

Oldest of all literary arts, storytelling still thrives. It has the virtue of direct communication: eye contact, vocal and body expression without intervention of print, and the excitement of seemingly spontaneous creation. Well-chosen stories told in vivid, concrete language with a sense of interaction between audience and storyteller give an excitement that other forms of literary experience seldom match.

Watching a great storyteller at work, you can understand how storytellers of old—and more recent practitioners such as Marie Shedlock, Ruth Sawyer, and May Hill Arbuthnot—could hold large audiences enthralled. The feat of sustaining attention is even more impressive when you realize that the storyteller's art is *not* that of dramatic performance. The storyteller is *not* an actor interpreting a role but, rather, an intermediary through whom the story speaks. This seems a slender thread; the storyteller must surely have great courage to trust it.

But don't let these remarks about great storytelling intimidate you! *Everyone* has sometime told a story and will do so again. "How I got myself into difficulty by borrowing a bicycle" is someone's story—and he or she will tell it well or poorly depending on how strongly the reality of the experience returns during the telling. "How as a child your age I—" marks the beginning of many a family story that builds ties to the past. Stories based on personal experience may or may not have literary value, but telling them gives practice and can lead to the telling of stories based on literary selection.

How do you begin? Personal-experience stories are one way to start. Another way to begin to get the feel of storytelling is to create a story in a spontaneous reaction to a picture or a suggested set of circumstances. Adults just starting their work with groups of children may gain confidence through creating such fragments. In many cases the interest of a child audience in these early attempts is surprising and heartening. You discover that children are starved for a story!

In like manner, encourage children themselves to explore storytelling. Wordless picture books by John S. Goodall, Mercer Mayer, and others are useful for early inspiration.[15] If you divide a large group into smaller groups of four or five, permitting each child in the group to tell a wordless picture book, the opportunity to initiate storytelling is increased.

Most storytellers recommend that you begin literary storytelling with folklore. The brevity and novelty of fables invite economy of style and good listening. Folk tales, too, are recommended. Their beginnings are direct. They leap into action. Their characters are limited in number and in subtlety so that rambling and confusion can be avoided. Their themes are universal so that, selecting from a variety of ethnic origins, you can convey universal human experience. Above all, they show ingenuity, an uncomplicated surprise over the ability of an unremarkable individual to achieve a remarkable outcome. Such qualities are sure-fire interest arousers if

---

[14] Ruth Sawyer, *The Way of the Storyteller*, rev. ed. (Viking, 1962), p. 71

[15] Examples: *Shrewbettina's Birthday* and *Paddy's Evening Out* by John S. Goodall; *Frog Goes to Dinner* by Mercer Mayer.

you, as intermediary, keep the story clear and do not overelaborate.

Remember that folk tales were originally told to the "folk"—to children and adults who received them with wonder and enthusiasm. Russian farmers took their grain to the mill that offered the best tale-teller; native American storytellers *owned* their story chants and were so respected that others were not allowed to tell a story they did not own; the High King in ancient Ireland required new stories of each clan's storyteller on pain of death. The folklore legends with their respect for history and tradition and the myths with their religious origins commanded honor as well as interest. To know something of the place these stories held in the lives of the people is to enrich the tone of such stories when you tell them. They are ageless—and they may be told to any age level, keeping in mind only that, for early childhood, a selection must not be confusing.

Should you *tell* stories from today's literature, written by authors who intend that their work be read? The integrity of the author's material and style is in question. For example, to change Hans Christian Andersen's style as handed us by a good translator is unfair to author and audience. Still, stories such as Andersen's may beg to be told, not read. If you love "The Darning Needle" or any richly written modern story, chances are that you can "own" it—you can learn it "by heart" and then learn to tell it well.

There are dangers in telling the memorized story. You may forget what comes next. Worse: you may forget to think and to feel, so that the story comes out like announcements at the airport. Nevertheless, the risk is worth taking if you are game to memorize. Despite some storytellers' warnings against memorization, you may find it a wonderful avenue for sharing the modern story.

Incidents from longer works, and sometimes summaries of whole books, broaden the scope of storytelling. I recall an exciting day some twenty years ago when Marguerite Henry told the entire narrative of her forthcoming *Cinnabar the One O'Clock Fox* to an audience of teachers and children. This was no "book report" intended to touch each base and hurry on. It was a full living of the tale replete with suspense, integrity of tone, and clarity of theme. Today, there are many books whose plots, part or whole, invite storytelling. The plot background for exploring the old house in Virginia Hamilton's *The House of Dies Drear* (pp. 646–55)—these and other works may at times be effectively told.

The sounds and rhythms of poetry are background music for storytelling, so include poetry in your repertoire. Quickly memorized by the "teller" and just as quickly and effortlessly memorized by children who listen to them, jingles and participation poems capture and hold attention. "Galoshes" (p. 103) invites the feet to move about in the slush: let your audience stand up and go through the motions. Recite "Girls and boys, come out and play" (p. 58) twice and you'll find your audience joining in, eager to feel the poem with their lips. The mood for a quiet story is established with singing lines, such as Robert Louis Stevenson's "When I was down beside the sea/ A wooden spade they gave to me/ To dig the sandy shore" or "Song of the Sky Loom" (p. 144). Narrative poems, the folk ballads, and modern story poems of every topic and hue, are story selections in themselves. For instance, "Macavity: the Mystery Cat" (p. 73) is a favorite of intermediate-age children. Such a poem tunes the ear to hear the less obvious cadences of story prose.

Once a selection is made, the important first step is to become totally familiar with it. Read it carefully several times. Read it aloud until its language seems natural to you. If a passage seems awkward or too difficult, try rewording without losing the story's tone.

Some people "see" a story through its incidents, its plot. Outline in your mind or on paper the progression of incidents. Or a story may be visualized as a sequence of scenes, the emphasis on settings. In this case, outline the scenes, filling in the movements and motives of characters.

If a story includes characters' speeches, your problem is to render them without breaking the storyteller's point of view. To attempt to impersonate a character completely, using the movements and voice of that character, is an actor's role, not that of a storyteller. You can *suggest* a character in speech and gesture without wholly imitating her or him—and this is usually a preferable technique.

During practice, it's a good idea occasionally to return to the story as a whole after experimenting with the telling of parts. The movement of the story from its introduction, usually brief, through its problem and climax to its resolution involves a revelation of theme and tone, and to give this movement unity requires your practice and concentration.

Spoken language is your medium. Strive for precision and economy of language. If Odysseus is "wily, daring, wise," speak with the variety in tone and emphasis to convey the meaning in each word. A short pause between each of those words will highlight them so that your listeners can deal with each concept as it sharpens the portrait of the Greek hero. Long descriptions slow a story; brief, precise descriptions clarify without losing the pace.

Some stories contain vocabulary or concepts that need explanation before you begin. Plan these explanations, sometimes using a picture or an object or a bit of action to help. Harriet Tubman's story (pp. 815–20) will be confusing if the Underground Railroad is visualized as a sort of subway built from North to South across the United States. So, before you begin to tell of Harriet Tubman, you may need to clarify the metaphor of the Underground Railroad. This does not mean that *every* difficult word you plan to use must be explained ahead of time. The story and the way you tell it should make meaning clear through context, building vocabulary as a valuable side benefit. A child may not be certain about the meaning of "wily" in the example in the preceding paragraph, but the way you speak the word and the way Odysseus bears it out as the story unwinds will help define it.

In many stories there is room for just a bit of ambiguity in the listener's reception of strange words or concepts. Don't try to avoid that ambiguity by watering down the vocabulary. Use the difficult word when it's needed; if necessary, explain it briefly. That will do more for language development than talking down or trying to use a "controlled vocabulary."

Spoken language does not live by words alone but by the "melody" you give it through variation in pitch, dynamics (loud and soft), rhythm, and rate. Good storytellers advise that you begin a story quietly and with low pitch so that you can build as you progress. Plan for variety in pace, too, and you'll find that the effect soon seems spontaneous. To start a story in high gear and tell it straight through, without pause for fear of losing attention, is likely to lose an audience midway.

A good way to improve storytelling, once you're launched into the experience, is to listen to good storytellers and to yourself. Tape record one of your performances and then listen critically. Initially, this can be a discouraging experience: you'll hear your faltering for words, your apparent lack of variety, your difficulty in sustaining the tone. Take heart. Record another time and find your improvements. Read Ruth Sawyer's account in *The Way of the Storyteller* of how she began less than perfectly—and the great satisfaction she felt when words began to flow and audiences began to respond.

None of these suggestions is secret lore. All can be shared with children as they also experiment with storytelling. In one school, fifth-graders selected and told stories to primary children once a week, critiqued their performances at weekly meetings, and vastly improved not only in storytelling ability but in listening to stories told by their teacher. Would that all children and adults who impart literature might do so well!

The effect of the art and a summary of the art is best conveyed in the words of a renowned storyteller three-quarters of a century ago: "I like to think of the storyteller as a good fellow standing at a great window overlooking a busy street or a picturesque square, and reporting with gusto to the comrade in the rear of the room what of mirth or sadness he sees; he hints at the policeman's strut, the organ-grinder's shrug, the schoolgirl's gayety, with a gesture or two which is born of an irresistible impulse to imitate; but he never leaves his fascinating post to carry the invitation farther than a hint." [16]

## Selected Bibliography for Storytelling

FEINSTEIN, BARBARA, "Storytelling for Remedial and Reluctant Readers," *Instructor* (April 1971) , pp. 64–65.

[16] Sara Cone Bryant, *How to Tell Stories to Children* (Houghton Mifflin, 1905) , pp. 102–03.

How older children help a transitional kindergarten class through storytelling.

GARTHWAITE, MARION, "Stories to Shorten the Road," *Elementary English* (April 1972), pp. 600–03. Suggestions and titles to aid you in selecting stories to tell.

GREENE, ELLIN, "The Preschool Story Hour Today," *Top of the News* (November 1974), pp. 80–85. Fifteen excellent suggestions and a peppering of good titles for storytelling.

MOORE, VARDINE, *The Pre-School Story Hour*, 2nd ed., Scarecrow, 1972. Participation games, ideas for using a story rug or telling stories in outdoor settings; useful story-title lists.

ROSS, EULALIE STEINMETZ, ed., *The Lost Half-Hour*, Harcourt, 1963. Procedure for starting and sustaining storytelling sessions; a plea for sincerity that surmounts mere technique.

SHEDLOCK, MARIE L., *The Art of the Storyteller*, 3rd ed., Dover, 1951. A classic to be owned and read often; first published in 1915; here is a storyteller who looked deeply into the well of literature and knew how to tell about it.

TOOZE, RUTH, *Storytelling*, Prentice, 1959. Examples and title lists, criteria for selecting stories to tell, a useful chapter on the teller's technique.

# DISCUSSION OF LITERATURE

*Questions for Eliciting Discussion*

"Did you think I didn't know the answer to *that?* Ask another," says Humpty Dumpty to Alice, who has been asking a great many questions. Her purpose is to find out where and in whose world she is.

The first questions in a discussion of literature ought to come from children who, like Alice in *Through the Looking-Glass,* are exploring a literary world. Don't block questions; invite them. Try starting a discussion with an invitation: "What did you wonder about as we read this selection?" or "Tell us about it." That's better than a mundane "Did you like this selection?"—a yes-no question that can cast a shadow over further discussion. Don't rush to judgment. "What part of this selection did you like best?" can come later. Begin broadly, invitingly. Then use children's questions and answers as indicators of what should follow in the discussion.

Sometimes it becomes evident through these beginning discussions that parts of a selection are unclear. Main ideas or sequence of events may need to be reviewed. For example, the sequence of events in "The Pride of the County" (p. 666) from *Queenie Peavy* includes Queenie's first encounter with her father after his release from the penitentiary, Queenie doing the chores and talking with the neighbor children, Queenie's lonely evening of study while her parents are out, the morning chores, and the climactic discovery that father has a pistol. Behind these scenes is the discovery that all is not well: prison has not changed the father's negligent and willful ways. But this discovery, and discussion leading up to it, is unlikely to take place until the main events are clearly in mind. Such clarification can be accomplished through questions such as these: "What is the first scene? What does Queenie invite her father to do?"

This is discussion on a *literal* level. These questions and answers are aimed at disclosing what the selection tells literally, not what it implies. It establishes the basis for higher level discussion, inviting conjecture about the implications and the significance of the work.

Discussion on a literal level is justified and sometimes necessary as a stepping stone to appreciating and understanding literature. Questions should not stop there. Unfortunately, they sometimes do. There is evidence that literal-level questions and empty evaluative questions ("Did you like the story?") comprise 85 percent of those asked about a literary selection.[17]

With this in mind, let's consider types of questions that lead to discussion on a higher level—those designed to get at the significance of a story, poem, or nonfiction selection. In most instances these will be *open* questions; that is, they invite a variety of answers, not one "right" answer. Their aim is to inspire *interpretation, creative response,* and *problem solving.*

Interpretation questions explore literary elements and their relationships. In respect to character, they help determine motives. *Why* does Queenie Peavy's father say those unfeeling things to his daughter? *Why* does he carry a gun when this is forbidden by the parole board? They explore the cause-and-effect within plot.

---

[17] Frank J. Guszak, "Teacher Questioning and Reading," *The Reading Teacher,* December 1967, pp. 227–34.

*If* Queenie's father continues to act as he does, *then* what is likely to happen? *If* Momotaro, the Boy-of-the-Peach (pp. 336–38), befriends the animals along his way, *then* how might those animals aid him on his mission to Ogre Island? They may help us infer the significance of setting. *How* does the rainy day affect "Vern" (p. 35) and the tears he must hide? What does the city setting have to do with James Douglas's troubles in "Trapped by the Gang" (pp. 633–38) from *How Many Miles to Babylon?* Ultimately, these questions lead to interpretation of theme. When we have discovered the reasons that cause Sam Gribley to select his tree home in "This Is About the Old, Old Tree" when we have seen the cause-and-effect of his attempts to carve out a home and find food, then we can understand his thematic statement: "And that was the first time I had planned ahead!"

Two requirements for good interpretation questions are that they be relevant to the selection and that they be concrete enough to promote specific response. "Being President can practically ruin your whole life," declares Theodore Roosevelt's son in *The One Bad Thing About Father* (pp. 838–40); but neither the tone nor the theme of this delightful selection warrants an interpretation question that takes the statement seriously. Instead, your questions might focus on the way the children's antics and their father's reactions show a pleasant if hectic sojourn in the White House. What evidence do you find to show what Theodore Roosevelt thought of his children? If you had visited the family for a day, what would you have observed? These items are more relevant to the tone and theme of the selection. If a question is too broadly stated, it will invite abstract answers that are lifeless. "What kind of man was Theodore Roosevelt?" may elicit a catalog of abstract qualities: "kind, busy, funny, impatient, nice, blustery." The question, although open, is too general to arouse thought and expression specific to the work.

Creative response questions may go beyond the selection itself to produce fluency and flexibility in creative thinking. Such questions may aim at production of many relevant answers (fluency). "Cynthia in the Snow" (p. 117) contains several made-up words to describe the snow, including "sushes" and "flitter-twitters." Using these as a base, ask for other made-up words to describe snow, encouraging quick, uncriticized response to make a long list. Gradually, this list may begin to change in point of view: the person lost in a blizzard, pelted by hard-driven snow, is unlikely to use "flitter-twitter" to describe the experience! Fluency can lead to and include flexibility as answers begin to differ from each other, to show a change in attitude or observation. In "An Afternoon with the Oldest Inhabitant" (pp. 627–33) from *The Middle Moffat,* Jane plays cards with a spry Civil War veteran to keep him safe and occupied. What else might she do to accomplish her purpose? Other games to be shared by young and old come easily to mind, but so do nongame activities such as writing a diary or working together to devise a way for Jane to select books to read in her thwarted attempt to read the whole library. . . . Hence, flexibility—the production of different *types* of answers—can be encouraged.

Creative responses may lead to production of an entirely new story or poem using one or more of the elements from the literary work itself. "Start telling a new story about someone who offended a water imp" might be a "question" to follow literal and interpretive discussion of "The Bride Who Out Talked the Water Kelpie" (pp. 166–71). The advantage in this activity is in the ready-made plot idea and character garnered from the story. Unless one is careful, however, the tone of the newly created story or poem may be at odds with the original, endangering the literary experience. So use the activity wisely—and sparingly.

Questions to inspire problem solving may be described as a combination of interpretation and creative response questions, although, in general, they are more highly structured than those. First of all, they help children focus on characters' problems within the plot. They guide the discussion toward a clear statement of the problem. Then they invite hypothesized solutions, and this is followed by discussion to test and evaluate the proposed solutions.[18] Simple exam-

[18] Sara W. Lundsteen, "Questioning to Develop Creative Problem Solving," *Elementary English,* May 1974, pp. 645–50

ples can be drawn from fiction selections with light tone. For instance, how can Homer Price stop the runaway doughnut-making machine? Solutions here might range from breaking the machine to using its precocious behavior for feeding a multitude! Folk literature, too, offers simple problem-solving material: how can the heroine find out the spinner's name in "Tom Tit Tot" (pp. 160–62), or how can an elephant earn money in "Granny's Blackie" (pp. 348–49)? Nonfiction often presents a central problem upon which discussion can be focused: how might people escape danger in the fog in "Hide and Seek Fog" (pp. 860–61)? At times, the problem-solving questions are posed in the midst of reading—before the selection moves on to present the author's solution. At other times, the discussion follows the reading as the author's solution is considered and evaluated.

When fiction has a serious tone and theme, problem-solving questions should follow suit. The theme statement in the title of "That a Man Can Stand Up" from *Johnny Tremain* (pp. 749–54) seems to contain the solution to the colonists' dilemma. Still the problem—how might the colonists react to British rule?—needs discussion, and the solutions aren't necessarily those chosen by Paul Revere and the others. Mary Stolz's unique pair of books presenting opposite points of view about the same set of incidents—*The Dog on Barkham Street* and *The Bully of Barkham Street*—are exciting material for problem solving. On one hand we have Edward's main problem: he's victimized by Martin. On the other hand we have Martin's problem: he can't seem to get along with people, especially his mother, especially Edward. Questions to define these problems more explicitly, then to figure out what Edward and Martin ought to do about them, can generate discussion that finds many parallels in children's lives. Look, too, at the growing body of serious historical fiction for problems to explore with the problem-solving kind of question. See, for example, *Sing Down the Moon* (pp. 767–70) and the Briton episode from Rosemary Sutcliff's *Capricorn Bracelet* (pp. 738–42).

With careful reading and a bit of practice, you won't find higher level questions too difficult to prepare. That, however, is only part of the task. Sometimes children ignore your well-prepared questions. Sometimes they hand you previously learned stock answers. Sometimes they tell you, "The story doesn't say."

Here are some suggestions for striking pay dirt in your use of higher-level questions. Design question clusters rather than a list of disconnected questions. One level of questioning should lead to another: your literal items become the base upon which interpretation and problem-solving questions and activities are built. By formulating several clusters, you can expect that one of them will catch fire, leading to an interchange that goes beyond the question framework and generates its own discussion.

Learn to *wait* after you ask a question, not rushing on to another without giving children a chance to speculate. Research by Mary Budd Rowe indicates that *wait time* of three seconds or more after a question is posed increases length and number of answers and raises levels of thinking from literal to interpretive to critical.[19]

Within each level of questioning there is room for questions of several types. One type is the *focusing* question to pinpoint the aspect of a selection that is to receive attention. From the initial focusing question you may need to *extend* or *clarify* the information through additional questions, then to *develop* the inquiry by more elaborate questions on the same level, and finally to *raise* the discussion by asking questions on a new level.[20]

Consider, for example, " 'Checking-In' at the Museum" (pp. 655–60). To examine the two characters' relationship, you might begin with focusing questions: "When do Claudia and Jamie agree? When do they disagree?" To extend and clarify the relationship, ask for additional instances. Is it likely, from this information, that the two runaways will have a serious quarrel, perhaps causing them to turn each other in or to stop the adventure? As discussion develops, you may raise the level to problem solving: "What will Claudia and Jamie do if they run out of money, or if they are discovered, or if something

[19] Mary Budd Rowe, *Teaching Science as Continuous Inquiry* (McGraw, 1973), p. 343
[20] Robert B. Ruddell, *Reading-Language Instruction: Innovative Practices* (Prentice, 1974), pp. 399–408

else unplanned happens in the museum? Which of the two is more likely to have a quick, workable solution to such problems—and why?"

To talk *about* Claudia is not to *be* Claudia, not to "get inside" the character. In such discussions as this one about Claudia and Jamie, try wording some of your questions so that answers will be in first person from a character's point of view. "Claudia, when did you and Jamie have your biggest disagreement?" is an example of a direct point-of-view question. Or, "What are the two of you going to do when you run out of money?" Sometimes the point-of-view strategy leads naturally to role playing.

There is more to discussion than questioning, although good question alternatives may be seen as the basis of planning. You need also to consider organizing for a discussion of literature and recognizing its outcomes. So, before you undertake your next discussion, read on. . . .

### Organizing for Discussion

As you plan for discussion of literature, you will be concerned with setting up situations for children to talk about books and with helping them to select appropriate material. If a discussion is to be successful, children will need some guidance in book selection so that the books have common elements. The most typical discussion situations are organized around a single piece of literature that is either read aloud by the adult or available in multiple copies for children to read independently. Material for successful discussion is of reasonable length, yet has characters and plot well enough developed to allow for reader interpretation of the major themes. Short stories or chapters from books in which each chapter is an episode are good selections to use, as are the *Anthology* selections. For example, you may have multiple copies available of *Roosevelt Grady* by Louisa Shotwell. A group of five or six children might read the book and meet to talk about their reactions to it. Or you may choose to read aloud the selection from *Roosevelt Grady* from the *Anthology* (pp. 695–98) and allow time afterward for discussion by the entire group. In either case, the discussion could focus on the kind of person

Roosevelt is and on the way he handles his problems.

A second scheme for selecting discussion material involves offering readers a choice of selections of a common literary type. For example, most biographies will deal with critical incidents in the person's life. They show how such incidents have helped to shape the individual's character and how that person has dealt with personal difficulties and disappointments. Each group member may be asked to select a biography of a famous person, from five or six books available. After a period of a week or so, the group meets to discuss the factors that seemed to shape the person's life and to compare the treatment given in the various books read. Folk tales have common elements of plot (repetition of incidents in three's, for example) and characterization (good versus evil) that provide a good basis for comparison of stories. Folk tales are especially useful for discussion with young children. You might read several versions of the same tale, such as "Cinderella" (pp. 210–13), "Tattercoats" (pp. 158–60), and "Little Burnt Face" (pp. 392–94). Children will find many ways in which these three stories are alike as well as ways in which they are different. They will also notice unique words and concepts in one version that suggest its origin as an American Indian tale. Other folk tales that can be compared are "Tom Tit Tot" (pp. 160–62) and "Rumpelstiltzkin" (pp. 197–99), "Mr. Vinegar" and "Gudbrand on the Hillside" (pp. 244–46), and "The Old Woman and the Tramp" and "Stone Soup."

Discussion formats that are most usable with elementary age children are the large group discussion guided by an adult, small group discussion guided by an adult or by a student leader using questions prepared beforehand or suggested by the teacher, and the panel discussion involving four to six students. The last of these is, of course, the most formal since panel members are presenting their ideas to the group. By contrast, group discussions involve interaction of all students.

If a group discussion is planned to follow oral reading of a story, tell the children in advance of the reading that they will talk about the story afterwards. If you want the discussion to focus on specific aspects of the story, such as characterization or plot, you may want to suggest that children listen to find out how a character changes during the story or that they listen to find out how the problem in the story is solved.

Discussions that are planned for a small group of children who have read different but related books require careful preparation. You need to decide, with the children, the type of book they want to read during the week that follows. Then you will probably want to develop some guiding questions for them to keep in mind as they read. For example, children reading fantasy should take note of means used by the author to produce the fantasy. Is it the characters who make this a fantasy, as in Mary Norton's *The Borrowers?* Are they small people, animals, or imaginary creatures? Has the setting of the story been placed in the future—or on another planet? What adventure did the story characters have? Were they ever in danger? If so, how did they escape? Would their escape have been possible in real life? Finally, ask the children to try to discover ways in which all of their books are alike. They should be aware of the elements of impossibility in each book and be able to determine similarities in the manner used to achieve the fantasy. Questions like the above could be adapted to panel discussions as well as to small group discussion.

Gifted children deserve special attention and they benefit from interaction with one another. You can provide such experience by helping them to select books and setting up weekly meetings so they can discuss the books. You will have to identify a type of book for each session that will interest most of the children and to help them find good selections. In preparation for a discussion of fantasy, children might choose to read Kendall's *The Gammage Cup,* Lloyd Alexander's *The Cat Who Wished to Be a Man,* C. S. Lewis's *The Lion, the Witch and the Wardrobe,* or Kenneth Grahame's *Wind in the Willows.* Younger children will enjoy *The Borrowers,* E. B. White's *Charlotte's Web,* Lorenzini's *The Adventures of Pinocchio,* Virginia Lee Burton's *The Little House,* and the Atwaters' *Mr. Popper's Penguins.* The "Modern Fantasy" sec-

tion of the *Anthology* includes selections from a number of other books that children enjoy and that would be appropriate for this assignment.

If you have only a limited amount of free time to conduct book discussions with small groups of children, you may want to ask parents or other adults to serve as discussion leaders. The main requirements for volunteers are a love of books and willingness to read and study the books to be used for discussion. Volunteers will usually appreciate it if you prepare guidelines for study of the book and suggested questions to be used during the discussion. A person who has not had much experience in leading discussion groups may find it easiest to deal first with a single book since preparation takes less time and responses to questions are more easily predicted. A good beginning experience would be for a volunteer to read aloud a story to a small group of children and to guide the story discussion immediately following, limiting the entire session to no more than thirty minutes. Many selections from the *Anthology* are good choices for this activity. Among them are any of the folk tales as well as stories like "Harriet Changes Her Mind" (pp. 676–79) from *Harriet the Spy,* "Edward Cleans His Room" (pp. 670–73) from *A Dog on Barkham Street,* "A Very Small Miracle" (pp. 641–44) from *Peter and Veronica,* "The Second Day" (pp. 705–708) from *From Anna,* "Boy into Man" (pp. 787–90) from *Benjamin Franklin,* or "Pupil and Teacher" (pp. 841–48) from *The Helen Keller Story.*

Librarians, familiar as they are with many books and often with the reading interests of individual children, are in a good position to encourage children to read and discuss books. Discussion groups, based on new books displayed in the library, are often effective in promoting wider reading and acquainting children with new materials. A worthwhile discussion can be held with a small group of younger children who have read the Caldecott Medal and Honor books for one year but have not been told which book was selected for the Medal. Each child decides which of the books he or she would choose for the nomination and the discussion centers on the relative merits of the books. You can guide children to look at the quality of the illustrations and judge their suitability to the style and structure of the story. In fact, the discussion can be based on criteria used in selection of award books. Similarly, older children can enjoy reading and discussing Newbery Award and Honor books to decide which one they think should have the award. The amount of time required for reading Newbery books is almost prohibitive for many children so you may want to concentrate on years when there were only three or four books honored. And consider the fact that the analysis called for requires fairly mature reading skills and may detract from the reading enjoyment of less able readers. Therefore, the discussions might best be reserved for superior readers and for gifted children, providing challenging reading experiences for those children who are capable of dealing with more sophisticated thinking skills than are provided in a typical classroom.

*Recognizing Response to Literature*

The role of an adult in guiding discussion of literature is demanding. Guidance must be subtle. If you talk too much and give too many opinions, children will very likely cease to offer their own ideas and simply agree with you. On the other hand, you know the special features of a story you feel should be discussed. With those important features in mind and some idea of the kinds of responses children are likely to make, you will be able to recognize increasing maturity in their responses.

"Troubles with a Penguin" from *Mr. Popper's Penguins* is well liked by second, third, and fourth grade children. They will often chuckle while it is being read. If you ask what made them laugh, some children will mention that it is funny because Mr. Popper wants a handle on the inside of his refrigerator (laughter at a surprising or incongruous happening). Others will describe the conversation between Mr. Popper and the repairman as hilarious because the repairman obviously thinks Mr. Popper is crazy and Mr. Popper seems unconcerned about that (laughter at a totally ridiculous situation). Responses may not be expressed in very sophisticated terms, but it is important to follow up, when possible, by asking children to think about

why the selection is funny or what the author did to create the humor. That will help to make them aware of some of the common elements of humor: laughter at a character, laughter at a surprising situation, laughter at the impossible, laughter at words, and laughter at the totally ridiculous situation.[21]

For most children, listening to a humorous story certainly involves an emotional response. Other examples of emotional response to literature are a child's remark that he or she has had the same kind of trouble a story character is having. On higher levels of empathy, a child tries to explain how he or she thinks a character must feel about something that has happened in the story. Young children often show emotional response by excitement over an event in the story or by showing anger at a character.

Interaction with a story may also involve response to literary elements such as characterization, plot structure, and style, or humor as we have discussed. Although it is not common practice to ask elementary children to consciously analyze those elements of a story, you will find it interesting to note that many of their responses reflect the early stages of literary awareness. The selection "Tom Tit Tot" (pp. 160–62) often evokes response to the style because of the many colloquialisms. Do not ask children to make value judgments about the language, but rather encourage them to appreciate it as most fitting to a tale which reflects the oral tradition of storytelling. Children who look surprised to hear a teacher or librarian read "put you them there pies on the shelf" at the beginning of the story will probably grin in appreciation of "Noo, that ain't" and "Noo, 'taint," repeated frequently as the tale develops. Your reading skill can help to create an appreciation for language and author's style that enhance a story. If children pick up some of the phrases and repeat them afterwards, you know that they are developing a feeling for the language.

Following a reading, children will sometimes respond to characterization, as when a child remarks, "I really liked Roosevelt (from *Roose-*

---

[21] Stephen Leacock, *Humour and Humanity* (Butterworth, 1937).

*velt Grady*). He's curious about lots of things and he asks questions even if he usually doesn't get answers. I feel that way sometimes, too." That response shows an emotional interaction with the story or, at least, with a story character. The child apparently felt a certain amount of empathy with Roosevelt. She may also have begun to respond to the author's skill in developing characterization, for she refers to one of the techniques used to show us the kind of a person Roosevelt was. It is not important for children to analyze the story or to study author's devices for building characterization. It is sufficient for an adult to recognize the understanding shown by such a response and to acknowledge it by saying, "Good. You are beginning to see how an author can make a character interesting and real to us." Over a period of time, such exchanges begin to develop readiness for more sophisticated literary analysis that will be studied in high school and college.

Children's responses to story material frequently show awareness of plot structure, especially in folk literature and in adventure or mystery stories. A child may notice that an incident is very often repeated three times in folk tales (see "The Three Bears," pp. 150–52, and "The Three Pigs," pp. 152–54) or that "rags to riches" is the basis for many a story ("Cinderella," pp. 210–13, "Momotaro, Boy-of-the-Peach," pp. 336–38 and "Hansel and Gretel," pp. 185–88). If you ask, at the close of an adventure story, whether the children were surprised at the ending, their responses may show that they noted clues to the story's solution and are quite prepared to explain how they were able to predict the story ending. Such responses are the essence of more mature literary analysis that comes in the upper grades.

We have looked at responses that show emotional involvement with the story or awareness of its literary qualities. Children's responses also frequently show that they are trying to make sense of the story, to interpret it. That may happen in a summing up as, "I think *Queenie Peavy* is about the way a girl learns to behave so that other people don't guess how sad she really feels," or "*The Incredible Journey* shows how three animals can learn to help each other because they all want to reach the same goal."

A more common response from young readers links the story characters, plot, or theme to happenings in their own lives. A child may try to interpret a story through his or her own experience, giving a response which is probably more an association with the story than interpretation of it. If you ask a young child why Peter in Keats's *Whistle for Willie* wanted to learn to whistle, the answer may be, "Well, I wanted to learn to ice skate because everyone else could." The child is really showing emotional involvement with a character at the same time that he or she is making an attempt at interpretation.

Children need experience to make sophisticated interpretations of stories and they also need to have some chances to evaluate stories. We must give them opportunity to say, "That isn't a good book" or "I don't like those pictures." A followup "Why?" from the teacher would allow a child to think out loud but should not force an answer. Accept, "I don't know. I just like ——— better." The child who says, "I don't think this book is right. I read another book about bats and it gave different information" is reading critically and should be encouraged to follow with a third source to determine which of the books is probably correct. Critical reading is crucial to literacy and should be fostered at every opportunity.

Watch for free responses that show children are emotionally involved with a story or with story characters or that they associate something in the story with their own lives. The involvement is healthy. Young people who respond emotionally to a story also tend to do a good job of evaluating its literary qualities.[22] In any case, we need to develop the affective response first. Encourage children to identify with characters, to see that their favorite story characters have problems similar to their own. Charley (in *Did You Carry the Flag Today, Charley?* pp. 605–608) has a problem that children can understand. He rarely does the "correct" thing. Eventually children will be able to see in such problems a sort of universal that is the building material of much good literature and, indeed, a part of their own daily lives.

[22] James R. Squire, *The Responses of Adolescents While Reading Four Short Stories,* (NCTE, 1964), p. 51.

Enjoyment, sympathy for a story character, emotional response, appreciation for illustrations—those are the most important reactions we can get from children. It is not important to ask them to analyze literature, though we may set up reading situations that will allow for spontaneous responses that show some skill in that area. Too much emphasis, however, is likely to inhibit enjoyment and emotional involvement which are the highest priority in the responses we can hope to get from elementary grade children.

### Selected Bibliography for Discussion of Literature

BINGHAM, JANE M., AND GRAYCE SCHOLT, "The Great Glass Slipper Search: Using Folktales with Older Children," *Elementary English* (October 1974), pp. 990–98. Gives the synopses of twelve variants of the "Cinderella" tale and points out the similarities and differences of the versions. Useful for guiding children in comparison of folk tales.

FEARN, LEIF, "Strategies for Involvement in Affective Conversation," *Elementary English* (March 1974), pp. 456–59. The leader uses open questions and silence to initiate discussion. Here are helpful hints on how to open the session.

FISHER, CAROL J., and PATRICIA A. LYONS, "Oral Interaction: Involving Every Child in Discussion," *Elementary English* (November/December 1974), pp. 1100–01. How to use children as question-askers in small-group discussion.

HUNKINS, FRANCIS P., *Questioning Strategies and Techniques,* Allyn & Bacon, 1972. A complete presentation of question types with help on how to evaluate the effect through analysis of responses.

LAZARUS, ARNOLD, "Performance Objectives in Reading and Responding to Literature," *English Journal* (January 1972), pp. 52–58. Describes objectives that might be set for six kinds of response to reading: valuing, describing, discovering relationships, discriminating, inferring, and evaluating.

PORTER, E. JANE, "Reflections of Life through Books," *Elementary English* (February 1973), pp. 189–95. Contains some good ideas for sharing books and creating interest in reading.

RICHARDSON, CARMEN, "A Thirst After Books," *Elementary English* (March 1974), pp. 345–47. Discusses books for eliciting sensory responses and books that evoke emotional response.

SEBESTA, SAM LEATON, "The Neglected Art: Thought Questions," *Elementary English* (December 1967), pp. 888–95. Four strategies, including direct point-of-view, for formulating questions about stories.

SMITH, RICHARD J., and THOMAS C. BARRETT, *Teaching Reading in the Middle Grades,* Addison-Wesley, 1974. Chapter Three presents Barrett's taxonomy for devising questions on appropriate comprehension levels: a useful device for *all* ages.

SQUIRE, JAMES, ed., *Response to Literature,* NCTE, 1968. Notes from the Dartmouth Conference in which British and American educators dealt with the need to develop response to literature, beginning with the early grades.

# SPECIAL TECHNIQUES FOR GAINING RESPONSE

A selection is read, recited, or told to the group. The pleasant tension of listening begins to subside. Oral interpretation, questions, and open discussion illuminate the work. What then?

The "what then" depends on time available, the decision whether or not to move to a different selection, the nature of the literary experience intended. Sometimes the "what then" calls for more active participation than listening, discussion, and recitation involve. In such cases, you and your group may choose to dramatize, to attempt written response, or to expand appreciation through music and art.

Whether such activities will really promote a love of literature depends very much on how you select and implement them. The good intent behind an invitation to "act out the story" will be subverted unless there is careful planning. Creative response, like literature itself, is structured: "All art is orderly; beneath every man's search for beauty in expression there is profound order."[23]

Let's do more, then, than merely list activities and their possible aid to literary experience. In the sections that follow, we'll consider ways to make these activities work for you in the pursuit of literature.

### Creative Dramatics

Enthusiasm is quickly generated by work with creative dramatics. To understand the process and its power, we recommend that you sample references cited on page 969. Here we'll cite some of its high points.

[23] Geraldine Brain Siks, *Children's Literature for Dramatization* (Harper, 1964), p. xvii

Creative dramatics is *improvisation*. While it does *not* involve use of a script or memorized speech, it *does* involve planning, practice, playing, evaluating, and replaying. Although the replaying often includes repetition of actions and speeches that have proved effective in prior performance, there is always room for on-the-spot creation. Thus, creative dramatics differs from children's theater, in which a carefully practiced product is displayed to an audience by actors, and it differs from an impromptu exercise in which almost anything goes. It is a process with emphasis on what it contributes to the participants, not on product or audience.

The process requires a spirit of cooperation and shared effort, qualities best developed gradually over a series of sessions. Two meetings each week, a half hour or so for each meeting, give opportunity for these attitudes to grow. Early sessions should focus on pantomime and rhythmic activity to establish body awareness. These, at first, may be based on first-hand experience: eating something with such precision that others can guess what it is, reacting to an imagined sound (an explosion, a cry for help, an invitation to go to the movies) so that others can guess the sound. Gradually, mime activities are directed toward literary characterization. Young children may mime a character from Mother Goose, Curious George, Babar, Anansi. Older children may mime a physically active character from recently shared literature, indicating the character through a crucial incident: Tom Sawyer whitewashing the fence, Pippi Longstocking making pancakes.

The leader's role is important during these early sessions. You need a ready set of suggestions—a sequence of pantomime ideas ranging from simple and short to difficult. You must help children critique their own performance (not that of others at this point) in order to refine their interpretation through movement. Ask, "What was good about what you did? How can you make it better? Next time what will you add?" You can encourage participants to talk about the characters they are trying to portray, a procedure that not only improves enactment but literary interpretation as well! You can model a pantomime, asking children to guess who you are portraying. In so doing, you

encourage the reluctant to try. You demonstrate the precision based on observation that good pantomime requires. If children fail to guess your character, you can remark, as one teacher has done, "I must not have made my pantomime clear enough to you. I'll concentrate a little harder and try again." [24] The "try again" is a tenet of dramatization—to be learned early in the sequence!

Finally, you can in these early sessions lay the groundwork for *respecting drama*. Early sessions may be filled with awkwardness and silence, or they may be bedlam. In either case, the *tone,* as you work together and refine your work, must shift to one of respect for what you are doing and, consequently, for the literary works that you are attempting to understand and illuminate. It may be a difficult time, but the sessions will improve.

When you first try creative dramatics with a specific story, select one with a dramatic line of action. Whatever the level, a folk tale is probably best in the beginning. Tell or read the story. Discuss it. Don't say at this point: "Let's act it out." Say instead, "Let's try on a character. Which of the characters do you want to try? What actions of this character are the ones we should try first?" Then let *every* child simultaneously mime the character, taking time to evaluate the outcome and try again. Slowly, tentatively, try out two or more characters and now you have the opportunity for dialogue. Let children play in pairs to try out dialogue—*not* the exact dialogue suggested in the telling of the story but child-created dialogue to be evaluated in terms of its "rightness" for characters and plot.

Now turn attention to plot. You'll need to divide the story into scenes, developing a sequence with a beginning, middle, and end. Planning scenes is in itself a useful lesson in literary form, although children needn't be aware of this side effect. Once the outline is completed, start again the process of playing, evaluating, and replaying. Note that some scenes play better than others. Would it be better, then, to play selected scenes, leaving others to a narrator

[24] Gwen Osten, "Structure in Creativity," *Elementary English,* April 1969, p. 440

or reader? This is a matter for you and your group to decide.

Before you end a session in which a story is played, it's well to critique the entire session with participants. Did it go well? What was learned? Did the enactment of the story *suit* the story? Would the writer or teller of the tale be pleased with the tone, the mood, the characterizations as these were presented? Occasionally, children will ask to repeat a story at later sessions. One group of first-graders insisted on playing *Drummer Hoff* and "Turnabout" twice a week for an entire six-week sequence! Such requests need at times to be honored, since they are part of the enthusiasm for the process. But move on. Give your participants the feeling of new frontiers in literature each time you meet. Begin with folklore but move on.

Warmup activities include movement to music and to brief rhythmic poems. Younger children listen as "Jump or Jiggle," "Tiptoe," and "Climbing" (p. 61) are read or recited. Then they are invited to join in, to feel the words on their lips. Finally, they try out movements described by the poems, often repeating the poems as they perform the movements. Older children listen to brief narrative poetry such as "Jabberwocky" (p. 76), then try out their own movement interpretation of the incidents. Not surprisingly, nursery rhymes provide miniature plots for quick, effective warmups. These have the virtue of familiarity. Older children respond to them happily if told to pretend that they are acting for the benefit of their juniors.

The advantages of folk tales for creative dramatics include good plot lines and simple characterization. Well-known cumulative tales invite dialogue as well as action; try, for instance, "Henny Penny" (pp. 154–55). Add to these some lesser known stories with clear plots: "The Great Tug-of-War" (pp. 318–21) and "The Tiger, the Brahman, and the Jackal" (pp. 350–51). In early sessions you may tell part of a story, encourage response through movement and dialogue, then return to the story so that episodes are interspersed with dramatic activity. Later, an entire story can be told or read, after which children begin by exploring a central incident through character portrayal. For example, let children choose playable incidents from "Snow-White and the Seven Dwarfs" (pp. 190–93), "Beauty and the Beast" (pp. 216–25), "Aladdin and the Wonderful Lamp" (pp. 302–10), "The Fire on the Mountain" (pp. 312–14), and "The Witches' Ride" (pp. 407–408).

When you move on to modern literature— and you should—a problem in selection arises. Some excellent literary pieces do not work well in creative dramatics. "Tolly's New Home" (pp. 535–39) from *The Children of Green Knowe* is one of these. It is beautiful to read and to imagine. It contains quiet suspense. But resolute action and character confrontation—attributes that inspire dramatic portrayal—are not present in this chapter. On the other hand, climactic scenes from later Green Knowe books, including *A Stranger at Green Knowe* and *An Enemy at Green Knowe,* may work very well.

Look for scenes containing comic action, high adventure, or the strong resolution of a character who then acts upon his or her resolve. "An Unexpected Party" (pp. 555–57) from *The Hobbit* is a natural for playing.

Some modern fiction, despite its dramatic appeal, should probably *not* be played. "Ellen Rides Again" (pp. 611–17) from *Ellen Tebbits* seems playable, but a closer look indicates that its wonderful humor derives from Beverly Cleary's ability to show us the inner feelings of Ellen caught in a web of misunderstanding spliced with a bit of vanity. The characterization is subtle enough to be joggled out of shape if we try to portray Ellen joggled on the horse's back. Better to read the selection well, enjoy its interpretation through oral reading and discussion, and then ask children to perform *their* parallel experience. Ask, "When have *you* bragged about something and later regretted that you did so? Show us." *This* session is truly improvisational, not an attempt at interpretation of the original.

After numerous sessions, a group involved in creative dramatics training will begin to select materials on its own. Members become adept at seeing dramatic possibilities in materials that seem unlikely—incidents from biography and from informational nonfiction. Your role now is to make materials available, help discuss dramatic possibilities in proposed selections, and focus evaluation when a session is completed.

## Other Types of Dramatization

As we've seen, some exciting literature does *not* fit the creative dramatics mode. Some may not fit the dramatic mode at all, though opinions differ on this matter. And some may be suited to dramatization with techniques more heavily prescribed than creative dramatics: specifically *children's theater, story theater,* and *role playing.*

Of the three, *children's theater* is by far the most difficult and least adaptable. It requires a script, talented actors, explicit staging, and rehearsal. The emphasis is upon product—the play performed from memory for the enjoyment of an audience.

In modern times, most adults (except professional theater people) have not promoted children's theater. The risk of stunting or magnifying the ego, the alleged waste of time, and the shortage of good scripts are against it. Yet the spirit of Jo March in *Little Women*, weeping over her scripts as she wrote them and bellowing forth her heroes as she played them, suggests that children's theater meets a need—a need that creative dramatics alone is not quite able to fulfill.

What is more, some recent writing for children lends itself to script-making. "Harriet Changes Her Mind" (pp. 676–79) from *Harriet the Spy* is explicit in speech and action; it is a script all in itself, suitable for children's theater. With a bit of ingenuity in staging, almost any of the episodes from *The Peterkin Papers* (pp. 568–70) can be played in children's theater; explicit dialogue and action comprise the writing of each story. And don't neglect the possibility of a series of fragments, each one the staging of a central incident from children's literature with the intent of stimulating readership: for example, try the script apparent in "A Yankee Meets a Young Confederate" (pp. 761–63) from *Jed.*

Since its appearance on Broadway in 1970, *story theater* has gained attention among theater groups.[25] You may find it useful and adaptable, especially to folk literature. In the original

format actors alternate between playing roles in which they speak characters' lines and serving as narrators to describe the action. An alternative is to have a narrator read the story while actors perform it and occasionally speak lines created on the spot or memorized. In addition, children play the scenery: they can become the house in "Bremen Town Musicians" or the brook in "Boots and His Brothers." One group of intermediate-graders reduced the story theater technique to three very useful "rules":

(1) *Volunteer*—whenever the story mentions a character or setting, someone must spring into action to create what is needed; (2) *Mime* when possible—show the meaning bodily as the narrator reads; (3) *Disband* as soon as the scene is over so that the stage isn't littered with discarded scenery and actors. A good selection for experimenting with story theater format is Maurice Sendak's *Where the Wild Things Are.*

The intent of *role playing* differs markedly from other dramatic types. Its focus is on a problem derived from an unfinished selection. Its aim is to develop problem solving through enacted decision making. To get a session in role playing underway, you read or tell a selection up to the point where a problem is disclosed. Then, through discussion, define the problem and encourage participants to suggest several solutions; then enact them to discover how well they work.

For example, read "Enter Melanie—and Marshall" (pp. 691–95) from *The Egypt Game,* stopping when Melanie and April first meet, just before Melanie speaks. Melanie has had high hopes for the meeting. Discuss the high hopes. Discuss, too, her surprise when she discovers April in her "fur thing" and false eyelashes. Then discuss April: what is she trying to do? What can the two girls say to each other? Is there any hope for a friendship?

The problem seems to be one of beginning a friendship under unusual circumstances—either that or rejection. Invite children to play the roles of Melanie and April, trying out hypotheses as to how the scene will be resolved. After each enactment, evaluation takes place: do the characters seem true to the tone of the story?

[25] Hear *Paul Sills' Story Theatre,* Columbia Records, SG30415. The script for this recording, *Story Theatre* by Paul Sills, is published by Samuel French, Inc.

Does the proposed solution work? After playing and discussing alternatives, children attempt to decide which decision would be best. In so doing, they receive practice in decision making and, in addition, gain practice in discerning cause-and-effect in literature. Needless to say, they are eager to hear the outcome of the story as the author wrote it: the ending of "Enter Melanie—and Marshall" (and the entire book) takes on special significance after role playing.

For initial role-playing sessions, use stories with not-too-serious problems. Later you should present problems that are not so easily solved. In "On Their Own" (pp. 732–35), the first chapter from John Rowe Townsend's *Trouble in the Jungle*, a family of children is deserted by Walter the father and his girlfriend Doris. What will the children do? How might they decide what to do? Again, the role-playing technique will help clarify alternatives and arouse eagerness to continue with the story. Problem-centered nonfiction can also be used as a basis for these later role-playing sessions.

Suitably used, role playing excites anticipation in the reading of literature. Its contribution to problem solving in real-life situations is convincingly discussed by the Shaftels in their book about the technique. In addition, this book gives extensive help in how to lead role-playing sessions.[26]

Each of the three types of dramatization discussed here should have roots in creative dramatics. The involvement of body language and created spoken language in response to literature is a facet of appreciation not to be overlooked.

### Selected Bibliography for Dramatics

HOETKER, JAMES, *Dramatics and the Teaching of Literature*, National Council of Teachers of English, 1969. A hard look at the evidence of drama's effectiveness here and abroad in harnessing drama and literature: the discussion includes mention of most promising techniques.

KEYES, G. E., "Creative Dramatics and the Slow Learner," *English Journal* (February 1965), pp. 81–84. The author evolved a high school literature program around creative dramatics.

PIERINI, MARY PAUL FRANCIS, *Creative Dramatics:*

*A Guide for Educators*, Herder and Herder, 1971. A complete sequence for creative dramatics sessions—from beginning pantomime through three-minute dialogues to enactment of stories, with an exemplary plan for playing James Thurber's *The Thirteen Clocks*.

SCHATTNER, REGINA, *Creative Dramatics for Handicapped Children*, Day, 1967. This book presents an inspiring set of ideas to show that wheelchairs and other accouterments of physical disability needn't dampen the joy of creative dramatization.

SHAW, ANN M., "A Taxonomical Study of the Nature and Behavioral Objectives of Creative Dramatics," *Educational Theatre Journal* (December 1970), pp. 361–72. A definitive study of the ways in which drama may contribute to human development.

SIKS, GERALDINE BRAIN, *Creative Dramatics: An Art for Children*, Harper, 1952. The complete guide, beautifully written, by a renowned teacher who knows children and books as well as drama.

STEWIG, JOHN WARREN, "Creative Drama and Language Growth," *The Elementary School Journal* (January 1974), pp. 192–95. Presents evidence from research that creative dramatics improves children's verbal and nonverbal communication as well as listening skills.

STEWIG, JOHN WARREN, "Drama: Integral Part of the Language Arts," *Elementary English* (January 1974), pp. 66–71. How to make the transition from interpretation questions to dramatic improvisation; the article includes numerous examples using folk literature.

STRATTON, LA VERNE, "What's Black and White and Moves All Over?" *Teacher* (October 1974), pp. 20–23. A unique idea: using newspapers as props and costumes to aid the imagination.

WAGNER, BETTY JANE, "Evoking Gut-Level Drama," *Learning* (March 1974), pp. 16–20. On-the-spot description of a drama session led by England's Dorothy Heathcote, with relevance to presenting complex literary selections.

WARD, WINIFRED, *Playmaking with Children*, 2nd ed., Appleton, 1957. The classic work on extemporaneous drama—its rationale, procedure, and literary examples.

### Puppetry

Children's experiences with puppets can provide satisfying interaction with books. Some children are released from shyness and embarrassment as performers when they interpret a character using a puppet. Inhibitions are forgotten and dialogue flows freely.

Good experiences with puppets require careful choice of story material. A story should have plenty of action, lively dialogue, and a limited number of characters so that not too many children are involved at one time. The plot should be simple enough so that children have no trouble carrying out the story line with improvised dialogue.

Because of the simple plot structure and generally strong contrast in characters, folk tales

26 Fannie R. Shaftel and George Shaftel, *Role-playing for Social Values* (Prentice, 1967)

adapt well for puppetry. There are a number of them in the *Anthology* that children enjoy and are able to work out with puppets. Among them are "The Four Musicians" (pp. 200–202), "Henny-Penny" (pp. 154–55), "Rumpelstiltzkin" (p. 197), "The Pancake" (pp. 238–40), and "Journeycake, Ho!" (pp. 365–67). Other story material and poems that can be used are "Little John and the Tanner of Blyth" (pp. 460–65) from *The Merry Adventures of Robin Hood,* "The Glorious Whitewasher" (pp. 673–76) from *The Adventures of Tom Sawyer,* "Motherless Lamb" from *The Good Master,* "Pinocchio's Ears Become Like Those of a Donkey" (pp. 496–98) from *The Adventures of Pinocchio,* and poems such as "The Pied Piper of Hamelin," by Robert Browning (pp. 16–20), "The Duck's Ditty," by Kenneth Grahame (p. 45), "The Duel," by Eugene Field (p. 71), and "Mrs. Snipkin and Mrs. Wobblechin," by Laura E. Richards (p. 82). All of these selections have in common strong characters that would make interesting puppets.

In preparation for a puppet presentation, children should first read through the story to determine the cast of characters. They must identify those characters that are essential to the story and decide on others they would add. In the tale "The Four Musicians" (pp. 200–202), the donkey, dog, cat, and rooster must be represented. Two or three robbers would also be required to make the production effective. Stage effects must be identified, too. In this case, the only essential is a frame of upright posts topped by a flat roof which may be placed to one side of the stage to give the illusion of the house where the robbers are dining.

Once the characters and setting have been established, children must determine the personality of each character. In "The Four Musicians" the donkey, dog, cat, and rooster have some common characteristics since all have been evicted from their homes because they are no longer useful. Except for the donkey, each animal is despondent until joining with the others. The personality change builds to a joyous mood as the four realize the power they all have over the robbers. To assist children in character analysis, you can develop a simple guidesheet like the one following:

| Name of character: | (donkey) | (dog) | (cat) | (rooster) |
|---|---|---|---|---|
| How does the character act when the story begins? | | | | |
| How does he/she change during the story? | | | | |

When children have studied the story and the characters carefully, they are ready to make the puppets. The key is to make the puppets look as though they represent the personalities of story characters and to make them flexible enough so that you can manipulate them to the positions and action needed for the play. Marionettes are rather difficult to handle, so puppets, particularly hand puppets, are recommended for young children. Papier-mâché fashioned onto a three-inch styrofoam ball, an inflated balloon, or some other such form is a popular material for puppet heads and can be modeled to produce distinctive features. The facial features can be proportioned according to the character being developed, whether troll, witch, or animal, and should begin with construction of an appropriate nose. Other features can be added in three-dimensional papier-mâché or simply painted on. Whatever technique is used, the features should be clear enough to show something of the personality of the character from some distance. A suitable costume must also be designed, cut long enough so that it will hide the hand and most of the arm of the puppeteer. It is fitted snugly at the base of the head. You must be certain that the puppet is the right size for the person who uses it and that it has a hole at the base of the head large enough for the entire index finger which serves as a support for the head.

Children will want to practice some simple movements as they get acquainted with hand puppets. You may need to remind them that the puppet should have personality, much as an actor does, and it should be able to express emotions and moods. With that in mind, children can practice head movements for "yes" and "no." They might also practice entering the stage with the puppet so that the audience is aware of the character as humorous, sad, angry, etc. From those movements, children can progress to more subtle motions that indicate fear, happiness, disapproval, or agreement with something proposed by another character. They may also practice various ways of moving the puppet so as to produce running, jumping, hopping, gliding, or weaving movements or movements using the puppet's arms as in hitting someone, waving, and beckoning.

The staging for a puppet production is quite simple. A table makes a fine stage if a floor-length cloth is put over the table to hide the puppeteers. When scenery is required, it can be drawn or painted by the children on shelf paper or mural paper and held or otherwise fastened in place. In order to give an impression that the puppet characters can cover great distances, the scenery can be placed on dowel rods and unrolled during the performance.[27]

A simple classroom or library presentation done by young children can make use of one child or an adult as narrator, thus freeing the other children to be responsible for manipulating the puppets. A more complicated presentation involves a narrator reading structural parts of the story and each puppeteer delivering the lines for his or her puppet in a freely adapted fashion, without memorization. The latter plan is more true to a professional puppet production, for it allows children to become involved with the characters as they attempt to make the appropriate vocal sounds and inflections for each one. With practice, children become adept at providing lines that are consistent with the story plot and with the characterization.

Puppets can also be used informally in the classroom to give children opportunity to extend their understanding of story characters' moods and motives. This occurs when a teacher makes up a new situation involving characters from a familiar story and asks how they think the characters would react. In a sense the use of puppets in this way provides an alternate to a typical book reporting situation, as will be shown in the section that follows.

## Book Reports

If you ask a group of children to make written book reports, chances are that you will see reactions ranging from acceptance of the assignment to outright unhappiness and rebellion. The fact is that many children who read willingly enough do not write with much facility and so they consider writing a chore. They need many well-planned experiences to help them overcome dislike for the writing task but those experiences should never be at the expense of reading enjoyment. Many boys and especially boys from lower socioeconomic levels apparently find writing so unpleasant that they will say they don't like a selection if liking it means they will have to write about it.[28] In the face of such a situation, we need to provide as many options as possible for reporting about books, realizing that some children may select a writing task, but that many will not.

If you start with the assumption that the purpose of reporting on reading is not to police the children's outside reading but to encourage their enjoyment and to sharpen their skills in evaluating—if you start here, then you should be eager to provide any activity that will accomplish this. What are some variations of written book reports that children enjoy? Older children like to adapt a short section of a story for Readers Theatre. To do this the reader must decide on a part of the story that would be suitable, prepare a script for use by the readers, and choose classmates to help with the performance. Younger children can adapt picture books and excerpts from longer stories for use in puppet shows, coordinating it with an art project to produce the puppets.

Written book reports are most worthwhile for children when their writing is read by others. For example, a book jacket project gives each child a chance to illustrate a jacket and write a brief resume of the book on the inside cover of the jacket. A critical comment can also be included, allowing children the experience of making value judgments and encouraging them to begin establishing taste for literature. Chil-

[27] Robert Whitehead, *Children's Literature: Strategies of Teaching* (Prentice, 1968), p. 234.

[28] Dianne Monson, "Children's Responses to Seven Humorous Stories," *Elementary School Journal*, April 1968, pp. 334–39.

dren who are discouraged by the amount of writing necessary to do a summary may, instead, want to write a lost or found advertisement for a person or object from the story. Other alternatives are:

> Write a letter to one of the story characters, as though you expected to get an answer. (Harriet in *Harriet the Spy*)
> Write a poem about the book.
> Write a newspaper article about something that happened to one of the characters. Begin with a good headline.
> Write about what you would have done if you were in the same situation as one of the characters.
> Write a part of the story as though you are seeing it through the eyes of a story character ("The Second Day" from *From Anna* told by Anna or "Willie's Bad Night" from *Rabbit Hill* told by Willie).

If several children have read the same story, they may enjoy each taking the role of a character and corresponding about something that took place in the story or they might write conversations that could take place between the characters.

Children can show understanding of a story graphically, with little or no writing required. A child may choose to build a scale model of something in the book and/or to write down instructions so that someone else can duplicate the model. Or a young child may make a picture book of the most important part of the story, first planning a sequence of pictures and then adding simple captions. Another child might prepare a poster to "advertise" the book interpreting a main theme in the picture. A mobile made of objects important to the story can also be an effective way for children to synthesize the main elements of a story. And children are discovering the value of a map in the front of a science fiction or fantasy story. Let them make maps to accompany favorite stories, making them available to other children who want to read the books. Picture maps are especially effective and fun to make.

The most important guideline in planning for book reporting is that the report, whatever its form, should be useful to someone. It should not be a meaningless exercise, done to please an adult, but should be used to give other children interest in and information about the book.

## Selected Bibliography for Puppetry/Book Reports

PASTON, HERBERT S., "Puppets Are Personalities," *School Arts* (November 1970), pp. 28–29. Suggests a way of making puppets that grow from character study and avoid a cartoonlike or stereotyped form.

PASTOR, CONSTANCE, "The New Alice in Wonderland," *School Arts* (June (1974), pp. 14–15. Clear pictures and descriptions of marionettes used for a production of *Alice in Wonderland*.

RYAN, FLORENCE HOLMES, "Taking the Boredom out of Book Reports," *Elementary English* (October 1974), pp. 987–89. Many good ideas for developing interesting book reporting activities.

WHITEHEAD, ROBERT, *Children's Literature: Strategies of Teaching*, Prentice, 1968. (Chapter 6) Suggestions for using drama, puppetry, and art to develop creative projects based on literature.

# LITERATURE AND THE ARTS

## Music and Literature

As with other activities related to and growing out of reading literature, your purpose in relating music and literature is to show children how both art forms give attention to mood, to elaboration of an idea, and to some delineation of style developed through rhythm and pacing of words or musical units.

You can begin by introducing children to poems that have musical settings.[29] "I Had a Little Nut Tree" has a lilting tune. In "The Nut Tree" the music suits the rhyme scheme with emphasis on the *ABCB* pattern. "The Grand Old Duke of York" (p. 60) is an excellent example of a tune that adds to interpretation of the poem because the melody builds to a high note at the phrase "top of the hill" and descends with the phrase "and he marched

[29] Two good sources are: William Engvick, ed., *Lullabies and Night Songs* (Harper & Row, 1965), and Margaret Bradford Boni, ed., *Fireside Book of Folk Songs*, (Simon and Schuster, 1974).

them down again." For older children, "The Raggle Taggle Gypsies" (p. 11) provides an excellent example of a tune in a minor mode that matches the sad, somewhat pensive tone of the ballad. All three of the song-poems mentioned here are effective with a simple guitar or autoharp accompaniment.

In addition to poems in the *Anthology,* there are a number of picture books based on familiar songs that can introduce children to rhyme and music in combination. Some of those are *Go Tell Aunt Rhody,* illustrated by Aliki, *The Fox Went Out on a Chilly Night,* illustrated by Peter Spier, *Always Room for One More* by Sorche Nic Leodhas, and *One Wide River to Cross* by Barbara Emberley.

Music can also be used to tell a story partially or completely. Two forms of musical storytelling that children can enjoy are ballet and opera. Folk tales have been adapted for use with both art forms. For example, "Cinderella" (pp. 210–13) and "The Sleeping Beauty" (pp. 207–10) have both inspired ballet music by Tchaikovsky. Rimsky-Korsakov wrote ballets based on "Sadko" (pp. 290–94) and "The Fire Bird" (pp. 294–99) and his "Scheherazade" was supposed to have told the tales of "The Arabian Nights," one of them "Aladdin and the Wonderful Lamp" (pp. 302–309). To introduce one of these ballets to children, read the story and give them a chance to talk about the mood of the story and the story characters who would be the dancers for a ballet version. Then play a portion of the music, encouraging them to imagine the kind of dancing they would expect to see in that scene. Several modern ballets are also interesting to children, particularly Aaron Copland's "Billy the Kid" and "Rodeo." They are quite short and are often available in library or public school record collections. Of course, Tchaikovsky's "Nutcracker" is a classic ballet which is familiar to many children because it is often performed by professional and community groups. It offers a good introduction to ballet if you tell or read the story of the "Nutcracker" [30] and follow the reading by playing one or two dances, perhaps "The Dance of the Sugar Plum Fairies" and

[30] Louis Untermeyer, adapter, *Tales from the Ballet,* (Golden, 1968).

"The Dance of the Reed Flutes." Allow time for children to talk about Tchaikovsky's use of tunes and rhymes to make the characters come alive.

Opera is somewhat more complex than ballet, yet children can enjoy hearing the stories of operas and learning to recognize some important themes or tunes. There are operas based on folk tales such as "Hansel and Gretel" by Engelbert Humperdinck, "Cinderella" by Gioacchino Rossini, and "William Tell" by Rossini. Two other operas by a modern composer are also popular with children: Gian-Carlo Menotti's "Help, Help, the Globolinks!" and "Amahl and the Night Visitors." The second of these, "Amahl," is one of the loveliest short operas available. It has been produced by numerous community groups and for years was given on television each Christmas season. If you want to give children an enjoyable first experience with opera, you might use "Amahl." It is the story of a poor, crippled shepherd boy. The three kings stop at his poor hut on their way to Bethlehem. As he listens to them talk of the gifts they are bringing to the child they hope to find, Amahl determines to send along the only thing he has of value, his crutch. When he makes the decision and presents his gift, he becomes able to walk again. The opera is lively, whimsical, and compellingly sad and Menotti's music depicts action and characters by means of rhythm as well as melody and tone quality. Children love to listen to the rhythm of the crippled boy's movements to and from the door as he tries to convince his mother that there are, indeed, three kings outside. The shepherds' dance adds charm and liveliness.

Children who develop a feeling for the tie between music and stories may enjoy planning their own musical accompaniment for puppet productions and for Readers Theatre presentations. A classic introduction to a musical puppet show is "Petrouchka" by Igor Stravinsky. It is the story of a puppet, Petrouchka, his love for the Ballerina, and his death by the hand of the Moor. The story is not too difficult for children and the music is beautifully suited to such contrasting characters as the clumsy puppet and the lovely Ballerina. Children might try to match "The Donkey Serenade" to "Pinocchio's

Ears Become Like That of a Donkey" (pp. 496–98), using a tape recorder to record only the most appropriate parts of the piece. With your help, they can also experiment with music to accompany "The Open Road" (pp. 487–93) from *Wind in the Willows*. Berlioz's "Harold in Italy" and Prokofieff's "Lieutenant Kije" are both blithe treatments of a wanderer's theme and are appropriate music. Children may also want to experiment with recording their own versions of folk songs as accompaniment.

## Selected Bibliography for Using Music with Literature

DEAN, LEIGH, adapter, Gian-Carlo Menotti's *Help, Help, the Globolinks!* McGraw, 1970. Colorful illustrations and parts of the musical score complement the contemporary dialogue in this story of invasion by creatures from another planet.

FUJITA, TAMAO, adapter, G. A. Rossini's *William Tell*, Gakken, Ltd., 1971. No music is included in this Japanese edition of the opera, but the story is faithful to the original and the illustrations are lovely.

LAWRENCE, ROBERT, *Hansel and Gretel: The Story of Humperdinck's Opera*, Grosset, 1938. A simple adaptation of the opera with melodies and words for the most familiar songs.

LAWRENCE, ROBERT, *Petrouchka: A Ballet by Igor Stravinsky*, Random House, 1940. The story is appropriate for intermediate-grade children. Illustrations show the major scenes clearly.

MANASEK, LUDEK, ill., *The Firebird*, Watts, 1969. A well-told version of the story with illustrations that clearly represent mood and action.

MONTRESOR, BENI, *Cinderella*, Knopf, 1965. A beautifully illustrated version of the Rossini opera by a Metropolitan Opera set designer who is also a noted illustrator and writer of children's books.

MORETON, JOHN, *The Love for Three Oranges*, Putnam's, 1966. A very readable version of this humorous opera.

SPENDER, STEPHEN, *The Magic Flute*, Putnam's, 1966. The plot is rather complex in this Mozart opera, but the version is suitable for intermediate-grade children. Interesting illustrations by Beni Montresor.

### *Visual Arts and Literature*

As we discussed earlier, the need for beauty and order is one of childhood's basic needs. The aesthetic need is central to human development for it is the need to grasp the significance of experience and to clarify one's values in living.

Literature itself serves this need. Its style, its manner of revealing a theme, the structure imposed by its author upon the experience portrayed—all of these and more are aesthetic concerns. Likewise, the contribution of literature to other arts is important to aesthetic development. We have discussed the relation of literature and music and we turn now to literature and the visual arts.

Of special interest are literary materials for children *about* art. Through illustrations and commentary, these materials present the products and process of art creation. The numerous slim volumes by Shirley Glubok contain well-selected representations of visual art products. These are accompanied by a brief, clear text that explains their significance in the cultures which produced them. To own Glubok's *The Art of Colonial America* (Macmillan, 1970), to examine the structure and detail of the objects and paintings it contains, is to grasp the aesthetic awareness of a struggling but self-confident people. The Glubok volumes deal with subsequent American history as well as ancient history and other cultures, including those of the Far East.

Despite appealing design and content, these and similar art books may be missed by children who lack guidance in how to use them. The art of active viewing rather than passive looking is difficult. Bombarded by pictures as we are, we may glance at items that really require unhurried scrutiny and imagination. Consequently, you may need to guide looking with questions: "What was this object used for? If this picture came to life, what would happen next in it? Be the artist and tell us what you thought about the person whose portrait you painted." Sometimes, too, a combination of items from a Glubok book will inspire pantomime or creative dramatics. They supplement information about setting when readers turn to historical fiction or nonfiction about a specific time and place.

Some insight into the art process is afforded by books that present contrasting treatments of similar subject matter. The opening chapter of *Looking at Art* by Alice Elizabeth Chase (Crowell, 1966) begins with a majestic photo of a lion and ends with Darrel Austin's enigmatic, vulnerable little tiger in "The Gathering Storm." Between the two is an array of painting, drawing, and sculpture, each item giving evidence of the infinite variety of ways artists help us see and interpret "cats." This is material for teaching what art means and how the process of creation goes beyond mere representation. Similarly, the fifteen artists whose biographies and work comprise Lillian Freedgood's *Great Artists of America* (Crowell, 1963) help extract the essence of art: the range from Washington Allston's romantic realism to Jackson Pollock's dribble design is a contrast to enlarge any child's concept of what art can do—and what art is about!

Biographies of artists ought to add to a child's understanding of the art process, too. Some of them do. The majority, perhaps by necessity, seem concentrated upon artists' outward struggles; the inward struggle to master skill and harness it to inspiration seems seldom to come to light. Yet Michelangelo agonized long months to find a way to transform an imperfect marble block into "David." America's Mary Cassatt, seeking freedom to express her vision of color without losing craft gained from the French impressionists, overcame a conflict much more important than the more obvious one of a woman artist struggling against public opinion. Yes, these are stories of inner struggle difficult to tell in words; yet they are integral to understanding artists and creativity. As a child reads an artist's biography, arrange it so that he or she can simultaneously examine a portfolio or large volume of the artist's work. Many libraries are well stocked with such material, although its appeal to children is often overlooked.

Perhaps a child moves even closer to the art process when books give opportunity to practice the craft. The "japanned toleware" of colonial times and the "Paul Revere lantern" can be constructed from directions included in *How to Make Whirligigs and Whimmy Diddles and Other American Folkcraft Objects* by Florence H. Pettit (Crowell, 1972). Scrimshawing, gilding, and mobile making are among the processes described in *21 Kinds of American Folk Art and How to Make Each One* by Jean and Cle Kinney (Atheneum, 1972). And both books contain a good deal of historical perspective, revealing how their art products fitted into American culture.

Finally, creating visual art to complement the reading of literature may be considered a way to enhance aesthetic experience. Here, as in any other "enrichment" or response activity, there is need for caution. "Now draw a picture of the story" has spoiled many a promising literary enterprise. Many selections are *not* enriched by making a picture!

As a rule of thumb, you and the children with whom you work need to decide whether picture-making will aid understanding and imagination when dealing with a specific literary selection. Will it help a reader or listener infer the setting and action? Will it aid interpretation? Might it first require discussion guided by open questions, dramatization, and sometimes research in order to have substance for the production of the visual art form? If a visual art activity seems valuable, what should that form be: a picture in what medium? a mural? a three-dimensional panorama? a display of objects? a puppet? a clay sculpture? a soap carving?

The possibilities are almost endless, and they are not interchangeable. A class project, rather than an individual one, consisting of brightly painted, inexpensive, large stuffed paper figures will liven many an animal folk tale.[31] The combination of visual and verbal images which you seek for lyric poetry such as "Silver" (p. 113), "The Mother's Song" and "Knoxville, Tennessee" (p. 129) may be more wisely done through a search for finely toned paintings or sculptures done by renowned artists rather than the assignment of the easel. These need not—and probably should not—be literal representations of the poems; they are selected to mirror the mood and sometimes the general topic or motif of a poem. Collages pieced from current magazines and newspapers may underline the currency and sharp humor of "Sonic Boom" (p. 53) and "Reflections Dental" (p. 79)—or the multi-mooded "We Real Cool" (p. 10). A posed photograph done by amateur shutterbugs may be just the right image for John Ciardi's "Mummy Slept Late and Daddy Fixed Breakfast" (p. 79) or Harry Behn's "Trees" (p. 129).

[31] Michael Foster, "Stuffed Paper Forms," *Arts and Activities,* September 1973, pp. 19–21

The selected bibliography which follows presents options in art forms, media, and techniques as well as things to consider in choosing whether, when, and how to use visual art production as a facet of literary experience.

## Selected Bibliography for Using Visual Arts with Literature

CHANDLER, MONTGOMERY, *Art for Teachers of Children,* Charles E. Merrill, 1968. Chapter Fourteen discusses combining of verbal and visual images, using visual art to accompany selections from Richard Lewis' *Miracles* poems.

FELDMAN, EDMUND BURKE, *Becoming Human Through Art: Aesthetic Experience in the School,* Prentice, 1970. A difficult but rewarding book, exemplifying aesthetic education as a search for the elements of beauty through all art forms.

GRIGSON, GEOFFREY and JANE, *Shapes and Stories— A Book About Pictures,* Vanguard, 1964. Drawings and paintings are related to folklore and epic. For instance, the powerful and imaginative detail from Paolo Uccello's "St. George and the Dragon" is coupled here with a brief but precise telling of the story.

MCFEE, JUNE KING, *Preparation for Art,* Wadsworth, 1961. Chapter Nine is a brief, trenchant guide to planning art lessons, using filmed folklore and other motivators derived from literature.

MOORE, JANET GAYLORD, *The Many Ways of Seeing,* World, 1968. An "interlude" of pictures and quotations in this book memorably illustrates the pairing of poetry and prose with fine art—for example, Wallace Stevens' "The Man with the Blue Guitar" and Picasso's "The Old Guitarist."

PECK, RUTH L., *Art Lessons That Teach Children About Their Natural Environment,* Parker, 1973. Excellent direct advice on how to set up lessons for a myriad of art experiences based on direct observation; the tie-in with literature is easily inferred.

SCHUMAN, JO, "Animals in the Art Room," *School Arts* (September 1973), pp. 26–28. For children who love to read about animals: an inspiring account of how a barred owl brought out the best in artistic response.

SMITH, JAMES, *Creative Teaching of the Creative Arts in the Elementary School,* Allyn & Bacon, 1967. Chapter Four contains well-explicated lists of common and not-so-common art experiences including "painting words" to strengthen verbal and visual art ties.

# ROLES AND RESPONSIBILITIES IN PRESENTING LITERATURE

### The Value of Literature

Can listening to books being read aloud increase children's reading and language skills?

Recent studies suggest that listening to literature can indeed bring about significant improvement in children's use of language. Stories read aloud on a regular basis can also influence reading achievement and increase independent reading. Teachers, librarians, parents, and even high-school students can contribute to the reading development of younger children by providing enjoyable listening experiences.

It is possible that attitudes toward members of minority groups may also be improved through a planned literature program, especially if the listening or reading experience is followed by discussion. Research is neither conclusive nor comprehensive. Findings do suggest, however, that it is important to choose worthwhile literature to use with children and, when the content merits it, to engage children in discussion of literature that has been read to them.

### The Challenge to Parents

In her book, *Bequest of Wings,* Annis Duff says:

> People have often said to us, "How does it happen that your children know so many books? Mine have never asked for them." It does not just "happen"; children seldom do *ask* for books, as an initial stage in learning to love them. Reading, for young children, is rarely a pleasure in isolation, but comes through shared pleasure and constant discerning exposure to books so that they fall naturally into the category of pleasant necessities, along with food, sleep, music and all out-of-doors. If the parents really want a child to have the fun of being a great reader, or if the child feels any need of it at all, I am fairly confident that it can be managed with a little intelligent effort. The important thing to remember, is that "you can lead a horse to water but you cannot make him drink." We have the greatest respect for a child's independence in his choice and judgment of books. . . .[32]

Material selected for home reading can be for oral reading by parents or for shared reading by several family members. A book, story,

[32] From *Bequest of Wings* by Annis Duff. Copyright 1944, Copyright © renewed 1972 by Annis Duff. Reprinted by permission of The Viking Press, Inc.

or poem to be read aloud by parents should be of interest to the child and should be well enough written so that it reads aloud smoothly. If the reading of the selection is to be shared by parents and children, a third criterion, readability, must be added. Here, parents may need to rely on books recommended by a librarian or teacher. Material that is very difficult for a child will not provide the most enjoyable reading experiences.

The selections in the *Anthology* offer parents an excellent source of material for home reading. Selections that prove to be favorites may be followed by oral reading of the entire book, since most of these selections are excerpts from books. Children will also enjoy reading other books and poems by their favorite writers.

When parents read to children, it should be done in a comfortable and relaxed atmosphere. If the reading is a continuation of a story from the previous day, you and your children might want to jointly "remember" what went on during the last episode of the story and to review what happened at the very end of the reading. Sometimes, as with mystery and adventure stories, children like to think ahead and suggest what they think will take place in the next section of the story. (This is good background for developing interpretation skills, for it encourages children to think beyond the literal meaning of what they read or hear.) You will want to determine a reasonable length of time to spend in reading aloud. Often a day's reading will be determined by the length of an episode or a chapter. Unless a section is very long, it is a good idea to read to the end so that children have a sense of satisfaction with the day's reading.

Reading *with* children is a somewhat different matter than reading *to* them. Here, you and your children share the reading. The sharing may be done by letting each person read a page or two or it may follow a more elaborate scheme, with each reader taking a different character part, as is done in Readers Theatre. The latter plan is enjoyed most by older children and depends on the use of material containing considerable amounts of dialogue. A note of caution on any reading *with* children: If the material is rather difficult, the child should probably scan it or read it silently first so that the act of reading aloud is enjoyable and not too frustrating. In the case of a story that is difficult but very interesting, a parent may want to do most of the reading, pausing at character or place names and other familiar words or phrases so that children can join in reading them. That gives good practice and, at the same time, keeps the reading free from pressure.

### The Roles of School and Public Librarians

If children are to have many experiences with books, it is evident that good books must be recommended and made available to them. Parents and teachers need to be made aware of public library services such as book talks and story hours which are ways to acquaint children with good books. Many librarians also make available lists of award-winning books and others that are highly recommended. Children's librarians are the acknowledged experts on juvenile book collections. For that reason, a good school librarian will be the primary source of information for people who want lists of recommended books to suit interests of children or to supplement textbook reading in social studies or science. Similarly, a public librarian with good knowledge of children's books will be the most accessible source of book information for parents. In districts where school library services are not well developed, teachers also rely on public libraries for short-term classroom book collections.

Teachers and parents can make very good use of book lists and other materials available from public libraries. For example, if the film of Ezra Jack Keats's book *The Snowy Day* is to be shown at a public library Saturday film session, the information should be well publicized so that teachers and parents can have that book and others by Keats available for children to read. The interest generated by filmed versions of books and by storytelling should be sustained after the children leave the library whenever possible.

Children's librarians also have an opportunity to make books available when a movie has been shown on television or at a local theater. The renewed popularity of Laura Ingalls Wilder's *Little House* books paralleled the introduction of a television series based on episodes from the books. Children who are familiar with the characters through media are eager to read about the family's other adventures. They may be chagrined to learn that the shows did not follow any one book accurately, but that is, after all, the beginning of critical reading and thinking.

Librarians have used many ingenious means to bring children together with books. In one school, a fall sharing of books is done by people in the community who know literature. Five or six people are invited for a morning and asked to share for fifteen minutes some books that they think children will enjoy reading. They are told to prepare for either primary children (one day) or intermediate children (another day) and are encouraged to include some new books in the presentation. Each presenter is given a classroom for the morning. Every primary (or intermediate) child is given a schedule telling which room he or she is to be in from 9:00–9:15 A.M., 9:25–9:40 A.M., etc., allowing ten minutes for travel between rooms and settling down. The response is very good. Many of the books "advertised" by the volunteers are requested from the library for months and are reported as gift requests to parents for birthday or Christmas presents.

Librarians and parents have also been successful in organizing book fairs, in cooperation with local book supply houses or book clubs. It is especially useful to hold such a fair during Book Week in November so as to stress the availability of books. A book fair, to which parents as well as children are invited, may culminate in an evening meeting with a local children's book author as guest speaker. An alternative is to have a panel of librarians, teachers, and parents present some new books to interest children.

Librarians recommend books to children in many ways, including the attractive display of interesting books in the library. Many librarians hold regular story hours for class groups and most school librarians advise and guide individual children in their reading. Book Week programs and book parties are important ways to involve children with good books. A party where children impersonate favorite book char-

acters can help to acquaint them with books their friends like. Since peers are recognized as a good source of information about books, this library activity is worthwhile.

### Teachers' Responsibilities

Many a teacher has suggested to parents that they give their children opportunities to read at home, especially during the summer. Too often, parents respond by asking that their children be allowed to bring home a school reader to use for the practice. Readers may be used, of course, but they will not provide the fresh experiences with new books that children need, nor will they allow the reading act to extend beyond what goes on during the school reading instruction. A resourceful teacher will have available a list of books that are of interest to many children in the class and not too difficult for most. The list is given to parents with two suggestions: (1) Visit your public library regularly with your children and help them select books. The books on this list are some they will probably like; and (2) If you want to buy books as gifts for your children, you might want to consider some from this list.

Many of the selections included in this *Anthology* would appear on a list of recommended books. For example, a teacher recommending books for fifth graders might suggest *America's Paul Revere* by Esther Forbes, *Crazy Horse* by Shannon Garst, *The Helen Keller Story* by Catherine Peare, *Queenie Peavy* by Robert Burch, *A Dog on Barkham Street* by Mary Stolz, *Harriet the Spy* by Louise Fitzhugh, *My Side of the Mountain* by Jean George, and *The Incredible Journey* by Sheila Burnford.

One of the important responsibilities adults have is to give students a sense of the joy to be gained from reading and the knowledge that interesting facts as well as fine stories are to be found between the covers of books. The ultimate objective of reading instruction must be to create a continuing desire to read, yet that often is one of the most difficult objectives to attain. Perhaps that is because too often children do not see adults as models of the behavior we so much want children to show. The most important role an adult plays may be that of a person who loves to read, reads for a purpose, and shares the results of reading with others. Adults who read aloud joyfully and well and who read their own books at school, in a library, or at home, especially when children are supposed to be reading, can make a real difference in the long-range reading habits of children.

### Selected Bibliography for Adult Responsibilities

ARMSTRONG, MARY K., "First Grade Lift-off with Library Books and Lots of Energy," *Reading Teacher* (May 1974), pp. 778–81. Describes a multi-media program for first-graders which combines library books with reading and writing projects.

CRISCUOLO, NICHOLAS P., "Parents: Active Partners in the Reading Program," *Elementary English* (September 1974), pp. 883–84. Recommendations for courses and workshops for parents and specific reading aid that parents can give.

HOUSEMAN, ANN LORD, "Tuned In to the Entire Family—a Book Festival," *Reading Teacher* (December 1973), pp. 246–48. Observations about a PTA-sponsored book fair and the potential it can have for uniting parents, children, and books.

LA BUDDE, CONSTANCE, and RICHARD J. SMITH, "Librarians Look at Remedial Reading," *Reading Teacher* (December 1973), pp. 263–69. Results of this study point to the important role a librarian can play in providing services for poor readers.

PIKULSKI, JOHN J., "Parents Can Aid Reading Growth," *Elementary English* (September 1974), pp. 896–97. Includes a good list of things parents can do to help children enjoy reading more.

SPENNATO, NICHOLAS A., "Cause: Project Literary Fair; Effect: More Eager Readers," *Elementary English* (September 1974), pp. 880–82. The suggested book fair could involve parents as well as librarians, teachers, and children.

# CHILDREN'S BOOK AWARDS

The awards and prizes given in the children's book field by organizations, schools, publishers, and newspapers, in the United States and other countries, has grown to a sizable number. Some of the best known and most prestigious are the Newbery and Caldecott Medals and National Book Award for Children's Literature, all given annually in the United States, and the Hans Christian Andersen Medal, an international award given biennially. In the case of all but the Andersen Medal, the awards are given for books published during the preceding year.

Following is a brief history of these four awards and a listing of the winners. Runners-up, or Honor Books, have usually been named but are not listed here.

## THE NEWBERY MEDAL

Frederic G. Melcher, American editor of *Publisher's Weekly,* created and named this award as a tribute to John Newbery (1713–1767), the first English publisher of books for children. Mr. Melcher proposed at an American Library Association Meeting in 1921 that an annual award be given for the most distinguished American children's book. Beginning in 1922 and every year since, the Newbery Medal has been given by an awards committee of the Children's Services Division of the American Library Association to the author of the most distinguished contribution to literature for children published in the United States during the preceding year. The author must be a citizen or resident of the United States, and announcement of the winner is made in early spring. Since Frederic Melcher's death, the award, a bronze medal, has been continued by his son.

1922    Hendrik Willem Van Loon, *The Story of Mankind,* ill. by author, Liveright

1923    Hugh Lofting, *The Voyages of Doctor Dolittle,* ill. by author, Stokes (Lippincott)

1924    Charles Boardman Hawes, *The Dark Frigate,* Little

1925    Charles Joseph Finger, *Tales from Silver Lands,* ill. by Paul Honoré, Doubleday

1926    Arthur Bowie Chrisman, *Shen of the Sea,* ill. by Else Hasselriis, Dutton

1927    Will James, *Smoky, the Cowhorse,* ill. by author, Scribner's

1928    Dhan Gopal Mukerji, *Gay-Neck,* ill. by Boris Artzybasheff, Dutton

1929    Eric P. Kelly, *The Trumpeter of Krakow,* ill. by Angela Pruszynska, Macmillan

1930    Rachel Field, *Hitty, Her First Hundred Years,* ill. by Dorothy P. Lathrop, Macmillan

1931    Elizabeth Coatsworth, *The Cat Who Went to Heaven,* ill. by Lynd Ward, Macmillan

1932 Laura Adams Armer, *Waterless Mountain,* ill. by Sidney Armer and the author, Longmans (McKay)

1933 Elizabeth Foreman Lewis, *Young Fu of the Upper Yangtze,* ill. by Kurt Wiese, Winston (Holt)

1934 Cornelia Meigs, *Invincible Louisa,* Little

1935 Monica Shannon, *Dobry,* ill. by Atanas Katchamakoff, Viking

1936 Carol Ryrie Brink, *Caddie Woodlawn,* ill. by Kate Seredy, Macmillan

1937 Ruth Sawyer, *Roller Skates,* ill. by Valenti Angelo, Viking

1938 Kate Seredy, *The White Stag,* ill. by author, Viking

1939 Elizabeth Enright, *Thimble Summer,* ill. by author, Rinehart (Holt)

1940 James Daugherty, *Daniel Boone,* ill. by author, Viking

1941 Armstrong Sperry, *Call It Courage,* ill. by author, Macmillan

1942 Walter D. Edmonds, *The Matchlock Gun,* ill. by Paul Lantz, Dodd

1943 Elizabeth Janet Gray, *Adam of the Road,* ill. by Robert Lawson, Viking

1944 Esther Forbes, *Johnny Tremain,* ill. by Lynd Ward, Houghton

1945 Robert Lawson, *Rabbit Hill,* ill. by author, Viking

1946 Lois Lenski, *Strawberry Girl,* ill. by author, Lippincott

1947 Carolyn Sherwin Bailey, *Miss Hickory,* ill. by Ruth Gannett, Viking

1948 William Pène du Bois, *The Twenty-One Balloons,* ill. by author, Viking

1949 Marguerite Henry, *King of the Wind,* ill. by Wesley Dennis, Rand

1950 Marguerite de Angeli, *The Door in the Wall,* ill. by author, Doubleday

1951 Elizabeth Yates, *Amos Fortune, Free Man,* ill. by Nora S. Unwin, Aladdin (Dutton)

1952 Eleanor Estes, *Ginger Pye,* ill. by author, Harcourt

1953 Ann Nolan Clark, *Secret of the Andes,* ill. by Jean Charlot, Viking

1954 Joseph Krumgold, *. . . and now Miguel,* ill. by Jean Charlot, T. Crowell

1955 Meindert DeJong, *The Wheel on the School,* ill. by Maurice Sendak, Harper

1956 Jean Lee Latham, *Carry On, Mr. Bowditch,* ill. by John O'Hara Cosgrave II, Houghton

1957 Virginia Sorensen, *Miracles on Maple Hill,* ill. by Beth and Joe Krush, Harcourt

1958 Harold Keith, *Rifles for Watie,* ill. by Peter Burchard, T. Crowell

1959 Elizabeth George Speare, *The Witch of Blackbird Pond,* Houghton

1960 Joseph Krumgold, *Onion John,* ill. by Symeon Shimin, T. Crowell

1961 Scott O'Dell, *Island of the Blue Dolphins,* Houghton

1962 Elizabeth George Speare, *The Bronze Bow,* Houghton

1963 Madeleine L'Engle, *A Wrinkle in Time,* Farrar

1964 Emily Neville, *It's Like This, Cat,* ill. by Emil Weiss, Harper

1965 Maia Wojciechowska, *Shadow of a Bull,* ill. by Alvin Smith, Atheneum

1966 Elizabeth Borton de Treviño, *I, Juan de Pareja,* Farrar

1967 Irene Hunt, *Up a Road Slowly,* Follett

1968 E. L. Konigsburg, *From the Mixed-Up Files of Mrs. Basil E. Frankweiler,* ill. by author, Atheneum

1969 Lloyd Alexander, *The High King,* Holt

1970 William H. Armstrong, *Sounder,* ill. by James Barkley, Harper

1971 Betsy Byars, *Summer of the Swans,* ill. by Ted CoConis, Viking

1972 Robert C. O'Brien, *Mrs. Frisby and the Rats of NIMH,* ill. by Zena Bernstein, Atheneum

1973 Jean George, *Julie of the Wolves,* pictures by John Schoenherr, Harper

1974 Paula Fox, *Slave Dancer,* ill. by Eros Keith, Bradbury

1975 Virginia Hamilton, *M.C. Higgins, The Great,* Macmillan

## THE CALDECOTT MEDAL

This award is named in honor of Randolph Caldecott (1846–1886), the English illustrator whose pictures still delight today's children. In 1937, Frederic G. Melcher, the American editor and publisher who had conceived the idea of the Newbery Medal some years earlier, proposed to the American Library Association the establishment of a similar award for picture books, and since 1938 the Caldecott Medal has been awarded annually, by an awards committee of the American Library Association's Children's Services Division, to the illustrator of the most distinguished picture book for children published in the United States during the preceding year. The award, a bronze medal, is limited to residents or citizens of the United States, and the choice is announced in early spring. Since Mr. Melcher's death, the award has been continued by his son.

If only one name is given, then the book was written and illustrated by the same person.

1938 Dorothy P. Lathrop, *Animals of the Bible,* text selected from the King James Bible by Helen Dean Fish, Stokes (Lippincott)

1939 Thomas Handforth, *Mei Li,* Doubleday

1940 Ingri and Edgar Parin d'Aulaire, *Abraham Lincoln,* Doubleday

1941 Robert Lawson, *They Were Strong and Good,* Viking

1942 Robert McCloskey, *Make Way for Ducklings,* Viking

1943 Virginia Lee Burton, *The Little House,* Houghton

1944 Louis Slobodkin, ill., *Many Moons,* by James Thurber, Harcourt

1945 Elizabeth Orton Jones, ill., *Prayer for a Child,* by Rachel Field, Macmillan

1946 Maud and Miska Petersham, *The Rooster Crows,* Macmillan

1947 Leonard Weisgard, ill., *The Little Island,* by Golden MacDonald, Doubleday

1948 Roger Duvoisin, ill., *White Snow, Bright Snow,* by Alvin Tresselt, Lothrop

1949 Berta and Elmer Hader, *The Big Snow,* Macmillan

1950 Leo Politi, *Song of the Swallows,* Scribner's

1951 Katherine Milhous, *The Egg Tree,* Scribner's

1952 Nicolas Mordvinoff, ill. (Nicolas, pseud.), *Finders Keepers,* by William Lipkind (Will, pseud.), Harcourt

1953 Lynd Ward, *The Biggest Bear,* Houghton

1954 Ludwig Bemelmans, *Madeline's Rescue,* Viking

1955 Marcia Brown, ill., *Cinderella,* by Charles Perrault, Scribner's

1956 Feodor Rojankovsky, ill., *Frog Went a-Courtin',* retold by John Langstaff, Harcourt

1957 Marc Simont, ill., *A Tree Is Nice,* by Janice May Udry, Harper

1958 Robert McCloskey, *Time of Wonder,* Viking

1959 Barbara Cooney, ill. and adapter, *Chanticleer and the Fox,* by Geoffrey Chaucer, T. Crowell

1960 Marie Hall Ets, ill., *Nine Days to Christmas,* by Marie Hall Ets and Aurora Labastida, Viking

1961 Nicolas Sidjakov, ill., *Baboushka and the Three Kings,* adapted by Ruth Robbins, Parnassus

1962 Marcia Brown, *Once a Mouse. . . ,* Scribner's

1963 Ezra Jack Keats, *The Snowy Day,* Viking

1964 Maurice Sendak, *Where the Wild Things Are,* Harper

1965 Beni Montresor, ill., *May I Bring a Friend?* by Beatrice Schenk de Regniers, Atheneum

1966 Nonny Hogrogian, ill., *Always Room for One More,* by Sorche Nic Leodhas, Holt

1967 Evaline Ness, *Sam, Bangs & Moonshine,* Holt

1968 Ed Emberley, ill., *Drummer Hoff,* by Barbara Emberley, Prentice

1969 Uri Shulevitz, ill., *The Fool of the World and the Flying Ship,* by Arthur Ransome, Farrar

1970 William Steig, *Sylvester and the Magic Pebble,* Windmill

1971 Gail E. Haley, ill. and adapter, *A Story—A Story,* Atheneum

1972 Nonny Hogrogian, *One Fine Day,* Macmillan

1973 Blair Lent, ill., *The Funny Little Women,* retold by Arlene Mosel, Dutton

1974 Margot Zemach, ill., *Duffy and the Devil,* retold by Harve Zemach, Farrar

1975 Gerald McDermott, ill. and adapter, *Arrow to the Sun, A Pueblo Indian Tale,* Viking

## THE HANS CHRISTIAN ANDERSEN AWARD

This award was established in 1956 by the

International Board on Books for Young People and is given every two years to one living author who, by his complete work, has made an important international contribution to children's literature. Since 1966 an artist's medal is also given. Each national section of the International Board proposes one author and one illustrator as nominees and the final choice is made by a committee of five, each from a different country.

1956 Eleanor Farjeon (Great Britain)
1958 Astrid Lindgren (Sweden)
1960 Erich Kästner (Germany)
1962 Meindert DeJong (United States)
1964 René Guillot (France)
1966 Author: Tove Jansson (Finland)
     Illustrator: Alois Carigiet (Switzerland)
1968 Author (tie vote): James Krüss (Germany)
     José Maria Sanchez-Silva (Spain)
     Illustrator: Jiri Trnka (Czechoslovakia)
1970 Author: Gianni Rodari (Italy)
     Illustrator: Maurice Sendak (United States)
1972 Author: Scott O'Dell (United States)
     Illustrator: Ib Spang Olsen (Denmark)
1974 Author: Maria Gripe (Sweden)
     Illustrator: Farshid Mesghali (Iran)

### THE NATIONAL BOOK AWARD

In March 1969, the National Book Awards included for the first time in its 20-year history a prize for Children's Literature. The $1000 prize, contributed by the Children's Book Council and administered by the National Book Committee, is presented annually to a juvenile title that a panel of judges considers the most distinguished written by an American citizen and published in the United States in the preceding year.

1969 Meindert DeJong, *Journey from Peppermint Street*, ill. by Emily A. McCully, Harper
1970 Isaac Bashevis Singer, *A Day of Pleasure*, photos by Roman Vishniac, Farrar
1971 Lloyd Alexander, *The Marvelous Misadventures of Sebastian*, Dutton
1972 Donald Barthelme, *The Slightly Irregular Fire Engine*, Farrar
1973 Ursula K. LeGuin, *The Farthest Shore*, Atheneum

1974 Eleanor Cameron, *The Court of the Stone Children*, Dutton
1975 Virginia Hamilton, *M.C. Higgins, The Great*, Macmillan

### THE CANADIAN LIBRARY AWARDS

Beginning in 1947, the Canadian Library Association has presented annually in May a bronze medal for the outstanding English-language children's book published in the preceding year and written by a Canadian citizen. Since 1954, a bronze medal has also been given for the outstanding children's book written in French.

1947 Roderick Haig-Brown, *Starbuck Valley Winter*, Collins
1948 Mabel Dunham, *Kristli's Trees*, Hale
1949 No award
1950 Richard S. Lambert, *Franklin of the Arctic*, McClelland & Stewart
1951 No award
1952 Catherine Anthony Clark, *The Sun Horse*, Macmillan of Canada
1953 No award
1954 No English award
     Emile S. J. Gervais, *Mgr. de Laval*, Comité des Fondateurs de l'Eglise Canadienne
1955 No awards
1956 Louise Riley, *Train for Tiger Lily*, Macmillan of Canada
     No French award
1957 Cyrus Macmillan, *Glooskap's Country*, ill. by John Hall, Oxford
     No French award
1958 Farley Mowat, *Lost in the Barrens*, drawings by Charles Geer, Little
     Béatrice Clément, *Le Chevalier du Roi*, Les Editions de l'Atelier
1959 John F. Hayes, *The Dangerous Cove*, Copp Clark
     Hélène Flamme, *Un Drole de Petit Cheval*, Editions Léméac
1960 Marius Barbeau and Michael Hornyansky, *The Golden Phoenix*, ill. by Arthur Price, Walck
     Paule Daveluy, *L'Ete Enchante*, Les Editions de l'Atelier
1961 William Toye, *The St. Lawrence*, Walck
     Marcelle Gauvreau, *Plantes Vagabondes*,

Centre de Psychologie et de Pedagogie

1962  No English award

Claude Aubry, *Les Iles du Roi Maha Maha II*, Editions du Pélican

1963  Sheila Burnford, *The Incredible Journey*, ill. by Carl Burger, Little

Paule Daveluy, *Drole D'Automne*, Les Editions du Pélican

1964  Roderick Haig-Brown, *The Whale People*, ill. by Mary Weiter, Collins Sons & Co. Canada Ltd.

Cécile Chabot, *Feerie*, Librairie Beauchemin Ltée.

1965  Dorothy Reid, *Tales of Nanabozho*, ill. by Donald Grant, Walck

Claude Aubry, *Le Loup de Noel*, Centre Psychologie de Montreal

1966  James Houston, *Tikta'liktak*, Harcourt

Andrée Maillet-Hobden, *Le Chêne des Tempêtes*, Fides

James McNeal, *The Double Knights*, Walck

Monique Corriveau, *Le Wapiti*, Jeunesse

1967  Christie Harris, *Raven's Cry*, ill. by Bill Reid, McClelland & Stewart

No French award

1968  James Houston, *The White Archer*, ill. by author, Longmans

Claude Mélançon, *Legendes Indiennes du Canada*, Editions du Jour

1969  Kay Hill, *And Tomorrow the Stars*, Dodd

No French award

1970  Edith Fowke, *Sally Go Round the Sun*, ill. by Carlos Marchioni, McClelland & Stewart

Lionel Gendron, *Le Merveilleuse Histoire de la Naissance*, Les Editions de l'Homme

1971  William Toye, *Cartier Discovers the St. Lawrence*, ill. by Laszlo Gal, Oxford

Henriette Major, *La Surprise de Dame Chenille*, Centre Psychologie de Montreal

1972  Ann Blades, *Mary of Mile 18*, Tundra

No French award

1973  Ruth Nichols, *The Morrow of the World*, Macmillan

Simone Bussières, *Le Petit Sapin Qui a Poussé Sur Une Étoile*, Presses Laurentiennes

1974  Elizabeth Cleaver, *The Miraculous Hand*, ill. by author, Holt

No French award

# BIBLIOGRAPHY

The numbers at the ends of the entries indicate the age range for the books, although adults should always remember that there are individual differences among children of the same age level and that what is appropriate, for example, for one ten-year-old may be too hard or too easy for another. Some out-of-print titles are included for the reason that they are classics and are still available in many libraries. The symbol ♪ denotes collections of folk songs with music or single songs in picture-book form. A list of publishers with their addresses appears on page 1061.

The Bibliography is organized under the same categories as the anthology with the addition of several groups of adult references. The table of contents below shows the organization and should help you find your way more easily through the following pages.

# ADULT REFERENCES
## General References

ARBUTHNOT, MAY HILL, *Children's Reading in the Home*, Scott, Foresman, 1969. Especially designed to help parents guide their children's reading.

ARBUTHNOT, MAY HILL, and ZENA SUTHERLAND, *Children and Books*, 4th ed., Scott, Foresman, 1972. A broad and comprehensive survey of children and all areas of children's books.

BRODERICK, DOROTHY M., *Image of the Black in Children's Fiction*, Bowker, 1973. A literary and historical analysis of the portrait of the black in children's books published between 1827 and 1967.

CHUKOVSKY, KORNEI, *From Two to Five*, tr. and ed. by Miriam Morton, Univ. of Calif. Pr., 1963. This work, by a great Russian educator, critic, and writer, was first published in Russia in 1925 and was addressed to teachers and parents. It stresses the importance of poetry, folk tales, and fantasy in the development of imagination and creativity.

COLBY, JEAN POINDEXTER, *Writing, Illustrating and Editing Children's Books*, Hastings, 1967. A look at children's book publishing from an editor's viewpoint.

DUFF, ANNIS, *"Bequest of Wings": A Family's Pleasures with Books*, Viking, 1944. A charming and intimate account of one family's experience with books. The discussion of poetry and fairy tales is of special value. The author also has much to say on reading aloud and discussing books with children.

EGOFF, SHEILA, G. T. STUBBS, and L. F. ASHLEY, eds., *Only Connect: Readings on Children's Literature*, Oxford Univ. Pr., 1969. A discriminating and often provocative selection of articles by and about illustrators and authors on a broad range of topics.

FISHER, MARGERY, *Intent upon Reading*, rev. ed., Watts, 1964. A work which discusses, with perception and great insight, every kind of fiction for children. The author was for many years a reviewer of children's books for a national magazine in England and mentions no book that she has not read. Bibliographies cover mainly the period from 1930 to 1960.

*Matters of Fact; Aspects of Non-Fiction for Children*, T. Crowell, 1972. A critic of international standing discusses the criteria for evaluation of nonfiction, examining critically books within each subject area. Useful information about the books discussed; firm guidelines for future book selection.

FRYE, NORTHROP, *The Educated Imagination*, Ind. Univ. Pr., 1964. A book concerned with the study and teaching of literature.

GERSONI-STAVN, DIANE, ed., *Sexism and Youth*, Bowker, 1974. An excellent variety of articles on social attitudes and sex roles in children's books.

HAVILAND, VIRGINIA, *Children and Literature: Views and Reviews*, Scott, Foresman, 1973. A choice collection of essays and criticism concerning trends and theories in children's literature.

*Children's Literature: A Guide to Reference Sources*, Library of Congress, 1966. An "annotated bibliography which describes books, articles, and pamphlets selected on the basis of their estimated usefulness to adults concerned with the creation, reading, or study of children's books" (preface) .

HAZARD, PAUL, *Books, Children and Men*, tr. by Marguerite Mitchell, 4th ed., Horn Book, 1960. An eminent member of the French Academy discusses national traits in relation to children's books and gives special attention to folklore, fairy tales, nursery rhymes, and poetry.

HUCK, CHARLOTTE S., and DORIS YOUNG KUHN, *Children's Literature in the Elementary School*, 2nd ed., Holt, 1968. A critique of books for children based on the psychology of child growth and development at different age levels.

JACOBS, LELAND B., ed., *Using Literature with Young Children*, Teachers College Pr., 1965. A collection of papers on relating literature to school experiences.

JORDAN, ALICE M., *From Rollo to Tom Sawyer and Other Papers*, decorated by Nora S. Unwin, Horn Book, 1949. A survey of American children's literature from early days through the nineteenth century.

KARL, JEAN, *From Childhood to Childhood*, Day, 1970. An editor of children's books brings together her personal views and values derived from twenty years of evaluating, editing, and publishing.

KIEFER, MONICA, *American Children Through Their Books, 1700–1835*, Univ. of Pa. Pr., 1970. This book will be of special value to students interested in the history of American books for children. Miss Kiefer's book is carefully documented and indexed.

MACCANN, DONNARAE, and OLGA RICHARD, *The Child's First Books; A Critical Study of Pictures and Texts*, Wilson, 1973. A perceptive and authoritative discussion of the qualities that make a picture book distinguished.

MEIGS, CORNELIA, ANNE THAXTER EATON, ELIZABETH NESBITT, and RUTH HILL VIGUERS, *A Critical History of Children's Literature*, rev. ed., Macmillan, 1969. A chronological survey of children's books in English from the earliest times to the present.

MORTON, MIRIAM, ed., *A Harvest of Russian Children's Literature*, Univ. of Calif. Pr., 1967. An outstanding effort to bring to children, librarians, and teachers of the U.S. a sampling of the reading of Russian children. One hundred selections published from 1825 to the present.

PELLOWSKI, ANNE, *The World of Children's Literature*, Bowker, 1968. Brings together annotated bibliographic references of monographs, articles, and periodicals that trace the development of children's literature in 106 countries.

PICKARD, P. M., *I Could a Tale Unfold: Violence, Horror, and Sensationalism in Stories for Children*, Barnes, 1961. This perceptive and scholarly account by a British psychologist deals with the relationship between the comics and traditional literature and with the child's need for stories of various kinds, including fantasies and tales with aspects of horror.

ROSENBLATT, LOUISE M., *Literature as Exploration*, rev. ed., Noble, 1968. Builds a rationale for using books to learn about self as well as about literature.

SMITH, DORA V., *Fifty Years of Children's Books*, Nat. Council of Teachers of English, 1963. A concise, readable account of children's book publishing between 1910 and 1960. Excellent references and bibliographies.

SMITH, LILLIAN, *The Unreluctant Years: A Critical Approach to Children's Literature*, ALA, 1953. An excellent book on all types of literature for children by a distinguished librarian.

TOWNSEND, JOHN ROWE, *Written for Children: An Outline of English Children's Literature*, rev. ed., Lippincott, 1975. "A brief, readable account of English prose fiction for children from its beginnings to the present day."

## BIOGRAPHICAL REFERENCES

BARNES, WALTER, *The Children's Poets*, World, 1924. Interesting notes about the older poets of childhood.

BENÉT, LAURA, *Famous American Poets*, ill. with photos, Dodd, 1950; *Famous Poets for Young People*, Dodd, 1964. Biographical sketches of American and British poets of the nineteenth and twentieth centuries.

COMMIRE, ANNE, *Something About the Author; Facts and Pictures About Contemporary Authors and Illustrators of Books for Young People*, Gale Research, Vol. I, 1971– Vol. VII, 1975. A series of biographical listings that includes other sources of information, examples of illustrators' work, photographs, references to work in progress, and a cumulative index.

DARTON, F. J. HARVEY, *Children's Books in England; Five Centuries of Social Life*, 2nd ed., Cambridge Univ. Pr., 1958. First published in 1932, this classic in the field of children's literature is primarily a history of children's books in England, but it also contains invaluable biographical information.

DE MONTREVILLE, DORIS, and DONNA HILL, *Third Book of Junior Authors*, Wilson, 1972. A supplement to the Kunitz and the Fuller titles, this includes biographical and autobiographical sketches for each author listed, and photographs.

DOYLE, BRIAN, ed., *The Who's Who of Children's Literature*, Schocken, 1969. The brief biographical entries consist primarily of British and American authors but include some European authors whose works have been translated into English.

FULLER, MURIEL, ed., *More Junior Authors*, Wilson, 1963. Short biographical sketches of authors who have become known since the publication of *The Junior Book of Authors*, ed. by Stanley J. Kunitz and Howard Haycroft (see below).

GREEN, ROGER LANCELYN, *Tellers of Tales: Children's Books and Their Authors from 1800–1968*, rev. ed., Watts, 1965. This survey of British authors of children's books gives an excellent historical perspective.

HOFFMAN, MIRIAM, and EVA SAMUELS, eds., *Authors and Illustrators of Children's Books; Writings on Their Lives and Works*, Bowker, 1972. A compilation of articles from magazines gives more depth than many of the briefer entries in other sources, although the coverage is not as broad. Editorial notes add information.

HOPKINS, LEE BENNETT, *Books Are by People*, Scholastic, 1969; *More Books by More People*, Citation Pr., 1974.

Informal, readable stories about the lives and work of contemporary authors and illustrators with emphasis on details that would interest young people. Photographs are included.

HÜRLIMANN, BETTINA, *Three Centuries of Children's Books in Europe*, World, 1968, first published in Switzerland in 1959, tr. and ed. by Brian W. Alderson. A historical survey that includes discussion of contemporary authors and illustrators as well as those of the past.

KINGMAN, LEE, ed., *Newbery and Caldecott Medal Books: 1956–1965*, Horn Book, 1965. A biographical sketch of each author or illustrator, along with his or her acceptance paper and related material from *The Horn Book*.

KUNITZ, STANLEY J., *British Authors of the 19th Century*, Wilson, 1936.

KUNITZ, STANLEY J., and HOWARD HAYCROFT, *American Authors, 1600–1900*, Wilson, 1938. A biographical dictionary of American literature, complete in one volume. *The Junior Book of Authors*, 2nd ed. rev., Wilson, 1951. Includes biographical or autobiographical sketches of authors of both classic and contemporary juvenile literature.

*Twentieth Century Authors*, Wilson, 1942. A biographical dictionary of modern literature. Gives information about writers of this century of all nations. First suppl. 1955.

MAHONY, BERTHA (Bertha Mahony Miller), LOUISE PAYSON LATIMER, and BEULAH FOLMSBEE, *Illustrators of Children's Books, 1744–1945*, Horn Book, 1947. Includes articles on illustration, biographical sketches, and bibliographies of authors and illustrators.

MILLER, BERTHA MAHONY, and ELINOR WHITNEY FIELD, eds., *Newbery Medal Books: 1922–1955*, Horn Book, 1957. In addition to a biographical note on each author, his or her acceptance paper and related material from *The Horn Book* are included.

*Caldecott Medal Books: 1938–1957*, Horn Book, 1957. In this volume, the biographical material is devoted to the illustrators, many of whom also were authors of the prize-winning books.

TOWNSEND, JOHN ROWE, *A Sense of Story: Essays on Contemporary Writers for Children*, Lippincott, 1971. Each of the nineteen essays on contemporary English-language writers for children is accompanied by a brief autobiographical note.

VIGUERS, RUTH HILL, MARCIA DALPHIN, and BERTHA MAHONY MILLER, *Illustrators of Children's Books, 1946–1956*, Horn Book, 1958. In the same format as the Mahony title cited above.

WARD, MARTHA E., and DOROTHY A. MARQUARDT, *Authors of Books for Young People*, 2nd ed., Scarecrow, 1971. Very brief biographical sketches.

### Book Selection Aids

### Review Magazines

*Appraisal: Children's Science Books*, Harvard Graduate School of Education, Cambridge, Mass. Published three times each year. Around 50 books reviewed in each issue, all rated on a five-point scale by both a librarian and a science specialist.

*The Bulletin of the Center for Children's Books*, Graduate Library School, University of Chicago. This is a highly selective list which does not hesitate to indicate books which are *not recommended*. The reviews are careful, authoritative, and based not only on the critical analyses by librarians but on the evaluations of classroom teachers and subject specialists. Published every month except August.

*Elementary English,* Nat. Council of Teachers of English. Besides a regular column reviewing children's books, this journal has articles on children's reading and related subjects.

*The Horn Book Magazine,* Horn Book. Devoted wholly to children's books, with many fine articles about writers, illustrators, and special areas of literature and reading. Many children's books are selectively reviewed. Published six times a year.

*In Review; Canadian Books for Children,* Provincial Library Service, Ontario, Canada. Published quarterly, a journal that reviews both recommended and not recommended books. Reviews are in English for English language books, in French for French language books.

*Kirkus Reviews,* The Kirkus Service. Punched loose-leaf sheets are published twice a month; reviews are divided and grouped by age level.

*The New York Times Book Review.* Many newspapers review children's books, such as *The Christian Science Monitor* and *The Chicago Tribune. The New York Times Book Review,* however, gives the widest and most regular coverage. There are often many special articles about children's books and other special features which make this a most valuable tool for keeping up.

*School Library Journal,* Bowker. A journal for librarians especially, it is published monthly, September through May. Approximately fifteen hundred titles are reviewed, sometimes with dissenting opinions. There are also many articles on library services, books, and reading for children and young people.

*Science Books: A Quarterly Review,* Am. Assoc. for the Advancement of Science. Reviews around 100 science and mathematics books, elementary through college and beyond. Reviews are by specialists in the field.

### Annual Booklists

*Children's Books,* Library of Congress. An annotated list of about 200 of the best books published during the year for preschool through junior high school.

*Fanfare: The Horn Book Honor List,* Horn Book. Books chosen by the editors of *The Horn Book Magazine* as the best books published during the preceding year. The list appears annually in the October issue of the magazine.

*Growing Up with Books,* Bowker. Two hundred fifty to three hundred best children's books are briefly annotated. Old and new books are included.

*Notable Children's Books,* ALA. Also appears in the April issue of the *ALA Bulletin.* Fifty or so titles are selected by a committee of the Children's Services Division as the best books for children published during the preceding year.

### Standard Lists

ARBUTHNOT, MAY HILL, et al., *Children's Books Too Good to Miss,* Case Western Reserve Univ. Pr., rev. ed., 1971. A reliable guide to new and old books for children.

It features sample illustrations from some of the more outstanding titles.

*The AAAS Science Book List for Children,* comp. by Hilary Deason, Am. Assoc. for the Advancement of Science, 3rd ed., 1970. Briefly annotated science and mathematics books for K–8 grades.

*Choosing a Child's Book,* Children's Book Council, 67 Irving Place, New York, N.Y. 10003. General lists and lists in specific categories. Regularly updated.

EAKIN, MARY K., ed., *Good Books for Children,* 3rd ed., Univ. of Chicago Pr., 1966. A collection of 1391 reviews of recommended books published between 1950 and 1965 as reviewed in *The Bulletin of the Center for Children's Books.* Grade levels are given, and a topical index aids in finding books for special interests.

HUUS, HELEN, *Children's Books to Enrich the Social Studies,* Nat. Council for the Social Studies, 1966. A graded, annotated list arranged under general topics with many subheads. Emphasizes nonfiction and books for younger children.

SUTHERLAND, ZENA, ed., *The Best in Children's Books; The University of Chicago Guide to Children's Literature 1966–1972,* Univ. of Chicago Pr., 1973. 1400 reviews selected from some of the best books reviewed in the *Bulletin of the Center for Children's Books.* Graded and annotated, with indexes to curricular uses and developmental values, reading levels, and types of literature.

### Storytelling and Reading Aloud [1]

BROWN, JENNIFER, "Reading Aloud," *Elementary English,* April 1973, pages 635–36. An annotated bibliography follows a discussion of the values of reading aloud.

CATHON, LAURA E., and others, eds. *Stories to Tell to Children,* 8th ed., Carnegie Library of Pittsburgh, 4400 Forbes Ave., Pittsburgh, Pa. 15213, 1974. "A selected list for use by libraries, schools, clubs, and by radio and television storytellers, with a special listing of stories for holiday programs."

CHAN, JULIE M. T., *Why Read Aloud to Children?* International Reading Association, 800 Barksdale Road, Newark, Delaware 19711.

GREENE, ELLIN, comp., *Stories; A List of Stories to Tell and to Read Aloud,* 6th ed., New York Public Library, 1972. An excellent aid for the beginning storyteller. Contains an annotated list of stories and their sources, a list of poetry and books for reading aloud, a bibliography for the storyteller, a subject index, and a name index.

HARDENDORFF, JEANNE B., ed., *Stories to Tell: A List of Stories with Annotations,* 5th ed., Enoch Pratt Free Library, 400 Cathedral St., Baltimore, Md. 21201, 1965. In addition to a well-annotated list of stories for telling, this book contains a list of picture books for TV storytelling, suggested programs for story hours, a list of stories by subject, and a list of poetry collections.

MOORE, VARDINE, *The Pre-School Story Hour,* 2nd ed., Scarecrow, 1972. Gives the basic necessities for planning and conducting story hours in all kinds of libraries. Especially useful for its listings of finger games, record-

[1] For additional discussion of storytelling and reading aloud, see the Arbuthnot and Sutherland, Duff, and Huck and Kuhn titles in "General References" (p. 986). Also consult the bibliographies for reading aloud and storytelling found on pages 949 and 957–58 in this book.

ings, and picture books. A practical and authoritative work, unfortunately marred by an abundance of typographical errors.

SAWYER, RUTH, *The Way of the Storyteller,* rev. ed., Viking, 1962. A great storyteller discusses the art and technique of successful storytelling and shares eleven of her best stories.

SHEDLOCK, MARIE, *The Art of the Story-Teller,* 3rd ed., bibl. by Eulalie Steinmetz, Dover, 1951. A master British storyteller discusses the techniques of storytelling and presents eighteen stories as she would tell them.

WILLCOX, ISOBEL, *Reading Aloud with Elementary School Children,* Teachers Practical Press, Atherton, 1963. Designed especially for the classroom teacher, this brief booklet discusses various aspects of reading aloud. In addition, it contains useful suggestions for scheduling and recommends appropriate post-reading activities.

## Sources of Audiovisual Materials

School personnel, librarians, and parents who wish to know what literature has been presented on recordings, films, or filmstrips often find it difficult to ascertain just what is available. Further, it is difficult to obtain information about its quality or the value it may have for the particular situation in which they propose to use it. Recently more periodicals have begun reviewing current productions, and *Previews,* published by R. R. Bowker from September through May, reviews nonprint software and hardware. Four basic types of listings which give information about media are available: producers' catalogs, indexes, bibliographies, and periodical reviews.

Producers' catalogs are usually free upon request and are easily kept up-to-date since the old catalog can be discarded when the new one arrives. As a source of information as to what is available they are moderately helpful. They generally describe the item quite accurately as to content, length of time, color, and other such details. However, no producer can be expected to give a dispassionate evaluative report on the product he is in business to sell. For the individual interested in keeping abreast of the total range of material, even in the field of literature, such catalogs soon become very cumbersome to search through. Catalogs from agencies that distribute materials from other sources give a broader range. Two useful ones are *Social Studies School Service,* distributed by the firm of the same name, and Baker & Taylor's *Guide to the Selection of Books and Media for the Elementary School Library;* both of these are revised annually. The *Media Review Digest* (formerly *Multi-Media Reviews Index*) is an annual volume published by the Pierian Press that culls and gives ratings to reviews from many periodicals.

Indexes are easier to use than producers' catalogs when one needs to locate and compare what is available on a certain topic or when one needs to locate all the forms in which a folk tale or work of literature has been presented. The *NICEM Indexes* published by the R. R. Bowker Company are designed to serve the media field in much the same manner in which *Books in Print* has served the book trade for many years. (NICEM is the acronym for National Information Center for Educational Media located at the University of Southern California.) The *Index to 16 mm Educational Films* (2nd ed.) lists more than 30,000 films; the *Index to 8 mm Educational Motion Cartridges* lists approximately 9000 films; and the *Index to 35 mm Educational Filmstrips* lists about 25,000 items. The annotations are descriptive, not evaluative, and the inclusion of an item in the index should not be considered an indication of quality or worth.

Another index which covers motion pictures and filmstrips since 1953 is the *Library of Congress Catalog: Motion Pictures and Filmstrips.* It is issued quarterly with quinquennial cumulations. Each volume is arranged alphabetically by title with a detailed subject index. Entries include a brief descriptive annotation. The *Library of Congress Catalog: Music and Phonorecords* has also been issued since 1953 and is similar in format to the motion-picture and filmstrip catalog.

Although parents and teachers may find relatively little need to consult the indexes described above they should be aware of them and of their usefulness in locating materials.

The bibliographies and catalogs described below are of greater value to those in search of material since they provide both description and evaluation of the items included. Indeed the fact of their inclusion is for most of the listings an evaluation since the compilers aim to include only worthwhile and high quality productions.

One of the best bibliographies of recordings is *An Annotated List of Recordings in the Language Arts,* compiled and edited by Morris Schreiber, published by the National Council of Teachers of English, 1964. This guide is divided into sections for elementary, secondary, and higher education. The 125 entries for elementary schools include poetry, rhymes, folk songs, literary fairy tales, folk tales, musical plays, and a few recordings for use with social studies.

*The Elementary School Library Collection; A Guide to Books and Other Media: Phases 1-2-3,* edited by Mary V. Gaver is published by the Bro-Dart Foundation and is revised annually. Each revision has included more entries for the various media. It is reassuring to note that media based on books are not included unless the book itself is recommended.

*Films for Children,* published by the Educational Film Library Association is a list of 272 16 mm entertainment films which includes among its thirteen categories those of: fables, legends, fairy tales, and story films.

*Films for Children: A Selected List,* prepared and published by the New York Library Association, lists 70 16 mm entertainment films which represent a wide range of subjects. The annotations also suggest books and recordings which may be used with a film to make a complete program.

*Folk Music: A Catalog of Folk Songs, Ballads, Dances, Instrumental Pieces and Folk Tales of the United States and Latin America on Phonograph Records* is a list of the choicest recordings in the Archive of Folk Song of the Library of Congress. The catalog is arranged by subject with various indexes. All recordings listed are for sale by the Library of Congress.

*Recordings for Children: A Selected List,* regularly revised and published by the New York Library Association, lists about 500 of the best recordings for home and recreational use. It includes among its many categories: spoken records of poetry, folk tales, fairy tales, as well as music.

*Spoken Records*, 2nd ed. by Helen Roach, Scarecrow Press, 1966, includes recordings of children's literature among its 500 entries. Inclusion on this list is based upon literary or historical merit, interest and entertainment values, and excellence of production.

Some periodicals which formerly reviewed only printed materials have broadened their coverage to include nonprint productions. *Booklist*, which is published twice monthly, except August, by the American Library Association, has included a quarterly review of films suitable for public library use for several years. In September 1969, it began coverage of 35 mm filmstrips and 8 mm motion film loops and in September 1970 began reviews of 16 mm films in each issue and also added nonmusical recordings (discs, tapes, and tape cassettes). The reviews include media in all fields: science, social science, literature, and the arts.

There are several periodicals devoted solely to audiovisual education and media which review new material. *Landers Film Review* covers from 50 to 60 current productions each month. The *Film News*, published bimonthly, has a regular "New Films" department which gives brief descriptive annotations of recent productions. It also provides coverage of filmstrips and recordings. The *Educational Screen and AV Guide*, published monthly, includes regular columns on motion pictures, recordings, and filmstrips. Among the periodicals that are devoted to the field of audiovisual materials are *Educational Technology*, the *Audio Visual Language Journal*, and *Audiovisual Instruction*, which occasionally publishes supplements to the *Media Review Digest* mentioned above.

In addition to the publications listed above there are many which give extensive coverage to a limited field. An example of such coverage is: *An Audio Visual Guide to Shakespeare*, or, *African Film Bibliography*. Readers who wish to learn more about the specialized lists available in the audiovisual field are advised to consult *Guides to Newer Educational Media*, 2nd ed. by Margaret Rufsvold and Carolyn Guss.

# POETRY

## Poets Children Enjoy

ADOFF, ARNOLD, *Black Is Brown Is Tan*, ill. by Emily McCully, Harper, 1973. 5–8

AIKEN, CONRAD, *Cats and Bats and Things with Wings*, ill. by Milton Glaser, Atheneum, 1965. 5–9

ALDIS, DOROTHY, *All Together*, ill. by Marjorie Flack and others, Putnam, 1952. 6–9

*Is Anybody Hungry?* ill. by Artur Marokvia, Putnam, 1964. 6–10

ARMOUR, RICHARD, *Who's in Holes?* ill. by Paul Galdone, McGraw, 1971. 8–10

BARUCH, DOROTHY, *I Would Like to Be a Pony, and Other Wishes*, ill. by Mary Chalmers, Harper, 1959. 5–8

BEHN, HARRY, *The Golden Hive*, ill. by author, Harcourt, 1966. 8–up

*The Little Hill*, ill. by author, Harcourt, 1949. 5–8

*Windy Morning*, ill. by author, Harcourt, 1953. 5–8

BENÉT, ROSEMARY and STEPHEN VINCENT, *A Book of Americans*, rev. ed., ill. by Charles Child, Holt, 1952. 12–up

BLAKE, WILLIAM, *Songs of Innocence*, ill. by Ellen Raskin, Doubleday, 1966. 9–up

BODECKER, N. M., *Let's Marry Said the Cherry and Other Nonsense Poems*, ill. by author, Atheneum, 1974. 9–11

BROOKS, GWENDOLYN, *Bronzeville Boys and Girls*, ill. by Ronni Solbert, Harper, 1956. 8–11

BROWN, MARGARET WISE, *Where Have You Been?* ill. by Barbara Cooney, Hastings, 1952. 4–6

BROWNJOHN, ALAN, *Brownjohn's Beasts*, ill. by Carol Lawson, Scribner's, 1970. 9–11

CARROLL, LEWIS, *Poems of Lewis Carroll*, comp. by Myra Cohn Livingston, ill. by John Tenniel and others, T. Crowell, 1973. 10–up

CAUSLEY, CHARLES, *Figgie Hobbin*, ill. by Trina Schart Hyman, Walker, 1974. 7–9

CHUTE, MARCHETTE, *Around and About*, ill. by author, Dutton, 1957. 4–7

*Rhymes About the City*, Macmillan, 1946. 5–8

CIARDI, JOHN, *I Met a Man*, ill. by Robert Osborn, Houghton, 1961. 4–6

*The Man Who Sang the Sillies*, ill. by Edward Gorey, Lippincott, 1961. 5–8

*The Monster Den*, ill. by Edward Gorey, Lippincott, 1966. 5–8

*The Reason for the Pelican*, ill. by Madeleine Gekiere, Lippincott, 1959. 7–9

*You Read to Me, I'll Read to You*, ill. by Edward Gorey, Lippincott, 1962. 6–9

CLIFTON, LUCILLE, *Some of the Days of Everett Anderson*, ill. by Evaline Ness, Holt, 1970. 5–7

COATSWORTH, ELIZABETH, *Down Half the World*, ill. by Zena Bernstein, Macmillan, 1967. 12–up

*Poems*, ill. by Vee Guthrie, Macmillan, 1957. 9–11

*The Sparrow Bush*, ill. by Stefan Morton, Norton, 1966. 8–12

CULLEN, COUNTEE, *The Lost Zoo*, ill. by Joseph Low, Follett, 1969. 7–12

DE GASZTOLD, CARMEN BERNOS, *Prayers from the Ark*, tr. by Rumer Godden, ill. by Jean Primrose, Viking, 1962. 12–up

DE LA MARE, WALTER, *Bells and Grass*, ill. by Dorothy Lathrop, Viking, 1963. 8–12

*Peacock Pie*, ill. by Barbara Cooney, Knopf, 1961. 9–11

*Rhymes and Verses*, ill. by Elinor Blaisdell, Holt, 1947. 9–12

*Songs of Childhood*, Dover, 1970. (Orig. pub. by Longmans, 1923) 9–12

DE REGNIERS, BEATRICE, *Something Special*, ill. by Irene Haas, Harcourt, 1958. 5–8

ESBENSEN, BARBARA JUSTER, *Swing Around the Sun*, Lerner, 1965. 10–14

FARBER, NORMA, *Where's Gomer?* ill. by William Pène du Bois, Dutton, 1974. 5–8

FARJEON, ELEANOR, *Around the Seasons*, ill. by Jane Paton, Walck, 1969. 5–8

*The Children's Bells*, ill. by Peggy Fortnum, Walck, 1960. 9–11

*Eleanor Farjeon's Poems for Children*, ill. by Lucinda Wakefield, Lippincott, 1951. 9–11

*Mrs. Malone*, ill. by Edward Ardizzone, Walck, 1962. 9–11

FIELD, EUGENE, *Poems of Childhood*, ill. by Maxfield Parrish, Scribner's, 1904. 6–10

FIELD, RACHEL, *Poems*, ill. by author, Macmillan, 1957. 5–8

*Taxis and Toadstools*, ill. by author, Doubleday, 1926. 8–12

FISHER, AILEEN, *But Ostriches . . .*, ill. by Peter Parnall, T. Crowell, 1970. 8–10

*Do Bears Have Mothers, Too?* ill. by Eric Carle, T. Crowell, 1973.                                    5–8

*Feathered Ones and Furry,* ill. by Eric Carle, T. Crowell, 1971.                                    8–10

*Going Barefoot,* ill. by Adrienne Adams, T. Crowell, 1960.                                    5–8

*In the Middle of the Night,* ill. by Adrienne Adams, T. Crowell, 1965.                                    5–8

*Listen, Rabbit,* ill. by Symeon Shimin, T. Crowell, 1964.                                    4–7

*Up, Up the Mountain,* ill. by Gilbert Riswold, T. Crowell, 1968.

*Where Does Everyone Go?* ill. by Adrienne Adams, T. Crowell, 1961.                                    5–8

FROST, FRANCES, *The Little Whistler,* ill. by Roger Duvoisin, McGraw, 1949.                                    4–8

*The Little Naturalist,* ill. by Kurt Werth, McGraw, 1959.                                    7–10

FROST, ROBERT, *You Come Too, Favorite Poems for Young Readers,* ill. by Thomas W. Nason, Holt, 1959.    10–14

FYLEMAN, ROSE, *Fairies and Chimneys,* Doubleday, 1920                                    9–11

GIOVANNI, NIKKI, *Ego-Tripping and Other Poems for Young People,* ill. by George Ford, Hill, 1974.    11–up

GRAVES, ROBERT, *Ann at Highwood Hall, Poems for Children,* ill. by Edward Ardizzone, Doubleday, 1964.    10–11

GREENAWAY, KATE, *Under the Window,* ill. by author, Warne, 1878.                                    4–8

HOBAN, RUSSELL, *The Pedaling Man and Other Poems,* ill. by Lillian Hoban, Norton, 1968.                                    8–12

HOBERMAN, MARY ANN, *Hello and Good-by,* ill. by Norman Hoberman, Little, 1959.                                    5–8

*Nuts to You & Nuts to Me,* ill. by Ronni Solbert, Knopf, 1974.                                    3–6

HOLMAN, FELICE, *At the Top of My Voice and Other Poems,* ill. by Edward Gorey, Norton, 1970.    5–10

*I Hear You Smiling and Other Poems,* ill. by Laszlo Kubinyi, Scribner's, 1973.                                    8–10

HOWARD, VANESSA, *A Screaming Whisper,* photos by J. Pinderhughes, Holt, 1972.                                    12–up

HUBBELL, PATRICIA, *The Apple Vendor's Fair,* ill. by Julie Maas, Atheneum, 1963.                                    6–12

*Catch Me a Wind,* ill. by Susan Trommler, Atheneum, 1968.                                    7–10

HUGHES, LANGSTON, *Don't You Turn Back,* selected by Lee Bennett Hopkins, ill. by Ann Grifalconi, Knopf, 1969.    10–14

*The Dream Keeper and Other Poems,* ill. by Helen Sewell, Knopf, 1945.                                    12–up

JACOBS, LELAND B., *Is Somewhere Always Far Away?* ill. by John E. Johnson, Holt, 1967.                                    5–8

KIPLING, RUDYARD, *Collected Verse of Rudyard Kipling,* Copp Clark, 1910.                                    all ages

KRAUSS, RUTH, *The Cantilever Rainbow,* Pantheon, 1965.                                    10–up

KUSKIN, KARLA, *Alexander Soames: His Poems,* ill. by author, Harper, 1962.                                    5–8

*In the Middle of the Trees,* ill. by author, Harper, 1958.                                    5–8

LEAR, EDWARD, *The Complete Nonsense Book,* ill. by Lady Strachey, Dodd, 1942.                                    9–11

*The Pelican Chorus and Other Nonsense Verses,* ill. by L. Leslie Brooke, Warne, 1954.                                    9–11

*The Scroobious Pip,* completed by Ogden Nash, ill. by Nancy Ekholm Burkert, Harper, 1968.                                    5–9

LENSKI, LOIS, *City Poems,* Walck, 1971.                                    5–8

LINDSAY, VACHEL, *Johnny Appleseed and Other Poems,* ill. by George Richards, Macmillan, 1928.    10–14

LIVINGSTON, MYRA COHN, *A Crazy Flight and Other Poems,* ill. by James Spanfeller, Harcourt, 1969.    9–12

*Happy Birthday,* ill. by Erik Blegvad, Harcourt, 1964.                                    6–8

*I'm Hiding,* ill. by Erik Blegvad, Harcourt, 1961.    5–8

*The Malibu and Other Poems,* ill. by James Spanfeller, Atheneum, 1972.                                    10–12

*The Way Things Are and Other Poems,* ill. by Jenni Oliver, Atheneum, 1974.                                    9–11

*Whispers and Other Poems,* ill. by Jacqueline Chwast, Harcourt, 1958.                                    6–10

*Wide Awake and Other Poems,* ill. by Jacqueline Chwast, Harcourt, 1959.                                    6–10

MCCORD, DAVID, *All Day Long, Fifty Rhymes of the Never Was and Always Is,* ill. by Henry B. Kane, Little, 1966.                                    11–14

*Away and Ago,* ill. by Leslie Morrill, Little, 1975.    8–11

*Every Time I Climb a Tree,* ill. by Marc Simont, Little, 1967.                                    5–8

*Far and Few,* ill. by Henry B. Kane, Little, 1952.    9–11

*Take Sky,* ill. by Henry B. Kane, Little, 1962.    9–11

MCGINLEY, PHYLLIS, *All Around the Town, a City Alphabet,* ill. by Helen Stone, Lippincott, 1948.    5–8

*Mince Pie and Mistletoe,* ill. by Harold Berson, Lippincott, 1961.                                    6–12

*A Wreath of Christmas Legends,* ill. by Leonard Weisgard, Macmillan, 1967.                                    6–12

MERRIAM, EVE, *Catch a Little Rhyme,* ill. by Imero Gobbato, Atheneum, 1966.                                    5–9

*Finding a Poem,* ill. by Seymour Chwast, Atheneum, 1970.                                    11–up

*Independent Voices,* ill. by Arvis Stewart, Atheneum, 1968.                                    9–12

*It Doesn't Always Have to Rhyme,* ill. by Malcolm Spooner, Atheneum, 1964.                                    10–14

*Out Loud,* designed by Harriet Sherman, Atheneum, 1973.                                    10–14

*There Is No Rhyme for Silver,* ill. by Joseph Schindelman, Atheneum, 1962.                                    7–11

MILLER, MARY BRITTON, *Jungle Journey,* Pantheon, 1959.

MILNE, A. A., *The World of Christopher Robin,* ill. by E. H. Shepard, Dutton, 1958. (*When We Were Very Young* and *Now We Are Six* combined in one volume)                                    5–10

MINARIK, ELSE HOLMELUND, *The Winds That Come from Far Away,* ill. by Joan Berg, Harper, 1964.    5–8

MOORE, JOHN TRAVERS, *Cinnamon Seed,* ill. by Trina S. Hyman, Houghton, 1967.                                    5–10

MOORE, LILIAN, *I Feel the Same Way,* ill. by Robert Quackenbush, Atheneum, 1967.                                    4–7

*I Thought I Heard the City,* ill. by Mary J. Dunton, Atheneum, 1969.                                    9–13

NEVILLE, MARY, *Woody and Me,* ill. by Ronni Solbert, Pantheon, 1966.                                    9–11

O'NEILL, MARY, *Fingers Are Always Bringing Me News,* ill. by Don Bolognese, Doubleday, 1969.                                    6–11

*Hailstones and Halibut Bones,* ill. by Leonard Weisgard, Doubleday, 1961.                                    6–11

*People I'd Like to Keep,* ill. by Paul Galdone, Doubleday, 1964.                                    9–up

*Words, Words, Words,* ill. by Judy Piussi-Campbell, Doubleday, 1966.                                    8–12

POTTER, CHARLES FRANCIS, *Tongue Tanglers,* ill. by William Wiesner, World, 1962.                                    8–11

*More Tongue Tanglers and a Rigamarole,* ill. by William Wiesner, World, 1964. 8–11

PRELUTSKY, JACK, *Toucan Two; And Other Poems,* ill. by Jose Aruego, Macmillan, 1970. 5–8

REEVES, JAMES, *Prefabulous Animiles,* ill. by Edward Ardizzone, Dutton, 1960. 6–10

*Ragged Robin,* ill. by Edward Ardizzone, Dutton, 1961. 6–10

RICHARDS, LAURA E., *Tirra Lirra: Rhymes Old and New,* ill. by Marguerite Davis, Little, 1955. 5–8

RIDLON, MARCI, *That Was Summer,* ill. by Mia Carpenter, Follett, 1969. 8–10

RIEU, E. V., *The Flattered Flying Fish and Other Poems,* ill. by E. H. Shepard, Dutton, 1962. 7–10

ROBBINS, PATRICIA, *Any Time at All,* St. Martin's, 1964. 6–8

ROBERTS, ELIZABETH MADOX, *Under the Tree,* ill. by F. D. Bedford, Viking, 1922. 5–8

ROETHKE, THEODORE, *Dirty Dinky and Other Creatures; Poems for Children,* selected by Beatrice Roethke and Stephen Lushington, Doubleday, 1973. 8–11

ROSSETTI, CHRISTINA, *Sing-Song,* ill. by Marguerite Davis, Macmillan, 1924. 5–8

SANDBURG, CARL, *Early Moon,* ill. by James Daugherty, Harcourt, 1930. 10–14

*Wind Song,* ill. by William A. Smith, Harcourt, 1960. 11–up

SILVERSTEIN, SHEL, *Where the Sidewalk Ends,* ill. by author, Harper, 1974. 8–11

SMITH, WILLIAM JAY, *Boy Blue's Book of Beasts,* ill. by Juliet Kepes, Little, 1957. 5–9

*Laughing Time,* ill. by Juliet Kepes, Little, 1955. 5–9

*Mr. Smith and Other Nonsense,* ill. by Don Bolognese, Little, 1968. 8–11

SNYDER, ZILPHA KEATLEY, *Today Is Saturday,* ill. with photos by John Arms, Atheneum, 1969. 8–12

STARBIRD, KAYE, *Don't Ever Cross a Crocodile,* ill. by Kit Dalton, Lippincott, 1963. 5–8

*Pheasant on Route Seven,* ill. by Victoria de Larrea, Lippincott, 1968. 12–up

*A Snail's a Failure Socially,* ill. by Kit Dalton, Lippincott, 1966. 10–12

STEARNS, MONROE, *Ring-A-Ling,* ill. by Adolf Zábransky, Lippincott, 1959. 5–8

*Underneath My Apple Tree,* ill. by Adolf Zábransky, Lippincott, 1960. 5–8

STEVENSON, ROBERT LOUIS, *A Child's Garden of Verses,* ill. by Tasha Tudor, Walck, 1947. (There are many other editions of this classic collection of poems.) 5–10

SWENSON, MAY, *More Poems to Solve,* Scribner's, 1970. 11–up

*Poems to Solve,* Scribner's, 1966. 12–up

TAGORE, SIR RABINDRANATH, *Moon, For What Do You Wait?* ed. by Richard Lewis, ill. by Ashley Bryan, Atheneum, 1967. 6–10

TEASDALE, SARA, *Stars To-night,* ill. by Dorothy Lathrop, Macmillan, 1930, 1954. 9–12

TIPPETT, JAMES, *I Live in a City,* Harper, 1927.

TORBERT, RUTH, *Snail Mail,* Hastings, 1958.

UPDIKE, JOHN, *A Child's Calendar,* ill. by Nancy Ekholm Burkert, Knopf, 1965. 6–9

### Mother Goose Editions of Special Interest

*Brian Wildsmith's Mother Goose,* ill. by Brian Wildsmith, Watts, 1965. Eighty-six rhymes illustrated with beautiful water colors.

DE FOREST, CHARLOTTE B., adapter, *The Prancing Pony, Nursery Rhymes from Japan,* ill. by Keiko Hida, Walker, 1968. The adapter has contributed English rhyme and meter to translations of very old lullabies and children's songs. 5–9

LINES, KATHLEEN, ed., *Lavender's Blue,* ill. by Harold Jones, Watts, 1954.

*Marguerite de Angeli's Book of Nursery and Mother Goose Rhymes,* ill. by Marguerite de Angeli, Doubleday, 1954.

MONTGOMERIE, NORAH, and WILLIAM MONTGOMERIE, eds., *A Book of Scottish Nursery Rhymes,* Oxford, 1965. A volume of real value to parents, nursery school, Headstart, and kindergarten teachers. The 200 rhymes are divided into categories such as: Handclapping, Head nodding, Finger pointing, and First singing games.

*Mother Goose,* ill. by Tasha Tudor, Walck, 1944.

*Mother Goose and Nursery Rhymes,* ill. by Philip Reed, Atheneum, 1963.

*Mother Goose in Hieroglyphics,* Houghton, 1962. A facsimile of a book of Mother Goose rhymes in rebus form, first published in 1849.

*Mother Goose Lost,* collected by Nicholas Tucker, ill. by Trevor Stubley, T. Crowell, 1971. A collection of unfamiliar rhymes supplements the standard collections. 2–5

*Mother Goose Nursery Rhymes,* ill. by Arthur Rackham, Watts, 1969. A reissue of a book first published in 1913.

*Mother Goose; Or, the Old Nursery Rhymes,* ill. by Kate Greenaway, Warne, 1881. A quaint and charming little volume.

*The Mother Goose Treasury,* ill. by Raymond Briggs, Coward, 1966. One of the liveliest and most interesting editions ever published.

OPIE, IONA and PETER, eds., *A Family Book of Nursery Rhymes,* ill. by Pauline Baynes, Oxford, 1964. Originally published as the *Puffin Book of Nursery Rhymes.* Verses are arranged by subject or form, not haphazardly as in most nursery rhyme books.

*The Oxford Nursery Rhyme Book,* ill. from old chapbooks with additional pictures by Joan Hassall, Oxford, 1955.

*The Real Mother Goose,* ill. by Blanche Fisher Wright, Rand, 1916, 1965. Golden anniversary edition with introduction by May Hill Arbuthnot.

*Ring o' Roses: A Nursery Rhyme Picture Book,* ill. by L. Leslie Brooke, Warne, n.d.

*The Tall Book of Mother Goose,* ill. by Feodor Rojankovsky, Harper, 1942.

WYNDHAM, ROBERT, ed., *Chinese Mother Goose Rhymes,* ill. by Ed Young, World, 1968. A beautifully illustrated book of riddles, rhymes, and games translated into smooth English verse.

### Poetry by Children

BARNSTONE, ALIKI, *The Real Tin Flower: Poems about the World at Nine,* ill. by Paul Giovanopoulos, Crowell-Collier, 1968. The sharp and perceptive poems in this slender book deal with the common experiences of children.

BARON, VIRGINIA OLSEN, ed., *Here I Am,* ill. by Emily McCully, Dutton, 1969. Subtitled, "An anthology of poems written by young people in some of America's minority groups." 6–up

CONKLING, HILDA, *Poems by a Little Girl* and *Shoes of the Wind,* Lippincott, 1920, 1922. Both books are now out of print but are occasionally found in libraries.   5–10

HOPKINS, LEE BENNETT, comp., *City Talk,* ill. with photos by Roy Arenella, Knopf, 1970. Forty-two cinquain verses by young authors from various parts of the U.S. reflect upon seasons in the city.   8–12

JORDAN, JUNE, and TERRI BUSH, eds., *The Voice of the Children,* Holt, 1970. Poems by black and Puerto Rican children in a creative writing workshop.   10–up

LARRICK, NANCY, comp., *Green Is Like a Meadow of Grass,* ill. by Kelly Oechsli, Garrard, 1968. Children whose ages ranged from six to thirteen wrote these seventy-four poems.   5–8
*I Heard a Scream in the Street,* Evans, 1970. Poetry by urban young people.   10–up

LEWIS, RICHARD, ed., *Miracles: Poems by Children of the English Speaking World,* Simon, 1966. Two hundred poems written by children between the ages of five and thirteen.   6–12
*There Are Two Lives,* tr. by Haruna Kimura, Simon, 1970. Poems by children of Japan. 8–10 *The Wind and the Rain,* ill. with photos by Helen Buttfield, Simon, 1968. Some of the poems in this volume were also published in *Miracles* but here they are given new life by photographs of exceptional beauty.   6–12

## Supplementary Anthologies of Poetry

ADAMS, ADRIENNE, comp., *Poetry of Earth,* ill. by comp., Scribner's, 1972. Poems about the beauty of nature.   8–10

ADOFF, ARNOLD, ed., *City in All Directions,* ill. by Donald Carrick, Macmillan, 1969. This exciting collection, drawn from many modern poets, portrays the city in all its diversity.   12–up
*I Am the Darker Brother,* ill. by Benny Andrews, Macmillan, 1968. Modern-day poems by black Americans with a foreword by Charlemae Rollins.   12–up
*My Black Me,* Dutton, 1974. A positive affirmation of blackness for younger readers.   8–11
*The Poetry of Black America; Anthology of the 20th Century,* Harper, 1973. Major and minor poets are well represented in a discriminating collection.   12–up

ADSHEAD, GLADYS L., and ANNIS DUFF, eds., *An Inheritance of Poetry,* Houghton, 1948. Chiefly for adolescents.

AGREE, ROSE H., comp., *How to Eat a Poem and Other Morsels,* ill. by Peggy Wilson, Pantheon, 1967. Subtitled, "Food poems for children," this collection centers upon a topic of interest to all children.   7–10

ASSOCIATION FOR CHILDHOOD EDUCATION, *Sung Under the Silver Umbrella,* ill. by Dorothy Lathrop, Macmillan, 1935.   4–9

BARON, VIRGINIA OLSEN, ed., *The Seasons of Time,* ill. by Yasuhide Kobashi, Dial, 1968. A fine collection of tanka and haiku poems arranged according to seasons. 12–up

BEHN, HARRY, trans., *Cricket Songs,* ill. with photos of Japanese prints, Harcourt, 1964. Beautifully translated haiku.

BELTING, NATALIA, comp., *Our Fathers Had Powerful Songs,* ill. by Laszlo Kubinyi, Dutton, 1974. Reverent poems from North American Indian tribes.   9–12

BIERHORST, JOHN, ed., *In the Trail of the Wind; American Indian Poems and Ritual Orations,* Farrar, 1971. Includes a glossary that gives facts about the North and South American tribes represented.   10–up

BLISHEN, EDWARD, ed., *Oxford Book of Poetry for Children,* ill. by Brian Wildsmith, Watts, 1964. Approximately one hundred sixty poems grouped under a variety of intriguing headings such as: "O'er Ditches and Mires," "Sweet Sprites," etc.   5–12

BOGAN, LOUISE, and WILLIAM JAY SMITH, eds., *The Golden Journey,* ill. by Fritz Kredel, Reilly, 1965. A great variety of poems selected by two distinguished poets.

BONTEMPS, ARNA, comp., *Hold Fast to Dreams,* Follett, 1969. A well-known author presents poems he "couldn't forget," collected over many years.   12–up

BREWTON, SARA and JOHN E., comps. The Brewtons have published many helpful anthologies, each focused upon a single topic. Most contain about three hundred poems and are suitable for use with children aged 9 to 13. *America Forever New,* ill. by Ann Grifalconi, T. Crowell, 1968; *Birthday Candles Burning Bright,* ill. by Vera Bock, Macmillan, 1960; *Christmas Bells Are Ringing,* ill. by Decie Merwin, Macmillan, 1964; *Laughable Limericks,* ill. by Ingrid Fetz, T. Crowell, 1965; *Shrieks at Midnight: Macabre Poems, Eerie and Humorous,* ill. by Ellen Raskin, T. Crowell, 1969.

COLE, WILLIAM, ed. Another anthologist whose compilations each focus upon a special topic. *Beastly Boys and Ghastly Girls,* ill. by Tomi Ungerer, Viking, 1966, ages 9–13; *The Birds and the Beasts Were There,* ill. by Helen Siegl, World, 1963, ages 9–11; *Book of Love Poems,* Viking, 1965, ages 12–up; *Book of Nature Poems,* ill. by Robert Parker, Viking, 1969, ages 11–up; *Humorous Poetry for Children,* ill. by Ervine Metzl, World, 1955, ages 9–11; *I Went to the Animal Fair,* ill. by Colette Rosselli, World, 1958, ages 5–9; *Oh, What Nonsense!* ill. by Tomi Ungerer, Viking, 1966, ages 5–11; *Poems for Seasons and Celebrations,* ill. by Johannes Troyer, World, 1961, ages 10–14; *Poems of Magic and Spells,* ill. by Peggy Bacon, World, 1960, ages 9–11; *Rough Men, Tough Men,* ill. by Enrico Arno, Viking, 1969, ages 12–up.
*Pick Me Up; A Book of Short Short Poems,* Macmillan, 1972. Useful for introducing poetry to those who aren't yet poetry-lovers.   9–up

COLUM, PADRAIC, ed., *Roofs of Gold: Poems to Read Aloud,* Macmillan, 1964. The editor's favorites from Shakespeare to Dylan Thomas.

DE LA MARE, WALTER, ed., *Come Hither,* ill. by Warren Chappell, Knopf, 1957. An entrancing collection.
*Tom Tiddler's Ground: A Book of Poetry for Children,* ill. by Margery Gill, Knopf, 1962. More good selections for all ages.

DOOB, LEONARD, ed., *A Crocodile Has Me by the Leg,* ill. by Solomon I. Wangboje, Walker, 1967. A slender compilation of poems from several African countries.   9–14

DOWNIE, MARY A., and BARBARA ROBERTSON, comps., *The Wind Has Wings: Poems from Canada,* ill. by Elizabeth Cleaver, Walck, 1968. Forty-eight poets are represented in this collection which portrays the range of Canada's history and diverse peoples.   9–12

DUNNING, STEPHEN, EDWARD LUEDERS, and HUGH SMITH, comps., *Reflections on a Gift of Watermelon Pickle . . . and Other Modern Verse,* ill. with photos, Scott, Foresman, 1966. An exciting collection for older children and youth.

DUNNING, STEPHEN, and others, comps., *Some Haystacks Don't Even Have Any Needle; and Other Complete*

*Modern Poems,* Lothrop, 1969. A splendid collection of poems complemented by reproductions of modern art in full color. 13–18

FERRIS, HELEN, comp. *Favorite Poems Old and New,* ill. by Leonard Weisgard, Doubleday, 1957. A varied selection of over 700 poems for children of all ages.

FLEMING, ALICE, comp., *Hosannah The Home Run! Poems About Sports,* Little, 1972. Varied in subject and mood. 10–up

HANNUN, SARA, and GWENDOLYN E. REED, comps., *Lean Out of the Window,* Atheneum, 1965. Carefully selected modern poems for young people.

HINE, AL, ed., *This Land Is Mine,* ill. by Leonard Vosburg, Lippincott, 1965. A unique collection of American verse with historic implications.

HOUSTON, JAMES, ed., *Songs of the Dream People,* ill. by author, Atheneum, 1972. Dignified, beautiful. 9–up

JONES, HETTIE, comp., *The Trees Stand Shining; Poetry of the North American Indians,* ill. by Robert Andrew Parker, Dial, 1971. Lovely paintings face each page of text. 8–11

LARRICK, NANCY, ed., *On City Streets,* ill. with photos by David Sagarin, Evans, 1968. Poems selected by young readers in city schools reflect the despair and loneliness of city life as do the photographs. 10–15
*Piper, Pipe That Song Again,* ill. by Kelly Oechsli, Random, 1965. Contains many poems which appeal to younger children. 5–10
*Piping Down the Valleys Wild,* ill. by Ellen Raskin, Delacorte, 1968. A treasury of favorites encompassing poets from ancient to modern times. 8–12
*Room for Me and a Mountain Lion; Poetry of Open Space,* Evans, 1974. Poems about nature and people's need for such beauty and space. 10–up

LEWIS, RICHARD, ed., *In a Spring Garden,* ill. by Ezra Jack Keats, Dial, 1965. A selection of twenty-three Japanese haiku, illustrated with glowing collage. 5–9
*The Moment of Wonder: A Collection of Chinese and Japanese Poetry,* Dial, 1964. Imaginative and beautiful poems from the Orient. all ages
*Out of the Earth I Sing,* Norton, 1968. These poems and songs were collected from primitive peoples of the world and are illustrated by photographs of primitive art. all ages

LIVINGSTON, MYRA COHN, comp., *Speak Roughly to Your Little Boy,* ill. by Joseph Low, Harcourt, 1971. An amusing collection of parodies, each paired with the original poem by an English or American poet. 11–up
*A Tune Beyond Us,* ill. by James Spanfeller, Harcourt, 1968. Poems selected from world literature, ranging from the eighth century to modern-day poets. 12–up

MCDONALD, GERALD D., comp., *A Way of Knowing: A Collection of Poems for Boys,* ill. by Clare and John Ross, T. Crowell, 1959. In spite of the subtitle, girls will like this collection of vigorous poetry as well as the boys do.

MCGINLEY, PHYLLIS, comp., *Wonders and Surprises,* Lippincott, 1968. Sixty-five poets, most of them modern, are represented in this collection. 12–up

MACKAY, DAVID, ed., *A Flock of Words: An Anthology of Poems for Children and Others,* ill. by Margery Gill, Harcourt, 1970. Poems from world literature and from ancient and modern writers, grouped by subject matter. 10–up

MOORE, LILIAN, and JUDITH THURMAN, comps., *To See the World Afresh,* Atheneum, 1974. Voices of today. 10–up

MORRISON, LILLIAN, ed., *Sprints and Distances,* ill. by Clare and John Ross, T. Crowell, 1965. Sports poetry especially attractive to older readers.

MORSE, DAVID, comp., *Grandfather Rock; The New Poetry and the Old,* Delacorte, 1972. Rock lyrics are paired with poems that speak to the same subject or emotion. 12–up

PARKER, ELINOR, comp., *The Singing and the Gold,* ill. by Clare Leighton, T. Crowell, 1962. Good selections for older children.

PECK, RICHARD, ed., *Mindscapes; Poems for the Real World,* Delacorte, 1971. Reflects the concerns of young people. 12–up
*Sounds and Silences; Poetry for Now,* Delacorte, 1970. 12–up

PLOTZ, HELEN, comp., *The Earth Is the Lord's; Poems of the Spirit,* ill. by Clare Leighton, T. Crowell, 1965. 11–up
*Imagination's Other Place; Poems of Science and Mathematics,* ill. by Clare Leighton, T. Crowell, 1955. 11–up
*The Marvelous Light; Poets and Poetry,* T. Crowell, 1970. Three excellent anthologies. 11–up

RASMUSSEN, KNUD JOHAN VICTOR, comp. and tr., *Beyond the High Hills,* ill. with photos by Guy Mary-Rousselière, World, 1961. A slender but memorable book notable for the beauty of the photographs as well as the poems collected among the Eskimos. 9–14

READ, HERBERT, ed., *This Way, Delight,* ill. by Juliet Kepes, Pantheon, 1956. A small, choice collection of authentic poetry from the Elizabethans to Dylan Thomas.

REED, GWENDOLYN, comp., *Bird Song,* ill. by Gabriele Margules, Atheneum, 1969. Eighty-one poems inspired by the crow, the crane, the crested hen, and other feathered creatures. all ages
*Out of the Ark,* ill. by Gabriele Margules, Atheneum, 1968. A group of animal poems for the more sophisticated reader already familiar with much good poetry. 12–up

REES, ENNIS, *Fables from Aesop,* Oxford, 1966. Forty-two of the fables appeared originally in *Poems,* Univ. of South Carolina Pr., 1964.

THOMPSON, BLANCHE JENNINGS, comp., *All the Silver Pennies,* ill. by Ursula Arndt, Macmillan, 1967. Combines *Silver Pennies* (1925) and *More Silver Pennies* (1938) in an enlarged format with new drawings. 6–10

TOWNSEND, JOHN ROWE, comp., *Modern Poetry,* Lippincott, 1974. Focuses on concerns of the years 1940–1970. 11–up

UNTERMEYER, LOUIS, ed., *The Golden Treasury of Poetry,* ill. by Joan Walsh Anglund, Golden Pr., 1959. A large, attractively illustrated collection of poetry, chiefly from the older poets. The comments add much to the text.

## Adult References: Poetry [2]

ABNEY, LOUISE, *Choral Speaking Arrangements for the Upper Grades,* Expression, 1952.

ARBUTHNOT, MAY HILL, and ZENA SUTHERLAND, *Children and Books,* 4th ed., Scott, Foresman, 1972. Part Six, "Techniques for Using Books with Children."

[2] In addition to the books listed here, many of the entries in "General References" (p. 986) include discussions specifically concerned with poetry. See especially the Arbuthnot and Sutherland, Chukovsky, Duff, Hazard, Huck and Kuhn, and Jacobs titles.

ARNSTEIN, FLORA, *Adventure into Poetry*, Stanford Univ. Pr., 1951. A teacher's careful record of her step-by-step procedures in conducting an experiment in creative writing with a group of elementary-school children. Sound literary taste, endless patience, and tact make this an invaluable study.
*Poetry in the Elementary Classroom*, Appleton, 1962. How the author encouraged children to write poetry.

AUSLANDER, JOSEPH, and FRANK ERNEST HILL, *The Winged Horse: The Story of the Poets and Their Poetry*, Doubleday, 1927. Written for young people, this book is good reading for adults.

BAMMAN, HENRY A., MILDRED A. DAWSON, and ROBERT J. WHITEHEAD, *Oral Interpretation of Children's Literature*, Brown, 1964.

BEHN, HARRY, *Chrysalis: Concerning Children and Poetry*, Harcourt, 1968. The author sets forth his beliefs on the importance of poetry for children and the emotions it should arouse in the reader or listener.

CONNOLLY, FRANCIS X., *Poetry: Its Power and Wisdom*, Scribner's, 1960. A perceptively written introductory textbook.

CROSSCUP, RICHARD, *Children and Dramatics*, Scribner's, 1966. Discusses dramatization of all forms of literature.

DREW, ELIZABETH, *Poetry: A Modern Guide to Its Understanding and Enjoyment*, Dell, 1959. The first sentence of the Foreword states: "Any book about poetry must be written in the hope that it will win new hearts and minds to both the pleasures and the profits in the reading of poems." This book should certainly accomplish its goal.

EASTMAN, MAX, *The Enjoyment of Poetry*, Scribner's new ed., 1951. Good reading; note especially the chapters on "Poetic People," which includes children, and "Practical Values of Poetry."

ERSKINE, JOHN, *The Kinds of Poetry and Other Essays*, Bobbs, 1920. Read the fine chapter on "The Teaching of Poetry."

GRIGSON, GEOFFREY, *Poets in Their Pride*, Phoenix House, 1962. A consideration of selected poets and their craft.

GULLAN, MARJORIE, *The Speech Choir*, Harper, 1937. Both an anthology and a methods text, with detailed advice on presentations of English and American poetry.

HIGHET, GILBERT, *The Powers of Poetry*, Oxford, 1960. A brief introduction to the oral-aural aspects of poetry, with delightful chapters on poets and types of poetry.

HUGHES, TED, *Poetry Is*, Doubleday, 1970. An introduction to poetry based on the author's B.B.C. programs.

ISAACS, J., *The Background of Modern Poetry*, Dutton, 1952. Scholarly first aid to adults who find modern poetry hard to take.

KOCH, KENNETH, *Rose, Where Did You Get That Red? Teaching Great Poetry to Children*, Random, 1973.
*Wishes, Lies, and Dreams; Teaching Children to Write Poetry*, Chelsea House, 1970.

OPIE, IONA and PETER, *The Oxford Dictionary of Nursery Rhymes*, Oxford, 1951. An exhaustive study of the origins and variants of nursery rhymes. A treasure of sources for students of this field.

PAINTER, HELEN W., *Poetry and Children*, International Reading Association, 1970. Suggestions for guidance.

RASMUSSEN, CARRIE, *Let's Say Poetry Together*, Burgess, 1963. Addressed to children directly.

SANDERS, THOMAS E., *The Discovery of Poetry*, Scott, Foresman, 1967. An introduction to the aesthetics of poetry, this book reveals how poetry is written and how it can be read in the same creative way.

TERRY, ANN, *Children's Poetry Preferences: A National Survey of Upper Elementary Grades*, National Council of Teachers of English, 1974.

WITUCKE, VIRGINIA, *Poetry in the Elementary School*, Brown, 1970. Outline of a poetry program.

# FOLK TALES

## *Worldwide Collections: General*

ASSOCIATION FOR CHILDHOOD EDUCATION, *Told Under the Green Umbrella*, ill. by Grace Gilkison, Macmillan, 1962. Twenty-six excellent tales for reading aloud or storytelling.     5–7

BAKER, AUGUSTA, comp., *The Golden Lynx and Other Tales*, ill. by Johannes Troyer, Lippincott, 1960.
*The Talking Tree and Other Stories*, ill. by Johannes Troyer, Lippincott, 1955.
The compiler, a storyteller of distinction, selected from her own repertoire and from out-of-print sources forty-four stories of proven interest to children.   8–11

CHILD STUDY ASSOCIATION OF AMERICA, *Castles and Dragons: Read-to-Yourself Fairy Tales for Boys and Girls*, ill. by William Pène du Bois, T. Crowell, 1958. Eighteen amusingly illustrated stories selected for their interest to the young independent reader.     9–12

DE LA MARE, WALTER, *Tales Told Again*, ill. by Alan Howard, Knopf, 1959. Felicitously worded versions of nineteen widely known stories. A valuable book for the storyteller.     9–12

FENNER, PHYLLIS R., comp., *Adventure, Rare and Magical*, ill. by Henry C. Pitz, Knopf, 1945.
*Giants and Witches and a Dragon or Two*, ill. by Henry C. Pitz, Knopf, 1943. Excellent collections for the reader and storyteller.     9–12

FILLMORE, PARKER, *The Shepherd's Nosegay, Stories from Finland and Czechoslovakia*, ed. by Katherine Love, ill. by Enrico Arno, Harcourt, 1958. Favorites selected from three of the author's out-of-print books.     9–13

JACOBS, JOSEPH, *The Pied Piper and Other Tales*, ill. by James Hill, Macmillan, 1963. An attractive edition with good illustrations and large print.   10–12

LANG, ANDREW, ed., *Fifty Favorite Fairy Tales*, ill. by Margery Gill, Watts, 1964. Selected from the many volumes collected by this great folklorist. (Andrew Lang's "color fairy books" are still in print and include such titles as *Blue Fairy Book, Crimson Fairy Book, Green Fairy Book,* and *Yellow Fairy Book.* McGraw-Hill and Dover have undertaken publication of facsimile editions of the twelve original titles. Users should be aware that a few stories in the original editions are unacceptable to minority groups.)     9–12

MANNING-SANDERS, RUTH, comp., *A Choice of Magic*, ill. by Robin Jacques, Dutton, 1971. Most of the tales, retold in fluent style, are from Europe.     9–11
*Tortoise Tales*, ill. by Donald Chaffin, Nelson, 1974. Short tales particularly useful for young children.   5–8

RACKHAM, ARTHUR, comp., *Arthur Rackham Fairy Book*, ill. by compiler, Lippincott, 1950. A famous artist chose his favorite stories to illumine with his matchless illustrations.     8–10

ROSS, EULALIE S., comp., *The Buried Treasure and Other Picture Tales*, ill. by Joseph Cellini, Lippincott, 1958. Twenty-two favorite tales from the out-of-print Picture Tales series.     7–10

*The Lost Half-Hour*, ill. by Enrico Arno, Harcourt, 1963. A collection of traditional and modern fanciful stories chosen for their appeal when told aloud.   9–11

SHEEHAN, ETHNA, comp., *Folk and Fairy Tales from Around the World*, ill. by Mircea Vasiliu, Dodd, 1970. Includes suggestions for the storyteller.   9–11

UNITED NATIONS WOMEN'S GUILD, *Ride with the Sun: An Anthology of Folk Tales and Stories from the United Nations*, ed. by Harold Courlander, ill. by Roger Duvoisin, McGraw, 1955. Each of the sixty tales included was approved by the U.N. delegate of the country from which it comes.   10–12

WIGGIN, KATE DOUGLAS, and NORA A. SMITH, eds., *The Fairy Ring*, rev. by Ethna Sheehan, ill. by Warren Chappell, Doubleday, 1967. Forty-six tales from fifteen countries are contained in this new edition of a time-honored favorite.   9–12

WITHERS, CARL, comp., *A World of Nonsense; Strange and Humorous Tales from Many Lands*, ill. by John E. Johnson, Holt, 1968. An outstanding collection of nonsense stories.   9–11

### Worldwide Collections: Special Topics

BELTING, NATALIA M., *Cat Tales*, ill. by Leo Summers, Holt, 1959.
*The Earth Is on a Fish's Back: Tales of Beginnings*, ill. by Esta Nesbitt, Holt, 1965.
Two excellent collections.   8–12

CARPENTER, FRANCES, *Wonder Tales of Dogs and Cats*, ill. by Ezra Jack Keats, Doubleday, 1955. The wit and wisdom of cats and dogs are well portrayed in this unusual collection of tales from seventeen nations.   9–12

DE LA MARE, WALTER, *Animal Stories*, Scribner's, 1940. This valuable collection for storytellers contains forty-two stories and forty-six rhymes and ballads about animals.   10–up

HARDENDORFF, JEANNE B., comp., *Tricky Peik, and Other Picture Tales*, ill. by Tomie de Paola, Lippincott, 1967. Tricksters from eight countries are introduced in this assemblage of tales from the out-of-print Picture Tales series. A valuable source for storytellers.   8–10

JAGENDORF, M. A., and C. H. TILLHAGEN, *The Gypsies' Fiddle and Other Gypsy Tales*, ill. by Hans Helweg, Vanguard, 1956. A unique and useful collection of stories gathered from Gypsy sources.   9–12

LEACH, MARIA, *How the People Sang the Mountains Up: How and Why Stories*, ill. by Glen Rounds, Viking, 1967. Imaginative tales from primitive cultures, retold by one of America's well-known folklorists. Sources and backgrounds are explained in the notes.   9–12

MANNING-SANDERS, RUTH, *A Book of Charms and Changelings*, ill. by Robin Jacques, Dutton, 1972.   9–11
*A Book of Dragons*, ill. by Robin Jacques, Dutton, 1965.
*A Book of Giants*, ill. by Robin Jacques, Dutton, 1963.
*A Book of Mermaids*, ill. by Robin Jacques, Dutton, 1968.
*A Book of Witches*, ill. by Robin Jacques, Dutton, 1966. Excellently illustrated collections.   8–12
*The Red King and the Witch: Gypsy Folk and Fairy Tales*, ill. by Victor G. Ambrus, Roy, 1965. Entertaining versions of familiar tales.   9–11

SAWYER, RUTH, *Joy to the World: Christmas Legends*, ill. by Trina Schart Hyman, Little, 1966.
*The Long Christmas*, ill. by Valenti Angelo, Viking, 1941.

Two fine collections of stories well told by a master storyteller.   8–12

SPICER, DOROTHY GLADYS, *13 Ghosts*, ill. by Sophia, Coward, 1965. This diverting collection presents tales of ghouls, ghosts, and other supernatural creatures.   9–11

## Europe

### Jewish Folk Tales

HIRSH, MARILYN, ad., *Could Anything Be Worse?* ill. by author, Holiday, 1974. A humorous tale of rabbinical wisdom.   5–8

ISH-KISHOR, SULAMITH, *The Carpet of Solomon; a Hebrew Legend*, ill. by Uri Shulevitz, Pantheon, 1966. An excellent retelling of the ancient legend in which King Solomon, exultant over his magic flying carpet, compares himself to God.   9–11

SIMON, SOLOMON, *The Wise Men of Helm*, ill. by Lillian Fischel, Behrman, 1945.
*More Wise Men of Helm; and Their Merry Tales*, ill. by Stephen Kraft, Behrman, 1965.
Funny tales about a mythical Jewish community in Poland.   10–12

SINGER, ISAAC BASHEVIS, *The Fools of Chelm and Their History*, ill. by Uri Shulevitz, tr. by the author and Elizabeth Shub, Farrar, 1973.   10–12
*When Shlemiel Went to Warsaw and Other Stories*, tr. by Elizabeth Shub and the author, ill. by Margot Zemach, Farrar, 1968. Eight lively, appealing stories. 9–up
*Zlateh the Goat and Other Stories*, tr. by Elizabeth Shub and the author, ill. by Maurice Sendak, Harper, 1966. Seven skillfully told stories.   10–up

### British Isles: General Collections

MANNING-SANDERS, RUTH, ed., *A Bundle of Ballads*, ill. by William Stobbs, Oxford (in U.S. by Lippincott), 1959. A fine compilation of ballads from the British Isles.   11–15

PICARD, BARBARA LEONIE, *Tales of the British People*, ill. by Eric Fraser, Criterion, 1961. Nine stories which represent the lore of the various peoples who invaded the British Isles.   10–12

RITCHIE, JEAN, *From Fair to Fair: Folk Songs of the British Isles*, photos by George Pickow, piano arrangements by Edward Tripp, Walck, 1966. Sixteen songs woven together by a story about Jock, a wandering minstrel. The piano and guitar arrangements add to the value of this volume.   9–13

### British Isles: Cornwall and Wales

JONES, GWYN, *Welsh Legends and Folk-Tales*, ill. by Joan Kiddell-Monroe, Walck, 1955. Retellings of ancient sagas as well as folk and fairy tales are included.   11–14

MANNING-SANDERS, RUTH, *Peter and the Piskies: Cornish Folk and Fairy Tales*, ill. by Raymond Briggs, Roy, 1966. A sprightly and diversified group of Celtic tales filled with the deeds of the spriggans, demons, knockers, piskies, and other supernatural beings.   8–11

PUGH, ELLEN, *More Tales from the Welsh Hills*, ill. by

Joan Sandin, Dodd, 1971. 9–11
*Tales from the Welsh Hills,* ill. by Joan Sandin, Dodd, 1968. Tales told by the author's grandmother and nicely adapted from Mrs. Pugh's notes. 9–11
SHEPPARD-JONES, ELISABETH, *Welsh Legendary Tales,* ill. by Paul Hogarth, Nelson, 1960. Well-told tales of mortals' encounters with mermaids, monsters, wizards, dragons, and other mythical creatures of Wales. 9–12
TREGARTHEN, ENYS, *Piskey Folk; A Book of Cornish Legends,* collected by Elizabeth Yates, Day, 1940. A rare compilation of Cornish tales. Although out of print, the book is available in many public libraries. 9–11
ZEMACH, HARVE, ad., *Duffy and the Devil,* ill. by Margot Zemach, Farrar, 1973. An entertaining Cornish version of "Rumpelstiltskin" and winner of the Caldecott Medal. 5–8

### British Isles: England

BROOKE, L. LESLIE, ed., *The Golden Goose Book,* ill. by editor, Warne, n.d. Contains "The Golden Goose," "The Three Bears," "The Three Little Pigs," and "Tom Thumb." 5–7
CHAUCER, GEOFFREY, *Chanticleer and the Fox,* adapted and ill. by Barbara Cooney, T. Crowell, 1958. Caldecott Medal. 6–9
CROSSLEY-HOLLAND, KEVIN, *The Pedlar of Swaffham,* ill. by Margaret Gordon, Seabury, 1971. A dream comes true. 9–11
*Dick Whittington and His Cat,* adapted and ill. by Marcia Brown, Scribner's. 4–8
GALDONE, PAUL, *The History of Mother Twaddle and the Marvelous Achievements of Her Son Jack,* ill. by author, Seabury, 1974. Rollicking verse, vigorous pictures. 5–7
JACOBS, JOSEPH, ed., *English Folk and Fairy Tales,* ill. by John Batten, Putnam, n.d.
*More English Folk and Fairy Tales,* ill. by John Batten, Putnam, n.d.
Good sources for the favorite tales, appealing in format and illustration. 9–12
*Mr. Miacca, an English Folktale,* ill. by Evaline Ness, Holt, 1967. 5–7
*Tom Tit Tot,* ill. by Evaline Ness, Scribner's, 1965. 5–8
♪*London Bridge Is Falling Down,* ill. by Ed Emberley, Little, 1967. The verses, the tune, the rules, and the historical background of this favorite game accented with glowing illustrations. 5–8
♪*London Bridge Is Falling Down!* ill. by Peter Spier, Doubleday, 1967. Eighteenth-century London lives again in this splendid picture book. 6–8
*The Old Woman and Her Pig,* ill. by Paul Galdone, McGraw, 1960. 3–6
SEWALL, MARCIA, ill. *Master of All Masters; An English Folktale,* Atlantic, 1972. The master's a Ms! 8–10
STEEL, FLORA ANNIE, *English Fairy Tales,* ill. by Arthur Rackham, Macmillan, 1962. First published in 1918. Although the style is somewhat more formal and literary than that of Joseph Jacobs, the book is an excellent one for both readers and storytellers. 9–12
*The Story of the Three Bears,* ill. by L. Leslie Brooke, Warne, 1934. 3–6
*The Story of the Three Little Pigs,* ill. by L. Leslie Brooke, Warne, 1934. 3–6

### British Isles: Ireland

COLUM, PADRAIC, *The King of Ireland's Son,* ill. by Willy Pogány, Macmillan, 1962, 1944, 1916. Each exciting story in this volume is concerned with the daring deeds of the King's son. 10–12
*The Stone of Victory and Other Tales of Padraic Colum,* ill. by Judith Gwyn Brown, McGraw, 1966. The author selected these stories from seven of his earlier works, six of which are no longer in print. 9–12
DANAHER, KEVIN, *Folktales of the Irish Countryside,* ill. by Harold Berson, White, 1970. Delightful style and wit, and a good source for storytelling. 10–12
HAVILAND, VIRGINIA, ed., *Favorite Fairy Tales Told in Ireland,* retold from Irish storytellers, ill. by Artur Marokvia, Little, 1961. 7–10
JACOBS, JOSEPH, ed., *Celtic Fairy Tales,* ill. by John D. Batten, Putnam, n.d.
*More Celtic Fairy Tales,* ill. by John D. Batten, Putnam, n.d.
Both volumes include Welsh, Scotch, Cornish, and Irish tales. 9–12
*Munachar and Manachar; An Irish Story,* ill. by Anne Rockwell, T. Crowell, 1970. Nonsense humor. 5–7
MACMANUS, SEUMAS, *The Bold Heroes of Hungry Hill,* ill. by Jay Chollick, Farrar, 1951.
*Hibernian Nights,* ill. by Paul Kennedy, Macmillan, 1963.
Fascinating tales which the author collected. Three out-of-print collections worth seeking in libraries are: *Donegal Fairy Stories, Donegal Wonder Book,* and *In Chimney Corners.* 10–up
O'FAOLAIN, EILEEN, *Children of the Salmon and Other Irish Folktales,* selected and tr. by the author, ill. by Trina Schart Hyman, Little, 1965.
*Irish Sagas and Folk-Tales,* ill. by Joan Kiddell-Monroe, Walck, 1954.
Two useful books. The cadence of the Gaelic has been preserved in the latter. 10–up
PICARD, BARBARA LEONIE, *Celtic Tales: Legends of Tall Warriors and Old Enchantments,* ill. by John G. Galsworthy, Criterion, 1965. Source and background are given for each story. 10–12
PILKINGTON, FRANCIS MEREDITH, *The Three Sorrowful Tales of Erin,* ill. by Victor Ambrus, Walck, 1966. The handsome illustrations match in mood and style these excellent retellings of third-century legends. 11–13
YOUNG, ELLA, *The Unicorn with Silver Shoes,* ill. by Robert Lawson, McKay, 1957. The tale of Ballor, the King's son, and his adventures in the Land of the Ever Young is told in beautifully cadenced prose. 9–12

### British Isles: Scotland

HAVILAND, VIRGINIA, ed., *Favorite Fairy Tales Told in Scotland,* ill. by Adrienne Adams, Little, 1963. Six action-packed stories retold with simplicity. 7–10
NIC LEODHAS, SORCHE (pseud. of LeClaire Alger), *By Loch and by Lin: Tales of the Scottish Ballads,* ill. by Vera Bock, Holt, 1969.
*Claymore and Kilt: Tales of Scottish Kings and Castles,* ill. by Leo and Diane Dillon, Holt, 1967.
*Gaelic Ghosts,* ill. by Nonny Hogrogian, Holt, 1964.
*Ghosts Go Haunting,* ill. by Nonny Hogrogian, Holt, 1965.

*Heather and Broom: Tales of the Scottish Highlands,* ill. by Consuelo Joerns, Holt, 1960.
*Sea-Spell and Moor Magic: Tales of the Western Isles,* ill. by Vera Bock, Holt, 1968.
*Thistle and Thyme: Tales and Legends from Scotland,* ill. by Evaline Ness, Holt, 1962. These delightful volumes have made a great body of Scottish lore accessible to children. 9–12 Sorche Nic Leodhas has also written for younger children four picture books based on folklore of Scotland: *All in the Morning Early,* ill. by Evaline Ness, 1963; *Always Room for One More,* ill. by Nonny Hogrogian, 1965; *Kellyburn Braes,* ill. by Evaline Ness, 1968; *The Laird of Cockpen,* ill. by Adrienne Adams, 1969. All published by Holt. 5–8
SHEPPARD-JONES, ELISABETH, *Scottish Legendary Tales,* ill. by Paul Hogarth, Nelson, 1962. An extensive compilation of stories about the fairy people and other small folk of Scotland. 10–13
WILSON, BARBARA KER, *Scottish Folk-Tales and Legends,* ill. by Joan Kiddell-Monroe, Walck, 1954. Contains examples of many types of Scottish folk tales. 11–13

### Finland

BOWMAN, JAMES CLOYD, and MARGERY BIANCO, *Seven Silly Wise Men,* from a tr. by Aili Kolehmainen, ill. by John Faulkner, Whitman, 1964. A picture-book version of a story often called "The Wise Men of Holmola." 5–8
*Tales from a Finnish Tupa,* from a tr. by Aili Kolehmainen, ill. by Laura Bannon, Whitman, 1936, 1964, An interesting group of Finnish tales. 10–14

### France

BERSON, HAROLD, ad., *How the Devil Gets His Due,* ill. by author, Crown, 1972. Adapted from the story in *Le Meunier Garçon,* this is a tale in which justice triumphs. 9–10
*The Thief Who Hugged a Moonbeam,* ill. by author, Seabury, 1972. First published in the 12th century, the story of a gullible knave trapped by his intended victim. 8–10
BROWN, MARCIA, *Stone Soup,* ill. by author, Scribner's, 1947. 5–8
COONEY, BARBARA, *The Little Juggler,* adapted and ill. by author, Hastings, 1961. A beautiful adaptation of the legend about the boy who was inspired to amuse the Virgin and Child with his best juggling act. 8–11
D'AULNOY, COMTESSE, *The White Cat and Other Old French Fairy Tales,* ed. and tr. by Rachel Field, Macmillan, 1967, 1928. A fine collection that has long deserved republication. 8–11
LANG, ANDREW, *The Twelve Dancing Princesses,* ill. by Adrienne Adams, Holt, 1966. This version of the tale, drawn from French sources, is more elaborate and fanciful in tone than that recorded by the Grimms. 5–9
PERRAULT, CHARLES, *Cinderella; or The Little Glass Slipper,* ill. by Marcia Brown, Scribner's, 1954. Caldecott Medal. 5–9
*Perrault's Complete Fairy Tales,* tr. by A. E. Johnson and others, ill. by W. Heath Robinson, Dodd, 1961. This edition is not very attractive to children, but adults should know of it because the "moralities" of

Perrault are included and the illustrations are excellent. 10–up
*Puss in Boots,* ill. by Marcia Brown, Scribner's, 1952. 6–9
*Puss in Boots,* adapted and ill. by Hans Fischer, Harcourt, 1959. 5–8
PICARD, BARBARA LEONIE, *French Legends, Tales, and Fairy Stories,* ill. by Joan Kiddell-Monroe, Walck, 1955. A rich source of French folklore. 10–14

### Germany

*A Boy Went Out to Gather Pears,* ill. by Felix Hoffmann, Harcourt, 1966. An outstanding pictorial interpretation of this cumulative verse-tale. 5–8
GRIMM, JACOB and WILHELM, *The Brave Little Tailor,* adapted by Audrey Claus, ill. by E. Probst, McGraw, 1965. 6–9
*The Complete Grimm's Fairy Tales,* ill. by Josef Scharl, Pantheon, 1974. A reissue of the 1944 edition based on the Margaret Hunt translation. Includes a full folkloristic commentary by Joseph Campbell, and is useful to adults as well as children. 9–11
*Fairy Tales,* tr. by Lucy Crane, Marian Edwardes, Mrs. Edgar Lucas, and others, ill. by Jean O'Neill, World, 1947. Sixty stories selected from the vast collection of the Grimms. 9–12
*The Fisherman and His Wife,* ill. by Margot Zemach, Norton, 1966. 6–8
*The Four Clever Brothers,* ill. by Felix Hoffmann, Harcourt, 1967. 5–8
*The Goose Girl,* a new tr., ill. by Marguerite de Angeli, Doubleday, 1964. 5–8
*Grimm's Fairy Tales,* based on the Frances Jenkins Olcott edition of the English translation by Margaret Hunt, Follett, 1968. This beautiful edition is notable for its illustrations, which were chosen from artwork submitted by children of many nations. Frances Clarke Sayers, author and storyteller of distinction, has contributed an eloquent foreword. 7–up
*Grimm's Fairy Tales,* tr. by Lucy Crane and others, ill. by Fritz Kredel, Grosset, 1945. Based on some of the best English translations of the tales, this edition is thoroughly satisfying to children. 9–12
*Household Stories,* tr. by Lucy Crane, ill. by Walter Crane, McGraw, 1966 (paperback ed., Dover, 1964). Unabridged republication of the work first published by Macmillan in 1886. 10–up
*The Juniper Tree and Other Tales from Grimm,* selected by Lore Segal and Maurice Sendak, tr. by Lore Segal with four tales tr. by Randall Jarrell, ill. by Maurice Sendak, Farrar, 1973. A two-volume edition distinguished both for the translations and the illustrations. 9–up
*Rapunzel,* ill. by Felix Hoffmann, Harcourt, 1961. 6–8
*The Seven Ravens,* ill. by Felix Hoffmann, Harcourt, 1963. 6–9
*The Shoemaker and the Elves,* ill. by Adrienne Adams, Scribner's, 1960. 5–9
*The Sleeping Beauty,* ill. by Felix Hoffmann, Harcourt, 1960. 6–11
*Snow-White and Rose-Red,* retold and ill. by Barbara Cooney, Delacorte, 1966. 6–10
*Snow-White and the Seven Dwarfs,* tr. by Randall Jarrell, ill. by Nancy Ekholm Burkert, Farrar, 1972. 8–11

*Tales from Grimm,* freely tr. and ill. by Wanda Gág, Coward, 1936. 8–11

JAGENDORF, M. A., *Tyll Ulenspiegel's Merry Pranks,* ill. by Fritz Eichenberg, Vanguard, 1938. A large collection of tales about the exploits of that legendary figure who championed the cause of the underdog and embarrassed his enemies with jokes and pranks. 9–11

PICARD, BARBARA LEONIE, *German Hero-Sagas and Folk-Tales,* ill. by Joan Kiddell-Monroe, Walck, 1958. Despite the title of this volume from the Oxford Myths and Legends series, the content is predominantly folklore. 10–12

VAN WOERKOM, DOROTHY, ad., *The Queen Who Couldn't Bake Gingerbread,* ill. by Paul Galdone, Knopf, 1975. A romping tale of role reversal, with amusing pictures. 5–8

## Italy

BASILE, GIOVANNI BATTISTA, *Old Neapolitan Fairy Tales,* selected and retold by Rose Laura Mincieli, ill. by Beni Montresor, Knopf, 1963. These stories are retold from a seventeenth-century collection, *Il Pentamerone.* Children will enjoy the variants of "Cinderella" and "Rapunzel." 8–10

CHAFETZ, HENRY, *The Legend of Befana,* ill. by Ronni Solbert, Houghton, 1958. An ancient Christmas legend well told and illustrated. 5–9

HAVILAND, VIRGINIA, *Favorite Fairy Tales Told in Italy,* ill. by Evaline Ness, Little, 1965. Two of the six tales in this collection are variations on the themes of "Cinderella" and "The Three Little Pigs." 7–11

JAGENDORF, MORITZ ADOLF, *The Priceless Cats and Other Italian Folk Stories,* ill. by Gioia Fiammenghi, Vanguard, 1956. An attractive, gaily illustrated collection which children will enjoy reading for themselves. 10–13

TOOR, FRANCES, *The Golden Carnation,* ill. by Anne Marie Jauss, Lothrop, 1961. Includes Italian versions of Greek myths, historic legends, and variations of well-known stories from other countries. 10–12

VITTORINI, DOMENICO, *Old Italian Tales,* ill. by Kathryn L. Fligg, McKay, 1958. Twenty short tales alive with humor and wisdom. 7–12

ZEMACH, HARVE, *Too Much Nose; an Italian Tale,* ill. by Margot Zemach, Holt, 1967. The theme of the three sons who set out to make their way in the world is again encountered in this highly entertaining book. 6–9

## Poland

BORSKI, LUCIA M., and KATE B. MILLER, *The Jolly Tailor, and Other Fairy Tales Translated from the Polish,* ill. by Kazimir Klepacki, McKay, 1928, 1956. An excellent source for the storyteller, but tales should be selected from this collection with discretion, for some may offend minority groups. 9–12

HAVILAND, VIRGINIA, ed., *Favorite Fairy Tales Told in Poland,* ill. by Felix Hoffmann, Little, 1963. Six stories which merit more attention in this country. 8–11

TURSKA, KRYSTYNA, ad., *The Woodcutter's Duck,* ill. by author, Macmillan, 1973. Nicely retold and beautifully illustrated, a story of virtue rewarded. 5–8

## Scandinavian Countries

ASBJÖRNSEN, PETER C., and JÖRGEN E. MOE, *East of the Sun and West of the Moon, and Other Tales,* ill. by Tom Vroman, Macmillan, 1963. The unsurpassed tales of Scandinavia that were collected in mid-nineteenth century by the scholarly authors and translated by Sir George Dasent. 10–14

*Norwegian Folk Tales,* tr. by Pat Shaw Iversen and Carl Norman, ill. by Erik Werenskiold and Theodor Kittelsen, Viking, 1960. Excellent stories and some of the incomparable illustrations of earlier Scandinavian artists. Invaluable to the storyteller. 10–up

*The Three Billy Goats Gruff,* ill. by Marcia Brown, Harcourt, 1957. 7–9

AULAIRE, INGRI and EDGAR PARIN D', eds., *East of the Sun and West of the Moon,* ill. by eds., Viking, 1969. Reissue of an earlier edition, also based upon work of P. C. Asbjörnsen and J. E. Moe. 8–12

FEAGLES, ANITA, *Autun and the Bear: An Old Icelandic Legend,* ill. by Gertrude Barrer-Russell, W. R. Scott, 1967. 7–9

HATCH, MARY C., *13 Danish Tales,* ill. by Edgun (pseud.), Harcourt, 1947.

*More Danish Tales,* ill. by Edgun (pseud.), Harcourt, 1949.

Two fine compilations of amusing and wittily illustrated stories. 9–12

JONES, GWYN, *Scandinavian Legends and Folk-Tales,* ill. by Joan Kiddell-Monroe, Walck, 1956. Contains a few well-known stories along with hero tales and some unusual examples of folklore. 8–12

LUNDBERGH, HOLGER, tr., *Great Swedish Fairy Tales,* ill. by John Bauer, Delacorte/Seymour Lawrence, 1973. The tales have a gentle quality that is echoed by the romantic pictures by one of Sweden's greatest illustrators. 9–11

OLSEN, IB SPANG, *The Marsh Crone's Brew,* tr. by Virginia A. Jensen, ill. by author, Abingdon, 1960. A fantastically humorous tale concerning the "little people" of Denmark. 6–8

THORNE-THOMSEN, GUDRUN, *East o' the Sun and West o' the Moon,* rev. ed., ill. by Gregory Orloff, Row, 1946. Though out of print, this book is included because it is an outstanding rendition of Norwegian folk tales by a storyteller who represented the highest and most artistic achievement in her field. It is available in many libraries. 9–13

UNDSET, SIGRID, ed., *True and Untrue, and Other Norse Tales,* ill. by Frederick T. Chapman, Knopf, 1945. Twenty-seven striking Norwegian tales based on the collections of Asbjörnsen and Moe. The foreword is especially valuable to adult students of folklore. 10–14

## Spain

BOGGS, RALPH STEELE, and MARY GOULD DAVIS, *Three Golden Oranges and Other Spanish Folk Tales,* ill. by Emma Brock, McKay, 1936, 1964. Romantic and exciting stories for older children. Includes one remarkable ghost story. 10–12

DAVIS, ROBERT, *Padre Porko, the Gentlemanly Pig,* ill. by Fritz Eichenberg, Holiday, 1948. The activities of the kindly pig who delights in helping his friends, both human and animal, are retold in eleven tales. 8–12

HAVILAND, VIRGINIA, ed., *Favorite Fairy Tales Told in Spain,* ill. by Barbara Cooney, Little, 1963. Six of the best-loved stories of the Spanish people.               7–10

## Turkey[3]

DOWNING, CHARLES, *Tales of the Hodja,* ill. by William Papas, Walck, 1965. Nasreddin Hodja, the invincible, half-wise, half-foolish personality from Turkey, is the hero of each of these short tales.               8–11

EKREM, SELMA, comp., *Turkish Fairy Tales,* ill. by Liba Bayrak, Van Nostrand, 1964. These twelve Turkish tales, never before published in the U.S., were heard by the Turkish-born author from her nurse in Istanbul.               9–12

ENSOR, DOROTHY, *The Adventures of Hatim Tai,* ill. by Pauline Baynes, Walck, 1962. Colorful, romantic tales about the legendary feats of Hatim Tai.               9–11

KELSEY, ALICE GEER, *Once the Hodja,* ill. by Frank Dobias, Longmans, 1943. Humorous tales about Nasr-ed-Din Hodja, who combines wisdom and foolishness but always manages to come out on top.               8–11

WALKER, BARBARA K., *Hilili and Dilili,* adapted from a tr. by Mrs. Neriman Hizir, ill. by Bill Barss, Follett, 1964. *Just Say Hic!* adapted from a tr. by Mrs. Neriman Hizir, ill. by Don Bolognese, Follett, 1965.               5–7
*The Round Sultan and the Straight Answer,* ill. by Friso Henstra, Parents, 1970. A humorous tale of sage advice.               5–8

## Union of Soviet Socialist Republics[4]

AFANASYEV, ALEXANDER, *Soldier and Tsar in the Forest; A Russian Tale,* tr. by Richard Lourie, ill. by Uri Shulevitz, Farrar, 1972. A lively adaptation.               5–8

ARTZYBASHEFF, BORIS, *Seven Simeons; a Russian Tale,* retold and ill. by author, Viking, 1961.               7–10

BLOCH, MARIE HALUN, ed., *Ukrainian Folk Tales,* tr. by editor from the original collections of Ivan Rudchenko and Maria Lukiyanenko, ill. by J. Hnizdovsky, Coward, 1964. These twelve short animal stories, rich with unforced peasant humor, will be new to most American children.               8–12

DANIELS, GUY, tr., *Foma the Terrible; A Russian Folktale,* ill. by Imero Gobbato, Delacorte, 1970. A merry tale adapted from the Afanasyev collection.               5–8

DEUTSCH, BABETTE, and AVRAHM YARMOLINSKY, eds., *Tales of Faraway Folk,* ill. by Irene Lorentowicz, Harper, 1952.
*More Tales of Faraway Folk,* ill. by Janina Domanska, Harpers, 1963.
These unique collections come mainly from Russia and other Asiatic lands.               7–11

DOWNING, CHARLES, *Russian Tales and Legends,* ill. by Joan Kiddell-Monroe, Walck, 1957. Authoritative versions of Russian tales.               9–11

DURHAM, MAE, *Tit for Tat and Other Latvian Folk Tales,* retold from the tr. of Skaidrite Rubene-Koo, ill. by Harriet Pincus, Harcourt, 1967. Twenty-two distinctive stories which portray the Latvian peasant's philosophy of life.               9–11

[3] Included in this section are stories from Asian Turkey.
[4] Included in this section are stories from Asian sections of the Union of Soviet Socialist Republics.

GINSBURG, MIRRA, tr., *The Kaha Bird; Tales from the Steppes of Central Asia,* ill. by Richard Cuffari, Crown, 1971. Non-Russian tales from Russia are told with vigor.               9–11

HOGROGIAN, NONNY, ill., *One Fine Day,* Macmillan, 1971. A cumulative tale with pictures, based on an Armenian tale, awarded the Caldecott Medal.               4–7

HUGGINS, EDWARD, ad., *Blue and Green Wonders and Other Latvian Tales,* ill. by Owen Wood, Simon, 1971. Told with true folktale cadence, a varied selection.               9–11

MAAS, SELVE, ad., *The Moon Painters; And Other Estonian Folk Tales,* ill. by Laszlo Gal, Viking, 1971.               9–11

RANSOME, ARTHUR, *Old Peter's Russian Tales,* ill. by Dimitri Mitrokhin, Nelson, 1917. This is the teacher's most practical source for the Russian tales.               8–12
*The Fool of the World and the Flying Ship; A Russian Tale,* retold; ill. by Uri Shulevitz, Farrar, 1968. Caldecott Medal.               8–11

REYHER, BECKY, *My Mother Is the Most Beautiful Woman in the World; a Russian Folktale,* retold; ill. by Ruth Gannett, Lothrop, 1945.               6–9

ROBBINS, RUTH, *Baboushka and the Three Kings,* ill. by Nicolas Sidjakov, Parnassus, 1960. Caldecott Medal.               5–9

TASHJIAN, VIRGINIA A., *Once There Was and Was Not,* based on stories by H. Toumanian, ill. by Nonny Hogrogian, Little, 1966. A captivating array of Armenian tales, all of which deserve to be better known.               9–12
*Three Apples Fell from Heaven,* ill. by Nonny Hogrogian, Little, 1971.               9–12

TOLSTOY, LEO, *Russian Stories and Legends,* tr. by Louise and Aylmer Maude, ill. by Alexander Alexeieff, Pantheon, 1967. Eight folk tales grouped around the theme of brotherhood.               10–up

WHITNEY, THOMAS P., tr. *Vasilisa the Beautiful,* ill. by Nonny Hogrogian, Macmillan, 1970. A version of the Cinderella story from the Afanasyev collection.               9–11

WYNDHAM, LEE, comp., *Tales the People Tell in Russia,* ill. by Andrew Antal, Messner, 1970. Told with gusto.               8–10

ZEMACH, HARVE, *Salt: A Russian Tale,* adapted from Benjamin Zemach's literal translation of the Russian of Alexei Afanasev, ill. by Margot Zemach, Follett, 1965.               6–8

## Other Countries of Europe

AMBRUS, VICTOR G., *Brave Soldier Janosh,* ill. by author, Harcourt, 1967.
*The Three Poor Tailors,* ill. by author, Harcourt, 1965. Two Hungarian tales. Both books are notable for glowing illustrations.               5–9

CURCIJA, PRODANOVIC NADA, *Heroes of Serbia,* ill. by Dušan Ristic, Walck, 1964. An excellent contribution to the study of folklore. Scholarly comments on background and sources.               11–up
*Yugoslav Folk-Tales,* ill. by Joan Kiddell-Monroe, Walck, 1957. One of the books in the Oxford Myths and Legends series.               10–14

DUVOISIN, ROGER, *The Three Sneezes, and Other Swiss Tales,* ill. by author, Knopf, 1941. Lively and humorous tales, many of them variants of stories from other countries.               9–11

FILLMORE, PARKER, *The Laughing Prince,* ill. by Jan Van Everen, Harcourt, 1921. This interesting group of Yugoslavian stories is full of fun, humorous inventions, and imaginative detail. 9–12

HAVILAND, VIRGINIA, ed., *Favorite Fairy Tales Told in Czechoslovakia*, ill. by Trina Schart Hyman, Little, 1966. Five Slavic tales in a volume attractive to the young reader and useful to the storyteller. 7–11

MANNING-SANDERS, RUTH, *Damian and the Dragon; Modern Greek Folk-Tales*, ill. by William Papas, Roy, 1966. Superior and extremely interesting retellings of several gay tales in which the brave, steadfast, and wise are aided by a variety of magical creatures. 9–11
*Gianni and the Ogre*, ill. by William Stobbs, Dutton, 1971. Eighteen tales from the Mediterranean area. 9–11

MÜLLER-GUGGENBÜHL, FRITZ, *Swiss-Alpine Folk-Tales*, tr. by Katharine Potts, ill. by Joan Kiddell-Monroe, Walck, 1958. One of the collections in the useful Oxford Myths and Legends series. 10–14

PRIDHAM, RADOST, *A Gift from the Heart: Folk Tales from Bulgaria*, ill. by Pauline Baynes, World, 1967. A good collection of tales that reflect the Oriental and Western heritage of the Bulgarian people. The introduction provides background for the stories. 9–11

STALDER, VALERIE, ed., *Even the Devil Is Afraid of a Shrew; A Folktale of Lapland*, ill. by Richard Brown, Addison, 1972. Told with quiet, sly humor. 5–8

## Africa

AARDEMA, VERNA, *Behind the Back of the Mountain; Black Folktales from Southern Africa*, ill. by Leo and Diane Dillon, Dial, 1973. Smoothly written, a varied collection. 9–11
*Tales from the Story Hat: African Folk Tales*, ill. by Elton Fax, Coward, 1960.
*More Tales from the Story Hat*, ill. by Elton Fax, Coward, 1966.
In West Africa the storyteller wears a broad-brimmed hat from which dangle tiny objects representing his tales of magic, wonder, and fun. 7–11

APPIAH, PEGGY, *Ananse the Spider: Tales from an Ashanti Village*, ill. by Peggy Wilson, Pantheon, 1966. These interesting stories are a trifle more formal than those of Courlander and will appeal to older readers. 11–14

ARKHURST, JOYCE COOPER, *The Adventures of Spider: West African Folk Tales*, ill. by Jerry Pinkney, Little, 1964. A book of amusing folk tales, dashingly illustrated, which many youngsters will be able to read for themselves. 7–10

ARNOTT, KATHLEEN, *African Myths and Legends*, ill. by Joan Kiddell-Monroe, Walck, 1963. Contains stories representative of nineteen African nations and of several tribes south of the Sahara. 9–12

BURTON, W. F. P., *The Magic Drum; Tales from Central Africa*, ill. by Ralph Thompson, Criterion, 1962. Thirty-eight tales heard from storytellers in Congo villages during the author's service as a missionary. 9–12

CARPENTER, FRANCES, *African Wonder Tales*, ill. by Joseph Escourido, Doubleday, 1963. Twenty-four tales from various parts of Africa. Includes a pronunciation guide for African names. 8–11

COURLANDER, HAROLD, *The King's Drum and Other African Stories*, ill. by Enrico Arno, Harcourt, 1962. 9–11

COURLANDER, HAROLD, and EZEKIEL A. ESHUGBAYI, *Olode the Hunter, and Other Tales from Nigeria*, ill. by Enrico Arno, Harcourt, 1968. 8–12

COURLANDER, HAROLD, and GEORGE HERZOG, *The Cow-Tail Switch, and Other West African Stories*, ill. by Madye Lee Chastain, Holt, 1947. 10–12

COURLANDER, HAROLD, and WOLF LESLAU, *The Fire on the Mountain and Other Ethiopian Stories*, ill. by Robert W. Kane, Holt, 1950. 10–14

COURLANDER, HAROLD, and ALBERT PREMPEH, *The Hat-Shaking Dance, and Other Tales from the Gold Coast*, ill. by Enrico Arno, Harcourt, 1957. 9–11
Harold Courlander and his collaborators on the volumes listed above have contributed greatly to our knowledge of African folklore and to our understanding of the great continent of Africa.

DAVIS, RUSSELL, and BRENT ASHABRANNER, *The Lion's Whiskers: Tales of High Africa*, ill. by James Teason, Little, 1959. Thirty-one tales from Ethiopia and its borderlands. 11–15

DAYRELL, ELPHINSTONE, *Why the Sun and the Moon Live in the Sky: An African Folktale*, ill. by Blair Lent, Houghton, 1968. 5–8

FUJA, ABAYOMI, comp., *Fourteen Hundred Cowries; And Other African Tales*, ill. by Ademola Olugebefola, Lothrop, 1971. An anthology of Yoruba tales. 9–12

GILSTRAP, ROBERT, and IRENE ESTABROOK, *The Sultan's Fool and Other North African Tales*, ill. by Robert Greco, Holt, 1958. Eleven stories concerned with the deeds of sultans, caliphs, camel drovers, merchants, and scheming wives. 10–12

GUILLOT, RENÉ, *Guillot's African Folk Tales*, ill. by William Papas, Watts, 1965. Tales of the days when men and animals, trees and plants, and the sun and the moon walked and talked with one another. 11–up

GUIRMA, FREDERIC, *Princess of the Full Moon*, ill. by author, tr. by John Garrett, Macmillan, 1970. Good triumphs over evil in a tale from the Upper Volta. 9–11

HARMAN, HUMPHREY, comp., *Tales Told Near a Crocodile: Stories from Nyanza*, ill. by George Ford, Viking, 1967. Tales gathered from the storytellers of six tribes who live in the vicinity of Lake Victoria. 9–11

HEADY, ELEANOR B., *Jambo Sungura! Tales from East Africa*, ill. by Robert Frankenberg, Norton, 1965. 7–11
*Safiri the Singer; East African Tales*, ill. by Harold James, Follett, 1972. 8–10
*When the Stones Were Soft; East African Fireside Tales*, ill. by Tom Feelings, Funk, 1968. 9–12
These collections feature stories about the animals of East Africa and contain some *why* stories of the region.

ROBINSON, ADJAI, *Singing Tales of Africa*, ill. by Christine Price, Scribner's, 1974. Tales from Sierra Leone and Nigeria. 9–11

## Asia

## General Collections

CARPENTER, FRANCES, *The Elephant's Bathtub; Wonder Tales from the Far East*, ill. by Hans Guggenheim, Doubleday, 1962. An entertaining group of twenty-four tales gathered from Oriental sources. Each carries the atmosphere of the country in which it originated. 9–11

COURLANDER, HAROLD, *The Tiger's Whisker and Other Tales and Legends from Asia and the Pacific*, ill. by Enrico Arno, Harcourt, 1959. Brevity and simple concepts make these tales suitable for telling to groups in which the children vary widely in age. 9–12

## Arabian Countries

BROWN, MARCIA, *The Flying Carpet*, ill. by author, Scribner's, 1956. 7–10

COLUM, PADRAIC, *The Arabian Nights: Tales of Wonder and Magnificence*, ill. by Lynd Ward, Macmillan, 1953. This attractive group of stories, selected by a noted storyteller, will appeal to older readers. 10–14

KELSEY, ALICE GEER, *Once the Mullah*, ill. by Kurt Werth, McKay, 1954. Stories told by the Mullah give insight into Persian life and folklore and are often exceedingly funny. 9–12

LANG, ANDREW, ed., *Arabian Nights*, ill. by Vera Bock, McKay, 1946. Attractive format, fine design and illustrations. 10–12

MEHDEVI, ANNE SINCLAIR, *Persian Folk and Fairy Tales*, ill. by Paul E. Kennedy, Knopf, 1965. Stories authentically Persian in their portrayal of character but universal in topic. 9–12

*The Seven Voyages of Sinbad the Sailor*, ill. by Philip Reed, Atheneum, 1962. A beautiful book, illustrated with handsome, colored woodcuts, brings interest to the tale of this extremely durable merchant. 7–10

SPICER, DOROTHY GLADYS, *The Kneeling Tree; and Other Folktales from the Middle East*, ill. by Barbara Morrow. Coward, 1971. Retold in a lively, fluent style. 9–12

## China

CARPENTER, FRANCES, *Tales of a Chinese Grandmother*, ill. by Malthé Hasselriis, Doubleday, 1937. Thirty folk tales, told with quiet charm, reveal customs, beliefs, and home life in the China of long ago. 8–11

HUME, LOTTA CARSWELL, *Favorite Children's Stories from China and Tibet*, ill. by Koon-chiu, Tuttle, 1962. Nineteen stories collected in China over a period of twenty years. Many familiar themes. 8–11

KNIGHT, MARY, *The Fox That Wanted Nine Golden Tails*, ill. by Brigitte Bryan, Macmillan, 1969. 7–10

LIN, ADET, *The Milky Way, and Other Chinese Folk Tales*, ill. by Enrico Arno, Harcourt, 1961. A collection of twelve stories translated from original sources. 9–12

MOSEL, ARLENE, *Tikki Tikki Tembo*, ill. by Blair Lent, Holt, 1968. 4–7

WYNDHAM, ROBERT, *Tales the People Tell in China*, ill. by Jay Yang, Messner, 1971. A varied collection. 9–11

## India

BABBITT, ELLEN C., *The Jataka Tales*, ill. by Ellsworth Young, Appleton, 1912.

*More Jataka Tales*, ill. by Ellsworth Young, Appleton, 1912.

These fables from India have more elaborate plots and characterization than Aesop's fables, and they are often rather humorous. 6–10

GRAY, JOHN E. B., *India's Tales and Legends*, ill. by Joan Kiddell-Monroe, Walck, 1961. Skillfully told and well-illustrated tales and fables from the ancient epics and folklore of India.

JACOBS, JOSEPH, ed., *Indian Folk and Fairy Tales*, ill. by John D. Batten, Putnam, n.d. First published in 1892 with the title *Indian Fairy Tales*. 9–11

MACFARLANE, IRIS, *Tales and Legends from India*, ill. by Eric Thomas, Watts, 1966. Tales retold with respect for their basic humor and the ancient oral tradition of the village storytellers. 8–11

QUIGLEY, LILLIAN, *The Blind Men and the Elephant*, ill. by Janice Holland, Scribner's, 1959. 6–9

REED, GWENDOLYN, *The Talkative Beasts: Myths, Fables, and Poems of India*, ill. with photographs by Stella Snead, Lothrop, 1969. The culture of India is reflected in this volume. All ages

SHIVKUMAR, K., *The King's Choice*, ill. by Yoko Mitsuhashi, Parents, 1971. An animal tale with a moral. 5–8

SPELLMAN, JOHN W., *The Beautiful Blue Jay, and Other Tales of India*, ill. by Jerry Pinkney, Little, 1967. Stories that mothers tell to their children, collected firsthand by the author. The first appearance in print for many of the tales. 5–8

## Indonesia

BRO, MARGUERITTE HARMON, *How the Mouse Deer Became King*, ill. by Joseph Low, Doubleday, 1966. An excellent collection of eleven stories about Kantjil, the mouse deer, Indonesian counterpart of Brer Rabbit. 9–11

COURLANDER, HAROLD, *Kantchil's Lime Pit, and Other Stories from Indonesia*, ill. by Robert W. Kane, Harcourt, 1950. Twenty-three tales with notes on their origins and a glossary and pronunciation guide. 9–11

DELEEUW, ADÈLE L., *Indonesian Legends and Folk Tales*, ill. by Ronni Solbert, Nelson, 1961. An enjoyable collection gathered from the storytellers of Indonesia. 10–11

## Japan

BARUCH, DOROTHY W., *Kappa's Tug-of-War with Big Brown Horse*, ill. by Sanryo Sakai, Tuttle, 1961. 6–8

CARPENTER, FRANCES, *People from the Sky; Ainu Tales of Northern Japan*, ill. by Betty Fraser, Doubleday, 1972. A contemporary storyteller, Ekashi, remembers the tales of his childhood. 9–11

ISHII, MOMOKO, *Issun Boshi, the Inchling, an Old Tale of Japan*, tr. by Yone Mizuta, ill. by Fuku Akino, Walker, 1967. 7–9

MCALPINE, HELEN and WILLIAM, *Japanese Tales and Legends*, ill. by Joan Kiddell-Monroe, Walck, 1959. Traditional tales of Japan's legendary past, folk tales, and the epic of the Heike. 10–15

MOSEL, ARLENE, ad., *The Funny Little Woman*, ill. by Blair Lent, Dutton, 1972. A Caldecott Award book. 5–8

PRATT, DAVIS, and ELSA KULA, *Magic Animals of Japan*, Parnassus, 1967. Twelve stories that describe the legendary animals of Japan. Decorated with handsome woodcuts. 8–10

STAMM, CLAUS, ed., *Three Strong Women: A Tall Tale from Japan*, ill. by Kazue Mizumura, Viking, 1962. Hilarious story of the wrestler who trained with three women of superhuman strength. 6–10

*The Very Special Badgers: A Tale of Magic from Japan*, ill. by Kazue Mizumura, Viking, 1960. 6–10

UCHIDA, YOSHIKO, *The Dancing Kettle and Other Japanese Folk Tales*, ill. by Richard C. Jones, Harcourt, 1949.

*The Magic Listening Cap*, ill. by author, Harcourt, 1955.

Tales in the two books are well told, moralistic, and full of magic. 9–12

*The Sea of Gold and Other Tales from Japan*, ill. by

Marianne Yamaguchi, Scribner's, 1965. A handsome book in which the tales reflect age-old concepts of morality. 9–11

YAMAGUCHI, TOHR, *The Golden Crane*, ill. by Marianne Yamaguchi, Holt, 1963. Allegorical story about a young deaf mute and his guardian who nurse one of the sacred cranes back to health. 9–10

YASHIMA, TARO, *Seashore Story*, ill. by author, Viking, 1967. 5–9

### Other Countries of Asia

HITCHCOCK, PATRICIA, *The King Who Rides a Tiger, and Other Folk Tales from Nepal*, ill. by Lillian Sader, Parnassus, 1966. A dozen Nepalese folk tales were selected and handsomely illustrated for this volume. 10–12

JEWETT, ELEANORE MYERS, *Which Was Witch? Tales of Ghosts and Magic from Korea*, ill. by Taro Yashima, Viking, 1953. Fourteen stories with sparkle and suspense, excellent for storytelling. 9–12

MERRILL, JEAN, *High, Wide, and Handsome*, adapted from a Burmese folk tale, ill. by Ronni Solbert, W. R. Scott, 1964. 7–9

*Shan's Lucky Knife*, ill. by Ronni Solbert, W. R. Scott, 1960. A Burmese folk tale. 7–11

SIDDIQUI, ASHRAF, and MARILYN LERCH, *Toontoony Pie and Other Tales from Pakistan*, ill. by Jan Fairservis, World, 1961. Twenty-two authentic tales from the regions of the Punjab and Bengal. 8–11

### Oceania and Australia

BATES, DAISY, *Tales Told to Kabbarli; Aboriginal Legends*, retold by Barbara Ker Wilson, ill. by Harold Thomas, Crown, 1972. Tales of the first humans on earth. 10–up

BROWN, MARCIA, *Backbone of the King*, ill. by author, Scribner's, 1966. Linoleum-block prints enhance this presentation of an old Hawaiian legend. 10–12

COLUM, PADRAIC, *Legends of Hawaii*, ill. by Don Forrer, Yale Univ. Pr., 1937. Nineteen tales, some selected from the author's *At the Gateways of the Day* and *The Bright Islands*. 11–up

HOLDING, JAMES, *The Sky-Eater and Other South Sea Tales*, ill. by Charles Keeping, Abelard, 1955. Tales of the origin of the moon, the mango, and the coconut, and other stories with the flavor of the South Seas. 6–9

PARKER, CATHERINE SOMERVILLE (FIELD), *Australian Legendary Tales*, collected by K. Langloh Parker, sel. and ed. by H. Drake-Brockman, ill. by Elizabeth Durack, Viking, 1966. Not suitable for children, but valuable for folklorists, teachers, and storytellers. Adult

ROCKWELL, ANNE, *Tuhurahura and the Whale*, ill. by author, Parents, 1971. Based on a Maori legend. 5–8

SECHRIST, ELIZABETH HOUGH, *Once in the First Times*, ill. by John Sheppard, Macrae, 1969. Fifty folk tales from the Philippine Islands. 8–12

THOMPSON, VIVIAN L., *Hawaiian Myths of Earth, Sea, and Sky*, ill. by Leonard Weisgard, Holiday, 1966. Twelve nature myths retold with artful simplicity. 8–10

### North and South America

### General Collections

COTHRAN, JEAN, *The Magic Calabash: Folk Tales from America's Islands and Alaska*, ill. by Clifford N. Geary, McKay, 1956. A useful collection of tales from Hawaii, Puerto Rico, the Virgin Islands, and Alaska. 8–10

LEACH, MARIA, *The Rainbow Book of American Folk Tales and Legends*, ill. by Marc Simont, World, 1958. Tall tales, Indian legends, and scary stories from all regions of North and South America. 9–12

### North America: Indian and Eskimo Tales

BAKER, BETTY, *At the Center of the World; Based on Papago and Pima Myths*, ill. by Murray Tinkelman, Macmillan, 1973. A reverent integration and interpretation. 9–11

BELTING, NATALIA, *The Long-Tailed Bear, and Other Indian Legends*, ill. by Louis F. Cary, Bobbs, 1961. Twenty-three animal legends retold from the lore of various Indian tribes. Bibliography and notes on tribal sources are included. 7–9

CHAFETZ, HENRY, *Thunderbird, and Other Stories*, ill. by Ronni Solbert, Pantheon, 1964. Three tales from American Indian mythology. The illustrations are reminiscent of Navaho sand paintings. 9–11

CURRY, JANE LOUISE, *Down from the Lonely Mountain: California Indian Tales*, ill. by Enrico Arno, Harcourt, 1965. Twelve tales concerning the creation, the way men obtained fire, and the outwitting of enemies. 8–10

FISHER, ANNE B., *Stories California Indians Told*, ill. by Ruth Robbins, Parnassus, 1957. Legends collected by an eminent anthropologist, Dr. C. Hart Merriam, who in turn related them to the author. 8–12

GILLHAM, CHARLES EDWARD, *Beyond the Clapping Mountains: Eskimo Stories from Alaska*, ill. by Chanimun, Macmillan, 1943. 9–10

*Medicine Men of Hooper Bay: More Tales from the Clapping Mountains of Alaska*, ill. by Chanimun, Macmillan, 1946. 9–11

Unusual and highly imaginative tales of the animals and folk heroes of the Eskimos. Unfortunately, the author's language tends to detract from the dignity of the stories.

HARRIS, CHRISTIE, *Once Upon a Totem*, ill. by John Frazer Mills, Atheneum, 1963. Five tales of the Northwest Indians which will help boys and girls understand an interesting people. 10–13

*Once More Upon a Totem*, ill. by Douglas Tait, Atheneum, 1973. Three additional tales. 10–13

HILL, KAY, *Glooscap and His Magic: Legends of the Wabanaki Indians*, ill. by Robert Frankenberg, Dodd, 1963. Amusing stories of the mythical Indian hero, his people, and his animals. 8–11

HILLERMAN, TONY, ad., *The Boy Who Made Dragonfly: A Zuni Myth*, ill. by Laszlo Kubinyi, Harper, 1972. Fact and myth woven into the story of the first Corn Priest. 10–12

HOFMANN, CHARLES, *American Indians Sing*, ill. by Nicholas Amorosi, Day, 1967. An excellent introduction to the ceremonials of American Indians by a collector of folk materials for the Library of Congress. Includes transcribed music and a recording. 10–14

HOUSTON, JAMES, *Tikta'liktak: An Eskimo Legend*, ill. by author, Harcourt, 1965.

*The White Archer: An Eskimo Legend*, ill. by author, Harcourt, 1967.

Stories that reflect the Eskimo's courage and his will to

survive adversity. 9–11

HUNT, WOLF ROBE, and HELEN RUSHMORE, *The Dancing Horses of Acoma, and Other Acoma Indian Stories,* ill. by Wolf Robe Hunt, World, 1963. Twelve legends and stories of the Pueblo Indians reveal the customs and character of a proud and complex people. 10–12

LEEKLEY, THOMAS B., *The World of Manabozho: Tales of the Chippewa Indians,* ill. by Yeffe Kimball, Vanguard, 1965. These stories retain the flavor of the original tales as told by Indian storytellers. 9–11

MCDERMOTT, GERALD, ad., *Arrow to the Sun; A Pueblo Indian Tale,* ill. by author. Viking, 1974. Caldecott Award. 5–8

MARTIN, FRAN, *Nine Tales of Coyote,* ill. by Dorothy McEntee, Harper, 1950.
*Raven-Who-Sets-Things-Right,* ill. by Dorothy McEntee, Harper, 1975.
The first volume draws upon the legends of the Nez Percé Indians; the second upon the tales which came via the Eskimos and Canadian Indians. 9–11

PARKER, ARTHUR C., *Skunny Wundy; Seneca Indian Tales,* ill. by George Armstrong, Whitman, 1970. Animal stories written by the grandson of a Seneca chief. 9–11

PENNEY, GRACE, *Tales of the Cheyennes,* ill. by Walter Richard West, Houghton, 1953. Long-ago legends explaining nature and customs, and a group of humorous tales. 10–14

REID, DOROTHY N., *Tales of Nanabozho,* ill. by Donald Grant, Walck, 1963. Twenty-one short Indian tales about the great creator-magician, Nanabozho (Hiawatha) of the Ojibwas. Pronunciation guide and extensive bibliography. 9–12

## Canada

BARBEAU, MARIUS, *The Golden Phoenix, and Other French-Canadian Fairy Tales,* retold by Michael Hornyansky, ill. by Arthur Price, Walck, 1958. These stories are quite easily recognized as variants of well-known European tales, and little about them is distinctively French-Canadian. 9–11

CARLSON, NATALIE, *The Talking Cat and Other Stories of French Canada,* ill. by Roger Duvoisin, Harper, 1952. This array of genuinely funny stories has been adapted from tales told within the author's family circle. 9–11

HOOKE, HILDA MARY, *Thunder in the Mountains; Legends of Canada,* ill. by Clare Bice, Walck, 1947. Seventeen tales which draw upon three major sources: Indian legends, stories of the coming of white men, and variants of European tales. 9–12

## Latin America

BARLOW, GENEVIEVE, *Latin American Tales: From the Pampas to the Pyramids of Mexico,* ill. by William M. Hutchinson, Rand, 1966. Most of these stories, translated from Spanish sources which are cited, come from the Indian tribes of South America. Four have not previously been published. 8–11

BRENNER, ANITA, *The Boy Who Could Do Anything, and Other Mexican Folk Tales,* ill. by Jean Charlot, W. R. Scott, 1942. These curious tales are distinguished for their authentic idiom. They evoke the setting and style of Mexico and its people. 9–11

CARTER, DOROTHY SHARP, ad., *The Enchanted Orchard; And Other Folktales of Central America,* ill. by W. T. Mars, Harcourt, 1973. A colloquial retelling, with notes. 10–12

FINGER, CHARLES J., *Tales from Silver Lands,* ill. by Paul Honore, Doubleday, 1924. Nineteen Indian legends and folk tales from South America transcribed as the author heard them on his travels. Newbery Medal. 10–12

JAGENDORF, M. A., and RALPH S. BOGGS, *The King of the Mountains: A Treasury of Latin American Folk Stories,* ill. by Carybé, Vanguard, 1960. An impressive gathering of sixty-five tales. 9–12

ROSS, PATRICIA FENT, *In Mexico They Say,* ill. by Henry C. Pitz, Knopf, 1942. Fourteen tales that reflect the social life and customs of Mexico. 9–12

♪YURCHENCO, HENRIETTA, *A Fiesta of Folk Songs from Spain and Latin America,* ill. by Jules Maidoff, Putnam, 1967. Over thirty folk songs and singing games from Spain and the Spanish-speaking American nations. Melody line and chords are indicated for accompaniment. 5–11

## United States: General Collections [5]

COTHRAN, JEAN, ed., *With a Wig, With a Wag, and Other American Folk Tales,* ill. by Clifford N. Geary, McKay, 1954. Fifteen stories gleaned from many parts of the United States, felicitously worded for telling or reading aloud. 8–10

FIELD, RACHEL, ed., *American Folk and Fairy Tales,* ill. by Margaret Freeman, Scribner's, 1929. A highly satisfactory collection of Indian legends, Negro stories, Louisiana folk tales, mountain stories, and tall tales. 12–13

JAGENDORF, MORITZ ADOLF, ed., *Folk Stories of the South,* ill. by Michael Parks, Vanguard, 1973. Broad humor. 9–12

*The Ghost of Peg-Leg Peter and Other Stories of Old New York,* ill. by Lino S. Lipinsky, songs of old New York selected by June Lazare, Vanguard, 1966. An amusing potpourri of tales about one of our greatest cities. 10–13

## United States: Black Tales

COURLANDER, HAROLD, *Terrapin's Pot of Sense,* ill. by Elton Fax, Holt, 1957. American Negro stories collected in several widely spaced rural areas of the U.S. Notes give sources of different versions of the stories. 8–11

FELTON, HAROLD W., *John Henry and His Hammer,* ill. by Aldren Watson, Knopf, 1950. 10–13

HARRIS, JOEL CHANDLER, *Brer Rabbit: Stories from Uncle Remus,* adapted by Margaret Wise Brown with the A. B. Frost pictures redrawn for reproduction by Victor Dowling, Harper, 1941. Twenty-four stories suitable for younger children. The dialect has been modified slightly to make it easier for the young reader. 8–11
*The Complete Tales of Uncle Remus,* comp. by Richard Chase, ill. by A. B. Frost and others, Houghton, 1955. A monumental collection of interest to folklorists and storytellers. Adult
*Uncle Remus: His Songs and His Sayings,* rev. ed., ill. by A. B. Frost, Appleton, 1921. This version of the

[5] Three books of Hawaiian tales are listed among the collections from Oceania and Australia (p. 1003).

Uncle Remus stories is more acceptable to children than the preceding volume, but probably only the best readers will tackle it. 10–up

LESTER, JULIUS, ad., *The Knee-High Man, and Other Tales,* ill. by Ralph Pinto, Dial, 1972. Six animal stories, retold with simplicity. 5–7

REES, ENNIS, ad., *Brer Rabbit and His Tricks,* ill. by Edward Gorey, Scott/Addison, 1967, and *More of Brer Rabbit's Tricks,* ill. by Edward Gorey, Scott/Addison, 1968. Rhyme without dialect, simple style, droll pictures. 5–8

## United States: Tall Tales

BLAIR, WALTER, *Tall Tale America: A Legendary History of Our Humorous Heroes,* ill. by Glen Rounds, Coward, 1944. The authenticity is questionable but this should not detract from enjoyment of the book. 10–14

BOWMAN, JAMES CLOYD, *Mike Fink,* ill. by Leonard Fisher, Little, 1957. 11–15
*Pecos Bill,* ill. by Laura Bannon, Whitman, 1937.
Collections of tales about two American superheroes whose folk origins are doubtful. 11–15

CARMER, CARL, *The Hurricane's Children,* ill. by Elizabeth Black Carmer, McKay, 1967. A reissue of an excellent collection of American tall tales first published in 1937. 9–11

CREDLE, ELLIS, *Tall Tales from the High Hills, and Other Stories,* ill. by Richard Bennett, Nelson, 1957. Twenty amusing tales from the Blue Ridge Mountains. 9–12

FELTON, HAROLD W., *Bowleg Bill, Seagoing Cowpuncher,* ill. by William Moyers, Prentice, 1957. 8–10
*Mike Fink, Best of the Keelboatmen,* ill. by Aldren Watson, Dodd, 1960. 10–12
*New Tall Tales of Pecos Bill,* ill. by William Moyers, Prentice, 1958. 10–13
*Pecos Bill, Texas Cowpuncher,* ill. by Aldren Watson, Knopf, 1949. 10–13

MC CORMICK, DELL J., *Paul Bunyan Swings His Axe,* ill. by author, Caxton, 1936. 9–11
*Tall Timber Tales; More Paul Bunyan Stories,* ill. by Lorna Livesley, Caxton, 1939.
Stories about the exploits of the legendary logger. 9–12

MALCOLMSON, ANNE, *Yankee Doodle's Cousins,* ill. by Robert McCloskey, Houghton, 1941. This is one of the finest and most satisfying collections of real and made-up heroes from all sections of the United States. 10–14

MALCOLMSON, ANNE, and DELL J. MC CORMICK, *Mister Stormalong,* ill. by Joshua Tolford, Houghton, 1952. Bulltop Stormalong's adventures at sea are told with verve and imagination. 9–12

PECK, LEIGH, *Pecos Bill and Lightning,* ill. by Kurt Wiese, Houghton, 1940. A brief edition with copious illustrations to aid and comfort the slow reader. 8–12

ROUNDS, GLEN, *Ol' Paul the Mighty Logger,* ill. by author, Holiday, 1949. Paul Bunyan stories retold with an earthy, exuberant zest. 10–adult

SHEPHARD, ESTHER, *Paul Bunyan,* ill. by Rockwell Kent, Harcourt, 1941. This is an early version of the Paul Bunyan epic. 10–14

STOUTENBERG, ADRIEN, *American Tall Tales,* ill. by Richard M. Powers, Viking, 1966. Covers many of the characters found in Malcolmson's *Yankee Doodle's Cousins* but is more modestly written. 9–11

## United States: Variants of European Folk Tales

BARTH, EDNA, *Jack-O'-Lantern,* ill. by Paul Galdone, Seabury, 1974. The Devil is outwitted by Mean Jack. 8–10

CHASE, RICHARD, ed., *Grandfather Tales,* ill. by Berkeley Williams, Jr., Houghton, 1948.
*The Jack Tales,* ill. by Berkeley Williams, Jr., Houghton, 1943.
Two fine collections of tales from the Southern mountains. Priceless contributions to American folklore. 10–up
*Jack and the Three Sillies,* ill. by Joshua Tolford, Houghton, 1950. 5–9

JAGENDORF, MORITZ ADOLF, *New England Bean-Pot; American Folk Stories to Read and to Tell,* ill. by Donald McKay, Vanguard, 1948. The dry humor characteristic of the New England people is found in these folk tales from six states. 10–13

SAWYER, RUTH, *Journey Cake, Ho!* ill. by Robert McCloskey, Viking, 1953. 6–10

## West Indies

BELPRÉ, PURA, *Perez and Martina,* new ed., ill. by Carlos Sanchez, Warne, 1961. A Puerto Rican folk tale. 7–9
*The Tiger and the Rabbit, and Other Tales,* ill. by Tomie de Paola, Lippincott, 1965. This book, originally published by Houghton in 1946, contains eighteen Puerto Rican stories which echo themes and characters from other national folklore. 9–11

CARTER, DOROTHY SHARP, ad., *Greedy Mariani; And Other Folktales of the Antilles,* ill. by Trina Schart Hyman, Atheneum, 1974. Marvelous style and humor. 9–11

COURLANDER, HAROLD, *The Piece of Fire: And Other Haitian Tales,* ill. by Beth and Joe Krush, Harcourt, 1964. Twenty-six tales which capture the humor and mischief of this island people. 9–11
*Uncle Bouqui of Haiti,* ill. by Lucy Herndon Crockett, Morrow, 1942. This delightful array of folk tales from Haiti is now out of print. It should, however, be available in some libraries and is well worth searching out, for the tales reflect the happy collision of African and European folklore. 9–11

SHERLOCK, PHILIP M., *Anansi, the Spider Man,* ill. by Marcia Brown, T. Crowell, 1954. These stories, told by Jamaicans, have their roots in Africa. 9–12
*The Iguana's Tail; Crick Crack Stories from the Caribbean,* ill. by Gioia Fiammenghi, T. Crowell, 1969. A group of humorous animal tales. 8–12
*West Indian Folk-Tales, Retold,* ill. by Joan Kiddell-Monroe, Walck, 1966. Twenty-one West Indian *how* and *why* stories, eight of them new tales about the wily spider man, Anansi. 9–11

## FABLES

AESOP, *The Miller, His Son, and Their Donkey,* ill. by Roger Duvoisin, McGraw, 1962. 5–9

ARTZYBASHEFF, BORIS, ed., *Aesop's Fables,* ill. by editor, Viking, 1933. Ninety fables selected by the editor-illustrator and embellished with beautiful wood engravings. 12–14
*The Book of Fables,* ill. by Will Nickless, Warne, 1963. An attractive selection, mainly from Aesop, but also

from later fabulists of England, France, Germany, Russia, and India. 9–11

BROWN, MARCIA, *Once a Mouse . . .*, Scribner's, 1961. A fable from *The Hitopadesa*, illustrated with vivid woodcuts. Caldecott Medal. 5–9

FRASCONI, ANTONIO, *The Snow and the Sun: La Nieve y el Sol*, ill. by author, Harcourt, 1961. 6–9

GAER, JOSEPH, *The Fables of India*, ill. by Randy Monk, Little, 1955. Selected from three collections of Indian fables—*The Panchatantra, The Hitopadesa,* and the *Jatakas.* 10–14

JACOBS, JOSEPH, ed., *The Fables of Aesop*, ill. by David Levine, Macmillan, 1964. Contains over eighty fables and Jacobs' history of them. 9–11

KENT, JACK, ad., *More Fables of Aesop*, ill. by author, Parents, 1974. Simple language, breezy pictures. 5–7

KRYLOV, IVAN ANDREEVICH, *Fifteen Fables of Krylov*, tr. by Guy Daniels, ill. by David Pascal, Macmillan, 1965. The translator has rendered these fables into sophisticated English verse. 12–up

LA FONTAINE, *The Hare and the Tortoise*, ill. by Brian Wildsmith, Watts, 1967.
*The Lion and the Rat*, ill. by Brian Wildsmith, Watts, 1963.
*The North Wind and the Sun*, ill. by Brian Wildsmith, Watts, 1964.
*The Rich Man and the Shoemaker,* ill. by Brian Wildsmith, Watts, 1966.
Each of the above fables is beautifully illustrated in glowing colors. 5–8

REEVES, JAMES, *Fables from Aesop, Retold*, ill. by Maurice Wilson, Walck, 1962. In this collection the narrator has chosen to have the animals speak. 8–12

SHOWALTER, JEAN B., *The Donkey Ride*, a fable adapted by author, ill. by Tomi Ungerer, Doubleday, 1967. 5–9

UNTERMEYER, LOUIS, ed., *Aesop's Fables*, selected and adapted by editor, ill. by Alice and Martin Provensen, Golden Pr., 1965. Forty fables in a large picture book with refreshing illustrations. 6–9

WERTH, KURT, *The Monkey, the Lion, and the Snake*, retold and ill. by author, Viking, 1967. 6–9

WHITE, ANNE TERRY, *Aesop's Fables*, retold; ill. by Helen Siegl, Random, 1964. These fables are retold in an easy, contemporary style. 8–10

# MYTHS, EPICS, AND HERO TALES

## General Collections

ASIMOV, ISAAC, *Words from the Myths*, ill. by William Barss, Houghton, 1961. Explains the mythological origins of many words in common usage and thus deepens the reader's understanding of the myths and their pervasive influence in literature and art. 9–14

BAUMANN, HANS, ed., *The Stolen Fire; Legends of Heroes and Rebels from Around the World,* tr. by Stella Humphries, ill. by Herbert Holzing, Pantheon, 1974. 9–11

GREEN, ROGER LANCELYN, ed., *A Book of Myths*, selected and retold by editor, ill. by Joan Kiddell-Monroe, Dutton, 1965. A useful reference for children because it gives parallels and variants of myths from many ancient lands. 9–12

HAMILTON, EDITH, *Mythology*, ill. by Steele Savage, Little,

1942. Probably the most valuable single source of information for the reader who needs background in the myths. 12–up

HAZELTINE, ALICE I., ed., *Hero Tales from Many Lands*, ill. by Gordon Laite, Abingdon, 1961. A judicious selection from well-known retellings of the stories about great epic heroes. Includes sources, background notes, a glossary, a pronunciation guide, an index, and a bibliography. 10–14

UDEN, GRANT, ad., *Hero Tales from the Age of Chivalry; Retold from the Froissart Chronicles,* ill. by Doreen Roberts, World, 1969. Twelve dramatic stories. 11–13

## Babylonian Epic

BRYSON, BERNARDA, *Gilgamesh*, ill. by author, Holt, 1967. An exceptionally fine retelling of the ancient story of the proud King Gilgamesh. 11–up

FEAGLES, ANITA, ed., *He Who Saw Everything: The Epic of Gilgamesh,* ill. by Xavier Gonzáles, W. R. Scott, 1967. This epic antedates the earliest Hebrew and Greek writers by at least fifteen centuries. 9–13

## Greek and Roman Myths and Epics

AULAIRE, INGRI and EDGAR PARIN D', *Ingri and Edgar Parin d'Aulaire's Book of Greek Myths,* ill. by authors, Doubleday, 1962. A book with appeal for younger readers. The Greek myths are told in a simple narrative beginning with the Titans and finishing with the heroes. A large volume illustrated with beautiful lithographs. 8–11

BENSON, SALLY, *Stories of the Gods and Heroes*, ill. by Steele Savage, Dial, 1940. A selection of stories from Thomas Bulfinch's *Age of Fable.* 10–12

BULFINCH, THOMAS, *A Book of Myths*, selections from Bulfinch's *Age of Fable,* ill. by Helen Sewell, Macmillan, 1942. Striking illustrations suggestive of ballet postures and movement distinguish this collection. 10–14

COLUM, PADRAIC, *The Children's Homer*, ill. by Willy Pogány, Macmillan, 1918, 1962. A distinguished version in cadenced prose. 10–14
*The Golden Fleece and the Heroes Who Lived Before Achilles,* ill. by Willy Pogány, Macmillan, 1962. A good-looking modern edition of this famous retelling. 11–15

COOLIDGE, OLIVIA E., *Greek Myths*, ill. by Edouard Sandoz, Houghton, 1949. A retelling of the most widely known Greek myths. Here the gods are not idealized—indeed the book opens with an unappealing tale of trickery—but the stories have authenticity. 10–14
*The King of Men,* ill. by Ellen Raskin, Houghton, 1966. A robust and absorbing narrative based on stories about Agamemnon. 12–15

DE SÉLINCOURT, AUBREY, *Odysseus the Wanderer*, ill. by Norman Meredith, Criterion, 1956. A lusty, modern retelling of *The Odyssey.* 12–up

GARFIELD, LEON, and EDWARD BLISHEN, *The God Beneath the Sea,* ill. by Zevi Blum, Pantheon, 1971, and *The Golden Shadow,* ill. by Charles Keeping, Pantheon, 1973. Myths woven together into a continuous story in each book, superb in style, cohesive and dramatic. 12–up

GRAVES, ROBERT, *Greek Gods and Heroes*, ill. by Dimitris Davis, Doubleday, 1960. This sardonic interpretation is excellent for young people who are familiar with the standard treatments of the myths. 12–up

HAWTHORNE, NATHANIEL, *The Complete Greek Stories of Nathaniel Hawthorne*, ill. by Harold Jones, Watts, 1963. 10–12

*Tanglewood Tales*, ill. by S. Van Abbé, Dutton, 1952. 9–12

*A Wonder Book and Tanglewood Tales*, ill. by Maxfield Parrish, Dodd, 1934. 9–12
Hawthorne's treatment of the myths, though often criticized, has helped to interest many children in mythology. His work is well presented in the editions listed above.

KINGSLEY, CHARLES, *The Heroes*, ill. by Joan Kiddell-Monroe, Dutton, 1963. Narrative versions of Hercules' twelve labors and of the legends about Perseus, the Argonauts, and Theseus. 10–14

*The Heroes*, ill. by Vera Bock, Macmillan, 1954. Thirty tales are beautifully retold and make a fine cycle for the storyteller. 10–14

MC LEAN, MOLLIE, and ANNE WISEMAN, *Adventures of the Greek Heroes*, ill. by Witold T. Mars, Houghton, 1961. Parents or teachers in need of simply written versions of the myths will find this book valuable. 8–11

PRODDOW, PENELOPE, tr., *Hermes, Lord of Robbers; Homeric Hymn Number Four*, ill. by Barbara Cooney, Doubleday, 1971. Smoothly told, handsomely illustrated. 9–11

SELLEW, CATHARINE F., *Adventures with the Gods*, ill. by George and Doris Hauman, Little, 1945. Sixteen popular myths are included in this volume. 9–11

SERRAILLIER, IAN, *The Clashing Rocks; the Story of Jason*, ill. by William Stobbs, Walck, 1964.

*A Fall from the Sky; the Story of Daedalus*, ill. by William Stobbs, Walck, 1966.

*The Gorgon's Head; the Story of Perseus*, ill. by William Stobbs, Walck, 1962.

*The Way of Danger; the Story of Theseus*, ill. by William Stobbs, Walck, 1963.
The handling of these legends is direct and vigorous, and the illustrations are dramatically strong. 10–up

TOMAINO, SARAH F., ad., *Persephone, Bringer of Spring*, ill. by Ati Forberg, T. Crowell, 1971. Dramatic. 8–10

### Norse Myths and Epics

ALMEDINGEN, E. M., *The Treasure of Siegfried*, ill. by Charles Keeping, Lippincott, 1965. This is an adequate version of the Niebelungenlied. It is faithful to the original plot, although the author has omitted some of the cruel and barbaric incidents. 11–14

AULAIRE, INGRI and EDGAR PARIN, *Norse Gods and Giants*, ill. by authors, Doubleday, 1967. Retells for younger children the dramatic, exciting, and often humorous tales of Norse mythology. 8–11

COLUM, PADRAIC, *The Children of Odin: The Book of Northern Myths*, ill. by Willy Pogány, Macmillan, 1920, 1962. This incomparable retelling of Norse mythology has been given a new format and new type, but the distinctive Pogány illustrations remain. 11–15

HOSFORD, DOROTHY G., *Thunder of the Gods*, ill. by Claire and George Louden, Holt, 1952. The author successfully combines the dramatic form of the folk tale and the formal language appropriate to the myths. 9–11

SELLEW, CATHARINE F., *Adventures with the Giants*, ill. by Steele Savage, Little, 1950. A discriminating selection of stories for younger readers. 8–11

*Adventures with the Heroes*, ill. by Steele Savage, Little, 1954. The Volsung saga retold in simple language. 9–12

### English Epics and Hero Tales

HIEATT, CONSTANCE, ad., *The Sword and the Grail*, ill. by David Palladini, T. Crowell, 1972. One of the best of Hieatt's Arthurian retellings is this tale of Percival. 10–12

HOSFORD, DOROTHY, *By His Own Might; the Battles of Beowulf*, ill. by Laszlo Matulay, Holt, 1947. A retelling especially suitable for children in upper grades of elementary school. 10–12

LANIER, SIDNEY, *The Boy's King Arthur*, ill. by N. C. Wyeth, Scribner's, 1942. An authoritative and popular version, the best one to use for reading or telling. 10–14

*King Arthur and His Knights of the Round Table*, ill. by Florian, Grosset, 1950. An attractive and inexpensive edition. 10–14

MAC LEOD, MARY, *The Book of King Arthur and His Noble Knights*, ill. by Henry C. Pitz, Lippincott, 1949. A version, faithful to the original, which presents the legend in an easily understood manner. (Other editions by this author were published by Dodd, 1953; Macmillan, 1963; World, 1950.) 9–13

♪MALCOLMSON, ANNE, ed., *Song of Robin Hood*, music arr. by Grace Castagnetta, ill. by Virginia Lee Burton, Houghton, 1947. A handsome book containing eighteen songs. 11–14

PICARD, BARBARA LEONIE, *Hero Tales of the British Isles*, ill. by John G. Galsworthy, Criterion, 1963. Eleven stories about the ancient heroes of the Isles. Helpful notes give perspective on each hero's place in history and folklore. 10–13

*Stories of King Arthur and His Knights*, ill. by Roy Morgan, Walck, 1955. An absorbing retelling that evokes the atmosphere and spirit of the Middle Ages without the use of archaic language. 10–12

PYLE, HOWARD, *The Merry Adventures of Robin Hood of Great Renown in Nottinghamshire*, ill. by author, Scribner's, 1946. This version has gone through many editions and remains a favorite with readers. A fine source for reading aloud. 12–14

*Some Merry Adventures of Robin Hood*, rev. ed., ill. by author, Scribner's, 1954. Twelve stories, each somewhat abridged, from the longer version above. 10–13

*The Story of King Arthur and His Knights*, ill. by author, Scribner's, 1903. One of the great versions of the Arthurian legends. Also available in paperback edition from Dover. 10–12

SERRAILLIER, IAN, *Beowulf, the Warrior*, ill. by Severin, Walck, 1961. One of the better versions, told in verse form. 12–14

SUTCLIFF, ROSEMARY, *Beowulf*, ill. by Charles Keeping, Dutton, 1962. The battles with Grendel and Grendel's mother, and the final combat with the fire-drake are covered in this account. 12–14

TREASE, GEOFFREY, *Bows Against the Barons*, ill. by C. Walter Hodges, Meredith, 1967. A newly illustrated reissue of a version published in 1934. Robin Hood is presented as leader of a band of serfs in rebellion against the feudal lords. 10–12

## Irish Epics and Hero Tales

HULL, ELEANOR, *The Boy's Cuchulain*, ill. by Stephen Reid, T. Crowell, 1910. This out-of-print version is often available in libraries and is included because it offers excellent material for the storyteller.  11–14

SUTCLIFF, ROSEMARY, *The High Deeds of Finn Mac Cool*, ill. by Michael Charlton, Dutton, 1967. A vivid recounting of the legends of the Fianna by a superb storyteller.  11–14

*The Hound of Ulster*, ill. by Victor Ambrus, Dutton, 1964. A finely written account which incorporates the many legends about Cuchulain into one consecutive narrative. (See p. 550.)  11–14

YOUNG, ELLA, *The Tangle-Coated Horse and Other Tales*, ill. by Vera Bock, Longmans, 1929. Tales of Finn told by one of Ireland's most gifted storytellers.  11–14

*The Wonder Smith and His Son, a Tale from the Golden Childhood of the World*, ill. by Boris Artzybasheff, McKay, 1957. Fourteen tales from the Gaelic told with incomparable verve and beauty by one who had the poet's touch.  10–13

## Other National Epics and Hero Tales

ALMEDINGEN, EDITH MARTHA, *The Knights of the Golden Table*, ill. by Charles Keeping, Lippincott, 1964. These twelve stories about Prince Vladimir of Kiev and his knights are filled with the color and flavor of early Russia.  12–14

BERTOL, ROLAND, ad., *Sundiata, the Epic of the Lion King*, ill. by Gregorio Prestopino, T. Crowell, 1970. Story of the founder of the African kingdom of Mali.  9–12

DAVIS, RUSSELL, and BRENT K. ASHABRANNER, *Ten Thousand Desert Swords: the Epic Story of a Great Bedouin Tribe*, ill. by Leonard Everett Fisher, Little, 1960. Eleven tales from the great group of legends surrounding the Bani Hilal, a powerful tribe of Bedouin warriors.  11–13

DEUTSCH, BABETTE, *Heroes of the Kalevala*, ill. by Fritz Eichenberg, Messner, 1940. A version with literary distinction and continuity.  10–14

GAER, JOSEPH, *The Adventures of Rama*, ill. by Randy Monk, Little, 1954. This is a retelling of one of the best-loved epics of India.  12–14

GOLDSTON, ROBERT C., *The Legend of the Cid*, ill. by Stephane, Bobbs, 1963. The adventures and brave deeds of this Spanish hero are presented in a simple prose narrative enhanced by strong illustrations.  10–13

SAWYER, RUTH, and EMMY MOLLÈS, *Dietrich of Berne and the Dwarf King Laurin; Hero Tales of the Austrian Tirol*, collected and retold by authors, ill. by Frederick T. Chapman, Viking, 1963. This intriguing hero tale, a complex blend of historical fact and legend, concerns Dietrich of Berne, who became Theodoric the Great, Emperor of Rome.  9–13

*The Song of Roland*, tr. by Merriam Sherwood, ill. by Edith Emerson, McKay, 1938. A version that begins with Ganelon's treachery and ends with the triumph of Charlemagne over the Saracens.  11–up

THOMPSON, VIVIAN L., ad., *Hawaiian Tales of Heroes and Champions*, ill. by Herbert Kawainui Kane, Holiday, 1971. Good style, this is also useful for storytelling.  9–11

## Adult References: Folk Tales, Fables, Myths, Epics, and Hero Tales [6]

AUSUBEL, NATHAN, ed., *A Treasury of Jewish Folklore*, Crown, 1948. A lengthy compilation of over seven hundred stories and seventy-five songs of the Jewish people.

BAUGHMAN, ERNEST, *A Type and Motif Index of the Folktales of England and North America*, Indiana University Pr., 1966.

♪BONI, MARGARET BRADFORD, ed., *Favorite American Songs*, arr. by Norman Lloyd, ill. by Aurelius Battaglia, Simon, 1956.  10–up

♪*Fireside Book of Folk Songs*, sel. and ed. by Margaret Bradford Boni, arr. by Norman Lloyd, ill. by Alice and Martin Provensen, Simon, 1947, 1966.  10–up

BOTKIN, BENJAMIN A., ed., *A Treasury of American Folklore*, Crown, 1944. The stories, ballads, and traditions of the people are grouped under such headings as "Heroes and Boasters," "Boosters and Knockers," "Songs and Rhymes."

*A Treasury of New England Folklore*, Crown, n.d.

*A Treasury of Western Folklore*, Crown, 1951.

*A Treasury of Southern Folklore*, Crown, 1949.

BRAND, OSCAR, *The Ballad Mongers; Rise of the Modern Folk Song*, Funk, 1962. An excellent historical survey.

♪BRAND, OSCAR, ed., *Singing Holidays*, music arr. by Douglas Townsend, ill. by Roberta Moynihan, Knopf, 1957. Ninety interesting folk songs for American holidays.  12–up

BRUNVAND, JAN H., *The Study of American Folklore, An Introduction*, Norton, 1968. A good text and bibliographies.

BULFINCH, THOMAS, *Bulfinch's Mythology: The Age of Fable; The Age of Chivalry; Legends of Charlemagne*, ill. by Elinore Blaisdell, T. Crowell, n.d., 3 vols. in 1. This adult work, first published in 1855, has much value as a basic reference.

♪CARMER, CARL, comp., *America Sings*, music arr. by Edwin John Stringham, ill. by Elizabeth Black Carmer, Knopf, 1942.  11–16

♪CHASE, RICHARD, *American Folk Tales and Songs*, New Am. Lib., n.d. This excellent contribution to American folklore, by a renowned collector and teller of tales, has been given new life by its recent reissue in a paperback edition.

COLUM, PADRAIC, ed., *A Treasury of Irish Folklore*, 2nd rev. ed., Crown, 1967. The legends, ballads, stories, and superstitions of the Irish people, compiled and edited by an eminent authority on the subject.

COOK, ELIAZBETH, *The Ordinary and the Fabulous; An Introduction to Myths, Legends, and Fairy Tales for Teachers and Storytellers*, Cambridge Univ. Pr., 1969.

♪DIETZ, BETTY WARNER, and THOMAS CHOONBAI PARK, eds.,

---

[6] In addition to the books listed here, many of the entries in "General References" (p. 986) include discussions specifically concerned with folk tales, fables, myths, and epics. See especially the Arbuthnot and Sutherland, Chukovsky, Duff, Hazard, Huck and Kuhn, Morton, Pickard, and Smith titles.

Numbers at the end of an entry marked ♪ in this section suggest the age level of the children with whom the songs in that collection can best be used.

*Folk Songs of China, Japan, Korea,* Day, 1964. A valuable volume for teachers and others who are interested in helping children understand the culture of the Orient. Many of the songs can be effectively used with the folk tales of the countries named in the title. 9–11

DORSON, RICHARD, *American Folklore,* Univ. of Chicago Pr., 1959. A volume in the Chicago History of American Civilization series, this work surveys the entire field of American folklore from colonization to mass culture. Based upon field collection and research, the text includes folkways, jests, boasts, tall tales, folk and legendary heroes, and ballads.

*Buying the Wind: Regional Folklore in the United States,* Univ. of Chicago Pr., 1964. A supplement to *American Folklore.* Includes the folklore of Maine Down Easters, the Pennsylvania Dutch, Southwest Mexicans, Utah Mormons, southern mountaineers, Louisiana Cajuns, and Illinois Egyptians. For each regional group, the text provides narratives, proverbs, riddles, beliefs, folk dramas, and folk songs.

See also Folktales of the World series, ed. by Richard Dorson, Univ. of Chicago Press. The series contains the following titles: *Folktales of China,* ed. and tr. by Wolfram Eberhard (1965) ; *Folktales of England,* ed. by Katharine M. Briggs and Ruth L. Tongue (1965) ; *Folktales of Germany,* ed. by Kurt Ranke (1966) ; *Folktales of Hungary,* ed. by Linda Degh (1965) ; *Folktales of Ireland,* ed. by Sean O'Sullivan (1966) ; *Folktales of Israel,* ed. by Dov Noy (1963) ; *Folktales of Japan,* ed. by Keigo Seki (1963) ; *Folktales of Norway,* ed. by Reidar Th. Christiansen (1964) . This series is of outstanding value to the adult who is interested in authentic versions of folk tales. The storyteller seeking new material from the countries represented will be well rewarded by study of these volumes.

EASTMAN, MARY HUSE, *Index to Fairy Tales, Myths, and Legends,* Faxon, 1926. First supplement, 1937. Second supplement, 1952. Useful for locating various sources in which individual tales may be found. There are geographical and racial groupings and lists for storytellers.

ƒENGVICK, WILLIAM, ed., *Lullabies and Night Songs,* music by Alec Wilder, ill. by Maurice Sendak, Harper, 1965. 4–8

ƒFELTON, HAROLD W., ed., *Cowboy Jamboree: Western Songs and Lore,* arr. by Edward S. Breck, ill. by Aldren A. Watson, Knopf, 1951. 9–15

ƒFUKUDA, HANAKO, comp. and tr., *Favorite Songs of Japanese Children,* ill. by Katsuya Kay Nishi, Highland Music Company, 1965. Fifteen delightful songs presented with dancing, dramatization, and games, just as they would be performed in Japan. 6–10

ƒGLAZER, TOM, comp., *Treasury of Folk Songs,* ill. by Art Seiden, arr. for piano by Stanley Lock and Herbert Haufrecht, Grosset, 1964. All ages

ƒHAYWOOD, CHARLES, ed., *Folk Songs of the World,* ill. by Carl Smith, Day, 1966. Songs in this global array are presented in their native languages and in English. Notes add commentary on the musical life of each country and a description of each song. Chords for instrumental accompaniment are also indicated. 10–up

ƒHURD, MICHAEL, *Sailors' Songs and Shanties,* ill. by John Miller, Walck, 1965. Includes a brief but informative discussion of the purposes and origins of various sea shanties. 10–up

ƒIVES, BURL, *The Burl Ives Song Book,* Ballantine, 1953.

ƒ*Sea Songs of Sailing, Whaling, and Fishing,* Ballantine, 1956. This collection is out of print but is available in many libraries.

ƒ*More Burl Ives Songs,* Ballantine, 1966.

JOURNAL OF AMERICAN FOLKLORE, *Folklore in America,* sel. and ed. by Tristram P. Coffin and Hennig Cohen, Doubleday, 1966. This interesting compilation of verified folk pieces, reprinted from the *Journal of American Folklore,* is divided into the following categories: tales, songs, superstitions, proverbs, riddles, games, folk dramas, and folk festivals.

JUNG, CARL, and others, eds., *Man and His Symbols,* Doubleday, 1964. The chapter "Ancient Myths and Modern Man" should be read for the insight which it gives into the importance of myth. This book serves as the best introduction to Jung's psychology to have appeared so far.

ƒKNUDSEN, LYNNE, comp., *Lullabies from Around the World,* arr. by Carl Bosley, ill. by Jacqueline Tomes, Follett, 1967. This very specialized collection is excellent for use with young children. Guitar and simple piano accompaniments are included, and a brief, informative introduction precedes each song. 3–6

ƒKRONE, BEA and MAX, *Cantemos, Ninos,* Neil Kjos, 1961. A compilation of folk songs, singing games, and dances. Lyrics are printed in Spanish and in English. Simple accompaniments and chords for guitar and autoharp are included. Excellent for use with stories from Spain and Latin American countries. 10–up

LEACH, MARIA, ed., *Funk and Wagnalls Standard Dictionary of General Folklore, Mythology and Legend,* 2 vols., Funk, 1949–1950. The tremendous extent and variety of the world's folklore is made known in this fine reference work which serves the general reader as well as the expert.

ƒLOMAX, ALAN, *The Folk Songs of North America,* Doubleday, 1960. 12–up

ƒLOMAX, ALAN, and ELIZABETH POSTON, *Penguin Book of American Folk Songs,* Penguin, 1964. 12-up

ƒLOMAX, JOHN A., ed., *Folk Song: U.S.A.,* Duell, 1948. 10–up

MUNCH, PETER A., *Norse Mythology, Legends of Gods and Heroes,* rev. by Magnus Olsen, tr. by Sigurd Hustvedt, Singing Tree, 1968. Material on sources.

OPIE, IONA and PETER, *The Classic Fairy Tales,* ill., Oxford, 1974. Although primarily for adult students of folk literature, the 24 stories can be used for children.

*The Oxford Dictionary of Nursery Rhymes,* Oxford, 1951. An authoritative and highly interesting work which gives much of the folklore surrounding the nursery rhymes.

ƒPAZ, ELENA, *Favorite Spanish Folk Songs,* Oak, 1965. Forty-five traditional songs from Spain and Latin America. Included are literal English translations, notes on the songs, and guitar chords. 10–up

ƒREYNOLDS, MALVINA, *Little Boxes and Other Handmade Songs,* ill. by Jodi Robbins, Oak, 1964.

ƒ*Tweedles and Foodles for Young Noodles,* Schroder Music Co., Berkeley, Calif.

These two books contain songs by a well-known ballad maker. Although they are not folk songs, they comment upon life and the social scene in much the same manner as folk songs. Not all songs in the first volume are suitable for use with children, but in many cases the author suggests variants. Songs in the second book were written especially for children. 8–up

RITCHIE, JEAN, *Folk Songs of the Southern Appalachians*, Oak, 1965. 10–up
*Jean Ritchie's Swapping Song Book*, piano arr. by A. K. Fossner and Edward Tripp, ill. by George Pickow, Walck, 1952. 9–12
*Singing Family of the Cumberlands*, Oak, 1963. 10–up
RYDER, ARTHUR W., tr., *The Panchatantra*, Univ. of Chicago Pr., 1925. Adult students will be interested in discovering in these Indian fables the sources of many Aesop and La Fontaine fables.
SACKET, S. J., *Cowboys and the Songs They Sang*, W. R. Scott, 1967. A group of familiar favorites from the West of the 1870's and '80's. The book is illustrated with photographs of the period and contains descriptive background on the songs. A book that should have special appeal for boys. 8–13
SANDBURG, CARL, ed., *American Song Bag*, Harcourt, 1927. *New American Song Bag*, Broadcast Music Inc., 1950. 10–up
SAWYER, RUTH, *The Way of the Storyteller*, Viking, 1942, 1962. The history and techniques of storytelling.
SEEGER, PEGGY, *Folk Songs of Peggy Seeger*, Oak, 1964. Over eighty traditional American folk ballads and songs from the repertoire of Peggy Seeger. Rare versions and unusual tunes. Guitar chords and introductory notes are included. 12–up
SEEGER, PETE, *American Favorite Ballads*, Oak, 1961. Eighty-four traditional songs as sung by this noted wandering minstrel. 12–up
SEEGER, RUTH CRAWFORD, *American Folk Songs for Children*, ill. by Barbara Cooney, Doubleday, 1948. 5–12
*American Folk Songs for Christmas*, ill. by Barbara Cooney, Doubleday, 1953. 5–12
*Animal Folk Songs for Children; Traditional American Songs*, ill. by Barbara Cooney, Doubleday, 1950. These three books should assuredly form the nucleus of any collection of folk songs for children. The tunes and piano accompaniments are simple and appealing. *American Folk Songs for Children* contains an especially helpful discussion on the values and uses of folk songs. Each book includes a classified index and an index of titles and first lines. 5–12
SHEDLOCK, MARIE, *Art of the Storyteller*, 3rd ed., Dover, 1951. Guide to selection and use of materials.
SHEKERJIAN, HAIG and REGINA, *A Book of Ballads, Songs and Snatches*, Harper, 1966. A book that is graphically beautiful and musically excellent. Many unusual and little-known songs can be found here. Piano arrangements are tasteful and guitar chords are given. The coverage is international. 10–up
SILBER, IRWIN, and E. ROBINSON, *Songs of the Great American West*, Macmillan, 1967. Each of eight chapters is prefaced by a short historical essay. In addition, documentary notes on sources are provided for the ninety-two songs, which cover the decades from 1840 through the 1920's. Adult
THOMPSON, STITH, *The Folktale*, Holt, 1960 (Dryden Pr., 1946). The author, one of the world's foremost authorities on the subject, discusses the universality of the folk tales, and analyzes types of tales and their place in a primitive culture. The final section concerns ways of studying the folk tale on a worldwide basis. *Motif-Index of Folk Literature*, ed. by Stith Thompson, rev. and enl. ed., 5 vols., Indiana Univ. Pr., 1955. A reference work valuable for analyzing and categorizing folk literature of the world. Volume I includes a bibliography of all works examined for motifs.
TOOR, FRANCES, *A Treasury of Mexican Folkways*, ill. by Carlos Merida, Crown, 1947. Although published over twenty years ago, this comprehensive book has much of value on the customs, myths, fiestas, dances, and songs of the Mexican people.
TOOZE, RUTH, *Storytelling*, Prentice, 1959. Suggests titles, methods, and criteria for selection.
VON SCHMIDT, ERIC, *Come for to Sing*, piano arr. by Robert Freedman, Houghton, 1963. An amusing collection of folk songs with easy piano arrangements and guitar chords. Pathways of Sound, Inc., has produced a recording of all songs in this book.
WEAVERS, THE, eds., *The Weavers' Song Book*, arr. by Robert De Cormier, Harper, 1960. 10–up
*Travelin' On with The Weavers*, arr. for piano and guitar by Herbert Haufrecht, Harper, 1966. 10–up
WHITE, FLORENCE, and KAZUO AKIYAMA, *Children's Songs from Japan*, ill. by Toshihiko Suzuki, Edward B. Marks Music Corp., 1960. Approximately fifty songs make up this interesting collection. 6–10
WINN, MARIE, and ALLAN MILLER, *The Fireside Book of Children's Songs*, arr. by Allan Miller, ill. by John Alcorn, Simon, 1966. 6–10
ZEITLIN, PATTY, *Castle in My City*, ill. by Lucille Krasne and the children in Watts, Golden Gate, 1968. A group of original songs composed and tested by the author in her nursery school classes. The title song refers to the famous Watts Towers in Los Angeles. Most of the songs are easy for young children to sing and will be very useful in connection with the story hour. 4–8

## MODERN FANTASY

ADAMS, RICHARD, *Watership Down*, Macmillan, 1974. 12–up
AIKEN, JOAN, *Black Hearts in Battersea*, ill. by Robin Jacques, Doubleday, 1964. *Nightbirds on Nantucket*, ill. by Robin Jacques, Doubleday, 1966. *The Wolves of Willoughby Chase*, ill. by Pat Marriott, Doubleday, 1963. In these three engagingly melodramatic and fantastic stories, the author demonstrates her mastery of a writing style which seems to poke sly fun at Victorian novels. 9–12
ALEXANDER, LLOYD, *The Book of Three*, Holt, 1964. *The Black Cauldron*, Holt, 1965. *The Castle of Llyr*, Holt, 1966. *Taran Wanderer*, Holt, 1967. *The High King*, Holt, 1968. These five spirited chronicles, set in the imaginary kingdom of Prydain, follow the adventures of Assistant Pig-Keeper Taran as he grows to manhood. *The High King* received the Newbery Medal. 10–up
*Coll and His White Pig*, ill. by Evaline Ness, Holt, 1965. Coll, once warrior, now farmer, wants only to be left to his garden. But when Hen Wen, a pig with oracular power, is spirited away, Coll sets out to rescue her from the land of death. This story is also set in the imaginary kingdom of Prydain. 7–9
*The Marvelous Misadventures of Sebastian*, Dutton, 1970. An amusing fantasy which tells of fourth-fiddler Sebastian's flight across a kingdom and into the heart

of a princess. National Book Award. 9–12

*The Truthful Harp,* ill. by Evaline Ness, Holt, 1967. Another story set in the kingdom of Prydain. 7–9

*The Wizard in the Tree,* ill. by Laszlo Kubinyi, Dutton, 1975. A small girl rescues the last wizard in the world. 9–11

ANDERSEN, HANS CHRISTIAN, *Andersen's Fairy Tales,* ill. by Lawrence Beall Smith, Macmillan, 1963. An attractive and useful edition containing sixteen stories. 8–11

*The Complete Fairy Tales and Stories,* tr. by Erik Christian Haugaard, Doubleday, 1974. A fine translation by an author equally fluent in Danish and English. 9–11

*The Emperor and the Nightingale,* retold and ill. by Bill Sokol, Pantheon, 1959. Retold with sensitivity and illustrated with striking pictures. 9–12

*The Emperor's New Clothes,* ill. by Virginia Lee Burton, Houghton, 1949, 1962. An enchanting edition of Andersen's funniest story. Children and adults find the pictures as irresistible as the story. 7–10

*Hans Andersen's Fairy Tales,* tr. by L. W. Kingsland, ill. by Ernest H. Shepard, Walck, 1962. Thirty-two of Andersen's stories, several of which are not usually found in other collections. 9–12

*It's Perfectly True: And Other Stories,* tr. by Paul Leyssac, ill. by Richard Bennett, Harcourt, 1938. This collection, translated by a well-known Danish actor, is most highly recommended for the storyteller. The tales are written in the conversational tone in which Andersen liked to tell his stories. 9–12

*The Nightingale,* tr. by Eva Le Gallienne, designed and ill. by Nancy Ekholm Burkert, Harper, 1965. A beautifully designed book in every detail. The translation flows smoothly, and the illustrations faithfully echo the gemlike quality of the story. 9–11

*Seven Tales,* tr. and adapted by Eva Le Gallienne, ill. by Maurice Sendak, Harper, 1959. Pleasant, appreciative versions of some of Andersen's simpler tales, illustrated in a medieval style. Large print and wide margins add to the appeal of this volume. 8–12

*The Steadfast Tin Soldier,* tr. by M. R. James, ill. by Marcia Brown, Scribner's, 1953. Beautiful pastel illustrations enhance this poignant tale. 6–10

*The Swineherd,* tr. and ill. by Erik Blegvad, Harcourt, 1958. 5–9

*Thumbelina,* tr. by R. P. Keigwin, ill. by Adrienne Adams, Scribner's, 1961. A delicate, appealing presentation of one of the author's most charming stories about the adventures of the feminine counterpart of Tom Thumb. 8–10

*The Wild Swans,* tr. by M. R. James, ill. by Marcia Brown, Scribner's, 1963. Excellent illustrations. 9–12

ANDERSON, LONZO, *Two Hundred Rabbits,* ill. by Adrienne Adams, Viking, 1968. A gentle, beautifully illustrated tale of a boy and his magical wooden whistle, which summoned all the rabbits in the wood to parade before the king. 5–8

ASSOCIATION FOR CHILDHOOD EDUCATION INTERNATIONAL, *Told Under the Magic Umbrella,* ill. by Elizabeth Orton Jones, Macmillan, 1962. A fine collection of modern fairy tales for storytelling or reading aloud. 6–9

AVERILL, ESTHER, *The Hotel Cat,* ill. by author, Harper, 1969. A gentle, humorous tale of the great star-dust ball planned by the Hotel Cat and his friend, Miss Wilkins. 5–8

BABBITT, NATALIE, *The Devil's Storybook,* ill. by author, Farrar, 1974. Ten brief tales about a plump, vain Devil. 9–11

*Kneeknock Rise,* ill. by author, Farrar, 1970. A lively, suspenseful fantasy which examines the nature of truth and its meaning for various people. 9–12

*The Search for Delicious,* ill. by author, Farrar, 1969. A lighthearted tale which centers upon a disagreement over the definition of *delicious.* 8–up

*The Something,* ill. by author, Farrar, 1970. What's the "something" a little cavedweller fears? A child of today, and they meet in dreams. 4–6

BAILEY, CAROLYN SHERWIN, *Finnegan II: His Nine Lives,* ill. by Kate Seredy, Viking, 1953. The story of how Finnegan II lost one after another of his lives in one short year but lived to scoff at the legend that a cat has only nine lives. 9–11

*Miss Hickory,* ill. by Ruth Gannett, Viking, 1946. The story of a homemade doll and her remarkable adventures in Boston. Newbery Medal. 9–11

BARRIE, J. M., *Peter Pan in Kensington Gardens,* retold by May Byron, ill. by Arthur Rackham, Scribner's, 1930. This is a simplified version. The illustrations are considered by some critics to be the richest and most imaginative work of this noted illustrator. 8–10

*Peter Pan,* ill. by Nora Unwin, Scribner's, 1950. Peter Pan, the boy who never grew up, and all his delightful companions are beautifully pictured in this edition. 9–12

BAUM, LYMAN FRANK, *The Wizard of Oz,* new ed., ill. by W. W. Denslow, Reilly, 1964. The story of Dorothy and Toto's visit to the Land of Oz is perennially popular with children since it was first published in 1900. Many sequels are also available from the publisher listed above. Other editions are available from Dutton and Parents Magazine Press and in various paperback versions. 8–11

BELLAIRS, JOHN, *The House with a Clock in Its Walls,* ill. by Edward Gorey, Dial, 1973. This and its sequel, *The Figure in the Shadows* (ill. by Mercer Mayer, Dial, 1974), describe the adventures of a boy who lives with an amiable uncle who's a wizard. 10–12

BIANCO, MARGERY WILLIAMS, *The Little Wooden Doll,* ill. by Pamela Bianco, Macmillan, 1925. A wistful, appealing tale reminiscent of Hans Christian Andersen. 6–10

*The Velveteen Rabbit,* ill. by William Nicholson, Doubleday, 1926, 1958. How a very old velveteen rabbit, with the aid of the Fairy of Old Toys, becomes real and goes off into the real world. 4–7

BIEGEL, PAUL, *The King of the Copper Mountains,* English version by Gillian Hume and author, ill. by Babs Van Wely, Watts, 1969. A series of tales told by animals help keep the King alive. Dutch Children's Book Award winner. 9–11

BISHOP, CLAIRE H., *The Five Chinese Brothers,* ill. by Kurt Wiese, Coward, 1938. Told in folk-tale style, this very funny story has been a favorite of kindergartners for many years. 5–8

BOND, MICHAEL, *A Bear Called Paddington,* ill. by Peggy Fortnum, Houghton, 1960. This and the subsequent five books in the series chronicle the adventures of Paddington, a Peruvian brown bear, whom the Brown family found wandering in Paddington Railway Station in London. He became a member of the family and complicated its life ever after. 6–10

*The Tales of Olga da Polga,* ill. by Hans Helweg,

Macmillan, 1973. A humorous tale of a guinea pig.
9–10

BOSTON, LUCY MARIA, *The Castle of Yew,* ill. by Margery Gill, Harcourt, 1965. This brief tale involves the imaginative play of two boys who suddenly find themselves small enough to inhabit the castle of a topiary yew chess set. This book is for children younger than the readers of the author's *Green Knowe* stories. 8–10
*The Children of Green Knowe,* ill. by Peter Boston, Harcourt, 1955. 9–11
*Treasure of Green Knowe,* ill. by Peter Boston, Harcourt, 1958.
*The River at Green Knowe,* ill. by Peter Boston, Harcourt, 1959.
*An Enemy at Green Knowe,* ill. by Peter Boston, Harcourt, 1964.
Beautifully written fantasies that skillfully blend present and past. 9–12
*The Sea Egg,* ill. by Peter Boston, Harcourt, 1967. A finely written fantasy woven around an episode in the lives of two boys on vacation at the seaside. The egg-shaped stone which they place in a tide pool disappears, and a few days later they observe a child merman playing with the seals. 8–10

BRAND, CHRISTIANNA, *Nurse Matilda,* ill. by Edward Ardizzone, Dutton, 1964.
*Nurse Matilda Goes to Town,* ill. by Edward Ardizzone, Dutton, 1968.
Although Nurse Matilda is not as attractive a character as Mary Poppins, she also has some marvelous ways of exacting obedience, and incredibly naughty children are soon brought into line. 7–10

BRENTANO, CLEMENS, *Schoolmaster Whackwell's Wonderful Sons,* retold by Doris Orgel, ill. by Maurice Sendak, Random, 1962. Five sons were sent out into the world for a year to find a vocation and develop their talents. When they returned home to report, they found that by combining their talents they could rescue a captive princess. 8–11

BRIGGS, RAYMOND, *Father Christmas,* ill. by author, Coward, 1973. A series of cartoon-style frames show a grumbling Santa making heavy weather of his job.
5–8

BRINK, CAROL R., *Andy Buckram's Tin Men,* ill. by W. T. Mars, Viking, 1966. Andy builds four robots to help with his routine farm chores. When danger threatens, the robots rise to the challenge and perform heroically.
9–11

BROCK, BETTY, *No Flying in the House,* ill. by Wallace Tripp, Harper, 1970. Half a fairy, Annabel can fly!
7–9

BROOKS, WALTER, *Freddy Goes to Florida,* ill. by Kurt Wiese, Knopf, 1927, 1949.
*Freddy and the Dragon,* ill. by Kurt Wiese, Knopf, 1958. Between these two books lies a long series (twenty-one titles) of *Freddy* stories that enjoy enormous popularity. 9–12

BRUNHOFF, JEAN DE, *The Story of Babar, the Little Elephant,* tr. by Merle Haas, ill. by author, Random, 1933. This delightful story about the young elephant who was reared by an elderly lady has long been a favorite with young children. Many titles follow in the series, but some lack the charm and appeal of the first. The author's son, Laurent de Brunhoff, has carried on the series and has added another memorable animal character—Serafina, the giraffe. 4–7

BUCHWALD, EMILIE, *Gildaen: The Heroic Adventures of a Most Unusual Rabbit,* ill. by Barbara Flynn, Harcourt, 1973. Magic and humor in a lively story. 9–11

BURNETT, FRANCES H., *Racketty-Packetty House,* ill. by Harrison Cady, Dodd, 1961. An old-fashioned story of dolls and their house. 6–9

BURTON, VIRGINIA, *Choo Choo,* ill. by author, Houghton, 1937.
*Katy and the Big Snow,* ill. by author, Houghton, 1943.
*The Little House,* ill. by author, Houghton, 1942. Caldecott Medal.
*Mike Mulligan and His Steam Shovel,* ill. by author, Houghton, 1939.
These four fanciful stories, which have as their real heroes a train, an enormous tractor, an old-fashioned house, and a steam shovel, respectively, have delighted two generations of children and will probably survive to amuse several more. 5–8

BUTTERWORTH, OLIVER, *The Enormous Egg,* ill. by Louis Darling, Little, 1956. A tale of the fantastic complications that develop for twelve-year-old Nate Twitchell when a baby Triceratops emerges from a giant egg found in the family henhouse. 9–11
*The Trouble with Jenny's Ear,* ill. by Julian de Miskey, Little, 1960. When her two brothers discover that Jenny has an unusually sensitive ear that can hear thoughts, they arrange her appearance on a TV quiz show. 9–11

CAMERON, ELEANOR, *The Beast with the Magical Horn,* ill. by Beth and Joe Krush, Little, 1963. With the help of a unicorn she has saved from the hunters, Allison fulfills an otherwise impossible task and in doing so, wins the handsome prince. 8–12
*The Court of the Stone Children,* Dutton, 1973. Mystery and fantasy deftly blended. National Book Award.
10–12
*The Wonderful Flight to the Mushroom Planet,* ill. by Robert Henneberger, Little, 1954.
*Stowaway to the Mushroom Planet,* ill. by Robert Henneberger, Little, 1956.
*A Mystery for Mr. Bass,* ill. by Leonard Shortall, Little, 1960.
*Time and Mr. Bass: A Mushroom Planet Book,* ill. by Fred Meise, Little, 1967.
These four books, which relate the adventures of David and Chuck on the Mushroom Planet, are an interesting mixture of fantasy and science fiction. 9–11
*The Terrible Churnadryne,* ill. by Beth and Joe Krush, Little, 1959. Fast-paced, suspenseful writing marks this story, which moves convincingly on the border between realism and fantasy. 9–11

CARLSON, NATALIE SAVAGE, *Alphonse, That Bearded One,* ill. by Nicolas (pseud. for Nicolas Mordvinoff), Harcourt, 1954. An amusing, intriguing tale of how a well-trained bear shouldered a gun and went off to take his master's place in the army. 9–11

CARROLL, LEWIS (pseud. for Charles Lutwidge Dodgson), *Alice's Adventures in Wonderland* and *Through the Looking Glass.* Many editions are available. 10–up

CERVANTES, MIGUEL DE, *The Adventures of Don Quixote de la Mancha,* adapted by Leighton Barret from the Motteux translation, ill. by Warren Chappell, Knopf, 1945, 1960. 12–up

CHASE, MARY, *The Wicked Pigeon Ladies in the Garden,* ill. by Don Bolognese, Knopf, 1968. A delightfully scary fantasy about a neighborhood pest and how she incurs the anger of seven evil sisters who haunt an abandoned mansion in the guise of pigeons. 9–12

*Loretta Mason Potts*, ill. by Harold Berson, Lippincott, 1959. An absorbing tale of a naughty child and the fantasy world which she inhabits. 9–12

CHRISMAN, ARTHUR B., *Shen of the Sea*, ill. by Elsie Hasselriis, Dutton, 1925, 1968. These original fairy tales, set in China, seem very similar to folk tales and are told with glee and subtle humor. Newbery Medal. 10–12

CHRISTOPHER, JOHN, *The Guardians*, Macmillan, 1970. Superior science fiction set in 21st century England. 11–14

*The Prince in Waiting*, Macmillan, 1970. First in a trilogy (*Beyond the Burning Lands*, 1971; *Sword of the Spirits*, 1972) of England returned to feudalism. 11–14

*The White Mountains* and its sequels, *The City of Gold and Lead*, Macmillan, 1967, and *The Pool of Fire*, 1968. Exciting science fiction. Supposedly, earth has been invaded from outer space, and men are controlled by means of wire-mesh caps permanently attached to their scalps at the age of fourteen. The books are concerned with the adventures of three boys who decide to evade the capping ceremony. 10–13

CLARKE, ARTHUR, *Dolphin Island*, Holt, 1963. 11–14

CLARKE, PAULINE, *The Return of the Twelves*, ill. by Bernarda Bryson, Coward, 1964. 10–12

CLEARY, BEVERLY, *The Mouse and the Motorcycle*, ill. by Louis Darling, Morrow, 1965. A delightful fantasy about a mouse who makes friends with a boy and learns how to ride a toy motorcycle. 7–9

*Runaway Ralph*, ill. by Louis Darling, Morrow, 1970. In this lively sequel to the book listed above, Ralph makes a daring bid for freedom. 8–10

COATSWORTH, ELIZABETH, *The Cat Who Went to Heaven*, ill. by Lynd Ward, Macmillan, 1930, 1967. A humble Japanese artist risks his future to include the portrait of his cat in a painting for the temple. A miraculous change in the picture rewards his unselfish act. Newbery Medal. 9–12

*Cricket and the Emperor's Son*, ill. by Juliette Palmer, Norton, 1965. Several of the delightful tales that Cricket, a poor lad, found on a magic paper which never ran out of stories, no matter how many he read to the Emperor's invalid, insomniac son. 9–11

COBLENTZ, CATHERINE CATE, *The Blue Cat of Castle Town*, ill. by Janice Holland, McKay, 1949. The blue Kitten, born under a blue moon, learned the river's song, "Enchantment is made of three things—of beauty, peace and content." 9–12

COLLODI, See LORENZINI

COOPER, SUSAN, *Over Sea, Under Stone*, ill. by Margery Gill, Harcourt, 1966. An unusual story which melds mystery, Arthurian legend, and allegory. Two children, aided by an old uncle, follow the clues found on an ancient parchment and find themselves involved in the age-old struggle between good and evil. *Greenwitch*, Atheneum, 1974, *The Dark Is Rising*, 1973, and *Grey King*, 1975, are sequels. 10–12

CORBETT, SCOTT, *Ever Ride a Dinosaur?* ill. by Mircea Vasiliu, Holt, 1969. Charlie rides a dinosaur whose one ambition is to see a museum dinosaur exhibit—which is easy if you can make yourself invisible. 9–11

*The Lemonade Trick*, ill. by Paul Galdone, Little, 1960. First in a series of "Trick" books about the magic powers of a chemistry set. All bouncy and amusing. 8–11

CRAIG, M. JEAN, *The Dragon in the Clock Box*, ill. by Kelly Oechsli, Norton, 1962. While not fantasy in the usual sense of the word, this is a highly fanciful story that is concerned with the amusing imaginative play of a child. 5–7

CRESSWELL, HELEN, *The Bongleweed*, Macmillan, 1973. Fantasy adroitly integrated with the reality of a family desperately resisting a plant that takes over. 9–11

CUNNINGHAM, JULIA, *Candle Tales*, ill. by Evaline Ness, Pantheon, 1964. A story within a story made up of the rhyming tales which six little animals tell to a rather crabbed candlemaker each evening. Happily, the lonely old man enjoys the stories so much that he invites the animals to live with him. 8–10

*Drop Dead*, ill. by James Spanfeller, Pantheon, 1965. A memorable story of an orphan boy who is sent from the orphanage to live with a seemingly pleasant carpenter. With growing terror the boy, Gilly, discerns that the carpenter's true purpose is to make him into an utterly submissive slave. A sharp mixture of hard reality and allegory well worth introducing to youngsters. 10–up

*Macaroon*, ill. by Evaline Ness, Pantheon, 1962. Macaroon, a somewhat selfish raccoon, avoids hibernating each winter by choosing a child to live with. Since he dislikes their tears when he departs each spring, he decides to choose a nasty, spoiled, impossible child whom he can leave without regret. 8–11

CURRY, JANE LOUISE, *Beneath the Hill*, ill. by Imero Gobbato, Harcourt, 1967. A group of Pennsylvania children attempt to aid Welsh elfin folk in their struggle against the evil forces released by a strip-mining operation. 9–11

DAHL, ROALD, *Charlie and the Chocolate Factory*, ill. by Joseph Schindelman, Knopf, 1964. Charlie, who lives in dire poverty, is one of five children chosen to visit a chocolate factory whose eccentric owner is seeking an heir. When tests finally eliminate the other children, Charlie is chosen to inherit the bizarre and wonderful factory. 10–11

*James and the Giant Peach*, ill. by Nancy Ekholm Burkert, Knopf, 1961. When his parents were devoured in "thirty-five seconds flat" by an angry rhinoceros, James was sent to live with two very unpleasant aunts. After three years of misery he made his escape across the Atlantic in a giant peach, which also carried some very strange insect companions. 9–11

*The Magic Finger*, ill. by William Pène du Bois, Harper, 1966. An original and intriguing fantasy in which an eight-year-old girl, whose right forefinger acquires magic powers whenever she becomes angry, turns a teacher into a cat and a family of hunters into the hunted. 8–10

DAUGHERTY, JAMES, *Andy and the Lion*, ill. by author, Viking, 1938. Young Andy had read about lions but never expected to meet one. The encounter ends in adventure for both of them and for the reader. 6–8

DE LA MARE, WALTER, *A Penny a Day*, ill. by Paul Kennedy, Knopf, 1960. Six tales of fantasy which offer choice reading aloud. Followed by a companion volume, *The Magic Jacket* (1962). 10–13

*The Three Royal Monkeys*, ill. by M. E. Eldridge, Knopf, 1948. Originally published as *The Three Mulla-Mulgars*, this distinguished fantasy is a long story of the adventures of three young monkeys who go in search of their father, a prince from the valley of Tishner. 12–up

*Mr. Bumps and His Monkey,* ill. by Dorothy Lathrop, Holt, 1942. The story of the monkey who came to London from Africa, learned to speak English, affected the dress of a British gentleman, and eventually became the toast of the theater. 8–11

DEL REY, LESTER, *The Runaway Robot,* Westminster, 1965. Convincing science-fiction account of a sixteen-year-old boy and his companion robot, Rex, who refuse to be separated when the boy's family is to be transferred back to earth. 12–15

DEUTSCH, BABETTE, and AVRAHM YARMOLINSKY, *The Steel Flea,* adapted from the Russian of Nicholas Leskov, ill. by Janina Domanska, Harper, 1964. A humorous account of the dancing steel flea that was made by English craftsmen for Alexander, Czar of Russia. 8–10

DICKENS, CHARLES, *Captain Boldheart and The Magic Fishbone,* ill. by Hilary Knight, Macmillan, 1964. Two comedies presented in picture-book format. Boldheart was certainly the bravest ten-year-old pirate ever to set foot on a ship. "The Magic Fishbone," the story of a princess and her eighteen brothers and sisters, will delight girls. 8–10
*A Christmas Carol,* ill. by Arthur Rackham, Lippincott, 1956. The story of Ebenezer Scrooge and his discovery of the true meaning of Christmas has timeless appeal for both young and old. 8–up
*The Magic Fishbone,* ill. by Louis Slobodkin, Vanguard, 1953. Slobodkin's illustrations enhance this charming fairy tale. 8–10

DICKINSON, PETER, *The Devil's Children,* Little, 1970.
*Heartsease,* ill. by Nathan Goldstein, Little, 1969.
*The Weathermonger,* Little, 1969.
A trilogy, set in England, which explores a future in which machines have been outlawed, superstitious belief in witchcraft is prevalent, and only the courage and faith of the young seem to hold promise for mankind. 10–14
*The Gift,* Little, 1974. Davy's Welsh grandmother has the gift, and he too can read minds—an ability that leads him into a dangerous adventure. 10–14

DOLBIER, MAURICE, *Torten's Christmas Secret,* ill. by Robert Henneberger, Little, 1951. This gay Christmas story involves Santa's toy factory, hard-working gnomes, lists of good and bad children, and lovely glimpses of Santa's frosty, sparkling Arctic world. 4–8

DRUON, MAURICE, *Tistou of the Green Thumbs,* tr. by Humphrey Hare, ill. by Jacqueline Duhème, Scribner's, 1958. 9–11

DRURY, ROGER W., *The Finches' Fabulous Furnace,* ill. by Erik Blegvad, Little, 1971. It's not easy to keep a family from learning that the furnace is really a very small, quite active, volcano. 9–11

DU BOIS, WILLIAM PÈNE, *The Alligator Case,* ill. by author, Harper, 1965. The story of an unusually alert boy detective who starts working on the case before the crime is committed. 8–10
*Bear Party,* ill. by author, Viking, 1951, 1963. A wise old koala bear gives a costume party which serves to reunite all the bears and make them stop quarreling. Delightful fantasy with allegorical overtones. 5–7
*Elisabeth the Cow Ghost,* ill. by author, Viking, 1936, 1964. The story of gentle Elisabeth, who decided to reveal her true, fiery nature after her death and returned to haunt her former master. 5–8
*The Great Geppy,* ill. by author, Viking, 1940. The Great Geppy, detective, is the only red-and-white-

striped horse in the world. When he attempts to solve the Bott Circus Case, the stripes are a great asset. 8–10
*The Horse in the Camel Suit,* ill. by author, Harper, 1967. The boy detective who solved the *Alligator Case* pits his skill against a troupe of entertainers who turn out to be horse thieves in disguise. 8–10
*The Twenty-One Balloons,* ill. by author, Viking, 1947. Newbery Medal. 11–up

DUVOISIN, ROGER, *Petunia,* ill. by author, Knopf, 1950.
*Petunia, I Love You,* ill. by author, Knopf, 1965.
Between these two titles the author has given us four other humorous stories about the doings of this adventurous and silly goose. 5–8
*Veronica,* ill. by author, Knopf, 1961. As with Petunia, the author has told the adventures of Veronica, an extremely versatile hippopotamus, in several amusingly illustrated picture books. 5–8

EAGER, EDWARD M., *Half Magic,* ill. by N. M. Bodecker, Harcourt, 1954.
*Magic by the Lake,* ill. by N. M. Bodecker, Harcourt, 1957.
*Magic or Not?* ill. by N. M. Bodecker, Harcourt, 1959.
*The Well-Wishers,* ill. by N. M. Bodecker, Harcourt, 1960.
Although the above titles do not comprise a series in the usual sense of the word, they do have many elements in common: lively, somewhat bookish children, humor, magic, and lighthearted satire of the current scene. 9–11

ENGDAHL, SYLVIA LOUISE, *Beyond the Tomorrow Mountains,* ill. by Richard Cuffari, Atheneum, 1973. A sequel to *This Star Shall Abide* (1972) continues the story of a young man's maturing in a world that is rebuilding after Earth is doomed. 11–14
*Enchantress from the Stars,* ill. by Rodney Shackell, Atheneum, 1970. An absorbing work of science fiction which portrays three worlds whose inhabitants are at different stages of mental and psychic development. 12–up
*Journey Between Worlds,* ill. by James and Ruth McCrea, Atheneum, 1970. A story of the pioneers of the future and their life on Mars. 12–14

ENRIGHT, ELIZABETH, *Tatsinda,* ill. by Irene Haas, Harcourt, 1963. This original, strikingly illustrated fairy tale on the topic of unreasoning conformity offers children penetrating social comment, coupled with the delight and suspense of a well-told tale. 8–11
*Zeee,* ill. by Irene Haas, Harcourt, 1965. Glowingly illustrated and expertly told, this humorous fairy tale with allegorical overtones concerns the efforts of an irritable fairy to find a suitable home. 7–9

ERWIN, BETTY K., *Aggie, Maggie, and Tish,* ill. by Paul E. Kennedy, Little, 1965. The story of three remarkable old women and their marvelous means of vanquishing space and time, solving the difficulties of children, and recovering lost belongings. 8–10

ESTES, ELEANOR, *The Witch Family,* ill. by Edward Ardizzone, Harcourt, 1960. The witches created by Amy and Clarissa with crayons and paper take on an independent life of their own. The result is a fine blend of reality and fantasy. 6–10

ETS, MARIE HALL, *Mister Penny,* ill. by author, Viking, 1935. Mr. Penny's good-for-nothing animals did nothing to help themselves or their master. But after they ate up old Thunderstorm's garden, they redeemed themselves and saved Mr. Penny from a life of toil. 6–8

*Mister Penny's Race Horse*, ill. by author, Viking, 1956. Further adventures of Mr. Penny and his animals. 6–8
*Mr. T. W. Anthony Woo*, ill. by author, Viking, 1951. Mr. Woo and his cat, dog, and mouse live together, but not too happily. When Mr. Woo's meddling sister moves in with the idea of reforming them, they unite against the common enemy and learn to live peacefully. Humorous pictures add to the fun. 7–9

FARJEON, ELEANOR, *The Glass Slipper*, ill. by Ernest H. Shepard, Viking, 1956. An extension of the story of Cinderella into a full-length book. 8–11
*The Little Bookroom*, ill. by Edward Ardizzone, Walck, 1956. Twenty-seven stories with the author's unique blend of reality and fantasy, humor and wisdom. Most of them are excellent for reading aloud. 6–10
*The Silver Curlew*, ill. by Ernest H. Shepard, Viking, 1954. An expansion of the story of Tom Tit Tot, to which Shepard's humorous illustrations add a great deal. 8–11

FARMER, PENELOPE, *Charlotte Sometimes*, ill. by Chris Connor, Harcourt, 1969. 9–12
*The Summer Birds*, ill. by James J. Spanfeller, Harcourt, 1962. The children of a small English village are faced with a difficult decision when the boy who has taught them to fly asks them to go with him to save his race from extinction. Followed by *Emma in Winter*, ill. by James J. Spanfeller, Harcourt, 1966. 9–12
*William and Mary; A Story*, Atheneum, 1974. Two children are transported to other times and places when they hold a magic shell. Fine style and characterization. 10–12

FATIO, LOUISE, *The Happy Lion*, ill. by Roger Duvoisin, McGraw, 1954. An unlocked gate inspires the amiable lion in a little French zoo to return the calls of the villagers. The results are amusing. Roger Duvoisin's drawings are humorous and full of atmosphere. This first story about the Happy Lion has been followed by others equally hilarious and popular: *The Happy Lion in Africa* (1955), *The Happy Lion Roars* (1957), *The Happy Lion's Rabbits* (1974), and others. 5–8

FIELD, RACHEL, *Hitty, Her First Hundred Years*, ill. by Dorothy P. Lathrop, Macmillan, 1929. Hitty was a doll of real character, and the adventures of her first hundred years are varied and satisfying to little girls. Newbery Medal. 10–13

FISK, NICHOLAS, *Grinny*, Nelson, 1974. The sweet old lady at Tim's door announces she's Great-aunt Emma but Tim's little sister calls her "Grinny" and suspects the malevolence of the lady with metal bones. 10–12
*Trillions*, Pantheon, 1973. One of the few science fiction books for children that have the theme of invasion from outer space. 11–13

FLACK, MARJORIE, *Walter the Lazy Mouse*, ill. by Cyndy Szekeres, Doubleday, 1939, 1963. A whimsical tale about a lazy mouse whose family forgot him when they moved. 6–8

FLEISCHMAN, SID, *McBroom Tells the Truth*, ill. by Kurt Werth, Norton, 1966.
*McBroom and the Big Wind*, ill. by Kurt Werth, Norton, 1967.
*McBroom the Rainmaker*, ill. by Kurt Werth, Grosset, 1973.
Tall tales spun by an author with a great sense of the ridiculous and the ability to make it seem plausible. 7–10

Although not strictly fantasy, the titles listed below border on the fanciful by reason of their wonderful exaggeration.
*By the Great Horn Spoon*, ill. by Eric Von Schmidt, Little, 1963. 9–12
*The Ghost in the Noonday Sun*, ill. by Warren Chappell, Little, 1965. 9–12
*Mr. Mysterious and Company*, ill. by Eric Von Schmidt, Little, 1962. 8–11

FLEMING, IAN, *Chitty-Chitty-Bang-Bang*, ill. by John Burningham, Random, 1964. The Potts, owners of a magic auto, took a sea voyage in it and stumbled onto a gangster's cave. When they were surrounded by danger, Chitty-Chitty-Bang-Bang took over. 9–11

FLORA, JAMES, *Grandpa's Farm*, ill. by author, Harcourt, 1965. This book is sure to bring chortles of delight from the children who hear about the time the cow's tail got cut off and Grandma's marvelous ointment, applied to each part, causes a new tail to grow on the cow and a new cow on the tail! 5–8

FREEMAN, BARBARA C., *Broom-Adelaide*, ill. by author, Little, 1965. A convincing tale of magic and mystery in which the evil powers of a feared and abhorred governess are revealed and destroyed. 8–10

FRITZ, JEAN, *Magic to Burn*, ill. by Beth and Joe Krush, Coward, 1964. An amusing tale, excellently illustrated, in which an English boggart causes his hosts much trouble when he decides to return to America with them. 9–11

GÁG, WANDA, *The Funny Thing*, ill. by author, Coward, 1920.
*Millions of Cats*, ill. by author, Coward, 1938.
*Nothing at All*, ill. by author, Coward, 1941.
These three picture books, by a noted author-illustrator, contain fun, suspense, and incredible happenings of great appeal to children. 4–9

GAGE, WILSON, *Miss Osborne-the-Mop*, ill. by Paul Galdone, World, 1963. When Jody accidentally turns her cousin into a squirrel, her magic powers seem quite delightful; but when a mop comes alive and begins to direct the children's activities, the youngsters take a different view. 9–11

GARD, JOYCE, *Talargain*, Holt, 1965. The story that Talargain, who wanders the seas as a member of a band of seals, tells to Lucilla, a young girl of today, concerns his life as a human in the seventh century. 11–up

GARNER, ALAN, *Elidor*, Walck, 1967. A convincing, eerie, atmospheric fantasy in which four English children are transported backward in time to a war-torn medieval kingdom and become involved with the forces of evil that are striving to destroy the realm. 9–11
*The Moon of Gomrath*, Walck, 1967. This original story has its sources in the mythology of the British, Celtic, and Scandinavian peoples. A child, aided by dwarfs and elves, battles against the evil forces called to life by the power of an ancient bracelet. 10–12
*The Owl Service*, Walck, 1968. A story of suspense and beauty in which three youths of today are caught up in the mystery of an ancient Welsh legend and are seemingly forced to reenact it. 13–up

GATES, DORIS, *The Cat and Mrs. Cary*, ill. by Peggy Bacon, Viking, 1962. A story which moves quite convincingly on the border between realism and fantasy. The only fantastic element is a talking cat who talks to no one but Mrs. Cary. 8–11

GEISEL, THEODOR SEUSS (pseud., Dr. Seuss), *And to Think That I Saw It on Mulberry Street*, ill. by author, Vanguard, 1937.

*Bartholomew and the Oobleck,* ill. by author, Random, 1949.

*The 500 Hats of Bartholomew Cubbins,* ill. by author, Vanguard, 1938.

*Horton Hatches the Egg,* ill. by author, Random, 1940.

*The King's Stilts,* ill. by author, Random, 1939.

This prolific author has written and illustrated more than twenty books for children. All feature improbable creatures performing incredible feats. Probably, Dr. Seuss will be remembered best for his imaginative use of language and his facility in inventing descriptive names for the creatures of his imagination. In general, his earlier books are superior to his later ones. The titles listed above are among his best.　　　4–10

GODDEN, RUMER, *Candy Floss,* ill. by Adrienne Adams, Viking, 1960. Candy Floss, a doll with compelling powers, is stolen by a spoiled child, but is eventually returned to the carnival worker to whom she belongs.　　7–10

*The Doll's House,* ill. by Tasha Tudor, Viking, 1962. A completely enthralling book about the adventures of Tottie, a Dutch farthing doll.　　　7–10

*The Fairy Doll,* ill. by Adrienne Adams, Viking, 1956. A perceptive and beautifully told story about a fairy doll and a seemingly stupid child.　　7–10

*Home Is the Sailor,* ill. by Jean Primrose, Viking, 1964. Another of this versatile author's skillful fantasies which can be read on several levels. The plot is concerned with the loss and recovery of three male dolls and their return to the doll household.　　8–11

*Impunity Jane,* ill. by Adrienne Adams, Viking, 1954. An excellent doll story that boys will enjoy.　　8–10

*Mouse House,* ill. by Adrienne Adams, Viking, 1957. An enchanting and brief story that tells how a little mouse, crowded out of the nest, finds a comfortable new home.　　　7–10

*The Story of Holly and Ivy,* ill. by Adrienne Adams, Viking, 1958. A fanciful tale of the fortuitous way in which a doll, an orphan, and a lonely woman are united at Christmas time.　　　7–10

GOODALL, JOHN S., *The Adventures of Paddy Pork,* ill. by author, Harcourt, 1968. This delightful fantasy depicts, without text, the adventures of a brash young pig who runs off to join the circus.　　　4–7

*The Ballooning Adventures of Paddy Pork,* Harcourt, 1969. Another picture story, this one showing the rescue of a pretty young piglet from the pot under which some cannibal gorillas are ready to light a fire.　　　5–7

GOUDGE, ELIZABETH, *The Little White Horse,* ill. by C. Walter Hodges, Coward, 1947. This memorable mystery story, set in the west of England more than a century ago, contains a rare blend of fantasy and realism.　　　12–15

*Linnets and Valerians,* ill. by Ian Robbins, Coward, 1964. A rather special concoction of witchcraft, fantasy, and reality. Four children run away from their stern grandmother, only to be taken in by their great-uncle who is equally strict in a different way.　　10–12

GRAHAME, KENNETH, *The Reluctant Dragon,* ill. by Ernest H. Shepard, Holiday, 1938, 1953. A subtly amusing tale about a boy who made friends with a dragon and contrived to have him meet and fight St. George.　10–12

*The Wind in the Willows,* ill. by Ernest Shepard, Scribner's, 1953.　　　9–12

GRAMATKY, HARDIE, *Hercules,* ill. by author, Putnam, 1940.

*Little Toot,* ill. by author, Putnam, 1939.

*Loopy,* ill. by author, Putnam, 1941. An ancient fire engine, a tugboat, and a very early model airplane are amusingly personified in these ever popular picture books.　　　4–9

GRAY, NICHOLAS STUART, *Mainly in Moonlight,* ill. by Charles Keeping, Meredith, 1967. A group of original stories with appeal for children who are a bit older than the usual fairy-tale age. The settings are traditional, but the language and colloquial expressions used are very modern.　　10–14

GRAY, GENEVIEVE, *Ghost Story,* ill. by Greta Matus, Lothrop, 1975. When a bum moves into the house they're haunting, Mama feels he's a bad influence on the kids. A blithe tale in breezy style.　　8–10

GRIPE, MARIA, *The Glassblower's Children,* tr. by Sheila La Farge, ill. by Harald Gripe, Delacorte, 1973. A tale of good and evil in the Gothic vein.　　9–11

GROSSER, MORTON, *The Snake Horn,* ill. by David Stone, Atheneum, 1973. Playing the tartöld, a snake-shaped horn, brought its owner from the 17th century into Danny's room.　　　10–12

HALE, LUCRETIA, *The Complete Peterkin Papers.* Houghton, 1960.　　　10–12

HARRIS, ROSEMARY, *The Moon in the Cloud,* Macmillan, 1968. A humorous, much-embroidered retelling of the story of Noah's ark.　　　10–up

*The Seal-Singing,* Macmillan, 1971. A smooth blend of realism and the supernatural, set in Scotland.　11–14

*The Shadow on the Sun,* Macmillan, 1970. In the sequel to the book first listed above, Reuben and Thamar return to Egypt for a visit.　　10–up

HAUFF, WILHELM, *Dwarf Long-Nose,* tr. by Doris Orgel, ill. by Maurice Sendak, Random, 1960. This is the well-known German fairy tale about the shoemaker's son who was "herb-enchanted" by an evil fairy. It is given new life by Sendak's illustrations.　　9–11

HEINLEIN, ROBERT A., *Farmer in the Sky,* ill. by Clifford Geary, Scribner's, 1950.　　　11–13

*Have Space Suit—Will Travel,* Scribner's, 1958.

*Podkayne of Mars; Her Life and Times,* Putnam, 1963. One of the few science fiction stories with a female protagonist, and a cracking good one.　11–14

*Rocket Ship Galileo,* ill. by Thomas Voter, Scribner's, 1947.

*Space Cadet,* ill. by Clifford N. Geary, Scribner's, 1948. All of Heinlein's science-fiction novels are written for the teen-ager or adult. Those listed above are also suitable for a younger age group.　　11–up

HENDERSON, LEGRAND. *See* LeGrand.

HOBAN, RUSSELL, *Bedtime for Frances,* ill. by Garth Williams, Harper, 1960. The first of a series of books about a small badger, all delightful.　　3–6

*The Mouse and His Child,* ill. by Lillian Hoban, Harper, 1967. A tender and delicate fantasy about a wind-up tin toy, a father and child with paws attached.　　　9–11

HODGES, ELIZABETH JAMISON, *Serendipity Tales,* retold; ill. by June Atkin Corwin, Atheneum, 1966. Seven well-written, carefully plotted fairy tales set in Persia. They recount the victories of faith, hope, and steadfastness over the worst deeds of men and gods.　　9–11

*The Three Princes of Serendip,* retold; ill. by Joan Berg, Atheneum, 1964. The three princes are sent into the world by their father to finish their education and to find a way of ridding the seas of monsters.　10–12

HOLMAN, FELICE, *The Escape of the Giant Hogstalk,* ill. by Ben Shecter, Scribner's, 1974. A blithe, nonsensical tale of a giant plant that runs amok. 8–11

*The Future of Hooper Toote,* ill. by Gahan Wilson, Scribner's, 1972. A very funny story about a boy whose feet just won't stay on the ground. 9–12

HOLT, ISABELLA, *The Adventures of Rinaldo,* ill. by Erik Blegvad, Little, 1959. A rather old and worn, albeit courageous, knight seeks and wins a wife and castle. A jaunty tale in the manner of *Don Quixote.* 10–13

HOOVER, H. M. *Children of Morrow,* Four Winds, 1973. Telepathy is used to rescue two children from a cruel culture in a fast-paced science fiction story. 10–13

HOPP, ZINKEN, *The Magic Chalk,* tr. from the Norwegian by Susanne H. Bergendahl, ill. by Malvin Neset, Mc-Kay, 1959. Translated into more than eight languages, this delightful tale of fun and fantasy tells of John Albert Brown Sunnyside, who found a piece of witch's chalk with which he could draw himself in and out of fabulous adventures. 7–10

HUNTER, MOLLIE, *The Haunted Mountain,* ill. by Laszlo Kubinyi, Harper, 1972. Brave McAllister defies the blind ghost that guards the treasure of the mountain. 10–12

*The Kelpie's Pearls,* ill. by Joseph Cellini, Funk, 1966. When old Morag saved the kelpie's life, she set in motion a chain of happenings. A convincing, suspenseful fantasy in which humane values triumph over fear and avarice. 9–12

*The Smartest Man in Ireland,* ill. by Charles Keeping, Funk, 1965. A modern fairy tale about a boaster who bragged that he was smart enough to outwit the little people. When they stole his son away, he had to make good on his boasting. 9–11

*The Walking Stones,* ill. by Trina Schart Hyman, Harper, 1970. Once a century, the stones walk, and an old Highlander staves off the building of a dam to let it happen just once more. Eerie yet convincing. 10–12

JANSSON, TOVE, *The Exploits of Moominpappa,* tr. by Thomas Warburton, ill. by author, Walck, 1966.

*Finn Family Moomintroll,* tr. by Elizabeth Portch, ill. by author, Walck, 1965.

*Moominland Midwinter,* tr. by Thomas Warburton, ill. by author, Walck, 1962.

*Moominpappa at Sea,* tr. by Kingsley Hart, ill. by author, Walck, 1967.

*Moominsummer Madness,* tr. by Thomas Warburton, ill. by author, Walck, 1961.

*Moominvalley in November,* tr. by Kingsley Hart, ill. by author, Walck, 1971.

*Tales from Moominvalley,* tr. by Thomas Warburton, ill. by author, Walck, 1964.

These highly imaginative fantasies have been largely ignored in this country. Since, however, the author received the 1966 Hans Christian Andersen Award, it is likely that more librarians and teachers will read these engaging stories and bring them to the attention of children. 9–12

JARRELL, RANDALL, *The Animal Family,* ill. by Maurice Sendak, Pantheon, 1965. A memorable story of a solitary hunter who takes unto himself some remarkable companions: a mermaid, a bear cub, a lynx, and a little boy. How they adjust to each other and become a loving family is perceptively told. 10–up

*The Bat-Poet,* ill. by Maurice Sendak, Macmillan, 1967. A beautiful tale about a little brown bat who does not conform to the habits of bats. Instead, he opens his eyes in the daytime and awakens to a whole world previously unknown to him. For the sensitive reader who likes to daydream. 10–up

JESCHKE, SUSAN, *Firerose,* ill. by author, Holt, 1974. A fresh, amusing tale of a foundling who can't be admitted to school because she has a dragon's tail. 5–8

JOHNSON, CROCKETT (pseud. of David Leisk), *Ellen's Lion,* ill. by author, Harper, 1959. Twelve whimsical stories about Ellen's conversations with her stuffed toy lion —talk which, though seemingly absurd, carries bits of wisdom. This author's stories about Harold, especially *Harold and the Purple Crayon* (Harper, 1955) and *Harold's Trip to the Sky* (Harper, 1957), are also popular with children. 5–8

JOHNSON, ELIZABETH, *The Little Knight,* ill. by Ronni Solbert, Little, 1957. An entertaining story about a princess who wanted to be a knight but discovered that it is better to have one than be one. 8–10

JOHNSON, SALLY PATRICK, ed., *The Harper Book of Princes,* ill. by Janina Domanska, Harper, 1964. Twelve enjoyable stories, each of which describes the training of the mind and heart of a prince and the testing of these qualities. The book contains biographical notes on each author. 9–12

*The Princesses,* ill. by Beni Montresor, Harper, 1962. Well-chosen selections, most given in their complete and original form, which encompass a variety of plots and styles. Includes biographical notes on each author. 9–11

JONES, ELIZABETH ORTON, *Big Susan,* ill. by author, Macmillan, 1967. An entrancing little story about the happenings in a dollhouse on the one night of the year when dolls can come alive and speak. 8–10

JUSTER, MORTON, *The Phantom Tollbooth,* ill. by Jules Feiffer, Random, 1961. An extensive, well-written fantasy with much clever play on words and ironic social comment. Milo, a very bored boy, puts together a gift, which proves to be a tollbooth. After he pays his toll, he finds himself in an exceedingly strange land where he encounters many unusual characters and has some extraordinary adventures. 10–up

KAHL, VIRGINIA, *Away Went Wolfgang!* ill. by author, Scribner's, 1954. Wolfgang was the least useful dog in an Austrian village, until the housewives discovered that when Wolfgang ran, he could churn a whole cartful of milk into butter! 5–8

*The Duchess Bakes a Cake,* ill. by author, Scribner's, 1955. A humorous, rhymed story of the duchess who was carried skyward atop the light fluffy cake she had baked. 6–10

*The Perfect Pancake,* ill. by author, Scribner's, 1960. A lighthearted rhymed story about the good wife who limited her "feathery, fluffy, and flavory" pancakes one to a person. 6–10

KÄSTNER, ERICH, *The Little Man,* ill. by Rick Schreiter, tr. by James Kirkup, Knopf, 1966. An extremely funny fantasy about a two-inch-high circus artist who plans not only his own rescue from kidnapers but also the subsequent arrest of his abductors. 9–11

*The Little Man and the Big Thief,* ill. by Stanley Mack, tr. by James Kirkup, Knopf, 1970. An interesting sequel which ties up some of the unsolved problems of the earlier book and introduces a possible wife for Maxie. 9–up

KENDALL, CAROL, *The Gammage Cup,* ill. by Erik Blegvad,

Harcourt, 1959. A compelling well-written fantasy about the Minnipins, or Small Ones, who dwell in the land between the mountains. 10–12

*The Whisper of Glocken,* ill. by Imero Gobbato. Harcourt, 1965. 10–12

KINGSLEY, CHARLES, *The Water Babies,* ed. by Kathleen Lines, ill. by Harold Jones, Watts, 1961. A judicious cutting of this lengthy, Victorian, moralistic fairy tale has resulted in a readable version for today's children. 8–12

KIPLING, RUDYARD, *The Jungle Book,* ill. by Philip Hays, Doubleday, 1964. Stories of India and the jungle life of the boy Mowgli, who was adopted by the wolf pack. 9–13

*The Jungle Books,* ill. by Robert Shore, Macmillan, 1964. A selection of fourteen stories from *The Jungle Book* and *The Second Jungle Book.* 9–13

*Just So Stories,* ill. by author and Joseph M. Gleeson, Doubleday, 1932. Other editions are available from various publishers. 7–10

*The Second Jungle Book,* ill. by J. L. Kipling, Doubleday, 1923, 1946. 9–13

KRAUS, ROBERT, *Leo the Late Bloomer,* ill. by Jose Aruego, Windmill, 1971. Some lion cubs start slowly but, like Leo, they soon can do everything. 3–5

*Owliver,* ill. by Jose Aruego and Araine Dewey, Windmill, 1974. An owlet with ambitious parents chooses his own surprising career. 3–5

KRÜSS, JAMES, *Eagle and Dove,* tr. by Edelgard von Heydekampf Brühl, ill. by Pat Kent, Atheneum, 1965. Eight wisdom-filled fables which the dove tells the eagle as she works to enlarge an escape hole. 8–10

LAGERLÖF, SELMA, *The Wonderful Adventures of Nils,* tr. by Velma Swanston Howard, ill. by H. Baumhauer, Pantheon, 1947. Nils rides astride the gray goose and so learns about the geography, customs, and folklore of his country, Sweden. 9–12

LAMORISSE, ALBERT, *The Red Balloon,* ill. with colored photos from the film of the same title, Doubleday, 1957. A captivating story about a little boy who catches a magic red balloon and pursues it through the streets of Paris. 6–10

LAMPMAN, EVELYN SIBLEY, *The City Under the Back Steps,* ill. by Honore Valintcourt, Doubleday, 1960. Jill and Craig suffer many indignities and adventures when they are reduced to ant size and taken prisoner by the ants. Scientific detail is accurate. 9–11

*The Shy Stegosaurus of Indian Springs,* ill. by Paul Galdone, Doubleday, 1962. The Brown twins renew their friendship with George, the shy stegosaurus, who is an English-speaking, modern dinosaur. Preceded by *The Shy Stegosaurus of Cricket Creek* (1955). 10–12

LANIER, STERLING E., *The War for the Lot: A Tale of Fantasy and Terror,* ill. by Robert Baumgartner, Follett, 1969. Alec strives to help defeat a horde of rats intent upon invading the territory of some small friends. A story of communication and rapport between men and animals. 8–12

LAUGHLIN, FLORENCE, *The Little Leftover Witch,* ill. by Sheila Greenwald, Macmillan, 1960. How a stubborn little witch, accidentally left behind on Halloween, is gradually transformed by the human family which takes her in. 7–9

LAURENCE, MARGARET, *Jason's Quest,* ill. by Staffan Torell, Knopf, 1970. An episodic, humorous tale of a band of animals who seek a cure for fatal ennui. 9–11

LAWSON, JOHN, *The Spring Rider,* T. Crowell, 1968. A fine, dreamlike fantasy in which a boy and his sister mingle with the soldiers who fought a Civil War battle on the area that is now farmed by their family. 12–14

*You Better Come Home With Me,* ill. by Arnold Spilka, T. Crowell, 1966. A fantastic tale which blends into the realistic setting of rural Appalachia as an orphaned boy seeks through the mountains for clues to his real identity. 10–up

LAWSON, ROBERT, *Edward, Hoppy, and Joe,* ill. by author, Knopf, 1952. When Edward, a rabbit, needed educating, Hoppy Toad and Joe Possum did plenty of mischief, but Benjamin Beaver came to the rescue and turned their pranks into constructive action. 6–8

*Mr. Revere and I,* ill. by author, Little, 1953. A unique view of some events of the American Revolution as related by Paul Revere's horse, Scheherazade. A good story for reading aloud. 9–12

*Rabbit Hill,* ill. by author, Viking, 1944. Newbery Medal. 8–11

*The Tough Winter,* ill. by author, Viking, 1954. Sequel to *Rabbit Hill.* This book carries the story of the animal inhabitants of Rabbit Hill through a long and severe winter during which the Big House is left in charge of a dour caretaker who owns a very mean dog. 8–11

LE GRAND (pseud. for LeGrand Henderson), *Cats for Kansas,* ill. by author, Abingdon, 1948.

*How Baseball Began in Brooklyn,* ill. by author, Abingdon, 1958.

*Why Cowboys Sing in Texas,* ill. by author, Abingdon, 1950.

Three tall tales with a folklore flavor. Good for reading aloud. 5–8

LE GUIN, URSULA K., *A Wizard of Earthsea,* ill. by Ruth Robbins, Parnassus, 1968. An extraordinary allegory that explores the nature of evil. Ged, a young apprentice sorcerer, unintentionally releases a malignant force, which he must then struggle to overcome. 12–up

*The Farthest Shore,* ill. by Gail Garraty, Atheneum, 1972.

*The Tombs of Atuan,* ill. by Gail Garraty, Atheneum, 1971.

Sequels to *A Wizard of Earthsea,* equally intricate. 12–up

LEICHMAN, SEYMOUR, *The Boy Who Could Sing Pictures,* ill. by author, Doubleday, 1968. A brief but profound fairy tale that explores the problems created for the unhappy citizens of a kingdom whose ruler fights a succession of "just wars." 8–11

L'ENGLE, MADELEINE, *A Wrinkle in Time,* Farrar, 1962. Newbery Medal. 11–14

LEWIS, CLIVE STAPLES, *The Lion, the Witch, and the Wardrobe,* ill. by Pauline Baynes, Macmillan, 1951. Other titles in the Narnia series, in order of appearance, are: *Prince Caspian* (1951), *The Voyage of the Dawn Treader* (1952), *The Silver Chair* (1953), *The Horse and His Boy* (1954), *The Magician's Nephew* (1955), and *The Last Battle* (1956). 9–13

LIFTON, BETTY JEAN, *The Cock and the Ghost Cat,* ill. by Fuku Akino, Atheneum, 1965. An outstanding book that tells of the sacrifice made by the cock to save his master from the demon cat. 6–10

*The Rice-Cake Rabbit,* ill. by Eiichi Mitsui, Norton, 1966. Despising his success as a baker of rice cakes, the rabbit became a swordsman, won a fencing contest, and was rewarded by being made Samurai of the Moon. 6–8

LINDE, GUNNEL, *The White Stone,* tr. by Richard and Clara Winston, ill. by Imero Gobbato, Harcourt, 1966. A white stone becomes a symbol which helps two imaginative children transcend the irritations of their everyday life. Although not fantasy in the traditional sense, this story, like *The Boy and the Whale,* by Sanchez-Silva, shows the highly fanciful play of two children. 9–11

LINDGREN, ASTRID, *Pippi Longstocking,* tr. by Florence Lamborn, ill. by Louis Glanzman, Viking, 1950. For sheer outrageous hilarity, Pippi the superchild takes all prizes. Sequels are: *Pippi Goes on Board* (1957) and *Pippi in the South Seas* (1959). 8–11

LIONNI, LEO, *Inch by Inch,* ill. by author, Astor, 1962. A truly distinguished picture book, with glowing illustrations, tells a clever tale of the inchworm who escaped great danger by literally measuring his enemies. 5–7

*Swimmy,* ill. by author, Pantheon, 1963. A picture book of flawless design. It tells how a little orphan fish finds a way to protect himself and his newly adopted family from the dangers of the deep. 5–7

*Alexander and the Wind-up Mouse,* ill. by author, Pantheon, 1969. An allegory of love and friendship in which a young mouse learns that real life with all its dangers is preferable to life as a toy. 5–8

LIPKIND, WILLIAM, *The Magic Feather Duster,* ill. by Nicolas Mordvinoff, Harcourt, 1958. The story of four brothers who covet a unique feather duster which can produce anything desired with but a flick. 5–8

LIPKIND, WILLIAM, and NICOLAS MORDVINOFF, *Finders Keepers,* Harcourt, 1951. Written in folk-tale style, this is the rollicking fable of two dogs who solve, with admirable commonsense, the problem of who shall keep the bone. 4–8

LITTLE, JANE, *Sneaker Hill,* ill. by Nancy Grossman, Atheneum, 1967. When Matthew's mother decides to take the test for membership in the Sisterhood of Witches before she is eligible, her owl, Shadow, Matthew, and his cousin Susan attempt to rescue the would-be witch. 9–11

LIVELY, PENELOPE, *The Ghost of Thomas Kempe,* ill. by Antony Maitland, Dutton, 1973. A mischievous ghost leaves notes for which poor James is blamed. Winner of the Carnegie Award. 9–11

*The House in Norham Gardens,* Dutton, 1974. Time-shift sequences are smoothly woven into the setting of an old house where Clare lives with two beloved great-aunts. 11–14

LOBEL, ARNOLD, *Frog and Toad Are Friends,* ill. by author, Harper, 1970. Five short stories, simple and charming, tell the ups and downs of friendship, as do those in its sequel, *Frog and Toad Together,* 1972. 6–7

LOFTING, HUGH, *The Story of Doctor Dolittle,* ill. by author, Lippincott, 1920.

*The Voyages of Doctor Dolittle,* ill. by author, Lippincott, 1922.

There are seven more books in the *Doctor Dolittle* series, but these first two remain the favorites. Some volumes include racially offensive material. 8–12

*The Story of Mrs. Tubbs,* Lippincott, 1923, 1968. 6–8

*Twilight of Magic,* ill. by Lois Lenski, Lippincott, 1930, 1967. Entirely different from the Dr. Dolittle tales, this story tells of a magic shell and its influence

upon two children of medieval days. 9–12

LORENZINI, CARLO, *The Adventures of Pinocchio,* tr. by Carol Della Chiesa, with ill. after Attilio Mussino, MacMillan, 1951. 9–11

MC CLOSKEY, ROBERT, *Burt Dow: Deep-Water Man,* ill. by author, Viking, 1963. This handsomely illustrated tall tale recounts the adventures of a weather-beaten fisherman who was lucky enough to catch a whale by the tail. 7–9

MAC DONALD, GEORGE, *At the Back of the North Wind,* ill. by Harvey Dinnerstein, Macmillan, 1964. A fine edition of this Victorian fairy tale, which tells of a little boy's relationship with the North Wind and of the many ways in which she appears to him. (Available in another edition, ill. by E. H. Shepard, Dutton.) 10–12

*The Light Princess,* ill. by William Pène du Bois, T. Crowell, 1962. The lovely pastel illustrations add greatly to the appeal of this whimsical story about the princess who floated away unless tied down. (Available in another edition, beautifully illustrated by Maurice Sendak, Farrar, 1969.) 7–11

*The Princess and Curdie,* ill. by Nora Unwin, Macmillan, 1954. Curdie, son of a silver miner, is commanded by a strange witchlike woman to seek the land of Gwyntystorm where the king is very ill. Along the way he encounters and overcomes much evil until at last the enemy is vanquished and justice established. *The Princess and the Goblin,* ill. by Nora S. Unwin, Macmillan, 1951, 1967.

Excellent editions of the two books immediately above are also available from Dutton, ill. by Charles Folkard. 9–11

MC GINLEY, PHYLLIS, *The Horse Who Lived Upstairs,* ill. by Helen Stone, Lippincott, 1944.

*The Horse Who Had His Picture in the Paper,* ill. by Helen Stone, Lippincott, 1951.

In the first book, a trip to the country teaches discontented Joey that he is a true city dweller at heart. The second book finds Joey again restless, this time yearning for publicity that will silence the policeman's boastful horse. The climax is utterly satisfying. 4–8

MAC GREGOR, ELLEN, *Miss Pickerell and the Geiger Counter,* ill. by Paul Galdone, McGraw, 1953.

*Miss Pickerell Goes to Mars,* ill. by Paul Galdone, McGraw, 1951.

*Miss Pickerell Goes to the Arctic,* ill. by Paul Galdone, McGraw, 1954.

*Miss Pickerell Goes Undersea,* ill. by Paul Galdone, McGraw, 1953.

Miss Pickerell is a plainspoken, elderly spinster with a remarkable flair for attracting adventure wherever she goes. The author combines some scientific information with suspense and nonsense in a way that pleases young readers. 9–11

MC HARGUE, GEORGESS, *Hot & Cold Running Cities,* Holt, 1974. An anthology of tales about the future. 11–up

MAC KELLAR, WILLIAM, *Ghost in the Castle,* ill. by Richard Bennett, McKay, 1960. The hero of the story did not believe in ghosts. To prove his point and to demonstrate his courage, he went to Craigie Castle—and came face to face with Mr. MacSpurtle, the ghost. 9–11

MC KENZIE, ELLEN K., *Taash and the Jesters,* Holt, 1968. A complicated and absorbing tale of adventure, witchcraft, and malice in an imaginary kingdom. By returning a kidnaped prince to the palace, Taash and his allies defeat the power of the witches. 9–12

MC LEOD, EMILIE, *Clancy's Witch*, ill. by Lisl Weil, Little, 1959. Nine-year-old Clancy has the startling experience of having a witch for a neighbor!                   7–10

MC NEILL, JANET, *Tom's Tower*, ill. by Mary Russon, Little, 1967. A beguiling fantasy with appeal for both boys and girls. The hero, Tom, is suddenly transported to a strange country where he is made to serve as guardian of the castle treasure.                   9–11

MAYER, MERCER, *The Great Cat Chase*, ill. by author, Four Winds, 1975. Raffish children, plenty of action in a wordless picture book.                   2–5

*Frog, Where Are You?* ill. by author, Dial, 1969. One of a series of very funny wordless books about a frog, a dog, and a boy.                   2–5

MAYNE, WILLIAM, *Earthfasts*, Dutton, 1966. An engrossing fantasy in which inhabitants of a sedate British community become involved with legendary characters from the past. Supernatural and everyday events are woven into an exciting, convincing tale with appeal for the above-average reader.                   10–14

*A Game of Dark*, Dutton, 1971. Time-shift at its eeriest, in a story with psychological depths.                   10–13

*A Grass Rope*, ill. by Lynton Lamb, Dutton, 1962. Four children follow clues in an old legend concerned with lost treasure and a unicorn, and solve a local mystery of long standing.                   9–12

*The Hill Road*, Dutton, 1969. Three contemporary young people, riding their ponies on the Yorkshire moors, become involved in the lives of ancient Britons and Saxons.                   10–up

MERRILL, JEAN, *The Pushcart War*, ill. by Ronni Solbert, W. R. Scott, 1964.                   10–12

*The Superlative Horse*, ill. by Ronni Solbert, W. R. Scott, 1961. An imaginative tale set in ancient China.                   9–11

MILNE, ALAN ALEXANDER, *The House at Pooh Corner*, ill. by Ernest H. Shepard, Dutton, 1961. Concerned with the adventures of Christopher Robin and all his toys: Eeyore, Tigger, Winnie-the-Pooh, and others. Full of the same whimsical humor as *Winnie-the-Pooh*.                   5–10

*Prince Rabbit and the Princess Who Could Not Laugh*, ill. by Mary Shepard, Dutton, 1966. Two amusing fairy tales, each a variation on the contest theme. In the first are tests of skill and intelligence. The second contains a trial for the hand of the princess.                   7–10

*Winnie-the-Pooh*, ill. by Ernest Shepard, Dutton, 1974.                   4–9

*The World of Pooh*, ill. by E. H. Shepard, Dutton, 1957. Distinctive color illustrations lend a festive air to this large-print volume containing *Winnie-the-Pooh* and *The House at Pooh Corner*.                   5–10

MINARIK, ELSE H., *Father Bear Comes Home*, ill. by Maurice Sendak, Harper, 1959.

*A Kiss for Little Bear*, ill. by Maurice Sendak, Harper, 1968.

*Little Bear*, ill. by Maurice Sendak, Harper, 1957.

*Little Bear's Friend*, ill. by Maurice Sendak, Harper, 1960.

*Little Bear's Visit*, ill. by Maurice Sendak, Harper, 1961. These are books for children in primary grades to read for themselves, but the stories are also worth reading aloud to the preschool child.                   4–8

MOON, SHEILA, *Knee-Deep in Thunder*, ill. by Peter Parnall, Atheneum, 1967. A most unusual fantasy in which the characters seem to have been brought together by some mysterious force in order to travel and struggle toward an unseen goal. Gradually a purpose is revealed to them, and when it is fulfilled, after much toil, pain, and death, each is released to go his way.                   12–up

MULOCK, DINAH M., *The Little Lame Prince*, ill. by John Nielsen, World, 1948. A fascinating tale, first published in 1893, in which a lonely prince visits strange lands and sees marvelous sights while wrapped within a wonderful traveling cloak.                   9–11

NESBIT, E., *The Enchanted Castle*, ill. by Cecil Leslie, Dutton, 1964. The story of a beautiful house and garden and of the many strange adventures caused by the power of a wishing ring.                   10–12

*The Story of the Treasure Seekers: Being the Adventures of the Bastable Children in Search of a Fortune*, ill. by Gordon Browne, Dover, 1958. Although the young Bastables have little success in regaining the family fortune, their quest offers the reader much amusement.                   8–10

This author also wrote a number of stories which feature plucky, resourceful children who find themselves in strange situations brought on by the forces of magic. The better-known titles are:

*Five Children and It*, Random, 1959; Dover, 1965.   8–up
*Harding's Luck*, ill by H. R. Millar, Dover, 1961.   8–10
*House of Arden*, Dutton, 1968; Dover, 1958.   8–13
*The Magic City*, Dover, 1958.   7–9
*The Magic World*, Dover, 1959.   7–9
*Wet Magic*, Dover, 1958.   7–9
*The Wonderful Garden*, Dover, 1959.   7–9

NICHOLS, RUTH, *A Walk out of the World*, ill. by Trina Schart Hyman, Harcourt, 1969. An absorbing fantasy in which a brother and sister are carried into the world of their royal ancestors and help bring about the end of a usurper's reign.                   10–12

NORTH, JOAN, *The Light Maze*, Farrar, 1971. A witty depiction of village life in England is a foil for a trip outside time and space.                   11–14

NORTON, ANDRE (pseud. of Alice Mary Norton), *Catseye*, Harcourt, 1961. This teen-age science-fiction story, set in the future, tells of the adventures of Troy Horan, who is demoted and exiled from his native planet.
                  11–14

*Key out of Time*, World, 1963. A group of Terran explorers are sent ten thousand years backward in time to probe the past of a beautiful but now uninhabited planet. Like the author's other science-fiction stories, this is a well-written, fast-moving adventure fantasy. Some other acceptable titles for the younger teen-age reader are:

*Dread Companion*, Harcourt, 1970.
*Fur Magic*, ill. by John Kaufmann, World, 1968.
*Ordeal in Otherwhere*, World, 1964.
*Quest Crosstime*, Viking, 1965.
*The X Factor*, Harcourt, 1965.                   11–15

NORTON, MARY, *Bed-Knob and Broomstick*, ill. by Erik Blegvad, Harcourt, 1957. The three Wilson children have some exciting times after they discover a lonely spinster who is studying to become a witch and who gives them some magic powers.                   8–11

*The Borrowers*, ill. by Beth and Joe Krush, Harcourt, 1953.                   8–11

*The Borrowers Afield, The Borrowers Afloat,* and *The Borrowers Aloft*, ill. by Beth and Joe Krush, Harcourt, 1955, 1959, and 1961. Sequels to *The Borrowers*.   8–11

NOURSE, ALAN, *Rx for Tomorrow; Tales of Science Fiction, Fantasy, and Medicine*, McKay, 1971. A varied anthology with emphasis on medicine, written by a physician. 11–15

OAKLEY, GRAHAM, *The Church Mouse*, ill. by author, Atheneum, 1972. Bland style, lively plot and humor. 5–7

O'BRIEN, ROBERT C., *Mrs. Frisby and the Rats of NIMH*, ill. by Zena Bernstein, Atheneum, 1971. Ex-laboratory rats try to improve their image. Newbery Medal. 9–11
*Z for Zachariah*, Atheneum, 1975. A taut science fiction story of the last people left in the world. 11–up

ORMONDROYD, EDWARD, *Broderick*, ill. by John Larrecq, Parnassus, 1969. A dashing mouse rides to fame by reason of his exploits on a surfboard. 5–9
*Castaways on Long Ago*, ill. by Ruth Robbins, Parnassus, 1973. A mystery-fantasy concocted with suspense. 9–11
*Time at the Top*, ill. by Peggy Bach, Parnassus, 1963. 11–13

PARKER, EDGAR, *The Enchantress*, ill. by author, Pantheon, 1960. A princess-enchantress, in the form of an owl, tries in vain to deter a young knight from performing three dangerous tasks in order to win her hand. A happy change from the standard fairy tale. 8–11

PARKER, RICHARD, *A Time to Choose; A Story of Suspense*, Harper, 1974. A nicely knit story of movement between two periods of time, one the far future. 11–14

PARRISH, ANNE, *Floating Island*, ill. by author, Harper, 1930. An unusually imaginative tale about the adventures of Mr. and Mrs. Doll and their family while shipwrecked on a tropical island. 8–12

PEARCE, ANN PHILIPPA, *A Dog So Small*, ill. by Antony Maitland, Lippincott, 1963. The child who is the central figure of the story lives in a dream world of his own devising. It is a world he has created by meticulous research, intense concentration, and the exclusion of everyday reality. In the end he returns to reality, slowly and painfully, as he recovers from an accident. 10–11
*Mrs. Cockle's Cat*, ill. by Antony Maitland, Lippincott, 1962. Mrs. Cockle's cat, Peter, deserts her because fish are scarce and too expensive for her to buy. Grieving for her pet, she grows extremely thin. One day a strong wind lifts her, along with the balloons she is trying to sell, into the sky. When the wind drops, Mrs. Cockle is unexpectedly reunited with Peter. 7–9
*The Squirrel Wife*, ill. by Derek Collard, T. Crowell, 1972. An original story in pure fairytale tradition, in which good and justice triumph. 8–10
*Tom's Midnight Garden*, ill. by Susan Einzig, Lippincott, 1959. 10–12

PECK, RICHARD, *The Ghost Belonged to Me*, Viking, 1975. Turn-of-the-century flavor, a restless ghost, and a boy with powers of precognition are merged in a lively and amusing story. 10–13

PEET, BILL, *The Wump World*, ill. by author, Harcourt, 1970. Through this story about the despoliation of an imaginary planet, the author provides effective satire and comment on the pollution of the earth. 6–up

PESEK, LUDEK, *The Earth Is Near*, tr. by Anthea Bell, Bradbury, 1974. A striking story of a Mars expedition, stressing the problems of the astronauts. 11–up

PEYTON, K. M., *A Pattern of Roses*, T. Crowell, 1973. This combines deftly the theme of adolescent independence and identification with a long-dead boy. 11–14

PICARD, BARBARA LEONIE, *The Faun and the Woodcutter's Daughter*, ill. by Charles Stewart, Criterion, 1965.
*The Goldfinch Garden*, ill. by Anne Linton, Criterion, 1965.

*The Lady of the Linden Tree*, ill. by Charles Stewart, Criterion, 1962.
Three books of delightful, original fairy tales with special appeal to slightly romantic little girls. 9–12
*The Mermaid and the Simpleton*, ill. by Philip Gough, Criterion, 1970. Beautifully written and carefully plotted, these fifteen original fairy tales are excellent for reading aloud. 10–13

POOLE, JOSEPHINE, *Moon Eyes*, ill. by Trina Schart Hyman, Little, 1967. An eerie, suspenseful tale of witchcraft in a modern English setting. The victims are a fifteen-year-old girl and her five-year-old mute brother. 10–12

POTTER, BEATRIX, *The Tale of Peter Rabbit*, ill. by author, Warne, 1903. A favorite nursery classic followed by many more books about the little animals which the author-artist observed so lovingly and reproduced in meticulous watercolors. 4–8
*The Fairy Caravan*, new ed., ill. by author, Warne, 1952. This amusing collection of stories tells about the adventures of an extremely long-haired guinea pig who joins a traveling circus. The delightful illustrations are in Potter's usual style, though only a few are in color. 8–10

PREUSSLER, OTFRIED, *The Little Witch*, tr. by Anthea Bell, ill. by Winnie Gayler, Abelard, 1961. Too young to join in the annual Walpurgis Night dance, the little witch sneaks in. As punishment she is sentenced to be a good witch all year. At the end of the time she finds herself a pariah because the only good witch is a bad witch. 7–10
*The Satanic Mill*, tr. by Anthea Bell, Macmillan, 1973. An evil magician traps all his apprentices until one escapes through the power of love. 11–14

PROKOFIEFF, SERGE, *Peter and the Wolf*, ill. by Warren Chappell, Knopf, 1940. This is a delightful version of the well-known story. 7–12

PROYSEN, ALF, *Little Old Mrs. Pepperpot*, tr. by Marianne Helwig, ill. by Björn Berg, Obolensky, 1959. 8–10
*Mrs. Pepperpot to the Rescue*, ill. by Björn Berg, Pantheon, 1964. An engaging story about the further adventures of an old woman who found herself shrunken to the size of a pepperpot at unexpected moments. 7–11

PYLE, HOWARD, *Pepper and Salt, or Seasoning for Young Folks*, ill. by author, Harper, 1885, 1923. This charming book of eight fairy tales, wittily retold and well-illustrated, is apt to be overlooked in the flood of new material that appears each year. However, it deserves continued use by teachers and storytellers. 9–11
*The Wonder Clock*, ill. by author, Harper, 1887, 1943. This volume of twenty-four delightful tales, "one for each hour of the day," is a companion volume to the one above. 9–11

RASKIN, ELLEN, *Figgs & Phantoms*, ill. by author, Dutton, 1974. Hilarious nonsense about a family of odd personalities moves into fantasy—or is it a dream? 9–11

REY, H. A., *Curious George Gets a Medal*, ill. by author, Houghton, 1957. Curious George, the little monkey hero of many popular tales, rockets into space and wins a medal for his courage. Other popular titles are *Curious George Rides a Bike*, Houghton, 1952, and by Margaret Rey, *Curious George Flies a Kite*, Houghton, 1958. 5–8

RODGERS, MARY, *Freaky Friday*, Harper, 1972. What would a girl do if she woke one morning and found she'd turned into her mother? Annabel tells us what. 9–11

*A Billion for Boris,* Harper, 1974. Annabel and her friend Boris find a television set that gives the news of the next day. Including stockmarket prices! 9–11

ROSS, EULALIE STEINMETZ, ed., *The Lost Half-Hour: A Collection of Stories,* ill. by Enrico Arno, Harcourt, 1963. This excellent collection, compiled by a noted storyteller, contains both traditional and modern fanciful stories, especially selected for their appeal when told aloud. 9–11

RUSKIN, JOHN, *The King of the Golden River, or the Black Brothers,* ill. by Fritz Kredel, World, 1946. A well-written, genuinely dramatic story in the old fairy-tale style. Other editions are available from various publishers. 10–14

SANCHEZ-SILVA, JOSÉ MARIA, *The Boy and the Whale,* tr. by Michael Heron, ill. by Margery Gill, McGraw, 1964. Santiago, small boy of Madrid, loved his imaginary whale very much and they had many wonderful adventures together before he swam away forever. 7–10

SANDBURG, CARL, *Rootabaga Stories,* ill. by Maud and Miska Petersham, Harcourt, 1936. 9–12
*The Wedding Procession of the Rag Doll and the Broom Handle and Who Was in It,* ill. by Harriet Pincus, Harcourt, 1967. One of Sandburg's delightful *Rootabaga Stories* has been transformed into an eye-filling picture book which captures the unique humor and invention of the author. 4–8

SAUER, JULIA L., *Fog Magic,* Viking, 1943. A sensitive and beautifully written story of a little girl who goes back in time to a people and a village which no longer exist. The day comes when she knows that her "fog magic" must end. 10–12

SAWYER, RUTH, *The Enchanted Schoolhouse,* ill. by Hugh Troy, Viking, 1956. A tale of the wonderful enchantment which an Irish leprechaun and a timid young immigrant worked on the town taxpayers. 9–11
*This Way to Christmas,* rev. ed., ill. by Maginel Wright Barney, Harper, 1967. When a stranded boy takes a fairy's suggestion that he visit each of his neighbors, he receives a wonderful Christmas gift from each of them. A fine Christmas story. 9–11
*The Year of the Christmas Dragon,* ill. by Hugh Troy, Viking, 1960. A charming original story concerning the origin of Mexican Christmas customs. The tale begins in China, where a small boy becomes friendly with a great dragon. Together they fly to Mexico, and there the dragon hibernates for hundreds of years. 8–11

SCHLEIN, MIRIAM, *The Raggle Taggle Fellow,* ill. by Harvey Weiss, Hale, 1959. Written in folk-tale style, this engaging story of Dick, a wandering musician, holds wisdom and entertainment for the story hour. 7–10
*The Big Cheese,* ill. by Joseph Low, W. R. Scott, 1958. A story about a farmer who made an excellent cheese and decided to take it as a gift to the king. Each of the many characters he met along the way persuaded him to part with a sliver, and in the end there was nothing left for the king. 5–8

SELDEN, GEORGE (pseud. of George Selden Thompson), *The Cricket in Times Square,* ill. by Garth Williams, Farrar, 1960. This engaging modern-day fantasy features Chester, a cricket with perfect pitch. Once this fact is discovered, he is launched on a concert career. 8–10
*Harry Cat's Pet Puppy,* ill. by Garth Williams, Farrar, 1974. Everybody but Chester Cricket is back in New York and preoccupied with a stray puppy. 8–11

*Tucker's Countryside,* ill. by Garth Williams, Farrar, 1969. Some of the engaging city-bred animals first met in *Cricket in Times Square* appear in this adventure set in rural Connecticut. 8–11

SENDAK, MAURICE, *Higglety Pigglety Pop: Or, There Must Be More to Life,* ill. by author, Harper, 1967. An extremely amusing tale of a Sealyham terrier, Jennie, who leaves home to go in search of EXPERIENCE. A playful use of language. 6–up
*In the Night Kitchen,* ill. by author, Harper, 1970. Mickey falls out of his bed and into the night kitchen, amid the singing bakers and their work. An unusual and highly fantastic story which provides a rich evocation of the sensory enjoyment to be found in the textures, tastes, and smells of food. 4–8
*Where the Wild Things Are,* ill. by author, Harper, 1963. This perceptively written and illustrated book portrays the fearsome monsters of a child's imagination. Caldecott Medal. 3–7

SEREDY, KATE, *The White Stag,* ill. by author, Viking, 1937. This hero tale of the founding of Hungary was awarded the Newbery Medal. Illustrated with interpretive drawings of great beauty. 9–12

SEUSS, DR. *See* Theodor Seuss Geisel.

SHARMAT, MARJORIE WEINMAN, *Walter the Wolf,* ill. by Kelly Oechsli, Holiday, 1975. Blithe style, vigorous pictures, and sly humor enliven the story of a *very* good wolf. 5–7

SHARP, MARGERY, *The Rescuers,* ill. by Garth Williams, Little, 1959. A clever fantasy concerning the adventures of three mice who attempt to rescue a Norwegian poet from the dungeon of a Black Castle. Adults catch the satire, while children enjoy the story. The charming drawings of the mice capture the essence of their courage and daring. Followed by: *Miss Bianca* (1962), *The Turret* (1963), *Miss Bianca in the Salt Mines* (1966). 9–up

SHURA, MARY FRANCES, *The Nearsighted Knight,* ill. by Adrienne Adams, Knopf, 1964. This easy-to-read fantasy features some improbable characters: a rotund witch, a congenial dragon, a homely princess, and the nearsighted knight. The plot is rather weak but beginning readers may enjoy it. 6–9
*Shoe Full of Shamrock,* ill. by N. M. Bodecker, Atheneum, 1965. Davie O'Sullivan, playing alone in Central Park, met a little man who insisted that Davie had found his leather pouch. Since Davie had heard of leprechauns from his father, he wisely gave up the pouch and was rewarded with a bit of advice that made his secret wish come true. 9–11
*Simple Spigott,* ill. by Jacqueline Tomes, Knopf, 1960. A friendly Scottish spook proves a wonderful guide and companion to three American children who visit Scotland. A first-person narrative that happily blends fantasy and realism. 7–10

SILVERBERG, ROBERT, *The Calibrated Alligator: and other Science Fiction Stories,* Holt, 1969. Nine imaginative tales in a varied collection. 11–15
*Time of the Great Freeze,* Holt, 1964. A story set in the ice age of the future, circa A.D. 2300. A seventeen-year-old boy accompanies his father, a scientist, and several other men on an expedition. They travel by solar-powered sled and hope to establish contact with other isolated communities of the world. 11–14

SINGER, ISAAC BASHEVIS, *The Fearsome Inn,* tr. by author and Elizabeth Shub, ill. by Nonny Hogrogian, Scrib-

magic and fast thinking. Beautifully executed illustrations. 7–11

SKURZYNSKI, GLORIA, *The Poltergeist of Jason Morey*, Dodd, 1975. Two girls find that the quiet young cousin who's come to live with them brings a destructive poltergeist along. 10–13

SLEIGH, BARBARA, *Carbonel, the King of the Cats*, ill. by V. H. Drummond, Bobbs, 1957. Humorous magical tale of two children who rescue the king of cats from the spell of an old witch. Followed by *The Kingdom of Carbonel*, ill. by D. M. Leonard, Bobbs, 1960. 9–12

SLOBODKIN, LOUIS, *The Space Ship Under the Apple Tree*, ill. by author, Macmillan, 1952, 1967. Things begin to happen when a strange little man is found in Grandmother's apple orchard. A good combination of activity, country fun, and pseudoscience. Followed by *Space Ship Returns to the Apple Tree* (1958) and *The Three-Seated Space Ship* (1964). 8–10

SLOBODKINA, ESPHYR, *Caps for Sale*, ill. by author, W. R. Scott, 1947. This merry little story, with its engaging monkeys, is always popular with younger children. 5–7

SMITH, DODIE, *The Hundred and One Dalmations*, ill. by Janet and Anne Grahame-Johnstone, Viking, 1957. When fifteen Dalmatian puppies are stolen to be made into a fur coat, all the dogs in England aid in recovering them. 8–10

SMITH, EMMA, *Emily's Voyage*, ill. by Irene Haas, Harcourt, 1966. An appealing short fantasy about a proper, respectable guinea pig who is periodically given to wanderlust. This tale is concerned with her adventures on a voyage which ended with shipwreck on a tropical island. 8–10

SNYDER, ZILPHA K., *Below the Root*, ill. by Alton Raible, Atheneum, 1975. A science fantasy set in a community of tree-dwellers has depths of meaning below the surface events. 10–12

*Black and Blue Magic*, ill. by Gene Holtan, Atheneum, 1966. Modern-day San Francisco is the setting for this story. Lonely, awkward Harry Houdini Marco meets a fascinating stranger who gives him a magic lotion that enables him to grow wings. His nocturnal wanderings are most amusing. 8–11

*Season of Ponies*, ill. by Alton Raible, Atheneum, 1964. Despite some weaknesses, this blend of gentle fantasy and realism has much to recommend it. A lonely girl, living with two aunts, meets a mysterious boy and helps him to care for his ponies. In the course of her adventures she learns a song of strength and goodness which helps her endure the reality of everyday life. 10–12

STEELE, MARY Q., *Journey Outside*, ill. by Rocco Negri, Viking, 1969. Dilar, a young boy who has always lived on a raft floating endlessly on a subterranean river, undergoes many trials and adventures when he leaves his people to search for a better place. 9–12

STEELE, WILLIAM O., *Andy Jackson's Water Well*, ill. by Michael Ramus, Harcourt, 1959. When a terrible drought hit frontier Nashville, Andrew Jackson, attorney-at-law, and his friend, Chief Ticklepitcher, went east to get water. Their hilarious and exaggerated experiences are told with dry humor. 9–14

*The No-Name Man of the Mountain*, ill. by Jack Davis, Harcourt, 1964. This hilarious tall tale may bring tears of laughter when read aloud. 9–up

STEIG, WILLIAM, *Dominic*, ill. by author, Farrar, 1972. Dominic is a dog with heart of gold and nerves of steel who swashes and buckles through a beguiling tale of derring-do. 9–11

*Sylvester and the Magic Pebble*, ill. by author, Simon, 1969. An amusing tale of a donkey who, while trying to escape from a hungry lion, uses a magic pebble to turn himself into a rock. Caldecott Medal. 5–7

STOCKTON, FRANK R., *The Bee-Man of Orn*, ill. by Maurice Sendak, Holt, 1964. Stockton's amusing story of the man who set out to discover his original form is given new life with Sendak's illustrations. 10–up

*Casting Away of Mrs. Lecks and Mrs. Aleshine*, ill. by George Richards, Meredith, 1933. The absurd adventures of two prosaic matrons on a desert isle, where they kept house with the same meticulous precision which had characterized their life in a New England village. 11–up

*The Griffin and the Minor Canon*, ill. by Maurice Sendak, Holt, 1963. A humorous tale about the friendship which develops between a young minor canon and a griffin who takes up residence in a cathedral town in order to observe his likeness over the church door. 8–10

*The Storyteller's Pack*, ill. by Bernarda Bryson, Scribner's, 1968. A collection of twenty short stories, representative of the author's best work. Includes ghost stories, comic fantasy, and fairy tales. 12–up

STOLZ, MARY, *Belling the Tiger*, ill. by Beni Montresor, Harper, 1961.

*The Great Rebellion*, ill. by Beni Montresor, Harper, 1961.

*Siri the Conquistador*, ill. by Beni Montresor, Harper, 1963.

*Maximilian's World*, ill. by Uri Shulevitz, Harper, 1966. These gently satirical little fantasies will amuse children on one level and adults on another. 7–10

*Frédou*, ill. by Tomi Ungerer, Harper, 1962. The story of a Parisian cat who manages a hotel and does it supremely well. 6–9

THACKERAY, W. M., and CHARLES DICKENS, *The Rose and the Ring; The Magic Fishbone*, ill. by W. M. Thackeray, John Gilbert, and Paul Hogarth, Dutton, 1959. In the Thackeray story, the fairy's gift of a "little misfortune" gives rise to one hilarious error after another in the Court of Paflagonia. "The Magic Fishbone" is also available in other editions. (See Charles Dickens.) 9–12

THAYER, JANE, *The Popcorn Dragon*, ill. by Jay Hyde Barnum, Morrow, 1953. When Dexter, a little dragon, made himself unpopular with the other animals by blowing smoke, he took refuge in a cornfield, where he soon discovered a way to restore his popularity. 5–8

THURBER, JAMES, *The Great Quillow*, ill. by Doris Lee, Harcourt, 1944. In this delightful story with an old, old theme, Quillow, the shortest man in town, triumphs over the giant, Hunder. 8–11

*Many Moons*, ill. by Louis Slobodkin, Harcourt, 1943. Told in fairy-tale style, this is the appealing story of a little princess who yearned for the moon but learned to be satisfied with less. Caldecott Medal. 7–10

*The White Deer*, ill. by author and Don Freeman, Harcourt, 1945. An amusing satire on red tape and official regulations. 10–up

TITUS, EVE, *Anatole and the Cat*, ill. by Paul Galdone, McGraw, 1957. An alert French mouse outwits the cat who interferes with his duties as Cheese Taster in M'sieu Duval's cheese factory. Other adventures of this dauntless mouse are related in: *Anatole* (1956), *Anatole and the Robot* (1960), *Anatole over Paris* (1961), *Anatole and the Poodle* (1965), *Anatole and the Piano* (1966).                                                       5–7

*Basil and the Pygmy Cats,* ill. by Paul Galdone, McGraw, 1971. The great mouse detective, Basil of Baker Street, hero of other breathless and nonsensical tales of brilliant snooping, goes to the Far East.     8–10

TODD, RUTHVEN, *Space Cat*, ill. by Paul Galdone, Scribner's, 1952. An amusingly illustrated story about Flyball, a daring kitten, and his adventures in space. Followed by: *Space Cat Visits Venus* (1955), *Space Cat Meets Mars* (1957), *Space Cat and the Kittens* (1958).     8–10

TOLKIEN, J. R. R., *Farmer Giles of Ham,* ill. by Pauline Diana Baynes, Houghton, 1962. The story of how Farmer Giles, the reluctant dragon hunter, subdues the dragon, gets a large share of his treasure, and manages peaceful coexistence with his erstwhile enemy.    10–up
*The Hobbit,* ill. by author, Houghton, 1938. An enthralling account of the great quest which took Bilbo Baggins from his comfortable Hobbit hole out into the great world of evil, danger, and magic.     10–up

TRAVERS, PAMELA L., *Mary Poppins*, ill. by Mary Shepard, Harcourt, 1934. The story of the many remarkable things that happened to Jane and Michael Banks while their wind-borne nurse, Mary Poppins, held sway in their nursery. These adventures are continued in the succeeding books: *Mary Poppins Comes Back* (1935), *Mary Poppins Opens the Door* (1943), *Mary Poppins in the Park* (1952).     8–12

TRESSELT, ALVIN R., *The World in the Candy Egg*, ill. by Roger Duvoisin, Lothrop, 1967. The magic world inside a spun-sugar Easter egg is witnessed first by the animals in a toy shop window, and finally by the small girl who receives the egg as a gift.     4–8

UNGERER, TOMI, *Crictor*, ill. by author, Harper, 1958. An original and very nonsensical tale about the boa constrictor who became a pet of Madame Bodot, schoolteacher in a little French town.     5–8
*Emile,* ill. by author, Harper, 1960. The originator of Crictor and the Mellops now introduces another uncommon picture-book character—an engaging octopus.     5–8
*Moon Man,* ill. by author, Harper, 1967. This oversize picture book, with special appeal for small boys, depicts the adventures of Moon Man on a visit to earth.     4–8

UTTLEY, ALISON, *A Traveler in Time*, ill. by Christine Price, Viking, 1964. A story set in a marvelous old manor house which Penelope, a girl of sixteen, comes to visit. Gradually she becomes aware that she is living in two worlds—the modern world and that of three hundred years earlier.     11–up

WABER, BERNARD, *"You Look Ridiculous," Said the Rhinoceros to the Hippopotamus*, ill. by author, Houghton, 1966. A hippopotamus grows more and more depressed as each of her animal friends tells her she looks ridiculous. They say this only because she does not possess the features which distinguish each of them.     5–7
Waber has created another remarkable and fantastic animal character, Lyle, the Crocodile. His adventures are related in: *The House on East 88th Street; Lyle, Lyle, the Crocodile; Lyle and the Birthday Party;* and *Lyle Finds His Mother,* ill. by author, Houghton, 1962, 1965, 1966, and 1974.     4–7

WALDEN, DANIEL, *The Nutcracker*, ill. by Harold Berson, Lippincott, 1959. This retelling of the familiar Nutcracker ballet is marked by grace and delicacy in both text and pictures.     8–12

WATSON, SALLY, *Magic at Wychwood*, ill. by Frank Bozo, Knopf, 1970. The Princess Elaine's search for magic shakes her royal family's composure. A story which has appeal for girls of all ages.     8–up

WERSBA, BARBARA, *The Brave Balloon of Benjamin Buckley*, ill. by Margot Tomes, Atheneum, 1963. Benjamin and his cat are stowaways on a balloon when it breaks loose and becomes airborne.     7–9

WHITE, ANNE H., *Junket*, ill. by Robert McCloskey, Viking, 1955. The story of a strong-minded airedale who succeeded in teaching the new city folks, who had purchased his master's farm, just how a farm should be run. Despite the new owner's verdict that there be no animals, Junket manages to have all the animals which had belonged to the farm returned one by one.     8–11
*The Story of Serapina,* ill. by Tony Palazzo, Viking, 1951. Serapina, the cat who could carry milk bottles with her tail, both disciplined and entertained the children. This is a modern tall tale of great originality. It is also very funny.     8–12

WHITE, E. B., *Charlotte's Web,* ill. by Garth Williams, Harper, 1952.     8–10
*Stuart Little,* ill. by Garth Williams, Harper, 1945. It is unusual for a mouse to be born to an apartment-dwelling Park Avenue family, but they make the best of it, and the mouse-son, Stuart, becomes a very interesting person.     9–11
*The Trumpet of the Swan,* ill. by Edward Frascino, Harper, 1970. Many complications ensue when Louis' father decides that he will steal a trumpet so that his son, who is mute, can lead a normal swan's life.     9–12

WIESNER, WILLIAM, *The Magic Slippers*, ill. by author, Norton, 1967. A story by Wilhelm Hauff provided the inspiration for this humorous picture book. It recounts the adventures of Hassan and his magic slippers in the service of the Caliph of Bagdad.     6–9

WILDE, OSCAR, *The Complete Fairy Tales of Oscar Wilde*, ill. by Charles Mozley, Watts, 1960. Nine original fairy stories by a noted nineteenth-century poet and author. They now seem somewhat dated but are nevertheless worth introducing to the better readers.     9–11

WILLIAMS, JAY, and RAYMOND ABRASHKIN, *Danny Dunn, Invisible Boy*, ill. by Paul Sagsoorian, McGraw, 1974. One of a series of Danny Dunn books, this is about an Invisibility Simulator via which Danny can sit in a laboratory yet be projected elsewhere.     9–11

WILLIAMS, URSULA MORAY, *Island MacKenzie*, ill. by Edward Ardizzone, Morrow, 1960. The two survivors from a shipwrecked pleasure cruiser find themselves on the same island. MacKenzie, the captain's cat, loves humans; Miss Pettifer, the other survivor, loathes cats. A fine mixture of humor, fantasy, and suspense in which MacKenzie remains true to his cat nature.     9–11
*The Moonball,* ill. by Jane Paton, Meredith, 1967. A group of resourceful English children appoint themselves protectors of the moonball—a weird, silky-haired, grapefruit-size, living object—which a professor wishes to subject to scientific investigation.     7–9

WINTERFELD, HENRY, *Castaways in Lilliput*, tr. by Kyrill Schabert, ill. by William Hutchinson, Harcourt, 1960. After being adrift on a rubber raft, three Australian children are cast ashore on fully modernized Lilliput. A good introduction to the Swift story.     9–13
*Star Girl,* tr. by Kyrill Schabert, ill. by Fritz Wegner,

Harcourt, 1957. Three children, gathering mushrooms in the woods, accept the explanation of a strange child that she is from the planet Asra (Venus). When they take her home with them, the adults refuse to believe her story and many complications ensue. 8–11

WRIGHTSON, PATRICIA, *Down to Earth*, ill. by Margaret Horder, Harcourt, 1965. 10–12

*The Nargun and the Stars*, Atheneum, 1974. An Australian boy discovers ancient creatures in the remote outback and learns that his elderly cousins have seen them too. 10–12

YAMAGUCHI, TOHR, *Two Crabs and the Moonlight*, ill. by Marianne Yamaguchi, Holt, 1965. A tale of unselfish and fearless loyalty in the face of near hopelessness. 6–10

YOLEN, JANE, *Greyling; A Picture Story from the Islands of Shetland*, ill. by William Stobbs, World, 1968. Based on the Scottish legend of the seal-boy. 8–10

ZEMACH, HARVE, *The Tricks of Master Dabble*, ill. by Margot Zemach, Holt, 1965. The clever Master Dabble takes in everyone with his tricks except the servant boy, Andrew, who unmasks him as an imposter. 5–8

ZINDEL, PAUL, *Let Me Hear You Whisper*, ill. by Stephen Gammel, Harper, 1974. An elderly cleaning woman can, by her kindness, get a laboratory dolphin to talk while the scientists fail. 12–up

ZION, GENE, *The Meanest Squirrel I Ever Met*, ill. by Margaret Bloy Graham, Scribner's, 1962. One must indeed be an M. O. (mean old) squirrel to trick a youngster out of his Thanksgiving dinner. However, the trickster repents in the end and becomes a friend of the defrauded young squirrel. 5–8

ZOLOTOW, CHARLOTTE, *Mr. Rabbit and the Lovely Present*, ill. by Maurice Sendak, Harper, 1962. A small girl gravely consults a distinguished rabbit regarding a present for her mother. The beautiful illustrations are in perfect harmony with the gentle story. 5–7

### *Adult References: Modern Fantasy* [7]

CAMERON, ELEANOR, *The Green and Burning Tree*, Little, 1969, Part 1, "Fantasy."

CARROLL, LEWIS, *Alice's Adventures Under Ground*, Dover, 1965 (paperback), McGraw, 1966 (clothbound). Facsimile of the author's manuscript book with additional material from the facsimile edition of 1886 and with a new introduction by Martin Gardner. This also contains a facsimile of Carroll's "Easter Greeting" and "Christmas Greetings," as published in the 1886 edition. Another facsimile of the manuscript was published by University Microfilms in 1964.

*The Annotated Alice: Alice's Adventures in Wonderland* and *Through the Looking Glass*, ill. by John Tenniel. With an introduction and notes by Martin Gardner, Potter, 1960. Gardner's notes in the margins of the pages clarify many allusions that are likely to mystify the modern reader.

*Claremont Reading Conference: Thirtieth Yearbook*, ed. by Malcolm P. Douglass, Claremont Graduate School Curriculum Laboratory, 1966. A compilation of the

[7] In addition to the books listed here, many of the entries in "General References" (p. 986) include discussions specifically concerned with modern fantasy. See especially the Arbuthnot and Sutherland, Chukovsky, Duff, Fisher, Frye, Hazard, Morton, and Smith titles.

addresses and discussions of the conference which had as its theme, "Beyond Literacy." The articles by Frank G. Jennings, Augusta Baker, and Mark Taylor deal with the profound need of children for literature which takes them beyond the confines of the here and now and gives wings to their imagination.

*Essays Presented to Charles Williams*, Eerdmans (paperback). A group of distinguished British authors who were friends of Charles Williams contributed to this memorial volume. Among the essays, those by C. S. Lewis and J. R. R. Tolkien are valuable for the reader who seeks understanding of the importance of the fairy tale.

HIGGINS, JAMES, *Beyond Words: Mystical Fancy in Children's Literature*, Teachers College Pr., 1970.

TOLKIEN, J. R. R., *Tree and Leaf*, Houghton, 1965. The first part of this slender volume provides a definition of fairy stories and discusses their origin and use. The remainder of the book is devoted to a short story, "Leaf by Niggle," which demonstrates the author's ability to imbue fantasy with the very texture of reality.

TOWNSEND, JOHN ROWE, *Written for Children*, Lothrop, 1967, Chapter 13, "Fantasy Between the Wars."

# REALISTIC STORIES

## *Animal Stories*

ANDERSON, C. W., *Billy and Blaze*, ill. by author, Macmillan, 1936. 4–8

*Blaze and the Forest Fire*, ill. by author, Macmillan, 1938. 4–8

*High Courage*, ill. by author, Macmillan, 1941. 10–14

*Salute*, ill. by author, Macmillan, 1940. 7–12

These are excellent horse stories for children, and the drawings that illustrate them are superb.

AVERILL, ESTHER, *Fire Cat*, ill. by author, Harper, 1960. An easy-to-read story about an adventurous cat who wasn't content to be a mere house pet. 6–8

BAUDOUY, MICHEL-AIMÉ, *Old One-Toe*, tr. by Marie Ponshot, ill. by Johannes Troyer, Harcourt, 1959. A French version of the hunted and the hunters with both fox and human characters warmly portrayed. 10–12

BIALK, ELISA, *Taffy's Foal*, ill. by William Moyers, Houghton, 1949. A little girl meets two major problems in one year—her father's second marriage and the death of her adored horse. 9–12

BORG, INGA, *Parrak, the White Reindeer*, ill. by author, Warne, 1959. A reindeer calf grows up to become herd leader. Brilliantly colored pictures of Lapland. 5–9

BROWN, MARCIA, *How Hippo!* ill. by author, Scribner's, 1969. Baby Hippo learns to roar most convincingly in this humorous little tale illustrated with striking woodcuts. 4–7

BUFF, MARY and CONRAD, *Dash and Dart, A Story of Two Fawns*, ill. by authors, Viking, 1942. The first year in the life of twin fawns is beautifully told and illustrated. The cadenced prose reads aloud well and the pictures in sepia and full color are exquisite. 5–8

*Hurry, Skurry, and Flurry*, ill. by Conrad Buff, Viking, 1954. Another beautifully illustrated book, this one about frolicking squirrels. 5–8

BULLA, CLYDE R., *Star of Wild Horse Canyon*, ill. by Grace Paull, T. Crowell, 1953. An easy-to-read western story. 7–9

BURNFORD, SHEILA, *The Incredible Journey,* ill. by Carl Burger, Little, 1961. 10–14

BYARS, BETSY, *The Midnight Fox,* ill. by Ann Grifalconi, Viking, 1968. 9–11

CALHOUN, MARY, *Houn' Dog,* ill. by Roger Duvoisin, Morrow, 1959. A warm and humorous tale that will be enjoyed by many young readers. 7–9

CHIPPERFIELD, JOSEPH E., *Wolf of Badenoch,* ill. by C. Gifford Ambler, McKay, 1959. Magnificent descriptions of nature highlight this perceptive story of sheepherding in Scotland. 12–15

CLARK, DENIS, *Black Lightning,* ill. by C. Gifford Ambler, Viking, 1954. Black Lightning, a black leopard, regains his jungle freedom after harsh captivity in a circus. 12–16

DE JONG, MEINDERT, *Along Came a Dog,* ill. by Maurice Sendak, Harper, 1958. 10–13

*The Easter Cat,* ill. by Lillian Hoban, Harper, 1971. Millicent is torn between love for the stray kitten she finds on Easter morning and concern for her mother's allergic reaction. 8–10

*The Little Cow and the Turtle,* ill. by Maurice Sendak, Harper, 1955. Humorous, read-aloud story about a frisky cow and her adventures. 8–12

*Smoke above the Lane,* Harper, 1951. Here is told an amusing and touching story of a strange friendship. 6–10

DELAFIELD, CLELIA, *Mrs. Mallard's Ducklings,* ill. by Leonard Weisgard, Lothrop, 1946. A beautiful picture book with interesting text of the seasonal cycle of ducks from egg to winter flight. 6–8

DILLON, EILÍS, *A Family of Foxes,* ill. by Vic Donahue, Funk, 1965. When four boys find two black foxes washed ashore on the Irish isle of Inishowan they know they must hide them from the adults who hate foxes. 10–12

DOTY, JEAN SLAUGHTER, *Winter Pony,* ill. by Ted Lewin, Macmillan, 1975. Two girls have the exciting experience of training a pony to pull an old-fashioned sleigh. 8–10

FLACK, MARJORIE, *Angus and the Ducks,* ill. by author, Doubleday, 1930.

*Story About Ping,* ill. by Kurt Wiese, Viking, 1933. Each story is unique, each has a well-defined plot, delightful style, and just enough suspense or surprise to keep children interested. 5–8

GAGE, WILSON, *Mike's Toads,* ill. by Glen Rounds, World, 1970. Mike's offer to take care of a neighbor's toads turns into a full-time project. 8–10

GEORGE, JOHN L., and JEAN GEORGE, *Masked Prowler: The Story of a Raccoon,* ill. by Jean George, Dutton, 1950. This is a story about Procyon, a young raccoon, and the dangers and joys he encounters in growing up. 11–15

*Meph, the Pet Skunk,* ill. by Jean George, Dutton, 1952. This is not only the story of a tame skunk but also the story of the reclamation of an eroded farm and its effect on an embittered farmer and his unhappy son. 11–16

*Vulpes the Red Fox,* ill. by Jean George, Dutton, 1948. The fascinating biography of a red fox and the skills he possesses to outwit the hunters. 10–14

GIPSON, FRED, *Old Yeller,* ill. by Carl Burger, Harper, 1956.

*Savage Sam,* ill. by Carl Burger, Harper, 1962. Two excellent stories of the importance of hound dogs in the lives of the frontier settlers. For mature readers. 12–16

GRIFFITHS, HELEN, *Just a Dog,* ill. by Victor Ambrus, Holiday, 1975. A unsentimental but touching story about a stray. 10–12

HALL, LYNN, *A Horse Called Dragon,* ill. by Joseph Cellini, Follett, 1971. Fictional framework for a sympathetic story of a real horse, a Mexican mustang. 10–12

HENRY, MARGUERITE, *Album of Horses,* ill. by Wesley Dennis, Rand, 1951. 8–14

*Brighty of the Grand Canyon,* ill. by Wesley Dennis, Rand, 1953. 9–12

*Justin Morgan Had a Horse,* ill. by Wesley Dennis, Rand, 1954. 9–12

*King of the Wind,* ill. by Wesley Dennis, Rand, 1948. Newbery Medal. 8–14

*Misty of Chincoteague,* ill. by Wesley Dennis, Rand, 1947. 8–12

*White Stallion of Lippiza,* ill. by Wesley Dennis, Rand, 1964. 8–12

Horse stories by this author are invariably dramatic and exciting but never sensational, and they are written with fidelity to the animal's nature. Most children, having read one, will read them all.

HOFF, SYD, *Julius,* ill. by author, Harper, 1959. The humorous account of a gorilla who makes friends with a small boy. A beginning-reading book. 6–7

JAMES, WILL, *Smoky, the Cowhorse,* ill. by author, Scribner's, 1926. One of the great animal stories for children, this poignant story is told in cowboy vernacular. Newbery Medal. 11–16

KJELGAARD, JIM, *Big Red,* ill. by Bob Kuhn, Holiday, 1956. 12–14

*Kalak of the Ice,* ill. by Bob Kuhn, Holiday, 1949. 10–14

These justly popular stories are well written, with plenty of action, and both human characters and animals are well drawn. Big Red is an Irish setter, the constant companion of Danny Pickett. Their adventures together climax in tracking down a huge outlaw bear. Kalak, known to the Eskimos as the "mist bear," is a heroic figure in her struggle to protect her cubs and survive.

KNIGHT, ERIC, *Lassie Come Home,* ill. by Marguerite Kirmse, Holt, 1940. A popular story of a collie's faithfulness to her master and her ability to track her way home over a great distance. 10–16

LATHROP, DOROTHY, *Who Goes There?* ill. by author, Macmillan, 1935. Exquisitely illustrated story about a winter picnic for birds and animals of the forest. 7–9

LIERS, EMIL, *A Beaver's Story,* ill. by Ray Sherin, Viking, 1958.

*A Black Bear's Story,* ill. by Ray Sherin, Viking, 1962.

*An Otter's Story,* ill. by Tony Palazzo, Viking, 1953. Three excellent animal biographies which depict the dangers facing each species from man as well as other animals. Exciting natural history. 9–12

LIPKIND, WILLIAM, and NICOLAS MORDVINOFF, *The Two Reds,* Harcourt, 1950. The two Reds, boy and cat, both city dwellers, were enemies because they both yearned for the same goldfish, but for different reasons. 4–8

LIPPINCOTT, JOSEPH WHARTON, *Gray Squirrel,* ill. by George F. Mason, Lippincott, 1954.

*The Wahoo Bobcat,* ill. by Paul Bransom, Lippincott, 1950. 12–15

Mr. Lippincott's tales of the wilderness life of hunted creatures are scientifically accurate, and in the process of reading them children develop understanding and sympathy for wild animals.

MC CLOSKEY, ROBERT, *Make Way for Ducklings*, ill. by author, Viking, 1941. Since this episode really happens in Boston each year, it is largely realistic with a few thoughts and words permitted the sagacious Mrs. Duck. Caldecott Medal. 4–8

MC CLUNG, ROBERT M., *Spike, the Story of a Whitetail Deer*, ill. by author, Morrow, 1952. A clear, factual story of the first year in the life of a whitetail deer. 5–10

*Stripe, the Story of a Chipmunk*, ill. by author, Morrow, 1951. These easy-to-read animal stories by a scientist and artist are well told, interesting to read to five-year-olds, and good reading for slow readers of nine and ten. 5–10

MEADER, STEPHEN W., *Red Horse Hill*, ill. by Lee Townsend, Harcourt, 1930. Bud Martin is happy when he wins a chance to work with horses in a New Hampshire village. In the process, he discovers a great racer. 11–16

MILES, MISKA, *Fox and the Fire*, ill. by John Schoenherr, Little, 1966. A suspenseful portrayal of the plight of a young fox fleeing a forest fire. 7–11

*Nobody's Cat*, ill. by John Schoenherr, Little, 1969. An unforgettable portrait of a rough, tough alley cat. 5–9

MONTGOMERY, RUTHERFORD, *Kildee House*, ill. by Barbara Cooney, Doubleday, 1949. A raccoon and some skunks enliven the home planned as a solitary refuge. 10–12

MOREY, WALT, *Kävik the Wolf Dog*, ill. by Peter Parnall, Dutton, 1968. A dog makes his way back from Seattle to the Alaskan home where he had first found love and kindness from a boy. 11–14

*Runaway Stallion*, Dutton, 1973. A runaway stallion and a lonely boy help each other adjust. 10–13

NAKATANI, CHIYOKO, *The Day Chiro Was Lost*, ill. by author, World, 1969. The busy city of Tokyo as seen from a dog's eye. 4–7

NEWBERRY, CLARE TURLAY, *April's Kittens*, ill. by author, Harper, 1940.

*Mittens*, ill. by author, Harper, 1936.

Clare Newberry's drawings of cats are so entrancing that the slight stories do not matter. 5–8

O'HARA, MARY, *Green Grass of Wyoming*, Lippincott, 1946. 12–adult

*My Friend Flicka*, Lippincott, 1941. 10–14

*Thunderhead*, Lippincott, 1943. 10–14

These books are a trilogy about the McLaughlin's horse ranch, where the problems are complicated by a bad wild-horse strain. Exciting reading.

PHIPSON, JOAN, *Birkin*, Harcourt, 1965. This is a story about a young calf, Birkin, who grows up into a monstrous steer. He and his owners lead an eventful life, and Birkin almost ends up as steak and roast beef. 10–12

PIATTI, CELESTINO, *The Happy Owls*, ill. by author, Atheneum, 1964. In a stunningly illustrated book, the owls try to explain to the quarreling barnyard animals the secret of being happy, but their wisdom is rejected. 6–8

RAWLINGS, MARJORIE KINNAN, *The Yearling*, ill. by N. C. Wyeth, Scribner's, 1939. This is a poignant story of growing up, when the boy Jody learns to accept the tragic necessity of disposing of his pet deer which has become a menace to the family's livelihood. 10–adult

ROBINSON, TOM, *Buttons*, ill. by Peggy Bacon, Viking, 1938. Wonderful picture-story of an alley cat who became a gentleman. 6–10

ROUNDS, GLEN, *The Blind Colt*, ill. by author, Holiday, 1960. A wild colt, blind from birth, is patiently trained

by a boy of ten. 9–11

*Stolen Pony*, ill. by author, Holiday, 1948. A moving story of a pony stolen by horse thieves and abandoned when it was found that he was blind. A faithful dog guides the pony home. 8–12

SCHOENHERR, JOHN, *The Barn*, ill. by author, Little, 1968. The life-and-death struggle between an owl and a skunk depicted in handsome drawings. 6–8

SEREDY, KATE, *Gypsy*, ill. by author, Viking, 1951. Children of any age and all cat-loving adults will enjoy Miss Seredy's magnificent pictures and simple account of a growing kitten. 4–up

STOLZ, MARY, *Emmett's Pig*, ill. by Garth Williams, Harcourt, 1959. A small boy is delighted with the gift of a real pig for a pet. 4–8

STONG, PHIL, *Honk: the Moose*, ill. by Kurt Wiese, Dodd, 1935. This is undoubtedly one of the most amusing animal tales we have. A hard winter drives a hungry moose into the cozy confines of a livery stable, and the problem is to get rid of him. 9–12

WALDECK, THEODORE J., *Jamba the Elephant*, ill. by Kurt Wiese, Viking, 1942.

*The White Panther*, ill. by Kurt Wiese, Viking, 1941. Authentic and exciting stories of wild animals. 10–14

WARD, LYND, *The Biggest Bear*, ill. by author, Houghton, 1952. The Orchard family said, "Better a bear in the orchard than an Orchard in a bear." But Johnny was bound to get a bear and he did. A prize tale with wonderful pictures. 4–8

## Life in the United States

BABBITT, NATALIE, *Goody Hall*, ill. by author. Farrar, 1971. A mystery-adventure story, both Gothic and humorous. 9–11

BENARY-ISBERT, MARGOT, *The Long Way Home*, tr. from the German by Richard and Clara Winston, Harcourt, 1959. Orphaned during World War II, thirteen-year-old Chris leaves his native village in eastern Germany to find a new home in the United States. 12–16

BINNS, ARCHIE, *Sea Pup*, Duell, 1954. Clint Barlow, an only child living with his parents in a remote region of Puget Sound, knows that he wants to be an oceanographer, and uses his wonderful outdoor life for observations which he carefully records. 9–11

BLUME, JUDY, *Are You There, God? It's Me, Margaret*, Bradbury, 1970. Eleven, Margaret is perturbed about religion (she has one Jewish parent) and about physical evidence of maturing. A warm, humorous story. 10–12

*Blubber*, Bradbury, 1974. Jill discovers what it's like to be a taunted outsider, and gains compassion. 9–11

*Tales of a Fourth Grade Nothing*, ill. by Roy Doty, Dutton, 1972. A very funny story about the troubles Peter has with an obstreperous two-year-old brother. 8–9

BONHAM, FRANK, *Durango Street*, Dutton, 1965. Rufus Henry has two choices: to become involved with a street gang and face being sent back to a home for delinquents or to get himself killed because he lacks gang protection. A realistic portrait of life in the Los Angeles slums. 12–15

BRADBURY, BIANCA, *Andy's Mountain Top*, ill. by Robert MacLean, Houghton, 1969. A story of a family, grandparents and two children, whose family solidarity is broken by eviction from their property. 10–13

BRINK, CAROL RYRIE, *Family Grandstand,* ill. by Jean M. Porter, Viking, 1952.
*Family Sabbatical,* ill. by Susan Foster, Viking, 1956.
These delightful stories tell of the activities of a professor's family in a Midwestern college town and during a year's trip to France.                                    9–12
BULLA, CLYDE, *A Ranch for Danny,* ill. by Grace Paull, T. Crowell, 1951.
*Surprise for a Cowboy,* ill. by Grace Paull, T. Crowell, 1950. Two stories of a city boy's adventures on his uncle's ranch where he learns how to be a cowboy.                    7–10
BURCH, ROBERT, *Queenie Peavy,* ill. by Jerry Lazare, Viking, 1966.                                               10–14
*Skinny,* ill. by Don Sibley, Viking, 1964. An eleven-year-old works in a hotel while waiting for admission to an orphanage.                                               9–11
*Tyler, Wilkin, and Skee,* ill. by Don Sibley, Viking, 1963. The three brothers in the title have grand times together; their relationships with each other and their parents are warmly portrayed, sometimes with humor, sometimes with poignancy.                            8–12
BYARS, BETSY, *Go and Hush the Baby,* ill. by Emily McCully, Viking, 1971. Will is asked to pacify a baby brother, and does so by telling an original fairy tale.                    2–5
*The House of Wings,* ill. by Daniel Schwartz, Viking, 1972. Sammy learns to love both his grandfather and the animals that have free rein in his home.          9–11
*The Summer of the Swans,* ill. by Ted CoConis, Viking, 1970. The climax of an unsatisfying summer for fourteen-year-old Sara is the disappearance of her retarded younger brother. A humorous and poignant story. Newbery Medal.                            12–15
CAMERON, ELEANOR, *A Room Made of Windows,* ill. by Trina Schart Hyman, Atlantic, 1971. A selfish adolescent girl gains in her understanding of the problems of others.                                               10–13
CAUDILL, REBECCA, *A Certain Small Shepherd,* ill. by William Pène DuBois, Holt, 1965. At six, Jamie still cannot speak. Then, on Christmas Eve, his father befriends a man and woman, and the mysterious power of love of one's fellow man goes to work and Jamie can talk. Moving without being overly sentimental.            5–8
*Did You Carry the Flag Today, Charley?* ill. by Nancy Grossman, Holt, 1966.                                    5–7
*A Pocketful of Cricket,* ill. by Evaline Ness, Holt, 1964. A tender story of a young boy who takes his pet cricket to school.                                            5–8
CHENERY, JANET, *Wolfie,* ill. by Marc Simont, Harper, 1969. An amusing story of two little boys and their efforts to protect the spider they are studying from their little sister.                                    5–8
CLARK, MARGERY, *The Poppy Seed Cakes,* ill. by Maud and Miska Petersham, Doubleday, 1924. A book of realistic, gay, and funny tales, told in a Russian atmosphere.                                               7–11
CLARKE, TOM E., *The Big Road,* Lothrop, 1965. A good book to give young people who scoff at their parents' tales of the Depression. It should help readers to see that America did not always have an "affluent society."                                               11–14
CLEARY, BEVERLY, *Ellen Tebbits,* ill. by Louis Darling, Morrow, 1951.                                          8–10
*Henry and Beezus,* ill. by Louis Darling, Morrow, 1952.
*Henry and Ribsy,* ill. by Louis Darling, Morrow, 1954.

*Henry Huggins,* ill. by Louis Darling, Morrow, 1950. Three of the many fine stories about one of the most believable young boys in all of fiction. Fun to read aloud to almost any age group, and nine- or ten-year-olds can read these books for themselves.          8–12
*Mitch and Amy,* ill. by George Porter, Morrow, 1967. Although they battle each other, the fourth-grade twins present a united front against a bully.              9–11
*Ramona the Brave,* ill. by Alan Tiegreen is a sequel to *Ramona the Pest,* ill. by Louis Darling (Morrow; 1975, 1968) and the hilarious stories of a kindergarten dropout who becomes a brave seven-year-old.      8–10
CLEAVER, VERA and BILL, *Ellen Grae,* ill. by Ellen Raskin, Lippincott, 1967.                                       9–11
*Grover,* ill. by Frederic Marvin, Lippincott, 1970. A penetrating look at Grover and his adjustment to life after his mother's suicide.                                9–12
*Where the Lilies Bloom,* ill. by Jim Spanfeller, Lippincott, 1969. The indomitable Mary Call Luther, fourteen, holds the family together when they are orphaned. A moving story set in Appalachia.                    11–14
CLEMENTS, BRUCE, *The Face of Abraham Candle,* Farrar, 1969. Abraham longs for his face to show age and wisdom and he gains a bit of the latter when he joins an expedition searching for Indian pottery.          11–13
CLYMER, ELEANOR, *My Brother Stevie,* Holt, 1967. Stevie is a problem to his older sister Annie. How Annie turns Stevie's energies from delinquent activities to constructive uses is a sensitively told, understated story.   9–12
CONFORD, ELLEN, *The Luck of Pokey Bloom,* ill. by Bernice Loewenstein, Little, 1975. Amusing incidents about an incorrigible contest-entrant; a good family story.   9–11
CORCORAN, BARBARA, *The Winds of Time,* ill. by Gail Owens, Atheneum, 1974. Running away from an uncle she dislikes, Gail stumbles into an odd household where she is given both freedom and concealment from authorities.                                          10–12
CORMIER, ROBERT, *The Chocolate War,* Pantheon, 1974. A strong indictment of power-hungry students and teachers in a boys' high school.                            12–up
CRAYDER, DOROTHY, *She, the Adventuress,* ill. by Velma Ilsley, Atheneum, 1973. Going alone from Iowa to Italy, Maggie proves resourceful during an exciting adventure.                                            9–11
CREDLE, ELLIS, *Down Down the Mountain,* ill. by author, Nelson, 1934. This story of two southern mountain children who yearn to own a pair of squeaky shoes has action and good humor.                            7–8
DE REGNIERS, BEATRICE, *A Little House of Your Own,* ill. by Irene Haas, Harcourt, 1955. Even a child needs privacy that is respected, and many an odd place becomes a house of his own.                            4–7
ECKERT, ALLAN, *Incident at Hawk's Hill,* ill. by John Schoenherr, Little, 1971. A child of six wanders off and is adopted by a badger. Touching, dramatic.      12–up
ENRIGHT, ELIZABETH, *The Four-Story Mistake,* ill. by author, Holt, 1942.
*The Saturdays,* ill. by author, Holt, 1941.
*Then There Were Five,* ill. by author, Holt, 1938.
One of the trilogy about the Melendy family, *The Saturdays* is set in New York City, where the children evolve a scheme for taking turns in spending their allowances; the other titles are set in the country.   8–12
*Thimble Summer,* ill. by author, Holt, 1938. A delightful story of the adventures of a little girl on a Wis-

consin farm. Newbery Medal. 8–12

ESTES, ELEANOR, *The Middle Moffat,* ill. by Louis Slobodkin, Harcourt, 1942.
*The Moffats,* ill. by Louis Slobodkin, Harcourt, 1941.
*Rufus M.,* ill. by Louis Slobodkin, Harcourt, 1943. The Moffat family is fatherless and bordering on real poverty, but the spirit is one of good humor and warm relationships. 9–12
*Ginger Pye,* ill. by author, Harcourt, 1951. The author's Newbery Medal book centers around the theft of a dog and the children's attempts to find the thief. 9–12
*The Hundred Dresses,* ill. by Louis Slobodkin, Harcourt, 1944. Children are not likely to forget Wanda, who was rejected by the group, nor the culprits who taunted her. 9–11

ETS, MARIE HALL, *Bad Boy, Good Boy,* ill. by author, T. Crowell, 1967. A sensitive, honest portrayal of a newly arrived Mexican family striving to adjust to life in a California town. 6–8
*Play with Me,* ill. by author, Viking, 1955. This is a charming picture-story of a little girl and all the little wild things she meets on a walk. 2–5

FALL, THOMAS, *Dandy's Mountain,* ill. by Juan Carlos Barberis, Dial, 1967. Between memorizing the dictionary and helping Bruce, her cousin who is trying hard to be a juvenile delinquent, rejoin the human race, Amanda "Dandy" Miller spends a memorable summer. A very funny but thoughtful book. 9–12

FENTON, EDWARD, *Duffy's Rocks,* Dutton, 1974. Tim Brennan goes from the dreary suburb of Duffy's Rocks to try finding his long-absent father. 11–13

FITZGERALD, JOHN, *The Great Brain Does It Again,* ill. by Mercer Mayer, Dial, 1975. Amusing episodes about an older brother who is a wheeler-dealer are told by a boy. 9–11

FITZHUGH, LOUISE, *Harriet the Spy,* ill. by author, Harper, 1964. 9–12

FLACK, MARJORIE, *Wait for William,* Houghton, 1935. This amusing circus story turns upon the most natural conflict in the world—a four-year-old's trouble with his shoelace and the older children's impatience with his slowness. 5–8

FOX, PAULA, *Portrait of Ivan,* ill. by Saul Lambert, Bradbury, 1969. When his photographer father decides to have his son's portrait painted, the lonely withdrawn boy begins to make new friends and become more sure of himself. 10–12
*The Stone-Faced Boy,* ill. by Donald McKay, Bradbury, 1968. A perceptive account of a timid middle child in a noisy, outgoing family. 8–12

GAGE, WILSON, *Dan and the Miranda,* ill. by Glenn Rounds, World, 1962. Humorous story of Dan's half-hearted attempts to do a project for the fifth-grade science fair. 8–11

GATES, DORIS, *Blue Willow,* ill. by Paul Lantz, Viking, 1940. The story of Janey Larkin, daughter of migrant workers, who longed for a real home. 9–12
*Sarah's Idea,* ill. by Marjorie Torrey, Viking, 1938. A girl's story of California ranch life and a coveted burro. 8–10

GEORGE, JEAN, *Gull Number 737,* ill. by author, T. Crowell, 1964. When birds cause a fatal plane crash, Dr. Rivers and his son Luke are called upon to help drive the birds from the runways. A natural science detective story with important human values. 12–14

*My Side of the Mountain,* ill. by author, Dutton, 1959. 11–14
*Who Really Killed Cock Robin?* Dutton, 1971. An ecology-minded small town learns that there are dire and complicated results to pollutants. 10–12

GREENE, CONSTANCE, *A Girl Called Al,* ill. by Byron Barton, Viking, 1969. A moving story of two girls growing in sensitivity and self-confidence as they cultivate a friendship with their apartment superintendent. 11–13
*The Unmaking of Rabbit,* Viking, 1972. Friendship brings courage to a shy boy who doesn't want to be called "Rabbit." 9–11

GUILFOILE, ELIZABETH, *Nobody Listens to Andrew,* ill. by Mary Stevens, Follett, 1957. A humorous sustained story for beginning readers. The title describes the grownups' reaction when Andrew tells them there is a bear in his bed. 6–7

HALL, LYNN, *Sticks and Stones,* Follett, 1972. A mature story about an adolescent who becomes the subject of malicious gossip due to an innocent friendship with another male. 12–15

HAYWOOD, CAROLYN, *"B" Is for Betsy,* ill. by author, Harcourt, 1939.
*Eddie's Valuable Property,* ill. by author, Morrow, 1975.
*Little Eddie,* ill. by author, Morrow, 1947.
*Penny and Peter,* ill. by author, Harcourt, 1946. Carolyn Haywood has written over two dozen books about the mild adventures of suburban children at home, at school, or in the community. Eddie has more humor in his life than the others. 5–9

HILDICK, EDMUND W., *Manhattan Is Missing,* ill. by Jan Palmer, Doubleday, 1969. English children vacationing in New York with their parents are involved in an exciting chase as they attempt to solve the mystery of a disappearing Siamese cat. 9–12

HODGES, MARGARET, *The Making of Joshua Cobb,* ill. by W. T. Mars, Farrar, 1971. An only child adjusts to preparatory school. 9–11

HUNT, IRENE, *Up a Road Slowly,* Follett, 1967. Julie Trelling, left motherless at age seven, is sent to live with her Aunt Cordelia and Uncle Haskell, who, between them, provide her with insight into the qualities necessary to became a mature, happy individual. Newbery Medal. 12–16

ISH-KISHOR, SULAMITH, *Our Eddie,* Pantheon, 1969. A penetrating study of the influence of a self-centered fanatical Jewish father on his son and other members of the family. 12–up

JACKSON, JACQUELINE, *The Taste of Spruce Gum,* ill. by Lillian Obligado, Little, 1966. A well-told story of eleven-year-old Libby and her adjustment to life in a lumber camp and her new father. 10–13

JOHNSON, ANNABEL and E. K., *The Grizzly,* ill. by Gilbert Riswold, Harper, 1964. A sympathetic story of eleven-year-old David, who is caught between an over-protective mother and an over-athletic father. 9–12

KERR, M. E., *Dinky Hocker Shoots Smack,* Harper, 1972. Dinky doesn't do it, but she paints that sentence on walls to make her parents realize that she has problems as well as the addicts they're helping. Perceptive writing. 12–15

KINGMAN, LEE, *The Peter Pan Bag,* Houghton, 1970. A girl of seventeen discovers more pathos than fun in urban communal living. 12–15
*The Year of the Raccoon,* Houghton, 1966. A percep-

tively written story of Joey, a boy struggling for identity and self-worth in the shadow of two gifted brothers and a dynamic father. 11–13

KONIGSBURG, E. L., *About the B'nai Bagels*, ill. by author, Atheneum, 1969. Mark thinks his troubles are unique: his mother is manager of his Little League team, his big brother is coach, and with all that he has to get ready for his Bar Mitzvah. 9–11
*Altogether, One at a Time*, ill. by Gail Haley et al., Atheneum, 1971. Four witty, perceptive short tales. 9–11
*From the Mixed-up Files of Mrs. Basil E. Frankweiler*, ill. by author, Atheneum, 1967. Newbery Medal. 10–12
*Jennifer, Hecate, Macbeth, William McKinley, and Me, Elizabeth*, ill. by author, Atheneum, 1967. The adventures of Elizabeth as apprentice witch under the tutelage of Jennifer, self-declared witch, are perceptively told and give us a memorable portrait of the friendship which develops between two ten-year-old girls. 8–10

KRASILOVSKY, PHYLLIS, *Benny's Flag*, ill. by W. T. Mars, World, 1960. The true story of how an Indian boy's entry in a flag contest came to be chosen as the official flag of Alaska. Striking illustrations of Alaska. 7–9

KRUMGOLD, JOSEPH, *Henry 3*, ill. by Alvin Smith, Atheneum, 1967. *. . . and now Miguel* is listed under Minority Groups in the United States since his Spanish-American heritage is central to the story.
*Onion John*, ill. by Symeon Shimin, T. Crowell, 1959. Andy Rusch, Jr., is a typical American boy growing up in a small town, devoted to his father who is his hero, but fascinated by Onion John, an eccentric town character. There is a father-son conflict which is more happily resolved than Onion John's problems when the town tries to civilize him. Amusing, and skillfully told. Newbery Medal. 10–14

LEE, MILDRED, *Fog*, Seabury, 1972. A compassionate picture of an unhappy first romance for Luke. 12–14

LENSKI, LOIS, *Cotton in My Sack*, ill. by author, Lippincott, 1949. A story of sharecropping in Arizona. 8–10
*Cowboy Small*, ill. by author, Walck, 1949. 3–7
*Strawberry Girl*, ill. by author, Lippincott, 1945. Set in rural Florida. Newbery Medal. 8–10
*The Little Airplane*, ill. by author, Walck, 1938.
*The Little Train*, ill. by author, Walck, 1940.
*Papa Small*, ill. by author, Walck, 1951.
It is hard to overestimate the appeal of Lenski's "little" books. Indeed, the Small Family has become a tradition for untold numbers of small children. 3–7

MC CLOSKEY, ROBERT, *Blueberries for Sal*, ill. by author, Viking, 1948. A picture story about Sal and her mother, who tangle with a bear and her cub. 3–7
*Homer Price*, ill. by author, Viking, 1943, 1963. 9–11
*Lentil*, ill. by author, Viking, 1940. Amusing story of a boy living in a small Midwestern town who saves the day with his harmonica. 6–9
*One Morning in Maine*, ill. by author, Viking, 1952. Another Sal story with glorious pictures of Maine woods and water. This time Sal has lost her first tooth, but after the inital shock, life goes on serenely. 3–7
*Time of Wonder*, ill. by author, Viking, 1957. In full color, McCloskey captures both the fun of a vacation in Maine and the power of a hurricane. Caldecott Medal. 6–9

MC GINLEY, PHYLLIS, *The Most Wonderful Doll in the World*, ill. by Helen Stone, Lippincott, 1950. A lost doll becomes more and more remarkable until the real doll is a shock when it is found. Gentle, humorous treatment of a common ailment. 7–9

MOSER, DON, *A Heart to the Hawks*, Atheneum, 1975. Fourteen and an ardent naturalist, Mike tries to save the woodland near his Cleveland home. The characterization is as strong as the message of conservation. 11–14

NEUFELD, JOHN, *Edgar Allan*, ill. by Loren Dunlap, Phillips, 1968. The reaction of townspeople, congregation, and family to the adoption of a black child by the minister and his wife is described by their elder son. 10–13

NEVILLE, EMILY, *Berries Goodman*, Harper, 1965. Sharply written story of the effects of anti-Semitism on the friendship of two suburban boys. 10–14
*It's Like This, Cat*, ill. by Emil Weiss, Harper, 1963. Dave Mitchell is an average fourteen-year-old trying to come to grips with himself and his family. This Newbery Medal book has depth and subtlety, humor and realism. 9–13

NORDSTROM, URSULA, *The Secret Language*, ill. by Mary Chalmers, Harper, 1960. 7–9

PECK, RICHARD, *Don't Look and It Won't Hurt*, Holt, 1972. A tender picture of a girl who assumes a protective role when her younger sister gets in trouble. 11–14
*Representing Super Doll*, Viking, 1974. A sensible girl chaperones a friend who wins a beauty contest. 11–13

PECK, ROBERT, *A Day No Pigs Would Die*, Knopf, 1972. A strong family story about a Shaker boy on a Vermont farm who must adjust to the death of a father. 12–up

PEVSNER, STELLA, *A Smart Kid Like You*, Seabury, 1975. Discerning treatment of a girl's adjustment to her father's remarriage. 10–12

PFEFFER, SUSAN BETH, *Marly the Kid*, Doubleday, 1975. A plump, plain adolescent finds more security with her father and stepmother than she had with her mother. Sensitive and witty. 11–14

REDFORD, POLLY, *The Christmas Bower*, ill. by Edward Gorey, Dutton, 1967. A department store family puts on a Christmas display of live birds. Result: riot. 10–12

ROBERTSON, KEITH, *Henry Reed, Inc.*, ill. by Robert McCloskey, Viking, 1958.
*Henry Reed's Baby-Sitting Service*, ill. by Robert McCloskey, Viking, 1966.
*Henry Reed's Journey*, ill. by Robert McCloskey, Viking, 1963.
Three very funny stories about a literal-minded boy who provides laughter for everyone but himself. 10–12
*In Search of a Sandhill Crane*, ill. by Richard Cuffari, Viking, 1973. From an elderly aunt and her Indian friend, a bored boy learns to appreciate wildlife. 10–13

ROSEN, WINIFRED, *Henrietta, the Wild Woman of Borneo*, ill. by Kay Chorao, Four Winds, 1975. Noisy and messy, Henrietta thinks she's rejected but finds how much her parents and her well-behaved older sister love her. 5–8

SACHS, MARILYN, *The Bears' House*, ill. by Louis Glanzman, Doubleday, 1971. The dollhouse with a bear family is Fran Ellen's escape from an intolerable home situation. 9–11
*Veronica Ganz* and *Peter & Veronica*, ill. by Louis Glanzman, Doubleday, 1968 and 1969. Two stories in which Veronica, long the bully of her class, meets her match

in undersized Peter and a painful friendship begins. 10–14

SAUER, JULIA, *The Light at Tern Rock*, ill. by Georges Schreiber, Viking, 1951. A Christmas story set against the wild beauty and isolation of a lonely seagirt lighthouse. The story is beautifully told and illustrated, and the moral problem involved makes it unusual. 9–12

SCHAEFER, JACK, *Old Ramon*, ill. by Harold West, Houghton, 1960. A convincing character study of an old shepherd who is wise not only in the ways of sheep but also in the ways of young boys. An effective read-aloud story. 10–14

SHARMAT, MARJORIE WEINMAN, *Gladys Told Me to Meet Her Here*, ill. by Edward Frascino, Harper, 1970.
*I'm Not Oscar's Friend Anymore*, ill. by Tony DeLuna, Dutton, 1975.
Two funny, touching stories of misunderstanding. 5–8

SHULEVITZ, URI, *Dawn*, ill. by author, Farrar, 1974. A truly beautiful book about two campers' dawn. 5–7

SLOTE, ALFRED, *Matt Gargan's Boy*, Lippincott, 1975. Danny learns that wishing isn't going to bring his divorced father back or keep a girl off the baseball team. 9–11
*My Father, the Coach*, Lippincott, 1972. Good baseball, a strong father-son relationship. 9–11

SMITH, DORIS BUCHANAN, *A Taste of Blackberries*, ill. by Charles Robinson, T. Crowell, 1973. A most moving story about a child's adjustment to his friend's death. 9–11

SNYDER, ZILPHA KEATLEY, *The Egypt Game*, ill. by Alton Raible, Atheneum, 1967. 9–12
*The Velvet Room*, ill. by Alton Raible, Atheneum, 1965. Mystery adds suspense to a story of migrant workers. 10–12

SORENSEN, VIRGINIA, *Miracles on Maple Hill*, ill. by Beth and Joe Krush, Harcourt, 1956. A warm story of a family's experiencing the wonder of woods and fields at all seasons. Newbery Medal. 9–12

SPYKMAN, E. C., *A Lemon and a Star*, Harcourt, 1955. The amusing adventures of four motherless Cares youngsters. For superior readers. 11–14

STAPP, ARTHUR D., *The Fabulous Earthworm Deal*, ill. by George Porter, Viking, 1969. Two young entrepreneurs begin a mail-order business in earthworms but fail to reckon with the law of supply and demand. 10–11

STOLZ, MARY, *The Bully of Barkham Street*, ill. by Leonard Shortall, Harper, 1963. An unusual companion volume to the title cited below, giving the same story from another view. *A Dog on Barkham Street*, ill. by Leonard Shortall, Harper, 1960. 9–12
*Noonday Friends*, ill. by Louis S. Glanzman, Harper, 1965. Being poor, wearing old clothes, and having a free lunch pass given to needy children nags at eleven-year-old Franny Davis. An inspiring book—sometimes funny, always perceptive in its sensitivity. 9–12

TAYLOR, MARK, *Henry the Explorer* and *Henry Explores the Jungle*, ill. by Graham Booth, Atheneum, 1966 and 1968. Two stories of a highly imaginative little boy, who might live in any small town, with a strong inclination to explore the surrounding countryside. 5–7

TRESSELT, ALVIN, *Follow the Wind*, ill. by Roger Duvoisin, Lothrop, 1950.
*I Saw the Sea Come In*, ill. by Roger Duvoisin, Lothrop, 1954.
*Sun Up*, ill. by Roger Duvoisin, Lothrop, 1949.
These picture-stories are little dramas of weather and seasonal changes. 4–6

TUNIS, JOHN R., *All-American*, Harcourt, 1942. No one writes better sports stories than John R. Tunis. In addition to sports, his books center on adolescent problems resulting from religious and racial prejudices. 12–14

TWAIN, MARK (pseud. for Samuel Clemens), *The Adventures of Huckleberry Finn*. 11–up
*The Adventures of Tom Sawyer*. 12–up
Both classics are available in many editions.

UDRY, JANICE, *The Moon Jumpers*, ill. by Maurice Sendak, Harper, 1959. The delight of playing in the moonlight out-of-doors is caught in the artist's luminous drawings. A rare book. 4–7

WERSBA, BARBARA, *The Dream Watcher*, Atheneum, 1968. A lonely, unhappy boy finds solace in a friendship with a very old woman. 11–14

WIER, ESTER, *The Barrel*, McKay, 1966. A well-told story of a boy forced to make a difficult adjustment to life in a Florida swamp and a hostile older brother. 10–13
*The Loner*, McKay, 1963. Boy has no family to help him survive the problems of being a migrant worker. He has had to learn to depend on himself and no one else, a kind of independence which enables him to survive while following the crops, but which causes trouble when he finds himself "adopted" by Boss, a tough old lady with rigorous standards. 10–12

YASHIMA, TARO (pseud. for Jun Iwanatsu), *Umbrella*, ill. by author, Viking, 1958. Day after day small Momo waited and hoped for rain so that she might use her bright red boots and new umbrella. Stunning illustrations. 5–8

ZOLOTOW, CHARLOTTE, *My Grandson Lew*, ill. by William Pène Du Bois, Harper, 1974. A boy and his mother fondly remember a loving grandfather. 3–7
*William's Doll*, ill. by William Pène Du Bois, Harper, 1972. Grandmother is the only one who understands that boys as well as girls can love dolls. 4–8

## Minority Groups[8]

ANGELO, VALENTI, *The Bells of Bleecker Street*, ill. by author, Viking, 1949.
*Hill of Little Miracles*, ill. by author, Viking, 1942.
In *The Bells of Bleecker Street* twelve-year-old Joey finds himself the accidental possessor of a toe from the statue of St. John. His struggles to return the toe, his adventures with his gang, and his father's return from the war make an amusing story and bring this Italian neighborhood vividly to life. *Hill of Little Miracles*

[8] Books about blacks are included here. However, recent publications in the area of inter-group relationships are listed in the "Life in the United States" section of the Bibliography because of the shifting focus found in these books. Teachers wishing comprehensive lists on inter-group relations are advised to consult the following publications:
Rollock, Barbara, *The Black Experience in Children's Books*, The New York Public Library, revised at regular intervals.
Crosby, Muriel, editor, *Reading Ladders for Human Relations*, Am. Council on Education, 4th rev. ed., 1963.
Rollins, Charlemae, *We Build Together*, Nat. Council of Teachers of English, 1967.

shows Ricco, who was born with one leg too short, starting on the road to normalcy. 10–14

ARMER, LAURA ADAMS, *Waterless Mountain*, ill. by Sidney and Laura Adams Armer, McKay, 1931. A poetic story of Navaho life containing little action and much mysticism. For the special reader. 12–14

ARMSTRONG, WILLIAM H., *Sounder*, ill. by James Barkley, Harper, 1969. A somber moving novel of a black sharecropper's family who surmount injustice with dignity. Newbery Medal. 11–up

ASSOCIATION FOR CHILDHOOD EDUCATION, *Told Under Spacious Skies*, ill. by William Moyers, Macmillan, 1952.
*Told Under the Stars and Stripes*, ill. by Nedda Walker, Macmillan, 1945.
The first book is made up of regional stories; the second book is an anthology of short stories about various minority groups in our cities throughout the country. 8–12

BAKER, BETTY, *And One Was a Wooden Indian*, Macmillan, 1970. A young Apache learns that he has the true vision of the shaman. 11–15
*Little Runner of the Longhouse*, ill. by Arnold Lobel, Harper, 1962. Easy-to-read story of an Iroquois boy and his New Year celebration. 6–7
*The Shaman's Last Raid*, ill. by Leonard Shortall, Harper, 1963. Very funny account of what happens when Great-Grandfather, who rode with Geronimo, tries to teach the old ways to modern Indian children. 8–12

BEIM, LORRAINE and JERROLD, *Two Is a Team*, ill. by Ernest Crichlow, Harcourt, 1945. Two little boys find that they get more done as a team than singly. That they are of two different races makes no difference; it's the team that is important. 5–8

BONHAM, FRANK, *Viva Chicano*, Dutton, 1970. A young Chicano on parole gets a second chance. 12–15

BRONSON, WILFRID S., *Pinto's Journey*, ill. by author, Messner, 1948. A fine adventure story about a Navaho Indian boy of modern times. Brilliant colored pictures. 8–10

BUFF, MARY, *Dancing Cloud, the Navajo Boy*, rev. ed., ill. by Conrad Buff, Viking, 1957. 9–10
*Hah-Nee of the Cliff Dwellers*, ill. by Conrad Buff, Houghton, 1956. 8–10
*Magic Maize*, ill. by Conrad Buff, Houghton, 1953. 9–12
Three fine Indian stories.

BULLA, CLYDE, *Eagle Feather*, ill. by Tom Two Arrows, T. Crowell, 1953.
*Indian Hill*, ill. by James J. Spanfeller, T. Crowell, 1963.
Bulla has a special touch which makes his easy reading books especially appealing to reluctant readers. 7–10

CHILDRESS, ALICE, *A Hero Ain't Nothin' but a Sandwich*, Coward, 1973. The story of a young drug addict, brilliantly told from his own and others' viewpoints, is candid and touching, with superb characterization. 11–14

CLARK, ANN NOLAN, *Blue Canyon Horse*, ill. by Allan Houser, Viking, 1954. A beautiful story of a young Indian boy and his horse. 8–10
*In My Mother's House*, ill. by Velino Herrera, Viking, 1941. This is a fine story written with simplicity and beauty about the Tewa Indian children. 8–12
*Little Navaho Bluebird*, ill. by Velino Herrera, Viking, 1943. The story of a little Navaho girl who loves her home and the old ways of life, but who learns to accept going to the white man's school. 8–12
*Year Walk*, Viking, 1975. A young Basque is on his own as a sheepherder in Idaho. 12–14

CLYMER, ELEANOR, *The Spider, the Cave, and the Pottery Bowl*, ill. by Ingrid Fetz, Atheneum, 1971. Each summer Kate returns to the Indian village where her grandmother lives. 8–10

DAVIS, RUSSELL G., and BRENT K. ASHABRANNER, *The Choctaw Code*, McGraw, 1961. The Choctaws granted a year of freedom to a man under the death sentence. This moving story recounts how youthful Tom Baxter learned to accept the inevitability of his friend's death. 10–14

DE ANGELI, MARGUERITE, *Henner's Lydia*, ill. by author, Doubleday, 1936.
*Skippack School*, ill. by author, Doubleday, 1939.
Two stories of life in a Mennonite community in Pennsylvania. 8–10
*Yonie Wondernose*, ill. by author, Doubleday, 1944. A favorite, especially when his "wondering" pays off and he proves his courage as well. There could hardly be a more appealing introduction to the Pennsylvania Dutch than Yonie. 6–9

ERWIN, BETTY K., *Behind the Magic Line*, ill. by Julia Iltis, Little, 1969. A well-told story of a close-knit black family in a midwest ghetto and their move to the northwest to begin a new life. 10–12

FAULKNER, GEORGENE, and JOHN BECKER, *Melindy's Medal*, ill. by C. E. Fox, Messner, 1945. A humorous and tender story of a little girl's achievement. 8–11

FIFE, DALE, *Who's in Charge of Lincoln?* and its sequels, *What's New, Lincoln?*, *What's the Prize, Lincoln?* and *Who Goes There, Lincoln?* ill. by Paul Galdone, Coward, 1965, 1970, 1971, and 1975. Lively, humorous stories about an imaginative black boy. 7–10

FITZHUGH, LOUISE, *Nobody's Family Is Going to Change*, Farrar, 1974. Emma's black and brilliant, but her father scoffs at her wanting to become a lawyer. 10–12

FOX, PAULA, *How Many Miles to Babylon?* ill. by Paul Giovanopoulos. White, 1967. 9–11

GREENE, BETTE, *Philip Hall Likes Me, I Reckon Maybe*, ill. by Charles Lilly, Dial, 1974. Funny, breezy story of a smitten black girl of eleven, Beth, whose mother knows she's bright about everything except That Boy. 9–11

GREENFIELD, ELOISE, *She Come Bringing Me That Little Baby Girl*, ill. by John Steptoe, Lippincott, 1974. Kevin's jealousy is assuaged by Mama's wise approach. 3–5

HAMILTON, VIRGINIA, *The House of Dies Drear*, ill. by Eros Keith, Macmillan, 1968. 9–12
*M. C. Higgins the Great*, Macmillan, 1974. The oldest boy in a mountain family, M. C. dreams of a better life for them all. Rich in setting and characterization, written with distinction. Newbery Medal. 11–13
*The Time Ago Tales of Jahdu*, ill. by Nonny Hogrogian, Macmillan, 1969. A small black inhabitant of Harlem is held in wonder by Mama Luka's tales of Jahdu. 6–9
*Zeely*, ill. by Symeon Shimin, Macmillan, 1967. A perceptive and sensitively written story with focus upon the problems of a young girl beginning to grow up. 9–11

HUNT, MABEL LEIGH, *Ladycake Farm*, ill. by Clotilde Embree Funk, Lippincott, 1952. This joyous story of a black family beginning a new life on a farm has its tragic moments, too. A delightful family group, and a first-rate story. 9–12

HUNTER, KRISTIN, *Guests in the Promised Land*, Scribner's, 1973. 11–14
*The Soul Brothers and Sister Lou*, Scribner's, 1968. A

memorable story of Louretta Hawkins and her singing group who take the tragic events which surround them in the ghetto and turn them into soul music. 12–15

JACKSON, JESSE, *Call Me Charley,* ill. by Doris Spiegal, Harper, 1945. The story of the ups and downs in a young black boy's friendship with a white boy in a white community. 9–12

JONES, WEYMAN, *The Edge of Two Worlds,* ill. by J. C. Kocsis, Dial, 1968. The story of an encounter between an aged, very ill Cherokee Indian and a white boy stranded in the wilderness and their gradual acceptance of the fact of their interdependence. 10–14

JORDAN, JUNE, *New Life: New Room,* ill. by Ray Cruz, T. Crowell, 1975. Three children in a black family resent having to share a room because another child is to be born, but find it's fun planning and rearranging. 5–8

KEATS, EZRA JACK, *Peter's Chair,* ill. by author, Harper, 1967.
*The Snowy Day,* ill. by author, Viking, 1964. Caldecott Medal.
*Whistle for Willie,* ill. by author, Viking, 1964.
Three beautifully illustrated stories about a little boy's adventures in the first snow; how, when he is a little older, he learns to whistle for his dog; and his final acceptance of his new little sister. 4–7

KINGMAN, LEE, *The Best Christmas,* ill. by Barbara Cooney, Doubleday, 1949. A simple, moving story of a Finnish-American family's Christmas. 8–11

KRUMGOLD, JOSEPH, *. . . and now Miguel,* ill. by Jean Charlot, T. Crowell, 1953. The story of twelve-year-old Miguel, who wishes to be accepted as a man, is told with humor and tenderness. Fine picture of sheepherding in New Mexico. Newbery Medal. 10–14

LAURITZEN, JONREED, *The Ordeal of the Young Hunter,* ill. by Hoke Denetsosie, Little, 1954. A distinguished story of a twelve-year-old Navaho boy who grows to appreciate what is good in the cultures of the white man and the Indian. 11–14

LEXAU, JOAN, *Benjie on His Own,* ill. by Don Bolognese, Dial, 1970. When his grandmother fails to pick him up after school, Benjie tries to find his own way. When he arrives home and finds her very ill, he must use even more initiative to get help. 5–7

LINDQUIST, JENNIE D., *The Golden Name Day,* ill. by Garth Williams, Harper, 1955. The delightful quest of a Swedish name day for a little American girl in the midst of her loving Swedish relatives. 8–10
*The Little Silver House,* ill. by Garth Williams, Harper, 1959. The mystery of a little silver house and a festive Swedish Christmas will please young readers in this sequel to *The Golden Name Day.* 8–10

LOWNSBERY, ELOISE, *Marta the Doll,* ill. by Marya Werten, McKay, 1946. Hanka, a little Polish girl, longs for a soft, cuddly doll such as her American cousins have. Her sister Marysia gives up a new skirt to buy the doll. Hanka and her doll Marta are inseparable and share the pleasant adventures of everyday living. 7–10

MATHIS, SHARON BELL, *The Hundred Penny Box,* ill. by Leo and Diane Dillon, Viking, 1975. Soft pictures of a wrinkled old black face and an eager young one echo the love that is the theme of this tender story. 8–10

MEANS, FLORENCE CRANNELL, *Great Day in the Morning,* Houghton, 1946. In this book a lovable black girl experiences the bitterness of racial prejudice but has the courage to go on. At Tuskegee she comes to know Dr.

Carver and decides to become a nurse. 12–14

MILES, MISKA, *Annie and the Old One,* ill. by Peter Parnall, Atlantic, 1971. A Navajo grandmother helps little Annie understand that death is an inevitable part of life. 8–10

MILHOUS, KATHERINE, *The Egg Tree,* ill. by author, Scribner's, 1950. This beautifully illustrated book of an Easter egg tree in rural Pennsylvania has started egg trees blooming all over the country. Caldecott Medal. 6–8

MOHR, NICHOLASA, *Nilda,* ill. by author, Harper, 1973. A somber but candid picture of life in Spanish Harlem. 11–14

MONTGOMERY, JEAN, *The Wrath of Coyote,* ill. by Anne Siberell, Morrow, 1968. A story which depicts the impact of the white man's civilization upon the Miwok Indians of Northern California. 11–14

MURRAY, MICHELE, *Nellie Cameron,* ill. by Leonora Prince, Seabury, 1971. Set in Washington, D.C., the story of a black child who overcomes a reading problem also presents a warm picture of family life. 9–11

NEWELL, HOPE, *A Cap for Mary Ellis,* Harper, 1953. Two young nursing students enter as the first black trainees in a New York State hospital. Their story is told with warmth and humor. 11–14

OAKES, VANYA, *Willy Wong: American,* ill. by Weda Yap, Messner, 1951. Here is the old struggle of a little Chinese boy to be accepted as a one hundred percent American. A good family story. 10–up

PALMER, CANDIDA, *Snow Storm Before Christmas,* ill. by H. Tom Hall, Lippincott, 1965. Two children in a middle-class black family go Christmas shopping. 8–10

POLITI, LEO, *A Boat for Peppe,* ill. by author, Scribner's, 1950.
*Juanita,* ill. by author, Scribner's, 1948.
*Little Leo,* ill. by author, Scribner's, 1951.
*Mieko,* ill. by author, Golden Gate, 1969.
*Moy Moy,* ill. by author, Scribner's, 1960.
*Pedro, the Angel of Olvera Street,* ill. by author, Scribner's, 1946.
*Song of the Swallows,* ill. by author, Scribner's, 1949. Caldecott Medal.
These appealing picture-stories have slight plots but a tender beauty that is unique. Pedro and Juanita show the Christmas and Easter customs of the Mexican colony on Olvera Street in Los Angeles. The swallows are the famous birds of San Capistrano Mission. Peppe takes part in the blessing of the fishing boats at Monterey, but Little Leo journeys to Italy and converts a whole village of children to the charms of playing Indian. Moy Moy, the little sister of three brothers in Chinatown, finds the New Year's festivities wonderful, and Mieko yearns to be queen of Nisei Week in Los Angeles. 5–8

ROSENBERG, SONDRA, *Will There Never Be a Prince?* ill. by Mircea Vasiliu, St. Martin's, 1970. A very amusing tale of a Jewish girl's adolescence, told partly in diary form. 11–14

SANDOZ, MARI, *The Horsecatcher,* Westminster, 1957. Compelling story of Young Elk, a Cheyenne, who faces disapproval because he would rather capture horses than kill men. 11–14

SHOTWELL, LOUISA, *Magdalena,* ill. by Lilian Obligado, Viking, 1971. Grandmother has old-fashioned Puerto Rican ideas, Magdalena feels, but they reach agreement. 10–12

*Roosevelt Grady*, ill. by Peter Burchard, World, 1963. 9–11

SONNEBORN, RUTH, *Friday Night Is Papa Night*, ill. by Emily McCully, Viking, 1970. Working at two jobs, Papa came home only on Fridays, so to Pedro it was the best time of the week. 5–7

STEPTOE, JOHN, *Stevie*, ill. by author, Harper, 1969. A vivid portrayal of the feelings of a young boy who resents the child his mother cares for during the week. 5–8

STERLING, DOROTHY, *Mary Jane*, ill. by Ernest Crichlow, Doubleday, 1959. A young black girl enrolls in a newly integrated junior high school where she is lonely and has problems to solve in winning friendship. 12–14

TALBOT, CHARLENE, *Tomás Takes Charge*, ill. by Reisie Lonette, Lothrop, 1966. Tomás and Fernanda, alone in New York, take refuge in an abandoned building rather than let the welfare authorities find them. 9–12

TAYLOR, SYDNEY, *All-of-a-Kind Family*, Follett, 1951. This is a heart-warming story of an affectionate Jewish family, living in the early 1900's. 9–12
*More All-of-a-Kind Family*, ill., by Mary Stevens, Follett, 1954. 9–12
*All-of-a-Kind Family Downtown*, ill. by Beth and Joe Krush, Follett, 1972. Another cozy story. 9–12

THOMAS, DAWN, *Mira! Mira!* ill. by Harold James, Lippincott, 1970. Ramon, newly arrived from Puerto Rico, is enchanted by his first snow. 5–7

UCHIDA, YOSHIKO, *The Promised Year*, ill. by William M. Hutchinson, Harcourt, 1959. A little Japanese girl and her cat learn to adjust to their new home and friends in California. 8–12

UDRY, JANICE MAY, *Mary Jo's Grandmother*, ill. by Eleanor Mill, Whitman, 1970. A small black girl copes resourcefully when the grandmother she's visiting has an accident. 5–8

### Life in Other Lands

### England, Ireland, Scotland

ARDIZZONE, EDWARD, *Little Tim and the Brave Sea Captain*, ill. by author, Walck, 1936. A picture-story book about life at sea with five-year-old Tim as the hero. 6–8
*Tim All Alone*, ill. by author, Walck, 1957. This is a story about a young seafaring lad who is the personification of achievement. 6–8

ARUNDEL, HONOR, *The Terrible Temptation*, Nelson, 1971. A freshman at Edinburgh University loses her boyfriend because of her self-centered behavior. 11–14

BAWDEN, NINA, *The Runaway Summer*, Lippincott, 1969. A finely drawn portrait of lonely Mary as she slowly adjusts to life after her parents' divorce. 9–11
*Squib*, Lippincott, 1971. An older girl loves an orphaned waif of seven who reminds her of the small brother who had died. Set in England. 10–11

BREINBURG, PETRONELLA, *Doctor Shawn* and *Shawn Goes to School*, ill. by Errol Lloyd, T. Crowell, 1975 and 1974. A small English boy plays doctor, and has his first day at nursery school; these are among the few British books with black characters. 3–5

BROWN, ROY, *The Day of the Pigeons*, Macmillan, 1969. As a reform school runaway searches London for his father he is drawn into the affairs of a group of children intent upon a search of their own. 10–12
*Flight of Sparrows*, Macmillan, 1973. Gang life in a squalid London neighborhood, tough but touching.
*The White Sparrow*, Seabury, 1975. Two of the characters from the first book go off on their own, and one finds a home with an understanding family. 12–14

DICKINSON, PETER, *Emma Tupper's Diary*, ill. by David Omar White, Atlantic, 1971. Planned as a quiet Highlands vacation, Emma's visit provides high drama. 11–14

DILLON, EILÍS, *The Coriander*, ill. by Vic Donahue, Funk, 1964. Set on the Irish island of Inishgillan, this story of a kidnaped doctor who reluctantly is pressed into service offers more than just an exciting plot. 11–14

GARDAM, JANE, *The Summer After the Funeral*, Macmillan, 1973. A wheedling mother arranges summer plans for her three children. Witty and perceptive. 11–14

GODDEN, RUMER, *The Kitchen Madonna*, ill. by Caro Barker, Viking, 1967. A tender little novel of two London children and their painstaking effort to create an acceptable Madonna for their homesick Polish-Ukrainian maid. 8–12

HILDICK, E. W., *Louie's Snowstorm*, ill. by Iris Schweitzer, Doubleday, 1974. One of a series of books about a British milkman and the boys who help him; here a plucky American girl helps during a Christmas snowstorm. 10–12

LINGARD, JOAN, *Across the Barricades*, Nelson, 1973. One of a trilogy, this describes the tragic tension between Protestant and Catholic children in Ireland. 11–14

MACKEN, WALTER, *The Flight of the Doves*, Macmillan, 1968. An exciting chase results when Finn Dove and his younger sister flee to relatives in Ireland to escape a vicious stepfather. 9–12

MC LEAN, ALLAN CAMPBELL, *Master of Morgana*, Harcourt, 1959.
*Storm over Skye*, ill. by Shirley Hughes, Harcourt, 1957. Two suspense-mystery stories which capture the fascination of the Isle of Skye. For better readers. 12–15

MC NEILL, JANET, *The Battle of Saint George Without*, ill. by Mary Russon, Little, 1968. A lively and believable story of some English children who conspire to save a derelict church from the wrecking crew. 9–12
*Goodbye, Dove Square*, ill. by Mary Russon, Little, 1969. In this sequel to the story listed above we see the same children two years later as they adjust to new homes in council housing and cope with the problems of adolescence. 11–14

MAC PHERSON, MARGARET M., *The Rough Road*, ill. by Douglas Hall, Harcourt, 1966. Readers may catch a vivid glimpse of another way of life in this account of an orphan boy on the Isle of Skye. 11–14
*The Shinty Boys*, ill. by Shirley Hughes, Harcourt, 1963. Earning money on the Isle of Skye is not easy, and the boys must earn fifty pounds over the summer if they are to keep their shinty team. 10–12

MADDOCK, REGINALD, *The Dragon in the Garden*, Little, 1969. It's new boy versus school bully in this story as Jimmy refuses to pay "protection money." 9–11

MAYNE, WILLIAM, *Royal Harry*, Dutton, 1972. Told with fluent grace, a mystery story in which a girl of twelve inherits a house and a mountain. 10–12

PEYTON, K. M., *Pennington's Last Term*, ill. by author, T. Crowell, 1971. The first of several books about a tough adolescent who becomes a concert pianist. 11–14

RANSOME, ARTHUR, *Swallows and Amazons*, ill. by Helene

Carter, Lippincott, 1931. This is the only title in a seven-volume series which is still in print. It is the story of a summer vacation spent on an island by a group of children. They are far enough from home to feel independent, but close enough to feel secure. A satisfying book for special readers.                    10–12

ROBINSON, VERONICA, *David in Silence*, ill. by Victor G. Ambrus, Lippincott, 1968. A memorable story, set in England, about a deaf boy and his attempts to join in the activities of normal children.          10–12

TOWNSEND, JOHN ROWE, *Good-Bye to the Jungle*, Lippincott, 1967. This fine novel about English slums is a sometimes amusing, sometimes sad, story of what happens to six people when they move into a new neighborhood.                              12–15
*The Intruder*, ill. by Joseph A. Phelan, Lippincott, 1970. An account of a psychopathic stranger's attempt to usurp the name and rights of a foundling lad in a British coastal village.                  12–up
*Pirate's Island*, Lippincott, 1968. Two children in a decaying neighborhood, a neglected girl and a fat overindulged boy, manage to resolve their personal problems and find friendship and adventure.        9–12
*Trouble in the Jungle*, ill. by W. T. Mars, Lippincott, 1969.                                       10–14

TUNIS, JOHN R., *Silence Over Dunkerque*, Morrow, 1962. This is a moving account of the events leading up to the evacuation of thousands of troops across the English Channel during World War II. The horrors of war as they touch the lives of young and old, people and animals, are recounted in quiet understatement.  12–15

TURNER, PHILIP, *Colonel Sheperton's Clock*, ill. by Philip Gough, World, 1966.
*The Grange at High Force*, ill. by W. T. Mars, World, 1967.
Although both books contain a slight element of mystery, it is the relationships among the three boys and between the boys and the adults which lend flavor to these pictures of small village English life.    12–14

VAN STOCKUM, HILDA, *The Cottage at Bantry Bay*, ill. by author, Viking, 1938. The escapades of the O'Sullivan children—Michael, Brigid, and the twins Francie and Liam—make a lively tale.                  10–12

### France

BEMELMANS, LUDWIG, *Madeline*, ill. by author, Simon, 1939. Madeline inhabits a French boarding school with "twelve little girls in two straight lines" doing everything in two straight lines, except the appendix that only Madeline had to have removed. The other *Madeline* books are equally as much fun as this one.    5–8

BERNA, PAUL, *The Horse Without a Head*, tr. from the French by John Buchanan-Brown, ill. by Richard Kennedy, Pantheon, 1958. The right combination of an exciting mystery and the French *joie de vivre* in a picture of lower-class children in France.        9–12

BISHOP, CLAIRE HUCHET, *Pancakes Paris*, ill. by Georges Schreiber, Viking, 1947. A half-starved postwar French child receives a miraculous package of American pancake mix. How he meets two American soldiers and gets the directions for the pancakes translated makes a heart-warming tale.                        8–12
*Twenty and Ten*, ill. by William Pène DuBois, Viking, 1952. During the Nazi occupation of France, nineteen

French children with their teacher were asked to feed and hide ten Jewish children. How these fifth-graders shared their food and managed with their teacher held in jail is a moving and satisfying story.        9–12

CARLSON, NATALIE SAVAGE, *The Family Under the Bridge*, ill. by Garth Williams. Harper, 1958.    8–10
*The Happy Orpheline*, ill. by Garth Williams, Harper, 1957. An imaginative and amusing story of twenty orphans, happy in their home outside of Paris, afraid only of being adopted.                        8–10
*A Brother for the Orphelines*, ill. by Garth Williams, Harper, 1959. A delightful sequel to *The Happy Orpheline*, this tells of the efforts of the orphans to keep a baby boy foundling left on their doorstep.    8–10

FRANÇOISE (pseud. for Françoise Seignebosc), *Jeanne-Marie at the Fair*, ill. by author, Scribner's, 1959.
*Jeanne-Marie in Gay Paris*, Scribner's, 1956.
*Noël for Jeanne-Marie*, Scribner's, 1956.
Popular picture-story book series about a sunny little French girl and her adventures.              5–7

### Holland

DE JONG, MEINDERT, *Far Out the Long Canal*, ill. by Nancy Grossman, Harper, 1964. At nine, Moona alone among his classmates cannot skate and his only dream is to learn.                                      10–12
*Journey from Peppermint Street*, ill. by Emily A. McCully, Harper, 1968. Siebren experiences three days filled with excitement and adventure on his first journey away from home. The author skillfully portrays the inner thoughts and feelings of the young boy. National Book Award.                           8–10
*The Wheel on the School*, ill. by Maurice Sendak, Harper, 1954. A tenderly told, warmly humorous story of how a Dutch fishing village brings back the storks to settle there again. Newbery Medal.           9–12

DODGE, MARY MAPES, *Hans Brinker; or the Silver Skates*, ill. by Hilda Van Stockum, World, 1946. Although still considered a classic, this lengthy story of Hans should not be a first choice for books about Holland.    10–12

KRASILOVSKY, PHYLLIS, *The Cow Who Fell in the Canal*, ill. by Peter Spier, Doubleday, 1957. Stunning picture book which combines humor with an accurate look at Dutch life.                                  5–8

### Italy

ANGELO, VALENTI, *The Honey Boat*, ill. by author, Viking, 1959. Friendly picture of an Italian family at work and play.                                     10–12

BETTINA (pseud. for Bettina Ehrlich), *Pantaloni*, ill. by author, Harper, 1957. This author-artist has never created more beautiful pictures than those for this appealing picture-story of an Italian boy's search for his dog.                                       5–9

### Mexico and South America

BEHN, HARRY, *The Two Uncles of Pablo*, ill. by Mel Silverman, Harcourt, 1959. The contrast between Pablo's two uncles creates a real problem for him. How he reunites the family is sensitively told. Fine reading aloud.  9–12

CLARK, ANN NOLAN, *Secret of the Andes*, ill. by Jean Charlot, Viking, 1952. In this Newbery Medal book, Cusi lives among the great peaks of the Andes Mountains, guarding a hidden herd of royal llamas and learning from old Chuto the sacred traditions of his Incan ancestors. 10–14

ETS, MARIE HALL, and AURORA LA BASTIDA, *Nine Days to Christmas*, ill. by Marie Hall Ets, Viking, 1959. Small Ceci enjoys her first posada in this Caldecott Medal book of present-day Mexico. 5–8

KALNAY, FRANCIS, *Chúcaro: Wild Pony of the Pampa*, ill. by Julian de Miskey, Harcourt, 1957. Excellent depiction of life on the Argentine pampas with a story that leaves the reader with much to think about. 9–12

O'DELL, SCOTT, *The Black Pearl*, ill. by Milton Johnson, Houghton, 1967. An unforgettable tale of Ramon Salazar, a pearl diver and his fortunes after he brings up to the surface a great black pearl. 11–14

RITCHIE, BARBARA, *Ramón Makes a Trade* (Los Cambios de Ramón), ill. by Earl Thollander, Parnassus, 1959. A picture-story with English and Spanish text which tells of an enterprising Mexican boy who succeeds in trading his pottery jar for a much-desired green parakeet. 9–10

SOMMERFELT, AIMÉE, *My Name Is Pablo*, ill. by Hans Norman Dahl, Criterion, 1965. Portrait of modern Mexico's poverty problem as seen through the eyes of Pablo, who is befriended by a Norwegian family. 10–12

STOLZ, MARY, *The Dragons of the Queen*, ill. by Edward Franscino, Harper, 1969. Two Americans meet a queenly old Mexican woman and are charmed by her. 10–12

*Juan*, ill. by Louis S. Glanzman, Harper, 1970. A poignant story of Juan who refuses to accept the fact that he is an orphan. 8–11

TARSHIS, ELIZABETH K., *The Village That Learned to Read*, ill. by Harold Hayden, Houghton, 1941. A robust story with humor and an amusing moral. Important for its focus on the national drive for literacy in Mexico. 10–12

VAN ITERSON, SINY, *Pulga*, tr. by Alexander and Alison Gode, Morrow, 1971. Pulga, or "flea," is a Colombian waif who has adventures on his first trip away from Bogotá. 11–14

## The Orient [9]

AYER, JACQUELINE, *NuDang and His Kite*, ill. by author, Harcourt, 1959.
*A Wish for Little Sister*, ill. by author, Harcourt, 1960. Colorful picture-stories of Thailand. 5–8

BUCK, PEARL, *The Big Wave*, prints by Hiroshige and Hokusai, Day, 1948. Significant story built around the theme that "life is stronger than death." Two Japanese boys adventure together, survive a terrible catastrophe, and begin life anew. 9–12

DE JONG, MEINDERT, *The House of Sixty Fathers*, ill. by Maurice Sendak, Harper, 1956. Set in China during World War II, this is the story of how Tien Pao and his pig, Glory of the Republic, were finally able to rejoin Tien Pao's family. 10–12

HANDFORTH, THOMAS, *Mei Li*, ill. by author, Doubleday, 1938. The pleasant adventures of a little Chinese girl at the fair. Caldecott Medal. 5–8

[9] Included in this section are stories of China, India, Japan, Thailand, Tibet, etc.

KIM, YONG-IK, *The Happy Days*, ill. by Artur Marokvia, Little, 1960. Modern Korea is a mixture of disappointments and happiness for orphaned Sang Chun. 10–12

LATTIMORE, ELEANOR FRANCES, *Little Pear*, ill. by author, Harcourt, 1931. 6–9
*Little Pear and His Friends*, ill. by author, Harcourt, 1939. 6–9
*Little Pear and the Rabbits*, ill. by author, Morrow, 1956. 6–9
Three adventure stories of a likable little Chinese boy.

LEWIS, ELIZABETH FOREMAN, *To Beat a Tiger*, ill. by John Heubnergarth, Holt, 1956. A devastating picture of the effects of poverty upon people. Although it has its hopeful side, it is for mature readers. 12–16
*Young Fu of the Upper Yangtze*, ill. by Kurt Wiese, Holt, 1932. This Newbery Medal book gives us a graphic picture of the inner strife and conflict in the life of a young Chinese boy. The details are Chinese, but Fu is any boy of any country trying to make his way in the world. 10–14

LINDQUIST, WILLIS, *Burma Boy*, ill. by Nicolas Mordvinoff, McGraw, 1953. An absorbing story of a boy's search for a lost elephant. 9–11

MARTIN, PATRICIA MILES, *The Pointed Brush*, ill. by Roger Duvoisin, Lothrop, 1959. Story of Chung Wee, small sixth son of the House of Chung, who goes to school only because he is least needed in the rice fields, and who convinces his family that "the man who knows the written word has strength." 6–8

MEHTA, RAMA, *The Life of Keshav, A Family Story from India*, McGraw, 1969. A novel in which a boy escapes crippling poverty, the slavery of caste, and makes his difficult way into the university. 12–14

MERRILL, JEAN, *The Superlative Horse*, ill. by Ronnie Solbert, W. R. Scott, 1961. When Po Lo, Chief Groom in Duke Mu's court, grows too old to retain his position, he recommends Han Kan, son of a fuel hawker, as his successor. Han Kan's test is to select one horse for the Duke's stable of already magnificent horses. 8–11

MUHLENWEG, FRITZ, *Big Tiger and Christian*, ill. by Rafaello Busoni, Pantheon, 1952. Here are nearly six hundred pages packed with adventure, people, and strange places in a story so unusual that no one who reads the first chapter will want to put it down. An English and a Chinese boy carry through a dangerous mission for General Wao in wartime China. 12–adult

SOMMERFELT, AIMÉE, *The Road to Agra*, ill. by Ulf Aas, Phillips, 1961. Thirteen-year-old Lalu's younger sister Maya is going blind, and he decides to take her to the UNICEF hospital in Agra. The trip is long and hazardous, and events depict the poverty of India's small villages and its effects upon people. 9–12

UCHIDA, YOSHIKO, *Sumi and the Goat and the Tokyo Express*, ill. by Kazue Mizumura, Scribner's, 1969. It is a most unusual day for Sumi and her classmates as Mr. Odo's goat stops the crack train to Kyoto. 6–9
*Takao and Grandfather's Sword*, ill. by William M. Hutchinson, Harcourt, 1958. One of a number of good stories by this author which depicts both modern Japan and its rich heritage. 8–10

WIESE, KURT, *Fish in the Air*, ill. by author, Viking, 1948. An amusing account of what happens to a small Chinese boy when he buys the largest kite in the market. Lovely, bright pictures. 6–8

YASHIMA, TARO (pseud. for Jun Iwanatsu), *Crow Boy*, ill. by author, Viking, 1955. This story of a small outcast

Japanese boy has unusual social values as well as great pictorial beauty.                                              6–8

YASHIMA, TARO, and HATOJU MUKU, *The Golden Footprints,* ill. by author, World, 1960. A beautiful story of the devotion of two foxes to their captured cub and how it affects a young Japanese boy. Excellent reading aloud.                                                  8–11

## Pacific Islands

CLARK, MAVIS T., *Blue Above the Trees,* ill. by Genevieve Melrose, Meredith, 1969. A memorable account of the Whitburn family's struggle to build a new life on a farm located in the rain forest of Australia.                11–13
*The Min-Min,* Macmillan, 1969. A troubled teen-ager and her younger brother leave home on a quest for the guidance and security not offered them at home. 11–15

OTTLEY, REGINALD, *The Bates Family,* Harcourt, 1969. An incredibly demanding way of life is pictured in this story of the Bates family and their struggle against drought and flood.                                    12–14
*Boy Alone,* ill. by Clyde Pearson, Harcourt, 1966. 10–12
*Rain Comes to Yamboorah,* ill. by Robert Hales, Harcourt, 1968. The final book of the trilogy which began with *Boy Alone.*                                        10–13
*Roan Colt,* ill. by Clyde Pearson, Harcourt, 1967. A very fine sequel to *Boy Alone.*                      10–13

PHIPSON, JOAN, *The Boundary Riders,* ill. by Margaret Horder, Harcourt, 1963.
*The Family Conspiracy,* ill. by Margaret Horder, Harcourt, 1964.
*Threat to the Barkers,* ill. by Margaret Horder, Harcourt, 1965.
These three fine stories are set in the back country of Australia and show how rugged life is in the wilds.                                                       10–12

SOUTHALL, IVAN, *Ash Road,* ill. by Clem Seale, St. Martin's, 1965.
*Hill's End,* ill. by Clem Seale, St. Martin's, 1963.
Two unforgettable stories from Australia about people under pressure from a disastrous fire and a flood. High drama at its best.                                    10–14
*Josh,* Macmillan, 1972. A city boy adjusts to rural life in Australia.                                        10–14

SPERRY, ARMSTRONG, *Call It Courage,* ill. by author, Macmillan, 1940. This Newbery Medal book is an exciting adventure story and also the tale of one boy's conquest of fear. Beautifully illustrated and poetic text.  10–12

WOOD, ESTHER, *Pedro's Coconut Skates,* ill. by author, Longmans, 1938. A lively story about a small boy of the Philippines whose curiosity often gets him into trouble, but whose determination to learn about things brings him a reward.                                       9–10

WRIGHTSON, PATRICIA, *A Racecourse for Andy,* ill. by Margaret Horder, Harcourt, 1968. A poignant story of a retarded boy, his loyal friends, and the events which follow his supposed purchase of a racetrack.       9–12

## Scandinavian Countries

ANCKARSVÄRD, KARIN, *The Mysterious Schoolmaster,* tr. from the Swedish by Annabelle Macmillan, ill. by Paul Galdone, Harcourt, 1959. A coastal village in Sweden provides the background for this captivating tale of two children who outwit an international spy.    10–12

*Robber Ghost,* tr. from the Swedish by Annabelle Macmillan, ill. by Paul Galdone, Harcourt, 1961. A sequel to the above, with numerous escapades.            10–12

BESKOW, ELSA, *Pelle's New Suit,* ill. by author, Harper, 1929. This beautifully illustrated picture book of how Pelle works for his new suit has acquired the status of a classic.                                          4–7

FRIIS-BAASTAD, BABBIS, *Don't Take Teddy,* tr. by Lise Sømme McKinnon, Scribner's, 1967. A retarded boy of fifteen is protected by a younger brother.        10–13

GRIPE, MARIA, *Hugo and Josephine,* ill. by Harald Gripe, Delacorte, 1969. A prize-winning story from Sweden of the mishaps and adventures of two children at home and school.                                        8–10
*The Night Daddy,* tr. by Gerry Bothmer, ill. by Harald Gripe, Delacorte, 1971. A young writer becomes a father figure to a child whose mother, a nurse, is on night duty.                                                 9–11

JANSSON, TOVE, *The Summer Book,* tr. by Thomas Teal, Pantheon, 1975. A lovely, lyric story about a child and her grandmother.                                    10–12

LINDGREN, ASTRID, *Rasmus and the Vagabond,* tr. from the Swedish by Gerry Bothmer, ill. by Eric Palmquist, Viking, 1960. Nine-year-old Rasmus runs away from the Swedish orphanage and meets Paradise Oscar, a lovable tramp. How he finds a home and happiness is well told in this touching tale.                           10–12

UNNERSTAD, EDITH, *The Spettecake Holiday,* tr. from the Swedish by Inger Boye, ill. by Iben Clante, Macmillan, 1958. A warm, humorous story of a little boy's summer on a Swedish farm.                                8–10

VESTLEY, ANNE-CATH., *Hello, Aurora,* ill. by Leonard Kessler, tr. by Eileen Amos, ad. by Jane Fairfax, T. Crowell, 1974.                                          8–10

## Switzerland

CHÖNZ, SELINA, *A Bell for Ursli,* ill. by Alois Carigiet, Walck, 1950. One of the most beautiful picture-stories to come out of Europe, this is also an exciting adventure story of a small Swiss boy's determination to have the largest bell to ring in the spring processional.   5–7

SPYRI, JOHANNA, *Heidi.* Any edition.                    9–11

ULLMAN, JAMES RAMSEY, *Banner in the Sky,* Lippincott, 1954. A dramatic and exciting story of young Rudi's determination to become a mountain climber and one day conquer the Citadel. Captures, as no other book does, the fascination of mountain climbing.      12–16

VAN DER LOEFF-BASENAU, ANNA RUTGERS, *Avalanche!* ill. by Gustav Schrotter, Morrow, 1958.                   11–13

## Eskimo Stories

FREUCHEN, PIPALUK, *Eskimo Boy,* ill. by Ingrid Vang Nyman, Lothrop, 1951. This epic tale, translated from the Danish, is the grimmest, most terrifying picture of Eskimo life we have had. It is the story of a boy's fight to save his family from starvation. The realistic details make it unsuitable for young children, but the heroism of the boy and his deeds are good for older children to read about.                                        10–12

GEORGE, JEAN CRAIGHEAD, *Julie of the Wolves,* ill. by John Schoenherr, Harper, 1972. A young Eskimo girl survives in the Arctic by living with a wolf pack after learning to communicate with the wolves. Newbery Medal. 10–13

GRIESE, ARNOLD, *At the Mouth of the Luckiest River,* ill. by Glo Coalson, T. Crowell, 1973. An Athabascan boy of the past creates a bond between his people and an Eskimo tribe they had feared. 9–11

HOUSTON, JAMES A., *Akavak, An Eskimo Journey,* ill. by author, Harcourt, 1968. A revealing portrait of Eskimo life is presented in this story of the struggle of a boy and his grandfather to reach their destination. 9–12

LIPKIND, WILLIAM, *Boy with a Harpoon,* ill. by Nicolas Mordvinoff, Harcourt, 1952. This, like Freuchen's book, should banish forever the igloo stereotype of Arctic life. An absorbing story of a boy's attempts to rid himself of a derogatory nickname and win a respected place in the community of men. 7–10

## Other Countries

ALMEDINGEN, E. M., *Young Mark: The Story of a Venture,* ill. by Victor G. Ambrus, Farrar, 1968. The author tells of her great-great-grandfather's trek from the Ukraine to St. Petersburg through Czarist Russia. 11–15

BENARY-ISBERT, MARGOT, *The Ark,* Harcourt, 1953. 12–14
*Castle on the Border,* tr. from the German by Richard and Clara Winston, Harcourt, 1956. 12–15
Two stories of life in postwar Germany and the problems encountered in rebuilding a normal life out of the ruins of World War II.

BLOCH, MARIE H., *Aunt America,* ill. by Joan Berg, Atheneum, 1963. Without moralizing, Bloch makes clear the meaning of freedom by depicting the lives of those who live in the Communist-dominated Ukraine. 9–12

CATHERALL, ARTHUR, *Yugoslav Mystery,* Lothrop, 1964. Within the framework of an exciting suspense story is an excellent portrait of an Iron Curtain country. 12–14

FEELINGS, MURIEL L., *Zamani Goes to Market,* ill. by Tom Feelings, Seabury, 1970. The story of a young Ugandan boy's first trip to market with his father and older brothers is well told and conveys the atmosphere of village life in Africa. 7–10

FROLOV, VADIM, *What It's All About,* tr. by Joseph Barnes, Doubleday, 1968. Contemporary life for Russian adolescents shows common concerns. 12–15

GEBHARDT, HERTHA VON, *The Girl from Nowhere,* tr. from the German by James Kirkup, ill. by Helen Brun, Phillips, 1959. An absorbing story of Magdalene, a nine-year-old from nowhere, who arouses wonder and suspicion among the children of a small German town. When she leaves, they find they are lost without her. 10–12

HÁMORI, LÁSZLÓ, *Dangerous Journey,* tr. from the Swedish by Annabelle Macmillan, ill. by W. T. Mars, Harcourt, 1962. The dramatic, but believable, story of two Hungarian boys who make their escape to freedom in Vienna. 10–12

HOLM, ANNE S., *North to Freedom,* tr. from the Danish by L. W. Kingsland, Harcourt, 1965. A tremendously moving story of young David's trip from a concentration camp to Denmark and freedom. Contrasts between the camp and life in the free world are excellently drawn and David's experiences arouse in the reader a new appreciation of a way of life we often take for granted. A unique book. 10–14

KASSIL, LEV, *Once in a Lifetime,* tr. by Anne Terry White, Doubleday, 1970. A Moscow girl of thirteen has a movie role, then decides to go back to school. 11–14

KINGMAN, LEE, *The Meeting Post; A Story of Lapland,* ill. by Des Asmussen, T. Crowell, 1972. A Lapp child, sent to a Finnish boarding school, adjusts to his new life. 8–10

KORINETZ, YURI, *There, Far Beyond the River,* tr. by Anthea Bell, ill. by George Armstrong, O'Hara, 1973. A Russian boy remembers the vitality and affection of a boisterous uncle. 10–12

KRUMGOLD, JOSEPH, *The Most Terrible Turk,* ill. by Michael Hampshire, T. Crowell, 1969. A warm story of the affection between a Turkish boy and his uncle. 7–9

LITTLE, JEAN, *From Anna,* ill. by Joan Sandin, Harper, 1972. 9–11
*Kate,* Harper, 1971, and *Look Through My Window,* ill. by Joan Sandin, Harper, 1970, to which it is a sequel, are about the friendship between two Canadian girls and the problems of one (Kate) who has one Jewish parent. 9–12

MIRSKY, REBA P., *Seven Grandmothers,* ill. by W. T. Mars, Follett, 1955.
*Thirty-one Brothers and Sisters,* ill. by W. T. Mars, Follett, 1952.
Two stories of Nomusa, a young Zulu girl. Warmly drawn picture of life in a Zulu kraal. 8–10

NAGENDA, JOHN, *Mukasa,* ill. by Charles Lilly, Macmillan, 1973. A good family story based on the author's childhood in Uganda. 9–11

POTTER, BRONSON, *Antonio,* ill. by Ann Grifalconi, Atheneum, 1968. A crippled boy who cannot become a fisherman wins a place in his Portuguese village by quick thinking and ingenuity during an emergency. 8–12

SEREDY, KATE, *Chestry Oak,* ill. by author, Viking, 1948. An involved and difficult story with a deeply significant theme—the fall of an ancient house and its rebirth in a new land. The boy Michael and his great horse Midnight are the central figures in the tale. 10–14
*The Good Master,* ill. by author, Viking, 1955. 10–12

SERRAILLIER, IAN, *The Silver Sword,* ill. by C. Walter Hodges, Phillips, 1959. An inspiring narrative of four courageous children of Warsaw after World War II. The three who have been separated from their parents set off to find them and are joined by a fourth child. Their journey covers three hard years, but their spirit never falters. 10–14

SHANNON, MONICA, *Dobry,* ill. by Atanas Katchamakoff, Viking, 1934. Beautifully written and rich in unique characters, this slow-moving story of a Bulgarian peasant boy may be more appealing to children if read aloud. Newbery Medal. 11–14

SLOBODKIN, FLORENCE, *Sarah Somebody,* ill. by Louis Slobodkin, Vanguard, 1970. A small girl delights in going to school in a Polish village at the turn of the century. A warm Jewish family story. 8–10

STEVENSON, WILLIAM, *The Bushbabies,* ill. by Victor Ambrus, Houghton, 1965. 11–14

STINETORF, LOUISE A., *Musa, the Shoemaker,* ill. by Harper Johnson, Lippincott, 1959. A lame Algerian boy, apprenticed to a shoemaker, grows up in a village of acrobats but achieves success with another skill. 9–11

TAYLOR, THEODORE, *The Cay,* Doubleday, 1969. After a ship is torpedoed in World War II, the survivors, a blinded white boy and a highly competent old black sailor, are stranded on a barren island in the Caribbean. 11–14

WATSON, SALLY, *The Mukhtar's Children,* Holt, 1968. Although their father does his best to prevent it, the children of an Arab village headman manage to make friends with the inhabitants of a nearby Jewish kibbutz.  9–12

WUORIO, EVA-LIS, *Save Alice!* Holt, 1968. Set in Spain, a lively and humorous mystery story involves British and American children in saving a white cockatoo.  10–12

## Historical Fiction

### American

ALCOTT, LOUISA MAY, *Little Women,* ill. by Jessie Willcox Smith, Little, 1934 (1868). Although this forerunner of modern realism for children and young people is chiefly a story of family life, it is also a story of life in Civil War times. There are numerous attractive editions available.  10–14

BACON, MARTHA, *Sophia Scrooby Preserved,* ill. by David C. White, Little, 1968. A rather romantic tale of a Zulu chieftain's daughter sold into slavery who triumphs over hardships to achieve success as a singer in London.  10–13

BAKER, BETTY, *A Stranger and Afraid,* Macmillan, 1972. A Wichita brave acts as guide to Coronado's men.  11–14

*Walk the World's Rim,* Harper, 1965. Chakoh, a young Indian, went to Mexico City with four Spanish survivors of a force of six hundred which had set out to search for gold in the sixteenth-century land of America.  10–12

BENCHLEY, NATHANIEL, *Only Earth and Sky Last Forever,* Harper, 1972. A young Cheyenne joins Crazy Horse.  12–15

*Small Wolf,* ill. by Joan Sandin, Harper, 1972. The eviction of native Americans from Manhattan Island.  6–8

BULLA, CLYDE ROBERT, *Down the Mississippi,* ill. by Peter Burchard, T. Crowell, 1954.  8–10

*The Secret Valley,* ill. by Grace Paull, T. Crowell, 1949. Just two of the more than thirty titles this author has produced for young readers. All of them are readable and all capture the atmosphere of times past.  8–10

BURCHARD, PETER, *Bimby,* ill. by author, Coward, 1968. One day in the life of a young slave boy as he tries to decide whether to make a break for freedom.  9–12

*Jed, The Story of a Yankee Soldier and a Southern Boy,* ill. by author, Coward, 1960.  10–12

CAUDILL, REBECCA, *Tree of Freedom,* ill. by Dorothy B. Morse, Viking, 1949. An outstanding pioneer story which gives a detailed picture of life in 1770, near Louisville, Kentucky. The story involves some stormy family relationships and appealing characters.  12–14

CLAPP, PATRICIA, *Constance; A Story of Early Plymouth,* Lothrop, 1968.  12–15

COATSWORTH, ELIZABETH, *Away Goes Sally,* ill. by Helen Sewell, Macmillan, 1934. The first of a series of historical stories about Sally, this one has to do with the migration of her whole family of aunts and uncles from Massachusetts to Maine after the American Revolution.  10–12

*Five Bushel Farm,* ill. by Helen Sewell, Macmillan, 1939. This book sees Sally's family established on their new farm and introduces Andy to her circle of friends.  8–10

COBLENTZ, CATHERINE CATE, *Martin and Abraham Lincoln,* ill. by Trientja, Childrens Pr., 1947.  7–10

COLLIER, JAMES LINCOLN and CHRISTOPHER, *My Brother Sam Is Dead,* Four Winds, 1974. A poignant story of a Connecticut family during the Revolutionary War.  11–14

CONSTANT, ALBERTA W., *Miss Charity Comes to Stay,* ill. by Louise Darling, T. Crowell, 1959. Lively, imaginative story of a young teacher in the Oklahoma Territory in 1893.  10–12

DALGLIESH, ALICE, *Adam and the Golden Cock,* ill. by Leonard Weisgard, Scribner's, 1959. A small boy faces a personal problem of divided loyalty when General Rochambeau's army comes to his Connecticut town during the Revolution.  7–9

*America Travels,* ill. by Hildegard Woodward, Macmillan, 1943.  9–11

*The Bears on Hemlock Mountain,* ill. by Helen Sewell, Scribner's, 1952. This adventure story is based on a historical episode. There weren't supposed to be any bears on Hemlock Mountain, but there *were,* as poor Jonathan proved. Jonathan's ingenuity in hiding from the bears will delight every young reader.  7–9

*The Courage of Sarah Noble,* ill. by Leonard Weisgard, Scribner's, 1954. "Keep your courage up, Sarah Noble," her mother had told her as she set off to the Connecticut wilderness to take care of Papa. A wonderfully warm story of courage.  7–9

DOUGLAS, EMILY, *Appleseed Farm,* ill. by Anne Vaughan, Abingdon, 1958. Ten-year-old Penny hears about a visit Johnny Appleseed once made to her family's Indiana farm.  8–10

EDMONDS, WALTER D., *The Matchlock Gun,* ill. by Paul Lantz, Dodd, 1941. A thrilling story of young Edward's courage in defending his home while his father is away fighting the Indians during the French and Indian Wars. Stunning illustrations capture the drama. Newbery Medal.  8–10

FALL, THOMAS, *Canalboat to Freedom,* ill. by Joseph Cellini, Dial, 1966. Benjamin Lown, a young Scotch boy, is apprenticed to Captain Roach, a hard-bitten canalboat captain on the Hudson and Delaware canals. On the boat Ben works side by side with a freed Negro, Lundius, learns about the Underground Railway, and encounters a tragedy involving Lundius, which teaches him that there are principles for which a man dies.  12–15

FIELD, RACHEL, *Calico Bush,* ill. by Allen Lewis, Macmillan, 1931.  12–14

FORBES, ESTHER, *Johnny Tremain,* ill. by Lynd Ward, Houghton, 1943. Newbery Medal.  11–14

FOX, PAULA, *The Slave Dancer,* ill. by Eros Keith, Bradbury, 1973. A white boy of 1840 is impressed into work on a slave ship. Newbery Medal.  11–14

FRANCHERE, RUTH, *Stampede North,* Macmillan, 1969. A lively account of life during the Klondike gold rush narrated by a fourteen-year-old boy who accompanies his father on a photographic tour of the camps.  11–13

FRITZ, JEAN, *And Then What Happened, Paul Revere?* ill. by Margot Tomes, Coward, 1973, and *Why Don't You Get a Horse, Sam Adams?* ill. by Trina Schart Hyman, Coward, 1974. Accurate, funny, delightful.  8–10

*Brady,* ill. by Lynd Ward, Coward, 1960. The Underground Railroad station in a small Pennsylvania town is endangered because Brady can't keep his mouth shut. A fine story of how a boy becomes a man when he learns that there are more important things in the world than his own well-being.  10–12

*The Cabin Faced West*, ill. by Feodor Rojankovsky, Coward, 1958. Appealing story of frontier life and of a little girl who learns to like being a pioneer.  9–12

*Early Thunder*, ill. by Lynd Ward, Coward, 1967. An outstanding novel set in pre-Revolutionary War days with both British and Colonial views presented objectively. Teen-age Daniel considers both sides but when the issues become clear to him he takes a stand.  11–14

GOBLE, PAUL and DOROTHY, *Red Hawk's Account of Custer's Last Battle*, ill. by authors, Pantheon, 1970. Seen from the viewpoint of a young Sioux, a brilliantly illustrated, dramatic story.  10–12

GREENE, BETTE, *Summer of My German Soldier*, Dial, 1973. A Jewish girl in a small southern town, unhappy at home, finds solace in helping a German war prisoner.  11–14

HALL, ANNA G., *Cyrus Holt and the Civil War*, ill. by Dorothy Bayley Morse, Viking, 1964. At first, life in the upstate New York small town goes on much as it had before the War. Slowly, the effects are felt and Cyrus Holt ceases to think of war as a joyful time.  8–12

HODGES, C. WALTER, *Columbus Sailed*, ill. by author, Coward, 1939. Fiction, but based on facts, and tremendously moving. This is a popular book.  12–14

HOLLING, HOLLING C., *Seabird*, ill. by author, Houghton, 1948.

*Tree in the Trail*, ill. by author, Houghton, 1942.

*Seabird* is a story of American ships in terms of one family of shipbuilders. In *Tree in the Trail*, a cottonwood tree on the Santa Fe Trail was a landmark for Indians and white men. Both books are superbly illustrated.  10–12

HUNT, IRENE, *Across Five Aprils*, Follett, 1964. Jethro is nine when the Civil War begins and he sees it in terms of parades and dashing soldiers marching in bright uniforms. When the war is over, Jethro knows better.  12–14

JOHNSON, ANNABEL and EDGAR, *Torrie*, Harper, 1960. Fourteen-year-old Torrie Anders travels by covered wagon from St. Louis to California in 1846. In the excitement of the adventure, she gains a new understanding of and admiration for her family.  12–16

*Wilderness Bride*, Harper, 1962. A realistic picture of the persecution of the Mormons, built around a moving love story.  12–16

KEITH, HAROLD, *Rifles for Watie*, T. Crowell, 1957. Jeff Bussey, Union volunteer at sixteen, gains insight into and sympathy for the problems and ideals of both the North and the South in this powerful Civil War story. Newbery Medal.  12–16

LAMPMAN, EVELYN, *Tree Wagon*, ill. by Robert Frankenberg, Doubleday, 1953. This journey to Oregon is a happy one for all concerned, including potential readers.  10–13

MC MEEKIN, ISABEL, *Journey Cake*, ill. by Nicholas Panesis, Messner, 1942. Six motherless children, in the care of an intrepid old free black woman, journey through the wilderness to join their father in Boone's Kentucky.  10–12

MEADER, STEPHEN W., *The Buckboard Stranger*, ill. by Paul Caile, Harcourt, 1954.

*The Fish Hawk's Nest*, ill. by Edward Shenton, Harcourt, 1952.

Exciting stories with historical background and usually an element of mystery, these and other books by this author are well written and exceedingly popular.  10–14

MEANS, FLORENCE CRANNELL, *A Candle in the Mist*, ill. by Marguerite de Angeli, Houghton, 1931. Pioneer life in a Minnesota settlement in the 1870's is difficult, but fifteen-year-old Janey faces it with high courage.  12–14

MEIGS, CORNELIA, *Covered Bridge*, ill. by Marguerite de Angeli, Macmillan, 1936.

*Willow Whistle*, ill. by E. B. Smith, Macmillan, 1931. These well-written stories of other days and ways are not easy reading, but they are rewarding books for the able child. Action and theme carry the interest.  10–14

MELTZER, MILTON, *Underground Man*, Bradbury, 1973. Based on the antislavery activities of Joshua Bowen, an exciting story set in 1835.  12–up

MONJO, F. N., *The Drinking Gourd*, ill. by Fred Brenner, Harper, 1970. An easy-to-read story of Tommy and his chance involvement in the activities of the Underground Railroad.  6–9

*The Secret of the Sachem's Tree*, ill. by Margot Tomes, Coward, 1972. Hallowe'en in colonial times.  7–9

MURRAY, MICHELE, *The Crystal Nights*, Seabury, 1973. Elly's father brings Jewish kin from Germany, during World War II, and she is baffled by their ingratitude.  12–15

O'DELL, SCOTT, *Island of the Blue Dolphins*, Houghton, 1960. An Indian girl shows remarkable courage and resourcefulness in living alone on an island off the coast of Southern California for eighteen years. An outstanding historical episode. Newbery Medal.  10–14

*The King's Fifth*, Houghton, 1966. A remarkable story of the power of gold to corrupt men. It is basically the story of young Esteban, who accompanies the Spanish in their search for the golden cities of Cibola.  12–16

*Sing Down the Moon*, Houghton, 1970.  11–14

RICHARD, ADRIENNE, *Pistol*, Little, 1969. A novel which evokes depression days in its depiction of the fortunes of a youthful horse wrangler.  12–up

STEELE, WILLIAM O., *The Buffalo Knife*, ill. by Paul Galdone, Harcourt, 1952.

*The Far Frontier*, ill. by Paul Galdone, Harcourt, 1959. Realistic stories of life on the frontier in which the heroes must learn that all goals are achieved at a price.  9–12

*Perilous Road*, ill. by Paul Galdone, Harcourt, 1958. A Civil War story in which youthful Chris learns that there is nothing simple about war.  9–12

UCHIDA, YOSHIKO, *Journey to Topaz*, ill. by Donald Carrick, Scribner's, 1971. A moving story of a Japanese-American family's evacuation and relocation during World War II.  10–12

*Samurai of Gold Hill*, ill. by Ati Forberg, Scribner's, 1972.  10–13

WIBBERLEY, LEONARD, *Peter Treegate's War*, Farrar, 1960. American Revolutionary days are vividly re-created as the background for the hero, a high-spirited sixteen-year-old boy, who attempts to resolve conflicting loyalties between his real and foster fathers. (Sequel to *John Treegate's Musket*, Farrar, 1959; followed by *Treegate's Raiders*, Farrar, 1962.)  11–14

WILDER, LAURA INGALLS, *By the Shores of Silver Lake*, ill. by Garth Williams, Harper, 1953.

*Farmer Boy*, ill. by Garth Williams, Harper, 1953.

*Little House in the Big Woods*, ill. by Garth Williams, Harper, 1953.

*Little House on the Prairie*, ill. by Garth Williams, Harper, 1953.

*The Long Winter,* ill. by Garth Williams, Harper, 1953.
*On the Banks of Plum Creek,* ill. by Garth Williams, Harper, 1953.
*These Happy Golden Years,* ill. by Garth Williams, Harper, 1953.
Originally published in the 1930's and reissued with completely new illustrations in 1953, these seven books cover the saga of a pioneer family and the childhood of the author to the time of her marriage. This is the family invincible, able to stand up to misfortunes and tragedies because it is strong in love and in loyalty. For most children the books are a totally satisfying reading experience.                                                    9–12

## European

AVERY, GILLIAN, *Ellen and the Queen,* ill. by Krystyna Turska, Nelson, 1975. A nine-year-old country girl has an unexpected meeting with Queen Victoria.     8–10

BALDERSON, MARGARET, *When Jays Fly to Barbmo,* ill. by Victor G. Ambrus, World, 1969. An excellent novel of a teen-age girl and her growth to maturity in occupied Norway during World War II.                          12–14

BAWDEN, NINA, *The Peppermint Pig,* Lippincott, 1975. A turn-of-the-century family story, written with grace.
                                                            9–11

BEATTY, JOHN and PATRICIA, *Master Rosalind,* Morrow, 1974.                                                  12–14

BUFF, MARY, *Apple and the Arrow,* ill. by Conrad Buff, Houghton, 1951. The stirring story of William Tell and his son Walter, with many dramatic illustrations by Swiss-born Conrad Buff.                          8–11

BURTON, HESTER, *Beyond the Weir Bridge,* ill. by Victor Ambrus, T. Crowell, 1970. A compelling story of 17th century Quakers in England.                  12–15
*In Spite of All Terror,* ill. by Victor G. Ambrus, World, 1969. A notable novel of England during the grim days of 1940.                                        12–14
*Time of Trial,* ill. by Victor Ambrus, World, 1964. A novel on the theme of freedom of speech is set in London in 1801. Carnegie Medal.                  12–15

CHUTE, MARCHETTE, *The Innocent Wayfaring,* ill. by author, Dutton, 1955. Fourteenth-century England brought vividly and authentically to life.     11–14
*The Wonderful Winter,* ill. by Grace Golden, Dutton, 1954. In 1596 Sir Robert Wakefield ran away to London to find work. His adventures included finding himself a happy part of an actor's family and, eventually, one of the boy actors in Will Shakespeare's own theater. A vivid picture of the Elizabethan theater.     11–14

COOPER, SUSAN, *Dawn of Fear,* ill. by Margery Gill, Harcourt, 1970. A World War II story, perceptive in depicting the effect of war on children.            9–11

DE ANGELI, MARGUERITE, *Door in the Wall,* ill. by author, Doubleday, 1949. When Robin is stricken with an illness that leaves his legs paralyzed and his back bent, it is brother Luke who helps him to find a "door in the wall" and nurses him back to strength and courage. A valuable addition to children's literature of the medieval period which should bring courage to handicapped children. Newbery Medal.                          8–10

ECKE, WOLFGANG, *Flight Toward Home,* tr. by Anthony Knight, Macmillan, 1970. Based on real experience, this story relates Peter's two-year struggle to find his grandmother after his flight from East Germany in 1945.                                                   11–14

FECHER, CONSTANCE, *Heir to Pendarrow,* Farrar, 1969. An exciting historical novel set in the England of 1558. The author has added a note to explain the amount of fictionalizing.                                         12–up
*The Leopard Dagger,* Farrar, 1973. A foundling boy who works at the Globe theater finds his mother. 11–13

GARDAM, JANE, *A Long Way from Verona,* Macmillan, 1972. A lively, funny story about a would-be writer of 13.                                              11–13

GARFIELD, LEON, *The Sound of Coaches,* ill. by John Lawrence, Viking, 1974. A picaresque romance of 18th century England has colorful period details.     12–up

GRAY, ELIZABETH JANET, *Adam of the Road,* ill. by Robert Lawson, Viking, 1942. When Adam, by mischance, loses both his father and his dog, he seeks them on the highways and byways of thirteenth-century England. Newbery Medal.                                           10–14

HARNETT, CYNTHIA, *Caxton's Challenge,* ill. by author, World, 1960. The scriveners of England saw the printing press as a manner of depriving them of a living, and they fought by fair means and foul to keep William Caxton from successfully operating his business. Exciting storytelling, excellent history.     11–14

HAUGAARD, ERIC CHRISTIAN, *The Little Fishes,* ill. by Morton Johnson, Houghton, 1967. The hapless condition of homeless children in World War II is shown as three children straggle northward from Naples to Cassino, Italy.                                      10–14

HUNTER, MOLLIE, *The Ghosts of Glencoe,* Funk, 1969. An absorbing story set against the massacre of Glencoe in 1692.                                            11–13
*The Lothian Run,* Funk, 1970. An action-filled historical novel of eighteenth-century Scotland.     11–15

KELLY, ERIC P., *The Trumpeter of Krakow,* ill. by Janina Domanska, Macmillan, new ed., 1966. Medieval Poland comes vividly alive in this tale of the youthful trumpeter who finishes the Heynal and prevents tragedy. Newbery Medal.                                     11–14

LEVITIN, SONIA, *Journey to America,* ill. by Charles Robinson, Atheneum, 1970. The story of a Jewish family's escape from Nazi Germany as told by one of the daughters.                                          10–13

LEWIS, HILDA, *Here Comes Harry,* ill. by William Stobbs, Criterion, 1960. Henry VI became King of England at the age of nine months and was thus deprived of anything resembling a normal childhood. Intrigues and power-manipulations surrounded him. All told through the eyes of Harry Rushden, a goldsmith apprentice and devoted follower.                                  12–15

PARKER, RICHARD, *The Sword of Ganelon,* ill. by William Ferguson, McKay, 1958. A remarkable and stirring tale of ninth-century England invaded by the Danes.  11–16

PEYTON, K. M., *Flambards* and *The Edge of the Cloud,* ill. by Victor G. Ambrus, World, 1968 and 1969. Two exciting novels which carry the same characters through the early days of flying in England during World War I.                                            11–14

PICARD, BARBARA L., *Ransom for a Knight,* ill. by C. Walter Hodges, Walck, 1956. After the English loss to the Scots at Bannockburn, young Alys sets forth to try and ransom her father and brother. Excellent picture of the times, combined with a fast-moving plot.     12–15

PLOWMAN, STEPHANIE, *Three Lives for the Czar,* Houghton, 1970. A colorful novel of the court of Nicholas II.
                                                          12–up

PYLE, HOWARD, *Men of Iron,* ill. by author, Harper, 1891.

The training of knights, the clash of battle, and all the glamor of feudal England under Henry IV. 12–14
*Otto of the Silver Hand,* ill. by author, Scribner's, 1888. The appealing story of a boy whose father, a German robber baron, places him in a medieval monastery to assure his safety. 10–12

REISS, JOHANNA, *The Upstairs Room,* T. Crowell, 1972. Based on the author's life, this is the taut, touching story of Jewish sisters who were hidden by a Dutch family during the Nazi occupation. 9–12

SUTCLIFF, ROSEMARY, *Eagle of the Ninth,* ill. by C. Walter Hodges, Walck, 1954. 12–15
*Lantern Bearers,* ill. by Charles Keeping, Walck, 1959. 12–15
*Silver Branch,* ill. by Charles Keeping, Walck, 1957. 12–15
Three magnificent novels about the Roman impact upon England, and the influence of England upon the conquerors.
*Warrior Scarlet,* Walck, 1958. This is a story about a young handicapped boy's long, painful struggle to become a great warrior, told in heroic language that captures the harshness and discipline needed to survive as a Bronze Age inhabitant of England. 12–15
*The Witch's Brat,* ill. by Richard Lebenson, Walck, 1970. A crippled boy helps found a hospital in Norman England. 12–14

SYMONS, GERALDINE, *Miss Rivers and Miss Bridges,* ill. by Alexy Pendle, Macmillan, 1972. Two lively girls join the suffragette cause in pre-World War I London. 11–13

TREECE, HENRY, *Perilous Pilgrimage,* ill. by Christine Price, Phillips, 1959. The Children's Crusade portrayed through exciting incidents and vivid prose. 11–14

VIVIER, COLETTE, *The House of Four Winds,* tr. and ed. by Miriam Morton, Doubleday, 1969. The story of a young boy's service in the resistance movement of Nazi-occupied Paris. 10–12

WALSH, JILL P., *Fireweed,* Farrar, 1970. A tender and sensitively written novel of two teen-agers adrift in London during the Blitz. 12–16

WAYNE, KYRA PETROVSKAYA, *Shurik,* Grosset, 1970. An orphaned boy is adopted by a nurse during the siege of Leningrad. A true story, fictionalized. 11–14

WILLARD, BARBARA, *The Iron Lily,* Dutton, 1974. Fourth in a series of books about the Medley family, this is a vivid story of Tudor England. 11–13

YEP, LAURENCE, *Dragonwings,* Harper, 1975. A Chinese boy comes to San Francisco just before the earthquake. 10–12

ZEI, ALKI, *Petros' War,* trans. by Edward Fenton, Dutton, 1972. 10–12
*Wildcat Under Glass,* tr. by Edward Fenton, Holt, 1968. The story of a Greek family whose home life is torn by the Fascists' rise to power in 1936. The author shows both the hidden and overt methods used by a totalitarian government to enforce conformity. 10–13

### Ancient Times

BFHN, HARRY, *Faraway Lurs,* World, 1963. A tenderly told story of tragic yet inspiring dimensions, of a girl of the Forest People who made the mistake of falling in love with a boy of the Sun People. 12–14

BENCHLEY, NATHANIEL, *Beyond the Mists,* Harper, 1975. A vivid tale of a young Viking's New World travels. 11–13

DICKINSON, PETER, *The Dancing Bear,* ill. by David Smee, Atlantic, 1973. A slave boy and his pet bear escape when the Huns sack Byzantium. 10–13

HAUGAARD, ERIK CHRISTIAN, *The Rider and His Horse,* ill. by Leo and Diane Dillon, Houghton, 1968. A story narrated by the main character, David Ben Joseph, tells of his struggle to find meaning for life in a country devastated by the Romans. 12–14

HUNTER, MOLLIE, *The Stronghold,* Harper, 1974. An evocative story of the struggle for power between a local chieftain, a Druid leader, and the Romans, set in ancient Scotland. 11–15

LAWRENCE, ISABELLE, *The Gift of the Golden Cup,* ill. by Charles V. John, Bobbs, 1960.
*The Theft of the Golden Ring,* ill. by Charles V. John, Bobbs, 1960. Twelve-year-old Atia and seven-year-old Gaius are two of Julius Caesar's relatives, and their adventures present a vivid picture of Roman life. 11–14

LINEVSKI, A., *An Old Tale Carved Out of Stone,* tr. by Maria Polushkin, Crown, 1973. An archeologist writes with fluency of a Stone Age tribe in Siberia. 12–15

MC GRAW, ELOISE JARVIS, *Mara, Daughter of the Nile,* Coward, 1953. Mara, a slave of the Egyptians, is promised every luxury and eventual freedom if she will spy for the Queen, the Pharaoh, Hatshepsut. But Mara also sells her services to the rival political faction which is trying to put the rightful heir, Thutmose, on the throne. Her decision to play both ends against the middle, as she puts it, leads to greater peril than she had expected. 13–17

MORRISON, LUCILE, *The Lost Queen of Egypt,* ill. by Franz Geritz, Lippincott, 1937. This story of ancient Egypt solves the mystery of the disappearance of the young queen when her husband Tutankhamen, king of Egypt, dies. 12–14

SNEDEKER, CAROLINE DALE, *The Forgotten Daughter,* ill. by Dorothy Lathrop, Doubleday, 1933. When Chloe's Greek mother died, she suffered many hardships until her Roman father remembered her and made a home for her in Rome. 12–14
*A Triumph for Flavius,* ill. by Cedric Rogers, Lothrop, 1955. The story of a young Roman boy who, in compassion for his Greek slave and teacher, works to secure his freedom. Interesting background of ancient Rome and early Christian days. 8–11

SUTCLIFF, ROSEMARY, *The Capricorn Bracelet,* ill. by Richard Cuffari, Walck, 1973. 11–14
*Heather, Oak, and Olive,* ill. by Victor Ambrus, Dutton, 1972. Three superbly written stories of ancient times, one set in ancient England, one in Britain during the Roman occupation, the third in Greece. 10–13

TREASE, GEOFFREY, *Message to Hadrian,* Vanguard, 1955. Young Paul must journey from England to Rome with a message for Emperor Hadrian if his friend Severus is to stay alive. Paul's trip is one headlong dash, reading like a modern spy thriller for all its historical accuracy. 11–14

WINTERFELD, HENRY, *Mystery of the Roman Ransome,* ill. by Fritz Biermann, tr. by Edith McCormick, Harcourt, 1971. The boys who turned sleuths in *Detectives in Togas* again become involved in an adventure. 10–13

# BIOGRAPHY

ADAMS, JOHN QUINCY (1767–1848)

Lomask, Milton, *John Quincy Adams, Son of the American Revolution*, Farrar, 1965. A readable, interesting biography of the sixth President of the United States. 12–14

ADAMS, SAMUEL (1722–1803)
Alderman, Clifford L., *Samuel Adams, Son of Liberty*, Holt, 1961. A vivid re-creation of prerevolutionary Boston and Adams' role in the Sons of Liberty. 11–14

ADDAMS, JANE (1860–1935)
Meigs, Cornelia Lynde, *Jane Addams, Pioneer for Social Justice*, ill. with photos, Little, 1970. The major emphasis in this work is upon Miss Addams' forty years at Hull House and her numerous crusades for reform and social justice. 12–16

AGASSIZ, LOUIS (1807–1873)
Tharp, Louise Hall, *Louis Agassiz, Adventurous Scientist*, ill. by Rafaello Busoni, Little, 1961. This Swiss-born immigrant raised natural science to an honored position in the United States. 10–12

ALCOTT, LOUISA MAY (1832–1888)
Fisher, Aileen, and Olive Rabe, *We Alcotts*, ill. by Ellen Raskin, Atheneum, 1968. 11–14
Meigs, Cornelia, *Invincible Louisa*, ill. with photos, Little, 1933. The life of the author of *Little Women*. Newbery Medal. 12–15
Peare, Catherine Owens, *Louisa May Alcott: Her Life*, ill. by Margaret Ayer, Holt, 1954. An easier-to-read version of the life of America's most popular nineteenth-century lady author. 9–12

ALEXANDER THE GREAT (353–323 B.C.)
Gunther, John, *Alexander the Great*, ill. by Isa Barrett, Random, 1953. All the excitement and danger in the life of a great conqueror who built the world's first empire. 10–14

ALLEN, ETHAN (1738–1789)
Holbrook, Stewart H., *America's Ethan Allen*, ill. by Lynd Ward, Houghton, 1949. Spirited illustrations add to the dramatic story of the "Green Mountain Boys" and their fighting leader. 10–14

ANDERSEN, HANS CHRISTIAN (1805–1875)
Collin, Hedvig, *Young Hans Christian Andersen*, ill. by author, Viking, 1955. Sensitively told story of the Danish writer from his unhappy childhood years to his first literary recognition. 10–13

ANDERSON, MARIAN (1902–     )
Tobias, Tobi, *Marian Anderson*, ill. by Symeon Shimin, T. Crowell, 1972. Softly drawn pictures add to the warmth of a simply written biography. 7–9

ARCHIMEDES (287?–212? B.C.)
Bendick, Jeanne, *Archimedes and the Door of Science*, ill. by author, Watts, 1962. A usable history of the life and achievements of the Greek physicist and mathematician. 11–14

ARMSTRONG, LOUIS (1900–1971)
Eaton, Jeanette, *Trumpeter's Tale: The Story of Young Louis Armstrong*, ill. by Elton C. Fax, Morrow, 1955. From New Orleans' slums to king of the trumpeters is the stirring story of "Louis the Lip." 12–16

ATATURK, KEMAL (Mustafa Kemal) (1881–1938)
Lengyel, Emil, *They Called Him Ataturk*, Day, 1962. A factual, realistic history of the great Turkish leader's career as well as a good description of life in Turkey from 1890 to 1938. 11–14

BALBOA, VASCO NUÑEZ DE (1475?–1519)
Mirsky, Jeannette, *Balboa, Discoverer of the Pacific*, ed. by Walter Lord, ill. by Hans Guggenheim, Harper,

1964. An interesting, sympathetically written account of Balboa's work from 1510–1519. 10–13

BANNEKER, BENJAMIN (1731–1806)
Lewis, Claude, *Benjamin Banneker: The Man Who Saved Washington*, ill. by Ernest T. Crichlow, McGraw, 1970. Story of the Afro-American scientist who helped survey and plan Washington, D.C. 11–14

BEETHOVEN, LUDWIG VAN (1770–1827)
Goss, Madeline B., *Beethoven: Master Musician*, ill. by Carl Schultheiss, Holt, 1946. A sensitive and thwarted genius portrayed with rare sympathy. 12–14

BELL, ALEXANDER GRAHAM (1847–1922)
Shippen, Katherine, *Mr. Bell Invents the Telephone*, ill. by Richard Floethe, Random, 1952. Alexander Graham Bell's achievement is doubly satisfying because of the disheartening failure that preceded his successful invention. 10–13

BERNSTEIN, LEONARD (1918–     )
Cone, Molly, *Leonard Bernstein*, ill. by Robert Galster, T. Crowell, 1970. An interesting short biography of one of America's most popular composers and conductors. 7–11

BETHUNE, MARY MC LEOD (1875–1955)
Peare, Catherine Owens, *Mary McLeod Bethune*, Vanguard, 1951. 12–14
Sterne, Emma Gelders, *Mary McLeod Bethune*, ill. by Raymond Lufkin, Knopf, 1957. 12–16
Two fine biographies of a great black educator who dedicated her life to her people.

BLACKWELL, ELIZABETH (1821–1910)
Baker, Rachel, *The First Woman Doctor: The Story of Elizabeth Blackwell, M.D.*, ill. by Corinne Malvern, Messner, 1944. Before Elizabeth Blackwell broke down the barriers, the medical profession was closed to women. Girls particularly should enjoy reading this book. 12–15

BLAKE, WILLIAM (1757–1827)
Daugherty, James, *William Blake*, with reproductions of drawings, Viking, 1960. A sensitive portrait of a great artist and poet whose *Songs of Innocence* still delight children. 12–16

BOONE, DANIEL (1734–1820)
Meadowcroft, Enid, *Holding the Fort with Daniel Boone*, ill. by Lloyd Coe, T. Crowell, 1958. An easy-to-read book which emphasizes the pioneers' struggles rather than details about Boone. 8–11

BRAILLE, LOUIS (1809–1852)
Neimark, Anne E., *Touch of Light, The Story of Louis Braille*, ill. by Robert Parker, Harcourt, 1970. A somewhat fictionized account of the life of an extraordinary man who succeeded in doing something worthwhile for other blind people. 8–12

BRONTË, CHARLOTTE (1816–1855)
Kyle, Elisabeth, *Girl with a Pen, Charlotte Brontë*, Holt, 1964. Fine biography of the author of *Jane Eyre*, from the age of seventeen through thirty-one. 12–15

BROWNING, ELIZABETH BARRETT (1806–1861)
Waite, Helen, *How Do I Love Thee?* Macrae, 1953. An absorbing story of the Victorian poetess, climaxed by her romance with Robert Browning. 12–16

BUDDHA (Gautama Siddhartha) (563?–483? B.C.)
Kelen, Betty, *Gautama Buddha in Life and Legend*, Lothrop, 1967. A carefully written story which discriminates between fact and legend surrounding this religious leader. 12–up

BUNCHE, RALPH J. (1904–1971)

Kugelmass, J. Alvin, *Ralph J. Bunche: Fighter for Peace*, rev. ed., ill. by Elton Fox, Messner, 1962. Reared in Detroit's slums, Bunche was one of America's most honored citizens and a winner of the Nobel Peace Prize. 12–16

BURROUGHS, JOHN (1837–1921)
Swift, Hildegarde Hoyt, *The Edge of April: A Biography of John Burroughs*, ill. by Lynd Ward, Morrow, 1957. Biography of John Burroughs, whose nature observations and writings made him a potent voice in the fight for conservation. 12–15

CABOT, JOHN (1450–1498)
Hill, Kay, *And Tomorrow the Stars*, ill. by Laszlo Kubinyi, Dodd, 1968. Carefully researched, dramatic, and written with vitality, this biography of the Venetian explorer received the Canadian children's book award. 12–up

CARNEGIE, ANDREW (1835–1919)
Judson, Clara Ingram, *Andrew Carnegie*, ill. by Steele Savage, Follett, 1964. The excellent story of America's great philanthropist who used his fortune that all people might live better lives. 10–13

CARSON, CHRISTOPHER (1809–1868)
Bell, Margaret, *Kit Carson, Mountain Man*, ill. by Harry Daugherty, Morrow, 1952. A short, dramatic biography with large print and lively illustrations. 8–11

CARSON, RACHEL (1907–1964)
Sterling, Philip, *Sea and Earth: The Life of Rachel Carson*, ill. with photos, T. Crowell, 1970. A well-documented account of the life of the conscientious civil servant who was one of the first to raise her voice against the despoiling of our planet. 13–up

CARTIER, JACQUES (1491–1557)
Averill, Esther, *Cartier Sails the St. Lawrence*, ill. by Feodor Rojankovsky, Harper, 1956. A fascinating and factual account of Cartier's three voyages to the New World. 10–14

CARVER, GEORGE WASHINGTON (1864?–1943)
Means, Florence Crannell, *Carver's George*, ill. by Harve Stein, Houghton, 1952. A moving account of the great black scientist from his tragic infancy to his triumphant old age, honored and beloved by the world. 10–14

CASSATT, MARY (1845–1926)
Wilson, Ellen, *American Painter in Paris; A Life of Mary Cassatt*, Farrar, 1971. A discerning portrait of the artist and the trends that influenced her work. 11–14

CATHER, WILLA (1876–1947)
Franchere, Ruth, *Willa: The Story of Willa Cather's Growing Up*, decorations by Leonard Weisgard, T. Crowell, 1958. A flowing narrative relates Willa Cather's early experiences in Nebraska and the influences which produced her adult novels.

CHAVEZ, CESAR (1928– )
Franchere, Ruth, *Cesar Chavez*, ill. by Earl Thollander, T. Crowell, 1970. A story for younger readers of biography with focus upon the early struggles and self-sacrifice of this resolute leader. 7–11

CHIEF JOSEPH (1840?–1904)
Davis, Russell, and Brent Ashabranner, *Chief Joseph —War Chief of the Nez Percé*, McGraw, 1962. The tragic story of a peace-loving chief forced into war as his people opposed the westward movement. 12–16

CHILD, LYDIA MARIA (1802–1880)
Meltzer, Milton, *Tongue of Flame*, T. Crowell, 1965.

The life story of the first American to write a book attacking slavery. 12–17

CHISHOLM, SHIRLEY (1924– )
Brownmiller, Susan, *Shirley Chisholm*, Doubleday, 1970. 10–14

CHURCHILL, WINSTON (1875–1965)
Coolidge, Olivia E., *Winston Churchill and the Story of Two World Wars*, Houghton, 1960. A view of the British statesman in relation to his times. 13–17
Wibberley, Leonard, *The Complete Life of Winston Churchill*, rev. ed., Farrar, 1968. An account of the life of one of England's greatest notables, told with humor and dignity. 12–16

CLARK, WILLIAM (1770–1838) (See Lewis, Meriwether.)

CLEMENS, SAMUEL LANGHORNE (see Twain, Mark.)

COCHISE (?–1874)
Wyatt, Edgar, *Cochise: Apache Warrior and Statesman*, ill. by Allan Houser, McGraw, 1953. Few readers will be unmoved by the betrayal of Cochise by the whites. Most readers will find themselves rooting for Cochise to win despite their knowledge of his defeat. 10–14

CODY, WILLIAM (1846–1917)
Aulaire, Ingri and Edgar Parin d', *Buffalo Bill*, ill. by authors, Doubleday, 1952. Colorful pictures highlight the enthralling story of a man who was a legend in his own time. 5–9

COLUMBUS, CHRISTOPHER (1446?–1506)
Sperry, Armstrong, *The Voyages of Christopher Columbus*, ill. by author, Random, 1950. A historically accurate account of the four important voyages undertaken by Columbus. 9–11

COOK, JAMES (1728–1779)
Latham, Jean Lee, *Far Voyager: The Story of James Cook*, maps by Karl Stuecklen, Harper, 1970. An engrossing narrative of the rise of a poor boy to officership in the British Navy and great achievement as explorer and scientist. 12–up

COPLEY, JOHN SINGLETON (1738–1815)
Ripley, Elizabeth, *Copley: A Biography*, Lippincott, 1967. Presents the life of the artist in alternating pages of text and pictures. 12–14

COURT, MARGARET (1942– )
Sullivan, George, *Queens of the Court*, ill. with photos, Dodd, 1974. Brisk, informative sketches of Margaret Court, Billie Jean King, and other tennis stars. 11–15

CRAZY HORSE (1844?–1877)
Garst, Doris Shannon, *Crazy Horse, Great Warrior of the Sioux*, ill. by William Meyers, Houghton, 1950. 12–14

CROCKETT, DAVY (1786–1836)
LeSueur, Meridel, *Chanticleer of Wilderness Road: A Story of Davy Crockett*, ill. by Aldren A. Watson, Knopf, 1951. Legends, tall tales, and facts are humorously woven together to produce a delightful book. 10–14

FATHER DAMIEN (1840–1889)
Roos, Ann, *Man of Molokai: The Life of Father Damien*, ill. by Raymond Lufkin, Lippincott, 1943. This tells of Father Damien's work with the lepers on the island of Molokai, for whom he gave his life. 12–14

DARROW, CLARENCE (1857–1938)
Gurko, Miriam, *Clarence Darrow*, T. Crowell, 1965. America's most famous trial lawyer's life is also the story of America's coming of age in many areas of social concern. 13–16

DEBS, EUGENE (1855–1926)

Selvin, David F., *Eugene Debs: Rebel, Labor Leader, Prophet*, Lothrop, 1966. Debs is the only man to run for President while in prison, a circumstance typical of this amazing man. 11–14

DICKENS, CHARLES (1812–1870)
Kyle, Elizabeth, *Great Ambitions: A Story of the Early Years of Charles Dickens*, Holt, 1968. This fictional biography covers Dickens' life from age twelve to twenty-seven and offers a valuable introduction to the author's books. 12–14

DICKINSON, EMILY (1830–1886)
Fisher, Aileen, and Olive Rabe, *We Dickinsons*, decorations by Ellen Raskin, Atheneum, 1965. An emotionally appealing book. The technique of having Emily's brother Austin tell the story is an interesting one for young people. 12–16

DOUGLASS, FREDERICK (1817–1895)
Bontemps, Arna, *Frederick Douglass*, ill. by Harper Johnson, Knopf, 1959. A vivid picture of the life of one of the most influential black leaders of the abolition movement. 10–14

DRAKE, FRANCIS (1540?–1596)
Syme, Ronald, *Francis Drake, Sailor of the Unknown Seas*, ill. by William Stobbs, Morrow, 1961. A highly abbreviated account of Drake's career from boyhood through the defeat of the Spanish Armada. 9–11

DREW, CHARLES (1904–1950)
Bertol, Roland, *Charles Drew*, ill. by Jo Polseno, T. Crowell, 1970. A story for younger readers about the pioneer blood researcher. 7–11

DU BOIS, WILLIAM EDWARD BURGHARDT (1868–1963)
Hamilton, Virginia, *W.E.B. Du Bois*, T. Crowell, 1972. A carefully researched and well-written biography of the eminent teacher, writer, and political leader. 12–15

DUNBAR, PAUL (1872–1906)
Gould, Jean, *That Dunbar Boy*, Dodd, 1958. A sympathetic biography of a great poet who showed the world that black people could write poetry. 12–16

EDISON, THOMAS ALVA (1847–1931)
North, Sterling, *Young Thomas Edison*, ill. with photos, decorations, diagrams, and maps by William Barss, Houghton, 1958. Warm biography of the scientific wizard. 10–14

EINSTEIN, ALBERT (1879–1955)
Levinger, Elma Ehrlich, *Albert Einstein*, Messner, 1949. A worthwhile account of the achievements and life of a great scientist despite the author's use of invented dialogue. 12–15

ELEANOR OF AQUITAINE, QUEEN OF ENGLAND (1122?–1204)
Konigsburg, Elaine, *A Proud Taste for Scarlet and Miniver*, ill. by author, Atheneum, 1973. This is highly and superbly fictionalized, it has elements of fantasy (most of the discussion takes place in Heaven), yet it is above all a delightful biography of the indomitable wife of Henry II. 11–up

FARRAGUT, DAVID GLASGOW (1801–1870)
Latham, Jean Lee, *Anchor's Aweigh: The Story of David Glasgow Farragut*, ill. by Eros Keith, Harper, 1968. The life of the great naval hero is presented with humor and compassion. 11–14

FORTEN, CHARLOTTE (1837–1914)
Longsworth, Polly, *I, Charlotte Forten, Black and Free*, T. Crowell, 1970. The daughter of a prominent black Philadelphia family describes her life during the Civil War period and Reconstruction. 11–14

FORTEN, JAMES (1766–1842)

Douty, Esther M., *Forten the Sailmaker, Pioneer Champion of Negro Rights*, ill. with photos, Rand, 1968. The life story of a man who battled for civil rights and freedom for his people. 11–14

FORTUNE, AMOS (1709?–1801)
Yates, Elizabeth, *Amos Fortune: Free Man*, ill. by Nora S. Unwin, Dutton, 1950. Moving story of a colonial Negro who spent his life buying freedom for other slaves, and eventually bought his own and died a free man. Newbery Medal. 11–14

FOSTER, STEPHEN (1826–1864)
Purdy, Claire Lee, *He Heard America Sing: The Story of Stephen Foster*, ill. by Dorothea Cooke, Messner, 1940. A sympathetic picture of America's first popular composer. 11–14

FRANCIS OF ASSISI (1182–1226)
Bulla, Clyde, *Song of St. Francis*, ill. by Valenti Angelo, T. Crowell, 1952. The appealing story of St. Francis presented in simple fashion for the youngest readers. 7–10

FRANKLIN, BENJAMIN (1706–1790)
Aulaire, Ingri and Edgar d', *Benjamin Franklin*, ill. by authors, Doubleday, 1950. 8–10
Daugherty, James, *Poor Richard*, ill. by author, Viking, 1941. A beautifully written and illustrated book which emphasizes Franklin's patriotic achievements. 12–16
Eaton, Jeanette, *That Lively Man, Ben Franklin*, ill. by Henry C. Pitz, Morrow, 1948. Franklin's many-sided career from printer to ambassador is well portrayed. 10–14

FREEMAN, ELIZABETH (?–1829)
Felton, Harold W., *Mumbet: The Story of Elizabeth Freeman*, ill. by Donn Albright, Dodd, 1970. The story of the first American black woman to win her human rights by court action. 9–12

FULLER, BUCKMINSTER (1895–    )
Rosen, Sidney, *Wizard of the Dome: R. Buckminster Fuller, Designer for the Future*, Little, 1969. Candid and vigorous, an interesting book about the inventor-architect. 12–up

GALILEI, GALILEO (1564–1642)
Rosen, Sidney, *Galileo and the Magic Numbers*, ill. by Harve Stein, Little, 1958. Absorbing accounts of Galileo's many discoveries and inventions presented in nontechnical language. 12–up

GANDHI, MOHANDAS (1869–1948)
Coolidge, Olivia, *Gandhi*, Houghton, 1971. Forthright and objective. 12–up
Eaton, Jeanette, *Gandhi: Fighter Without a Sword*, ill. by Ralph Ray, Morrow, 1950. A fine biography of the Hindu nationalist who worked for the political independence of his people. 12–15

GARIBALDI, GIUSEPPE (1807–1882)
Syme, Ronald, *Garibaldi*, ill. by William Stobbs, Morrow, 1967. A competent, easy-to-read story of the brilliant man who succeeded in freeing and uniting Italy. 9–12

GARRISON, WILLIAM LLOYD (1805–1879)
Faber, Doris, *I Will Be Heard*, ill. with portraits, Lothrop, 1970. A well-written account of Garrison's life with much attention to his work in the abolitionist movement. 10–14

GERONIMO (1829–1909)
Wyatt, Edgar, *Geronimo: The Last Apache War Chief*, ill. by Allan Houser, McGraw, 1952. Unlike most Indian chiefs, Geronimo lived a long and peaceful life

after being defeated by the whites.                10–14

GERSHWIN, GEORGE (1898–1937)
Ewen, David, *Story of George Gershwin*, ill. by Graham Bernbach, Holt, 1943. Memories of an American composer of popular music by a personal friend.        12–15

GORGAS, WILLIAM CRAWFORD (1854–1920)
Judson, Clara Ingram, *Soldier Doctor: The Story of William Gorgas*, ill. by Robert Doremus, Scribner's, 1942. A lively account of the man whose work against yellow fever made possible the building of the Panama Canal.        9–12

GRANT, ULYSSES S. (1822–1885)
Kantor, MacKinlay, *Lee and Grant at Appomattox*, ill. by Donald McKay, Random, 1950. Excellent portraits of two very different men, focusing upon the last weeks of the war and the surrender.        10–14

GRIEG, EDVARD HAGERUP (1843–1907)
Kyle, Elizabeth, *Song of the Waterfall*, Holt, 1969. The story of the composer and his wife and their musical world.        12–15

HAMILTON, ALEXANDER (1755–1804)
Lomask, Milton, *Odd Destiny: A Life of Alexander Hamilton*, Farrar, 1969. A vivid portrayal of Hamilton and his relationships with Washington, Jefferson, and Burr.        12–14

HAMILTON, ALICE
Grant, Madeleine P., *Alice Hamilton: Pioneer Doctor in Industrial Medicine*, Abelard, 1968. The inspiring story of a woman whose career encompassed both science and social reform.        12–14

HAMMARSKJÖLD, DAG HJALMER (1905–1961)
Simon, Charlie May, *Dag Hammarskjold*, Dutton, 1969. A book which offers a personalized view of the statesman through use of excerpts from his diary and speeches.        12–14

HANDY, WILLIAM CHRISTOPHER (1873–1958)
Montgomery, Elizabeth Rider, *William C. Handy; Father of the Blues*, ill. by David Hodges, Garrard, 1968. A simply written biography of the Negro composer and music publisher.        8–11

HAUTZIG, ESTHER (1930–      )
Hautzig, Esther, *The Endless Steppe: Growing Up in Siberia*, T. Crowell, 1968. A Polish-Jewish family is sent to Siberia in 1941, when Russian troops took over Vilna. Stark, gripping, and touching.        11–14

HENRY, PATRICK (1736–1799)
Campion, Nardi Reeder, *Patrick Henry: Firebrand of the Revolution*, ill. by Victor Mays, Little, 1961. A fascinating and well-documented biography that never glosses over the weaknesses of its hero.        12–up
Daugherty, Sonia, *Ten Brave Men*, Lippincott, 1951.        10–12

HOLMES, OLIVER WENDELL (1841–1935)
Judson, Clara Ingram, *Mr. Justice Holmes*, ill. by Robert Todd, Follett, 1956. A wonderfully exciting book about a great Supreme Court judge whose legal opinions were always tempered with a sense of humanity.        12–16
Meyer, Edith Patterson, *That Remarkable Man, Justice Oliver Wendell Holmes*, ill. with portraits, Little, 1967. A well-written, objective account of the life of America's great champion of freedom of expression.        13–up

HUGHES, LANGSTON (1902–1967)
Walker, Alice, *Langston Hughes, American Poet*, ill. by Don Miller, T. Crowell, 1974. A candid and sympathetic biography for younger readers.        7–9

HUTCHINSON, ANNE (1591–1643)
Crawford, Deborah, *Four Women in a Violent Time*, Crown, 1970. Anne Hutchinson, Mary Dyer, Lady Deborah Moody, and Penelope Stout were four independent, courageous women of colonial times whose paths crossed and whose stamina and bravery are beautifully described.        12–15

ISHI (1861?–1916)
Kroeber, Theodora, *Ishi; Last of His Tribe*, ill. by Ruth Robbins, Parnassus, 1964. The touching story of the last surviving member of the Yahi tribe.        12–up

JACKSON, ANDREW (1767–1845)
Foster, Genevieve, *Andrew Jackson: An Initial Biography*, ill. by author, Scribner's, 1951. This excellent biography provides insight into the character of Jackson.        8–10

JACKSON, MAHALIA (1911–1972)
Jackson, Jesse, *Make a Joyful Noise Unto the Lord!* ill. with photos, T. Crowell, 1974. A biography that really captures the vitality and dedication of the beloved gospel singer.        11–14

JEFFERSON, THOMAS (1743–1826)
Judson, Clara Ingram, *Thomas Jefferson, Champion of the People*, ill. by Robert Frankenberg, Follett, 1952.        10–14
Lisitzky, Gene, *Thomas Jefferson*, ill. by Harrie Wood, Viking, 1933.        12–16
Both titles capture the essence of this brilliant and great American.

JOAN OF ARC (1412–1431)
Fisher, Aileen, *Jeanne d'Arc*, ill. by Ati Forberg, T. Crowell, 1970. A short, beautifully illustrated and accurate account of the life of the young saint.        8–10
Paine, Albert B., *Girl in the White Armor*, Macmillan, 1964. An historically accurate yet passionate portrait of the Maid of France.        11–14

JONES, JOHN PAUL (1747–1792)
Syme, Ronald, *Captain John Paul Jones, America's Fighting Seaman*, ill. by William Stobbs, Morrow, 1968. A balanced history of the naval hero's life.        9–11

JUÁREZ, BENITO (1806–1872)
Syme, Ronald, *Juárez; The Founder of Modern Mexico*, ill. by Richard Cuffari, Morrow, 1972. Not only a good biography, this is also an excellent history of Mexico in the nineteenth century.        10–13

KELLER, HELEN ADAMS (1880–1968)
Bigland, Eileen, *Helen Keller*, ill. by Lili Cassel-Wronker, Phillips, 1967. A fine treatment of the subject's life from early childhood to old age.        12–14
Peare, Catherine Owens, *The Helen Keller Story*, T. Crowell, 1959.        11–14

KING, MARTIN LUTHER, JR. (1929–1968)
Preston, Edward, *Martin Luther King: Fighter for Freedom*, Doubleday, 1968. A simply written narrative of King's life with emphasis upon the period from 1954 until his death in 1968.        9–12

LA FLESCHE, SUSETTE (1854–1903)
Crary, Margaret, *Susette La Flesche; Voice of the Omaha Indians*, Hawthorn, 1973. As an Indian woman of her time, Susette La Flesche had no legal rights, but she fought all her life for reform and justice.        10–14

LEE, ROBERT E. (1807–1870)
Commager, Henry Steele, *America's Robert E. Lee*, ill. by Lynd Ward, Houghton, 1951. Lee is a hero all America should be proud of, and this biography shows why.        11–15

LEEUWENHOEK, ANTON VAN (1632–1723)
Payne, Alma S., *Discoverer of the Unseen World: A Biography of Antoni van Leeuwenhoek,* ill. by Donn Albright, World, 1966. Solidly researched, readable biography of the self-educated Dutchman whose work with the microscope opened up new vistas for other scientists. 11–14

LEWIS, MERIWETHER (1774–1809)
Daugherty, James, *Of Courage Undaunted,* ill. by author, Viking, 1951. One of the most exciting books in any library, this account, with its subtitle, "Across the Continent with Lewis and Clark," makes clear the courage and resourcefulness demanded of the men who explore the unknown. 10–14

LINCOLN, ABRAHAM (1809–1865)
Aulaire, Ingri and Edgar Parin d', *Abraham Lincoln,* ill. by authors, rev. ed., Doubleday, 1957. 5–9
Daugherty, James, *Abraham Lincoln,* ill. by author, Viking, 1943. 12–16
Foster, Genevieve, *Abraham Lincoln,* ill. by author, Scribner's, 1950. 8–11
Meadowcroft, Enid, *Abraham Lincoln,* ill. by Kurt Wiese, T. Crowell, 1959. 9–12
Sandburg, Carl, *Abraham Lincoln Grows Up,* ill. by James Daugherty, Harcourt, 1928. 11–14
Each of these books has its own approach to Lincoln, and the range of reading difficulty offers something for almost everyone.

LIND, JENNY (1820–1887)
Benét, Laura, *Enchanting Jenny Lind,* ill. by George G. Whitney, Dodd, 1939. The romantic and appealing story of the "Swedish Nightingale," who won the hearts of the world in the nineteenth century. 12–14

LITTLE, MALCOLM (1925–1965)
Adoff, Arnold, *Malcolm X,* ill. by John Wilson, T. Crowell, 1970. An easy-to-read account which sketches the events which influenced Malcolm X from childhood on and plainly sets forth his importance as a black leader. 8–10
Curtis, Richard, *The Life of Malcolm X,* Macrae, 1971. 11–14

LONGFELLOW, HENRY WADSWORTH (1807–1882)
Peare, Catherine Owens, *Henry Wadsworth Longfellow: His Life,* ill. by Margaret Ayer, Holt, 1953. The life of the poet who immortalized both the village blacksmith and Paul Revere. 9–12

LUTHER, MARTIN (1483–1546)
McNeer, May, and Lynd Ward, *Martin Luther,* ill. by Lynd Ward, Abingdon, 1953. Luther's fighting spirit makes his complex life both difficult and thrilling. 12–14

MARSHALL, THURGOOD (1908–     )
Fenderson, Lewis H., *Thurgood Marshall: Fighter for Justice,* ill. by Dave Hodges, McGraw, 1969. A lively narrative of Marshall's private and public life from childhood until his appointment to the Supreme Court. 8–10

MARTÍN DE PORRES, SAINT (1579–1639)
Bishop, Claire Huchet, *Martin de Porres, Hero,* ill. by Jean Charlot, Houghton, 1954. Moving story of the Peruvian mulatto boy who, despite poverty and the racial taunts of other children, grew up to be filled with love for his fellow men. 9–12

MAUD, QUEEN OF ENGLAND (1102–1167)
Trease, Geoffrey, *The Seven Queens of England,* Vanguard, 1953. 12–16

MENDEL, GREGOR (1822–1884)
Sootin, Harry, *Gregor Mendel: Father of the Science of Genetics,* Vanguard, 1958. A straightforward biography of the scientist who explained the laws of heredity. 12–16

MICHELANGELO (1475–1564)
Ripley, Elizabeth, *Michelangelo, A Biography,* ill. by Michelangelo, Walck, 1953. One of more than a dozen biographies of famous artists by this author. All are illustrated by the artist's work and represent landmarks in the artist's life or his artistic development. 12–14

MOSES (c. 1200 B.C.?)
Shippen, Katherine B., *Moses,* Harper, 1949. The story of a great leader's sense of dedication to his people and to God. 12–16

MOZART, WOLFGANG AMADEUS (1756–1791)
Komroff, Manuel, *Mozart,* ill. by Warren Chappell and by photos, Knopf, 1956. 10–14
Mirsky, Reba Paeff, *Mozart,* ill. by W. T. Mars, Follett, 1960. 9–12
Komroff's book is an outstanding example of the best in musical biography. Mirsky, while basically accurate, is more fictionalized and is for a younger audience.

MUIR, JOHN (1838–1914)
Swift, Hildegarde Hoyt, *From the Eagle's Wing: A Biography of John Muir,* ill. by Lynd Ward, Morrow, 1962. Very readable biography of the Scotch immigrant whose writings on nature helped the United States recognize the need to conserve its natural resources. 12–15

NEHRU, JAWAHARLAL (1889–1964)
Lengyel, Emil, *Jawaharlal Nehru; The Brahman from Kashmir,* Watts, 1968. A careful examination of Nehru's life from childhood to old age. Good explanations of Indian culture and customs. 12–15

NEWTON, ISAAC (1642–1727)
Tannenbaum, Beulah, and Myra Stillman, *Isaac Newton: Pioneer of Space Mathematics,* McGraw, 1959. Newton's personal life and his contributions to scientific knowledge are well combined in this science biography.

NIGHTINGALE, FLORENCE (1820–1910)
Nolan, Jeannette Covert, *Florence Nightingale,* ill. by George Avison, Messner, 1947. This warm, readable biography of the "Lady with the Lamp" stresses her work rather than her personal life. 11–14

PADEREWSKI, IGNACE (1860–1941)
Kellogg, Charlotte, *Paderewski,* Viking, 1956. An unforgettable picture of the great Polish musician and statesman. 14–16

PAINE, THOMAS (1737–1809)
Coolidge, Olivia E., *Tom Paine, Revolutionary,* Scribner's, 1969. The life and significant writings of the famous revolutionary are objectively presented in this work. 13–up
Gurko, Leo, *Tom Paine: Freedom's Apostle,* ill. by Fritz Kredel, T. Crowell, 1957. Exciting portrait of the man whose writings helped prove the power of the pen. 12–16

PANKHURST, EMMELINE (1858–1928)
Noble, Iris, *Emmeline and Her Daughters; The Pankhurst Suffragettes,* Messner, 1971. 11–15

PARACELSUS, PHILIPPUS (1493?–1541)
Rosen, Sidney, *Doctor Paracelsus,* ill. by Rafaello Busoni, Little, 1959. Excellent biography of the sixteenth-century Swiss-German physician and alchemist who

challenged the medical superstitions of his time. 12–16

PARKS, ROSA (1913–    )
Greenfield, Eloise, *Rosa Parks,* ill. by Eric Marlow, T. Crowell, 1973. A competent book about the quiet woman whose sense of justice precipitated the Montgomery bus strike.                                              7–9

PASTEUR, LOUIS (1822–1895)
Wood, Laura Newbold, *Louis Pasteur,* ill. with photos, Messner, 1948. The story of one of the world's great scientists whose experiments and research made tremendous contributions to modern medicine.              12–14

PENN, WILLIAM (1644–1718)
Gray, Elizabeth Janet, *Penn,* ill. by George Whitney, Viking, 1938.                                                  11–14

PICASSO, PABLO (1881–1973)
Greenfeld, Howard, *Pablo Picasso,* Follett, 1971. Illustrated with examples of the artist's work, this is as perceptive in revealing the man as it is knowledgeable about his role in art history.                          7–10

POCAHONTAS (1595?–1617)
Aulaire, Ingri and Edgar Parin d', *Pocahontas,* ill. by authors, Doubleday, 1949. Large, colorful pictures make this story of the Indian maid who saved John Smith's life useful for reading aloud to young children.       5–9

POTTER, BEATRIX (1866–1943)
Aldis, Dorothy, *Nothing Is Impossible, the Story of Beatrix Potter,* ill. by Richard Cuffari, Atheneum, 1969. Depicts the events in the author's life and the atmosphere of her family in an excellent way.                8–12

REVERE, PAUL (1735–1818)
Forbes, Esther, *America's Paul Revere,* ill. by Lynd Ward, Houghton, 1946.                                      8–11

ROBESON, PAUL (1898–    )
Hamilton, Virginia, *Paul Robeson; The Life and Times of a Free Black Man,* ill. with photos, Harper, 1974. A perceptive, detailed biography that also gives a good picture of the period and of the struggles of the black performer.                                              12–up

ROBINSON, JACK (1919–1972)
Rudeen, Kenneth, *Jackie Robinson,* ill. by Richard Cuffari, T. Crowell, 1971. A balanced treatment of Robinson's baseball career is brisk and candid.    7–9

ROOSEVELT, ANNA ELEANOR (1884–1962)
Goodsell, Jane, *Eleanor Roosevelt,* ill. by Wendel Minor, T. Crowell, 1970. An easy-to-read story of the courageous humanitarian woman who became a legend in her own lifetime.                                    7–11

ROOSEVELT, FRANKLIN D. (1882–1945)
Johnson, Gerald White, *Franklin Delano Roosevelt: Portrait of a Great Man,* ill. by Leonard E. Fisher, Morrow, 1967. An objective view of Roosevelt and his role in domestic and world affairs.                    11–14
Peare, Catherine Owens, *The FDR Story,* T. Crowell, 1962. A remarkably perceptive biography of Roosevelt as an individual and as a political figure.           12–15

ROOSEVELT, THEODORE (1858–1919)
Foster, Genevieve, *Theodore Roosevelt,* ill. by author, Scribner's, 1954. Simply written story of the weakling who grew up to lead his country in its early days as a world force.                                              8–12
Judson, Clara Ingram, *Theodore Roosevelt, Fighting Patriot,* ill. by Robert Frankenberg, Follett, 1953. A work which discusses Roosevelt's work for conservation of natural resources as well as his political and military achievements.                                     12–up
Monjo, Ferdinand, *The One Bad Thing About Father,*

ill. by Rocco Negri, Harper, 1970.                    7–8

SALOMON, HAYM (1740?–1785)
Fast, Howard, *Haym Salomon: Son of Liberty,* ill. by Eric M. Simon, Messner, 1941. A moving story of the Polish immigrant who helped finance the American Revolution, using his own fortune and cajoling others into giving more money than they wanted to.    12–16

SCHWEITZER, ALBERT (1875–1965)
Manton, Jo, *The Story of Albert Schweitzer,* ill. by Astrid Walfard, Abelard, 1955. Fine biography of the man who gave up a comfortable life to work as a missionary in Africa.                                      12–16

SCOTT, SIR WALTER (1771–1832)
Gray, Elizabeth Janet, *Young Walter Scott,* Viking, 1935. Even readers who are bored by Scott's novels will enjoy this portrait of the author.                    12–15

SHACKLETON, ERNEST HENRY (1874–1922)
Bixby, William, *The Impossible Journey of Sir Ernest Shackleton,* Little, 1960. A dramatic and informative account of Shackleton's trans-Antarctic expedition, 1914–1917.                                            11–13

SINGER, ISAAC BASHEVIS (1904–    )
Singer, Isaac Bashevis, *A Day of Pleasure: Stories of a Boy Growing Up in Warsaw,* ill. with photos, Farrar, 1969. Intimate glimpses of the author's boyhood in the Warsaw ghetto before the first World War. National Book Award.                                          11–15

SMITH, ELISABETH (1898–1937)
Moore, Carman, *Somebody's Angel Child; The Story of Bessie Smith,* T. Crowell, 1970. The sad and dramatic life of the great blues singer is told with skill and candor.                                            11–14

SQUANTO (?–1622)
Bulla, Clyde R., *Squanto, Friend of the Pilgrims,* ill. by Peter Burchard, T. Crowell, 1954. Easy-to-read story of the Wampanoag Indian who gave aid to the Plymouth colonists.                                          8–10

STEINMETZ, CHARLES (1865–1923)
Lavine, Sigmund, *Steinmetz, Maker of Lightning,* ill. with photos, Dodd, 1955. A happy combination of good characterization and scientific information.          12–14

STEVENSON, ROBERT LOUIS (1850–1894)
Proudfit, Isabel, *Treasure Hunter: The Story of Robert Louis Stevenson,* ill. by Hardie Gramatky, Messner, 1939. A full-length biography of a favorite children's author.                                              12–16

SUN YAT-SEN (1866–1925)
Spencer, Cornelia, *Sun Yat-sen: Founder of the Chinese Republic,* ill. with photos, Day, 1967. A well-documented telling of the sources of the Chinese revolutionary movement and Sun's role within it.              12–14

TALLCHIEF, MARIA (1925–    )
Tobias, Tobi, *Maria Tallchief,* ill. by Michael Hampshire, T. Crowell, 1970. Of Osage and Scots-Irish heritage, Maria Tallchief became one of our country's outstanding prima ballerinas.                              7–9

TERESHKOVA, VALENTINA (1937–    )
Sharpe, Mitchell, *"It Is I, Sea Gull," Valentina Tereshkova, First Woman in Space,* ill. with photos, T. Crowell, 1975. Despite weaknesses of style, this is a fascinating account of the first woman cosmonaut
                                                        11–15

THOREAU, HENRY DAVID (1817–1862)
North, Sterling, *Thoreau of Walden Pond,* ill. by Harve Stein, Houghton, 1959. A biography which begins with the boyhood of the great independent thinker and ends

with his death. 12–15

TOUSSAINT L'OUVERTURE (1743–1803)

Syme, Ronald, *Toussaint the Black Liberator*, ill. by William Stobbs, Morrow, 1971. An interesting biography that is candid and authoritative. 10–13

TRUMAN, HARRY S. (1884–1972)

Hayman, LeRoy, *Harry S. Truman; A Biography*, ill. with photos, T. Crowell, 1969. A history of Truman's life, personal and public, from childhood until the end of his presidency. 10–14

TRUTH, SOJOURNER (1797?–1883)

Barnard, Jacqueline, *Journey Toward Freedom*, ill. with photos and engravings, Norton, 1967. Though born in slavery, Sojourner Truth earned her freedom and went on to champion the rights of labor, women, and Blacks. 12–16

TUBMAN, HARRIET ROSS (1821?–1913)

Epstein, Samuel and Beryl, *Harriet Tubman, Guide to Freedom*, ill. by Paul Frame, Garrard, 1968. An easy-to-read episodic story of the life of the dauntless woman who guided hundreds of her fellow slaves to freedom. 8–10

Petry, Ann, *Harriet Tubman, Conductor on the Underground Railroad*, T. Crowell, 1955. 12–16

TURNER, NAT (1800–1831)

Griffin, Judith Berry, *Nat Turner*, ill. by Leo Carty, Coward, 1970. A brief but dignified biography of the slave who led a rebellion. 8–10

TWAIN, MARK (1835–1910)

Eaton, Jeannette, *America's Own Mark Twain*, ill. by Leonard Everett Fisher, Morrow, 1958. 10–13

VERNE, JULES (1828–1905)

Freedman, Russell, *Jules Verne*, ill. with old photos and drawings, Holiday, 1965. Well-written account of the first genuine science-fiction author. 12–16

VINCI, LEONARDO DA (1452–1519)

Hahn, Emily, *Leonardo da Vinci*, ill. by Mimi Korach, Random, 1956. 10–13

Ripley, Elizabeth, *Leonardo da Vinci, A Biography*, ill. by Leonardo, Walck, 1952. 12–14

These three books taken together make a beginning at capturing the genius of Leonardo. Ripley's has more art criticism than the others.

WALD, LILLIAN (1867–1940)

Block, Irvin, *Neighbor to the World; The Story of Lillian Wald*, ill. with photos, T. Crowell, 1969. An account of the remarkable woman who introduced the concept of public nursing. 10–14

WASHINGTON, GEORGE (1732–1799)

Aulaire, Ingri and Edgar Parin d', *George Washington*, ill. by authors, Doubleday, 1936. 5–9

Eaton, Jeanette, *Leader by Destiny*, ill. by Jack Manley Rosé, Harcourt, 1938. 12–16

Judson, Clara Ingram, *George Washington, Leader of the People*, ill. by Robert Frankenberg, Follett, 1951. The nation's first President emerges as very human in these excellent books. 10–12

WHITMAN, NARCISSA (1808–1847)

Eaton, Jeannette, *Narcissa Whitman: Pioneer of Oregon*, ill. by Woodi Ishmael, Harcourt, 1941. Inspiring story of a great pioneer woman, based on early letters and memoirs. 12–15

WHITMAN, WALT (1819–1892)

Stoutenberg, Adrien, and Laura N. Baker, *Listen America*, Scribner's, 1968. An objective view of the life of one of America's greatest poets. Many of his poems

are included. 13–16

WILDER, LAURA INGALLS (1867–1957)

Wilder, Laura Ingalls, *West from Home; Letters of Laura Ingalls Wilder, San Francisco, 1915*, ed. by Roger Lea Macbride, Harper, 1974. A vivid evocation of place and period as well as a delightfully intimate picture of the author. 11–up

WILLIAM THE CONQUEROR (1027–1087)

Costain, Thomas B., *William the Conqueror*, ill. by Jack Coggins, Random, 1959. An excellent appraisal of William and of the events which preceded and followed his conquest of Britain. 12–15

WILLIAMS, ROGER (1603?–1683)

Eaton, Jeanette, *Lone Journey*, ill. by Woodi Ishmael, Harcourt, 1944. Williams' fight for religious freedom remains one of the stirring moments in early American history. 12–15

WILSON, WOODROW (1856–1924)

Peare, Catherine Owens, *The Woodrow Wilson Story: An Idealist in Politics*, T. Crowell, 1963. Objective but sympathetic biography of the college president who made good in politics. 12–16

WREN, SIR CHRISTOPHER (1632–1723)

Weir, Rosemary, *The Man Who Built a City; A Life of Sir Christopher Wren*, Farrar, 1971. Well-researched, solidly written, and informative. 11–14

WRIGHT, FRANCES (1795–1852)

Stiller, Richard, *Commune on the Frontier; The Story of Frances Wright*, ill. with photos, T. Crowell, 1972. The unusual story of a wealthy young Scotswoman who was an atheist, an abolitionist, and founder of a commune in Tennessee. 12–14

WRIGHT, WILBUR (1867–1912) and ORVILLE (1871–1948)

Glines, Carroll V., *The Wright Brothers, Pioneers of Power Flight*, Watts, 1968. A factual recounting of the Wrights' experiments and the reaction of the public to their work. 11–14

ZENGER, PETER (1697–1746)

Galt, Tom, *Peter Zenger: Fighter for Freedom*, ill. by Ralph Ray, T. Crowell, 1951. Freedom of the press in America begins with Peter Zenger, who was a hero almost by accident. 11–14

# INFORMATIONAL BOOKS

ABERNATHY, ROBERT G., *Introduction to Tomorrow: The United States and the Wider World, 1945–1965*, Harcourt, 1966. A lucid survey of events and ideas of twenty years of crisis and change. Biographies of central historical figures are woven into the text. 12–16

ADKINS, JAN, *The Craft of Sail*, ill. by author, Walker, 1973. Useful for the would-be sailor, a book that is detailed in explanation and illustration. 11–up

*How a House Happens*, ill. by author, Walker, 1972. Describes the process from consultation to completion. 10–12

ADLER, IRVING, *The Sun and Its Family*, rev. ed., ill. by Ruth Adler, Day, 1969. A clear presentation of the history of astronomical knowledge. A few chapters contain new scientific knowledge gained in the ten years since the first publication. 10–13

*Time in Your Life*, rev. ed., ill. by Ruth Adler, Day, 1969. A clear and accurate explanation of the development of clocks, watches, and calendars, with some discussion of nature's rhythms. 10–14

*The Tools of Science*, ill. by Ruth Adler, Day, 1958. A

discussion of the tools, apparatus, and instruments used by scientists to observe, measure, or manipulate parts of the universe and its elements. 11–14

ADRIAN, MARY, *A Day and a Night in a Forest*, ill. by Genevieve Vaughan-Jackson, Hastings, 1967. A book which focuses upon the balance of nature. The ways in which forest creatures pursue their separate yet interdependent ways is shown. 7–9

*Fiddler Crab*, ill. by Jean Martinez, Holiday, 1953. The life story of a crab shown in illustration in proportion to other beach life. Scale is stated when such proportion is not observed. Text is factual and direct, but not oversimplified or monotonous. 9–12

ALIKI, *Fossils Tell of Long Ago*, ill. by author, T. Crowell, 1972. Discusses formation of fossils and how to find them. 7–8

ANDREWS, ROY CHAPMAN, *Exploring with Andrews*, Putnam, 1938. Thirteen selections for young readers drawn from three of the great explorer's adult books: *On the Trail of Ancient Man, Ends of the Earth*, and *This Business of Exploring*. 12–up

*In the Days of the Dinosaurs*, ill. by Jean Zallinger, Random, 1959. The author, former director of the American Museum of Natural History, discusses authoritatively and simply the types of dinosaurs and their world and tells about a fossil hunt he led in Asia. 8–10

ASIMOV, ISAAC, *ABC's of the Earth*, Walker, 1971. Photographs and text are nicely integrated in an alphabetical arrangement of brief topics. 8–10

*Building Blocks of the Universe*, Abelard, 1957. In his usual entertaining, readable style, the author discusses the chemical elements out of which the universe is built—their discovery and naming, their uses, their place in the periodic table. 12–16

*Great Ideas of Science*, ill. by Lee Ames, Houghton, 1969. 11–14

*The Shaping of England*, ill., Houghton, 1969. Excitingly written and lucidly organized, this history begins with tribal England and ends with the signing of the Magna Charta. 13–up

BAITY, ELIZABETH C., *America Before Man*, ill. by C. B. Falls, Viking, 1953. The evolution of life on this continent from the earliest single-cell forms to the primitive people who first came here. A section of suggested readings is included. 12–16

*Americans Before Columbus*, rev. ed., ill. by C. B. Falls, Viking, 1961. The story of the Indians of North, Central, and South America from the last ice age to the time of Columbus. Includes thirty-two pages of photographs. 11–16

BAKER, LAURA NELSON, *A Tree Called Moses*, ill. by Penelope Naylor, Atheneum, 1966. The Moses tree is an actual tree, estimated to be 2500 years old, growing near Sequoia National Forest in California. A vivid recounting of all its struggles to live. 9–12

BAKER, LIVA, *World Faiths, A Story of Religion*, ill. with photos and art reproductions, Abelard, 1966. A highly interesting work which treats major world religions covering their beliefs, sacraments, holidays, history, scriptures, and artistic expressions. 12–16

BARR, GEORGE, *Fun and Tricks for Young Scientists*, ill. by Mildred Waltrip, McGraw, 1968. Clear instructions for performing a variety of safe tricks based on scientific principles. Included are riddles, puzzles, and jokes. Readily available materials. 9–12

BARTH, EDNA, *Lilies, Rabbits, and Painted Eggs; The Story of the Easter Symbols*, ill. by Ursula Arndt, Seabury, 1970. Describes rites, customs, and symbols. 8–10

BAUMANN, HANS, *The Caves of the Great Hunters*, tr. by Isabel and Florence McHugh, ill., Pantheon, 1954. Four boys and their dog discover the Lascaux cave paintings and are informed by Abbé Breuil, a famous archaeologist, of the historical significance of their discovery. Many of the illustrations are reproductions of the cave paintings. 9–11

*Lion Gate and Labyrinth*, tr. by Stella Humphries, ill., Pantheon, 1967. The archaeological discoveries of Troy, Crete, and Mycenae are described along with some of the history, myths, and legends of those civilizations. Includes color plates of archaeological sites and finds. 12–15

BEALER, ALEX, *Only the Names Remain; The Cherokees and the Trail of Tears*, ill. by William Bock, Little, 1972. Interesting, accurate, and poignant. 9–11

BEELER, NELSON F., *Experiments in Sound*, ill. by George Giusti, T. Crowell, 1961. This study of sound approaches its subject in a scientific manner by providing numerous simple experiments to accompany the informal, readable text. 8–12

BELL, THELMA HARRINGTON, and CORYDON BELL, *The Riddle of Time*, ill. by Corydon Bell, Viking, 1963. The question of what time is seems at first simple but, as the authors show, time is a difficult concept. This book deals with scientists' efforts to theorize about it, from Aristotle to Einstein, and discusses efforts to measure time. 12–16

BENDICK, JEANNE, *Why Can't I?* ill. by author, McGraw, 1969. Children learn about the reasons why they cannot do some of the things animals can do. 5–7

*The Wind*, ill. by author, Rand, 1964. Offers a simple explanation of the nature and measurement of wind, windstorms, and the influence of wind upon weather. Also includes superstitions, myths, and sayings about the wind. 7–10

BERGAUST, ERIK, and WILLIAM O. FOSS, *Oceanographers in Action*, ill., Putnam, 1968. A brief survey of research and study projects and an outline of requisites for a career in oceanography. 10–14

BILLINGS, HENRY, *All Down the Valley*, ill. by author, Viking, 1953. A fascinating blend of engineering, history, economics, and sociology awaits the reader in this story of the TVA. 12–up

*Bridges*, ill. by author, Viking, 1956. From covered bridges to arches of steel and concrete. Clear diagrams show how bridges do their work. 12–15

BILLINGTON, ELIZABETH T., *Understanding Ecology*, ill. by Robert Galster, Warne, 1968. An introduction to ecology that includes practical projects for young people to sharpen their awareness of nature's relationships. 12–up

BLEEKER, SONIA, *The Pygmies: Africans of the Congo Forest*, ill. by Edith G. Singer, Morrow, 1968. A sympathetic account of the tribal culture and society of the Pygmies. This author has written a series of books about American Indian and African tribes. 9–12

BLOUGH, GLENN, *Discovering Insects*, ill. by Jeanne Bendick, McGraw, 1967. Good basic introduction to insects, well illustrated. Suggests many ways young readers can study and collect insects themselves. 6–9

*The Tree on the Road to Turntown*, ill. by Jeanne Bendick, McGraw, 1953. The life story of a tree is related to the lives of the organisms which in their turn affect the life of the tree. 6–9

BONTEMPS, ARNA, *Story of the Negro*, rev. ed., ill. by Raymond Lufkin, Knopf, 1960. This very readably written history tells the story of the earliest tribes in Africa, the crossing of slave ships to the new world, the early struggles for freedom and those of the post-Civil War period up to the emergence of Martin Luther King in Montgomery. 10–13

BOVA, BENJAMIN, *Workshops in Space*, Dutton, 1974. 11–14

BRADFORD, WILLIAM, and EDWARD WINSLOW, *Pilgrim Courage*, adapted and ed. by E. Brooks Smith and Robert Meredith, ill. by Leonard Everett Fisher, Little, 1962. William Bradford's history, for which he used his own journal and that of Edward Winslow, has been edited to a dramatic, colorful, and often humorous account of the Pilgrims' difficulties and adventures. 10–up

BRANDHORST, CARL T., and ROBERT SYLVESTER, *The Tale of Whitefoot*, ill. by Grambs Miller, Simon, 1968. Nature's unending cycle of life, death, and renewed life is presented in this story of a whitefooted mouse. A fine blend of sensitive writing and scientific observation. 8–12

BRANLEY, FRANKLIN M., *Eclipse: Darkness in Daytime*, ill. by Donald Crews, T. Crowell, 1973. Explains lucidly the phenomenon of the total solar eclipse. 7–9

*Experiments in Sky Watching*, ill. by Helmut K. Wimmer, T. Crowell, 1959. The author provides clear directions for constructing some simple pieces of apparatus and then gives directions for using them to locate and study heavenly bodies. 12–14

*The Mystery of Stonehenge*, ill. by Victor G. Ambrus, T. Crowell, 1969. "Its mysteries may be locked forever within the silent stones" is the concluding sentence in this description of the efforts of anthropologists, engineers, historians, and astronomers to solve the mystery that, thus far, is still unsolved. Illustrations provide beauty as well as information. 10–12

BRENNER, BARBARA, *A Snake-Lover's Diary*, ill., Young Scott, 1970. A great deal of scientific information is woven into this account of a young boy and his reptile collection. 8–12

BRIDGES, WILLIAM, *The Bronx Zoo Book of Wild Animals, A Guide to Mammals, Birds, Reptiles and Amphibians of the World*, ill. with photos, Golden Pr., 1968. Begun as a guidebook of the Bronx Zoo, this book became a reference book on 2000 mammals, birds, reptiles, and amphibians. Illustrations are photographs, in black and white as well as color. Excellent index. 10–14

BRONOWSKI, J., and MILLICENT E. SELSAM, *Biography of an Atom*, ill. by Weimar Pursell and with photos, Harper, 1965. The life of a carbon atom is described from its explosive birth in a star, billions of years ago, until it becomes part of the earth and finally part of a human being. 8–12

BRONSON, WILFRID, *Beetles*, ill. by author, Harcourt, 1963. A thorough introduction to the subject of beetles (nearly a third of a million are known!) which describes the varieties, how they are formed and work. Information on collecting and preserving specimens is included. 10–14

BROWN, LLOYD ARNOLD, *Map Making: The Art That Became a Science*, ill. by Aldren A. Watson, Little, 1960. The art by which ancient people mapped discoveries or conjectures about the world and the advances in map making over the centuries. 12–16

BUEHR, WALTER, *Automobiles, Past and Present*, ill. by author, Morrow, 1968. Covers the history of the automobile in the United States, basic mechanical principles, assembly line production, and the importance of experimental autos. 9–12

*Strange Craft*, ill. by author, Norton, 1962. Unusual ships designed over the centuries. 8–12

BUELL, HAL, *The World of Red China*, ill. with photos, Dodd, 1967. A description of life in mainland China today with a brief overview of Chinese history. 9–12

BUFF, MARY and CONRAD, *The Colorado: River of Mystery*, ill. by Conrad Buff, Ritchie, 1968. The geological and human history of the Colorado River with a description of Powell's exploration. 8–10

*Elf Owl*, ill. by Conrad Buff, Viking, 1958. Drama of desert life as seen by an elf owl who lives in a saguaro cactus. The illustrations and text give the story a poetic quality. 6–8

BULLA, CLYDE ROBERT, *Flowerpot Gardens*, ill. by Henry Evans, T. Crowell, 1967. Easy instructions for starting and growing twenty common plants indoors. 8–10

BURTON, VIRGINIA LEE, *Life Story*, ill. by author, Houghton, 1962. The evolution of the earth is presented in lucid text and unusual format. Excellent for reading aloud. 8–10

CARSON, RACHEL, *The Sea Around Us*, adapted by Anne Terry White, Golden Pr., 1958. This young reader's edition lacks some of the beauty of the original work but retains the fascinating aspects of the story of the sea. 12–16

CARTEY, WILFRED, *The West Indies; Islands in the Sun*, ill. with photos, Nelson, 1967. This book describes the geography, history, and discovery of the Caribbean Islands. The author has a warm appreciation for the islands' beauty and diverse peoples. 12–up

CHARLIP REMY, MARY BETH, and GEORGE ANCONA, *Handtalk; An ABC of Finger Spelling & Sign Language*, Parents, 1974. Superb photographs and a minimum of text show the signs for words and letters; an adventure for the child who hears, a necessity for the child who doesn't. 8–up

CHASE, ALICE ELIZABETH, *Famous Paintings: An Introduction to Art*, rev. ed., ill., Platt, 1962. Almost 200 pictures, some in full color, of all periods and styles provide an introduction to art appreciation. The author discusses all the examples and, although the text is brief, gives information on techniques, historical periods and styles, and the artists themselves. 8–up

*Looking at Art*, ill., T. Crowell, 1966. How artists throughout the centuries have looked at the world around them and pictured it. The author takes several aspects of the artist's craft, such as perspective, and shows how each has been used in different times and cultures. 10–14

CHUBB, THOMAS CALDECOTT, *The Byzantines*, ill. by Richard M. Powers, World, 1959. An absorbing account of the Byzantine Empire from about 300 A.D. to 1500. The colorful detail brings this history to life. Included is a chronological chart that correlates events in the Byzantine Empire and the rest of the world. 12–up

CLARK, ANN NOLAN, *Along Sandy Trails*, photos by Alfred A. Cohn, Viking, 1969. A small Indian girl walks across the desert as this author's poetic prose and Alfred Cohn's incomparable color photographs inform the reader of desert life. A glossary identifies the eleven desert plants pictured. 7–9

CLARKE, ARTHUR C., *The Challenge of the Sea*, ill. by Alex Schomburg, Holt, 1960. An exciting book about resources of the sea, their exploration, and their possible future uses as mineral and food sources. 12–up

CLARKE, CLORINDA, *The American Revolution 1775–83, a British View*, ill. by H. Toothill and H. S. Whithorne, McGraw, 1967. 10–14

CLEMONS, ELIZABETH, *Shells Are Where You Find Them*, ill. by Joe Gault, Knopf, 1960. A simple identification book of the commonest shells on our ocean beaches gives the areas where the shells can be found and the scientific names as well as the common ones. Advice on how to clean, catalog, and mount them. 8–11
*Waves, Tides and Currents*, ill., Knopf, 1967. The author acknowledges much expert help on this explanation of the causes, characteristics, and uses of waves, tides, and currents. Photographs, diagrams, charts, glossary, bibliography, and index facilitate use as a reference book. 9–11

CLYMER, ELEANOR, *The Second Greatest Invention: Search for the First Farmers*, ill. by Lili Réthi, Holt, 1969. This account of archaeologists' search for the first farmers is distinguished for both its writing and its illustration. Concluding chapters discuss today's food production problems. 10–13

COHEN, ROBERT, *The Color of Man*, ill. with photos by Ken Heyman, Random, 1968. A survey of the facts known about skin color and the development of prejudice. The need for racial understanding is stressed. Magnificent photos. 10–12

COIT, MARGARET L., *The Fight for Union*, ill., Houghton, 1961. A vivid story of the heroes who tried to avert the Civil War. 12–up

COLMAN, HILA, *Making Movies; Student Films to Features*, ill. by George Guzzi, World, 1969. Career-oriented, this gives a broad picture of opportunities in the field. 12–15

CONKLIN, GLADYS, *The Bug Club Book: A Handbook for Young Bug Collectors*, ill. by Girard Goodenow, Holiday, 1966. In a chatty, informal style the author gives general information and activities which are appropriate for the solitary collector as well as for groups. Tells how to organize a bug club. 8–12

COOLIDGE, OLIVIA, *The Golden Days of Greece*, ill. by Enrico Arno, T. Crowell, 1968. An authority on the Egyptian, Greek, and Roman worlds, this author has written here a simplified version of her earlier *Men of Athens*. In the simplifying, however, she has not sacrificed accuracy, nor does she write down to the reader. 9–11

COOMBS, CHARLES, *Be a Winner in Baseball*, Morrow, 1973. Lively style, good coverage, sensible advice. 10–12
*Cleared for Takeoff; Behind the Scenes at an Airport*, ill. with photos, Morrow, 1969. Description of the operation and problems of the three busiest U.S. airports (Los Angeles, Chicago, and Kennedy in New York) with a look to the future. 11–14
*Spacetrack, Watchdog of the Skies*, ill. with photos and diagrams, Morrow, 1969. Since humans are cluttering space with an average of six objects a week put into orbit, *Spacetrack* tells the story of attempts to keep track of this debris. 11–14

COOPER, ELIZABETH, *Science in Your Own Back Yard*, ill. by author, Harcourt, 1958. No one could resist becoming a "scientist" after reading this book. 4–6

COSGRAVE, JOHN O'HARA, *America Sails the Seas*, ill., Houghton, 1962. American ships from the Indian canoe to the Polaris submarine are described; over 200 ships are pictured; and well-labeled diagrams help explain the parts and construction of ships. 9–13

COSGROVE, MARGARET, *A Is for Anatomy*, ill. by author, Dodd, 1965. Focus is upon the human body as a "machine" perfectly adapted for the tasks it must perform. 10–up
*Bone for Bone*, ill. by author, Dodd, 1968. This well-illustrated introduction to comparative anatomy explores relationships in three ways: comparison of today's vertebrates, study of fossils of yesterday, and study of embryos. 10–14
*Eggs—and What Happens Inside Them*, ill. by author, Dodd, 1966. The complicated subject of embryology is explained in clear text and detailed drawings. Different types of eggs are discussed and scientific methods of investigation are explained. 8–11

COTTRELL, LEONARD, *Crete: Island of Mystery*, ill. by W. T. Mars, Prentice, 1965. The account by a distinguished British archaeologist of this early Greek civilization gives also an excellent picture of the workings of archaeological sciences. 12–14
*Digs and Diggers: A Book of World Archaeology*, ill. with photos, World, 1964. This book ranges from European prehistory to the great cultures of pre-Columbian America, from the Middle East and Egypt to China and India. The author is well known for his work in this field and has written a comprehensive introduction to archaeology. 12–up

COY, HAROLD, *The Americans*, ill. by William Moyers, Little, 1958. A breezily written history of the United States telling about the beginnings of "democracy, ice cream, free schools, railroads, skyscrapers, bathrooms, automobiles, movies, airplanes, social security, penicillin, and atomic energy." A bibliography for each chapter and an extensive index make this a handy reference book. 11–14

CZAJA, PAUL, *Writing with Light; A Simple Workshop in Basic Photography*, Chatham/Viking, 1973. There's information about a camera, instructions for making pictures without one, and an encouragement of observation and imagination. 11–up

DALGLIESH, ALICE, *The Thanksgiving Story*, ill. by Helen Sewell, Scribner's, 1954. A simple telling for young readers of the founding of Plymouth and the celebration of the first Thanksgiving. 6–8

DARLING, LOUIS, *The Gull's Way*, ill. with photos, Morrow, 1965. The author gives a sensitive report on a summer's observations of herring gulls on a Maine island. 9–12
*Kangaroos and Other Animals with Pockets*, ill., Morrow, 1958. The evolution of the unusual marsupial mammals and their isolation in Australia are explained. 8–10

DARWIN, CHARLES, *The Voyage of the Beagle*, abr. by Millicent E. Selsam, ill. by Anthony Ravielli, Harper, 1959. Each chapter of this excellent abridgement has an introduction that clarifies the following material and that helps tie together the text preceding and following. Included are biographical information and suggestions for further reading. 12–up

DAUGHERTY, JAMES, *Of Courage Undaunted: Across the Continent with Lewis and Clark*, ill. by author, Viking, 1951. A spirited account of the Lewis and Clark expedition that is excellent for reading aloud. 11–13

DAY, BETH, and DR. MARGARET LILEY, *The Secret World of the Baby*, ill. with photos, Random, 1968. Factual, simple, effective account of the baby's growth from conception through about the first year. 10–12

DE BORHEGYI, SUZANNE, *Ships, Shoals and Amphoras; the Story of Underwater Archaeology*, ill. by Alex Schomburg, Holt, 1961. The preparations for an underwater exploration are described, as are famous underwater archaeological finds around the world. 12–16

DENNY, NORMAN, and JOSEPHINE FILMER-SANKEY, *The Bayeux Tapestry; the Story of the Norman Conquest: 1066*, ill., Atheneum, 1966. A great art masterpiece, in color, section by section, with a brief text that tells what is happening in each. Explanation, speculation, and commentary in smaller print accompany each picture and give a good notion of the process of historical interpretation. 10–13

DIETZ, BETTY W., and MICHAEL B. OLATUNJI, *Musical Instruments of Africa: Their Nature, Use, and Place in the Life of a Deeply Musical People*, ill. by Richard M. Powers and with photos, Day, 1965. The vital significance of music in African life is emphasized in this book about the musical instruments, how they are made and how they are played. Includes music of African songs and a record of examples of music. 10–12

DOWNER, MARION, *Roofs over America*, ill. with photos, Lothrop, 1967. Two or three paragraphs on each page, accompanied by full-page photographs, introduce thirty-two roofs: saddle, gambrel, overhang, gabled, dormer, paperfold, etc. No other technical vocabulary is used in this unified treatment of American architecture from the Plymouth Colony to the present. 10–14
*The Story of Design*, ill. with photos, Lothrop, 1963. The instinct of design has dominated human life since primitive time. Sensitive text and numerous fine photographs illustrate the use of design. 10–14

DUGGAN, ALFRED, *Growing Up in 13th Century England*, ill. by C. Walter Hodges, Pantheon, 1962. A very readable account of what it was like in thirteenth-century England as the child of an earl, of a country knight, of a peasant, of a rich merchant, and of a craftsman. 11–14

EARLE, OLIVE, *Praying Mantis*, ill. by author, Morrow, 1969. The life cycle of the praying mantis is described in detail carefully delineated by words and illustration. Anecdotes about the author's own pet mantis add interest to this careful scientific description. 6–10
*The Strangler Fig and Other Strange Plants*, ill. by author, Morrow, 1967. A simply written discussion of such parasites, epiphytes, and saprophytes as Spanish moss, orchids, mistletoe, and mushrooms. Excellent drawings and large print make this volume attractive for younger readers. 9–11

ERDOES, RICHARD, *The Sun Dance People*, ill. by author, Knopf, 1972. A sympathetic overview of the Plains Indians, their history and way of life. 11–up

ESKENAZI, GERALD, *Hockey*, ill. by photos, Grosset, 1973. Despite the lack of index, this is a survey superior to most, comprehensive but informally written. 11–14

EVANS, EVA KNOX, *People Are Important*, ill. by Vana Earle, Capitol, 1951. The differences among the people of the world are described in simple text that shows how a person is related to one's culture. 5–8

FAIRSERVIS, WALTER A., JR., *India*, ill. by Richard M. Powers, World, 1961. This well-written introduction to a complex subcontinent concentrates on the historical forces that have shaped it. 12–16

FENNER, CAROL, *Gorilla Gorilla*, ill. by Symeon Shimin, Random, 1973. Accurate and straightforward, a description of a gorilla in the wild and in captivity. 8–10

FISHER, AILEEN, *Valley of the Smallest; the Life Story of a Shrew*, ill. by Jean Zallinger, T. Crowell, 1966. A dramatic, beautifully illustrated story of this tiny creature. We learn about some of the other animals that inhabit its world and how all contribute to a larger natural plan. 10–13

FISHER, LEONARD EVERETT, *The Potters*, ill. by author, Watts, 1969 (Author's Colonial American Craftsmen series). A brief history of pottery making in colonial times, along with the author's unique combination of text and simply detailed illustration to describe the potters' craft. Includes index and listing of colonial American potters and potteries of the seventeenth and eighteenth centuries. 9–11

FLANAGAN, GERALDINE LUX, *Window into an Egg*, ill. with photos, Young Scott, 1969. A clearly written, detailed account of the development of a chicken within its egg from fertilization to the twenty-first day when it breaks out. 10–13

FOSTER, GENEVIEVE, *Birthdays of Freedom: America's Heritage from the Ancient World*, 2 vols., ill. by author, Scribner's, 1952 and 1957. Great historical events in man's struggle for freedom, from prehistoric times to July 4, 1776. 12–15
*George Washington's World*, ill. by author. Scribner's, 1941. 10–13
*The World of Columbus and Sons*, ill. by author, Scribner's, 1965. The world of Columbus is portrayed in a series of episodes that give a broad picture of the important people and events of that time. Very informative. The author has written a book for younger readers, *Year of Columbus: 1492* (1969). 12–15

FREEMAN, MAE BLACKER, *Finding Out About the Past*, ill. with photos, Random, 1967. An excellent introduction to archaeology which shows how this study is conducted and how it helps us learn about the people of the past. 7–10

FROMAN, ROBERT, *The Many Human Senses*, ill. by Feodor Rimsky, Little, 1966. Basic information, clearly written, on the traditional five senses and other obscure senses, such as ESP. Up-to-date scientific research in different areas is discussed. 10–14

GALLANT, ROY A., *Exploring the Universe*, rev. ed., ill. by Lowell Hess, Doubleday, 1968. One of the best introductions to astronomy, this book explains what scientists believe were the origins of the stars, the sun, and the planets, provides a brief history of the development of astronomy, and discusses many astronomical terms and phenomena. Helpful illustrations. 10–14
*Man Must Speak; The Story of Language and How We Use It*, ill., Random, 1969. Beginning with a discussion of what has been learned about animal language, the author goes on to describe theories about the origin and development of human language and the later development of writing. 12–up

GEKIERE, MADELEINE, *Who Gave Us . . . Peacocks? Planes? & Ferris Wheels?* ill. by author, Pantheon, 1953. International interdependence is introduced in this original picture book. 5–8

GEORGE, JEAN CRAIGHEAD, *Spring Comes to the Ocean*, ill. by John Wilson, T. Crowell, 1965. Spring comes as emphatically to the ocean as it does to the land, and this book poetically describes the changes that come to the animal and plant life. 12–15

GLUBOK, SHIRLEY, *The Art of India,* ill. with photos, Macmillan, 1969. The three major religions of India, illuminated through a study of art throughout the years, helps us understand the present. See, also, other books in this author's series: *The Art of Africa,* Harper, 1965; *The Art of Ancient Greece,* Atheneum, 1963; *The Art of Ancient Peru,* Harper, 1966; *The Art of America in the Early Twentieth Century,* Macmillan, 1974. 11–14

GLUBOK, SHIRLEY, ed., *Home and Child Life in Colonial Days,* abr. from *Home Life in Colonial Days* (1898) and *Child Life in Colonial Days* (1899) by Alice Morse Earle, photos by Alfred Tamarin, Macmillan, 1969. Browsing in the index reveals the fascinating content of this meticulously written and illustrated book on the colonial period: Bathing, infrequency of; Betty lamps; Corncobs, uses of; Diseases among children; Girls, importance of erect bearing; Names for children; Rattlewatch; Stone bee; Voider; and Whispering sticks. Excellent reference source. 11–up

GORODETZKY, CHARLES, and SAMUEL CHRISTIAN, *What You Should Know about Drugs,* Harcourt, 1970. Simply written but dignified enough for adults, this is objective in tone and comprehensive in coverage. 10–up

GOUDEY, ALICE E., *Butterfly Time,* ill. by Adrienne Adams, Scribner's, 1964. The simple text and detailed illustrations make this an excellent introduction to butterflies for the youngest. 4–7
*Here Come the Dolphins!* ill. by Garry MacKenzie, Scribner's, 1961. 7–9
*Houses from the Sea,* ill. by Adrienne Adams, Scribner's, 1959. In a context young children can identify with, information about shells with careful labeling of each is presented. Illustrations supply information beyond textual content. Good to read aloud to pre-readers. 4–7

GUILCHER, JEAN MICHEL, and ROBERT HENRY NOAILLES, *A Fruit Is Born,* ill., Sterling, 1960. The simple text and superb photographs explain the development of different kinds of fruits. 9–11

HADER, BERTA and ELMER, *The Big Snow,* ill. by authors, Macmillan, 1948, 1962. How the small animals on a country hillside survive a heavy snow-storm. Caldecott Medal. 4–7

HALACY, DANIEL, *The Energy Trap,* Four Winds, 1975. A competent assessment of the complex problems of energy needs and population pressures. 12–15

HALL, LYNN, *Kids and Dog Shows,* ill. by photos, Follett, 1975. Facts on grooming, training, judging, and all the small details of canines in the ring. 10–14

HAMBLIN, DORA, *Pots and Robbers,* Simon, 1970. True stories about some of the more dramatic aspects of archaeology are written with wit and vigor. 12–up

HARRIS, JANET, *The Long Freedom Road; The Civil Rights Story.* McGraw, 1967. 11–15

HARRIS, JANET, and JULIUS W. HOBSON, *Black Pride, a People's Struggle,* ill., McGraw, 1969. From Dred Scott to Eldridge Cleaver this account of activist blacks tells the story of the long struggle for freedom from the point of view of opponents on nonviolence. 12–14

HARRIS, LOUISE and NORMAN, *Flash: The Life Story of a Firefly,* ill. by Henry B. Kane, Little, 1966. Interesting and accurate scientific observation in this story of Flash, who is born a glowworm and turns into a firefly. 8–10

HARTMAN, GERTRUDE, *Medieval Days and Ways,* ill., Macmillan, 1937. A wide and varied picture of many facets of life in the Middle Ages. The author goes beyond the description to discuss our heritage from that period. 10–15

HASKINS, JAMES, *The Consumer Movement,* Watts, 1975. 12–up

HILTON, SUZANNE, *The Way It Was—1876,* Westminster, 1975. Comprehensive and witty, with a touch of nostalgia, this describes and pictures aspects of daily life. 11–up

HIRSCH, S. CARL, *The Globe for the Space Age,* ill. by Burt Silverman, Viking, 1963. A well-written history of globe-making—from the first crude model made in 150 B.C. to the accurately detailed globes in the U.S. space program—with much interesting related information. 10–14
*The Living Community; A Venture into Ecology,* ill. by William Steinel, Viking, 1966. 11–14
*Meter Means Measure; The Story of the Metric System,* Viking, 1973. Historical background prefaces an appreciative description of the advantages of the system. 11–15
*This Is Automation,* ill. by Anthony Ravielli, Viking, 1964. A book which deals with the social aspects of automation. There is a brief explanation of binary mathematics but no attempt to explain how computers work. 9–14

HOAG, EDWIN, *American Houses: Colonial, Classic, and Contemporary,* ill. with photos, Lippincott, 1964. The story of the development of American houses. The author shows how the houses reflect the historical events and trends of their times and how the house reflects the people it contains. 12–16

HOBAN, TANA, *Look Again!* Macmillan, 1971. 2–4
*Shapes and Things,* Macmillan, 1970. 2–5
The first book uses photographs and cut-out portions of the page, the second uses pictures made without a camera, to show new ways of looking at familiar objects.

HODGES, C. WALTER, *The Spanish Armada; the Story of Britain,* ill. by author, Coward, 1967. Well-illustrated and well-written book that takes account of the Spanish viewpoint in the battles between the English and the Spanish Armada in 1588. 10–13

HOGBEN, LANCELOT, *The Wonderful World of Energy,* rev. ed., ill., Doubleday, 1968. A dramatic history of people's efforts to harness power from the prehistoric use of fire to the development of today's atomic power. An illustrated glossary is included. 10–13

HOGG, GARY, *Deep Down, Great Achievements in Cave Explorations,* Criterion, 1962. The dramatic stories of eight important speleological expeditions. Among them the discovery of Carlsbad Caverns, the Lascaux cave paintings, and the Eisriesenwelt ice caverns. 12–up

HOLLING, HOLLING C., *Paddle-to-the-Sea,* ill. by author, Houghton, 1941. An Indian boy carves a toy canoe and sets it afloat in a stream in Canada. Its travels through the Great Lakes and down the St. Lawrence to the sea are an opportunity to tell much about the geography, the industry, and the history of the areas with full-page illustration and text. 10–12

HOLME, BRYAN, *Drawings to Live With,* ill. with reproductions, Viking, 1966. Each chapter of this book offers a different aspect of drawing. By the end of the book the reader will have learned about drawings, art techniques, art history, and artists, too. 10–14

HORVATH, JOAN, *Filmmaking for Beginners*, Nelson, 1974. Clear explanations of every part of the process.  11–15

HUGHES, LANGSTON, *The First Book of Rhythms*, ill. by Robin King, Watts, 1954. A beautifully written book showing how rhythms are to be found in all aspects of life. An excellent introduction for young readers to an awareness of the harmonies around them.  10–14

HUTCHINS, ROSS E., *The Amazing Seeds*, photos by author, Dodd, 1965. Superb close-up photographs and lively text tell the story about seeds plus some unusual facts about them.  9–12

*Travels of Monarch X*, ill. by J. P. Connolly, Rand, 1966. A true story of the migration of a tagged Monarch butterfly from Canada to Mexico. Well documented, handsomely illustrated, overall pleasingly designed.  8–10

HYDE, MARGARET O., *Animal Clocks and Compasses*, ill. by P. A. Hutchinson, Whittlesey, 1960. The fascinating natural rhythms by which animals live and travel are explored. A section of science projects is included. 9–12

JANSON, H. W., and DORA JANE JANSON, *The Story of Painting for Young People; from Cave Painting to Modern Times*, ill. with reproductions, Abrams, 1952. The history of how painting began and how it developed through the ages, with 245 reproductions. The authors convey successfully how artists have chosen to express themselves differently in different periods.  12–16

JENNESS, AYLETTE, *Dwellers of the Tundra: Life in an Alaskan Eskimo Village*, photos by Jonathan Jenness, Crowell-Collier, 1970. A sympathetic account of the lives of 150 Eskimos who live in Makumiut on the Bering Sea by an author and photographer who lived with them for more than a year.  12–16

JOHNSON, ERIC, *Love and Sex in Plain Language*, rev. ed., ill. by Edward C. Smith, Lippincott, 1974. Outstanding for its dignity, informality, and candor.  12–15

JOHNSON, GERALD W., *America, A History for Peter*, 3 vols., ill. by Leonard Everett Fisher, Morrow, 1959–1960. A readable, easily understood history which makes clear the issues and underlying causes of the events chronicled. (The Peter of the title is the author's grandson.)  12–14

*The Congress*, ill. by Leonard Everett Fisher, Morrow, 1963. In this and two companion volumes (*The Presidency*, 1962, and *The Supreme Court*, 1962), the author presents authoritative, informative overviews of the three branches of the federal government. A related volume is *The Cabinet*, 1966.  11–13

KAREN, RUTH, *Song of the Quail; The Wondrous World of the Maya*, Four Winds, 1973. Excellent photographs enhance a text that gives facts about the rich culture of the Maya.  11–up

KAVALER, LUCY, *Dangerous Air*, ill. by Carl Smith, Day, 1967. A succinct discussion of the causes of air pollution beginning with the discovery of fire and what government, industry, and individuals must do to eliminate this danger.  12–up

*The Wonders of Algae*, ill. with photos and with drawings by Barbara Amlick and Richard Ott, Day, 1961. Molds, mushrooms, the fermentation process, uses of algae as food and as a potential staple for space travel.  10–13

KIRK, RUTH, *The Oldest Man in America: An Adventure in Archeology*, photos by Ruth and Louis Kirk, Harcourt, 1970. Fascinating description of the findings at a dig in the state of Washington.  10–14

KUMIN, MAXINE, *The Beach Before Breakfast*, ill. by Leonard Weisgard, Putnam, 1964. A grownup and a child dig clams on a beach at sunup. Text, meant for a young child, uses a style somewhat awkward for reading aloud but ideal for talking about the full-page illustrations that invite looking and relooking.  6–8

KURELEK, WILLIAM, *A Prairie Boy's Summer*, ill. by author, Houghton, 1975, and *A Prairie Boy's Winter*, Houghton, 1973. A Canadian painter describes in text and handsome pictures his childhood on a Manitoba dairy farm.  8–10

LAFFIN, JOHN, *Codes and Ciphers: Secret Writing Through the Ages*, ill. by C. de la Nougerede, Abelard, 1964. A history of codes and ciphers from ancient to modern times makes fascinating and exciting reading. At the end of the book are cipher messages that the reader should be able to break.  11–15

LATHROP, DOROTHY P., *Let Them Live*, ill. by author, Macmillan, 1951. The disasters that can occur when people interfere with the balance of nature are forcefully presented in a group of essays.  8–12

LAUBER, PATRICIA, *Bats; Wings in the Night*, ill. with photos, Random, 1968. Up-to-date, extensive study of types of bats and their eating and living habits. Excellent photographs.  8–12

LAWSON, ROBERT, *They Were Strong and Good*, ill. by author, Viking, 1940. The author's own ancestors provide the opportunity to move from the present to long ago in a simple, personal approach to "history" for younger children. Caldecott Medal.  7–10

*Watchwords of Liberty: A Pageant of American Quotations*, rev. ed., ill. by author, Little, 1957. A collection which highlights important occasions in American history. Background and circumstances surrounding each quotation are explained.  8–12

LEHR, PAUL E., *Storms: Their Origins ana Effects; Forecasting and Weather Lore*, ill. by Harry McNaught and Nino Carbe and with photos, Golden Pr., 1966. The author, a meteorologist with the U.S. Weather Bureau, describes all kinds of storms, storm patterns, and frontal storms. Included is a discussion of famous winds of the world and of weather lore.  9–12

LESTER, JULIUS, *To Be a Slave*, ill. by Tom Feelings, Dial, 1968. A collection of published and unpublished reminiscences by ex-slaves weaves a moving history of black Americans from their abduction from Africa through slavery, the Civil War, and its aftermath.  12–16

LEY, WILLY, *The Meteorite Craters*, ill. by John Bierhorst, Weybright, 1968. The story of the origins and history of discoveries of meteorite craters is told in relatively untechnical language with the help of numerous diagrams, charts, photographs, and maps.  11–14

LIFTON, BETTY JEAN, *Return to Hiroshima*, photos by Eikoh Hosoe, Atheneum, 1970. This picture book records Hiroshima as it is 25 years after the atomic bomb blast—the survivors, the Peace Museum, and so many chilling reminders of the past.  10–15

LIPSYTE, ROBERT, *Assignment: Sports*, Harper, 1970. A compilation of colorful articles about diverse sports. 10–up

LISTON, ROBERT A., *Downtown: Our Challenging Urban Problems*, ill. with photos, Delacorte, 1968. The author looks soberly at the problems facing our cities, explains how these problems developed, and considers the variety of solutions suggested.  12–up

LUBELL, WINIFRED and CECIL, *Green Is for Growing*, ill., Rand, 1964. Without attempting to be comprehensive,

this beautiful book discusses the plant kingdom and the classification of groups, giving some examples. The importance of plant life to humankind is made clear.
8–12

MACAULAY, DAVID, *Cathedral; The Story of Its Construction*, ill. by author, Houghton, 1973. Superbly illustrated, this describes—step by step—the building of a Gothic cathedral.
11–up
*City; A Story of Roman Planning and Construction*, ill. by author, Houghton, 1974. An engrossing and detailed account of the planning and building of a Roman city.
11–up

MARCUS, REBECCA B., *Prehistoric Cave Paintings*, ill., Watts, 1968. The discovery and subsequent study of Cro-Magnon cave art in France and Spain. The author includes discussion of various theories about the purposes of the paintings.
10–13

MARRIOTT, ALICE LEE, *Indians on Horseback*, rev. ed., ill. by Margaret Lefranc, T. Crowell, 1968. The author describes how the first Indian tribes settled along the edges of the Great Plains and later, with the coming of horses, moved into that area to live and hunt. These people came to be called Plains Indians and this book provides a very thorough history of their customs, government, arts, and religion.
10–14

MATTHEWS, WILLIAM H., III, *The Story of the Earth*, ill. by John E. Alexander, Harvey, 1968. An introductory book on geology, straightforward, simple. Includes glossary of geological terms.
9–12

MAY, JULIAN, *Why the Earth Quakes*, ill. by Leonard Everett Fisher, Holiday, 1969. The clear drawings and simple text clarify the causes of earthquakes.
7–10
*Before the Indians*, ill. by Symeon Shimin, Holiday, 1969. This picture book with only a few lines of text per page is not as simple as it appears. It presents an excellent picture of the work of archaeologists who, in this case, are piecing together the story of pre-Indian inhabitants of the Americas.
8–10

MC CLUNG, ROBERT M., *Black Jack, Last of the Big Alligators*, ill. by Lloyd Sanford, Morrow, 1967. A realistic narrative, illustrated with many accurate drawings, of the life cycle of an alligator in the Okefenokee Swamp.
9–11
*Lost Wild America, The Story of Our Extinct and Vanishing Wildlife*, ill. by Bob Hines, Morrow, 1969. About half of this book tells the history of the destruction and virtual extinction of wildlife in America and the beginning of conservation. The second half is a "field guide" to species endangered today, concluding with man himself. Index and bibliography make this a very useful reference.
12–15

MC COY, J. J., *The Hunt for the Whooping Cranes; A Natural History Detective Story*, maps and drawings by Ray Abruzzi, Lothrop, 1966. A suspense story about the eleven-year search by naturalists and conservationists for the Canadian nesting grounds of the whooping cranes, a search which was undertaken to save them from extinction.
12–16

MC NEER, MAY, *The American Indian Story*, ill. by Lynd Ward, Ariel, 1963. The life and history of the American Indians are told in a series of dramatic anecdotes and vigorous pictures.
10–14

MEAD, MARGARET, *People and Places*, ill. by W. T. Mars and Jan Fairservis and with photos, World, 1959. An extensive and exciting picture of the anthropologist's profession.
12–16

MELTZER, MILTON, *Brother, Can You Spare a Dime. The Great Depression 1929–1933*, ill. with contemporary prints and photos, Knopf, 1969. "How it started and why and what it felt like . . ." is what this book tells about "the human side" of the Great Depression as it affected auto workers, wheat farmers, clerks, secretaries, miners, teachers, sharecroppers, and doctors. Much documentation is from newspaper headlines, articles, cartoons, and pictures from periodicals, from art, literature, and songs of this period.
12–14
*Remember the Days; A Short History of the Jewish American*, ill. by Harvey Dinnerstein, Doubleday, 1974. Broad in coverage, serious and well-researched.
12–up

MELTZER, MILTON, ed., *In Their Own Words: A History of the American Negro*, 3 vols., ill. with facsimiles and portraits, T. Crowell, 1964, 1965, 1967. A unique history told through excerpts from documents, journals, letters, diaries, and speeches. Background information and sources are given for each item.
12–up

MELTZER, MILTON, and AUGUST MEIER, *Time of Trial, Time of Hope; The Negro in America, 1919–1941*, ill. by Moneta Barnett, Doubleday, 1966. One of a series commissioned to present historically the contribution made by minority groups to the development of the United States. The print size, illustration, and writing style invite the average or below average adolescent reader of any race to understand and appreciate the black during the heights of the 1920's and the depths of the 1930's.
12–16

MOORE, JANET GAYLORD, *The Many Ways of Seeing; An Introduction to the Pleasures of Art*, ill. with reproductions and photos, World, 1968. In the first half of this book the author discusses how artists see things in different ways and suggests ways of sharpening one's perception in art. Following a collage of pictures and quotations, the author suggests simple exercises to investigate some of the ideas and terms used earlier. A simple, personal, and enthusiastic presentation.
12–16

MORISON, SAMUEL ELIOT, *The Story of the "Old Colony" of New Plymouth*, ill. by Charles H. Overly, Knopf, 1956. Thoroughly familiar with his subject, this writer, well known for his historical works for adults, continues the story of the Pilgrims beyond Plymouth Rock and the first Thanksgiving. He writes authentically and with humor about the everyday lives of these people, as well as about the more conventional historical events.
12–16

MORRIS, RICHARD, and JAMES WOODRESS, eds., *Voices from America's Past*, 3 vols., ill. with photos and prints, Dutton, 1961, 1962, 1963. The history of America told by eyewitnesses and participants through their diaries, letters, memoirs, and other contemporary accounts. 12–16

MORRISON, SEAN, *Armor*, ill. by author, T. Crowell, 1963. In a lively style the author describes the armor of the ancient and feudal worlds and the men who wore it. Detailed and careful illustrations.
12–16

MURPHY, E. JEFFERSON, *Understanding Africa*, ill. by Louise E. Jefferson, T. Crowell, 1969. The author dispels stereotypes about Africa and its people. A general overview of the geography, people, and history, mainly of that part of Africa south of the Sahara Desert. 12–14

MURPHY, ROBERT, *A Heritage Restored; America's Wildlife Refuges*, ill. with photos and maps, Dutton, 1969. An introduction to America's wildlife and its unfortunate past history. The author describes representative refuges in the national system of refuges.
12–up

NEWMAN, ROBERT, *The Japanese: People of the Three Treasures*, ill. by Mamoru Funai, Atheneum, 1964. The three treasures—the Mirror, the Jewel, and the Sword —are central to the myths in which Japanese culture is steeped. The author shows the Japanese throughout their history as a people whose character is a blending of what the Three Treasures represent.            12–16

NICKEL, HELMUT, *Arms and Armor in Africa*, Atheneum, 1971. Objects described by the Curator of Arms and Armor at the Metropolitan Museum are related to tribal cultures.            10–14

PACE, MILDRED, *Wrapped for Eternity; The Story of the Egyptian Mummy*, ill. by Tom Huffman, McGraw, 1974.            10–14

PAINE, ROBERTA M., *Looking at Sculpture*, ill. with photos, Lothrop, 1968. Nearly a hundred works of sculpture, ancient to modern, are shown and discussed. Biographical information on the artists is included along with a glossary and suggested reading list.            12–16

PATON, ALAN, *The Land and People of South Africa*, rev. ed., ill. with photos, Lippincott, 1964. The author makes very clear his views of South Africa's racial problems but also states fairly the opposite point of view. A thought-provoking study of the geography and the various racial groups.            12–16

PERKINS, CAROL MORSE, and MARLIN PERKINS, *"I Saw You from Afar": A Visit to the Bushmen of the Kalahari Desert*, ill. with photos, Atheneum, 1965. The daily life of the bushmen in photographs and simple text. The treatment is sympathetic and dignified.            8–11

PETERSON, ROGER TORY, and the Editors of *Time-Life Books*, *The Birds*, ill. with photos and drawings, Time Inc., 1967 (Young Readers Edition). An outstanding book with beautiful color photos. *The Mammals* (1967) is another excellent book in this series of Young Readers Editions of *Life Nature Library*.            10–16

PETTIT, FLORENCE, *How to Make Whirligigs and Whimmy Diddles; and Other American Folkcraft Objects*, ill. by Laura Louise Foster, T. Crowell, 1972. Useful for the hobbyist, entertaining for the general reader.            12–up

PLACE, MARIAN T., *American Cattle Trails, East and West*, ill. by Gil Walker, Holt, 1967. An account of the cattle industry in prerailroad days which centers upon the movement of cattle from farm and ranch to market.            10–12

POLGREEN, JOHN and CATHLEEN, *The Stars Tonight*, ill. with photos, Harper, 1967. Descriptions of constellations and their legends, galaxies, and nebulae are all accompanied by charts to help locate them in the sky.            10–14

PORTAL, COLETTE, *The Beauty of Birth*, ill. by author, ad. by Guy Daniels, Knopf, 1971. A French artist's lovely watercolors and her reverent text show the development of a newborn from insemination.            8–11

PRICE, CHRISTINE, *Made in the Middle Ages*, ill. by author, Dutton, 1961. This is a book about the craftsmen and their products in a period that produced so many splendid objects. See, also, *Made in the Renaissance*, 1963, and *Made in Egypt*, 1970.            12–16

PRINGLE, LAURENCE, *Dinosaurs and Their World*, ill., Harcourt, 1968. One of the best books on dinosaurs with explanatory illustrations. Readable text includes descriptions of field work and museum study methods.            7–10

RAVIELLI, ANTHONY, *From Fins to Hands: An Adventure in Evolution*, ill. by author, Viking, 1968. A well-illustrated account of the human hand through the stages of fin, paw, and claw with emphasis upon the period from early primates to humans.            8–12

*Wonders of the Human Body*, ill. by author, Viking, 1954. An attractive, clear study of anatomy which portrays the body as a perfect machine. Simple analogies describe parts of the body and their functions.            8–12

*The World Is Round*, ill. by author, Viking, 1963. Diagrams and pictures with simple text explain how the ancient Greeks inferred that the earth is round and how today, for the first time, people can actually see its shape from outer space.            6–8

REED, W. MAXWELL, *Patterns in the Sky: The Story of the Constellations*, ill. by D. F. Levett Bradley, Morrow, 1951. The constellations are located in the sky with the help of charts, and the origins of their names are explained.            8–12

REED, W. MAXWELL, and WILFRID S. BRONSON, *The Sea for Sam*, rev. ed. edited by Paul F. Brandwein, Harcourt, 1960. Originally written in the 1930's for the nephew of W. Maxwell Reed, astronomy professor at Harvard, this edition has been revised and checked by authorities. Most photographs are new and the whole book has been redesigned. See, also, *The Earth for Sam* and *The Stars for Sam*, both similarly updated by Paul F. Brandwein.            11–14

REISS, JOHN, *Colors*, Bradbury, 1969. Identifying captions are the only text for Reiss' stunning pictures. An excellent first book for small children. See also *Numbers*, 1971, and *Shapes*, 1974.            2–6

RIPPER, CHARLES L., *Bats*, ill., Morrow, 1954. Clear text and drawings tell the life cycle and habits of bats the world over. Corrects some misconceptions.            10–12

ROCKWELL, ANNE, *Temple on a Hill; the Building of the Parthenon*, ill. with line drawings, Atheneum, 1969. A good deal of history is included with the account of the building of the Parthenon.            10–14

*The Toolbox*, ill. by Harlow Rockwell, Macmillan, 1971. A simple text and clear, spacious pictures show basic tools and their uses.            5–7

ROOSEVELT, ELEANOR, and HELEN FERRIS, *Partners: United Nations and Youth*, ill. with photos, Doubleday, 1950. The story of United Nations agencies' efforts to help children and young people around the world, made more dramatic by numerous true anecdotes.            12–14

ROSEN, ELLSWORTH, *Spiders Are Spinners*, ill. by Teco Slagboom, Houghton, 1968. Accurate information about spiders and their habits is presented in sprightly verse and attractive illustrations.            4–8

ROSENBERG, NANCY, and LOUIS Z. COOPER, *Vaccines and Viruses*, Grosset, 1971. An authoritative and smoothly written review of research in the field.            12–14

ROSS, FRANK, JR., *Transportation of Tomorrow*, ill. with drawings by the author and photos, Lothrop, 1968. Different modes of future transportation, some of almost science-fiction sort, are discussed, but the author is very conscious of the social usefulness and reality of what he describes.            10–14

ROUNDS, GLEN, *Rain in the Woods: And Other Small Matters*, ill. by author, World, 1964. In a personal and informal style, the author reveals his amazement at small events in nature. His appealing approach provides information as well as enjoyment.            9–12

RUCHLIS, HY, *Bathtub Physics*, ill. by Ray Skibinski, Harcourt, 1967. This book shows how some everyday laws of physics can be discovered in the bathtub. Each chapter includes brain teasers and investigations for the reader to pursue for oneself. 10–14

SANDERSON, IVAN T., *The Continent We Live On*, adapted by Anne Terry White, ill. with photos, Random, 1962. In this special edition for young readers, a naturalist gives an ecological interpretation of the life and weather of the North American continent. Numerous beautiful photographs. 12–16

SASEK, MIROSLAV, *This Is the United Nations*, ill. by author, Macmillan, 1968. An excellent, bright picture book that brings the U.N. vividly to life. Other books in this author's series about the great cities of the world include *This Is London*, 1959; *This Is Paris*, 1959; *This Is Rome*, 1960. 8–10

SAVAGE, KATHERINE, *The Story of Marxism and Communism*, ill. with photos and maps, Walck, 1968. The author traces the philosophical origins of communist thought, describes the creation of a communist state in Russia, and provides vivid portraits of the men who shaped it. She also describes the other Eastern European communist states and communist China's divergent path. 12–16

SCHALLER, GEORGE B., and MILLICENT E. SELSAM, *The Tiger: Its Life in the Wild*, ill. with photos and drawings, Harper, 1969. The author's firsthand experiences give excitement to this complete account of a great deal that is known about tigers. Myths about these animals are also recounted. 9–14

SCHECHTER, BETTY, *The Peaceable Revolution*, ill. with photos, Houghton, 1963. The nonviolent way of solving human problems is traced through the perspective of history: Thoreau, Gandhi, and into today's civil rights movement. 12–16

SCHEELE, WILLIAM E., *Prehistoric Animals*, ill., World, 1954. A well-written account of animal life during the first five million years of life on the earth. The locations of fossil finds and museums in which fossil remains may be found are included. 9–14

SCHEFFER, VICTOR, *Little Calf*, ill. by Leonard Everett Fisher, Scribner's, 1970. Adapted beautifully by Scheffer from his adult title, *The Year of the Whale*, this is as accurate as it is imaginative. 12–up

SCHELL, ORVILLE, and JOSEPH ESHERICK, *Modern China; The Story of a Revolution*, Knopf, 1972. Lucid and objective, a thoughtful analysis of China today. 11–up

SCHNEIDER, HERMAN and NINA, *How Big Is Big? From Stars to Atoms*, ill. by Symeon Shimin, W. R. Scott, 1946. Relativity of size is treated in this picture book with its pleasant illustrations and easy text. Included is a list of the approximate measurements of the things compared in the text. 6–9

*How Your Body Works*, ill. by Barbara Ivins, W. R. Scott, 1949. The parts of the body and their different functions, the nervous system, the senses are all described. 8–12

*Rocks, Rivers, and the Changing Earth*, ill. by Edwin Herron, W. R. Scott, 1952. A simple book about geology designed to help young readers understand the message given in rivers, moutains, and other geological formations. 9–12

*You Among the Stars*, ill. by Symeon Shimin, W. R. Scott, 1951. A clever approach introduces the young child to the wonders of astronomy. 8–10

*Your Telephone and How It Works*, 3rd ed., ill. by Jeanne Bendick, Whittlesey, 1965. An easily understood explanation of the workings of the telephone with helpful diagrams. 10–13

SCHWARTZ, ALVIN, *The City and Its People*, photos by Sy Katzoff, Dutton, 1967. Amply illustrated with photographs, this book describes a real modern city, Trenton, New Jersey, with its urban renewal, poverty, city court, garbage removal, traffic, etc. 11–14

*The Night Workers*, ill. by Ulli Steltzer, Dutton, 1966. Each hour from 6 P.M. to 6 A.M. is represented by a night worker whose work is often unknown to day people: newspaper pressman, night-school teacher, produce-market workers, disc jockey, jazz musicians, and many others—all are shown at work in photographs taken in a big city setting. 8–11

SCOTT, JACK DENTON, *That Wonderful Pelican*, photos by Ozzie Sweet, Putnam, 1975. A photo-essay, detailed and authoritative, on every aspect of pelican life. 10–up

SEEGER, ELIZABETH, *The Pageant of Chinese History*, McKay, 1934, rev. ed., 1962. This social, cultural, and political history from 3000 B.C. to the present time appears formidably thick and detailed, but with the help of its excellent index, can be an accurate and readable resource on the Chinese people. 12–14

SELSAM, MILLICENT E., *All Kinds of Babies*, ill. by Symeon Shimin, Four Winds, 1969. Very brief text with beautiful illustrations gives this picture book special appeal for young children. Develops two concepts very clearly, related to both familiar and less familiar animals: every living thing makes more of its own kind and babies look like their parents. 5–8

*Benny's Animals; And How He Put Them in Order*, ill. by Arnold Lobel, Harper, 1966. 6–8

*Birth of an Island*, ill. by Winifred Lubell, Harper, 1959. The evolution of a volcanic island is described in simple, lucid language from the initial eruption to the time when a variety of plant and animal life occupy it. 7–9. See, also, *Birth of a Forest*, 1964. 8–10

*How Animals Tell Time*, ill. by John Kaufmann, Morrow, 1967. With her usual clarity and directness the author discusses the biological clocks that seem to be a part of all animal life. In conclusion she mentions some of the experiments going on that may answer many remaining questions. 8–12

*Plants That Heal*, ill. by Kathleen Elgin, Morrow, 1959. A brief history of man's use of plants for medicine. Covers such topics as herbs used by medicine men, plants which made medical history, and plant medicines now in use. 11–14

*The Plants We Eat*, ill. by Helen Ludwig, Morrow, 1955. A brief history of people's use and cultivation of plants, along with a discussion of the types of plants used for food and how they are grown. See, also, *Plants That Move*, 1962. 9–13

*See Through the Forest*, ill. by Winifred Lubell, Harper, 1956. Plant and animal life at various levels of the forest, from the ground to the treetops, is described in this author's usual simple and accurate style. See, also, *See Through the Sea*, 1955; *See Through the Jungle*, 1957; *See Through the Lake*, 1958. 7–10

SHIPPEN, KATHERINE B., *The Great Heritage*, ill. by C. B. Falls, Viking, 1947; rev. ed., 1962. One by one this author looks at the natural resources—fur, timber, iron, gold, wheat, corn, etc.—that constitute the heritage for which the people of the U.S. are responsible. 12–16

*Men, Microscopes, and Living Things*, ill. by Anthony Ravielli, Viking, 1955. At least twenty pioneers in biology are discussed in this outstanding account of how our understanding of living things has changed over the centuries. The scientists' own writings are woven into the text. 12–16

*New Found World*, ill. by C. B. Falls, Viking, 1945. A history rich in detail of the people, Indians and Spaniards, who have lived in Central and South America from the coming of prehistoric people through the Second World War. 12–16

SHIPPEN, KATHERINE BINNEY, and ANCA SEIDLOVA, *The Heritage of Music*, ill. by Otto van Eersel, Viking, 1963. This history of the development of Western music concentrates upon major composers and their contributions. A helpful glossary of musical terms is included. 12–16

SHOWERS, PAUL, *Use Your Brain*, ill. by Rosalind Fry, T. Crowell, 1971. A fine introduction, clear and simple. *Where Does the Garbage Go?* ill. by Loretta Lustig, T. Crowell, 1974. Conservation and recycling are seen from the child's point of view. 7–8

SHUTTLESWORTH, DOROTHY, *All Kinds of Bees*, ill. by Su Zan N. Swain, Random, 1967. In this simply written, clearly illustrated book, the author describes the different families of bees and the ways they live. 8–10

*Clean Air—Sparkling Water: The Fight Against Pollution*, ill., Doubleday, 1968. The author describes the growth of a fictional city to explain the steady increase in water and air pollution. She goes on to describe worldwide problems and control efforts. 8–10

SILVERBERG, ROBERT, *The Auk, the Dodo, and the Oryx: Vanished and Vanishing Creatures*, ill. by Jacques Hnizdovsky, T. Crowell, 1967. A well-written plea for conservation is included in this book which uses eyewitness accounts from persons who saw the animals described in this volume. 11–13

*Vanishing Giants; the Story of the Sequoias*, ill. with photos, Simon, 1969. This story of the redwoods concludes with an account of the numerous efforts to save the trees through the establishment of national parks. 10–14

SILVERSTEIN, ALVIN, and VIRGINIA B. SILVERSTEIN, *A Star in the Sea*, ill. by Symeon Shimin, Warne, 1969. The dramatic telling of the life cycle of a starfish named Stella, from her hatching in a tidal pool through such dangers as storms and attacks by gulls to her laying her eggs and the beginning of the cycle anew. 6–10

*Unusual Partners: Symbiosis in the Living World*, ill. by Mel Hunter, McGraw, 1968. An excellent study of a variety of symbiotic relationships which can be related to the study of ecology. 8–10

SIMON, HILDA, *Insect Masquerades*, ill. by author, Viking, 1968. The unusual and wonderful shapes and colors that camouflage some insects are described. The book concludes with a chapter "Nightmare Insects" for which no explanation of natural selection seems adequate. 10–14

*Snakes; The Facts and the Folklore*, ill. by author, Viking, 1973. Meticulously detailed drawings add to the usefulness of an excellent text. 10–14

SIMON, MINA LEWITON, *Is Anyone Here?* ill. by Howard Simon, Atheneum, 1967. Creative language and excellent illustration are combined with accurate scientific observation of the seaside environment in this picture book for young readers. 5–9

SIMON, SEYMOUR, *The Paper Airplane Book*, ill. by Byron Barton, Viking, 1971. A book that describes the principles of flight as well as giving instructions for making paper airplanes. 8–11

*The Rock-Hound's Book*, ill. by Tony Chen, Viking, 1973. A fine book for the beginning collector. 9–11

SPENCER, CORNELIA, *Made in Japan*, ill. by Richard M. Powers and with photos, Knopf, 1963. A very readable book about the architecture, the crafts, the visual arts, literature, and music of this country. Includes a section of photographs. See, also, *Made in Mexico*, 1952; . . . *Italy*, 1957; . . . *Thailand*, 1964. 12–16

STERLING, DOROTHY, *Caterpillars*, ill. by Winifred Lubell, Doubleday, 1961. A zestful, well-written book about caterpillars—the life cycles of many species, the differences between moths and butterflies, and instructions for keeping caterpillars. 8–10

*Forever Free; The Story of the Emancipation Proclamation*, ill. by Ernest Crichlow, Doubleday, 1963. A comprehensive, well-written history of slavery in the United States with information on famous as well as little-known fighters for freedom. 12–16

*Tear Down the Walls! A History of the American Civil Rights Movement*, ill., Doubleday, 1968. Moving episodes from the black's struggle in America for equality. Explores some of the causes of today's anger. 12–up

STEVENS, CARLA, *The Birth of Sunset's Kittens*, photos by Leonard Stevens, W. R. Scott, 1969. Clear photographs show each step of the ever-miraculous birth process. 5–8

STEVENS, LEONARD, *The Town That Launders Its Water*, Coward, 1971. An engrossing report on a California town that learned to reclaim sewage-laden water. 11–up

STEVENSON, JANET, *Women's Rights*, Watts, 1972. 10–13

STONE, A. HARRIS, *The Chemistry of a Lemon*, ill. by Peter P. Plasencia, Prentice, 1966. A group of simple experiments leads the young reader to apply methods of scientific research and thinking to discover certain chemical principles for oneself. 8–11

STONE, A. HARRIS, and IRVING LESKOWITZ, *Microbes Are Something Else*, ill. by Peter P. Plasencia, Prentice, 1969. An excellent book of meaningful activities to be conducted with a microscope which will lead one to discover some fascinating facts about microbes. 8–12

SUTTON, ANN and MYRON, *Animals on the Move*, ill. by Paula A. Hutchison, Rand, 1965. Animal migration has always been a fascinating mystery and this book discusses the superstitions, guesses, and scientific information on the subject. 8–10

*Exploring with the Bartrams*, ill. by Paula A. Hutchison, Rand, 1963, reprint by Hale, 1966. The story of John and William Bartram, two of America's greatest botanists. To their credit are many "firsts" in the field of American botany. 12–16

SWIFT, HILDEGARD, *North Star Shining*, ill. by Lynd Ward, Morrow, 1947. One of the earlier accounts of black contributions to United States history. 10–14

TAYLOR, THEODORE, *Air Raid—Pearl Harbor! The Story of December 7, 1941*, ill. by W. T. Mars, T. Crowell, 1971. Well-documented, a vivid account of the events that led up to Pearl Harbor is told from both the Japanese and the American viewpoint. 11–14

TREASE, GEOFFREY, *This Is Your Century*, ill., with photos, maps, and drawings, Harcourt, 1965. Beginning with Queen Victoria's death in 1901 and going through 1964, this fascinating history introduces young people to the events and people who have shaped today's world. 12–16

TRELEASE, ALLEN, *Reconstruction; The Great Experiment*, Harper, 1971. Objective in tone but dramatic in treatment, an outstanding book about the post–Civil War years in the United States. 11–14

TRESSELT, ALVIN, *The Beaver Pond*, ill. by Roger Duvoisin, Lothrop, 1970. The story of the cycle of a beaver colony also gives an introduction to a balanced ecology. Beautiful. 5–8

*Hide and Seek Fog*, ill. by Roger Duvoisin, Lothrop, 1965. 5–8

*Rain Drop Splash*, ill. by Leonard Weisgard, Lothrop, 1946. Description of a rainfall beginning with a few drops and ending with the water flowing into the sea. The brief text and lovely illustrations create the mood of a rainy day. 5–7

*White Snow, Bright Snow*, ill. by Roger Duvoisin, Lothrop, 1947. The simple and quiet text evokes the feeling of the first snowfall and the landscape, describes people's activities, and concludes with the return of spring. Caldecott Medal. 5–7

TUNIS, EDWIN, *Chipmunks on the Doorstep*, ill. by author, T. Crowell, 1971. The author's experiences taming chipmunks. 10–up

*Colonial Craftsmen and the Beginnings of American Industry*, ill. by author, World, 1965. The comprehensive, lucid text and the excellent illustrations make this a very useful book for the study of crafts and industries in the New World. 10–13

*Colonial Living*, ill. by author, World, 1957. This first-rate reference book provides a detailed look at life in the United States in the seventeenth and eighteenth centuries. See, also, *Frontier Living*, 1961. 8–12

*Shaw's Fortune: The Picture Story of a Colonial Plantation*, ill. by author, World, 1966. Almost everything you read in the text of this book you can find illustrated by the full-page facing picture or the small, well-labeled drawings filling margins and unused portions of the page. An excellent example of a picture book appropriate for all age groups, it covers over 100 years of the Shaw family's living, up to 1752. 9–12

*The Young United States, 1783 to 1830*, ill. by author, World, 1969. A superb book that captures an overall feeling of these early years, the diversity of views, activities, and people. 10–13

TURNBULL, COLIN M., *The Peoples of Africa*, ill. by Richard M. Powers, World, 1962. An informative survey of the basic tribal cultures of Africa by the Curator of African Ethnology at the American Museum of Natural History. 12–16

*Tradition and Change in African Tribal Life*, World, 1966. An anthropologist looks at the institutions of tribal life in an effort to see how they meet the needs of people. The survey includes the fishers, desert hunters, forest hunters, and mountain farmers of various parts of Africa. 12–up

UDEN, GRANT, *A Dictionary of Chivalry*, ill. by Pauline Baynes, T. Crowell, 1968. More than a thousand entries, many with detailed illustrations, provide a very thorough picture of the world of knighthood and chivalry. 11–up

UNGERER, TOMI, *Snail, Where Are You?* ill. by author, Harper, 1962. Not a word of text is needed to make the simple point that spiral shape and form are everywhere around us. 5–8

USHINSKY, K., *How a Shirt Grew in the Field*, adapted from the Russian by Marguerita Rudolph, ill. by Yaroslava, McGraw, 1967. When originally written over a hundred years ago, this account of a Russian peasant boy's watching his shirt "grow" from seeds to finished product was an authentic picture of living in the Ukraine before modern machinery and factory-produced textiles. Both adapter and illustrator have Ukrainian connections and have designed this book with loving care for authenticity as well as beauty. 5–7

VALENS, EVANS G., *Wingfin and Topple*, ill. by Clement Hurd, World, 1962. A good read-aloud picture book with lovely illustrations describes the adventures of a flying fish. 4–7

*Me and Frumpet: An Adventure with Size and Science*, ill. with photos, Dutton, 1958. A boy's play with his model railroad and a pipecleaner man is the vehicle for familiarizing the reader with the kind of reasoning in such scientific concepts as relativity. 7–9

VAN LOON, HENDRIK WILLEM, *The Story of Mankind*, ill. by author, Boni & Liveright, 1926. Newbery Medal. 12–15

VARNER, VELMA, *The Animal Frolic*, ill. by Toba Sojo, Putnam, 1954. A twelfth-century Japanese scroll, showing small animals, can be studied section by section in a modern picture book. 8–12

VIERECK, PHILLIP, *The New Land; Discovery, Exploration, and Early Settlement of Northeastern United States, from Earliest Voyages to 1621, Told in the Words of the Explorers Themselves*, ill. by Ellen Viereck, Day, 1967. 14–up

VLAHOS, OLIVIA, *African Beginnings*, ill. by George Ford, Viking, 1967. Anthropological and archaeological discoveries of Africa's past bring the reader to understand some of the differences between today's Africa and Western society. The author gives a very complete account of the many African tribes and kingdoms that arose before much contact with the West. 12–16

VON HAGEN, VICTOR W., *The Incas; People of the Sun*, ill. by Alberto Beltrán, World, 1961. The story of the Inca Empire is told through the eyes of a fictional young boy, Huamán. The authenticity and vigor of the text and illustrations make this a distinguished book. 12–16

*South American Zoo*, ill. by Francis Lee Jacques, Messner, 1946. Scientific information supplemented by illustration tells about animal life in different geographic areas of South America. 8–12

VON WARTBURG, URSULA, *The Workshop Book of Knitting*, Atheneum, 1973. Clear directions and a progression of projects from simple to difficult are provided, as well as advice on materials. 10–up

WARREN, RUTH, *The Nile: The Story of Pharaohs, Farmers, and Explorers*, ill. by Victor Lazzaro, McGraw, 1968. A well-written overview of the history and geography of the Nile region from the time of the Pharaohs to the Aswan High Dam. 10–14

WATERS, BARBARA and JOHN, *Salt-Water Aquariums*, ill. by Robert Candy, Holiday, 1967. Detailed guide to setting up a salt-water aquarium, ranging from the simplest type to the very complex. Advice is included on handling small marine animals and performing harmless but instructive experiments with them. 6–up

WEISS, HARVEY, *Pencil, Pen, and Brush*, ill. by author, W. R. Scott, 1961. Instructions in basic drawing techniques combine with illustrative examples from the masters. See, also, *Sticks, Spools, and Feathers*, 1962; *Ceramics: from Clay to Kiln*, 1964; *Paint, Brush, and Palette*, 1966; and *Collage and Construction*, 1970. 10–up

*Sailing Small Boats*, ill. by Peter Barlow, Young Scott, 1967. Brief history of sailing, description of various types of boats, and instructions for building a sailboat. Includes definitions of nautical terms. 10–15

WHITE, ANNE TERRY, *Lost Worlds: Adventures in Archaeology,* Random, 1941. A description of the discovery of four ancient civilizations: Troy and Crete, Egypt, Assyria, and the Mayan Indian of Central America. 13–16 *Prehistoric America,* ill. by Aldren Watson, Random, 1951. A simple account of prehistoric times told through the discoveries of bones, fossils, and other remains. 9–11

WIDDER, ARTHUR, *Action in Submarines,* Harper, 1967. A history of submarines and their crews from the earliest to the nuclear-powered giants of today. A discussion of the bathyscaphe, trieste, and other experimental craft is included. 11–up

WILLIAMS, SELMA, *Kings, Commoners, and Colonists; Puritan Politics in Old and New England, 1603–1660,* Atheneum, 1974. A fine analysis of Massachusetts politics and England's reaction. 12–up

WOLF, BERNARD, *Don't Feel Sorry for Paul,* photos by author, Lippincott, 1974. A sympathetic documentary about a severely handicapped child. 8–11

ZIM, HERBERT S., *Blood,* ill. by René Martin, Morrow, 1968. A clear explanation of the composition of the blood and the processes by which the body makes and uses it. Also discussed are blood groups and the uses of vaccines and antitoxins. 8–12

ZIM, HERBERT S., and SONIA BLEEKER, *Life and Death,* ill. by René Martin, Morrow, 1970. A dispassionate survey of aging, death, and funeral practices of other times and places as well as our own. 9–12

ZIM, HERBERT S., and JAMES R. SKELLY, *Hoists, Cranes and Derricks,* ill. by Gary Ruse, Morrow, 1969. In simple language the authors describe these three machines and the work they do. 8–10

ZOLOTOW, CHARLOTTE, *The Storm Book,* ill. by Margaret Bloy Graham, Harper, 1952. The effect of a summer storm on the country, the city, the ocean, and the mountains is shown without being frightening. 4–7

## PUBLISHERS AND PUBLISHERS' ADDRESSES

ABELARD. Abelard-Schuman, Ltd. See T. Y. Crowell Co., Inc.

ABINGDON. Abingdon Pr., 201 Eighth Ave. S., Nashville, Tenn. 37202

ABRAMS. Harry N. Abrams, Inc., 110 E. 59th St., New York, N.Y. 10022

ADDISON. Addison-Wesley Pub. Co., Inc., Reading, Mass. 01867

ALA. American Library Assoc., Pub. Dept., 50 E. Huron St. Chicago, Ill. 60611

ALDINE PRESS, 529 S. Wabash Ave., Chicago, Ill. 60605

AM. ASSOC. FOR THE ADVANCEMENT OF SCIENCE. 1515 Massachusetts Ave., N.W., Washington, D.C. 20005

AM. COUNCIL ON EDUCATION. 1 Dupont Circle, N.W., Washington, D.C. 20036

APPLETON. Appleton-Century-Crofts, 292 Madison Ave., New York, N.Y. 10017

ARIEL. Ariel Books. See Farrar

ASHANTILLY. Ashantilly Pr., Darien, Ga. 31305

ATHENEUM. Atheneum Pubs., 122 E. 42nd St., New York, N.Y. 10017

ATHERTON. Atherton Pr., Inc. See Aldine Pub. Co.

ATLANTIC. Atlantic-Little. See Little, Brown & Co.

BALLANTINE. Ballantine Books, Inc. See Random House

BARNES. Barnes & Noble Books. See Harper & Row Pub.

BASIC. Basic Books, Inc., 10 E. 53rd St., New York, N.Y. 10022

BEHRMAN. Behrman House, Inc., 1261 Broadway, New York, N.Y. 10001

BOBBS. Bobbs-Merrill Co., Inc., 4300 W. 62nd St., Indianapolis, Ind. 46268

BOND WHEELWRIGHT. The Bond Wheelwright Co., Porter's Landing, Freeport, Maine 04032

BONI & LIVERIGHT. See W. W. Norton and Co., Inc.

BOWKER. R. R. Bowker and Co., 1180 Ave. of the Americas, New York, N.Y. 10036

BRADBURY. Bradbury Pr., Inc. 2 Overhill Rd., Scarsdale, N.Y. 10583

BRO-DART PUB. Co., 1609 Memorial Ave., Williamsport, Pa. 17701

BROWN. William C Brown Co. Pub., 2460 Kerper Blvd. Dubuque, Ia. 52001

BURGESS. Burgess Pub. Co., 7108 Ohms Lane, Minneapolis, Minn. 55435

CAMBRIDGE UNIV. PR., 32 E. 57th St., New York, N.Y. 10022

CAXTON. The Caxton Printers, Ltd., Caldwell, Idaho 83605

CHATHAM/VIKING. See Viking Press

CHELSEA HOUSE PUBS., 70 W. 40th St., New York, N.Y. 10018

CHILDREN'S BOOK COUNCIL, INC. 67 Irving Pl. New York, N.Y. 10003

CHILDRENS PR. Childrens Press, Inc., 1224 W. Van Buren, Chicago, Ill. 60607

CHILTON. Chilton Book Co., Chilton Way, Radnor, Pa. 19089

COLLINS. William Collins & World Pub. Co., Inc. 2080 W. 117 St., Cleveland, Ohio 44111

COPP CLARK. Copp Clark Ltd., 517 Wellington St. W., Toronto, Ont. M5V IGI

COWARD. Coward-McCann and Geoghegan, Inc., 200 Madison Ave., New York, N.Y. 10016

COWLES. Cowles Book Co. See Henry Regnery Co.

CRITERION. Criterion Books. See T. Y. Crowell Co.

CROWELL-COLLIER. Macmillan, Inc., 866 Third Ave., New York, N.Y. 10022

T. CROWELL. Thomas Y. Crowell Co., Inc., 666 Fifth Ave., New York, N.Y. 10019

CROWN. Crown Pubs., Inc., 419 Park Ave. S., New York, N.Y. 10016

DAY. The John Day Co., Inc., 257 Park Ave. S., New York, N.Y. 10010

DELACORTE. Delacorte Pr. See Dell

DELL. Dell Pub. Co., Inc., One Dag Hammarskjold Plaza, New York, N.Y. 10017

DEVIN. Devin-Adair Co., Inc., 143 South Beach Ave., Old Greenwich, Conn. 06870

DIAL. The Dial Pr., Inc. See Dell

DODD. Dodd, Mead & Co., 79 Madison Ave., New York, N.Y. 10016

DOUBLEDAY. Doubleday & Co., Inc., 245 Park Ave., New York, N.Y. 10017

DOVER. Dover Pubns., Inc., 180 Varick St., New York, N.Y. 10014

DUELL. Duell, Sloan & Pearce. See Meredith

DUFOUR. Dufour Editions, Inc., Chester Springs, Pa. 19425

DUTTON. E. P. Dutton & Co., Inc., 201 Park Ave. S., New York, N.Y. 10003

EDUCATIONAL FILM LIBRARY ASSOC., 250 W. 57th St., New York, N.Y. 10019

EDUCATIONAL SCREEN AND AV GUIDE, 434 S. Wabash, Chicago, Ill. 60605

EERDMANS. William B. Eerdmans Pub. Co., 255 Jefferson Ave., S.E., Grand Rapids, Mich. 49502

EVANS. M. Evans & Co., Inc., 216 E. 49th St., New York, N.Y. 10017

EXPRESSION. Expression Co., 155 Columbus Ave., Boston, Mass. 02116

FARRAR. Farrar, Straus & Giroux, Inc., 19 Union Sq., W., New York, N.Y. 10003

FAXON. F. W. Faxon Co., Inc., 15 Southwest Park, Westwood, Mass. 02090

FERNHILL. Fernhill House, Ltd. See Humanities Press, Inc.

FILM NEWS, 250 W. 57th St., New York, N.Y. 10019

FOLLETT. Follett Pub. Co., 1010 W. Washington Blvd., Chicago, Ill. 60607

FOUR WINDS. Four Winds Pr. See Scholastic

FUNK. Funk & Wagnalls Pub. Co., Inc. See T. Y. Crowell

GALE RESEARCH CO., Book Tower, Detroit, Mich., 48226

GARRARD. Garrard Pub. Co., 1607 N. Market St., Champaign, Ill. 61820

GOLDEN GATE. Golden Gate Junior Books. See Childrens Press

GOLDEN PR. See Western Pub. Co.

GREENWILLOW. Greenwillow Books. See William Morrow

GROSSET. Grosset & Dunlap, Inc., 51 Madison Ave., New York, N.Y. 10010

HALE. E. M. Hale & Co., 20 Waterside Plaza, New York, N.Y. 10010

HARCOURT. Harcourt Brace Jovanovich, Inc., 757 Third Ave., New York, N.Y. 10017

HARPER. Harper & Row, Pubs., 10 E. 53rd St., New York, N.Y. 10022

HARVEY. Harvey House, Inc., 5 S. Buckhout St., Irvington-on-Hudson, N.Y. 10533

HASTINGS. Hastings House Pubs., Inc., 10 E. 40th St., New York, N.Y. 10016

HAWTHORN. Hawthorn Books, Inc., 260 Madison Ave., New York, N.Y. 10016

HILL. Lawrence Hill and Co., Pubs., Inc., 150 Fifth Ave., New York, N.Y. 10011

HOLIDAY. Holiday House, Inc., 18 E. 53rd St., New York, N.Y. 10022

HOLT. Holt, Rinehart & Winston, Inc., 383 Madison Ave., New York, N.Y. 10017

HORN BOOK. Horn Book, Inc., 585 Boylston St., Boston, Mass. 02116

HOUGHTON. Houghton Mifflin Co., 1 Beacon St., Boston, Mass. 02107

HUMANITIES PRESS, INC. Atlantic Highlands, N.J. 07716

IND. UNIV. PR., Tenth and Morton Sts., Bloomington, Ind., 47401

KNOPF. Alfred A. Knopf, Inc., 201 E. 50th St., New York, N.Y. 10022

LANDERS FILM ASSOC., Box 69760, Los Angeles, Calif., 90069

LAWRENCE. SEYMOUR LAWRENCE, INC., 90 Beacon St., Boston, Mass. 02108

LERNER. Lerner Pubns. Co., 241 First Ave. N., Minneapolis, Minn. 55401

LIBRARY OF CONGRESS. Supt. of Documents, U.S. Govt. Printing Office, Washington, D.C. 20402

LIPPINCOTT. J. B. Lippincott Co., E. Washington Sq., Philadelphia, Pa. 19105

LITTLE. Little, Brown & Co., 34 Beacon St., Boston, Mass. 02106

LONGMANS. Longmans, Green & Co. See McKay

LOTHROP. Lothrop, Lee & Shepard Co. See William Morrow

LUCE. Robert B. Luce, Inc., 2000 N. St., N.W., Washington, D.C. 20036

MCGRAW. McGraw-Hill Inc., 1221 Ave. of the Americas, New York, N.Y. 10020

MCKAY. David McKay Co., Inc., 750 Third Ave., New York, N.Y. 10017

MCKINLEY. McKinley Pub. Co., P.O. Box 77, Ocean City, N.J. 08226

MACMILLAN. Macmillan, Inc., 866 Third Ave., New York, N.Y. 10022

MACRAE. Macrae Smith Co., 225 S. 15th St., Philadelphia, Pa. 19102

MESSNER. Julian Messner, 1 W. 39th St., New York, N.Y. 10018

METHUEN. Methuen Pubns., 2330 Midland Ave., Agincourt, Ont. MIS 1P7

MORROW. William Morrow & Co., Inc., 105 Madison Ave., New York, N.Y. 10016

NAT. COUNCIL FOR THE SOCIAL STUDIES. National Education Assoc., 1201 16th St., N.W., Washington, D.C. 20036

NAT. COUNCIL OF TEACHERS OF ENGLISH, 1111 Kenyon Rd., Urbana, Ill. 61801

NATURAL HISTORY PR. Am. Museum of Natural History, Central Park W. at 79th St., New York, N.Y. 10024

NELSON. Thomas Nelson, Inc., 407 Seventh Ave., S., Nashville, Tenn. 37203

NEW AM. LIB. New American Library, 1301 Ave. of the Americas, New York, N.Y. 10019

NEW YORK LIBRARY ASSOC., P.O. Box 521, Woodside, N.Y. 11377

NEW YORK PUBLIC LIBRARY. Fifth Ave. and 42nd St., New York, N.Y. 10018

NOBLE. Noble & Noble, Pubs., Inc. See Dell Pub. Co.

NORTON. W. W. Norton & Co., Inc., 500 Fifth Ave., New York, N.Y. 10036

O'HARA. J. PHILIP O'HARA, INC., PUB. 20 E. Huron, Chicago, Ill. 60611

OXFORD. Oxford Univ. Pr. Inc., 200 Madison Ave., New York, N.Y. 10016

PANTHEON. Pantheon Books, 201 E. 50th St., New York, N.Y. 10022

PARENTS. Parents Magazine Pr., 52 Vanderbilt Ave., New York, N.Y. 10017

PARNASSUS. Parnassus Pr., 4080 Halleck St., Emeryville, Calif. 94608

PHILLIPS. S. G. Phillips, Inc., 305 W. 86th St., New York, N.Y. 10024

PLATT. Platt & Munk, Inc., 1055 Bronx River Ave., Bronx, N.Y. 10472

POTTER. Clarkson N. Potter, Inc., 419 Park Ave. S., New York, N.Y. 10016

PRENTICE. Prentice-Hall, Inc., Englewood Cliffs, N.J. 07632

PRINCETON UNIV. PR., Princeton, N.J. 08540

PUTNAM. G. P. Putnam's Sons, 200 Madison Ave., New York, N.Y. 10016

RAND. Rand McNally & Co., P.O. Box 7600, Chicago, Ill. 60680

RANDOM. Random House, Inc., 201 E. 50th St., New York, N.Y. 10022

REGNERY. Henry Regnery Co., 114 W. Illinois St., Chicago, Ill. 60610

REILLY. Reilly & Lee Books, 114 W. Illinois St., Chicago, Ill. 60610

RITCHIE. The Ward Ritchie Pr., 474 S. Arroyo Pkwy., Pasadena, Calif. 91105

ROW. See Harper & Row

ROY. Roy Pubs., Inc., 30 E. 74th St., New York, N.Y. 10021

ST. MARTIN'S. St. Martin's Pr., Inc., 175 Fifth Ave., New York, N.Y. 10010

SCARECROW. The Scarecrow Pr., 52 Liberty St., Metuchen, N.J. 08840

SCHOLASTIC. Scholastic Book Services, 50 W. 44th St., New York, N.Y. 10036

W. R. SCOTT. William R. Scott, Inc. See Addison-Wesley Pub. Co.

SCOTT, FORESMAN. Scott, Foresman and Co., 1900 E. Lake Ave., Glenview, Ill. 60025

SCRIBNER'S. Charles Scribner's Sons, 597 Fifth Ave., New York, N.Y. 10017

SEABURY. Seabury Pr., 815 Second Ave., New York, N.Y. 10017

SIMON. Simon & Schuster, Inc., 630 Fifth Ave., New York, N.Y. 10020

SINGING TREE. See Gale Research Co.

STANFORD UNIV. PR. Stanford, Calif. 94305

STERLING. Sterling Pub. Co., 419 Park Ave. S., New York, N.Y. 10016

STOKES. Frederick A. Stokes Co. See Lippincott

TAPLINGER. Taplinger Pub. Co., Inc., 200 Park Ave. S., New York, N.Y. 10003

TEACHERS COLLEGE PR. Teachers College, Columbia Univ., 1234 Amsterdam Ave., New York, N.Y. 10027

TIME INC. Time-Life Books, Time-Life Bldg., Rockefeller Center, New York, N.Y. 10020

TOWER. Tower Pubns., Inc., 185 Madison Ave., New York, N.Y. 10016

TUTTLE. Charles E. Tuttle Co., Inc., 28 S. Main St., Rutland, Vt. 05701

UNIV. OF CALIF. PR. 2223 Fulton St., Berkeley, Calif. 94720

UNIV. OF CHICAGO PR. 5801 Ellis Ave., Chicago, Ill. 60637

UNIV. OF PA. PR. 3933 Walnut St., Philadelphia, Pa. 19104

VANGUARD. Vanguard Pr., Inc., 424 Madison Ave., New York, N.Y. 10017

VAN NOSTRAND. Van Nostrand Reinhold Co., 450 W. 33rd St., New York, N.Y. 10001

VIKING. Viking Pr., Inc., 625 Madison Ave., New York, N.Y. 10022

WALCK. Henry Z. Walck, Inc. See David McKay

WALKER. Walker & Co., 720 Fifth Ave., New York, N.Y. 10019

WARNE. Frederick Warne & Co., Inc., 101 Fifth Ave., New York, N.Y. 10003

WASHBURN. Ives Washburn, Inc. See McKay

WATTS. Franklin Watts, Inc., 730 Fifth Ave., New York, N.Y. 10019

WESTERN PUB. CO., 1220 Mound Ave., Racine, Wis. 53404

WESTERN RESERVE PR. 3530 Warrensville Ctr. Rd., Cleveland, Ohio 44122

WESTMINSTER. The Westminster Pr., Witherspoon Bldg., Philadelphia, Pa. 19107

WESTON WOODS STUDIO. Weston, Conn. 06880

WEYBRIGHT. Weybright and Talley, Inc. See McKay

WHITE. David White Co., 60 E. 55th St., New York, N.Y. 10022

WHITMAN. Albert Whitman & Co., 560 W. Lake St., Chicago, Ill. 60606

WHITTLESEY. Whittlesey House. See McGraw-Hill

WILSON. H. W. Wilson Co., 950 University Ave., Bronx, N.Y. 10452

WINDMILL. Windmill Books, Inc., 201 Park Ave. S., New York, N.Y. 10010

WORLD. See Collins

YALE UNIV. PR., 302 Temple St., New Haven, Conn. 06511

YOUNG SCOTT. Young Scott Books. See Addison-Wesley Pub. Co.

# GLOSSARY AND PRONUNCIATION GUIDE

The following list contains foreign words and phrases and the names of authors, places, and story characters selected from Parts One, Two, Three, and Four. Words that can be found in a standard college dictionary are not included. Definitions are limited to those that apply in this book and are given only if meanings have not been supplied in context.

Symbols used in the pronunciation are as follows: a as in *hat;* ā as in *age;* ã as in *care;* ä as in *father;* e as in *let;* ē as in *see;* ėr as in *term;* i as in *pin;* ī as in *five;* o as in *hot;* ō as in *go;* ô as in *order, all;* oi as in *oil;* ou as in *house;* th as in *thin;* ŦH as in *then;* u as in *cup;* u̇ as in *full;* ü as in *rule;* ū as in *use;* zh as in *measure;* ə as in the unaccented syllables of *about, taken, pencil, lemon, circus;* H as in the German *ach;* N as in the French *bon* (not pronounced, but shows that the vowel before it is nasal); œ as in the French *peu* and the German *könig* (pronounced by speaking ā with the lips rounded as for ō); Y as in the French *du* (pronounced by speaking ē with the lips rounded as for ü). All other symbols represent the consonant sounds that they commonly stand for in English spelling.

AFANASIEV (ä fä nä'syif)

AICHINGER (ī'kin jėr)

AIX (eks)

ALDIS (ôl'dis)

ALEIAN (ä'lā an), a plain in Lycia

ANANSI (ə nan'sē)

ANTEA (an tē'ə)

ANTIGONE (an ti'gō nē)

ARDIZZONE (är di zō'ni)

ARHA (är'hä)

ARMAND (är män')

ARRA (ar'ə), a mild Irish expletive, equivalent to "Really!"

ARRIETTY (ãr'i e tē)

ARTZYBASHEFF (är tsi ba'shif)

ASBJÖRNSEN (äs'byėrn sen)

ASIMOV (a'si mov)

AULNOY, D' (dō nwä' or dôl nwä')

BALLAGHADEREEN (bä lä hä'də rēn)

BARBEAU, MARIUS (bär bō', ma'rē ys)

BARGI (bär'gē), grandmother

BÄRLI (bär'lē)

BARTEL (bär'tel)

BASILE, GIAMBATTISTA (bä zē'lā, jäm'bät tēs'tä)

BEAUMONT, DE (də bō môN')

BEEREEUN (bā rā ün′)
BEHN (bān)
BELLOC, HILAIRE (bel′ok, hi lär′)
BENÉT (be nā′)
BEWICK (bū′ik)
BIALKA (byäl′kä)
BIDPAI (bid′pī)
BINGAWINGUL (bing′ə wing′əl), an Australian shrub; scrub
BLANID (blô)
BLASS (bläs)
BLEGVAD (bleg′vad)
BOADAG (bō′ag)
BOGATIR (bō gä tēr′), hero; valiant knight
BOONDI (bün′dē), a club-headed weapon
BORSKI, LUCIA MERECKA (bōr′skē, lü′syä mə res′kä)
BOULANGER (bü län zhä′)
BOUQUI (bü kē′)
BOVA (bō′vä)
BRANDIS (bran′dis), a three-legged iron stand used to support a cooking vessel over a fire; a trivet
BREIDABLIK (brī′də blik)
BRICRIEU (brik′rü)
BUDULINEK (bə dü′lə nek)
BULLAI BULLAI (bul′ī bul′ī)

CAMILLE (ca mēl′)
CARABAS (ka′rə bas)
CARIGIET, ALOIS (cä rē zhē ā′, al wä′)
CAUDILL (kô′dl)
CELEUS (sē′lē əs)
CETHERN (kär′ən)
CHAYOTE (chä yōd′ē), the fruit of a tropical vine of the cucumber family, used as a vegetable
CHEELD-WHIDDEN (chēld′ hwid′ən), baby
CHINKERINCHEE (ching′kə rin′chē), South African perennial with starry white blossoms; commonly known as star-of-Bethlehem
CHUI (chü′ē)
CHUKOVSKY, KORNEI (chu kôf′skē kôr nā′)
CHURA (chü′rä)
CHUTE, MARCHETTE (chüt, mär shet′)
CIARDI (chär′dē)
CLOAM (klōm), earthenware
CLYTIE (klī′tē)
COLUM, PADRAIC (kol′um, pôd′rig)
COMENIUS (kə mē′ni us)
CONALL (kon′əl)
CONNLA (kon′lə)
CONTES DE MA MERE L'OYE (kônt də mä mär lwä)
COOLABAH (kü′lə bä), eucalyptus
CORAN (kō′rən)
CORNCRAIK (kôrn′krāk), a hand rattle used to frighten birds from sown seed or growing corn; also, the European land rail, a bird with a harsh grating voice heard among the grain fields
CROOM (krüm), crumb
CROOM OF A CHEELD (krüm əv ə chēld), a very small child
CUCHULAIN (kü hul′in)
CUROI (kü′roi)
CURRAGH (kér′əH or kér′ə), an open boat made of skin or canvas
CYANE (sī′ə nē)

DAEN (dä′ən), an aborigine of Australia
DASENT (dā′sənt)
D'AULAIRE (dō lär′)

DEALGAN (däl′gən)
DE ANGELI (də an′jel ē)
DEENYI (dēn′yē)
DE GASZTOLD, CARMEN BERNOS (də gaz′tōl, bér′nōs)
DEJONG, MEINDERT (də yung′, min′dért)
DE LA MARE (dě la mär′)
DÈMI (dem′ē)
DE REGNIERS (də rän′yä)
DEUTSCH, BABETTE (doich, bab et′)
DINKY (ding′kē), very small; a small creature, i.e., fairy
DODGE, MARY MAPES (māps)
DOOLOOMAI (dü′lü mī′)
DOON-GARA (dün′gä rä)
DOOWI (dü′wē), dream spirit
DRAUPNER (droup′nér)
DREXEL (drek′səl), threshold
DRUON (drü an′)
DU BOIS, PÈNE (dœ bwä′, pen)
DUIRMUID (dir′mid)
DUMMUTS (dum′its), twilight
DŪN (dün), fort
DURRI (dur′ē), cake of grass-seed flour
DUVOISIN (dœ vwä zaN′)

ECRETTE (e kret′)
EE (ä), yes
EEHU (ē′hü)
EER-DHER (ēr′ᵗᴴer)
EICHENBERG (ī′ken bérg)
ELIL, refers to rabbits in Watership Down by Richard Adams; no authoritative pronunciation available.
EMAIN MACHA (em′ôn ma′hä)
ENCELADUS (en sel′ə dəs), in Greek mythology, a hundred-armed giant
ENKIDU (en′kə dü)
ENNA (en′ə), in Greek mythology, the vale of Enna was Persephone's home on earth
ERYX (er′iks), a city and mountain in Sicily
ESU (ä′sü), an African interjection, equivalent to "Good!" or "Wonderful!"
EUMÊLUS (yü mē′ləs)

FALADA (fä lä′dä)
FARJEON (fär′jun)
FIONN (fin)
FY (fī), faith
FYLEMAN (fīl′man)

GÁG (gäg)
GAGNON (ga nyōN′)
GALLAND, ANTOINE (gə läN′, äN twoN′)
GATLESS (gat′lis or gôt′lis), shiftless; careless; thoughtless
GIDYA (gid′yä), a shrub of the genus Acacia, which gives off a sickening odor in damp weather or when in bloom
GILGUY HOLE (gil′gī hōl), a water hole
GIOCONDO DE' FIFANTI (jō con′dō dä fi fän′tē)
GIUFA (jü′fə)
GIUSEPPE (jü zep′pē)
GLEED (glēd), a glowing coal
GOO-GOOR-GAGA (gü′gür gä′gä), an Australian bird with a raucous cry, commonly known as laughing jackass
GOOLA-GOOL (gü′lä gül′)
GOOLAY-YALI (gü′lä yä′lē)
GOOMBEELGA (güm bēl′gä)
GOOWEERA (gü wē′rä)
GOTHEL (gôt′əl)

GOUDEY (gou′dē)
GRAINNE (grôn′yə)
GRANDMERE (grän mãr′)
GUDBRAND (gud′bränd or gud′bränt)
GUINEDA (gē nā′də)
GUITERMAN (git′ĕr mən)
GURAGÉ (gü′rä gä′), a group of people in central Ethiopia
    and the region in which they live

HAILU (hī′lü)
HAPTOM HASEI (hap′təm hä sē′)
HAZARD, PAUL (a zar′, pōl)
HEIDI (hī′dē)
HEINLEIN (hīn′līn)
HELHEIM (hel′hām)
HERMOD (her′müd or her′məd), a son of Odin
HIISI (hī′si), in Finnish folklore, the Evil Power
HIITOLA (hī′tō lä), the dominions of Hiisi
HOCH (hōch)
HODER (hō′dĕr)
HOLLE (hôl′lə)
HOMILY (hom′i lē)
HUNG VUONG (hun vwun)
HYRROKEN (hī′rō kin)

INJERA (in jā′rä), a pancake-style bread
IOBATES (ī ob′ə tēz)
ISKWAO (isk wā′ō)
ISMARUS (is′mə rəs)
ISS (is), yes
ISS FY (is fī), by my faith

JANCSI (yan′sē)
JANSSON, TOVE (yän′sən, tō′vä)
JATAKA (jä′tə kə)
JEAN LEBLANC (zhän lə blän)
JOAQUIN (wä kēn′)

KALASHNIKOFF (kä läsh′ni kôf)
KIBOKO (ki bō′kō), a rhinoceros-hide whip
KJELGAARD (kel′gärd)
KNOWE (nou or nō), knoll
KOBI (kō′bē)
KOICHI (kō′i chi)
KONIGSBURG (kō′nigs bĕrg)
KOPPIE (kop′ē), hill
KRYLOV (kril ôf′)
KWAKU ANANSI (kwa′kü ə nan′sē)

LAERY (lē′rē)
LAIVA (lī′vä)
LEDOUX (lə dü′)
LE GALLIENNE (lə gal′yən)
LENSKI (len′skē)
LING BROOM (ling brüm), a broom made of heather
LIONNI (lē ō′nē)
LIU (lyü)
LOKE (lō′kē)
LÖNNROT, ELIAS (lĕrn′rôt, ə lī′əs)
LORENZINI (lô ren tsē′nē)

MAEVE (māv)
MALI (mä′lē)
MALICE (mä lēs′)
MÄRCHEN (mãr′Hən)
MARMOT (mar mō′)
MAROOSIA (mä rü′sēə)

MBWEHA (əm bwã′hä)
MEDIO POLLITO (mã′dē ōpō lyē′tō)
METANIRA (met ə nī′rə)
MICHEL MELOCHE (mē shel′ mä lôsh′)
MILNE (miln)
MJOLNER (myôl′nĕr)
MOE, JÖRGEN (mōə, yer′gən)
MONTRESOR, BENI (mōn′trə sôr, bã′nē)
MUHINDI (mü hin′dē)
MUNARI, BRUNO (mü nä′rē, brü′nō)
MUNGU (mün′gü)
MURTHEMNEY (mir them′nē)
MUSTAPHA EFFENDI (mus′tä fä i fen′di)
MUTUNYEUSI (mü tün yeü′sē)
MUZUNGU (mü zün′gü)
MY CHAU (mē jou)

NAGY (nod′yə or noj)
NANNA (nä′nä)
NASR-ED-DIN HODJA (näs′red din′ hôd′yə)
NICHET (nē shā′)
NIC LEODHAS, SORCHE (nik lē ō′əs, sôr′ä)
NIKOLAI (nē kō lī′)
NINA-CUX (ni ña-cux)
NUNKU (nun′kü)
NUNNOOS (nun′üs)
NYODU (nə yō′dü)

O′FAOLAIN (ō fwã′lôn)
OISIN (u shēn′), great legendary Irish hero who went to the
    Land of the Ever Young
OJIISAN (ō jē sän)
OKEI (ō kē′)
ORGEL (ôr′gel)
ORMANINI (ôr′mä nē′nē)
ORMONDROYD (ôr mond roid)

PADRE PORKO (pä′thre pôr′kō)
PANCHATANTRA (pän chə tän′trə)
PARRA, NICANOR (pä′rä, nē′kä nôr)
PENTAMERONE (pen tä mä rō′nä)
PERRAULT, CHARLES (pe rō′, sharl)
PETROS (pe′trōs)
PIACEVOLI NOTTI, LE (lä pyä chã′vô le nôt′tē)
PICARD (pē kar′)
PIES (pyesh)
PIRENE (pī rē′nē)
POLYIDUS (pol′ē ī′dəs)
PRELUTSKY (pre lut′skē)
PROETUS (prô ē′təs)
PROYSEN, ALF (proi′ sən, älf)

RAPUNZEL (rə pun′zəl), rampion, a European plant having
    a tuberous root used for salad
RIEU (rü)
RINTARO (rin tä′rō)
ROETHKE (ret′kē)
ROJANKOVSKY (rō jan kôf′skē)
ROSLIE (rōs′lē)

SADKO (säd′kô)
SAINT-EXUPÉRY, ANTOINE DE (san tāg zœ pä rē, än twän′ də)
SARETT (sä ret′)
SCHWÄNLI (shwän′lē)
SEANACHIE (shän′ə hē)
SÊCHE (sesh)

SELSAM (sel′səm)
SEMAMINGI (sā mä min′gē)
SEREDY (shär′ə dē)
SHMELKA (shmel′kä)
SHMELKICHA (shmel′ki chä)
SILFLAY, see ELIL
SKILLY-WIDDEN (skil′i wid′ən), a Piskey baby
SLEIPNER (slāp′nir), the eight-legged steed of Odin
SLOAN (slōn), sloe, the fruit of the blackthorn
SLOOGEH (slü′gə), Saluki, the long-eared desert hound
SMOLICHEK (smol′i chek)
SON TIEN (shun tin)
SOTIRIS (sō ti′ris)
SPIEWNA (shpyev′nä)
SPYRI, JOHANNA (shpē′rē, yō hä′nä)
STOLZ (stōlts)
STRAPAROLA (strä pä rō′lä)
SUNGURA (sün gü′rä)

TAILLEFER (tä′yə fär′)
TASHJIAN (täs jun)
TENNIEL (ten′yel)
THOK (łhôk)
THORNE-THOMSEN, GUDRUN (tôrn tom′sen, gü′drun)
THRYM (łhrim or trēm)
THUY TIEN (tù′ē tin)
TIMO (ti mō)
TIRE-WOMAN (tīr′wùm′ən), one who sells and provides headdresses
TISTOU (tē stü′)
TMOLUS (tə mō′ləs)

TOIVO (toi′vō)
TOLKIEN (tôl′ken)
TRESSELT (tre′selt)
TUNIS (tū′nis)
TUPA (tù′pä)

UATH (ü′ä)
UCHIDA, YOSHIKO (ü chē dä, yō shē kō)
ULI (ü′lē)
URASHIMA TARO (ü rä shē mä tä rō)
URUK (ü′ruk), an ancient Sumerian city
USNA (us′nə)

VAN DER LOEFF (van′ dėr ləf)
VENDLA (vend′lä)
VIERECK (vēr′ək)
VILLENEUVE (vēl nœv′)
VLEI (flā), meadow; marsh

WEEDAH (wē′dä)
WIRINUN (wir′ē nun), sorcerer; medicine man
WOMBA (wom′bä)

YASHIMA, TARO (yä′shi ma, tä′rō)
YEVTUSHENKO, YEVGENY (yĭv tù shěn′kō, yĭv gä′nyē)
YGDRASIL (ig′drə sil), in Norse mythology, the world tree in Neflheim which binds together heaven, earth, and hell
YHI (yē)

ZEMACH (zē′mak)
ZHENYA (zhä′nyə)

# SUBJECT MATTER INDEX

This subject index has been developed to meet the needs of potential users of the *Anthology*. It reflects, within reason, the content of the majority of entries in the *Anthology*.

A major goal of the index is to bring together the different literary genres about the same subject. Thus, under CATS, for example, are found poems, fairy tales, and historical fiction, Not all headings will reflect a similar range of material, but many do.

The majority of headings are those found in most library tools. However, there are deviations, and the user is encouraged to browse through the index for ideas not usually reflected in traditional indexes. One example of this is the heading CINDERELLA THEME. A teacher who wants to help children understand how different cultures develop a similar theme should find the heading helpful.

A beginning has been made toward developing headings that treat of concepts as well as specifics. *Snow-White and the Seven Dwarfs* is listed under PRIDE AND VANITY since the Queen's motivation to kill Snow-White stems from these personal characteristics.

The headings used for the excerpts from whole books refer to the selection within the *Anthology* and not to the entire book. *Harriet the Spy* is not basically about DANCES AND DANCING, but the selection included here is.

Finally, the index is not definitive, but it should provide a starting point for users interested in interrelating the literary genres within the *Anthology*.

# INDEX OF TITLES, AUTHORS, AND ILLUSTRATORS

Brief biographical information, when available, is provided for all authors and illustrators represented in the *Anthology*. Page references in roman type refer to selections and illustrations; page references in italic type refer to editorial discussion. Entries in this index have been alphabetized word-by-word.